Ref.
801.95
Hall.

P9-BIJ-016

Property
Ithaca High School Library
Ithaca, Michigan

Contemporary
Literary Criticism
Yearbook 1985

Guide to Gale Literary Criticism Series

When you need to review criticism of literary works, these are the Gale series to use:

If the author's death date is: **You should turn to:**

After Dec. 31, 1959
(or author is still living)

CONTEMPORARY LITERARY CRITICISM

for example: Jorge Luis Borges, Anthony Burgess,
William Faulkner, Mary Gordon,
Ernest Hemingway, Iris Murdoch

1900 through 1959

TWENTIETH-CENTURY LITERARY CRITICISM

for example: Willa Cather, F. Scott Fitzgerald,
Henry James, Mark Twain, Virginia Woolf

1800 through 1899

NINETEENTH-CENTURY LITERATURE CRITICISM

for example: Fedor Dostoevski, George Sand,
Gerard Manley Hopkins, Emily Dickinson

1400 through 1799

LITERATURE CRITICISM FROM 1400 TO 1800
(excluding Shakespeare)

for example: Anne Bradstreet, Pierre Corneille,
Daniel Defoe, Alexander Pope,
Jonathan Swift, Phillis Wheatley

SHAKESPEAREAN CRITICISM

Shakespeare's plays and poetry

Antiquity through 1399

CLASSICAL AND MEDIEVAL LITERATURE CRITICISM

for example: Dante, Plato, Homer, Sophocles, Vergil,
the Beowulf poet

(Volume 1 forthcoming)

Gale also publishes related criticism series:

CHILDREN'S LITERATURE REVIEW

This ongoing series covers authors of all eras. Presents criticism on authors and author/illustrators who write for the preschool through high school audience.

CONTEMPORARY ISSUES CRITICISM

This two volume set presents criticism on contemporary authors writing on current issues. Topics covered include the social sciences, philosophy, economics, natural science, law, and related areas.

ISSN 0091-3421

Volume 39

Contemporary Literary Criticism

Yearbook 1985

The Year in Fiction, Poetry, Drama,
and World Literature and the Year's
New Authors, Prizewinners, Obituaries,
and Works of Literary Biography
and Literary Criticism

Sharon K. Hall

EDITOR

Gale Research Company
Book Tower
Detroit, Michigan 48226

STAFF

Sharon K. Hall, *Editor*

Lisa M. Rost, *Senior Assistant Editor*

Derek T. Bell, Sandra J. Crump, Anne Sharp, *Assistant Editors, Yearbook*
Joyce A. Davis, *Senior Research Assistant, Yearbook*

Melissa Reiff Hug, Molly L. Norris, *Assistant Editors*

Sheila Fitzgerald, Sharon R. Gunton, *Contributing Editors*

Lizbeth A. Purdy, *Production Supervisor*
Denise Michlewicz Broderick, *Production Coordinator*
Eric Berger, *Assistant Production Coordinator*
Kathleen M. Cook, Maureen Duffy, Sheila J. Nasea, *Editorial Assistants*

Linda M. Pugliese, *Manuscript Coordinator*
Donna Craft, *Assistant Manuscript Coordinator*
Maureen A. Puhl, Rosetta Irene Simms, *Manuscript Assistants*

Victoria B. Cariappa, *Research Coordinator*
Maureen R. Richards, *Assistant Research Coordinator*
Daniel Kurt Gilbert, Kent Graham, Michele R. O'Connell, Keith E. Schooley,
Filomena Sgambati, Vincenza G. Tranchida, Mary D. Wise, *Research Assistants*

Jeanne A. Gough, *Permissions Supervisor*
Janice M. Mach, *Permissions Coordinator, Text*
Patricia A. Seefelt, *Permissions Coordinator, Illustrations*
Susan D. Battista, *Assistant Permissions Coordinator*
Margaret A. Chamberlain, Sandra C. Davis, Kathy Grell,
Josephine M. Keene, Mary M. Matuz, *Senior Permissions Assistants*
H. Diane Cooper, Colleen M. Crane, Mabel E. Schoening, *Permissions Assistants*
Margaret A. Carson, Helen Hernandez, Anita Williams, *Permissions Clerks*

Special recognition is given to Jean C. Stine for her editorial contributions.

Frederick G. Ruffner, *Publisher*
Dedria Bryfonski, *Editorial Director*
Ellen Crowley, *Associate Editorial Director*
Christine Nasso, *Director, Literature Division*
Laurie Lanzen Harris, *Senior Editor, Literary Criticism Series*

Since this page cannot legibly accommodate all the copyright notices,
the Appendix constitutes an extension of the copyright notice.

Copyright © 1986 by Gale Research Company

Library of Congress Catalog Card Number 76-38938
ISBN 0-8103-4413-0
ISSN 0091-3421

Computerized photocomposition by
Typographics, Incorporated
Kansas City, Missouri

Printed in the United States

Contents

Preface vii

Authors Forthcoming in *CLC* xi

Appendix 493

Cumulative Index to Authors 509

Cumulative Index to Critics 561

The Year in Review

The Year in Fiction.............................3
   John Blades

The Year in Poetry 6
   Dave Smith

The Year in Drama............................15
   Gerald Weales

The Year in World Literature 18
   William Riggan

New Authors

Isabel Allende 1942- 27

Carolyn Chute 1947- 37

Pam Durban 1947- 44

Fernanda Eberstadt 1960- 48

Clyde Edgerton 1944- 52

Bret Easton Ellis 1964- 55

Carlo Gébler 1954- 60

Molly Giles 1942- 64

Amy Hempel 1951- 67

Alexander Kaletski 1946- 72

Nancy Lemann 1956- 75

Ed Minus 1938- 79

Lorrie Moore 1957- 82

T. R. Pearson 1956- 86

Joan K. Peters 1945- 91

Cecile Pineda 1942- 94

Mary-Ann Tirone Smith 1944- 97

Norman Williams 1952- 100

Prizewinners

Literary Prizes and Honors Anounced in 1985.....105

Prizewinners Featured in 1985 Yearbook 109

Prize Commentary 111

Don DeLillo 1936- 115

Louise Erdrich 1954- 128

Maria Irene Fornes 1930- 135

William Gibson 1948- 139

Robert Hass 1941- 145

Robert Holdstock 1948- 151

Barry Hughart 1934- 155

Keri Hulme 1947- 158

Carolyn Kizer 1925- 168

James Lapine 1949-
   see James Lapine and Stephen Sondheim

James Lapine and Stephen Sondheim 172

Alison Lurie 1926- 176

Sharon Olds 1942- 186

Richard Rosen 1949- 194

Bob Shacochis 1951- 198

Claude Simon 1913- 202

Neil Simon 1927- 216

Josef Škvorecký 1924- 220

Stephen Sondeim 1930-
   see James Lapine and Stephen Sondheim

Richard Stern 1928- 234

Ross Thomas 1926- 246

Judith Thompson 1954- 250

Robert Penn Warren 1905- 254

August Wilson   1945- 275

Tobias Wolff   1945- 283

Obituaries

Necrology....................................289

Heinrich Böll   1917-1985 291

Basil Bunting   1900-1985 297

Taylor Caldwell   1900-1985 301

Italo Calvino   1923-1985 305

Robert Fitzgerald   1910-1985 318

Robert Graves   1895-1985 320

Geoffrey Grigson   1905-1985 330

Philip Larkin   1922-1985 333

Helen MacInnes   1907-1985...................349

Josephine Miles   1911-1985 352

Shiva Naipaul   1945-1985....................355

Theodore Sturgeon   1918-1985 360

E.B. White   1899-1985 369

Literary Biography

Louise Bogan: A Portrait
    Elizabeth Frank........................383

Along with Youth: **Hemingway,** *the Early Years*
    Peter Griffin.............................398

Into Eternity: The Life of **James Jones,** *American Writer*
    Frank MacShane 404

Mailer: *His Life and Times*
    Peter Manso 416

Hemingway: *A Biography*
    Jeffrey Meyers 427

Agatha Christie: *A Biography*
    Janet Morgan 436

The Kindness of Strangers: The Life of **Tennessee Williams**
    Donald Spoto 444

Literary Criticism

The Flower and the Leaf: A Contemporary Record of American Writing since 1941
    Malcolm Cowley.........................457

Plausible Prejudices: Essays on American Writing
    Joseph Epstein...........................463

Enlarging the Change: The Princeton Seminars in Literary Criticism, 1949-1951
    Robert Fitzgerald 470

Habitations of the Word
    William Gass 477

Occasional Prose
    Mary McCarthy 484

Preface

Every year, an overwhelming number of new publications and significant literary events confront the reader interested in contemporary literature. Who are the year's notable new authors? What dramas have been introduced on the New York stage? Who won the literary world's most prestigious awards? What noteworthy works of literary criticism have been published, and how have they been received? Which authors have been the subjects of significant new literary biographies, and what approach did the biographer take—factual, interpretive, psychological, critical? Finally, who among our best-known contemporary writers died during the year, and what is the reaction of the literary world?

To answer such questions and assist students, teachers, librarians, researchers, and general readers in keeping abreast of current literary activities and trends, the *Contemporary Literary Criticism Yearbook* is being published as part of the *Contemporary Literary Criticism (CLC)* series.

Standard *CLC* volumes provide readers with a comprehensive view of modern literature by presenting excerpted criticism on the works of novelists, poets, playwrights, short story writers, scriptwriters, and other creative writers who are now living or died after December 31, 1959. Works covered in regular *CLC* volumes are those that have generated significant critical commentary within recent years, with a strong emphasis on works by established authors who frequently appear on the syllabuses of high school and college literature courses.

To complement this broad coverage, the *Yearbook* focuses in depth on a given year's literary activity and highlights a larger number of currently noteworthy authors and books than is possible in standard *CLC* volumes. The *Yearbook* provides critical overviews of the past year's works in various genres, supplies up-to-date critical commentary on new authors and prizewinning writers whose publications have made recent literary news, and marks the deaths of major contemporary literary figures. In addition, the *Yearbook* expands the scope of regular *CLC* volumes by presenting excerpted criticism on the works of such nonfiction writers as literary biographers and critics, whose growing importance in the literary world warrants increased attention. The *Yearbook* is, in short, a valuable supplement to the regular *CLC* volumes in its comprehensive treatment of the year's literary activity. Since the majority of the authors covered in the *Yearbook* and regular *CLC* volumes are living writers who continue to publish, an author frequently appears more than once in the series. There is, of course, no duplication of reprinted criticism.

Scope of the Work

CLC Yearbook 1985 includes excerpted criticism on over 75 authors and provides comprehensive coverage of the year's significant literary events. As with the regular volumes of *CLC,* the authors covered include those who are now living or who died after December 31, 1959. In addition, the *Yearbook* also includes essays commissioned exclusively for this publication. The *Yearbook* is divided into six sections: The Year in Review, New Authors, Prizewinners, Obituaries, Literary Biography, and Literary Criticism.

The Year in Review—This section includes specially commissioned essays by prominent literary figures who survey the year's new works in their respective fields. In *CLC Yearbook 1985* we have the advantage of viewing "The Year in Fiction" from the perspective of John Blades, literary critic, reporter, and columnist for the *Chicago Tribune.* Blades, who serves on the board of The National Book Critics Circle, was one of three judges in Fiction for The American Book Awards in 1985. "The Year in Poetry" is presented by Academy-Institute Award-winning poet Dave Smith, who has published several poetry collections and who reviews poetry for many literary journals. In 1985 Smith published a new poetry collection, *The Roundhouse Voices,* and an essay collection, *Local Assays: On Contemporary American Poetry,* and also edited *The Morrow Anthology of Younger Poets* with David Bottoms. "The Year in Drama" is reviewed by Gerald Weales, a winner of the George Jean Nathan Award for drama criticism and an author of numerous books on drama and film, including his recently published *Canned Goods As Caviar: American Film Comedies of the 1930s.* Weales is a theater critic for such journals as *Commonweal* and *The Georgia Review;* his survey is reprinted from *The Georgia Review.* Finally, "The Year in World Literature" is discussed by William Riggan, who as associate editor of the quarterly *World Literature Today* is in a unique position to comment on important international literature; Riggan specializes in Third World, Slavic, and Anglo-American literatures. These annual survey essays on fiction, poetry, drama, and world literature are a special feature of the *Yearbook* and provide a focus that is outside the scope of our regular *CLC* volumes.

New Authors—*CLC Yearbook 1985* introduces eighteen writers whose first book, or first book in English-language translation, was published during 1985. Authors were selected for inclusion if their work was reviewed in several sources and garnered significant criticism. Although the regular *CLC* volumes often cover new writers, the *Yearbook* provides more timely and more extensive coverage of authors just coming into prominence. This expanded coverage includes writers of poetry, short stories, and novels. *CLC Yearbook 1985,* for example, presents the poet Norman Williams, short story writers Molly Giles, Amy Hempel, Lorrie Moore, and Pam Durban, the newly translated novelists Isabel Allende of Chile and Alexander Kaletski of Russia, as well as new American novelists such as Carolyn Chute, who brings to life the poor in backwoods Maine, and T.R. Pearson, who paints an amusing portrait of a small town in North Carolina.

Prizewinners—This section of the *Yearbook* begins with a list of Literary Prizes and Honors Announced in 1985, citing the award, its recipient, and the title of the prizewinning work. *CLC Yearbook 1985* then highlights twenty-four major prizewinners who will be featured in this volume. A Prize Commentary follows and discusses each award that is featured in the *Yearbook;* the Prize Commentary indicates the year the award was established, the reason it was established, the awarding body, how the winner is chosen, and the nature of the prize (money, trophy, etc.). After the Prize Commentary, entries on individual award winners are presented. Recipients of established literary honors, such as the Pulitzer Prize, are included as well as authors who have won less established but increasingly important prizes, such as the PEN/Faulkner Award for Fiction, the only award given by writers to writers. In addition to the winners of major American awards, recipients of several outstanding international prizes are also covered. Thus we include England's distinguished Booker-McConnell Prize, awarded to Keri Hulme, and Canada's Governor General's Literary Awards, presented to Josef Skvorecky for Fiction and Judith Thompson for Drama. We have, of course, also featured the literary world's most prestigious award, the Nobel Prize in literature, bestowed on French fiction writer Claude Simon.

Obituaries—This section begins with a Necrology of *CLC* authors. Following the Necrology, individual author entries are included for the more prominent writers whose influence on contemporary literature is reflected in the obituaries, reminiscences, tributes, or retrospective essays included in their entries. *CLC Yearbook 1985,* for example, presents entries on Heinrich Boll, Italo Calvino, Robert Graves, Philip Larkin, and E.B. White, among others.

Literary Biography—Since literary biographies are outside the scope of works covered in regular *CLC* volumes, the *Yearbook* provides an opportunity to offer comprehensive commentary on these prominent and popular works. This part of the *Yearbook,* then, is devoted to criticism on literary biographies of authors who are within the *CLC* time period. We do not, therefore, include biographies of authors of the early twentieth century or of previous centuries. Besides giving a biographical perspective on the authors who are the subjects of the literary biographies, this section also introduces readers to today's biographers, their methods, styles, and approaches to biography. This *Yearbook* discusses seven literary biographies, including Peter Manso's celebrated biography of Norman Mailer, *Mailer: His Life and Times,* Janet Morgan's "authorized" biography of Agatha Christie, and two biographies of Ernest Hemingway: one by Jeffrey Meyers, *Hemingway: A Biography,* which is only the second full-scale biography on Hemingway to have appeared since his death in 1961, and the other biography by Peter Griffin, *Along with Youth: Hemingway, the Early Years,* which is the first of a projected three-volume work.

Literary Criticism—While the works of several major literary critics have been covered periodically in regular *CLC* volumes, the new *Yearbook* format allows us to devote an entire section to this important genre. In this section we focus on noteworthy works of literary criticism published in the past year, both important works devoted to a single author in the *CLC* time period and general works that reflect contemporary theories or analyses of literature. *CLC Yearbook 1985* considers five such studies, including works by the venerable critics Malcolm Cowley and Mary McCarthy. This comprehensive treatment of works of literary criticism is another special feature of the *Yearbook.*

Format of the Book

With the exception of essays found in The Year in Review section, which are original survey essays written for this publication, the *Yearbook* is comprised of excerpted criticism. There are approximately 575 individual excerpts in

CLC Yearbook 1985 taken from hundreds of literary reviews, general magazines, distinguished newspapers, and scholarly journals. The excerpts included reflect the critical attention the authors and their works have received by critics writing in English and by foreign criticism in translation; critical books and articles not translated into English have been excluded.

Since the *Yearbook* is designed to complement other *CLC* volumes, *Yearbook* entries generally follow the same format with some variations and additional features. *Yearbook* entries variously contain the following elements:

- The **author heading,** which is included in entries in the New Authors, Prizewinners, and Obituaries sections, cites the author's full name. The portion of the name outside the parentheses denotes the form under which the author has most commonly published. If an author has written consistently under a pseudonym, the pseudonym will be listed in the author heading and the real name given on the first line of the author entry. Also located at the beginning of the author entry are any important name variations under which an author has written. For New Authors and Obituaries, the author's name is followed by the birth date, and, in the case of an obituary, the death date. Uncertainty as to a birth or death date is indicated by question marks. For Prizewinners, the author's name is followed by the title of the prizewinning work and the award received.

- The **book heading,** which is included in entries in the Literary Biography and Literary Criticism sections, cites the complete title of the book followed by the biographer's or critic's name. In cases where there is an editor of a book as well as an author, the editor's name is also given.

- A brief **biographical and critical introduction** to the author and his or her work precedes the excerpted criticism in entries in the New Authors and Prizewinners sections.

- **Cross-references** have been included in entries in all sections, except The Year in Review, to direct the reader to other useful sources published by the Gale Research Company: *Contemporary Authors* now includes detailed biographical and bibliographical sketches on more than 82,000 authors; *Children's Literature Review* presents excerpted criticism on the works of authors of children's books; *Something about the Author* contains heavily illustrated biographical sketches on writers and illustrators who create books for children and young adults; *Contemporary Issues Criticism* presents excerpted commentary on the nonfiction works of authors who influence contemporary thought; *Dictionary of Literary Biography* provides original evaluations of authors important to literary history; and the new *Contemporary Authors Autobiography Series* offers autobiographical essays by prominent writers. Previous volumes of *CLC* in which the author has been featured are also listed. Cross-references are provided for both the authors and subjects of literary biographies and literary criticism when applicable. In *CLC Yearbook 1985,* for example, the entry on Janet Morgan's *Agatha Christie: A Biography* cites additional sources of information on both Morgan and Christie.

- A list of **principal works,** including the author's first and last published work and other important work, is provided in entries in the Obituaries section in order to reflect the author's entire literary career. The list is chronological by date of first book publication and identifies the genre of each work. In the case of foreign authors where there are both foreign language publications and English translations, the title and date of the first English-language edition are given in brackets. Unless otherwise indicated, dramas are dated by first performance, not first publication.

- A **portrait** of the author is included, when available, in entries in the New Authors, Prizewinners, and Obituaries sections; in the Literary Biography section, **illustrations** of the subject, representing different stages in his or her life, are included whenever possible.

- Illustrations of **dust jackets** are included, when available, to complement the critical discussion in entries in The Year in Review, Prizewinners, Literary Biography, and Literary Criticism sections.

- An **excerpt** from the author's work is included, when available, in entries in the New Authors, Prizewinners, Literary Biography, and Literary Criticism sections, in order to provide the reader with a sampling of the author's theme and style.

- The **excerpted criticism,** included in all entries except those in The Year in Review section, represents essays selected by the editors to reflect the spectrum of opinion about a specific work or about an author's writing in general. The excerpts are presented chronologically, adding a useful perspective to the entry. All titles featured in the entry are printed in boldface type, which enables the reader to easily identify the works being discussed.

• Selected critical excerpts are prefaced by **explanatory notes** that give important information regarding critics and their work and also provide a summary of the criticism.

• A complete **bibliographical citation** designed to help the user find the original essay or book follows each excerpt. An asterisk (*) at the end of a citation indicates the essay is on more than one author.

Other Features

• A list of **Authors Forthcoming in CLC** previews the authors to be researched for future volumes.

• An **Appendix** lists the sources from which material in the volume has been reprinted. Many other sources have also been consulted during the preparation of the volume.

• A **Cumulative Index to Authors** lists all the authors who have appeared in *Contemporary Literary Criticism* (including authors who are the subjects of works of literary biography and literary criticism covered in the *Yearbook*); *Twentieth-Century Literary Criticism, Nineteenth-Century Literature Criticism,* and *Literature Criticism from 1400 to 1800,* along with cross-references to other Gale series: *Children's Literature Review, Authors in the News, Contemporary Authors, Contemporary Authors Autobiography Series, Dictionary of Literary Biography, Something about the Author,* and *Yesterday's Authors of Books for Children.* Users will welcome this cumulated author index as a useful tool for locating an author within the various series. The index, which lists birth and death dates when available, will be particularly valuable for those authors who are identified with a certain period but whose death date causes them to be placed in another, or for those authors whose careers span two periods. For example, F. Scott Fitzgerald is found in *Twentieth-Century Literary Criticism,* yet a writer often associated with him, Ernest Hemingway, is found in *Contemporary Literary Criticism.*

• A **Cumulative Index to Critics** lists the critics and the author entries in which the critics' essays appear.

Acknowledgments

The editors wish to thank the copyright holders of the excerpted articles included in this volume for permission to use the material and the photographers and other individuals who provided photographs for us. We are grateful to the staffs of the following libraries for making their resources available to us: Detroit Public Library and the libraries of Wayne State University, the University of Michigan, and the University of Detroit.

Suggestions Are Welcome

The editors welcome the comments and suggestions of readers to expand the coverage and enhance the usefulness of the series.

Authors Forthcoming in *CLC*

Contemporary Literary Criticism, Volumes 40 and 41 will contain criticism on a number of authors not previously listed and will also feature criticism on newer works by authors included in earlier volumes.

To Be Included in Volume 40

Brian Aldiss (English novelist, short story writer, critic, and editor)—A Hugo and Nebula Award-winning science fiction author, Aldiss recently published *Helliconia Winter*, the third novel in his series about a remote planet called Helliconia.

Jorge Amado (Brazilian novelist and nonfiction writer)—Amado is recognized as one of Brazil's greatest writers, and his works have been translated into over forty languages. He is best known for his novels *The Violent Land, Gabriela, Clove and Cinnamon, Dona Flor and Her Two Husbands,* and the recently translated *Pen, Sword, Camisole.*

Ann Beattie (American novelist and short story writer)—In her fiction Beattie records the disillusionment of the "Woodstock generation" as her protagonists come to terms with middle age and a suburban, middle-class lifestyle. Her latest works include *The Burning House* and *Love Always.*

Marguerite Duras (French novelist, dramatist, short story writer, and filmmaker)—Internationally recognized for her mastery of several genres, Duras is perhaps best known for her work in film and her application of cinematic techniques to the novel. Her recent prizewinning novel, *The Lover,* has furthered her reputation as an important contemporary author.

William M. Hoffman (American dramatist and editor)—Hoffman's controversial play *As Is* has been praised for its sympathetic treatment of the tragic effects of AIDS on a homosexual couple.

Garrison Keillor (American novelist and essayist)—Host of the popular radio program "A Prairie Home Companion," Keillor gained widespread recognition and praise for his best-selling novel, *Lake Wobegon Days.*

Etheridge Knight (American poet, short story writer, and editor)—Knight published his first collection of poetry, *Poems from Prison,* while serving a sentence in the Indiana State Prison. The poems in this and subsequent volumes are rooted in oral tradition and feature common, colloquial language through which Knight conveys messages of social protest.

Tim O'Brien (American novelist)—Winner of the National Book Award for his novel *Going After Cacciato,* O'Brien focuses on the theme of nuclear annihilation and social issues of the post-World War II era in his latest work, *The Nuclear Age.*

Konstantin Paustovsky (Russian fiction and nonfiction writer)—Paustovsky's six-volume autobiography, *The Story of a Life,* received considerable attention in both the Soviet Union and the West. This work chronicles his life against a historical background that includes World War I, the Bolshevik Revolution, and the Stalin purges.

Muriel Spark (Scottish-born novelist, short story writer, poet, and nonfiction writer)—Spark is best known for her witty satires which probe themes related to morality. Her recent novels include *Loitering with Intent* and *The Only Problem.*

Kurt Vonnegut, Jr. (American novelist, short story writer, and critic)—This prolific and popular author of the novel *Slaughterhouse-Five* satirizes contemporary America and Darwinism in his recent novel, *Galapagos,* which several critics consider one of his finest works.

Diane Wakoski (American poet and critic)—In her poetry Wakoski often depicts an ongoing search for fulfillment that frequently leads to loss and betrayal. Her latest books include *The Magician's Feastletters* and *The Collected Greed: Parts 1-13.*

Reinaldo Arenas (Cuban novelist and poet)—Censored by the Cuban government for his controversial fiction and poetry and for his homosexuality, Arenas now lives and works in the United States. His recent acclaimed novel, *Farewell to the Sea,* recounts the psychic struggles of a disillusioned writer and his wife.

Ray Bradbury (American short story writer, poet, scriptwriter, novelist, dramatist, and author of children's books)—Best known for his popular and acclaimed science fiction and fantasy short stories, Bradbury recently published a detective story, *Death Is a Lonely Business*, which is his first novel in twenty-three years.

Moerly Callaghan (Canadian novelist, short story writer, essayist, and dramatist)—Described by Edmund Wilson as "perhaps the most unjustly neglected novelist in the English-speaking world," Callaghan has been active in literature for over sixty years. His latest novel, *Our Lady of the Snows*, like much of his work, is characterized by its journalistic prose style, ironic tone, and moralistic themes.

T.S. Eliot (American-born English poet, critic, dramatist, and essayist)—One of the most important literary figures of the twentieth century, Eliot is recognized as a major contributor to the modern age in poetry and criticism. The twentieth anniversary of Eliot's death has sparked renewed evaluation of his achievements.

Carlos Fuentes (Mexican novelist, dramatist, short story writer, essayist, and critic)—In his internationally acclaimed works, Fuentes draws upon Mexican history and legend to explore and define the identity of his homeland. Among his most recent novels are *The Old Gringo* and *Distant Relations*.

Eugene Ionesco (Rumanian-born French dramatist, essayist, scriptwriter, and novelist)—One of the most renowned exponents of the Theater of the Absurd, Ionesco employs exaggeration and black humor to explore the alienation of individuals searching for meaning in an irrational and meaningless world.

Peter Levi (English poet, novelist, travel writer, and editor)—A former Jesuit priest whose poetry often employs such Elizabethan and classical forms as the sonnet and the elegy, Levi has also written two adventure novels, *Head in the Soup* and *Grave Witness.*

Janet Lewis (American novelist, poet, short story writer, dramatist, and author of children's books)—The author of *The Wife of Martin Guerre* and other acclaimed historical novels, Lewis has also gained considerable respect for her poetry about the Ojibway and Navajo tribes of North America.

Ross Macdonald (American novelist, short story writer, essayist, and autobiographer)—A prolific and popular author of detective fiction, Macdonald is best known as the creator of sleuth Lew Archer. In his recent volume of essays, *Self-Portrait: Ceaselessly into the Past*, Macdonald examines his long career and the geneses of his novels.

Boris Pasternak (Russian poet, novelist, short story writer, essayist, and autobiographer)—Best known in the United States for his novel *Doctor Zhivago,* Pasternak is also highly regarded for his poetry, which is often associated with the Symbolist and Futurist movements.

Anne Rice (American novelist and critic)—The author of the popular novel *Interview with the Vampire*, Rice has recently published *The Vampire Lestat,* the second installment of *The Vampire Chronicles.*

Nayantara Sahgal (Indian novelist, short story writer, autobiographer, and nonfiction writer)—Sahgal's writings are noted for their insightful portraits of life in contemporary India. Her recent novels, *Rich Like Us* and *Plans for Departure*, are considered important additions to her canon.

The Year in Review

The Year in Fiction

by John Blades

Judging strictly by the headlines, 1985 couldn't have helped but be disheartening—even distressing—for those who put a high value on fiction as an art rather than a commodity. As never before, American publishers seemed to be gripped by the profit motive, determined not only to produce blockbusters but to launch them with maximum impact.

The biggest of these was Jean M. Auel's *The Mammoth Hunters,* the third in her series of "Earth's Children" novels. The news about Auel's fiction was not so much whether it was good or bad—though critics did seem to agree that it was eons away in quality from her first Cro-Magnon epic, *The Clan of the Cave Bear*—but that it had set a publishing record with a first printing of a million copies. In the process, Auel's novel beat—by 250,000 copies—the previous record-holder, James Michener's equally mammoth diorama, *Texas,* published a few months earlier. Meantime, Bantam Books was claiming yet another record—the $1 million they paid Sally Beauman for her first novel, *Destiny,* was claimed to be the highest for a writer without a "track record."

But American publishers weren't so bewitched by the forces of commerce (or darkness) as the evidence superficially seemed to indicate. The real bottom line is that there were more good works of fiction in 1985—short story collections as well as novels—than anyone had reason to expect. If Auel's book, for example, ended the year on a mercenary note, it began with the publication of two novels of exceptionally high quality, one by an unknown, the other by a writer who had been producing exceptional novels for more than a decade.

The first of these was Carolyn Chute, whose *The Beans of Egypt, Maine,* was a horrifyingly funny detour into the backwoods of modern New England, a region the author herself calls home. Chute's episodic story and her savage but empathetic portraits of the rural poor didn't please everyone, especially not her neighbors; but whatever the book's imperfections, there was no contesting the force and prodigality of the author's writing talents.

The veteran novelist was Don DeLillo, whose *White Noise* was considered his finest work by most critics, including judges of The American Book Awards, who gave him the top prize in fiction. Like Chute's novel, this combined sobering realism with savage satire, but the characters and the milieu could scarcely have been further apart. Set on a Midwestern campus, the book dealt with the high-tech anxiety and death obsessions of a professor of Hitler studies, his wife and children, and various academic colleagues, during a "toxic event" (a deadly gas leakage).

The excellence of DeLillo's book was also recognized by the National Book Critics Circle, whose membership nominated it as one of the five most distinguished novels of 1985. The award itself, however, went to Anne Tyler, another novelist many felt had reached her apogee, in this case with *The Ac-cidental Tourist,* the story of a travel writer whose eccentricities lead him down an offbeat romantic path, after a painful marital breakup and the even more painful death of his son. While written with Tyler's customary economy and skill, and displaying her customary affection for her odd characters, the book was not received with universal affection; a good many critics found it painfully contrived and full of artificial sweeteners, a situation tragicomedy.

A strong runnerup in the NBCC judging was Larry McMurtry's *Lonesome Dove,* his longest, most ambitious, and, by consensus, best novel. Among other things, it proved that there's still plenty of life and energy left in the old-fashioned Western, supposedly a moribund genre for at least a decade. This long, tall tale of a cattle drive from Texas to Montana was crowded with stock characters—hard-riding Texas Rangers, drunken gamblers, deadly Indians, pure-hearted whores—and cliche situations, but McMurtry managed to make it all seem original and convincing, not to mention funny and moving, unlike Michener's dead-in-its-tracks *Texas*.

Yet another remarkable frontier novel was Hugh Nissenson's *A Tree of Life,* though it couldn't have been more different, in size or scope, from either the McMurtry or the Michener books. In fact, it was less an historical than a spiritual novel. Set in a much earlier American West (Ohio during the early 19th Century), this was a bleak, spare, humorless book that took the form of a journal, in which a farmer/minister recorded not just the external details of pioneer life (the price of nails, for example) but his own internal anguish—a crisis of faith, the temptations of the flesh, and other Bergmanesque concerns.

There were several other historical novels worthy of mention; John Calvin Batchelor's *American Falls,* a straightforward but stylish story of espionage during the Civil War; and Cormac McCarthy's *Blood Meridian,* a disturbing and ultraviolent tale of Indian warfare in the 1850s Southwest. Skipping many decades ahead into a much more placid era of America's past, there was E. L. Doctorow's autobiographical novella, *World's Fair,* about a boy (named Edgar) growing up in the Bronx at the time of the 1939 exposition. It was well reviewed, but its slender charms and consciously prosaic writing made the book seem nearly weightless in comparison to the versatile Doctorow's more substantial and poetic work, such as *The Book of Daniel* and *Loon Lake*.

Richard Powers also drew on historic materials—most obviously a classic pre-World War I photograph by August Sander—as the foundation and inspiration for his *Three Farmers on Their Way to a Dance,* perhaps the year's most impressive first novel (and the single one to be nominated for an NBCC fiction prize); with its three intersecting stories and extensive moral/philosophical/historical digressions, however, the book often seemed disjointed and ruminative, for all its brilliant prose and intellectual legerdemain.

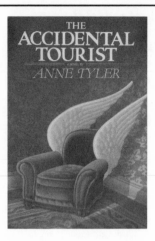

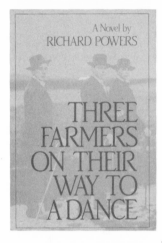

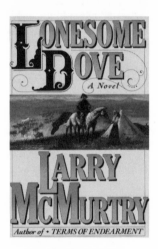

Dust jacket of Blood Meridian; or, The Evening Redness in the West, *by Cormac McCarthy. Random House, 1985. Courtesy of Random House, Inc. Dust jacket of* Lonesome Dove, *by Larry McMurtry. Simon and Schuster, 1985. Copyright © by Larry McMurtry. Courtesy of Simon & Schuster, Inc. Dust jacket of* Three Farmers on Their Way to a Dance, *by Richard Powers. Beech Tree Books, 1985. Courtesy of Beech Tree Books (A Division of William Morrow & Company, Inc.). Frontispiece © The Estate of August Sander. Courtesy of The Sander Gallery, New York, NY. Dust jacket of* The Accidental Tourist, *by Anne Tyler. Knopf, 1985. Courtesy of Alfred A. Knopf, Inc.*

Powers's unassuming book took critics by surprise, which was not the case with award-winning short story writer Bobbie Ann Mason's *In Country,* one of the year's most heralded first novels. All the advance publicity may have been counterproductive, however, because this honest, touching but somewhat drab and enervated story—which dealt with a teen-aged girl's attempt to find some meaning in the Vietnam War—earned respectful but not overwhelmingly enthusiastic critical notice.

Ann Beattie, whose incisive short stories have made her one of the most admired (and imitated) writers of her generation, was not at her best, either, with the novel, *Love Always;* indeed, she seemed distinctly out of her element in this mock soap-operatic farce that centered around a dizzy, advice-to-the-lovelorn columnist and her colleagues on a slick exurban-living magazine. Yet another distinctive writer of short stories, Frederick Barthelme, published a brisk novella, *Tracer,* and even

though the characters had a bizarre charm, as they acted out assorted marital and extramarital misadventures at Florida resorts, the story didn't have much tensile strength when stretched to book length.

While temporarily forsaken by such accomplished practitioners as Mason, Beattie, and Barthelme, the short story was scarcely allowed to fall into neglect; if for nothing else, 1985 was distinguished for the abundance and variety of its short fiction. Perhaps the most distinguished of these was *The Old Forest and Other Stories,* a generous sampling from Peter Taylor, whom many readers consider the grandmaster of the form. These were archetypal Taylor stories, stately, traditional, centered on highly cultivated members of the upper or upper-middle classes, usually in Memphis or St. Louis, grappling with economic, social, domestic, and, occasionally, psychological problems.

For some modern readers, Taylor's stories are *too* stately and traditional, to the point of monotony and dullness. Neither of these, however, are criticisms that could be applied to George Garrett, another older master whose **An Evening Performance and Other Stories** brought together his best short work of 30 years, which seemed nearly infinite in voice and subject: from Gothic comedy to Faulknerian tragedy to both rural and urban alienation.

Another highly unconventional writer, Grace Paley, published her third collection, **Later the Same Day,** which was immediately recognizable for its breezy language and quirkily appealing characters, especially Paley's alter ego, Faith. While it was generously praised, many critics seemed to feel that it wasn't quite as captivating or consequential as her previous two books.

Mid-Air marked the return of Frank Conroy, twenty years after his autobiographical landmark, **Stop-Time,** with stories that seemed to reinforce, rather than enlarge upon, themes of that earlier book. In her second book of stories, **The Bus of Dreams,** Mary Morris gave us understated portraits of youthful lovers and middle-aged dreamers, glimpses of what one critic called "pent-up romantic longing."

Perhaps the most successful debut of the year in the short story was that of Bob Shacochis, whose **Easy in the Islands** not only brought him comparisons with Conrad and Graham Greene, among others, but an American Book Award for first fiction. Alice Adams' **Return Trips** represented some of her finest short work, stories of characters struggling to make sense of their pasts.

However, the charmingly erratic Barry Hannah simply seemed erratic in **Captain Maximus,** a book that one critic called a "publishing mistake." Among the other collections that helped prove the vitality of the short story were those by Tobias Wolff (**Back in the World**), Amy Hempel (**Reasons to Live**), Stephen King (**Skeleton Crew**), Sharon Sheehe Stark (**The Dealer's Yard**), T. Coraghessan Boyle (**Greasy Lake**), and Lorrie Moore (**Self-Help**), to cite only a few.

Shifting the focus back to longer fiction, 1985 was a vintage year for vintage writers, whose new work may not have made readers forget previous triumphs but was welcome and worthwhile nonetheless. Foremost among these was Kurt Vonnegut, whose **Galapagos** was not only a healthy best seller but an evolutionary tour de farce that took readers a million years into the future, a post-apocalyptic vision that was more whimsical than depressing. In **The Call,** John Hersey returned to his birth-

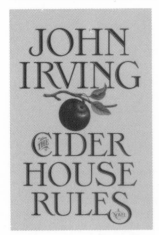

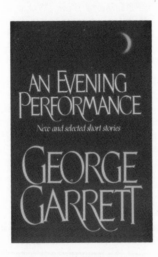

Dust jacket of The Cider House Rules, *by John Irving. Morrow, 1985. Copyright © 1985 by Garp Enterprises Ltd. Courtesy of William Morrow & Company, Inc. Dust jacket of* The Bus of Dreams, *by Mary Morris. Houghton Mifflin, 1985. Jacket illustration copyright © 1985 by David Tamura. Used by permission of Houghton Mifflin Company. Dust jacket of* The Old Forest and Other Stories, *by Peter Taylor. The Dial Press, 1985. Dust jacket of* An Evening Performance, *by George Garrett. Doubleday, 1985. Both reproduced courtesy of Doubleday & Company, Inc.*

place, China, to tell at great length the story of the country's entry into the 20th century, as seen by an American missionary couple. Herman Wouk's *Inside, Outside* was also autobiographical fiction, relating the author's upward struggle from Bronx ghetto to Columbia University to naval duty in World War II.

If for no other reason, William Gaddis's *Carpenter's Gothic* was remarkable for its brevity; at 200 pages it was little more than a broadside by comparison with the author's other monuments, *The Recognitions* and *JR;* but it had numerous other virtues: an expressionist, claustrophobic, inhuman comedy, it was also a furious and splenetic denunciation of all that is wrong with contemporary America, and much of the world.

Russell Banks, a fine if not sufficiently appreciated writer, had one of the year's most deservedly praised novels with *Conti-*

nental Drift, which told of a tragic convergence in the lives of a Florida charter-boat captain and a Haitian refugee. After the nearly insufferable whimsy of his previous novel, *The Hotel New Hampshire,* John Irving's *The Cider House Rules* seemed especially engaging and amiable, even though it was set in a New England orphanage and was concerned, to a great degree, with abortion. Stanley Elkin took considerable risks with *The Magic Kingdom,* which followed seven fatally ill children through Disney World, a novel that mixed pathos, comedy, and grotesquerie, not always successfully.

For many, Mary Gordon's *Men and Angels* was even better than her celebrated first novel, *Final Payments;* this was an unusually (but, for Gordon, typically) somber work that ranged over questions of maternity, art, and religious obsessions. Obsessions of another kind—those of a young girl for a woman who almost unwittingly becomes her tutor—dominated Gail Godwin's *The Finishing School,* a psychological detective story with (deliberate?) overtones of Daphne DuMaurier. Ursula LeGuin's staggering *Always Coming Home,* packaged with a complementary audiocassette recording of songs and poetry, was undeniably impressive—it was nominated for an American Book Award—but more as a work of fictional anthropology than as anthropological fiction.

Jay McInerney's second novel, *Ransom,* was a best-selling paperback original, like his first, *Bright Lights, Big City,* a seriocomic excursion through New York's cocaine culture; *Ransom,* however, was a world apart in style and locale, a martial-arts melodrama set in Japan. An old hand at melodrama, Elmore Leonard, scored with what the publishing industry likes to call a "breakthrough" book, *Glitz,* a best-selling revenge story that was written with the author's flawless ear for tough-guy idiom and with his unerring skill at creating believably creepy villains.

Ray Bradbury published his first novel in more than a quarter-century, not science fiction but a detective story, *Death Is a Lonely Business,* which was less successful as a mystery than an homage (occasionally an unintentional parody) of Raymond Chandler and other Southern California *noir* novelists.

Garrison Keillor's first novel, *Lake Wobegon Days,* besides being a huge best seller was a skillful recycling and elaboration of material developed on his popular National Public Radio show, the *Prairie Home Companion*: homespun satire but with a scattering of dark threads.

There was so much remarkable fiction published during 1985 that it seems necessary to conclude by merely listing a few of the more remarkable books, an honor roll that includes Gloria Naylor's *Linden Hills,* Julius Lester's *Do Lord Remember Me,* Tom Robbins's *Jitterbug Perfume,* Denis Johnson's *Fiskadoro,* Lee Smith's *Family Linen,* Elizabeth Tallent's *Museum Pieces,* Thomas Berger's *Nowhere,* Joyce Carol Oates's *Solstice,* and, finally, four books of uncommon interest from Chicago writers: Lore Segal's *Her First American,* Charles Dickinson's *Crows,* Jan Novak's *The Willys Dream Kit,* and James McManus's *Chin Music.*

It would, no doubt, be just as easy to draw up a dishonor roll of 1985 fiction, but in a year with so much to sing about, why end on a downbeat note?

　　　　　　　　　　　　　　　　　　　　　　　Book Critic
　　　　　　　　　　　　　　　　　　　　　　Chicago Tribune

The Year in Poetry

by Dave Smith

One hundred years ago, in 1885, Ezra Pound was born to tell poets "make it new." The Modernists, William Carlos Williams (b.1883) and T. S. Eliot (b.1888) especially, whom Pound spoke for, faced a radically changed and changing world. In the end, these writers proved as thoroughly modern as Millie and as revolutionary as Rotarians: if they roared forward to claim the "new," they faced backward to secure a heritage. They questioned the nature and function of poetry itself, seeking a right form in all the facsimiles. To understand their anxiety we need only look at our own age: technology is replacing television, telephones, records, automobiles, and hand-delivered mail; our bodies become bionic; our lives grow extended, eased, enhanced. Yet everywhere wars, guerilla lunacy, disease, poverty, spiritual hunger, and fear dominate. Everything we have known blurs. Can poetry express this world?

In 1985 poets stand again at the edge of joyful possibility and dismal sameness. But ours is not a climate of the "new" in poetry; rather, a conservatism grips us in form and vision. Reminiscent of the quiet 1950s, the 1980s appear to prefer a poetry of rationality, subdued emotion, disengagement from public issues, with a "disappeared" speaker whose voice is startlingly metrical, stanzaically sculpted and tidy, whose great concern is domestic tranquillity. The wildly various poetries of the 1960s-70s decade which enfranchised all causes, all forms, and all ethnic sides seems safely sequestered. While many books continue to deliver the jolting beauty and truth we expect, many others lack passion and content themselves with a miniaturist art whose appeal is primarily to small, esoteric audiences. In these the heroes of consciousness remain, ironically, revolutionary poets, painters, musicians who have become the tradition. The books I have reviewed below are only a portion of those submitted to me from the 1985 crop, representing those I consider the best poetry, not most exemplary of these trends. Those listed as "Recommended" were, I thought, worthy of mention but less compelling than those reviewed.

Younger American Poets

The youngest poets are ordinarily the brash, the restless, the idealistic who are furious with the energies of change in a callously indifferent universe. Arthur Smith, winner of the 1984 Agnes Lynch Starrett Poetry Prize for *Elegy on Independence Day* (University of Pittsburgh Press), shows the surprising quietism in favor with "It is good, I think, / To be sitting in a warm room / While the lawn whitens with frost." If, despite Coleridge, this is banal, Smith's elegiac gift remains seductively celebrative in poems like "Twelve Pole" and "Hurricane Warning." In *Henry Purcell in Japan* (Knopf) Mary Jo Salter proves the prototype new poet. Her Anglicized diction prefers "queing" to the American "standing in line." Pentameter pages, fastidious bric-a-brac scenic descriptions, and sentimentality (a bee's death is called "murder") suggest the chat up character of English verse that has little subject and less force, though parlors-full of skill and grace. Kathy Fagan's

The Raft (Dutton), one of five National Poetry Series winners, views poetry as something much more flexible, something that drifts more than finishes. Every poem has sharp intelligence and talent, but too many wind up posturing, wanting things like "the withheld breast that is this life" and moaning over its absence. Matisse is her painter. Monet is Janet Sylvester's. *That Mulberry Wine* (Wesleyan University Press), like Fagan and Salter, sometimes lapses into a humm, but it has an unusual punch in wry fables of a resilient woman who has survived family, sexual initiation, physical abuse, and travels in the country. This is a fine first collection.

Three first books from 1985 favor traditional verse but employ it to achieve original expression. *The Unlovely Child* (Knopf) is an auspicious debut by Norman Williams, a lawyer by trade. He makes verse a liberator of feeling and turns a trip to a barber shop into a ritual experience. His descriptions of smelt-fishers are runic and sharp as fresh-minted brail. Still, Williams's strength, a historical consciousness, sometimes suckers him into easy generalization. Eric Pankey has the same problem in a more untraditional verse. His *For the New Year* (Atheneum) won the 1984 Walt Whitman Award. Often reminiscent of Norman Dubie, Pankey writes anecdotal narratives which turn out to be private meditations with a sly and ghostly compulsion the reader follows as effortlessly as a bird's flight. "The Guard: 1934" is a haunting look at responsibility. In *Saints & Strangers* (Houghton Mifflin) Andrew Hudgins shows a fine ear for memorably pulsed traditional verse but, like Eric Pankey, he joins this to invented dramatic monologues (Sidney Lanier, Audubon, Zelda Fitzgerald, etc) which sometimes seem more precious than pressured. His painter is, gulp, Botticelli. Granting his first-book infelicities, Hudgins, I think, sees a deeper, more complicated world than most, wants to say it accurately, and knows whatever we yearn for comes only at cost, if at all. His gift seems Bosch-like:

> The birds outside the stained-glass windows
> brawl and copulate beneath the eaves—
> what dark spasmodic shapes they make
> behind the thieves and bright crucifixion!
> "The Stoker's Sunday Morning"

Many poets hope for successively better books and few are so rewarded. Rodney Jones's *The Unborn* (Atlantic Monthly Press) shows how hard work makes luck. His second book, *The Unborn,* combines countryman wit, narrative ease, and a superior clarity to make memories become metaphors. Poems about Edison, Thoreau, laundromats, and unpainted houses suggest he can write about anything. Baron Wormser's gifts make him a satiric moralist whose second collection, *Good Trembling* (Houghton Mifflin), is cunning, funny, and sharply epigrammatic ("Poems are gestures swallowed by history"). His painter is Matisse. Elizabeth Spires is not a verse poet and shows no favorite painter in *Swan's Island* (Holt Rinehart Winston), although a culture consciousness is pronounced in her work.

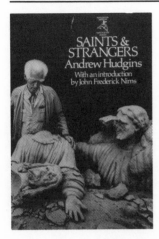
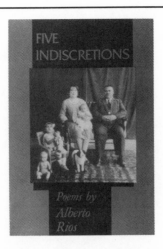

Dust jacket of Saints & Strangers, *by Andrew Hudgins. Houghton Mifflin, 1985. Jacket photo: Vandalized sculpture of "The Last Supper." Bibleland, California, 1979. Tom Kasser © 1980. Dust jacket of* Five Indiscretions, *by Albert Rios. Sheep Meadow Press, 1985. Courtesy of The Sheep Meadow Press. Dust jacket of* Henry Purcell in Japan, *by Mary Jo Salter. Knopf, 1985. Jacket typography by Candy Jernigan. © 1985 Alfred A. Knopf, Inc. Dust jacket of* The Unlovely Child, *by Norman Williams. Knopf, 1985. Jacket design by Francine Kass. Jacket painting by Joseph Whiting. © 1985 by Alfred A. Knopf, Inc. Both reproduced courtesy of the publisher.*

Spires's second book is attractively readable and more than accomplished, but one does grow wearied by relentless art appreciation. If she gives good art, Alberto Rios gives poetic prose that often rises to poetry in his *Five Indiscretions* (Sheep Meadow Press). A salute to Chicano culture as much as a quest for identity, his tales are quasi-mythical venerations of heros—boxers, wrestlers, wise elders, lovers—who compose a darker romance than any ethnic experience. Marilyn Nelson Waniek knows and dramatizes black American life in *Mama's Promises* (Louisiana State University Press). Extremely lyrical, drawn from dreams and memories, her poems are as prosy as those instructional fables from our childhood—and as sweetly elegaic. They praise the mothers of the earth and compose a kind of gospel in which feeling and dignity are *the* civic virtues, a gospel of preparation, not salvation. Waniek's home-songs are wise and beautiful in *Mama's Promises.*

Paula Rankin's *To the House Ghost* (Carnegie-Mellon University Press) catalogs the insults to the soul that come with contemporary life. This third collection is her best. Bruce Wiegl's fourth collection, *The Monkey Wars* (University of Georgia Press) focuses those insults on the effect of industrial society upon people and the natural world. He shows an expanded range, increased technical skills, and a wholly winning lyric tenderness. More than anyone, he has become the poetic voice of the Vietnam memory with such powerful poems as "Burning Shit at An Khe" and "Song of Napalm." Yet he is never a poet of accusation or polemic, constructing his poems as near-confessions whose effect is to celebrate the individual and lonely wars of all creatures to survive:

> You lie back on the stoop and hear the evening
> Of birdsong rise and fall
> And only a few black wings roll past.
>
> 　　　　　　　　　　　　　　　"The Ghost Inside"

The Monkey Wars is among the most distinguished of 1985's collections of poetry. Another in that category is Carole Oles's *Night Watches* (alicejamesbooks). Oles investigates the spirit of the nineteenth-century astronomer and Vassar professor, Maria Mitchell, through a sequence of historically informed but "invented" moments which, not surprisingly, look to the stars for truths. *Night Watches* joins two visionaries to create a heroic tale of feminist consciousness and the result is first-rate poetry. Michael Harper's chronicle of insults is viewed through the lens of blackness in his eighth collection, *Healing Song for the Inner Ear* (University of Illinois Press). Harper's poems throb with anger at social injustice, lash out at their enemies, but do not sloganeer. Beneath them is a Whitmanic tenderness that links the embattled Black to the soul beyond color. Harper has never been sharper.

Larry Levis, a leading voice of his generation, reveals a Whitmanic line that loops, sprawls, and veers through poems of narrative cores fused into lyrical riffs in *Winter Stars* (University of Pittsburgh Press). His poetry of race tracks, jazz clubs, and American dreams may prove too thickly textured for some, but it is a complex, moving art which demands hearing. David St. John's *No Heaven* (Houghton Mifflin), a third book, offers narrative similar to Levis's but in more privately patterned language—like a telephone conversation breaking up with static. St. John is a musical and meditative poet, one for whom meeting Lenny Bruce is not a matter of what happened but of what it felt like. His is a singular voice, sometimes the symphony, sometimes the tuning up. That obliquity purified to passionate reticence characterizes Louise Glück in *The Triumph of Achilles* (ECCO). In her art we are moved by speech before we understand it. The poems brood with a sexual-intellectual energy as bright as hard polyurethane. This energy is delivered by cadences of curt, clipped lines that draw us to her, then push us away. This is a poetry of flirtation teasing up a deep and paralyzing subject, the constant struggle of hungers—"one serves the other, one is less than the other"—which is the dynamic of all human relationships. Flesh works to possess flesh; art works to know truth. So Glück implies. But, bitterly, she foreknows truth as illusory and flesh as fatal. In the end this chilling, calculating, obdurate, extraordinarily fine poet labors for and indicts love, the human weakness. She says, "I lie awake; I feel / actual flesh upon me, / meaning to silence me." *The Triumph of Achilles* shows why few of her generation rival her.

RECOMMENDED: John Allman, *Clio's Children* (New Directions); Ralph Burns, *Any Given Day* (Univ. of Alabama

Press); Christopher Jane Corkery, *Blessing* (Princeton Univ. Press); Ken Gerner, *Throwing Shadows* (Copper Canyon Press); Linda Gregg, *Alma* (Random House); William Hathaway, *Fish, Flesh, & Fowl* (Louisiana State Univ. Press); Jonathan Holden, *The Names of the Rapids* (Univ. of Massachusetts Press); Linda McCarriston, *Talking Soft Dutch* (Texas Tech Univ. Press); Richard Michelson, *Tap Dancing for the Relatives* (Univ. of Florida Press); Peggy Shumaker, *Esperanza's Hair* (Univ. of Alabama Press); Nancy Simpson, *Night Student* (State Street Press); Bruce Smith, *Silver and Information* (Univ. of Georgia Press); Gary Soto, *Black Hair* (Univ. of Pittsburgh Press); Jeanie Thompson, *How to Enter the River* (Holy Cow! Press); Michael Rosen, *A Drink at the Mirage* (Princeton Univ. Press)

Contemporaries

By "contemporaries" I refer to those poets above the age of 45 who have what is called a secure reputation for poetry. John Updike, the novelist, writes poems as apparently playful entertainments. *Facing Nature* (Knopf), his fifth collection, teases us with Rockettes, rot, riddles, and generally debunks writerly suffering. Still, Updike's is a relentlessly nasty world barely confronted through wit, leer, and intelligence. "Another Dog's Death" and "Accumulation" show him to be a poet who writes some fiction. Frederick Turner's *The New World* (Princeton University Press) invites fiction to wear poetry's clothes in an epic that, as Dr. Johnson said of *Paradise Lost,* none would wish longer. Descended from weird tales, science fiction, and horror movies, *The New World* comes admirably ambitious, impressively coherent, and often neatly laid. But, less cosmic than comic in Darth Vader's shadow, this volks-hymn is sometimes metaphorically plodding. A new world. Sort of. James Merrill's magnum opus, *The Changing Light at Sandover,* swept American awards in poetry. It combined literary mugging, graphic hocus pocus, and a talking ouija board for an epic vision of our century. Some said. Others allowed Merrill transformed poetry to a parlor game as boring as charades. The same opinions fit *Late Settings* (Atheneum), a book remarkable for resourceful rhymes, predictable tunes, a surprising snappishness, and two memorable poems—one about a manatee, one about a collapsed table. Merrill resembles an aging athlete: great technique, grace abounding, but moves that lack consequence. Or do they?

The punch of consequence is Faye Kicknosway's intention in *Who Shall Know Them?* (Viking), poems about characters "imagined from the photos of Walker Evans." As the verbal equivalents of Evans's images of raw experience, these poems at first move us but their hectoring, patchy language fades like a country fighter with a boxer. That's why Kicknosway's art can't, finally, make us know these people as people. Maxine Kumin does that in *The Long Approach* (Viking), her seventh collection, with superior ancestor-portraits, some near-condescending snapshots of Southern grits, and more of her mea culpa hymns to nature. Kumin, a terrific poet, is sometimes a driven apologist whose lyrics wobble under their burden of righteousness before age, disease, anti-Semitism, racism, poverty, rudeness, crudeness, insensitivity, etc. She wants us to do right, so lectures—but sings in "My Elusive Guest," "The Long Approach," and a few more. The large hurts she feels in her large way are more personal in Carl Dennis's *The Near World* (William Morrow), his fourth book. In "Puritans" he says "They wanted the big prize, bliss everlasting, / And knew they couldn't earn it, being human." His soft-spoken narrative scenes consistently reveal him caught in that trap and looking around with steady love, humor, and a scrupulous courage.

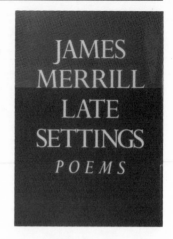

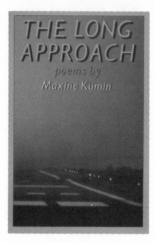

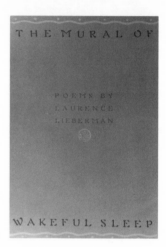

Dust jacket of The Long Approach, *by Maxine Kumin. Viking, 1985. Jacket photograph by Charles Feil. By permission of Charles Feil. Dust jacket of* The Mural of Wakeful Sleep, *by Laurence Lieberman. Macmillan, 1985. Jacket © 1985 Macmillan Publishing Company, a Division of Macmillan, Inc. Used by permission of Macmillan Publishing Company. Dust jacket of* Late Settings, *by James Merrill. Atheneum, 1985. Copyright © 1985 James Merrill. Reprinted with the permission of Atheneum Publishers, Inc. Dust jacket of* Facing Nature, *by John Updike. Knopf, 1985. Jacket design by John Updike and Francine Kass. © 1985 Alfred A. Knopf, Inc. Courtesy of the publisher.*

Dennis is a true poet. Linda Pastan writes brief poems and lines. Like headlights they flare and leave the mind slowly. *A Fraction of Darkness* (Norton), her sixth book, is less narrative, more image-centered than previous volumes. Pastan treats language like an old vacuum cleaner that still works—it's plain but functional. Always a poet of ironic edges, of griefs, she writes increasingly of sickness, the dead, the loving company in the memory, the world that betrays its promises when "the sun drops / its rusted padlock / into place."

Among poets in mid-career in 1985, five speak what has been called a midwestern voice (see Lucian Stryk, *Heartland I & II*). An intense awareness of land, weather, and human fragility, a celebration of common virtues, a straining against inevitable limitations, an imagistic and texture-stripped free verse mark a poetry rich in the rebukes and aspirations of a historical consciousness. What is the nature of this place? This life? these poets ask. Ted Kooser, an insurance executive, praises "God / walking the bean rows" in his *One World at a Time* (University of Pittsburgh Press). Constance Urdang's *Only the World* (University of Pittsburgh Press) ironically notes "This is the country. Of everyone's dreams, from which there is no escape." Donald Finkel's most lyrical collection, *The Detachable Man* (Atheneum), echoes Urdang, his wife, when he describes "the St. Louis of the soul" and says "All day the sun gleams on the parching cornfields / like a fat gold tooth in a sky-blue grin." The historical inhabitants of that midwestern space have long been Thomas McGrath's subjects, as well as the North Dakota ancestral spirit he evokes when "Dreaming . . . / waking . . . / I hear a distant animal voice— / Either a farmhouse dog or a night-beast deep in the woods." Parts three and four of his long poem *Letter to an Imaginary Friend* (Copper Canyon) compose a welcome report for many readers who dote on his long-lined, near-mythical, sonorous travelogue. Yet it cannot be more welcome than John Knoepfle's *Poems from the Sangamon* (University of Illinois Press). Knoepfle (pronounced No-full) is absolutely unpretentious, has an ear finely tuned to the ironies and idioms of men and women, and writes with an efficient precision that is wonderful. Of the subdivisions gobbling up midwestern plains: "country trail subdivision / sign says it sucks"; of a concert of unimaginative musicians: "they ping and ping and ping / ping ping and ping"; of ordinary responsibility: "let us stand with anybody / who stands right"; and of the candidate for princess of the county fair, the sap and truth of our spirit:

> I am the gnawed bone of my
> fathers desire the starlight
> of my mothers dreaming
> I am the bean blossom of their
> happy needfulness

Sap and truth might be the very words to describe Laurence Lieberman and Philip Levine, also midwesterners. Lieberman's *The Mural of Wakeful Sleep* (Macmillan) is perhaps the surprise of poetry's year. His best book, it fuses the travelogue's eye for detail, color, and idiosyncracy with poetry's patterns as the poet passes through Jamaica, Nassau, Barbados, St. Lucia, and elsewhere. The title poem, about a huge church mural done by a native artist overcomes the plangency that threatens Lieberman's poems and soars as a hymn to art and joy. In a quite different form, Philip Levine's "Sweet Will" and "A Poem with No Ending" show another hymn to joy. Levine is our acknowledged voice of the City of Engines, the soul of toughness. He is best with an anger that modulates to declarations of solidarity, even love. The poems of *Sweet Will* (Atheneum), his eleventh collection, have less anger, more contentment, and seem not always sure of what they are—like a man in sneakers and three-piece gray. Similarly, the scenes vacillate from Detroit to Europe, but nod toward California. In many ways a transitional book, *Sweet Will* is nevertheless the work of an American master.

Another master, Galway Kinnell, seemed to some not so magical with *Mortal Acts, Mortal Words,* then won the Pulitzer in 1983 for his *Selected Poems,* an unquestionably right choice. His ninth collection, *The Past* (Houghton Mifflin), will surely remove anyone's reservations. Excepting his *The Book of Nightmares,* this is Kinnell's best book. His poetry is, as always, serious, sometimes solemn, but marked with a new sense of humor, relaxed. He gives splendid vignettes and natural scenes without the salinity of his New England morality. He is that knight of the spirit we expect in lovely elegies for

Richard Hugo and James Wright, although Kinnell the piously stiff still lingers—"Our spouses weaken at the same rate we do." Nevertheless, these lyrical meditations show a man with the world against his skin. He simply overwhelms us with his marriage of word and feeling. Poems big and little ("The Seekonk Woods" and "The Shroud") suggest he may be our preeminent poet. Here's a small sample:

PRAYER

> Whatever happens. Whatever
> *what is* is what
> I want. Only that. But that.

RECOMMENDED: Hayden Carruth, *Asphalt Georgics* (New Directions); Raymond Carver, *Where Water Comes Together with Other Water* (Random House); Leo Connellan, *The Clear Blue Lobster-Water Country* (Harcourt Brace Jovanovich); Patricia Goedicke, *The Wind of Our Going* (Copper Canyon); Robert Hazel, *Soft Coal* (Countryman Press); Cynthia Macdonald, *Alternate Means of Transport* (Knopf); Paul Mariani, *Prime Mover* (Grove Press); Dennis Schmitz, *Singing* (ECCO); John Stone, *Renaming the Streets* (Louisiana State Univ. Press); Anne Waldman, *Skin Meat Bones* (Coffee House Press)

Selected/ Collected

Lorine Niedecker, who died in 1970, was a protegé of Louis Zukofsky's minimalist aesthetics. Her selected poems, *The Granite Pail* (North Point), edited by Cid Corman, sometimes seems 111 pages of smudges on white space, yet she has the remarkable clarity of a water-colorist in work that "took a lifetime / to weep / a deep / trickle" and will, perhaps, now win an audience she has deserved. Robert Hayden died in 1980, widely recognized as America's dean of black poets. His *Collected Poems* (Liveright) ought to be required reading in public schools for the lessons in patience, courage, outrage, civilization, and art which it manifests. Hayden's practice was always "complex and not for the fearful, / simple and not for the foolish." His range was large, his form was classical, and his subject was ordinary people. Readers will find here the masterpieces—"Those Winter Sundays," "Frederick Douglass" and others—but there are marvels among the twenty-four new poems of "American Journal" which ought to become anthology staples, including "The Prisoners," "Double Feature," "Ice Storm," and "Astronauts." Like Niedecker and Hayden, Wendell Berry is a pastoral elegist ("though the green fields are my delight, / elegy is my fate.") Berry's *Collected Poems* (North Point) is ripe with the forces of nature: wind, soil, water, sun, birds. But the poet especially favors cycles of effort, both those of nature and people,—which are planting and harvesting as emblems of a right relationship in the world. Berry hates the corruptive industrial world and proselytizes in poetry that occasionally and bombastically lapses into simplistic agrarian nostalgia, if not politics. Still, he is an enormous lyric talent who when resisting his weaknesses makes art a reified vessel of celebration. No reader will be untouched by his wisdom, clarity, or passion.

More than forty years of poetry are packed into Howard Moss's *New Selected Poems* (Atheneum), where the arcane and the ordinary walk together toward revelation. Moss always means to make the reader *see*. Given a certain elegance, he sounds like a tourist guide and a detective (Poiret), but his voice versatility covers more than bumps in the night and arias of joy. His incredible tote of subjects includes birds, artists, waters, murderers, wigs, cities, trains, magic, mail, money, flowers, family. . . . It's endless. Little wonder he says "I am only trying to teach you / What pleasure is, and also about / The end of things. . . .'' Moss makes writing a kind of brave living, all avuncular, comely, welcome, and surprising as a new discovery. Who else might speak of ''Pollock's wounded linoleum'' or ''the rainpipe drip of snow''? Moss is, as this book shows, a major poet.

Robert Penn Warren is, however, *the* major living American poet. Warren's *New and Selected Poems 1923-1985* (Random House) covers sixty-two years of his poetry and is dominated by poems written in his late seventies. The book asks us to pay keen attention to the elder Warren, to poems of early psychological events, of memories, and to poems narrating the lyrical and dangerous moments of late life—of mountain climbing and swimming and hiking. One expects such poems in young poets, expects bullish vigor, but one yields to it with surprise and delight in Warren the octogenarian. Then one finds, behind the new work, the poetic history of the twentieth century, a history that Warren both lived and made. He began

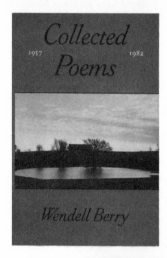

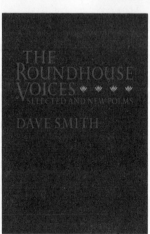

Dust jacket of Collected Poems 1957-1982, *by Wendell Berry. North Point Press, 1985. Jacket design by David Bullen. Jacket photograph © Guy Mendes. Courtesy of North Point Press. Dust jacket of* New Selected Poems, *by Howard Moss. Atheneum, 1985. Copyright © 1985 Howard Moss. Reprinted with the permission of Atheneum Publishers, Inc. Dust jacket of* The Roundhouse Voices, *by Dave Smith. Harper & Row, 1985. Courtesy of Harper & Row, Publishers, Inc.*

publishing while Thomas Hardy lived. Hardy, Yeats, Eliot, Hopkins, Tate, Ransom—these voices echo in Warren as he sweeps forward to find his own sonic character in *Promises* and perfects it in the magnificent *Audubon*. There are those who complain that his newest decade's work sputters, repeats itself, bullies, and settles for platitudes. Truly his latest forty-nine poems, though not the previous three collections, suffer from a decline, yet as part of his *New and Selected Poems,* even the work of ''Altitudes and Extensions'' records the shape of a man's life and the astonishing timbre of a poetry that will cry through many distant woods. Warren should be read as one experiences the ocean or a mountain peak, taken in, known, loved. He is a force of beauty, of courage, of humility before life's grand enigmas:

> You stand in the dark, heart even now filling, and think of
> A boy who, drunk with the perfume of elder blossoms
> And the massiveness of moonrise, stood
> In a lone lane, and cried out,
> In a rage of joy, to seize, and squeeze, significance from,
> What life is, whatever it is. Now
> High above the maples the moon presides. The first bat
> Mathematically zigzags the stars. You fling down
> The cigarette butt. Set heel on it. It is time to go in.
>
>   ''Rumor at Twilight''

RECOMMENDED: Robert Bringhurst, *The Beauty of the Weapons* (Copper Canyon); Kenneth Koch, *Selected Poems* (Random House); Leonard Nathan, *Carrying On: New & Selected Poems* (Univ. of Pittsburgh Press); Dave Smith, *The Roundhouse Voices: Selected and New Poems* (Harper & Row); John Tagliabue, *The Great Day: Poems 1962-1983* (Alembic Press)

Non-American English-Speaking Voices

The books we have received for this review, from the publishers of British and Irish poets, suggest 1985 was a less than luminous year. The British still favor uninspired metrical speech. Andrew Young's *The Poetical Works* (Secker & Warburg), edited by Edward Lowbury and Alison Young, is formally dominated by Thomas Hardy but substitutes for his dark honesty the sweetness of the Georgians and his own pastoralizing god-fear. Young seems never to have heard Pound say ''Make it new'' and neither has Cliff Ashby whose *Plain Song* (Carcanet), a thin collected poems, muddles between god-and-garden chatter and a loose awareness of Philip Larkin as the avant garde. In Ashby one does find an attractive humor, even a lyrical affection—the jazz elegy ''In Memory of Lester Young'' is lovely—but he is wildly uneven, if never so smug and tight as Young. We do not expect humor or affection but the slate chill of God in R. S. Thomas, the Welsh clergyman. That is exactly what the *Poems of R. S. Thomas* (University of Arkansas Press) gives us. Thomas has never had more than an underground American audience for his thirteen previous books, all represented here, with forty-three new poems, but this should now change. His fierce, metallic, almost Viking view of a world ruled by an enigmatic deity seems to ask constantly *Why?* Father Hopkins would have admired Thomas's control, precise phrasing, special gifts for images of scope, and withering self-scrutiny all in service of a world-class passion. ''Thirteen Blackbirds Look at a Man'' shows he has an unexpected humor. Some.

Alison Fell, like R. S. Thomas, rejects the programmatic English sound in *Kisses for Mayakovsky* (Virago). A Scot and a virulent feminist, she echoes the first-person anecdotal poem that is Sylvia Plath's American legacy yet shows a tenderness that sometimes undercuts her message-mongering. Carol Rumens's **Direct Dialing** (Chatto & Windus) is less fleshy, less angry, less free-lance in form but gives a memorable portrait of what Thoreau called the lives of "quiet desperation." Michael Hulse, like Fell and Rumens a younger poet, sometimes affects a Larkinesque cool in **Propaganda** (Secker & Warburg). Alternatively, he marries brutal/vulgar scenes with firm stanzas of rhymed verse as a way of showing the sweet-and-sour of life. He resembles, erratically I think, both James Fenton and Paul Muldoon, but often enough he is himself and is among the most interesting new voices.

Carcanet (distributed by Humanities Press, Atlantic Highlands, NJ) appears to be the most active English poetry press. In 1985 they released C. B. Cox's **Two-Headed Monster,** John Heath-Stubbs's **The Immolation of Aleph,** and Brian Jones's **The Children of Separation.** All are servants of verse, decorous men for whom Prufrock's question of daring would produce, one suspects, a demurral. Cox and Heath-Stubbs are funny, learned, sometimes endearing. Jones is the only contemporary sensibility of the three.

Carcanet's significant gift to readers, however, is something it calls "Poetry Signatures"—a paperback series of the "Selected Poems" (all carry the same title) by Gillian Clarke, Edwin Morgan, Ian Crichton Smith, and Jeffrey Wainwright. Clarke says "My head is full of sound, remembered speech" and it's the speech of her late countryman Dylan Thomas. A compulsive poet, she manages a greater statemental clarity than Thomas while still giving herself to the slip-slide of poetry's music. She is also more introspective, with a foreboding quality that reminds me of Ted Hughes. A pleasant surprise altogether. Edwin Morgan surprises no one, having since 1952 done eleven collections. He adds five new poems here. A Scot, Morgan's formal behavior seems as eccentric and various as his subjects remain predictably historical, literary, or mythical. His poems are like magic—a lot of smoke, a few instants of dazzle. Ian Crichton Smith, another Scot, says his people have "no place for the fine graces / of poetry." He means they (and he) want meat, not puffery. But forewarned of this toughness, we often get polish and intellectual posturing. Smith favors Modernist poems of elliptical form and sequences. Like Whitman, he contradicts himself. But he is not the great graybeard. Jeffrey Wainwright's offering is the thinnest. Also the most oblique, intense, and mannered. Wainwright yearns for lambent purity of speech and has the odd effect of making him sound, regardless of subject, like a half-translated Geoffrey Hill. Still, at best, Wainwright is a remarkable poet, clear and terse and ambitious: "We wade so deep in our desire for good." Sometimes he wades out with the goods.

No one in 1985 claimed more goods than the Canadian Michael Ondaatje in his **Secular Love** (Norton), a solid knockout book. Ondaatje has shown a talent for mixing poetry and prose in his novel, **Coming through Slaughter,** and in the poetry of **The Collected Works of Billy the Kid.** His attraction to blurring generic distinctions represents a boundary-testing akin to his making the psycho-mythic outlaw William Bonney into a hero of sorts. Ondaatje wants poetry loosened up. Sometimes he wants to play the class clown. In **Secular Love** (Norton) he breaks the rules of genre as well as of convention and effectively sets himself outside "real life" where "men talk about art / women judge men . . . ," and he succeeds in creating a voice that is wholly believable. This "voice" tells a love tale

wherein he is bruised, liberated, and disoriented, a condition reinforced by booze consumed and poetics spouted. Ondaatje fuses narrative thrust with lyric receptivity to engender what is in fact a metaphor itself—the book. Inside this outlaw composition one finds tender homages to such poetic precursors as James Wright, Robert Creeley, Lorca, and Rilke. John Wayne and Bogart are thrown in for—well, you know what for. Ondaatje has done what all poets hope to do, taken the oldest and most mysterious subject—love and pain—and made it shimmer with fresh brilliance. If you read poems, you should read **Secular Love.**

Anthologies, Criticism, & Etc.

Anthologies represent windows erected by editors: what you get is only what they saw. **The Morrow Anthology of Younger American Poets** (William Morrow Co.), edited by Dave Smith and David Bottoms, collects 104 poets forty-five and younger and may be viewed as a group portrait of America's best hopes in poetry. **The Bread Loaf Anthology of Contemporary American Poetry** (University Press of New England), edited by Robert Pack, Sydney Lea, and Jay Parini, collects 72 poets who have been associated with the Bread Loaf Writers Conference in Vermont. Most controversial of the new anthologies is **The Harvard Book of Contemporary American Poetry** (Harvard University Press), edited by critic Helen Vendler. Beginning with Wallace Stevens, it collects only 35 poets, excludes Levine, Kinnell, Warren, Kumin, Van Duyn, Kizer, etc, to end with Rita Dove. Vendler's choices are, well, her choices. Stephen Berg's **Singular Voices** (Avon) features 31 poets with a poem and an essay by each. Some of the poems are tedious; some of the essays are hoots; a few of both sparkle. From the ghosts, spoofs, and patriotic shills of American forebear-poets to Wilbur, Roethke, and X. J. Kennedy, one reads **The Oxford Book of Children's Verse in America** (Oxford University Press) with a grin. Editor Donald Hall's contemporary choices seem sparse and uninspired, however. He might have consulted **Light Year '86** (Bits Press), edited by Robert Wallace. As with all light verse collections, some is funny; some is not. The 1985 Pulitzer Prize winner Carolyn Kizer, in her "Woman Poet," tells us why: "It's not easy—washing out poems / And writing underwear at the same time."

The compulsion of poets to record and speculate about the art produces the "Poets on Poetry" series published by the University of Michigan Press. This year's crop includes **No Evil Star,** by Anne Sexton, **Writing Like a Woman,** by Alicia Ostriker, **A Ballet for the Ear,** by John Logan, and **A Local Habitation** by John Frederick Nims. Anne Sexton, plainly, was neither a skilled essayist nor thinker but a gifted gab-maker. Her life is found in her self-interviewing poems. Ostriker is a serviceable writer who sees her art as sexually-biased. That thesis is her critical lens for seeing Sexton, Plath, Swenson, and Rich. She has little subject otherwise. John Logan's volume, edited by A. Poulin, Jr., comes as a nosegay of Logan's essays, interviews, reviews, and poems. In everything Logan says a huggy love dominates. It's sometimes tender, sometimes bilious, and always blurs any difference between prose and poetry. But Logan does, in fact, set the ear and the imagination dancing. John Frederick Nims's **A Local Habitation** voyages widely in poetics, corvettes inlets of 1950s craft wisdom (irony/paradox), and ventures bays inhabited by Dante, Yeats, Frost, Joyce, Ovid, displaying always a ship-shape erudition. He startles, amuses, and educates with the nearest thing to a reference text among the four. Nims has a classical perspective that makes him, with Howard Nemerov, one of the grandparents

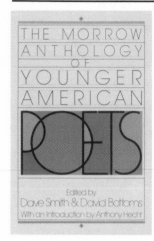

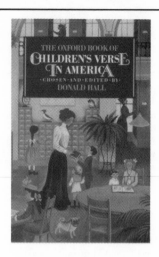

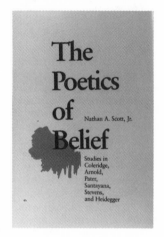

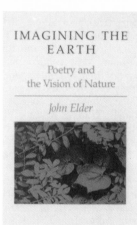

Dust jacket of Imagining the Earth: Poetry and the Vision of Nature, *by John Elder. University of Illinois Press, 1985. Reprinted by permission of the University of Illinois Press. Dust jacket of* The Oxford Book of Children's Verse in America, *edited by Donald Hall. Oxford, 1985. Jacket design by Honi Werner. Reproduced by permission of Oxford University Press, Inc. Jacket illustration originally from* Miss Rumphius, *by Barbara Cooney Porter; copyright © by Barbara Cooney Porter. Reprinted by permission of Viking Penguin Inc. Dust jacket of* The Poetics of Belief: Studies in Coleridge, Arnold, Pater, Santayana, Stevens, and Heidegger, *by Nathan A. Scott, Jr. Design by Patrick O'Sullivan. Copyright 1985 The University of North Carolina Press. Reprinted by permission of the publisher. Dust jacket of* The Morrow Anthology of Younger American Poets, *edited by Dave Smith and David Bottoms. Morrow, 1985. Cover design by Jacqueline Schuman. Be permission of William Morrow & Company, Inc.*

of the current re-verse in American poetry. Nemerov lays that grid on the poem in *New & Selected Essays* (Southern Illinois University Press) and is sometimes guilty of an intellectual hatred. But "The Poet and the Copywriter: A Dialogue," "On Metaphor," and "Poetry and Meaning" remain clear thinking and well said.

Emily Dickinson's obliquity, fecundity, and enigmatic clarity encourage critics to seek continuously for principles of cohesion in her poetry. She often seems more modern than citizen of the nineteenth century, yet two recent studies locate her in one of Romanticism's central currents, the quest romance. Jane

Donahue Eberwein's *Dickinson: Strategies of Limitation* (University of Massachusetts Press) considers the quest for Godhead as she considers the limitations of Dickinson's synthetic imagery. Greg Johnson's *Emily Dickinson: Perception and the Poet's Quest* (University of Alabama Press) follows the quest shape through to realization of consciousness by which the nineteenth century internalized the paradigm of progress, reversing the religious and secular. William H. Shurr's *The Marriage of Emily Dickinson* (University of Kentucky Press) is, like Eberwein and Johnson, a sort of form criticism. He thinks Dickinson's manner of binding her poems reveals a more worldly quest: a disguised love affair with a married man to whom Dickinson imagined herself, by love, formidably married. Using the recently published manuscripts—"fascicles,"—he shows a startlingly erotic pattern of imagery which he tries to collate to known biographical details. Is it true? She was not entirely innocent—Dickinson assisted her brother Austin's affair with Mabel Loomis Todd. Still, Shurr's evidence is circumstantial and enigmatic.

Modernism's equally mysterious nature continues to attract scholars like the blind men in the Zen parable seeking to name the elephant, mistaking the part for the unseen whole. Stuart Y. McDougal's *Dante among the Moderns* (University of North Carolina Press) gathers nine essays which emphasize the heritage-seeking aspect of Modernism, or the search for visionary form. Modernism is the umbrella-term for the climate of change in art and thought which convention dates roughly 1875-1945. Two helpful studies of nineteenth-century poetics are Nathan A. Scott's *The Poetics of Belief* (University of North Carolina Press) and John Elder's *Imagining the Earth: Poetry and the Vision of Nature* (University of Illinois Press). Scott is particularly good examining the roles of imagination and religious belief as they build toward the waste land. John Elder is slightly more ecological and less supernatural as he surveys the altering face of Nature in poetry. Both suggest Modernism's yearning for certainty in vortices of change that are, with fine succinctness, described by Sanford Schwartz's *The Matrix of Modernism* (Princeton University Press). He concludes: "the modern artist no longer *represents* a preexisting reality but *presents* a new set of relations, a 'model' through which to order the world anew." That is, of course, a form definition, and it is form obsession which dominates the twenty statements gathered by Monique Chefdor, Ricardo Quinones, and Albert Wachtel in *Modernism: Challenges and Perspectives* (University of Illinois Press). In contrast to McDougal, *Modernism* emphasizes a future-seeking aspect. What, then, is Modernism? Martin Esslin writes that is like asking "How long is a piece of string?" This text is certain to be the favorite of scholars though how new is new remains an open question.

Emphasis on the new characterizes *The Art of Seamus Heaney* (Poetry Wales Press), essays edited by Tony Curtis, only in that this is an updated version of the 1982 original collection. Harriet Davidson's *T.S. Eliot and Hermeneutics* (Louisiana State University Press) sounds like a rock group and is sometimes as unbearably opaque. She is interested in the meaning of "The Waste Land"—what it asserts and lacks—as seen through the lens of late French thinking. Her case for Eliot's originality seems finally credible but vastly overwrought. And late. Neal Bowers has convinced himself he understands and admires James Dickey's poetry. Yet *James Dickey: The Poet as Pitchman* (University of Missouri Press) is an innuendo-ridden snarl that concludes "a Dickey poem is usually intended to sell God." Bowers has missed Dickey's ecstatic animism and is flatly wrong more often than right. This is irresponsible crit-

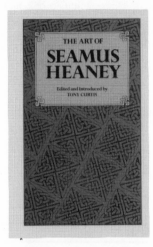

Tate, and Warren, but as something less than poets. This is response-summary thinking from old class notes and a need to pigeonhole. Poetry isn't taken seriously perhaps because as the Southern Critic said in *Southern Literary Study* (1975) "lyric poetry always has less to do with social issues and the family." Aside from that wrongheadedness, you often get what you look for. Hence there's no mention of writers under 40; here's a social standard subbed for a literary standard of evaluation; and here's the redefinition as Southern of Maryland's John Barth and Oklahoma's Ralph Ellison. One almost survives the gluey catalog prose, the distortions, the omissions, then comes the mind of the South. *History of Southern Literature* notes widespread courses in Southern literature and adds: "A great many of these institutions are outside the South, a clear sign that the study of Southern literature is entirely free of its provincial beginnings. . . ." Aha! Entirely?

Dillon Johnson's *Irish Poetry after Joyce* (Notre Dame University Press) could show the *History of Southern Literature*'s

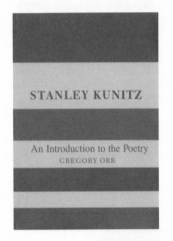

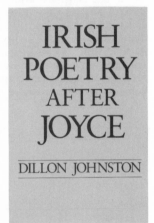

Dust jacket of Modernism: Challenges and Perspectives, *edited by Monique Chefdor, Ricardo Quinones, and Albert Wachtel. University of Illinois Press, 1985. Reprinted by permission of the University of Illinois Press. Dust jacket of* The Art of Seamus Heaney, *edited by Tony Curtis. Dufour Editions, 1985. Courtesy of Dufour Editions, Chester Springs, PA. Dust jacket of* T. S. Eliot and Hermeneutics, *by Harriet Davidson. Louisiana State University Press, 1985. Courtesy of Louisiana State University Press. Dust jacket of* The Matrix of Modernism: Pound, Eliot & Early 20th-Century Thought, *by Sanford Schwartz. Princeton, 1985. Copyright © by Princeton University Press. Reproduced by permission of Princeton University Press.*

icism. In *Stanley Kunitz* (Columbia University Press), Gregory Orr, a poet of consequence himself and an ex-student of Kunitz's, argues that Kunitz is an under-recognized major poet whose elaboration of thematic continuities—especially the search for a father—is the most significant archetypal art. Orr's credible, loving study is worthy of Kunitz who, at 80, remains a lively American eminence.

I wish that was true of *The History of Southern Literature* (Louisiana State University Press), edited by Louis Rubin, Jr., Blyden Jackson, Rayburn S. Moore, Lewis P. Simpson, and Thomas Daniel Young. *History of Southern Literature* is unquestionably welcome particularly for its sweeping vista; there is no one-stop rival for provisioning lectures. But wishing won't make this text lively. Two-thirds of *History of Southern Literature* survey the twentieth-century poets such as Ransom,

Dust jacket of Irish Poetry after Joyce, *by Dillon Johnston. University of Notre Dame Press, 1985. Cover design by Margaret Gloster. By permission of the publisher. Dust jacket of* Stanley Kunitz: An Introduction to the Poetry, *by Gregory Orr. Columbia University Press, 1985. By permission of the publisher. Dust jacket of* Local Assays on Contemporary American Poetry, *by Dave Smith. University of Illinois Press, 1985. Reprinted by permission of the University of Illinois Press.*

editors how and why to write about poetry and parochial vision. This splendid study demonstrates that when a poet and his audience no longer share cultural values and reference points, the poet must invent a language, a form of expression, which can revivify the triangular relationship of poet / poetic object / audience. Obviously not just an Irish phenomenon, this displacement and consequent shift leads to, as Johnson says, the poem controlled by "tone." The poem is no longer a static presentation of meaning but a dynamic act of experience where tone manages reader participation. Johnson's shift also indicates the poem moves from lyric toward narrative, from image toward rhetoric. Behind everything is the poet's impulse to escape a vision that is merely provincial and to cultivate a view which is local in heritage and universal in experience. Both Yeats and Joyce serve this need as analogues but Johnson's choice of Joyce, at first surprising, seems ultimately right. He applies his concept of the Irish poet seeking a new speech and a new identity to Clarke, Kinsella, Kavanagh, Heaney, Devlin, Montague, MacNeice, and Mahon, glancing at selected younger poets, and concludes with Paul Muldoon, whom he presents as an innovator who has freed himself from tradition's dead hand. Johnson is a spirited, readable, wise critic in a book that illuminates the nature and progress of any poetry written after World War II. His work emulates his poets in trying to compose a language by which and through which passionate communication of all that has been known and might yet be known remains possible. *Irish Poetry after Joyce* shines.

RECOMMENDED: (Anthologies) James Berry, *News for Babylon: The Chatto Book of Westindian British Poetry* (Chatto & Windus); W. D. Ehrhart, *Carrying the Darkness* (Avon); Paul & Hualing Engle, *Writing from the World* (International Writing Program Press); Raymond Garlic & Roland Mathias, *Anglo-Welsh Poetry* (Poetry Wales Press); Bonnie Bilyeu Gordon, *Songs from Unsung Worlds* (Birkhauser); Bill Mohr, *"Poetry Loves Poetry"* (Momentum Press); William Jay Smith & Dana Gioia, *Poems From Italy* (New Rivers Press); (Criticism) Edward J. Brunner, *Splendid Failure: Hart Crane and the Making of The Bridge* (University of Illinois Press); Albert Cook, *Figural Choice in Poetry and Art* (University Press of New England); Neil Fraistat, *The Poem and the Book* (University of North Carolina Press); Jean Gould, *Modern American Women Poets* (Dodd, Mead); Edwin Honig, *The Poet's Other Voice: Conversations on Literary Translation* (University of Massachusetts Press); Bruce K. Martin, *British Poetry Since 1939* (Twayne); Timothy Materer, *The Letters of Ezra Pound and Wyndham Lewis* (New Directions); Diane Middlebrook and Marilyn Yalom, *Coming to Light: American Women Poets in the Twentieth Century* (University of Michigan Press); Peter Stitt, *The World's Hieroglyphic Beauty* (University of Georgia Press); Thomas Daniel Young and George Core, *Selected Letters of John Crowe Ransom* (Louisiana State University Press).

Virginia Commonwealth University

The Year in Drama

by Gerald Weales

[Both Neil Simon and David Rabe] are represented on Broadway this season by serious (or presumably serious) comedies. Rabe's **Hurlyburly** came by way of the Goodman in Chicago and a successful off-Broadway run, and Simon's **Biloxi Blues** arrived after warm-ups in Los Angeles and San Francisco. According to *Variety*'s summary of the season (5 June 1985), their plays make up half of the slim four productions to become hits (i.e., to recover their investments) on Broadway this season (Whoopi Goldberg's one-woman show and the revival of *The King and I* are the other two). They were critically as well as commercially well-received. . . . Simon won [the Tony award] and—understandably—made a wryly snide acceptance speech about finally being honored for his twenty-second play. If it had been up to me, I would have given the prize to **Hurlyburly**; so I will begin this year's look at American drama with Rabe's play.

Hurlyburly is set in the Hollywood Hills in a house shared by two men, visited frequently by two others and by the women the four of them pass around. All the men work in the movies or in television in jobs that presumably interest them so little that they spend their waning energy trying to escape the meaninglessness of their lives in drink, drugs, and sex, or to reestablish meaning through pointless and often aggressive talk—salvation by platitude. Most of the disquieting comedy in the play comes out of that talk; there is, for instance, a scene between Eddie, the protagonist, and Darlene, the most introspective of the women, which is so funny that I wanted to burst into tears listening to it. "What Eddie's struggling with," Rabe says in *The New York Times Magazine* interview, 26 May 1985 (in a sentence that looks as though it will never end), ". . . is how to organize his life and his feelings, and how many feelings to have and who can he trust, and does he have to be boss to survive, what'll happen to him if he loses control." Rabe says that the audience at a play should identify with the main character ("if I go to see 'Medea,' I'd better identify with Medea"), but what we are asked to identify with in **Hurlyburly** is control that has become icy cruelty, intelligence that has dwindled to verbal games-playing, and compassion that has become ritual response to causes that are safely at a distance. Medea at least has passion. Although I do not identify with Eddie (or I resist identifying with him), I recognize him and even find him charming in his desiccated way. . . .

Back in 1950, Garson Kanin wrote a play called *The Live Wire* about a group of young actors living together; as one would expect of a playwright of Kanin's generation, there were good guys and bad guys—one who sacrificed friendship for stardom—and a moral was spun among the jokes. There are no live wires in **Hurlyburly**; even a *macher* like Artie, the butt of most of the gags, is treading water. *The Rat Race,* Kanin called another of his plays in 1949, but that was a long time ago, and Rabe's rats do not run at all. In fact, they are not even rats—only sometimes dangerous mice in a maze which is uncomfortably familiar despite the Hollywood trappings. Although

Hurlyburly is a comedy and often a funny one, it is set in the dark country that Rabe has been mapping since his first play.

Perhaps it was inappropriate to introduce Kanin's comedies into a discussion of **Hurlyburly,** for the latter is so clearly a contemporary play—discursive, ironic, inconclusive. It is **Biloxi Blues** that has a 1940's look about it. It is the further adventures of Eugene Morris Jerome, the Neil Simon surrogate whom we met as an adolescent in *Brighton Beach Memoirs*. Simon presumably wanted some of the gently attractive tone he managed in the latter, but he pulls out similar sentimental and comedic stops to little effect. Mine is a minority report on a play which has been showered with rave reviews and prizes, but it looks to me like a collection of army clichés that were not all that appealing thirty-odd years ago when we had them in *At War with the Army* and *Time Out for Sergeants*. **Biloxi Blues** is a maturation play in which the hero loses his virginity to a sympathetic whore, falls chastely in love with a good girl, and takes his first tentative steps toward becoming a writer by discovering that words can hurt and that a sharp eye and tongue are not always tools to understanding and accuracy. A pre-opening interview in the *Times* (24 March 1985) made clear that, for Simon, the seriousness in the play lies in Eugene's unwillingness to identify with the insistent Jewishness of another recruit, a reluctance that feeds the anti-Semitism in the barracks. In the 1940's, such a theme would more likely have been treated in a drama than in a comedy (see Arthur Laurents' *Home of the Brave*), but its presence here does not alter the old-fashioned look of the play; the only slightly up-to-date note is the introduction of homosexuality into the ingredients of the standard army play.

Simon, who went into the army in 1945, moves the action here back to 1943, presumably for his final catalogue of losses and injuries which puts the little war in the barracks into larger perspective. Like so much in the play, this final sequence actively annoyed me. Perhaps I have reached an age when I feel protective of my youth, but I do not believe that what we see on stage has much connection with Simon's fellow recruits of 1945 or my own of 1943. Whatever the autobiographical elements in it, the referents for **Biloxi Blues** are purely theatrical. This was made particularly clear in . . . Eugene. . . . [The] device of Eugene's journal allowed [the character] to come directly to the audience, caressing them with his calculated cuteness. . . .

The other nominees for the best-play Tony were August Wilson's **Ma Rainey's Black Bottom,** which came to Broadway from the Yale Repertory Theatre, and William M. Hoffman's **As Is,** which moved uptown from the Circle Rep. Both are plays of substance with something serious to say and with the theatricality and the intensity to hold audiences. Wilson's play takes place during a recording session in which Ma Rainey is cutting a record for the "race" division of Paramount Records, an operation that found it profitable to market black performers

15

for black audiences. The flamboyant side of the play is the presentation of Ma Rainey, who uses her star status to show her black bottom to the white businessmen (represented in the play by her long-suffering agent and the studio owner) to whom she is both a necessity and a burden. The irony is that, for all her glitter, she is only a product to them, useful so long as there are buyers out there; it is an irony that is not lost on her because she is the play's chief voice for getting while the getting is possible.

Although Ma Rainey is the play's dominant figure and she provides the occasion for the action, the heart of the play lies with the musicians, the back-up band that her old friend Cutler has brought together for the recording. They spend much of their time waiting and talking, but one of the most impressive things about *Ma Rainey* is the way in which their desultory chat creates an ensemble effect as though their divergent voices, like their instruments, could be brought together to form a whole....

The effect I am imperfectly describing was not consistent when I saw *Ma Rainey* in Philadelphia, a way station between New Haven and New York, but the fault was not in the production so much as in the play itself. Wilson, who has a remarkable ear for the intricacies of ordinary speech, violates the ensemble he creates by a presumed need to give biographical background to Levee, the play's protagonist. His raped mother and murdered father, however true to the uglier aspects of black history in America, are not necessary to the dramatic and ideational point of the play. Levee, who wants a band of his own to play his own music, believes the casual promise of the studio owner and, with a sense of self not unlike Ma's, manages to get himself fired by the singer who sees him not only as a pushy sideman with a lech for her girlfriend but as a potential danger to her kind of song. When the studio owner brushes him aside at the end, offering him five dollars a song as a favor, he vents his frustration by stabbing one of the musicians who steps on his new shoes. The trivial accident which so infuriates Levee masks—for him, certainly—that the victim is Toledo, the autodidact whose earlier conversations keep returning to the meaning of being black in America. As Gorky indicates in *Mother,* when the oppressed is unable to reach his oppressor, he often takes his anger out on his family, his friends, his group. I would have preferred to see this theme grow out of the musicians' talk as it wended its circular way to the final explosion—a song of sorts to work in unhappy counterpoint to the mocking defiance of "Ma Rainey's Black Bottom," which they are recording. I seem to be on the point of rewriting Wilson's play for him—a critic's trick that I abhor—but it is a way of saying that the best of *Ma Rainey* is much more effective than the conventional horror story of Levee's family history. . . .

This season's musical about race and show business is *Grind,* with a book by Fay Kanin which reminds us—here come the 1940's again—that she wrote the benignly liberal *Goodbye, My Fancy* (1948). Set in a burlesque house in Chicago in 1933—based apparently on a real theater that offered separate black and white shows—*Grind* tells how an alcoholic ex-IRA gunman is saved by the love of a good black woman (how did Sean O'Casey get in here?), a plot line that brings the two races together in time for the finale. But for all its good intentions, *Grind* hardly belongs in the company of . . . *Ma Rainey's Black Bottom.*

William Hoffman's *As Is* is one of the two plays about AIDS which have drawn a great deal of attention this year; the other is Larry Kramer's *The Normal Heart. As Is* is about a man who faces the fact that he has AIDS with the support of his former lover, to whom he returns, and of his brother who overcomes both his fear of the disease and his discomfort about the dying man's homosexuality. The personal story is acted out within a larger context—a great many characters played by a handful of performers—which emphasizes the effect of the disease on the gay community. A similar story lies at the center of *The Normal Heart,* but that play is primarily an angry agitprop accusing New York and Mayor Koch, the Federal government, the medical establishment (predictably, the good doctor is a wheel-chair bound woman), and the gay community itself for not doing enough to recognize, publicize, and combat the disease. Richard Goldstein had an interesting article in a recent *Village Voice* (2 July 1985) in which he tried to explain why Kramer's play was better received by straight critics than by those writing for gay papers. It is perceived by the latter as self-advertisement for the author, who has been considered an anti-gay gay since the publication of his novel *Faggots* in 1978, and as an attack on homosexuality itself. The play does advocate continence as a preventative, but to anyone not involved in the running argument with Kramer, the playwright can easily be seen as sympathetic to the anguish of the gay activist of the 1960's who suddenly finds the social and sexual victories of that decade threatened by AIDS. If *As Is* is a touch too sentimental as an AIDS variation on the acceptance-of-death play (for a finer example of the genre, see Ronald Ribman's *Cold Storage,* in which cancer is the killer), and if *The Normal Heart* seems too preoccupied with internecine politics and the self-righteous virtues of its author-surrogate protagonist, both are strong theatrical statements to which audiences, straight and gay, have responded with enthusiasm.

The grandest—and most disappointing—gathering of playwrights was in *Faustus in Hell,* a tedious pastiche Nagle Jackson put together for the McCarter Theatre in Princeton. Marlowe, Goethe, and Molière were joined by seven dramatists, each commissioned to do a sin—Amlin Gray ("Greed"), John Guare ("Gluttony"), Romulus Linney ("Wrath"), Jean-Claude van Itallie ("Pride"), Edward Albee ("Envy"), Christopher Durang ("Sloth"), and Joyce Carol Oates ("Lechery"). They ranged in quality and inventiveness from van Itallie's witty contribution to Oates's leadenly obvious monologue, but even the best of them could not survive Jackson's mishmosh. Many of these playwrights were busy in and out of New York with more substantial works, but the only one I saw was Amlin Gray's *The Fantod,* which finally opened off-Broadway after a busy life in the regional theaters; it is an amusing parody melodrama which I suspect is trying to use the dark underside of Victorian manners to say something serious about sexuality and repression.

Elsewhere, the range was wide and the quality mixed.

Dennis McIntyre's *Split Second,* in which a black policeman decides to defend with a lie his killing of an abusive white thief, is an interesting consideration of situation ethics *vs.* the rigidity of received morality; its problem as a play is that after an electric opening it gives way to a series of scenes that sound like seminar demonstrations.

Herb Gardner's *I'm Not Rappaport* is a performers' vehicle which gives two comparatively young actors . . . a chance to strut their stuff as eighty-year-olds; it toys with a serious problem—the difficulty and dangers of city living for the very old—but, as is characteristic of Gardner's work, it pulls back to give audiences a wryly upbeat ending.

Unlike *Rappaport,* which does have great charm, *Taking My Turn* brings aging performers back to the stage in what purports to be a musical celebration of vitality in the old but which is as lugubrious as a lecture on aging; it needs some of the bite of the John Kander-Fred Ebb *70 Girls 70,* still the funniest and toughest work of this genre.

Martin Sherman's *Messiah,* set in 1665, uses the coming of a false messiah to examine the ways in which several characters respond, socially and sexually, to a release—tentative and fatal in one case—from the restrictions of a legalistic religion; although it has a number of strong scenes, it is too dependent on direct address to God and somewhat confusing in some of its emotional shifts.

The Miss Firecracker Contest is another of Beth Henley's slapstick descents into bittersweet Southern grotesquerie, which has Gothic echoes in Heather McDonald's *Faulkner's Bicycle* (from the Yale Rep) and John Erlanger's *God's Attic* (in the Philadelphia Festival Theatre for New Plays). McDonald is Canadian and Erlanger a beginning playwright, so there may still be a chance to save them from a South that seems to have sprouted from a misreading of Eudora Welty.

The most interesting new play to turn up in the Philadelphia Festival is Bayldone Coakley's *Side Effects,* in which a somewhat scatterbrained psychologist and a very clever would-be delinquent spar with one another until they realize that they are allies in a world that sets limits to imagination; a predictable ending, but getting there is where the fun lies.

David Wiltse's *Doubles* is a locker-room comedy in which an opinionated WASP is finally made one of an otherwise Jewish tennis foursome; considering that it encompasses infidelity, bad marriages, unemployment, white-collar crime, and a heart attack, it is remarkably funny. Although P. J. Barry's *The Octette Bridge Club* ups the ante—eight women to *Doubles'* four men— it is not even half as amusing, a lost opportunity both as a vehicle for talented performers and as a statement about the stress beneath the chipper surface of the relationships among eight sisters.

Larry Shue's *The Foreigner* is an effective farce in which a shy Englishman, pretending to be a visitor from a country whose language no one speaks, finds his confidence at a fishing lodge in Georgia and with the good folks defeats the malevolent Klan villains. Joseph Dougherty's *Digby* is a comedy about a young man who insists that friendship between a man and a woman is more important than casual sex and who is, of course, rewarded for this revolutionary insight by winning the heroine; the satirical material on advertising and the current art scene is fairly conventional, but Dougherty shows his skill as a comic writer in the lines he provides for his protagonist. . . .

Since I used the Tony awards as a device to open this survey, let me temper any seriousness implied in my remarks on these awards by pointing out that the whole process was something of a joke this season. The televising of the awards has moved the emphasis from plays to musicals, and this year there were no musicals of any distinction. The Tony mavens had to toss out a number of categories, and the four nominations for best musicals, including *Grind,* were ludicrous.

Big River won a basketful of awards and may get a run as a result, but despite its origin in the neighborhood of Harvard (at the American Repertory Theatre in Cambridge), it is *Huckleberry Finn* as it might have been conceived by Tom Sawyer. With songs by Roger Miller and a book by William Hauptman, it slides over the harsher elements in Mark Twain's novel, using classy scenic effects and show-business cuteness to cuddle up to its audience.

Singin' in the Rain does better by an American classic than *Big River* does. The new version adds nothing interesting (including Twyla Tharp's additional choreography) to the Gene Kelly film on which it is based, but it does attempt (or did when I saw it: the opening was frequently postponed so the current version may not resemble the one I saw in preview) to reproduce the four best known musical numbers from the original. "Make 'Em Laugh," "Moses Supposes," and "Good Mornin'" were still a little uncertain when I saw the show, but the film's most famous number, "Singin' in the Rain," was—to my surprise—a fine recreation of (and homage to) the original, Don Correia's echo of Gene Kelly exact and loving.

Harrigan 'n Hart, which came to New York from the Goodspeed Opera House and deservedly died within the week, did nothing for the celebrated nineteenth-century theatrical team; their lives were reduced to schmaltz and their material was so tackily staged that it is impossible to know whether or not there is anything retrievable in once-famous shows like *The Mulligan Guard Ball* (although an off-off-Broadway production I saw in 1977 suggested not).

Leader of the Pack is about and with Ellie Greenwich, but it may be a little early to celebrate the author of "Do Wah Diddy" as a cultural giant. A social point might have been made—but was not—about a successful composer of the 1960's who never noticed the Vietnam war or any of its domestic offspring.

Quilters is based on an unusual idea: to dramatize the place of women in the settling of the American West, using the quilt as an image of female inheritance within the family and the community. Unfortunately, the individual numbers ran more to cliché than to discovery. The night I saw *Quilters* there was nothing on stage as compelling as the display of quilts on exhibit in the lobby of the theater.

My One and Only, an amusing parody of the 1920's musicals built around the songs of George and Ira Gershwin, uses "Strike Up the Band" to bring down the curtain of both acts. Anyone who saw the revival of the Gershwin-Kaufman musical in which the song first appeared (at the 1984 American Musical Theater Festival held in Philadelphia) knows that the song, in its proper context, is harsh antiwar satire and that its bowdlerization in *My One and Only* is a sign of that show's likable innocuousness. Still, given this season's musical offerings, even a laundered "Strike Up the Band" sounds good.

Reprinted from The Georgia Review, *Fall, 1985*

The Year in World Literature

by William Riggan

At the recent PEN congress in New York, the official theme of "The Writer's Imagination and the Imagination of the State" sparked far more political boilerplate than the memorably imaginative prose or speeches that might have been expected from such an assemblage of the world's finest writers, translators, editors, and critics. Interestingly, some of the most insightful and intelligent remarks on the subject came from writers whose lives and works have been strongly affected by government control, principally in Central and Eastern Europe: former Nobel laureate Czeslaw Milosz, the exiled Lithuanian writer Tomas Venclova, and the Russian émigré novelist Vassily Aksyonov. This circumstance provided a fitting postlude to the literary year 1985 internationally, for the same East European region furnished perhaps the finest set of first-rate new works to be found anywhere during the year.

Among the Russians, for example, Aksyonov published his second long novel since his 1980 emigration, *Skazhi izium* (**Say Cheese**), which focuses on several photographers involved in the compiling of an "unofficial" photo collection, a situation in which readers will doubtless see many parallels to the author's own participation in the ill-fated *Metropol'* almanac affair of 1979 that led to his loss of Soviet citizenship. *Surplussed Barrelware* presents readers of English with several of Aksyonov's previously untranslated short stories and novellas, all written between 1968 and 1979, and many of them are heavily annotated here to give some indication of just how much in the way of verbal and cultural allusions is lost in rendering his highly original prose into another langue. Sergei Dovlatov, in *Remeslo* (**The Craft**), paints a more realistic and perhaps more directly informative picture of the Soviet émigré author (in this case, a journalist as well) via a largely autobiographical narrative tracing the protagonist's adventures and misadventures in cofounding a second Russian-language newspaper in New York: as one critic notes in answer to the central figure's rhetorical closing question, the work is "*about* both Russia and America, and *for* both the Russian and American reading public." An English translation will no doubt soon emerge.

In the Soviet Union, major works by at least two of this half-century's most noted Soviet writers head the year's list. The late Nikolai Tikhonov, whose poetic career paralleled and to some extent chronicled his nation's emergence from revolution and civil war, through pogroms and world war, to the Cold War years and the nuclear age, was honored by the issuance of *Kak pesnia molodoĭ* (**Young Like a Song**), a collection of his early verse from the years 1916-35, which provides not only authoritative versions of his published work of that period but a number of previously unpublished pieces as well. Yevgeny Yevtushenko, long the more or less official national poet with occasionally outspoken liberal views on delicate sociopolitical matters, continued his recent turn to prose with the novella *Ardabiola,* almost immediately translated into English under the same title, which refers to a wondrous new cancer-curing plant developed by a brilliant young Soviet geneticist;

the socialist-realist happy ending and obligatory bows to Gorky and Mayakovsky (as well as Lenin) do not obscure the book's enriching echoes of Pasternak and Bulgakov and the candid treatment of such topics as pandemic Soviet alcoholism, widespread abortion, and bureaucratic oppression of individual creativity. Elsewhere, Western readers are given further tastes of two other fine Soviet authors in poet-songwriter Bulat Okudzhava's novel *Poor Avrosimov* and in the late Kirghiz novelist and filmmaker Vassily Shukshin's admirable collection of short stories, *Roubles in Words, Kopecks in Figures*.

In Central Europe, the sad state of contemporary Czech literature was strikingly demonstrated in 1985 with new publications by four of its leading writers: the fact that all the works had to appear outside Czechoslovakia, with translations often preceding the originals in print, speaks volumes. Bohumil Hrabal, whom no less a figure than the émigré novelist Milan Kundera terms the most original and authentic Czech author of the postwar period, saw two of his unpublished short novels brought out together in France as *La petite ville où le temps s'arrêta, suivi de Moi qui ai servi le roi d'Angleterre* (**The Small Town Where Time Stood Still, and I Who Have Served the King of England**), both written in the sixties and circulated clandestinely in his homeland but never published there: like much of his work, these two explore what Kundera calls "le burlesque quotidien," the better to express the native wisdom, lucidity, and contrived simplicity that are his characters' best weapons against overt aggression and pervasive ideology. Ivan Klíma, another important Czech figure who chose to stay in his homeland despite political obstacles, was represented with two new works as well: *Moje první lásky* (**My First Loves**), a collection of short fiction issued by an émigré press in Toronto, shows Klíma's deft touch and bemused stance to excellent advantage in stories largely about adolescent loves amid frightening yet fascinating sociopolitical realities; *My Merry Mornings* makes another, similar collection from 1979 available to readers of English in a scrupulously faithful translation. Kundera's own latest novel, *The Unbearable Lightness of Being,* finally appeared in the original Czech after publication a year earlier in English, French, and German, and bolstered his growing reputation as a world author of the very first rank; Czech reviewers were startled primarily by the much rawer, more concrete quality of the prose in comparison to the elegant smoothness of the English and French versions in particular. Ota Filip, who emigrated to Munich in 1974, brought out his latest novel, *Café Slavia,* in German, with the Czech version presumably to follow soon; the work traces Czech cultural and political history from 1910 to 1968 through the life and experiences of a protean nobleman and his numerous progeny.

Like its southern neighbor, Poland itself produced little of literary note in 1985, though an important new collection by one of its most outstanding poets, Zbigniew Herbert, did appear in translation in the West; *Report from the Besieged City*, principally representing Herbert's most recent writing, bears po-

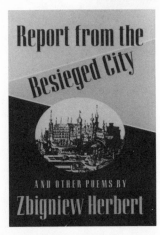

Dust jacket of Café Slavia, *by Ota Filip. S. Fischer, 1985. By permission of S. Fischer Verlag GmbH, Frankfurt am Main. Dust jacket of* Report from the Besieged City, *by Zbigniew Herbert. The Ecco Press, 1985. © Cynthia Krupat. By permission of the publisher. Dust jacket of* My Merry Mornings, *by Ivan Klíma. Readers International, 1985. By permission of Readers International/Jan Brychta.*

etic-philosophical witness to his countrymen's bitter fate and attempts a reply, through the poet's persona Mr. Cogito, to what he variously terms "the bitter question" and the "monster"—the large-scale manipulation of information and ultimately of reality. Far less bleak is the situation in Yugoslavia, where Serbian writers such as Danilo Kiš and Dobrica Ćosić continue to benefit from a recent cultural liberalization. Kiš, who alternates residence in Belgrade with long stays in Paris, published translations of two major novels, *Encyclopédie des morts* (**Encyclopedia of the Dead**) and *Hourglass,* in France and the U.S. And Ćosić brought out the year's biggest popular success, *Grešnik* (**The Sinner**), the story of a political assassination told in the didactic and romantic-nationalist manner and compelling tone of Dostoevsky and other nineteenth-century writers: critical reception has been mixed, due to the novel's polemical and somewhat iconoclastic tendencies in respect to ideological and historical dogma.

Writers from the marginal or smaller regions and languages of Europe were reasonably well represented in 1985, though their names will be less familiar to Westerners than the aforementioned Slavs and their works perhaps less immediately accessible. The Greek authors Yannis Ritsos and Vassilis Vassilikos will be the most readily recognizable of this lot—Ritsos through the many translations from his enormous poetic output, and Vassilikos from the successful film version of his novel *Z* two decades ago. *O yérontas me tous hartaetoús* (**The Old Man with the Kites**) continues Ritsos's recent experiments with prose; nominally a novel and the fifth in a five-part series, the work is more properly the fictional diary of a respected older writer with a somewhat embarrassing passion for building and decorating kites as a diversion from his obsession with words, memories, and ruminations on death and esthetics. In *Exile and Return* we are given a new set of Ritsos poems in translation, elegantly rendered by Edmund Keeley. The two récits of *Le dernier adieu suivi de Foco d'amor* (**The Last Adieu, with Fire of Love**) evoke the memory of Vassilikos's late wife, mixing past and present in what French critics have labeled a "veritable descent into hell, giving birth to a novel of despair, more somber than the works of the author's exile years [1967-74], more personal, more lyrical, and more disconcerting than any he has written before." The reputations of Hungary's Miklós Radnóti, Finland's Veijo Meri, and Albania's Ismail Kadare benefited from new releases in 1985 as well, though none has attained anything like a breakthrough among the English-reading public. Radnóti comes closest of the three, and *Under Gemini,* containing "a prose memoir and selected poetry," will certainly add to his small but growing renown in the West. Kadare continued to enjoy the benefits of French patronage during the year with the publication of two more books in Paris. *Qui a ramené Doruntine?* (**Who Brought Back D.?**), an exotic, adventure-packed historical novel of the kind he has become famous for in France and Albania; and *Invitation à un concert officiel* (**Invitation to an Official Concert**), a collection of novellas and short stories offering what one reviewer lavishly terms "a multicolored, kaleidoscopic efflorescence" of mythic themes and settings as farflung as old Peking and the Ottoman Empire of the eighteenth century. Meri's *Novellit* (**Short Stories**), by contrast, presents more rough-hewn, realistic accounts of rural episodes and folksy types, often in wartime settings; these are leavened by several fantasies and fabliaux, as well as by at least two bittersweet autobiographical accounts featuring young love and the death of a beloved relation.

The major West European literatures enjoyed an only modestly successful year, at best. The situation in the Germanic countries was typical. The appearance of Heinrich Böll's last novel, *Frauen vor Flußlandschaft* (**Women in Front of a River Landscape**), shortly after the former Nobel laureate's death in July certainly ranks as a literary event of magnitude, concluding his exemplary career of forty years; but the novel itself, a vast prose drama about Bonn political life composed entirely in monologues and dialogues taking place on a single day but covering forty years of history, ultimately proves excessively ponderous in construction and melodramatic in plotting. Another posthumous publication is the early novel *Ingrid Babendererde* by the émigré novelist Uwe Johnson who died in 1984. The novel reveals just how mature a talent this young author was already in the 1950s, before his most famous works began to appear; his account of adolescent love, the cultural conflict between rival youth organizations in the new East German state, and the dilemma of young dissidents and emigrants in those years shows all the human sensitivity, political astuteness, and modernistic style of the later Johnson.

Martin Walser, with *Messmer's Gedanken* (**Messmer's Thoughts**) and *Brandung* (**Surf**), and Peter Härtling, with *Felix Guttmann,* also contributed significant new novels to the year's production in the Federal Republic, as did Gabriele Wohmann with her latest short-story collection, *Der Irrgast* (**The Errant [or Mad] Guest**). In Austria, the most notable publication was Thomas Bernhard's new novel, *Alte Meister* (**Old Masters**), the dark comedy of two elderly esthetes and their discovery of the ultimate imperfection and imperfectibility of all artistic endeavor. The best of a slack year in East German writing was the elderly Stefan Heym's novel *Schwarzenberg,* a fictive account of a small region on the Czech border that stands as a paradigm of the author's utopian idealism and touching political naïveté in the face of twentieth-century historical fact. The Swiss playwright and novelist Friedrich Dürrenmatt offered the well-crafted novella *Justiz,* whose title and story cunningly play on the fine distinction between due legal process and true justice. From the outlying Germanic areas, mention should be made of the Dutch author Willem Brakman's novel *De bekenntnis van de heer K.* (**The Confession of Mr. K.**), an imaginative sequel to Kafka's *Trial* in which K. escapes execution and then writes an account of his travails, filled with intricate plots, subplots, anxieties, and an overriding aura of perceived guilt.

A year that includes new works with bylines such as Robbe-Grillet, Michaux, Proust, Sollers, Modiano, Le Clézio, and Clavel can scarcely be termed inconsequential, and the French reveled in the variety and quality of 1985's production. The greatest excitement was created by the appearance at long last, after nine years, of Alain Robbe-Grillet's imagistic autobiography, *Le miroir qui revient* (**The Reflecting Mirror**), a unique composite of mirror images, interlocking visions, and recurrent prismatic refrains, wherein we learn of his childhood loves and fears, his parents, fellow writers and critics such as Sartre and Barthes, and his ideas on e.g. truth and dogma and the problematics of writing style; the blend is a wonderfully felicitious and frequently provocative one. Henri Michaux's verse collection *Déplacements, dégagements* (**Displacements, Disengagements**), the final one he had a hand in assembling before his death in late 1984, maintains the "curiously uncongealed, unbound quality, the exploitation of shifting phenomena" characteristic of his previous work, as he ranges over such matters as his reactions to a film, a visit to a friend in Belgium, the drawings of children, and an accidental narcotic episode. The twelfth volume of Proust's correspondence draws exclusively from the year 1913, taking us through the many tribulations, delays, and redoubled efforts involved in actually getting the author's masterwork into print; admirers and specialists will not want to miss it.

Three sophisticated exercises in post-New Novel *écriture* highlighted the year for French readers with more contemporary tastes. Patrick Modiano's sleek, multilayered novel *Quartier perdu* (**Lost District**) superimposes Parisian *haute culture* of twenty years ago onto today's literary scene and intertwines the wealthy and famous of yesteryear in a long-undetected murder only now brought to light, with unsettling consequences for the returned expatriate author who chances to uncover the whole matter. Luc Estang weaves a haunting psychological mystery in *Le loup meurt en silence* (**The Wolf Dies in Silence**), as a son gradually comes to terms with his long-absent father and with his own misconceptions of family, sacrifice, love, and "silence." Philippe Sollers offers a quasi-fictionalized memoir in *Portrait du joueur* (**Player's Portrait**), creating as a persona a quirky *homme de lettres* who slips easily into and out of a bewildering array of roles and poses, ruminates on an equally wide range of topics, and will strike readers as either infinitely charming or unbearably fatuous. In another vein,

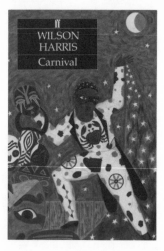

Dust jacket of Carnival, *by Wilson Harris. Faber and Faber, 1985. Jacket design by Pentagram. Illustration by Chris Brown. Reprinted by permission of Faber and Faber Ltd. Dust jacket of* Historia de Mayta, *by Mario Vargas Llosa. Seix Barral, 1985. Dust jacket of* Collected Poems 1948-1984, *by Derek Walcott. Farrar, Straus and Giroux, 1985. Jacket painting copyright © 1986 by Derek Walcott. Design by Cynthia Krupat. Reproduced by permission of Farrar, Straus and Giroux, Inc.*

Emmanuel Roblès, with *Le chasse à la licorne* (**The Hunt for the Unicorn**), J. M. G. Le Clézio, with *Le chercheur d'or* (**The Gold-Seeker**), and Bernard Clavel, with *L'or de la terre* (**The Earth's Gold**), exemplify the recent turn in French literary taste toward quality romantic fiction. Roblès's love story takes on the heroic aura of the mythical emblematic creature whose name it invokes; Le Clézio's solitary hero survives the horrors of World War I, only to discover that his idyllic prewar paradise in far-off Mauritius no longer exists as he once knew it: and Clavel's work continues his saga of the Canadian gold rush in an epic style that ably matches the beauty and grandeur of its northern frontier setting.

Hispanic letters, by comparison, made a relatively unimpressive showing in 1985. Of considerable historical importance is the first publication ever of the complete text of *Guerra en España* (**War in Spain**) by the late Spanish Nobel laureate Juan Ramón Jiménez, a series of reports, impressions, and documentary materials compiled by the famed writer on the vicious civil war and its aftermath. Spain's finest living novelist, Juan Goytisolo, departs from his recent spate of alternately pitiless and scandalous fictional attacks on traditionalist Spain and, in *Coto vedado* (**Game Reserve**), offers what one critic aptly terms ''an essay in understanding, a tranquil autobiographical survey of childhood [and] self-discovery''; the book is also ''a memorable description of how a typical bourgeois Catalan family was shattered by ideology and social forces it was fated to defend, [and] a fine description of the traumatic generation gap which opened between pro-fascist parents and their radicalized, educated offspring.''

 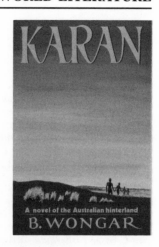

The year's most interesting Spanish-language fiction, however, came from Latin America, in new novels on somewhat similar themes by Mexico's Carlos Fuentes and Peru's Mario Vargas Llosa. Fuentes's short novel *El gringo viejo* (translated as *The Old Gringo*) reconstructs the final months and days of the aging American writer Ambrose Bierce, whose disappearance during the Mexican Revolution sometime after 1910 has never been solved; the writing is imaginative, as always with Fuentes, but is perhaps overburdened by literary referentiality and conscious mythmaking. In Vargas Llosa's *Historia de Mayta* (Eng. *The True Life of Alejandro Mayta*) the novelist's persona has sought out the still-living leader of an abortive 1958 revolt in Peru and reconstructed the story of his uprising and its ultimate failure; the work does not match the author's best efforts, but neither does it diminish his high reputation. Also of note, finally, is the posthumous publication of two late plays by the self-exiled Argentine writer Julio Cortázar, the one-act *Nada a Pehuajó* (**Nothing to Pehuajó**) and the dramatic sketch *Adios, Robinson:* valuable because they presumably now complete the Cortázar canon, and fascinating as texts, the two unfortunately also reveal the author's limitations as a dramatist.

Elsewhere in the Romance-language world, the 1985 literary harvest was quite respectable, even excellent. The late Mercé Rodoreda, termed by some ''the greatest contemporary Catalan novelist and possibly the best Mediterranean woman author since Sappho,'' was introduced to American audiences in the collection *My Christina and Other Stories,* providing a good indication of her range and versatility. Natalia Ginzburg, who ranks among Italy's leading fiction writers of today, brought out *La città e la casa* (**The City and the House**), an epistolary novel centering on a lonely, alienated, but unself-pitying Italian expatriate in America. And from Brazil came two examples of quality historical fiction in Nélida Piñon's novel *A república dos sonhos* (**The Republic of Dreams**), describing the ''Movimento de '30'' which swept Getúlio Vargas to power, and *Os tambores de São Luis* (**The Drums of São Luis**), an epic account that surveys three centuries of black participation in Brazilian history.

The appellation ''Third World'' covers an enormous geographic expanse, and the range of new works produced by Third World writers in 1985 was almost as great. From the West Indies came the *Collected Poems* of Trinidadian poet and playwright Derek Walcott, drawing on nearly forty years (1948-84) of creative activity variously evoking the landscapes and dialects of his homeland, the vastly different environs of London and New York, and the tensions he feels between the several worlds in which he moves and lives; his originality of language, virtuosity of style, and thoroughgoing honesty of tone make Walcott one of world literature's finest all-around poetic voices in English. Wilson Harris of Guyana confirmed his reputation as a skillful and highly innovative writer of fiction with the publication of *Carnival,* a dizzying and Dan-

Dust jacket of The Sea-Crossed Fisherman, *by Yashar Kemal. Braziller, 1985. Reprinted by permission of the publisher George Braziller, New York. Dust jacket of* Maiba: A Novel of Papua New Guinea, *by Russell Soaba. Three Continents Press, 1985. Courtesy of the publisher. Dust jacket of* Karan, *by B. Wongar. Dodd, Mead, 1985. Jacket design by David Gatti. Reprinted by permission of Dodd, Mead & Company, Inc.*

tesque journey into the life of one Everyman Masters that leads to a kind of transcendent resonance amid the ritual Caribbean carnival of masks. In *Pays rêvé, pays réel* (**Dreamed Land, Real Land**) the poet-novelist Edouard Glissant of Martinique constructs a lengthy baroque narrative poem on the African origins of his island nation's culture, replete with mythical figures of the Old World's folklore and fictional characters from his own earlier novels and plays.

In Africa itself, the year's sparse production was distinguished by one new work in English and one in French. Christopher Hope's novel *Kruger's Alp* is unique in its extraordinary comic treatment of South African history and politics, casting its story in the form of a *Pilgrim's Progress* dream about a search for the fortune in gold reputedly spirited away by President Paul Kruger to a private enclave in Switzerland after the Boer defeat: effectively laying a curse on all the political houses in his native land, Hope successfully creates a complex and open-ended fictional analogue to South Africa's complex and maddeningly intractable political dilemma. Sony Labou Tansi of Congo-

Brazzaville offers a similarly comic portrait of politics and history in *Les sept solitudes de Lorsa Lopez* (**The Seven Solitudes of L.L.**), a fablelike narrative on ''the silence of History'' toward even the most outrageous acts of regimes and individuals—in this case, the wholesale removal of a country's government from one city to another, and Lorsa Lopez's brutal, calculated murder of his wife; it is the latter event which finally provokes resistance in the form of an organized cadre of women with the courage both to speak out about the formerly unspeakable and to oppose by force such direct affronts to their honor and their fundamental rights.

The Near East furnished a strong slate of new works in 1985, both at home and abroad. Yashar Kemal, Turkey's (and probably the region's) perennial Nobel candidate, continued to be favored by Western publishers and readers, this time with **The Sea-Crossed Fisherman**, perhaps the wildest in his long line of colorfully exotic novels and stories of Anatolian village life; the entwined destinies of a simple fisherman and a petty criminal are the main focus of a chaotic plot aimed ultimately at savaging Turkey's present-day social structure, particularly exploitative capitalism and the widespread corruption that is seen to accompany it here. Egypt's three leading literary lights—Naguib Mahfouz, Yusuf Idris, and Tawfiq al-Hakim—were also represented with translations of recent works during the year. Mahfouz, in fact, scored a triple with the publication of three novels: the stream-of-consciousness narrative **The Thief and the Dog;** the novel **Wedding Song,** a study of time's impact on the features and hearts of the four protagonists; and **Impasse des deux palais** (**Impasse of the Two Palaces**), the first volume in a trilogy that traces the history of interwar Egypt through the fortunes of a single Cairo mercantile family. Al-Hakim, the Arab world's lone playwright of international stature, followed two earlier U.S. editions of his selected plays with the 1985 publication of **The Tree Climber,** an unusual and slightly absurdist drama about murder and philosophy, set in a suburb of modern Cairo. Idris was represented by **Rings of Burnished Brass,** a selection of short stories and novellas that offers an excellent overview of his skill as a craftsman of short fiction.

The war in Lebanon provided the impetus for the year's other two Arabic works of note, both by women: **Zahra** (the central character's name, which means ''flower''), by the Lebanese author Hanan el-Sheikh, recounts the story of a young Shi'ite girl from southern Lebanon who escapes her authoritarian home and the implacable law of her society through love and political commitment, ultimately blossoming (in the work's central image) like a flower in the desert. Less schematic and far more complex in both style and content, the Lebanese-Egyptian writer Andrée Chedid's novel *Le maison sans racines* (**The House without Roots**) vividly and imaginatively portrays the hellish Christian-Muslim battleground of present-day Lebanon; from one central flash point—the presumed random sniper-shooting of two friends before the eyes of the protagonist, the fiftyish grandmother Katya, and her attempt to leave her apartment and walk to the scene in order to learn their fate—the novel moves backward and forward in time, delineating her own past as well as that of her troubled nation. It is a work not to be missed by all interested in the Near East. Another side of the conflict in Lebanon was touched on by such Israeli writers as the poet Yehuda Amichai, but the year's best work in Israel came from the novelist Amos Oz, whose **Menukha nechona** (Eng. **A Perfect Peace**) furnishes an ironic and insightful study of contemporary kibbutz life using the examples of three young characters, who by novel's end achieve a relative peace with themselves and their lives that is, however, far from perfect.

The year's biggest literary news from Asia and the Pacific was of course Keri Hulme's receipt of both the Pegasus Prize (U.S.) and the Booker Prize (U.K.) for her remarkable novel, **The Bone People** (discussed in the Prizewinner's section in this volume of the *Yearbook*). Two Australians, David Malouf and B. Wongar, also produced first-rate new works that attracted overseas attention. Malouf's novel **An Imaginary Life** betrays the hand of a poet throughout its sensitively imagined account of Ovid's life in exile among the barbarians, whereas Wongar's **Karan** (the word means ''soul'') vividly portrays the devastation wrought upon the aboriginal tribes of the primitive bush country by the advance of technological civilization—here, principally uranium mining and atomic-weapons testing. Along similar lines, Russell Soaba's **Maiba,** only the second full-length novel from Papua New Guinea ever published (the first was his **Wanpis,** 1977), recounts the efforts of the daughter of

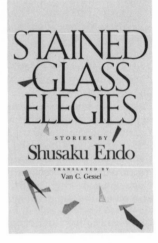

Dust jacket of Stained Glass Elegies, *by Shusaku Endo. Dodd, Mead, 1985. Jacket design by Claire Counihan. Reprinted by permission of Dodd, Mead & Company, Inc. Dust jacket of* The Fall of the House of Nire, *by Morio Kita. Kodansha, 1985. Reprinted with permission from Kodansha International © 1985. Dust jacket of* Trees on the Mountain: An Anthology of Chinese Writing, *edited by Stephen C. Soong and John Minford. University of Washington Press, 1985. By permission of the publisher. Dust jacket of* Naomi, *by Junichirō Tanizaki. Knopf, 1985. Jacket art by Yumeji Takehisa. Jacket design by Naomi Osnos. © 1985 Alfred A. Knopf, Inc. Courtesy of the publisher.*

a village's last traditional chief to defuse an imminent violent confrontation between her community and the forces of modernity and change, thus holding her people together despite its weaknesses. The Philippine author Linda Ty-Casper, a long-time resident of the United States but a frequent visitor to her native country as a lecturer and writer in residence, had the good fortune of bringing out two major works in 1985: the novella *Fortress in the Plaza* uses the experiences of a small-town politician to trace the events leading to the grenade attack on several VIP's at an opposition rally in Manila's Plaza Miranda on 21 August 1972, which prompted the establishment of martial law; and the novel *Awaiting Trespass,* set in 1981 (the year martial law was lifted), conveys rich social satire through its account of events surrounding the wake for an aging playboy who died under rather mysterious and possibly scandalous circumstances.

Japanese authors continued to make a growing impact on world letters in 1985 through the increasing dissemination of their writing in the West. The major earlier work *Naomi* by Junichiro Tanizaki, adjudged by many as Japan's finest modern novelist, amply displays his stylistic brilliance and charm as well as his penchant for perversity and bitter social comedy in a tale of a Pygmalion experiment gone miserably awry. Among the more contemporary authors, Shusaku Endo continues to stand out, most recently through his first collection of short stories to reach Western readers, *Stained Glass Elegies. The Fall of the House of Nire*, Morio Kita's sequel to his earlier success, *The House of Nire,* draws his saga of a family dynasty to a ruinous end amid Japan's collapse at the close of World War II. Toyoko Yamasaki's novel *The Barren Zone* approaches the topic of Japan's defeat via another avenue: the story of a military man's eleven years of incarceration in the Soviet Gulag following his army division's capitulation on the Russian front; the officer is a prime example of the traditional Japanese hero and of what has been labeled ''the nobility of failure,'' but the work has met with opposition from forces representing Japan's resurgent national pride in the wake of the country's phenomenal economic success.

Two 1985 anthologies of recent fiction and poetry advance the steady flow of current Chinese writing to the West. *Contemporary Chinese Literature* presents what the subtitle designates as simply ''An Anthology of Post-Mao Fiction and Poetry'' from the People's Republic, much of it quite accomplished, with only an occasional selection marred (for Western tastes) by excessive sentimentality or overwrought contrivance. *Trees on the Mountain* ranges more widely to include writers from Taiwan and Hong Kong as well as from the mainland and also offers criticism and drama in addition to fiction and verse; the quality is, if anything, consistently higher than that of its companion volume.

Closing out this survey of the year 1985 in world literature are two new works on the Vietnam War and its aftermath—by Vietnamese authors. *Bāo nôi* (**Tempest Brewing**), part 2 of a planned tetralogy by Nguyen Mong-Giac titled *Mùa biên dông* (**Season of Rough Seas**), continues part 1's account of Vietnamese life as experienced by the author's generation, which came of age around the time of the Diem government's collapse in 1963; the third and fourth installments will take the account respectively through the 1968 Tet offensive and the 1975 fall of Saigon. Hà Thúc Sinh's *Dai-hoc máu* (**Blood University**) complements Nguyen's sweeping tetralogy with an almost naturalistically detailed recounting of the author's fifty-five-month detention in the infamous reeducation camps that were instituted by the communists for all former South Vietnamese military officers and civil servants. If and when these two works, and others like them now being published by the Vietnamese émigré communities of Southern California in particular, are translated, their perspectives on the war and on its prelude and aftermath will doubtless prove most revelatory reading for American audiences.

World Literature Today
University of Oklahoma

New Authors

Isabel Allende

1942-

Chilean novelist, journalist, dramatist, and juvenile fiction writer.

Allende's first novel, *La casa de los espiritus* (1982; *The House of the Spirits*) draws deeply on its author's family history and the political upheaval in modern Chile. Allende is the niece of former Chilean president Salvador Allende, who was murdered during August Pinochet's right-wing military coup in 1973. Allende, who shares her uncle's socialist views, says that she envisions her life divided into two parts: before and after Pinochet's takeover. As a young girl, Allende lived for a time with her maternal grandparents, who serve as the models for Esteban and Clara, patriarch and matriarch of the Trueba family, whose history is chronicled in *The House of the Spirits*. Allende describes her grandfather as "a conservative, a patriarch, a very violent person, but he was adorable in many ways, and I loved him dearly. And I had a grandmother who was a very sweet, gay, incredible woman. She liked spiritualism and astrology and tarot. . . . She was always telling me stories. . . ." After an adolescence spent in Bolivia, Europe, and the Middle East with her mother and diplomat stepfather, Allende worked with journalists at the United Nation's Food and Agriculture Organization in Chile. Eventually, she herself became a journalist for television and newsreels, as well as a writer for a radical feminist magazine. She also wrote plays and short stories for children.

After Pinochet seized power, Allende, her husband, and children went into exile in Venezuela. "When I left Chile, I didn't dare tell my grandfather," Allende recalls. "I went the day before and wanted to tell him that I was leaving, but I couldn't. I couldn't find the words." Years later, in 1981, the grandfather, who was by then nearly a hundred years old, telephoned from Chile to inform her that he was about to die. "I wanted to tell my grandfather that I was never going to forget him, he would never die, just as my grandmother had never died. . . . And I started writing a letter, telling him the same things he had told me when I was a child." The letter, never sent, evolved into Allende's first novel. "That's why at the beginning of the book Alba [the granddaughter of Clara and Esteban] writes to keep alive the memory of her past and to survive her own terror. That's how I felt. I wanted to survive the terrible experience of exile, and I wanted to keep alive the memory of the past—the house that I lost, the people that are dead, those that disappeared, the friends that were scattered all around the world."

The House of the Spirits gathers the recollections of its three main characters. Accounts of incidents in the Trueba family during the earlier part of the twentieth century are drawn from Clara's diaries. Later, Alba recounts her nightmarish experience during a military coup in which she is tortured as a left-wing counterrevolutionary. Interspersed with their recollections are those of Esteban, whose expressions of sentiment win him reader sympathy in spite of his crude, violent character. Although *The House of the Spirits* evidently takes place in

© *Jerry Bauer*

Chile, Allende never uses proper names which might identify her setting. She refers to Salvador Allende as "the President," and to Pablo Neruda, whom she quotes in her introduction to the novel, as "the Poet." Critics, many of whom expected a socialist harangue from Salvador Allende's niece, praise Allende's subtle working of her political message into the body of the novel. Most critics compare *The House of the Spirits* to Gabriel García Márquez's *One Hundred Years of Solitude*. Although Allende denies having deliberately used that novel as a model, reviewers point out several likenesses: the family chronicle structure, the magic realist technique, and the resemblance between Clara's sister, the ethereal Rosa, and Márquez's Remedios the Beauty. Despite these similarities critics find in Allende's novel an authorial voice which, if not as great as that of Márquez, is nevertheless authentic and original in its own right. In the earlier chapters of *The House of the Spirits*, Allende uses a Márquez-like magic realism to impart a legendary quality to events in the far past of the Trueba clan. As the story draws to a climax, Allende reverts to a more straightforward journalistic style to the events leading up to the military coup and its aftermath. Throughout, critics find, Allende relies on well-rounded characters and a succession of compelling images, rather than a schematic plot, to hold reader interest. Allende has written a second novel, *De amor y de sombra* (1985), also dealing with right-wing abuses in Chile, which will also be published in English translation. She is currently at work on a third novel.

LORI M. CARLSON

There is a lot of love in *The House of the Spirits*. The love-making of powerful men and naive women, worn-out married couples and anxious rebels might even conjure up the reader's personal experience. But there is another kind of love in this book with which the reader cannot identify. It is a kind that requires forgiving the person whose torturous hand has shoved your face into a bucket of excrement. A spiritual force that can overcome a world sutured with evil, to beget art.

Isabel Allende . . . tells in this, her first novel, a vibrant story of struggle and survival dedicated to her mother, grandmother and "other extraordinary" women in a country unnamed. Given the descriptions of events and people in the book, however (i.e., the Poet whose funeral "turned into the symbolic burial of freedom"), Chile quickly comes to mind.

Politics count here. There are the haves and have-nots, those who impose their will and those who whimper on cue. But what is assuring about this dynamic is the way life gives and takes from both sides, making the distance equal between each of them and happiness. In this novel, by love's own measure, the strong and weak are the same: scared souls, faulty human beings who have the ability, if nudged by the right spirits, to care sincerely.

Fortunately, the spirits in the "big house on the corner" are fashioned of benevolent stuff. When stupidity and hatred collaborate to destroy the mansion's family, Clara—matriarch and central figure—works wonders talking to her kindly ghosts. The family is blessed by this nimble, radiant woman. She is especially precious to Esteban Trueba, her husband, Blanca, her daughter, and Alba, her granddaughter.

In terms of human passion and need this story is simple. A man and woman marry, have children and watch them fall in love. But it is the clash of mismatched personalities—Clara's propensity to help the downtrodden versus Esteban's hunger for power and money—framed by their country's political growing pains that cause sorrow for their loved ones. A future of revolution, torture and murder awaits them.

Lack of refuge is their *cri de coeur*. Although the family has two houses, in neither do any of the characters seem complete individuals—a reflection on Chileans today having lived in two sad houses. . . .

Esteban, despite his callous resistance to the needs of those around him, first to those of his ailing mother, then to those of his family and ultimately as a senator to those of his countrymen, is given sight—is redeemed—by his wife's and grand-daughter's love for him. Redemption through woman's love is a familiar cliché in Hispanic literature; but here it takes on a new significance.

Esteban's fattened existence is just as dissatisfying as the lives of the wretched characters who tread Allende's pages: among them his son's Haight-Ashbury-type girlfriend and the wiry activist his daughter eventually marries. Jaime and Nicolás, Esteban's own twin sons, however, aimlessly dawdle between his world and the counterculture. Somehow these figures never take root in the story. We are distracted by their lazy constitution. Meager figures they are and after a certain point irritating.

Actually the host of individuals doing and saying could have resulted in showy display. The characters could have become allegorical figures instead of finely hewn personalities if it weren't for Allende's precise structuring of character development. She is careful to give each major personality the limelight. Thus we become familiar with the quirks of each, the reactions and actions that have little to do with dogma, but everything to do with plain human nature.

Multivocal patterning, third-person omniscient narration threaded with first-person testimonies, establishes their credibility. Esteban elicits our sympathy in spite of his disagreeable behavior, because we hear his heartbeats. Were it not for his sorrowful confessions, the female characters of this novel would have been overpowering. His strong voice balances the story.

There are constant reminders, too, of *One Hundred Years of Solitude*—too many in fact, since the reader cannot finish one chapter without thinking of García Márquez's Buendía family. Allende's novel does remain compelling, nevertheless. Technique is polished, imagination full. (p. 77)

Rich in description the story is "divided according to events and not in chronological order," so that acts of horror and warped desire become comprehensible, at least somewhat, to us. Says Alba, the inheritor of the family's curses and blessings and presumably the "writer" of this history:

> I write, she [Clara] wrote, that memory is fragile and the space of a single line is brief, passing so quickly that we never get a chance to see the relationship between events; we can not gauge the consequences of our actions, we believe in the fiction of past, present and future, but it may also be that everything happens simultaneously. . . . That's why my grandmother Clara wrote in her notebooks, in order to see things in their true dimension.

The tenor of the narrator's voice in the epilogue, now Alba's voice, brings us face to face with the valiant spirit of the women Allende places in relief against the grimness of her country. Their strength to endure imprisonment, starvation, humiliation and the loss of their loved ones is what she has honored. If she has hinted at her admiration for these brave souls in the chapters preceding the last two, it is to make us work at comprehending the indomitable, silent force that finally is defined here. We have come to understand what she believes: "that the days of Colonel García and all of those like him are numbered, because they have not been able to destroy the spirit of these women." Bravo to them and to her. (p. 78)

Lori M. Carlson, in a review of "The House of the Spirits," in Review, *No. 34, January-June, 1985, pp. 77-8.*

PUBLISHERS WEEKLY

A runaway bestseller in Europe, this accomplished first novel [*The House of the Spirits*] is a richly symbolic family saga by the niece of Chile's assassinated President Salvador Allende.

It is both an engrossing narrative and an impassioned testimony to the people of Chile, oppressed for centuries by rich land-owners, briefly freed by the election of a socialist government, and now crushed by a brutal, murderous dictatorship. Because of its supple integration of the supernatural with the real, the book will be compared with Gabriel García Márquez's *One Hundred Years of Solitude*. Allende has her own distinctive voice, however; while her prose lacks the incandescent brilliance of the master's, it has a whimsical charm, besides being clearer, more accessible and more explicit about the contemporary situation in South America.

The story concerns the del Valle and Trueba families, united in the union of gentle, clairvoyant Clara del Valle and autocratic, emotionally violent Esteban Trueba, *pátron* of a huge hacienda whose peasants he controls with implacable tyranny. Through three generations of vividly portrayed characters we are given a strong, compassionate picture of the social and political conditions in Chile (though the country is never named) from the turn of the century to the present day. It is a world of sharp contrasts: between opulent wealth and soul-grinding poverty, between barbaric political chicanery and self-sacrificing, pure idealism.

Allende's richly and meticulously detailed narrative moves with the slow power of legend as she chronicles the rise and fall of the Truebas and the ideological chasm that sunders man from wife and children from parents, as the irrevocable revolution arises, lives briefly and is crushed by those who confuse traditional class divisions with patriotism and who are themselves betrayed by forces of tyranny. The family is the paradigm of the nation: old Senator Trueba is an arch-conservative who plots with the CIA to overthrow the socialist government and its president; the latter is a close friend of Truebas's son Jaime, who is murdered by agents of the military coup his father has set in motion; in the anarchy that follows, Senator Trueba's beloved granddaughter aids the guerrilla resistance and comes in for her own share of suffering.

As Allende recounts her country's "unending tale of sorrow, blood and love," the initial mood of mysticism is overcome by a tide of bitter tragedy. The book, heavy with portent and irony, grows in power and significance.

A review of "The House of the Spirits," in Publishers Weekly, *Vol. 227, No. 9, March 1, 1985, p. 70.*

CHRISTOPHER LEHMANN-HAUPT

Within a couple of dozen pages, Isabel Allende's extraordinary first novel, *The House of the Spirits,* found several ways to antagonize this reader.

First, it seems to be an openly ideological novel. Set in an unnamed South American country, it is obviously going to tell the story of Chile's peaceful socialist revolution and violent militaristic counterrevolution—the author being a Chilean now living in Caracas, and, not incidentally, the niece of former President Salvador Allende Gossens. Moreover, it is obviously going to tell Chile's story from a point of view not exactly sympathetic to the present ruling junta. The reader may not be exactly sympathetic to the present ruling junta either, but he doesn't need a novel to lecture him about political repression.

Second, *The House of the Spirits* seems guilty of that extravagant and whimsical fabulousness so dear to the imagination of many South and Central American fictionalists. Within the first few dozen pages of *The House of the Spirits,* we have a

horse-sized dog named Barrabás who likes ham and "every known type of marmalade," an uncle named Marcos who flies off into the clouds with the aid of a mechanical bird he has built, and a clairvoyant child named Clara who decides to become mute upon witnessing her green-haired sister's autopsy. In the land of repression, magic sometimes sounds like hysteria.

But while novels of this length and variety often erode the reader's patience, *The House of the Spirits* has the effect of wearing down one's resistance. True, it's full of one-dimensional characters of excessive good or evil, and you can bet that none of the reactionaries are nice. But the Clara, Blanca and Alba Trueba—the mother, daughter and granddaughter who successively preside over the House of the Spirits—are complex and vivid women. And the story's dominant character, the tragically ill-tempered Senator Esteban Trueba, is so appalling and appealing that he easily transcends ideology.

Yes, there are patches of simplistic writing: "The relationship between" Clara and Blanca "underwent no major changes with the girl's development, because it was based on the solid principle of mutual acceptance and the ability to laugh together at almost everything." But most of the prose is sharply observant, witty and eloquent. An assessment of the Truebas more typical of the novel's style is Clara's remark to her granddaughter Alba that there are no crazy people in the family because "here the madness was divided up equally, and there was nothing left over for us to have our own lunatic."

And certainly, the details of Isabel Allende's story continue throughout to be bizarre and exaggerated. Clara the clairvoyant grows up to be a seer and necromancer who is often observed by her family floating about the house in a chair. She is attended by a devoted sister-in-law who ends up putting a curse on the master of the house, the irascible Esteban Trueba, that causes him gradually to shrink.

Yet for every fabulous detail there is elaborate psychological underpinning. Moreover, the degree of the whimsy is a function of history: it is the distant past that is suffused with magic dogs and flying uncles; the present time is all too drearily deterministic. And finally, what is fabulous in the story works to give it its extraordinary character. The book's all too predictable message may be that the evil forces of the right cannot crush the people's revolutionary spirit. But that spirit is also the "spirits" in the title—the indomitable women who rule Senator Trueba's mansion, as well as the benign ghost world that gives them their unique power. It is also these spirits that help to lift the novel out of the realm of local political allegory, and lend it a feeling of extraterritorial truth.

I still have my quarrels with *The House of the Spirits*. One never stops feeling impatient with the symmetry of good and evil; except for Senator Trueba—so big a character that he exists in an extra dimension—there are simply no good right-wingers and no bad revolutionaries. More seriously, the real evil of repressive police states seems trivialized by the cheap psychology rung in to explain the story's grand inquisitor, Col. Esteban García, the policeman-torturer who is Senator Trueba's bastard son. The message implied is that we should only be kinder to the children we thoughtlessly spawn. Somehow, that won't really do.

But judged by the standards of the mainstream of historical fiction, *The House of the Spirits* has to be considered powerful and original. Just like Esteban Trueba's relationship with the young revolutionary who loves his daughter, I began by wanting to kill the book and ended up with deep respect for it.

Christopher Lehmann-Haupt, in a review of "The House of the Spirits," in The New York Times, *May 9, 1985, p. 23.*

JONATHAN YARDLEY

This first novel [*The House of the Spirits*] by a Chilean journalist comes to the United States after a great success, both commercial and critical, in Europe. At first glance it is tempting to suggest that this is explained by the author's minor celebrity . . . but the novel itself indicates otherwise. *The House of the Spirits* does contain a certain amount of rather predictable politics, but the only cause it wholly embraces is that of humanity, and it does so with such passion, humor and wisdom that in the end it transcends politics; it is also a genuine rarity, a work of fiction that is both an impressive literary accomplishment and a mesmerizing story fully accessible to a general readership.

Like so many other writers now at work in Latin America and elsewhere in the "third" world, Isabel Allende is very much under the influence of Gabriel García Márquez, but she is scarcely an imitator. Like García Márquez, she has created a world that interweaves the real and the fantastic, she has devised a colorful, ironic language with which to describe it, and she has addressed herself to the contemporary Latin American political and social situation. But her narrative method is more conventional, her prose is less flamboyant, and her politics are less insistent. She is most certainly a novelist in her own right and, for a first novelist, a startlingly skillful, confident one.

Her story takes place in a "country of catastrophes," a "half-forgotten country at the end of the earth" that could be Chile or just about anywhere else in Latin America; like García Márquez' Macondo, it is a Latin everyland where the wildness and mystery of nature are always close at hand, where the very rich and the very poor coexist in an uneasy intimacy that constantly threatens to dissolve into open conflict. The very rich in this story are the family of Esteban Trueba, an energetic, willful man whose "most salient trait was his moodiness and a tendency to grow violent and lose his head"; the very poor are the peasants who farm his lavish estate in the countryside, for whom "time was measured in seasons, and thought by generations," who have been taught by hard experience "that in the end the fox always eats the hens, despite the subversive ballads that were traveling from mouth to mouth preaching just the opposite."

Esteban is the only character who lasts through the novel's beginning around the turn of the century until its conclusion sometime near the present, yet he is not really its central character. That distinction is shared by three women: his wife, Clara, his daughter, Blanca, and his granddaughter, Alba. They are an extraordinary trio, of whom Clara is the most extraordinary. She is possessed of supernatural powers and as a girl is known as Clara the Clairvoyant because, among other things, she can "interpret dreams," "predict the future and recognize people's intentions," and "move objects without touching them." What is more extraordinary about her, though, is her character, which is compounded out of such seemingly contradictory elements as resilience and ethereality, playfulness and silence, dependency and unconventionality.

As did her mother, an outspoken suffragette, Clara exists in a world of macho dominance yet refuses to accept its dictates uncritically. Within her marriage, Esteban may contribute the sound and fury but she is clearly the stronger partner; while she had determined to marry a man she did not love, "Esteban Trueba's exaggerated love for her was without a doubt the most powerful emotion of his life, greater by far than his rage and pride," thus rendering him helpless before her whim. Esteban is a thundering leader of the Conservative Party, stubbornly upholding the old order; Clara quietly tells him that "you can't keep the world from changing." (p. 3)

Allende has both the tolerance and the wisdom to understand that there is lamentable human loss when any world crumbles, even if it was not a good one, and thus the cantankerous Esteban emerges at last as a deeply sympathetic figure.

It is this desire of Allende's to understand all people, and if possible to love them, that allows *The House of the Spirits* to rise far above its evanescent political concerns. It is a novel not about ideas or causes but about people, who move "down through the centuries in an unending tale of sorrow, blood and love." For all the elements of fantasy and magic with which Allende has imbued them, they are as real a group of people as one could hope to meet—and there are many more of them than have been mentioned here. Every bit as real is the world in which they live, a world Allende has created out of the reality of Latin America and the fecundity of her own imagination. The result is a novel of force and immediacy, compassion and charm, spaciousness and vigor. It can only be hoped that American readers will respond to it as enthusiastically as those in Europe already have. (p. 4)

Jonathan Yardley, "Desire and Destiny in Latin America," in Book World—The Washington Post, *May 12, 1985, pp. 3-4.*

ALEXANDER COLEMAN

With this spectacular first novel [*The House of the Spirits*], Isabel Allende becomes the first woman to join what has heretofore been an exclusive male club of Latin American novelists. Not that she is the first contemporary female writer from Latin America (I think immediately, for instance, of Luisa Valenzuela and Cristina Peri Rossi)—but she is the first woman to approach on the same scale as the others the tormented patriarchal world of traditional Hispanic society and to argue that the enraged class violence in Latin America is a debate among men who are not only deaf but who have fixed and unalterable ideas on all subjects. And she has done all this in an absorbing and distinguished work that matches her predecessors' in quality as well as scope.

Her world, like that in the novels of the male writers who have preceded her, is a world ruled by men. It is haunted by the figure of the hyperbolic *macho,* an authoritarian force in the family and in the national political structure. Such a man glories in his ability to command submission, to flaunt his gigantic ambition, usually at the immediate expense of the women who surround him. For Miss Allende, this reality is already written in the social history of the Latin American past and cannot now easily be given another direction. As she said in a recent interview with Marjorie Agosín in the journal *Imagine:* "I wanted to show that life goes in a circle, events are intertwined, and that history repeats itself, there is no beginning and no end."

That does sound a bit like the philosophy of history that governs the bleak final meaning of all of Gabriel García Márquez's novels, but Miss Allende is in no sense fatalistically resigned to the phenomenon of violence in Latin America. Quite the contrary—*The House of the Spirits* is a novel of peace and reconciliation, in spite of the fact that it tells of bloody, tragic events. The author has accomplished this not only by plumbing her memory for the familial and political textures of the continent, but also by turning practically every major Latin American novel on its head. Rarely has a new novel from Latin America consciously or unconsciously owed more to its predecessors; equally rare is the original utterance coming out of what is now a collective literary inheritance.

In ways that North American literature over the years has never had to face, Latin American literature has been and still is a kind of writing directly related to social concerns. It has a sense of mission that puts estheticism in its rightful place. More often than not, *pace* Jorge Luis Borges, the writer has a political function within his culture as voice for freedom and social justice. Gabriel García Márquez's *One Hundred Years of Solitude,* generally regarded—with justification—as the big daddy of the contemporary Latin American novel, was not just the family saga of the Buendías, but had larger ambitions as an epic tale of the founding, rise and decline of the family and of the mythical region of Macondo. (pp. 1, 22)

There are many variants on such grand "imaginative biographies" in individual national literatures. The novels of the Chilean José Donoso, for instance, in such works as *The Obscene Bird of Night,* give us a more marked urban setting, containing telling descriptions of the "upstairs-downstairs" world of the ancient family manse. . . . The "big house" is a constant in contemporary Latin American letters, for it signifies the class structure of an entire continent. Carlos Fuentes and Juan Rulfo of Mexico and Mario Vargas Llosa of Peru have written on the theme as well.

Isabel Allende combines this central theme of Latin American fiction with autobiography in complex ways. She is the niece of Salvador Allende Gossens, the President of Chile last seen alive on Sept. 11, 1973, wearing a helmet and with a pistol in his hand while the tanks and soldiers of Gen. Augusto Pinochet surrounded the presidential palace in Santiago. Before the coup, she was a popular journalist who specialized in barbed ridicule of the male establishment. She was close to her uncle—he stood in for her father at her wedding. After the coup, she and her husband spread out a map before them; they chose Caracas, Venezuela, where she now makes her home with her family. She avoids mentioning her connection to the late President, but the family name, which she has kept, carries tremendous emotional weight as a symbol not only for the Chilean cataclysm, but also for the struggle over the definition of social justice in Latin America.

The House of the Spirits draws on this experience, though always in veiled terms. A meticulously detailed family saga spanning four generations, the novel is set in a mythified land of volcanoes, earthquakes and hurricanes, peopled by characters who seem to derive their extravagance from their natural surroundings. The founder of the Trueba clan, Esteban Trueba, is yet another exaggeration of the classic Hispanic father, admirable in his consistency and stubbornness, it is true, but a homicidal dictator, an enemy of the common people, a violator of submissive women. . . .

Alba is the survivor-narrator of the novel. She is generous and feisty, having inherited her mother Blanca's rebellious nature.

Like her mother, she takes a lover from another class—Miguel is "one of those fatal men possessed by a dangerous idealism and an intransigent purity." It is because of him that she is jailed, and it is she who brings together all the strands of this dynastic history in the stunning final pages, a remarkable meditation on the carnage caused by her grandfather and his class, and by the equally militant determination of the Socialists to oppose a return to oligarchy.

Thus the narrative focuses on the evolution of feminine consciousness over the generations and on the gradual acquisition of self through social action and humane concern, an evolution accomplished in the face of traditional authority. Yet it is also the story of the failure to temper that power: Chapter 12, "The Conspiracy," and Chapter 13, "The Terror," describe in excruciating detail the end of democracy in a nation like Chile; when, after the wracking power and horrific bestiality of the scenes in the dungeons of the new dictator, Alba is set free, hers is a voice speaking from a society in ruins. (p. 22)

It is, finally, the pressure of such events that gives Isabel Allende's book its force and individuality. In its closing pages, *The House of the Spirits* takes on a darker, firmer tone, as if the literary models were gradually and imperceptibly abandoned under the weight of remembered experience. Miss Allende has credibly maintained that she was not specifically thinking of *One Hundred Years of Solitude* when she wrote the work. The first half of the novel does read like a direct prolongation or ramification of Gabriel García Márquez's masterpiece; he and all the other contemporary novelists are alive and present to Miss Allende's voracious imagination. But in the end texts and politics add up to one reality. As she has said, "It is not worth the trouble to make a boundary between events that occur within pages and those that take place outside . . . if something is not true at this moment, it may be true tomorrow."

The House of the Spirits, with its all-informing, generous and humane sensibility, is a unique achievement, both personal witness and possible allegory of the past, present and future of Latin America. It is also a moving and compelling first novel, translated with grace and accuracy by Magda Bogin; one would have to be a most recalcitrant reader not [to] be swept up by it. (p. 23)

Alexander Coleman, "Reconciliation among the Ruins," in The New York Times Book Review, *May 12, 1985, pp. 1, 22-3.*

BRUCE ALLEN

[*The House of the Spirits*] offers further proof, if any were needed, that the most exciting fiction being written these days comes from that embattled continent energized by the pressures of poverty and despair and ablaze with revolutionary ardor. It is another masterly vision of the phantasmagoric place we've come to know best through the "magical realism" practiced by Gabriel Garcia Marquez and his peers and imitators—and I think it deserves comparison with the major work of Mario Vargas Llosa, Julio Cortazar and, yes, Garcia Marquez himself. . . .

It is a richly imaginative story, a kind of Marxist epic or romance, set in a world where impossible events occur routinely, where the dead casually commune with the living, and there appears to be an ongoing "state of emergency and upheaval in the laws of physics and logic." Though it expresses the resigned certainty that the same kinds of social failures and political injustices are doomed to recur, this is at the same time a pointedly hopeful book, a celebration of the collective instinctual energies that fuel such troubled societies and, more specifically, an original feminist argument that suggests women's monopoly on powers that oppose the violent "paternalism" from which countries like Chile continue to suffer. (p. 37)

The story's climax and finale include the surprising election of an unnamed Socialist "Candidate" [whom the younger Truebas support], his regime's replacement by the military coup that the conservatives unwisely encourage, and the bloody aftermath, during which Alba works as a guerrilla, aiding this newest government's Marxist "enemies." Allende's gift for dramatic detail is used magnificently in the moving passages that describe how the military junta transforms and terrorizes the country. A sequence of prison scenes is especially splendid; again and again, Allende rises to the challenges she has set for herself.

The very end concentrates on Sen. Trueba's chastened recantation of his elitist ideals—and on Alba's serene survivor's determination to remember everything they've lived through and preserve the lesson for later generations. The story she begins writing is the one we are just finished reading.

What unifies this novel, and produces its considerable emotional power, is Allende's demonstration of how families as well as countries become hopelessly divided. When Clara Trueba dies, "detaching herself from the world," she's confirming her alliance with "a world of apparitions" that has nothing to do with her husband Esteban's compulsion to possess her absolutely; it's his destiny to control, hers to escape and transcend.

The novel is filled with such contrasts and tensions. "Liberal" sentiments keep infiltrating the family—partly because of the dispossessed bastard children Esteban keeps fathering. Daughter Blanca is a talented potter; her "mania for clay" symbolizes her commitment to common life. Son Nicolas, a befuddled communicant of various Eastern religions, founds a "millennial organization" that loudly opposes his father's profit-making practices. And his twin, Jaime, together with granddaughter Alba, steals provisions from the old man's hoard, to sustain the workers' needs.

The endurance of the major women characters seems to me to suggest that they're free of the mercenary and proprietary passions that drive the men. Clara/Blanca/Alba: They aren't blank or vacant; rather, it's as if each is a *tabula rasa,* a moral whited sepulcher that's open to all experiences and receptive to all claims.

The most remarkable feature of this remarkable book is the way in which its strong political sentiments are made to coexist with its extravagant and fascinating narrative. If the final pages are more overtly political, less "magical" than their earlier counterparts, there's nevertheless a more-than-compensatory gain in dramatic focus and thematic intensity. Once you're into the final 75 pages, it's impossible to stop reading.

How good is *The House of the Spirits*? Despite its undeniable debt to *One Hundred Years of Solitude,* this is an original and important work; along with Garcia Marquez's masterpiece, it's one of the best novels of the postwar period, and a major contribution to our understanding of societies riddled by ceaseless conflict and violent change. It is a great achievement, and it cries out to be read. (p. 38)

Bruce Allen, "A Magical Vision of Society in Revolt," in Bookworld, Chicago Tribune, *May 19, 1985, pp. 37-8.*

An Excerpt from *The House of the Spirits*

"Let's open it up, son. I want to see Rosa," I told Jaime.

He didn't try to talk me out of it, because he recognized the tone that creeps into my voice when I've made an irrevocable decision. We angled the lantern just so, and he loosened the bronze screws that had grown dark with time. We lifted the top, which was as heavy as a piece of lead, and in the white light of the carbide lantern I saw Rosa the Beautiful, with her orange-blossom crown, her green hair, and her unruffled beauty, just as I had seen her many years before, lying in her white coffin on my in-laws' dining room table. I stared at her in fascination, unsurprised that time had left her intact, because she was exactly as I'd seen her in my dreams. I leaned over and, through the glass covering her face, placed a kiss on the lips of my immortal beloved. At just that moment a breeze crept through the cypresses, slipped through a crack in the coffin, which until that instant had remained hermetically sealed, and in a flash the unchanged bride dissolved like a spell, disintegrating into a fine gray powder. When I raised my head and opened my eyes, the cold kiss still on my lips, Rosa the Beautiful was gone. In her place was a skull with empty sockets, a few strips of marble-colored skin clinging to its cheekbones, and a lock or two of moldy hair at its nape.

Jaime and the guard quickly slapped the coffin lid back on, placed Rosa in a wheelbarrow, and took her to the place that had been readied for her next to Clara in the salmon-colored mausoleum. I sat down on a grave in the middle of the cypresses and looked up at the moon.

Férula was right, I thought; I've been left all alone and my body and my soul are shriveling up. All that's left for me is to die like a dog.

PATRICIA BLAKE

Chopin performed on the piano by invisible hands, a horse-size dog with crocodile claws who feeds on marmalade, chairs that dance and saltcellars that scamper across the dining table. These are some of the fantastic images in *The House of the Spirits,* a first novel by Isabel Allende that has captivated readers in Latin America and Western Europe. . . .

Allende has self-consciously modeled her novel on Gabriel García Márquez's *One Hundred Years of Solitude,* a four-generation family chronicle set in a nonexistent town. Allende's Rosa the Beautiful is obviously a stand-in for García Márquez's Remedios the Beauty, famed for her spectacular ascension to heaven with the family laundry. The job-hopping Nicolás in *The House of the Spirits* doubles for *One Hundred Years'* mad inventor, José Arcadio Buendía, who strives to manufacture the philosophers' stone and photograph God.

Allende is not just an epigone of García Márquez. Writing in the tradition of Latin America's magic realists, she has a singular talent for producing full-scale representational portraits with comic surreal touches. Her rendering of the Trueba patriarch Esteban and his wife Clara is a hilarious display of mismatching. While the crude, commonsensical Esteban is doomed by nature to cause constant offense to his wife, Clara the Clairvoyant irritates her spouse by her perpetual whispered concourse with the spirits.

Esteban's efforts to please Clara prove disastrous. After their wedding he can think of nothing better to present to his bride than the hide of her beloved dead dog Barrabás, turned into a rug and laid out at the foot of the marriage bed. "His two glass eyes stared up at her with the helpless look that is the specialty of taxidermists." Esteban's insensitiveness toward his wife extends beyond the grave. When Clara dies, the inconsolable widower begins wearing a suede pouch hanging under his shirt. "In it were his wife's false teeth, which he treated as a token of good luck and expiation." Indeed, he had knocked out her teeth in a quarrel years earlier. . . .

The antic narrative is carried along by Allende's natural sense of fun until her characters reach the 1970s. At this juncture the Truebas are drawn into the violent confrontations between oligarchs and socialists that have afflicted modern Chile. The author here begins to exercise her skills as a journalist as she evokes the turbulent events she witnessed during the Marxists' electrifying rise and precipitous fall. Not surprisingly, magic subsides and realism takes over. Allende deftly turns her characters into archetypes of Latin America's left and right.

Allende's most persuasive pages describe the coup that felled her uncle and the terror that followed as it hits all the members of her fictional family, whatever their politics. Hers is an even-handed account told with much poignancy. Regrettably, however, the novel stumbles to a close when the author falls back upon one of García Márquez's hoariest literary devices: the discovery of an old manuscript that predicts the family's whole history. Though Allende's debut is full of promise, she still needs to break away from the domination of her unwitting mentor before she can fully display her distinctive voice.

Patricia Blake, "From Chile with Magic," in Time, *Vol. 125, No. 20, May 20, 1985, p. 79.*

ENRIQUE FERNÁNDEZ

Salvador Allende's niece? The first woman in the Fuentes/García Márquez/Vargas Llosa club? Spare me the radical chic hype and the "feminist" good conscience. Isabel Allende has written a book [*The House of the Spirits*] that is neither as good as the critics have claimed nor as bad as I'd like it to be so I could show them up by tearing into it. It's an okay read, just the right hefty size for summer. And it tells a contemporary holocaust tale worth recalling: Chile's passage from democracy to butchery. But it's no masterpiece. Only the dullest reader can fail to be distracted by the shameless cloning from *One Hundred Years of Solitude:* characters (like Rosa the Beautiful from Remedios) and stylistic idiosyncrasies (García Márquez's accumulation of fabulous anecdote, surreal hyperbole, and eccentric personages that turns each sentence into a complete short story). What was a dazzling style in *One Hundred Years* can sound annoying in a knockoff. Allende writes like one of the many earnest minor authors that began aping Gabo after his success, except she's better at it than most. . . .

Today, once again, Latin America is on the map, and if politics dominates the headlines, there's no longer any doubt that the brilliant constellation of boom writers has created a new con-

sciousness about their part of the world—in fact, sometimes it's these artists who write the headlines, as in Vargas Llosa's recent Nicaragua article for *The New York Times Magazine*. Since most of those writers were male, the road has been paved for an Isabel Allende, for a woman, to rewrite Latin America's patriarchal history in a big, ambitious novel.

If only she were better at it. For one, she's telling it with a straight face, as if it hadn't been told before, as if García Márquez had never written a word, as if such resources as irony and parody were not at her disposal. I'm all for sending up the boys in the Latin literary band, but Allende is not the great female hope. I don't think she realizes that instead of copying the masters she could be jiving them. Still, *The House of the Spirits* is not badly written. Once the echo-chamber effect of her imitative prose wears off, the reading flows. The last chapters are especially moving (though this is due to the tragic Chilean history she's retelling as much as to her narrative powers). And there is a structuring intelligence behind her vast panoramic tale. It's just that Allende's predecessors did so much more: they turned the fabric of the novel inside out; they made time flow backward and forward at will; they tapped the loquaciousness of the dead; they sent narrative discourse on a dizzying roll and made it pirouette, explode.

Latin American women have not been silent. The novel may not have been their most characteristic genre, but from Sor Juana Inés de la Cruz to the present, Latin letters have borne proud female inscriptions. Many of the great poets of the region have been and are women, including one Nobel Prize winner, Gabriela Mistral. It's true that novels are the necessary corrective to history and Latin history needs female chroniclers, someone to tell what happened besides the quests of our bold conquerors, brave chiefs, noble patriots, monstrous generals and feverish rebels. Allende tries. But she stays on the surface of both literature and life, revealing nothing new about either. She fails to explore the psychology of her characters, and her narrative voices are indistinguishable and archaically omniscient. If she persists in this trade—she's already a very successful journalist in Venezuela—Allende may become what Matthew Arnold was to his age and language: our best second-rate writer.

Since novelists reach a wider audience than poets, I can see why a Latin American woman would want to muscle into this all-too-male genre. Isabel Allende has done it. Everyone's reading *The House of the Spirits*. Which means, of course, that everyone's *buying* it. The rush to crown Allende queen of Latin fiction is good for business, hers and her publishers'. She probably deserves her own private boom. Her book is as engaging as most on the market, and it calls attention to the unresolved plight of her country. But it's a best seller. Period.

Enrique Fernández, "Send in the Clone," in The Village Voice, *Vol. XXX, No. 23, June 4, 1985, p. 51.*

Property Ithaca High School Library Ithaca, Michigan

HERMIONE LEE

[Even] for devotees of enchanted labyrinths, *The House of the Spirits* looks, at first, too much to swallow: the all-purpose, cut-out Latin American magical realist novel, written, what's more, by a relative of Salvador Allende, with impeccably heroic socialist and feminist credentials. There may be some reluctance, then, as we enter what Clara's granddaughter Alba calls 'the world-without-return of the imagination.'

But a world without return it does turn out to be: slowly, this fine, stirring, generous novel casts its powerful spell. It is a much more redoubtable and complex narrative, and much more grimly truthful, than at first appears.

What looks like a magic world is overtaken, with no change of tone, by the realities of Chilean history. Fictional characters overlap with legendary heroes, 'The Poet' (Neruda) and 'The Candidate' (Allende). . . .

This bitter chronicle is partly told by Esteban, a splendidly ferocious reactionary patriarch who at the very last understands the monsters his anti-Marxism has unleashed. Esteban overshadows the other political males: Pedro the guitarist, a peasant hero of the people and the life-long love of Clara's romantic daughter Blanca; Jaime, Esteban's compassionate socialist doctor son; Miguel, Alba's student anarchist lover, and Captain Garcia, Esteban's bastard son, whose vindictive revenge on his father's family embodies (perhaps too tidily) the brutalities of the military regime.

But there is an alternative narrative to Esteban's, pieced together from Clara's kaleidoscopic notebooks and from Alba's prison stories, which speaks not of politics but of magic, love and survival. It is the women—not just the family line of Rosa, Clara, Blanca and Alba, but all kinds of others: servant, prostitute, spiritualist, peasant, prisoner—whose spirits, we are finally told, cannot be destroyed by dictatorship and oppression. So magic, at first apparently an indulgence, becomes at the last a form of resistance, a way of reclaiming the past and overcoming fear.

Some reservations linger. I wasn't quite convinced by Esteban's first-person intrusions: they seemed a crude way of ensuring sympathy for him. The women's choice of the personal over the political was sometimes sentimental (though Isabel Allende writes marvellously about the pleasures of love). And I found the transformation of an ostensibly baroque, extravagant narrative into a relentless chain of linked events a little too schematic. But it seems petty to quibble, when there is such cause for celebration and delight.

> Hermione Lee, "Chile Con Carnage," in The Observer, *June 7, 1985, p. 21.*

ROBERT WILSON

The Truebas [in *The House of the Spirits*] represent two cultures that are about to be superseded, at least temporarily, by the political victory of the Salvador Allende character. Esteban's is the patriarchal world of the rich landowners and the extreme poverty on which their power is based. Clara's animism is equally a throwback to a vanishing rural society. As one of Esteban's co-religionists wrongly predicts, "Marxism doesn't stand a chance in Latin America. Don't you know it doesn't allow for the magical side of things? It's an atheistic, practical, functional doctrine. There's no way it can succeed here!"

When it does succeed, when Isabel Allende brings her story up to the events of recent decades, the magic goes out of her narrative just as it goes out of the lives of her characters. Her intentions are no longer novelistic but journalistic. No doubt she intends simply to report the stirring, then tragic, then horrifying nature of her uncle's rise and fall, and of Augusto Pinochet's reign of terror.

But it seems to me an easy way out for a novelist. She leaves her characters—Esteban, his daughter Blanca and her daughter

Alba, who narrates the story—suspended, so that when she returns to them in the end, their fate seems less significant than it would have if she had stuck with them.

Alba uses the house in the city to hide the endangered enemies of the military dictatorship; who would expect to find them in the home of the right-wing Sen. Trueba? It is once again a house of the spirits, protecting these lost souls of the left. But Alba is caught, and Esteban finds that he is powerless to prevent the torture she must endure.

You see that it's a complicated story, made more complicated, I think, because it lacks the clear themes that would give it coherence. The novel's pedestrian translation doesn't help, either.

But now and then *The House of the Spirits* soars, and the success it has already had abroad suggests that Isabel Allende will write other books. They will be welcome.

> Robert Wilson, "A Latin Epic of Marxism and Magic," in USA Today, *June 7, 1985, p. 4D.*

MARION GLASTONBURY

Following the election of a popular government [in *The House of the Spirits*], festive crowds watch the panic-stricken rich storming the banks to reclaim their money, and the effects of economic sabotage are soon evident: overnight queues outside empty shops, crops rotting in the fields, highways blocked by the abandoned trucks of striking teamsters. Despite the systematic 'stockpiling of hatred by the Right', witnesses are unprepared for the sudden eruption of cruelty at the moment of the coup, the talent for torture instantly flowering among those in uniform.

To account for this, the author traces the heritage of oppression through the saga of the Trueba family, whose children are inured to terror. Hurricane-voiced Esteban, landowner and senator, finds the blows he has inflicted on the peasants redounding on the heads of his posterity, while his visionary women, living up to the purity of their names—Nivea, Clara, Blanca and Alba, recognise that the poor need justice, not charity. This hardly amounts to clairvoyance, yet magical powers proliferate and become something of a bore. I suppose a symbolic resonance might be claimed for premonitions and poltergeists and Gothic mayhem generally; yet the disembowellings, dismemberments and disinterrals seem to be there for the sake of sensation rather than sense. No doubt necrophily and necromancy sell well, but they are not what Isabel Allende does best. It is the growth of a shanty town, the spread of a plague, the ravages of an earthquake that suit the galloping momentum of her rhapsodic style.

> Marion Glastonbury, "States of Emergency," in New Statesman, *Vol. 110, No. 2833, July 5, 1985, p. 29.**

ROBERT M. ADAMS

Two bitter twists for the Trueba family [in Isabel Allende's *The House of the Spirits*] connect that domestic chronicle with the larger disaster of the nation. Old Esteban Trueba, though passionately anticommunist and active in planning the coup that overthrew The Candidate, finds himself neglected and despised by the new regime—as did, apparently, many reactionaries in Chile itself. (Once in power, fascist regimes have no use for mere parliamentarians, no matter how conservative.) And in a climactic turnabout, old Trueba's adored granddaughter Alba is savagely tormented and brutally raped by a police officer who is no other than one of Trueba's own bastard children, sadistic as an infant and bestial as an adult. Even if a bit mechanically, this turn of the story works out the notion of retribution, and ties the gruesome ending of the novel into at least symbolic relation with the first part.

In that more purely novelistic first part, Allende rightly pays more attention to the women of the Trueba clan than to the inflexible, almost mechanistic, males. The spiritualist readings of the ladies, their fortune-telling enterprises, their attachment to fads, faiths, and folk remedies are explored in endearing particularity. Viewed with skeptical affection, they are entertaining creatures; but after a couple of hundred pages, the reader is likely to develop an irritating sense that Isabel Allende doesn't really know what to do with this cast of picturesque eccentrics. They are often silly, usually sensitive, mostly unpredictable, and therefore (in the pages of a novel) likable; but directed energy they do not have. The ladies of the clan build, or cause to be built, a big town house; they decorate it elaborately according to their tastes of the moment; they enlarge it to accommodate guests or hobbies, let it disintegrate, restore it, hide in its multiple recesses during the bad days. This is the house that gives its title to the novel; it is largely the creation and the concern of the women, scarcely less fragile and evanescent than their fantasies in a male society of rock-hard realities.

Allende has clearly profited from her reading of Gabriel García Márquez; though a little more equivocal than he about the various preternatural deeds and beliefs of her characters, she uses them to lay a dusting of legendary and mythical feeling over her story. About the only narrative tricks to which she resorts are occasional brief passages written from the point of view of Esteban Trueba himself. A long-withheld explanation in the book's final pages informs us that these are the result of a collaborative effort in reconstructing the past from Clara's diaries; the joint editors of the material have been the embittered patriarch and his ravaged granddaughter Alba. Thus the novel belongs among those that build toward an explanation of their own existence. Apart from that traditional mark of closure, the final pages develop a mood of reconciliation, even after the horrible events of butchery, rape, and terror that mark the coup. Allende's novel suggests in its closing pages a serenity that is achieved with some difficulty. (p. 21)

Robert M. Adams, "The Story Isn't Over," in The New York Review of Books, *Vol. XXXII, No. 12, July 18, 1985, pp. 20-3.**

PAUL WEST

Behind its flash, the boom in Latin American fiction is merely that continent's version of the copious documentary practiced by Arnold Bennett and deplored by Virginia Woolf in her famous essay "Mr. Bennett and Mrs. Brown," Except for the work of Carlos Fuentes, whose ebullient mind urges him toward the impossible, the undone, there is little in recent Latin American fiction that bears comparison with the innovations of authors as diverse as Samuel Beckett, Maurice Blanchot and Alain Robbe-Grillet. Instead, the boom is thickset family chronicle, done with much the same enticing garrulity that Gabriel García Márquez attributes to his favorite aunt, who told him stories nonstop.

The Latin Americans who have been most celebrated have given the world yet another good solid read, whereas the truly inventive Latin American writers—from Jorge Luis Borges, José Lezama Lima, Julio Cortázar and Mario Satz to the Brazilians Joao Guimaraes Rosa, Mário de Andrade and Osman Lins—find a smaller public, fewer major prizes and a discerning readership akin to the one that gave the French *nouveau roman* more serious attention in the United States than it initially got in France. It was ever thus. Rossini is not Ives.

Family chronicle reassures us, of course. It teaches us that this thing that we curse and yet prize is really the main stuff of life, the source of endurance and mutation, the irreducible focus and context, the dimension in which all things happen. In the family the human being is at his or her most commonplace, and it is against a family background that black sheep must be savored. And family, happy or unhappy, is the team version of existential pain, the theatrical version of something most grievously expressed by loners and pariahs or by the fierce paucity of so unpeopled a fiction as Beckett's *How It Is*. The act of reading is a lonely one, and perhaps lonely readers, or at any rate readers who are by themselves, prefer something chummy before their eyes—some festive, uproarious knockabout to distract them from the knowledge that the family of man is truly the loneliest individual of all, a hapless sacrificial animal on the altar of zealous militarism. As my mother used to say during the blitzkrieg, as we crouched under the kitchen table (until we got an air raid shelter), "If we go we'll go *together*." The thing she abhorred, on behalf of the rest of us, was any one of us having to go it alone. In this sense, the family novel is a talisman.

Perhaps this explains the runaway vogue of Isabel Allende's first novel [*The House of the Spirits*], which has been translated into at least a dozen languages. The author happens to be the niece of the slain Chilean President, but even that fateful connection can hardly account for the response to this ably done variant of the typical recent Latin American novel, one formula for which might run: while moving elastically about in time, heap up incongruous juxtapositions (a block of ice in the jungle, Márquez; a mouse trapped inside a worn corset, Allende) and encrust the characters with eccentric surface. Many times over, convey the notion of plenty, and overanimate everyone to fever pitch. Make the baggy monster spill over. Make it groan and seep like the exploding gourmand in a recent Monty Python movie. Suggest the swarmingness of things to give the impression, as the poet Diane Ackerman puts it, that we are "sucking on jungle."

There is much to be said for this attitude to people and their mores. At least it requires that the novelist be observant and inventive; at most it requires what many novelists lack, a surfeit of material. The boom novelist must appear to be immersed in life, a life more garish and more intense than most folk know. Here are glimpses at random from the opening pages of *The House of the Spirits*. While the household tries to sleep, Uncle Marcos drags his suitcases up and down the halls, tooting on barbaric musical instruments. He takes off aboard a mechanical bird with an eagle's face. . . . There is more—from an idiot tethered in a courtyard, beating his enormous penis on the ground, to a mother whose legs resemble "bruised, elephantine columns covered with open wounds in which the larvae of flies and worms had made their nests."

Images this lurid suit me. Something is making full use of my mind's eye, a rare thing in contemporary English or American fiction. But such images do blot out what goes on among the characters. I found myself bored by the family to and fro, what I could discern of it, and eager for the next sensational tableau.

I had to keep reminding myself that this is the saga of the Trueba family, that Clara and Esteban have a daughter Blanca and two twins, Nicholás and Jaime, who get involved with a socialist leader called the Candidate. As *The House of the Spirits* advances, it calms down into the book Allende probably wanted to write, and would have had she not felt obliged to toe the line of magical realism. Hers is a realism learned from models and ritually imposed from without: heraldic, not sociological. As the book begins to get allegorical, through the introduction of a murdered poet of world stature and a murdered president, Allende begins the diatribe she no doubt had in mind all along.

If you recall the opening of *One Hundred Years of Solitude* (''Many years later, as he faced the firing squad, Colonel Aureliano Buendía was to remember that distant afternoon when his father took him to discover ice''), you may hear echoes in this book, as in ''At the end of his life, when his ninety years had turned him into a twisted fragile tree, Esteban Trueba would recall those moments with his granddaughter as the happiest of his whole existence.'' Such echoes are bows, perhaps, but a book of bows becomes a bow-wow. (pp. 52-3)

> *Paul West, ''Narrative Overdrive,'' in* The Nation,
> *Vol. 241, No. 2, July 20 & 27, 1985, pp. 52-4.**

D.A.N. JONES

It is obvious that Isabel Allende's novel about Chile, *The House of the Spirits,* has something about it that appeals to women readers: but I cannot imagine what that something is. 'Magical realism' is the vogue-word: but this seems to me a farrago of fantasy-triggers. I was astonished when Marina Warner asserted on television that the book 'gives you an astonishing understanding of a political situation'. On the same day, Marilyn Butler was equally effusive on Radio 3 and Hermione Lee assured us in the *Observer* that the author has 'impeccably heroic socialist and feminist credentials' [see excerpt above]. My daughter-in-law brought home *Cosmopolitan* with a long extract, prettily illustrated, and an astounding comment from Emma Dally: 'Although it is not a ''women's novel'', the strength of the female characters is quite astounding.' Isabel Allende herself on television has described these figments as 'strong women who are somehow opposite to violence and torture, all this male world'. They had struck me as rather ineffectual ladies.

The grandmother, mother and daughter in this ninety-years-long family chronicle are called Clara, Blanca and Alba—names which, Isabel Allende explains, stand for whiteness and purity. Their principal man is Esteban, the grandfather, a landowner and Conservative senator, with his own peculiar regard for whiteness: he is made to say, during Chile's democratic period, that his nation can 'set an example for this continent of Indians and Negroes who spend their time making revolutions. Here the Conservative party wins cleanly and openly . . .' . . . . This boringly stupid and vicious man is treated with great tolerance by the author and by the ladies of his house, as if sighing sweetly: 'You know what men are!'

Esteban spends much of his time brutally raping the daughters of his peons; sometimes he goes to brothels instead, to be coddled by lovable whores. The ladies of his house don't seem to mind. Esteban might plead in mitigation that his wife, the pure Clara, no longer sleeps with him, preferring to cuddle up with his sister. . . . Clara is too pure to concern herself with her sons or with any domestic duties: after all, she has servants and Esteban pays them when he is not raping their daughters. Clara prefers dealing with the ghosts in her house, including those of some old South American mummies, almost the only local product: everything else seems to have been imported.

Clara's magical powers are strengthened by books left her by her uncle Marcos, an intrepid explorer who used to fly about in a vintage airplane shaped like a bird with flapping wings. This magically unrealistic uncle also left her a horrid dog, caked with excrement and urine, which grew to be as big as a horse: this dog could carry a bitch around town, 'impaled on his immense masculinity', until the pair were hosed down by the servants, whereupon the poor bitch was left to die in the courtyard. The ladies of the house couldn't care less. Clara's daughter, Blanca, has a blank marriage with an effeminate Frenchman who reads Sade in bed and enjoys erotic murals in his private room. So Blanca's daughter, Alba, is fathered by another man, a political activist whose left-wing aspirations are expressed by singing a song about hens ganging up on a fox. Esteban wants to kill this left-winger and is guided to his hideout by his illegitimate grandson: but the old fool only manages to cut the chap's fingers off. Later, Esteban makes his grandson into a policeman, hoping he will use his authority for the benefit of the Conservative Party: but this plan goes awry when Pinochet seizes power in 1973, for the young policeman decides to arrest Esteban's legitimate granddaughter, and she is raped and tortured most horridly, in the style we expect from Pinochet's men . . .

Pinochet? But he's *real*. What is he doing in this farrago of feminist 'magical realism'? A plain man's irritation must be expressed. . . . Isabel Allende presents her novel as 'a portrait of Latin America, not only Chile'—and that means the same old Hollywood film-set, populating an enormous . . . continent with ferocious rapists on horseback and lovely ladies in black lace dresses with big red roses in their hair. The hair is green nowadays, to accord with the feminist aspect of magical realism. The trouble with this book's political stance is that it gives the impression that nothing can be done about Chile's notorious government—you know what South Americans are like, ha ha!—and that Pinochet's regime is no worse than its predecessors. This is surely untrue.

From a more literary point of view, we might complain that the book, though 'packed with incident', is not well packed. The bizarre little fantasies come sputtering out with an inconsequential brevity, like ideas thrown up at a script conference for a Latin American soap opera or horror film. Some of the ideas, if properly developed, might make a film story: directors could introduce a sense of place and actors could put some flesh on the bones of the characters. But it would be as well to keep real-life politics out of it. (p. 26)

> *D.A.N. Jones, ''Magical Realism,'' in* London Review of Books, *August 1, 1985, pp. 26-7.**

Carolyn Chute

1947-

American novelist, short story writer, and journalist.

Chute has spent most of her life amidst the bleak rural poverty she depicts in her first novel, *The Beans of Egypt, Maine* (1985). After a relatively sheltered childhood in Cape Elizabeth, Maine, she dropped out of school at the age of sixteen to marry. Divorced three years later, Chute struggled to support herself and a young daughter, relying on government assistance between working as a domestic, picking potatoes, and other low-paying jobs. During this time, Chute acquired her high school diploma and, when she could afford it, took courses in psychology, sociology, and writing at the University of Maine. Chute says that she wrote stories as a girl, but was never ambitious about it: "I didn't think of a writer as something you grew up to be. It wasn't a thing I could aspire to. I didn't know any writers. Folks never had any books in their houses." She adds, "I knew about the concept of stories because my father and my grandmother were good storytellers, that's all." As an adult, she worked as a correspondent for the *Portland Evening Express* and the *Courier Free Press*. She has also contributed short fiction to *Ploughshares, Ohio Review, Shenandoah, Grandstreet*, and *Agni Review*.

Chute says that she began writing *The Beans* in 1980 as a way of recovering from the loss of her second child, who died in infancy. She explains how she devised the fictional setting of Egypt, Maine, where her heroine, Earlene Pomerleau, grows up across the street from the Bean family's trailer camp: "I drew a map of it—a little trailer home, the right-of-way, a big barn across the street and then the house." Chute's second husband, Michael, a "mountain man" who never learned to read or write, nevertheless helped with the writing process by listening to her read the manuscript aloud, then discussing with her the plot, the characters, and various details. Their collaboration resulted in a stark, vivid portrait of the Beans, a brutish backwoods tribe that critic Bertha Harris describes as "infernally white trash." Chute resents this and other derogatory attitudes towards her creations; for her, such opinions are a reflection of the bigotry that she and her family have endured from a society that willfully misunderstands or ignores the poor. At the same time, she deliberately refrains from making any social commentary in *The Beans*. "I don't feel it's the place of fiction to make judgments or prescribe changes," she comments. "I think ever since the beginning of time, and until the world ends, there will be some people who will get everything and others that don't. It's just nature."

Although critics have repeatedly compared the Beans to William Faulkner's Snopses, Chute never read Faulkner until her novel had been published. "He uses a lot of big words," she says, comparing Faulkner's extravagant language to her own concise, colloquial style. "And his sentences run from here back to the airport. I couldn't make a sentence that long. I'd forget what the first part of it was." When critics compare Chute to Faulkner, Erskine Caldwell, or Alice Walker, they

Photograph by Christopher Little

generally refer to the similarity of the authors' subject matter. As for Chute's style, some found her episodic, disjointed narrative a distraction. In general, however, critics praised her skill in evoking the claustrophobic world of the uncouth, violent, and incestuous Bean dynasty. Chute's book provoked furious rebuttals from various parts of Maine, where Bean is a common family name. Chute reports that her next novel will be set in a junkyard based on the one in Gorham, Maine, where Michael once worked. "I used to spend time there eavesdropping," she remarks, in a letter to her publisher. "It's a great place."

PUBLISHERS WEEKLY

Like the Snopes clan of Faulkner's Yoknapatawpha, the Beans of Egypt, Maine, know a stark poverty that discolors every part of their lives. The difference in the Beans, who with this book [*The Beans of Egypt, Maine*] may take their place in the literature of rural America, is that they are on the very bottom; each family member is uniformly devoid of the desire or will to rise above the sordid legacy, and they drag others inexorably down with them.

Earlene Pomerleau begins life across the road from the Beans, in a shack shared with her small, frail father, an unemployed carpenter, and her Gram, a sour woman who evokes the name of Jesus at every turn. [Earlene] witnesses the Beans' inexplicable ways, despising them for the hugeness of the men and the fertility of the women. But in later years she finds herself in the unbreakable cycle, impregnated by and then married to Beal Bean, living amidst his squalor. Her children have "foxcolor Bean eyes"; they take on the worst traits of their elders, while Earlene assumes the desperate Christian convictions of her dying Gram. Beal, laid off from the mill, explodes in violence and is killed by the police—angels of mercy for Earlene. As she is getting comfortable with her widowhood, however, Beal's cousin Rubie returns from prison to degrade her further and to continue the downward spiral.

Chute tells her story with a subtlety and power scarcely matched by writers of the educated world. There are layers of Christian symbolism here, in perverted form, plumbed by few since Faulkner, and a portrait of a woman as dehumanized and brutalized, yet alive, as the women of Alice Walker's *The Color Purple*. Chute seems not to bear the influence of anyone in her writing, though; she is startlingly original. No self-pity nor muffled cry for social justice is present in this short book—just fiction at its most involving, resonant and clear.

> *A review of "The Beans of Egypt, Maine," in* Publishers Weekly, *Vol. 226, No. 20, November 16, 1984, p. 53.*

D.J.R. BRUCKNER

Sympathy is out of the question for the characters in *The Beans of Egypt, Maine*. Salvation seems beyond them and Carolyn Chute sometimes seems to adopt the view of Uncle Loren in the novel. He says: "Sweetheart, pigs and hogs is superior to folks. Folks are ratty messed-up back-stabbin' sons-a-whores. I'd rather be a born-once hog than a born-again Christian any day."

Some of the folks are funny people, especially two Bean women who set out to seduce elusive men with very different results—one gets daily boxes of doughnuts for her crop of babies and the other gets one kiss from a terrified junkman who had been imprisoned in a bathroom by a dog. Those hilarious deflations of sexual romance are welcome interludes in the chronicle of the Beans.

The Beans are an incest-infested brood; the men, when they are not working, join all the other Beans in the clan's principal occupations—eating, having sex and shooting animals. The senior Beans live in a trailer from which the family fans out like an ineradicable growth all over the town of Egypt. Next door to the patriarchal trailer the Pomerleaus—Earlene and her father—live in a house the father surrounds with signs warning Beans to keep out.

But he cannot keep Earlene in. She runs away from home as a teen-ager and ends up with young Beal Bean. Beal is one of many male power symbols in the novel; he reproduces not only with Earlene but with one of his aunts and many other women. . . .

The plot might be Earlene's descent into the Bean inferno; the image of descent is conjured up repeatedly. But a descent from what? Her father is a little man intent on replacing God's creation with his own—tiny figures he whittles day and night. Her addlebrained mother is absent except for one visit. Her slowly dying grandmother, in despair, uses hair-raising biblical verses to condemn almost everyone. The one lasting legacy Earlene gets from her family is the habit of passing judgment in the tongues of prophets. . . .

The poverty of all these people is evident everywhere—in their clothes, houses, trailers, junked logging rigs and cars, and in the hordes of children and even the animals that often seem to have more character than the children. Mrs. Chute's sensuous language makes one aware of it also in the way the characters are perceived—noisy, crude of feature and reeking.

All Egypt smells. Beal brings with him the scent of pine from the logs, or just the outdoors. A junkman smells like the underside of a car and fills whole rooms with the odor. A woman who appears to produce children by the litter fools men's noses into thinking they are sniffing the great earth mother.

This first novel is an impressive performance. But there is a serious underlying fault. Its tales are of women and men, all told from women's points of view. Eventually, all the women's views are drawn together in Earlene, but her view is disorienting. She is captivated by her father (there is more than a mere hint of incest here). She kisses Beal's filthy feet in the presence of her daughter. Later her caring for Reuben suggests something just a little short of worship. In a sense she defeats them all, but she cannot resist them.

When the novel opens Earlene, who shares the role of narrator throughout with the author, gives us a vision of the big men and women of her world as they appear to a little girl. One has to suspect that, although she grows eventually, her vision doesn't. The patriarchy of her abysmal universe is mean, oppressive, brutal and repulsive. But the men who occupy its seats, or beds, of power are objects of terrible adoration.

Possibly, the problem lies in the imaginative source of the story. The book's dedication reads: "In memory of real Reuben. Who spared him this occasion? Who spared him rage?" If the epigraph applies to anyone in the novel, it is not to Reuben, but to Beal, or even to Earlene's father, both of whom are compassionately drawn while Reuben is only a figure in a morality play. The reader cannot but feel there is a disjunction between the emotional force of Mrs. Chute's writing and the story she is telling. But that force is considerable. By the end, she has made one feel that life, even the earth itself, is to be mourned.

> *D.J.R. Bruckner, in a review of "The Beans of Egypt, Maine," in* The New York Times, *January 4, 1985, p. C28.*

BERTHA HARRIS

Carolyn Chute's infernally white-trash Beans of Maine have taken a chunk out of the literary turf formerly owned and operated by Jeeter Lester of *Tobacco Road* and the more grotesque of Faulkner's Mississippians. The Beans have in common with their Southern kin tribal decrepitude, personal degeneracy and unrelieved squalor. But their particular claim is based on incest. The Beans' favorite way of breeding more Beans is the first tenet of family pride, and they even seem to have elaborated the oldest crime against nature into a metaphysic.

In her startling and original first novel [*The Beans of Egypt, Maine*], it is clear that it's the metaphysics of incest—and of father-daughter incest particularly—that interests Mrs. Chute. Bean incestuousness is almost never described by the writer but is a kind of subtext of sensibility. Many of our perceptions of Bean mating habits will depend on getting past the author's diversionary tactics. These tactics include the use of a highly lyrical prose and frequent and effective quotation from the King James Version of the Bible. What emerges is a kind of religious formulation—part myth, part hellfire fundamentalism. . . .

Earlene (who shares the narration with the author) opens the novel in the fake-ingenuous style of child actors transmitting sexual innuendo. In the beginning (and from the vantage of the lonely, repressive Pomerleau way of life), little Earlene sees her neighbors as no more than exotics. . . .

According to Daddy, ''what the Beans do inside their mobile home would make a grown man cry.'' In spite of Daddy's protestations, the ancient apologia for incest (if you ain't good enough for your own family, who are you good enough for?) probably applies to Pomerleaus too. Though Mrs. Chute, via Earlene, is coy about what the Pomerleaus do inside their ranch house, it's clear that Daddy sleeps in the same bed with Earlene.

In obedience to the author's scheme of like calling implacably to like, Earlene shortly finds an excuse to reject her little Daddy and make a religious-sexual move upmarket by going off with Beal Bean. (In this novel's scheme of things, which seems to make a sacrament of what is usually considered a social evil, Earlene's degradation is progress toward a higher good.) Earlene's marriage to Beal is a submission to rape, impregnation, the birth of two Bean babies, catatonic depression, destitution and servitude. Eventually, Beal, chronically jobless and crazed by poverty, goes on a doomed rampage, shooting out the windows of a nearby house. When Beal dies, Earlene just takes up with his cousin Reuben, now back from prison.

Earlene doesn't have real life choices; she lives in a religious drama. Mrs. Chute grants an ardor to Earlene's uninterrupted transition usually reserved for sacred texts. But at the end of the novel, Earlene is a half-mad conglomeration of two incompatible theologies.

Mystical conflicts aside, Mrs. Chute often enough abandons the portentous and is deliberately funny about the Beans. They are endlessly slamming doors, dropping food in their beards, moaning, stomping, snorting and unzipping. But other matters that may appear funny or pathetic to the reader are solemn affirmations of Beanness to Mrs. Chute. Bean women are always pregnant or about to become so, but they are earth goddesses, not victims or fools. Bean men are ever at the ready for the call of the wild Bean womb, but they are neither villains nor buffoons—they're dark, priapic gods.

The trouble is knowing what Mrs. Chute thinks. Does she really believe that Earlene's degradation has a kind of holy beauty— that civilization is merely an overlay of hypocrisy and repression? A careful reading of *The Beans* reveals beneath the comedy and the religious interplay a relentlessly bleak vision. But vital clues to the novel's meaning might easily escape the reader who stops to laugh or gag or figure out who belongs to whom— or make a moral or political judgment.

The unstated object of Earlene's life with Beal Bean is to rid herself of all the influences of the false father—the puritanical

Lee—so she can find her eventual apotheosis in the arms of the true pagan patriarch, Reuben Bean himself, who may be her actual father. The cleansing medium is humiliation. . . .

The Beans, it seems, are of royal descent. This novel's locale is not an accident of whimsy. Half-hidden in the father-daughter sexual fantasy and Bean rambunctiousness is a fantastic comparison of the Beans of Egypt, Maine, with the Egyptian dynasties. While this analogy goes some distance in explaining, for example, why we hear Bean babies so frequently ''hiss'' (they are like sacred serpents), it functions specifically as Mrs. Chute's ultimate excuse for incest. The Beans are merely exercising their royal prerogative.

Mrs. Chute has a gift for humor and image making. If it weren't for the hocus-pocus Egyptology and Earlene's degradation, it would be tempting to read *The Beans of Egypt, Maine* as a talented attempt to recreate the ''something nasty in the woodshed'' of Stella Gibbons's hilarious 1932 novel, *Cold Comfort Farm*. But there is Earlene, and Carolyn Chute is dead serious about Earlene. What happens to Earlene inside this novel would make a grown woman cry.

> Bertha Harris, ''Holy Beauty or Degradation?'' in The New York Times Book Review, *January 31, 1985, p. 7.*

SUZANNE FREEMAN

By now, as readers, we have come to know the trademarks of backwoods poverty—Southern backwoods poverty, that is: junked cars and weary women, barking dogs and barefoot children, shotguns and whiskey and hope, all run dry. These things have pretty much held true from Yoknapatawpha, Mississippi to Chattahoochee, Georgia to Dogpatch. And now, in her first novel [*The Beans of Egypt, Maine*], Carolyn Chute gives us a Northern territory to add to the list. Egypt, Maine may not be found on any map, but we can guess that it lies not far from the real-life towns of Poland, Peru or China, Maine, and we can see, for certain, that it's close to the bone for Carolyn Chute. ''This book was involuntarily researched,'' reads a quote from Chute on the cover, ''I have lived poverty. I didn't CHOOSE it. No one would choose humiliation, pain and rage.''

It's fair to say that not even the Beans, Egypt's prevailing overgrown, hulking, low-life family would CHOOSE humiliation, pain and rage, but, if that's all life dishes out to them, they'll slurp it right up and, maybe, even thrive on it. (p. 3)

Chute takes us right to the innards of the family secrets and what we find there is every bit as messy as we might have expected: incest and brutality and monumental ignorance. Chute does not gloss over any of it, but what she does do is handle it with astonishing humor and good grace. In scene after scene, her vision, which is both knowing and funny, sustains us. (pp. 3, 8)

In general, the Beans are not what we would call good-looking. They have massive bodies, small heads, bad teeth and ''fox color'' eyes. Their complexions are hardly peaches and cream. But Chute takes care to give them a wonderful, low, brutish appeal. There is a kind of thrilling strength in their shoulders and arms and big hands. And, when their logging trucks rumble down the road, the whole earth seems to shake. It's not surprising, then, that as clean little Earlene Pomerleau grows up, she finds herself watching big, sweaty Beal Bean from a distance and thinking the unthinkable: she wonders for instance, if it's possible to tell just where his beard ends and his chest hair begins.

Finally, after her daddy has washed out her mouth with soap once too often, Earlene runs off with Beal. Eventually she becomes a Bean herself and bears big Bean babies with fox-color eyes. And her life with Beal turns out to be pretty much everything her daddy might have predicted: it's degrading and impoverished and, in the end, disaster strikes. But, this time, we see it all differently. Because, like Earlene Pomerleau, we're no longer looking at Bean life from across the right-of-way. Chute has moved us into the tumble-down house and we have watched, in the night, as Earlene unlaces her husband's worn work boots and kisses his big, tired feet. What Chute has given us is an inside look at Bean love and it's changed our focus for good.

One of the trickiest bits in writing a regional novel must be getting the dialect to ring true. Chute does a fairly credible job, but, after a while, it just gets a trifle much, contemplatin' all those dropped g's. And the funny part of it is that Maine backwoods dialect, in print, seems generic, like those junked cars and weary women. It reads just like Southern backwoods dialect. Still, we're never left doubting that this is Chute's own turf. She has staked it out and we look forward to visiting it again. Carolyn Chute may well have lived in poverty, but what we learn here is that she has a wealth of knowledge about the human spirit. (p. 8)

Suzanne Freeman, "Down East Gothic," in Book World—The Washington Post, *February 17, 1985, pp. 3, 8.*

ELLEN LESSER

What Faulkner did for Mississippi, Chute does for Maine. [*The Beans of Egypt, Maine*] is regional writing at its most evocative. Chute's Maine is a cross between New England primitive and New England tacky. . . .

The novel is written in sections alternately titled "Earlene" and "The Beans." Earlene's sections are told in first-person, in the dialect of Egypt, Maine: "dinnah," "downcellah," "eyup," "no-suh," "wicked glad." For the Beans, Chute uses a third-person narrator and an idiom that stands a bit apart from the characters. In both voices she writes with tremendous vigor and precision, rendering Egypt and its inhabitants with a stark but lyrical poetry.

Part of Chute's considerable accomplishment is that she makes the reader see the Beans as people, not animals. Even before Earlene becomes a Bean by marriage, Chute brings us into the turquoise mobile home, into Aunt Roberta Bean's "wee blue house" to show with a meticulous humanity the reality beneath the stereotype. Sensitive young Beal, teased and tormented, sometimes "wishes he had no face at all, just a soft white empty place like the sky." Beal flees the mobile home for Aunt Roberta's house, seeking the comfort he never got from his own idiot mother. His visits yield another string of inbred Bean babies, and Roberta vacillates between rejecting and embracing him. Wherever the towering Roberta goes, she is surrounded by children, clinging to her boots, climbing her legs, "eyes wrinkled up with love"—"forever close, madly close."

Chute never shies away from the brutal or ugly, as when Rubie Bean—the black sheep of this dark family—beats the game warden until "he cannot distinguish himself from the pinespills and mud he is bleeding into." Yet her vision also has scope

for lust among the soil and squash vines, for tenderness, for dreams, for the grace a woman like Roberta Bean carries amid the populous squalor. . . .

To make a reader feel at home in Rubie Bean's Egypt is no mean feat, but Carolyn Chute does just that. It is a place not easily forgotten.

Ellen Lesser, "No Deliverance," in The Village Voice, *Vol. XXX, No. 8, February 19, 1985, p. 58.*

PETER S. PRESCOTT

To a callous eye, Carolyn Chute's characters [in *The Beans of Egypt, Maine*] might appear prime candidates for compulsory sterilization. Cousins to Faulkner's Snopeses and Caldwell's Lesters, the prolific Bean family subsists in poverty and squalor in Maine's logging country. . . . This is an episodic first novel, and Earlene is its pivotal character; she narrates half the stories through which the narrative advances over a decade. Earlene's about 10 when the story starts; in time, she will marry Beal Bean, a backward, useless but not unsympathetic fellow who exercises his uncontainable sexuality on his unmarried, uncommonly fertile aunt.

Does this sound grim beyond enduring? It's not. Chute's novel pulses with kinetic energy. It seizes the reader on its opening page with a rhythm, a language, a knock-about country humor unmistakably its own: "My heart feels like runnin'-hard shoes," says Earlene. It's instantly clear that Chute knows exactly what poverty is—the pain and anguish of being unable to take charge of one's life—and the frustration, humiliation and rage that the stress of poverty provokes. Her story deals with what remains of humanity when family feeling, even human communication, has been reduced to minimum efficiency; its strength derives from its guarded optimism and from a pathos unmarred by sentimentality.

Peter S. Prescott, in a review of "The Beans of Egypt, Maine," in Newsweek, *Vol. CV, No. 8, February 25, 1985, p. 86.*

An Excerpt from *The Beans of Egypt, Maine*

The McKenzies' car toots as it buzzes away into the slanted storm. I carry Dale and his new brown shoes. Bonny Loo smashes at the snow, trying to get room to open the piazza door.

"What's these footprints?!" she cries out. Her frozen breath is a chain like paper dolls dancing out of her mouth. She presses her bare palms together as if in prayer. "COMPANY!"

I murmur, "That's our footprints when we came out."

"No-SUH!" she screams. "These are NEW!"

We stomp our boots inside the piazza.

Through the door glass, I can see somebody at our supper table! He handles part of a gun, his fingers long and short. One fingernail is just a claw. He looks up at us through the glass, lookin' in at him. His mouth is shut up on a wooden match. Seethin' over the mouth is an untrimmed mustache of black. Some gray cuts through.

It's the ghost of my dead husband, Beal Bean.

Pinkie butts at the man's new yellow work boots, butts hard with his head.

The right boot shoves him away.

At first, I guess I just stand there with my mouth open, but now I'm moving through the kitchen that smells of WD-40, of toast he has made in the oven, of hot peanut butter. He has lit the lamp to make a coarse light over the guns on the table. He watches me go into the hall, carrying Dale.

Bonny Loo says, 'Hi!''

When I come back, I says, ''Bonny Loo, shut the door, for cryin' out loud!'' I take off my coat, hang it, start a pot of tea. My hands aren't shakin'. I'm proud of how steady my hands do these things.

Pinkie is back at the boots, rubbin' and purrin'. The boot draws up and kicks, knocks Pinkie into a skid.

His voice, hoarser than Beal's, is tellin' Bonny Loo that if these weapons ain't oiled, they'll pit up . . . and you can't knock the friggin' sights . . . an' who's been fuckin' around with his guns while he was gone? Around these words his mustache rolls.

I fit myself on the stool in the corner, my back to the wall, clumps of snow droppin' from my pant legs. I light up a Kent.

I say, ''You're Rubie, ain't you?''

Bonny Loo's eyes widen.

''That ain't the question,'' he says hoarsely, workin' his fox-color eyes over the bolt and spring in his hands. ''The *real* question is, *who* are *you?*'' The tops of his hands, softly haired, crisscrossed with roused arteries, are the hands of Beal. No difference. No difference. In my throat, something growing to the size of an egg crowds my windpipe.

''Beal's wife,'' I say.

He grunts.

I clutch my knees. ''You can call me Earlene.''

HUGH M. CRANE

Chute's first novel [*The Beans of Egypt, Maine*] suffers primarily from its divided structure—part portrait of the unsavory Bean family, part biography of neighbor Earlene Pomerleau. Until Beal Bean becomes Earlene's husband, we are given mystifying stories without a story and characters who engage or outrage our sympathies, then recede. Chute vividly evokes the substitutions rural poverty must make for everything from drinking glasses to romance, yet her imaginary Egypt can also echo with Old Testament allusions. The writing is uneven: sometimes striking and provocative, but mainly hovering uncomfortably between (perfectly caught) rural Maine speech patterns and a more literary spareness. The result will appeal more to readers of *Ploughshares* and other little mags than to the *Yankee* audience.

Hugh M. Crane, in a review of ''The Beans of Egypt, Maine,'' in Library Journal, *Vol. 110, No. 4, March 1, 1985, p. 101.*

ANNABEL EDWARDS

The cover design and style of *The Beans* is straight from the children's bookshelf; its content is sufficiently full of poverty, squalor, violence and incest to turn a social worker's stomach. At first sight Carolyn Chute's novel is confusing.

The narrative, which spans about twenty years, does not really have a thread. It consists of isolated incidents and dead ends, with sub-plots appearing and fading in a matter of pages. Through this series of random events Carolyn Chute convincingly builds up a picture of the lifestyle of a very poor rural community in Maine, north-eastern USA. . . .

The book is split into sections, some narrated by Earlene Pomerleau and some told in the third person, but nowhere is there any sign of an omniscient authorial voice, no moral judgement is made and the reader is not invited to make one either. In this harsh, impoverished world a woman is supposed to find herself a man and stick with him, ignoring his infidelities, however violently or coarsely he treats her—a strange but effective form of self-preservation on the women's part. Illegitimate babies appear to unattached women with barely a question asked and one of the Bean women, Roberta, takes unmarried motherhood to an almost mythic level—a strange, tall woman always followed by an ever increasing swarm of spewing, mewling babies apparently possessed of a collective consciousness. . . .

The characters are trapped by the brutality of life at subsistence level and there are only occasional interlopers who enter this claustrophobic world. Strangers approach with suspicion, like March Goodspeed ''the celebrated highway engineer'', who interprets the present of rabbit meat that Roberta leaves at his door as some kind of sinister threat. Earlene's daughter seems to be the only character likely to escape—a dispassionate, self-educating scientist and pragmatist of startling precocity who conducts endless experiments with mouldy doughnuts and small dead animals. But even she, by the end of the book, has retired to her bedroom to chain smoke cigarettes in adolescent despair. (p. 30)

Annabel Edwards, ''Squalor, and Incest,'' in Books and Bookmen, *No. 354, April, 1985, pp. 30-1.**

ANN MARIE CUNNINGHAM

In her vivid first novel [*The Beans of Egypt, Maine*], Carolyn Chute, born and still living in Maine, writes both darkly and hilariously about her relatives, neighbors, and acquaintances, who bear the outward signs and inner scars of rural poverty. There is no Operation Bootstrap in Egypt, Maine, and even if there were, Chute believes, her characters could not take advantage of it.

This is not the Maine that summer people see. The countryside matches the characters' meager circumstances and spirits: it's almost always ''a cold damp day, the hardwoods iron color, still leafless.'' . . .

Unlike, for example, Alice Walker's heroines in *The Color Purple*, Chute's characters make no attempt to transcend their circumstances. Men find something on which to vent their rage; women duck or, if they're luckier, stand watching.

Feminist readers have been puzzled by Chute's portrait of Earlene's downward spiral and deepening passivity. ''The trouble,'' writes critic Bertha Harris [see excerpt above], ''is knowing what Mrs. Chute thinks'' about her heroine, who progresses from "a childhood dominated by God-fearing Gram and Gram-fearing Daddy to a worse subjugation—through marriage—as a woman among the Beans." In a recent interview with *Ms.*, Chute replied that she is accurately depicting the condition of the poor, and "women are the ones who tend to be poor. When I haven't had any money at all, I've felt helpless and withdrawn. The smallest task seemed overwhelming." . . .

Chute is trying to show that men and women who have no desire or talent for the American dream are of value. Rather than offering solutions to Earlene's plight, she wants readers to contemplate it, to know what it feels like to be poor. "Some people are like the first puppy out of the box; they leap over barricades," said Chute. "But some people are too meek or awkward to do that." The jobless Beal and Earlene, two puppies who remain in their box, are finally done in. Beal goes on a rampage and is shot down by the police. At the novel's close, the widowed Earlene seems about to marry violent, unstable Reuben Bean, the darkest of her dark gods. Chances are, Chute has said, that Earlene "will be a battered wife, will be poor, and probably will have four to eight more kids. Because that's (more children) what's good, and that's what's everything in Egypt, Maine."

Such a devastatingly pessimistic portrait of the cycle of rural poverty is enormously disturbing to any reader who believes in organizing, not agonizing: you just want Earlene's degradation to *stop*. Chute simply seems to be urging compassion for those who cannot help themselves.

The gratifying part about the Beans is that they firmly establish Carolyn Chute as a powerful writer. Unlike another equally poor state, Mississippi, Maine has been celebrated mostly by out-of-staters, not homegrown talent. All along, however, there has been great folk material in Maine for the taking, as Sarah Orne Jewett recognized in 1896 when she recounted a middle-aged rural woman's stories in *The Country of the Pointed Firs*. In *The Beans of Egypt, Maine,* another gifted native daughter—an eavesdropper with an uncanny ear for dialogue—is once again doing the storytelling.

> Ann Marie Cunningham, "Carolyn Chute: Down East
> Daughter," in Ms., Vol. XIII, No. 10, April, 1985,
> p. 17.

MEGAN MARSHALL

Since novel-writing rarely offers a living wage, novelists have long been drawn from the aristocracy. They are the only ones who can afford the luxury. But occasionally a writer emerges from the working class to affirm our democratic belief that art can be made of anything and by anyone. Dickens was such a writer, and so was Mark Twain. Their accurate portrayal of the everyday lives of common people brought them a popularity largely unknown to novelists whose material and means came from the world of privilege.

Carolyn Chute may well be the latest in this line. As many news accounts have made clear, Chute has lived the rural poverty she describes in her first novel, the instantly popular *Beans of Egypt, Maine*. . . .

The Beans is written in Chute's own Down East dialect which, with its combination of wit and naive insight, is cousin to Huck Finn's Mississippi drawl. Its tribe of brutish characters ("If it runs, a Bean will shoot it! If it falls, a Bean will eat it!") is a backwoods American version of the Jellybys of *Bleak House*. Reviewers have compared her fictional Maine wilderness to

Faulkner's Yoknapatawpha County, and the resemblance is there—in the primitive residents, the raw natural beauty, and in the power of the author's voice, although Chute claims never to have read Faulkner until the reviews started coming in.

But don't get me wrong: [*The Beans of Egypt, Maine*] is not literary. Its only allusions are to the Sunday comics. One character shows off a bicep tattooed with Donald Duck "in midquack." Another, the towering Roberta Bean, closely resembles Popeye's sweetheart Olive Oyl, with her pin head, fist-sized black bun, and squeaky high-pitched voice. And in Egypt, Maine, as in Popeye's Sweet Haven, emotions are acted on as soon as they are felt. In Egypt, however, where people live in trailers and on foodstamps, the most common emotion is anger, and that means men beating up other men, men beating their women, women beating their children, children beating their dogs. . . . (p. 25)

More often than not, women consent to sex simply in order to calm their violent-tempered men. Sexual violence—either in the form of rape, or in the brutalizing poverty women enter as a result of unwanted pregnancies—is the dark side of life in Egypt. And it is what sets [*The Beans of Egypt, Maine*] apart from the male tradition of fiction about the poor—from Twain to Dreiser to Faulkner—where poverty's chief damage is to the spirit, its greatest wrong, stifled opportunity.

Original and energetic as her writing is, Chute cannot seem to find what Faulkner saw as "the love and honor and pity and pride and compassion and sacrifice" in the lives of the poor. She shows us there is nothing uplifting or even dignified in their tragedies—the payoff we can safely expect in Dickens or Twain. The Beans are stuck, their tiny homes claustrophobic, their only comforts perverse.

But then, unlike Twain or Dickens or Faulkner, Chute has lived her entire life amidst the poverty she writes about. If Mark Twain had not had a man's freedom to leave it all behind, he might have written differently about life on the Mississippi. While Huck Finn lights out for the territory, Earlene spreads her legs for yet another of the Bean men she relies on to support her children and provide a bit of companionship. She takes up the fundamentalist religion that Huck derided in his guardian, the Widow Douglas. And she uses it in the way poor women must, for the strength she is too tired and hungry and sick to find on her own. "REUBEN," she whispers to her new lover in a gasping last line, "YOU ARE GOIN' TA BURN IN HELL." (p. 26)

> Megan Marshall, in a review of "The Beans of Egypt,
> Maine," in Boston Review, Vol. X, No. 2, April-
> May, 1985, pp. 25-6.

CHRIS VINCENT

Carolyn Chute's first novel [*The Beans*] arrives from the States trailing clouds of superlatives: "a literary Diane Arbus" (Vogue); "the most powerful voice yet heard from the depths of Reagan's America" (the publisher); even our own Angela Carter announces disarmingly "I haven't enjoyed a novel more for years".

In a recent interview with the author, it was suggested that the book's phenomenal success in America could be attributed as much to liberal, middle-class guilt about the extremes of poverty and wealth to be found in that country, as to any literary merit.

Certainly, this novel's strength is in its evocation of what it feels like to be poor. The writer's main concern appears to be the *texture* of her material: the smells of an overcrowded, poorly ventilated "mobile home"; the flavour of cheap, badly-cooked food; above all, the effect on human beings of generations of deprivation and neglect.

It is a claustrophobic, inward-looking world. The novel opens with a young girl's observations of her feckless, racketty neighbours, the Beans, with their hordes of unwashed children, ever-pregnant women and brawling, good-for-nothing men; it ends with the same character, Earlene, looking back on her disastrous marriage into the Bean tribe.

There is little to suggest that her characters are living in the twentieth century, or even that anywhere exists at all, outside of "Egypt, Maine", and its collection of ramshackle houses and mobile homes. It is perhaps the continued existence of such isolated communities, and the poverty and insularity they engender, which is the true legacy of Reagan's America.

Chris Vincent, "Reagan's True Legacy," in Tribune, *Vol. 49, No. 35, August 30, 1985, p. 13.**

VALERIE MINER

The Beans are a large, in fact innumerable, family who live and work cramped together in Egypt, Maine. To middle-class outsiders, they are a repulsive, undisciplined lot. To their young neighbour Earlene, growing up in a rigid Fundamentalist family, they are romantic iconoclasts. They move with spirit and humour, indifferent to their neighbours' judgments about cleanliness, order or sexuality.

Earlene has seen her mother go crazy and be banished to an asylum. In comparison, the Beans' maverick responses to their environment seem, at times, heroic. Earlene watches the Beans with wide eyes and eventually becomes inextricably bound to them. One day, Earlene ventures too close. She becomes pregnant by a Bean; she has her baby, goes mad like her mother before her, and suffers her father's oppressive religiosity. Finally she is rescued by one Bean. Then by another.

Carolyn Chute tries here to shake up bourgeois expectations, to shock readers into a recognition of their own inhibitions and prejudices. *The Beans* offers no sentimentality about poverty; there is, rather, an unblinking exposure to hardship. The Beans survive on the raw edge of humanity. Clearly Chute knows Maine and its people. She is at her best when evoking the unemployment and fierce climate that serve to make the region one of the poorest states in New England: the pain lies close to the surface. Ultimately, though, Chute's writing subverts itself with veiled self-hatred, a voyeuristic tone and the compulsive acceleration of grotesquerie. The Beans become caricatures of themselves. Chute wanders over the border from irony to ridicule, and gets lost.

The novel has five alternating sections told in two voices: "Earlene", narrated in the first person, and "The Beans", in the third person. Perhaps the Earlene chapters are more effective because they are more clearly written. It is easier, too, to identify with a narrator-protagonist's intimate voice than with the assortment of protagonists in "The Beans" sections, in which experiences turn into antics and Chute succeeds only in creating a sense of morbid, puerile curiosity. The book becomes an exhausting exercise in pushing back the boundaries of repulsion. . . .

The most interesting aspect of this book is not the writing—which shows talent and courage as well as inexperience—but the publicity it has received. The novel and the forthcoming film have been promoted as the homespun product of a new writer, herself a formerly poor Maine woman. Americans have a stunted imagination about class. They have little tradition—except in Black literature—of working-class characters identifying with a sense of community and pride. American culture fosters the illusion that everyone is potentially middle-class, except for a few unfortunate victims or retrograde souls, and *The Beans* reinforces this illusion by portraying poor people treading comfortably in their own squalor.

Valerie Miner, "Homespun Grotesquerie," in The Times Literary Supplement, *No. 4314, December 6, 1985, p. 1406.*

Pam Durban

1947-

American short story writer and journalist.

All Set About with Fever Trees (1985), Durban's first collection, brings together seven short stories, six of them previously published in *Tri-Quarterly, Epoch, Ohio Review, Crazyhorse,* and *Georgia Review*. In these tales Durban, a South Carolina-born teacher and journalist, describes crises and conflicts within family relationships. Reviewers praise her lyrical expression of her characters' emotions, as well as her evocation of distinctively Southern settings.

PUBLISHERS WEEKLY

The fever trees in the long title story [in *All Set About with Fever Trees*] grow in what was once the Belgian Congo, where the narrator's Grandmother Mariah of Macon, Ga., went on impulse to teach the children of missionaries. Reflecting on the eccentric lady, the once-fascinated child, now herself grown to motherhood, learns some eternal truths about life and death. **"Notes Toward an Understanding of My Father's Novel"** tells of the narrator's father's life and of his obsession with his military experience in World War II. Again, the girl will learn after attaining womanhood that life is process and that its meaning lies in living it. The seven stories in this first work, set in the South, tell tales of family, of the turbulence of love, of survival and affirmation. Typically the tempo is deliberate—slow and fitful; Durban's considerable gifts are lyric, descriptive, stylistic rather than dramatic and narrative.

A review of "All Set About with Fever Trees," in Publishers Weekly, *Vol. 227, No. 24, June 14, 1985, p. 61.*

KIRKUS REVIEWS

Most of the seven stories in this first volume [*All Set About with Fever Trees*] rest on the tired stuff of good intentions, but near the end there is a sharpening of judgment that results in some fine moments, indeed. The next-to-last story, **"Notes Toward an Understanding of My Father's Novel,"** is a poised and moving achievement.

The earlier pieces have more about them of the writing-seminars than of life. **"This Heat"** works conscientiously toward its culminating symbols in a story of grief among mill hands, but it remains more literary and rhetorical than moving. **"World of Women"** is the story of a boy's awakening to sex, done capably but not freshly. **"In Darkness,"** which looks at a marital crisis through the eyes of a ten-year-old daughter, declines at crucial moments into the greeting-card sentiment of words that merely blather on ("You had to be brave . . . a

Photograph by Frank Hunter

special kind of bravery and love that kept you standing in the dark, in the silence, looking for the light inside you, believing it was there").

The final two stories, however, for the most part leave the dross behind and give a hard clear light by themselves. The title story ["**All Set About with Fever Trees**"], about a girl growing up, comes to life thanks in part to a grandmother who at 60 leaves Georgia for a mission in the Belgian Congo. But the big difference is that Durban's eye has sharpened and become her own. **"Notes Toward an Understanding . . ."** may be one of the best stories we have of WW II—confident, alert, and unfalsified. A father has been marked for life by the war he fought in as little more than a boy. "The wind was blowing toward us," says his daughter, 40 years later, in the back yard, "blowing his pant legs flat against him, and I noticed that one leg was thinner than the other and my heart hammered. I might as well have come across him naked, and I looked away."

A book two-thirds undistinguished, but that rises in the end to that genuine, wonderful thing, real fiction.

A review of "All Set About with Fever Trees," in Kirkus Reviews, *Vol. LIII, No. 12, June 15, 1985, p. 543.*

ROBB FORMAN DEW

In a recent interview William Styron is quoted as saying, "This, it seems to me, is an era of witnesses. We no longer trust the voice of the omniscient." But I think it is not so; I think that given any voice at all that has power and integrity, a reader will abandon his soul to it, and there is such a voice to be found in *All Set About with Fever Trees,* this first book of collected stories by Pam Durban.

Though most of the seven stories are set in the South it would be a mistake to label this regional fiction, because these tales are enriched by, but not dependent on, a sense of place. Besides, regional has become a derogatory designation for fiction these days, almost always meaning Southern, almost always meaning insignificant. This book should not be insignificant to any reader, because Pam Durban ranges up and down the social spectrum and in and out of dangerous emotional territory to tell her stories. By the very nature of their particular persuasiveness they often demand an omniscient narrator. When an author with a vision as powerful as hers tries to convey the essence of lives lived in ways other than those of her readers, she must also tell the story in language that is not that of her characters, a language that makes a bridge of empathy between audience and material. *She,* then, is the witness, and within a paragraph we know she is trustworthy.

In **"This Heat,"** the protagonist is a mill worker in Georgia who is trying to come to terms with her own grief at a long-expected tragedy. She is called to school for what she believes will be yet another bureaucratic confrontation about her child. "And that's how she learned that Beau Clinton, her only son and the son of Charles Clinton, was dead.

"From then on it was just one amazement after another. She was amazed to find the day just as hot and close as it had been when she'd gone inside the school building. Everything should have been as new and strange as what had just happened. But the dusty trees stood silent against the tin sky, and below, in the distance, Atlanta's mirrored buildings still captured the sun and burned. Then the word *dead* amazed her, the way it came out of her mouth as though she said it every day of her life. . . . She was surprised by her sister's voice, how it boiled on and on shaped like questions." There is such a remarkable wealth here of intention and consequence. And, although in this story Pam Durban is at her most colloquial in her use of language, there is no sense of voyeurism or condescension. This author is entirely engaged with her characters.

The title story ["**All Set About with Fever Trees**"] is a complex and fascinating delineation of family ties, familial love and the dangers that lie within a shared history. "The stories they told were about each other, but it seemed to me that they all shared a common center. They were about the past but not the whole past, just special moments, those moments I was looking for, times that had been dilated somehow by a mysterious richness." The intricate relationships within this family and its evolution by the time we leave it will evoke an aching melancholy and a nod of acknowledgment.

Throughout this collection the reader is privy to an uncanny visual intelligence—a perception recreated through language of the image the eye takes in—made hauntingly resonant by the careful examination of the emotional context. But the luxury of Pam Durban's language and the generosity of her vision are both wonderful and, now and then, a bit excessive. The reader balks at being made to imagine every single thing, every little bit of getting from here to there. Perhaps the author could let some things just pass by.

However, she has such a compelling new voice that her minor excesses are easily dismissed. In **"World of Women,"** the 10-year-old protagonist muses that "the choir at school had practiced and practiced . . . trying to get it right. They'd adjusted, readjusted, bass voices holding, sopranos ringing clear, then they'd hit upon it all at once: a shared constellation of notes, the center of the notes itself a note that nobody sang but everybody heard all around them so that they were no longer outside, they were inside something larger." And just so does Pam Durban envelop the reader in these extraordinary and mesmerizing stories.

*Robb Forman Dew, "Family Ties, Family Perils,"
in* The New York Times Book Review, *October 13,
1985, p. 13.*

An Excerpt from *All Set About with Fever Trees*

Our town was home to many of these men, Papa's friends, survivors of the Bataan Death March, survivors of the Air Force or the infantry. They greeted each other on the streets with clasped handshakes. They marched together on Veterans Day; their faces slid by, eyes fixed beyond the crowd. It was after one such parade that I left home for the final time.

I had made a mistake, a miscalculation of loyalty, and had come home after college to teach in the local high school. I was dying there. I don't regret that it happened, I only wish it had gone by faster and cleaner than it did. On the day of the parade that year, three of us, who called ourselves refugees, climbed into the second story of a deserted building on Main Street and unfurled from the window the biggest, rattiest American flag we could find. For every star, there was a matching hole. But every one of the vets who looked up saluted grimly— what else could they do to a flag?—as we cheered and waved the flag and showered them with soap bubbles.

"What have I raised?" my father demanded to know when he caught up with me after the parade. "Tell me, what in hell have I raised?" He was wearing his khaki uniform; silver bars gleamed on his cap, the Purple Heart on his chest, the lieutenant's chevron on the sleeve.

"Your daughter," I said. "Me. Annie."

"My daughter doesn't mock me," he said. His eyes were red-rimmed, hard.

"I'm not mocking you."

He pointed to the flag draped over my arm. "Then what the hell were you doing?"

"Papa," I said, but he wheeled and hurried off down the street. I cannot speak for my father but I know what I saw that day—I saw a man who had been betrayed, for whom betrayal was like death, whom I had killed this time, I had cut a thread—call this one loyalty—that holds the world together.

ELLEN LESSER

Pam Durban grew up in South Carolina, and it shows—not only in the subtle Dixie charm of her diction, the ambience that rises from the humid heat, choking kudzu vines, and broad sluggish rivers, but in a Southern kind of ampleness, generosity. Durban is a storyteller who's not afraid to put her feet up on the porch railing and linger. Her tales are substantial, like gracious country meals; the seven gathered in *All Set About with Fever Trees* make for an unusually satisfying collection.

Ruby Clinton, heroine of **"This Heat,"** is a mill worker from Cotton Bottom. Ruby has always been a fighter—by day she matches the furious, deafening pace of the spooling machines, and at night beats back the devil at prayer meetings, hitting the tambourine "so hard that no one could stand close to her." Ruby's strength is mightily tested by her son, Beau, who was born with a weak heart and grew up a delinquent. When Beau collapses in the high school gym, his death hits Ruby harder than she expected, and her pain turns bitter with the appearance of her long-absent husband and his new wife. Durban sees Ruby through the funeral, evoking the claustrophobic press of memory and a houseful of mourners. Ruby's grief nearly drags her under, but listening to the pastor at Beau's grave site, she thinks his words are not the real prayer: "The prayer was [Beau's] life that she couldn't save, and the prayer was her own life and how it continued. And the prayer never stopped; lives began and ended, but the prayer never stopped."

Durban's stories rely on language and imagery more than startling turns of plot; their power builds with the accumulation of detail, insight, and atmosphere. This is particularly true of the long title story ["**All Set About with Fever Trees**"]. Annie's grandmother, Mariah, announces that she's heard a "clear call," and travels to Africa to teach missionary children. Believing Mariah has special powers, Annie respects that call. She remembers the night Mariah read her Kipling's *Just So Stories,* transporting her to the "banks of the great, grey green, greasy Limpopo River, all set about with fever trees, where life first stirred and crawled from the mud." That night, Annie floated close to sleep and felt herself "rising out through the roof and flying over the planet." She expects Mariah to return from Africa miraculously transformed, but she comes back the same—only 30 pounds heavier. Annie grows into a young woman listening for her own call, but never hears it; after Mariah's death, she questions her trust in fate and the future. Durban closes with a metaphor, recalled from Mariah's Congo days: an enormous anaconda killed and cut open to reveal an antelope fawn it had swallowed. Annie imagines telling the story to her own daughter—"It stood up trembling, Jesse. . . . Yes. Down inside that dark old snake, it was alive as you or me."

Death and survival, loss and love, disillusionment and desire: these are the poles along which Durban's stories align themselves. Whether it's a country singer throwing away her big chance on a quart jar of clear whiskey, a woman tracing the meaning of her father's life to his Pacific soldier days, or a preadolescent boy discovering the **"World of Women,"** Durban works through her characters toward a larger vision. Along the way she's liberal with her gifts—a lush, resonant prose and a knack for illuminating the "whole dense web" of experience.

> *Ellen Lesser, "Southern Comforts," in* The Village Voice, *Vol. XXX, No. 49, December 3, 1985, p. 68.*

LESLIE PIETRZYK

The seven stories in Pam Durban's first collection, *All Set About With Fever Trees and Other Stories,* share a concern with beginnings and endings—of life, of relationships, of brief epiphanies—and the circular trip between the two.

In the title story (easily the most accomplished in the book and a real stunner) Annie contemplates her maverick grandmother, now somewhat debilitated by old age:

> I thought I understood a little more about what people mean when they say, "This person is alive." They mean that the circle curves, unbroken, between what is visible and what cannot be seen, and you know of its existence the same way you knew currents in water by watching a boat or currents in the sky by seeing the way a hawk holds tight to the wind.

Movement becomes not a way to get places, but rather a way to see and to understand what it is you are traveling through.

This idea is put to metaphorical use in **"World of Women,"** in which Sara teaches seventh-grader Mark how to swim. Mark's strokes through the water are not an effort to reach the other side of the deep end—the goal Sara has set—but a way for him to feel close to Sara. He treasures their time in the pool together and tries desperately to prolong the swimming lessons—partially a refusal to be forced to acknowledge his semiconscious sexual desire by actually learning to swim in a grownup fashion. The association between swimming and sexuality proves a recurrent one for Mark, and Durban includes one scene of an adult Mark in which the hypnotic, endless strokes of swimming come back to him. He sees "that the world where women live has no end, it is round, it has only beginnings and everything comes back to the place where it began."

"Notes Toward an Understanding of My Father's Novel" is about a different Annie, and her father, a World War II veteran. At one point he tells his daughter about his 22nd birthday, spent in New Guinea during the war, and an encounter with a wounded soldier:

> I kept my hand on the boy's shoulder until he was gone. . . . And you know, I *knew* when he was gone. . . . I didn't have to see anything to let me know, just all of a sudden there was nothing under my hand any longer and that's when I realized there had been *something* there before.

This startling realization of the realness of life hits hard: He flees, first literally, then figuratively throughout the story. He is no longer able to take the idea of living for granted, so he runs from the thought of kowtowing to any sort of weakness, including emotional closeness and physical fragility. Annie reflects on her father: "I kept thinking of his hand, how it had rested there on the man's shoulder, a link in a circle that joined his own spared life to the finished life of the other, and how, brought into that circle, he must have felt his own life come onto him, real as fire, real as water, as certain to disappear."

It seems appropriate that stories exploring the continuity between beginnings and endings should have, overall, such astonishing openings and closings. The first story, **"This Heat,"** pulls us in with a bald statement—"In August, Beau Clinton died"—followed by a whirlwind paragraph mirroring the scattered emotions felt after such a sentence. I consider **"Made to Last,"** about a divorcing couple, one of the minor samples of

Durban's work, save for the final paragraph, when the husband and wife actually sign the dissolution papers: "'Did you see where we both signed them?' she says. 'Down there at the end. Did you see what we've done?'" A simple closure yet one that reverberates.

Occasionally Durban's mystical prose style becomes burdensome, and one story, **"In Darkness,"** is far too coy and preachy for my taste. The best stories are grounded in incident, with abstractions taking on comprehensible metaphors. Even so, this is not a book to read while riding the commuter train to your office. I would allow an eight-day week—one day for each of the seven stories and the final day to contemplate the trip.

> *Leslie Pietrzyk, "The Circle Unbroken," in* Belles Lettres, *Vol. 1, No. 4, March-April, 1986, p. 8.*

Fernanda Eberstadt

1960-

American novelist.

Eberstadt, the daughter of novelist Isabel Eberstadt and grand-daughter of poet Ogden Nash, has demonstrated her own distinctive literary voice in her first novel, *Low Tide* (1985). Eberstadt started writing *Low Tide* as a nineteen-year-old student at Magdalen College, Oxford. She finished the first draft in six weeks, then spent five years revising it. A published novelist at twenty-four, Eberstadt is cautious about her early success: "I want to do it slow and right. I want to avoid the *Wunderkind* syndrome." Her articles on history and literature have appeared in *Commentary* and other English and American periodicals.

Low Tide is the feverish confession of Jezebel, a wealthy adolescent obsessively infatuated with a bizarre young man named Jem. While disappointed with *Low Tide*'s meager plot line in which Jezebel follows Jem from New York to London and Mexico, most critics find Eberstadt's lush prose intriguing and energetic. Eberstadt uses startlingly original imagery and word-play, reviewers observe, to express Jezebel's surging emotions and exotically poetic view of the world.

KENDALL MITCHELL

The best thing about Fernanda Eberstadt's first novel [*Low Tide*] is her impressive, sometimes dazzling, command of the language; she is intrepid in her use of worldly allusion and vivid imagery. It is a rich, often tasty, international brew, but *Low Tide,* as a novel, is very often out of focus. It jitters about through past and present, from New York to Oxford to rural Mexico, in the wake of its narrator, Jezebel Western, but it's never clear what she wants or what all this racketing about means.

Not rich or famous, not cruel or vicious, the characters are chiefly bright, dubious, sophisticated flotsam—"landed, salt-dried, and petrified in our monstrousness," left in the low tide of the contemporary world.

Jezebel is herself 17 and for much of her life in New York with her divorced mother, she has been intrigued and fascinated by Jem, the son of her English father's friend who now lives outside Oxford. Jezebel goes to England for the summer and her interest in Jem turns to obsession. He is unattractive, unstable, sullen and lost. They go to Mexico where his dead mother grew up on an isolated plantation in the southern mountains. The final pages are finely wrought, the focus is sharp at last, but it's rather too late.

© Jerry Bauer

Kendall Mitchell, in a review of "Low Tide," in Bookworld, *Chicago Tribune, September 8, 1984, p. 37.*

PUBLISHERS WEEKLY

[Eberstadt] is a clever writer who has achieved a stylish prose. It is employed, however, in a narrative so mannered in tone, with characters so disagreeably eccentric, that the reader [of *Low Tide*] is at first turned off and at last supremely bored. Rich, spoiled, willful, restless with wanderlust and lack of purpose, the teenage protagonists, Jezebel and Jem, are locked in a cold, chaste, doomed attraction that ends in melodramatic tragedy. . . . The two, and others in the book, converse in brittle, insolent interchanges, aimed to convey the lack of warmth and emotional security in their lives. As a tale of self-destructive obsession, the book is more bizarre than *Endless Love;* as a chronicle of angst and alienation afflicting the young and privileged, it is even more depressing than Lisa St. Aubin de Téran's *The Slow Train to Milan.* One hopes that Eberstadt will turn her considerable skills to a more engaging narrative next time.

A review of "Low Tide," in Publishers Weekly, *Vol. 227, No. 5, February 1, 1985, p. 350.*

MARY ELLEN QUINN

Eccentric teenager Jezebel [in *Low Tide*] lives sometimes with her eccentric mother in New York and sometimes with her eccentric father in London. They also have eccentric friends, including Professor Chasm and his family. Jezebel's obsession with the professor's son, Jem, forms the core of this distinctive first novel. Unfortunately, the characters never quite overcome their oddities and affectations, making it difficult for the reader to care much about what happens to them; this is a book without a heart. Still, it should be read for its many strange and startling images and its very careful use of words. Eberstadt is a writer to watch; despite its flaws, her initial effort shows considerable promise.

Mary Ellen Quinn, in a review of "Low Tide," in Booklist, *Vol. 81, No. 15, April 1, 1985, p. 1098.*

EDMUND MORRIS

"Youth," sighed Shaw, "is wasted on the young." Any writer *d'un certain age* must have similar emotions when he sees youthful talent squandered as recklessly—and enchantingly—as here by Fernanda Eberstadt, in her first novel. *Low Tide* is a slender sapling of a book, but it has enough sap rising to foliate an orchard. No doubt the time will come when Miss Eberstadt too will feel wistful for "the force that through the green fuse drives the flower." Her only problem now is to control this force, and channel it upward, rather than outward in all directions.

One does not doubt that she will succeed, because while *Low Tide* is mostly about passion, it is also about self-restraint. There is an austere, if overwhelmed intelligence behind the riotous sensibility. Her protagonists are young and very rich, yet they disdain drugs; they are beautiful and full of sex, yet they understand the value of chastity.

A glance at the back cover tells us the plot of the novel. Here, in profile, sits a graceful young woman. She looks both sensuous and devout. Huge eyes—Spanish eyes; a plain gold ring. Five lines of copy drop the necessary words: New York, the Brearley School, Magdalen College, Oxford. Unsurprised, we begin to read inside about the large-eyed child of an East 94th Street brownstone, who goes to Oxford and meets a young man so extraordinary that she is "seized by a trembling crazy exaltation such as I had known only before God." The world around her, hitherto comfortably diffused by old money, leaps into focus and bright color, like an El Greco shoved in her face.

So far, so much Henry James. But James would not have called his heroine Jezebel, nor brought her to catharsis, fewer than 200 pages later, in Mexico. It soon becomes apparent that Miss Eberstadt's real mentor is Evelyn Waugh.

Jem Chasm ("You and I—they named us both slave names," he tells Jezebel when bound to her) is demonstrably Sebastian Flyte, with his "tormented exquisite look" and eyes like "wet jewels—eyes the color of an oil spill, petrol-green," his monochromatic clothes and eccentric diet—bread and olive paste, chocolates and Armenian champagne—his nimbus-like charm, which everywhere attracts a retinue, his monastic yearnings

(Sebastian retreats to Morocco, Jem to Salamanca) and bouts of black depression, eyes "guttered out."

This is not to deny his originality as Miss Eberstadt's own creation. Jem is a sharper, more masculine personality than Waugh's epicene enigma, made flesh by a writer who is feminine to her fingertips. Uninhibited, she (or Jezebel) can rejoice in Jem utterly, and reveal her own soul in a succession of ravishing images. . . .

It is Miss Eberstadt's imagery, indeed, that proclaims her a major talent. Waugh said of Wodehouse, "One has to call anyone Master who manages, on average, three quite original metaphors per page." Actually Waugh was exaggerating. Old Plum valued his currency too much to spend it so wastefully: and here is where Miss Eberstadt betrays her youth. She *can* manage three original metaphors a page—sometimes in a single paragraph—but she cannot suppress the lesser, to enhance the best. Her flowers are too copious and too various; the sapling bends under their weight, their combined perfume chokes us. On page 17, for example, we have several tarot symbols, then a Scarlet Whore, a boy with "buccaneer looks and wandering fingers . . . [and] a girl in every port," "late arctic light" in the middle of English summer, a mythical mother grieving for a soldier, and "books piled vertically in a shaky avenue of pagodas [that] looked as if they might walk away at night, leaving behind them unpaid bills." Of these images, only the buccaneer boy and the pagodas seem worth preserving, and even they should be further pruned, the former losing its cliché and the latter its silly conclusion (pagodas do not walk, nor leave behind unpaid bills).

Perhaps it is unjust to select for criticism such a weak page, when there are so many more—the majority—that show abundant strength. Flicking at random, we come upon a rotting tree house "like a crazed aircraft pitched among the weeds," three Spanish sisters moving with "cheetah graces," Jem prancing down the Banbury road ahead of Jezebel, "doubling back like a kite on a string, recalled." (p. 9)

These images, lovely as they are, would not alone make Miss Eberstadt a novelist of rich promise. She has another essential gift: power of characterization. All the figures in this book are grotesques—Jezebel calls them (and herself) low-tide creatures, "salt-dried, petrified in our monstrousness." She is wrong: they live and breathe lovably. Meet ageless Eustacius, her mother's Cajun cook, in his kitchen full of hot fetishes; randy, Red-baiting Professor Chasm, who disappears beneath dinnertables for serious conversation with children; Jezebel's art-dealing father, "this pink-and-gold flit"; old Mrs. Palafox, subsisting on black coffee and yogurt and "screeching her memoirs at the secretary." Most attractive of all is Jem's brother Casimir, the buccaneer boy, with whom we rather hope Jezebel will end up.

This reviewer looks forward to more novels by Miss Eberstadt. She will soon learn from Waugh that profundity is impossible without lucidity; from Molly Keane how to interweave humor and cruelty; from Thomas Beer how to combine color and speed; from Hemingway when to be violent (although her climax in this book is so well timed as to make the reader shout with alarm). And these older writers, or their shades, will learn again from her that there is nothing as beautiful as youth bursting with talent and love of life. (pp. 9, 12)

Edmund Morris, "The Young in One Another's Arms," in Book World—The Washington Post, *May 12, 1985, pp. 9, 12.*

An Excerpt from *Low Tide*

When we were alone, Mummy said with inexhaustible good nature, "Tell me what's on your mind, dumpling. You'll feel better for getting it out of your system. Curse me out if it would make you feel better. Just don't bottle it up."

But how could you bottle up nothing? Nothing was what I was butting my head against. Nothing was the manacles and the fetters. There was nothing under the sun, nothing as far as the eye could see, and beyond, world after world, of nothing. Sometimes I sniveled a little, sometimes I scowled. You see, it was only Jem who had finally got me to talk, and when he left, he took his bag of tricks with him. Before, I could hold inspired conversations in my head, but face to face it had always been pictures on the floor traced with the toe of my shoe, and silences that extended to deserts without oases. It was only Jem whose talk had made words rise to the tongue like greedy trout the way they did in dreaming, and silences cavort like porpoises in the lucid depths of the unspoken—the unspoken no longer a burden, but possibly our future. . . .

Eustacius, addressing me directly, said that I was coming apart at the seams. "You hair's a rat's nest. You shoes all broken and you clothes raggle-taggle." ("She's gone with the raggle-taggle gypsies-oh," went my favorite song when I was little, about a young lady who left her fine lord on a stormy night. "What care I for my silken bed? With the sheets turned down so bravely-oh? For tonight I will sleep in a cold dark field / Along with the raggle-taggle gypsies-oh.") "Honey, the hem of you dress all coming down in back. Now you get inside you head and you do a little housekeeping inside there."

How do you tidy a ravine? How do you send darkness to the dry cleaners? Those mustard-colored children shuffling on their knees across the floor, asking their father for forgiveness for being born, were more real to me than I was. Airline hostesses advertising cheap fares in old magazines I leafed through were more real. No one was as worthless.

LISA ST. AUBAN DE TERAN

Fernanda Eberstadt's first novel [*Low Tide*] is something of an original. It starts like a send-up of a bodice-ripper. Told in a cloying gush, the opening scene presents us with a precocious 10-year-old, Jezebel, locked in the dream of a rotting Southern mansion and flirting with an Oxford University professor under the dining room table. ("I love you better than anything in the world," she tells him. "Better than your daddy?" he asks.) It ends in a tight-lipped splatter of blood and Raymond Chandler. . . .

This is not an easy book to categorize or one dominated by a story line. The rather skeletal boy-meets-girl plot—in which Jezebel jets back and forth between Jem and her father in England and her mother in New York—could use a bit more substance. The story is always on the verge of collapsing into bathos or boredom. But Miss Eberstadt manages a skillful

series of death-bed resuscitations bestowing the kiss of life on her thin theme with a flashing variety of memorable phrases.

Not all these rescues work. Sometimes the lily is gilded as in "A fuchsia-lipped girl in a turquoise New Look dress with rosebudded stilettos." "Fuchsia-lipped" is excellent the first time round and then fractionally tarnished after "rosebudded stilettos." Two reds, unlike two heads, are not always better than one. But the hit-or-miss effect is appropriate, arguably, in a prose aiming to be as grossly fertile as the tropical bayou in which the moods of Jem and Jezebel seem to have been brewed.

"Steamy" is a word we associate with the coarser elements of sexuality, and this book fastidiously avoids any tint of porn; but steamy it nevertheless is, in the high-temperature way of a mangrove swamp, or an overcrowded Mexican hammock. We view the action through a veil of sweat and tears, licking our lips so as not to miss the salt.

The action, of course, traces Jezebel's obsession—"waiting for Jem, whose gruesome beauty was a hum in my blood." Gruesome would seem to be the word. "He looked like a child with rickets; the thin greenish arms riddled with scars, the stalk legs, a face dominated by a great bee-stung mouth." Are we to see the fascination with such a distorted physique as other than infatuated? I think not. Miss Eberstadt consciously degrades her hero, Pan dipped in acid, to highlight the monstrous growth and almost jungle-like extravagance of her heroine's interest in him. We have something of a Krafft-Ebing study of a woman adoring the most extreme thing the world can offer. . . .

The book remains a portrait, and a successful one, of an individual soul in torment, a young woman who has undeniably pinned her flag to the mast of Mr. Wrong. At this level it drips with a convincingly festering sap.

In many ways, though, this is a bouillon cube of a book; it's so condensed. I would like to have known more, for instance, about the *Gone With the Wind* mansion in Louisiana, "a tottering Third Empire delirium of glory-be, giddy with pinnacles and cupolas." More, too, about the old Creole servant Eustacius ("Heady," said Eustacius. "That soup real heady.") in the earlier days of his three wives and his love for Jezebel's Aunt Celestine, "who came to him at night chattering like a macaw." But there is a virtue in condensation. Add your own imagination and this book makes a meal for six. There are occasional excesses of tropicality—where is the dry season to counter the rains and drain the swamps? Nevertheless, despite the excessive sophistication of Jem's mind, and a rather too abrupt ending, *Low Tide* is a book that leaves its mark.

Whether the mark is a bruise or an insect bite one isn't sure. But that soup real heady, Miss Eberstadt.

> *Lisa St. Auban de Teran, "The Hum in Her Blood,"
> in* The New York Times Book Review, *May 26,
> 1985, p. 13.*

LAURA FURMAN

Low Tide is a love story about two privileged young bohemians, Jem Chasm and Jezebel Western, the beautiful daughter of a vaguely insane Louisiana mother and a cool English father, who abandons ship early on. . . .

Her mother and Eustacius are stuck in a paralysis of nostalgia for their old Louisiana home. Jezebel is stuck in her youthful world-weariness. . . .

Very little happens in this first novel until the final third, when the narrator lets go her hammerlock on the reader and allows scenes to take place. Until then, the book's energy goes into recounting old stories and making sophisticated pronouncements. . . .

The publisher compares Jem and Jezebel with Charles and Sebastian of *Brideshead Revisited*. I think they aren't even distant cousins.

Low Tide is by and large a work that hasn't hatched. As Jezebel herself says: "The gasping shortcomings of what language can express. Before the catch, it screams to a halt, its exaggerations vapid, devalued currency." The reader is told about a lot, but given the chance to experience very little. One feels strained, as if forced to listen to someone who is talking into a mirror.

Low Tide wants to have voice and feeling, but it seems that it wishes more than anything to be admired. It is a relief when the narrative relaxes enough to do what the reader wanted it to do all along—just tell the story.

> *Laura Furman, in a review of "Low Tide," in* Los Angeles Times Book Review, *June 2, 1985, p. 9.*

Clyde Edgerton

1944-

American novelist and short story writer.

Edgerton is a North Carolina native whose first novel, *Raney* (1985), details a marriage between two young Southerners of very different backgrounds. Raney, a charming, provincial Baptist from rural North Carolina, narrates a humorous account of her first two years of marriage to Charles, a priggish but liberal-minded librarian from Atlanta. The one sustaining force in the union of Raney and Charles is their mutual love of music—a subject Edgerton knows well, as he plays five-string banjo in both a bluegrass and a rhythm-and-blues band. Edgerton taught English at Campbell College for several years before taking a post at St. Andrews Presbyterian College in 1985. Edgerton's former colleagues at Campbell, a Baptist institution, reportedly objected to Edgerton's playful portrayal of Raney's narrow-minded religious fundamentalism.

Critics note that the character Raney, despite the prejudices that dominate her thinking at the start of the novel, manages to endear herself to the reader with her simple wisdom and the gradual softening of her rigid attitudes towards race relations and sexual experimentation. Critics praise Edgerton's mastery of Southern dialects, particularly his well-sustained portrayal of Raney's own ungrammatical idiom, and his thoughtful character development, which inspires sympathy for Raney and Charles despite their faults. Edgerton, whose stories have appeared in *Old Hickory Review, Just Pulp, descant, Forms, The Lyricist,* and *Pembroke Magazine,* is currently at work on two new books.

Courtesy of Clyde Edgerton

understanding to a young couple whose problems are neither epic nor earth-shaking but very much like our own.

A review of "Raney," in Publishers Weekly, Vol. 227, No. 1, January 4, 1985, p. 60.

PUBLISHERS WEEKLY

With very little plot and no pretension, this charming vignette [**Raney**] about the marriage of Raney, a smalltown Southern Baptist, to Charles, a biggertown Southern Methodist with a B.A., makes you smile at the artful innocence of the bride and the smart-aleck liberalism of the groom. All the usual adjustment crises of the newly married are chronicled: his scorn of the humdrum complacency of her parents' lives; her timidity before his schoolteacher mother, who is not only a vegetarian but an Episcopalian; his predilection for wine, yes, and whiskey, and, secretly, dirty pictures; her aridly conventional view of sex. These burdens on their union must be removed, along with her implacability about black people, one of whose number is Charles's closest friend. The couple consult a marriage counselor, whose style is reasonable, gentle and not without humor and whose contribution to their future consists in teaching them to listen to each other. Edgerton's ear for idiom is exact, the two central characters perceptibly develop and the other members of the small cast are given dimension and personality. Few readers will fail to respond with sympathy and

GENE LYONS

There's a song on the radio these days that tells us the surest way to a life of country-and-Western bliss is to "get you a redneck girl." What it don't say, as Raney Bell Shepherd, redneck bride and narrator of Clyde Edgerton's warmly funny first novel [**Raney**] would put it, is what else you get in the bargain. Like Mama, Aunt Naomi, Aunt Flossie and them. Blood kin every one, and Free Will Baptists too. Among a whole lot of other attributes, folks in Bethel, N.C., know exactly what they think. When Mrs. Shepherd, the Atlanta schoolteacher who's the mother of the bridegroom, comes to town, she wants to go to a restaurant "but Aunt Naomi strongly suggested the K and W. She said the K and W would be more reasonable and the line wouldn't be long on a Thursday. So we ate at the K and W."

Mrs. Shepherd's not just an Episcopalian; she's a vegetarian, of all things. So when the conversation gets a little sticky, Raney seizes upon her Aunt's cold and subtly changes the subject: "We'd finished eating so I said, 'Aunt Naomi, you get more nose blows out of one Kleenex than anybody I've ever seen in my life'." That's pretty much how it goes in this affectionate, loosely plotted little comedy of manners about the first two years of marriage between a spunky girl whose daddy runs a general store and a warmhearted and mildly obtuse liberal academic who are drawn to each other by their love of music. Edgerton can be patronizing now and then, and he does tend to lay it on a bit thick where race is concerned. ("Charles, that is disgusting," Raney says on their embarrassing wedding night. "That is something niggers would do.") But in general, he's in perfect command of Raney's voice, provides wonderful small surprises throughout, and by the night of their sweet reconciliation in Daddy's store ("I just don't know how to explain this, but I wanted to sit on a feed bag in my underwear . . .") has made us care for his characters and wish them well.

Gene Lyons, in a review of "Raney," in Newsweek, *Vol. CV, No. 8, February 25, 1985, p. 86.*

WANDA URBANSKA

Bethel, N.C., is the small-town home of the small-minded title character of **Raney,** Clyde Edgerton's first novel. Raney is an old-fashioned, bigoted Mama's girl whose roller-coaster ride begins when she marries Charles, a priggish but liberal-minded Atlantan who has migrated to this backward community to play bluegrass music and read books undisturbed.

Charles' feathers are quickly ruffled when he realizes that Raneys' family's attitudes are as fixed as the menu down at Penny's Grill. And for Raney's part, she can't understand how Charles can prefer reading books to visiting with her folks. The novel is a romp through the couple's tumultuous first year of marriage, detailing their every domestic squabble.

At age 24, Raney seems to entertain thoughts no loftier than whether one should or should not pull the stopper from the kitchen sink, and she draws the line at calling a black a "nigger" only when addressing him to his face and at that not if "the nigger acts like one." Charles, whose best friend happens to be black, is horrified by his wife's bigotry, as well as the clutchy family that constantly surrounds her and from which she appears to have sprung full-grown. Marital conflict escalates when Charles protests Raney's mother's habit of making herself at home, in their home, when they're not home. When Raney's uncle commits suicide and Charles suggests that family problems are partially to blame, Raney packs up and leaves.

The couple reconcile, of course, and begin visiting a marriage counselor. At the book's climax, Raney has begun to ease off the blinders of her constrictive world view, to remove the kitchen cabinet doors from their hinges (because she feels like it), and to drop her panties, voluntarily, for some down-home good "luvin'."

"What it all came down to is I was trying too hard to feel what I was supposed to feel," she comes to realize.

Edgerton is an idiosyncratic writer of real talent who has taken on the formidable task of making sympathetic a self-absorbed young Southerner who is given over to lengthy digressions on minor matters. Though Raney's story is truthful, in the end, it seems trivial.

One ends hoping for a larger subject in Edgerton's next book.

Wanda Urbanska, in a review of "Raney," in Los Angeles Times Book Review, *June 23, 1985, p. 3.*

An Excerpt from *Raney*

Charles got out of the car not saying a word and started for the house. I was about three feet behind, trying to keep up. The front door was wide open.

Charles stopped just inside the door. I looked over his shoulder and there was Mama coming through the arched hall doorway. She stopped. She was dressed for shopping.

"Well, where in the world have you all been?" she says.

"We been to eat," I said.

"Eating out?"

"Mrs. Bell," says Charles, "please do not come in this house if we're not here."

I could not believe what I was hearing. It was like a dream.

Mama says, "Charles son, I was only leaving my own daughter a note saying to meet me at the mall at two o'clock, at the fountain. The front door was open. You should lock the front door if you want to keep people out."

"Mrs. Bell, a person is entitled to his own privacy. I'm entitled to my own privacy. This is my—our—house. I—"

"This is my own daughter's house, son. My mama was never refused entrance to my house. She was always welcome. Every day of her life."

I was afraid Mama was going to cry. I opened my mouth but nothing came out.

"Mrs. Bell," says Charles, "it seems as though you think everything *you* think is right, is right for everybody."

"Charles," I said, "that's what everybody thinks—in a sense. That's even what *you* think."

Charles turned half around so he could see me. He looked at me, then at Mama.

Mama says, "Son, I'll be happy to buy you a new monogrammed glass if that's what you're so upset about. Naomi didn't mean to break that glass. I'm going over to the mall right now. And I know where they come from."

Charles walks past me and out the front door, stops, turns around and says, "I didn't want any of those damned monogrammed glasses in the first place and I did the best I could to make that clear, plus that's not the subject." (I gave him a monogrammed blue blazer for his birthday and he cut the initials off before he'd wear it.)

So now Mama's at the mall with her feelings hurt. Charles is in the bedroom with a blanket over his head, and I'm sitting here amongst eleven broken monogrammed glasses, and every door and window locked from the inside.

Evidently Charles throws things when he's very mad. I never expected violence from Charles Shepherd. Thank God we don't have a child to see such behavior.

CAROL VERDERESE

When Raney Bell Shepherd, a Free Will Baptist from North Carolina and narrator of Clyde Edgerton's first novel [*Raney*] marries Charles Shepherd, a liberal Episcopalian from Atlanta, neither one is prepared for the compromise in store. While they literally make beautiful music together—she is a singer and he plays guitar and banjo—the discordant notes in their marriage abound. Religion, sex, the family, race relations and even the English language are all cause for disagreement between Raney and Charles. While Charles believes sexual experimentation is healthy, Raney feels "some things are natural, and best left alone." Of the Episcopal Church service, Raney observes, "the priest had a yellow robe with a butterfly on the back. Now that is plum sacrilegious. . . . A house of worship is no place to play Halloween." In response to Charles's intellectualism, Raney says, "He'd rather read a book, written by somebody he don't know, than to sit down and talk to a live human being who's his neighbor." When Charles finally suggests they see a marriage counselor, Raney concedes, "I'm willing to try anything—even a psychiatric. I figure a psychiatric might be able to explain to Charles at least some of what he did wrong." Raney grows during her first year of marriage and many of her views soften; however, it is difficult to hold her opinions against her, no matter how outrageous. Like Charles, we are both appalled by Raney's provincial attitudes and awed by her simple wisdom. She is ingenuous but not naïve, and her exploration of life's limitations and possibilities is as poignant as it is funny. Utterly beguiling, Raney lives beyond the pages of this short novel. (pp. 20-1)

> *Carol Verderese, in a review of "Raney," in* The New York Times Book Review, *June 23, 1985, pp. 20-1.*

GEORGE CORE

When this reviewer was last seen in *Book World,* he was reporting on new novels, two of which, *The Watermelon Kid* and *The Whisper of the River,* happened to be comic. Since then he has read four more good novels in this vein, including Charles Dickinson's *Crows* and Hilary Masters' *Clemmons. Raney,* a splendid first novel, and *I Am One of You Forever* . . . stand tall in this distinguished company.

Both novels are Southern; both are written in the first-person vernacular mode that harks back to Mark Twain; and both should be read in a rush—a sitting or two. The comedy in both ranges from the quick thigh-slapping humor of the guffaw to the slow and indirect response of the faint smile. . . .

Raney begins with the marriage of Raney Bell, a Free Will Baptist from Bethel, N.C., to Charles Shepherd, a Methodist (who yearns to become an Episcopalian) from Atlanta. The only thing the couple has in common is music. Raney is a lively but inhibited small-town girl whose behavior is circumscribed by her family and her church. Charles, an only child, thinks that sweet reason is the answer to everything. Charles is a product of the modern world who holds great faith in psychology. Raney comes from a matriarchy; Charles is not worldly enough or advanced enough to see women as the equals of men. On these considerable differences the action turns. The result is a playful and humorous war of the sexes, what James Thurber might have written had he lived in North Carolina rather than Connecticut. How this gentle comedy could have gotten its author in trouble with the administration of the Baptist university where he teaches—his contract for [1986] was held up and an expected raise was denied—only its members and God could possibly know.

Despite Edgerton's being a professional educator, he has not only learned the English language but mastered its conversational idioms. Listen. Charles: "I have had one conversation with Mrs. Moss and one conversation with Mrs. Moss is enough. I am not interested in her falling off the commode and having a hairline rib fracture." Raney: "This is one of the areas of life Charles does not understand . . . Charles thinks old people are all supposed to grace him with a long conversation on psychology."

> *George Core, "Tall Tales, Guffaws, and Sly Southern Humor," in* Book World—The Washington Post, *June 30, 1985, p. 11.*

COMMENTS OF CLYDE EDGERTON TO *CLC YEARBOOK*

Asked if *Raney* was autobiographical, Edgerton replies: "Certain facts about my background could be used as tools in telling my story. However, no characters are based on real people. It's much more interesting, and makes for better writing, to let your characters grow into real fictional people rather than, as a writer, writing about real real people."

Edgerton also comments on the experience of writing and publishing *Raney:* "The book started as two short stories with the same characters. It grew into a book of 30,000 words. I sent it to Sylvia Wilkinson, a novelist, to read. She read it, liked it, and said to double the length. I did, although I hadn't thought I could (she was encouraging). . . .

"Several agents and publishers rejected it. I was a reader of the work of Louis Rubin and appreciated what he wrote about Southern writing. I also knew he liked baseball. I wrote him and told him if he would read one chapter of my book, I'd send him a good book I was reading on baseball. He agreed. I sent him two chapters. He read them, told me he was starting a publishing house, and asked me to send the complete ms. to the fiction editor, Shannon Ravenel. She liked the book, suggested revisions, and Algonquin published it." Edgerton further credits Ravenel "because of her ability to know 'when it's right' and to know what to say to me so that I can 'get it right'."

Bret Easton Ellis
1964-

American novelist.

Less than Zero (1985) both horrifies and fascinates with its depiction of wealthy, degenerate Los Angeles teenagers obsessed with mood-altering drugs and violent debaucheries. This first novel brought much media attention to its author, Ellis, partly due to the sensational aspect of a talented, articulate senior at Bennington College writing knowledgeably about such squalid matters as narcotics addiction and gang rape. Ellis is familiar with the adolescent subculture he chronicles in *Less than Zero,* as he grew up in suburban Los Angeles. "It can be taken, I guess, as a piece of sociology," Ellis has commented. "A lot of teenagers hunger to be in that kind of group." The novel's eighteen-year-old narrator, Clay, attends a prestigious Eastern college; but home on vacation, he wallows in a mindless, thrill-seeking life-style.

Although he acknowledges stylistic debts to Ernest Hemingway and credits Joan Didion with influencing his attitudes about southern California, Ellis is viewed by critics as the voice of a new generation. Critic John Rechy labels *Less than Zero* "the first novel of MTV," referring to its subject matter: white adolescent male fantasies acted out to an accompaniment of rock music. Ellis says he deliberately patterned the "staccato pace, the rapid layering of image upon image" of his novel after the aesthetics of a rock video. "My generation is really the first to have grown up in the shadow of the video revolution," he explains. "Being bombarded all the time by music videos, you tend to think of things, stories, in purely visual terms." Ellis makes liberal use of metaphor to express his subjects' pathological cravings and personal disintegration, especially in his choice of characters' names, and allusions to suggestive commercial slogans and rock band titles.

Ellis reports that he wrote the first draft of *Less than Zero* in eight weeks, then reworked the novel over the next two years. Critics commend Ellis's prose, in which he achieves a cool and distant tone by presenting his narrator, Clay, as affectless, self-absorbed, and without comment on the appalling incidents he relates. Ellis is also praised for his fine ear for language evidenced in his capable rendering of the banal and inarticulate speech of these "lost" suburban youths. Some reviewers observe that because Clay's story delivers shock after shock, the reader grows inured to the atrocities described, to the point of boredom or disbelief; but other critics contend that this is a carefully engineered effect meant to parallel the inertia experienced by Clay and his jaded companions. Ellis is writing a second novel, tentatively titled *The Rules of Attraction,* as his senior thesis at Bennington.

© *Jerry Bauer*

KIRKUS REVIEWS

The over-familiar emptiness and super-decadence of L.A.—witnessed, this time around [in *Less than Zero*], by a very young semi-outsider. Clay is 18, home for Christmas break from college in New Hampshire. And he quickly finds himself in the swim of life such as it is in his circle: movie-industry parents, ubiquitous cocaine, Valium, MTV, bisexuality, anorexia, Mercedes cars—and a daily round of numbing, inconsequential acts. . . . After . . . vacant days, the nights are devoted to partying: the in-group gatherings sometimes involve the screening of snuff films; on one occasion an actual murder-mutilation occurs. So, though Clay does do some running with a crowd that is into male prostitution (to support drug-habits), he eventually backs away from all the sub-zero sleaziness. Throughout, first-novelist Ellis and narrator Clay register everything here with utter coolness: there is no inflection, no viewpoint; you're supposed to simply sponge up all the horror. Unfortunately, however, the effect is one of overkill—like a Soviet propaganda film about the murderous effects of too much wealth. And you never experience revulsion, only eventual boredom. In sum: a flat Cook's tour of kiddie-depravity in Lotusland—with a pounding beat, no zing, and only some marginal voyeur-interest for the insatiably curious.

A review of "Less than Zero," in Kirkus Reviews, *Vol. LIII, No. 6, March 15, 1985, p. 233.*

ELIOT FREMONT-SMITH

"I suppose the first thing people are going to notice is my age," sighs Bret Easton Ellis, author of a remarkable first novel, *Less than Zero*. . . . "There's no way to avoid that, but I hope the critics are able to look past that and judge the book on its own terms, for what it says." . . .

For myself, I'll say that Ellis, at 20, has seen and done and/ or imagined an awful lot, and not all of it from MTV; that he has a very fine ear and perhaps overcalculating talent, and that *Less than Zero* (dumb title) is sexy, sassy, and sad, even as it becomes an increasingly heavy trip. It's a teenage slice-of-death novel, no holds barred; eventually the shocks run out and not even melodrama can save it or us from the rack of inertia. But that's its whole . . . point, of course.

Clay, 18, a freshman at a New Hampshire college and narrator of the novel, has come to L.A. for the month-long Christmas holidays. . . .

[Names] are pretty much the plot—elegant names of stores (Camp Beverly Hills, Parachute, Privilege), restaurants (Chasen's, Trumps), discos, hang-out clubs, and bars (Hard Rock, The Edge, The Roxy, The Wire, The New Garage, Land's End, Nowhere Club), drugs (Valium, coke, pot, acid, smack, meth, Nembutal, Thorazine, speed, Quaaludes, Preludin, Desoxyn, Perrier-Jouet champagne), and rock groups.

I count 22 groups in *Less than Zero,* from Human League to Prince, from the Eagles to XTC (my favorite is Killer Pussy, of "Teenage Enema Nurses in Bondage" fame). Unfortunately, the kids in the book are too young or dragged out to have developed much sense of humor.

Drinking, drugging, partying, shopping, remembering trade names, and keeping their bodies tan, blond, Nautilized, and otherwise "totally gorgeous" occupy all their attention. Which is not to say that their attention on anything is more than vague and fleeting. It's a desperate quest these people are on, from one sensation to another, to prove themselves alive, if without purpose.

We are also to understand that the process toward jadedness starts very early. (p. 20)

Less than Zero is a killer, dispiriting and exhausting. . . . [It] may not be wholly "real," but the feel of it—this rich, frenetic, repetitive, yuppie-punk video madness—hits where it hurts. It will, I suspect, be much discussed, and dope, California, affluence, narcissism, rock and roll, the movie biz, divorced and uninterested parents, and the whole, sick, aimless culture will be viewed anew with alarm. . . .

For a long time, the theme seems to be human disconnection and spiritual disintegration through drugs and (perhaps) the high-contrast surface escapism of video and disco life—with the villains being factors of a strictly contemporary culture.

Toward the end, the novel seems to veer into a specific attack on these youths' parents. And then Clay's increasingly frequent and italicized memories of visiting his grandparents in Palm Springs carry the indictment back into the past. His grandfather, rich on Nevada hotels, sits around in his jockstrap and

drinks too much, while his grandmother, dying of cancer, hums to herself "On the Sunny Side of the Street" and nobody cares at all. And then one learns that Clay's great-grandfather died alone in Las Vegas. And so, it is hinted, the decay and unhappiness go way, way back, perhaps forever.

I think this sense of vague, timeless, and inevitable sin, even more than Ellis's brutally undifferentiated shocks . . . is what makes *Less than Zero* so despairing. But also of more than passing "first voice of a new generation" interest. (p. 21)

Eliot Fremont-Smith, "The Right Snuff," in VLS, *No. 35, May, 1985, pp. 20-1.*

RAY OLSON

[The narrator of *Less than Zero*] discovers his friends deeply sunk in cocaine, heroin, male prostitution, and sadistic sex, caroming wildly from party to drug connection to rock club. It's a sleazier, all-American rich kids' *Dolce Vita,* and to his credit, young Clay is at last disgusted by it. His self-told tale speaks with the grim determination of a stunned disaster survivor's report. He is too desiccated to speak with Holden Caulfield's tang, too naive to achieve Jake Barnes' devastating innuendos, too horrified to essay the wild humor of a William Burroughs mouthpiece. Yet Salinger, Hemingway, and Burroughs all echo in Ellis' prose. This 20-year-old first novelist, however, seems equally influenced by Fitzgerald's wounded temperament and the staccato style of TV cop shows. A youthful sweetness seethes beneath the surface, though, offering hope for Ellis' development as a writer. (p. 1294)

Ray Olson, in a review of "Less than Zero," in Booklist, *Vol. 81, No. 18, May 15, 1985, pp. 1293-94.*

JOHN RECHY

The 20-year-old author of this pruriently violent book [*Less than Zero*] is being widely vaunted as the voice of his generation. The voice is one of traumatized self-pity, passivity and blind self-absorption as heard in this chilly novel about teenage males.

It is certainly the first novel of MTV—rampant with aimless rage and symptomatic images and attitudes that it does not quite understand, symbols of fascism, women crawling as slaves, homosexuality derided while courted by imitation. . . .

Authenticity is essential in a novel purporting to illuminate unexplored territory. Ellis knows the world of ample wealth. But in certain essential areas, the book suggests the possibility of sensationalized distortion. Some incidents are staples of "creep chic," horrible rumors spread by a few morbid college students swearing to know "someone who saw" the snuff movie, other ugly outrages.

The only plot line is blatantly contrived, involving the mysterious activities of Clay's best friend. Julian becomes a homosexual prostitute because he has an expensive drug habit—and his family has canceled his bank account and credit cards, and it would be a "bummer" to sell his gorgeous Porsche! Julian takes Clay to meet his pimp at a most propitious time. "You bringing your friend here might be a good thing," says the pimp, because a client "wants two guys, one just to watch. Of course." Of course. This artificial device allows Clay to witness what he considers "the very worst"—an act of male prostitution that he watches, for money he does not need.

Beyond sensational content, what of literary quality? As a first novel, it is exceptional, exhibiting notable potential. The best writing describes violence—the tortured death of a coyote under the wheels of a car, every twist rendered in sexual detail. Expertly, Ellis captures the banality in the speech of his teenagers. His cool, languid prose is impressive but slides into self-parody: "Angel was supposed to go with us tonight, but earlier today she got caught in the drain of her Jacuzzi and almost drowned." There are more desultory cigarette lightings than perhaps in any other book ever published. "Suddenly," "and then," "for some reason," "missing a beat"—these occur singly or together with dogged persistence.

In a recent essay, Joyce Carol Oates takes exception to the growing notion that sanity lies in "the capacity to assimilate horrors without comment." One might infer that Ellis intends to present objectively for indictment by the reader this world of opulent decay, except that Clay chooses his lacerating judgments and exonerations too carefully. They are delivered in the book's last paragraph.

Los Angeles: Guilty! People are "driven mad by living in the city." Parents: Guilty! They are "so hungry and unfulfilled they ate their children." And Clay and the teen-agers preying on those younger than they? Not guilty: They are merely "looking up from the asphalt and being blinded by the sun." With that lofty, vague phrase, Clay releases himself and his malicious friends from all responsibility. Corrupt as the parents may be, nothing conveyed about them here approaches the ancient depravity of these male teen-agers. They arouse not pity but an extending fear, because they will inherit the power and wealth of the parents they despise. (pp. 1, 11)

> *John Rechy, in a review of "Less than Zero," in* Los Angeles Times Book Review, *May 26, 1985, pp. 1, 11.*

An Excerpt from *Less than Zero*

I'm sitting in my psychiatrist's office the next day, coming off from coke, sneezing blood. My psychiatrist's wearing a red V-neck sweater with nothing on underneath and a pair of cut-off jeans. I start to cry really hard. He looks at me and fingers the gold necklace that hangs from his tan neck. I stop crying for a minute and he looks at me some more and then writes something down on his pad. He asks me something. I tell him I don't know what's wrong; that maybe it has something to do with my parents but not really or maybe my friends or that I drive sometimes and get lost; maybe it's the drugs.

"At least you realize these things. But that's not what I'm talking about, that's not really what I'm asking you, not really."

He gets up and walks across the room and straightens a framed cover of a Rolling Stone with Elvis Costello on the cover and the words "Elvis Costello Repents" in large white letters. I wait for him to ask me the question.

"Like him? Did you see him at the Amphitheater?

Yeah? He's in Europe now, I guess. At least that's what I heard on MTV. Like the last album?"

"What about me?"

"What about you?"

"What about me?"

"You'll be fine."

"I don't know," I say. "I don't think so."

"Let's talk about something else."

"What about me?" I scream, choking.

"Come on, Clay," the psychiatrist says. "Don't be so . . . mundane."

NEW REPUBLIC

Twenty-year-old Bret Easton Ellis's first novel [*Less than Zero*] paints a grim picture of the lives of L.A.'s overprivileged children. But who cares? Readers with a degree in pharmacology may find the chemical catalog diverting (marijuana, coke, Quaaludes, Valium, Nembutal, lithium, ether, acid, heroin, methadone, novocaine, Decadron, Celestone, and Percodan), but the rest of us probably prefer to read stories about people than about powders or pills. Written in the inarticulate style of a petulant suburban punk, this novel strains to capture the genuine despair in some rich kids' lives, but ends up only superficially reporting their tedious hedonism. Reading it is like watching MTV. Each of the brief, videoesque vignettes that make up the book hints at depths never explored. There's a glimpse of real feeling; then, click, it's onto the next episode of ennui. . . .

> *A review of "Less than Zero," in* The New Republic, *Vol. 192, No. 23, June 10, 1985, p. 42.*

PAUL GRAY

This decidedly offbeat first novel [*Less than Zero*] offers a mixed message to all those who might be worried about contemporary teenagers. On the one hand, the example of its author looks hopeful: Bret Easton Ellis, 21, is . . . obviously an enterprising and successful young man. But the story he tells about members of his generation is lurid in the extreme. Most readers who are not helplessly zonked on sex, drugs and rock 'n' roll will finish *Less than Zero* with the conviction that they have not fretted over the current condition of young people nearly enough. . . .

Ellis conveys the hellishness of aimless lives with economy and skill; his efforts to distance Clay, the narrator, from all the other zombies is unsuccessful. True, he has a few scruples. He does not mainline heroin, he walks out before the end of an apparently genuine snuff film, and he refuses an obliging friend's invitation to rape a drugged and trussed up twelve-year-old girl. He is also sensitive. The crying jag he experiences at his psychiatrist's office may suggest some inner anguish, although it might just as easily occur because he spends so much time drugged to the eyeballs.

Ultimately, Ellis' novel is anchored to a hero who stands for nothing. How Clay managed to muster the energy to go to college in the first place remains mysterious; so do the forces that made him so passive and world-weary at age 18. That such questions about the central character seem important is a tribute to Ellis' talent; his refusal to address them is thus all the more unsettling. In spite of its surface vitality and macabre glitter, *Less than Zero* offers little more than its title promises.

Paul Gray, "Zombies," in Time, *Vol. 125, No. 23, June 10, 1985, p. 80.*

MARY JO SALTER

There seems little joy in the world of Bret Easton Ellis, unless it's the delight he takes in christening his creations: names like Blair, Kim, Chris, Lee and Lindsay, which suggest in their androgyny the indifference of most of the characters about the sex of their bed partners; and names like Rip, Spit, Spin, Finn, Fear, Dead and X, which suggest the drugged stupor in which these people conduct their lives. . . . Clay unlike anyone else in [*Less than Zero*], has the tattered remnants of a personality. Once he even chides others for their inconsiderateness: "I don't think it's right," he proposes to his friends who are raping a 12-year-old girl they have shot up with heroin. Finally, he feels just enough longing for a meaningful life to drift back to college. The other partygoers in this novel are so incapable of moral or critical thought that the reader may be numbed into an inability to judge it as literature. I hated reading the book for more than 20 minutes at a stretch, but that was partly because Mr. Ellis succeeded in making its world hellish. The novelist . . . has precociously fashioned, despite an obvious stylistic indebtedness to writers from Hemingway to Joan Didion, a tone so distant that he almost seems to write by remote control. That is control of a kind, and augurs well. May he write more novels—next time about people not too burnt out to change.

Mary Jo Salter, in a review of "Less than Zero," in The New York Times Book Review, *June 16, 1985, p. 24.*

DAVID LEHMAN

[In *Less than Zero*, Ellis] relies on short takes and dangling conversations in lieu of a conventional plot. There's plenty of writing on the wall: "Gloom Rules," announces a bathroom mirror; "Disappear Here," the legend on a roadside billboard, pops up again and again as a leitmotif. Despite Ellis's shrewdly understated style, the metaphors frequently scream out at us. When Clay gets a leather-bound date book for a Christmas gift and knows it will sit on his desk "unused, blank," we've got a pretty strong idea of what he thinks his future holds.

Less than Zero is almost more interesting as a cultural document than as a novel; no doubt that's why it's now all the rage in Los Angeles. Ellis gives us the seamy underside of the preppy handbook. "Living wretchedly is the best revenge," might well be the motto of his self-destructive non-rebels without a cause. The private eye in Arthur Lyons's *Three With a Bullet*, surveying similar wreckage, says it best. "How could they look so tired and jaded at seventeen?" he wonders. "It had taken me thirty years to get that look in my eyes."

David Lehman, in a review of "Less than Zero," in Newsweek, *Vol. CVI, No. 2, July 8, 1985, p. 70.*

JAMES M. MILLIKEN, JR.

Bret Easton Ellis' novel [*Less than Zero*] is a debut for a possibly bright new talent. . . .

The first nine-tenths of the story seem to be just a sullen parade of debauchery (and it's a tribute to the author's command of the language that he maintains the reader's avid interest). At the end, however, we see that Ellis has not merely been impressing upon us the emptiness of this L.A. fantasy world: he gradually adds just enough extra detail to carry us along and to prepare us for the conclusion. The final realization of the inhumanity that Clay's society spawns is all the more shocking because it follows so logically from what seems at first to be harmless (if disgusting).

There are flaws in the book, the greatest of which is a certain heavy handedness. The observation that "People are afraid to merge on freeways in Los Angeles" is sufficient to alert us to the fact that this is a story of alienation, and the author needn't have spent a whole page on it. There are numerous other instances of bludgeoning us with symbolism, and the sheer extent of the characters' shallowness and amorality sometimes stretches the reader's credibility.

Less than Zero is no *Catcher In the Rye* (although the liner notes assure us otherwise), but it is a well written, cleverly structured novel. Its flaws might well be the result of over-eagerness on the part of a young author. If so, we should expect to see some very good things from him in the future.

James M. Milliken, Jr., in a review of "Less than Zero," in Best Sellers, *Vol. 45, No. 5, August, 1985, p. 166.*

ALAN JENKINS

Though [*Less than Zero*] deals with terminal boredom and mindless repetition, it is not quite boring or mindless. In the cinematic arrangement of the short scenes, the threading of leitmotif phrases ("People are afraid to merge", "Wonder if he's for sale", "Disappear here") through the narration, the carefully unmodulated switches from catalogues of brand-names to gang-rape and the other uses of Bain de Soleil lotion, there is evidence of a concern for form and of a genuine instinct for literary "cool", for understatement or non-statement. Ellis catches some things very well: the background of rock-lyric sentiments to adolescent life (Clay's hero is Elvis Costello, from one of whose songs the title *Less than Zero* is taken), the vacuities of what passes in this world for conversation, the all-pervadingness of savagery and fear, the nameless menace of the surrounding desert encroaching on the no less inhuman city—a scream heard in the night, cars burning on the roads, the sound of glass breaking "in the hills", a coyote prowling a suburban street. Violence takes over too explicitly, and too suddenly, in the closing sections, but it is at such moments that Clay's stunned inner world seems most to reflect an appropriately played-down respect for the facts (the horrors evoked here are, apparently, the facts). In italicized, highly descriptive, sensuous passages recalling childhood days spent with a comparatively united family at a Palm Springs holiday house, or, for once roused to rage, putting his appalling psychiatrist straight, or shuffling bewilderedly around his on-off, unsatisfactory, failing attachment to Blair, his girl (who seems momentarily to share with him the merest inkling of something better, a glimpse of love, commitment, mutuality that premature world-weariness and self-loathing cut them off from), Clay is sympathetic, even touching. At the close, a song provokes him to some kind of insight: "The images I had were of people being driven mad by living in the city. Images of parents who were so hungry and unfulfilled that they ate their own children. . . . Images so violent and malicious that they seemed to be my only point of reference for a long time afterwards.'' A reviewer ought to be able to end by comparing him to Holden Caulfield and this book to *Catcher in the Rye,* but it's not really on.

Less than Zero will no doubt make, has already made, its author a great deal of money, but the price will have been too high if its success commits him to repeating the tone of ambiguous nihilism he sustains here. And the question remains how far that tone, thoroughly self-conscious performance though it seems, is a conscious achievement, how far it believes it is something else.

> *Alan Jenkins, ''Back Home with the Tan Blond Boys,'' in* The Times Literary Supplement, *No. 4326, February 28, 1986, p. 216.*

DARRYL PINCKNEY

[*Less than Zero*] is not really a punk novel (the title comes from Elvis Costello's *Trust*). There are no crash pads, safety pins, monumental mohawks, buzz cuts, or rock bands in the garage. The outrageousness is all in the lack of restraint, in the consumption. This is light years away from New Wave's roots as depicted in *The Punk* (1977), the underground novel Gideon Sams published in London when he was fifteen. Not that *Less than Zero* lacks violence. But it depicts the casual violence of kids toward themselves. The novel is not about youth lost in the world. In fact, Ellis's characters have no contact with the world. The eighteen-year-olds of *Less than Zero* keep apartments with Jacuzzis on Wilshire just to be close to class, but no one attends. USC is the ''University of Spoiled Children'' and then there is ''Jew.S.C.'' and ''Jew.C.L.A.'' Mostly the kids hang out and nod out in many mansions from Beverly Hills to Malibu to Palm Springs. They are on their own so much that the book resembles a *Peanuts* cartoon—the adults seem to speak from off-frame. These kids are alone with Pac Man and large wardrobes, alone except for nameless, faceless Hispanic maids or blond hangers-on who seem to answer doors only in briefs with tan lines showing. The aim of life is not to miss a beat while crying, mainlining, snorting, skin-popping, or free-basing to keep from laughing, as in been-rich-so-long-it-feels-like-poor-to-me. . . . (p. 33)

Less than Zero is not pornographic, though it uses the pornographic method of inviting the reader to voyeurism. Ellis is at pains to free his narrator of any stain by inserting passages of longing for happier summers with his grandparents in Palm Springs, by making Clay appropriately queasy, and by including brief scenes with an authority figure, a shrink, who is, predictably, a fool. Endless, aimless hanging out does not require justification, but Ellis does not seem to want to place the narrator too far beyond the pale.

A recent Gallup Poll concluded that the number of books sold to Americans between the ages of eighteen and twenty-four dropped 6 percent from last year. This raises the question of who is reading *Less than Zero* and other works in what could

be called the youth-novel genre. It's hard to believe that any of the hyped-up kids outside rock clubs like CBGB or Save the Robot want to be home reading about MTV viewers, and in this sense some of the works written by the young must truly be messages for the grown-ups.

Youth has dominated popular culture since the Beatles. Some analysts now predict that the baby boom generation will become the most important voting bloc for the next twenty years. Does this mean that by the next election people who can recall the Davy Crockett fad will be crowding in the same boat with voters born in 1970? A part of the Sixties legacy is the tendency to view youth as a homogenous group, as if it were a permanent class. No one seems to get kicked upstairs into adulthood anymore and those involved in the youth industry or dependent on the image seem like committee members who vote themselves into office year after year. How long can Mick Jagger go on? As long as he likes.

> Man and boy stood cheering by,
> And home we brought you shoulder-high

David Leavitt published an article recently about ''The New Lost Generation'' in *Esquire*, rather in the way Joyce Maynard came forth more than a decade ago to explain youth after the generation of the Sixties had moved on to greener pastures. ''We hit our stride in an age of burned-out, restless, ironic disillusion,'' Leavitt writes of his generation. ''We don't pretend we're not wearing costumes.'' Leavitt convincingly describes the difference in sensibility between those who grew up in the Seventies and those who came of age in the Sixties. What Leavitt does not say is that the Sixties, with its moral imperatives and social consciousness, imposes something of a burden on the young who have followed.

It is not so much that contemporary fiction by young writers describes a reconciliation between the young and society, as that that fiction defies nostalgia for the Sixties and insists on its own distinct and separate identity. . . . [Novels like *Less than Zero*] are written from the inside of youth, not about it. The slang and drug of choice may differ, but the tone today is not far from that of the generation of *This Side of Paradise*, the atmosphere of romance. (p. 34)

> *Darryl Pinckney, ''The New Romantics,'' in* The New York Review of Books, *Vol. XXXIII, No. 9, May 29, 1986, pp. 30-4.**

❝

COMMENTS OF BRET EASTON ELLIS TO *CLC YEARBOOK*

Ellis observes that *Less than Zero* is ''not very'' autobiographical, ''though people always seem to think it is—which is part compliment and part insult. Complimentary in the sense that they find the voice so overwhelmingly persuasive. An insult in the sense that the narrator is a WRETCH.'' The audience he hopes to reach, ''because I'm writing about my generation,'' would be ''young people—people who normally wouldn't read but are interested in someone chronicling their lives.''

Carlo (Ernest) Gébler

1954-

(Born Carlos Gébler) Irish novelist.

Memories of summer visits to his grandparents in rural Ireland inspired Gébler to write his first novel, *The Eleventh Summer* (1985). The novel begins and ends with scenes of middle-aged Paul Weismann returning to his grandparents' home in the Irish countryside, where he had spent his childhood summers. Through flashbacks to his eleventh year, Paul recalls the painful incidents that initiated his passage from childhood to adolescence, which forms the heart of the story. Reviewers note that in *The Eleventh Summer* Gébler creates an authentic portrait of childhood, rich in sensation and atmospheric detail. Because of the unpleasant nature of many scenes and events, critics especially admire Gébler for his unsentimental tone and fresh approach to the traditional rite-of-passage novel.

Born in Ireland, Gébler has lived in London since the age of five. His parents, now divorced, are the writers Edna O'Brien and Ernest Gébler. Carlo Gébler claims to have read only one of his mother's novels. However, he adds, "If you live with writers, you absorb the character of their work from their conversation, you absorb the atmosphere in the house; it's an osmotic process. Also, I now see that my reluctance, or disinclination, to read my mother's work could have sprung from a feeling that if one day I was going to write myself, I'd be better off without that primary influence." Gébler says he began writing in childhood, but school had a stifling effect on his creativity: "The whole process of education and the way we were streamed made me feel very stupid; and that sort of atmosphere gave the sense that any kind of artistic endeavor was going to be beyond me." Eventually, Gébler found his first satisfactory educational experience through postgraduate studies at the National Film and Television School. He now makes television documentaries as well as writing fiction. "Writing is private and solitary and you have complete control," observes Gébler, "and there's nothing to beat that pleasure. But making films brings quite a different set of joys: companionship, getting something done against the odds. I'm interested in both because of the way they complement each other."

Gébler completed a second novel, *August in July* (1986), which involves a theme similar to that of *The Eleventh Summer*. In it, a Polish exile living in London records in a diary recollections of his boyhood in Warsaw. Gébler is working on a third novel, tentatively called *Work and Play*. Gébler reports, "This owes its inspiration to Antonioni and his description of his life (in his films) as a process of endless detection. To the hero, people and events are mysteries and he can only at best have a fragmentary understanding of what is going on around him. The book is set in London in 1986, and in it I am trying to describe modern metropolitan life."

© Jerry Bauer

HUGH BARNES

On the face of it, Carlo Gebler owes much to Laurie Lee's *Cider with Rosie*. It's safe to say the definitive work will be regularly, and irresistibly, invoked reading **The Eleventh Summer**. But comparisons are odious, and too persuasive. Gebler's narrative, its main business at least which is an eleven-year-old's holiday out, is sandwiched by tableaux, prologue and epilogue, of adulthood. Paul Weismann takes time out from prosperity and middle age to retrace a journey made years earlier, to his grandparents' Red House in rural Ireland.

For much of the time, Paul has the advantage over us, his innocent witnesses. Sensations precede explanation. It becomes clear towards the end that, mother dead, Paul rebounds between an unsympathetic father and the older, homelier generation. Granny is an awesome figure of authority, chaotically steering an even-ish keel through hard times and Grandpa's hazardous obsessions. He is consumed by a love of horses, racing ones; also, when they don't come in, by a consolatory love for the bottle. Paul offers him companionship and, precociously, supervision. After a particularly unlucky streak at the track, Grandpa slips the leash, disappearing for a fortnight, until he is discovered unconscious in a Cork boarding house. Finally, convalescing after a riding accident, he incinerates himself with fag ash.

Trials and tribulations, beautifully conjured, but perhaps the boy's passion for his cousin Philomena identifies the novel's truest moments. *The Eleventh Summer* is a notable achievement, childhood seen through spectacles which are tinted, yes, but not unduly rosy.

Hugh Barnes, "Enchanted Gardens," *in* Books and Bookmen, *No. 353, February, 1985, p. 26.*

RICHARD DEVESON

The Eleventh Summer, Carlo Gébler's first novel, has an Irish setting and, like much writing about Ireland, is a Chekhov-ish amalgam of melancholic sensibility, apparent plotlessness and meticulously placed dialogue. It contains Russo-Irish elderly eccentrics, drunkards, grandmotherly grandmothers, peasantry, rural decay, characters given to grand but hollow gestures and to intimations of transcendence that are liable to degenerate into seizures of sentimentality. The events of a summer are seen exclusively through the eyes of a boy, Paul Weismann: so exclusively that we never fully learn about the events which lead the cold and tyrannical non-Irish father of this sensitive only child to park him on fond but disaster-prone Irish grandparents.

As tends to happen in novels, Paul has a lot of half understood but highly maturational experiences in rather rapid succession: fire, illness, death, sexual fumblings with a girl cousin, glimpses of sexual fumblings between adults, glimpses of adults stricken by grief and despair. The tone, however, is not remotely melodramatic. Paul's world is delicately built up out of a mass of precise physical detail: colour, touch, smell and taste; strange Irish brand names and trademarks; the sensation of getting lost in a daydream over a comic book; the sound of two old women standing up after praying, 'their knees creaking like corks being pulled from bottles'. It is a remarkably good picture of the mind of a child, for whom, in his solitariness and vulnerability, one feels considerable compassion. (p. 33)

Richard Deveson, "High Energy," *in* New Statesman, *Vol. 109, No. 2811, February 1, 1985, pp. 32-3.*

CHRISTOPHER HAWTREE

The slim first novel about the long, lyrical summers of childhood has died out in recent years; aspirants, frightened off by the clichés, perhaps, have turned to palpably grittier themes. It might seem that Carlo Gébler was deliberately flying in the face of fashion by choosing to write such a novel [*The Eleventh Summer*], but his prose, which is successful on a number of levels, has such an assurance that the story bears no traces of hesitant catharsis.

Aged eleven, Paul Weismann "had already started the retreat from life back into himself, by which the passage to adulthood is achieved". The novel opens and closes with brief sections in which the narrator, adulthood long since reached, broods on this transformation and the attitudes that it creates. These

jar a little, but such jolts are a necessary part of troubled reminiscence. The inward journey has been precipitated by his mother's death (perhaps even S-U-I-C-I-D-E, as it is patronizingly spelled out within his supposedly ignorant earshot). A more tangible journey is the one that he has made to a village somewhere in the Irish countryside in order to live with his grandparents so that his severe, atheistic father can be left free to go about his business for the summer.

As the weeks go by the balance of Paul's mind tips from innocence to knowledge, and at the same time the disinterestedness of his young eyes reveals the absurdities and ignorance of adulthood. The grandfather is blessed with more than his share. The summer begins with an incident which in lesser hands might have been a set-piece, but is here effortlessly assimilated into the whole: Paul accompanies his grandfather to the races, where the horse which carries their insurance money on its back tumbles "as if she had collided with an invisible stone wall". The vet arrives and the horse "shrieked again and struggled to get to her feet. It was as if she knew what fate awaited her." A pistol shot rings out and she leaves the world in a more dignified way than that in which the grandfather consoles himself for the loss at an inn on the way back. (On an earlier expedition he had escaped to a hotel room and left it in such a state that an outside cleaner had to be summoned.)

Money, whether sixpences passed in soiled handkerchiefs and hoarded in buried jam-jars or the large sums offered by a German industrialist for the surrounding land, recurs in these pages. It takes its place amid such details as the keys hidden beneath the soap-dish, *Beano* annuals, unsavoury chamberpots and Perpetual Lights, which together form a strange, recognizable world. In a bucket Paul finds "a John West's salmon tin and an empty salmon paste jar. Bridget had supplemented the salmon with paste, he guessed. That explained the strange taste."

Acute observation and an abundance of telling, unobtrusive metaphor enable Gébler to carry the reader through page after page in which nothing much happens; the more startling incidents which punctuate this life are of a piece with all that has gone before. Enigmas remain—did Paul, as he lay in a convalescent bed, really hypnotize Philomena before she took off her clothes? Why did his father address the grandmother in that odd way?—and transport one back, much as they do the narrator, to an Ireland, without a sergeant-major or terrorist in sight, that has perhaps not been as sharply and variously evoked since J. G. Farrell's *Troubles*.

Christopher Hawtree, "The Journey Inward," *in* The Times Literary Supplement, *No. 4270, February 1, 1985, p. 110.*

An Excerpt from *The Eleventh Summer*

The light inside the church had a blue tinge to it on account of where the ceiling was painted blue between the rafters. The colouring always gave him the feeling of being underwater.

He discreetly surveyed his relatives, stiff in their mourning clothes beside him; granny, uncles James and Thomas; their wives, aunties May and Pat; and his auntie Bridget at the end. He had been hoping that Philomena would come, but she was too young, everyone had said, for such a sad occasion. For him it was his second funeral, so different from the first, and he was able to look about with a certain detachment. Around the eyes of everyone lined up beside him he saw there was a glaze of tears trapped there by the wrinkles. Father Murphy's rapid Latin echoed around the walls. Behind his bare knees he could feel the always damp, always sticky wooden pew.

His granny turned her head and looked down at him. She was wearing a black hat held in place with a black-ended pin and a piece of black veiling hung over her face. Her eyes were grey and wet. She took out a small sodden hankerchief from the sleeve of her jacket and wiped her nose, red and chafed from having been wiped so many times before. Then she nodded her head in the way she always did when she thought manners were slipping and he turned his attention to the front again.

Father Murphy was tall in white and purple. His nose was purple too, swollen and fascinating like an obscure vegetable. The coffin lay behind on rough trestles. The wood was the dark colour of whiskey and the handles were shining brass. Once they got it into the ground and buried, grandfather would be gone for ever, his secret about the fire would be safe and he and granny would go an live in old Andy's cottage together, now that old Andy had gone to the hospital where he would stay until he died. Wicked as it was, he knew, to think it, it was a glorious future that was going to begin once the last spadeful of earth went on. He looked up and saw the pale, pained face of Jesus looking down, the mysterious initials INRI on the scroll at his feet. Granny had once told him that Jesus could read the thoughts of any man if he chooses to do so. But as there were so many men's thoughts to be read in the world, he hoped his own would be passed over.

VALENTINE CUNNINGHAM

Carlo Gébler's [*The Eleventh Summer* is a] pared-down, bony encounter with a temporary Irish boyhood. . . . Revisiting Ireland, middle-aged Paul Weismann recalls with aching precision his very unpastoral eleventh summer there when he was dumped on his grandparents after his mother's suicide.

What he was put through amounts to a classic of Black Irishness. His racehorse-training grandad went in for protracted messy drunkenness and raw gropings of his wife. Paul had unsatisfying physical engagements with little Philomena and awesome encounters with ticks on the testicles, a coach-load of hapless lunatics, a runaway horse, a labourer with a ghastly facial strawberry-mark, and finally grandad's burning corpse. All pretty distasteful stuff, but which Gébler has an extraordinarily powerful way with. Puke that looks like nougat is the sort of image he relishes.

He also has an engaging eye for calamitous farce, such as the battery-flat hearse that the mourners need to push to the cemetery. Here is an Ireland eager to serve its turn as Joyce's green snot-rag of the bard. It's no accident that young Paul is re-

markably obsessed by phlegm and mucus and what's dried on to his elders' grotty handkerchiefs. Ireland's unfailing gruesomeness and menace prove, once more, undeniable.

Valentine Cunningham, "The Ties that Bind," in The Observer, *February 3, 1985, p. 51.**

KIRKUS REVIEWS

Gebler . . . makes a less than auspicious debut with this novel [*The Eleventh Summer*] about a child's loss of innocence. As 31-year-old Paul Weismann journeys from his London home to Ireland (the country of his childhood), memories crowd in. The remembered events are narrated from the child Paul's point of view—in a style so terse and flat, and with characters so familiar, that the story fails to become engaging. . . .

The unique flavor of Ireland and the Irish is strangely missing from this book. Despite his efforts, the conscientious author provides neither lyricism nor rueful humor—qualities that have distinguished so many others in this genre, and from this place.

A review of "The Eleventh Summer," in Kirkus Reviews, *Vol. LIII, No. 15, August 1, 1985, p. 728.*

ROBERT O'MEALLY

At his grandfather's burial site, Paul guiltily overhears two gravediggers talk: "'There's nothing in that coffin that just went down, only a handful of cinders.' . . . 'No peace for the wicked.'" Grandfather died in a fire that burned the house down, a fire caused by one of his unextinguished cigarette matches, flicked by the old man while in an evil stupor following one of his drunken rampages. Dreamy, sensitive Paul would conceal forever his fear that *he* had caused the fire that lit up his unforgettable 11th year, his "eleventh summer." This is Paul's summer in the country where The Young Man lives through an unusually painful series of initiatory upheavals. . . . Told as a flashback sparking more flashbacks by now grownup Paul, [*The Eleventh Summer*] starts slowly and—perforce its wit and its carefully measured poetic diction—gains momentum. It is a fine debut by a skillful young writer with much eloquence. (pp. 28-9)

Robert O'Meally, in a review of "The Eleventh Summer," in The New York Times Book Review, *October 6, 1985, pp. 28-9.*

COMMENTS OF CARLO GÉBLER TO *CLC YEARBOOK*

"My childhood forms the basis of the novel," says Gébler, commenting on the origins of *The Eleventh Summer*, "but I was inspired to write about it . . . in the following way. An Irish newspaper asked me to photograph the reunion of four siblings who had been brought up in separate orphanages. Their conversations about their memories of childhood and rural Ireland triggered me off.

"I wrote the first chapter as a short story and then realized it was a novel. I showed it to an editor at Hamish Hamilton who commissioned two further chapters. On the basis of those, he commissioned the rest. I was very lucky in that I experienced no difficulties in getting this novel published.

''I wrote the book in the traditional longhand manner page by page. Each chapter went through at least 5 drafts. The first stage was fast and exciting, but the revision was slower and more painstaking. As I advanced through the book I had no sense of what would follow, but I knew that there were various climaxes which I had to aim for.''

Asked what motivates him to write, Gébler responds, ''From the earliest age I wanted to be a writer. Unless I write I find my life without purpose. I don't see my work as being motivated by any particular desire but rather as arising from compulsion. What I hope to achieve are perfectly realized imaginary worlds in which the reader is completely involved.''

*Property
Ithaca High School Library
Ithaca, Michigan*

Molly Giles

1942-

American short story writer.

Several of the stories in *Rough Translations* (1985), Giles's first collection, were previously published in *North American Review, Ascent, Redbook,* and *Playgirl*. Giles, who teaches creative writing at San Francisco State University, takes as her subjects the everyday lives of contemporary women. Most of the stories in *Rough Translations* dramatize troubled relationships in which efforts at communication have failed. Critics observe that Giles's sharp, engaging style avoids sentimentality while offering insight into her characters' mental and emotional lives.

© 1986 Jay Daniel

A review of "Rough Translations," in Kirkus Reviews, *Vol. LIII, No. 5, March 1, 1985, pp. 188-89.*

KIRKUS REVIEWS

Marriage, divorce, and motherhood—those are the reasonable enough preoccupations of this debut collection of stories [**Rough Translations**], latest winner of the Flannery O'Connor Award for Short Fiction. Some of these brief pieces don't attempt much more than a plain, gently ironic recording of contemporary social situations: a divorcee's hopeful night and disappointing morning-after amidst the singles scene; another divorced woman's dalliance with her remarried ex-husband (not worth the trouble, she realizes); and **"What Do You Say"** if you happen to be sitting near your ex-husband's father (fallen on hard times) in a coffee shop? Elsewhere, Giles can be more than a little heavyhanded. **"Baby Pictures"** leans obviously on a married woman's conflict between career (photography) and motherhood—especially with a less-than-supportive husband. Three stories rather crudely sketch in the quasi-feminist disillusionments of marriage: in **"Heart and Soul,"** newly pregnant Joan and banker-husband John (a would-be songwriter) buy a used grand-piano—in a transaction that reveals John's crass, cynical side; in **"Chocolate Footballs,"** Joan realizes that macho-insensitive John is "cruel," with a similar fate likely for her young son ("The men have been feeding Jeffie chocolate footballs and he already has a brown mustache around his mouth that makes him look like a miniature man himself"); **"Peril"** finds Joan later in unhinged despair. And, even in this slight volume, Giles repeats herself too much—the story that follows **"Peril"** presents a woman in virtually the exact same state as Joan's—though she does also deal with death (in two stark pieces) and psychic phenomena (in the lightly whimsical **"Old Souls,"** narrated by the one down-to-earth type in a family of mystic romantics). Thin and uncommanding work, then, but a likable debut nonetheless—flecked with humor and insight, largely uncontaminated by the arch/sentimental mannerisms that frequently go with younger marriage/divorce material. (pp. 188-89)

PUBLISHERS WEEKLY

While [**Rough Translations**] is nominally a collection of short stories, a current as irresistible as the tides flows through and unifies them. Their common theme is the struggle to communicate, to make "rough translations" of the words the heart speaks. The same people, recognizable instantly, turn up in several stories: Joan, watching John dicker over a piano he wants to buy in **"Heart and Soul,"** asks a question whose answer tells her more than she wants to know; later, in **"Chocolate Footballs,"** when life with John has settled into a predictable groove, Joan sees that the marks, the twin prints of the groove, have etched themselves like stigmata around her mouth; finally, in **"Peril,"** ostensibly a story about Joan's houseful of cats, John once again goes to the piano, intent on working out the difficulties in one of his musical compositions but playing notes that echo the chaos in Joan herself. In **"Pie Dance,"** Pauline spars with her husband's new wife, with her three children, with her ambiguous ex, and ends up dancing to reggae music on the radio with the only straightforward creature in the house, her scruffy dog Stray. [The story **"Rough Translations"**] sums it all up: an old woman lies dying, trying to plan her own funeral, reconcile her children to herself and each other, writing her wishes and her dreams on a piece of paper that is crumpled and tossed into the air at the moment that her spirit leaves her body. The funeral is a great success; the woman has failed. These stories do not fail; they carry you with wit and compassion into corners of the mind and heart that most writers neglect to enter.

> *A review of "Rough Translations," in* Publishers Weekly, *Vol. 227, No. 11, March 15, 1985, p. 101.*

ROBERTA GRANT

The title of Molly Giles's first collection of short fiction [*Rough Translations*] reflects her attempt to capture in layered phrases and fresh, sharp dialogue the timely theme of human connections gone bad, broken or missed altogether. Written most often in the first person, these 12 stories confront their main characters with the large-scale drama of cancer in loved ones or their own deaths—or, more simply, with a subdued shift in perception that guarantees estrangement from a lover or loss of an old way of life. Mrs. Giles's tone is often fashionably deadpan, but her characters live on hope and are firm believers in their own spunk. In **"What Do You Say?"** and in the title story, the author poignantly juxtaposes memory and reality. Listening to the youthful inner voice of an old woman planning her funeral or observing a remarried woman struck dumb by the sight of her former father-in-law, we are privy to interplays of time and desire that leave the characters stymied but the reader highly gratified. However, at other moments Mrs. Giles translates her characters' anxieties and longings with far too much clarity. Overly articulate pronouncements of self-knowledge hoist a red flag in front of the readers' eyes: writer at work. Also, in several stories she exploits the first-person voice to reveal key emotional shifts rather than showing them through action, dialogue or detail. But Mrs. Giles . . . seems too accomplished a writer to carry these flaws with her for long.

> *Roberta Grant, in a review of "Rough Translations," in* The New York Times Book Review, *May 12, 1985, p. 18.*

ELLEN LESSER

The narrator of **"Old Souls,"** the opening story in Molly Giles's first collection [*Rough Translations*], works as an X-ray technician. Her patients ask, "Am I going to die?" And she thinks, "Of course you're going to die. Is that being too hard? We're all going to die." In *Rough Translations,* . . . Giles takes an approach as pragmatic and unsentimental as the technician's.

The 12 stories in this collection belong to the women Giles tracks across a scarred domestic terrain. Three of them follow Joan Bartlett through a decade and a half of marriage, charting the emptiness at the center of the relationship. When they go for a drive, Joan "hopes something interesting will appear outside the window so she can think of somthing interesting to say." By 24, she has wrinkles—the Avon lady calls them "anxiety lines"—mixed with occasional acne. She relies on John to reassure her she's beautiful, to answer the question "Do you love me?," which "shames and obsesses her." Joan has nothing "real" to complain about—just her solitude, the

conjugal silence, the accumulation of small disappointments and hurts. After a fight, she thinks of running away but knows "She'll give in, she'll give up, she'll give out, she'll give. . . . She will start to flow into him as she has always flowed and . . . nothing anyone can ever do or say will change the regret she feels in this ignoble flowing . . ."

"Peril" finds the Bartletts still angry, estranged, with two older children, Jeffery and Jillian. Joan is afraid John will leave her, Jillian reject her, Jeffrey replace her, "and she thinks all these things are going to happen soon, before she is ready, if anyone can ever be ready, ever, for disaster. Because disaster, Joan thinks . . . is always out there, waiting to fall down on somebody's head." In that kind of world, happiness is too much to ask for; survival is enough of a miracle.

The young mother in **"Baby Pictures"** wants to be a photographer, but all she has in her portfolio are shots of her son. Her friend, Leslie, a mother, a jogger and jewelry maker, complains about her husband's stasis, his paunch: "But I can't stop growing. I can't go backwards. I have to go forward. What else is there?" The would-be photographer wants to tell Leslie, "There is the second in between backwards and forwards that sometimes blazes and can sometimes be captured." That's the moment Giles often captures—her characters may have a fix on their problems, but they're not ready to change. At the end of the story, the woman shoots one more baby picture.

A few heroines do take the first steps, however small, toward altering their situations. **"Self Defense"** is narrated by the single mother of a 17-year-old who flunks drivers' ed and reads suicide poetry. She passes up a date to drive her daughter, Amanda, to self-defense class, but later acknowledges she has to begin her own life. After the class, she forces Amanda into the driver's seat. "'This is going to take a long, long time,' Amanda warns. Arms crossed, tired to the bone, I tell her that's fine; time means nothing to me." It's as close as Giles gets to a happy ending.

The dying Ramona, in [**"Rough Translations"**], could be any one of these women in her last days. She surveys with regret the legacy of her marriage and mothering: her children dislike her and each other; she's not even sure her husband would want her buried next to him. The unfinished novel lying in a cardboard box, the paintings lining the garage walls reproach her. She tries to tell her daughter about the "important and beautiful" things she's had to do with her life, but after a stroke, her speech is incomprehensible. On her deathbed Ramona reflects that she's "never said anything right"—has only managed "rough translations of a foreign language" she hears but cannot master. In less skillful hands, the stymied lot of Joan or Ramona might make for bleak reading, but Giles's sharp perceptions keep the stories engaging. She also knows how to get in and out quickly; her tales average 10 or 12 pages, which may be about as long as you'd care to spend with these characters. One can't help wondering what Giles will do next—move her heroines forward or keep her focus on these freeze-frame lives?

> *Ellen Lesser, in a review of "Rough Translations," in* VLS, *No. 36, June, 1985, p. 3.*

An Excerpt from *Rough Translations*

"You know who I admire?" she said to Potter as she joined him in the kitchen for dinner. "Junie Poole. Junie sat down in the hall outside the coroner's office one night and tried to kill herself by drinking a thermos of gin mixed with pills. When they arrested her she was too drunk to talk, but they found this note pinned to her mink coat saying she hoped her children would appreciate the fact that she had at least taken herself to the morgue. Of course, no one's appreciated anything Junie's ever done, before or since, but that's not the point. The point is that she did try to make things easy for her family. I want to make things easy too.'' She picked up her fork and looked down at her plate. "Liver? Won't Nora be impressed." She tried to eat a little. But when she saw the cat, in the corner, licking from an identical plate, she put the fork down and regarded Potter, who had done this to her before, once with canned salmon and once with pickled herring. He was either trying to be very economical or his values were more confused than she suspected. "Potter," she said, watching the old gray cat huddled murmurously over its plate, "do you think I should just crawl off to the woods?"

"There aren't any woods within crawling distance," said Potter. Ramona smiled; Potter did not. "I think . . ." Potter began. He stopped. Ramona folded her hands and waited. Potter, born when she was over forty, had been a talkative child, full of ideas and advice and so original that even Hale had paid attention, but Potter had stopped talking years ago, at least to her. "I think," Potter repeated, one thin hand fluttering before his downcast face, "that you are using this funeral to mask your real feelings."

Ramona waited, her own head bent. "And what are my real feelings?" she asked at last.

"Rage," Potter said, his shy eyes severe behind his smudged glasses. "Terror. Awe. Grief. Self-pity."

"Heavens," said Ramona. She was impressed. Once again she wished she were the mother her children deserved, and once again she found herself having to tell them she was not. "I'm afraid, Potter," she said, "you give me credit. I don't feel any more of those 'real' feelings now than I ever have. What I feel now is a sort of social panic, the same old panic I used to feel when Hale wanted me to give a dinner party for his clients and the guests would arrive and I'd still be in my slip clutching a bucket of live lobsters. I'm sorry dear, I can't eat this. I'm too nervous."

EILEEN KENNEDY

The very contemporary, even trendy characters in these stories [*Rough Translations*] are often deep in second marriages; they go to abortion clinics; they read Yeats in intimate bars and pick up strangers; they are would-be photographers, sketchers of witty cartoons, and rescuers of stray animals; they believe their lives will be changed if they change their hair styles or make-up. For the most part, the narrators or major characters are nearly all women who are vulnerable, decent, even kind, but

who make faulty connections in their love lives or marriages. They emerge bruised but not maimed, emotionally shaken but not mentally unbalanced. They go on, planting some winter carrots or teaching an unrealistic selfish daughter to drive.

The title of this collection takes its name from the final story, **"Rough Translations,"** in which a dying woman briefly and bitterly despairs over the fact that she has never been able to express what she thinks and how she feels toward her former husband and her two adult children. All the things she has done, she thinks, are "rough translations of a foreign language I hear but cannot master." Most of Molly Giles's major characters do try these raids on the inarticulate, but their hearers, those to whom they are bound up in close relationships—a husband, a sister, a woman friend—do not understand and so they must go on alone. The point is strongly made in the opening and perhaps finest story in the book, **"Old Souls."** The narrator, thoughtful, loving, and sensible, realizes how different she is from her sister who believes in fortune tellers, her mother who plays a Ouija board, her grandmother who thought God called her by name—and yet because of family bonds she is permanently tied to these women for whom she is the insensitive outsider.

Molly Giles is a perceptive writer, with an eye for the concrete detail that creates a realistic scene and makes the moment of realization credible. Her characters, heedless of the bigger world or their role in society, take the meaning of existence solely from emotional relationships. The stories are extended snapshots of caring, fragile, fearful women, and an occasional man, who somehow make it through the rough crossings of life.

> *Eileen Kennedy, in a review of "Rough Translations," in* Best Sellers, *Vol. 45, No. 4, July, 1985, p. 125.*

MICHAEL J. CARROLL

This slim volume of short stories [*Rough Translations*] . . . is populated by strangers, by the kind of people that we encounter in Laundromats, who—knowing we will never meet again—bare their souls, then pass out of our lives forever. Giles' people are real people, and Giles wisely allows them the freedom to be themselves. We meet a woman so desperate for companionship that she turns every stranger into a potential husband, falls for the illusion and totally misses the reality. There is a wife whose seeming defensive passivity is really a brutal aggression with which she diminishes her husband, herself and their marriage. Many of Giles' population are mean-minded and self-centered; some are growing, or coming to terms with themselves. A middle-aged woman realizes that she must take her own and her daughter's lives in hand, that she cannot waste any more precious time, even if it means giving a midnight driving lesson. Giles is a perceptive writer with a fine ear for the psyche's voice. The strangers to whom she introduces us become real. We may feel relief when they leave us to continue our separate lives, but we will have been touched.

> *Michael J. Carroll, in a review of "Rough Translations," in* Los Angeles Times Book Review, *August 11, 1985, p. 4.*

Amy Hempel

1951-

American short story writer.

Hempel is currently a contributing editor at *Vanity Fair,* where some of the stories in her first collection, *Reasons to Live* (1985), originally appeared. A resident of California since her teens (she was born in Chicago), Hempel attended four different colleges, including Whittier and San Francisco State—''your basic non-linear education''—before moving on to New York and a professional writing career. Some unhappy experiences from those early, wandering days—traumatic accidents, the tragic deaths of family members—resurface in *Reasons to Live,* as her characters, often wounded or bereaved, struggle to keep their wits amidst the bizarre, alienating environment of California culture. ''I am really interested in resilience,'' Hempel told the *New York Times Book Review.* ''Dr. Christian Barnard said, 'Suffering isn't ennobling, recovery is.' If I have a motto for this particular bunch of stories, that's what it is.''

The fifteen brief stories in *Reasons to Live* are products of a fiction workshop Hempel attended at Columbia University in 1982. Her instructor Gordon Lish, a novelist and editor at Knopf, later arranged the book's publication. Hempel cites Lish as a special influence on her work, as well as ''Mary Robison, Barry Hannah, Leonard Michaels, Raymond Carver—contemporary short story writers who 're-invent' the language, who tell the truth in shocking ways.'' These writers, she believes, use ''a kind of compression and distillation in their work that gets to the heart of things and gives the reader credit for being able to keep up without having everything explained.''

Similarities between Hempel and Californian Joan Didion have been noted by critics, particularly in the use of a certain California setting, rich in detail, that points up the characters' shallow and alienated lives. In prose style, however, Didion is viewed as a more accomplished ironist. Reviewers note, though, that Hempel's spare prose and curt, witty tone effectively convey her sensibility—an anguished, at times sentimental, voice with a detached and absurd world view. Critic Dawn Ann Drzal comments: ''To her credit, Ms. Hempel continually strives for and sometimes manages to find, the poetry and raw humor in meaninglessness.''

Copyright © Daniel Mularoni

KIRKUS REVIEWS

Fifteen tiny stories, some only a few paragraphs long—in a slight collection (less than 100 pages of text) that features, principally, the adolescent-*angst* sensibility of strung-out young women living in southern California. Hempel's narrators [in *Reasons to Live*] murmur about lost childhoods, rotten men, adored pets; they deliver routine one-liners—about TV commercials, award-shows, and other minor cultural manifestations. Sometimes, as in the similarly thin work of Lorrie Moore (*Self-Help* . . .), there are rueful little instructions on how to deal with all the anxiety: ''Here is what you do. You ease yourself into a tub of water, you ease yourself down. You lie back and wait for the ripples to smooth away. Then you take a deep breath, and slide your head under, and listen for the playfulness of your heart.'' (Here, and elsewhere, Hempel—occasionally in bald, hollow imitation of Joan Didion—strains for a severe sort of lyricism.) But, though the recurring theme of grief (mourning a broken marriage, a death, the past, etc.) provides a hint of resonance, too often the approach is cheaply manipulative, an artsy equivalent to tabloid sensationalism—as in **''When It's Human Instead of When It's Dog''** (about the sad carpet stain in a fancy home that marks the spot where the lady-of-the-house died). And only two pieces really attempt to go beyond the studied juxtaposition of whimsical/portentous anecdotes, ironic observations, and refrigerated self-pity: **''Beg, Sl Tog, Inc, Cont, Rep''** presents the familiar setup of two friends, one about to give birth and one recovering from an abortion, with knitting as an over-obvious symbol of both pulling-oneself-together and rejected/frustrated maternal yearnings; **"In the Cemetery Where Al Jolson Is Buried"** is somewhat more successful—layering the plainly affecting story of a friend's death with dark jokes and self-deprecation . . . though here too the central sentiment is unnecessarily, moistly emphasized. ("Baby, come hug, Baby, come hug, fluent now in the language of grief.") Borrowed mannerisms for the most part, with only a few glimmers of emotional substance or fresh voicing.

A review of "Reasons to Live," in Kirkus Reviews, *Vol. LIII, No. 4, February 15, 1985, p. 151.*

PUBLISHERS WEEKLY

Spare, droll, elliptical—these 15 stories comprising Hempel's fiction debut [*Reasons to Live*] have a familiar contemporary hard edge—but a surprisingly sentimental and moving interior. Two themes run parallel throughout the collection: an intense regret at life's missed connections and might-have-beens, plus a sharp—and wittily observed—sense of just what it takes to survive. In the risible **"Nashville Gone to Ashes,"** the widow of a veterinarian nicknamed "Flea" muses over his love for their outrageous assortment of animals—and his failure to love her; in **"The Cemetery Where Al Jolson Is Buried,"** the best friend of a terminally ill patient wonders at her own desperate need to affirm life after a visit to the hospital; and in **"Today Will Be a Quiet Day,"** a father finds that an off moment with his children takes on a deeper meaning. If there is a fault with these stories, it lies in Hempel's use of a first-person narrator who often seems to be the same character. But Hempel's many gifts, including her deliciously absurd sense of the trivia we all carry around with us and her comic obsession with animals, more than make up for this small lapse. Hers is a talent to watch.

A review of "Reasons to Live," in Publishers Weekly, *Vol. 227, No. 9, March 1, 1985, p. 69.*

MICHIKO KAKUTANI

"The test of a first-rate intelligence is the ability to hold two opposed ideas in the mind at the same time, and still retain the ability to function," wrote F. Scott Fitzgerald. "One should, for example, be able to see that things are hopeless and yet be determined to make them otherwise."

This is a view of life shared by nearly every character in Amy Hempel's astringent new collection of short stories [*Reasons to Live*]. Scarred by love and loss, attuned to natural disaster (both the geological sort, like earthquakes and floods, and the more personal variety), and given to feeling overwhelmed by the intractable facts of daily life, these people nonetheless keep searching for reasons to live. They are too wise, too damaged or maybe just too skeptical to hold out for anything so luminous as hope or faith. What they want, simply, is something—a sign, a person, a perspective, a joke—that will help alleviate the pain, enable them to continue, to go on to the next day.

Most of them try to function by thinking up ways to make the time pass: They enter sweepstakes (which, as one character points out, are less risky than contests, which actually require the exercise of certain intelligence), knit sweaters, watch dumb television shows and teach their pets stupid tricks. . . .

Making jokes, for Miss Hempel's characters, is one way of coping with life, and even though their humor's often defensive—a way of mocking themselves as well as others—their

laughter can also be redemptive. Miss Hempel's own tart, tingly wit meshes incongruously but neatly, like a well-cut jigsaw-puzzle piece, with her gift for empathy, and her pointed sense of the grotesque (the body at the bottom of the scenic overlook point, the blood stain on the freshly vacuumed rug, the late arrival of flowers sent by someone who has died). Held together in the nubbly matrix of the author's narrow, conversational prose, these qualities announce not only the presence of a sharply defined sensibility, but also that rarer thing—a distinctive and finely tuned literary voice.

There are moments when that voice falters. Such slighter stories as **"The Man in Bogotá," "Celia Is Back"** and **"When It's Human Instead of When It's Dog"** are no more than odd, contrived fragments of overheard dinner-table conversation—awkwardly and unprofitably stretched out into narratives. And Miss Hempel's efforts to evoke a particular kind of California malaise (its symptoms include thinking about earthquakes and fault-lines, and driving the highways, aimlessly, at night) can sound like dull, tinny echoes of Joan Didion.

For Miss Hempel, as for Miss Didion, the tacky, ahistorical landscape of Southern California, with its parking garages, fake Spanish colonial condominiums and fast-food joints, provides the perfect backdrop for her characters' alienated lives. "We live the beach life," says a character in **"Tonight Is a Favor to Holly,"** and by that she means not the life with "sunscreen and resort wear," but the easy, buoyant life of living by the ocean—sitting around languorously in the sun, waiting for something—anything—to happen.

Some of Miss Hempel's people are car-accident victims; some are recovering from abortions or the death of someone they loved; most, however, are suffering from a more insidious spiritual affliction that makes them feel boring and inert. Everyone she knows, says one narrator, falls into one of two categories: "those who are going under and those who aren't moving ahead." About the one thing that these characters do seem to do—and with great frequency—is move from apartment to apartment, town to town; but this changing of places only accentuates their feelings of disconnectedness. Because they are disaffected, these people feel like doing nothing; and because they do nothing, they feel even more disaffected. It is, to say the least, a very vicious circle.

In the end, though, each of them does find some reason to go on, if not to climb out of their despair. Sometimes, it's a question of tricking themselves into not feeling scared: one woman, to get to sleep after her husband's death, takes to sleeping in his bed so that "the empty bed I look at is my own." Others try to find substitutes, placebos, for the love or security they lack in their lives: they talk to their pets and slip quarters into phony evangelist shrines. Like methadone users, they get by, for the time being, with substitutes for what they really need.

Rather than trivializing their efforts to get by, Miss Hempel writes of her characters with charity and understanding. Indeed, she suggests that even the smallest act, the tiniest gesture—knitting a new pattern in a sweater, making sure the cat gets water and food it likes, even refusing payment for a job undone—can be an act of courage. Such acts, she implies, at least hold the promise of beginning, of establishing some connection—and, probably, that is the most we can do. "We give what we can," says the narrator of **"Nashville Gone to Ashes,"** and "that's as far as the heart can go."

Michiko Kakutani, "Uphill Battles," in The New York Times, April 13, 1985, p. 14.

RAY OLSON

[Reasons to Live] introduces a writer able to meld almost hallucinatory anguish with uproarious wisecracking, everyday anxiety with ordinary goofing. In an age of black humorists, this may not seem like much, but Hempel's curt yet uncallous style breaks down resistance to the extreme and banal situations she has her personae endure. She limns the strange details of dull lives with a vocabulary honed just this side of abstraction. It allows her to trace, with illuminating insight rather than sentimental coziness, the day in which a single father gets back in touch with his two teenagers ("Today Will Be a Quiet Day"). Without descending totally into the bizarre, she can also expose the daffiness of a veterinarian's widow ("Nashville Gone to Ashes") who continues tending a legacy of abandoned pets until they, too, pass on. Although Hempel fails occasionally by nearly telegraphing instead of writing a story ("Celia Is Back"), she mostly yields affecting vignettes that cry to be read aloud.

Ray Olson, in a review of "Reasons to Live," in Booklist, Vol. 81, No. 16, April 15, 1985, p. 1160.

An Excerpt from Reasons to Live

Dale Anne wanted a nap, so Dr. Diamond and I went out for margaritas. At La Rondalla, the colored lights on the Virgin tell you every day is Christmas. The food arrives on manhole covers and mariachis fill the bar. Dr. Diamond said that in Guadalajara there is a mariachi college that turns out mariachis by the classful. But I could tell that these were not graduates of even mariachi high school.

I shooed the serenaders away, but Dr. Diamond said they meant well.

Dr. Diamond likes for people to mean well. He could be president of the Well-Meaning Club. He has had a buoyant feeling of fate since he learned Freud died the day he was born.

He was the person to talk to, all right, so I brought up the stomach pains I was having for no bodily reason that I could think of.

"You know how I think," he said. "What is it you can't stomach?"

I knew what he was asking.

"Have you thought about how you will feel when Dale Anne has the baby?" he asked.

With my eyes, I wove strands of tinsel over the Blessed Virgin. That was the great thing about knitting, I thought—everything was fiber, the world a world of natural resource.

"I thought I would burn that bridge when I come to it," I said, and when he didn't say anything to that, I said, "I guess I will think that there is a mother who *kept* hers."

"*One* of hers might be more accurate," Dr. Diamond said.

SHEILA BALLANTYNE

Minimalism has its uses, and can achieve surprisingly varied effects: it can allude and expand, as well as leave out and compress. At its most reductive or repetitive, it can induce corresponding states of boredom or trance. There is a kind of writing that masks a lack of substance by itself posing as substance. Rushing to fill that void, a reader must project his own meaning, or assume the presence of some meaning that eludes his grasp. At its worst, minimalism is a kind of fraudulent tic that serves to hide a vacuum or defend against feeling. At its best it can, with economy and restraint, amplify perception and force meaning to leap from the page. In most of the stories that make up this first collection [Reasons to Live], Amy Hempel has succeeded in revealing both the substance and intelligence beneath the surface of a spare, elliptical prose.

Some of the one-page pieces in Reasons to Live are so truncated and incomplete they are interesting only as snapshots. Sometimes a vignette is just a vignette, a sketch a sketch. There are other misses here and there, gags that fall flat. But at their best these stories are tough-minded, original and fully felt. Some—in particular the wrenching "In the Cemetery Where Al Jolson Is Buried," which describes a friend's dying; and the equally haunting "Beg, Sl Tog, Inc, Cont, Rep" (which takes its title from the conventions of knitting instructions), have a kind of effortless, unconscious integrity. They can take your breath away, so in tune are their resolutions with everything that has gone before. . . .

It is tempting to think of this collection as a "California book" because many stories seem to spring directly from that soil like native plants: highly colored and direct. The details are perfectly rendered, quintessential California clichés; and yet they are also the truth. They establish the emotional climates in which these characters survive. A peculiarly California kind of drifting is exemplified by the narrator of "Tonight Is a Favor to Holly":

"Four days a week I drive to La Mirada, to the travel agency where I have a job. It takes me fifty-five minutes to drive one way, and I wish the commute were longer. I like radio personalities, and I like to change lanes. And losing yourself on the freeway is like living at the beach—you're not aware of lapsed time, and suddenly you're there, where it was you were going."

You can almost hear her gum crack as she speaks. Still, small slips betray a vestigial identity, a wish not to blend, but to stand out: of the beach in the morning, she says, "I like my prints to be the first of the day."

True, too, are the details of California overabundance: "Everything there is the size of something else: strawberries are the size of tomatoes, apples are the size of grapefruits, papayas are the size of watermelons." But alongside the particulars that anchor the stories to a place, there are intimations of a growing homogenization of scene. . . .

A subtle universality of feeling infuses the more fully realized stories, transcending the cliché—or forcing it to underscore and serve a greater truth. Waiting helplessly for her friend to die, the narrator of **"In the Cemetery Where Al Jolson Is Buried,"** in a displacement of hallucinatory intensity, envisions a simple beach ("The beach is standing still today. Everyone on it is tranquilized, numb, or asleep") as the locus of destruction; then transmutes the scene again, observing the way terror can transform itself into desire—the other side of death. . . .

These stories, more than half of which have never been published before, are conspicuously contemporary—both the abbreviated one-page sketches and the more extended pieces of five or six; feeling is always contained, never explicit. Yet this is a kind of minimalism that robs us of nothing, that has room for the largest themes; the best of these stories have a compression that seems to capture it all.

Sheila Ballantyne, "Rancho Libido and Other Hot Spots," in The New York Times Book Review, *April 28, 1985, p. 9.*

MARCIA TAGER

Amy Hempel's stories [in **Reasons to Live**] are like candid snapshots. They capture people in authentic detail in a splinter of reality. She gives a bare minimum of information about her characters but they are meticulously placed in an external landscape which reflects their inner reality.

The landscape is that of California, where everything is "the size of something else: strawberries are the size of tomatoes, apples are the size of grapefruits, papayas are the size of watermelons." It is always "earthquake weather" and "The sand on the beach will all of a sudden suck down like an hourglass. The air roars. In the cheap apartments on-shore, bathtubs fill themselves and gardens roll up and over like green waves." In this shifting terrain, where nothing is what it seems, Hempel's characters are taking their own pulse. . . .

In the story **"In The Cemetery Where Al Jolson Is Buried"**, we are given two young women, seriously injured, in Isolation in the hospital. By indirection only, the reader understands that one young woman will die and be moved from the hospital to the cemetery where Al Jolson is buried. But how the young women came to be where they are, what happened to them, is only implied. As in minimalist art, implication and suggestion are all. Reading Hempel is like reading a heart-stopping telegram and one measure of her art is that, like the child delaying bedtime, one longs to cry, "Tell me more. Tell me the rest."

Marcia Tager, "Witty Stories Mask Pain," in New Directions for Women, *Vol. 14, No. 4, July-August, 1985, p. 16.**

DAWN ANN DRZAL

The most basic aim of psychoanalysis, Freud said, is "transforming hysterical misery into common unhappiness." While this formulation may seem harsh and hopeless, the characters in [**Reasons to Live**] . . . would be more than willing to settle for it.

Most of the stories in **Reasons to Live** open after a crisis to find the narrator standing, shell-shocked, amidst the rubble of her life. Although the tone of Hempel's spare, first person narratives (the exception is the third person **"Today Will Be a Quiet Day"**) varies from the almost Southern Gothic flavor of **"Breathing Jesus"** to the silly/surreal **"Celia is Back"** to the full and touching **"In the Cemetery Where Al Jolson Is Buried,"** they share a veneer of detachment. The alternately wise and wise cracking narrators provide ironic commentary, letting us in on the action and on a store of little-known facts: that Bob Dylan's mother invented White-Out, that insects fly between raindrops, that blue-eyed white cats are usually deaf, and cats that can hear will yawn when you run your finger along the teeth of a comb (this doesn't work; I tried it).

This obsessive collection of facts can be seen as a key to Hempel's sensibility. Her narrators are collectors of small, ironic tidbits, and Hempel seems to put forth the theory that the world is just a random assemblage of these trifles—some poignant, some beautiful, some amusing, but none deriving meaning from their arrangement. . . . Can sanity exist in a senseless world? For Hempel, the answer is obvious.

While it is sometimes witty, the view of the world as absurd deprives the stories of emotional power. Some of them seem merely to be vehicles designed to transport us to the oracular punchline, but fail to lend it resonance along the way. Even at its best, Hempel's prose lacks the neurasthenic charge of Joan Didion's. Didion uses the agglomeration of concrete details to much the same end, but manages to infuse the facts themselves with a simultaneous wonder and irony, to convince the reader that everything she describes, from a hydraulic power plant to a waiter in Zipaquirà, Colombia, is a singular phenomenon with its own body of lore.

Hempel's successes come from another direction. In her one fully-realized, moving story, **"In the Cemetery Where Al Jolson Is Buried,"** and to a lesser extent in the fine **"Beg, Sl Tog, Inc, Cont, Rep"** (knitting instructions), her disaffected tone works to lend depth to her narrator. In the former story, we suffer along with a woman visiting her best friend, who is dying of cancer, in a California hospital room. Only because we suffer with her can we come to understand and pardon the tactics she uses to avoid feeling pain, but we do come to understand. We believe in her fear, her love of life, and her psychological fragility. The cool monologue is revealed for what it is—noise to drown out pain and fear. The stories are less successful when we have to piece together the events from driblets and hints. The trouble with many of Hempel's aimless heroines (and occasional heroes) is that they're too strong to let themselves go and too cynical to believe in strength. If, as in **"Beg, Sl Tog, Inc, Cont, Rep,"** an energizing crisis arrives and anomie slips into madness, the heroine just bobs up again into common unhappiness: she has a psychological air bladder that floats her to the surface but no further. Limbo seems like the only honest place to be in these stories. They take place in earthquake and landslide country, where stability is revealed to be a necessary delusion. To her credit, Ms. Hempel continually strives for, and sometimes manages to find, the poetry and raw humor in meaninglessness. (pp. 505-06)

Dawn Ann Drzal, "An Assemblage of Trifles," in Commonweal, *Vol. CXII, No. 16, September 20, 1985, pp. 505-07.**

COMMENTS OF AMY HEMPEL TO *CLC YEARBOOK*

Hempel traces her inspiration for *Reasons to Live* back to ''several 'lost' years spent in San Francisco and Los Angeles. I began the book after leaving California for New York—all of the stories are set out West, and come from missing the west coast, trying to find value in the time spent there.'' The stories are ''very'' autobiographical—''or, if not from my life, then there are composites of people I know. I said in the *Times Book Review*, 'The whole book is true.' Which is different from 'the whole book is autobiographical.' I was making notes on things that happened many years before I started to write, though at the time I did not know why.''

Alexander Kaletski

1946-

Russian novelist.

Metro: A Novel of the Moscow Underground (1985) is Kaletski's fictionalized memoir of his days as a young actor in the Soviet Union. In the early seventies Kaletski was a successful performer in Russian theater, film, and television; in addition to acting, he was a folksinger and songwriter, painter, and graphic artist. Dissatisfaction with government policies led him to appear in clandestine shows featuring his anti-Soviet songs and artwork. In 1975 he obtained permission to emigrate and has since lived in New York City.

Metro is "ninety percent my life story," comments Kaletski. Sasha, Kaletski's fictional counterpart in the novel, narrates a first-person reminiscence of his youth, from his apprenticeship at the Moscow Theatre and Film Institute to his final departure from Russia. The overall anti-Soviet tone of *Metro* reflects Kaletski's dissident background. However, critics observe that *Metro* is positively lighthearted in comparison with the work of other Russian emigrés. Sasha's narrative focuses on his friends—rowdy, dissipated artists—who are more interested in obtaining black market food and liquor than in improving their society. Critic William Grimes suggests that *Metro*'s relatively cheerful depiction of these wastrels is a throwback to certain Russian novels of the 1920s, which goodnaturedly satirized the discrepancies between the Bolsheviks' ideal of Soviet society and the less inspiring reality. *Metro* demonstrates how poverty and repression can warp promising young people. Kaletski designed and illustrated the dust jacket for the Viking edition of *Metro*, as well as illustrating his text with photocollages and line drawings. He is writing a sequel to *Metro*, which will describe Sasha's experiences in America.

Photograph by Basha Szymanska. Courtesy of Alexander Kaletski

---

PUBLISHERS WEEKLY

[In ***Metro***, Kaletski] has created a headlong, vivid first novel of what sounds suspiciously like his own life: successful young actor rebelling against the constraints of Soviet life and finally emigrating (in the book, it's done by faking a Jewish aunt in Israel). His Moscow circle, characterized in broad strokes, drinks constantly (aviation alcohol, if necessary), fornicates freely, dreams of emigration or, failing that, at least an apartment, and in general behaves like bohemian groups in Russian novels for 100 years—the manic, mostly cheerful kind rather than the brooding, suicidal kind. Grimmer notes are struck from time to time, including a climax involving the hijacking of a subway train and a shootout with the KGB; but the predominant impression is of a group of high-spirited, often foolish youngsters living lives completely warped out of shape by their constant struggles with officialdom. At one stage hero Sasha travels to the U.S. with a theater group, and the material

there is lively enough to arouse keen anticipation of a promised sequel. Kaletski wrote the book in Russian, then translated it himself; he has astonishing mastery of a dashing, colloquial style, adding another dimension to this lively, often eye-opening read.

A review of "Metro: A Novel of the Moscow Underground," in Publishers Weekly, Vol. 227, No. 11, March 15, 1985, p. 103.

MARY F. ZIRIN

The attractive narrator, Sasha, and the description of the roadblocks the USSR puts in the way of energetic and creative people make ***Metro*** worthwhile for general readers. Stylistic aspects are less successful. The English is clumsy and at times distracting. Kaletski is not yet skilled enough in the craft of fiction to bring anything new to Sasha's depiction of the grotesque "underground" of violence and drunkenness that is rapidly becoming a commonplace in novels by recent emigrés, although some of his pop-porn anecdotes are quite funny. A promising start, but one hopes that next time Kaletski finds a stronger editor.

Mary F. Zirin, in a review of "Metro: A Novel of the Moscow Underground," in Library Journal, *Vol. 110, No. 9, May 15, 1985, p. 80.*

GINA KOVARSKY

In the 1920's Soviet satire unveiled a hectic world overrun with con men, raconteurs, womanizers and alcoholics bribing their way past rules apparently meant to be broken; readers saw a chasm between the splendid simplicity of revolutionary slogans and the scrambled realities of everyday life. This appealing but flawed first novel [*Metro*] by a Russian émigré reveals a similar chasm. Sasha, the young semiautobiographical hero, escapes the provinces and heads for Moscow to study acting. He soon meets a cast of broadly drawn and none-too-endearing characters, including Andrewlka, the lucky inheritor of a two-room Moscow apartment; Stas, a practical joker; and Toilik, Sasha's alcoholic landlord, for whom drinking is a revolutionary protest (he falls out of bed each morning bellowing the "Internationale"). Sasha dreams of nearly unobtainable privileges, such as permission to live and work in the capital, exemption from military service and a chance to travel to the glamorous, nearly mythological West. He realizes all three ambitions, but he and his wife encounter injustice and brutality along the way, and so apply for emigration. Alexander Kaletski spices his narrative with allusions to personalities prominent among Moscow's elite, but gossip mixes strangely with his portentous portrayal of their milieu. Sasha sees the endless escalator of the Moscow metro and exclaims, "The path was long, like life." Although the author manipulates a number of tones—melodrama, lyricism, black comedy—his devices fail to draw the reader to Sasha. But those who can take their champagne flat may enjoy this glimpse of Moscow's underground "other half," and appreciate the thought of the caviar, sausages and tangerines known as "Kremlin health food."

Gina Kovarsky, in a review of "Metro," in The New York Times Book Review, *June 30, 1985, p. 20.*

An Excerpt from *Metro: A Novel of the Moscow Underground*

I couldn't believe my eyes—right there in front of me stood the last bottle of beer. I touched its warm neck. I hugged it tenderly and headed for the door. . . . I leaned against the train door, took a key out of my pocket, and slowly started to open my darling. I placed the key beneath the wavy cap, hooking the notch to the edge, and cautiously pulled up. The bottle whispered and bubbled.

I eased the key under another notch and another. The cap went flying; foam burst out of the bottle and, just as I raised the bottle to my mouth, I felt somebody tapping me on the shoulder. I stiffened. A controller? I turned slowly, expecting to see the stern face of authority. But no, it was a bearded, little man with a kepi on his head, dangling a tiny fish in front of my face.

"Listen, let's make a deal, huh? I'll give you the tail and fins, you give me a glass of beer, huh? No good, huh? Okay, if there's any roe inside, you get that too, huh? No? Come on. Okay, let's go halves—half a fish for you, half a bottle for me, huh? Hey, it's a real live dried fish . . . Wait, don't drink. Okay, you win. I'll give you half a fish and some vodka. Yeah, you heard me, vodka! Anyway, I can't drink vodka without beer. Let's make a 'yorsh.'"

I said nothing. I didn't want to draw any attention so I let the little man have his way. He quickly shoved two glasses at me, poured out his vodka and added my beer, bit into the tail of the fish and split it down the middle. What could I do? We clanged glasses and drank.

"Yorsh" goes two ways—the vodka goes straight to your head; the beer to your feet. It felt good. We smiled at each other and pressed our foreheads against the windowpane. Through the glass, amid the starting drizzle, flew the incomparable Soviet landscape—mostly billboards of Lenin's sayings alternating with his slogans in red stones on the hills:

> COMMUNISM WILL BE THE HAPPY FUTURE OF ALL HUMAN BEINGS
>
> COMMUNISM = THE SOVIET REGIME PLUS ELECTRIFICATION OF THE COUNTRY
>
> THIS GENERATION WILL WITNESS COMMUNISM

"Listen, my friend," the stranger said, breathing on the glass. His cap, pressed against the window, was standing up revealing a bald spot. "What's your name, huh?"

"Sasha."

"What do you think, Sash, which generation did Lenin have in mind when he said, 'This generation will witness communism,' the one that lived back then; my generation; or yours?"

"I've never given it much thought," I said tentatively. One doesn't discuss politics with strangers. Sometimes, one shouldn't discuss politics even with friends.

We continued to drink as we stared out the window.

The rain was coming down harder, and the drops were running in diagonals on the outside of the window. On the inside, the glass was fogged up by our breath, and the red sayings were turning into a blur:

> EVERY DAY, LIFE IN THE SOVIET UNION GETS BETTER AND . . .
>
> STUDY, STUDY, AND ONCE AGAIN . . .

WILLIAM GRIMES

The USSR we get in *Metro* is a nation of sublimely corrupt bureaucrats, wheezing alcoholics, black-market hustlers, and Party stooges. Everyone is on the take, or the give and take; virtually every waking moment is devoted to obtaining such exotica as a pair of blue jeans or a tangerine. Which leaves little energy to pursue the Soviet Dream: live in Moscow, avoid the draft, and travel abroad.

Metro is subtitled "A Novel of the Moscow Underground," but that's a bit of a tease. Sasha and cohorts are not so much political dissidents as high-spirited troublemakers who enjoy tweaking the bulbous nose of Soviet officialdom. It's almost as if the USSR were an awful high school, with Lenin as the venerable principal. The kids smoke dope, spray paint the walls, play hooky, and crack Lenin jokes, all the while keeping an eye out for the KGB's hall monitors. Politics has little meaning beyond providing a vocabulary for humor.

Although Kaletski never even hints at the existence of a politically conscious dissident movement, he does zero in on one hotbed of countercultural activity—the apartment of Toilik, Sasha's landlord, where a disciplined cell of alcoholics gather to protest an increase in the price of vodka from 3.12 to 4.12 rubles per bottle. . . .

Kaletski is no fan of the Soviet Union, but he remains rather good-humored about the trials and tribulations of his hero. Sasha's reaction to the wage scales at his first theatrical job is characteristic: "I started out as a street cleaner, at a salary of 120 rubles a month, was made a stagehand, at 90 rubles a month, and finally became an actor, playing Lenin's brother, whose salary was 75 rubles a month. So, in this way, I climbed the ladder of success." Such wry commentary on the absurdities of Soviet existence gives the novel its pungency and verve.

Kaletski's high-speed brand of comedy whisks the reader past some linguistic and structural problems. *Metro* was written in Russian, then translated by the author into English—no mean feat, but what is doubtless some fairly juicy Russian speech remains tantalizingly just out of earshot. And there are times when the book lurches from incident to incident. Yet at its best, *Metro*'s drunken ramble through a Russia of crooks, confidence men, and fat officials harks back to the freewheeling Soviet satire of the '20s. Evidently Kaletski has noticed an absurdity or two in our own society, since a sequel is already in the writing. To his credit, the prospect of a follow-up volume feels like a promise, not a threat.

William Grimes, "Prank Amateurs," in The Village Voice, *Vol. XXX, No. 32, August 6, 1985, p. 50.*

FRANK WILLIAMS

"I love the Moscow metro", says Sasha on the first page of Alexander Kaletski's novel *Metro.* And if some sing the praises of the Taj Mahal, in Moscow there is "a Taj Mahal at every station". Speaking of the Circle line, Kaletski's hero's own favourite, he is not, in a perverse kind of way, all that far off the mark. In the stations of the Circle line the Stalinist decorative arts reach a peak of splendid, bravura absurdity—polished marble, chandeliers, sculptured ensembles, glittering mosaics and all the other paraphernalia designed to impress impoverished workers and peasants with the glory of the proletarian state. Sasha also gawped in wonder as a small provincial boy on his first visit to the capital; he is still under the spell of the metro when he returns to Moscow as a recalcitrant student escaping to the Theatre Institute from the draft and a future in Tula's munitions factories.

However, it is neither the metro nor the Theatre Institute that is the true focus of *Metro.* That is provided by Sasha's circle of friends—Lena, whose aunt dines exclusively off champagne and caviare from the Kremlin stores and who becomes his wife;

his childhood friend Boris, an architecture student; Youssuf, an African diplomat's son, also an architecture student, whose idea of monumental sculpture is a poured concrete erect phallus; the larger-than-life homosexual Stas, who makes a speciality of wrecking his friends' lives; finally, Andrewlka, loafer and part-time KGB informer, whose chief merit is that he is perhaps the only unmarried man in Moscow to have a two-room flat of his own, placing him in an exceptional position of influence and power.

Kaletski received a thorough grounding in the Stanislavsky method (like his hero, the author trained as an actor in Moscow), though *Metro* owes more to caricature and the techniques of the American comedy sketch. Sasha's teachers are talentless decrepits, his drunks heroic, his film makers lecherous, his lovers pure and passionate. Sasha and his friends race through a sequence of drunken binges, cadged train rides, sexual escapades, dissident demonstrations, black market dealings, theatrical disasters, the hi-jacking of a metro train and ultimately, in what must be the most unbelievable episode yet to emerge from the pen of a Soviet-born author, a shoot-out with the KGB from which Sasha emerges unscathed and unpunished. Sasha leads a charmed existence. He gets the girl of anybody's dreams, he succeeds in outwitting the military authorities to dodge the draft, manages to tour with his theatre company to the United States, obtains a Moscow residence permit and flat. On top of that he manages to wangle an invitation from a fictitious relative for himself and Lena to go to Israel, and then is given the visas, despite the obvious fraud. (It is the height of détente and the KGB, ever sensitive to the demands of *realpolitik,* closes its eyes to the deception.)

So, a novel which begins with the arrival of a provincial greenhorn in Moscow ends with his departure, older and wiser, though perhaps no less starry-eyed about his destination, for New York. In the exploits of Sasha and company the sceptical will no doubt catch a whiff of good old-fashioned Russian *vranyo* or leg-pulling, a fine form of self-defence against the bleakness of much of Soviet life—poor health care and living conditions, the Catch-22 of the residence permit (no residence permit—no job; no job—no residence permit). Kaletski packs in instances of these and many other contemporary tribulations. The list is long and familiar—too familiar, in fact, from other writers of greater weight who have explored roughly the same territory. Kaletski, though, has written his novel to entertain and he seems to have judged his market shrewdly.

Frank Williams, "Charmed Greenhorn," in The Times Literary Supplement, *No. 4315, December 13, 1985, p. 1433.*

COMMENTS OF ALEXANDER KALETSKI TO *CLC YEARBOOK*

Kaletski explains why he wrote *Metro:* "My goal was to tell Americans the truth about the Soviet regime, to paint a clearer picture of everyday life in Russia and to speak for those who don't have the freedom to speak for themselves.

"I never expected that writing a book required so much discipline and hard work. I came through hell trying to stretch my creative limits to meet my own artistic standards."

Nancy Lemann

1956-

American novelist.

Lives of the Saints (1985) is a lyrical evocation of the city of New Orleans, of Southern gentility, and of the South's fading aristocracy. Lemann, a native of New Orleans, notes that the motivation behind her novel was "to depict great men I have known, to hold up their qualities to offer hope." She selects for her chronicle three males in an eccentric, and sometimes endearing family of the old South: they are the father, Louis, and his two sons, Claude and Saint. The novel's narrator, Louise Brown, steadfastly admires Claude Collier, the gentle, charming, yet lost son of the Collier family, and it is around their relationship that the story revolves. Claude has been likened by a few critics to Walker Percy's alienated southern heroes in *The Moviegoer* and *The Last Gentleman,* an appropriate comparison since Lemann has called Percy her "literary idol." Lemann attributes her esteem for Percy to his "greatness both in style and content, equally," and because "his is an enterprise mounted in hope."

Reviewers comment that *Lives of the Saints,* which is set in contemporary New Orleans, is not so much a plotted novel as it is a romantic and comic tale told through a series of social events, among them a wedding and a funeral. Critics praise Lemann for her lyrical and luxurious prose, her mannered speech, and her effective use of repetition, which together create a languid, almost hypnotic portrait of a place and of a people.

© 1986 Thomas Victor

PUBLISHERS WEEKLY

We are plunged, in this distinctive but soon wearisome novel [**Lives of the Saints**], into a wedding reception in New Orleans, where the guests are drunk, maudlin, soggy with perspiration and endeavoring to maintain their Southern femininity or gallantry. "Normal" behavior is impossible in this upper-class society, we soon discover, because everyone is subject to Breakdowns, Weird Depressions, Hysterical Fits or other Major Catastrophes brought on by debauchery, boredom or drink—and usually all three. Louise Brown, the narrator, speaks in a voice heavy with portent, aphorisms ("nuts make life worth living"), deliberate repetition of words, and quotations from the poets. Her tale focuses on the Collier family and the members she idolizes: Claude, the vague, gentle, good-natured wastrel and college dropout whom Louise adores but who never seems the least bit charming to the reader; his three-year-old brother, Saint, who has bloody accidents and eventually falls out of a tree; and their father, Saint Louis, whose "interest in the lives of the saints was, like his other eccentricities, the refuge and the consolation of the solitary." There is a funeral as well as a wedding in this novel, both endured in the New

Orleans humidity that makes everyone lethargic. Unfortunately, this lethargy soon claims the reader.

A review of "Lives of the Saints," in Publishers Weekly, *Vol. 225, No. 17, April 26, 1985, p. 69.*

MICHIKO KAKUTANI

"Then I climbed the sharp hill that led to all the years ahead"—the epigraph that Nancy Lemann has chosen for her first novel comes from Evelyn Waugh, and it turns out to be a fitting choice indeed. If the first portion of **Lives of the Saints** recalls such early satirical works as *Vile Bodies* and *Decline and Fall*—a giddy, madcap chronicle of giddy, madcap people—its second half aspires to be nothing less than an American version of *Brideshead Revisited*. In chronicling the dissolution of an aristocratic and gloriously eccentric family, **Saints**—like Waugh's famous novel—becomes a lovely, grave elegy for lost innocence, for lost youth and a vanished world.

Miss Lemann's setting is not prelapsarian England, but the contemporary South; and her narrative resonates delicately with memories of that region's faded glory, its loss of the war, its sense of being a place apart. There's a vaguely anachronistic feel to the world Miss Lemann has created—the girls here still have debutante balls; the boys still dress up in white tie and tails, and they all like to refer to themselves as "wastrel youth" or victims of "youthful folly." Many of the people have so much family money that they need never find a profession; and even those who do have jobs seem quite happy to stay up till 4 in the morning, sipping gin and tonics in the dark shade of a summer garden.

Although Louise Brown, the narrator of *Lives of the Saints,* has gone East to college, she's returned home to New Orleans—tired of being "an obscure provincial" in New York. She now spends her days as a proofreader in a law office, her nights and weekends going to parties, where she feels vaguely like an outsider. At first, the reader is apt to find Louise's voice—and Miss Lemann's prose style—annoyingly mannered. Louise has a baroque way of talking, breathy and tongue-in-cheek at the same time: She likes to accent emotion with capital letters—as in "he was acting Extremely Peculiar" or "their family was always having Breakdowns"—and she tends to repeat aphoristic clichés and trivial observations to the point of distraction.

As the novel progresses, however, a design slowly emerges. Miss Lemann has written a dense, musically patterned novel, in which repetitions of scenes, images and phrases—varied by mood and time—acquire a cumulative power: An exchange of non sequiturs at a party that seems silly, even pointless, on first hearing, can reverberate with much darker tones when it surfaces again later. There is also, it appears, some method to Louise's idiosyncratic style. Her tendency to alternate between detachment and gushy emotion, to jump back and forth in time, to replay certain experiences again and again in her mind—all are strategies engaged by her to hold onto feelings for a place, memories of individuals.

What Louise wants, most of all, is to set down in words a portrait of one Southern gentleman named Claude Collier, and to convey to us, a sense of how her impossible love for him deepened and evolved over a space of years. Kind, selfless and unrequitedly charming, Claude is sort of a combination of Waugh's ruined innocent, Sebastian Flyte; and Binx Bolling, the disaffected hero of Walker Percy's *Moviegoer.* He's one of those effortlessly sociable fellows, adept at becoming best friends with strangers in bars and trains, someone who has led a riotous, hectic life—partying with other young aristocrats, as well as winos and seedy race-track types—and yet managed to remain undamaged. "He was what you would call a sterling character," says Louise. . . .

Page by page, Louise's portrait of Claude and her own youth takes form out of fragments of bad jokes ("I'm not so hot— I have a cold"); bits of remembered emotion, and poetic images lodged in the imagination. . . .

In the end, it is a resonant, loving portrait that Louise assembles; and in telling *her* story, Miss Lemann has succeeded in creating not only a finely etched picture of the South, but also a lyrical prose poem about a young woman's coming of age.

> Michiko Kakutani, "Family in Decline," in The New
> York Times, *May 25, 1985, p. 13.*

ANNE TYLER

Maybe the scenes in *Lives of the Saints* could have happened someplace else, but it's difficult to think where. There is a sense of New Orleans as a kind of drug, an ether. Its citizens are dazed with heat and with the constant flow of alcohol and the smell of tropical flowers. They are determinedly Southern: gentle, courtly, funny, charmingly hopeless. They are always "falling apart." (p. 36)

[A] wedding opens the book, and when you read about it you're not yet in step. You imagine something will come of it, that there's a reason for the breakdowns and for mentioning the wedding and so forth. Well, there's not. Bit by bit you catch on; you relax; you become a little dazed yourself. And that's when you start to have fun.

Think of *Lives of the Saints* as a long poem—a hysterically funny poem that is also beautifully written, if you can imagine such a thing. It doesn't exactly tell a story. It violates all kinds of rules. (The narrator, for instance, is part of the events but never fully explains herself; she's both there and not there, and on at least two occasions describes scenes from which she was absent.) Even so, the book works—perhaps because of its sheer exuberance, its enthusiasm for its characters, its peculiarly Southern habit of telling us not so much *what* happened as to *whom.*

Each person here has one special quality—one mania or comic flaw to which he clings as if it were his most precious personal possession—and this quality is unchanging. If a woman is known to be fond of discussing the hat she wore when she was 16, then any time we read of her she will be discussing that hat. It's a form of characterization that's larger than life; it's what gives the book its dash. (pp. 36-7)

Nancy Lemann's writing style . . . uses repetition to great advantage. . . .

The effect is to deepen our sense of the lush, sleepy atmosphere. The extravagant language deepens it further: that "small, bloody, hilarious child," for instance, or the "wildly crestfallen" expression on a woman's face, the "violently pretty" spot on the corner of Indulgence and Religion Streets, the "madcap palm trees." Words are slung about recklessly, piled in staggering heaps, and what emerges from them is an almost hypnotic portrait of unforgettable people in a strange and magnificent city. (p. 37)

> *Anne Tyler, "Down in New Orleans," in* The New
> Republic, *Vol. 192, No. 25, June 24, 1985, pp. 36-8.**

An Excerpt from *Lives of the Saints*

The reception was drawing vaguely to a close.

In the garden, there were gin and tonic and lemons and limes all lined up neatly in rows on a table, in readiness, and empty chairs—in the garden in the glittering night, under the monumental palms and oaks. Of that neighborhood, I could never tire. The antebellum houses— stony, impassive, still—and the monumental palms and oaks gave the place an unrelenting beauty.

They say April is the cruelest month—and maybe it is so. But it is not so in the tropics. It is not like the North, where spring comes like an idiot whose wake is strewn with garish flowers. The New Orleans spring is more subtle, and gentle to bear. Everything remains the same throughout the year, overgrown and green.

Then I saw Mary Grace in her traveling clothes, standing under the oaks in the garden, appearing to be having some sort of breakdown. Claude was standing there with her, with that stricken look on his face that he got when people were having breakdowns. I heard her say things only a drunk girl would say. Only a girl who was very drunk would say them. It was one of those swift and irrevocable moments during which someone's whole life is ruined. But Claude stood there stalwart and tall, with something understated in his eyes.

He took her face in his hand and said something, which I could not hear, but I do not doubt that he gave her kind advice, and that he wished her well. . . .

In Napoleon House, with the crumbling walls, the "Hallelujah Chorus" was playing when we walked in, by the portraits of Napoleon brooding while his soldiers sack the Tuileries. The night was fairly balmy. No one was there. The waiter knew us. It was very pleasant. Until some got too drunk and threw their coats down in the gutter and had no cash and I had to stop the order for more champagne and became alarmed. But some decaying social conservatives in seersucker suits in the back room saved us and took care of the bill.

There was some sort of jazz revolution going on in Armstrong Park, formerly Congo Square, with black men in gold suits with sequins or dapper summer whites. A black man in a white suit came across the lagoon in a pirogue, standing up and playing a mournful trumpet solo in the night, and then he landed over at the Gospel Tent. There were rickety old black men in pink ruffled suits with jazz umbrellas, dancing for the crowd—and you felt that if at least you were near to people like that, then maybe you were not weak, if you could even be near to such as them.

Summer whites, green gardens, Mississippi, white summer suits and seersucker suits, those were the sights. In the Garden District, Claude stopped and pointed out the jasmine and the cicadas in the night. That was his innocence to me. He had the sweetness of the town itself and broke my heart completely into a million pieces on the floor, as he himself would say, for he touched my heart, to such degree, that I had to steel myself, or my heart would break, like his, into a million pieces on the floor. For in Claude Collier I saw my very youth, a fateful green garden, parades on the Avenue, an orchestra on a bandstand, my youth in New Orleans.

I knew him so well that I knew him in my bones, and I saw, among other things, that in him. But at the end of the night what I did not see was that Claude sat with a bottle and was unable to lay his head down, went back out dancing until dawn, back to the party on St. Claude and Desire, and got in a minor car wreck on the bridge over the Industrial Canal on the way home, and had to go to Night Court in Araby.

But there he could talk to his friends, no doubt, in Central Lock-Up.

JAMES WOLCOTT

Prefaced with a quotation from Evelyn Waugh, *Lives of the Saints* smarts with raw irritation as the vile bodies of New

Orleans society remove themselves from the lawn ("Tom, the bride's old flame, was strewn upon the ground, tangled up in the wires of his Walk-Man, passed out underneath his car"). But where Waugh in his early novels is savage and jaunty, Lemann seems anchored to her peeves; she keeps poking her stick at the hornet's nest, courting a rash of stings. Yet her sulkiness, like Waugh's briskness and aplomb, is spikily comic. Put upon, Louise seems capable of shooting BB's from her narrowed pupils. . . . If Louise and Anthony Powell's Pamela Widmerpool were ever to meet, they could blow clouds of smoke into each other's faces. It's difficult to imagine, however, that Pamela Widmerpool would second Louise's notion that "nuts made life worth living." To Pamela Widmerpool, nuts are for crushing.

After a chain of nervous breakdowns (Lemann's wedding bash is equal to the best parties in Powell's *A Dance to the Music of Time*), *Lives of the Saints* becomes a bit too dawdling and dreamy. It could use a little nutcracking. Nancy Lemann is expert and original when she's standing back and taking beady aim, but as the novel fidgets along she tends to dote on Louise's beau, Claude, tenderly mussing his hair and maintaining the shine on his halo even after he gets involved in shady activities (including a race-track scandal). Claude begins to poke around the house in an old bathrobe and crummy slippers, "eating pathetic wilted cheese sandwiches," yet he never loses a certain doomed courtly glamour. He succeeds Walker Percy's Will Barrett as the South's last gentleman, making a bad-movie exit into the wet streets of tomorrow: "With his hands in his pockets and his collar turned up against the rain, my beloved Claude receded—and disappeared for years." (You can almost see the credits coming up in white letters as a lone saxophone mourns.) But what's pleasing about the book, aside from the dragon-puffs of humor and annoyance, is its sense of southern charm and redolence gone slightly tilt.

> We went to the country to Perseverance and Souvenir. The grace of Perseverance set a calm into my heart—the famous avenue of oaks, the gardenia and banana trees. We sat on wrought-iron chairs painted green, looking out to the avenue of oaks. The men wore seersucker suits and horn-rimmed glasses and the matriarchs were the salt of the earth who exhibited untold charm and mirth through such adversities as seven pregnancies. . . .

It's like a self-tranquilizing sigh, this voice. This is how Blanche DuBois talked before the lampshade was torn away and life became lit with a naked bulb. (p. 34)

> *James Wolcott, "Southern Discomfort," in* The New York Review of Books, *Vol. XXXII, No. 11, June 27, 1985, pp. 33-4.**

VALERIE MARTIN

[In *Lives of the Saints*] Claude Collier is a dazed, useless young man, the scion of an aristocratic New Orleans family, who has outraged decency (though not his father) by refusing to go to law school. . . . Louise narrates Claude's history with a strange combination of passion and insouciance. She disregards ordinary syntax and is given to stunning oversimplifications about the nature of humanity and the meaning of honor. "There are two kinds of people in the world," Louise informs us, "the kind who would never sit around talking about honor because they intrinsically have it, and then there is the type who would sit around talking about honor all the time, but who does not actually have it.'' Despite her disjointed narrative (or perhaps because of it), Louise is a more interesting character than the one she is so eager to describe. Her determination to believe that Claude is a saint never falters, though he continually presents her with evidence that he is not. *Lives of the Saints* is not about saints, or innocence or even decadence, though; it is about the persistent attraction of all three. Much of the action in this first novel takes place at parties and funerals, at which everyone but Louise is drunk. Nancy Lemann is at her best in these scenes, particularly in evoking her characters' confusion amid the lush variety of the New Orleans setting. This luxuriant city is the other object of Louise's affection and in the end it seems more worthy of her than Claude or the other members of the aimless Collier family.

> *Valerie Martin, in a review of "Lives of the Saints,"* in The New York Times Book Review, *June 30, 1985, p. 20.*

FLORENCE KING

Nancy Lemann has taken the South away from the Sun Belters and returned it to a clutch of New Orleans natives who know how to give decadence a good name. Her hero, Claude Collier, is no ''underachiever'' but a bona fide professional ''ne'er-do-well,'' a.k.a. a ''Complete Wreck,'' a man ''who can be found in the bar in the Lafayette Hotel at four in the morning on a weeknight.'' . . .

Lemann wastes no time on Freudian explanations of why Claude is the way he is, preferring the Southerner's recumbent Q.E.D., ''That's just the way he is.'' This regional tolerance for eccentricity is evident on every page. . . .

One of the nicest things about this novel is that there isn't a career woman in it. Lemann gives us instead that quintessential Southern type, the post-deb with a double name who lives in a perpetual state of hysteria: ''Mary Grace Stewart was the type of girl you see being dragged screaming from a convertible

sports car outside of the bar at the Lafayette Hotel at three in the morning by her father and brothers.'' . . .

Lemann has a gift for freshness that is almost eerie—when a servant wanders in and announces, ''There's a man on the phone who says his name is immaterial,'' we laugh anyway despite the hoary host of dire straits/fine fettle jokes that must have inspired the line. As comical as she is, she is also reverent in her treatment of the Western world's last gentle knight, the Southern gentleman, and in her lush descriptions of her beloved New Orleans, where ''the graves are above ground, whitewashed vaults in the heat.''

If the Crescent City should find itself in the grip of a population explosion, they can blame Nancy Lemann for making her readers want to move there. I want to have a drink at that Lafayette Hotel.

> *Florence King, in a review of "Lives of the Saints,"* in Los Angeles Times Book Review, *July 28, 1985, p. 5.*

COMMENTS OF NANCY LEMANN TO *CLC YEARBOOK*

Commenting on the process of writing and publishing *Lives of the Saints*, Lemann says, ''Actually, I wrote the book 7 years ago; it took 3 months to write and 7 years to find a publisher. So for me it was extremely difficult to break into the profession. Some say it grows increasingly hard for a first novel to find a publisher; this was certainly true in my case. . . . Only one person, Gordon Lish at Knopf, famous fiction editor, would take a chance on me.

''Writing is the thing above all things that I would most prefer to spend my time doing, so I am the more grateful to finally be allowed to follow my chosen profession. . . . As Walker Percy says, writing is 'an enterprise mounted in hope' and I write to address that part of the heart of any reader that is inconsolable, to offer hope, toward their secret sorrow, as well as toward my own. So I write about characters who have greatness, for this is the hope I see.''

Ed Minus

1938-

American novelist, short story writer, and poet.

Minus, a native of South Carolina, has contributed short stories and poems to the *New Republic, Atlantic Monthly, New England Quarterly, Boston Phoenix,* and *Georgia Review.* His first novel, *Kite* (1985), tells the story of an orphaned adolescent boy who spends a brief summer with relatives in rural South Carolina. Reviewers note that some plot elements are unresolved or implausible, but they are impressed with the novel's characterization and its evocation of atmosphere. Critics praise, for example, the character of Kite, the orphan, as an appealing and realistic portrait of an adolescent. They commend too, Minus's use of fresh, sensitive language to depict the South Carolina countryside as an Eden for Kite, a metaphor that Minus works subtly and admirably into the novel.

© Jerry Bauer

A review of ''Kite,'' in Kirkus Reviews, *Vol. LIII, No. 5, March 1, 1985, pp. 196-97.*

KIRKUS REVIEWS

[In *Kite*] Kite Cummings, 15, is an orphan reclaimed, so to speak, when his aunt and uncle—the Hamptons, peach-growers in South Carolina—ask him to come live with them. Mr. and Mrs. Hampton have lost their only child in an accident; Kite is only happy to be whatever substitute he can manage—even though leaving the orphanage means leaving the sexual comforts of Jarlene, another orphan. And, with the Hamptons, Kite finds an Eden of kindness and sadness and security—as well as mountains (Kite can see them out his bedroom window), new friends, and the general goodness of small-town/rural life. Like St. Augustine, however, Kite feels like the dirtiest thief in the garden, feels that his unruly adolescent sexual urges—dirty pictures and thoughts, masturbation, a great attractiveness for the local girls—will somehow mess it all up. So the worse he feels (and fears) about himself, the better Kite tries to be—while confronting strange, peripheral, undermining forces: a shadowy, perhaps retarded, black man named Boydy; a magical glass panel found in Boydy's house; an earthquake; a near-drowning in the washing room of the peach orchard; and—ultimately—Kite's own departure from this Eden . . . when he's forced to go back and marry Jarlene (who has declared herself pregnant). First-novelist Minus, with an utterly unaffected, unassuming style and pacing, has thus written a version of the Adamic myth—with a spareness that lets us feel it all anew. The storytelling is bathed in general amity, evoking the peaceable kingdom of goodness with unforced credibility; the Biblical echoes are subtle, virtually invisible at first; and, whether or not the reader consciously follows the Eden parallels here, this fine debut—deeply moving in its rendering of a paradise gained and lost—is quiet, resonant, richly satisfying fiction. (pp. 196-97)

PUBLISHERS WEEKLY

This first novel [*Kite*], by a published poet and short story writer, strongly suggests the author's other métiers. It is carefully and evocatively written, full of atmosphere and summer languor—but it is also episodic to a fault, building to mini-climaxes that are never quite resolved. Even the final fade-out, with its chilling implications, seems rather perfunctory. Nevertheless, there is a great deal to enjoy, particularly in the personality of Kite Cummings, the 15-year-old hero. Kite is perpetually horny (as he would put it), a dedicated masturbator who is yet capable of subtle shades of feeling toward the three women who enter his life, first in the South Carolina orphanage where he has been brought up, later in the home of an uncle and aunt who adopt him. The ways in which Kite struggles with sexual temptation—trying always to be ''good''—and finally accepts adult responsibilities are utterly convincing and touching. Subplots involving a mysterious black man and his

·strange house in the woods and a rival for one of Kite's girl-friends are just left dangling, however, as if the author is interested in things other than story-telling. Minus is clearly a born writer, and in everything other than its shaping of narrative, *Kite* is triumphantly alive.

A review of "Kite," in Publishers Weekly, *Vol. 227, No. 11, March 15, 1985, p. 103.*

BILL CHAPLA

Writing a notable novel about adolescents specifically for the adolescent reader takes a special talent—a talent possessed by the likes of Paul Zindel and S. E. Hinton who can actually tap into the teenage heart and mind because they themselves are still sensitive to the teenage world. But writing a notable novel about adolescents specifically for the adult reader takes a bit more. It takes that same astute understanding of teenagers, but it also takes a unique awareness of the adult world. Ed Minus must have exactly what it takes, for this coming-of-age tale [*Kite*] is quite moving and quite mature and reminds one very much of J. D. Salinger's *The Catcher In the Rye.*

Raised in a Baptist orphanage and hampered by a limited view of the world, fourteen-year-old Kite Cummings is adopted by an aunt and uncle after their own small boy is recently killed in a mysterious accident on their South Carolina farm. Placed in this entirely new rural [setting] Kite immediately begins to experience the restorative qualities of the fields, orchards, woods and rivers of the pristine piedmont countryside. Like Adam in the garden of Eden, Kite discovers a true sense of pleasure and freedom—the pleasure of a real home and real friends and the freedom to choose. Becoming increasingly more aware of his own sexual identity amid the rigid morality of southern country folk in the 1950's, Kite begins to realize how serious some choices can be, especially when they involve either exercising freely or restraining his overactive teenage libido. Ironically, it is a choice from the past that destroys Kite's new-found freedom and banishes him from paradise to the premature world of adulthood.

Ed Minus writes in an unassuming and evocative style blending stark realism with romantic imagery. His narrative is simple and riveting; his protagonist is complex and alive. With *Kite*, less is not more. Less is magnificent.

Bill Chapla, in a review of "Kite," in Best Sellers, *Vol. 45, No. 4, July, 1985, p. 129.*

An Excerpt from *Kite*

Halfway through the cake, Kite stopped eating long enough to take his shoes and socks off. Then he sat with his back against the headboard and rubbed his feet up and down on the tufted bedspread. He could not remember ever sleeping in a room by himself, and it felt strange and unreal—as if he was another person, somebody he had known a long time ago but had not been with for many years and did not know how to talk to. He wished that Jimmy was there. Or Jarlene. He wished that Jarlene was there, just to talk to; he would not even want to do it to her right now—though that would be nice, sometime, in this big bed. They never had done it in a bed. But he mainly just wanted somebody to talk to. . . .

Some noises came from downstairs for a while; then the house got very quiet. The only sounds were the cicadas. And dogs barking far off in the distance. And those sounds somehow made the silence even louder. He took the plate, glass, and fork into the bathroom and rinsed them off. He tried to be as quiet as possible, but every sound seemed to echo. He opened his suitcase and hung his Sunday coat and pants, his white shirt, and two other pairs of pants in the wardrobe. His other shirts and his underwear and socks he put in the chest.

In the bottom of the suitcase was a spiral notebook, and in the notebook were a dozen or more pictures of naked or nearly naked women, pictures he had torn out of magazines or dirty books. He had thought about leaving those pictures behind. Had even wanted to—in a way. He had told himself that he was going to be starting a clean new life where he would no longer have any need or use for pictures like that. But he had not convinced himself. I can always get rid of 'em when I get up there, he had decided. Without opening the notebook, he slid it under his socks and underwear. Then he took it out again and put it under the tissue paper that lined the drawer. He took his toothbrush, toothpaste, hairbrush, and comb into the bathroom and brushed his teeth, watching himself in the mirror.

He pulled the spread back to the bottom of the bed and folded back the sheet. Then he turned out the lamp. He felt his way over to the back windows and looked out, but all he could see were masses of shadows, very still and quiet; the moon was gone.

He moved back to the bed and knelt beside it and said one of the children's prayers he had been taught at Brightwood, and added, "Please bless my friends and teachers and Dr. Sills down at Baptist Home. Especially Jimmy and Jarlene. Please help Jarlene not to miss me too much. Please bless Aunt Ruth and Uncle Hampton. And please help me to be the kind of boy they want me to be. Amen."

RONALD FLORENCE

Kite is a boy/man of 14 spending his first summer outside the orphanage that has been his only home. As one of his female admirers describes him [in *Kite*], he is the "cutest and sweetest boy" anyone has ever known. He also is delightfully over-sexed, a veritable virtuoso of masturbation.

A scrap of old newspaper is on the floor, Kite spots an advertisement for an adults-only movie, and for days he cannot get the image of the tawny heroine out of his mind. If he goes to a store, he cannot resist stealing a men's magazine, hiding it inside a *Saturday Evening Post* that he buys, like Woody Allen in *Bananas* hiding raunchy magazines under the high-brow magazines he buys to impress a woman.

The novel follows Kite through a summer in rural South Carolina, a world of "big noonday meals" and "suppertime," of swimming holes and front porches with gliders, of boys swimming in their cut-offs, constantly worried whether their erections show, of thick slices of cake and a glass of milk at bedtime. Ed Minus captures the language of this rural world and the feel of the countryside beautifully. We can taste an ice-cold watermelon on a steamy day, watch shadowy sunlight play through the lush foliage, see the unexpected colors of distant mountains.

Only occasionally does the prose stray too far. A boy feels the sun "smiting" his back. When Kite is working at a conveyor belt in a packing shed, stamping peach crates, he feels "like Charlie Chaplin in a scene from a silent movie he had seen once on television." *Modern Times* on television in the '50s?

The lapses are minor blemishes. It is the character of Kite, not the plot, that draws us into this world; and not until a third of the way into the book does Minus introduce the imagery of the fall from innocence that becomes his theme. When the hints of Adam and Eve and Milton come, they are a flood: page after page of snakes; Kite and one of his girlfriends lying amid flowers and trees, tempted; a cataclysmic earthquake; fat, juicy, tempting watermelons. Fortunately, the imagery is not heavy handed. Minus resists the temptation of first novelists who fear that a reader will not make the connection and feel compelled to toss in a superfluous "Like Adam and Eve. . . ."

If there is any criticism to be made of this lovely little book, it is that Minus, like so many authors, has been ill-served by the designer of the book jacket, who has painted a character that looks not at all like the attractive Kite, and who evokes weird psychological imagery that has little to do with Minus' subtle portrait of lost adolescent innocence.

> *Ronald Florence, in a review of "Kite," in* Los Angeles Times Book Review, *July 14, 1985, p. 8.*

DAVID GUY

Fourteen-year-old Kite Cummings has spent nearly his whole life in orphanages but is suddenly told that his aunt and uncle have lost their young child in an accident and want Kite to come live with them. It is a wonderful opportunity—they have a house near the mountains in South Carolina—but also a frightening one. He is not sure he will be able to adjust.

What is remarkable about this first novel [*Kite*] is that it does not follow a stereotype from there. Kite is not a hardened young thug who has become embittered by his experience but an ordinary boy who tries to love an aunt and uncle who are essentially strangers to him, who has been raised in a fundamentalist faith but finds himself in adolescence as randy as any other youth.

This novel is at its best in its leisurely early sections—Kite gets settled in his new home, sees the mountains for the first time, makes friends with the neighbor boys, explores the woods and streams, does heavy manual labor in his uncle's peach-packing business and falls for a local girl. Mr. Minus is a splendid descriptive writer who structures his scenes deftly and never lets his voice obtrude on the beauty and simplicity of his situations.

As the novel progresses and he tries to force a plot on it, Mr. Minus gets in trouble. Instead of letting his story's natural conflicts play themselves out, he drags in implausible events—a timely minor earthquake, an accidental death, an appendicitis attack—that rob him of his best narrative opportunities. The conflict between Kite's raging sexuality and the narrow tenets of his church is an obvious problem throughout the book, but Kite never takes the obvious step of questioning his faith, and it is only in the novel's final pages that the church suddenly reveals itself to be full of hypocrisy.

Ed Minus is a talented writer with a wonderful sensitivity to nature. When he gains enough confidence in his material, he will write better novels.

> *David Guy, "Coming of Age in Carolina," in* The New York Times Book Review, *September 15, 1985, p. 21.**

Lorrie Moore

1957-

(Born Marie Lorena Moore) American short story writer.

In her first collection of short fiction, *Self-Help* (1985), Moore explores themes of love and anguish from the point-of-view of the contemporary woman. Her narratives are often deceptively light in tone, full of urbane witticisms. Beneath the surface, however, are powerful emotions, as her characters face problems ranging from unhappy love affairs to terminal cancer. Moore cites Margaret Atwood as an influence because Atwood has written "fiction about women who were not goddesses or winners. In some ways they were victims, but they weren't wimps. They were stylish about their victimization." Although Moore's heroines suffer, the author emphasizes their efforts to cope, to practice "self-help."

In six of the nine stories in this collection, Moore borrows narrative devices from psychological self-help manuals, among them the second person imperative: "Understand that your cat is a whore and can't help you," begins one story. While a few critics find the self-help approach in telling a story to be a tiresome gimmick, most find it an ingenious technique that allows Moore to create the emotional distance and ironic tone that is characteristic of the collection. Moore, commenting on this device, reports: "The first story I wrote was 'How' in 1980 and was, I thought, going to be my sole experiment in second-person, telling a how-to that, of course, is a how-not-to. I wanted to appropriate a vernacular form (the instruction manual, the self-help guide) and see what it could be made to do. I found myself returning to this voice in subsequent stories, as if the voice were insisting on further use, further experimentation. My concerns in working with it had to do with whether it was supple enough for storytelling and whether the uneasy place between reader and writer in which this narrative 'you' resided was, in fact, *too* uneasy, *too* disconcerting."

Besides her self-help stories, Moore has included three other stories that also reveal her acute observation and verbal wit in examining human dilemmas; these are rendered in a more lyrical tone but evidence the same compassion for her characters found in the "how-to" stories. Moore, who teaches English at the University of Wisconsin in Madison, plans to publish her first novel in 1986.

(See also *Contemporary Authors*, Vol. 116.)

KIRKUS REVIEWS

In this flimsy, strained collection of nine short stories [*Self-Help*], young writer Moore offers, for the most part, variations on a single gimmick and two limited situations. The gimmick? Stories in the form of self-help/instruction manuals—written in the second person, with a mannered veneer of ironic wise-

© *Jerry Bauer*

cracks to half-mask the essential sentimentality beneath. The situations: a young woman caught in an unhappy, no-win romantic relationship; and a young woman's recollections of her unhappy, unstable mother. . . . And when Moore abandons this tinker-toy formula, the results are only slightly more interesting: **"What is Seized"** gives conventional, first-person/montage treatment to memories of a miserable, mad, now-dying mother—but with too much stagy whininess to be affecting ("And when your mother starts to lose her mind, so do you"); **"Go Like This"** is an artsy exercise, a monologue for a terminally ill woman planning her suicide; and the longest story, **"To Fill,"** is likewise a studied assemblage of distressed streams-of-consciousness—as a married woman verges on breakdown amid recollections of passion (*"How we loved each other with forks"*), mordant wisecracks, and pseudo-profundities. ("Life is a pun, I say. It's something that sounds like one thing but also sounds like even means like something else.") A few glimmers of talent here and there—but maudlin/juvenile work overall: boutique fiction at its most cutesy-poo.

A review of ''Self-Help,'' in Kirkus Reviews, *Vol. LIII, No. 2, January 15, 1985, p. 58.*

RAY OLSON

Six of the nine stories in this absorbing debut collection [*Self-Help*] are cast in the instructional present tense of the how-to manual, with the second person singular the understood subject of most sentences. Since Moore's material—love affairs and marriages in trouble, the deaths of mothers, a child adjusting to divorce—is fraught with emotion, perhaps this technique is a strategy for avoiding bathos. It allows her to be distant and ironic, implying that her stories reflect what little bits of hell are like for anyone, not just for her particular characters. Unfortunately, the instructive voice also seems to release Moore from the challenge of rendering strong emotion at all. However, in **"What Is Seized,"** a daughter's memoir of her recently deceased mother, Moore uses the usual past and present tenses with first or third person singular subjects and achieves an emotional masterpiece as powerful as, say, Tillie Olsen's best work. For this fine story, and for many funny and sharp lines and effects in others, *Self-Help* is definitely recommended.

Ray Olson, in a review of "Self-Help," in Booklist, *Vol. 81, No. 1, March 15, 1985, p. 1031.*

JAY McINERNEY

The current epidemic of self-improvement manuals, ostensibly nonfiction, may tell us as much about ourselves as Horatio Alger novels tell us about the prelapsarian American dream. We devour books that show us how to be our dog's best friend, how to fornicate, find a mate, divorce a mate and feel O.K. about ourselves in transit. In *Self-Help,* the collection of short stories that is her first book, Lorrie Moore examines the idea that lives can be improved like golf swings and in so doing finds a distinctive, scalpel-sharp fictional voice that probes, beneath the ad hoc psychic fixit programs we devise for ourselves, the depths of our fears and yearnings.

The women in these stories know they should be their own best friends, but it doesn't help much. They are mothers whose husbands have left, daughters who are only interested in the men they can't have. They are witty and intelligent, addicted to wordplay and other forms of verbal self-defense, but they know their wit and intelligence can't save them from love, loss of love, death. This fictional terrain and the brisk, ironic tone of these stories is somewhat reminiscent of Grace Paley, although Miss Moore's voice is very much her own.

"Understand that your cat is a whore and can't help you," one story begins. In another the narrator coaches herself, "Remember what Mrs. Kloosterman told the class in second grade: Just be glad you have legs." The humor here is equivalent to the nitrous oxide that precedes root canal work. Go ahead—laugh while you can. The joke behind the how-to format is that the answer is always—"No way." Your lover is dumb and nice or smart and nasty, and one of you is about to split with the best books and records under your arm; your mother and father are either dead or ungracefully dying. . . .

Romantic love in these stories is like the dying downtown of a Northeastern city; everyone is nostalgic for it, but no one spends his money there. . . .

Haunting the romantic quests of most of Miss Moore's narrators is the complex puzzle of maternal love. Several of these stories are concerned with a mother's death, a daughter's terrible ambivalence about the woman she may become. The splendid **"How to Talk to Your Mother"** moves backward, in sections dated by year, from a mother's death through the daughter's

adolescence and childhood to the moment of birth, when the mother "knows it when you try to talk to her, though this is something you never really manage to understand."

In **"What Is Seized,"** the daughter says, "The touches and the words and the moaning the night she dies, these are what you seize, save, carry around in little invisible envelopes, opening them up quickly, like a carnival huckster, giving the world a peek. They will not stay quiet."

In this story and several others, Miss Moore departs from the how-to format, enriching the collection with tones other than the wryly comic, probing the cavities that require laughing gas and demonstrating that the range of her verbal dexterity extends into the lyrical. In **"What Is Seized,"** she evokes the childhood of a brother and sister: "James and I shared the large bed in the lakeside room upstairs, in the morning often waking up staring into each other's eyes, and at night spending hours listening for the underwater world in the lake to come magically to life, when no one was looking, when it was pitch black and still except for the quietest rocking, and the good, shy fish would put on pink and orange jackets and smile and go to balls, with violins and oriental fans."

Occasionally irony clashes with pathos, as in the story **"Go Like This,"** about a middle-aged woman with cancer who decides to commit suicide, the cancer being reductively compared to "a clumsy, uninvited guest who is obese and eats too much."

All of Miss Moore's tones and thematic concerns are deployed in **"To Fill,"** the concluding story of the collection, in which a middle-aged woman named Riva begins to come apart, convincingly and hilariously, stealing money from the department store where she works and overeating in a desperate attempt to compensate for the seepage of love from her marriage and the encroaching senility of her mother. "There is no dignity in appetites," she realizes, but she goes on trying to fill herself, dreaming of a former lover or husband, Phil, who comes to stand for what is missing in her life.

Lorrie Moore is very talented, and *Self-Help* is a funny, cohesive and moving collection of stories. The title is not, perhaps, totally ironic. From its beginnings fiction has pretended, among other things, that it is good for us. Think of Richardson and Fielding. Self-improvement, instruction in manners and morals, was the ingenious defense of readers and writers accused of idling. The current wisdom is that fiction is not supposed to do anything, it's just supposed to be, but a book like *Self-Help* does, in fact, instruct us in our current and abiding dilemmas. It may even be good for us.

Jay McInerney, "New and Improved Lives," in The New York Times Book Review, *March 24, 1985, p. 32.*

JENNIFER CRICHTON

Baby-boomed American women have it tough and maybe Lorrie Moore, who is 28, knows why. Every emotional landmark we and her characters [in *Self-Help*] reach—being the other woman, being cheated on, falling out of love—is clichéd; we've already read about it or seen it on television, but that doesn't stop us from actually being there, clumsy emotion skimmed over by glib awareness. This can be funny. Kind of. It is, at any rate, when Moore writes about it. Her stories are observations cobbled together (as in Renata Adler's *Speedboat*), fresh and snappy like bites from a green apple. And they're often in second-person narrative: You. As in: "After four movies, three concerts, and two-and-a-half museums, you sleep with him. It seems the right number of cultural events." (This from **"How to Be an Other Woman."**) Could be a device to distance Moore from the intimate nuisance of the autobiographical "I," especially when the stories skate over fiascos in love with we'll-laugh-about-it-someday irony. But then again, maybe you *is* you. Whatever it is, it works—for you, for me, for Lorrie Moore.

Jennifer Crichton, in a review of "Self-Help," in Ms., *Vol. XIII, No, 12, June, 1985, p. 68.*

An Excerpt from *Self-Help*

Moss Watson, the man you truly love like no other, is singing December 23 in the Owonta Opera production of *Amahl and the Night Visitors*. He's playing Kaspar, the partially deaf Wise Man. Wisdom, says Moss, arrives in all forms. And you think, Yes, sometimes as a king and sometimes as a hesitant phone call that says the king'll be late at rehearsal don't wait up, and then when you call back to tell him to be careful not to let the cat out when he comes home, you discover there's been no rehearsal there at all.

At three o'clock in the morning you hear his car in the driveway, the thud of the front door. When he comes into the bedroom, you see his huge height framed for a minute in the doorway, his hair lit bright as curry. When he stoops to take off his shoes, it is as if some small piece of his back has given way, allowing him this one slow bend. He is quiet. When he gets into bed he kisses one of your shoulders, then pulls the covers up to his chin. He knows you're awake. "I'm tired," he announces softly, to ward you off when you roll toward him. Say: "You didn't let the cat out, did you?"

He says no, but he probably should have. "You're turning into a cat mom. Cats, Trudy, are the worst sort of surrogates."

Tell him you've always wanted to run off and join the surrogates.

Tell him you love him.

Tell him you know he didn't have rehearsal tonight.

"We decided to hold rehearsal at the Montessori school, what are you now, *my* mother?"

In the dark, discern the fine hook of his nose. Smooth the hair off his forehead. Say: "I love you Moss are you having an affair with a sheep?" You saw a movie once where a man was having an affair with a sheep, and acted, with his girlfriend, the way Moss now acts with you: exhausted.

Moss's eyes close. "I'm a king, not a shepherd, remember? You're acting like my ex-wife."

His ex-wife is now an anchorwoman in Missouri.

"Are you having a regular affair? Like with a person?"

"Trudy," he sighs, turns away from you, taking more than his share of blanket. "You've got to stop this." Know you are being silly. Any second now he will turn and press against you, reassure you with kisses, tell you

oh how much he loves you. "How on earth, Trudy," is what he finally says, "would I ever have the time for an affair?"

ROBERT TOWERS

Not unrelated to Grace Paley in sensibility, Lorrie Moore is one of those young writers—Amy Hempel and David Leavitt are others—whom Knopf has been publishing in rapid succession as if to dispel forever the old notion that no one wants to buy a first collection of short stories by an unknown author. However these books have done commercially, they have certainly demonstrated the vitality and attractiveness of the short form as it is shaped by talented young writers.

Lorrie Moore composes "how-to" stories: **"How to Be an Other Woman," "The Kid's Guide to Divorce," "How to Talk to Your Mother (Notes)," "How to Become a Writer,"** and one simply called **"How."** Collectively, these and the other pieces that make up *Self-Help* present a dismal account of failed relationships, disappointed yearnings, dying, crazy, or senile mothers and neurotic daughters, loose ends, and the ongoing battle between the sexes. While no one wins, it is the women who are the biggest losers. Yet Lorrie Moore is no soured feminist. She is funny and inventive, and the impact of her stories is often as exhilarating as it is dismaying. (p. 28)

The story called **"Go Like This"** is not really a manual of self-instruction but a powerfully imagined first-person narrative of what it would be like for a young woman with cancer to decide to kill herself on a certain day (Bastille Day, in fact). She announces her intention to her husband, who has withdrawn from her sexually since her operation, and then assembles her friends for a public announcement. They react in ways that reveal not only their characters but an assortment of possible responses—responses that again reflect the prevailing clichés of our time. Some are, like her husband, supportive, telling her that she is doing a beautiful, creative thing. The Catholic couple flee in dismay, leaving their umbrellas behind. Another friend, Olga, insists on eroticizing the encounter with death; advising delay, she says, "You haven't earned your death yet. You want the orgasm without the foreplay." The play of ironies enlivens the course of the story without, in this case, mitigating its essential grimness.

The emotional range of *Self-Help* is narrow. The "how-to" device becomes, after two or more examples, something of a gimmick. Yet Lorrie Moore's wit, her psychological acuity, and the deadly accuracy of her social observation are such that one looks forward to what she will write next. (pp. 28-9)

Robert Towers, "Moveable Types," in The New York Review of Books, *Vol. XXXII, No. 13, August 15, 1985, pp. 26-9.**

DAWN ANN DRZAL

The stories [in *Self-Help*] are ironic because they teach you what you already know and wish you didn't: how to fall out of love, how to avoid talking about your parents' divorce, how to watch your mother grow frail and die. Moore's heroines, like [Amy] Hempel's, know better, but it doesn't do them much good either. They are intelligent, clever women one imagines as compulsive takers of magazine quizzes—"What's Your Love Quotient?"—even though they know how silly they are. Also like Hempel's heroines, they are smartasses, addicted to, even controlled by, obsessive wordplay. For them wordplay is a mental tic, a diversion, a spillway for unassimilable pain.

The six how-to stories are told in the second person and derive much of their narrative tension from the pull between the general and the specific inherent in the second person. This conflict can never be resolved fully because "you" means "you, the reader," and there is no avoiding the recognition that "you, the reader" are not participating in the events of the story but only in the emotions they arouse. Therefore, the stories prevent the full suspension of disbelief and strike the reader as artful, as less than wholly "true." This emotional distance is compensated for by the appeal to the reader's vanity. "This story is about me," some part of you says, "it must be interesting."

The combination of the second person and the present tense adds another, unexpected, dimension to the stories. A strange alchemy results in something resembling the future tense that lends them an odd feeling of cause and effect. "Begin by meeting him in a class, in a bar, at a rummage sale," is the opening line of **"How."** Something is about to happen; the story is unfolding just as you read it. Only when you've reached the end does it become clear that the story has unfolded as it always has, and you have had no effect on it at all. Very artful, indeed.

These stories seem to present their heroines with a variety of options, but they zero in to invalidate all but the chosen one. The large wheel of life is turning and within it the small cog of the heroine's psyche. No matter how many ways she turns a phrase, no matter how many points of view she assumes, she can make only one choice, but that doesn't mean she'll feel it was the right one, or even the only one. No, she is doomed to be both determined and doubt-ridden. The clever wordplay in these stories is a defense doomed to failure—life goes on, her mother will grow senile with age, her husband will leave her or she will leave him. The heroines know it; the people who know them know it. When Trudy in **"Amahl and the Night Visitors: A Guide to the Tenor of Love"** finishes a humorous monologue about slippers, her boss comments succinctly, "You're depressed." Still, she continues to banter even though she knows why she's doing it: it keeps her mind off the abyss. (pp. 506-07)

Self-Help is a funny, compassionate course in what you can't help knowing no matter how hard you try. The hope in these stories springs from the same source as their hopelessness— the irrevocability of the cycle, which may trap you but keeps going on. That's what Moore's characters try to do, love and work as best they can and keep going on. Even Freud said that's all anyone can ask for. (p. 507)

> *Dawn Ann Drzal, "An Assemblage of Trifles," in* Commonweal, *Vol. CXII, No. 16, September 20, 1985, pp. 505-07.**

GEOFF DYER

Lorrie Moore's stories [in *Self-Help*] are dazzling exercises in an ingenious wisdom. Written, for the most part, as omniscient but partial instructions for modern women these stories have a deadly accurate clairvoyance; every couple of pages you're jolted by Moore's intimate knowledge of the not-so-spontaneous choreography of romance.

Clichés, says the narrator in one of the stories, can take on epiphanic dimensions with some people. That's how Moore works. Her stories delight in their own glossiness but are all the time controlled by her sense of the dangerous edge of things. . . .

Reading Moore you simultaneously recognise and realise for the first time (that, for example, the problem with cold men is that 'they never learn the beauty or value of gesture'). These stories hurt: not because they clout you in the nose—it's more like bumping your face in a mirror. They're funny as well.

> *Geoff Dyer, "Clear-Sighted," in* New Statesman, *Vol. 110, No. 2844, September 27, 1985, p. 34.**

COMMENTS OF LORRIE MOORE TO *CLC YEARBOOK*

In response to the question of whether *Self-Help* is autobiographical, Moore commented: "This work is not at all autobiographical if by autobiographical one means an account of things that really happened to the author. None of these fictional events happened to me, except in my imagination—which, of course, is nonetheless a powerful way of having something happen. There are relationships and other aspects of the stories that embrace a certain autobiographical spirit or tone or emotion, perhaps even to the point of becoming 'metaphors of self' (I'm not quoting anyone in particular here). And a few of the specifics I hauled in willy-nilly from the real world, like a junk collector. Most, however, were invented."

Asked about her motivations for writing, Moore responded, "Everyone has already said 'to teach and delight,' so I will add 'to confide inventively and likewise console.' I think that when you write you should have the feeling that you're creating something brand new, something that doesn't already exist in the world. . . . The intimacy that can be established between reader and writer is one of words and imagination only, yet it is miraculous in its powers. The writer says 'Here are some things I care about; here are some friends I've invented for both of us,' and the power of these literary inventions, these fictional confidences, to bring people together, to reveal our common humanity, is an astonishing and moving thing."

T(homas) R(eid) Pearson

1956-

American novelist and short story writer.

Pearson describes his first novel, *A Short History of a Small Place* (1985), as "the first thing I've written that I really liked." Pearson, a native of North Carolina, started writing short stories when he was eighteen. "I was trying to write what I thought publishers wanted," he recalls, "which mostly was what I was reading. I would read the *New Yorker* and write something about angst in Manhattan." Each story he submitted for publication was rejected. After teaching English at North Carolina's Peace College and Pennsylvania State University, Pearson went to work as a painter and carpenter and started writing his first novel. *A Short History* was completed in December 1982. Over the next year, Pearson submitted it to publishers, who, claims Pearson, turned down the manuscript at the rate of one rejection per week. In 1983, the editor of the *Virginia Quarterly Review* published an excerpt from the novel. He also referred Pearson to a New York literary agent, who told the author that the novel was "too slow and indirect and oblique." "That," Pearson observed, "was exactly what I intended. . . ." Nevertheless, he wrote a second novel, *Off for the Sweet Hereafter* (1986), deliberately adding "a little more velocity to it." This novel, he says, is "set pretty much in the same place, but about a lower class of people altogether. It's pretty much in the same style, but not with the same organization. It's not so broken apart." Another agent at the same agency arranged for the publication of both novels by Simon and Schuster's Linden Press.

The narrator of *A Short History* is Louis Benfield, Jr., a fifteen-year-old resident of Neely, Pearson's fictionalized version of a small town in North Carolina. While recounting the events that led to the suicide of a Miss Myra Angelique Pettigrew, Louis adds numerous anecdotes to his narrative, resulting in a composite picture of the entire Neely community. Many of Louis's anecdotes are based on stories Pearson heard as a child in Winston-Salem and in his visits with relatives in Reidsville. "A lot of things were things my parents told me," he comments. "Others were stories people told me, not knowing that I was going to do anything with them or was even paying attention."

Critics are generally impressed by *A Short History*'s distinctly Southern pacing and flavor and commend Pearson for his mastery over his material. Reviewers compare Louis's narrative with that of Huckleberry Finn, noting beneath Pearson's rampant hilariousness a poignant and compassionate vision of humanity. Some critics fault Pearson's slow-paced method of storytelling, with its many digressions and repetitions. Pearson claims his technique is simply rooted in Southern oral tradition. "When Southerners set out to tell a story," he explains, "they always start in the middle, thinking they are starting at the beginning, because once you start to telling a story, you realize you have to go backward." Pearson has completed a third

© *Jerry Bauer*

novel—modeled after *A Short History* and also featuring Louis Benfield, Jr.—and is at work on a fourth.

KIRKUS REVIEWS

As the title [*A Short History of a Small Place*] suggests, the town of Neely, North Carolina, is the main character of this colorful, often amusing, but ultimately frustratingly episodic novel. The changes in Neely's fortunes, and those of its several notable residents, are recounted by young Louis Benfield, who arrives at his own droll version of truth from two versions: his Momma's romanticized, charitable one, and his Daddy's sardonic, plain-spoken one.

The story loosely centers around the waxing and waning of the fortunes of the Pettigrew family, Neely's most prominent and admired residents, beginning with the reclusive Miss Myra Angelique Pettigrew's rare public appearance on her front lawn in the center of town, draped in a bedsheet, enacting the part of Antigone, while her pet chimpanzee, Mr. Britches, capers around the front yard. A few days after this demonstration that Miss Pettigrew has become "Not Right," she throws herself to her death from the water tower at the edge of town.

The funeral, the auction of the Pettigrews' effects, the destruction of the house by fire, the purchase of the empty lot for a bank's branch office—with digressions into the doings of some of Neely's less august but still colorful denizens—make up the rest of the novel. As the yarn spins on, however, interest in this by-now somewhat familiar brand of southern small-town oddness begins to give way to curiosity about what the book's true aim was, and then to disappointment as it becomes evident that this aim has been too loosely defined to give *A Short History* . . . the main satisfaction most readers seek in a novel: a sense of deepening and change in the main character. Pearson has not been able to bring off the formidable feat of making a town be a protagonist. The natural expectation that grows in the reader is that young Louis Benfield will step to center stage at some point, but he remains merely a passive recorder of events.

The pleasures here are considerable: Pearson has a strong sense of place, a fine ear for speech, a confident, old-fashioned way of storytelling, and a subtle, disarming humor expressing itself in throwaway lines that surprise laughter again and again. He also has an evident compassion and liking for even his screwiest characters.

Overall, this is a promising, if not fully accomplished, first effort by a talented writer, to whose future offerings one looks with hope. (pp. 343-44)

> *A review of "A Short History of a Small Place," in Kirkus Reviews, Vol. LIII, No. 8, April 15, 1985, pp. 343-44.*

PUBLISHERS WEEKLY

Pearson's first novel [*A Short History of a Small Place*] is as wise as it is funny. Narrated by young Louis Benfield, it is the story of Miss Myra Angelique Pettigrew, sister of the late mayor of a small Southern town, who is elegant and beautiful and has gone quite mad. After many years of seclusion, she finally emerges from her home to jump to her death from the water tower. In the process of telling his tale, Louis offers vignettes about other residents of Neely, N.C., and their strange habits and activities. Among them are: Pinky Throckmorton, whose sole pleasure in life is taking those who cross his path to court in order to satisfy his dignity; little Jack Vestal, who tried to bury his guinea pig, Artemus Gordon, in Mr. Zeno's coffin so that it too would be assured of some portion of saintliness; and Peahead Boyette, who was fined for catching catfish with a telephone (slightly modified to produce a lethal electric shock—certainly the easiest way to fish). Wry observations by Louis's father provide much of the humor, while Louis's own innocent outlook serves to make some incisive statements about life. Pearson's writing is both smooth and hilarious. He creates crazy situations and presents them in a wandering prose that reflects Southern speech patterns, ending each idea with a punchline. This is an original and wonderful novel, an auspicious debut. (pp. 221-22)

> *A review of "A Short History of a Small Place," in Publishers Weekly, Vol. 227, No. 19, May 10, 1985, pp. 221-22.*

JONATHAN YARDLEY

A Short History of a Small Place is an absolute stunner, the work of a writer who may be young but whose command of his material never falters, who knows exactly what he is doing and does it with the sure hand of one far older and more experienced.

Because Pearson is indeed young there is evidence in his work of the influence of others, but his literary bloodlines are excellent to say the least. In his exuberant storytelling there's more than a trace of Sut Lovingood and Huckleberry Finn, of the comical Faulkner of *The Hamlet* and *The Reivers,* of the similarly comical Welty of *Losing Battles,* the book that *A Short History* most closely resembles. There are hints of the language of all three of these writers in Pearson's prose, but you can also detect Ring Lardner in his use of the vernacular as well as W. C. Fields in his owlish humor; his eye for the vainglorious could be Mencken's, his nose for the ludicrous could be Thurber's.

He's all of these and none, because mainly Pearson is Pearson, disguised as a 15-year-old boy named Louis Benfield Jr. who is the novel's narrator or, perhaps more accurately, amanuensis. What he records is not so much his own observations and experiences as the talk of a town in which gossip is the principal local business. In particular he records the talk of two people: his father, the wry, sardonic and loving "Daddy," and Mrs. Philip J. King, a neighbor whose capacity for nosing into the affairs of others is limitless. Ostensibly all this talk is about the legendary life and spectacular demise of Miss Myra Angelique Pettigrew, a once-beautiful and wealthy spinster who had been for the town the embodiment of elegance and sophistication. But talk about Miss Pettigrew merely leads, as talk is likely to do, to other things. . . . (p. 3)

On and on the talk goes, winding its sinuous way from Pinky and Mr. Britches—not to mention Judge Mortenson and Mr. Curtis Amos' straw fedora—to the scandalous behavior of Miss Sissy Nance, and the great duck war between the Nances and the Gottliebs, and the general disputation over the precise nature of the relationship between Miss Pettigrew and Mr. Alton Nance, and the expiration of the saintly Zeno Stiers, and the appearance of Mr. Conrad Rackley, who hails from the West Virginia end of Kentucky. One after another the shaggy-dog stories come, and just when you think it is entirely impossible for Pearson to top himself he turns right around and does just that—right to the end, when Miss Pettigrew is lowered into the ground after obsequies by, among others, the Reverend Holroyd, the Reverend Mr. Richard Crockett Sheldon and the Reverend W. B. Red Hamilton.

If it all weren't so incredibly funny it would be inestimably sad, which is precisely Pearson's point. The human comedy—and in the truest sense of the term, *A Short History of a Small Place* is just that—always is laughter beneath which lurk sorrow and loss, and so it is in the rich layers of this novel. What young Louis Benfield is receiving, as he recites the history of a place in which lunacy seems to prevail, is an education in life's hard realities, an education both practical and moral. In the story of Miss Pettigrew he learns something about love and betrayal; in that of Pinky Throckmorton, something about the true nature of dignity; in that of the dead sister he never knew, something about "fate and courage and the trials of existence." Not to mention what he learns from the death of Mr. Zeno Stiers:

It was a sorrowful few days in Neely after Mr. Zeno passed away. Stierses converged on Lamont Street from all over the southeast and most everybody from one end of town to the other went around with Mr. Zeno's virtues on their lips. Of course it was an exceedingly black time for chickens as well. Legions of them got fried and roasted while a considerable few showed up in pot pies and casseroles boiled off the bone. . . . Daddy said once he had shaken hands with near about twenty Stierses he dished himself up an assortment of prepared poultry and was coming up fast on the cobblers and the pound cakes when he noticed, with measurable awe and trepidation Daddy called it, that he was sharing the dining room with perhaps the largest collection of deviled egg plates ever assembled under one roof. Daddy says it was a somewhat sobering revelation to him. Here he was enjoying a bounteous meal at Mr. Zeno's house while Mr. Zeno himself was off at the mortuary being siphoned. But Daddy says he simply decided that is the way things are on God's earth—the dead get embalmed and the living get seconds.

So pass the pot pie and have another deviled egg; life goes on, fragile and heartbreaking though it can be, and each moment should be treasured because "this will never happen just this way again." For Louis that is the lesson that counts above all others, and for Pearson's wonderful novel it is the theme that echoes on every exuberant page. In a small place in North Carolina, Pearson has found the stuff of life, and thus has given us a world that is both his own and ours. (p. 8)

Jonathan Yardley, "Tale of a Tarheel Town," in Book World—The Washington Post, *June 16, 1985, pp. 3, 8.*

CHRISTOPHER LEHMANN-HAUPT

Unlike the blood of aristocrats, that remarkable Southern gift for talk seems to get thicker as it gets passed down through the generations since William Faulkner. One of the many places it has coagulated is in this first novel by T. R. Pearson, ironically (given its length) called *A Short History of a Small Place*, which recounts yet again the decline of Southern nobility and the rise of the riffraff, but in a voice that makes it all seem slapstick and zany, as if Quentin Compson had stepped in a bucket of paint on his way to the Charles River and Benjy the idiot had run off and joined the pro golf tour.

What gets Mr. Pearson's intricate narrative voice started is the suicide of Miss Myra Angelique Pettigrew. . . .

Behind Miss Pettigrew's suicide lie overrefinement, violated honor, the premature deaths of beloved relatives, and too many years of living alone with her monkey and a loyal servant—in short, the familiar Southern gothic baggage. But these gloomy facts become almost incidental to the elaborate episodes in which the young narrator, Louis Benfield, becomes hopelessly and charmingly entangled. . . .

[There] is the episode of Reverend Shelton's 1962 Christmas pageant, which went awry when the Virgin Mary, in her agitation at seeing Miss Pettigrew in attendance, dropped the baby Jesus, whose porcelain head made a sound that scared the goats into breaking a lamp and setting the manger on fire. "The wise men bolted off in one direction, Joseph cleared out in the other, and the Virgin Mary crept backwards into the stable with her hands over her mouth until she stepped on the camel's hindquarters, which caused him to jump up and start barking."

As the narrator keeps adding these brushstrokes, the camera slowly backs away to reveal a mural so colorful and elaborate that we can no longer find in it the tragic decline of the Pettigrews. Instead, we see a sociological Rube Goldberg machine, or a Jackson Pollock as executed by a cornpone Walt Disney.

Some readers will be charmed to the point of falling in love with Mr. Pearson's prose. Others will begin after a while to sense the tedium of self-indulgence. This reviewer ended up at a point somewhere in between—where he laughed out loud every now and then, but also found himself occasionally gritting his teeth.

What ultimately elevates *A Short History of a Small Place* are the rare moments when the narrator's own voice interrupts the grown-up gossip he is so adept at reporting. In one curious passage, Louis describes the experience of seeing his mother turn on the porch light as he and his father are leaving their house: "And I said to myself without really saying it but just knowing it right off, this is the sort of thing that sets me apart from Daddy and him from me and both of us from everybody else, not simply that I saw the porch light come on and he didn't and nobody else would care anyway, but more that Momma could switch on a single bulb and switch on something in me with it, something of sadness and grief and shot through with the melancholy of twilight, something I could not be sure Daddy would know as I knew it, feel as I felt it."

Such a passage, so at odds with the novel's relentless hyperbole, makes one wonder if in writing this novel Mr. Pearson hasn't been acquitting himself of an obligation to his ancestry. It's as if he has been stuffed with the oral tradition of his region and been compelled by the weight of history to give voice to it. But now that the grownups in his head have had their say, the child may be ready to begin. Finally, what keeps Mr. Pearson's novel alive is not so much precocious articulateness and compulsive animation, but more the tension created by what young Louis Benfield holds back.

Christopher Lehmann-Haupt, in a review of "A Short History of a Small Place," in The New York Times, *June 20, 1985, p. C24.*

An Excerpt from *A Short History of a Small Place*

Mr. Small pointed up to the rung of the ladder from which Miss Pettigrew's breadsack still dangled and he counted down four rungs from that one and said, "There. That's where she stood." Then he indicated the rung above the one with the breadsack on it and said, "There. That's were she held on." He was not so precise with Mr. Britches and his "There" took in about a fifteen-foot section of ladder. "That's where that monkey hung from," he said, "sometimes headfirst and gripping with his feet." Then Mr. Small told how Miss Pettigrew did not pitch herself off from the ladder but simply let go and fell over backwards, and he said she did not for a moment tend towards tumbling but remained in the horizontal all the way to the ground. Mr. Small said she almost gave the impression of flight, an observation which caused Daddy and Mr. Newberry to look at each other and say more or less at the same time, "Flight?"

Mr. Small was emphatic about Miss Pettigrew's line of descent and he traced it for us with his finger from the breadsack down through the railing and into the rosebush, choosing not to respond to Daddy's question concerning crosswinds. Miss Pettigrew's encounter with the section of fence was given a full reckoning by Mr. Small. He told exactly how she hit it and which pieces she caused to fly up and which pieces she caused to fly out and which pieces she caused to fly down, and then he made a very harsh, unpleasant noise in his throat and said, "There. That's what it sounded like when she landed in the rosebush," which prompted one of the lady customers to pipe in and say yes, she had heard it just that way, precisely that way. Then Mr. Small told how he bolted across the street and discovered that Miss Pettigrew, although noticeably dead, did not appear disfigured or brutalized at all except for the scratches from the rose thorns, and he said it was next to miraculous to him how Miss Pettigrew's hat had managed to remain in its proper place atop her head. "All in all," Mr. Small assured us, "she looked very presentable."

Daddy and Mr. Newberry agreed that Mr. Small's version of what Daddy called Miss Pettigrew's departure from this life was the most satisfying to be had. We heard several afterwards, all of which were secondhand and delivered by men who Daddy said had sat at the feet of Mr. Small, and pretty soon it got to the point that you couldn't turn around without seeing somebody's raised finger caught up in the business of tracing Miss Pettigrew's path to glory. However, no matter how lively and colorful the various accounts we sampled, Daddy and Mr. Newberry stuck by Mr. Small's version. The others did not differ considerably from the original except in authority, but Daddy said that makes a world of difference in this sort of thing.

FRAN SCHUMER

A Short History of a Small Place is regional fiction, but not in the superficial sense the word "regional" has come to connote these days—all those characters running around the K-Mart, quoting Phil Donahue and living in apartment complexes with kidney-shaped pools. The author does not simply toss in references to Moon Pies and then disappoint us with characters who might just as easily have grown up in New York. After finishing this novel, you could say "It could only have happened there," and you would be right.

"There" is Neely, a speck on the map in North Carolina, and the narrator is Louis Benfield, a youth not as wry as Holden Caulfield, but certainly as observant, and with a bigger, even sadder, heart. . . .

And yet despite being mired in melancholy, this is a remarkably funny book. Mr. Pearson even manages to make a suicide, the novel's central action, seem as cheerful as a romp through the park. But this may have to do with Daddy's perspective. "Most people supposed you had to be weak and cowardly to take your own life; Daddy said you had to be brave. . . . I always got

the feeling Daddy would have tried it himself if he didn't have to die from it."

Miss Myra Angelique Pettigrew leaps from the top of the town's water tower to her death, and from there the novel takes off. . . . It is not tragic love that kills Miss Pettigrew, who is less deluded but no less vulnerable than Blanche DuBois. It is betrayal, and this is where the novel gains depth. Only on one level is it a hilarious regional farce. On another, it is about corruption and about people losing heart.

The story survives an unconscionable number of plot twists, but it is the meandering that leads us to the book's heart, which is in each of the pixilated Neelyites. There are the Epperson sisters, who passed from "reasonably normal to unquestionably insane without ever pausing at peculiar"; Uncle Warren, who believed himself to be the King of Prussia until a doctor informed him there was no Prussia anymore and so there was no need for a king (the doctor "called it therapy"); and Casper Epps, who was bad but at least colorful until "salvation and clean living . . . thoroughly washed all the appeal out of him." Miss Bambi Kinch is the anchorwoman from Action News Five, and the way she bungles a story ought to be studied in journalism schools, and probably is; she gets all of the facts but nothing of the truth. (The author is never wicked but does engage in a bit of wrist slapping; therapists, journalists and holy men have their wrists slapped the most.) . . .

There are flaws in *A Short History of a Small Place.* The plot is so encumbered by tangents that a reader is likely to lose sight of the central theme. And the author is so skilled at keeping out of the way that he leaves us hungering for more details about the narrator's life. It would be nice to know why Bumpins died and more about Louis in the chapter entitled "Me." And yet this is more than an impressive debut; it is an accomplishment. If there is some benign God watching over us, we want Him to look upon us with the wisdom and compassion with which Mr. Pearson views his world. The world about Neely is mean and nasty and bitter; that we know. But Mr. Pearson makes it funny and, at worst, only a little sad.

> Fran Schumer, "Crazy Nights and Days in Neely," in The New York Times Book Review, *July 7, 1985, p. 4.*

LINDA BRINSON

By writing an unabashedly Southern novel that is clearly tied to a place and a culture, Tom Pearson has made himself a possible target of sharp criticism from at least two directions.

On the one hand, *A Short History of a Small Place* might not win the hearts of some Yankee critics, who may almost need a translator as they work their way through the easy-going, talkative meanderings. No matter that the publishing establishment has for years, without apology, offered up books that were just as clearly tied to and in the idiom of such worlds as middle-class New York Jews or the Newport summer set. Some New York reviewers already have chastized Pearson for being self-indulgent and a prisoner of his childhood memories, apparently without realizing that most first novelists are.

On the other hand, and perhaps more demanding, will be those readers who are of Pearson's world, those who feel that he is writing their story. I, because I grew up and still live near Pearson's small place, am in this group. I loved the book, I was exasperated by it, I grew impatient with it, I quibbled with it and, by the end, I loved it again. . . .

It took me only a few pages with their generous sprinkling of real place names and highway numbers to know that Neely is in Rockingham County. A few pages more, and I had it narrowed down to a fictitious Reidsville.

A Short History is a comedy, at times to the point of being absurd. Its wild tales and sometimes tongue-in-cheek Southernisms produce many chuckles, a few guffaws and some disbelieving head-shaking. Yet, just as less fragrant elements of life lurk beneath the South's honeysuckle and wisteria, so do some more serious truths lie behind Pearson's zany stories and outlandish characters. . . .

All of this, and a great deal more, is told in a wide-eyed style strongly reminiscent of Huck Finn. The stories unfold in ornate, old-fashioned words in convoluted phrases strung together with lots of whiches and ands and wheres and whiles.

The book is good. It is funny, lively and poignant. As a first novel, it is highly impressive, and Pearson will be an author to watch. The book is not, however, perfect.

It can be overwhelming, and may be best read as what it almost is: a collection of loosely connected short stories. Even a Rockingham County native, steeped in the vernacular, can become dizzy reading too much of *A Short History* in one sitting. There were times when I wanted to throw up my hands and yell "Stop! Enough!" and other times when I found myself wondering how in the world we came to be in the middle of one side story or another.

Now for the quibbles of one who is close to the story: I wish Pearson had not so clearly spelled out the time period of the novel, because it does not ring true. He sets his tale almost in the present, with events happening through the 1970s, and some remembered back into the '60s. The language and some of the mannerisms and events, however, seem of an earlier era.

Louis Jr., for example, often uses the verb "commence." This is a word I remember being uttered by my grandmother and my most elderly aunt, back in the 1960s, but one that I have not heard used in everyday conversation since.

He also talks about the town's Negroes, rather than blacks. I doubt that anyone of the Benfields' social status in Reidsville or Rockingham County or just about anywhere in North Carolina has used that term in conversation since about 1970.

A minor but annoying flaw is his apparent carelessness with a few place names. Having decided to use real places—the state zoo for example—he should have spelled them right. The zoo is at Asheboro, not Ashboro.

Finally, the worst affront to me, a native of Madison, is Pearson's repeated references to Madison-Mayodan. . . .

Madison and Mayodan, the towns, will always be without a hyphen and remain separate because they are just different, Mayodan being a textile mill town and Madison being a tobacco market and shopping sort of town, even if the country club out near Stoneville has sort of brought together the rich people from both towns, not to mention those who would like to be rich. But that's another story.

Small places can be great fun, and, as T. R. Pearson well knows, there's always another story.

I'll be eager to hear him tell them.

> *Linda Brinson, "Wild Tales, Southern Style," in* Winston-Salem Journal, *July 14, 1985, p. C8.*

TOM NOLAN

The chief explainer and first-person tour guide throughout [*A Short History of a Small Place*] is a boy named Louis Benfield, born in 1963. . . . "According to Daddy," the junior Louis will say, or, "Daddy said," or, "As Daddy recalled it"—a conversational tic that never ceases even in the midst of the most complicated and baroquely detailed anecdote, this being only one of a whole repertoire of regional affectations and storytelling mannerisms that more than occasionally inspire the urge to grab the speaker by the scruff of the neck and shout, "Say it! Say it! Say it! Say it!"

But Neelyites are not to be rushed. They live life at their own strange thoughtful pace—observing, reflecting, gawping, absorbing—savoring every nuance of event. This creates a curious tension, a motion at once pulling backward and forward. Neelyites are like distance swimmers battling a tide of molasses. Neelyites live in their own timeless self-contained world—a tiny town sealed inside of a bell jar, where everyone's a bit giddy and simple from lack of air. . . .

But not to exaggerate the threads of insanity running through this crazy quilt, I hasten to say that drollery is more common here than dementia; hilarity, not hysterics, is the Neely norm. And *A Short History* is a veritable gallimaufry of piney-woods humor. A cast of about a hundred demonstrates great talent for idiosyncrasy, and several extended set pieces are laugh-out-loud funny: church services and afternoon socials that gallop out of control like an Oldsmobile with a chimp at the wheel.

The tone is sustained to near perfection; Pearson's control of his material is almost absolute. Once or twice the tomfoolery descends to the level of Lum 'n' Abner slapstick, but most often the apt comparison is Twain.

Some things, though, like Miss Pettigrew's fatal leap, cannot be laughed away. It comes to seem as if the most sensitive folk in Neely—young Louis and his parents, say—are sometimes maybe chuckling just to keep the sobs or sighs or screams from seeping out. In the end, all the narrator's father can tell him is, "Louis, you have to bend some. . . . You have to sway a little every now and again, don't you know." Beyond that, young Louis—like all of us—will have to figure out the rest for himself.

> *Tom Nolan, in a review of "A Short History of a Small Place," in* Los Angeles Times Book Review, *September 8, 1985, p. 3.*

Joan K. Peters

1945-

American novelist.

In *Manny & Rose* (1985), a first novel set in 1970s-era Manhattan, Peters dramatizes the physical and emotional decline of Manny, a retired accountant, after the death of his wife Rose. Contrasted with Manny's reaction is that of his daughter Ellen, who retreats to a local Indian ashram. Reviewers were particularly impressed by Peters's realistic and compassionate portrayal of Manny, whose grief leads to his gradual withdrawal from life. Critics observe that in combining a simple structure with well-drawn characters Peters has created a moving story.

PUBLISHERS WEEKLY

Bits of septuagenarian Manny Herman slip away [in *Manny & Rose*], as he tries to recapture the once-overpowering presence of his wife, Rose, dead now of cancer. His stock of memories dwindles and he is left only with his diminished self: an accountant no longer concerned with the net worth of his clients; a father unrelated to a daughter with a revolutionary worldview and a penchant for transcendental meditation; a grandfather chanting lullabies in Yiddish to a granddaughter who laughs uncomprehendingly. His realities amount to a handful of embroideries left by Rose, and buck-toothed Miss Liu, Rose's Chinese nurse. But Miss Liu is going back to Taiwan, Ellen is spending a month in an ashram, his secretary and two business partners are on vacation. Manny's existence condenses to a walk to the park, a piece of fruit for nourishment; his life force ebbs. By the time Ellen rushes home from the ashram, it is too late to restore him to the world. The novel, simply and movingly told, etches itself on the heart; Manny and his family cannot be forgotten.

A review of "Manny & Rose," in Publishers Weekly, *Vol. 227, No. 15, April 12, 1985, p. 89.*

KIRKUS REVIEWS

After Rose Herman dies following a terminal illness, cast adrift are her husband, 74-year-old accountant Manny, and her social-worker daughter Ellen. But the family bonds, however close, were never harmonious. Rose was contentious, moody, quick-tempered, and despairing; Manny was and is resentful (and half-relieved at her going); and Ellen—who's never quite found peace in her own husband and child, and who's turned to study with a guru—is the last triangulation point in a constellation of incessant mutual disappointment and familial chafe.

Peters, in her first novel [*Manny & Rose*], does a number of thorny things quite well. The scenes of acrimonious shiva-sitting in Manny's Queens apartment after Rose's death are splendid, rich with emotional posturing and the settling of old scores. Manny's new widowerhood (destined not to last long:

© Jerry Bauer

he'll die soon after Rose, lost utterly into memories less than fully nourishing) is credibly seedy, specific, and sad. A general mood of strain impresses, of blood lessons that might yet be learnt . . . and aren't.

So heralded here is a feeling-filled (and brave-feeling) fiction writer. As a novel, Peters' debut is less than perfect, though: it's got something too stretchy about it, too pulled: the sections about Ellen's abdication to the upstate N.Y. ashram, leaving her father and her husband and her daughter at a most painful moment of aftermath, don't feel of a piece with the rest of the story, and contribute little tension or drive. Two-thirds, then, of a promising and vivid novel—one third filler. (pp. 442-43)

A review of "Manny & Rose," in Kirkus Reviews, *Vol. LIII, No. 10, May 15, 1985, pp. 442-43.*

JENNIFER CRICHTON

Set in the mid-70s, [*Manny & Rose*] carries a sense of that decade's malaise with it. Rose, a domineering wife and mother, dies as the novel opens. Manny, a passive accountant who has never managed to please his wife, daughter, or self, slips into old age with that death. And Ellen, her back turned on her parents' suffocating life, pursues salvation fruitlessly in yoga ashrams and spiritual masters; rejection of her parents is as oppressive as acceptance. What one might have expected—a grudging resolution, a coming to terms—never actually occurs. Peters' depiction of Manny at death's door is moving and her gift as a writer is such that we feel as trapped as Ellen in her parents' stuffy apartment and wish Ellen could break through into light, air, humor, if only so that we might escape with her.

Jennifer Crichton, in a review of "Manny & Rose," in Ms., *Vol. XIII, No. 12, June, 1985, p. 68.*

ALISON B. CARB

Manny & Rose is a stirring first novel about the foundering relationship between a 73-year-old accountant named Manny and his radical daughter, Ellen, who confront each other after the death of his wife and her mother, the overpowering Rose. . . . Joan K. Peters develops her characters nicely, even minor ones like Ellen's best friend, Kirstan, and her acquaintance at the commune, Jyoti. The novel's imagery is sensual and poetic. Striving to recapture her mother's presence, Ellen sits on the grass near a rosebush and "touched the flesh of a bud, its yellow skin so intimate, she leaned over and kissed its lip-smooth perfect petal." Generally such lyrical passages are juxtaposed with sharp dialogue. The book's major imperfection is its tendency to be a bit too sentimental at times, as in Ellen's observation about the frailty of human bonds: "So many things seemed to slip away and finish, leaving nothing in their place." The few attempts at humor are flat; the book needs comic relief. But despite some blemishes, this is a timely novel in our era of disintegrating families.

Alison B. Carb, in a review of "Manny & Rose," in The New York Times Book Review, *July 7, 1985, p. 16.*

An Excerpt from *Manny & Rose*

In his green chair, he waited for six o'clock, then hurried down the hall to the Goldfarbs' door. Before he arrived, he was already nervous about having to leave and what he would do by himself. Sylvia was a bit formal, he thought, but they talked about Pittsburgh. They had seen their new grandchild, they had taken the kids to a fancy restaurant on a mountain overlooking the city, they'd sat in a park where two rivers came together. Mac somehow got on to his father, who was sick and couldn't get out to play cards any more. Then Manny told about how his father had won a hundred dollars in the numbers once. "My mother," he said, "set him straight. My mother could have set Attila the Hun straight, believe you me." Sylvia and Mac laughed and slapped their cheeks. He knew he couldn't stay much longer and got nervous again. Did they know they had musicians on the street now and actors sometimes? There's a man who plays the saxophone and someone who does pantomime on the steps of the Forty-second Street Library. He saw a girl on the train with a hand like an ape. Sylvia put the coffee cups in the sink. There's a man on his corner near work who

talks about a planet where everyone is blue. Mac mumbled that they should be locked away.

Manny was relieved when Mac offered him some schnapps and blurted out that Ellen had gone to a religious community while her husband Mark and Lizzie went to the Grand Canyon. What did they think? What would they do? Sylvia said she wouldn't know. Her daughter lived eight blocks away. "Those gurus make $40,000 a year and drive around in Cadillacs," Mac said. He'd read it in the papers. No one spoke. Manny was sorry that he'd said anything. It made them uncomfortable.

"Thank you," Manny said. Sylvia seemed especially appreciative he was leaving early. She came running toward him with a package in a supermarket bag.

"Here, take this," she said. "It's a sirloin steak. You'll put it under the broiler tomorrow. I bought too much for us." The brown bag was moist from the refrigerator. Manny saw that Sylvia was letting him know that he wouldn't be eating with them every night. He cradled the package and padded back down the hall.

The apartment was dark. He hadn't turned the lights on before he left. He thought he saw his father staring blankly out the window. A wave of panic passed through his body. He threw the package into the kitchen sink and went into the bedroom. Peeling off his clothes, he heard Dr. Katz' voice: "You have to begin again, Manny." Liu sat with her teacup. "But I am going home soon." Rose's frightened eyes followed him everywhere. Ellen was marching in a procession in the oriental mountains. Without switching on the air conditioner, Manny slipped into bed and pulled the comforter over him.

JACQUELINE AUSTIN

Having sighed and laughed over Philip Roth and Saul Bellow, I'm finding it a bit difficult these days to be thrilled by new American Jewish Novels, especially those that explore the relationships of adult children with elderly parents, and those about coming to terms with one's identity in the '60s or '70s. Many recent AJNs have seemed slight, bitter, derivative, or pretentious. As Ted Solotaroff once said in an essay on Jewish camp, "This fiction, so its reputation goes, is full of 'invention' (imagination, vitality, wildness, etc.) and it is 'human' (compassionate, loving, radiant with insight, etc.). Since genuine vitality and humanity are in short supply these days in fiction, as everywhere else, one can understand why they should be so much appreciated and why pretensions to them should be so easily confused with the real thing."

So why get all excited about *Manny & Rose?* It's in many ways a standard AJN: Mom dies, Pop mourns, sarcastic daughter attempts to deny her heritage, trots off to find herself in a commune. Present and accounted for all those various muttering *Tantes,* glowing *maidelehs,* and folksy co-workers without which an AJN just would not fly, as well as a complete and representative AJN supporting cast including a Chinese nurse, an awkward hubby, a consciousness-raising best buddy, a wise old guru, a handsome six-foot-tall male flower child with whom sarcastic daughter can have affair, plus assorted New York townsfolk for added local color. Yet *Manny & Rose* is a bona fide treat. It shines with invention and humanity, minus the quotation marks, and its attitude of imaginative compassion is real, not superimposed.

The novel is simple in structure. Rose Herman, wife of Manny and mother of Ellen, has just died of cancer at Mount Sinai Hospital. Manny mourns, not the way people generally mourn in novels, but the way they do in life, with irreverent reflections ("Dark hair had grown in her mustache"), euphoria ("As for why he was chuckling he didn't know but he felt oddly cozy"), annoyance at the interruption of his routine ("In the months Rose had been there, Manny realized, the hospital had become his home"). Peters uses more conventional traits—numbness, time compressions, flashbacks, displacement of feeling for the deceased onto others—to construct a long opening chapter which encapsulates much of the rest of the novel from Manny's point of view. Later, daughter Ellen goes through her own idiosyncratic process of bereavement. Having rejected Rose while she lived, Ellen slowly comes to accept that her mother meant a great deal to her. After immersing herself in work, neglecting Manny, and running for psychic help to her swami, she finally returns, too late, to help her father, who dies.

The thing that's immediately wonderful about **Manny & Rose** is its grace. This is a first novel that finds itself on Page 1, Sentence 1 ("Someone murmured 'Mr. Herman' twice, three times, but Manny sank back into the rock of sleep"), and manages not to lose itself at any time along the way. Peters balances herself between intimacy and distance, melodrama and restraint. She winds in and out of everyone's minds with taste, verity, and a fine sense of timing; she doesn't miss a beat. Manny's progression through shock, bereavement, and self-imposed starvation seems not only natural, but inevitable—to be accepted, even laughed with, if sadly. Peters never turns her characters into camp, though in a clumsier or snider writer's hands they might be easily exploitable as jokes. She loves her characters, and lives with them, but manages not to sink with them.

The emphases on family and death are both classically AJN, as is the tone of affectionate sarcasm, at once biting and gentle, with which characters are presented. What is unusual here is the depiction of change. Ellen and her husband Mark, at the book's opening, are selfish and generous, conciliatory and argumentative. At the end, they let themselves be carried away by Manny's death: "She got up and they hugged without kissing, her arms under his, clasped around the back. With one hand, he stroked her hair. . . . They did not move, except for his hand." Manny, after Rose's death and before his own, changes even more radically: he mourns, liberates himself (he thinks) from Rose, falls in love, abandons work. Unlike many characters in AJN novels, Peters's people rise to their occasions.

Given the quantity of AJNs and the nauseating smugness of many new AJN writers, it's more than heartening to find a member of the species who declines to sneer, either at herself or others, and who permits her entities the same latitude of action that she would presumably want for herself. May Peters write forever. May she never descend to camp.

Jacqueline Austin, "Death in the Family," in The Village Voice, *Vol. XXX, No. 31, July 30, 1985, p. 49.*

*Property
Ithaca High School Library
Ithaca, Michigan*

Cecile Pineda

1942-

American novelist, dramatist, short story writer, poet, and essayist.

Face (1985), Pineda's first novel, is an allegorical exploration of the fragile nature of human identity. Pineda was the founder of the San Francisco-based experimental Theatre of Man ensemble, and for twelve years worked with the troupe as a writer, director, and producer. She states that her literary influences are "metaphysical writers; that is to say that under the apparent surface of their narrative, there is a reflection of the ultimate things. Their concerns leave questions reverberating in the mind long after the book is closed once more. Questions having to do with who are we, and why are we here, and how are we here? And how does it come to be that this is the way of things? And, if so, why not another?"

Face is a fictionalized retelling of a newspaper item Pineda discovered in 1977, about a grievously disfigured barber from the Brazilian slums. Denied recourse to conventional plastic surgery, the barber performs reconstructive operations on his own face. Pineda presents the barber's story in a series of brief segments interspersed with dreams and flashbacks. While observing that Pineda does not fully exploit the artistic possibilities of her subject, critics acknowledge the competency of the medical details presented and credit the author for attempting this real and symbolic tale of identity. Commentators note that, although stark and unrelenting, Pineda's depiction of the barber's sufferings emerges as a suprising affirmation of spiritual strength.

Pineda reports that she is currently working on her second novel, *Frieze,* set in Java and India during the ninth century: "Like *Face,* it is a parable, but whereas *Face* has seven levels of meaning and a structure patterned on damped oscillations, *Frieze* has fewer layers of meaning, and is patterned on a circle."

© 1986 Thomas Victor

KIRKUS REVIEWS

[In *Face,*] Helio Cara, a 36-year-old Brazilian barber, is unimaginably disfigured in a fall down some harbor steps: he's left virtually without a face—and the rest of his life soon disappears as well. The crude rubber mask they give him at the hospital is unwearable; in quick succession he loses his job, his girlfriend, his shack in the slums. He batters and rapes the girlfriend in frustration; he rummages for food at night, becoming a completely underground creature—virtually invisible, except for his hat and the white handkerchief he wears over his destroyed visage. True, after terrible bureaucratic coldness, Helio does at last discover a plastic surgeon who agrees—for free—to experimentally reconstruct the face. But, by this time, poor Helio is exhausted, homeless, at wit's end, and—not very plausibly—he refuses the surgeon's offer. Instead, he leaves Rio to go home to the country—where his mother is now dead, where no one is likely to know him by sight any more. And, after securing subsistence wages by becoming a water-bearer, Helio sets out—with some success—to perform rudimentary plastic surgery (first scar excision, then actual reconstruction) on *himself*. First-novelist Pineda, with details (the use of lidocaine) and background texture (Helio's barbering expertise), manages to make this self-surgery seem at least semi-convincing. Unfortunately, however, she doesn't quite have the narrative skills to convey the intensity of this potentially remarkable story: her chapters are too short, and the horror is compacted into melodramatic cadences that never really build or intensify. ("What pain would he have to accept to remake it? Was his pain enough to make that pain less? Everywhere he went, he had been searched out, found out, smoked out like vermin in rotting wood.") Stark and disastrous in outline, but without the compelling or affecting power that such extreme subject-matter should generate in fiction form.

A review of "Face," in Kirkus Reviews, *Vol. LIII, No. 3, February 1, 1985, p. 108.*

PUBLISHERS WEEKLY

This thoughtful, well-written first novel—[*Face*] doesn't quite live up to its considerable ambitions, but it's a promising debut for a talented writer. . . . The theme of devising a new identity is compelling, and Pineda handles it well, but the subsidiary tale of Helio's parents isn't closely enough integrated with the main story of Helio's degradation and redemption. Nonetheless, *Face* grapples with important issues in an interesting way.

> *A review of "Face," in* Publishers Weekly, *Vol. 227, No. 6, February 8, 1985, p. 70.*

DIANE COLE

Cecile Pineda's *Face* gives us nothing if not a nightmare vision of the world. Helio Cara falls from a Brazilian cliff and awakens to discover that his face has been disfigured beyond recognition. Kafkaesque insurance regulations disqualify him from plastic surgery, and so he is given a rubber mask to wear—he soon replaces this with a plain white handkerchief—and is carelessly discharged from the charity hospital.

The story, based on a true incident, resonates as metaphor: without a face to identify him, Helio loses his identity as a human. Before long his neighbors, friends, and colleagues begin to shun him as a monstrous outcast, an animal in human form. But the human spirit does not die so easily. Against all odds, Helio escapes to an inland village and there, with stolen medical manuals, secretly begins the work of reconstructing his face and his life.

Pineda, who has previously worked in the theater rather than with the printed word, adds poignance and avoids melodrama by revealing the story gradually, through a series of brief, understated, dreamlike fragments and flashbacks. There is dignity and beauty in these spare scenes. Only a tendency to be self-consciously "poetic" mars the book: "The questions dangle unanswered like paper stars suspended in a ballroom firmament, always unanswered." The story speaks powerfully enough for itself. (p. 15)

> *Diane Cole, "The Pick of the Crop: Five First Novels," in* Ms., *Vol. XIII, No. 10, April, 1985, pp. 14-15.**

CATHY COLMAN

Cecile Pineda's lucid first novel [*Face*] explores the darkness of human nature. Helio Cara's real-life nightmare begins with a fall from a cliff . . . that leaves him horribly disfigured. In a mirror, "someone stands weaving before him on unsteady legs, something without nose or mouth, eyes dark purple splotches, sealed almost shut. . . . *Not me! Not me!*" He could emerge from this ordeal transformed and triumphant, or be left to die in despair. Transfixed by Miss Pineda's mixing of past and present, dream and reality, we follow Cara after his fall, symbolically a fall from innocence, as he comes to know evil and brutality. . . . Using medical manuals, razor blades and local anesthetic, he begins to reconstruct his face. It is here that the author reveals the immense power of human will and obsession. The rhythms of the author's language invoke the way Cara's thoughts oscillate between terror and illumination. Had Miss Pineda created for Cara a central relationship with another character (even an antagonistic one) during his attempt to heal his physical and spiritual wounds, the novel would have had greater resonance. Yet taking off from a brief account of

an actual incident, she has achieved an original, complex portrait of survival.

> *Cathy Colman, in a review of "Face," in* The New York Times Book Review, *April 28, 1985, p. 24.*

An Excerpt from *Face*

In the street he wears the white handkerchief. He has worn it for—how long? A month? Since the first stone seemed to fly through his window of its own accord one morning. It was not to be the last.

He sits on the step overlooking the bay. From here he can see the stairs. Was it raining then? He still has trouble remembering. There was a wind. Of that he is certain. From the top he could see the bay, grey then, grey sky, water color of lead. He remembers the feeling he had of being pressed. Was there a letter, perhaps? Or a telegram? At first he only vaguely remembers. Later it seems to him as though someone had died.

Why was he unable to remember clearly? Had he been thinking at all in the first days as he lay in his cocoon of bandages? Or were his thoughts of a different kind? Was he perhaps without consciousness for a very long time? Or only sleeping? Was it the pain that allowed him to wake only for brief moments at a time? And where were the days that were lost to him, the ones that occupied his memory only by their absence? Had he perhaps died a little?

He could imagine taking his life—the old one, before—taking it off like a coat and leaving it, on this step perhaps, high, overlooking the bay, and quite calmly walking away, leaving it there, still warm. Would someone find it, try it on perhaps, enter it seamlessly, wear it like a sleeve—Lula, the barber shop—without thinking about it? Perhaps even now there was someone inhabiting his old life, someone other than he, before this had happened to him; someone with a face, not even necessarily much like his had been before, but a face that could be worn, even in daylight—at noon perhaps—in the street.

What if it had been that way? No pain. Removing it, peeling it from him like a layer of being, leaving it sprawled on a bench. And what was left of his old life before the fall? The barber shop, the boss, Mario, they had all vanished. They were carrying on without him, had been now for nearly a season. And the boss must be cleaning up. With the apprentice there was even less to pay. And his mother? Had he ever known her to live anywhere else? Yet now, in the high village of the Interior, her wooden shack gaped empty, the shell of her passing. And somewhere in the Capital, sprawling there far below him, probably without giving him a passing thought, Lula. . . .

The sky turns wet. Cold seeps through his shirtsleeves. The clouds still melt.

SHELLY LOWENKOPF

In this stark, relentless tale [*Face*] Cecile Pineda, a new American novelist, transforms our dread fears of disfigurement and ugliness into a plangent epiphany of human spirit. (p. 2)

Because of the Brazilian setting, the lean prose, and the subtextual anguish shouting like macaws in a tropical jungle, Pineda will be compared to Cortazar, Borges and Marquez. Compare away, if you must; if Pineda is like any Latin, she is like Manuel Puig, who squeezes the forces of life from his themes. Pineda, a San Franciscan, has had considerable experience with the stage, which should be given its proper due in noting her evocative, nonjudgmental prose, which clings to our sensibilities the way Cara's rubber mask clung to his face in the oppressive Brazilian humidity.

Pineda picked up the concept for *Face* from a media account. But she has breathed the life of drama, the morality of the novel, and her own special grace into what she found. Cheers to her. (p. 10)

> *Shelly Lowenkopf, in a review of "Face," in* Los Angeles Times Book Review, *June 23, 1985, pp. 2, 10.*

JOHN CLUTE

Cecile Pineda cannot be accused of lacking ambition. In *Face*, her first novel, she plunges headlong into a metaphysical and poetic assault on the theme of identity, as her title hints forthrightly. She has not brought much that is new to the topic, but the story she tells is of some interest. . . .

The implications of the tale [of Helio the barber] are all too clear, and it must be said that in novels like *The Face of Another*

(1964) and *The Box Man* (1973), the Japanese novelist Kobo Abe has gone a long way towards exhausting them. Pineda is no more than competent in presenting the technology of the re-creation of the human face; in any of a half-dozen or more science fiction novels, this technology, and the questions surrounding its use, have been treated with more sophistication. The humid density of Pineda's Brazil is occasionally gripping, and the poetic earnestness of her identification with the young barber sometimes touching; but even he remains, in more senses than the literal, a man without a face.

> *John Clute, "Stitched Up," in* The Times Literary Supplement, *No. 4315, December 13, 1985, p. 1434.*

COMMENTS OF CECILE PINEDA TO *CLC YEARBOOK*

Pineda comments on the process of writing *Face:* "The writing stood in place of journal entries I might make. There were fallow periods, but apart from them, most of the writing occured from 4 A.M. to dawn; the time of day is reflected in the narrative. Many of the protagonist's dreams were my own dreams during and before the period of writing. Others, of course, were invented."

Asked about her motivation for writing, Pineda responds: "Life and the living of it prompts the writing, an attempt to make sense of an alien, chaotic, exterminating world.

"Although I don't believe the human imagination will ever have the kind of perverted power we see, for example, among politicians and generals, responsible writing can remind us of what it must have been like to be human, of what it might have been like to belong to a blessed community."

Mary-Ann Tirone Smith

1944-

American novelist.

The heroine of Smith's first novel, *The Book of Phoebe* (1985), endeared herself to many critics with her wit, courage, and irrepressible verve. In her own words Phoebe relates how at nineteen she left Yale for Paris, ostensibly on a study trip, in order to give birth to an illegitimate baby. Interspersed with her narrative are diary entries written by Phoebe as a thirteen-year-old in which she records her campaign to get help for her neglected schizophrenic cousin Tyrus, who believes he is General Patton, among others. "The character Tyrus is based on my brother, Tyler Besette Tirone," Smith says, "who also thought he was any number of World War II military leaders. I was usually the target of his bombing raids. Many incidents which took place in my extended family were transferred to *The Book of Phoebe*." Several critics observe that Phoebe's adventures, particularly her idealized romance with a Parisian painter, weaken the novel by portraying wish-fulfillment fantasies rather than realistic possibilities. Most writers, however, praise Smith's humorous, affecting characterization of the spirited Phoebe.

Smith, who attended Central Connecticut State University, the University of Hawaii, and Columbia University, spent two years in West Cameroon as a Peace Corps volunteer before settling in Connecticut, where she now teaches at Fairfield University. Asked about her future publishing plans, Smith replied, "I wrote a terrific mystery, *No Reckoning with the Dead,* but no one knows what to do with it because I'm not Norman Mailer." She describes her novel-in-progress, *Innocents and Sharks,* as a story "about two women from the time they meet at age 13 in 1956 and what happens to them until 1988. The backdrops are: Norwalk, CT, Bryn Mawr, the University of Hawaii, Columbia U., West Africa, Italy, and the Palestinian refugee camps of Beirut."

© Jerry Bauer

KIRKUS REVIEWS

At its best this first novel [*The Book of Phoebe*] is spirited and amusing in a smart-alecky way, the first person story of a young student at Yale, who discovers she is pregnant and, ditching her "shit-heel" lover, goes to Paris for six months to have the baby and find a good home for it. At its worst, it is glib and facilely plotted, sentimental, trading in stereotypes.

Phoebe, the heroine, gets in touch with her childhood friend, Marlys, now a star at the Folies Bergere. Marlys is black, and—an example of the book's glibness—consequently has a debt of gratitude to discharge to Phoebe: "This is your turn to be a pest," she says, "which will never make up for all the times I came up to your room and cried about the torment that goes along with being black and you took all my misery so seriously."

Unfortunately, Marlys turns out to be of minimal help to Phoebe, being surrounded constantly by photographers, magazine writers, and other hangers-on befitting her stardom. Not to mention the fact—an example of the book's tendency toward cliché—that she is protecting a secret: the naked glamour girl, lusted after by men by the thousands every night, turns out to be in love with her prim secretary Barbara.

But Marlys does do her friend the favor of setting her up with a place to live, with one Ben Reuben, an American painter. Needless to say, the inevitable happens, with implausible swiftness, mutuality and totality. Ben and Phoebe are instantly lovers, and she takes him into her confidence about a part of her past that we are to believe has always haunted her, and constituted one of the main reasons why she did not abort the baby she is carrying. We learn about this episode from Phoebe's journal, in which she recounts her single-handed attempt, at age 13, to "mainstream" her mentally limited cousin, Tyrus, who had never in thirty-nine years left the attic in which he grew up. Phoebe believes herself to be responsible for his death

. . . and believes that the child she is carrying will, in some mystical manner, allow him to be born again. Her guilt is that she lured him from his attic out into the real world, and in a climactic and hard-to-swallow scene, she and Tyrus took over Grant's Tomb, an event televised nationwide. Phoebe demanded to speak with Sargent Shriver and to him she stated the purpose of this media stunt: for Tyrus to go, all expenses paid, to the best mental health facility available. Shriver obliged her.

Inevitably, by failing to make us fully believe in the events of her story, the author has also failed to make us care much. Breezy, Salinger-ish (not coincidentally, Phoebe is named for Holden Caulfield's sister), and rife with easy sentimentality, this book would probably be most appealing to mid to late teens, if the sex and profanity didn't make that a somewhat dicey proposition. (pp. 346-47)

A review of ''The Book of Phoebe,'' in Kirkus Reviews, *Vol. LIII, No. 8, April 15, 1985, pp. 346-47.*

PUBLISHERS WEEKLY

If Holden Caulfield's sister had written a book, this [*The Book of Phoebe*] would be it. In *Catcher in the Rye,* her name was Phoebe too, and this Phoebe, whose intuitive grasp of emotional nuance and sense of humor sustain her through the wrenching experiences of unplanned motherhood, dropping out of Yale, and falling in love with an artist on the banks of the Seine, could be she, grownup and groping, but never at a loss for the irreverent. This first novel by Smith is no imitation of Salinger, however. It's an original, engaging and very funny story of a young woman whose sharp mind fashions verbal adventure out of her unhappy encounters and makes some impossible situations bearable with wit and insight. In Paris, where she goes to wait out her pregnancy and escape a lover, Phoebe finds something to believe in again, even if she is left with a familiar bittersweet aftertaste. An accomplished writer is at work here; Phoebe—vibrant, gallant, vulnerable—is a character we will not easily forget.

A review of ''The Book of Phoebe,'' in Publishers Weekly, *Vol. 227, No. 17, April 26, 1985, p. 69.*

DONNA KITTA

[In *The Book of Phoebe*] Phoebe Desmond is a plucky, ''gifted'' Yalie who gets pregnant by a casual, dislikable lover. She takes a semester off, goes to Paris (where her girlhood friend Marlys Hightower lives), has the baby, and gives it away. Marlys not only arranges for Phoebe to stay with a fabulously wealthy, gentle, and virile painter who falls madly in love with her, but also finds a perfect French couple to adopt the baby. This ease and dazzle is in brilliant contrast to the other *The Book of Phoebe,* which consists of long sections of the heroine's alleged childhood journal. By far the strongest half of this remarkable first novel, Phoebe's journal tells of her kidnapping by an eccentric yet kind band of thieves and of her patient, bold love for the mad, attic-bound Tyrus. Mary-Ann Tirone Smith writes with an X-acto blade wit, feisty assurance, and timing that rivals that of the best stand-up comedians; her cleverness and finesse, however, are not mere artifice. She treats birth, war, death, love, and risk with a fresh, potent mix of femininity, verve, and imagination. A very special literary debut.

Donna Kitta, in a review of ''The Book of Phoebe,'' in Booklist, *Vol. 81, No. 18, May 15, 1985, p. 1274.*

An Excerpt from *The Book of Phoebe*

With my dad gone, my mother didn't cry. ''You haven't grown up yet, have you, Phoebe? After all these years you're going to pull one of your silly stunts that could ruin your entire life.''

''Ma, Paris isn't a silly stunt. I'll get some course credit. I'll be back at Yale in February.''

''Your Great-aunt Virginia's son left college and never went back.''

''Virginia's son enlisted in the Navy. Rest assured I will not choose the Navy over Yale.''

''You'll miss your graduation ceremonies.''

''I'll get you tickets, anyway. You'll never miss me. Oh, Ma, this is important. I will broaden my perspective in Paris. It's time I left this country and looked at things from an international viewpoint.''

My dad stuck his head in the doorway, ''What's wrong with this country?''

''Who cares, Dad? Listen, I don't have to tell you all this. I'm doing it to be civil. I have a full scholarship to Yale, and I work for my expense money.''

''You've been living under my roof all summer.''

''You sound like Ann Landers. Throw me out. I'll find a place to stay till I go.''

''Where? Or have those queers asked you to live with them?''

''What's wrong with that? I should think that would make you happy. I could walk around naked in front of them, and all they would say is 'Oh, yuck!' '' . . .

My mother sighed. ''Phoebe, I've never worried about your being unable to take care of yourself, but Paris . . . and that Marlys! She leads a wild life now.''

''We don't know that, Ma. She's a dancer. An especially illustrious one. If the jet set or whatever chose to adopt her, she's still my old pal Marlys. This is very generous of her. I can't pass up such an opportunity. Yale thinks it's wonderful.''

''Yale does? Oh. Well, maybe it will help you decide what you want to do with your life once your education is through.''

My dad was back. ''If it's ever through.''

I ignored him. ''Maybe, Ma. Maybe I'll find my destiny in Paris. In fact, I hope so. I really do.''

''Phoebe?''

''Yeah, Ma?''

''I hope you won't be a dancer.''

''You have to be beautiful to dance, Ma, otherwise you look like an idiot.''

''You are beautiful, Phoebe.''

"Thanks, Ma, but I'm not." Some day, though, I will be. Right now I couldn't handle beautiful. Gifted is plenty. Pregnant, more so.

REBECCA GOLDSTEIN

Holden Caulfield, the hero of what was *the* coming-of-age novel for several generations, had a little sister named Phoebe, of whom he was touchingly proud. She was only 10 years old, but already she was writing books—which she never finished— and seemed an appealingly quirky little kid. Phoebe Desmond's mother took *The Catcher in the Rye* so to heart that it determined her first child's name. And this first novel [*The Book of Phoebe*] is that child's own coming-of-age story, told in a voice one could easily imagine as the precocious Phoebe Caulfield's own. At least there is something more than faintly reminiscent of Holden's voice, with the achingly sensitive passivity replaced by a confident activism. But there is the old Caulfield impatience with phoniness, which, together with an adolescent awkwardness and gaucheness, provide much of the humor of this very funny book.

Phoebe Desmond is such an activist that at the age of 13 she takes over Grant's Tomb together with her disturbed cousin, Tyrus, to call attention to the plight of the mentally handicapped. And she is so confident that when she learns she is pregnant, at the age of 19 and three weeks into her first love affair, she takes a leave of absence from Yale and goes to Paris to have the baby. She is determined no one will know of its existence, most particularly, the father, who turns out to be undeserving of both Phoebe and their progeny: "Falling immediately out of love with him, I looked into his sly hazel eyes for the last time, and I will go to the grave knowing that he'll never know he had a baby."

Phoebe chooses to hide out in Paris because her very best friend, Marlys, lives there. Phoebe counts on Marlys to help her through the pregnancy, and Marlys is clearly a woman who can get things done. She is, like Phoebe, gifted. (*This* Phoebe, having no older brother to sing her praises, must tell us herself, and often, how smart she is.) But instead of going to Yale or Harvard, Marlys, who is black, decided to chuck it all and go to Paris, where in less than six months she becomes a famous American expatriate. The star of the Folies-Bergère, she is "the toast of the town; the Josephine Baker of the eighties." Because Marlys is so busy, she arranges for Phoebe to live with a young artist named Ben Reuben, with whom Phoebe immediately falls in love: "A person like me who tends to fall victim so effortlessly to love at first sight also tends not to learn from experience. At Yale it had taken two meetings. In Paris it was taking two seconds." Fortunately for Phoebe, Ben also falls effortlessly in love.

When Ben asks Phoebe why she hadn't chosen to have an abortion we learn of the sad and funny friendship of a younger Phoebe and the mad middle-aged Tyrus. She hands Ben a journal. He reads, and so do we. The inventive 13-year-old had turned the facts of the story into wild fiction—as if the facts weren't wild enough—so that her aunts and uncles and cousins become crooks and kidnappers. But Phoebe swears to Ben that all the facts about Tyrus are true. He had been kept hidden in the family attic since he was 9 years old and there occupied himself listening to polka records, reading heavy tomes about the Second World War and believing himself to be Gen. George Patton and other sundry World War II characters. The family loves and protects him but thinks he's retarded. Phoebe tries to explain to them that retarded people don't spend all their time reading. His delusions are quite funny, of course, but there is nothing mean-spirited about the laughter they provoke. Just like Phoebe, one smiles at Tyrus with a tug at the heart for he is as trusting and vulnerable as a child. Or, as the young Phoebe herself puts it: "It's my belief that kids and mentally ill people have quite a lot in common." The sad ending of the tale of Tyrus explains why Phoebe decides to carry her baby to term.

Ben doesn't read the journal at one sitting, so the story of Phoebe and Tyrus is interspersed with the story of Phoebe and Ben. It is probably a measure of my involvement in both tales that I found myself becoming annoyed each time Ben either takes up or leaves off reading the journal. The technical difficulties involved in weaving together the two tales are for the most part worked out quite neatly. Paramount among these, perhaps, is adjusting Phoebe's two voices so that the reader believes the 13-year-old in the diary could grow up to be the 19-year-old who runs off to Paris. I'm not sure this problem is worked out entirely. The younger Phoebe's powers of expression are so extraordinary for a child of her age that, despite self-avowals of giftedness, they approach the borders of unbelievability. The elder Phoebe does not seem to have made any substantial progress beyond her former precocious self. Where, we might ask, are the signs of the three and a half years she has studied at Yale? *What* was she studying? A smart kid like Phoebe should have got a lot more out of a first-class education.

At the end of the book, having undergone various growing experiences, which include, most importantly, carrying and giving birth to a child she knows she cannot keep, Phoebe knows what she wants to be when she grows up. And so we are left with a first novel very much like its heroine: extremely likable and filled with the promise of a perhaps even brighter future.

> *Rebecca Goldstein, "Holden Caulfield's Kid Sister Gets Pregnant," in* The New York Times Book Review, *July 14, 1985, p. 11.*

COMMENTS OF MARY-ANN TIRONE SMITH TO *CLC YEARBOOK*

Smith reflects on *The Book of Phoebe:* "Writing this book was my ultimate joy in life. There were two major obstacles, Jene, then aged 8 and Jere, then aged 5. The other obstacles were, in order of size: laundry, meals, unmade beds, chicken pox, three cats, five generations of gerbils and all my friends who don't write."

Asked why she writes, Smith responds, "Some nameless inner drive I was born with motivates me. The accomplishment I dreamed of—seeing a book I wrote on a library shelf—I've accomplished. In all my writing, I plead for justice. That is the theme of my next book."

Norman Williams

1952-

American poet.

Williams impressed critics with his American sensibility in this unusually masterful first poetry collection, *The Unlovely Child* (1985). In these poems Williams explores both the small towns and prairies of his native country as well as European settings. Reviewers praise the poet's direct, controlled style, which captures the essence of his subjects in simple, yet telling portraits.

JOSEPH A. LIPARI

Williams's collection [*The Unlovely Child*] surveys a wide panorama. Geographically, the poems move east from the Kansas prairies to the slums of Florence. Thematically, they compare the American necessity to make a home in a "bare region of the earth" with the "ancient rites and mysteries" of the Old World. As might be expected in a first book, Williams sometimes allows influences to intrude. For example, his use of Elizabethan syntax and diction to describe an American landscape is jarring: "the mists and fog / Seemed special envoys of the fall / Forced, before their time, from earth." Altogether, though, the craftsmanship and flashes of "foreign, swift, expanded sight" here raise uncommon hopes for future work.

Joseph A. Lipari, in a review of "The Unlovely Child," in Library Journal, *Vol. 110, No. 1, January, 1985, p. 88.*

PUBLISHERS WEEKLY

If we can define a classic as a book that, once read, seems to the reader to have always existed, then Williams's book [*The Unlovely Child*] is something on that order. As a title for his work, the poem **"The Genius of Smalltown America"** seems apt. Williams's evocation of the Midwest is vivid in its particulars and wholly painterly. Even in the poems that explore different European national characters, Williams's American sensibility is paramount. He goes abroad only to find slight variations on the genius of small towns like his own. Each of his poems is complete, self-contained and satisfying, and if the ultimate effect is poignant, it is achieved only through self-restraint. Above all, Williams accomplishes the difficult task of writing poems that are ambiguous and exploratory even as they are revelatory, concrete and modestly bardic. This is a small book, a likely sleeper, but a definite, unforgettable gem.

A review of "The Unlovely Child," in Publishers Weekly, *Vol. 227, No. 2, January 11, 1985, p. 69.*

© Kelly Wise

JANE COOPER

Norman Williams gives the impression—awesome in one who has just published his first book—of doing almost nothing by accident. *The Unlovely Child* opens with his characteristic grave sweep and extended syntax:

> In the dark morning when most chil-
> dren are born,
> When only a few all-night lights star
> the prairie
> And the east shifts slowly from black
> to blue,
> When farm wives have their worst
> and most accurate dreams,
> The girl in danger inside the only
> bright house
> Believes with all her strength there
> are in the sky
> Planets crossing. . . .

So the poem moves in through time and space to face the puzzle of our expectations, how we always believe that *this* child will be the miraculous one and are thwarted. Just at the end the poet brings himself in as neutral witness: "Or so I imagine it must have been . . ." The tone is quiet yet capable not only of irony but of a certain grandeur. There is a lot of space in this book, the space of the grand sky over the burnt-out fields of the Midwest, the space accorded even to disappointment by a historical consciousness. Williams is a poet who can summon up the ghosts of unremarkable people and make them significant, just as he summons up the ghosts of things, the 19th-century tool chest with its "unimpeachable odor of ancestral Bibles, / Antique dolls, or the undergarments of old women." And the book is beautifully structured, as gradually the bankrupt figures of those "giants of the Midwest" give way to the tawdry revelation of the personal bankruptcy of the poet's parents, and finally he is released to travel east and so to Europe. Actually, most of the European poems don't have the resonance for me of the American ones, but I was moved by how the same themes are rediscovered in **"The Dream of South"** and especially **"Ancient Rites and Mysteries."** Williams may have to watch out not to repeat himself, but this is a memorable debut.

> *Jane Cooper, "Words of Distance and Intimacy,"*
> in Book World—The Washington Post, *August 25,*
> *1985, p. 4.*

An Excerpt from *The Unlovely Child*

In Florence, early, a stooped man moves down the
   alleys
Waiting for the rinds to be set out for the pigeons,
And, at dawn, swallows wheel from the eaves and
   campaniles
Crying out a call of pain peculiar to this city.
One thinks of the plague that moled through these
   cellars
Six centuries ago, and of the beggars that begot these
   beggars
Rolling off their women to shuffle past the merchants'
   doors.
Though a sculptor, here and there, may have succeeded
At converting their bald pain into a kind of sorrow,
It lives still, an heirloom of back rooms and old
   piazzas,
And is first cousin to a suffering I used to think
Belonged to the Midwest alone, where I grew up,

Observing its essential rules: that men edge off
Just when their help is needed most, and that
A person, almost always, will starve before abandon
The land and circumstances of his birth. But more,
I saw that in Florence, too, a woman in a dusty dress
Will sometimes lean against a door she's leaned against
A thousand times, watching her child chase balking
   chickens,
And with her darkened teeth will smile
The selfsame smile that I have seen and wondered at
Among the plywood shacks of Kankakee or Peotone.

JAMES BESCHTA

[**The Unlovely Child**] is a book of powerful poetry. It relies on language that is direct and deceptively simple. Williams describes characters and places in words that have grown out of ordinary people and the land. He knows the secret of language, that it is adapted perfectly to the needs of the people who use it. Only on second reading, especially if reading aloud, does the reader become aware of the subtle poetic control Williams exercises, of the hidden alliteration or periodic rhyme.

In these poems there is strength and truth instead of eloquence and ornamentation. Williams' stark concrete images share his visions, demand audience involvement and subtly direct our judgments. Yet he never imposes his conclusions on us.

Though the poems included here are worldwide, this is a book of American poetry. Williams captures the spirit of America in an uncanny way, especially when dealing with the sombre Midwest in which he grew up, the prairies of Kansas where houses float in loneliness and memories, the western shores of Lake Michigan where people wait as they've always waited, the small towns where

> The beak-nosed men walk head-up and proud,
> Convinced, against all evidence, that what
> They've planted, built or reared is theirs, . . .

This is a striking first book, powerful, sensitive and moving. Based on this work, Williams could well become a major voice in American poetry. (pp. 31-2)

> *James Beschta, in a review of "The Unlovely Child,"*
> in Kliatt Young Adult Paperback Book Guide, *Vol.*
> *XIX, No. 6, September, 1985, pp. 31-2.*

Prizewinners

Literary Prizes and Honors

Announced in 1985

ACADEMY OF AMERICAN POETS AWARDS

FELLOWSHIP OF THE ACADEMY OF
AMERICAN POETS
 Maxine Kumin
THE LAMONT POETRY SELECTION
 Cornelius Eady, *Victims of the Latest Dance*
IVAN YOUNGER POETS AWARD
 *Diane Ackerman, Michael Blumenthal,
 Richard Kenney*
WALT WHITMAN AWARD
 Christianne Balk, Bindweed

**AMERICAN ACADEMY AND INSTITUTE OF
 ARTS AND LETTERS AWARDS**

GOLD MEDAL FOR POETRY
 Robert Penn Warren
AWARD OF MERIT
 Richard Stern
AWARDS IN LITERATURE
 Alan Dugan, Maria Irene Fornes, George Garrett,
 Carolyn Kizer, Gilbert Sorrentino, Paul West, John
 Williams, Paul Zinner
HAROLD D. VURSELL MEMORIAL AWARD
 Harriett Doerr
JEAN STINE FICTION AWARD
 George W.S. Trow
MORTON DAUWEN ZABEL AWARD
 Stanley Clavell
RICHARD AND HINDA ROSENTHAL
FOUNDATION AWARD
 Janet Kaufman
ROME FELLOWSHIP IN LITERATURE
 Oscar Hijuelos
SUE KAUFMAN PRIZE FOR FIRST FICTION
 Louis Erdrich
WITTER BYNNER PRIZE FOR POETRY
 J.D. McClatchy
SPECIAL CITATION
 William Shawn

THE AMERICAN BOOK AWARDS

FICTION
 Don DeLillo, *White Noise*
FIRST FICTION
 Bob Schacochis, *Easy in the Islands*
NONFICTION
 J. Anthony Lukas, *Common Ground*

BOLLINGEN PRIZE IN POETRY
 John Ashbery and Fred Chappell

BOOKER McCONNELL PRIZE FOR FICTION
 Keri Hulme, *The Bone People*

COMMONWEALTH POETRY PRIZE
 Lauris Edmonds, *Selected Poems*

**DELMORE SCHWARTZ MEMORIAL POETRY
AWARD**
 Edward Hirsch

DRUE HEINZ LITERATURE PRIZE
 W.D. Wetherell, *The Man Who Loved Levittown*

EDGAR ALLEN POE AWARDS

BEST NOVEL
 Ross Thomas, *Briarpatch*
FIRST NOVEL
 Richard Rosen, *Strike Three You're Dead*
SHORT STORY
 Lawrence Block, "By Dawn's Early Light," in *Playboy*
 and *The Eyes Have It*
CRITICAL/BIOGRAPHICAL
 Mike Weiss, *Double Play: The San Francisco City
 Hall Killings*
GRAND MASTER AWARD
 Dorothy Salisbury Davis
ELLERY QUEEN AWARD
 Joan Kahn

**GEORGE JEAN NATHAN AWARD FOR
 DRAMATIC CRITICISM**
 Jan Kott, *The Theater of Essence*

GEORG BÜCHNER PREIS
 Heiner Muller

PRIX GONCOURT
 Yann Queffelec, *Les Noces Barbares*

GOVERNOR GENERAL'S LITERARY AWARDS
FICTION
 Josef Škvorecký, *The Engineer of Human Souls*
DRAMA
 Judith Thompson, *White Biting Dog*
POETRY
 Paulette Jiles, *Celestial Navigation*

HUGO AWARDS
NOVEL
 William Gibson, *Neuromancer*
NONFICTION
 Jack Williamson, *Wonder's Child: My Life in Science Fiction*
NOVELLA
 John Varley, "Press Enter," in *Isaac Asimov's Science Fiction Magazine*
NOVELLETTE
 Octavia E. Butler, "Bloodchild," in *Isaac Asimov's Science Fiction Magazine*
SHORT STORY
 David Brin, "The Crystal Spheres" in *Analog*

JAMES TAIT BLACK MEMORIAL PRIZES
FICTION
 J.G. Ballard, *Empire of the Sun*
POETRY
 Angela Carter, *Nights at the Circus*
BIOGRAPHY
 Lyndall Gordon, *Virginia Woolf: A Writer's Life*

JERUSALEM PRIZE
 Milan Kundera

JOHN DOS PASSOS PRIZE FOR LITERATURE
 Russell Banks

LENORE MARSHALL/NATION POETRY PRIZE
 John Ashbery, *A Wave*

LOS ANGELES TIMES BOOK AWARDS
FICTION
 Louise Erdrich, *Love Medicine*
POETRY
 X.J. Kennedy, *Cross Ties*
BIOGRAPHY
 Michael Scammell, *Solzhenitsyn*
HISTORY
 Evan S. Connell, *Son of the Morning Star*

THE NATIONAL BOOK CRITICS CIRCLE AWARDS
FICTION
 Louise Erdrich, *Love Medicine*
POETRY
 Sharon Olds, *The Dead and the Living*
CRITICISM
 Robert Hass, *Twentieth Century Pleasures: Prose on Poetry*
BIOGRAPHY
 Joseph Frank, *Dostoevsky: The Years of Ordeal, 1850-1859*
NONFICTION
 Freeman Dyson, *Weapons and Hope*

NEBULA AWARDS
NOVEL
 William Gibson, *Neuromancer*
NOVELLA
 John Varley, "Press Enter," in *Isaac Asimov's Science Fiction Magazine*
NOVELLETTE
 Octavia E. Butler, "Bloodchild," in *Isaac Asimov's Science Fiction Magazine*
SHORT STORY
 Gardner Dozois, "Morning Child," in *Omni*

NEW YORK DRAMA CTITICS CIRCLE AWARD
 August Wilson, *Ma Rainey's Black Bottom*

NOBEL PRIZE IN LITERATURE
 Claude Simon

OBIE AWARD
 Maria Irene Fornes, *The Conduct of Life*

O. HENRY AWARDS
 Stuart Dybek, "Hot Ice" and Jane Smile, "Lily"

PEN AWARDS
PEN/FAULKNER AWARD FOR FICTION
 Tobias Wolff, *The Barracks Thief*
ERNEST HEMINGWAY FOUNDATION AWARD FOR FIRST FICTION
 Josephine Humphreys, *Dreams of Sleep*
PEN MEDAL FOR TRANSLATION
 Richard Howard, for entire career
PEN TRANSLATION PRIZE FOR POETRY
 Seamus Heaney, *Sweeney Astray*
PEN TRANSLATION PRIZE FOR PROSE
 Helen R. Lane, *The War of the End of the World,* by Mario Vargas Llosa

PULITZER PRIZES

FICTION
  Alison Lurie, *Foreign Affairs*
POETRY
  Carolyn, Kizer, *Yin*
DRAMA
  James Lapine and Stephen Sondheim, *Sunday in the Park with George*
BIOGRAPHY
  Kenneth Silverman, *The Life and Times of Cotton Mather*
HISTORY
  Thomas K. McCraw, *The Prophets of Regulation*
NONFICTION
  Studs Terkel, *The Good War: An Oral History of World War II*

TONY AWARDS

BEST PLAY
  Neil Simon, *Biloxi Blues*

WORLD FANTASY AWARDS

NOVEL
  Robert Holdstock, *Mythago Wood*
  Barry Hughart, *Bridge of Birds*
NOVELLA
  Geoff Ryman, "The Unconquered Country"
SHORT STORY
  Scott Baker, "Still Life with Scorpion"
  Alan Ryan, "The Bones Wizard"
LIFETIME ACHIEVEMENT
  Theodore Sturgeon

YALE SERIES OF YOUNGER POETS AWARD

  George Bradley, *Terms to be Met*

Prizewinners

Featured in 1985 Yearbook

Don DeLillo
White Noise
The American Book Awards: Fiction

Louise Erdrich
Love Medicine
The National Book Critics Circle
    Award: Fiction

Maria Irene Fornes
The Conduct of Life
Obie Award

William Gibson
Neuromancer
Hugo Award
Nebula Award

Robert Hass
*Twentieth Century Pleasures: Prose
    on Poetry*
The National Book Critics Circle
    Award: Criticism

Robert Holdstock
Mythago Wood
World Fantasy Award: Best Novel

Barry Hughart
*Bridge of Birds: A Novel of an
    Ancient China That Never Was*
World Fantasy Award: Best Novel

Keri Hulme
The Bone People
Booker-McConnell Prize for Fiction

Carolyn Kizer
Yin: New Poems
Pulitzer Prize: Poetry

James Lapine
Stephen Sondheim
Sunday in the Park with George
Pulitzer Prize: Drama

Alison Lurie
Foreign Affairs
Pulitzer Prize: Fiction

Sharon Olds
The Dead and the Living
The National Book Critics Circle
    Award: Poetry

Richard Rosen
Strike Three You're Dead
Edgar Allan Poe Award:
    Best First Novel

Bob Shacochis
Easy in the Islands
The American Book Awards:
    First Work of Fiction

Claude Simon
Nobel Prize in Literature

Neil Simon
Biloxi Blues
Tony Award

Josef Škvorecký
The Engineer of Human Souls
Governor General's Literary Award:
    Fiction

Richard Stern
American Academy and Institute of
    Arts and Letters: Award of Merit
    for Fiction

Ross Thomas
Briarpatch
Edgar Allan Poe Award:
    Best Novel

Judith Thompson
White Biting Dog
Governor General's Literary Award:
    Drama

Robert Penn Warren
American Academy and Institute of
    Arts and Letters: Gold Medal for
    Poetry

August Wilson
Ma Rainey's Black Bottom
New York Drama Critics Circle
    Award: Best Play

Tobias Wolff
The Barracks Thief
PEN/Faulkner Award for Fiction

Prize Commentary

American Academy and Institute of Arts and Letters: Gold Medal

The Gold Medal, established in 1909, is the most prestigious award given by the American Academy and Institute of Arts and Letters. Each year the prize is given in two separate categories of the arts and these categories are repeated every six years; in all, twelve categories of the arts are recognized, including architecture and history, poetry and music, drama and graphic arts, criticism and painting, biography and music, and fiction and sculpture. The award honors the recipient's entire body of work and can be given to a member of the Institute as well as to other individuals.

American Academy and Institute of Arts and Letters: Award of Merit

The Award of Merit, established in 1942, is one of the most prestigious prizes bestowed by the American Academy and Institute of Arts and Letters. Rotating annually, the prize consists of a medal and 1,000 dollars and recognizes outstanding achievement in painting, sculpture, fiction, poetry, or drama. The award is given to individuals who are not members of the award-giving body and recognizes their entire work.

The American Book Awards

Administered by the Association of American Publishers, The American Book Awards, which were revised in 1984, are given annually "to honor and promote books of distinction and literary merit." Books written by American citizens and published in the United States are submitted by publishers and reviewed by the nominating committees; three titles are nominated in each of the three categories: fiction, nonfiction, and first work of fiction. The winner in each category is judged by the Academy of The American Book Awards. Nominees receive 1,000 dollars, and winners receive 10,000 dollars. The American Book Awards were established in 1980 and are the successors of the National Book Awards, which were established in 1950 by the National Book Committee.

Booker-McConnell Prize

Britain's most important prize for fiction, the Booker-McConnell Prize is awarded to the writer of the year's most distinguished full-length novel written in English by a citizen of the British Commonwealth and published in the United Kingdom. Publishers submit the books for consideration and a five-member committee selects the winner of the 10,000 pound award. The prize was established in 1968 by the international food company Booker-McConnell Limited and is administered by the National Book League.

Edgar Allan Poe Awards

Informally known as the "Edgars," the Edgar Allan Poe Awards were established in 1945 by the Mystery Writers of America and are given annually for the year's outstanding works in the mystery genre. The winners are selected by the General Awards Committee from works submitted by publishers. Scrolls are awarded to all nominees, and the winner in each category receives a ceramic bust of Edgar Allan Poe.

Governor General's Literary Awards

Established in 1936 by the Canadian Authors Association, the Governor General's Literary Awards are now administered through the Canada Council. The prize is given for superior works of fiction, poetry, drama, and nonfiction published during the year by Canadian authors. Awards are given both for works in English and works in French, bringing the total annual number of awards to eight. The winners, who are chosen by an eighteen-member committee, receive a specially bound copy of the award-winning work in addition to a cash prize of 5,000 dollars.

Hugo Awards

The Hugo Awards, established in 1953, are sponsored by the World Science Fiction Society and are chosen through the vote of the people who attend the Annual Science Fiction Convention. The Hugo is awarded for notable science fiction works in several categories. Each winner receives a trophy of a chrome-plated Rocket Ship. Informally named after Hugo Gernsback, an early publisher of science fiction, the award's official title is the Science Fiction Achievement Award.

Lenore Marshall/Nation Poetry Prize

Established in 1974 and sponsored by The New Hope Foundation and *The Nation* magazine, the Lenore Marshall/Nation Poetry Prize honors the writer of the year's outstanding collection of poems. The winner, who must be a living American writer, is chosen by one or more poets appointed as judges by the Foundation and is awarded a 5,000 dollar honorarium. The prize was formerly co-sponsored by *The Saturday Review.*

The National Book Critics Circle Awards

Awarded for books published in the previous year, The National Book Critics Circle Awards honor superior works by American authors. The purpose of The National Book Critics Circle, which was founded in 1974, is "to raise the standards of the profession of book criticism and to enhance public appreciation of literature"; awards are bestowed for the best fiction, poetry, biography, criticism, and nonfiction. The winners are judged by the twenty-four members of the National Book Critics Circle Board of Directors; each winner receives an honorary scroll.

Nebula Awards

Established in 1965 and bestowed by the Science Fiction Writers of America, the Nebula Awards merit significant works in several categories of the science fiction genre that are published in the United States during the previous year. Winners are nominated and chosen by the organization's membership. The trophy awarded is a lucite sculpture embedded with a Nebula formation.

New York Drama Critics Circle Awards

The purpose of the New York Drama Critics Circle Awards is to encourage continued excellence in playwriting by recognizing the year's best play (American or foreign), best foreign play (when the "best play" is American), and the best musical. Eligible dramatists are those who have had a new play produced during the year on or off Broadway in New York City; winners are chosen by the vote of members of the Circle. The award has been given by the New York Drama Critics Circle since 1935 and includes a scroll and 1,000 dollars for the best play and a scroll for the other playwrights.·

Nobel Prize in Literature

One of six Nobel Prizes given annually since 1901, the Nobel Prize in Literature is generally considered to be the highest recognition a writer can receive. Established under the terms of the will of the Swedish-born Alfred Bernhard Nobel, the Nobel Prizes are given to those "who, during the preceding year, shall have conferred the greatest benefit on mankind." Nobel willed the literary portion of the award to go to "the person who shall have produced in the field of literature the most outstanding work of an idealistic tendency." The award recognizes the author's entire body of work and is open to writers of any nationality. The Nobel Committee of the Swedish Academy nominates candidates and selects the winner. The

Nobel laureate receives a gold medal, a certificate, and a honorarium that varies each year but always exceeds 100,000 dollars. The awards are presented in Stockholm, Sweden.

Obie Awards

Established in 1956 by the Plumsock Fund and *The Village Voice,* the Obie Awards recognize excellence in off Broadway and off-off Broadway theater productions. The awards are given in various categories and a panel of jurors, experts in the field, select the winners from the year's productions. The prize consists of a certificate and 500 dollars.

Pen/Faulkner Award for Fiction

The PEN/Faulkner Award for Fiction, sponsored by the PEN South and the PEN American Center in New York—organizations comprised of writers—is judged and mainly supported by writers. First presented in 1981, the award recognizes the year's superior work of fiction by an American writer and continues the tradition of William Faulkner who donated funds to the Nobel Prize to help honor other writers. Each nominee receives 1,000 dollars, while the winner is awarded 5,000 dollars. To emphasize the national nature of the prize, the award committee moved its offices to the Folger Shakespeare Library in Washington, D.C.

Pulitzer Prizes

The Pulitzer Prizes were established in 1904 by Joseph Pulitzer, founder of the *St. Louis Post Dispatch,* and have continued through his willed endowment since 1917. Administered by the Graduate School of Journalism at Columbia University, the prizes recognize outstanding American works that address some aspect of American life; they are awarded in various categories within journalism, music, and literature. The fifteen-member Pulitzer board receives nominations from the separate juries of each category. The winner in each category is awarded 1,000 dollars.

Tony Awards

Formally titled the Antoinette Perry Awards, the Tony Awards were founded in 1947 by the American Theatre Wing "to award the achievement of excellence in the theater" and are administered by the League of New York Theatres and Producers. The awards recognize the year's best play produced at one of the eligible Broadway theaters and also honor many other categories related to dramatic production. From a list of nominees, winners are selected by some 560 people involved in various aspects of the theater. The award itself bears images of the masks of comedy and tragedy on one side and the profile of actress Antoinette Perry on the other.

World Fantasy Award

The World Fantasy Awards, established in 1975, honor outstanding writers and publishers in the fantasy genre. Works of original fiction are eligible for awards in three categories: novel, novella, and short story. The award statuette is the sculptured metal caricature of horror writer Howard Phillips Lovecraft; informally, the prizes are known as Howards. Like the older Science Fiction Achievement Awards, or Hugos, the Howards are connected with a prestigious annual convention. Each year registered members of previous World Fantasy Conventions nominate their award candidates by mail-in ballot. A panel of five distinguished judges is chosen each year to select the winners, who are announced at the next convention.

Don DeLillo

White Noise

The American Book Awards: Fiction

(Also writes under the pseudonym Cleo Birdwell) American novelist and short story writer.

DeLillo enjoys a reputation as a preeminent satirist of contemporary American life. Some critics regard his novel *White Noise* as his most engaging and provocative work to date. DeLillo directs his satire at such phenomena of mass culture as football and supermarkets, analyzing how these institutions function and what purpose they serve. A similarly academic approach is evident in other aspects of his writing. Commentators note that he has a linguist's fascination with the meaning and usage of words and a penchant for explaining the metaphysical implications of everyday matters. As a result, critics charge that his characters, such as fourteen-year-old Heinrich Gladney in *White Noise,* often sound more like philosophy professors than the average citizens they are meant to represent. While humor plays an integral role in his work, DeLillo is considered a serious social critic. Television, the CIA, and the dehumanizing aspects of American consumer culture are favorite DeLillo topics that resurface in *White Noise.*

Mortality and the life-denying effects of technology are the themes of *White Noise.* The narrator-protagonist, Jack Gladney, is the death-obsessed chairman of Hitler Studies at a midwestern university. Jack, his equally anxious wife, Babette, and their children live in a farce of Middle American philistinism, yet DeLillo portrays them as an appealing, affectionate family. Their security is threatened by two outside forces. One is an experimental drug that is purported to relieve the fear of death. The other is an industrial accident that releases a lethal cloud of insecticide, from which the Gladneys flee but cannot escape unharmed. Critics note the uncanny coincidence of the novel's publication with the poisonous gas leakage at a pesticide plant at Bhopal, India that killed and injured thousands of people.

DeLillo comments on the novel's origins: "I thought of a college that had a department of Hitler Studies and that led to death as a subject. I haven't a clue where that thought came from, but it seemed innately comic, and everything sprang from it. I never felt that I was writing a comic novel before *White Noise.* Maybe the fact that death permeates the book made me retreat into comedy." He explains how the basically sympathetic protagonist became founder of Hitler Studies: "Only Hitler is large enough and terrible enough to absorb and neutralize Jack Gladney's obsessive fear of dying—a very common fear but one that's rarely talked about." Although some critics view *White Noise* as apocalyptic fiction, DeLillo says this was not his intention: "It's about death on the individual level."

While critics universally praise the virtuoso style and thematic unity of *White Noise,* some believe that DeLillo has created a facile political tract that lacks the heart of successful fiction. Detractors charge that DeLillo's characters are mere mouthpieces, the dialogue rhetoric, and the plot a contrivance. "DeLillo is an excellent ventriloquist," according to Thomas M. Disch,

© 1986 Thomas Victor

"but when he tries to operate a puppet theater he gets tangled in the strings." In contrast, other critics view the Gladney family as memorable characters who invest the novel with the substance and sympathy that DeLillo's previous works lack. These critics commend *White Noise* as not only a brilliantly realized black comedy and social satire, but a fully integrated work of fiction.

(See also *CLC,* Vols. 8, 10, 13, 27; *Contemporary Authors,* Vols. 81-84; and *Dictionary of Literary Biography,* Vol. 6.)

JOHN BROSNAHAN

The chairperson of the department of Nazi studies at a midwestern college aches to escape the inevitable path of decline and death; a "toxic event" that releases a dangerous cloud of pollution gives him the chance to break free in previously uncontemplated ways. The appeal of this novel [*White Noise*] lies not in its narrative strength—which in truth wastes away like the professor's own progressive disintegration—but in the individual moments in which DeLillo captures the restless essence of modern lives: sibling terrorism and counterintelligence; academic one-upmanship among the researchers of popular culture; the careers of former spouses that have blossomed in unexpected but thoroughly predictable ways; the supermarket as a reassuring microcosm of American culture; the enforced tedium of mandatory family television viewing; and the lure of an experiment that promises not freedom from death, only freedom from the fear of dying.

John Brosnahan, in a review of "White Noise," in Booklist, Vol. 81, No. 5, November 1, 1984, p. 322.

CHRISTOPHER LEHMANN-HAUPT

White Noise, the title of Don DeLillo's eighth and latest novel, refers to death. (Jack Gladney: "What if death is nothing but sound?" Babette Gladney: "Electrical noise." Jack: "You hear it forever. Sound all around. How awful." Babette: "Uniform, white").

Jack Gladney, who is chairman of the department of Hitler studies at the College-on-the-Hill in the town of Blacksmith, is afraid of death. So is Babette, who "gathers and tends" the children, teaches a course in posture in an adult education program, and reads once a week from *The National Enquirer* and similar publications to a blind person known as Old Man Treadwell, "as if he were a landmark, a rock formation or a brooding swamp."

Also afraid of death, one suspects, is Jack's son, Heinrich Gerhardt Gladney, whose best friend, Orest Mercator, is training to break the world endurance record for sitting in a cage full of deadly snakes for the *Guinness Book of Records.* (Why a cage full of deadly snakes? Orest Mercator: "They're the best at what they do. I want to be the best at what I do.")

That Hitler and death and poisonous snakes are so prominent in *White Noise* does not prevent it from being one of Don DeLillo's funniest novels to date. And—as readers of such earlier DeLillo novels as *End Zone* or *The Names* will easily understand—that *White Noise* is so funny doesn't mean it isn't eerie, brilliant, touching and as serious as death and puff adders.

In *White Noise* for a change—indeed for the first time in any of his fiction—at least as far as I can recall—Mr. DeLillo tells a story that is slightly more than just a vehicle for his brilliant writing and his gags. This is appropriate to his theme. "To plot is to live," Murray Jay Siskind, a visiting professor on living icons, tells Jack Gladney. "We start our lives in chaos, in babble. As we surge up into the world, we try to devise a shape, a plan. There is dignity in this. Your whole life is a plot, a scheme, a diagram."

Anyway, while Jack is trying to learn German in preparation for an upcoming Hitler conference scheduled at the College-on-the-Hill ("Actual Germans would be in attendance.") and Babette is lecturing on good posture, a tank car gets punctured at the local train yards, releasing some Nyodene Derivative, which grows quickly from "a feathery plume" to "a black billowing cloud" to "the airborne toxic event." Unfortunately, while Jack is evacuating his family to an abandoned Boy Scout camp, he is forced to refuel his car, exposing himself to the "event" long enough to elicit "bracketed numbers with pulsing stars" on a computer screen. ("What does that mean?" "You'd rather not know.")

Meanwhile, Babette has secretly answered an advertisement in *The National Examiner* and become a guinea pig for a company experimenting with a drug called Dylar, which is supposed to counteract the fear of death. Dylar hasn't worked for Babette. But now that he has been contaminated by the "toxic event" and is "tentatively scheduled to die," Jack wants to try it. Babette won't reveal her source ("You want to ingest. No good, Jack. Dylar was my mistake. I won't let you make it yours as well.") The struggle is joined.

Some expressed strong opinions on the matter. Winnie, a neurochemist, asks, "Isn't death the boundary we need? Doesn't it give a precious texture to life, a sense of definition? You have to ask yourself whether anything you do in this life would have beauty and meaning without the knowledge you carry of a final line, a border or limit."

Murray Jay Siskind, the lecturer on living icons, points out that Jack's basic problem has been his dependence on Hitler. "Helpless and fearful people are drawn to magical figures, mythic figures, epic men who intimidate and darkly loom," he explains. "Some people are larger than life. Hitler is larger than death. You thought he would protect you. I understand completely."

Others simply babble. "There are more people dead today than in the rest of world history put together," Orest Mercator, the snake man, tells Jack and his son Heinrich.

Jack's narration continues:

> I looked at my son. I said. "Is he trying to tell us there are more people dying in this twenty-four-hour period than in the rest of human history up to now?"
>
> "He's saying the dead are greater today than ever before, combined."
>
> "What dead? Define the dead."
>
> "He's saying people now dead."
>
> "What do you mean, now dead? Everybody who's dead is now dead."
>
> "He's saying people in graves. The known dead. Those you can count."
>
> I was listening intently, trying to grasp what they meant.

We listen intently, too, trying to grasp what Mr. DeLillo means. As far as I'm concerned, in *White Noise* he means more than he's ever meant before. In the final scene of the novel, Jack's and Babette's youngest child, Wilder, tries to cross a four-lane highway riding his plastic tricycle. I don't really understand what draws Mr. DeLillo to children on tricycles. (One of his earlier novels, *Ratner's Star,* ended with the boy protagonist pedaling madly into the landscape.) But I do know that the final scene in *White Noise* is heart-stopping. The boy Wilder is the Gladney's main comfort in the face of death. To trifle with his life seems positively overheated for a sensibility as icily intelligent as Mr. DeLillo's has always seemed. It is almost as if we were listening to a massive glacier breaking up. The scenery may be arctic, but the noise is not in the least white.

Christopher Lehmann-Haupt, in a review of "White Noise," in The New York Times, January 7, 1985, p. C18.

TOM LE CLAIR

Union Carbide in Bhopal, India, has given us a new way to die. Don DeLillo in *White Noise* imagines how an American family and community live through a huge "airborne toxic event." Coincidence or prophecy or both, this kind of present-time connection between death and art is DeLillo's signature, the result of his placing the novelist's sensors in the most threatening places.

Jack Gladney, his wife, Babette, and their four children from several marriages live in a Midwestern town.... For Jack, who narrates the book, this little family in a little place is a defense against large "city" dangers: violence, intrigue, knowledge. Only when the professor, whose academic specialty is killing, is forced to evacuate his home and is exposed to the "toxic event" does he understand that no place or self is safe.

For DeLillo, the billowing cloud is both suspenseful plot device and analogue for other toxic excess: the incessant gabble of TV and talk radio in the background, the trivia-mongering of Gladney's university colleagues, the power jargons of science and medicine, the needless expertise of the "helping professions," the supermarket's barrage of pitch and glitter, as well as the random hum and blurt that penetrate Gladney's home and head. All this is "white noise"—sound without significance, the poisonous distractions that William Gaddis made into his prize-winning novel *JR*. DeLillo is an equal authority on waste.

For Jack and Babette, the toxic event is reason to admit what they have most concealed: their fear of death. Babette secretly and briefly participates in a testing program for Dylar, a drug that supposedly inhibits this fear. In the novel's second half, Jack plots a way to get the drug for himself; such a thing may be worth killing for in a toxic environment. Dylar is, of course, just one more toxin as DeLillo draws his ironic circle tight: That which we desperately take in (or build up) to fight our fear of death brings us closer to that death. Thomas Pynchon's *Gravity's Rainbow* draws a similar self-destructive arc. *White Noise* is the accessible, "domestic" version of Pynchon's worldwide vicious zero.

Despite its subjects and its similarities to these monumental novels, *White Noise* is not a forbidding book. DeLillo's sorrow and rage at what we do to ourselves are mixed with his usual wit and, here for the first time, close and often original observations of family life, "the one medium of sense knowledge in which an astonishment of heart is routinely contained." The Gladneys' kids are wised-up TV creatures, but not without a canny innocence. Jack and Babette could be figures from what DeLillo has criticized as the "around-the-house-and-in-the-yard" school of fiction, a *New Yorker* realism; but they are given secret pockets beneath their tweeds and running suits.

White Noise is also full of wonderful comic set pieces: a back-to-college caravan of station wagons carrying consumers in training; a lecture-duel between Gladney's Hitler and a colleague's upstart culture-hero Elvis; confusion in the supermarket when shelves are changed and goods are moved; a visit from Babette's father, a tool-wise and gun-carrying anachronism in electronic America; an adolescent's doctrine of absolute relativism, bolstered by the newest science in which people become TV sets.

And in this novel that had as one working title *The American Book of the Dead*, DeLillo ends with what can only be called a minor miracle. Another working title was *Panasonic*, the

wide range of sound. Mystery and authority: These are the elements of DeLillo's achievement in *White Noise*, a work of high art for our survival kit.

> *Tom Le Clair, "A Nightmare Novel of Stunning Sweep," in* USA Today, *January 11, 1985, p. 3D.*

TOM LE CLAIR

Don DeLillo knows our secrets—American anxieties, obsessions and dread, our silent spaces and the noise of entertainment and explanation we use to fill them. No wonder that, despite publishing seven widely praised novels since 1971, DeLillo has to be "discovered" with each new book. This Samuel Beckett of Americana we'd just as soon forget.

DeLillo knows, too, that secrets help preserve us from what he calls the "mass anesthesia" of consumerism. From the early '70s football star of *End Zone* and the rock star of *Great Jones Street* to the more recent yuppies of *Players* and the American businesspeople abroad in *The Names,* his characters resist and pursue a personal mysteriousness, their spiritual voiceprint in a world of preconditioning and tabloid solace.

DeLillo disturbs because he can be read by anyone. The Thomas Wolfe journey of *Americana,* the science fiction of *Ratner's Star,* the espionage of *Running Dog,* and the "disaster novel" drama of the new *White Noise* solicit readers before conducting them to secret uncertainties. DeLillo's sentences have the sound of Hemingway's—if Hemingway's precision had taken in higher mathematics, anthropology, linguistics and the language of the urban mad.

Like a mobile CAT scanner, DeLillo sees through every pretense to the human quiver—by turns frightening and funny. With DeLillo's recent induction into the American Academy and Institute of Arts and Letters and the republication by Vintage of his work in a uniform paperback edition, there remains only one question about this major American novelist: "Do we dare?"

> *Tom LeClair, "Discovering DeLillo, Our Own Beckett," in* USA Today, *January 11, 1985, p. 3D.*

JONATHAN YARDLEY

Don DeLillo is a prodigiously gifted writer. His cool but evocative prose is witty, biting, surprising, precise. Here's a characteristic passage, describing the faculty of "the popular culture department, known officially as American environments," at a middle western institution called College-on-the-Hill, where DeLillo's new novel [*White Noise*] takes place:

> A curious group. The teaching staff is composed almost solely of New York emigres, smart, thuggish, movie-mad, trivia-crazed. They are here to decipher the natural language of the culture, to make a formal method of the shiny pleasures they'd known in their Europe-shadowed childhoods—an Aristotelianism of bubble gum wrappers and detergent jingles....
>
> (p. 3)

That is splendid stuff; not merely are its wit and glitter distinctive, but it is *true*—it describes, with sympathetic but devastating finality, an academic subspecies that any habitué of the campuses will immediately recognize. DeLillo spills out passages like that with seeming effortlessness, and *White Noise* is loaded with them. For lovers of pure prose the novel is a trip; the trouble is that when you step back from it and view it clinically, it proves to be a trip to nowhere—yet another of DeLillo's exercises in fiction as political tract.

This is what makes DeLillo so irritating and frustrating: he's a writer of stupendous talents, yet he wastes those talents on monotonously apocalyptic novels the essential business of which is to retail the shopworn campus ideology of the '60s and '70s. Like his contemporary Robert Stone, whose abilities are comparable, he's more interested in the message than the medium. He knows how to shape a novel and tell a story, but he's a pamphleteer, not a novelist; he's interested in ideas and institutions (especially malign ones), but not in people. The result is that he writes books that, while their sheer intelligence and style are dazzling, are heartless—and therefore empty—at their core.

White Noise, though arguably DeLillo's best novel, is a case in point. Its narrator, Jack Gladney, teaches "Advanced Nazism, three hours a week, restricted to qualified seniors, a course of study designed to cultivate historical perspective, theoretical rigor and mature insight into the continuing mass appeal of fascist tyranny, with special emphasis on parades, rallies and uniforms, three credits, written reports," and right away you can figure out that Jack Gladney is far less important than the various messages affixed to him. He's hung up on all things German—he's even named his young son Heinrich—in which he sees the roots of modern evil, but he's also hung up on technology, which he considers to be the American Nazism: "Man's guilt in history and in the tides of his own blood has been complicated by technology, the daily seeping falsehearted death."

Technology is everywhere, transmitting "waves and radiation" that carry with them the death-in-life of modern society. The television set, throbbing in the living room, brings daily calamity into the American household: "That night, a Friday, we gathered in front of the set, as was the custom and the rule, with take-out Chinese. There were floods, earthquakes, mud slides, erupting volcanoes. We'd never before been so attentive to our duty, our Friday assembly. . . . Every disaster made us wish for more, for something bigger, grander, more sweeping." Could there be a more predictable catalogue of trendy political themes: radiation, addiction to violence, television as religion, the trivialization of suffering, the vulgarity of America?

All of this being the case, it will not surprise you to learn two things. The first is that all four of Jack's previous, unsuccessful marriages were to women who had one connection or another to espionage; the CIA is as essential to novelists of the fashionable left (DeLillo, Stone, Didion) as shredded bodices are to the authors of Harlequin romances. The second is that a "toxic event" takes place; a tank car carrying a lethal chemical overturns, and a killer cloud slowly begins to work its way toward the town of Blacksmith, where the Gladney family lives. An evacuation is ordered:

> The enormous dark mass moved like some death ship in Norse legend, escorted across the night by armored creatures with spiral wings. We weren't sure how to react. . . . This was a death made in the laboratory, defined and measurable, but we thought of it at the time in a simple and primitive way, as some seasonal perversity of the earth like a flood or tornado, something

> not subject to control. Our helplessness did not seem compatible with the idea of a man-made event.

There you have it: fiction as op-ed material. As such, to give DeLillo his due, it is very effective. DeLillo constructs a powerful case against a great many things it's extremely easy to be against: the numbing and corrupting influences of technology, the dehumanization of modern society, nuclear war, all the usual suspects. But upon these unrelievedly familiar themes he has constructed a novel that simply doesn't work as *fiction,* which is the novelist's first artistic obligation. None of the characters acquires any genuine humanity because each exists solely to represent something; there's too much chatter, too much of which is merely brittle; the tank-car accident isn't an event but a *deus ex machina;* the conclusion—DeLillo often has trouble winding things up—is contrived.

Listen: Don DeLillo can *write,* and attention therefore must be paid. He's also smart, perceptive and clever. But that's not enough. Until he has something to say that comes from the heart rather than the evening news, his novels will fall far short of his talents. (pp. 3, 10)

> *Jonathan Yardley, "Don DeLillo's American Nightmare," in* Book World—The Washington Post, *January 13, 1985, pp. 3, 10.*

RICHARD EDER

[In *White Noise*] Don DeLillo assembles a scene of contemporary American well-being out of the civilized customs of a college town; and contaminates it. . . .

It is a novel of disintegration, of familiar things hijacked and spoiled, of nature, love and civility leached and estranged the way a familiar face grows strange in a dream. It is a novel of hairline prophecy, showing a desolate and all-too-believable future in the evidences of an all-too-recognizable present.

The wonder, though, is the sense of well-being that steals around us as we read it. It is the feeling of being in the best of hands. The author is Charon as a master mariner; his flame, like Quevedo's, knows how to swim the icy water. He brings us across the Styx in a lilting maneuver that is so adept that we can't help laughing as we go. Indeed, *White Noise,* besides being prophetic and sad, is very funny.

Jack Gladney, his wife Babette, and four children by various marriages live in the bucolic Midwestern town of Blacksmith. They are a tender, nervy bunch: they cherish and surprise each other, and DeLillo portrays them with an endearing warmth.

They live the normalcies of an academic community, yet all these normalcies have a wild, parodic edge to them. . . .

Toward the end, DeLillo lets the wildness go briefly out of control, but this is a minor defect in a stunning book. The author has engaged us thoroughly with his Gladneys; we adopt them as our Noahs; we register the damage when the contamination and alienation of a society past human control mark them, and we cheer their struggles to resist.

As the Gladney children rattle on knowledgeably about ionization and advanced biochemistry, Jack and Babette recite to each other the schoolroom verities of their youth: the three kinds of rock, the square of the hypotenuse, where the battle of Bunker Hill was really fought. There has been an avalanche of scientific discovery, Jack reflects, but people do not possess it the way they possess a much smaller body of knowledge in the past.

"What good is knowledge if it just floats in the air?" he wonders. "It goes from computer to computer. It changes and grows every second of the day. But nobody actually knows anything."

The toxic cloud, terrifyingly described, is the central symbol of humanity's inability to master its knowledge. But, through tenderness, wit and a powerful irony, DeLillo has made every aspect of *White Noise* a moving picture of a disquiet we seem to share more and more.

> *Richard Eder, in a review of "White Noise," in* Los Angeles Times Book Review, *January 13, 1985, p. 5.*

JAYNE ANNE PHILLIPS

[*Phillips, an American novelist, short story writer, and critic, earned an enthusiastic following with her short story collection* Black Tickets *(1978) and her novel* Machine Dreams *(1984). Phillips's fiction, set in her native West Virginia, frequently portrays people in fear-provoking or shocking situations. In the following excerpt Phillips admires DeLillo's method of documenting the alienation and anxiety experienced by modern Americans.*]

The fiction of Don DeLillo is no longer the well-kept secret of a dedicated following. In such novels as ***Ratner's Star, Great Jones Street*** and ***The Names,*** Mr. DeLillo has dealt not so much with character as with culture, survival and the subtle, ever-increasing interdependence between the self and the national and world community. The he-man against the elements, the outlaw, the superhero exist only as myths in the modern world; we are nature's elements, a technologically oriented people nonetheless caught in the sieve of history. There are suspense and an urgent intelligence to Mr. DeLillo's writing, a sense of the widening gyre and the tight-drawn net. *White Noise,* his eighth novel, is the story of a college professor and his family whose small Midwestern town is evacuated after an industrial accident. In light of the recent Union Carbide disaster in India that killed over 2,000 and injured thousands more, *White Noise* seems all the more timely and frightening—precisely because of its totally American concerns, its rendering of a particularly American numbness. (p. 1)

This is an America where no one is responsible or in control; all are receptors, receivers of stimuli, consumers. Some join Simuvac, which signs up local school children as volunteer victims in simulated evacuations ("Some people," Gladney tells his daughter in response to a question about the Nazis, "put on a uniform and feel bigger, stronger, safer"). . . .

Children, in the America of *White Noise,* are in general more competent, more watchful, more in sync than their parents; emotionally, they constitute a kind of early-warning system. The novel's first short section informs us that "homemade signs concerning lost dogs and cats are posted on telephone poles all over town"—signs often handwritten by children. Indeed, the children seem the only ones still attuned enough to the natural world to be concerned about dogs and cats. But children are not merely guardians of the heart; they are the targeted audience, the frequency to which the advertising industry and the vast construct of the media are tuned. The professors at the College-on-the Hill speak of a "society of kids" and tell their students they are "already too old to figure importantly in the making of society. . . . It is only a matter

of time before you experience the vast loneliness and dissatisfaction of consumers who have lost their group identity."

Group identity is a "white noise" in itself, the white noise of history. "Crowds came to hear Hitler speak," Gladney points out in his classes, "crowds erotically charged, the masses he once called his only bride. . . . There must have been something different about those crowds. What was it? . . . Death. Crowds came to form a shield . . . to become a crowd is to keep out death." Academia is trying, too; Hitler studies shares a building with the popular culture department, officially known as American environments, "an Aristotelianism of bubble gum wrappers and detergent jingles." Murray J. Siskind, a shining, somewhat shunned star of the department, is a former sportswriter from New York who studies American culture with the doomed glee of a Dr. Strangelove and the reverence of a Buddhist monk. "You've established a wonderful thing here with Hitler," he tells Gladney. "You created it, you nurtured it. . . . He is now your Hitler. I marvel at the effort. It was masterful, shrewd and stunningly preemptive. It's what I want to do with Elvis." If white noise heralds death, Murray maintains, it also hints at the secrets of the (technologically transformed) universe, a modern music of the spheres.

White Noise finds its greatest distinction in its understanding and perception of America's soundtrack. White noise includes the ever-present sound of expressway traffic, "a remote and steady murmur around our sleep, as of dead souls babbling at the edge of a dream." Television is "the primal force in the American home, sealed-off, self-contained, self-referring . . . a wealth of data concealed in the grid, in the bright packaging, the jingles, the slice-of-life commercials, the products hurtling out of darkness, the coded messages . . . like chants. . . . Coke is it, Coke is it, Coke is it." Television, Murray Siskind asserts, "practically overflows with sacred formulas." White noise includes the bold print of tabloids, those amalgams of American magic and dread, with their comforting "mechanism of offering a hopeful twist to apocalyptic events." Fast food and quad cinemas contribute to the melody, as do automated teller machines. Nowhere is Mr. DeLillo's take on the endlessly distorted, religious underside of American consumerism better illustrated than in the passage on supermarkets.

Jack Gladney:

> Everything seemed to be in season, sprayed, burnished, bright. . . . The place was awash in noise. . . . The toneless systems, the jangle and skid of carts, the loudspeaker and the coffee-making machines, the cries of children. And over it all . . . a dull and unlocatable roar, as of some form of swarming life just outside the range of human apprehension.
>
> (p. 30)

Americans in *White Noise* do well to study their supermarkets closely, since death is edging nearer, anonymous, technical, ironically group-oriented. Menacing signs appear—reports of various toxic waste disasters are broadcast frequently; the local grade school is evacuated ("Investigators said it could be the ventilating system, the paint or varnish, the foam insulation, the rays emitted by microcomputers"), and a man dies during the inspection of a second-floor classroom.

Finally, after "a night of dream-lit snows," an "airborne toxic event" originates in a rail accident at a nearby train yard. The dark billowing cloud is full of Nyodene D, a chemical familiar to Heinrich ("It was in a movie we saw in school on toxic wastes. These videotaped rats''). The radio quotes a series of symptoms ranging from sweaty palms to *déjà vu* (''Death in the air,'' Murray explains, ''liberates suppressed material'') to coma. ''I'm the head of a department,'' Gladney tells Heinrich, ''I don't see myself fleeing an airborne toxic event. That's for people who live in mobile homes out in the scrubby parts of the county, where the fish hatcheries are.''

Nevertheless, Gladney finds himself joining an exodus familiar from disaster movies, directed by amplified voices over loudspeakers. (pp. 30-1)

After nine days, the Gladneys return home. Normalcy resumes. Men in protective suits and German shepherd dogs ''trained to sniff out toxic material'' patrol the town. Sunsets last for hours; silent crowds watch the spectacular colors from overpasses. Gladney secretly visits a think tank diagnostic center that confirms the presence of Nyodene D in his blood.

Babette admits to taking Dylar, moved by her constant anxieties to answering a tabloid ad: ''Fear of Death? Volunteers wanted for secret research.'' Following test after test, she is judged one of three most fearful finalists, but the ''small firm doing research in psychobiology'' decides not to use human subjects. Desperate, Babette makes a private arrangement with the project manager, a shadowy figure she will reveal to Gladney only as ''Mr. Gray.'' For several months, she has met him in a motel room, offering herself (''It was a capitalist transaction'') in exchange for drugs.

Gladney, ''scheduled to die'' himself, is moved equally by rage and fear. He tells Babette he wishes to contact Gray only to get Dylar. In fact, he evolves a plan to kill Gray, and the book reaches its least convincing twist with a comic near-murder. Gladney takes his victim to a hospital and has a conversation about belief with a nun called Sister Hermann Marie: ''You don't believe in heaven?'' he asks. ''Your dedication is a pretense?'' ''Our presence is a dedication,'' she responds. ''As belief shrinks from the world, people find it more necessary than ever that *someone* believe . . . Nuns in black. . . . Fools, children. We surrender our lives to make your nonbelief possible. . . . There is no truth without fools.'' ''I don't want to hear this,'' Gladney protests. ''This is terrible.'' ''But true,'' she answers.

''What good is my truth?'' Heinrich asks Gladney early in the novel. ''My truth means nothing. . . . Is there such a thing as now? 'Now' comes and goes as soon as you say it.'' Babette has observed of her husband that it is his nature ''to shelter loved ones from the truth. Something lurked inside the truth.'' It is in documenting such epidemic evasiveness and apprehension, such lack of connection to the natural world and to technology, such bewilderment, that *White Noise* succeeds so brilliantly. ''The nature of modern death is that it has a life independent of us,'' Mr. DeLillo asserts. This truth, in itself, has indeed forever altered ''man's guilt in history and in the tides of his own blood.'' What belief can correspond to a fact so irrevocable? *White Noise* offers no answers, but it poses inescapable questions with consummate skill. (p. 31)

Jayne Anne Phillips, ''Crowding Out Death,'' in The New York Times Book Review, *January 13, 1985, pp. 1, 30-1.*

WALTER CLEMONS

Don DeLillo's eighth novel [*White Noise*] should win him wide recognition, till now only flickeringly granted, as one of the best American novelists. Comic and touching, ingenious and weird, *White Noise* looks, at first, reassuringly like an example of a familiar genre, the campus novel. It opens with the return of students in the fall and ends with a glorious sunset. The cozy family kitchen and the local supermarket are central locales. But domestic scenes are invested with an uneasiness that recalls a line of Auden's, ''The crack in the tea-cup opens / A lane to the land of the dead.'' . . .

White Noise tunes us in on frequencies we haven't heard in other accounts of how we live now. Occult supermarket tabloids are joined with TV disaster footage as household staples providing nourishment and febrile distraction. Fleeting appearances or phone calls from the Gladneys' previous spouses give us the start of surprise we experience when we learn that couples we know have a previous family life we haven't heard about.

Forgetfulness has become a sinister preoccupation since the discovery and publicizing of Alzheimer's disease. *White Noise* suggests that filtering, denial, blackout are widely diffused characteristics of everyday behavior. Both death-ridden parents adore Babette's preschool son, Wilder, an enchanting child who doesn't yet talk. ''I liked being with Wilder,'' says Jack. ''The world was a series of fleeting gratifications. He took what he could, then immediately forgot it in the rush of a subsequent pleasure. It was this forgetfulness I envied and admired.'' The homey comedy of *White Noise* invites us into a world we're glad to enter. Then the sinister buzz of implication makes the book unforgettably disturbing.

Walter Clemons, ''At the Edge of Dreams,'' in Newsweek, *Vol. CV, No. 3, January 21, 1985, p. 69.*

R. Z. SHEPPARD

Unrelieved worry about self-preservation is one of life's more depressing preoccupations. DeLillo illustrates this sad fact [in *White Noise*] and attempts to lift the dread with satire and comic invention. An expert explains the poison cloud that threatens Iron City: ''This is Nyodene D. A whole new generation of toxic waste. What we call state of the art.'' There are lampoons (if that is possible) of occult tabloids: ''From beyond the grave, dead living legend John Wayne will communicate telepathically with President Reagan to help frame U.S. foreign policy. Mellowed by death, the strapping actor will advocate a hopeful policy of peace and love.'' In what may be regarded lightly as a plot, Gladney searches for the source of Dylar, an experimental drug that allegedly cures fear of death.

The ''distinguished thing'' yields to no potions or megadoses of prose. DeLillo's gifts are lavish, but his vision is a bit facile. The white noise of the title is electronic static forced into symbolic service as some sort of universal death rattle. Throughout, technology is depicted as the ominous messenger of our common fate; even the price scanners in supermarkets are spooky. Discovering malevolence in things and systems rather than in people is a little callow, especially when DeLillo's solemn moralizing overruns his comedy. Perhaps that is why, after eight books, he still seems like a writer making a debut. (p. 73)

R. Z. Sheppard, ''Death 'n' Things,'' in Time, *Vol. 125, No. 3, January 21, 1985, pp. 71, 73.*

Dust jacket of White Noise, *by Don DeLillo. Viking, 1984. Jacket design by Neil Stuart. By permission of Viking Penguin Inc.*

THOMAS M. DISCH

[*Disch is an American novelist, short story writer, poet, librettist, editor, critic, and juvenile fiction writer whose elegant prose style is evident in both his science fiction and mainstream writings. His horrific fantasy novels, including* The Genocides *(1965),* Camp Concentration *(1968) and* The Businessman: A Tale of Terror *(1984), also function as satirical commentaries on the human condition. In the following excerpt Disch observes that DeLillo's distanced attitude towards death and suffering in* White Noise *undercuts the novel's dramatic impact. Nevertheless, he praises DeLillo's perceptive and amusing portrayals of American mass culture.*]

White Noise is as funny and as dramatically satisfying as a collection of the year's best *New Yorker* cartoons. It is a rum-soaked fruitcake packed with comic monologues, one-liners and shticks, all delivered in the same droller-than-life tone of mock-intellectual aphorizing. This uniform style of dialogue becomes as characteristic and signatory as the cartooning style of Charles Addams, Roz Chast or George Booth. . . .

The media are a pervasive presence in *White Noise,* and may indeed be its true subject (rather than death and the apocalyptic imagination, its ostensible subject). DeLillo shrewdly delineates the way the modern mind adjusts to a daily infusion of bad news, from the death of God to the slow metamorphosis of the nation into one big Love Canal. Comedy this black can always be accused of callousness, and history has underscored this for DeLillo by producing, simultaneously with his book, an "airborne toxic event" in India that will inevitably shape readers' responses to DeLillo's depiction of a similar crisis in an American suburb. (p. 120)

It is hard not to contrast this chimerical crisis to events in Bhopal. That DeLillo's cartooned catastrophe survives the comparison as well as it does is due to his insistence on showing the sense in which all public events are merely a branch of show business—until one's own eggs are scrambled. And even then . . . But DeLillo is always his own best explainer. Here is his view of the matter, as delivered by Alfonse Stompanato, the chairman of the department of American environments at an imaginary university (Stompanato has been asked why "decent, well-meaning and responsible people find themselves intrigued by catastrophe when they see it on television"):

> Because we're suffering from brain fade. We need an occasional catastrophe to break up the incessant bombardment of information. . . .
>
> The flow is constant. . . . Words, pictures, numbers, facts, graphics, statistics, specks, waves, particles, motes. Only a catastrophe gets our attention. We want them, we need them, we depend on them. As long as they happen somewhere else. This is where California comes in. Mud slides, brush fires, coastal erosion, earthquakes, mass killings, et cetera. We can relax and enjoy these disasters because in our hearts we feel that California deserves whatever it gets. Californians invented the concept of life-style. This alone warrants their doom. . . .
>
> Japan is pretty good for disaster footage. . . . India remains largely untapped. They have tremendous potential with their famines, monsoons, religious strife, train wrecks, boat sinkings, et cetera. But their disasters tend to go unrecorded. Three lines in the newspaper. No film footage, no satellite hookup. This is why California is so important.

In the category of oft-thought-but-ne'er-so-cruelly-expressed, *White Noise* offers literally hundreds of passages as quotable as the foregoing, and if you have enjoyed this sampling, you'll surely enjoy the book. But don't expect a story. By relegating pain and death to the category of media events, DeLillo has painted himself into a dramaturgical corner that inhibits all large gestures. In a comic showdown with a villain who has remained an offstage presence until the penultimate chapter, DeLillo strives for the kind of black farce patented by Nabokov, but the scene is a fiasco. DeLillo is an excellent ventriloquist, but when he tries to operate a puppet theater he gets tangled in the strings.

A worse blemish, because it is not confined to a single chapter, is the narrator's expressed (but not communicated) fear of death, a fear that becomes the prevailing metaphor of the last half of the book. Death, however, has lost most of its sting in DeLillo's postmodern cartoon landscape, where no character could say *"Timor mortis conturbat me"* without feeling obliged to follow up with a wisecrack. Basically, DeLillo has too hearty an appetite for the junk food of modern life for death to be a serious bother to him. He would seem to believe, with Roosevelt, that we have nothing to fear but fear itself, a very cheering and American sentiment which he has expressed in a cheering and very American book. (pp. 120-21)

Thomas M. Disch, "Maximum Exposure," in The Nation, *Vol. 240, No. 4, February 2, 1985, pp. 120-21.*

JAY McINERNEY

Yeats once remarked that sex and death were the proper concerns of literature. Don DeLillo's abiding concerns are technology and death, and in this he may be one of our few truly postmodern writers. . . . He is a virtuoso systems analyst, exploring the increasingly complex strategies we deploy in our attempts to beat back primal fears. In DeLillo's universe, technology is both cure and disease, the doomed master plot against death. DeLillo's novels not only have plots, they are about plots. He is a conspiracy theorist. The hazy and rigorous world of espionage is his central metaphor for all systems. The lover's deceptions are of a kind with the scheming of intelligence agents.

In his last novel, *The Names,* DeLillo worked on a global scale, juxtaposing the manipulations of multinational corporations and the C.I.A. with the primitive quest of a cult group dedicated to restoring lost innocence by killing victims on the basis of the letters of their names. In *White Noise,* his eighth novel, the setting is middle America. (p. 36)

[Jack Gladney, the narrator] wants a plotless existence. "All plots tend to move deathward," he tells the students in his advanced Nazism seminar, not quite sure what he means. "This is the nature of plots. Political plots, terrorist plots, lovers' plots, narrative plots, plots that are part of children's games. We edge nearer death every time we plot." When the novel opens he is healthy and has every reason to expect a long life, but Gladney is obsessed with his own mortality. (p. 37)

The black cloud, the "airborne toxic event" [that overtakes his town] is the objective correlative of Jack's fear. It is also the nightmare counterpart of the hypnotic, omnipresent white noise of the title, the banal surface of technology: "the jingles, the slice-of-life commercials, the products hurtling out of darkness, the coded messages, endless repetitions, like chants, like mantras. *Coke is it; Coke is it; Coke is it.*" Watching [his daughter] Steffie sleep in the evacuation shelter, Jack leans close when she begins to mutter something, hoping to be initiated into a mantra of innocence. The words she says are "Toyota Celica." (p. 38)

White Noise is a stunning performance from one of our finest and most intelligent novelists. DeLillo's reach is broad and deep, combining acute observation of the textures of American life and analytic rigor. The accumulation of evidence is sometimes indistinguishable from burlesque as, for example, when DeLillo gives all three of Gladney's wives CIA connections. Although DeLillo consciously, and for the most part deftly, mixes modes, occasionally we see the seams between the real and the surreal; at times the observation seems a little too consciously shaped in the service of thematic impulses. But at his best DeLillo masterfully orchestrates the idioms of pop culture, science, computer technology, advertising, politics, semiotics, espionage, and about 30 other specialized vocabularies. An official in charge of a program to simulate disaster evacuation complains to Gladney about the messiness of the real thing: "The insertion curve isn't as smooth as we'd like. There's a probability excess. Plus which we don't have our victims laid out where we'd want them if this were an actual simulation." Because he is so deadly serious, it is not said often enough that DeLillo is tremendously funny. *White Noise* is one of his most accessible novels. Access and interface with it immediately. (pp. 38-9)

Jay McInerney, "Midwestern Wasteland," in The New Republic, *Vol. 192, No. 5, February 4, 1985, pp. 36-9.*

An Excerpt from *White Noise*

I followed him into the supermarket. Blasts of color, layers of oceanic sound. We walked under a bright banner announcing a raffle to raise money for some incurable disease. The wording seemed to indicate that the winner would get the disease. Murray likened the banner to a Tibetan prayer flag.

"Why have I had this fear so long, so consistently?"

"It's obvious. You don't know how to repress. We're all aware there's no escape from death. How do we deal with this crushing knowledge? We repress, we disguise, we bury, we exclude. Some people do it better than others, that's all."

"How can I improve?"

"You can't. Some people just don't have the unconscious tools to perform the necessary disguising operations."

"How do we know repression exists if the tools are unconscious and the thing we're repressing is so cleverly disguised?"

"Freud said so. Speaking of looming figures."

He picked up a box of Handi-Wrap II, reading the display type, studying the colors. He smelled a packet of dehydrated soup. The data was strong today.

"Do you think I'm somehow healthier because I don't know how to repress? Is it possible that constant fear is the natural state of man and that by living close to my fear I am actually doing something heroic, Murray?"

"Do you feel heroic?"

"No."

"Then you probably aren't."

"But isn't repression unnatural?"

"Fear is unnatural. Lightning and thunder are unnatural. Pain, death, reality, these are all unnatural. We can't bear these things as they are. We know too much. So we resort to repression, compromise and disguise. This is how we survive in the universe. This is the natural language of the species."

I looked at him carefully.

"I exercise. I take care of my body."

"No, you don't," he said.

He helped an old man read the date on a loaf of raisin bread. Children sailed by in silver carts.

"Tegrin, Denorex, Selsun Blue."

Murray wrote something in his little book. I watched him step deftly around a dozen fallen eggs oozing yolky matter from a busted carton.

"Why do I feel so good when I'm with Wilder? It's not like being with the other kids," I said.

"You sense his total ego, his freedom from limits."

"In what way is he free from limits?"

"He doesn't know he's going to die. He doesn't know death at all. You cherish this simpleton blessing of his, this exemption from harm. You want to get close to him, touch him, look at him, breathe him in. How lucky he is. A cloud of unknowing, an omnipotent little person. The child is everything, the adult nothing. Think about it. A person's entire life is the unraveling of this conflict. No wonder we're bewildered, staggered, shattered."

"Aren't you going too far?"

"I'm from New York."

"We create beautiful and lasting things, build vast civilizations."

"Gorgeous evasions," he said. "Great escapes."

DIANE JOHNSON

[*Johnson is an American novelist, critic, and biographer whose novels, such as* The Shadow Knows *(1974), focus on the personal and social alienation of modern women. She served as a judge on the American Book Award panel that chose* White Noise *as its fiction prizewinner for 1985. In the following excerpt Johnson defends DeLillo against critic Jonathan Yardley (see excerpt above) who charged that DeLillo neglects plot and character in* White Noise *in favor of "trendy political themes."*]

The horrors of 1984 did not emerge quite in the form that Orwell imagined, reminding us that novelists are usually more gifted with hindsight than with prescience. Many novelists confess to feeling that there are certain things they dare not write, for fear they will come true, and can tell you of things they have written which have afterward happened, proving, if not prescience, the power of wishes. Novelists stay away from prediction. Not to make too much of the "airborne toxic event" in Don DeLillo's new novel, *White Noise,* and the Bhopal tragedy it anticipates, but it is the index of DeLillo's sensibility, so alert is he to the content, not to mention the speech rhythms, dangers, dreams, fears, etc., of modern life that you imagine him having to spend a certain amount of time in a quiet, darkened room. He works with less lead time than other satirists, too—we should have teen-age suicide and the new patriotism very soon—and this must be demanding. But here, as in his other novels, his voice is authoritative, his tone characteristically light. In all his work he seems less angry or disappointed than some critics of society, as if he had expected less in the first place, or perhaps his marvelous power with words is compensation for him.

White Noise is a meditation on themes of whiteness—the pallor of death, and white noise, the sound, so emblematic of modern life, that is meant to soothe human beings by screening out the other, more irritating noises of their civilization. . . .

As we read fiction, we are always aware of the operative formal principle—it's either "life" (meandering, inconclusive) or "plot," as in this novel, where the fortune or fate of an individual is opposed to a conspiracy, to a plot within the plot, which serves as a metaphor for the world itself, organized against you, clever, wickedly determined on its own usually illegal ends, and in this mirroring the illicit desires of our own hearts. Thus the pirates, spy rings, smugglers, dope pushers, CIA, criminal organizations, high-up secret governmental department, terrorist cadre, heartless chemical industry we find in some of the most interesting recent fiction, conspirators

representing in microcosm the hostile confusion and formless menace of the big world. A novel whose plot contains a plot might be *the* postmodern novel, an adaptation of an earlier model of fiction, from before the era of the fiction of the self, when we had novels of the person in society or the universe, making his or her way, and making judgments on it. It is a distinguished tradition from Gulliver to Greene, but harder than ever to succeed in, now that plots demand an extreme imagination if they are to surpass what is furnished by mere reality. (p. 6)

All of Don DeLillo's fictions contain these conspiratorial models of the world. In *Players* two Yuppies get mixed up with urban terrorists. In *Running Dog* a porn ring tries to get its hands on a dirty home movie reputed to have been made *in the bunker.* In *Great Jones Street* a drug syndicate pursues a depressed rock star who unwittingly possesses their stash. Chemical substances and commodities, like the conspiracies, and like the dustheaps in Dickens, embody the moral defects of the society that produces them.

In *White Noise* the conspirators try to find a drug that will take away the fear of death from a society that is fixedly preoccupied with producing death, but the motive is profit. Sometimes the desire for power, or to possess the substance for its own sake, moves the plot, but the Dickensian themes of mistaken, lost, or found identity, themes that have dominated novels ever since the nineteenth century, are deliberately effaced—another gloss on the modern situation. Perhaps a vestige of the struggle for place, that other Victorian obsession, can be seen in Jack's efforts to stake out an academic niche for himself as chairman of Hitler Studies.

One finds these plots, these themes, in other contemporary novels—by Robert Stone, or Gore Vidal (in his *Duluth* or *Kalki* mode), or Joan Didion, and however one might long for the affirmative charm of, say, Grace Paley, one can't but admit that these are powerful observers. . . . Of course people are by no means agreed that the world is a suitable subject for fiction. The distinguished *Washington Post* critic Jonathan Yardley objects to DeLillo's topical agenda [see excerpt above]: "Could there be a more predictable catalogue of trendy political themes: radiation, addiction to violence, television as religion, the trivialization of suffering, the vulgarity of America?" But is topicality only transmogrified into art by the passage of time? Without a willingness to engage the problems of the world around him, we would not have the novels of Dickens, just as, without an acid tone and interest in abstraction, we would not have the novels of Voltaire, or Peacock, or Huxley. Yardley complains, like others, about "fiction as op-ed material. . . . a novel that simply does not work as *fiction,* which is the novelist's first artistic obligation." The difficulty seems to lie in the definition of fiction: "None of the characters acquires any genuine humanity."

Along with the novel of plot and the novel of character, certain old-fashioned theorists of the novel would sometimes speak of the novel of ideas, implying that it was a special taste, and that there is something distinct, if not antithetical, about ideas and the kind of narrative pleasure one derives from less abstract and more simply suspenseful stories: what will happen next? Perhaps the novel of ideas cannot be as exciting, if the ideas demand, like badly brought-up children, to be noticed. Perhaps, even, the reader's awareness of the restless and skeptical intelligence of the author may in some absolute sense operate against such reader responses as sympathy and identification. One is always slightly too aware of the efforts of, say, Bellow, another novelist of ideas, to try to combat their effect by putting in charming human touches, and DeLillo certainly tries to do that here, strewing the text with kids and endearing details of family life.

A first-person protagonist is at least a concession to our old-fashioned wish for heroines and heroes, somebody to stumble through the narrative, thinking the thoughts, experiencing the emotions, more reassuringly human than in satires like Vidal's equally trenchant but chillier *Duluth,* for instance, where all the jokes are the author's. Authors in their omniscience can be intimidating, and perhaps should be advised to conceal their intelligence, the way girls used to be advised to do. Anyhow, we are happy to have Jack Gladney, a diplomatic creation on DeLillo's part, and necessary to a fiction that could otherwise seem too programmatic or too abstract, a regular guy who, because an airborne toxic event and the fear of death are part of his life, convinces us that these unwelcome universals will soon be part of ours.

A more conventional hapless hero, like Jay McInerney's in his recent *Bright Lights, Big City,* may make us laugh by doing a bunch of bad-boy dumb things—too much cocaine before an office deadline—but he does them with minimum self-awareness, and a kind of irritating (male?) confidence in the total indulgence of his readers, among whom the men are expected to identify with him, the women forgive. But Gladney disarms by his penetration, even if he is a five-times married academic who goes around wearing his robe and dark glasses and has to pretend to know German. ("I talked mainly about Hitler's mother, brother and dog. His dog's name was Wolf. This word is the same in English and German. . . . I'd spent days with the dictionary, compiling lists of such words.")

All the characters are infected by Jack's high interrogative style. The novel is entirely composed of questions, sometimes ones you'd like to know the answers to: "Were people this dumb before television?" "Does a man like yourself know the size of India's standing army?" "What if someone held a gun to your head?" "What if the symptoms are real?"

What accounts for the charm of these serious novels on dread subjects? Perhaps Jack's eloquence is such that we are a little less harrowed by his author's exacting and despairing view of civilization. And he is very funny. Besides, there is the special pleasure afforded by the extraordinary language, the coherence of the imagery, saturated with chemicals and whiteness and themes of poisons and shopping, the nice balance of humor and poignance, solemn nonsense and real questions:

> "What do I do to make death less strange? How do I go about it?"
>
> "I don't know."
>
> "Do I risk death by driving fast around curves? Am I supposed to go rock climbing on weekends?"
>
> "I don't know," she said. "I wish I knew."

(pp. 6-7)

Diane Johnson, "Conspirators," in The New York Review of Books, *Vol. XXXII, No. 4, March 14, 1985, pp. 6-7.*

ANNA SHAPIRO

You do not at first think you will be able to take a character like Jack a.k.a. J.A.K. Gladney—divorced both from Janet

Savory a.k.a. Mother Devi and from Tweedy Browner—seriously. Nor do you think you will need to, since Jack seems to take himself pretty lightly, running the Hitler department at the College-on-the-Hill, driving his charmingly frowsy current wife, Babette, to her posture class, or exchanging flashy aphorisms with his colleagues in the popular culture department, particularly Murray Jay Siskind, who describes himself as "the Jew. What else would I be?" But then Jack encounters the "airborne toxic event," a cloud of "Nyodene D," and discovers that Babette is taking a mystery drug called Dylar, after which he has to take everything seriously. The Dylar comes in capsules engineered like spaceships that release the drug evenly and continuously through a laser-drilled hole. This might be a model for the book and everything in it, all of which revolves around man-made disaster and natural pleasure. *White Noise* is swoopingly elegant, releasing its opaque insights in a continuous stream of glossily rendered close observation. As with any good novel—as with Dylar—it distances you from death and other personal fears by delivering them through the characters. It is funny. It is irritating. It is baffling. It is clever, modern and celebratory in a downbeat fashion. And like Dylar, it implodes when finished.

Anna Shapiro, in a review of "White Noise," in Saturday Review, *Vol. 11, No. 2, March-April, 1985, p. 65.*

THOMAS DE PIETRO

Don DeLillo's centerless novels everywhere threaten to deconstruct. No character or idea—and his clever novels abound in both—appears more privileged than the next. He parts company, though, with other technicians of uncertainty—Pynchon or Barth, say—in that his work poses an urgent and admirable challenge: to locate ourselves within the heightened reality he so accurately records. . . . (p. 219)

Everyday life [in *White Noise*] for Gladney, his wife Babette, and their children from previous marriages has always proceeded randomly, defined by media-created images, full of "vague forebodings" and "nameless dread." The "dark black breathing thing of smoke" wafting from the train yard seems to be merely another occasion to ponder death in the abstract—a subject of endless fear and fascination for Gladney and Babette, whose daily quibbles result from simple questions: which toothpaste should they buy? who will die first?

This juxtaposition of consumption with death may be funny, but it's no joke. The peace and security found in malls and supermarkets, where many of the lives in *White Noise* unfold, calm palpitating hearts and cool sweaty palms. Numbing flourescent light seems to stave off death. "We don't die," a character says strolling the aisles, "we shop." The mantra-like chants of product names which punctuate DeLillo's manic narrative promise his characters "a fullness of being that is not known to people who need less, expect less, who plan their lives around lonely walks in the evening."

But DeLillo's penchant for waxing theoretical about consumption is itself consumed in parody. Everywhere in the novel popular culture assaults with its overripe imagery and everywhere a colleague of Gladney's is there to interpret it for us: Alfonse (Fast Food) Stompanato on prewar soda pop bottles, Murray Jay Siskind on car crashes in the cinema, Dimitrios Cotsakis on Elvis. These iconologists and mythographers of "the American mystery" caricature the kind of high-minded defenses of mass culture common among pundits and professors. The reverential awe and academic solemnity Gladney's buddies bring to their wacky subjects throw into doubt their genuine insight into the "only avant-garde we've got"—the culture of consumption. (pp. 219-20)

Concocted images of more than just death saturate the world of *White Noise*—a world coterminous with our own—until the point of mass skepticism. The most articulate skeptic here is Gladney's precocious son Heinrich, a fourteen-year-old deconstructionist, whose philosophical playfulness rivals that of Jacques Derrida. In one particularly Kantian aside, Heinrich calls into question his father's idle speculation on the weather: "Our senses are wrong more often than they're right. This has been proved in the laboratory. Don't you know about all those theorems that say nothing is what is seems? There's no past, present, or future outside our own minds." Heinrich gives voice to the collapse of object into subject which everyone else in *White Noise* experiences silently. What further distinguishes DeLillo from other postmodern explorers of subjectivity is his determination to discover the social consequences of his abstract idea.

The most immediate consequence is a world in which no one is sure how to function. Babette's classes in sitting, standing, and walking—she's to begin teaching one in eating and drinking—together make up a technology of everyday survival. Gladney's fascination with fascism derives from a similar impulse; the holocaust becomes a metaphor for quotidian helplessness and victimization—a metaphor deflated by DeLillo's piercing wit.

In DeLillo's truly Swiftian social satire, we're never sure what he himself believes or what he thinks of his characters. As in Swift, we're instead forced to rely on ourselves, to measure literary experience against our own sense of reality. For DeLillo, a novelist of questions, there is no clear winner in the struggle between randomness and order. In this case, Gladney's crazed pursuit of the drug Dylar (an antidote to the fear of death) gives shape to the chaos everywhere imminent in the novel. Death too pervades *White Noise,* on the air (televised catastrophe), in the air (the toxic cloud) and in the title itself ('What if death is nothing but sound? . . . Uniform, white"). The only relief is laughter, pure and unabated—the kind DeLillo induces with apparent effortlessness. What we laugh at is ourselves in constant fear of oblivion. From the accumulation of consumer rot, DeLillo manufactures a wonderfully comic apocalypse—a genuine revelation. (p. 220)

> *Thomas De Pietro, "Laughing through the Malls,"* in Commonweal, *Vol. CXII, No. 7, April 5, 1985, pp. 219-20.*

ALBERT MOBILIO

In Don DeLillo's first novel, *Americana,* published in 1971, a television producer embarked on a cross-country trip, camera in hand, from Madison Avenue to Dealey Plaza. His desire to nail down the gas-driven, motel-housed American soul indicated the scope of DeLillo's ambition and established one of his abiding themes: Americans' fondness for their own reflection. In seven subsequent novels he's watched us watch ourselves, measuring in keenly observant prose the depth and cost of that self-absorption. His richest conceit in developing this vision has been technology's ability to project the reassuring likeness—hence television's status as a character in many books. But broadcast waves just mediate the fascination; the mirror game is a human one. Its motivation is expressed without

embarrassment by *Americana*'s narrator: "When I began to wonder who I was, I took the simple step of lathering my face and shaving. It all became so clear, so wonderful. I was blue-eyed David Bell. Obviously my life depended on this fact."

Working a territory thick with social critics, DeLillo spares us the polemics. In the current *New Criterion* [April 1985], he's accused of passing cynical judgments, but criticism of that sort misinterprets his tone. His tack is inquisitive, almost anthropological, as he serves up a variety of American specialties like college football (*End Zone*), leftists and the CIA (*Running Dog*), rock music (*Great Jones Street*), and Wall Street (*Players*). An intensely visual writer, DeLillo can locate and dissect the telling freeze—porchfront cocktails on a suburban Sunday or downtown Manhattan's rush-hour ballet. He illuminates the idiosyncrasies of our tribal life with an indulgent grace that imparts a sense of communality where none was ever imagined. Yet the darker side of such attachments, the subterranean warfare Americans wage against their own cultural and ideological inventions, inspires his shrewdest insights.

What sets DeLillo apart from moralists like Heller or Bellow is an understanding of the complicitous bond between individual and institution. His novels actually celebrate the confusion over personal responsibility for public madness. To this end he turns the trick of making Wall Street or the CIA objects of wondrous contemplation, splicing a clipped lyricism with technical detail to produce descriptions of labyrinthine toys, exaggerated sums of private fears.

While DeLillo's Americans nurse paranoias large and small, they're most frightened of themselves. Apprentice schizophrenics living in willful isolation, these characters still maintain a practiced cool. Thinking tends to occur in quotation marks, acute self-awareness permitting only laconic assessments of surface activity. Their cramped, often abstract dialogue suggests that words aren't quite up to the job of saying what's felt. Sex is rendered topologically, in terms of tensed arcs and shifting planes: a poetry for wind-up romance. The implacable aloneness and emotional confinement surface repeatedly as amply qualified passion: "He was lean and agile. She found herself scratching his shoulders, working against his body with uncharacteristic intensity. Who is this son of a bitch, she thought." The narcissism is corrosive, potentially terminal; these people worry themselves to death.

DeLillo's new novel, *White Noise,* takes that possibility seriously, exploring the narcissist's inevitable trap: a preoccupation with dying. (pp. 49-50)

For solace, [Jack Gladney] turns to his family, a middle ground between fervent isolation and mass hysteria. A family took center stage in DeLillo's last novel, *The Names;* he examined its emotional strategies and hermetic codes with sympathetic insight absent from his earlier books. In *White Noise* he extends this evocation of the complex, colloquial textures of contemporary family life. . . .

DeLillo's surgical analysis of their domestic rituals uncovers the irresistible force proximity exerts on personality, a force that fuels Gladney's obsession. When infant son Wilder begins crying inexplicably and continues for hours, Gladney hears "an anguish so accessible that it rushes to overwhelm whatever immediately caused it. There was something permanent and soul-struck in this crying. It was the sound of inbred desolation." What he hears, of course, is his own unvoiced pain. Every embrace he and Babette share is followed by a silent refrain: Who will die first? This unrestrained projection of despair seems to bear out faculty friend Murray Siskind's remark that "the family is the cradle of the world's misfortune." But ultimately DeLillo sees these human connections as too vital and necessary to be easily dismissed. In counterpoint he's drawn a compassionate picture of a primitive refuge in a modern "world of hostile fact." . . .

In the book's closing scene Gladney describes son Wilder pedaling his tricycle through four lanes of highway traffic. The child, oblivious to the danger, arrives safely on the other side, where he slips in a puddle and only then begins to cry.

The coda affirms the workaday usefulness of faith, however naive or contrived, and recalls its primal, complementary link to mortality. In the emergency room Gladney quizzes a nun who denies believing in heaven. She tells him, "Our pretense is a dedication. Someone must appear to believe. Our lives are no less serious than if we professed real faith, real belief. As belief shrinks from the world, people find it more necessary than ever that *someone* believe." This resolution, no doubt equivocal, still offers some possibility of escaping the self's prison. Indeed, it is the author's most optimistic reading of the situation yet.

In light of this, *White Noise* can be taken as a terse summa of DeLillo's work. Again he shows Americans to be a damaged breed, carnivores devouring their own tails. Our peculiar brand of extinction—which, as Gladney points out, deserves an aerosol spray can for a tombstone—embodies our deepest wishes. The technological prowess evidenced by carcinogens, television, and the fantasy drug Dylar serves a consumptive, and therefore fatal love of self. Its death rattle is heard in TV's electronic din, the book's "white noise." DeLillo, it seems, may lean a bit too hard here. While his grasp of television's fluid grammar and mime of broadcast patter are first-rate, perhaps he's come to regard the box as too sinister, too important. Granted, it lulls us with "coded messages and endless repetitions," and attractive footage of downed jets and hostage shoot-outs offers intimate knowledge of death. But by trying to prove such knowledge makes us "strangers in our own dying," DeLillo appears to be straining. If death has been wrung free of mystery and meaning, larger factors must weigh in alongside the evening news as culprits.

This slight imbalance aside, the novel is perceptively targeted—and the writing, as usual, is sharp as cut glass. DeLillo becomes increasingly elliptical with every book, as if he's paring his prose to the style of a scientist's notebook. Paradoxically, the distillation is matched by a more subtle and convincing treatment of his characters' inner lives. This broadened emotional vocabulary charges *White Noise* with a resonance and credibility that makes it difficult to ignore. Critics who have argued his work is too clever and overly intellectual should take notice: DeLillo's dark vision is now hard-earned. It strikes at both head and heart. (p. 50)

> *Albert Mobilio, "Death by Inches," in* The Village
> Voice, *Vol. XXX, No. 18, April 30, 1985, pp. 49-50.*

ROBERT PHILLIPS

Don DeLillo's eighth novel [*White Noise*] is not extremely long; it just seems that way. Book after book has been greeted by critics as "a novel of ideas." Finally, however, the ideas have overwhelmed the novel. Quite possibly DeLillo—like James Baldwin, Mary McCarthy and Gore Vidal—would be more at home with the personal essay form than the novel. One wonders

how many more times, in how many fictional guises, his characters can tell us that life in America today is boring, dehumanized and dangerous. . . .

Among the many enemies in this novel are television, plastic furniture, spray mists, automated teller machines, sugarless gum and churches located in mobile homes. The chief dread, however, is an "airborne toxic event." . . .

This is original and promising material. But DeLillo's style has hardened into predictable mannerisms that stand between him and the reader. One is his penchant for rhetorical questions. All his characters launch into interminable tirades, even Heinrich, Jack's adolescent son. When asked what he wants to do in life, he replies: "Who knows what I want to do? Who knows what anyone wants to do? How can you be sure about something like that? Isn't it all a question of brain chemistry, signals going back and forth, electrical energy in the cortex? How do you know whether something is really what you want to do or just some kind of nerve impulse in the brain?" And so on. If only Heinrich spoke this way, you might take him for either a genius or a nut. But every character speaks this way. Whenever they are not speculating or philosophizing, they engage in improbable exchanges, such as when Jack meets a colleague in the supermarket. "How are you, Jack?" the other asks. "What did you mean, how are you?" Jack wonders. Sure.

The problem is, DeLillo loves language and cuteness at the expense of probability and characterization. He falls in love with a phrase like "fluctuating plane" and makes it the very music of existence. The two words he places in the mouth of a disturbed daughter talking in her sleep are: "Toyota Celica."

Consequently, *White Noise* has no characters, only mouthpieces for Don DeLillo's rather tired world view. Oh, I'm wrong. There is one character: a dog who thinks he is a space alien. He stares out of windows—but not just any window. He trots up to the attic, places his elbows on the sill to look out the highest window, as if waiting for instructions from above. Now *there's* a character.

> *Robert Phillips, in a review of "White Noise," in*
> America, *Vol. 153, No. 1, July 6-13, 1985, p. 16.*

ROZ KAVENEY

When Jack Gladney, head of a prestigious University Department of Hitler Studies where he teaches Advanced Nazism, is faced with the potential social embarrassment of hosting a conference in his field while having no German, our response is merely to shake our heads and say "That so, that so". This comic effect, our belated recognition that our outrage has been disconnected, is one that has long been familiar to American comedians, and a few of Don DeLillo's throwaways [in *White Noise*]—"There is no Hitler building as such"—have the air of out-takes from a Mel Brooks film. There is a sense in much modern life that almost anything, perhaps especially anything horrid, that might be imagined will turn up as a logical and unforeseen consequence of earlier social trends; DeLillo takes this and builds round it a gentle fiction dominated by the appropriate lack of surprise, even by bland resignation. He used similar effects less well in an earlier novel, *Running Dog,* where they were combined with a parody of spy thrillers; in that particular genre, moral sensibilities have a tendency to be so blunted already that parodic use of it is no longer a forceful way of making the point.

White Noise is more in the mainstream of contemporary American fiction; the principal characters are academics or their children by previous marriages. Much of it is concerned with the mundane—though at times the mundane is turned to worrying confusion, as when, in a stunning coda to the novel, the local supermarket rearranges its shelves, and regulars mill around, uncertain as to the location of scouring pads and cream of wheat. When this world is disrupted by the melodramatic (Gladney's shooting of the scientist who has abused his research in order to seduce Gladney's wife Babette) or the apocalyptic (the menacing of the town in general and Gladney in particular by a cloud of toxic waste), the tone continues to be one of routine coping, and of mild intrigued amusement. Gladney is an attractive protagonist because his responses are all of a piece; he makes no exceptions to his moral and emotional detachment, neither for his own approaching death nor for Babette's use of dangerous experimental medication, hardly even for their toddler son's crossing of the local freeway on his plastic tricycle. There are metaphysical aspects to all of this (Babette is trying to cure herself of the fear of death, even at the risk of dying; the chemicals that are killing Gladney may well take more than his natural life-span to do so), but they have no resonance in this muted atmosphere of intellectual cool.

DeLillo does not make the mistake of resting on the power and validity of these ideas and observations, or of embodying them only in staccato one-liners. His prose is as coolly observant of concrete detail, as obsessed with intellectual balance, as his central character is, whether the matter to hand is a technique for administering drugs or the arrival of students in an endless line of station wagons full of commodities. In the stripped, mocking dialogue of precocious children, we hear a hint of silent and accustomed familial affection and regard: this is an alternative and unsentimental focus of our response to the novel.

Roz Kaveney, "The Disconnected View," in The Times Literary Supplement, *No. 4320, January 17, 1986, p. 56.*

Louise Erdrich

Love Medicine

The National Book Critics Circle Award: Fiction

American short story writer, novelist, and poet.

Erdrich grew up near the Turtle Mountain Chippewa Reservation in North Dakota, the setting for her first novel, *Love Medicine* (1984). Both her parents—her father was German-born and her mother a Chippewa Indian—worked for the Bureau of Indian Affairs, and Erdrich often visited her maternal grandparents on the Chippewa Reservation. When she went to Dartmouth College in 1972 Erdrich met her future husband and literary collaborator, anthropologist Michael Dorris, who is also part Indian and who heads the Native American Studies Program at Dartmouth. Erdrich's short stories have appeared in several journals, including *The New England Review, Kenyon Review, Chicago, Atlantic Monthly,* and *American Indian Quarterly*. Her short story "Scales" was anthologized in *Best American Short Stories 1983,* and "Saint Marie" was selected for *Prize Stories: The O. Henry Awards 1985*. Though Erdrich has written much short fiction, the stories that make up *Love Medicine* are her first attempt to deal with her Chippewa heritage in fictional form. Erdrich recalls: "I tried to write about it, but I just wasn't able to address that part of me, to speak in that voice. It was difficult. It forced me to come to terms with who I am." Erdrich credits her husband with helping her conceive and edit the stories that evolved into *Love Medicine*. While Erdrich does all the writing, both she and Dorris discuss the plots and characters; Dorris also acts as her agent.

Love Medicine is not a novel in the traditional sense, but a set of fourteen interconnected short stories, narrated by seven different members of the Kashpaw and Lamartine families. Each story is self-contained, but refers to characters and incidents mentioned elsewhere in the book. These dramatic vignettes cover a fifty-year time span beginning in the 1930s and involve a complex network of characters, each a richly drawn individual, yet adding to a total portrait of the Turtle Mountain Chippewa community. Some reviewers find Erdrich's handling of her characters confusing, especially at the book's beginning when a plethora of information about familial and sexual interrelationships is introduced. Noting her fine poetic gift—Erdrich also published a collection of poems, *Jacklight* (1984)—critics observe a lyric quality in her prose that emphasizes the moments of joy and beauty in her subjects' lives, otherwise blighted by poverty and racism. Erdrich's decidedly literary approach in emphasizing the universal, legendary qualities of her stories makes *Love Medicine* more than an exposé of life on Native American reservations. This novel is the first installment of a tetralogy planned by Erdrich; she is working on a second volume, *The Beet Queen*.

(See also *Contemporary Authors,* Vol. 114.)

© Jerry Bauer

KIRKUS REVIEWS

Called a novel, Erdrich's book of powerful stories [*Love Medicine*] interlocks the lives of two Chippewa families in North Dakota, the Kashpaws and the Lamartines (though some are Morrisseys too, and Nanapushes)—a tribal chronicle of defeat that ranges from 1934 to the present. Illegitimacy, alcoholism, prison, and aborted dreams of something better mark both clans; and the fluidity of exchange between them is echoed by poet Erdrich's loose, time-shifting approach—an oblique sort of narration that sometimes makes it difficult to remember who's who among the characters. Even when hard to follow, however, this web of stories keeps its theme vividly in focus: the magical haunting that reminds the various generations of the families of their basic identity. And, whether the haunting comes in the form of nightmares or supernatural powers, Erdrich convinces us that these people, sunk as low as imaginable, retain *powers,* the "love medicine" of the title. . . . Erdrich fuses mystery and violence, exaltation and deepest despair—so poetically that the rich prose sometimes clots. But, despite flaws and excesses, this is a notable, impressive book of first fiction: the unique evocation of a culture in severe social ruin, yet still aglow with the privilege and power of access to the spirit-world. (pp. 765-66)

A review of "Love Medicine," in Kirkus Reviews, *Vol. LII, No. 16, August 15, 1984, pp. 765-66.*

CYNTHIA KOOI

Louise Erdrich's first novel [*Love Medicine*] is a beautifully written, realistic account of the lives of two Chippewa Indian families. Told from multiple points of view, with members of the Kashpaw and Lamartine families as narrators, the book spans the time from 1934 to 1984. Erdrich creates characters who are loving in their desperation and who reveal the differences between individuals by the similarities of their society—their spare existence forces Marie to hard work, but inspires Lulu to plant an enviable flower garden. Such characters as June, a woman who flaunts beauty with a smile, and Nector, a stately Indian whose picture once hung in North Dakota's state capitol, intertwine the two families through their greed for love, giving birth to children who late in life discover their heritage. The book poignantly reflects the plight of contemporary Indians and at the same time depicts people the reader wants to be with a little bit longer.

Cynthia Kooi, in a review of "Love Medicine," in Booklist, *Vol. 81, No. 1, September 1, 1984, p. 24.*

JEANNE KINNEY

The critic and novelist Tom Wolfe said recently: "The U.S. is afflicted with 'cultural amnesia' . . . much of the will of a nation is comprised of memory and memories have to be brought alive by artists. That is one of the great forgotten roles of artists."

In *Love Medicine*, Louise Erdrich's first novel, the memory of Native American life on a reservation in North Dakota is brought to life. Character after character tell their individual stories until at the end we readers have circled and entered the world of two Chippewa extended families. By showing their world impinging on the white world that surrounds them and by showing the white world impinging on them, the author leads us into another culture, her own. The stories, beautifully crafted, lead to the conclusion that in not knowing this people before we have truly impoverished our land.

Louise Erdrich's stories celebrate the ordinary parts of life. Like many women authors, she seems to appreciate the balance between the commonplace and the sensational. At age thirty, by capturing the depth of spirit of the Native through her artistry, she leaps into the role of major American novelist on her first try. . . . She does so by stringing together a series of characterizations connected only by relatives from one story wandering into another, as happens in small-town life anywhere, yet in this piece of North Dakota reservation she uncovers a foreign culture—that's been here all along but is foreign to us white invaders.

The Catholic Church too has its foreign culture. The convent where the nuns live appears in a couple of stories as a house of horrors and as the house on the hill where one goes for charity and white approval. I remembered the African missionaries who found it necessary to incorporate and blend the natives' concept of God into their proselytizing to be successful. Native Americans also have much to tell us about God, a God close to nature.

The third-world aspect of these stories is not prominent, except that Native Americans share many of the trials that oppressed people share everywhere: generations of men relying on alcohol and sex for esteem, rather than deeds of greatness or money making capability; and generations of women coping with little money and many children and questionable fidelities. Like poor everywhere they are people-rich and land-poor, sharing with one another and hoping the eternal hope of a better life.

These stories point out that the native Americans share the same troubles as the rest of us—senility in old parents, veterans of war unable to forget, and children getting into trouble.

These pages open up for us a new type of compassion, forgiveness, and strength. Nice people. Happy to know you at last. (pp. 324-25)

Jeanne Kinney, in a review of "Love Medicine," in Best Sellers, *Vol. 44, No. 9, December, 1984, pp. 324-25.*

D.J.R. BRUCKNER

There are at least a dozen of the many vividly drawn people in [*Love Medicine*] who will not leave the mind once they are let in. Their power comes from Louise Erdrich's mastery of words. Nobody really talks the way they do, but the language of each convinces you you have heard them speaking all your life, and that illusion draws you quickly into their world, a place of poor shacks stuck amid the wrecks of old cars and other junk made beautiful in Miss Erdrich's evocation.

The voice of the narrator intervenes only a few times in the novel. Otherwise, seven characters tell theirs and one another's stories at different times of their lives; many of their tales have the structure and lyric voice of ballads. Miss Erdrich is a skilled poet and the voices she creates in her novel are distinct; it is when they quote one another that her art shows (once in a while she is a bit too clever), and when they make random remarks to one another the way members of a family do, the reader cannot quite remember what he was told that makes him understand them. . . .

[The] characters are mostly Chippewa Indians or, like the author, a mixture of European and Chippewa descent. But Miss Erdrich is not out scouting Indians. Their culture and beliefs are in the background but it is with real surprise that one realizes eventually that these people are different.

At the outset a woman who has been having a fling in town sets out to walk back to her reservation and dies in a blizzard on the way. Suddenly her niece is telling of a family gathering later that ends in a fight as comically mean and memorable as those in some of Sam Shepard's plays. Along the way, in less than 30 pages, she has given us all the main characters and the beginnings of the many plots.

That girl's grandmother tells of entering a convent 50 years before as a teen-ager; she barely escaped alive from a nun who was hot on the tracks of the devil, but she has survived triumphant. Not 200 yards into her flight she meets the man she will marry and their encounter is at once appalling and funny (Miss Erdrich has a keen, and classical, sense of humor about sex). Then the different characters unfold a score of interleaved stories of love, mystery, death, adventure, tragedy and hope in what all but a few of them see as lives without fate, destiny or providence.

Almost everyone in *Love Medicine* is related to everyone else. It would take genealogists or canon lawyers to track the consanguinity, but the blood tie is essential to the transformation of their tawdry stories from roadhouse tragedies into legends. Many are familiar legends, including the one that leads to the novel's climax—a young man's search for his real father, which involves his painful recognition of who his real mother was. Miss Erdrich's confident use of such legends is canny; her strange and sometimes wild characters are on quests we all know, from the past and from deep inside ourselves.

Every detail in this novel counts and eventually they all come together. The man who throws himself on the girl fleeing the convent is carrying wild geese he has shot, birds that play a comic role in his awkward lovemaking. The hearts of wild geese are love medicines to these Indians. When that suddenly-joined couple's grandson tries to reconcile them with the same medicine 50 years later the geese won't cooperate and what he substitutes for their hearts proves fatal to his grandfather. But his account of the incident makes one laugh out loud. There is a lot of honest laughter here, and most of it comes at just such moments; one laughs and blushes for it.

In the end the troubling emotions Miss Erdrich has drawn from one also come together in two great reconciliations. Two old women, one who had eight children by eight fathers and the other, the girl who fled the convent, whose husband was one of those fathers and whose own family had swelled with uncounted orphans and castaways, come to an understanding of one another's lifetime loves that defeats words but goes right to the heart. And the young man finds his father in a place of terror from which they escape in a bright red car with blue wings painted on the hood (cars are real characters in this novel; they reveal a lot about the souls of people), taking a journey to understanding that puts one in mind of the lines of the poet John Wieners: "The beauty of men never dies / It drives a blue car through the stars."

> *D.J.R. Bruckner, in a review of "Love Medicine," in* The New York Times, *December 20, 1984, p. C21.*

MARCO PORTALES

Ethnic writing—works that focus on the lives and particular concerns of America's minorities—labors under a peculiar burden: only certain types of people are supposed to be interested. Louise Erdrich's first novel, *Love Medicine*, . . . dispels these spurious notions.

The story opens in 1981 when June Kashpaw, an attractive, leggy Chippewa prostitute who has idled away her days on the main streets of oil boomtowns in North Dakota, decides to return to the reservation on which she was raised. Before leaving Williston, N.D., however, June takes on one more client and, afterward, decides to walk back to her home. En route she dies in the freezing Dakota countryside. But her memory and the legacy she passes on to her family prompt various relatives and acquaintances to recall their relationships with her and to reminisce about their own lives. June's death is thus the event that fires *Love Medicine*.

The novel is composed of 14 chapters in which seven narrators relate particulars of the American Indian experience. This structure allows Miss Erdrich to present a variety of voices: each forceful in its own way, each adding a different dimen-

sion—cruel, somber, humorous—to what is cumulatively a wondrous prose song. . . .

[The] characters might be unfamiliar to most readers, but Miss Erdrich makes us understand and care for them through her selection and skillful presentation of the events, details and attitudes that each of her well-conceived narrators relates. At one point, for instance, Nector says that he was fond of reading the "story of the great white whale," Moby-Dick. "What do they get to wail about, those whites?" his mother says. And Miss Erdrich can bring an element of poetic stylishness to descriptions of ordinary events such as digging up dandelions: "Outside, the sun was hot and heavy as a hand on my back. I felt it flow down my arms, out of my fingers, arrowing through the ends of the fork into the earth."

Love Medicine is finally about the enduring verities of loving and surviving, and these truths are revealed in a narrative that is an invigorating mixture of the comic and the tragic. Miss Erdrich . . . is a careful writer. Each word, each sentence seems perfectly placed to achieve her desired effect. "The Beads," to my mind, is the best chapter in the book, mainly because it is sedately narrated by wise old Grandma Kashpaw. But the engaging starkness of the short "Wild Geese" section, told by Grandpa Kashpaw, is also handled extremely well, and there are numerous other scenes, set pieces, that sparkle.

If there are flaws in the novel, one is that the otherwise excellent chapter "Saint Marie," which appeared in *The Atlantic*, ends a bit flatly. Another is that Miss Erdrich might have written more expansively about the younger generation of her characters, such as Albertine and Lipsha. The depiction of Albertine Johnson—who is particularly intriguing because she represents the modern Chippewa woman faced with an undefined life whose shape she must determine—is not rendered with enough depth. We are shown what happens to Indians of the older generation but are left guessing about the futures of Miss Erdrich's younger characters. Are they to spend their lives disturbingly poised between their nation's proud past and the unpromising, uncertain future suggested?

But these are minor objections that do not detract from Miss Erdrich's clear success in portraying the lives of characters to whom most Americans are oblivious. *Love Medicine* . . . is an engrossing book. With this impressive debut Louise Erdrich enters the company of America's better novelists, and I'm certain readers will want to see more from this imaginative and accomplished young writer.

> *Marco Portales, "People with Holes in Their Lives," in* The New York Times Book Review, *December 23, 1984, p. 6.*

An Excerpt from *Love Medicine*

Grandma tried to get me to put the touch on Grandpa soon after he began stepping out. I didn't want to, but before Grandma started telling me again what a bad state my bare behind was in when she first took me home, I thought I should at least pretend.

I put my hands on either side of Grandpa's head. You wouldn't look at him and say he was crazy. He's a fine figure of a man, as Lamartine would say, with all his hair and half his teeth, a beak like a hawk, and cheeks like the blades of a hatchet. They put his picture on all the tourist guides to North Dakota and even copied his face for artistic paintings. I guess you could call him a monument all of himself. He started grinning when I put my hands on his templates, and I knew right then he knew how come I touched him. I knew the smokescreen was going to fall.

And I was right: just for a moment it fell.

"Let's pitch whoopee," he said across my shoulder to Grandma.

They don't use that expression much around here anymore, but for damn sure it must have meant something. It got her goat right quick.

She threw my hands off his head herself and stood in front of him, overmatching him pound for pound, and taller too, for she had a growth spurt in middle age while he had shrunk, so now the length and breadth of her surpassed him. She glared up and spoke her piece into his face about how he was off at all hours tomcatting and chasing Lamartine again and making a damn old fool of himself.

"And you got no more whoopee to pitch anymore anyhow!" she yelled at last, surprising me so my jaw just dropped, for us kids all had pretended for so long that those rustling sounds we heard from their side of the room at night never happened. She sure had pretended it, up till now, anyway. I saw that tears were in her eyes. And that's when I saw how much grief and love she felt for him. And it gave me a real shock to the system. You see I thought love got easier over the years so it didn't hurt so bad when it hurt, or feel so good when it felt good. I thought it smoothed out and old people hardly noticed it. I thought it curled up and died, I guess. Now I saw it rear up like a whip and lash.

She loved him. She was jealous. She mourned him like the dead.

And he just smiled into the air, trapped in the seams of his mind.

JASCHA KESSLER

I am glad to report that in 1984 a really first-rate novel by a young woman named Louise Erdrich appeared, and I think it is a book that everyone on the lookout for good, imaginative, rewarding writing will enjoy and admire. It is called *Love Medicine*. . . . Louise Erdrich . . . has had enough of the direct knowledge of the people she writes about with such tender penetration, such objective and ferocious intensity, an intensity of love and sympathy, as well as an objective view of their plain humanity and striking differentation from the rest of America's peoples. It's easy enough to be polemical, political, or philosophically sentimental about Native Americans, even if you are a writer with some personal attachment to a tribe, that is some blood-relationship to Indian people; it's much harder to come up to the standards that really good fiction requires, partly because it's so hard to be responsible and loyal to one's racial past, and at the same time be able to speak in the language of art, which always tells too much that the relatives don't like to hear.

There have been some notable books of poems and novels by young Native American writers since the 1970's, artists like James Welch and Leslie Silko, and they have not stopped at showing us the hard and painful sides of the life that Indians have to lead, both on and off the reservations. But their works, like Erdrich's *Love Medicine*, are full of revelations of the mysteries of the Indians' rich and strange, and always bitterly humorous, interior lives, and they tell us stories that show us true human beings, and not the exotics, and not the aliens, those idealized Indians, both "good" and "bad" savages that European literature has been stuffed full of since Columbus came to the New World. In short, what the new Native American writers have been doing for the last decade or so, is part of the maturation that we have seen in the past of other ethnic writers, and writers of some of the many races who have been part of the American mosaic: they are giving a voice, in lovely, accomplished poetry and prose, to their peoples, a voice that somehow, though speaking in the American language, conveys the magic, the ancient mysteries and lore, the inner heart of the religious and of the traditional ways of thought and feeling of groups who have never been part of the European cultural experience.

Erdrich's novel is made up of what really seem like overlapping short stories about two intertwined families, the Kashpaws and the Lamartines, often stories about the very same events as told from the points of view of men and women, grandparents, parents, and the boys and girls themselves—the "Rashomon" technique, you might say—so that the fullest picture of the messy, the comical, the sad, and the always passionate lives of two dozen or so relatives comes through to us, full of surprises and full of disasters that are, it seems, typically Indian, and a world away from the usual life of Americans. And yet that world is here, right next door, and very much part of our national consciousness, or it should be, which is what good writing can do for us. But, rather than go on heaping up praises for Louise Erdrich, I will say simply that she has come on the scene like a new star being born, and with her first novel, a book that will surprise and delight us for a long time, or so I'm willing to predict.

Jascha Kessler, "Louise Erdrich: 'Love Medicine'," in a radio broadcast on KUSC-FM—Los Angeles, CA, January, 1985.

HARRIETT GILBERT

When Grandma Kashpaw tries to refocus her husband's drifting affections by serving him up for his dinner, uncooked, the monogamous heart of a wild, male goose, she has the discretion to garnish the organ with lettuce leaves and boiled peas. Louise Erdrich's *Love Medicine*, in which the incident occurs, is a similarly thoughtful concoction: a tragedy made ingestible by its author's humour, tenderness, perceptiveness and restraint.

These qualities extend themselves most obviously to her characters: the inhabitants of a North Dakota reservation for Native Americans. The Kashpaws and the Lamartines are no one's idea of 'good' Indians (for a start, they're defiantly alive) but, and this is Erdrich's question, why the hell *should* they be good? Dispossessed of land, culture, religion and economic power—dragged into the American Nightmare of Christian sado-masochistic guilt, consumerism and war in Vietnam—that these few survivors of genocide drink, fight, destroy themselves and sell each other out is scarcely a matter for wonder.

Anger is what it more properly evokes and Erdrich, a Native American herself, might well have chosen to hurl that emotion like vitriol in our eyes. Instead, she offers us the same consideration that she tends to Grandma Kashpaw and her magic, to the errant husband Nector, chairman of the tribe and as weak-willed in politics as love, to gloriously fecund Lulu Lamartine, to simple-minded Lipsha Morrissey. Largely using her characters' own voices, she washes their stories backward and forward in rollers of powerful, concentrated prose through half a century (1930s to now) of loving, hating, adapting, surviving and tragically failing to survive.

If, to begin with, there are moments of confusion as to when is when and who is who, by the end the reader is soaked in the history and viewpoints of the reservation. Too soaked to leap up and act? Well, this certainly isn't a Native Americans' *Uncle Tom's Cabin* (if only because it's too complex a novel to work well as propaganda) but what kind of action, in any case, would resurrect a massacred race, an annihilated culture?

*Harriett Gilbert, "Mixed Feelings," in New States-man, Vol. 109, No. 2812, February 8, 1985, p. 31.**

GENE LYONS

The first thing readers ought to be told about Louise Erdrich's novel ***Love Medicine*** . . . is that no matter what the dust jacket says, it's not a novel. It's a book of short stories. Interlocking short stories, thematically related short stories—but short stories. And as unpleasant as it is to say so, Erdrich's 14 tales of life in and around an Indian reservation of North Dakota between 1934 and the present are so self-consciously literary that they are a whole lot easier to admire than to read. . . . [Erdrich] has plenty of stories to tell, and a fine poetic gift. Consider this scene from "Crown of Thorns," one of the best stories

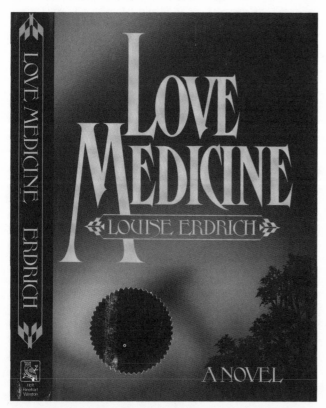

Dust jacket of Love Medicine, *by Louise Erdrich. Holt, Rinehart & Winston, 1984. Jacket design by Honi Werner. Courtesy of Holt, Rinehart & Winston, Publishers.*

in the book. A Chippewa named Gordie Kashpaw, blind drunk and mourning his ex-wife's death (she got lost in a snowstorm while walking home from a one-night stand with an oil-rig worker), runs down a doe on the highway. Thinking to trade the carcass for liquor, he hauls it into the back seat. But the animal is only stunned and sits up, her eyes meeting his in the rearview mirror: "Her look was black and endless and melting pure. She looked through him. She saw into the troubled thrashing woods of him, a rattling thicket of bones. She saw how he'd woven his own crown of thorns. She saw how although he was not worthy he'd jammed this relief on his brow. Her eyes stared into some hidden place but blocked him out. Flat black." Fine writing, yes. But that's not a real deer in that back seat, it's a symbolic one.

Erdrich does a good job evoking her characters' conflicting feelings of pride and shame, guilt and rage—the disorderly intimacies of their lives on the reservation and their longings to escape. But her inexperience as a storyteller shows throughout. *Love Medicine* has as many as a half dozen first-person narrators, and several stories are told in the third person. No central action unifies the narrative, and the voices all sound pretty much the same—making it difficult to recall sometimes who's talking and what they're talking about. (pp. 70-1)

Gene Lyons, "In Indian Territory," in Newsweek, Vol. CV, No. 6, February 11, 1985, pp. 70-1.

VALENTINE CUNNINGHAM

Right from the start, . . . what's shown happening to Louise Erdrich's complex cousinhood of Kashpaws and Lamartines [in *Love Medicine*] is an aweing tale of violence—personal, social, ideological.

Over the generations these men and women have been smashed up, locked up, shot up, moved on, pushed around. In State penitentiaries, in Vietnam, in convents, they've been the victims. Their frequent response has been to smash up others, motor-cars, themselves. A nun burns the devil out of a small girl with hot metal. A returned soldier bites his lip during telly-casts from Vietnam until the blood runs down his chin on to his piece of bread.

But survival is also shown to hinge on the more admirable resilience of sisterly love, brotherly affection, the solidarities of kin. We're made to admire the way a tribe's fierceness and chauvinism have lasted, but also to be gladdened that the white man didn't manage to bury every bit of heart at the Wounded Knees of the Indian past.

*Valentine Cunningham, "A Right Old Battle-Axe," in The Observer, February 24, 1985, p. 27.**

ROBERT TOWERS

Love Medicine . . . is very much a poet's novel. By that I mean that the book achieves its effect through moments of almost searing intensity rather than through the rise, climax, and closing of a sustained action, and that its stylistic virtuosity has become almost an end in itself. The prose indeed has remarkable energy and sensuousness. But I found ***Love Medicine*** a hard book to penetrate. The episodes, most of them dramatic monologues, are loosely strung together and the relationships of the various narrators and characters are so confusing that one must constantly flip back to earlier sections in an effort to get one's bearings. The reader who perseveres will undergo an imaginary adoption into a nearly forgotten American Indian tribe.

The subject has much documentary interest. Louise Erdrich . . . has created a scroll-like account of the often squalid, demoralized, but at times rhapsodic lives of the Kashpaws, Lazarres, Lamartines, Nanapushes, and Morrisseys—Indian and part-Indian families living on a Chippewa reservation in western North Dakota. . . .

Sooner or later nearly every member of this cast steps forward to participate in a moment of drama or self-revelation. From the medley of individual faces and voices a few generic, or tribal, features gradually emerge. The men get drunk as often as possible, and when drunk they are likely to be violent or to do wildly irresponsible or self-destructive things. Even Grandpa Kashpaw (Nector), the most able and ambitious of the lot, achieved his political standing in the Chippewa community only because Marie repeatedly dragged him back from the bootlegger's and sometimes sat "all night by the door with an ax handle so he would not wander off in search of liquor." Self-destructiveness leads in several instances to suicide. Meanwhile the women, with the exception of the stalwart Marie, are likely to take up with any man who comes along. . . .

On the face of it, the factual details presented by Louise Erdrich combine to give an appalling account of the lives of contemporary Indians on a reservation—impoverished, feckless lives far gone in alcoholism and promiscuity. Bitter pride alternates with shame; away from the reservation some of them try to account for their dark complexions by claiming to be "French" or "Black Irish." By implication, *Love Medicine* delivers an irrefutable indictment against an official policy that tried to make farmers out of the hunting and fishing Chippewas, moving them from the Great Lakes to the hilly tracts west of the wheat-growing plains of North Dakota. But the author's intentions are more lyrical or rhapsodic than polemical. The pervasive sadness of the Indian condition is offset by proclamations of joy, wisdom, and reconciliation that might go a long way toward making the account more palatable to a sentimental reader. . . .

Alas, the love medicine does not always work, though Louise Erdrich applies it thickly to the wounds and abrasions that her characters suffer. At times the language becomes overwrought to the point of hysteria or else so ecstatic that the reader may feel almost coerced into accepting a romanticized version of a situation—a version that the hard facts belie. But at its best, the writing is admirably graphic, full of unexpected and arresting images and brilliantly dramatized small scenes. Louise Erdrich is in any case a notably talented writer whose first novel, despite its structural problems and stylistic excesses, clearly merits much of the praise it has received. (p. 36)

> Robert Towers, "Uprooted," in The New York Review of Books, *Vol. XXXII, No. 6, April 11, 1985, pp. 36-7.**

ELAINE JAHNER

[*Jahner, an American educator, edited* Lakota Myth *(1983) by James R. Walker. She teaches in the English and Native American Studies Departments at Dartmouth College, where Erdrich was a writer-in-residence during 1981; Erdrich's husband, Michael Dorris, is chairman of Dartmouth's Native American Studies program. In the following excerpt Jahner praises* Love Medicine *for its humane depiction of a changing Native American culture.*]

The restlessness so endemic to American society today proceeds in part from a vague intuition of impending change. This sense of change seems to drive people to whatever they perceive as sources of security at the same time as they grope towards the individual and collective transformations that must occur if we are to emerge from crises threatening planetary life. Novels have a place in helping people move into the momentary security of invented worlds to learn the feeling of alternative ways of living. Obviously, novels complex enough to affect consciousness in any significant way and compelling enough to attract a wide readership are far too infrequent. Louise Erdrich's *Love Medicine* is one such novel.

Erdrich's novel derives much of its complexity from its truth to the culture of the Turtle Mountain Chippewa Tribe in North Dakota, but its compulsive fascination comes from the fact that she knows how to tell grand stories about characters whose intensity shatters banality and leaves us rethinking the whole matter of being human.

Some basic knowledge about the Turtle Mountain band of Chippewa can be useful to readers of *Love Medicine* although it is not essential for responding to the novel's immediacy. Erdrich depicts a culture that found the sources of its energy and its unique identity amidst cataclysmic changes affecting other Native American and European cultures, changes that forced individuals into new territory to shape a way of life that is perhaps most usefully capsulized through a description of the language these people evolved. It is one in which most verbs are derived from Chippewa, and most nouns from French, with other Native American and European languages leaving less easily identifiable traces. The rest of the cultural fabric is similarly woven of diverse national and cultural strands, yet all these people are direct descendants of individuals who refused to give up just because their security was yanked out from under them. The importance of this cultural dimension of the novel is best assessed after encountering the range among Erdrich's characters. (p. 96)

The incident that refers directly to the novel's title features Lipsha Morrissey, Marie's grandson. Even in old age, Marie requires undivided loyalty from her husband; and when his attentions seem to stray, she decides to try one last desperate remedy, traditional Chippewa love medicine. No one of her trusted acquaintances knows how to make love medicine anymore; but, she feels Lipsha must have special powers of some kind and she persuades him to try to prepare it. The results are totally unpredictable, hilarious, and genuinely touching. Finally, in spite of the consequences, we realize that the effort was absolutely necessary and that the novel redefines love medicine somewhat, or, more appropriately, it expands the traditional sense so that the term applies to the healing powers of all forms of love.

Love has many modalities, but the one that gives the book its particular force is delight. For anyone tempted to see delight as one of love's weaker forms, Erdrich's novel should prove otherwise. Delight is never a turning away from the pain that stalks the days and nights. It isn't even a shield to be held against pain. Rather, it springs from the act of staring down pain, holding one's ground in spite of pain, with the full and certain knowledge that suffering has an inevitable role in shaping the universe, but that is all. Life still has much that is good; indeed, delightfully good.

Undoubtedly, as *Love Medicine* finds its many publics there will be discussion of its specifically tribal aspects; scholars will find traces of tribal ritual in style and plot, proving the continuity of mythic traditions. Such scholarship will have its value but hopefully it will not overshadow the book's basic insights which apply to any culture. Whatever may have happened in the past, people like Erdrich's characters are stubbornly alive and magnificently self-possessed because they are not self-obsessed. Erdrich's novel needs to be placed in the large context of contemporary writers who are helping us rethink the concept of self that has dominated so much of this century. She shows us how the crucible of Plains history is part of the redefining process, and that geographical locale points to a sort of marvelous accidental symbolism. The Turtle Mountain Chippewa Reservation is near the International Peace Garden; it is also near the line of Intercontinental Ballistic Missile silos strung across North Dakota. This contextual dimension of the novel helps us realize why the tenacity, caring, and humor Erdrich depicts constitute the love medicine we all need to help us face the stunning contrasts between missiles and a peace garden. (pp. 98, 100)

> *Elaine Jahner, in a review of "Love Medicine," in* Parabola, *Vol. X, No. 2, May, 1985, pp. 96, 98, 100.*

CAROL HUNTER

In her first novel [*Love Medicine*] Louise Erdrich, a reputable poet, has created a challenging experience in reading. Using an autobiographical technique in the Faulknerian mode of narrator-and-reader relation, Erdrich spans fifty years and three generations in the lives of the Kashpaws, Morrisseys, Lamartines, and Lazarres. The setting is a rural community on the Chippewa Indian reservation in North Dakota. Erdrich, herself of Chippewa heritage, gives depth to her characters' personalities through her poetic sensibility toward language, using a vernacular diction, funny analogies, and epithets that evoke laughter rather than pathos for these mixed-blood Chippewas struggling with their disillusionments and shallow existence. The novel is structured primarily around seven characters, who relate the life history of the related families and at the same time convey their own needs, experiences, perceptions, complaints, and excuses in a *Spoon River* manner.

In the tradition of popular American Indian writers, Erdrich also uses the oral technique for written fiction. Other contemporary Indian authors have intertwined historical and mythical contexts from tribal oral literature that conveys a spiritual message for a modern world . . . ; Erdrich's novel does not contain such elements, but instead falls into the category of modern black humor and indicates an existential philosophy. Through the inner thoughts of the narrators, the reader is given insight into personal illusions and individual motivations amidst interactions of human relations. In each narrative the reader learns how the lives of the individuals were changed by some unplanned event.

Love Medicine is a love story about the ties that bind kinship and "blood relations" in a rural community—in this particular instance, the Chippewa reservation. The novel's title is based on the Chippewas' folk medicine, in particular on the belief in a love potion that can cast a spell, causing its victims to fall in love. In the novel this belief relates to a love triangle between Nector Kashpaw, his wife Marie, and Lulu Lamartine. After almost fifty years of marriage and "seventeen come and go children," Nector, who has lusted after Lulu since he was a teen-ager but is married to Marie by fault, is discovered trying to seduce Lulu in the laundry room of the elders' nursing home. Lulu, described as "a cat loving no one only purring to get what she wanted," relates earlier in the novel her story of how she seeks revenge for having been jilted by Nector and how after their five-year illicit love affair he accidentally burned her house down. Toward the end of the novel, when Lipsha, the grandson, sees Lulu and Nector in the laundry room "wooing," for the sake of his grandmother's feelings he makes a love potion from goose hearts and slips it into Nector's baloney sandwich. Nector chokes on it and dies, leaving Lipsha with a guilty conscience.

This account, related by Lipsha, is but one of the tragicomic narratives told by the Kashpaw grandchildren. Each of the autobiographies is an indication of Erdrich's astute insight into personalities. Above all, her sense of humor and skill with language make *Love Medicine* a dynamic novel.

> *Carol Hunter, in a review of "Love Medicine," in* World Literature Today, *Vol. 59, No. 3, Summer, 1985, p. 474.*

Maria Irene Fornes

The Conduct of Life

Obie Award

Cuban-born American dramatist.

Fornes is among the avant garde dramatists who created the world of off-off-Broadway in the 1960s. Unlike most of her contemporaries she has remained working there for the past twenty-five years. In 1972 Fornes helped to found the New York Theater Strategy—an organization that produced the work of experimental American playwrights—and served in various roles from bookkeeper to president until the organization dissolved in 1979. She currently works at the Theater for the New City. *The Conduct of Life* (1985) has earned Fornes her sixth Obie Award, the highest recognition for off-Broadway productions and a fitting tribute to one so dedicated to the non-Broadway theater. The only dramatists to equal this Obie award-winning record are Samuel Beckett and Sam Shepard.

Despite her achievements, Fornes has not received significant notoriety; her plays are neither widely attended nor extensively reviewed. In an interview Fornes pointed to the reason her plays receive so little recognition: "Most critics and theatergoers," she explained, "are so used to seeing plays in only one way—What is the dramatic conflict? What are the symbols?—that they go through their entire lives looking for the same things. If they don't find what they expect, they're disconcerted. But I can't 'plant' things that way, like a treasure hunt where you need a map. To me, a play is more like a path I just follow never knowing where it's going to end up, letting the material guide me step by step." In her plays Fornes works closely with the actors, usually directing her own productions.

Fornes was born in Cuba and came to the United States in 1945, when she was fifteen years old. She began a career as a painter but decided to devote her life to playwriting after attending Zero Mostel's *Ulysses in Nighttown* and Roger Blin's 1954 Paris production of Beckett's *Waiting for Godot*. Of the performance of the Beckett play Fornes says, "I didn't know a word of French. I had not read the play in English. But what was happening in front of me had a profound impact without even understanding a word. Imagine a writer whose theatricality is so amazing and so important that you could see a play of his, not understand one word, and be shook up. When I left that theater I felt that my life was changed, that I was seeing everything with a different clarity."

Fornes's plays are unconventional in their structure, dialogue, and staging. Emphasizing neither plot nor character development, the plays are often symbolic rather than realistic and at times contain both brutality and slapstick humor. Fornes is mainly concerned with human relationships, though a social and political consciousness is also evident in many of her plays. In her first important play, *Tango Palace* (1964), Fornes presents two men, ill-fated lovers, who create their own world wherein they enact the roles of seducer-seduced, father-son, teacher-pupil, masculine-feminine, each engaged in a metaphysical power struggle. In *The Successful Life of 3: A Skit for Vaudeville* (1965), for which Fornes received her first Obie

Photograph by Marcella Scuderi

Award, the symbolic names He, She, and 3 represent the nature of the characters. They are involved in a love triangle that is established in a series of scenes unconnected to particular times or places, a device that adds to the sense that the relationship of these characters is archetypal; this device also brings the dynamics of the relationships to the fore. Similarly, *Promenade* (1965), another Obie Award-winner, uses representative characters called prisoner 105 and prisoner 106 in a comedy of manners where the prisoners are exposed to the world of the rich and the poor; the escaped prisoners eventually choose to return to the "freedom" of their cells.

Fefu and Friends (1977) marked a change for Fornes to a more realistic approach in her drama. Fornes described *Fefu* as a breakthrough, explaining, "My style of work in *Fefu* was very different from my work before. I hadn't been writing for a few years. When you start again something different is likely to happen. The style of *Fefu* dealt more with characters as real persons rather than voices that are the expression of the mind of the play. In *Fefu* the characters became more three-dimensional." Fornes's innovative staging is the highlight of the Obie Award-winning *Fefu and Friends,* a play about the tension building among a group of female friends that eventually ends in violence. Set in a New England country house, scenes of the play takes place in different rooms simultaneously; the audience, which is split into groups, physically moves from room to room. Only the opening and closing scenes are shown to the audience as a whole. The Obie Award-winning *Mud* (1984) also uses a realistic setting: here Fornes employs the backdrop of a farm to explore the relationships between a woman, her husband, and a second man who becomes the woman's lover when her husband is crippled in a farm accident. Though some critics have called *Fefu* and *Mud* feminist plays, Fornes argues that the protagonist of a play can be a woman or a man, that it may be natural for a woman playwright to have a female protagonist, however, it is personal vision and imagery that are central to a play: "When we start respecting imagery and sensibility, which are unique, the gender of the writer will be the last thing we think of."

Like some of her earlier plays, *The Conduct of Life* does not rely on theatrical conventions. Instead it presents a series of seemingly unrelated scenes that focus on the interior life and the relationships of a few characters. It also reflects Fornes's realistic style in that it deals with a politically timely subject and creates believable characters. Taking place in an unknown Latin American country, *The Conduct of Life* concerns an army captain whose duty it is to torture prisoners for his military government. Rather than showing the audience the particulars of the captain's job, however, Fornes conveys his heartless temperament by depicting his violent treatment of his wife and female servant. Through the link between the captain's private and public lives Fornes comments on the brutality of political oppression. *The Conduct of Life* has received critical approval for its avoidance of didacticism and for its strong theatrical impact.

Since January of 1985 Fornes has begun to receive notable recognition beyond the supporters of the off-Broadway theater. The American National Theater has commissioned a play, calling Fornes a "national treasure," and the American Academy and Institute of Arts and Letters selected her for an Academy-Institute Award to encourage her creative work. Fornes, both pleased and surprised by unexpected attention, maintains her proven philosophy: "The longevity of a playwright depends on having a place where his or her work will be performed with love and trust, a place that is not filled with terror and fear of collapse. A place that would rather collapse than give up the idea that there is such a thing as art."

(See also *Contemporary Authors*, Vols. 25-28, rev. ed. and *Dictionary of Literary Biography*, Vol. 7.)

MARILYN STASIO

As a rule, playwrights make awful mudpies when they try to direct their own work. Not Maria Irene Fornes. Her new play, *The Conduct of Life* . . . is a stunning piece of theater that owes much of its impact to the playwright's own direction.

Set in an unnamed country in Latin America, the play takes place in the household of an army captain who handles the dirty job of "interrogating" prisoners for his military government. We never see him at work, but his brutality is evident

from the way he humiliates his wife and abuses a young woman whom he keeps in the house as a sexual prisoner.

Although the play is structured around the captain's moral deterioration, it is the women of his household who are written and played with the most insight and compassion. . . .

Another director, however, might have shown the playwright that her men are weakly drawn and indifferently acted. The captain, in particular, is an unrelieved brute whose pre-fiend state is alluded to, but not dramatized. The horrid causes of his inhumanity are well told, but we are shown only their result, in a character too far gone for us to care about.

> Marilyn Stasio, "'Life', a Stunning Show," in New York Post, *March 9, 1985.*

THE VILLAGE VOICE

Maria Irene Fornes's [*The Conduct of Life*] is a stunning and major piece of work, both as important and as entertaining as any you're likely to see this year. The topic is Latin American politics, but the focus is human and domestic. The hero is an army man in some unspecified country who joins the torture squad as career move upward. There's neither torture nor political sermonizing onstage, however—the play takes place in his home, centering on his changing relations with his wife and mistress. . . .

> A review of "The Conduct of Life," in The Village Voice, *Vol. XXX, No. 12, March 19, 1985, p. 73.*

THE VILLAGE VOICE

Irene Fornes is America's truest poet of the theater. With *The Conduct of Life,* she takes on a subject so close to the bones of our times you'd think it unapproachable: the home life of a Latin American army captain who is a professional torturer and a domestic sadist. Fornes's freedom from psychological, naturalistic, and didactic conventions lets her explore what happens to this man, his wife, his young mistress, his childhood pal, and his servant without exploiting subject or audience. The events are as direct and mysterious as life, and as surprisingly funny. There's nothing goody-goody or hectoring about this most ethical play, and despite its surface simplicity I am still . . . finding new possibilities in the web of class, sex, and character she has woven.

> A review of "The Conduct of Life," in The Village Voice, *Vol. XXX, No. 13, March 26, 1985, p. 85.*

PAUL BERMAN

What is the spirit of the time? In his book *The Conduct of Life*, Emerson answered that the question is too broad. Better to ask, How shall I live? Because in examining the conduct of life we come as close as we can to discovering the spirit of our time.

I wonder if Maria Irene Fornes, she of the five Obies, meant to invoke Emerson in her own *The Conduct of Life*. . . . Her setting is Hispano-fascist, her characters more Dostoevskian than transcendental. An army officer is mad for power and might get some if he can control his vices and corrupt his fellow officers. His wife is beside herself with suspicion that he tortures prisoners and rapes the servant girl in the basement. The whole of society looks maggoty and illegitimate in her eyes. She would happily give away her wealth to those who need it. Her husband disgusts her. All is sinking into a black pit of moral despair.

This is curious to see. We don't think of the fascist classes in Latin America bothering with disgust or introspection or moral concern, only with Miami bank accounts. Of course that is stupid of us. The Hispanic fascist classes have obviously been tormenting themselves morally for many years now, since a portion of those classes has been defecting to the left-wing opposition. So they do ask, How shall I live?—naturally they do, and no doubt they ask much the way Fornes shows this officer's unhappy wife asking in *The Conduct of Life,* with agonies of soul and eventually with a gun. And what is this, by the way, if not the spirit of our time?

The play conjures a lot of tension, mostly by keeping the scenes tight and disciplined and unsettlingly short. The dialogue and staging seem almost to have been cropped too close at the top or bottom, like those paintings by Philip Pearlstein where the nude's head or leg has been cropped off the edge. Sometimes the cropping pares away everything but the musing of a single voice, and these monologues are the most effective aspect of all. The cook spends the better part of a scene describing her day. She lists her tasks, the precise timing and planning they require, the coordination, concentration and energy she must command, and though she never gets much further than break-fast, we get a vision not just of woman's work but of patience, suffering, dignity. It is a working person's answer to "How shall I live?" . . . In another monologue the servant girl . . . describes life in less than a shanty with her indigent grandpa, then her kidnapping and rape by the army officer. . . . (p. 412)

The play as a whole falls short of its high points. Just as there are horse operas, space operas and oil operas, *The Conduct of Life* threatens to become a fascist opera. . . . [It] seemed pos-sible that Fornes's direction perhaps lacked some of the pre-cision of her writing. It is an uneven play and was an uneven production—yet *The Conduct of Life* is incomparably more serious than any of the new plays on Broadway and will surely stand out in memory as a bright spot of the season. A quick revival is in order. (pp. 412-13)

Paul Berman, in a review of "The Conduct of Life," in The Nation, *Vol. 240, No. 13, April 6, 1985, pp. 412-13.*

An Excerpt from *The Conduct of Life*

OLIMPIA: Where is your grandpa?

NENA: I don't know. (*They work a little in silence.*) He sleeps in the streets. Because he's too old to remember where he lives. He needs a person to take care of him. And I can take care of him. But I don't know where he is.—He doesn't know where I am.—He doesn't know who he is. He's too old. He doesn't know anything about himself. He only knows how to beg. And he knows that, only because he's hungry. He walks around and begs for food. He forgets to go home. He lives in the camp for the homeless and he has his own box. It's not an ugly box like the others. It is a real box. I used to live there with him. He took me with him when my mother died till they took me to the home. It is a big box. It's big enough for two. I could sleep in the front where it's cold. And he could sleep in the back where it's warmer. And he could lean on me. The floor is hard for him

because he's skinny and it's hard on his poor bones. He could sleep on top of me if that would make him feel comfortable. I wouldn't mind. Except that he may pee on me because he pees in his pants. He doesn't know not to. He is incontinent. He can't hold it. His box was a little smelly. But that doesn't matter because I could clean it. All I would need is some soap. I could get plenty of water from the public faucet. And I could borrow a brush. You know how clean I could get it? As clean as new. You know what I would do? I would make holes in the floor so the pee would go down to the ground. And you know what else I would do?

OLIMPIA: What?

NENA: I would get straw and put it on the floor for him and for me and it would make it comfortable and clean and warm. How do you like that? Just as I did for my goat.

OLIMPIA: You have a goat?

NENA: . . . I did.

OLIMPIA: What happened to him?

NENA: He died. They killed him and ate him. Just like they did Christ.

OLIMPIA: Nobody ate Christ.

NENA: . . . I thought they did. My goat was eaten though.—In the home we had clean sheets. But that doesn't help. You can't sleep on clean sheets, not if there isn't someone watching over you while you sleep. And since my ma died there just wasn't anyone watching over me. Except you.—Aren't you? In the home they said guardian angels watch your sleep, but I didn't see any there. There weren't any. One day I heard my grandpa calling me and I went to look for him. And I didn't find him. I got tired and I slept in the street, and I was hungry and I was crying. And then [Orlando] came to me and he spoke to me very softly so as not to scare me and he said he would give me something to eat and he said he would help me look for my grandpa. And he put me in the back of his van . . . And he took me to a place. And he hurt me. I fought with him but I stopped fighting—because I couldn't fight anymore and he did things to me. And he locked me in. And sometimes he brought me food and sometimes he didn't. And he did things to me. And he beat me. And he hung me on the wall. And I got sick. And sometimes he brought me medicine. And then he said he had to take me somewhere. And he brought me here. And I am glad to be here because you are here. I only wish my grandpa were here too. He doesn't beat me so much anymore.

OLIMPIA: Why does he beat you? I hear him at night. He goes down the steps and I hear you cry. Why does he beat you?

NENA: Because I'm dirty.

OLIMPIA: You are not dirty.

NENA: I am. That's why he beats me. The dirt won't go away from inside me.—He comes downstairs when I'm sleeping and I hear him coming and it frightens me. And he takes the covers off me and I don't move because I'm frightened and because I feel cold and I think I'm going to die. And he puts his hand on me and he recites poetry. And he is almost naked. He wears a robe but he leaves it open and he feels himself as he recites. He touches himself and he touches his stomach and his breasts and his behind. He puts his fingers in my parts and he keeps reciting. Then he turns me on my stomach and puts himself inside me. And he says I belong to him. (*There is a pause.*) I want to conduct each day of my life in the best possible way. I should value the things I have. And I should value all those who are near me. And I should value the kindness that others bestow upon me. And if someone should treat me unkindly, I should not blind myself with rage, but I should see them and receive them, since maybe they are in worse pain than me. (*Lights fade to black.*)

SUSAN SONTAG

Mud, The Danube, The Conduct of Life, Sarita—four plays, recent work by the prolific Maria Irene Fornes, who for many years has been conducting with exemplary tenacity and scrupulousness a unique career in the American theatre. (p. 7)

Fornes [is] an autodidact whose principal influences were neither theatre nor literature but certain styles of painting and the movies. But unlike similarly influenced New York dramatists, her work did not eventually become parasitic on literature (or opera, or movies). It was never a revolt against theatre, or a theatre recycling fantasies encoded in other genres.

Her two earliest plays prefigure the dual register, one völkisch, the other placeless-international, of all the subsequent work. *The Widow,* a poignant chronicle of a simple life, is set in Cuba, while *Tango Palace,* with its volleys of sophisticated exchanges, takes place in a purely theatrical space: a cave, an altar. Fornes has a complex relation to the strategy of naivete. She is chary of the folkloristic, rightly so. But she is strongly drawn to the pre-literary: to the authority of documents, of found materials such as letters of her great-grandfather's cousin which inspired *The Widow,* the diary of a domestic servant in turn-of-the-century New Hampshire which was transformed into *Evelyn Brown,* Emma's lecture in *Fefu and Her Friends.*

For a while she favored the musical play—in a style reminiscent of the populist parables in musical-*commedia* form preserved in films from the 1930s like René Clair's *A Nous la Liberté.* It was a genre that proclaimed its innocence, and specialized in rueful gaiety. Sharing with the main tradition of modernist drama an aversion to the reductively psychological and to sociological explanations, Fornes chose a theatre of types (such personages as the defective sage and the woman enslaved by sexual dependence reappear in a number of plays) and a theatre of miracles: the talking mirror in *The Office,* the fatal gun wound at the end of *Fefu and Her Friends.* Lately, Fornes seems to be eschewing this effect: the quotidian as something to be violated—by lyricism, by disaster. Characters can still break into song, as they did in the dazzling bittersweet plays of the mid-1960s, like *Promenade* and *Molly's Dream* and *The Successful Life of 3.* But the plays are less insistently charming.

Reality is less capricious. More genuinely lethal—as in *Eyes on the Harem, Sarita.*

Character is revealed through catechism. People requiring or giving instruction is a standard situation in Fornes's plays. The desire to be initiated, to be taught, is depicted as an essential, and essentially pathetic, longing. (Fornes's elaborate sympathy for the labor of thought is the endearing observation of someone who is almost entirely self-taught.) And there are many dispensers of wisdom in Fornes's plays, apart from those—*Tango Palace, Doctor Kheal*—specifically devoted to the comedy and the pathos of instruction. But Fornes is neither literary nor anti-literary. These are not cerebral exercises or puzzles but the real questions, about . . . the conduct of life. There is much wit but no nonsense. No banalities. And no non sequiturs.

While some plays are set in never-never land, some have local flavors—like the American 1930s of *Fefu and Her Friends.* Evoking a specific setting, especially when it is Hispanic (this being understood as an underprivileged reality), or depicting the lives of the oppressed and humiliated, especially when the subject is that emblem of oppression, the woman servant, such plays as *Evelyn Brown* and *The Conduct of Life* may seem more "realistic"—given the condescending assumptions of the ideology of realism. (Oppressed women, particularly domestic servants and prostitutes, have long been the signature subject of what is sometimes called realism, sometimes naturalism.) But I am not convinced that Fornes's recent work is any less a theatre of fantasy than it was, or more now a species of dramatic realism. Her work is both a theatre about utterance (i.e., a meta-theatre) and a theatre about the disfavored—both Handke *and* Kroetz, as it were.

It was always a theatre of heartbreak. But at the beginning the mood was often throwaway, playful. Now it's darker, more passionate: consider the twenty-year trajectory that goes from *The Successful Life of 3* to *Mud,* about the unsuccessful life of three. She writes increasingly from a woman's point of view. Women are doing women's things—performing unrewarded labor (in *Evelyn Brown*), getting raped (in *The Conduct of Life*)—and also, as in *Fefu and Her Friends,* incarnating the human condition as such. Fornes has a near faultless ear for the ruses of egotism and cruelty. Unlike most contemporary dramatists, for whom psychological brutality is the principal, inexhaustible subject, Fornes is never in complicity with the brutality she depicts. She has an increasingly expressive relation to dread, to grief and to passion—in *Sarita,* for example, which is about sexual passion and the incompatibilities of desire. Dread is not just a subjective state but is attached to history: the psychology of torturers (*The Conduct of Life*), nuclear war (*The Danube*).

Fornes's work has always been intelligent, often funny, never vulgar or cynical; both delicate and visceral. Now it is something more. (The turning point, I think, was the splendid *Fefu and Her Friends*—with its much larger palette of sympathies, for both Julia's incurable despair and Emma's irrepressible jubilation.) The plays have always been about wisdom: what it means to be wise. They are getting wiser. (pp. 8-9)

Susan Sontag, in a preface to Plays: Mud, The Danube, The Conduct of Life, Sarita *by Maria Irene Fornes, PAJ Publications, 1986, pp. 7-12.*

William Gibson

Neuromancer

Hugo Award
Nebula Award

American short story writer and novelist.

Gibson's first novel, *Neuromancer* (1984), is a science fiction crime thriller of corporate intrigue, describing urban life in a future dominated by multinational corporations and computer technology. Critics praise Gibson for his believable creation of a high-tech world in which the criminals are industrial technological spies and information is the valued object. Though reviewers find his characterization weak, Gibson is acclaimed for his descriptive style and his awareness of contemporary issues and sensibilities, which infuse his work with a vigor and depth often lacking in traditional science fiction.

Gibson followed *Neuromancer* with a second novel, *Count Zero* (1986), and a short story collection, *Burning Chrome* (1986). Both works are written in the gritty futuristic style Gibson introduced in *Neuromancer,* for which his admirers have coined the term "cyberpunk."

Photograph by Charles N. Brown

PUBLISHERS WEEKLY

Case [the protagonist of *Neuromancer*] is a computer jock, a "console cowboy" who leaves his body behind when he plugs in and soars through the inner world of cyberspace. In plainer language he's a thief for hire, one of today's whiz kids grown up and wised up. His criminal underworld of the near future has supplemented the staples of drugs and sex with illegal neurosurgery and stolen data, all loosely controlled by the Yakuza. It is a world furnished from a melange of movies; the computer folklore of *Tron* and *WarGames;* the rundown high-tech look of *Blade Runner* and the moral ambience of '40s *film noir*. Movies also provide the book's caper plot, in which criminal misfits are recruited for their special abilities. Gibson describes his world in a hyped-up prose thick with jargon, slang and neologisms. Despite the interesting idea and some striking scenes, the style often floats free of the story, leaving the reader wondering what if anything is happening.

A review of "Neuromancer," in Publishers Weekly, *Vol. 225, No. 21, May 25, 1984, p. 57.*

LAWRENCE I. CHARTERS

The press release claims *Neuromancer* is Gibson's first novel. If you read the release after reading the novel, you'll probably be inclined to call the release fiction and the novel fact. Gibson has created a rich, detailed, and vivid near-future, populated with uncomfortably realistic characters. Without sacrificing clarity, Gibson also manages an amazingly complex novel; some will enjoy it as a fast-paced, exciting adventure; others

will claim it's actually a very subtle, clever mystery; still others will see it as a thought-provoking social discourse. . . .

Gibson will have a difficult time as a new novelist; his first effort is superb, and so expectations for future efforts may be unreachably high. *Neuromancer* is a major novel, difficult to compare with other works for the simple reason that it really is new, and different. Terry Carr, in his introduction, congratulates himself on finding it. The congratulations are deserved; the novel is highly recommended.

Lawrence I. Charters, in a review of "Neuromancer," in Fantasy Review, *Vol. 7, No. 6, July, 1984, p. 39.*

DEBRA RAE COHEN

I first ran across William Gibson through his fever-bright stories **"Johnny Mnemonic"** and **"Burning Chrome"** in *Omni* magazine, and have since burrowed through old *Universes, Omni* best-ofs, and lesser-known periodicals, unwilling to miss a single published word. Gibson's stories plunge you into a coherent universe, a world of the not-too-far future that's urgent and hyperventilation-close—like the visuals in *Blade Runner*—through its sheer mass of vivid detail. Like Texan Bruce Sterling, . . . Gibson delineates a world split by attitudes toward pervasive technology. Like K. W. Jeter, . . . he sketches a new urban underworld, black-marketing microchips and body modifications, laser weaponry and bootleg pharmaceuticals refined by control of the body's own drugs. But where Sterling's intricate "Shaper/Mechanist" stories depend on external tension and street-level philosophical debate, Gibson's high-tech, high-tension work crawls in the cracks of a "well-regulated" world. Where Jeter's jousts between computer-augmented evangelism and black-market braggadocio are limited by their L.A. insularity, Gibson offers a world internationalized by money and information; interlocking data nets serve as ceiling to the underworld, jungle gym for computer cowboys in search of a line in and a leg up. Most sf writers spell out a world and then color it in; Gibson shows us corporate monoliths and looming power from below, through a roiling mixture of black leather and chrome, personal weapons surgically installed, cybernetically boosted cosmetic changes, Yakuza enforcers and coffin-stacked flophouses. His world is gradually assembled from the multiple-angled snapshots of his stories, each crisply focused and individual as survival. Gibson's first novel, *Neuromancer*, . . . like all his work, is unforgettable. Through his characters' squints at the main chance—the scams and hustles, big and small, of a thousand scrabbling one-shots—Gibson distills a technopunk sensibility with the kick of white lightning and the clarity of white light.

*Debra Rae Cohen, in a review of "Neuromancer,"
in* The Village Voice, *Vol. XXIX, No.. 27, July 3,
1984, p. 52.*

CHARLES PLATT

William Gibson's first novel, *Neuromancer* . . . is an amazing, virtuoso performance. Kaleidoscopic, picaresque, flashy and decadent, it is reminiscent of Alfred Bester's classic early science fiction. Indeed, Gibson is the nearest we have to an Alfred Bester of the 1980s.

The novel uses standard plot elements borrowed from the espionage/suspense genre to sustain an episodic trip through vivid landscapes of the next century. The protagonist, Case, is a high-tech criminal whose special talent is cracking electronic security systems; after double-crossing his previous employers, he has been stripped of his semi-psychic ability to key his consciousness into "cyberspace," and winds up in a futuristic skid row on Tokyo Bay, where "gulls wheeled above drifting shoals of white styrofoam," and "the sky above the port was the color of television, tuned to a dead channel."

An enigmatic, surgically reconstructed special-forces veteran rescues Case, gets him off drugs, restores his talents, and teams him with a beautiful, biologically engineered female assassin. Their mission is to crack computer security in a space colony; subsequent revelations lead us, with some predictability, to the inevitable super-computer that's running things—or trying to.

What sets this book apart from all other current science fiction is its totally modern orientation. Most writers in this field have middle-aged tastes and style; they dress, act, and write as if the 1960s never happened. Nor is this effect ameliorated when an elder statesman such as Robert Heinlein tries to tackle "taboo" themes, in the embarrassing manner of a retired colonel dancing at a discotheque to prove he's still hip.

Of the few who have demonstrated any real contemporary awareness, Harlan Ellison, Samuel R. Delany, and Norman Spinrad are probably the best-known names, though they have now been with us for 20 years or more. Gibson's technique can be as melodramatic as Ellison's, but is closely controlled, carefully rewritten, allowing no lapses into excess. His descriptions are as stylized as Delany's, but free from far-fetched metaphors and awkward syntax. His style owes debts to Bester and perhaps William Burroughs, but the result is synergy, a totally new voice.

The images are densely packed, and there are numerous little tableaux, such as:

"Ratz was tending bar, his prosthetic arm jerking monotonously as he filled a tray of glasses with draft Kirin. He saw Case and smiled, his teeth a webwork of East European steel and brown decay. . . . His ugliness was the stuff of legend. In an age of affordable beauty, there was something heraldic about his lack of it."

The book's faults are glibness and a gimmicky use of farfetched gadgets. Gibson is no engineer, and doesn't even try to explain his pseudoscience. In visualizing the human impact of high technology, however, he is brilliantly perceptive. The resulting society is dehumanized and even repellent, but always derived from trends that are becoming apparent today.

If science fiction is to have any real worth, it must be consistent with the way the world really works, as opposed to how it used to work, or how we wish it would work. The future in *Neuromancer* satisfies this criterion perfectly. This cosmopolitan insight, combined with eloquent writing talent, transmutes category fiction into fine art. *Neuromancer,* in every sense, is state-of-the-art.

Charles Platt, in a review of "Neuromancer," in
Book World—The Washington Post, *July 29, 1984,
p. 11.*

COLIN GREENLAND

On the whole, science fiction's anticipations of the computer were simplistic, envisaging it as a machine rather than a system, and missing altogether the implications of the microcircuitry predicated by all those androids. In *Neuromancer* William Gibson imagines a future pervaded by micro-processes, electronic and surgical, in which information is the prime commodity. Cowboys like Henry Dorsett Case make their living rustling data for unscrupulous employers, cracking "ice" ("Intrusion Countermeasures Electronics") as conventional burglars crack safes. They plug their own brains directly into their computers, to penetrate a shared dream-world where information exchange and its protective ice appear as tangible, luminous blocks, like geometric skyscrapers.

All this technical wizardry, its copious jargon, skewed professional ethics and social consequences Gibson renders plausible, with panache and without tedious explanation. In his lurid, grim future most of the Eastern USA is one giant city, much of Europe radioactive rubble, and Japan a "neon forest", corrupt and gleaming, where a personality is the sum of its vices. . . .

Neuromancer is a hard-boiled crime thriller, both terse and baroque, as the genre demands. It stimulates the requisite adrenalin without bypassing the intellect. Gibson has the glamour of Samuel Delany and the vertigo of Philip K. Dick, and better organization than either; and this is only his first novel.

THE NOVEL OF THE YEAR!
1984 NEBULA AWARD—BEST NOVEL
1984 PHILIP K. DICK AWARD

EDITED BY TERRY CARR
THE NEW ACE SCIENCE
FICTION SPECIALS

NEUROMANCER
WILLIAM GIBSON

Cover of Neuromancer, *by William Gibson. Ace Science Fiction Books, 1984. Copyright © 1984 by William Gibson. Cover art by James Warhola. Reprinted by permission of The Berkley Publishing Group.*

Colin Greenland, *"Possess, Integrate, Inform," in* The Times Literary Supplement, *No. 4262, December 7, 1984, p. 1420.**

An Excerpt from *Neuromancer*

Two blocks west of the Chat, in a teashop called the Jarre de Thé, Case washed down the night's first pill with a double espresso. It was a flat pink octagon, a potent species of Brazilian dex he bought from one of Zone's girls.

The Jarre was walled with mirrors, each panel framed in red neon.

At first, finding himself alone in Chiba, with little money and less hope of finding a cure, he'd gone into a kind of terminal overdrive, hustling fresh capital with a cold intensity that had seemed to belong to someone else. In the first month, he'd killed two men and a woman over sums that a year before would have seemed ludicrous. Ninsei wore him down until the street itself came to

seem the externalization of some death wish, some secret poison he hadn't known he carried.

Night City was like a deranged experiment in social Darwinism, designed by a bored researcher who kept one thumb permanently on the fast-forward button. Stop hustling and you sank without a trace, but move a little too swiftly and you'd break the fragile surface tension of the black market; either way, you were gone, with nothing left of you but some vague memory in the mind of a fixture like Ratz, though heart or lungs or kidneys might survive in the service of some stranger with New Yen for the clinic tanks.

Biz here was a constant subliminal hum, and death the accepted punishment for laziness, carelessness, lack of grace, the failure to heed the demands of an intricate protocol.

Alone at a table in the Jarre de Thé, with the octagon coming on, pinheads of sweat starting from his palms, suddenly aware of each tingling hair on his arms and chest, Case knew that at some point he'd started to play a game with himself, a very ancient one that has no name, a final solitaire. He no longer carried a weapon, no longer took the basic precautions. He ran the fastest, loosest deals on the street, and he had a reputation for being able to get whatever you wanted. A part of him knew that the arc of his self-destruction was glaringly obvious to his customers, who grew steadily fewer, but that same part of him basked in the knowledge that it was only a matter of time.

STEVE CARPER

In some ways *Schismatrix* [by Bruce Sterling] and ***Neuromancer*** and others of their ilk are the books John W. Campbell would have demanded were he a young editor today. Their extrapolative powers make Heinlein look stodgy, the density of their wide canvases makes Asimov's universe look cramped, and they put Van Vogt to shame by ringing his changes an order of magnitude faster and slipping in a new technological plot point every 80 words. They are the Jack Kemps of science fiction, forward-looking conservatives for a conservative age. At least they have forever destroyed the sterility of Heinlein space, the cardboard fantasyland of cleanliness without detail that was the implicit backdrop of every outer space epic we were brought up on. (p. 25)

Steve Carper, *"Sterling Tries but Fails," in* Fantasy Review, *Vol. 8, No. 7, July, 1985, pp. 24-5.**

ORSON SCOTT CARD

One of the most common complaints about artsy-fartsy stories is that the hero is a jerk. And it's a valid complaint. Still, the jerk hero is a natural reaction against the pristine Galahad of the pure romance. To make the hero believable and interesting, the writer has to vary the hero to some degree from perfection.

This can range from Hercule Poirot's annoying vanity and Nero Wolfe's invariable habits to the painful introspection of Spenser and Fletch's cheerful opportunism-verging-on-amorality.

It's no accident that my examples are drawn from mystery fiction. The most delicate and difficult task for the creator of a mystery series is to come up with a protagonist who is interesting and yet whose life is unstructured enough to allow him to get involved in an endless series of adventures. This task of differentiating the protagonist from all other protagonists gets more intense the farther the writer removes himself from the plain tale well told. Until sometimes the hero gets to be so ugly-looking and loathesome-of-soul that Jack Nicholson can be cast in the part.

Sometimes, though, the ugly hero crosses an invisible line and becomes, instead, the tragic hero. Macbeth is as vile as any artsy-fartsy anti-hero you could ever hope to find, and yet we have seen him become a murderous tyrant without ever really wishing to, and with terrible remorse and self-loathing. The result, ironically, is an ennobling story instead of a debasing one.

I dislike William Gibson's novel *Neuromancer* for the very good reason that it never passes from ugly to ennobling. The protagonist has all the good qualities of a turd. In the whole novel, he never makes a single decision on his own initiative. He never *acts*. He is self- and other-destructive. Only two characters in the whole novel *did* have any initiative, and both of them existed only as electronic life—the one, an artificial intelligence; the other, a computer simulation of a once-living man. And what infuriated me most was that Gibson had the only genuinely living characters in the book *wishing for death*. This was obviously a conscious decision on his part, and it was subverted at every turn by his unconscious choices: almost every piece of information, almost every original act in the whole book came from these supposedly death-wishing creatures.

The result was that, despite Gibson's brilliant creation of a milieu, despite the excellent action-adventure writing, despite the dazzling language, despite the fact that I couldn't put the damn thing down, the novel left me with a gnawing pain, a deep anger, because the book obviously wanted me to care about the protagonist, and there was nothing there to care about.

I know it won the Nebula. I know it won the Dick. It can win the Nobel and the Pulitzer for all I care. Flash and dazzle can't compensate for the fact that any person with enough bonding drive, enough social impulse to write a novel cannot be autocentric and isolate enough to believe in the pursuit of death for its own sake. Gibson *doesn't* believe in it. But for whatever reason (and I suspect, with no justification whatsoever, that the reason is that Gibson was sucked into fashionable existentialism just enough to pervert his book) Gibson chose to make his book say something he doesn't believe. In literary terms, I call that a lie, and I think it's just about the worst thing a storyteller can do.

I include this gentle criticism of *Neuromancer* so that you'll know that I am not an uncritical fan of William Gibson's work. (pp. 24-5)

> *Orson Scott Card, "You Got No Friends in This World: A Quarterly Review Essay of Short Science Fiction," in* Science Fiction Review, *No. 56, Fall, 1985, pp. 22-30.*

GERALD JONAS

I have to apologize for failing to review William Gibson's *Neuromancer* . . . when it appeared [in 1984]. What put me off, I think, was the title, which struck me as an ungainly play on words, hinting at some trendy hybrid of sword-and-sorcery fantasy and high-tech adventure, with perhaps a bit of heavy-breathing sex thrown in. I was led to believe I had done Mr. Gibson an injustice when this novel (the author's *first*) won both of the important 1984 best-of-the-year awards in science fiction: the Nebula (voted by members of the Science Fiction Writers of America) and the Hugo (voted by the fans). Now that I have read the book, I would like to cast a belated ballot for Mr. Gibson.

The 21st-century world of *Neuromancer* is freshly imagined, compellingly detailed and chilling in its implications. The theme is power. Advances in computer technology and bioengineering have made it possible to create human beings of preternatural strength and agility. Mr. Gibson's protagonist, known only as Case, is one of a new breed of "cyberspace cowboys," computer hackers who plug into their machines so intimately that they experience the electronic transmission and storage of data as physical sensation—mostly visual, but also tactile and olfactory. Like everyone else in his world, Case can think of nothing to do with his talent except sell it to the highest bidder, which inevitably turns out to be one of the giant corporations whose no-holds-barred rivalries transcend nationality, ideology and even the normal constraints of space and time: "Viewed as organisms, they had attained a kind of immortality."

Mr. Gibson's style is all flash, and his characters are all pose without substance; but the emphasis on surface seems more a statement about Case and Case's world than an attempt to manipulate the reader. The story moves faster than the speed of thought, but even when I wasn't sure what was happening, I felt confident that Mr. Gibson would pull me through, and he did. The "cyberspace" conceit allows him to dramatize computer hacking in nontechnical language, although I wonder how much his somewhat florid descriptions of the "bodiless exultation of cyberspace" will mean to readers who have not experienced the illusion of power that punching the keyboard of even a dinky little word-processor can give. (P.S. I *still* think *Neuromancer* is a terrible title.)

> *Gerald Jonas, in a review of "Neuromancer," in* The New York Times Book Review, *November 24, 1985, p. 33.*

TOM MADDOX

[*Maddox is an American critic and short story writer specializing in science fiction. The essay excerpted below was first presented at the International Conference on the Fantastic on March 15, 1986. In the following excerpt Maddox identifies three distinctive characteristics of Gibson's fiction, citing examples from* Neuromancer.]

In terms of the esteem of his peers and the fans, William Gibson was the most successful science fiction writer of 1985. His first novel, *Neuromancer*, published in 1984, won the Philip K. Dick, Nebula and Hugo Awards, as well as the Ditmar, the top award given in Australia. *Neuromancer* tapped the source, hit a nerve. To many of those who voted for it or just read and admired it, the book seemed to manifest a new set of possibilities for sf.

The questions naturally arise, what are the characteristics of Gibson's work and what is its novelty by the standards of sf? The primary difference, especially in terms of reader response, is that—untypically in sf—the ideas are *not* the hero. Rather, line for line his narratives contain a precise and detailed inventory of perception. Also, they are built around the narrative conventions of the thriller and executed with an intensity not seen in the genre since Alfred Bester's *The Stars My Destination* and *The Demolished Man*. Finally, Gibson's fiction is an art of collage, assembled fragment—the work of a junkman and vandal: post-apocalypse biker rooting through Bloomingdale's for a piece of fine lace to hang from his sleeve.

Gibson claims not to invent anything. He says he just looks around. If that's the case, it's weird in here. Altered states of being, rewritten flesh—in sum, technology redoing fundamental ways of human life. Perhaps Gibson is right: perhaps he's extrapolating, not inventing. The concentrated tunnel vision of the videogames player mutates into *cyberspace*, the audio-visual intensity of color television and Walkman earphones into *simstim*, the password and data encryption programs of telecommunications into *ICE*, the Atlantic corridor into the *Sprawl*. Just extrapolating—as surpassing the speed of sound just required speeding things up a bit.

In fact, the essence of Gibson's technique is not dependent upon any sf device. He can work his effects with objects we can obtain here and now. Here, chosen more-or-less at random, is an example:

> She brought an oblong box from beneath the counter. The lid was yellow cardboard, stamped with a crude image of a coiled cobra with a swollen hood. Inside were eight identical tissue-wrapped cylinders. He watched while mottled brown fingers stripped the paper from one. She held the thing up for him to examine, a dull steel tube with a leather thong at one end and a small bronze pyramid at the other. She gripped the tube with one hand, the pyramid between her thumb and forefinger, and pulled. Three oiled, telescoping segments of tightly wound coilspring slid out and locked. "Cobra," she said. (*Neuromancer*. . . .)

Though there's nothing to mark this passage as sf, the presence of Samuel Delany comes through strongly in the insistently precise visual images. One could slide this paragraph into *Dhalgren* without creating a ripple.

Gibson constantly pushes forward. There are indeed other technologies to explore. For instance, there is cyberspace:

> And in the bloodlit dark behind his eyes, silver phosphenes boiling in from the edge of space, hypnagogic images jerking past like film compiled from random frames. Symbols, figures, faces, a blurred, fragmented mandala of visual information.
>
> Please, he prayed, *now*—
>
> A gray disk the color of Chiba sky. . . .
>
> *Now*—
>
> Disk beginning to rotate, faster, becoming a sphere of paler gray. Expanding—
>
> And flowed, flowered for him, fluid neon origami trick, the unfolding of his distanceless home, his country, transparent 3D chessboard extending to infinity. Inner eye opening to the stepped scarlet pyramid of the Eastern Seaboard Fission Authority burning beyond the green cubes of the Mitsubishi Bank of America, and

> high and very far away he saw the spiral arms of military systems, forever beyond his reach.
>
> And somewhere he was laughing, in a white-painted loft, distant fingers caressing the deck, tears of release staining his face. (*Neuromancer*. . . .)

There are also styles—of clothing, architecture, cosmetic surgery, drugs, sex—on and on, a veritable catalog of apparently disconnected items which seem part of an unnamed, probably unknown gestalt whose structure shifts with every moment.

What is this structure? What is the nature of its elements? Gibson himself provides the clue. In an interview given to the British sf magazine *Interzone*, he says, "I see myself as a kind of literary collage-artist, and sf as a marketing framework that allows me to gleefully ransack the whole fat supermarket of 20th century cultural symbols." The "fat supermarket" is of course itself a powerful cultural symbol—one can see Gibson as the winner in a mad gameshow competition which allows him to wheel his basket through the store and take anything he wants.

More precisely and comprehensively, he is talking about semiotics—signs, symbols, signifiers. As Umberto Eco says, in *A Theory of Semiotics*, everything that can be used to *lie*. As the twentieth century has gone on, and the means for producing and distributing signs have proliferated wildly, our environment becomes evermore densely layered with them. From the viewpoint of semiotics, human culture is seen as a vast assemblage of signs, shifting in meaning from moment to moment, place to place; both structuring and structured by human understanding and emotion. In some ways, the study of culture has become the study of signs. . . . (p. 46)

Granted the semiotic supermarket as the source of his loot, Gibson is then confronted with the question, in what form should these elements be presented? His answer to this question emerged with **"Johnny Mnemonic"**—which stands to the Gibson cosmos as the Big Bang does to our own. The form Gibson chose is, of course, the hard-boiled thriller.

Though the elements of hard-boiled fiction vary, certain constants remain. The primary one is affect: the writing must be intense, the action violent, the atmosphere erotically charged. Hard-boiled fiction can be crude and direct, as in early Dashiell Hammett; ornate and meditative, as in the Philip Marlowe novels of Raymond Chandler; extravagant and hallucinatory as in William Burroughs. If the 20th century has a distinct narrative voice, this is it.

The version of hard-boiled that Gibson employs has proven one of the most durable: the cosmopolitan, great game narrative. First seen in primitive form in Somerset Maugham's *Ashenden*, it became widely known in the works of Graham Greene and Eric Ambler, and has served authors as various as John Le Carre and Robert Stone. In it, the hard-boiled atmosphere is made more complex by the presence of what we might call vast powers. The British Secret Service has provided a flexible and eloquent framework for many writers—its antagonisms span decades and range from Nazis to Russians to traitors within. But always, whoever is doing the writing and in whatever context, the narratives are figured by what a character in **Count Zero**, Gibson's second novel, calls an "articulate structure," an "unnatural field." . . . . It is created by vast power or vast wealth—governments, their secret services and hidden armies, industrial combines licit and illicit, families and individuals whose wealth elevates them to these precincts. As

Thomas Pynchon showed in *V., The Crying of Lot 49*, and *Gravity's Rainbow*, the intuited presence of such forces is the characteristic 20th century paranoia. Thus, as in Elizabethan drama, we have a sense of the familiar and profound—of a whole literary style, yes, but more: of a metaphysics of 20th century life.

Behind all I have said about Gibson thus far remains a fundamental fact about his work that is extremely difficult to talk about analytically, and yet is central to it. Reading Gibson is an intensely involving, sometimes exhausting experience. The constant flow of sensual detail embedded in an unfamiliar, often grotesque technology makes for a quintessential sf experience, but for some people the experience is either too intense or too unrelenting. For instance, I know of several people whose response to *Neuromancer* went something like, "It's really well done, but I got tired of it towards the end." Then usually comes an addendum to the effect, "I couldn't get involved with the characters."

In old-fashioned terms, this is a sensible response. It is a call for "rounder" characters, more believable plot lines, and so on. However, I think the response is also quite mistaken. For a cautionary instance, one can look at Kim Stanley Robinson's *The Wild Shore*, which succeeds in precisely these old-fashioned ways, and also succeeds in seeming irrelevant, unexciting—sf by a serious, well-intentioned 50s writer, someone on the order of Louis Auchincloss.

In this light, I think that critics or reviewers who are waiting for Gibson to make some radical move outside this narrative framework are simply kidding themselves. For him to do so would be no more or less unexpected than for Robert Stone or John Le Carre. And no more or less ill-advised. If Gibson is going to *go* anywhere, he cannot relinquish the values of the hard-boiled thriller.

My point is this: much of contemporary art is strenuous, but we have learned to meet its demands. So my advice to the reader of *Neuromancer* is simply *read it again*. Its supposed flaws—plot fatigue, weak character development—are in fact manifestations of its strength and modernity.

Semiotic fragments, then, caught in the thriller's web—here we have essential Gibson. One other element remains to be discussed: Gibson's characterization of himself as a "collage artist." A recent story, **"Winter Market,"** features a character who puts together constructions out of junk of all sorts. The story's narrator says he is "a master of . . . garbage, kipple, refuse, the sea of cast-off goods our century floats on. *Gomi no sensei*. Master of junk." However, as the narrator also recognizes, our century poses a difficult question: "Where does the *gomi* stop and the world begin?" The answer the narrator seems to give is that there is no separation, not if one understands *gomi* correctly. There is the *gomi* which the Japanese have piled in Tokyo Bay and named "Dream Island," and

there is the *gomi* which is the entire collection of human symbols, conscious and unconscious—semiotics in its entirety. Here is Gibson as post-modernist: cultural vandal, junkman, boxmaker.

He makes even more explicit his ancestry in the visual arts, in references to Marcel Duchamp and Joseph Cornell. In *Neuromancer,* Molly passes through the Tessier-Ashpool family's art gallery and without comment or recognition sees "a shattered, dust-stenciled sheet of glass" (*Neuromancer* . . .) with an inscription in French which translates, "The bride stripped bare by her bachelors, even." This is of course the legend on Marcel Duchamp's "Large Glass," one of the first pieces of assemblage art and perhaps still the most influential. Gibson has appropriated yet another semiotic element from the cultural store—through implication he has invoked Dada and Surrealism and has claimed allegiance to that form of the avant-garde which continues today in painting, sculpture, dance, music, and performance art combining any number of these elements. *Neuromancer*'s "Big Scientists" are a tribute to Laurie Anderson, the New York City musician and performance artist who works in the musical tradition of Philip Glass and Robert Wilson's more recent *Einstein on the Beach*. . . . (pp. 47-8)

Finally, there is a minor but persistent theme in Gibson's work which can serve as a coda. It is this: technology produces results different from and more radical than the intent of its creators. In **"New Rose Hotel"** (*Omni*, July, 1984), the narrator says, "Nothing here seems to serve its original purpose." . . . In **"Winter Market"** the *gomi no sensei*—master of junk—says, "Anything people build, any kind of technology, it's going to have some specific purpose. . . . But if it's new technology, it'll open areas nobody's ever thought of before." One of Gibson's primary obligations is to portray these "new areas," to show the capable human monkey at its elaborate, everchanging play; in the process he has perhaps used sf in new ways.

As I indicated at the beginning of this paper, he has been wellrewarded so far. However, sf's honeymoon with Gibson will end, and other writers with other concerns will be spotlighted. It is the way of things in our culture. To quote *Neuromancer,* "Fads swept the youth of the Sprawl at the speed of light; entire subcultures could rise overnight, thrive for a dozen weeks, and then vanish utterly." . . . But Gibson has also received Molly Millions' warning: "You can't let the little pricks generation-gap you." . . . And he won't. Like the *gomi* master he will continue to pick through our culture's semiotic junk, looking for "things that fit some strange design scrawled on the inside of his forehead by whatever serves him as a muse." (p. 48)

Tom Maddox, "Cobra, She Said: An Interim Report on the Fiction of William Gibson," in Fantasy Review, *Vol. 9, No. 4, April, 1986, pp. 46-8.*

Robert Hass

Twentieth Century Pleasures: Prose on Poetry

The National Book Critics Circle Award: Criticism

American poet and critic.

While *Twentieth Century Pleasures: Prose on Poetry* is Hass's first collection of criticism, he had gained recognition as an important new poet over a decade earlier with his first volume of poetry, *Field Guide* (1973), for which he won the Yale Series of Younger Poets Award. With his collected criticism, Hass has again attracted attention. The National Book Critics Circle offered this enthusiastic praise: "In *Twentieth Century Pleasures* [Robert Hass] brings a poet's sensibility to powerful readings of Lowell, Rilke, and other central figures of our century, combining deep learning with passionate conviction. The criticism, like Hass' poetry, is robust, engaged, and utterly lucid."

A native Californian, Hass studied briefly with Yvor Winters, who is associated with the New Critics and is a proponent of the moral role of poetry. Both Winters and Kenneth Rexroth, who was part of the San Francisco Renaissance, are cited as influential in Hass's poetic development. Another interest apparent in his work is Asian poetry, especially Japanese haiku with its purity of observation, a form popular on the West Coast during Hass's developing years. Hass commented on his poetic influences in a 1981 interview: "I think very much the influence for me in poetry is poetry. Specifically Wordsworth and Pound and through them Snyder and Whitman and others. . . . I guess there is not one model. What I seem to return to most is Pound in the late *Cantos,* and Wordsworth's blank verse." Hass is also learned in Slavic languages and along with Robert Pinsky translated Czesław Miłosz's *The Separate Notebooks*.

Called both a painterly poet and a meditative poet, Hass in his collections *Field Guide* and *Praise* (1979) excels in descriptions of natural landscapes and at the same time presents thoughtful dialectics on desire and despair, nature and imagination, meaning and mystery, life and death. An intellectual writer, he fills his poems with references to books, films, paintings, and music—all used by the poet to interpret his experiences. These discursive meditations are matched with a richness of sensory experience and human feeling that led critic Stanley Kunitz to describe Hass as "a poet who sits easy in his skin."

Hass's love of poetry as well as his own poetic style are evident in his criticism. *Twentieth Century Pleasures* comprises ten essays and four reviews; several essays are appreciations of American and international poets, including Robert Lowell, James Wright, Tomas Tranströmer, Stanley Kunitz, Czesław Miłosz, Rainer Maria Rilke, and others. In discussing writers, Hass locates them in the context of their time and place in order to more fully consider their artistic vision, and, in some cases, to revise current assumptions about an author or a work. The collection includes, too, an autobiographical piece on the San Francisco Bay area and three meditative essays: on poetic form, on prosody and rhythm, and on images (particularly the

© 1986 Thomas Victor

imagery of the Japanese haiku masters and the use of this haiku form by contemporary American poets).

Critics note that Hass writes in a relaxed, narrative style and that his essays often include more personal stories, which, though not integral to his argument, make his essays more immediate and human. Critics also observe that Hass's discussions on writers and on the status of contemporary poetry are compelling and illuminating. These essays were originally published in a variety of literary journals, but they are marked by a unified sensibility: a devotion to poetry and an abiding faith in poetry's importance to self-knowledge, to existence. In the words of critic Edward Hirsch, "*Twentieth Century Pleasures* is informed by a deep faith that the greatest poems can capture the numinousness of the world and ultimately it is this faith which makes Robert Hass a critic—as well as a poet—of praise."

See also *CLC,* Vol. 18 and *Contemporary Authors*, Vol. 111.)

CLAYTON ESHLEMAN

Fifty years ago such a collection [*Twentieth Century Pleasures*] might have been called "Cherished Hours With Favorite Authors."

In many of these pieces, Hass shares aspects of his own life with the reader in an attempt, I believe, to make a connection between the life lived and, through his authors, the life imagined. While such "sharing" gives a friendly, personalized quality to the writing, much of it does not seem necessary to the textual commentaries. Hass, who is careful never to offend (even when he is presenting writing that in part appalls him), seems to be weaving a sympathetic picture of himself into his criticism, to draw the reader into an acceptance of his literary positions.

Page for page, about half of the book is devoted to commentary on foreign poetries, mainly Rilke, Milosz, Transtromer and Japanese haiku. The long essay on Rilke is the most thorough piece in the collection (although it is packed with hindsight) and would serve as a fine introduction to the most translated European poet of this century.

Hass often fails to distinguish between serious writing and doggerel in what he quotes, and this problem undermines his writing on Czeslaw Milosz. Near the end of this 40-page essay, Hass states that what he has come to love about Milosz's work is that he is an erotic poet; yet what he quotes in no way confirms such a statement.

The divergence between what is quoted and what Hass makes of the quote—or infers from it—is one of the main problems of the book. To a certain extent, I am sympathetic with the problem; it often comes up as a result of Hass' enthusiasm for poetry. He writes with a laconic gusto; his dedication is unquestionable, and his range of reading has a wide generosity. However, his tendency to aggrandize what he quotes with associations from other sources can be irritating. Having quoted a Buson haiku—"Nothing moves; / frightening! / the summer grove"—Hass comments: "This is the Pan of panic, the old terror of the woods that somehow became for the Greeks a god of wine and sap and semen and breast milk. Birth, death, growth, madness, mistakenness, beauty, sadness, curiosity. They are all there, as one might turn from Ceres to Cybele to Apollo to Thor, each power acknowledged and given full weight."

Of the pieces on American poets, the ones on James Wright and Robert Creeley are the most penetrating.

Clayton Eshleman, "*A Poet in Praise of Other Poets,*" in Los Angeles Times Book Review, *November 18, 1984, p. 8.*

An Excerpt from *Twentieth-Century Pleasures: Prose on Poetry*

It seems to me that we all live our lives in the light of primary acts of imagination, images or sets of images that get us up in the morning and move us about our days. I do not think anybody can live without one, for very long, without suffering intensely from deadness and futility. And I think that, for most of us, those images are not only essential but dangerous because no one of them feels like the whole truth and they do not last. Either they die of themselves, dry up, are shed; or, if we are lucky, they are invisibly transformed into the next needful thing; or we act on them in a way that exposes both them and us.

Literature is a long study of instances. Stephen Dedalus growing up and into some imagination of the life of an artist. Emma Bovary's fatal imagination of herself and of the promise of her life. Gatsby and the light on the dock. Rilke and his angel. The difference between Rilke and Gatsby is something to pause over, for Gatsby is a study of an appalling literalization of the image, and Rilke with his extraordinary subtlety and dramatic quickness of imagination located the power of the image completely outside himself, as a beautiful being, absolutely real and indifferent to him. The *Duino Elegies* are a record of that face-to-face encounter with the deliteralized power of the image. The danger there is personal, spiritual: it is not Gatsby's danger or Emma Bovary's which is a danger to others as, say, Pol Pot's image of justice was dangerous to the people of Cambodia or Ronald Reagan's image of good and evil is dangerous to the people of Central America. Images are powers: it seems to me quite possible that the arsenal of nuclear weapons exists, as Armageddon has always existed, to intensify life. It is what Rilke says, that the love of death as an other is the great temptation and failure of imagination.

Speaking of Rilke and Gatsby, of course, I begin to mix up art and life, since Gatsby himself is an image—perhaps for Fitzgerald an image created to control and deliteralize the image of the light at the end of the dock, the fatal and absolute yearning through which psychic energy that does intensify the world comes pouring into it. But that confusion of art and life, inner and outer, is the very territory of the image; it is what an image is. *And the word was made flesh and dwelt among us.* Someone defined religion as communal worship centered on a set of common images of the mystery, and it has always seemed to me a useful definition. It distinguishes religion from art on the one hand and madness on the other, from that psychotic literalization of images we glimpse in others from time to time. The young woman on the bus with a ravaged face and the intense eyes of some very beautiful species of monkey who turned to me and said, "I think I'm getting a sore throat. Can you feel it?"

Images in art, or maybe I should say images in great art, differ from religious images in that they are personal rather than communal. Though having been personal, they can become communal: some man or woman may have lived on the earth and looked at women and the rounded middenheaps out of which the human cultivation of the earth evolved and fashioned the Venus of Willendorf as an image of Ge, of the earth mother herself, and having made that image so powerfully, it may have passed into other images and entered the human imagination, in the way that some forms do, as a collective symbol; myself and my classmates in high spring carrying in procession our garlands to the statue of the Virgin in the schoolyard and singing shrilly:

> Oh Mary we crown thee with blossoms today,
> Queen of the rosary, Queen of the May.

The nuns looking on, mothers looking on as we made our adorable, brief passage through the matriarchy. But each of those successive images of the earth mother was, first of all, an individual act of imagination.

EDWARD HIRSCH

"Images haunt," Robert Hass tells us in *Twentieth Century Pleasures*. They are also, by their very nature, phenomenal, standing for nothing else but themselves, reaching down into the well of being and affirming, *this is*. It is a permanently startling fact that language can give us back parts of our own world, full-bodied. "Images are powers," Hass also writes, emphasizing that they are metonymic glimpses, fundamental acts of imagination, moments of pure being. The image is the primary pigment of the lyric poet and in its purest form it is the enemy of time, of discourse, of all narratives that seek to surround and distill it. . . . Yeats claimed that the intensity of images actively bordered on the visionary, an intersection between two worlds. In a different tradition, one of Tu Fu's colleagues told him, "It is like being alive twice."

The nature of the image—its surprising fullness of being and phenomenological significance—is one of the leitmotifs of *Twentieth Century Pleasures,* Robert Hass's collection of prose pieces about poetry. The book brings together ten essays and four reviews, all of which were commissioned by various editors over the past five years, and consequently it has the character of an omnibus, weaving together a number of essays about individual poets—Lowell, Wright, Tranströmer, Kunitz, Milosz, Rilke, and others—with a memoir about the San Francisco Bay Area as a cultural region and three larger meditations about poetic form, prosody and rhythm, and images. Most of these essays are what used to be called "appreciations"—if we mean by the term something along the order of Randall Jarrell's essays on Frost, Auden, and Whitman. Like Jarrell, Hass is often at his best when he is both reconsidering a poet's work and rescuing it from a myriad of surrounding assumptions. His extended meditation on "The Quaker Graveyard in Nantucket," for example, should forever lay to rest the received opinion that Lowell's early poems "clearly reflect the dictates of the new criticism" while the later ones are "less consciously wrought" and "more intimate." In a somewhat different vein, his indispensable essay on James Wright helps to define the inward alertness, luminous intelligence, and clarity of feeling in Wright's work; but it also unmasks some of the unspoken assumptions and limitations in his aesthetic, in particular the unconscious insistence on a "radical and permanent division between the inner and outer" worlds. For Hass, this Calvinist division—which is anyway denied by Wright's best work—is one of the recurrent problems in American poetry. Indeed, *Twentieth Century Pleasures* is held together not only by Hass's uniquely personal and unified sensibility, but also by his ongoing conviction that the division between inner and outer can be healed in post-romantic poetry and that human inwardness needs to find a viable shape in the external world. One of his persistent concerns is the relationship between looking and being, his sense of how the image comes together and how the mind—through the medium of the lyric poem—recovers and creates form.

Hass is the most intimate and narrative of critics—each of his essays begins with a personal example or story—and he writes with an unusually vivid sense that "Poems take place in your life, or some of them do, like the day your younger sister arrives and replaces you as the bon enfant in the bosom of the family. . . ." So, too, he writes always as a man situated in a particular place at a particular time, a Wordsworthian poet, only partially off-duty, who is taking a specific occasion—a symposium, the publication of a book—to think about his art. As a native Californian with a formalist training (Kenneth Rexroth and Yvor Winters are two California presences who

shaped his sensibility), Hass often seems to be standing at the edge of the continent, facing west. Throughout *Twentieth Century Pleasures* the Japanese haiku poets serve as his primary touchstones and models. Thus Chekhov's notebook entries are praised for being "close to the temperament" of Japanese poets, and Whitman's "Cavalry Crossing a Ford" is demonstrated to be "in the spirit" of Buson; Gary Snyder's "August on Sourdough, A Visit from Dick Brewer" is located in a tradition of Oriental leave-taking poems, and James Wright's "Outside Fargo, North Dakota" is compared to a haiku by Bashō which gets at the same feeling. Hass's essay on **"Images"**—which is the concluding and arguably the most important piece in the book—weaves together a series of radiant personal memories with a mini-discussion of Japanese poetics. Poems by Buson, Issa, and Bashō are the essential examples in his argument that images are not so much "about" anything as they are things-in-themselves, "equal in status with being and the mysteriousness of being." At times Hass sounds like an intuitive Bachelard, a phenomenologist transplanted to California and turned into a mid-century American poet.

One recurrent problem for modern poets is the relationship between image and discourse, epiphanic moment and narrative time, song and story. Hass is particularly alert to the issue, noting in one piece that "The *Cantos* are a long struggle between image and discourse" and in another that "Winters never solved for himself the problem of getting from image to discourse in the language of his time." The problem is crucial for poets who seek to transcend Imagism (and deep Imagism) and want to carve forms in time, to build from the individual to the community and to incorporate into their work aspects of natural, social, political, and historical life. The "perilousness of our individual lives," Hass declares, "is what makes the insight of the isolated lyric untenable." One of the secondary dramas in *Twentieth Century Pleasures* is watching the essays circle the problem of image and discourse, finding different solutions in different poets. Thus, Hass argues that Tranströmer's *Baltics* solves the problem through a series of wandering fragments or islands, Wordsworth's *Prelude* by knitting together being and looking, giving the poet's own inwardness "a local habitation and a name." He finds that Rilke finally lets the world come flooding through him in the *Duino Elegies* and that Milosz circumnavigates the problem in *Separate Notebooks,* continually returning to the issue of "whether one should try to rescue being from the river of time by contemplating or embracing it." The Japanese haiku poets serve as another type of model by organizing their anthologies seasonally; as a result each poem reaches out "toward an absolute grasp of being" but also takes its place in a larger seasonal cycle. In this way the stillness of the moment is given special poignance by the velocity of time. What is crucial to Hass in all of these works is the basic idea of poetic form, the mind making connections, creating rhythmic texture and shape out of diverse fragments.

Twentieth Century Pleasures begins by discussing the difficulty of talking about favorite poems, and it ends by affirming "the fullness and emptiness of being." Its very title sets itself against our twentieth-century experience of fragmentation, and one of the book's key subjects is the mind's capacity for "wonder and repetition," the way the best poems can focus an attentive and self-forgetful consciousness. Hass's own most successful poetic mode has been the meditative lyric which, as he notes in an essay on Stanley Kunitz's work, "can step a little to the side and let the world speak through it, and the world has no need to cry 'Let be! Let be!' because it is." Hass has an acute sense of the perils of twentieth-century history, but this is

Dust jacket of Twentieth Century Pleasures: Prose on Poetry *by Robert Hass. The Ecco Press, 1984. Jacket © Cynthia Krupat. By permission of the publisher.*

always tempered by his abiding faith in "the absolute value of being." He has a long memory for happiness and returns often to experiences of well-being, radiance, fullness, health. As his most well-known poem, **"Meditation at Lagunitas,"** puts it: "There are moments when the body is as numinous / as words, days that are the good flesh continuing. . . ." *Twentieth Century Pleasures* is informed by a deep faith that the greatest poems can capture the numinousness of the world and ultimately it is this faith which makes Robert Hass a critic— as well as a poet—of praise. (pp. 345-48)

Edward Hirsch, "Praise," in Poetry, Vol. CXLV, No. 6, March, 1985, pp. 345-48.

ANTHONY LIBBY

Twentieth-century pleasure is not precisely what we expect from a book of criticism, which often has a distinctly 19th-century quality and offers secondary pleasures at best. But as the California poet Robert Hass recounts and analyzes his complex joy in poets from Basho to Rilke to James Wright, he creates [in *Twentieth Century Pleasures: Prose on Poetry*] a very special pleasure of his own. This results partly from the almost fictional tendencies of his criticism. As Mr. Hass tends to locate

poets in their times and places, so he locates his reading for us, giving up the illusion of objectivity to place the reading in his life. In a piece about Robert Lowell, Mr. Hass complains about the difficulty of judging the value of poetry "when it's gotten into the blood. It becomes autobiography then." So his criticism contains many snatches of autobiography, for instance as he introduces a study of the poetry and politics of Czeslaw Milosz with a memory of participating in a 1966 antinapalm demonstration or when he begins a piece on prosody with a quick, funny glance at dirty saloon repartee. Conversely, he writes only one overtly autobiographical piece for this collection, and it is mostly about poetry.

Mr. Hass's complexity shows not so much in his autobiographical gestures as in his thinking about the poems. We are conscious of a whole mind before us, presented in a style that is both elegant and plain, enlivened by a freely metaphorical imagination and magisterial one-liners. (About rhythm: "The first fact of the world is that it repeats itself.") Deep intelligence and wide knowledge serve Mr. Hass's particular vision of poetry, a vaguely Tory one that has been unfashionable for much of the past two decades, though it is coming dramatically into its own now.

Unlike the early modern Imagists and such recent neo-Surrealists as Robert Bly, Mr. Hass cares more for the line than the image. Not that he opposes Surrealism, but he argues that what is genuinely basic, what gets to the unconscious, what defines "revolutionary ground," is rhythm more than visual representation. Mr. Hass admits that "images haunt," but he remains clearly less drawn to pictures than to ideas. This inclination has one unfortunate effect: the piece called **"Images,"** despite some thoughtful meditations on haiku, is less compelling than the others. Even the tone of its personal reminiscences—which are too obviously rhetorically calculated, habitual—seems askew.

Another, more interesting effect of Mr. Hass's interest in thought is his ambivalence about modernism, partly an inheritance from the poet and critic Yvor Winters, with whom he briefly studied. But Mr. Hass moderates Winters's rather ill-tempered scorn for everything Romantic or post-Romantic. (He also does a little restorative work on Winters's image as a poet, trying in one review to remember "the fierce old curmudgeon of Palo Alto" as a young Romantic.) Whatever his position in the poetry wars, Mr. Hass remains devoted to the massive poems of modernism, like Lowell's *Quaker Graveyard in Nantucket* or Rilke's *Duino Elegies*. But because of his interest in the moral implications of ideas and because he locates poetry so squarely among the central experiences of existence, he worries about modernism's infatuation either with intense self-examination or with the inhuman—the darkness of instinct, not the light of reason, and finally death.

Mr. Hass argues with a rationalist's insistence on the value of reason as opposed to more mysterious ways of knowing. But unlike excessively rationalist critics, he understands precisely the appeal of mystery and admits the esthetically generative power of dark forces in the self. Even while amusing himself by accusing Mr. Bly of describing "imagination as a kind of ruminative wombat," he tends to grant the general validity of Mr. Bly's Romantic insistence on the deep roots of poetry— though Mr. Hass insists that "the imagination is luminously intelligent." But there remains a problem. As he says in a moment of impatience in his wonderful essay on Rilke, at times he feels "a sudden restless revulsion from the whole tradition of nineteenth- and early-twentieth-century poetry'' because of its narcissistic obsession with inwardness and death.

The great skill of this critic is his willingness to entertain such judgments, as well as many small, fair, precise judgments of individual poems. His final intention is not merely to judge but to give a picture of the writer's mind. He begins with a balanced assessment of flaws in a particular vision and articulates a complex understanding of the way those flaws are inseparable from—genius. Among the transcendent contradictions of poetry, human or even esthetic weakness can be one of the springs of esthetic power.

Because he is so concerned with the absence of human relationships in so much poetry, Mr. Hass sometimes tends to welcome suggestions of sexual desire with an uncharacteristically uncritical enthusiasm. He is a stern judge of Surrealist sentimentalism about darkness and otherness, but when he finds traces of the erotic, Mr. Hass sometimes lets sentimentalism pass (in James Wright, for instance), and he does not always see the dangers of narcissism in the contemplation, especially male and abstract, of the sexual other. But it seems unduly crabby to insist on this small failing; let me suggest, as Mr. Hass does when he points to poetic flaws, that it is in ways inseparable from the strengths of Mr. Hass's own luminous sensibility.

Because of the range of that sensibility, many of these essays, especially the introduction to Rilke but even the rather too long discussion of prosody, are both interesting enough for a general audience and rigorous enough for professionals. Correspondingly, Mr. Hass's style balances conversational directness and eloquent complexity. However readers might argue with the details of his responses, his writing appeals. That comes naturally—if his highly self-conscious rhetoric can be described as natural—from his pleasure in poetry and in talking about poetry, always frankly mixed with enjoyment in talking about the self. The two are indivisible. Mr. Hass believes that poetry is what defines the self, and it is his ability to describe that process that is the heart of this book's pleasure.

Anthony Libby, "Criticism in the First Person," in The New York Times Book Review, March 3, 1985, p. 37.

DICK DAVIS

We enter a different world, and one I think most readers of poetry would much rather live in, when we open Robert Hass's *Twentieth Century Pleasures;* his first sentence, ''It's probably a hopeless matter, writing about favourite poems'', establishes the tone—colloquial, welcoming, inviting complicity; and if you don't have favourite poems read no further. Hass is a poet himself and it shows; his love for poetry, his intimate awareness of how it is made and the kinds of effects it is capable of, are obvious on almost every page. [This book] . . . constantly sent me back with fresh understanding to poems I thought I knew, and in search of poems I had not known before.

The writing is relaxed, almost belletrist, certainly free of jargon: there are some brilliantly illuminating passages—the comparison of a James Wright poem with Truffaut's *L'Enfant Sauvage*, for example, and the scansion of a poem by Snyder. It may be that the writing will prove too personal for some readers (we learn a great deal about Hass's children in the course of the book), but the personal moments are often the most telling, as in the essay describing his own discovery of poetry during adolescence. An adolescent hunger for poetry is something he values and he quotes Octavio Paz with evident approval: "Young boys read verse to help themselves express or know their feelings, as if the dim intuited features of love, heroism or sensuality could only be clearly contemplated in a poem"; out of his own hunger a fine critical intelligence has grown. The book is helped by the fact that Hass writes almost entirely about poems and poets he likes: often his assurance is a little breathtaking (he confidently discusses poems he can read only in translation) and some of his aphorisms can seem more glib than true (particularly his dismissal of Herrick) but these are minor cavils. One reads here the prose of an intelligent man who wishes to serve poetry—not appropriate it or crow over it or show off at its expense—and this is a rare enough experience to arouse gratitude and admiration. (pp. 293-94)

Dick Davis, "Arguing in Unknown Quantities," in The Times Literary Supplement, No. 4276, March 15, 1985, pp. 293-94.*

MARIANNE BORUCH

Gertrude Stein's belief that we all have two literatures inside us—the way it really happened, and the way it is a history of our knowing it—is the two-hearted intelligence guiding these essays [in *Twentieth Century Pleasures*.] ''You can analyze the music of poetry,'' Hass writes at the start of his tangled and generously lit piece on Robert Lowell, ''but it's difficult to conduct an argument about its value, especially when it's gotten into the blood. It becomes autobiography there.'' Personal stake, image, eccentricity: it is this insistence, probably, that makes these essays feel sophisticated and ingenuous at once. All bear the mark of ordinary circumstance, human days and nights spent badly or well. They lull, startle, and (much of the time) convince because of their continual visible motion: one man thinking about matters he finds both natural and urgent.

One urgency is form—how swiftly content figures it in a poem, in a lifetime, in any genuine moment of comprehension. Yes, it is Williams, and of course, it is Olson, but however dogeared a notion by now, in these hands it is not predictable because Hass resists reduction in his analysis—striking, in most cases, past the single portable idea. There is the young Lowell, for instance—who perhaps never had a more able or loving visitor in his Quaker graveyard—losing himself, by that poem's second section, in a syntax as wrenching as the imagery, a movement which, as Hass observes, swells and gathers toward violence like the waves themselves. ''Surrealism,'' he adds suddenly, ''. . . is syntax: not weird images but the way the mind connects them.'' This is criticism sprung from an earlier age into this one by sheer restlessness before the thing itself, before the infamous static ritual of wood and stone and darkness in contemporary work. This is reverence for essence: how it comes about through shape, forces us back into memory, and carries us past memory into history.

Hass's memory, how fluid it is. In beginning the essay **''One Body: Some Notes on Form,''** he taps the wonder of his children's obsession with repetition—in language, daily habit, weather—that brings forward a major use of poetry: security, and beyond that, identity. Then, cross repetition with variant (and here he recalls Creeley, who himself is busily recalling Pound) and at once daring is pitted against safety, escape against rescue, until poetry begins to feel like poetry: that sensible, daredevil flight. Where history enters, the essay widens to contain it, gracefully but with the quirky relief of details pocketed like keepsakes—knowledge as Frost would have it, sticking like burrs to the pant leg. Why, Hass wonders, this amazing thing: that nineteenth-century men would actually begin *to hear* differently. Where they understood "the power of incantatory repetition before, they now heard its monotony." Why, seemingly out of nowhere, did we have free verse? Look to democracy—of course. But rake that landscape again: balloon-frame construction—quick and elegant without the tedious mortise and tenon—or the Windsor chair, or the clapboard house, repeated beyond fad into icon. America. *Leaves of Grass* with its sudden and superb impatience.

Which is to say, this is part of the charm of these essays: how they follow their own fascinations, the boy genius of the class refusing the common homework, and working all night on the extra-credit project that has everything and nothing to do with the topic. Definition. Redefinition. If these essays recall the pleasures of a century's poetic thinking, then here at the garden's center is Hass, naming and renaming in Adamic fever.

In a crucial way every piece in this collection returns, like music haunted by a single theme, to form, to the idea that a poem is merely "the shape of its own understanding." How that understanding moves beyond the single work to a body of work is the focus of several essays, as Hass takes on the living and the dead: Milosz, Kunitz, Wright, Rilke, and others. Yet if, as he observes, not all poems in a lifetime are "equally poems," then these essays are not all equally essays, and at least two of his subjects—Milosz and Kunitz—suffer for it. In the case of Kunitz (**"What Furies"**) the discomfort is clear enough. He is trapped from the start by a seemingly neat comparison with Wallace Stevens—"*Beyond, beyond,* Stevens says. *Into, into,* says Kunitz"—and by it, Hass is eager to grant Stevens his place as a meditative poet, and Kunitz his as a dramatic lyricist. Both labels, being true, have a tendency to tyrannize our thinking, narrowing our notion of both poets. One thinks of John Barth's Jake Horner muttering that things are not "just true" but "also true." The problem with Hass's handling of Milosz is less artificial, and moves, I think, from a very real enthusiasm, unfortunately made tedious as the essay progresses by an amazing accumulation of historical detail. Milosz is a complex writer and within him lives the beauty and terror of what has perished and what has survived. But in Hass's zeal, one finds the myopia of too careful a translator. He wants to lay everything before us—the literary, political, social, and religious seizures of the European century—all the while throwing the development of this poet against it; a clear point of view, the entry, is somehow lost, and with it a living sense of one man within, keeping the house whole.

To give us the time and the poet: this is the dual ambition surfacing almost everywhere in this volume, and it is Rilke who arrives before us most fully—and strangely—intact. We begin, typically, with Hass himself, this time in Paris at the onset of pilgrimage, seeking out a breakfast spot of Rilke from some fifty years before. That Hass finds the place now thickened with generations of façade, and renamed King Kong, *does* seem to matter, does beg another way into Rilke more appropriate than tracing daily habit. "Wandering the empty Sunday-morning warren of streets off Boulevard St.-Michel," he writes, "remembering how passionately Rilke had argued that the life we live every day is not life, I began to feel that looking for him in this way was actively stupid." From here, the impossibility of *placing* Rilke becomes not the limit to our grasp of him but—to use Hass's idea again—the actual shape of our understanding of his life, his work, and ultimately the larger turning of a nineteenth-century sensibility into a twentieth-century mind. Thus we are launched into **"Looking for Rilke"** as the essay's title modestly declares, and our travel is pulled forward, and rewarded, by a studied meander of historical and textual detail. Finally, Hass insists, it is the "persistent strangeness of Rilke's imagination"—rootless, obsessive, and luminous—that shapes a poetry absolutely "given over to the moment of its making." So Hass defines an approach peculiar to our time, and in laying this foundation stone of twentieth-century work, he locates for us in Rilke's poems the actual excitement of watching the building rise: from the *New Poems* through the elegies at Duino and, in a stunning rush, the *Sonnets to Orpheus.*

Although these essays have fluidity, moving swiftly through time and text, they also hold stubbornly to a personal witnessing of what poems make clear in the life of a real child growing into husband, father, poet. Criticism itself—like Hass's (and Stephen Dobyns') idea of metaphor—becomes a "participatory act" which surprises the hearer and, one suspects, the speaker, into self-knowledge. The edges blur and with them any sense that poetry is apart, defused by success, sorrow, or time. "Images haunt," Hass declares. "On an August night . . . curled leaves from a Benjamin fig on the floor of the dining room, and a spider, in that moonlight, already set to work in one of them. . . . It is possible to feel my life, in quiet ecstatic helplessness, as a long slow hurtle through the forms of things."

An irresistible example. It is our lives, after all, that poems enter; and we take them in, happily or out of politeness. But Hass wants no part of that politeness. He is speaking here of pleasures, the most gradual kind: literature which finds its way, as he says, into the blood; autobiography discovering in itself a culture. (pp. 205-07)

Marianne Boruch, in a review of "Twentieth Century Pleasures: Prose on Poetry," in The Georgia Review, *Vol. XXXIX, No. 1, Spring, 1985, pp. 205-07.*

Robert (P.) Holdstock
Mythago Wood
World Fantasy Award: Best Novel

(Also writes under pseudonyms of Chris Carlsen and Robert Black) English novelist, short story writer, nonfiction writer, and editor.

Holdstock's novel *Mythago Wood* (1984) evolved from a novella by the author that appeared in the *Magazine of Fantasy and Science Fiction* in 1981. The author, who holds a master's degree in medical zoology from the London School of Hygiene and Tropical Medicine, worked as a medical researcher for four years before embarking on a full-time writing career. Best known as a science fiction and fantasy writer, Holdstock has become increasingly fascinated by mythology, particularly Celtic folklore, as evidenced, for example, in an earlier novel *Earthwind* (1977), and in the short story collection *In the Valley of the Statues* (1982). *Mythago Wood*, which tied with Barry Hughart's *Bridge of Birds* for the World Fantasy Best Novel Award, uses Jungian theories of archetypes and the collective unconscious to create a magical English forest in which the mythic figures in the minds of three men come to life and engage in an epic struggle. Critics find *Mythago Wood* an original and compelling fantasy that represents Holdstock's finest work to date.

BRANDON RUSSELL

Robert Holdstock's latest book is indescribably enchanting, though I suspect he may be a Zen Buddhist. **Mythago Wood** is a fantasy which celebrates the immensity of love. Simultaneously, it is a celebration of fantasy: of the generation and regeneration of legends (e.g. a Chinese folktale), a dissection by analogy (with the forest) of the mythic process, returning man to the most elemental and primitive state.

The Huxleys live in uneasy harmony on the edge of Ryhope Wood in Herefordshire. While just over six miles in circumference, the wood *within* is free from the confines of time and space and the seasons, and has a separate reality. It is a repository of 'hope' figures, or 'mythagos'—'the image of the idealised form of a myth creature'.

George Huxley, the father, becomes obsessed with the wood and what it signifies. His search for the archetypal mythago ultimately destroys him (it has alienated him from his family and caused his wife's suicide), but not before he has transferred his obsession to his son, Christian. They struggle over a shared urge to possess Guiwenneth, a female mythago of incredible beauty, having a thousand manifestations and whom the second son, Steven, comes to love. Then Guiwenneth is kidnapped by Christian, and the wood's mounting attraction for Steven becomes a compulsion while he, in turn, enters the myth.

'The form of the idealised myth, the hero figure, alters with cultural changes, assuming the identity and technology of the time.' Creatures from every period exist in the forest. They are there to aid or hinder Steven as he traverses the power zones protecting the heartwoods, the place where he must do battle with Christian. It is an epic struggle in a book which should be read several times. (p. 34)

Brandon Russell, "Fantasies," *in* The Spectator, *Vol. 250, No. 8150, September 15, 1984, pp. 33-4.**

CHRIS MORGAN

Robert Holdstock has written a complex and compelling book—certainly one of the best fantasy novels of the year. **Mythago Wood** was a British Fantasy award-winning novelette which appeared in *The Magazine of Fantasy & Science Fiction* in 1981; the novel version is not only a great deal longer, it is more satisfying and does justice to the author's marvelously original idea.

He postulates a patch of ancient English woodland, untouched since the last Ice Age, which supposedly has an area of only three square miles but, like Dr. Who's Tardis, is much bigger inside than out. The wood itself is semi-sentient, turning away all but the most determined explorers; it is inhabited by mythagos (= myth imagos), flesh and blood images of mythical heroes of the past. These images are formed from racial memories lingering in the minds of the people who live near the wood—even when all conscious memory of the particular hero has gone. Thus although the wood may contain Robin Hood and King Arthur, most of the action concerns mythagos of prehistoric origin—magnificent, wholly believable creations.

The story is told by Steven Huxley, a young man who returns to his family home, adjacent to the wood, in the late 1940s, after war service. His father, recently dead, has spent decades trying to understand the wood and its mythagos. His elder brother, Christian, is already obsessed by the wood's secrets, and Steven cannot help following the same path. This is the situation in the original novelette, the first part of the book. In part two Steven has a love affair with one of the mythagos, Guiwenneth—the archetypal warrior maiden. Part three is a superbly written quest into the depths of the wood.

It must be stressed that at no time is **Mythago Wood** a simple adventure tale. The wood itself is clearly intended to be analogous to a human mind; inside it time flows faster, and the deeper one goes the more ancient are the mythagos living there. Right to the end the novel is always surprising, always more complex than one has imagined.

Steven's narration is gripping rather than elegant. It is aided by extracts from the notebooks of his father and by legends told to them by some of the mythagos. Holdstock shows himself to be expert at myth creation. Although better known as a science fiction writer, Holdstock has, in recent years, been attracted towards myth, particularly Celtic myth. This is evidenced by his story collection, **In the Valley of the Statues,** if one reads it chronologically.

Mythago Wood's faults are minor: for example, there is insufficient sense of the late 1940s in its setting, Steven seems to possess no friends or points of contact with the outside world, and in one place the month of July immediately follows the month of August. What really matters, though, is that this is a deep and highly original novel—the best work so far of an outstanding young author. (pp. 25-6)

> *Chris Morgan, "One of the Year's Best Fantasy Novels," in* Fantasy Review, *Vol. 7, No. 74, December, 1984, pp. 25-6.*

COLIN GREENLAND

It is characteristic of inner space to be at once fixed and fluid, bound and unbound. Looking-Glass Land, for example, is as regular as a chessboard, but incoherent as a nightmare. Broceliande, Charles Williams's symbol of the subconscious as savage land, is a forest that is also an ocean. J. G. Ballard's terminal landscape, concrete bunkers lined up among shifting sands, modernizes the image. The visitor, or dweller, in inner space knows that there are laws, but experiences chaos. In Robert Holdstock's *Mythago Wood* a gentleman scientist sets out to map an oakwood at the edge of his property in Herefordshire. The wood resists him; it may hardly be penetrated. Once inside, George Huxley discovers that the normal laws of space and time do not prevail there. The wood gets larger as he goes inwards. Time accelerates, so a week in the wood may be only a day outside. He develops a new science to measure the wayward energies of the place: his charts of the edgewood are marked with leys, the "spiral vortex", the "oscillating traverse zone".

Among the trees, vagrant figures appear, of various epochs and cultures. These Huxley terms "mythagos", myth imagos, archetypes generated by the wood itself in response to his own psychic states. Alone, he walks into a great green womb of Creation, peopled with his dreams. Huxley is the traditional lost pilgrim, astray in the greenwood; there is even a belle dame there who bewitches his heart. Precision yields to passion as he forsakes his family to pursue his obsession. After his inevitable death his sons Christian and Steven inherit the mystery, and become ensnared in their turn.

Thus Holdstock re-imagines inner space in terms of the wildwood, a symbol that was already sophisticated when the Gawain poet wrote. His shrewdest decision was to base his novel in 1947, when national sensitivity to natural heritage was enhanced by raw memories of loss and devastation; and the very last time when it was possible for an individual to advance the frontiers of science with a theodolite in one pocket and a notebook in the other. *Mythago Wood* is sonorous, vivid and utterly enthralling. Holdstock's narrative powers have matured greatly.

> *Colin Greenland, "Operations in Inner Space," in* The Times Literary Supplement, *No. 4276, March 15, 1985, p. 284.* *

KIRKUS REVIEWS

[*Mythago Wood* is a] striking and original fantasy that opens with quiet confidence, unfolds into a wealth of absorbing ram-

Dust jacket of Mythago Wood, *by Robert Holdstock. Arbor House, 1984. Jacket design by Dorothy Wachtenheim. Jacket illustration by Christopher Zacharow. Courtesy of Arbor House Publishing Company.*

ifications, and finally subsides into rather unsatisfying, flat-footed symbolism.

Steve Huxley, after a long recuperation from WW II wounds, returns to Oak Lodge, the family seat, only to find his elder brother Chris degenerating physically and mentally; Chris has become obsessed with nearby Ryhope Wood (it may be the last patch of primeval forest left in England) and the weird creatures that live there. According to George (the brothers' late, unloving, preoccupied father), minds interact with the psychic forces of the wood to generate archetypal characters— "mythagos"—from the human racial unconscious; among the beings described in George's cryptic diary are Guiwenneth, a lovely, red-haired warrior-princess, and the huge, powerful, nightmarish Urscumug.

Deep inside the forest, space and time are distorted, and mythagos from both historical and prehistorical times are created spontaneously. Moreover, those who enter the forest are changed in unpredictable ways. So when Guiwenneth reappears— George's version having been killed by a Robin Hood mythago—the brothers each find her as irresistible as George did. Thus the stage is set for fierce sibling rivalries and a final showdown deep inside the forest—with both brothers threatened by the looming, sinister Urscumug, a mythago-embodiment of their dead father.

The approach could have been more felicitous, but Holdstock's fantasy-idea is one of the most exciting and arresting in years. All in all, an impressive advancement on [Holdstock's novel] **Eye Among the Blind** (1977). (pp. 1048-49)

A review of ''Mythago Wood,'' in Kirkus Reviews, Vol. LIII, No. 19, October 1, 1985, pp. 1048-49.

An Excerpt from *Mythago Wood*

''It's the old man's mythago,'' [Christian] said. ''He brought it into being in the heartwoods, but it was weak and trapped until I came along and gave it more power to draw on. But it was the old man's mythago, and he shaped it slightly from his own mind, his own ego. Oh God, Steve, how he must have hated, and hated *us,* to have imposed such terror on to the thing.''

''And Guiwenneth. . . .'' I said.

''Yes . . . Guiwenneth. . . .'' Christian echoed, speaking softly now. ''He'll revenge himself on me for that. If I give him half a chance.''

He stretched up to peer through the bramble covering. I could hear a distant, restless movement, and thought I caught the sound of some animal grumbling deep in its throat.

''I thought he'd failed to create the primary mythago.''

Christian said, ''He died believing that. What would he have done, I wonder, if he'd seen how successful he'd been.'' He crouched back down in the ditch. ''It's like a boar. Part boar, part man, elements of other beasts from the wildwood. It walks upright, but can run like the wind. It paints its face white in the semblance of a human face. Whatever age it lived in, one thing's for sure, it lived a long time before man as *we* understand 'man' existed; this thing comes from a time when man and nature were so close that they were indistinguishable.''

He touched me, then, on the arm; a hesitant touch, as if he were half afraid to make this contact with one from whom he had grown so distant.

''When you run,'' he said, ''run for the edge. Don't stop. And when you get out of the wood, don't come back. There is no way out for me, now. I'm trapped in this wood by something in my own mind as surely as if I were a mythago myself. Don't come back here, Steve. Not for a long, long time.''

''Chris—'' I began, but too late. He had thrown back the covering of the hole and was running from me. Moments later the most enormous shape passed overhead, one huge, black foot landing just inches from my frozen body. It passed by in a split second. But as I scrambled from the hole and began to run I glanced back and the creature, hearing me, glanced back too; and for that instant of mutual contemplation, as we both moved apart in the forest, I saw the face that had been painted across the blackened features of the boar.

The Urscumug opened its mouth to roar, and my father seemed to leer at me.

PUBLISHERS WEEKLY

Holdstock's fantasy of a surviving primeval forest where legends and tribes of different ages coexist [*Mythago Wood*] draws power from the myths, archetypes and literary conventions it embodies. The long, Wellsian introduction to the Huxley family and their fascination with Ryhope Wood slowly moves toward a civilized British confrontation with the wilderness and savagery. . . . Although it takes its time getting started, and occasionally reminds us that it was expanded from a short story, this is a winning novel with a fine feeling for the interface between airy dreams and sweaty reality.

A review of ''Mythago Wood,'' in Publishers Weekly, Vol. 228, No. 14, October 4, 1985, p. 71.

ROLAND GREEN

Holdstock, an English fantasy and horror writer not nearly as well known on this side of the Atlantic as he deserves to be, has produced an exceedingly fine fantasy novel with strong overtones of horror [*Mythago Wood*]. In a remote corner of England, in three square miles of undisturbed virgin forest, mythical beings maintain a real existence. The continuous juxtaposition of this legendary nightmare with contemporary England recalls Stephen King at his best. As such, the book is more than likely to engage the sustained interest of both fantasy and horror readers.

Roland Green, in a review of ''Mythago Wood,'' in Booklist, Vol. 82, No. 6, November 15, 1985, p. 468.

ROBERT A. PARSONS

An unusually strong tension between earthy reality and ethereal fantasy is *Mythago Wood*'s most striking feature. The novel opens in a thoroughly mimetic setting: Oak Lodge, a family estate in a remote corner of England to which Steven Huxley returns from post-war France after the death of his apparently eccentric father. The older brother, Christian, has inherited the father's obsessive fascination with Ryhope Wood, a small primeval forest that borders Oak Lodge. Intrigued by unexplained apparitions, and alarmed at the bizarre behavior of Christian, who disappears for increasingly long stretches into the primitive woodlands, Steven begins a painstaking investigation of his father's arcane journal entries and a timid exploration of the forbidding forest's outer fringes.

He is slowly convinced of the woodland's magic; here dwells an array of strange and terrifying peoples and beasts that draw their existence from psychic energy and take the forms of legendary and mythic heroes and heroines. Some, such as Robin Hood, are embodiments of historical-legendary figures residing in or near the conscious levels of the mind. Others, Neolithic tribes, for instance, who communicate with animal-like grunts and pre-linguistic gutteral noises, take their substance from human archetypes buried in the depths of the subconscious. Within the confines of the woods both time and space are drastically distorted, and all inhabitants are real and potentially dangerous.

Sibling rivalry for Guiwenneth, a mythical huntress and ''mythago,'' or prehistorical psychic substantiation who has ventured to the forest's periphery in different forms to love both brothers, is the central conflict and the motive for Steven's reluctant entry into the forbidden realm in pursuit of Christian, who has kidnapped Steven's version of the huntress.

Allegorical patterns come into sharp focus in the novel's final sections. Pawns of the inscrutable forces of the woodlands, the brothers are forced into predetermined roles in a ritualistic drama. They transmogrify into powerful and savage replicas of one another as tension builds toward the inevitable confrontation of doubles. The outcome is mysteriously influenced by a terrifying primitive mythago form that embodies the diffuse psychic power of the father, who thereby competes in the quest for the archetypal huntress.

I found the final third of the novel, the allegorical pursuit and confrontation, a bit tedious in parts and somewhat, though never totally predictable. Still, Holdstock has achieved a remarkable blend of the mythical, the historical, the archetypal, the fantastic, and the real. *Mythago Wood* provided the vehicle for one of the finest flights of fantasy I have ever taken. (pp. 409-10)

> *Robert A. Parsons, in a review of "Mythago Wood,"*
> *in* Best Sellers, *Vol. 45, No. 11, February, 1986,*
> *pp. 409-10.*

Barry Hughart

Bridge of Birds: A Novel of an Ancient China That Never Was

World Fantasy Award: Best Novel

American novelist.

Bridge of Birds: A Novel of an Ancient China That Never Was (1984), Hughart's first novel, tied with Robert Holdstock's *Mythago Wood* for the World Fantasy Best Novel Award. This quest novel, set in a mythical seventh-century China, combines Chinese religious myth and folklore with realistic period details, plus some fanciful inventions by Hughart. The author became interested in Asian culture during military duty in Japan; he was particularly impressed by the fact that many Chinese deities were introduced as characters in novels. Critics praise *Bridge of Birds* for its humor and inventiveness, as well as its authentic representation of Chinese traditions. Hughart plans to use the settings and characters of his first novel in future writings.

Courtesy of Barry Hughart

KIRKUS REVIEWS

With comic-book characters, echoes of Lewis Carroll, and Sinological trappings galore [*Bridge of Birds* is] a "Novel of an Ancient China That Never Was"—featuring the quest for the Queen of Ginseng, a magical root needed to cure the cataleptic children of the village of Ku-fu. The heroes are the stalwart young narrator, Lu Yu (Number Ten Ox), and the sage Lio Kao—cunning, resourceful, alcoholic. Their complicated adventures bring them up against the satanic Duke of Ch'in, who guards the Great Root of Power and is all but invulnerable because his heart has been removed for safekeeping in a burglar-proof casket at the bottom of a spirit-infested frozen lake. Furthermore, the Duke inhabits an impregnable fortress, with a lethal labyrinth, innumerable boobytraps, and an army of bloodthirsty myrmidons. Still, if Lu Yu and Li Kao can somehow slay him, they will not only save the children but break the spell binding the Princess of the Birds—a lovely mortal separated from her divine lover, the Star Shepherd, when the Duke stole from her the three feathers of immortality. The story combines Disney Studios, the Brothers Grimm, and Dungeons & Dragons in roughly equal proportions, with some random sex to liven up the show—which ends on a note so ecstatic it makes *Snow White* look like a tragedy. But at least Hughart has no pretensions. He's laughing all the way, and readers who like their fantasy in generous, self-mocking doses may laugh along with him. (pp. 314-15)

A review of "Bridge of Birds," in Kirkus Reviews, Vol. LII, No. 7, April 1, 1984, pp. 314-15.

PUBLISHERS WEEKLY

In an imagined China of the seventh century, cast in the classic mold of the legendary journey in quest of a magical key, two companions [in *Bridge of Birds*] set out in search of the Great Root of Power, which alone can release the enchanted children caught in a drugged slumber. Li Kao and Number Ten Ox are an odd couple indeed: the former is a cunning, ancient wise man with an amiable weakness for wine, and the latter a young idealist as decent as he is ingenuous. It is the way of such fables that en route to their appointed end, the two will encounter the world for good and ill, beauty and squalor, spirit and flesh; and encounter it they do, traversing an eerie landscape rising out of dream, nightmare, fantasy, fairy tale. They press onward among talking flutes, mammoth bamboo dragonflies, wicked dukes and winsome maidens, castles and labyrinths, underground caverns full of corpses and ghosts, hairraising escapes, gold and silver and mountains of jade and pearls. Hughart's wit, invention and narrative skill dextrously save the story from dissolving into foolishness or parody.

A review of "The Bridge of Birds," in Publishers Weekly, Vol. 225, No. 14, April 6, 1984, p. 67.

ANN MAXWELL HILL

[*Bridge of Birds*] is a magical tale of a quest, a search for an antidote for poison that has paralyzed the children of Ku-fu village. Set in seventh century China, the story leads two heroes through a series of adventures and encounters with characters from Chinese mythology and history. The heroes are two stock figures in Western fiction about China: the strong, earthy, boneheaded peasant and the wily old sage.

The author clearly is familiar with some aspects of Chinese culture and esoterica and, I suspect, has been to more than a few Chinese movies, the Shaw Brothers classics with sword-fights and flying Taoist adepts. Surely there is material here for entertaining fiction or fantasy appealing to Western readers. VanGulick's tales, for example, of the Tang dynasty magistrate, Judge Dee, have entertained generations of Americans.

However authentic *Bridge* may be as a piece of orientalism, it is not a very interesting story. Its conventional plot is encumbered by characters with little to distinguish one from the other. The peasant narrator does an adequate job of setting the scenes, but seems to possess only one feeling—that of awe in the presence of monsters and fair ladies alike. The humor that might have enlivened the story is corny—a Chinese princess who calls all her lovers "Boopsie," for example.

Readers with a real yen for adventure stories in a Chinese setting would be better off with any of the excellent translations of Chinese novels and epics. *Monkey* and *The Romance of the Three Kingdoms* are fascinating tales readily available in English. (pp. 126-27)

> *Ann Maxwell Hill, in a review of "Bridge of Birds," in* Best Sellers, *Vol. 44, No. 4, July, 1984, pp. 126-27.*

An Excerpt from *Bridge of Birds: A Novel of an Ancient China That Never Was*

"Thirty years ago, at a price of three hundred talents, which I cannot possibly believe, a Root of Power was sold to the Ancestress," said the abbot, looking up from his lists. "There is no further mention of it, and I assume that it is still in the dear lady's possession."

Li Kao looked as though he had bitten into a green persimmon.

"If that woman laid eyes on me, she'd have my head in two seconds," he said sourly. Then he had second thoughts. "Come to think of it, it would be a miracle if she recognized me. She couldn't have been more than sixteen when I was summoned to the emperor's palace, and that was a good fifty years ago."

"Master Li, you were summoned by an emperor?" I asked with wide eyes.

"Several, but this particular one was old Wen," he said. "In the carefree days of my youth I once sold him some shares in a mustard mine."

We stared at him.

"A mustard mine?" the abbot said weakly.

"I was trying to win a bet concerning the intelligence of emperors," he explained. "When I was summoned to court I assumed that I was going to be rewarded with the Death of Ten Thousand Cuts, but Emperor Wen had

something else in mind. Oddly enough, it was sericulture. Some barbarians were trying to learn the secret of silk, and the emperor thought that they might be getting close to the truth. 'Li Kao,' he commanded, 'sell these dogs a mustard mine!' It was one of the most ghastly experiences of my life." . . .

"I had to turn their brains to butter with strong wine, and every morning I pried my eyelids open and glared at red-bearded barbarians who were snoring in puddles of vomit," he said. "They had the constitutions of billy goats, and it was a month and a half before I was able to persuade them that silk is extracted from the semen of snow-white dragons that breed only in caverns concealed in the mysterious Mongolian glaciers. Before sailing away with the sad news, their leader came to see me. He was an oaf named Procopius, and the wine had not improved his appearance. 'O great and mighty Master Li, pray impart to me the Secret of Wisdom!' he bawled. A silly smile was sliding down the side of his face like a dripping watercolor, and his eyeballs resembled a pair of pink pigeon eggs that were gently bouncing in saucers of yellow wonton soup. To my great credit I never batted an eyelash. 'Take a large bowl,' I said. 'Fill it with equal measures of fact, fantasy, history, mythology, science, superstition, logic, and lunacy. Darken the mixture with bitter tears, brighten it with howls of laughter, toss in three thousand years of civilization, bellow *kan pei*—which means "dry cup"—and drink to the dregs.' Procopius stared at me. 'And I will be wise?' he asked. 'Better,' I said. 'You will be Chinese.'"

NAOMI GALBREATH

The children of Ku-fu village [in *Bridge of Birds*] are dying, victims of a poison so virulent and rare that an antidote exists only in rumor and myth. Sturdy, ingenious Number 10 Ox finds help in Li Kao, an ancient, wily scholar who has much experience of the world and its rampant evil.

Pleading ghosts, divinities wonderfully human, and even the Jade Emperor of Heaven all take an urgent interest in the quest. Slowly Li Kao and Number 10 Ox realize that more than the fate of the children depends on their success. Slowly a cosmic drama unfolds.

The flavor of this tale is deeply, accurately, Chinese. Barry Hughart has steeped himself in the folklore and tradition of old China, and his fantasy makes liberal use of the mystery, richness, and method of old Chinese tales. At times, one wonders what is lore and what is Hughart. Old folktales, mandarin tongue twisters, a drunken presentation of a classic poem are all woven gracefully through the plot.

Intricate and imaginative, compassionate and funny, *Bridge of Birds* is highly recommended.

> *Naomi Galbreath, "The Lore of Old China," in* Fantasy Review, *Vol. 8, No. 9, September, 1985, p. 19.*

ALGIS BUDRYS

[*Bridge of Birds* is] a fantasy subtitled "A Novel of an Ancient China that Never Was," and there I would quibble. It's a novel set in an ancient China that I suppose never was, but it is a

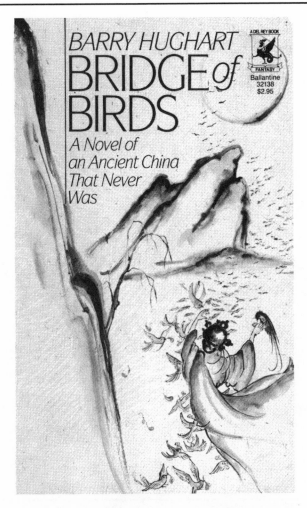

Cover of Bridge of Birds: A Novel of an Ancient China That Never Was, *by Barry Hughart. Ballantine Books, 1984. Copyright © 1984 by Barry Hughart. Courtesy of Random House, Inc.*

novel of universal things that clearly are: Greed, love, faith, honor, opportunism, *joie de vivre*, rascality, courage, and the many faces of honesty, to name some of them. (p. 25)

[Hughart's] book is couched in terms of the quest shared by the strong, sincere young man called Number Ten Ox, and the ancient master Li Kao with a slight flaw in his character. The children of Ox's village have been poisoned by the intricate greedy scheme of Pawnbroker Fang and the merchant called Ma the Grub, and only the Great Root of Power can revive

them from their coma before they are lost forever. Finding the Great Root will consume the entire book.

In the best-plotted quest novels, not a word is wasted; every step leads into greater complications, every bland assertion of fact conceals some fresh pitfall, and the straightforward solutions are always disastrous. You may not have noticed that yet, because in our contemporary plethora of quest novels, you can go miles before encountering one that approaches this ideal. *Bridge of Birds* embodies it; Hughart may not have written much before this, but he has assuredly been thinking.

In the most attractive quest novels, however, it is advisable to show full-bodied characters moving swiftly and speaking charmingly through an eye-catching array of quasi-medieval scenery and furniture. This is what people think the story is about, and what creates the pictures in their minds, one hopes enduringly. It is a good idea to incorporate at least one raffish principal character, and to make the maidens ravishing, the rascals convincingly shrewd but terminally mistaken, and the central villain a truly monstrous figure. In addition, a thread of pure romance is always a good thing to weave into the fabric. Hughart knows this, too, and very rarely falters. This is an area in which intelligence and doing your homework will not quite substitute for experience, but even so *Bridge of Birds* is a wonderfully told story, packed with charming incident and spiced with laughter.

The "Chinese" setting—which I must judge almost entirely on the basis of the settings in fiction by Jack Finney, Stephen Becker and Richard McKenna, plus some travelogues—strikes me as marvelously facilitative. Where it has to be realistic, it can be about a real place that is not like our real place. Where it has to stretch credulity—as in introducing a gunpowder-powered bamboo helicopter of enormous range and carrying capacity—it can shift over into the milieu of brushstrokes on silk or pottery, so that although one cannot actually see the fire-cart bearing its three heroes safely away from monstrous peril, one can readily visualize the painting in which this scene is depicted.

Hughart takes full advantage of this metamorphic capability; one moment we are enmeshed in a tale of struggle and alarm on the nitty-gritty level, and the next we are delicately and deftly transported into a universe where myth becomes reality becomes myth. In the grip of this engaging will-o'-the wisp effect, it becomes unnecessary to even guess at how much of this is China and how much of it is not; it is the universe within the tale. And in that universe move characters we will long remember. (pp. 25-6)

Algis Budrys, in a review of "Bridge of Birds," in The Magazine of Fantasy and Science Fiction, *Vol. 69, No. 3, September, 1985, pp. 24-6.*

Keri Hulme
The Bone People

Booker-McConnell Prize for Fiction

New Zealand novelist, poet, and short story writer.

Hulme, a native of Christchurch, New Zealand, identifies strongly with the Maori, the Polynesian racial group indigenous to New Zealand, as she is one-eighth Maori. Her own version of Maori myth plays a major role in her first novel, *The Bone People* (1981). The novel rejects the social realism favored by contemporary New Zealand writers and reflects instead Hulme's subjective poetic vision. Its subject matter evolved from a short story, "Simon Peter's Shell," that Hulme wrote when she was eighteen. While "perfectly dreadful" in itself, Hulme says it contained three characters that would continue to intrigue her: "It was really about myself, cunningly disguised as Kerewin Holmes, a person of vast wealth and great skills. . . . Oh, there was a rather unruly kid running around in it who didn't talk, and a kind of background ogre called Joe." Over the next twelve years, Hulme worked with these characters, even painting their portraits as a way of visualizing Kerewin, the mute child Simon, and his violent stepfather Joe Gillayley. Her completed project, *The Bone People,* uses the interrelationships of these lonely, troubled individuals to explore some of Hulme's concerns as a mature artist. She explains: "What I was doing in *The Bone People* was getting my head straight on questions like: What happens to outcasts? Is there any point to life? What would happen if a Maori spiritual presence was resurrected in this land of ours?" She describes her story as "a deliberate attempt to manufacture New Zealand myth," to blend real and invented Maori legends with European literary style, harmonizing both of her country's cultural influences.

After holding a succession of menial jobs, Hulme has since age twenty-five devoted herself to writing. Among her published works are *The Silence Between: Moeraki Conversations* (1982), a book of poetry, and *The Wind Eater* (1982), a short story collection. *The Bone People* was initially rejected by three publishers, mainly because Hulme refused to consider editorial changes; she vowed she would entomb her 400-odd page manuscript in resin and use it as a doorstop before she would alter or delete a word. In 1981 a small feminist publishing collective, Spiral, was formed by a woman enthusiastic about *The Bone People;* the novel was then printed in its unedited form. *The Bone People* eventually received several honors, including the Booker-McConnell Prize. Though initially stunned at the response *The Bone People* received, Hulme imagines that the time had come for the ideas presented in the novel: exploitation of the land, family violence, and the regeneration of Maori spirituality.

The Bone People can be described as a vivid, exotic prose poem with no real beginning or end. Critics most often praise Hulme for her imaginative and powerful style that blends reality and myth in a simple, yet serious, narrative; they note that the themes of love, violence, national identity, and social responsibility are compellingly examined through the relationships of the three main characters. Some commentators suggest that the

NYT Pictures

work suffers from an unequal development of these characters, particularly Joe, and from an excessive prose that is sometimes melodramatic and sometimes difficult, as when the Maori language is used. A few reviewers also express concern over the novel's treatment of violence. "I became aware, very early in my childhood, of the beauty and the horror of the world," Hulme has said. "I have never developed an adequate shell against it." Though Hulme has created a personal retreat in her isolated home in New Zealand, she explores "the horror of the world" unflinchingly in her writing. Undoubtedly provocative, Hulme's novel received this accolade from the Booker-McConnell Prize jury: "*The Bone People* gives a deep insight into human nature and breaks new literary ground."

PUBLISHERS WEEKLY

A first novel of distinct originality, *The Bone People* (they are Hulme's ancestral Maoris) tumbles out in an energized spill of narrative, poetry, dream and tribal lore. . . .

Hulme's rough, hacked-out tongue, highly individual and eloquent, at times superbly vulgar, feisty, and unkempt, can also be pure and glowing. Her gifts of language sidetrack her into self-indulgent verbiage, challenging one's patience. Still, she has abundant, enticing stories to tell of culturally split lives; these draw the reader willy-nilly into *The Bone People*'s tangled web.

A review of "The Bone People," in Publishers Weekly,
Vol. 228, No. 11, September 13, 1985, p. 124.

KIRKUS REVIEWS

Kerewin Holmes [in *The Bone People*] is a female (but quite unsexed) New Zealand hermit painter (she made what she needs to live by winning the lottery) whose self-sufficient, vaguely mystical rhythms of life are broken into when she discovers a small boy, Simon, on the beach near her hut, apparently having survived a shipwreck. After nursing him back to health, Kerewin eventually relinquishes Simon (who seems like he can't—and certainly won't—speak) over to a foster father, a Maori man named Joe Gillayley; and though Joe loves Simon fiercely, he doesn't react well to Simon's frequently contrary and maddening behaviors—reactions which too often end up in brutal beatings (one is nearly fatal).

Kerewin tries to step in, threading the needle between her real affections for Simon and Joe both—a situation that novelist Hulme tries unsuccessfully to stretch over the length of nearly 500 pages, hoping it will become a plot. It never happens. Stylistically, it's a very homemade-feeling book, hippy-ish, filled with elaborate Maori references (a glossary in back is indispensable, too indispensable), inner thoughts, goopy lyricism, and torrents of inner thinking that are clumsy and unconvincing.

In all, a slow slog through a good deal of self-congratulatory spiritual homeopathy, with only the smallest smidge of story thrown in.

A review of "The Bone People," in Kirkus Reviews,
Vol. LIII, No. 18, September 15, 1985, p. 967.

C. K. STEAD

[Stead is a Modernist critic from New Zealand whose The New Poetic: Yeats to Eliot *(1964) is regarded as a standard work on Modernism. His other critical writings include* The Glass Case: Essays on New Zealand Literature *(1981). He has published short stories, novels, and poetry collections, as well as editing a number of anthologies, including* World's Classics: New Zealand Short Stories, *second series. As chairman of the New Zealand Literary Fund Advisory Committee from 1972 to 1975, Stead was instrumental in obtaining for Hulme two government grants that paid for the initial publication of* The Bone People. *In the following excerpt Stead disputes some ideas prevalent in New Zealand literary circles about Hulme and her work and offers his own insights into* The Bone People. *This essay was reprinted in a slightly abridged form as a letter to the editor in the* London Review of Books *of December 5, 1985.]*

Great excitement has attended the publication of this novel in New Zealand. So far, nothing I have seen written about *The Bone People* could be described as "critical." It has been received with acclamation. The *New Zealand Listener* gave it not one review but two—both by women, one Maori, one Pakeha (European). As far as I can recall both were direct addresses to the author. They told her she had spoken for us

all, or for all women, or all Maoris; but it was impossible to guess what kind of novel was being reviewed. (p. 101)

Criticism is always a dialogue. One seldom has the chance to speak first, and what the critic says is always partly in answer to what has been said already. In the case of Keri Hulme's novel "what has been said" is largely a babble of excited voices in public places. *The Bone People* touches a number of currently, or fashionably, sensitive nerves. New Zealand intellectual life, limping along in the wake of the world, has been lately lacerating itself into consciousness that racism and sexism exist. Where they don't exist, zealots nonetheless find them. Keri Hulme, a woman and, let's say for the moment, a Maori, her novel published by a "feminist collective" after being "turned down" by three others—this is the stuff for those zealots! As in the case of most books which take off publicly like rockets, a lot of the energy has nothing to do with the quality of the work. It is, however, the quality of the work that will determine what future the book is to have.

For the record let it be said first that of the three who were offered the novel before Spiral saw it, one was a feminist publisher who thought it insufficiently feminist for her list; another was a woman publisher who thought the book needed more work before it was ready for publication; and the third was a commercial publisher who was anxious about the novel's length and its prospects in the market-place. The latter two deny having "turned it down." They wanted more work done on it. From a purely commercial point of view it could be said they made a mistake in not accepting the book as it was when the author declined to make cuts and revisions. From a literary point of view I think the author made a mistake in rejecting all advice about how the typescript might be edited and improved. (pp. 101-02)

If *The Bone People* is not in any very obvious way a "feminist" novel, in what sense is it a Maori novel?. . . If any modern literary writing has been done in the Maori language, none has been published; and that is likely to continue to be the case. For the present, anyway, all Maori writers of any consequence write in English; and probably few of them know more than a little of the Maori language. (pp. 102-03)

Of Keri Hulme's eight great-grandparents one only was Maori. Hulme was not brought up speaking Maori, though like many Pakeha New Zealanders she has acquired some in adult life. She claims to identify with the Maori part of her inheritance—not a disadvantageous identification at the present time—but it seems to me that some essential Maori elements in her novel are unconvincing. Her uses of Maori language and mythology strike me as willed, self-conscious, not inevitable, not entirely authentic. Insofar as she is an observer of things outside herself, Hulme has observed Maoris and identified with them. If that is what constitutes a "Maori" writer, however, then Pakeha [European] writers like James K. Baxter and Roderick Finlayson (to name two obvious cases) could be said to have been more successfully "Maori" than Keri Hulme. (pp. 103-04)

The Bone People is a novel about violence. It is also about love and about identity. The love and the violence have a common source. All three of the main characters, a woman, a man, and a child, could be described as violent, though the propensity exhibits itself in different ways. All three are strong characters. All three, but especially the woman and the child, are sharply portrayed. They form a close unit. What is interesting about the novel is that their bonds exist outside biology. It is the biological pattern imitated. The man's own wife and child have died. The boy he acts as father to comes as from nowhere, born out of the sea. And although a bond like sexual love grows between the man and the woman, there is no physical contact. That, I think, is the imaginative strength of the work—that it creates a sexual union where no sex occurs, creates parental love where there are no physical parents, creates the stress and fusion of a family where there is no actual family.

Interviews with Keri Hulme have shown how closely her central character, Kerewin Holmes, is based on herself. Both the novelist and her character describe themselves as sexless, sexually drawn neither to male nor female, "neuter."

> I spent a considerable amount of time when I was, o, adolescent, wondering why I was different, whether there were other people like me. Why, when everyone else was fascinated by their developing sexual nature, I couldn't give a damn. I've never been attracted to men. Or women. Or anything else. It's difficult to explain, and nobody has ever believed it when I have tried to explain, but while I have an apparently normal female body, I don't have any sexual urge or appetite. I think I am a neuter.
>
> (pp. 104-05)

This is Kerewin Holmes speaking. Most of it, almost word for word, Keri Hulme has said of herself in a television interview.

Many—perhaps most—works of fiction are fuelled by sexual energy. Here is a novel fuelled by its lack. What for most of us would be merely the domestic subject is for Keri Hulme, I think, the equivalent of romance—the realm of the unattainable. I mean this in no derogatory sense. Whatever confusions of motive and propulsion there may have been in responses to this book (and I think it is worthwhile attempting to unravel some of them) it is not for nothing that there has been so much excitement. *The Bone People* is at the core a work of great simplicity and power.

The narrative creates a simple pattern. The three principal characters are drawn slowly together to form a strong unit, though one in which negative forces are working. A catastrophe occurs which blows them apart. Each, alone, is driven by circumstances, through pain and suffering, to the edge of destruction. Each of the two adults has been partly to blame for the catastrophe, and each is saved from death by the intervention of what appears to be a force from the lower echelons of the Divine. At the end the three come together again, purged, and certain of their need for one another.

To recognize this pattern in which are mixed, not always successfully, a remorseless realism with elements of the mythical, the magical and the mystical, one must stand off at some distance from the novel. Seen from a nearer point of focus it is likely to be described in sociological terms. Joe Gillayley loves his adopted child dearly, but is subject to pressures he cannot quite recognize or control. He drinks, beats the child, and finally very nearly kills him.

Simon, the child of unknown parentage, survivor of a wreck, with the marks still on him of beatings previous to those inflicted by Joe, never speaks, but is able to write and signal messages, and to communicate his love, his rages, and his intelligence. His love for Joe is almost unwavering, despite the beatings. Simon is a major fictional character, the most

complete, convincing, and fascinating of the three, and all the more remarkable in that his personality has to be conveyed to us without spoken language.

Kerewin is the isolated artist who has run out of inspiration. She lives, literally, in a tower of her own making, which (again quite literally) has to be broken down before she can paint again. The obviousness of the symbolism doesn't detract from the authenticity of the portrait. Kerewin, one feels, is bold enough and innocent enough to live by her symbols, as Yeats did when he bought a tower from Ireland's Congested Roads Board for £35 and restored it so he could write of himself "pacing upon the battlements." In fact Kerewin strikes me as more Irish than Maori, word-obsessed, imaginative, musical, unstable, something of a mystic, full of bluster and swagger, charm and self-assertion. All this is shown, not from the outside, but from within, so the novel partakes of Kerewin's strengths but is not detached from her weaknesses. Like its central character, *The Bone People* seems at times disarmingly, at times alarmingly, naive.

The novel is successful from the start in portraying the character of Simon and the way he insinuates himself into Kerewin's isolated life. Joe, on the other hand, strikes me as a character who is never quite perfectly formed in the novelist's imagination, and there are times when his cast of mind and turn of phrase seem to belong to Kerewin rather than to himself. The relationship between the two is less than convincing in its early stages; and though it becomes more real as the novel continues, this reader, at least, never felt entirely secure in his "suspension of disbelief." To give only one example: Joe is represented as physically powerful, a fairly traditional Maori male, though with more education than most. He is kind, affectionate, but with a dangerously short fuse, precarious pride, and a propensity for violence. Yet when an argument between him and Kerewin turns into a fight, Kerewin, who has learned something like kung fu during a visit to Japan, beats him effortlessly, a beating which he accepts with great good humour and with no apparent damage to his ego. That is not the only point at which the reader is likely to feel the novel has taken a dive from reality into wishful daydream.

Worse, however, is the sequence in which Joe comes close to death and then is rescued by an old Maori man who has waited his whole lifetime under semi-divine instruction to perform just this rescue, so he can pass on to the man he saves proprietorial rights over a piece of land and the talisman in which its spirit is preserved. There would be no point in recounting in detail the physical and mystical experiences which make up this section of the novel. It should be enough to say that I found it, read either as Maori lore or as fiction, almost totally spurious. There is a parallel set of events in which Kerewin, who appears to be dying of cancer, is saved by the intervention of an old woman and a magical, or simply herbal, potion.

From the first time I read letters Keri Hulme addressed to the Literary Fund Advisory Committee requesting assistance (that was more than ten years ago) I have never doubted that she has a powerful and original literary talent. I have admired some of her stories published in *Islands*. And I was sure Auckland University Press made the right decision when it accepted her collection of poems, *Moeraki Conversations,* for publication. Her talent is abundantly clear in *The Bone People*. But all the indications are that, for reasons which are not strictly literary, the achievement of this novel is going to be inflated beyond its worth. I'm glad *The Bone People* has been written and published. I'm sorry it wasn't revised, decently copy-edited, and presented to better advantage. I'm sure its author will go on to better things. But I have to admit that when I stand back from the novel and reflect on it there is, in addition to the sense of its power, which I have acknowledged, and which is probably the most important thing to be said about it, a bitter aftertaste, something black and negative deeply ingrained in its imaginative fabric, which no amount of revision or editing could have eliminated, and which, for this reader at least, qualifies the feeling that the publication of this book is an occasion for celebration.

I'm not sure whether I should even attempt to explain to myself what it is constitutes that negative element, or whether it should simply be mentioned and left for others to confirm or deny. But I suspect it has its location in the central subject matter, and that this is something it shares (to give another point of reference) with Benjamin Britten's opera *Peter Grimes,* a work which also presents extreme violence against a child, yet demands sympathy and understanding for the man who commits it. In principle such charity is admirable. In fact, the line between charity and imaginative complicity is very fine indeed. (pp. 105-08)

> *C. K. Stead, "Keri Hulme's 'The Bone People,' and the Pegasus Award for Maori Literature," in Ariel, Vol. 16, No. 4, October, 1985, pp. 101-08.*

ANGELA HUTH

Bone People, by Keri Hulme, is a very depressing book indeed. New Zealand critics afforded it all sort of superlatives, so I began in hope. But the tedious prose soon produced such torpidity I was unable to finish, even in the course of duty. In her preface Miss Hulme explains: 'Maybe the editors were too gentle with my experiments and eccentricities. Great! The voice of the writer won through.' Those editors did her a great disservice.

Kerewin, the middle-aged virgin heroine, is a frosty painter who befriends a sad, mute little boy, who is beaten up by his father, Joe, who loves Frosty—God knows why, she is 'neuter', 'dead inside' and given to much boring soul-searching. This simple tale is inflated to nearly 500 pages with endless descriptions of vomit, violence, drink, dreams, plus Maori words and embarrassing poems. But there *is* something of the experimental in Miss Hulme's writing which must have caused a gleam in the judges' eyes. Experiments such as sentences printed like this:

> If only I had
> Shut up.
>
> (p. 33)

> *Angela Huth, "The Booker Club," in The Listener, Vol. 114, No. 2932, October 24, 1985, pp. 33-4.**

RHODA YERBURGH

[*The Bone People*] is quite a first novel. The ending is revealed at its mysterious beginning; exotic line breaks and poetic punctuation put off at first but gradually become the best way to tell the tale; the Maori vocabulary is interwoven with contemporary British, Australian, and American idioms; and the New Zealand sea- and landscape vibrate under fresh perception. Hulme shifts narrative points of view to build a gripping account of violence, love, death, magic, and redemption. A silverhaired, mute, abused orphan, a laborer heavy with sustained

loss, and a brilliant introspective recluse discover, after enormous struggle through injury and illness, what it means to lose and then regain a family.

> *Rhoda Yerburgh, in a review of "The Bone People," in Library Journal, Vol. 110, No. 18, November 1, 1985, p. 110.*

MICHIKO KAKUTANI

Though it's a huge, ambitious work that aspires to portray the clash between Maori and European cultures, even as it attempts to mythicize the lives of its three peculiar heroes, *The Bone People* never quite lives up to its billing. It's not so much that the novel offers "a taste passing strange," as the author notes in the preface—interior monologues, disjointed narratives and vulgar language, after all, are hardly news these days. It's more that the novel is unevenly written, often portentous, and considerably overlong.

With some judicious pruning, the book might well make a powerful visionary fable—about love and redemption, violence and renewal. As it is, though, *The Bone People* feels too much like a grab-bag stuffed with weird dreams (a woman dreams that her teeth have turned into bloody stumps; a man dreams that he is kissing a fat, furry moth), intriguing talismans (an antique rosary, a necklace made from a lock of hair, a mysterious earring) and lots of willfully symbolic events (a lonely artist's tower is burned to the ground; a shipwrecked boy is rescued from the sea; a man, wandering in the wilderness, is granted a wondrous vision). If such images attest to the prodigality of Miss Hulme's imagination, their rampant profusion also indicates a certain reluctance, on her part, to exercise the critical faculties of selectivity—to shape the design of her narrative with some vision in mind. Instead, the reader increasingly feels that strange incidents have been included simply for the sake of their strangeness, and as a result begins to tire of the novel's italicized emotions.

Indeed, *The Bone People* is most effective when it is not trying to address large social and spiritual questions, but when it is simply chronicling the complicated relationships that develop among three outcasts brought together by chance: Kerewin, a painter, who leads a hermetic, solitary life, convinced that art, not people, is sufficient to sustain her and that friendships can only lead to pain; Simon, a mute child of 6, who apparently has suffered some terrible wound in the past, and his adoptive father, Joe, a laborer with a nasty temper.

Shifting from one point of view to another, Miss Hulme carefully delineates each character's thoughts and feelings, each one's simultaneous desire to connect and fear of becoming dependent on another human being. She has a sure understanding of ambivalent emotions—or rather the coexistence of two contrary emotions at the same time—and an ability, too, to portray this anomalous state of mind through both action and extended monologues.

The language employed by Miss Hulme's characters tends to range, back and forth, from the lyrical to the crude—even the mute 6-year-old thinks in extraordinarily dirty phrases—and slangy bits of bar talk. ("Time to hit the road, Holmes. Time to get gone") can alternate with passages of incantatory verse ("watching the blood sky swell and grow, dyeing the rainclouds ominously, making the far edge of the sea blistered and scarlet"). There is a pleasing, musical attention to the sound and rhythms of words in this novel, though Miss Hulme also seems to possess a rather decided penchant for heavy, cliché-ridden prose ("In the beginning, it was darkness, and more fear, and a howling wind across the sea"), which, instead of lofting the narrative up into the territory of legend, simply has the effect of dragging it all down.

As for the story itself, it takes the overall form of a Shakespearean comedy: the characters move from a state of unhappy isolation, through a period of turmoil, into a new world that holds the promise—or at least the possibility—of harmony and redemption. In the process, various dark secrets about the characters are suggested or revealed. Kerewin, it seems, has had some sort of terrible falling out with her family that has turned her into a misanthropic hermit, and her seclusion, in turn, has curdled her artistic talent. Simon, it turns out, is really something of a juvenile delinquent, given to stealing and vandalism, and his foster father, who has been beating him regularly, soon comes close to pummeling him to death.

That event—described in startling, graphic terms—sends the characters spinning away from each other, the tentative bonds that might make them a family seemingly dissolved. In fact, only by undergoing a kind of ritual catharsis are they able to find the self-knowledge that will eventually enable them to accept each other's love. It is in the final chapters of *The Bone People,* which detail this spiritual rebirth, that Miss Hulme finally succeeds in finding a voice capable of welding together her inclinations toward the mythic and the naturalistic, the surreal and the mundane. And it is these pages that testify to her considerable, if unfulfilled, gifts as a writer.

> *Michiko Kakutani, in a review of "The Bone People,"* in The New York Times, *November 13, 1985, p. C23.*

CLAUDIA TATE

In the preface to *The Bone People,* the New Zealander Keri Hulme addresses her American readers, who she suspects may regard her first novel as a big, strange book, by encouraging them to taste a strange, new food. "To those used to one standard," she writes, "this book may offer a taste passing strange, like the original mouthful of kina roe. Persist. Kina can become a favourite food." The "passing strange" taste of this novel is unforgettably rich and pungent. . . .

Set on the harsh South Island beaches of New Zealand, bound in Maori myth and entwined with Christian symbols, Miss Hulme's provocative novel summons power with words, as in a conjurer's spell. She casts her magic on three fiercely unique characters, but reminds us that we, like them, are "nothing more than people," and that, in a sense, we are all cannibals, compelled to consume the gift of love with demands for perfection. But they, and perhaps we too, are capable of change.

The story centers on three broken people: Joe, a Maori factory worker who sacrifices ties to his culture in order to secure material comfort; a female aikido fighter, Kerewin, who is a pakeha (or part-European) artist; and Simon Peter, a mute "spider-child" who is washed ashore, a lone survivor of a shipwreck. All conceal painful pasts that have severed them from their families, from the nurturing heritage of their tribes, pasts that they try to conceal from themselves with hard drinking and gluttony. As their stories unfold, the mysteries of their former lives slowly take shape in experiences that oscillate between conscious events and dreams, in prose that is alter-

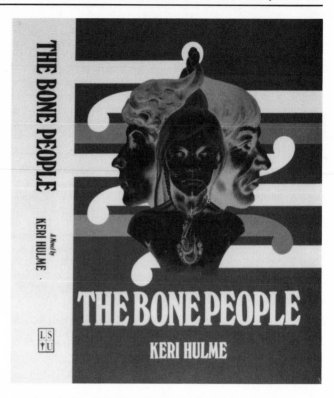

Dust jacket of The Bone People, *by Keri Hulme. Louisiana State University Press, 1984. Reprinted by permission of Louisiana State University Press.*

nately lyrical and coarse and in dialogue that is quixotic and commonplace—all steeped in Maori folklore and expressions.

Thrown together when Simon and his foster father, Joe, interrupt Kerewin's self-imposed exile, the three form a unit beautiful and terrifying, which Keri Hulme repeatedly refers to as a trinity, held taut by love and pain. But self-inflicted violence tears their tenuous bond apart, and separately they travel to the threshold of death, which the author portrays with such emotional intensity that we too are swallowed up in the characters' excruciating pain. When death becomes their only relief, the bone people appear. They are enchanted healers, ghosts of Maori ancestors so distant they encircle past and future. They mend the three, leaving behind scars as signs of human frailty and strength; they infuse them with the life force of hope and direct them homeward by empowering them with the vision of a new life. Reconciled, they are "toughened, different, an annealed steel, triple-forged." Bound together, they can endure anything. But, if they were alone, apart, they would not find "it is dawn, and bright broad daylight braiding our home."

> *Claudia Tate, "Triple-Forged Trinity," in* The New York Times Book Review, *November 17, 1985, p. 11.*

ELIZABETH WARD

Since there is in a sense no beginning and no ending to this huge and extraordinary novel *The Bone People* from "good old Godzone" (God's own country, New Zealand, Aotearoa, "the shining bright land"), it is difficult to choose a starting point for an introduction. . . .

The reason for the novel's fairytale success is that it is an original, overwhelming, near-great work of literature, which does not merely shed light on a small but complex and sometimes misunderstood country, but also, more generally, enlarges our sense of life's possible dimensions. So Godzone is made flesh, all irony momentarily transcended, as New Zealand's Maori heritage is brought to life. ''O Thou art beyond all good but truly this land and sea is your dwelling place. . . .''

First novel it may be, but there is nothing timid or derivative about *The Bone People.* It is a work of immense literary and intellectual ambition, that rare thing, a novel of ideas which is also dramatically very strong. ''It's all here, alive and salt and roaring and real.'' The drama is naturally what pulls you in first, then, once hooked, you are more subtly mesmerized by the novel's spiralling inner structure or design. There is no way out of *The Bone People* but through: reading it becomes an act of catharsis.

The plot is compressed and intense, despite the novel's length. At center is the character of Kerewin Holmes (the name suggests she both is and is not the author), an artist, wealthy, reclusive, clever, coarse, with a coruscating wit, ''a woman of the sea and the fire,'' who has retired to a remote coastal town in the South Island and built herself a tower, that most symbolic of dwellings, in which to paint, sculpt and meditate. (p. 1)

Her voluntary isolation is suddenly and rather rudely shattered by the arrival at her tower of the small boy, Simon, blond, charming, lawless and mute, ''a right stubborn illnatured mess of a child,'' and his Maori stepfather, Joe, alternately violent and loving. . . .

The relationships among these three—man, woman and child; Maori, mixed-race and Pakeha—tighten, loosen, break and re-knit to form the strong thread upon which Keri Hulme's ideas are strung. ''Webs of events that grew together to become a net in life'', reflects Kerewin. ''Life was a thing that grew wild. She supposed there was an overall pattern, a design to it.'' But ''she'd never found one.''

Life is certainly wild in *The Bone People,* but both artistically and philosophically, Hulme has also found an ''overall pattern'' to it, the concept or symbol of the spiral, which recurs over and over in the novel. ''On the floor at her feet was an engraved double-spiral, one of the kind that wound your eyes round and round into the center where surprise you found the beginning of another spiral that led your eyes out again to the nothingness of the outside. Or the somethingness . . . The spiral made a useful thought-focus, a mandala . . . It was reckoned that the old people found inspiration for the double spirals they carved so skilfully, in uncurling fernfronds: perhaps. But it was an old symbol of rebirth, and the outward-inward nature of things . . .''

So, too, the novel as a whole moves between ''something'' and ''nothingness,'' between the limitless richness and variety of life attested to by Kerewin's own lively mind and the black hole at the heart of the book which is the physical abuse of the child, Simon. ''The drone of flies gets louder. The world goes away. The night has come.'' But a mere turn of the spiral can bring us suddenly to a quite different perception of ''nothingness,'' life given a fresh start. ''The rain has ceased . . . The wind is gone. The air is very still: the sea roar is magnified and easy birdcall is piercingly clear.''

In the same way the novel shifts from Kerewin's sterile isolation in the tower to the community of sorts she forms with Simon and Joe, and from their horribly violent splitting-up to the final tenuous reunion. *''E nga iwi o nga iwi,''* says Joe, invoking in this untranslatable phrase ''the bones of the people or the people of the bones,''—his Maori ancestors, for whom community meant, simply, survival. And the child: ''We have to be together. If we are not, we are nothing. We are broken. We are nothing.'' Because Joe is Maori, Simon Pakeha and Kerewin mixed-race, the pressure towards union throughout the novel probably has an allegorical import, bearing on questions of race-relations and conservation in New Zealand today which lie beyond the scope of this review. But from a purely literary point of view, the union of ''Maoritanga'' (Maori culture) and the English language in Keri Hulme's own novel is itself a powerful argument for her vision of unity. ''They were nothing more than people, by themselves. Even paired, any pairing, they would have been nothing more than people by themselves. But all together, they have become the heart and muscles and mind of something perilous and new, something strong and growing and great. Together, all together, they are the instruments of change.''

The Bone People does have its failings. The exuberant prose occasionally lapses into mawkishness or gush. The last third of the book, especially the semi-mystical invocation of the ''Maoritanga,'' is too schematic. And Joe remains a tantalizingly undeveloped character compared with Kerewin. But the sheer flow of language and ideas sweeps you on. The novel might even be thought of as, itself, ''something perilous and new,'' and therefore a very exciting event, in the field of New Zealand literature and beyond. (p. 4)

> *Elizabeth Ward, ''A First Novel of Sweeping Power,''* in Book World—The Washington Post, *December 1, 1985, pp. 1, 4.*

SUSAN BROIDY

Keri Hulme's Booker Prize-winning novel, *The Bone People,* . . . leaves me, as a New Zealander, with a sense of painful recognition and of deep disappointment. Is this the best that New Zealand can offer the world? It is a world that is vitally aware of race relations and of national identities, and of the dehumanising elements within society which produce such phenomena as baby-battering. We are also aware of the need to conserve and protect the environment. All these issues are Keri Hulme's concern, yet they are handled with none of the insight we might expect from a New Zealander whose country is now seen as a David fighting against the Goliath of European nuclear interests.

Instead, she reflects the inward-looking nature of our country and the oppressive nature of its geograpical isolation. The sense of place can be suffocating in New Zealand, and there is no escaping the feeling of being poised on the rim of the known world: to the South lies the wasteland of Antarctica and to the North is America and Europe—the only way ahead. At the same time, there is always the feeling that New Zealand is God's own country, and that its very remoteness gives it the distance necessary for the creation of a utopian state. This feeling of being separate, special and different brings with it a complexity of psychological problems, notably a reluctance to relinquish an obsession with self and to accept adult responsibilities. (p. 4)

Keri Hulme writes from the viewpoint of the Maori, a name which includes those of mixed European (Pakeha) and Maori blood. The novel's spokeswoman says: "If I were in America, I'd be an octoroon . . . I am but an eighth Maori, by heart, spirit and inclination I feel all Maori—or I used to—the Maoritanga has got lost in the way I live.' Maoritanga—Maoriness, as the necessary appendix tells us—pervades the book in the blurred consciousness of Kerewin Holmes, artist and obvious self-portrait of Keri Hulme, novelist, who is quoted as saying that her novel was 'home-grown' and that it took her 12 years to write. Perhaps this interval reflects the difficulty of expressing or achieving a national voice when the national identity in question is confused, diffused and derivative.

The use of the thinly disguised author's name for the central consciousness of the novel is a device which evades the honest 'I' and has the effect of disconcerting the reader's expectations to an extent I do not think the author intended. There is an uneasy blend of two cultures in the one personality, and the authorial voice tends to become like that of some short-sighted social worker who argues that Joe could not help his brutal drunken battering of the small orphaned boy because society put him up to it. Joe's self-destructive drinking may have been due to loneliness after the death of his wife and child, but is no excuse for his savage attacks on the small boy, whose only crime is to remind Joe of his guilt and inadequacies. Similarly, Kerewin's attitude is at fault, for her obsession with her identity, and her inability to love or to create, have blocked her comprehension of reality: like Joe, she retreats into drunken oblivion to avoid responsibility. On the one hand, we are offered a parable of the child healing the broken adult, and then the adult becomes in turn the destroyer. The paradox is explained in the title: the Maori phrase *E nga iwi o nga iwi* means both bones of the people or ancestors, and people of the bones—that is, the beginning people or progenitors. The constant tension evoked by this inherent paradox produces a lack of focus, and the author has to retreat into a lame ending with a Maori phrase which translates: "The end—or the beginning'.

There is an attempt to allow Joe a form of redemption by linking him to his ancestral past, but it fails to impress. Joe has served a term in prison, and the novelist then shows him in retreat. His meeting with a dying mystic, the old Maori man, brings him more closely in touch with his heritage. The romance convention offers him the chance to be guardian of a buried tribal treasure—a decaying canoe and a little stone god, or mauriora. The old man has believed it to be a symbol of the rebirth of the Maori nation as something 'special and different'.

Joe retreats into a reverence for old burial customs and Kerewin has also retreated—to the mountains this time instead of the sea. In the high McKenzie country, sub-alpine sheep lands of wind-swept tussocks, she undergoes a dark night of the soul as she prepares to die alone from suspected stomach cancer. But she is returned to life again, and she sets herself to rebuild a dilapidated Maori meeting-house. This is to re-create the marae, the heart of the Maori community, and she announces to herself that she will concentrate on seven directions: recovery, renewed talent, rebuilding, tying up loose ends, trying not to dodge responsibilities, going into the world rather than moving against it, and, finally, 'I will go when it is time—no choice!—but now I want life.'

The ending is a reunion of Joe, Kerewin and the child in a drunken, incoherent, sentimental coming-home: 'all good cheers, and covered tears and matey friendship'. Kerewin has made peace with her estranged family and everyone is 'aching with

love to give, smothered by love in return'. There is no examination of the uncomfortable truths which haunt this book and which haunt New Zealand. Beneath all this togetherness, and the notion of a racial or cultural solidarity which accompanies it, there seems to be a dangerous exclusiveness. The sterility of the island mentality is not confined to places like New Zealand, of course—it exists in inner cities throughout the civilised world. But I would have thought that if this novel depicts the present state of its nation, then New Zealand still has some spiritual growing-up to do. (p. 5)

Susan Broidy, in a letter to the editor in London Review of Books, *December 19, 1985, pp. 4-5.*

DIANE JACOBS

"Passing strange," observes Keri Hulme, in the preface to this bold and luxuriant *Pilgrim's Progress* of a first novel; but to her credit, **The Bone People** is no more passing strange than it is slyly, often brilliantly scrupulous. The eponymous Bone People are Hulme's own New Zealand Maoris, whose tribulations and renascence are the subtext of her tale. The setting is Whangaroa, a South Island town so small the telephone operator can tell you everybody's whereabouts, not to mention their business. Blocked painter Kerewin Holmes, clearly the voice of the author, sums up a typical "shit of a day" in Whangaroa as "a sort of dreary combination of the murderous and the domestic, you know?" And except for the "dreary," this nicely defines the book's soap-operaish plot.

The resonances of racial identity are deftly probed by Hulme, whose main characters are Kerewin, a Pakeha (New Zealander of European descent); Joe, a Maori widower; and Joe's charge, Simon, a pasty white mute child, washed ashore in a shipwreck like Ishmael and similarly livid with history. "To care for anything deeply is to invite disaster," announces Kerewin, who has built herself a secluded tower festooned with Maori talismans after a bitter rift with her family. A determined loner, Kerewin doesn't suffer children gladly. "Made yourself thoroughly at home, haven't you, guttersnipe? Well, you're about to get the boot," she thinks when wild child Simon first wanders into her tower. Nor has she the remotest sexual attraction for the boy's handsome, seemingly gentle father, with whom she shares sumptuous teas and marathon drinking bouts.

Kerewin offhandedly invites Joe and Simon to go fishing at her family's deserted Moerangi beach house. Just before they leave, she discovers weltering scars on Simon's back, and thus the fact that Joe is also a rageful man who often straps his curiously unresentful son. When she confronts Joe, he acknowledges his guilt and promises forbearance. Kerewin flirts with committing herself to the child, but shortly afterwards Joe beats him again, even more viciously, and Kerewin shies from responsibility. Simon barely survives, Joe is stripped of his custody and sent to prison, Kerewin sacrificially burns her tower and steals away with a lump that feels (a bit conveniently) like cancer in her intestines. What follow, in the book's final section, are mythically rich descents into hell and redemptions of a sort for all.

While Hulme's plot is almost myopically domestic, her style is lush, and ranges in dauntingly swift progression from elegiac chant to blistering description, from mystical asides ("O me killer instinct, riding high on my shoulders, wide with teeth and smiling") to slangy musings on the here and now. At first, the plenitude is overwhelming. And then, through an accretion of striking images, through superb formal inventiveness and painstaking rhythmic control, Hulme proves her skill and originality. What is most remarkable about *The Bone People* is its sustained contradictoriness. Kerewin is as much a lusty skeptic as she is a seeker after Truths. A sentence that begins with an incantation will most likely end comically with an oath. Yes, Kerewin explains the spiritual values of Aiki to Joe, but first she uses Aiki skills to beat him up.

I have a few cavils: the characters of Simon and Joe are never as full-bodied as the superbly evoked Kerewin, whose lilting and distinctively cranky voice they often borrow. And Kerewin's asexuality seems calculated—a device that lets Hulme claim she is "Of indeterminate sex. Of indeterminate race." Yet these are minor deficiencies indeed in a book so multifarious and compelling. As in Maxine Hong Kingston, Hulme's earthily evoked present seamlessly intersects with a rawer and more exhilarating ancestral past. As in Alice Walker, her ethnographer's zeal is politically resonant and always tempered by commitment to the living. Kerewin's fascination with the appurtenances of Maori warrior tradition, for instance, inspires her passionate revolt against Pakeha ecology and social hegemony in New Zealand today.

The Bone People is a spiritual quest, a meditation on racial identity, and a celebration of social responsibility—portrayed through Kerewin's metamorphosis from recluse to parent and born-again painter. On its surface the story of a man, woman, and child defying conventional definitions of familyhood to make themselves a home, *The Bone People* is an affirmation of the larger families we are born into—of Joe's Maori ancestors, Kerewin's fiercely longed-for parents and siblings, even the nefarious underworld of Simon's drug-dealing parents. Early on, Kerewin tells Simon, "A family can be the bane of one's existence. A family can also be most of the meaning of one's existence." By the swelling conclusion, Kerewin has so enlarged her vision that she can embrace family without sacrificing solitude. Hulme's dialectic is at times naive, but her articulation is unerringly artful, rich, and revealing of a mature and provocative talent. (pp. 67-8)

Diane Jacobs, "Search for Tomorrow," in The Village Voice, *Vol. XXX, No. 52, December 24, 1985, pp. 67-8.*

An Excerpt from *The Bone People*

Kerewin, beneath the distant luminous dust of stars: so that's what there is to know of Gillayleys in their queer strait antiseptic haven. She stretched her arms, wide as a cross, and something small and bony snapped in her chest.

She swore, and closed her arms in a hurry.

Snapped a wishbone without a wish . . . what would I wish for anyway? A return of the spirit of joy? It won't come back by wishing . . . Maybe, considering this rintin shambles of a night, I should wish something for them . . . for Simon, what? A real name? No, something better. A shield to raise against his dreams, and for the other, a relief of that need he shows so plainly, for dead wife and dead child. But there's only one way to do that, send him to them. . . .

Anyway to hell, I forgot to wish.

She walked on, her bare feet sinking in the sand. There was a crust on it from the past night's rain. No-one walked on this beach much.

O chief of my children, primate of woes, come sink in the fleece of your old mother, Earth . . . but seriously Holmes, there is something wrong with the brat, beyond what Joe says. For that matter, there's something wrong with the fella as well.

Chanting into the night,

"O all the world is a little queer, except thee and me, and sometimes, I wonder about thee."

I know about me. I am the moon's sister, a tidal child stranded on land. The sea always in my ear, a surf of eternal discontent in my blood.

You're talking bullshit as usual.

Only what to do about the urchin's bitter dreams? Or the man's evil shadows—the ghosts riding on his shoulders? The miasma of gloom that shrouded his lightning smile?

ROD EDMOND

Why is Karl Stead [see excerpt above] so narked by *The Bone People*? His [essay] . . . reads strangely from this side of the world, where many, perhaps most, reviews of Keri Hulme's novel have been unenthusiastic. The story of its publishing history has, of course, raised interest, and several reviewers have hinted that the book's reputation rests on extra-literary factors. *Private Eye* offered the most reductive account of this kind. Stead's letter is a subtler, sometimes contradictory version of this response. He seems to imply that some of the book's success lies in its 'fashionable' association with feminism and 'Maori-ism'. Feminism, he then concedes, is hardly an issue. The only obvious sense in which *The Bone People* is feminist is that it has a strong, active heroine. This, however, would also make *Pride and Prejudice* a feminist novel. In fact, *The Bone People* is conspicuously empty of women. Its 'Maoriness', however, is central. Stead describes one distinctively Maori section late in the novel as 'spurious', and more generally seems to imply there is something opportunist in its use of Maori elements. This is neither fair nor accurate. New Zealand is a mixed society, Maori and European. Keri Hulme has written a novel in which one of the central characters is mainly Maori but part-European, a second is mainly European but part-Maori, and the third, the child Simon, is a strange kind of European immigrant. This configuration is used to explore tensions in New Zealand's mixed, and mixed-up culture. There can obviously be disagreement as to whether or not Joe's rescue and redemption by the Kaumatua works. But the Maori-European theme is neither spurious nor opportunist. It is very serious, and toughly presented. There is no idealisation of the central Maori character. Joe Gillayley is responsible for repeated violence and the eventual maiming of the European child. One could imagine a hostile Maori reaction to this depiction. . . .

I described Stead's letter as contradictory because, having suggested there is something meretricious about the novel's success, he then offers an interesting, often sympathetic reading, pointing, for example, to its careful patterning, something most reviews I've seen have missed. But then, in his final paragraph, he buries the novel. There is 'something black and negative deeply ingrained in its imaginative fabric', and this is because it 'presents extreme violence against a child, yet demands sympathy and understanding for the man who commits it'. Understanding is one thing and sympathy another. I learnt something about the intertwining of love and violence from this novel, but it certainly did not make me come to love violence. For all its violence, I find something hopeful, even pacific, ingrained in its imaginative fabric, and this seems to me a measure of its extraordinary power. There is a lot 'wrong' with *The Bone People,* as analysis of the kind Stead performs in the middle sections of his [essay] can show, but in the end this hardly seems to matter. I'm fascinated by the way that, for me, its flaws make no difference to its overall effect. I can think of very few novels of which this is true. Perhaps it is here, rather than with paranoia about its feminist and Maori credentials, that serious discussion of *The Bone People* should continue.

Rod Edmond, in a letter to the editor in London Review of Books, *January 23-30, 1986, p. 5.*

JOHN T. SULLIVAN

[*The Bone People*] sets ambitious goals for a first novel, yet its long term progress makes these objectives seem unduly modest. The themes of feminism, single parenting and child abuse, while dexterously handled, become almost secondary to a story which is much more than the sum of its parts.

The synergistic energy of the work is effortlessly exuded, but the effort put into it could not have been easy. The book is a tribute to the people and culture of New Zealand, the author being a product thereof. This background lends an amount of flavor to the story, with the only drawback being the inconvenience of looking back to the glossary to translate the odd but seldom important Maori phrase.

The story involves three characters with all others playing bit (though well-explained) roles. There are the father and the mute foster son, the latter rescued by the former from a capsized boat. The accident leaves the child with no one and no discernible past. Joe, the man, takes the child in as his own, only to be later widowed and to lose his own natural child. Joe and the orphaned child, Simon, develop an unrelenting love for each other—as they are both "orphans"—strong enough to withstand the horrific beatings Simon must endure for his own often malevolent spirit.

Into this explosive relationship is drawn Kerewin Holmes, who, we can only assume, has more in common with the author than just their names. Estranged from her family, she gives new meaning to the idea of an independent woman. Despite unending hesitation, she is unable to resist the attractive qualities of Joe and Simon. Taking a seaside vacation with the two, she learns more and more of them. But in the end, it is she whom she learns about the most.

Readers should be advised that the story, like its heroine, takes its time finding itself . . . but once found, increases its crescendo while making relevant detours. Getting there, however, is more than worth the while. (pp. 406-07)

John T. Sullivan, in a review of ''The Bone People,'' in Best Sellers, *Vol. 45, No. 11, February, 1986, pp. 406-07.*

D. J. ENRIGHT

In *The Bone People,* . . . nature will fight back valiantly, but the opening pages are all artifice, dispiritingly so. The stoutest reader must quail when he reads in the preface that the short story which the novel began as (and really ought to have stayed) was typed on the author's first typewriter, a present from her mother. . . .

There are good things in the novel, even some original things, which I shall note later. Unfortunately they will be spotted only by readers of enormous patience and long-suffering, or possibly by those who, unaware of the ancient modes of modernism, are fired by the conviction that Keri Hulme has invented a brand-new style for herself. Swift remarked long ago that something can pass as wondrous deep for no better reason than that it is wondrous dark.

The narrative is chiefly mediated, directly or indirectly, through the central character, Kerewin Holmes, a one-eighth Maori woman very much of our time in being or seeking to be self-sufficient: a loner, a painter, a guitar player, wised-up in the fashionable naïvetés, aikido, the Diamond Sutra, the Sufis, mandalas, the *I Ching*. Scraps of undistinguished verse, identified only by the layout, alternate with scraps of Maori, direct speech with meandering rivulets of consciousness.

> She stares at the screaming painting.
> The candlelight wavers.
> The painting screams silently on.
> She hates it.
> It is intensely bitter.
>
>> O unjoy, is that all I can do? Show
>> forth my misery?

The portentous alternates with the Joycean coinage ("She is immune to the eyesting of onionjuice"), the oddly ejaculatory ("Sweet apricocks and vilest excreta"), and the whimsically colloquial ("Me image hath gone down the drain").

> Aue and ach y fi, the cold and my chilblains.
> And that bloody little bugger upstairs. All miseries hemming me in together.

No wonder that Simon, the little bugger upstairs, asks himself, "What does she talk like that for? To fool me?"

Simon, or Haimona, is the easiest character to get along with. He is mute: a weird silver-blond boy of six or seven, either distinctly backward or precociously forward, orphaned in a shipwreck and adopted, though not legally, by a half-Maori called Joe Gillayley. We begin to warm to Kerewin when, meeting Joe for the first time, she says she had expected something big and blond and "dumb and boisterous to boot," then remembers that Simon is present and rushes to explain that by "dumb" she meant "stupid."

Yet there is a sort of innocence about the prose and its overwriting, whether affectedly tough-guy or affectedly profound. Keri Hulme is not being modish; she is simply—though at excessive length—being herself. The setting is the South Island of New Zealand, and the natural and animal side of the book, its earthiness and marine life, is impressive, shining brilliantly through the verbiage. The accounts of fishing trips attest to professional know-how, and the scenes in bars, occasionally reminiscent of Joyce again, are authentic and lively. Striking too are the passages concerning Maori beliefs, Maori imagination and magic. (The scraps of Maori language elsewhere are no doubt in place, but I had the impression that they were meant to add "significance" to the book rather than contribute to actuality.)

The story of **The Bone People** is minimal, deriving from a somewhat static triangular relationship, a relationship in which a British reviewer more suspicious than the present one saw an attempt to foist on us an allegorical Holy Family. Kerewin is an educated and well-to-do woman, hating to touch or be touched though able to outdrink and outfight most men, a virgin and sexually a neuter. (It is one manifestation of originality that she is not in for an "awakening" on this score.) Yet this tough nut has a soft center, and she is drawn against her will to the mysterious Simon.

Simon, an enterprising variation on the wolf-boy theme, is disobedient, and steals, and is subject to fits of destructive rage, behavior which (we assume) is caused by his dumbness, too commonly taken for stupidity, or by the experience of shipwreck and the loss of his parents. Joe loves him, but in uncontrollable fits of violence, due (we assume) either to his inability to communicate fully with Simon or else to the death of his wife and baby, he beats the boy: he doesn't know why. That for some time Kerewin fails to realize what is happening, despite the broken teeth and the scars, cannot be blamed on the author, since similar failures even among trained social workers to recognize gross cases of child abuse have occurred recently in Britain and the US.

What is less understandable is that when Joe almost kills the boy—breaking his nose and jaw, smashing in the side of his skull, and reducing him to deafness as well as dumbness—he is merely sent to prison for three months. No one thinks much the worse of him. "Home is Joe, Joe of the hard hands but sweet love": this is Simon, a child, reflecting during his convalescence. But there seems to be a general tacit agreement that you can smash a child up just as long as you love it in some strange, powerful way. With its debased memories of *Wuthering Heights* this belongs, at best, to the darker side of novelette writing. I would say it is positively immoral; I don't recall such acquiescence displayed by Dickens or any other portrayer of times supposedly less tender.

Yet the author even manages to contrive a happy ending, or nonending. In the grip of cancer, Kerewin is miraculously cured by a brew of red currant juice provided by a mysterious visitant of indeterminate age and sex. Joe is returned, somewhat cloudily, to his Maori roots—the novel embraces two popular themes, roots and rootlessness—to the ancestors of the book's title. We must hope for Simon's sake that he has been miraculously cured of his violent temper. For the boy escapes from the home for the handicapped where he has been sent, and the three of them are reunited, to be—we gather from the prologue, "The End At The Beginning"—in some undefined way "the instruments of change." The novel's last words are "TE MUTUNGA—RANEI TE TAKE": translated in the glossary as "The end—or the beginning." Sentimentality has been lurking throughout, and now it surges to the surface. (p. 16)

D. J. Enright, "Worlds of Wonder," in The New York Review of Books, *Vol. XXXIII, No. 3, February 27, 1986, pp. 16-18.**

Carolyn (Ashley) Kizer

Yin: New Poems

Pulitzer Prize: Poetry

American poet, translator, and editor.

Kizer's poetry is marked by technical elegance, an unsentimental attitude, and a woman's consciousness. It is her female sensibility that comes to the foregound in *Yin: New Poems* (1984), Kizer's fourth collection. Reviewer Robert Phillips comments that *Yin*'s "goddesses, muses, mothers, wives, and daughters coalesce in the mature voice of Carolyn Kizer."

Kizer was born in Spokane, Washington, raised in Los Angeles, and graduated from Sarah Lawrence College in New York. Her father was a lawyer and author and her mother a biology professor who taught Kizer to love nature even in its most unattractive states. Kizer's involvement with poetry began early and spans more than four decades. Her first poem appeared in the *New Yorker* in 1942, when she was only seventeen, and in the early 1950s Kizer participated in Theodore Roethke's Washington University poetry workshop. In 1959 she cofounded the quarterly *Poetry Northwest* and was its editor until 1965. Interested in foreign cultures and literatures, Kizer has traveled extensively throughout Europe, Japan, China, and Pakistan, among other countries, and has translated poetry from Chinese and Urdu into English. A professor and guest lecturer in literature, Kizer has also served as the director of literary programs for the National Endowment for the Arts and as a U.S. State Department specialist in Pakistan.

Critics have noted an evolution in Kizer's work from the harsh imagery and the poems of parody and satire evident in her early collections to the more contemplative nature of her later works. Throughout all her poetry, however, Kizer has evidenced a sense of irony and restrained emotion wedded to a mastery of form both traditional and free.

In her first work, *The Ungrateful Garden* (1961), Kizer used repelling imagery to examine the conflicts that individuals face with nature and with one another. Refusing to romanticize nature, neither does Kizer bemoan its frequent ugliness or its inaccessibility; rather, she presents a stoical acceptance of life. But, Kizer suggests, although we may be alienated from such traditional sources of comfort as nature, some reprieve from life's terrors and hardships may be found in poetry and other art forms, and, perhaps, in human relationships.

Knock Upon Silence (1965) continues Kizer's relentless observation of the human condition and introduces her interest in Oriental poetry. Some critics suggest that Kizer's outlook was influenced by the Chinese poets whose works she translated; some of those translations appear in this volume as well as a number of Kizer's own poems in the section "Chinese Imitations." *Knock Upon Silence* also contains one of Kizer's best-known poems, "Pro-Femina," in which the poet emphasizes the importance of creative women adhering to their arts and their true womanhood, in spite of the obstacles inherent in a male-dominated culture.

© 1986 Thomas Victor

Kizer's poetic style continued to mature in *Midnight Was My Cry: New and Selected Poems* (1971). While maintaining the same technical control and admiration for human resilience, Kizer shifted her subject matter from nature and love relationships to contemporary social and national issues prominent throughout the 1960s. She employed free verse and everyday idiom where previously she had only used formal verse. The collection witnesses her mastery of various types of poems: narrative, contemplative, love, and Oriental.

Yin is a natural outgrowth of Kizer's earlier works. The title is the Chinese word for the feminine principle and many of the poems in *Yin* examine female perceptions, instincts, and creativity: "Semele Recycled," for example, is a metaphorical poem about a woman who is broken into pieces, like the mythical Semele, and then unified again; "A Muse," a poem cited by critics as one of the collection's best, recounts Kizer's childhood impressions of an over-zealously supportive mother; and "Fanny," another poem singled out by critics, focuses on the wife of Robert Louis Stevenson as she nurses her husband through the last years of his life. With *Yin* Kizer's objectivity is again admired, as is her tempering of bleakness with humor.

Critics also remark on the variety of voices and tones in *Yin*, ranging from the wise to the witty and the affectionate to the sardonic. Kizer has recently published *Mermaids in the Basement* (1984), a collection of poems from her earlier works, including some from *Yin*.

(See also *CLC*, Vol. 15; *Contemporary Authors*, Vols. 65-68; and *Dictionary of Literary Biography*, Vol. 5.)

JOSEPH PARISI

Though she has titled her fourth book **Yin,** Kizer might well have considered *Yin and Yang*, the range of emotions here expressed is so wide. Two loving and lovely poems celebrate her joy in her adult daughter, as does the long prose memoir of her early life with her greatly accomplished and ambitious mother, toward whom her emotions are more mixed. Likewise, her vivid memories of growing up middle-class and Catholic in **"Running Away from Home,"** while wickedly funny and evocative (many a reader will share similar recollections), reveal equal amounts of bitter resentment for adolescent suffering and regret for those less-fortunate boys and girls who, unlike the author, did not escape a stifling culture. But with her intelligence and poetic gifts, Kizer cannot help but see, and speak, sharply. Acute but acid, her vision and voice are both witty and wise—and may provoke the more middle-of-the-road reader with their pungency. Still, whether tender or biting, Kizer's poems will demand the kind of attention that other informed hearts can understand.

> *Joseph Parisi, in a review of "Yin: New Poems,"*
> *in* Booklist, *Vol. 80, No. 21, July, 1984, p. 1512.*

SUZANNE JUHASZ

Kizer's new collection [*Yin*] is a mixed bag, or blessing. Her wise laughter is an ever-present virtue, the uncompromising clarity of her line a pleasure to anticipate. At times they find just the right object: her long poem **"Fanny"** is tough, tense, and sure; her prose piece about her mother, **"Muse,"** stands both within and without her childhood self to make poignant sense out of memory; shorter pieces like **"Children"** and **"Dream of a Large Lady"** are likewise both witty and moving. At other times, however, her skills are dissipated when she claims for an idea or a subject more than she delivers: poems like **"Food for Love," "The Dying Goddess,"** or the ambitious **"Running Away from Home"** are too predictable, and a letdown.

> *Suzanne Juhasz, in a review of "Yin," in* Library
> Journal, *Vol. 109, No. 12, July, 1984, p. 1333.*

JOEL CONARROE

In **Yin** we find a funny childhood reminiscence called **"The Muse,"** a prose poem in which the poet describes a kind of show-business mama smothering her precocious offspring with encouragement: "Why was I chosen to live the life she wanted . . .?" Only with the woman's death does the speaker's serious life as an artist begin, since now she can write without pressure, "without the hot breath of her expectations. I wrote the poems for her. I still do." This is a lovely tribute.

"Yin" refers to the feminine principle, and not surprisingly the book contains several poems about the female sensibility, including an imaginative narrative, **"Semele Recycled,"** about a woman symbolically broken in pieces and later made whole. **"The Blessing"** is one of two lyrics addressed to the poet's daughter, who, more like a mother, helps the poet through her "difficult affairs." . . .

The affectionate tone of these personal messages, utterly at odds with the hard-boiled, abrasive voice of the satires and parodies, is also evident in a dramatic series of diary entries called **"Fanny."** The speaker, or diarist, is Robert Louis Stevenson's wife, Frances, writing in Samoa during the last year of his life. As her husband works in his study, Frances laboriously clears the land and plants cocoa, custard apples, pumpkin, whatever will grow. At 50, past childbearing, she is nevertheless an earth mother, and Stevenson, 10 years her junior, comments on her "fever of planting." . . .

The long poem is Keatsian in the sensuousness of its imagery, the laughing of its odors and textures. Kizer gives a shattering sense of a woman's sacrifice and isolation while communicating vividly the terrible beauty of the woman's obsession with her husband's health and with the plenitude of her gardens. The conclusion is affecting. . . .

Although **"Fanny"** is the most impressive poem in **Yin,** it is certainly not the book's only triumph. For nearly 25 years Carolyn Kizer has been writing poetry that is imaginative, moving, and funny, and it will come as no surprise to her admirers to hear that she is still writing at the top of her powers. This is a wonderful book. (p. 3)

> *Joel Conarroe, "Poets of Innocence and Experience," in* Book World—The Washington Post, *August 5, 1984, pp. 3, 11.**

An Excerpt from *Yin: New Poems*

The Dying Goddess

The love goddess, alas, grows frailer.
She still has her devotees,
But their hearts are not whole.
They follow young boys
From the corners of their eyes.
They become embarrassed
By their residual myths.
Odd cults crop up, involving midgets,
Partial castration, dismemberment of children.
The goddess wrings her hands; they think it vanity,
And it is, partly.

Sometimes, in her precincts
Young men bow curly heads.
She sends them packing
Indulgently, with blown kisses.
There are those who pray endlessly,
Stretched full-length with their eyes shut,
Imploring her, "Mother!"
She taps her toe at these. A wise goddess
Knows her own children.

On occasion, her head raises
Almost expectantly: a man steps forward.
She takes one step forward,
They exchange wistful glances.
He is only passing.

When he comes to the place
Of no destination
He takes glass after glass
As her image wavers.
In her own mirror the image wavers.
She turns her face from the smokeless brazier.

PATRICIA HAMPL

Yin is a collection of new poems, some of them also found in *Mermaids in the Basement.* But the most striking offering, a real find, is the prose memoir, **"A Muse."** This piece, about Miss Kizer's extraordinary mother, is not only a fascinating portrait, but a model of detachment and self-revelation.

Her mother, who had led a vivid intellectual life until her late marriage, settled herself into motherhood with her only child in her mid-40's as into a new, absorbing career. When her small daughter laboriously formed the letters A, R, T with a crayon, she decided this ("Her first word!") meant she was "fated to become an artist."

Miss Kizer "was entirely aware at the time that the conjunction of the letters . . . was wholly accidental." But like Sartre's account of how his family turned him into a miracle child in *The Words,* the great family creation had begun.

It is a testimony to Miss Kizer's generosity of spirit that her account of this relationship is not bitter, but astonished. The humor here is certain of its territory, and the tone modulates beautifully, arriving at a tenderness and acquiescence that are moving and memorable. If only it were longer; this is a story to read and read.

> *Patricia Hampl, "Women Who Say What They Mean,"*
> *in* The New York Times Book Review, *November 25, 1984, p. 36.**

ROBERT PHILLIPS

One could never say with certainty what "a Carolyn Kizer poem" was—until now. *Yin,* her fourth collection, is her most unified, original, and personal. Now we know a Kizer poem is brave, witty, passionate, and not easily forgotten.

As title, she takes the traditional Chinese symbol for the feminine principle; usually conceived as the "passive" half, it is the dark half as well. But Kizer's attitudes are never passive, and the blackness is mitigated by high humor. Feminism is explored with humility. . . .

[Hers] is a poetry of rhetoric and tone rather than imagery. Many of the poems are built on single extended metaphors. These include **"Semele Recycled,"** in which the dismembered goddess is a figure for personal dissociation; **"Exodus,"** a Felliniesque vision of the Last Days; **"Food of Love,"** on total possession of the Other; and **"Running Away from Home,"** a 40-stanza, 160-line poem, sometimes rhymed, which relates in anecdote and pun the claustrophobia of growing up in the Northwest and its damaging effects, particularly the wrongs inflicted in the name of the Catholic Church. An even longer poem, the 224-line **"Fanny,"** purports to be diary entries by Mrs. Fanny Osbourne after her marriage to Robert Louis Stevenson, a record of how Fanny self-sacrificially kept the consumptive R.L.S. alive for five years while he wrote his unfinished masterpiece.

Cover of Yin, *by Carolyn Kizer. BOA Editions, 1984. Cover drawing by James Johnson. Copyright © 1984 by James Johnson. Reprinted with the permission of Carolyn Kizer and BOA Editions, Ltd.*

Creativity and will are the themes of the book. Its goddesses, muses, mothers, wives, and daughters coalesce in the mature voice of Carolyn Kizer. A dozen years in the making, *Yin* is a marvelous book. (pp. 350-51)

> *Robert Phillips, in a review of "Yin," in* Poetry,
> *Vol. CXLV, No. 6, March, 1985, pp. 350-51.*

JUDITH BARRINGTON

As a feminist reader, I find *Yin* less exciting than *Mermaids,* though it is hard to fault either volume. Kizer's writing about her mother is especially potent, making *Yin* particularly valuable for its inclusion of **"A Muse"**—a prose memoir. Kizer is such an accomplished exponent of the craft of poetry that I would encourage any reader interested in the form to read and savor both volumes. (p. 5)

> *Judith Barrington, "Kizer: Feminist Poet Pre-Feminism," in* MOTHEROOT *Journal, Vol. 6, Nos. 1 & 2, Summer, 1985, pp. 1, 5.*

GRACE SCHULMAN

Carolyn Kizer's new collection, *Yin* (Chinese for the female, negative, dark, evil principle), has few traces of the emblematic feminine selfhood Carolyn Kizer projected in *The Ungrateful Garden* (1961) and especially in *Knock Upon Silence* (1965), with its memorable **"Pro Femina."** What does survive is her wisdom; her wry wit; her alternating public and private voices, often with personae; and her use of models from the remote past.

One poem that displays many of these characteristics is **"Fanny,"** written beautifully in Roman hexameters. In this, the poet identifies so closely with her character as to speak for her: she is Fanny Stevenson, who, in the 1890s, kept a diary of how she nourished her husband, Robert Louis Stevenson, in Samoa for eight years, having removed him from London's harsh winters that had threatened his life. (p. 102)

"Fanny" is a modern portrait of a late nineteenth-century woman, somewhat reminiscent of the narrative techniques in novels by Ford, Conrad, and Fitzgerald, in that the central character, who refers to various historical and literary events, knows less of those incidents than does the reader. Instead, she is obsessed by her planting, and by her family (who are, themselves, seen aslant, from a distinctive point of view). The triumph of this poem is that Fanny is presented in precise, minute detail but as a particular person, remote from our own lives. Nevertheless, the more unusual her portrayal, the more she tells us of ourselves.

To be sure, there are other remarkable poems in this book. I like best those in the personal voice, with personae, such as **"Semele Recycled,"** spoken by a modern version of the goddess who was destroyed at the sight of her lover; or without personae, as in **"Antique Father,"** a delineation of a reserved, now silent, parent, and his inquisitive child who implores him to be heard. . . .

Reading *Yin,* I search for poems of this caliber, find them (in **"Three from Tu Fu," "Running Away from Home,"** among others), wish for more, and feel grateful for what the poet has achieved. (p. 103)

Grace Schulman, in a review of "Yin: New Poems," in Poetry, *Vol. CXLVII, No. 2, November, 1985, pp. 102-03.*

James Lapine
Stephen (Joshua) Sondheim
Sunday in the Park with George

Pulitzer Prize: Drama

Lapine—American dramatist.

Sondheim—American dramatist, lyricist, and scriptwriter.

Sunday in the Park with George (1984) is the first collaboration between Lapine, who wrote the musical's book and directed its Broadway premiere, and Sondheim, who composed its music and lyrics. Lapine, who started his career as an artist and photographer, became interested in drama when he worked as a graphic designer for the Yale Repertory Theatre. He went on to write plays, including the Obie award-winning *Photograph* (1978). Whereas Lapine is a relative newcomer to Broadway, Sondheim started his controversial career in the American musical theater as a lyricist for the critically acclaimed musical *West Side Story* (1957). *Sunday in the Park with George* resembles two early collaborations between Sondheim and producer-director Harold Prince, *Company* (1970) and *Follies* (1971), in that its action centers on a single concept rather than a conventional plot.

The concept of *Sunday in the Park with George,* originated by Lapine, reflects Lapine's background in the visual arts. In two parallel vignettes presented as separate acts, the musical demonstrates how an innovative artist creates. The first vignette shows nineteenth-century French painter Georges Seurat as he conceives and executes his famous pontillist work, ''A Sunday Afternoon on the Island of La Grande Jatte.'' The second vignette, set in the 1980s, involves the creative struggles of George, a fictional American descendant of Seurat who is an avant-garde laser artist. Lapine's book and Sondheim's lyrics dramatize the conflict between Seurat, who is obsessively devoted to his artistic principles, and the art critics of his era who called his work clever but emotionally lifeless. Several reviewers of *Sunday in the Park with George* observe that these same charges have been repeatedly made against Sondheim's musicals, the dilemmas of both artists are being explored. Sondheim has anticipated the critics' reaction to his latest achievement and reflects on the challenges to the artists in his song ''Lesson #8.'' Most negative comments on the play are directed towards what reviewers claim are uninspired dialogue and lyrics and characters who fail to come to life. Nevertheless, critics who reviewed *Sunday in the Park with George* favorably, as well as a few who did not, credit Lapine and Sondheim with an ambitious innovation in American musical theater. Within the musical genre they have fashioned a work whose vision encompasses the struggles of a pioneer artist, the actual creation of a work of art, and the enduring importance of art to humanity.

(For Stephen Sondheim: see also *CLC*, Vol. 30 and *Contemporary Authors*, Vol. 103.)

Courtesy of Stephen Sondheim

DAVID STERRITT

Georges Seurat completed only a handful of paintings during his brief life, and he failed to sell a single one. Yet his fame and influence have been enormous. Even casual art-watchers know ''A Sunday Afternoon on the Island of La Grande Jatte,'' an 1886 pointillist masterpiece shaped not from traditional brushstrokes but from multitudinous specks of color.

The contrast between Seurat's quiet, hardworking life and his largely posthumous celebrity is the kind of irony Broadway and Hollywood love to explore and it's one theme of *Sunday in the Park With George*. . . .

In concocting this entertainment writer-director James Lapine and composer Stephen Sondheim have in effect opened up Seurat's greatest painting, inviting us inside for a rather meditative tour. During the first half of the evening, the stage mimics ''La Grande Jatte,'' complete with pointillist trees and dogs. Many of the figures come to life, chatting or arguing with the painter. While the second act takes place a century later, it explores similar themes, just as much contemporary art is an echo of past explorations.

The trouble with the show is not a lack of imagination but rather a basic conflict between its style and substance. The character Seurat . . . keeps repeating his artistic watchwords: order, design, harmony, and so forth. They perfectly suit the stately, orderly, supremely composed world of "La Grande Jatte."

By themselves, however, they don't particularly suit (and aren't successfully made to suit) the needs of a stage musical. . . . *Sunday* hovers between the formal elegance of "La Grande Jatte" and the living, breathing, potentially fascinating life of Seurat himself—but partakes fully of neither. . . .

At other moments, . . . Sondheim and Lapine find strong links between their subject and their stagecraft. But too often the characters are stereotypes in trite situations. . . .

> David Sterritt, "Sondheim Musical Explores an Artist's Life and Work," in The Christian Science Monitor, *May 3, 1984, p. 27.*

DOUGLAS WATT

Sunday in the Park With George is pretty; trouble is, you can't simply pass on to the next gallery after a bit and take in another show. The new Stephen Sondheim musical . . . doesn't bear looking at or listening to for very long.

James Lapine, who has provided the static and even foolish book, has tried to peek into the lives of those idling 19th century holidayers in Georges Seurat's pointillistic masterpiece, "A Sunday Afternoon on the Island of La Grande Jatte." Unlike Alice through the looking glass, he has found little of genuine interest there. (p. 283)

Sondheim's inspiration seems to have been at a low ebb most of the time, his enormous talent shining through only in brief flashes. . . . Sondheim seems merely to be repeating himself.

During the first act, Seurat . . . is seen mostly sitting around in the park (the island is on the Seine just outside Paris) absorbedly drawing figures on his sketchbook for his grand canvas. The principal figure is his . . . model-mistress, named Dot (possibly a pun on his painting technique, for his real mistress, who bore him a son, was named Madeleine). Seurat has little time for Dot even in his studio where, painstakingly applying thousands of little dots or strokes of color, the whole blending to produce a shimmering effect when observed from a proper distance, he ignores her pleas to take her nightclubbing. She winds up marrying a baker, a congenial chap who takes her and her infant (by Seurat) to Charleston, S.C. Seurat, by the way, died at 31, having completed only seven works in this style.

In Act Two, we meet Seurat's great-grandson and his grandmother, the infant grown up . . . in a 1983 gallery where he has created, with the help of a humorless SoHo-type composer . . . a "Chromolume" show honoring Seurat and made up of darting laser beams and photo projections on the globular head of an object resembling a "Star Wars" robot. Mesmerized by his great-grandmother's diary, he returns to the island, now spiked with high-rise apartments in place of the earlier trees—there to meet with the original Dot, bustle and all, and to stroll off with her, arm in arm. (pp. 283-84)

[The] painting itself says far more about the people in it than the show does. Sondheim, as usual, is to be admired for taking on a challenging subject, but he was barking up the wrong tree, or trees, this time. (p. 284)

> *Douglas Watt, "'Sunday in the Park' Is Pretty . . . ," in* Daily News, *New York, May 3, 1984. Reprinted in* New York Theatre Critics' Reviews, *Vol. XXXXV, No. 7, Week of April 16, 1984, pp. 283-84.*

CLIVE BARNES

Personally I was nonplussed, unplussed, and disappointed by *Sunday in the Park With George,* the new James Lapine and Stephen Sondheim musical. . . .

It is not simply that it tells us more about the short, uneventful life of the painter Georges Seurat than many of us may wish to know.

It is not even that it persists in offering a somewhat simplistic and bathetically pretentious course in art appreciation.

The difficulty with the show is that . . . it simply doesn't sing.

Sunday in the Park never really takes off. It just lies there like an expensively ornamental paperweight, or a cuckoo clock that has lost its cuckoo.

The idea, which apparently first came to Lapine, who wrote the book and directed the show, is audaciously ambitious. It is to show us the creation of a work of art, the formulation of an artistic style based on scientific principles, and to reveal, in passing, the struggles of an artist for recognition.

Now this is not your run-of-the-mill subject for a musical. It is attempting to say something of moment about the actual process of creation, and is using as its starting and finishing points an actual painting, Seurat's remarkable and well-known "A Sunday Afternoon on the Island of La Grand Jatte," a work that took two years to paint and is recognized as a landmark in modern art. . . .

But one can hardly make a musical out of a *tableau vivante,* however adroit and diverting that may be, and Lapine has been constrained to construct a plot. Unfortunately the plot thins.

The idea is to have Seurat more obsessed with science and his work than with his model-mistress, who has been given the pleasantly pointillist name of Dot.

Dot, impregnated by Seurat, is married off to an obliging painter and bundled off to America. In the second act—and at times I wondered why there was a second act—the time is the present, and Seurat's daughter and great-grandson . . . are involved in a lecture at an art institute.

After some satirical digs (more pokes than digs) at the art establishment, the scene returns to La Grand Jatte, where the young Seurat returns on pilgrimage, only to find the place overgrown with ugly buildings. But don't worry, the painting wins out in time for the finale.

In most ways this seems to be far more Lapine's musical than Sondheim's, and Lapine's book does, in my view, trivialize and vulgarize art and artist alike.

As a sample of the vulgarity let me cite an American tourist couple, having a homesick couple of days in Paris, who are last seen carting off a couple of Renoir paintings as souvenirs. A small visual joke—but a cheap one.

There is triviality in some aphorisms—such as "jealousy is a form of flattery"—but worst of all, art itself is trivialized. A museum director, in charge of the laser show and faced with a power cut, announces: "Unfortunately, no electricity, no art—there is no juice!"

That comes unfortunately close to describing *Sunday in the Park With George,* but there are, of course, the music and lyrics by Stephen Sondheim. . . .

[But] the overall flavor and texture of the music is not especially distinctive, while even in the lyrics Sondheim's normally felicitous verbal facility seems to have temporarily deserted him. (p. 284)

[When] all is said and sung, . . . it might be better to go to the park with anyone than to spend it boringly in the theater with George. (p. 285)

> *Clive Barnes, "Grass Could Be Greener in Sondheim's Sunday Park," in* New York Post, *May 3, 1984. Reprinted in* New York Theatre Critics' Reviews, *Vol. XXXXV, No. 7, Week of April 16, 1984, pp. 284-85.*

HOWARD KISSEL

It is easy to see why Stephen Sondheim should have been attracted to the idea of creating a musical about Georges Seurat, whose career is a way of discussing some of the dilemmas that confront the contemporary artist. Since the 19th century, "serious artists" have brought themselves to the attention of the "serious public" by flouting the conventional taste of the day. Once having achieved recognition, they are in the unenviable position of having to fend off the derisive Philistines on one hand and the sycophantic trendies on the other.

Several times in the course of *Sunday in the Park With George,* . . . Sondheim alludes openly to the awkwardness of his own position, most touchingly in a song entitled **"Lesson #8,"** in which an artist ponders what direction his work should take.

Elsewhere in the show Sondheim strikes a touchy, defensive note, as when Seurat's detractors describe his work as "so drab, so cold, and so controlled," terms that have been used to describe Sondheim. In the same song the detractor declares, "It has no presence, no passion, no life," and one can only think Sondheim wanted to get the jump on his critics and forestall such attacks by implying that only the superficial would see no more in his work than that. The sad fact, however, is that despite his obvious intention to treat the subject in a mode as experimental as it deserves, . . . *Sunday* is a thin and lifeless evening.

In the first act Sondheim and his collaborator, James Lapine, try to sketch the disparate lives that Seurat brings together in his great painting, "Sunday Afternoon on the Island of La Grande Jatte." It is possible that if we really had a sense of the classes of 19th-century Paris Seurat portrayed, the final moments of the act, in which all the characters assume the positions they have in the painting might be intensely dramatic. But all Lapine has given us is cliche characters, so their convergence has no drama at all. (The most offensive of his stereotypes is that of some vulgar American tourists—if Americans of this epoch were so stupid, how does it happen that so many major works of French art of the period, including *Sunday,* are in American rather than French collections?)

Lapine's and Sondheim's Seurat is a humorless, dour man always trying to break reality down into its component colors. . . .

What are we to do with Sondheim? Encourage his self-absorption, bitterness and musical preciosity on the grounds it "advances" the art of the musical? Chide him for being an elitist in an essentially popular medium? Pretend that his work is avant-garde and stimulating when it is mainly contrived? *Sunday* is too tepid even to occasion outrage or anger. It makes you nostalgic for *Merrily We Roll Along.*

> *Howard Kissel, in a review of "Sunday in the Park with George," in* Women's Wear Daily, *May 3, 1984. Reprinted in* New York Theatre Critics' Reviews, *Vol. XXXXV, No. 7, Week of April 16, 1984, p. 285.*

JACK KROLL

The theater can coddle you or challenge you, it can treat you like a tired businessman or an alert citizen. Composer-lyricist Stephen Sondheim is a challenger, not a coddler. And *Sunday in the Park with George,* the new musical he's created with writer-director James Lapine, may be his biggest gamble. That harmless-sounding title masks more daring and surprise than the American musical stage has seen in a long time. George is Georges Seurat, a painter as revolutionary as any in the last hundred years. With Seurat as their central figure, Sondheim and Lapine have fashioned not only a musical about an artist but a musical about art, about its triumphs, pains and its inescapable necessity.

To say that this show breaks new ground is not enough; it also breaks new sky, new water, new flesh and new spirit. In the astonishing first act, as compact and complex as a novella by Henry James (with music), we watch George . . . create his monumental painting, "A Sunday Afternoon on the Island of La Grande Jatte." This painting is one of those works, like Beethoven's "Eroica" or Joyce's *Ulysses,* that change the metabolism of culture. Sondheim and Lapine make its creation as exciting as the discovery of a new world. . . . [We] see George as a single-minded genius whose "scientific" technique of pointillism, in which he covers his canvas with a myriad of dots of pure color that fuse in the viewer's eye, is really his way of controlling his passion for seeing and shaping the world. . . .

Sondheim and Lapine have imagined who Seurat's subjects might be with great charm and insight: a nurse and her elderly charge who turns out to be George's mother; a pair of soldiers . . . cruising a couple of pretty shopgirls; a resentful boatman who puts down George as an arrogant snob; a snooty, successful painter and his snooty, silly wife, and, most important, George's chief model and mistress. . . . (p. 83)

It seems clear that Sondheim identifies in many ways with Seurat. Throughout his career the extravagantly gifted Sondheim has been accused of emotional coldness and other associated syndromes. . . . But Lapine and Sondheim show that George's scientific rigor conceals strong emotional force. When Dot accuses George of hiding behind his art, he answers: "I am not hiding behind my canvas, I am living in it." Clutching his sketchbook like a lover, George both records and empathizes with his subjects in a long song chain called **"The Day Off."** He even gets inside the heads of two dogs, the boatman's mutt and a lady's lap dog, who make a witty embodiment of class distinction as George sings to them, imagining their lives in a whimsical doggerel that includes splendid arpeggios of barks, yelps, growls and sniffs. (pp. 83-4)

The second act leaps forward a century after Seurat's tragic death at 31. We're given an ironic contrast between the two eras, a contrast expressed in the satiric **"Putting It Together,"** in which what is put together is no longer the work of art but the deal making of the modern art establishment. The song is delivered by a new George . . . , who may be a great-grandson of the original George. At least his 98-year-old grandmother . . . says so as she sings a song called **"Children and Art"** that makes a touching connection between the twin legacies of love and art.

For all its uncertainties of focus, this second act is indispensable to the play's vaulting vision of art as a human glory. The new George doesn't make paintings but machines called Chromolumes . . . , and if that sounds like a mere jargon word, it helps if you know that Seurat preferred to call himself a Chromo-Luminarist. So Lapine and Sondheim take us full circle, implying that there's still hope for vision in a high-tech world and that art and love may be two forms of the same energy. That difficult but noble thesis, in this show of beauty, wit, nobility and ardor, makes this Sondheim's best work since *Company* and *Follies,* his classic collaborations with Harold Prince. (p. 84)

Jack Kroll, "Sondheim Paints a Picture," in Newsweek, *Vol. CIII, No. 20, May 14, 1984, pp. 83-4.*

Alison Lurie (Bishop)

Foreign Affairs

Pulitzer Prize: Fiction

American novelist, nonfiction writer, children's writer, and critic.

For more than two decades Lurie has been exploring in her fiction the world of the American middle class, especially its academic world. Lurie provides a social history of the post 1950s era and exposes the pretensions of her characters with satirical wit. Lurie is herself an academic—a Professor of English at Cornell University where she teaches classes in creative writing, folklore, and children's literature. Lurie shares several similarities with Vinnie Miner, the heroine of her prizewinning novel, *Foreign Affairs;* Vinnie, too, is a middle-aged professor, an instructor in children's literature, and a confessed anglophile. Lurie, who spends a month in London every year, has seen her reputation grow on both sides of the Atlantic. *Foreign Affairs* is her first book, however, with a London setting. Though the novel is characteristically witty and ironic, it is cited by critics as her most compassionate work to date—a departure for the author dubbed by Gore Vidal as "the Queen Herod of Modern Fiction."

Beginning with her first novel, *Love and Friendship* (1962), Lurie has continuously wedded brilliant technique to her examination of contemporary manners and institutions. The institution of marriage and the practice of adultery are frequently subjects of Lurie's scrutiny: *Love and Friendship* recounts the romantic fling of a young faculty wife at a New England college; *The Nowhere City* (1965) follows an Eastern academic couple transplanted to California with its atmosphere of license; and the bestselling *The War between the Tates* (1974) portrays the dissolution of an academic marriage against the background of the troubled Vietnam War era. In *Imaginary Friends* (1967) and *Real People* (1969) Lurie challenges the perception of reality. In the former, Lurie satirizes two sociologists who are studying a bizarre religious cult in upstate New York, while in the latter, she examines the relation of art to reality as she presents a writer who has retreated from life to an artists' colony. Besides her fiction, Lurie has written several works for children and the nonfiction *The Language of Clothes* (1981), a discussion of fashion and the relation of color and style to character. The revealing details of clothing is, in fact, a technique employed by Lurie in *Foreign Affairs,* and several reviewers note its effectiveness.

Foreign Affairs follows two American professors of literature through their respective romances when each travels to London on sabbatical leave. The book is typical of Lurie's work in its well-planned structure as well as in its satiric examination of human fallibility. Some critics have likened *Foreign Affairs* to a fairy tale for its allusions to children's classics, especially in its theme of the transforming power of love. Other reviewers note a Jamesian influence in the idea of American innocents abroad in a wizened, decadent Old World, and, indeed, the protagonist Fred frequently makes direct comments about being inside a Jamesian story. Still other reviewers see likenesses to

© 1986 Thomas Victor

Jane Austen, particularly in the novel's examination of manners and its omniscient narrator who comments on the unfolding story. No matter where reviewers tend to see allusions, they usually find Lurie's writing rich in literary resonances.

Lurie's narrative technique is often discussed in reviews of *Foreign Affairs*. Although the adventures of the two professors are not directly connected with one another, their stories are interwoven in alternating chapters. The narrator provides a thematic connection between them as well as a running commentary on other subjects, including food, culture, and travel. The mechanical structure of the novel is described by Christopher Lehmann-Haupt as "almost musical" in form. A few critics contend that Lurie's characters—especially Fred and Rosemary who create the alternate love story—remain shallow or uninteresting, partly because they are undeveloped. Even reviewers who fault Lurie's choice of development of characters, however, agree that her interplay of plots is technically superb. Her story is told with the satiric, self-conscious wit that is typical of her work and further enhances her reputation as an acute observer and able literary writer.

(See also *CLC*, Vols. 4, 5, 18; *Contemporary Authors*, Vols. 1-4, rev. ed.; *Contemporary Authors New Revision Series*, Vol. 2; and *Dictionary of Literary Biography*, Vol. 2.)

CHRISTOPHER LEHMANN-HAUPT

It's amusing enough simply to recall some of the events of *Foreign Affairs*, the seventh and latest work of fiction by Alison Lurie, who teaches English at Cornell University and has quietly but surely established herself as one of this country's most able and witty novelists.

At the beginning, Virginia (Vinnie) Miner, a tiny spinsterish Ivy League professor of children's literature, boards a plane for a six-month period of study in her beloved England, trailed by an imaginary mutt "known to her privately as Fido and representing self-pity." Fido will shortly be howling and putting his paws on Vinnie's lap, for not only has she just discovered a paragraph disparaging her in a magazine of national circulation, but she is about to be accosted conversationally by a folksy sanitary engineer from Tulsa, Okla., against whose friendliness her only defense is the copy of *Little Lord Fauntleroy* she offers to lend him.

The possibilities of this situation will develop beyond our most intricate imaginings. It will be helped along by a younger colleague of Vinnie's named Fred Turner, an excessively handsome young man who is visiting England to do research on the 18th-century poet and dramatist John Gay, and who, in chapters that alternate with those recounting Vinnie's triumphs and tribulations, gets steadily more involved in a Jamesian love affair with a beautiful and aristocratic English television actress.

But besides amusing us with its story, *Foreign Affairs* is wonderfully stimulating for its sheer performance as a novel. Perhaps by stressing this I'm admitting nostalgia for a classical approach to literature, but as I read *Foreign Affairs* I couldn't help visualizing a diagram with the rise of Vinnie's fortunes superimposed on the decline of Fred Turner's. There's something almost musical in the way the two plots interplay, like two bands marching toward each other playing consonant music.

I have the urge to digress on Miss Lurie's treatment of the classic themes of love and illusion, of innocents abroad (as well as the guilt-ridden), and of American boosterism colliding with Anglophilia. I want to take apart her marvelous language and see what makes her witty metaphors tick. I'd like to paint a map of her London, for she has taken its familiar features and made them glow with the special colors of her art.

I will take as a sample of the novel's technique one passage in which Professor Miner assays her future. As she sits on a bench outdoors in London, having been released anew into physical passion, she realizes not only that she is free of the "demanding and defining voices of her colleagues and students and friends," but also that "English literature, to which in early childhood she had given her deepest trust, and which for half a century has suggested what she might do, think, feel, desire, and become, has suddenly fallen silent. Now, at last," she continues to ruminate, "all those books have no instructions for her, no demands—because she is just too old."

"In the world of classic British fiction," she reflects, "almost the entire population is under fifty, or even under forty—as was true of the real world when the novel was invented." Even today, in most novels "it is taken for granted that people over fifty are as set in their ways as elderly apple trees, and as permanently shaped and scarred by the years they have weathered. The literary convention is that nothing major can happen to them except through subtraction."

But in real life—or the real life of Alison Lurie's fiction—Vinnie has many years to live and much to experience. Why, therefore, she concludes, should she "become a minor character in her own life? Why shouldn't she imagine herself as an explorer standing on the edge of some landscape as yet unmapped by literature, interested, even excited—ready to be surprised?"

This passage works in several different ways. First, it is interesting as an observation about literature. Second, being typical of the way Vinnie Miner thinks, it contributes to our interest in her as a character. (Fred Turner, her foil, also has an original turn of mind.) Third, the passage is typical of the way the novel calls attention to what it is up to—for indeed the book is unusual in the way it focuses on a person "over fifty" without patronizing or pitying her. But more important still is how by calling attention to itself the scene reminds us of the book's self-consciousness and thereby highlights not only its dazzling artistry but also the highly artificial world in which both its major characters are living.

Finally, the passage resonates because, with irony characteristic of the book, its insight comes too late for Vinnie. Unknown to her, a tragedy has occurred. Except it somehow isn't tragic. With Alison Lurie's alchemy it is transmuted into comedy. So deft is the touch of her intricately playful fiction—so securely fixed are her characters at just the right distance between the pathetic and the ridiculous—that we can both like them and laugh at them.

I forgot to mention that it's at the London Zoo that Vinnie Miner realizes she has been freed from the constraints of literature to express her physical being. On the outer hand, she happens to be watching the polar bears at the time. In *Foreign Affairs* no detail lacks its special piquancy. And none can be savored without leaving you with a mouthful of barbed hooks.

> *Christopher Lehmann-Haupt, in a review of "Foreign Affairs," in* The New York Times, *September 13, 1984, p. C21.*

ANNE BERNAYS

Foreign Affairs is an intelligent novel whose female protagonist, Virginia—Vinnie—Miner, a 54-year-old English professor, is described as "elderly." She is, I'm afraid, less a woman with heartbeat, appetite and particularity than she is Miss Lurie's abstract notion of an "aging," solitary female who "for nearly forty years . . . has suffered the peculiar disadvantages of the woman born without physical charms." On a transAtlantic flight to England, where Vinnie plans to continue her lifelong study of children's rhymes, she meets "Chuck" Mumpson, whose "dress and speech proclaim him to be, probably, a Southern Plains States businessman of no particular education or distinction; the sort of person who goes on package tours to Europe."

Alas, Chuck, too, must bear the weight of his creator's preconceptions and this is simply too heavy for him; he's flattened.

"Metchoo on the plane last month. Chuck Mumpson," he says, reintroducing himself to Vinnie. "'Hey, did you see those guys?' Mumpson says in a loud whisper, jerking his head back at the small table . . . where two Fortnum's employees in Regency dress are having tea and playing chess. 'Weird.'" Thus does Miss Lurie load the dice against a character who would have fared better if she had let him have his head.

Meanwhile, as Vinnie and Chuck become improbable lovers, Fred Turner, a disconcertingly handsome young American who teaches in the same department of the same university as Vinnie, arrives in London in order to continue his research on John Gay, for a biography he intends to write about the 18th-century poet. Fred is separated from his wife, Roo (who appeared as a minor character, a child, in *The War Between the Tates*). Adrift, Fred meets Rosemary, an aristocratic television actress somewhat his senior. He falls desperately in love with her and they begin an affair. Rosemary introduces Fred to her fast-track London set: "In the last few weeks Fred has entered a world he had before only read of: a world of crowded, electric first nights, leisurely highbrow Sunday lunches in Hampstead and Holland Park; elegant international dinner parties in Connaught Square and Chester Row." Miss Lurie knows her London and its social layers.

In what I think is the novel's best scene, sharp, funny and relatively free of authorial comment, Fred discovers at a house party in the country what British upper-crust morality is all about. But Rosemary, like Chuck, never springs to life; she seems stagey and unreal, like the shallow character she represents on the tube.

The tangling and untangling of these two sets of lovers—Vinnie and Chuck, Fred and Rosemary—make up the rest of Miss Lurie's novel, including a bizarre episode in which the true identity of Rosemary's housemaid is revealed as in a melodrama, at disproportionate length and with old-fashioned relish.

Foreign Affairs is not a simple book. The reader is meant to infer several things, among them that Fred Turner is a sort of Macheath, because his love life "follows one of the classic literary patterns of the eighteenth century in which a man meets and seduces an innocent woman, then abandons her." Also, that how one feels affects how one views the world. Disappointed in love, Fred decides that "London especially—like Rosemary—seems to him alternately false and mad." And finally, that people need each other: "Like the Miller of Dee, as long as she [Vinnie] didn't really care for anyone, the fact that nobody cared for her could not trouble her."

These inferences and others are perfectly valid and fitting. The problem is that too often we draw them because of what the author tells us, rather than from what her characters say and do. There is a sense, in this book, of crude manipulation, of the author as a director unwilling to leave the stage when the curtain goes up.

The omniscient author always takes a risk: the temptation to jump in and give the reader a piece of one's mind is sometimes too great to withstand. In earlier novels Miss Lurie played the omniscient role impeccably, energetically, with self-control and delicacy. Not so in *Foreign Affairs*. Which makes this novel merely intelligent.

Anne Bernays, "What to Think about Chuck and Vinnie," in The New York Times Book Review, September 16, 1984, p. 9.

WALTER CLEMONS

Alison Lurie's wit is robust enough to give the so-called academic novel a good name. The two principal characters in *Foreign Affairs* teach in the same English department, and both come to London on sabbatical. . . .

Lurie traces their unsuitable love affairs in alternating chapters; Henry James looms in the background. A BBC serial of a James novel is turned on in one scene and recurs to Fred when he's invited to a house party James might have relished. This is a wonderful comic idea. The Jamesian expatriates who once had the money to trip through British society have become academics, on limited budgets, whose heads are stuffed with literary notions of England as The Great Good Place.

Foreign Affairs is good enough to argue with. One of the pleasures of Lurie's fictions is her habit of commenting tartly on her story in Jane Austen's peremptory manner. But some of her asides on the love affair of Vinnie and Chuck have the schoolmarmy click of a pointer tapping on a blackboard: "The media convention is that people like Chuck and Vinnie—especially Vinnie—don't enjoy sex very much or experience it very often . . . In books, plays, films, advertisements, only the young and beautiful are portrayed as making love. That the relatively old and plain do so too, often with passion, is a well-kept secret." Isn't that just a little preachy?

Another objection: at the climax of Fred and Rosemary's love affair, Lurie explodes a plot contraption that has been so elaborately prepared that one applauds its cunning instead of wholly believing in it. It involves a charwoman named Mrs. Harris, a boldly Dickensian clue. I confess I was had. I was so busy spotting Eng. Lit. references in the higher realm of Henry James that I was hit in the back of the knees when Lurie snuck up and pulled a piece of Agatha Christie humbuggery. High and low, this is a *very* literary comedy. . . .

But it's an ingenious book and, surprisingly for Lurie, a touching one. She has not been famous for mercy. I liked *The War Between the Tates* for its fury, which won her Gore Vidal's accolade as "the Queen Herod of modern fiction." Here she does a magnificent number on an awful baby as terrible as the monstrous teen-age children of the Tates. But acidulous, snobby Vinnie Miner is granted a moving acknowledgment of love. Vinnie is an entirely successful creation, Chuck almost as good. Rosemary is an unstable compound. A plain woman's (Lurie's) meditation on the problems of beauty, she has a stinging scene with Vinnie. "You think a lot of men want to sleep with me," says Rosemary. "Men don't want to sleep with me, they want to have slept with me." While I don't quite buy what Lurie finally does with Rosemary, I keep thinking about her. I'll be surprised if another novel this year amuses and bothers me so.

Walter Clemons, "Lovers and Other Strangers," in Newsweek, Vol. CIV, No. 13, September 24, 1984, p. 80.

JOEL CONARROE

The title of Alison Lurie's latest comedy of manners [*Foreign Affairs*] does not refer to the machinations of our State Department but to the amorous adventures of some Americans living abroad. . . .

In the novel's clash of cultures, the Yanks (naive, forthright, vulgar) get the better of their Old World cousins (cultivated, dishonest, effete), though in the grand tradition of satirical demolition nobody comes off terribly well. . . .

The novel's dramatic finale points up by contrast the leisurely nature of the earlier chapters. Interspersed among lively conversations about tourism, aging, popular culture, and other worthy topics are scenes in which characters engage in earnest discussions about who is doing what (or not doing what) with whom. These scenes every now and then evoke thoughts of afternoon television, a response also prompted by the sudsier passages in **Real People** (1969), Luries's unpleasant *roman à clef* about the artists' colony at Yaddo, and **The War Between the Tates** (1974), her best-selling gloss on love and squalor in upstate New York. For the most part, though, given its general level of literacy, **Foreign Affairs** causes one to think not of TV serials but of Jane Austen.

It is Henry James, however, who comes to Fred Turner's mind. After witnessing some upper-class hijinks (and on other occasions as well), he wonders if he has somehow got into one of that author's novels. But which novel? Where Philip Roth weaves a specific James tale into *The Ghost Writer,* thereby adding allusive richness to his text, Lurie chooses simply to drop a few sentences about the Master's mannered elegance and move on. Although her plot is concerned with the confrontation of American naiveté and European sophistication, a major Jamesian theme, she resists the temptation to explore various levels of ironic correspondence.

I hasten to add, however, that Lurie is a writer on whom little is lost, and resonant details can be found in abundance in this novel. It is satisfying, for example, in the light of her 1981 book on the language of clothes (what the clothing we wear says about us), to see how she dresses her characters and especially to see the symbolic weight she attaches to such seemingly ordinary things as a furled umbrella, a green plastic raincoat, and a pair of scuffed loafers. Not surprisingly, she also perceives a great deal about the language of food. And she cleverly uses speech patterns (the language of language?) to reveal character, though some of her examples lack subtlety, as when a young American arrives at Vinnie's flat and commits not only ''hopefully'' but also ''finalize,'' ''y'know,'' and ''Have a nice day!'' One half expects to see a smile button.

Vinnie's own language is puzzling. She has a pedant's impatience with split infinitives and other grammatical lapses of ''half-literate middle Americans,'' yet though she generally thinks and speaks with chiseled precision, she also says things like ''data has'' and ''no one likes their own voice.'' Is the author having a bit of fun at the grammarian's expense? If so, this would explain some figurative language that is not exactly Jamesian. Her ex-husband, Vinnie reveals, ''was on the tearful rebound from a particularly aggravating beauty and, like a water-logged tennis ball, had rolled into the nearest hole.'' Even leaving aside the sexual innuendo, this description is bizarre. ''Rebound'' relates to billiards, not to tennis. And while pool balls (and golf balls) roll into holes, tennis balls, water-logged or dry, do not. I don't mean to make a mountain out of a mole hole; I want simply to suggest that here, as elsewhere, Professor Miner gets a C-minus for accuracy.

And Professor Lurie? Her novel earns an A. It also earns the gratitude of all of us who admire literacy, wit, and the underrated joys of ironic discourse.

> *Joel Conarroe, ''Footnotes to Lovenotes,'' in* Book World—The Washington Post, *September 30, 1984, p. 6.*

MAUREEN CORRIGAN

> There was an old woman called
>   Nothing-at-all
> Who lived in a dwelling exceedingly
>   small;
> A man stretched his mouth to its
>   utmost extent,
> And down at one gulp house and old
>   woman went.
>
>   (Anon)

Poor Vinnie Miner has devoted most of her 54 years to studying children's folk rhymes, and she's taken their message sternly to heart. Those taunting couplets of yore often celebrate the maiming and murder of homely spinsters, like herself, who foolishly search for love. Long after the schoolchildren have thrown down their jump ropes and quit the playground, Vinnie broods over the rhymes, arranging them into chapters for future books and cautionary maxims for her life. With the exception of one impetuous marriage that sizzled out faster than witches' spittle, Vinnie has remained cloistered within a charmed circle of literary friends. But, by the end of **Foreign Affairs,** she's leapt out of these intellectual confines and joyously tumbled into the maws of a slobbering, all-consuming love. It's not that Vinnie has been misinterpreting her rhymes all along; she's been concentrating on the wrong material. Like an agnostic obsessively reading *Faust,* she's favored a literature that confirmed, not dispelled, her worst fears. Alison Lurie's latest novel investigates how choosing the wrong research topic can warp and even destroy one's life.

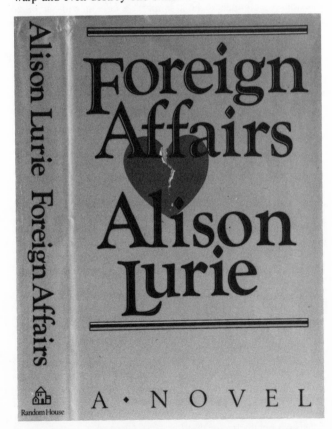

Dust jacket of Foreign Affairs, *by Alison Lurie. Random House, 1984. Jacket design and illustration by Wendell Minor. © 1984 Random House, Inc. Courtesy of the publisher.*

In *Love and Friendship* and *The War Between the Tates,* Lurie wickedly contemplated affinities between the world of the child and the scholar: both, she maintained, are populated by whiny smart alecks. *Foreign Affairs* (an awful title for this genuinely funny, emotional book) multiplies the dimensions of the metaphor. Not only is Vinnie a colicky little grind, but her field is "Literature and the Child"—and, best of all, the story of her transformation reads like a fairy tale. Brewing an atmosphere from equal parts of the Brothers Grimm and *A Midsummer Night's Dream,* Lurie playfully regards characters as asses, serpents, Druids, dust, and replaces the familiar green world of committee meetings, research sabbaticals, and cocktail parties with a golden world of endless possibility.

Even Lurie's white magic isn't potent enough to work these wonders at Vinnie's University of Corinth, so—presto!—a travel grant whisks her off to England. The plot borrows generously from "The Frog Prince," which Bruno Bettelheim classifies with those fairy tales centering on "the shock of recognition when that which seemed animal suddenly reveals itself as the source of human happiness." The friendly animal in this version is seated next to Vinnie on her BOAC charter flight. Chuck Mumpson, a retired waste disposal engineer, does everything but croak to announce his frog prince potential: he's plump, balding, leathery, and dresses in string ties with turquoise clasps and a green plastic raincoat. (Lurie's appreciation for the details of self-decoration, evident in *The Language of Clothes,* adds zest to these descriptions.) To any veteran fairy tale reader, Mumpson would be immediately suspect; but to Vinnie, who's been brainwashed by sneering folk rhymes and academic pretensions of eloquence, he's simply "a person without inner resources who splits infinitives." In the original, the princess reluctantly sleeps with the frog, he loses his warts, and she loses her virginity. Vinnie's no innocent—she's had a score of casual lovers (mostly caught on the rebound from prettier women) and has often supplemented that list with imaginary beaux: M. H. Abrams, John Cheever, Robert Lowell, Walker Percy, Lionel Trilling, Robert Penn Warren. But Mumpson is the first man who really loves Vinnie, and his love educates her out of her worst scholarly immaturities: self-pity, Anglomania, and the conflation of the mind with the sex organ.

Mumpson metamorphoses into such an enchanting yet pitiable character that whenever he's absent—as in the alternating chapters on Vinnie's junior colleague, Fred Turner, who's also having a London love affair—the magical aura of the story diminishes. (To accept, as we must, that two members of the same English department would simultaneously be granted six months' leave in London and that they would actually break ranks and socialize while there requires a whopping suspension of disbelief but, hey, this *is* a fairy tale.) In a witty and woeful inversion of Vinnie's story, young, handsome, but penniless Fred experiences the nightmare aspect of academe, London, and fairy tales. After wasting bleak months in the British Museum (redubbed the Bowel Movement—he often "has to wait up to four hours for the constipated digestive system of the ancient library to disgorge a pathetic few of the volumes whose numbers he has copied from the complex, unwieldy catalogue"), Fred scampers back to Corinth and, while he's been most amusing, he's not overly missed. From his first appearance, Fred was marked as the expendable ritual victim and, even though he's saved by Mumpson at the 11th hour, he's a bit too sympathetic for comfort.

Fairy tales and academic adventures complement each other marvelously, not only because they assume the same degree of maturity in their characters and audience, but—as Kingsley Amis demonstrated 30 years ago in *Lucky Jim*—because an academic novel with a happy ending is necessarily something of a fantasy. Mumpson and Vinnie cannot live happily ever after since his demigod powers would corrode on the caustic intellectual battleground of Corinth. Foreseeing the inevitable, Mumpson leaves Vinnie with an amulet which will remind her to seek out happiness without him. His gift, an 18th century engraving of Mumpson the Wise Hermit, is comically fierce enough to ward off both depression and its gnomic academic attendants in the green world. In many ways, *Foreign Affairs* fulfills the same function.

> *Maureen Corrigan, in a review of "Foreign Affairs," in VLS, No. 29, October, 1984, p. 5.*

DOROTHY WICKENDEN

In *Foreign Affairs,* although Lurie leaves her American setting behind and ventures into the bowels of the British Museum and the drawing rooms of country estates, she carries along many of her old belongings. The two characters at the center of the story, Vinnie Miner and Fred Turner, are by now familiar types in her fiction: professors from Corinth University who are painfully aware of their own provincialism, but seemingly incapable of overcoming it. (p. 35)

There is potential here for the kind of sharp social satire Lurie excels in, and the novel contains flashes of her distinctive wit and style. But *Foreign Affairs,* like its two protagonists, is hampered by an inability to surmount its own pettiness. The plot is mechanical and cluttered with unpolished jottings on everything from tourist disorientation to the ways in which specialists in Vinnie's field relate to real children; and the characters are both overwrought and undeveloped. Even Lurie's keen ear for colloquial speech and her eye for revealing mannerisms frequently fail her: in characterizing Chuck and Rosemary, Lurie vacillates between joining Vinnie and Fred in their crude typecasting—Chuck talks in an exaggerated Western twang; Rosemary flutters and giggles and pouts—and taking them to task for it.

All of Lurie's novels are programmatic: like most comic writers she relies upon formal contrivances to heighten irony, to create startling juxtapositions, to make a larger point about the individual's accommodations to the demands of society. In *The War Between the Tates* Erica and Brian's marital battles were punctuated by a sonorous voice-over narration which compared them to the social and political upheavals accompanying the Vietnam War. In *Only Children* Lurie failed in her occasional attempts to blend the naïveté of two little girls with her own stinging cynicism. But Erica and Brian were energetically and realistically drawn; and Lolly and Mary Ann, if somewhat limited as narrators, brought a fresh glimpse into the old themes of marital boredom and infidelity. In both novels Lurie credibly evoked a chapter on American social history. Alas, in *Foreign Affairs* the characters are so unappealing and the contrivances of plot so labored that the ironies are leaden rather than leavening. And, its title notwithstanding, the only affairs she addresses here are carnal.

As for the lessons Lurie lays out, they are of the most rudimentary sociopsychological sort. Yet these two reputable professors are maddeningly slow learners. Fred, filled with self-love, can't find happiness until his obsession with what Lady Rosemary represents is replaced by a clear-eyed recognition of what she is. . . . It is during a game of charades—what else?—that he has his first vague glimmerings that Rosemary is not quite the fragile English flower she seems. Suddenly she and her cultivated friends appear raucous, even depraved. . . . Vinnie, for her part, filled with self-hate, must not only cease to see Chuck Mumpson as a source of revulsion and pity, but herself as well. . . . In the end, of course, it becomes clear to Fred that Lady Rosemary, far from representing "the best of England," actually embodies the destructive self-indulgence of a decadent class society; and to Vinnie that Chuck, who reminds her of all that's shameful and ugly in America, in fact personifies American openness and stolid decency.

Still, simplicities and stereotypes aside, Lurie is as deft as ever when she turns to the mortifications of romance. She is an uncannily accurate observer of the ambivalent emotions that enter into unconventional sexual alliances, and when she abandons her gimmicky plot devices and moral posturing, *Foreign Affairs* is funny, touching, and even suspenseful. As Fred's affair with Lady Rosemary is being consumed in horror (the final revelation scene is a weirdly appropriate combination of Hitchcock suspense and Lurie humor), Vinnie's affair with Chuck is being consummated in a moment of poignant farce. This odd couple is finally brought together thanks to a suitably ludicrous matchmaker: Chuck's plastic fold-up raincoat.

At last, a character with integrity. This homely garment not only has a perverse charm of its own, it also helps to transform Vinnie, the perpetually peevish man-hating snob, into a flustered, touchingly vulnerable woman. When Vinnie and Chuck first bump into each other in London, she disdainfully notes that he is wearing "a semi-transparent greenish plastic raincoat of the most repellent American sort," and registers it as an emblem of his personality: coarse, tasteless. Yet the raincoat comes to show Vinnie more about her own shortcomings than it does about Chuck's. Her hatred of it festers over the weeks, and she turns on it in furious embarrassment after Chuck's first bumbling embrace in her tiny kitchen, in which he knocks a bowl of watercress and avocado soup over them both: "If he only had a decent raincoat instead of that awful transparent plastic thing—she gives it a nasty look as it hangs in the hall—then he could wear that while his clothes dried, or even go home in it." In several quick scenes the raincoat explains Vinnie's social pretensions and fragile dignity; and in the scenes that follow, it gives credence to the evolution of her contempt for Chuck into tolerance, affection, and—most remarkably of all—hearty sexual appetite.

In *Foreign Affairs* Lurie shows once again that she is a far-sighted observer of human fallibilities, but an odd kind of moralist. Hers is a particularly brutal form of mockery: she forces her characters into compromising positions and then denies them any real escape. The end of the novel superficially follows the traditional comic pattern—the characters are sent back home; the social order resumes—but Lurie doesn't think much of spiritual regeneration. (pp. 35-6)

Of course, neither Fred nor Vinnie has essentially changed at all: he is still impossibly obtuse, she has reverted to whining self-pity. This elaborate novel is more of an exercise in verbal and structural ingenuity than it is a full-fledged comedy or melodrama. The snugness has become oppressive, and the secrets Lurie invites us to share, no longer enticing, are for the most part trivial, sordid, and sad. (p. 36)

Dorothy Wickenden, "Love in London," in The New Republic, *Vol. 191, No. 15, October 8, 1984, pp. 34-6.*

CHARLES CHAMPLIN

In her new novel, *Foreign Affairs,* Lurie follows Virginia Miner, a spinster professor of English, specializing in children's literature at a New York state university suspiciously called Corinth (ah, Ithaca), who is off to London to research children's rhymes. . . .

Vinnie Miner is accompanied by a small, invisible dog that is the tangible embodiment of her self-pity (an allowable conceit in an imaginative 54-year-old academic, I expect, although I didn't so much accept it as admire Lurie's daring in making it almost credible.) . . .

Lurie's real focus, just beyond Vinnie herself, is the small segment of English society in which Vinnie and Fred move. Fred stumbles into an affair with an English actress, flaky as a baklava, named Rosemary Radley, daughter of an earl, star of a sitcom, scandalous and untidy, spiderlike at the center of a salon that is insubstantial as a web.

As she was good, and lethal, about some of the excesses of Los Angeles in the '60s, Lurie is wonderful, sharp and satiric, about present London and its trendiness, its fringe of short-time celebrities and savants, its snobberies and posturings, its clingings to a national and literary past that seems more distant all the while. Even the valorous Britain of wartime seems longer ago (Fred was there as a child) than the decades would indicate.

Lurie uses the present tense for present time, which can sometimes be awkward but is particularly useful here because both Vinnie and Fred carry uncommon loads of memory that fall nicely and clearly into past tense. (p. 1)

Lurie is a polished and sharp-eyed watcher of manners and mores, and *Foreign Affairs* is streaked with deft passages of insight and malice, comic but stopping short of farce and with an underlying regard for her principals. An everyday London of bus queues and rain is evoked without sentiment but with an implicit affection that Lurie could not quite summon for Los Angeles.

The novel is eventful and, beneath its rather oblique and subdued telling, even dramatic. (Rosemary is a case history.) Yet somehow the whole, on consideration, lacks the vigor of the parts, like a holiday that begins well and ends with four days of cold and damp. Vinnie heads home, her silent companion once again nipping at her heels. We have come to know the lady extremely well and by her nature we probably should have expected no more than a freshened stock of footnotes anyway. She is disappointed and so are we.

Just as Antonioni's motion pictures have sometimes demanded the question whether films about boring and bored people can themselves avoid being boring, *Foreign Affairs* invites speculation whether largely bloodless and unassertive characters can be made compelling company. The answer is less cheering than I wish it were. (pp. 1, 12)

Charles Champlin, in a review of "Foreign Affairs,"
in Los Angeles Times Book Review, *October 21,*
1984, pp. 1, 12.

An Excerpt from *Foreign Affairs*

It is 12:39 by the poison-green light of the digital alarm clock. Vinnie sighs and turns over in bed again, causing her nightgown to twist itself round her into a tight, wrinkled husk that resembles her thoughts. With an effort she revolves in the opposite direction, unwinding herself physically; then she begins to breathe slowly and rhythmically in an attempt to unwind herself mentally. One-out. Two-out. Three-out. Four—

The telephone rings. Vinnie startles, lifts her head, crawls across the bed, and gropes in the dark toward the extension, which rests on the carpet because her landlord has never provided a bedside table. Where the hell is it?

"Hello," she croaks finally, upside down and half out of the covers.

"Vinnie? This is Chuck. I guess I woke you up."

"Well yes, you did," she lies; then, abashed at the sound of this, adds, "Are you all right?"

"Yeh, sure."

"I hope you're not still upset about what I said. I don't know why I blew up like that; it was rude of me."

"No it wasn't," Chuck says. "I mean, that's why I called. I figured maybe you were right: maybe I oughta give London another chance before I lie down in front of a bus . . . Wal, so, if you're free sometime this week, I'll take you anywhere you say. You can pick a restaurant. I'll even try the opera, if I can get us some decent seats."

"Well . . ." With considerable difficulty Vinnie rights herself and crawls backward into bed, dragging the telephone and the comforter with her. "I don't know." If she refuses, she thinks, Chuck will go back to Oklahoma with his low opinion of London and of Vinnie Miner intact; and she will never see him again. Also she will miss a night at Covent Garden, where "decent seats" cost thirty pounds.

"Yes, why not," she hears herself say. "That'd be very nice."

For heaven's sake, what'd I do that for? Vinnie thinks after she has hung up. I don't even know what's on this week at Covent Garden. I must be half asleep, or out of my mind. But in spite of herself she is smiling.

MALCOLM BRADBURY

A critic once divided American writers into two camps, the Palefaces and the Redskins. The Redskins looked west, toward the frontier, responded to the more physical and natural aspects of life, and often wrote in a style which expressed raw experience rather than literary form. The Palefaces looked east, wrote of those peculiarly elusive areas in American life, society and manners, and were preoccupied with craft and formal brilliance.

British readers, often baffled in front of the Redskins, have been persistently attracted to the Palefaces, clasping some, like Henry James, firmly to their bosoms. Paleface writers may now be in decline in America, but there are a few left, one of the most finished and brilliant being Alison Lurie.

It is appropriate that her work, with its sharp observant comedy, great intelligence and exacting and satirical view of human nature, has always been well received in Britain. Her books are formidably well made, though that phrase is uncomfortable and can make her sound dangerously old-fashioned.

So does another phrase which reviewers have favoured, "novelist of manners", and she confesses that it causes her embarrassment. Nonetheless it remains useful, for her seven novels . . . collectively form a biting record of American social, moral and sexual mores from the early 1960s (her first novel, *Love and Friendship,* appeared in 1962) to the present. . . .

It is therefore no surprise that the dustjackets of her books usually compare her with Jane Austen, Henry James and Edith Wharton. But the older novels of manners were written in periods of relative social stability. The elusiveness and volatility of modern manners make them far harder to fix. We buy and spend history at a remarkable rate, and this challenges not just the observation but the endurance of the novelist. . . .

Satire, done well, is usually a product of a very precise literary skill and a good deal of rigorous intelligence. Lurie's novels please by having both. She might be called an academic author; she studied at Radcliffe, wrote a thesis on Jacobean comedy, spent much time in academic life and is still a part-time Professor of English at Cornell University. . . .

It so happens that Cornell has been a stronghold of structuralism and deconstruction, those two powerful movements in criticism and philosophy that have reshaped the spirit of many English departments in the direction of an organized rigour that has not always been entirely favourable to the study of literature as an act of constructive intelligence. A few cunning asides about all this are to be glimpsed in *Foreign Affairs.* Alison Lurie also reveals here a pleasure in teaching that comes partly from establishing the writer as a real presence and writing as a considered and deeply professional activity. . . .

Mrs Lurie's novels explore the dangerous relations between the imaginary and the real with exact observation and cunning intelligence. Perhaps it is these qualities, not in enormously long supply in contemporary fiction, which help her books travel the Atlantic so readily. Alison Lurie herself travels it fairly regularly, living part of the year in Ithaca, New York, when she is teaching, part in Florida and part in a flat somewhere behind Lord's cricket ground in London.

Her own international theme becomes the subject of *Foreign Affairs* in which an untypical heroine, a 57-year-old professor of children's literature—the kind of person who in stories does not deserve a story—encounters in a more or less contemporary London the contradictory nature of British images and the confusions of British manners.

The book is discreet and in some respects deliberately low-key, just like its heroine. Romance is what fiction gives us all too easily. Lurie's famous observation has to take purchase on material which, as she readily confesses, is harder to handle than American material. As Henry James said, the American observing British life often has a sense of too much of the superfluous and not enough of the necessary. But Mrs Lurie's venture on to the vaunted scene of Europe is cunningly contemporary.

As *The Nowhere City* caught the cultural conflict between the American East and California, *Foreign Affairs* looks again at an old map of literary and emotional relations and revises them with the usual rigour. *Foreign Affairs* is Mrs Lurie's inquiry into the romance of Europe, from a writer who knows that romance is the one thing we all need but can never trust. And rightly so; in an age of soft dreams, we need her hard edge.

Malcolm Bradbury, "The Paleface Professor," in The Times, *London, January 19, 1985, p. 6.*

RICHARD BOSTON

As a novelist in the line of Henry James (though, thank goodness, without James's stylistic convolutions) [Alison Lurie in *Foreign Affairs* makes it] clear from the start that we are in for a tale about the cultural clash as west meets east. But will the encounter go to show again the innocence of the American abroad and the corrupting decadence of the Old World, or will Lurie come up with a new twist?

The first of the marvellously differentiated Americans we meet (the lady boarding the plane) is self-pitying, very little, dowdy, unmarried—"the sort of person that no one ever notices", Lurie comments in her brutally reductionist Jane Austen manner.... England is for her "the imagined and desired country", formed over [a] quarter of a century from such ingredients as the books of Beatrix Potter, Anthony Powell and Masefield's *The Box of Delights*. Even frequent visits to the imagined country have failed to alter this image. By contrast, other Americans, teachers of English, to be met in the book "with the bitterness of disillusioned lovers . . . complain that contemporary Britain is cold, wet and overpriced: its natives unfriendly . . . past her prime . . . worn out and old: and, like most of the old, boring."

What is odd about this comment (about most of which one can agree or disagree to taste) is the verifiable fact implied in the word "overpriced". For some years now the poor old pound has been in such a bad state against the dollar that American professors on sabbatical have been able to spend money like drunken sailors, and without the penalty of a financial hangover. Yet in this book the Yanks seem to be really quite hard up. This strange state of affairs gives me the feeling (rightly or wrongly) that the book was written some time ago and only recently revised.

Not only do the exchange rates seem unfavourable to the Americans in a way we have not known for years, but also the prices seem rather odd. Is it possible to buy a theatre programme in London for ten pence? . . . Even the Americans themselves seem rather old-fashioned. Vinnie Miner's chance travel companion, Chuck Mumpson, is at once splendidly comic and strangely sympathetic, but with his Wild West clothes, fringed jacket, shoelace tie and all, bandoleered with cameras, and wearing a transparent plastic raincoat (which Vinnie likens to a male contraceptive) he surely comes from the imagery of cartoonists of more than 20 years ago.

The book is full of such strange little puzzles. The suitably Jamesian name of Virginia (or Vinnie) Miner nudges the reader's thoughts towards virginity (which suits her celibate state) while Miner suggests not only smallness (as in minor) but also the diligent mole-like mining of the researching scholar. She writes under the name of V. A. Miner. One does not have to be a virtuoso crossword-puzzle solver to spot that V. A. Miner is an anagram of Minerva, the Roman goddess of wisdom.

But what's the point? Is this a true clue or a red herring? Will V. A. Miner prove exceptionally wise, or is the name an example of that commodity so highly prized by academic critics, irony? The answer, as far as I can see, is neither. She turns

out to be sometimes wise, sometimes a little foolish, in fact more like the rest of us than the goddess Minerva.

Perhaps I've missed something. Alison Lurie is such a meticulous writer that one can normally assume that when she does something it is for a reason. . . .

[The] book does have errors of detail that are surprising in such a sharply observant writer, and we are left with a lot of loose ends that reinforce my uneasy feeling that *Foreign Affairs* is somehow incomplete. As expected, there are some nicely sharp-clawed observations of English behaviour (rather in the manner of early Angus Wilson) but I was a little disappointed at how lightly we were let off compared with, say, the Californians of *The Nowhere City*. Perhaps Alison Lurie, too, like Vinnie Miner, is a little starry-eyed about England.

Richard Boston, "Minerva in London," in Punch, *Vol. 288, No. 7520, January 23, 1985, p. 52.*

LORNA SAGE

[*Foreign Affairs* is] warm, clever and funny—the kind of novel that elicits a conspiratorial glow from the start because it flatters the reader unmercifully. You're assumed to be witty and literate, you're told (indirectly, of course) how very wide awake you are, and you're congratulated for being (on the other hand and after all) so sensible as to prefer your metafiction in traditional form. In short, the reader turns out to be a nicely rounded character, well-buttered with irony.

The plot is about being on sabbatical. Two American academics, neatly contrasted and with a distinctly Jamesian aura about them, are on study leave in London. . . . Though Vinnie and Fred work at the same Ivy League college, they have little to do with each other. Their point is to set up a pattern of symmetries and oppositions—pretty and plain, male and female, naïve and knowing, young and oldish, (possible) hero and (probable) minor character, and so forth. . . .

What Alison Lurie is up to is taking an eccentric (Dickens, not Austen) comic character, and making her indecorously, inventively changeable. The traditional types haven't gone away, they're being put together differently. So following on the farewell to English literature we're offered tongue-in-cheek a George Eliot optics metaphor ("each of us is always a central point round which the entire world whirls in radiating perspective"). And indeed "semi-literate" Chuck (who is looking for ancestors in the West Country) has already been given a Hardy-style monologue about the reality of unhistoric lives: "they grew up and plowed and milked and cut the hay and ate dinner and drank the local beer at the Cock and Hen; and they fell in love. . .".

This kind of double-take is what gives the novel its conspiratorial quality. The plot takes both Vinnie and Fred (who turns out to be very much the minor character, of course) back to America, and to their American-ness. At the same time, the writing echoes and re-echoes with the (English) literary past, transformed but not jettisoned. Miss Lurie's characters smuggle enormous amounts of overweight baggage back with them—though (like Fido) it's all in the mind. *Foreign Affairs* is a novel that doesn't exactly embody the continuities it is about; rather, it proposes them, fleshed out in fancy. . . .

[Alison Lurie has] extraordinary powers of collusion—so that (for instance) you find yourself at times knowing the plot in advance (I'm thinking of a particularly Dickensian bit involving a phantom cleaning lady called Mrs Harris) and not minding, feeling instead rather pleased, as though you made it up yourself. And if this writer/reader relationship remains (as ever) unconsummated, if the future of Anglo-American literary relations stays in the future (''Why shouldn't she imagine herself as an explorer standing on the edge of some landscape as yet unmapped by literature . . .?'')—then that too has its point. Isn't the ''special relationship'' just like that, at once embarrassingly intimate and unreal?

Lorna Sage, "Adventures in the Old World," in The Times Literary Supplement, *No. 4270, February 1, 1985, p. 109.*

MARILYN BUTLER

Foreign Affairs is probably Alison Lurie's best novel to date, certainly it is a triumph, and much of its success stems from its accomplished plotting. Lurie has known from the first how to tell a story brilliantly through the consciousness of a woman who in type and circumstance resembles the author herself. The classic Lurie heroine is attractive, intelligent, well-intentioned, but also very fallible, which becomes clear as she is subjected to an alert, wry appraisal. But problems arise from Lurie's tendency to rely on what is really an extended character-portrait as the vehicle of narration. This led in some earlier books to a slow development of plot, at times to virtual stasis, and—in spite of the presence of issues like campus demonstrations, the Vietnam War and the emergence of feminist protest—to a narrowing of social horizons. It was hard to maintain the early novels' intended critiques of the mental horizons of the educated middle-class American woman while the narrative remained spoken in the voice of such a woman; the hippy generation and the hardernosed academic were heard all right in the dialogue, but the heroine's insistent Ivy League tones easily drowned them. Here the use of a double plot neatly resolves that difficulty. Fred's more active and varied love-affair makes the novel funnier, brighter, more compellingly readable than the early Luries. And instead of distracting the reader from Vinnie's emotional experience, which should and does remain the heart of the book, the presence of the Fred plot helps to focus it. We have an unusually objective view of the heroine, who through the conversations of Rosemary's friends evolves for us into a quaint, eccentric middle-aged American, not the double of the English lady she herself likes to imagine. This means that she grows more endearing to the reader, who also gives her credit for being more reflective and self-critical than Fred, a more fully-engaged researcher and a more committed lover. Vinnie's affair and its dénouement would not move us as it does if the love-affair of the more presentable couple had not been developed first.

Not that the Fred plot is essentially conventional or naturalistic, as the early Lurie plots tended rather flatly to be. Just as Fred's adventures land him in a Jamesian country house party, where charades are played as an elegant cover for sexual misdemeanours, so they also take him back into a world reminiscent of the 18th-century London he is supposed to be working on. Gay is the author of 'Town Eclogues', anti-pastorals set in a fallen, seedy urban world, and, more famously, of *The Beggar's Opera,* whose hero Captain Macheath lives among villains and loves two women, who each love him more faithfully in return. Rosemary resembles not Lucy Lockit so much as Fielding's corrupt society woman Lady Bellaston: though, as an actress, and also as it turns out a schizophrenic, she can shift-shape into one of the grotesque and sexually predatory

older women beloved of 18th-century literature and caricature, a Wishfort or Slipslop or Mother Needham. (pp. 5-6)

The nuanced and naturalistically-observed middle-aged love-affair between Vinnie and Chuck shows the kind of writing Lurie still perhaps does best, but her bold and freely-handled alternative plot enormously widens its range of suggestion. Released from programmatic naturalism, she can introduce characters who contrast strongly with one another, while the naturalistic novel demands that characters who are supposed to be denizens of the same social world should seem broadly alike. Though as usual her protagonist is genteel, Vinnie's gentility and that of her world repeatedly come up against the philistinism of Chuck and his daughter Barbie, or seem far away from Fred's wife Roo, whose marital offence was to feature several penises, only one of them her husband's, in an exhibition of her photographs. Rosemary, the stereotypical lady, hitherto a model for Vinnie, can drunkenly insult her, and put Fred off by having unflushed turds in her lavatory. Equally different from what Vinnie believes in and usually persuades herself to see are the novel's children, disagreeable variants on the picturesque figures of folktale: the Vogelers' charmless one-year-old Jakie, a 'retarded infant troll', or, in his regulation toddler overalls, 'a dwarf railway engineer', and, more disturbing to Vinnie, the pubescent Camden Town schoolgirl Mary Mahoney, a punk goblin who demands payment before she will recite her obscene playground rhymes. Not only is this variety of tone a relief: it operates cunningly as the objective correlative of the psychic drama inside Vinnie Miner-Minor's head, as she tries to sustain her childhood and to defend her priorities.

Foreign Affairs is a novel of economical and effective dialogues, and of insights into British linguistic and social practice, the conceit of the young, handsome and sexually successful, the snobberies of, say, theatre people, and London literary journalists, and American academics. It is also an urbane but unironic study of that Murdochian topic, sexuality in clever older people. In short, the structure and method are in most respects like the opening scene, deeply conventional—and not necessarily the worse for that. For, however we may praise originality, it is at least as important that art should be conventional. . . .

If, asked to say what *Foreign Affairs* is about, you replied by narrating the romance of Vinnie and Chuck, you would have told a sentimental tale apparently designed to prove that simple people can be nicer than clever people, and that real life matters more than pretence. No one reading the Vinnie episode alongside the Rosemary plot would interpret the whole novel as having so banal a message, but some may reasonably suspect that here a literary conservative is making a case for a naturalistic method, and an old-fashioned moralist for humane values. More, and worse, she seems to insist on something nowadays intellectually unfashionable: on the existence outside the confined world of her fiction, not of a proliferating series of fictions, but of a stable and knowable real world. And if the world as Chuck knows it can be allowed to disperse Vinnie's elaborately-built fantasies, the plot conveys a view of reality which does not flatter artists and writers. To put it in an old way, if all everyone can ever do is to make mental constructs of reality, artists as the most dedicated system-builders become leading citizens: but if, as Plato proposed, the 'real' in some sense exists, and artists merely fake it, then there is no place for them in the ideal republic. A number of arguments can be tried to defend the 'truth' of what the artist does, but most high-minded claims are out for the naturalist, whose object is to copy mundanity and trivia. It's hard to tell whether the present low critical repute of naturalism really stems from its being too indulgent to society, as Roland Barthes maintained, or from its being (as observation suggests) less than indulgent to art. At any rate, it is in the anti-professional underground that Lurie has enlisted, by claiming the freedom to continue working with plots in which artists and academics fail to score. *Foreign Affairs* does what many intelligent works do: it writes a commentary on its own mode, and makes space in the future for more books of this mixed but predominantly traditional kind. At the same time it imposes the burden of the exceptionally good book upon its author: next time she will have to do better still, and out performing the Lurie of *Foreign Affairs* is not going to be easy. (p. 6)

> *Marilyn Butler, "Amor Vincit Vinnie," in* London Review of Books, *February 21, 1985, pp. 5-6.*

JAMES LASDUN

The very same formula that won Anita Brookner's *Hotel du Lac* its Booker Prize seems to have worked its magic again for Alison Lurie in *Foreign Affairs*. The acclaim has been lavish and unanimous, beginning with the back-cover puffs; John Fowles awards it a position on the same shelf as Henry James and Edith Wharton, Mary Gordon notes its brilliant depiction of a new, post-Jamesian generation of Americans in England, and Gabriele Annan remarks on "the discreet brilliance with which the author chooses every word."

It is difficult to challenge such plaudits without overstating the case against them. I would certainly not wish to imply that *Foreign Affairs* is ever less than an entertaining, finely constructed novel. (p. 49)

Alison Lurie skilfully milks [the] brush between American academics and the English smart set for its yield of cross-cultural tensions and misunderstandings, generating from it a plot that is consistently absorbing, a series of vividly described British scenes (the Country House party, tea at Fortnum's, drinks in Mayfair . . .) and a collection of well-drawn, if familiar, English and American types.

A polished, engaging novel then. But despite its very visible aspirations to something grander than that (one of its characters repeatedly imagines himself to be inside a Henry James novel—a piece of authorial presumption that John Fowles *et al.* seem to have accepted with amazing lack of protest), it doesn't, I think, amount to a particularly significant work of art. Aside from the dubious worth of even *trying* to write like Henry James almost a century after the event, and the unlikeliness of producing anything other than pastiche, there is too much in the book that is either clumsy in a way that James could never be, or quite simply *wrong*.

Alison Lurie's last book was an examination of the meaning of dress, and she appears to pride herself on a depth and precision in her cultural detailing. She cares about getting people's clothes, accessories, mannerisms, speech habits, and so forth, exactly right. Even more, she cares about the way in which these things differ in England and America. When she *is* right, however, she tends either to be ploddingly so (for example, taking the reader doggedly through the various colours of the London telephone directories), or else to sound like a prim guide to British etiquette for socially ambitious American visitors—"Most of the guests, as is usual at warm-weather London parties, are drinking white wine"; "the polite British are taught as children that it is rude to stare." She slips into tourist-brochure language in some of her descriptions of places—"the old-fashioned British elegance of Wheeler's", and into the rag-trade's debased vocabulary, for clothes—"the coat she's wearing now, with its romantic gathered hood. . . ." And then there are the mistakes: a cockney houskeeper, as impersonated by the aristocratic actress, using the Americanism "faggots"; a child's game called "cops and villains"; a snobbish littérateur referring to one of his titled friends as "Lord George" (intimacy with the Grand is implied precisely by *omitting* the title, rather than mentioning it). . . .

Minor solecisms perhaps, but in a book where the complexities of social minutiae are given a great deal more attention than those of individual characters (all of whom are stock-in-trade regulars, with countless appearances in novels of this nature), such carelessness is at best irritating, at worst a sign of fatally undependable powers of observation. (pp. 49-50)

> *James Lasdun, "The Great or the Good," in* Encounter, *Vol. LXV, No. 2, July-August, 1985, pp. 47-51.**

Sharon Olds

The Dead and the Living

The National Book Critics Circle Award: Poetry

American poet and critic.

In her two poetry collections, *Satan Says* (1980) and *The Dead and the Living* (1984), Olds candidly recollects her harrowing childhood while confronting such issues as sexuality, power, and anger. In graphic physical and emotional detail, Olds's confessional poems tell of a cruel grandfather, a drunken, violent father, an embittered mother, and an abusive sister. Critics suggest that in this unflinching probe of personal traumas, Olds is fuelled by a drive to exorcise and transmute her experience—to see and to celebrate the victim who has become the survivor. While some critics have placed Olds in the tradition of Sylvia Plath, both in her haunting focus on the family, especially the father, and in her comparisons of political crimes to personal sufferings, they also note that Olds's strong, proud tone is less tormented than that of her predecessor and that her poetry is more accessible.

The Dead and the Living is divided into two sections: "Poems for the Dead" contains imagistic poems, many of which are based on photographs of public atrocities; "Poems for the Living" focuses on familial relationships and experiences. The sections are thematically related, pointing out the universality of violence, injustice, and suffering. But through the poems about motherhood and her children, Olds suggests the human potential for warmth, understanding, and affirmation.

Olds uses a direct, powerful idiom, often employing graphic details of violent and erotic acts. While some critics noted excesses of shocking language in *Satan Says,* they generally concur that in *The Dead and the Living* Olds has gained control of her emotional subject matter, creating a more restrained yet disturbing vision of humanity. Although some critics believe that the connections Olds makes between public and private cruelties are underdeveloped, most agree that Olds's poems about her family are powerfully evocative. *The Dead and the Living* is highly regarded for the humor that tempers the work's darker aspects; as the National Book Critics Circle remarked in its announcement of Olds's award: "Olds writes of private and public traumas with a fierce commitment to the vulnerable—and with a saving wit. Hers is a voice like no one else's."

(See also *CLC,* Vol. 32 and *Contemporary Authors,* Vol. 101.)

LINDA McCARRISTON

Content is what will draw strongly positive or negative first reactions from readers of **The Dead and the Living,** especially in the poems about family, such as **"Possessed,"** which is addressed to the speaker's parents: ". . . I can look in the eyes of any stranger and / find you there, in the rich swimming bottom-of-the-barrel brown, or in the / blue that reflects from

© 1986 Thomas Victor

the knife's blade, / and I smell you always, the dead cigars and / Chanel in the mink. . . ." In this and other reproachful childhood reminiscences, Olds gives us the heart of her book, the seminal experience out of which a victim has created a survivor.

Though timeliness of theme must account in part for the success of . . . [*The Dead and the Living*], the work's wholeness transcends the limitations of any patently confessional or political mode. Refusing to stop at "her pain" or "her group's pain," Olds presses outward to an inclusive understanding of suffering in the nuclear family. We endure reading the most painful of these poems because we hear in them not the voice of the victim—the child—but that of the adult daughter with children of her own, looking both forward and back, demanding justice.

Justice, however, with a difference. The moral intelligence that is at work here—lucid, aggressive, unfashionably opinionated—offers a lavish eroticism that embraces family, friends, strangers, *and* self. This leonine maternalism/sexuality rights the wrongs done to Eros by uniting sexuality and justice as if the two had never parted company in the first place. Thus *people* are loved in these poems, specifically and vividly, located and known by their textures and smells, their ripening and decay. (p. 899)

In *The Dead and the Living,* family becomes an analogue to a larger world. Extending pity and outrage to the most distant victims of oppression, she likewise extends these feelings, and demands them, under her own roof: relationships of power, Olds argues, though peopled with different figures, are everywhere the same. The volume opens with a series of set pieces from photographs of anonymous individuals suffering acts of political violence in remote times or places. In each of these the reader senses the poet envisioning her own child or husband, or herself. By the close of the book—in the tumble of her son and daughter, asleep in the car's back seat, their heads together ". . . in the dark solitary / power of the dream—the dream of ruling the world,"—the political paradigm has been brought to its nearest, smallest enactment.

Though this consciousness is acutely political, it is not theoretical. No aphorism nor generalization undermines the authority of each life and act in the book. . . . The poems reside in the power of the self-evident, and the plumb of their emotional logic is inevitable.

The work's indigenous feel, coupled with its ingenuous assumption of its own "universality," will be taken by some as its major flaw. Others may find the emotional/moral position of the speaker insupportable—judgmental, self-righteous. But tired of irony and ethical ennui, tired of the impressive, forgettable poem, I welcome the integrity of Olds's voice: a poet's poems here become people's poems; dogma returns to its proper residence in the feeling flesh; love and power lose themselves in a sexual embrace and bring forth justice. No ideas but in beings. (pp. 899-900)

> *Linda McCarriston, in a review of "The Dead and the Living," in* The Georgia Review, *Vol. XXXVIII, No. 4, Winter, 1984, pp. 899-900.*

DAVID LEAVITT

Many of the poems in *The Dead and the Living* . . . describe with acute precision an image or situation so startling that I was inclined to turn my eyes from the page. Olds shies away from nothing: not the grisly torture of a Chilean child in front of his parents; not the "dark, scalloped shapes" of a fetus in a toilet; not the incipient sexual smell, "like peach brandy," of her adolescent daughter's pajamas. As she writes in **"The Issues,"** a poem about a Rhodesian baby sliced by a bayonet, "Don't talk to me about / politics. I've got eyes, man." Her poetry focuses on the primacy of the image rather than the "issues" which surround it, and her best work exhibits a lyrical acuity which is both purifying and redemptive. In **"The Takers,"** the narrator recalls her older sister seizing her bed, straddling her body, and peeing on her, "the dark gold / smell of her urine spreading through my room." This is a harrowing memory, and Olds spares herself and her readers no sensual detail. She sees description as a means to catharsis, and the result is impossible to forget.

In **"The Eye,"** one of her "Poems for the Dead," Olds writes of "My bad grandfather," who

> . . . wouldn't give my
> sister any supper, he wouldn't give us
> any
> light to read by. He sat alone
> in front of the hearth, and drank

Olds recalls the grandfather's glass eye,

> and how at night in the big double bed
> he slept facing his wife, and how the
> limp
> hole, where his eye had been, was open
> towards her on the pillow . . .

This image suggests a staring contest between the poet and the gaping horror of that "limp hole," a battle to see who will look away first. But the poet's anger empowers her not to give in to her fears and in the end provides escape from them:

> somewhere in me too is the path
> down to the creek gleaming in the dark,
> a way out of there.

"Son," one of the "Poems for the Living," employs a different kind of frankness. "Coming home from the women-only bar," the narrator is drawn to her son's bedroom, where she watches him as he sleeps. Her pleasure in him leads to the prayer with which the poem concludes:

> Let there be enough
> room for this life: the head, lips,
> throat, wrist, hips, cock,
> knees, feet. Let no part go
> unpraised. Into any new world we
> enter, let us
> take this man.

The narrator drinks in her son's masculinity (an implicit confirmation of her own female fertility) almost as an act of replenishment. Once again, it is not an idea (of a women-only bar or a world without men) which concerns her, but a revivifying image.

Sharon Olds is enormously self-aware; her poetry is remarkable for its candor, its eroticism, and its power to move. But I suspect that her impulse to stare down and articulate painful images masks a less intelligible response. I miss the inchoate and the ineffable, those moments when one senses that the poet herself may not know what she's saying. Olds's poems tend to be so complete that they leave the reader little to question or ponder. In her universe, anything can be understood if one only stares at it long enough; I kept wanting a glimpse of the unknowable. (pp. 4-5)

> *David Leavitt, in a review of "The Dead and the Living," in* VLS, *No. 24, March, 1984, pp. 4-5.*

PAULA BONNELL

Sharon Olds writes about a woman's life as women have always known their lives—in relation to other lives—and she does it in verse so plain, so dark, so touched with gleams of light, so simple in its candor as to seem inevitable. The central truth around which [the poems in *The Dead and the Living*] collect is that to be human is to hurt and be hurt, whether in the public way by war and political violence, or in the dark private stairwells and dully glowing firesides of the family.

Her book includes such darkly funny poems as **"Rite of Passage"** (about a six-year-old's birthday party with the boys portrayed as "short men," "small bankers," "Generals") and **"Bestiary"** (in which a child and mother discuss people mating with animals) and also poems of harsh and tender beauty: **"Ecstasy," "My Father's Breasts."** But no one poem—be it such a wrenchingly sweet poem as **"New Mother"** (about desire and forbearance) or such a powerful and funny poem as **"Sex Without Love"**—presents her full power. That power results in part from the accumulation of emotional force around her key words of "dark," "gold," "red," "glittering," "gleaming," "glistening," and "glowing," and her key figures of fish, eggs, burning, cutting, and stroking. Together these portray the chiaroscuro of human relations, the dependence and power that are the cross currents resolved in neither her work nor our lives.

> *Paula Bonnell, in a review of "The Dead and the Living," in* Ms., *Vol. XIII, No. 1, July, 1984, p. 34.*

MARY KINZIE

[The] poems in Sharon Olds's **The Dead and the Living** are univocal, swift, impassioned, completely "sincere," and eminently public poems. Her sort of brevity and cruel punch will appeal to that large public who do not as a rule read poetry, hence have toughened sensibilities and a short attention span. But her virtues in this regard, in getting through and making an impression, are also her dangers. Although the poet's language is meager and hard and especially well adapted, with its tough, conversational sound, for declaring incontrovertible fact, it tends to be unrhythmical; the sentences repeatedly stiffen toward the same sorts of climactic statements about guilt, savagery, and pain. She is clearly writing in the tradition of Sylvia

Cover of The Dead and the Living, *by Sharon Olds. Knopf, 1984. Courtesy of Alfred A. Knopf, Inc.*

Plath *(Ariel)* and Louise Glück *(First-born)*, although she is yet more stylized, reduced, simplified, and in a curious way purer than either.

But despite the intensity of her rage, the nice shock of the eroticism, and the severity of the acts against human flesh that everywhere threaten—all of which suggest burden and struggle—I am not entirely convinced that the poet's approach is not too easy, automatic, even soft. She becomes sentimental about the penis, "eager and so / trusting you could weep." She is so keen to merge with the bodies of all relatives and beloveds that she wants to *be* her grandparents' act of copulation, and somehow to embody the physical brunt of her bearish alcoholic father even as she and her husband make love (this creates difficulties: "you / enter him as a woman, my sex like a / wound in his body"). And she makes the error of concrete transfer, confusing minuteness of particulars with accuracy of characterization: really, her parents' smoking bowels and pearly glands might just as well belong to her grandparents or next-door neighbors; anatomy is neither distinct personality nor even material energy. The spiritual component of being in her poems is even perhaps too often left to strong visual tableau, the poetic text relegated to a passive lens, and the moment of truth, a snapshot of victim (or oppressor) gazing right into the camera. Nevertheless, it were churlish to ignore their stricken appeals. Two men in a turn-of-the-century photograph taken after the imperial Boxer Uprising against the West and before Sun Yat-Sen's populist revolution (although their allegiance is not clear) have been nailed to two horrifying contraptions that cause their bodies to twist into painfully grotesque postures. Then their crucifixes have been leaned against a wall in a pre-performance gloom like garden tools or stage props. One of them is asleep. They are awaiting execution:

> They'll be shouldered up over the crowd and
> carried through the screaming. The sleeper will wake.
> The twisted one will fly above the faces, his
> garment rippling.
> Here there is still the backstage quiet,
> the dark at the bottom of the wall, the props
> leaning in the grainy half-dusk.
> He looks at us in silence. He says
> *Save me, there is still time.*

The poem ["**Ideographs**"] bears the epigraph, "a photograph of China, 1905," which makes the temporality of the last appeal particularly rending.

Olds explores that threshold of sentient adult behavior just prior to the stage of concerted thought about being-in-the-world. She takes everything personally. She makes the world-beyond an analogy illustrated from her local experience. After a time spent upon this threshold, where the open sensibility of the woman to her private relationships is carried over to public attitudes, humanizing, domesticating, and bringing home the implications of geopolitics for the starving child in Turkey or Russia, for the southern black, the condemned Chinese men, and the Chilean dissenter, she begins to translate the exorbitant automatic hatred one feels when the weak and tender are violated by "Forces" beyond one's grasp, back to the domestic realm. The enmity, now no longer directed against even so unspecified and amorphous a villain as that violating the men in **"Ideographs,"** is transformed into a rage against the household oppressors. Thus the domestic emotions, sources of nascent political response, are channeled back roughly and prematurely into the family romance before having taken on breadth or sophistication, as in the poem ["**The Departure**"] comparing her father to the puppet Shah of Iran:

> You knew us no more than he knew them,
> his lowest subjects, his servants, and we were
> silent before you like that, bowing
> backwards, not speaking, not eating unless we were
> told to eat, the glass jammed to our
> teeth and tilted like a brass funnel in the
> soundproof cells of Teheran.

The tenor of the comparison somewhat trivializes the enormous vehicle.

Not only do public and private mirror each other, they implicate the same evil, although the poet cannot quite name it. The closest she comes to evoking the monster of Force is to imagine the guard, historically German, currently, Latin American, to and by whom all atrocity is permitted and craved. In this, the poet follows the sensationalist novel of Robert Stone, *A Flag for Sunrise,* and the more parabolic J. M. Coetzee's *Waiting for the Barbarians.* Doubting her own bravery even when her children are threatened ("It is all I have wanted to do, / to stand between them and pain"), she unwittingly concentrates on the victim from the tormentor's point of view. The transfer from victim to tormentor is most evident in "**Things That Are Worse Than Death**" when she ponders the information given her by Margaret Randall, editor, poet, and longtime resident of Mexico, about Chilean guards torturing members of a young family in front of each other "'as they like to do.'" The eyes of each family member in turn rest upon the guards' acts— tableau, paralyzed stasis, stunned vision, and harsh gazing reach their most electric form here, as the way the helpless gaze touches the hurt ones parodies the unmentionable brutalities that touch, press upon, and invade the victims like sewage (Olds's simile), like something worse than death.

Rhetorically and imaginatively the poems in the volume are dependent on the frisson, when more violent suffering subsides. It is as if Sylvia Plath's "Cut" were the model for the sudden little thrill, when, owing to its extreme pitch and prolonged siege, Plath's poem "Lesbos" could no longer be borne. Like Plath and Louise Glück, Sharon Olds turns the skills of cooking and nurture against her tribal tutors in metaphors of occasionally devastating success. "**Burn Center**" is illustrative, about a hospital ward the rich mother has donated, where children luckier than the speaker can be salved, bathed, cooled, quenched, and made whole again. She, however, because of the years spent next to the "hot griddle" of her mother's affection in "the burning / room of her life," was one of the walking wounded, her flesh coming off her like well-done pork meat, "and no one gave me / a strip of gauze, or a pat of butter to / melt on my crackling side." A stunning metaphor, but after so many single-explosion poems, the question of redundancy of effect arises, as does the further question about the straitened scope of the individual poem and its straitened prosody (which is to say, its lineation). Sharon Olds has adapted with great success several basic techniques of dramatizing metaphor and closed the door to the rest of aesthetic possibility. Nor can we argue that there would be a *better* way to frame or to narrate or to lineate these poems, because such arguing ignores the compositional process in which the making of tropes, the use of the lexicon, the complexity and variety of the sentences, and the lines themselves—all operate simultaneously, in a kind of tightly variable musical suspension. We can only say that, in reading this volume, we do not quite enjoy the sense of a full keyboard in use. (pp. 41-3)

Mary Kinzie, in a review of "The Dead and the Living," in The American Poetry Review, *Vol. 13, No. 5, September-October, 1984, pp. 41-3.*

JAMES FINN COTTER

Confessional poetry becomes *True Confessions* in Sharon Olds' [*The Dead and the Living*]. Her book presents a cycle of public and private instances of suffering and death, but it exploits the people it describes and sensationalizes events, although her family must be a real rogue's gallery of weirdos. Grandfather and father were hate-filled drunks and their wives their bitter opponents. The author writes of her own children carrying the same seeds of self-destruction which she is intent on rooting out before they grow up poisoned. In many poems sex organs keep popping up, menstrual blood flows, copulation thrives, girls pee on one another and boys play war games. Everything is physical—which is good—but these bodies have no souls. Olds keeps upping the stakes but her bluff doesn't work. The symbolic stuff of literature, its grace and strength are missing; she ends by bringing to poetry the personal violence that already perverts so many other areas of our culture. (p. 503)

James Finn Cotter, "Poetry Marathon," in The Hudson Review, *Vol. XXXVII, No. 3, Autumn, 1984, pp. 496-507.**

LINDA GREGERSON

The pleasures of [*The Dead and the Living*]—those it takes in the world and those we take in the poems—are frankly erotic. The imagery is voluptuous and near-at-hand, the voice direct and richly modulated, the conceits—of mountain climbing in "**Ecstasy**" or grade-school mathematics in "**The One Girl at the Boys' Party**"—are limpid and readily assimilable. The background narrative, as in Olds's first book, belongs to family romance and sexual coming of age. The body is her credo and her inexhaustible source of metaphor. None of its dramas— puberty, aging, childbirth, hunger, mutilation, miscarriage, sleep, arousal—is beyond her clear-eyed powers of transcription: even a child lost in the fourth week of pregnancy can find a body in these poems, can float for its wrenching moment as "dark, scalloped shapes" "in the pale/green swaying water of the toilet." . . . Olds is an eloquent celebrant—I know no contemporary her equal here—of sexual love and its extrapolation in a mother's erotic ties to her children. She also, perhaps inadvertently, records the radical invasiveness of erotic proprietorship: Olds takes in these poems an owner's liberties with her son's erections and her daughter's immanent pubescence. Such causes and such a gift for celebration are enviable, and are meant to be: much of this poet's work might be described as a poem in her previous volume was titled—"**The Language of the Brag**." Displaying a connoisseur's way with the sensuous image, an unabashed advocacy of the flesh, and a seemingly uncensored penetration of domestic life and its progressive revision of female consciousness, these poems can afford to be free with their clarity, as a beautiful woman can afford to be free with photographers.

In the first of five sections in *The Dead and the Living*—the "Public" half of "Poems for the Dead"—immediacy and passion afford insufficient guidance, despite the white heat of the poet's protest over a murdered Rhodesian mother and child: "Just don't tell me about the issues . . . I've got eyes, man." . . . Few readers would wish to tamper with the general lines of partisanship in these anti-elegies, espousing as they do the victims of famine, of war, of political torture (in Iran, in China, in Chile), of racial hatred, and of sexual exploitation (**"The Death of Marilyn Monroe"**), but our ready-made consensus is somehow part of the problem. These poems anthologize approved causes; their repeated origin in photographs merely enhances the discomfiting impression of scrapbook pages. If their purpose can be neither to proselytize (we already agree) nor to inquire (they explicitly disavow "the issues"), their primary work, by design or by default, is to set the stakes for the book they introduce, to make an implicit claim for the stature of subject matter and the moral authority to come. And as if to betray such a self-serving project, the poet/persona later compares her cruel father to Nixon resigning from office in shame and to the murderous Shah of Iran; she portrays her bullying older sister for a full poem's length as Hitler invading Paris. The "public" poems wish to cast off all issues but those of human suffering and its deep counter-argument, the stubborn faith and sublime intelligence of the human body, its survival and its eloquent reproduction (in children, in photographs, and in imagination). But the opportunistic deployment of public figures in "private" poems reminds us that passionate advocacy cannot suspend "the issues" indefinitely. When poetry taps and exploits the charged realms of human extremity and public opinion without taking on the real burden of history and choice, it willy-nilly evolves a politics of its own, and one that can only be called exploitative. Olds's portraits of individual anguish in Chile or in racially splintered Tulsa gain much of their momentum, after all, from the increments of public opinion they claim to transcend.

We badly need an intelligent political poetry in America. In *The Dead and the Living,* I find the most convincing political formulations in poems to the living family, where Olds is willing to anatomize the workings of power and principle and partisanship before our eyes. "Coming home from the women-only bar" in one poem, she confronts the contrary claims of her beloved, sleeping son: "Into any new world we enter," she writes, "let us / take this man." The moment is a small one as world government goes. . . . The competition between gender loyalty and family loyalty and strategies for the mutual liberation of the sexes constitute less momentous dilemmas, no doubt, than genocide and mass starvation, but they are worthy issues, nevertheless, and they are the issues more deeply interrogated in this book. (pp. 36-7)

Linda Gregerson, in a review of "The Dead and the Living," in Poetry, *Vol. CXLV, No. 1, October, 1984, pp. 36-7.*

RICHARD TILLINGHAST

[*Tillinghast is an American poet with an independent voice and an experimental approach. His three published collections,* Sleep Watch *(1969),* The Knife and Other Poems *(1981), and* Our Flag Was Still There *(1985), evidence his skill with free and formal verse as well as his varied poetic styles, including Surrealism, Symbolism, and, like Olds, confessional and political poetry. In the following excerpt Tillinghast points out flaws in Olds's work but admires its overall impact.*]

A brutalized childhood is the storm center around which the poems in Sharon Olds's second book, *The Dead and the Living* . . . , furiously revolve. The actors in the drama are indelibly drawn. (p. 361)

Olds's attempts, however, to establish political analogies to private brutalization . . . are not very convincing. For one thing,

Sylvia Plath did the same thing earlier, and did it better. In **"The Departure,"** Olds asks her father, "Did you weep like the Shah when you left?" And in **"The Victims,"** she writes:

> Then you were fired, and we
> grinned inside, the way people grinned
> when
> Nixon's helicopter lifted off the South
> Lawn for the last time.

This becomes a mannerism, representing political thinking only at the most superficial level. Was Nixon ever really thought of as a father, for example, with the instinctual trust and love that implies? Were his crimes ever as intimate and damaging to any of us as child abuse would be? There is, in short, less political insight here than meets the eye.

While reading this book I found myself thinking both of Sylvia Plath and of *Wuthering Heights.* Olds has without a doubt been influenced deeply by Plath's poetry. Love and hatred of the father are major preoccupations for both writers, and both equate violence within the family with violence within the state and between nations. But there are important differences. The father in Plath is essentially a fantasy, the creation of a mind hovering on the edge of madness. Olds is, one feels certain, recording an actual story. The thrill of horror one often feels while reading Plath is produced less by some apparently real-life situation than by the workings of a brilliant mind out of control: "the autobiography of a fever," as Robert Lowell put it. But *The Dead and the Living,* like Olds's first book, *Satan Says,* has the chastening impact of a powerful documentary. It is for this reason, too, that the comparison with *Wuthering Heights* breaks down. Sadism within the family, the spectacle of the victim becoming the victimizer—those are present in both works. But because there is no romantic masochism in Olds, or—more accurately—none that has not been closely examined, her book is not a family romance but a photographic view of a family tragedy.

While her first book was impossible to ignore because of its raw power, *The Dead and the Living* is a considerable step forward. Her earlier impulse was to turn her pain and anger into myth, analogy, metaphor, as in **"Love Fossil"** from *Satan Says*—perhaps because of the difficulty of facing it head-on:

> My da on his elegant vegetarian ankles
> drank his supper. Like the other dinosaurs
> massive, meaty, made of raw steak,
> he nibbled and guzzled, his jaw dripping weeds and
> bourbon,
> super sleazy extinct beast my heart dug for.

This grips and shocks, yet its tone of hysterical excess reflects something of the psychic damage that the speaker has sustained. In her new book the repulsion has lost none of its intensity, witness a detail such as "the black / noses of your shoes with their large pores." But the poet—and presumably also the person one glimpses fleetingly behind the work—seems more in control of the experiences that have clearly obsessed her for most of her life. In both her books, that obsessiveness is a strength and a weakness. Even in the second, many readers will feel overwhelmed by Olds's dogged insistence on reliving and rethinking her childhood traumas.

She must have sensed as much herself, because this book moves—perhaps a bit too schematically—through sections titled "The Dead," "The Living" and "The Children," from the past into the present. Olds is a keen and accurate observer of people. Still bearing the scars if not the wounds of childhood, she is not prone to sentimentality: "It's an old / story—the oldest we have on our planet— / the story of replacement," whereby as the daughter grows up, she replaces her mother. Sharon Olds is a tough, clear-eyed survivor. (pp. 361-62)

Richard Tillinghast, "Blunt Instruments," in The Nation, Vol. 239, No. 11, October 13, 1984, pp. 361-63.*

An Excerpt from *The Dead and the Living*

Sex without Love

How do they do it, the ones who make love
without love? Beautiful as dancers,
gliding over each other like ice-skaters
over the ice, fingers hooked
inside each other's bodies, faces
red as steak, wine, wet as the
children at birth whose mothers are going to
give them away. How do they come to the
come to the   come to the   God   come to the
still waters, and not love
the one who came there with them, light
rising slowly as steam off their joined
skin? These are the true religious,
the purists, the pros, the ones who will not
accept a false Messiah, love the
priest instead of the God. They do not
mistake the lover for their own pleasure,
they are like great runners: they know they are alone
with the road surface, the cold, the wind,
the fit of their shoes, their over-all cardio-
vascular health—just factors, like the partner
in the bed, and not the truth, which is the
single body alone in the universe
against its own best time.

CAROLYNE WRIGHT

[*Wright is an American poet whose poems from her collections* Stealing the Children *(1978),* Returning What We Owed *(1980),* Premonitions of an Uneasy Guest *(1983), and* From a White Woman's Journal *(1984) have won numerous awards. Wright sees her poetry "as a lyrical and imagistic means of telling the truth," a belief apparent also in Olds's poetry. In the following excerpt Wright compares* Satan Says *to* The Dead and the Living *and praises Olds's control of powerful emotions in the latter, as well as her ability to face the darkness in her family and in humanity and yet maintain a spirit of affirmation.*]

[*The Dead and the Living*] is a powerful follow-up to *Satan Says,* fulfilling all the expectations that first book raised. Grace Paley has said in an interview that "the act of illumination is political . . . the act of bringing justice into the world a little bit": by bringing into the light lives that have been (to use Paley's words) "unseen, unknown, in darkness," Olds has both revealed and redeemed the most painful portions of her private and public lives, and celebrated that which has brought her a palpable, full-bodied joy. By confronting her own "darkness" fairly, Olds has affirmed the humanity of those who engendered that darkness, and shown herself, in these days of sensationalized telling-all for lucrative book contracts, to be a

poet of affirmation. To draw a parallel with non-fiction, we could say that Olds' poetry about family is more in the spirit of Geoffrey Wolff's *The Duke of Deception* than of Christine Crawford's *Mommie Dearest.*

As is already apparent, Olds' focus in these new poems is on themes which continue to preoccupy her—familial relationships, both those in which the speaker is daughter or granddaughter, and those in which she is wife and mother. In spite of many celebratory and humorous poems (especially in the sections of the book devoted to her chosen family—her husband and children), the dominant impression of the collection's first half is somber-hued, like that of a gallery of Old Master family portraits darkening with age. In what must have been poems difficult to write, Olds gives us, in passages seasoned with anger and leavened with compassion, the cruel, hard-drinking grandfather; the submissive grandmother; the elder sister who shockingly tormented her when they were children, knowing their mother "would never believe [the] story"; the brother who as an adult is still "sending his body to hell," in a protracted attempt at suicide; the mother who "took it and / took it in silence, all those years, and then / kicked [her husband] out, suddenly, and her / kids loved it"; and the father himself, especially the father, with his double bourbons and child abuse—tying his daughters to chairs, denying his son dinner, slapping the glasses off their faces. In the magnitude of what she has to forgive, and the courage, honesty, and gentleness with which she treats the details of the familial nexus, Olds brings a little more justice into the world, and also provides us with a sympathetic view of human love persisting in spite of cruelty and emotional trauma. There is much in the complexity of nuance and interrelation of characters, moreover, in these poems, that reminds us of a good collection of short fiction; as such, these poems are accessible and believable in the same way that fiction is. Olds does not stand outside or above the people in her poems; she speaks out but does not condemn; she is part of the same emotive fabric as they are, and this identification lends the work much compassion. . . . (pp. 151-52)

The preoccupation with the father figure points to the truth of the love-hate relationship, in the nearly equal degree of energy the speaker devotes to those two emotions; and we see the peculiar way in which one transforms to the other, as [in **"Fate"**] the speaker gives up the attempt to be *other* than the object of fascination, and "becomes her father"—as we all are mysteriously inseparable from our earliest origins, and are most truly ourselves when we recognize and accept this truth. There are undertones of the Oedipal complex here—in the bowing to whatever is inevitable about the identity of parents and children, the nature we are perhaps fated to possess—but here the realization of such is less immediately terrifying, more immediately a source of redemption and psychic peace.

What makes these poems gripping (I read the galley proof straight through in one sitting) is not only their humanity, the recognizable and plausibly complex rendering of character and representative episode, but their language—direct, down to earth, immersed in the essential implements and processes of daily living. . . . (pp. 152-53)

Concern for the fundamentals, however, does not mean that the poems are devoid of wit, intellect, or extended figurative play. . . . (p. 153)

Olds is not hesitant about dealing with violence or sexuality; she neither aggrandizes these concerns nor self-consciously flaunts them. Her treatment of physical love is direct, unembarrassed, and affectionate, as in this poem to her husband ["**New Mother**"]:

> A week after our child was born,
> you cornered me in the spare room
> and we sank down on the bed.
> You kissed me and kissed me, my milk undid its
> burning slip-knot through my nipples,
> soaking my shirt . . . I began to throb:
> my sex had been torn easily as cloth by the
> crown of her head, I'd been cut with a knife and
> sewn, the stitches pulling at my skin . . .
> I lay in fear and blood and milk
> while you kissed and kissed me, your lips hot and
>   swollen
> as a teen-age boy's, your sex dry and big,
> all of you so tender, you hung over me . . .

Sensuality is heightened here by the impossibility of consummation, the tension between the couple's passion and present constraints; but it is the sensuality Olds affirms of happily married love. She can also be gently humorous, especially with that most evident of male totems, treating it neither with pre-Freudian awe nor post-Freudian resentment. Her humor, rather, bespeaks familiarity that breeds appreciation. . . . (pp. 154-55)

If I were to fault this book in any way, it would be for one aspect of the same urge toward clarity that makes Olds' work accessible: a tendency in places to overwrite, to overdescribe or explain beyond what would suffice. The language here is generally looser, more narrative than that of *Satan Says,* and several poems could benefit from cutting of excess adjectives and explanatory phrases. . . .

There are many poems, nonetheless, with the same ironic tautness, the same perceptive rigor, as those in *Satan Says*. One of my favorites is "**Rite of Passage,**" an observation of small boys at a party already practicing their adult masculine roles as aggressors. . . . (p. 156)

I have been focussing so far principally upon "Poems for the Living," the second half of the collection, in which Olds recollects her difficult past with relative tranquility and generosity, and celebrates her own married life and the lives of her two children. But it is the opening, "Public" section of the book's first half, "Poems for the Dead," which is likely to capture critical attention above all. These are poems based on news photographs, visual documentations of the grisly effects of civil and international conflict, and the hapless victims thereof—starving Russian and Armenian children, dead civil rights protestors, Chinese and Iranian revolutionaries, and an address, in the manner of Carolyn Forché's poems to those struggling in El Salvador, to activist poet Margaret Randall. . . . (p. 157)

Although Olds has not gone abroad to witness or participate personally in the resistance in El Salvador, Nicaragua, Chile, or elsewhere, the reality of that which is worse than death has entered her life as fully as it has the lives of those who have been present. She is just as engaged, her poetic reportage is every bit as impassioned—every line says, "I have been there, in mind and heart." She has not merely looked at, but truly *seen* the victims in the photographs—photos in the magazines we all flip through, photos in the archives we all have access to—and has responded in a way that many of us have not, although in theory we are all capable of doing so, if Kierkegaard's notion of actualizing potential is to be believed. Olds knows that we do not need to join the Peace Corps, work as overseas correspondents, or volunteer for partisan armies abroad

in order to respond as human beings to man's own inhumanity, and to speak out and act upon what we have seen and heard. . . . (p. 158)

What is signal about Olds' approach is a fidelity to detail that amounts to a modified naturalism: if she tells accurately what she sees (after selecting the most affectively pertinent details, just as the photographer has originally singled out *that* image, *that* angle and shutter speed and focal length, out of all possible subjects and treatments), the "message" implicit in the composition will stand forth on its own, as much as is possible in the inescapable contrivances of art. The speaker's stance toward her material is evident in the tone—"Just don't tell me about the issues"; "Things that are worse than death"; "I've got eyes, man";—but her attitude emerges from and is justified by the patent horror or pathos of what she shows us. Attention to detail has its ironic function as well, to point out the beauty or economy of the implements of oppression, the skill of those who devised them. . . . (p. 160)

Olds' confidence in the power of detail, and her concomitant refusal to show off verbally, to interpose a display of verbal or prosodic pyrotechnics between subject and reader, make for clarity, a style very much at the service of the subject. In her own way, Olds has heeded Stevens' aphorism in *The Necessary Angel*—poetry as an act of the mind engaged in finding "what will suffice," to do justice to what she shows us. In a sense, then, her style at its best becomes "invisible," unobtrusive except for those moments in which the desire for clarity works against itself in an excess of adjectives or descriptive phrases. But these less effective passages do not unduly distract from the power of the poems.

I am stimulated by this book—by its fulfillment of earlier promise, and by the potential it suggests both for Olds' own future work and for American poetry in general. Once again we have an example of our common ability to embrace the world "out there"—we need not remain, mentally or aesthetically, in our suburbs and literary ghettoes, writing only about ourselves. What we turn our attention to in our respective "private sectors" can and does have relation to the public realm, and to the lives of others. Truly "political" poetry—that which has to do with the *polis,* the community—can function as an aesthetic semi-permeable membrane, where the personal and the public inform and interfuse each other, where we private citizens can respond as individual human beings to the fate of others across socio-economic and national boundaries. Whatever the controversies raging in the journals about the possibility for and validity of political poetry, Sharon Olds has shown us that she, at least, is able both to focus on her own family and to avail herself of information accessible to all of us to enact in literature a concern for the larger family of humanity. (p. 161)

> *Carolyne Wright, in a review of "The Dead and the Living," in* The Iowa Review, *Vol. 15, No. 1 (Winter), 1985, pp. 151-61.*

STEPHEN C. BEHRENDT

The cover [of *The Dead and the Living*] features Frank Eugene's 1910 photograph, "Adam and Eve," a starkly moving print based upon the iconographic tradition of the Expulsion from Eden. It is at their expulsion, after all, not at their discovery of their nakedness, that Adam and Eve most fully comprehend their fallenness, their displacement into a wilderness both material and psychological. . . . Sharon Olds's poems reveal narrative consciousnesses at work reclaiming the wilderness, not wallowing in it, salvaging the ruins to begin constructing a new emotional Eden.

These poems are set at the crossroads of several generations, several time-frames. . . . (pp. 101-02)

[In] ''Poems for the Living,'' we move from childhood recollections of the immediate family of parents and cruel sister through more recent views of the men who include lovers and husband and finally on to observations of the children, in which latter poems we see the transmutation of the themes of repression, suffering, and even death into images of growth, fertility, and life. It is a genuinely forward-looking concluding section, a culmination to what is clearly a deliberate mental effort to spare the children the horrors the narrator has experienced both firsthand and vicariously. The young son and daughter of these poems are perhaps the most lovingly treated I have encountered in any recent volume of poems: the narrator's awe at their simple/complex Edenic beauty and at the miraculous regenerative power of humanity they both represent and portend is everywhere in this final section. Yet never is this awe overworked or played for effect; it comes as the logical culmination of the process of growth embodied in the narrative voice.

Perhaps it is the fact that this volume is so effective in a cumulative fashion that accounts for the difficulty of discussing particular poems adequately. More than is usually the case with a collection, these poems work in what is best described as a ''symphonic'' sense, with themes and motifs employed from section to section in the complex fashion of a late Romantic composer like Mahler, so that even as one appreciates the essential newness of each succeeding poem she or he recognizes as well the presence of threads from previous poems. The overall effect upon the reader is, I think, a powerful one. Still, a word or two on the general style of *The Dead and the Living* may be appropriate. The carefully-manipulated diction and syntax contribute throughout the volume to the interiority of the poems. The lines tend to be rather longer than in much of contemporary poetry, employing complex internal rhythms and grammatical compounding and series-making as a means of slowing the reader's pace. A single example [from **''The Guild''**] may suffice to suggest both the manner and its effect:

> Every night, as my grandfather sat
> in the darkened room in front of the fire,
> the liquor like fire in his hand, his eye
> glittering meaninglessly in the light
> from the flames, his glass eye baleful and stony,
> a young man sat with him
> in silence and darkness, a college boy with
> white skin, unlined, a narrow
> beautiful face, a broad domed
> forehead, and eyes amber as the resin from
> trees too young to be cut yet.

This kind of painstaking recreation of the past as a means of liberating not only that past but the future as well through a complex series of sharp, clear images internally mediated and elegantly articulated characterizes this carefully crafted volume. It is fine, sensitive poetry, warm with a sense of the genuine, and certain to reward anew with each rereading. (pp. 102-03)

Stephen C. Behrendt, in a review of ''The Dead and the Living,'' in Prairie Schooner, *Vol. 59, No. 1, Spring, 1985, pp. 101-03.*

MICHAEL J. BUGEJA

In the cacophony of claims among contemporary poets as to which are the ''best'' poetic voices, the difficulty of choice is in part related to the diversity of values by which to make such a judgment: imagery, metrics, numbers of publications, prestigious awards, etc. Each of these, and combinations of them, might throw up different familiar candidates. If universality were the primary criterion—the ability to appeal to baker and bricklayer, as well as to scholar and fellow poet—then the list is considerably shortened, and one name, above all, stands out: Sharon Olds.

Olds communicates. In my office in the mass communication building, I have plastered my walls with her poems, along with the work of others. I bait my newswriting students with them, students who never read poetry unless forced to in literature classes, who like so many journalists think poetry is sissy or sentimental. But they read everything on walls. When they come across Olds' yet uncollected poems, **''When,''** and **''Greed and Aggression,''** they experience for the first time what many poets take for granted: the understanding of metaphor, the tingle of it in the veins, the spark that goes off in the head. They leave with desire to read poetry, knowing for the first time that a poem like **''When''** doesn't have to mention nuclear holocaust to be about one, and a poem like **''Greed and Aggression''** doesn't have to be about those abstractions; it could be about sex. Olds speaks in their language, a diction devoid of poetic cliches. . . . (pp. 61-2)

[*The Dead and the Living*] is divided into two sections, ''Poems for the Dead'' and ''Poems for the Living.'' The first section has two divisions, ''Public'' and ''Private''; the second, three divisions, ''The Family,'' ''The Men,'' ''The Children.'' This format allows the narrator first to focus upon the universal dead and then upon her private history, a descent that continues into the next section. The tension is greatest in ''The Family,'' poems that unveil a personal tragedy of cruelty and alcohol. Yet those who have read *Satan Says* know that Olds is a survivor, and when this theme is touched on again in ''Poems for the Living,'' we anticipate ascent and reaffirmation. It is a masterful performance that only a full reading can convey. However, representative poems from each division can indicate how Olds communicates with precision and how her work appeals to all levels of audience. (p. 62)

The Dead and the Living shines with myth and metaphor. In poem after poem, Olds proves she not only can return to the same creative well that produced *Satan Says,* but can do so with more precision and intensity. Her clear, powerful poetry communicates on all levels. Her diction, wit, and imagery lure non-poetry readers into the fold. As Marilyn Hacker so aptly puts it, Olds' work ''affirms and redeems the art.'' Olds is by anyone's standard among the best poets writing today. By my standard, she is the best. (p. 65)

Michael J. Bugeja, in a review of ''The Dead and the Living,'' in Open Places, *No. 40, Fall-Winter, 1985, pp. 61-5.*

Richard (Dean) Rosen

Strike Three You're Dead

Edgar Allan Poe Award: Best First Novel

American essayist, scriptwriter, novelist, journalist, critic, and poet.

While *Strike Three You're Dead* (1984) is Rosen's debut fiction, it is not his first work; Rosen is an accomplished writer whose eclectic interests have taken him into diverse forms. Rosen first published poetry as a student at Harvard, then followed with journalism at the *Boston Phoenix* where he served as arts editor, book review editor, and restaurant reviewer, among other assignments. He has also published two nonfiction works, *Me and My Friends, We No Longer Profess Any Graces* (1971), a collection of essays chronicling culture in the 1960s, and *Psychobabble: Fast Talk and Quick Cure in the Era of Feeling* (1977), a critique of psychotherapy, including its language—the word psychobabble, coined by Rosen, has become a popular term for psychological jargon. More recently as a TV writer and producer for PBS (WGBH in Boston), Rosen has contributed many humorous and documentary pieces, and his spoof "The Generic News," in which he also acted, was aired on PBS in December, 1983.

Rosen says he started writing *Strike Three* during the 1981 major league baseball strike: "In the absence of actual baseball, I would create my own team, the Providence Jewels." The result is as much an inside view of baseball as it is a murder mystery. In *Strike Three* Rosen draws together many of his interests and experiences. It is set, for example, in Providence, Rhode Island, where Rosen was a student at Brown University before transferring to Harvard. It also reflects Rosen's first-hand experience of playing organized ball in his early college years. But most notably, it exhibits his work in film production, for reviewers note that many of his scenes are compressed in description and action. "I don't understand writing which uses pages of narrative to set up the scene," comments Rosen. "I wanted the book to be edited like a film, entering scenes before the crucial action." Indeed, most reviewers praise *Strike Three* for its fast-paced action, as well as for its realistic dialogue and well-developed characters. Rosen's interests in psychology and sports are also well represented in *Strike Three:* Rosen addresses male/female roles and careers through the protagonist Harvey Blissberg, the center fielder for the Jewels and their resident philosopher, and his lover, the female sportscaster Mickey Slavin. Harvey has ample opportunity to muse on the meaning of his experiences as he attempts to solve the murder of his friend Rudy Furth, the relief pitcher.

Reviewers commend Rosen for his knowledge of baseball and for offering a sustained mystery story. "I'm particularly pleased with the Edgar," comments Rosen, "since *Strike Three* does not follow some of the conventions of the [mystery] form." Rosen has chiefly expanded the mystery genre by portraying a very realistic sleuth who does not have the vast and unique range of knowledge and skills possessed by most detectives. Rosen plans to publish a sequel to *Strike Three,* entitled *Fadeaway,* in 1986. It will again feature amateur sports de-

© 1986 Thomas Victor

tective Harvey Blissberg, this time in a basketball-oriented plot.

PUBLISHERS WEEKLY

As the title [*Strike Three You're Dead*] indicates, this entertaining mystery is as much about baseball as murder. Rosen chronicles one season in the life of the Providence Jewels, a new and not very successful expansion team. When relief pitcher Rudy Furth is found dead in the whirlpool bath, his roommate, center fielder Harvey Blissberg, attempts to assist the police in discovering the murderer's identity. As he investigates, Blissberg uncovers secrets about his friend's past that may involve the team's players, management and owner, and even the mob. Of course, Blissberg himself eventually is in danger, too. Despite all the hinted-at intrigue, Rudy's life turns out to have been pretty dull after all. More interesting than the unraveling of the mystery is the baseball action, as the team tries

194

to keep from sinking to the bottom of the standings in the aftermath of the murder. The book's climax, a wildly unbelievable man-versus-baseball encounter in an empty stadium, is quite exciting despite the contrivances that bring it about.

A review of "Strike Three You're Dead," in Publishers Weekly, *Vol. 225, No. 19, May 11, 1984, p. 263.*

BOB WIEMER

In his first mystery novel, R. D. Rosen takes his readers on a tour of professional baseball's locker rooms, barrooms and bedrooms. He does this skillfully and with enough wit to make the book, ***Strike Three You're Dead*** . . . , the literary equivalent of an in-the-park home run.

Rosen has a deadly eye for detail. He does not have to tell the reader that Det. Sgt. Linderman, a bumbler, has a pot belly. Instead, he notes in one scene that Linderman is wearing a "navy blue polo-shirt with little sailboats all over it." And then adds: "Where his stomach was, the boats sailed farther apart." Rosen's fictional American League expansion team, the Jewels, is based in Providence, R.I., summed up by Rosen as seeming "to consist entirely of outskirts."

The real detective in this story is not Linderman: It's Harvey Blissberg, the Jewels' center fielder. He majored in history in college and later made the mistake of letting his teammates spot him reading books. That earned him the locker room sobriquet, "professor."

Blissberg's roommate, relief pitcher Rudy Furth, is found bludgeoned to death in the team's whirlpool bath. Linderman suspects Blissberg because both men were reportedly interested in the same woman, a local television sports reporter. Out of a combination of self-interest and loyalty to his departed friend, Blissberg feels impelled to begin his own investigation. He does this while managing to continue to hit .300 even as the team goes into a monumental slump.

As the Jewels move through their schedule, the reader becomes as interested in the outcome of their season as in the outcome of the murder investigation. The plot is adequate; the characterization is sharp, and the setting is both believable and delightful.

Bob Wiemer, "Some Deadly Doings around the Diamond," in Newsday, *August 19, 1984, p. 18.**

LES DANIELS

[Daniels is a book reviewer for the Eagle, *the local paper in Providence, Rhode Island, the city in which* Strike Three You're Dead *takes place. In the following excerpt Daniels comments on Rosen's use of the city for his setting as well as on the writer's knowledge of baseball.]*

"Even on a Friday evening, the city seemed barely alive."

That's the way R. D. Rosen describes Providence in his new crime novel ***Strike Three You're Dead.*** For years, authors of detective stories have been describing sinister cities corresponding to what poet W. H. Auden described as "The Great Wrong Place," and now Rosen, in his first mystery, has made Our Little Towne into one of them.

A former resident who subsequently fled to Boston, Rosen writes about Providence with the affectionate contempt that

familiarity with the city has inspired in so many. The plucky heroine, who has an upscale job and a dusting of freckles on her nose, says "I have this fantasy that I'm going to look at a map of New England one day and it's not going to be there. And no one will miss it."

Of course Rosen doesn't go as far as H. P. Lovecraft, who depicted the state capital as a metropolis populated by fiends and ghouls, but his general attitude has some of the same entertainment value. On the bright side, Rosen has decided that Providence is about due for a major league baseball team, the Jewels; naturally they're kicking around the bottom of the league and getting murdered on top of it. The novel is about the great American pastime more than it is about Rhode Island, and fans of the sport will discover that Rosen has a feel for it, and a plot which really uses the details of the game to unravel the detective story. . . .

He has written a funny novel with a strong dramatic finish, and he'll be returning to Providence again with a sequel about more crime and depravity.

Les Daniels, "The Great Wrong Place," in The Eagle, *Providence, R.I., October 21, 1984.*

NEWGATE CALLENDAR

Mr. Rosen knows his baseball. He is probably one of those types who can tell you who participated in the first-ever triple play, who had the most fouls in a season, who led the league in being hit by pitchers in 1904 and which left-handed pitcher

Dust jacket of Strike Three You're Dead, *by R. D. Rosen. Walker & Company, 1984. Jacket illustration by James Forman. By permission of the publisher.*

who hit right-handed had the most broken shoelaces over a five-year period.

Strike Three is an entertaining and well-written book. It introduces Harvey Blissberg, a former Boston Red Sox center fielder who now plays for the Providence Jewels, the newest addition to the American League Eastern Division. The Jewels are in a determined fight for last place. Harvey is no Willie Mays or Joe DiMaggio, but he is having a good season, hovering around a .300 batting average. He is also the club veteran and philosopher—a college graduate (history major) who reads books and knows which fork to use.

His roommate gets murdered in the clubhouse, brained by a bat. The entire team goes into a tailspin, Harvey included. Could the killer have been one of the Jewels? Harvey pokes around. Some people get the idea he knows more than he actually does, and a hood warns him off. The policeman in charge of the case is not too smart or anxious to stir himself. Finally Harvey figures it out and barely escapes with his life. The confrontation with the killer in the clubhouse and later on the playing field is a real thriller.

Mr. Rosen can write. His dialogue is smart and sophisticated and his characters altogether three-dimensional. Clearly the author loves baseball, but he does not get sentimental about it. His approach is entirely professional. Has he done some playing himself? Anyway, the last game of the season has the Jewels against the Yankees, and New York must win to tie for first place. All readers will be satisfied with the way that things work out. In his first mystery, Mr. Rosen has hit a home run.

> *Newgate Callendar, in a review of "Strike Three You're Dead," in* The New York Times, *October 28, 1984, p. 39.*

An Excerpt from *Strike Three You're Dead*

"So you didn't have time to call and tell about Rudy Furth?" a voice said.

"Hi, Mom. I was going to, but it's been too crazy around here."

"What kind of sport is that, a person gets murdered?"

"I don't know, Mom."

"Play something less dangerous. Not baseball."

"Too late, Mom."

"Harvey, he was murdered just like that? What do they do now, give you a new roommate?"

"From now on I think I'll take a single room on the road."

"That's good. So tell me—have you found anyone yet?"

"Anyone what?"

"Anyone special, that's what."

"Nothing's changed since last week, Mom. You asked, and I told you I was seeing a woman who's a sportscaster on the news here."

"What is she, a tomboy?"

"She's a very successful journalist, Mom."

"Maybe you should marry her, dear."

"Would you like that?"

"You mention a girl once over the phone and I'm supposed to know if she'll make you a nice wife? What am I, a prophet? Mrs. Bernstein's daughter lives in Providence, Harvey, a nice girl."

"No, thanks, Mom."

"Maybe you're too picky. Norman's married."

"I'm not Norman, Mom. Norman's also an English professor, which I'm not."

"You could have been a history professor."

"I could have been an astrophysicist, too, but I'm a baseball player. Anyway, I make four times as much money as a professor."

"Since when is money everything? Is that how we brought you up? A good thing Big Al's not around to hear you talk like that. In three years, you're not going to be a baseball player. Then what?"

"Seven years ago you said the same thing to me, and I'm still playing."

"That's because you choked up and learned how to hit on the average."

"*For* the average, Mom."

"On, for, it's not easy telling people my son is thirty years old and plays baseball."

"Look at the bright side, Mom. Not everyone has a son who's batting three hundred in the majors."

"Well, excuse me. I didn't realize I could be so lucky. Here I was all these years, thinking how nice it would be to have a son who used his head for a living, who healed the sick, who taught the uneducated, even, God forbid, who could draw up a will or help with the income taxes. All along, I was ashamed he wore a uniform with the name of a city on the front. And a three hundred average! This I didn't know what a thing this was! 'Mrs. Blissberg, so how is Harvey doing these days?' 'Fine, Mrs. Schottsky. My son is now hitting three hundred. And how is your son?' 'Oh, David is all right, I guess. He just found the cure for cancer.' So forgive, Harvey, I didn't know you were such a big deal. I see you're playing in Boston this week. What night are you coming out for dinner?"

KATHLEEN MAIO

Rosen sets his mystery [*Strike Three You're Dead*] in Providence, Rhode Island, a locale he claims looks "like a place you ended up when they kicked you out of everywhere else." Proud citizens of the Ocean State may resent Rosen's repeated jabs at their capital, but baseball buffs will especially enjoy this tale of murder in the clubhouse of the newest team in the American League East, the Providence Jewels.

Rosen's central character and amateur detective is center fielder Harvey Blissberg, who feels obliged to investigate when his friend and road-roommate, pitcher Rudy Furth, is slugged to death in the team whirlpool. The investigation gives him insights of friend Furth, and numerous opportunities for a little wiseacre humor. Rosen handles comedy, suspense, and even Blissberg's romance with a local sportscaster with the skill of a seasoned pro. *Strike Three You're Dead* is a winning rookie effort. (p. 212)

> Kathleen Maio, "Murder in Print," in Wilson Library Bulletin, *Vol. 59, No. 3, November, 1984, pp. 212-13.**

JEAN M. WHITE

Even those unfortunate readers who are not fans and cannot share the delights of the game can enjoy a nifty mystery puzzle and the roster of colorful characters in *Strike Three, You're Dead*. . . .

Rosen knows his way around the baseball field and the clubhouse. The talk is gamey. The players are real guys, not the Robert Redford folk hero of *The Natural*. They worry about a hitch in their batting swing, bicker with each other, and grow moody on a losing streak.

It helps to know and like baseball to savor all the nuances of *Strike Three, You're Dead*. ("But extra-marital affairs were as common as 6-4-3 double plays.") The vital clue does come from the statistics that dedicated baseball fans cherish.

But there is much beyond the baseball background to appease and attract nonfans. Rosen . . . writes brightly and sharply. Providence is a little-used setting for mystery novels. Then there is a humdinger of a chase-confrontation scene in the clubhouse and on the baseball field with all the excitement of a 3-2 pitch with two out and the winning run at third base.

> Jean M. White, "Murder on the Mound," in Book World—The Washington Post, *January 20, 1985, p. 9.*

JEREMIAH TAX

Rosen knows something about baseball as well as good writing. In [*Strike Three You're Dead*], he has devised a plot that keeps you turning through 234 pages. . . . My only serious objection to *Strike Three* is that as the curtain is falling, so to speak, he explains more than he needs to, apparently trying to avoid the accusation that he has left a few loose ends. Otherwise, the book is full of bright banter between Harvey and his TV-reporter lady friend. There's a whiff of resemblance between his dialogue and the laconic lingo that enlivens the Spenser private-eye novels by Robert B. Parker. If the similarity is deliberate, Rosen has chosen a fine model. Harvey's friend is no mere sex object or background embroidery. Her career is constructed to conflict with Harvey's—so that you're sure to notice it—and proof is offered throughout the book that she's a genuine newshound and not just a pretty face reading stuff off a ticker.

Harvey himself is an introspective sort, given to meditations on the nature of his game. Here's how he feels about his job playing center: "Being alone with all that grass calmed him. Even as a kid, when other Little Leaguers wanted to play only shortstop or pitch, Harvey had played centerfield. Green, spacious, removed from the crowded, dusty infield, center had all the virtues of a desirable suburb." . . .

As Harvey stumbles in his efforts to solve Rudy's murder, he faces moments of despair as well as danger. In one of his down periods, he is interviewed by a somewhat unlikely reporter who expresses the hope that someone really feels a *personal* responsibility for nabbing the killer. He tells a story to illustrate what he means: A wedding was planned in a small town and each of the guests was asked to bring a bottle of vodka and pour it into a barrel from which all would drink. One guest figured, "With all this vodka, who will know if I put water in my bottle?" When all the bottles were poured into the barrel, "the first man drew a glass. . . . He brought it to his lips and he drank it. It was water. The whole barrel was water." Harvey gets the point. "Somebody," he says, "has to bring the vodka." He continues groping for a solution.

He arrives at one, but it is not the ending. Rosen offers a series of these, and the final wrap-up, though contrived, is satisfying. If you've been reading carefully, you will have sorted through enough red herrings to have only solid suspects, motives and methods left in your net.

> Jeremiah Tax, "By Solving His Teammate's Murder, a Centerfielder Becomes the MVP," in Sports Illustrated, *Vol. 62, No. 14, April 8, 1985, p. 24.*

Bob Shacochis

Easy in the Islands

The American Book Awards: First Work of Fiction

American short story writer.

Most of the stories in Shacochis's first collection of short fiction, *Easy in the Islands* (1985), relate the adventures of white American men in the West Indies. Shacochis gathered material for the stories while living in the Caribbean, between his university studies in the United States and serving as a Peace Corps volunteer. The heroes of *Easy in the Islands* are usually rough-and-ready men caught in absurd predicaments that the author treats with deprecating humor. Shacochis contrasts the wide-eyed tourist's view of the tropics with a cynical insider's knowledge of the ugliness and frustrations of island life. Though critics observe that Shacochis is not successful with every story, they find his vivid evocations of the book's tropical settings a strong point of the collection. Shacochis, whose stories have appeared in a number of periodicals including *Paris Review, Esquire,* and *Playboy,* is writing a novel set in the Caribbean.

© 1986 Thomas Victor

PUBLISHERS WEEKLY

The "islands" in this collection of nine stories [*Easy in the Islands*], Shacochis's first book, are the West Indies, where the local dialect, like the local characters, has a distinctive rhythm and lilt not quite like any other and the living *seems* to be easy to the imperceptive tourist's eye. In ["**Easy in the Islands**"] an American expatriate hotel owner who wants simply to bury his mother, dead of causes beyond the powers of the incompetent and corrupt native medical examiner to diagnose, becomes hopelessly ensnarled in the inscrutable, venomous local bureaucracy and mystifying folkways of native institutions. Finally, at the end of his tether, he casts her body from a plane into the sea, without ceremony or proper authority. The story, for all its possibilities, begins to sag and waver early on and never strikes a steady course: distractions and digressions fracture the narrative and the author succumbs to the fatal temptations of bursts of inappropriate and false lyricism, over-figurative writing, verbosity and the syncopated beat of island speech for its own sake. Local color, however exotic the setting, does not a story make, nor does accurately transcribed speech, however vivid. In this case, they attest to the author's gift of ear and eye, and his promise as a storyteller, but these tales are too contrived and labored to be entirely successful. (pp. 81-2)

> *A review of "Easy in the Islands," in* Publishers Weekly, *Vol. 226, No. 22, November 30, 1984, pp. 81-2.*

MARY ELLEN QUINN

The title story in this collection [*Easy in the Islands*] sets the trend for the rest. The setting is the Caribbean, the central character is an outsider with no close ties, identified only by his last name; the images are vivid, and the contrast between life in the tropics and life in the States is an important element. The stories are populated by calypso singers, Rastafarians, exciting women, and cynical men making a bid for independence and adventure. The author tends to romanticize the tropics, yet he maintains an ironic stance towards his Hemingway-type heroes. Despite a certain repetitiveness, good storytelling and vibrant imagery make this a strong first collection.

> *Mary Ellen Quinn, in a review of "Easy in the Islands," in* Booklist, *Vol. 81, No. 7, December 1, 1984, p. 484.*

KIRKUS REVIEWS

Shacochis' debut story-collection [*Easy in the Islands*] presents its shiny talents confidently and quickly. The stories are set in the Bahamas and other Antilles islands, on shore and off—but these are no tropicalia-angst concoctions (*à la* Thomas Mc-Guane): they are as firmly grounded in indigenous custom, in place and politics (civil and sexual), as are the best works of Robert Stone and V. S. Naipaul. [**"Easy in the Islands"**]—about a tourist-hotel owner trying to dispose of his visiting mother's freezered corpse—is jaundiced, comic, remarkably unforced (if conventionally predictable at the close). In **"Lord Short Shoe Wants The Monkey,"** sexual viciousness and revenge are arranged into a cynical tableau in a calypso bar. And perhaps best of all—in its sweetness and comic stamina—is **"Redemption Songs"**: two black revolutionaries-*manque* get way over their heads in astonishingly successful trouble. Other stories, which feature white men as observers or inept participants, knot up less well; they sometimes have a slightly sophomoric edge. And none of these pieces is a moral tale with the weight of prime Stone or Naipaul. Still, even at his weakest, Shacochis writes from fresh angles, with a strong sense of narrative surprise—and ever-bright prose. ("I steered for an hour while Champ played below and let me tell you, it's a fine feeling to captain a ship, a liberation to power it over the depths, surely a magic, like flight. The horizon writhes. You go on and on. The horizon writhes, now brassed with daybreak, now colorless and baleful with the coming of night, and the distance irons out in your wake.") An exciting introduction to a highly promising writer. (pp. 1116-17)

A review of "Easy in the Islands," in Kirkus Reviews, *Vol. LII, No. 23, December 1, 1984, pp. 1116-17.*

CAROL VERDERESE

In **"Easy in the Islands,"** the title story in Bob Shacochis' first collection of short stories, the narrator—who is harboring his mother's corpse in a hotel freezer to keep it from the clutches of inept authorities—thinks of an average day in the Caribbean as an accumulation of "event upon event . . . until it was overrich, festering or glorious, never to be reproduced so wonderfully." Shacochis' stories mirror this description. Those that succeed are quirky and quite wonderful, while those that fail struggle under the weight of overripe prose.

Shacochis' Caribbean is a land that challenges the ambivalence and vain piety exhibited by many of his characters.

Shacochis skillfuly explores the tension between pride and survival in male-female relationships in **"Dead Reckoning"** and **"The Heart's Advantage,"** using the navigation of a boat on turbulent seas as his central metaphor. **"The Heart's Advantage"** founders, however, as does the only other non-Caribbean story in the book. **"Hot Day on the Gold Coast,"** encumbered by lines like "the terry knot bulged with the foretelling of permanence." Still, Shacochis' Caribbean stories reveal the islands unlike any travel brochure, evoking their ruthless beauty with intriguing realism.

Carol Verderese, in a review of "Easy in the Islands," in Saturday Review, *Vol. 11, No. 1, January-February, 1985, p. 79.*

An Excerpt from *Easy in the Islands*

"I don't believe it," the new man said in an aside to Tillman as he checked them in. "The skycaps at the airport whistled at my wife and called her a whore." His wife stood demurely by his side, looking a bit over-whelmed. He could see the dark coronas of nipples under her white muslin sundress.

"Hey, people here are more conservative than you might think," Tillman told the couple, and to the woman he added, "Unless you want little boys rubbing up against your leg, you shouldn't wear shorts or a bathing suit into town."

"But this is the tropics," the woman protested in an adolescent voice, looking at Tillman as if he were only being silly.

"Right," Tillman conceded, handing over the key. He escorted the couple to their room, helping with the luggage, and wished them well. Wished himself a dollar for every time their notion of paradise would be fouled by some rudeness, aggression, or irrelevant accusation.

He crossed back over the veranda out onto the cobbled drive, past the derelict stone tower of the windmill where every other Saturday the hotel sponsored a goat roast that was well attended by civil servants, Peace Corps volunteers and whatever tourists were around, down the glorious green lawn crazy with blossom, down, hot and sweaty, to the palm grove, the bamboo beach bar on its fringe, the lagoon dipping into the land like a blue pasture, Tillman walking with his hands in the pockets of his loose cotton pants, reciting a calypso and feeling, despite his troubles, elected, an aristocrat of the sensual latitudes, anointed to all the earthly privileges ordinary people dreamed about on their commuter trains fifty weeks a year. No matter that in a second-class Eden nothing was as unprofitable as the housing of its guests. Even loss seemed less discouraging in the daily flood of sun.

PATRICIA MOLLOY

Shacochis's first collection of short stories [*Easy in the Islands*] does capture the lilt and ease that make the Caribbean islands into a vacationers' paradise, but he focuses on the underside of island life: Rastafarianism, reggae, and revolution; smuggling; the often tense relationships between blacks and whites. Although not every story is successful, the comic touch and well-drawn characters in the best ones (**"Lord Short Shoe Wants the Monkey," "Hot Day on the Gold Coast," "Redemption Songs"**) make for laugh-out-loud quality.

Patricia Molloy, in a review of "Easy in the Islands: Stories," in Library Journal, *Vol. 110, No. 2, February 1, 1985, p. 114.*

CHERI FEIN

Bob Shacochis's collection of short stories [*Easy in the Islands*] definitely places him with the guys. While women's fiction remains a hot topic, of late the critical spotlight has not been focused on fiction such as Mr. Shacochis's that, well, could only have been written by a man. It's no mistake that many of these stories were first published in *Playboy* and *Esquire*. Their main characters are outlaws of sorts, white men living in Florida and the Caribbean, where the exotic lushness of island life makes it difficult to find peace but "easy to catch hell." With a "why me?" shrug and an absurdist edge, that's exactly what occurs.

Tillman, the argumentative owner of Rosehill Plantation, finds his mother, who had been in bed reading Colette and eating canned peaches, dead. The authorities refuse to let Tillman speedily dispose of the corpse, so, frustrated, he resorts to rash measures. His actions are not triggered by grief or love, but simply by his annoyance at a dead body that must be dumped. This is the title story and the first in the collection, and it sets up the accurate expectation that **"Easy in the Islands"** means something quite different to us tourists than it does to Mr. Shacochis's full-time residents, islander and white man alike.

The white men who choose to live in the tropics are "at home with grime and knuckle-busting," yet retain a James Bondian veneer, along with uppercrust names like Davis, Sims, Weber or Harter (first names or last we are never told). They are mad for sailboats, fishing and freedom. As Davis proclaims, "Let me tell you, it's a fine feeling to captain a ship, a liberation to power it over the depths." And yet, when it comes down to it, these guys are always blundering through extraordinary disasters and scratching their heads in sheer amazement.

I suspect that Mr. Shacochis means for us to take the souls of his white men quite seriously while chuckling at their antics. His airbrushed picture of male bonding is pure fantasy, although it often works. The stories are generally amusing. Who could help but laugh at the pot-bellied dope pusher in **"Hot Day on the Gold Coast"** who decides to go jogging in Palm Beach wearing only his boxer shorts and ends up on a boat loaded with Haitian aliens and a mad fisherman?

As for the women, they are as necessary as shoes and usually worn as hard. Inevitably, to the men's surprise, though not their obvious distress, they eventually leave. In only one instance, the lyrical and complex **"Lord Short Shoe Wants the Monkey,"** does a sensuous woman use her considerable powers to get the better of two boorish men who have bartered her favors for a monkey. The story is a witty triumph for both Mr. Shacochis and the wronged woman, though once again the white man is allowed to regain his cool and depart intact.

The indigenous island men are a different lot altogether, more philosophical and dignified and human. In **"Redemption Songs,"** Glasford, recently returned from New York, has caught the fire of revolution, which he imparts to his easygoing friend, Fish. Together they set out on a night of adventure, an innocent enough rampage. Home again, Fish realizes that for him a more powerful position in life will not bring greater contentment. It is a wise self-realization, juxtaposed against Glasford's unfocused rage.

The message of these stories is simple enough: the islander belongs where he is and will live out his days in a dignified if sometimes foolish manner, while the white interloper, overly confident of his supremacy even on foreign turf, bluffs or bullies his way, often with charm but never with character. As in life, the macho stance works both for and against Mr. Shacochis's characters. While their "manliness" satisfies certain fantasies, it blocks these men from becoming true heroes or even truly human—and these stories from giving more than temporary gratification.

> Cheri Fein, "Free, White and Hairy-Chested," in The New York Times Book Review, *February 17, 1985, p. 13.*

PAUL GRAY

It happens every winter. When the winds howl and the snow drifts, TV screens across the U.S. bloom with images of sway-

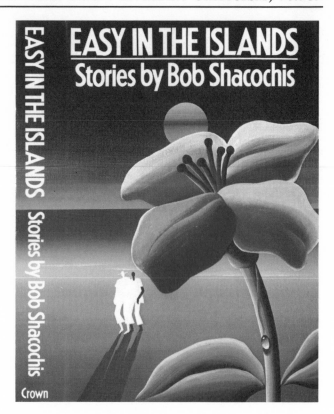

Dust jacket of Easy in the Islands, *by Bob Shacochis. Crown, 1985. Copyright © 1985 by Bob Shacochis. Jacket illustration by Alain Gauthier. Reprinted by permission of Crown Publishers, Inc.*

ing palms, emerald waters and undulating swimsuits. The islands beckon; come to the Caribbean. Not everyone has the time or money to heed the call, but stay-at-homes this year may console themselves with this collection of nine stories [*Easy in the Islands*]. In his first book, author Bob Shacochis not only offers some beguiling tropical tours, he also shows how living in Eden can be considerably harder than jetting into and out of it.

The hero of [**"Easy in the Islands"**], for example, has nothing but problems. As the reluctant inheritor of a deteriorating resort hotel, Tillman quickly learns that he should have left most of his expectations back home in the States: "The terms of life in the islands were that nothing ever made sense, unless you were a mystic or a politician, or studied both with ambition." When Tillman's mother dies, of no visible cause, in her hotel room, petty annoyances assume the dimensions of conspiracy. The black authorities seem determined to find evidence of foul play. The hotel bartender, who hates whites in general and Tillman especially, feels free to slander the dead woman: "Daht ol boney-bag he call his muddah grabbin aht every blahck boy on de beach." As bad feelings spread and red tape unreels, the proprietor must store his mother's body in the kitchen freezer, prompting a walkout by the staff.

Such impasses are common in these stories, the residue of cross purposes and overstrained racial tolerances. In **"Dead Reckoning,"** a woman sets out on a sailboat with a new boyfriend. When they reach Nevis, she thrills to "my first true touch of paradise." Before long, her companion is locked in a battle of wills with a black beggar boy, who redoubles his efforts every time he is rebuffed. Soon the visitors are made to feel unwelcome, the woman especially so; she decides to abandon both the island and her partner. Her decision reminds her of an earlier tale; "I saw, like Eve, that paradise had become just another place to leave behind."

Proprieties tend to wilt in the pervasive heat. In **"Lord Short Shoe Wants the Monkey,"** a rising calypso singer strikes a deal at a Barbados nightclub with a white man who owns a trained monkey; the performer gets the onstage use of the animal, and the owner gets a night with a stunning black woman in the singer's entourage. Overhearing this transaction, an American visitor solemnly interrupts: "Gentlemen, forgive me. You cannot trade a woman for a monkey."

Nothing is that clear-cut in the world of these stories. Shacochis shows a keen awareness of lush disparities. He evokes the allure of a village marketplace, "the air luscious with the smells of spices, of frying coconut oil and garlic and cumin, the scents of frangipani and lime." The counterimage appears in a neighborhood of ghetto shanties, where everything "smelled like rotting fruit and kerosene, urine and garlic." In **"Hunger,"** a lone white works alongside a team of black fishermen; near the end of their labors, they all retire to a deserted beach for an extended evening feast. The outsider marvels at the smells that begin simmering from the cooking pots. He also recoils when he sees a comrade slice the neck of a live hawksbill turtle and use the dying creature's blood to flavor the stew.

Three of these stories first appeared in *Playboy* and two others ran in *Esquire;* the remainder made their debuts in quarterlies or little magazines. That parlay of the slick and scholarly is unusual, particularly for a beginning writer. Odder still, only a peek at the copyright page can confirm just which stories reached the mass or middling audiences; *Easy in the Islands* is a whole unified by consistent parts. . . . Shacochis has had the commerical prudence to learn and write about an uncommonly fascinating part of the hemisphere. Better still, his talent seems more than a match for the subjects at his hand.

Paul Gray, "Paradise Lost," in Time, *Vol. 125, No. 7, February 18, 1985, p. 100.*

Claude (Henri Eugéne) Simon

Nobel Prize in Literature

French novelist, essayist, and dramatist.

Simon is commonly identified as one of the first of the French New Novelists. Like Alain Robbe-Grillet, Nathalie Sarraute, Michel Butor, and others connected with the New Novel movement that emerged after World War II, Simon does not attempt to impose artistic order on the chaos of human experience. Instead, his works reflect the fragmented, disordered nature of reality. In his major novels, including *Le vent* (1957; *The Wind*) and *La route des Flandres* (1960; *The Flanders Road*), Simon dispenses with conventional narrative structures and concentrates on the essential processes of language, memory, and perception. The destructive effects of war, as well as the ravages of time itself, are themes repeated throughout his work. In awarding Simon its Prize, the Nobel committee paid this tribute: "Claude Simon's narrative art may appear as a representation of something that lives within us whether we will it or not, whether we understand it or not—something hopeful, in spite of all the cruelty and absurdity which . . . seem to characterize our condition and which is so perceptively, penetratingly, and abundantly reproduced in his novels."

Simon, who studied art in his youth, claims to have adapted the methods of proto-cubist painter Paul Cézanne for his own literary experiments. Indeed, critics frequently point out the influence of visual aesthetics, such as those borrowed from painting or cinema, in his novels. After abandoning his brief career as a painter, Simon fought with the Republicans in the Spanish civil war, but became disillusioned with the cause. Later, as a cavalryman in World War II, he was one of four French survivors of the Battle of the Meuse in 1940. This experience was especially significant to Simon, as it happened on the same field where, sixteen years earlier, his father had died in a cavalry battle. Simon wrote about this incident in *The Flanders Road*, which many critics consider his finest novel. Taken prisoner by the Germans, Simon managed to escape, and spent the rest of the Occupation working as a Resistance fighter. During this period, he also completed the novel *Le tricheur* (1945), which he had started before the war. After the Liberation, Simon retired to his ancestral country estate in the south of France and devoted himself exclusively to writing.

"In one sense, my novels are autobiographical," Simon said in an interview. "At least as far as the material. But where is truth? To begin with, our perception of the world is deformed, incomplete. Then, our memory is selective. Finally, writing transforms. One doesn't reproduce, one produces something that relates to what one has lived, but also to language itself. It's the moment when I begin to battle with words that something comes to me." Simon's first four novels, *Le tricheur*, *La corde raide* (1947), *Gulliver* (1952), and *Le sacre du printemps* (1954), are his most conventional, although they evidence Simon's disregard for linear plot in favor of evocative descriptions full of sensory details. These novels have not been

© Lütfi Özkök

widely read in recent years and have not been translated into English. In the second phase of Simon's career, he produced what most critics consider his finest novels: *The Wind, L'herbe* (1958; *The Grass*), *The Flanders Road,* and *Le palace* (1962; *The Palace*). All four novels are interconnected by shared characters and incidents and draw heavily on Simon's war experiences. They represent a development in Simon's prose style, including the experimental use of punctuation and chapter-length sentences, which has pleased, bored, or infuriated numerous critics. After a fallow period of five years, Simon began the third major phase of his work. These later novels, including *Histoire* (1967; *Histoire*), *La battaile de Pharsale* (1969; *The Battle of Pharsalus*), and *Les georgiques* (1981), take Simon's exercises in literary cubism even further, as Simon adopts a new method of composition. Working from separate visual images, Simon weaves a series of associations between them, to form a unified narrative. In order to organize these complex word tapestries, Simon reportedly uses colored pencils, color-coding each narrative strand as he writes. In *Orion aveugle* (1970) Simon set forth his literary manifesto, using pictures as well as words to explain his theories.

Critics have debated whether or not Simon should be categorized as a New Novelist. Simon himself dislikes the label, and, technically, his experiments in *Le tricheur* predate by several years the avant-garde novels of Robbe-Grillet, Sarraute, Butor, and others more closely identified with the New Novel. The majority of commentators, like Simon himself, maintain that the author's true literary connections are with the stream-of-consciousness pioneers Marcel Proust and James Joyce, as well as William Faulkner, whose abstract narratives and sentence structures are echoed in Simon's prose. Critics agree that, beyond the question of influences and alliances, Simon has developed a unique style in his fiction that, while often frustrating or obscure, is rewarding to readers able to share Simon's experimental visions. Simon reported in a 1986 interview that he is writing a new novel, tentatively titled *Complément d'information.* "Yes, I am always at work," he commented. "Anyone can do what I've done as long as he's willing to work as hard as I do. I repeat: *anyone* can do what I've done."

(See also *CLC*, Vols. 4, 9, 15 and *Contemporary Authors,* Vols. 89-92.)

LEON S. ROUDIEZ

[*Roudiez is an American critic and editor specializing in contemporary French literature. His critical works include a study of French New Novelist Michel Butor published in 1965 and* French Fiction Today *(1972). Roudiez also served as editor and managing editor of* French Review *from 1953 to 1965. In the following excerpt Roudiez chronicles the evolution of Simon's style from his relatively conventional early works to his later experiments with new narrative structures.*]

Surveying the ten works of fiction Claude Simon has published so far, one becomes aware of several stages in his esthetic development. In his earliest work, which is relatively conventional, from *Le Tricheur* (1945) to *Le Sacre du printemps* (1954), he appears to be searching for the right focus and style to give to his work. With *Le Vent* (1957) he seems to have found it, at least temporarily, and the next three books, through *Le Palace* (1962), reveal a highly disciplined concentration on a single character, theme, or setting, and a distinctive style. Meanwhile, *La Route des Flandres* (1960) had begun to evidence a preoccupation with textual matters. *Histoire* (1967), which came out after a five-year silence, shows a confident and relaxed Simon—he knows he can allow his fiction to become more complex, letting textual and thematic developments intermingle, without having to fear its getting out of focus. Finally, *La Bataille de Pharsale* (1969), with its emphasis on textual operations, was the sign of yet another renewal, as it aligned itself with the most recent trends in French writing.

Critical recognition came to Simon only after *Le Vent.* While feeling no compulsion to attempt a rehabilitation of his previous works, some of which read like dry runs for later ones, I believe they are well worth examining, both in the context of their author's developing craft and in the context of their times. Of the writers who have found eminence after the end of the Second World War, he is almost alone in allowing history as such to intrude into his fiction. . . . [In] some of Claude Simon's books historical events, like the Spanish civil war, function as they did in Malraux's a generation earlier—and not at all as they do in Sartre's fiction and drama. In spite of chro-

nology, Malraux actually might be said to stand at mid-point between Sartre and Simon in this respect. Sartre is interested in a man's "project," his existential choice when confronted with an historical situation; Malraux is more concerned with using the situation in order to give meaning to a person's life; and Simon emphasizes the situation mainly as it fills one's consciousness.

During Claude Simon's first two stages, his fiction could be characterized as being structured by time. But in the time-space equation, it is the spatial element that receives the most attention. Rather than progressing in linear fashion, gathering experience as they go, his characters seem more like giant, interlocking receptacles: time fills them relentlessly, and there comes a moment when they can take no more. A balance is destroyed and they come crashing down, carrying others with them or, at the very least, damaging the equilibrium of the structure of which they are part. The past is felt as a material presence that can be inventoried. There is no need to go in search of lost time, for it weighs on characters only too heavily.

Seen in retrospect, it is no gratuitous impulse that triggers the very first act of the main character in *Le Tricheur:* he throws his watch away. A denial of conventional chronology, characteristic of all of Simon's work, is already in evidence in the jumbled narrative sequences of that text. The protagonist is a man who refuses to be governed by chance. He takes matters involving life and death into his own hands, and that can be described as a form of cheating—hence the title. There is much that is traditional here, especially in the handling of both narrative and descriptive sequences, much also that is typical of the later Simon, although sometimes only in embryonic form. Thematically, of course, it cannot be separated from what follows. But while the performance is a creditable one, such that a lesser writer might justifiably be proud of, the master's imprint is not sufficiently strong to make a detailed examination as rewarding as it will be in the case of *Gulliver.*

The setting of *Gulliver* (1952) is postliberation France. Its mood is one of disillusionment and cynicism, reflecting the mood that prevailed in the country after the initial euphoria had subsided. . . . Not sympathy but bitterness pervades Simon's book, and its title refers to the tone of Swiftian satire, not, as I see it, to any particular detail of the fiction. (pp. 152-54)

The opening lines of *Gulliver,* "At *apértif* time, on Monday evening, in a small café in the neighborhood of the station, three regular customers were seated," are as old-fashioned as anything that could be found in a novel by Paul Bourget. When the first few sentences of *Le Vent* (1957)—a work that owes a great deal to *Gulliver*—are compared with them they provide a most striking contrast: "A fool. That's all. And nothing else. And everything people have been able to tell or invent, or try to deduce or explain, that can only confirm what anything could see at first glance. Just a plain fool." We are not only plunged *in medias res*, a commonplace in fiction today, but we are given no immediate indication as to the identity of the speaker. We know neither about whom or to whom he is talking. The words pour out, almost compulsively, breathlessly, and continue to do so with minor variations in intensity, carrying with them images of people and events, until the end of the book some 230 pages later. They are like the wind, which gives its title to the book, blowing fiercely through the southern French town where the action takes place, "an unleashed force, aimless, condemned to exhaust itself endlessly, with no hope of ending." . . . The style of *Le Vent,* developed in the fiction of the middle period and emphasizing continuity and accumulation, is one of the techniques Simon was searching for. Like the symbol of the unrelenting wind, it is part of a structure that aims at creating within the reader a sense of the past's dynamic pressure. But this style did not originate in *Le Vent*. There are many pages in *Gulliver*, especially those describing the more significant episodes, that show Simon's ability to write in such a manner, almost, one might say, naturally. His problem was one of unity. In *Le Vent*, it was solved by having the story told in the first person by a narrator who has put together information gathered from the main character and a number of others with whom he happened to be acquainted. Claude Simon pays his respects to conventional verisimilitude, for the author's surrogate teaches in a *lycée* and is doing research on Romanesque churches in the region. He is well qualified to assemble the various pieces of the puzzle created by the sudden appearance and strange behavior of the protagonist in the town. (pp. 157-59)

The relationship between this work and the earlier one becomes apparent. *Le Vent* represents a refining, perhaps even a sublimation of a pattern encountered in *Gulliver*. At first a variation on the theme of the prodigal son, it now appears as a veiled allusion to the life of Christ. Set in the context of Simon's other works, however, the value of such cultural references diminishes to a large extent. At least a change of emphasis should take place. The absence of the prodigal son, Christ's stay in Egypt and Galilee, both serve to establish a distance. Translated into Claude Simon's fiction, it becomes the distance between generations, between youth and old age, promise and fulfillment, innocence and corruption. The cry of Christ on the cross, "Why hast thou forsaken me?" could be uttered by any number of Simon's characters, especially by older ones addressing their former selves.

The reappearance of the son in *Gulliver* and *Le Vent* reflects the same theme as the confrontation between son and stepfather in *Le Sacre du printemps* or between the protagonist and his younger self in *Le Palace*. It is expressed again in capsule form in the description of an old photograph in *L'Herbe*, contrasting "the well-behaved child with gnarled knees . . . and the old man, overrun, crushed, smothered". (pp. 159-60)

Not at all concerned by Nathalie Sarraute's condemnation of "the monotonous, clumsy, 'said Jeanne,' 'answered Paul,' with which dialogue is usually strewn," he keeps the device and modifies it for greater effectiveness. He uses it not only in run-in dialogues, as Faulkner does, where it is perhaps less noticeable, but also in indented forms, where he appears to flaunt it at the reader. Using no verb, only a conjunction and a pronoun, Simon appears to consider them substitutes for the traditional French dash that precedes indented fragments of conversation. But since he also uses the dash on occasion, it would seem that the sequence "And he: . . . / And she: . . ." serves an emphatic purpose, characterizing those exchanges in which there is opposition or a momentary emotional clash between two characters. The device is both unrealistic and effective. Another feature of Claude Simon's dialogues is that they are often interrupted, not merely in the middle of a sentence, but also in the middle of a word. While it could be argued that this realistically reflects what happens in rapid-fire conversation, at least for the first kind of interruption, such a chopping-off process relates to the refusal to accept a linear concept of time. It is in harmony with the "breathless" impression created by Simon's style in this group of works and mirrors the constant accumulation of experience within a consciousness, ever increasing and ever present.

Neither of these aspects of dialogue originated with *Le Vent*. Fragmentation was already present in *Gulliver* and, in one instance, in *Le Tricheur;* emphatic dialogue-identification appeared in *Le Sacre du printemps,* which embodies a different approach to the problem Simon was attempting to solve. It is also the forerunner of *Le Palace* (1962), for in both instances we are dealing with a Spanish civil war experience confronted with a much later situation. Simon must have sensed that a temporary esthetic salvation lay in the direction of the first-person narrative, but perhaps he did not realize that the traditional, plausible first-person narrative was only one of several possibilities. He was still, in part, a victim of the realistic fallacy.

Le Sacre du printemps focusses on the early fifties and a young man named Bernard. In the background loom his stepfather and the Spanish war. Essentially, the book describes a confrontation between the two men, a clash between two receptacles of experiences. . . . What interest there is in this book emerges from the situation created by Bernard, that is, by the sum of his experiences, even more so by his lack of them (for, in some ways, he, too, prefigures Montès), when confronted by a no-longer so innocent outside world. The Spanish experience appears to obsess Simon. To him, it may be a necessary ingredient of consciousness, but in the story it is esthetically superfluous. Or else, Bernard's experience was superfluous: each one obliterated the other. In *Le Palace,* the conflict is resolved by fusing the two consciousnesses into one, and the same person confronts his own civil war experience in Spain with the total experience of what he has become many years later.

The narrative elements in *Le Palace* are more closely woven together. A Frenchman goes to Barcelona, has a glass of beer in a café across the street from a modernistic bank building. Where the bank now stands there used to be a luxury hotel, the "palace" of the title, which burned down during the final stages of the Spanish war. As he looks at the bank and thinks back to the few days he had spent in the hotel, apparently as a volunteer for the loyalists, when it was requisitioned by the republican forces, he re-experiences both the events and the material objects of that particular past. (pp. 163-64)

The palace is both a correlative to the war and to his consciousness. The narrative is so structured as to make of the war not an outside reality, an absolute that might be used as a standard by which past actions might be evaluated, but a fragmented series of events, of which several become the components of an inner reality.

In similar fashion, *La Route des Flandres* (1960) is not about the French army retreat in 1940; rather, it describes the attempt by one participant to make some sense out of the life and death of another (a death that occurred during the military rout of 1940, a time of intense psychological stress). As in *Le Palace,* the historical event is viewed from a later point in time, on the occasion of a purely personal experience that releases a previously repressed trauma. What in the later piece of fiction triggers an inventory of the past is an emotional shock, but also a somewhat arbitrary one: the Frenchman did not have to return to Barcelona. The catalytic event of *La Route des Flandres* is deliberately sought by George, who is the central consciousness of this story. He thinks sleeping with Corinne, the dead man's widow, will provide him with certain clues he is looking for—although he does not realize how much his own memory will yield on that occasion. From that point of view, it is almost a necessary event and one to which the narration comes back regularly. That is one of several reasons that leads me to place this book a few rungs above *Le Palace,* which follows chronologically.... What may have happened is that Simon was becoming gradually more and more interested in textual motifs but had not yet found an effective way of weaving them into the fictional architecture, as he later succeeded in doing in *Les Corps conducteurs.*

The success of *La Route des Flandres* is in large part the result of Simon's having built a very rigorous architecture for his narrative. He was thus able to achieve a more complex interweaving of thematic elements than the fundamental plot of *Le Palace* allowed. (pp. 165-66)

La Route des Flandres ... exhibits a tripartite confusion affecting narrator, narration, and listener, destroying the three indispensable elements of traditional story-telling. What remains is no longer a story, properly speaking, but something that one might conveniently call a text—an assemblage of words that functions according to linguistic laws. As Bernard Pingaud wrote about one of its features, "transition from fictitious scene to real scene (and vice versa) is in most instances effected by surprise, the narrative turning not on a fact, not even on an analogy (thereby giving up all logical links), but on a word, as in music a simple chord is enough to indicate modulation." Going one step further, Jean Ricardou gave such pivotal words the designation of "structural metaphors," since what enables the transition to take place is often the shift from one meaning of that word to another. The most striking example he gives concerns the references to *traditions ancestralement conservées comme qui dirait dans la Saumur* ("traditions ancestorially preserved as if they had been soaked in brine"), where the meaning "brine" immediately gives way before "French officers' cavalry school," located in the town of Saumur (which lacks the final "e" of *saumure,* meaning "brine").

Claude Simon had previously published *L'Herbe* (1958), not as accomplished as *La Route des Flandres* but a text in which his concept of time is given clear emphasis. Aspects of style, dialogue, and narrative technique previously noted are present here to the extent and quality one might expect, considering the chronological position of this work in relation to others. (pp. 168-69)

The entire emphasis of *Histoire* is on integrating the architecture of the narrative into a natural framework, something *La Route des Flandres* had already attempted and partially accomplished. The basic unit here is a day in the narrator's later years, from early morning until after midnight.... If we consider the day of the narrative to constitute the present time of the fiction, the first and last chapters then belong outside of time and serve a purpose similar to the corresponding chapters in *Gulliver.* The second chapter starts with the awakening of the narrator; the eleventh chapter closes as he watches the stars from his bedroom window. In the meantime he has gone out into the street, encountered a former beau of his mother's, visited his bank, had lunch in a restaurant.... A completely uninteresting day, a mere canvas on which to weave the drama of a single person against the backdrop of history. Colonialism, two world wars, the Russian revolution, and the Spanish civil war are inescapably present throughout the pages of *Histoire.*

What sets things in motion is the narrator's decision to sell a chest of drawers and the ensuing necessity to empty it of its contents—the mass of postcards. They are sent by various members of the family, but those that spur his memory most were mailed to his mother from all over the world by his father

before their marriage. Much of his life is resurrected in the process, modified by present obsessions. That, at least, is how things appear to the reader; but if one looks at this work with the insight gained from reading subsequent ones, he sees a need to modify the order of those events. If one will refrain from allegorizing, from attempting to fit matters into a plausible story, and remain on the textual level, he should realize that the postcards are at the very source of the fiction. Their aggregate has generated the chest of drawers and the reason for its being where it is. Each individual card has generated an incident or series of incidents that eventually create the narrator's life and all the aspects of the fiction.

To go back to the narration and the fable it allows readers to elaborate, one does not get the impression of a series of flashbacks as in the preceding books; the narrative seems closer to an interior monologue.... As the day of the narrative unfolds, the narrator's life is spread out before us, some of it in chronological order. There are actually three planes of development: the present time, the narrator's life, and incidental forays into the past. The first two constitute the fixed, arbitrary elements of the architecture, which nevertheless corresponds to biological realities. The third is, esthetically speaking, a chance element; it is the one more obviously determined by the reality of the thought process, that is, by the nature of language. That sort of freedom under a close-fitting harness is an essential virtue of this book.

As in previous works, the theme of *Histoire* is the accumulation of time, its accelerating encroachment upon innocence and life, the increasing weight it places upon a person until it eventually destroys him. A concomitant theme is that of decay. (pp. 170-73)

Histoire seemed such a felicitous culmination of Simon's writings, it restated and related so many of the earlier themes, that it was hard to visualize the work that might follow. This is *La Bataille de Pharsale* (1969), a text that heralds the appearance of a third stage in his fictional development. One of a number of factors that apparently prompted the change was Simon's first visit to the United States, especially to New York, which he made in the fall of 1968. There he was struck by the kaleidoscopic variety of the metropolitan area—lower Manhattan, Brooklyn Heights, industrial areas of New Jersey, fall colors in Bear Mountain Park and in Westchester, various lookout points and bridges over the Hudson and other waterways, which he saw in quick succession and also telescoped together from the top of the Empire State building. Another factor has been a growing interest in the thought process that Claude Lévi-Strauss has called *bricolage* (the act of pottering, of making objects with whatever materials are at hand).... (pp. 174-75)

The new manner revealed in *La Bataille de Pharsale* does not signify a complete break with his previous fiction, for one of its important features was already noted in connection with *La Route des Flandres.* The work is a text, not a linear narrative but an assemblage of words ruled by linguistic laws rather than by those of plausibility and everyday logic. An indication of the evolution that has taken place since *Le Palace* may be conveyed in the contrast between "Inventaire," a chapter heading from that book and "Lexique," the title of the second chapter of *La Bataille de Pharsale.* The shift is from representation of an objective exterior reality as absorbed by a subjective consciousness to a display of the reality of language as constituting the subjective world of an individual. (pp. 175-76)

There are several major narratives in *La Bataille de Pharsale.* One describes war episodes that could have been inserted in

La Route des Flandres without startling the reader. Another centers in an affair with a painter's model named Odette (the Proustian overtone is surely not accidental). A third tells of an auto trip to Greece and the site of the battle of Pharsalus. A fourth depicts a boy struggling with his Latin homework dealing with that same battle. A fifth involves a train trip through Italy. There are also detailed descriptions of lovemaking and battle scenes evidently based on sculptures and paintings. Narratives and descriptions are broken up and their fragments juxtaposed, sometimes even interwoven. In the process, images of intense jealousy and death are set up against a foil of indifference on the part of those not directly involved. Various references, such as the one to "Uncle Charles," might lead one to assume that there is a narrator who is identical with the one in *Histoire,* but even more than in that work this text acquires an autonomy of its own and tends to push such an imagined narrator into the background if it does not destroy him utterly. He is no longer the actor; he is the stage upon which the action takes place. He is also the observer (of which there may well be more than one). As we learn in the last section of the second chapter, he is designated by the letter O, which is also the symbol for zero, that is, nonexistence. The initial O designates not only the observer but also the object being observed (a duality already hinted at in *Histoire*). In addition, O is the first letter of the name Odette, the model whose representation in the text could perhaps be seen as correlative to that of ancient Rome, for whom Caesar and Pompey were fighting (as two men appear to be currying favor with Odette)—a struggle culminating in Pompey's defeat during the battle of Pharsalus.

If *Histoire* ends with a word that challenges the identity of the author of *Le Tricheur,* thus completing a rather wide circle, *La Bataille de Pharsale* achieves another kind of circularity, not unique in postwar fiction, by ending with the very sentence that set it in motion. This recalls a statement from the diary of Maurice Merleau-Ponty, in connection with the language of both Simon and Butor: "Such uses of language may be understood only if language is conceived as a being, a world, and if Speech [*la Parole*] is thought of as the circle."

Claude Simon's most recent book, *Les Corps conducteurs* (1971), has a history that enables one to grasp in more concrete fashion the writing process characteristic of his third manner. He had been asked to contribute a text to the Skira collection called "The Paths of Creation." That text, published as *Orion aveugle,* came with a preface in which he explained how he writes. "From my point of view, there are no paths of creation other than those one clears step by step, that is, word after word, through the treading of the pen itself." . . . To which he added: "Before I start setting down signs on paper, there is nothing—aside from a formless mass of more or less confused sensations, of more or less precise memories; and a vague, a very vague project." The painting by Nicolas Poussin, "Paysage avec Orion aveugle," serves as a metaphor for the writing activity, which has become, at this stage of Simon's evolution, nearly identical with the one described by Blanchot. The writer is blind to the extent that, having nothing to communicate, driven by a need to say "something," he proceeds without knowing whither such a need might take him.

In the case of *Orion aveugle,* it began with the desire to put "something" together (*bricoler*), using as a point of departure a few paintings that he liked—in particular, "Charlene," by Robert Rauschenberg—which brought forth other images or representations of the American continent. . . . The text of *Or-*

ion aveugle was then published, lavishly illustrated with reproductions of many of the generators that set it in motion, and itself standing as an illustration of a specific approach to fiction writing. The initial purpose having been fulfilled, Simon felt he needed to pursue his work. "And it now seems as though the path cleared by *Orion aveugle* should lead somewhere." . . . That "somewhere," however, does not designate the traditional kind of ending one expects in a narration, for the emphasis is on the text rather than the anecdote. Consequently, the path followed by the writer "can have no other end than the exhaustion of a traveller exploring that inexhaustible landscape." The landscape he has in mind is that of man's language. At such a time of "exhaustion," a piece of fiction comes into being, "which will not tell the exemplary story of some hero or heroine, but that very different story constituted by the singular adventure of the narrator who never abandons his quest, discovering the world gropingly, in and through the written language." . . . (pp. 177-80)

"Pottering" might be basic, but it is not sufficient for Claude Simon. He needs to weld things together within a unifying architecture. What Poussin's painting and the resulting symbolism did for *Orion aveugle* is not enough for the organization of this developing fiction. The basic generative elements being linked with the American continent, it seemed natural enough to center the various textual products of such elements describing the brief stay of a traveller in a large American city. (The city is easily identifiable as New York, in spite of the insertion of a number of European items that emerged out of the writer's consciousness). The parallel between physical travel and a writer's "adventure" in language is obvious enough. (p. 180)

Leon S. Roudiez, "Claude Simon," in his French Fiction Today: A New Direction, *Rutgers University Press, 1972, pp. 152-82.*

JOHN FLETCHER

[Fletcher is an English critic and editor who specializes in French literature. He has written and coauthored several studies of Samuel Beckett, including The Novels of Samuel Beckett *(1964) and* A Student's Guide to the Plays of Samuel Beckett *(1978). His other works include* New Directions in Literature: Critical Approaches to a Contemporary Phenomenon *(1968) and* Alain Robbe-Grillet *(1983). In the following excerpt Fletcher examines the influences of Joseph Conrad, Marcel Proust, and William Faulkner on Simon. He then analyzes three aspects of Simon's mature work: his fascination with the concept of time, his use of the narrator, and specific characteristics of his style and narrative technique.]*

Like his coeval Camus [Simon] has been profoundly affected by Dostoyevsky, by the unique density and intensity of his novels which are features (all proportions kept) of Simon's writings also. But a more specific influence can be discerned in his early books. The second he published, *La Corde raide,* takes its epigraph from Dostoyevsky; novels like *Le Tricheur* and *Gulliver* could be said to be rather sombre in their Dostoyevskian preoccupation with mystery and sensational crime, and their concentration on dark and even evil forces at work in human affairs, corrupting, polluting and destroying people's feeble attempts to achieve happiness and tranquillity; and *The Wind*'s hero is a kind of Dostoyevsky innocent, a Simonian 'Idiot'. But after *The Wind* this influence fades as the mature writer outgrows the young man's literary enthusiasms; for what he tried to imitate in Dostoyevsky was an atmosphere, the rather feverish tone, without at the same time sharing the religious and social assumptions underlying the original. In so far as they possess a Dostoyevskian flavour, Simon's early works do not rise much above laboured pastiche.

From Joseph Conrad, on the other hand, Simon learned something much more lastingly important: how to construct a fiction. The books of his apprentice years all show him exploring and developing techniques copied from the Polish master, who is for him 'the father of the kind of novel which has freed itself from extra-literary preoccupations like message, realism and psychology', . . . and he refers interviewers to the preface of *The Nigger of the Narcissus* which he believes to be a text of crucial importance in his own development. (pp. 43-4)

Simon shares completely the emphasis Conrad lays upon visualization, on making palpable, on creating a sensuously experienced world, rather than on conveying a message. In his own case, he is not concerned in *The Flanders Road* to analyse the political and moral dilemmas of the period, the sort of thing which occupies nearly all of Sartre's attention in *Roads to Freedom;* nor, in *The Palace,* does he go in for the sort of ideological conversations which take up so much space in Malraux's novel *Days of Hope.* On the contrary: in the first book he reconstructs, even reconstitutes, a moment on a road in the war zone with such vividness that not only did one of the participants recognize it at once after twenty years, but the rest of us who were not there carry the feel of it in our imagination long after reading about it. And in *The Palace* the requisitioned luxury hotel of the title is faithfully resurrected before our eyes by such details as the 'huge couch . . . upholstered in faded red or rather pinkish moiré silk, still in rather good condition along the back, but worn on the seat, frayed in ladders of parallel fibres fine as hairs' . . . which is soon stained with grease when one of the characters leans his rifle against it.

More concretely, we find Simon in *The Wind* adopting the sort of devices of narrative reconstruction (it is not for nothing that the novel is subtitled 'Attempted Restoration of a Baroque Altarpiece') elaborated by Conrad in *Under Western Eyes* and other works. In *Lord Jim,* as in *Heart of Darkness,* Marlow is the narrator, but he is not omniscient. Indeed, in *Lord Jim* he is not introduced until the fourth chapter, and some of his information is gleaned only 'a long time after' from 'an elderly French lieutenant' whom he met 'by the merest chance', 'one afternoon in Sydney', and whose story is related in chapter twelve. Similarly, in *Under Western Eyes* Conrad's narrator, the ageing teacher of languages, is by no means in full possession of all the information needed to tell Razumov's story. He acquires this only gradually, from a variety of sources, one of which is Razumov's personal diary, but part of the truth is revealed only at the very end of the novel when, the narrator tells us, 'I heard for the first time of Razumov's public confession in Laspara's house', a crucial episode about which only a 'very summary' version had been available. This is very like the technique Simon's schoolmaster narrator adopts in *The Wind:* he picks up information, from which the story is built up, in a variety of ways. He learns a lot, of course, from the protagonist Montès, but other people, like the lawyer, tell him things too. The very Conradian device of situating a marginal observer, like Marlow or the language-teacher, within the narrative, and making him its principal constructor, is seen operating at its purest in *The Wind,* which is for that reason still a rather derivative novel. But by *The Grass* Claude Simon reveals that he has transcended and absorbed this very necessary and fruitful influence. He will still employ time-shifts like

Conrad, unfolding his narrative in piecemeal fashion as memory or association dredges up fragments of information buried in the narrator's consciousness; he will continue to follow Conrad's example and employ dialogue, or free indirect speech, as a vehicle for conveying facts about the situation; and, like Conrad introducing Nostromo almost surreptitiously, he will still slip in vital details amongst a lot of secondary material. But he will no longer employ, as a kind of safety net, an omniscient narrator of the kind that has to tell us about Decoud's end in *Nostromo* since in the nature of things no one else could have observed it. *The Grass* is transitional in this regard: although the whole story is told very closely from Louise's point of view, her consciousness does not constitute the sole theatre in which the story is enacted. Although the next novel, *The Flanders Road,* alternates between first- and third-person narration (between 'I' and 'Georges'), nothing occurs outside Georges's mental sphere. And in *The Palace,* the whole novel is enacted in the student's mind, and is compounded of his memories of the past and his impressions of the present. Thus by the early 1960s Simon had fully absorbed the lessons of Conrad, and had begun to surpass them.

The other influences which Simon sustained are more obvious and more generally shared with other 'new novelists'. Proust's flexible construction of time in *La Recherche,* where he moves over long stretches with few temporal indications to give an impression of generality is widely followed today, not least by Claude Simon in a novel like *Histoire* which covers half a century of human history. Just as in his account of Swann's love affair with Odette Proust ranges over months and even years of time, or in his later volumes glides freely between the Dreyfus case and the occupation of eastern France by the Germans in 1914-18, so *Histoire* moves us from the narrator's father penning laconic postcards for his fiancée, the narrator's future mother, to the hero himself trying to sell the chest in which the cards have been stored all those years. There is a distinction, of course: Proust is genuinely vague about time, even indifferent to matters of chronological exactitude, partly because the writing of his novel was spread over many years, whereas Simon deliberately adopts imprecision from the outset. The result, aesthetically speaking, may be similar, but the intention is different.

Simon is quite overt about his debt to Proust. He quotes him frequently (in *The Battle of Pharsalus* even systematically, as part of the plot, using a technique dubbed 'intertextuality'), and his style presents some analogies with Proust's; they both use long, complex periods for instance, and where Proust subordinates, Simon tends to parenthesize, so that the cumulative effect of such syntax will often sound very similar. (pp. 44-7)

Again like his contemporaries, Simon has derived great benefit from a study of narrative methods, especially interior monologue, as practised by Virginia Woolf and James Joyce; of Joyce, in particular, much could be said: Simon always mentions his name admiringly, and *Ulysses* seems to be affectionately parodied in *Histoire*. . . . The raising of the pun (above its status in *Tristram Shandy* as a mere embellishment) to high art in *Finnegans Wake,* where it becomes an integral and all-embracing element of total structure in fiction, was probably just as inspiring an example to Simon as *monologue intérieur* which, in common with many others of his generation, he imitated from *Ulysses.* Joyce's later verbal profusion lies behind several contemporary works, not least Simon's recent novels, where the proliferative potential of linguistic components is exploited to the full. (p. 49)

This self-consciousness of fiction in fiction is what is archetypally modernist. Shem is writing a book which is the *Wake* itself; this is the case with Proust's narrator, too, of course, but Joyce goes further in offering the 'parody of a parody'. Such are Nabokov's *Pale Fire,* Robbe-Grillet's *Project for a Revolution in New York,* and Simon's *The Battle of Pharsalus* in which the central figure O. is alternately author of and protagonist within the fiction, in a text that presents itself as being, so to speak, 'self-generated'. This is what I understand by Hassan's term 'parodic reflexiveness' in which 'the genre, with its multiple, fractured and ambiguous perspectives' comes of age. Of course, there may be drawbacks in Joyce's method and in its imitators'; Hassan's rhetorical question, 'Without hope of redemption, will not such ('lapsarian') irony turn secretly into despair or even malice?' commands an answer which it is yet too early to give. But Hassan himself indicates the possible alternative tradition within modernism, Picasso's 'pagan wit'. I think we have some of that in Simon's baroque, pantheist side, his sheer celebration of life's processes in spite of their tragic destination. But he gives his sensuous impulse rigour by sharing with other post-modernists in continuing the Joycean heritage of proposing rational control of the pullulating and effervescent energies of the world.

Simon owes, too, a general debt to French pathfinders in the modern like Louis-Ferdinand Céline and Michel Leiris. But, more markedly than any of his colleagues, he has been profoundly influenced by William Faulkner; so much so, in fact, that some critics have tended to dismiss his work as little more than pastiche of the great Southern writer. In reality, Simon probably owes no more to Faulkner than he does to Conrad, but because the latter's style is not so obviously personal it is harder to accuse Simon of copying it. He admires Faulkner primarily for developing the 'sensorial' rather than the 'intellectual' possibilities of literary creation, but he has his reservations, in particular over Faulkner's habit of delivering himself of moral observations of 'staggering banality, of lamentable conformity'; 'it would be interesting', he says, 'to separate out in Faulkner's work the admirable passages in which he wrote so superbly (about people, things, animals, smells . . .) from those in which he philosophizes and moralizes'. . . . (pp. 50-1)

These objections, together with the gradual and necessary quality of the evolution of Simon's style over the years . . . makes it very improbable that anything like pastiche is a satisfactory description of the connection between the two writers. There may, however, be a case for supposing unconscious imitation, even in such a selfconscious novelist. It is true that Simon shares certain technical devices with William Faulkner and may have derived them from him. Random soundings in one of Faulkner's most characteristic works show his fondness for colons and parentheses, both of which are standard features of Simon's practice. (p. 51)

Simon was clearly impressed by American writing, and by Faulkner's in particular, like many other French novelists of his generation; it will be remembered that Sartre devoted early essays to *Sartoris* and *The Sound and the Fury,* and Camus's admiration led to an adaptation of *Requiem for a Nun.*

The obvious occasional similarities between Simon's style and French versions of Faulkner should not, however, blind us to the differences. For all its elaboration, Faulkner's writing—compared with Simon's—is relatively unselfconscious. It has a deceptive spontaneity lacking in Simon. It does not attempt to be 'intellectual', but only to imitate the thought processes and speech rhythms of Southern people. Simon's language on

the other hand is a highly imaged artefact, deliberately and painstakingly developed for a purpose which owes little to any other writer (except, marginally, to Proust in the matter of time and memory). In any case he has shown in his most recent works—*Les Corps conducteurs* and *Triptyque*—that his style is not static and immutable, and that he is able to discard the long, sinuous periods of his middle novels when his thematic interests change. . . . (pp. 53-4)

Nevertheless, it is clear from an investigation of Claude Simon's sources and debts that, like other neo-modernist writers, he has self-consciously carved out a place for himself in the fictional tradition he shares with his contemporaries. Like them, he builds on what has gone before; like them, too, he modifies and develops his inheritance. In extending what he has learned from the practice and example of the great modernists he has created a fictional oeuvre which is uniquely personal. It presents similarities, of course, with the work of other *nouveaux romanciers,* but cannot be confused with their explorations. What Simon has created, he has created alone. Like all great artists, he has fashioned his own instrument by trial and error in the never-ending task—and never-satisfied ambition—of expressing his own vision of reality in the universal medium of language. (p. 54)

Claude Simon is, first and last, a novelist. What he has written or published outside the canon of his fiction is of little significance. But, for the record, this is what it appears to be made up of. There are the interviews, replies to literary *enquêtes* and questionnaires, public lectures and so on, which constitute an unsystematic and partial exposition of the theory, or aesthetic, of the kind of novel-writing Simon practises; but he is not a propagandist or polemicist like Robbe-Grillet or even Nathalie Sarraute, and so far he has shown no interest in collecting these scattered pieces. I doubt even whether he attaches very much importance to them; they were all produced in response to a stimulus exerted from outside (a journalist's questions, an invitation to lecture) and were not, like Robbe-Grillet's statements, provoked by any inner compulsion to make explicit what have been called 'les sentiers de la création'. In fact, in his contribution to a series bearing that title, published by Skira, Simon writes: 'As far as I am concerned, the only "paths of creation" are those opened up step by step, that is word by word, by the very progression of the writing'. . . . In other words, for Claude Simon the act of writing alone can uncover, and then only partially, the principles which govern its functioning, so that all 'theory' is inevitably *post hoc,* descriptive of a state of affairs that lies already behind in the past. Hence no doubt the fact that Simon sees no utility in giving these utterances a more permanent form.

Apart from composing theoretical statements, Simon has had one play performed. It was called *La Séparation;* it was based on *The Grass;* it consisted, drama critic Jacques Lemarchand writes, of 'four interwoven monologues' and was not very effective theatrically; it was staged at the Théâtre de Lutèce, a small experimental playhouse in Paris, in the spring of 1963, was taken off after a few performances, and has not been published; nor is it likely to be. Like Henry James, Simon writes superb dialogue in his novels, but he has no sense of theatre, no feeling for ways of filling a stage with movement and life. Although he would like to write a filmscript, no one has yet invited him to do so, and he has done nothing in this medium at all.

The only other published works, apart from the novels, and a kind of prose poem called *Femmes* which was illustrated by

Joan Miró, are the early essay in autobiography *La Corde raide* . . . , various pre-publication fragments from the novels (these appeared in various journals—*Tel Quel, Lettres Nouvelles,* and so on—and rarely show variants of any significance); and a rather indifferent short story called "**Babel**" which Simon now repudiates. And that is all.

The novels, then (and even so not the entire canon, of course), are what really count, and they alone are the subject of the present study. Since there are now almost a dozen of them, it would help, I think, if I suggested certain broad groups or categories into which they appear naturally to fall. The first remark that has to be made is that all Simon's fiction is based, to a greater or lesser extent, on his personal experience: he has declared, not quite truthfully, that he is unable to invent anything by himself. As a reading of *La Corde raide* and acquaintance with the basic facts of his biography make clear, he certainly exploits personal memories in his novels, but refracts and distorts these, often in quite radical ways. He takes full advantage, in fact, just as Proust did, of the artist's prerogative to modify and adapt reality to fit his aesthetic purposes. Just as Proust's Combray is an idealized, even mythified version of Illiers, and his Balbec resembles the real Cabourg only in incidentals, so Claude Simon charges places, people and real occurrences with a significance quite transcending that which they originally represented. His setting for *The Palace* is and is not Barcelona; *The Wind* may be located in Perpignan, but it need not be; *The Grass* is based, like *Histoire,* only partially on family documents and souvenirs; and *The Flanders Road* draws only fragmentarily on Claude Simon's own war experiences (there is nothing about his successful escape, for instance: Georges spends the whole period in captivity). But, when that is said, the fact of an at least partial degree of personal experience does enable us to place the novels into three broad groups, as follows: firstly novels dealing with the period immediately preceding and that immediately following the Second World War (*Le Tricheur, Gulliver, The Wind*); these are perhaps the least 'personal' works in Claude Simon's fictional output, and so it is not surprising if they read occasionally as if they were written to a formula, a pattern imitated from Simon's acknowledged masters in the art of the novel; secondly novels dealing with the Spanish civil war (*Le Sacre du printemps, The Palace*); these draw so obviously on Simon's own experience that little comment is needed, except (as Leon S. Roudiez has perceptively pointed out [see excerpt above]) *Le Sacre* is really just a first draft for *The Palace,* which makes a much better book 'by fusing the two consciousnesses into one [so that] the same person confronts his own civil war experience in Spain with the total experience of what he has become many years later'; thirdly novels dealing with the period during and after the Second World War, with particular reference to the fortunes of the narrator's family; all the other works enter this category more or less directly. (pp. 57-9)

As to how the progression in these works figures itself in the author's own mind, Simon has been quite explicit. Interviewed by Ludovic Janvier, he spoke of his 'slow, groping evolution'; he saw his first phase as ending with *The Wind;* a second period was inaugurated by *The Grass,* and ended with *Histoire;* and a third began with *The Battle of Pharsalus,* in which for the first time he allowed himself to be governed not by what he himself wished to say but by what the writing itself said, by its own 'internal dynamic'. We might see the first phase as being apprenticeship, in which he tried a number of different plots and situations in his attempts to find an authentically individual voice of his own. For this reason, these novels are

not discussed in any great detail in this study. The second period can be seen as maturity, when Simon had not only established his characteristic manner, but had also started to mine the rich vein of family history that I have just discussed. In my view, these novels—especially *The Grass, The Flanders Road* and *Histoire*—constitute his highest achievement as of now, the early 1970s. His more recent works—particularly *Les Corps conducteurs*—I am less happy about. They seem to me to betray uncertainty, and to be excessively influenced by theories (picked up from others, Jean Ricardou in particular) of the alleged autogeneration of texts. Nevertheless Claude Simon is still in the prime of life, and out of his current restless experimentation an altogether new manner may evolve. He has done it before; by dint of patience and constant trying he found, with *The Grass,* how to transcend the category of the talented but minor novelist in which his early books put him. Perhaps, in much the same way, texts of the *Corps conducteurs* variety will enable him to pull off that most difficult of artistic feats, a complete self-renewal and the creation in a quite different idiom of another series of masterpieces. If this does happen, Simon will quite clearly become one of the great novelists of this century, and take his place naturally among the masters he reveres: Joyce, Faulkner, Beckett and Proust.

But for the present such considerations must be speculative. . . . I should like us to consider . . . , in synoptic fashion, three important aspects of the fiction: how it handles the theme of time, which is so central to it; how the narrator operates in the novels; and what the characteristic features of Simon's style and narrative technique are. (pp. 62-3)

Simon would agree that the past is like a spectre, one that cannot be exorcized. 'There is a profound tension in his novels,' John Sturrock writes [see *CLC,* Vol. 15], 'between the urge to reconstruct the past as densely and plausibly as possible, and the perpetual recognition that any sort of certainty dies with the event.' This is because, when things are perceived by man, that act of perception itself deforms what is perceived; and when perceptions are remembered later, the act of memory deforms those perceptions too; and, finally, when the memories are written down, the very act of writing deforms further what has twice been deformed already. . . . [Simon's] treatment of time and of the way human memory and perception attempt to control and organize it reveals a profound scepticism about the nature of reality. The novels are usually articulated around an event which is only half-remembered, and at least partially imaginary; this is then painfully reconstructed in a narrative process which invariably omits to do more than confirm a rather hopeless quest. This occurs in *The Flanders Road,* where Georges's sexual failure with Corinne is paradigmatic of his wider failure to reconstruct the past as it was, and in *The Palace,* where the middle-aged hero is compelled to accept the impossibility of recreating the Barcelona he knew so intimately as a young revolutionary in 1936.

Time attracts a surprisingly extensive range of epithet in Simon's writings: it is at various points described as 'solid' or 'rigid', 'gelatinous' and 'liable to putrefy', 'stagnant' and 'viscous' like sludge or a thick clay 'in which the instant resembles a spade slicing the dark earth and revealing the myriad wriggling worms' (*The Wind*) . . . and—of course—'inexorable', 'mechanical', its progress as irreversible as the hands of antique clocks jumping forward with the staccato rhythm imposed on every second by the action of the pendulum and giving the impression that time consists of a conglomeration of solid lumps, a 'succession of solidified fragments' or 'of fixed, frozen, motionless images' (*The Palace*). . . . This dual aspect of duration—its liquid, mobile quality, its resemblance to haemorrhage, ceaseless flow, and its divisible, fragmentary nature—is continually insisted upon. (pp. 64-5)

The issue of the status of the narrative voice in fiction—of the '*voix-qui-parle*'—is central to the modernist novel, and Simon's work is no exception. Like other writers, he probes the ambiguous relationship between author and narrator which is so typical a feature of modernism, but he extends the investigation to include perception of flux and change, a perception which is characteristically his own.

On a purely technical level, Simon moves from the kind of fiction which employs a plausible narrator, such as *The Wind* where a *lycée* teacher, rather like Conrad's teacher of languages in *Under Western Eyes,* supplies an objective but not omniscient point of view, to a new form of novel in which the reader is addressed by the text itself. Leon S. Roudiez [see excerpt above] discerns the origins of this evolution as early as *The Flanders Road;* certainly it comes to the fore in *The Battle of Pharsalus* and dominates *Les Corps conducteurs* and *Triptyque.* And we have indeed come a long way from the rather unsubtle use of younger and older variants of the same person's point of view in *Le Sacre du printemps* when we pass, via the gradually revealed narrator of *The Wind,* to the complex 'observer observed', the narrator called O. who is also an actor (and sometimes actress) in the drama of *The Battle of Pharsalus.* (pp. 69-70)

Simon brings the situation of the narrator into line with the general perception of mobility and change which lies at the heart of his vision. Over the years he has moved from traditional-style narrators, which are necessarily rigid by definition, to a position in which extremely volatile and fluid narrational situations are the norm. Whether such a development makes for fiction of real quality is a moot point, but what is certain is that Simon has revealed an impressively consistent impulse over the years, as well as a will to self-renewal which does him great credit. In common with all modern writers, Claude Simon is very self-conscious about his art and what he is trying to attain in writing novels, though like most writers he stresses that the final elaborated product goes far beyond anything he had originally in mind. I propose here to look more closely at the question of style and narrative technique in order to illustrate how Simon's aesthetic operates on the level of the text we are presented with. (pp. 73-4)

As Simon himself has argued, the texture of the writing is not just an involved way of saying something basically quite simple, but the most straightforward manner he can find of conveying something highly complex. His early novels are naive affairs, and the style is similarly embryonic. But his later fictions are profound and subtle meditations on time, memory and the aesthetic act itself, for which an organic narrative manner, rich in synonyms, amplifications, qualifications and illustrative analogies, is indispensable. In evolving that style Claude Simon has shown himself to be one of the most inventive prose artists of our time. (pp. 82-3)

In terms of plot, the early novels employ a technique—derived variously from Simon's literary masters—which consists of deferring information or temporarily interrupting the action to bring up elements of a side- or sub-plot, or in order to introduce, via a flashback or a supplementary narrative, information which explains an earlier dramatic episode whose cause, at the time, was obscure. (p. 83)

Another feature of Simon's plots—and all this of course concerns only the work up to the early sixties, after which date plot ceases to be a factor of any importance in his fiction—is the gradual revelation by fits and starts of a story, for example the theft of jewels in *The Wind,* or their loss on a railway track in *The Grass;* in both novels the text returns frequently and often unexpectedly to events like these which are of dramatic interest and, in *The Wind* at least, of serious consequence. Sometimes aspects of a story are told from more than one point of view; either the narrative is continued from another person's angle without much interruption in the progression . . . , or the same events are repeated in a different register of discourse. (p. 84)

In the later novels the notion of reconstitution, which formed the basis of *The Wind,* comes to the fore as the major structural principle. In *The Battle of Pharsalus,* the publisher's blurb says, 'an observer himself observed seeks to reconstitute something which is ultimately revealed as being constituted solely by the quest itself in its progression, its hesitations and its meanders.' And in Simon's most ambitious exploration of the fictive process to date, *Triptyque,* three separate and distinct stories are told, not consecutively as in Flaubert's volume *Three Tales,* but concurrently, with little to indicate that the text has switched gear. The unprepared reader is all the more likely to be misled because the book is divided into three parts; but these are purely arbitrary divisions and bear no relation to the subject-matter. In fact, one might claim that after the early novels—say up to and including *Le Sacre du printemps*—in which the chapter-break retains its traditional dramatic value as a suspense creator or as a way of modulating to another level of the plot or to another point of view, the reason for which the prose is cut up in sections is mere convenience. The chief exception is *The Palace,* where each of the five parts (which are linked together by the last phrase of the one being repeated at the start of the next) corresponds to a different episode, or at least aspect, of the fiction. . . . (pp. 85-6)

In all the later novels the reconstitution is provoked and pressed forward by generative elements. In *Histoire* the postcards fulfil this function, and *The Battle of Pharsalus* is at least partially generated by the photograph of Uncle Charles in the Dutchman's studio which perhaps lay among the family papers that the narrator of *Histoire* clears out of the chest he is selling to the antique dealer. Such a link between one novel and its successor would be fully characteristic of Simon's method. When the generators are not external objects like these, the text develops according to the changing associations in the narrator's mind; in *Les Corps conducteurs,* for instance, there is fertile confusion between a woman's boa, a serpent, and the serpentine meanders of a great river seen from the air. . . . Similarly in *The Grass* Louise's consciousness jumps from her frenzied attempts to unbutton her lover's shirt to the grotesque struggle in the bathroom next to her own when Pierre catches Sabine tippling . . . , and in *The Flanders Road* the descriptions of POWs in a meadow lying exhausted head to foot jumps straight to Georges engaged in cunnilingus with Corinne. . . . Jean Ricardou . . . has made much of puns and anagrams as a structural factor in Simon's prose. More obvious than Ricardou's sibylline exegetic is the fact that newspaper headlines provoke particular resonances in Simon's texts. . . . Perhaps Simon acquired his interest in newspaper headlines from the collage artists he admires, from Braque to Rauschenberg; but however that may be, there is no question about the powerful associative role such elements play in his work. . . . (pp. 86-7)

Simon's debt to the cinema is . . . immense throughout his career. His novels are full of analogies and metaphors of cinematographic origin. . . . Reading one or two of the early novels, especially *Le Sacre du printemps,* I occasionally think what a good film it would make: the cutting script seems already to exist in embryo and the dialogues are already written out, so that the transition to *mise en scène* would be smoothly accomplished; even the short-focus work and the close-ups are specified in *The Wind* . . . [and] the flashback is a basic structural feature of both *Le Tricheur* and *Gulliver.*

More than this, Simon appears to build his later novels according to a principle very like that of montage. He has himself said that *The Flanders Road* is 'composed essentially of a sequence of images', written in fragments which he later put together 'by means of connectives provided by associations or by contrasts of feelings, emotions, words or sounds'. In order to keep these strands distinct, he has said elsewhere, he used different coloured pencils, mapping out his text as a director might the varied sequences which make up his film. *Histoire* is obviously constructed according to similar principles. (pp. 89-90)

A subsidiary feature of film art is suspense, and here again Simon has learned from the practice of movies. In *Le Sacre du printemps,* for instance, he cleverly conceals the existence of the ring and thus maintains doubt about it until the very end of the novel, the last words of which describe its discovery; in fact the whole rhetoric of the book is converging on this one point, so that the text closes on the two significant syllables, 'la bague', the ring. (p. 91)

But Claude Simon himself would claim, I suspect, that his fiction owes more to the visual arts than to the film. It was noted at the conference on the new novel held in Cerisy-la-Salle in 1971 that Simon tends to visualize his intentions more than his colleagues, and the novelist himself has stated that 'plastic imperatives' must be allowed to predominate in the art of fiction. For this reason he intends his novels should give the reader plenty to 'see'; and it is for this reason that his methods have been compared to those of the pointillistes, and also of the cubists. But these are at best only metaphors for his activity; painting and writing are such different media that analogies made between them must be tenuous (the same is not true of the film since this art, like the novel, narrates fictions in the dimension of time). Simon has a trained eye for art, and has in a sense 'dedicated' some of his novels to painters he admires. Thus *Les Corps conducteurs* is written under the aegis of Robert Rauschenberg, and *Triptyque* is an act of homage to the great triptychs of Francis Bacon. It is just possible to see influence in these cases; the *objets trouvés* aspects of Rauschenberg's art, the collage and sculptural qualities present in his work, are roughly paralleled in the collage devices of *Les Corps conducteurs.* Similarly *Triptyque*'s structure offers some analogies with Bacon's three-panelled works, but they do not extend very far, since as I have shown, the three sections into which the novel is divided do not correspond to three aspects of a single narrative, as tends to be the case with Bacon. It would, in fact, be difficult to parallel in [pictorial] form the structure of *Triptyque* in which the three elements interweave continuously.

There is, however, one aspect of Simon's fiction which clearly owes something to the plastic arts, and that is the occasional tendency of his scenes to 'freeze' into static sculptural or graphic representation. An example of the first is the way the lovers become statuesque in *The Battle of Pharsalus,* petrified into

immobility in the frenzied energy of their erotic activity; and examples of the second are the cartoons into which scenes dissolve in *The Palace* . . . and *Triptyque.* (pp. 92-3)

[Claude Simon's] example is supremely relevant in the consideration of the avant-garde's contribution to the expression of our tragic condition. For when all is said and done, the only justification for fictional experiment, for the restless dissatisfaction with pre-existing forms and modes of expression, must be the more precise and exact formulation of what Claude Simon calls, in the dedicatory note in *La Corde raide,* 'la tragica i dolorosa inquietud' . . . in so far as it besets mankind at every moment. For Simon eschews two extremes, set out on the one hand by Alain Robbe-Grillet when he says that by repudiating communion with the world of things man can escape tragedy, and on the other by George Steiner who has drawn attention to the tempting blandishments of what he calls in an arresting phrase 'the suicidal rhetoric of silence'. Simon has not succumbed to this rhetoric; nor has he fallen either for Robbe-Grillet's easy optimism. 'Life is tragic for Claude Simon', writes Laurent LeSage, 'because human existence counts for so little in the universal order of things', and he compares Simon's vision to that of Ecclesiastes. There is in both works, LeSage argues, a perception of the essential vanity of human activity coupled with a strangely satisfying emphasis on the cyclical perenniality of the natural world in which 'to every thing there is a season . . . a time to be born, and a time to die'. . . . And Jean-Luc Seylaz has drawn attention to a fertile paradox in Simon's fiction between an impulse towards complete reconstitution and a tendency to nihilistic destruction, and between a powerfully evocative vision and hesitations about the solidity of things.

It is this dual perception which drives Claude Simon to write novels in a vain (though for us fortunate) attempt to reconcile the conflict between the sceptical pessimism of the intellectual and the confident optimism of the artisan, between the Diogenes and the Daedalus aspects of his nature. It is this which causes him willy-nilly to explore the major permanent themes of the western novel in the wake of his masters, Dostoyevsky and Conrad. (pp. 218-19)

It is this dual perception of tragic absurdity which makes Simon's vision not only unsentimental but fully relevant to contemporary concerns. He is part of the avant-garde . . . , but he is also preoccupied with the major themes of the humanistic novel since its rise in the eighteenth century. He pursues technical perfection because he is a moralist who wishes to convey intuitions about the human condition in a form that can command respect and admiration in today's world. He does not cultivate art for art's sake, but art for life's sake. What makes him a great novelist, what causes him to tower above most other writers of his generation, is that he has not impoverished the novel inherited from his forbears, but, on the contrary, enriched it. What Conrad did for the novel of the early 1900s, Claude Simon has done for the novel of the mid-century; he has enlarged its aesthetic range and has developed new possibilities of realism, but he has not caused it to abandon its permanent vocation: to exalt, in spite of everything, the heroic stature of man, and so help us to understand our life, and come to terms with our death. (pp. 226-27)

John Fletcher, in his Claude Simon and Fiction Now,
Calder and Boyars, 1975, 240 p.

RANDOLPH STOW

Claude Simon has never been an easy writer, but he has not seemed before to flaunt his difficulty quite so uncompromisingly as in this latest novel [*Les Géorgiques*] published in his sixty-eighth year. . . .

Simon has often been accused of imitating his junior, Alain Robbe-Grillet, which is perhaps unfair. It might be truer to say that he became a convinced member of a movement. But in *Les Géorgiques* there are unmistakable signs of a more overwhelming influence—that of Faulkner—and this debt has been damaging, perhaps fatally so. One battles continually through sentences half a dozen pages long, struggling to retain the drift while being diverted into parentheses (containing other parentheses) more extended than most contemporary novelists' paragraphs. Not all the strain is on the reader. It is clear that the author too has had his struggles, which show in the way in which passages of vivid and exact description trail away into the same vague, high-flown hollowness which one regrets in Faulkner. Adjectives, adverbs, and participles pile on top of one another as Simon strives to be absolutely precise, and succeeds in being just the opposite.

Not that this striving after precision never succeeds. Far from it: there are many long passages of description to which one can imagine oneself returning, to admire their felicities in isolation. One of the few short enough to quote is the end of a description of some farm-horses, perhaps descended from the chargers of knights long ago, placidly surviving a bitter winter in the fields. To the defeated and idle cavalrymen of 1940, whose own horses are ailing, they seem "comme des animaux à la fierté héraldique, doux, pensifs, fabuleux et sauvages".

This is rather touching, as Claude Simon, absolutely unsentimental, often is. Better, probably, than any other living writer except the author of *Cancer Ward* he conveys the pathos of very tough and not at all imaginative men. . . .

But it is very difficult to know quite what the whole long book adds up to. There are three intersecting stories: a device which Simon has used before, but which (except in *Triptyque*) has always seemed a little too arbitrary, and certainly seems so here. . . .

Though I find the book quite unreasonably difficult, so that its undeniable power is dispersed in verbiage, I expect to return to it. But more rarely than I shall return to *Leçon des choses*, which makes many of the same points more accessibly.

> *Randolph Stow, "Of O. and the General's Stock,"*
> *in* The Times Literary Supplement, *No. 4105, December 4, 1981, p. 1412.*

LEON S. ROUDIEZ

The Spanish Civil War and the 1940 disaster are among the major traumatic events that marked the lives of Frenchmen of Claude Simon's generation. Indeed, they suffuse the texture of several novels of his, including the most recent one [*Les Géorgiques*] but without necessarily furnishing the sole significance of any individual work.

Alongside the defeat of democracy at the hands of fascism in Spain and France, there now looms the quasi-mythical memory of the birth of democracy in the late eighteenth century. For many, such a myth was rekindled and transmitted through the imaginative prose of Michelet's *Histoire de la révolution française*. Somehow its spirit seems inseparable from that of Simon's *Les Géorgiques*. . . .

One might say that, as Vergil sought, in his own *Georgics*, to extol the virtues of an earlier Roman age, Simon's novel maintains, in opposition to twentieth-century failures, the presence of earlier victories achieved against overwhelming odds. Such an "inspirational" effect, however, no matter how many readers experience it, is a spin-off rather than the main enterprise. A more literal analogy with the *Georgics* is also provided by one of the characters' almost obsessive preoccupation with seasonal caretaking, planting and reaping on his estate.

The writing (and reading) process is a central concern. How experience is communicated, how communication modifies action; how the shape of writing is patterned after the form of experience, how writing and action proceed, subject to irrational, hidden forces as well as to rational, overt intentions—such are the things that matter. A short preliminary section epitomizes it; we read the description of a pencil drawing of an older man, seated at his desk, reading a communication that has been delivered by a younger one, still standing nearby. Throughout the five subsequent chapters of the novel a narrator, who is writing the intricate narrative we are reading, is himself reading, almost simultaneously, a) papers dating back to the French Revolution, which enable him to relate episodes in the life of a general serving the government of the emerging republic and eventually the empire; b) the mental text of his own memories both as a child and (mainly) as a cavalryman in the "phony war" and the ensuing rout of 1940; and c) an experience of the Spanish Civil War, mediated through the mind of an English writer who has gone to Spain, joined the Republican forces but with what turns out to be the "wrong" party, and later attempts to account, in writing, for what happened. The narrator may well identify with the general to the point of losing his own individuality, and he may be unable to dissociate himself from the person of the English writer; as to his own memories, they could in a number of instances be indistinguishable from those of the writer Claude Simon, who orchestrates the several sets of narratives—but such speculations need not detain the reader too long.

The novel begins to function as words interact within each narrative and between the sets. Several types of interaction are in evidence. For instance, the names of two strategically located rivers, the Sambre and the Meuse, are in one sequence drawn together to form a cultural unit; "Sambre et Meuse" evokes a stirring military march, a former department extending over a part of what is now Belguim, and the site of a significant victory for the French revolutionary armies; the same rivers are mentioned in the narrative involving the 1940 disaster, but separately—and at the same time the reader is led to recall their conjunction and to contrast the spirit of 1939-40 with that of 1792. (p. 301)

Still other modes of interaction could be enumerated. What I have just alluded to is perhaps sufficient to give one an idea of the complexity, scope and richness of *Les Géorgiques*. Probably the most ambitious novel Claude Simon has written so far, it is an engrossing one that should not disappoint admirers of his earlier books; in all likelihood, it will spawn new ones. (pp. 301-02)

> *Leon S. Roudiez, in a review of "Les Géorgiques,"*
> *in* World Literature Today, *Vol. 56, No. 2, Spring, 1982, pp. 301-02.*

DAVID CARROLL

[*In his* The Subject in Question: The Languages of Theory and the Strategies of Fiction *(1982), American critic Carroll uses Simon's fiction as a model for examining the influence of semiotics on contemporary literature. In the following excerpt from* The Subject in Question, *Carroll discusses Simon's theoretical approach to history, as well as the aesthetic problems encountered by authors who use structuralist theory as a starting point for their fiction.*]

My claim for Simon's importance at the present historical conjuncture is simply this: his fictions are especially rich because of the intricate ways they raise, formulate, and confront questions of theory as part of their thematics and form. They are one of the places, though not the only one, where such a forceful confrontation occurs. . . .

My interest in Simon is largely due to the fact that in his novels he continually confronts and questions the problem of history (even in the novels' most "formalist" moments) in contrast to so many contemporary novelists and theoreticians who have ignored it. And need I add that history is ignored either when it is taken as a given, the simple, unquestioned ground for everything else, or when it is simply opposed, suppressed, or considered irrelevant? The rethinking and reformulation of history and historical discourse and methodology is one of the most pressing of contemporary theoretical problems, and I shall argue that one of the most powerful aspects of Simon's novels is the critical rethinking and reformulation of history they propose. (p. 5)

All of the novels of Claude Simon are marked by a fundamental uncertainty concerning the workings and sense of history, an uncertainty which permeates all levels of reality, all forms of knowledge, and all action. This uncertainty is first of all due to the fact that the traditional foundations for history, the epistemologies, ideologies, and narrative techniques used to order, form, and make sense out of the past and relate it to the present, prove themselves to be contradictory and reductive in dealing with the complexity of the past. In Simon's novels there seems to be no solid foundation on which to construct an historical order—both the subject and the referent of history are pictured as being deficient in various ways and are repeatedly undercut in the novels as the origin or foundation of history. The concepts of progress, development, continuity, enlightenment, rationality, etc. which constitute and give direction to traditional history are presented in Simon's novels not as innocent, metahistorical assumptions underlying the course of history and determining its sense and narrative form, but rather as naive ideals which restrict the form of history to that of a continuous *récit* and in the process suppress the deviations, contradictions, and gaps from within the narration of history. Simon's novels attempt to resist this form of historical-narrational reductionism by continually multiplying the ways any (hi)story is told, by contradicting with an opposing version any (hi)story which takes itself to be definitive. (pp. 126-27)

If history has traditionally been thought of either as the presentation of an accurate picture of the past, "things as they really were" in Ranke's phrase, or as the determination of well-defined historical periods within the continuous movement of a positivist evolution toward an end, then there is nothing further removed from this concept of history than the novels of Claude Simon. Discontinuous, contradictory, intermixing fact and fiction, fantasy and reality, as well as past and present, Simon's novels state clearly and repeatedly that they are unable to resolve the historical questions which haunt them. If history is supposed to determine a *knowledge* (even an "archeology of knowledge"), then Simon's novels are "failures" as history, unable to determine and represent the truth of the past they question. The questions asked of history in the novels in fact produce no valid, uncontradicted responses—history in its dispersive multiplicity, is continually falling back into fiction, unable to establish itself against fiction as *the form* of true discourse.

Insomuch as they raise fundamental historical questions, rather than being opposed to historical investigation as both a narrow historicism and formalism might claim, I would argue that the novels of Claude Simon have an important place within the ongoing critique and rethinking of both history and the novel. The historical uncertainty at the basis of his novels takes the form of a narrative uncertainty affecting history and fiction at the same time and in the same ways. This means that in Simon's work the initial disorder or "debacle" of history is never completely overcome, never effectively made to conform to any other, supposedly more fundamental order—neither to a metaphysical order nor to an empirical one, and certainly not to any order of discourse or language which might be claimed to underlie them both. The "order of discourse" is no more certain, no more systematic, no more totalized, and no more fundamental and determining than the traditional "orders of history" explicitly put into question. The problem then is more complicated than replacing one order with another, than arguing that one order is more essential than another. (pp. 127-28)

Simon's novels, then, assume a radically critical position on history, inserting negativity where it is repressed; complexity, conflict, and contradiction where they are supposedly surpassed. Loss, destruction, and defeat at the same time constitute and interfere with Simon's narratives; and this produces a continual process of reconstruction, reordering, and reinscription. A superficial reading might lead one to believe that Simon views history as cyclical, in the sense of an eternal return of the Same (of an historical identity or essential subject). But the form and sense of history in Simon's novels is, . . . repetitive and not cyclical, the return of difference rather than identity. Each repetition and return produces new conflicts and contradictions and never results in their simple resolution. Without the assumptions which would determine the institution of Order (social, temporal, linguistic, or ontological), repetition and plurality are the basic characteristics of Simon's narratives, of the *histoires* which constitute his texts. An order, then, cannot be found or posited *in, under, around* or *above* the debacle.

If the Simonian novel is haunted by historical questions, it ultimately returns these questions to history without a solution but with a difference—for it reinscribes them in a space which is not that of traditional history. By their radical critical perspective on these questions, by their continual undercutting of all historical finalities, and by their contradictory formal complexity, Simon's novels demand that history do more than simply provide answers to them. They demand that history also investigate continually how and in terms of what system (what order) it provides these answers and in whose interests it imposes an order on the debacle. Finally, they demand that history begin to question itself as a particular narrative form, not only in terms of what is accepted (written down) as history, but also in terms of what does not fit into any "continuous" narrative form, what is "lost" or rejected but nevertheless "written" in the blank spaces of history, in its margins. The questions of history, as they are returned to history by Simon's novels, demand, then, not *an answer,* a resolution of the debacle and an imposition of order, but rather that history assume a critical perspective on itself: that it not be content to be the simple narration of "what happened," that it not accept as such any sense, order, or form as definitive or fundamental.

Simon's novels from the beginning have included within them, as elements of fiction, theoretical questions, speculations about the nature of fiction and demonstrations of how fiction is formulated in terms of these questions. What is different in Simon's recent novels (and in other contemporary novels) is that the theoretical questions have become more and more "dogmatically" formalist and faithful to Ricardou's theory of the novel and the structuralist heritage it continues. It is not the interpenetration of theory and fiction that is the problem here; this has always been one of the most interesting aspects of Simon's work. . . . The problem is rather the monolithic nature of the theory now confronted in the novels or, more accurately, the lack of confrontation between theory and practice and the agreement and harmony reached between them. The problem is one of the *programming* of fiction after an ultraformalist theory of fiction, for such a structuralist (or post-structuralist) form of fiction is too predictable. In following closely the development of Ricardou's theoretical position and analyzing the form it takes in the recent fictions of Simon, my purpose is to make clear the limitations of the position and to situate and undermine its "dogmatism." Fiction, when it pretends to generate its own theory of itself and to master itself totally is just as "dogmatic" as any theory supposedly originating "outside" which has as its goal the total explanation and mastery of fiction. "Dogmatism" is not then an attribute of any theory or group of theories alone, but it can also be characteristic of the speculative, theoretical side of fiction as well—and most certainly of fiction which claims to engender and figure both itself and its own theory of itself. (p. 170)

The new break instituted by *Pharsalus* is due not to this novel being of a fundamentally different nature than those that came before it but, rather, to the growing consciousness Simon began to have of the "internal dynamics of writing." From this point on in his writing, he tried to interfere less with what writing said on its own and to follow it more rigorously. The contradiction in such statements is quite evident: if "one never writes— one never says—anything except what occurs at the *present moment* of writing," how can Simon talk about substantial breaks in the evolution of his own writing? What does it mean to have "let oneself be guided more by what writing *was saying*—or discovering—than by what one wants to *make it say*," if all fiction is in fact basically what "writing says?" What Simon really means is that in *Pharsalus* and in the novels following it he will make repeated attempts to eliminate from his fictions anything that cannot be made to originate from within fiction itself; not just to make fiction work the way it will work no matter what he wants or does, but to have the subject fiction as *the only subject* of fiction.

Fiction as an operation of pure productivity, as the uninhibited play of language, supposedly remains within itself and is (even more?) only itself. The purity of the productive system or instrumentality, as well as the uninhibited nature of the play of the signifier, come into question because they are products of an inhibition or exclusion, of a "sacrifice" as Simon puts it: "It is always necessary to sacrifice the signified to plastic necessities or, if you prefer, to formal ones." . . . The "free play" is not free but limited in theory to one level of the text to the exclusion of all others. In order to have his texts conform exactly to the theory used to interpret them, in order that this theory and his texts say the same thing, and in order that his fictions represent only themselves and the theory of themselves they contain within them, the "sacrifice" of the signified to the dictates of the signifier is necessary. The gradual elimination of all problems of the signified (of representation, his-

tory, sense, etc.) alone can guarantee that fiction is really what this theory and practice project it as being, but the consequences of such a "sacrifice" are evident within both the theory and practice of such fictions.

The Battle of Pharsalus, however, is not yet the ideal, totally self-enclosed, self-reflexive, self-generated text that *Fiction* is supposed to be, even if Ricardou's analysis "La Bataille de la Phrase" at times reads as if it were. For no fiction can ever attain this formalist ideal, no matter how much it sacrifices the signified. Perhaps there is a simple explanation as to why this particular fiction fails to attain the ideal which has nothing to do with the ideal itself. Perhaps it is due to a confusion of motives on the part of the author, resulting in a plurality or mixture of contradictory programs engendering the novel. Perhaps Simon still interfered too much with the workings of fiction itself. As Simon says in an interview the novel had a complex and multiple (even contradictory, one could say) origin. It was engendered not simply from within itself but from various "outsides," from a complex intertextual network (Simon's other fictions, his readings, history, his experiences, his "life," etc.). And in another interview, when asked how a more recent novel, *Triptych,* was "engendered," Simon replied: "That's a very difficult question to answer: so many factors play a part in the engendering of a text." . . . But it is only when these "other factors" are eliminated or when the intertextual, historical "outside" is overcome or neutralized by the text itself that there is true self-engenderment. Simon's anecdotal references to personal experience as the source, or at least as one of the sources of *The Battle of Pharsalus,* may seem to many to be theoretically naive; but they are in fact no more naive than Ricardou's reduction of the process of engenderment to that of the text totally engendering itself from itself—a position which Simon will soon make his own. When the only experience engendering a text is the experience of the text of itself, both experience and the text have been seriously reduced. (pp. 177-78)

> *David Carroll, in his* The Subject in Question: The
> Languages of Theory and the Strategies of Fiction,
> *The University of Chicago Press, 1982, 231 p.**

PUBLISHERS WEEKLY

This difficult and very disturbing book [*The World about Us*] is based upon Simon's experiences in the French Army in 1940. Dazed soldiers, suffering from nervous exhaustion and holed up in a crumbling building, provide one of the focal points in this montage of images. As Mark W. Andrews mentions in his preface, Simon originally studied to be a painter: "His painter's eye first came into its own in the *chosisme* or verbal descriptions of objects." Utilizing a flat, dispassionate style, Simon plays with the reader's perceptions by juxtaposing disparate scenes. Pictures come alive: a gunner looks at an illustrated book with chapters on building a house, thus introducing the workmen who provide another focus for the narrative. The label on a box of Havana cigars, a calendar reproduction, a can of sardines and a picture on a cast-iron plate behind a fireplace are described so meticulously that they seem to have their own vitality. Perhaps Simon's stylistic intention is best reflected by the most haunting image in the novel, that of a gull giving the illusion of stillness whilst in flight: "Soundlessly, effortlessly, it remains there, a living, magnificent thing, born up by nothing, like a kind of challenge not only to the laws of gravity but also to the impossible marriage of motionlessness and motion."

A review of "The World about Us," in Publishers Weekly, *Vol. 223, No. 14, April 8, 1983, p. 54.*

ROBERT P. HOLLEY

This short narrative [**The World about Us**] by a well-known French "new novelist" intermingles three separate slices of the "world about us": a group of French soldiers wait for attacking Germans; a couple's walk along a cliff ends in a graphic seduction scene; two workmen demolish a partition. Simon refuses either to confirm or deny the existence of a narrative structure, challenging us with abrupt jumps from one story line to another—without paragraphs—and stream of consciousness sections. The sophisticated reader attempting to weave these disparate parts into a coherent whole will alternately be confused and intrigued.

Robert P. Holley, in a review of "The World about Us," in Library Journal, *Vol. 108, No. 9, May 1, 1983, p. 921.*

ALAN CHEUSE

This nine-year-old novel [**The World about Us**] from one of France's leading contenders for the Nobel Prize could well serve as a handbook for the author's major esthetic obsession. The book takes the form of a highly stylized elementary school primer in which the nature of ordinary things is explored. . . . Simon's *trompe l'oeil* world is our own under a magnifying glass, a universe of fierce brush stroke and sparkling points of color, all surface and sometimes motion. In it, seemingly fixed, frozen sounds and odors emanate throughout a time and space unnaturally elongated or tragically foreshortened. There is little resembling conventional characterization or plot here, but the prose, as a result of the writer's sometimes nearly pathological concern for things in themselves, is highly emotive. **The World about Us** is not Mr. Simon's most ambitious work but this translation by Daniel Weissbort provides an opportunity for serious readers new to Mr. Simon's style to make his acquaintance. (pp. 22-3)

Alan Cheuse, in a review of "The World about Us," in The New York Times Book Review, *April 1, 1984, pp. 22-3.*

A. OTTEN

Although published recently in book form, Simon's brief text [**La chevelure de Bérénice**] had previously appeared in 1966 in a limited edition that included reprints of paintings by Miró under the title **Femmes** at the Editions Maeght. Even more than other Simonian productions, **La chevelure de Bérénice** is verbal painting.

In the opening two pages we see a woman dressed in black, lying on the beach, set off against a gray sky. In the background is a dune, consisting of two soft hills divided by the horizontal line of the gray sea. Clouds have pale bellies, the dune a sleek flank, and the wind traces sketches in the sand that look like veins. On a piece of wood we observe undulating patterns like "hair." The woman also has black undulating hair, and when she enters the sea, water sketches an undulating line on her skirt. If we remember that Simon spoke of "words with their undulations" in **La Bataille de Pharsale,** then we realize even more the harmonious flow of images and text.

In **La chevelure de Bérénice** Simon projects the human drama and the beauty of the world against the background of the moving sea and the seeming constancy of the stars. There we behold Comet Berenice, a comet north of Virgo, with its luminous, hairlike rays. Undulating patterns in a dune, a woman's body, wood, and a star show us a world in flux. There is also the play of colors, day and night, and the hint of life and death. In this slender volume, more than elsewhere in his fiction, Simon has emphasized movement and expressed it in words with their own undulations.

A. Otten, in a review of "La chevelure de Bérénice," in World Literature Today, *Vol. 59, No. 1, Winter, 1985, p. 56.*

(Marvin) Neil Simon

Biloxi Blues

Tony Award

American dramatist and scriptwriter.

Throughout his career, Simon has enjoyed tremendous popularity with audiences, yet he has experienced a precarious reputation among critics who remain skeptical about the significance of his art, even though they consistently applaud his unique comic vision. Although the critical debate over Simon's artistic talent is not resolved in discussions of *Biloxi Blues,* many reviewers believe that the play represents a new direction in the author's career—an integration of comedy with more serious themes. Based on Simon's own experience as an army draftee in training, the play is a comic portrayal of a young man's first real confrontation with anti-Semitism and moral responsibility.

Simon began his career as part of a comedy writing team with his brother Danny. The pair wrote for radio and television until 1956 when Danny began directing. Simon continued to write for television until his career shifted with the opening of his first play, *Come Blow Your Horn* (1961). The production was well received, although some critics observed that the constant stream of jokes detracted from the development of the characters. Eager to be relieved of the pressures of writing comedy on command, Simon left television and began writing full time for the theater, which provided him with more independence and greater artistic satisfaction. Simon's other early works, including *Barefoot in the Park* (1964) and *The Odd Couple* (1966), were described as more substantial than *Come Blow Your Horn,* but critics again noted Simon's reliance on gags to fill in for character development. Many of his scripts, including *Barefoot in the Park* and *The Sunshine Boys* (1973), have been adapted for film.

Several commentators attribute Simon's success to the white middle-class appeal of his humor and maintain that the playwright compromises dramatic quality in order to accommodate the demands of the Broadway audience. Other critics, however, insist that Simon's distinct style of comedy has depth and substance and that it has survived because the author offers significant insight into human relationships. The depth of Simon's vision as a dramatist, they suggest, is revealed in his sensitivity to human vulnerability and his ability to inspire laughter in tragic situations.

Biloxi Blues is the second play in what many reviewers anticipate will be a trilogy reflecting Simon's life. Its predecessor, *Brighton Beach Memoirs* (1983), portrays life in Brooklyn, New York in the 1930s and the aspirations of a young Jewish boy, Eugene, who is Simon's alter ego. In *Biloxi Blues* Eugene is a young man entering army training and forced for the first time to confront the immorality of his fellow recruits and officers. While *Brighton Beach Memoirs* is often considered Simon's most serious play, reviewers have found that *Biloxi Blues* is the playwright's most successful attempt at combining his characteristic sense of humor with a more probing approach to underlying issues and the dynamics of character interaction.

© Jay Thompson

Through Eugene's observations, and his interactions with his forthright friend Arnold Epstein, Simon addresses anti-Semitism and moral responsibility. Eugene questions his role as a naive observer of unjust behavior and begins to realize that he must act on the courage of his convictions. Some critics suggest that Eugene's growing sense of moral responsibility implies a parallel change in the playwright's attitude towards his own career. After years of quietly succumbing to his expectant audiences, these commentators assert, Simon is discovering his own dramatic conscience.

(See also *CLC,* Vols. 6, 11, 31; *Contemporary Authors,* Vols. 21-24, rev. ed.; and *Dictionary of Literary Biography,* Vol. 7.)

DOUGLAS WATT

Blues, indeed. The perils of Eugene are wearing very thin in *Biloxi Blues.* . . . A sequel to *Brighton Beach Memoirs,* it has its funny lines and scenes, but the strain shows as the playwright tries to freshen up subject matter—those loveable, laughable G.I.s in basic training during World War II—that was already stale by the late 1940s.

Eugene Morris Jerome, whom we met as a pubescent Brooklynite in the earlier comedy, has now joined the Army and been shipped to Biloxi, Miss. It is 1943. Still jotting down his ''Memoirs'' in the hope of someday becoming a writer, Eugene and five other assorted enlisted men suffer humiliation at the hands of a severe top sergeant, confront the daily ''mess'' served up at the mess hall and, of course, join together in a visit to a local whore, who succeeds in initiating the panicky Eugene. A little later on he finds pure love in the chaste person of a Catholic girl at a church dance. Then, his training over, it's goodby Biloxi.

What can Simon do to make all this worn-out junk seem new again? Nothing, really. Not by delving into sexual habits and filling the air with scatological jokes that could never have found their way into those old movies. Not by dragging in racism; Eugene and one of the other fellows are Jews. And not by melodramatic flourishes, as when he has the top sergeant, gone haywire with drink, come near blowing out the brains of Pvt. Arnold Epstein. . . .

The war at home—that is, the training part of it in the States— is so far behind us that Simon has trouble at times even in recapturing the flavor and proper usages. There are many Simon-pure laughs in *Biloxi Blues;* still the play remains almost a dead weight.

> Douglas Watt, ''It's Taps for 'Biloxi Blues','' in Daily News, *New York, March 29, 1985. Reprinted in* New York Theatre Critics' Reviews, *Vol. XXXXVI, No. 5, Week of April 8, 1985, p. 323.*

CLIVE BARNES

Biloxi Blues is a fine comedy, top drawer Simon, and another step in the process of making Simon neither so simple, nor so simplistic. With Neil Simon it is not the plot that is thickening, it is the playwright. And to advantage. (p. 323)

As his unusually successful career whirligigs on, he more and more discards the wisecracking style that, in part, made, if not his reputation, his image, and concentrates on a realistic comedy of the heart.

To be sure *Biloxi Blues* is funny, often heart-rendingly funny, but nowadays Simon will not compromise character for a laugh, and never inserts deliberate jokes that could have, without any more than a blush of pride, come straight off Johnny Carson.

Simon's six recruits and a drill sergeant (brain-damaged, psychotic yet cunning) are a pretty typical rookie group; and their troubles with discipline, drill, latrines, chow, and women are scarcely unusual.

Yet Eugene, who started his life as an observer in the earlier play, has now got it down to a fairly calculated art, and those powers of observation are often turned upon himself.

Of course, as a Jew, he is shocked by the Army's racism and anti-Semitism. But he is almost more horrified—and this will touch a common chord—by his own failure to defend a fellow Jew, by his complaisant willingness to ''remain neutral, like Switzerland.''

In this account of anti-Semitism can be seen something of those World War II Army horrors recounted in such postwar novels as Saul Bellow's *The Adventures of Augie March,* but in a Simon comedy it touches a darker note than the playwright normally ventures.

Oddly enough the play is at its strongest and its weakest in its treatment of Eugene. At times there is an accuracy of observation here so sharp that it is poignant.

Take for example, the explanation to his new girlfriend for his shyness, which draws a firm distinction between ''Jerome the writer, and Jerome the talker.'' And indeed these two scenes of first love, like Jerome's very different loss of virginity with a kindly whore, are realized with compassionate affection.

Yet Jerome is still far, far too cute a dramatic characterization. Does he have to be so adorable? So moral that even his failings, frankly acknowledged, are panoplied in virtue? . . .

Biloxi Blues is an engrossing play, whether it is taken as a walk through memories or a journey to history, and it has much the same quality that we define in a novel as ''a good read.''

At its initial level, at its moment of intake as it were, Simon's latest charms, amuses, and even fascinates. But it also leaves feelings to savor as an aftertaste, and it is this aftertaste that makes *Biloxi Blues* so deliciously rewarding, and a big gun in the already impressive Simon canon. (pp. 323-24)

> Clive Barnes, ''Atten-Hut!! 'Biloxi Blues' Marches In,'' in New York Post, *March 29, 1985. Reprinted in* New York Theatre Critics' Reviews, *Vol. XXXXVI, No. 5, Week of April 8, 1985, pp. 323-24.*

FRANK RICH

Although the laughter rarely stops in *Biloxi Blues,* Neil Simon's joyous and unexpectedly rewarding new comedy, the most surprising line of the evening by far is not a joke, but a reprimand. The reprimand is delivered to the young hero, Eugene Jerome . . . who has now graduated from the Depression adolescence of Mr. Simon's previous autobiographical play, *Brighton Beach Memoirs,* to basic training in the wartime Army of 1943.

Eugene is still an aspiring writer, fond of scribbling his every private observation into a composition book. But at this moment in *Biloxi Blues,* he censors those observations: He rips a completed page out of the journal and throws it away. It's then that Eugene's best friend in the platoon, a high-minded Jewish intellectual named Arnold Epstein . . . , lets him have it. ''Once you start compromising your thoughts,'' Arnold tells Eugene, ''you're a candidate for mediocrity.''

What makes the line so startling is that it applies not only to the apprentice Neil Simon, as represented by Eugene, but also to the latter-day Neil Simon, as represented by his recent unfulfilled plays and mechanical screenplays. And as Arnold's sharp warning makes a strong impression on the hero, so the playwright seems finally to be heeding the same warning in the new play. . . . Gone from *Biloxi Blues* is the self-congratulatory air of *Brighton Beach Memoirs* and *Chapter Two*— works in which Mr. Simon presented himself as a near-saint and invoked death and disease to prove he was writing with a new seriousness. This time, the writer at last begins to examine himself honestly, without compromises, and the result is his most persuasively serious effort to date—not to mention his funniest play since the golden age bordered by *Barefoot in the Park* (1963) and *The Sunshine Boys* (1972).

There is no contradiction in that assessment: When a playwright is writing honestly, he writes in his own voice—and Mr. Simon's honest voice is not the official, middlebrow tone he's adopted over the last decade but the comic vernacular of his first hits. In *Biloxi Blues,* we can feel Mr. Simon's exhilaration at giving that voice full vent again. . . .

Act I, in which Eugene and his fellow "dogfaces" get acclimated to Army discipline at their Mississippi training post, is service comedy as Broadway probably hasn't seen since *No Time for Sergeants.* Eugene, leaving Brooklyn for the first time, must contend not only with a sergeant . . . who in no way resembles the kindly taskmasters he's anticipated from James Stewart movies, but also with an entire new gentile world: hick bunkmates with low I.Q.'s and high incidences of tooth decay, parochial-school girls, and goyishe mess-hall foods with exotic names like creamed chipped beef.

Eugene has a sharp riposte for every new jolt. Listening to his lines in Act I of *Biloxi Blues* is like watching a graceful basketball player sink shot after shot. Every joke hits its exact mark, none are wasted. As befits the setting, many of the gags are of the locker room-and-latrine variety, but others dramatize the hero's predicament as a Jew in an alien land: Hard-pressed, Eugene will invent a new High Holiday to escape the chow line. While Mr. Simon's brand of Jewish humor has often occupied a safe, bland middle ground between the poles occupied by his fellow one-time Sid Caesar writers Mel Brooks and Woody Allen, here he merrily embraces both low Brooks and neurotic Allen.

For once the playwright also lets his plot develop from character rather than the other way around. When we first meet Eugene, he explains that he has three goals in the war—to become a writer, stay alive and lose his virginity. The second of these goals is reached by one of the evening's final jokes, the last by a priceless variation on the standard boy-meets-prostitute scene. But the story of how Eugene becomes a writer is Mr. Simon's true passion, and it's what gives *Biloxi Blues* its affecting bite.

The playwright unfolds the tale by really giving his hero something to write about in his journal. Eugene witnesses the anti-Semitic and anti-homosexual humiliations of fellow recruits. Yet Mr. Simon's plan is not, as one might fear from past efforts, to write a gratuitous problem play about prejudice in the World War II armed forces. Quite the contrary: The author unearths some human qualities in the play's ignorant bigots and reserves his harshest judgments for his hero, who stays meekly on the sidelines of the conflicts around him.

Mr. Simon's real subject is not prejudice, but how Eugene perceives prejudice. As the ever-instructive Arnold explains, Eugene is too much an ingratiating, naïve observer, neatly reducing other people's dramas to clever diary entries. If he is to become a real writer, he cannot forever remain "neutral, like Switzerland." He will have to stop making peace and jokes and start entering the battles worth fighting, whether for principle or love. It's a lesson that Mr. Simon seems to be learning along with his protagonist, and we soon watch Eugene grow up as no other Simon character has.

Frank Rich, "'Biloxi Blues,' Neil Simon's New Comedy," in The New York Times, *March 29, 1985, p. C3.*

An Excerpt from *Biloxi Blues*

EUGENE You win, Arnold. It's your money.
(EPSTEIN *starts for the money*)

WYKOWSKI It never fails. It's always the Jews who end up with the money. Ain't that right, Roy?

SELRIDGE Don't ask me. I never met a Jew before the army.

WYKOWSKI They're easy to spot. (*To* EPSTEIN) There's one . . . (*To* EUGENE) . . . And there's another one. (*To all*) They're the ones who slide the bacon under their toast so no one sees them eat it. Ain't that right, Jerome?

EPSTEIN (*Calmly*) I'm tired of taking that Jew crap from you, Wykowski. I know you can probably beat the hell out of me, but I'm not going to take it from you anymore, understand?

WYKOWSKI Sure you will. You'll take any shit from me . . . Come on. Come on. Let's see how tough you are. I'll knock the Alka-Seltzer right out of your asshole.

HENNESEY Cut it out, Kowski. What difference does it make what religion he is?

WYKOWSKI I didn't start it. Epstein's the one who thinks he's too good to take orders, isn't he? Well, I'm not doing a hundred push-ups for any God damn goof-up anymore. If he doesn't shape up, I'll bust his face whether he's got a Jew nose or not.
(*They both go for each other, but are restrained by the others*)

CARNEY (*Seeing* TOOMEY *coming*) Ten-HUT!
(*Suddenly* SERGEANT TOOMEY *appears in his pants and an undershirt. All snap to attention*)

TOOMEY What the hell is going on here?

HENNESEY Nothing, Sergeant.

TOOMEY What do you mean nothing? I heard threats, challenges and an invitation to bust the nose of members of minority races. Now are you still telling me that nothing was going on here?

HENNESEY Yes, Sergeant.

TOOMEY I think you'd better sleep on that answer, boy. And to make sure you get a good night's sleep, you get yourself good and tired with one hundred push-ups. On the floor, dogface, and let me hear you count, (HENNESEY *gets on the ground and immediately starts to do push-ups*) If I hear any more racial slurs from this platoon, some dumb bastard is going to be shoveling cow shit with a teaspoon for a month. Especially if I hear it from a Polack! LIGHTS OUT!!
(*The lights suddenly go out, leaving only a tiny spot on* EUGENE)

EUGENE (*To the audience*) . . . I never liked Wykowski much and I didn't like him any better after tonight . . . But the one I hated most was myself because I didn't stand up for Epstein, a fellow Jew. Maybe I was afraid of Wykowski or maybe it was because Epstein sort of sometimes asked for it, but since the guys didn't pick on me that much, I figured I'd just stay sort of neutral . . . like Switzerland . . . Then I wrote in my memoirs what every guy's last desire would be if he was killed in the war. I never intended to show it to anyone, but still I felt a little ashamed of betraying their secret and private thoughts . . . Possibly the only one who felt worse than I did was Hennesey on the floor.

HOWARD KISSEL

Arnold Epstein, one of the pivotal characters in Neil Simon's *Biloxi Blues*, . . . is thin—the kind of thin that makes you nervous, an ascetic, neurasthenic thinness, like that of a Russian Orthodox monk or an evangelical vegetarian. Worse yet, Epstein is a Jew, thoroughly uncompromising in his commitment to his own intellect and to certain principles, which might be admirable in many situations but is prickly in an Army barracks during World War II.

Epstein so antagonizes his fellow soldiers that we are not really surprised when, toward the end of the first act, he has a monolog describing an awful humiliation he experiences doing latrine duty. The monolog is harrowing in its own right, more so because the soldier he tells is the only other Jew in the outfit, a more naive, ingratiating sort, whose pity is mingled with a certain anxiety that he can't feel more compassion for the man whose arrogance so unnerves him.

There are several remarkable things about this moment. One is the frankness with which Simon comes to terms with his Jewishness. In his 1981 *Fools,* based quite obviously on the Chelm stories, nothing in the text indicated that the characters or the mentality was Jewish, leading to a vagueness that rendered the play bland and basically unfunny. His 1983 *Brighton Beach Memoir* was set quite clearly in Jewish Brooklyn, but not one actor on the stage was Jewish—it was again a cosmeticizing of Simon's experience that may have been one of the reasons the play seemed to go nowhere. The confrontation between the two Jews in *Biloxi* gives the play an arresting, haunting focus—for the first time Simon seems willing to look at his experience directly, even harshly.

More important he does not try to minimize the situation with irrelevant humor, which marred even the better moments in *Brighton Beach.* He is willing to risk the chill that runs through the theater after the latrine monolog—he does not trivialize a man's anguish with easy laughs.

Biloxi Blues begins with five young recruits on a dismal train carrying them from Fort Dix to Mississippi. The first scene is full of jokes about flatulence and body smells, certainly appropriate but suggesting a typical Simon yock-filled evening. By the end of the play, when the men are bound for the Atlantic coast and ultimately the war in Europe we feel each of the characters has become someone about whom we know—and care—a great deal. . . .

Biloxi Blues is certainly Simon's best play, to my mind the first in which he has had the courage to suggest there are things that matter more to him than the reassuring sound of the audience's laughter. My admiration for the play is deep and unqualified.

> *Howard Kissel, in a review of "Biloxi Blues," in* Women's Wear Daily, *March 29, 1985. Reprinted in* New York Theatre Critics' Reviews, *Vol. XXXXVI, No. 5, Week of April 8, 1985, p. 326.*

WILLIAM A. HENRY, III

In contrast to the confident, even cocky kid of *Brighton Beach,* the Eugene of *Biloxi Blues* knows how little he knows. He is aware enough of the larger world to realize how many perils, including the war, may bar his path to glory. And through the nudging of his wise and principled friend Arnold Epstein. . . . Eugene begins to grasp that his charm and amiability may mask the moral flaw of self-absorption. When Arnold stingingly accuses Eugene of being "a witness," devoid of passion and commitment, the insight may make an audience reconsider its feelings about the character and also its author, who appears to be musing self-critically about three decades of often bland ingratiation on Broadway, in Hollywood and on TV.

Nonetheless, the jokes keep on coming. Titters resound even in what are meant to be grim moments: the exposure and imprisonment of one of Eugene's barracks mates as a homosexual; a nervy confrontation between a drunk drill sergeant wielding a loaded pistol and a raw recruit whom the officer despises. The detached Eugene, moreover, proves Arnold's attack true by being offstage during these scenes; he is so passive that the viewer may long for a play that focuses more on Arnold. Inevitably, the sequel lacks some of the roundedness and universality of *Brighton Beach:* a military stopover cannot encompass the complex, cumulative relationships of a family. Still, it stands with the most telling statements of the World War II generation, or any generation that loses many of its young in battle, about how much of life is luck. After a fall and winter of disappointment, *Biloxi Blues* ranks as the best new American play of the Broadway season.

> *William A. Henry, III, "Bawdy Rites of Passage," in* Time, *Vol. 125, No. 14, April 8, 1985, p. 72.*

Josef (Václav) Škvorecký

The Engineer of Human Souls: An Entertainment of the Old Themes of Life, Women, Fate, Dreams, the Working Class, Secret Agents, Love, and Death

Governor General's Literary Award: Fiction

Czechoslovakian-born novelist, editor, translator, short story writer, poet, essayist, dramatist, and scriptwriter.

Škvorecký, who now lives in Canada, made his mark on Czechoslovakian literary history with the publication of his first major novel, *Zbabělci* (1958; *The Cowards*), an irreverent work that defied the Communist Party's call for socialist-realist literature and told instead a story revolving around the tabooed subject of American jazz, using an unprecedented colloquial dialogue. Several of Škvorecký's subsequent works, including the novels *Tankový prapor* (1971) and *Mirákl* (1972) and the novella *Bassaxofon* (1977; *The Bass Saxophone*), continue the saga of Danny Smiřický, the mischievous, semi-autobiographical protagonist of *The Cowards*. *Příběh inženýra lidských duší* (1977; *The Engineer of Human Souls: An Entertainment of the Old Themes of Life, Women, Fate, Dreams, the Working Class, Secret Agents, Love, and Death*), translated in 1984, represents the latest work available in English of the Smiřický saga. A derisive parody of Josef Stalin's reported proclamation that ''as an engineer constructs a machine, so must a writer construct the mind of the New Man,'' *The Engineer of Human Souls* denounces dogma of any kind.

In his native Czechoslovakia Škvorecký lived under the successive totalitarian regimes of the German Nazis and the Soviet Communists. Because of the strict censorship of literature under these regimes, Škvorecký did not attempt to publish many of his works until years after he had written them, at intervals when the political climate was less restrictive. *The Cowards,* although not published until ten years after it was written, caused such a stir in the government that not only was the book banned and Škvorecký demoted from his post as editor-in-chief of *Světová literatura,* a review of foreign literatures, but a subsequent tightening of governmental controls resulted in the dismissal of many other artists in various fields. Škvorecký, however, had gained a large popular following. Also politically unacceptable in Czechoslovakia are Škvorecký's many translations of American fiction, including works by Ernest Hemingway and William Faulkner, both of whom greatly influenced Škvorecký's prose style. Despite repression Škvorecký acted as a member of the central committees of the Czechoslovak Writers' Union and the Czechoslovak Film and Television Artists. When the months of relaxed governmental controls known as The Prague Spring ended with the Soviet invasion of Czechoslovakia in August 1968, Škvorecký immigrated to Canada where he became a professor of American literature. His Czechoslovakian citizenship has since been revoked. In addition to teaching, Škvorecký helps operate the publishing house founded by his wife Zdena Salivarová. Named Sixty-Eight Publishers, the press upholds the freedom of speech that Czech writers experienced in 1968, just prior to the Soviet invasion, and publishes works by banned Czech writers. Several of Škvorecký's own works were originally published through this

Photograph by Layle Silbert © copyright 1986

press. In 1980 Škvorecký was awarded the Neudstadt International Prize for Literature.

In *The Engineer of Human Souls* protagonist Danny Smiřický has followed Škvorecký's path of immigration to Canada and professorship at a small college within the University of Toronto. By juxtaposing his life in Czechoslovakia with letters from other dissidents and émigrés, and current experiences with his students and members of the Czech community in Toronto, Smiřický presents impressions about both the injustices of totalitarianism and the naïveté of Western attitudes towards politics. The main theme of the oppressiveness of dogmatic thinking is interspersed with the additional themes of eroticism, loss, displacement, and the connection between art and life, all of which are highlighted in Professor Smiřický's lectures on the works of American and English authors. These lectures actually serve to divide the book into thematic sections. Though literature is the unifying motif in *The Engineer of Human Souls,* jazz music appears, as in the earlier Smiřický novels, as a metaphor for the individualistic, antiestablishment attitude held by Škvorecký's protagonist. Škvorecký's use of this metaphor stems from his personal interest in music; in Czechoslovakia

Škvorecký was an amateur saxophone player and at one time a disc jockey for a jazz radio station.

Although *The Engineer of Human Souls* is an anguishing examination of oppression, the work is notably humorous. Polish critic Jan Kott observes that "it is not 'black humor' or 'laughter through tears.' It is plain, ordinary, and hearty laughter...." Kott goes on to explain that in the face of bleak circumstances such as those the Czechs have experienced, all that may remain is humor: "When there is no hope or consolation, there is still laughter—bawdy laughter." Indicative of the humor in *The Engineer of Human Souls* is its subtitle: "An Entertainment of the Old Themes of Life, Women, Fate, Dreams, the Working Class, Secret Agents, Love, and Death."

Škvorecký describes the writing process of *The Engineer of Human Souls* as one in which he literally pieced together episodes he had written down on strips of paper and thus formed the basis of a story; of the disjointed episodes Škvorecký writes, "I grouped them by contrasts, by similitudes, linked them by tone and meaning, I tried to create a world out of the mess of my life in our messy country. Finally some sort of pattern emerged." While some critics believe the frequent alternation between past and present in *The Engineer of Human Souls* confuses the plot, others find it an interesting and successful method of conveying a person's total experience. Most critics concur, though, in their high opinion of Škvorecký's various characterizations, which according to critic Eva Hoffman show Škvorecký's "acceptance of [the] diversity of human souls."

Already internationally recognized, Škvorecký is now gaining the attention of his adopted country, Canada, especially as his writing begins to reflect his experiences there. Several critics claim that it is the assimilation of his two heritages that has made *The Engineer of Human Souls* Škvorecký's most successful work to date.

(See also *CLC*, Vol. 15; *Contemporary Authors*, Vols. 61-64; *Contemporary Authors New Revision Series*, Vol. 10; and *Contemporary Authors Autobiography Series*, Vol. 1.)

PETER Z. SCHUBERT

You know them all. The protagonists of this latest sequel to Škvorecký's cycle about Danny Smiřický are not new to the reader. Either they appear in the other five books of the cycle, or you can meet them in the streets of Toronto. Josef Škvorecký's depiction of the characters is so realistic that, although their names have been altered, the reader has no difficulty recognizing their true identities. The selection and delightful portrayal of the protagonists are among the chief assets of *Příběh inženýra lidských duší (The Story of an Engineer of Human Souls)*.

In this extensive book, up to now the longest novel by Škvorecký, the action progresses on two temporal levels. One is during the Bohemian and Moravian Protectorate, where it centers around a sabotage in a plane factory—not seen, however, in the "anti-Nazi resistance literature" tradition, but through the eyes of the saxophonist Danny. The other is in contemporary Canada, where the Czech exiles are described from the point of view of the same character. The latter level is complemented by depiction of life at a Canadian college. Both streams of action are connected by a series of letters received by Danny from some of his friends of both sexes and of varied social standing and fate in the quarter-century separating the past and the present of the novel. These letters reveal the personal tragedies of some Czechs of the narrator's generation (1920s) as, for instance, the fate of Rebekka Ohrenstein, known to the reader from *Sedmiramenný svícen (The Seven-Armed Candelabrum)*.

The subtle portrayal of Rebekka's or Přemek Skočdopole's tragic life alone makes the book worth reading. Enjoyable are Škvorecký's literary allusions. His Czech, however, leaves much to be desired. This fault is accentuated by the mutilated language as spoken by the characters. In the narrator's account there are far too many grammatical mistakes, not to speak of the mutilated words and mistakes in the other languages used (English, French). On page 161 of the first volume Škvorecký directly contradicts this practice, as he claims that normally he does not use foreign words. These shortcomings, however, should not dissuade the reader from enjoying this book, which is one of Škvorecký's best.

Peter Z. Schubert, in a review of "Příběh inženýra lidských duší," in World Literature Today, *Vol. 52, No. 4, Autumn, 1978, p. 655.*

MARK CZARNECKI

As an exhaustive, insightful document of modern society in both East and West, [*The Engineer of Human Souls*] has no equal. For encyclopaedic sensibility and daunting erudition, Skvorecky easily keeps company with Joyce, Barth, and Pynchon. But his focus on the all-embracing paranoia induced by totalitarianism is unique, and that obsession is all the more noteworthy since he angrily rejects political solutions. Skvorecky's opening epigram from Blake—"To Generalize is to be an Idiot. To Particularize is the Alone Distinction of Merit"—announces his dominant leitmotiv. Later, he notes, "Meaning is a compulsive neurosis." All man's constructs, whether mythical or ideological, are false; to survive we must "live simply for life itself".

The man who survived two totalitarian occupations flogs political fanaticism with cutting, Rabelaisian wit. Little in his previous work has prepared readers for this scintillating cascade of scatological, sexual, and political anecdotes, all jumbled together with a vigorous disregard for plot of any kind. Skvorecky's metaphor is jazz, his method, improvisation. Professor Smiricky's prolonged seduction of his student Irene constantly evokes the loves of his youth, inspiring him to leap decades in a single sentence: "Literature is forever blowing a horn," Skvorecky wrote in *The Bass Saxophone* . . . in 1977. "Singing about youth when youth is irretrievably gone, singing about your homeland when in the schizophrenia of the times you find yourself in a land . . . where your heart is not."

Exiles live in the past; having survived a translation in space, they are doomed to an external translation in time. Locked into that rhythm, they endure a sterile present rendered bleaker by nostalgia. As Smiricky stares out his window at the flat Ontario landscape, he imagines Poe's raven pecking at the snow: despite Skvorecky's repeated affirmation of immediate experience, and the exuberant vitality of his satire, his heart is in the homeland. The tragedy of *Engineer* is the impotent wisdom of old age: the romantic idealism of Smiricky's past may ultimately be wrong, even fatal, but then he was truly, passionately alive. Now, secure in democracy, experience palls. "It is always too late for everything," Daniel says and, towards the end, section after section simply finishes with a shrug: "So what?"

Engineer's most stunning achievement is its exhilarating verbal virtuosity. Although Skvorecky's syntax stays sober, Paul Wilson's masterful English translation, like the original, is strewn with Latin epigrams, quotations in Russian and, occasionally, entire passages in German. Furthermore, true to his dictum that "the only authors whose work remains alive are those who transfer language to the page in its natural form", Skvorecky's Czech original defies the formalism so dear to totalitarian governments by its copious use of slang and a constant admixture of English, the language of freedom.

Engineer, therefore, places enormous demands on the translator, but Wilson admirably matches slang for slang; his English is much looser than the Czech, but what he loses in pungency he gains in clarity. Ultimately, however, no rendering could adequately communicate the political defiance inherent in Skvorecky's free-wheeling style, a defiance to which only those "over there" can truly respond. As the saying has it, something always gets lost in translation; especially in a work that is about translation in the most profound sense. A complex, challenging analysis of contemporary politics and society, *The Engineer of Human Souls* will become a milestone in the evolution of world literature.

> Mark Czarnecki, *"Skvorecky Engineers a Milestone of World Literature,"* in Quill and Quire, *Vol. 50, No. 5, May, 1984, p. 30.*

RICHARD EDER

Skvorecky calls *The Engineer of Human Souls* an entertainment. It is, in places, so entertaining that it would be dangerous to read it without laughing aloud; in other places it is sad or dismaying. What he has really written, though, is an epic of his country and its exiles.

Epic is a foreboding word. But Skvorecky has accomplished it with all the talent that he and his fellow Czech writers seem to possess for the particular, for a fruitful irony, for an indignation teetering upon a sense of its own absurdity, and for a meditative discursiveness that fixes both sides of our world's political equation with a mild but pitiless clarity.

Both sides. The New World, the free West, offers a lavish hope to the exile, opportunities of all kinds, a truce with his fellows; everything that the human requires, in fact, except memory. The struggles of the old country, the defeats, despairs and oppressions are to be rejected for every possible reason, except one: memory, again.

The novel is long, spans 40 years and shifts, sometimes within a single sentence and usually without warning, from the Second World War to the present and halfway back to the post-Stalinist thaws. Skvorecky has centered on a calm, middle-aged novelist-professor, comfortably settled outside of Toronto. His name is Smiricky, and the resemblance to the author is not coincidental.

Smiricky is a kind of revolving lantern, picking out his past and his present. He ruminates on the heroisms and mock-heroics of his friends and antagonists, their short and long terms, the finely winding path that so many have traced between expedience and resistance, between a hopefulness that finds itself contaminated by opportunism and a principled refusal that coarsens into despair. . . . (p. 1)

Smiricky teaches literature to university students whose minds are as new-minted as their stereos, though less distinctly voiced. Discussing *The Confession,* the Costa-Gavras film about Stalinist purges of Eastern European Communist leaders, Smiricky mentions that he knew the wife of one of the characters. "Was she an actress too?" a student asks. History has no more weight to these young people than its representation in a movie or a TV show.

And yet, he loves his Canada: the ease, the hopefulness, the decency, the abundance; he falls in love with the glossiest of his students. "I feel wonderful. I feel utterly and dangerously wonderful in this wilderness land," he says. And when a student, caught plagiarizing, miserably awaits punishment, he reflects:

> Life had long since immunized me against the temptation to inform on anyone, regardless of what authority demanded it. My reluctance is as impregnable as the Iron Curtain. I lived too long in a country where even the most pristine truth, once reported to the authorities, becomes a lie.

That may come closest of anything said or written in these 20 years to defining the peculiar temper of the Czechoslovak flowering; both in its pre-1968 stages and, later, in the literature of exile. No other Western people has wielded truth with such modesty; none other has discovered so precisely the moral dimension of the elbow—just how far it is licit to poke it without committing an affront to the neighbor. ("Licit" is not the same as "permissible." That a particular and far more powerful neighbor had quite different criteria is another matter.)

Over the 40 years of Smiricky's memories, everything and everyone is transformed. A priest he goes to for refuge after his anti-Nazi sabotage is discovered, rebuffs him; years later he turns up as a captain in the Communist secret police. The Nazi factory commandant who catches him, on the other hand, turns out to be a member of the resistance. Pro-Nazi collaborators emerge as Communist apparatchiks.

Mostly, though, people avoid such extremes. A young firebrand who resists the Nazis and then the Communists, ends up as a laborer in Australia. A minor poet, horrified by the death scenes under the Nazis, embraces Socialist Realism for a while; and Skvorecky manages remarkably to show its allure. Others float and prosper, no matter what.

Perhaps the sharpest and most comical portraits are those of the exiles. They are divided dozens of different ways; the single funniest passage in the book concerns a furious debate over an underground book. (pp. 1, 10)

There are perpetual schemes. One exile dreams of persuading everybody in Czechoslovakia to buy 10 boxes of matches at the same time; this, he thinks, would wreck the year's economic plan. Tourists pour through from Prague, and many of them are amateur spies, blackmailed by the police, and laughably incompetent. There are those who flourish and, without forgetting, come to terms with their new life; there are others who can't manage it.

The most moving personage is about not managing. Veronika is a student, attractive, intelligent and witty. She is taken up by rich Canadian friends, becomes the girlfriend of their son; but she cannot get 1968 out of her mind. She is sad and bitter; she conducts absurd acts of protest such as releasing a noise-making balloon at a Russian folk concert. And finally, almost against her own will, she returns. The last word from her—possessing an endless echo—is a telegram received by Smiricky:

Im a fool stop veronika.

The Engineer of Human Souls—the title is an ironic reference to the Stalinist notion of the writer's function—is a treasure, but has its flaws. In form it is an accumulation of materials set, apart from skips backward and forward, in chronological order. The accumulation is massive, and it tends to be repetitious and excessive.

At its best, Skvorecky's irony is silvery and delicate; but sometimes it can become heavy-handed. And the narrator's various loves enjoy great attention without being very interesting. With the exception of Veronika, who is not really his love, and a touching portrait of a whole-hearted village girl, his young women are dolls, but not quite living dolls.

Within this excessive length and detail, though, the author has set his lives bobbing midway between memory and the present. He refuses to spare us a choice between the first, which is unbearable, and the second which, rejecting the first, is empty. (p. 10)

Richard Eder, "Exiles' Epic as an Entertainment," in Los Angeles Times Book Review, *July 1, 1984, pp. 1, 10.*

EVA HOFFMAN

If E. M. Forster's injunction, "Only connect," is a prescription for an expanded sympathy, then Josef Skvorecky, a writer who was born in Bohemia and emigrated to Canada . . . , fulfills it with an unusual amplitude. And if a tragic understanding of the complexities of our time, leavened with an acute sense of perennial human comedy, is a sign of a ripened vision, then this nourishing, serious and wonderfully entertaining novel [*The Engineer of Human Souls*] is one of the more mature works to have appeared recently on our literary horizons.

Not that the connections Mr. Skvorecky makes are of a willfully systematic kind. On one level, *Engineer* is a novel of ideas, but if it has any underlying argument, it is against the tyranny of any obsessional Idea—against all dogmas and orthodoxies that, in the service of unifying the world, reduce and suppress its dappled variety. Like many writers from Eastern Europe, Mr. Skvorecky reserves some of his most passionate polemics for those who think they are in possession of an exclusive historical Truth—whether they are representatives of Fascism in German-occupied Czechoslovakia or Soviet-style Communism.

But to emphasize the novel's argument would be to belie its own variety, its playful inventiveness. In one sense plotless, *Engineer* proliferates with enough stories—funny, improbable, dramatic, sly, erotic—to fill several lesser novels. Its action moves effortlessly between contemporary Canada, where Danny Smiricky, the novel's protagonist, teaches English at a small Ontario college, and wartime Czechoslovakia, between high literature and popular culture . . . ; between the large canvas of history and intimate vignettes of love and eroticism.

Among the novel's several settings and its plethora of vividly drawn characters, there is Edenvale College, with Danny Smiricky's endearingly or impossibly naive students, and his almost equally benighted colleagues (one of whom wants to suspend

parachutes from classroom ceilings "to help nervous students let themselves go"). There is the small town of Kosteletz, where the young Danny falls in love with a tubercular peasant girl, Nadia, a sort of central, uncompromisingly simple conscience of the novel; where he indulges in his first experiment in antiwar heroics, experiences his first taste of truly mortal and truly instructive fear, and hangs around with a group of some of the more sophisticated and irreverent adolescents to grace the pages of any fiction.

There is also the Czech emigré community in Toronto, with its cast of eccentrics, heroines, vamps and fanatics. . . .

Paradoxically, it is the acceptance of this diversity of human souls that gives *Engineer* its geniune connectiveness, its sense that life can be found anywhere. Over the years, Danny Smiricky says of himself, "I have grown used to the fact that almost everything can mean many things, but that the primal, the real meaning, the concrete reality, is ultimately the best. The most beautiful. The most valid." It is Danny's relish for the concrete that gives his perceptions their zest and enables him to extend his sympathies and ironies with a remarkable even-handedness—to find mocking pleasure in the absurdities of his friends, or to feel a kind of comraderie with a young Arab student whose pamphlet-fed revolutionary fervor he finds dangerously reductive.

Like many writers in exile, Mr. Skvorecky is aware of the often radical disjunctions between the two worlds he has known. But unlike writers who emphasize the damage that can proceed from a fragmented life, he is also intent on giving meaning to those moments of happiness, or winsomeness, or surreal surprise, that are independent of any ideology or culture.

Such moments can proceed from something as insubstantial as the sense of safety which overcomes Danny as he drives on a wintry Canadian highway, or from the high comedy of human behavior, or from "the truly erotic art of conversation." But there is also another important source of both meaning and connectedness—and that is the art of literature itself.

The chapters in *Engineer* are entitled "Poe," "Hawthorne," "Twain," "Crane," "Fitzgerald," "Conrad" and "Lovecraft." Mr. Skvorecky, like his protagonist, teaches English at Erindale College, University of Toronto—and among its other riches, the novel contains literary criticism of a rare elegance, intelligence and originality (anyone contemplating a new study of Conrad should look at Professor Smiricky's disquisition on the harlequin as the key to *The Heart of Darkness*).

For Danny, "the relevance" of literature is palpable everywhere—from his friends and lovers who repeat fictional characters as if through magical recurrence, to his own, Eastern European history, which he finds prophesied in American fiction with uncanny accuracy. The multiplicity of human forms, Mr. Skvorecky seems to say, is apprehended and shaped by literature; and in turn, literature illuminates and joins that multiplicity. Mr. Skvorecky's own novel, with a capacious flexibility, encompasses them both. It is a difficult work to summarize; it is a deep pleasure to read.

Eva Hoffman, in a review of "The Engineer of Human Souls," in The New York Times, *July 23, 1984, p. C16.*

PAUL WEST

Told first-person by a Czech novelist teaching American literature at "Edenvale College" in Toronto, *The Engineer of*

Human Souls makes one wonder all over again if novels about novelists must always be a bore. No, not if the mind on show is interesting, and the heart behind it ample....

The Engineer might have shown a dry, sly, sardonic, sad literary refugee fingering the detritus of his past, his childhood among Nazis, his manhood among Reds, and Canada might have figured only in glimpses: the source of many an anticlimax, maybe, but never of a trauma. Indeed, it might be argued that the émigré's special gift is not social documentary at all, but the creation of composite and intricate limbos: verbal (Nabokov), alcoholical (Lowry), infernal (Beckett), relativistic (Cortazar), narcissistic (Goytisolo), and so on. What you have lost, or been forced out of, makes you need to concoct something wholly your own—a dimension of the mind, a country of only you and those like you.

Well, Skvorecky is his own man. He gives us Edenvale College and Toronto and Canada in abundance . . . , eager to test the New World against the Old, to posit his long novel on a series of cultural collisions, and his hero is not so much an innocent abroad as a man of almost terminal experience among innocents whose notion of tragedy begins and ends with the death of Janis Joplin.

Professor Danny Smiricky finds Canada baffling, but it entertains him too. He plugs away, even organizing his novel after the pattern of his courses into sections headed Poe, Hawthorne, Twain, Crane, Fitzgerald, Conrad and Lovecraft. There is even a hint here of what John Stuart Mill called the healing power of literature; Smiricky has come from abroad to teach bright tadpoles about stuff they will never fathom until they are 20 years older, but he gets something from the rough and tumble of classroom talk. He twitches back to life again. Smidgens of his students' impetuous energy rub off on him as, banned at home, he grows affable, slangy, boozes it up, swaps wisecracks and dirty stories, and strives to push beyond the clique of transplanted Czechs. The whole of Canada is eligible to become his family, his toy, his dream, his tribe.

It's a winning enough idea, insofar as it sets up harsh and unusual contrasts; but Toronto is over-documented here when it might have been the eye of a needle through which Danny passes the gruesome gamut of life back home. As it is, life under two successive totalitarian regimes does appear in flashbacks which have a weight, a density, a mortal bite that the many Toronto scenes lack, for all their mellow plenitude. It's almost as if an Elie Wiesel had handed over part of his book to Peter De Vries. I wonder why Skvorecky, with so much pain at his disposal, so strong a tendency to the discursive within him (like his expatriate countryman Kundera), and so many examples of the highly evolved 20th-century novel around him, turns his alias into such a plodder. Maybe the point is that Danny has been tempted and corrupted by some vision of The Great North American Novel. Skvorecky's much praised *The Bass Saxophone*—swift, epitomistic, mercurial—was nothing like this....

At his most moving and compelling, Smiricky-Skvorecky sails with Jules Verne over a blue-black sea, evokes a hangman who made the condemned shave beforehand and then almost always postponed the execution, and relays the yarns of a professional hyperbolist who specializes in how people buried alive manage to subsist on worms. Every now and then, something more than the merely jocose heaves into view and floods the text with keen remembrances of family, lovers, and friends, but not often enough. The novel takes its dominant tone from scenes, funny enough, with condoms, suckling pigs, ketchup on fries, a cropduster plane loaded with dung to dump on the Bratislava May Day military parade.

Skvorecky has a forthright sense of humor. The book has charm and point, but it is too unwieldy, too garrulous, to slice unforgettably home. "An entertainment" it undoubtedly is, most of all if you relish a vision of the end of the world to an accompaniment of cracking bubblegum. Ironists sometimes overdo the easy opposite of what gets them on the raw, leaving the reader to infer volumes of anger, pain, or grief, and I think that's what's happened here.

> *Paul West, "Last Tango in Toronto," in* Book World—The Washington Post, *July 29, 1984, p. 10.*

MICHAEL HENRY HEIM

[*Heim is an American professor of Czech and Russian literature and the English translator of Czech novelist Milan Kundera's* The Unbearable Lightness of Being *(1984). In the following excerpt Heim discusses* The Engineer of Human Souls *in the light of Škvorecký's emigration and especially praises the author's blend of Czech and Canadian culture.*]

Ours is a time of massive migration. In the works of some of the century's greatest writers—Conrad, Joyce, Nabokov, Beckett—the sense of loss and displacement that comes from leaving native soil acquires general significance: it represents a modern everyman's clichéd but nonetheless substantial sense of alienation. Josef Skvorecky, a prominent Czech novelist, essayist and translator who left his homeland after the 1968 Soviet invasion, is no Pollyanna, but he has something refreshingly positive to say about the fate of the emigrant and perhaps, by extension, about our provisionally alienated everyman. His latest novel, *The Engineer of Human Souls,* is not merely a medium for this message; it is to some extent the message itself. For Skvorecky is one of those rare birds who still believes in the connection between literature and life.

To begin with, Skvorecky's novel boasts the subtitle "An Entertainment on the Old Themes of Life, Women, Fate, Dreams, the Working Class, Secret Agents, Love and Death." And in fact it swings effortlessly back and forth between the hilarious and the serious, the randy and the chaste....

In *The Engineer of Human Souls,* memories form several separate but parallel story lines: Danny's teen-age life and loves as a conscripted laborer during the Nazi occupation; Daniel's life and loves as a "bourgeois element" during the early years of the Communist regime; and the experiences of various of his friends—related here primarily through personal letters—during the Stalinist 1950s, the liberal 1960s and the "normalized" 1970s. "Associations—the essence of everything," [Danny] Smiricky muses. "Associations in time, in appearance, in theory, in the heart, omnipotent and omnipresent."

Within the context of the novel these associations take on a new dimension. When Smiricky free-associates, he links his pre-emigration and postemigration lives, re-establishing contact with himself. The move from Czechoslovakia to Canada is no final rift; it is a new stage in the same life. Not surprisingly, Smiricky is a conservative, but he is one in the etymological sense of the word: he has a strong need to conserve what he feels to be worthwhile, and he accordingly counsels the West to pay closer attention to the past. Released from the burden of the "scientific"—that is, Marxist—world view, he feels "dangerously wonderful" in Canada, *dangerously* because he recognizes the jeopardy involved in going too far in the direction of ''unscientific'' hedonism: of letting everything lose meaning by living life only for itself. (p. 86)

Smiricky takes literature seriously. When Hawthorne asks, ''Cannot you conceive that a man may wish well to the world, and struggle for its good, on some other plan than precisely that which you have laid down?'' Smiricky applies the question to the ideology he has lived under. And when Hawthorne's Hollingsworth calls mankind ''but another yoke of oxen, stubborn, stupid and sluggish,'' waiting to be goaded, Smiricky sees Hollingsworth as a preincarnation of Lenin and his ''method of scientifically exploiting false consciousness.'' Later, when discussing Conrad's *Heart of Darkness* with the class, he sets forth a detailed analysis of the work as a prescient vision of Soviet society.

Of course, Smiricky has no intention of forcing his interpretations on the students. He wishes to show them how literature, real literature, deals in images and ideas that go beyond the immediate issues; he wishes to encourage them to apply what they read to their own lives. By the end of the novel he seems to be making progress even with an American draft resister; in one of his associative flashbacks, the American falls together with a Czech secret service man who once upbraided Smiricky for singing ''Annie Laurie'' immediately after the ''Internationale.''

The Engineer of Human Souls is an intensely literary work. The title itself is a tongue-in-cheek reference to Stalin's definition of the writer: ''As an engineer constructs a machine, so must a writer construct the mind of the New Man.'' Each chapter is named for and discusses the author Professor Smiricky happens to be taking up in class at the time; each is prefaced by a galaxy of epigraphs from Czech, Anglo-American and French literature. And many of the Czech characters in the novel—notably the narrator, Daniel Smiricky, and the characters he summons up by association or by letter—have appeared before in Skvorecky's works. They thus not only refer to other works; they owe their very existence to them.

Skvorecky's first novel, *The Cowards*, is seminal in this process. Written just after the war, it could not be published in Czechoslovakia until 1958, and even then it caused an immediate scandal: Danny and his pals in provincial, war-time Kostelec were more concerned with American saxophonists than Soviet liberators, and although they sabotaged munitions in the plants where their German overlords forced them to work, they did so as much to play up to their girls as to bring down the Reich. ''There was so much to remember about Kostelec,'' Smiricky/Skvorecky thinks years later in Canada, as he incorporates the gang's new adventures into *The Engineer of Human Souls* and brings their stories up to date. The result is a rich, multilayered narrative that juggles an amazing variety of characters and events with admirable clarity and finesse.

In a sense, then, the novel belongs equally to Czech and to Canadian literature. (Special praise is due Paul Wilson for a stunning translation that perfectly matches the verve and ebullience of Skvorecky's style.) On the one hand, it is the high point of one side of Skvorecky's prodigious Czech output and shows him at his sparkling best; on the other, it places him in the forefront of the cultural life of the new, ''ethnic'' Canada.... (pp. 86-8)

By combining the Czech and Canadian worlds so deftly, by molding them in such a way that they complement each other

and work together, Skvorecky demonstrates emblematically, as it were, the *value* of emigration....

''I carry my native land in my heart,'' Smiricky soliloquizes near the end of the novel. ''National in form, international in feeling.'' If he and his maker have come through the ordeal of emigration so unscathed, is it not because they have turned misfortune to advantage by becoming not merely multilingual but multicultural? Literature plays an almost sacral role in *The Engineer of Human Souls,* but Skvorecky insists again and again on the connection between literature and life. He chides a student for dismissing the bullets in Crane's *The Red Badge of Courage* as mere figments of naturalism; he would probably chide us for dismissing any of the injustices and griefs that abound in *The Engineer of Human Souls.* They are real and they are gruesome. And yet we put the novel down with a sense of joy at the plenitude of life. Old-fashioned, perhaps. Against alienation. But surely what we hope for from ''An Entertainment on the Old Themes of Life, Women, Fate, Dreams, the Working Class, Secret Agents, Love and Death.'' (p. 88)

Michael Henry Heim, ''Dangerously Wonderful,'' in The Nation, *Vol. 239, No. 3, August 4 & 11, 1984, pp. 86-8.*

An Excerpt from *The Engineer of Human Souls: An Entertainment on the Old Themes of Life, Women, Fate, Dreams, the Working Class, Secret Agents, Love, and Death*

Outside the window, which is high, narrow and gothic, the cold Canadian wind blends two whitenesses: snowflakes sifting down from lowering clouds and snowdust lifted and whirled by the wind from the land stretching southwards to Lake Ontario. The snow swirls through a white wasteland broken only by a few bare, blackened trees.

Edenvale College stands in a wilderness. In a few years the nearby town of Mississauga is expected to swell and envelop the campus with more variety and colour, but for the time being the college stands in a wilderness, two and a half miles from the nearest housing development. The houses there are no longer all alike: people have learned something since George F. Babbitt's time. Perhaps it was literature that taught them. Now there are at least four different kinds of bungalow spaced at irregular intervals so that the housing development looks like a Swiss village in one of those highly stylized paintings. It is pretty to look at.

But I see it only in my mind's eye, as I look out on the white, cold, windy Canadian landscape. Often, as my thoughts flow, I conjure up again the many wonderful things I have seen in this country of cities with no past. Like the Toronto skyline with its black and white skyscrapers, some plated with golden mirrors, thrusting their peaks into the haze, glowing like burnished chessboards against the evening twilight above the flat Ontario landscape, and beyond them a sun as large as Jupiter and as red as an aniline ruby sinking into the green dusk. God knows why it's so green, but it is. The Toronto skyline is more beautiful to me than the familiar silhouette of Prague Castle. There is beauty everywhere on earth, but there is greater beauty in those places where one feels that sense of ease which comes from no longer having to put off one's dreams until some improbable future—a future inexorably shrinking away; where the fear which has pervaded one's life suddenly vanishes because there is nothing to be afraid of. Gone are the fears I shared with my fellows, for although the Party exists here, it has no power as yet. And my personal fears are gone too, for no professional literary critics in Canada will confine me in arbitrary scales of greatness. My novels, published here in Czech by Mrs. Santner's shoestring operation, are widely read by my fellow Czechs but hardly ever reviewed, because there is no one to review them. There are those two or three grateful laymen who lavish praises on them in the émigré press, their flatteries sandwiched between harvest home announcements and ads for Bohemian tripe soup; they are literate, but they do not understand literature. Then there is Professor Koupelna in Saskatchewan. Every once in a while Passer's mail-order firm in Chicago sends him one of my books as a free gift along with his order of homemade jelly and Prague ham. The book arouses a savage and instinctive outrage in the good professor which he mistakes for the spirit of criticism and he fires off a broadside to the journal of the Czechoslovak Society for Arts and Sciences in America. Fortunately, his attack is launched from such a pinnacle of erudition that most Society members find it repellent. And his erudition has so many gaps in it that even those who are not repelled remain unconvinced.

I feel wonderful. I feel utterly and dangerously wonderful in this wilderness land.

ROBERT TOWERS

[Skvorecky has] published a huge, multifaceted novel that seems to be no less than a compendium of the writer's experience of two worlds: the tragi-farcical world of the police state he left and the safe, prosperous, shallow, world without history in which he presently lives and teaches.

By choosing to write copiously about his experience rather than distilling it, Mr. Skvorecky has endowed *The Engineer of Human Souls* with a superabundance of content (often rich and delectable) while burdening it with problems of shape and momentum that have not, in my opinion, been adequately resolved....

What is almost an embarrassment of riches in *The Engineer of Human Souls* is accompanied by a degree of formlessness that I find damaging. The thematic structure, though often interesting, even provocative, in its own right, is insufficient to keep the novel from sagging under its vast accumulation of character and incident. The ghosts of earlier writers evoked at the beginning of each chapter cannot do the formal work required. While a presiding image (like Günther Grass's tin drum in the novel of that name) or a set of recurring motifs might give a satisfactory shapeliness to a more expressionistic work, what an essentially realistic novel of great length badly needs is a strong, centralized action to supply not only coherence but movement. In the absence of such an action, one incident, no matter how vivid, is simply replaced in the reader's consciousness by the next, and that by the next, until a blurring of both content and outline occurs.

As if to enter a plea against such criticism, Mr. Skvorecky assigns these words to one of Danny Smiricky's correspondents, the poet Jan: "There is something that falls short of perfection in every book, without exception, something influenced by the age, even something ridiculous; just like everyone, without exception, has weaknesses . . . and may even be ridiculous. But if he is an honorable man and if it is an honorable book, no one has the right to ridicule it or heap contempt on it. Genuine lovers of literature will instead feel sorry that the author was not up to some things, and will look for the remains of the golden treasure in that shipwreck on the bottom of the sea of criticism."

Salutary advice. Mr. Skvorecky is indeed an honorable writer—large-souled, passionate in his response to the atrocities and absurdities of the age, a writer who never loses sight of what is concretely human beneath the abstractions of history and ideology. And *The Engineer of Human Souls* is an honorable book, a work that makes one regret that so much of its wealth has been squandered by an inadequate attention to what might be called its sculptural dimension....

> Robert Towers, "Pursuer of Lost Maidens," in The New York Times Book Review, *August 19, 1984, p. 9.*

JAN KOTT

[*Kott is a Polish-born critic and professor of English and comparative literature now residing in the United States. In his critical study* Shakespeare, Our Contemporary, *originally published in Polish as* Szkice o Szekspirze (1964), *he interprets several of Shakespeare's plays as presenting a tragic vision of history. Kott calls this historical pattern the "Grand Mechanism," and he also finds it evidenced in* The Engineer of Human Souls. *In the following excerpt Kott praises the effectiveness of Škvorecký's tone and technique in conveying the experience of the emigrant.*]

[*The Engineer of Human Souls*] does not seem to fit into the category of either autobiography or novel, which accounts for its originality. Yet the communication of an experience and its scope is far more important than artistic innovation.

In *The Engineer of Human Souls,* there is a present time and many past times. The present time takes place in the mid-1960s in the Canadian vale of Eden in Toronto. The past times encompass the '40s, '50s, and '60s in Czechoslovakia. But these pasts do not organize themselves chronologically, nor are they rendered as a steady stream of reminiscences. Instead the book unexpectedly cuts away, like a camera, to foreign landscapes and other times. The constant jumping back and forth from one time to another seemed to me, at first reading, to be an overwrought narrative sophistication, a needless obstacle for the reader to overcome in following the vicissitudes of the characters. Later I realized that the author was right. The past always remains in the memory in a tangled synchrony. And an emigrant's past, more than anyone else's, is a second present time. It keeps opening, like a badly healed wound.

The past also returns in another way: in letters. The narrative in Skvorecky's novel, from the first chapter to the last, is constantly being interrupted by letters from Czechoslovakia and the four corners of the earth, to which all his old friends and acquaintances have been scattered. These letters, too, seemed schematic and superfluous at first, an interference with the narrative; again, about halfway through the book, I had to admit that the author was correct in including this minor epistolary novel in his work. The biographies of each of us emigrants—

and this is even more true of emigrant writers—are discontinuous, as if they were cut off midway and made up of two sections which do not want to grow together. And the biographies of our friends, of those friends who remained behind and of those who left, are also discontinuous. They are full of blank pages, empty years. It is only in letters that the stories of their lives merge and form one collective destiny.

But past time returns not only in letters. Acquaintances come to visit, sometimes only the acquaintances of acquaintances; musicians or actors on tour; the Czech, Polish, and Hungarian wives of foreigners; provocateurs; informers; police agents of both sexes on special assignment. The past of the political émigré is never quite closed or written off as a loss once and for all. There are always some unsettled accounts that are usually quite personal and quite common. Each letter from the homeland fills one of these blank pages, as does each encounter.

At all those emigrant gatherings in all the vales of Eden, the New Havens or Stony Brooks, the conversations are carried on in the native tongue of the particular group. In the first hour, before the bottle of slivovitz or vodka is emptied, every second sentence is patiently translated into broken English for the Canadian husbands or American boyfriends. (What for? They don't understand a thing, anyway!) The emigrants talk about nothing but their native land. How it had been there, and how it will be in the future. You really think that it could happen one more time? In *our* lifetime? Each person tells his own story; the life stories of the emigrants are a chapter out of the collective history of that country. The weaving of a collective destiny from incoherent and astigmatic scraps of reminiscences, pieces of paper, and eternal conversations: these are the only things that make up the "recovered time" of the emigrants. (pp. 34-5)

Before the war, [Rebecca Silbernaglova] and the narrator used to go swimming together. It is likely that she had a crush on him. In the novel, we read only her letters. The first is from January 1944 from a camp in Terezin before she is transported out. She asks that he keep a miniature portrait of her mother. After the war, she is brought back on a stretcher, an expiring skeleton. She had been in Auschwitz to the very end, but had somehow survived. The next letter is from Braunau in 1953. Her husband has been arrested on charges of being a Zionist, and she works in a textile plant, the new labor camp. She cannot take a day's leave and has no money. She asks for Swiss medicine for her ailing son. The next letter, seven years later, is from Israel. Rebecca is living with her son in a kibbutz. And after another seven years, in 1967:

> Daniel, I only hope the peace lasts ten years at least. But our Slavonic brothers will certainly do their best to ensure that it won't last that long. So I'll hope for at least five years. At least five.

Her last letter is from Tel Aviv in 1974. Her son and daughter-in-law die when a bomb planted in the center of the city explodes.

> For the first time in my life I've said to myself what the women in Auschwitz would say when their husbands, their children, their families, everyone was killed: Why couldn't I have gone up that chimney too?

In *The Engineer of Human Souls,* individual fates make up the common lot. They are instances of the Great Mechanism: the steamroller crushing the ants. Skvorecky is interested in exemplary lives. He is shamelessly real, like Solzhenitsyn. The most astonishing thing in this epic novel about the annihilation of people, however, is the laughter. It is not "black humor" or "laughter through tears." It is plain, ordinary, and hearty laughter—Schweik's laughter, which rings out in Skvorecky as it does in Kundera. When there is no hope or consolation, there is still laughter—bawdy laughter. This slightly archaic word "bawdy," bawdy but never indecent, seems appropriate here for Skvorecky. Bawdy laughter is good medicine, as the old carnival wisdom teaches. And it is not an accident that many scenes in *The Engineer of Human Souls* take place, as in Jaroslav Hasek's *The Good Soldier Schweik,* in the latrine. In 1936 when I was in the army, I was taught: "Only the house is peaceful evermore, which has never known the state of war." Conversations in the army, camp, or factory latrine, are always full of civilian wisdom. In times of war and terror, the only refuge of civilized conversation is the latrine, the only place free from fear.

The most characteristic feature of Polish theater and Czech prose of the last quarter century is the presence in them of a menace which is nevertheless ludicrous. This is not the comic terror so often invented by Western writers of the absurd; it is an observed fact. It is not surrealism; it is superrealism. Kundera, and Mrozek in Poland before him, are peerless in their demonstrations of the absurdity of the menace; but no one will be able to outdo Skvorecky.

The last of the emigrants to show up in Toronto is Dr. Toth, a decent, kindhearted, and nonparty electrical engineering specialist. A year earlier he is officially sent to attend an international conference in London. He returns according to plan, sleeps off the trip, and the next day, after a hot bath and coffee with milk, he puts on his slippers and opens the newspaper *Rude Pravo*. On the first page is an article, "The Story of a Traitor." The article is about him, about how he had gone to London for a conference, how he had met each day with the head of the Soviet delegation to get instructions for the following day, how he had read two papers . . . Everything was accurate except that he had not returned and that he had had an interview with the capitalist press about his not returning. Sweet, honest Dr. Toth wipes his glasses and re-reads the article. He keeps telling himself that this could, conceivably, be about someone else, but his name and titles stand out in very bold print.

He quickly runs over to the editorial office of *Rude Pravo*. The senior editor is an old acquaintance and receives him immediately. The editor looks at him and then very carefully at the front page of his newspaper, as if he were looking at it for the first time. Then he says: "Indeed, Citizen Professor, if you are here now, then it seems that you are not in London. But . . . there must be something to this, because we got the information from the Ministry and we didn't change a word of it, except for," and here he smiles knowingly, "correcting the spelling errors."

Dr. Toth then runs over to the appropriate ministry. This time he waits longer, but the chief of the ministry receives him in person. He looks his petitioner up and down carefully and then says: "Indeed, Citizen, if you are here then it seems that"— and here he throws him another scrutinizing look—"you did not remain with the capitalists. But . . . there must be something to this. The information," and here he lowers his voice, "remember, this is a secret, was received from our embassy in London. . . . But don't worry, everything will eventually be explained. Return to your home and workplace."

At the Institute where Dr. Toth had worked, no one would speak to him any longer. Only his faithful secretary would occasionally sneak him a glass of pale, already cooled tea. His phone was bugged and it seemed that someone was always following him. And perhaps someone was. After six months of this, he applies to go abroad on a skiing trip to the Austrian Alps. He uses all of his savings to buy two pairs of skis, a knapsack, sleeping bag, and ski jacket. He never uses the skis, but within a month's time he finds himself in Canada.

The story of the Prague electrical engineering specialist who was declared a defector before he defected is straight out of Kafka's world, in which "the cage seeks a bird" and the punishment is proof of the guilt. Yet in Skvorecky's work one hears Gogolian laughter (as in *The Inspector General,* where the servant's widow beaten by police has "whipped herself") more than one hears Kafka. That absurd Gogolian dread, which strikes even though it never stops being ridiculous, is not only a characteristic of a specific literary genre; it is also a characteristic of a specific system of repression in which contempt for the party apparatus is stronger than fear, and those in power are grotesque and ridiculous because they have come to believe their own lies.

Among Skvorecky's literary affiliations, we should name one more: Nabokov. Nabokov was also an emigrant writer, even though he belonged to another epoch, and hailed from a separate cultural sphere. He was a great emigrant in two literatures: Russian and English. He wrote about Russian literature from a Western literary perspective and about English and French classics from the perspective of a Russian writer—a comparatist in the fullest sense of the word, because he was an emigrant in the fullest sense of the word. Skvorecky's hero reads Poe's "The Raven" to his students, but first in Russian, in Jesenin's well-known adaptation:

> Kak to noch-yu v chas terrora . . .
> Karknul Voron: *Nevermore!*

And then in his own translation: "Once at night in time of terror . . ." And he concludes with a surprising, startling interpretation which equals Nabokov in its mastery of style: "We have always been surrounded by terror and by the beauty that is an inseparable part of it."

In this Canadian present time of the novel there is also the narrator's romance with his 20-year-old pupil who is fascinated by his lectures on literature. These are not the best pages of *The Engineer of Human Souls.* The girl is the daughter of extremely wealthy Swedish emigrants and has the beauty of a northern goddess. The first love scene takes place on her parents' barge which is moored at lakeshore:

> . . . she seems made of alabaster. She glows
> like the white goddess in *Trader Horn,* and
> around her head a golden halo of blonde hair
> and in the female centre of her body a mag-
> nificent golden thicket . . .

She loses her virginity a little later, on the folding seat of her father's Cadillac. The whole romance abounds in clichés, which range from the unbearably sentimental to the even more unbearably vulgar, and its model seems to be the worst of American soap operas. The flatness of these episodes is even more apparent when compared with the wartime love scenes in which

there is tenderness and harshness, the smell of flesh and earth, real landscapes and feelings. Long after one has shut the book, one recalls Nadia, a worker in the same military factory in Kostelec, in oversized men's boots and raglan, the latter probably sewn long before she was born. Nadia is always hungry, and kisses with a mouth still full of the pancakes which the narrator's mother sends him from home.

Of all the times past that are evoked in *The Engineer of Human Souls,* the fullest is the last year of the war, and of all the places recalled, Kostelec is the most distinct. Emigration is always (and not just metaphorically speaking) an emigration from the land of one's childhood and youth. *The Engineer of Human Souls* is a settling of accounts with all the past times of the emigrant. Yet since Josef Skvorecky and Danny Smiricky, author and narrator, emigrated not from Kostelec in 1946, but from Prague in 1968, the absence of the "Prague spring" in this novel written by a political emigrant may seem somewhat odd. But the "Prague spring" only *seems* absent from Skvorecky's novel. It is not there in description or in action, but it is always present as an undercurrent in the narration, in the hope and despair of the refugees. ". . . we need them both, Prague and freedom," says Veronika, the youngest of the refugees, "but the way things are, we can't have both. It's either-or." Prague returns for the last time, via Paris, at the end of the novel. Paris is the first stop in flight from Soviet tanks.

> I remember Paris in 1968. We were standing
> in front of *Les Deux Magots* like poor relations
> whose house had just burned down and Milan
> Kundera said, "I only hope I die soon. There's
> been too much of everything. How much longer
> do you think we can last?" I too had felt the
> longing for death. The Death Wish. The tanks
> had suddenly turned a theoretical Freudian con-
> cept into a real feeling. . . .

One of the most anguished poems in Polish literature was written in the 1830s by the Polish poet, Adam Mickiewicz, in exile in Paris:

> While my body sits here among you,
> Looks you in the eye and talks aloud,
> My soul leaves and wanders far, o far away,
> It roams about and wails, o how it wails.

The Engineer of Human Souls, written 150 years later, is a novel about the same experience. (pp. 36-7)

> *Jan Kott, "The Emigrant as Hero," in* The New Republic, *Vol. 191, No. 9, August 27, 1984, pp. 34-7.*

SAM SOLECKI

Unlike Solzhenitsyn, who is also chronicling and correcting Eastern European history, Skvorecky, a great comic writer and superb story teller, seems a reluctant participant in the imaginative recreation of what Milan Kundera calls "the tragedy of central Europe." In the best of all possible worlds Skvorecky would probably have been a Chaplin of the pen, writing about youth, swing jazz and love, about lives beyond politics and ideology. In that impossible ideal world where central Europe would not have been God's playground, Danny Smiricky [the protagonist of *The Engineer of Human Souls*] could have played his tenor saxophone, listened to Chick Webb and Ella Fitzgerald *(I've Got a Guy)* and pursued the love of his youth—the always beautiful and out of reach Irena. Skvorecky's fiction is haunted both by this image of the past as might-have-been and by the tragic history that was. Milosz's comments about his own life in Poland could easily have been written by Skvorecky:

> Like many of my generation, I could have wished that my life had been a more simple affair. But the time and place of his birth are matters in which a man has nothing to say. The part of Europe to which I belong has not, in our time, met with good fortune.

The idea of *belonging* to a nation, the awareness of history as an everyday fact of life and not just an intellectual abstraction, the quiet authority with which Milosz shifts from his particular situation to a generalization—all of these are also part of the texture of Skvorecky's style and vision. But it's the wry and poignant understatement in the last sentence, in which the razing of Warsaw, the Holocaust, Lidice, and Soviet totalitarianism are tacitly and unemotionally summed up, that could pass for a line from one of Skvorecky's novels.

Just beyond the complex tone of such a sentence is a dark humour that takes its hue from overwhelming, often absurd historical events. It's justifiably absent, for the most part, from those stories and novels (*The Swell Season, The Bass Saxophone* and *The Cowards*) dealing with Smiricky's youth. . . .

But the darkness, of both humour and vision, is certainly present in *The Engineer* which, with its ominous title taken from that other Josef's morbidly ironic description of writers, juxtaposes the war years with Smiricky's later life in contemporary Canada. The two periods, each with its own distinguishing style and emotional tone, are joined by two similar love stories and a series of letters. These letters to Smiricky inform us about the lives of his friends over a 30 year period and allow Skvorecky to offer voices and commentary on various events and places—from concentration camps to collectives—not experienced or seen by Smiricky. (p. 39)

If from one point of view *The Engineer* can be seen as bringing the Smiricky cycle to a close—he's nearly 60, lives in exile and has lost several friends—from another angle this is a crucial transitional novel for Skvorecky, in which we see him extending his imagination beyond his Czechoslovak past while still including it. This is worth emphasizing because at some point every émigré writer confronts the problem of how to write about the present. Almost as important as subject matter is the question of audience. Censorship may condemn a writer to an underground existence but it can't make him irrelevant in the community about which he writes and which he's addressing; exile can. (pp. 39-40)

The Engineer, like *Mirakl,* is haunted by the possibility that the novelist writing in exile is inevitably condemned to his own particular kind of silence. In one of the novel's most poignant scenes, Smiricky is the only person listening to a Czech song broadcast on the college radio station, a Czech girl "sending her . . . message into the empty cafeteria to fall at best on the uncomprehending ears of Italian cleaning ladies." Substitute a Czech novel for the Czech song and English speaking Canadians for Italian cleaning ladies and you have Skvorecky tacitly asking whether there exists outside the émigré community an audience for his work. But the question also implies a judgment on a society so naive and complacent in its prosperity, values, and sense of history that it lacks the historical imagination to recognize the importance of what happened in Eastern Europe.

The extended but very lively classroom dialogues between the mournful Professor Smiricky, who admits to never having failed anyone, and his politically naive students, about writers as different as Poe, Hawthorne, Twain, Fitzgerald, Conrad and Lovecraft, are really occasions for Smiricky's provocative, occasionally preachy, reflections on the nature of fascist and communist totalitarianisms. They are also, of course, challenges to the reader's ideas about political systems. The method isn't quite Socratic, since the reader can't answer and the students aren't Smiricky's intellectual equals, but it works as fiction.

While the scenes dealing with the war years are, for the most part, lighter in tone, often playfully comic and even on occasion farcical, the letters dealing with contemporary Czechoslovakia and the scenes set in Toronto tend to be much darker, the humour more satirical, the ironies more bitter. The chronologically earlier scenes are almost devoid of explicitly ideological content; when politics and ideas enter the scene they are treated casually, with a youthful irreverence. The Edenvale scenes, by contrast, show Skvorecky more committed to the novel of ideas, to taking risks with his medium in moving toward a more insistently didactic mode of writing. It is in these scenes at the college that *The Engineer* becomes most obviously a novel with something to say. There is an insistent monitory and polemical edge here that will surprise those who know Skvorecky only through his earlier work, yet it's in keeping with his essentially liberal defence in those works of the individual's right to live beyond and without political ideologies.

At the heart of Skvorecky/Smiricky's defence of the self is the novel's critical engagement with Marxism, presented as a philosophy of history and an economic and social theory leading inevitably to totalitarianism. Whatever one may think of the argument or Skvorecky's refusal to disengage Marxism from Soviet Marxism, his thesis is internally coherent and consistent with some of the critiques offered by academic Marxists. More important from the artistic point of view, this discussion is fully integrated into the texture of the novel by means of letters, dialogues and reflections. Without resorting to allegory or extended monologues Skvorecky also manages to embody ideologies in characters so that we see ideas expressed as individual attitudes to historical and mundane experiences, as a concrete part of the felt texture of social life. Since the novel is narrated by Smiricky and is organized around a large number of often short scenes, it is easy to overlook that it deals with several dozen characters from all classes and several nationalities, and that its action takes place in at least half a dozen countries. This comprehensiveness is essential to this often very funny yet finally almost despairing novel about what at one point Smiricky calls "the fall of the Western world."

A significant part of the novel's gloom comes from Smiricky's complex response to his personal situation (his aging and exile) and Czechoslovakia's historical one (in half a century his native country has passed from one totalitarianism to another, and the current Husak regime is hardly cause for general rejoicing). But some of the sadness also seems to come from Skvorecky's doubts that his writing will change anything. Smiricky points out to his students that writing rarely improves or changes the world because the "men and women of the pen" speak a different language and seek a different truth from "the men and women of action." To put it in Stalin's terminology, the writer "engineers" human souls in ways very different from those of the politician. It's significant that Smiricky, also a writer, does little serious creative work in this novel; similarly his friend Jan Prouza, who remained in Czechoslovakia, tells him in 1970 that ''I no longer write even for myself, 'for the desk drawer.''' In both cases silence is near despair.

Some of the novel's emotional and intellectual despair may also come from the overall terms or concepts within which Skvorecky frames his discussion of history and politics. *The Engineer* allows Smiricky (and the reader) only two choices: the communist society of the East or the present-day capitalistic, democratic society of the West (which looks better from Kostelec than from Toronto). Within this almost Manichean pairing the West is obviously preferable but choosing it leaves Smiricky in an awkward position when he finds himself criticizing the West's myopic vision of history (''For these beautiful children 'our times' began with the death of James Dean, no, Janis Joplin''), the endless self-indulgence brought on by post-war prosperity, and the decline of public values. . . . Appalled by North American political innocence, contemptuous of Marxism, suspicious of all ideologies and ''isms,'' Smiricky is left clinging to the status quo even as he realizes that he despises it. He's the émigré as dangling man, committed by his memories to a society that no longer exists, by circumstances to another whose language he will always speak with an accent. Ultimately he belongs nowhere.

Smiricky's real and symbolic inbetweeness has interesting implications for the reader's final view of the novel and its author. Attacked and later banned in Czechoslovakia for being avant-garde, ''lewd,'' too modern, overly influenced by western writers, and for showing ''revisionist tendencies,'' Skvorecky may appear to western readers of *The Engineer* as an often curiously conservative, even reactionary figure (I'm referring here, I hope it's obvious, to Skvorecky the imaginative writer and not to the controversial public figure who, often speaking out on national and international affairs, has been referred to by one Parisian writer as ''le petit Solzhenitsyn.'') Our impression of the novel's conservatism in attitude and politics may be due in part to the dual nature of satire, which can be simultaneously **subversive** and fundamentally conservative (think of Swift and Zinoviev). It is also related to the fact that while dealing critically with history and politics Smiricky holds no defined position of his own and leaves us, in the end, with a detached attitude to reality. I suspect that, in self-defence, Skvorecky might point to a quotation from Evelyn Waugh cited by his hero during one of his dialogues with the students. According to Waugh, ''An artist *must* be a reactionary. He has to stand out against the tenor of the age and not go flopping along; he must offer some little opposition.''

That's as good a way as any of situating this funny, despairing, satirical, compassionate, sprawling, gloomy, provocative, prophetic, angry, and entertaining book. One of the most important novels ever written in Canada, *The Engineer of Human Souls* offers ''some little opposition'' not just to ''the tenor of the age'' but also to all political ideologies and social attitudes that intrude on personal relationships and what Skvorecky calls ''the most important things in life.'' Youth, friendship, art, love and freedom—these constitute Skvorecky's simple constellation of values, and his life's work is an impassioned artistic celebration and defence of them. (pp. 40-1)

Sam Solecki, ''The Laughter and Pain of Remembering,'' in The Canadian Forum, *Vol. LXIV, No. 741, August-September, 1984, pp. 39-41.*

JASCHA KESSLER

Skvorecky's latest book . . . is titled *The Engineer of Human Souls,* a sobriquet that belongs to none other than Stalin himself. It is a peculiar sort of phrase, an oxymoron if you will, suggesting that under the positivist dogma of Marxist-Leninism it is quite possible to arrange society rationally in order to ensure that not only society, and not only the individual, but the human soul itself can be ''engineered.'' Of course, the notion is comical, and Skvorecky is nothing if he is not a comic novelist, as so many Czechoslovak writers have been. (p. 2)

I don't know whether the reevocation of the narrator's lucky escapes during his youth from both the Nazis and his various amorous entanglements, which occupies about a third of the book's pages, or the incredibly funny passages of wild discussions in the factory's toilet, where the various young men spend a lot of time talking about life and the world, are better than the pictures of the narrator's current problems in Canada, but I think that this novel manages to convey a lot of teaching about the abyss between the goodwilled, innocence of people in the New World and those among them, the refugees from the East, whose lives have been disrupted forever, and whose adaptation to North America is really a crazy kind of maladaptation, full of humor and bittersweet sorrows.

If one function of the novel remains to teach us about reality, then we have a lot to learn from this marvellous writer. Not every exiled writer is a deadly-serious, ambitiously-furious prophet like Alexander Solzhenitsyn; the Hungarians, the Yugoslavs, and the Czechs tend to be mordantly satiric and wildly comic. Skvorecky, unlike Kundera, is not a dreamer-philosopher, but an earthy realist, and quite unique. . . . I think that

Dust jacket of The Engineer of Human Souls, *by Josef Škvorecký. Knopf, 1984. Jacket illustration and design by Fred Marcellino. © 1984 Alfred A. Knopf, Inc. Courtesy of the publisher.*

Josef Skvorecky should be *must* reading for anyone who enjoys the human comedy, which would be a title that could suit this novel well.

Jascha Kessler, ''Josef Skvorecky: 'The Engineer of Human Souls','' in a radio broadcast on KUSC-FM—Los Angeles, CA, September 26, 1984.

D. J. ENRIGHT

Jazz, loved by both narrator [Danny Smiricky] and author [Josef Skvorecky], gives offense to both Nazis and communists—as demonstrated in Skvorecky's novella of 1977, *The Bass Saxophone.* There, a band got away with playing ''Tiger Rag'' under the Third Reich by calling it ''The Wild Bull''; here [in *The Engineer of Human Souls*], the number features in the program as ''Red Flag.'' Danny's earnest friend Jan, who strives to reconcile literature with the requirements of socialism and is eventually found hanged, mentions a picture in an exhibition of Soviet art called ''The Defence of Sevastopol''; it shows a handful of idealized Russian soldiers fighting off a horde of villainous Germans. He realizes that he has already seen a specimen of Nazi art in which a scattering of noble German soldiers were dispatching a mob of degenerate Russians; the title was ''The Conquest of Sevastopol.'' *Plus c'est la même chose* is heaped on *plus ça change,* and the last instance, at least, may be thought both banal and inartistically neat. Yet banality and inartistic neatness are part of the story. Such *exempla* contribute to the dense texture of the novel, and it is hard to say what we would rather be without.

I could also forgo some of the lavatory scenes and smells—including a ludicrous and protracted episode in which a smuggled manuscript is surreptitiously handed over in a Toronto comfort station—and the tall horror-stories with which a youth transferred from Dresden regales the Messerschmitt workers. Svejkian, all too Svejkian! I could dispense too with much of the what-abouting that passes between the native Canadian intellectuals and the émigrés: What about Angela Davis? What about the Rosenbergs? What about Sacco and Vanzetti? Once democracy insists that people must be free to hold opinions, there will be no holding them and their opinions. That we know well. I was reminded of Saul Bellow's story ''Cousins,'' in which the narrator customarily gives more information than his questioner can possibly have any use for; he takes every opportunity, he explains, of transmitting his ''sense of life,'' and ''such a habit can be irritating.''

Some such complaint can be made of Günter Grass, another master of the epic canvas, and of Hasek's *The Good Soldier Svejk,* which the present novel rivals in scatology but outdoes in sexual zest. Skvorecky's slogan, one thinks at times, could well be Sex Conquers All. . . . But there is love here, also: in the refusal to despair, present too in Milosz's poetry of Poland and his memories of good things as well as of bad, and specifically in the figure of Nadia, the book's finest character, truest love of the great lover Danny, the factory girl who died young of tuberculosis. ''How she would lick her lips with her unfussy little tongue, how she was simple as a clarinet counterpoint in a village band and yet full of surprises . . . how she had displayed the wisdom of a beautiful mayfly who is crushed under foot before she can fulfil the one meaning her life has. But no. Nadia's life had a different meaning. It was more than mere biology—.'' . . .

''Every serious novel,'' the Professor tells his students, ''is *à thèse.* But the thesis is always the same, except in novels *à thèse.''* And the thesis is: *Homo sum; humani nil a me alienum puto.* All the same, some things strike us as more alien than others. We doubt that Goethe was wholly sincere when he said, of his *Wilhelm Meister,* that a rich manifold life brought close to our eyes ought to be enough without any express tendency. (Though it is the sort of remark a writer does well to throw in the face of the thesis-hunter.) Decent writers veer away from the role laid down for them by Stalin, for example: to engineer, as it were, the soul of the New Man. Still, one way of suggesting an implication, if not a thesis, is to invoke some other literary work whose tendency is itself not all that express. *The Engineer of Human Souls* brings to mind an authorial comment in *Middlemarch:* ''There is no general doctrine which is not capable of eating out our morality if unchecked by the deep-seated habit of direct fellow-feeling with individual fellow-men.'' What better check on general doctrine than the poet's and the novelist's ''small stories,'' the kind that Josef Skvorecky recounts with such verve and generosity? (p. 50)

D. J. Enright, ''Home from Home,'' in The New York Review of Books, Vol. XXXI, No. 14, September 27, 1984, pp. 49-50.

ANTHONY BURGESS

[An English novelist and critic, Burgess is well known for his satires of contemporary society in which he uses black humor—the most famous of these is his novel A Clockwork Orange *(1962). Burgess's experimentation with language is widely acclaimed, and his interest in linguistics is reflected in his critical studies of James Joyce, including Burgess's popular* Here Comes Everybody: An Introduction to James Joyce for the Ordinary Reader *(1965; published in America as* Re Joyce, *1965). In the following excerpt Burgess discusses what he considers a basic weakness in Škvorecký's novel.]*

Skvorecky has a mass of things to entertain us with [in *The Engineer of Human Souls*]; his problem is finding a shape. What he does is divide the book into seven large chapters, each named for an author. . . .

But all the attempts to impose shape on the sprawl are sadly ineffectual. The conversations are prolix, anecdotes go on for too long, there is just no narrative drive. There is so much to say and yet so little seems to be said. Perhaps, sadly, political satire is a dead scene. A Soviet writer once boasted to me that it was impossible to produce science fiction in Russia: the technological reality too swiftly overtook even the wildest imaginative flight. Similarly the maddest satire is deflated by political reality.

I'm not disposed to make little of a book of which Milan Kundera says: ''It is magnificent! A magnum opus.'' And I'm oppressed by the shame that genuinely oppressed East Europeans and South Americans are imposing on us bland British: we haven't suffered enough, therefore we can't produce significant fiction.

But it's instructive to contrast this book with Nabokov's *Pnin,* which is also about an émigré professor in North America, is not one word too long, and says everything about nostalgia and the great human wrongs without mentioning them. You can only write about the futility of ideologies and the tyranny of dictators by not writing about them. This means Kafka.

Professor Skvorecky has known suffering I haven't and it is an act of courage, or a quirk of the Czech temperament, to be able to offer this impressionistic record as an entertainment. I get all the entertainment I need these days in trying to find the Overseas BBC on a waveband choked with Soviet propaganda. No unemployment in the USSR. The Russians invented truly progressive jazz. The snowdrops are budding in Siberia. I wish I found it easier to laugh.

> Anthony Burgess, *"Laughing It Off,"* in The Observer, *March 3, 1985, p. 26.*

MELVIN MADDOCKS

[*The Engineer of Human Souls*] spins its story from the torn entrails of Central Europe. Yet what emerges is comedy—black, grimacing and explosively funny, as peculiarly Middle European as the despairing wit of Prague's own Franz Kafka. Skvorecky has mixed history with high unseriousness before—notably in *The Bass Saxophone,* about a Czech youth playing in a German dance band during the war—but his latest work is unquestionably his masterpiece of that modern specialty, the heartbreaking belly laugh.

Skvorecky's alter ego is Danny Smiricky, 48, a Czech émigré professor at a college very like Skvorecky's academic home for some 15 years, the University of Toronto. . . .

Skvorecky handles the young Danny with a gentleness that borders on the romantic, but not for long. Juxtaposed with the bygone scenes of adolescence are contemporary letters to the middle-aged Danny that trickle in from his Kostelec friends. Prema, the young resistance fighter, loses his focus after the war and drifts to Australia, dying a pointless death in a hurricane. Rebecca, the idealist, ends up in a kibbutz, shattered and alone after her son is killed by a bomb in an Israeli café. Jan, the poet, remains in Czechoslovakia. Blacklisted into silence, he commits suicide. As a self-described "raconteur of cynical tales," Danny concludes that the only meaning to life is that there is no meaning. "History that repeats itself is a farce" becomes his fancy way of translating Huck Finn's cry from the heart: "I been there before."

Amid this chaos and despair, the professor irrationally hopes. A mad, glorious scene near the end captures Danny's self-contradiction. At a wedding reception in Toronto, the guests become obsessed with recalling gallows-humor stories about a Kostelec hangman who forced condemned prisoners to shave, and shave again until the blood trickled from their chins as they mustered to face their doom. Then he would shout: "Back to your cells, gentlemen. The execution is postponed!"

Meanwhile, the band strikes up. The bride smiles radiantly. The dance goes on, and even as he braces himself to insist that life is simply biology's *la ronde,* Danny—and certainly Skvorecky—joins in the dance.

What his personal history has cost Skvorecky, only he can measure. But in the process of recording his pain he lends a keen zest to the act of living and writing. So this is what the novel has been! So this is what the novel can still be! Readers for whom contemporary fiction has meant obligatory searches for self-fulfillment or another go-around at suburban malaise may never be the same.

> Melvin Maddocks, *"Comic Exile in Three Worlds,"*
> in Time, *Vol. 124, No. 5, July 30, 1985, p. 97.*

JAMES LASDUN

There's a remark by Silone to the effect that the one book every writer carries within him, writing and rewriting it all his life, is nothing less than the image of his own soul. A fanciful way of putting things, but the truth it undoubtedly contains accounts more accurately than any amount of aesthetic criticism for the fact that Josef Skvorecky's *"magnum opus"* (Milan Kundera's tribute) is not a Great Novel: not quite.

It *ought* to be a great novel. Like most Czechs, Skvorecky's life, of which *The Engineer of Human Souls* is a fictionalised rendering, has been lived close to the epicentres of the century's more significant upheavals. . . .

A life suffused in the glamour of history, then. And Skvorecky's gifts as a writer are more than equal to the epic scale of his subject matter; of that there is no doubt. A conventional realist at heart, though somewhat in flight from his own conventionality, he organises his subject into a dozen or so straightforward, well-executed stories of love, war, campus life and so forth, splicing them together with a deliberate disregard for narrative sequence. The cutting method is crude but effective. Sometimes it operates as a simple suspense technique, abandoning the reader at a series of cliff-edges. More interestingly, it produces a structure which is peculiarly well-adapted to illuminating the Czech political experience of "recurrences with variations": unfettered by the demands of a linear plot, Skvorecky is free to jump back and forth in time, grouping disparate incidents for the sake of the patterns they reveal in human affairs. (p. 47)

It takes a formidable historical sense to sculpt with time in this way; and on a more detailed, technical level Skvorecky is also abundantly gifted. Witty, erudite, his lively, garrulous prose can accommodate everything from the most rarefied of philosophical arguments to the lower depths of scatological farce. He has a light touch with weighty ideas, that yields pithy turns of phrase—"Why bother to conceal the nakedness of power with a whore's G-string of ideology?"—and he has, too, a poet's transformative eye that can, for example, evince the tension of a family squabble in a candle-lit room with a single, perfect image—"The ordinary little flames on the expansive candles registering it all like the hands of a seismograph."

But for all that, there is something less than satisfactory—at times even unlikeable—about the book. The company of Skvorecky/Smiricky is not an unmitigated pleasure. Quite why is difficult to say; an accumulation of questionable attitudes smuggled through in the diplomatic bag of dissident status, rather than a single glaring vice. There's an implicit contempt for Western liberals evident in some rather savage caricatures, which is disagreeable, not because it is unjustified, but because it is presented in a way that somehow casts the dissenting reader into the role of brainwashed ideologue. Skvorecky is not prepared to countenance the relativity of his own point of view: despite his affable manner, he seems fundamentally short on tolerance and magnanimity; one would not relish having him in a position of power. Then, too, there is a hint of smugness in the way he adduces personal experience as a series of points scored against his naive students—"Higgins has not, as I have, carried a man in German uniform on a stretcher through a parched May afternoon . . ."—and when this is coupled with his gleeful relish of the sexual opportunities his position as teacher affords him, it becomes somewhat objectionable. And finally there is something self-regarding in the sheer space he devotes to propping up the authority of his enterprise: large chunks of the book, in the form of drawn-out anecdotes illustrating indirectly (but unmistakably) the narrator's political wisdom, and long letters defending the literary methods he favours, serve little purpose other than to conscript the reader's acquiescence in the author's vision.

With Ignazio Silone's help, I have argued myself into the strangely pious position of criticising a writer for what amounts to a defect of soul. All I really mean to express by it is a vague disappointment with a book that has all the trappings of magnificence, but falls short, and for reasons that strictly *literary* criticism is ill-equipped to define. (pp. 47-8)

> *James Lasdun, "The Great or the Good?" in* Encounter, *Vol. LXV, No. 2, July-August, 1985, pp. 47-51.**

Richard (Gustave) Stern

American Academy and Institute of Arts and Letters: Award of Merit for Fiction

American novelist, short story writer, essayist, editor, and dramatist.

Stern is noted for his superb style, skillful characterization, and above all the sense of wry intelligence that pervades his work. Critics compare him in tone, technique, and theme to better-known contemporaries such as Saul Bellow and Bernard Malamud. But reviewers also observe Stern's meticulous prose and the well-wrought themes of his six novels recall the elegance and wit of late nineteenth-century works, particularly those of Henry James. This similarity is enhanced, critics note, by Stern's treatment of sophisticated moral questions in addition to the Jamesian theme of Americans abroad. Unlike many American postwar novelists, Stern eschews confessional and experimental approaches to fiction, and he has criticized the type of novel that he terms a "roller coaster of distress and sympathy, love and desire." Stern continually attracts serious critical attention, though he is not widely read. A longtime Professor of Literature at the University of Chicago, Stern is generally admired as a moral realist and acknowledged as a "writer's writer."

Stern's fiction characteristically casts the protagonist, whom Stern calls a "coreless" middle-aged man, into a situation that forces him from his complacency and demands that he examine the morality of his own and others' actions. While his characters usually encounter ambition, treachery, and betrayal, their plunge into society also becomes a baptism of self-discovery. Stern's first novel, *Golk* (1960) places Hondorp, a near-recluse, on the staff of a television program styled after "Candid Camera." The formerly mild-mannered Hondorp becomes engaged in increasingly aggressive exposé tactics, which eventually result in a political scandal that leads Hondorp to betray his director and to lose his job. The portrayal of Hondorp's fall becomes a black humor satire on network executives and the phenomenon of American television.

In subsequent works, Stern often moves his protagonists abroad. Though he is not as overtly concerned with social satire as in *Golk,* he invests all his works with the gentle mockery that some critics consider his hallmark. In *Europe; or, Up and Down with Schreiber and Baggish* (1961) a retiring elderly gentleman and a young scoundrel in Europe are pitted in a moral conflict in which youth prevails. *In Any Case* (1963) portrays an innocuous man who ventures throughout the Continent to clear the name of his dead son, who he'd inadvertently learned was a traitor, not a hero, in World War II. Stern again examines treachery in *Stitch* (1965). Set in Venice, this novel centers on a character modeled after Ezra Pound, the American poet accused of treason in the 1940s. Stern's most recent novels focus more on emotional betrayal and self-discovery than political matters. An aging, habit-driven professor in *Other Men's Daughters* (1973) leaves his wife and children for a woman the age of his eldest child, while in *Natural Shock* (1977) a dispassionate journalist becomes emotionally involved when

Photograph by Layle Silbert © copyright 1979

he writes the story of a dying young woman. Several of the short stories in *Teeth, Dying, and Other Matters, and The Gamesman's Island: A Play* (1964), *1968: A Short Novel, an Urban Idyll, Five Stories, and Two Trade Notes* (1970), and *Packages* (1980) continue the themes of confrontation and betrayal.

Critics generally agree that Stern's greatest strengths are his fluid, flexible style and the power of his allusive and highly literate intellect. Some, however, assert that Stern exploits these features at the expense of structure and, sometimes, characterization. Particularly in *Stitch* and the novella "Veni, Vedi . . . Wendt," included in the collection *1968,* reviewers contend that the elements of story and character are overwhelmed by wordplay and displays of learning. Some critics suggest that Stern is merely showing off or engaging in intellectual name-dropping rather than constructing successful fiction. Similarly, *Natural Shocks,* praised for the wide-ranging subjects it explores and the beauty of its prose, is considered by some too structurally diffuse to be satisfying. *Other Men's Daughters,* which combines complex emotional and moral issues with sympathetic characters in a simple, solid plot, is cited by many as Stern's most fully realized work of fiction to date.

(See also *CLC*, Vol. 4; *Contemporary Authors*, Vols. 1-4, rev. ed.; and *Contemporary Authors New Revision Series*, Vol. 1.)

JAMES KELLY

As the television folks have demonstrated through the use of their prying-eye camera, people like to laugh at other people during private moments of frustration, small contretemps, shattered dignity. A keyhole can be more fun than an open door, so to speak, and it is the principle which Richard Stern extends to first-novel length in *Golk*. With sardonic relish and unhampered imagination, he fashions a little gothic grotesquerie of what could happen when the candid camera begins to stick its zoomar into forbidden places. A very funny idea for those readers who thought Orwell's Big Brother was cute and still get a chuckle out of the paintings of George Grosz.

To clarify matters, Golk is the name of an evil Blob Man who has invented a television show called "You're on Camera" which is designed to stick pins into unsuspecting gullibles for public entertainment. On his staff, he includes an Amoeba Man named Herbert Hondorp who is sort of human; a renegade socialite named Jenny Hendricks who is not; a beauteous Negro girl named Elaine who knows what she wants from life; an assortment of Television Types. The surrounding landscape includes ominous network owners and hatchet-men, a few television-oriented characters like Hondorp's father (who broods over questions like "Who's the real brains, Tex or Jinx?") and the hapless targets of the program's episodes.

What emerges from all this is a handbook on how to trap people. You catch a victim where he is and shoot him as he is. Or capture a moment of terror. Or turn him inside out, from laughs to weeps to laughs. Or find a double-take. Or work up to situations which involve real social criticism, the most dangerous one for the trapper. "There are two pivots to the golks we're doing these days," said Golk. "The hook in the worm is one. You dangle the prize before a victim, play him like a hooked carp, and while he watches, turn the prize to dust. The other kind is stepping in between a man and his legitimate pleasures. We thwart a man from the satisfaction of the appetites he's entitled to."

The people in this novel are not to be confused with anybody living or dead, and it is not likely that they will be. Mr. Stern's sole purpose seems to be to sustain an eerie effect and unload pungent observations about topical mores, which he manages to do with considerable style. A good ear for human speech and a clear eye for New York's sights and sidewalks help him to escape briefly from the plot gimmick. There is even some suspense during final episodes when Golk reaches beyond pure entertainment and untidily disintegrates. This reviewer fears, however, that not many readers, even admitting the validity of the Message, will find *Golk* palatable or arresting enough to stay to the end.

One hopes that Mr. Stern's next outing will find him advancing upon the abundance of human targets without camera or other mechanical device, relying only upon his manifest talent as a novelist.

James Kelly, "Handbook on How to Trap People," in The New York Times Book Review, *May 1, 1960, p. 34.*

CHARLES MONAGHAN

Golk is a novel notable for a consistent and pleasant lightness of tone that never degenerates into frivolousness, for intriguing characterization and plotting, and for a clean and efficient prose style. These are admirable qualities, especially in a first novel. . . . (pp. 188-89)

Mr. Stern, thank heaven, is not out to score easy points at the expense of television. He does indulge in some mild satire of network executives, but his main interest is in his central characters and their fates. Hondorp and Hendricks are themselves "victims" of "You're On Camera" before joining Golk. But both are also victims of their own backgrounds. Hondorp, though thirty-seven years old, never worked until meeting Golk, living in complete dependence on his father, while Hendricks is scarred by a lurid bohemian past. Both derive their new existence from Golk, and deprived of him, they return to mediocrity.

Their betrayal—accepting the chance to take over the program—is the key to their downfall. They fail not only in loyalty but in intelligence, not realizing how much the program is dependent on Golk's vision and dedication. Power—which spurs Golk on to better things—corrupts Hondorp and bores Hendricks.

The one weakness of the novel lies in its failure to provide complete characterizations of Golk, Hondorp and Hendricks. They have a modernistic attractiveness, all angles and edges, but they lack the full dimension which their key roles in the novel demand. Golk and Hondorp remain enigmas and Hendricks verges on being a cliché, a sort of American Brett Ashley.

Golk shares certain characteristics with some of the finest writing of recent times, especially that of Bellow, Nabokov, William Gaddis and J. P. Donleavy. The one unifying fact about the world views of these writers seems to be that they are in revolt against the simplistic conception of man and his problems that has come down to us from the thirties. The dreary seriousness of the thirties' tradition is answered with lightness of tone and treatment; its emphasis on things political is countered by ignoring politics and concentrating on personal moral questions; and that tradition's black-and-white conception of human nature draws forth a spate of half-heroes whose goodness is mired in lust or pride.

Golk shares all of these characteristics. So light is the tone that the casual reader might be deceived into thinking that it is frivolous. It isn't. *Golk* is a short novel which brilliantly describes the effects of its leading characters on one another. If Mr. Stern learns to make these characters come fully alive in their own right, he will surely gain election to that select circle to which he is prematurely assigned by *Golk*'s book jacket. (pp. 189-90)

Charles Monaghan, "New Traditions," in Commonweal, *Vol. LXXII, No. 7, May 13, 1960, pp. 188-90.*

PETER BUITENHUIS

Sam Curry, an American long resident in France, receives a book in the mail. It is by a former member of the Resistance, now a monk. The corner of one of the pages is turned down. On that page it states that Sam's son, Robert, a member of an intelligence group organized by the British in France, had betrayed his network to the Germans. Sam, who had been informed three years earlier of his son's death in a German concentration camp, is certain of his Robert's loyalty and bravery. He sets out to clear his name.

This is the basic pattern of Richard G. Stern's . . . novel [*In Any Case*]. It is his third, and it reveals the growing maturity of his vision, the expanding richness of his style. The pattern is used, as it should be, not simply as a means of setting the plot in motion but as a device to explore character and to establish meaning. Mr. Stern has combined two familiar conventions (that of the spy story and that of detective fiction) into one and given his book that extra dimension of substance and imaginative technique that makes for a true novel.

Curry is in business, a man about many towns, a connoisseur of women and food. The book is told by him in the first person. It begins: "I was a terrible father to my son, at least until it was too late for him to know otherwise." As the reader can see, the novel is also a confession. As the trail from loyalist to collaborator, from agent to double-agent, lengthens, it also becomes entwined with Curry's own past, his failures and his conquests, his individualism and his self-indulgence.

In the end, it becomes a pilgrimage of self-discovery as well as a search for a son, a speculation about the meaning of love as well as of espionage. It explores relationships as well as towns, ideas as well as bars and restaurants. Curry is a hedonist, but he also has an irritable American conscience. He demonstrates his nationality too in his tendency to take a moral tone about the actions of others, even when his own are far from blameless.

Mr. Stern's complex plot is occasionally hard to accept. This is especially true when it takes a reverse Oedipal twist—that is, when Curry falls in love with the unresisting former Resistance mistress of his son. The trouble stems, I think, from the author's attempt to project himself into a viewpoint character whose experience seems to be larger than, and alien to, his own. The attempt is praiseworthy because most American novelists rely on autobiography and, as a result, either repeat themselves or dry up. It may be, however, that Mr. Stern went too far afield for his protagonist. Some of the material in the book has that "got-up" or researched quality that recalls the novels of Zola.

As a result, the authority of the main character is not quite to be trusted. Being aware of this, perhaps, and trying to escape from his dilemma, the author falls back on that old standby, coincidence. The device turns his plot in on itself instead of outward toward experience. The experience itself is sometimes philosophized about instead of being felt.

In spite of this, however, the novel seldom flags in its narrative pace and excitement. Mr. Stern has the skill of a born storyteller as well as a highly literate, allusive mind. He sees clearly and can convey sensation, whether it be the enjoyment of a lobster bisque or an embrace.

> *Peter Buitenhuis, "A Pilgrimage of Self-Discovery,"*
> in The New York Times Book Review, *October 14,*
> *1962, p. 5.*

SAUL MALOFF

Richard Stern established himself as a comic novelist with an impressive first book, *Golk*—a harrowing portrait of carnivo-

rous egotism and its destructive radiating effects. Then he secured that reputation with a second novel, *Europe: or Up and Down with Schreiber and Baggish,* which, while it attempted more than it fully achieved, exploded with verbal and imaginative energy. What struck one from the first was Stern's command of the novelist's resources: an ample and supple language, a lively, vigorous narrative style, a sense of character and scene, of place, person and significant action.

In his new novel, *In Any Case,* Stern writes in a new key and in an unexpected voice. Yet however bold his choice of theme is, the theme itself is formidably complex and the manner of narration by which he chooses to complicate and reveal it is, in part at least, so burdened by sub-literary associations as to incur very great risks.

For at the center of this novel lies a mystery-and-spy thriller; and into this center moves the protagonist as detective seeking to solve an enigma which is ultimately his own. As he is forced back upon himself, the novel becomes one of the protagonist's quest for his own nature and moral center.

The narrator-protagonist is Sam Curry, an American businessman in his late fifties who has lived in France, the scene of the action, for nearly all his adult life. A widower, he had married a Frenchwoman, and by her had a son, now also dead. His son had been an agent in Occupied France for British Intelligence and is accused, in a book written several years after the war by a fellow-agent, of having betrayed the organization to the Nazis. To accept this charge, Curry feels, is to accept his own complicity in his son's guilt, the child being both issue and father of the man. To learn the truth thus becomes the occasion of the action. On a deeper level, it is a search for the meaning of love and the failure of love, of guilt and responsibility, and of the ways in which we betray and may redeem one another. . . .

Curry moves back and forth during much of the novel, in typically alternating chapters, from the present quest into his son's past, to an introspective quest into his own—moving, that is, from the suspenseful present to the quieter despair of his own reflections upon himself.

Stern beautifully sustains his difficult themes, creating an atmosphere where nothing is clear, where motive and act are never discernibly related, because we cannot locate and define even the act, let alone the motive. Only occasionally does Stern yield before the excesses of his own striking gifts, and then the novel, even when it is most strongly controlled, indulges in brilliant superfluities. But when the tension is no longer sustained—about at the point when Curry falls in love with his son's former mistress, thus betraying him again, and in death—the novel cracks under its burdens, and becomes something else. How it does so constitutes both its vigor and its failure.

Possibly the failure has to do with the very nature of the problem: how does one dramatize ambiguity? (p. 319)

Yet Stern's conception seems adequate to the meaning he seeks even when his novel enters upon its greatest difficulties: Curry is employed by his son's (possible) betrayer and killer, who is really the nicest sort of man, and who is also the lover of Curry's mistress—a woman who restores Curry to something like life, though she may lie down "with every operator in France," and though the child she will bear may not be his own, and though the man she loved was his own son.

The conception is a brilliant, if melodramatic one. The strongest parts of its execution could have been achieved only by a novelist of the most authentic and exciting talent. Yet just where the meanings, however ambiguous, must be made to emerge from the action and interaction of characters who shape and convey meaning, other characters evacuate the scene, and the action buckles and drifts into the wings, coming to us by hints and rumors. The ruminative voice of Curry, as spectator of his own fate—now all the action there is—seeks, without success, to force the meaning and fill the void. At the end he is left with a small, qualified, ambiguous triumph—he is now sixty-two, and is alive, and someone's child is about to be born. But it is a triumph that looks like, and smells of, defeat. (pp. 319-20)

Saul Maloff, "A Personal Quest," in Commonweal, Vol. LXXVII, No. 12, December 14, 1962, pp. 319-20.

STEPHEN DONADIO

[*Teeth, Dying and Other Matters*] consists of thirteen stories, a play, and an essay. The play and the essay are expendable: the stories are what count, and they are, generally, fine examples of economy, intelligence, and literary tact. Mr. Stern is a compassionate and careful writer, able to distinguish between his subjects and limitations, sure of his intentions.

Although all are executed skillfully, these stories span a period of roughly fifteen years, and the most recent are, in general, the best: ("**Teeth**," "**Wanderers**," and "**Dying**"). They are concerned, more or less, with people in a fix. In "**Wanderers**," for instance, Mr. Stern deals with Miss Swindleman's awakening. A cashier in a West Side "transient and permanent" hotel, for years she has imagined herself representing "rules" and gentile stability to the unsettled Jews, who keep sending her postcards (which she organizes into a collection). Invulnerable to experience, she cannot understand them; then, too late, her closed mind opens: "An opening had been made. What does one do about an opening? Send a postcard of the Empire State Building to oneself? . . . The opening was a wound in Miss Swindleman. Days passed, and embarrassment . . . was all she could stuff in to stop the raw ache. She was altered, but the alteration had nowhere to go."

Managing a desperate but gentle humor, Mr. Stern discovers unexpected states of our sophisticated minds. The only fault worth noting in these stories is a certain tendency to favor grace at the expense of weight. Engaging in formalities, the author sometimes risks patness; intent on his detachment from his characters, he occasionally robs these stories of the moral energy and substance which a closer, less provisional commitment would allow.

Nevertheless, the general orientation of his writing is one that makes literature possible and more than self-expression, something other than one's private odds and ends. . . . Mr. Stern is aware of the difference between personal and artistic necessity. He knows that to project internal disarray upon the limitations of the world is an activity of more interest to psychologists than to readers of fiction. (p. 303)

Stephen Donadio, "The In Way Out," in Partisan Review, Vol. XXXII, No. 2, Spring, 1965, pp. 299-303.*

GEORGE P. ELLIOTT

Stern's people [in the stories in *Teeth, Dying and Other Matters*] have little power in their world, which is also our city world;

or if they have some power, we are not shown them in the exercise of it. (Odd how few talented fiction writers nowadays, beyond O'Hara, Cozzens, and Auchincloss, take the most powerful social class seriously into account in their stories.) Moreover, Stern's stories are so artfully constructed that they do not merge together in the reader's mind to make a landscape of their own. By choosing with great accuracy just enough experience to fit the form of each story, the author has kept the stories separate by reason of their very elegance; the hedges that define them keep them apart. "**Dying**," for example, does not show us more experience than a twelve-page story can accommodate gracefully; it shows, with wit and sardonic understatement, not a dying man but a man two removes from a person who is dying. A botanist who has published a few poems is approached by a businessman whose mother is dying and who works on the botanist-poet to write a four-line epitaph for her tomb. The comedy of the story is both pathetic and satiric—humane. Clearly Stern is a real artist of the short story; he knows how to make us look in a certain manner at those byways of the world he chooses to take us along. The comic intelligence of the looking is what matters most. (pp. 112-13)

George P. Elliott, "Exploring the Province of the Short Story," in Harper's Magazine, Vol. 230, No. 1379, April, 1965, pp. 111-16.*

THE CHRISTIAN SCIENCE MONITOR

In *Stitch* . . . Richard Stern has written still another novel about Americans in Europe crying out "Who am I, father?" to the stones of the Old World. (In this case, it is the stones of Venice that hollowly echo back.)

To give his novel an even more usual look, Mr. Stern has supplied it with familiar protagonists. The title character is an American sculptor, a venerable priest of art who does indeed know who he is—and understands not only how he fits into the present, but how he is related to the past. He is quite unable to pass on this sense of identity to his surrogate son—an even more familiar figure: the middle-aging, second-rate esthete in flight from a successful career in advertising.

The whole concept of *Stitch* is almost ceremonial in its deliberate usualness. But there is little usual about Mr. Stern's treatment. To the prescribed problems of Americans abroad he often brings writing and thinking as fresh as if Henry James had never existed. Like James, but unlike most James disciples, he cuts through to the fundamental problem: flawed character. This means that he offers no glib answers for the people in conflict with their place, their time, and themselves. But he raises questions with more passion and more discrimination than all but a very few of his contemporaries.

For his essential seriousness, one forgives Mr. Stern a lot: his knowledgeableness that not only shows but sometimes shows off; his inability to put the components of his novel finally together; the lapses both in taste and style that reflect this failure.

"Innocents Abroad," in The Christian Science Monitor, December 9, 1965, p. 19.*

DANIEL STERN

Something odd is happening in the evaluation of contemporary writing. It's getting so you can't review a serious novel without taking up the whole question of Man in the Universe. It's a ridiculous notion, but I'm afraid in a subtle sense it applies. There is a patronizing tone that has crept into literature since the advent of the age of the common man. The anti-hero is at least a heroic attempt to demolish the débris of convention; the nonhero poses much more serious problems.

The characters in Richard Stern's . . . novel, *Stitch,* are mediocrities with little to recommend them to any reader's attention—all except the intentionally ''fabulous'' protagonist. He is a major character, yet he fails to compel belief. The others merely fail to compel interest.

The place is Venice, the time is the present. The people are Edward, an ex-public relations man and ''amateur scholar''; Nina, an unpublished poet in self-exile, and the world-renowned Stitch, a great sculptor whose creations grace a special island given him by the Italian government. Stitch's work is clearly meant to represent the artistic achievements and failures of the twentieth century. The figure he most recalls is Ezra Pound.

The encounter between Edward, Nina, and Stitch constitutes the main action. Edward is leading a pointless expatriate life; Nina is laboring on a book for an American university press. Their affair is, or is made to seem, a trivial one. This effect is reinforced by the author's tone and selection of characteristics for Nina and Edward. Stern does have a clever and observant eye; but it is as if (to paraphrase Peter de Vries on Katherine Anne Porter) in seeing through people he misses seeing what is inside them.

The portrait of the aging sculptor is heavy with portentous interior monologue. He is presented as a sort of repository for the crisis-culture of the Western world. The result, instead of being moving or even intellectually stimulating, is pedantic and self-conscious.

Had Stitch reached the size his author intended for him, one could have overlooked the cold eye focused on the little people who occupy the rest of the novel. But, failing this, to engage our minds and feelings on behalf of a man of whom we read: ''The world's Edwards, men of minimal accomplishments and fair intelligence, were always mercurial . . . '' is an impossible job. This sentence appears, it is true, in the thoughts of Edward's biased wife. But the reader, or at least this reader, has long since come to share that evaluation.

It must be said in Mr. Stern's defense that he writes well and builds scenes skillfully. Thus his stance toward his characters is clearly one of choice, not the result of limited ability. Of course no one may dictate his stance to a writer. It may be heroically affirmative; it may be utterly contemptuous; it may be one or more of a thousand attitudes. But it is equivocal and patronizing at a terrible risk.

> *Daniel Stern, "Portrait of an Artist," in* Saturday Review, *Vol. XLVIII, No. 50, December 11, 1965, p. 80.*

PETER BUITENHUIS

Whatever else Richard Stern intends to do, he is apparently not going to repeat himself. His novels and stories display a wide variety of subjects and an almost equal number of different techniques in which to express them. His willingness to keep reaching makes *Stitch,* his fifth book, a challenging, if sometimes infuriating, novel.

As I see it, Mr. Stern has attempted to catch the fragmentation of our culture through the variously prismatic or astigmatic visions of several people living in Venice. The magnificent decay of the city itself seems to stand for an order now gone. The characters are attempting to live there happily; but their failings, partly personal, partly cultural, variously incapacitate them.

The title figure himself, Thaddeus Stitch, a kind of combination Frank Lloyd Wright and Ezra Pound, is a crusty sculptor who spends a good deal of his time raging against the weakness of old age. His references to his ''friends'' summarize much of the artistic history of the West in the last 65 years.

The Stitch sections of the novel are usually stream-of-consciousness in form and Poundian in content: ''Evil communication rots everything. Yes, that was not from the Oriental side of wisdom. Clarity, the clear word, the well-cut stone, the adjustment to light, the clear mind, the ordered file, the, the . . . '' Stitch's reflections break off, partly because of the wreck of age, but also because of the failure of the tradition. His masterwork, an eclectic mass of figures and abstractions on an island in the lagoon, is his attempt to give historic form to the great tradition. But he sometimes reflects bitterly that it will all perish as the level of the water rises and the island sinks beneath the sea.

The central figure of the novel is not, however, Stitch, but a more representative mid-century man, Edward Gunther. He is an advertising copy-writer who has sold everything to leave Chicago to live in Venice with his wife and three children. Edward is a messy creature, idle, vain, bungling, who helplessly watches his savings drain away as he lives it up in Italy. Seeking out Stitch in the hope of getting answers to his problems, he gets insults instead. He gets little more satisfaction from the third major figure in the novel, Nina Callahan, who becomes his mistress. Nina is an American poet living in Venice on practically nothing. She is trying to write an epic about women (and here the novel moves dangerously close to the ridiculous). Nina is attracted to Stitch, too, but the old man, after hearing the first part of the epic, tells her what's wrong with her poetry and her life. It lacks love—which seems likely.

These three characters weave in and out of the story, having more or less unsatisfactory encounters with each other, going to parties, riding in the *vaporettos,* drinking in bars and eating in restaurants. Much of the novel takes place in winter when Venice, empty of tourists, is full instead of chilled life, biting winds and the smell of poverty.

It doesn't seem like a very satisfactory existence for any of the characters, each of whom makes the momentous discovery that it's as possible to be as bored and frustrated in Italy as it is anywhere else. Some of this sense is, unfortunately, conveyed to the reader, impossible as it is to write of boredom without boring. Similarly, the essential lack of contact between the characters is expressed in the author's technique in which unrelatedness sometimes dissolves into total obscurity.

The descent into disintegration is accelerated at the end of the novel, after Edward returns to the United States. Separated from his wife and children and living on the California coast, he watches the funeral of President Kennedy on television. Outside his window, the young surfers go through their tricks as if nothing had happened. ''Their memory was yesterday's waves,'' Edward reflects. ''Was it what Stitch was getting at, what made him so gloomy? . . . Was this what he meant by the death of Europe? The death of transmission? Of memory?''

The main trouble with this book is that Mr. Stern seems to have been swallowed up by the general gloom that it diffuses. For all the wide range of learning and sophistication that he shows, his lack of detachment has prevented him from giving expressive form to *Stitch*. It remains a striking mass of fragments, like his own fictional sculptor's work on the island in the rising lagoon.

Peter Buitenhuis, "Italy Can Be Boring, Too," in The New York Times Book Review, *December 19, 1965, p. 14.*

D. A. N. JONES

In one of Richard Stern's seven tales which, with two essays, make up *1968,* there is a man called McCoshan, "a gentleman out of sympathy with the times," who drops ideas, large generalizations, at breakfast-time, when he "uncovers for his wife the terrible configurations beneath the newspaper facts." This is surely what Stern himself is trying to do, in what he calls "a diverse collection commenting on contemporary life." (p. 26)

According to Stern's publishers, his ambition is much like that of his own McCoshan: he wants to "wrench current dilemmas into patterns that clarify" and to "evoke the misery and comedy of the crucial year of mid-century America." He has not succeeded. His publishers are nearer the mark when they flaunt a review of his earlier work: "Enough to frighten a rustic." Stern's English is Butch Academic, allusive and exclusive, mingling a studied demotic with a little learning, none too lightly worn, so that each sentence seems designed to impress rather than communicate. Newspaper tragedies are made subjects for epigram; of more real concern are newspaper reviews, articles in the London *Times Literary Supplement,* or Mailer on masturbation:

> "Why the author who strokes himself more publicly than any writer since Whitman should have this terrible bug about the most economical of pleasures, this old economist knoweth not."

> Dugan disliked such subjects, had to force hearty interest.

> "When a man's work is done to corral nookie, and Mailer must get plenty, he's naturally going to crow over poor lugs like you beating their meat to Judy Collins. If he ate shit, he'd be knocking hamburgers."

> "It's more complicated than that. The guy hates solipsism. . . ."

This fairly lucid and amusing example of Stern's writing comes from his tale, **"Idylls of Dugan and Strunk."** But his donnish, nervously bawdy whimsicality and his desperate search for *mots justes* can become a strain, especially when he strays into the world of physical action and attempts to remain knowing.

> Dugan is too busy to shift historic furniture. His quarry is very present-tense indeed. . . . "I'm not much on sarcophagi. I'm only at the *Titus Andronicus* stage of my life." . . . A clot of teenagers looked across the iron-pillared, El-shadowed street. The horn yowled on. Dugan felt his old street-fighter's click.

What is happening is that two university prosers—Strunk, the old economist who knoweth not, and Dugan, the one who forces hearty interest—have got involved in a street riot. The tale concludes with an uncontrolled, page-long, prose-poem-type sentence (which means "Pow!") and finally leaves the prosers' car "winging by glaring incarcerated eyes toward the light, toward the open green and light of the Midway, toward the gray university towers."

If the author had allowed Dugan and Strunk to admit that they are very feeble and boring people, they might, I suppose, have proved as interesting as Beckett's characters; but Dugan and Strunk seem to be thought worthy of respect and sympathy.

The same applies to the tedious musician, Wendt, hero of the novella, **"Veni, Vidi . . . Wendt,"** who offers musical examples composed for Richard Stern by his friend, Easley Blackwood. Wendt's ruminations are stiff with capital letters, famous names put slickly in their place. On a single page we are told about Schoenberg, Lehar, Berg, Mann, Ravel, Stravinsky, Pound, Beethoven, Joyce, Giacometti, Michelangelo, Mozart, and Shakespeare, among others, and also "those elegant books of R. Craft." Elsewhere, we are told of A. von Webern, Dr. S. Johnson, and H. Morgenthau. But we are not told very much, despite R. Stern's air of knowingness. The frightened rustics may excuse his breathlessness, assuming that new insights bubble up so fast in him that he cannot stop to develop them into argument or realize them as fiction. But, if that were so, he would not repeat himself so often.

We may allow that many good writers have revealed something of themselves by repeating their favorite jokes in different works. If we are dropping names in this chummy way, I have noticed that B. Jonson's favorite joke is about people selling their farts; O. Wilde's is about ugly old mothers; G. Byron's is about women longing to be raped. R. Stern's favorite joke is about Martin Luther King being a Jesus looking for a Judas, a joke which does not amuse me at all. He also twice quotes Tacitus's joke, *"capax imperii, nisi imperasset,"* but does nothing with it, except to show it off. (It is a joke against the emperor Galba and means, roughly, "an emperor with a great future behind him.") Stern's Latin tags are overfamiliar to those who read Latin, annoying to those who cannot, and too inaccurately spelled to be helpful to the autodidact. (pp. 26, 28)

D. A. N. Jones, "Pow! Now," in The New York Review of Books, *Vol. XV, No. 3, August 13, 1970, pp. 26, 28-30.**

STEPHEN WALL

Richard Stern's *1968* consists of "a short novel, an urban idyll, five stories, and two trade notes," and, as the sub-title indicates, it makes a scrappy impression. The best piece by a long way is the novella **"Veni, Vidi . . . Wendt,"** an account of the Pacific coast vacation of a middling composer during which he gets on quite well with the first draft of an opera about Horace Walpole.

The irritating distractions of family are offset by a couple of heroic spells of motel adultery. Wendt tends to think of himself as up there with "Arnold Prettymount, Igor the Penman, my dear Webern (the musical laser), plus a bit of Elliot C. and Pierre B.," and this cultural allusiveness and overweening reminds one of the hero of Richard Stern's novel *Stitch.* But to recall that book is to have it made clear that the present performance is on a smaller and less interesting scale.

Wendt does, however, have a manner; the rest of the pieces in this collection seem only to have mannerism. Treatment takes precedence over subject, as if we were expected to be more interested in Mr Stern than in what he writes about.

Stephen Wall, "Californian Castaway," in The Observer, March 21, 1971, p. 37.*

THE TIMES LITERARY SUPPLEMENT

Richard Stern's prose is as dazzling as early sunshine in cloudless winter: it makes you blink. "Too clever by half"—that odd and characteristic British snub—might perhaps be thrown at it, but couldn't in the main be made to stick. What the reader gets here is word-play raised to stature and substance, and what the patterns and gyrations are about doesn't perhaps matter all that much, even though Mr. Stern does sometimes seem to get a bit punch-drunk himself in company with his sparring partner, the hazed reader. (Where does it get you to call Shakespeare "clipped, snubbed, shunted, but world-relaxed"?)

Unless you are one of the 600 million Chinese you may, of course, tire rather quickly of fireworks. This means that Mr. Stern is a splendid man to read over short stretches, and so this book [*1968*], which contains eight short pieces and one short novel, suits his method. The novel, on the perennial American theme of the middle-aged, far-from-stupid man engaged in a Laocoön-type struggle with his own sexuality, is brilliant. The other pieces go fizzingly, too—until the last couple. These are mercifully very short indeed, but nevertheless *1968* would be much better without them.

"Full-Range Fireworks," in The Times Literary Supplement, No. 3612, May 21, 1971, p. 581.*

ANATOLE BROYARD

The middle-aged man and the young girl are becoming an archetypal theme in American fiction. In *Other Men's Daughters,* Richard Stern hasn't exactly "made it new," but neither has he worn it thin. Mr. Stern has a distinctive style, curiously laced with scientific references drawn from physics and physiology, though he is in fact a professor of English. While many of these allusions, which amount to a sort of universal metaphor, may be beyond the layman's comprehension, they still give the texture of the writing a kind of cachet. You feel that the author is bringing new instruments to bear on his familiar material.

Robert Merriwether, his hero, is an M.D. who teaches biology at Harvard and hasn't slept with his wife, Sarah, in years. Though he keeps asking her, she refuses. She is naturally warm, she claims, but it is clear to her that he doesn't want her as a person, only as the nearest woman available. As far as one can tell from the evidence, she is mistaken. Merriwether may be a bit abstracted, but he seems to be actually aware of who Sarah is and to value her for it. While she is not the kind of militant woman who feels that staying home and caring for children is demeaning, she doesn't seem satisfied with it either, referring to herself as a broom or vacuum cleaner. . . .

As an outlet for her repressed feelings, [Sarah] has hardly any choice but to hate her husband. Hating isn't one of his talents, however, so she can't even share this with him.

When Merriwether, who is 40, enters into an affair with Cynthia, who is 20, even the most partial reader will have to admit that he has not sought it and that he does everything he can to discourage Cynthia, in spite of her rather improbable array of appeals. She is beautiful, witty, intelligent, understanding, well-educated and wholly in love with him. She is the aggressor in initiating the affair, and for months he maintains his self-deprecating pose. "I don't think the love system functions usefully after 30," he tells Cynthia. "Real love comes at your age. I mean, the early, parent-child structure of love is matched in the late teens or early twenties by the great transference. By the time you're my age, it's but a combination of lust and nostalgia. There's no room for new roots."

This much is fresh, at least, in contrast to the cries of rejuvenation we've heard so often. When Merriwether does admit the affair into his head, his analysis of it is interesting, if characteristically oblique. "The neural complex was so staggering," he muses, "a statistical case could be made for the absolute uniqueness of every human feeling and event. . . ."

[Merriwether] discovers that his feeling for Cynthia enlarges his feelings for other things. Perhaps he can really do something profound with himself. Perhaps his old way of life was only "a domestic vaccine," as a colleague suggested. Freed from his ancestral home, from his strict history, he might conceivably manage to rise from his own ashes and take flight.

It must be a bitter pill for women that, in so many novels of divorce, the children monopolize the most poignant scenes. Mr. Stern is not guilty here: he reviews Sarah and grieves over her, too. Though he is learning to hate her, he refuses to devalue her. It is she who forces the divorce. Of course, this may be blamed on the fact that he has a lover—but, in a sense, she has one too. She loves her hatred with a sexual intensity. . . .

His only consolation lies in "the depth of love after loss," and the fact that he asks for so little that the likelihood of disappointment is proportionately reduced. He sees himself and Cynthia as "self-catalytic forms, fed by errors, and so perpetuated." Whatever he is to find in her and in his laboratory, Mr. Stern has found what he was searching for in *Other Men's Daughters*—a final fusion of romanticism and irony, a new leap for our synapses.

Anatole Broyard, "New Leap for Our Synapses," in The New York Times, October 16, 1973, p. 41.

MICHAEL WOOD

Where all comment is tactless, a personal style must be a cruel luxury, an affront to all those who live not so much without style as below it. Richard Stern's practice suggests the opposite view: style is what saves buried lives from extinction, style is the mark of an exceptional and delicate attention. Reality in general may refuse names, but small pieces of the world can still be held in language if we choose carefully enough and if our touch is light enough, if we can catch our piece of world without crushing it beyond recognition. Stern has a style in a perfectly old-fashioned sense, and *Other Men's Daughters* is an old-fashioned novel, an impressive plea for the private life as a continuing subject for serious fiction. "A statistical case could be made," Stern's hero thinks, "for the absolute uniqueness of every human feeling and event."

The risk of having this kind of style is that it will deteriorate into a manner, and Stern's does at times. He masters his fragile and banal subject—the love affair of a settled, married Harvard professor of medicine and a golden-haired young summer-school student—by means of a fierce, precise, compressing intelligence, and this can result in a brittle wit (''He was wearing a dark tweed suit, the only one in sight not in summer clothes. It was like a coffin coming through a circus'') or in ugly, mind-stopping epigrams (''Somewhere in the schedule sits life'') or in a sort of crowding in the sentences (''Even then much more of the world was in their heads than in talk with each other''). Far more often, though, indeed for most of the book, it yields fluent, sharp prose like this:

> That double vision of the mind which *knows* but cannot feel or act its knowledge, which squats behind its own bones and measures everything from within those slats, which, at five o'clock, takes the long view of its own troubles like a surveying god, and at five-fifteen shrivels into a nut of egotism; human duplicity with its sparkling outer and inner crepuscular brains, cortical light dazzling over opaque old fear. . . .

Other Men's Daughters is certainly literary, full of allusions; even academic, because Stern has slightly overdone his homework in medicine. But if we use those terms as serious pejoratives, indeed as anything other than means of pointing to certain characteristics of the work, we shall miss the urgency and the distinction of Stern's treatment of his profound theme: the necessary end of particular seasons in our lives, the pain and confusion and exhilaration of leaving safe old places when they have become truly uninhabitable. The novel closes on a small evolutionary hope: we survive, we climb into our futures on the falling scaffolding of our past habits. (p. 19)

> Michael Wood, ''Where the Wolf Howls,'' in The New York Review of Books, *Vol. XX, No. 20, December 13, 1973, pp. 19-23.*

THE TIMES LITERARY SUPPLEMENT

As its title suggests, *Other Men's Daughters* deals with ''one of the most familiar bond-pairs of the new age: the young girl and the middle-aged man'', and, as such categorization implies still further, deals with it with more scrutiny than passion. A Harvard Professor of Physiology, Robert Merriwether is of course accustomed to the clinical perspective; he is father, doctor and teacher, and Cynthia, the liberated lunar beauty who accuses him of the ''masculine dysfunction'' of naming things—''to limit your feeling for them''—is child, patient and pupil. He is decent, kindly and modest, she is eager, intelligent and sad, and without his wife or her father their relationship would have no problems—unless one perversely concludes that without these problems there would be no relationship, a view Merriwether himself seems to have some time for. As with the characters—and perhaps necessarily in this Harvard environment of ''fluent passivity'' and with no wider objectivity than their own—so with the novel. In spite of its intelligence and its many virtues, there is a weakness here, an incompleteness of vision only reinforced by the author's attempt to thematize it, fitting round his scheme of things a sense of acquiescence in the unsatisfactorily resolved. . . .

[Merriwether's] separation from old commitments finally complete and himself one of those ''self-possessed dispossessed'' whose bizarre exhibitions of youth he had earlier envied and puzzled over, Merriwether comes to see himself, and not without a certain logical complacency, as a survivor among the weak. Although this conclusion is undoubtedly right, it is so

in a way which serves curiously to upset the balance of sympathy for our fatherly prescriber of pills. Described by his dominated and unpleasant wife as an ''inhuman tyrant'', this ''hysterical'' verdict gains quiet validity from the consideration that his new strength and freedom have, after all, been drawn from the now exhausted vitality of the two women whose emotional enslavement made it possible. Merriwether himself, adept at ''clarifications'', is even able to see that this is so: Cynthia is ''the classic girl of high intelligence rocked by, well, yes, males like himself—and worse''; his tyranny is precisely this ability to escape explaining things causally. Unfortunately, the author too, at whatever cost in deadness of style, seems content to leave it at that.

Writing his new book, Merriwether feels that ''there was a void in his conception of it: he did not know what it was'', and the novel too conveys this same disappointing sense of the peripheral.

> *''A Physiological Affair,'' in* The Times Literary Supplement, *No. 3766, May 10, 1974, p. 493.*

ANATOLE BROYARD

Richard Stern is brilliant enough to write a novel about almost anything, and I'm afraid that in *Natural Shocks* he has. Perhaps his plan stretches farther than my imagination, but when I had finished the book I felt that it did not cohere. How much coherence you need in order to be happy is one of the difficult questions raised by modern fiction.

I liked Mr. Stern's last novel, *Other Men's Daughters,* better than any of his others [see excerpt above by Broyard]. It seemed to me the most fully realized of all, but that may be another way of saying that I realized what he was doing. *Natural Shocks* takes up so many questions and so many people that I had to keep suspending my opinion of what the book was about. And that is all I got in the end: a hung-up feeling.

There are novelists who would be satisfied with such a response, who are content to conduct their readers to a sort of esthetic limbo and leave them there. They remind me of people who are intense about traveling and say, ''You really must go to Jakarta.'' But while he drops a surprising number of exotic place names, I don't believe that Mr. Stern is one of these types.

I had looked forward to *Natural Shocks* and I was unhappy about my disappointment in it. I reread the jacket copy, which sounded to me as if Mr. Stern had given that writer some clues as to how to take the book. I compared the dust jacket's claims to my own impressions and wondered whether, in reading the book so closely, I might have failed to see it in perspective. With this in mind, I read it again, more quickly, trying to take it in as a whole.

Well, if I can't, I can't. As far as I am concerned, Mr. Stern has a lively mind and a loose grip on his novel. There are too many themes here for 260 pages, and I could not get, or stay, interested in these themes because they do not seem to me to supplement one another. They are not even all that interesting in their own right.

Fred Wursup, the protagonist of *Natural Shocks,* is a highly successful journalist who has just divorced his wife, Susannah, because she has ''a fanatic's serenity'' and ''lives by exclusion.'' Fred lives with Sookie Gumpert, ''with whom he shares 10,000 signals,'' who excites him and satisfies him in every way, despite the fact that he will not admit that he loves her. Wursup takes on an assignment to write an article on dying and, in the course of his research, meets, and develops ineffable feelings about, a 22-year-old girl named Cicia, who has cancer.

When I had read this far, I felt a pleasant sense of anticipation. I foresaw a significant equation between life-denying Susannah, life-enhancing Sookie and Cicia, who could throw still another sort of light on the business of being alive. I saw these questions as congenial to Mr. Stern's talent and turn of mind. Yet, as the book progressed he seemed reluctant to focus on them.

I suffered through a long digression about a political magazine for which Susannah works, and which has just printed a piece about someone named Doyle. Wursup feels he must write a rejoinder to this piece, and for this he must go to Rome, where Doyle now is. Besides Doyle there is a mutual acquaintance named Knoblauch, as well as a hotel keeper who speaks comical English and who has a daughter who has a lover, who in his turn has a peculiarity I can no longer recall.

Then there is Cicia's father, who is writing a double autobiography together with a professor who fails to do his share. And there is Cicia's friend Tina, who writes poetry and who has an Indian lover who wants to go home. Wursup has a father who writes doggerel and who, against all expectations, commits suicide with his mistress, Mona. Wursup also has three elderly aunts who live in his neighborhood. He gets tangled up, in Europe again, with a stupid airlines stewardess, who seizes a statue ''in a hammerlock'' in a museum and is flatulent in her sleep.

Then too, there is a playwright named Blick, who commits suicide, and a man Susannah marries. Wursup has two sons, who occasionally flicker through his thoughts. Wursup's mother lives in Florida, and we are given 10 years of her life in 10 lines. A man who worked with Wursup's father at People's Gas reminds Wursup of a Central Asian mountain chief he interviewed nearly 20 years earlier, and we get a page or two about Pathans. It almost begins to seem as if the author were deliberately teasing us, as if all these digressions—there are more—are some sort of practical joke or satirical comment on the modern novel.

When it is all over, Cicia is dead, but she has fallen ''as apples fall, without astronomy,'' as a poet put it. Wursup is called back from a solitary stay on an island off the coast of Maine, where he is happily planning an assignation with an old girlfriend who happens to be nearby. This one is doing research on sleep.

On the last page of *Natural Shocks* Wursup returns home. Not expecting him, Sookie is at her own apartment, which they both feel she should keep. Although he has not seen her for some time and values her as much as ever, Wursup does not call her, because ''he wasn't hungry, thirsty, tired or lonely.''

He's a better man than I am. After hanging around with him for a day and a half, I was all those things. (pp. 12, 21)

> *Anatole Broyard, ''One Critic's Fiction,'' in* The New York Times Book Review, *January 1, 1978, pp. 12, 21.**

CHRISTOPHER LEHMANN-HAUPT

Richard Stern's . . . work is not as well known as it ought to be. . . . Like all accomplished works of art, *Natural Shocks*

moves along so easily and spontaneously that it virtually resists close examination. Besides, its surface pleasures are easy to describe, and what more do we need to know? It has a superstructure that is as solid and timeless as a folktale: Fred Wursup, an internationally famous journalist now biding his time in New York, is asked, between assignments, to do an article on death, still ''undiscovered country,'' as his editor puts it. While Wursup, in his globe-trotting, has seen almost every face of death, never before has it touched him personally. Now, having taken on the assignment, he finds death all about him, coming steadily closer to home.

And characters—the novel fairly teems with vividly realized men and women. . . . [Upon] finishing *Natural Shocks,* I could instantly call to mind almost two dozen of its characters, which seems extraordinary for a novel of only 260 pages.

And prose—energetic, muscular, intelligent, playful prose, bristling with epigrams and allusions, yet never distracting from the onward rush of the story it unfolds. . . .

Yet when you finish reading *Natural Shocks* and idly wonder how Mr. Stern managed to work so many characters into his story, or how he succeeded in keeping the plot so vigorous, or even how the many subplots interlink so naturally, you begin to see the complexity of the novel's structure. Of course, Mr. Stern is a practiced craftsman: he is at home with the simple but often neglected trick of planting a character firmly in the reader's mind by describing him or her from several other characters' point of view; or with the century-old device of building interest in a plot development by postponing its immediate outcome until the beginnings of another incident have been nursed along.

It may be faintly intimidating to discover from the back of the novel's dust-jacket that Mr. Stern is much admired by the likes of Saul Bellow, Richard Ellman, Mordecai Richler, John Cheever, and Thomas Berger. But if Stern is a writer's writer, it is because he is a craftsman *par excellence,* not obscure.

But look deeper into the well of the novel's meaning and see the thematic complexity down there. The book is about death, yes, but more than that, it is about the deaths of fathers and children and lovers and mentors. And it is about journalism—public events viewed by public men for the consumption of the public. And about the relationship between the public and the private. So that Frederick Wursup's journey from life into death is not so much a matter of tempting fate (as in the old folktale about the three men who go in search of death) as it is a voyage from the public realm into the private, where natural shocks hurt more than cataclysms.

But none of this really matters to an appreciation of Mr. Stern's novel. It is only at the end—when Cicia Buell has died of her cancer and Wursup's ex-wife has remarried and moved away, and Wursup climbs to his rooftop one last time to view through his binoculars the darkness that was once his home—that you realize he has experienced even more than the death of several loved ones. That's when you begin to wonder how Mr. Stern accomplished so much. And by then the visceral pleasure of reading his novel is past.

> *Christopher Lehmann-Haupt, in a review of ''Natural Shocks,'' in* The New York Times, *January 9, 1978, p. C29.*

ROGER SALE

We can say that Stern . . . may simply be interested in too many things [in *Natural Shocks*] to try to write a coherent narrative. We can add that everything in the book is connected with dying or with News as Gospel, and that Stern has a range of styles to adapt for his large cast of characters. The book is good page by page, but it never avoids giving the sense that it is a little indulgent, about all the people and events Stern can think of when he contemplates certain subjects.

For instance, at one point Wursup is lying in bed in Bruges, next to a woman he has picked up for the trip, contemplating the word he has just received that his father and his father's companion-housekeeper have committed suicide:

> Under the sheet Gretchen slept. Vines knocked the wooden shutters, leaves chattered, boats moaned in the canal; voices talked of Burgundy, Charles the Bald, Van Eyck, Memling. The little room thickened with absence. Gretchen grew noisier. A human bassoon. Under the sheet, skin to skin, Wursup thought if only one of her sounds could come from his father's body now, it would undo the universe. His father was gone. And great-bottomed Mona, with all her languages. Little Poppa, who gave him cells, his fat nose, and archless feet. Poppa and Mona, two of the four billion, paying nature's debt before it was due. (Perhaps.)

The writing is flexible and moving, but it also takes on the central themes of the novel all too easily. Why is Wursup in Bruges? Why did his father and his father's mistress kill themselves? So that Stern could write this paragraph? One hardly wishes it unwritten, good as it is, but it seems to float arbitrarily on the page.

Passages like the one above suggest to me a stylistic relation with Bellow. Some later scenes in the book—good scenes, too—in which Wursup goes back to his father's funeral could fit easily into *Herzog* or *Humboldt's Gift*. At certain points during *Natural Shocks* I felt sure Stern was trying to show he could outdo Bellow at Bellow's kind of novel by being less omnivorous, more restrained; at others I felt he had just fallen victim to the master's touch. In any event, strange things happen before Wursup climbs up on the roof of his apartment for the last time, things so strangely assorted that I cannot see how Stern could have been satisfied with their lack of connection. Nonetheless, *Natural Shocks* has intelligence and energy, and Stern . . . deserves to be taken more seriously than he has been. But I hope he doesn't try this kind of mixture again. (p. 44)

> *Roger Sale, "Picking Up the Pieces," in* The New York Review of Books, *Vol. XXV, No. 2, February 23, 1978, pp. 42-4.**

JULIAN BARNES

Richard Stern . . . is the author of ten books, each garlanded with praise by his fellow-writers (Roth, Bellow, Cheever, Malamud, Mailer, Southern). Yet the handicaps he carries make it unlikely that he'll ever come into his rightful fame. For a start, his fiction has no desire to hector or bemuse. He writes an elegant, witty and self-aware prose: an obstinate and selfish attachment to lucidity debars his work from the attention of problem-solving academic critics; while his tense intelligence discourages holiday skimmers. His novels are studded with intriguing, unpredictable bits of technical, political and intellectual information; but the learning is worn shamefully lightly. His characters, unpopularly, belong to the cosmopolitan profes-

sional class: the sort who keep *The Penguin Book of Latin Verse* as lavatorial reading, and who get itchy if they aren't allowed to spend at least one chapter in Paris or Rome. Stern is Jewish, but this potential plus is cancelled out by the fact that he finds Jewishness only as interesting as a range of other subjects. Finally, he has the misfortune to be a Professor of English at the University of Chicago, and the podium there is already fully occupied. The result is that Stern, like Cheever, is comparatively neglected (not necessarily a matter for complaint—and comparative neglect in America is quite well rewarded anyway): and, causing no huge stir in the States, he is less likely to cause even a medium one here [in England]. (p. 377)

Natural Shocks is easier to enjoy than summarise; perhaps it's best described as a novel about the onset of doubt, informed everywhere with Stern's quizzical mixture of sadness and knowing wit. It's entirely characteristic that when, at the end, Wursup invokes Beethoven's last quartet and the *muss es sein* on the score, he notes (is it scholarship or invention?) that the answering *es muss sein* is 'a joke about the landlady's call for the rent'. (p. 378)

> *Julian Barnes, "Trick or Treat," in* New Statesman, *Vol. 96, No. 2479, September 22, 1978, pp. 377-78.**

PETER S. PRESCOTT

It is probably too easy to say, but I will say it anyway, that loneliness is a theme more suitably exercised in a short story than in a novel. The reason is purely technical. A lonely person, as a rule, requires the slimmest of supporting casts. A novel, as a rule, requires more characters than a short story, and more human connectedness than simple loneliness can sustain—which is why novels about loneliness tend to be about psychopathology as well. In fiction, as in life, plain loneliness becomes boring over the long haul and is best left to those who don't prolong the anguish. . . .

[In the short stories of *Packages*] Richard Stern evokes a precise sense of familiar situations; dry, witty and economical, he writes often about the relation between loneliness and love.

That relation can prove as sticky as your kid nephew with a jar of peanut butter. Stern, however, never lets sentiment succumb to sentimentality, in which an occasion is afflicted by excessive or unearned emotion. In his first story, a teacher muses over students who have passed from his care, some into alarming lives, and realizes how much he has loved them and teaching. In his last, a very old man, his mind unmoored by age, comes to understand that his younger wife is dying. Plenty of tear-tugging opportunities in both tales, but Stern turns them deftly aside: he upsets his teacher on an icy path, and reduces his old man's vocabulary to the language of bridge.

These two stories bracket others that are less tender, more acerb. In ["Packages"], the narrator reflects upon his father's degeneration ("Senility is too part of life, one of the few remaining middle-class encounters with the Insoluble") and his mother's cremation. What remains of the package that once contained [her] is now packaged in an urn which he throws to the revolving blades of a sanitation truck. He listens to one of Bach's cello sonatas "until it overflows my capacity . . . Is the idea to reduce vastness into something portable? A package." And in the book's most brilliant story, a comedy of unfulfilled sexual desire called **"Lesson for the Day,"** a failed professor of English professes his lust for his neighbor's wife.

At a critical moment he quotes from one of the Earl of Rochester's bawdy poems, ''The Imperfect Enjoyment.'' Stern, however, does not offer the title; perhaps to name the poem would be to define too clearly what his story is about.

Stern's stories are crisp, mundane, occasionally optimistic. ''The moral,'' says one of his people, ''was keep looking and waiting and maybe push it a little here or there, there's enough somewhere to celebrate.''

Peter S. Prescott, "Lonely Lives," in Newsweek, *Vol. XCVI, No. 18, November 3, 1980, p. 88.**

NICHOLAS SPOLIAR

A good short story is apt to resemble one of those card tricks in which the unassuming card that we had been expecting turns out, when uncovered, to be the ace. We find ourselves wondering how it is that something we were sure would be slight can appear to contain so much, and practitioners of the genre from Chekhov and Maupassant to William Sansom have exploited its brevity by finding ways of transcending it. The title of Richard Stern's [*Packages*] suggests brevity rather than transcendence, but the best stories in it have something of both qualities (the very best story, moreover, is by far the shortest). As the title also suggests, Stern is as deft as an old-time grocer in his control over his material: he both packs his punches and packages them.

The packages are intended to ''reduce vastness into something portable'', without really reducing it, and in [''**Packages**''] the hero's feelings about his recently dead mother are sparked off by a small package ''wrapped in brown paper tied with a strand of hemp which broke when I hoisted it''. The contents of the packet are a matter for conjecture, but there is a paradoxical boast implicit in the story's title: it is not the mother's mortal remains that are important—they are got rid of as unceremoniously as possible—but the story itself, the real ''package'', in which the mother is effectively memorialized.

Memories play an important part in most of these tales, and an unaccidental reference to Proust in the title-story shows the way ahead, or rather backwards. The first two stories are built around, respectively, a professor's recollection of many years of students, and a collection of letters to a poet-cum-cartographer going back twenty years. In a sense both stories are about needs: the professor depends on his students almost as much as they depend on him (''Can you guess how I've grown to love you?'', he asks his class, before launching into reminiscence). In the end, he *is* his memories, while the cartographer is grateful for being taken as a poet. In another story, **''Double-Charley''**, one of the Charleys of the title can write music only to the other man's lyrics, though it is so long since they have written a hit that their music appeals only to nostalgia, which mocks at memory. Memory is even more effectively mocked by one of the Charley's discovery of his wife's infidelity with his collaborator.

Several of these stories are about marriages, mostly failed ones. In **''Troubles''** a young woman keeps an embarrassingly pretentious diary in an attempt to reconstruct past events and find out what has gone wrong. In **''Lesson for the Day''** what has gone wrong is ''WE—Woman's Era'', as we discover through a series of meditations and flashbacks in the hero's mind. Neither of these stories altogether succeeds: they suffer from cliché and whimsy. But one that does succeed is **''Riordan's Fiftieth''**, the account of a man's rather melancholy birthday,

passed in the somewhat spiky bosom of his family. George Riordan is a sympathetic character with a highly unsympathetic wife: he knows that ''if he got a greeting out of her it would leak out of the side of her moon face and make him feel 'Who're you, Riordan, that anyone in the world should care you've weighted the planet fifty years?' '' Not the kind of consolation a man deserves on such an occasion. Stern makes the reader care about Riordan through an astute use of language (that nicely unpleasant ''leak out'', for example) and through detail—what there is for dinner, who serves whom, who wins the baseball game, all things that are made to count for us.

Richard Stern who, as the dust-jacket informs us, is Professor of English at the University of Chicago, is as verbally dexterous as one might expect. Riordan, with a ''pug's nose'' and a ''chin like a boat-keel'', looks in his mirror and sees ''Just George Riordan on his fiftieth. His own birthday cake''. This is the only cake he gets, and the pun is typical of a writer who can have ''Smoke Gets in Your Eyes'' played at a funeral parlour. In the last, and in some ways best, story, an old man uses bridge language as an idiolect, so that food becomes ''clubs'', eyes ''spades'', or at other times something else—no one can be sure. Stern can be funny on the subject of communication, but also moving: the old man's effort to speak normally to his fading, hospitalized wife is touching and nicely judged. Not all the stories work as well as this, and some of the writing is clumsy and overblown. A couple of characters lead a ''rodent life on the periphery of lofty mentality''. The heroine of **''A Recital for the Pope''** thinks of herself, incongruously, as a ''citizen of time, not space''. ''Her country'', Stern says, ''was Poetry'', and one feels that he is taking her pretensions altogether too seriously (just as his own stories are spattered with references to the literary good and great, not to mention Bach and the troubadours). *Packages* remains an interesting collection, however, and the best stories in it are excellent—inventive and economical.

Nicholas Spoliar, "Letters on Brown Paper," in The Times Literary Supplement, *No. 4051, November 21, 1980, p. 1342.*

DAVID KUBAL

Richard Stern is enamored by cities, specifically Chicago and New York, because in them he finds humankind in all its variousness. At the beginning of the first of this . . . collection of stories [*Packages*], the narrator, Professor Wissler, intones the singular names of his students: ''Miss Fennig. Mr. Quincy. Mr. Parcannis. Miss Shimbel. Ms. Bainbridge. . . . Miss Vibsayana. . . . Miss Glennie, Mr. Waldemeister.'' Later he says: ''I love individuals, yes, and I stay aware of clothes, bodies, gestures, voices, minds, but it is the class itself I love. The humanscape. The growth of the unique molecule of apprehension and transmission. From the first tense, scattered day through the interplay, the engagements, the drama of collective discourse to the intimate sadness of the last class. How complicated the history, the anatomy, the poetry of such a body.'' At the center of Mr. Stern's love for the ''humanscape,'' moreover, is a large sympathy for the individual caught in a world too narrow for his energies and talents. The sadness emerges then not only because the ''class'' ends, the body broken up and scattered; it also resides in the realization that the whole cannot answer the needs of the single part. In **''Troubles,''** a story of a seedy graduate school marriage, Hanna, the neglected wife, comes to understand that her discontents have no identifiable source—they ''were deep structures. Or structural defects. Deep, confusing, hard to assign. Cagey. Uncageably cagey''—and that there is no cure—''Energy, talent and hope warred with her life; no relationship and no institution could help. She had the isolation of a pioneer in the circumstance of a soap opera. The only axe she had was the knowledge she was in trouble, that she was down there with the others.'' Hanna's life is part of a package for which she must accept delivery, even if she is, like another character, ''Immense, passionate'' and unable to be ''contained by any métier.''

This double vision, entailing the perception of the self's scope and the limitations imposed by nature and society, informs the eleven small dramas, the ''Packages,'' of the book. To Mr. Stern's credit he sustains the tension, resisting the easier responses of pity or rage or cynical irony. Holding hard to both truths, he rather prefers an accommodating, gentle humor; although no one is condescended to—whether it is a Chicago bus driver, neglected by his wife and family on his fiftieth birthday; or a son who disposes of his mother's cremated remains in a city garbage can; or a group of academics and their infantile lusts and ambitions. Mr. Stern's lucidity, together with his capacity for affection and the comic, are very rare qualities, shortages in contemporary literature. The informed reading public, at least, wants its fictive realities uncontaminated by an author's suggestion that human character is greater than its circumstances, or that the condition itself has its goodness, or that anyone should be forgiven or tolerated. That Mr. Stern continues to offer these consolations in a body of work, which now contains nine major fictions, tells us of his artistic integrity. (pp. 458-59)

> *David Kubal, in a review of ''Packages,'' in* The Hudson Review, *Vol. XXXIV, No. 3, Autumn, 1981, pp. 458-59.*

GEOFFREY WOLFF

Richard Stern has been writing crafty fiction for a quarter of a century, and he knows his apples about the voices of educated Americans who have come up, Augie March-like, from down there. . . .

Family is [the subject of his novel, *A Father's Words*], and particularly the idiom of a particular family, particularly American: ''Riemers are athletes of the mouth.'' Wisecracking wisdom, [the narrator] Cy Riemer remarks that ''Tolstoy's wrong about happy families.'' Was he ever wrong! What could be more peculiar, more singular, more remarkable than a happy family?

Alas for the Riemers and literary novelty, this is not a happy family, though it often tries to be, and the trying always is interesting. But it seems that the energy of a novel comes from friction rather than from the sun, that oppositions almost inevitably provoke its motions and noises. Clash is surely the fuel by which this novel runs.

A Father's Words are uttered to four children, and most potently and cruelly to a son, Jack, a relentless failure. ''All I know,'' the father says, knowing much more, ''is I can't tolerate the way he acts and looks. After all, he's mine. I helped shape him. His life's a rebuke to mine.''

Those are not my words or Richard Stern's; they belong to Cy Riemer. Yet knowing this, I find them as painful to type now as to read then. The pain is the fruit of Stern's masterful calculation of an offhanded grammar for a cataclysmic repudiation. Not far into *A Father's Words*, Riemer talks to his son, delicately knocking Jack off balance with light jabs almost dreamily delivered, deflating the boy's (perhaps) ill-considered enthusiasms: ''After I rock him back and forth like this, I hate myself.''

The very *rock* is the crusher, pulling from some distant channel the blurry memory of a child rocked for comfort in a father's arms. Not that Jack isn't a royal pain, a slippery customer. . . .

Still, Cy Riemer's disapproval of Jack is out of all ratio to the offenses that putatively provoke it. His other three children see this, as Stern and his readers see it, and the delicate manipulation of a smart, sane, self-justifying narrator, who is not the character he wishes his audience to see and believe (''For me, family counted . . .''), is not the least of Stern's achievements in this delicate fabrication of tough prose and tender adjustment of sentiment. (It comes to break a reader's heart to hear Jack, or Riemer's daughter Jennifer, call out to this father: ''Hi, Dad.'') . . .

As Tolstoy said, right on the button in the second half of his formulation, unhappy families are indeed unhappy each in its own way. . . .And isn't that the saddest damned thing? Except that it's a fact that makes novels as good as *A Father's Words*.

> *Geoffrey Wolff, in a review of ''A Father's Words,'' in* Los Angeles Times Book Review, *May 9, 1986, p. 1.*

Ross (Elmore) Thomas

Briarpatch

Edgar Allan Poe Award: Best Novel

(Also writes under pseudonym of Oliver Bleeck) American novelist and scriptwriter.

Briarpatch (1984) is Thomas's twentieth novel and his second Edgar winner; *The Cold War Swap* (1966), with which Thomas began his mystery-writing career, won the Edgar Allan Poe Award for Best First Novel. Before turning to fiction writing, Thomas worked as a journalist, public relations agent, and government consultant in the United States, Europe, and Africa. His books frequently draw on his knowledge of politics and his interest in corruption in public and private life. In the nearly two decades between Edgars, Thomas has written many political thrillers under his Ross Thomas signature; under the pseudonym of Oliver Bleeck he has published five novels featuring the character Philip St. Ives, a professional ransomer of stolen valuables and kidnapped people. In spite of his long career, Thomas has yet to win a wide audience; he has, however, achieved popularity with crime fiction buffs who appreciate his consistently well-crafted, intelligent, and humorous suspense novels. Some reviewers have expressed hope that *Briarpatch* might win Thomas the readership that he deserves.

Critics observe that *Briarpatch*, the latest of his political thrillers, bears all the familiar Thomas trademarks: careful pacing, an engaging plot full of wry twists, convincing setting, fine characterization, and smart, witty dialogue that together make a first-rate mystery. The book's title refers to an unnamed city in the southwest that bears a noted resemblance to Oklahoma City, where Thomas was born and raised. Ben Dill, a Washington congressional investigator, returns to his rustic hometown after his police detective sister, Felicity, is murdered. A typically worldly, cynical Thomas hero, Ben is nevertheless shaken when evidence connects both Felicity and Ben's boyhood friend, Jake, with graft, mysterious killings, and the unsavory dealings of local police. Thomas usually offers social commentary in his works, and reviewers note that *Briarpatch* is no exception. Besides exposing corruption, Thomas examines personal dilemmas as his protagonist is forced to make the painful choice between loyalty to Jake and his late sister or his professional duty as a crimefighter. As critic Jonathan Yardley remarks, *Briarpatch* "is quintessential Thomas—and that, in my judgment, is about as high a compliment as a piece of popular fiction could be given."

(See also *Contemporary Authors*, Vols. 33-36, rev. ed.)

© Jerry Bauer

KIRKUS REVIEWS

Thomas fans who have come to dote on his whimsically tangled plots and black-comic absurdities may be a little disappointed by this new thriller [*Briarpatch*]—a somber, relatively *(relatively)* straightforward murder-mystery, notwithstanding some CIA complexities and a few dashes of prime-Thomas repartee. Rising police-detective Felicity Dill dies in a car-bomb explosion in a southwestern city—and her beloved older brother Ben, a Congressional investigator, leaves Washington to return to his home town and look into the matter. Was Felicity's death connected to a case she was working on? Or to her love-life—which included a spurned suitor and a married cop-fiancé? And why did Felicity have two apartments—one where she *seemed* to live, one where she really lived? Could it be—as the evidence starts suggesting—that Felicity was on the take? Dill finds that hard to believe, as does his new love-interest: Felicity's lawyer Anna Maude Singe. Meanwhile, however, Dill must also do some Washington-assigned work: dealing for information with an old buddy of his—Jake Spivey, an ex-CIA type who made a fortune in illegal arms-deals and is now sitting pretty in a local mansion. And eventually Dill starts wondering if Felicity's death could somehow be connected to this illegal-arms subplot—which also includes Spivey's ex-partner (now a ruthless fugitive), blackmail secrets, and police corruption. There's another corpse (the spurned suitor), lots of wire-tapping, a little action, and a lot of amorality from the assorted government officials involved . . . before the final twist and windup shootout. But it's only Thomas' sure, sharp-edged style that lifts this above the humdrum—with just enough smart/nasty dialogue to keep Dill (an unusually earnest Thomas hero) and his quest from turning soggy or murky.

A review of "Briarpatch," in Kirkus Reviews, *Vol. LII, No. 18, September 15, 1984, p. 876.*

BILL OTT

Ross Thomas has been writing high-quality thrillers for many years. Although he has developed a loyal audience, he has yet to take that next step into bestsellerdom. Eventually Thomas will write his breakthrough novel, and *Briarpatch* just might be it. Thomas specializes in world-weary, cynical heroes who thrive on the edges of politics. Ben Dill is typical of the breed: consultant to a congressional committee, he makes contacts, sets up meetings, cuts deals. Only this time he has two problems that threaten to knife through his hard edge of cynicism: his sister, a police detective in his hometown, has been murdered, and his oldest friend, an ex-CIA agent and arms dealer, is the object of a congressional investigation. . . . Thomas entertains with witty (but not *too* witty) dialogue, fast-moving action, and that familiar world-weary tone. Ben Dill is competent at what he does, but being so tires him out. Not many thriller writers are that honest in portraying their heroes.

Bill Ott, in a review of "Briarpatch," in Booklist, *Vol. 81, No. 4, October 15, 1984, p. 265.*

JONATHAN YARDLEY

One of the oddities of contemporary culture is that American writers have defaulted, almost to a man, on their obligation to provide readers with witty, literate and intelligent popular fiction. American fiction these days is divided between the devil and the deep blue sea: between the cynical purveyors of exploitation fiction on the one hand, and the ivory-tower academic novelists on the other. There seems hardly any middle left at all. For fiction that means primarily to entertain, but that assumes its audience to be reasonably sophisticated and alert, we must turn to the British, whether for novels of manners (Barbara Pym and Isabel Colegate) or for thrillers (John le Carré and Len Deighton). Apart from John D. MacDonald and Elmore Leonard, there's hardly an American writer alive who writes escapist fiction that a person of discrimination can read without wincing.

But there *is* Ross Thomas, and it is about time that he got the large, enthusiastic readership he deserves. *Briarpatch* is his 20th book, a well-rounded milestone that, if there is any justice left, should get him over the hump and onto the best-seller lists. Whether writing under his own name or that of the pseudonymous Oliver Bleeck, Thomas consistently turns out novels that, while providing the requisite amounts of suspense to qualify as genre fiction, are distinguished by expert prose, penetrating social commentary and—bless you, sir—a marvelous sense of humor.

All of which are abundant in *Briarpatch*. I can't say that it's the best of Ross Thomas because I haven't read all the others, but it certainly is quintessential Thomas—and that, in my judgment, is about as high a compliment as a piece of popular fiction could be given. To begin with, it amply fulfills the first requirement: you can't put the damned thing down. Its char-

Dust jacket of Briarpatch, *by Ross Thomas. Simon and Schuster, 1984. Copyright © 1984 by Ross Thomas. Designed by Karolina Harris. Courtesy of Simon & Schuster.*

acters are real, and interesting, and there's not a piece of cardboard in the lot. Its setting—"the capital of a state located just far enough south and west to make jailhouse chili a revered cultural treasure"—is depicted with an impressive eye for small but telling detail. And there are enough laughs, including the funniest CPR rescue ever written, to make a happy evening for the speed-reader or a gleeful week for the dawdler.

Among the many pleasures of reading it, one of the most satisfying is simply to watch Thomas juggling—and never once dropping—two complicated plots that for over 300 pages seem to have nothing to do with each other except that both involve the central character. His name is Benjamin Dill, he is 38 years old, and he works on Capitol Hill as a $168-a-day consultant to "an obscure three-member Senate subcommittee on investigation and oversight." He is a native of the aforementioned state capital, to which he is drawn back by terrible news: the murder of his 28-year-old sister, a homicide detective in the municipal police department, in a car-bombing. So long as he is going there, and so he can put the trip on his expense account, the minority counsel suggests he interview a former CIA operative whose affairs the subcommittee is looking into.

Thus we have the two mysteries: the murder of Felicity Dill and the tangled past of Jake Spivey. As is always the case in the best suspense fiction, though, there is more to these matters than at first meets the eye. For openers, as Dill begins to look into his sister's life he discovers that there was a great deal about it she never told him: that she'd had a love affair with a former pro-football player turned private eye, for example, but that she'd broken it off for a fellow cop whom, before her death, she had said she would marry. More than that, as Dill observes: "She was leading a pretty strange life before they blew her away. She bought a duplex she hardly lived in with money she didn't have. She took out a two hundred and fifty thousand dollar life insurance policy, paid cash for it, and died three weeks later—right on schedule. Doesn't anyone wonder . . . where the hell the money was coming from?''

By the time matters are more or less sewn up just about everyone is asking that question, or trying to avoid answering it, and a great many people are in a great deal of trouble, some of it of the fatal variety. Not merely are there Dill and the woman lawyer he has fallen for and a spaced-out fellow with a genius for electronics and the ex-footballer and a nasty old newspaperman and enough cops to populate *Hill Street Blues;* there are also all those "renegade spooks" whom Dill is trying to track down. Chief among these is Spivey, who was Dill's closest boyhood friend and who remains, their conflicting interests notwithstanding, a person about whom he cares deeply. Spivey made himself a fortune in Vietnam after the war by co-founding with another apostate CIA agent a company "that bought surplus equipment from the new Vietnamese government and sold it on the open market to whoever wanted to buy it"—equipment along the lines of "defensive weaponry, transportation, communications." Now Spivey is wanted by Dill's subcommittee, either for his own suspected violations of the law or as a witness against even bigger miscreants.

It's a difficult position for Dill, one that forces him, as his lover the lawyer puts it, "to choose between your friend and your government." As much as anything, that's what the novel is about: friendship and loyalty, the ties that bind people to each other and that can make life unbearably complicated when other considerations enter the picture. Whatever Dill's frailties, and they are not inconsiderable, he is a principled man; his deepest loyalties, he discovers, are to his sister and his friend, and it is to the memory of one and the future of the other that he dedicates himself—although even this dedication must ultimately be compromised, in the higher interests of self-preservation.

This is serious stuff, but Thomas doesn't let himself get too serious about it. One of the most appealing characteristics of his work is that it never lets you get very far from the knowledge that all this foolishness is just that: foolishness. Thomas is always there in the background, though never obtrusively so, making wry, deflating comments on his characters, exaggerating things a bit just to emphasize their silliness, poking fun at the vainglorious and pompous. Certainly there are more certifiably "serious" American writers than he, but there's no one who gives more pleasure to the page. Ross Thomas is a craftsman, a professional in the most admirable sense of the word, and he does what only the best writers can: he leaves you wanting more. (pp. 3, 12)

Jonathan Yardley, "Ross Thomas with a Double Twist," in Book World—The Washington Post, *October 28, 1984, pp. 3, 12.*

An Excerpt from *Briarpatch*

The bedroom was not quite as large as the living room because its size had been reduced by the addition of a large closet. There were pretty yellow curtains on the windows and a cheerful white-and-brown rug on the floor. The bed was of the three-quarter kind, quite large enough for one and even for two, providing number two didn't plan to stay the night.

The bedroom also contained an old-fashioned chaise longue, which gave it the air of boudoir. A card table, bridge lamp, portable electric typewriter, and director's chair gave it the air of Felicity Dill.

Dill crossed to the closet and slid one of its doors back. The closet was filled with women's clothing, all neatly hung on hangers with winter clothes in plastic bags and summer clothes ready to hand. Dill shoved the hung clothing to one side to see if there was anything else worth noting and discovered the man at the back of the closet. The man had a long narrow face that wore a foolish smile. His eyes were a yellowish brown and looked trapped. Dill thought they also looked clever.

"Who the hell are you, friend?" Dill said.

"Lemme explain," the man said.

Dill stepped back quickly, looked around for something hard, spotted the windowsill, and smashed the beer bottle against it. It left him with a weapon formed by the bottle's neck and three or four inches of sharp jagged green glass.

"Explain out here," Dill said.

The man came out of the closet carrying a small toolchest and still wearing his fool's smile.

"I'll tell you exactly what I want you to do," Dill said. "I want you to put that chest down very carefully, then reach into a pocket just as carefully—I don't care which one—and come out with some ID. If you don't, I'm going to cut your face."

"Take it easy," the man said, still smiling his fixed smile. He put the toolchest down as instructed, reached into a hip pocket, and brought out a worn black billfold. He offered it to Dill.

"Give it to her," Dill said.

The man offered the billfold to Anna Maude Singe. She approached him warily, almost snatched the billfold from his hand, and hurriedly stepped back. She opened it and found a driver's license.

"He's Harold Snow," Singe said. "I remember that name."

"So do I," Dill said. "You're Cindy's roomie, aren't you?"

"You know Cindy?" the man said, his tone puzzled, the fool's smile still trying to please.

"We met," Dill said.

"Harold's the tenant," Singe said. "At the duplex. His name was on the lease."

"I know," Dill said.

Harold Snow's foolish smile finally went away. The yellowish-brown eyes stopped looking trapped and began looking wily instead.

"You guys aren't the cops then," he said in a relieved tone.

"I'm worse than that, Harold," Dill said. "I'm the brother."

JOHN SUTHERLAND

A new novel by Ross Thomas is hardly a news event; not because Thomas doesn't write good thrillers (he does), but because they come round as regularly as January sales. . . . At Thomas' industrial rate of production, consistency matters more than one-off triumphs.

Category fiction comes apart easily in the reader's hands, and the best way to assess this season's offering [*Briarpatch*] is to dismantle it into standard thriller components. First, plot: Ben Dill, a smart Washington lawyer, is called back to his hometown (the briarpatch where he was "bawn en bred") for his sister's funeral. She, a homicide detective, was murdered by a car bomb. Circumstances are suspicious; she had amassed more money than a virtuous policeperson should. The main strand of narrative has to do with unraveling the twin mysteries of whodunit and how she got it. On the way, Ben falls in love with his detective sister's glamorous lawyer (no gender stereotypes here) and has some problems with dishonest local cops and politicians (plenty of stereotypes here). Suspense is efficiently maintained, although *Briarpatch* causes no page-turning frenzy. By the time the last chapter comes round, the reader will either have guessed or won't care who the arch-villain is. There are, as I calculate, five violent deaths and some torrid but very straight bedroom sex.

Next, setting: *Briarpatch* employs the familiar convention of the wanderer returned. Thomas coyly keeps the identity of the revisited city secret. In fact, one doesn't have to know the author's own regional background to figure out that the briar-patch must be Oklahoma but that he (or his publisher) is wary of lost sales. For intensification, *Briarpatch* uses the hoary device of a mounting heat wave, which breaks with the denouement of the mystery. On the whole, atmosphere is well done, though one tires of recurrent references to the time-and-temperature display over the First National Bank.

Third, theme: *Briarpatch* is more ambitious than many of its ilk and in places, verges on the portentous (usually a mortal failing in the thriller). The hero is placed in the classic Forsterian dilemma: loyalty to country or to his oldest hometown friend? A senate investigation with which he is coincidentally involved is close to indicting said friend. After much moral writhing, Ben makes the proper betrayal. Thematically, *Briarpatch* bites off more than Thomas' functional technique can comfortably chew.

Finally, what new twists does Thomas offer? The modern taste is for political relevance in our escapist fiction. Here—by rather forced contrivances—Watergate is made to figure in the action. But the best new twist in *Briarpatch* is in its opening chapter, where for three or four pages, Thomas brilliantly traps the reader into sexual-chauvinist prejudice. (The trick turns on what one sees in one's mind's eye on reading the first sentence, "The redheaded homicide detective stepped through the door.")

Briarpatch does a good three-quarters of what we expect a thriller to do. Its principal weakness is in the character of Ben Dill. The narrative makes us share his point of view, but we don't really feel close to him nor much care about his lone quests against Washington venality and hometown corruption. What works best in this novel is the pace, which is brisk, and the dialogue, which crackles.

> *John Sutherland, "The Dead Detective Was Female," in* Los Angeles Times Book Review, *December 2, 1984, p. 17.*

Judith Thompson
White Biting Dog

Governor General's Literary Award: Drama

Canadian dramatist.

Both of Thompson's plays, *The Crackwalker* (1981) and *White Biting Dog* (1984), are characterized by abrasive imagery and wildly imaginative situations reminiscent of the startling techniques of the Theater of the Absurd. In *The Crackwalker* Thompson explores life in an Ontario slum by focusing on two slow-witted couples, one of whom kills its own baby. The award-winning *White Biting Dog* combines farce, romance, realism, and fantasy to examine death and decay and to question conventions of language, viewpoint, and lifestyle, particularly as these relate to families.

White Biting Dog revolves around a family that is broken by the mother's adultery and darkened by the father's imminent death. The words and actions of the characters are often symbolic of their physical conditions and their unconscious attitudes. The father who is dying of cancer, for example, is fond of dropping peat moss wherever he goes, symbolizing his state of decay, while the words of a talking white dog reflect the son's intuited solution to the family's problems. Because in life people do not usually express their feelings and attitudes in such graphic detail, *White Biting Dog* creates unsettling effects in the theater.

Critics have had mixed reactions towards Thompson's sometimes grotesque imagery, but most praise the idiosyncratic imagination and the theatrical energy evident in *White Biting Dog*. Her dialogue is commended for its rhythmic use of language that is described as both musical and mesmerizing. Commentators note, too, Thompson's successful creation of an absurd world with its own convincing logic.

Thompson graduated from Queen's University in Ontario and from the acting program of Canada's National Theatre School, and she has performed as an actress in Manitoba and Toronto. With the production of *The Crackwalker* Thompson was recognized as a promising new talent. She is now considered one of her country's most important young dramatists, having, in the words of reviewer Carole Corbeil, "the best ear of any playwright now writing in Canada."

RAY CONLOGUE

The wild imagination of Judith Thompson is on the loose again.

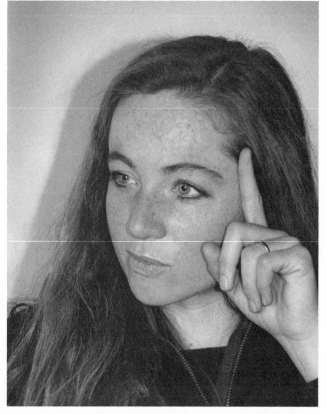

© Paul Till/Now

It is filling the Tarragon Theatre with a quantity of prodigiously original jokes and beatific fallings-out in the bosom of a very peculiar family.

The Race clan, around whom her new play **White Biting Dog** is built, are about the shabbiest gentry you would ever want to meet. Dad is upstairs dying, which he illustrates every so often by coming out and shaking peat moss from under his shirt. "Feel like a rotten tree," quoth Dad, who is also called Glidden.

Mom, meanwhile, has run off with the latest in a string of lovers, this one a new waver named Pascal whose topknot jiggles in time with his drug-induced jitters; but they've had to come home because their hotel burnt down. Mom, whose name is Lomia, is still wearing a satin slip and an air of sensuous *noblesse oblige*.

The son, whose name is Cape (Cape Race?), is trying to keep his father alive and figures the best way is to arrange a reconciliation between him and Lomia. In this endeavor Cape has a helper, a former ambulance attendant named Pony who has shown up on his front step. She is a queer bird, which means they understand each other perfectly.

And moreover, Cape was, at some earlier date, apparently dissuaded from jumping off the Danforth viaduct by the arguments of a small talking dog which appeared out of nowhere. This dog apparently belonged to Pony ("I had one just like that, especially the talking"), which explains her appearance on Cape's Forest Hill front stoop. . . .

[The] kind of play we are seeing [is] a comic romance. This isn't obvious right off the top. There's a lot of dirty talk and emotional violence à la kitchen-sink realism, more than a touch of desperate absurdity, and a lot of bloody spatters on Pascal's punker leathers.

But there's also more than a bit of magic. Not only the talking dog, but the peculiar exuberance of Cape and Pony as they fall in love with each other. They do it on a rush of words and shared experience which is almost psychic, and when they make love it's like being "upside down together in one of those Nova Scotia waves." It's a case of Puck meets Ariel; they are almost spirits.

Well, not completely; they are not immune from death, it appears. And unlike the case in most romances, the separated lovers—Mom and Dad—don't quite make it back together, though they nearly do. Mom at least breaks out of her enchantment.

But, the frozen dachshunds in the freezer downstairs do get a proper burial. The dachshunds, along with a torrent of suchlike slightly morbid but incredibly funny minutiae, make up the moment-to-moment flow of this wickedly amusing play.

> *Ray Conlogue, "Funny, Exuberant Spirit Fills 'White Biting Dog'," in* The Globe and Mail, *Toronto, January 13, 1984, p. E10.*

MARK CZARNECKI

[*White Biting Dog*] is a disorienting example of theatre of the absurd. It attempts to yoke pungent realism with airy fantasy: a prophetic talking dog figures prominently in Thompson's hostile and often tedious enigma. But . . . [it also has] poignant moments.

White Biting Dog is a morality play performed by a lunatic Toronto household. Mortality has cast a pall on the Race family. In a second-floor bedroom full of sickly light, Glidden . . . crawls from his deathbed and showers himself with peat moss. Glidden's son Cape . . . vows to redeem his own wasted life by saving his father's: a talking dog told him that Glidden would live if his adulterous wife, Lomia . . . , returned home. Pony . . . , a young psychic from Kirkland Lake who inexplicably turns up at the Races' front door, confirms the dog's prognosis. When Lomia suddenly arrives with her punk lover, Pascal . . . , Cape and Pony successfully conspire to alienate him from Lomia. The dying man's wife finally decides to stay with him, but her conversion comes too late—Glidden and Pony learn that the price of redemption is still mortality.

Only the plot of *White Biting Dog* is simple. Much of the first act is boring gibberish spiced only by Thompson's acid one-liners and disturbingly inventive imagination—Cape at one point

accuses Lomia of storing his childhood nosebleeds in jam jars. Family members remain ciphers, especially Cape, whose sole purpose in the play is to provide a plot, such as it is. . . . But the second act brings strange revelations. The characters' long soliloquies, on the surface as nonsensical as before, begin to exhibit their own emotional logic. When [Lomia] can utter the line, "I am not a dust storm—I am a carrot with its head chopped off," and move an audience with it, both actress and playwright have achieved a theatrical triumph.

Without the irritating first act to tear down "normal" social and dramatic conventions, the second act would degenerate further into perplexing anticlimax. . . . Judith Thompson has worked her minor miracles in truly mysterious ways, but she runs the risk that few of the congregation will stay to witness them.

> *Mark Czarnecki, "A Drama of Weird Skills," in* Maclean's Magazine, *Vol. 97, No. 5, January 30, 1984, p. 51.*

CAROLE CORBEIL

Judith Thompson's *White Biting Dog* . . . is orgiastic and poetic in its use of language, excessive in its theatricality, and achieves its power by an accretion of extraordinary images. . . .

In *White Biting Dog,* all is disorder. All bonds are broken—the mother has left the father for a punk rocker, the son hates the mother for having left his father, and he has left his own wife in order to save his father. In terms of dialogue, however, the most important bond that is broken is physiological. *White Biting Dog* is about many things, and it would be impossible to do justice to Miss Thompson's imagination in such a short space, but the dominant metaphors of her language are physiologically based; this play, on some level, is an extraordinary poem on cancer, on the knowledge of mortality, on the physiological base of every emotion. What is extreme about Miss Thompson's approach is that her characters say everything— what can be spoken and what is usually merely thought. They, in other words, take their own temperatures all the time.

The father is dying; in Miss Thompson's theatrical scheme, which is farcical as well as absurd, he drops peat moss from his belly. But every character is obsessed by the decay of his or her own body, and other people's bodies. Some, like the son and the mother, are completely hermetic in their obsessions. Miss Thompson tries to set up a parallel here, of mother and son being essentially creatures who are unable to feel, and so must use others as extensions. But this schematic-thematic attempt is not what is interesting in *White Biting Dog;* it is actually an indication of one of Miss Thompson's weaknesses—too much self-conscious cleverness mars her writing. She robs herself of her own effects by piling it on. Miss Thompson has the best ear of any playwright now writing in Canada. She does not need to outdo herself.

Any play, however, which pushes against the limits of theatrical naturalism has to accomplish one very difficult thing: it has to create its own world. Miss Thompson, in *White Biting Dog,* does this. And that is an amazing accomplishment.

> *Carole Corbeil, "The Observer: Plays in Which a Family Is Trapped in Its Own Creation; Variations on a Cliche," in* The Globe and Mail, *Toronto, February 23, 1984, p. E4.**

An Excerpt from *White Biting Dog*

GLIDDEN: (stands up violently) POP POP POP POP
ROCK ME TO GRAVENHURST ROCK
ME TO GRAVENHURST ROCK ME TO
GRAVENHURST ROCK ME TO GRAV-
ENHURST (opens eyes wide) I'M NOT
A ROCK CONCERT NOT A ROCKA-
BYE ROCK, NOT A ROCKABYE,
ROCKABYE CONCERT, ROCK ME TO
GRAVENHURST, ROCK ME TO . . .

(GLIDDEN passes out. CAPE
catches him and puts him over
his shoulder)

CAPE: Gravenhurst is where the family's all
buried this is it! It's all over there
is no way out.

(CAPE dumps GLIDDEN on his bed,
comes out, returns to throw bag
of peat moss into his father's
room, comes out again)

Hear that? Hear that? That's the . . .
grinding of teeth again—I—I bet
it's the devils that my great aunt told us
about, under the Don Valley Parkway,
that's THEIR way of laughing, GRIND-
ING their teeth—they're laughing
because they think that they have me but
they don't—they don't, do they?
'Cause the white dog is coming, she's
coming now oh somebody tell her tell
her I'm in trouble, tell her to
HEEEEEEEEEEEELLLLLLLLLLLP!!—the
drums. Maybe she'll hear the drums (starts
drumming) white dog, dog from the bridge
oh QUEEN of dogs oh please oh help oh
help oh (stops) It's not working.
What'll I do what'll I—A SONG! A song,
yes, they sing in CHURCH (sings, to the
melody of *Agnus Dei*) A—ahhhhhhhhh
laaaaaaa whiiiiitee dog pleeeeeeeeeease . . .

Cover of White Biting Dog, *by Judith Thompson. Playwrights Canada, 1985. Cover photo and design by E. J.
Powers. Courtesy of Playwrights Canada.*

Thompson is a mesmerizing writer much of the time, with a
voice that is all her own. ***White Biting Dog*** doesn't always
work, but I can't think of another recent Canadian play like
it, either in ambition or tone.

> *Jon Kaplan, in a review of ''White Biting Dog,'' in*
> NOW, *September 27-October 3, 1984.*

JON KAPLAN

Judith Thompson's ***White Biting Dog*** . . . emphasizes the poetry
and expansiveness of the language of the characters. . . . ***White
Biting Dog*** takes Toronto family life into the weirdness of
hallucination.

Cape Race feels he must save his dying father Glidden—and
himself—by bringing Lomia, his wandering mother, back to
the family. But she's living with a punker named Pascal, and
Cape needs the help of the psychic Pony (maybe the owner of
the dog of the title) to set it all right.

Cape is alternately fascinated and repelled by his mother. . . .
She is the erratic anchor . . . , dragging all the other characters
behind her instead of giving them some kind of grounding.

The second act of the play seems to wander away from the
points made in the first, but there are still some riveting scenes.

PAUL WALSH

Judith Thompson's ***White Biting Dog,*** winner of the 1984 Gov-
ernor-General's Award for Drama, is also a love-story of sorts,
though a love-story of twisted absurdity and bitter cynicism.
Cape Race, a seductive young lawyer who has cracked, or
pretended to crack, under the pressures of life, was standing
on the wall of the Bloor viaduct preparing to jump when he
was given a mission by a small white dog: ''You're living in
hell, 'cause you ain't done your mission . . . To save your
father from death.'' (p. 145)

White Biting Dog is an improvisational piling up of incidents
and images that, deep down, reminds one of a nineteenth-
century melodrama. Brooding with predictability on a bed of
old answers, it uses extreme situations and hyperbolic images
to dramatize a situation gone wrong. What is reinforced in the
process are the absent norms that these extremes violate. If the
story of the mission is not just a pretense for the explosive

confrontation of eccentric characters, then behind the straw dogs of excess that clutter the stage stand the familiar values of patriarchal authority, of duty and restraint, industry and patience, and, above all, responsibility and guilt. Unfortunately, the play seems unaware of its own ideological commitments, and this tension tears it apart.

Perhaps it is the unexplored conflict between a desire for formal innovation and an acquiescence to a perniciously powerful ideology of conservative authority that explains the bitter cynicism of this play and its structural ambiguities. The play is troubling and engenders a passionate response, but ultimately it is deeply unsatisfying in the warning it issues against both passion and concern. In the end we are left with a grim morality of good and evil, summarized by Pony in one of the play's several superb monologues: "I was invaded, Dad," she says in a post-mortem wrap-up for her absent father, "*filled* by the worst evil . . . you ever imagined—I guess it happened when I fell in love, on account of I had to open my mouth so wide to let the love in that the evil came in, too." Pony is destroyed; Glidden is destroyed; even Pascal, who turns out to be plain "Gordon from Oakville" is destroyed. And we are left unmoved and unconvinced by the fairy-tale suggestion that the sacrifice of their loved ones might somehow be sufficient to melt the stone hearts of Cape and Lomia. Brrr. (pp. 145-46)

> *Paul Walsh, in a review of "White Biting Dog," in* Canadian Theatre Review, *No. 45, Winter, 1985, pp. 145-6.*

RICHARD PAUL KNOWLES

Judith Thompson's **White Biting Dog** is poetic drama of a very different kind, by one of English Canada's most exciting new dramatic voices. . . . Judith Thompson is a street poet, sensitive to the musicality of everyday speech; in fact she is so concerned with the sound of the words that the printed text is prefaced by a note warning that

> any attempts to go against the textual rhythms, such as the breaking up of an unbroken sentence, or the taking of a pause where none is written in are DISASTROUS. The effect is like being in a small plane and suddenly turning off the ignition. This play must SPIN, *not* just turn around.

White Biting Dog is concerned with salvation through sacrificial love, and its symbolic underpinnings are Christian. The dog of the title (God spelled backwards?) is love, and his intervention at the outset precipitates the action of the play. The symbolism is never heavy-handed, however, and the play's affirmation of life is achieved as much through its almost manic energy, its theatricality, and its stimulating use of language, as through its steady accretion of compelling images. Following in the wake of her first highly successful play, **The Crackwalker**, **White Biting Dog** confirms Judith Thompson as a unique new voice in Canadian drama, and a leader in the country's new generation of playwrights. (pp. 85-6)

> *Richard Paul Knowles, "Dramatic Work: Retrospectives and New Directions," in* The Fiddlehead, *No. 143, Spring, 1985, pp. 84-7.**

RICHARD PLANT

Carole Corbeil has written in the *Globe and Mail* of **White Biting Dog**'s "orgiastic and poetic" qualities [see excerpt above], and of Thompson's attempt to escape the confinement of a realistic mode, possibly of the kind she used in **The Crackwalker**. And to be sure, the play moves from one metaphor to another in a string of densely packed images apparently meant to illuminate the characters and action. (However, Thompson surely cannot mean for the characters and action to be as self-consciously symbolic as they seem.) . . .

I feel elfish suggesting this, but there is a current running through the play that urges me to see it all as comic. The stronger impression, however, is that Thompson meant to be serious. On either ground we can applaud her vigorous imagination, her theatrical sensibility, and her poetic gift—which is largely undisciplined in this play.

White Biting Dog is so overburdened with imagery that it is finally inaccessible. We can see the elaborate and convoluted metaphor struggling to express Cape and Lomia's flood of elemental feelings—sexual, moral metaphysical—which are brought to a crisis point by the impending, then actual death of the father/husband. Unfortunately, the imagery exists as a cloak, hiding the reality Thompson seems to want to explore, rather than as a metaphorical force organic to the subject. (p. 23)

> *Richard Plant, "Opening Lines," in* Books in Canada, *Vol. 14, No. 3, April, 1985, pp. 22-4.**

Robert Penn Warren

American Academy and Institute of Arts and Letters: Gold Medal for Poetry

American poet, novelist, short story writer, dramatist, essayist, and critic.

Warren is widely acclaimed as one of the most distinguished writers and critics of contemporary American literature. In 1986 Warren was named America's first Poet Laureate (an annual appointment made by the Librarian of Congress in which the poet acts as a consultant to the Library of Congress). In addition to this recent accolade, Warren has received numerous awards, including the American Academy and Institute's prestigious Gold Medal for Poetry. Warren previously won The National Book Award for his collection *Promises: Poems 1954-1956* (1957), and he is the only writer to have received a Pulitzer Prize in both fiction (for *All the King's Men*, 1946), and poetry (one for *Promises* and one for *Now and Then: Poems, 1976-1978*, 1978). After the publication of *Selected Poems: 1923-1943* (1944) Warren produced no more verse until *Brother to Dragons: A Tale in Verse and Voices* (1953), which many critics consider one of the finest long poems in American literature. Warren's popular reputation is due mainly to his novels, especially *All the King's Men,* a probing examination of the evil inherent in political demagoguery. His reputation as a critic is also firmly established. As the author with Cleanth Brooks of a series of textbooks on literature and writing, *Understanding Poetry* (1938) and *Understanding Fiction* (1943), Warren is largely responsible for introducing several generations of college teachers and students to the theories of the New Criticism, and he was a founding editor of *Southern Review,* an influential literary journal that served as a forum for the New Criticism from 1935 to 1942. Through the years Warren has also published several highly respected critical studies on such major authors as Joseph Conrad, Ernest Hemingway, and William Faulkner. Despite his achievements in fiction and criticism, Warren is primarily dedicated to the writing of poetry; when asked in an interview whether he would rather be remembered for his fiction or his poetry, Warren answered that he would choose his poetry as "representing me more fully, my vision and my self." Though after more than fifty years of publication he could rest comfortably on his reputation, Warren continues to produce significant works of poetry. With the recent publication of *Being Here: Poetry 1977-1980* (1980), *Rumor Verified: Poems 1979-1980* (1981), *Chief Joseph of the Nez Perce: Who Called Themselves the Nimipu "The Real People"* (1983), and *New and Selected Poems: 1923-1985* (1985), Warren continues to evolve as a poet and to capture critical recognition for his evocative verse.

Born and raised in Kentucky, Warren was instilled from an early age with traditional agrarian values and a love of storytelling. Warren attributes much of his knowledge about history, poetry, and the oral tradition to his maternal grandfather, Gabriel Thomas Penn, with whom Warren spent his childhood summers. Warren dedicated *Being Here* to Penn and pays tribute to his grandfather's influence on him with the following dialogue on the dedication page: "OLD MAN: You get old

© 1986 Thomas Victor

and you can't do anybody any good any more. BOY: You do me some good, Grandpa. You tell me things." Warren also acknowledges the positive effects of his well-read parents and his traditional education, which included the memorization and recitation of poetry. Warren planned to attend a military academy for his higher education, but his future changed at age fifteen when an accident caused the loss of sight in his left eye.

At Vanderbilt University in Tennessee, Warren studied under John Crowe Ransom and became the youngest member of the Fugitive Movement, which brought him into contact with such noteworthy poets and critics as Donald Davidson, Allen Tate, and Stark Young. The Fugitives upheld the values of their Southern agrarian culture against the North's encroaching industrial economy and its presumed capitalistic values. In their writings these poets and critics honored classical literature and metaphysical poetry and called for formal diction and meter in works of verse. After receiving his M.A. from the University of California in Berkeley and studying at Yale and Oxford in England, Warren joined the faculty at Louisiana State University. It was there that Warren and Brooks wrote their textbooks based on the theories of the New Criticism, which favored close literary analysis and derived, in part, from the discussions held by the Fugitives and the group that evolved from them known as the Agrarians.

All of Warren's books of poetry and fiction, which number over thirty, have some connection to history. The poems are often based on a historical event or legend and are recounted in narrative, but it is not the events themselves that concern Warren; rather, he concentrates on the universal moral issues that surround those events and with the immutable nature of history. An exemplary early poem is ''The Ballad of Billie Potts,'' which Warren bases on the legend of a son who after a period of wandering and financial success returns home only to be murdered by his parents, who fail to recognize him. The event itself is used as a prototypical example of the innocent who, through seemingly uncontrollable forces, is pushed towards evil and death. This conception of Original Sin—the belief that a progression from innocence to knowledge and evil is inevitable—recurs throughout Warren's poetry, as well as much of his fiction. Warren holds that this progression is true of both an individual and a society and is the moving force behind such historical events as the Civil War and the violent settling of the American West—the subject of his long poem *Chief Joseph of the Nez Perce*. Equally apparent is Warren's emphasis on the importance of nondiscriminatory love and hospitality, the necessity for self-knowledge, and each person's responsibility for the world's evil. Among the numerous poems that address these issues are ''Original Sin: A Short Story,'' a paradigmatic poem; *Brother to Dragons*, a versification of the story of Thomas Jefferson's nephew who savagely murdered a slave; and *Audubon: A Vision* (1969), a verse dramatization that praises the artist's ability to transform the brutality of nature into beauty through imagination. Landscape and nature imagery are prevalent elsewhere in Warren's poetry. In his descriptions of nature, Warren makes clear that we may identify with the environment, but we can never become one with it. He also points out the paradox that when nature's potential destructiveness is controlled, the result is sterility and stifling predictability. Many of the poems in *Thirty-Six Poems* (1935), *Eleven Poems on the Same Theme* (1942) and *Rumor Verified* center on these concerns.

Consistent as his ethical convictions have been, Warren's treatment of his themes has changed considerably throughout his career. In his earliest poetry, collected in *Thirty-Six Poems* and *Eleven Poems on the Same Theme*, Warren used the impersonal tone valued by the Fugitives. He later adopted a more immediate tone characterized by his use of the ego-personae ''You'' and ''R.P.W.'' Critics also note a looser metrical style evident in his use of broken rhythms rather than regularly stressed meters and deliberate contrast between controlled eloquent language and long pauses. But most notable is Warren's gradual shift in emphasis from narration to introspection. Though Warren made philosophical observations in his earliest poetry, after his ten-year abstinence from poetry-writing the reflective nature of his work became more central. In *Brother to Dragons* Warren advanced the narrative through discussions between and among the poem's characters, rather than recounting the action directly. This allowed him to move from a temporal novelistic framework to a more meditative poetic one. In his poems since *Promises: Poems 1954-1956* Warren has almost completely subordinated narration to reflection. Thus, his recent works, especially *Being Here* and *New and Selected Poems* offer candid speculation on the essential issues long implicit in his poetry: As defined by critic Peter Stitt those issues are ''the

meaning of life, the relentless process of time, the function of memory, the possibility of knowing truth.''

While recognizing the weightiness of Warren's themes, Warren's detractors claim that his treatment of those themes is marred by lofty language and a platitudinous, didactic tone. However, even his detractors acknowledge Warren's diversity and evolution as a poet, and he remains one of the most honored writers of the second half of the twentieth century. Not only is he recognized for the insight he offers his readers, Warren is praised for the influence he has had on several generations of younger poets as well. As his student poet Robert Lowell described him in a poem, Warren is ''an old master still engaging the dazzled disciples.''

(See also *CLC*, Vols. 1, 4, 6, 8, 10, 13, 18; *Contemporary Authors*, Vols. 13-16, rev. ed.; *Contemporary Authors New Revision Series*, Vol. 10; *Dictionary of Literary Biography*, Vol. 2; and *Dictionary of Literary Biography Yearbook*, 1980.)

PAUL BRESLIN

Mr. Warren has sometimes been compared with Hardy and Yeats, poets who also did some of their finest work in old age. Though not quite ready to rank him in such exalted company, I find the comparison with Hardy suggestive. Like Hardy, Mr. Warren was best known in middle age as a novelist but has devoted his later years (so far, at least) to his poetry. His work, like Hardy's, is deeply rooted in a regional tradition. And some of his strengths and weaknesses are Hardy's also. T. S. Eliot's remark on Hardy actually becomes more just when applied to Mr. Warren: ''He wrote sometimes overpoweringly well, but always very carelessly; at times his style touches sublimity without ever having passed through the stage of being good.'' All but a few of Mr. Warren's new poems [in *Being Here: Poetry 1977-1980*] are marred by outbreaks of bombast and clumsy prosody, but so many of them are touched with pure magic that one forgives him. The inspired moments usually come when the poet is looking at a landscape, especially one with plenty of open space:

> Have you—scarcely more than a boy—been
> The last man afield, the old binder
> Dragged off, sun low? Have you stood
> Among shadowy wheat shocks, the tips
> Of stalks showing gold in that last light? Beyond
> Shorn earth the sun sags slow red. In distance
> One cowbell spills
> The empty tinkle of loneliness. A bullfrog,
> Brass-bellied, full-throated,
> Accents the last silence.
>
> Long later, the owl.

In passages such as this one, the music of the poetry is as extraordinary as its imagery. Here the repetitions of ''last,'' spaced just far enough apart to avoid being obvious, lead to the rush of *l* sounds in the last few lines and contribute to the sense of closure and repose in ''Long later, the owl.'' Unabashedly obvious, but very powerful, is the massing of sibilants and stresses in ''Beyond / Shorn earth, the sun sags slow red.''

We will just have to accept the fact that Mr. Warren, though capable of effects like these, is also capable of the worst sort of rant about Time, God, History and Identity. . . .

Mr. Warren (in this respect quite unlike Hardy) has no interest in the possibilities of understatement. He also does very strange things with accentual-syllabic prosody. He often writes in what is clearly intended as an iambic meter, with frequent anapestic substitutions. But then he starts demoting the stress of heavily-accented syllables in order to fit them into the anapestic rhythm. One quickly becomes uncertain where the accents should be placed. . . . The diction is that of an original and gifted poet, but the prosody, taken in isolation, is that of doggerel.

But enough carping; we must take Mr. Warren's book as we find it. For the beautiful meditations on the relationship between consciousness and nature in poems such as **"Platonic Drowse"** and **"Timeless, Twinned,"** for the novelistic fullness of detail in poems such as **"Filling Night With the Name: Funeral as Local Color"** and **"Recollection in Upper Ontario, From Long Before,"** and for the many superb descriptive passages scattered through the book, there can be only praise. (p. 12)

Paul Breslin, "Three Poets," in The New York Times Book Review, *November 2, 1980, pp. 12, 28-30.*

SANDRA PREWITT EDELMAN

If it has not been suggested elsewhere, I am suggesting here that poets set names to wounds. Perhaps, to be less inclusive, I ought to say they set uncommon names to common wounds: failures of love, failures of courage, early rejections and denials—disorder and early sorrow. It is not by the state of woundedness that poets are set apart (if, indeed, they are set apart at all), but by the depth of the wound, the poet's inner response to it, and the outer manifestation of that response, which is to say the poem. (p. 215)

Wheat is discernible from chaff . . . not by the wound (which we cannot know in its entirety) but by the response. Depending on our outlook, the wound can either prove to be our salvation, or it can, as an analyst friend of mine put it, "cut us off at the ankles." It can drive us to look for answers, developing the best of our capacities for love, sensibility, and acceptance, or it can drive us into a raging, confused, and unfulfilled old age. In short, in its extreme expression, the wound can make us healers or it can make us cripples. Most of us fall somewhere in between. And most of us, I believe, if we read poetry at all, and if we think long enough about why we read it, will find that one of our reasons is to discover some kind of healing. We come to poetry, if not for answers, for the old questions put in a new and healing light. For the restoration of some tribal or private myth. For the sharing of power; because when a poet bleeds, the blood runs with healing. (pp. 215-16)

Robert Penn Warren, three-time winner of the Pulitzer Prize, once the youngest of the Fugitives, is now seventy years old. The fifty poems [in *Being Here*] were written during the three years just passed, and constitute, according to their author, a "shadowy autobiography." Threading with some dominance through the collection is the need to inventory, weigh, and reiterate the questions that become inevitable for us all: what have I done, who am / was I, what has it all been about. In the process, wounds are exposed: the pain and anger at discovering one's ineluctable mortality, the failures of love, and perhaps the worst of all, going into night without quite knowing who one is.

Much as I might wish to do so, I cannot set these poems on the side of the healer. The wounds are raw and gaping, and

the poetry which is their vessel fails artistically. Warren seems to have written this collection in somewhat the same spirit as a man whips a horse; one finishes reading out of breath, not from exaltation but because there are no measures of grace and play, no long strides or canters; the poems have been ridden at a gallop, as though they might otherwise languish and die before the last word leaves the pen.

Partly responsible for this pell-mell effect are Warren's unabashed and old-fashioned use of alliteration ("how soundless crunch / Cloud cobbles of bright cumuli" is a typical example) and his unending reliance on hyphenation—presumably in an effort to wrench the language into new anatomies, the result of which makes one think of nothing so much as egg pudding with too many raisins. Thus, . . . (the only four-raisin line in the book) "From bough-crotch to bough-crotch, the moon-eyed tree-toad utter . . ."

Yet another culprit in the race for breath is Warren's habit of breaking lines willy-nilly. A good many contemporary poets do this now, as though it were *de rigueur*, and it is a contrivance which not only makes no sense to me but is downright annoying. The lacuna developed out of oral tradition and represents an organic break in the line, a place where the singer needed to take a breath, or where emphasis was appropriate, or where a unit of meaning had been created. Poets have used this natural consequence of semiotic and human physiognomy to enhance and / or create image, music, and meaning, but what used to be a felicity has become a cheap trick. Warren employs it repeatedly, as in "But at / That instant . . ." but nowhere more maddeningly than in a poem he labels as having been written in octosyllabic lines and which on close inspection turns out to be a hunk of prose broken after each set of eight syllables, even if the break happens to fall in the middle of a word.

There are other failures. Of musicality. . . . Of tone. . . . Of taste and sensibility, as in a longish poem titled **"Recollection in Upper Ontario, from Long Before,"** dedicated to Richard Eberhart. Here the voice of the poem sees a woman crushed and mangled to death by a train. Later he recalls the porter having said, with reference to the remains, "Hell—it's hamburger now," and immediately after, in the next line, says, "I wonder what's coming for supper." (The juxtaposition reminds me of the kind of low-level schoolboy attempts at gothic humor we were treated to in Coppola's film, *Apocalypse Now*. . . .)

In **"Cocktail Party,"** Warren writes ". . . you try / To speak, an urgency like hard phlegm / In your throat." It's as though he had written the critic's epitaph for his own collection, because the phrase bespeaks a man exhausted by seven decades of questioning, angry that the answers still elude him, much of grace and love sapped away. In that sense, too, the poetry is failed poetry. The wounds may run deep, but the response seems only just beneath the skin. The poems look outward for answers and find none; look inward and find empty rooms. They reiterate the age-old solopsism we all commit when we demand infinite answers to finite questions. They remind us that without some healing, we lose the knack of putting the right questions in the right way. (pp. 216-18)

Sandra Prewitt Edelman, "The Poet as Healer," in Southwest Review, *Vol. 66, No. 2, Spring, 1981, pp. 215-19.*

WILLIAM H. PRITCHARD

[Pritchard is an American critic, biographer, and professor of literature. He has written several books on contemporary poets

and poetry, including Wyndham Lewis: Profile in Literature *(1972),*
Lives of the Modern Poets *(1980), and* Frost: A Literary Life
Reconsidered *(1984). In the following excerpt Pritchard evaluates
the strengths and weaknesses of Warren's prosody in* Being Here.]

In his introduction to the recent *New Oxford Book of English
Light Verse,* Kingsley Amis refers at one point to the opposite
of such verse and instead of opting for the demeaning "heavy"
(Who would want to be known as a writer of heavy verse?)
chooses the adjective "high." Whatever one calls it, a prime
contemporary example of unlight verse is the work of Robert
Penn Warren. As was the case with respect to his last volume
(*Now and Then,* 1978) nobody goes on about Mr. Warren for
very long without reaching for the word "powerful." Harold
Bloom, who has been touting Warren's later poetry as America's central contemporary instance of the High Romantic Sublime (Bloom touts the Sublime generally) finds it "deeply
moving." But what is there to be said about an ordinary reader's experience of this powerful, sublime, deeply moving voice,
varying little from poem to poem, speaking always as if propelled by some elemental force which throws up memories and
scenes from the past and is never at a loss for words to describe
them?

Since it is an excellent idea to be on the alert whenever one
is placed in the neighborhood of something deeply moving
(especially if it's the Sublime) we may remark first on the
extreme ease with which Warren summons up the language in
poem after poem. Wyndham Lewis once accused Faulkner of
possessing a "whipporwill tank" to which he had frequent
recourse when his prose threatened to flag. Mr. Warren owns
something like a Time and History tank. [*Being Here*'s] three
epigraphs all refer to Time, and the tank is repaired to on
numerous occasions in the poems themselves:

So dressed now, I wandered the sands, drifting on
Toward lights, now new, of the city afar, and pondered
The vague name of Time,
That trickles like sand through fingers,
And is life

There are many more, and a similarly large selection could be
made of his employment of "Truth." I do not mean to be
perverse in saying that when I come to these patches in Warren's writing—

Time died in my heart.
. . .
So I stood on that knife-edge frontier
Of Timelessness,

—I am not at all deeply moved, but depressed rather at the
mechanical cranking-out (or bucket gone to the well once more)
of an old tune. It's not so much High as it is Heavy verse.

Surely the co-author of *Understanding Poetry* knows more about
prosody than I, and there may be richly interesting prosodic
feats in these poems I'm not hearing. What I do hear is a voice
that has decided to rear back and let go as if, having attained
the age of seventy-five, Mr. Warren feels he's earned the right
to behave as he likes. He is certainly no searcher for the *mot
juste;* the ease with which "like a" this or that comes to his
pen suggests something other than Flaubertian fastidiousness.
I think rather that his appeal—and many of these poems are
indeed appealing—stems from the universality of the situation:
an old man looks back, encourages his childhood to cry out to
him, asks unanswerable questions about *why* (the favorite first
word in these poems), and then wrestles with the big, impossible questions which have none, or only one, answer. His is

not a poetry of ideas, although concepts are always popping
up; it is the poetry of emotions rather, high-pitched and poignant. The self these poems speak to is one which given a
chance will eagerly indulge in thoughts that lie too deep for
tears. (pp. 107-09)

William H. Pritchard, "Weighing the Verse," in
Poetry, *Vol. CXXXVIII, No. 2, May, 1981, pp.
107-16.*

PHOEBE PETTINGELL

In *Rumor Verified: Poems 1979-1980* . . . [Robert Penn Warren]
has, for the moment, laid aside the colloquial free style of his
recent verse to return to the more formal language and syntax
that marked his contributions to the *Fugitive* during the early
1920s. Led by Allen Tate and John Crowe Ransom, the writers
associated with this journal were fleeing from the prettified
motifs and sugared pretenses of Southern poetry on the one
hand, and the sterile, abstract theology of Yankee industrialism
on the other. They concentrated on violence, starkly confronting a life that is all too often nasty, brutish and short. The
uncompromising posture produced a wild romanticism as Tate
declaimed, "The poet is he who fights on the passionate / Side
. . . There is an infallible instinct for the right battle / On the
passionate side." In *Rumor Verified,* Warren takes one more
stand in this just war.

His vigor leads him to search for a way out of the fear that we
are aliens, estranged from Nature, leading purposeless or destructive lives. Increasingly, he tries to capture the glimmering
of an answer. "But what can you do?" he asks in the title
poem. "Perhaps pray to God for strength to face the verification / That you are simply a man, with a man's dead reckoning, nothing more."

In "Afterward," the death of someone once loved yet mis-
treated drives the "You" addressed in the poem into a depression; it seems that the "unimaginable expanse of polar / Icecap
stretching forever in light of gray-green ambiguousness" may
be "the only image of eternity." Instead, the poet offers the
solace that comes from the presence of objects worn down by
loneliness and time: "Ah, menhirs, monoliths, and all / Such
frozen thrusts of stone, arms in upward anguish of fantasy,
images / By creatures, hairy and humped, on heath, on hill,
in holt / Raised!" Warren suggests that despairing people, after
acknowledging this not very prepossessing picture of man and
his art, ought to be laughing with rueful self-recognition and
not brooding in isolated pride.

Sustained by irony and compassion for the absurdity of the
human condition, Warren pushes on, writing spirited, glowing
poetry. By the time we reach "Fear and Trembling," the
lovely conclusion of this book, questions themselves have become a kind of reply. Musing on whether autumn can serve
as a correlative for our own decay, he is disturbed by illusions—
destroying doubts about language's ability to really represent
what it purports to describe. Is it only babble? And though we
project our emotions upon our surroundings, how can inanimate
objects be anything except indifferent to us? Such queries threaten
to bring the whole artistic house of cards down about our ears
in an instant, but Warren always finds hope at the bottom of
every Pandora's Box:

Can the heart's meditation wake us from life's long
sleep,

And instruct us how foolish and fond was our labor
  spent—
Us who now know that only at the death of ambition
  does the deep
Energy crack crust, spurt forth, and leap
From grottoes, dark—and from the caverned
  enchainment?

To me, the cave evoked at the end is Plato's, with its implication that whatever we see may be only the shadow of that
reality awaiting us one day.

The epigraph to *Rumor Verified,* taken from the last verse of
Dante's *Inferno,* reads (in my paraphrase of the Italian) "I saw
these lovely things that are of Heaven / through a round opening
from which we came forth / again to see the stars." Warren
has kept alive a rhetorical grandeur that is rare in modern
poetry, and his vitality has influenced and encouraged many
younger poets. But he remains more powerful than any of his
progeny. (p. 17)

Phoebe Pettingell, "Fathers and Children," in The
New Leader, *Vol. LXIV, No. 23, December 14, 1981,
pp. 16-17.**

JAY PARINI

[*Parini is an American poet, critic, and novelist, and a frequent
contributor to literary journals. His poetry is classic in form,
serious in tone; his subject matter—as evidenced in his recent
collection,* Anthracite Country *(1982)—is personal. Among the
many influences on his artistry are Seamus Heaney, John Crowe
Ransom, and Warren. Parini dedicates his poem "High Gannet"
from* Anthracite Country *to Warren and evidences the older poet's
influence in the poem's observations and speech. In the following
excerpt Parini comments on the three most recent collections of
Warren's poetry,* Now and Then, Being Here, *and* Rumor Verified.]

Robert Penn Warren has stepped out boldly as a major poet,
publishing four strong books of new verse in seven years. *Now
and Then* (1978) established his position by astonishing readers
with its ferocity and grandeur, and that memorable volume has
not been surpassed by *Being Here* (1980) or his latest collection
Rumor Verified. Nevertheless, these last three collections are
of a piece, and Warren has emerged at the front of a field
noticeably lacking in major figures since the death of Robert
Lowell.

At the age of seventy-six, Warren seems literally pressed by
time. This pressure has led to what some critics regard as overproduction, and some of these poems do read like rough drafts.
In a sense, we have been given entry to Warren's workshop;
the poet tries out the same poem many different ways, narrowing in on the final version, which is usually stunning. A
fair number of these works take the form of the descriptive
poem in which a (presumably) older man climbs a hill in Vermont or stands overlooking a seascape, having come to a specific point and place in nature, whereupon he is overwhelmed
by questions of time and identity.

Even Warren's worst poems are interesting for the way they
grope towards the better work, struggling for clarification. In
the best of them, such as **"Heart of Autumn"** in *Now and
Then,* **"Acquaintance with Time in Early Autumn"** in *Being
Here,* or **"Mountain Mystery"** in *Rumor Verified,* Warren makes
us vividly aware of ourselves as creatures caught in the thresh
of time. He sees the need to ask the right questions even while
he dangles before us the insufficiency of any answers we might

obtain. "If this is the way it is", he writes in a new poem
called **"If",** then "we must live through it". . . .

In his later work, Warren has rescued many of the virtues found
in his early poems: wit, a muscular intellect, and a longing to
get rapidly to the heart of things. He has added a clamorous
urgency, an intensity occasioned by age, and a turn to what
might be called autobiographical verse. The road was opened
for him by Lowell, Snodgrass, and others, who made confessional poems respectable. Yet Warren has gone beyond confession, reaching through mere personal fact to impersonal truth;
he has taken on the mantle of the vatic poet and turned his
own life into an exemplar. The lyric "I" in these poems is
simply man at his best: simple, learned, loving, and completely
human. This man, faced with "the terror / Of knowledge" in
the title poem, asks: "But what can you do?" Warren answers:
"Perhaps pray to God for strength to face the verification /
That you are simply a man, with a man's dead reckoning,
nothing more."

A genuine humility informs these poems and saves them from
pretentiousness. And Warren's predilection for grand philosophical speculation is held in check by the autobiographical
mode, which insists that each poem be founded on an incident
or place. Thus, having evoked his climb up a seawall beside
the Mediterranean, the poet can get away with talk about "the
agony of Time". We can absorb his question—"What lies in
the turn of the season to fear?" in a poem called **"Vermont
Ballad: Change of Season"** because he has rendered so concretely the transformations of autumn, the "fitful rain" which
has "wrought new traceries, / New quirks, new loveknots,
down the pane". Indeed, the title poem, **"Rumor Verified",**
is an ode to humility, a poignant confession of moral inade-
quacy.

Jay Parini, "The Vatic Mantle," in The Times Literary Supplement, *No. 4113, January 29, 1982, p.
113.*

JASCHA KESSLER

[*Kessler is an American poet, short story writer, critic, editor,
translator, novelist, dramatist, and scriptwriter. In his short stories and poetry, Kessler focuses on everyday people and events,
envisioning them within a larger framework of human significance. Drawing on individual experience, he creates universal
resonances. In the following excerpt Kessler reviews Warren's
collection* Rumor Verified, *praising the poet's articulate and candid view of himself and his world.]

The poems in [*Rumor Verified: Poems 1979-1980*], both in
quantity and quality, are just about at the same high level as
Penn Warren offered us in his *Now and Then: Poems 1976-1978,*
and his *Being Here: Poetry 1977-1980.* I would not want to say
that there is really any refining, any sharpening or intensifying,
any further penetration into the psychological depths, spiritual
tangles or complexities of advancing age, nor will I suggest
that the language of this new book represents any kind of
advance or discovery of new powers. Such sorts of praise are
unnecessary for this poet, who long [ago] established his tone
of voice, his approach to the world and to himself, and the
conventions of his form and diction. Nor will I say of Penn
Warren that his powers are increasing or even decreasing, and
that, should these be among his very last poems, he will have
shown himself to us in a sunset blaze of glory. I don't think
Penn Warren needs—what with all the honors lately accumulating to him—either our praise or half-hearted acceptance

(and this new volume has not received many enthusiastic reviews). What he asks us for, I think, is our attention. And that, he very much merits: *Rumor Verified* is a most absorbing book, in fact.

Penn Warren has always been a writer insisting upon a candid, secular and intensely reflective psychological analysis. In these books written in his 70's, he has worked with what remains to him, as a man and as a poet who contemplates life spiritually, but without religion: a secular and honest man. His honesty consists, I would say, in his adherence to the beautiful natural world, as it exists, and to the experience of the sensitive, self-aware person wandering in it. Now, in this book, as in the others, Penn Warren seems to be rummaging in what's left to him, mostly the past, and every day less of even that past seems to be available to his recollections. Having been a novelist and a playwright, most of his poems take the form of narrations of events in certain strange hours of his childhood and his manhood, events that stamped themselves into permanence by means of terror, dread, passionate sexual love and passionate losses of love, choices fortunate or disastrous, moments of death and scenes of mysterious encounters. The poet often enough tells us about the terrors of insomnia, of hauntings in the dark hours of the sleeping house, of sleepless, and often anguished vigils. Of course, we are all familiar with the complaints of the old: how often have we heard from them of their restless, light sleep, their nightly anguish and their confusions between what is long past, if not buried, and their patient, sometimes, bored, endurance of the tedium of each day, which may or may not be their last. What we seldom hear however, because so few of the old are poets, is their thoughts, the content of their long, dark lonely vigils.

In *Rumor Verified*, however, we can listen to a powerful and eloquent nature, a poet long-trained in self-observation and self-analysis, uttering his sorrow, and his ecstasy too. The sorrows of so many poems in this book came from his failure to be reconciled with the wrongs he himself committed, or from the long-buried and never-expiated guilts of a life full of passionate argument and action. Sometimes they are not exactly sorrows, but melancholies surrounded [by] the re-evocation of frights and terrors in boyhood, mysterious things that happened, that can be replayed in memory, but never changed or solved, accidents and encounters that must have marked his life and changed its course, somehow weaving themselves into the story of his life, but incomprehensibly. Such poems are confessions of the deepest anguish, although as puzzling to the poet, it seems, as to anyone else. In other words, Penn Warren is able to confess them because he sees them objectively, as belonging to someone himself yet no longer himself somehow. And the ecstasies come from remembered moments of triumph, of achievement, as, for example, a landscape spread out before him after an arduous hike or climb, or a scene of sexual climax that, remembered now, fills all the past and the present with meaning. There is, in short, a sequence of poems in this book in which good and evil, the ugly and the beautiful are mixed and tangled in such complex ways that even his careful meditation and analysis cannot solve, let alone *absolve*, the poet of his guilt and his grief. They do not, and cannot add up to what we sometimes hope a full life might reward us with: wisdom. The more Penn Warren knows the less comfort comes of it, and certainly less understanding, even of the difference between truth and vanity, illusion and revelation. But courage and honesty are required of us all—to the end, and that is what I believe Penn Warren is trying to show us. (pp. 1-3)

I hope that this poet will work on, because the pictures of himself offered in this new book are not yet completed, not everything has been said that he can say, and seems to be willing to say about himself and the world: one feels that the tensions surrounding this book like an aura of summer lighting remain undischarged. (p. 6)

Jascha Kessler, "Robert Penn Warren: 'Rumor Verified: Poems, 1979-1980'," in a radio broadcast on *KUSC-FM—Los Angeles, CA, March 31, 1982.*

PETER STITT

Robert Penn Warren is not so much a metaphorical writer, nor yet quite a symbolist, although his poetry does very much investigate the relationship between what we see and what we don't see, between objects and their significance, between events and their meaning. It would probably be most accurate to call him a mythic poet, for it is not so much the images of objects that signify in his work as it is the incidents, the stories, the happenings. What ultimately carries the meaning is the pattern of events, which is the way myth works. In *Rumor Verified* (as in all Warren's books) are poems which comment, directly or obliquely, on the poet's method. Toward the beginning of **"Minneapolis Story,"** for example, we find these lines: "every accident / Yearns to be more than itself, yearns, / / In the way you dumbly do, to participate / In the world's blind, groping rage toward meaning." He then goes on to tell a story that tends towards meaning, though precisely what meaning is never specified. Again, in the poem **"Twice Born,"** which tells of lightning striking a tree just outside the speaker's window and setting it afire, Warren theorizes: "all / At once, I knew. I knew / The storm, and all therewith, but as / A metaphor. / It was, I knew, / A metaphor for what, long back, I / Had undergone. I saw the fact of that." We are never told exactly what the earlier experience was—but again we see the doubling method, wherein understanding emerges from event.

The relationship between poetry and reality, poetry and event, is even more profoundly treated in a poem called **"The Corner of the Eye."** . . . (p. 191)

In terms of theme, this book is not very different from Warren's other recent volumes, though the emphasis has changed slightly. Warren remains a philosophical writer in search of the meaning of life, injecting sly metaphysical hints and undertones into many of his poems. But a contrary, earth-bound tendency is also at work: about the other world, the unseen world, there is no way to be certain, but about this world, the physical one we so solidly inhabit—of this one we can be sure. Thus the wisdom that Audubon arrives at in *Audubon: A Vision* is simply to "continue to walk in the world. Yes, love it!" *Being Here,* similarly, arrives at a profound appreciation for the significance of pure being. In *Rumor Verified,* the philosophical emphasis is upon the miracle of life within a basically inert, inanimate universe. Thus just living may be the most profoundly meaningful act, the deepest form (if you will) of prayer. This is the wisdom Warren arrives at in the volume's concluding poem, paradoxically entitled **"Fear and Trembling."** . . . The issue is a large and ancient one—the relation between language and reality. Warren turns it slightly by wondering about the language of nature as opposed to the language of man, asking at a middle stage in the argument if man couldn't do this nature's way: "Can one, in fact, meditate in the heart, rapt and word-less?" The poem concludes:

Can the heart's meditation wake us from life's long
    sleep,
And instruct us how foolish and fond was our labor
    spent—
Us who now know that only at death of ambition does
    the deep
Energy crack crust, spurt forth, and leap

From grottoes, dark—and from the caverned
    enchainment?

What this expresses is precisely a meditation implicit not in word but in action—or, for man, not in prayer but in pure essence of being. In enunciating such a stand, this book carries a theme generally present in Warren's work forward just far enough. It may be that *Rumor Verified* does not contain as many truly outstanding poems as some of Warren's earlier volumes do, but this is not to voice a significant criticism; the book still presents more excellent poems than most writers produce in a lifetime. (pp. 192-93)

> Peter Stitt, "Problems of Youth . . . and Age," in
> The Georgia Review, *Vol. XXXVI, No. 1, Spring,*
> *1982, pp. 184-93.**

FLOYD C. WATKINS

[*Watkins is an American professor of English and American literature who has written several books on Southern literature. Among his works are* The Literature of the South *(1952) and* Old Times in Faulkner Country *(1961), which he wrote with John B. Cullen. In addition, Watkins edited with John T. Hiers* Robert Penn Warren Talking *(1980), a collection of interviews with Warren. In the following excerpt taken from his book* Then & Now: The Personal Past in the Poetry of Robert Penn Warren *(1982), Watkins describes the autobiographical nature of Warren's poetry.*]

Besides Warren, no poet that I know of in the English language has written numerous poems that can be arranged to form a chronological account of much of the poet's life from youth to age. Tennyson perhaps did it, but always in a lyrical mode—never with clearly recognizable event and character. Some of Whitman's poems follow such a pattern in a loose fashion. Warren, however, has written poems that can be considered biographical not only about himself but also about his father, his mother, and his friend—or the poetic counterparts of these people. The biographical poems—much true and much imagined and designed—begin far back in talk and legend and proceed to the late moments of the poet's life in his most recent poems.

A number of complex structures simultaneously govern Warren's poetic accounts of his past. The interlockings of the poems are intricate. Within one poem there may be, for example, small parts designated with Arabic numbers; the small piece may be a section of a larger poem identified with a Roman numeral; the latter, in turn, may be part of a still larger work with a title to identify it. Warren writes some poems in "suites of three or four units." Even the titled long poem may be part of a book. Twenty-four separate poems are at once individual works and a unified book that Warren says in *Or Else—Poem/ Poems 1968-1974* "can be considered a long poem, or it can be considered a group of short poems." In the complexity of Warren's own organization of his poetry, it is possible to read the poems in many ways. All kinds of threads unify a single perspective in a diverse conglomerate.

The arrangement here is roughly chronological, beginning with the earliest events and proceeding to the poem about that latest event (or memory). All derives from Warren's personal or poetic past, springing from his childhood, proceeding to his poetic meditations at the time of the composition of the poem, and sometimes extending the subject of one poem into another piece written at a later date. One can follow the life of the father through three major poems, *Brother to Dragons* (the first extensive treatment in the poetry of any close member of Warren's family) to "**Mortmain**" to "**Reading Late at Night, Thermometer Falling.**" Ruth Warren, the mother, died many years before her husband. With the passing of time, she became less a factor in the poet's day-to-day thoughts. But she appears in the poems, and she is often portrayed in her relationships with other people around her, or in less detailed characterizations than the father. The intensity of the emotions—given the distance of time—may be less, but not a great deal, and her early death seems to be the reason for the blurring.

The brother and sister of Warren appear in random glimpses and brief scenes or actions, never with characterizations in depth. Early in her young womanhood the sister, Mary, seems to have separated herself from the family, and she hovers as a remembered child over the poems but never as a living figure. Thomas was only nine years old when Warren went to Clarksville, and brothers separated by several years seem to develop close relationships only after a few decades have passed. Yet in many of the poems Thomas is there as a significant and silent figure, never speaking. Warren has said in his essay on Jefferson Davis and in personal letters that he and Thomas sit together, hunt together, and visit in silence—communicating deeply but without words.

Along with the Warrens and the members of the family of Grandfather Penn, one other person emerges intimately from the personal past—a silent friend, Kent Greenfield, star baseball player, hunter and fisherman, drunk, but a kindly child and a gentle man, who spoke with an old fashioned gentility. He first appears as the protagonist in a short story, "**Goodwood Comes Back**," but he is also in a marvelously inexplicable vignette when he kills a goose in *Brother to Dragons*. In *Now and Then* Warren writes a poem of broad reference, "**American Portrait: Old Style**"; the portrait is of Kent. A trip home usually meant a short visit to Kent, and a reminiscence of childhood and Guthrie in Warren's writings often contains an allusion to that boyhood playmate. In the essay on Jefferson Davis (1980) Robert and Thomas stand not only at the graves of their parents but also at the grave of Kent.

Moving through the narrative and meditations on intimates of Guthrie days is the character of Warren himself. He has written as many narrative poems as any major American poet. A Southerner, he is a born and bred and practicing teller of tales. But he is also one of the most explicitly meditative and lyrical poets in America, one of the most personal. He mixes his meditations on those close to him with overviews of the entire range of American history.

Though these autobiographical poems are not formally linked, no one of them can be fully appreciated in isolation. With sufficient annotation and explication, one might work out T. S. Eliot's "Mr. Eliot's Sunday Morning Service" for himself so that he might come to understand what happens as the persona sits in his pew and contemplates the actions of the priests and Sweeney in his bath. The poem does not require a knowledge of Eliot's religious beliefs and his biography. But that is not true of "**Mortmain,**" because it involves Warren's actual father, the father in other poems, the father in the course of nearly a century of American history, the father as a meditator and even a would-be poet himself, and the diverse moods and meditations of Warren as son and as poet on the subject of his father.

A traditional poet may become intensely engaged in an attempt to penetrate the unfathomable past in a search for historical truth so far as it can be known. A descendant of an ancient New England family, Warren's friend Robert Lowell (an admirer of the Fugitives—especially of Allen Tate) has elaborately studied his heritage in such poems as ''The Quaker Graveyard in Nantucket'' and ''For the Union Dead.'' But the relevance of Lowell's past for the poet's present is generally left mysterious, certainly not clearly stated by Lowell himself. Warren's fellow Fugitive, Tate, pursues the past, its meanings, and the search for self-assurance as strenuously and relentlessly as any modern poet. His poems go back to the origins of human awareness and consciousness (''The Wolves''), back to the classical past and relevance of the ancients especially to the modern South (''The Mediterranean,'' ''Aeneas at Washington''), and to the American past, which just might supply a meaning necessary for a poet who can define neither his world nor himself (''The Ancestors,'' ''Mother and Son''). As a rule Tate and Ransom write about their ancestors in their poems, but not about their parents.

Warren's poetry about his personal and family past, on the other hand, is extensive and detailed. He writes about himself, his parents, and his grandparents. Grandfather Penn talks about American history, especially the Civil War. The poet looks with his grandfather's and his own perspectives on the ancient American past. They arrive at decisions about the meaning of the world, and the absence of them. (pp. 122-26)

The time span—from just after the Civil War perhaps until the moment when Warren's pen is stilled—is less extensive than the saga of Faulkner. But, as poetry, they are more compact, even than Faulkner. At first glance, Warren seems to explicate his own writing, even to moralize, but lasting contemplation produces statements, concrete and abstract, general and specific, as puzzling as the contents of that unopened box under the Christmas tree. The connections between Warren's poems have never been explicitly stated in his volumes of poetry; they may only be deduced by a reader or a critic. Nevertheless they assume a unity from the singularity of the life of the poet, from a consistent tone and subject matter, from progressions of chronology in the lives of a family and a nation, and from the meaning of an endless and insatiable thirst for knowledge and search for truth. To treat the poems as something of a unit, as here, is unquestionably a momentary violation of the unity of each distinct work of art and, perhaps, sometimes of the whole body of Warren's work. They are like, say, an experimental and looseleaf French novel. However the pages are shuffled and ordered, they come out with oneness as well as separateness. The intentional fallacy may work (or fail) from two perspectives. If one cannot measure a work by the author's intent, he also cannot deny the truth though it was not conscious or intended. Thus literature is pervaded by the unintentional truth as much as criticism is by the intentional fallacy. That truth in the separate poems about Warren's family, his friend, and his self is a unity of spiritual search.

Robert Penn Warren is a major poet by any standard—perhaps even a prophet in some meanings of the word. (pp. 168-69)

In the family and community poems . . . , Warren has created a complex and extensive world. No American author seems to have started out with a design for the creation of his own literary community in several works, but many there are who have persistently developed works about their cultures and their places. Warren's people—even in this imaginary Kentucky community without a name—derive from and represent a world as recognizably Warren's as Yoknapatawpha is Faulkner's or Winesburg, Ohio, is Anderson's. The community exists in Warren's poetic works, although neither poet nor critic can pinpoint the time when he came to recognize its existence.

The poetic chronicle of Warren's family has a scope of more than a hundred years, not less than the time span of the Gant (or Webber) and Sartoris and Compson families or of the political and literary sagas of the Lowells and the Adamses. The joys and sorrows of the Penns and the Warrens are created with lyrical intensity and with national and historical implications.

What Faulkner was perhaps groping for when he wrote *Flags in the Dust* is reflected in a different form in Warren's poems of the personal and community past.

The community past and the family past give the poems a texture different from that usually found in the fiction. The poems about the past reveal that the deep feelings almost always concealed beneath the hard exteriors of the narrators in Warren's best novels are indeed related to the personal and lyrical feelings of the poet.

In the diverse poems, the dominant theme seems to be the desire to know. The effectiveness of this motif is due in part to its final failure. There are moments of joy and even of reconcilement, but one cannot achieve ultimate joy in the labor of the frontier, the relationships of the family, the completeness of knowledge, and the beauties of art, or in the knowledge of the amazing grace of personal or religious salvation. (pp. 169-70)

> *Floyd C. Watkins, in his* Then & Now: The Personal Past in the Poetry of Robert Penn Warren, *The University Press of Kentucky, 1982, 184 p.*

JOHN BOENING

Robert Penn Warren has established an astonishing pace in his recent output of poems, and just when we reviewers, nearly breathless, think we've caught up with the old fellow, out comes another book [**Rumor Verified: Poems 1979-1980**]. . . . One's first reaction to each new collection is awe: not only in the face of Warren's prodigious energy, but also awe at his range, his virtuosity and his capacity for the integration of experience and sagacity. For the reviewer playing catch-up, however—or for the admiring reader trying to get and keep a grip on the themes and images which move through Warren's recent work—these rapid-fire collections are not all joy to deal with. For one thing, there is hardly time to savor the pleasures of rereading, rethinking and reevaluating one cluster of poems before another collection alters, modifies or tempers the canon, before we must read an earlier poem through a later one. A more disorienting (if it weren't all such dizzy fun, one would say disturbing) feature of these recent volumes is that they overlap in time of composition; in the case of some individual poems there is even overlap in the dates of original publication. An image one thought was isolated turns out to have been used in a whole group of poems; a theme, a ''concern,'' a line of development becomes blurred. . . . (p. 110)

All that and its attendant frustration out of the way, a reviewer can still praise famous men. Many of the poems in **Rumor**

Verified are of a quality equal to the best of Warren's recent work. A few, including the title poem, are not. The most arresting are still those which combine an almost biblical diction and cadence (or is it a Southern diction and cadence?) with the names of natural things and the (seeming) informality of a country conversation. The four poems in the cycle "Glimpses of Seasons" are gems of this order. **"Snow Out of Season"** and **"Redwing Blackbirds"** especially; so are the poems of **"Paradox of Time."** The opening pieces, two poems set in/ on a Mediterranean world that seems strangely both younger and older than its geography, are difficult and somewhat opaque; they would be mythopoetic, but the allusions seem elusive, or mingled in mysterious ways. The coda, a poem called **"Fear and Trembling,"** is, by contrast, too outspoken, too translucent. A stronger, more representative coda would have been the one preceding it, **"Afterward,"** which particularizes, as only Warren's strong poems can, the pincer-press of mortality and morality. (p. 111)

John Boening, in a review of "Rumor Verified: Poems, 1979-1980," in World Literature Today, *Vol. 57, No. 1, Winter, 1983, pp. 110-11.*

SEAN WILENTZ

> As my grandfather said, there were only two
> benefits of modernity. One was fly screens, and
> the other was painless dentistry, and I think he
> was right.
>
> —Robert Penn Warren

American historians have ceased to be poets; long ago, they broke W. H. Auden's commandment: Thou shalt not commit a social science! More irksome still, American poets have ceased to be historians. The great exception is Robert Penn Warren.

Warren has written 10 novels, 15 volumes of poetry, and nine nonfiction books; the antimodernist passion behind this prodigious output provokes ambivalence. On one side is Warren's shrewdness about the tricks of historical memory and his profound critique of capitalism's moral and material destructiveness; on the other, his utter condemnation of "modernity" mixed with a kind of grim fatalistic irony. It's a combination that can be pretty discouraging. But Warren has become a stronger poet as he's gotten older: now nearly 80, he can suffer contradictions in himself and the rest of the world, revise his opinions, and still look for truths. *Chief Joseph of the Nez Perce,* a vivid 64-page narrative, restates Warren's lifelong concerns with history, memory, and irony, and contains some of his biggest surprises yet.

Modern America, with its peculiar mixture of self-interest and squander, was born in 1877. In the South, a political deal removed the last federal troops, ended Reconstruction, killed the hopes of a generation of blacks, radicals, and reformers. In the North, labor disputes along the railways turned into the first mass strike in our history, a literal insurrection. (The troops called in to crush the strike included some of those taken from the South.) Meanwhile, in eastern Montana, the U.S. Army, under the command of General O. O. Howard (late head of the Freedmen's Bureau in the South), finally tracked down Chief Joseph and his band of Nez Perce. Warren has chosen his subject wisely; shifting the locale from his native South, he has found a web of historical circumstances well suited to his Jeffersonian instincts.

Joseph's was one of the saddest chapters in the brutal history of subjugation that had turned vicious with Jackson's persecution of the Cherokees and would end in 1890 with the Wounded Knee massacre. Breaking an 1855 treaty and an 1873 presidential agreement, the government ordered Joseph's band to the reservation. Joseph did not understand the settlers' eagerness: "For all things live, and live in their nature, / But what is the nature of gold?" The Nez Perce, unaccustomed to war, sent out a white flag, which was met by a bullet. . . .

For three months, Chief Joseph and his people evaded capture, in a masterpiece of maneuver. In September, ill, hungry, and outnumbered, they gave up. Joseph delivered his famous surrender, "I will fight no more forever." General Howard allowed a subordinate to set the terms, which turned out surprisingly generous—but the agreement proved unacceptable to military brass and was scrapped. The last of the Nez Perce left for the reservation. The man giving the orders was the Commanding General of the U.S. Army, William Tecumseh Sherman—whose name bore tribute to a slaughtered Indian warrior. In captivity, Joseph became something of an American hero, according to the fashion of the Gilded Age. . . .

Joseph died on the reservation in 1904—the death certificate said of a broken heart. He remained a fabled figure, but Warren sees through the accolades with a Southerner's knowledge of defeat and hypocrisy: "Great honor came, for it came to pass / That to praise the red man was the way / Best adapted to expunge all, all, in the mist / Of bloodless myth."

Thus far, the poem is classic Warren, in the Romantic style of his recent work but with a twist. The obliteration of a precapitalist agrarian order by the blue-bellies and the greedy, the treachery of the victor's myths, irony after irony in the legacy of the Civil War—all are classic Warren themes. The twist is in the subject. Maybe now that Warren is writing about the Indians and not the Confederacy, Yankee critics can better understand (without condoning) the conservative agrarian Warren of the '20s and '30s, and better appreciate the writer Warren has become. No apologist for slavery or racism, he's more like a genuine but disillusioned upcountry Populist, saddened by America's course since the Civil War but tempered by 20th-century fears of unintended consequences and by a deep pessimism about the prospects for change.

Warren's big surprise comes when he tells of his pilgrimage to Joseph's monument at Snake Creek. He saw, as all tourists do, the plains' vastness, thought once again of the "squirming myriads" at his back:

> But suddenly knew that for those
> sound
> Of heart there is no ultimate
> Irony. There is only
> Process, which is one name for
> history. Often
> Pitiful. But sometimes, under
> The scrutinizing prism of Time,
> Triumphant.

In an instant the awesome ironies dissolve—the pessimistic, immobilizing ironies that spelled the end of an older idealism to Warren, as well as to a generation of fiercely modernist historians who came of age during the political traumas of the 1940s and '50s. To be sure, there is no absolute Good or Evil, even in this grotesque saga: Warren makes it clear that to imagine otherwise is as dangerous as it is foolhardy. But all does not end in ambiguity and irony, as one might expect from a Warren poem; the victory of what he calls modernity is not so overwhelming or one-sided that we are left only with grave laments and wry jokes about fly screens and laughing gas. In Joseph's story, and in the myriads of eternity, we can find the strivings and conflicts of the once-defeated, a living presence.

And, perhaps, we can find more, not all of it to our liking. Warren the antimodernist is still troublesome. The stubborn, truly traditionalist features of Warren's sensibility persist in *Chief Joseph,* his veneration of fatherly authority, his rage at modern life. Yet there is also much that inspires: apart from the poetic vindication of Joseph, there is Warren's vision of historical change—a vision not of some flight from "modernity," but of a retrieval of the more humane virtues of an earlier (and in some ways nobler) civilization, as part of a continuing development.

With this vision, and with the end of irony, it is possible to find some courage for the future. All master civilizations, all great empires have considered themselves the culmination of history, after which would come the barbaric deluge. Such claims by today's masters, East and West, are more persuasive and terrifying than any that have come before. But if history can be called process, if like Warren we can still see Chief Joseph in our own hearts and minds, then history may not be over after all.

> *Sean Wilentz, "The End of Irony," in* The Village Voice, *Vol. XXVIII, No. 40, October 4, 1983, p. 57.*

CAROLYN KIZER

[*Kizer is an American poet and the founder of the literary journal* Poetry Northwest, *which she edited from 1959 to 1965. Her works, which include* The Ungrateful Garden *(1960),* Midnight Was My Cry: New and Selected Poems *(1971), and* Yin *(1984), often focus on the settings and themes of the northwestern United States and take a radical political stance. In the following excerpt Kizer denounces the language Warren attributes to the Indian chief in* Chief Joseph of the Nez Perce.]

Robert Penn Warren is full of years, and honors and great works, so it pains me to have to say that [*Chief Joseph of the Nez Perce*] is a mistake. Perhaps I take more than usual umbrage here, because Mr. Warren is writing about my Northwest and my Indians. Chief Joseph was only a shade less eloquent than Chief Sealth (Seattle). . . .

Mr. Warren writes his poem from Joseph's point of view. Unfortunately, the language he puts in the great chief's mouth sounds more like Tonto than Cicero. Two painful quotes to show what I mean:

> But what is the nature of gold?
>
> In the deepest dark what vision may find it?
> On its stone-bed of vision what secret name be divulged?
> If it could dance in the name-dance, what
> Name would gold dance. Would it be—
> 'Death-that-in-the-darkness-comes-smiling'?
>
> Or is it man's nature this thing not to know?

And here Joseph waxes philosophic again, 40 pages later:

> but what is a man? An autumn-tossed aspen,
> Pony-fart in the wind, the melting of snow-slush?
> Yes, that is all. Unless—unless—
> We can learn to live the Great Spirit's meaning . . .

Mr. Warren's impulses in writing this poem were clearly all of the best, and, one honors him for them. But, oh, I wish he hadn't done it! Ugh. I have spoken.

> *Carolyn Kizer, in a review of "Chief Joseph of the Nez Perce Who Called Themselves the Nimipu 'The Real People'," in* Book Week—The Washington Post, *November 13, 1983, p. 8.*

ROBERT PETERS

I would like to say that [*Chief Joseph of the Nez Perce*] is a noble failure. Certainly the tragic history of Chief Joseph and his people, of their betrayals and decimations at the hands of the U.S. Grant administration, has the scope of an epic. Warren's treatment, alas, is ill-felt, ill-thought-out, and ill-executed. In his favor (and he is almost an octogenerian, and has won just about every literature prize going, plus others invented for him), he is on the right side: he ennobles, if meekly, the great chief. And there are moments when the writing manages a brief splendor. Let me be specific.

Warren floats over this turbulent history, giving the barest hints of events. He assumes his image of an eagle (borrowed from Tennyson?), adrift in the sky, casting its glance over the immense landscape. He sails too swiftly to take in much that transpires on the ground. Superficialities abound. The Indian mind is cluttered with cliches about forked tongues, Great White Fathers, and commonplace flora and fauna. When Warren seeks to encompass the white mind (he zings from one figure to another, like a bee taking small sips before buzzing off), he imagines the most obvious preoccupations of that mind— much as comicbook figures would think them. And the very last section of the book is a disaster. Warren moves to 1981, when he visits the site near Snake Creek where many of the Nez Perce died, leaves a pair of friends and their Honda behind, and peregrinates off to find a "vision." The vision of Chief Joseph he pretends to seems entirely manufactured: "in fanatic imagination," Warren resorts to quasi-primitive talk: "I see lips move, but / No sound hear." The abstractions (they are a pustulance throughout) betray his forcings: "I saw," he continues, "Vastness of plains lifting in twilight for / Winter's cold kiss, its absoluteness."

Warren's fatigued imagination also mars his language. His Indians speak a mix of verse reminiscent of Longfellow and Tennyson (with an occasional Transcendental sentiment tossed in from Emerson and Thoreau). They are fond of the archly literary periodic line, viz., "We touch not the locks of the honored dead"; "There, southward, a steel pipe, / With marker screwed on, defines the spot / Of the tepee of Joseph." . . . (pp. 3-4)

We never see, taste, hear, smell the crucial battle; we are given, instead, an alliterative line suitable for a typing exercise manual.

Another of Warren's unhappy devices is that of including cut-out moments from histories and communiques. These serve as transitions and excuse Warren from the demanding chore of writing transitions himself. The effect is deadening—too often the uninspired verses seem merely repetitions of the prose. A recurring theme is "manhood," another simplification, I think, about the Indian mind. Perhaps what Warren is really writing about is the lessoning of his own manhood via aging. And he dedicates the book to James Dickey, the manliest man-poet of us all.

Warren's poem will undoubtedly be praised by adulators. But I can't imagine Simon Ortiz, Wendy Rose, Joy Harjo, or a host of other Native American writers will be pleased at seeing their magnificent history reduced to cardboard, to coloring-book history. I can see *Chief Joseph* adapted by some junior high school class, as a pageant; I can't see it inspiring many dedicated poetry readers. And I may be trashed for daring to write so negatively about so revered an American institution as Warren. (p. 4)

Robert Peters, in a review of "Chief Joseph of the Nez Perce," in The American Book Review, *Vol. 6, No. 1, November-December, 1983, pp. 3-4.*

MICHIKO KAKUTANI

"We shall come back, no doubt, to walk down the Row and watch young people on the tennis courts by the clump of mimosas and walk down the beach by the bay," Robert Penn Warren wrote in *All the King's Men.* "But that will be a long time from now, and soon now we shall go out of the house and go into the convulsion of the world, out of history into history and the awful responsibility of Time."

Published back in 1946, those beautifully resonant final words, with their delicate echoes of Milton's *Paradise Lost,* would not only sum up the preoccupations of Mr. Warren's most famous novel, but they would also delineate the ongoing concerns of his poetry, both early and late: man's exile from Edenic innocence; his groping search for knowledge and love; and his attempts, as a creature caught in history and the particular excesses of this "maniacal century," to connect time present with time past.

As this splendid new selection [*New and Selected Poems: 1923-1985*]—which includes such early classics as **"Bearded Oaks"** and **"Original Sin: A Short Story,"** as well as a generous helping of recent work—so vigorously demonstrates, Mr. Warren remains one of our pre-eminent poets, a poet blessed with a passionate moral intelligence and a huge abundance of verbal gifts. By turns lyrical and plain-spoken, earthy and cerebral, Mr. Warren writes with the fluency of a great, instinctive talker: he seems equally at home with the narrative story-poem (**"The Ballad of Billie Potts," "Rattlesnake Country"** and **"New Dawn,"** to name a few, are as dense with incident, character and landscape as any naturalistic novel), and more abstract, philosophical verse. He can use the sound and pacing of words to achieve sensuous, musical effects. . . .

Although he occasionally invokes awkward and willfully poetic terms—words like "orchidaceous," "marmoreal" and "gracility" tend to be more distracting to the reader than evocative—Mr. Warren possesses a wonderful ability to smoothly transit the gap between the down-home, just-folks vernacular of his native South and the more allusive, self-consciously literary language of traditional British-American poetry. He mixes up allusions to Shakespeare, Eliot and Auden with references to folk ballads and old Kentucky tales, and peoples his poems with characters ranging from Tiberius, Elijah and Gibbon to "Laughing Boy" and "Dollie-May."

Whatever form or historical back-drop they happen to employ, Mr. Warren's poems almost always return to that central myth of man's expulsion from the Garden, his fall into a world subject to death and the wasting effects of time. It is a violent, dangerous world that Mr. Warren's characters inhabit: rattlesnakes lie in wait, for the helpless infant, on the lovely green lawn; a pheasant flies, pell-mell, into an oncoming car, spattering the windshield with blood; a gunshot rings out, and someone, animal or human, lies dying in the dark. Sometimes, the evils is momentous—a bomb, waiting to be dropped over Hiroshima—but more often, the loss of innocence is ordinary, mundane; a child speaks a harsh word to his mother and realizes the terrible ambiguities of love, or two old friends meet and discover that time has whirled them, forever, apart.

Mostly, the terror that Mr. Warren's poems investigate has to do with our existence in the world of nature, a world that often feels "God-abandoned" or at least indifferent to our little problems, and in the end, profoundly unknowable—inaccessible to understanding. "The heart cries out for coherence," Mr. Warren writes in **"Tale of Time,"** but while man spends his days trying to discover the secret logic of the world, he is granted, at best, only glimpses—moments "non-sequential and absolute"—of God's master blueprint. Like half-remembered fragments from a dream, reality gleams, glitters and is gone, eluding the grasp of imagination, and leaving us unsure of our place in "nature's flow and perfection."

Mr. Warren's characters often seem amazed by the speed with which their lives unspool. They have difficulty connecting the child they were with the person they are today, and they labor to come to terms with the losses—of friends, of children, of physical vigor—that the passing years have brought. Some, as Southerners, seek parallels between their own lost youth and the faded glory of their homeland; others find reminders of their own mortality in everything from the downward flow of a river to the yellowing of old newspaper pages. For them, even memory proves an insufficient tool for holding on to the swiftly receding past.

In the later poems, particularly, there are recurrent images of aging and death—the word "dark" is used so many times it becomes a kind of refrain—and a sense of regret is expressed over "nameless promises unkept, in undefinable despair." Still, the poet's faith in the world's "tangled and hieroglyphic beauty" never diminishes, and he can end by embracing the limitations of man's condition, the fullness of our nature "for good and for evil," the fact that we are "only ourselves," "only human."

Just as his hero in **"Audubon: A Vision"**—the famous naturalist, portrayed as a sort of American Adam, who exchanges radical innocence for knowledge of love and evil—earns a kind of final redemption, Mr. Warren, too, appears to achieve a sense of grace, a wondrous, hard-won acceptance of the "human bumble and grind." "I love the world even in my anger," he writes in **"American Portrait: Old Style."** "And that's a hard thing to outgrow."

Michiko Kakutani, in a review of "New and Selected Poems: 1923-1985," in The New York Times, *April 24, 1985, p. C19.*

WILLIAM H. PRITCHARD

> From the deep and premature midnight
> Of woodland, I hear the first whip-o-will's
> Precious grief, and my young heart,
> As darkling I stand, yearns for a grief
> To be worthy of that sound.

These lines are from Robert Penn Warren's **"Boyhood in Tobacco Country,"** a poem originally published in his *Being Here: Poetry 1977-1980,* and one of many that readers will find missing from Mr. Warren's [*New and Selected Poems: 1923-1985*].... Ten years ago, when his [*Selected Poems: 1923-1975*] appeared, the pruning of earlier volumes was evident, but the losses did not seem so prominent: generous samples were still present from such earlier books of the 1950's and 60's as *Promises*, *You, Emperors, and Others*, *Tale of Time* and *Incarnations*. Now, the 165 pages representing these poems in the volume of 10 years ago have been trimmed to 50, and the trimming has not been confined merely to those poems Mr. Warren wrote two and three decades ago. Recent volumes, such as *Now and Then*, *Being Here* and *Rumor Verified*, many of whose poems have been highly admired by reviewers eager—like Harold Bloom and Stanley Plumly—to assert the preeminence of Mr. Warren's later poetry, have also met the axe. One looks in vain in the new book for **"Speleology," "No Bird Does Call," "Passers By on a Snowy Night," "Vermont Thaw"** and **"Millpond Lost,"** just to mention some of the ones I had put checks next to when encountered in their original habitats.

The "New and Selected Poems" idea, with the new poems placed first and the selection of previous work following them, has been, I think, a fairly recent publishing phenomenon (there was no "New and Selected" Wordsworth or Browning), and in Mr. Warren's case it is worth attending to for two reasons. First, because it teases us into wondering whether the stern winnowing he has performed is merely at the behest of exigency (his publisher wants the book to stay under 350 pages), or whether and to what extent it represents an act of critical discrimination designed to indicate an oeuvre: *these*, at the age of 80, are the poems on which I make my claim as a poet. Second, because the new poems in this volume (the section titled "Altitudes and Extensions") occupy roughly a quarter of it, and all date from the last five years. Could it be, the skeptic might wonder, that Mr. Warren upon entering his ninth decade has been bemused by his most recent work, to the extent of critically misrepresenting himself?

The answer to the skeptic's question seems to me to be decidedly no, even though my acquaintance with these new poems has been of relatively short duration. But from the very first one in the book—a tripartite piece titled **"Three Darknesses"**—one is engaged by a voice that is wonderfully expressive, as first it remembers watching a bear at the zoo in Rome (surely Mr. Warren has more bears—and not just metaphysical ones—in his poems than any other American poet)

> ... big as a grizzly, erect, inde-
> structible,
> Unforgiving as God, as rhythmic
> as
> A pile-driver—right-left, right-left
> Slugged at an iron door.

The bear, so the speaker eventually decides, is trying to enter into darkness, into a cave containing "the darkness of wisdom." Later, in the poem's third section, a man, a "You" (often a stand-in for R.P.W.) lies in the darkness of his hospital room, thinking about the "trivial" operation he is to undergo in the morning:

> A dress rehearsal,
> You tell yourself, for
> The real thing. Later, Ten years? Fifteen?

In this darkness (is it of wisdom?) he reaches out and flicks on the television to an "old-fashioned western" where "Winchester fire flicks white in the dream-night." Both the bear in

his pile-driving actions and the man flat on his back in the grip of thoughts are helplessly doing what they have to do, and Mr. Warren gives them to us without a hint of condescension or pity.

One notes that this opening poem establishes contours of altitudes and declensions, light and darkness, to be met more than once in the volume. Yet, as with so much of Mr. Warren's recent verse, what fascinates him and his readers is (in the language of **"Rattlesnake Country,"** a poem of 10 years back that has survived) "The compulsion to try to convert what now is *was* / Back into what was *is*." This compulsion can be seen from titles like **"Old-Time Childhood in Kentucky"** and **"Reinterment: Recollections of a Grandfather,"** or by the question asked in **"Covered Bridge."** ... These moments I judge to be Mr. Warren at his finest, converting "was" into the "is" of presence, the present. (p. 8)

Other things from the past, like the whistle of the 3 A.M. train, or a youthful picnic, or listening to a coyote howl in the Arizona night, are summoned into presence through accurately rendered sensations and the urgency of Mr. Warren's demanding voice.

In his published interviews he quotes his old student Randall Jarrell's insistence about being a poet, that "You've got to be there when the rain hits you." As in his title *Being Here*, Mr. Warren has persisted in being here and there, very much out in the rain, for the six decades spanned by this new book. Along with Jarrell, he seems to me pre-eminently our poet of fierce nostalgia, of a driven, often harsh desire to convert past into present. Yet as the new poems demonstrate, he is no one-note dweller on remembrance: **"Mortal Limit"** shows the visionary-metaphysical singer; the long and remarkably successful **"New Dawn"** converts the excruciating and delicate details of the bombing of Hiroshima into a gripping piece of writing; while **"After the Dinner Party,"** my now-favorite poem of Mr. Warren's, gives us a couple sitting late at the dinner table, drinking the last of the wine after the guests have long gone and the logs burn down. One hand reaches out for the other, as they speak of "the absent children, whose bright gaze / Over-arches the future's horizon." Finally it is time to make an end:

> The last log is black, while ash beneath displays
> No last glow. You snuff candles. Soon the old stairs
> Will creak with your grave and synchronized tread as
> each mounts
> To a briefness of light, then true weight of darkness,
> and then
> That heart-dimness in which neither joy nor sorrow
> counts.
> Even so, one hand gropes out for another, again.

(p. 10)

William H. Pritchard, "The Past in the Present Tense," in The New York Times Book Review, *May 12, 1985, pp. 8-10.*

HAROLD BLOOM

[*Bloom is a prominent contemporary American critic and literary theorist. In* The Anxiety of Influence (1973), *Bloom formulated a controversial theory of literary creation called revisionism. Influenced strongly by Freudian theory, which states that "all men unconsciously wish to beget themselves, to be their own fathers," Bloom believes that all poets are subject to the influence of earlier poets and that, to develop their own voice, they attempt to overcome this influence through a process of misreading. By misreading, Bloom means a deliberate, personal revision of what has been said by another so that it conforms to one's own vision. In this way the poet creates a singular voice, overcoming the fear of being inferior to poetic predecessors. Bloom's later books are applications of this theory, extended in* Kabbalah and Criticism *(1974) to include the critic or reader as another deliberate misreader. In addition to his theoretical work, Bloom is one of the foremost authorities on English Romantic poetry and has written widely on the influences of Romanticism in contemporary literature. In the following excerpt taken from a review of Warren's* New and Selected Poems, *Bloom examines Warren's evolution as a poet, praising the intensity and durability of Warren's works.]*

Robert Penn Warren, born April 24, 1905, in Guthrie, Kentucky, is at the age of eighty our most eminent man of letters. His position is the more remarkable for the extraordinary persistence with which he has made himself into a superb poet. A reader thinks of the handful of poets who wrote great poetry late in life: Browning, Hardy, Yeats, Stevens, Warren. Indeed, **"Myth of Mountain Sunrise,"** the final poem among the new work in [*New and Selected Poems: 1923-1985*], will remind some readers of Browning's marvelous "Prologue" to *Asolando,* written when the poet was seventy-seven. . . .

The epigraph to the new section of this [*New and Selected Poems*] is from Warren's favorite theologian, St. Augustine: "Will ye not now after that life is descended down to you, will not you ascend up to it and live?" One remembers another epigraph Warren took from the *Confessions,* for the book of poems **Being Here** (1980): "I thirst to know the power and nature of time." At eighty Warren now writes out of that knowledge, and his recent poems show him ascending up to living in the present, in the presence of time's cumulative power. Perhaps no single new poem here quite matches the extraordinary group of visions and meditations in his previous work that includes **"Red-Tail Hawk and Pyre of Youth," "Heart of Autumn," "Evening Hawk," "Birth of Love," "The Leaf," "Mortmain," "To a Little Girl, One Year Old, in a Ruined Fortress,"** and so many more. But the combined strength of the eighty-five pages of new poems that Warren aptly calls "Altitudes and Extensions" is remarkable, and extends the altitudes at which perhaps our last poet to attempt the ultimate questions of life and death continues to live and work. (p. 40)

Warren's poetry began in the modernist revival of the metaphysical poets, as a kind of blend of Eliot's *The Waste Land* with the gentler ironies of Warren's teacher at Vanderbilt, John Crowe Ransom. This phase of the poetry took Warren up to 1943, and then came to an impasse and, for a decade, an absolute stop. *At Heaven's Gate, All the King's Men,* and *World Enough and Time* belong to that decade of poetic silence, and perhaps the major sequence of his fiction usurped Warren's greater gift. But he was certainly unhappy in the later stages of his first marriage, which ended in divorce in 1950, and it cannot be accidental that his poetry fully resumed in the late summer of 1954, two years after his marriage to the writer Eleanor Clark.

The book-length poem, *Brother to Dragons* (1953, revised version 1979), formally began Warren's return to verse, and is undoubtedly a work of considerable dramatic power. I confess to admiring it only reluctantly and dubiously, ever since 1953, because its ideological ferocity is unsurpassed even elsewhere in Warren. This ferocity is manifested by its implicit assertion that Thomas Jefferson is somehow affected by the barbaric act of his nephews in butchering a black slave. Much improved in revision, it remains unnerving, particularly if the reader, like myself, longs to follow Emerson in forgiving himself, if

not everything, then at least as much as possible. But Warren— unlike Emerson—does not wish us to cast out remorse. Like his then master, Eliot, though in a more secular way, Warren was by no means reluctant to remind us that we *are* original sin. **Brother to Dragons** is rendered no weaker by its extraordinary tendentiousness, but it is not necessarily persuasive, if you happen not to share its moral convictions.

Warren's shorter poems, his lyrics and meditations, evolve impressively through three subsequent volumes: *Promises* (1957), *You, Emperors and Others* (1960), and [*Selected Poems: New and Old, 1923-1966*] (1966), where the new work was grouped as "Tale of Time." I recall purchasing these volumes, reading them with grudging respect, and concluding that Warren was turning into a poet rather like Melville (whom he was to edit in a *Selected Poems of Herman Melville,* in 1971) or the younger Hardy. Warren's poems of 1934 through 1966 seemed interestingly ungainly in form, highly individual in genre and rhetoric, and not fundamentally a departure from Eliot's high modernist mode. A poetry of moral belief, with some of the same preoccupations as the *Four Quartets,* I would have judged it, rather dismissively, and not of overwhelming concern if a reader was devoted to Hart Crane and Wallace Stevens. Such a reader would also have preferred contemporary volumes like Elizabeth Bishop's *Questions of Travel* (1965) and John Ashbery's *Rivers and Mountains* (1966), which were in the poetic tradition of Crane and Stevens, of visionary skepticism rather than Eliot's poetry of belief in the "truth," whether moral or religious. I could not foresee the astonishing breakthrough that Warren, already past the age of sixty, was about to accomplish with *Incarnations* (1968) and *Audubon: A Vision* (1969).

Other critics of Warren's poetry see more continuity in its development than I do. But in 1968 I was a belated convert, transported against my will by reading *Incarnations,* and able at least to offer the testimony of a very reluctant believer in his poetic strength, a strength maintained by Warren throughout these nearly two decades since he began to write the poems of *Incarnations* in 1966.

Incarnations opens with a closely connected sequence of fifteen poems called "Island of Summer," which is the volume's glory. Unfortunately, Warren has included only five of these in his [*New and Selected Poems: 1923-1985*], but they are the best of a strong group, and I will discuss only those five here, since Warren subtly has created a new sequence or a condensed "Island of Summer." Like the original work, the sequence is a drama of poetic incarnation, or the death and rebirth of Warren as a poet. In what is now the opening meditation, **"Where the Slow Fig's Purple Sloth,"** Warren associates the fig with fallen human consciousness and so with an awareness of mortality:

> When you
> Split the fig, you will see
> Lifting from the coarse and purple
> seed, its
> Flesh like flame, purer
> Than blood.
>
> It fills
> The darkening room with light.

This hard, riddling style is now characteristic and has very little in common with the evocations of Eliot in his earlier verse. **"Riddle in the Garden"** even more oddly associates fruits, peach and plum, with negative human yearnings, suicidal and painful; with a horror of inwardness. A violent confrontation, **"The Red Mullet,"** juxtaposes the swimming poet and the great fish, eye to eye, in a scene where "vision is armor, he sees and does not / Forgive." In a subsequent vision of **"Masts at Dawn,"** the optical effect of how: "The masts go white slow, as light, like dew, from darkness / Condensed on them" leads to what in some other poet might be a moment of illumination, but here becomes a rather desperate self-admonition, less ironic than it sounds: "We must try / To love so well the world that we may believe, in the end, in God." This reversed Augustinianism is a prelude to a burst of Warren's poetic powers in the most ambitious poem he had yet written, **"The Leaf."**

When he was fifteen, Warren was blinded in one eye by a sharp stone playfully thrown by a younger brother, who did not see that Warren was lying down on the other side of a hedge. Only after graduating from Vanderbilt did Warren get around to having the ruined eye removed and replaced by a glass eye. Until then, the young poet suffered the constant fear of sympathetic blindness in his good eye. There may be some complex relation between that past fear and Warren's remarkable and most prevalent metaphor of redemption, which is to associate poetic vision both with a hawk's vision and with a sunset hawk's flight. This metaphor has appeared with increasing frequency in Warren's poetry for more than half a century, and even invades the novels. (pp. 40-1)

"The Leaf" centers upon an image of redemption, that of a hawk's flight, with the difference from earlier poems of Warren being in the nature of the redemption. Opening with the fig again, seen as an emblem of human mortality and guilt, and of "the flaming mullet" as an encounter in the depths, the poem proceeds to an episode of shamanistic force. . . .

Nothing in Warren's earlier poetry matches [the hawk episode of **"The Leaf"**] in dramatic intensity, or in the accents of inevitability, as the poetic character is reincarnated in him by his sacrificial self-offering "near the nesting place of the hawk." Much of the guilt and sorrow in Warren's earlier life come together here, with beautiful implicitness: the fear of blindness, the decade of poetic silence, the failure of the first marriage, and most mysteriously, a personal guilt at having become a poet. . . .

Warren's father died in 1955, at the age of eighty-six. Robert Franklin Warren, who wanted above everything else to be a poet, became a banker instead, solely to support not only his own children, but also a family of young children bequeathed to him by his own father, who had married again and then died. Reflecting upon all this, Warren has said: "It's as if I've stolen my father's life," somberly adding: "If he had had the opportunity I did, with his intelligence and energy, he'd have done a lot better than I did." This is probably part of the sorrow heard in: "I, / Of my father, have set the teeth on edge." From Warren's own account, one might think it the larger part of the sorrow, but imaginatively the heavier burden may have been his poetic inheritance, the influence of Eliot, which Warren here almost involuntarily disavows and overcomes. Eliot's "not the cicada" from *The Waste Land* becomes [in the next movement of **"The Leaf,"** which includes the line "My father's voice, in the moment when the cicada ceases, has called to me"] the moment when Eliot's presence in Warren's voices ceases, to be replaced by the poetic voice that Robert Franklin Warren had to abandon. The return of the father's voice becomes the blessing of Warren's new style, the gift given by Warren in his father's name. (p. 41)

From this poem on, Warren rarely falters, whether in *Audubon: A Vision* or in the half-dozen books of shorter poems (or new sections in selected volumes) that have followed. The achievement throughout these books necessarily is mixed, but there are several score of poems that manifest all the marks of permanence.

I want to look at just one of these poems, because it raises again, for me and for others, the ancient problem of poetry and belief. The poem is **"A Way to Love God"** from "Can I See Arcturus From Where I Stand?," the section of new poems in [*Selected Poems, 1923-1975*, which] preceded the book under review. I quote only the poem's final vision, which is no grislier than the ones preceding it:

> But I had forgotten to mention an
>   upland
> Of wind-tortured stone white in
>   darkness, and tall, but when
> No wind, mist gathers, and once on
>   the Sarré at midnight,
> I watched the sheep huddling. Their
>   eyes
> Stared into nothingness. In that
>   mist-diffused light their eyes
> Were stupid and round like the eyes
>   of fat fish in muddy water,
> Or of a scholar who has lost faith in
>   his calling.
>
> Their jaws did not move. Shreds
> Of dry grass, gray in gray mist-light,
>   hung
> From the side of a jaw, unmoving.
>
> You would think that nothing would
>   ever again happen.
>
> That may be a way to love God.

By loving God, Warren appears to mean loving what he calls "the truth," which is that all human beings are dreadfully involved in sin. This is an ancient and Augustinian polemic in all his work, poetry and prose, and does not pretend to settle what "truth" is, but rather asserts a necessarily personal conviction. Warren, despite the critical efforts of his more pious exegetes, is a skeptic and not a believer, but he is a Bible-soaked skeptic. His way of loving God is to forgive himself nothing, and to forgive God nothing.

The aesthetic consequences of this position, in the poetry written since 1966, seem to me wholly admirable, while the spiritual grimness involved remains a formidable challenge for many readers, myself among them. Missing from [*New and Selected Poems: 1923-1985*] is a notorious sequence, **"Homage to Emerson, On Night Flight to New York,"** to be found in the "Tale of Time" section of *Selected Poems: 1923-1975*. I don't regret its deletion, but it has considerable value in clarifying Warren's lifeling distaste for Emerson. . . .

[The] entire poem vigorously thrashes Emerson for his supposedly deficient sense of fact. Accusing Emerson of an abstract heart is not original with Warren, but I wince properly at the effective anti-transcendentalism of: "At 38,000 feet Emerson / Is dead right." At ground level, I believe Emerson to be dead right also. "His Smile" [the first part of **"Homage to Emerson, On a Night Flight to New York"**] is a good polemic, and should be admired as such.

The vexed issue of poetry and belief arises rather when I reread a poem like **"A Way to Love God,"** which is an impressive nightmare from my perspective, but a truth from Warren's. A secularized conviction of sin, guilt, and error is an obsessive strand in Warren's work, and for him it helps to create a position that is more than rhetorical. However, the effect is only to increase the rich strangeness of his poetic strength, which is wholly different from that of the best living poets of my own generation: Ashbery, Merrill, Ammons, and others, and from their precursor, Stevens.

Ideological ferocity never abandons Warren, but he passionately dramatizes it, and he has developed an idiom for it that is now entirely his own. He would appear to be, as I have intimated elsewhere [see *CLC*, Vol. 8], a sunset hawk at the end of a great tradition. Because of our increasing skepticism, I doubt that we will ever again have a poet who can authentically take this heroic a stance. He has earned, many times over, his series of self-identifications with the flight of the hawk, or an aspect of the truth. The second new poem in [*New and Selected Poems: 1923-1985*], **"Mortal Limit,"** is a sonnet celebrating again his great image of the hawk. . . .

So long as he abides, there will be someone capable of asking that grand and unanswerable question: "Beyond what range will gold eyes see / New ranges rise to mark a last scrawl of light?" (p. 42)

Harold Bloom, *"The Flight of the Hawk,"* in The New York Review of Books, *Vol. XXXII, No. 9, May 30, 1985, pp. 40-2.*

DAVE SMITH

[*Smith is an American poet, critic, editor, and novelist. An heir to the Romantic tradition, Smith holds an exalted conception of the purpose of poetry—for him, critic Robert De Mott notes, "poetry is a redemptive act," and "a poem is a moral act." Smith's many poetry collections, including* The Fisherman's Whore *(1974),* Cumberland Station *(1976),* Goshawk, Antelope *(1979),* Southern Delights *(1984), and* The Roundhouse Voices *(1985) evidence a sensibility informed by geography, community, family, and inner states and a verbal energy expressed in narrative and meditative pieces of passionate humanity. In the following excerpt from a talk given by Smith on the occasion of Warren's eightieth birthday, Smith pays tribute to Warren, citing his important influence on younger poets.*]

[Mr. Warren] begins and ends as a writer to whom nothing is so sacred or orthodox it cannot be tested, remeasured. (p. 574)

His energy, imagination, and vision make Mr. Warren a hero to younger poets. His poem is not reality's mirror but its body, whether gorgeous or grotesque. No body was ever more fecund or compelling. He celebrates dignity and possibility; he rejects cynicism and ignorance. Asking "Have I learned to live?" his poems dream large and well. They teach us to ask "For what is man without magnificence?" Surely this is what Emerson meant when he said, "The world is upheld by the veracity of good men; they make the earth wholesome."

One figure is central to Mr. Warren's poetry: it is the boy at the foot of the grandfather whose memory is full of passionate sparks. In Warren's early poem **"Court-Martial"** the grandfather draws civil war campaigns in the summer dust and the boy learns that "life is only a story" which he calls "the *done* and the *to-be done*." Mr. Warren has spent more than sixty years attending to what rises out of that dust, the story of what

happens and why, and younger poets have paid their attentions to him. (pp. 574-75)

Mr. Warren's effect, his presence, is his poems, and in them the gift of continuity, of a tradition that civilizes the life of a people and insists on the radiant wildness of each individual heart. This is the writer's tradition, one well described by his wife, the novelist Eleanor Clark, who says:

There are after all only two requirements for being a decent writer: one is to have a total passion—meaning a readiness to give up anything for it, rather than expecting to get anything out of it; the other is to spend your life at it, working like hell.

Because he has worked like hell, he can be read by tobacco farmers and aestheticians alike. No one makes a hag in the woods, a masturbating novelist, the eye of a hawk or mullet, or an old mule cart full of junk so interesting as he does. When he speaks of stars grinding or a mad woman "legs spread, each ankle / shackled to the cot-frame" or scares us with Dragon Country's unkillable beast, we can hear the awful breathing of the world. Yet bursting forth like life itself is that grandfatherly voice saying:

But let us note, too, how glory, like gasoline spilled
On the cement in a garage, may flare, of a sudden, up,

In a blinding blaze, from the filth of the world's flare.

He throbs with desire for the big look at life that each heart and each moment can yield. That's what he pleads for in the American masterpiece, **Audubon: A Vision,** when he says "Tell me a story of deep delight."

Emerson said of Goethe that he "strikes the harp with a hero's strength and grace." I don't know a better way to proclaim what Warren's presence is. This harp-striking is a man's struggle to imagine and pursue fullness of spirit with courage and humility, to complete himself. In an early poem Warren wrote "Past silence, sound insinuates / Past ear into the inner brain." Well, we all know some sound does that and some does not. Why is Mr. Warren's sound so unmistakably his and so compelling? I suspect it is the broken ballad form and the Anglo-Saxon stress energy, those calls to action, that hover adventurously in each of his poems. It is also the mannerly, gentlemanly tale of counsel that bears the flesh and feel of one life in one place. Yet there is something more, something harder to name. That is, I think, the rhythmic pressure and plain honesty of humility and conviction that proceeds from a fundamental belief that each of us has worth, is capable of worth. (pp. 576, 78)

Perhaps what is most remarkable about Mr. Warren as poet, as an architect of New Criticism, is that the urgent experience of language is meaning. The poem embodies both truth to be sought and the truth as it is lived. Though he has loved as much as anyone the verbal and technical pretties of poetry, he has by main force wrestled into the poem what he once called the world of prose and imperfection—warts, wens, politics, infidelities, Times Square, Iwo Jima, telephone screech, solitary walks. His language has been as unpredictable and immediate as the life in and of the vision, hence the whipsawing suspensions of sentence, razoring phrases, and cadences so intimate with the heart they shock. He has refused the poem of approximate speech and tried continuously to say the thing itself straight and right. He has been a skeptic, a hunger artist denying abstraction, anonymity, and the narcosis of relativism whose end is "I'm ok; you're ok."

Behind Mr. Warren's language is another compulsion, the dream of freedom. In and out of poetry, he believes, freedom exists in human acts attentively scrutinized, in the witness of a man who stands somewhere, believes in something, and willingly pays with his life the costs of that existence. Let me recall the image of the boy and his grandfather. That world drawn in the dust is a dream but it is also the enactment of generations of truth, not truth as homily but as experienced, felt, comprehended as "the human scheme of values." Encompassing this story is love: the boy loves without knowledge, the grandfather loves in spite of knowledge. That world in the dust is inevitable, flawed, but by both it is forgiven, accepted because that is the only way to live with purpose. The man or woman who lives with purpose is already free. We honor Mr. Robert Penn Warren because his tales of heroism, his stories of deep delight may yet shake us to know that—if only that. It is this Robert Lowell recognizes in a poem about Mr. Warren that speaks of "an old master still engaging the dazzled disciples." And another younger poet, James Dickey, says "He gives you the sense of poetry as a thing of final importance to life: as a way or *form* of life."

Few are given to live long and few are given to write well. We know how rare is the one who writes grandly "though in years"—a Whitman, a Yeats. No one disputes the astonishing brilliance, the great and responsible dream of freedom in Robert Penn Warren's last decade. He has, like our Southern flowers, poked his head up, higher and more dangerously, to take hold of the air and the sun. His affect on the younger poet has been to prove the possibility of that life. (pp. 578-79)

> Dave Smith, "Robert Penn Warren: The Use of a Word Like Honor," in The Yale Review, Vol. 74, No. 4, July, 1985, pp. 574-80.

PETER STITT

Robert Penn Warren's *New and Selected Poems: 1923-1985,* especially when considered along with Harold Bloom's review of it in *The New York Review of Books* [see excerpt above], raises a couple of important issues. The one of these that concerns the book specifically as a selection of a lifetime's work I will reserve until the end of my discussion. For now I would like to consider a fundamental issue about Warren's thinking and, in the process, air my disagreement with Professor Bloom, who insists upon divorcing Warren from the great tradition of American transcendentalism. In his review, Bloom discusses Warren as a moralist "who forgives himself nothing," an ironist who "nevertheless so loves the world that he will forgive it nothing," and "like Eliot, . . . an idealogue" whose "temperament is far more ferocious than Eliot's." These three aspects of Warren's work are so closely related as to be one; in Bloom's eyes, Warren is a fierce moralist committed to a vision of abiding original sin.

In support of his view, Bloom discusses the poem **"A Way to Love God,"** from the sequence "Can I See Arcturus From Where I Stand?" The series of nihilistic visions of earthly life presented by the poem concludes with a portrait of a herd of sheep that stands "unmoving" in the night, "stupid," like "a scholar who has lost faith in his calling." At the very end of the poem, dry grass is seen hanging "From the side of a

jaw. . . . You would think that nothing would ever happen again. / / That may be a way to love God." Warren the ironist is bitterly in command here, implicitly condemning a god who would allow not just evil to exist (as we see in so many other poems) but empty faithlessness, Kierkegaardian despair.

What seems obvious from such a poem—and many others like it—is the poet's intense preoccupation with the idea of God. This, however, is not what Bloom sees here:

> By loving God, Warren appears to mean loving what he calls "the truth," which is that all human beings are dreadfully involved in sin. This is an ancient and Augustinian polemic in all his work, poetry and prose, and does not pretend to settle what "truth" is, but rather asserts a necessarily personal conviction. Warren, despite the critical efforts of his more pious exegetes, is a skeptic and not a believer, but he is a Bible-soaked skeptic. His way of loving God is to forgive himself nothing, and to forgive God nothing.

Two of the words in this passage are problematical. I find it difficult to think of Warren as a "skeptic," one who dryly doubts the existence of God. That he questions God, is exasperated with Him, even refuses to forgive Him—so much is clear. But underlying all of these attitudes is an implicit acceptance of the root notion, God. Further, when Warren uses the word *God* he does not mean what Bloom suggests—that "all human beings are dreadfully involved in sin." The best definition of Warren's usage that I have seen is that made by Samuel Lloyd in his study "Robert Penn Warren: In the Midst of the World": "'God' is a word for the sense of awe and holiness the speaker feels in his experience of the world." . . . (p. 645)

Bloom's own disagreement with Warren is represented in his review by their different reactions to Emerson. Bloom speaks of "Warren's lifelong distaste for Emerson"; the poet "thrashes Emerson for his supposedly deficient sense of fact." Indeed he does. Emerson essentially denied the existence of evil in the world, and Warren has found this hard to swallow. . . . [In an interview, Warren spoke] of Emerson as having the "modern disease—self-righteousness, the idea of natural virtue. I think he just has a basic idiocy in him, the old Emersonian disease." Bloom does not agree with Warren's condemnation; he speaks of a "reader" who "like myself, longs to follow Emerson in forgiving himself, if not everything, then at least as much as possible."

Because of Bloom's preoccupation with the question of morality, he is curiously blind to another aspect of Emerson's thinking, one that is far more important to Warren's poetry. Emerson believed in the underlying goodness of the physical universe because he saw it not as composed of inert matter but as a manifestation of the Oversoul. Matter thus is sacred, in Emerson's eyes. Of course he did not stop there but charged ahead into the Platonic view that matter does not even exist as matter; it is an illusion; spirit is all. Warren has also questioned Emerson's transcendentalism: "I'm not a transcendentalist. I find that kind of talk just doesn't make sense to me—well, in some ways. I'll put it this way: I *hope* we can find meanings in nature. . . ." Putting this statement together with one quoted earlier ("I am a man of religious temperament in the modern world who hasn't got any religion"), it would be easy to conclude that if Emerson had not gone Platonic—that is, had he stopped with the notion that something spiritual inhabits the material universe—then Warren would have found his thinking a whole lot easier to accept.

Warren's poems are absolutely saturated with the notion of an immanent meaning that hovers within the real, just beyond man's grasp. The problem is that, in a secular and fallen world, man lacks the means to perceive such a truth. Often—as in **"Muted Music,"** one of the new poems in this volume—Warren expresses this idea in terms of sound and hearing; his speaker's dream is:

> To hear at last, at last, what you have strained for
> All the long years, and sometimes at dream-verge
> thought
>
> You heard—the songs the moth sings, the babble
> Of falling snowflakes (in a language
> No school has taught you), the scream
> Of the reddening bud of the oak tree
>
> As the bud bursts into the world's brightness.

Warren explains passages like this one in his poem **"Code Book Lost,"** from *Now & Then*: "Yes, message on message, like wind on water, in light or in dark, / The whole world pours at us. But the code book, somehow, is lost."

Better than twenty-five percent of Warren's *New and Selected Poems: 1923-1985* . . . , is devoted to work written since 1980, when *Being Here* was published. In terms of philosophy— indeed, in terms generally of content—the newest poems do not differ significantly from those in earlier collections. If there is a stylistic change it is that the newer poems are generally somewhat more literal, somewhat less figurative, than the older ones. Note, for example, this philosophic passage—"Since my idiot childhood the world has been / Trying to tell me something. There is something / Hidden in the dark"—which exhibits a directness not often present earlier.

Elsewhere, however, Warren's customary power is triumphantly present. The second of the **"Three Darknesses,"** for example, is a masterpiece of detail and timing. . . . (pp. 646-47)

As he did in his previous selected volumes, Warren here has placed his newest poems first and worked backwards to those of 1923. The reader thus finds his appetite whetted by many wonderful and characteristic new works—for example, **"Three Darknesses," "Mortal Limit," "Immortality Over the Dakotas," "Hope," "Old Photograph of the Future," "The Place,"** and **"Question at Cliff-Thrust"**—and looks forward eagerly to rereading poems he has loved for years. Which raises the second of the two issues I mentioned earlier. So that many new poems could be accommodated in this selected volume, many older poems were left out. For example, the magnificent sequence *Or Else* has been cut from its original twenty-four sections plus eight "Interjections" down to twelve sections and no interjections. Of those included, the **"Homage to Theodore Dreiser"** has been cut from three parts to one. Among the omitted poems are **"Times as Hypnosis"** and **"A Problem in Spatial Composition,"** neither of which would I leave out of a fifty-page pamphlet containing the best American poems of the century. And *Being Here*, a fifty-poem sequence that many consider Warren's best and most tightly structured, is represented here only by ten scattered poems.

In short, the book comes nowhere near representing Robert Penn Warren at his best, and I think it could have a seriously negative effect upon his reputation. A "selected poems" tends to set the canon; because the selection has been made by the author himself, most readers will assume that the very best work has been included. If this is not the case, new readers will not be seduced by the selected volume into reading further. Robert Penn Warren is the most important American poet of the second half of the twentieth century, and one of the five most important of the entire century. It is nothing less than shocking that the magnificent output of his entire lifetime should be represented by this volume. What is needed now is not another new and selected poems; what is needed is a Collected Poems containing *all* of the best work in its entirety. (p. 648)

> *Peter Stitt, "Tradition and the Innovative Godzilla,"* in The Georgia Review, *Vol. XXXIX, No. 3, Fall, 1985, pp. 635-48.**

PETER STITT

Critics are in general agreement that Warren's poetry showed a profound change with the publication in 1958 of the volume *Promises: Poems 1954-1956*. Warren had never been what we would call a nihilist, but it is fair to say that before *Promises* he was more a poet of despair and alienation than one of joy and union, a writer influenced (along with his fellow fugitive poet, Allen Tate) by the early T. S. Eliot. With *Promises*, as the title certainly indicates, a sense of hopefulness emerged within Warren's work, and this sense has dominated his poetry since then. What we see in the later work is the poet questing to define, to understand, to apprehend, somehow to seize, the meaning of the joyous promise he senses.

This general quest—which is pursued in all of Warren's most recent work—appears in two slightly different but closely related forms, depending upon the primary goal of the individual manifestation of the quest. One of these versions seeks understanding or hope within a metaphysical realm; it is a quest with quasi-religious implications. The other version is more time-bound and has as its goal an understanding of life within this world. . . . The metaphysical aspect of the quest . . . [is apparent in] several poems from the volumes *Now and Then: Poems, 1976-1978* and *Or Else: Poem/Poems, 1968-1974*. In order to illustrate Warren's quest within time (which, to be sure, yearns toward the eternal as well) I will discuss in detail the more recent volume, *Being Here: Poetry, 1977-1980*. Because the latter of these patterns is the more dominant one within Warren's mature work, I will devote most of my attention to it.

Robert Penn Warren is emphatically a philosophical poet. (p. 215)

Warren does not approach reality with the intention of imposing a preconceived system of values upon it. Rather, he prefers to search through the raw materials presented by the world in the hope of arriving at some understanding, some meaning. With specific reference to his own work, Warren has described this method in an interview: "For me, the process of writing . . . is to grope for the meaning of the thing, an exploration for the meaning rather than an execution of meanings already arrived at. . . . the poem has to start with something concrete and not with an abstract idea." . . . It is for this reason that concrete imagery is so important a component of the poetry of Robert Penn Warren; only by immersing himself within the rich fabric of reality, "life's instancy," does he feel he can arrive at abstract understanding, "the astrolabe of joy."

The same reason—this deep and abiding sense of love for physical reality, for the texture of "the world's body"—also explains why Warren's poems are nearly always narrative in structure; the philosophy is grounded in the telling of a story. (p. 216)

The passion that gives both emotional force and intellectual structure to Warren's late poetry is a powerful sense of yearning, a longing to understand the meaning of the world that surrounds us. . . . To want something, to sense its presence, but not to know its name, is to desire to render a felt truth into language, into literature.

That there is a metaphysical, a transcendent, a quasi-religious dimension to this quest is evident from the definition of his sense of longing that Warren gave in an interview: ''I am a creature of this world—but I am also a yearner, I suppose. I would call this temperament rather than theology—I haven't got any gospel. That is, I feel an immanence of meaning in things, but I have no meaning to put there that is interesting or beautiful. I think I put it as close as I could in a poem called **'Masts at Dawn'**—'We must try / To love so well the world that we may believe, in the end, in God.' I am a man of religious temperament in the modern world who hasn't got any religion.'' . . . I call this sense of yearning ''quasi-religious'' because it so obviously operates within the realm of the religious—that is, it addresses the same questions that religion sets out to answer, but does so without recurrence to any established theology. (p. 217)

The metaphysical concerns so present in *Or Else* are not abandoned in the later volume, *Being Here: Poetry, 1977-1980,* though they are reduced in importance. In the more recent book, Warren chooses to deal with the here and now, hoping to arrive at an understanding of life as it is lived within the world of physical reality. . . . It is characteristic of Warren as philosopher to say that ''meaning is . . . more fruitfully found in the question asked than in any answer given''; *Being Here* is a speculative and hopeful volume, incandescent with felt nuances, but without absolutes. No ultimate answer is furnished by these poems—what we find inside is what we are promised on the cover—it is a matter of *Being Here.*

Thus it is appropriate that the ''thematic order'' (meaning) of the volume should be presented through a ''shadowy narrative, a shadowy autobiography.'' The structure of the volume loosely parallels the structure of life: it begins in childhood (section 1), moves through impetuous youth (2), cynical middle age (3) and speculative, searching middle age (4), then finishes with the summations and vague hopes of old age (5). The question that Warren raises in his phrase ''shadowy autobiography''—Just how autobiographical is this book?—he answers both in his ''Afterthought'' and in the poems themselves. There is a strong sense of distance built into the poems. We never feel (as we so often do when reading the confessional poets) that we are peeking into the secret inmost recesses of the poet's life. The most intimate moments presented are those in which the speaker (certainly Warren himself) feels on the verge of a revelation, generally of a quasi-mystical sort. At such times he is not in the process of getting drunk or seducing someone else's wife; we see him alone instead, in the woods, on the beach, or in the mountains.

In addition to this, certain techniques of narration employed by Warren also have the effect of distancing the reader from a sense of intimacy with what is revealed. Many experiences, for example, are presented as dreams the aged speaker has of his earlier life; we thus are doubly distanced from this material—distanced by the passage of time, distanced by the process

of dream. Further, Warren has refined his use of the word *you*—which in the past has often been used to refer to the reader and to other characters in the poems. Here, the word refers almost exclusively to the speaker himself and is used in poems detailing the intimate experiences just mentioned. Warren addresses himself as ''you'' when speculating on the meaning of an event or questioning his earlier behavior. In either case, the effect is to distance both author and reader from the material. Finally, when Warren refers to the ''shadowy autobiography'' of the volume as ''a fusion of fiction and fact in varying degrees,'' we are emphatically put off the confessional trail. Warren is not talking only about an individual life—he is talking about the process of life as all thinking people know it. His story thus expands outward to embrace us all, becoming almost mythical, almost, indeed, a ''supreme fiction.''

The structure of *Being Here* is both linear and circular. As indicated above, Warren approaches time primarily in a narrative fashion, his ''shadowy autobiography'' moving chronologically toward old age. The ''thematic order'' is more nearly circular; each of the five sections has its own particular area of thematic concern, but these concerns appear in other sections as well. Moreover, as the book progresses, we see more and more connections between the various concerns, so that ultimately they come to coalesce, forming one large circular pattern. It is my intention here to approach the book through its structure, taking up the thematic concerns as they occur. (pp. 223-25)

A central preoccupation of Warren's has always been the nature of time; all three epigraphs to *Being Here* are concerned with this topic. (p. 225)

The issue of time for Warren, . . . is not unitary but dual—there is time and there is eternity. *Being Here* as a whole is built upon this polarity, which carries with it several additional paired concepts, paired sets of images, paired settings, situations, experiences, even paired characters. The volume achieves its dynamic, thematic energy from its use of the notion of the quest, which appears on two levels, one aimed at eternity, one rooted within time. The larger or higher quest spans the entire volume, the entire life—it is imagistically described as a path, the metaphorical trail we follow through the thicket (or snowfield) of life. (pp. 225-26)

Eternity is always vague in Warren; it is not where we live, not something we can see or exactly experience in and of itself. As suggested earlier, it is given imagistic, metaphorical representation in the poetry, and exists in contrast to the rather more obvious images associated with the here and now—time, earth, and life as we know it. The places of eternity in *Being Here* are known on earth, but are distant and rarified—the sky, snow, stars, mountains (crags, ledges, scarps), brightness, the color white. This is a silent realm; when birds appear, they are seen against the sky and we cannot hear their song, if any. The realm of time is relatively darker, more colorful. Its places and objects cling to or penetrate the earth—trees, streams, caves, grasses, oceans, lake, and pools. Birds here roost and sing, sometimes mournfully. The settings of time, its landscapes, have movement and tend to flow; the settings of eternity are static, frozen. Each of these realms has its truth or truths; as its goal the path has the truth of eternity, while the individual quests seek the truth/truths of earth.

The volume begins and ends with poems that are separate from the five sections—one a kind of preface, the other a kind of epilogue. Taken together, they measure the distance traveled by the speaker, just as they indicate the direction in which he moves. The first, **"October Picnic Long Ago"** . . . , is set in the timelessness of pretime; so young is the speaker that he is not yet aware that time passes and measures our place. . . . The concluding poem, **"Passers-by on Snowy Night"** . . . , is a set piece, almost a parable, and defines as clearly as anything in Warren the notion of the path. (pp. 226-27)

Another aspect of the prefatory poem also demands consideration. The October picnic is a family outing; the people on it who most interest the speaker are his parents, whom he uses to help define his concept of the two sides of time. . . . The mother, and by extension the feminine, is associated with the realm of time, the realm of earth, while the father, the masculine, is linked to the future, perhaps by extension to eternity. (p. 227)

The time of narration for the poems in this volume is nearly always the time of their writing—that is, now. Within a poem, the speaker will return through memory or dream to the time of the event he relates, and at the end he will carry us forward again into the present. In so doing, he generally speculates both on the meaning of the experience itself and on its relevance to his thinking now. In terms of both time and theme, section 1 picks up where the prefatory poem leaves off—the speaker's thinking is dominated by the figure and meaning of the mother as he reviews certain events from his boyhood. When his two structures—time and theme—conflict with one another, Warren is most likely to prefer the latter over the former; thus, two of these poems relate events rather far removed from the speaker's boyhood, but they are included here because they are concerned with the mother. **"The Only Poem"** tells of a visit the speaker—now grown—and his middle-aged mother make to see the baby grandchild of a friend. The episode illustrates a newly recognized dimension of this woman's love, as her son sees how strong in her is the mothering impulse—which he knows turns back toward himself. The other of these out-of-time poems is **"Grackles, Goodbye,"** an elegy addressed to the mother, which ends: "only, / In the name of Death do we learn the true name of Love". . . . Two other poems seem, at first glance, alien to the thematic thrust of the section, though their action occurs in its time. However, both **"Filling Night with the Name: Funeral as Local Color"** and **"Recollection in Upper Ontario, from Long Before"** are concerned with women—beloved at least by someone, at least one time—who die. We see then that the intertwined concepts of woman and love and death are crucially central here. (pp. 227-28)

In the beginning of the book, it seems to the speaker that union with woman is ultimate and mystical, equivalent to union with God. This notion is expressed in the only poem from section 1 not previously mentioned here—**"When Life Begins"**—which tells the wonderful boyhood times the speaker spent on his grandfather's farm. We find this stanza:

> And the old man, once he said
> How a young boy, dying, broke into tears.
> "Ain't scairt to die"—the boy's words—"it's jist
> I ne'er had no chance to know what tail's like."

At this stage in the volume, such lack means an unfulfilled life. Later, women lose their mystery, their mystical dimension, though there is one poem in section 2 where the notion of union with or perception of the all is linked with sex (if not precisely woman). In **"Preternaturally Early Snowfall in Mating Season"** . . . , the speaker camps on a mountainside and is surprised by an unexpected and heavy snowfall, which comes

during the night. Sometime before dawn, he is awakened by the furor of two deer mating; it is an impressive experience for him. The trip out takes "two days, snowshoeing, . . . / And rations short the second." Malnutrition and exhaustion put the speaker in another trancelike state, though awake. It is then that he feels he almost sees "the guessed-at glory"—almost, but not quite. The juxtaposition of the mating with the near vision is causal and illustrates the power woman and sex still have over the young man.

Beyond this point, however, the speaker cannot be so swayed by these paired forces; the most telling poem in this regard is **"Part of What Might Have Been a Short Story, Almost Forgotten"** . . . , from section 3. The poem is complex, beautiful, and long; briefly, it tells of the end of a love the speaker finds ultimately and finally (for it has been a long relationship) unfulfilling. . . . [It] is only in section 1 that woman—the mother and the womb—is used consistently as a means towards and an image for union with the all. What the speaker takes with him from childhood is the vague memory of (and consequent longing for) such experience throughout the rest of his life.

In section 2 of *Being Here* we see the speaker in his youth, restless, searching for something he can perhaps name but cannot define. The title of the first poem is indicative of the kind of action that takes place throughout this section: **"Youthful Truth-Seeker, Half-Naked, at Night, Running Down Beach South of San Francisco."** Every one of the poems here involves a quest and a longing for union or truth. Some occur within the realm of time and some rely on landscapes that suggest eternity; but none is successful at reaching the goal, which Warren describes in **"Youthful Truth-Seeker . . .":**

> You dream that somewhere, somehow, you may embrace
> The world in its fullness and threat, and feel, like Jacob, at last
> The merciless grasp of unwordable grace
> Which has no truth to tell of future or past—
>
> But only life's instancy, by daylight or night,
> While constellations strive, or a warbler whets
> His note, or the ice creaks blue in white-night Arctic light,
> Or the maniac weeps—over what he always forgets.

Warren's localized quests, those that occur mostly in the middle parts of the book, always return him to the present moment. There is not the power here to transcend time in either direction—neither towards union with the "all" in the past, nor towards eternity in the future. In his early childhood, the speaker was still close, in time and location, to an archetypal experience of union (that with the mother in the womb). Thus, he was able without much effort to create a near approximation of that satisfying state, as in the cave. When he arrives at old age—in the final section—we will again see him on the verge of such satisfaction. Here, however, he is trapped within time, with both consciousness and understanding consumed by the present moment, "life's instancy." (pp. 229-31)

Section 3 is, emphatically, the portion of this book devoted to the pursuits of "day," although a careful distinction has to be made at this point. I have said that Warren associates darkness with the realm of time, while white and brightness are associated with the realm of eternity. This is true as far as it goes—that is, when these qualities or tones are applied to individual images or objects (trees, streams, and fields, as opposed to snow, stars, and single white clouds). When darkness and brightness are generalized states (that is, when they refer to the relative lightness of night or day), then a reversal of sorts takes place. In darkness, things may happen or be achieved that we would naturally associate with the more metaphysical of the two realms, that of eternity. Conversely, unless the landscape is covered in snow, nothing mystical is likely to occur during day. Ordinary daytime is not just of the realm of time as I have been using the term (for there is a certain exaltedness in that concept); it defines for itself a realm of the mundane, even of the debased. And so section 3 is where Warren attends to the base nature of mankind, including himself. It is a bit disconcerting to find this material at the heart of a book that plays elsewhere so seriously with mystic intonations, sacred undertones. But that is precisely the point— man's life is debased, comical, so far from perfection even in the best cases as to make the word *perfection* laughable. There is no point in promising man redemption if you have to deny human nature to deliver; Warren is a realist, not a dreamer: he justifies the promises he makes by admitting the truth of what we are.

He bares this truth in nearly every poem in section 3, showing the secret stealth of illicit lovers, the "haze," the "personal ambition," the "beast in shadow" that inhabit a **"Cocktail Party"** . . . , even the arrogance of those (the speaker and his friend) who would rid the earth of evil by killing cottonmouth snakes. This is the surrounding reality, and yet Warren can still see the possibility of redemption. In **"Function of Blizzard"** . . . , he explicitly associates snow with eternity ("God's goose, neck neatly wrung, is being plucked") and shows how it can lend grace to man's lowest endeavors: "Black ruins of arson in the Bronx are whitely / Redeemed." Among those in need of grace, he places himself. . . . We seem to end this section with time and death ascendant over man and God. This shows Warren the realist, Warren the ironist, at work. Although the volume as a whole comes to a positive conclusion, that conclusion remains tentative, besieged on all sides by less attractive but still viable possibilities. It is here, in section 3, that he lays the firmest grounding for the darker alternatives. We are reminded again that meaning in this book, "as in life," may be "more fruitfully found in the question asked than in any answer given."

I want to return briefly to the image of circularity that was posited as a model for the thematic order or structure of *Being Here*. Sections 1 and 5 of the book blend together on one side of the circle—each suggests a tentative answer, acceptable to the speaker, to the underlying question of the book. These answers exist, alternatively, within the timelessness of "part of all" and the womb, and within eternity. Sections 2, 3, and 4 investigate possibilities within the realm of time. Section 3 is farthest from sections 1 and 5—spiritually (there is little or no spirituality in 3), spatially (on the circle as clock's face, section 1 would come at 6 A.M., section 5 at 6 P.M., and section 3 at high noon), and in terms of time/light (morning and evening—the envelopment of near darkness; noon—the harsh brightness of day). Sections 2 and 4 are found on opposite sides of the circle, but occupy analogous positions. Their light is softer—that of day, but with interesting shadows; the angle of the sun at 9 A.M. and 3 P.M., as it were, lends a teasing texture to the landscapes of the earth. In terms of theme, these two sections complement one another much as do question and answer. Section 2 sets out the compulsive habit of questing— within the realm of time, upon the face of earth. It is the function of section 4 to define the hoped-for goal (or at least the general area in which the goal might be found) of that kind of questing.

The poems in this penultimate section are all concerned with varieties of sound—most of them natural, some of them human, some from objects or machines. Whereas the process of the quest as presented in section 2 is vague and frustrating (not only because an answer is not found, but also because the speaker is unsure even where he should search), section 4 attempts to solve at least that part of the problem by focusing on the potential of sound. Thus, we find poems with such provocative titles as **"Language Barrier"** and **"What Is the Voice That Speaks?"** Even here the search uncovers no ultimate answers and at times is even downright frustrating:

> What grandeur here speaks? The world
> Is the language we cannot utter.
> Is it a language we can even hear?

However, there is one type of sound that turns out to be more promising than the others. Warren draws it to our attention in a poem that, through its title, is paired in importance with what probably is the central poem in section 2—**"Why Have I Wandered the Asphalt of Midnight?"**

The new poem is called **"Tires on Wet Asphalt at Night"** . . . , and it presents our speaker once again in a meditative state near sleep:

> As my head in darkness dents pillow, the last
> Automobile, beyond rhododendrons
> And evergreen screen, hisses
> On rain-wet asphalt.

Warren proceeds to imagine a life for the imagined occupants of the car—a man and woman who may later seek truth in the false quest of sex:

> . . . the old
> Mechanic hope of finding identity in
> The very moment of paradox when
> There is always none.

Then the sound he has heard possesses his imagination and determines the rest of the poem:

> I think of the hiss of their tires going somewhere—
> That sound like the *swish-hiss* of faint but continual
> Wavelets far down on the handkerchief beach-patch
> In a cove crag-locked and pathless, slotted
> Only to seaward and westward, sun low. And I
> Felt need to climb down and lie there, that sound
> In my ear, and watch the sun sink, in its blaze, below
> The blind, perpetual, abstract sea.

The language and action are those of the typical quest—but the importance given to sound in this poem draws our attention to it as a new and potent element.

Of course this isn't just any sound; it is the whisperlike *"swish-hiss"* sound made by tires on wet pavement and waves on a beach. In the poem **"August Moon"** (section 2) Warren rather baldly states the thematic or conceptual or abstract basis for the importance he places on this particular sound; the setting is yet another quest—

> We walk down the woods-lane, dreaming
> There's an inward means of
> Communication with

That world whose darkling susurration
Might—if only we were lucky—be
Deciphered.

Warren partly hides his concept within the unusual word *susurration,* which means rustle or whisper. But what he is talking about is the goal of all his speaker's quests: he seeks some knowledge of the innermost secret truth of the "world," of earth.

Once this sound has been noticed, we are able to find it in many, crucial passages and poems. For example, in **"Speleology"** the underground stream makes its own sound, "A silken and whispering rustle." . . . The many individual quests in this book have as their desired end some apprehension of earth's truth, the meaning of creation. But while the sound that might contain this knowing is heard, it is not translated into meaning; our speaker is left again with his questions and longing, the conviction that something is there—But what is it?

The question or problem of death, just beneath the surface for most of this book, emerges into prominence in section 5. The power of time, of course, pushes man relentlessly towards death—and it is with death in mind that the question of eternity becomes so crucially important. It is only to be expected that a philosophical poet such as Robert Penn Warren should, in his seventy-fifth year, devote considerable thought to this final event. Many images, passages, and whole poems throughout the volume suggest that this may be the central topic of the book. Even in the earliest poems, time has its lethal dimension. . . . (pp. 232-37)

There are also entire poems that can be read as the speaker's description of his own imagined death—for example, **"Dreaming in Daylight"** and **"Better Than Counting Sheep."** These poems, which come in earlier sections, do not suggest any solution to the approach of death—indeed, the speaker ends **"Dreaming in Daylight"** in a state bordering on panic. Section 5 attempts to provide some possible solution by bringing to fusion and conclusion certain thematic and imagistic patterns begun earlier. (p. 237)

There remains a word to say on how this affects the ultimate "payday, the payment"—death itself. The first poem in section 5, **"Eagle Descending"** . . . , a poem "To a dead friend," is an elegy as much addressed to the hopes of the self as to the memory of the friend. Once again, Warren's imagery contrasts the realms of time and eternity; the eagle is emblematic of the dead friend, who has passed forward to eternity from the vale of time:

Beyond the last flamed escarpment of mountain cloud
The eagle rides air currents, switch and swell,
With spiral upward now, steady as God's will.
Beyond black peak and flaming cloud, he yet
Stares at the sun—invisible to us,
Who downward sink.

This one image, this powerful, transcendent bird, embodies once again—like the hawk in **"A Problem in Spatial Composition"**—all of the promises that have filled Warren's work since his own rebirth into poetry in 1954. The poem ends with earth and its minions in darkness, and the bird "Alone in glory":

The twilight fades. One wing
Dips, slow. He leans.—And with that slightest shift,
Spiral on spiral, mile on mile, uncoils

The wind to sing with joy of truth fulfilled.

In line with his questioning method, Warren stops short of absolute assertion—and of course there are the ironic countermovements noted above. And yet we know that Warren always presents his greatest truths through suggestion and image—and this is the logical conclusion reached by all of the various questioning strains in this book: time is united with eternity, darkness with light, feminine (mother and womb) with masculine (father and God), sound with silence, the quest with the path. The circle of theme is closed at the end of the book's extended biographical line. (pp. 239-40)

Peter Stitt, "Robert Penn Warren: Life's Instancy and the Astrolabe of Joy," in his The World's Hieroglyphic Beauty: Five American Poets, *The University of Georgia Press, 1985, pp. 215-40.*

August Wilson

Ma Rainey's Black Bottom

New York Drama Critics Circle Award: Best Play

American dramatist and poet.

Wilson, a published poet and the author of several plays, was unknown until his discovery by Lloyd Richards, who directed the original Broadway production of Lorraine Hansberry's *A Raisin in the Sun;* Richards is both the dean of the Yale School of Drama and director of the Yale Repertory Theater. Upon reading the script for *Ma Rainey's Black Bottom* (1984) in 1981 Richards recalls, "I recognized it as a new voice. A very important one. It brought back my youth. My neighborhood. Experiences I had." Richards also points out that Wilson's talent is "not for the black theater or the green theater or the blue theater but for the American theater." *Ma Rainey's Black Bottom* enjoyed a highly successful run at Yale before moving on to Broadway.

Since his childhood in Pittsburgh, Wilson had dreamed of being a writer. At the age of twelve, when he discovered the literature of such black writers as Ralph Ellison and Langston Hughes, Wilson realized it was possible for blacks to be successful in artistic endeavors. Wilson's first experience with the theater was in the 1960s when, as a member of the black power movement, he formed an activist dramatic troupe in his hometown. Later, when he moved to St. Paul, Minnesota, Wilson wrote historical plays for one of the city's museums and was also the artistic director of a black theater there. Wilson began writing *Ma Rainey's Black Bottom* in 1976 after hearing a recording of Gertrude (Ma) Rainey, the legendary black singer regarded by some as the mother of the blues. Speaking of the impact of that album on him Wilson says, "When I listened to Ma Rainey it suddenly—or not so suddenly—occurred to me how full and rich my grandmother's life had been in the South. It dawned on me that both her life and my life had value. That was something I hadn't realized before. So I wanted to get behind that music. I am not an autobiographical writer, but I assure you that what's up on that stage is part of my life."

Set in the 1920s *Ma Rainey's Black Bottom* is based on an imaginary episode in the life of Ma Rainey, whose successful career set an example for following generations of black performers. The action takes place in a recording studio and focuses mainly on Ma's four musicians who are waiting for her arrival in a band room to the side of the recording room. As the details of the musicians' lives unfold, the audience becomes aware of the struggle against racism that these successful black performers have had to face as their careers developed. The actions and attitudes of the group's white manager and the owner of the studio, however, show that this struggle has not yet ended, that Ma and her band continue to be exploited despite their demonstrated talents. This exploration of the effects of racism reaches its climax when one of the musicians, Levee, vents his frustrations on the others.

In *Fences* (1985), a play he wrote after *Ma Rainey,* Wilson again examines the destructive and far-reaching consequences of racial injustice on its victims. Instead of music, however,

Photograph by William B. Carter

athletic competition is the arena where the protagonist, Troy, is prevented from excelling because of his race. Describing the two plays, Wilson has commented, "My concern was the idea of missed possibilities. Music and sports were the traditional inroads for blacks, and in both *Ma Rainey* and *Fences,* with both Levee and Troy, even those inroads fail."

Critics consistently praise Wilson for the vitality of *Ma Rainey's Black Bottom.* Many believe that one element contributing to this overall effect is the thorough development of the black characters, each of whom is an individual, non-stereotypical personality. Also applauded is the play's authentic, lively dialogue that conveys the eloquence of black diction and brings to life the black experience. It is largely due to such dialogue, critics believe, that Wilson is able to blend wit with the weighty theme of racism.

The play's structure, however, is a matter of critical dispute. Some critics find the play's ending to be contrived. Also, while a number of reviewers believe that there is too much dialogue, tending towards the didactic, and not enough dramatic tension, others contend that this flow of dialogue is essential to the play's overall effect. But even of those critics who are dissatisfied with some of the play's dramaturgical devices, most agree that *Ma Rainey's Black Bottom* is a striking piece of writing that, in the words of reviewer Frank Rich, "sends the entire history of Black America crashing down on our heads."

(See also *Contemporary Authors,* Vol. 115.)

JOEL SIEGEL

Ma Rainey's Black Bottom, a first play by the talented August Wilson, uses the place and the time and the musicians' easy-going camaraderie and undeniable artistry to chart black America's search for success and identity. The musicians are wonderfully written. Wilson hears dialogue in perfect pitch.

He writes funny. In fact, he's more comfortable with comedy. When he has a serious point to make he changes gears so quickly you need a seat belt. Dialogue becomes monologue. Gimmicks—a stuttering nephew—are added. Actors, for no reason, start exposing physical and psychological scars.

As a play *Ma Rainey* has flaws. But . . . as theatre this is fireworks.

> *Joel Siegel, in a television broadcast on WABC-TV—New York, NY, October 11, 1984.*

DOUGLAS WATT

Ma Rainey's Black Bottom . . . is both stirring and entertaining much of the time. But despite its length, this work by August Wilson is more in the nature of a padded out, though vivid, slice-of-life than a full-fledged play.

The time is 1927, and we're in the "race" division of a Chicago recording studio, a section where "race" records, made by black performers and almost exclusively for the black pockets of the population, were produced. Though limited, the market was large enough to be profitable for the white entrepreneurs and managers who paid the artists as little as possible.

Nevertheless, Gertrude (Ma) Rainey, the first of the famous blues singers (the great Bessie Smith was her protege), was successful enough to be able to retire in 1933 in considerable comfort. Thus, her story lacks the tragic dimensions of those of Smith, Billie Holiday, and so many others.

But *Ma Rainey's Black Bottom* (the catchy title is a reference to one of her numbers, though not one of her biggest hits) isn't really about Ma Rainey. It's about the four musicians who back her up and who are observed during most of the evening in the grubby rehearsal room adjoining the studio.

Wilson's colorful play . . . , takes us deep into the lives and personalities of the four musicians as they rehearse, fool around, reminisce and quarrel, (violently in the melodramatic finish). . . .

The popular music business, whether in publishing or recording, has always consisted of the exploitation of the artist, whether writer or performer, until he or she gained a foothold. But the condition of the black artist (or black athlete, for that matter) was considerably worse. And once Wilson has established that, he must fall back on related aspects of black life, remembered incidents interlaced with occasional confrontations leading up to the melodramatic finish. And while Wilson's dialogue is

brightly authentic, his play does mark time a good deal, especially in the second half. And in addition to that questionable figure of Ma's toy doll (the one who goes for Levee), there is a musical ambivalence here as jazz is placed in a kind of limbo, Levee referring to Ma's preferred arrangements as "jug" music, whereas he likes to swing and improvise on themes (after all, this 1927, when Louis Armstrong was already recording, or had been, with Rainey, and when, incidentally, the DeSylva-Brown-Henderson hit "Black Bottom" was already a year old). . . .

Ma Rainey's Black Bottom is a superb production in all respects, and its tendency toward wordiness, or filling, is largely overcome by the striking characterizations.

> *Douglas Watt, "'Ma Rainey's': Mostly, It Swings," in* Daily News, *New York, October 12, 1984. Reprinted in* New York Theatre Critics' Reviews, *Vol. XXXXV, No. 12, Week of September 17, 1984, p. 197.*

CLIVE BARNES

It is a strange kind of play, *Ma Rainey's Black Bottom.* . . . (p. 197)

Perhaps it is not so much a play as a slice of life, or an exposition of the black experience—the black experience between the wars, around the end of the 1920s. . . .

The play does have something to do with the legendary Rainey, and, rather more, the relationship between the black artist and the white, exploitative world of his or her time.

For this is essentially a political play, and although Ma Rainey—and perhaps her singing of the blues and the very blues spirit—inspired Wilson's work, Ma is not even the principal character at her own session.

The focus is on the four musicians that the singer had as her accompaniment. (pp. 197-98)

Much is explained, but—and this is the crucial fault of the play—nothing much happens. Until right at the end, when, as if Wilson who had scarcely started his play suddenly found he had run out of time and had to finish it, there is an eruption of sorts, feasible in life but scarcely credible in the tidier domain of drama.

The dialogue is racy, salty, pertinent—but it hangs in the air, its social content being so much more evident than its dramatic context.

The characters—both black and, to a lesser extent, white—are fine. For the most part the writing avoids cliche and stereotype, although the white cop on the take, and the white studio owner on the make, veer close to the danger zone.

Yet the imperious Ma, high-handed, shrewd, proud, and even jealous of her rival Bessie Smith, and Ma's motley crew—sharply representative of their race, time, and profession—are drawn with the observation of life. . . .

Ma Rainey's Black Bottom might yet wriggle its way to glory. But watch out for that ending, friends! (p. 198)

> *Clive Barnes, "'Ma Rainey'—The Black Experience," in* New York Post, *October 12, 1984. Reprinted in* New York Theatre Critics' Reviews, *Vol. XXXXV, No. 12, Week of September 17, 1984, pp. 197-98.*

FRANK RICH

Late in Act I of *Ma Rainey's Black Bottom,* a somber, aging band trombonist . . . tilts his head heavenward to sing the blues. The setting is a dilapidated Chicago recording studio of 1927, and the song sounds as old as time. "If I had my way," goes the lyric, "I would tear this old building down."

Once the play has ended, that lyric has almost become a prophecy. In *Ma Rainey's Black Bottom,* the writer August Wilson sends the entire history of black America crashing down upon our heads. This play is a searing inside account of what white racism does to its victims—and it floats on the same authentic artistry as the blues music it celebrates. Harrowing as *Ma Rainey's* can be, it is also funny, salty, carnal and lyrical. Like his real-life heroine, the legendary singer Gertrude (Ma) Rainey, Mr. Wilson articulates a legacy of unspeakable agony and rage in a spellbinding voice. . . . (p. C1)

Mr. Wilson's characters want to make it in white America. And, to a degree, they have. Ma Rainey (1886-1939) was among the first black singers to get a recording contract—albeit with a white company's "race" division. Mr. Wilson gives us Ma . . . at the height of her fame. A mountain of glitter and feathers, she has become a despotic, temperamental star, complete with a retinue of flunkies, a fancy car and a kept young lesbian lover.

The evening's framework is a Paramount-label recording session that actually happened, but whose details and supporting players have been invented by the author. As the action swings between the studio and the band's warm-up room . . . Ma and her four accompanying musicians overcome various mishaps to record "Ma Rainey's Black Bottom" and other songs. During the delays, the band members smoke reefers, joke around and reminisce about past gigs on a well-traveled road stretching through whorehouses and church socials from New Orleans to Fat Back, Ark.

The musicians' speeches are like improvised band solos—variously fizzy, haunting and mournful. . . . Gradually, we come to know these men, from their elusive pipe dreams to their hidden scars, but so deftly are the verbal riffs orchestrated that we don't immediately notice the incendiary drama boiling underneath.

That drama is ignited by a conflict between Ma and her young trumpeter Levee. . . . An ambitious sport eager to form his own jazz band, Levee mocks his employer's old "jugband music" and champions the new dance music that has just begun to usurp the blues among black audiences in the urban North. Already Levee has challenged Ma by writing a swinging version of "Ma Rainey's Black Bottom" that he expects the record company to use in place of the singer's traditional arrangement.

Yet even as the battle is joined between emblematic representatives of two generations of black music, we're thrust into a more profound war about identity. The African nationalist among the musicians, the pianist Toledo . . . , argues that, "We done sold ourselves to the white man in order to be like him." We soon realize that, while Ma's music is from the heart, her life has become a sad, ludicrous "imitation" of white stardom. Levee's music is soulful, too, but his ideal of success is having his "name in lights"; his pride is invested in the new shoes on which he's blown a week's pay.

Ma, at least, senses the limits of her success. Though she acts as if she owns the studio, she can't hail a cab in the white city beyond. She knows that her clout with the record company begins and ends with her viability as a commercial product: "When I've finished recording," she says, "it's just like I'd been some whore, and they roll over and put their pants on." Levee, by contrast, has yet to learn that a black man can't name his own terms if he's going to sell his music to a white world. As he plots his future career, he deceives himself into believing that a shoeshine and Uncle Tom smile will win white backers for his schemes.

Inevitably, the promised door of opportunity slams, quite literally, in Levee's face, and the sound has a violent ring that reverberates through the decades. Levee must confront not just the collapse of his hopes but the destruction of his dignity. Having played the white man's game and lost to its rigged rules, he is left with less than nothing: Even as [he] fails to sell himself to whites, Levee has sold out his own sense of self-worth.

In a rare reflective moment, [Ma Rainey] explains why she sings the blues. "You don't sing to feel better." . . . "You sing because that's a way of understanding life."

The lines might also apply to the play's author. Mr. Wilson can't mend the broken lives he unravels in *Ma Rainey's Black Bottom.* But, like his heroine, he makes their suffering into art that forces us to understand and won't allow us to forget. (pp. C1-C3)

> *Frank Rich, "Wilson's 'Ma Rainey's' Opens," in* The New York Times, *October 12, 1984, pp. C1, C3.*

HOWARD KISSEL

At times Wilson's humor [in *Ma Rainey's Black Bottom*] seems stereotyped, at others sharp and poignant. Throughout the play the dialog has a clear musical shape, a good-natured wit and a disarming, moving authenticity—many recent black plays have been built from jargon. Perhaps because of its period setting, Wilson's avoids such problems, striking the ear as fresh and authoritative.

Ma Rainey . . . and her immediate entourage . . . seem like stock characters, although the performances have vitality and charm. . . .

The characters Wilson seems to love best are the four jazzmen, beneath whose banter we sense the pain of the black experience—even Ma Rainey's. . . .

Ma Rainey is a play of great power mounted with sensitivity and uncommon grace.

> *Howard Kissel, in a review of "Ma Rainey's Black Bottom," in* Women's Wear Daily, *October 12, 1984. Reprinted in* New York Theatre Critics' Reviews, *Vol. XXXXV, No. 12, Week of September 17, 1984, p. 200.*

BRENDAN GILL

Ma Rainey's Black Bottom . . . is an excellent melodrama, and I am all the more eager to recommend it because it is the first New York production of a play written by a poet, August Wilson, hitherto unknown to me. Mr. Wilson gives every indication of being a born dramatist; we are sure to hear from him again. In such cases, it is always a welcome task to make the earliest possible acquaintance with the playwright's work and to follow it as it develops over time. *The Glass Menagerie* startled us when it first came to Broadway—startled us not least because of the ease with which it proved capable of moving us in spite of certain awkward dramaturgic mishaps on the part of its youthful author. *Ma Rainey's Black Bottom* is also startling, and in something like the same fashion. Mr. Wilson has mingled farce and tragedy in oddly unequal proportions, and there are moments when we observe him wrestling with that bugbear of any beginning playwright: how to get his characters plausibly on and off the stage when it is indispensable for him to do so. No matter! This is a genuine work of art, every turn of whose little plot we follow with interest (a pair of new shoes proves to be every bit as important in the telling of the story as Queequeg's sea chest is in *Moby Dick*), and its climax, unlooked-for and of extreme violence, is a stunning one. . . .

Much of the play is devoted to the conversation of the four backup men as they desultorily rehearse the numbers that Ma Rainey is about to sing. The four have been brilliantly drawn by Wilson, each of them being totally unlike his colleagues and yet in close rapport with them. Each has suffered from his blackness in a white society, and each has survived at a cost that we perceive only gradually, behind the funny and harsh insults and reveries that make up their badinage.

Brendan Gill, "Hard Times," in The New Yorker, *Vol. LX, No. 36, October 22, 1984, p. 152.*

JACK KROLL

Ma Rainey's Black Bottom sneaks up on you like the anger, pain and defiance that rides on the exultant notes of the blues. In this extraordinary Broadway debut by a new playwright, August Wilson, we're in a seedy recording studio in Chicago in 1927. Four black musicians and two white men are waiting for Gertrude (Ma) Rainey, the great blues singer, to arrive for a recording session. Ma is taking her time, and meanwhile the musicians swap stories and the white men—one the studio owner, the other Ma's manager—commiserate with each other and decide they'd just as soon be in the textile business. The stories are funny and the atmosphere seems casual: we're waiting for the star, and this play is going to be about her, Ma Rainey, the "mother of the blues." But with jolting dramatic irony Wilson subverts our expectations. These backup musicians are thrust forward as the recording session becomes a microcosm of the subjugation of black Americans.

Not that this is a grim and depressing play. It's a fierce and biting one, mixing the savage inevitability of black rage with the shrewd humor of jazz itself. That long wait for Ma is like a vamping introduction to a blues number, and the play tears through the dancing flesh of jazz to show us the tormented spirit inside.

Jack Kroll, "So Black and Blue," in Newsweek, *Vol. CIV, No. 17, October 22, 1984, p. 106.*

An Excerpt from *Ma Rainey's Black Bottom*

MA RAINEY: It sure done got quiet in here. I never could stand no silence. I always got to have some music going on in my head somewhere. It keeps things balanced. Music will do that. It fills things up. The more music you got in the world, the fuller it is.

CUTLER: I can agree with that. I got to have my music too.

MA RAINEY: White folks don't understand about the blues. They hear it come out, but they don't know how it got there. They don't understand that's life's way of talking. You don't sing to feel better. You sing 'cause that's a way of understanding life.

CUTLER: That's right. You get that understanding and you done got a grip on life to where you can hold your head up and go on to see what else life got to offer.

MA RAINEY: The blues help you get out of bed in the morning. You get up knowing you ain't alone. There's something else in the world. Something's been added by that song. This be an empty world without the blues. I take that emptiness and try to fill it up with something.

TOLEDO: You fill it up with something the people can't be without, Ma. That's why they call you the Mother of the Blues. You fill up that emptiness in a way ain't nobody ever thought of doing before. And now they can't be without it.

MA RAINEY: I ain't started the blues way of singing. The blues always been here.

CUTLER: In the church sometimes you find that way of singing. They got blues in the church.

MA RAINEY: They say I started it . . . but I didn't. I just helped it out. Filled up that empty space a little bit. That's all. But if they wanna call me the Mother of the Blues, that's all right with me. It don't hurt none.

DAVID RICHARDS

In a Broadway season notable only for what appears to be terminal anemia, *Ma Rainey's Black Bottom* . . . is not just a shot in the arm. It amounts to a veritable transfusion.

Throbbing with vitality and the kind of dialogue that burrows into the marrow, August Wilson's drama charts the storms that erupt one day in 1927 in a Chicago recording studio, where Ma Rainey, the legendary blues singer, is cutting such songs as "The Black Bottom" and "Moonshine Blues." Going behind the scenes to reveal the nuts and the bolts of show business as they come together—or come loose—has always been a particularly theatrical tactic. But if Wilson is opening doors generally closed to the public, it's not just to catch performers with their public masks down.

This is the "race division" of a white-owned and white-run recording company. And while the business at hand is getting Ma Rainey's voice on wax—and her signature on the mandatory release forms—the real dramatic business is the growing sense of checkmate that weighs on Ma and the four members of her backup band. All of them know instinctively that their usefulness, and whatever momentary civilities are being extended, will come to an end as soon as the afternoon session does.

Like Charles Fuller's *A Soldier's Play*, Wilson's play builds to a particularly violent revelation of the boomerang effects of racism. The whites in *Ma Rainey's Black Bottom* are all out of reach. The blacks must deal among themselves with the frustrations and injustices regularly meted out by a society that uses them only to make a buck. At the end, a knife flashes in the dank basement that passes for the musician's warm-up room. Black lashes out at black, stupidly, unknowingly, because there's no other target in sight. No other target is permissible. (p. H1)

Other plays have come to such bloody, melodramatic ends. What is remarkable in Wilson's work, his first for the stage, is the richness of its texture and the variety of its tone along the way. If the humor is savage in places, it is frankly robust in others. Red-hot anger exists alongside cool irony. The edginess overtaking the musicians as they wait in the basement for one of Ma Rainey's purposeful tantrums to pass does not preclude a farcical episode once they all get back up in the studio itself, and Ma insists that her nephew, a hopeless stutterer, speak the introduction to one of her numbers.

To Wilson's characters, music is music, but so is talk, and their banter ranges freely from the trivial to the blasphemous. So authentic does it sound coming from the mouths of a superlative cast that Wilson is already being hailed as a major new "voice" in the American theater.

The evidence is persuasive. The only thing that holds **Ma Rainey's** power partially in check is the work's rambling stop-and-go structure. Wilson seems at times to have written two plays and not been able to marry them as firmly as he wished. . . .

Wilson's play is ruled by two equally commanding creatures, each battling it out on separate turf. Although Ma Rainey and her musicians come together periodically for the actual recording sessions . . . the traffic between their two worlds is minimal. The power generated in the studio does not necessarily carry over into the band room, and vice versa. Repeatedly, the play halts here, so it can begin anew over there. Divided in its loyalties, it ends up dividing its impact. . . .

Even in the best of years, **Ma Rainey** would command attention. But at a time when Broadway can muster no more than a couple of openings a month . . . it stands out, and very nearly alone, for its integrity and its insight. It may be premature to hail Wilson as the next savior of the American theater, as more than a few New York critics have already done. But it is undeniable that he has redeemed what, up to now, has been a shockingly bankrupt season. (p. H4)

> *David Richards, "Look! Ma!: 'Rainey' Brings Life to Tired Broadway," in* Book World—The Washington Post, *November 18, 1984, pp. H1, H4.*

SYLVIE DRAKE

There is such a dearth of new plays on Broadway this season— the slowest season in years—that anything of some quality is received with fanfare and celebration.

That's partly what happened to **Ma Rainey's Black Bottom,** the freshest old-fashioned play to hit Broadway since *Ceremonies in Dark Old Men*. That it is yet another slice of realism about being black and disenfranchised in America becomes secondary to the play. The point is that it's tackled with skill, a sparkling grasp of language and potent dramatic values by August Wilson—a playwright who's been around and whose time hadn't come until now.

Everything about **Ma Rainey** sounds hackneyed. It takes the single instance of a recording session in—yup—the "Race" division of a 1927 Chicago studio to illustrate how Whitey exploits the black man—or woman. Ho-hum.

Yet, as always, plot is only a device. (You could say *Hamlet* is about an unstable son who can't adjust to his mother's new marriage.) **Ma Rainey** works because Wilson transcends its cliches. Incident is the springboard for creative talk by astutely drafted characters whose interaction illuminates a whole history of misplaced angers. It *feels* new even when it isn't. (p. 1)

Far from making music, **Ma Rainey** is about discord under the harmony. It's about partnerships of convenience and internalized fury that unleashes itself on the wrong target when the compression gets to be too much to bear.

Outwardly, then, **Ma Rainey** packs a wallop. But Wilson, who writes largely by implication, has created a subtle treatise on confrontational politics. It's about power and powerlessness: Ma vs. the studio, Levee vs. his peers, Ma vs. Levee, white against black, black against black.

However talky the play—and it is—the laconic dialogue is paradoxically brisk. It wraps itself around rivalries, uncovers sores, scours lingering hatreds and becomes this melodrama's single strongest asset. . . .

Oddly, what distinguishes **Ma Rainey** as a singularly moving experience is not its departures from, but its similarities to the best of black theater in America: a melding of sentimentality, sweetness, anger, violence and grace. (p. 3)

> *Sylvie Drake, "'Rainey': A Verbal Jam Session," in* Los Angeles Times, *November 24, 1984, pp. 1, 3.*

PAUL BERMAN

American culture contains only so many myths or stories of central importance, and one of those is surely the story of black music and its fate in the white world. Black musicians invent a certain style, demonstrate its brilliance and get clobbered for their efforts, is roughly how the story goes. You don't see it all that frequently in American literature, but on the stage it is a staple. (p. 626)

The appeal of the black music story is so obvious there's no point in spelling out its elements A to Z. But perhaps I'll go as far as D or E. The story has simplicity but also depth, which is why it qualifies as myth. It conjures a simple sympathy for the victims of bigotry, since musicians are by definition an inoffensive class, and if they are discriminated against, the injustice is undeniable. No explanation need be made about how these are well-behaved, decent musicians, as opposed to nasty, thuggish ones who deserve what they get. Then again, the story is not so simple and shows aspects of racial prejudice that can be harder to detect than straight-out Jim Crow injustice. (Jim Crow, by the way, was a nineteenth-century black minstrel dancer, and I wonder if he didn't play a role in one of the earliest versions of the black music story.) The story is very good, for instance, at showing the sometimes subtle snobbism in American life—snobbism, that most insidious of prejudices—that makes people foolishly denigrate black music as crude and unserious. (pp. 626-27)

At a deeper level, the black music story shows bias and bigotry in a dialectical light, every oppression matched by some form of resistance—usually, resistance that is moral and esthetic. The musicians are victims, but they are not only victims. The world has pretty much come to agree by now that black music is one of the glories of American culture, and even a tin-ear musician is likely to reflect some of the collective triumph.

"Extraordinary...a major find for the American theatre."
—Frank Rich, The New York Times

Ma Rainey's Black Bottom

A Play By
August Wilson

PLUME Ⓟ

Cover of Ma Rainey's Black Bottom, *by August Wilson. New American Library, 1985. Cover photograph by George G. Slade. Reproduced by permission of George G. Slade.*

Needless to say, the black music story doesn't bother with tin-ear musicians anyway. What it shows is black music blossoming magnificently before your eyes, and you come to feel that however downtrodden the musicians may be, they are better people with bigger souls and bigger talents than their oppressors. But it's true that the triumphal aspect of the story usually runs in a tragic vein. At perhaps its deepest level the story shows how the pressure of bigotry and the resulting sense of powerlessness among blacks produces the most awful violence, black against black. . . . And to mention one more trait, the story has an unusual quality among the great American myths: it is made for the stage.

Ma Rainey's Black Bottom offers a classic version of the black music story and does it from the moment the curtain goes up. The white owner of a record company ascends to his glass-enclosed control room and glowers at the studio floor below, where Ma Rainey and her band are going to cut a record. You notice immediately that here is a picture of how life appears to an ordinary black musician. The musician is down below actually making the music, and white society lurks above, isolated behind glass, controlling events for its own purposes. The four band members come in and spend their time warming up and hanging out in the rehearsal room, waiting for Ma to arrive so they can record. She does arrive, delays occur, they

perform, tensions produce a climax—and in the course of these events, each level of the classic story takes shape upon the stage. We see the straight-out Jim Crow bigotry, mostly through long monologues by the band members, who recall things that happened long ago. We see the more subtle bias, the denigration of the music by the man who is prospering from it, the record company owner, who hopes to get into a line that's more "respectable" than issuing blues records. We see how casually and callously the musicians are exploited.

We also see—and this is the strongest, most theatrical part of the play—how the musicians resist by affirming their superiority over the white powers-that-be. Ma enters the studio dressed like the Queen of England, trailing her retinue of a nephew and a lesbian lover, in an obvious challenge to the authority of her dour white manager and the equally dour studio owner. She behaves outrageously. She holds up the session while someone fetches her a Coke. And for a moment—so carefully are Ma and her challenge presented—we're not sure how to judge her. Maybe the owner is right and she is an impossible, disrespectful fool. But then we remember that Ma is the Mother of the Blues, that she's a great artist, that she can do things the owner could never dream of doing. We remember that Ma has been the meat and potatoes of this record company. Or never mind remembering, she tells us. And why shouldn't she hold up the works while someone runs out to fetch her a Coke? It may be that her imperial authority doesn't extend very far in white society, and that not even Ma Rainey can hail a taxi in the streets of Chicago. So what? She's still the Mother of the Blues. And having watched all this, and listened to her sing, we also watch the last and most terrible level of the black music story unfold, and we see the toll that resistance of this sort takes on the black world.

Now, not everything in *Ma Rainey's Black Bottom* is presented as well as one might wish. My colleague from *The Village Voice* Julius Novick has been railing against the naturalist clichés in *Ma Rainey,* and he's got a point. The long monologues by the trumpet player introduce the traumas of his childhood, the action introduces the traumas of his adulthood, and no one will fail to guess that a violent explosion is on its way. It arrives—boom!—but it can't help sounding like bombast. (pp. 627-28)

The music is another problem. . . . The whole play is designed to prevent the actors from having to perform more than an occasional note, and when the recording session finally begins, a rather well-done tape takes over and the actors merely pretend to play. But the few notes they offer in warming up fail to prepare us for that tape. The trumpet and trombone players have bad tones; they play tentatively. Yet the tape is smooth and professional. Nor do the actors behave like musicians. Real musicians love their "axes" and find it hard not to play them. But these stage musicians spend a couple of hours fingering their axes without much urge at all to tootle a few bars. The scene would be more convincing if the actors left their instruments alone instead of using them so promiscuously as props. In fact, the play would have been much better if it had been cast with actors who are also musicians, not an impossible combination, or if the band had been expanded to include a couple of real musicians. That way the play wouldn't be so frustrating to blues lovers who, when they see a blues band standing around with instruments in hand, want to hear, after all, the blues, and would prefer it live.

Too much is missing from *Ma Rainey* because the music is missing. We should feel that Ma and the band are great musicians not only because the playwright means us to feel this, and not only because they eventually do perform a first-rate blues number with the aid of tape and loudspeakers, but also because throughout the play this fact is evident, as it would be with real musicians. There is a subtheme, too, that might have been made more prominent. The trumpet player has turned against Ma's music, which he derides as jug-band stuff, and says he has developed a more modern style. A tiny hint of this style appears on the tape, and you are meant to feel that the trumpet player is on to something, perhaps that he's extremely talented. (The real Ma Rainey's trumpet player for some of her 1920s sessions was Louis Armstrong.) But even if he's not supposed to be a titan of jazz, you should feel in this trumpet player's pressure for innovation some of the dynamic of jazz development, the excitement of a musical genre being developed before your eyes. You should be able to see and not just deduce that Ma and her band figure in an important cultural movement, that these people aren't the humble offhand musicians you might take them for. But this is something the production can't deliver.

So *Ma Rainey's Black Bottom* stumbles where it should fly. Still, it remains a better play than its flaws might lead you to think—better because the black music story is such a powerful one, and better because of the sharp ear and trusty instinct Wilson . . . [brings] to black speech. There is a sweet slowness to the dialogue in *Ma Rainey* that is characteristic of a certain kind of Southern talk. Nothing clichéd about this aspect of the play, and as the dialogue circles around, now indulging a monologue, now bantering back and forth in the rehearsal room, you get the feeling that the play as a whole is a kind of blues song: relaxed, colloquial, deep, punctuated by solos, shaped by a pattern of theme, repetition and climax. . . . And since the play is the first by August Wilson to arrive in New York, one can say that it contains an additional element of suspense, a sort of suspended dominant chord at the end containing the question, What will his next play be like? (pp. 628)

Paul Berman, in a review of "Ma Rainey's Black Bottom," in The Nation, *Vol. 239, No. 19, December 8, 1984, pp. 626-28.*

STANLEY KAUFFMANN

The title is arresting—*Ma Rainey's Black Bottom*. The author, August Wilson, is black. There was a real Ma Rainey who made a record of that name in 1927. The program tells us that the setting is the Chicago studio where that record was cut. All these matters whet our appetite for social ironies. In proof, the promise is bigger than the fulfillment, but Wilson's play certainly has some rewards and encourages some hope. . . .

The first people to enter, opening the premises as well as the play, are the owner of the record company, who will go into the booth to monitor the sound, and Ma Rainey's manager. Both men are white, and both, as characters, are quickly discouraging. The owner is peevish about Ma's possible tardiness and tantrums, and the role continues at that one tonal level throughout. The manager, too, continues at one level throughout, conciliatory, pleading. They are clichés, the nervous impresario and the maneuvering agent, whom we have met in countless plays and films.

But the black characters, who soon begin to appear, tingle with some life. In essence they are familiar, too, from the sage old trombonist to the queenly Ma, but Wilson's writing shows a knowledge of them, an intensity, that makes them vital. This

vitality, more than anything that is explicitly said or thematically implied, is the play's best asset. . . .

Ma, too, is a familiar figure, the stout, domineering black queen, but she, too, is touched to vitality by Wilson's concern.

Still Wilson's intensity can't heal a central flaw. His work is split figuratively, just as the set is split literally, between the musicians and the star. The four men reveal themselves, with differing degrees of submission, as victims of the racial situation in America. Throughout the play, they use the word "nigger" to one another with grim self-mockery. The group's leader, the elderly trombonist . . . has seen so much injustice that, without ceasing to hate it, he has learned to live with it. It is he who gives the beat to the band whenever they start a number, and each time he starts them off with a phrase that comes to have a mordant ring, "A-one, a-two, y'all know what to do." *He* knows what to do; life has taught him.

The bassist . . . burdened though he is with his own painful memories, has converted his life into a pleasure machine. The pianist . . . , the thinker of the group, berates his friends for not reading, for not planning to change black conditions. The trumpeter, . . . is simultaneously the most hedonistic and the most cynical of the four. (p. 83)

Yet, on the other side of the stage, there is Ma . . . an absolute monarch whose idlest wish is law obeyed by white men and black. The play's action—its chief action *in the present tense*—lies in Ma's regal behavior. That present-tense action simply doesn't dramatize what the play is supposed to be about; what we see is the opposite of what we hear.

Ma says that when she makes a record she feels like a whore who is used and paid off, but surely that reaction isn't limited to black performers. And if Wilson intends us to view Ma's arrogance as symbolic revenge for the impotence of the musicians in the bandroom, he confuses this intent with another conflict. The trumpeter wants his version of "Black Bottom" used for the record. Ma refuses. He becomes insistent, and she fires him. He resents this hotly, and this heat sparks the play's explosive close, but the injustice he thinks he has suffered was at the hands of another black.

Further, the play has some clumsy construction which seemingly asks to be overlooked because of the grave theme. During one recording session, [Levee, the trumpeter,] . . . gives Ma's girlfriend the eye. Later, while they're all taking a break, the girl wanders down to the bandroom where [Levee] is alone at the time, so patly that we know exactly what's going to happen. And when [Levee] begins to move in on her, assuring her that no one will disturb them, we know that intimacy is being set up for interruption. The worst of the play's mechanics is the explosion at the close. After Ma fires [Levee], the studio owner pays him peanuts for the rights to two of his songs. (But we feel that this is not racist, that this man cheats everyone.) [Levee] is further heated. Then [Slow Drag, the bassist,] accidentally steps on [Levee's] new shoes. [Levee] almost deliberately whips himself into a manic fury so that he can stab [Slow Drag], as a release. That catastrophe, the killing of black by black, is clearly what Wilson wanted for his curtain, but he makes it much too clear that it's what he wanted. He contrives and shoves in order to get it.

Ma Rainey's Black Bottom, though not nearly the masterwork that a famished theater has called it, demonstrates a sharp eye for dramatic metaphor and dialogue that frequently flies. *Ma Rainey* is Wilson's first major production. He is thirty-nine, young enough for a long career, old enough to distill experience maturely. What he needs now, and what we have some right to hope for in him, is the art to match his human sympathies and his theatrical invention. (pp. 83, 90)

Stanley Kauffmann, "Bottoms Up," in Saturday Review, *Vol. 11, No. 1, January-February, 1985, pp. 83, 90.*

ROBERT LEITER

The language in *Ma Rainey's Black Bottom*—whether spoken or sung—is one of this fine first play's strong points. August Wilson is a poet as well as a playwright and the street patois he has devised for his characters sounds absolutely right. But even more unusual, he has conceived his play both as realism and metaphor (the title announces this predisposition) and both imaginative levels work without betraying one another. We believe what we see and hear, and it all resonates. (p. 299)

It is Levee who brings the play to its unfortunate melodramatic finale; by then we have realized that the character's long speeches have been grafted onto the action to justify his murderous rage.

In this respect, Wilson lacked the courage to let the metaphor at the heart of his play guide him. Apparently, he felt obligated to "create" a plot, and all his maneuvering seems to come straight out of some textbook idea of character motivation and play construction. Both acts are marred by too many broad comic moments and there is some unnecessary underlining of the play's theme throughout. All the talk of the "white man" and his oppression—when . . . the action just stops—is superfluous because the play, simply by "being," dramatizes the idea. Wilson should have trusted his metaphoric imagination more and used the blues to comment on the action. But this would have made the play less old-fashioned in design, perhaps harsher, more Brechtian, less willing to satisfy the expectations of a Broadway audience.

But these are minor faults. *Ma Rainey* plays exceedingly well, and Wilson is to be commended for his economy of means. . . . *Ma Rainey,* despite some lapses in judgment, hasn't an ounce of fat on it. (p. 300)

Robert Leiter, in a review of "Ma Rainey's Black Bottom," in The Hudson Review, *Vol. XXXVIII, No. 2, Summer, 1985, pp. 299-300.*

Tobias (Jonathan Ansell) Wolff

The Barracks Thief

PEN/Faulkner Award for Fiction

American short story writer, novelist, editor, and journalist.

Wolff's novel *The Barracks Thief* (1984) received little critical notice until it was awarded the PEN/Faulkner Award. Wolff, who was educated at Oxford and Stanford and currently teaches literature and creative writing at Syracuse University, has won two O. Henry prizes for his short stories. His first collection of stories, *In the Garden of North American Martyrs* (1981), received scattered but praiseworthy reviews for its compact prose and lucid characterizations. Wolff was compared, on the basis of this first collection, to his colleague at Syracuse, the short story writer and poet Raymond Carver, with whom he shares a stark vision of everyday life and ordinary people.

Like Wolff's shorter works *The Barracks Thief* delineates its characters and their experiences in a terse but powerful prose. In this story of three stateside paratroopers during the Vietnam War who are bonded together through a shared experience of self-imposed risk, Wolff concentrates on the thoughts and motivations of the characters rather than on their actions. The story is narrated primarily by Bishop, one of the paratroopers, but also includes passages that convey the viewpoints of the other characters. Wolff, who served in the army with a year's duty in Vietnam, notes that his experience in Vietnam has shaped his fiction. "I'll always in one way or another return to it in my writing," he comments. "It bent me a certain way— I don't mean misshaped me—and it put a kind of depression in my mind in which things gather occasionally, slide in, so I am compelled to return to it from time to time, without actually writing about Vietnam myself, which I find really hard to do." He further explains, "I seem to need to approach it from an oblique angle. Maybe some day I'll actually write about my experience in Vietnam itself, when I find a way to do that that makes me feel like I'm really telling the truth."

Critics commend *The Barracks Thief* for its tolerance and understanding for its characters, who often allow chance to direct their lives. Though showing the dark side of the personality, Wolff does not moralize or pass judgment. In an interview Wolff commented, "I don't see my people as being without insight or heart, or without nobility. But they are people who aren't what they dreamed they would be, and aren't what they still wish they were. I sympathize with them because—I suppose these things all come in some way from our own history— my own family had ups and downs, mostly downs, and I don't believe in security."

Since the publication of *The Barracks Thief*, Wolff has published a second collection of short stories, *Back in the World* (1985), which is similar to his earlier works in that the stories are succinct commentaries on human strengths and weaknesses, or, as reviewer Mona Simpson described them, "stripped-down moral fables." Like *The Barracks Thief*, some of the stories in *Back in the World* also treat the experience of American soldiers in Vietnam.

© *Mike Okoniewski*

(See also *Contemporary Authors*, Vol. 114.)

DON G. CAMPBELL

Three young paratroopers waiting to be shipped out to Vietnam—not really liking each other very much—share an experience guarding a fire-threatened ammunition dump in the deep South one steamy afternoon. It is a brush with danger and violence that is to mark them forever. In his thin novella, *The Barracks Thief* . . . , Tobias Wolff strips the souls bare of these three undistinguished young men. Back in the tedium of their barracks existence, a sudden rash of petty thefts throws everyone under suspicion and the camaraderie that has grown out of their dangerous afternoon together begins slowly unraveling. The dark sides of the three young men—their fears, uncertainties, tangled loyalties and instincts for betrayal—come sharply into focus.

Don G. Campbell, in a review of "The Barracks Thief," in Los Angeles Times Book Review, *July 29, 1984, p. 8.*

ANDRE DUBUS

Most of the action of **The Barracks Thief** occurs at Fort Benning, Ga., where the protagonist is undergoing paratrooper training before going to Vietnam. It is not a story of training: Remarkably, Wolff limits actual training scenes and focuses instead on the more significant and universal actions and complex motivations and desires of three men. Not since Conrad's *The Nigger of the Narcissus* have I read such an excellent dramatization of the singularity and therefore isolation of men who are otherwise joined together by male work: joined ephemerally before the final rending. If words on paper could make sounds, you would hear me shouting now, urging you to read this book right now.

Andre Dubus, in a review of "The Barracks Thief," in America, *Vol. 151, No. 5, September 1-8, 1984, p. 109.*

WALTER KENDRICK

"He said that a barracks thief was the lowest thing there was. A barracks thief had turned his back on his own kind. He went on like that." A first sergeant is about to retire, after 20 years of faithful service, and his final Army days have been soured by such a tawdry, disgraceful incident. A month or so later, dressed in garish, ill-fitting civilian clothes, the first sergeant (he has no other name) drives away from his last post without a word or a wave. "There goes a true soldier," remarks a pompous second lieutenant whom the enlisted men usually ignore. This time, however, Philip Bishop listens: "the lieutenant meant what he said, and I thought he was right."

The first sergeant's dismay is a peripheral matter in *The Barracks Thief,* Tobias Wolff's short, incisive first novel.... Most of our attention is focused on Bishop and his friends Hubbard and Lewis, airborne trainees at Fort Bragg, N.C., in the summer of 1967. But it is typical of Mr. Wolff's command of eloquent detail that, though we are told next to nothing about the first sergeant, a few sentences serve to delineate his proud past, sad present and uncertain future. The mood is typical, too: neither the first sergeant nor the lieutenant, nor even Bishop himself, is a particularly likable character, yet they all are portrayed with clear-eyed generosity.

Bishop plays a minor role in the events that give **The Barracks Thief** its title, but the novel is principally his story; it begins with a sketch of his frustrated, empty childhood and ends with his reflections, nearly two decades later, on what meaning, if any, those events possess. Young Bishop's father has left home, his mother is near hysteria all the time, and his brother is fast turning into a stoned dropout; a mortifying encounter with his repentant father leads Bishop to decide that he has no choice but to join the Marines—which he cannot manage because the recruiting office is closed when he arrives. So, with no more forethought than that, he walks up the street and joins the Army instead. Like Mr. Wolff's other characters, though less disastrously than most, he lets accident and inadvertence run his life for him.

At Fort Bragg, surrounded by cynical Vietnam returnees who sneer at his inexperience, Bishop is naturally thrown together with other greenhorns—or "piglets," "warts" and "toads,"

as the first sergeant calls them. The slow, stumbling process by which Bishop becomes friends with Hubbard and Lewis is told with remarkable delicacy and convincingness. They are unlovely creatures, devoid of wit, and Lewis might even be crazy; but they are human, and Mr. Wolff treats their awkward, vague emotions as fully worthy of respect on that account.

A decisive incident occurs on a sweltering Fourth of July afternoon, when the three are assigned guard duty at an ammunition dump 30 miles from the post. A forest fire breaks out nearby, and the local police arrive to rescue the endangered soldiers. The first sergeant, however, has ordered them to shoot anyone who comes too near. In the crisis, each reveals himself: "Back off," Lewis keeps repeating, aiming his rifle at an astonished policeman; hesitant at first, Hubbard finally sides with Lewis; Bishop, the observer, remains neutral. Their rescuers flee, and the fire dies out; nothing, after all, has happened. But bonds have been formed.

Most of **The Barracks Thief** is told from Bishop's point of view, but at times Mr. Wolff's narrative turns more fluid, portraying the thoughts and experiences of several characters, giving the reader fuller knowledge of the course of events than any participant possesses. In less skillful hands, this technique might have been merely tricky, but Mr. Wolff makes it work to his advantage.

The pathos of these people (it is too muted to be called tragedy) resides in the way they blunder from one mistake to another, ignorant of their own motives and blind to consequences. Just as Bishop joins the Army because his father has embarrassed him, so Lewis becomes a despicable barracks thief because he stings his hand on nettles at the ammunition dump. The intricate chain of events that leads to Lewis's disgrace proceeds independently of anyone's will, as if some vengeful god were forging it. The atmosphere recalls Thomas Hardy, but Hardy is seldom generous, while Mr. Wolff has boundless tolerance for the stupid sorrow of ordinary human entanglements.

Exposed, Lewis breaks down, is beaten by his former buddies (excluding Bishop and Hubbard) and disappears from Bishop's life. Not long thereafter, Hubbard deserts to Canada, and Bishop loses track of him, too. Seventeen years later, married and a father, Bishop has become "a careful man, addicted to comfort, with an eye for the safe course." He would never do anything so foolish as he and his two friends did one Fourth of July long ago.

Yet the memory endures: "Three men with rifles," he keeps thinking, "three crazy paratroopers inside the fence." The mere absence of a spark from that forest fire has produced, by inexorable logic, his current placid state; but he might—just might—have gone out with a bang: "They'd have heard the blast clear to Fort Bragg. They'd have seen the sky turn yellow and red and felt the earth shake. It would have been something."

Mr. Wolff does not editorialize. We are left to make up our own minds whether it is better to die spectacularly or to dribble on for decades in safe conventionality. The world of *The Barracks Thief* contains no answers, even when—and this is rare—its inhabitants gain enough perspective to pose coherent questions. It is a bleak place, short on joy and very long on undeserved suffering; when happiness briefly flares up, redoubled misery quickly quenches it.

Mr. Wolff's grim vision is relieved only by the simple fact that he grants his characters the dignity of telling their story—

without hope, perhaps, but also without apology or complaint. And there are splendid moments, like the night of July 4, 1967, when three crazy paratroopers, too elated for sleep, sit on the steps of the orderly room: "Hubbard suddenly threw his hands in the air. In a high voice he said, 'Boys, be reasonable,' and we all started laughing. I was in the middle. I didn't think about it, I just reached out and put my arms on their shoulders. We were in a state."

Walter Kendrick, "Men with Rifles," in The New York Times Book Review, *June 2, 1985, p. 42.*

An Excerpt from *The Barracks Thief*

"You're a smart boy," the man said. "I can see that. Use the brains God gave you. Just put one foot in front of the other."

"You've been told to back off," Hubbard said. "You won't be told again."

"Boys, be reasonable."

Hubbard swung his rifle up and aimed it at the man's head. The motion was natural. The other man leaned out the car window and shouted, "Come on! Hell with 'em!" The deputy chief looked at him and back at us. He took his hands away from the fence. He was shaking all over. A grasshopper flew smack into his cheek and he threw up his arms as if he'd been shot. The car horn honked twice. He turned and walked to the car, got inside, and the two men drove away.

We stood at the fence and watched the car until it disappeared around a curve.

"It's no big deal," I said. "They'll put the fire out."

And so they did. But before that happened there was one bad moment when the wind shifted in our direction. We had our first taste of smoke then. The air was full of insects flying away from the fire, all kinds of insects, so many it looked like rain falling sideways. They rattled against the buildings and pinged into the fence.

Hubbard had a coughing fit. He sat on his helmet and put his head between his knees. Lewis went over to him and started pounding him on the back. Hubbard tried to wave Lewis off, but he kept at it. "A little smoke won't hurt you," Lewis said. Then Lewis began to cough. A few minutes later so did I. We couldn't stop. Whenever I took another breath it got worse. I ached from it, and began to feel dizzy. For the first time that day I was afraid. Then the wind changed again, and the smoke and the bugs went off in another direction. A few minutes later we were laughing.

The black smudge above the trees gradually disappeared. It was gone by the time the first sergeant pulled up to the gate. He only spoke once on the drive home, to ask if we had anything to report. We shook our heads. He gave us a look, but didn't ask again. Night came on as we drove through the woods, headlights jumping ahead of us on the rough road. Tall pines crowded us on both sides. Overhead was a ribbon of dark blue. As we bounced through the potholes I steadied myself with my rifle, feeling like a commando returning from a suicide mission.

BRUCE ALLEN

This remarkable short novel [*The Barracks Thief*], virtually unnoticed by reviewers (including this one) when it appeared, . . . was recently named the winner of the PEN Faulkner Award for the year's most distinguished work of American fiction. It is a more than worthy choice, and a powerful reminder to those of us who think we know the literary territory that every serious book has a claim on us, and that there really isn't any substitute for reading everything, or at least trying to.

The story begins in Seattle in the mid-1960s, focusing on a soon-to-be-broken family, the Bishops, and following the beginning military career of their eldest son, Philip, a confused and angry boy drifting away from family and toward nothing in particular. Philip joins the Army as a paratrooper trainee, and the quiet, rather flat omniscient narrative describes his basic training experiences in Georgia and North Carolina preparatory to a tour of duty in Vietnam.

Then, by way of a daring and surprising shift in viewpoint, we enter the mind and feelings of a parallel character—one of

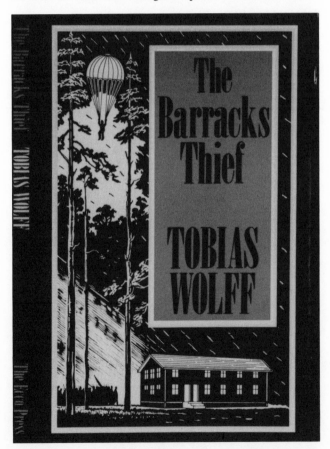

Dust jacket of The Barracks Thief, *by Tobias Wolff. The Ecco Press, 1984. Jacket design © Reg Perry. By permission of the publisher.*

Philip's Army buddies. Their separate stories cohere, stunningly (though Wolff never forces the connections), and confer real power on the ending that shows Philip in later life, long after Vietnam, having become ''a careful man'' and now remembering ''how it felt to be a reckless man with reckless friends.''

The Barracks Thief is a moving and original rendering of antagonisms and apprehensions probably peculiar to youth at any time, but intensified in the twin contexts of ongoing war and a culture that seems to view separation, even alienation, as available social options.

Wolff displays his characters' ennui and semi-despair in abrupt Hemingway-like scenes that understate strong emotion and slowly draw us deep inside these embryonic lives struggling toward maturity and completion.

There are several fully rounded, moving scenes: Philip rejecting his estranged father's ardent efforts to reconnect; a confrontation between soldiers on parade and a cadre of war protesters; a hallucinatory extended description of three soldiers guarding an ammo dump as a nearby fire intensifies. In fact, so many recognizable longings and fears are packed into this taut book's brief compass that we come away from it scarcely believing how much its people, and we, have been through.

> *Bruce Allen, ''Nam Book Year's Best,'' in* The Christian Science Monitor, *June 7, 1985, p. B7.*

WILLIAM L. TAZEWELL

The Barracks Thief is about three paratroopers in the 82nd Airborne Division at Fort Bragg. The chance of military service has thrown them together. One steals the second's wallet; the third is the narrator who tells what happened. It is a novella, or long short story, suggesting the dimensions of the nine-tenths of the iceberg that is underwater, the novel unwritten. It's not much more than an hour's reading, but it stays with you. It is a book of high intensity, told in a voice with near-perfect pitch. In many respects—length, subject, style, tensile strength—it is similar to *The Long March,* the 1952 novella by William Styron, the best book he has written.

> *William L. Tazewell, ''Writers' Prizes: A Positive View,'' in* The Virginian-Pilot and The Ledger-Star, *June 9, 1985, p. C6.**

MONA SIMPSON

[In the novella *The Barracks Thief,*] about three young paratroopers waiting to be shipped to Vietnam, Wolff once again deftly stages a small-scale moral drama. A mysterious series of thefts occur within their company, involving each of the three boys: thief, victim, and bystander. Our narrator, neither the thief nor the victim, at first feels guilt, as if he may have somehow committed the crime without knowing it. When the thief is caught, the protagonist swells with the idea of revenge, though years later he confesses that he is uneasy with his ostensibly firm moral convictions. ''I didn't set out to be what I am,'' he says at the book's close. ''I'm a conscientious man, maybe even what you'd call a good man—I hope so. But I'm also a careful man, addicted to comfort, with an eye for the safe course.'' Again, the story is told by the good man, neither the victim nor the perpetrator—ironically, the only one of the three who ultimately goes to Vietnam. (p. 38)

> *Mona Simpson, ''The Morality of Everyday Life,'' in* The New Republic, *Vol. 193, No. 24, December 9, 1985, pp. 37-8.*

Obituaries

Necrology

Riccardo Bacchelli . . . . October 8, 1985

Alvah Bessie . . . . July 21, 1985

Heinrich Boll . . . . July 16, 1985

Basil Bunting . . . . April 17, 1985

Taylor Caldwell . . . . August 30, 1985

Italo Calvino . . . . September 19, 1985

Salvador Espriu . . . . February 22, 1985

Robert Fitzgerald . . . . January 16, 1985

Robert Graves . . . . December 7, 1985

Geoffrey Grigson . . . . December 6, 1985

James Hanley . . . . November 11, 1985

Alex LaGuna . . . . October 11, 1985

Philip Larkin . . . . December 2, 1985

Helen McInnes . . . . September 30, 1985

Josephine Miles . . . . May 11, 1985

Elsa Morante . . . . November 25, 1985

Shiva Naipaul . . . . August 13, 1985

F.R. Scott . . . . February 8, 1985

Theodore Sturgeon . . . . May 8, 1985

E.B. White . . . . October 1, 1985

Heinrich (Theodor) Böll

December 21, 1917 - July 16, 1985

(Also transliterated as Boell) German novelist, short story writer, essayist, dramatist, and translator.

(See also *CLC*, Vols. 2, 3, 6, 9, 11, 15, 27 and *Contemporary Authors*, Vols. 21-24, rev. ed., Vol. 116 [obituary].)

PRINCIPAL WORKS

Der Zug war pünktlich (novella) 1949
  [*The Train Was on Time*, 1956; also published in *Adam and the Train: Two Novels*, 1970]
Wanderer, kommst du nach Spa (short stories) 1950
  [*Traveler, If You Come to Spa*, 1956]
Wo warst du, Adam? (novel) 1951
  [*Adam, Where Art Thou?*, 1955; also published in *Adam and the Train: Two Novels*, 1970; and as *And Where Were You, Adam?*, 1974]
Und sagte kein einziges Wort (novel) 1953
  [*Acquainted with the Night*, 1954]
Haus ohne Hüter (novel) 1954
  [*Tomorrow and Yesterday*, 1957; also published as *The Unguarded House*, 1957]
Das Brot der frühen Jahre (novel) 1955
  [*The Bread of Our Early Years*, 1957; also published as *The Bread of Those Early Years*, 1976]
Irisches Tagebuch (travel essays) 1957
  [*Irish Journal*, 1967]
Doktor Murkes gesammeltes Schweigen, und andere Satiren (satires) 1958
Billard um Halbzehn (novel) 1959
  [*Billiards at Half Past Nine*, 1961]
Ein Schluck Erde (drama) 1962
Ansichten eines Clowns (novel) 1963
  [*The Clown*, 1965]
Entfernung von der Truppe (novella) 1964
  [*Absent without Leave* published in *Absent without Leave: Two Novellas*, 1965; also published in *Absent without Leave and Other Stories*, 1967]
Ende einer Dienstfahrt (novel) 1966
  [*End of a Mission*, 1967; also published as *The End of a Mission*, 1968]
Gruppenbild mit Dame (novel) 1971
  [*Group Portrait with Lady*, 1973]
Die verlorene Ehre von Katharina Blum; oder, Wie Gewalt entstehen und wohin sie führen kann (novel) 1974
  [*The Lost Honor of Katharina Blum; or, How Violence Develops and Where It Can Lead*, 1975]
Was soll aus dem Jungen bloss werden? oder, Irgendwas mit Büchern (memoirs) 1981
  [*What's to Become of the Boy? or, Something to Do with Books*, 1984]
Fürsorgliche Belangerung (novel) 1982
  [*The Safety Net*, 1982]
Frauen vor Flußlandschaft (novel) 1985

© Lütfi Özkök

The Collected Stories of Heinrich Böll (short stories and novellas) 1986

ANNA TOMFORDE

Heinrich Boell, who was not only West Germany's best-known novelist but also often referred to as the country's literary conscience because of his critical involvement in every stage of its postwar development, died [July 17] at the age of 67.

Mr. Boell, the author of more than 40 novels, short stories and works of nonfiction, was awarded the Nobel Prize for Literature in 1972. . . .

Mr. Boell's social conscience, strong moral courage and deep-seated hatred of militarism, war and totalitarianism, led him to defend human and civil rights for people as far apart as Russian dissidents and West German Baader-Meinhof terrorists.

As a writer, he began to make his mark after 1947 with short stories, radio plays and novels. Most contained a strong streak of social satire, describing how Germans experienced the war, were caught up in Naziism and later adjusted to the postwar society.

Mr. Boell's best-known novels included *Billiards at Half Past Nine, The Clown,* and *Group Portrait with Lady.*

Short stories such as **"Something Must Happen"** parodied postwar West German mania for efficiency in the workplace that characterized the republic's "economic miracle."

His stubborn nonconformity and relentless questioning led to his enjoying greater recognition abroad than in his native country, where his reputation declined after he accused the authorities of "hysteria" in their fight against the terrorist wave of the 1970s, and warned against increased state control of the critical individual.

But the writer had already withdrawn from active support for the established political setup, after his disenchantment with day-to-day Social Democrat policies, after Willy Brandt, for whom he had earlier campaigned, was returned to power in 1972.

He focused his attention on the new social movements arising in West Germany, the citizens' groups, the antinuclear movement and later, the Green Party. Mr. Boell joined thousands of young protesters who squatted outside the US Army Base at Mutlangen in the fall of 1983, to express their opposition to Pershing II missiles.

During his rare public appearances in recent years, Mr. Boell gave the impression of a lonely man, and yet, it was to him that the young were looking for guidance in determining Germany's place in superpower politics 40 years after the war.

"I think the Germans are discovering something akin to patriotism. They realize that the next war will take place on their territory, and that Germany could be reunited on the battlefield," he said in 1983, giving his reasons for the widescale opposition to the deployment of new American medium-range missiles here.

But despite his increasingly bitter attacks on US policy, in Europe and in the Third World, Mr. Boell never lost his reputation for balance and integrity.

His involvement on behalf of Russian dissidents—he received Alexander Solzhenitsyn when he emigrated from his homeland in 1974, and was similarly active in the continuing efforts to secure freedom for Andrei Sakharov—earned him scathing comments in Communist East Germany, and support among West Germany's intellectuals.

The son of a sculptor, he began as an apprentice in the book trade in 1937. He went into military service in World War II and was wounded three times. In the immediate postwar years, Mr. Boell studied German linguistics at Cologne University. In 1947 his short stories started appearing in various newspapers and on radio programs. His first novel, *The Train Was on Time,* was published in 1949.

> *Anna Tomforde, "Heinrich Boell, Author, Known as 'Literary Conscience' of W. Germany," in* Boston Globe, *July 17, 1985.*

LOS ANGELES TIMES

An outspoken and often controversial proponent of leftist causes, Boell published more than 40 novels, short stories and radio plays. His works were translated into 45 languages, including Russian.

He was awarded the Nobel literature prize in 1972, the first German to be presented the honor since Thomas Mann received it in 1929.

In presenting the award, the Swedish Academy of Arts and Sciences cited Boell "for his writing which, through its combination of its broad perspective on his themes and a sensitive skill in characterization, has contributed to a renewal of German literature."

In accepting the award, Boell told of his struggles as a disillusioned, war-weary veteran who, he later recalled, had been burdened "by the frightful fate of being a soldier and having to wish that the war might be lost."

He told the Nobel Prize ceremony: "The way has been long for me here. Like millions of others I came home from the war with empty hands. But I had the passion to write and keep on writing."

Boell's major works included *The Lost Honor of Katharina Blum,* which critics suggested reflected the lives of the notorious Baader-Meinhof urban guerrilla group that terrorized West Germany in the 1970s. The book was seen as a reflection of Boell's concern over moves to suppress civil rights in the effort to crush urban terrorism.

Boell's first short novel was *The Train Was on Time* (1947), which chronicles the last days in the life of a young German soldier who returns to the Russian front after a furlough. Resigned to his death, the soldier tries to live as intensively as possible beforehand.

Born Dec. 21, 1917, in Cologne, the youngest of eight children of a sculptor and cabinetmaker, Boell ranked as West Germany's first angry young man, and many considered him the republic's conscience.

He was drafted into the German army in 1938 after he had worked in the book trade for a year. He fought on both the Western and Eastern fronts and was wounded three times.

The American Army captured him in 1944. After his release following the war, Boell returned to Cologne and worked as a cabinetmaker and began writing.

In the immediate postwar years, Boell studied German linguistics at Cologne University. In 1947 his short stories started appearing in various newspapers and on radio programs.

He founded a film society in 1971 and was the publisher of works by Soviet novelist Alexander I. Solzhenitsyn in 1974.

Having won a reputation for his anti-war books, Boell turned his critical eye on West Germany's startling economic recovery, with a satirical collection of short stories titled *Dr. Murke's Collection of Silences, and Other Satires.*

Billiards at Half Past Nine followed and many critics considered it Boell's best book. It tells the story of three generations of a family of German architects. The central character, Robert Faehmel, by destroying an abbey built by his father, protests what he believes to be the Catholic Church's tolerance of the Nazis.

Boell was a longtime supporter of the nation's Social Democratic Party, and in 1983 caused a stir when he announced he would vote for the radical environmentalist Greens party.

At the time, Boell said he felt that the Greens' fresh, unorthodox approach should be represented in Parliament. He added that he was perplexed by the hostility to intellectuals he had found in the country's mainstream political parties.

Boell joined West Germany's anti-nuclear movement in the 1980s, campaigning against deployment of new U.S. missiles.

"Nobel Laureate Heinrich Boell Dies at 67," in Los Angeles Times, *July 17, 1985, p. 14.*

ERIC PACE

Mr. Böll, a corporal in the German infantry during World War II, returned to his native Cologne in late 1945, when much of Germany and German cultural life lay in ruins, and began his career as a writer. Over the years, in the words of his Nobel Prize citation, his novels and short stories "contributed to a renewal of German literature" through their "combination of a broad perspective on his time and a sensitive skill in characterization."

At the time Mr. Böll received the prize—he was the first German citizen to win it since Thomas Mann in 1929—his popularity and prestige in Europe were phenomenal. More than any other German writer, he constituted a link between capitalist West Germany, where he was a best-selling author, and Communist East Germany, where his works came to be the best-selling West German fiction; when he gave readings in East Berlin, the auditoriums were packed.

His work was praised by Marxist critics throughout the Communist bloc, despite the fact that, though he left the Roman Catholic Church in 1976, he remained an intensely moral Christian. He was as popular in Poland as in Sweden, and in the Soviet Union he was the best-selling contemporary non-Soviet author.

Some of his work, which included essays, articles and radio and stage plays, was translated into many languages, and millions of copies of his books were sold, including, by one estimate, as many as four million copies in the Soviet Union.

Mr. Böll also won international reknown as a champion of writers' freedom. He used his personal prestige and position as president, for several years, of the international PEN club, the writers' organization, to try to help suppressed and oppressed East European writers in various ways. In 1974, when Aleksandr I. Solzhenitsyn was expelled from the Soviet Union, his first refuge was Mr. Böll's farmhouse.

As an activist and as a writer, Mr. Böll was a perennial critic and foe of establishments, bureaucracies and inhumane rules—of any kind of oppressive institutionalized power. In 1979, when the West German Government awarded him a medal, he refused to take it, saying: "Medals don't suit me. I'm not that kind of guy."

Mr Böll's manner and appearance were appropriately easy-going and rumpled, and he almost never wore a tie. He was 5 feet 10 inches tall, mostly bald, with brown eyes set in an amiable, ordinary face.

Much of Mr. Böll's literary output—a score of books by him appeared in German and more than a dozen in English—was set in the Rhineland, where he was born and where he spent

most of his life. Cologne, the great Rhine river port near the Dutch and Belgian borders, was the setting for his 1971 novel, *Group Portrait With Lady,* which the Nobel Prize committee called his "most grandly conceived work." Its main character, a debt-ridden widow, was the focus for a survey of German life during five decades.

Praising the book, Richard Locke wrote in *The New York Times* that the writing had "an exemplary moral directness."

Mr. Böll also came in for criticism. Some critics termed some of his writing boring, too sentimental, two-dimensional in its characterizations and too harsh in its depiction of certain elements in West German society, notably the police and the hierarchy of the Roman Catholic Church.

Heinrich Theodore Böll—the pronunciation falls between Bohl and Bell—was born Dec. 21, 1917, in Cologne, the last of eight children born to Viktor Böll, a cabinetmaker and sculptor, and Maria Hermanns Böll.

Some of young Heinrich's earliest memories were of buying candy with banknotes, given him by his father, that were emblazoned with many zeroes. Severe inflation was racking the country, and a handful of candy, Mr. Böll recalled vividly in middle age, cost 1 billion marks or more.

As a student in a Cologne secondary school, Mr. Böll was one of the few boys in his class who did not join the Hitler youth. He spent his spare time writing poems and stories, and formed a harsh view of the education of that day.

"The Nazi period could have happened only in Germany," he said years later, in part "because the German education of obedience to any law and order was the main problem."

He graduated from secondary school in 1937, briefly worked in a bookstore and studied philology for a few months. With the outbreak of World War II, he was assigned to a frontline infantry unit. He served on Germany's East and West fronts, was repeatedly wounded and, as he later recalled, "became convinced of the almost total senselessness of the military life."

In April 1945, while on the Western front not far from Cologne, Corporal Böll was taken prisoner. "I will never forget the moment when I was liberated by the American Army," he wrote years later.

Released, he matriculated at the University of Cologne and began writing. His first novel, *The Train Was on Time,* appeared in 1949 and was widely praised. Written in a blunt style that contrasted with the bombast of the Nazi era, it was about the last days of a sensitive young German soldier returning to the front. His second book, the short-story collection *Traveler, If You Come to Spa* (1950), was about people whose lives are scarred by the war and the early postwar period. The 1951 novel *Adam, Where Art Thou,* about officers and soldiers of a German army unit, was strongly antiwar.

Mr. Böll won particularly high praise for *Billiards at Half-Past Nine* (1959), a panoramic work about three generations in a family of German architects, and *The Clown* (1963), a study of an outsider condemned to live in a sterile hypocritical world.

A perennial gadfly in West Germany's public life, Mr. Böll campaigned for its Social Democratic Party in 1972, but later became disillusioned.

Mr. Böll's 1979 satirical novel, which came out in the United States with the title *Safety Net,* was praised by the *Times Lit-*

erary Supplement in London as helping "to throw a sharp and revealing light on important aspects of life in West Germany."

Mr. Böll's other last works included the memoir *What's to Become of the Boy? or: Something to Do With Books* [*Was soll aus dem Jungen bloss werden?; oder, Irgendwas mit Büchern*], which first appeared in 1981.

Joan Daves, who has represented Mr. Böll in the United States for 33 years, said yesterday that a new novel by him will be published in West Germany this fall. Carol Janeway, a vice president at Knopf, said her publishing house would bring out a translation of the novel in 1986. It is about women in a West German political setting, she said, and was finished by Mr. Böll this spring.

In 1942, Mr. Böll married Annemarie Cech, who collaborated with him in translating works of J. D. Salinger, Bernard Malamud and other English-language authors into German.

> Eric Pace, "Heinrich Böll, West German Novelist, Dead at 67," in The New York Times, *July 17, 1985, p. A20.*

THE TIMES, LONDON

Heinrich Böll, who died [July 17] at his home in the Eifel Mountains aged 67, was a writer in the mainstream of European humanism, a Catholic and a Socialist who in 1972 became the first German to win the Nobel Prize for Literature since Thomas Mann. Encompassing both the disorientation of defeat and the complacency of affluence, Böll's work offers a subtle, compassionate and wholly individual portrait of German society since 1945.

Born in 1917 in Cologne, where he lived and worked for most of his life, Heinrich Theodor Böll was the sixth son of a cabinet-maker and woodcarver of British descent. After Gymnasium he was apprenticed to a bookseller in the city before being conscripted and serving through the war, chiefly on the Russian Front. He was wounded four times, and remained a corporal.

When he began writing he faced the huge task of cultural regeneration common to all German artists at the time. No words were safe. Language had been debauched by twelve years of dictatorship, and it was one [of the] aims of the *Gruppe 47* writers, whom he joined in 1950, to rebuild the German language into what Böll himself defined as a new vehicle of "monologue, dialogue and prayer".

German critics compared the plain, laconic speech of the common soldiers in Böll's first stories—*Der Zug war pünktlich* (1949, *The Train was on time*); *Wanderer, kommst du nach Spa* (1950, *So, Traveller, if you come to Spa*); and *Wo warst Du, Adam?* (1951, *Adam, where art thou?*) to that of Hemingway. But plain speech alone could not contain the irrational elements in modern German history, and Böll's talent for social realism was equalled, if not at times surpassed, by his sharp, poetical eye.

Reminiscence haunted his fiction. Echoing Yeats (he sustained strong affinities with Ireland, translated Behan and Synge, owned a house there for many years, published an Irish journal and wrote with intelligence about the North) he defended memories and beliefs as sacred dreams and, whilst occasionally employing the kind of elaborate allegory whose resonance does not survive translation, came increasingly to evoke what one critic called "the intrinsic strangeness of familiar things": a pale square on a classroom wall where the Führer's portrait used to

hang; a thin red line of ink through the name of a boy who has fallen through the third floor of a bombed house, together with the washing machine he had been sent up to save (*The Bread of Those Early Years,* 1955, translated 1977).

Drawing on the prevalent language of the Absurd in the Fifties, he wrote one story about silences lovingly cut and spliced from his own tapes by a desperate radio producer, and another about a critic who became so neurotic about undoing books for review that he reviewed the parcels themselves and placed them on the shelves of his library unopened.

The stories are funny, the metaphors speak of a country tiptoeing round a void. "A global catastrophe can serve many purposes", wrote Theodor Haecker in a passage quoted at the head of *Wo warst Du, Adam?* in its second English translation (1975).

"One of them is to provide an alibi when God asks "And where were you, Adam?" "I was in the war.""

Böll was by no means the only—nor, after the emergence of Günter Grass in 1959 the most gifted—writer dedicated to piercing the collective amnesia which settled over the Nazi years after the war, but he was unusually successful in showing that public responsibility and personal freedom were not merely compatible with one another, but were inseparable halves of the same thing: individual conscience.

A steady stream of radio plays, stories, novels, lectures and reviews made the point with quiet consistency and mounting anger for nearly thirty years—among them *Billard um halbzehn* (1959, *Billiards at half-past nine*), *Ansichten eines Clowns* (1963, *The Clown*), *Entfernung von der Truppe* (1964, *Absent Without Leave*) and *Ende einer Dienstfahrt* (1966, *End of a Mission*)—and when the intellectual unrest of the late 1960s and the urban terrorism of the 1970s challenged Böll's definition of conscience in the most direct and painful way he was thrust into a position of moral leadership he had never sought but which he filled, so far as could be seen from outside Germany itself, with fierce integrity and noble courage.

The award of the Nobel Prize and the Presidency of International PEN (1971-4) merely placed him more clearly in the enemy's sights and he had the distinction of being savaged by both *Literaturnaya Gazeta* in Moscow, for his defence of dissident writers, and by *Quick* magazine at home, for seeking to temper the reactionary stampede that threatened to follow the kidnap of Hanns-Martin Schleyer in 1977.

To the astonishment of his admirers in Britain, who had grown steadily since the early 1970s, this shy, benevolent and humorous man was reviled as "a spiritual instigator of terrorism". Apart from his friend Solzhenitsyn, for whom [he] carried manuscripts out of the Soviet Union and who turned to him first on his expulsion to the West in 1974, it is hard to think of any European writer whose moral stature stood so high at the end of that hard decade for writers.

Böll's humanitarianism was felt and expressed on behalf of the inarticulate and disadvantaged, the "People" for whom at various times the Baader-Meinhof gang, the German tabloid Press, his own Catholic Church (whose role in the war he came increasingly to attack) and Brandt's Social Democratic Party, for whom he actively campaigned in 1972, all claimed to speak. He once divided human society into "buffaloes" and "lambs", exploiters and exploited, and whilst siding with the lambs, he realized that they too had often learned nothing from the disasters of Weimar, Hitler and Year Zero except that they must never go hungry.

Latterly he had supported the Green party and joined demonstrators blockading American bases in Germany.

Exploiters and exploited were at least alike in wishing to be freed from their guilt in the past, and when their own innocence was denied them they could turn viciously on anyone who withheld it—anyone suspected of the slightest association with terrorism, for example, like the heroine of *Die Verlorene Ehre von Katharine Blum* (1974, *The Lost Honour of Katharina Blum* (1975) or the passive innocent who drifts instinctively through a world of deceit in his longest and most ambitious novel *Gruppenbild mit Dame* (1971, *Group Portrait with Lady*) the achievement which was probably decisive in getting him the Nobel Prize.

His finest work, however, is on a denser, smaller scale, in short stories or novellas like *The Clown*—or indeed in *Katharine Blum,* which distils the bitter experiences of the Seventies in a short and brilliantly reconstructed witchhunt, full of public destruction and private grief. It was successfully filmed in 1977.

Böll's work was widely available and popular in the German Democratic Republic and at least until recent years, in Russia. He received, among many awards, the Georg Büchner Prize (1967), and in 1973 was made an Hon LittD of Trinity College, Dublin, HonDSc at the University of Aston and HonDTech at Brunel. In the same year he was also given a Scottish Arts Council Fellowship to meet and talk with Scottish writers.

"Heinrich Böll: Novelist in the Humanist Tradition," in The Times, *London, July 17, 1985, p. 14.*

BART BARNES

The first German author to win the Nobel Prize since Thomas Mann in 1929, Mr. Boell wrote dozens of essays and translated such writers as George Bernard Shaw, J. D. Salinger and Brendan Behan into German. He was sometimes described as "the conscience of his country," as Mann had been, and many of Mr. Boell's literary themes—the absurdity of war, the dehumanization of the individual in a materialistic environment, and the corruption of Christianity by ecclesiastical hierarchies—evoked Mann's writings. . . .

Mr. Boell came into literary prominence as his country was emerging from the physical and spiritual devastation of World War II, and much of his writing reflected the war's legacy. The critic Paul Bailey observed that he wrote of "depressed innocents trying to live decently in an indecent world. Enemies loom everywhere, men and women who have surrendered their humanity. . . ."

Despite the "wounds and wrenchings in their lives," said critic Edwin Kennebeck, and a "milieu that is predominantly stultifying, dreary, cynical—a defeated nation after a war of unspeakable horror"—there are characters in Mr. Boell's novels who are capable of an extraordinary depth and range of human feeling.

In many respects, Mr. Boell's themes were similar to those of Russian dissident Alexander Solzhenitsyn, a fellow Nobel laureate, who wrote of the dehumanization of the individual in the Soviet Union. Mr. Boell was a friend and staunch supporter of Solzhenitsyn's, who was his house guest in Germany on the first night of his exile from Russia in 1974.

Mr. Boell was said by the critics to have been a master of the art of storytelling, and one who did not obscure the moral of his tales in myth or history. He wrote instead about contemporary Germans, many of them from lower-middle-class families like his own. His characters often were ordinary workers in run-of-the-mill jobs or romantics who burned out early and spent the rest of their lives in boredom.

But Mr. Boell sometimes was faulted, however, for what some critics regarded as lapsing into acute sentimentality or introducing wildly improbable situations into otherwise realistic contexts.

Politically, Mr. Boell was an antimilitarist and a defender of the rights of West Germany's left-wing intellectuals. A 1975 novel, *The Lost Honor of Katherine Blum,* was said to have been an attack on the West German press magnate Axel Springer, and it caused a controversy in West Germany when critics found similarities between the main characters in the novel and the Baader-Meinhoff urban guerrilla band. Mr. Boell's detractors said the book reflected his sympathies for the group, which was then on trial for a series of bombings and murders.

Born in Cologne on Dec. 21, 1917, the youngest of eight children, Mr. Boell received a diploma from the local gymnasium. With the support of his family he resisted pressures to join the Hitler Youth organization. He was conscripted into the Nazi government's labor corps in 1938, then discharged in the spring of 1939 to study at the University of Cologne. Reared as a Roman Catholic, Mr. Boell broke with the church in 1976. . . .

Mr. Boell's first short novel, *The Train Was on Time,* appeared in 1949, and it told in detail of the last days in the life of a young German soldier returning to the Russian front after a brief furlough. A year later there appeared a collection of his short stories, *Traveller, If You Come to Spa,* which dealt with the uprooted victims of the war and its aftermath.

Among his best known novels in the United States are *Billiards at Half Past Nine* (1962), and *The Clown* (1965). The former is the story of three generations of a family of prominent German architects from the years before World War I to the 1950s, with the Abbey of St. Anthony as the central symbol of the book. The abbey is built by the father, demolished by the son as a protest against the church's toleration of Hitler, then rebuilt by the grandson.

The Clown is a caustic commentary on contemporary German society and the Roman Catholic establishment through the monologues of its main character, a 27-year-old entertainer who has been jilted by his mistress, alienated from his relatives and frustrated in his work. . . .

When he received the Nobel Prize, Mr. Boell said, "The way here has been long for me. Like millions of others, I came home from the war with empty hands. But I had a passion to write and keep on writing. . . ."

Bart Barnes, "Heinrich Boell, Author, Dies; Nobel Prize Winner in 1972," in The Washington Post, *July 17, 1985, p. C11.*

D. J. ENRIGHT

[*Enright is an English poet, novelist, and critic who has lived abroad for more than twenty years, teaching English literature at universities in Egypt, Japan, Berlin, Thailand, and Singapore. His poetry is noted for its conversational style, and it frequently expresses empathy for the victims of betrayal, as does his fiction. In his criticism Enright often questions the conventional interpretations of literature. In the following excerpt Enright pays tribute to Böll, commenting on the role Böll played as the conscience of post-Nazi Germany and showing how his sense of moral responsibility affected Böll's fiction.]*

Since Günter Grass soon showed himself rather too fantastical for the part, it was Heinrich Böll who by natural process became the conscience of post-war Germany, attacking complacent amnesia concerning the past and complacent pride concerning the present.

Yet, while Germany provided the local habitation and the name, in its gently ironic way his best writing is universally and timelessly pertinent. A fine story, **"Murke's Collected Silences,"** tells of a radio talks editor who is so sickened by the high-flown guff he deals with that he cuts out the bits of tape where the speaker has paused for a rare moment, splices them together, and preserves his sanity by playing back the tape at home in the evenings.

The "clown" in the moving and trenchant novel of that name is a mime who could make a rich living in Leipzig with his "Board Meeting" act and in Bonn with his "Party Conference Elects its Presidium"—except that he sees no point in this, and wants to perform the first in Bonn and the second in Leipzig.

And in *Group Portrait with Lady,* Böll's most sustained and complex novel, the all-important question is raised: "What has happened to justice?" For some women are rewarded with villas and cars and large sums of money for providing the same service which brings other women merely a cup of coffee and a cigarette. One woman lies in hospital with venereal disease, caught from a foreign statesman whom, on official instructions, she won round to a "treaty mood," an act which benefited the society which despises her. She dies, not of the disease, but of blushing; she was a modest woman.

Böll's passionate sympathy—at times a little too overt perhaps, but often conveyed in deceptively comic guise—is for the un-derdog, the victim of bureaucracy, of ideologies political, social or religious, of those big words that Stephen Dedalus feared. The heroine of *The Lost Honour of Katharina Blum* is punished for shooting an obnoxious and lecherous reporter by having her reputation and, worse, her privacy torn to shreds by the media: the killing of a reporter is in a different category from that of a bank manager or shopkeeper; it is virtually a ritual murder. Friends who describe Katharina as "cool and level-headed" find their words transmogrified into "ice-cold and calculating." The quality papers are more restrained, but—she comments ruefully—the people she knows all read the other ones.

We may have faint doubts even about the charming Katharina, and we may suspect that even exposing the sins of capitalism in a capitalist theatre can be a little too easy, or *de rigueur.* There is a price to pay for being—and being conscious of being—a national conscience, on top of Nobel laureate and president of International PEN. So many good causes to espouse, so many big words to speak, such anxiety to be always and scrupulously fair (having searched the faces of the Soviet troops in Prague in 1968, Böll reported that they "did not seem imperialistic"). . . .

It was ironical, yet inevitable, that the loving champion of the private person should have become himself a public figure. Yet the writer remained firmly private, and his fiction will surely live and last by virtue of its unique blend of qualities not unique in themselves: tenderness, anger, humour, shrewdness, pathos and cheerfulness, an earthy humanism and a persistent strain of religious feeling, plus the ability to tell a good story while enlightening and instructing.

There is no post-war European novelist who could seriously be considered his equal as a writer about and for the so-called "common man," that ill-done-by but resilient creature.

D. J. Enright, "Heinrich Böll," in The Observer, *July 21, 1985, p. 21.*

Basil Bunting

March 1, 1900 - April 17, 1985

English poet, editor, journalist, and critic.

(See also *CLC,* Vol. 10; *Contemporary Authors,* Vols. 53-56, Vol. 115 [obituary]; *Contemporary Authors New Revision Series,* Vol. 7; and *Dictionary of Literary Biography,* Vol. 20.)

PRINCIPAL WORKS

Redimiculum Matellarum (poetry) 1930
Active Anthology [editor, with Ezra Pound] (poetry) 1931
Poems 1950 (poetry) 1950
The First Book of Odes (poetry) 1965
Loquitur (poetry) 1965
Ode II/2 (poetry) 1965
The Spoils (poetry) 1965
Briggflatts (poetry) 1966
Two Poems (poetry) 1967
What the Chairman Told Tom (poetry) 1967
Collected Poems (poetry) 1968
Descant on Rawley's Madrigal (Conversations with Jonathan Williams) (poetry) 1968
Collected Poems (poetry) 1978

© 1986 Thomas Victor

THE TIMES, LONDON

Basil Bunting, the poet, died in Hexham, Northumberland on April 17. He was 85.

When Ezra Pound's seminal *Guide to Kulchur* appeared in 1938 it bore a joint dedication to Basil Bunting and Louis Zukofsky, "strugglers in the desert". The desert in which Bunting had struggled up to that date, and in which he was to continue struggling until the mid-sixties, was essentially that of being himself *terra incognita.*

As might be supposed from the dedication, and from other hints and tips in Pound's published letters, Bunting was a Poundian, a young disciple, one of those who learned technique from the master in Rapallo in the 1930s, but exactly what he was capable of in his own right did not become apparent until much later.

There was a tendency in those early days, if Bunting's name was mentioned, to regard him as perhaps a minor aberration of Pound's.

It was only in the 1960s that his true worth gained him a rather more general recognition.

Basil Bunting had been born in Scotswood on Tyne, England, in 1900, and educated at a Quaker public school, and the London School of Economics. During the First World War, he was jailed as a conscientious objector. He lived abroad for considerable periods—in Paris in the 1920s, in Italy until 1933, and then in the United States for some while. In each of these periods he had definite cultural interests, which viewed in retrospect, can be seen as stages in his self-education as a poet.

In Paris in the 1920s, he was assistant editor of the *Transatlantic Review;* after this, he was music critic of *The Outlook,* London; and then Persian correspondent after the Second World War for *The Times.* His journalistic experience was varied and professional—later on, he spent twelve years as a sub-editor of the *Newcastle Evening Chronicle.*

In all these places, and at all these stages in his career, Bunting was writing verse. The earliest specimens of it appeared in ***Redimiculum Matellarum,*** published in a limited edition in Milan in 1930, and now one of the rare sought-after books of the modern movement.

After that, so far as publishing went, there was a twenty year silence until ***Poems (1950).*** . . . Neither of these volumes attracted any attention in England.

It was the publication of ***Loquitur*** (1965), ***The First Book of Odes*** (1965), and ***Briggflatts*** (1965) . . . which really put Bunt-

297

ing on the map. Here, the critics realised, was an interesting and accomplished practitioner who had learned his trade slowly and for himself, who wrote a literate and sometimes erudite poetry, referring sometimes for its resonance to Persian originals and always infused with a keen awareness of musical forms—a whole group of his poems called "Sonatas" bearing a much more rigorous relationship to that shape than is usually the case with words: yet a poet who in all his wayward sojourning, and his further journeys of the mind and spirit, had remained essentially at home in the Northumbrian landscape of his youth.

Collected Poems (. . . 1966) merely confirmed what the volumes of 1965 had suggested: that Basil Bunting was a poet uncompromisingly married to the modern movement as that movement had first defined itself in the poems of Pound and Eliot in the 1920s, but who had brought the sometimes facile eclecticism of his masters under dour North Country control, and discovered in his native place a local habitation and a name for what is often in Pound and Eliot a spiritual expression of a sense of exile.

Bunting, it was seen, was a rooted poet and a strangely English one. Even when he adopted a persona, as in **"Villon"**, it was in order to explore certain possibilities of his own experience. The sympathy felt with the French poet as one outlawed and imprisoned is the sharper and more tender for the Englishman's remembering his time in jail as a conscientious objector. But the scrupulous mastery of form allows for no intrusive self-pity.

He went on publishing volumes of verse—*What the Chairman Told Tom* (1967) and *Descant on Rawley's Madrigal* (1968) may be mentioned, although his taste for out-of-the-way American publishers made . . . these books difficult to lay hold of in England. He was also a fairly regular contributor to the poetry magazine *Agenda* in London.

None of his later work surpassed *Briggflatts* in its appeal to a younger generation of readers, however. This autobiographical testament, hailed by Cyril Connolly as "the finest long poem to have been published in England since *Four Quartets*", elegiacally celebrates the poet's own life in lines stripped to a lyric intensity that achieves maximum effectiveness where a certain Northumbrian roughness or looseness of speech-texture is allowed to poke through, as the writer expresses and rejects what he has learned about his nature over the years. Absolutely modern, it is also local: that is its rarity.

Bunting was an Hon DLitt of the University of Newcastle of which he was also made an Hon Life Visiting Professor. He was President of the Poetry Society, 1972-76, and of Northern Arts, 1973-76.

He was twice married.

> "*Basil Bunting: Poet of Unique Strengths*," *in* The Times, *London, April 19, 1985, p. 14.*

THE NEW YORK TIMES

Basil Bunting, a British poet who was a friend of W. B. Yeats and Ezra Pound, died [April 17] in a hospital near his home in Hexham, Northumberland. . . .

Mr. Bunting was best known for a long poem he wrote in 1965 called *Briggflatts,* an autobiographical work that identifies with Northumberland legends, names, language and myths.

In a review of Mr. Bunting's poetry in *The New York Times* in 1969. Thomas Lask wrote, "Mr. Bunting will be a pleasure to all who cherish the craft of verse. His is not the kind of poetry that wears away with a single reading."

> "*Basil Bunting,*" *in* The New York Times, *April 20, 1985, p. 28.*

AUGUST KLEINZAHLER

The last of this century's great poets writing in English died Wednesday, April 17, 1985 in Hexham, England. Basil Bunting was 85 years old. The *New York Times* gave Mr. Bunting 120 words for his obituary [see excerpt above], misspelling Hexham and mistaking the name of his American publisher, the space afforded Bunting being somewhat more than to the editor of *Popular Mechanics* and to the singer Ethel Waters' accompanist, while somewhat less than to the illustrator of Captain Marvel, the comic book hero, and about half as many words as to one Li Boxhao, dramatist and wife of a Chinese Politburo official.

Though more influenced by than influential as Yeats, Pound, Eliot, and Williams, Basil Bunting wrote the finest long poem of the century, *Briggflatts* and a magnificent, condensed version of Kamo-No-Chomei's *Ho-Jo-Ki,* which he rendered, in turn, from an Italian translation of the medieval Japanese classic. These two poems, along with a dozen or so shorter, lyrical poems he called *odes,* and several handsome versions (what he called *overdrafts*) of Horace and the great Persians, Firdosi, Rudaki and Manuchehri, comprise a corpus that places Bunting among the finest lyric poets of the language.

In 1971-72 I had the great good fortune to study and spend time with Mr. Bunting at the University of Victoria in British Columbia, and with a few other students at his cottage several miles down the road by the water. He was already into his 70's, but apart from a nagging cigarette cough he was a hale, splendidly lucid man of understated but proud bearing. I recall two things—or two things come to mind—from that time: he usually had the Penguin translation of *Njal's Saga* in his coat pocket, and he could often be seen on a bench near the small place he rented looking out on the Strait of Juan de Fuca.

He wasn't a man comfortable in an academic setting, and he was treated abominably by the *creative writing* faculty, who were jealous of him as only provincial hacks can be of a distinguished outlander they can't fathom and who doesn't give a tinker's damn about them. The regular English faculty would try to chat him up for tasty anecdotes about Yeats, Pound, Eliot, etc., but they were sent away disappointed on every occasion. Mr. Bunting was always rather old-fashioned about telling tales outside of school. I rather suspect his *attitude* cost him along the road—in fact, it cost him dearly. But he did like young people, and Mr. Bunting tried to give us what he felt we were able to digest of the important moderns, many of whom were friends. As teacher he instilled in his students the notion that poetry is the most rigorous of disciplines and has little to do with self-expression. Just as Picasso complained about there being too many artists and not enough painters, Mr. Bunting believed that the world was lousy with geniuses, *sensitive flowers* and great souls while short, very short, on men and women who knew how to write. He further warned us to take our material from life not books, as his generation—Pound, Eliot, Joyce, David Jones, Zukofsky, himself—did, encumbering their work with too much literary allusion and esoteric learning.

He liked to say there's no excuse for literary criticism—considerable though his regard for Kenneth Cox and Hugh Kenner was—and read to us: Yeats, H.D., Williams, Pound (*Homage to Sextus Propertius, Hugh Selwyn Mauberley,* and hour upon hour, weeks on end, from *The Cantos*), Marianne Moore and Eliot; but also Lorine Niedecker, David Jones, Zukofsky, and Hugh MacDiarmid, the first experience of these writers for most of us. When he tired of reading, he played for us recordings of Dowland, Morley, Byrd and others so that we might hear all the rhythms possible in English, which he felt were contained in the Renaissance madrigal and compositions for lute. Mr. Bunting regarded himself as a minor poet ("not conspicuously dishonest") but a good one, whose work would hold up.

His poetry is, of course, better than that. I suspect he knew it. When I rudely—as a younger man is rude—asked him one day if it bugged him that he wasn't famous like Ted Hughes or Robert Lowell, he answered easily and with equanimity, "No, not really. My work will be read long after I'm gone."

Spenser, Wordsworth, and Pound were the writers in English Bunting valued most highly. *Briggflatts* is very much the flower of Pound's legacy, and in many regards the poem Pound never developed a human enough voice to achieve. The concentration of image and emotion, the strength and variety of tone and rhythm, the wedding of these elements, are like nothing else in the language. To hear him read the poem was overwhelming—as if no one else had tapped so rich a vein of word and music before. It's something you don't forget; and afterwards almost everything, especially one's own work, seems broken-backed and threadbare.

"It is time to consider," Bunting writes in *Briggflatts,* "how Domenico Scarlatti / condensed so much music into so few bars / with never a crabbed turn or congested cadence, / never a boast or a see-here; . . ." It's time for a new generation of writers to get past the natter and posturings and to explore how a poet like Bunting was able to get so much poetry into so few lines, his line never faltering, his heart and eyes open to the world and its difficult beauty.

Basil Bunting was a wonderful man, quite apart from his poetry, however diligently he tried to play the curmudgeon. He led a fascinating, eventful life, and not on other men's money as Byron did. The stories and praises will spring forth. We usually like our poets dead before honoring them.

> The sheets are gathered and bound,
> the volume indexed and shelved,
> dust on its marbled leaves.

We'll not see his like again. (pp. 4-6)

August Kleinzahler, "Basil Bunting," in Sulfur 13, *Vol. V, No. 2, 1985, pp. 4-6.*

CONNIE PICKARD

[*Pickard, an English editor, organized poetry readings at Morden Tower in Newcastle from 1964 to 1976; Bunting, a friend of Pickard's, read his own poetry there. Pickard, along with her husband Tom and Richard Hamilton, published Bunting's long poem* The Spoils *(1965), as well as a magazine dedicated to the poet,* King Ida's Watch Chain. *In the following excerpt Pickard recounts her memories of Bunting, including his reading at Morden Tower and his process of composing the poem* Briggflatts.]

Gateshead, Tyne and Wear. It is 26th April and ten days since the death of the poet Basil Bunting. Sitting at the typewriter I can hear the wind in the back lane. The notes on my table tell of a friendship between three unlikely people, bits of shared experience, a few entries from a few diaries.

In the early days Basil, who was sixty-five before a book of his poetry was published in Britain, hated the idea of interviews, personal anecdotes, letters—anything about the poet that took away attention from the work itself. I didn't keep a continuous diary. There are not many entries, but I am glad there are some notes to act as remembrancers. Forgive me, Basil. (p. 8)

Both Basil and Tom Pickard had been born in Scotswood. In 1900 this part of West Newcastle was still quite rural, still a residential area for well-known Quaker families. By the nearby pit Basil's father was the miners' doctor. By the time Tom was born forty-six years later, Scotswood had become a slum. About the time Tom's family were moving into their house on one of the new post-war estates on the outskirts of the town, Basil would have been returning to England after being expelled from Persia.

We all finally met in Wylam, further up the Tyne, in a beautiful and substantial house overlooking the river. We sat in the garden, in Sima's domain full of raspberries and other good things. Sima was Basil's second wife, whom he had met in Persia. On that day she had just been playing tennis; her long black hair was tied in a pink scarf and her eyes sparkled. The Bunting children were quite young: Tom very plump, and Maria an exquisite figure from a Persian miniature. In the background Basil's mother, then in her nineties, fussed over the poet, calling him Son in a broad Northumberland accent. There were one or two Persian students and lots of animals in that big household. Sima cooked us a great spaghetti dinner and afterwards Basil made Turkish coffee.

On that first evening in Wylam, Basil, you read us some of your poems. We were amazed and delighted: **"Let them remember Samangan," "Mesh cast for mackerel,"** but the revelation was **"Chomei at Toyama."** In 1931, when it was written, the story of the devastation of a city must have seemed something remote:

> To appreciate present conditions
> collate them with those of antiquity.

Tom and I were a very odd couple. Tom was eighteen and had recently published a piece called "Workless Teens" in *Anarchy.* I was older. I came from a pit village and had graduated from King's College (now the University of Newcastle upon Tyne) and then taught until I was expecting Matthew. I was living with Tom, but as I was not yet divorced from my first husband I was naturally asked to leave my job; in fact, it was suggested that I should go and live in another town—advice which people still tend to give me. Good advice, but impossible. When some superannuation money I had applied for miraculously turned up—a whole £180—we decided we would start a bookshop. Crazy. I managed to persuade the City Fathers to let me rent a medieval tower in a very unsalubrious back lane in downtown Newcastle for ten bob a week. When publishers' reps used to call they suggested that a better idea would be to keep pigeons. Basil thought all this was a hoot, but he did not discourage us.

By chance Tom had met Pete Brown while hitchhiking to London, and Pete had invited himself to read in the Tower when he was to pass through Newcastle in a few weeks' time. We asked Basil to come to Pete's reading and were amazed when he said he would. A few years before, poetry and jazz had come to the town, announced when the immortal words "Bird Lives" started to appear on walls among the graffiti. Our friends Tony Jackson and Roy Robertson were reading Rexroth, Patchen and Snyder. At that time we had still read only one poem of Basil's, **"The Complaint of the Morpeth-shire Farmer,"** and had been expecting someone quite different, so that we were very pleased to find Basil shared our enthusiasm for Snyder. He introduced us to William Carlos Williams and Zukofsky.

When Basil himself finally read in the Morden Tower he had a great appeal for the young people. He could not understand this. But just imagine him as he was then, his face quite thin, almost wolfish, or cadaverous, reading Villon with the intensity of his own experience; add the fact that many of the people who came to the Tower had faced arrest in peace demonstrations, and some were lads who themselves had seen the inside of prison because of trivial offences. Also, it could be quite chilly sitting on the floor of a medieval tower. One begins to understand that Basil's reading was an impressive experience.

But it was not always solemn. Basil had a strong sense of humour and sometimes reminded us of Groucho Marx. Someone was always requesting **"An arles, an arles for my hiring."** And we wondered who had been the original Margaret Dumont for whom it had been written. There was another occasion. During Allen Ginsberg's first reading in Newcastle he had dedicated to Basil the poem "To an Old Poet in Peru." After the reading Basil retaliated by out-singing "The Howling King of the Beats" (as Allen had ludicrously been described in the local evening paper). For every mantra that Allen performed Basil would sing a sweet Purcell aria or a lovely song of Campion's—the strong voice getting stronger and stronger in tone, the centuries rolling away, till after some very stern Victorian ballads we all collapsed laughing, and Allen fell with his head on Basil's knee.

Some years later there was another good day with Allen when he wanted to visit Durham Cathedral. Basil, I remember you both discussing prayer very learnedly in the cloisters, discussing the way Buddhist or medieval Christian monks dealt with wool-gathering. Allen was obviously never guilty of wool-gathering, because he quoted the inscription on Bede's tomb even before we reached: *Hac sunt in fossa Baedae venerabilis ossa.* After we had also paid our respects to Cuthbert's bones, Allen noticed the little fossil remains of the sea lilies in the Frosterly marble pillars. Allen had a broken leg, and your eyes, Basil, were not too great, but in no time at all we were clambering into your jalopy, driving over hill and dale and walking through fields until we came to the old working of the quarries

of Frosterly. It was a day of huge time-scales. Often it seemed that we had stepped into eternity with you.

There were other times like that—when, for instance, you were writing *Briggflatts* sitting in St. John's churchyard and you read out some lines that you were really pleased with:

> You who can calculate the course
> of a biased bowl,
> shall I come near the jack?
> What twist can counter the force
> that holds back
> woods I roll?

Until then I had thought that when Pound had addressed you and Zukovsky as strugglers in the desert he was talking about the difficulties poets face in making a living or getting accepted. It was only then that I realised it was something quite different: it was about the seriousness of the work in itself.

I love *Briggflatts,* not only because it is a great poem but also because we were privileged to be around you while you were writing it, and I can see that it is only fitting that your ashes should be scattered over the meeting-house in Briggflatts. Indeed, that they should also go to America. However, it is Chomei that keeps coming into my mind. It could almost have been written for 1985.

> Fathers fed their children and died,
> babies died sucking the dead.
> The priest Hoshi went about marking their foreheads
> A, Amida, their requiem . . .

Anyone wishing to know what you were like in the last few years need only read the last few verses of that poem.

> The moonshadow merges with darkness
> on the cliffpath,
> a tricky turn near ahead.
>
> Oh! There's nothing to complain about,
> Buddha says: 'None of the world is good.'
> I am fond of my hut . . .
>
> I have renounced the world;
> have a saintly
> appearance.
>
> I do not enjoy being poor,
> I've a passionate nature.
> My tongue
> clacked a few prayers.

Requiescat in Pace Basil Bunting, Great Northumbrian poet. (pp. 8-11)

Connie Pickard, "Basil Bunting, 1900-1985: A Personal Memoir," in Stand Magazine, *Summer (1985),* pp. 8-11.

(Janet Miriam) Taylor (Holland) Caldwell

September 7, 1900 - August 30, 1985

(Also wrote under pseudonym of Max Reiner) English-born American novelist and autobiographer.

(See also *CLC*, Vols. 2, 28; *Contemporary Authors*, Vols. 5-8, rev. ed., 116 [obituary]; and *Contemporary Authors New Revision Series*, Vol. 5.)

PRINCIPAL WORKS

Dynasty of Death   (novel)   1938
The Eagles Gather   (novel)   1940
The Earth Is the Lord's: A Tale of the Rise of Genghis Khan
   (novel)   1941
Time No Longer [as Max Reiner]   (novel)   1941
The Strong City   (novel)   1942
The Arm and the Darkness   (novel)   1943
The Final Hour   (novel)   1944
This Side of Innocence   (novel)   1946
There Was a Time   (novel)   1947
Let Love Come Last   (novel)   1949
The Devil's Advocate   (novel)   1952
Never Victorious, Never Defeated   (novel)   1954
Dear and Glorious Physician   (novel)   1959
A Pillar of Iron   (novel)   1965
Dialogues with the Devil   (prose)   1967
Testimony of Two Men   (novel)   1968
Great Lion of God   (novel)   1971
On Growing Up Tough: An Irreverent Memoir   (memoir)
   1971
Captains and the Kings   (novel)   1972
The Romance of Atlantis [with Jess Stearn]   (novel)   1975
I, Judas [with Jess Stearn]   (novel)   1978
Answer as a Man   (novel)   1981

TED THACKREY, JR.

Taylor Caldwell, the best-selling author whose more than 30 historical and romantic novels made her the darling of booksellers—and the bane of critics both literary and political—for nearly half a century, has died at her home in Greenwich, Conn.

Medical Examiner Dr. Hugo Virgilio said Ms. Caldwell, 84, died [August 30] of pulmonary failure caused by advanced lung cancer.

She had been almost deaf since 1967 and had suffered two strokes that deprived her of the ability to speak. Ms. Caldwell's health had been in decline for more than five years, members of the family said.

"But she never stopped working, never stopped trying, never gave in," said Robert Prestie, her manager and fourth husband, who was with her at the time of her death.

"She was always game for a fight," added J. J. Harris, a friend and former editor.

It was an ending entirely in character for a woman whose life had been a constant, and largely successful, battle against the odds.

Over the years, Taylor Caldwell's literary output had led opponents to call her everything from "feminist revolutionary" to "right-wing hack" while earning her a fortune from book sales that evoked the words "miracle" and "Godsend" and "master storyteller" from publishers and the reading public.

Her private life was no less contentious.

Taylor Caldwell was a lifelong and self-acknowledged hypochondriac; her first and third marriages ended in divorce; her works were ignored and unpublished until she was 38 and the wealth generated by her success finally led to a bitter legal battle with her elder child.

"Nobody ever helped me. Nobody ever gave me anything. Nobody ever left me anything. Everything I have, I earned myself," she told an interviewer in 1976.

And that seemed to be accurate.

Janet Miriam Holland Taylor Caldwell was born Sept. 7, 1900, in Manchester, England.

"I never had a childhood, never had an adolescence," she said in later years, adding that she did not recall any open—or, indeed, covert—show of affection from her parents, who saw to it that her schooling began when she was 4.

"There was no nonsense about kindergarten or finger painting or hot lunches," she recalled. "And believe me, within six weeks you *had* to know how to read and write. . . ."

Yet there was a certain pride in her recounting of that era— and an admission that this learning, far from being a burden, became her prime absorption in the years that followed.

When she was 6 her father, a commercial artist, moved the family from England to Buffalo, N.Y., the city that was her home for the next seven decades, and Janet (the name by which she was always known in private) began to write books.

"I illustrated them too," she said, "and the very first was a fairly lurid tale of seduction in the time of Nero—you know, the kind of thing I still like best—copiously and luridly illustrated. My father read it, an early critic, looked at the drawings, picked up the whole armful and disappeared in the direction of the furnace.

"But I didn't care.

"I've always lost interest in anything I write as soon as it's done. I went right on to the next book and kept turning them out at the rate of nine or 10 a year pretty much until the time of my first marriage."

That was when she was 18; she wed William Fairfax Combs, whom she later described as "shiftless" because she was required to contribute to the support of the family (she had one daughter, Mary Margaret, by Combs) through a succession of jobs as a stenographer and court reporter.

That marriage continued, however, until 1931, when Ms. Caldwell (who had been taking night courses at Buffalo University) finally obtained three bits of paper she called "my passports to freedom."

One was her bachelor of arts degree, one a decree of divorce from Combs and one was a certificate of her marriage to Marcus Reback, who had been her boss at the U.S. Immigration Department office in Buffalo.

"That began the happy years. For a while," she said.

The Rebacks were not rich, but they could afford to let the wife and mother spend what little free time she had (another daughter, Judith Ann, was born to the second marriage) in literary pursuits. Nonetheless, it was 1939 and Janet Caldwell Reback had "dozens" of unpublished books behind her before she received her first check as a novelist—and acquired the name by which she would be known to the reading public.

Scribners liked *Dynasty of Death,* her huge and somewhat contrived first published novel about the doings of the munitions-making Barbour and Bouchard families, but found it difficult to believe that it had been written by a woman.

"Too masculine," said editor Maxwell Perkins; besides, publishers of the era felt that the public simply did not buy books by women. So Perkins came up with a solution that was both technically honest—and intentionally deceptive.

"Use the Taylor part of your name," he said. "Taylor Caldwell. That's a good, commercial name, and . . . oh, yes . . . don't use a picture of the author."

Which is just what happened. *Dynasty of Death* drew mixed reviews (although Ms. Caldwell and Perkins had the private pleasure of noting that some well-known critics took it for the work of a seasoned male novelist) but was a blockbuster in the stores.

"It's addictive," Perkins said. "That's the whole thing—Taylor Caldwell is a story-teller first, last and foremost, and once you begin reading one of her books, you can't help finishing it. Let the literary people sneer all they want. I'll wager not one of them could help reading the whole thing!"

Ms. Caldwell continued writing—and selling—without letup over the next few years.

A sequel to *Dynasty, The Eagles Gather,* arrived on the stands in 1940, followed by *Earth Is the Lord's* in 1941, *Time No Longer* (under the pseudonym of Max Reiner) in 1941 and *The Strong City* in 1942.

Other novels included *This Side of Innocence* (1946), *Let Love Come Last* (1949), *Never Victorious, Never Defeated* (1954), *Dear and Glorious Physician* (1959), *Testimony of Two Men* (1968), *Great Lion of God* (1971), *Captains and the Kings* (1972) and *Answer as a Man* (1981).

She also collaborated with Jess Stearn on *A Romance of Atlantis* in 1975 and *I, Judas* in 1978.

Her second marriage ended with Reback's death in 1970, and a third, in 1972 to William E. Stancell, was dissolved by divorce the next year. She was married to Prestie in 1978—and her family's adverse reaction to this added to a thunderhead of troubles that had been steadily accumulating.

Originally perceived as a feminist (after the gender of "Taylor Caldwell" became known) the Buffalo author provoked screams of distaff outrage with her repeated public proclamations that a woman's place "is in the kitchen and the bedroom."

These sounds were promptly drowned, however, in the chorus of protest that attended publication of such works as *Captains and the Kings,* which purported to connect the French Revolution, the Civil War, the Spanish-American War, the New Deal and the Kennedy family assassinations as an ongoing "plot" hatched and moved forward by a consortium of bankers, industrialists and international financiers.

Not all the reaction was hostile, of course: Taylor Caldwell became a policy board member of the extreme right wing Liberty Lobby and the darling of the John Birch Society, which honored her with a plaque as a great "American Patriot and Scholar."

But there was no doubting the continuing hostility of critics:

"Verbose" and given to "literary furbelows," they said, while granting a grudging nod to her storytelling gifts.

And there was no mistaking the anger of her elder daughter over her mother's fourth marriage.

Two years after becoming Mrs. Prestie, she suffered the first of her strokes and moved with her husband to Greenwich—an action that led to filing of a $5-million lawsuit by daughter Mary Margaret, who charged that Ms. Caldwell had been taken to Greenwich against her wishes.

She asked that she be named conservator of her mother's multimillion-dollar estate.

The Presties promptly countered with a $5-million lawsuit of their own, Ms. Caldwell publicly denied that she was being held against her will ("Greenwich is a civilized place to live," she said) and after 18 months of legal wrangling, both actions were dropped.

Hostilities—professional, political and personal—continued to dog Taylor Caldwell through her remaining years. But she seemed hardly to notice.

Doctor's orders to give up cigarettes (she had consumed three to four packs daily through most of her adult life) appeared to irritate her more than troubles with offspring or critics.

"Time's running out," she sighed, shortly before a second stroke deprived her of speech.

But the words were followed by a deep chuckle.

Taylor Caldwell didn't believe a word of it. . . . (pp. 3, 18)

Ted Thackrey, Jr., "Taylor Caldwell, Controversial but Popular Novelist, Dies," in Los Angeles Times, *September 2, 1985, pp. 3, 18.*

THE NEW YORK TIMES

Taylor Caldwell, one of the world's most prolific best-selling authors, died of pulmonary failure on [August 30] at her home in Greenwich, Conn. She was 84 years old and suffered from lung cancer.

Miss Caldwell had a stroke in May 1980 that left her paralyzed and speechless. She had by then written more than 30 novels.

Her 1981 best-seller, **Answer as a Man,** published after her stroke, was a story of a rags-to-riches rise against great odds; it made *The New York Times* best-seller list before its official publication date, and partly fulfilled a two-book, $3.9 million contract she had signed in 1980 with G. P. Putnam's Sons.

She was described by Orville Prescott in *The Times* in 1945—only seven years after the publication of her first novel in 1938—as "one of the most industrious of our contemporary novelists." "Each year sees a new book fresh from her smoking typewriter," he wrote, adding that her novels were "more than life size but far from natural."

Her first published novel, immediately successful, was **Dynasty of Death,** about a dynasty of munitions makers; she ultimately wrote three novels concerning this imaginary family, and other books on dynasties whose fortunes were based on steel, textiles and railroading.

The getting and spending of large sums of money was a principal preoccupation of her novels. Other subjects were historical figures, such as Cardinal Richelieu and Genghis Khan.

Three of her books—including **Dear and Glorious Physician,** based on the life of St. Luke—are among the best-selling religious novels of all time.

Not sweet romance but melodrama was her stock in trade, laced increasingly with her own conservative political opinions. Two of her novels—one of them **Captains and the Kings,** the saga of an Irish-American highly reminiscent of Joseph P. Kennedy—became the bases for television mini-series.

Miss Caldwell, who said that her greatest inspiration was "the anticipation of big checks," was enormously popular with readers.

By 1980, one paperback house alone had published 25 million copies of Caldwell books—including **Captains and the Kings,** which sold 4.5 million copies. Back in 1946, **This Side of Innocence** set a record for Literary Guild selections, selling more than one million copies.

She was as predictably panned by the critics as she was purchased by her reading public.

"Steamroller" was the adjective for her prose used by one critic; another reviewer noted that she tooled on timelessly, "hardly shifting gears from one volume to the next."

Orville Prescott, however, in a review of **The Wide House** in *The Times* in 1945, wrote that while its style was creaking and antiquated, the book was "still surprisingly effective." He noted that while the author's "characters may be caricatures, they never lack vitality and force."

"Her story may be fantastic, but there is plenty of it," he wrote. "Things keep happening in these tumultuous pages."

To achieve this, Miss Caldwell generally wrote through the night, working in nightclothes at her electric typewriter. Her success began at the age of 38, after years of what she later described as excruciating efforts and disappointments—years

so painful that she maintained her outlook on life was permanently clouded. They were, she said in 1976, "endless years of writing."

In fact, she wrote her first novel, she recalled, at the age of 12, a futuristic opus called **The Romance of Atlantis.** This was six years after she had moved with her family to Buffalo, N.Y., where she lived the rest of her life. . . .

Miss Caldwell was an outspoken conservative, politically, and was a founding sponsor of the Conservative Party in New York State. She was at one time a board member of the Liberty Lobby, and the John Birch Society honored her with a plaque describing her as a "Great American Patriot and Scholar."

Although Miss Caldwell said that she never had to rewrite, she added that her long years of effort left her permanently somber.

"Only we writers know of the agony and frustration and despair," she wrote. "I can only say that my health is permanently ruined and my outlook on life permanently somber and depressed, because of those years of wretchedness."

"Taylor Caldwell, Prolific Author, Dies," in The New York Times, *September 2, 1985, p. 26.*

RICHARD PEARSON

Taylor Caldwell, 84, the best-selling author of more than 30 books, including **Dear and Glorious Physician,** and **Captains and the Kings,** which have been translated into 11 languages, and whose historical novels may have been lightly regarded by some critics but were found entertaining by millions of readers, died [August 30] in Greenwich, Conn. . . .

Miss Caldwell's novels, most of them set in the dramatic past, dealt with epic personalities or times of enormous significance. Her books were intricately plotted and filled with suspense and vitality. When critics found fault, it was often with the credibility of her characterization.

Her first novel, **Dynasty of Death,** published in 1938, began a saga concerning the lives and times of the Barbours and the Bouchards, wealthy families engaged in the manufacture of munitions. This story was continued in two sequels, **The Eagles Gather,** published in 1940, and **The Final Hour,** in 1944.

Others of her books published in the 1940s included **The Earth Is the Lord's,** concerning the life of Genghis Khan, **Time No Longer,** set in Nazi Germany, **The Arm and the Darkness,** set in France in the 1500s, and **This Side of Innocence,** set in New York's Gilded Age.

Books that she published in the 1950s included **The Devil's Advocate, Never Victorious, Never Defeated,** and **Dear and Glorious Physician.** The 1960s saw her publish **A Testimony of Two Men, A Pillar of Iron,** which was a fictional biography of Cicero, and **Dialogues with the Devil,** a book containing comments on the modern world and revealing her conservative political bent.

During the 1970s, her works included **Captains and the Kings,** which was adapted for a television serialization, and **Great Lion of God. Answer as a Man,** published in 1981, told the rags-to-riches tale of an American at the beginning of the 20th century.

Her increasing illness did not cause [Caldwell] to abandon her craft; Prestie, who was his wife's manager before their 1978 marriage, said he remembered her sitting at a typewriter every evening. He told a reporter that she sometimes stayed up all night finishing a chapter or two. And in most cases, he said, except for a word or two, the final text would be identical to the first draft.

Janet Miriam Taylor Holland Caldwell was born on Sept. 7, 1900 in Manchester, England, and came to this country in 1907. She grew up Buffalo, N.Y. It has been said that her father had a "strange antipathy for almost everyone but Scotsmen, Presbyterians, and Caldwells."

Miss Caldwell characterized hers as a violently conservative, British home with "books, arguments, boiled beef, and cabbage."

She began to exhibit a literary talent at an early age. When she was 9 years old, she began to write and illustrate her own books. One of the first included a graphic love scene set in Nero's Rome and included illustrations that were as numerous as they were anatomically accurate.

Miss Caldwell said that she wrote about 10 books a year and gave them to her parents. A remembered sight, she once said, was her father who "frequently disappeared furnaceward with armfuls" of her work.

She attended night school and in 1931 earned a bachelor's degree at the University of Buffalo. She was a Navy yeomanette during World War I. Between the early 1920s and early 1930s she worked in Buffalo for the New York State Department of Labor and then the U.S. Immigration and Naturalization Service, as a stenographer and court reporter.

She began writing seriously during her years with the government, finally getting her first work published in 1938. She began publishing under the name "Taylor Caldwell" after her editor, the legendary Max Perkins, said her writing was too "forceful" and "masculine" to be published under an obviously female name.

Be that as it may, she had some rather forceful views on women and modern times. As early as 1940, she said that both politics and the professional world had enough women, questioned their intelligence in general, and said education for women had become too universal.

During the 1960s, she served on the board of the Liberty Lobby and contributed articles to *American Opinion,* a John Birch Society publication. She also served as president of the National Coordinating Committee for Friends of Rhodesian Independence, a group supporting the all-white, breakaway regime of Ian Smith.

Miss Caldwell told one interviewer that her life lacked excitement and that her fondest wish was to enter a convent. She said that another ambition, with which she was having no luck, was to produce an absolutely pink petunia using Mendelian laws.

Richard Pearson, "Novelist Taylor Caldwell Dies at 84," in The Washington Post, *September 2, 1985, p. B6.*

Italo Calvino

October 15, 1923 - September 19, 1985

Italian novelist, short story writer, translator, essayist, editor, and journalist.

(See also *CLC*, Vols. 5, 8, 11, 22, 33 and *Contemporary Authors,* Vols. 85-88, 116 [obituary].)

PRINCIPAL WORKS

Il sentiero dei nidi di ragno   (novel)   1947
  [*The Path to the Nest of Spiders,* 1956]
La formica Argentina   (novella)   1952
  [*The Argentine Ant* published in *Adam, One Afternoon and Other Stories,* 1957]
Il visconte dimezzato   (novel)   1952
  [*The Non-Existent Knight* published in *The Non-Existent Knight and The Cloven Viscount,* 1962]
Fiabe Italiane: Raccolte dalla tradizione popolare durante gli ultimi cento anni e trascritte in lingua dai vari dialetti [editor and adaptor]   (fables)   1956
  [*Italian Fables,* 1959; also published as *Italian Folktales,* 1980]
La nuvola di smog   (novella)   1958
  [*Smog* published in *The Watcher and Other Stories,* 1971]
I racconti   (short stories)   1958
Il cavaliere inesistente   (novel)   1959
  [*The Cloven Viscount* published in *The Non-Existent Knight and The Cloven Viscount,* 1962]
La giornata d'uno scrutatore   (novel)   1963
  [*The Watcher* published in *The Watcher and Other Stories,* 1971]
Marcovaldo ovvero le stagioni in città   (short stories)   1963
  [*Marcovaldo: The Seasons in the City,* 1983]
Le cosmicomiche   (short stories)   1965
  [*Cosmicomics,* 1968]
Ti con zero   (short stories)   1967
  [*t zero,* 1969]
Il castello dei destini incrociati   (novel)   1969
  [*The Castle of Crossed Destinies,* 1977]
Gli amori difficili   (short stories)   1970
Le città invisibili   (novel)   1972
  [*Invisible Cities,* 1974]
L'entrata in guerra   (short stories)   1974
Se una notte d'inverno un viaggiatore   (novel)   1979
  [*If on a Winter's Night a Traveler,* 1981]
Palomar   (novel)   1983
  [*Mr. Palomar,* 1985]

© 1986 Thomas Victor

HERBERT MITGANG

Italo Calvino, the master of allegorical fantasy who became Italy's leading contemporary novelist, died [Sept. 19] in a hospital in Siena, Italy, from the effects of a stroke he suffered on Sept. 6. He was 61 years old.

Mr. Calvino was among the handful of major novelists of international standing and was to have delivered the prestigious Norton lectures at Harvard this fall.

John Updike commented yesterday: "Calvino was a genial as well as brilliant writer. He took fiction into new places where it had never been before, and back into the fabulous and ancient sources of narrative. His human warmth as well as his super-human ingenuity will be greatly missed."

Mr. Calvino was attracted to folk tales, knights and chivalry, social allegories and legends for our time: Fabulous and comic memory chips, slightly askew, seemed to be imbedded in his unprogrammed mind. His characters defied the malaise of daily life in the modern world.

When the *New York Times Book Review* asked him last December what fictional character he would like to be, Mr. Calvino revealed himself and his artistic intentions in his answer:

> Mercutio. Among his virtues, I admire above all his lightness in a world of brutality, his dreaming imagination—as the poet of Queen Mab—and at the same time his wisdom, as the voice of reason amid the fanatical hatreds of Capulets and Montagues. He sticks to the old code of chivalry at the price of his life, perhaps just [for] the sake of style, and yet he is a modern man, skeptical and ironic—a Don Quixote who knows very well what dreams are and what reality is, and he lives both with open eyes.

Mr. Calvino has two books coming out in the United States this month. His new novel is **Mr. Palomar.** The title character, with a name that recalls the famous telescope, is a quester after knowledge, a visionary in a world sublime and ridiculous. He is impatient and taciturn in society, preferring to spin inner dialogues and listen to the silence of infinite spaces and the songs of birds.

The second book . . . is a trade paperback edition of earlier stories titled **Difficult Loves.** Its characters include a soldier caught up in a private world of seduction and a middle-class woman who discovers she has lost the lower half of her bikini while swimming.

In addition, a bilingual edition in English and Italian of an unpublished story, **Before You Say ''Hello,''** will appear in a signed, limited edition this month, put out by Richard-Gabriel Rummonds, Plain Wrapper Press, University of Alabama, Tuscaloosa.

Mr. Calvino's other works include **The Baron in the Trees, The Path to the Nest of Spiders, The Castle of Crossed Destinies, Invisible Cities, Italian Folktales, Cosmicomics,** and **If on a Winter's Night a Traveler** and **Marcovaldo.** The subjects range from takeoffs on Tarot cards to satires of literary styles.

For a while after World War II, he tried to write realistic stories. His early novel, **The Path to the Nest of Spiders,** described his experiences while fighting with the partisans against the Nazis and Fascists in the mountains of Liguria. Eventually, he came to realize that the only way for him to write was to invent. Straight science fiction seemed too remote. In **Cosmicomics** he came close to science fiction, inspired by the workings of the universe.

Thereafter, he began to grapple with modern events in his own way through fables that often crisscross time. ''If the reader looks,'' he said, ''I think he will find plenty of moral and political ideas in my stories. I suffer from everyday life. When I'm depressed, I start with some euphoric image that transmits itself. Anyway, I'm sure that I'm a man of my times. The problems of our time appear in any story I write. Knights and chivalry—they are related to today's wars. No, I'm not writing in a vacuum. The fables just make use of a different language. Politics is marginal, but literature moves along by indirection.''

By contrast to his own work, Mr. Calvino ridiculed commercial fiction, including American novels. In **If on a Winter's Night a Traveler,** he invented a group called the Organization for the Electronic Production of Homogenized Literary Works. He said it was inspired by the market research conducted by the television networks and some book publishers to determine what audiences wanted to see and read—and then to manufacture it.

The Baron in the Trees is about a young Italian nobleman in the 18th century who rebels against parental authority and lives for the rest of his life in ''an ideal state in the trees.'' Louis Malle, the film director, has said he has long dreamed of turning the novel into a movie.

To help preserve literary traditions and promote new writers, Mr. Calvino edited a fiction series called ''Cento Pagi'' (One Hundred Pages), short novels that are published by Giulio Einaudi in Turin. He explained: ''Italian literature today does not have any real school or current but only complex personalities of writers who are so different. But difference is what is worth encouraging.''

Italo Calvino was born on Oct. 15, 1923, in Santiago de Las Vegas, Cuba, of Italian parents, both of whom were tropical agronomists. Several years later they returned to San Remo, on the Italian Riviera. Mr. Calvino enrolled at the University of Turin, intending to study agronomy. After Italy's entry into World War II, as a compulsory member of the Young Fascists, he participated in the Italian occupation of the French Riviera, but in 1943 he joined the Italian Resistance and fought the Germans in the Ligurian mountains.

In 1945, he joined the Communist Party and began contributing to party journals. With the writers Cesare Pavese and Elio Vittorini, he shared an involvement in Socialist politics and in the neorealistic literary vogue. ''The Communist Party seemed to have the most realistic program for opposing a resurgence of Fascism and for rehabilitating Italy,'' he said, ''but I left the party in 1957, and today I am apolitical.''

In the opinion of his fellow-writers and critics, Mr. Calvino was a world-class author. His stories and especially his folk tales were translated in many countries.

Margaret Atwood, the novelist, compared Mr. Calvino's urban landscapes to ''the early Fellini films.''

Ursula K. Le Guin, the American novelist whose work includes science fiction and fantasy, said, ''One of the innumerable delights of **Italian Folktales** is its mixture of the deeply familiar with the totally unexpected. He is one of the best storytellers alive telling us some of the best stories in the world—what luck!''

Commenting on the same book, Anthony Burgess, the British novelist, said, ''Calvino has performed a valuable service to his own culture and, by extension, to our own. Reading his book, we are confirmed in our belief that human aspirations are everywhere much the same.''

Of Mr. Calvino's **If on a Winter's Night a Traveler,** Michael Wood, the critic, wrote, ''Architect of scrupulously imagined, apparently fantastic, insidiously plausible words, Calvino occupies a literary space somewhere east of Jorge Luis Borges and west of Vladimir Nabokov. Borges dreams of libraries and Nabokov texts and commentaries, but Calvino pictures acres of vulnerable print, gathered into volumes but constantly menaced with dispersion or vertiginous error.''

Mr. Calvino himself talked enigmatically about his writing.

''When I'm writing a book I prefer not to speak about it,'' he said, ''because only when the book is finished can I try to understand what I've really done and to compare my intentions with the result.''

While he was writing *Mr. Palomar* two years ago, Mr. Calvino said, "What can I say of the book I'm working on now is that it is a quite different one, but it also deals with the relations between man and nature. Here the hero is called Mr. Palomar, like the astronomical observatory, but he observes only the nearest things around him."

> Herbert Mitgang, *"Italo Calvino, the Novelist, Dead at 61," in* The New York Times, *September 20, 1985, p. A20.*

LOS ANGELES TIMES

Neo-realist novelist Italo Calvino, who fashioned such fairytale characters as knights cut in two by a sword or young noblemen who ascend trees and spend the rest of their lives there, died [Sept. 19 at a hospital in Siena, Italy]. . . .

Calvino, 62, was stricken with a brain hemorrhage and lapsed into unconsciousness Sept. 6. He was considered one of Italy's most prestigious modern writers.

In a *New York Times Book Review* article, the late John Gardner once called Calvino "possibly Italy's most brilliant living writer" and classed him with Kobo Abe, Jorge Luis Borges and Gabriel Garcia Marquez.

Other critics place him in the intellectual school of writers that includes Franz Kafka, Luigi Pirandello, Vladimir Nabokov and Alain Robbe-Grillet.

Novelist Alberto Moravia said the death of his "dear friend" and fellow neo-realist leaves "a great emptiness" in Italian letters.

Calvino began his writing career after World War II, one of a new breed of writers.

"We had survived the war, and the youngest of us partisans . . . did not feel crushed, conquered or 'burned,' but victors, propelled by a driving task of the battle just concluded," he wrote of the neo-realists.

Out of his experience in the Resistance, fighting German occupation soldiers in northern Italy, came his first novel, *The Path to the Nest of Spiders*.

Unlike most of his contemporaries, Calvino told his story of the Resistance not through an adult character but in the voice of a young boy forced by the war to grow up quickly. It became Calvino's last realistic novel.

The works for which he won his international reputation became literary experiments combining fantasy, folklore, philosophy and science.

They include *The Nonexistent Knight and the Cloven Viscount, The Baron in the Trees*—published together in English as *Our Ancestors—Cosmicomics, The Castle of Crossed Destinies* and *Marcovaldo, or the Seasons in the City.* He also edited *Italian Folktales.*

The Baron in the Trees is about a 12-year-old, 18th-Century nobleman who decides to live his life in the treetops, and *The Nonexistent Knight* is about a Crusader who is split in two and returns home with only his wicked half.

One of his most exotic works was *Invisible Cities,* in which a young Marco Polo entertains the aged Kublai Khan with fantastic descriptions of places that exist everywhere and nowhere, in the past, present, and future.

Author Gore Vidal called the novel "perhaps his most beautiful."

Calvino had emerged from the war a communist. He moved into an unheated garret, went to work for the new publishing house of Giulio Einaudi and began writing.

He resigned from the Communist Party after the Hungarian uprising of 1956 and withdrew from active politics.

Italian President Francesco Cossiga said Calvino's death "deprives our country of a spiritual presence, creative and stimulating, of a voice among the most free and coherent of this century, of a poetic intellect who, as few have, knew how to express the truth of universal man."

In recent years, Calvino's reputation grew abroad, especially in the United States. The author lectured at Harvard and held writing seminars at Columbia University. He was to have lectured again at Harvard this fall.

> *"Italian Novelist Italo Calvino Dies at 62," in* Los Angeles Times, *Part IV, September 21, 1985, p. 7.*

LORNA SAGE

Italo Calvino was asked earlier this year by the French paper *Liberation* why he wrote, and answered: 'Because I'm never satisfied with what I've already written, and would like . . . to make it better, completed, propose other endings. . . .' This offers some clue perhaps to the special gift—the imaginative climate of tension, intimacy, freedom—he shared with his readers.

He was born in 1923 (his patriotic Christian name comes from the Fascist era) and grew up in San Remo on the Italian-French border. During the war he fought with the Partisans; he studied at Turin, and did a thesis on Joseph Conrad; and he became a writer, and worked for the publishers Einaudi, where he signed up (among others) Malamud, Bellow, and Cortazar. He did try his hand at social realism briefly, but even in early stories the speculative sense of other worlds sneaked in.

For Einaudi he made a collection [*Italian Folktales*], translated out of their various dialects into his own marvellously lucid Italian—and it's that kind of tradition (not the grim Gothic tales of the north, nor the realist solidities of the novel 'proper') that stands behind his fiction, with all its sharpness and sophistication.

Invisible Cities (1972) was, I think, the book that first brought him large-scale international acclaim. He proved to be brilliantly 'translatable'—not only because of the simplicity of his style (deceptive anyway) nor because he'd found an excellent and congenial translator in William Weaver, but because his themes were a distillation, a kind of epitome of the histories (the realities or rather the stories about the realities) we'd laboured through before.

When Marco Polo describes to Kubla Khan the myriad cities he's seen, as one fantastic and recognisable, mythic and merely human, you find yourself on a tour of the possible. There's a marvellous fertility of invention, yes, and pleasure (the pleasure principle comes into its own everywhere in his work), but accompanied by a daunting and ironic awareness of limits.

There was something of the anthropologist about Calvino, perhaps—at least in the sense that his self-consciousness (the century's legacy) wasn't narcissistic, but anxious and curious: in fact, not entirely unlike the meditative, exacting trait he invented for the comic hero of his story sequence *Mr Palomar*. . . . It ends, by a gloomy coincidence, with a story called "Learning To Be Dead" and suggests (Calvino was no author-God, though a great magician) that one cannot learn, one just does it.

His premature passing has naturally made headline news in the Italian Press. . . . Alberto Moravia has talked of the enormous gap he'll leave, in the world of Italian letters—'un grande vuoto'—and that goes for the world outside, too.

> Lorna Sage, "Tribute to Italo Calvino," in The Observer, September 22, 1985, p. 25.

PATCHY WHEATLEY

Calvino's death occurred two weeks after he had suffered a stroke in the garden of his summer villa in Tuscany. The news for me was both saddening and disturbing. I had just spent four weeks watching him walk around that garden without mishap on a film screen at the BBC. In the editing-room it is easy to believe in the illusion of immortality which film bestows on its subject.

The film I was making included the first, and now the only, English television interview Calvino gave about his work. Calvino disliked recorded interviews of any kind. 'I always have a problem with speech,' he says in the film. 'Not only in a foreign language, but also in my own language . . . I always need to write to express myself completely.' It took some negotiation to persuade him (at one point, with a typical mixture of whimsy and seriousness, he suggested a silent interview), but he finally agreed to be filmed in conversation with *Bookmark*'s Ian Hamilton.

Calvino had always said in the past that he wanted to hide himself behind his work and, indeed, the dazzling variety of fictional styles and voices he produced over the years kept the author well screened from his readership. But his last book, *Mr Palomar*, . . . is somewhat different. Philosophical, poetic, touchingly humorous, it is about only one man—one man's mind, in fact; and the workings of that mind are so minutely drawn that it is tempting to make connections.

When I spoke to Calvino about this, I was surprised that he didn't object—he even suggested we film him as Mr Palomar on his private beach, and explained that the settings in which Palomar conducts his inquiries into the nature of the world are precise reconstructions of Calvino's own—his beach, his lawn, his flat in Rome.

On my first visit to Tuscany, I had lunch at the villa with Signor and Signora Calvino. She was energetic, talkative and treated him with the affectionate bossiness usually reserved for a dreamy child. Calvino fitted the part. It seemed entirely possible that, if asked to fetch a knife from the kitchen, he would return with the pepper pot because the pepper had unleashed an infinite trail of Palomar-like speculation.

Calvino's death is a great loss. But we can be thankful that he gave us what he did: in the last chapter of *Mr Palomar*, called "Learning to be Dead", Palomar speculates on the nature of being dead and decides that it is 'himself plus the world minus him'. In Calvino's case, the world is left a splendid literary legacy.

> Patchy Wheatley, "The World Minus Calvino," in The Listener, Vol. 114, No. 2928, September 26, 1985, p. 9.

UMBERTO ECO

[*An Italian scholar known primarily for his work in the fields of semiotics and medievalism, Eco gained wide attention with the publication of his first novel,* Il nome della rosa *(1980;* The Name of the Rose). *Critics praised this intricately plotted murder mystery, set in a Benedictine abbey in northern Italy in 1327, as a success on many levels: at once a gothic thriller, a novel of ideas, and an evocation of medieval life, politics, and religion. In the following excerpt Eco recounts the effect of Calvino's artistic innovations on his own work and that of other young writers and expresses gratitude for the encouragement Calvino gave them.*]

When Italo Calvino's *The Baron in the Trees* was published, we understood—we who were 10 years younger than he—that we had in him the writer of our generation. Later—when I made his acquaintance—his evasive and sardonic smile, his way of lowering his eyes when he spoke so as to conceal the flashing irony, could have misled me. But on reading his *The Watcher*, I understood that in that little book this author, so near in spirit to the Encyclopedists, had given us one of the loftiest, largest religious texts I had ever encountered.

It was the story of a man on the left in charge of counting the vote in a polling place located inside the Cottolengo, the immense hospital/asylum where a pitying Church took in those whom other charitable institutions had rejected: the homeless, the deformed, the crippled, the incurable. The protagonist of the story experiences at first the irritation of a secular man at seeing these poor wretches, incapable of comprehension or choice, exploited for electoral purposes, steered toward hope by the same nuns who, each day, clean up their slobber and their soil.

In the course of the day, however, he thinks about evil, about sorrow, about charity. He wonders with a certain puzzlement whether these strange voters are not, after all, paying their debt to the only beings who have taken any care of them.

I do not want to speak of Calvino the writer; the whole world is doing that these days. I want to talk about the Calvino who used to go to hear avant-garde musicians—Berio, Maderna, Boulez; the man who put out the review *Menabo* with Elio Vittorini, trying to open a dialogue between the neo-realism of the traditional left and the currents of the new experimental literature; the Calvino who was attentive, respectful and curious about precisely those of whom he did not approve.

Or again of the Parisian Calvino, who followed structuralist research on the grammar of narrative with the excited attention of a student and who, after the lapse of some years, declared himself the pioneer of a self-interrogating, "other" narrative technique (*If on a Winter's Night a Traveler*). Of that Calvino who, with Perec and the Oulipo group, took part in language games, knowing that a game can also be a mission.

In his relations with others, he always seemed ill at ease and eager to withdraw into himself as quickly as possible. But, behind the mask, he was always listening. As consultant to the Einaudi publishing house, he showed himself a generous discoverer of new talent, who knew how to work on others' manuscripts with the same excitement he brought to his own.

I cannot, here, avoid a personal recollection. In 1959, shortly after we became acquainted, he told me that he had just read in a music review an article on "Open Work." He asked me to write a book on this theme, which he found interesting. I wrote the book, though, for circumstantial reasons, it appeared with another publisher. Without Calvino's encouragement, I would never have begun it.

I mention this to show how, behind his mask of detachment and absence, Calvino knew how to be present to others, to encourage them, to help them create.

The imaginary cosmos of Italo Calvino was poised, in a subtle equilibrium, between Voltaire and Leibniz. At the moment when I learned he was gone, I was reminded of a page in one of his works on which he seemed to speak to us of the passage into other universes. I speak of *T Zero,* one of his most philosophical narratives, a meditation on Zeno of Elea and his eternally immobile arrow:

> What I ask myself is whether, seeing that at this point we have to go back in any case, it wouldn't be wise for me to stop, to stop in space and in time. . . . What, after all, is the use of continuing if sooner or later we will only find ourselves in this situation again? I might as well grant myself a few dozen billion years' repose, and let the rest of the universe continue its spatial and temporal race to the end, and wait for the return trip . . . or else let time go back by itself and let it approach me again while I stand still and wait—and then see if the right moment has come for me to make up my mind and take the next step, to go and give a look at what will happen to me in a second, or on the other hand if it's best for me to remain here indefinitely.

> *Umberto Eco, ''Ex Libris,'' translated by Jack Miles,*
> *in* Los Angeles Times Book Review, *October 20, 1985, p. 15.*

THE NEW YORKER

In September, the Italian writer Italo Calvino died, aged sixty-one, from the effects of a stroke. A few months before, when I last saw him, at my apartment in New York, he was bustling: having completed a novel, **Mr. Palomar,** he had now turned to the Charles Eliot Norton Lectures, which he was to deliver at Harvard this year. Calvino was bustling, that is, in a Calvino way. **Mr. Palomar** he admitted to be ''perhaps good,'' and the Norton Lectures were difficult. ''I am having terrible problems with them,'' he said. That meant he was thoroughly enjoying himself. By the last day of his visit, he wanted to celebrate. . . .

The Calvinos took great pleasure in young people, the age of their own daughter, Giovanna—boys and girls fresh from college, who dreamed without embarrassment and were untainted by literary politics. The Calvinos infinitely preferred their company to that of the famous and the influential. Gathered in my living room, therefore, were a young carpenter, a young woman who worked at the Metropolitan Museum, a young dancer, and a young poet. Calvino had taken to the poet when the young man said easily to him a year before, ''I have never read any of your books. What would you suggest I begin with?'' If interviewers asked Calvino what he considered his ''most important work,'' he often responded with silence. That time, however, the reply had come as comfortably as the question was asked: the young man might try **Cosmicomics** and **t zero.** These were the books in which he felt he had begun to write a new kind of novel. The ''hero'' of **Cosmicomics,** for instance, is a protean being named Qfwfq, present from the Big Bang on to the mid-nineteen-sixties; unlike most science fiction, these novels are experiments in how to describe the wondrous. It was natural for him to move from Qfwfq to tales of medieval

knights, and to make his famous collection of **Italian Folktales;** his curiosity was provoked by fables, and he wanted to discover new, unusual ways to tell them. **Mr. Palomar** continued this kind of research. Now, a year later, the young poet was reporting that he had read almost everything. Calvino flushed; he hated the idea of disciples. But he had chosen his young friend well. ''I think you are wrong about your work,'' the poet said. ''**Invisible Cities** is better, though there are still problems.'' Calvino smiled; Chichita beamed. They were not going to be imprisoned within the cage of deferential respect.

The dancer, a young man, suggested we go to an Ethiopian restaurant in SoHo; the Calvinos were delighted. (Chichita is from Argentina, and Calvino's father, an agronomist, had spent many years in Cuba and Mexico, so they considered themselves more living in Italy than Italian.) The Calvinos said that they would not mind eating with their hands and drinking honey wine. In the restaurant, as we plunged our fists into the fiery food, the dancer asked Calvino if he had fought with the Italians in Ethiopia—this young man was ''hazy'' about the dates and what had happened. I wondered if Calvino would tell him; he was as far away and as safe with these young Americans as he would ever be. But he replied merely that he had been too young for Mussolini's campaign, and that later he had been forced to join the Army but had deserted and joined the Italian Resistance. What his brief reply left out is the youthful drama that I believe shaped the course of Calvino's writing. From modesty, he omitted facts attested to by people who knew him then. He said nothing about having courageously faced mortal danger many times as a member of the Partisans. He did not speak of nightmares he still suffered from, which recalled those days—images of famine, torture, and fear. He did not mention the idealism that led him to join the Communist Party after the war, or the disillusion that prompted him to leave it in the nineteen-fifties. These events led Calvino to attempt realistic writing, so that he might bear witness to his time: the subject of his first novel, **The Path to the Nest of Spiders,** is his experiences as a Partisan. The attempt failed—but for him, not for us; the novel is superb. ''In my imagination,'' he once said to me, ''I wanted to find something to set against the Fascism, the Communism.''

I never believed the claim that he had become an ''apolitical'' writer. His fables, his other experiments with narrative are all essays in freeing the imagination. There was an urgency behind his invention of his fictional worlds—his playfulness was serious. Liberty through fantasy: in this manner Calvino indeed sought his alternative to the totalitarianism he had known as a youth. This also explains why he was so ''friendly'' an avant-garde writer. He wanted people to enjoy his books and thus share his sense of freedom. Fantasy is not ordinarily what we think of as socially engaged or political writing, but then Calvino had found conventional politics deadly. It was characteristic of the man never to explain himself. When people insisted on a guided tour of his literary experiments, he genuinely believed that it could only be because the writing had failed. And I think his extraordinary affinity with young people came from a related impulse: his own youth was incommunicable in its terrors; he hoped theirs might be different; and he would meet them, if he could, on the ground of a common pleasure in stories—in a newly created world. (pp. 26-7)

> *''Notes and Comments,'' in* The New Yorker, *Vol. LXI, No. 36, October 28, 1985, pp. 25-7.*

CONSTANCE MARKEY

With his untimely death at age 62, Italo Calvino's latest book, **Mr. Palomar,** abruptly became his last. Through the penetrating gaze of the central figure, named for the telescope at Mt. Palomar in Southern California, the novel unflinchingly scans the future.

With uncanny accuracy, it foretells Calvino's dying, just as surely as his earlier fairy tales had anticipated his living and discovering for us the magic lands of cloven viscounts and invisible cities.

In those days, even without a telescope, Calvino was already a wise, perceptive observer of humanity and human mores. He was a natural explorer, endowed with a rich legacy of Renaissance enthusiasm for new inventions and fresh worlds. Unlike his favorite discoverer, Marco Polo, however, Calvino preferred staying at home.

Timid, even awkward in society, he was instead, like Palomar, an armchair voyageur who let curiosity travel for him. Eagerly he steeped himself in world literature, history, biology and even astrophysics, using each of these tools as a springboard to a good yarn. A consummate storyteller, a cynical philosopher and a roguish literary trickster, there was no gamble, no game he would not dare in the name of a new story. As a result he wrote something for everyone and something of everything: science fiction, spy sagas, political satire, slice of life and, best of all, satirical fairy tales.

Among those works for which he will best be remembered is *The Castle of Crossed Destinies,* a brilliant ensemble of moody chivalric tales. Fashioned from the adventures of heroes admirable and ignominious, each brief story unfolds as a mini-medieval quest, rich in adventure and dark humor.

Like Calvino's earliest fantasy trilogy, *Our Ancestors, Castle* transports the reader back through time only to use that romantic epoch to lampoon this present Palomar age of machines and mass madness. The result is a masterpiece that combines the best of two Calvinos: the fantasy conjurer, the realistic social critic.

A second memorable novel is *Invisible Cities,* a fragile tapestry of mood pieces that has enjoyed wide success in this country, despite the elusiveness of its delicate framework. Defying labels, *Cities* hardly can be called fiction, at least not in a traditional sense, because it holds no intrigue and tells no stories.

Instead, it unfolds as a quiet dialogue in which two voices, presumably that of Marco Polo and Kubla Khan, meditate on the emperor's once wondrous but now decaying realm. Fabulous visions of each of the Khan's cities are raised and then quickly shattered beneath the ever-watchful Palomarlike eye of Marco Polo.

Portraits are drawn of exotic beauty and grim ugliness, of utopia and dystopia. The city of Clarice is "a gem" and "a nest of huts and hovels." Marozia too is a frustrating enigma, a twin city, "one of the rat, one of the swallow." All the cities call up not deeds, but dreams, perhaps even nightmares. To Calvino these illusive images represented what he himself quite simply called "my petits poemes."

To American readers, however, the cities struck a tender nerve, evoking the duplicity of the American metropolis: its gleaming steel surface barely concealing corroded underpinnings.

Perhaps still best loved in his native Italy are Calvino's earliest short stories, only recently published in English under the titles *Difficult Loves* and *Marcovaldo.*

Special tenderness has been lavished on Marcovaldo, a bumbling buffoon whose well-meaning misadventures can lead him on rooftop rabbit hunts or to joust with soap bubbles. He is a small dreamer, as insignificant, vulnerable and lovable as Chaplin's "little fellow."

Recalling Chaplin and other of today's comic heroes, Marcovaldo inevitably dramatizes the bittersweet plight of modern humankind, recounting the petty saga of our mechanical lives and shrinking individuality. Like Kurt Vonnegut's Billy Pilgrim, for example, Marcovaldo would place his trust in an impossible dream rather than face the drab sameness of his everyday factory existence. Like a typical Woody Allen misfit, Marcovaldo is a loner, an onlooker who lives on the edge of life owlishly peering in and gamely trying to make sense of it.

Palomar is another one of life's game losers who for some time has realized that "things between him and the world are no longer proceeding as they used to." In the manner of all Calvino characters, he too is a spectator, a stargazer, "looking at things from the outside." For all his greater sophistication, he has a lot of Calvino's earlier Marcovaldo life in him. At times it seems almost as if the author in this, his final work, has come full circle, has come home at last.

An ominous note—his age—distinguishes Palomar from Marcovaldo. Whereas Marcovaldo is forever young, innocent and comforted quickly in his little hopes, Palomar is older and wiser, realizing now that his dreams are behind him, "all in the past."

Whereas Marcovaldo sees his future in survival, Palomar, through his telescope, sadly contemplates the limitless expanse of an eternity that the world will spend without him and "to which he can add nothing."

Mr. Palomar, for all its gentle whimsy, is not a book for light reading nor is it the fantasy tale advertised on its glossy cover. On the contrary, it is exactly what Palomar tells us it is: uncompromisingly realistic and a "difficult step in learning how to be dead." With somber wit, so reflective of Calvino's pensive humor in his final years, the aging Palomar reviews his life, its pleasures and pains, its successes and failures, its silly moments and serious ones.

With simple candor he confesses himself no more than an individual "made up of what he has lived and the way he lived." Purposefully, perhaps, he goads the reader to take a hard look at his own worst fears, to reckon with himself, and examine boldly the journey's end. The result is a touching novel that provides an intimate portrait of Calvino the writer as well as a tender and fitting eulogy for the man.

Constance Markey, "Last Work Offers an Inward View of Writer, Person," in Chicago Tribune, *November 10, 1985, p. 38.*

GORE VIDAL

[The author of such works as Visit to a Small Planet *(1956),* Myra Breckenridge *(1968),* Burr *(1973), and* Lincoln *(1984), Vidal is an American novelist, short story writer, dramatist, and essayist. He is particularly noted for his historical novels and his iconoclastic essays, but his writing in all genres is marked by his urbane wit and brilliant technique. In his work Vidal examines the plight of modern humanity caught in a valueless world amid corrupt institutions. In the following excerpt Vidal, a friend of Calvino, credits himself with introducing the author to an American audience. He also reflects on Calvino's personal and artistic nature,*

particularly as it is expressed in Calvino's last novel, Mr. Palomar.]

On the morning of Friday, September 20, 1985, the first equinoctial storm of the year broke over the city of Rome. I awoke to thunder and lightning; and thought I was, yet again, in World War II. Shortly before noon, a car and driver arrived to take me up the Mediterranean coast to a small town on the sea called Castiglion della Pescáia where, at one o'clock, Italo Calvino, who had died the day before, would be buried in the village cemetery.

Calvino had had a cerebral hemorrhage two weeks earlier while sitting in the garden of his house at Pineta di Roccamare, where he had spent the summer working on the Charles Eliot Norton lectures that he planned to give during the fall and winter at Harvard. I last saw him in May. I commended him on his bravery: he planned to give the lectures in English, a language that he read easily but spoke hesitantly, unlike French and Spanish, which he spoke perfectly; but then he had been born in Cuba, son of two Italian agronomists; and had lived for many years in Paris.

It was night. We were on the terrace of my apartment in Rome; an overhead light made his deep-set eyes look even darker than usual. Italo gave me his either-this-or-that frown; then he smiled, and when he smiled, suddenly, the face would become like that of an enormously bright child who has just worked out the unified field theory. "At Harvard, I shall stammer," he said. "But then I stammer in every language."

Unlike the United States, Italy has both an educational system (good or bad is immaterial) and a common culture, both good and bad. In recent years Calvino had become the central figure in Italy's culture. Italians were proud that they had produced a world writer whose American reputation began, if I may say so, since no one else will, in these pages when I described all of his novels as of May 30, 1974. By 1985, except for England, Calvino was read wherever books are read. I even found a Calvino coven in Moscow's literary bureaucracy; and I think that I may have convinced the state publishers to translate more of him. Curiously, the fact that he had slipped away from the Italian Communist party in 1957 disturbed no one. Then, three weeks short of Calvino's sixty-second birthday, he died; and Italy went into mourning, as if a beloved prince had died. For an American, the contrast between them and us is striking. When an American writer dies, there will be, if he's a celebrity (fame is no longer possible for any of us), a picture below the fold on the front page; later, a short appreciation on the newspaper's book page (if there is one), usually the work of a journalist or other near-writer who has not actually read any of the dead author's work but is at home with the arcana of Page Six; and that would be that.

In Calvino's case, the American newspaper obituaries were perfunctory and incompetent: the circuits between the English departments, where our tablets of literary reputation are now kept, and the world of journalism are more than ever fragile and the reception is always bad. Surprisingly, *Time* and *Newsweek*, though each put him on the "book page," were not bad, though one thought him "surrealist" and the other a "master of fantasy"; he was, of course, a true realist, who believed "that only a certain prosaic solidity can give birth to creativity: fantasy is like jam; you have to spread it on a solid slice of bread. If not, it remains a shapeless thing, like jam, out of which you can't make anything." This homely analogy is from an Italian television interview, shown after his death.

The New York Times [see excerpt above], to show how well regarded Calvino is in these parts, quoted John Updike, our literature's perennial apostle to the middlebrows (this is not meant, entirely, unkindly), as well as Margaret Atwood (a name new to me), Ursula K. LeGuin (an estimable sci-fi writer, but what is she doing, giving, as it were, a last word on one of the most complex of modern writers?), Michael Wood, whose comment was pretty good, and, finally, the excellent Anthony Burgess, who was not up to his usual par on this occasion. Elsewhere, Mr. Herbert Mitgang again quoted Mr. Updike as well as John Gardner, late apostle to the lowbrows, a sort of Christian evangelical who saw Heaven as a paradigmatic American university.

Europe regarded Calvino's death as a calamity for culture. A literary critic, as opposed to theorist, wrote at length in *Le Monde*, while in Italy itself, each day for two weeks, bulletins from the hospital at Siena were published, and the whole country was suddenly united in its esteem not only for a great writer but for someone who reached not only primary school children through his collections of folk and fairy tales but, at one time or another, everyone else who reads.

After the first hemorrhage, there was a surgical intervention that lasted many hours. Calvino came out of coma. He was disoriented: he thought that one of the medical attendants was a policeman; then he wondered if he'd had open-heart surgery. Meanwhile, the surgeon had become optimistic; even garrulous. He told the press that he'd never seen a brain structure of such delicacy and complexity as that of Calvino. I thought immediately of the smallest brain ever recorded, that of Anatole France. The surgeon told the press that he had been obliged to do his very best. After all, he and his sons had read and argued over *Marcovaldo* last winter. The brain that could so puzzle them must be kept alive in all its rarity. One can imagine a comparable surgeon in America: only last Saturday she had kept me and my sons in stitches; now I could hardly believe that I was actually gazing into the fabulous brain of Joan Rivers! On the other hand, the admirer of Joan Rivers might have saved Calvino; except that there was no real hope, ever. (p. 3)

As we drove north through the rain, I read Calvino's last novel, *Palomar*. He had given it to me on November 28, 1983. I was chilled—and guilty—to read for the first time the inscription: "For Gore, these last meditations about Nature, Italo." "Last" is a word artists should not easily use. What did this "last" mean? Latest? Or his last attempt to write about the phenomenal world? Or did he know, somehow, that he was in the process of "Learning to be dead," the title of the book's last chapter?

I read the book. It is very short. A number of meditations on different subjects by one Mr. Palomar, who is Calvino himself. The settings are, variously, the beach at Castiglion della Pescáia, the nearby house in the woods at Roccamare, the flat in Rome with its terrace, a food specialty shop in Paris. This is not the occasion to review the book. But I made some observations; and marked certain passages that seemed to me to illuminate the prospect.

Palomar is on the beach at Castiglion: he is trying to figure out the nature of waves. Is it possible to follow just one? Or do they all become one? *E pluribus unum* and its reverse might well sum up Calvino's approach to our condition. Are we a part of the universe? Or is the universe, simply, us thinking that there is such a thing? Calvino often writes like the scientist that his parents were. He observes, precisely, the minutiae of nature: stars, waves, lizards, turtles, a woman's breast exposed on the beach. In the process, he vacillates between macro and micro. The whole and the part. Also, tricks of eye. The book is written in the present tense, like a scientist making reports on that ongoing experiment, the examined life.

The waves provide him with suggestions but no answers: viewed in a certain way, they seem to come not from the horizon but from the shore itself. "Is this perhaps the real result that Mr. Palomar is about to achieve? To make the waves run in the opposite direction, to overturn time, to perceive the true substance of the world beyond sensory and mental habits?" But it doesn't quite work; and he cannot extend "this knowledge to the entire universe." He notes during his evening swim that "the sun's reflection becomes a shining sword on the water stretching from shore to him. Mr. Palomar swims in that sword. . . ." But then so does everyone else at that time of day, each in the same sword which is everywhere and nowhere. "The sword is imposed equally on the eye of each swimmer; there is no avoiding it. 'Is what we have in common precisely what is given to each of us as something exclusively his?'" As Palomar floats he wonders if he exists. He drifts now toward solipsism: "If no eye except the glassy eye of the dead were to open again on the surface of the terraqueous globe, the sword would not gleam any more." He develops this, floating on his back. "Perhaps it was not the birth of the eye that caused the birth of the sword, but vice versa, because the sword had to have an eye to observe it at its climax." But the day is ending, the wind-surfers are all beached, and Palomar comes back to land: "He has become convinced that the sword will exist even without him."

In the garden at Roccamare, Palomar observes the exotic mating of turtles; he ponders the blackbird's whistle, so like that of a human being that it might well be the same sort of communication. "Here a prospect that is very promising for Mr. Palomar's thinking opens out; for him the discrepancy between human behavior and the rest of the universe has always been a source of anguish. The equal whistle of man and blackbird now seems to him a bridge thrown over the abyss." But his attempts to communicate with them through a similar whistling leads to "puzzlement" on both sides. Then, contemplating the horrors of his lawn and its constituent parts, among them weeds, he precisely names and numbers what he sees until "he no longer thinks of the lawn: he thinks of the universe. He is trying to apply to the universe everything he has thought about the lawn. The universe as regular and ordered cosmos or as chaotic proliferation." The analogy, as always with Calvino, then takes off (the jam on the bread) and the answer is again the many within the one, or "collections of collections."

Observations and meditations continue. He notes, "Nobody looks at the moon in the afternoon, and this is the moment when it would most require our attention, since its existence is still in doubt." As night comes on, he wonders if the moon's bright splendor is "due to the slow retreat of the sky, which, as it moves away, sinks deeper and deeper into darkness or whether, on the contrary it is the moon that is coming forward, collecting the previously scattered light and depriving the sky of it, concentrating it all in the round mouth of its funnel." One begins now to see the method of a Calvino meditation. He looks; he describes; he has a scientist's respect for data (the opposite of the surrealist or fantasist). He wants us to see not only what he sees but what we may have missed by not looking with sufficient attention. It is no wonder that Galileo crops up in his writing. The received opinion of mankind over the centuries (which is what middlebrow is all about) was

certain that the sun moved around the earth but to a divergent highbrow's mind, Galileo's or Calvino's, it is plainly the other way around. Galileo applied the scientific methods of his day; Calvino used his imagination. Each either got it right; or assembled the data so that others could understand the phenomenon.

In April 1982, while I was speaking to a Los Angeles audience with George McGovern, Eugene McCarthy, and the dread physical therapist Ms. Fonda Hayden, "the three 'external' planets, visible to the naked eye . . . are all three 'in opposition' and therefore visible for the whole night." Needless to say, "Mr. Palomar rushes out on to the terrace." Between Calvino's stars and mine, he had the better of it; yet he wrote a good deal of political commentary for newspapers. But after he left the Communist party, he tended more to describe politics and its delusions than take up causes. "In a time and in a country where everyone goes out of his way to announce opinions or hand down judgements, Mr. Palomar has made a habit of biting his tongue three times before asserting anything. After the bite, if he is still convinced of what he was going to say, he says it." But then, "having had the correct view is nothing meritorious; statistically, it is almost inevitable that among the many cockeyed, confused or banal ideas that come into his mind, there should also be some perspicacious ideas, even ideas of genius; and as they occurred to him, they can surely have occurred also to somebody else." As he was a writer of literature and not a theorist, so he was an observer of politics and not a politician.

Calvino was as inspired by the inhabitants of zoos as by those of cities. "At this point Mr. Palomar's little girl, who has long since tired of watching the giraffes, pulls him toward the penguins' cave. Mr. Palomar, in whom penguins inspire anguish, follows her reluctantly and asks himself why he is so interested in giraffes. Perhaps because the world around him moves in an unharmonious way, and he hopes always to find some pattern to it, a constant. Perhaps because he himself feels that his own advance is impelled by uncoordinated movements of the mind, which seem to have nothing to do with one another and are increasingly difficult to fit into any pattern of inner harmony."

Palomar is drawn to the evil-smelling reptile house. "Beyond the glass of every cage, there is the world as it was before man, or after, to show that the world of man is not eternal and is not unique." The crocodiles, in their stillness, horrify him. "What are they waiting for, or what have they given up waiting for? In what time are they immersed? . . . The thought of a time outside our existence is intolerable." Palomar flees to the albino gorilla, "sole exemplar in the world of a form not chosen, not loved." The gorilla, in his boredom, plays with a rubber tire; he presses it to his bosom by the hour. The image haunts Palomar. "'Just as the gorilla has his tire, which serves as tangible support for a raving, wordless speech,' he thinks, 'so I have this image of a great white ape. We all turn in our hands an old, empty tire through which we would like to reach the final meaning, at which words do not arrive.'" This is the ultimate of writers' images; that indescribable state where words are absent not because they are stopped by the iron bars of a cage at the zoo but by the limitations of that bone-covered binary electrical system which, in Calvino's case, broke down September 19, 1985. (pp. 3, 6)

Among the tombs, I am interviewed. How had I met Calvino? A few drops of warm rain fall. A cameraman appears from behind a family chapel and takes my picture. The state television crew is arriving. Eleven years ago, I say, I wrote a piece about his work. Had you met him *before* that? Logrolling is even more noticeable in a small country like Italy than it is in our own dear *New York Times*. No, I had not met him when I wrote the piece. I had just read him, admired him; described (the critic's only task) his work for those who were able to read me and might then be inclined to read him (the critic's single aim). Did you meet him later? Yes, he wrote me a letter about the piece. In Italian or English? Italian, I say. What did he say? What do you think he said? I am getting irritable. He said he liked what I'd written.

Actually, Calvino's letter had been, characteristically, interesting and tangential. I had ended my description with "Reading Calvino, I had the unnerving sense that I was also writing what he had written; thus does his art prove his case as writer and reader become one, or One." This caught his attention. Politely, he began by saying that he had always been attracted by my "mordant irony," and so forth, but he particularly liked what I had written about him for two reasons. The first, "One feels that you have written this essay for the pleasure of writing it, alternating warm praise and criticism and reserve with an absolute sincerity, with freedom, and continuous humor, and this sensation of pleasure is irresistibly communicated to the reader. Second, I have always thought it would be difficult to extract a unifying theme from my books, each so different from the other. Now you—exploring my works as it should be done, that is, by going at it in an unsystematic way, stopping here and there; sometimes aimed directly without straying aside; other times, wandering like a vagabond—have succeeded in giving a general sense to all I have written, almost a philosophy—'the whole and the many,' etc.—and it makes me very happy when someone is able to find a philosophy from the productions of my mind which has little philosophy." Then Calvino comes to the point. "The ending of your essay contains an affirmation of what seems to me important in an absolute sense. I don't know if it really refers to me, but it is true of an ideal literature for each one of us: the end being that every one of us must be, that the writer and reader become one, or One. And to close all of my discourse and yours in a perfect circle, let us say that this One is All." In a sense, the later Palomar was the gathering together of the strands of a philosophy or philosophies; hence, the inscription "my last meditations on Nature." (p. 8)

For the last year, Calvino had been looking forward to his fall and winter at Harvard. He even began to bone up on "literary theory." He knew perfectly well what a mephitic kindergarten our English departments have become, and I cannot wait to see what he has to say in the three lectures that he did write. I had planned to arm him with a wonderfully silly bit of lowbrow criticism (from *Partisan Review*) on why people just don't like to read much anymore. John Gardner is quoted with admiration: "'In nearly all good fiction, the basic—all but inescapable—plot form is this: a central character wants something, goes after it despite opposition (perhaps including his own doubts), and so arrives at a win, lose or draw.'" For those still curious about high, middle, and lowbrow, this last is the Excelsior of lowbrow commercialities, written in letters of gold in the halls of the Thalberg Building at MGM but never to be found in, say, the original *Partisan Review* of Rahv and Dupee, Trilling and Chase. The PR "critic" then quotes "a reviewer" in *The New York Times* who is trying to figure out why Calvino is popular. "If love fails, they begin again; their lives are a series of new beginnings, where complications have not yet begun to show themselves. Unlike the great Russian and French

novelists" (this is pure middlebrow: *which* novelists, dummy! Name names, make your case, *describe*), "who follow their characters through the long and winding caverns [!] of their lives, Calvino just turns off the set after the easy beginning and switches to another channel." This sort of writing has given American bookchat (a word I coined, you will be eager to know) a permanently bad name. But our PR critic, a woman, this year's favored minority *(sic)*, states, sternly, that all this "indeterminancy" is not the kind of stuff real folks want to read. "And Calvino is popular, if at all, among theorists, consumers of 'texts' rather than of novels and stories." I shall now never have the chance to laugh with Calvino over this latest report from the land to which Bouvard and Pécuchet emigrated. (pp. 8-9)

On the drive back to Rome, the sun is bright and hot; yet rain starts to fall. Devil is beating his wife, as they say in the South. Then a rainbow covers the entire eastern sky. For the Romans and the Etruscans, earlier inhabitants of the countryside through which we are driving, the rainbow was an ominous herald of coming change in human affairs, death of kings, cities, world. I make a gesture to ward off the evil eye. Time can now end. But "'If time has to end, it can be described, instant by instant,' Palomar thinks, 'and each instant, when described, expands so that its end can no longer be seen.' He decides that he will set himself to describing every instant of his life, and until he has described them all he will no longer think of being dead. At that moment he dies." So end "my last meditations on Nature," and Calvino and Nature are now one, or One. (p. 10)

Gore Vidal, "On Italo Calvino," in The New York Review of Books, *Vol. XXXII, No. 18, November 21, 1985, pp. 3, 6, 8-10.*

JAMES GARDNER

An ancient adage counsels us to speak only well of the deceased, and the recent and untimely death of Italo Calvino, at the age of sixty-one, has provoked in almost all quarters a confirmation, if not an escalation, of the enthusiasm that greeted his work for over a generation. It is fitting that Calvino's death should sadden us, because his writings were characterized by a broad humanity, a compelling ingenuity, and above all the constant promise, while he lived, that he might finally consolidate within a single work of art those scattered passages of excellence that are present in all his works.

Since only a very few writers in any generation are treated to the degree of adulation that Calvino enjoys at this moment, it must be the purpose of any critical essay to test whether indeed his virtues reside in those elements of his work that have been praised, whether such praise has been excessive, and, most disturbing of all, whether the universal enthusiasm for Calvino's writing did not in fact undermine his artistic integrity. Such has been the exuberance of the praise with which Calvino's writings have been received that any critic who demurs from total capitulation to this author's mystique, especially in the present circumstance of his death, is likely to seem something of a crank. (p. 6)

It must seem almost inconceivable to anyone acquainted with only the rarefied fictions of *Cosmicomics* (1965) or the structuralist experimentation of *The Castle of Crossed Destinies* (1969) that their author could ever have announced, as he did in 1955, that "We are in a state of emergency. Let us not exchange the terror *(terribilità)* of writing for the terror of reality; let us not forget that it is against reality that we must fight, even if we avail ourselves of the weapons of words.'' How different is even the style of this prose from that measured stasis of Calvino's more recent writing; a whole culture is reflected in the strident cadences of its declamation, echoing as it does back to the oratory of Mazzini and Garibaldi, translated into the postwar idiom of the Neo-Realists, and suffused with all the urgency of Camus. Is this truly the utterance of a man who in less than a generation would be signing his name to pallid Barthesian essays on Groucho's cigar or Saul Steinberg's pen?

Yet the reputation that Calvino enjoys in this country is founded almost entirely upon these later writings, which might be characterized as ''deconstructionist,'' since their matter seems inextricably involved with the act of reading, and the same currents that have made fashionable the philosophy of Jacques Derrida are largely responsible for causing Calvino to appear as a significant spokesman for a certain way of conceiving the universe. The same people who have found so much to like in his later writings have been slightly embarrassed by what Calvino was doing in the first half of his creative life, since this would seem to be so very much at odds with what he would go on to do as to make it impossible for a proponent of one period to have much use for anyone who favored the other. Indeed, unless a reader had already been tipped off, it is unlikely that he would ever realize that works as disparate as *La giornata d'uno scruttatore* (1963) and *Cosmicomics* could have proceeded from a single imagination, although in fact only two years divide them.

The reason for which the early fiction of Calvino has constituted an embarrassment to many of his admirers on this side of the Atlantic, who came into the act in time to adore only his more recent efforts, is the boldness and obviousness with which these first endeavors pose political and social questions. In these early works the freewheeling imaginativeness that has endeared him to many American readers in recent years is but rarely in evidence. The literary tradition into which Calvino emerged in adulthood, that of Neo-Realism, was one to which he would have been predisposed by inclination as well as by education. His father was active in various anarchist movements early in the century, and in his youth Calvino, by indulging Communist ideas, registered a similar disrelish for the extreme Right that was then in power. But the application of these ideas to his literature was always fairly casual, and his political impulses seem in the main to spring from the implicit but indestructible conviction, which pervades everything he ever wrote, that man is essentially good. Whether he seeks to expose the fatuity of the fascists, as in those early stories in the volume *L'entrata in guerra*, or to celebrate that Adamite freedom so dear to the hearts of anarchists and nudists, as in some of the still earlier stories included in *Difficult Loves* (1970), or finally to simplify human existence through a poetic system, as in *Invisible Cities* (1972) or *Mr. Palomar* (1983), Calvino still advocates throughout the profoundly if sometimes disastrously political position that all men are good, and that, left to their own devices, they will band together in choirs of fraternity. (pp. 6-7)

As is evident in the sense of urgency with which they are so often filled, [*The Path to the Nest of Spiders* (1947)] and other early writings in his Neo-Realist phase reflect the influence of philosophical movements, like existentialism, which were in vogue in the years immediately after the Second World War. But they also presage the more dulcet and graceful tendencies that would evolve only much later in Calvino's career, and which it may be accurate to consider more essentially his own. These proclivities are present in some of his earliest short

stories, as in those contained in the two volumes *Ultimo viene il corvo* (1949) and *I racconti* (1958), which were published together in the volume *Difficult Loves.* Here he indulges, even if at a humbler level, in those tricks that would later make him famous. One of these is the inverted perspective, whereby he, the author, adopts the point of view of the character who is narrating the tale, even when that viewpoint is diametrically opposed to his own. In ''A Goatherd at Luncheon,'' for instance, Calvino relates an incident that occurs within an affluent and upper-middle-class family, when the overly exuberant father invites a peasant to dine with them. This story is related from the perspective of the younger son of the household, who looks with a mixture of horror and condescending pity upon the downtrodden representative of the lower classes. This tale is surely one of very few in the canon of modern literature in which the story is told entirely from the point of view of the snob, who is made to appear as rational as can be, and who, above all, instinctively assumes that the reader, to whom he is telling the story, could not possibly feel otherwise. Thus the traditional reader of modern fiction, who is most comfortable seeing things from the perspective of the underdog, especially in Neo-Realist fiction, is here co-opted against his will into company in which he feels sure he doesn't belong. Similarly, in ''A Ship-load of Crabs,'' we are made to see things from the point of view of very young children, to share in their conflicts, and once again to feel as our own those tribulations which we thought we had overcome when we turned ten. This technique, which approaches stream of consciousness, is present in works as disparate as *The Path to the Nest of Spiders,* his foremost Neo-Realist work, with its adolescent protagonist Pin, and the much more recent *t zero* (1967) with its postmodern narrator Qfwfq. Calvino has achieved this more through sympathy than through mimicry, for mimicry has never been one of his strong points; and although he is constantly passing judgment, this judgment is always benign. (pp. 7-8)

The *Stories of Love and Sickness* (1949), which were included in *I racconti,* are interesting in the history of the oeuvre of Calvino, since they would seem to announce a tendency that became of major importance for him later on. This volume comprises eight tales, and their titles, such as ''The Adventure of a Poet'' and ''The Adventure of a Clerk,'' have a decidedly Chaucerian ring to them. Indeed, they are even narrated in that deadpan poker-faced tone, at once familiar and distant, that Boccaccio introduced into Italian literature. It is in these works that we see the origins of an interest that would later induce Calvino, in the mid-Fifties, to take on the task of editing and rephrasing two hundred Italian fables [in *Italian Folktales*], as well as paraphrasing Ariosto's *Orlando Furioso.* This fabulistic tendency is present in many of the later works, like *The Castle of Crossed Destinies,* and especially in the three imaginative works from the 1950s that have been published together in Italy under the title *I nostri antenati* (1960), and that have been translated into English as *The Baron in the Trees, The Cloven Viscount,* and *The Nonexistent Knight.* What links all these works, and constitutes an implicit attack upon the aesthetic of Neo-Realism, is the fact that they all take place in the past, in the eighth, seventeenth, and eighteenth centuries, and in a context not of the lower and middle classes but rather of the feudal aristocracy, who are as remote as could be from adolescent heroes like Pin. Furthermore, the heroes are the recipients of a curious and even supernatural destiny, by which their lives are irreversibly altered. (p. 8)

These three works struck their first critics as signaling a decidedly radical departure from the style of writing that one had come to associate with Calvino, and it was easy to believe, with the publication of such sturdily Neo-Realist works as *La Nuvola di Smog* and *La Formica Argentina,* both from 1958, and *La giornata d'uno scruttatore* and *La speculazione edilizia,* both from 1963, that those three earlier works had been merely an aberration which might yet be accommodated within a larger and more traditional context. But in fact, as is now well known, the three novels comprised in *I nostri antenati* are really presentiments, if not fulfillments, of a tendency which would become more and more dominant in Calvino's writing as the years went on, and which, as we have seen, had its origins in his very earliest short stories.

As has already been suggested, it is the growing interest in science which informs the shorter fiction in *Cosmicomics* and *t zero,* although these works are in effect the translation into a more exotic vocabulary of the earlier Neo-Realist short stories whch Calvino had written in the Forties. They express the same very human longings and frustrations that were found in the early fiction, and the title under which these earlier works were collected, *Difficult Loves,* would serve to describe them as well.

Despite the presence in *Cosmicomics* and *t zero* of a profusion of scientific references, and chic effusions in the manner of Barthes and Derrida, Calvino was really an unsystematic thinker at best, and he has used these borrowings most effectively where they serve only to underscore or to enhance the emotional content that was equally present, if in another form, in his Neo-Realist works. Calvino was by nature a timid and introspective intelligence. For many years he served in the capacity of editor at the important Italian publishing firm of Einaudi in Turin, and this fact, combined with his native, if desultory, inquisitiveness, brought him into contact with works on many different subjects. But as far as can be deduced from his fiction and his occasional forays into expository prose, neither his knowledge nor his thought was ever especially profound or brilliant, although they often provided the context and the form for a sensibility that could go quite deep. . . . Calvino's knowledge of the sciences is characterized in the highest degree by superficiality, which it is important to bear in mind, considering that many people place him on a higher level of scientific sophistication. He has merely applied to a modern context (though one that even now is becoming slightly dated) the imaginative exorbitancies of older poets like Boiardo and Ariosto, whose *Orlando Furioso,* as we have seen, he prepared in an updated version for Einaudi. What the world looked like before the advent of color, or what the fish were thinking as they began their trek onto the dry land upon which they would become in due course lizards and birds, are the sort of questions that poets rather than scientists ask. Nor is this merely to chastise Calvino for not being more of a scientist, or for being in fact a pseudo-scientist. It is to insist that the mystique and vogue that this pseudo-methodology takes should not be allowed, as they usually are, to enter into our assessment of his literary worth. Calvino is never especially good at considering a scientific fact in its natural context; he is able to appreciate it only in its phenomenal nakedness. Essential to the scientific method is a complete confidence in the laws of cause and effect, and these Calvino makes no effort to understand. This is not to criticize him for misapplying these laws or standing them on their head, though this he occasionally does, so much as to insist that he abstains from their application almost altogether.

In his earlier scientific fiction (for it is not "science fiction") he was content merely to stand the reality of science on its head, cooking up an engagingly imbecile story-line around the colorful facts that he had at his disposal. But in one of his most recent books, and the one most recently translated into English, *Mr. Palomar,* he has rejected the principles of causation altogether. He has done this by cataloguing the naked facts of reality, rather than forcing them into a relationship like that of cause and effect, in which facts lose their individuality and autonomy, by being perceived as only parts in a new and larger whole. And in this as well Calvino shows the influence of recent philosophers, like Jacques Derrida, who have criticized the traditional paradigms of science, and have sought to go "beyond" cause and effect, by creating "texts" that subsist under a category of mind different from that of traditional Western science. This is surely the reason for which a novel like *Mr. Palomar* seems so fiercely contemporary, and one of the reasons for which it will probably come in a very short while to seem very dated indeed. (pp. 9-10)

The inspiration for a work like *Mr. Palomar* will doubtless become much clearer when his most recent book, which appeared in Italy late last year, is rendered into English. This work, titled *Collezione di Sabbia (A Collection of Sand),* brings together Calvino's more recent essays, mostly from the early 1980s. In addition to its containing essays . . . in which the author aspires to the universal culture that Barthes at least aspired to in his *Mythologies,* Calvino has included what are really descriptions of strange and curious collections that have been amassed over the years, collections of different kinds of sand, of maps, alphabets, and physical deformations, all described in that soft-spoken and understated prose that has characterized his writing for almost two decades now. These forays into history and science are, to use the structuralist jargon by which the author was probably inspired, synchronic rather than diachronic, that is, they perceive all the data of traditional historiography and science as existing, not in hierarchical relations of causes to effects, but rather in terms of the contemporaneous juxtaposition of random and provocative facts. As it occurs in the latter writings of Calvino, this critique of contemporary science, for such indeed it is, goes beyond the willful rejection of the traditional scientific method. In a field of inquiry that can go only forward and never backward, Calvino seems to me directly to confront science's native progressiveness by professing an exaggerated affection for the obsolete artifacts of an earlier science. He examines with a thoroughly unscientific pleasure the craftsmanship of old maps, astrolabes, and preposterous contraptions. He has Mr. Palomar enter a cheese shop, which he typically calls a cheese museum, with all that that implies of neurotic methodology and classification, and then a butcher shop, where he soon becomes lost in baroque reveries about the infinite varieties of those commodities he has come to purchase.

Perhaps the most sustained exercise in this sort of cataloguing technique is to be found in *Invisible Cities.* . . . (p. 10)

But if Calvino does not show much interest beyond a very superficial one in the explicatory powers of the scientific or historical method, he shows scarcely greater interest in the rigorous method of those philosophers who influenced his writings, especially in later years. In his writings from the late Sixties and the early Seventies one finds the influence of thinkers like Barthes and the theoreticians of the Nouveau Roman, and thereafter he becomes interested in, or at least breathes the same spirit as, Jacques Derrida and the Tel Quel writers. And yet, he seems only to share in their spirit in a very casual way, and it is difficult to imagine Calvino sitting down with the texts of Barthes's more scientific inquiries into the nature of narrative, or with Derrida's impenetrable *De la grammatologie.*

It is perhaps safest to say that Calvino is very much inspired with the *Zeitgeist,* although it must be stated in his behalf that he did much to form it into its present shape. Whether he is the cause or the effect of certain of those tendencies with which he is associated is a question that is outside of the scope of the present essay, although it is my suspicion that the form itself that Calvino's writing and his thoughts took, especially most recently, will be found to have a Frenchman behind every one. But Calvino had neither the inclination nor the cast of mind truly and thoroughly to assimilate these foreign importations, any more than he had the diligence to acquire the basic principles of the scientific method. They are present merely as ornaments that decorate his native inclinations, or as vaguely construed ideas that inspire him to attempt bold literary experiments which really have little to do with what had been intended by the originators of those systems. (p. 11)

The tone of the scientific writings of the Sixties was not only very human but also touched with that gentle good humor which Calvino revealed so often and so refreshingly throughout his career. But in more recent works, which were inspired by the French and which might be considered scientific or at least "methodological" in the rigor with which they unfold, this characteristic humor is lacking and we are faced with that dour sobriety that had not been seen since *La speculazione edilizia* and *La giornata d'uno scruttatore* a decade earlier. It is not unworthy of consideration that perhaps these late works, which have been held up often enough as paragons of inventiveness and zestful caprice, are in fact the results of a partial and momentary exhaustion which manifested itself in their mirthlessness. For although it may be debated to what degree the invention of a narrative system is an artistic act comparable with that of narration itself, the fact remains that it would have been possible for someone who was not in the mood for creativity, by applying the systems used in these two works, to wind up with a novel of the required length. In *Invisible Cities* . . . the plot reduces itself to a dialogue between Marco Polo and Genghis Khan, interspersed with, and dominated by, the description, one after the other, of fifty-five cities. These descriptions are often quite inventive and beautiful, but the plot really does not carry itself with conviction, and a sense of sluggish homogeneity begins to set in early on, as it did in Calvino's collection of Italian fables. If it is the cataloguing method that inspires this work, his next work, *The Castle of Crossed Destinies,* is a boring application to the short story of the narrative principles which the structuralists would have us believe to inhere in some important sense in a pack of tarot cards. By drawing from the deck, Calvino explains in a pedantic epilogue, he was provided with the general outlines for the plots. If these stories were successful, and I do not feel that they were, they would be so for a few beautiful descriptions or for a dramatic scene for which the tarot had provided the context—in other words, for reasons entirely different from those of narrative technique, which are ostensibly the innovations that made the work sell to those more avant-garde readers who mistook and still mistake novelty for consequence. (pp. 11-12)

We should be thankful . . . that in his two final works of fiction, *If on a Winter's Night a Traveler* (1979) and *Mr. Palomar,* although Calvino was inspired ostensibly by post-structuralist principles not unlike those of the two works that preceded them, still, he has leavened these last two books, especially the earlier one, with a genuine and pungent sense of humor. In *If on a Winter's Night a Traveler,* this takes the form of an inquiry into the ways in which we read a novel, for instance, the novel called *If on a Winter's Night a Traveler.* A long and engaging series of reversals and *mises en abîme* keep the narrative moving pleasantly through ten simulated novels, and it is to the author's credit that he has kept this from becoming boring, which it would almost certainly have done in the hands of a less skilled artist. The system of **Mr. Palomar** is divided into three sections, each with three chapters, each of which in its turn has three sub-chapters marked 1, 2, and 3. These latter chapters are supposed to correspond (they "tend" to correspond, to use Calvino's revealing expression of methodological laxness) to sensory experience in the first part, linguistic data in the second, and speculative questions in the third. It is obvious that in order to achieve this clear schema, Calvino has almost surely had either to eliminate material that simply would have run over, or to include superfluous material merely to fill in the holes in the grid. But in addition to composing some attractive prose passages, he has managed to create an appealing and pitiable personality in the eponymous hero, and, insofar as novel writing concerns the creation of memorable personalities, Calvino has at least that much of traditional achievement. It is also worth remarking that in the hierarchy implied in the ordering of 1, 2, and 3 he seems to have placed spiritual and religious questions above those of language and structure. Is this not the earliest, the truest Calvino emerging once again? In certain circles of his admirers, this fact, if it were ever to be fully appreciated, would have to be understood as a kind of apostasy.

Although the quality of Calvino's output varies considerably, he is never conspicuously bad, just as he is never truly great. That he is never conspicuously bad is, of course, only of biographical interest; in an assessment of a man's creativity, it is the possibility of excellence that alone commands our attention, and in application to Calvino the consequences of such an examination may be very sad indeed. For it is by no means impossible that Calvino might have become a much finer novelist than he turned out to be, if he had ever managed to combine in a single work the inventiveness of *If on a Winter's Night a Traveler* with the poetic beauty of *Invisible Cities* and the warmth of the earliest stories in **Difficult Loves. The Baron in the Trees** comes closer to this imaginary novel than does any of Calvino's other works, but still it is not a great novel, and even if it were, this fact probably would not justify the praise almost universally paid to Calvino's entire output. If the reception that Calvino received had been a bit more critical perhaps he might have gone on to create a work of such sustained excellence. But he did not achieve this, and since, in a sense, he could not help responding, especially later on, to the applause that he was receiving from all sides, and since he might have been tempted by this enthusiasm to provide his glamorous public with exactly what it wanted, in order to win still more applause, is it not possible that that adoring and insincere public has participated in neutralizing a great talent? We have seen this before and we will see it again. Surely this is one of those occasions Eliot had in mind when, as he lamented, "fools' approval stings and honor stains"! (pp. 11-12)

James Gardner, "Italo Calvino, 1923-1985," in The New Criterion, *Vol. IV, No. 4, December, 1985, pp. 6-13.*

TERESA DE LAURETIS

The death of a writer is like the death of a sun, in a way. It leaves us, readers, dazzled and sad with incomprehensible finality, beyond vision or speech. It is a death without regeneration or rebirth. It is for ever.

"Before birth," Italo Calvino wrote, "we are part of the infinite possibilities that may or may not be fulfilled; whereas, once dead, we cannot fulfill ourselves either in the past (to which we now belong entirely but on which we can no longer have any influence) or in the future (which, even if influenced by us, remains forbidden to us)." This rational or historical-materialist sense of death as the end of infinite possibilities—whether realized or not doesn't matter—is much more difficult to accept than the mystical or mythic sense of death as the closure of a cycle, which contains promises of regeneration. For the death of the writer, like the death of a sun, has shrunk our universe by putting an end to those "infinite possibilities" and preempting all the possible worlds which that writer alone, and no other, could have illuminated. Nor does it help, right now, to think that, though the writer will write no more, still the texts written will live on, open, as all texts are, if not to infinite at least to as yet indefinite possibilities of interpretation.

Calvino, the brilliant creator of constantly diverse and always uncanny fictional worlds, died . . . September 19th of a cerebral hemorrhage that struck him two weeks earlier, in his summer home of Castiglione della Pescaia (Siena), while he was working on a series of lectures he had been invited to give at Harvard University during the coming fall and winter.

Born in Santiago de las Vegas (Cuba), where his parents worked for a brief period as agronomists, Calvino grew up near Genoa and then lived in Turin, Paris, and lastly Rome. Since the beginning of his career as an intellectual, a critic, and a creative writer, Calvino took an active role in the making of Italian cultural history. The early years were spent in the most radical literary and political milieu of postwar Italy, the Einaudi publishing company in Turin, where Calvino worked as an editor. But even before, at the age of 20, he had joined the partisans of the Italian Resistance in 1943, and two years later the Communist Party (which he left in 1957, as did many other Italians, after the Soviet invasion of Hungary). As it was for Cesare Pavese and Elio Vittorini, his distinguished fellow writers and editors at Einaudi's, the Resistance came to mean for Calvino more than a single historical event or political action. It meant the total renewal of a cultural tradition that had worn itself out and disastrously shipwrecked on the shores of Fascism.

The Resistance, which shaped the landscape of Calvino's first novel, *The Path to the Nest of Spiders* (1947), represented the opening up of a stifling provincial culture to influences from the great world outside: the myths of America, Hemingway, Melville, the immense frontier and ever-expanding horizon, and of Soviet Russia, the people's revolution, Marxian praxis, socialist utopia. At the same time, the Resistance created a new national heritage, the basis of different values, myths, memories, and aspirations for the people of Italy. Thus, the task of Calvino's early stories in the '50s (some only recently translated, in *Difficult Loves*), his "Ancestors" trilogy (*The Cloven Viscount, The Baron in the Trees, The Nonexistent Knight,* 1951-59), as well as his collection and transcription of Italian

folktales (1956), was to recuperate and integrate with the new post-war culture a great popular-literary tradition dating back to the Middle Ages.

In the '60s and '70s, responding to the growing international concerns with space, scientific exploration, genetic engineering, communication technologies, and theories of meaning (linguistics and semiotics), his stories took on a more specifically S-F quality. Whether set in geological time or intermolecular space (*Cosmicomics* and *t zero,* 1965-1967), whether inscribed in the combinatory figures of a tarot deck (*The Castle of Crossed Destinies,* 1969) or in the voices of Marco Polo and Kublai Khan dialoguing across the centuries of Western civilization (*Invisible Cities,* 1972), these works were all highly imaginative, scientifically informed, funny and inspired meditations on one insistent question: What does it mean to be human, to live and die, to reproduce and to create, to desire and to be?

Meditations these, but in the form of fiction, in the style of a consummate narrative art that is conscious of being at once fantasy and reality, that is conscious of being artifice, constructed and socially produced, yes, but no more so or no less so than human life is and, for that matter, nature itself. Not coincidentally, then, Calvino's last two novels, *If on a Winter's Night a Traveller* (1979) and *Palomar* (1983), were also keenly self-conscious meditations, on the telling and the reading of stories and on the observation of nature as self and other respectively. There, too, as in all of his works, theoretical sophistication in matters scientific or philosophical was firmly grounded in a profound, genuine respect for everyday life and for popular culture in the broadest sense of the term.

If the trajectory of Calvino's writing, from the neo-realism of his early tales to the S-F and meta-narrative modes of his later fiction, can be said to reflect the major shifts that have occurred over four decades in contemporary poetics, and is thus a sign of his uncommon literary and historical awareness, it is all the more extraordinary that he did remain, amid such wealth of invention and expressive variety, so perfectly consistent in his own poetic vision and so faithful to his craft, storytelling.

Calvino knew that stories are instruments for the obliteration of time, and this is why we love them: stories construct time in order to negate it. But he also knew that neither storytelling nor writing can ultimately defer that moment of dazzling and incomprehensible blankness that marks the end of all possibilities. The passage I quoted above is from the chapter in his last book of fiction, *Palomar*, entitled "Learning to Be Dead." And if I may be allowed to honor him by a very personal statement, I would recall his reply to a letter I sent him almost 10 years ago, wherein I observed that his stories had the effect of annulling death as well as time. He was flattered, he said, by my attributing to him such powers, but believed that those powers were in me—in my ability to find them in myself. Only now do I fully understand how generous his answer had been. (pp. 97-8)

Teresa de Lauretis, "Italo Calvino: In Memoriam," in Science-Fiction Studies, *Vol. 13, No. 1, March, 1986, pp. 97-8.*

Robert (Stuart) Fitzgerald
October 12, 1910 - January 16, 1985

American translator, poet, editor, and critic.

(See also *Contemporary Authors,* Vols. 2, rev. ed., 114 [obituary]; *Contemporary Authors New Revision Series,* Vol.1; and *Dictionary of Literary Biography Yearbook: 1980.*)

PRINCIPAL WORKS

Poems   (poetry)   1935
Alcestis [translator, with Dudley Fitts]   (drama)   1936
Antigone [translator, with Dudley Fitts]   (drama)   1939
Oedipus at Colonus [translator]   (drama)   1941
A Wreath for the Sea   (poetry)   1943
Oedipus Rex [translator, with Dudley Fitts]   (drama)   1949
In the Rose of Time: Poems 1931-1956   (poetry)   1956
The Odyessy [translator]   (verse)   1961
Spring Shade   (poetry)   1971
The Iliad [translator]   (verse)   1974
The Aeneid [translator]   (verse)   1983
Enlarging the Change: The Princeton Seminars in Literary Criticism, 1949-1951   (criticism)   1985

HERBERT MITGANG

Robert Fitzgerald, Emeritus Boylston Professor of Rhetoric and Oratory at Harvard, whose translations of the Greek classics became standard works for a generation of scholars and students, died [January 16] at his home in Hamden, Conn. after a long illness. He was 74 years old.

As a poet, critic and translator, Mr. Fitzgerald wore a mantle of authority. His current book, ***Enlarging the Change,*** was reviewed in the [*New York*] *Times Book Review.* . . . The critic, Martin Duberman, called the work "an unexpectedly ingratiating account of an intrinsically arcane subject"—literary criticism. "It is an invaluable, unique resource."

Mr. Fitzgerald's translations of Sophocles' *Oedipus at Colonus* (1961), Homer's *The Odyssey* (1961), *The Iliad* (1974) and *The Aeneid* (1983) became widely admired and accepted. Collaborating with Dudley Fitts, he also produced translations of Euripedes' *Alcestis* (1935) and Sophocles' *Antigone* (1938) and *Oedipus Rex* (1948).

Because he was a poet himself, his translations were bold and hard-edged in their clarity. He avoided the literalness of traditional translators. For example, his translation of the first lines of Book Eleven of *The Odyssey* begins:

> We bore down on the ship at the sea's
> edge
> and launched her on the salt immor-

© 1986 Thomas Victor

> tal sea,
> stepping our mast and spar in the
> black ship;
> embarked the ram and ewe and went
> aboard
> in tears, with bitter and sore dread
> upon us.

For his version of *The Odyssey,* Mr. Fitzgerald received the first Bollingen Award for translation of poetry in 1961. He worked on the translation while living for a decade in Italy with his family beginning in 1953.

Robert Stuart Fitzgerald lived in Springfield, Ill., until he was 18, went to the Choate School for a year, then entered Harvard in 1929. Two years later, a group of his poems were published in *Poetry* magazine. After graduating from Harvard in 1933, he worked as a reporter for the *New York Herald Tribune* for a year and later at *Time* magazine for several years.

During World War II, he served in the Navy in Guam and Pearl Harbor. In the postwar years, he was an instructor at

318

Sarah Lawrence and Princeton and also served as poetry editor of *The New Republic.*

A collection of his own poems, **Spring Shade,** came out in 1971. He also edited *The Collected Poems of James Agee* (1968) and *The Collected Short Prose of James Agee* (1969). His other translations included Paul Valery's *Three Verse Plays* (1960) and St. John Perse's *Chronique* and *Birds* (1965).

In the 50th anniversary report of Harvard's Class of '33, Mr. Fitzgerald summed up his philosophy:

"So hard at best is the lot of man, and so great is the beauty he can apprehend, that only a religious conception of things can take in the extremes and meet the case. Our lifetimes have seen the opening of abysses before which the mind quails. But it seems to me there are a few things everyone can humbly try to hold onto: love and mercy (and humor) in everyday living; the quest for exact truth in language and affairs of the intellect; self-recollection or prayer; and the peace, the composed energy of art."

> *Herbert Mitgang, "Robert Fitzgerald, 74, Poet Who Translated the Classics," in* The New York Times,

January 17, 1985, p. B8.

TIME

Robert Fitzgerald [was a] poet, critic and translator whose own beautifully crafted, formal verse was overshadowed by his magnificent translations of the Greek classics, notably Homer's *Iliad* and *Odyssey,* in which his flexible meter, vigor of language and deep feeling for the supernatural serve to render all the clangor and eloquence of Homer into fast-paced, idiomatic yet poetic English.... A sometime journalist (at *Time* and elsewhere), he began in the 1930s to collaborate with the late Dudley Fitts on translations of Sophocles' and Euripides' plays. Largely on the strength of the 1961 *Odyssey* translation, on which he worked for eight years, he was named in 1965 Boylston Professor of Rhetoric and Oratory at Harvard, where he befriended aspiring young writers, completed his translations of the *Iliad* (1974) and other works and edited the short prose and poetry of his longtime friend (and *Time* colleague) James Agee.

> *"Milestones: Robert Fitzgerald," in* Time, *Vol. 125, No. 4, January 28, 1985, p. 75.*

Robert (von Ranke) Graves

July 24, 1895 - December 7, 1985

English poet, novelist, critic, historian, autobiographer, biographer, translator, mythographer, editor, essayist, short story writer, juvenile fiction and nonfiction writer, and dramatist.

(See also *CLC*, Vols. 1, 2, 6, 11; *Contemporary Authors*, Vols. 5-6, rev. ed.; *Contemporary Authors New Revision Series*, Vol. 5; and *Dictionary of Literary Biography*, Vol. 20.)

PRINCIPAL WORKS

Over the Brazier (poetry) 1916
Fairies and Fusiliers (poetry) 1917
On English Poetry (criticism) 1922
John Kemp's Wager: A Ballad Opera (drama) 1925
Poetic Unreason, and Other Studies (criticism) 1925
Poems 1914-1926 (poetry) 1926
Lawrence and the Arabs (biography) 1927
Good-bye to All That: An Autobiography (autobiography)
    1929
Poems 1926-1930 (poetry) 1931
Poems 1930-1933 (poetry) 1933
Claudius the God (novel) 1934
I, Claudius (novel) 1934
Collected Poems 1938 (poetry) 1938
Count Belisarius (novel) 1939
Sergeant Lamb of the Ninth (novel) 1940
Proceed, Sergeant Lamb (novel) 1941
The Story of Marie Powell: Wife to Mr. Milton (novel)
    1943
The Golden Fleece (novel) 1944; also published as
    Hercules, My Shipmate, 1945
Poems 1938-1945 (poetry) 1945
King Jesus (novel) 1946
The White Goddess: A Historical Grammar of Poetic Myth
    (criticism) 1947
Collected Poems, 1914-1947 (poetry) 1948
The Common Ashpodel: Collected Essays on Poetry,
    1922-1949 (criticism) 1949
Seven Days in New Crete (novel) 1949; also published as
    Watch the North Wind Rise, 1949
The Nazarene Gospels Restored [translator, with Joshua
    Podro] (gospels) 1953
Collected Poems 1955 (poetry) 1955
The Greek Myths. 2 vols. (mythology) 1955
Jesus in Rome: A Historical Conjecture [with Joshua Podro]
    (history) 1957
They Hanged My Saintly Billy: The Life and Death of Dr.
    William Palmer (biography) 1957
Collected Poems 1959 (poetry) 1959
The Big Green Book (juvenile fiction) 1962
The Siege and Fall of Troy (juvenile history) 1962
Collected Short Stories (short stories) 1964
Hebrew Myths: The Book of Genesis [with Raphael Patai]
    (criticism) 1964

© Rollie McKenna

Man Does, Woman Is (poetry) 1964
Collected Poems 1965 (poetry) 1965
Love Respelt (poetry) 1965
The Original Rubaiyyat of Omar Khayaam [translator, with
    Omar Ali-Shah] (poetry) 1968
New Collected Poems (poetry) 1977

WOLFGANG SAXON

Robert Graves, the English poet, novelist and classical scholar, died [December 7] at his home in Deyá, a fishing village on the island of Majorca. He was 90 years old and had been living in seclusion since failing health stayed his pen 10 years ago.

Reports from Majorca said Mr. Graves died with his wife and other family members at his bedside. He had been bedridden for several months.

Church bells on the island rang out with a traditional song of mourning at the news of his death. The local parish priest, the Rev. Ignacio Montojo, said Mr. Graves, an Anglican, wished to be buried in the village. The burial took place [December 7] in the presence of family members and neighbors.

Robert Graves was an enormously prolific and astonishingly versatile writer. Best known here for such prose works as *I, Claudius* and *The White Goddess,* he was first and foremost a poet who regarded his other writings as the means of supporting that impecunious vocation. ''Prose books,'' he said, ''are the show dogs I breed and sell to support my cat.''

His range of subject matter was staggering. Prehistoric Greece, the life of Imperial Rome, Cromwellian England, revolutionary America, the Spain of the Conquistadors and Lawrence of Arabia were some of his chosen topics. In addition, he translated works from Greek, Latin, French, German and Spanish and offered his opinions on just about everything from mushrooms to myths.

The ideas he propounded often bore the mark of dazzling scholarship. But, often considered heresies, they inevitably raised the hackles of scholars in one quarter or another. Thus he concluded from his research that Jesus survived the crucifixion, that the Emperor Claudius was a mild man and quite a good administrator rather than a despicable tyrant, and that Homer probably did not write the *Odyssey*.

A gregarious, tall, strong-bodied man, Mr. Graves chose to live simply but freely, away from the stress of modern society. His compulsion, he admitted, was writing. His output comprised more than 130 volumes of poetry, fiction, essays, criticism and lectures.

This steady stream of work spanned more than half a century, and Mr. Graves was an author to be reckoned with for almost that long. The attacks on his unorthodoxies notwithstanding, there were few who would not rank him among the finest practitioners of the English language today.

His style in verse and prose was plain, sinewy and forceful; for all the millions of words he published, Mr. Graves shunned verbosity. What the reader could hardly notice behind the seamless finished product was his habit of revising his longhand scripts over and over again until he was satisfied.

His erudition was legendary and nearly encyclopedic. He also did his homework well, so gainsayers among the historians, theologians, classicists and literati he angered could not dismiss him as an eccentric trespasser lost without a compass in their fields of specialization.

Iconoclastic though he could be in other fields, his verse was traditional in form. He believed that meter was an indispensable element in poetry, and that the primary function of language, in poetry no less than in prose, was to convey meaning.

This meant that he was not in any blatant sense a modernist. But he was modern none the less, in his tone and temper. His romanticism had been toughened by his experiences in the trenches; his poetry brought back to English verse a colloquial vigor and a sardonic, hard-bitten wit that had been largely missing for generations.

It was virile poetry—oddly (or perhaps not so oddly) for a poet who dedicated himself to serving and celebrating a female Muse. It also showed great variety, ranging from the terse, staccato lyrics in which he revived and adapted the meters of the Tudor poet John Skelton, to the rich, fully orchestrated style of **"To Juan, at the Winter Solstice."**

He could be equally forceful whether he was being satirical or reflective, whether he was devising epigrams or dramatic monologues or miniature myths. But he was above all, increasingly in his later years, a love poet. In the opinion of many critics, his love poems were the finest written in English in the 20th century, apart from those of W. B. Yeats.

He stood apart from fashions and never quite secured a central place in the pantheon of poets who emerged in the 1920's and 30's. But from the 1950's onward an increasing number of younger poets, and younger readers, saw in his work an important alternative to the Eliot and Auden tradition. His admirers included such figures as Randall Jarrell in this country and Philip Larkin in Britain.

This is how Mr. Graves once limned himself in a poem, **"The Face in the Mirror"**:

> Gray haunted eyes, absent-mindedly
>   glaring
> From wide, uneven orbits; one brow
>   drooping
> Somewhat over the eye
> Because of a missile fragment still
>   inhering,
> Skin deep, as a foolish record of old-
>   world fighting.
> Crookedly broken nose—Low tack-
>   ling caused it;
> Cheeks furrowed; coarse grey hair,
>   flying frenetic;
> Forehead, wrinkled and high;
> Jowls, prominent; ears, large; jaw,
>   pugilistic;
> Teeth, few; lips, full and ruddy;
>   mouth, ascetic.
> I pause with razor poised, scowling
>   derision
> At the mirrored man whose beard
>   needs my attention,
> And once more ask him why
> He still stands ready, with a boy's
>   presumption,
> To court the queen in her high silk
>   pavilion.

In fact, the fractured nose Mr. Graves acquired by tackling low in a rugby game helped make him look like a rugged, athletic character well into his old age. Over 6 feet tall, he had the aspect of a man of action, with deep-set gray eyes, a high forehead fringed with white hair and a large, arresting head, usually deeply tanned from the sun of Majorca, the Spanish island where he made his home many years ago.

Robert von Ranke Graves was born in London on July 24, 1895. His father was Alfred Perceval Graves, an Irish poet and ballad writer. His mother, Amy von Ranke, was the daughter of a German professor of medicine and directly related to the great German historian Leopold von Ranke.

Young Robert had an enriching childhood, with mountain-climbing holidays in Germany and Wales, amid a large and talented family that had few money worries and many influential contacts, and a large library that provided much of the boy's early education.

He was sent to six preparatory schools before 1914, when he entered the Charterhouse and made a reputation for himself as a boxer. But he also started writing poetry in his teens, some of it good enough to be included in his later collections.

When war broke out in Europe, Mr. Graves joined the Royal Welch Fusiliers and served as an officer in the same regiment as Siegfried Sassoon, who inspired him to write poetry in earnest. Before the war was over, the young officer had published three volumes.

But Captain Graves was severely wounded in 1916. In fact, he first was listed as killed in action, and his family received notice of his death on his 21st birthday.

He recovered from his wounds. But the agonies he had witnessed as a platoon and company leader in the front lines scarred him for life. The war, he said later, changed his entire outlook on the world, and he joined those who felt that his generation had been sold by generals and men of wealth.

After the war, he went to Oxford and married Nancy Nicholson, the daughter of Sir William Nicholson. They started out poor, for his published poems brought him little money. For a while, the couple ran a shop, not very successfully, while Mr. Graves attended St. John's and edited *Oxford Poetry 1921* with Alan Porter and Richard Hughes.

It was not until 1926 that Mr. Graves received his Bachelor of Literature degree and won appointment as professor of English literature at the newly founded Egyptian University in Cairo. The salary was a then princely $7,000 a year, but upon his return to England in 1927 he vowed never to take another job for the rest of his life.

Working 18 hours a day, he took two months to write a biography of his friend T. E. Lawrence, *Lawrence and the Arabs,* which by Christmas 1927 was selling 10,000 copies a week. It brought him the financial success his poems had missed, for all the critical acclaim heaped upon them.

He and his wife had two daughters and two sons, one of whom would be killed in Burma in World War II. But the marriage was disintegrating and ended in unhappiness in 1929.

That year he took the advice of Gertrude Stein and moved to Majorca, the largest of the Balearic islands, to find the right atmosphere for a writer to work and thrive. Except for the years of the Spanish Civil War and World War II, he kept his home there in the small, flowering hillside village of Deyá until his death.

Before leaving for his Mediterranean retreat, he wrote an autobiography, *Good-bye to All That,* published in 1929. Its account of his experiences in the Great War—some horrifying, others comic—made an enormous impression on a reading public that was just beginning to come to terms with the realities of the war. Fifty years later it has lost none of its impact, and it is generally regarded as a classic.

On the island, Mr. Graves first conducted the Seizin Press with Laura Riding. The two wrote several critical books in collaboration, and many of his books were published by the press.

I, Claudius, appeared in 1934 and won him the Hawthornden and the James Tait Black Prizes for that year. It also suddenly made him a novelist of stature. The book and its sequel, *Claudius the God,* were hailed as brilliant reconstructions of Roman life in which Mr. Graves succeeded in breathing extraordinary life into an ancient cast of characters.

The books—together they served as the basis of the enormously successful British television series *I, Claudius,* broadcast in the United States by the Public Broadcasting Service in 1978—were written in an easy, unpretentious and often witty style that quickly gained popularity. While historians found much to disagree with in the author's version of that Roman era, others considered it an ingeniously accurate reconstruction, actually helped along by poetic license.

A later novel, *Count Belisarius,* won the Femina-Vie Heureuse Prize in 1939.

King Jesus, published in 1946, challenged widely accepted religious dogma with its bold but erudite interpretation of the life of Jesus. It asserted that he had not died on the cross but had lived out a natural life as a Jewish layman.

The following year, Mr. Graves distressed anthropologists and scholars of poetic myth with *The White Goddess,* in which he traced the cult of the lunar maternal deity all over Europe.

Mr. Graves retold the story of Jason and the Golden Fleece in *Hercules, My Shipmate,* and he imaginatively reconstructed Milton's first marriage to Mary Powell in *Wife to Mr. Milton.*

He wrote an emphatic defense of Dr. William Palmer, who was hanged for murder in 1856, with his *They Hanged My Saintly Billy.* For a complete contrast of locale and theme, he produced two novels on the experiences of a British soldier in the American Revolution, *Sergeant Lamb of the Ninth,* and *Proceed, Sergeant Lamb,* written in 1940 and 1941.

In 1964 Mr. Graves "translated" Shakespeare's *Much Ado About Nothing* by replacing now obscure Elizabethan words and phrases with others easily understandable today. "A remarkable thing about Shakespeare," he said at the time, "is that he is really very good in spite of all the people who say he is very good."

His effort was not universally appreciated, but the reaction was nothing compared to the controversy he aroused a few years later with a new translation of the *Rubaiyat of Omar Khayyam.* It was Mr. Graves's contention that Edward FitzGerald had mistranslated the 12th century Persian author from a 15th century manuscript; Mr. Graves said he had found a more authoritative 12th century text.

Mr. Graves lectured at the Massachussetts Institute of Technology in 1963 and in England at Trinity College in 1954 and as professor of poetry at Oxford from 1961 to 1966. None of these stints kept him long from his cluttered study in Majorca, where he worked unconcerned by the household noises and disruptions around him.

The people of Deyá honored him by declaring him an adoptive son of their village, and his many other honors included the Queen's Gold Medal for Poetry, which he received in 1968.

He made no bones about intending his prose works to serve as moneymakers. "This is to be said for the money motive," he once wrote, "that an eye to salability of work obliges a writer to take some thought for his readers, and may even help him cultivate a clear, vigorous, economical style."

Lecturing at City College of New York one day, he told students about a banker who had warned him that one could not grow rich writing poetry: "I replied that if there was no money in poetry, there was certainly no poetry in money, and so it was all even."

Mr. Graves's second marriage was to Beryl Pritchard, daughter of Sir Harry Pritchard, and that union produced three more sons and one daughter. (pp. 1, 19)

Wolfgang Saxon, "Robert Graves, Poet and Scholar, Dies at 90," in The New York Times, *December 8, 1985, pp. 1, 19.*

LAURENCE MARKS

Robert Graves, one of the most distinguished English poets of the twentieth century, died [December 7] at his home in Majorca. He was 90.

He had lived there since 1929 in a self-imposed exile interrupted only by the Spanish Civil War and the Second World War. His daughter Catherine said: 'My father died at home, surrounded by his family.'

He was the third distinguished English poet to have died within a week. The others were Geoffrey Grigson and Philip Larkin.

Graves's first collection of verse, *Over the Brazier,* was published in 1916. But it was not until the publication in 1929 of *Goodbye to All That,* an account of his experiences in the Great War, that he became widely known. Four volumes of *Collected Poems* were published in 1948, 1959, 1969 and 1975—in each case excluding much of his previous work from the canon.

His best known novels were *I, Claudius* and *Claudius the God,* which were adapted as a BBC TV serial. He was a classical and biblical scholar who wrote books about the Greek and Hebrew myths and the life of Jesus, and translated Apuleius, Suetonius, Lucan and Terence.

Graves was the third of five children of a school inspector and his German wife. He was educated at Charterhouse and St John's College, Oxford. He served in the Royal Welch Fusiliers, Siegfried Sassoon's regiment, but wrote relatively little war poetry. He disliked Virgil because, he explained, he had never done military service.

His first wife, Nancy, daughter of the painter Sir William Nicholson, was an ardent feminist. They had two sons and two daughters. During the 1920s, they formed a celebrated *ménage à trois* with the American poet Laura Riding, by whom Graves was embroiled in a literary quarrel with W. H. Auden, whom Riding accused of borrowing her poetic style. Graves succeeded Auden as Professor of Poetry at Oxford in 1960. . . .

He lived quietly in his later years, writing in a fisherman's hut by the ocean, a familiar figure in the streets of Deya with his black felt hat and cane, rolling his own cigarettes, refusing to have a telephone, a typewriter or a car—'the last of the old-fashioned men-of-letters,' as he described himself.

Three of his fellow-poets spoke of his death. . . .

Stephen Spender said: 'Of all the poets of his time, he is the one who, without solemnity but with total dedication, has kept the idea of poetry sacred.'

Gavin Ewart said: 'At his best, he was a first-class poet, as good as Auden, Eliot or Yeats.

'His love poems were much admired in the Sixties, but I think many of them are less good than his socially critical verse and the grotesques he called "poems written with the left hand," like **"1905"** (about Nelson's funeral) and **"Lollocks"** (about invisible spirits that are in league with housewives).

'He was very idiosyncratic. He wrote an entire book, *They Hanged My Saintly Billy,* attempting to prove that Palmer the Poisoner, one of the guiltiest criminals in the annals of English crime, was innocent.

'He refused to support the petition to secure Ezra Pound's release from prison after World War II, saying that he could not respect Pound as a poet.'

Peter Levi: 'He was a very endearing man, but he had few imitators among the young because his poetic style was so very pure and personal, like polished steel. He was a remarkable combination of intellectual wildness and extreme precision as a poet.'

In Deya, church bells tolled. 'He was a much loved man here. He was not Roman Catholic but the Bishop gave us permission to ring the Bells for him,' said Fr Ignacio Montojo, the parish priest.

'He was part of the town. He wanted to be buried at our cemetery like any other villager,' he said.

Laurence Marks, "Robert Graves, Poet in Exile, Dies at 90," in The Observer, *December 8, 1985, p. 1.*

JOHN CAREY

Robert Graves was unique. He followed no fads and set no fashions. He had a mind like an alchemist's laboratory: everything that got into it came out new, weird and gleaming.

In *I, Claudius* and *Claudius the God* (1934), he renovated the historical novel, populating ancient Rome with a set of cynical up-to-date degenerates. In *King Jesus* (1946) he turned Jewish and Christian notions of the Messiah upside down. In *The White Goddess* (1949), a mammoth magic and make-believe work, he cast world mythology into undreamed-of shapes.

"It is good," he once wrote, explaining his passion for rock-climbing, "to stand somewhere on the earth's surface where nobody has stood before." That's where his poems stand. His Clark Lectures, given at Cambridge in 1954, mocked all the modern masters—Yeats, Eliot, Auden, Pound, and "sick, muddle-headed, sex-mad D. H. Lawrence."

He was born in Wimbledon in 1895. His father was Irish, and a poet, which as Graves later remarked "at least saved me from any false reverence for poets." Always fascinated by the past, real or imaginary, he traced his pedigree to a French knight who landed at Milford Haven with Henry VII. On his mother's side he came from a family of Saxon country pastors: Leopold von Ranke, the first modern historian, was a great-uncle. When young Graves went to Charterhouse with a classical scholarship, he found that his German connections gave offence. His study was frequently wrecked. Accordingly he took up boxing and, fortified by some cherry whisky which the house butler smuggled in, knocked out both his opponents in the school championship. After that his racial peculiarities were tolerated.

In 1913 he won a classical exhibition to St John's College, Oxford, but instead of taking it up volunteered for military service as soon as war came, and went to France as a subaltern with the Royal Welch Fusiliers. He was bucked to find himself in so fine a regiment, and revelled in its traditions—the 29 battle honours, the raw leeks eaten to a roll of drums on St David's night, the black ribbons worn behind the collar to commemorate the old tarred military pigtail. The soldierly part of Graves, which treasured such things, always survived side by side with the seer and the magus.

He fought in the Battle of Loos, a bloody fiasco described in appalling detail and with perfect sang froid in his autobiography *Goodbye to All That* (1929). Later, during the early stages of the Somme offensive on July 19, 1916, one third of the Royal Welch was wiped out by German gunfire before the attack began, and Graves was among the casualties with a shell splinter through his lung. There was apparently no hope, and his CO wrote to Mrs Graves telling her that her son had died of wounds. The announcement of his death in the *Times* coincided with his 21st birthday. Obstinately alive, he was shipped home to England, but soon persuaded the doctors to send him back to the fighting.

When Siegfried Sassoon, a brother officer in the Royal Welch, made his famous public declaration against the war in 1917, Graves pulled strings to save him from court martial. He himself gave evidence before Sassoon's medical board, and broke down in tears three times during the course of it. He accompanied Sassoon to Craiglockhart, the hospital for shell-shock cases near Edinburgh, where Wilfred Owen was also a patient. For the next ten years Graves was to suffer from nightmares and hallucinations: shells burst on his bed at night; corpses and ghosts filled the streets.

In 1918 he married Nancy Nicholson, sister of Ben, the painter, and decided to take up his Oxford place, chiefly because students came high on the demob list. He spent most of his undergraduate career running a general store on Boar's Hill, and didn't finish his degree, but was allowed to write a B.Litt. thesis on The Illogical Element in English Poetry instead. This gained him a job as Professor of English at Cairo University—a farcial institution, which he soon left. Colonel Nasser, he later learnt, had been among his students. Meanwhile Nancy and he had four children, but in 1929 the marriage broke up and Graves went to Majorca with the American poet Laura Riding, with whom he lived till 1938.

In his poetry of these years he turned and faced his inner terrors. He had learnt about Freudian dream-analysis from a doctor at Craiglockhart, WHR Rivers, and the poems use the monsters and demi-gods of myth and fairy tale—trolls, ogres, lollocks—to explore the war-damaged depths of his mind. The modish social and political themes of between-the-wars poetry had no appeal for him. He despised boy Bolsheviks of the Auden stamp, particularly after Auden had abandoned his own country for the USA during the Second World War. In later life Graves would describe Auden curtly as "a traitor."

Typically, he returned to England himself in 1939. Three of his children joined the armed forces, and his eldest son David died fighting with the Royal Welch in Burma. He was, as his father records with pride, posthumously recommended for the VC [Victoria Cross]. Having been rejected for active service on grounds of age, Graves retired to a Devonshire village for the duration of the war. He married again—and went back to Majorca, his permanent home, in 1946.

About this time he found a new and vital poetic impulse—love. As might be expected he reached it by a craggy, erudite, untrodden route, which began with his attempt to reconstruct the beliefs of Bronze Age matriarchial societies. In three weeks of intense work he finished the first draft (70,000 words) of *The White Goddess,* the eternal woman who creates, fulfils and

destroys man. "All true poetry," Graves now declared, celebrates some part of her story.

He had always distrusted the intellect, and had become disillusioned with masculine values, perceiving that women were more in touch with intuitive truths. Now he had found a seemingly historical basis for his romanticism. The result was a new burst of poetry celebrating woman and love, and Graves's late flowering as a love poet lasted for three decades, the poems becoming more calm and joyous as the years passed.

Occasionally he visited England—to give his lectures as Professor of Poetry at Oxford in 1961-66; to receive the Queen's Gold Medal for Poetry in 1968; to take a look at his old college, St John's, which made him an Honorary Fellow in 1971. But his roots were in Majorca—literally as well as metaphorically. He grew his own oranges, lemons, olives and vegetables (potatoes, he took especially seriously); he would grumble about the difficulty of getting olives pressed, and boast that the oldest Malvoisie vine in the world grew near his house. It had been there since 1229, and had supplied wine for James of Aragon when he went off to fight the Saracens.

His physique inspired awe: six-foot-two, ramrod back, a massive head with a sunburst of thick white curls. Meeting him, you felt you'd come up against some wayward and unpredictable Mediterranean god, on tour from his island shrine. He wore magic rings. One, amber-coloured, large and oval had an Arabic inscription which, a Sufi friend had told him, actually referred to Graves, though Graves had bought the ring by chance. Another, greyish and transparent, had a carved bird and he had found the same bird, carved by the same hand, on a cornelean on a London stall.

The rings, he said, "worked" for friends who were ill. His talk was a staggering cascade of erudition, authoritative and utterly unbelievable. The Etruscans, he would explain, had discovered nuclear radiation, hence the hardness of their clay. The mazes at sites such as Lemnos were connected with the disposal of nuclear waste, and, he suspected, of contaminated workers. Hephaistion, the limping god, had really been maimed in nuclear work. Once he produced a meteorite from his pocket, a bluish, veined stone, which, he said, revealed wondrous properties under a microscope. He later told me that the people at the Victoria and Albert Museum had pronounced that it wasn't a meteorite. He seemed to pity their ignorance, and had let them have a wish with it nevertheless.

You were never quite sure whether he was pulling your leg. He once said that the supreme gift bestowed on the poet by the Muse was that of poetic humour, and that in its final draft a poem would become so perfectly ambivalent as to make him wonder whether the insertion of a simple "not" wouldn't perhaps improve it. He seemed amused and intense, detached and earnest, at the same time: eyeing you with what looked disconcertingly like humour when making his most serious point. It was partly this agile front which made him seem so vital, even in advanced age. The announcement of his death is saddening, as was that earlier announcement of it in 1916, but he will certainly outlive it, as he did then.

> *John Carey, "Goodbye to All That," in* The Sunday Times, *London, December 8, 1985, p. 10.*

RICHARD PEARSON

Robert Graves, 90, the noted British classical scholar, poet and translator who was perhaps best known for his novels *I,*

Claudius and *Claudius the God,* and his classic 1929 auto-biography, *Good-bye to All That,* died Dec. 7 at his home on the Mediterranean island of Majorca. He had arteriosclerosis.

His *Claudius* novels are brilliant reconstructions of ancient Rome, as seen through the eyes of the Emperor Claudius I. While most historians have portrayed Claudius as something of a mad dictator, Mr. Graves tells the story of a gentle man who surprised the Roman military establishment that enthroned him and became a wise and competent ruler of a violent society.

Both novels were published in 1934, becoming best-sellers and reaping literary prizes. They gained new generations of readers in the 1970s—when John Mortimer adapted them to the London stage in 1972 and when the BBC and PBS produced a 13-part television epic based on the works.

But Mr. Graves was not a man for one season. He wrote an estimated 140 books and some 800 shorter works. His literary scope, versatility, and audacity could be breathtaking. He translated works into English from Greek, Latin, German, Spanish and French. Among his more popular translations was the *Twelve Caesars* by Suetonius. He also stirred up hornets nests with two works in which he functioned as cotranslator.

In the early 1950s, he and Talmudic scholar Joshua Podro published *The Nazarene Gospels Restored,* a reconstruction of the New Testament, and in 1967, with Omar Ali-Shah, he rendered in blank verse *The Rubaiyat of Omar Khayyam.* In addition to the *Claudius* books, his novels included *Sgt. Lamb of the Ninth,* the story of a British soldier in the American Revolution, and *Wife to Mr. Milton,* which was an unflattering portrait of poet John Milton as "narrated" by the wife. His *King Jesus,* published in 1946, brought charges of blasphemy from some shocked Christians who took offense at his fiction-alized account.

In the 1960s, he wrote two children's books, *The Big Green Book,* which was illustrated by Maurice Sendak, and *Two Wise Children.* He also published works of criticism and studies of myths. His *New Collected Poems* was published in this country in 1977. He also published works dealing with the social history of Britain and rare stamps, and rewrote works of both Shakespeare and Dickens.

Yet, he once wrote, "Since the age of 15, poetry has been my ruling passion. Prose has been my livelihood."

He became recognized as a master of English lyric poetry, blending word-perfect diction with sensuous imagery. This poetry was dominated by the theme of man's quest for chaste and romantic love.

In *The White Goddess,* his 1948 study of Celtic and Mediterranean mythology, he published his own statement of poetic faith. He argued that all true poetry was written by man to his "white goddess," the muse of his imagination, and that "the main theme of all poetry is, properly, the relations of man and woman" and "the practical impossibility, transcended only by belief in miracle, of absolute love continuing between man and woman."

In "Woman and Tree," a poem first published in the *New Yorker* in 1956, he wrote of his feelings for the quest:

> To love one woman, or to sit
> Always beneath the same small
>   tree,
> Argues a certain lack of wit
> Two steps from imbecility . . .

In *Good-bye to All That,* he wrote that poetry was "first a cathartic for the poet suffering from some inner conflict, and then as a cathartic for readers in similar conflict."

He continued to write and publish poetry until he was in his late seventies, writing in a shepherd's hut on a lonely hillside. He rolled his own cigarettes, and never learned to drive a car or use a typewriter. "I seem," he once said, "to be the last of the old-fashioned men of letters."

Robert Ranke Graves was born in Wimbledon, England, in July 1895. His father was a Scotch-Irish schools inspector and his mother a member of a learned German family. Mr. Graves attended Charterhouse before enlisting in the British Army during World War I.

A captain in the Royal Welch Fusiliers, Mr. Graves became friends with a fellow officer-poet in the regiment, Siegfried Sassoon. After two years in the trenches, Mr. Graves was wounded in the chest and groin while serving on the Somme in July 1916. His injuries were so extensive that he was reported dead. He read his own obituary, somewhat prematurely, in the *Times* of London.

While still on active duty, Mr. Graves had three volumes of poetry published. After leaving the Army, he went up to Oxford University to study literature. He graduated in 1926, while afflicted with poverty and recurring visions of horror and flashbacks of his days in the French trenches. His reputation as a writer of the first rank and a degree of financial independence came with the publication of *Good-bye to All That,* which told of his war.

While at Oxford, the legendary author and military personage T. E. Lawrence introduced him to Ezra Pound, correctly predicting, "Graves . . . Pound. Pound . . . Graves. You'll dislike each other."

Perhaps Lawrence was of greater service to his friend when he helped secure Mr. Graves a post as professor of English literature at the University of Cairo, where Mr. Graves spent the academic year 1926 to 1927. His students included a future president of Egypt, Gamel Abdul Nasser. By 1929, Mr. Graves was in Majorca, where he was to spend most of the rest of his life, writing poetry for love and prose for money.

His personal life was as epic as nearly any poem. In 1918, he married Nancy Nicholson, the feminist daughter of painter William Nicholson. They had four children, separated after 11 years and later divorced. In 1926, he met the eccentric American poet Laura Riding, who moved in with Mr. Graves and his first wife.

The trio became a foursome when an Irish journalist named Geoffrey Phipps joined in what came to be known as the "Free Love Corner." On April 27, 1929, after an all-night confrontation among the four, Miss Riding drank Lysol and jumped from a fourth-floor window saying, "Goodbye, chaps." Mr. Graves then dove out a third floor window. Both wound up in the hospital, but only Miss Riding, who suffered a spinal injury, was seriously hurt.

In 1939, he married the former Beryl Pritchard, by whom he had four more children. . . .

Richard Pearson, "Scholar, Author, Poet Robert Graves Dies," in The Washington Post, *December 8, 1985, p. C10.*

DAVID REMNICK

Robert Graves, whose heart gave out at age 90 [December 7], was buried . . . in the small fishing village of Deyá on the island of Majorca. In a way he had experienced his own death once before.

As a captain in the Royal Welch Fusiliers, he was badly wounded in the chest and groin during the trench warfare of World War I. On his 21st birthday his family read his obituary in the *Times* of London.

"The experience," Graves said, "permanently changed my outlook on life."

Though he was plagued for years by bloody flashbacks that persisted "like an alternate life," Graves embarked on a singular career as a man of letters, producing 140 books of poems, fiction, mythology, history and a volume of autobiography, ***Good-bye to All That.***

Graves said, without reservation or embarrassment, that he wrote under the inspiration of the Muse, a persistent phenomenon he described in his great grammar of poetic myth ***The White Goddess.*** He was driven by magical sources, an adherence to traditional forms and an idiosyncratic view of the past.

"Graves alone among contemporary poets seems to live, as Coleridge did," wrote critic Peter Davison, "in a world of naked-breasted sirens and reptilian enemies, of substitutions and transformations, in a universe of metaphor."

In an interview 16 years ago with the *Paris Review,* Graves described the writing of ***The White Goddess*** more as an act of discovery than the rehashing of given fact: "Suddenly I was answering ancient Welsh and Irish questions that had never been answered, and I didn't know how or why. It terrified me. I thought I was going mad. But those solutions haven't been disproved.

"Then someone sent me an article on the Irish tree alphabet, and the footnote referred to Graves but not to me. It was my grandfather! And I hadn't even known he had investigated such things. I believe in the inheritance of skills and crafts—the inheritance of memory. They find now that if a snail eats another snail it gets that second snail's memory." (pp. C1, C10)

[December 1985 was] cruel to the conservative impulse in literature and to the English language in general.

First came the loss of Philip Larkin, Britain's poet of loneliness. And [then] Graves, who lived nearly all his life in Deyá in the company of his wife Beryl Pritchard, a few hundred Spanish natives and a vast library of classical literature. Majorca, which was recommended to him by Gertrude Stein, had declared him an adopted son.

The conservatism Larkin and Graves shared was principally esthetic, a terrific impulse to preserve traditional forms. Larkin ruled by acerbic remark, dismissing the radical innovations of Ezra Pound or Charlie Parker or Pablo Picasso with a one-liner and an Anglo sniff.

Graves was an equally unsparing and eccentric presence but a far more comprehensive thinker. He cared deeply about history, albeit an extremely idiosyncratic view of it. His sympathetic vision of the Roman emperor Tiberius Claudius—the main character in his novel *I, Claudius*—came as a shock to orthodox classical scholars who had portrayed Claudius as a mad autocrat.

He had an abiding belief in the practical and natural origins of traditional verse forms. In his lecture **"Harp, Anvil, Oar,"** he spoke admiringly of how "Marvan, the 7th-century poet of Connaught, revealed to the professors of the Great Bardic Academy how the poet's harp originated: namely when the wind played on the dried tendons of a stranded whale's skeleton . . . And how metre originated: namely in the alternate beat of two hammers on the anvil."

Graves loved such ideas, even if they were "challengeable" by an orthodox reading of the facts. He loved to assert that "Anglo-Saxon poetry is unrhymed because the noise of rowlocks does not suggest rhyme" or that the rhythms of Greek poetry are "linked to the ecstatic beat of feet around a rough stone altar . . . and the sound of the dactylic drum played by a priestess or a priest."

In poetry Graves believed in the importance of magical inspiration over technique. His description of the White Goddess as the central "monomyth" before the rise of patriarchal society was dismissed by some academics as "unsound." He based his career and art on it.

For Graves, poetry was "a way of thought—non-intellectual, anti-decorative thought at that—rather than an art." And he believed in a single subject—"one story and one story only"—the love between man and woman.

Among his contemporaries he found satisfaction in the work of Robert Frost and Thomas Hardy, not in the avatars of modernism, Ezra Pound and T. S. Eliot.

Graves worked in a kind of tropical isolation away from the "nasty mess" of urban life. His house was surrounded by a lawn of Bermuda grass, a vegetable garden and an orchard with 15 varieties of fruit trees. He worked in a study crammed with books, tobacco tins, porcelain clown heads, African figurines and a piece of wood from a tree in Shakespeare's yard.

Graves worked at exactly one job: He was a professor of English literature for a year at the University of Cairo in the mid-1920s. From then on he worked as an independent writer, supporting his poetry with translations, textbooks and more saleable literary projects such as *I, Claudius* and *Good-bye to All That.*

He was, according to Davison, "more purely poet than anyone else alive." Though Graves' reputation as a poet was eclipsed by several of his contemporaries, no one lived more single-mindedly and passionately for his art or more concertedly against the current of fashion and critical dogma.

"The very idea of a public, unless one is writing for money, seems wrong to me," he once said. "Poets don't have an 'audience': they're talking to a single person all the time. What's wrong with someone like Yevtushenko is that he's talking to thousands of people at once. All the so-called 'great artists' were trying to talk to too many people. In a way, they were talking to nobody."

Though he celebrated persistence, he understood that history was marked by the rise and fall of different cultures. He lived far from its political center, but Robert Graves was fundamentally pessimistic about the persistence of contemporary life. The crisis was comprehensive.

"Civilization has got further and further from the so-called 'natural' man who uses all his faculties: perception, invention, improvisation. It's bound to end in the breakdown of society and the cutting down of the human race to manageable size.

That's the way things work; they always have. My hope is that a few cultural reservations will be left undisturbed.'' (p. C10)

David Remnick, ''Magical Sources,'' in The Washington Post, December 9, 1985, pp. C1, C10.

STEPHEN SPENDER

[Spender, an English poet and essayist, belonged to the influential literary-political ''Oxford Group'' of the early 1930s, along with W. H. Auden and C. Day Lewis. His poetry, in such collections as Ruins and Visions (1942) and The Generous Days (1969), reflects a nostalgic, prewar style of lyrical romanticism. In later decades, his critical writings, including The Making of a Poem (1955), have overshadowed his accomplishments as a poet. He has edited a number of anthologies and translated works by writers such as Rainer Maria Rilke and Georg Büchner, among other literary endeavors. In the following excerpt Spender offers interviewer Nick Worrall his opinions on Graves's poetry and relations with women.]

Within a single week, three important British poets died: Geoffrey Grigson, Philip Larkin and Robert Graves. Sir Stephen Spender paid this tribute to Robert Graves in an interview with Nick Worrall. 'He regarded himself simply as a poet. He disliked the idea of poets claiming to greatness; he disliked Virgil, he disliked Milton, he disliked Wordsworth, he disliked Eliot, he disliked Auden, because he regarded all of them as having attempted to be major poets. All that you had to do that was important was to write poetry.'

'He was also very critical of other poets and many of his contemporaries for the poetry they actually wrote,' said Worrall. 'How did people regard him?' 'I think people regarded him in that respect rather as a joke. I don't think that people took his judgments very seriously. I think that Graves was a very self-centred man and particularly self-centred about his own work—and he really only approved of his own work.'

'He was a man who, in spite of his buoyancy and grand manner, was mysterious in a great many respects—certainly as regards poetry. In his relationships with women, for instance—some of them were just women, others were white goddesses or they were muses of the white goddess. He regarded poetry as something separate and sacred—he probably had quite a lot of affairs but they were really not scandalous. They were all according to his system of muses, and if he found a lady who was a muse he presumably had an affair with her, but not necessarily. I don't think from one or two things that he said to me that sex was very important to him: love was important to him and I think that he did realise that if you have love for a woman, sex comes into it.

'I think that a great deal of his poetry is very beautiful and that he was a wonderful, a miraculous poet at his best—very pure and quite unlike anyone else. It was very important to him, of course, that poetry should be honest.

'It suited Graves very much to be a kind of local deity. Majorca was exactly the right setting for him. There he was, like a statue, a shrine, which people from all over the world, especially American girls, visited. This was all in a kind of rhetorical style, with a certain amount of noble self-worship about it.'

Stephen Spender, ''Graves and the Muses,'' in The Listener, Vol. 114, No. 2940, December 19 & 26, 1985, p. 40.

JEFFREY HART

Several years ago, [a National Review] senior editor was teaching a course in the literature arising out of World War I. He knew that Robert Graves, then in his eighties, had lived on Majorca for years, and he asked a colleague whether it might not be a fine idea to fly Graves over to talk about the war, poetry, and so forth.

The answer, alas, was no. Though Graves was of sound enough body, age had eaten away at his mind. He spent his Majorca days in his garden, contentedly, but he could not remember his writing, and in fact he could not remember World War I.

The shock of the Western Front produced major poetry in many who were not major poets, and afterward many of them produced little of interest. Siegfried Sassoon and Edmund Blunden, for example, wrote impressively about the war, but not much poetry that mattered later on. It is unlikely that Wilfred Owen or Isaac Rosenberg, who were killed in France, would have found a suitable subject in the 1920s. Rupert Brooke, on the other hand, who died of blood poisoning on the way to Gallipoli, was already an established poet in 1914, with impressive technical equipment and a wide range of poetic interests. His loss was major.

Robert Graves emerged as a ''war poet,'' and a good one. Here is a typical short poem called **''The Last Post,''** written in June 1916:

> The bugler sent a call of high romance—
> ''Lights out! Lights out!'' to the deserted square:
> On the thin brazen notes he threw a prayer,
> ''God, if it's *this* for me next time in France . . .
> O spare the phantom bugle as I lie
> Dead in the gas and smoke and roar of guns,
> Dead in a row with the other broken ones,
> Lying so stiff and still under the sky,
> Jolly young Fusiliers, too good to die.''
> The music ceased, and the red sunset flare
> Was blood about his head as he stood there.

But Graves's extraordinarily restless intelligence expanded far beyond war's emotions. Indeed, with ironic distance, he said good-bye to the war as well as to much else in his classic memoir, *Good-bye to All That* (1929), the opening sentences of which spoof the conventions of nineteenth-century autobiography: ''As proof of my readiness to accept autobiographical convention, let me record at once my two earliest memories. The first is being loyally held up at a window to watch a procession of decorated carriages and wagons for Queen Victoria's Diamond Jubilee in 1897. . . . The second is gazing upward with a sort of despondent terror at a cupboard in the nursery, which stood accidentally open, filled to the ceiling with octavo volumes of Shakespeare.'' Good-bye to all that.

Graves joined the army in 1914, in order to avoid going to Oxford, and after the war he became extraordinarily and eccentrically learned, as well as, many think, a great poet. A succession of novels, beginning with *I, Claudius* in 1934, won him wide readership and made use of his erudition. An autodidact and archetypal British individualist, he developed quirky theories and supported them learnedly. He thought that Christ had lived through the Crucifixion. He reinterpreted the Greek myths as an allegory of the prehistoric struggle in which a ''White Goddess'' and a matriarchal order were overthrown by the forces of patriarchy. No professional anthropologists agreed with Graves's theories about this, but, like Yeats's theories of history, supposedly dictated by his wife while in a trance, they provided a mythical framework for much powerful poetry, including some of the best love poetry of the twentieth century.

During the 1950s, Graves's verse became an important literary influence, a more traditional alternative to the modernist verse of Eliot, Pound, and Stevens, and gave writing room to such poets as Randall Jarrell and Philip Larkin.

As professor of poetry at Oxford from 1961 to 1966, Graves was a favorite with the undergraduates, and indeed became something of a legend. "Mr. Graves is immensely valuable," a Magdalen College undergraduate remarked to a visitor in 1966. "In fact, he is infallible. Every one of his judgments is wrong. You can count on it, and move on from there."

Twenty years after the Great War, and on the threshold of another and long-expected one, Graves had the poet's awareness of the effects of time. In **"Recalling War"** he wrote:

> Entrance and exit wounds are silvered clean,
> The track aches only when the rain reminds . . .
> What, then, was war? No mere discord of flags
> But an infection of the common sky.

He died at ninety and is buried on Majorca. (pp. 18-19)

Jeffrey Hart, "Robert Graves, RIP," in National Review, *Vol. XXXVII, No. 25, December 31, 1985, pp. 18-19.*

FLEUR ADCOCK

[*Adcock is a New Zealand-born poet, editor, and translator. In her poetry collections, including* Tigers *(1967) and* High Tide in the Garden *(1971), she deals mainly with familiar, domestic subjects, although an occasional bizarre image emerges. In the following excerpt Adcock discusses Graves in relation to her own work.*]

Someone told me, when I was in my twenties, that I had been influenced by Robert Graves. Slightly surprised, I turned to his **Collected Poems** (1959). Never mind about the content—I had other sources for my classical references, fairy-tale props and obsession with love—but here were bits of what I had thought to be my own diction glaring at me, together with familiar constructions, mannerisms, and even rhythms. I hastily composed a deliberately Gravesian poem about the Muse, dedicated it to my newly identified master, and hoped I had exorcized him. I was wary of stylistic influences, nervously picking over my verses for signs of Eliot, Yeats and other heavies, but it had not occurred to me that Graves *had* a style: I thought what he wrote was just poetry—a pure substance like distilled water, safely nonaddictive.

This is a view he might have endorsed. He was full of idiosyncrasies, and some of his most memorable poems are the odder ones (**"Warning to Children"**, **"Welsh Incident"**), but their oddness lies in their conceptions, not in their language, which is clear, precise, classical (even when using colloquial speech), and unaffected by what he called "the whore of contemporary fashion". The single-minded dedication to poetry which led him to live abroad, away from literary society, and to earn his living only by writing, is reflected in the untiring scrupulousness with which he revised each poem. He was almost never careless, and always, until late in life, self-critical. In his seventies he published too many poems and their content became (by deliberate policy) repetitive, but until then he pruned

each successive **Collected Poems** down to something like the size of its predecessor.

A happy side-effect of his vow to be "nobody's servant" is the bulk and variety of his prose writings. Everyone knows about *I, Claudius,* but there were nearly twenty other novels, as well as criticism (some of it wonderfully or, when it punctures a cherished favourite, alarmingly subversive), history, mythology and autobiography. All this is admirable; but what most people find hard to take is, of course, **The White Goddess,** that obsessed interweaving of Greek, Hebrew and Celtic mythology with occult alphabet-lore and much else into a ruling philosophy. The true poet, Graves insisted, must be literally in love with the White Goddess (the Lunar Muse), in a succession of her human incarnations: "the main theme of poetry is, properly, the relations of man and woman". The poems he himself wrote on this theme include some of the most haunting and durable love-lyrics of this century—for example, **"Sick Love"** and **"The Sea Horse"**—but a thesis which excludes everyone but heterosexual males from the status of poet simply will not do.

By 1970, when I heard Graves read his poetry at the Mermaid Theatre in London, my early admiration had given way to an amused although fond irritation at his persistence in his folly ("I would always rather be a Court Fool than a Laureate", he once said), but like the rest of the audience I was charmed by his act—the almost arrogantly casual reading of the poems, the joky anecdotes, the somewhat woolly but still radiant air of authority. Two years later, in Mallorca, I seized greedily at an invitation from friends who had literary business with him to accompany them to Deya. It was tricky to organize—Graves had no telephone, he had been ill, time was short—but it happened. We walked up through the garden and there coming to greet us, wearing the famous black hat, was Graves. He discoursed with predictably bizarre erudition on curious artefacts in his study, he made us join him in a ritual curse on a publisher, and when he gazed into my eyes and flattered me I felt for one hypnotized moment that to be a "Muse" might not be entirely unrewarding. His own Muse had led him into a poetic marsh in the end; but great poets, in old age, ought to be eccentric, and Graves was close to being a great poet.

Fleur Adcock, "Robert Graves, 1895-1985," in The Times Literary Supplement, *No. 4320, January 17, 1986, p. 59.*

PETER KEMP

For its obituary homage to Robert Graves, *Bookmark* drew on four of his televised interviews from 1959 to 1969. . . .

Graves, army captain and father of a teeming family, was seen silhouetted against Majorca's sun-rippled sea and olive groves, wild-haired and with silk scarves flamboyantly knotted round his neck. . . .

Very much a haste-and-paste job, the programme made use of sizeable snippets from Graves's interviews, most of which revealed him in his magus vein, expatiating on muses, magic and mystic forces. As if influenced by this, *Bookmark*'s survey laid most emphasis on **The White Goddess** side of Graves's imagination, with his prose masterpiece, **Good-bye to All That,** rating little more than a mention. What made this particularly regrettable was that it is the searing experiences documented in the latter book that fused that amalgam of tenderness, trauma and toughness that gives Graves his distinction. *Bookmark,* though, skipped unnoticingly past the formative phases in his life. It was mentioned that Graves was unhappy at Charterhouse, but no real indication was offered of the factors contributing to this—his social background, candour, sexual decency and artistic tastes—nor of the intense and long-lasting misery generated (half a century later, he'd still wake sweating from nightmares that he was back at the school). When war broke out in 1914, Graves welcomed it, as he had dreaded going up to Oxford, "which promised to be merely a more boisterous repetition of Charterhouse".

As it transpired, he found regimental life often as rebarbative as the regimented life of public school, being again ostracized as a "rotten outsider", an outlandish breacher of the communal code. None of this emerged from *Bookmark*'s cursory inspection of Graves's war experiences. Likewise, the links were missed between that early male-dominated period of his life, his subsequent bruising experiences with female partners like Nancy Nicholson and Laura Riding, and the eventual romantic masochism of his White Goddess theories. Ignoring connecting traits, *Bookmark* made Graves's work—which it depicted as a motley-looking sprawl—seem far less coherent than it is. Also, missing the way he was tugged between opposing impulses—meekness and assertiveness, visions and revision, the fantastic and the factual—it never touched on the tension that keeps his writing taut and vibrant.

Peter Kemp, "Living on the Edge of Things," in The Times Literary Supplement, *No. 4321, January 24, 1986, p. 89.*

Geoffrey (Edward Harvey) Grigson
March 2, 1905 - November 25, 1985

English poet, editor, critic, anthologist, nature writer, journalist, scriptwriter, juvenile fiction writer, nonfiction writer, and autobiographer.

(See also *CLC,* Vol. 7; *Contemporary Authors,* Vols. 25-28, rev. ed.; and *Dictionary of Literary Biography,* Vol. 27.)

PRINCIPAL WORKS

The Year's Poetry [editor, with others] (poetry) 1934
Several Observations: Thirty-Five Poems (poetry) 1939
Under the Cliff, and Other Poems (poetry) 1943
The Isles of Scilly, and Other Poems (poetry) 1946
The Harp of Aeolus, and Other Essays on Art, Literature, and Nature (criticism) 1947
The Crest on the Silver: An Autobiography (autobiography) 1950
Essays from the Air (broadcasts) 1951
A Master of Our Time: A Study of Wyndham Lewis (criticism) 1952
The Collected Poems of Geoffrey Grigson 1924-1962 (poetry) 1963
Shapes and Stories: A Book about Pictures [with Jane Grigson] (juvenile nonfiction) 1964
The Shell Nature Book (nonfiction) 1964
A Skull in Salop, and Other Poems (poetry) 1967
Ingestion of Ice Cream, and Other Poems (poetry) 1969
Poems and Poets (criticism) 1969
Discoveries of Bones and Stones, and Other Poems (poetry) 1971
The Gambit Book of Popular Verse [editor] (poetry) 1971; also published as *The Faber Book of Popular Verse*
Unrespectable Verse [editor] (poetry) 1971
The Faber Book of Love Poems [editor] (poetry) 1973
Sad Grave of an Imperial Mongoose (poetry) 1973
Angles and Circles, and Other Poems (poetry) 1974
The Penguin Book of Ballads [editor] (ballads) 1975
The Fiesta, and Other Poems (poetry) 1978
The Faber Book of Nonsense Verse [editor] (poetry) 1979
The Oxford Book of Satirical Verse [editor] (poetry) 1980
The Private Art (notebooks) 1982
Collected Poems 1963-80 (poetry) 1984
Persephone's Flowers (poetry) 1986

THE TIMES, LONDON

Geoffrey Grigson, the poet, anthologist, editor and journalist died on November 25 at the age of 80.

Fay Godwin's Photo Files

Though not perhaps a major poet, he may well be an underrated one. His ***Collected Poems*** of 1963 did not demonstrate the best he was capable of but ***Collected Poems 1963-80*** (1984) with its robust, idiosyncratic qualities, indicated that he had latterly had much more to give.

His impact as a poet was always under the shadow of other literary activities in which he was prolific. He was an adroit anthologist and compiler; a critic who seldom left his readers unmoved; and, in the broadest sense, a man of letters who put his gifts at the service of a whole spectrum of interests ranging from a dictionary of plant names and Shell guides through the many excellent selections of verse he edited; to the literary journalism for which he was most immediately known to the public.

Grigson was probably the best literary journalist of his time, with a prose style at once abrupt and fluent, condensed and relaxed, briskly impatient and boyishly enthusiastic. His manner was immediately recognizable even in an anonymous front-page article in *The Times Literary Supplement* on the letters of Dylan Thomas, and yet, though extremely individual, it never degenerated into mannerism.

His period of greatest literary influence was during the 1930s when he combined the editorship of the periodical *New Verse*, many of whose contributors were very far to the left, with the literary editorship of the extremely conservative *Morning Post*.

His deeper interests, however, were in English romantic painting and poetry, especially in its relationship to landscape and natural history, and in the English countryside generally. He edited the poems of John Clare's asylum years, the poems of William Barnes, and discovered an excellent and forgotten early 18th century nature poet, William Diaper.

Himself an excellent botanist, he was a little apt to judge poets by the accuracy or sloppiness of their natural history.

He loathed anything that struck him as gaudy or inane, and thus tended to be as ferocious in his attacks on poets like the Sitwells and Dylan Thomas as he was sensitive and exact about poets whose work sprang from a rootedness in the English countryside.

Though he had a wide knowledge of Europe and European literature, he was, in his sense of place and atmosphere, and in his temperamental mixture of harsh prejudice, quick impatience, and warm generosity, very much an old-fashioned John-Bullish Englishman.

Grigson's reviews had often a ferocity and personal animus foreign to the general, indulgent tone of modern criticism. Meeting him, therefore, was a surprise. Tall, handsome, he had a warm and charming smile and gentle and considerate manners.

The bitter tone of some of his writing may have sprung partly from the comparative nonrecognition of his poetry. His voice, so inimitable in prose, became rather flat and muted in verse.

His industry as a writer, compiler, and anthologist was extraordinary and included to enumerate only literary compilations, the enormously popular *Faber Book of Popular Verse, Unrespectable Verse, Faber Book of Love Poems, Penguin Book of Ballads, Faber Book of Nonsense Verse,* and *Oxford Book of Satirical Verse*.

If his essays and reviews could be collected into a substantial volume, he would be revealed as something like a modern Hazlitt and the autobiographical **The Crest on the Silver** is outstanding. In prickliness, enthusiasm, prejudice, a love of painting, he resembles Hazlitt more than other of his predecessors in the higher English journalism. And like Hazlitt on his deathbed, he might have said: "Well, I have had a happy life."

Grigson was born in Cornwall, on March 2, 1905, the son of a country clergyman. He was educated at Leatherhead and at Oxford. After the folding up of *The Morning Post* in the late 1930s, he devoted himself to free-lance writing and journalism, and lived mainly in the country.

His combative nature did not prevent him from making many friends, even among writers like Edwin Muir, who had been the victims of his written asperities. It was impossible to meet him intimately, even once or twice, and not like him.

He was three times married; firstly to Frances Galt, who died in 1937, by whom he had one daughter; secondly to Berta Kunert, this marriage, of which there were a son and a daughter, being dissolved; and thirdly to Jane Grigson, the well known writer on cookery.

*"Mr Geoffrey Grigson: Poet and Man of Letters,"
in* The Times, *London, November 30, 1985, p. 10.*

GAVIN EWART

[*Ewart, an English poet and editor, writes light satirical verse in the style of W. H. Auden. He first gained recognition with his collection* Poems and Songs *(1939). After a twenty-five year period in which he did not write, he again started publishing poetry collections, including* Pleasures of the Flesh *(1966) and* All My Little Ones *(1978), as well as editing the* Penguin Book of Light Verse *(1982). As editor of* New Verse, *Grigson published poems by the seventeen-year-old Ewart. In the following excerpt Ewart discusses Grigson's career and recalls encounters with the older poet.*]

Geoffrey Grigson had several claims to fame. He was, first of all, the pioneering editor of *New Verse*, the most interesting poetry magazine of the Thirties—which he founded in 1933 with the express intention of publishing the poetry of Auden, in whose honour he actually produced an Auden Double Number.

Next, he was certainly the best anthologist of our times, with a real talent for spotting out-of-the-way material. In the main, these were poetry anthologies—the list is a long one—but he also excelled at 'guidebook' writing and he had a real feeling for the local and the particular. The Shell Guides are a good example of this. In the same sort of spirit, he would resurrect poets, like Cotton, that he particularly liked. A Penguin selection of a forgotten eighteenth-century poet might not be very high on the Common Reader's library list, but the merit of such undertakings is undeniable.

Grigson had very good taste. I can't myself think of any writer he liked who was not at least interesting. I'm not a great fan of Wyndham Lewis, as he was, but at least a liking for Lewis's books is justifiable (*The Apes of God* and *One-Way Song* were the two that appealed to me), and, likewise, it's not everyone who would say, of Stevie Smith, that when she was good she was good, but when she was bad she was bloody awful.

However, I think he was quite right about Edith Sitwell; apart from "Façade," her output is pretty dismal. One must remember that in the Twenties and for much of the Thirties she had tremendous prestige. Grigson was very rude about her (perhaps adopting his anti-Sitwell attitudes from Wyndham Lewis) but some courage was needed to stand up to that powerful clique, however rich and silly and snobbish they now must seem to a lot of people.

Most important of all, and last of all, is the recognition he won from the literary world for his poetry. This began rather feebly, in the *New Verse* days—he used the pseudonym Martin Boldero to conceal himself; but after the war, and particularly in the 1950s, the Wallace Stevens-William Carlos Williams touch is no longer distinguishable, and what reviewers call 'his own voice' can be clearly heard. He excelled, as one would expect, at topographical miniatures; but he could also write very telling nursery-rhyme-like short poems that were often both satirical and neatly made. Internal rhymes gave these a very distinctive air.

The topographical verse, people as well as places featuring in it, could give an oblique view of mutability, old age and death. It was never merely pretty. I prefer, as perhaps a poet would, the poetry to the prose; but there's no doubt that his critical remarks, of the notebook-like kind that he favoured, do tell the reader a lot about the appreciation and the nature of literature.

Grigson was the kind of writer who is always an interesting companion, however angry, brutal and dismissive. As a man, everybody who knew him seems agreed that the aggressive slayer of Sitwell was not one of the personalities on show in his private life. I knew him only slightly before the war, when as a schoolboy of 17 I had my first poems published in *New Verse*. Grigson liked these, I am sure, because I made them as like Auden's poems as I possibly could. A very young writer of any talent can reproduce a style—as Debussy in his youth reproduced the style of Wagner. Every writer has to begin somewhere; and, usually, he or she begins by imitating the predecessor who is most admired.

The *New Verse* parties were my first introduction to the literary life, on its social side. As well as Auden, Spender, MacNeice, there were older literati—Edwin and Willa Muir and Herbert Read, for example. In my adolescent shyness, I was of course an onlooker, and very withdrawn and untalkative. It's always good, though, for writers to meet other writers (whether they like them or not); and friendships of a literary kind can do good, as they reduce the sense of isolation that can afflict the lonely poet—and the equally lonely novelist.

I last saw Grigson at the Poetry Society's celebration of his eightieth birthday. This was the first time I had seen him since 1939, when I was staying for a night in John Piper's house near Henley. He seemed remarkably *compos mentis*, although I think he had fairly recently had a series of strokes.

With Peter Reading, I read some of his poems; Richard Boston read a selection of the prose. In his speech of thanks, Grigson was very genial. He described, among other things, how my poem "Miss Twye" arrived one morning at his breakfast table, and he quoted it, with only one small inaccuracy. I think he was really pleased that after so long his own poetry was recognized for what it is—miniature but marvellous.

Gavin Ewart, "Angry Old Man of Letters," *in* The Observer, *December 1, 1985, p. 8.*

PETER READING

[*Reading is an English poet whose collections include* Water and Waste *(1970) and* Tom O'Bedlam's Beauties *(1981). In the following excerpt Reading comments on Grigson's astute observations on nature, art, and literature.*]

Geoffrey Grigson was a national monument when I was an art student over twenty years ago. Three early issues of *New Verse*, which I'd bought on a youthful bibliophilic spree, contained contributions not only by the legendary but also by one Ewart, who was at that time (the saucy Sixties) re-emergent.

I thought of Grigson then as an editor, critic, English amateur natural historian—I didn't know much of his poetry. I read him on Ben Nicholson and Henry Moore and a painter I'd hitherto regarded as a clumsy eccentric—Samuel Palmer (whose pictures have seemed magical to me ever since). I was first and permanently attracted to the poems of William Barnes by Grigson's enthusiastic commentary on them. His topographical

and historical guides had the same quality of pointing out something good one had somehow missed. His accounts of flora and fauna were knowledgeable and not poetically twee. His reviews amused me greatly; exposing humbuggery, spotting talent, valuing sense, zapping bunkum. They were healthy, good fun to read (though the dissected probably didn't relish them), and the attendant whines of "cruelty" from the anti-vivisection lot were entertaining. In this desultory way many of us have learned from Grigson.

The verse has the same diversity of interests, enthusiasms, ferocities. There are mortal broodings and celebrations. The value of good things is Grigson's continual theme. He is insistent that certain things or people are excellent, and those, therefore, that aren't, provoke his satiric flourishes. "Another verse-reviewing squirt" is neatly dispatched in one squib as a sacrifice to precisely the same cause as that which engenders the celebratory, haikuesque:

> An item of best being is
> Halving this pear and in its
> Ivory seeing this black
> Star of Seeds.

"Items of best being" are what he was good at guiding us towards. It is his gratitude for these which lends tension to his elegiac strengths:

> You are young, you two, in loving:
> Why should you wonder what endearments
> Old whisper still to old in bed,
> Or what the one left will say and say,
> Aloud, when nobody overhears, to the one
> Who irremediably is dead?

The poems got better and their author more prolific towards the end of his life (a new collection, ***Persephone's Flowers***, will be published in June 1986). At their most impressive they have a Hopkins-like concision and cohesion brought about by an individual, subtle internal homophony.

The poet's notebooks, ***The Private Art*** (1982), are unassumingly wise and useful. In these, as in all his writing, he finds things for us that we didn't know—a botanical observation, a painter's quality, an anonymous gravestone poem, a new insight to Quasimodo's "And suddenly it's evening".... There's an implicit generosity in a writer's sharing these items of best being—which quality also served to make Grigson the superlative anthologist he was.

Geoffrey Grigson was rare—a writer who, by affecting what one saw and thought, affected one's life. What he wrote of dead Auden is applicable to himself:

> You are not. But time, after you, by you
> Is different by your defiance.

Peter Reading, "Geoffrey Grigson, 1905-1985," *in* The Times Literary Supplement, *No. 4320, January 17, 1986, p. 59.*

Philip (Arthur) Larkin

August 9, 1922 - December 2, 1985

English poet, novelist, critic, editor, and essayist.

(See also *CLC*, Vols. 3, 5, 8, 9, 13, 18, 33; *Contemporary Authors*, Vols. 5-8, rev. ed.; and *Dictionary of Literary Biography*, Vol. 27.)

PRINCIPAL WORKS

The North Ship (poetry) 1945
Jill (novel) 1946
A Girl in Winter (novel) 1947
XX Poems (poetry) 1951
The Less Deceived (poetry) 1955
The Whitsun Weddings (poetry) 1964
All What Jazz: A Record Diary, 1961-68 (criticism) 1970
The Oxford Book of Twentieth Century English Verse
    [editor] (poetry) 1973
High Windows (poetry) 1974
Required Writing: Miscellaneous Pieces, 1955-1982
    (criticism) 1983

Fay Godwin's Photo Files

BURT A. FOLKART

Philip Larkin, whose reclusive life style and limited poetic output earned him the sobriquet "hermit of Hull," died [December 2]. . . .

He was 63 and his death was attributed to breathing difficulties after throat surgery. He died in Nuffield Hospital in Hull, a small northeast English town where he led a secluded life as a librarian living in a simple house darkened by drawn shades that protected his cherished books.

At his death his influence was felt far beyond the four slim volumes of poetry, two novels and two collections of essays that comprised his written legacy.

When the post of poet laureate became vacant in 1984 after the death of Sir John Betjeman, 30%—a plurality of the 120 British poets polled by the *Times* of London—favored Larkin.

But Larkin turned the job down, saying he had published only the four volumes of poetry between 1945 and 1974 and none in the last 10 years.

Larkin later told an interviewer he sometimes dreamed about being poet laureate and having to write verses for ceremonial occasions. He would "wake up screaming."

And of his slim output, he said: "I didn't give poetry up, it gave me up."

Despite his limited production he was England's best-selling poet after Betjeman. When his last volume, *High Windows*, was published in 1974 it sold 6,000 copies in three weeks.

High Windows included the poem **"Cut Grass,"** illustrative of Larkin's simple style in which he composed sparse stanzas for ordinary folk:

> Cut grass lies frail
> Brief is the breath
> Mown stalks exhale
> Long, long the death.

Jonathan Barker, poetry librarian of the British Arts Council told the Associated Press that "one of the most extraordinary things about him [Larkin] was that his poems held the attention of people who didn't read much poetry. . . . He wasn't like those modernists who want the reader to work hard to understand the poem."

The tall, bespectacled and balding poet was born in Coventry, the son of the city treasurer. He once described his boyhood as an agony "of forgotten boredom."

His native shyness was further complicated by a stammer that sometimes forced him to communicate by written notes.

As a youngster he became interested in jazz, and his written criticisms for the *London Daily Telegraph* outnumbered by far his verses. He had been the newspaper's primary jazz critic for the last decade.

In that role he was taken with the jazz traditionalists much as he was with orthodox poets and much preferred Louis Armstrong, Duke Ellington and Bix Beiderbecke to the progressive musicians of his time whom he found "pinched, unhappy and febrile."

As a young poet he fell under the influence of William Butler Yeats, but abandoned that infatuation after he found he could not adapt his homelike phrasing to the Irish poet's style. More recently he listed Thomas Hardy, Dylan Thomas and Betjeman among his idols.

Sadness and failure permeated his works, which included *North Ship, The Less Deceived* and *The Whitsun Weddings.*

"Deprivation is for me what daffodils were for Wordsworth," he once said.

A bachelor, Larkin was a librarian all his life in such towns as Shropshire, Leicester and finally Hull, where he had been at the unversity for 30 years.

"I don't really notice where I live," he once said. He also refused to attend the readings or deliver the lectures expected of successful poets.

"I couldn't bear that," he said several years ago. "It would embarrass me very much. I don't want to go around pretending to be me."

> Burt A. Folkart, "*Poet, Jazz Critic Philip Larkin Dies at 63*," in Los Angeles Times, *Part II, December 3, 1985, p. 2.*

JO THOMAS

Philip Larkin, reclusive librarian who was one of Britain's best-loved poets, died early [December 2]. He was 63 years old.

He had lived for almost 30 years in Hull, a northeastern city sufficiently out of the way, he once noted, that importunate visiting Americans usually decided to bother someone else. He refused to give poetry readings, shunned interviews, and when asked by Kingsley Amis if he thought about becoming Poet Laureate, replied: "I dream about that sometimes—and wake up screaming. With any luck they'll pass me over." . . .

He had never married, lived alone, and insisted to the last that he was happy. But "it's very difficult to write about being happy," he told *The Observer* in one of his few extended interviews, in 1979. "Very easy to write about being miserable.

"I think writing about unhappiness is probably the source of my popularity, if I have any—after all, most people are unhappy, don't you think?" He continued: "Deprivation is for me what daffodils were for Wordsworth."

Sometimes the deprivation is visible ("Their nippers have got bare feet," he wrote of the unemployed, "Their unspeakable wives / Are skinny as whippets"), but more often, it is the unseen torment of disappointment and desolation.

"In everyone there sleeps / A sense of life lived according to love," he wrote in **"Faith Healing."** "To some it means the difference they could make / By loving others, but across most it sweeps / As all they might have done had they been loved. / That nothing cures."

Philip Arthur Larkin was born Aug. 8, 1922, the son of Coventry's city treasurer. He later described his childhood as "a forgotten boredom." His father, who twice took the family to visit Germany, left his son with a lifelong aversion to travel. "I wouldn't mind seeing China," he told *The Observer,* "if I could come back the same day." Novelists, he said, need to travel. Poets re-create the familiar.

He stammered badly, from childhood to the age of 30, and by the time he reached St. John's College, Oxford, hoping at that time to be a novelist, already had thick glasses and receding hair. "Like a balding salmon," he once said when asked how he thought he looked.

He was declared unfit for military service and joined the staff of a small Shropshire public library. In the evenings, he wrote. If he had tried to live by writing in those years, he said later, "I'd have been a heap of whitened bones long ago."

His first book of poems, *The North Ship,* was published in 1945. Two novels, *Jill* and *A Girl in Winter* followed, and although he tried to write a third, he found fiction "just too difficult."

He worked at universities in Leicester and Belfast. In 1955, with the publication of *The Less Deceived,* his reputation as a poet was made, and he went to Hull University as librarian and remained. His next book, *The Whitsun Weddings,* was published in 1964. His last collection, *High Windows,* was published in 1974. Two collections of essays have also been published, one, *All What Jazz,* an anthology of his work as the jazz critic for *The Daily Telegraph.*

"Truly, though our element is time," he wrote in **"Reference Back,"** a poem about playing some old jazz records, "We are not suited to the long perspectives / Open at each instant of our lives. / They link us to our losses: worse, / They show us what we have as it once was, / Blindingly undiminished, just as though / By acting differently we could have kept it so."

A poem, Mr. Larkin told *The Sunday Times* of London a year ago, "represents the mastering, even if just for a moment, of the pessimism and the melancholy, and enables you—you the poet, and you, the reader—to go on."

> Jo Thomas, "*Philip Larkin, Poet and Librarian, Dies at 63*," in The New York Times, *December 3, 1985, p. B12.*

A. N. WILSON

[*Wilson is an English novelist and biographer and the literary editor of* The Spectator. *His novels are usually satires of life in modern England, as exemplified by* The Sweets of Pimlico (1977); *his biographies include studies of Hilaire Belloc, John Milton, and Sir Walter Scott and are noted for their scholarly attention to detail and their bold critical interpretations. In the following excerpt Wilson offers his personal recollections of Larkin.*]

There are many ways of judging poets. One sure test of their personal appeal is how many lines of their poetry you can remember. Not only can I remember a lot of Larkin, I find that it has sunk very deep, and become part of my private language. This is true both of his funny stuff—

> My wife and I have asked a crowd of craps
> To come and waste their time and ours . . .

and also the jokey sadness of

> What else can I answer,
> When the lights come on at four
> At the end of another year?
> Give me your arm, old toad,
> Help me down Cemetery Road.

or the tenderness of **"The Arundel Tomb"** or the sheer bleak despair of **"Dockery and Son"** or **"Aubade"**. One will never forget such poems, and perhaps the reason Larkin made such a great name from so small an *oeuvre* was that he so exactly caught the mood of so many of us. One of the symptoms of the decline of our society is that we distrust fine expressions and rhetoric. Since the death of Yeats, there has been no poet who could *quite* manage a high style. Larkin found the perfect voice for expressing our worst fears. All the other papers will have articles explaining why he was such a good poet, and trying to 'place' him in the History of Eng. Lit.

I am not competent to do that, nor to praise his achievements as a librarian. Doubtless at some later date I might be able to fathom out what *happened*: why he stopped being able to write. Did the poetry dry up because of his relentlessly negative view of things?

> Man hands on misery to man,
> It deepens, like a coastal shelf.
> Get out as early as you can
> And don't have any kids yourself.

Or was it much more a technical matter? He often described the dawning of poems to me. He said that it was like music in the head, always accompanied by a sense of excitement and exhilaration. 'I went to the doctor and said it's years since I heard a bird sing. He said, "That's not surprising. You've gone deaf."' The silencing of the inner music was even more crushing to him than the deafness.

In his writings, and in the various profiles, interviews and so on, Larkin was always represented as a crushingly sad man. ('Oh!' he exclaimed late one night, 'I hate being fat, I hate being deaf, I hate not being able to write any more, I hate having a stammer! You can't imagine how much I hate it!') Doubtless he was sad. I remember his saying to me that he really believed the last four lines of **"Dockery and Son"**, and that he was prouder of having written them than of anything else he'd done. . . .

But it was not sad being with him. For someone who made such a thing of his social awkwardness, he actually had great conversational gifts, and although he tried to make himself sound like a cynical old brute, he actually had great tenderness and sympathy. His friendships often started with his taking the initiative, and once formed they were a great source of mutual pleasure. To say that he had a sense of humour would be to imply that he sometimes said things which it was safe to take wholly seriously. ('I know how to stop unemployment. Stop unemployment pay.') His pessimism, and the Toryism which was its concomitant, were tinged with irony. One often laughed at things he said, not because they were preposterous, but because of how they were expressed. 'But I really mean it,'

he would have to add, having reduced his company to laughter by some confession of distaste for the Young or the Left.

When Betjeman died, it was natural that Mrs Thatcher should offer him the Laureateship. Not only was he fervently patriotic, and filled with a sense of place; his tone of voice was untranslatably English. Given the fact that the poetry had stopped, however, it was not surprising that he said no. 'I never want to see my name in the papers again,' he said after the speculations about whether he would succeed Betjeman, adding, with characteristic candour '(Not quite true)'. Now that one knows how short a time he had to live, it is hard not to wish that Larkin had accepted the Laureateship, just for a year. I even had a superstition then—which is still stronger now—that he would have been able to write verse to order; that, as it were, Mrs Thatcher would have been able to succeed where the Muses failed.

Larkin had an absolute conviction that death was nothing but extinction. It was a fact which filled him with terror and gloom. Religion was completely unable to console him. Last year he read through the Bible from cover to cover. He had a large lectern-size Bible and he read it while he was dressing. When he had finished it, I asked him what he thought. 'Amazing to think anyone once believed it was true,' was his only comment. Yet many of his closest friends were religious, and he shared the wistfulness of one of his favourite poets, Thomas Hardy, about his inability to believe. Needless to say, I hope that he is now blinking his eyes on the edge of paradise, perhaps responding as when I urged him to try out an exotic high church not far from his house in Hull: 'I finally attended Evensong at St Stephen's—I say finally because after meeting Mr B (the vicar) I've had it in mind to do so. I'm far from being a church-taster, so I suppose it was just curiosity. However I was much impressed. The congregation numbered seven, but the service was as splendid as if there had been 70. Of course I was pretty lost—"no church-goer he"—but I tried to be devout, and really quite enjoyed it.'

Meanwhile, for his friends, there is a dreadful silence. He was not looking forward to old age. He hated the modern world. He had been ill. So perhaps one ought to be glad 'for his sake' that he is gone. But with him has gone one of the most distinctive sensibilities of the age. He was right, in some famous lines, to suggest that 1963, was 'much too late' for him. He seemed like a living embodiment of something which had died out in the Fifties—a world of intelligent provincials who had their suits made for them, and distrusted London and foreigners in almost equal doses. Not long ago, I lent him the diaries of Major Warren Lewis, and in his description of what he liked about them, he seemed to encapsulate something of himself: 'a bygone bachelor world—sticks in the vanished hall stand, lodgings, walking tours, pubs, discomfort—women as nuisances—books, irritation. And of course tremendous inarticulate love.'

A. N. Wilson, "Philip Larkin," in The Spectator, *Vol. 255, No. 8213, December 7, 1985, p. 24.*

KINGSLEY AMIS

[*Amis made his reputation as a rebel against the postwar English intellectual establishment with his sardonic first novel,* Lucky Jim *(1954). Although best known for his satirical fiction, he has written poetry, science fiction, criticism, and articles for periodicals including the* Spectator, New Statesman, *and the* Observer. *Amis met Larkin at Oxford, and they remained close friends;* Lucky

Jim is dedicated to Larkin. In the following excerpt Amis reminisces about Larkin and comments on the distinction of his poetry.]

I met Philip Larkin in my first week at Oxford in the spring term of 1941. In what was to me an outlandish milieu he struck me at once as entirely affable, someone who erected no barriers. Partly perhaps through having been at the place since the previous October he moved in it without awkwardness, even with a touch of the spectacular to be seen in his style of dress: bow ties, check shirts, plum-coloured trousers—no commonplaces then.

I was wise enough to know, or thought I knew, that this sort of thing was no sign of any particular artistic bent. Indeed even in our college, St John's, there were almost enough velvet-waistcoated barbarians to suggest the opposite.

In a group, which was where I usually saw him, Philip's manner was sociable, talkative, sometimes noisy, scattered with bursts of laughter and imitations of Oxford stereotypes we had developed in common. (One of these, the Yorkshire Scholar, got into *Jill* under the name of Whitbread.) In fact to passing acquaintance Philip must have looked and sounded rather like a stereotype himself, the generic Oxford undergraduate of that day or possibly the one before.

His activities and attitudes ran in a similar direction. Drinking was important—beer if available; if not, through wartime shortage, then whatever was there. It went down accompanied by plenty of swearing, belching, and hostile accounts of most of the components of our world: dons, porters, lectures, essays, college life, landladies, rationing and all the encroachments of the war. Work, English literature according to the English faculty, was a matter for evasion and fraud, confidence trickery to filch a degree. Even a meeting of the English Society, though requiring attendance, was seen largely as an episode in another beery evening or scope for more derision.

Philip's exterior of a non-games-playing hearty wobbled rather over jazz. I was ready to meet him half way, having like most youngsters of the period come as far as Benny Goodman, Artie Shaw, Fats Waller and the lesser works of Louis Armstrong without really noticing. With Philip the music was a preoccupation, one I quickly shared. A form ideally suited to those with enough—but no more—music in them to respond intensely to a few strong, simple effects? A world of romance with no guide, no senior person to point the way? Both, no doubt; in any case a marvellous bond and one that endured for many years. With me that youthful 'craze' has never gone away; with Philip, sadly, it dimmed in his last years.

Extra-curricular poetry, in the persons of Hardy, Yeats, Auden and—a recent find—Betjeman, was a permitted subject, and I saw at once that Philip was much more closely concerned with it than I had been, but it was to be mentioned, taken for granted, not discussed. And I was well enough aware that he wrote poetry, but so did I, so did half the people one talked to—superficially, it was no more than might be expected from the likes of us. Even his poems in undergraduate magazines hardly suggested there might be another Philip from the one I had seen.

What brought that home to me was reading *Jill*. The experiences of the hero, John Kemp, in wartime Oxford were instantly attributable to the visible Philip; Kemp's fantasy life, dreamy, romantic, sensitive, seemed the work of a different person. I found them impossible to reconcile—well, so had the author.

This set me pondering, and I have hardly finished doing so yet. Only in these past few days have I finally decided that at times there was something strained and overdone about what I saw of Philip at Oxford. He might have been seeing to it that he could not possibly be mistaken for someone inviting intimacy. There was something else about him, a barrier not of his making, that hindered that: his stutter, severe enough in those days to impede conversation, at least in my own case, to discourage, for instance, the asking of questions less straightforward than 'What do you think of Tolkien's lectures?' or 'Are you a Sidney Bechet fan?'

One day it might be fair to speculate about that childhood of his which he famously called 'a forgotten boredom.' It can be said now that he was and remained a man much driven in upon himself, with increasing deafness from early middle age cruelly emphasising his seclusion. In some ways this may almost have suited him; in others it ran strongly against his remoteness. He was too warm, too humorous, too genuinely sociable—as well as having been a little awkwardly so—to settle into withdrawal. That would have required some degree of self-delusion and Philip was capable of none of that. He extended to himself that sometimes frightening honesty which marked all his dealings with the world and, more even than delicacy of feeling, was a distinctive glory of his poetry.

After the middle of 1942, when I left Oxford for military service, I saw Philip on visits, never prolonged, shorter and rarer as time passed and he settled down in Hull. I never saw enough of him. He remained my best friend and his company brought a jovial reassurance, a sense that the fools and charlatans, the Ponds and Picassos and many of their living heirs were doomed by their own absurdity. But for 20 years and more our chief contact was by letter. Those of his to me brought a tiny, unfading sample of his company lit up by an affection he rarely did more than imply face to face. No wonder he was always the best letter-writer I have known, or that what I will miss most immediately is the sudden sight of the Hull postmark.

But of course, permanently and universally, his poetry tells us everything about him as well as all the other things it does. Visible Philip is there and no mistake—**"Toads," "I Remember, I Remember," "A Study of Reading Habits," "Posterity," "This Be the Verse"** with its over-quoted mum-and-dad opening—and invisible Philip too, strongly, unparaphrasably personal but never self-centred, often amazingly remote and distanced from any interest of his own that could reasonably be inferred by any outsider: **"Wedding Wind," "Deception," "At Grass," "MCMXIV"**—all about those men, nothing about him at all—**"First Sight"**—about the lambs in the snow, **"The Explosion."**

Poems like these reduce the rest of us to cloddish wonderment that a man such as we know him to have been should have been able even to think of things like that, let alone set them down with such fidelity, precision and tact: that worthwhile secret is something that neither his poetry nor anything else is ever going to tell us about him. But then this kind of bafflement is a normal response to an artist of the first rank.

Will his work live, will it last? Yes, no doubt about it, if anything does from this barren time, as, along with much more in the same strain, I wish I could have told him.

Kingsley Amis, "Farewell to a Friend," in The Observer, *December 8, 1985, p. 22.*

BLAKE MORRISON

For friends and admirers, one of the saddest things about Philip Larkin's death is knowing how much he feared dying and how wretchedly he spent his last few months. The usual consolatory props are not available—his great poem, **"Aubade,"** knocks them down one by one.

We mourn him especially on this paper [*The Observer*]. Since 1980 he had enjoyed a close relationship with us, reviewing up to half a dozen titles annually (a prolific output by his standards) and on one occasion even *asking* to review a book about the Powys Brothers, an unprecedented act from someone who gave his collected reviews the grudging title ***Required Writing*** and who would usually receive what he called our 'bullying' solicitations with a groan.

> Blake Morrison, *"Unrequired Writing," in* The Observer, *December 8, 1985, p. 22.*

IAN HAMILTON

[*An English author of several volumes of poetry, Hamilton is best known for his criticism of modern and contemporary poetry, which he writes for British periodicals and which is collected in his book* A Poetry Chronicle: Essays and Reviews *(1973). Hamilton is the founder and editor of the poetry journal* New Review, *and he has also edited numerous poetry anthologies. In the following excerpt Hamilton describes Larkin's poetry, especially its somber point-of-view, and comments affectionately on the poet.*]

Philip Larkin worked hard at not looking or behaving like a poet, but it is likely that future generations will value him as one of the most hauntingly "poetic" artists of this century. More often than any other English poet since the war, Larkin gave us lines that it is unlikely we'll be able to forget, lines that now have to carry an extra weight of loss:

> Life is first boredom, then
> fear.
> Whether or not we use it, it
> goes,
> And leaves what something
> hidden from us chose,
> And age, and then the only
> end of age.

Larkin is his own elegist, and has been for some 30 years. Intimations of mortality touch even his most jocular, debunking pieces of "light verse". In the larger, more sustained works, death is omnipresent—almost Larkinesque. It is hard to see an ambulance race down someone else's street without being jolted by his cordial reminder that "In time all streets are visited". And few Larkin readers can walk past a hospital without imagining

> The unseen congregations
> whose white rows
> Lie set apart above—women,
> men;
> Old, young; crude facets of
> the only coin
>
> This place accepts. All know
> they are going to die.
> Not yet, perhaps not here,
> but in the end. . . .

Larkin was a marvellous poet of natural description but he looked at nature through train windows, mostly, as a citizen temporarily caught between two dismal towns. His love poems—if one can call them that—are often almost heart-breaking in the force with which they yearn for that "much-mentioned brilliance" and yet they are always ready to redirect themselves back to the realm of canniness, and final solitude:

> Just think of all the spare
> time that has flown
> Straight into nothingness by
> being filled
> With forks and faces, rather
> than repaid
> Under a lamp, hearing the
> noise of wind,
> And looking out to see the
> moon thinned
>
> To an air-sharpened blade.
> A life, and yet how sternly it's
> instilled
>
> All solitude is selfish

Is solitude selfish—selfish *and* painful? The question recurs in Larkin's work. He never married, and for most of his life he lived alone, shuttling from his flat in Hull to the University where he served as the Librarian. It was a life that he enjoyed making no claims for, but it certainly belonged to him. I remember once asking him if he could ever imagine himself writing a pure, unfettered love lyric, an offering from the heart that didn't feel inhibited by "common sense". He looked at me as if I had suggested something thoroughly low-grade; he wouldn't even think of doing such a thing, he said, unless he was (at the very least) prepared to marry the girl to whom the protestations were addressed.

This was not, luckily, a test that Larkin applied to other people's verse (indeed, the poets he liked were often the soft-hearted rather than the clever sort), but he was deeply suspicious of all art that strayed beyond the reach of English irony. In the same interview, I asked him if he read much foreign verse: his indignant riposte—"Certainly not!"—soon passed into legend.

There was a measure of affectation in all this—an inheritance from the post-war, "come-off-it" generation he belonged to—but he also genuinely enjoyed teasing his detractors. To those who berated him for his thin-bloodedness, his disengagement, he would present himself as the gloomy opponent of all emotional excess; to left-wingers, he would become ever more tauntingly right-wing; to hard-up poets looking for assistance from the State, he would be the heavy nine-to-five bureaucrat—if he could do it, why can't they?

Part game; part deadly serious. Few poets can balance the two dispositions—in their lives or in their works. With Larkin, though, even his most sombre pieces carry at least two good jokes—and the tone doesn't seem to falter. And it is here that his extraordinary technical prowess comes into play: supremely among recent poets, he was able to accommodate a talking voice to the requirements of strict metres and tight rhymes, and he had a faultless ear for the possibilities of the iambic line: "Just think of all the spare time that has flown!", "Not yet, perhaps not here, but in the end".

The high skill never distances Philip Larkin's human presence. On the contrary: he is one of the very few artists of our time for whom we feel both admiration and affection—and this, I feel sure, goes for readers who never had the luck to know him.

Ian Hamilton, "Philip Larkin," in The Sunday Times, *London, December 8, 1985, p. 34.*

PATRICK GARLAND

[*Garland is an English dramatist, poet, short story writer, and editor. He is best known as a producer and director of plays for stage, cinema, and television. In 1964 he directed a documentary, "Down Cemetery Road," for BBC television about Larkin and poet John Betjeman. In the following excerpt Garland discusses the friendship that developed between himself and Larkin during the filming of the program.*]

'It is kind of you to ask about any post-*Whitsun Weddings* poems, but I have nothing to offer,' Philip Larkin wrote to me in 1966. 'The *Monitor* programme and the Gold Medal crowned and terminated my poetic career, as I knew they would . . .' Mercifully, of course, that was not true, because *High Windows* emerged a few years later.

The *Monitor* programme was a film we made in the summer of 1964 with John Betjeman, and it was shown in December of the same year. The planning and execution of the film occupied only a few weeks in June, and, of course, Philip being as is well known not so much a recluse as a private person, we rarely met afterwards. However, that brief episode brought us all closely together, and a firm affection remained.

Recently I have been working with Alan Bates on a kind of anthology-biography of Larkin—a map of the Larkin planet, perhaps—and in spite of Philip's illness, we had corresponded and spoken on the telephone. In fact, because he was always so precise and polite a correspondent, I wondered that my letter of last month—a few questions, news of a possible interest from the National Theatre, an article about the Jinlin Jazzband in Peking I thought he'd like, and a glorious misprint about 'a hereditary poetress' in the *Daily Mail* Diary—they meant peeress—had received no reply. Now I know why.

The last time we met was a rather funny and uncomfortable occasion, when we had dinner at an hotel in Beverley. He had refused to come to York (who can blame him?), where I was directing the medieval Mystery Plays in St Mary's Gardens: 'Two hours before the first drink, and then another two hours, and in the open air, to say nothing of the subject matter . . .' So we settled on a nice commercial travellers' pub in Beverley, and at the end of it he very kindly inscribed my copy of *High Windows* with 'a few last creaks of an old gate'. I say the evening was uncomfortable because I had failed to realise how increasingly deaf Philip had become, especially in a public place. The guests at dinner were fairly taciturn, and their dismay can be imagined as Philip launched into a characteristic barrage of literary raunchiness, just like his poems—'Any news of that bugger so-and-so?'—and then repeated several very comical Kingsley Amis anecdotes, while I yelled back equally indecent yarns about Auden. We sounded a couple of name-shouters, I'm afraid. 'How is John getting on?' Not too well, I told him; he had already had the first symptom of Parkinson's Disease, and we were both saddened.

Things had been so different, so little time before. During the filming of the programme John Betjeman urged us all to stay at the Railway Hotel at Hull, which we happily did, while he extolled the virtues of the Station Building with its classical portico, and the outlines of the old canals, and the rich Victorian merchants' houses by Pearson Park where Philip had a flat at that time.

I don't remember how I succeeded in conquering Philip Larkin's legendary resistance to the idea of the programme, as I have a letter in front of me addressed politely to "Dear Garland', but resolutely refusing the idea—and the next one is a card after the event saying 'Suggest you retitle the film "To Hull with John Betjeman"', so there must have been a change of heart. His reasons for refusal were, primarily, that he always *did* refuse 'to rave, read, recite and madden round the land on the grounds that I am very shy and very busy and so on . . .' and, secondly, that 'I am not a particularly impressive personality and had always believed that it is best to leave oneself to the reader's imagination . . .' He had said earlier that the number of writers who enhanced their reputation by public appearances was very small indeed (he excluded Vernon Watkins and Dylan Thomas) and that he was among the majority. He agreed that if he had the beauty of Rupert Brooke or the ugliness of Auden, he might make an exception—'but I seem such a dull old bird'.

The film turned out well, thank heaven: Philip Larkin is somebody, like Jane Austen, whose disapproval one would least like to earn. '*Monitor* was nearly the price of me on Tuesday,' he wrote, 'as I had to drive six miles into the country to see it, get three-quarters drunk in order to withstand its impact and drive back in even thicker fog than had reigned earlier. All in all it's a wonder I'm still alive . . . I have heard a lot of praise for the film work as opposed to the poems or my own thrilling appearance.' He went on to regret that some of the sequences, for the habitual reasons of time, had been cut out. He ended with a graceful compliment: 'You can certainly refer any future subject to me for a reference on the comparative gentlemanliness of the operation . . .' But he wrote to my splendid assistant, Ann James: 'I still remember Patrick's steely politeness with a shiver.'

One valuable fragment that got lost in the rejected wild-tracks (a film-crew jargon-word, along with brutes, sun-guns, dingle, spiders, etc. which both Larkin and Betjeman delighted in) was a conversation in which he and I talked about his single state ('Like all bachelors I'm rather romantic about marriage'): 'The marital history of writers as a class is particularly discouraging, I would say. It would be a very interesting subject for research—one might get a PhD on it.'

We also talked about the spontaneity of writing poetry as opposed to anything else: 'Well, the impulse that you can't turn on, that you can only ask for, yes, that is spontaneous. The rest of it, I think, is sheer hard work, trying night after night to advance it a little further. You know the old tag about genius being 99 per cent perspiration and one per cent inspiration. I think it's perfectly true, but that suggests the perspiration is more important. I don't think it is. I mean, it's like saying that at the Cup Final there are 100,000 people and 22 players and one ball; but they'd look very silly without the ball, wouldn't they?'

He repeated his wish that I'd cut out a tracking shot in the library: 'That bloody walk through the Reading Room looked like a Fritz Lang sequence of a deranged rapist feeling everyone's eyes are on him. Do cut it!!' he urged. 'Otherwise all my memories are happy ones . . . The programme undoubtedly helped to sell the book, *Whitsun Weddings,* especially in Hull, where it is regarded as "that book about Hull" much to my fury and alarm. It might as well be called a book about Sunny Prestatyn!'

Just before the transmission, he wrote to me suggesting how he imagined the film would emerge from the 'inexplicable scraps' I had brought back with me to Lime Grove. 'I can see it taking shape: Hull! The New Orleans of Yorkshire . . . ! And dwelling in the Basin Street of the North-East is colourful, balding book-basher Philip Larkin, who . . .'

After John Betjeman died last year, I spoke to Philip, who appeared so prominently on television attending the Memorial Service: as I suspected, the whole thing had affected him deeply, and he missed Betjeman, as did I, as a presence as well as poet. It had been an event not unmixed with a bleak moment of humour rather appropriate to the Laureate's sense of fun. The oddest of misprints turned up in the programme, and instead of *Ave Verum* by Elgar, the composer credited was Albert Ketèlbey. 'So we got as well,' said Philip, 'Edward Elgar's "In a Monastery Garden"—very pleasant, as one so seldom hears it these days.'

A similar incongruity, on television news on the day Philip died, was when the telly-presenter announced: 'And now, after the break, why the secret plans for the keel of a British yacht went missing, British government awards ten million to the Health Service to combat AIDS, and the man said to be the best Poet Laureate Britain never had dies in Hull.' Philip would have enjoyed that.

Patrick Garland, "'Colourful, Balding Book-basher'," in The Listener, *Vol. 114, No. 2939, December 12, 1985, p. 22.*

WILLIAM H. PRITCHARD

[*Pritchard is an American critic, biographer, and professor of literature. He has written several books on modern poets and poetry, including* Wyndham Lewis: Profile in Literature *(1972),* Lives of the Modern Poets *(1980), and* Frost: A Literary Life Reconsidered *(1984). In the following excerpt Pritchard quotes passages from Larkin's later work that illustrate the poet's style and attitudes.*]

The recent death of Philip Larkin at age 63 not only deprived us of the finest poet writing in English, but of a particularly resourceful imaginer of the idea of death. He was also a resister of death as a fact; his great friend Kingsley Amis (*Lucky Jim* was dedicated to Larkin) wrote a novel titled *The Anti-Death League,* and Larkin was a charter member of that organization. "Beneath it all, desire of oblivion runs," ran a line from his first mature book of poems, **The Less Deceived** (1955). From the beginning Larkin was exceptionally sensitive to, and moved by, the oblivion into which things fall, while the "all" continues on its way. His poems were acts of resistance directed at that oblivion, from which (in **"Maiden Name"**) he beautifully rescued such things as a married woman's former name ("Now it's a phrase applicable to no one") by affirming eventually that "It means what we feel now about you then: / How beautiful you were, and near, and young." Or, in the final poem from **The Less Deceived** (**"At Grass"**), he contemplated racehorses 15 years past their prime: "Do memories plague their ears like flies? / They shake their heads"—but shake them, not in response to the question, only against the flies. Thus it is left for the poet to memorialize them: "Almanacked, their names live; they / Have slipped their names, and stand at ease . . . And not a fieldglass sees them home."

I first became aware of Larkin sometime in the middle 1950s, when I had worn out both my record of Dylan Thomas reading his poems and most of my enthusiasm for Dylan Thomas. Thomas was certainly full of stirring challenges and directives to death with a capital D ("And Death Shall Have No Do-

minion," "Do Not Go Gentle Into That Good Night"), but the music was too loud, the voice too thrilling for its own good. Without raising his voice, Larkin spoke about death (in his poem **"The Old Fools"**) with a small d, in a tone of regretful evenhandedness, making his subject all the more inescapable and unarguable with, even as he argued about it:

> At death, you break up: the bits that
>   were you
> Start speeding away from each other for
>   ever
> With no one to see. It's only oblivion,
>   true:
> We had it before, but then it was going
>   to end,
> And was all the time merging with a
>   unique endeavour
> To bring to bloom the million-petalled
>   flower
> Of being here. . . .

No one has said anything truer and wiser about the difference between birth and death: between the "unique endeavour" that someone—a mother, a father, a doctor—is there to see, and the much later lonely breaking up of that "million-petalled flower" we scarcely knew we were part of in being here.

Like Hardy, the poet of all poets he admired most, Larkin wrote rhymed verse, and when the occasional poem didn't rhyme it only proved the rule. Like Frost, he would as soon have written free verse as played tennis with the net down (though I doubt that he played tennis) and would as soon have written poems that delighted in not making "sense" (John Ashbery's delight) as he would have visited a foreign country, say the United States ("And of course I'm so deaf now that I shouldn't dare. Someone would say, What about Ashbery, and I'd say, I'd prefer strawberry, that kind of thing"). For Larkin, rhyme and stanza and making sense were the cement that held together both the poem and the poet's relation to his reader, as in the following lines from **"Aubade,"** published a few years after his last book of poems, *High Windows,* appeared in 1974. This is a different, grimmer song than the aubades sung at dawn, usually to a lover; here the man wakes at 4 a.m., in the grip of "unresting death, a whole day nearer now," the dread of which "Flashes afresh to hold and horrify." He goes on to explore this "special way of feeling afraid / No trick dispels":

> Religion used to try,
> That vast moth-eaten musical brocade
> Created to pretend we never die,
> And specious stuff that says *No
>   rational being
> Can fear a thing it will not feel,* not
>   seeing
> That this is what we fear—no sight, no
>   sound,
> No touch or taste or smell, nothing to
>   think with,
> Nothing to love or link with,
> The anaesthetic from which none come
>   round.

The specious stuff of religion and philosophy is dismissed, but there is nothing specious about the rhyming, especially the double one of "think with" and "link with," which touchingly links itself with the reader who both sees and hears a life-affirming connection made in the midst of death.

Larkin loved American jazz of the 1920s and 1930s (before Charlie Parker): Armstrong and Fats Waller, Sid Catlett and especially Pee Wee Russell, who figured for him and Amis and their Oxford pals as "mutatis mutandis, our Swinburne and our Byron." He concluded his introduction to *All What Jazz,* the just-reprinted collection of his reviews, by imagining the audience to whom this music could speak:

> Men whose first coronary is coming like Christmas; who drift, loaded helplessly with commitments and obligations and necessary observances, into the darkening avenues of age and incapacity, deserted by everything that once made life sweet.

One almost yearns to be such a man, just to live up to that prose, or to the figure in one of the last poems he published, **"Continuing to Live,"** in which life as it continues is seen as "nearly always losing, or going without":

> This loss of interest, hair, and
>   enterprise—
> Ah, if the game were poker, yes,
> You might discard them, draw a full
>   house!
>   But it's chess.

And, the poem continues, "Once you have walked the length of your mind / What you command is clear as a lading-list." I think that Larkin felt he had walked the length of his own mind, that he had no more—or hardly any more—poems to write, and that the only profit of continuing to live was that, in the poem's words, we may in time "half-identify the blind impress / All our behavings bear." Yet—it concludes ruefully—

>   . . . to confess
>
> On that green evening when our death
>   begins,
> Just what it was, is hardly satisfying,
> Since it applies only to one man once,
>   And that one dying.

Cold comfort farm. One likes, nevertheless, to think Larkin may once or twice have had an inkling of how much pleasure and satisfaction he gave to readers, most of them not aging men headed for coronaries, but younger readers of both sexes who, in the words of his best-known poem, **"Church Going,"** recognize in themselves "A hunger . . . to be more serious." He was passed over for Poet Laureate, but like his beloved Hardy, Larkin was something better. (pp. 41-2)

> *William H. Pritchard, "The Least Deceived," in* The New Republic, *Vol. 194, Nos. 1 & 2, January 6 & 13, 1986, pp. 41-2.*

JOHN BAYLEY

[*Bayley, an English critic, poet, essayist, novelist, and editor, is best known for such criticism as* Tolstoy and the Novel *(1966) and* Shakespeare and Tragedy *(1981). He has written poetry, essays, and a novel,* In Another Country *(1955). In the following excerpt Bayley offers an overview of Larkin's career.*]

Philip Larkin's death at the age of sixty-three not only means a sad day for English poetry but echoes the deaths of poets in a more romantic era—Shelley drowned, Keats dying of consumption. Larkin was not a young poet cut short in the fullness of his creative life—far from it—and yet something of their legend hangs about him. Like Housman he was a Romantic born out of his age; and it is ironic that his poetry was nonetheless identified, not long since, as wholly in keeping with the drab, diminished, unillusioned spirit of postwar Britain, a poetry of low-keyed vernacular honesty, whose every line seemed to be saying: "Come off it."

It must have given Larkin some wry amusement to have been hailed at that time as "the laureate of the housing estates." He was an expert showman, and he knew it, and like all showmen he knew how to seem wholly in touch with his public. He was also a connoisseur of classical jazz, and this gives a clue to the sense in which he lived in the past. In England many people do, and of Larkin's poetry if could be said—as he himself wrote in an introduction to the American edition of John Betjeman's poems —"it could only happen in England." For the greater irony is that in England his poetry had the popularity associated with other kinds of late Romanticism—Housman's Shropshire Lad and Barrie's Peter Pan and Betjeman's Joan Hunter Dunn. Like theirs, Larkin's poetic image sold in thousands, achieved a kind of plangent-comic national status.

Yet he was a very private man, and his private world was quite another one. If he touched the national nerve and appealed to the common reader, it was because he could be felt to be leading a double life—again as most people do. Behind the unsentimental directness and the refusal to play the part of poet or intellectual there was a quietly erudite and intensive inner life, a reticent romanticism. Larkin makes the "one life one writing" formula of a Lowell or a Berryman seem all surface exposure, a too coherent and explicable unity. Though he seemed so direct Larkin hated to explain. And he had nothing in common with the poets who write for academics and for other poets, the university-funded tribes of Ben with their handouts from government culture and their eagerness to explain on the radio and television what their poetry is trying to do.

A possible key to Larkin's inner world is that he did not want to be a poet so much as a novelist. While still at Oxford in wartime he wrote a novel called *Jill,* which is about a young man at Oxford. For comfort and protection against the dauntingly upper-class life around him he invents a fantasy girl called Jill, whose style and attraction he describes to his friends. Then he sees the actual Jill of his imagination riding past him on a bicycle. He gets to know her, with sad and comical results. Slight as it is the novel is saturated in the Larkinian style of poetry, although at the time that poetry hardly existed and he had found no voice of his own. Later poems were to evoke a Jill-like figure, wearing a bathing suit in **"Sunny Prestatyn,"** an image defaced on a billboard ("She was too good for this life"), or the model girl of a cigarette brand—"that unfocused she / No match lit up nor drag ever brought near"—who visits the dying smoker

>   newly clear,
> Smiling, and recognizing, and going
>   dark.

An ironic image, in view of the lung and throat cancer that killed Larkin.

Jill was followed by *A Girl in Winter,* which is a real masterpiece, a quietly gripping novel, dense with the humor that is Larkin's trademark, and also an extended prose poem. The author was still only twenty-one. Neither novel made any stir at the time and Larkin wrote no more novels, though he began and abandoned several. Like Keats he had written his "Lamia" and his "Eve of St. Agnes" (which the two stories curiously resemble: Larkin read the English course at Oxford), and creative impulse in that direction seems to have dried up. The novelist Kingsley Amis, who was at the same Oxford college and had been a close friend since their undergraduate days, suggested that Larkin was too diffident and conscious of possible failure to thrive in the cut and thrust of the novelists' world. His marvelous sense of things and people (**"Mr. Bleaney,"** **"Dockery and Son"**) became the luminous mirror for a poem rather than being pursued in a more extrovert way through the events of an extended history. However that may be, a poet was born to succeed the aborted novelist.

Gestation will still slow, although a first collection, *The North Ship,* contained some hints of what was to come. Over the years Larkin was working as a librarian, successively at the universities of Leicester, Belfast, and Hull, and short books appeared at ten-year intervals—*The Less Deceived* (1955), *The Whitsun Weddings* (1964), *High Windows* (1974). Though he unforgettably imaged regular work as a toad ("Why should I let the toad *work* / Squat on my life?") he performed it faithfully and with his own kind of drive, needing it as Wallace Stevens needed his insurance office, and ruefully admitting as much in **"Toads Revisited."**

> Give me your arm, old toad;
> Help me down Cemetery Road.

The toad could turn into Larkin's muse, was perhaps the same creature in disguise, and the idea of such visitation—like the moon goddess visiting Endymion—was unexpectedly appropriate for his poetry. In spite of its memorableness and popularity there is always something mysterious about it, and when in the last years of his life Larkin virtually ceased to write poetry he remarked: "I didn't abandon poetry. Poetry abandoned me."

With a sensibility as individual and as original as Betjeman's, he and his poems nonetheless hugged a persona of depression, sterility, absence. "Deprivation is for me," he once observed, "what daffodils were for Wordsworth." A sardonic enemy of the Good Life, he never took holidays abroad, never visited America, spoke of "foreign poetry" as something quite outside his taste and experience. Yet his book of essays and reviews, *Required Writing,* reveals wide sympathies, deep and trenchant perceptions, a subterranean grasp of the whole of European culture. And indeed the cult of "deprivation" in his verse has as much animation and relish in it as has Baudelaire's cult of spleen: the authentic and in both cases wholly personal note of Romanticism finding the fattest reward for poetry in its own sense of the unfitness of things.

One of Larkin's last, uncollected, poems begins, "I work all day and get half drunk at night," and goes on to descant with an almost joyful eloquence on the fear of death and the terror of extinction. The fear is all too genuine but the fact of the poetry overcomes it—a very traditional feat—as it overcomes the emptiness it evokes so majestically at the end of **"Dockery and Son."** . . . (pp. 21-2)

Such unforced majesty and scope of emotion in poems like **"The Building"** and **"The Old Fools"** have hardly been heard in English poetry since the great requiem of another Romantic—Wilfred Owen's war poem "Strange Meeting"—and about Owen Larkin wrote a moving tribute.

But his personality has no hint of Owen's priggishness. His sanity and pleasure are in very ordinary life and doings, about which he throws off phrases of devastating memorableness ("Glaring at jellies"; "an awful pie"). No modern poet has been more free of cant—political, social, or literary—than Larkin. His humor and common sense are very like Barbara Pym's, whose novels he deeply admired, helping to rescue her in the Sixties (that ill-omened epoch) from the neglect of publishers convinced that her books were not at all the thing for the modern world. In neither artist is there any question of the "major" or the "minor," although neither would be likely to have been awarded the Nobel Prize. Both are completely though unpretentiously themselves, and, as the poet said of the novelist, in its art such an achievement "will not diminish." (p. 22)

John Bayley, "On Philip Larkin," in The New York Review of Books, *Vol. XXXII, Nos. 21 & 22, January 16, 1986, pp. 21-2.*

PETER KEMP

What hounded Larkin was mortality, intimations of which never stop trembling through his verse. So it seemed appropriate that his interviewer in [a 1966 *Monitor*] film should be Betjeman, another death-possessed poet, and that much of their conversation should take place in a cemetery, where with a kind of grave companionableness they exchanged views, sitting among the tombs, weathered angels, and headstones proclaiming "In The Midst Of Life We Are In Death". Explaining his penchant for frequenting graveyards, Larkin declared: "It gets my worries into perspective." It was instructive to hear him, at that stage of his life, speaking of mortality as a helpful consideration, something far removed from the fearsome fact it later became for him—and which he memorialized with lapidary chill in what is surely poetry's last word on death, his terminal piece **"Aubade".**

"Everything I write, I think, has the consciousness of approaching death in the background", Larkin told Betjeman. Death, though, is only the most drastic of those loppings-off of life's possibilities he sees everywhere. At one point, with his usual alertness to restrictions, he remarked on the folly of critics who urged him to write other than he did, for "What one writes is based so much on the kind of person one is and the kind of environment one's had and has." What made *Monitor*'s film so fascinating was the light it cast on these shaping factors. Besides setting Larkin's personality before you, it prowled perceptively round his habitat, pouncing on correspondences between places and the poems they'd helped give rise to. As Betjeman recited **"Here"**—Larkin's long-lined survey that winds around all aspects of Hull—the camera closed in on "domes and statues", "ships up streets, the slave museum, / Tattoo shops", even one of the "grim head-scarfed wives". **"Church Going"** was accompanied by shots of Larkin—bicycle-clipped and hunched inside a damp-shouldered mac—on one of his Sunday afternoon outings to deserted or derelict churches.

Repeatedly, you were made aware of the match between Larkin's milieu and his poetry and personality. Like his verse, Hull showed itself robustly remote from the modish and metropolitan, harbouring a low-key, low-expectation life, keeping down-to-earth realities to the fore, but still offering vistas of classic elegance, and capable of being irradiated by sudden bursts of natural beauty (such as its spectacular sunsets across the Humber which Larkin expressed his admiration for, and whose suffusing of flat outlooks with transient, poignant glamour calls to mind those wellings out of lyricism that so often light up his final lines). Even the fact that the film was shot in black-and-white seemed apposite for a poet who so rarely uses colour words—and then mainly to suggest the synthetic or sinister: "the lemons, mauves, and olive-ochres" of **"The Whitsun Weddings"**, the "red stretcher-blankets" of **"Ambulances"**.

Peter Kemp, *"Living on the Edge of Things," in* The Times Literary Supplement, *No. 4321, January 24, 1986, p. 89.**

DONALD HALL

[*Hall is an American poet, critic, editor, biographer, and author of short stories for adults and children. He has written over ten books of poetry and is the recipient of numerous literary awards. Hall conducted television interviews with poets in the 1970s and has recorded poetry by several writers. In addition he has written and edited many books on poets and poetry, including* The Harvard Advocate Anthology *(1950) and* Contemporary American Poetry *(1962). In the following excerpt Hall reflects on Larkin's career and literary style.*]

Unless there is a cache of poems secreted somewhere in Hull, which we may doubt, the poet Philip Larkin died before the man. As far as I know, his last poem was **"Aubade,"** published in the *Times Literary Supplement* almost a decade ago. It begins:

> I work all day, and get half drunk at night.
> Waking at four to soundless dark, I stare.
> In time the curtain-edges will grow light.
> Till then I see what's really always there:
> Unresting death, a whole day nearer now,
> Making all thought impossible but how
> And where and when I shall myself die.

The fear of dying, daily companion of many, found its Homer, Dante, and Milton in Philip Larkin. His post-religious, almost Roman skepticism looks forward only to "total emptiness for ever, / The sure extinction that we travel to." As in his early **"Church Going,"** his language acknowledges religious feeling without diluting skepticism, sentimentalizing loss, or asking for pity. Larkin is resolute, forthright, witty, and gloomy. This is the man who famously said that deprivation was for him what daffodils were for Wordsworth. Yet surely the results of this life, in the shape of his poems, are gifts, not deprivations.

The Less Deceived announced Philip Larkin in 1955. As a young man he had published *The North Ship,* poems lyrical and Yeatsian and not yet Larkinesque. The early work resembled other young Englishmen: neo-Romantic, even a bit *wet* . . . By the time I found him he had acquired Philip Larkin's voice. I heard him first on John Wain's BBC program, "New Soundings," in 1953—where I also first heard Kingsley Amis telling about *Lucky Jim.*

Larkin's quality was clear; it was also clear that something new was happening. Although *The Less Deceived* was a small press book—published by George Hartley who ran the Marvell Press and edited *Listen,* the best literary magazine of its time—it was published with a list of subscribers which included almost all English poets under forty: Amis, Bergonzi, Boyars, Brownjohn, Conquest, Davie, Enright, Hamburger, Hill, Jennings, MacBeth, Murphy, Thwaite, Tomlinson, Wain. (Thom Gunn was in California; Ted Hughes was not yet Ted Hughes.) And

there were dons: Bateson, Dobree, Dodsworth, Fraser, Kermode, Leishmann.

It was not long before Larkin became a popular poet in England, second only to Betjeman in public affection. When a good poet becomes popular there is always some silly reason as well as recognition of excellence. Dylan Thomas became a bestseller in this country—surely the obscurest poet ever to sell ten thousand copies—because tales of drunkenness and irreverence sold copies. With Robert Frost, the carefully cultivated rural manner—gussied up by the Luce publications until he resembled Scattergood Baines—sold copies and had little to do with the real man.

With Larkin and his English readers, the silliness which helped to make him popular was his genuine, uncultivated, sincere philistinism. In his prose he wrote disparagingly of painters who put two noses on one face and sculptors who carved holes through bodies; he lectured us on the *ugliness* of modernism, most especially the three P's: Pound, Picasso, and (Charlie) Parker. In the United States the terrorists of modernism have frightened the semi-educated middle class into accepting anything that carries the Avant-garde Seal of Approval. In England the middle classes are not so gullible; many remain secure in the conviction that Picasso is a fake, and that good painters can be defined as the ones who make horses that look like horses. When he made an anthology, Larkin's *Oxford Book of Twentieth Century English Verse* was a monument to modesty and amateurism: Sir John Squire and yards of doggerel. Doubtless it is the *worst* anthology of modern poetry, with the possible exception of Yeats's . . .

Larkin's poetry of course is another matter. There is nothing modest or amateur about **"The Whitsun Weddings"** or **"Aubade."** *The Less Deceived* was a superb volume, with three or four of Larkin's best poems and two dozen fine ones. Some are corny but splendidly achieved: **"At Grass"** is the best horse picture ever painted. Back in the mid-Fifties, the jocular and tough-minded **"Toads"** stood out. Gradually, the softer and more ruminative **"Church Going"** seems more to represent Larkin's best. In his second volume, *The Whitsun Weddings,* the title poem may be the finest moment in all his work. Characteristic in the place it is spoken from—a little to the side of life, watching, commenting—it is both empathetic and aloof, both superior and wistful. It ends:

> I thought of London spread out in the sun,
> Its postal districts packed like squares of wheat:
>
> There we were aimed. And as we raced across
>   Bright knots of rail
> Past standing Pullmans, walls of blackened
>   moss
> Came close, and it was nearly done, this frail
> Travelling coincidence; and what it held
> Stood ready to be loosed with all the power
> That being changed can give. We slowed
>   again,
> And as the tightened brakes took hold, there
>   swelled
> A sense of falling, like an arrow-shower
> Sent out of sight, somewhere becoming rain.

Look at the way sentences curl down the page. Who else among us has made such motions?

The answer, I think, is Robert Frost, but I do not suggest direct influence. If there is influence, Frost to Larkin, it comes by way of Edward Thomas, whom Frost instructed. Although Thomas Hardy is Larkin's master—the only earlier twentieth-century poet clearly superior (and Geoffrey Hill the only contemporary)—the comparison with Frost remains useful. Frost loved to play the English sentence across the English line, usually pausing to rhyme on the way, mimicking what he called "sentence sounds." These sentence sounds show themselves by phrase-pitch and perform a sophistication of syntax. At the end of **"Mr. Bleaney,"** from *Whitsun Weddings,* we can see Larkin using the imitative gesture of syntax as well as Frost did it.

> But if he stood and watched the frigid wind
> Tousling the clouds, lay on the fusty bed
> Telling himself that this was home, and
>   grinned,
> And shivered, without shaking off the dread
>
> That how we live measures our own nature,
> And at his age having no more to show
> Than one hired box should make him pretty
>   sure
> He warranted no better, I don't know.

This awkward, difficult-to-say sentence mimics the reluctance of the mind to reach conclusion about its own worth or lack of worth. The muscular gestures of its hesitation express, by form and mimickry of grammar, the state of mind that the language describes. In this coincidence of manner and matter is a good portion of Larkin's genius.

But not only here. In an interview Larkin spoke about his reputation as a melancholy man, and protested that he thought he was rather funny, actually. True enough: "Sexual intercourse began / In nineteen-sixty-three / (Which was rather late for me)— / Between the end of the *Chatterly* ban / And the Beatles' first LP." But something besides humor redeems the gloom of Philip Larkin. His poetry is beautiful, which gives us deep and abiding pleasure, however melancholy a paraphrase may be. At the end of **"Aubade,"** Larkin makes a metaphor, appropriately sinister, in a gorgeous pentameter line:

> Meanwhile telephones crouch, getting ready
>   to ring
> In locked-up offices, and all the uncaring
> Intricate rented world begins to rouse.
> The sky is white as clay, with no sun.
> Work has to be done.
> Postmen like doctors go from house to house.

Doubtless the poem is *deprived* enough . . . but if you don't walk out of the theater humming the tune, you don't read poetry. (pp. 10-12)

> Donald Hall, "Philip Larkin, 1922-1985," *in* The New Criterion, *Vol. IV, No. 6, February, 1986, pp. 10-12.*

ROBERT RICHMAN

Of the many articles that have appeared in the newspapers on the sad occasion of Philip Larkin's death, at sixty-three, none dealt adequately with his poetry. The writers of these articles expressed admiration for Larkin's oeuvre, but more for its popularity than for its poetic qualities. Predictably, the poet's non-poetic characteristics were given the spotlight: his career as a librarian, his famous anti-social attitudes, and his "prickly, anti-cultural *persona,*" as an anonymous writer in the *Times*

of London put it. "He never married," Ian Hamilton reminded us in the *Sunday Times* [see excerpt above], "and for most of his life he lived alone, shuttling from his flat in Hull to the University where he served as the Librarian. It was a life that he enjoyed making no claims for. . . ." The daily *Times* also focused on the aspect of Larkin's life he "made no claims for" by reprinting a piece Larkin wrote in 1977 on his career as a librarian. Larkin's famous philistinism about modern art and literature was discussed at length. In *The Observer* Larkin's old friend Kingsley Amis recalled how the poet's "company brought a jovial reassurance, a sense that the fools and charlatans, the Pounds and Picassos and many of their living heirs were doomed by their own absurdity" [see excerpt above]. The author of the *Times*'s obituary agreed: "In reality he was the last neo-Georgian." (This author also retailed Larkin's "eccentric" views on marriage and sexual relations.) The obituary in *The New York Times* for the most part consisted of a string of quotations from Larkin's poetry and prose on just these subjects [see excerpt above].

It was to be expected, of course. Larkin himself spent the last years of his life conscientiously enhancing his reputation as an ordinary chap who hated children and modernity equally. In 1973, Larkin published his infamous *Oxford Book of Twentieth Century English Verse.* This fat anthology pretended for the most part that modern poetry did not exist, and earmarked its editor as an avowed enemy of modernism. Larkin's collection of critical prose, *Required Writing,* which appeared in 1983, was a virtual compendium of reactionary views on art, literature, and jazz. Larkin solidified his anti-modernist position by publishing, in 1985, an updated edition of his collection of jazz reviews, first brought out fifteen years ago, entitled *All What Jazz.* Then there were the interviews Larkin granted, after having refused to consent to one for so many years, to *The Observer* in 1979 and to *The Paris Review* in 1982. (Both are reprinted in *Required Writing.*) These confirm and elaborate not only Larkin's philistinism but his "eccentric" views on marriage, women, and social life. In a review of Henry de Montherlant's novel *The Girls,* Larkin reports that every page of the book has at least one choice nugget for a quote-a-day Misogynist's Calendar. In fact it is Larkin's interviews that are the best source for such a calendar. Marriage should be shunned, Larkin tells us, because it means "putting yourself at the disposal of someone else, ranking them higher than yourself." And: "there is a limit to what you can get from other people." In these interviews Larkin is so proudly devoid of illusions that he seems almost incapable of love.

One result, then, of Larkin's testimony, in the last decade or so of his life, to his own narrowness of mind and feeling has been the tendency to see the poetry strictly as versified versions of Larkin's prose statements. There are plenty of lines in the Larkin oeuvre that seem to be just that, of course. "Oh, no one can deny / That Arnold is less selfish than I" (from **"Self's the Man"**), "Get stewed: / Books are a load of crap" (from **"A Study of Reading Habits"**), and "They fuck you up, your mum and dad" (from **"This Be The Verse"**) are only a few of the more famous ones.

Yet in fact Larkin's poetry amounts to much more than this. For a proper understanding of that poetry, it is necessary to place him in the tradition of English poetry of the last century. Larkin always considered himself a member of the "English line" of verse. This tradition was said to include such writers as Thomas Hardy, A. E. Housman, and Edward Thomas—all poets of empirical doubt and stoical remove. Larkin's youthful infatuation with Yeats—the "foreign," Symbolist-inspired Romantic whose work is perceived to be the antithesis of that of the "English line" poets—was clearly seen in Larkin's first book of poetry, *The North Ship,* published in 1946. His abandonment of Yeats, quick on the heels of *The North Ship,* was, in the poet's own words, "undramatic, complete, and permanent." It is more likely, however, that it was dramatic, incomplete, and impermanent. For despite Larkin's claim to being "less deceived" (the words he would use as the title for his second book of poetry, published in 1954) by Yeatsian illusions of poetic transcendence, traces of Larkin's first master persist throughout his poems. In the concluding essay of the anthology called *Larkin at Sixty* (1982), Seamus Heaney characterizes Larkin's poetic career—correctly, it seems to me—as a quarrel between the visionary impulse of Yeats and the earth-bound mundanity of Hardy. Heaney finds, in lines such as "O wolves of memory! Immensements!" (from **"Sad Steps,"** in Larkin's last collection, *High Windows,* published in 1974) and, in **"Water,"** from *The Whitsun Weddings* (1964)—

> And I should raise in the east
> A glass of water
> Where any-angled light
> Would congregate endlessly.

—the "symbolist transports" we normally associate with a poet like Yeats. These "epiphanies," as Heaney calls them, inject elements of hope throughout a book that would otherwise be almost all bleakness, despair, and bitterness.

We see this struggle best in two poems not discussed by Heaney. In **"The Old Fools"** (from *High Windows*), an empirical, "Hardyesque" speaker muses on approaching death:

> . . . It's only oblivion, true:
> We had it before, but then it was going to end,
> And was all the time merging with a unique
>   endeavour
> To bring to bloom the million-petalled flower
> Of being here. Next time you can't pretend
> There'll be anything else. . . .

Larkin appears to take Hazlitt's wonderful remark about death ("There was a time when we were not: this gives us no concern—why then should it trouble us that a time will come when we shall cease to be?")—certainly one of the most consoling and happily "deceived" in all of English literature—and deals it a crushing blow. But does he? Larkin summons some distinctly Romantic language—"To bring to bloom the million-petalled flower / Of being here"—to make his very un-Romantic point. The result is an attitude of some ambiguity.

Another ambiguous poem is the well-known **"Days,"** from *The Whitsun Weddings,* quoted here in full:

> What are days for?
> Days are where we live.
> They come, they wake us
> Time and time over.
> They are to be happy in:
> Where can we live but days?
>
> Ah, solving that question
> Brings the priest and the doctor
> In their long coats
> Running over the fields.

The question of the here-and-now empiricist—"Where can we live but days?"—is exploded by the illogical, nightmare image

in the last two lines. The anti-rational imagination Larkin spurns in the first stanza (not to mention throughout his prose writings) is here given equal weight with the voice of detached intelligence. This brief poem throws into relief the conflicting impulses at the core not only of Larkin's poetic sensibility but of the entire tradition of the "English line" as well.

"Days" and **"The Old Fools,"** however, were written years ago. The sad truth is that Larkin published little poetry in the last decade of his life. The few poems he did publish show him no longer as inclined to be "deceived" by images of transcendence as he once had been. The conflict which had persisted in his verse grew dimmer as his poetic impulse waned, and what replaced it was the sheer fear of death. Thomas Hardy had managed to waylay his fear of death when he was old by inventing an obsession for a dead wife he had shown no affection for while she was alive. One can only wonder how Edward Thomas would have coped with old age, had he survived the First World War. Larkin seemed constitutionally incapable of harboring any forgetful illusion as Hardy did. He certainly foreswore the visionary splendor of his earlier poems. His last published poem, **"Aubade,"** which appeared in 1977, is as devoid of any "hopeful" transcendent impulses as anything Larkin had ever written.

In reply to the question why he wrote poetry, Larkin said: "You want [your poems] to be seen and read, you're trying to preserve something. Not for yourself, but for the people who haven't seen it or heard it or experienced it." *Not for yourself, but for the people who haven't seen it or heard it. . . .* The man speaking these words is the real Larkin, the Larkin we shall remember, the Larkin who wrote the last line of the poem **"An Arundel Tomb"** (from *The Whitsun Weddings*)—a line which could easily serve as Larkin's epitaph: "What will survive of us is love." It is, precisely, this elusive "love" that lies behind every line Larkin strove to perfect for us, his readers. (pp. 13-15)

*Robert Richman, " 'Trying to Preserve Something',"
in* The New Criterion, *Vol. IV, No. 6, February, 1986, pp. 13-15.*

X. J. KENNEDY

[*Kennedy is an American poet, editor, textbook and juvenile fiction writer, and lyricist. He has written several poetry collections, including* Nude Descending a Staircase *(1961) and* Celebrations after the Death of John Brennan *(1974), and was poetry editor of the* Paris Review *from 1961 to 1964. Like Larkin, he prefers to write poetry within the traditional framework of rhyme and meter. In the following excerpt Kennedy both praises Larkin for his modesty and precision as a poet and reviews his own favorites among Larkin's poems.*]

It had to be, in the end, a common cancer that bore off Philip Larkin. He could hardly have died with a flourish, like Saint-Exupéry, by charging off into the sky on a mission of reconnaissance only to vanish; or like Hemingway, by blowing out his brains. Nor could he go, like Matthew Arnold, in a burst of joy that stopped his heart in midair while leaping a fence to welcome a granddaughter. No, the dismal ordinariness of life, which Larkin so fondly celebrated, had to bring him down by its own dull strategies.

As a critic, to be sure, he delighted in being a curmudgeon. The gist of his message, given in his introduction to a sheaf of record reviews, *All What Jazz,* is that art, unless it helps us to enjoy and to endure, is nothing at all. In deliberately cultivating a stance of reaction—blaming Picasso for placing two eyes on the same side of a face, Henry Moore for perforating his figures, Samuel Beckett for setting out his actors with the trash—Larkin seems hardly a serious foe of modernity. But for the great modern artist's hordes of inferior imitators, he is a dangerous critic to meet in a dark alley. What refreshes in Larkin's complaint isn't its querulous tone, but its brash willingness to risk the charge of philistinism. Here, he implies, am I, a reasonably intelligent man willing to utter the worst doubts of the man in the street. And along with this trusty consumer, Larkin distrusts jazz that tends toward a shrill scream, the canvas that stays empty, the poem that in matter and form seems a mere accidental array of beardmutterings.

Like John Betjeman, whom he admired, Larkin achieved a poetry from which even people who distrust poetry, most people, can take comfort and delight. Surely it is the poetry that seems his enduring testament: only 105 pages, not counting *The North Ship,* an early collection of Yeats-imitations that the author came to disparage. Yet what a monolith, those 105 pages! In it, Larkin performs the feat of transfixing drab, awful postwar England: the seediness of Mr. Bleaney's room, with its fusty bed and a souvenir saucer in which to snuff out cigarettes, a window-view of ''a strip of building-land, / Tussocky, littered.'' It is the run-down boarding-house scene of *Lucky Jim,* whose anti-hero, the cynical little twit pretending to be a scholar, Kingsley Amis is supposed to have modeled after Larkin.

But Larkin was no Lucky Jim. Had Amis's Jim won the job of university librarian at Hull, he would quickly have sold the library's Second Folio, replaced it with a facsimile, and taken off with the proceeds to Aruba. Larkin stayed at his post for thirty years, presiding over the transformation of a small provincial library into a very nearly great one, increasing its collections fourfold and directing a staff that grew from a dozen to more than a hundred. He mounted a successful campaign to help Britain hang on to its literary manuscript holdings. In life, he was a man who shouldered with good grace crushing responsibility.

Still, it is the voice of some unlucky Jim that addresses us in Larkin's best-known early poems: **''Toads,''** in which the speaker wishes he might instantly blarney his way to fame, love, and money, but knows he won't; **''Poetry of Departures,''** with its mingled envy and contempt for those who have ''chucked up everything / And just cleared off.'' Any of these poems follows an order almost like a formula, as does the still more celebrated **''Church Going.''** The speaker confesses himself torn between two attractive and irreconcilable attitudes (faith and doubt, or whatever), wrestles with an insoluble ethical dilemma, and in the end imposes a quick solution on it. I like these poems, but not nearly so well as certain other, deeply compassionate poems, in which Unlucky Jim falls mute: **''Wedding-Wind,''** a marvelous act of female mimicry, seemingly written to show that the poet can imagine passionate fulfillment, if he so wants; or **''At Grass,''** that superb evocation of old race horses put out to pasture—

> Do memories plague their ears like flies?
> They shake their heads. Dusk brims the
> shadows.
> Summer by summer all stole away,
> The starting-gates, the crowds and cries—
> All but the unmolesting meadows.

That doesn't budge from memory. Nor does the wry and heartily envious title poem [**''The Whitsun Weddings''**] of *The*

Whitsun Weddings, with its affectionate view of newly married proletarians; neither does **''An Arundel Tomb,'' ''Broadcast,''** nor in the last collection, *High Windows* of 1974, **''Vers de Société,''** that frank and funny meditation on the pleasures and pains of bachelor solitude, nor **''Cut Grass,''** a lyric that defies the reader's fear that nothing good can come of rhymes so trite (*breath/death, hours/flowers, June/strewn*). In what quiet triumph this last poem ends, with a view of

> White lilac bowed,
> Lost lanes of Queen Anne's lace,
> And that high-builded cloud
> Moving at summer's pace.

Clearly, these are stupendously well-made poems, sometimes pursuing patterns so ingenious that the reader is hardly aware of their ingenuity—the alliterative l-sounds there, the rhyme-schemes that seem worked out on a calculator. In all great metrical poets from Wyatt to Hardy, I suspect, there is an element of self-flagellation: of setting oneself impossible goals, and winning through to them at terrible cost in time, toil, and spirit. In such poems, Larkin shows, I think, as keen a sense of rhyme as we can find in the work of any English-speaking poet; and, of all English and American poets of our time, perhaps rivaled only by Frost, he shows the best sense of the pulsebeat that resides in idioms. His language, however ordinary, is chosen brilliantly (''a snivel on the violins''), and it is woven together so well that it seems not likely to unravel.

Unlike the typical American orphic bard of the moment, Larkin never says, ''Behold! I am one hell of a brilliant visionary, and my life is the most important thing in the world—admire me, damn you, or die.'' By contrast, the voice of Larkin, modest and clear and scrupulous, is that of a man who sees himself as just a bit silly: the amateur student of architecture who, entering a church, takes off his cycle-clips ''in awkward reverence.'' In the end, I think, we love Larkin for admitting to a quality we recognize in ourselves—a certain dull contentment with our lives, for all their crashing ignobility. (pp. 16-17)

> *X. J. Kennedy, ''Larkin's Voice,'' in* The New Criterion, *Vol. IV, No. 6, February, 1986, pp. 16-17.*

ANDREW SULLIVAN

Philip Larkin makes a somewhat incongruous saint for the contemporary literary world. He managed to oppose almost all the artistic movements of the past century, was a firm opponent of all subsidies for the arts, had strong misogynist tendencies and described Liberalism as a combination of ''greed, idleness and treason''. He advocated self-repression, moderation, reverence, propriety and cultural insularity. . . .

He refused to take himself seriously, in public at least. His attitude was one of permanent self-mockery and self-deprecation. Any statement was followed by an ''All very unfair, I'm sure'', as if to disclaim it. Pomposity was hardly his forte: he got drunk too often for that.

But putting himself down was more than just an occasional slip. It served as the archetypal ''voice'' of his writing, and made a point in itself. The whole tenour of Larkin's work is that of an irrelevant and impotent spectator, whose anger and cynicism can be forgiven because they belong to a man unquestionably on the losing side.

In **"Going, Going,"** for example, the premise of the poem is that nothing can be done about the destruction of the natural beauty and cultural inheritance of England in the pursuit of economic growth. It is as if great evil is inevitable, and opposition can only be recorded in writing, never translated into action. Decay is unstoppable. We can only observe.

> Most things are never meant.
> This won't be most likely: but greeds
> And garbage are too thick-strewn
> To be swept up now, or invent
> Excuses that make them all needs.
> I just think it will happen soon.

Here this hopelessness, this self-deprecation has a surprising effect. It makes us care more, rather than less about the picture of decline Larkin is painting. In a curious way, it increases the power of his polemic. (p. 8)

Attack elsewhere comes in searing sarcasm:

> When I see a couple of kids
> And guess he's fucking her and she's
> Taking pills or wearing a diaphragm,
> I know this is paradise
>
> Everyone old has dreamt of all their lives

What is undeniable in these poems is the seriousness of intent with which Larkin is grappling with large social, political and moral concerns. His self-deprecation should not blind us to this fact, but rather suggest that he is no crude or trite preacher. In the last poem, for example, we have the sense that as well as being helpless in the face of moral decay, Larkin is also complicit in it. He is actually attracted to the very contraceptive-laden abyss he wants so much to resist.

Such compromised resistance constantly recurs. He mercilessly scorns the "old fools" only as he knows that one day he will become one of them; the mindless socialisers of **"Vers de Societe"** may be contemptible, but "Only the young can be alone freely. / The time is shorter now for company, / And sitting by a lamp more often brings / Not peace, but other things." Larkin's misanthropy is merely a smoke-screen for a larger concern: his subtler and more trained focus is fixed on a further enemy—change itself.

This sense of trauma at something so inescapable links Larkin's persistent terror of death with his social conservatism. Social and physical decline horrify him as he is drawn again and again to images of obsolescence and death: derelict churches, outdated combine harvesters, skin, cut grass, abandoned rooms. . . . (pp. 8-9)

That this despair in face of change, this resentment yet complicity in Modernity should have touched so many chords in England is hardly an accident. For the English—in particular the middle-class English—even at the height of their industrial power and energy, have never fully reconciled themselves to the doctrine of change, especially when it has come to be associated with the cultural and moral abyss that it seems to generate. In this way Larkin has spoken to the English in language they can readily understand of the profound self-doubt that this century has given them. He was, of all English poets, a laureate too obvious to need official recognition.

Imagine, for a moment, the full English experience from the bombed-out decay of the war years of *Jill* to the affluent, if slightly seedy atmosphere of **'High Windows'**. The undeniable fact is that what it means to be English has been transformed.

Politically, of course, this means one overwhelming fact: that England, after a supreme war-effort, has become at the same time a socialist and also a much less powerful country. These facts are not meant to be necessarily connected, but what does connect them is a sense of paralysis and dismay among the thinking middle-classes, of whom Larkin is a particularly eloquent member.

> England ceased to stand for an idea, a social structure or a mission, all at the same time. As she failed to uphold the illusions of class order, or a meaningful aristocracy, she gave up directing the world into the Victorian dining room of constitutional government. As the English abandoned their pretence at Whig world leadership, they plunged (for compensation?) into a domestic dream of egalitarian welfare, led by methodist public schoolboys and sustained by Tory patriarchs. And as they tore down their architectural inheritance, laid waste to their countryside, changed their currency, renamed the counties, entered the Common Market and giggled at the Commonwealth, they finally assaulted the very social fabric of their manners: in the sixties and eighties, it was the English who led the way in sexual permissiveness, youth excess and violent revolt.

This understanding of post-war English history is the essential context for Larkin's social commentary. In it a general dislike of change is intensified by the way in which this particular period of history has attacked Larkin's world specifically. Vulgarity, greed and garbage came to replace a world where the gardens were kept tidy and the marriages lasted just a little while longer. (p. 9)

[Larkin] is aware that a revival of a lost way of life, of a common moral order, is an impossibility. It is indeed the most powerful irony of both Thatcherism and Reaganism that in attempting to "Bring America/Britain Back", they have used the very weapons of materialist individualism that took them away in the first place. Larkin has seen through this conservative illusion even as he feels the need to affirm it. There can be no return.

This cultural and personal conservatism without hope is of course a recipe for permanent depression, and it would be unfair to deny that it is this mood which dominates Larkin's work. This may be simply because writing is the most immediate release from such a trap and therefore disproportionately reflects Larkin's gloom. He rarely felt the need to write when he was happy. But the tension lifts from time to time, often by being horribly funny:

> They fuck you up, your mum and dad.
> They may not mean to, but they do.
> They fill you with the faults they had
> And add some extra, just for you.

At other times, his gift for satire saves us. He writes of his jazz criticism readers in Britain's largest selling quality newspaper, *The Daily Telegraph*:

> My readers . . . Sometimes I wonder whether they really exist . . . Sometimes I imagine them, sullen fleshy inarticulate men, stockbrokers, sellers of goods, living in thirty-year old detached houses among the golf courses of Outer

London, husbands of ageing and bitter wives they first seduced to Artie Shaw's "Begin the Beguine" or the Squadronnaires' "The Nearness of You"; fathers of cold-eyed lascivious daughters on the pill, to whom Ramsay Macdonald is coeval with Rameses II, and cannabis smoking jeans-and-bearded sons whose oriental contempt for 'bread' is equalled only by their insatiable demand for it . . . men whose first coronary is coming like Christmas; who drift, loaded helplessly with commitments and obligations and necessary observances, into the darkening avenues of age and incapacity, deserted by everything that once made life sweet. These I have tried to remind of the excitement of jazz, and tell where it still may be found.

This passage is both very funny and gently moving, lucid prose that is never bland, rocking with an acerbic rhythm that is up to Orwell's journalism at its best. I think Larkin is a great journalist, and critic: singling out with great elegance and constantly strong independence of judgement a whole range of writers ignored or looked down upon: Hardy, Rupert Brooke, early Auden, and, of course, Barbara Pym.

This raises the question perhaps of why Larkin found his most successful literary "voice" in poetry rather than in prose of whatever variety. He originally intended to be a novelist, preferring in principle the more ambitious scope of a multi-faceted analysis to the individual insight. Yet poetry is undoubtedly, after the less than completely successful early novels *Jill* and *A Girl in Winter,* the mode into which he most naturally slipped.

This seems to me to be explicable in two ways. Firstly, even in his prose, it is the elliptical and surprising turn of phrase, in short the unprosaic aspects of his writing that make the difference. Short paragraphs reveal a lyricism that is unmistakably poetic:

> These, then, were his cups and plates: his cof-
> fee strainer (choked with tea-leaves); his shin-
> ing kettle blackened by the fire. His breadnife,
> his sugar basin.

This, of course is not to say that Larkin's technical brilliance in his poetry (his versatility is only matched by the way form never draws attention to itself) is merely glorified prose, but exactly the reverse. Who but a poet could write prose that links coronaries and Christmas, in an introduction to Jazz criticism?

But perhaps, too, poetry is the natural medium for deprivation and depression, which comes for Larkin, as for most of us in a single wave of experience, often inexplicable, often inexpressible. Larkin's own description of the occasion of writing seems to affirm just that. For him, the feeling and the execution of the poem are one inextricable motion; he does not have a thought, then think how to express it. It is one movement, one instinct, one act. (pp. 9-11)

Moreover, the choice of poetry highlights a further paradox of Larkin's work and personality. Poetry is a medium particularly suited to self-confession, of an immediate honesty and frankness. Yet Larkin, of all people, might seem averse to such direct communication. It seems unthinkable that the stammering semi-recluse, with his few friends, allergy to the mass media and terror of embarrassment should yet unburden himself so fully in public, should leave himself so naked, should be so honest—and for anyone to know or read.

But the subject matter of his poems is often intensely personal. We catch sight of him looking in at dancing girls, and debating the possibilities of sex; he openly discusses his own loneliness, his failure to communicate, his fear of death, his social awkwardness—and all in the first person. A striking number of poems are set in bed. And he is keen to tell us about himself, not others: even the novels are heavily autobiographical. It is a tale of personal confession, spoken as a man talks to himself. It is almost as if this bespectacled and awkward bachelor releases himself only fully on the written page; and only so fully there because in everyday life these emotions are kept in reserve, disciplined and ordered and English. The release is the only escape from an otherwise intolerable burden. But there are other consolations.

Nature, in particular, is a saving grace, a redeeming libation. The human world becomes bearable if we look beyond it to the endurance and renewal of natural forces. Here change can be borne, because it is part of a cycle that is unchanging. Unlike human society, nature lasts.

In "Trees" the consolation is doubly moving, soothing as it does Larkin's twin obsessions, change and death:

> Is it that they are born again
> And we grow old? No, they die too.
> Their yearly trick of looking new
> Is written down in rings of grain.
>
> Yet still the unresting castles thresh
> In fullgrown thickness every May.
> Last year is dead, they seem to say,
> Begin afresh, afresh, afresh.

This is Larkin's perception of the divine, of the spiritually saving, and, in common with millions of his fellow countrymen, it is to nature that he looks for resuscitation. (p. 11)

Of course we look to nature for a response that is not our own, yet is authoritative. It is, at its profoundest, an alternative to God, or to another's love. That seems to me to be the reason for its revival in English sensibility in recent years and also for its extraordinary celebration in Larkin. But even here there are complications. The premise of his entire experience, it seems, is one of the insignificance of the individual will, even when the natural world arbitrarily but magnificently lifts man up on its shoulders. The joy of Spring, in the poem just cited, meets man in a compromised way, because man is compromised, almost unworthy of the beauty of creation. In this way, it seems, even nature is not free from irony:

> And those she has least use for see her best,
> Their paths grown craven and circuitous,
> Their visions mountain-clear, their needs immodest.

Even here in the simplest and freshest of human relationships: nature and man, the conversation has misfired, the timing wrong, the plan botched. Only those who can no longer enjoy Spring appreciate what there is to rejoice in her and no effort of the will can overcome that failure. She passes on, oblivious of that small man in the park with the glasses and the traces of an old stammer, and his love for her is forever complicated by that irony.

It also seems that the "she" metaphor for Spring is not entirely accidental: there is lurking behind so much of Larkin's writings a repeated refrain about the traditional subject of unrequited love. This in turn becomes a more general statement about the difficulty of anything but awkwardness and misunderstanding in human relationships. It is there at the beginning in the novel *Jill* when John Kemp's only fruitful love is that with someone he completely invents: creating her in writing and eventually merging her in his imagination with an actual girl with whom he falls awkwardly and inexpressibly in love. But all the moments of reciprocation, of special understanding, of joy, are only possible in his imagination. In real life, his final desperate attempt to say or do anything about this emotion is greeted with appalling results:

> John stood back. In the weak light his face was quite expressionless. Everything seemed at the moment clear and restful. As Jill came level, he took her quietly in his arms and kissed her.
>
> Elizabeth gasped something.
>
> Christopher ran lightly down a few steps, pulled John forcibly round, and hit him hard in the face.
>
> John twisted away, falling crookedly among the drunks, whose cries met over his head. Fighting to get a grip on him, they carried him into the darkness. The trombone crowed triumphantly.

This direct and frightening prose was written the year after Larkin left Oxford where the novel is set. It reads unmistakably as a diary, and, as such, starts a story of isolation which makes any perusal of Larkin's four slim volumes of poetry oddly moving. The spurned John Kemp, grown much older and wiser in the third major work of poetry, muses gently over a medieval Arundel tomb and notices particularly the tiny detail that the two conjugal figures in stone lying side by side are still touching each other by the hand:

> The stone fidelity
> They hardly meant has come to be
> Their final blazon, and to prove
> Our almost-instinct almost true:
> What will survive of us is love.

This is a brave statement from someone who never claimed to know love himself, and intensifies the pain of death—since nothing of him will be left behind.

Larkin said in an interview that "Deprivation is for me what daffodils were for Wordsworth" and the deprivation is, I think, conceived, on one important level, in terms of love. For even at the peak of his cynicism, Larkin's genuine celebration of love, like Barbara Pym's, is uncompromised by any world-weariness. (pp. 11, 35)

[The] supremacy of human love, especially in a man who could not contemplate with any certainty the possibility of divine love, together with the fact of its unfulfilment helps us to see into the Hull librarian, listening to his jazz, working through the days, getting half-drunk at night and being unable to sleep for fear of death. The man known as the "fuck-poet" was above all concerned with love.

This craving for love is perhaps something which speaks even to Larkin's unlikeliest admirers. It may not simply be ignorance or hypocrisy or deference which attracts so large a respectful audience. It may be that Larkin's fear of apparently irrational change, his scepticism of "progress," his fear of death and his inability to be comfortable in a world which has lost any moral order, are more widely felt than those who lambast him as a cranky reactionary want to believe.

In the Hull librarian more lives than we may care to think of are summed up. Neither power nor human love can quite satisfy him, yet they are perhaps the only two things our world has now to offer. (pp. 35-6)

Larkin's recourse . . . is to that 'rough-tongued bell' of Art, "which insists that I too am individual". This is his legacy at least: his art. It is rare that any writer can touch chords as directly and as honestly as Larkin, and his freedom from the cant and obscurantism of much modernism has enabled him to describe more clearly than almost anyone else the world that "modernism" has created. His writing alone, the possibility even now of honesty and of clear and unpretentious artistry may be enough to relieve the displacement and incomprehension for us.

The tragedy is that ultimately, it did not seem to do the same for him. The "rough-tongued bell" fails him in that dawn of **"Aubade"** when death coldly closes in. No jazz is played then, no poems are read, no season uplifts, no lover comforts. We are left with his last option: the painful demand to be honest with ourselves, and to see in that our possible redemption. . . .

Larkin, for all his self-mockery, is a poet for the serious. And for that reason alone the underlying current of despair in his work cannot be shaken off lightly. Finally, even the trees desert us. Finally the prediction for our society and for us is unmistakable:

> There is an evening coming in
> Across the fields, one never seen before,
> That lights no lamps.

Philip Larkin's death, like one of his last lines, refuses to leave us in peace. (p. 36)

Andrew Sullivan, "Philip Larkin: Legacy of the Almost-Instinct," in The Harvard Advocate, *Vol. CXIX, No. 4, May, 1986, pp. 8-11, 35-6.*

Helen (Clark) MacInnes

October 7, 1907 - September 30, 1985

Scottish-born American novelist, scriptwriter, and dramatist.

(See also *CLC*, Vol. 27; *Contemporary Authors*, Vols. 1-4, rev. ed.; *Contemporary Authors New Revision Series*, Vol. 1; and *Something About the Author*, Vol. 22.)

PRINCIPAL WORKS

Above Suspicion   (novel)   1941
Assignment in Brittany   (novel)   1942
The Unconquerable   (novel)   1944; also published as *While Still We Live*, 1944
Horizon   (novel)   1945
Friends and Lovers   (novel)   1947
Rest and Be Thankful   (novel)   1949
Neither Five nor Three   (novel)   1951
I and My True Love   (novel)   1953
Pray for a Brave Heart   (novel)   1955
North from Rome   (novel)   1958
Decision at Delphi   (novel)   1960
Home Is the Hunter   (drama)   1964
The Venetian Affair   (novel)   1964
The Double Image   (novel)   1966
The Salzburg Connection   (novel)   1968
Message from Malaga   (novel)   1971
The Snare of the Hunter   (novel)   1974
Prelude to Terror   (novel)   1978
Ride a Pale Horse   (novel)   1985

© 1985 Nancy Crampton

EDWIN McDOWELL

Helen MacInnes, whose 21 novels established her as the queen of international espionage fiction, died [September 30] at New York Hospital, from the effects of a stroke she suffered three weeks [before]. She was 77 years old and lived in Manhattan.

"She is recognized as the creator of acute, exciting novels set against backgrounds of meaningful present-day events," said Julian P. Muller, a vice president at Harcourt Brace Jovanovich and Miss MacInnes's editor for about 25 years. "Her purpose always was to strike at authoritarian governments. In the genre of highly literate suspense she is considered unrivaled."

Miss MacInnes's books sold more than 23 million copies in the United States alone, Mr. Muller said, and they have been translated into 22 languages. Her latest novel, **Ride a Pale Horse,** appeared on the *New York Times* paperback best-seller list for the first time on [September 29].

Miss MacInnes was born in Glasgow and graduated from the University of Glasgow. There she met and in 1932 married Gilbert Highet, a classics scholar who in that year was ap-

pointed to a fellowship at St. John's College, Oxford. In 1937 he was invited to teach for a year at Columbia University, and soon accepted a professorship of Greek and Latin at Columbia, later holding the Anthon Professorship of the Latin Language and Literature.

On their honeymoon in Bavaria, the Highets were disturbed by the activities of the Nazis, and Miss MacInnes kept a diary filled with examples of Nazi violence and the Hitler menace. A few years later she fashioned her notes into the novel *Above Suspicion*, the story of a young British couple who sought a British anti-Nazi agent in Germany in the summer of 1939 while seemingly on a vacation. An immediate best seller, the book was made into a 1943 motion picture starring Joan Crawford and Fred MacMurray.

Her next book, *Assignment in Brittany* (1942), a tale of espionage in Nazi-occupied Brittany in the summer of 1940, was also made into a movie. . . . Two other MacInnes novels were made into films: *The Venetian Affair* . . . and *The Salzburg Connection*. . . .

In the 1940's, the villains in Miss MacInnes's books were Nazis; in later years they were often Communists. "I'm against totalitarians in general—national or religious, extremists of the right or left,'' Miss MacInnes said in a 1978 interview. ''If I can be labeled anything, I am a Jeffersonian Democrat.''

She authenticated many of the locales in her books from extensive travels throughout Europe, and many of her plots were derived from actual events. But she took pains to point out that the stories were largely inventions. To be a creative writer, ''we should create,'' she said, emphasizing the last word. ''I think it was E. M. Forster who said creative writing was like lowering a bucket into a well. You'd never know what would come up.''

The Highets, who lived in Manhattan and had a summer home in East Hampton, became American citizens in 1952. Mr. Highet died in 1978.

Edwin McDowell, ''Helen MacInnes, 77, Novelist and Specialist in Spy Fiction,'' in The New York Times, October 1, 1985, p. B6.

THE TIMES, LONDON

Helen MacInnes, who died in New York on September 30 at the age of 77, was a writer whose novels of international espionage won her immediate and immense popularity. From the moment her first book *Above Suspicion* appeared in 1941 Miss MacInnes captured a large following and the success of her 21 novels which sold more than 23 million copies in the United States alone, earned her the title ''Queen of International Espionage Fiction''.

In a field in which men tended to predominate she produced novels noted for their literate qualities, the authenticity of their settings and the acuity of their perceptions about current affairs.

Helen Clark MacInnes, was born in Glasgow on October 7, 1907, and educated at The Hermitage School, Helensburgh; and the High School for Girls, Glasgow, before going on to Glasgow University, where she took her MA.

In 1932 she met and married Gilbert Highet, a classics scholar and it was while on honeymoon with him in Bavaria that she filled a diary with those impressions of the sinister details of nascent Nazism which were several years later to provide her with the material for her first novel.

In 1937 Gilbert Highet was invited to teach at Columbia University, New York, where he was to make an international reputation as a classicist, and from that point on he and his wife were virtually Americans though they did not actually become nationalized until the 1950s.

Helen MacInnes began writing in the Second World War during which her husband had volunteered for service with the British Army. *Above Suspicion,* which was about a young British couple looking for an anti-Nazi agent in Bavaria, became an immediate success.

Its translation into a film . . . in 1943 added impetus to her reputation which had already been enhanced by *Assignment in Brittany* (1942), a tale of espionage in occupied France which was itself to receive film treatment in 1943. Other novels to be filmed were *The Venetian Affair* and *The Salzburg Connection.*

Miss MacInnes's typical protagonist tended to be an innocent or naive American caught up in a web of intrigue and espionage woven by enemies who had started out as Nazis, but as the years went by became Communists. There were some, even

among her staunchest admirers who feared that her politics—staunchly anti-totalitarian as she admitted—were occasionally in danger of triumphing over her creative impulses. Her latter novels tended in a somewhat black and white manner, to pit a scheming and malign Soviet Union against a United States of candid and generous impulses.

However her invention never flagged, nor did her popularity wane. Her books were translated into 22 languages and her latest, *Ride a Pale Horse* had featured in the *New York Times* paperback best seller list. . . .

''Miss Helen MacInnes,'' in The Times, London, October 2, 1985, p. 12.

BART BARNES

''Take away the sense of adventure from man, and you have flab,'' Miss MacInnes once said.

In a career that spanned more than four decades, her imaginary heroes and heroines battled Nazis during the 1940s and communists thereafter, and their adventures were followed faithfully by a global network of mystery buffs. . . .

Miss MacInnes was said by critics to have had few equals in the mystery writer's art of unraveling the details of stories bit by bit, quickly enough to keep readers' interest, but not so fast as to tip a hand too soon.

She usually followed a basic and time-honored stratagem: an ordinary person, possibly an architect, lawyer or historian, is suddenly swept up in a vortex of international espionage and skulduggery by dint of some commonplace action, picking up a wrong raincoat at an airport, for example.

Allen Dulles, former head of the CIA, said Miss MacInnes was a ''natural master of the thriller,'' and he included a selection from her second book, *Assignment in Brittany,* in his anthology, *Great Spy Stories From Fiction.*

Known for a highly literate style, Miss MacInnes found the ideas for many of her stories in her travels and in real-life events. Her encounters with Nazis during her honeymoon in Bavaria during the 1930s provided much of the material for *Above Suspicion,* for example. A newspaper account of a diving operation in a Czechoslovakian lake to recover boxes sunk by the retreating Nazis became the inspiration for *The Salzburg Connection,* which was published in 1969 and also was made into a movie.

She was on vacation in Greece when she got the idea that led to *Decision at Delphi,* a 1960 best seller. ''I don't pick the settings for my books. The places seem to pick me,'' she said. ''They tap me on the shoulder and say, 'Hey! Helen.' ''

She was a diligent researcher who made the settings for her stories come alive with authentic background details, and she was widely acknowledged to be perceptive in her handling of political issues.

''I'm a research historian,'' she once said. ''I went to the trial of Col. (Rudolf) Abel [the Soviet spy exchanged for Francis Gary Powers in 1962] to study the eyes, expressions. I want hard facts, want to know what I am writing about.''

Born in Glasgow, Miss MacInnes met her husband, Gilbert Highet, while at the University of Glasgow, and she came to the United States with him in 1937 when he accepted an appointment to the classics faculty at Columbia University. . . .

As the young bride of an Oxford don, she had thought of writing a novel even before coming to the United States, and one night in New York in 1939 as their infant son was hospitalized with a ruptured appendix, Highet picked up a pad of notes and commentary Miss MacInnes had been keeping on contemporary politics and the rise of Hitler.

''Helen, dear, I think you are now ready to write your novel,'' she recalled him saying after he had read her notes.

''So he gave me a yellow pad and two sharpened pencils. That's how it began. I got myself a clipboard and said, 'I'm going to tell myself a story.' ''

Above Suspicion was followed in short order by ***Assignment in Brittany,*** a tale of World War II espionage that also became a movie, and there followed a novel every two or three years.

Among Miss MacInnes' other well-known novels are ***The Venetian Affair,*** which was also made into a movie, ***The Snare of the Hunter, Double Image*** and ***Message from Malaga.***

> *Bart Barnes, ''International Spy Novelist Helen MacInnes Dies at 77,'' in* The Washington Post, *October 2, 1985, p. B7.*

Josephine (Louise) Miles

June 11, 1911 - May 12, 1985

American poet, critic, and editor.

(See also *CLC*, Vols. 1, 2, 14, 34; *Contemporary Authors*, Vols. 1-4, rev. ed., 116 [obituary]; and *Contemporary Authors New Revision Series*, Vol. 2.)

PRINCIPAL WORKS

Lines at Intersection   (poetry)   1939
Poems on Several Occasions   (poetry)   1941
*Pathetic Fallacy in the Nineteenth Century: A Study of a Changing Relation between Object and Emotion (criticism)   1942
*Wordsworth and the Vocabulary of Emotion   (criticism) 1942
Local Measures   (poetry)   1946
*Major Adjectives in English Poetry from Wyatt to Auden (criticism)   1946
After This Sea   (poetry)   1947
**The Primary Language of Poetry in the 1640's (criticism)   1948
**The Primary Language of Poetry in the 1740's and 1840's (criticism)   1950
**The Primary Language of Poetry in the 1940's (criticism)   1951
Prefabrications   (poetry)   1955
Eras and Modes in English Poetry   (criticism)   1957; revised edition, 1964
House and Home   (drama)   1960
Poems, 1930-60   (poetry)   1960
Renaissance, Eighteenth-Century, and Modern Language in English Poetry: A Tabular View   (criticism)   1960
Ralph Waldo Emerson   (criticism)   1964
Civil Poems   (poetry)   1966
Style and Proportion: The Language of Prose and Poetry (criticism)   1966
Bent   (poetry)   1967
Kinds of Affection   (poetry)   1967
Saving the Bay   (poetry)   1967
Fields of Learning   (poetry)   1968
American Poems   (poetry)   1970
Poetry and Change: Donne, Milton, Wordsworth, and the Equilibrium of the Present   (criticism)   1974
To All Appearances   (poetry)   1974
Coming to Terms   (poetry)   1979
Working Out Ideas: Essays in Composition   (essays)   1979
Collected Poems, 1930-83   (poetry)   1983

*These works were published as *The Vocabulary of Poetry: Three Studies* in 1946.

**These works were published as *Continuity of Poetic Language: Studies in English Poetry from the 1540's to the 1940's* in 1951.

Courtesy of University of California, Berkeley

CHICAGO TRIBUNE

Josephine Miles, a poet and longtime professor at the University of California, Berkeley, has died of pneumonia. She was 73.

Miss Miles, who died [May 12], was professor emeritus of English at the Berkeley campus and 1 of only 12 faculty members in the nine-campus school system to hold the title of "university professor."

Miss Miles, severely handicapped since childhood with rheumatoid arthritis, won dozens of scholarly and literary awards. She was the first woman to win tenure, in 1947, in the Department of English at the Berkeley campus, and until recently was the only female university professor, an honor bestowed on her in 1972.

Her *Collected Poems, 1930-1983* won *Nation* magazine's Lenore Marshall Poetry Prize in 1983 and nearly won the Pulitzer Prize [in 1984]. It was one of three finalists. It was the last of two dozen books of verse and criticism written or edited by Miss Miles in her nearly 50-year career.

Her students have published more than 50 volumes of poems and won at least two National Book Awards.

Her critical works traced the changing language patterns in poetry over four centuries.

Among other national awards, she was inducted as a member of the American Academy of Arts and Sciences and the American Academy and Institute of Arts and Letters.

She received a Guggenheim Fellowship in 1948 and a Fellowship for Distinguished Poetic Achievement from the American Academy of Poets in 1978.

Born in Chicago on June 11, 1911, she graduated Phi Beta Kappa from UCLA, earned her master's and doctorate degrees at the Berkeley campus and joined the faculty there in 1940.

> *"Josephine Miles, Poet and Teacher,"* in Chicago Tribune, *Section 4, May 15, 1985, p. 11.*

THE NEW YORK TIMES

Josephine Miles, a poet and member of the American Academy and Institute of Arts and Letters, died [May 12] at her home in Berkeley, Calif. . . .

Miss Miles wrote a number of volumes of poetry and jointly edited with Mark Schorer and Gordon McKenzie *Criticism: The Foundations of Modern Literary Judgment,* a collection of essays by T. S. Eliot, W. H. Auden, Henry James and Lionel Trilling. In 1935, she won the Shelley Memorial Award, an honor previously won by Conrad Aiken, Archibald MacLeish and Stephen Vincent Benet.

Her first volume of poetry, *Lines at Intersection,* was published in 1939. Her other volumes include *Local Measures, Prefabrications* and *Kinds of Affection.* Reviewing the latter book in *The New York Times* in 1968, Hayden Carruth wrote, "Her poems, most of them very short, are glimpses into the drama of ideas and perceptions played by an agile intelligence."

> *"Josephine Miles Dies: A Poet and Professor,"* in The New York Times, *May 17, 1985, p. D20.*

LOS ANGELES TIMES

Josephine Miles, a well-known West Coast poet and the first woman granted tenure in the University of California's English department, is dead at age 73. . . .

At her death she was professor emeritus of English at the Berkeley campus and one of only 12 faculty members in the nine-campus school system to hold the prestigious title of University Professor. The honor is bestowed each year on one senior faculty member in the statewide system.

Her *Collected Poems, 1930-1983,* won *Nation* magazine's Lenore Marshall Poetry Prize in 1983 and was one of three finalists for last year's Pulitzer Prize in poetry. It was the last of two dozen books of verse and criticism authored or edited by Miss Miles in her nearly 50-year career. She was known for writing of the things and places around her, often interspersing the names of neighborhood streets and stores in her poems. . . .

"Jo Miles was an extraordinary teacher and a wonderful inspiration of courage and creativity who lived and cherished

every moment of life," said UC Berkeley Chancellor Ira Michael Heyman.

> *"Josephine Miles, UC Berkeley Poet and Scholar, Dies,"* in Los Angeles Times, *Part IV, May 18, 1985, p. 7.*

R. E. NOWICKI

Jo Miles has to be one of the most courageous people we've ever met. To live in constant pain, as she did, the result of rheumatoid arthritis, is bad enough, but to have to be carried about in public, as she was for the last years of her life, would have broken the spirit of even the most stouthearted person. But not Miles, the Poet. The few times we met and saw her at lectures and seminars, she was always carried in by an attendant who waited patiently by the door until Jo signalled that she wished to leave.

In 1984 she received the Fred Cody Memorial Award for Lifetime Achievement from the Bay Book Reviewers Association. She was very moved by the outpouring of emotion from the audience, and later said it was one of the great moments of her life. . . .

Her presence on the Bay Area—as well as on the national—poetry scene will be greatly missed. But at least she has left us the legacy of her exquisitely crafted poems and the memory of one courageous woman.

> R. E. Nowicki, *"Josephine Miles (1912-1985),"* in San Francisco Review of Books, *May-June, 1985, p. 5.*

JACK MILES

[Miles is book editor of The Los Angeles Times. *At one time, he and the poet considered the notion that they might be distant relatives, because of shared family names and geographical backgrounds. In the following excerpt Miles offers anecdotes about the poet's career as an educator at the University of California at Berkeley.]*

One of the several book prizes that the *Los Angeles Times* confers each fall is the Robert Kirsch Award for lifetime achievement by a writer living in or writing on the West. There is nothing in any bylaw governing the award that prevents its conferral upon a young writer. John Keats surely had a lifetime of achievement behind him when at just 25, he ceased to be. In retrospect, we may judge that an award given him in his 24th year would not have been premature. In prospect, however, we all expect an American Keats to live into masterful middle age and then into sage seniority and only then to harvest his lifetime achievement award. It is for this reason, I suspect, that the Kirsch Award winners have all been in the autumn of their years.

If a small injustice has thus been perpetrated against accomplished younger writers, a larger one may have been perpetrated against a few accomplished older writers, who might well have won had they but lived a little longer. The Robert Kirsch Award, you see, does bear one condition: It may not be awarded posthumously. I have all this in mind, for one of my perennial candidates for the award has just died.

Josephine Miles died in Berkeley on May 12, 1985, at age 73. Above all else a poet, Miles was also professor emerita at Berkeley, the first woman to win tenure there in English, and one of only a dozen "university professors" in the nine-campus University of California system. When you are a university professor, you get to go to any campus you choose and talk about anything you please, but Miles did not travel much: She had been severely handicapped since childhood with rheumatoid arthritis. If that handicap was her hermitage, the pilgrims who sought her out were many. She was not only a poet but the teacher of poets. One of her students—A. R. Ammons—won the National Book Award.

Miles was the author of two dozen volumes of verse, including a 1983 *Collected Poems* (University of Illinois), and of various volumes of learned criticism, including a series entitled *The Primary Language of Poetry in the 1640s, The Primary Language of Poetry in the 1740s and the 1840s* and *The Primary Language of Poetry in the 1940s* (University of California, 1948, 1950, and 1951). What lay ahead for Miles when she got past the 1940s?

Why, the 1950s! Allen Ginsberg showed her his "Howl" before it was published. She was included in a landmark 1957 issue of *Evergreen Review* with Ginsberg, Jack Kerouac, Robert Duncan, and others. If she was no San Francisco Beat, she was at least the Beats' Berkeley connection to the 1840s, the 1740s, and the 1640s. I once asked a writer loosely of that North Beach company whether Josephine Miles was a Beat poet. "No," he said, "she was a Bent poet." The remark was simultaneously a comment on her twisted physical condition and an allusion to her 1967 collection, *Bent*. A cruel crack? Perhaps, but I imagine her laughing at it.

In a previously sealed oral history, just released for use by Berkeley's Bancroft Library, Miles remembers the 1960s as the best years of her teaching life. The 1970s were less good, a time of panic: "panic over jobs and panic over grades that lead to jobs. It's very hard to teach people that have to have A's." Miles wanted students whose desire to know was as disinterested and unrestricted as her own.

Denis Donoghue once applied to Miles Samuel Johnson's words about Alexander Pope: She was, he said, "an intelligence perpetually on the wing, excursive, vigorous, and diligent." There is indeed about this poet's work a certain tirelessness of wings. Like a small sea bird many leagues from the nearest shore, she hangs aloft. Nothing is beneath her notice, nothing too little to be thought about, stayed by, lived with till it yields its prize of sense, and sound.

Miles and I were not related. The surname is too common for consanguinity ever to be presumed among its bearers, and I had presumed the opposite. A few years ago, however, I saw a picture of her for the first time, and it bore a more than passing resemblance to an aunt of mine. I sent Miles a snapshot of my aunt, and there followed a brief correspondence that ended with Josephine convinced that we were indeed related. We were both from Chicago. We both had Montana in the family history. Why doubt it?

Miles was a woman who suffered such fools gladly. "What is one fool more or less among all the other suffering?" That seemed to be her attitude. She believed that madmen move the world forward, even as they move poetry. "They have some axe to grind," she wrote, "and they are better at the grinding than at the poetry." But often too they have more to teach than "major" poets, who "tend to use most fully the emphases already accepted and available to them in the poetry of their time." San Francisco Beats, madmen with axes to grind, supposititious cousins, imperious professors at the bureaucratic counsels she so often wrote about—if any of them had something to teach, he had in Miles someone who would learn.

One of her saddest poems, **"Away,"** tells the life story of an aging teacher in a few unsparing lines:

> What is my life but your leaving?
> Giving a brief biography of my life,
> I say
> Each year they are off, all of them,
> Goodbye, goodbye,
> Yet here I stay
> As in 1940, 41, 58, 60, 70,
> Now again they are going away.

But a better vespers than that one comes from **"For Futures,"** the selection with which Donoghue closed his appreciation:

> When the lights come on at five
> o'clock on street corners
> That is Evolution by the bureau of
> power,
> That is a fine mechanic dealing in
> futures:
> For the sky is wide and warm
> upon that hour,
> But like the eyes that burned once
> at sea bottom,
> Widening in the gloom, prepared
> for light,
> The ornamental standards, the
> glazed globes softly
> Perceive far off how probable is
> night.

Farewell, Josephine, and please accept this last, lost letter in lieu of more official homage.

Jack Miles, "End Papers," in Los Angeles Times Book Review, *July 7, 1985, p. 10.*

Shiva(dhar Srinivasa) Naipaul

February 25, 1945 - August 13, 1985

Trinidadian novelist, journalist, essayist, and short story writer.

(See also *CLC*, Vol. 32, and *Contemporary Authors*, Vols. 110, 112, 116 [obituary].)

PRINCIPAL WORKS

Fireflies (novel) 1970
The Chip-Chip Gatherers (novel) 1973
The Adventures of Gurudeva (short stories) 1976
North of South: An African Journey (travel diary) 1978
Black and White (journalism) 1980; also published as
    Journey to Nowhere: A New World Tragedy, 1981
Love and Death in a Hot Country (novel) 1983; also
    published as *A Hot Country,* 1983
Beyond the Dragon's Mouth (essay and short stories)
    1984

© *Jerry Bauer*

THE NEW YORK TIMES

Shiva Naipaul, the Trinidad-born author and journalist, died of a heart attack [on August 13] in London, where he lived. He was 40 years old.

Although his work was less well-known than that of his brother, V. S. Naipaul, the novelist, he was considered by many in Britain to be one of the most talented and wide-ranging authors of his generation.

In his journalism and travel writings, Mr. Naipaul often reported candidly about what he considered the shortcomings of life in the third world. His 1979 book, ***North of South,*** about an African journey through Kenya, Tanzania and Zambia, includes descriptions of his hapless encounters with immigration officials and people he portrays as racists.

Reviewing the book in *The New York Times Book Review,* John Darnton commented: ''***North of South*** is superbly written, even in the evocation of the scenery that Mr. Naipaul finds uninspiring. Many of the points are well taken, if not altogether new—that independence has primarily benefited a black elite'' and that ''the continent craves the material goods of the West.''

Mr. Naipaul's first novel, ***Fireflies,*** published in 1971, was acclaimed critically and won four literary prizes, including the *New Statesman* award in Britain. His second novel, ***The Chip-chip Gatherers,*** also had a Trinidad background and won the 1973 Whitbread award. His bitter 1984 novel, ***Love and Death in a Hot Country,*** was set on an imaginary ''sloping shoulder of South Africa.'' It described the effect that its atmosphere had on the English expatriates living there.

His most recent work, ***Beyond the Dragon's Mouth,*** published here by the Viking Press in March, included both stories and articles. In the introduction, he talked about growing up as an East Indian in the West Indies, rising above what he saw as the squalid life there, and becoming a man of letters in England.

After attending St. Mary's College in Trinidad, he won a scholarship to Oxford, where he studied Chinese. He wrote in ***Beyond the Dragon's Mouth*** that, because of his ethnic and national background, ''every day, I have to redefine myself.''

One of his reporting books, ***Journey to Nowhere,*** published here in 1981, described the mass suicide of the followers of the Rev. Jim Jones in the jungles of Guyana.

> *''Shiva Naipaul Is Dead at 40: Wrote Books on Third World,'' in* The New York Times, *August 16, 1985, p. D15.*

THE TIMES, LONDON

Shiva Naipaul, the West Indian writer and younger brother of the eminent novelist, V. S. Naipaul, died in London on August 13 at the age of 40.

His bold first novel *Fireflies,* which was published when he was only 25, had gained him several prizes, including the Royal Society of Literature's Winifred Holtby Memorial Prize. But though he produced some distinguished travel books and pieces of journalism he had not so far fulfilled his early promise as a novelist.

Shivadhar Srinivasa Naipaul was born in Port of Spain, Trinidad, on February 25, 1945, into a Hindu family. He was one of seven children. He was educated at Queen's Royal College and St Mary's College before going on to University College, Oxford, where he took a degree in Chinese.

Fireflies appeared in 1970. It was a striking, although misanthropic work, dealing with the gradual weakening of the power of the leaders of the Hindu community in Trinidad. What it lacked in subtlety or understanding was in some measure compensated for by Naipaul's clever plotting and sure depiction of squalor and bad faith.

Sociologically, the novel was remarkably accurate. But it also displayed a memorable contempt for the weak and stupid.

The successor to this work, *The Chip-Chip Gatherers* (1973), was rather less successful, though it won the Whitbread Literary Award. This, too, was set in Trinidad, and skilfully suffused with naturalist gloom, but its impact was lessened by an outdated social Darwinism in which only the most unpleasant were allowed to be "the fittest".

Though oppressive, however, it was a book which left no doubt at all of its author's capabilities and talent. Had he lived to work out this bitterness to the full, he might have achieved remarkable results.

He did not immediately follow it up, but turned, first, to the short story with *The Adventures of Gurudeva* (1976), and then to travel diaries (*North of South: an African Journey,* published in 1978) and journalism. In 1980 he published *Black and White,* a perceptive account of the mass suicide at Jonestown, Guyana.

In 1983 he made a welcome return to the novel with *A Hot Country,* and in the following year he published a number of short pieces and stories in *Beyond the Dragon's Mouth.* He had recently been commissioned to write a book about Australia. But he appeared to be faced with a perhaps temporary block in the development of his undoubted creative abilities.

> *"Shiva Naipaul: West Indian Writer of Unfulfilled Promise," in* The Times, *London, August 16, 1985, p. 12.*

DAVID REMNICK

Shiva Naipaul, whose searching novels and reportage about his native Trinidad and other countries in the Third World were widely celebrated, died of a heart attack Aug. 13 in London. He was 40 years old.

Although the works of his older brother, V. S. Naipaul, are better known, both men wrote with an exile's sensibility. Born of Indian parents in Trinidad, both left for Oxford and settled in London.

Shiva Naipaul first gained attention with two novels, *Fireflies* (1970) and *The Chip-Chip Gatherers* (1973). Both books were set in Trinidad and explored class differences and family customs on the island. After publication of *The Chip-Chip Gatherers,* Martin Amis wrote in *The New Statesman* that Mr. Nai-

paul's "next novels will establish him as one of the most accomplished, and most accessible, writers of his generation."

But there would be only one more novel, [1983's] *Love and Death in a Hot Country.* The story is set in the fictional South African state of Cuyama, a desperate place where politics have become "banditry, cynicism and lies" and architecture has become "archways leading nowhere."

Such was Shiva Naipaul's sensibility: critical, severe, penetrating. Like his brother, he was obsessed with the theme of identity, of belonging to a country, a race, a people. Partly in pursuit of those themes, the Naipauls traveled all over the Third World.

While V. S. Naipaul traveled to India, Iran, Indonesia, Malaysia and elsewhere to produce, among other books, *India: A Wounded Civilization* and *Among the Believers,* Shiva Naipaul went to Kenya, Tanzania and Zambia to write *North of South* (1979), and to Guyana to describe the mass suicide of the followers of the Rev. Jim Jones in *Journey to Nowhere* (1981). Some reviewers found Shiva Naipaul's generally bleak view of the Third World unsympathetic and unsparing.

His most recent book was *Beyond the Dragon's Mouth* [1984]. . . . In that collection of articles and essays, he described his journey from Trinidad to Britain and a career as a writer.

> *David Remnick, "Shiva Naipaul, 40, Author of Third World Novels, Essays," in* The Washington Post, *August 17, 1985, p. B6.*

MARTIN AMIS

[*Amis, an English novelist and journalist and the son of novelist Kingsley Amis, is a satirist of contemporary life. In his novels, including* The Rachel Papers *(1973),* Dead Babies *(1975), and* Money: A Suicide Note *(1985), Amis uses black humor as he explores his themes of alienation, the breakdown in communication, and the superficiality of sex. In a 1981 interview Amis commented, "I'm more obsessed by down-and-outs and the griefs of ordinary people than in the life at the top end of the scale." In his journalistic pieces, Amis, as a staff writer for the* London Observer, *specializes in American culture. In the following excerpt Amis offers his impressions of Naipaul, both as a greatly admired fellow writer and as a personal acquaintance.*]

Anyone who knew—or read—Shiva Naipaul will feel horribly robbed and violated by his death [August 13] at the age of 40.

The moment I finished his first novel, *Fireflies,* I felt delight in being alive at the same time as such a writer. I passed the book round to friends (I must have bought half a dozen of those Penguins) and there are many people with whom I can initiate a long train of quotations—and laughter—from that book alone: Ram Lutchman's torments at the hands of his hobby, photography (he takes to developing his own film, under the bed: 'There go another sonofabitch! Is like a goddam lake in here'); his subsequent refrain, at any humbling reverse in his troubled and frustrated life: 'Is just like that sonofabitch camera'; and the ostracism his wife Baby must endure from her family, having settled on the lowly Ram: 'It was generally agreed that Baby was being deliberately awkward, "too big," as Urmila had put it, "for she boots."' I quote from memory. Perhaps this is what one is always obliged to do with the dead— 'from memory.'

The second novel, *The Chip-Chip Gatherers,* fully maintained the great promise, and the great achievement. I got to know him about that time (the early Seventies), a humorous, recalcitrant, and denunciatory figure. He was still not yet 30. Many people felt impatience at the turn his career then took. His travel books, *North of South* (Central Africa) and *Black and White* (Jonestown, Guyana) were brilliant, and characteristically brilliant; but where were the novels?

The novels were simmering away. Shiva's third, *A Hot Country*, signalled a change of direction and a toughening-up, a wheeling round of the guns. In losing him, we have lost 30 years of untranscribed, of vanished genius: the hard political intelligence, and the beautiful comedy, which dealt in the most forgiving pathos and irony, as bearish and affectionate as the man himself.

With Shiva, you usually found yourself having ebullient five-hour sessions in exasperated but needy Greek restaurants. I once asked him what he thought of an editor we both knew, an editor I liked. 'To kill such a man,' smiled Shiva, 'could not be accounted murder.' It turned out that this editor had once cut three lines of Shiva's copy, or had been a day late with payment. Such vehemence was partly play, for he was a gentle presence. He loved gossip, but soon turned the subject back to Life.

The other day I parped my horn as I drove past him in the street, and saw him wave and smile and level his accusing eyes. I felt more warmth for him than for people I know far better. He had a talent for warmth, and for much else. He was one of those people who caused your heart to lift when he entered the room.

> Martin Amis, "A Talent for Warmth," in The Observer, August 18, 1985, p. 19.

THE TIMES, LONDON

Your somewhat lowering obituary notice of Shiva Naipaul [see excerpt above] underestimated the achievements of a novelist and journalist whose output, including six books and many thousands of words of journalism, far from indicating "unfulfilled promise", in fact represented an extremely respectable output from a writer who died young and in who perfectionism and fastidiousness competed against the tyranny of publishers, editors and deadlines.

It is a tribute to Shiva that he was never overawed by the success already achieved by his distinguished brother, V. S., thirteen years his senior, but established his own independent reputation.

Two years ago he was named as one of the best of young British novelists, a recognition of his distinctive and individual voice, quite unlike that of any of his contemporaries, a voice that was developing in power and confidence with each of his three novels.

If he took a gloomy view of the state of race relations in Britain, while rejecting (to their dismay) the orthodox pieties of the liberal establishment, he could call on his own early experiences as a brown man in London's Earl's Court—readers of *The Times* of last Saturday will recall the memorable complaint, from his last book, *Beyond the Dragon's Mouth:* "Sufficient unto any man the handicap of being straightforwardly Indian or straightforwardly West Indian. But to contrive somehow to combine the two was a challenge to reason. An Indian from the West Indies! I was guilty of a compound sin."

Shiva Naipaul possibly because of the tenuous position of the community in which he was brought up was a sharp observer of the barbarous and the primitive, whether such characteristics were to be found among Australian aborigines, or in post-colonial Africa, the doomed American cultists in Guyana, or the confused Rastafarians in Brixton. He was also unusually a man of detachment, an occasionally abrasive voice in British journalism, capable of saying some painfully true things about our society.

There was, however, another dimension to the man. He had a gift for friendship, for companionability and for love which earned him an especially warm place in the affections of friends and colleagues. He was supported by the extraordinary devotion of his wife, Jenny, daughter of the BBC's Douglas Stuart, from his Oxford days onward, and both delighted in the son Tarun.

Nevertheless, there was always a rootlessness about Shiva Naipaul, a sense of belonging nowhere in particular, which afforded the stout independence, together with an edge and an extraordinary clarity to his writing, which will ensure that he is not forgotten.

> "Shiva Naipaul," in The Times, London, August 21, 1985, p. 14.

ALEXANDER CHANCELLOR

[*Chancellor, an English journalist, is the editor of* Time and Tide, *as well as an assistant editor of the* Sunday Telegraph. *He also writes a television column for the* Spectator, *a newspaper that he edited from 1975 to 1984. He met Naipaul through Naipaul's wife Jenny, a member of the* Spectator's *editorial staff. In the following excerpt Chancellor offers a biographical sketch of Naipaul, highlighted by his personal recollections of the writer. Like Martin Amis, Chancellor observes that Naipaul's brooding literary persona was totally unlike the writer himself, a warm and affable man.*]

If, like me, one has never been to Trinidad, and perhaps even if one has, it is extremely difficult to imagine the circumstances in which Shiva Naipaul grew up. He has described them often enough, and with great eloquence, but his story still has about it the quality of a fairy tale. Most of the Indians in Trinidad before the first world war had come there as 'indentured labourers', arbitrarily transferred from one end of the British Empire to the other to work in the sugar plantations. Shiva's grandfather was one of them. His father, however, contrived to escape from this wretched environment. He became a journalist (working for the *Trinidad Guardian*), married into a family of Indian landowners, and settled eventually in the Trinidadian capital, Port of Spain, where Shiva was born, one of seven children, on 25 February, 1945.

Three years ago, Shiva returned to Trinidad to make a television programme for the BBC. In it he described the life that might have been his:

> My father's family lived in darkest Caroni, Trinidad's Indian heartland. They worked on the sugar estates, lived in mud huts, kept cows and goats and chickens: men and women with rough hands, who smelled of dust and sugar-cane and—all too often—of rum: an authentic peasantry whose existences were very different from my own and yet, ancestrally, so close. Only a kind of magic separated me from them; a kind of luck I could not understand. It was out of this background that my father emerged,

managed somehow to get an education—English was a language he had to acquire—and eventually was able to turn himself into a journalist and writer of short stories. Looking back, it seems a miraculous achievement.

I could so easily have been exactly like my country cousins: labouring in the canefields and ricelands, taking cows out to pasture, bringing bundles of firewood home at dusk. I could, I suppose, have been married off at 17 or 18; become father to a child or two by the time I was 20. I might have drunk away the wages of the sugar harvest in the local rum shop and regularly beaten my wife. My childish ears picked up rumours of all these horrors. As it was, I lived in Port of Spain. I was a town boy, having a reasonably good education drummed into me, driven by quite other impulses and ambitions.

Among the bright Indian boys of Port of Spain, these impulses and ambitions had a single objective: escape. For the poor among them, who included Shiva, the only possible escape route was to Oxford University through one of the four 'island scholarships' awarded each year. His elder brother, V. S. Naipaul, had already achieved this dazzling goal. He was in London, working for the BBC, becoming a writer. Now it was Shiva's turn. 'Education under these circumstances,' said Shiva, 'became a barely controlled form of frenzy shared by parents and offspring alike.' It was a conventional English education imposed with the ruler and the leather strap. At one time the misery was so great that Shiva played truant for a month, roaming the slums around the Central Market. At another time, against his own inclinations and aptitudes, his parents decided he should be a doctor—the most prestigious career open to a Trinidadian Indian—and put him into the science stream of his school, with near-disastrous consequences. But, returning to the more 'humane' branches of study, he finally obtained his 'island scholarship' and, at the age of 18, triumphantly boarded the banana boat for Avonmouth and Oxford, leaving an island he had found tawdry, confining and alien.

'Trinidad calls itself a nation,' Shiva has said. 'But Trinidadians have no genuinely collective existence. We are merely a random collection of different races thrown together by outside forces for purposes quite alien to our well-being.'

It was to be a voyage of no return, or at least of no permanent return. 'Having to return to Trinidad—to St James (Shiva's home district of Port of Spain)—nearly always fills me with alarm. It brings on this nightmare—that, having once arrived there, I may never be able to get out again. I imagine myself trapped there for ever,' he wrote in a long autobiographical essay published [in 1984] in the *New Yorker* and reprinted in his last book, a collection of stories and pieces called *Beyond the Dragon's Mouth*. . . . For most of the next 22 years, until the tragedy of his sudden death [August 13], he was to live in England. But he was never to regard England as home. He was by now convinced that he was incapable of allegiance to any community, or indeed of any normal social existence. He had left Trinidad, so he wrote, 'haphazardly cobbled together from bits and pieces taken from everywhere and anywhere'. Lacking, so he believed, any coherent identity, he felt obliged to 're-invent' himself every day. Oxford, which had been the miraculous fulfilment of a great dream, did nothing to change this idea he had of himself. 'The magic of Oxford had not

rubbed off on me,' he wrote in an article for the *Sunday Telegraph* seven years ago. 'I had no splendid conversations that went on all night, no intellectual or spiritual revelations. The University cannot be blamed for this. It belonged to a tradition, a civilisation, concerning which I had only the most primitive notions.' When he left Oxford, with a degree in Chinese and a young English wife, it was in a very gloomy state of mind. 'I had no vision of myself: I would have to start afresh; to discover, unaided, my human possibility. In my meagre baggage was the beginning of a novel, the outlines of which had occurred to me one bilious and despairing afternoon as, sick in mind and body, I gazed at the mossy apple tree that grew in the unkempt garden of the flat I had been renting. It wasn't much to be taking away after four years, but it was better than nothing: it gave me, however unreliably, a reason to go on living.'

The portrait of Shiva that emerges from his own writings is one of a remarkable, exceptionally gifted man, but possibly of a man one would not care to know, of a solitary, gloomy, self-obsessed person, lacking the gift of companionship. It is a portrait in this last respect so misleading that it fairly takes the breath away.

What keeps coming back to me at the moment is his laugh: high, rasping and infectious. Writing may have been his main 'reason to go on living'—indeed, I believe that it was—but he was one of the most companionable people I have ever met. The headline over Martin Amis's appreciation of him in [the August 18] *Observer* was 'A Talent for Warmth' [see excerpt above.]. It was exactly the right headline, because it was—to those who did not know him—the most improbable of Shiva's qualities.

I first met him about ten years ago after he had already written two prize-winning novels, both set in Trinidad: *Fireflies* (1970), and *The Chip-Chip Gatherers* (1973). I had read neither of them. Indeed, I knew very little about him. I had just been appointed editor of the *Spectator* and had advertised for a secretary. I interviewed about 30 candidates, but one was quite obviously much better qualified, much more intelligent, and very much nicer than any of the others. She turned out to be Shiva's wife, Jenny. Jenny quickly became far more than a secretary, though she was brilliant in that role. She became (and still is) an indispensable member of the editorial staff, the person with whom our contributors most liked to communicate. I was sometimes quite jealous of her in this respect. I was even more jealous of Shiva. However petty his needs might have seemed in comparison with mine, he always came first. Working for an 'island scholarship' is clearly a full-time occupation. So far as I could tell, Shiva had failed to master even the most elementary of practical skills. He couldn't boil an egg or mend a fuse. If a tap was dripping, so to speak, he would telephone Jenny at the office and she would rush home immediately to deal with it. She would deal with everything. He couldn't possibly have coped without her. If, in his literary persona, he tended to ignore her existence, his dependence on her was nevertheless absolute.

One of the things Jenny did was to introduce Shiva to the *Spectator*. More than half the non-fictional pieces in *Beyond the Dragon's Mouth* were first published in this paper, as were parts of his 1978 African travel book *North of South*. These articles were, without exception, excellent. As a writer dedicated to his craft, he devoted much more time to them than most journalists do. He refused to be rushed. He would only deliver his pieces when he felt they were right. He brought to them not only his rare skills as a writer and his novelist's powers of observation, but an independence of mind which came from his own sense of belonging nowhere. One might be tempted to call it detachment, but that would not be right. He minded very much about things and about people. What he minded most of all was the way in which fools and bigots would misrepresent reality. He was a genuine seeker after truth.

But the main thing now is to recall those qualities which he seemed not to realise he possessed—warmth, good humour, and an exceptional capacity for friendship. He was much too obsessed with his lack of 'a collective consciousness'. It made him think he was much unhappier than he was. I believe he had recently become quite happy, with his large and comfortable new flat in Hampstead, with his growing success as an author, with his circle of devoted friends—not to mention his extraordinary good fortune in his wife and son, Tarun. Had he lived, he would not only have written more marvellous books; he would soon have been ready to call England his home. Or so I believe. His death was an appalling tragedy. His loss is even harder to understand than his extraordinary life. (pp. 17-18)

Alexander Chancellor, "Shiva Naipaul," in The Spectator, *Vol. 255, No. 8198, August 24, 1985, pp. 17-18.*

Theodore Sturgeon

February 26, 1918 - May 8, 1985

(Born Edward Hamilton Waldo; also wrote under the pseudonyms of Frederick R. Ewing, E. Hunter Waldo, and E. Waldo Hunter) American short story writer, novelist, scriptwriter, dramatist, essayist, and critic.

(See also *CLC*, Vol. 22; *Contemporary Authors*, Vols. 81-84; and *Dictionary of Literary Biography*, Vol. 8.)

PRINCIPAL WORKS

Without Sorcery (short stories) 1948
The Dreaming Jewels (novel) 1950; also published as *The Synthetic Man*, 1957
E Pluribus Unicorn (short stories) 1953
More than Human (novel) 1953
Caviar (short stories) 1955
A Way Home (short stories) 1955; also published as *Thunder and Roses*, 1957
The Cosmic Rape (novel) 1958
A Touch of Strange (short stories) 1958
Aliens 4 (short stories) 1959
Beyond (short stories) 1960
Venus Plus X (novel) 1960
Some of Your Blood (novel) 1961
Sturgeon in Orbit (short stories) 1964
The Joyous Invasions (short stories) 1965
Starshine (short stories) 1966
Sturgeon is Alive and Well (short stories) 1972
To Here and the Easel (short stories) 1973
The Golden Helix (short stories) 1980
The Stars are the Styx (short stories) 1979
Visions and Venturers (short stories) 1979
Godbody (novel) 1986

BOB COLLINS

[Collins is editor-in-chief of Fantasy Review. *In the following excerpt he offers a biographical sketch of Sturgeon.]*

On Sunday, May 5, Theodore Hamilton Sturgeon said goodbye to close friends, by telephone from his apartment in Springfield, Oregon. His lung condition (an effect of cystic fibrosis) had worsened, so that he could utter only a few syllables at a time. A few hours later he entered the local hospital with terminal pneumonia.

There was a gathering of the clan (Ted had five marriages and eight children). On Wednesday evening, May 8 (''I think he was just waiting for all the family to arrive,'' said a neighbor) Sturgeon ceased his efforts to breathe at 8:15 p.m., Pacific Coast time. He was 67.

Photograph by Jay Kay Klein

Ted was born Edward Hamilton Waldo in Staten Island on February 26, 1918; his parents were a Protestant Episcopalian couple, Edward and Christine Waldo. The marriage was a failure: Ted saw his father only once a week at Sunday dinner. When he was nine, divorce brought him a stern and unsympathetic Scottish stepfather, employed as a teacher at Drexel College in Philadelphia, who gave him little more than a new surname.

His earliest dream, of a career as a circus trapeze artist (he was a star gymnast in high school, and had been promised an athletic scholarship at Temple University), was destroyed by a bout of rheumatic fever at 15 that left him with an enlarged heart. Always an erratic student, Ted's attitude worsened, and his stepfather refused to send him to college. Instead, partly with a small bequest from his grandmother, he was enrolled in Penn State Nautical School, but after a term there he ran away to sea as an engine-room wiper.

During his years in the Merchant Marine he began selling short fiction to McClure's newspaper syndicate. When a Brooklyn couple showed him a copy of John Campbell's *Unknown* he set out to write for that market. His ''first sale'' was **"God in** a Garden" to *Unknown,* but **"Ether Breather"** in *Astounding* was published earlier (1939); these sales began his first highly productive period (**"Shottle Bop," "Microcosmic God," "Nightmare Island"**) during which he used the pseudonyms "E. Hunter Waldo" and "E. Waldo Hunter" to allow multiple stories in the same issue of *Astounding.*

Flushed with new success, in 1940 he married Dorothy Fillingame, his high school sweetheart, over her parents' objections. On his honeymoon he wrote that early classic of the macabre, **"It,"** which established his reputation as a stylist. But World War II was just around the corner: caught in the British West Indies, where he had gone to manage a resort hotel to supplement his writing, Sturgeon found himself managing army properties instead. One of these was a tractor lubrication center, where Sturgeon learned to operate bulldozers and loved it. This stint inspired the only story he completed during the war, **"Killdozer"** (published in *Astounding,* 1944, filmed for television in 1974).

Sturgeon's long spell of writer's block undermined his confidence, and Dorothy's. She divorced him in 1945, keeping the children (Colin, Patricia, Cynthia), and he returned to New York in a daze. Sharing an apartment with L. Jerome Stanton, assistant editor of *Astounding,* he let [John W.] Campbell coax him gradually out of his depression. In 1946, while writing again for Campbell, Sturgeon also tried agenting (for Pohl, Chandler, Merrill, etc.) and found some new markets, notably *Weird Tales,* which took many stories rejected by Campbell. Meanwhile he submitted **"Bianca's Hands,"** a story of obsessive, fetishist passion, which kinky American editors shunned it, to a story contest in the British magazine *Argosy,* and won! (1947). The same year his **"Thunder and Roses,"** a powerfully pacifist atomic war story, suddenly captured the imagination of fans at the Philadelphia Worldcon. There he met his second wife Mary Mair, a showgirl who sang the "title song" from his story. Sturgeon's confidence was restored.

Although the marriage to Mary was brief and childless, through Jerome Stanton he soon met his third wife, Marion, with whom he lived for 18 years, producing Robin, Tandy, Noel and Timothy.

Meanwhile, Prime Press issued Sturgeon's first hardcover anthology, **Without Sorcery** (1948) and Horace Gold founded *Galaxy,* which was to be Sturgeon's major market over the next decade. There he published **"Baby Is Three,"** his most famous short story, which he expanded in 1953 to **More Than Human,** a blockbuster novel which got simultaneous hardcover and paperback distribution, beating Alfred Bester's *The Demolished Man* for the International Fantasy Award (the best then going) in 1954. The earliest and best exploration of the "gestalt mind" concept, it has remained in print, a classroom classic, ever since.

During the 50s Sturgeon produced a series of important novels (**The Dreaming Jewels, The Cosmic Rape, Venus Plus X, Some of Your Blood,** the last a vampire tale) and a host of representative stories (**"The Sex Opposite," "The World Well Lost," "The Silken Swift,"** . . . **"And My Fear is Great"**) as well as several story collections. In 1962, *The Magazine of Fantasy & Science Fiction* devoted a special issue to him, and he was Guest of Honor at the 20th Worldcon in Chicago, where he delivered a memorable speech outlining his philosophy of love.

(By 1969, career conflict had ended this third marriage in favor of a union with Wina Golden, who bore his last son, Andros.

Then, a decade later, with that union gone flat, he married his surviving wife, Jayne.)

In retrospect, we can see that Sturgeon's most important work had been done by 1962. Yet the power of his mind and personality remained unimpaired though relatively unused. His infrequent contributions in later years (**"If All Men Were Brothers. . . ,"** for Harlan Ellison's *Dangerous Visions,* 1967; **"Slow Sculpture,"** winner of Hugo and Nebula Awards, 1970, **"Why Dolphins Don't Bite,"** written for Ellison's *Medea: Harlan's World,* but first serialized in *Omni,* (1980) are still among the very finest stories in the genre. Yet, as E. F. Bleiler remarked, the moral of **Venus Plus X** (1960), that "even if there were a way to human salvation, humans would refuse to take it," seems to have been Sturgeon's final position. All of his subsequent work has reflected it.

His legacy, however, is unique. More than any other figure in Science Fiction's "Golden Age" he consistently attempted profound themes, in the belief that science fiction should be "an instrument of progress . . . an active participant in the dynamics of social change" (Bleiler). The kind of progress that interested him was moral rather than material. He anticipated the "Love, not War" ethos of the 60s Flower Children by at least a decade; unlike them he never abandoned belief in the therapeutic power of love. His assault upon the irrational taboos of human society included empathic treatments of such "deviant behavior" as homosexuality, incest, and cannibalism; even his unfinished novel, **Godbody,** an attempt to restore the primitive link between sex and religion, was based on the conviction that cultural frustration and exploitation of human sexuality is at the root of all evil. (pp. 6, 32)

> Bob Collins, "Theodore Sturgeon: 1918-1985," in *Fantasy Review, Vol. 8, No. 5, May, 1985, pp. 6, 32.*

JAMES GUNN

[*Gunn is an American novelist, short story writer, editor, nonfiction writer, dramatist, and scriptwriter who works in the science fiction genre. His novel* The Immortal *(1962) was made into a television series; other works include* Alternate Worlds *(1975), an illustrated history of science fiction, and* Isaac Asimov: Foundations of Science Fiction *(1982). Gunn, who has known Sturgeon since the early 1950s, conducted seminars in science fiction at the University of Kansas; Sturgeon was a regular instructor at these seminars. In the following excerpt Gunn shares some personal memories of Sturgeon.*]

Every member of the science-fiction community is irreplaceable, but some are more irreplaceable than others. We will never replace Theodore Sturgeon. He was unique.

I did not know Ted as well as others have known him, who met him as a young man in New York in the early days of his self-discovery as a writer. My first contact with him was the result of a telephone call from Horace Gold. Horace said he would buy my short novel *Breaking Point* if I would let Ted cut it by a third. I had such admiration for the author of most [of] the stories I liked best in *Astounding* and *Unknown* and later in *Galaxy* that I agreed without hesitation. Then, when I visited New York in November of 1952, having decided to return to freelance writing after learning about the sale of four stories, I visited Ted in an unusual house built by a retired sea captain on a hill overlooking the Hudson. He drew me in to the circle of people he thought mattered, and he showed me Ted Sturgeon: personal magnetism, an interest in others, an intense involvement with words and writing, and a generous admiration for the accomplishments of others.

Later I met him occasionally at science-fiction conventions, most notably in Philadelphia in 1953, when I heard him announce Sturgeon's Law (''ninety percent of everything is crud'') and sing ''Strange Fruit.'' But I got to know him best in his later years, when he was not doing much writing any more, when he answered my appeal to help with the Intensive English Institute on the Teaching of Science Fiction—my decade-long effort to teach the teachers of science fiction.

Ted arrived for the second Institute (as did Fred Pohl); only Gordon Dickson had a longer tenure, and Ted came last year when Gordon could not come. Last year Ted was watching his health, wearing a monitor on his wrist to check his pulse and having some difficulty with hills, and that was frightening, because Ted had seemed always so wiry and inexhaustible that we all thought he would go on forever.

Ted would arrive and immediately begin to charm everyone around him. Ted cared about people, anybody, everybody. One student enrolled in the Institute only because Ted would be there, and within hours she had poured out to him the intimate tragedies of her life. Ted was like that; he didn't so much invite intimacy as draw it into him with every breath, the breath that must have become so difficult for him at the end. People wanted to do things for Ted, just as he was willing to do anything for them. They would meet him at the airport, write to him, seek him out. One fan came to the Institute just to sit with his wife's young child (and later returned to participate in the Institute). Another, when his wife (whom he always called ''Lady Jayne'') could not afford to come took up a collection to fly her to the Institute as a surprise.

Ted loved to come to Lawrence. So did Jayne. They told me so often and were willing to do anything they could to help the Institute, to keep it going. I always wondered whether he loved to go anywhere he could find people to talk to, people to bring into his magic circle, but it may have been the special kind of people who came to the Institute that drew him. They were involved people, teachers most of them, and special teachers at that, because they were willing to experiment, and Ted knew that through teachers he could influence thousands of young minds.

He wanted the teachers to understand what he thought was important. That was writing. He wanted them to love words the way he did. He wanted them to love the right words and the right way to put them together, and he wanted them to pass the loves of his life along to their students. One evening he would talk almost entirely about his discovery of what he called ''metric prose,'' the author's conscious choice of a particular poetic foot for passages in which the author wanted to achieve special effects. But he always insisted (I can hear him now in his intense, musical voice) that the reader must never become conscious of the technique or the game is lost.

He would spend another evening discussing style and reading a particular favorite or two among his own work. But he would spend most of the time reading from the English translation of a French author who told the same ridiculous story in dozens of different styles, Ted chortling over each discovery, as if he were enjoying it for the first time, and then leafing further into the slender volume to come upon another. Once he forgot the book and wrote some examples of his own; they were far more interesting because he was a far better writer, but I never could convince him of that. He liked his French author because it

showed that somebody else had discovered, before he had thought of it, a beautiful way to reveal the power of words and style.

Ted loved finding new writers or admiring the new work of older writers. He fell in love with them and his love overflowed into the reviews he wrote for *The New York Times* and other journals. He may not have been the best critic in the field, because he hated to give a work a bad review, but he was the best-loved critic. Dozens of important authors will never forget the encouragement he gave them.

Ted also wanted people to live, which meant to not be afraid to enjoy life and to be eternally curious, as he was. Fred Pohl says that every novel is about ''how to be more like me.'' That certainly was true of Ted's stories, which had more of himself in them than might be said about the work of any other author I know, but it was also true of his life. In that, too, he said ''how to be more like me.'' Each summer we would ask our guest writers to give a public lecture, and Ted would tell the audience to ''ask the next question,'' for which a fan had made up a symbol for him as a medallion he wore around his neck: a ''Q'' with an arrow horizontally through it. And he would always end with the statement that ''you must never stop asking the next question, because if you do that, you're dead.'' I hope Ted, wherever his questing intelligence has come to rest, is still asking the next question.

If there is a great deal in this reminiscence about love, it is for a good reason. Ted loved life, loved people, and loved writing. He particularly loved outsiders, the unfortunate, the despised and the downtrodden. The superhuman gestalt in *More than Human* was made up of outcasts, the refuse of traditional society. For good reason: Most of his fiction involved those kinds of characters because they were his special people.

He believed that we should love everybody, but particularly the unloved and those who placed themselves beyond scorn or beneath contempt, often by their practices or appetites. His favorite title among his own works was **''If All Men Were Brothers Would You Let One Marry Your Sister?''**

One of the insights that came to me in the early days of the Institute was that many science-fiction authors (maybe all of them) can be differentiated by what they think is the single change that will solve the world's problems: ''everything would be wonderful, *if* only. . . .'' Isaac Asimov might complete it ''. . . people behaved rationally''; Robert Heinlein, ''. . . the incompetent people let the competent people solve the problem''; A. E. Van Vogt, ''. . . people could use their hidden powers.'' For Ted it had to be ''. . . people loved each other.''

If there is an afterlife, Ted now must be afloat in a sea of love. If there isn't, he left much behind, both in the people whose lives he touched and the books and the stories that distilled his message into fiction that continues to ask the next question.

James Gunn, ''I Remember Ted,'' in Fantasy Review, *Vol. 8, No. 5, May, 1985, p. 7.*

GARY K. WOLFE

[*Wolfe, an American short story writer and novelist, is best known for his wryly humorous science fiction stories. He has also written novels, including* Killerbowl *(1975) and* The Resurrectionist *(1979). In the following excerpt Wolfe comments on the contributions Sturgeon made to science fiction as well as to mainstream culture.*]

"We shall never see him again. There will be no more arguments, no more pleasant thinking with Eudiche," mourned Torth to the other Titan.

"Come now. Don't be so pessimistic," said Larit, stroking the machine. "The idea of dissociation has horrified you, that's all. There is every chance that his components will fuse."

This passage, from a not-too-well-known story by Theodore Sturgeon called **"Make Room for Me"** (1951), may not seem much of an epitaph for the man himself. There is, after all, little to be said about Sturgeon by way of praise that hasn't been said during his life by his fellow writers: "the finest conscious artist science fiction has ever had" (James Blish), "the finest of us all" (Alfred Bester), etc. But later in **"Make Room for Me,"** we learn more about the departed Eudiche, an alien who has saved Earth from conquest by his own race. He has "imbalanced," we find. "'He suffered from an overbroadening of the extrapolative faculty. We call it empathy. It need not concern you. It is an alien concept and a strange disease indeed.'"

Perhaps more than any other writer of his time, Theodore Sturgeon brought this strange disease to science fiction. It may be what caused him to view the genre in unusual ways and what in turn made him hard to categorize for critics; of all the undeniably major figures in the field, Sturgeon has perhaps received the least critical and academic attention. He saw the science in science fiction as meaning "wisdom" rather than technology, and he explored themes that other writers would "invent" decades later. He was an unabashed stylist and romantic during a time when science fiction was characterized first by technology and later by social satire; neither was his forte. And to make matters worse, he made people uncomfortable—but more about that in a moment.

Because of his oblique perspective, he sometimes had to look for new words and concepts to express his concerns. Some of his phrases, like the famous "Sturgeon's Law," have become cliches of fandom. Others, like the "Prime Directive" which he formulated for the *Star Trek* TV series, have even entered the vocabulary of management and educational research, and are widely used by people who have never heard of Sturgeon. But I am referring mainly to the peculiar words that he made his own—words like "syzygy," borrowed from biology to become a magical image of an impossible spiritual and physical union; or "infrarational," which he defined as "that source of belief, faith, and motive which exists beside and above reason." Or even "extrapolation," a term he didn't invent but that he used as the title of a story which I guarantee will forever change your notions of what this most overused of science fiction concepts really implies.

I sometimes wonder what readers who came to the genre late make of Sturgeon. The impact of a story like **"The World Well Lost"** appearing in a 1953 issue of *Universe Science Fiction* is hard to recapture for someone weaned on Le Guin and Delany. Perhaps the most commonly cited example of Sturgeon's being ahead of his time is his use of sexuality and love; how often have I read about the controversy surrounding *Venus Plus X,* with its depiction of a bisexual society a decade before *The Left Hand of Darkness.* And this, of course, brings us back to the question of why Sturgeon, even today, makes readers uncomfortable.

I don't think it's sexuality by itself that is the source of this discomfort. I think that Sturgeon, more than any other writer in the field, was determined to make us aware of our bodies—and as simple as that sounds, it's something that few writers can get away with. Sturgeon's work is full of bodies in strange permutations—bodies that fly and vanish, bodies that can shed their skins, deformed bodies with appallingly sensual hands, bodies inhabited by sentient digestive tracts, bodies that sweat and smell and get dirty and that, one way or another, have to be dealt with. I leave it to some future scholar to explore this in more detail, with footnotes, but for now let me merely urge you to think about how much most science fiction really tells you about the flesh which you inhabit.

As one of the most sensuous of writers, Sturgeon knew things that the rest of science fiction is still only beginning to discover. As a master of the most important arts of science fiction, he knew things that "mainstream" writers have only rarely discovered. Writers as diverse as Bradbury, Vonnegut, and Delany have learned from him, and any final assessment of his impact on literature will have to go well beyond the boundaries of science fiction and fantasy. In time, there is every chance that his components will fuse.

Gary K. Wolfe, "Eudiche: Theodore Sturgeon," in
Fantasy Review, *Vol. 8, No. 5, May, 1985, p. 8.*

S. P. SOMTOW

[*Somtow, an American novelist and essayist, is the author of the science fiction novel* Vampire Junction *(1985). In the following excerpt Somtow expresses his sense of personal loss over the death of Sturgeon, whom he acknowledges as a major influence on his own writing.*]

I have been promising [Bob] Collins I would return to the pages of his august magazine [*Fantasy Review*] for some time. I had hoped to make my comeback with some apocalyptic, biting satire, but it is not to be. Two weeks ago I was visiting Los Angeles, attempting to peddle "high concepts" in Hollywood. I was going to do this silly, witty article about it. But instead, I'm sitting at the keyboard contemplating a week of grief, both for myself and for the world of science fiction. It's been rough, my friends.

It's obvious that I'm going to talk about Ted Sturgeon. It seems that I was among the last people to talk to him,. . . May 5 when I received a message from Sharon Webb, who suggested that I call the Sturgeons. "I think he's dying," she told me. "I just spoke to him, he sounded as if he was saying goodbye." When I phoned him in Oregon, he spoke breathlessly, panting between words. I told him that my new book, *The Darkling Wind,* was dedicated to him. I had meant it to be a surprise, when it came out, but I knew it would be too late. Ted said, "I love you very much." "I love you too," I said. He said, "I know." Then he said, "Good-bye." I talked to Jayne for a while longer, but I was barely coherent from weeping. I heard his voice in the background; "Tell him, 'Thanks for the S. P. Phonecall.'" He was still making puns, weakened though he was. Only a few hours after I talked to him, I discovered later, his already critical lung condition became complicated by pneumonia, and he went into the hospital. He died three days later. His youngest son Andros told me, "I was there and it was beautiful."

I had known Ted peripherally for about seven years, and been close to him only for the last year of his life. But I can barely remember a time when I had not heard of Theodore Sturgeon. His is the single most important influence on my own work. The earliest science fiction story I can remember reading is **"The Skills of Xanadu,"** a story so rich in resonance that I based an entire tetralogy on its premise. Another seminal work of his, the novella *Some of Your Blood,* was the structural, thematic and conceptual inspiration for my novel *Vampire Junction,* which is nothing more or less than a remake of and a homage to, his book. As always, he said it all in about a twentieth of the time it took me.

I have promised to write a short eulogy for Charlie Brown's *Locus.* It will represent, as befits the stature of that magazine, a more public sort of mourning. Ted Sturgeon was, and always will be, one of the most significant figures in our field, and in a way it is hard not to find one's personal sense of loss subsumed in the far greater awe at a great man's passing.

S. P. Somtow, "Worst Week of My Life," in Fantasy Review, *Vol. 8, No. 5, May, 1985, p. 9.*

BURT A. FOLKART

Theodore Sturgeon, a prolific science fiction writer credited with humanizing that genre at a time when it was obsessed primarily with wars between worlds, died [May 8] in a Eugene, Ore., hospital. . . .

"He was an influence on most of us science fiction and fantasy writers," said Ray Bradbury, who wrote the introduction to the first of Sturgeon's nearly 30 books, **Without Sorcery,** in 1948.

The stepson of a university professor who established a daily compulsory reading program for his new son, Sturgeon became instead an indifferent student, and with his brother spent free time devouring the pulp adventure stories popular in the 1930s.

His stepfather next enrolled him at a Pennsylvania nautical school but instead of studying, Sturgeon went to sea as a laborer. It was during that subsequent three-year period that he first began to write.

By 1939, he was contributing articles to *Unknown,* a New York-based magazine that published stories of the supernatural and whose editor, John W. Campbell, was publishing and encouraging such future giants of science fiction writing as Robert A. Heinlein and Isaac Asimov.

In 1941, he published **"Microcosmic God,"** a tale of an inventor who creates a race of small creatures that quickly become more advanced than their propagator. It was his first popular success.

He eked out a living writing throughout the 1940s, and in 1952, published **More Than Human,** considered the best of his novels. It was hailed, reported the *Dictionary of Literary Biography,* for its "discovery of an ethical sense which will insure not merely its benevolence but its survival." It was awarded the International Fantasy Award.

Sturgeon brought a stream-of-consciousness technique to his characters, and his writings were compared to those of William Faulkner and James Joyce, although Sturgeon's troubled souls were found in far-flung worlds.

Some critics found him a forerunner of the New Wave generation, with his emphasis on the alienation, loneliness and eventual self-discovery of adolescents.

He also painted word portraits of women struggling for a sense of self, when few male authors were at work in that field. Homosexuals and other sexual minorities were also part of his novels and stories.

Other books by Sturgeon include **Venus Plus X, Some of Your Blood** and **The Dreaming Jewels.** Among his last was **The Golden Helix** in 1980.

In 1966-67 the television series *Star Trek* produced two of his scripts, **"Shore Leave"** and **"Amok Time."** In 1970 he won both the Hugo and Nebula (science fiction) awards for his short story **"Slow Sculpture."**

Burt A. Folkart, "Theodore Sturgeon: Noted Science Fiction Writer," in Los Angeles Times, *Part IV, May 11, 1985, p. 7.*

STEPHEN KING

[*King, an American novelist, short story writer, scriptwriter, and essayist, is an immensely popular and prolific author of horror and suspense fiction. Among his works are the novels* Carrie *(1974),* The Shining *(1977), and* Pet Sematary *(1983), the short story collections* Night Shift *(1978) and* Skeleton Crew *(1985), and a collection of essays on the horror genre,* Danse Macabre *(1981). Many of King's novels and stories have been adapted for film and television. In the following excerpt King praises Sturgeon as a stylistic innovator who raised the level of science fiction writing, and whose work compares favorably with that of mainstream writers.*]

Not many newspapers have Sunday book sections these days; a couple of brief reviews courtesy of the wire services is usually the extent of it. Not many of those that do have such sections will have anything to say about the work of Theodore Sturgeon, who died of lung disease [May 8]. Sturgeon, after all, was only a science fiction writer. In the pantheon of modern fiction, where distinctions of subject have hardened into a critical mindset almost as arbitrary and complex as the Hindu caste system, that means Sturgeon occupied a place on the literary ladder one rung above writers of westerns and one rung below the writers of mysteries.

Only a science fiction writer. But his often tender explorations of alien minds were as carefully worked out as Faulkner's exploration of the mind of Benjy, the idiot in *The Sound and the Fury.* Sturgeon's emphasis on psychology instead of blasters prepared the way for such modern masters of the genre as Robert Silverberg, Gregory Benford, John Varley, Kate Wilhelm. When science fiction made its crucial shift from pulp action to a careful consideration of what the future might hold for the emotions and the psyche as well as for the techno-toybox, Sturgeon was in the van.

Only a science fiction writer, but in **"Baby is Three"** (part of **More Than Human**) and **The Dreaming Jewels** he brought Joycean stream-of-consciousness techniques to a field which until 1954 or so had considered the prose styles of such stalwarts as E. E. "Doc" Smith and Ray Cummings perfectly adequate.

Sturgeon and Philip José Farmer (who is also only a science fiction writer) broke the sex barrier almost by themselves during the 1950s—almost alone of their kind they dared propose that the sex life of science fiction might be more than cover deep. Sturgeon did it with **Some of Your Blood,** a giddy bravura tale of a vampire who drinks not from the jugular to kill but from the menstrual flow . . . as an act of love.

His stories in fact defy categorization—beyond that implied by the Richard Powers paperback covers or the Virgil Finlay magazine illustrations, that is. He did in fact write horror stories as well as science fiction; long before Steven Spielberg's *Duel* or my *Christine*, Ted Sturgeon had linked the power train of an engine to fantasy in the nightmarish **"Killdozer."** He wrote social comedy satirizing the racial strife of the 1950s and early 1960s by creating love affairs between earthlings and aliens. He fulfilled the pulp dictum to create story before all else but the stories he created were told in an often transcending prose that almost sang as well as simply telling.

Only a science fiction writer was all Theodore Sturgeon was. Check the obits and see if I'm not right. But he also entertained, provoked thought, terrified, and occasionally ennobled. He fulfilled, in short, all the qualifications we use to measure artistry in prose.

Perhaps the best comment on how quietly such a fine writer can pass from us—like an intelligent and witty guest who slips from a party where many less interesting folk are claiming greater attention by virtue of greater volume—is this: *Book World* okayed a piece by Ray Bradbury, Harlan Ellison or me. By someone better known than Ted himself. A noisy party guest.

Considering the fact that he was only a science fiction writer, Theodore Sturgeon left exceedingly fine work behind him. Who knows? That work may be read and enjoyed long after the category itself has ceased to guarantee instant dismissal. That would be very fine.

> Stephen King, "*Theodore Sturgeon (1918-1985)*," in Book World—The Washington Post, *May 26, 1985, p. 11.*

IAN BALLANTINE

[*In 1952 American publisher Ballantine founded Ballantine Books, the first prestigious science fiction publishing company. Among the major authors published by Ballantine were Arthur C. Clarke, Frederik Pohl, and Sturgeon. In the following excerpt Ballantine outlines Sturgeon's publishing history with Ballantine Books.*]

Theodore Sturgeon had a blazing, wild talent. It was most tempting for a publisher to attempt to be of help to an author whose short stories and short novels were so very good. Besides, Ted Sturgeon was fascinating company. He was a brilliant conversationalist. His domestic complications were not without drama. One could not publish [his work] and not participate fully in Ted's life.

Ballantine Books had begun the regular publication of original science fiction both in paper and in cloth simultaneously. Major houses—Bantam and Dell—announced that the field was too limited to be of interest to them. Ballantine made modest advances against a better rate of royalty. These advances were not enough to keep a family going. When we commissioned Ted Sturgeon to amplify his prize-winning short novel **"Baby Is Three,"** Ted wrote two more short novels which he hoped to sell to the S.F. magazines. The three short novels together are the novel. Ted had the brilliance to make it work. . . .

Ted was ready to take on commissions. Having been brought up in Woodstock, New York, I have had—still do—an interest in the artistic creative process. I asked Ted for a short novel that gave the reader insight into the creative process. Ted wrote *To Here And The Easel*, published in *Star Short Novels* edited

by Fred Pohl in 1954. The short novel was not completely successful. On the other hand, it had many useful insights. There are very few writers who would accept that order of problem.

Ted Sturgeon moved up to Woodstock. One morning I encountered him in the local grocery store. He said that he had just completed a novelization of a movie script, *Four Kings and A Queen*, for Dell. He thought the story very dull. I was inspired to tell him about a non-fiction account of a modern-day vampire that had been delivered to us but which could not be published as non-fiction. I asked him to do a novelization as I believed that Ted's particular talents could relate the story of the vampire sympathetically from the vampire's point of view. Ballantine Books published *Some Of Your Blood* in 1961. It is brilliant.

Ted had moved on to work with other publishers. The whole science fiction field was enjoying unprecedented success. From my point of view Ted Sturgeon helped to create that success. It was a joy to have with Ted the excitements of imagination winning over routine.

> Ian Ballantine, "*Ted Sturgeon Eulogies: Ian Ballantine,*" in Science Fiction Chronicle, *Vol. 6, No. 10, July, 1985, p. 30.*

ROBERT BLOCH

[*Bloch is an American short story writer, scriptwriter, novelist, essayist, and editor, specializing in horror and suspense fiction. As a teenager Bloch started a friendly correspondence with his idol H. P. Lovecraft, who encouraged Bloch to write horror fiction. Bloch has published numerous short story collections, including* Sea-Kissed *(1945) and* Mysteries of the Worm *(1981), and several novels, notably* Psycho *(1959). In the following excerpt Bloch recalls his impressions of Sturgeon and expresses regret that Sturgeon's career was interrupted by writer's block.*]

Theodore Sturgeon is gone.

He was sixty-seven when he succumbed to pneumonia in Oregon on May 8th. So much for the vital statistics.

But no statistics can convey what was really vital about Ted Sturgeon. Even the details of his life—his many colorful occupations in adolescence and early manhood, his numerous marriages and divorces, a listing of his surviving offspring—would not be genuinely vital. Theodore Sturgeon's true vitality lies in his work.

His professional writing career began in 1937, accelerating during the twenty years which followed. The many short stories and all-too-few novels he produced firmly established him as one of the great talents of science fiction's Golden Age. But the man himself remained a mystery.

I first encountered Ted Sturgeon in print in the pages of *Unknown Worlds, Astounding, Weird Tales* and *Galaxy*. What I read impressed me greatly, but didn't prepare me for our first meeting in the flesh. The year was 1952; the occasion, the science fiction convention in Chicago. My introduction took place in John Campbell's suite where this personable young man with the neatly-trimmed goatee sat crosslegged on the floor, singing and playing the guitar while surrounded by an audience of admirers. He didn't seem like the kind of person who could write **"It," "Killdozer," "Microcosmic God"** or *More Than Human*. It wasn't until we met alone later that I became aware of him as a writer rather than merely a smiling, soft-spoken charmer.

We met in Chicago again, ten years later. Once more he was at a convention, accompanied by a wife and children and minus the guitar. He had, he confided, been in a writing slump for several years, and regarded his appearance as Guest of Honor at this World Science Fiction Convention as a shot in the arm that would renew the creative flow.

More than a decade passed when, in Hollywood, I found myself walking a Writers' Guild strike picket-line with Richard Matheson and Ted Sturgeon. There was a touch of grey in his beard now and a touch of melancholy in his smile, but the intellectual brilliance remained apparent on the verbal level even though it was seldom manifested in print. Subsequently, over the next two decades, we met at conventions; each time he expressed the resolution to resume fulltime writing. But he published only a few highly-acclaimed tales, and after sporadic ventures into television scripting he then devoted himself almost entirely to book reviews, teaching, lecturing and convention appearances.

For many ordinary writers in the *genre* this would mark the end of the road. But Ted Sturgeon was no ordinary writer. Thanks to its unique vitality his work endured, regularly reprinted in anthologies and collections. And it endures today, so that readers who were not yet born when his classic creations first appeared are presently discovering and delighting in Sturgeon's magic mastery of style, his compelling and compassionate explorations of human and non-human relationships.

One may damn his death, damn the writing block that robbed us of more opportunities to enjoy his consummate craftsmanship. But the literary legacy he left will, I predict, continue to enchant future generations. He has earned a permanent place in the pantheon of fantasy and science fiction immortals because the truths he tells are timeless, his insights eternally alive.

Theodore Sturgeon is *not* gone. And he will not be forgotten. (pp. 30, 32)

> *Robert Bloch, "Ted Sturgeon Eulogies: Robert Bloch," in* Science Fiction Chronicle, *Vol. 6, No. 10, July, 1985, pp. 30, 32.*

DAVID G. HARTWELL

One of the significant writers of the century is dead and the science fiction field that gave him a home should pay tribute to a man who was always ahead of his time. Famous for his writer's blocks, he nevertheless produced more than one hundred seventy-five stories and seven or more novels (depending upon how you count), as well as a significant body of reviews (I suspect that Sturgeon's Law and its corollaries will be quoted and mis-quoted for years to come) and, from the 1940s through the present, his influence as a teacher on generations of writers is incalculably great.

Ted had the advantage of making it to legendary status early on, sometime between the publication of *Without Sorcery* (1948), with its laudatory introduction by the (then) new superstar, Ray Bradbury, and the publication of *More Than Human* (1953). And it is the particular nature of Sturgeon's legend, of the SF writer as artist, that I find most significant. Because Ted Sturgeon was always a loyal and vocal member of the SF community (blocks, but no retirements or resignations) and always a literary artist. He not only taught other SF writers technique,

he stood for the idea that literary technique is worth striving for in SF. Jim Blish called him the finest self-conscious literary artist the SF field has yet produced. Samuel R. Delany has pointed out that Sturgeon was the first SF writer to stand for revision as a virtue. . . .

That Sturgeon often wrote horror or fantasy or poetry or just plain fiction (e.g., *Some Of Your Blood, Sturgeon's West*) never took him out of the SF field as a person. Here he lived and here he belonged, with all his eccentricities, friends, lovers, wives, and fictions, for nearly fifty years. He was a kind man, sincere and humane, given to passionate enthusiasms; he could sing and play the guitar; when he erred, it was on the side of sentiment. His characters are, as a group, the best yet written in SF. Robert Scholes, in *Structural Fabulation*, used a piece of Sturgeon's Nebula-winning **"Slow Sculpture"** to show a literary style functioning perfectly in place in a science fiction story.

The first time I met him I loaned him $200.00 and he repaid me promptly. The first SF paperback I ever bought was *More Than Human* (actually I bought *Childhood's End* at the same time)—a stroke of luck that is partially responsible for me being here today writing this eulogy.

Ask the next question. That was Ted's motto in later years . . . a good one for a science fiction person. Perhaps Ted is the closest one to a Slan living among us we have yet experienced. He showed us ourselves, he showed us the way to the future, he left us a rich and immense legacy in his works, he left us his love.

> *David G. Hartwell, "Ted Sturgeon Eulogies: David G. Hartwell," in* Science Fiction Chronicle, *Vol. 6, No. 10, July, 1985, p. 32.*

DAMON KNIGHT

[*Knight is an American science fiction critic, editor, novelist, short story writer, translator, and biographer. His critical writings, represented in his collection* In Search of Wonder: Essays on Modern Science Fiction *(1956), are known for their harsh, uncompromising demand for higher literary standards in science fiction. In the following excerpt Knight praises Sturgeon as an innovator and utopian visionary.*]

We began hearing his unique voice in 1939 when his first two stories were published, one in *Astounding,* the other in *Unknown:* **"Ether Breather"** and **"A God in a Garden."** Through the forties his work appeared often in *Astounding,* although he was going his own way even then and was never in philosophy a member of Campbell's group. Some of his most compelling works were fantasies—**"It,"** for example, and **"Bianca's Hands."**

Sturgeon showed us that prose can be something more than a blunt instrument, even in science fiction. He worked lovingly with the sounds of words and their rhythms, and taught more by example than the rest of us by precept. In the fifties he was the star turn of the brilliant circus assembled by H.L. Gold for *Galaxy,* with stories like **"Rule of Three,"** **"The Other Celia,"** **"Saucer of Loneliness,"** and **"The Stars Are the Styx."** *Galaxy* also published **"Baby Is Three,"** the first segment of his award-winning novel *More Than Human.*

Those were the years when he was taking love apart to see what made it tick—not just the conventional kind of love, but all the other kinds too. His **"The World Well Lost,"** published in 1953, was almost certainly the first sympathetic treatment of homosexual love in science fiction. "It is fashionable," he wrote, "to overlook the fact that the old-shoe lover *loves* loving old shoes."

He was bearded and sandaled long before it was fashionable to be so; over the years his appearance grew more Christlike, and there was always something messianic in what he wrote. Love was his theme, not repentance; he also played the guitar and sang bawdy songs.

He had a lifelong glimpse of a way people could live better together. He tried to put it into practice and did not always succeed, because other people did not rise to his standards, but he never wavered and never gave up. (pp. 32, 34)

> Damon Knight, "*Theodore Sturgeon: February 26, 1918—May 8, 1985*," *in* Science Fiction Chronicle, *Vol. 6, No. 10, July, 1985, pp. 32, 34.*

THOMAS D. CLARESON

[*Clareson, an American critic and editor, has focused his career on science fiction is such works as* Some Kind of Paradise: The Emergence of Science Fiction *(1985). He has edited many anthologies, including the series* Voices for the Future: Essays on Major Science Fiction Writers *(1976, 1979, 1983), and is editor of* Extrapolation, *a scholarly journal devoted to the genre. In the following excerpt Clareson recalls some remarks Sturgeon made at a session of the 1979 MLA Convention.*]

One of the disadvantages of editing a quarterly [*Extrapolation*] is the time lag. Consequently, because I want to say something about Ted, I have decided to let him speak for himself. At the MLA meeting in 1979 I had the privilege of chairing a session in which Ted talked about his work and the field of science fiction in general. It was the longest of a number of interviews/dialogues I had with Ted. It should have been transcribed and presented as an article, for as always, Ted said many things well. . . .

At one point he praised Joan Vinge's *The Snow Queen* and referred to Joanna Russ's *The Female Man* as a "healthy, angry book, justifiably so." He singled out the time travel stories of Robert Silverberg and called Clifford D. Simak's *City* "beautifully written and beautifully conceived." He called science fiction his "best friend and worst enemy" because of the problems a writer of science fiction has in gaining critical recognition, and he suggested that neither serious critics nor the popular audience had permitted science fiction to have the "spectrum of excellence" every other field of fiction is allowed. As might be guessed, considering the date and the substance of Sturgeon's fiction, he spoke of the fact that "women (have been) ghettoized so long" that they have had to develop sensitivities which men—who "have guns"—may not have. *Venus Plus X* grew out of his concern for "sexuality and the use of sexuality in our culture." Throughout his remarks a single theme dominated: the need for individuals and political philosophies to grow and change. He admitted, too, to being "preoccupied with love." In discussing **More Than Human** and referring to the first Milford Conference, where James Blish had asserted that each writer has a central theme, he suggested that throughout all of his work he had been "searching for the optimum human being" whose "internal ecology is beautifully balanced." Theodore Sturgeon (1918-85) was a writer, teacher, and beautifully human. (pp. 179-80)

> Thomas D. Clareson, "*The Launching Pad,*" *in* Extrapolation, *Vol. 26, No. 3, Fall, 1985, pp. 179-80.*

RODGER RAPP

[*Rapp is a contributing editor of* The Bloomsbury Review *and managing editor of* Satellite World, *an international cable and satellite communications guide. In the following excerpt Rapp, who was a friend of Sturgeon and his family, offers anecdotes about Sturgeon's life and writings.*]

Theodore Sturgeon . . . was a Writer, God bless him, and he left you, The Reader, a thought-provoking, sometimes confrontational literary legacy atypical of a genre, a country, and an age lusting afer escapist entertainment.

His many works of speculative fiction—the bastard begot of classics initially force-fed by his mother and professor stepfather, and the secretly read pulp magazines and novels of the Great Depression—are well wrought mental-interior tales denuded of snobbish moral aphorisms. *Some of Your Blood,* for example, a novel written in Woodstock, New York (Ted left the town, four children, and his second wife and headed for Hollywood years before the concert to end all concerts), is much more than an old-fashioned set-of-missals novel. Robin, Ted's first-born son, told me his father locked himself in his room for a week and lived off bottled milk and fresh blueberry pies when he wrote it; Ted didn't remember it that way.

The letters in the novel concern a military psychiatrist's analysis of a quiet private who struck his sergeant when questioned about a line in a letter he'd written. (*Dear Anna: I miss you very much. I wish I had some of your blood.*) The tale proper closes with the good doctor's disquieting discovery: the patient equates love with warm, preferably human, thicker-than-water fluids.

The italicized closing, the alien magic of canted Roman letters, is as comforting as the introduction. In the end, Ted says, The Reader is free to choose from a number of divergent fates for the confused bloodsucker, ranging from he and the girl back home got hitched and lived happily ever after, to the system righteously fried his twisted brain and locked him up for the rest of his cursed life. Or, the author suggests, one can choose to call the tale fiction, shut the book, and forget the whole thing . . . take your pick.

Ted liked to say that there is more "room" in inner space than in outer space. He put a lot of himself into his work, and he often felt drained. For Ted, and his big heart, introspection was a deep but sometimes dry well. In May of 1984, when I last sat down and talked with him—in Vail, Colorado, before the opening of a SF convention at which he was the guest of honor—we did not discuss writer's block or the stories and novels about incest, playing God, the healing power of love, murder, possession, and all the other themes a friend-of-the-family-turned-interviewer could have shamelessly plowed into.

No, while Jayne Enelhart, his companion of eight years (they met at another SF convention), served up instant coffee and Ted's tired lungs struggled with the rarified high-altitude atmosphere, he talked about gymnastics, failing high school, hitchhiking, life in the merchant marines, John Campbell, how he learned to type and later to operate heavy machinery, his first sale (a short, twisted tale about a "perfect" insurance scam that he had carefully researched but decided not to attempt), and much more. I soon found myself answering *his* questions. He mostly talked about the four children (of seven) and the ex-wife (of three) who are my friends. Jayne, and Ted's Woodstock family—Marion, Robin, Tandy, Noel, and Timothy—were among those with him in Eugene, Oregon, when those same tired lungs finally gave out [in 1985].

Ted won the International Fantasy Award in 1954 for *More Than Human,* a novel about a "homo-gestalt," comprising a set of mentally, emotionally, and physically crippled individuals who could best survive as an interlocking unit. **"Slow Sculpture,"** a tale that likens growing up and growing older to the Japanese art of bonsai, received the Nebula Award in 1970 and the Hugo Award in 1971. He also wrote numerous stories under the pseudonyms "E. Hunter Waldo" and "Frederick R. Ewing."

After Ted moved to California, he wrote scripts for *Star Trek, The Invaders,* and *Wild Wild West.* Although a number of production companies periodically bought the film rights to many of his works, the movies were not good to Ted. **"Killdozer,"** a successful if not impressive short story about an earth machine under the control of an alien intelligence pitted against a group of construction workers, was turned into a coarse, mechanical rendition of a Godzilla rampage; the actors' lips, unfortunately, were in synch with the poorly "translated" dialogue.

Orson Welles had great plans for **More Than Human,** but he soon got bogged down in plotting the cinematics of his spring-time opening sequence. After Ted saw a movie made with a new color process and was impressed with its tonal affinity to old-master paintings, he asked Welles to see it, but the self-styled old master replied, "I never watch another man's movie." While they were friends, said Ted, Welles never visited anyone in the hospital either.

Like his Woodstock friend and fellow speculative fiction writer, the late Edgar Pangborn, Ted wrote as if fiction was a mirror for observers. As he matured as a writer, however, he evolved his own notion of what a story should accomplish. As a storyteller, he compared H. G. Wells to Robert Louis Stevenson, but he described Wells' oft-repeated notion of the cataclysmic crisis as the only miracle that would unify mankind as "pitiful." Ted's characters are not cardboard-cutout heroes. They are ordinary people like you and me—some likable, some despicable—caught up in "what-if" situations while "running up the stairs in the dark, expecting a sixth step when the architect only put in five."

Rodger Rapp, "E Pluribus Unicorn: Theodore Sturgeon, 1918-1985," in The Bloomsbury Review, *Vol. 6, No. 3, February, 1986, p. 23.*

E(lwyn) B(rooks) White

July 11, 1899 - October 1, 1985

American essayist, juvenile fiction, sketch, and handbook writer, editor, and poet.

(See also *CLC,* Vols. 10, 34; *Children's Literature Review,* Vol. 1; *Contemporary Authors,* Vols. 13-16, rev. ed., Vol. 116 [obituary]; *Contemporary Authors New Revision Series,* Vol. 16.; *Something About the Author,* Vols. 2, 29; and *Dictionary of Literary Biography,* Vols. 11, 22.)

PRINCIPAL WORKS

Is Sex Necessary? or, Why You Feel the Way You Do [with James Thurber] (essays) 1929
The Lady Is Cold (poetry) 1929
Quo Vadimus? or, The Case for the Bicycle (sketches) 1939
One Man's Meat (essays) 1942
Stuart Little (juvenile fiction) 1945
Charlotte's Web (juvenile fiction) 1952
The Second Tree from the Corner (prose and poetry) 1954
The Elements of Style [with William Strunk, Jr.] (handbook) 1959
The Points of My Compass: Letters from the East (essays) 1962
The Trumpet of the Swan (juvenile fiction) 1970
Letters of E. B. White (letters) 1976
Essays of E. B. White (essays) 1977
Poems and Sketches of E. B. White (poetry and sketches) 1981

Photo © 1980 Jim Kalett

KEITH LOVE

E. B. White, one of America's foremost essayists, author of classic children's books and a guiding influence at *The New Yorker* magazine from its earliest days, died [October 1] at his farm in Brooklin, Me.

He was 86. J. Russell Wiggins, publisher of a local newspaper and a longtime friend, said White had been suffering from Alzheimer's disease.

"A few months ago, he said he had so much to tell and so little time to tell it," recalled Wiggins, a former U.S. ambassador to the United Nations who had known White since the late 1940s.

White was familiar to millions on various levels. He was the author of *Charlotte's Web, Stuart Little* and *The Trumpet of the Swan,* children's books that have also delighted adults. He was well known to writers for his updating of *The Elements of Style,* a highly praised guide to writing and English usage written by one of White's college professors, Will Strunk.

He was probably at his best, however, in his essays on American life, both urban and rural, many of which appeared in *The New Yorker.* White also wrote editorials for *The New Yorker.* And more than any other writer associated with the magazine since its founding in February, 1925, he helped set its tone and style.

White was curious but rarely passionate, intelligent but never intellectual, modern but never faddish or stylish, a city man who wrote some of his best essays about rural life.

And he was often very funny.

The magazine bought some of his light verse in 1925, and by 1929, he was given a small salary and an office. White rarely kept regular hours and would be just as likely to write from Maine as from his apartment in New York.

One of White's closest friends was James Thurber, with whom he shared an office at *The New Yorker* in the magazine's early days. It was White who taught Thurber how to write the magazine's "Talk of the Town" pieces and who helped launch Thurber's career as a cartoonist.

Thurber could not get his drawings published until 1929, when he and White collaborated on a humorous book, *Is Sex Necessary? Or Why You Feel the Way You Do.* According to White's biographer, Scott Elledge, the editor of the book trusted White's intuition that Thurber's drawings would be well received. They were so well received that Thurber was an overnight sensation as a cartoonist.

At *The New Yorker,* White was one of the first—and best— writers of witty tag lines for "news breaks," the filler items selected from American newspapers because of their typographical errors or odd statements.

In his 1984 biography of White, Elledge recounted some of White's best tag lines for news breaks, including one written for an advertisement someone spotted in a Pittsburgh newspaper. The ad read: "Gent's laundry taken home. Or serve at parties at night." White's tag line was, "Oh, take it home."

It was White who wrote the caption for the now legendary *New Yorker* cartoon showing an angry little girl at dinner with her mother. When the mother insists that the dish before her is broccoli, the child replies, "I say it's spinach, and I say the hell with it."

Although he was long associated with rural life in Maine, where he had his farm near Brooklin, Elwyn Brooks White was born July 11, 1899, in the city of Mount Vernon, N.Y., the youngest of six children whose father was president of a piano-making firm in New York City.

He attended Cornell University on a scholarship, leaving briefly during World War I to serve as a private in the Army.

It was at Cornell that White got the nickname "Andy." The school's first president had been named Andrew White, and E. B. White's classmates decided he should be called "Andy" as a prank. For the rest of his life, E. B. was known to friends and associates as Andy White.

After college, White toured the west in a Model A Ford and spent a year writing for a Seattle newspaper. He was not very happy with daily newspapering and once explained why in a letter to one of his brothers:

> I discovered . . . that writing of the small things of the day, the trivial matters of the heart . . . was the only kind of creative work which I could accomplish with any sincerity or grace. As a reporter I was a flop because I always came back laden not with facts about the case but with a mind full of the little difficulties and amusements I had encountered in my travels. Not until *The New Yorker* came along did I ever find any means of expressing these impertinences and irrelevancies.

At *The New Yorker,* White not only charmed readers with reports on life at his Maine farm or his experiences in New York, he also wrote eloquently about the evils of totalitarianism, about the need for a world government after the invention of the nuclear bomb and about the dangers of censorship.

During World War II, White joined other writers and artists on the Writers' War Board and, when assigned to define democracy in a pamphlet, he wrote:

> Surely the board knows what democracy is. It is the line that forms on the right. It is the word 'don't' in don't shove. It is the hole in the stuffed shirt through which the sawdust slowly trickles; it is the dent in the high hat. Democracy is the recurrent suspicion that more than half of the people are right more than half of the time. It is the feeling of privacy in the voting booth, the feeling of communion in the libraries, the feeling of vitality everywhere. Democracy is a letter to the editor. . . .

White won the National Medal of Literature in 1971 and a Pulitzer Prize special citation in 1978 for the body of his work.

He created a major flap in 1976, when he publicly challenged *Esquire* magazine's plan to let corporations pay writers directly for pieces in the magazine. Xerox had just paid Harrison Salisbury $55,000 for an article in *Esquire* about America at age 200.

White said, "A writer ought to be paid by the paper which is publishing the piece—that's fundamental. Otherwise, you won't know what you are reading." Xerox decided that White was right. *Esquire* dropped the experiment.

Most of White's essays were published in book form, and among the best-known collections are *The Essays of E. B. White* (1977), *The Second Tree From the Corner* (1954) and *One Man's Meat* (1942). The latter was a collection of columns White wrote in the late 1930s for *Harper's* magazine while he was living in his 160-year old clapboard farmhouse in Maine and only occasionally traveling to New York City.

From Maine he wrote about hatching goslings, the peculiarities of Maine speech, training a dog and getting ready to own a cow. He wrote that buying a cow was inevitable, because he had found a milking stool when he bought the farm and it was "handmade, smooth with the wax finish which only the seat of an honest man's breeches can give to wood."

Stuart Little was the first of White's books for children. It was about a mouse born into a human family.

His children's story, *Charlotte's Web,* about a spider who saves a pig's life by helping make it a tourist attraction, was so popular that White said it had "kept me alive, been my bread and butter."

One of White's most famous essays was entitled **"Here is New York"** (1948). In it he offered his observations about the city that both delighted and confounded him:

> On any person who desires such queer prizes, New York will bestow the gift of loneliness and the gift of privacy. . . . It can destroy an individual, or it can fulfill him, depending a good deal on luck. No one should come to New York to live unless he is willing to be lucky.

About the art of writing essays, White once wrote, "The essayist is a self-liberated man, sustained by the childish belief that everything he thinks about, everything that happens to him, is of general interest."

In his updating of *The Elements of Style,* White added a chapter called "An Approach to Style" in which he expanded on such admonishments as "place yourself in the background," "write in a way that comes naturally" and "do not affect a breezy manner."

Some years ago, White surprised many of his fans when he revealed that he rarely read books. In a later interview he elaborated:

> I've never been much of a reader. Most of my 'enrichment' did not come from reading but from other pursuits, like netting a turtle or milking a ewe. I would like to be able now, at the age of 82, to catch up with my reading, but I'm out of luck—my eyes have had it. . . .

When he received the National Medal for Literature, White said of his craft: "Writing is an act of faith, nothing else. And it must be the writer, above all others, who keeps it alive—choked with laughter or with pain." (pp. 1, 20)

> Keith Love, "New Yorker's E. B. White Dies," in Los Angeles Times, *October 2, 1985, pp. 1, 20.*

HERBERT MITGANG

E. B. White, the essayist and stylist who was one of the nation's most precious literary resouces, died [October 1] at his home in North Brooklin, Me., where he had lived for half a century. He had Alzheimer's disease and was 86 years old. . . .

William Shawn, editor of *The New Yorker,* said . . . :

> E. B. White was a great essayist, a supreme stylist. His literary style was as pure as any in our language. It was singular, colloquial, clear, unforced, thoroughly American and utterly beautiful. Because of his quiet influence, several generations of this country's writers write better than they might have done. He never wrote a mean or careless sentence. He was impervious to literary, intellectual and political fashion. He was ageless, and his writing was timeless.
>
> Watched over and inspirited by *The New Yorker*'s founding editor, Harold Ross, he and James Thurber were the writers who did most to determine the magazine's shape, tone and direction. Even though White lived much of his life on a farm in Maine, remote from the clatter of publicity and celebrity, fame overtook him, fortunately leaving him untouched. His connections with nature were intimate and ardent. He loved his farm, his farm animals, his neighbors, his family and words. . . .

He could be outspoken and passionate on subjects that were especially close to his heart—the freedom and integrity of the press, personal privacy and liberty, the intrusion of advertising, market surveys and commercialism into everyday living, the conservation of nature, the need for some form of world government. His opponents often succumbed before the force of his purity, ridicule, regret and common sense.

Mr. White's strength as a writer was rooted in his respect for his audiences—children, adolescents and adults—regardless of what the pollsters and market surveys declared as scientific truth, "No one can write decently who is distrustful of the reader's intelligence," he said. "Television has taken a big bite out of the written word. But words still count with me."

His *Elements of Style,* which he updated from the privately printed notes made in 1918 by Mr. Strunk, his former professor at Cornell, and revised several times since for new editions, has sold millions of copies. The White-Strunk book was ignored at peril by students ever since it first appeared some three decades ago. It is considered one of the most enduring and most readable books on American English usage.

The wisdom in the book is both analytical and practical. In it he says: "Vigorous writing is concise. A sentence should contain no unnecessary words, a paragraph no unnecessary sentences, for the same reason that a drawing should have no unnecessary lines and a machine no unnecessary part. This requires not that the writer make all his sentences short, or that he avoid all detail and treat his subjects only in outline, but that every word tell."

In the latest edition, more than before, words tell. For example, Mr. White called "offputting" and "ongoing" newfound adjectives to be avoided because they are inexact and clumsy.

"Ongoing is a mix of continuing and active and is usually superfluous, and offputting might mean objectionable, disconcerting or distasteful. Instead, select a word whose meaning is clear. As a simple test, transform the participles to verbs. It is possible to upset something. But to offput? To ongo?" . . .

Talking about the surprising acceptance of *The Elements of Style,* he said: "It's a funny little book, and it keeps going on. Occasionally I get irate letters from people who find a booboo in it, but many more from people who find it useful. The book is used not only in institutions of learning, but also in business places. Bosses give it to their secretaries. I guess someone in the office has to know how to write English." . . .

Mr. White was born in Mount Vernon, N.Y., on July 11, 1899. His parents had moved there from Brooklyn, he later surmised, "because Mount Vernon sounded tonier." After serving as editor in chief of *The Cornell Sun,* he worked for the United Press in New York for a year, became a reporter for *The Seattle Times* for two years, tried his hand in an advertising agency as a production assistant and copywriter, and then found his niche as a contributor to *The New Yorker* in 1927.

Recalling his early tenure at the magazine, he said, "The cast of characters in those days was as shifty as the characters in a floating poker game. Every week the magazine teetered on the edge of financial ruin. It was chaos but it was enjoyable. James Thurber and I shared a sort of elongated closet. Harold Ross fought with Raoul Fleischmann and erected an impenetrable barrier between the advertising department and the editorial department. It was known as the Ross Barrier."

A friend who visited Mr. White at home in Maine several years ago found him in good spirits. He looked like his sentences: straightforward, yet elegant.

"Don't say I live exactly in North Brooklin or buses will show up—a few have already—loaded with schoolchildren and their teachers looking for 'Stuart Little,' 'Charlotte's Web' and 'The Trumpet of the Swan,'" he said. "Maybe you can say 'somewhere on the Atlantic Coast.' If you must, make the location the way the property appears on nautical maps—Allen Cove. That way no one will be able to find it except by sailboat and using a chart."

So many letters from children are addressed to Mr. White (as well as to Stuart Little and Charlotte, his fictional creations) that Harper & Row, his publisher, has a printed reply of thanks and explanation from Mr. White. Part of his form letter goes:

Are my stories true, you ask? No, they are imaginary tales, containing fantastic characters and events. In *real* life, a family doesn't have a child who looks like a mouse; in *real* life, a spider doesn't spin words in her web. In *real* life, a swan doesn't blow a trumpet. But real life is only one kind of life—there is also the life of the imagination. And although my stories are imaginary, I like to think that there is some truth in them, too—truth about the way people and animals feel and think and act.

After having lived in Manhattan in the 1920's and 1930's, Mr. White and his wife, Katharine, sought privacy in Maine. They bought the roomy old farmhouse in 1933 and lived in it almost continuously beginning in 1938.

Their lives were linked with *The New Yorker,* where they first met in 1926. He said that Katharine Sergeant Angell was considered "the intellectual soul" of the magazine, serving as fiction editor and encouraging many gifted writers.

They were married in 1929. Mr. White later said, "I soon realized that I had made no mistake in my choice of a wife. I was helping her pack an overnight bag one afternoon when she said, 'Put in some tooth twine.' I knew then that a girl who called dental floss tooth twine was the girl for me."

They were married for 48 years, and Mr. White never quite got over her death in 1977. When her book, *Onward and Upward in the Garden,* based on her *New Yorker* pieces, came out in 1978, with an introduction by him, he wrote, "Life without Katharine is no good for me."

Until illness slowed him down, Mr. White usually rose at 6 in the morning, started the wood fire in the black four-lidded kitchen stove, checked the action in the birdfeeder dangling outside the living-room window of the 19th-century farmhouse and peered with a Maineman's eyes at the broken clouds.

When the sun broke through without advance notice, the pencils, pens and typewriters (the portable one down at the boathouse, the upright Underwood in the workroom) went into action. Mr. White turned out some of the most moral, living prose produced by hand in the country.

Even in speaking, Mr. White seemed to have the right phrase at hand. Fiddling with a thick log in the fireplace, he made it flare up quickly—more a countryman's than an author's fire.

Mr. White liked to sip a vermouth cassis before lunch. "It's a French taxi-driver's drink," he said.

Walking with a visitor over to the general store, he took a bottle of orange juice to the counter. "Hi, Al," he said to the proprietor. "Hi, Andy," the proprietor replied, and at the same time handed him a copy of the local paper, *The Ellsworth American,* published by his longtime friend J. Russell Wiggins. Now and then, he would contribute a letter or essay to the paper.

Driving on a few miles, he stopped at the boatyard run by his son, Joel, a naval architect from M.I.T. and studied the small boats jiggling on the windy waters. In a cavernous boatshed, he climbed aboard the 19-foot sloop Martha, named after his granddaughter, which his son built for him. He sailed these waters, with friends and family, most of his life.

He pointed to the carved dolphins, four on each side of the bow, that he designed and decorated in gold. Like Louis the

trumpeter swan in his book "who thought how lucky he was to inhabit such a beautiful earth," E. B. White was on the side of good luck and the angels.

Back at Allen Cove, he spotted the geese on the pond below the farmhouse and barn. He picked up some apples and waved them aloft, inviting the geese to have a snack before dinner. "Geese are the greatest clowns in the world," he said. "I wouldn't be without them."

To followers of Mr. White's work, his Maine home was historic literary territory. The barn inspired many of the characters in his stories for children. In a corner of a cellar window a spider spun a web but, he said, it was a different species from the large gray spider that lived here with Wilbur the pig in *Charlotte's Web.*

In his small gray boathouse facing the cove, he wrote *One Man's Meat,* most of *Charlotte's Web* and, he said "10,000 newsbreaks."

These are the satirical and humorous observations that round off the columns in almost every issue of *The New Yorker.* Although uncredited, they bore the White imprint for many years. Their headings became part of the language: "Neatest Trick of the Week"; "Go Climb a Tree Department"; "Letters We Never Finished Reading"; "Our Forgetful Authors"; "Funny Coincidence Department"; "Wind on Capitol Hill."

Until recently, *The New Yorker* sent him a package of news items every week. "I like doing the breaks because it gives me a feeling of holding down a job and affords me a glimpse of newspapers all over the country," Mr. White said. "I turned in my first one 50 years ago. Everybody in the shop used to do them. One day I got a call from Harold Ross asking where I was. I said I was home with the chicken pox. And he said, 'I finally get someone who can do these breaks, and he gets the chicken pox.'"

For his contribution to American letters, Mr. White was awarded the National Medal for Literature in 1971. In 1963, President Kennedy presented him with a Presidential Medal of Freedom. He was elected to the 50-member American Academy of Arts and Letters and, in 1973, received its gold medal for essays and criticism. In 1978, he received a special Pulitzer Prize for the body of his work.

Two years ago, after he had begun to slow down, he typed, with his usual good humor, a long letter to a friend: "I have a first degree heart block, have lost the sight in my right eye because of a degenerated retina, can't wind my wrist watch because my fingers have knuckled under to arthritis, can't tie my shoelaces, am dependent on seven different pills to stay alive, can't remember whether I took the pills or didn't.

"On the other hand, I am camped alone here at Bert Mosher's Camps on the shore of Great Pond which I first visited in 1904. I have my 15-foot green Old Town canoe with me, which I brought over on the top of my car. I sat out a New England boiled dinner this noon by anticipating it with martinis and cheese-and-crackers before walking up to the farmhouse, and after dinner (or lack of same) went fishing for bass in my canoe.

"There is a certain serenity here that heals my spirit, and I can still buy Moxie in a tiny supermarket six miles away. Moxie contains gentian root, which is the path to the good life. This was known in the second century before Christ, and it is a boon to me today."

Herbert Mitgang, "E. B. White, Essayist and Stylist, Dies," in The New York Times, October 2, 1985, p. B9.

LESLIE HANSCOM

He was a "goodbye sayer," E. B. White observed of himself, a man who was inclined to deliver "noisy and ill-timed farewells." It was in that spirit that he quit *The New Yorker* in 1937 and went for good to live on a farm on the coast of Maine. In extenuation of this trait, he added, however, that he was also "like a drunk at a wedding he is enjoying to the hilt and has no real intention of leaving."

White died [October 1] in Maine, leaving behind him a personal imprint on the American language which makes his habit of farewells hollow of meaning. It looks from here as though he has no chance of really going away.

Even if he should cease to be read as the master essayist he was, he will live on in the influence he exerted on the way other writers write. White was the writer whom every journalist conscious of the delicacy and potency of language aspired in some way to resemble. He showed us that the British don't own English. In his hands, English with a distinctively American accent was as comely a thing as English written at the source.

He was a writer who never wrote a novel, or a history or a work of systematic ideas. He wrote journalistic essays, light verse and books for children. In the modesty of his themes, he was a minor writer, but not in the artistry with which he executed the work. The language of White had the loveliness of a Shaker chair, wrought with a simplicity which puts all fanciness to rebuke. A sentence written by him was taut and spare and gave the feeling that, . . . if you took hold of it and stretched it to arm's length, it would inevitably snap back into precisely the same shape.

To try to write about him is a nervous and self-conscious act, because he is part of the conscience with which one writes. He wrote, one wants to say, with an impregnable perfection, but a phrase like that would never get past his editorial pencil. Come off it, he would say, perfection is perfection; you don't need to decorate it with an adjective. White's way of creating an image with words was to write of his geese in winter walking on "their orange snowshoes" which for giving a picture to the eye is as good as any camera.

The great presence which he made of himself in journalism began to be felt all of 60 years ago, when he started contributing sketches to *The New Yorker* the year it was founded. The next year, 1926, he joined the magazine's staff as a writer and editor. His performance in both jobs made him responsible, probably more than any other individual—including Harold Ross, the founding editor—for establishing *The New Yorker*'s unique tone. It was a blend of urbanity, gentle skepticism, playfulness and common sense, all of which traits corresponded to the personality of E. B. White. As a contributor to the magazine's Notes and Comments department, he wrote unsigned pieces. They didn't need a byline. The voice was unmistakable.

It balanced elegance with down-home colloquialism and spoke in direct statement. . . .

In later years, when he published *The Elements of Style,* a revised and expanded set of instructions for writers, first devised by his old Cornell professor, William Strunk Jr., it was

that kind of plainness which he recommended to others. "Place yourself in the background," he counseled, "write in a way that comes naturally; work from a suitable design; write with nouns and verbs; revise and rewrite; do not overwrite; do not overstate; avoid the use of qualifiers; do not affect a breezy manner."

He practiced a literary manner which was always on guard against eccentricity, but in his personal makeup, he was not without quirks. There is a story that Harold Ross once observed White, with his *New Yorker* colleagues, James Thurber and Wolcott Gibbs, pausing at a curbside. To a companion, Ross remarked that such were the people he had to work with—one of them (Thurber) too blind to cross the street, another (Gibbs) too drunk to cross the street and the third one afraid to cross the street. White, who was a consummate hypochondriac, lived in a world full of menace. It was to nurse his delicate health and find a tranquil place to die that he left *The New Yorker* after a dozen years of brilliant service and moved with his wife to Maine, where he was to live and do productive work for almost another half century.

White had been born in the New York suburb of Mount Vernon, but that was one of destiny's mistakes. The coast of Maine, where the natives use words sparingly and relish the humor of understatement, was the place where he should have been from, and it was the place from which he never again moved. He liked being out of the way and warily guarded his privacy.

Garrison Keillor, the radio humorist and *New Yorker* writer of a later era, remarked on the air . . . that the one reason White ranked first among his heroes was that, unlike Keillor, he never showed himself in public except, very reluctantly now and then, to accept an honorary university degree.

The honors he couldn't escape. When he published **One Man's Meat,** a collection of essays he had written for *Harper's* magazine during World War II, it won the Gold Medal of The Limited Editions Club as "a work most likely to attain the stature of a classic."

One award which was notably appropriate in light of the veneration which fellow journalists felt for him was the Page One Award of the Newspaper Guild, given to him in 1954 for **The Second Tree from the Corner,** a collection of his periodical pieces over the past 20 years. It was this book which inspired the philosopher Irwin Edman to write, "It is high time to declare roundly what a good many people have long suspected; E. B. White is the finest essayist in the United States."

Literary reputations being wayward, especially in the period shortly following an admired author's death, it would be rash to predict whether Edman's words are an unalterable statement. White, however, in his canny way, put a couple of props under his name which give it extra promise of lingering with us. Nothing is more durable than a classic children's story, and in **Charlotte's Web,** White wrote one. Legions of children who were read to sleep with this seductive tale of a pig and a wise barn spider feel bound to read it to their own children. The other work which promises to keep White's name to the front is the guide to writing already cited.

After decades of teaching others how to write by force of example, White in 1959 put out the now standard reference work in which he at last taught by precept. In **The Elements of Style,** there is no formula for enabling anybody else to write like E. B. White, but it enables anybody who has something to say to say it well. The book contains what is probably the one best piece of advice ever given to users of language. When you want to say something, White instructs, make sure you have said it, because your chances of having done so are only fair.

In his retreat in Maine, White outlived his wife by seven melancholy years and, contrary to his expectations, outlived the majority of human beings. Some time ago, when an editor of this newspaper asked him to write a piece on old age, he declined, using old age as the excuse, but told the editor what longevity felt like. "I feel like a young man," he said, "with something terribly wrong with him." . . .

In the wake of White's death, no American similarly stands for integrity in the use of the language of reporting. It almost seems there needn't be. To older journalists, White will always be here looking over our shoulders. For those to come, he will probably be here too, but, as White would caution, don't over state.

Leslie Hanscom, "A Master of Plain Speech," in Newsday, *October 2, 1985.*

HENRY MITCHELL

E. B. White . . . took pains not to be grand and all for naught; he wound up grand for all his avoidances of grandeur, and the more he avoided noble and elevated style the more convinced his readers were that he was noble—a word not always trotted out for writers of short and casual pieces.

He joined *The New Yorker* in 1926 (it was founded in 1925) and his work was often unsigned, as in his "Talk of the Town" sketches. His work was better than that of most others at the magazine, and readers soon started pawing through the pages for traces of E. B. White and were commonly rewarded.

But he did not assume superstar status and while there was, of course, a slight letdown when one passed from him to other writers equally full of comment, still his writing was a garland for the team, you might say, rather than a spotlight so blinding that the others looked poor.

He has been called the best American essayist of the century, though most of his readers possibly have wondered who the competition was supposed to be.

His work was civil and polite; he either had no gift of vitriol or else never felt any. He was commonly funny, never in the high breathtaking way of an Aristophanes and never in the sparkling knock-'em-dead manner of the century's favorite one-line wits.

He gave the impression of getting through the day like an ordinary hard-pressed man trying to remember the hour of a meeting and the need to pick up dog food before the store closed, but then retiring for a time to think what the hell is *this* all about.

He achieved answers, and one of them was not to get carried away with words, to seem to feel more than he felt, and not to feel (in writing) in the first place without thinking it over a spell.

The trouble with many potentially nice writers is that once they think about things they either conclude (often correctly, no doubt) they have nothing to say and therefore write nothing, or they bull it through anyway to the temporary dazzlement of the easily dazzled, but not to the sustenance or delight of the civilized.

Nobody who only met and talked with White through a long and golden day at his house in Maine has any real idea of his life, however gratifying to see the deep courtesy and affection shown his wife of many years and his near-adoration of a rather grim and almost certainly brain-damaged terrier named Jones who despised the world and everything in it except his master whom he had conveniently converted to slavery. To love an unlovable dog suggests depths of commitment worth remarking.

White was a lyrical man in the sense that if wonder is lacking it is impossible to write at all, but because he was polite and therefore restrained and because he descended from respectable people who had an iron vase on the lawn and doubtless thought well of Emerson, he distrusted a too-easy loveliness and mush in general, first, because he wished to be honest all the way through and not to paint things sweeter than those things are, and second, because he had sufficient technical competence to notice that rhapsodies defeat the lofty effect aimed at.

He was not sentimental, or his work was not. He liked taking care of sheep partly because he simply loved animals, partly because he loved the bondage animals incur—lambs are invariably born at disgusting cold seasons and during prolonged and inconvenient hours—and partly, one may guess, because he liked to think of himself as a new Hesiod, bound through the night by the requirements of the beasts and through the day by the routine of the farmer's lot. He did not fool himself he was a plain farmer or did the hard work of a farmer, but he took extraordinary care to keep in touch with the cycling of the sun and the reality of growth and death.

Things must have welled up in him not just sometimes but most of the time. He had a powerful sense of life's sweetness and took the risk (a risk for a writer) of letting it show. He liked to set the stage by opening one of his pieces in a matter-of-fact way, forecasting in only the most tenous way how the piece would end:

> To perceive Christmas through its wrapping becomes more difficult with every year.

He speaks of those ear trumpets hunters can buy to hear the otherwise inaudible and distant music of the hounds, and says something of the kind would help us hear Christmas. But, alarmed this might seem a little too sweet, he follows it:

"We rode down on an escalator the other morning . . ." just to show you he does not avoid commonplace things or ugly words like escalators. Then he dares an emotional charge again, but damps it down at once, but goes on to prepare for the climax by orderly reasoning and useful but not blinding images. He remains conversational, casual, letting the effect of brooding build up very gradually, alluding to rabbit tracks, rocket travel, packages of energy and so on, to show you this is only ordinary thought and ordinary stuff. Then the thing he has with difficulty been holding back and is now ready to let fly:

> This week many will be reminded that no explosion of atoms generates so hopeful a light as the reflection of a star seen appreciatively in a pasture pond. It is there we perceive Christmas—and the sheep quiet and the world waiting.

Intellectually it may make no great sense; Christmas is not perceived by anything in any pond, but what he really wants to get to is "and the sheep quiet and the world waiting," and by the time he gets you to it there are few readers whose throats have not got tense.

One of his funny masterful wrenching sketches concerned a wimp's visit to a psychiatrist, during which he felt nervous, afraid, a general incompetent mess. He goes out on the street and something magical happens; he sees trees on the street and focuses on the second one from the corner. White wants to say what the Damascus Road is like, and how the soul can leap from a dingy cave to the high clear ether in a bound, but he will show it, not talk about it. He will show it funny, pathetic, stupid—he will sketch us as we are most of the time. He will also show the transcendent minute in which the wimp looks at the ordinary tree of a city street, and after the nonsense of his psychiatric session and its attendant confusion and garble about what he really wants, he looks at the tree:

> "I want the second tree from the corner, just as it stands," he said, answering an imaginary question from an imaginary physician. And he felt a slow pride in realizing that what he wanted none could bestow, and that what he had, none could take away. He felt content to be sick, unembarrassed at being afraid; and in the jungle of his fear he glimpsed (as he had so often glimpsed them before) the flashy tail feathers of the bird courage.

Then he winds up with a paragraph of funny letdown. Only not before attempting and achieving in a mere handful of paragraphs a stunning salute to the soul of man in a way that makes nobody wince at the gush, and in a way that makes anybody proud to be a poor bifurcated simian and immortal diamond.

Never mind the "classic" children's books so lavishly praised, and rightly praised. Turn to *The Second Tree From the Corner,* a good start and a good finish to the man or to any man.

Virgil reported on the kingdom of the dead and Socrates, too, modest to claim any knowledge of it, yet looked forward to speaking there with the heroes, arguing the sweet day long. They wrestle (Virgil assures us) on the yellow sands in sport. And there are the sons of Teucros, they are not without beauty.

White's sad and grateful readers may in their own vision see that wrestling on that yellow sand today. Dear Lord, if it isn't E. B. White and his dachshund Fred, the one so interested in the farm pigs, the one so full of mischief (White used to go visit his grave) and with whom White could not romp for all these recent years. Look at them going at it. They are not without beauty. (pp. D1, D14)

> *Henry Mitchell, "The Man Behind the Mastery," in* The Washington Post, *October 2, 1985, pp. D1, D14.*

THE NEW YORKER

This page, our Notes and Comment page, belongs to E. B. White. He began writing our editorials under that heading some months after Harold Ross, our first editor, founded the magazine in 1925, and he continued to write them week after week, with an endless flow of ideas and an unflagging spontaneity, for thirty years. He died on his farm in Maine [October 1], at the age of eighty-six. As an essayist, as a humorist, as a stylist, he was one of America's masters. In his paragraphs here he developed a new literary form: brief personal essays, conversational, lyrical, idiosyncratic, yet somehow capable of striking some chord common to all of us. He took events as they came along—ordinary household events, farm events, national and world events—and, sifting them through his odd, playful mind, came out with conclusions and observations that were sensible to the point of genius. He was not a man for profundities or large abstractions; he stayed with the details of everyday living, which necessarily included tragedies and calamities of every kind—wars and political and social upheavals and natural disasters, and the rest—but he remained calm through it all, and even unreasonably optimistic, without ever lapsing into frivolity or foolishness. He never raised his voice, in or out of print, but he had a lively conscience and he was an early and brave defender of civil liberties, social justice, and the environment. His softspoken eloquence was heard. Humor pervaded whatever he wrote; the touch remained light; he ran counter to our century's fashion for literary despair, and did not try to tamper with his inexplicably sunny inclinations. For that matter, he sometimes seemed unaware of the very intellectual and literary fashions he was resisting. This most companionable of writers kept to himself in his personal life: a private man who, when he was not at his typewriter, did farm chores and spent fond hours with his wife (on whom he doted) and children and grandchildren and great-grandchildren and neighbors. He kept busy, too, with his own thoughts, which must have been as unexpected and pleasurable to him as to his readers, for, renowned as his writing was for its simplicity and its clarity, his mind constantly took surprising turns, and his peculiar mixture of seriousness and humor could not have failed to astonish even him.

Whether he was writing Notes and Comment regularly, as he did until 1955, or sporadically, as he did after that, Andy White also managed to provide the magazine with countless humor pieces, short stories, poems, and tag lines for our newsbreak fillers, taking time out to compose a series of marvellous essays for *Harper's* and to write three children's books—*Stuart Little, Charlotte's Web,* and *The Trumpet of the Swan*—which became classics. In his Comment pieces and his other writings, he did as much as any other single writer to set the tone and create the spirit of *The New Yorker.* Like his unforgettable mentor, Harold Ross, he left his mark on every page of the magazine, and his presence continues, and will always continue, to be felt in our pages. Ross was so enchanted with White's work that he had moments when he wished that all writers were E. B. White. In his more restrained moments, he was content to welcome the diverse styles and diverse interests of his other writers and to accept White as just the model. For White did serve as a model, not only at *The New Yorker* but for many, if not most, of our country's writers. Other writers took their bearings from him, and learned from him a respect for craft and discipline and the language. Because so many writers have acknowledged his influence, it seemed to us appropriate to ask two writers who themselves have contributed greatly to the magazine to speak about Andy White here, each in his own way. What follows is what they have said.

. . . . .

White had abundantly that most precious and least learnable of writerly gifts—the gift of inspiring affection in the reader. Affection and trust, for the writer we like is the one who never gives us anything less than the trustworthy truth, in his version of it, delivered up without fuss or shame. For some reason, I keep thinking back to White's version of his own career, transparently fictionalized as that of a Mr. Volente in a story called **"The Hotel of the Total Stranger."** It all began when a waitress in a Childs restaurant spilled a glass of buttermilk down his blue serge suit: "Mr. Volente had written an account of the catastrophe at the time and had sold it to a young and inexperienced magazine, thus making for himself the enormously important discovery that the world would pay a man for setting down a simple, legible account of his own misfortunes." The magazine, of course, was this one, and for more than half a century after that spilled buttermilk White's confessions, observations, poems, and stories awakened the laughter and enhanced the alertness of its readers. Elsewhere, too—in other magazines and in surprising forms, in his three classic short novels for children and in the revisions of a Cornell professor's guide to English usage—his intensely lucid brand of simple legibility sparkled. He would try anything, from a rondeau to a cartoon caption, from collaborating with James Thurber on a book ostensibly about sex to collaborating with his goddaughter on a non-posthumous volume of his own letters; and everything in his widely assorted works is lit from within by a certain bold and jaunty restlessness. Though timid about air travel, he moved nimbly on land and, in one series of essays for *The New Yorker,* dispatched letters from all points of the compass. He ranged far in his quest for artistic freedom. His young life was animated by a number of sudden excursions and departures. Mr. Volente recalls with pleasure "the renewal of liberty" that comes with quitting a job: "The sense of the return of footlooseness, the sense of again being a reporter receiving only the vaguest and most mysterious assignments, was oxygen in his lungs." Young and aspiring in an era when urban gaiety was plentiful, and witty humorists were common, he became a humorist, and, with his fastidious verbal timing and frequent sensations of bemusement, one of the best; but he was a humorist with broad perspective, a light-verse writer who could also ask, in the poem **"Traveler's Song,"** "Shall I love the world That carries me under, That fills me full Of its own wonder And strikes me down With its own thunder?" White was a man in love with beauty, with nature, and with human freedom, and these concerns lifted his essays to an eloquence that could be sombre and that sets them on the shelf with those of Thoreau. The least pugnacious of editorialists, he was remarkably keen and quick in the defense of personal liberty and purity of expression, whether the threat was as overt as McCarthyism or totalitarianism or as seemingly innocuous as the Xerox Corporation's sponsorship of an *Esquire* article or Alexander Woollcott's endorsement of a brand of whiskey. American freedom was not just a notion to him; it was an instinct, a current in the blood, expressed by his very style and his untrammelled thought, his cunning informality, his courteous skepticism, his boundless and gallant capacity for wonder.

• • • • •

Last August, a couple of sailors paid an unexpected visit to my summer house in Maine: *young* sailors—a twelve-year-old girl and an eleven-year-old boy. They were a crew taking part in a statewide small-boat-racing competition at a local yacht club, and because my wife and I had some vacant beds just then we were willingly dragooned as hosts. They were fine company—tanned and shy and burning with tactics but amenable to blueberry muffins and our exuberant fox terrier. They were also readers, it turned out. On their second night, it came out at the dinner table that E. B. White was a near neighbor of ours, and our visitors reacted to the news with incredulity. "No!" the boy said softly, his eyes travelling back and forth over the older faces at the table. *"No-o-o-o!"* The girl, being older, tried to keep things in place. "He's my favorite author,"

she said. "Or at least he was when I was younger." They were both a bit old for *Stuart Little, Charlotte's Web,* and *The Trumpet of the Swan,* in fact, but because they knew the books so well, and because they needed cheering up (they had done badly in the racing), arrangements were made for a visit to E. B. White's farm the next morning.

White, who had been ill, was not able to greet our small party that day, but there were other sights and creatures there to make us welcome: two scattered families of bantam hens and chicks on the lawn; the plump, waggly incumbent dog, name of Red; and the geese who came scuttling and hissing up the pasture lane, their wings outspread in wild alarm. It was a glazy, windless morning, with some thin scraps of fog still clinging to the water in Allen Cove, beyond the pasture; later on, I knew, the summer southwest breeze would stir, and then Harriman Point and Blue Hill Bay and the islands would come clear again. What wasn't there this time was Andy White himself: emerging from the woodshed, say, with an egg basket or a length of line in his hand; or walking away (at a mid-slow pace, not a stroll—never a stroll—with the dog just astern) down the grassy lane that turns and then dips to the woods and shore; or perhaps getting into his car for a trip to town, getting aboard, as he got aboard any car, with an air of mild wariness, the way most of us start up on a bicycle. We made do without him, as we had to. We went into the barn and examined the vacant pens and partitions and the old cattle tieups; we visited the vegetable garden and the neat stacks of freshly cut stovewood; we saw the cutting beds, and the blackberry patch behind the garage, and the place where the pigpen used to be—the place where Wilbur was born, surely. The children took turns on the old single-rope swing that hung in the barn doorway, hoisting themselves up onto the smoothed seat, made out of a single chunk of birch firewood, and then sailing out into the sunshine and back into barnshadow again and again, as the crossbeam creaked above them and swallows dipped in and out of an open barn window far overhead. It wasn't much entertainment for them, but perhaps it was all right, because of where they were. The girl asked which doorway might have been the one where Charlotte had spun her web, and she mentioned Templeton, the rat, and Fern, the little girl who befriends Wilbur. She was visiting a museum, I sensed, and she would remember things here to tell her friends about later. The boy, though, was quieter, and for a while I thought that our visit was a disappointment to him. Then I stole another look at him, and I understood. *I think* I understood. He was taking note of the place, almost checking off corners and shadows and smells to himself as we walked about the old farm, but he wasn't trying to remember them. He looked like someone who had been there before, and indeed he had, for he was a reader. Andy White had given him the place long before he ever set foot on it—not this farm, exactly, but the one in the book, the one now in the boy's mind. Only true writers—the rare few of them—can do this, but their deed to us is in perpetuity. The boy didn't get to meet E. B. White that day, but he already had him by heart. He had him for good.

Like some other people in my line, I suppose, I still remember the struggles I endured in my twenties, and even into my thirties, when I was trying to find my feet as a writer. What I was looking for, without quite knowing it, was a tone of voice—a way of getting words down that seemed to suit not just the story at hand but me, the person who was trying to tell it. I kept getting it wrong, because I thought it was incumbent on me to sound like a writer; I think I half believed that if some editor or reader caught a glimpse of me in the underbrush of my own prose he would order me out of there forth-with, because the world of letters was posted. It belonged to authors—the landed literary, whose tweeds and gestures and tones of voice were known to us all, and copied, of course, by those of us who secretly wanted to belong. For a long time, then, I dressed up in the styles of my time: terse and brave, like Hemingway; rough and low-down, like O'Hara; sad and windy, like Wolfe. I wasn't happy in these disguises, of course, but I didn't know any better; young writers have more sense about this today, I suspect. It was White who set me straight. I'd been reading him right along, to be sure, but the qualities of *One Man's Meat* and *Quo Vadimus?* and the Comment pieces and **"The Fox of Peapack"** and **"Here Is New York"** and the rest were so plain and so clearly pleasurable—a glass of cool water, a breeze on one's face—that they did not feel like lit-erature. A man who set down words that way, who obviously wrote only as he spoke, which is to say clearly and quietly by habit, and who seemed to finish many of his sentences with a shrug or a smile, a shy fellow, always on the point of sidling out of the room—well, he was there to be liked and befriended but surely not to be emulated. It took me a while to see how foolish this notion was, but when I did see, I stopped imitating other writers (even E. B. White), and tried instead to be clear, the way he was. If I could do only that—how hard it turned out to be!—I might have a voice of my own after all, and perhaps even a style in the end, too, for I would be simply myself: my one and only. I think that this is White's special gift to us all. Almost without our noticing it, he seemed to take down the fences of manner and propriety and pomposity in writing, and to invite the rest of us, readers and writers alike, to walk the fields and spinneys and weedy pathways of our own thoughts and experiences, shadowed or shining, and to enjoy the outing and the day.

E. B. White was admired and loved by readers of all ages, but, like other splendid donors, he found some critics as well. It was said of him once that you could read his entire works and never know that Freud or Marx had ever lived. The barb glitters as it flies through the air, but somehow it leaves the man untouched. He would agree, one senses—another smile, another small shrug—but he would not then set about becoming more political or more at one with his psyche. He never wished his readers to think him deeper or wiser than he found himself to be. Relieved of that frightful burden, he got more of himself onto paper in a lifetime than most writers come close to doing. Our knowledge of him seems wonderfully clear, like the view back down a series of steep meadows climbed on a cool day in autumn; and, looking back over that long path, one cannot imagine a leaf or a word that might have made it better. (pp. 31-3)

> "E. B. White," in The New Yorker, *Vol. LXI, No. 34, October 14, 1985, pp. 31-3.*

PAUL GRAY

Imagine a house filled with books, and then try to track down the one bearing his name. *The Elements of Style* should be somewhere by the desk where the letters get written. The clutter of the children's rooms ought to yield dog-eared copies of *Charlotte's Web, Stuart Little* and *The Trumpet of the Swan.* The *Essays* and *Letters* are both within easy reach of the over-stuffed armchair in front of the fireplace. For *A Subtreasury of American Humor,* the best bet is probably the bedside table in the guest room, where Aunt Mary left it a month or so ago.

E. B. White's death [October 1] at 86, was cause for sadness in many spots in millions of homes. . . .

Because he so consistently favored straight talk over polemics and specific details over abstractions, White has been dismissed in some quarters as a miniaturist a little too long on charm and short on substance. It is true that big ideas seldom engaged him unless they could be broken down into parts that made clear and common sense. His response to the hue and cry for loyalty oaths during the Communist witch hunts in the early 1950s was typical. He ignored ideology and compressed the body politic into a single form: "If a man is in health, he doesn't need to take anybody else's temperature to know where he is going."

Since he so carefully watched and reported the small workings of nature, nothing that White wrote is very far removed from the central subject of life and death. In the long run, if there is one, *Charlotte's Web* should overshadow any number of manifestos. The story of how Wilbur the pig was saved by the unusual weaving skills of Charlotte the spider has taught count-less children, many of them now middle-aged, how to weep and exult at the same moment. Wilbur's tribute to his departed benefactor bears repeating, with a nod to the man who created them both: "It is not often that someone comes along who is a true friend and a good writer."

> *Paul Gray, "A Master of Luminous Prose," in* Time, *Vol. 126, No. 15, October 14, 1985, p. 105.*

JOSEPH EPSTEIN

[Epstein is an American essayist, nonfiction writer, critic, and editor. His books include Divorced in America: Marriage in an Age of Possibility *(1974) and* Plausible Prejudices: Essays on American Writing *(1985). Since 1975 he has edited* American Scholar, *the Phi Beta Kappa publication. He has also contributed essays and articles to publications such as* Commentary, *the* New Criterion, *and the* New Yorker. *In the essay from which the following excerpt is taken, Epstein presents a lengthy biography of White and discusses the troubled, gloomy side of the author's personality.]*

I have recently been reading through the works of E. B. White, a writer of whom I hitherto had a most blurry and inexact picture, and the one thing that can be unequivocally said about him is that one has to search very sedulously indeed to find a gloomier writer than E. B. White. The gloom is not merely incidental but pervasive in his writing. He is, moreover, a relentless preacher, as perhaps befits one whose own favorite writer was that consummate American preacher in prose, Henry David Thoreau. Isaac Rosenfeld's review of *Wild Flag,* a 1946 collection of White's "Notes and Comment" editorials from the *New Yorker,* was entitled "Chopping a Teakettle," from the Yiddish phrase *hacken a tcheinik.* "Not only does he chop away with an unfailing stroke," Rosenfeld wrote, "but he manages to keep a cloud of steam issuing from the spout as he works." The editorials in *Wild Flag* are about world gov-ernment, but before he lays down his ax, White has worked on several teakettles: the environment, bureaucracy, the horrors of modern life. He turns out to be something of a Jeremiah, but with a plain prose style.

This is not the figure, the precious literary resource, most people think of when they think of E. B. White. Most people, I suspect, think of E. B. White as the archetypical *New Yorker* writer of the early days of that magazine; not quite so anarchical in his humor as James Thurber, or so wickedly witty as Wolcott Gibbs, but very clever, always in good taste, and never heavy—

a White Lite, to adapt both the concept and the spelling favored by the American low-calorie beer industry. Later, when White removed himself from New York to live on a farm on Allen's Cove, near North Brooklin, Maine, he became a naturalized New Englander, a man who, it was believed, lived close to the earth and whose prose, it was also believed, took on some of the good sense that comes from plain living among plain people. His success with his children's books served to enhance his reputation—and, into the bargain, to authenticate his sensitivity. You cannot, after all, fool children about these things, can you? There was, then, something of a saintly aura about White, and the older he grew, the more honored he became, the saintlier he seemed. "I wouldn't mind being as old as E. B. White," said Kurt Vonnegut, "if I could actually *be* E. B. White."

E(lwyn) B(rooks) White was born in 1899, the sixth, the last, and the late-life child of an upper-middle-class family in Mount Vernon, New York. He was brought up in a rambling Victorian house. His father, who had begun to prosper when White was born, was the general manager and vice-president of Horace Waters & Company, a firm that sold musical instruments. The single blot on White's otherwise pacific childhood was that his father was charged with, but later acquitted of, fraud in connection with a stock transaction—an event he harks back to in *The Trumpet of the Swan,* the last of his children's books.

From his father, who each summer took the family on vacation to Maine, White acquired a love of the natural world and a respect for order and precision. (In the White family, when a child did not know the meaning of a word, he was sent upstairs to consult *Webster's Unabridged Dictionary.*) From his mother, whose own father was a painter, he acquired a respect for art, shyness, and a strong strain of hypochondria that was never to leave him. (Interesting, is it not, that hypochondriacs seem to be so long-lived?) The large house in Mount Vernon had an expansive lawn, a fine garden, servants, animals—all the things, together with parental love, that ought to make for boyhood happiness, but in E. B. White's case did not, or at least not quite.

Scott Elledge, E. B. White's biographer, begins the second chapter of his book by remarking, "White was born lucky, as he has often said, but he was also born scared. . . ." And it is true that in his portraits of and random comments about his youth, a combination of melancholy and anxiety hangs over everything. (p. 49)

Although he was of the generation of E. E. Cummings and Edmund Wilson, Wallace Stevens and William Faulkner, high art was never the name of his desire. He had no wish to write the intricate poem or the experimental novel, and so far removed from great artistic ambitions was he that (he once claimed) it took him fully fourteen months to read *Anna Karenina.* What did attract him was the world of smart journalism, the world of H. L. Mencken and Don Marquis and Christopher Morley and F.P.A., in whose New York *World* column, "The Conning Tower," White had published an occasional squib. These were the days, recall, of the wits of the Algonquin round table: Robert Benchley, Alexander Woollcott, Dorothy Parker, Heywood Broun, Frank Sullivan, and Ring Lardner. It was in the atmosphere of smart journalism, and through the efforts of such writers, that Harold Ross planned and brought to fruition his dream for the weekly magazine first published on February 19, 1925 and known as the *New Yorker. . . .*

[The] marriage of E. B. White with the *New Yorker* was perhaps the most crucial event in the magazine's history.

Although the *New Yorker* has accommodated in its pages writers as various in style and intellectual range as Hannah Arendt and S. J. Perelman, A. J. Liebling and Kenneth Tynan, Harold Rosenberg and Garrison Keillor—its editorial capaciousness has been part of its genius—it is the magazine's tone that has been chiefly responsible for its success. That tone was early set by E. B. White, and even today, decades after White ceased regularly to supply the magazine with the editorials known as "Notes and Comment," the reigning tone of the *New Yorker* remains White's. The tone itself is an attempt at a compound of whimsy and common sense, modesty and decency, from which pretentiousness and heavy-handedness generally are extruded. The tone shimmers with an implied sensitivity, the chief implication being that we readers are ourselves highly sensitive characters—intelligent, good-humored, tasteful. (p. 50)

By the mid-1930's E. B. White's fame, though more than intramural, was not yet anything like national in the way it was one day to become. He had published a collection of his *New Yorker* pieces, along with a few volumes of light verse and a collaboration with James Thurber entitled *Is Sex Necessary?* Around New York he was thought of as a pro—a man of modest but real talents who could get the job done. (p. 51)

In the summer of 1937, at the age of thirty-eight, E. B. White awarded himself a year's sabbatical. *Time* magazine, noting his departure from the *New Yorker,* remarked that he was giving "himself time to think about progress and politics, whether to get out of their jumpy way or try to catch up with them." But *Time* was mistaken. White had taken leave to devote himself to a lengthy writing project. A bad idea whose time never came, this project was to be a long autobiographical poem, but White was able to make no headway with it, which redoubled his frustration. "I have made an unholy mess out of this 'year off' business," he wrote to Thurber. He spoke of envying those people who could write without being lashed to deadlines. Never quite comfortable in Manhattan, he now moved permanently to his farm in North Brooklin, Maine. He yearned to make something of his life; he yearned to be more than a mere journalist; he yearned—though he never used the word—for significance.

Although E. B. White continued to do various editorial chores for the *New Yorker* and would go on writing for it until the last few years of his life, in 1938 he made what appeared to be a break when he signed on to contribute a monthly essay of 2,500 words to *Harper's.* (pp. 51-2)

The break, less than complete though it was, could not have been all that easy for White, even if he was eager to put an end, as he said, to "his long apprenticeship in the weekly gaiety field." Well before Heisenberg discovered it, uncertainty was a principle for E. B. White, who felt himself not only something of a lightweight but a sad failure as well. When, in 1938, he wrote a letter of general self-deflation to James Thurber, putting himself down for his own insignificance, Thurber responded that, in the present tumultuous age, the need for humor was all the greater, and that White ought not to be ashamed of providing some of it. . . .

To the gloominess of the times—the civil war in Spain, the ascendancy of Hitler in Germany and Mussolini in Italy, the entry of the United States into World War II—White joined his own gloominess of temperament. When he became a full-blown essayist, at least partially free from "the gaiety field," the "I" who emerged from the "we" of the editorialist was more melancholic, dark, and depressed than most of E. B. White's earlier readers would have been likely to suppose....

While life in Maine for White was less anxious than life in New York—about which he had written a famous essay—he was still able to discover the cloud in every silver lining. Read cumulatively, the *Harper's* essays (brought together in a book entitled *One Man's Meat*) are dark indeed. (p. 52)

Owing to a strong attack he had written for *Harper's* on Anne Morrow Lindbergh's *The Wave of the Future,* a book arguing the isolationist case against America's entry into World War II, and other pieces he had written against fascism and on behalf of democracy, White had become something of a spokesman for what in bygone days used to be called "the American way of life." (As an opponent of fascism, White, it is worth noting, early condemned the Nazis' savage treatment of Jews in Germany.) Evidence of his new and greatly enhanced reputation is that, in 1941, Archibald MacLeish, the director of the government Office of Facts and Figures, asked White to join Max Lerner, Reinhold Niebuhr, and Malcolm Cowley in collaborating on a propaganda pamphlet on "The Four Freedoms"; he, White, was to write on freedom of speech and then to serve as rewrite man for the entire project. He was offered—and refused—a judgeship at the Book-of-the-Month Club. Around this time Irwin Edman asserted of White's *Harper's* essays that they contained "the poetry of observation and the philosophy of shrewd, usually gentle, sometimes biting moral insight." From such items are the altars of middlebrow gurus constructed.

How seriously did E. B. White take himself as a spokesman, guru, thinker? Elledge acknowledges that White "seldom commanded the patience and the intellectual staying-power needed for arguments involving a knowledge of history and the formulation of complex ideas." From his own letters one gets a sense that White was aware of his own intellectual indigence. On the dust jacket of *The Wild Flag,* his book of editorials on world government, White himself must have written: "Mr. White does not regard himself as a Thinker and says he feels ill-at-ease writing editorials on massive themes. He regards himself as a clown of average ability whose signals got crossed and who found himself out on the wire with the Wallendas." Yet though he kept no bees on his farm, E. B. White would from time to time get a bee in his bonnet, and then his confidence in his powers of intellect could be very great. A case in point is, precisely, world government—a subject that he took up in the late 1930's and retained an interest in to the end of his days....

Although White wrote about world government in some of his *Harper's* essays, it was in the "Notes and Comment" section of the *New Yorker* that he really chopped away at this particular teakettle. Elledge maintains that, after White's return to the *New Yorker,* "beginning with the issue of April 10, 1943, and continuing for the next four years, nearly one-third of White's weekly 'Notes and Comment' included at least one paragraph on the subject [of world government]." It is a tribute to Harold Ross's regard for White that he allowed him to editorialize so relentlessly on a subject that he, Ross, was not at all interested in. White's editorials did nothing, of course, to bring world government any closer to realization—neither, after all, has the United Nations—but they did have the effect of opening the *New Yorker's* pages to issues of social and political significance; they cleared the way for the magazine's political phase, which it has never left, so that today, in its "Notes and Comment" section, one can be almost certain of finding a weekly sermon on Nicaragua, or Star Wars, or fresh malfeasance on the part of the CIA. (p. 54)

He worried (in print) endlessly about the future, yet seemed only to love the past. He claimed not to have understood the meaning of life, yet was full of advice for the living. E. B. White was a pessimistic utopian, a despairing optimist, a sour idealist, a man reputed to be a humanitarian who, when one got right down to it, was made edgy by most human beings.

These contradictions were not always apparent in E. B. White's writing, and for at least two reasons. The first is that, as an essayist, he was not a writer one was likely to read *en bloc,* and so one took him piece by piece and could not be expected to discover his inconsistencies. (It may well be that he himself never discovered them.) The second reason is his prose, which was clear, often shyly eloquent, and immensely seductive. All writers seek to seduce their readers, with reason or charm or brilliance, or a combination of the three. White did it mostly on charm, but charm of a special kind: self-derogating, homey, sensitive. He was the ostensibly bashful boy who sets out to win the hand of the beauty queen.

White wrote in what, technically, is known as the plain style. His specialty was the declarative sentence: subject, predicate, direct object, indirect object, in that order. His sentences contained few subordinate clauses, inversions, semicolons, or dashes. His vocabulary was also plain: no foreign words, no arcane words, almost no abstract words, only occasionally a slang word like "dippy" or "loopy" that has its own charm. For the most part, an E. B. White essay is composed of plain words arrayed in plain syntax forming plain declarative sentences, one after another, back to back, on and on. In a prefatory note to his essay on William Strunk, the original author of *The Elements of Style,* White, after citing his uneasiness about "posing as an expert on rhetoric," said, "the truth is I write by ear, always with difficulty and seldom with any exact notion of what is taking place under the hood." That is the characteristic E. B. White tone.

White did have a fine ear for prose cadence. He also knew that the best-made sentences are those that have a small surprise waiting at their close. "In the still air," he wrote, describing a war-bond rally, "under the hard sun, gleamed the flags and the banners and the drum majorette's knees." Or, again, this time describing that moment in high summer when one realizes that autumn will soon follow: "The tides run in and out, clams blow tiny jets of seawater up through the mud, a white line of fog hangs around the outer islands, days tumble along in cool blue succession, and I hate the word September." This last sentence is perhaps, in Harold Ross's term, "writer conscious"—by which Ross meant artificial in the way that only an exhibitionist writer can be—but there is no denying White's descriptive powers. He was quite wonderful at describing buildings at dusk, snow in the bright sun, a lake in the rain.

Even with the plain style, variations exist. George Orwell used the plain style to convey that he, a man of plain words, could not be conned by fancy or false words. Behind E. B. White's plain style is the quiet but firm insistence that White was an unpretentious and sensitive man. One of the chief services performed by writers who project their own sensitivity—along with E. B. White, E. M. Forster and J. D. Salinger are two other such writers—is that (as I remarked earlier about the *New Yorker* in general) they make their readers feel that they, too, are sensitive. Yet sensitivity can easily slide into sentimentality. Often it did in the work of White, who, in his editorial for the *New Yorker* on the death of Franklin D. Roosevelt could invoke the guns fired at the dead President's grave and ''Fala's sharp answering bark,'' or could write at the death of John F. Kennedy: ''It can be said of him, as of few men in a like position, that he did not fear the weather, and did not trim his sails, but instead challenged the wind itself, to improve its direction and to cause it to blow more softly and more kindly over the world and its people.'' How sonorous, how beautiful, how not especially true!

Was E. B. White a great essayist? I, for one, think he was at his best when he was not preaching—when he set the teakettle aside and laid down his ax. But he was preaching a good deal of the time. Although he is now generally regarded as a cheery American writer . . .—White was by nature gloomy and at his most moving when he gave way to his fear and sadness. To my mind easily his most beautiful essay is **''Once More to the Lake,''** which is about his return in 1941, along with his eleven-year-old son, to the lake in Maine where White's own father used to take him and his family beginning in 1904. It is an essay that shimmers like a perfect poem; everything in it clicks.

In the essay White recalls the lake he once knew and now sees again through the eyes of his young son, who does everything at the lake that he did as a boy more than thirty years earlier:

> I began to sustain the illusion that he was I, and therefore, by simple transposition, that I was my father. This sensation persisted, kept cropping up all the time we were there. It was not an entirely new feeling, but in this setting it grew much stronger. I seemed to be living a dual existence. I would be in the middle of some simple act, I would be picking up a bait-box or laying down a table fork, or I would be saying something, and suddenly it would be not I but my father who was saying the words or making the gesture. It gave me a creepy feeling.

''Once More to the Lake'' is about generation, about birth and rebirth and death. White was fascinated by generation and haunted by death. Both obsessions come through brilliantly in this essay, where through his own son he relives his father's life and previews his own death. In the essay's closing paragraph, his son, after a rain shower, wrings out his bathing suit before going in for an afternoon swim. White writes: ''Languidly, and with no thought of going in, I watched him, his hard little body, skinny and bare, saw him wince slightly as he pulled up around his vitals the small, soggy, icy garment. As he buckled the swollen belt, suddenly my groin felt the chill of death.'' This essay is dazzling and devastating, art of a heightened kind that an essayist is rarely privileged to achieve.

One does not usually think of E. B. White as a man writing out of his obsessions, yet obsessional he was, and perhaps nowhere more so than in his books for children: *Stuart Little, Charlotte's Web, The Trumpet of the Swan.* Children adore these books, and yet one wonders what they make of them. Children love living things and have their own fascination with the animal world—a love and fascination which White, clearly, shared. Yet children have this advantage over adults: they are permitted to love things they do not understand. But coming to these books as an adult, and loaded down with knowledge

of their author's life, with its longings and fears, one cannot avoid reading them as fables about E. B. White's own life.

I hope I may be allowed to forgo a full-dress exegesis comparing E. B. White's life with that of the mouse Stuart, the pig Wilbur, and the swan Louis. But this much does require saying: all three are characters in need of rescue. Stuart is a mouse born to human parents who finds city life among human beings hazardous and indeed terrifying; Wilbur is a pig being fatted for slaughter; Louis is a trumpeter swan who is born mute and hence cut off from all communication. In these books Stuart is impelled on a quest after a bird who is very much like a muse; Wilbur is saved by a spider named Charlotte who can write; and Louis learns to play the trumpet, a talent which allows him to find a mate and also earn enough money to redeem the reputation of his father, who broke into a music store to attain the trumpet through which Louis learned to speak and eventually to live a fairly normal life.

I hope, again, that I do not betray the dreariness of my symbol-minded literary education when I suggest that Stuart's quest for the bird Margalo mirrors White's own quest in departing New York and journalism for art (at one point in the story Stuart is given charge of a class, and the lesson he teaches it is on the need for something suspiciously like world government); and that, at the close of *Charlotte's Web,* when Wilbur remarks of the spider who saved him that ''It is not often that someone comes along who is a true friend and a good writer,'' White has in mind his wife, who was the mainstay of his always shaky life; and that Louis's attempt to make good his father's theft at the music store refers to the charges of fraud brought against White's own father at the Horace Waters musical instrument firm.

In a letter, E. B. White reported that when Edmund Wilson, his colleague at the *New Yorker,* read *Stuart Little,* he announced to White: ''I read that book of yours. I found the first page quite amusing, about the mouse, you know. But I was disappointed that you didn't develop the theme more in the manner of Kafka.'' But in fact White did develop his books for children in the manner of Kafka, if in a somewhat enfeebled and oddly American way; these books are Kafkaesque but with the American twist that they are Kafka with happy endings, and in their own manner they fulfill the prescription of William Dean Howells, who once remarked that what the American public wanted ''was a tragedy with a happy ending.''

A tragedy with a putatively happy ending might well stand in as a description of E. B. White's own life and career. His was a life led in fear—''Everything scared me in those days,'' he wrote in an essay about his apprenticeship as a reporter in Seattle, ''and still does''—and on the rim of nervous breakdown. His was a career that strained after significance; but despite all the honors he won, he himself was never quite convinced he had achieved it. The obituarists and eulogists (they were one and the same) who wrote about him at his death both praised and buried him, obscuring, in their exaltation of him as ''a precious natural resource'' and a man of ''inexplicably sunny inclinations,'' both the man he was and the writer he wished to be. To be a writer vastly overrated and mostly misunderstood—this, for now, will have to pass for a happy ending. (pp. 55-6)

Joseph Epstein, ''E. B. White, Dark & Lite,'' in
Commentary, *Vol. 81, No. 4, April, 1986, pp. 48-56.*

Literary Biography

Louise Bogan: A Portrait

by Elizabeth Frank

(For Louise Bogan: see also *CLC*, Vol. 4; *Contemporary Authors*, Vols. 25-28, rev. ed., 73-76; and *Dictionary of Literary Biography*, Vol. 45.)

An Excerpt from *Louise Bogan: A Portrait*

[Louise] saw a small glass vase into which someone had placed a casual bunch of French marigolds. They had dark yellow petals with brown blotches and speckles, amidst a few "carrot-like leaves." So far Louise had never been especially fond of flowers. She liked the yellow daisies, black-eyed Susans, and cinquefoil growing in the mill towns, and she liked tansy, chicory, jill-over-the-ground, and weeds, but the French marigolds had quite another effect upon her. . . .

These flowers, as she saw them and responded to them, reflected the essence of every line of poetry and prose Louise Bogan was ever to write. It is not merely that in the moment's illumination she discovered taste and found its power jolting. An awakening took place: she became an artist before she could know it and before ambition and knowledge could bring their influence to bear upon her choices. Against her mother's ill-health and infidelity, against the family fighting and lower-middle-class constraints, against the imperious banality of the Yankee world, and against the enmity or indifference of others, she could now carry "the sudden marigolds" as a shield to deflect the cold light of estrangement and dread into warmer illuminations of mystery and form. Collecting shells later in life, keeping flowers in a vase or, when she couldn't afford flowers, lemon or rhododendron leaves, she remained faithful to the marigolds, to what they had brought forth in her. Dreary, ordinary, puzzling life as it simply *was* could never wholly trap her again.

SUZANNE JUHASZ

This long-awaited biography of Louise Bogan [*Louise Bogan: A Portrait*] is rich in personal, social, literary, even political detail, providing an abundance of essential information, well researched and engagingly presented. It is a major contribution to our knowledge about this important poet. And yet the book remains as tantalizing as it is informative. The dominant characteristic of Bogan's life and work, its profound privacy, creates a problem that Frank herself acknowledges at the outset: "Privacy that is violated for the sake of literary and cultural history remains violated, and the innermost secrets of a proud and dignified spirit have a way of retreating when too strenuously pressed." Nevertheless, the outline drawn so carefully around a space does help us to see the space; it is one way—

in Bogan's case, probably the only way possible—to make a portrait. (pp. 2145-46)

Suzanne Juhasz, in a review of "Louise Bogan: A Portrait," in Library Journal, *Vol. 109, No. 19, November 15, 1984, pp. 2145-46.*

KIRKUS REVIEWS

Moving back and forth between earnest, half-probing biography and conscientious, uninspired close-textual-analysis [in *Louise Bogan: A Portrait*], Frank offers a long, detailed, yet largely uninvolving portrait of poet/critic Bogan (1897-1970)—a "tough, witty, elegant apostle of endurance." Growing up in New England, witnessing her mother's infidelities and violent parental squabbles, the very young Louise found a "shield" from life's woes and banalities in art and beauty; but Frank's discussion of these early years is too vague and iffy to shore up the semi-psychoanalytic discussions that pop up throughout Louise's neurosis-plagued life. . . . Frank is less than persuasive as she charts the ups and downs of Bogan's "divided nature" and "psychic fissures"—especially when suggesting that psychiatry cured her neurosis but killed her creativity. Considerably better, though often over-decorous, are Frank's treatments of Bogan's aesthetic feuds (Allen Tate, Archibald MacLeish), her prickly friendships (Edmund Wilson, William Maxwell), her "feisty opposition" to the literary left, her role at *The New Yorker*. And, with long excerpt-chunks, Frank doggedly examines all the poems, fiction, memoirs, and criticism—noting influence (Rilke, Auden), analyzing prosody and form (the compression of fierce feelings into the formal lyric), tracing themes, and always (to uneven effect) finding autobiographical parallels. Without the narrative shape to attract a non-aficionado audience, without the critical or psychological authority to support a 500-page biography—but a solid, literate, reasonably balanced, fully committed study for enthusiasts and specialists. (pp. 26-7)

A review of "Louise Bogan: A Portrait," in Kirkus Reviews, *Vol. LIII, No. 1, January 1, 1985, pp. 26-7.*

JOYCE JOHNSON

[*Johnson, an American biographer, editor, and critic, won The National Book Critics Circle Award for* Minor Characters *(1983), her biography of Jack Kerouac. In the following excerpt Johnson observes that Frank's thematic focus on the origins of Bogan's creative block considerably narrows the scope of her biography.*]

For over 30 years Bogan herself struggled, in various pieces of memoir, to reexamine the difficult truths of her past and finally could not bear to complete the task Elizabeth Frank has now taken up [in *Louise Bogan: A Portrait*]. Admittedly, Bogan's biographer has been left with dauntingly fragmentary material to work from. As if Bogan's reluctance to look back were not enough for Frank to contend with, a fire in 1929 destroyed all the personal papers Bogan had kept since 1912, as well as many of her first unpublished poems and stories. . . .

It is no wonder that with so little to go on, Frank became pervasively obsessed with Bogan's failure to complete her memoirs. "Something stopped Louise Bogan dead in her tracks not once but many times," Frank laments. "Until we discover this principle of arrest, even the most copious supply of documentation and the most perceptive psychological guesswork will be of little advantage in our attempt to enter the sanctuaries of either the life or the work." Interpretation of the few available facts, of the psychological reference concealed in Bogan's works, nearly overwhelms this biography, even though much of it is valuable. Frank's "portrait" of Bogan is not so much a portrait as a study in what Leon Edel calls "tristimania"— the "persistent sadness of the artist" that is both the wellspring of creativity and, quite possibly in Bogan's case, the silencer of it as well. Discovering her "principle of arrest" in Bogan's earliest experiences, Frank applies it all too single-mindedly throughout. It becomes the formula which explains everything, and though it no doubt explains much, its effect in the end is curiously reductive. . . .

Louise Bogan spent her earliest conscious years in a series of shabby households in New Hampshire milltowns, households so poisoned by "secret family angers and secret disputes" that the child once went blind for two days. . . .

By 15, as a precocious student in Boston's Girls' Latin School, Bogan had found escape in the transmutation of poetry, studying Swinburne and the French symbolists, seeking in art the perfection, the harmony, that life denied her. At 19 she gave up a scholarship to Radcliffe for a precipitous and ill-fated marriage to an Army officer named Curt Alexander, who took her away from her parents, first to Greenwich Village, then to Panama. Yet, as Frank shows us over and over again in this book, Bogan would never outgrow her obsession with betrayal, neither in her life nor her work. "Poetry in form," Frank writes in one of her most illuminating passages, "must always have required from her a severity of unity, a repudiation of union with the object, or the person, who had driven her to utterance. To form attachments was thus hazardous, for the very feelings they produced would lead, as it were, to the need to write poetry, and poetry . . . inevitably exacted some sort of emotional violence toward the attachment." . . .

[By 25, the poet] had made a trip to Vienna and published her first collection of poems, *Body of this Death*. A brief, disastrous affair with an eccentric young man named John Coffey seems to have troubled her far more than it should have. On the whole, unfortunately, her biographer seems to have been able to unearth exceedingly little information about her during this period, and we read with some initial surprise about the violent extremes of emotion she experienced in her relationship with the writer and editor Raymond Holden, whom she married in 1925. A person who can trust neither herself nor anyone else is a person condemned to despair, rage and solitude. Bogan's relationship with Holden would become the supreme testing ground of truth—as treacherous and potentially deadly as a minefield. In the end Bogan's uncontrollable jealousy would become a self-fulfilling prophecy: Holden would leave her for another woman.

"A woman writes poetry with her ovaries," Bogan once told the poet John Hall Wheelock. When the sexual life that had cost her so much agony ended in her mid-forties, her poetry

died a simultaneous death. Although Frank tries to "prove" this connection—indeed it becomes her major concern—there are so many blank spaces in this account of Bogan's life that we must accept this final extension of Frank's "principle of arrest" almost on faith. . . .

Frank works all too scrupulously from Bogan's few existing papers. She seems curiously unwilling, or unable, to find ways of seeing around her subject; she makes little attempt to place her in relationship to the times in which she lived (a period in which women's lives underwent profound, confusing changes). The people who were important in Bogan's life remain shadow figures, summarized rather than portrayed. Only Bogan's own occasional words bring them to life. But Frank has set herself to solve mysteries rather than to recreate.

In her book *Silences,* the novelist Tillie Olsen quoted a phrase from one of Bogan's letters that has haunted me ever since I read it: "the knife of the perfectionist attitude in art and literature." Like Olsen herself, Bogan was always a perfectionist. Could this have blocked her from writing poetry, particularly during her middle years, when writing so much criticism in order to earn a living may have made her agonizingly self-conscious about her own work? Can we allow ourselves to view women's art from vantage points other than sexuality?

As for the real mystery of Bogan's life—it is what we might ask about any creative artist, male or female: What made her a poet? That is a question no one can yet answer definitively, not even Sigmund Freud. We might theorize, as Frank does, that the necessity to create may be connected with the inability to do "griefwork." Still the mystery remains. Why should the impulse toward perfection, toward wholeness, come to so few of us and not others? A child named Virginia Woolf saw a plant in a flowerbed and thought, "That is the whole," and knew this was an illumination she would have to come back to later. Another child named Louise Bogan experienced a similar early intimation of the poetic imagination. Looking at a bunch of marigolds in a glass jar standing next to a bunch of roses an admirer had sent her mother, she "suddenly . . . *recognized* something at once simple and full of the utmost richness of design and contrast that was mine. A whole world, in a moment, opened up. . . . The sudden marigolds."

Joyce Johnson, "Louise Bogan and the Poet's Vocation," in Book World—The Washington Post, *February 4, 1985, p. 5.*

JOHN GROSS

Louise Bogan, who died in 1970, disapproved of the self-dramatizing confessional poetry that she saw coming into vogue in her last years. Not only was she naturally reticent; she also believed that the true poet "represses the outright narrative of his life." Instead of exploiting his personal history, he uses his art to set it at a distance; subjective feeling is recast as seemingly objective myth. And this was an ideal that she did her best to live up to in her own work. She had set down her experience, she once wrote, "in the closest detail. But the rough and vulgar facts are not there."

To reconstruct such a life is a difficult task. It calls for exceptional empathy and insight, and for the ability to set imaginative work in its biographical context without reducing it to mere documentation. Fortunately, Elizabeth Frank, who teaches at Bard College, has risen admirably to the challenge. [*Louise*

Bogan at age eleven.

Bogan: A Portrait] is a model of its kind, and one that does full justice to a remarkable woman.

What were the "rough and vulgar facts" that are the biographer's business, if not the poet's? The most devastating of them were beyond doubt the events of Louise Bogan's childhood. She was born of Irish stock in Maine in 1897 and grew up in a succession of rooming houses and temporary homes. Her parents were ill-matched; there were fearsome quarrels, and her mother not only had a long series of lovers, but—impelled by who knows what twisted motives—took her small daughter along with her to her trysts. Louise loved her and felt an urge to protect her, but she also suffered permanent damage. For much of her life, she was to be racked by rage and jealousy, to alternate between tenderness and sudden spasms of cruelty.

Yet the sources of her strength showed themselves in childhood as well. Early on—she may have been as young as 8 at the time—the sight of a vase in which someone had placed a bunch of marigolds gave her an overwhelming sense of illumination. She understood the impulse of pleasure that lay behind the way the flowers were arranged. "And I knew the flowers—their striped and mottled elegance—forever and for all time, forward and back. They were mine, as though I had invented them."

In other words, she had grasped the possibilities of art. She went on to start writing poetry, and by her mid-teens it was

becoming clear that she had found her vocation. She had a knack for drawing, too, and she idolized her art teacher until the fatal afternoon when she caught sight of her "with a greasy paper bag in one hand and a half-eaten doughnut in the other." Her romantic ideal had been betrayed, and "with perfect ruthlessness I rejected her utterly."

After a year at Boston University, she dropped out in order to get married, but in spite of having a daughter to whom she remained closely attached, she was soon at odds with her husband. By 1919, she was living by herself in Greenwich Village and embroiled in a love affair with a young Irishman who felt he had a mission to call attention to the needs of the poor by shoplifting and then testifying in court to their plight. He was eventually committed to an insane asylum, but malicious gossip about the episode kept cropping up for years and adding to her sense of vulnerability whenever it did.

Her second marriage, to the writer Raymond Holden, lasted much longer than her first, but it was increasingly punctuated by fights and outbursts of jealousy, and Holden's devotion to her couldn't make up for—indeed, tended to underline—the relative weakness of his personality. Within a few years, she was showing distinct signs of paranoia, and in the early 1930's she spent two spells in the hospital under psychiatric care.

She emerged from the second of them a good deal mellower, and "as cured as she was ever likely to be." But old griefs and afflictions were always liable to flare up again. When she visited Ireland in 1936, for instance, she was seized with a sense of horror; it never seems to have occurred to her, as Elizabeth Frank says, that the conspiratorial faces she thought she saw on every side were ghosts from her mother-dominated past.

At least the episode had a happy outcome. The man who came to her rescue while she was on her travels—an electrician from Inwood in Upper Manhattan—became her lover, and their affair lasted eight years. She regarded it as a success, although she seldom mentioned it and never introduced him to her friends.

Painful though her life often was, it is much less gloomy to read about than a bare outline might suggest. It was lightened by friendships with such notable figures as Margaret Mead (who wrote a poem about her) and Edmund Wilson (who set her off on a long and distinguished career as a reviewer); by her fairly cheerful affair with Theodore Roethke, 10 years her junior, and by the tough humor of such things as her account of James Thurber, who met her at a party and told her they ought to see more of each other. "He has a glass eye, poor dear. Anyone who falls for me is sure to have something missing."

Above all, of course, there is the poetry, which Miss Frank analyzes at length, and with considerable skill. When she compares it to that of George Herbert or Gerard Manley Hopkins, she claims far too much for it. But at its best, in such poems as **"Hypocrite Swift"** or **"Song for the Last Act,"** it bears the impress of a formidable personality, who has now been commemorated in a biography of the caliber she deserves.

John Gross, in a review of "Louise Bogan: A Portrait," in The New York Times, *February 15, 1985, p. C32.*

APRIL BERNARD

[Louise Bogan] has never suffered from too large a reputation. During her life she was probably best known as a critic: she wrote for several publications and was *The New Yorker*'s poetry critic for more than 30 years, rustling a semiannual "round-up" for that magazine. Her reviews were catholic in range and stern in judgment. They lost her friends and won her as many. She had the anti-intellectualism of the autodidact, buttressed by a sympathy at all times for the "felt." To erstwhile friend Allen Tate, who had written to express his annoyance at a review, she replied: "I was reviewing a book of poetry which aroused in me respect and irritation in about equal measure. If you objected to the tone of my review, I objected, straight down to a core beyond detachment, to the tone of some of the poems."

Bogan's own poetry was read and admired—and of course also attacked—within the narrow circle of poetry's cognoscenti. Auden hailed her as one of the best poets writing, and her lyric verse won her Guggenheims, membership in the Academy of Arts and Letters, and a host of other honors from her peers. But her output was not enormous, and her poems remain difficult—chiseled, often bitter little riddles in which the poet's rational mind makes cynical (or resigned or brave) sense of the vagaries of the human heart. For all her poetry's well-tailored chic, its unmistakable power inheres in its resistance to its own good manners. But however remarkable her poetry, today not many remember, if they ever knew, who Bogan was.

Elizabeth Frank's biography [*Louise Bogan: A Portrait*] contributes much to our knowledge, though rather less to our understanding, of Bogan. Her childhood, which was the source of incredible trauma, exerts a grim fascination, something like the morbid chill of a Lizzie Borden trial as told in newspaper accounts of that time. Nothing quite so sensational afflicted Bogan's small, lower-middle-class family, but her mother did take lovers, which the child was aware of, and she did muster about her a circle of furtive confidantes whom the child despised and feared. The father was foreman in innumerable paper mills; the family moved often, perhaps one step ahead of scandal, from one New England manufacturing town to another. Louise was sent to one of the best preparatory schools in Boston, Girls' Latin, and she entered Boston University in 1915. After one year, against her parents' wishes and throwing over a scholarship to Radcliffe, she married a soldier and abandoned her formal education for good.

The biography is also valuable for its chronicling of Bogan's life in literary New York, where she moved in 1920 after her first marriage ended in divorce. One of her closest friends of the 1920s and 1930s was Edmund Wilson, and she was also friendly with Margaret Mead, Eleanor Wylie, Malcolm Cowley—the whole group. (Later important associations included Theodore Roethke, Morton Zabel and John Hall Wheelock, her editor at Scribner's for many years.) Wilson was a mentor and a goad, and in later years Bogan liked to tell the story of how he had locked her in a room and forced her to write her first critical essay. She was beautiful, tall, thin and high-strung, alternately charming and abrasive, hard-working but also beset by self-doubt. She worried about her personal life, as a succession of love affairs culminated in a stormy, decade-long marriage to the writer and editor Raymond Holden. And she worried about her poetry, which emerged only slowly and painfully.

Bogan's troubles prompted her to seek psychiatric help, and on a few occasions she was hospitalized for the depression that dogged her all her life. Her emotional instability contributed in large part to the jealous rages that marred her marriage, but it is clear from Frank's portrait that Bogan's anger had a positive function as well. Two extracts from Bogan's journals: "I

can feel rage, but I am never humiliated, any more." "Do not shrink from your hatreds. They may be a cover for other emotions—let that also stand. If I did not hate, if I had not hated pretense and falsehood in others, how false, how pretentious I should have been myself!" Anger and hatred provided a backbone for this vulnerable woman and fueled her relentless efforts to distinguish the true from the sham. With all her faults placed squarely before the readers of this book, Bogan emerges troubled, tormented and cruel. (That she is also vindicated, at least in this reader's eye, is more or less in spite of the treatment she receives here.)

Where Frank's biography fails—and its failure is substantial—is in its woolly lack of purpose. This is what led, I am sure, to the meticulous over-documentation that drones through rich and bare patches alike. In a spasmodic way, Frank exerts a certain amount of "critical" authority, pausing now and again to interpret Bogan's verse, usually by means of tediously detailed correspondences between the "subject matter" of the poems and the poet's life at the time they were written. Taken too seriously, this method is perilous, especially in the case of a writer like Bogan, whose poems attempted, and often achieved, transcendence through thought imposed on feeling. Criticism that insists on linking the work to the life does an implicit disservice to such poems. There is much more to be said about Bogan's poetry, but it does not get said here.

Frank is also impeded by an unavoidable reliance on letters, diaries and memoirs. Excepting the criticism and the badinage in some letters, Bogan's prose is labored and often boring. This liability would have weighed on any biographer.

Rather like a teacher's "topic sentence" tacked to a young student's paper, this biography does claim to have a purpose. In the foreword, Frank asserts that "something stopped Louise Bogan dead in her tracks, not once but many times," and she proposes to discover "this principle of arrest." But by the end of this thoroughly long book, the search has failed on two scores: Frank never broaches a coherent answer to her question, and it becomes clear that the question of poetic "arrest" was not the right one to have posed.

Why a biography at all? So many biographies seem gratuitous, but the fault does not lie with the genre. To look at a few relatively recent examples of successful biographies, Richard Sewall's of Emily Dickinson and Walter Jackson Bate's of Samuel Johnson are enthralling because the authors were driven by a passionate engagement with their subjects. (pp. 215-16)

Bad biography, on the other hand, is always looking for an excuse. One prevalent type uses a life to prove a point—either Freudian or sociological. The subject is sacrificed for the greater good of theory, and the only thing to be said in favor of such exercises is that they usually remain mercifully short on documentation, since too much detail throws the game. Other sorts of weak biography may begin with good intentions—fulfillment of a dissertation, say—and even a measure of passion, but somewhere in the course of research the biographer loses the spark and comes to feel saddled by the life being chronicled; the result shows all the signs of familial exasperation. You can choose your lovers but not your relatives, and such a biographer no longer feels he has the freedom to cast his subject aside. (p. 216)

Elizabeth Frank has fallen into this trap. Although she expresses admiration for Bogan, it does not seem to be particularly deep. Her overpowering wish that Bogan had been *more* productive, *less* troubled, is that of a hand wringer at the graveside. Frank writes: "The possibility, often said to be feared by people who are both creative and neurotic, that psychiatric treatment would cure their neurosis but in the process kill their creativity, may well have been, for Louise Bogan, uncannily close to the truth." If there were only one or two such passages in the book, one might discount them as a mild complaining to which the author was entitled. But they are legion. Perhaps I do Frank an injustice, but the flat, querulous tone does not suggest anything like a "felt" response to the poet or her work. *Louise Bogan: A Portrait* begins in enthusiasm for the woman and condescension for her early writing. It ends with praise for what work there was and with contempt for the woman. (The harsh way in which Frank disposes of Bogan's final days is ugly to read.) In this way, the book mirrors the habit of the world, to love the young only for what they cannot help being, and to love the old only for what they have done.

Is this book the appropriate vehicle for bringing the poet back into our gaze? How dare anyone blame such a writer for what she did *not* do? Bogan's poems will survive, and *The Blue Estuaries: Poems 1923-1968,* the definitive collection of more than a hundred poems spanning her career, is still in print. Read **"After the Persian," "To Be Sung on the Water," "Men Loved Wholly Beyond Wisdom," "If We Take All Gold"**— read them all. Here is the final verse from **"Roman Fountain"**:

> O, as with arm and hammer,
> Still it is good to strive
> To beat out the image whole,
> To echo the shout and stammer
> When full-gushed waters, alive,
> Strike on the fountain's bowl
> After the air of summer.

We must, for now, content ourselves with that, and that is much. (pp. 216-17)

> *April Bernard, "Arresting, Not Arrested," in* The Nation, *Vol. 240, No. 7, February 23, 1985, pp. 215-17.*

ALICIA OSTRIKER

[*Ostriker is an American poet, essayist, critic, and editor whose poetry collections include* Songs *(1969) and* A Woman under the Surface *(1982). In the following excerpt she commends Frank for balancing her portrait of Bogan's troubled life with a thoughtful analysis of her poetry.*]

Between the two world wars there appeared a body of American lyric poetry worthy of comparison with Elizabethan song in beauty and intensity. It was written by Sara Teasdale, Elinor Wylie, Edna Millay, Léonie Adams, Genevieve Taggard, H.D. and of course Louise Bogan (1897-1970)—a turbulent woman whom Auden in the 1940's considered "the best critic in America" and one of its best poets, and who contributed "a dozen or more to our small stock of memorable lyrics," according to Malcolm Cowley. Like the reputation of the long-neglected H.D., Bogan's reputation is on the rise. In part this is because of her sheer poetic mastery, in part because women poets today have discovered in her a key ancestress. I remember encountering Bogan's **"Cassandra"** as a student with the shock of recognition I later experienced reading Sylvia Plath. Here was a female voice, demonic and proud, like an inner submerged self.

Louise Bogan: A Portrait is the thoughtful biography that lovers of Bogan need. Unlike certain recent writers on H.D., Eliza-

Bogan with her daughter, Maidie, in 1922. Courtesy of Maidie Alexander Scannell.

beth Frank avoids reducing her subject to a titillating love life or a neurosis, though the material for that kind of treatment is not lacking in Bogan's life. Miss Frank plainly admires both the poet's art and her life, and enables us to see how they illuminate each other, triumphantly and tragically.

That a distinct though often disparaged tradition of women's poetry exists we now know, thanks to scholars who have unearthed and described it. Its dominant themes are the perennial ones of love and death, joy and suffering, but with some feminine twists. Women poets are often acutely ambivalent on subjects like love, power and femininity. And due to what Sandra Gilbert and Susan Gubar have dubbed the female "anxiety of authorship"—the result of women's awareness that they are supposed to be less ambitious than men— disguises, duplicities and ironies have always been central to them.

As Miss Frank's biography makes clear, Bogan's writing belongs firmly in this long tradition, as well as in the more immediate matrix of the "strict, austere, fire-and-marble poetry" women were writing in her youth. For in the words of a late poem, she was a "masked woman." She disliked public appearances, found herself unable to write an autobiography friends urged her toward and said of her highly coded poems, "I have written down my experience in the closest detail. But the rough and vulgar facts are not there." (pp. 1, 30)

For much of her life, Bogan struggled against depression and breakdown, and at times against poverty and near-poverty. Twice, she committed herself to a mental hospital. But with the help of therapy, friendships, the discipline of work and the emotional self-control she required of herself, she kept her head mostly above water. After the breakup with [her second husband], she had a successful eight-year love affair with an electrician from Inwood, in Manhattan. It was to be the first of several sensible instead of destructive love affairs. She also managed to maintain a close relationship with her daughter. Miss Frank demonstrates that the transformation of life into pure art we see in Bogan's poems is the objective correlative of a difficult personal self-conquest.

The cost was a gradual loss—though with many remissions—of the ability to feel largely and to write passionately. Bogan composed criticism through thick and thin, but less and less poetry, though some of her very late poems are among her finest. As a critic, she wrote poetry surveys for *The New Yorker* for 38 years, and her *Achievement in American Poetry: 1900-1950* is still a wise and balanced guide to that explosive period. Her tastes were eclectic, her standards high. She saw literature as a distillation and criticism of life, demanding of the artist both passion and craft in a way we have almost forgotten. "Innocence of heart and violence of feeling are necessary in any kind of superior achievement; the arts cannot exist without them," she wrote. Of a Rilke poem, she advises the young Theodore Roethke, "Now a poem like that cannot be written by technique alone. It is carved out of agony, as a statue is carved out of marble." The words might usefully appear on the lintels of many a creative writing classroom. She loved Goethe, Baudelaire, Colette, Mozart, Dickinson, James, Yeats, Hopkins, Auden and a host of others. She hated academic pretension and jargon, mistrusted the "life of literary gentility," and despised the growth of leftist orthodoxy among the literati of the 1930's—three aversions that combined to isolate her through her middle years.

About the issue of "the woman writer," Bogan blends pride and defensiveness much as many women writers do today. On the one hand she asserts in *Achievement in American Poetry* that the revitalization of American poetics at the turn of the century "was accomplished almost entirely by women poets through methods which proved to be as strong as they seemed to be delicate.... The line of poetic intensity which wavers and fades out and often completely fails in poetry written by men, on the feminine side remains unbroken." Her own work anticipates the exploration of female violence that erupted decades later in poets like Plath and Adrienne Rich. The much-anthologized **"Women,"** Miss Frank observes, reveals an "envy of maleness" that the poet also expressed to close friends like Edmund Wilson and Rolphe Humphries. Intellectual force and sexual liberty were expected of them, discouraged in her, she felt. Nevertheless, when asked to edit an anthology of poetry by women, she "turned this pretty job down; the thought of corresponding with a lot of female songbirds made me acutely ill."

Often competitive with her peers, Bogan could be warmly generous toward the talented young. At 38 she wrote Edmund Wilson, then traveling in Persia, "I, myself, have been made to bloom like a Persian rose-bush, by the enormous love-making of a cross between a Brandenburger and a Pomeranian, one Theodore Roethke by name." Cautiously, she let this affair cool, but for years helped Roethke overhaul his poems word by word, admonishing and encouraging him to more hard work and less self-pity. Roethke in return wrote that her poems demanded "the emotional and spiritual response of the whole man.... And the best work will stay in the language as long as the language survives." Later, William Maxwell and May

Sarton were her disciples and Sarton wrote that she was "a source of humility and joy, a pure standard."

Journey Around My Room, a mosaic of Bogan's autobiographical writings published in 1980 by her literary executor Ruth Limmer, is an engaging but radically incomplete version of the poet's life. *Louise Bogan: A Portrait* supplies facts and interprets riddles. It is important, for example, to understand the mother-daughter dimension of **"The Sleeping Fury,"** the genesis of the joyfully erotic-artistic **"Baroque Comment"** in the Roethke affair, and the source of **"Little Lobelia's Song"** in the weeping spells of Bogan's old age, when she was visited—apparently—by the ghost of her own childhood.

At times Miss Frank's readings may be slightly off, at others they seem repetitive. But she helps us understand the complex fusions of obsession and art in the poet who wrote the arrogant and admirable lines about poetic reputation and poetic value, **"Several Voices Out of a Cloud"**:

> Come, drunks and drug-takers; come, per-
>   verts unnerved!
> Receive the laurel, given, though late, on
>   merit;
>   to whom and wherever deserved.
> Parochial punks, trimmers, nice people,
>   joiners true-blue,
> Get the hell out of the way of the laurel. It is
>   deathless. And it isn't for you.

(p. 30)

Alicia Ostriker, "Innocence of Heart and Violence of Feeling," in The New York Times Book Review, *March 3, 1985, pp. 1, 30.*

RICHARD HOWARD

[*Howard is an American poet, critic, and translator. His most notable book of criticism is* Alone with America: Essays on the Art of Poetry in the United States Since 1950 *(1969). As a translator Howard is credited with introducing modern French fiction to the United States, and he has also won recognition for his poetry, receiving the Pulitzer Prize in 1970 for his collection* Untitled Subjects *(1969); his other works include* Fellow Feelings *(1976) and* Lining Up *(1984). In the following excerpt Howard commends Frank for her sensitive, nonjudgmental depiction of Bogan's struggles to overcome depression and writer's block.*]

It is a brave, indeed a dogged, biographer, and perhaps an obsessed one—a biographer with *corresponding recognitions*—who would undertake, given the documents already before the public or behind the private accounting, a portrait of this sternly lyric poet [Louise Bogan]. Consider the circumstances likely to dissuade a delineating pursuit: Bogan's poems have been several times collected, and in 1968, two years before her death at 73, they were once again published, as *The Blue Estuaries* . . .—some 100 poems of a relentlessly topiary art. Bogan's criticism was collected in 1955 and, one might say, recollected 15 years later in *A Poet's Alphabet*—chiefly the articles on poetry from 38 years of semiannual reviews in *The New Yorker*. Bogan's letters (the lioness's share) were published in 1973, articulating in the liveliest terms her friendships with Edmund Wilson, Theodore Roethke, Rolfe Humphries, Morton Zabel, and William Maxwell, as well as her loyalties to Yeats, to Auden (a mutual admiration), and most significantly to Rilke, who for her was the consummate poetic identity. Elizabeth Frank puts it nicely when she says that Bogan recognized herself in Rilke as "anarchic, submissive, patient, and finally ecstatic in the face of pleasure or pain.'' Then in 1980 Ruth Limmer, who had edited the letters and the criticism, stitched together Bogan's prose (all except her short stories, which remain scattered in *The New Yorker*'s files) into *Journey Around My Room,* a ''mosaic'' of autobiographical fragments that complement the letters with an inward version of the outward vision. With all this in hand, if not in mind, much as in the case of Virginia Woolf on even more extravagant terms, who needs a biography?

The answer is that Elizabeth Frank needed such a thing, which is why her ''portrait'' is the finely shaded and impassioned production that it is. Though she has been scholarly and even scrupulous in her sleuthing, Frank is after some larger image than interviews and three-by-five cards could produce. (For example, the composite figure of Wallace Stevens lately offered by Peter Brazeau: mercilessly heterogeneous, such compilations make us realize that biography without passion is a hard-boiled egg without salt.) What is vouchsafed here, I find, is a careful cartography of a woman's struggle to become what she knew was in her to be, against baffling odds of psychological abuse.

The wound seems to have been inflicted at once, by what the psychotherapist calls the parental situation, and Bogan spends a good deal of her poetic wealth in accounting for the pain. ''The young will be broken,'' she declares, ''and all time to endure. . . .'' and again, discovering the division that crippled her marriages, her motherhood, and even—and most of all— her solitude: ''the gentle self splits up / into a yelling fiend and a soft child.'' Extraordinarily sensitive to Bogan's own report of the conflict, Frank speaks of the young poet's gifts as having the inextinguishable strength of all powers ''as natural as they are compensatory,'' and states, with absolute trust in her informant (Bogan herself, I mean), that

> by the age of eight, or even perhaps as early as five or six, Louise Bogan was an exile from conventional life, and had become ''what I was for half my life: the semblance of a girl, in which some desires and illusions had been early assassinated: shot dead'' . . . In the end she forgave herself her own failures of love and judgment, as well as those who had failed her. Her darkest secrets she kept even from herself, giving them to her poetry, in which they remain sealed forever against direct inspection.

Thereby the portrait-painter suggests how she will read the poems—not for evidence, not for confirmation, but as a mystery ''sealed'' and therefore sustained, to be honored and respected *as* a mystery. It seems to me Frank ranks Bogan too high, and praises her poems too lavishly (though all ''ranking'' is a convenience merely, and like all conveniences doomed to supersession). Still, that is irrelevant; she has written one of the very few life-studies of an artist—a woman, an intellectual outsider, a traumatized imagination—that seek to follow the impulses toward survival and productivity, and that trace the choking-off, the subsidence into bitterness and *ressentiment,* with vigilant patience. Frank, who says ''I'' for the first time on page 285, is focused on how the spirit prevails, where it prevails, over its cankers and corruptions; how ''what had been the means of escape would have to become the means of return.'' Her subject (never her object: Frank is careful to avoid the easy detractions of psychoanalytic inquisition) is forever resolving to do better, writhing in the coils of her parental python:

I cannot become (she wrote in 1933, when she was about as old as Emily Brontë writing ''Cold in the Earth''), all at once, a detached, self-delighting individual. My own ideas are steeped in a romantic brew, however much I hate the color and the stain. I was fed on 19th-century literature, on symbolist poetry, on provincial morality. My two defences against the nonsense in myself and in others are my realism and my wit. Perhaps I can keep some inner balance with the help of these two, and with the help of routine and *willed* creation.

As Elizabeth Frank shows us, this admirable self-knowledge was frustrated by precisely what it knew: Bogan's peculiar rage for order in her making—''my gift depends on the flash—on the *apercu* . . . One can only remain open and wait''—was defeated by the notion that her poems must happen to her, must well up from within like an unopposable tide. All else would be trivial, even the ambition of assured talent (''ambition is automatically stopped by the thought of death; it becomes trivial and vulgar''), even her impatience with the world's mediocrity and mendacity (''by hatred of others' faults let me be cured!''). The last 30 years of this tormented life (high-spirited, certainly, as the letters reveal, but for the most part doomed and doom-acknowledging)—the years when a Colette and a Hannah Arendt were doing their finest work against psychic odds quite as repressive—were starved, soured, and silenced. ''The mystery draws in,'' she wrote at the end, from what seems an absolute loneliness: ''One needs the help of the imagination to die.''

How politely Elizabeth Frank puts the case for the obstacles and embarrassments of this self-harassing intellect:

> With those she considered better educated than herself she was fiercely, furiously competitive, simultaneously defensive and aggressive, blindly judging the use of philosophical discourse in criticism as intellectual fakery and exhibitionism, and greatly oversimplifying the virtues of criticism which instead incorporated 'images' . . . She thought of Burke, Blackmur, Ransom, Tate, even Eliot, Richards and Empson—perversely, defiantly, even desperately—as an encroaching phalanx of abstract, over-ingenious and deliberately obscure mandarins, out to safeguard their academic and social prestige by demonstrating the need for a priestly class of explicators and interpreters.

She had the arrogance of the self-educated, which in her case was not so much protective as aggressive, and I believe—on Frank's showing, if not from the warrant of the poems—that her anger with the literary world, which she believed regarded her as a ''dumb Mick,'' with her parents who left her unable to trust others, with herself most of all, brought her poetry to its unrealized end. ''I don't want to confess,'' she wrote to William Maxwell in 1945, ''I want to create; and the hatred of confessing has been one thing that has held me up all these years.'' The ambiguity of ''held me up''—sustained/defeated—is here agonizingly apt. Cautiously, sometimes reading so closely as to be invisible, Elizabeth Frank is astonishing in her capacity to take this up, to understand how the life played itself out:

> The woman who found it so difficult to write her autobiography was able, when she *trans-*

lated her knowledge of herself into her appreciative knowledge of others, to put her life to account, and moreover to keep faith with art in the process . . .

Frank has written a book no reader of Bogan's published work and remains could have imagined. It is a tragic account, and the more exceptional for being patient with the tragedy, not hot in pursuit of easy diagnoses, of replacement strategies. In 1941, when she had written what were essentially her last poems, Auden wrote Louise Bogan: "Unless you lose your head, your poetic career is only just beginning . . . What you do now depends on nothing except your talent." I am calling it a tragedy that Bogan could not acknowledge a dependence on talent as the reason for writing poetry. Unless she could transcend (and subvert) talent with each poem, she would choose silence over mere gift, and that is the choice Elizabeth Frank, with passionate originality in her method, searches out. She does not "judge" Bogan, whom she describes as "cherishing the notion that a deep affinity existed between the artist and the criminal," but she offers her life, and her "task of dissembling confession through symbol and form," as a cautionary emblem. The triumphs of Bogan's poetry, and of her spirit, are shown to be won over and from the indissociable disgraces of her character (self-confessed, homemade, ultimately cherished). This is not a work of literary criticism only, or of biographical exposure merely. It is a meditation on how to live, traced through the agon of a difficult woman's art. (pp. 34, 36-7)

> Richard Howard, "Yelling Fiend, Soft Child," in *The New Republic, Vol. 192, No. 12,* March 25, 1985, pp. 34, 36-7.

ELIZABETH WHEELER

[In *Louise Bogan: A Portrait,* Elizabeth Frank] uses Bogan's work to find her ideas, and she uses the ideas to theorize intelligently about those events in Bogan's life that can be documented.

This combination of intimate familiarity with the work and balance in the analysis makes this a fine biography. It is, and appropriately so, a mildly feminist and sympathetic view of Bogan, locating much of her chronic discontent in the traditional nature of interaction between men and women, especially women of intellectual depth and talent. It is not surprising that Frank finds that many of Bogan's difficulties come from a longstanding tradition of sexism—female biographers and biograhers of females frequently reach that conclusion these days—but . . . she does not seem to be taking any liberties with the material to draw that judgment. . . .

Using Bogan's work as the key to unlocking the secrets of her life has another advantage. It makes this biography almost a classic "life and works" and, as such, it should do modern readers the service of calling or recalling to their attention the poetry of Louise Bogan, with its painful insights into the nature of life, the condition of men and of women. (p. 15)

> Elizabeth Wheeler, in a review of "Louise Bogan: A Portrait," in Los Angeles Times Book Review, March 31, 1985, pp. 1, 15.

GLORIA BOWLES

Even the feminist movement in criticism has been slow to recognize [Louise Bogan]. There are several reasons for this neglect. "Her poetry is limited by its bitterness," a graduate student said to me years ago; and more recently, a colleague asked if I "liked" Bogan. "Like" is not what one feels about this *oeuvre:* what one gets from it is the wisdom of a woman who has been to hell and back in her personal life and her career. Moreover, Bogan's poetry is of the difficult modernist kind and—most damaging for her contemporary reputation— her poem **"Women"** was included in several of the anthologies of women's poetry which began to appear in the seventies. ("Women have no wilderness in them, / They are provident instead, / Content in the tight hot cell of their hearts / To eat dusty bread.") This poem, with its assessment of women's fears and limitations, was labelled "anti-woman" by the new feminist generation.

A decade later, we are able to understand the poem for its social accuracy and its record of a woman writer's ambivalent relationship to her own sex. We can also see it in the context of an entire and admirable body of writing. For Bogan is central to the female tradition in poetry. She published three major volumes: *Body of This Death* (1923), *Dark Summer* (1929) and *The Sleeping Fury* (1937). She wrote relatively little after these three books; her remaining poems were published in *Poems and New Poems* (1941), *Collected Poems* (1953) and the final complete poems, *The Blue Estuaries* (1968). This last slim volume of 105 poems is Bogan's *oeuvre* as she wished to present it. Not prolific, and a perfectionist, she did not want to be thought of as a woman poet. In her view, this appellation reduced her achievement; moreover, it placed her among the lachrymose poetesses of the nineteenth century and the twenties whose sentimental songs she detested. Bogan's work has the passion of the nineteenth century and some of its resignation, as Cheryl Walker has pointed out; but it also reflects modern reticence and control. There are some subjects—self-pity is one of them—she did not admit to poetry; she felt no imperative to write "happy" poems. She believed poetry ought to come out of real, lived experience. She did not advertise her personal life. . . .

Yet there is so much obscurity in the poems that we need something of the life to understand them. In the seventies, the only path to that life was through the letters (*What The Woman*

Bogan in 1933 in the south of France. Courtesy of Maidie Alexander Scannell.

Lived, 1973) edited by Ruth Limmer, and through Limmer's piecings of unpublished fragments and poems (*Journey Around My Room: The Autobiography of Louise Bogan, A Mosaic,* 1980). *A Poet's Alphabet* (1970), edited by Limmer and Robert Phelps, gave us a selection of Bogan's critical writing. To Limmer's prodigious work we owe the slow coming to recognition of this major poet. . . .

In her own time, she was known as a poet's poet. She has been neglected in ours. Those courses in modernist literature taught at the universities would be enriched by the inclusion of poets such as Bogan and H.D., who bring a female definition of modernism. (p. 8)

Bogan has been lucky in her biographer: Elizabeth Frank has written a splendid work [*Louise Bogan: A Portrait*]. She has avoided the usual pitfalls of the biographer who, overwhelmed by the subject, often gives us stilted, boring speech. Frank is eloquent. To write of a poet is unusually delicate and difficult, and while Bogan's outer life has its interests it is her inner life that matters. Frank gives it all: the affairs, the marriages, the mothering, the breakdowns; she also interprets the poems, linking the art and the life. This biographer is sympathetic to her subject even as she recognizes how very "difficult" she was. (She points out Bogan's culpability for the failure of her second marriage, for example, and chronicles her husband's happiness in a later marriage.) Her interpretation is primarily psychological. In the Foreword, she writes that "something stopped Louise Bogan dead in her tracks, not once but many times," and she sets out to discover "this principle of arrest." I think she finds many principles of arrest in the course of her narrative; and while I would come down more decisively on gender as one of the principles, I think that those principles of temperament and milieu and "psychology" which Frank locates are also extremely important in understanding Bogan.

Those of us who know a great deal about Bogan's life from Limmer's earlier books will find in this one the answers to many little questions we had wondered about; readers who are utterly unacquainted with Bogan will want to move back and forth between the poems and the biography. For the life does inform the art, and vice versa. No one of us, I think, is writing criticism or biography for the sake of criticism or biography alone. For the point is to send you to the complete poems— that slim accomplished volume *The Blue Estuaries,* where the principles of arrest and creativity join in magnificent tension. (p. 9)

> Gloria Bowles, "The Pursuit of Perfection," in The Women's Review of Books, *Vol. II, No. 10, July, 1985, pp. 8-9.*

KATHA POLLITT

[*Pollitt is an American poet and critic whose first poetry collection,* Antarctic Traveller *(1982), received* The National Book Critics Circle Award. *Pollitt's poems, in both free and formal verse, reflect on pastoral, urban, and domestic landscapes and are noted for their polished style and economy of expression. In the following excerpt Pollitt praises Frank for her "generous, scholarly, and unflaggingly sympathetic" portrait of Bogan.*]

"The poet represses the outright narrative of his life. He absorbs it, along with life itself. The repressed becomes the poem. Actually, I have written down my experience in the closest detail. But the rough and vulgar facts are not there." This passage, which Louise Bogan confided to her journal in the early 1930s, could have hung over her desk as a personal and artistic credo. Almost every word is revealing. There's the grand, unarguable ring of the first three sentences, with their high-minded commitment to an art of strict excision, of reticence embraced, rather than examined—this from a woman who was in therapy for years and who repeatedly tried and failed to complete a recalcitrant autobiographical manuscript. There is the use of the masculine pronoun by a woman poet who habitually grouped writers by sex. There is the odd, almost violent fastidiousness of those adjectives: the "facts" of one's life might be boring or commonplace, but "rough" and "vulgar"? Why not "vital" and "unique"? The adjectives seem odder still when you consider Bogan's love of Yeats and Auden, both of whom freely plundered their lives for literary material. Surely Bogan knew that "the poet," given enough talent, could get away with almost anything?

Maybe, but she stuck to her credo. Her poems permit us to gather only a few factual crumbs. . . . On a deeper level, a psychoanalytically inclined reader might speculate that at some point an emotional blow had been dealt and never overcome: the poems are full of words like "fiend," "demon," "grief," "rave," "dark," "tears," and "fury." But what sort of blow? From whose hand?

That the poems scorn such questions is part of their power. Bogan's distinctive tone comes from her use of a pure, elegant, and traditional symbolic vocabulary (flower, leaf, flame, lamp, star) in verse that while formal is also abrupt and disjunctive and therefore recognizably modern:

> The bee's fixed hexagon;
> The ant's downward tower;
> The whale's effortless eating;
> The palm's love; the flower
>
> Burnished like brass, clean like wax
> Under the pollen. . . .
>
> ("'Come, Sleep . . .'")

The emotional content of the poems is stripped of autobiographical baggage the way the rhythms are stripped of padding and the diction of words like "refrigerator" or "newspaper."

As we learn from Elizabeth Frank's fine biography [*Louise Bogan: A Portrait*], however, Bogan's reserve was less an artistic choice than an obsession. That is why, in the journal passage quoted above, she could speak of "repressing" the outright narrative of one's life, applying to the most ordinary facts the verb usually reserved for dire and dangerous psychic material. For Bogan, it was *all* dangerous. In the 1920s, many of her close friends did not know that she had a small child; twenty years later, they were not permitted to meet the local electrician with whom she had a satisfying eight-year love affair.

Given all this, there must have been moments when Frank felt Bogan's shade reaching out with ghostly hands to throttle her— and moments when most biographers would surely have wished to return the favor. Not Frank, who spent ten years researching this generous, scholarly, and unflaggingly sympathetic—one might even say empathetic—account of a brilliant, difficult, and complicated woman. (pp. 596-97)

[Bogan's was a] sad life. . . . But in the hands of another biographer, the life might have looked sadder still. Frank, however, has identified with her subject to a degree one rarely finds in the three-by-five-card world of biography. Because she sees so clearly how all-but-overpowering Bogan thought her demons were, Frank is able to present Bogan's life, for all its arrestedness, as mostly a story of gallantry, humor, and spiritual growth. Bogan's struggles—to write her *New Yorker* reviews, to give public readings, to write those never-to-be-written childhood memories, to understand herself—are evoked with an almost maternal warmth and tenderness. Frank doesn't gloss over Bogan's faults—the hostility that damaged her criticism, especially as she got older; the arrogance and spite and vanity. But we are never allowed to lose sight of the wounded psyche those faults protected.

There are other ways, though, of thinking about Bogan. If she can be seen as a gifted writer obstructed by early trauma, she can also be seen in the light of her cultural situation—that of women poets in the first half of the twentieth century.

The women who began publishing after World War I faced formidable difficulties. They were entering a field in which, with few exceptions, women were considered at best minor and at worst—a far more frequent worst—ridiculous. They had no real picture of a woman poet maturing as an artist over a lifetime, growing in power and mastery. They were subject to contradictory and debilitating notions about how they should write and what they should write about. Love, for example, was supposed to be their subject—but how were they to write about love in a way that was neither mawkish nor bawdy, trivial nor high-flown? The wild popularity of Edna St. Vincent Millay, who managed to achieve all four of these reprehensible qualities at once, only gave serious critics more "proof" that women were barred from the grand tradition of poetry. (pp. 598-99)

Seen against this background, Bogan's peculiarities look less strange. Her perfectionism, her inhibitions, her refusal to apply to her poetry the discipline she used on her bread-and-butter writing (she always spoke of poems as "arriving" or "occurring") can all be connected to an intense anxiety about self-expression and self-presentation. Even her famous reserve was not so singular: Sara Teasdale, H.D., and Marianne Moore (not to mention Emily Brontë, Emily Dickinson, and Christina Rossetti) were similarly afflicted.

What *is* striking is the degree to which Bogan accepted the received notions of her day. She too mocked women poets—they were "feminine sonneteers," "female songbirds," "Oh-God-the-pain girls." All her life she believed that the intellect was a male property, that "ardor" was woman's small offering at the shrine of poetry, that many sorts of language—from dirty words to Surrealism—were simply out of bounds for women. "There are so many ways one can't let oneself feel in poetry," she wrote Rolfe Humphries in 1937, the beginning of the "serene" years. Elsewhere she wrote, "Mine is the talent of the cry or the cahier"—the brief, intense lyric or the prose fragment.

Bogan's earliest poems are full of anxiety about being a woman. The poet-priestess speaker of the much-anthologized **"Cassandra"** explicitly places her gifts in opposition to her femininity. Another anthology favorite, **"Women,"** is a virtual catalogue of female shortcomings: women "have no wilderness in them"; they are blinded by hot, narrow emotions; they have no sphere of competence:

> They cannot think of so many crops to a field
> Or of clean wood cleft by an axe.
> Their love is an eager meaninglessness
> Too tense, or too lax.

It is interesting that Bogan liked **"Women"** enough to include it, forty-five years later, in her selected poems, *The Blue Estuaries,* but never published the marvelous **"Portrait of the Artist as a Young Woman,"** in which she gives a spirited, angry, and very disabused vignette of the young woman who wrote that early poem:

> Sitting on the bed's edge, in the cold lodgings, she
>   wrote it out on her knee
> In terror and panic—but with the moment's courage,
>   summoned up from God knows where.
> Without recourse to saints or angels: a Bohemian,
>   thinking herself free—
> A young thin girl without sense, living (she thought) on
>   passion and air.

As Frank points out, what distinguishes **"Women"** from its predecessor, Lizette Woodworth Reese's poem of the same title, is its obvious envy of men. Here is Bogan at twenty-four writing to Rolfe Humphries:

> O, you great male poets! Think of the life ahead
> of you, Rolfe! No rest! No hope! I should think
> you'd shudder at the thought of being 83, with
> no relief in sight. You'll fall for a girl of 19,
> at 83 (vide Goethe) whom you'll see one morn-
> ing chasing the ducks, you will leap out of bed,
> write an immortal sonnet, clutch the grizzled
> throat, and breathe your last.

The grim view of her own future implied here only deepened with time. "Women collapse so thoroughly, so soon"; "There can be no new love at 37, in a woman"—her letters and journals are full of such statements. "A woman writes poetry with her ovaries," she quipped at forty-three: no lyrics after menopause. "Has there ever *been* an old lady poet?" she wondered at sixty-one, after an astrologer predicted a long life.

I do not wish to reduce Bogan's complex nature to a set of beliefs about gender, but it does seem more likely that her ideas about the relative abilities and freedoms of men and women did not serve her well as an artist. Certainly they damaged her as a critic. Bogan was always a tough reviewer, and in the 1950s and 1960s she became a downright nasty one, but she was tougher on women than on men. In men she could admire genius: she was one of Auden's earliest American defenders and helped bring Rilke to American awareness. In women, however, she preferred the neglected minor talent—Viola Meynell, Abbie Huston Evans, Dorothy Richardson. Virginia Woolf was her *bête noire,* partly because of Woolf's feminist and leftist sympathies, and partly because of Woolf's social standing, but mostly she was just jealous. Woolf claimed for herself exactly those freedoms Bogan believed women could not, should not have: to be intellectually wide-ranging, ambitious, and prolific; to murder the inhibiting censor and say what she pleased; to work on a grand scale and, perhaps most important, to enjoy thoroughly the act of writing. Bogan almost never seems to have done so.

During her later life, Bogan came to feel that her moment had passed. Frank gives a touching picture of the poet looking up her name in the card catalogue of the Boston Public Library in 1964 and finding that none of her books were listed. When *The Blue Estuaries* came out four years later and failed to make a splash, she knew it was her last chance to see herself acknowledged as a figure to be reckoned with in modern poetry.

Interest has grown since her death. *The Blue Estuaries* has been reprinted by Ecco Press; her funny, witty, wonderfully written letters have been published to great acclaim; a selection of her uncollected work—journals, memoirs, poems—has appeared, albeit in mutilated form, as *Journey Around My Room,* a ''mosaic'' edited by Ruth Limmer. With Frank's painstaking life added to the shelf, all the materials for a Louise Bogan revival are now before the public.

I wonder if that revival will take place. Frank clearly hopes it will, but who will take on the task? Feminist scholars, who have done so much for H.D.'s reputation, are not likely to adopt Bogan: her spiky, dark, recalcitrant lyrics resist being read as foreshadowings of feminist progress (or indeed any other kind of progress, a concept in which Bogan did not believe); they work better as negative examples, and do, in fact, turn up here and there as textbook cases of this or that bad feminine attitude. Other critics have even less reason to see her as other than gifted but essentially minor, an odd duck who spent a great deal of her poetic energy striving for a musicality that no one cares much about these days.

Does it matter where critics place her? It is terrible to think how much it cost her to ''wait'' for those hundred-odd poems to ''arrive.'' Richard Howard has called Frank's biography ''a meditation on how to live'' [see excerpt above], that is, on how *not* to live. But I don't think we undervalue either her struggles or her achievement if we find ourselves wanting not to grapple with her poems as an oeuvre but simply to admire them one by one. That, at any rate, is the spirit in which I find myself rereading **''After the Persian,'' ''Roman Fountain,'' '''Come, Sleep . . .','' ''The Crossed Apple,'' ''The Sleeping Fury.''** As Auden said, Bogan belongs to the English tradition of pure song in poetry; her true predecessors are Thomas Campion, the anonymous Elizabethan songwriters, Christina Rossetti. A biography—even one as loving as Frank's—can't help but draw our attention to what her poems leave out, to the poems that didn't get written, to the blocks, the silences, the psychic panic, the rage. But the poems themselves stand apart from all that, because of their purity of feeling and the sheer loveliness of their sound:

> The cold remote islands
> And the blue estuaries
> Where what breathes, breathes
> The restless wind of the inlets,
> And what drinks, drinks
> The incoming tide;
>
> . . . .
>
> —O remember
> In your narrowing dark hours
> That more things move
> Than blood in the heart.
>
> (**''Night''**)

That, I suspect, is exactly what Louise Bogan wanted. (pp. 599-602)

Katha Pollitt, ''Sleeping Fury,'' in The Yale Review, *Vol. 74, No. 4, July, 1985, pp. 596-602.*

WILLIAM MAXWELL

[Maxwell is an American novelist, critic, editor, short story writer, and nonfiction and juvenile fiction writer. In his novels, such as The Folded Leaf *(1945) and* So Long, See You Tomorrow *(1980),*

Bogan in 1951 at age 53. © Rollie McKenna.

he creates gentle, witty portraits of rural Midwestern life. From 1936 to 1976 he was on the editorial staff of the New Yorker; *since then the magazine has published many of his stories and book reviews. Maxwell was a friend and disciple of* New Yorker *contributor Bogan. In the following excerpt Maxwell praises Frank's scholarly approach to her subject and recounts details of Bogan's life.]*

Elizabeth Frank says in the foreword to her biography *Louise Bogan: A Portrait* . . . that Miss Bogan seldom talked about her life: ''To those correspondents who committed the blunder of asking for biographical information, Bogan would reply—when she bothered to reply at all—that there were certain details, possessing 'tragic interest alone, and these I never describe or explain.' . . . Self-revelation she equated with confession; and . . . in her view, to confess was to ask for pardon, an act she considered as useless as it was ignoble.'' What was it she didn't care to go into? Her childhood, probably. Her forlorn first marriage. Her emotional dependence on a man she could not trust and unwillingly loved. Her struggle to forgive her own failures and those of the people who had failed her. Her periods of severe depression. The withdrawal, for years at a time, of her poetic gift.

As a schoolgirl she used to go home in the afternoon and write poems in the manner of Swinburne and William Morris and the Rossettis. The headmaster, noticing that her verse or prose compositions appeared in almost every issue of the school magazine, sent for her mother and told her to warn Louise that no Irish girl could expect to be editor of *The Jabberwock.* (''It was borne in upon me, all during my adolescence, that I was a 'Mick,' no matter what my other faults or virtues might be. It took me a long time to take this fact easily, and to understand the situation which gave rise to the minor persecutions I endured at the hands of supposedly educated and humane people.'')

Her paternal grandfather emigrated from Londonderry as a boy, before the Potato Famine, and settled in Maine, became a captain of sailing vessels, and built a big house in Portland. He had twelve children. The oldest, Daniel, Miss Bogan's father, went with him as cabin boy on a voyage to South America that lasted several years. The ship was called the Golden Sheaf. His father kept a parrot in a cage in the saloon, and at the end of the voyage the boy discovered that cigars, rum, and Panama hats were hidden under the floorboards.

Miss Bogan's maternal grandfather was a schoolteacher whose last name was Murphy. He married a Dublin woman. Louise Bogan said, in a letter to a friend, ''My maternal grandmother once picked up her mother-in-law, and was restrained only with some difficulty from dropping her down a stair-well.'' When and why they came to New England Miss Frank was unable to learn. He enlisted or was conscripted into the Union Army and was killed in battle. Either because his wife died or because she was destitute, their only child, named Mary Helen and called May, was adopted and raised by a Mr. and Mrs. Shields, who ran a saloon in Portland and were fairly prosperous. Miss Frank thinks that Louise Bogan never knew them. The adopted child was much loved and fussed over, and a great deal of attention was paid to the way she was dressed. She was sent to a convent school, and taught to sing and play the piano and other accomplishments expected of a young lady. At seventeen she married Daniel Bogan. He was twenty-one, and his copper-plate handwriting had got him a job as a clerk in a paper mill. They were both the same height—five feet four inches—but he had finished his growing and she grew another five inches and towered over her husband. She was impulsive, high-spirited, and a beauty. She loved clothes, especially large hats with veils. When she was nineteen she gave birth to a son and thirteen years later, in 1897, to a daughter, the subject of this biography. Between them there was another child, a boy, who only lived four or five months.

Like the heroine of *Madame Bovary* May Bogan was a romantic, married to a man who bored her, and trapped in a world of the commonplace. As he worked his way up from clerk to superintendent, they lived in one ugly New England mill town after another—sometimes in a house of their own, sometimes in a hotel or a boarding house. ''At some point,'' Miss Frank says, ''Louise became aware of . . . whisperings and intrigues at whose center her mother occupied some dread-inspiring role; conversations excluded her; secret signals were exchanged in her presence.'' The waitresses in the hotel dining room knew. And a woman who used to come to see her mother, one of her confidantes, who had the angry face of the queen of spades. The child went blind and then two days later suddenly saw the gas light in its etched glass shade, and knew that her sight had come back. Her father threatened to kill her mother, and her brother fought with him. On at least one occasion May Bogan took her small daughter with her to an assignation. As a grown woman Louise Bogan wrote, ''As I remember my bewilderment, my judgment even now can do nothing to make things clear. The child has nothing to which it can compare the situation. And everything that then was strange is even stranger in retrospect. . . . The door is open, and I see the ringed hand on the pillow; I weep by the hotel window as she goes down the street with *another;* I stare at the dots which make up the newspaper photograph (which makes me realize that I then had not yet learned to read). The

chambermaid tells me to stop crying. How do we survive such things? But it is long over. And forgiven . . .''

Erratically, during a good part of her life, Miss Bogan kept a journal. In it she wrote, ''The poet represses the outright narrative of his life. He absorbs it, along with life itself. The repressed becomes the poem. Actually, I have written down my experience in the closest detail. But the rough and vulgar facts are not there. At the same time, the desire (and need) remains to write of a time which has disappeared, and cannot be seen again, except in memory. . . . A few old stories. . . . But not egoistic or *minor* ones.'' She referred to the journal as her ''long prose thing'' and thought of publishing it as fiction, with the title ''Laura Daly's Story.'' At the time of her death, fifteen years ago, it amounted to about seventy handwritten pages. It is in the main about remembered details of her childhood—sights and sounds, impressions, memories: the mill flume; her mother's character; a moment of illumination brought on by seeing a bouquet of French marigolds in a hospital room; a boarding house where for the first time she experienced true order; her brother's crippling attachment to her mother; and so on. Without it, no really adequate biography would have been possible. Again and again in these fragments she approaches the hurdle that she clearly intended to take, and at the last minute turns aside, and it is this turning aside that, finally, says all there is to say: What was unbearable once is unbearable still.

The journal was published in the January 30, 1978, issue of *The New Yorker,* under the heading **''From the Journals of a Poet.''** In 1973, Ruth Limmer, Miss Bogan's literary executor, brought out a volume of her selected correspondence (*What the Woman Lived*) and, in 1980, a book of excerpts from the journal and from Miss Bogan's stories, poems, letters, and literary criticism. The title, *Journey Around My Room,* was borrowed from the title of her best short story. The subtitle, *The Autobiography of Louise Bogan,* is a misnomer. My copy of *Webster's New Collegiate Dictionary* defines ''autobiography'' as ''A biography written by the subject of it; memoirs of one's life written by oneself.'' This was a paste-up job, with a biographical end in view. It contained information at the time not generally known and of considerable interest, but until now Louise Bogan's life and work had not been subjected to the careful and intelligent scrutiny of a dispassionate mind.

''The innermost secrets of a proud and dignified spirit have a way of retreating when too strenuously pursued,'' Miss Frank says. ''Nevertheless, something stopped Louise Bogan dead in her tracks, not once, but many times. Until we discover this principle of arrest, even the most copious supply of documentation and the most perceptive psychological guesswork will be of little advantage in our attempt to enter the sanctuaries of either the life or the work. What we must do, instead, is to look at them long and hard, until, as Bogan herself learned from Hopkins and Rilke, they begin to look back at us.''

The biography is divided into alternating sections of narrative and literary analysis. Miss Frank is equally well equipped for both. The book's only shortcomings are extremely minor ones: it suffers from the occasional repetitions of a manuscript long worked on, which Miss Frank's editors should have caught, and from a rather inconvenient arrangement of the footnotes, and I would have liked a fuller index.

When Louise Bogan was eight years old she was sent for two years to the same convent school her mother had gone to. For reasons Miss Frank could not discover, she was kept out of school for a year. Then the family moved to Boston, and her mother placed her for the next five years in the Girls' Latin School, in Roxbury, where, Miss Frank says, she received "the best classical education then available to girls in this country." The local branch of the Boston Public Library subscribed to *Poetry* and she read it closely. She had, she says, "the double vision of the born reader, from the beginning." By the age of eighteen she had "learned every essential of my trade . . . I had no relations whatever with the world about me: I lived in a dream, populated by figures out of Maeterlinck and Pater and Arthur Symons and Compton Mackenzie . . . and H. G. Wells and Francis Thompson and Alice Meynell and Swinburne and John Masefield and other oddly assorted authors."

In her freshman year at Boston University she fell in love with Curt Alexander, a corporal in the Army. He was born in Breslau and trained as an architectural draftsman, and he became a soldier because he couldn't find a job in his chosen profession. He was nine years older than she was, tall and blond and handsome in a proud way. Her mother did not want her to repeat the mistake she herself had made, and Alexander struck her father as "very German and 'Achtung'!" She was nineteen when she married him, in 1916. He was transferred from New York City to Panama when the United States entered the First World War, and, four months pregnant, she followed him there on a troopship. She was so seasick that she had to be carried from the ship on a stretcher. She hated Panama. Her shoes were always moldy and her dresses stuck to her. She could not talk to the other Army wives. Or to her husband; they played cards, being unable to think of anything to say. "It had become clear to her," Miss Frank says, "that she and Alexander had nothing in common, a fact that was all the more apparent after the baby's birth, when Alexander inexplicably ceased to desire sexual relations."

She stuck it out for a year, and during that time two of her poems were published in a little magazine edited by Alfred Kreymborg. Then she took her daughter and went home to her parents. Her brother, fighting with the American Army in France, was killed a few weeks before the Armistice. After the war, she and Alexander lived together in various Army posts. Alexander was promoted to lieutenant, then captain. Once when they were living in an Army base off Portland, she telephoned from the mainland during a bad storm to say that she thought it would be better to spend the night where she was, and he told her to come right home with the baby and cook his dinner. His wants came before all other considerations. She said long afterward to Ruth Limmer, "What could I do. One must break free. One must burst forth." She left him again, this time for good. Alexander died of pneumonia after an operation for gastric ulcer, at the age of thirty-two.

Her parents looked after the baby for her, so that she could support herself. She worked first as a clerk in Brentano's and then in various branches of the New York Public Library.

In a species of questionnaire that the mature Louise Bogan put to herself she wrote:

> *Did you ever seek God?*
> No.
>
> *What is it that you sought?*
> I sought love.
>
> *And you sought love for what reason?*
> Those about me, from childhood on, had

sought love. I heard and saw them. I saw them rise and fall on that wave. I closely overheard and sharply overlooked their joy and grief. I worked from memory and example.

At a fund-raising party in a bookstore, the poet Raymond Holden saw her, was struck by her beauty, and went up to speak to her. He had a wife and children but was living apart from them, in his Washington Square house. After a few weeks he and Louise Bogan began living together. "Holden quickly learned," Miss Frank says, "that there were at least two Louises: one a tender, passionate, intensely sexual being, and the other a violent, cruel, and deeply suspicious fiend, who couldn't stand being loved and did everything possible to test and invalidate Raymond's feelings for her." She was twenty-five and he was twenty-nine. Two years later, when his wife divorced him, they were married.

He was witty and charming and the physical attraction between them was very strong. He was a loving father to her child. He came of a well-to-do family, but little by little his inheritance slipped through his fingers. He also had a tendency toward what he called "passionate renewing delight" and Louise Bogan called "Shelleyism." "By whatever name," Miss Frank says, "this was an addiction to romantic love. Raymond had grown up reading *The Idylls of the King* . . . and his hunger to do and risk all for love, to be perpetually scaling its heights and plunging into its depths, was insatiable." That he was by no means as good a poet as his wife he apparently failed to recognize.

During the period of the greatest happiness of their marriage they were living in the country, in an old farmhouse they had bought and fixed up, in Hillsdale, New York. Such times of happiness, Miss Frank observes, "seem so certain to go on forever, since nothing about them even hints at a built-in flaw in their design." The house caught on fire and burned to the ground. They moved back into the city. He went to work as managing editor of *The New Yorker*. She published short stories, reviews, a Profile of Willa Cather. She and Holden led a fairly social life. It was still Prohibition, and the gin was homemade. She was intensely jealous and accused him of having designs on other women, was sure that they had designs on him, and would not believe anything he said in his own defense. Her paranoid suspicions were not totally without foundation. Sometimes on the way home from a party they would engage in shouting matches in the street. Once in a moment of anger she threw a pot of hot coffee at him. On another occasion he knocked her down a flight of steps and injured her eye. "She was caught," Miss Frank says, "in a fatal paradox of simultaneously desiring and fearing the emotional violence she had always known." Without pushing things or asking the reader to accept suppositions that are unsupported by any real evidence, Miss Frank shows the effect of childhood shock working its way up through and ultimately destroying the marriage.

In the critical part of the book Miss Frank moves from poem to poem, right straight through the published work, identifying the voice, decoding the symbols, making the connection between a given poem and the same or similar ideas in poems that have come before, establishing the literary influence when there is one. It suggests many years of thoughtful reading, but in any case for the first time the whole run of the poems, so moving and beautiful even when one only partly understands them, opens out and becomes clear. A single example—part of Miss Frank's consideration of **"The Sleeping Fury"**—will perhaps give some idea of how secure her exegesis is. Having explained that in the spring of 1933 Louise Bogan saw in Rome, in the Museo Nazionale delle Terme, a head of one of the Erinyes, Miss Frank goes on to say, "While she gazed at the sculptured head in Rome and then (that is to say, months later) at the postcard with its image, and then at the image which her memory preserved, the figure became detached from all the occasions of viewing, turning from an object into a symbol that she consciously placed within a geography familiar from her earlier work. In her 1935-36 journal she wrote, 'To trace the dream-landscape that has grown inside me every night, all my life, along with daylight reality, and which has mountains, ruins, islands, shores, cities, and even *suburbs* and summer "resorts" *of its own,* related to one another and, many times, recurrent (almost in the sense of revisited).' The setting of **"The Sleeping Fury"** is this region fused with details picked up from the *Encyclopaedia Britannica* entry about the Furies. Thus the New England of Bogan's childhood becomes transposed to a land in which the most primitive cruelty and the most serene tenderness coexist."

In her journal Louise Bogan wrote, "The continuous turmoil in a disastrous childhood makes one so tired that 'Rest' becomes the word forever said by the self to the self. The incidents are so vivid and so terrible that to remember them is inadequate: they must be forgotten." When it is not done effortlessly, without the person's knowledge, the act of forgetting can be, of course, as difficult as the act of remembering. In 1931, a year and three months after the fire, she committed herself to a psychiatric hospital for treatment of depression. From the Neurological Institute she wrote to John Hall Wheelock, who was her editor at Scribners and her friend, "I refused to fall apart, so I have been taken apart, like a watch." Two years later she went to Europe for five months on a Guggenheim fellowship, and when she got home she discovered that Holden had been living with a woman in their apartment. And again had to put herself under treatment.

For thirty-eight years she covered the poetry scene for this magazine [*The New Yorker*]. She looked down her nose at Surrealism, thought T. S. Eliot's *Four Quartets* as beautiful as anything he had ever written and that they showed what he could do "in the province of pure emotion when all irony has been eliminated." She loathed the New Criticism, and saw in the poetry of John Berryman and Robert Lowell an exploitation of personal trauma that was relentless and theatrical. She was a pacifist, and during the time that Communism was stylish was never drawn to it. Her own identification with the working class was nonideological; she had lived through the nightmare of being dispossessed and seeing her furniture on the street.

Sometimes poets took offense at her chiselled opinions, but it is also true that many of the people she thought of as her enemies were not. With certain younger writers whose talent she believed in—Theodore Roethke was one of them—her patience and generosity were extraordinary.

After her mother's death, in 1936, she made a sentimental pilgrimage to Ireland. It was not a success. The faces in Dublin were, she wrote to her daughter, the faces of conspirators. She grew frightened. Afterward she wrote to the critic Morton Zabel, who was perhaps her closest friend, "There must be a God, Morton, for on the Southampton boat-train, there appeared a tall thin man who proceeded to take care of me like a baby. (No, Morton: it's not another of those things. This was probably, is,—the Angel Gabriel in disguise!) . . . He says *Nuttin* when he means *Nothing;* his parents came from Sligo

. . . I told him the whole story the second day out, and he nursed me along even more tenderly, thereafter. He laughed me out of it; he tricked me into deck chairs; he brought me lots of rye when the panic became too bad. But for that touch of human understanding, I should certainly have started gibbering." The relationship lasted for eight years. Though she mentioned him to her friends, she did not allow any of them to meet him.

She was devoted to her daughter, and her friendships were important to her, but as she grew older she felt less and less need for human company. People who wanted to see her for one reason or another—because they loved her or admired her or in some important way felt forever indebted to her—were usually put off with postponements or "visits to the dentist" too consistent to be plausible.

She had a third breakdown in her middle sixties. It was brought on by a brief period of living in Boston, when she was teaching at Brandeis University. Old experiences long laid to rest now rose to haunt her, and she saw herself living out her days in some shabby Boston boarding house. The therapy, which included a brief series of electroshock treatments, was only partly successful. She had weeping spells in the morning.

In her journal she wrote:

> Surely I have acted in a consistently *optimistic* fashion, ever since the 1933 breakdown.—I have surmounted one difficulty after another; I have *worked* for life and "creativity;" I have cast off all the anxieties and fears I could; I have helped others to work and hold on. Why this collapse of psychic energy? . . .
>
> *Who* have I become? *What* has me in hand? . . .
>
> What am I afraid of?
>
> *Death*—for one thing. Yes, that is part of it.— These deaths that are reported in the newspapers seem to be all my age—or younger.
>
> But people keep hopeful and warm and *loving* right to the end—with much more to endure than I endure.—I see the old constantly, on these uptown streets—and they are not "depressed." Their eyes are bright; they have bought themselves groceries; they gossip and laugh— with, often, crippling handicaps evident among them.
>
> Where has this power gone, in my case?

Miss Frank says that for twenty years she "had not permitted herself to feel (as far as anyone can know) new or rekindled love, for anyone or anything. Her carefully erected, thoroughly adult maturity had at last engendered its own defeat by refusing to countenance its opposite: the eternal, hungry, clamoring, yearning, angry, weeping child. . . . She could not feel, she could not give. Since the last depression she could not even listen to music."

But more poems did come. A few. And very beautiful and strange they are. Consider **"Masked Woman's Song,"** which she placed at the end of her final collection, *The Blue Estuaries:*

> Before I saw the tall man
> Few women should see
> Beautiful and imposing
> Was marble to me.

> And virtue had its place
> And evil its alarms,
> But not for that worn face,
> And not in those roped arms.

"Darkness was her fate," Miss Frank says, "what she knew best. . . . In this last poem . . . the known world is broken, and nothing can ever be the same again."

She died alone in her apartment on West 169th Street, of a coronary occlusion, at the age of seventy-two. In a commemorative tribute delivered before the American Academy of Arts and Letters, W. H. Auden said, "By temperament she was not a euphoric character and in her life she had much to endure. What, aside from their technical excellence, is most impressive about her poems is the unflinching courage with which she faced her problems, her determination never to surrender to self-pity, but to wrest beauty and joy out of dark places. . . . It was a privilege to have known her." (pp. 73-6)

> *William Maxwell, "Louise Bogan's Story," in* The New Yorker, *Vol. LXI, No. 23, July 29, 1985, pp. 73-6.*

Along with Youth: Hemingway, the Early Years

by Peter Griffin

(For Ernest Hemingway: see also *CLC*, Vols. 1, 3, 6, 8, 10, 13, 19, 30, 34; *Contemporary Authors*, Vols. 77-80; *Dictionary of Literary Biography*, Vols. 4, 9; *Dictionary of Literary Biography Yearbook:* 1981; and *Dictionary of Literary Biography Documentary Series*, Vol. 1.)

An Excerpt from *Along with Youth: Hemingway, the Early Years*

The last Sunday in October, Kate Smith invited Ernest and Bill to a party at the Belleville, as her brother Kenley's apartment on East Division Street was called. Dress was informal; there would be plenty of liquor and many guests they both knew. Besides, Kate said, she had invited a school friend from St. Louis, Elizabeth Hadley Richardson. She had spoken of her before, Kate said— the girl with the beautiful hair.

Ernest and Bill, "well-oiled" after an afternoon at the Venice Cafe, got to the Belleville while the party was still new. With the elegant manners of drunks, they acknowledged acquaintances, agreed with everyone in abstruse discussions of the new poetry of Ezra Pound and T. S. Eliot, looked over the strange apartment (a half-dozen small rooms off a long corridor), and conceived an aversion to one of the four young men boarding with Kenley and Doodles. His name was Don Wright, but everyone called him "Dirty Don," ostensibly because of the way he left the bathroom. Ernest told Bill he disliked Wright's attempt at suave gentility and the petty, calculating expression in his eyes.

Sometime in the midst of the party, when everyone else had caught up with Ernest and Bill, Kate Smith gave her friend from St. Louis a general introduction. Hadley, or Hash as she was called, was taller than Kate, with softer green eyes and thick auburn hair pulled back to a knot. Slouching a bit to conceal a full breast, she gave a practiced smile and looked bitten by each word Kate said. That night, Ernest saw little of Hadley Richardson. She was taken up by Don Wright and several of his friends. But the next day, after another long afternoon at the Venice, Ernest made his way back to the Belleville.

During his hours with Hadley, Ernest was loquacious and opinionated. He spoke as a veteran of the wars, as a cognoscente of the arts, as an intimate of the low-life in the toughest town in America—Kansas City. Hadley, although she was eight years older, was struck by Ernest's knowledge of the world and by his delicate vitality. They went to dinner, then to a movie. Later, they talked for hours (Agnes Kurowsky's name came up all too frequently for Hadley) at the Red Star Cafe. On the station platform, Sunday night, Hadley felt she hadn't known anything before she met Ernest. But, for some reason, he said accusingly she knew too much.

MARCUS CUNLIFFE

[*Cunliffe, an American scholar and critic, writes frequently about political, sociological, and cultural developments in the United States. He is best known for his study* The Literature of the United States *(1954), which he updates periodically. In the following excerpt Cunliffe states that Griffin's biography lacks substantial analysis of Hemingway's life and work, and he questions Griffin's authority and reliability as a biographer.*]

[In **Along with Youth: Hemingway, the Early Years**, Griffin] reprints the apprentice poetry and prose with a sort of proprietary pride but with meager analysis. His observations sometimes leave the impression that his knowledge of Hemingway stops short around 1920, when this volume ends. For instance, in the **"Buckley at Mons"** vignette from **in our time,** when a British officer says Germans looked "awfully surprised" at being shot, Griffin's comment is that "Ernest mocked the clipped British fashion of speaking." Mocked? He and Hadley, in their letters, used a semi-English with "awfully" as a standard non-humorous adverb. **The Sun Also Rises** is only one of the key Hemingway works that show a liking for slangy British understatement. "Chink" Dorman-Smith, a British regular officer and pukka sahib, became a friend as early as 1918. During the 1920s an acquaintance described Hemingway as "more European than American in get-up. Could have been taken as a young Guards officer." Again, Griffin is not always explicit enough. A sentence on the Hemingways as a young married couple in Paris reads: "Each morning, Ernest rose at dawn, emptied his chamber pot, and cooked his breakfast eggs in it." Why?—poverty, *la vie de Bohème?* We are left to guess, if we feel like it.

These are smallish affairs. A worse fault is Griffin's tendency to treat a fictional account as equivalent to straight autobiographical testimony. He has Hemingway eat spaghetti "very quickly and seriously" because that is how Lieutenant Henry eats it in **A Farewell to Arms.** When Henry is wounded by an Austrian mortar-bomb, "I tried to breathe but my breath would not come . . ." Griffin reproduces the passage unquestioningly as Hemingway's own memoir (except that he makes the phrase read "I tried hard to breathe").

Peter Griffin is not then altogether reliable or authoritative. (pp. 1, 14)

Marcus Cunliffe, "Ernest Hemingway: The Life behind the Legend," in Book World—The Washington Post, *November 3, 1985, pp. 1, 14.*

ARTHUR WALDHORN

Hemingway always insisted that he had the obligation to withhold his work from public view till it satisfied his standards. In a slender volume that traces Hemingway from boyhood through World War I and his first marriage [*Along with Youth: Hemingway, the Early Years*], Griffin ignores those standards, printing for the first time five inept, occasionally silly pieces of post-adolescent fiction, only one of which (**"Crossroads"**) even hints at Hemingway's mature genius. Griffin's other contribution is biographical. He establishes that Hemingway indeed had affairs with his wartime nurse, Agnes; and, while engaged to his first wife, with their mutual friend, Katy Smith. Otherwise, Griffin adds little of critical, interpretative, or biographical merit—and does so without stylistic grace.

> *Arthur Waldhorn, in a review of "Along with Youth: Hemingway, the Early Years," in* Library Journal, *Vol. 110, No. 19, November 15, 1985, p. 90.*

BILL RAYBURN

Along with Youth, the first installment of a projected three-volume work, began as Griffin's Ph.D. dissertation. It can be viewed as official, in that he had the blessings of Mary Welsh, Ernest's fourth wife and widow. Jack Hemingway, Ernest's son by his first wife, Hadley Richardson, has furnished a foreword and made his mother's vast correspondence available to Mr. Griffin. Bill Horne, Ernest's close friend from the First World War, also permitted access to letters, photographs and memorabilia. Thanks to these two sources, we now have the fullest account of Hemingway's formative years, told with depth and wealth of detail.

Early on, Hemingway knew he was going to be a writer, and the book contains many examples of his work, including excerpts from an incomplete novel, and five unpublished short stories. While these stories are hardly the work we would later come to expect, some flashes of style and substance are already apparent. A paragraph from **"The Mercenaries"** reads like Certified Old Ernest:

> It's all lemon orchards and orange groves along the right-hand side of the railway, and so pretty that it hurts to look at it. Hills terraced and yellow fruit shining through the green leaves and darker green of olive trees on the hills, and streams with wide dry pebbly beds cutting down to the sea and old stone houses, and everything all color.

Working first as a cub reporter for the Kansas City Star, Ernest then went off to the Great War; when he returned from Italy, he took a newspaper job at the *Toronto Star* in February 1920. In mid-May he left the paper for Walloon Lake, then moved to Chicago in October.

When he was introduced to Elizabeth Hadley Richardson at a party that fall, he knew he was going to marry her. At 29, she was eight years older than Hemingway. They were married on Sept. 3, 1921, in the Methodist Church at little Horton Bay in the Upper Peninsula [of Michigan] and took an apartment in Chicago.

Ernest had wanted to return to Italy, but Sherwood Anderson persuaded him to go to Paris, which he said was a civilized, free and tolerant city. Ernest and Hadley said farewell to Chicago just before Thanksgiving, 1921. They lived first at the Hotel Jacob, then settled in a dreary flat at 74 rue du Cardinal Lemoine. This was indeed the end of something. Old friends and familiar faces, along with youth, were now in the past. It was a beginning, too, for the Hemingways were entering that time of their lives that would be, to Ernest—looking back just before his death—"how Paris was in the early days when we were very poor and very happy."

Despite its rather flat tone, Griffin's work is the result of painstaking research and dedication, and is worth the reading.

> *Bill Rayburn, "A Couple of Clean, Well-Lighted Books on Hemingway," in* The Detroit News, *November 17, 1985, p. 2F.**

RAYMOND CARVER

[*Carver is an American short story writer and poet whose works include the poetry volume* At Night the Salmon Move *(1976) and the short story collections* Will You Please Be Quiet, Please? *(1976) and* Cathedral *(1983). His highly acclaimed stories, which often portray ordinary people frustrated by their inability to communicate, evoke the isolation of modern life. In the following excerpt Carver evinces his own regard for Hemingway and praises Griffin's "wonderful and intimate" portrayal of the author.*]

In the years since 1961 Hemingway's reputation as "the outstanding author since the death of Shakespeare" (John O'Hara's wildly extravagant assessment in praise of *Across the River and*

Hemingway in upper Michigan in 1917. From Along with Youth: Hemingway, the Early Years, *by Peter Griffin. Oxford University Press, 1985.*

Into the Trees) shrank to the extent that many critics, as well as some fellow writers, felt obliged to go on record that they, and the literary world at large, had been bamboozled somehow: Hemingway was not nearly as good as had been originally thought. They agreed that at least one, maybe two, of the novels (*The Sun Also Rises* and, possibly, *A Farewell to Arms*) might make it into the 21st century, along with a handful, five or six, perhaps, of his short stories. Death had finally removed the author from center stage and deadly "reappraisals" began taking place.

It is not entirely coincidental, either, that soon after his death a particular kind of writing began to appear in this country, writing that stressed the irrational and fabulous, the antirealist against the realist tradition. In this context, it might be worthwhile to remind ourselves what Hemingway believed good writing should do. He felt fiction must be based on actual experience. "A writer's job is to tell the truth," he wrote in his introduction to **Men at War.** His standard of fidelity to the truth should be so high that his invention, out of his experience, should produce a truer account than anything factual can be." And he also wrote: "Find what gave you the emotion, what the action was that gave you the excitement. Then write it down making it so clear that . . . it can become a part of the experience of the person who reads it."

Given his stature and influence, maybe the sharp reaction after his death was inevitable. But gradually, especially within the last decade, critics have been better able to separate the celebrity big-game hunter and deep-sea fisherman, the heavy-drinking bully and brawler, from the disciplined craftsman and artist whose work seems to me, with each passing year, to become more durable.

"The great thing is to last and get your work done," Hemingway said in *Death in the Afternoon.* And that, essentially, is what he did. Who was this man—by his own admission, "a son of a bitch"—whose novels and books of short stories changed forever the way fiction was written and, for a time, even the way people thought about themselves?

Peter Griffin's wonderful and intimate book, *Along with Youth: Hemingway, the Early Years* (the title is from one of Hemingway's early poems), supplies some of the answers. Mr. Griffin was a young Ph.D. student at Brown University when he wrote a short letter to Mary Hemingway telling her how important Hemingway's work had been to him at a difficult time in his life. She invited him to visit and promised full cooperation in writing this book, the first of three biographical volumes. Working a territory where a regiment of literary scholars and specialists have gone before, Mr. Griffin has uncovered a significant amount of new and revealing information. (Five previously uncollected short stories are also included.) Several chapters deal with Hemingway's early family life and relationships. His mother was an overbearing woman with pretensions to being a singer; his father was a prominent doctor who taught Hemingway to hunt and fish and gave him his first pair of boxing gloves.

But by far the larger and more important part of the book is devoted to Hemingway's coming-of-age as a reporter for the *Kansas City Star*, then as an ambulance driver for the Red Cross in Italy, where he was seriously injured by an Austrian mortar shell and machine-gun bullets. There is a long section devoted to his convalescence in a military hospital in Milan. While there he fell in love with a nurse from Pennsylvania named Agnes Kurowsky, who became the model for Catherine

Barkley in *A Farewell to Arms.* (She jilted him for an Italian count.)

In 1919 he returned home to Oak Park, Ill., wearing "a cock-feathered Bersaglieri hat, a knee-length officer's cape lined with red satin, and a British tunic decorated with ribbons of the Valor Medal and the War Cross." He had to use a cane to walk. He was a hero, and he signed up with a lecture agency to talk to civic groups about his experiences in the war. When he was finally asked to leave home by his angry and bewildered parents (Hemingway didn't want to work at a job, liked to sleep in late and spend his afternoons shooting pool), he went to the peninsula country in upper Michigan and then to Toronto, where he accepted room and board and $80 a month from a wealthy family to tutor and "make a man out of" the family's retarded son.

From Toronto he moved to Chicago, where he shared rooms and a bohemian life with a friend named Bill Horne. He worked at a magazine called *Commonwealth Cooperative,* for which he wrote, in his words, "Boy's Personals, The Country Division, Miss Congress's fiction, bank editorials, children's stories, etc." At this time, Hemingway began meeting literary people like Sherwood Anderson and Carl Sandburg. He liked to read aloud and explain the poems of Keats and Shelley and once, in the company of Sandburg, who praised his "sensitive interpretation," he read from "The Rubaiyat of Omar Khayyam." He was crazy about dancing and won a dance contest with a woman friend named Kate Smith. (She later married John Dos Passos.) In October 1920, he met another woman, eight years older than he, who would become his first wife—the remarkable Elizabeth Hadley Richardson.

In the nine months of their courtship—she was living in St. Louis while Hemingway was living and working in Chicago—they each wrote over 1,000 pages of letters. . . . The passages Mr. Griffin quotes are intelligent, witty, often moving, and show her offering a shrewd and perceptive response to the stories, sketches and poems that the 21-year-old Hemingway was sending her every week.

In one of the letters, she contrasts her own writing with his. She knew, she said, that her writing was filled with abstractions, whereas his was not. But there was something more. In all of Ernest's sentences, "the accents fell naturally on the correct quantitative place . . . *I* have to scratch lines under important words." She praised his intuitive sense: "It is a most lovely thing—intuition—inside dead sure of stuff. A very obvious example of it is ideas just appearing in your mind that make you understand the way things are." It was, she felt, the basis for his work. She encouraged their plan to go to Europe and felt it would be just the thing for his writing: "Why, you will write like a great wonderful breeze bringing strong whiffs from all sorts of interior places. You'll give birth before I will, and for you Paris is the place to do it."

At the end of April 1921, Hemingway told her he was beginning his first novel, a book with "real people, talking and saying what they think." The young man who was the hero of the novel would be called Nick Adams. (pp. 3, 51)

Mr. Griffin's biography closes just as the newly married couple, armed with letters of introduction to Gertrude Stein and Ezra Pound, are about to sail for France. It brings to life the young Hemingway with all his charm, vitality, good looks, passionate dedication to writing, like nothing else I've ever read about the man. (p. 51)

Raymond Carver, "Coming of Age, Going to Pieces," in The New York Times Book Review, *November 17, 1985, pp. 3, 51-2.**

R.W.B. LEWIS

[*Lewis is an American critic who has written and edited many works on American literature and literary figures, including a biography of Edith Wharton and the landmark critical work* The American Adam: Innocence, Tragedy and Tradition in the Nineteenth Century *(1955). In the following excerpt Lewis describes Griffin's technique and expresses dissatisfaction with his casual approach.*]

[In *Along with Youth*] Griffin puts before us a series of short fictional workouts by Hemingway in 1919 and 1920, dug out of the Hemingway collection now in the John F. Kennedy Library in Boston. They involve assortments of violence, eccentricity, lovemaking, and standing tall. One of them, **"Crossroads,"** consists of quick glimpses of half a dozen rural individuals in or just after some little moment of crisis, and it has, so to say, the promise of a promise. But as a cluster, the stories are of minimal interest, and serve mainly to make more arresting the progress reflected a few years later in the vignettes for the original or lowercase **in our time.** Of measurably greater value are the many letters from Hadley Richardson to Ernest—about 1,000 pages in all, as we gather—also found in the Kennedy Library and effectively deployed by Griffin to give

Hemingway at The American Red Cross Hospital in Milan. From Along with Youth: Hemingway, the Early Years, *by Peter Griffin. Oxford University Press, 1985.*

the wayward courtship saga a palpable poignancy, as well as a sort of sexual vibrance: the best and richest portion of the book. In addition, Griffin has brightened the atmosphere of his tale by folkloristic anecdotes picked up in conversations with Jack Hemingway, the novelist's first-born son, who contributes an appreciative foreword; and Bill Horne, a lifelong friend whom Hemingway came to know in New York while waiting to be shipped overseas. (p. 32)

Malcolm Cowley has called the most important single event in Hemingway's life his wounding by a mortar shell on July 8, 1918, at Fossalta di Piave in the Italian Veneto. Hemingway bicycled out to the frontline trenches near the Piave River on a warm moonlit evening, carrying cigarettes and chocolate, and crept forward to a listening post 150 yards away, manned by two Italian soldiers. Griffin's account continues:

> As Ernest and the two soliders lay hunched against the rim of their hole, they heard across the river a "cough," then a "chuh-chuh-chuh-chuh," then a long descending roar. "Then there was a flash, as when a blast-furnace door is swung open, and a roar that started white and went red and on and on in the rushing wind." Ernest "tried to breathe but my breath would not come and I felt myself rush bodily out of myself and out and out all the time bodily in the wind. I went out swiftly, all of myself, and I knew I was dead and that it had all been a mistake to think you just died. Then I floated and instead of going on I felt myself slide back. I breathed and I was back."

One of the two soldiers had his legs blown off and was dead. The other was badly wounded but alive; Ernest slung the man over his shoulder and staggered back toward the trenches. On the way, he was hit by machine-gun fire in his right foot and knee, but he made it to the trench before collapsing.

There appear to have been three Italian soldiers, not two; and by Hemingway's own testimony (to Cowley) the one Hemingway was carrying died before the command post was reached. But what is notable is that the heart of the experience, from "cough" and "chuh-chuh-chuh-chuh" through ". . . and I was back," is taken, not from Hemingway's letters or reminiscences, but from a work of fiction, *A Farewell to Arms*, of 1929. Hemingway's fictional writings are put to service on other occasions: Ernest's feelings about playing football in high school, and his reactions to wartime Paris, are borrowed intact from *The Torrents of Spring*. These sources are scrupulously acknowledged in the back; but the assumption that the novelistic wording of an experience can be accepted as strict historical fact is an exceedingly risky one. The American in *A Farewell to Arms* is a creature of the imagination called Frederick Henry; it is Henry and not "Ernest" who "tried to breathe" and so on. For sound aesthetic reasons, his terrible misadventure occurs in the summer of 1917, some months before the rain-swept retreat from Caporetto; and the quoted narrative language participates in and grows out of the larger thematic and imagistic patterns of one of the most poetically designed novels ever written.

Griffin is not engaged in a "critical" biography, and may perhaps be excused from observing niceties of distinction. Even so, the literary aspect of *Along with Youth* is oddly displaced. A 2,500-word letter of 1919, which shows Hemingway finding his personal voice and (in a clear anticipation of **"Big Two-**

Hearted River'') his characteristic assuagements for pain and loss, is simply inserted verbatim into the text without the hint of a comment. A literary sensibility enters the biography at points outside the narrative proper: in chapter titles—''Disorder and Early Sorrow,'' ''A Boy's Will,'' ''War is Kind''; in captions for photographs—''Ernest good-humoredly playing the role of a naive hobo (a role he would recreate for Nick Adams in **''The Battler''**)''; and in the prefatory remarks to the chapter-by-chapter list of notes in the back of the book. These begin as plain indications of sources, but by chapter eight they have become diagnostic: ''Ernest Hemingway's un-published **''Crossroads''** expresses the theme of this chapter . . . Ernest is indeed at the crossroads of his young life.'' By the epilogue, the remarks faintly and rather appealingly resemble the titles in silent movies: ''They had made many plans during their nine-month marriage; they had many dreams. Now it was time, they felt, for Ernest to start his career.'' (pp. 32-3)

R.W.B. Lewis, ''Who's Papa?'' in The New Republic, *Vol. 193, No. 23, December 2, 1985, pp. 31-4.**

MATTHEW J. BRUCCOLI

[*An American biographer, editor, and bibliographer, Bruccoli is probably best known as an authority on F. Scott Fitzgerald and his contemporaries. His numerous publications include* Scott and Ernest: The Authority of Failure and the Authority of Success *(1980) and* Fitzgerald/Hemingway Annual, *which he coedits. In the following generally laudatory review, Bruccoli refutes charges by such critics as R.W.B. Lewis and Jeffrey Meyers that the early Hemingway stories included in* Along with Youth *were not worth publishing.*]

Peter Griffin has been the recipient of unwarranted abuse because he prints five unpublished apprentice works by Hemingway [in his ***Along with Youth: Hemingway, the Early Years***]. The abusers have opaquely charged that this material is bad and not worth resurrecting: the familiar complaint about ''wastebasket scholarship.'' Mr. Griffin makes no claims for the merit of these stories; he presents them as evidence of how Hemingway learned to refine his technique and find a controlling point of view. Their very badness—with anticipatory flashes of later achievement—renders them instructive. The ponderous facetiousness of ''When you enter the room, and you will have no more chance than the zoological entrant in the famous camel-needle's-eye gymkhana of entering the room unless you are approved by Cambrinus, there will be a sudden silence'' provides a gauge of how far and how rapidly Hemingway developed. Yet the vignettes in **''Crossroads''** are so good that one wonders if Mr. Griffin has misdated them; they seem to belong with the style-forging Paris work of the early Twenties rather than with the 1919 imitative pieces. The detailed account of Hemingway's courtship of Hadley Richardson, with generous excerpts from their love letters, is a valuable gap-filler, pointing out the need for a comprehensive edition of Hemingway's correspondence. (p. 58)

[Peter Griffin accepts] the widely held explanation that the Hemingway code and ultimately the Hemingway canon grew out of his World War I initiation experiences—his exposure to violent death and his own wounding. Yet the evidence indicates that this . . . was another exercise in Hemingway's self-mythologizing. He arrived at the Italian front in early June 1918; he drove a Red Cross ambulance for three weeks; he then distributed chocolate, postcards, and tobacco on the front

lines for seven days; and on July 8 he was wounded by a Minenwerfer while in a forward observation post. He was not in combat. He was never even a soldier. The theory that this accident shaped his character and art seems distorted. All the interpretations of the traumatic consequences of the event derive from Hemingway's testimony. Since he was an inveterate fabricator and self-aggrandizer about everything else, it is difficult to accept his claims on this matter. The Great War did not test him and form him, although it educated him. . . .

[This admirable biography reaffirms] the instruction in reading about Hemingway's most interesting fictional invention. As he said of another writer in *A Moveable Feast,* ''. . . when he was lying, he was more interesting than many men telling a true story.'' (p. 60)

Matthew J. Bruccoli, ''Portrait of the Writer as a Liar,'' in National Review, *Vol. XXXVIII, No. 1, January 31, 1986, pp. 58, 60.*

JEFFREY MEYERS

[*A prolific author and editor, Meyers has written several literary biographies, including* Hemingway: A Biography, *which appeared in 1985 simultaneously with Griffin's* Along with Youth. *In the following review of Griffin's book, Meyers asserts: ''Both the method and the accuracy of this biography are radically flawed.''*]

Hemingway and Hadley. From Along with Youth: Hemingway, the Early Years, *by Peter Griffin. Oxford University Press, 1985.*

He challenges Griffin's factual accuracy and critical judgment and questions the value of including Hemingway's apprentice fiction. Matthew J. Bruccoli (see excerpt above) defended Griffin on the latter charge.]

The publisher claims that *Along with Youth* "promises to become the definitive Hemingway biography." Griffin's two important discoveries are Hemingway's letters to his Red Cross friend Bill Horne and new information about their commanding officer, Captain Jim Gamble. In the late 1970s, Mary Hemingway allowed Griffin to remove five early stories from the Hemingway Collection at the Kennedy Library and to print them in this book.

Hemingway's apprentice fiction was not good enough to publish in his lifetime. These stories, mixed in with Griffin's own text, bring his limping narrative to a halt. Though Griffin does not actually discuss these stories, he unconvincingly claims that Hemingway's style and vision were formed before he went to Paris. Just as birth anticipates death, so, for Griffin, everything written in youth "anticipates the mature Hemingway voice." Hemingway's style was not modeled on Tolstoy, Kipling, Crane, Stein, Joyce, and Pound, but on the "unaffected in tone, sonorous, rhythmical" letters of his first wife, Hadley, which "set a standard for Ernest." Since dozens of Hadley's repetitious letters are quoted, we can judge how characteristic sentences—"I wanted to run down and holler my undying affection in your too distant ear" and "I love you so highly and lowly and like a boy and girl warmly"—influenced her husband.

Both the method and the accuracy of this biography are radically flawed. Based on a dissertation, it is amateurishly padded with long and sometimes pointless quotes. Griffin, with a keen eye for the non-essential, spends two full pages on an uneventful train ride from Chicago to New York. He cannot distinguish between petty and significant detail, or, when presenting evidence, between fact, fiction, and fantasy. Though dissatisfied with Carlos Baker's biography, he lacks Baker's originality and precision, repeats all his faults, and presents a compendium of trivial facts—without analysis, interpretation, or insight. He maintains that Hemingway's father gave "a rousing speech about adolescent sexuality," although we know that Clarence Hemingway was extremely reticent about sex. He unaccountably calls *Death in the Afternoon* Hemingway's "own *Life on the Mississippi*" (on another page, he refers to

Twain's book as *Old Tunes on the Mississippi*). And he completely misreads the character of Hemingway's first love, the sophisticated nurse Agnes von Kurowsky, by stating she was not "a serious, intelligent woman."

Griffin also makes numerous factual mistakes. Hemingway's mother's temporary blindness was not related to scarlet fever; Hemingway's left eye was defective from birth, not from boxing with his son Jack; the family cottage was named after an English lake, not in appreciation of Sir Walter Scott; Hemingway was never a lieutenant in the Italian army; Jim Gamble did not save his life. Hemingway, while earning $50 a week and saving for a trip to Italy with Hadley, did not lose $700 on the Carpentier-Dempsey fight. His close friend Chink Dorman-Smith was Irish, not Scottish, and was not (like Griffin) credulous about Hemingway's sexual adventures. Griffin states, without evidence, that Hemingway had sexual relations with Indian girls, was actually engaged to the actress Mae Marsh, was seduced by a rich, beautiful woman in Paris in 1918 (a fantasy from *The Torrents of Spring*), and was the lover of his childhood friend Kate Smith. In "**Summer People**," his story about Kate, as in *A Farewell to Arms* and *Across the River,* Hemingway portrays fictional sex with women he never managed to sleep with in real life.

Griffin describes in excruciating detail the buds and lawn in Oak Park and the kinds of apples at Walloon Lake, a sister's dress and a walk to a dance, an uncle's handkerchief and the temperature in Kansas City, what Hadley made for breakfast and wore on her honeymoon. But he does not fully discuss the influence of the Civil War, the church and high school in Oak Park, the marriage of Hemingway's parents and Hemingway's conflict with them, his writing for papers in Kansas City, Toronto, and Chicago, the psychological effects of his wound, his friendship with Chink Dorman-Smith, and, most importantly, how the dominant traits of his character emerged from his early life. Griffin's laundered Hemingway is a conventional chap who shows no indication of future greatness. This portrait is likely to please the immediate family (Jack writes a laudatory preface), but few others. If Griffin plans to continue this ambitious project, he will have to raise his standards. (pp. 60-1)

Jeffrey Meyers, "A Conventional Chap," in National Review, *Vol. XXXVIII, No. 1, January 31, 1986, pp. 60-1.*

Into Eternity: The Life of James Jones, American Writer
by Frank MacShane

(For James Jones: see also *CLC*, Vols. 1, 3, 10; *Contemporary Authors*, Vols. 1-4, rev. ed., Vols. 69-72 [obituary]; *Contemporary Authors New Revision Series*, Vol. 6; and *Dictionary of Literary Biography*, Vol. 2. For Frank MacShane: see also *Contemporary Authors*, Vols. 11-12, rev. ed. and *Contemporary Authors New Revision Series*, Vol. 3.)

An Excerpt from *Into Eternity: The Life of James Jones, American Writer*

In the increasingly monastic Handy household, Jones was aware that he had "renounced society." Yet the regimen of yoga and philosophy was beginning to have useful literary consequences. He now saw how far he had gone astray in early drafts. He had been "trying to associate Prewitt with myself, and *was trying to make him a Hero*. Every line I wrote was forcing me further back, because I wanted thru Prewitt to be accepted as a Hero." Now he had a new perspective. Once he recognized that with Prewitt and Warden he had been "trying to make them both Jim Jones," he knew that he would have to give them their independence. He would have to see them as he now saw himself, without illusions or pretensions. Conceiving them as real people, he could "just put them together" and "they will make their own plot and it will be life and not formula."

The routine of life and work in the Handys' house suited Jones. "I have a fine place to work, and comforts here that I could never have in New York by myself," he informed Maxwell Perkins. But the work itself worried him. "I sometimes despair of ever learning technique," he wrote, "so I can just sit down and write. I have trouble with transitions in the middle of chapters." Perkins responded with gentle praise, urging flexibility. "A deft man may toss his hat across the office and hang it on a hook if he just naturally does it, but he will always miss if he does it consciously."

Jones quickly got the point and told his brother that learning how to write seemed to be "the development of a particular set of muscles, and thats all it is; just like with an auto mechanic or high jumper. When you can admit that to yourself, you will be there, all the way." He was also beginning to see that with writing, "no one can help you. A writer is alone with it, by the nature of it."

Perkins was useful, however, when Jones began to think of a title for the book. He had been considering *Old Soldiers Never Die*, *If Wishes Were Horses*, and *They Merely Fade Away*. But he settled on *From Here to Eternity* when he heard the refrain of the famous song

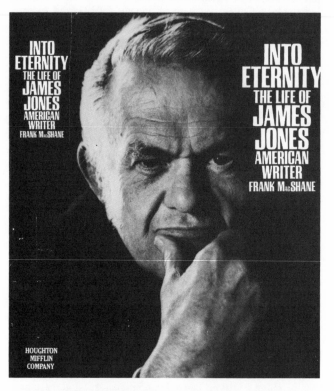

Dust jacket of Into Eternity: The Life of James Jones, *by Frank MacShane. Houghton Mifflin, 1985. Courtesy of Houghton Mifflin Company. Jacket photograph © 1985 Nancy Crampton. By permission of Nancy Crampton.*

sung by the Yale Whiffenpoofs. Perkins pointed out that the words came originally from Rudyard Kipling's "Gentlemen Rankers" in the *Barrack-Room Ballads*, and Jones was somewhat chagrined by his ignorance.

KIRKUS REVIEWS

MacShane's fourth biography [*Into Eternity*] (the others treated Ford, Chandler, and O'Hara) is a slack, puffy piece of business—reading half like an official Soviet biography of a peasant farm-hero, half like a too-slick apology for its subject's shortfallings.

And Jones, as a subject for a straight literary bio (unlike Leggett's cautionary tale *Ross and Tom* of some years ago), had shortfallings aplenty. His was the story, basically, of an *unlikely* writer. A Midwestern bruiser of a kid raised by a failed dentist-father and cruel, cold mother, enlisting in the Army right after high school, exposed to the work of Thomas Wolfe, wounded at Guadalcanal, discharged, taken up by a mother/lover-figure from his home town who painstakingly (and fairly psychotically) fashions him into a writer through intimidation, Jones' life thereafter was fairly free of incident other than a startling first success, followed by a long decline on the strength of ever less-good novels.

When the strongest first adjective a biographer can find for his writer-subject is "vital"—MacShane uses it within the first few pages—you sense you're in trouble. MacShane is unable to shake from his own recounting the literary inferiority Jones felt all his life. His education was minimal, his style primitively gross or overmuch, his artistic tastes schlocky—but, in his first and best book, *From Here to Eternity,* the raw pressures of a complex experience—the needs of soldiers at peace—were effectively rendered. You keep waiting for MacShane to play up this strongest moment of Jones' career with some intelligent analysis; but he mostly gives plot summary and then lets it rest. Nor does he ever stand back and squint critically at the oddest, most fascinating part of the life: Jones' thralldom to his Illinois witch/muse Lowney Handy, an Oedipal tragicomedy if there ever was one. Jones' life was basically the attempt of industry, of hard work, to overcome a small store of native talent—and MacShane, though scrupulously noting every fact and source, seems to let the *shape* of this life and career totally drift by him. Which is maybe why the book seems so official, so stiffly "authorized," hanging anxiously and uncritically to every thread no matter how weak or dull. It leads MacShane into ridiculousnesses: "He would also go to Orient Point, on the very end of the north fork of Long Island, and from the rocky, windswept beach look out over the water toward Plum Island. With the wind smacking him in the face, he would think of his own destiny." Oh.

As a vehicle for rehabilitating Jones' gutted literary reputation, this sluggish and unconscious book won't do. What it does for MacShane's own reputation as a serious biographer is also open to question. (pp. 1066-67)

> *A review of "Into Eternity: The Life of James Jones, American Writer," in* Kirkus Reviews, *Vol. LIII, No. 19, October 1, 1985, pp. 1066-67.*

ROBERT PHILLIPS

[Phillips, an American advertising executive, has also pursued a literary career in poetry, criticism, and fiction. His poems, in collections such as Inner Weather *(1966) and* Running on Empty: New Poems *(1981), tend to focus on small town life and grotesque characters. He has written several books of criticism, mostly on modern poets, and edited* Last and Lost Poems of Delmore Schwartz *(1979) and the* Letters of Delmore Schwartz *(1985). In the following excerpt Phillips commends MacShane for writing a balanced biography that offers an explanation for the uneven quality of Jones's work.]*

Has any other modern American novelist received the barrage of bravos and brickbats accorded James Jones? Unlikely. His first novel, *From Here to Eternity* (1951), was universally cheered. The *New York Times Book Review* called it "A major contribution to literature." His second, *Some Came Running* (1958), was called "befuddled" by Edmund Fuller and "a monstrosity" by Granville Hicks. And so it was throughout his writing career. It is just eight years since Jones's death, too early to predict accurately his place in American literature; but it seems safe to say that on the strength of his war trilogy,

he will be seen as one of the significant writers of his generation.

Jones's reputation should be helped by this balanced critical biography [*Into Eternity*]. Author of previous biographies of Ford Madox Ford, Raymond Chandler and John O'Hara, Frank MacShane, who is director of the Translation Center at Columbia University and a professor in the School of the Arts there, shows us why Jones's output was so terribly uneven. From 1958 until 1974, Jones, his wife and two children were in Paris living out the American dream. Not unlike Scott and Zelda Fitzgerald, James and Gloria Jones were recognized as celebrities and lived as such, traveling and frequently entertaining. More and more of Jones's time was squandered in correspondence with film agents, producers, lawyers and publishers. He agreed to write two nonfiction books, *Viet Journal* (1974) and *WWII* (1975). He wrote screenplays.

The author helps us to understand why Jones succumbed to such financial and social demands. Having grown up a deprived child in Illinois, he was determined—even driven—to give his family the best. His generosity to family was, apparently, equaled by his generosity to fellow writers. At one point he paid the poet Delmore Schwartz's hospital bills. He also gave 10 percent of his earnings to support a writers' colony.

The colony was run by a woman called Lowney Handy, who was as determined to be a famous midwife to literature and new writers as Jones was to become a famous novelist. Jones loved Lowney more than she did him, which he saw as an advantage in a way: "I desire to be a great writer more than anything on earth; and because of that, would stay with her; deliberately seeking not to be satisfied in love."

Gloria Jones survived this, and much more. She is the book's true heroine. Beautiful, earthy, wise—with a sense of humor that was to become her survival kit—she emerges as the wife every uncertain writer should have. As Irwin Shaw described her, "She was the candle that kept the house alight."

The biography is chronological and concise, yet Mr. MacShane manages to examine the man from many angles. It is surprising to discover that one of the tough-guy Jones's favorite writers was the lyric poet Edna St. Vincent Millay, and that he was passionate about modern painting and sculpture. His knowledgeable pronouncements on Alexander Calder seem at odds with the primitive image the novelist cultivated.

Mr. MacShane sees Jones as one of the few American writers who treated lower-class characters as human beings, giving them dignity without resorting to sentimentality. Mr. MacShane discusses each book, speculating on why some are successful and others fail. Of *Some Came Running,* Jones's novel of life in a small Middle Western town, he concludes:

> A theme of this kind, even though tragic, could be treated in a comic manner with the gusto that eighteenth-century novelists brought to novels of amorous adventure, but *Some Came Running* has little of the light touch of *Tom Jones.* It is more like a nineteenth-century novel, infused with social consciousness and sympathy for the characters. The reader therefore does not know whether to take the story straight or to accept its basic absurdity.... Jones's error ... is one of conception, for his intentions are not clearly executed, and the scope of his book suggests a straight social study rather than a

burlesque. Not by nature a satirist who could dispense with human folly in a brief story, Jones had too much feeling for the slow, drawn-out agony of his characters.

Such incisive evaluation makes this more than a biography. It is a guidebook to the works, accomplishments and failures of an American writer who was not afraid to take chances—a writer for whom the importance of art was that, like the war which was his most successful subject, it took risks.

> *Robert Phillips, ''Blood, Guts and Edna Millay,'' in* The New York Times Book Review, *November 10, 1985, p. 61.*

CHRISTOPHER LEHMANN-HAUPT

At first, the story of James Jones's life (1921-1977), as told by Frank MacShane in *Into Eternity,* makes for absorbing reading. One is curious to learn how Jones overcame the wounds inflicted upon him in childhood—his parents' fall from middle-class respectability because of the Great Depression, his father's subsequent decline into alcoholism, his mother's loss of health and withdrawal into religiosity, and his own growing disenchantment with a small-town Middle Western community from which he could barely wait to escape.

One reads of his enlistment in the United States Army in 1939 knowing that out of the experience that will shortly follow will come the material for his four best novels, *From Here to Eternity* (1951), *The Pistol* (1959), *The Thin Red Line* (1962), and *Whistle* (1978). A little more than a third of the way into Mr. MacShane's biography, with *From Here to Eternity* perched atop the fiction best-seller lists and the equally successful film version well into production, one has witnessed one of the more exhilarating success stories in the history of American letters.

But from that point on, this account of James Jones's life seems to lose its bearings. One's first inclination is to blame the biographer. Mr. MacShane . . . seems not to know what to make of Jones's life after the success of *Eternity.* He mounts flabby defenses of Jones's worst creative mistakes, the overlong and clumsy *Some Came Running* (1957) and *Go to the Widow-Maker* (1967), arguing that reviewers failed to understand what Jones was trying to do in these novels.

Jones in study where he wrote From Here to Eternity. *Photograph by Sally Jones.*

He wanders somewhat aimlessly through Jones's Paris years, 1958 through 1974, giving us parties, friendships, screen-writing assignments and even pets, instead of any compelling sense of how Jones's imagination was developing. And where he does pause to look at Jones's work, his observations often misfire. ''It is rich material for literature,'' he writes of the material in *Go to the Widow-Maker,* as if the subject of scuba diving had ever enlivened anything above a James Bond thriller or a television documentary.

And to explain why Jones once belched in the face of ''a beautiful and delicate young Israeli actress,'' he offers the following over-obvious analysis: ''It was as though, in comparing her beauty and grace with his momentary idea of himself as a monster, he allowed his feelings of inferiority to manifest themselves.'' All this for a burp.

But on closer examination, it would seem to have been James Jones's own fault that his life story sags at the point that it does. ''A man with the most ordinary of names,'' Mr. MacShane observes while introducing his subject, ''he was interested in the most ordinary of people—soldiers, small-town shopkeepers, teen-age children.'' It was no wonder then that in 1958, when he was looking around for a place to live with his new wife, Gloria Mosolino, he rejected New York for being ''just a hotbed of literary coteries and self-promoters.''

Yet in settling on Paris as his residence—ostensibly to acquire culture and not incidentally to take advantage of tax benefits and the favorable rate of exchange—he would seem to have gone where the soil was equally conducive to literary cabal, albeit one that he could more easily dominate. Certainly, Paris had little to do with his work or his interest in ''ordinary people.'' Even he admitted as much when he eventually chose to give it up. According to Mr. MacShane: ''As the time approached for leaving, he saw how artificial his relationship to France had been. He had surrounded himself, he said, 'with a sort of balloon, cushioning air,' in which he could live and work.''

But not enough happened inside the balloon, at least as far as serious work was concerned. Both *Go to the Widow-Maker,* with its undersea setting, and *The Merry Month of May,* with its background of the 1968 student uprisings in Paris, are novels in which the environments are trumped up and the protagonists are alien to those environments. Both novels collapse under the strain of trying to fit together mismatched parts.

The only worthwhile work that James Jones did in Paris was the writing of *The Thin Red Line,* the second volume of his World War II trilogy, and that, like the third volume, *Whistle,* was done from memories of the earlier period of his life. No wonder, then, that *Into Eternity* begins to drift. The life itself wandered off its course.

On the other hand, it is difficult to imagine any other route that Jones could have followed after his experience of the war. As with so many of his generation, the banks of his memory were filled early in his life, and he could have drawn on them just as well wherever he lived. The way to read his biography, then, is to read the first half of Mr. MacShane's *Into Eternity.* But from 1958 on, the real story of Jones's artistic development lies in his two final war novels, *The Thin Red Line* and the uncompleted *Whistle.* The rest was parties, international celebrity, and his two precipitous declines into ill health, and death.

Christopher Lehmann-Haupt, in a review of "Into Eternity: The Life of James Jones, American Writer," in The New York Times, *November 11, 1985, p. 19.*

GERALD NICOSIA

[*Nicosia, an American biographer and critic, is the author of* Memory Babe: A Critical Biography of Jack Kerouac *(1984). In the following excerpt Nicosia compliments MacShane for his sympathic portrait of Jones. At the same time Nicosia observes that MacShane failed to explore the many contradictions in Jones's character.*]

James Jones may well be the most paradoxical modern American novelist. He was not a conventionally successful writer. His books sold millions of copies despite a steady onslaught of terrible reviews, which by all rights should have buried him soon after the initial enthusiastic reception accorded his first blockbuster best seller about the peacetime Army in Hawaii, *From Here to Eternity,* published in 1951.

Nor was he a conventionally good writer. Almost wholly self-taught, he developed a style more clumsy and verbose than any major author since Theodore Dreiser, and at times he seemed to challenge grammar, piling two or three adverbs in succession—*pitifully awfully terribly.* As for his female characters, they seldom showed more individuality than a Playboy foldout; their dialogue usually consisted of male-fantasy lines such as "I never knew it could be like this." Yet Jones managed, through three decades of enormously dedicated work, to chronicle the influence of World War II on American society, and the American psyche, better than almost any writer of his generation.

Perhaps most remarkably, as a writer whose reputation was forged primarily as a war novelist, Jones consistently exposed the insanity of modern warfare. His purpose was not to glorify the courage of the warrior who takes on the irrational horror as a challenge to his masculinity, *a la* Rambo, but rather to show that fighting for any mass cause is bound to rob the individual of his conscience, his values and everything else he holds dear.

On top of all these contradictions, Jones, whose views were both traditionally humanitarian and amazingly prophetic in the light of the voluminous antiwar literature that came out of Vietnam, was not a very likable fellow. He was a drunk and a tough guy who enjoyed punching out anybody who might contradict him in ordinary barroom banter, and his self-pity was unquenchable. His income averaged nearly $200,000 a year for more than a decade; and yet, living in his luxury house on the Ile de St. Louis in Paris, he was forever crying over the hard lot of the American writer.

It is the great virtue of Frank MacShane's biography of Jones, *Into Eternity,* that it manages to build sympathy for Jones almost from the first few pages about his boyhood in Robinson, Ill. Here, in Jones' predictable conflicts with small-town authority and bigotry—as later, in Jones' stint in the Army [from which he received a psychiatric discharge], and in the pre-fame years, when Jones wandered the country like a shiftless outcast or lived off the bounty of his considerably older, wealthy, married mistress, Lowney Handy—MacShane reveals how Jones' ambivalences, especially his impossible attachment to both pioneer optimism and post-war cynicism, were rooted in the American heritage itself. Jones, MacShane argues, could not have been a truer product of a country that honors only success, but which accepts dishonor as a matter of course in attaining

it. But unlike many other writers who sell out (and Jones did sell out, unfortunately, writing trashy movie treatments and scripts to support his arrogantly high lifestyle), Jones at least had the honesty and the guts to question the worth of the American dream that had victimized him.

MacShane carefully traces the maturation of Jones' novelistic point of view. From the very beginning, Jones had been cursed with the disease, endemic to American novelists, of living his life in a perpetual search for *material* for his writing. Long before he was shipped into actual combat at Guadalcanal, Jones was recording interesting slices of military life in notebooks and letters to his brother, for future use in the novel he planned to write about the coming war. We see how the cockiness and offhand irreverence of the early drafts of *From Here to Eternity* changed and grew at Scribner's under the expert editorial guidance of Maxwell Perkins and, after Perkins' death, Burroughs Mitchell, to a far more sophisticated appraisal of the trauma of living under armed force. Jones had learned, in his own words, "to present life moving pictorially like a movie, but tied closely to the mental life which moves right with it."

Jones did not attempt to build upon *Eternity*'s immense popularity with a cautious sequel, but rather struck out into new territory in *Some Came Running,* an overwritten but ambitious dramatization of the hopeless attempts of returning veterans to adjust to the relatively unscarred American civilization that had blithely shipped them off to an inferno of destruction.

Certainly the awkward mixture of comic and sordid scenes contributed to the critics' scorn, but a great deal of the hostility toward the novel was actually generated by Jones' assumption that war veterans are a permanently cracked lot, bound to have an explosive and degenerative effect on their complacent fellow citizens. It was this apparently unpatriotic stance (and in truth a deep-rooted pacifism that Jones could never quite own up to) that offended Ernest Hemingway, who accused Jones of being a "whimpering neurotic" whose books would "do great damage to our country."

Eventually Jones completed his World War II trilogy with *The Thin Red Line,* which followed the innocent and unprepared "pineapple Army" into the murderous nightmare of taking the Pacific Islands back from Japan; and with *Whistle,* which dealt with the hollow homecoming of the physically and mentally crippled vets to a hospital in Tennessee, where death becomes their unshakable obsession. It is this trilogy that gives Jones his permanent place in American letters. But MacShane, while quite candid about the superficiality of Jones' several potboilers, makes us admire the willingness to experiment that led Jones to embark on novels about the perils of scuba diving (*Go to the Widow-Maker*) and about the youth rebellion of the '60s (*The Merry Month of May*).

In addition, *Into Eternity* ranks Jones among his contemporaries—not only Hemingway, whose hardboiled heroes Jones found both inspiring and ridiculous, but also Norman Mailer, who had far less ability to laugh at himself than Jones, and such fellow expatriates as James Baldwin, Irwin Shaw and William Styron. Still, one wishes MacShane had ventured to compare Jones with Beat novelists of the same period, such as Burroughs and Jack Kerouac, whom Jones evidently scorned, but with whom he shared many attitudes, including a preference for underdogs and a universal distrust of authority.

The one area MacShane fails to explore sufficiently is the contradiction in Jones between the macho brawler and the shy, scholarly man who would spend many hours alone every day in his study, and often go far out of his way to avoid arguments. At the very end, MacShane quotes Jones' friend Willie Morris that ''he knew so much about human cruelty in all of its manifestations, but as a human being was so lacking in cruelty himself.'' But one can't help suspect that this basic irresolution in Jones—an attraction to apocalypse combined with a repulsion for the disorder of modern life, both typically smalltown and Midwestern—was the wellspring of his creativity. (pp. 41-2)

> *Gerald Nicosia, ''James Jones, a Warrior Who Saw the Insanity of War,'' in* Chicago Tribune, *November 17, 1985, pp. 41-2.*

JAMES KAUFMANN

''He didn't talk theories, ideas, social stuff the way our crowd liked to do. He wasn't a do-gooder, a bleeding heart, a seeker after social justice. He was a kind of literary hardhat who talked facts, people, things, the everyday human conflict. He didn't use phrases like 'the human condition.' It was refreshing.''

The speaker is Budd Schulberg (*What Makes Sammy Run?*), and his subject is James Jones, the man who wrote *From Here to Eternity, The Thin Red Line, Whistle,* and eight other books; the man who in his time was considered by such (difficult and competitive) friends as William Styron, Norman Mailer, and Irwin Shaw as perhaps the best of the postwar novelists.

Now, of course, few people read Jones; his reputation is, to put it charitably, in eclipse. But in 1951, the year *From Here to Eternity* exploded onto the literary scene, things were entirely different.

Jones finished *From Here to Eternity* in a trailer park in Arizona, and Scribner's promoted the novel with ferocity. It was published on Feb. 26, 1951, quickly moved to the top of the best-seller list, eventually selling over half a million hard-cover copies and over 5 million in paper. It won the American Book Award, then the Pulitzer. Then came the film; it won Oscars. Jones was famous.

Jones grew up unhappily, writes Frank MacShane in *Into Eternity,* in Robinson, Ill., a small town 40 miles southwest of Terre Haute, Ind. He enlisted in the Army in 1939 at the age of 18, and stayed in until 1944. He spent most of his time on Hawaii, some in the Pacific Theater; he was injured by mortar fire at Guadalcanal.

After the war, he became the protégé/part-time lover of Lowney Handy, who, says Mr. MacShane, was ''primarily interested in developing his talent.'' Theirs was an extremely complicated

Jones and Lowney (seated left) in Illinois, where they established The Handy Colony for writers. Photograph by Pete Purinton.

and not altogether healthy relationship, but it did provide Jones with the support and time he needed to write.

Others recognized his talent, too. The legendary book editor Maxwell Perkins corresponded with Jones, and the young writer "would sometimes take out Perkins's letters and read them over," an act, wrote Jones, after which "I experienced such a feeling of joy as is hard to describe without exaggeration."

In 1957, he met and soon married Gloria Mosolino. Their relationship was passionate, if frequently incendiary, and always, for better or worse, exciting—as MacShane makes clear in *Into Eternity.* They moved to Paris in 1958 and enjoyed their celebrity—entertaining the likes of Lauren Bacall, John Kenneth Galbraith, Sargent Shriver, Kurt Vonnegut, Mary McCarthy, Françoise Sagan, and Jean Seberg. They returned to the United States in 1974, three years before Jones died.

Into Eternity, like most biographies, is dedicated in part to the restoration of Jones's reputation, and MacShane, like most biographers, is a bit overprotective of his subject. Passages like "Once again, most of the fury seems to have been generated by the reviewers' failure to understand what Jones's intentions were" appear more than once. There are also times when events could be more clearly dated.

Still, this is a fine biography, in a class with MacShane's studies of Raymond Chandler and John O'Hara. MacShane writes lively prose, is a thorough researcher, avoids lengthy summaries of Jones's novels, and his effort may—and probably should—boost Jones's literary stock.

Yet even those who consider Jones a minor novelist—and there are many who do—will find this biography pleasurable, for his life was as dramatic and absorbing, perhaps more so, than his work. (pp. 37, 44)

> *James Kaufmann, "Restoring the Reputation of a 'Literary Hardhat'," in* The Christian Science Monitor, *December 2, 1985, pp. 37, 44.*

EDMUND WHITE

[*White, an American novelist, dramatist, and nonfiction writer living in Paris, is noted for his impressionistic style and luxurious prose. Both in his fiction and nonfiction, which are informed by his own homosexual sensibility, White focuses on the life-style of the upper-middle-class homosexual. In the following excerpt White, by way of introduction, recounts a personal encounter with Jones's family; White then offers his own observations on Jones's career while praising MacShane for writing a truthful, balanced portrait of the author.*]

The people on the Île St. Louis still remember James Jones as a man who looked like a commando, but upon acquaintance revealed an extraordinary sweetness. His appearance suited the French preconception of how an American writer should look— an inspired savage, usually drunk—whereas his real gentleness disarmed them utterly. When I mentioned to the people who run the Brasserie St. Louis that I brought them greetings from my former writing student, Jones's daughter Kaylie, they went into raptures over the great man who'd used their restaurant as his living room; they even had to summon their daughter and her new baby from some inner recess to meet the man who'd known *les Jones.*

In fact I'd never known James Jones, although his daughter did once bring her mother, Gloria, to an end-of-the-semester party I gave for my Columbia fiction workshop. When I politely asked Mrs. Jones (who once worked as a stand-in for Marilyn Monroe) what she was doing for Doubleday, she replied, "I fuck writers." She then asked me why I was gay and wanted to know if I was afraid of women, had I ever tried one, did I think there were teeth down there. . . . I suddenly felt terribly prissy and *dépassé,* not at all the sort of writer James Jones, in his frank, searching way, would have liked.

Gloria was the great love of Jones's life—she and his writing. Once, when he thought he might die, Jones left a note for Gloria: "I've always loved you an awful lot. More than I've ever loved anything or anybody. Maybe my own work I've loved as much." The letter is pure Jones in its sincerity, its sacrifice of eloquence to the graceless truth, its egotism, and its generosity.

Despite his macho exterior, Jones had none of Hemingway's alternating sadism and self-hatred. He liked to help other writers and was extremely friendly with, among others, Irwin Shaw, Peter Matthiessen, Norman Mailer, James Baldwin, Willie Morris, William Styron, and Mary McCarthy. Jones would have been incapable of displaying the malice Hemingway evinced when Scribner's asked him for a comment on *From Here to Eternity.* Hemingway said of Jones:

> Things will catch up with him and he will probably commit suicide. . . . To me he is an enormously skillful fuck-up and his book will do great damage to our country. . . . I hope he kills himself as soon as it does not damage your or his sales. If you give him a literary tea you might ask him to drain a bucket of snot and then suck the puss out of a dead nigger's ear.

So much for the literary life.

Unlike Hemingway, Jones was concerned with analyzing the relations between men and women. His later books, so often misunderstood, can best be read in this light, especially *Go to the Widow-Maker* and *Whistle.* As Frank MacShane writes in his analysis of *Go to the Widow-Maker,* Jones researched that book by examining

> the lumpen world of male America as he found it in the West Indies. Consisting mainly of self-made men, it is a world of sports, drinking, and crude language. The men have no interior lives and spend most of their time together. Their sexual lives are unsatisfactory and most of them are maladjusted. Either they cannot perform at all or dissociate feeling from sex and settle for sensation.

Jones equated Hemingway's "big masculine bullshit" with people's need for dangerous but consoling myths—the same need that had engendered "heroes, great generals, and war." Despite this rejection of Hemingway's influence, however, Jones recognized his talent as a writer and made his Florida workshop read *The Sun Also Rises.*

Like Hemingway, Jones was born in an Illinois town. Both writers were sons of professional men (a doctor in Hemingway's case, a dentist in Jones's) and both had Christian Scientist mothers they despised. And in both cases their fathers committed suicide by shooting themselves. It occurs to me that one could build a case that the best American writers of this century have been the children of that endangered species, the small entrepreneur or self-employed professional—precisely the class to which the most had been promised by free-enterprise rhetoric and less and less delivered. Thomas Pynchon, that foe of corporate internationalism, seems to belong to this class.

Like Hemingway, Jones left the States for Paris, but Jones's Paris was less artistic than his predecessor's, and far more luxurious and worldly. Jones's large art nouveau house on the Île St. Louis, with its view of Notre-Dame and the Left Bank, became a sort of canteen for visiting American writers. But after Jones had to stop drinking, he and Gloria cultivated an ultra-chic set of the established rich, a group typified by Ethel de Croisset, a New York heiress who married a French aristocrat and still lives in the Seizième surrounded by Matisses and Giacomettis. Of all rich crowds in the world, this is the one most responsive to artists; frequenting artists (and supporting them when necessary) is as obligatory for the Paris *gratin* as charity work is for their New York counterparts.

Such a milieu could not have stood in greater contrast to Jones's background. Jones had grown up in Robinson, Illinois. As a boy he failed to distinguish himself in sports or academic work and frequently picked fights. He entered high school in 1935, during the heart of the Depression. His father was a drunk who lost all his money and spent most of his time away from home, indulging in self-pity at the local bar. His mother once warned her son that if he masturbated his hand would turn black—and she went so far as to paint his hand while he slept in order to prove her theory.

The Army freed Jones from his dismal home life. He'd enlisted first in the air corps, but he later transferred to the famously tough 27th Infantry Regiment. He participated in the Battle of Guadalcanal. While in the Army he also discovered the novels of Thomas Wolfe, which served as his main inspiration to write—and as a model for many passages in his first published novel, *From Here to Eternity*. That Maxwell Perkins, Wolfe's editor at Scribner's, took an early interest in Jones only confirmed this association.

From Here to Eternity took four years to write; in the process Jones tore up three-quarters of everything he put on paper. During this long period of composition, just after his Army discharge, Jones lived back in his native Robinson with an older woman, Lowney Handy, who fed him, occasionally slept with him, and submitted him to her bizarre and thoroughly American philosophy drawn from bits of Zen, Emerson, xenophobia, and anti-intellectualism. She detested other women, and felt certain women always kill the artist in a man. (It never occurred to her that a woman herself might be an artist.)

Lowney believed in cold showers, early to bed and early to rise, a long morning's work on an empty stomach, and other spartan deprivations. She encouraged her disciples (for she eventually founded a writers' colony) to use double negatives and coarse language, and to copy out long passages from such manly native writers as Hemingway and Dos Passos. She forbade her boys to read the "effete" authors she referred to as "Walter Stevens," "Kafkia," and "Dieland Thompson."

Jones, an intensely loyal person, put up with Lowney's eccentricities—until his marriage to Gloria precipitated a crisis. Gloria tried to live at the Handy Colony, and at first Lowney was cool and correct with her, and with Gloria's niece Kate, who was visiting. But as MacShane recounts [in *Into Eternity*]:

> One afternoon, while sitting in the living room with Kate, Gloria heard a loud crash. Lowney had just smashed through the screen door and

was standing in the living room, beside herself with rage. "The only reason Jim married you," she shouted, "is that you're the best cocksucker in New York!" Gloria sent Kate out of the room, and then Lowney lunged at her with a bowie knife. Gloria and Lowney rolled around on the floor, scratching and punching, until Jones came in and separated them.

After the violence and deprivations and philistinism of the Handy Colony, Paris must have seemed a refreshing change.

Despite his years in France, Jones remained the quintessential American writer. If he often recalls Wolfe, he is just as apparently a descendant of Whitman, as can be seen in page after page of *From Here to Eternity*. . . . His sympathy for the average guy, his impeccable ear for the American dialect ("Draft or no draft, they'll never get me back"), even his patient piecing together of the autodidact's "philosophy of life," make Jones the most representative spokesman of his generation. Even his omnivorous and pressing drive to narrate suits his subject—and his readers.

In his stories he reached back to his childhood, to its humiliations and bleak joys. With a sure sense of which details would "tell," he composed this passage in **"The Valentine,"** for instance, about a paperboy awakening before dawn:

> Outside it was steely cold and the handlebars and sprocket of his bike creaked with frost when he moved them. The air burned his nose like dry ice, and as he tucked the scarf up over it and put on his goggles, his eyes were already watering. The freezing cold air flushing the last threads of sleepiness and of reluctance out of his mind, he took off on his bike, giving himself joyously up to, and embracing happily, the discomfort which always made him feel important and as though he were accomplishing something, riding the bike downtown along deserted streets of darkened houses where nothing moved or shone and people slept except for a few boys like himself, scattered across town, converging on the Newsstand where the city papers would already have been picked up by the owner of the train.

In his *Viet Journal,* written during the closing days of the war, Jones speaks with lucid objectivity of the farce being played out around him—yet without ever losing sympathy for the American soldiers involved. His self-created Illinois childhood and his own military service gave him that sympathy; his years as a famous writer in Paris provided the objectivity, as did his profound skepticism about politics. He summarized his view of the war by remarking, "They're shits and we're shits so we might as well be for us as for them."

Frank MacShane's biography never forces Jones into a Procrustean bed of preconceptions (one of the biographer's chief temptations), nor does it condescend to its subject (the other temptation). Jones's virtues (his intense loyalty, his burrowing intelligence, his fortitude under hostile criticism, his genuine curiosity about other people) are as graphically presented as are his shortcomings (his clumsy style, his alcoholic rages, his often unrealized artistic intentions). Best of all, the book gives a sense of the animal reality of the man with "his thick neck, broad shoulders, Western clothes and turquoise bracelets," and his peculiarly penetrating independence of mind. After all, it

Jones with Gloria on a quai overlooking the Seine River. Photograph by Sam Shaw. Courtesy of Gloria Jones.

was Jones who made this complex observation: "The middle class rejects anything that is dishonest. Thus they miss the whole language of the common man—the rich texture of it." Only an uncommon man could have grasped that slippery truth about the elegance of falsehood. (pp. 31-4)

> *Edmund White, "Keeping Up with Jones," in* The New Republic, *Vol. 193, No. 24, December 9, 1985, pp. 31-4.*

SEYMOUR KRIM

[*Krim is an American essayist, editor, and contributor to* Village Voice, Chicago Tribune, Washington Post, *and other periodicals. In the 1950s Krim was greatly influenced by the Beat writers; he abandoned his formalist literary criticism to focus on personal revelations of his life and of American contemporary culture. Working as an editor, he was successful in extending the influence of the Beat writers and of the New Journalists who were dedicated to engaging art with day-to-day existential life. Krim's edited anthology* The Beats (1980) *included such writers as Jack Kerouac, Allen Ginsberg, Lawrence Ferlinghetti, and Norman Mailer. In the following excerpt Krim, who knew Jones when he lived in Paris, calls MacShane's biography of Jones uninspired. He suggests that as a "cultivated New Yorker" and intellectual academic, MacShane may have been uncomfortable with the bawdy details of Jones's life.*]

Right now [*Into Eternity*] is the most valuable book we have on James Jones because the author has done indefatigable legwork—201 individual names, by my count, appear in the Ac-

knowledgements alone. Frank MacShane has practically stood on his head and whistled "Dixie" to do right by his "true American primitive," as Budd Schulberg not unlovingly dubbed Jones. But the unfortunate truth is that this is not an inspired critical biography. The reasons are several, as I will try to show, but everyone who has read MacShane's corking *Life of Raymond Chandler* (1977) will know immediately what I mean. When a biographer has once hit the jackpot, we can never forget the freshness of the experience. This worthy effort seems plodding and dutiful by comparison.

The troubles begin, as they have in all previous biographical work on Jones, with the hovering family that the novelist left behind. They (read Gloria Jones, the writer's widow and keeper of the flame) "authorized" this book, and in spite of MacShane's obvious probity and track-record as an independent biographer, one feels that his very sense of responsibility to others has taken some of the joy out of his work. Nor does this mean to suggest that he was in any sense explicitly handcuffed in delicate areas; given the sexual worldliness and irreverence of both Jones and his wife, plus their 16 years of doing an updated Scott-and-Zelda turn in Paris, it is unthinkable that any thou-shalt-nots would be put on his reporting.

But it does mean that when MacShane has to poke into Jones' rumored bisexuality, Gloria's extensive pre-Jones literary bedlife, and so forth, he is conspicuously undetailed and discreet. It might even be, in a broader sense, that he is not entirely comfortable with the subject of James Jones and the raw erotic and scatological obsessions that were fundamental to his life.

I mean this quite neutrally and without value judgment: Jones, in spite of having written a great realistic novel about the peacetime Army, *From Here to Eternity,* and two follow-up novels deserving of high respect, was not the kind of man or even writer (too unsubtle?) that one would ordinarily think Frank MacShane would identify with. MacShane, a cultivated New Yorker with an Oxford PhD who until recently ran the Graduate Writing Program at Columbia, is almost a walking incarnation of all of James Jones' defensive prejudices about "the eastern intellectual establishment." To think of the two of them joined in this probably well-intentioned but temperamentally mismated project is to conjure up a literary Mutt and Jeff image that just won't go away.

However, since he did get into it, and even though I feel that his tight, lean style loses its edge with the burden of this job, MacShane lays out the groundwork of Jones' almost mythic *lumpen* American life with his usual assurance. We all more or less know the story by now: the smalltown boy from southeastern Illinois whose family tumbled from privilege and who was forced to enlist in the peacetime Army in 1939 instead of becoming a day laborer. It was, of course, a tremendous decision for both our literature and our popular culture: no one before or since has written with such feeling about the American Army from the inside. An entire world that had been hidden from most educated Americans before World War II was brought to such unexpected life that it remains indelible, both for the generation that fought the war and for the national memory.

It is in Jones' struggle to write that first sweeping revelation, and to survive both the Army and the opening campaign in the Pacific (where he was lightly wounded) in order to do it, that MacShane is especially valuable. James Jones loved the Army; but he hated its regimentation from the first day, and even finally cracked up during his reassignment back in the States in 1943. He had already started writing while in the service, was absolutely consumed with his sense of mission, and was ready to go AWOL in a desperate frenzy when he met the woman who was to be his teacher and mistress for the next 13 years—Mrs. Lowney Handy.

It is impossible to think of the writing of *Eternity,* and then later the overambitious *Some Came Running,* without the tutelary presence of this tough, courageous, unconventional woman who was 17 years older than Jones and had the encouragement of her husband in one of the strangest arrangements on record. With Jones' financial help, Lowney Handy went on to found a writing colony in Marshall, Illinois, which she ran like a literary boot camp, and many of her stubborn ideas (copying out the work of established masters, not inhibiting taboo body noises at table, using four-letter words rather than 10-letter ones, etc.) were to remain with Jones for a lifetime. She remains a startling enigma to this day, very much entitled to a biography of her own, and when Jones had to cut the cord and married the younger, more glamorous Gloria Mosolino in 1958, Handy quickly deteriorated and died six years later. But she was a powerful, magnetic presence in the first and undoubtedly most crucial half of James Jones' artistic life, a determined, "liberated" woman out of sync with her time and place, and she paid the bitter price.

The second half of both the book and the life is a more star-studded, gossipy chronicle if only because Jones found himself in a unique position, a little like a literary John L. Sullivan. With his first book he had made it on all fronts—artistic, financial, social—hitting practically every level of society, and

when he and Gloria moved their operation to Paris they were the toast of the town for all expatriate Americans. Jones was a sort of democratic king, and Gloria a populist queen, in their big, spectacular apartment overlooking the Seine. These were indeed warm occasions (I myself was there), but at this point MacShane's portrait of the authentic American original has to take a back seat to all the famous names that come to call. In fact this becomes the story, along with the Jones' two young additions to the family (Kaylie and Jamie), because as our biographer rightly says, "most of his writing did not achieve the intensity of his earlier books." High living, opportunistic movie-work to pay the bills, opportunistic topical novels like *The Merry Month of May*—the life itself seemed to lose purpose when Jones strayed too far from war and men bearing arms. "Death was his business," said Mary McCarthy in one of those brilliant remarks that stop all discussion.

The Joneses, of course, came home for the three years remaining to the author, where he all but wrapped up the last book of his war trilogy, *Whistle* (1978) after ducking it for years. Then his old business partner, Death, claimed him.

It is this reviewer's strong feeling that a good deal of time will now have to pass before we can get a totally unfettered, new look at James Jones' life and work. MacShane faithfully recounts all the main quantifiable materials—who was at this or that dinner, what the size of an advance was, that "he had Pierre Cardin jackets but he also wore cotton chino trousers," etc.—but I hungrily miss any sense of irony and absurdity in his narrative, any deep or even astonished sense of personal involvement. This was one larger-than-life, not unlike Orson Welles, and he can't be contained by the facts alone. Just by themselves—in the second half especially—they're about as thrilling as reading an overpriced menu written with the sobriety of a Bible study. (pp. 5-6)

> *Seymour Krim, "James Jones: Novelist of the Enlisted Man," in* Book World—The Washington Post, *January 5, 1986, pp. 5-6.*

IRVING MARDER

"Things will catch up with him and he will probably commit suicide. . . . I hope he kills himself as soon as it does not damage your sales. . . ."

Not, all things considered, anything you'd want to use in a blurb, which is what Scribner's had in mind when—with astonishing naivete—they sent an advance copy of their new hopeful's novel to their old star. That was one of the few printable sections of Hemingway's notorious 1951 letter to Charles Scribner.

"Hemingway understood courage," James Jones remarked mildly in conversation with this reviewer, who knew him slightly in Paris, "but he didn't understand people." It seems, in retrospect, a generous view. But it also seems likely that Jones missed the mark almost as widely as Hemingway had. Even allowing for hysteria and wishful thinking, as a connoisseur of courage, Hemingway could not have been wronger about Jones.

Frank MacShane, the author of widely praised biographies of John O'Hara, Ford Madox Ford, and Raymond Chandler, has taken on a tougher customer in James Jones [*Into Eternity*]. Predictably, the cheap-shot marksmen have already entered the gallery: A feline reviewer in the *New Republic* bagged the novelist's widow with his opening volley [see excerpt by Edmund White above].

But nothing, after all, could be easier: James Jones' defects are mostly on the surface. Is there a worse American writer who has written as good a book as *From Here to Eternity*?

MacShane does not confront this paradox until we are more than 200 pages into the biography. "Jones' difficulties with language," he says, "also contributed to his problem. Writing came hard to Jones. He would take an immensely long time with his paragraphs and had no facility with language. Writing letters, he often became embroiled in syntactical and grammatical errors. 'Can you explain my stylistic flaws,' he asked Burroughs Mitchell (his editor at Scribner's) 'which are frequent and annoying?' He had a good ear for dialogue and colloquial English, but he was often verbose and repetitive. . . . Yet if he wished to, he could write elegant and even witty prose. . . .''

Life being short, we are willing to take MacShane's word that Jones could write "elegant and even witty prose" when he wanted to. Elsewhere, he quotes Jones as saying he often wrote awkwardly on purpose—when it was in character. This, of course, leaves intact the problem of telling *exactly* when Jones is writing badly on *purpose*. He also relays Jones' complaint that his critics failed often to grasp his "intentions"—though one must assume that MacShane knows, if Jones did not, that what counts is what is on the printed page.

If MacShane falls too often into the biographer's trap of becoming an *advocate* for his subject rather than a detached commentator, he has nonetheless written, within self-imposed limits, an admirable book about an important American writer: the best American war novelist of his generation. But presumably he had hoped to do more—to present Jones in a wider literary context: to go, that is, beyond Norman Mailer and Irwin Shaw. As the biographer of Ford Madox Ford he might, for example, have had some interesting views on the war novels of this least-military of soldiers as compared with those of the Dogface's bard. Or on James' put-down on Remarque's *All Quiet on the Western Front*—a great war novel, as opposed to a good, or great, *American* war novel. Or about the apparently iron law that the best war novels are always written by the *losers*—which is why some of us are waiting impatiently for a look at Heinrich Böll's *The Train Was on Time*, published in 1947 but available only now in English translation.

MacShane notes Jones' affinity with Rudyard Kipling. Both were outsiders—nearsighted, undersize men who loved soldiers and soldiering but never made the A-team. Kipling, despite lyrical gifts and imaginative powers miles ahead of Jones', got his material mainly at secondhand. Jones, aching to prove himself, transferred from the Army Air Corps to the infantry, followed the big boys and ended up in the bloodbath of Guadalcanal. It was the crucial experience of his life, as it was for many others of his generation. He never got over it but in the process of trying, he wrote about it in a series of books that told his own stories and those of his inarticulate comrades-in-arms. They were not really, contrary to patriotic legend, the best or the brightest of soldiers, but they understood what he was saying.

Writers come in all shapes and sizes. Was there ever a less martial one than, for example, T. S. Eliot? Yet even he could lament, in gaunt cadences, his absence at "the hot gates." The Jones boy was there, and he wrote about it memorably.

Jones with friends Willie Morris and Irwin Shaw. Photograph © 1985 Nancy Crampton.

Irving Marder, in a review of "Into Eternity: The Life of James Jones, American Writer," in Los Angeles Times Book Review, *January 26, 1986, p. 14.*

TERRY TEACHOUT

This is a lousy time to be a compulsive reader. It's not just that we're going through what Joseph Epstein likes to call "a bad patch" in our serious fiction. Our popular fiction has also become horribly debased. It used to be possible for a first-rate book reviewer to read a new novel every day without going crazy in the process. (Diana Trilling used to keep that kind of schedule forty years ago when she wrote her "Fiction in Review" column for the *Nation,* and it doesn't seem to have done her any lasting harm.) Lots of bad novels got written and published, of course, but quality control in the popular fiction business was still significantly tighter. Veteran craftsmen like John P. Marquand were writing novels that could be taken more or less seriously by the intelligent reader; even the steamy blockbuster novel could be counted on more often than not for a good read. Remember *A Rage to Live*? Or *From Here to Eternity*? Compared to the reeking garbage in which our great publishing houses currently specialize, those old war horses look better and better with each passing bestseller list.

The trick, of course, is not to go too far with this line of reasoning. Mrs. Trilling certainly didn't, not even after reading several tons of junk. . . .

The absence of this sane and judicious perspective is all too typical of a distressing new phenomenon on the American literary scene: the current group of academic biographers who cull the checklists of our second-string novelists with unseemly enthusiasm. Witness Frank MacShane . . . whose new book, *Into Eternity: The Life of James Jones, American Writer,* opens with the profoundly wrong-headed pronouncement that James Jones "deserves to stand in the first rank of American writers in the second half of the twentieth century." Nor is Mr. MacShane at a loss for superlatives in subsequent pages:

He had appeared like a comet from the heart of America, and he wrote with a directness and truthfulness that recalled such distinctly American writers as Walt Whitman and Mark Twain.... His whole life was an education in books, and in the work of such writers as Teilhard de Chardin, Stendhal, Conrad, and Yeats he searched for an understanding of life. His reading nurtured his philosophical nature, and without cant or illusion he confronted the nature of love, sex, and mortality.

That's pretty strong stuff, especially when applied to the man whom Wilfrid Sheed once described as "the king of the good-bad writers" and whose eleven books are studded with hideous examples of paralyzing syntax. ("The unspeakable loneliness of self-pity that is blind and tongueless rose up hot in her, trying to bring tears.") But Frank MacShane can almost always be relied on to get the facts straight, and he has done so once again with this book. As an example of the critical biography as high art, *Into Eternity* is nothing special; as a secondary source of factual information about the author of *From Here to Eternity* and *The Thin Red Line,* it is a solid, eminently reliable performance.

Which begs the question: why would anyone want to read a three-hundred-page biography of James Jones in the first place? The details of his life—a rough childhood, a miserable stretch in the Army, a tempestuous but happy marriage, a disastrous second novel, a tour of duty as Parisian expatriate, an early death brought on by the excessive consumption of alcohol—have the vaguely familiar ring of a dozen other literary lives. The really remarkable thing about Jones, one feels after reading *Into Eternity,* was the distance he was able to travel on sheer nerve alone. One day he read *Look Homeward, Angel* and concluded, like so many other sensitive young men before him, that "I had been a writer all my life without knowing it or having written." Unlike most of those other young men, though, he promptly sat down and started to act on this wildly optimistic conclusion. The result was a long, clumsy, enthralling novel about the peacetime Army that is still in print after thirty-five years, one surprisingly good Hollywood adaptation, and God only knows how many copies sold.

From Here to Eternity is a textbook example of the very best sort of popular novel, the kind that went out with Brylcreem and the nuclear family. The plot is solid, the detail convincing, the macho romanticism smoky and fragrant. (It isn't surprising that Jones, a devotee of the hardboiled detective story, actually broke down and wrote one when he needed extra money to keep his Paris residence afloat.) Hearteningly ambitious in its scope, *From Here to Eternity* is warmed by a dignity so transparently authentic that Whittaker Chambers was moved to comment:

> To my grotesque way of thinking, one of the great moral moments in current U.S. writing is the quarry scene in *From Here to Eternity*—the scene in which one of the prisoners takes his crowbar and, on request, breaks the arm or leg of a fellow prisoner. That is the moment for which the great muck heap of that book exists.... *From Here to Eternity* is essentially a moral book.

The problem is that Frank MacShane is either unable or unwilling to make this kind of distinction in his critical discussions of Jones's work. His treatment of *From Here to Eternity* is all too typical: he ranks it above *Guard of Honor* and *The Naked and the Dead* as the "most successful" American novel to come out of World War II. For most readers, the very thought of ranking *From Here to Eternity* anywhere near a masterpiece like *Guard of Honor* will be jolting. Jones's gauche prose style is enough to prevent all but the most committed Dreiserites from taking him seriously as a "great" writer. (Norman Mailer once called Jones "the worst writer of prose ever to give intimations of greatness.") And as good as it is, *From Here to Eternity* is still a piece of *popular* fiction, an amalgam of middle-period Hemingway and fondly remembered thirties movies marred by a truly corny whore-with-a-heart-of-gold subplot introduced in all seriousness as a philosophical statement about the nature of romantic love.

In the end, *Into Eternity* serves chiefly as a distressing reminder of the runaway inflation which mars the American literary scene today. Scholarly biographies are pulling down six-figure advances; serious fiction is in a slump of unprecedented magnitude; charming lightweights like Jay McInerney are being touted as voices of a generation; nervous academics, having run out of new things to say about Kafka, are falling on the likes of James Jones like a ton of bricks. No doubt one of Mr. MacShane's students is about to give us the lowdown on yet another forgotten American. Herman Wouk? John Hersey? Whoever it may be, you can count on one thing: he'll emerge from this thoughtful new revaluation as an underrated classic. After all, how else is a starving young assistant professor going to get tenure these days? (pp. 51-2)

> Terry Teachout, in a review of "Into Eternity: The Life of James Jones, American Writer," in The American Spectator, Vol. 19, No. 2, February, 1986, pp. 51-2.

JEFFREY MEYERS

[*Meyers is an American critic, literary biographer, and professor of English. Among his many books are biographies of Wyndham Lewis, Katherine Mansfield, D. H. Lawrence, and Ernest Hemingway, bibliographies of George Orwell and T. E. Lawrence, and several critical studies of contemporary authors, most notably,* Wyndham Lewis: A Revaluation *(1980). In the following excerpt Meyers credits MacShane's biography of Jones as a fair appraisal and offers his own summary of the novelist's career.*]

On the Greek island of Skiathos, in the late 1960s, an ape-like man with protruding ears and a prognathous jaw swaggered up to our café table and claimed he was a writer. When I skeptically asked if he had published anything, he replied: "*From Here to Eternity.*" Despite the tough-guy manner adopted from Hemingway—the bad grammar, the words spat out of the side of his mouth—James Jones was gentle and genial. He had rented a huge villa, with private beach and boat, and invited us to drink his case of whisky. He had achieved commercial success despite devastating reviews, craved academic recognition, and urged me to write scholarly articles about his work.

Frank MacShane's lively and interesting narrative [*Into Eternity*] is sympathetic to Jones, captures the essence of the man, and offers a fair appraisal of his extremely uneven work. Though he mentions Jones's connections with Mailer, Styron, Shaw, Baldwin, and (rather improbably) Mary McCarthy, he does not describe their conversations or illuminate the nature of their friendship.

Jones was a Midwestern country bumpkin, a child of the Depression and World War II. He grew up in Robinson, Illinois, forty miles from Terre Haute, the son of a diabetic harpy and of a drunken dentist who had lost everything in the Wall Street crash and shot himself in 1942. After drug addiction and an attempted suicide, Jones's sister died of a brain tumor at the age of 27. Rejected by his coevals at school, Jones enlisted in the Army in 1939, was sent to Schofield Barracks in Honolulu, and served ingloriously as a clerk. He spent a good deal of his early life in whorehouses and bars, and fantasized about his sexual exploits. Slightly wounded in the head by a random mortar shell soon after he arrived at Guadalcanal, he was discharged in 1944 after injuring his ankle playing football.

After the war Jones became the lover, foster son, and literary protégé of an unattractive, peculiar, and devoted older woman, Lowney Handy. He published his first stories in the *Atlantic* and *Harper's* in 1949, finished *Eternity* in a trailer park in North Hollywood, and achieved immediate critical and popular success. He earned $178,000 the first year, received another $82,000 for film rights, and eventually sold half a million copies in hardcover.

Irwin Shaw noted that Jones ''grappled with the ghost of Hemingway all his life, excoriating him, mocking him, worried about what Hemingway meant to him.'' MacShane quotes Hemingway's manic, vituperative, and pathological attack on *Eternity* in a letter to Charles Scribner, but does not explain that it was inspired by profound insecurity about his own literary stature. After the failure of *Across the River*, Hemingway had a deep-rooted fear of younger literary rivals who challenged him by writing about the War.

Mailer thought *Eternity* was better than *The Naked and the Dead*. Styron, throwing his arms around Jones and Mailer,

exclaimed: ''Here we are, the three best writers of our generation, and we're all together!'' But their intense rivalry and sense of art as a lethal game led to Mailer's attack on his contemporaries in *Advertisements for Myself*. As Mailer and Styron matured as artists, Jones remained static and feared he had lost his ''drive to write because of being successful.''

Jones compared **Some Came Running** to *War and Peace,* but its commonplace plot and boring characters were condemned by the critics. In 1958, after his marriage to sexy Gloria Mosolino, a bit-part actress from a criminal clan in Pottsville, Pennsylvania, Jones escaped to Paris. There he became the perfect philistine, collecting knives and using a pulpit as a bar. He wrote lucrative scripts for films that were never made, consorted with wealthy expatriates and courtiers. After 16 years in Europe, he remained an ignorant, apolitical tourist, with scant knowledge of French language and culture. Jones died of heart disease after dictating the end of **Whistle** from his hospital bed.

Jones had unpromising origins, no education, limited intelligence, and a crude style. Driven by a powerful urge to write, he had nothing much to say, produced closely autobiographical novels, and was essentially a one-book author. John Aldridge demoted Jones to the ranks of Uris, Ruark, and Robbins; Wilfrid Sheed (using Orwell's phrase) called him the ''king of the good-bad writers''; and Mailer convincingly stated that he was ''the worst writer of prose ever to give intimations of greatness.'' (pp. 54-5)

Jeffrey Meyers, ''The Vulgar Streak,'' in National Review, *Vol. XXXVIII, No. 3, February 28, 1986, pp. 54-5.*

Mailer: His Life and Times

by Peter Manso

(For Norman Mailer: see also *CLC,* Vols. 1, 2, 3, 4, 5, 8, 11, 14, 28; *Contemporary Authors,* Vols. 11-12, rev. ed.; *Dictionary of Literary Biography,* Vols. 2, 16, 28; *Dictionary of Literary Biography Yearbook:* 1980, 1983; and *Dictionary of Literary Biography Documentary Series,* Vol. 3. For Peter Manso: see also *Contemporary Authors,* Vols. 29-32, rev. ed.)

An Excerpt from *Mailer: His Life and Times*

DIANA TRILLING Norman had sent me a copy of *Ancient Evenings* and asked me to read it and tell him whether or not the book had succeeded. His note said that he knew that he could count on me to tell him the truth. It was extraordinary. I mean, it was an extraordinary request to make of someone to whom you had hardly spoken over the last six years. It happened to come at a time when my eyes had been giving me great trouble; that's an awful lot of book to read—it's all I can manage to keep up with my own work. I think I wrote that to Norman. But even were my eyes not bothering me, I couldn't undertake to meet that request. What I'm trying to say is that he didn't have the right to put such a large burden of proof upon me. There had been too much failed faith between us.

I suppose that in a sense I had always thought of Norman as someone who could free me from the excesses of my own strictness of standard, introduce me to or at least allow me some new kind of personal authenticity. Yet, of course, at the same time I would be countering his influence with its opposite. These were the two sides of my nature that existed in conflict. He was to speak his side in my interior dialogue. Whoever doesn't understand that dialogue isn't worth bothering about.

My superego friends could use the correction in Norman just as Norman needed the principle of control which they might teach him. He is not, in my view, the writer he could and should be for that very reason, because he has never achieved that delicate balance. Still, though he has had so uneven a career, I continue to feel he is the best writing artist of our time. I have never read *The Executioner's Song.* I was afraid to read it when I was doing my *Mrs. Harris* book because its style was so insidious: I was afraid I would try to imitate it. And now, as I say, my reading is very restricted. But friends whom I trust tell me it's one of his best works. Whether or not, I still think of him as having far and away the most literary talent now going. Actually, I once asked him when he was going to write his *War and Peace.* He wasn't thrown by the question, nor by its elaboration: I went on to say that his *War and Peace* should be a novel of middle-class life, firmly rooted in established society, but that where Tolstoy had made his excursions into history, Mailer should make his excursions into dissidence.

Which, of course, is what I'd really like him to do, and it doesn't necessarily have to be a novel; it could be another *Armies of the Night,* or even autobiography. When you can see that somebody has the capacity to do something so uncommonly good, then you have to hold onto that and say, "Oh boy, please, please come through."

BARRY GEWEN

Peter Manso's **Mailer: His Life and Times** . . . cries out for comparison with Jean Stein's *Edie*—alas! Both are oral-history biographies, spliced together from hundreds of snippets of interviews the "authors" conducted with their subjects' friends, relatives and acquaintances; in Manso's case, over 200 people were taped, some for as long as 10 hours, producing almost 20,000 transcript pages of material. Besides format, the books share a "look." They have brief bios of the contributors at the end, together with elaborate family trees of Mailer and Edie Sedgwick, respectively. Loads of photographs are sprinkled throughout.

The interview technique was perfect for the life and death of a debutante-decadent, since everything anyone wanted to learn about her was right there on the surface. It is much less effective in the case of Mailer—not merely because, as a writer with a pronounced philosophical bent, he has made ideas central to his concerns, but also, and quite simply, because he is still very much alive. Wasn't it Camus who said we never know who a person is until he is dead?

Mailer's career has run in phases. The newest has come only in the last few years. With **The Executioner's Song** in 1979, he produced his best work in a decade, possibly his finest to date, achieving a stylistic transformation that may equal in importance the earlier breakthrough of **Advertisements for Myself.** The publication two years ago of his Egyptian novel, **Ancient Evenings,** signaled the start of a grandiose three-volume project that may evoke mixed feelings in his readers yet will alter our perception and judgment of his entire *oeuvre.* Thus, whereas Manso's opening chapters form natural set-pieces—Mailer in Brooklyn, Mailer at Harvard, Mailer in the Army—his book loses all focus as it approaches the present. By the end, it is sputtering along like an old car in need of a tune-up. **Mailer** is an unfinished work, premature, promising great things from the author in the future—and, then again, maybe not. Manso was so eager to pull this pie out of the oven, he hasn't even bothered to include a complete list of the writings.

Somewhat surprisingly, the theme that emerges most strongly is Mailer's Jewishness. Almost everyone Manso talked to seems to have something to say about it. Cousins describe his Bar Mitzvah, when he offended the congregation with a speech on Spinoza. College roommates remember "a little boy from Brooklyn." Former wives are said to have groused about having to visit his family every Friday night. Diana Trilling, James Baldwin and Joe Flaherty note the element of over-compensation for his Jewish background in his public persona. Literary critics rebuke him for ignoring his heritage. . . .

Indeed, it is hard to escape the thought that *Mailer* is an account of the 20th-century American Jew's eruption from parochialism to a position of cultural eminence. (p. 3)

In perhaps his most unjustly criticized book, *The Prisoner of Sex,* Mailer, writing brilliantly of D. H. Lawrence, says: "He was a momma's boy, spoiled rotten. . . . His mind was possessed of that intolerable masculine pressure to command which develops in sons outrageously beloved by their mothers. . . . Hitlers develop out of such balance derived from imbalance, and great generals and great novelists (for what is a novelist but a general who sends his troops across fields of paper?)." We suspected then, now we know, that Mailer was talking about himself. . . .

Fanny Schneider Mailer dominates Manso's volume. Her presence is so thermonuclear that she reduces the savagery of Philip Roth's and Bruce Jay Friedman's fictional Jewish mothers to the colorless ash at ground zero. This is an instance where art cannot hope to compete with life. Young Norman, in his mother's eyes, was a genius who could do no wrong. . . .

Bequeathed by his mother an assurance more valuable than any preppy's trust fund, Mailer traveled the light years from Brooklyn to Harvard, where, as a freshman, he decided he would be a writer. Naturally, nothing less than greatness would do. . . .

After the War, working at white-hot speed, he produced *The Naked and the Dead,* the best-seller that assured his never having to look back again. It launched the Norman Mailer everyone knows, the one who is forever forcing himself to live up to his willed identity.

Most of *Mailer* is crowded with the public figure. As a perpetual celebrity, he has moved among numerous worlds—politics, Hollywood, sports, high society, the arts. There is no lack of individuals eager to have their say about him. Nor is there any denying that he possesses a truly remarkable personality, the stuff of literary legend. Even those who despise him do so with fascination. Mailer is capable of charming anyone he meets, and of inspiring a loyalty so intense that it sometimes tests the bounds of good sense. . . .

From [various] comments, a picture emerges of an extremely controlling person who is himself a bit out of control. Based solely on the evidence presented in the interviews, a jury might well convict Mailer of being scarcely more than a beery and unpredictable rogue. What redeems the life is the work, the books that swallow contemporary America whole as no others have done. Since these are necessarily diminished in an oral biography, *Mailer* ultimately, if unintentionally, belittles its subject. It is a lamentable tribute to a great writer. (p. 4)

> Barry Gewen, "*Mailer's Jewish Mother,*" in The New Leader, *Vol. LXVIII, No. 6, April 22, 1985, pp. 3-4.*

CHRISTOPHER LEHMANN-HAUPT

There is a sense in which Peter Manso's mammoth *Mailer: His Life and Times* seems just plain ridiculous. Over 150 people talking for nearly 700 pages about a single American writer whose work is still far from completed (or so one hopes)! Rehashings of such desperately trivial issues as why alpha stopped speaking to beta, or what delta really said about epsilon. Still more contemplation of the wives, the babies, the book contracts, the fisticuffs, the bitten ear and the stabbing. And everywhere the writer's mother, Fanny Schneider Mailer, chiming in as if she were a Greek chorus doing a parody of a Jewish mother.

And yet try dipping into Mr. Manso's interviews without at once becoming addicted. Try just skimming the text without getting hooked in the stage-by-stage unfolding of Norman Mailer's career. You can't. There's stuff here you never knew even if you've read everything that's ever been written by or about the man. . . .

Is it mostly gossip? Maybe so; but it is gossip of a somewhat higher order to learn why Mailer and Norman Podhoretz fell out over the former's review of the latter's *Making It;* or why Mailer scaled down the enthusiasm of his blurb for Diana Trilling's collected essays, *We Must March My Darlings.* After all, these incidents impinge on the culture of our recent past, at least the hothouse of recent New York City culture, which has bred shoots of ideas that may well have shaped the national agenda, as well as maggots of sectarian ideology. One feels, at least as a New Yorker, that one's life is passing before one's eyes.

And does it tell us anything serious about Norman Mailer? There are persisting themes—the man's professionalism and dedication to the job of writing, his loyalty to friends, the gentleness of his private persona as opposed to the raucous exhibitionism of the clown he has so often played in public. There are also the dubious questions of courage and masculinity, of sex and being its prisoner, and of the sponsorship of the writer-criminal Jack Abbott. Some witnesses think he'll never write the "big" book he's been promising us. Others insist that the life he has lived amounts to the great American novel.

I was troubled throughout by a peculiar fantasy. For some reason, I kept visualizing the kitschy apocalyptic ending of the movie *Raiders of the Lost Ark,* where the ark's ghostly spirits disintegrate the gathered Germans and suck their remains into heaven as if they were the plate's last strand of spaghetti. This may not be altogether silly. And it isn't only that one fears some sort of retribution for watching Mr. Manso and his witnesses taking the lid off Norman Mailer and looking inside him for some sort of divine message. One also has visions of an Old Testament God made angry by the excesses of Jewish assimilationism, which Norman Mailer's life can arguably be said to represent.

This is a theme that is insufficiently explored by Mr. Manso. True, several witnesses comment on Mailer's peculiar relations with Judaism. Norman Podhoretz, his old "foul-weather friend" and recent antagonist, observes that "the older I get, the more peculiar I think he was—and is—in his whole relationship to Jewishness." He adds: "That a man of his curiosity and energy would show so little interest about something so close to him, something that is in his blood, is extraordinary. Just the fact that he's never gone to Israel is in itself suspicious."

And Alfred Kazin, a critic of Mailer's through the book, comments: "Norman's not a prisoner of sex, he's not the prisoner of Jack Abbott. He's a prisoner of Jewish history, and no matter how gifted you are, how courageous, you always feel you're under wraps. Carrying what happened to us in the Second World War, we've felt this restraint very bitterly. So I understand it when I see him break against that restraint, only there's also a positive side to being Jewish, which he hasn't begun to acknowledge."

But this reader kept recalling Mailer's maternal grandfather, Chaim Yehudah Schneider, the unofficial rabbi of Long Branch, N.J. (unofficial because the community was too poor to support a rabbi full time). Lovingly recalled by Mailer's oldest cousin as the source of "all the brains and talent," he is introduced in the opening pages of the book and then never mentioned thereafter. But it is Chaim Yehudah's unacknowledged spirit in the book that makes one see Mailer's life as a drama of assimilation.

Would he have disapproved of his grandson's tempestuous career? Maybe so, maybe not. As Mailer's cousin puts it, "Although" Chaim Yehudah Schneider "was ordained, he never wanted a *shtetl*—a pulpit or congregation—because he said that rabbis were *schnorrers,* and he wouldn't live that way. So he was not only serious and well educated and brilliant but also honorable and principled. He was a Talmudic scholar all his life."

Perhaps he would be appalled by Norman Mailer. Or perhaps he would see in his grandson his own life raised to the next power.

> *Christopher Lehmann-Haupt, in a review of "Mailer: His Life and Times," in* The New York Times, *May 13, 1985, p. C20.*

BARBARA GOLDSMITH

[*Goldsmith, an American journalist, columnist, and editor, is the founding editor of* New York *Magazine and a regular contributor to such periodicals as* Harpers Bazaar, Esquire, *and* New York *Magazine. Her chronicle of the custody case of Gloria Vanderbilt,* Little Gloria . . . Happy at Last *(1980), highlights the life of a celebrated family and presents the social history of a period—the 1930s; both of these features are found in Manso's work. In the following excerpt Goldsmith evaluates Manso's "celebration of celebrity."*]

Norman Mailer's career has been accompanied by a torrent of print: more than a dozen books about Mailer, innumerable magazine and newspaper profiles, reviews, hard news stories, gossip column items. It is impossible to calculate how much of this attention is due to Mailer's celebrity and how much to his art. There is little doubt, however, about Peter Manso's *Mailer:* it is the quintessential celebrity biography. . . .

Unfortunately, the meretricious aspects of our society so adroitly dealt with by Mailer are nowhere in evidence in Mr. Manso's oral biography. The more than 200 tape-recorded interviews with Mailer and his friends and relatives, publishers, writers, actors, sports figures, socialites, politicians and gossip columnists have been cut up and patched together in roughly chronological fragments. As these voices speak, celebrity names proliferate. . . .

Continuity, sense of time and place, Mailer's ability to transform his experiences into art are all sacrificed to the "item" or anecdote. Lillian Hellman's story of how Dashiell Hammett

locked her in his bedroom so she could not bring money to Norman Mailer when he was in Bellevue Hospital is typical. It is fascinating but hardly relevant. Several of the interviewees use the book as an opportunity to affirm or deny the images Mailer has created for himself, while simultaneously stroking their own egos. . . .

The most disconcerting note in the book is the tendency to speak of Mailer as if [he] were dead. Allen Ginsberg asserts, "I think Norman loved Kerouac. Although he'd have difficulty showing his love. . . . I think he felt more hard and sophisticated and worldly." . . .

The most interesting parts of the book are when Mailer speaks about the images of Mailer he has created. His observations are clear, cool, artistic and objective. His *mea culpa* for his actions is appealing. Also, the book contains a great deal of informative talk about the publishing industry and about money, notably in Adeline Lubell Naiman's account of the how Little, Brown & Company lost the chance to publish *The Naked and the Dead* and in Lawrence Schiller's frank discussion of the transformation of material concerning Marilyn Monroe and Gary Gilmore into books.

The book's early portions, dealing with the time before Mailer achieved celebrity, as well as the voices of those who have had in-depth relationships with him, rise above the general self-aggrandizing tone. The relationship between Mailer and Francis Irby Gwaltney—Fig, the novelist from Charleston, Ark., who became Mailer's Army buddy and friend of four decades— is rich. The letters between them that appear here and to my knowledge have never before been published deal with honest emotions and intellectual concerns. . . .

The edited tape recording or oral biography is a special kind of book. The work of Studs Terkel epitomizes the excellence that can be achieved with taped and edited material. In Mr. Terkel's books, what the interviewees say captures a sense of truth and tells how the pressure of the times played on their lives. Each voice carries the same weight, anonymous people become Everyman. In *Mailer,* however, the egos of the celebrities take over, exploding like a Fourth of July fireworks display in the many episodes that flash for a moment on our consciousness. . . .

The assumption seems to be that either the reader has total recall about Mailer's books, or that the scanty reviews of, and excerpts from, them presented here will suffice. Mailer's writing is discussed as if the reader were conversant with every character. We find ourselves dealing once again with Lieutenant Hearn, Sergeant Croft and Private Valsen. Even the most avid Mailer reader must struggle to dredge up memories of *The Naked and the Dead,* published 37 years ago.

Mailer is repetitious in the extreme. Mr. Manso, a journalist, informs us that he gives multiple versions of events because "one can assume there is more truth in a montage than in a monolith." However, the differing versions usually concern small quibbles. . . . There is little continuity; an episode or period seems to end, but then we find it discussed by another interviewee totally out of context. We are given a location or a year, but then there is a sudden transition to another location or year. Nonintegrated observations on Mailer's character even appear in some of the notes on the contributors. In what one presumes is a technique to heighten tension, Mr. Manso frequently places opinions of an event before an explanation of what happened.

Some will be tempted to compare *Mailer* with *Edie: An American Biography* by Jean Stein, edited with George Plimpton. *Edie* was artfully edited, the distillation of a mass of material was excellent. Edie Sedgwick, a flamboyant member of Andy Warhol's coterie, was an excellent subject for an oral biography. She was a clean canvas on which each person she became involved with painted his own picture, a vulnerable, confused creature destroyed by a fantasy forced on her. On the other hand, Mailer has imposed his powerful voice on the American consciousness. He is a master manipulator of the news media. His persona and work are inextricably connected. The canvas that is his life and times is complicated, paradoxical, chaotic.

In dealing with "close to twenty thousand pages" of transcript, Mr. Manso has produced a sprawling, diffuse book in which the potential for a coherent analysis of Mailer's work and his impact on our society is lost in an unabashed celebration of celebrity.

> *Barbara Goldsmith, "Lion in a Kaleidoscope," in* The New York Times Book Review, *May 13, 1985, p. 9.*

GEOFFREY WOLFF

Whatever the consequences on Mailer's self-cultivated legend of Peter Manso's biography by compilation [*Mailer: His Life and Times*] . . . , the object of this relentlessly thorough exegesis holds himself at a becomingly novel distance from its process of judgment. If he has let himself be interviewed about the phenomenon Norman Mailer, his conclusions are moderate, even tentative, as though at last he has decided to leave some apprehensions to others, as though he might have calmed himself some, as though he were no longer willing to devote himself to showoff nonsense.

To understand why Mailer would in any way collaborate with someone else's spin on the accumulated choices and mischances that have in sum made Mailer's self, his bread and wine as an artist, listen to him speak in the final few pages of this tome: ". . . I'm a little rueful that I'm not as competitive as I used to be. But you have to ebb a bit as you get older. What I'm concerned with now is how many books I have left

Mailer with running mate, Jimmy Breslin, conceding defeat, June 18, 1969. AP/Wide World Photos.

to write. It's no longer a question of Is one the champ? I'm a writer like other writers, either better or less good than I think I am. But in the meantime I have a life to work at. And how do I want to lead that life in the time remaining to me? In other words, no more stunts."

Pardon the reservations of a cynic, but I've read and written about many Norman Mailers, and while this elder statesman is among the more attractive of his populous tribe, of a piece with the reflective and deliberate craftsman recently interviewed by John Leonard on television, there is a core fact about Norman Mailer once (and brilliantly) declared by Norman Mailer, almost 30 years ago:

"To write about myself is to send my style through a circus of variations and postures, a fireworks of virtuosity designed to achieve . . . I do not even know what. Leave it that I become an actor, a quick-change artist, as if I believe I can trap the Prince of Truth in the act of switching a style" ("First Advertisement for Myself").

Mailer has always been justly preoccupied with his voice, whatever its imperfect dialects and shifty properties, first-person singular or third-person royal. (pp. 1, 10)

If it has been his credo that upon the anvil of personality (the sum of enactments and ruminations) style is beaten into shape, style for Mailer has until recently been the sounds of his voices. Not until *The Executioner's Song,* the first section of which is first among my own Mailer favorites, has he been certain enough of the power, perhaps even the existence, of his own voice to let another speak within his hearing, to imagine a voice not his own, to create the sound of someone else speaking, thinking, being.

His collaboration with Peter Manso's enterprise is another instance of a writer secure in his gift easing his grip on it, listening, watching others watch him. . . .

Such a biography, in which the interviewer and his questions disappear, and the responses to those questions are arranged in categorical mosaics, is an exercise in point of view. Many voices, many vantages, many partialities contribute to (and contend for) the truth of Mailer's experience at Harvard, for example, or as a soldier, friend, political partisan, professional writer. . . .

It would be wrong to underestimate the value of this testimony. Many among these 150 have been angry at Mailer, have felt themselves the victims of small (and larger) betrayals, have despised his courtship with extreme people who commit extreme acts that draw blood. But no one can read this account—page upon page of recollections by people famous and unknown, grave literary personages and trivial sycophants and social climbers, beings up the greasy pole and ignorant of its existence—without noting Mailer's bedrock decency, a steadfast commitment to his friends and his calling that transcends calculation, or any ambition, including the ambition to be good, or to be loved. Call the collective effect love: for Mailer, and if not for Mailer for what he has tried, and if not for what he has tried for what he has made others wish to try. (p. 10)

> *Geoffrey Wolff, "Norman Mailer as Others See Him," in* Book World—The Washington Post, *May 19, 1985, pp. 1, 10.*

ELIOT FREMONT-SMITH

Peter Manso's *Mailer: His Life and Times* . . . is, in some scheme of things, grotesque, a monstrous tributhon or roast,

700 pages of this-is-your-life recollections and interpretations by former and current friends, relatives, colleagues, hangers-on—151 interviewed contributors not counting Norman Kingsley Mailer himself, plus letters, reviews, salient quotes from the Works, etc.—all assembled chronologically, *Edie*-style, and the man not yet dead.

One can, of course, decline this celebration, change the channel, let the book go by. Mailer, too, will pass; it is an illusion of the book that all attention is riveted on him. Open *Mailer* anywhere, and the illusion reaches out and drags you in and under; you can bob up for a breath of air and a look-around any time, but may not want to. It isn't a matter of assault (though people will so complain) but of being willingly seduced (for whatever reason, by whatever means); assault is a compelling and relentless subject of the book—sexual pugilism, physical politics, the stabbings—but not its nature....

Nor is every subject thoroughly accounted for. The children are at very best glossed. The books are treated (appropriately) not in terms of themselves—in many cases just snippets of reviews—but in terms of what they reveal about Mailer and for their immediate personal and cultural effect. And the sex—well, a lot of talk up-front, and almost no actual description. Mailer as a lover remains an enigma, his shlong (one of the more promoted and conjectured about in literary history) wrapped in modesty. Which is probably just as well, the legend should live on. But for most of the rest, the book is frank, detailed, outspoken, funny, horrifying, fascinating, ludicrous, awesome, irreverent, brave, hypnotic, petty, dramatic, adroit, and unseemly—a whirligig of ambition, passion, and disaster. One thing about *Mailer:* it will make you forget your troubles. One thing about Mailer: he's got as many lives as Nixon. And is a lot more entertaining.

The book abounds in theory. Everybody has his or her say about why Mailer is the way he is, writes the way he writes, does the things he does. There is the doting mother theory, which has a great deal going for it. There is the virility-on-the-march theory. There is the good-little-Jewish-boy-from-Brooklyn-turned-narcissist theory and the rabbi theory and the *naïf* theory and the Hemingway theory and the-insatiable-hunger-for-attention theory and the he-really-likes-women theory and the loner theory and the competitive theory and the theory theory, to explain why Mailer tries to elevate everything to theory. There is not the mean little bastard theory, which I find tempting more than once....

There is also the talent theory, which makes sense to me (to begin with, Mailer had a grade school IQ of 165, as the principal proudly announced on graduation day—"the highest IQ we've ever had at P.S. 161"), and the disciplined hard work theory. Mailer notes that *The Naked and the Dead* was preceded by nearly a million words, mostly written at Harvard, including numerous stories (one won the then-important *Story* magazine prize), three apprentice novels (*No Percentage,* about a rich hitchhiker, for which he took a trip hitching south, making Fan "sick"; *A Calculus at Heaven,* which contains a burn-victim scene probably researched at the 1942 Coconut Grove fire in Boston; and *A Transit to Narcissus*), and a play entitled *The Naked and the Dead,* which, like *Transit,* was based on a brief summer job at a state mental hospital. And all the while he majored not in English but in engineering—the famous Lego city of the late 1960's had its antecedents in a boyhood passion for giant model airplanes. Mailer was always *doing,* and doing big. Everyone remarks on his energy. George Plimpton: "There's definitely a very large electrical field that comes off Norman.

Even sitting with him when he's absolutely at his ease, the energy is there, something almost palpable, and I've never known a person who had it to such a degree."

The discipline is interesting, since so much of Mailer's life seems chaotic, courting of violence and destruction. Amid all the booze and marijuana and mayhem and catastrophes—some of them comical, but absolutely ego-shattering to ordinary mortals—Mailer has time and again been able to pull himself together. Or been *driven* to pull himself together, as if he had no choice, as if instinct were a huge psychic gyroscope that simply gathered strength in adversity. This is, I suppose, the destiny theory, which I don't like on moral grounds, but find suggestive in this case. (p. 49)

There are quiet moments (usually either desperate or foreboding), but the book is never dull. Nor it is solely about Mailer; it is literary and cultural (and sexual, political, psychological) history of a fascinating order, approve of it or not, recounting the more idealistic and wrenching ideas, events, and terrors of the last three decades, approve of them or not. There are wonderful, funny, painful scenes (*The Prisoner of Sex* Town Hall imbroglio is a gas), and some very neat sniping among the contributors, and the candor, the courage of it, is itself moving.

It's kind of stupid, not knowing what he cut, to say that Manso has done a great job of editing; but he sure got people talking, and the book envelopes no matter where you enter it. I myself began with the stabbing, then the shambles of a birthday celebration; then Jimmy Breslin—or was it Joe Flaherty?—recalling who wanted what deleted from which manuscript, then Alfred Kazin on Jewish heritage à propos Mailer's concept of "fucking," then Midge Decter on how Diana Trilling's perception of proper behavior among intellectuals may be slightly less than 20/20—and so on, not always happy, but very definitely hooked. And with this weird sense of Mailer (or Mailer's mother) watching *me;* he is a doer, a worker, an actor (as much as anything else, his strange put-on accents, not all of them playful, give rise throughout the book to questions of his sanity), and, as proved beyond dispute, a penetrating and adroit critical observer.

As to whether you need *Mailer*—the sun will rise without it. As to the *Edie* effect on biography, I leave that to others—though I must say it's a generous way of going about a life, and freeing for the reader. As to the theories about who or what Mailer is and why, I like each one, depending on its angle of attack—though in the end, of course, a great writer is a great writer, as can also be said of pot roast. (p. 52)

Eliot Fremont-Smith, "Norman Mailer and the Pot-Roast Theory," in The Village Voice, *Vol. XXX, No. 21, May 21, 1985, pp. 49, 52.*

ANTHONY BURGESS

[*An English novelist and critic, Burgess is well-known for his satires of contemporary society in which he uses black humor—the most famous of these is his novel* A Clockwork Orange *(1962). Burgess's experimentation with language is widely acclaimed, and his interest in linguistics is reflected in his critical studies of James Joyce, including Burgess's popular* Here Comes Everybody: An Introduction to James Joyce for the Ordinary Reader *(1965; published in America as* Re Joyce, *1965). In the following excerpt Burgess points out the shortcomings of Manso's "pseudo-biography" and the strengths of Mailer, the writer, particularly his style and originality.*]

Mailer during the early 1980s. Photograph © 1983 Nancy Crampton.

Norman Mailer's fame is large and his immortality assured. But for precisely what is he famous and immortal? (p. 100)

[It] is, in fact, as a stylist that Mailer deserves his fame and his immortality. Whereas Hemingway created the "simple, declarative sentence," which was apt for an age that wanted no more of the bloated, periodic rhetoric of a discredited liberalism, Mailer restored the baroque and salted it with new and dangerous condiments—existential violence, anal magic, Brooklyn street-boy expletives. But whether he was ever again, after his first book, to be regarded as a novelist—promising or achieved—should never really have been the point. Give him a subject—the battle of the sexes, the moon shots, Marilyn Monroe, Vietnam, the mindless violence of a Utah hoodlum and his opting for an outmoded lethe, ancient Egypt—and you can be sure of getting a rare and inimitable prose, which, like D. H. Lawrence's, takes mad chances and risks silliness to gain new tonalities and resonances.

Whether Mailer is an intelligent writer is another matter. He is certainly—again, like Lawrence—not a rational writer. As Lawrence located reality in the loins, Mailer, on the evidence of both *An American Dream* and *Ancient Evenings,* finds it in the anal tract. He has made some dangerous constatations, like that early one, vaguely Camusian, about the possibility of finding the moment of truth in an "existential" killing. He has been too fond of the term *existential,* and Iris Murdoch . . . failed to put him right as to its meaning. It is probably impossible to argue with Mailer, as it was with Lawrence. He has convictions in his gut, or lower, and for good or ill these make him what he is. . . .

Like Hemingway before him, Mailer has wanted the nonliterary world to take him seriously; like Fitzgerald before him, he has been a cause of scandal. His public personality has rubbed onto his art, which is very un-European and probably harmful. . . . That he has not been destroyed, as either a man or a writer, by his engagement with the dirty world is a testimony to his Brooklyn Jewish toughness and his basic literary integrity.

And now—a little too soon, I would have thought—we have his biography, or rather a do-it-yourself kit for the making of a biography [*Mailer: His Life and Times*]. I cannot sufficiently deplore the production of biographies when their subjects are still alive. . . . Mailer is a mere child, aand his biography can be no more than a kind of interim report. The subject of a life should sit still, or lie still. Moreover, he should have done his work, and a life's pattern ought to be discernible. (pp. 100, 102)

Manso has not written this book. He has filled leagues, miles, versts, kilometers, of recording tape with reminiscences and observations from the people in Mailer's life. Because, in the manner of speech, this material is repetitive, vague, sometimes inaccurate, frequently slangy, and often obscene, Manso has done some editing, but he has not done much checking on matters of reliability. (p. 102)

It is the lack of a pattern that damages Manso's collocation of ana (Johnson's term), and it is the lack of time to reconsider that damages certain dicta—for example, Alfred Kazin's observation to the effect that Jews divorce more because they are richer. The only contributor who emerges as wholly serious, compassionate, intelligent, and objectively critical is Diana Trilling.

If Mailer is primarily a writer, which he is, we need more about his writing than can be conveyed by snippets from reviews. The reviews themselves are nearly all from American periodicals, and Mailer's world status deserved a sampling from the world's critics, especially those British ones who were quicker to see his distinction than many of their American counterparts. There is often a sense, not only in respect of literary matters, that the reader is expected to come to the book equipped with the knowledge that it is the duty of a biographer to provide, and that he should be satisfied with the kind of commentary appropriate to journalism or gossip. It is rather like prolonged and rambling dinner-table conversation with no dinner. The primary task of a biographer is to provide a biographical narrative.

I am especially annoyed with this bound file of minutes on Mailer because the possibility of creating a useful biographico-critical work on the man (a kind of expansion of the brief book that has already appeared in the Modern Masters series) seems thus foreclosed. . . . And the nature of this pseudo-biography is such that Manso has effectively preempted the materials from which another biographer, meaning a genuine one, could hack out, with the appropriate literary pain, a work worthy of its subject. Let us have no nonsense about this. Biography is art and can be great art. But the bogus claims of taped "immediacy" may well in this electronic age prevail over the approach that was good enough for Boswell and, for that matter, Ellmann.

Sighing, I admit that some sort of "portrait" comes out of this rough, synoptic gallimaufry. It is an image of an American intellectual . . . trying to cope with life in the United States. . . . The urge to be a kind of prophet—Lawrence's near undoing—explains Mailer's ventures into journalism and his hectoring, with jokes in doubtful taste, from various platforms. Add serial polygamy, multiple alimony, depression, pot, booze, scandal, and you have a fairly standard contemporary American literary life.

America is to Mailer, as his French friend and translator Jean Malaquais says, "cancerous" but the one mistress "to whom he remains faithful in a perennial love-hate affair." In his recent *Tough Guys Don't Dance* we have the telling phrase "I wanted my country on my cock," which may be taken as meaning a desire to love or rape his country, probably anally, into a sense of its destiny.... Why he spent a decade on a novel about ancient Egypt has never been made fully clear (it was one of the jobs of this biography to give us at least the intimation of a reason), but the novel is surely partially about the problems of American rule, the importance of the irrational in American culture, and why great empires rise and fall. What is still awaited from him is a work of Tolstoyan weight, as opposed to mere Tolstoyan wordiness.... As for what he's actually doing, John Leonard, a very honest and perceptive critic, says the right things:

> I can imagine everything Bellow and Updike and other writers are telling me, but what's so characteristic of Mailer is that he's finding something, telling me something I couldn't have imagined beforehand. Which is why I trust him. He continues to astonish.

The capacity to astonish is precisely what is not featured in this loose, multivocal survey. What we chiefly have is the capacity to hit the headlines, shock with routine modes of polemical violence, and behave like any mixed-up American in an age that is hard enough, God knows, to understand but perhaps willing to yield its secrets to a sensibility like Mailer's. It was an unworthy thing to unleash so much mere gossip on that sensibility. (pp. 103-04)

> *Anthony Burgess, "The Prisoner of Fame," in* The Atlantic Monthly, *Vol. 255, No. 6, June, 1985, pp. 100, 102-04.*

SEYMOUR KRIM

[*Krim is an American essayist, editor, and contributor to* Village Voice, Chicago Tribune, Washington Post, *and other periodicals. In the 1950s Krim was greatly influenced by the Beat writers; he abandoned his formalist literary criticism to focus on personal revelations of his life and on American contemporary culture. Working as an editor, he was successful in extending the influence of the Beat writers and the New Journalists, including Mailer, who were dedicated to engaging art with day-to-day life. Krim's edited anthology* The Beats *(1980) includes such writers as Jack Kerouac, Allen Ginsberg, Lawrence Ferlinghetti, and Mailer. Mailer wrote the foreword to Krim's autobiographical essays* Views of a Nearsighted Cannoneer *(1968). In the following excerpt Krim praises Manso for his deft use of interviews in preparing this "communal 'confession'" and also admires Mailer for his dedication and achievement as a writer.*]

Even though Hilary Mills did a very competent biography of Norman Mailer in 1982, you just can't beat 151 live human beings rapping away about one of the most incendiary Americans on the scene today [in *Mailer: His Life and Times*]. Yes, some of the testifiers in this book-length revival meeting do become self-serving and irritatingly "New Yorky," but the steady fascination of Peter Manso's wicked tape recorder lies in the fact that the witnesses reveal themselves quite as much

as they cast light on Mailer. They all become characters in a huge living novel, and we measure them as they squirm, flatter or berate the magnetic ringleader who has invaded all their lives....

Manso's method is to collect a ton of quotes from people who knew Mailer at each stage of his life: growing up in Brooklyn and Long Branch, N.J., then Harvard, after that the Army and the Pacific campaign, then publication of his first novel, the triumphal reception in Paris, etc. But Manso is a shrewd collagist of the spoken word, he doesn't squander what his interviewees say all at once. Instead, he cuts up the tapes and inserts relevant and even sheer gossipy information in the appropriate slots, shifting from one voice to another in order to keep the action going. The result is fast-paced variety and often contradiction, the very qualities that are an indigenous trademark of Mailer's psychic arsenal.

As we follow the novelist climbing the American success ladder and then being booted off because he refuses to play by anyone else's rules, the comments by the oversized chorus begin to shift from uncelebrated friends and family to a beehive of well-known names....

By and large, he comes off this griddle a little toasted, perhaps, but crisp and well-buttered in other people's estimation. Mailer's mysterious scope and complexity have been able to absorb humiliating attacks and terrible downers—like his stabbing of his second wife, Adele Morales Mailer, in 1960, and his incarceration in Bellevue—without ever permanently smearing his image. His resiliency has been little short of incomprehensible when you think of the mental, physical and financial pounding (six wives, nine children) he has taken over the years.

Finally, though, it is the novelist lodged inside the man who ought to be given credit for Norman Mailer's durability and the grand challenge that he always poses to the rest of us. Were Mailer merely the self-aggrandizing imperialist that critics in this book and elsewhere suggest, his credit rating would have been cut off long before now. But, so far, no true fix ultimately has been put on him, probably because the cape-twirling ego that arouses the troops works as a concealment for a persistent dedication that goes about its business on stealthy cat's feet.

So—if there is any misguided emphasis in this otherwise flagrantly readable communal "confession," it might be this: Rambunctious as Mailer's outer life has been, it doesn't hold a candle to what goes on where the klieg lights don't shine. Even Peter Manso's remarkably insinuating microphone can't burrow that craftily.

> *Seymour Krim, "Mailer in the Raw: A Tape Collage Brings Him Roaring to Life," in* Chicago Tribune, *Section 14, June 16, 1985, p. 35.*

LOUIS MENAND

It has always been Norman Mailer's literary gambit to present his reputation as a problem to be solved by those who wish him well. He is a writer who has gone far by making things difficult for his admirers.... [These] are not such happy times for controversialism. This big book [*Mailer: His Life and Times*] once again flings the familiar basket of contradictions in the public's face, but one of the lessons of the rather indifferent reception it has so far been accorded appears to be that Mailer's reputation is no longer a problem anyone feels much like solving. And if we are not quite sure what to make of Mailer these days, it seems that Mailer, whose self-image has always depended on the reactions he provokes, is not entirely sure what to make of himself.

Mailer: His Life and Times is a frustrating literary object. It is too long, and like most books that are too long, it cannot seem to make up its mind about what it wants to say. (p. 29)

Still, with all this material to work with, Manso has naturally had some successes. Mailer's mother, for instance—by all accounts a woman of extraordinary character—steals several scenes as only a mother can. . . . And the chapter on the 1950s includes an absorbing stretch in which the writing collected in *Advertisements for Myself* is made the center of a lengthy back-and-forth between various of the New York intellectuals (Irving Howe, Norman Podhoretz, Diana Trilling) and the Beats (Allen Ginsberg, Michael McClure)—a kind of ad hoc debate about the origins of the 1960s. This imaginary dialogue is a remarkable feat of editing, but it requires more than a hundred pages to work itself out—a hundred pages one can't help feeling would have been refined, with not much lost that matters, to no more than 30 in a more traditional history. Manso cannot afford to be this generous with the intellectual life of other periods, and when he gets to the 1960s, the memories tend to revolve around the thumb-wrestling and the amateur pugilism and the cars and the stars and the many, many bars.

Mailer is, in any case, a nearly impossible subject for a biographer. Who could hope to improve on the account he has provided himself? Mailer's life and times are, after all, Mailer's great subject and if one were to string together his omnibus collections . . . , one would have a history hard to beat for completeness and impossible to beat for moral nuance. For Mailer at his best is a writer in possession of an honesty once nicely described by Richard Gilman as "ravishing." . . .

Mailer's honesty, of course, has seemed to many people a literary excuse for poor judgment and for a hopeless incapacity for self-restraint, and it is on this issue that Mailer's admirers have had their work cut out for them. Conventional criticism prefers to keep what is written separate from what was lived—it's one of the ways of making the work of art a kind of risk-free zone for the dramatization of ideas and impulses thought to be too dangerous to be tried out in ordinary life. But it has also seemed like a way of making art inconsequential, and, as Diana Trilling observed many years ago, it is one of the critical decorums Mailer has done his best to ignore. He wants, like any strong moralist, to have his metaphors taken literally.

It is not easy to know how to respond to this challenge. We might want to say that if someone were not willing on occasion to play the fool, we would not have a very precise sense of the limits of civility. . . .

The feature of Mailer's thought that has given the most trouble to readers who have wanted to take him as seriously as he asks to be taken is his fascination with the psychopathic personality. (p. 30)

Mailer's status as a cultural figure is also something of a problem these days for the ironic reason that the popular culture's taste for behavioral extremes has now far outstripped his own. Ideas that were part of a new and difficult moral vision in 1959 have become the stock-in-trade of the purveyors of commercial culture. . . . Mailer is a thinker who needs a wall of provincialism to bounce his ideas off; but where there is no sin, there is no mystery, and polite curiosity has replaced shock as the culturally indicated response to an outrageous suggestion.

But if Mailer is a writer who commands large funds of forgiveness, it is a grace well-earned, for he has been more than generous with his talents for many years. He is one of the few real virtuosos of American letters. He has left his mark on nearly every literary form—on not only the novel in most of its contemporary guises, but even more dramatically on the literature of fact, where the range and variety of his achievements are unequaled.

The most influential of his work may be the political reportage—influential both because it showed other writers what could be done by describing the *experience* of covering a political event, and because it taught a new generation of readers how to look at a politician. We ordinarily think of the New Journalism as involving some sort of crossing of fact with fiction in violation of the laws of genre; but Mailer has made sporadic efforts over the years to dissociate his own political writing from this conception. His own intuition, he says, was that "the world (not the techniques but the *world*) of fiction can be brought to the facts of journalism," by which he appears to mean not that he invented what he could not see (he is, it hardly needs to be repeated, the most scrupulous of observers), but that he found characters and plots where there had once been only spokesmen and agendas. (pp. 31-2)

[It] is the description of Lyndon Johnson . . . that deserves to live in every memory book of the 1960s:

> [He] had compromised too many contradictions and now the contradictions were in his face: when he smiled the corners of his mouth squeezed gloom; when he was pious, his eyes twinkled irony; when he spoke in a righteous tone, he looked corrupt; when he jested, the ham in his jowls looked to quiver. He was not convincing.

One therefore knew exactly what Mailer meant when he offered, in *The Village Voice*, this sentence as his explanation for his decision to vote for Bobby Kennedy instead of Kenneth Keating: "He has finally a face." It is a new language for politics, the language not of the editorial page or the lectern but of the street corner and the bedroom: it is the language of love.

Everything in Mailer's writing seems charged in this way because he has the optimism of the apocalyptic imagination: he can imagine a time when everything will no longer be the same, and all his plots, novelistic and journalistic, end up pointed toward some enormous possibility whose features are not quite legible. It is a habit of mind that sometimes leads to self-parody ("the Beatles," he muses somewhere, "—demons or saints?"). But Mailer is usually at his sharpest when he catches a glimpse of his own obsessions at work and makes the recognition a part of his anger—at the world for being less than his best thoughts would wish it, and at himself for being foolish enough to care so much.

With *Ancient Evenings* Mailer's career has taken a curious turn, and the last chapter of Manso's book makes an unsettling finish to the story. Mailer's social life these days is centered on the Upper East Side, where he has evidently been found a congenial ornament for the dinner table. . . . And the last series of interviews in the book is with Jason Epstein, Mailer's editor at Random House, where he has a four million dollar contract for his next four novels; Walter Anderson, the editor of *Parade* magazine, for which Mailer has lately written some pieces; and Leo Lerman, who as editor of *Vanity Fair* paid $50,000

Mailer with his mother, Fanny. © 1986 Thomas Victor.

for the serial rights to Mailer's most recent novel, **Tough Guys Don't Dance.** It is the consensus among these observers that Mailer is now entering the most fruitful phase of his career.

Who would want to disagree? "People think they've found a way of dismissing me," Mailer warned an interviewer a few years ago, "but, like the mad butler—I'll be back serving the meal." What will he serve, though? Perrier with a twist? These are clean-living times, and clean living has not been a subject Mailer has usually given his best attention to. Still, even the most self-satisfied of times have their stories, and it does not seem too improbable an expectation that Mailer may somehow find a way to tell them. He has, after all, a face. (pp. 32-3)

> Louis Menand, "Advertisements for His Self," in The New Republic, *Vol. 192, No. 25, June 24, 1985, pp. 29-33.*

MARTIN AMIS

[Amis is a young English novelist and journalist and a satirist of contemporary life. In his novels, including The Rachel Papers *(1973),* Success *(1978), and* Money: A Suicide Note *(1985), Amis uses black humor as he explores themes of alienation, the breakdown in communication, and the superficiality of sex. In a 1981 interview Amis commented, "I'm more obsessed by down-and-outs and the griefs of ordinary people than in the life at the top*

end of the scale." In his journalistic pieces for the London Observer, *Amis specializes in American culture; Mailer is one of his favorite subjects. In the following excerpt Amis views Mailer's life as a microcosm of American life of the period: violent, strident, and ridiculous.]*

This 700-pager is an oral biography, or better say a verbal one. Peter Manso provides no links, no introduction; after his epic jugglings with the tapes and transcriptions, he was presumably hard-pressed to manage the acknowledgments and the dedication. Even in America the book has been sniffed at as a by-blow of the new barbarism, but I think there is an appropriate madness in Manso's method. What's so great about the literary biography, anyway? **Mailer** intercuts about 150 voices: family, friends, peers, onlookers, enemies. It is deeply discordant, naggingly graphic and atrociously indiscreet. No living writer, you'd have thought, could have more to lose by such an exposure. But then, programmatic self-destruction has always been the keynote of Mailer's life and times.

'Do things that frighten you,' is one of Norman's pet maxims. Needless to say, in real life, doing things that frighten you tends to involve doing things that frighten other people. For some reason or other, Mailer spent the years between 1950 and 1980 in a tireless quest for a fistfight. He liked his dirty-talking, hellcat women to fight too, teaching them how and egging them on. 'Drinking runs through this whole story,' as one of his wives remarks, 'drinking, drinking, drinking.' . . .

Irving Howe once said that Mailer risked becoming 'a hostage to the temper of his times.' But he was a willing hostage, and in fact he normally behaved more like a terrorist. 'For I wish to attempt an entrance,' wrote Mailer in 1959, with typical pomp, 'into the mysteries of murder, suicide, incest, orgy, orgasm and Time.' He was referring to his work rather than his life, but the two activities (like bar-room brawlers) were hard to keep apart.

The book is strewn with vicious confrontations, drunken couplings, ostentatious suicide bids, cruel human manipulations, incessant violence—and incessant cant. It is like a distillation of every Sixties hysteria, every radical-chic inanity. . . .

There is a fair bit to be said on the credit side. And, after all, better writers have behaved worse. There is manifest charm, strong loyalty, an absence of snobbery, the novelist's gift of finding interest everywhere (even in bores and boredom), the enviable—if not admirable—shamelessness, and above all the selective but delightfully strident honesty. . . .

In secure retrospect, Mailer's life and times seem mostly ridiculous: incorrigibly ridiculous. Some observers talk of his 'great huge ambition,' his 'great grace and correctitude'; others just lick their wounds. A devout immoralist, he always veered between the superhuman and the subhuman, between Menenhetet I and Gary Gilmore. Like America, he went too far in all directions, and only towards the end, perhaps—with no more drink and 'no more stunts,' dedicated to his work and to a noncombatant sixth wife—has he struck a human balance.

> Martin Amis, "Norman and the Women," in The Observer, *July 28, 1985, p. 25.*

CHRIS VINCENT

The personality which emerges from this multi-faceted account [**Mailer: His Life and Times**] is not so much that of the "psychic outlaw" Mailer sees himself as, but that of a little boy, performing for his doting family. There is an air of calculation about much of it—as if the hell-raising persona were a kind of fictional alter-ego.

Norman Mailer's big problem is that he isn't Ernest Hemingway; although to judge by this catalogue of boozing, brawling womanising and all the rest of what Ginsberg calls "that macho heterosexual bullshit", he has a damn good try. The difference is that, for all his absurd tough-guy posturing, Hemingway was a fine writer, whereas Mailer's novelistic efforts seem little more than extensions of his own fantasy.

In fact what comes across most strongly in his novels is his contempt for—and underlying fear of—women, an attitude substantiated time and again in the pages of his biography. . . .

Whatever one's attitude to the man—or his writings—there is no doubt of his importance as a figure in post-war American literature, one of the "prima donnas" of the American novel, in Alfred Kazin's phrase. Where Mailer displays true genius is as a self-publicist. He is an adaptor of current fashions in ideas—never an innovator. In the fifties, after the success of *The Naked and the Dead*, he enjoyed a brief flirtation with radical politics, and fraternised with the likes of Kerouac, Ginsberg and Burroughs. His naive romanticisation of violence amused them; as Ginsberg put it: "the whole notion of being smarter, more psychotic . . . was no longer of interest."

In the sixties, when he wasn't playing at being the psychic outlaw, Mailer threw in his lot with the anti-war movement; one of his finest pieces of journalism, the Pulitzer prize-winning *Armies of the Night* was written at this time.

His twin obsessions with sex and violent death surfaced, in the seventies, in the biographical fictions he wrote about Marilyn Monroe (1975) and Gary Gilmore (1979). . . .

What emerges most strongly from his biographical account is the extent to which Mailer is the central figure in his own fictions, assigning himself, and those he comes into contact with, particular roles in his private theatre. Not for nothing is one of his books of essays entitled *Advertisements For Myself*.

> Chris Vincent, "Mailer: Machismo Meets Little Boy,"
> in Tribune, Vol. 49, Nos. 32 & 33, August 9 & 16,
> 1985, p. 8.

ANDY STARK

In her *New York* review of *Mailer: His Life and Times,* a new "oral biography" by Peter Manso, Rhoda Koenig remarks on the vast voyage Norman Mailer has undertaken in order to get from "nice Jewish boy" to "romantic outlaw"—the point from which he has always operated as a writer. (Koenig then expresses her wish that Mailer, and men in general, settle on some point in between.) Yet over its six-hundred-odd pages, the book under review (which is a compendium of personal reminiscences about Mailer) sounds a recurring, disturbing demurral about both the wisdom and the success of Mailer's voyage. . . . Some of his closest friends, apparently, suspect that Norman Mailer has never actually negotiated the passage from intellectual, bespectacled, cautious Jew to violent, head-butting sexual adventurer. Yet it is as the latter, and with the latter's assumed experience, that Mailer has always written.

Arguably, then, Norman Mailer's life has been inauthentic as experience, and consequently his fiction has been inferior as art. But before one can draw this conclusion, it is necessary to come to grips with this so-called and obviously widely assumed gulf between Jewish experience and literary sensibility

on the one hand, and the life and art of sex and violence on the other. . . .

Many postwar critics and writers who have made it their business to effect rapprochements between sexuality and Jewishness, or to note points of contact between violence and the children of Israel, also abjure Mailer. They attack him, though, not for failing to honor the irreconcilability of the two realms, and so, as a Jew, necessarily writing inauthentically about sex and violence. Rather, they attack him for the opposite: for failing to honor the unity of the two realms, and so doing the American Jew a disservice by ignoring his darker side of sex and violence. (p. 44)

As with the gulf between sex and Jewishness, so with that between violence and Jewishness. There is a perception that Mailer has been oblivious to a postwar *convergence* of the two, and has consequently chosen to embrace violence and renounce his Jewishness. . . .

Everyone has his own agenda in these discussions, of course, which accounts for the contradictions in criticism. Nevertheless, since no one else is doing so, let me take up the defense of Norman Mailer, first against those who accuse him of having ignored the convergence between sex, violence, and the postwar American Jew, and then against those whose criticism relies on the underlying divergences between the romantic, the outlaw, and the Jew. To Philip Roth, on the marriageability of sexuality and Jewish heroes: Anybody could, in 1969, have created an erstwhile *yeshivabokher* who ploughs through shiksa after shiksa. It's another thing to have created, as Norman Mailer did in 1959, a frigid nineteen-year-old Jewish girl who becomes the ultimate object of the lust of a blond blue-eyed Catholic Greenwich-Village bull-fighting instructor. A lusted-after Jew. A defiled Jew. Here is Jew as believable *object* of *goyische* lust, not subject—I can't think of one by Philip Roth.

On violence: While Alfred Kazin has been busy grieving over the postwar migration of the Jew from the cowardices and courages of the victim, to the cowardices and courages of the violent, Norman Mailer has been end-running him. For Mailer has spent much of his time questioning almost every accepted connection between courage, cowardice, violence, and victimhood. This is an endeavor about which there should be absolutely no question as to its central importance for postwar Jewish self-understanding. For example, Mailer wrote in "The White Negro" (1957):

> It can of course be suggested that it takes little courage for two strong eighteen-year-old hoodlums, let us say, to beat in the brains of a candy-store keeper, and indeed the act . . . is not likely to prove therapeutic, for the victim is not an immediate equal. Still, courage of a sort is necessary, for one murders not only a weak forty-year-old man, but an institution as well; one violates private property, one enters into a new relation with the police and introduces a dangerous element into one's life. The hoodlum is therefore daring the unknown, and so no matter how brutal the act, it is not altogether cowardly. . . .

Tellingly, Philip Roth wrote of this very passage that "these few lines . . . should make it clear why Jewish cultural audiences, which are generally pleased to hear Saul Bellow and Bernard Malamud identified as Jewish writers, are perfectly content that by and large Norman Mailer . . . should go forth onto the lecture platform and the television shows as a writer *period*.'' Perhaps. Or perhaps Jewish cultural audiences recognize in such a passage not a siding with the violent hoodlum against the Jewish property-owner, but an exploration of the very ideas of victimhood, violence, courage, and cowardice which, however wrongheaded, fully engages them as Jews, because these ideas are central to their experience. (p. 45)

In his own mind, at least, Mailer has not fled from Jewish experience; rather, his view is that postwar American Jewish experience has itself been a flight from Jewish experience. To ignore ''Jewishness,'' and to concentrate on those aspects of American life that Jews have long quested after and are now winning, is to be keenly faithful to postwar Jewish experience.

As far as his stylized masculinity is concerned, Mailer's first use for it has been neither as substitute for real experience, nor as subject of his art. Rather, it has rested between the two. . . . Mailer's masculinity is practiced and stylized precisely because it is a practice, it is a style. It is part of the discipline of writing. What he sees as the masculine qualities—courage, love of danger, relentlessness—are necessarily first and foremost those of the artist, not of the man. Mailer thus does not have a false life's experience as a pretended romantic outlaw, nor is he really nothing but a bespectacled Jewish writer. Rather, by his own lights, Mailer is a Brooklyn Jew in his experience, which is the experience of a non-experience, and a romantic outlaw as a writer, because that is what a writer must be.

It is hard, though, not to note one imbalance between life and art in Norman Mailer. It has to do with time: I had a friend in graduate school whose dissertation was on a particular historical event; the dissertation takes longer to read than the event itself took to happen. One finds this affliction, if it is an affliction, all too often in Mailer's prose about sex. I would like to propose a neoclassical unity of time for fiction analogous to the classical unity of time for drama: A description of, or an allusion to, a given act should not take longer to read than the act takes to perform.

According to this unity, that writer approaches perfection in conveying his particular vision of the acts of sex as he manages to capture them in fewer and fewer words. Ideally, one word will make it, and the greatest of all writers about sex have found their word. . . . Lawrence . . . used only one word, so that while Mailer offers us an endless cascade of words which drown and disfigure and distract from the act he is describing, Lawrence made that one word into a jewel reflecting every reader's experience of the act back to him. This is not because the suggestive is necessarily more exciting than the explicit. It is because the symbolic is more powerful than the literal and belabored. This is why Lawrence is a far greater writer about sex than Mailer.

At this stage, then, if we judge Norman Mailer on criteria against which he would want to be measured—not by the fidelity of his art to his life, but by the light his art shines on life itself—he is good. But he has taken the road not chosen by the greatest. (pp. 45-6)

Andy Stark, in a review of ''Mailer: His Life and Times,'' in The American Spectator, *Vol. 18, No. 11, November, 1985, pp. 44-6.*

Hemingway: A Biography

by Jeffrey Meyers

(For Ernest Hemingway: see also *CLC*, Vols. 1, 3, 6, 8, 10, 13, 19, 30, 34; *Contemporary Authors*, Vols. 77-80; *Dictionary of Literary Biography*, Vols. 4, 9; *Dictionary of Literary Biography Yearbook: 1981;* and *Dictionary of Literary Biography Documentary Series*, Vol. 1. For Jeffrey Meyers: see also *Contemporary Authors*, Vols. 73-76.)

An Excerpt from *Hemingway A Biography*

Stein was the Amy Lowell of Paris: she weighed two hundred pounds and was ugly, rich, poetic and domineering. Though Hemingway later compared her to a monolithic Buddha, called her "Lard-Ass" and speculated that each of her great breasts must weigh at least ten pounds, he found her attractive when they first met. He transformed her from a Jew into an Italian and concentrated—as he always did with women—on her sensual hair: "Miss Stein was very big but not tall and was heavily built like a peasant woman. She had beautiful eyes and a strong German-Jewish face that also could have been Friulano and reminded me of a northern Italian peasant woman with her clothes, her mobile face and her lovely, thick, alive immigrant hair." Hadley thought Stein's dark-skinned, prune-faced, hairy-lipped companion, Alice Toklas, resembled "a little piece of electric wire, small and fine and very Spanish looking, very dark, with piercing dark eyes."

Stein, like Hemingway's father, had been trained as a doctor, though she did not complete her medical degree. But the striking resemblance to his mother made the presence of Grace immediately apparent. Grace was born in 1872; Gertrude, who was old enough to be his mother, in 1874. Both had the same imposing, statuesque appearance. Both, according to Hemingway, had emotional problems that were connected to their change of life and that provoked their quarrels with him. His comment on Stein applies perfectly to Grace, for he said that he had been loyal to that old bitch until the menopause affected her judgment and she threw him out of the house. Both women had formidable, overbearing characters: Stein "had such a personality that when she wished to win anyone over to her side she would not be resisted." Both were highly talented and extremely egocentric. Both were frustrated artists who felt irritated by their thwarted careers and lack of recognition. Stein had managed to publish only three of her books since 1909 and her magnum opus, *The Making of Americans*, had remained in her desk drawer since 1911. Both women competed with Hemingway (always a mistake) and were angry when he surpassed their achievement. Grace rejected him in 1920; Gertrude rejected him in 1925. Hemingway regretted

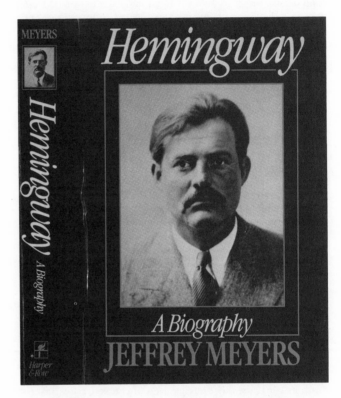

Dust jacket of Hemingway: A Biography, *by Jeffrey Meyers. Harper & Row, 1985. Courtesy of Harper & Row, Publishers, Inc.*

their quarrels and even remembered them fondly after Gertrude died in 1946 and Grace in 1951. Most significantly, Hemingway tried to work out with Gertrude some of the strong Oedipal feelings he had for Grace: "I always wanted to fuck her and she knew it and it was a good healthy feeling and made more sense than some of the talk." Such forbidden desires could be safely expressed because he knew he could not actually sleep with a lesbian any more than he could sleep with his mother.

KIRKUS REVIEWS

His *Toronto Star* editor once said of Hemingway: "A more weird combination of quivering sensitiveness and preoccupation with violence surely never walked the earth." The best thing about [*Hemingway: A Biography*] is the liberal supply of such vivid firsthand reminiscences by Hemingway's friends and associates. A serious weakness, however, is the failure of the biographer's expository skills to do full justice to his colorful subject.

Meyers summons his data briskly—and that's the problem. His implied judgments often need more amplitude of discussion to be persuasive, as in his skewed discussion of Hemingway's literary enemies and allies. Wyndham Lewis (the subject of two earlier biographies by Meyers) is praised as an author of classic stature, while Gertrude Stein is ungenerously (and inaccurately) depicted as a bad writer who lost her reputation as soon as she began to publish. In an early discussion of Hemingway's dislike of his given name, Meyers refers to the ''naive, even foolish hero'' of Wilde's *Importance of Being Earnest*—a farce with two ''Earnests'' but surely no ''hero.'' Meyers, however, drops this misreading into a sentence as though it were fact and proceeds. Such minor lapses create doubt about the accuracy of Meyers' equally abrupt decisions on more central matters, such as the literary quality of Hadley's letters, the attitude of Mary Hemingway (who does not appear to have been consulted) about the suicide of her husband, or young Ernest's attitude towards his domineering father.

The roistering, exuberant ''Papa'' of popular legend—the man who reportedly retaliated against Stein's attacks on him by wiring her ''A bitch is a bitch is a bitch''—makes few appearances in these pages. Meyers offers Hemingway at a sober middle distance—say, 20 yards or so—yet often fails to achieve the balanced perspective that should have resulted from this scholarly reserve.

A review of "Hemingway: A Biography," in Kirkus Reviews, Vol. LIII, No. 17, September 1, 1985, p. 939.

CHRISTOPHER LEHMANN-HAUPT

It is surprising to realize that despite the flood of memoirs and studies that have been written about Ernest Hemingway, Jeffrey Meyers's *Hemingway* is only the second full-scale biography to have appeared in the quarter-century since the novelist's death in 1961, the other having been of course Carlos Baker's *Ernest Hemingway: A Life Story*, published in 1969.

And what a relief this new biography seems after Professor Baker's shapeless gathering of a million facts. A professor of English at the University of Colorado who has written some 20 books on modern literature, including the lives of Katherine Mansfield and Wyndham Lewis, and *Hemingway: The Critical Heritage,* Jeffrey Meyers has produced just the book one wished Professor Baker's had been.

He has divided Hemingway's life into 27 chapters, most of which cover no more than a year or two. While the larger design of the book is chronological, the chapters are subdivided into an average of four or five sections, each of which focuses on a single subject like Hemingway's rivalry with his father, or his relationships with other writers in the early Paris years, or the best of the pieces in a given collection of writing, or the evolution of his esthetic theories.

While this determinedly selective approach produces some odd transitions and occasional confusions of time sequence, it allows the author to sharpen several important perspectives. He is able to illuminate what he considers the major turning points of Hemingway's life—his wounding at Fossalta di Piave in 1918, his divorce from Hadley Richardson in the 1920's, his participation in the Spanish Civil War in the 1930's, and his African plane crashes in the 1950's.

We are reminded what an appealing figure the Hemingway of the 1920's was, before ''the flawed public persona of the older writer'' took over. And we understand for perhaps the first time his work as a European reporter in the early part of that decade—particularly on the Genoa Conference in April 1922, the Greek-Turkish War and the Lausanne Conference later that year, and conditions in the French-occupied Ruhr in April-May 1923—and the role of that reportage in his later writing.

This topic-by-topic organization also allows Professor Meyers the leverage to straighten out the record on certain points. He stresses Hemingway's political perceptiveness and ideological courage. He calls *Across the River and Into the Trees* the most underrated of the novels and *The Old Man and the Sea* the most overrated. He suggests that nobody who attended Hemingway seems to have understood the real nature of his mental decline, and he speculates that the worst damage done to his mind may have been caused by the electric-shock therapy administered at the Mayo Clinic just before his suicide.

The result is an absorbing tragic portrait of the man that Professor Meyers ultimately pronounces ''the most important American novelist of the twentieth century as well as a seminal influence on the modern American character.'' Yet there is a major flaw in some of the author's key revisionist assertions. For instance, he rejects any link of Hemingway's ''assertive masculinity to the feminine finery of his infant years.'' As he concludes, ''though Ernest's long hair was not cut until 1906, it seems clear that he graduated into boy's clothing before he was aware of being dressed as a girl,'' as if a 6-year-old would be oblivious of his sexual identity.

Elsewhere, Professor Meyers announces that Hemingway's ''aggressive masculinity, his preference for exclusively male company, his occasional impotence, his sexual boasts, and his hostility to inverts'' were not signs of covert homosexuality. This suspicion, he avers, ''is as unconvincing as the theory that Don Juan is a homosexual because of his obsessive need to prove his virility. Despite all the theorizing, there is not a shred of real evidence to suggest that Hemingway ever had any covert homosexual desires or overt homosexual relations.''

Aside from lacking airtight logic in themselves, such statements do not exactly square with all the evidence Professor Meyers later presents of his subject's ''hair fetishism'' and fantasies of sex-role changes. It is almost absurd the way he first denies Hemingway's awareness of having had long hair as a child, and then later writes: ''Hemingway's fascination with hair probably began in childhood. His mother had long thick hair and'' his sister ''Marcelline remembered, from her girlhood, 'the light tickling wisps of the curls of her hair touching my face. . . .'''

In fact, an all-too-clear psychological portrait can be drawn from Hemingway's masculine assertiveness, his hatred of his mother in particular and hostility toward women in general, his aversion to psychoanalytic insight and the self-destructiveness manifest in his alcoholism, his proneness to accident, and his suicidal tendencies.

This is not to say that such an obvious portrait is necessarily the correct one. But Professor Meyers expends far more energy in simply denying that portrait than he does in confronting his own evidence for it. This peculiar bias not only confuses his picture of Hemingway, it also leaves a gaping hole at the very heart of his otherwise impressive treatment.

Christopher Lehmann-Haupt, in a review of "Hemingway: A Biography," in The New York Times, October 21, 1985, p. C22.

ARTHUR WALDHORN

What [Meyers] lacks in grace [in *Hemingway: A Biography*] he makes up for with scrupulous honesty. Where Carlos Baker withheld information or veiled its implications, Meyers details fully. The portrait is not flattering but it is always believable and often pitiable. "A man is essentially what he hides," Meyers writes, arguing that beneath the mask resided a "reflective man of innate sensitivity." Many will agree; at its best, Hemingway's prose supports that view. To prove his thesis, Meyers proceeds chronologically, interpolating special analyses ranging from literary battles to influences; from ethnic and sexual prejudices to religious beliefs; from parental relationships to the complex involvement with wives and mistresses. Occasionally, Meyers enthralls, as when he records the FBI's "pursuit" of Hemingway. Too often, however, we learn too little that is new or insightful. Within its limits, Meyers's bulky volume nevertheless deserves attention and respect.

Arthur Waldhorn, in a review of "Hemingway: A Biography," in Library Journal, Vol. 110, No. 19, November 15, 1985, p. 90.

Hemingway in 1937, returning to America from Spain's war front. UPI/Bettmann Newsphotos.

BILL RAYBURN

Now we have Jeffrey Meyers to thank for his *Hemingway,* and thank him we should, for it is a massive, eminently readable work of constant revelation and delight.

The first complete and critical biography to appear since Carlos Baker's monumental *Ernest Hemingway* (1969), it is written in a sure, authoritative style that urges the reader onward to the end. Meyers has had the benefit of numerous personal interviews and the use of previously suppressed material that enrich the work.

The outlines of Hemingway's life and career as artist, journalist, soldier, adventurer, bully and braggart, husband, father, patriot and expatriot are exhaustively filled in by Meyers. He believes that the war wound, the divorce from Hadley, his participation in the Spanish Civil War, and the African plane crashes were the major influences and turning points in Hemingway's life.

He shows Ernest as a reporter and a wounded war hero at 19; in an unhappy love affair at 20; married at 22; a foreign correspondent at 23; a father and published author at 24; a master before 30.

As a youth, he easily befriended such older, established writers as Fitzgerald, Ford Madox Ford and Stein, and they helped him in his career. He later broke with them just as easily, as he feared the personal obligation to others that his character would not permit him to fulfill. While he could be generous when it moved him, he was cruel to his friends, ruthless and relentless to his perceived enemies, and impaled them in print. By 1937, he no longer counted artists and writers as friends. He replaced these with millionaires, actors, soldiers, sportsmen, and sycophants, and became "Papa"—his own worst invented character.

He lost touch with his genius and his gradual decline began. His drinking increased dramatically in the 1940s, and he succumbed to the occupational disease of writers, chronic alcoholism: "His physique and character were at their very best during the years before he achieved literary fame. He was then quite a different man from the swaggering hero of the '30s, the drunken braggart of the '40s, or the sad wreck of the late '50s. The flawed public persona of the older writer is so well known that readers scarcely recognize the early Hemingway."

But above all else, he was dedicated to his craft, and he would be honored with the Pulitzer Prize in 1953, the Nobel Prize in 1954. In 1959, he was paid the incredible sum of $15 a word for an article in *Sports [Illustrated].* That he was as productive as he was almost to the very end is a tribute to his enormous recuperative powers. He never fully recovered from the air crashes in Africa in 1954, became at odds with signs of his own mortality and was often erratic and out of control.

When he died in 1961, a private man who had led a very public life, he was not simply the most renowned American writer, he was one of the most famous people in the world. Meyers concludes: "Hemingway has survived his decline, his death and his detractors. He is now recognized as the most important American novelist in the twentieth century as well as a seminal influence on the modern American character."

We will never see another like him in our time.

Bill Rayburn, "A Couple of Clean, Well-Lighted Books on Hemingway," in The Detroit News, November 17, 1985, p. 2F.

RAYMOND CARVER

[*Carver is an American short story writer and poet whose works include the poetry volume* At Night the Salmon Move *(1976) and the short story collections* Will You Please Be Quiet, Please? *(1976) and* Cathedral *(1984). His stories often portray ordinary people unable to communicate, caught in a dehumanizing, hostile society. In the following excerpt Carver expresses dissatisfaction with Meyers's approach, especially his lack of sympathy for his subject. For a rebuttal from Meyers see Meyers's excerpt below.*]

Mr. Meyers, a scholar and professional biographer, has written books on T. E. Lawrence, George Orwell, Katherine Mansfield, Siegfried Sassoon, Wyndham Lewis and D. H. Lawrence, to name a few. [For *Hemingway: A Biography* he] seems to have read everything ever written on Hemingway and interviewed many of Hemingway's family members (with the notable exception of Mary Hemingway, who, quite tellingly, I think, refused to cooperate) as well as friends, cronies and hangers-on.

Adulation is not a requirement for biographers, but Mr. Meyers's book fairly bristles with disapproval of its subject. What is especially disconcerting is his strong belief that, "like his heroes Twain and Kipling, [Hemingway] never fully matured as an artist." This is more than a little dispiriting to read, but it's one of the premises of the book and it is sounded repeatedly as one reads dazedly on. Mr. Meyers talks briefly, and disapprovingly, about *Death in the Afternoon* (though he calls it "the classic study of bullfighting in English"), *Green Hills of Africa, Winner Take Nothing, Men Without Women, To Have and Have Not, Across the River and Into the Trees, Islands in the Stream, A Moveable Feast* (which he nonetheless maintains was Hemingway's "greatest work of nonfiction") and *The Old Man and the Sea.*

By and large the rest of the work, according to Mr. Meyers, is ruined by "a pervasive display of vanity and self-pity . . . an inability to create a reflective character, a tendency to act out fantasies." What's left? *The Sun Also Rises,* a dozen short stories (among them *"The Short Happy Life of Francis Macomber"* and *"The Snows of Kilimanjaro"*) and maybe *A Farewell to Arms* and *For Whom the Bell Tolls.* He seems to find it lamentable that Hemingway was not killed in one of the

Hemingway and his wife, Martha Gellhorn, in 1942. The Granger Collection, New York.

African crashes. Had he died, Mr. Meyers says, "over a cataract or among wild elephants, his reputation would have been even greater than it is today. He would have gone out in a literal blaze of glory . . . before he began to decline and waste away."

While the biographer doesn't, thank Heaven, mention fishing rods and penis envy in the same breath, his interpretation of Hemingway and the man's work is strictly Freudian. There is plenty of talk of "wounds"—not only the physical injuries Hemingway suffered, beginning with the shrapnel and machine-gun bullets in Italy in 1918, but the "wound" he sustained when jilted by Agnes Kurowsky. Another "wound" occurred when a suitcase of Hemingway's early work was stolen from Hadley's compartment while she was on a train from Paris to Switzerland, according to Mr. Meyers: "The loss was irrevocably connected in Hemingway's mind with sexual infidelity, and he equated the lost manuscripts with lost love."

It was an unfortunate and dismaying accident, but to the biographer it's clear that as a result Hadley was about to become the former Mrs. Hemingway. Yet not without guilt on Hemingway's part and guilt's sometimes exceedingly strange manifestations. Mr. Meyers writes: "Hemingway had three accidents, probably connected to his guilt, during the first year of marriage to Pauline [Pfeiffer]." And then this amazing statement: "Hemingway—like many ordinary men—had been engaged in an Oedipal struggle against his father for the possession of his mother. If the bullfight symbolizes sexual intercourse, as it clearly does in *The Sun Also Rises* ('the sword went in, and for just an instant he and the bull were one'), then the matador's triumphant domination of the bull at the moment of orgasmic death represents a virile defense against the threat of homosexuality."

Moving from Freud and the unconscious to the mundane (and flat-footed), consider some of these sentences: "Hemingway made a successful assault on the literary beachhead soon after reaching Paris." "Hemingway had a short fuse and a bad temper, liked to be considered a tough guy rather than a writer." "He was selfish and always put his books before his wives." "The two sides of Ernest's character came from his two parents." "Hemingway had four sisters (and, later, four wives)." "The world of war was attractive to him because it removed women, the greatest source of anxiety." There are hundreds more like these, of similar perspicacity. The book is very tough going indeed.

After his move to Key West in 1931 and the publication of *Death in the Afternoon,* Hemingway adopted the macho stance so often associated with the man and his work. He killed lions, water buffaloes, elephants, kudus, deer, bears, elk, ducks, pheasants, marlin, tuna, sailfish, trout. You name it, he caught it or shot it—everything that flew, finned, scooted, crawled or lumbered. He began to bluster and posture, encouraged people to call him "Papa," got into fistfights, became merciless to friends and enemies alike. Fitzgerald remarked perceptively that "Hemingway is quite as nervously broken down as I am but it manifests itself in different ways. His inclination is toward megalomania and mine toward melancholy." Damon Runyon said, "Few men can stand the strain of relaxing with him over an extended period."

Reading the depressing account of Hemingway's middle and late years, from 1940 on—the years of decline, as Mr. Meyers calls them—the reader is left to wonder not so much that he wrote anything of merit (Mr. Meyers thinks he did not, after

For Whom the Bell Tolls), but that he was able to write at all. He suffered numerous serious accidents and was subject to serious and debilitating illnesses, including alcoholism. (His son Jack says his father drank a quart of whisky a day for the last 20 years of his life.) There is a three-page appendix cataloguing major accidents and illnesses, including five concussions; a skull fracture; bullet and shrapnel wounds; hepatitis; hypertension; diabetes; malaria; torn muscles; pulled ligaments; pneumonia; erysipelas; amebic dysentery; blood poisoning; cracked spinal disks; ruptured liver, right kidney and spleen; nephritis; anemia; arteriosclerosis; skin cancer; hemochromatosis; and first-degree burns. Once he shot himself through the leg trying to shoot a shark. At the time of his admission to the Mayo Clinic he suffered from "depression and mental collapse."

One grows weary of and ultimately saddened by the public Hemingway. But the private life of the man was no more edifying. The reader is battered with one display after another of meanspiritedness and spite, of vulgar and shabby behavior. (After his break with his third wife, Martha Gellhorn, Hemingway wrote a scurrilous poem about her, which he liked to read aloud in company.) He carried on adulterous liaisons and, in his 50's, had embarrassing infatuations with girls not yet out of their teens. At one time or another he quarreled and broke with nearly all his friends, with members of his family, his former wives (with the exception of Hadley; he was still writing love letters to her years after they had divorced) and his sons and their wives. He fought bitterly with each of his sons; one, Gregory, he said he'd like to see hang. In his will he left an estate of $1.4 million, and disinherited the sons.

It is almost with a sense of relief that one reaches that awful morning of July 2, 1961, when Hemingway, recently released for the second time from the Mayo Clinic (against his wife's wishes; she felt he had "conned" his doctors), locates the key to the locked gun cabinet. By now everyone has suffered enough.

There's little in this book that Carlos Baker, in his 1969 biography, didn't say better. And Mr. Baker, despite his blind spots, was far more sympathetic to the work and, finally, more understanding of the man. It may well be that another full-scale biography needs to be written to augment Mr. Baker's and Mr. Meyers's work, but I don't think so. At least I for one am going to pass on reading it.

The only possible antidote for how you feel about Hemingway after finishing this book is to go back at once and reread the fiction itself. How clear, serene and solid the best work still seems; it's as if there were a physical communion taking place among the fingers turning the page, the eyes taking in the words, the brain imaginatively recreating what the words stand for and, as Hemingway put it, "making it a part of your own experience." Hemingway did his work, and he'll last. Any biographer who gives him less than this, granting the chaos of his public and personal life, might just as well write the biography of an anonymous grocer or a woolly mammoth. Hemingway, the writer—he's still the hero of the story, however it unfolds. (pp. 51-2)

> Raymond Carver, "Coming of Age, Going to Pieces," in The New York Times Book Review, *November 17, 1985, pp. 3, 51-2.*

R.W.B. LEWIS

[*Lewis is an American critic who has written and edited many works on American literature and literary figures, including a* biography of Edith Wharton and the landmark critical work The American Adam: Innocence, Tragedy and Tradition in the Nineteenth Century *(1955). In the following excerpt Lewis describes the areas of Hemingway's life that are illuminated by Meyers's biography.*]

[In *Hemingway: A Biography* Meyers's tone] is relatively detached and judicious; his narrative has an air of scholarly assurance, as befits the author of some 20 books, among them biographies of Katherine Mansfield and Wyndham Lewis and studies of George Orwell, T. E. Lawrence, and D. H. Lawrence. . . .

Meyers regularly summarizes and recapitulates, sometimes as though laying it out in a lecture to undergraduates. ("Hemingway tended to form four kinds of friendships. . . ." "There are four reasons why [*Across the River*] received an intensely hostile reception. . . .") He is also given to making lists, which he does admirably and relevantly: the unending series of accidents that befell Hemingway; the literary friends and precursors he turned against or denied; the disastrous endings to the lives of Hemingway's relatives and associates—one of his sisters, two of his sons, one of his inamoratas, and one of his memoirists were suicides, as were Hemingway's father and Hemingway himself. . . .

[In this biography, Meyers also] brings to bear a fairly massive amount of new source materials—for example, a thorough review of the intricately sordid incident in Kenya in 1909 on which Hemingway, who heard of it from his guide on a 1934 safari, based that superlative story **"The Short Happy Life of Francis Macomber."** Meyers also seems to enlarge the inventory of Hemingway's certified partners in sex, while confirming the fact that the relationship with Adriana Ivancich, the svelte original for Renata in *Across the River and into the Trees,* was purely Platonic. For the most part Meyers fleshes out, often substantially, matters that Carlos Baker told about more briefly. In a typical instance, Meyers draws on State Department archives and the like to describe Hemingway's forays into Nazi spyhunting in Havana during the second war. He details the FBI's opposition to this half-serious and half-farcical enterprise, and explains Hemingway's enlistment of the help of the former Spanish Loyalist officer Gustavo Durán. (He also appends an account of the later career of the now-naturalized Durán, his splendid services with the United Nations, and his persecution by Senator McCarthy and other congressional witchhunters.) Meyers's life story thus arrives at a certain completeness, but my personal sense is that Baker's biography, into which I have been dipping again, remains the more prehensile and authoritative. (p. 32)

An appraisal of Hemingway's literary accomplishment, and the tone and temper of it, cannot, humanly speaking, be dissociated from a verdict on the man, though many would suppose it ought to be. . . . [The] man who comes gradually into perspective in Meyers's presentation is, as Edmund Wilson said as early as 1939, "not only incredible but obnoxious," a performer who was Hemingway's own "worst-invented character." . . .

Explanations for such noisome antics abound: the pressures of enormous celebrity, severe wobbling of talent, fear of failure, spiteful reviews. There were those who found the behavior entertaining, and dined out on tales about it. At the same time, Meyers offers evidence that Hemingway, nearly to the end, could have spurts of generosity and kindness, and that with male companions (for instance, the urbanely observant Charles Collingwood) his presence could be a memorably enlivening

Hemingway on safari in Kenya, 1953. Photograph by Earl Theisen.

one. But with his incessant rages and quarreling, his cruelties, his stupefyingly boring literary and sexual boasting, Hemingway emerges as perhaps the least simpatico figure in the annals of 20th-century letters. So much so, indeed, that he poses a question remotely like the one forced on us by Ezra Pound's diverse bigotries. To what degree does the quality of the work make up or atone for the personal life? . . .

Hemingway was without question one of the foremost among those who have made the American language live in our epoch. Did he write well enough—invent, imagine, compose, express—to be pardoned by history for his sins against the human? *Should* he be so pardoned? . . . The answer comes slowly, but as one thinks over the writing—''imperishable'' is the only word for some of it—the answer must surely be in the affirmative. (p. 34)

> *R.W.B. Lewis, ''Who's Papa?'' in* The New Republic, *Vol. 193, No. 23, December 2, 1985, pp. 31-4.*

IRVING MARDER

[In *Hemingway: A Biography,*] the first ''big'' Hemingway book since the weighty 1969 biography by Prof. Carlos Baker, Jeffrey Meyers, professor of English at the University of Colorado, takes the ''warts-and-all'' treatment somewhat further—and some of the warts are indeed big enough to hang a hat on. Certainly the Baker approach can stand a corrective—our guard went up with his opening sentence: ''As soon as it was safe for the boy to travel, they bore him away to the northern woods. . . .'' Was this the tone of biography or of *liturgy?*

But Meyers, if not quite as awe-struck, has his own problems: One is a style so graceless and so imprecise that, at crucial points, there is only ambiguity. We slog ahead, wincing periodically over the accumulation of the kind of detail that tends to make American literary scholarship an international joke. Among Carlos Baker's contribution to the Legend was the fact that Hemingway, during one stressful period, had 150 bowel movements in a single day (is this a record?). Meyers, not a

man to take this lying down, tells us about Hemingway's maternal *grandfather,* Ernest Hall, who ''had some comical troubles with constipation on the ship that brought him from England in his late teens.''

Meanwhile we are trying to keep in focus the first major writer whose work is almost inseparable from hype—a man whose personality engulfed his work in an almost unprecedented way. A writer who once said in effect, echoing the ancient epigram, ''Everything I say is a lie.''

How much this mattered, in relation to his *art,* can be debated endlessly. At first he was able, so to speak, to keep tabs. But at some point, the confusion of true and false became part of the madness that destroyed him. (pp. 2, 6)

> *Irving Marder, in a review of ''Hemingway: A Biography,'' in* Los Angeles Times Book Review, *December 8, 1985, pp. 2, 6.*

JEFFREY MEYERS

[*In the following excerpt, taken from a letter to the editor, Meyers refutes the arguments made by Raymond Carver in his review of* Hemingway: A Biography *(see excerpt above).*]

At least four factual points made by Raymond Carver in his irresponsible attempt to butcher my *Hemingway: A Biography* [see excerpt above] . . . demand response. He states that Mary Hemingway ''quite tellingly, I think, refused to cooperate'' and implies she sensed my book would be bad and chose to remain aloof. This is unwarranted and malicious speculation on Mr. Carver's part. In fact, Mrs. Hemingway has been quite ill, requires 24-hour nursing care and has not granted interviews to anyone for a number of years. Many of her close friends told me there was no point in interviewing her and I did not attempt to do so.

He states that I talk ''briefly, and disapprovingly,'' about a number of Hemingway's works, including *Across the River and Into the Trees.* In fact, I devote a 25-page chapter to this underrated novel, show for the first time that it is based on the military career of Hemingway's old friend Chink Dorman-Smith and argue that ''the most personal and revealing of all Hemingway's novels . . . has considerable interest and would have been hailed as impressive if it had been written by anyone but Hemingway.''

Mr. Carver states that I think Hemingway did not write ''anything of merit'' after *For Whom the Bell Tolls.* In fact, I wrote: ''*A Moveable Feast,* infinitely superior to all his postwar books, was his greatest work of nonfiction. The memoir decisively showed that Hemingway had arrested his decline and regained the full force of his literary power only months before he entered the Mayo Clinic.''

Finally, he claims: ''There's little in this book that Carlos Baker, in his 1969 biography, didn't say better.'' In fact, there is a great deal of material in my book that is new or scarcely mentioned by Carlos Baker: Hemingway's quarrel with his sister Carol and his son Gregory, his affair with Jane Mason, Dr. Lawrence Kubie's suppressed psychoanalytic essay on Hemingway, his political ideas, the F.B.I.'s attempt to destroy him, his relations with the bullfighters Dominguín and Ordó-ñez, the details of his medical treatment at the Mayo Clinic, the aftermath of his suicide and his literary influence. Unlike Carlos Baker (who had considered Hemingway's art in a previous book), I relate the life to the books and provide new interpretations of several major works.

The first duty of a reviewer is to provide an accurate, unbiased account of the book. Raymond Carver has clearly failed to do this.

Jeffrey Meyers, "Hemingway's Biographer," in The New York Times Book Review, *December 8, 1985, p. 85.*

ROBERT GORHAM DAVIS

As the overwhelming detail of [*Hemingway: A Biography*] demonstrates, we now know more about Ernest Hemingway than about any other modern writer, more even than about Henry James, D. H. Lawrence, André Gide, and Virginia Woolf. This is not only because what Hemingway acted out, as opposed to what those mentioned thought and felt, was so spectacular, violent and gross—almost unbelievable in its excesses—that it evoked a flood of memoirs (17 at present count) by people who knew him. There are moral and literary dimensions to Hemingway's story that make the sensational aspects critically relevant and raise some deep, troubled thoughts concerning violence in history and literature's long, rather admiring involvement with it back to Trojan times.

It is true that Henry James never went into the bush alone to finish off a wounded lion. Virginia Woolf never killed sharks with a machine gun. D. H. Lawrence never recited obscene poems about his wife to drunken cronies. André Gide never butted open the jammed door of a burning airplane with his head. None of the four was wounded in war or enjoyed the purgative ecstasy of what Albert Camus called "the one absolute freedom, the freedom to kill."

The conventional response is to say, "What of it? Who wishes them to have done such things? The four had finer and more original minds than Hemingway. They had their own kind of courage. So far as writing is concerned it does not matter one whit that they never risked their own lives in trying to kill others."

But the issue is not so simple, as Jeffrey Meyers shows us in discussing some of Hemingway's models, such as Stephen Crane and Joseph Conrad. It does matter in the totality of literature that Stendhal took part in the Napoleonic retreat from Russia and that Dostoevsky faced a firing squad prior to his years of imprisonment in Siberia. If truth to experience counts in literature we must have the testimony of writers who, having passed tests of courage in extreme circumstances, possess a consequent sense of themselves and others that can be acquired in no other way. Before that knowledge, those of us who lack it must always be a little uneasy, as Henry James was before returned Civil War heroes. (pp. 6-7)

In story after story Meyers shows specifically how Hemingway transformed private history not only for literary effect but to fulfill wishes or assuage guilt. . . .

Though Meyers is not so sensitive a writer as Carlos Baker, this volume is a marked advance on Baker's pioneering 1969 biography, both in all the new personal material it contains— some of it pretty horrifying—and in the detailed biographical/ critical analyses of individual works. By articulating Hemingway's usually difficult relations with his creative peers and quoting freely at key points from critics like Lionel Trilling, Mark Schorer, Alfred Kazin, and especially Edmund Wilson,

the author makes his work an indispensable literary history of the period.

Meyers has written or edited some 20 books. A number of them—*Fiction and the Colonial Experience, Disease and the Novel, Homosexuality and Literature, 1890-1930*—bear directly on the material of the present biography, as do his studies of George Orwell, Wyndham Lewis and T. E. Lawrence. In tackling his latest subject, though, Meyers faced a huge mass of materials difficult to assess fairly. Hemingway was a voluminous correspondent, given to extreme changes in mood. Interviewing a large number of those still living who had known Hemingway well, Meyers found them reacting so intensely in love or hate that it was impossible to make their impressions jibe. Some of the memoirists were as prone to lies and posturing as Hemingway himself. (p. 7)

Meyers' biography is the dramatic story of how much Hemingway saved from [his early experiences] and how much he wantonly wasted, especially how many people close to him he destroyed in the course of destroying himself. Shocking though some of the personal scandals may be, they bear directly on any estimation of Hemingway's art. He himself made them so by his malicious obiter dicta in *Death in the Afternoon* and *Green Hills of Africa,* the notorious portraits of old friends in *A Moveable Feast,* and the autobiographical moments slightly changed into fiction in such stories as **"Cat in the Rain."** . . .

[What do the details of Hemingway's excesses] have to do with the best of the writing? A great deal, if we recognize that at

Hemingway in 1960, the year before his death. UPI/Bettmann Newsphotos.

the time of its biggest impact Hemingway's fiction affected the life-attitudes of his most devoted readers in ways that were far more than literary. Much that is worst in Norman Mailer's fiction and demonstrative public displays has come from his own excess in taking on the Hemingway persona. The question, therefore, is whether the values that dominated Hemingway's writing, including the emphasis on male heroism, are separable from the darker aspects of the life as Meyers records it.

"No man is an island unto himself." Neither is a book. There have been in recent decades a spate of literary biographies. Some merely record the disorder of the lives in implied contrast to the order of the work. In the best of them, like Leon Edel's massive *Henry James* and the present study by Meyers, when books are put together with the events they were drawn from, facts both about human nature and art emerge that go beyond what can be discovered in the books alone, yet without impairing their integrity as art. (p. 8)

Robert Gorham Davis, *"Everything in Excess,"* in The New Leader, *Vol. LXVIII, No. 16, December 16 & 30, 1985, pp. 6-8.*

WILFRID SHEED

[*Hemingway: A Biography*] is splendidly organized. The author has licked the chronology vs. structural theme question by giving us a bit of both. For instance, Hemingway's various feuds are laid out neatly in a row and an impressive crew they make *en masse*: thus accumulated, they look less like isolated quarrels than like a willful sustained effort by Ernest to purge his life of *all* literary friendships. Having crashed Paris in a few golden months, *El Toro* crashed on out again in a shower of broken glass, and Mr. Meyers's arrangement makes this seem like one sustained sequence. Yet at no stage are we left wondering what year it is or what ever became of so and so. Although neatness may not be the first thing any author wants to be praised for, it is also much too rare to pass unnoticed. Since Mr. Meyers also writes a great deal less laboriously and more engagingly than Carlos Baker, the official biographer and quarry at large, he manages to make his heavy freight of research fairly rattle along.

One quality that grates seriously in Mr. Meyers's book, however, is his somewhat proprietary attitude toward his subject. In his brief bibliography, fifteen of the thirty-six items listed are by himself, so that there can be no question about whose turf we're dealing with. And in the text proper, although he doesn't hesitate to scold Ernest, he can be distinctly peevish with anyone else who attempts to. Having just waded through three different accounts of Hemingway's childhood, one would think that the last thing Ernest needed was another mother, but there are pages here where he almost seems to be getting one anyway.

Take, for instance, the notorious Lillian Ross interview in *The New Yorker* of 1950: Papa, by now firmly entrenched in his own driver's seat, with the boy wonder nowhere in sight, came to town for a few days in 1949, got and stayed plastered the whole time and talked gibberish, and Ross wrote it all down. It might have been kinder of her not to, but mere abdication isn't nearly enough for Mr. Meyers. In his view, what happened is that "Hemingway put on a performance for Ross, expected her to see through his act and show the highbrow readers of her magazine the man behind the rather transparent mask."

But why on earth should she have done all that? ... Ross didn't pull any tricks on Papa; he knew he was being interviewed, and the performance he gave was strictly up to him, and he gave a pathetic one. (pp. 8, 10)

Throughout Mr. Meyers's book we have seen the subject, time and again, talk and wriggle his way out of embarrassments, yet on this one the author takes him at his word and piles his wrath on the messenger. . . .

[Whatever] Hemingway's first reaction to the piece may have been, he was much more forgiving about Miss Ross later than his champion Mr. Meyers can bring himself to be. While Papa continued to correspond warmly with Lillian Ross almost to the day he died, Meyers has only this to say, or rather sniff, about her: She "repaid his generosity with meanness and established her reputation at his expense."

How much justice can one expect in other matters from an officer of the court who leaps down from his bench like this and starts pounding the witness with his gavel? Well, it varies from case to case. Meyers is particularly tender about the Ross affair because he believes it gave the signal for the bloodhounds to rip into **Across the River and into the Trees,** a book which he has made his special cause. Rehabilitating this turkey would certainly be a breathtaking coup for Meyers as a literary critic-biographer, but to get there he must first undertake an awesome amount of demolition work, not only of double agent Ross but of the whole literary consensus of the period.

Mr. Meyers sets about his task nothing if not manfully. The novel, he says, while not Hemingway at his best (one has to concede the utterly indefensible) "has been misinterpreted and maligned for purely external reasons." In other words, the critics *in toto* were incapable of reading a given text on its merits because of extraneous considerations. (Some bunch of critics.) Meyers then gives four reasons for the book's disastrous reception, and naturally, the first of them is "Hemingway's alienation of the critics," who presumably hunt in packs and decide among then selves in semaphore when and whom to attack.

Now I suppose it's perfectly all right, if not inevitable, for a novelist to view critics in this embattled way, even if he's had as easy a ride as Hemingway had till then. But when a biographer does so as well, it rather looks as if he's lost his bearings. Mr. Meyers has apparently so identified himself with his subject that he can suggest with a straight face that the critics of two nations (the British were even worse) were swayed from their professional duties by personal animus and whatever "alienation" is supposed to entail. As a biographer, Meyers seems to have strayed quite some distance from his own preserve in order to insult someone else's. And all for the sake of the sly, sodden old Hemingway, who certainly knew how to make an apologist sweat.

Anyhow, let us suppose that, however clumsily, the demolition has succeeded, and that all the other judges have been disqualified. Unfortunately, Mr. Meyers is left alone with the book itself. What sparks can he make fly from this weary bag of wind, which E. B. White once compared to "the farting of an old horse"? Well, the novel is "confessional" and that's something. It is also another "performance"—by chance the same one he gave for Miss Ross. Again the bumbling critics have failed to see what Hemingway was really up to, and have amateurishly identified the performance with Papa himself. But as before, this still leaves us with the performance itself to dispose of: never mind if we were fooled by it—was it a good one or a bad one? And here Mr. Meyers seems to encounter difficulties. He concedes that the book's tone is "similar to the exhibitionistic hunting and fishing articles that appeared in *Esquire* in the mid-1930s . . . a series of smug disquisitions," etc. Exhibitionist performance? Any connection? And can anyone still remember what we are arguing about at this point, or why the author seems so steamed up over it? (p. 10)

I have lingered over the *Across the River* fiasco only to show what can happen to a critic who tries to ride a hobbyhorse to glory, and also the dangers of hanging around Hemingway too close and too long. When Meyers talks of *To Have and Have Not* as having possibly influenced the tough-guy style of Dashiell Hammett we have to wonder if our author has ceased paying proper attention to the world outside Papa. Hammett had written all his novels and short stories well before *To Have and Have Not* came out, and was a fecund influence in his own right—possibly even on *To Have and Have Not*. For all his great gifts, Papa did not invent the twentieth century.

Curiously enough, Mr. Meyers is not such a bad conventional critic when he stops trying to shoot the moon and when he sticks to scholarly business and soberly investigates Hemingway's own influences, tracing the debts to Twain, Kipling, Crane, et al., with concentration and sense. He is particularly good on Kipling, whose soldierly ethic was so close to Hemingway's that a stranger might have difficulty guessing which of them first called courage "grace under pressure." (p. 12)

Wilfrid Sheed, "A Farewell to Hemingstein," in The New York Review of Books, *Vol. XXXIII, No. 10, June 12, 1986, pp. 5-6, 8, 10, 12.**

Agatha Christie: A Biography

by Janet Morgan

(For Agatha Christie: see also *CLC*, Vols. 1, 6, 8, 12; *Contemporary Authors*, Vols. 19-20, rev. ed., Vols. 61-64 [obituary]; *Contemporary Authors New Revision Series*, Vol. 10; and *Dictionary of Literary Biography*, Vol. 36. For Janet Morgan: see also *Contemporary Authors*, Vols. 65-68.)

An Excerpt from *Agatha Christie: A Biography*

In her childhood there was plenty of fuel for those who were entertained by mysteries and paradoxes, for the end of the nineteenth century and the beginning of the twentieth saw the publication of an increasing number of ever more ingenious detective stories. . . .

It was while they were discussing one of these detective stories that Madge had challenged Agatha to write one herself. This suggestion was at the back of Agatha's mind when dispensary work began to become monotonous and she decided to try, adopting what was to become her standard practice: beginning by deciding upon the crime and settling on a procedure which made it particularly hard to detect. What she sought was a plot that was simultaneously commonplace and surprising: 'I could, of course, have a very *unusual* kind of murder for a very *unusual* motive, but that did not appeal to me artistically.' She wanted a riddle: 'The whole point was that it must be somebody obvious but at the same time, for some reason, you would then find that it was not obvious, that he could not possibly have done it. But really of course he had.' She next settled on the characters, discovering the difficulty of basing fictional characters on people she knew and breaking the creative log-jam only after seeing some striking people in a tram. It was not so much that they were odd-looking; rather, as with the three people in the Gezirah Hotel who had been the models in *Snow Upon the Desert,* that their relationship and their behaviour made Agatha begin to speculate.

Next came the question of the detective. She wanted someone like Rouletabille, a detective of a type which had not been used before. She eventually decided that he should be a Belgian refugee; as she recalled in a memorable sentence of her autobiography, Torquay was full of Belgian refugees, bewildered and suspicious, who wanted to be left alone, 'to save some money, to dig their garden and manure it in their own particular and intimate way.' The detective was to be clever, meticulous, with an impressive name and some knowledge of crime and criminals. Agatha made Hercule Poirot a retired Belgian police officer. . . . Belgians, at the time of Poirot's first manifestation, were the object both of respect ('gallant little Belgium', overrun by Germany) and of some condescension, being thought to be neither as

Dust jacket of Agatha Christie: A Biography, *by Janet Morgan. Knopf, 1985. Jacket design by Paula Scher. Courtesy of Alfred A. Knopf, Inc.*

intellectual as the French nor as commercially astute as the Dutch. Poirot was clever, and equipped with a pompous character, ridiculous affectations, a luxuriant moustache and a curious egg-shaped head—in contrast to Rouletabille's bullet-shaped one. His creator could admire him without having to be so deferential that she felt unable to manipulate him. It does not matter whether certain of Poirot's features were derived, a fragment here, a morsel there, from other works that had contributed to the rich mulch in Agatha's subconscious; in his extravagance of personality he was sufficiently plausible to stand and survive by himself.

T. J. BINYON

At first sight Janet Morgan does not seem the obvious person to choose as the official biographer of Agatha Christie. She describes herself on the jacket of [*Agatha Christie: A Biography*] as a 'writer and consultant,' who now 'advises governments, companies and other organisations on long-range strategic planning, new technology and different approaches to whatever they find themselves doing.' She has written on politics and broadcasting and was, of course, the editor of the four-volume edition of Crossman's diaries. All this is a world away from M. Poirot or Miss Marple, and internal evidence suggests, too, that she has no particular knowledge of, or liking for, the detective story. But on the whole this is a solid and sensible life—if sometimes annoyingly vague on detail and dates—which complements and expands Agatha Christie's posthumously published autobiography. It is also annoying that it should not contain a chronological list of her work: that one is available elsewhere is no excuse for the omission. But the biography certainly fulfils what was presumably the family's main aim: it lays, once and for all, the malicious rumours and vulgar gossip put about by other writers on the subject of Agatha Christie's ten days' disappearance in 1926, providing an authoritative, as well as authorised, explanation for the event. (p. 13)

In 1926 [Agatha] became famous. In the spring of that year she published *The Murder of Roger Ackroyd,* a book based on an idea suggested to her independently by her brother-in-law and by Lord Louis Mountbatten and which certainly has claims to be the most ingenious of her novels. At 11 p.m. on Friday 3 December she came downstairs, got into her car, drove off into the darkness and vanished. The car was discovered abandoned the next morning at Newlands Corner, near Guildford. For the next ten days the Police scoured the Downs, dragged pools and streams, investigated reports of sightings. The press muddied the issue with far-fetched rumours and fabricated stories. On 12 December a 'Great Sunday Hunt for Mrs Christie' was organised. The *Evening News* advised 'anyone who may have bloodhounds . . . to bring them along.' Men should wear thick boots; women Russian boots and tweed skirts. An aeroplane flew overhead. Meanwhile the Yorkshire Police had come to suspect that a Mrs Theresa Neele, who was staying in a seven-guinea-a-week room at the Hydropathic Hotel in Harrogate, might be the missing novelist. On the evening of Tuesday 14 December Archie [Agatha's husband] identified Mrs Neele as his wife, though Agatha appeared to be less sure of him. 'She seemed to regard him as an acquaintance whose identity she could not quite fix,' reported the hotel manager. 'It was sufficient, however, to permit of her accompanying her husband to the dining-room.'

Ms Morgan has obviously put a great deal of research into disentangling this episode. She has read all the newspaper reports, consulted a lot of private papers, and spoken to all those who might have relevant knowledge. There is no reason to believe that anything—other than, perhaps, the odd minor detail—can be added to her account, or that her interpretation of events is likely to be superseded.

In the summer of 1926 Clara, Agatha's mother, had died. After the funeral Agatha went down to Torquay and spent a depressing and exhausting six weeks clearing out the family house, crammed with the accumulated debris of three generations. In August Archie and Rosalind [Agatha's daughter] arrived. Archie seemed unlike his usual self: pressed, he admitted that he had fallen in love with his golf partner, Miss Nancy Neele. An impossible three months followed. Archie blew hot and cold, moving from his London club to Styles, and then back to the club. Agatha's only friend was her wire-haired terrier, Peter. In December she cracked. Packing a suitcase with an odd assortment of effects, and putting on a money belt con-

taining several hundred pounds, she drove south. At Newlands Corner she seems to have had a slight accident. Leaving her car, she walked to Guildford and took a train to Waterloo. She was wearing a skirt and cardigan and had blood on her face. She went by taxi to Whiteleys, bought a coat and other necessities, and then took a train to Harrogate, where she checked in at the Hydropathic. There she led a quiet life for ten days, doing crosswords in the drawing-room, retiring to the conservatory in the evenings, and occasionally having a rubber of bridge with the other guests. Ms Morgan has no doubt—and we must undoubtedly follow her in this—that the behaviour is entirely consistent with genuine amnesia. She suggests that in Agatha's case it might be that rarer and more complex type of memory loss known as a 'hysterical fugue,' in which 'a person experiencing great stress flees from intolerable strain by utterly forgetting his or her own identity.' She puts forward, with less persuasiveness, the theory that Agatha might have belonged to the class of 'somnambules': people who can 'induce independently experiences of the kind produced by hypnosis: hallucinating, amnesia and so on . . . they have a strong propensity to fantasise . . . and as adults claim to spend much of their everyday life in the world of imagination, even when their normal daily tasks require concentration.' There's an attraction to this theory, in that it connects Agatha's behaviour with her imagination as a writer, smuggling in through the back door of neuropsychiatry the old Romantic myth of the artist's madness. Its weakness, obviously, is that she never again behaved somnambulistically, as she surely would have done if she belonged to the type, while the evidence Ms Morgan adduces from the work is flimsy and unconvincing, to say the least. For the reader, though more than half the book is still to come, everything after this event seems something of an anti-climax. (pp. 13-14)

Most years [Agatha] would publish two, sometimes even three books. The vast majority were detective stories or thrillers, but occasionally there would be a straight novel, under the name of Mary Westmacott, or even a book of poems such as *The Road of Dreams,* published at her own expense in 1924, copies of which were still available in the Sixties. In 1930 her first play, *Black Coffee,* was performed; she was gradually to become more and more interested in writing for the theatre: an interest which culminated in the unbelievable success of *The Mousetrap,* still going strong in its 32nd year. . . .

Ms Morgan's main concern in dealing with Agatha Christie's work is to tie it in with the life—which she does more than adequately. She says little, and on not much more than a superficial level, about her methods, or the books and plays themselves. But a biographer is not obliged to be a critic, and it is a more serious fault that one gets very little feeling of Agatha Christie's character; only in one respect does she come completely to life—her naked and unashamed love of food. 'Though rain pours down, eating is always eating,' she writes to Edmund Cork. As a child she forms a taste for Devonshire cream which lasts throughout her life; on her 80th birthday there's 'half a cup of neat cream for ME while the rest had Champagne'—she never drank. But she has more sophisticated tastes as well. In 1943 she celebrates the opening of *Moon on the Nile* with a dinner at which rationing seems to have been forgotten: 'Party at Prunier's afterwards. Smoked salmon and oysters, hot lobster Thermidor and chocolate mousse.' . . .

Perhaps the most interesting and instructive element in the book, though it is treated as no more than a subtext, concerns her relations with her publishers and with the income tax authorities. Immediately after acquiring an agent, she moved from the Bodley Head—who had been rather too sharp in dealing with her—to Collins. Their behaviour, towards an author who must have done them better than almost anyone else, is a revelation. She complains continually, and usually justifiably, about cover designs, blurbs, proofs and misprints. Even in the Seventies they were designing covers which made the tiny Poirot look six feet tall. In 1940, after she has complained about the cover of *Sad Cypress,* Edmund Cork writes that 'Collins think it would be unpatriotic to destroy 15,000 copies of a jacket in these times of paper shortage.' No doubt, but why didn't they consult her first? As late as 1967 a proof-reader is taking it upon himself to alter her sentences. When they keep printing, in the list of her previous books, *Death on the Hill* instead of *Death on the Nile,* with the result that fans complain that this title is unavailable, Billy Collins apologises and sends her . . . a book on roses. Collins's editor calls *They Came to Baghdad* 'far-fetched and puerile . . . it is difficult to believe that Mrs Christie regards this as more than a joke.' American sales outstrip those of any other Christie. Collins fear that *Passenger to Frankfurt* will be a disaster. It is a sensational best-seller in England and America. 'I am rather anti-Collins . . . such a thick-headed lot,' she writes, after Edmund Cork has persuaded her not to move to Gollancz. . . .

Her dealings with the income tax, and her financial affairs generally, are no less striking. In 1938, a Court of Appeals in the United States ruled that the author Rafael Sabatini, though residing in England, was liable for American tax on his earnings in the States. In the light of this judgment, Harold Ober engaged an eminent US tax lawyer, Howard E. Reinheimer, to look after Agatha's affairs. Ten years later Reinheimer managed to reach a settlement with the IRS for the years 1930 to 1941. Meanwhile, with her American earnings frozen, she found it impossible to meet the demands of the Inland Revenue. 'There seems little likelihood of Mrs. Mallowan avoiding bankruptcy,' Cork was writing to Ober in 1948. Fortunately, in this instance, he was mistaken. Patriotically, but probably mistakenly, she always refused to move to a tax haven, and in the Fifties, on Cork's advice, a number of trusts were set up which controlled the copyrights of her work and paid her an annual salary. . . . In the Sixties a subsidiary of Booker McConnell acquired a majority holding in the trusts, took over the copyrights, and lent Agatha the amount required to meet the tax assessments on the security of the copyrights she has reserved for herself.

'At last she was clear, if in debt,' writes Ms Morgan, and a little later: 'She could enjoy the real fruits of success: peace, privacy, the company of her family, friends and the dogs, delicious food and drink, and books.' It's impossible to detect even a tinge of irony here: yet Ms Morgan is referring to the world's best-selling author writing in the English language, whose works had sold, between the publication of *The Mysterious Affair at Styles* and 1980, over four hundred million copies. In the last three years the trust controlling her copyrights has had an annual turnover of over a million pounds. No wonder Agatha Christie was heard to remark wistfully towards the end of her life: 'If I'd been an opera singer, I might have been rich.' (p. 14)

> *T. J. Binyon, "At the Hydropathic," in* London Review of Books, *December 6 to December 19, 1984, pp. 13-14.*

OWEN DUDLEY EDWARDS

Agatha Christie's value to the historian is of three kinds. Firstly, as a best-selling author in Britain for the last sixty years and

Christie as a girl

in the USA since the Second World War, the picture of society she conveys is of importance to what her contemporaries made of their present and what ours make of the period 1925-55, after which her appeal was obviously nostalgic. Then, she has merits as historical witness. Dorothy Sayers' *Murder Must Advertise* is useful for admanship between the wars, Ngaio Marsh throws light on inter-war theatre and on Antipodean attitudes to Anglo-Saxony, but Christie's expertise is wider. On village life she observes keenly and instructively, as Richmal Crompton does, before, during and just after the Second World War (notably in *The Murder at the Vicarage, The Moving Finger* and *A Murder is Announced*); but she is also trustworthy on xenophobia, journalistic harrassment, nursing, archaeological expeditions, the British abroad and the military in civilian life during the years of her prime. Finally, she offers some lessons in the practice of history, if less profoundly than Conan Doyle. Her emphases on the most likely person as the probable criminal once camouflage has been determined and discarded, and on comparative human data (Miss Marple's 'village parallel' for all walks of society), are well worth bearing in mind.

Janet Morgan has been given a host of personal reminiscences and the fullest access to the Christie archive for her biography [*Agatha Christie*]. It narrates the facts of Christie's life in interesting if not enthralling fashion. Unfortunately the biographer has omitted any discussion of the nature of the source-material at her disposal beyond casual reference to individual notebooks, nor is there any indication of its ultimate destiny. (p. 56)

Dr Morgan makes use of the nondetective novels and of the autobiographical writings to assist her study, but she is fumbling on the detective stories themselves, inaccurate on several of them, and contributes little to analysis of the origins of their observation. Christie through the mouth of a satirical self-portrait in **Death in the Clouds** (Mr Clancy) indicated that she enjoyed putting persons who annoyed her into her stories: much could be made of this. (Her most odious detective officer, Inspector Slack, was created after the disappearance: Dr Morgan conveys how egregious was the conduct of Superintendent Kenward in that event, but makes little effort to show his relationship or that of the rest of the episode to the subsequent literary achievement. Miss Marple, too, makes her *début* at this juncture, much more unflatteringly than in subsequent work, her rather poisonous gossip hinting at her capacity for wreaking havoc in the private lives of many more persons than murderers.)

The book nevertheless is an important contribution to the cultural history of inter-war Britain, not least in its revelation of Christie's American antecedents. (pp. 56-7)

Owen Dudley Edwards, "A Talent to Observe," in History Today, *Vol. 35, March, 1985, pp. 56-7.*

KIRKUS REVIEWS

Invited to write this "authorized biography" by Christie's daughter, Morgan had access to the private Christie papers—letters, manuscripts, diaries, etc.—and to previously un-forthcoming interview subjects. But, while the result is thickly detailed and occasionally intriguing, there's little new light shed [in **Agatha Christie: A Biography**] on the subjects of greatest interest or importance: the sources of Christie's fearsomely lethal imagination, the reasons for her work's phenomenal success, and the truth about her famous disappearance. In documenting Agatha's Victorian childhood (so gorgeously evoked in AC's *Autobiography*), Morgan does come up with a few teasing, unexplored clues: her older sister's "passion for disguise," her father's love of amateur theatricals, the feeling that this serene childhood "was vaguely, but not unmanageably, disturbed beneath" the surface. When it comes to that 1926 *scandale*, Morgan reviews all the evidence, considers every theory, and settles on the most commonly held view (nervous breakdown, genuine temporary amnesia)—while railing at the "greedy, sensational, and importunate" press. And some of Christie's recurring themes—in the revealing Mary Westmacott novels as well as the mysteries—are remarked upon: maternally possessive love, evil and innocence, mirrors, disguise. Unfortunately, however, though Morgan uses the AC notebooks to provide a glimpse of a Christie plot's development from first notion to finished puzzle, her commentary on the mysteries is painfully thin: there's virtually no attempt at critical assessment; only the most obvious life/work parallels are noticed; faulty generalizations abound ("Her books do not make the blood run quicker"); the few strong insights are duly credited lifts from Robert Barnard's *A Talent to Deceive*. Nor is there anything surprising in the portrait of Agatha herself: industrious, good-natured, insular (the anti-Semitism), "self-protective." And the bulk of this biography, especially in later chapters, is devoted to the minutiae of travel, publishing, playwrighting, and domestic life. In sum: a valuable gathering of facts, documents, and testimony—but too superficial to please serious students of the genre, too lumbering to engage most fans (who'll prefer to stick with the imperfect yet irresistible *Autobiography*). (pp. 323-24)

A review of "Agatha Christie: A Biography," in Kirkus Reviews, *Vol. LIII, No. 7, April 1, 1985, pp. 323-24.*

JOHN GROSS

"I chiefly associate her with fluffy wool," Agatha Christie once told an admirer who had asked her about Miss Marple. And what does one associate with Agatha Christie? Flowered chintz, French windows, a twin set of pearls, sensible shoes? With all the appurtenances of a country lady, at any rate, a representative figure of her time (born 1890) and place (southern England) and class (upper middle).

In some ways she was as much of a stock character as the men and women in her novels, and though she shunned publicity, most of her readers must feel they have a pretty clear idea of what she was like. Sensible but superficial, brisk and humorous, invincibly respectable, stoutly English—never more so than when she was on her travels abroad or roughing it with her archeologist husband in Iraq.

This picture was largely confirmed by the autobiography that was published (in a heavily edited version) in 1977, the year following her death. It is a coherent picture, as far as it goes; but can it be the whole truth? Surely, the most successful mystery writer of the century ought to have been just a little bit more mysterious herself. Such a feeling has prompted a good deal of biographical speculation, and some out-and-out fantasy, particularly about the one undeniably melodramatic episode in her career, the 10 days in 1926 when she disappeared and became the object of a nationwide search.

In 1980, her family decided that the time had come for an authorized biography, and entrusted the job to Janet Morgan, a writer previously best known for her four-volume edition of the posthumous diaries of the Labor politician Richard Crossman—one of the most revealing works about British politics to have appeared in recent years. It was an imaginative choice, and it has proved a highly successful one. [In **Agatha Christie: A Biography**] Miss Morgan writes with clarity and wit, she organizes her material with a deft touch, and she brings to life vanished worlds with a sure sense of social nuance.

There is an excellent account, for a start, of the comfortable south coast resort of Torquay where the young Agatha Miller grew up. We are given just the right amount of detail, not too little and not too much, about her easy-going family (complete with an amiable scapegrace of a brother called Monty—it seems the right name for him) and her American connections, which seem to have counted for less in later life than you might have supposed. (Her father, who came from New York, was in the "Social Register;" one of her aunts was related by marriage to the Pierpont Morgans.)

We learn, too, about her avid childhood reading, her early ambition to be a singer, her shyness, her literary beginnings; and about the round of dances and country-house weekends during which she met Archie Christie, a regular soldier turned aviator who had already begun to make a name for himself as a Royal Flying Corps ace by the time she finally married him, after a turbulent courtship, on Christmas Eve 1914.

Rosalind, Mathew, Oliver Gurney, and Christie in 1948. From Agatha Christie: A Biography, *by Janet Morgan. Alfred A. Knopf, 1985.*

The same skill is deployed in telling the story of her second, much happier marriage at the age of 40 to Max Mallowan, 15 years her junior, quintessentially English in manner (though both his parents were in fact Austrian), in due course to become one of the leading British archeologists of his generation. And Miss Morgan is equally effective in plotting the graph of Agatha Christie's career as an author and describing her working habits, her tangled finances, her attempts to cope with the micro-idiocies of publishers and the macro-idiocies of film companies, her ventures into the theater, the mountainous success of *The Mousetrap.* There are plenty of good anecdotes, and a steady supply of entertaining Christie trivia—a droll consideration of Lord Mountbatten's claims to have devised the plot of *The Murder of Roger Ackroyd,* for example.

There are only a few passages in the book, however, where we feel that we are in the presence of a less straightforward personality than the Agatha Christie of legend. One, naturally enough, is the account of her disappearance; another is the account of a recurrent childhood dream in which she was stalked by a figure she called the "Gun Man," who was frightening not so much because he carried a gun but because of the strange way he stared at her with his pale blue eyes.

She recalls this dream in her autobiography, adding that in later life it took the form of dreaming that she was among friends or family and suddenly sensing that one of them was really the

Gun Man; but Janet Morgan points out that in a novel she published under the name "Mary Westmacott" the manifestation is described in more specific and more terrifying terms: "You looked up in Mummy's face—of course it was Mummy—and then you saw the light steely blue eyes—and from the sleeve of Mummy's dress—oh, horror!—that horrible stump."

If this reads like an open invitation to psychoanalysts, Miss Morgan's account of the disappearance frequently strikes a satirical note. Rightly so; the popular press turned the episode into a carnival, with many attendant absurdities. But there can be no doubt that Agatha Christie herself suffered a serious breakdown at this time, triggered off by learning that her husband had fallen in love with another woman—though it also seems of some relevance that her mother had died not long before.

In the end, despite the occasional dark aspect, she remains an obstinately unmysterious figure. If there are still things to be learned about her, it is probably by looking into her work rather than the outward circumstances of her life that they will be found. But meanwhile the story of that life has now been told in an authoritative and highly readable fashion.

John Gross, in a review of "Agatha Christie: A Biography," in The New York Times, *May 21, 1985, p. C14.*

*Christie with her husband, Sir Max Mallowan. Snowdon/
Camera Press.*

PAUL GRAY

Once, after reading in a magazine that she was "the world's
most mysterious woman," Agatha Christie complained to her
agent: "What do they suggest I am? A Bank Robber or a Bank
Robber's wife? I'm an ordinary successful hard-working author—like any other author." Her success was not exactly
ordinary. She produced nearly 90 novels and collections of
stories in a lifetime that spanned 85 years. One of her plays,
The Mousetrap, opened in London in 1952 and is still running.

She refined and left a lasting imprint on the detective formula.
An "Agatha Christie" became a shorthand description for an
unadorned display of crime unmasked by perceptive and relentless logic. She dared readers to outwit her, and few resisted
the challenge. Shortly after her death in 1976, one estimate
put the worldwide sale of her works at 400 million copies.
Given such glittering evidence and the clues provided by her
fiction, a mystique was bound to develop around the one whodunit: Agatha the enchantress, the proper Englishwoman with
a power to murder and create. When she insisted that the truth
was far less exotic, armchair sleuths who had been trained by
her books recognized a false lead when they saw one.

She was right, of course, as this biography [*Agatha Christie*],
the first written with the blessings of Christie's heirs and estate,
conclusively proves. Author Janet Morgan does a thorough job

of getting the facts in the Christie case straight and on the
record. But the story, even when demystified, seems almost
as unbelievable as the guessing games it prompted.

Her childhood could have been written by Jane Austen. Agatha
Miller, beloved by her parents and an older sister and brother,
grew up in an English seaside village surrounded by Edwardian
privileges and leisure. Her American father lived off a trust
fund that dwindled steadily, and his death when Agatha was
eleven left family finances ever more unsteady. Still, breeding
and manners meant as much as money, and the young woman,
largely educated at home, moved in a circle of eligible bachelors. She turned down three proposals and took a flyer instead.
After a stormy courtship, she married Archie Christie, a dashing aviator with few expectations of living through World War I.

While he fought, his new bride stayed home, working in a
hospital. Her sister suggested that Agatha, who was both exhausted and bored during her free time, try to write the sort
of detective novel they both enjoyed reading. She did, but by
the time *The Mysterious Affair at Styles* appeared in print, the
war was over and Agatha had a daughter, and a husband,
grounded at last, who seemed chiefly interested in making
money and playing golf.

The year 1926 changed her prospects and her life. For one
thing, she published *The Murder of Roger Ackroyd,* which caused
a stir because it broke the rules of detective fiction: the narrator
did it. Something more shocking followed. In December Agatha left her husband and child and disappeared for ten days,
setting off a nationwide search and a carnival of speculation.
Morgan's re-creation of this drama is meticulous, but it lacks,
perhaps unavoidably, the tight resolution that Christie gave her
invented plots.

Grieving over the death of her mother and staggering under
the burden of sorting out the estate, the heroine learns from
her husband that he is in love with another woman. She drives
off one night; her abandoned car is discovered the next morning. Questions multiply. Is she seeking publicity, has she joined
her lover, is she embarrassing her husband, or has she been
murdered?

When she is discovered at a Yorkshire hotel, registered under
the last name of the woman Archie now wants to marry, Agatha
Christie has nothing to say. Her biographer gives all the available details but suspends judgment: "There are moments in
people's lives on which it is unwise, as well as impertinent,
for an outsider to speculate, since it is impossible to be certain
about what actually took place or how the participants felt about
it."

Neither Miss Marple nor Hercule Poirot would accept such an
alibi, but truth is messier than fiction. Whatever may have
happened to Christie in 1926, she recovered admirably. Two
years after her divorce, while visiting friends on an expedition
in Iraq, she met Max Mallowan, an archaeologist nearly 14
years her junior. Eventually he proposed, fretting at the same
time that she might find his line of work boring. She reassured
him: "I *adore* corpses and stiffs." They lived happily ever
after.

Morgan is candid about the weaknesses in her subject's work.
Christie's stories were ingenious but her writing was pedestrian. She intentionally offered stereotypes instead of rounded
characters and grew annoyed when Poirot, her Belgian detective, began to assume a life of his own in the popular imagination. She once privately described him as "an ego-centric

creep.'' She constructed puzzles, not literature; she devoted what energies she could spare from a busy life to craft rather than art. To list real liabilities in this manner is, ultimately, to beg a question: Why, among so many talented competitors in a small field, did Agatha triumph? Responsible biography can suggest but never prove the probable verdict: she was the best at what she chose to do.

> Paul Gray, '' 'I Adore Corpses and Stiffs' ,'' *in* Time, *Vol. 125, No. 21, May 27, 1985, p. 85.*

SARA PARETSKY

After her death in 1976, Christie's family did not want to release her papers to biographers. Her popularity was such that they knew demands would continue. In Janet Morgan, the family found a sympathetic speaker to tell Agatha Christie's story, one that would not probe behind their image of an English country lady devoted to garden, to husband and child, who was a best-selling novelist, but shy and without ambition. . . .

[In *Agatha Christie: A Biography* many] facts are detailed by Janet Morgan. It is almost as though, overwhelmed by Christie's papers, she felt compelled to give us every moment of every day of the lady's long life. In one page, Morgan recounts the news of Christie's sister's death, the celebration of her 60th birthday, the way she spent the summer of 1950, her visitors at her country home and the completion of a novel she wrote under the pseudonym of Mary Westmacott.

This approach makes it hard to pursue the thread of Christie's life, so caught up are we in its details. Morgan will further frustrate mystery fans as she introduces facts without giving the reader prior clues. For example, during the unhappy period of Christie's life when her first marriage was breaking up, Morgan writes:

> Agatha was in despair but it would be wrong to imagine that she ever seriously contemplated suicide. . . . [It] would have been wholly contrary to her strong religious beliefs.

Christie may have had strong beliefs, but this is our first exposure to them. The description of her upbringing, during which her mother experimented with Catholicism, Unitarianism, Theosophy and other religions, gives no clue to any regular religious training or belief.

We are told that Christie was unambitious about her work, pursuing it almost as a sidelight to her second marriage to archeologist Max Mallowan. Yet she retained the name Christie, since that was how her fans knew her. She also demanded the final say over every jacket cover, going back to her first Poirot novel. Such decisions are wrested from the publisher only by a most determined, involved author. . . .

Morgan tells us that the themes of possessive love and relations between mother and daughter recur in Christie's work. In discussing *A Daughter's a Daughter,* a Westmacott novel that deals heavily with both issues, Morgan assures us that ''[t]he relationship she described here had nothing to do with herself or Rosalind. . . .''

Rosalind, Christie's only child, was left from the age of 2 with relatives and governesses while Agatha wrote and traveled. Christie's own mother seems to have been quite demanding. Perhaps that's why she spent so little time with Rosalind, and then had to keep exploring the relationship in different books.

Another biographer will have to look at that and other personal issues of Christie's life.

Morgan's biography will undoubtedly please the Christie/Mallowan families, for it does no impertinent prying. But for those mystery writers and readers who would like to understand the most popular writer of our age, the book will leave many important questions not only unanswered but unasked.

> Sara Paretsky, ''Agatha Christie Remains Mystery to Her Biographer,'' *in* Chicago Tribune, *June 9, 1985, p. 27.*

ANTONIA FRASER

[*Fraser is an English biographer, novelist, scriptwriter, and short story writer. Though she has written mysteries, Fraser is best known for her biographies of Mary Queen of Scots, Oliver Cromwell, King James VI, and Charles II. Critics note that Fraser's focus is to humanize her subjects, which often results in a revised image of these historical figures. In the following excerpt Fraser commends Morgan for her revealing portrait of Christie, but questions the biographer's decision to refrain from speculating on aspects of Christie's life.*]

What was she like, the woman born Agatha Miller in a modest villa in a seaside town in Devon in 1890, who ended up the wife of the distinguished archeologist Sir Max Mallowan, having in between as Agatha Christie (the surname came from her first husband) generated this extraordinary industry? Was she like Miss Marple for instance, that shrewd old lady detective,

Christie in her later years. Snowdon/Camera Press.

solving the world's problems from the vantage point of her ostensibly tranquil village of St. Mary Mead? As Christie grew older, many people made this identification. Now we have the official biography, *Agatha Christie,* by Janet Morgan, to tell us, among a host of other fascinating things, exactly how wrong that identification was. (Nor was Dame Agatha much like Hercule Poirot.)

This is an official biography in the sense that the author has had the full cooperation of Agatha Christie's family and full access to her papers, including the notebooks in which she plotted the stories. But she makes it clear that she was in no sense subjected to censorship, so that we have here an example of the new kind of official biography (Philip Ziegler's brilliant *Mountbatten* is another) where access to the papers has not inevitably resulted in hagiography. The result is a vigorous, lucid and highly readable book that will tell Christie fans what they have long wanted to know. I think it will also provoke still further discussion about the true nature of the Christie appeal.

So what was she like? The answer to the first question, Was she like Miss Marple? is an emphatic no. According to this biography, Agatha Christie was a passionate, vulnerable, instinctive woman who hardly resembled the wry Miss M. at all.

The second question most readers will want answered concerns the celebrated mystery of Christie's disappearance in 1926, when she was still married to her first husband, Col. Archibald Christie. In her own autobiography, published after her death in a heavily edited version, Agatha Christie summed up this disappearance and the events that led up to it in a simple sentence: "So ended my first married life."

But the story itself was a great deal more fascinating, and a great deal more heart-rending, than that simple sentence would seem to indicate. (pp. 8-9)

I have one criticism of Mrs. Morgan's handling of all this, although I freely admit that I may be writing here as an old codger of a biographer myself (this is Mrs. Morgan's first biography). She writes that it would be "impertinent" to speculate on the details of Agatha Christie's marriage to Colonel Christie. Mrs. Morgan has brilliantly edited the diaries of the late Labor Party politican Richard Crossman, which contained quite a few "impertinent" details (if of a political rather than a personal nature). She will shortly embark on the official biography of Lady Edwina Mountbatten, once again at the request of the family. With this in mind, I will suggest that the biographer can never actually be "impertinent" when speculating on matters vital to the subject in hand; tasteless in expression, yes, overfanciful, possibly, but in a quest for the truth, impertinence is a category that surely goes by the board.

Perhaps finally Mrs. Morgan was won over by Agatha Christie's own desire for privacy. Despite this minor restraint, this is still an excellent book. (p. 9)

> Antonia Fraser, "Who Created Roger Ackroyd?" in The New York Times Book Review, *June 23, 1985, pp. 8-9.*

WALTER KENDRICK

[Why] did Janet Morgan write *Agatha Christie: A Biography*? Morgan doesn't let on, except to say in her preface that, in 1980, Christie's daughter "invited" her to do so. Rosalind's motive seems to have been that despite Christie's posthumously published *Autobiography* (1978), the world was still hung up on the idea that the immemorial deviser of fiendishly clever crimes must have had something fiendish in her own composition. We should have known all along she didn't. . . .

I can't say it's boring to read, because Morgan writes so well that she imparts charm to matters which, in less accomplished hands, would amount to dust and ashes. Christie loved to eat, especially seafood and thick cream. . . . Slim in youth, in middle age Christie grew distinctly foursquare; but she didn't seem to mind, and Morgan's warm, smooth prose conveys the innocent pleasure that obesity used to provide as a sign of gustatory well-being. The biography of any fat Englishwoman, of course, might have done the same. The dismaying fact is that Christie, like writers of a stature far greater than hers, left no traces in her day-to-day existence of where her art came from. Unless the weird dreams spawned by a surfeit of *moules mariniéres* are a source of literary genius, *Agatha Christie: A Biography* contributes nothing to our understanding of a writer whose popularity is rivaled only by Shakespeare and the Bible.

As far as Morgan's book goes, that's no problem. Its subject could have been Jane Doe, and its absorbing, slightly drowsy appeal would remain. I'd hoped for better, though.

> Walter Kendrick, "Banal Retentive," in The Village Voice, *Vol. XXX, No. 27, July 2, 1985, p. 55.*

The Kindness of Strangers: The Life of Tennessee Williams
by Donald Spoto

(For Tennessee Williams: see also *CLC*, Vols. 1, 2, 5, 7, 8, 11, 15, 19, 30; *Contemporary Authors*, Vols. 7-8, rev. ed., 108 [obituary] *Dictionary of Literary Biography*, Vol. 7; *Dictionary of Literary Biography Yearbook: 1983;* and *Dictionary of Literary Biography Documentary Series*, Vol. 4. For Donald Spoto: see also *Contemporary Authors*, Vols. 65-68 and *Contemporary Authors New Revision Series*, Vol. 11.)

An Excerpt from *The Kindness of Strangers: The Life of Tennessee Williams*

Nowhere was the art more confessional than in *Suddenly Last Summer,* in which Tennessee Williams gave as clear a perception of derailed creative energies and the abuse of love as any moralist could ever proclaim. Obsessed with what the play calls "the trails of debris" that he believed had characterized so much of his life in the 1940s and 1950s, he wrote a play that wept for the waste—most of all because he felt that he had abused the freedom of the creative life, and of life itself. He had squandered what had been denied to his sister. He always knew that the only thing that kept him from sharing Rose's fate was the hair's breadth of accident; they had, after all, both endured breakdown. According to the artist Vassilis Voglis, who had by this time known Williams socially for several years and would see him frequently to the end of his life, "He was devoted to Rose, but in a way she was an extension of himself. *He* could have had the lobotomy. *He* felt the outsider, marred in some way. He really cared for her, and perhaps he never really cared for anyone else in this life, ever. And I think he knew it."

Sebastian Venable's exploitation of others, his empty, decreative life, and his abuse of his cousin Catharine were for Williams the clearest portrait he could draw of his own remorse. The play is, then, both confession and act of penance. He perhaps misjudged his own best gifts and the healing effects of those gifts when he told the interviewer that he hoped to have done with violence, and to write with serenity. "*Suddenly Last Summer* is a play he would have liked to have back—as if he regretted writing it," said Joseph L. Mankiewicz, who directed a brilliant film of it the following year. "There is something not only of confession in the play, but of wish-fulfillment, too. Tennessee might have liked to have a garden with statues like Sebastian's, a study with paintings like Sebastian's. If he had a distaste for anything, it was for his own aging and his own humble background and circumstances. *Suddenly Last Summer* enabled him to have what he despised, in a way. And Mrs. Venable is certainly a composite of the women who defended and accompanied him all over the world."

FRANK RICH

As the plays of Tennessee Williams are likely to live for as long as there is an American theater, so may the fabled drama of the man himself. Donald Spoto, the author of the first serious Williams biography since the playwright's death, is only a shade hyperbolic when he characterizes his subject as "a man more disturbing, more dramatic, richer and more wonderful than any character he ever created." Williams's life was lived almost entirely at the extremes embodied by Blanche DuBois and Stanley Kowalski. He was at once a man of frail sensitivities and brutal hungers—a moth dancing in his own flame. And, as surely as Stanley must smash Blanche, so Williams was inevitably driven to self-destruction.

It is not a pretty story that Mr. Spoto tells in *The Kindness of Strangers*. The son of a Mississippi rector's puritanical daughter and a shoe salesman who fell in love with long distances, Thomas Lanier Williams endured a sickly, rootless childhood (more than 16 family residences in his first 15 years) that he would re-enact for the rest of his life. Hating his callous father (who dubbed him "Miss Nancy") and wary of his volatile, genteel mother, he rarely trusted the affection of others: throughout his adulthood, he drove away most of the people who cared about him, from his most devoted lover, Frank Merlo, to Audrey Wood, the agent who nurtured his career from the days of his apprenticeship to boom times and creative drought. Even when Williams made millions, he continued to live the itinerant existence of his youth. Compulsively restless, he would always rather be on an airplane or in a hotel room than in his nominal, ill-maintained "permanent" residences of Key West, Fla., and New York City. Nor did he ever exorcise the guilt he felt over his inability as a young man to prevent his hysterical mother from subjecting his beloved sister, Rose, to a prefrontal lobotomy. Williams became a chronic hypochondriac who always saw himself, like Rose, at either the asylum's or death's door.

That hypochondria, as Mr. Spoto explains, eventually found its outlet in drug dependence. *The Kindness of Strangers* leaves little doubt that it was Williams's chemical addictions, rather than literary burnout, that effectively destroyed his career during the two decades between *The Night of the Iguana* in 1962 and his accidental death in a New York hotel room in 1983. In that grotesque final period, Williams indiscriminately swallowed or injected nearly every pharmaceutical he could find. Not only were the dosages of staggering proportions, but the various amphetamines and barbiturates mixed explosively with each other—as well as with the large quantities of alcohol that Williams consumed.

Amazingly enough, he kept writing. No matter how much he had abused his body or spirit the night before, he would somehow get up each morning to peck away at his typewriter for several hours, often working on several projects at once, frequently rewriting plays again and again after their increasingly brief New York runs. The output never slackened—only its quality. One is left with the poignant image of an artist whose creative reflexes kept functioning well after most of his organs, his brain included, had deteriorated. It is not inconceivable that a detoxified Williams might have produced as many lasting plays in the second half of his career as he did in the first.

Mr. Spoto lays out this chronicle dutifully and, as best one can tell, accurately. Readers familiar with the existing public record—the Williams-Donald Windham letters (1977), the memoirs and biographies of Williams associates and relatives, Williams's own somewhat scurrilous **Memoirs** (1975), the voluminous journalistic profiles of the playwright—will not find many major surprises here. But the author does reconcile conflicting versions of events, add footnotes and flesh out familiar anecdotes with fresh, if mostly unexamined, observations from surviving Williams friends.

Yet enemies rarely speak up, and neither, in a way, does Williams himself. **The Kindness of Strangers** is an unauthorized biography, as was Mr. Spoto's 1983 life of Alfred Hitchcock, **The Dark Side of Genius.** But in this book, unlike the last, the subject's presence is elusive. Although the author had access to the many Williams papers at the University of Texas at Austin, as well as other collections, we rarely hear the playwright's distinctive, often humorous voice in these pages. Mr. Spoto's flat journalistic prose and routine analysis cannot fill the vacuum. The reportage, more facile and seemingly more hurried than that of the Hitchcock book, is only rarely its own reward.

Mr. Spoto does have his theories and conceits, but they do not answer the central questions raised by his narrative. He leans too heavily on generalizations about ''the Dionysian or Bacchic impulse'' to explain his subject's artistic personality. Nor does he convincingly unravel what he calls the ''brutal paradox'' of a shy, sensitive man who, for all his identification with the vulnerable and dispossessed, tirelessly pursued sex ''for its own sake, as a quick, anonymous diversion.'' And what are we to make of the book's last-minute speculation—suggested by others and left uninvestigated by the author—that Williams's unquenchable thirst for male bodies masked a deep-seated hatred of homosexuality?

The discussion of the plays is, if anything, less illuminating. As the book's all-too-predictable title might indicate, Mr. Spoto often assumes an unsophisticated reader; at this late date, he mounts a strenuous defense against now-forgotten critics and public bluenoses who attacked Williams's work for its ''sensationalism.'' Moreover, the plays are laboriously dissected for what autobiographical nuggets they might contain, and they are schematically contrasted with the works of Williams's favorite writers. (*A Streetcar Named Desire,* we are told, has ''a certain nostalgia that testifies to its author's veneration of Chekhov and his tragic seagull.'') Mr. Spoto's critical vocabulary is meager. *Iguana* is commended for its ''human warmth'' and ''tragic serenity,'' and *Streetcar* for ''its tragic grandeur and its sharply etched portraits of men and women in conflict.'' In general, the best Williams plays are called ''great'' and the best film adaptations of them ''brilliant.'' Similarly, Williams's various lovers are characterized as either ''strikingly

handsome'' or ''dazzlingly handsome'' or, in the autumnal years, merely ''tall, handsome and alert.''

What **The Kindness of Strangers** most lacks, however, is passion—for Williams, for the theater, and for the language and telling scenes a literary biography requires. The only time Mr. Spoto gets worked up is when he is fuming about the paid and unpaid ''personal assistants'' who attached themselves to Williams at the end. The author describes this ''coterie of young men'' with ever-angrier invective—from ''social carnivores'' to ''glamor-hungry jackals who used sex like a fly-swatter''—but without revealing exactly who these people were or how and why the playwright needed them. Grateful as we can be that Mr. Spoto has done the spadework, someone else will have to dig far deeper to produce the biography that matches the size and drama of Williams's life and art. (p. 3)

> *Frank Rich, ''Half Blanche and Half Stanley,'' in*
> The New York Times Book Review, *April 21, 1985,*
> *pp. 3, 48.**

EDMUND WHITE

[*White, an American novelist, dramatist, and nonfiction writer, is noted for his impressionistic style and luxurious prose. Both in his fiction and nonfiction, which are informed by his own homosexual sensibility, White focuses on the lifestyle of the upper-middle-class homosexual. In the following excerpt White reflects on the personal and public life of Williams and on the dramatist's most memorable plays.*]

Rose before her lobotomy. Photography Collection, Harry Ransom. Humanities Research Center, The University of Texas at Austin

Donald Spoto comments extensively on Williams's vast oeuvre—his 25 full-length plays, more than 40 short plays, his volume of memoirs, two novels, 60-odd short stories, some hundred poems, published letters, and occasional pieces. Although Williams was immensely noticed during most of his writing career (there are 33 volumes of collected reviews of his work), *The Kindness of Strangers* is the first biography. I tired of the show-bizzy "philosophy" of Spoto's text, the "she-was-a-warm-wise-wonderful-human-being" kind of prose; but I do admire the book's thoroughness and its obvious affection for its subject. Williams is a man any lesser spirit would have quickly come to detest (the occupational hazard of most biographers). But Spoto never loses sight of Williams's genius, and never lets his excessive knowledge of the playwright's failures as an artist or man lead to condescension. (pp. 33-4)

Williams and Kerouac are among the few writers I know of who didn't read much. Despite this lack of curiosity, Williams did manage early on to discover both Strindberg and Chekhov, who influenced his major plays. The violent confrontations of Strindberg's unhappy couples in his realistic plays and the symbolic fantasies of his dream plays surface in Williams's work. So does the poetic realism of Chekhov's lovable incompetents in minutely observed, tightly structured but apparently disorganized dramas, so unstable in their shifts of tone from comedy to tragedy, from wisdom to banality. . . .

[Williams] first received recognition as a poet, although today his poems read like a blend of A. E. Housman and Sara Teasdale, a fusion that isn't admirable but is certainly likable. He was living at home and looking on as his mother encouraged "gentlemen callers" to visit her terrified, fragile daughter Rose. Both of the older children, exposed to their parents' quarrels and the gibes of working-class neighbor kids, showed signs of strain. Tom had a shocking anxiety attack and Rose began her decline into insanity. By 1936 Rose was being counseled by psychiatrists—to no avail. The next year she witnessed her drunk father beat her mother; when he then made a pass at Rose, she became hysterical for several days. Foreshadowing Stella's rejection of Blanche in *A Streetcar Named Desire*, Mrs. Williams, unable to accept Rose's allegation against her father, gave permission for Rose to be lobotomized. For the rest of her long life, Rose was to be institutionalized except for brief stays with Tom. (p. 34)

A consolation prize in a literary contest led Williams to his agent, Audrey Wood; and she, after a long struggle, managed to launch her client into stardom. By the time he was in his thirties, Williams was an international celebrity with *The Glass Menagerie* (1944), soon followed by *A Streetcar Named Desire* (1947). More than any other American playwright, Williams wrote plays that were not only hits but also enduring works of the repertory. They include *Summer and Smoke* (1948), *The Rose Tattoo* (1951), *Cat On a Hot Tin Roof* (1955), *Baby Doll* (1957), *Suddenly Last Summer* (1958), *Sweet Bird of Youth* (1959), and *Night of the Iguana* (1961).

Williams was an early master of publicity. In the sixties, when his talent was drying up, he was turning himself—his excesses and reverses—into an eye-catching product. Only Andy Warhol and Norman Mailer understood as well as he how to give good interviews. On the Sunday before a new play would open, Williams would write in *The New York Times* about his disputes with his psychoanalyst—confessions that were fatally readable. Or he'd announce his conversion to Catholicism—and then, a year later, his disillusion with the church. Or he'd tell an interviewer, "I'm a built-in definition of hysteria. I hate my-self. I feel I bore people—and that I'm too physically repulsive." Of course the slipping in of the word "too" suggests comic perspectives, and indeed in his later writings Williams was often comically grotesque, obscenely gothic.

A persistent sentimentality haunts even the most successful of Tennessee Williams's plays. If sentimentality means unearned and unrendered emotion, then we must find sentimental his habitual recourse to such an automatic bid for sympathy as madness (an undefined, "pure" state of madness), just as his invariable linking of madness to sexual frustration (or, conversely, to sexual violation) seems blandly and routinely Freudian. Sympathy for the crazed sex victim is the expected audience response in *The Glass Menagerie, A Streetcar Named Desire*, and *Summer and Smoke*.

But if such expectations give these plays their lurid appeal, as irresistible as a Sousa march, their enduring value lies elsewhere—in their ventriloquism. Williams recognized that great theater begins with great talkers, and that great talkers obey two rules: they never sound like anyone else and they never say anything directly. (pp. 34-5)

Amanda, Blanche, Serafina (in *The Rose Tattoo*), Big Daddy (in *Cat on a Hot Tin Roof*)—these are only some of the great talkers Williams invented and recorded. Here's Big Daddy: "I haven't been able to stand the sight, sound, or smell of that woman for forty years now!—even when I *laid* her!—regular as a piston." Like a line in W. S. Merwin, "even when I laid her!" modifies both the phrase that precedes and follows it. (pp. 35-6)

Many of Williams's intimates (as well as his biographer) ascribe his decline to the death of his lover Frank Merlo in the early sixties. Merlo, a New Jersey-born Navy veteran and a second-generation Sicilian, had been Williams's long-suffering companion for 15 years, someone who had never flattered the master but rather evaluated his work with acuity and lent his chaotic, peripatetic life some dignity and stability. And Merlo was the one with the charm. People took up with the couple because they were attracted by Williams's fame, but if they stuck around they did so because they were seduced by Merlo's easygoing amiability. . . .

Spoto includes a touching anecdote about Rose. In the autumn of 1949, when Rose was already 40, Tennessee visited her at her hospital in Ossining, New York. When he came back to the car, the multimillionaire was clutching a ten-dollar bill. Rose had given him the money as he was leaving.

"Tom," she had whispered, "I know how hard you are working at the shoe warehouse. I know you want to be a poet, and I believe in you. I have been saving some change for you, and I hope this will help things to be a little easier. If you will just be patient, I know good things will be ahead. Always remember I believe in you." (p. 36)

Edmund White, "Writer on a Hot Tin Roof," in The New Republic, *Vol. 192, No. 19, May 13, 1985, pp. 33-6.*

RUSSELL DAVIES

Donald Spoto is the man who recently exposed all manner of lurking turpitudes in the life of Alfred Hitchcock. The news that he had been let loose on the vices and vagaries of Tennessee Williams seemed to promise a feast of scandal bordering on the unprintable. . . .

Spoto has taken the other course, producing a mild tranquilliser of a book [*The Kindness of Strangers*], consolidating his claims to be a 'serious' biographer capable of actually toning down his subject's more sensational escapades.

The fact is that the life of Thomas Lanier Williams (who, had he pen-named himself in honour of his home state, would have been known as Mississippi Williams) was not a very complex structure. His behaviour may have caused a thousand complications, but the underlying psychic machinery that propelled his life forward was of no great intricacy. Most of its moving parts were set up before he was born, when Cornelius Coffin Williams won the hand of Edwina Estelle Dakin.

Edwina was the kind of fragile-tough, self-destructively prim, born-too-late Southern belle that Tennessee Williams later made so familiar on stage and screen, a Scarlett O'Hara caught somewhere in the process of becoming a Miss Havisham. Cornelius, to put it as baldly as would seem appropriate to his glistening scalp, was a roistering shoe-salesman whose sexual adventures were less embarrassing than his alcoholic binges only because he brought the effects of the latter home to the family. . . .

Most of the themes and preoccupations of [Williams's] work can be seen already sprouting from this early life. The hurtfulness of familiar intimacy; the semi-accidental amputation of emotional possibilities; the fateful attractiveness that attaches to even the most reprehensibly bullying masculine presence—all these notions were thrust into Williams's hands. Their potential dismalness is obvious, and it was an act of intellectual heroism on the playwright's part to wrest something positive from them. Yet he added only one real development—or solution, or escape route, what you will—of his own, and that was sex. . . .

Spoto never gives us a very intimate idea of how far Tennessee Williams sank in pursuit of his urge. . . . What's more, Spoto registers puzzlement over the 'brutal paradox' of Williams's habit of quick, anonymous sex, when within himself he was 'most deeply sensitive to the inequities, illusions and potential exploitations in intimate relationships.' But, pretty obviously, it was only by feeding the beast, treating sex as a daily, fast-food diet, that Williams was able to keep his imaginative and emotional faculties free and unencumbered for the subtler purposes of his writing. (It worked, of course, only for a time; gradually characters began appearing in his plays who would settle for orgiastic gratification just as he had.)

To the end of his life, Williams retained some vestige of his talent for fusing the caressing cadences of poetic diction with the corrosive inelegance of popular speech. But once he had exhausted, in his mid-life plays, the permutations of his given family material, he was reduced to beating the old routines into life with bunches of roses. . . .

In the last years, we saw quite a lot of a very fuddled Williams. He was said to hold the record for Atlantic crossings by Concorde. But the ceaseless movement fooled nobody. For many years his soul had been sunning itself in some sad garden, at Rose's side.

> *Russell Davies, "The Trouble with Tennessee," in*
> The Observer, *June 2, 1985, p. 23.*

JOHN SIMON

[Simon is an American critic known primarily for his film and theater reviews. He has written on literature and the arts for several popular magazines and newspapers, including Commonweal, Esquire, *the* New York Times, New Republic, *and* New York *magazine. His first published book,* Acid Test *(1963), is a collection of his critical essays on a variety of topics. His subsequent books, including* Singularities: Essays on Theatre, 1964-74 *(1976) and* Something to Declare: Twelve Years of Films from Abroad *(1982), focus more on movies and drama. Simon is known for his spirited yet discriminating criticism. In the following excerpt Simon faults Spoto for his failure to provide an interpretation of Williams's personality and a critical appraisal of his works.]*

Donald Spoto's book, bearing the threadbare title *The Kindness of Strangers,* is sedulous, pretentious, pedestrian, erratically researched, pontifical, and hopelessly shallow. . . . You cannot always trust Spoto, who is clearly too dull-witted for the task at hand. . . .

There are three main troubles with Spoto. First, he has no qualifications whatever as a critic or literary historian, despite many hollowly grandiose gestures in that direction. (Even his books on Hitchcock, his specialty, are paltry stuff.) . . . Second, he writes in an exceedingly flat, unsyntactical style that comes to grief whether it sinks to lower-than-sea-level platitudes or circuitously ascends into the cloudily opaque. Third, he harps on his moral disapproval of Williams' sexual indulgences (one mention would be quite enough), yet at other times he attempts to justify the playwright's worst excesses with such empty terms as "Dionysian or Bacchic impulse," to which he resorts some dozen times; but he is incapable of an incisive and convincing psychological interpretation of his subject. (p. 17)

Although Spoto finds merit in several of the later critically and financially unsuccessful works, he . . . portrays the middle-aged and older Williams as a man suffering from hypochondria, paranoia, erotomania, dromomania, fateful fascination with all sorts of perversion, drug addiction (vast excesses of medicines, stimulants, depressants, and one mention of cocaine), and schizophrenia. . . .

At the end of [Gore Vidal's essay-review in the *New York Review of Books* (see excerpt above)] Tennessee and Gore are on a restaurant terrace in Key West in the early '50s, and the playwright—martini in hand, bare feet on the terrace railing—smilingly declares, "I like my life."

No doubt there is truth to this picture too, particularly for the younger Williams in his artistic and vital prime, the years of Vidal's closest fraternization with him. Still, things cannot be that simple for someone who feels he is simultaneously "entirely natural" and "evil, sick, vicious." Vidal concedes hypochondria alone from the above-cited nosology, but something like manic depressiveness emerges from his description and, *a fortiori*, from those of Spoto and [Dotson] Rader. Even assuming much of this may have been drug-induced, what induced the drugs? Every account indicates periods of raucous euphoria, plus others of crushing depression, and if perhaps "not unuseful" to the writer, they were surely not unharrowing to the man and those around him who became the butts of his rages. In later life he changed agents almost as fast as friends, and friends nearly as often as shirts, possibly more so, considering his slovenliness and the filth in which he often lived. (p. 18)

A manifest memoir like Rader's does not require a critical stance; a biography like Spoto's, with self-professed critical standards and assessments, does. In its place, we get: "What was new in Tennessee Williams was his rhapsodic insistence that form serve his utterance rather than dominating and cramping it." Note the faulty parallelism along with the platitudinous

Williams with Frank Merlo, Elia Kazan, and Charles Feldman. Photography Collection, Harry Ransom. Humanities Research Center, The University of Texas at Austin.

insight and the historical absurdity. "New"? Had not Chekhov, Ibsen, Strindberg, O'Neill—Williams' models—done the same thing? Or consider: "*Iguana* was becoming a journal of Williams' soul passed through the prism of his poetic-dramatic art." Greater mastery of truism is unimaginable. Or this: "*Summer and Smoke* is one of Tennessee Williams' masterworks for the stage, a play of the eternal conflict between flesh and spirit—although these are often schematically represented." A schematic masterwork—that is certainly something new. And further: " 'The tables have turned with a vengeance,' Alma observes, in Tennessee Williams' most poignant assertion that balanced unions between right mates are very rare indeed." And just how does a seven-word utterance consisting of not one but two clichés become "most poignant"? Pathetic, perhaps.

Pathetic as well—beyond the bad thinking, the ungrammatical writing, the appallingly scrambled images ("Williams was surrounded by a pack of glamour-hungry jackals who used sex like a flyswatter"), the clichés paraded as deep insights, the total irresponsibilities (the "plays" of Kurt Weill!)—is Spoto's need to impress us with his threepenny erudition. (pp. 19-20)

On Williams the writer neither Spoto nor Rader can come up with anything approaching the following simple, compelling insight from Vidal: "Just as Williams never really added to

his basic repertory company of actors: Cornelius and Edwina, Reverend Dakin and [grandmother] Rose, himself and [sister] Rose, he never picked up much information about the world during his half-century as an adult. He also never tried, consciously at least, to make sense of the society into which he was born." He remained throughout his life the man who, having at age 10 discovered Existentialism, did not need to read Sartre or anyone else. Yet by turning his world into a sealed-off, stifling, exacerbating hothouse, he was able to convey with steamy intensity his moving but limited vision. No wonder that after two or three powerful plays Tennessee Williams was irreversibly depleted. (p. 20)

John Simon, "Life of an Antihero," in The New Leader, *Vol. LXVIII, No. 8, June 3 & 17, 1985, pp. 17-20.*

GORE VIDAL

[*Vidal is an American novelist, short story writer, dramatist, and essayist. He is particularly noted for his historical novels and his iconoclastic essays. In his work Vidal examines the plight of the modern human who exists in a valueless world amid corrupt institutions. Vidal's work in all genres is marked by his urbane wit and brilliant technique. In the essay from which the following excerpt is taken, Vidal relates anecdotes from his long friendship with Williams, whom he nicknamed "the Glorious Bird." He also theorizes on Williams's ongoing challenge to society's version of what was acceptable.*]

[*The Kindness of Strangers*] means to shock and titillate in a *responsible* way (drink, drugs, "wildly promiscuous sex"); that is, the author tries, not always successfully, to get the facts if not the life straight. . . .

Mr. Spoto begins at the beginning, and I found interesting the school days, endlessly protracted, of Thomas Lanier Williams (he did not use the name Tennessee until he was twenty-eight). The first twenty years of Williams's life provided him with the characters that he would write about. (p. 5)

Just as Williams never really added to his basic repertory company of actors: Cornelius and Edwina, Reverend Dakin and Rose, himself and Rose, he never picked up much information about the world during his half-century as an adult. He also never tried, consciously at least, to make sense of the society into which he was born. If he had, he might have figured out there is no such thing as a homosexual or a heterosexual person. There are only homo- or heterosexual acts. Most people are a mixture of impulses if not practices, and what anyone does with a willing partner is of no social or cosmic significance. (p. 6)

Both *The Glass Menagerie* and *A Streetcar Named Desire* opened during that brief golden age (1945–1950) when the United States was everywhere not only regnant but at peace, something we have not been for the last thirty-five years. At the beginning, Williams was acclaimed by pretty much everyone; only *Time* magazine was consistently hostile, suspecting that Williams might be "basically negative" and "sterile," code words of the day for fag. More to the point, *Time*'s founder, Henry Luce, had been born in China, son of a Christian missionary. "The greatest task of the United States in the twentieth century," he once told me, "will be the Christianization of China." With so mad a proprietor, it is no wonder that *Time-Life* should have led the press crusade against fags in general and Williams in particular.

Although Williams was able to survive as a playwright because he was supported by the reviewers of *The New York Times* and *Herald Tribune,* the only two newspapers that mattered for a play's success, he was to take a lot of flak over the years, often from Jewish journalists who employed—and employ—the same language in denouncing fags that sick Christians use to denounce Jews. After so much good-team propaganda, it is now widely believed that since Tennessee Williams liked to have sex with men (true), he hated women (untrue); as a result, his women characters are thought to be malicious caricatures, designed to subvert and destroy godly straightness.

But there is no actress on earth who will not testify that Williams created the best women characters in the modern theater. After all, he never ceased to love Rose and Rose; and his women characters tended to be either one or the other. Faced with contrary evidence, the anti-fag brigade promptly switch to their fallback position. All right, so he didn't hate women (as real guys do—the ballbreakers!) but, worse, far worse, *he thought he was a woman.* Needless to say, a biblical hatred of women intertwines with the good team's hatred of fags. But Williams never thought of himself as anything but a man who could, as an artist, inhabit any gender; on the other hand, his sympathies were always with those defeated by "the squares"; or by time, once the sweet bird of youth is flown. Or by death, "which has never been much in the way of completion." (p. 8)

All his life, Tennessee wrote short stories. I have just finished reading the lot of them, some forty-six stories. The first was written when Tom was seventeen: a sister avenges her brother in lush prose in even lusher Pharaonic Egypt; and published in *Weird Tales*. The last is unpublished. "**The Negative**" was written when Tennessee was seventy-one; he deals, as he so often came to do, with a poet, losing his mind, art; at the end, "as he ran toward this hugely tolerant receiver, he scattered from his gentleman's clothes, from their pockets, the illegibly scribbled poetry of his life."

To my mind, the short stories, and not his *Memoirs,* are the true memoir of Tennessee Williams. Whatever happened to him, real or imagined, he turned into prose. Except for occasional excursions into fantasy, he sticks pretty close to life as he experienced or imagined it. No, he is not a great short story writer like Chekhov but he has something rather more rare than mere genius. He has a narrative tone of voice that is wholly convincing. In this, he resembles Mark Twain, a very different sort of writer (to overdo understatement); yet Hannibal, Missouri, is not all that far from St. Louis, Missouri. Each is best at comedy and each was always uneasy when not so innocently abroad. Tennessee loved to sprinkle foreign phrases throughout his work, and they are *always* wrong. . . .

Tennessee could not possess his own life until he had written about it. This is common. To start with, there would be, let us say, a sexual desire for someone. Consummated or not, the desire ("something that is made to occupy a larger space than that which is afforded by the individual being") would produce reveries. In turn, the reveries would be written down as a story. But should the desire still remain unfulfilled, he would make a play of the story and then—and this is why he was so compulsive a working playwright—he would have the play produced so that he could, at relative leisure, like God, rearrange his original experience into something that was no longer God's and unpossessable but *his*. The Bird's frantic lifelong pursuit of—and involvement in—play productions was not just ambition or a need to be busy; it was the only way that he ever had of being entirely alive. (p. 9)

I had long since forgotten why I called him the Glorious Bird until I reread the stories. The image of the bird is everywhere in his work. The bird is flight, poetry, life. The bird is time, death: "Have you ever seen the skeleton of a bird? If you have you will know how completely they are still flying." In "**The Negative**" he wrote of a poet who can no longer assemble a poem: "Am I a wingless bird?" he writes; and soars no longer.

Although the Bird accepted our "culture's" two-team theory, he never seriously wanted to play on the good team. . . . (pp. 9–10)

The squares had indeed victimized the Bird but by 1965, when he came to write *The Knightly Quest,* he had begun to see that the poor squares' "virulent rage" is deliberately whipped up by the rulers in order to distract them from such real problems as, in the Sixties, the Vietnam War and Watergate and Operation Armageddon then—and now—under way. In this story, Tennessee moves Lyndon Johnson's America into a near future where the world is about to vanish in a shining cloud; and he realizes, at last, that the squares have been every bit as damaged and manipulated as he; and so he now writes an elegy to the true American, Don Quixote, an exile in his own country: "His castles are immaterial and his ways are endless and you do not have to look into many American eyes to suddenly meet somewhere the beautiful grave lunacy of his gaze." Also, Tennessee seems to be trying to bring into focus the outlandish craziness of a society which had so wounded him. Was it possible that he was not the evil creature portrayed by the press? Was it possible that they are wrong about *everything?* . . .

In story after story there are handsome young men, some uncouth like Stanley Kowalski; some couth like the violinist in **"The Resemblance Betweeen a Violin Case and a Coffin."** Then, when Tennessee produced *A Streetcar Named Desire,* he inadvertently smashed one of our society's most powerful taboos (no wonder Henry Luce loathed him): he showed the male not only as sexually attractive in the flesh but as an object for something never before entirely acknowledged by the good team, the lust of women. In the age of Calvin Klein's steaming hunks, it must be hard for those under forty to realize that there was ever a time when a man was nothing but a suit of clothes, a shirt and tie, shined leather shoes, and a gray felt hat. If he was thought attractive, it was because he had a nice smile and a twinkle in his eye. In 1947, when Marlon Brando appeared on stage in a torn sweaty T-shirt, there was an earthquake; and the male as sex object is still at our culture's center stage and will so remain until the likes of Boy George redress, as it were, the balance. Yet, ironically, Tennessee's auctorial sympathies were not with Stanley but with his "victim" Blanche. . . .

I did not see much of him in the last years. I don't recall when he got into the habit of taking barbiturates (later, speed; and

Williams posing. Photograph by Alex Gotfryd.

worse). He certainly did his mind and body no good; but he was tough as they come, mind and body. The current chroniclers naturally emphasize the horrors of the last years because the genre requires that they produce a Cautionary Tale. Also, since the last years are the closest to us, they give us no sense at all of what he was like for most of his long life. Obviously, he wasn't drunk or drugged all that much because he lived to write; and he wrote, like no one else.

I remember him best one noon in Key West during the early Fifties (exact date can be determined because on every jukebox "Tennessee Waltz" was being mournfully sung by Patti Page). Each of us had finished work for the day. We met on South Beach, a real beach then. We made our way through sailors on the sand to a terraced restaurant where the Bird sat back in a chair, put his bare feet up on a railing, looked out at the bright blue sea, and, as he drank his first and only martini of the midday, said, with a great smile, "I like my life." (p. 10)

> Gore Vidal, *"Immortal Bird," in* The New York Review of Books, *Vol. XXXII, No. 10, June 13, 1985, pp. 5-6, 8-10.**

GERALD WEALES

[*Weales, an American drama critic, is a winner of the George Jean Nathan Award for drama criticism and the author of numerous books on drama. He has also served as a theater critic for such journals as* Commonweal *and* The Georgia Review. *His books include, among others,* Tennessee Williams *(1965),* The Jumping-Off Place: American Drama in the 1960s *(1969), and his most recent work* Canned Goods as Caviar: American Film Comedy in the 1930s *(1985). In the following excerpt Weales cites Spoto's work as a conventional and useful biography, but one that nevertheless fails in its critical analysis of Williams's works.*]

The first biography off the presses after Tennessee Williams's death, on February 25, 1983, was the one subtitled *An Intimate Biography,* by the playwright's brother, Dakin, and Shepherd Mead. An accidental instance of the funeral baked meats, it was to have been released before Williams's death but was postponed so that a few paragraphs could be added about that grotesque and unhappy event. After Williams published *Memoirs,* in 1975, the adjective "intimate" held out small promise of titillation, and it was generally assumed that Dakin's book would be an answer to the angry accusations his brother had heaped on him for his part in the hospitalization that may have saved the dramatist's life in 1969. The book is self-justification to some extent, but it is also straightforward biography which, since Williams did not cooperate in any way, leans heavily on previously published works. . . . It does offer Dakin Williams's view of the family that, in various guises, peopled his brother's plays and fiction (Dakin assumes that it was a casually cruel remark of Tennessee's that finally "separated" their sister Rose "from her sanity") and there is some new material, but for the most part the book covers familiar ground. It has little of value to say about Williams's work. . . .

[In *The Kindness of Strangers*] Spoto lists Dakin as the "most important" of the many people he interviewed, although the bulk of the material he quotes could have been taken from the Williams-Mead book if it were not that Spoto regularly prefers his own interviews to published sources. . . .

He has consulted whatever records he could find and has attempted to sort out the facts of Williams's family background and of his unhappy years in St. Louis from Williams's somewhat mythical re-creations, which were presumably true for him emotionally and which were certainly important in his work. Spoto has identified the anonymous and pseudonymous men who pass in and out of **Memoirs** as they did of the playwright's life. He has conducted interviews with Williams's friends, former friends, associates and acquaintances, and has used these as his chief sources. They form the most valuable part of the book but also the most vulnerable, because, like Williams's remarks about himself, they are subject to the vagaries of memory, special interest, partial vision. There are obvious errors (the Group Theatre did not produce *Bury the Dead,* and Williams did not speak at the University of Pennsylvania in 1979) which would be unimportant blemishes if it were not that, although quotations are documented, presumed factual comments are not. Toward the end of the book, I began to have doubts about the accuracy of details. . . .

Williams became one of the best and most celebrated American playwrights, but his success, his fame, his money, gave him little peace. He was driven by his sexual needs, his hypochondria and his real illnesses, his fear of death, his guilt about the past, his sense of failure—driven literally, since he wandered the world restlessly in search of a cocoon he could call home. He had to be stroked, physically and spiritually, and by the end of his life his paranoia (its most public manifestations were his diatribes against critics) had pushed most of the strokers away. (p. 54)

In the midst of all this disorder and early (and late) sorrow, he remained an indefatigable worker who believed that a writer had to write. He also, at least intermittently, remained the charming, witty, sympathetic, understanding, affectionate man who over the years had made so many people love and want to protect him. Williams, who could make us feel both the cruelty and the helplessness of Blanche, her pain and her misused power, needs a biographer who can do him the same service. Spoto is not up to it. The last section of the book should have wiped me out with the horror of it all; instead it weighed me down with a stockpile of insecurities which finally made me understand the insensitive remark in the Williams-Mead book about the playwright's constant, loud announcement of impending death: ''He died only when he had nothing better to do.''

At the beginning of **The Dark Side of Genius,** Spoto says that while researching Alfred Hitchcock's life, he realized that the director's films ''were indeed his notebooks and journals.'' Given that approach, it is hardly surprising that he sees Williams's plays and stories primarily as reflections of his life. Perhaps that is what a biographer should do, but **The Kindness of Strangers** could use more acute comments on the works themselves. At least Spoto recognizes that it is Williams's work that makes a biography of the man desirable. (p. 55)

Until Williams gets a biographer who can treat his work with sympathy and acuity, his admirers may want to avoid both the naughty gossip books and the ''and then he went back to his home in Key West'' narratives and stick with revivals of his plays. After all, that is where he lives. (p. 56)

Gerald Weales, ''Funeral Baked Meats,'' in The Nation, *Vol. 241, No. 2, July 20 & 27, 1985, pp. 54-6.*

IRVING WARDLE

[Wardle is an English theater critic, dramatist, and biographer. In his The Theatres of George Devine *(1978), Wardle combines the life of theater director George Devine with a history of British theater from the 1930s to the present. In the following excerpt Wardle expresses his dissatisfaction with Spoto's biography and takes a different view of the dramatist's drug use.]*

What you get from **The Kindness of Strangers** (as that title promises) is the middlebrow academic line on Williams. It goes without saying that he was a great writer (so the claim never gets properly examined): on the other hand, what a disreputable and self-destructive life he led—and perhaps, in his heart of hearts . . . he really disapproved of homosexuality. The interdependence of creativity with sex and drugs remains unexplored; and likewise the transformation of people in Williams's life to the people in his plays. The autobiographical originals of Kowalski, Serafina and the rest are simply noted, so as to drag the plays down to the level of literal transcription. There is no evidence that Mr Spoto has ever set foot inside a theatre. Nor does he offer many personal close-ups of his subject, or long-range attempts to place it in cultural perspective. Instead, we get a dull, middle-distance narrative, veiling wild nights in Key West under words like 'bohemian', and chronicling events in deadpan sequence rather than organising them within a governing pattern. . . .

The fact remains that Mr Spoto has covered the ground. He is not much of a guide to the plays, nor to why they catapulted Williams into fame and riches beyond those of any other American playwright. But he has read all the material, interviewed all the available survivors, and assembled the only comprehensive account of what—by any standards—was a heroic life. (p. 8)

Williams was an extreme case of the writer as self-therapist. He identified with his sister to the extent of believing that, but for his portable typewriter, he too would have been institutionalised. Hence his refusal ever to forgive his brother Dakin for committing him to hospital for drug rehabilitation. The action may have saved his life, but Williams saw it as the ultimate treachery, as it denied his own powers of self-preservation and reduced him to the same helpless condition as his sister. To complete Vidal's statement: 'Above all, he is a survivor'.

When it comes to drugs, Mr Spoto is a mine of information: itemising the awesome intake of amphetamines, barbiturates, and novelties like glutethimide, washed down with gin, that headed the shopping list during the years (1963-69) which Williams later described as his 'stoned age'. As Mr Spoto views it, this is further evidence of his self-destructive nature, and another reason for equating him with the characters in his plays. It strikes me as much more likely that drugs—far from being a weak-natured indulgence—formed an essential instrument in his strategy of survival: and that, having worked his autobiographical sources dry in **Night of the Iguana** (1961), he turned to chemicals to keep his creative motor running. To write, he had to feel well; and any sacrifice was worth while if it gave him a few good hours at the typewriter every morning.

Physically, he came through the ordeal remarkably unimpaired. (His autopsy revealed a heart in Olympic condition). His loss, as Gregory Mosher points out, was that when he came to, 'he never really understood the changes in the American theatre', and awoke like Rip van Winkle into a strange world of resident theatres and non-profit production remote from his memories of all-powerful commercial producers and pre-Broadway tryouts.

In that sense perhaps he was lost. But that is no reason for associating him with the 'little company of the lonely and the lost' who appear on his stage. Writers figure prominently in Williams's plays; but none of them is a playwright. From *The Glass Menagerie* to *Vieux Carré* the writer is always a poet, and, one feels, a poet nobody will ever want to read.

Williams was such a poet himself: and generations of critics have saluted him as a 'lyrical' artist as though there were no difference between his stage work and his sub-Lawrentian outpourings in *Androgyne, Mon Amour.*

At this late date, the point still needs to be made that, so far as the theatre is concerned, Williams was and publicly proclaimed himself to be a comic writer. His work is entirely free from the airlessly confined atmosphere of McCullers, Faulkner and other Southern colleagues. From Tom's gloriously funny speech in *The Glass Menagerie*—imagining his mother astride a broomstick scouring the St Louis area for gentlemen callers—Williams declared himself a liberator, who could see around his characters and sustain mischief and irony with no loss of sympathy; and who, whatever his wounds, was always capable of taking wing. (pp. 8-9)

> *Irving Wardle, "Taking Wing," in* Books and Book-men, *No. 358, August, 1985, pp. 8-9.*

THOMAS MALLON

[*An American critic and professor, Mallon is the author of* A Book of One's Own *(1984), an informal study of the genre of literary diaries. In the following excerpt Mallon points to the enduring life of Williams's characters.*]

Donald Spoto did not win a reputation for gentlemanly restraint when he published his biography of Alfred Hitchcock (*The Dark Side of Genius*) a while back, which is why the general grace and judiciousness of *The Kindness of Strangers* may come

Williams in his later years. © 1986 Thomas Victor.

as a surprise to some readers. This is a thoughtful and well-proportioned book that celebrates Williams's "great period, 1944 to 1961" and attempts to explain the creative and personal slide that followed. (pp. 44-5)

Spoto's book, like Williams's life, is not solely about doom. There is intermittent amusement (what could be *more* amusing than knowing that Mary Martin and Gregory Peck were once mentioned as possibilities for Blanche DuBois and Stanley Kowalski?), and there is anecdotal glee: Williams is walking in London with the actress Sylvia Miles. She spots an emaciated girl and whispers to him, "Oh, Tennessee, look—anorexia nervosa." To which he replies: "Oh, Sylvia, you know everybody!"

What finally saves this book—what saved this life—from gloom and futility is not the odd anecdote or amusement, of course, but the work. If Spoto has committed any superfluity, it's in giving plot summaries of plays like *Streetcar* and *Glass Menagerie,* works that any remotely literate American mind now carries as part of its stock. There is something so powerfully living in Blanche and Amanda and Big Daddy and Maggie and Maxine that they can force belief from us even when they're set walking on the stages of a local dinner theater or community college. (p. 45)

Williams sends all of them, the men and women, toward clammy second-act hells. He has them sweat it out and battle back. Some of them make it. Hannah and Maggie drag Shannon and Brick home. Big Daddy fools cancer and lets out "a sigh of relief almost as powerful as the Vicksburg tornado." What finally happens to Blanche is questionable; Laura breaks like glass. But every one of them, so extraordinarily exaggerated, so prone to takeoff and imitation, remains firmly believable. Williams's heir to preeminence in the American theater is probably Sam Shepard, but to compare Williams's creations to Shepard's is to compare humans to humanoids. Shepard, for all his brilliance, likes to rob his characters of the last ten percent of real breath it would take to make us believe in them. There is finally a kind of heartlessness and perversity to much of what he writes. There is neither in Williams. The literal meaning of perverted is "turned the wrong way." It is perhaps the word most frequently applied—and most inappropriate—to this gifted and harrowed man, who in fact looked right at real human beings and came back with extraordinary news. As "the South's other great writer" might put it: He endures. (p. 46)

> *Thomas Mallon, in a review of "Kindness of Strangers: The Life of Tennessee Williams," in* The American Spectator, *Vol. 18, No. 9, September, 1985, pp. 44-6.*

TERRY TEACHOUT

Though he is by common consent America's leading modern playwright, many literate Americans remain highly uncomfortable with even the best work of Tennessee Williams: its Gothic subject matter, its emotional extravagance, its humid air of unreality. And they are just as uncomfortable with Williams the drug-sodden public figure, author of a squalid autobiography. Stanley Kauffmann once called Williams "a man who, although a giggling, silly, bitchy voluptuary, is the second most important dramatist this country has produced."

Donald Spoto faces this enigma head-on in *The Kindness of Strangers: The Life of Tennessee Williams.* In his preface, Mr. Spoto claims the status of "great art" for six of Williams's plays, rejects Williams's own *Memoirs* as a reliable primary source of information on the playwright's "deepest life," and depicts him as "a man more disturbing, more dramatic, richer, and more wonderful than any character he ever created." Mr. Spoto, then, has chosen to act as counsel for the defense; for him, there is no "Williams problem," only a solid body of work that, up through *The Night of the Iguana,* belongs "among the great literary and dramatic accomplishments of our time."

The first thing wrong with this approach is that Mr. Spoto has not taken the time to make his critical points. He devotes comparatively little space to any serious discussion of the plays themselves: The major ones get anywhere from five pages (*The Glass Menagerie*) to a page and a half (*The Night of the Iguana*). Moreover, he is simply not a very good critic, as his commentary on *The Glass Menagerie* shows:

> Transmuted through his memories of Rose's
> own glass collection is the purest poetic light—
> an arc of forgiveness (of fate and his mother),
> a ray of apologetic celebration of his sister's
> tragedy, a beam of understanding for himself
> and his own painful needs.

If *The Kindness of Strangers* strikes out as critical biography, how does it stand up as biography of record? Among other things, we are told nothing of Williams's reaction to the 1977 publication of his letters to Donald Windham; the summaries of critical responses to the various Williams plays make no mention of such key reviews as Stark Young's *New Republic* piece on *The Glass Menagerie* or Mary McCarthy's lethal *Partisan Review* article "A Streetcar Called Success"; and Mr. Spoto is inconsistent about supplying performance annals for the major plays. None of these omissions deprives the reader of essential information, of course, but the overall pattern suggests a lack of scholarly rigor—an impression strongly reinforced by the absence of even a token checklist of works and reviews.

The Kindness of Strangers, then, is a *popular* biography of Tennessee Williams, a book that must succeed or fail on its evocation of a personality. And it fails. The facts are here, and they are presented in a readable and orderly way; the voice of Williams himself, however, is absent. Quite literally so: *The Kindness of Strangers* contains no verbatim quotations whatsoever from Williams's correspondence—not even the published letters to Windham. Instead, we are given scattered remarks drawn from various newspaper and magazine interviews; when a Williams letter is mentioned, it is invariably paraphrased. Since Mr. Spoto does not trust *Memoirs* and tends to be sparing in his quotations from the plays and fiction, we are left wondering how we can apprehend the personality of an ostensibly great writer when his words are scarcely present. (p. 54)

[It] strikes me as a remarkable act of biographical arrogance for Mr. Spoto to have made so little use of *Memoirs* (seven citations in the index, most of them trivial) in a book that purports to reveal the "deepest life" of its subject. And it seems to me that Mr. Spoto's distrust of *Memoirs* is wrapped up with his diffidence in dealing with the central issue of Williams's sexuality.

This is not a matter of Mr. Spoto's trying to conceal the all too obvious: We are given names and dates in profusion. But it rarely goes further than that; Mr. Spoto evidently considers Tennessee Williams's sexual identity so peripheral that he is capable of waiting until page 320 to make the following comment:

> There was a negative quality, and an underlying
> resentment, to Williams's attitude to homosex-
> uality in his work. And Christopher Isherwood,
> Paul Bigelow, and Meade Roberts are among
> many who had the distinct feeling that Ten-
> nessee Williams in fact hated homosexuality,
> hated being homosexual, and could never ac-
> cept those who could come to peaceful terms
> with being one of a sexual minority.

The fact is that Williams's homosexuality, far from being a peripheral issue, is the key to any proper understanding of his dramatic world. Mr. Spoto, for example, appears to read *A Streetcar Named Desire* as a great play about realistically portrayed heterosexuals. The overwhelming impression created by the play in performance, however, is very different. Stanley, for all his vulgarity, is manifestly a symbol of perfect masculinity; Stella thrives by surrendering all of her traditional values to the "honesty" of a purely sensual relationship with Stanley; Blanche goes mad because (despite her own promiscuity) she is unable to see such a relationship as anything but "unnatural." Being a great playwright, Williams is able to give an electrically ambiguous surface reality to the characters of *A Streetcar Named Desire* and their sordid milieu; being an unhappy homosexual, he causes these "real" characters to interact in unreal and exaggerated ways that arouse the antagonism of ordinary viewers. Mary McCarthy said that "Dr. Kinsey would be interested in a semi-skilled male who spoke of the four-letter act as 'getting those colored lights going.'" It is exactly this kind of thing that (I suspect) makes most of us so uncomfortable with the imaginative world of Tennessee Williams.

Dr. Johnson, in words that deserve to be endlessly recalled, claimed that great literary art consists of "just representations of general nature" rather than "irregular combinations of fanciful invention." This is the Tennessee Williams problem compressed into a single sentence; it is a problem of which Donald Spoto seems to be unaware. Tennessee Williams at his best has a matchless ability to seize our attention; this is the gift of a truly great man of the theater. It's what he *does* with our attention that matters in the long run, though, and *The Kindness of Strangers* might have been a much better book had its author been better able to distinguish one kind of greatness from another. (pp. 54-6)

Terry Teachout, "Irregular Combinations," in National Review, *Vol. XXXVII, No. 20, October 18, 1985, pp. 54-6.*

Literary Criticism

The Flower and the Leaf: A Contemporary Record of American Writing since 1941

by Malcolm Cowley

An Excerpt from *The Flower and the Leaf: A Contemporary Record of American Writing since 1941*

Many American novels of the last twenty years, especially those by young men, are written in an exaggeratedly simple style, full of "ands," "all rights," and "anyways," full of accurate notes about the physical actions of the characters and flat statements about the way they felt. Book reviewers call it "the Hemingway style." Literary historians explain that it began as a combination of what Hemingway learned from Gertrude Stein and Sherwood Anderson with his oral memory of Midwestern speech. The truth is that it goes back much farther into the American past.

It began long ago as an attempt to reproduce the actual words and intonations of the American frontiersmen. Its earliest appearance was in humorous writing, and notably in the great collection of tales that gathered round David Crockett, the congressman from the canebrakes. Robert Montgomery Bird, of Philadelphia, was possibly the first to use something like the real language of frontiersmen in the dialogue of a novel: *Nick of the Woods,* published in 1837. Mark Twain, of Missouri, was the first to write a whole book and a serious book in the new style: of course it was *Huckleberry Finn.*

It was published in 1884, with an introductory note explaining that several dialects were used in it: "the Missouri Negro dialect; the extremist form of the backwoods Southern dialect; the ordinary 'Pike County' dialect; and four modified versions of the last." All the dialects are exactly rendered, when the characters start talking, but that isn't the important feature of the book, even from the standpoint of style. Its importance there is that Huck tells the story in his own words and that, besides being a modified version of the Pike County dialect, those words are also a literary medium capable of being used for many different effects: not only backwoods humor but also pity and terror and the majestic sweep of the river. Ernest Hemingway would say, many years later: "All modern American literature comes from one book by Mark Twain called 'Huckleberry Finn.' . . . There was nothing before. There has been nothing as good since."

There has been, however, a further development of this Mid-American style as a literary language. In a sense, Mark Twain had apologized for using it, by putting it into the mouth of an illiterate hero; it was not at all his own manner of speech. The next step was for an educated author to write the style when talking in his own person. That was the step taken by Gertrude Stein in her first

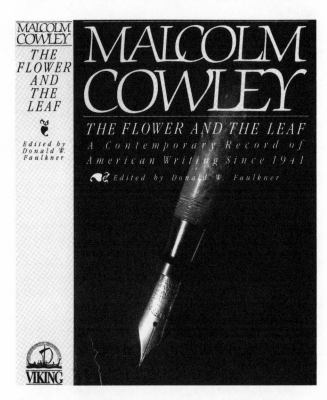

Dust jacket of The Flower and the Leaf: A Contemporary Record of American Writing, since 1941, by *Malcolm Cowley. Viking, 1984. Jacket design © Robert A. Reed, 1984. Jacket photograph © Jay J. Smith, 1984. By permission of Jay J. Smith.*

book, *Three Lives.* No publisher would accept the manuscript and she had to pay for having it printed; but the printer hesitated to do the work, even when payment of his charges were guaranteed. He sent an emissary to Miss Stein in Paris, to learn whether she was really illiterate. "You see," her visitor said hesitantly, "the director of the Grafton Press is under the impression that perhaps your knowledge of English . . ."—"But I am an American," said Gertrude Stein, as if that explained her whole manner of writing.

JONATHAN YARDLEY

Malcolm Cowley is now well into his 87th year, and the last thing he needs is an impertinent book reviewer barely half his age nipping at his heels over the shortcomings of his latest book. So let's get them out of the way at the outset. *The Flower and the Leaf* is a collection of odds and ends, mostly essays and reviews, several of which are excellent but many of which seem dated and, after all these years, thin. By contrast with Cowley's splendid volumes of memoirs and literary history, much of what is collected herein looks hasty and insufficient; a short review of a dreadful novel called *Women and Thomas Harrow,* for example, hardly serves as Cowley's summary pronouncement on the work of John P. Marquand, yet it is presented as such. Compared with *Exile's Return* or *A Second Flowering, The Flower and the Leaf* is in large measure a paste-up job.

Still, the writer being pasted up is Malcolm Cowley, and that alone is reason to pay respectful, admiring attention. These essays and reviews add little new to what Cowley has already told us about the generation of which he has been a principal chronicler—the generation that, in the 1920s, produced the "second flowering" of American literature—but they provide a welcome opportunity to read examples of Cowley's work that otherwise would remain buried in the back-issue files of the magazines and literary supplements in which they were originally published. The sum of all these parts is not very large, but the parts themselves are often enticing and agreeable.

Cowley's appearances as a book reviewer are infrequent these days, but in the '40s and '50s he was a formidably active critic who appeared regularly in *The New Republic, The Nation* and other magazines. He is quoted by his editor, Donald Faulkner, as saying of this period: "The relatively short book review was my art form for many years; it became my blank-verse meditation, my sonnet sequence, my letter to distant friends, my private journal. . . . As writers tend to do with any form imposed upon them by accident, I poured into it as much as possible of my adventures among events and opinions." This meant a certain amount of writing about books with political or social overtones, but primarily it meant passing judgment on the literary work of his contemporaries; at this he was astute, clear-eyed and outspoken.

For Cowley the reviewer nothing was so sacred as to be spared mordant commentary, and he seems never to have shied from writing against received opinion. In 1945, for example, he spoke highly of Gertrude Stein's *Wars I Have Seen,* but tempered his praise as follows:

> the great mystery about Gertrude Stein is how this woman with a real influence on American prose, so that her first book marks an era in our literature; this woman famous for her conversation, able to change the ideas of other writers, able to hold and dominate big audiences when she lectures, should at the same time have written books so monumental in their dullness, so many pyramids and Parthenons consecrated to the reader's apathy.

Similarly, here he comments on the work and personality of Ezra Pound:

> Spoiled work: that is the phrase for most of Pound's poems and I think for all the Cantos; they are never cheap or easy, never lacking in new phrases, but they are spoiled—and spoiled by vices that are inseparable from the virtues of his poetry; spoiled like the man himself by arrogance, crotchets, self-indulgence, obsessive hatreds, contempt for ordinary persons, the inability to see the world in motion (everything

in Pound's poems is frozen, as in a gallery of broken plaster casts), and finally by a lack of constructive power that keeps him from building his separate perceptions into unified works of art.

Both of these passages suggest what may be Cowley's greatest virtue as a reviewer: his capacity to see a writer's work in whole, to recognize both its strengths and its weaknesses and to give them proper weight. His comment on Theodore Dreiser is perfectly on target: "Dreiser is the clearest example in American literature, and perhaps in American life, of a man who possessed genius in its raw state, genius almost completely unfortified and unrefined by talent." Writing about Sinclair Lewis, he makes the accurate judgment that his novels after 1930 were pale imitations of the major work of the '20s, but also gives Lewis full credit for refusing to "write easy books after *Main Street*" and for serving as "the acknowledged center of a whole galaxy of gifted writers, the leader, so to speak, of a new generation." Marquand he describes as "a professional entertainer, and one of the best," but also gives him full credit as a student of "social stratification."

There is not a great deal of commentary in these pieces on broad literary questions, but such as is to be found is often telling. An excellent essay called **"The Limits of the Novel"** makes the point—you'd be astonished how many novelists ignore it—that "the novelist is compelled to meet only two stipulations," those being that "he must present characters in whom the reader can believe, and he must create a mood of expectancy." In some instances he displays a prescience that borders on the extraordinary; writing in 1954, for example, he remarks, "Unable to support themselves by writing books, many authors have been taking refuge in the universities, and that . . . might prove to be a danger to American writing."

In a way this comment echoes another that Cowley had made more than a decade earlier, when he bemoaned "the divorce of contemporary literature from contemporary life." This is a point to which he returns over and again—that literature must not retreat into the cloister, but reach out to the larger world in which it is situated—and one that has acquired special pertinence now that the university has become the cloister in which American fiction is hidden. By contrast with the prevailing opinion in today's literary climate, Cowley is an advocate of literature that seeks to embrace a large audience and to connect with it; he is out of fashion, perhaps, but he is right.

So it is good to have another book from him, even a paste-up job. As he wrote in 1954, while McCarthyism still seethed, "In our age of suspicion and intolerance we need more voices speaking for decency (not merely of language), good manners, and good sense." Malcolm Cowley's, need it be said, is precisely such a voice.

> *Jonathan Yardley, "The Critical Malcolm Cowley,"
> in* Book World—The Washington Post, *January 20,
> 1985, p. 3.*

ROBERT M. ADAMS

Though Malcolm Cowley's new book [*The Flower and the Leaf*] is subtitled "A Contemporary Record of American Writing Since 1941" and everything in the book was written in the last four decades, its roots go back at least 20 years earlier to the great transition of the 1920's. During that decade the last shaky props collapsed beneath the so-called genteel tradition and the whole bogus structure disintegrated. Its demise was largely the byproduct of independent and unrelated events. World War I and its disillusions, Prohibition and its absurdities, separate intellectual movements such as Freudianism, Marxism, Surrealism and Futurism (the latter experienced chiefly as a distant rumble from the Continent) cracked the facades of American respectability, provincialism and complacency.

A new generation of American writers, building on the work of the 1890 realists but responding to distinctively new social realities, exercised powerful and growing influence. The so-called "lost generation" may not have been lost in the sense of bewildered; but many of them felt so alienated from dominant American values that the sense of having lost the only war that counted was strong in them. Their challenge to the genteel tradition was direct and timely. After Judge Woolsey's 1933 decision lifting the ban on *Ulysses* and the almost simultaneous repeal of the Volstead Act, the walls had been breached, and the American citadel (once impregnable in its virtue) was open to all the variations on "modernism," "postmodernism" and cosmopolitan skeptical sophistication for which we haven't to this day settled on a proper terminology. After the mid-19th-century flowering, the change had been one of the two great turning points in American literary history.

From just about the beginning, Malcolm Cowley (born in 1898) was part of this tremendous transition, both as an observer and, to a lesser extent, as a participant. His sojourn in France just after the Armistice gave him a continuing interest in French writers and French culture; more important, it led to personal acquaintance with just about all the expatriate writers who clustered in Paris during the early 20's. (Eliot as a Londoner was something of an exception, and to Pound, Mr. Cowley was, as he remains, temperamentally antipathetic; but other than these, he knew just about everybody.) Then, starting around 1930, Mr. Cowley's return to America led to a career of literary journalism, mainly as weekly commentator for *The New Republic* and frequent contributor to *The New York Times Book Review*. For nearly 40 years he continued in this capacity, writing over 500 pieces, dealing perforce with the current run of literary production, but also consistently urging the case of the "new" writers, and interspersing his journalistic work with occasional volumes of more extended studies. Now that he is retired from regular service to the press, having long outlived his contemporaries and many of his juniors, he continues to bring out, from time to time, a collection of his old pieces.

The Flower and the Leaf is either the fourth or the fifth of this series, depending on how one defines the 1973 volume, *A Second Flowering*. (It is based on magazine articles, but much reworked and expanded; it is also, and incidentally, a splendid volume, perhaps Mr. Cowley's best.) All of these books deal primarily with American writing, to a considerable extent with American writers of Mr. Cowley's generation, and frequently with writers of his personal acquaintance. Invariably they are smoothly written, good-humored, more biographical than critical, modest in their methodological machinery and limited (quite apart from their original 1,200-word dimensions) by Mr. Cowley's polite and dryly skeptical sense of proportion.

Anyone who has written much literary commentary for periodical publication soon comes to appreciate the full meaning of the word "ephemeral." What one says drops silently and permanently into a yawning vacuum, where it is promptly joined by most of the books one has occasion to discuss. Things get written on the basis of an author's first book which will reveal themselves in a whole new light when he has written

his second or third. One doesn't have, in general, the blessed benefits of hindsight, nor, very often, the chance to do all the background reading and rereading one would like. The remarkable thing about Mr. Cowley is not that he wrote so frequently for so long, but that so many of the things he wrote have proved worth resurrecting.

To be sure, cultivating a limited field over a long period of time, he has not always avoided the peril of self-repetition; and the steady, sensible drift of his mind has not often led him off in pursuit of unfamiliar, "experimental" authors, or along the paths of abstract speculation. After a brief manic Marxist phase, fortunately unrepresented here, Cowley's admirations drifted slowly in a conservative—not quite a genteel—direction. In *The Flower and the Leaf* he has words of warm admiration for James Gould Cozzens and John O'Hara, only a little less enthusiasm for J. P. Marquand; one finds, on the other hand, no mention of Saul Bellow, Vladimir Nabokov, Jorge Luis Borges or Robert Lowell—not to mention movements like existentialism and the several intellectual strands that came together as structuralism. Black authors have never enjoyed the encouragement of his notice, and female writers—with a few exceptions—receive short shrift. Mr. Cowley's real heroes are the members of his own generation, to whose work he has continually recurred—Fitzgerald, Hemingway, Wilder, Cummings, Faulkner, Thomas Wolfe and Hart Crane. They were all white, male and middle-class; they were all imbued with a spirit of rather truculent honesty, and with that puritan work-ethic that invites an artist to treat himself as an engine in the hands of his literary calling. When Mr. Cowley departs from their company, he tends to look further backward, to Hawthorne, Twain and Whitman, rather than forward to writers such as Barth, Pynchon, Updike, and even wilder indigenes like Burroughs et al.

For, fundamentally, Mr. Cowley's talent in criticism has lain in the gift of friendship. With critical theories and nuances of technique he has never been much at home; rather, his talent lies in interpreting his friends (including some whom he knew only on the printed page) to a suspicious and grudging American public. The phrases recall his own appraisal of Van Wyck Brooks, and the larger comparison makes itself. They both campaigned long and hard to win recognition for an authentic American tradition in literature.

One aspect of Mr. Cowley's gift for friendship calls for special comment; surely his association with Kenneth Burke must qualify for the Guinness Book of Records. They first knew one another at the age of 3 or 4, and are still amicable acquaintances as 90 looms just around the corner. In the present volume, fidelity to old friends and old enemies leads to the occasional odd effect. Anno Domini 1985, one is surprised to find Mr. Cowley harking back to Bernard DeVoto—whose controversial book, *The Literary Fallacy*, appeared almost half a century ago and has not been much studied since—in an article taking him to task for his injustices to the authors of the 1920's. These echoes of distant wars (the flap over Pound's Bollingen award, the fuss over Mr. Cowley's 1949 appointment as visiting lecturer at the University of Washington) have a historical interest these days amounting almost to quaintness. But a reader's memory is likely to linger just as long, or longer, on a gentle vignette of a Connecticut village during World War II; an affectionate tribute to Thurber, or an image of Maxwell Perkins defending to old Mr. Scribner Hemingway's use of a word that Perkins couldn't bring himself to pronounce or even write on a pad of paper.

As if to emphasize the personal element, the last part of *The Flower and the Leaf* consists largely of brief elegiac tributes to departed friends. They are simple, quiet, individual statements, serene in their dignity, and retrospective rather than judgmental. No doubt it's premature to declare *The Flower and the Leaf* a valedictory, but if it should prove so, the ceremony will have been completed with grave decorum. (pp. 16-17)

Robert M. Adams, "He Knew Them All," in The New York Times Book Review, *February 10, 1985, pp. 16-17.*

JAMES R. MELLOW

[Malcolm Cowley] is perfectly aware of the cold wars of the literary life, the rivalries and backbiting of the profession. In a neatly turned summary of the position of the aged-man-of-letters, he writes:

> Ambitious writers, painters, lawyers, scientists and politicians have lived among professional jealousies since their apprentice days; they are used to being politely stabbed in the back; but if they survive to a fairly advanced age they find that most—not all—of the old vendettas have been interred.

The writer who escapes the paranoia that is one of the occupational hazards of the profession commands respect. The essays of *The Flower and the Leaf,* shrewdly selected by Donald W. Faulkner to show the range of the author's interest, constitute one of the best collections of Cowley's journalistic criticism yet published.

The essays span the years from World War II to the present. The style is easy and conversational—even confidential; the opinions and evaluations of the literary and social scene are remarkable for their sanity and even-handedness. As a critic, Cowley is still the man "of good will"; he brings love and dedication to the task. Only seldom does he use the cutting edge—and then, usually, for good reason.

The book is full of wonderful surprises; a remarkable essay, for instance, on **"The Middle-American Prose Style,"** prompted by, of all things, Gertrude Stein's vivid memoir of life in occupied France, *Wars I Have Seen.* Cowley's own wartime essays, particularly **"Town Report: 1942,"** are full of accurately drawn vignettes of that time in American life.

There is a long essay on Nathaniel Hawthorne and his bride, Sophia Peabody—a cautious couple passing their middling age—honeymooning blissfully at the Old Manse in Concord. American literature of the "first flowering" is still very much part of Cowley's territory, and there are interesting studies on Whitman and Poe.

In a 1954 essay, **"Some Dangers to American Writing,"** written during the great public advent of television, Cowley warns against the narrowing of focus of academic criticism, of the "specialized bureaucracy" of the scholar-writer: "Today for the first time we have to admit the possibility of a situation in which American writing would be confined to an elite of scholars, in which it would become as elaborate and dead as late-Roman writing, and in which the public would find its esthetic satisfactions in bang-bang gunsmoke on the television screen."

Cowley's prophecy may have been a bit too dire. Like several of the literary alarms and fads of the postwar years—remember the death of the novel, the greening of America, the apocalyptic

visions of Marshall McLuhan with his message that "The medium is the message"?—the Great Divide between the writer and the American public-at-large has not occurred, though there are, to be sure, some visible cracks.

Some of the most incisive of Cowley's reviews in *The Flower and the Leaf* are the later, briefer ones: a dissenting opinion on H. L. Mencken, a reappraisal of John O'Hara's novels. Even the retrospective essays on writers such as Fitzgerald and Hemingway about whom Cowley has written often have something more to say to a younger generation of readers.

In a reversal of the usual trend, Cowley seems only to have sharpened his wits on old age. And, gratifyingly, his enthusiasm for the subjects to which he has dedicated a literary lifetime—the power of writing, the link between literature and life, his pride in American achievement—is still untarnished.

James R. Mellow, "Cowley Provides Guide to Survive Literary Cold Wars," in Chicago Tribune, *March 3, 1985, p. 25.*

BRUCE ALLEN

Malcolm Cowley's many books and essays on domestic literary subjects entitle him to the status of spokesman for what he calls "a great period in American letters"—the 1920s partway into the '30s. It was a time dominated by Hemingway, Fitzgerald, Wolfe, and Faulkner, among others; they were Cowley's revered contemporaries and, in some cases, his friends as well.

This new collection of Cowley's occasional writings [*The Flower and the Leaf*] shows that his range extends rather beyond the period with which he is usually identified. There are knowledgeable essays here on classic American writers and a few vivid pieces focused on British and European writers and topics. What all these writings reveal is a relaxed and plain-spoken prose style and an impressive attentiveness to the social and political dimensions of the literary works that compel Cowley's interest. The best of these pieces (cut, of course, to fit editorial word limits) are frustratingly brief. We sense Cowley's deep and sympathetic interest in everything he writes about and, almost always, wish his essays were longer.

Part 1, "The War Years and After," includes miscellaneous reviews of biographies and memoirs describing how World War II was experienced at home and abroad. It also speculates at length about writers' difficulties with rendering the war. Cowley offers personal testimony on the postwar "loyalty crusades" that pretended to find subversive opinions everywhere, and "the atmosphere of anti-intellectualism" that clouded the early 1950s.

In Part 2, "The Usable Past," Cowley examines earlier American writers, literary movements, and styles. There's a charming portrayal of Nathaniel Hawthorne as devoted lover and husband, and a keen reading of Walt Whitman's 1855 first edition of *Leaves of Grass,* the definitive version graced by "all the gay impudence and vivid Yankeeisms that were excised from later editions."

In **"The Middle American Prose Style,"** Cowley traces one dominant strain in our writing from the frontier humorists through Twain, Hemingway, and Gertrude Stein. And the superb **"Hemingway at Midnight"** persuasively places that figure among the "haunted" writers Poe, Hawthorne, and Melville. (Hemingway's heroes, Cowley observes, "live in a world that is like a hostile forest, full of unseen dangers.")

Part 3 includes "Assessments and Retrospections," both of more recent writers and of older ones completing their careers. Examples are:

● Cowley's generous readings of Thornton Wilder's novel *The Eighth Day* and Faulkner's flawed completion of his Snopes trilogy, *The Mansion*.

● A lively remembrance of **"Ken Kesey at Stanford,"** when he was Cowley's writing student.

● And a moving memoir of the career of John Cheever, whom Cowley knew first as a brash beginning writer adrift in New York City, then, half a century later, as a chastened old man quietly facing death.

All the essays display Cowley's lightly worn learning and gift for resonant statement. He's the sort of critic who can suggest that Thomas Wolfe "saved his discarded scenes as plumbers save length of pipe, and eventually fitted them into other novels." He's also widely read enough to note (in an essay on James Thurber) "a curious similarity between one type of fantastic American humor and the current in European poetry that is represented in various phases by Rimbaud and Lautréamont, by expressionism, dadaism, and surrealism."

The book is adroitly edited and arranged by Donald Faulkner so that its contents in sequence observe, not just a formal logic, but also a rising interest and tension that evoke the pleasures of reading an absorbing novel. I don't know when I have so enjoyed a volume of criticism, and I can recommend this one without reservation.

> *Bruce Allen, "A Critic's Plain-Spoken Views of American Literature since 1941," in* The Christian Science Monitor, *May 1, 1985, p. 28.*

HANS BAK

The pertinence of [critic James Michael Kempf's] claim that "Cowley's literary beliefs in mid-career were an outgrowth of the beliefs with which he started" is amply proven by *The Flower and the Leaf,* a compilation of Cowley's uncollected essays and reviews since 1941. A sequel to *Think Back On Us . . .* (1967) and a companion volume to *A Many-Windowed House* (1970), it makes available another important segment of his writings hitherto buried in the backfiles of magazines. These essays and reviews form but a fraction of Cowley's literary output of the last forty years; much of his best critical, historical, and memoiristic writing was incorporated in the ten books that have seen the light since the revised edition of *Exile's Return* (1951). Given the limits to the editor's freedom of selection—he had to make a responsible choice out of five hundred articles, the best of which were no longer available to him—Donald Faulkner has done a perceptive and praiseworthy job. Though the present collection is less unified and homogeneous than its two predecessors, Faulkner has learned from Cowley the value of arranging seemingly disparate pieces within a roughly chronological or thematic framework so as to make visible certain recurrent leitmotifs.

These fifty-five articles are diverse in kind and quality, ranging from the short review to the examination of a whole career or oeuvre, from the broad survey of the literary landscape to the affectionate personal memoir. Collectively, they illuminate the versatility of Cowley's functions and concerns as critic, literary historian, teacher, editor, and "middleman" of letters, even as they display his special talents: an uncanny sense of social and historical context, a predilection for narrative in criticism, an ability to see a writer's life and writings as an organic whole, a poet's capacity for singling out a writer's strength or weakness in fresh, startling imagery, and an almost sacred respect for his readers.

The Flower and the Leaf testifies how, after the failure of his radical hopes and his break with politics in 1942, Cowley continued to record the changes in the literary landscape and to stand guard over the writing profession. Having settled his intellectual accounts in a sober investigation of the failure of Communism (**"Communism and Christianity"**), he remained sensitive to the social and historical ramifications of American writing, but avoided political controversy and aimed to survive the expected counter-purge with grace and self-respect. Much more so than the Hitler-Stalin Pact, it was the Fall of France in June 1940 that had a traumatic impact on Cowley and destroyed the last vestiges of his faith in the radical movement. In several articles he made a painful effort to understand why and how his beloved "second country" had surrendered and plunged into a state of "lethargic despair." In a beautiful essay on the wartime poetry of a one-time Dada friend, Louis Aragon, he discussed the role played by writers in the rebirth of French patriotism; a labor of love, the essay stood as proof of his continued allegiance to French culture.

Cowley was moved by the fate of European refugee writers and intellectuals. He found American writers shirking the social and political dilemmas of contemporary reality, and he scolded them for neglecting a chief duty: to make an effort towards "intellectual and emotional understanding of what was happening in the world." In the 1940's and 1950's Cowley consistently exhorted writers in a similar vein, hoping to avert what he saw as a fatal "divorce of contemporary literature from contemporary life."

From his early acquaintance with the French, Cowley retained a feeling for the unity of culture and the interrelatedness of all aspects of the literary trade; he wrote with equal expertise on the "business" of literature, the sociology of the writing profession, and the state of the publishing world. Thus, it was only natural for him to be sensitive to the significance of an editor like Maxwell Perkins and to write a classic profile, **"Max Perkins in 1944."** Cowley's awareness of the literary profession as "interdependent at all its levels" prompted him to speak up in its defense whenever he saw it threatened. He was skeptical about the inroads made into the writing trade by commercialism and collectivization, and he feared that writers might lose their status as "independent craftsmen" to become officials in a bureaucratic structure, possessing technical virtuosity but paralyzed by timidity, conventionality, and lack of personal courage. During the McCarthy years he was disturbed by the pervasive (and popular) mood of anti-intellectualism, by the decline of the reading habit, and by the potentially dangerous effects of an alliance between creative writing and academic careerism.

Cowley's humanism, pluralism, and eclecticism are apparent throughout *The Flower and the Leaf.* Always sensitive to the diversity of American writing, he has resisted any monolithic or reductive approach, whether exemplified in the distortions of literary nationalism (as in Bernard De Voto's *The Literary Fallacy*) or in the psychoanalytic reductivism of Leslie Fiedler's *Love and Death in the American Novel*. Consistent with his early ambiguity about a modernist aesthetics, Cowley continued to urge young writers to meet the challenges of contemporary reality, to find new forms, and to speak in their own voices. By the mid-1950's, however, the newer forms of fiction were not much to Cowley's liking. Though his conception of the novel remained open and flexible enough—witness his efforts on behalf of Kerouac's *On the Road*—it insisted too strongly on a mimetic, realistic, humanistic art to accommodate the bulk of postmodernist experimentalism. Rather, Cowley found himself attracted to an unclassifiable master craftsman like Thornton Wilder or conservative writers who intuitively grasped the shaping force of social reality in individual life—writers such as Marquand, O'Hara, or Cozzens ("the greatest architect in contemporary American fiction").

Cowley's later reviews lack the exhilarating sense of drama and discovery that marked his short writings in the 1930's and 1940's. At some point in the late 1950's his role as the barometric chronicler of his literary time lost its dramatic momentum. He was now an official member of the literary establishment, although he resisted becoming enshrined and continued to play an active role in the "commonwealth of letters." He remained generous and open to young writers—as scout and editorial adviser to Viking Press and as a lecturer and teacher at writers' conferences and in academia. The account of his writing class at Stanford in 1960 (including Ken Kesey, Larry McMurtry, and Peter S. Beagle) illustrates his role as a confidant, adviser, and exhorter of new talent.

From the first Cowley has conceived of American writers as a community of individual craftsmen, each fiercely devoted to his or her special talent and vision, yet all engaged in a united literary endeavor. For Cowley, as for Edmund Wilson, the advancement of literature has been "in great part a collaborative venture." Like Allen Tate's, his "true home" has been in the timeless and placeless Republic of Letters, but also in close touch with the American soil he loves. His republic is a realm which he likes to define, in typical pluralistic fashion, as a "loose federation composed of many dukedoms and principalities." In recent years Cowley's lifelong loyalty to his friends (here apparent in pieces on Kenneth Burke, Conrad Aiken, Allen Tate, Robert Penn Warren, Edmund Wilson, and John Cheever), has also given him another and sadder role in the republic of letters: more than anyone else he has become its retrospective celebrant and elegiac poet-in-prose, its memoirist and obituarist.

The Flower and the Leaf is Cowley's ninth book to appear in nineteen years. Though not his best, in my opinion, it forms an impressive testimony to his ongoing critical vitality and his sustained capacity for growth and productivity. Cowley deserves to be seen, as his editor here rightly claims, not as a "museum piece" of the Lost Generation, but as a living and vigorous writer whose words have a continuing relevance. (pp. 652-54)

Hans Bak, "Malcolm Cowley and the Rehumanization of Art," in The Georgia Review, *Vol. XXXIX, No. 3, Fall, 1985, pp. 649-54.*

Plausible Prejudices: Essays on American Writing

by Joseph Epstein

(See also *Contemporary Authors,* Vol. 112)

An Excerpt from *Plausible Prejudices: Essays on American Writing*

Book reviews are among those things people who write books despise but find it difficult to live without. Edmund Wilson, in his essay "The Literary Worker's Polonius," noted: "For an author, the reading of his reviews, whether favorable or unfavorable, is one of the most disappointing experiences in life." Yet in *Upstate,* a collection of journal entries from his last years, Wilson remarked that "getting older, for a writer, did not necessarily give you self-confidence. . . . I sometimes got up at four o'clock in the morning to read old reviews of my books." The worst of writing, as more than one writer has written, is that one depends so much on the opinions of others. . . .

Perhaps I ought to make a distinction between good reviews and reviews that sell books. The best book reviews are only rarely what the publishers can call "sell reviews." Sell reviews tend to be blurby: "Don't exhale till you have read this." Good reviews can sell books, yet sell reviews are not usually good. Sell reviews are a part of advertising, and it is always a bit embarrassing witnessing a good writer setting out to write one. Even Edmund Wilson was not above this sort of thing. It is sad to read his review of Svetlana Alliluyeva's *Only One Year,* for instance, which will take its place, Wilson tells us, "among the great Russian autobiographical works: Herzen, Kropotkin, Tolstoy's *Confession.*" I don't know why Wilson wanted to give a push to the feeble literary effort of Stalin's daughter, but push, clearly, he did, for the line I have quoted is, along with not being true, sheer *blurbissimo.*

What is a good book review? A first-blush answer is, I suppose, the product of an interesting mind thinking about a book. But there is more to it than that. A reviewer has certain obligations to the book he's reviewing and to his own readers: he must report what the book is saying; he must make a judgment about how well the author gets it said; and he must determine if what has been said was worth saying in the first place. Not to be dull, not to be fearful, not to scamp the duties of clear summary—these are the minimum requirements that a good book reviewer must meet.

Yet another quality ought to be part of his temperamental equipment, and this is a controlled anger aroused by breaches in literary justice. When bad writers are praised or good writers neglected or ill-understood, he should

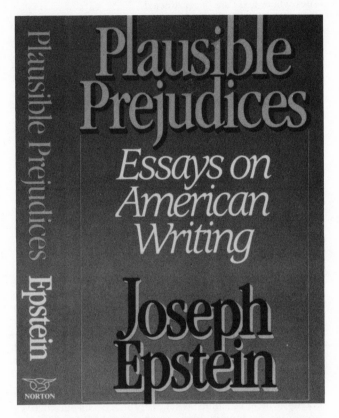

Dust jacket of Plausible Prejudices: Essays on American Writing, *by Joseph Epstein. Norton, 1985. Copyright © 1985 by Joseph Epstein. Jacket design by Terry Fehr. By permission of W. W. Norton & Company, Inc.*

feel personally offended. His pique, though, ought to be more than personal. Judging books correctly is of the utmost seriousness to him; misjudging a novel is of no less consequence than, say, misjudging a friendship.

STEVENSON SWANSON

In the last four or five years, Joseph Epstein's most interesting work has been his literary criticism. As the fiction critic for *Commentary* and, more recently, as a contributor to the *New Criterion,* he has—to borrow his description of the book critic's tasks—remarked upon unappreciated writers, let the air out of many inflated reputations, opposed several literary tendencies he has found pernicious, and called to the fore essential but neglected traditions. That his literary essays were worth preserving in a book has never been in doubt.

Epstein, who teaches at Northwestern University and edits the *American Scholar*, writes pieces of lasting interest because he uses a passing moment—the publication of a book—as the occasion for an evaluation of the author's work up to that moment, a method borrowed from Edmund Wilson, one of Epstein's heroes. Following Wilson's example, Epstein reads an author's works, identifies the common elements and themes, leavens criticism with biography, and tries to place the writer in his time and in the larger tradition of literature. In Epstein's work, there are no safaris in search of symbols, no demolition sites where texts are deconstructed.

But one of Wilson's most important aims, the explaining of the methods and purposes of Modernism, is not, understandably, on Epstein's critical agenda. As literature waits to be led out of the cul-de-sac that Modernism has become, Epstein takes his main jobs to be the upholding of standards and the restoration of literature to its former place of importance. They are not jobs for the faint-hearted, as he makes clear in his introduction [to *Plausible Prejudices: Essays on American Writing*]:

> My case is that literature is going through a very bad patch at present—that there is something second-rate about it. I find the case I have to make extremely sad because I believe that literature, considered as an institution, is in important respects a barometer that measures the quality of the culture as a whole. I also believe that literature can be a joyous thing in and of itself and that of late, in this regard, it has been failing its audience badly.

Appearing on stage to Epstein's boos are such fashionable writers as John Updike, Ann Beattie, Norman Mailer, Philip Roth, Bernard Malamud, John Irving, Renata Adler and Joan Didion. An "older crowd" of writers receives his applause: Edmund Wilson, Van Wyck Brooks, Willa Cather, A. J. Liebling, John Dos Passos and, most impressively, James Gould Cozzens, whose reputation Epstein attempts to resurrect in the best essay of the collection.

The best novelists, he believes, have a quality that he calls gravity, which, he admits, is not easily understood but "derives from a serious literary mind, unencumbered by the cliches of the day, at work on serious matters." It is not a quality in conspicuous abundance nowadays. "Among living writers, I would say Aleksandr Solzhenitsyn has it; so, when they are writing well, do V. S. Naipaul and Saul Bellow and I. B. Singer. John Updike and Gabriel Garcia Marquez do not, and Norman Mailer never will."

Epstein's long practice in writing familiar essays for the *American Scholar* has given his literary criticism a jauntiness that makes *Plausible Prejudices* enjoyable but less plausible because the tone of authority that is indispensable to a critic on the attack is weakened. The people who need to be convinced by this book may instead dismiss Epstein as a lightweight—which he is not—who cannot stand the unpleasant truths of modern life—which he can. They will be all the more tempted to dismiss him because of his tendency not to give supporting quotations or to expand on ideas that are provocative but not self-evident; when he writes that criticism must turn to biography to have serious standing as literature, the reader wants more to help him understand and judge the idea.

But the main thing is that the reader wants more rather than less. After finishing *Plausible Prejudices*, one wants to know what Epstein thinks of other American writers; Saul Bellow would make an excellent subject. And what are his opinions of English novelists? The great Victorian writers? American writers of the 1920s? In fact, what does Epstein think of every writer who has ever lived?

Stevenson Swanson, "Epstein: Jaunty 'Prejudices' from Deflationary Critic," in Chicago Tribune, February 24, 1985, p. 32.

RICHARD EDER

Yeats wrote of a generation that felt "more passion in our enmities than in our loves." Joseph Epstein doesn't quite convince us of the passion in his enmities, but he certainly gets a lot of fun out of them; more fun, I believe, than out of his loves, which seem blurry.

Editor of *The American Scholar*, Epstein writes about literature for a number of other publications, notably *Commentary* and the *New Criterion*. They inhabit what is known as the New Right, and so, I suppose, does Epstein. At times, he manages to button up with the best of that buttoned-up crowd, but there is considerable laughter at work and the buttons keep popping off.

His mother never raised him to be a critic, belonging to the generation and neighborhood that held that if you couldn't say something nice, you shouldn't say anything at all. But a critic he turned out to be, a shrewd, outspoken and often wrongheaded one.

In this latest collection of essays [*Plausible Prejudices: Essays on American Writing*], he is once again the Sword of Justice against literary liberalism, trendiness and all the main currents of the past decades. He calls himself a sheriff whose job is to head off writers at the pass. The sword doesn't hold quite steady, though; there is too much disarming wit and sneaky fair-mindedness at work. He looses off terrible volleys, but shoots more to startle than to kill.

The theme, or ostensible theme, for *Plausible Prejudices* is enunciated by Epstein as follows: "American writing itself has never seemed less important and more lost than it does now." I say "ostensible theme"; in fact, it is a set of colors that Epstein pins to his helmet so as to obtain the maximum possible amount of combat in the literary jousts that he so plainly enjoys.

Some of the essays, in fact, devote more energy to the literary wars than to the literature. Epstein denounces a politics that he claims favors liberal and left-wing writers at the expense of conservatives. When under full battle steam, he tends to treat writers in terms of how they are treated; he will have at Updike or Renata Adler or Joan Didion for the inflated quality of the reviews they get or a pretentious pose in a publicity shot.

He can be ferocious with other critics. As to the writers themselves, there is an odd and winning disparity between the war cries he broadcasts into the air, as it were, and the sensitivity he demonstrates to the work of those of whom, theoretically speaking, he disapproves.

Epstein comes close, in fact, to a marvelously unreasonable formula. The writers he dislikes, he dislikes. The writers he likes, he dislikes—for not writing better. He is ferocious with Philip Roth's solipsistic sexual bravura. "Roth can describe sex as easily as Dickens could describe London, though the views Dickens offers are more interesting."

He is almost equally, and, to my mind, much more obtusely hard on Updike. He can be funny about some of the writers' stylistic flourishes: "In Updike, there is always time to type out a bit of tapestry." But he pretty well ignores the achievement of *Couples* and the Rabbit trilogy, treating them largely in terms of sexual display. He seizes on one of Updike's weakest books—*Marry Me*—to make a general case. "Why would a novelist write such a book?" he demands; which is like asking, "Why would a playwright write *Titus Andronicus*?"

But more usually, with Adler, Didion, Ann Beattie, Robert Stone, his stand against liberal trendiness is undermined by his appreciation for the writers' talents and strengths. They are spoiled, he more or less argues, because they fall short at some point, but he has transmitted his pleasure too convincingly for the demure to have much weight. "He is, in the strict sense of the word, marvelous," he writes of the left-leaning Gabriel Garcia Marquez. "The pity is that he is not better." Mt. Aconcagua is high, in other words; the pity is that it is not higher.

There is some absurdity in this, yet, it is an absurdity I rather like. Epstein's love of battle continually comes up against a sensitive and honest critical mind. He is cantankerous and outrageous, sometimes, but he is not usually mean, and he scolds John Simon, his fellow Tory, for "free-floating nastiness" and adds that "he is the sort of writer who, when one finds oneself agreeing with him, makes one instantly want to reconsider one's own position."

In fact, for all of Epstein's wit and high spirits, you wonder at times what he is defending. It is clear what he is attacking. He is against hype, pretentiousness and knee-jerk liberalism. He is also, quite rightly, against critical inflation—the kind of thing that regularly discovers a new masterpiece every four weeks.

But, what remains after all of Epstein's targets are targeted? Who has been unfairly savaged by the liberal cabal? He mentions James Gould Cozzens and the later, conservative John Dos Passos. Yet, when he comes to deal with their work, his sensibility forces him to concede that Dos Passos' later work was mediocre and to give a decidedly mixed analysis of Cozzens. He tries to like Van Wyck Brooks for the liberal attacks upon him, but he doesn't really manage.

Epstein's ideological dislikes are scintillating. His ideological enthusiasms are non-contagious. One wonders where his real enthusiasm is.

For contention, clearly. For literature, also clearly. And more clearly still, for a delight in writing with wit and revelry.

> Richard Eder, "*Of Enmity without Passion*," in Los Angeles Times Book Review, *February 24, 1985, p. 7.*

WILLIAM PRITCHARD

[*Pritchard is an American critic, biographer, and professor of literature. He has written several books on modern poets and poetry, including* Wyndham Lewis: Profile in Literature *(1972) and* Lives of the Modern Poets *(1980). Pritchard is also the author of a biography of Robert Frost titled* Frost: A Literary Life Reconsidered *(1984). In the following excerpt Pritchard summarizes and evaluates Epstein's main arguments.*]

Joseph Epstein believes, and asserts more than once in the essays collected [in *Plausible Prejudices: Essays on American Writing*], that literature should deal with "life" and deal with it in ways both grave and joyous. By a similar token, literary criticism should hold to standards in a disinterested way. So as not to be overwhelmed by last month's latest great novel, it should demand from literature what Matthew Arnold (about whom Mr. Epstein has written with admiration) called high seriousness. Mr. Epstein's writing—five books in 10 years—is characterized by a sprightly, idiomatic irreverence toward established or (he would say) "liberal" pieties, and as he exposes false gods, an irrepressible wit is constantly breaking into his own high seriousness. His penchant for killer one-liners makes it impossible for him to go on about anything for very long without making a joke.

Over the last 10 years he has published five books and edited an excellent group of essays (*Masters*) on great teachers. Last year he published **The Middle of My Tether,** a consistently entertaining collection of his essays from *The American Scholar,* of which he is the editor. In one of these, **"Balls-Up,"** he describes his passion for amateur juggling and assures us that to practice this art it is unnecessary to dress up in fancy clothes: "I myself, when juggling, wear the simplest costume: buskins turned up at the toes, gold pantaloons, a leathern jerkin, and a cap with bells." The new book of essays on American writing is as complicatedly at ease: each piece in its four sections is written in a relatively informal, anti-pompous style that accommodates words like "zippy" while fending off—with the most scornful of quotation marks—words like "viable," "supportive" or "experience" used as a verb.

Like his "simplest" juggling costume, Mr. Epstein's informal style is not all simple, as may be seen from the following sentences about two contemporaries:

> I do not have the attention span to sustain a lengthy depression, but I have of late been reading two novelists who do: Renata Adler and Joan Didion. I think of them as the Sunshine Girls, largely because in their work the sun is never shining. If weather reports were offered in novels, in their novels the forecast would almost always be gray, mostly cloudy, chill winds, with a strong chance of rain. They seem, these two writers, not really happy unless they are sad. They keep, to alter the line from an old song, a frown on their page for the whole modern age. Muriel Spark once wrote an interesting book entitled *Girls of Slender Means*. Miss Adler and Miss Didion are slender women who write slender books heavy with gloom.

"Criticism is prejudice made plausible," runs the book's epigraph from H. L. Mencken. The above paragraph seems to me a plausible beginning for a critical account of Renata Adler and Joan Didion, and not the least for its "zippy" inventions of the Sunshine Girls, the weather report, the alteration of the popular song and the play with "slender" ("sexism," a voice will surely pronounce). These inventions are amusing and satisfying not in themselves, but because they issue from a relevant response to the novels of Miss Adler and Miss Didion. They organize our previously unformulated sense of the two writers by making us recognize something we didn't know we knew.

The book's main prejudice, which it bids to make plausible through repeated demonstration, is that American literary culture is in bad shape. In an essay-review of an already justly forgotten book, *The Harvard Guide to Contemporary Litera-*

ture, Mr. Epstein argues that "American writers have never received so much attention or been so institutionally well supported—and never has contemporary literature seemed quite so besides the point, so peripheral, so trivial." It lacks the "high and undeflected seriousness" he finds in such writers as Alexsandr Solzhenitsyn, V. S. Naipaul and Marguerite Yourcenar (the last a particular favorite of his). While our literary culture shows a few graceful poets (about whom Mr. Epstein does not write), it lacks a "towering literary figure." Some of its most admired novelists—Norman Mailer, Philip Roth, John Updike, Bernard Malamud—get poor grades from Mr. Epstein, while younger ones like Robert Stone, Ann Beattie and John Irving (the last is nicely skewered here) are chastised, respectively, for having simple-minded politics, for writing for the "Hippoisie," or for uniting "the cute and the loathsome."

There are other, related aspects to this decline: the overestimation, by university English departments, of contemporary writing; the ubiquity, in those same departments, of arcane procedures such as literary theory and deconstructionism; the increasing politicizing of art (Adrienne Rich drawing great crowds at her poetry readings); the frequent compartmentalizing of books into categories such as Black, Women, Homosexual, with a corresponding overrating of their individual value; the cheapening in worth of literary prizes; the paucity of good bookstores where new books get the chance to stay on the shelves for a while; the eclipse of New York City as a healthy place for novelists to do their work (Mr. Epstein lives in the Evanston-Chicago area and likes to tease the Big Apple).

These aspects of our literary culture lead Mr. Epstein to assume the role of critic-as-sheriff, "part of a posse to head writers off at the pass." (Though the pay is low, he adds, you're never out of work.) Of course this aggressive stance makes the sheriff a marked man, but since I share many of Mr. Epstein's prejudices, I don't aspire to gunning him down.

Mr. Epstein may be less than candid in not calling attention to the less-than-disinterested nature of his own critical operation. He deplores the politicizing of literature, yet the bulk of these essays were published in *Commentary* and *The New Criterion,* journals, it is fair to say, of the political and cultural right. And since sheriff-critics are not known for their dispassionateness, there is a certain amount of headhunting going on, particularly in the section on American novelists. When it comes to dead writers he admires—like Willa Cather and James Gould Cozzens—Mr. Epstein is concerned mainly to rescue them from cultural lefties who would try to appoint Cather an "honorary lesbian," or who reject Cozzens as socially conservative or reactionary. (The essay on Cozzens, incidentally, is a first-rate appreciation, book by book, of this interesting writer.)

As for the living (his motto is, in accord with Van Wyck Brooks, to be kind to the dead, hard on the living), I find him too hard on novelists I admire—John Updike, Philip Roth, Robert Stone and Ann Beattie. Though each is praised at some point for their prose (Mr. Stone's is "strong and flexible"; Miss Beattie's has "a deadly eye for right details") the overall account tilts too far toward the negative. In the interests of cudgeling Mr. Updike for an excessive interest in sexual detail, Mr. Epstein doesn't seem to me to weigh heavily enough the fine things in the Rabbit books (particularly *Rabbit Is Rich*) about time, change, death; nor does he bring out enough the distinction of *Of the Farm,* or the Olinger and Maples collections of stories (see "The Happiest I've Been" and "Separating").

In the interests of showing that Philip Roth lacks a "generous spirit" and that his books are intolerably self-regarding, Mr. Epstein fails to praise adequately the beautiful fourth section of *Zuckerman Unbound,* or the parts about university teaching in *The Professor of Desire.* In describing Ann Beattie's limitations as a "generation writer," he does not do justice to the frequent brilliance of *Falling in Place.*

Or so one might argue, since he is the sort of writer who writes, in part, to be argued with. His adverse judgments on contemporary writers goad a reader like myself into making better arguments for why those contemporaries are worth reading, and why the American novel is still more lively and nourishing than he judges it to be. Concurrently, his work throughout the collection shows there is more to literary criticism, to book reviewing, than the "rhinestone" quality he finds sadly prevalent in America today. Although he asserts that criticism is in decline, it cannot be in decline merely, when provocative critics like himself are on the scene. Let Mr. Epstein keep the sheriff badge if he chooses, but let him also be assured that he is not alone—that the posse may just be larger than he realized.

> *William Pritchard, "Kind to the Dead, Hard on the Living," in* The New York Times Book Review, *February 24, 1985, p. 8.*

ROBERT WILSON

Joseph Epstein has the knack for writing interestingly on a good many different subjects. One I wish he would drop is contemporary fiction.

Consider the writers he dismisses in separate essays in his new collection [*Plausible Prejudices: Essays on American Writing*]: Gabriel Garcia Marquez, Norman Mailer, John Updike, Bernard Malamud, Philip Roth, Cynthia Ozick, Joan Didion, Robert Stone, John Irving and Ann Beattie. There is no essay written in praise of a living writer.

You might agree with him about one or two of the above, as I do, or even as many as half. But if you reject all these writers, you should consider the possibility that you are not a very good reader of fiction, or that you bring to your reading prejudices that are far from plausible, to borrow from H. L. Mencken, via Epstein.

If Epstein has considered those possibilities, he has, of course, dismissed them, too. His conclusion is that the fault is not in himself, but in the age. As he writes in his introduction, "My case is that literature is going through a very bad patch at present—that there is something second-rate about it, especially in America, though not here alone." By "present" he means the last quarter century.

As it happens, Roger Sale, a respected reviewer who, like Epstein, has academic credentials and affiliations but is not an academic critic, has declared the same era to be "The Golden Age of the American Novel." Who is right? Probably neither, but at least Sale's enthusiasm for the age is tempered by the severity with which he criticizes certain writers. If Epstein could find *someone* who measures up, it would give him a little more credibility.

In a section of the book titled "The Older Crowd," Epstein does find writers to praise, among them the novelists James Gould Cozzens and John Dos Passos (in his later phase). This is telling. Both of these writers, in the estimation of Epstein and others who wish to reduce literature to politics, are conservatives. The living writers above are liberals, in this same reductive sense. Epstein wrote these essays primarily for conservative journals, *Commentary* and *The New Criterion*.

None of this would much matter, except that Epstein himself condemns many of these writers for, as he sees it, allowing their politics to get in the way of their artistic responsibilities. "Politics," he writes, "is part of the business of literature—it is, that is to say, an altogether proper subject for writers—but literature ought not to be part of the business of politics."

He's right, of course, but to my mind, Epstein's criticism is political and not aesthetic. Its insidiousness is that he masks his opinions as something else. He comes on as a critic with the longest possible view of literature. In fact, his view is not for the ages, but for the immediate consumption of his ideological audience.

> *Robert Wilson, "Rejecting the Major Writers of Our Time," in* USA Today, *March 15, 1985, p. 3D.*

EDMUND FULLER

[*Fuller is an American writer of fiction, history, religion, and criticism, and an editor of numerous literary anthologies. His best known work of literary criticism is* Man in Modern Fiction: Some Minority Opinions on Contemporary American Writing *(1958). In the following excerpt Fuller outlines Epstein's critical philosophy, showing approval for Epstein's approach.*]

Not originally expecting to become a book critic and reviewer, Joseph Epstein explains that above all he is "A reader; not someone who merely takes pleasure in reading—though I do take passionate pleasure in it—but someone for whom reading has been one of the main experiences in his life." Later, he says: "Good readers . . . read not only intelligently—with mental acuity, an ardor for language, a sense of humor—but also in the hope of having their souls stirred by literature."

Those are among a wealth of succinct observations in Mr. Epstein's *Plausible Prejudices: Essays on American Writing*. . . . In terms of money (a subject that Mr. Epstein believes some Americans are more shy of talking about than sex), when you have read the introduction and **"The Literary Life Today"** at the start of these 27 diverse pieces, you will already have your investment back. The rest is metaphorical capital gain.

It is a bit daunting to review Mr. Epstein's book after reading him on **"Reviewing and Being Reviewed,"** but since he has to run the risks of the process, so must I. . . .

Mr. Eptstein believes that "literature is going through a very bad patch at present—that there is something second-rate about it, especially in America, though not here alone." Those qualities of writing likely to stir the soul always are rare, but they are what we expect from greatness. What Chesterton scorned as "private lunacies" preoccupy many of the writers most esteemed by today's literary "establishment"—those writers and reviewers who talk to and about themselves.

On the subject of obsessions with sex, about which Mr. Epstein is shrewdly funny and never puritanical, he remarks: "To restrict myself to American novelists alone, I can think of three prominent figures who, but for the opportunity that the contemporary novel allows them to write about sex, would probably have to go into the drycleaning business: John Updike, Philip Roth, and Norman Mailer." Also, he holds in low esteem others whom some circles place high: John Irving, E. L.

Doctorow, Joan Didion, Robert Coover, Renata Adler and Ann Beattie among them.

He makes a bold assertion that will affect some sensitive skins like poison oak: ". . . as I look about me I find that culture today in the United States is much in thrall to political liberalism." That is true of the aforementioned "literary establishment," which, he argues, is not centered in New York or elsewhere but is widely dispersed, "a center without a center." He asserts: "Over the past 30 years the greatest single change in literary life in this country has been the gradual usurpation of literature by the university." Remember that Mr. Epstein not only teaches in a university but has been a visiting speaker in English departments all around Robin Hood's barn. He knows the terrain and the tribes.

Apart from trying to make universities the literary court of last appeal, some of their people also write "the English Department Novel" of a kind which "no one outside an English department would for a moment consider reading."

That is one contributor to the politicization of the novel, though there are more. Universities have nurtured special interests in their general curricula as well as in the critical biases of English departments. "Because universities are disposed to this general view, literature under their auspices has come to look a little like the Democratic Party under George McGovern."

Of course, this does not exclude politics from the novel, whether in Dostoevsky, Orwell, Silone, or the Koestler of *Darkness at Noon*. Mr. Epstein develops the distinction that such authors "wrote on political subjects with the authority of literature behind them." E. L. Doctorow, Robert Coover, et al., by contrast write "with the authority of politics behind them; for them the novel is politics by other means."

This book is broad in scope. About trends in biography, he observes there are "many would-be Boswells, and no Dr. Johnsons whatsoever." In a fine essay on Willa Cather, he defends her invaded right of privacy and that of other men and women in a day when biographers often advance currently fashionable interpretations of character on scanty or no hard evidence. He credits Cather with "a love of magnanimity, of the fine and generous gesture." She could "make goodness utterly believable." Those are rare gifts.

He restores justly the reputation of the late Van Wyck Brooks as critic and American literary historian, not omitting his possible faults, but defending him from academics (he was not one) and others who would not forgive him for changing his mind on some subjects—that is to say, for growing.

Much in this graceful, sometimes robustly funny, wisely perceptive book cannot be squeezed into this review. He puts high value in fiction on the quality of "gravity" that "derives from a serious literary mind, unencumbered by the cliches of the day, at work on serious matters." In a good essay, he attributes this quality to James Gould Cozzens. He says Solzhenitsyn has it, sometimes I. B. Singer and Saul Bellow. Willa Cather had it and I would credit it to Flannery O'Connor and the best of Walker Percy.

> *Edmund Fuller, "Reviewing the Reviewer," in* The Wall Street Journal, *April 2, 1985, p. 26.*

L. S. KLEPP

It might be said that we live in an Age of Criticism. More literary criticism is being written than ever before. On the other hand, less of it is being read than ever before. This is because so much of the criticism being published today has more to do with the requirements of academic life than with literature.

But there are still a few critics, both in and out of the universities, who are inspired by a love of literature rather than a hope of tenure. Instead of trying to cow the reader with opaque prose, they write clearly, even gracefully. Instead of an elaborate theoretical apparatus, they rely on a few touchstones and basic principles, along with instinct and common sense.

They are, in other words, the heirs of Addison and Johnson, Hazlitt and Arnold. They once would have been called men of letters, but that term has fallen into disuse, if not disrepute. But it is hard to think of a better one to describe the more versatile sort of critic such as, for instance, Joseph Epstein. He is an essayist, editor of *The American Scholar*, teacher of literature at Northwestern University, and author of **Plausible Prejudices**. (The title comes from H. L. Mencken's definition of criticism as prejudice made plausible.)

In a more settled literary period, I imagine Mr. Epstein would be content to spend his time writing his familiar essays and occasional appreciations of favorite writers. There is one pure appreciation here, of A. J. Liebling, and several embattled appreciations in which the author defends writers (such as John Dos Passos and James Gould Cozzens) against what he regards as critical injustice. There are fine essays on language and, appropriately, on writing essays.

But about half the essays are attempts to deflate contemporary reputations. For as Epstein cogently argues in an essay called **"The Literary Life Today,"** we are going through a period of rampant cultural inflation. In some periods, the critic's task is to smooth the way for new writers. But, as Epstein says in his introduction, the present age requires "critics who function rather more like sheriffs, who stand ready to apprehend delinquent writers. Without consciously setting out to do so, I seem . . . to have become such a sheriff."

So he has. But, in a way, this is even odder than Henry Kissinger's description of himself as a lone gunman. Epstein doesn't have the severe, dogmatic manner of a literary policeman. His prose is as imperturbably urbane as that of Max Beerbohm, one of his literary models. Unlike Bryan Griffin, from whose shrill polemics he distances himself in the essay **"It's Only Culture,"** Epstein brings in his delinquents with finesse and wit.

Epstein's usual procedure is to go carefully through a writer's work, noting strengths and weaknesses, giving credit where it is due, making his way gradually toward its moral center. What he looks for there is an appreciation of, and an engagement with, life in all its complexity and diversity. This is a quality he calls "gravity," which "derives from a serious mind, unencumbered by the clichés of the day, at work on serious matters." What he finds there, in contemporary literature, is mostly the clichés of the day.

Specifically, he finds political clichés (Robert Stone, E. L. Doctorow, Gabriel García Márquez), passivity and fatalism (Anne Beattie, Renata Adler, Joan Didion), sex obsession (Mailer et al.), self-obsession (Roth et al.), or not much of anything except a desire to write (John Updike). In most of these writers, he also finds things to praise—style, observation, invention, characterization—but he concludes that their purely literary virtues aren't enough.

Compared with the major writers of the past (or even some of the minor ones), there is, he believes, something narrow or hollow about these writers, a lack of intellectual curiosity and spiritual vitality. Most contemporary novelists and their reviewers have succumbed to a fashion mentality, he says: "Of clear distinctions, of questions of good and bad, of how things really are, the fashionable mind could hardly care less. It never asks of itself, what do I really think, . . . but instead, what ought I to think, what can I get away with appearing to believe?"

Readers will undoubtedly disagree with some of Epstein's conclusions about particular writers. But it is hard to disagree with his bleak assessment of our literary climate. The evidence of cultural inflation can be acquired at any newsstand. What makes these mostly pessimistic essays palatable and plausible, though, is that they are triumphs of style and wit.

L. S. Klepp, "Literary Criticism for Readers—Not Academics," in The Christian Science Monitor, *April 17, 1985, p. 22.*

GEORGE SIM JOHNSTON

Viewing the overproduction of books and pamphlets in his own day, Samuel Johnson complained of "an epidemical conspiracy for the destruction of paper." Joseph Epstein, who as a critic has much in common with the man who told Boswell to "clear your mind of cant," feels the same way about the volume of literary criticism today. Fortunately, however, for those who care about the quality of our literary culture, Mr. Epstein has not abstained from swelling the torrent of critical prose. *Plausible Prejudices* is a collection of his occasional literary writings. . . . But the word "occasional" hardly does justice to the sort of reviews and essays that Mr. Epstein writes. Like any first-rate critic, he has a larger purpose than simply turning over the book at hand. Even when he reviews a dim novel by Philip Roth or John Irving, we get a charming and perspicacious discussion of the novelist's *oeuvre* and the cultural issues that it raises. Epstein's charm, however, does not belie the severity of his views about contemporary literature. . . . Mr. Epstein, of course, is not the only critic to be embarrassed by what passes these days for serious writing. But I don't know of any other writer who can explain with such lucidity why our cultural life has come to such a pass.

Epstein is a man with an argument, and the point he drives home again and again is that much of our literature has been reduced to a flea market of received ideas. He blames this on the intrusion of politics, not specifically the electoral kind, but any scheme of ideas—Marxism, feminism, Freudian psychology—which tries to reduce human reality to simple formulas. . . .

When you sit down to read a contemporary novel, Epstein points out, too often you have to agree with the politics of the author in order to enjoy the book. This is not true of the great novelists of the past; it is not necessary to subscribe to the virulent opinions of Dostoyevsky or Malraux in order to enjoy *The Possessed* or *Man's Fate*. When these men picked up a pen, they were artists first and pamphleteers second. But contemporary novelists do not seem able to transcend ideology when they turn on their word processors. . . .

Lionel Trilling, in a famous phrase, talked about the "bloody crossroads where politics and literature meet." Epstein—quite against his will, it seems to me—stands at those crossroads and says with a shrug "Well, a man is entitled to his opinions." Epstein is a conservative, but he does not judge a writer by his politics; he prefers, for example, the work of the early left-wing Dos Passos to that of the right-wing Dos Passos; but he rightly condemns any writer who cannot free himself of ideology. He is concerned with politics only to the extent that they trivialize a writer's work. This being the case, I find the following complaint by William Pritchard, in his review of this book in the *New York Times Book Review* [see excerpt above], hard to fathom: "Mr. Epstein may be less than candid in not calling attention to the less-than-disinterested nature of his own critical operation. He deplores the politicizing of literature, yet the bulk of these essays were published in *Commentary* and the *New Criterion,* journals, it is fair to say, of the political and cultural right.... There is a certain amount of headhunting going on."

Professor Pritchard fails to make a distinction between leftists who happen to be critics, and a critic who happens to be a conservative. In the first category are writers like Malcolm Cowley and Dwight Macdonald, whose literary judgments are often vitiated by political motives. Their politics—which, in Cowley's case, involved at one time the most embarrassing infatuation with Stalinism—are stamped like a watermark on every page they wrote. This is not true of Epstein, who simply objects to the invasion of a writer's imagination by politics of any kind. I don't believe we would hear from him on the subject if the other side kept its politics to itself. I imagine that he feels like the narrator of a recent novel by Alasdair Gray: "I am very sorry. . . . I would like to ignore politics but POLITICS WILL NOT LET ME ALONE." It is the left, not the right, which has politicized our culture, and you cannot fault a critic— one who is not peddling a program and simply wants to enjoy a book for its own sake—for trying to clear the air of political fumes. And, contrary to the implication of Pritchard's remarks, Epstein always makes full disclosure of his political opinions.

Next to politics, in Epstein's view, the university earns the largest share of blame for the decline of American letters....

Other items on Epstein's list of baleful influences are the "normalization of alienation" (a.k.a., the Void)—which, he argues, is based on a selective understanding of modernism— and the decline of places like New York and Chicago as centers of literary culture. He might also have pointed out that those American novelists who have not left the city for the university have left it for the sticks. (p. 42)

Epstein's main concern is with the novel; a large section of *Plausible Prejudices* comprises reviews of living novelists, and Epstein's discussions are both comprehensive and just. His essay on Garcia Marquez is far and away the best treatment I have read of that Colombian artificer. Epstein is fully appreciative of Marquez's great gifts, but he is also the only critic I know to put his finger on the flaw that keeps Marquez out of the big leagues: ". . . Oddly, in Garcia Marquez's fiction morality is never an issue; Garcia Marquez himself seems little interested in moral questions, or in the conflicts, gradations, and agonies of moral turmoil. The reason for this, I suspect, is that for him the moral universe is already set—for him, as

for so many revolutionary intellectuals, there are the moral grievances of the past, the moral hypocrisies of the present, and, waiting over the horizon, the glories of the future, when moral complexity will be abolished." Politics, again, has done its corrosive work.

I do have some complaints about this part of the book. Epstein's reaction to a writer like Updike could be more modulated. True, Updike has never come close to writing an important novel, but he has produced some wonderful short stories and essays, including one of the best pieces ever written about baseball, "Hub Fans Bid Kid Adieu." Also, the group of novelists to whom Epstein gives extended treatment is somehow selective. They are all writers who have in some way misused their gifts and thus illustrate Epstein's "case." Where are I. B. Singer, Eudora Welty, J. F. Powers, Milan Kundera, Saul Bellow, and V. S. Naipaul? How about a younger writer like Mark Helprin? He alludes favorably to some of these writers in passing, but I think a full discussion of one or two of them would have made the collection more rounded.

Then, there is another kind of omission in Mr. Epstein's dealings with the novel. His approach to literature is essentially Augustan—meaning that he looks primarily for moral seriousness and intellectual gravity in a work of art—and this is fine so far as it goes, particularly given the antinomian strain in much contemporary writing. But it does have its limitations when it comes to writing about the novel. There is a line (to borrow F. R. Leavis's favorite word) in the history of the form which runs from *Tristram Shandy* through *At Swim-Two-Birds* and the novels of Ronald Firbank; it is full of freaks and gargoyles and is utterly lacking in seriousness; its practitioners approach the novel as a sport, not as moral gymnastics. Augustan strictures do not suffice when dealing with this kind of work. "Nothing odd will do long. *Tristram Shandy* did not last," Johnson remarked to Boswell. But it did last, and I see no evidence in Epstein's writing of an allowance for this element of play in the novel. What does he make of Thomas McGuane's *The Bushwacked Piano* or Donald Barthelme's short stories? There is little gravity in these works—but we do not wish them other than they are. And what about less-than-major writers who fully realize their gifts within strict, self-imposed limits? It seems to me that there is a distinction to be made between "minor" and "second-rate" when discussing the novel, and that Epstein does not make it.

This is but a cavil. I have not touched on half of Joseph Epstein's virtues as a critic and essayist. He complains in one essay that of the three hundred odd reviews his books have received, none contained any constructive criticism, so I am trying to oblige. His books are a pleasure to read, and now that he has flung his literary criticism between hard covers, readers of the contemporary novel have a place to go for intelligent talk about the boys and girls (as Epstein calls them), as well as the few grownups, who now write American fiction. (pp. 42-3)

George Sim Johnston, in a review of "Plausible Prejudices: Essays on American Writing," in The American Spectator, *Vol. 18, No. 6, June, 1985, pp. 42-3.*

Enlarging the Change: The Princeton Seminars in Literary Criticism, 1949-1951

by Robert Fitzgerald

(See also *Contemporary Authors*, Vols. 2, rev. ed., 114 [obituary]; *Contemporary Authors New Revision Series*, Vol. 1; and *Dictionary of Literary Biography Yearbook: 1980*.)

An Excerpt from *Enlarging the Change: The Princeton Seminars in Literary Criticism, 1949-1951*

Auerbach ended by discussing the question as to whether Emma [Bovary] could be considered a tragic heroine. He thought not. Neither author nor reader could ever feel sympathetic or at one with her, he said, because the style itself judged her silly as well as wretched. Balzac invested Père Goriot with tragic dignity, as Stendhal made Julian Sorel a tragic hero. Flaubert's attitude and tone were quite different and should be called, Auerbach said, quite simply "objective seriousness."

In the general talk that followed, various people seemed uneasy as they tried to match Auerbach's ever-incisive formulae with the novel as they knew it. Fergusson wanted to know if there was not something tragic in Flaubert's style itself. Curtius objected to the whole category of "realism" as applied to Flaubert, observing that Flaubert himself explicitly disavowed the intention of realism. He went on to say, even more cantankerously, that the critical study of the history of literature uses terms that won't bear examination; we should dispense with these venerable terms.

Auerbach (stung): Why question the characteristic things called realism in the textbooks?

Curtius (Olympian): Because the textbooks are all wrong.

Auerbach (fighting back): Isolated, the term has no meaning, but it is sufficiently understandable in the context—French nineteenth-century realism. No matter if Flaubert did not want to be called realist; he worked the same way whether he liked it or not. . . .

As to the matter of tragic tone, Gauss severely interposed that Emma was not tragic because the tragic are those who deserve to live, and deserve to live Emma did not. Curtius returned to the attack on the category of "realist," remarking that it was very interesting (that is, nonsense) that Stendhal, Balzac, and Flaubert should all be lumped in one category; did not Balzac and Stendhal enjoy life while on the contrary Flaubert was a prey to despair? What was important was not what novelists have in common but their differences. Auerbach mildly replied that you couldn't get at the individual in Flaubert without historical common denominators. Fergusson and Curtius tried again to slit the straightjacket in which they evidently felt that Auerbach had encased a living work of art. Borgerhoff, having thought the matter over, disputed one of Auerbach's principal points; the judgment in Flaubert's presentation of Emma and Charles at table, he said, was *sympathetic* to Emma; the reader shared Emma's feeling. Moreover—and this was Borgerhoff's liberating stroke—there was other evidence of the novelist's sympathy for Emma:

"Remember how Flaubert shows her at the time of extreme unction. . . . That is sad. To me, there is a quality like the ballads: something is celebrated, and properly."

Dust jacket of Enlarging the Change: The Princeton Seminars in Literary Criticism, 1949-1951, *by Robert Fitzgerald. Northeastern University Press, 1985. Copyright © 1985 by Robert Fitzgerald. Courtesy of Northeastern University Press.*

D.J.R. BRUCKNER

William Hazlitt thought "the conversation of authors is not so good as might be expected, but, such as it is (and with rare exceptions) it is better than any other." He did not include critics, but he might now. Among those gathered for two years of conversations about literature in Princeton, N.J., from 1949 to 1951 were Francis Fergusson, John Berryman, Delmore Schwartz, R. P. Blackmur, Ernst Robert Curtius, Erich Auerbach, Jacques Maritain, Rene Wellek and Allen Tate. They were terrific talkers, discussing literature, and the record of their talk [*Enlarging the Change*] might well make one impatient of other people's conversation for a while. Here their talk is recounted by Robert Fitzgerald, the poet and translator, who knows how to say what he wants to.

From the excitement of his account one might guess Mr. Fitzgerald thought the high point was Mr. Fergusson talking about Dante but he says it came with Maritain on the origins of poetry, presentations that eventually turned into the book *Creative Intuition in Art and Poetry*. Maritain's eloquence may have been even more brilliant in his seminars than in that great book. "Poetry proceeds from the totality of man, sense, imagination, intellect, love, desire, instinct, blood and spirit together. In what sense, then could poetry be called a form of knowledge?" "'The poet,' he said, 'knows himself only on the condition that things resound in him, and that in him, at a single awakening, they and he come forth together out of sleep.'" "The essential emotion, he said, was not an emotion to be expressed but an emotion *which causes to express*." Maritain unfolding the process of creation, and insisting on the primacy of the unconscious intuitions, in front of argumentative critics and poets is a scene as exciting as a hero negotiating his way through a gantlet of adversaries in a thriller.

By the time we reach Maritain, the book is resonant and we can hear echoes of previous sessions, most notably an earlier seminar in which Mr. Wellek had brilliantly surveyed European criticism in the 19th century (his seminar talks were also growing into a book), and had cited Schiller saying: "In experience the poet begins with the unconscious and he must consider himself lucky, if the clearest consciousness of his operations allows him to find again the first dark total idea of his work unweakened in the finished labor."

It is the resonance that makes the last series of seminars, on Thomas Mann's *Doctor Faustus*, the most fascinating to read about. By then one is aware of many understandings shared among the participants. All but one of the Faustus discussions are strikingly fresh—Erich Kahler wonders whether Mann identified himself with the hero of the novel and raises questions about Mann's hidden life we are only now beginning to find answers to in his letters. Joseph Kerman simply demolishes Mann's pretended understanding of music; Edmund King demonstrates that the real, hidden, tragic hero of the novel is Germany, and Mr. Fergusson exposes as a kind of treachery Mann's elaborate ironies which keep the novel's reader continually off balance.

There are enough fertile ideas in this small volume to keep a clever mind occupied for a long time, but there is also rich entertainment, in lightning glimpses of the seminar participants. One evening several people disputed Auerbach's interpretation of a Baudelaire poem and John Berryman exploded at all of them: "Either I do not understand this poem or there has been a series of violent misconceptions. . . . Here is my interpretation for what it is worth, though I do not see how it can be wrong." Auerbach, whose passion, Mr. Fitzgerald says, was "to make understandable the immediate human thing," often confronted the equally learned Curtius. Mr. Fitzgerald gives Blackmur's summary: "Curtius is, relative to Auerbach,

a deep anarch of the actual. Every blow he struck at Auerbach was meant to break down the formulas whereby we see how unlike things are like."

Even Mr. Fitzgerald can cut. He refers to one young philosopher who evidently annoyed him as "gadfly-in-chief" and later characterizes a talk by him as "modest points briskly made," and he calls a presentation by Mark Schorer "a loose end and a dead end." One attendant at a Schorer seminar on novels was much more pointed in his opinions. After the session John O'Hara "was heard briefly to express a story writer's attitude toward criticism in general and Schorer's in particular: he observed that The Novel was obscenity; obscenity The Novel, he advised."

This extraordinary manuscript was found in carbon copy in a file. Mr. Fitzgerald wrote it 33 years ago as a report for the seminars' sponsors—the Institute for Advanced Study in Princeton, Princeton University and the Rockefeller Foundation (these sessions were the forerunners of the well-known Gauss seminars which still go on at Princeton). It must be the most unusual, certainly the most eloquent, report sent to sponsors in our time. One of Mr. Fitzgerald's friends resurrected it recently and Northeastern University Press grabbed it. It is a great find.

D.J.R. Bruckner, "Conversations of Critics," in The New York Times, *January 1, 1985, p. 25.*

THOMAS D'EVELYN

This book [*Enlarging the Change*] must be read by everyone who considers himself a friend of the humanities in America. Chronicling a gathering of men of letters—some émigrés, some natives—who met under the auspices of the Rockefeller Foundation and the Institute for Advanced Studies and Princeton University, *Enlarging the Change* offers far more than a digest of literary evenings distinguished by a certain Old World delicacy. It offers, thanks to the running ruminations of the chronicler himself, a meditation on the very possibility of humanistic exchange.

Now that everybody seems to be alarmed by the decline in the status of the humanities in higher education in the United States, we have this book to show us just what did happen when certain prominent underwriters made possible an occasion that should have furthered the exchange of ideas between the two cultures—the humanities and the sciences.

Before he became involved in the seminars, Robert Fitzgerald thought of the Institute for Advanced Studies "as a preserve of scientists and mathematicians of whom the most famous was Albert Einstein." Robert Oppenheimer was the director at the time. Mr. Oppenheimer in fact continued and tried to expand the policy of his predecessor, Frank Aydelotte, from whom he took over in 1947, to include the humanities. Mr. Aydelotte had set up a School of Humanities at the institute in 1939. But during the seminars that school was dispensed with on a vote of the democratically run institute, Oppenheimer's wishes notwithstanding.

It is the sad burden of these pages to convey that even under Oppenheimer the institute failed to show good faith toward the scholars and poets whom Oppenheimer had attracted there, some of them as participants in the seminars.

T. S. Eliot, Erich Auerbach, and Ernst Robert Curtius, among others, met with a less than warm reception from members of the institute. Fitzgerald does not say the rejection was blatant in form, only that, once these and other humanists were present at the institute and the opportunity for keeping them there at hand, the institute, as a body, failed to seize the opportunity.

There were other failures to seize the opportunity to advance the cause of literature, and these Fitzgerald lays at the door of the seminar members themselves. This countertheme appears now and again, adding a poignance to the recapitulation of lectures and discussions which, we note with admiration, have withstood the test of time and the onslaught of changes in fashion literary and academic.

For we have in *Enlarging the Change* a record of works in progress by some of the best literary minds of the day. Auerbach, Francis Fergusson, Fitzgerald himself, Rene Wellek, and Jacques Maritain, among others, contribute here to the permanent discussion that is the lifeblood of literature. Perhaps one of the lessons of these seminars is the unintended one that literary criticism is not really a collaborative effort, but essentially a personal one.

The members of the now famous roll call lacked, as Fitzgerald with rueful amusement comments from time to time, solidarity. The distinguished chairman failed to show up on the night when his distinguished colleague made his contribution; the philosopher failed to attend the admirable evening supplied by an honored guest because he was busy preparing for his own.

In a particularly caustic mood, the writer remembers that "the rumble of falling facts continued to echo in the discussion periods, and very little good talk got started."

Besides being a record of what was said, Fitzgerald's book is a memoir, and a personal one. It began as a report commissioned by the faculty committee directing the seminars and by the Rockefeller Foundation. It now appears, beautifully published by Northeastern University Press. We are fortunate to have it. We need it now more than ever. The diversity as well as the quality of discourse among these almost mythical figures is recorded—*registered* is more like it. For Fitzgerald is our clear-eyed and solicitous cicerone throughout, filling in with memorable detail and arched eyebrows the significance of it all.

Fitzgerald's own seminar happens to have been my favorite, dwelling with fond emphasis on some pages of Aristotle that still offer a rare and most sensible starting point for poet and critic alike. And that chapter on his own performance includes the delicious moment when:

> The writer found himself under interrogation by Harold Cherniss, the classical scholar from the Institute, a pleasantly skeptical, weathered and seasoned Hellenist whose life work was a study of the relationship between Aristotle and the Academy. Cherniss had evidently surmised that the interpretation (given by Fitzgerald) lacked any underpinning from the great Arabic commentators. The writer indicated that the support was there, though slender, and invited Cherniss to strengthen it, whereupon the direction of the wind became noticeable as Cherniss remarked that he hadn't come "to give a speech."

One surmises that the members of the institute had had enough of speeches long before the seminars were over.

The scene gives a much-needed case study of the interaction one can expect between institutions and humanists, and even between scholars and poets. It offers little consolation to those who think the humanities flourish under institutional support. Yet this is a gracious book and a fitting cadenza, full of subtle invention and scholarly finesse, to a career distinguished by purity and generously single-minded service to the muses.

First known as the translator of Homer, then of Virgil, and himself a fine poet, Robert Fitzgerald now gives us his memoir of several evenings years ago, a book as precious as it is accurate, an herbal with real herbs growing in it, aromatic, pungent, and salubrious. (pp. 21-2)

> *Thomas D'Evelyn, "When Poet Meets Scientist," in*
> The Christian Science Monitor, *January 2, 1985, pp. 21-2.*

MARTIN DUBERMAN

[*Duberman is an American historian, dramatist, biographer, critic, essayist, and editor. In such historical works as his* Black Mountain: An Exploration in Communication *(1972), he adopts a frankly personal point of view, dispensing with the conventional historian's illusion of objectivity. His concern for civil rights is reflected in his play* In White America *(1963), which dramatizes the history of black Americans, using quotes from letters, diaries, and other documentary material. In the following excerpt Duberman praises Fitzgerald for providing an entertaining and accessible record of a significant event in literary criticism.*]

Robert Fitzgerald, the noted poet and translator, has written an unexpectedly ingratiating account [*Enlarging the Change*] of an intrinsically arcane subject—the Princeton seminars in literary criticism held in 1949-1951, a forum in which he was participant and official scribe. A book recounting the discussions of a literary seminar might not be expected to hold much interest for the general reader—particularly when the seminar concerns such esoterica as the stylistics of Pascal. But it does—and that is a mysterious and noteworthy accomplishment.

Enlarging the Change is based on Mr. Fitzgerald's original transcriptions which lay forgotten in his files for 30 years. His opinions seem not to have changed too much. He still holds in high regard the scholarship of Francis Fergusson and Jacques Maritain, still differs sharply with Erich Auerbach, Mark Schorer and René Wellek. With remarkable skill he recreates the discussions of these and other midcentury literary luminaries, vividly bringing their words back to life, unearthing treasured bits that might otherwise have been lost.

Here, for example, is Schorer on the novel: "Plot, in a great novel, is not first of all a means to demonstrate a view of life, but rather of forcing characters into positions where they will experience life at its fullest, its most intense and crucial, under the particular social circumstances. . . . *Tested* morality requires sustained *pressure* and *crisis.*"

Many of the participants were engaged at the time of the seminars in works of wide literary interest and importance—John Berryman's *Stephen Crane,* Irving Howe's *Sherwood Anderson* and Delmore Schwartz's *Vaudeville for a Princess* were all about to be published. Auerbach's *Mimesis* had not yet been published in English. Maritain's papers became his Andrew Mellon Lecture papers and, later, his acclaimed *Creative Intuition in Art and Poetry.* Delmore Schwartz, daunted by the reception of his seminar presentation as "thin and even weak," never published his study of T. S. Eliot, one which in crucial ways inspired his own career.

Simply and modestly, "the writer" reports on the triumphs and deflations, the petty politics and intellectual flights of the personalities, great and not so great, who attended the seminars. Scholars interrupt scholars. "But where is literature?" one asks, impatiently cutting off a thought on Pascal's Christianity. Auerbach isn't interested in Baudelaire's soul. Mr. Wellek disparages the visualizing power of Henry James—"There was a kind of roughness" in that, notes the writer. Auerbach never comes back after his own readings, except once for one by his friend Fergusson.

Mr. Fitzgerald recounts many instances of annoying academic certitudes, high-toned vagaries and unembarrassed arrogance in outlining "correct" critical standards—the denigration of D. H. Lawrence, the stress on "conscious reason" and the intellect's "superior intuition." William Meredith was "unable to discuss a second-rate mind in a great poem, such as some by Tennyson and Hugo." But the smug assertions were not unchallenged. Mr. Fitzgerald calmly records the frequent and angry objections that played off as subtheme to the confident—at times even fatuous—tone which dominated the gatherings.

Mr. Fitzgerald's book shows how much more confidence existed in 1950 than today about the possibility of literary absolutes. And we cannot help but feel envy. Scrupulously evoking the earlier era, the account makes our nostalgia not only palpable, but justified. He invites us to tally what has been lost and gained in the years since—modesty, perhaps, on the one hand, certitude on the other. But however stifling or narrow or arrogant that community was, the current anomie attendant on the loss of community is, by contrast, even more debilitating. This is perhaps the tacit message behind the reportage.

Many of the luminaries reintroduced here have since fallen from fashion, their literary criticism dismissed as antiquated. Thanks to this account, we can measure the changes that time and changing fashions have wrought. And when critical standards again shift, we will have at hand this book as a guide for re-evaluating literary theories once dominant—Schorer's overview, say, on the English novel, Auerbach's analysis of *Madame Bovary* or Ernst Robert Curtius's wide-ranging and much underrated opinions. For these purposes, ***Enlarging the Change*** will be an invaluable, unique resource.

> Martin Duberman, "Literary Summitry," in The New
> York Times Book Review, *January 13, 1985, p. 39.*

HARRY LEVIN

[*Levin, a former classmate and colleague of Fitzgerald at Harvard, is a professor of comparative literature. In 1961 he presented a series of papers at Princeton's Gauss seminars, which evolved from the literary discussions recorded in* Enlarging the Change. *In the following excerpt Levin offers some historical background on the Princeton seminars and reflects on the merits and shortcomings of the program.*]

"But are not those old occasions ghostly now? Have not those who took part in them faded into impalpability . . .?" These are poignant questions for a classmate and colleague to read, in the preface to a volume [***Enlarging the Change***] that—as it turns out—has reached publication during the very month of the author's death. His characteristic answer is a qualified affirmation: "Yes and no. Ghostliness and permanence both

are of the nature of good literature, and persons devoted to it partake of both. We have indeed seen changes of manners." Certainly Robert Fitzgerald will continue to be a presence, most widely felt through our most accessible translations of the three major classical epics. (It is not their least distinction that his Virgil sounds different from his Homer.) His uniquely discriminating ear for poetic effect, in his own and other languages, had also made him an ideal translator not only from Greek tragedy, but from such moderns as St. John Perse. That he was himself a gifted poet is manifest in the quality and individuality of the elegant lyrics he has left us, as they have been collected in *Spring Shade*.

Moreover, if we still have men of letters in this country, or anything like a literary community, it is thanks to such careers as Fitzgerald's. His gift for friendship, in journalistic days, made him a mentor for James Agee, Flannery O'Connor, and other fellow writers. Through his teaching years at Harvard and elsewhere, he discerned and fostered younger talents. He must indeed have seen a change of manners, in moving from *Time* magazine into "a fresh humanistic adventure," which could hardly have hoped for a more perceptive rapporteur. His last book consists essentially of his direct report, commissioned then by the Rockefeller Foundation, declassified a generation afterward, and published now with a certain amount of updating explanation. It is based upon full participation during the second year, and on a reconstruction of the first from partial attendance, relayed notes, and interviews. As "the writer," Fitzgerald engages and charms us with third-person Jamesian diffidence. Toward the interlocutors he is generous and sympathetic, personally if not always ideologically. His chronicle is all the richer because it so often discloses tastes and opinions, reservations, and pieties of his own.

The absorbing experiment to which it bears witness, and which has been successfully carried on into the present, inaugurated what have come to be known as the Gauss Seminars—after a warmly remembered dean who played a helpful part in the original sessions. It may be significant that the scene was Princeton, a somewhat more aloof and rarefied setting than Harvard or Yale would have been, and therefore probably more fallow ground for such colloquies. The Institute for Advanced Studies, recently settled nearby, had imported a cosmopolitan note by welcoming scientists out of the great European diaspora. Having sponsored a pilot course by Kenneth Burke, it was expected to collaborate with the university in sponsoring the seminars. But, despite the interest shown by its director, J. Robert Oppenheimer, it seems gradually to have withdrawn from joint patronage of this project. That was a serious loss for interdisciplinary expectations. On the other hand it could be said that, within the sphere of literature itself at mid-century, artists and universities stood at some distance from one another, and the seminars did much by bringing them together.

This edgy coalition, as Fitzgerald reminds us, had been celebrated by R. P. Blackmur in an article entitled "A Featherbed for Critics." Blackmur had been brought to Princeton to assist Allen Tate in creative writing—the same arrangement that would bring Fitzgerald there as assistant to Francis Fergusson in 1950-51. Fergusson, the first director of the seminars, would be succeeded by Blackmur, even as the latter had succeeded Tate in the writing program. Tate and Fergusson both had far more professional credentials; yet neither was what Blackmur soon became, an academic politician and foundation diplomat. As a professor without a college degree, his position was ironically unique. It had been quite creditably grounded on pioneering studies in New Criticism, some of the earliest close readings of important American poets, written with the oblique penetration of a painstaking autodidact. His association with the colloquium encouraged him to pontificate, on the basis of a wider knowledge than he could control. Fitzgerald cites an essay on *Madame Bovary* that was prompted by such a discussion, but charitably forbears to point out that it begins and ends with mistakes in elementary French.

The first two years set the pattern: four seminars per year, six weekly meetings per seminar, an hour on each occasion for a paper, plus another hour for questioning and comment. The select audience, 20 to 30 invited listeners, would then become active participants. Some of them were drawn from the institute, such as Erwin Panofsky, others from Princeton's changing constellation of visiting writers, such as John Berryman, with differences of temperament and background that stimulated lively dialogue. Some members of the faculty attended, while certain others stayed away rather pointedly. (Such regulars as Américo Castro and Erich Kahler were still attending, much to my gratification, when I presented a series of papers in 1961.) To conduct these eight conferences, Fergusson had lined up an exceptionally interesting and varied procession of spokesmen, who could speak for Europe and America, theory and practice, philosophy and theology, philology and history, poetry and fiction. Talk went "as the spirit spiraled," in Fitzgerald's phrase. If it did not pursue "that purposive logic that leads to decision," it did provide a showcase for work-in-progress, a sounding board for developing ideas.

The auspicious point of departure served the additional purpose of introducing Erich Auerbach, "the superlatively good European" who had just arrived from the University of Istanbul. His magisterial sequence of textual analyses, *Mimesis,* had appeared in German three years before and would be brought out in English translation four years later by the Princeton University Press. His subtle explication of suggestive texts by Pascal, Baudelaire, and Flaubert was well devised to enkindle arguments here. As chance would have it, Ernst Robert Curtius, another grand master of *Romanistik,* was present, and the situation briefly savored of continental polemics. An American remonstrance was that Auerbach's stylistics, while proceeding with structural acumen from sentence to sentence, scanted "the organization of the whole." But his inspiration lasted into the second seminar—along perhaps with Burke's "dramatistic" concepts—when the director took his turn by interpreting the *Purgatorio.* Having underscored the ritualistic elements of drama in his notable *Idea of a Theatre,* Fergusson now went on to elicit the "histrionic" features of *The Divine Comedy.* The resulting book, *Dante's Drama of the Mind,* was worked out through a dialectical process.

This sense of interaction stands in marked contrast to the account of a subsequent contribution by René Wellek: a preview of chapters on Johnson, Lessing, and other leading figures ("lectures indeed") from the two forthcoming volumes of his monumental *History of Modern Criticism.* Fitzgerald shows due respect for Wellek's intelligence, but seems slightly put off by his learning, reductively alluding to footnotes, filing cards, and stacks. Though one may sympathize with an aversion to the pedantries of graduate study, it seems only fair to remember that Wellek's (and Austin Warren's) *Theory of Literature* was designed precisely to correct them, rather than to become "a *PMLA* to end all others."

Fitzgerald himself, in the following seminar, earnestly proposed to bridge the "discursive" and the "creative" attitudes,

with Aristotelian support in epistemology and ethics as well as in poetics, and observations on the coalescence of *sophia* (wisdom) with *techne* (art). He was aware of the paradoxical hazards in defending and dignifying poetry by equating it with philosophy. Modestly and candidly he registers disagreements. He might have got further with his hearers by speaking more directly from the standpoint of the artist.

He might likewise have had the concurrence of the next—and for him the climactic—speaker, if Jacques Maritain had not been absent, immersed in the preparation of his own seminar. Certainly there is a continuity, reinforced by Hellenic and neo-Thomist authorities. As a religious apologist, Maritain had displayed a supple insight into all the nonscientific aspects of intellectual activity. His *Art and Scholasticism* (1920) had broken down earlier barriers between the Catholic tradition and the modernist esthetic. These new and more elaborate discourses would be further elaborated into his Mellon Lectures, *Creative Intuition in Art and Poetry* (1953), where distinct artistic and literary sensibilities are concretely framed at a high level of abstract generalization. A later generation of uncommitted readers may not feel the need or relevance of such ramifying conceptual apparatus. Fitzgerald reports that there was "almost no memorable interchange . . . between the philosopher and his listeners." It is not clear whether they were spellbound by a revelation or bemused by a language that was scarcely theirs. Yet Maritain, as the senior seminarist, could sustain a flair for universals and talk unabashedly about beauty.

Two of the first-year seminarists had been accomplished practitioners, yet they seem to have exercised less of an impact than their more theoretical colleagues. Delmore Schwartz may already have entered his unhappy second act. His subject was his concern, described by an auditor as "obsessive," with the circumstances of T. S. Eliot's career. In this case the reception, as Fitzgerald remarks, had the effect of arresting rather than fostering a book. Mark Schorer focused his expertise and experience on a dozen standard English novels. Despite the familiarity of the genre, its critical recognition—as a serious object of craftsmanship or a vehicle of moral consciousness—had been relatively belated. Henry James had given precept and example for a sophisticated conception of "the well-made novel," with its own technical terms and artistic criteria. Schorer could apply these retroactively and suggest some strategic revaluations. But Fitzgerald was frankly outraged to watch this progression lead up to D. H. Lawrence, in whom "an artist" had been spoiled by "a seer." For a seminar considering Jane Austen and George Eliot, or a first year that had dealt with Dante and Baudelaire, that was an anticlimax.

The second year, and the period covered by these annals, concluded with a symposium. As a test-case for methods and standards, it was agreed to discuss a current novel by "a man of letters of the heaviest calibre." Thomas Mann's *Doctor Faustus* (1948) proved a highly discussable choice, admittedly "a valedictory fable of the artist's life and Germany together," problematic even within the canon of so consciously problematic a novelist. Fitzgerald is perfectly forthright in confessing a general bias, if not a blind spot. The six symposiasts, though open-minded enough, were nothing if not critical. (The present reviewer, who reviewed the work when it came out, was inclined to share some of their doubts.) The most illuminating commentators were Joseph Kerman on the implications of the musical allegory, Kahler on the diabolic motifs from German legend, and Fergusson himself with a peroration that points up Mann's peculiar irony, the habit of having everything both ways. There may have been an extraneous irony, which seems to have gone unnoted by the seminars, in the fact that Mann and Eliot had both been dwelling and writing at Princeton shortly before.

There is a brief and tentative conclusion to Fitzgerald's book. The real conclusion, however, must be the long chain of sequels that by now have extended these hearings into their 36th year. (Are they still held on Thursday evenings in the poetry room of the Firestone Library?) Fergusson and Blackmur, after their respective tours of duty, were followed by Joseph Frank and currently Victor Brombert, distinguished scholar-critics strongly oriented toward modern languages, comparative literature, and the history of ideas. Like their predecessors, they have been both pluralistic and ecumenical in inviting guests from the many mansions within the house of criticism. Literary studies, when they are institutionalized, all too frequently tend to contract and harden into self-promoting, contentious, and doctrinaire schools of thought. Doctrines, by definition, have something to teach. But more is to be learned from juxtaposing them critically—"so Truth be in the field"—than by imposing one doctrine or another, whether it be neo-Aristotelianism or Post-Structuralism. Princeton has thus done better than Chicago did, or than Yale has been doing, in living up to the title Fitzgerald has borrowed from Wallace Stevens: in recognizing change and seeking enlargement. (pp. 35-7)

> Harry Levin, "Of Books and the Man," in The New Republic, *Vol. 192, No. 11, March 18, 1985, pp. 35-7.*

GABRIEL JOSIPOVICI

[*Josipovici, a French-born resident of England, is best known for such novels as* The Inventory (1968) *and* Migrations (1977), *and for his plays, including* Evidence of Intimacy (1970). *He has also written and edited collections of literary criticism, among them* The Modern English Novel: The Reader, the Writer, and the Work (1986). *In the following excerpt Josipovici observes that the exciting literary debate recorded in* Enlarging the Change *reflects the necessarily adversarial nature of modern criticism.*]

In 1949 the Princeton Institute for Advanced Study invited a group of scholars and writers to gather for a series of seminars. . . . Robert Fitzgerald, then a young poet and classicist, was invited to act as the official scribe. For years his notes on the first two years of the seminars lay in the Princeton files, until, not very long ago, a friend asked to see them and immediately realized that they were of more than antiquarian interest. ***Enlarging the Change,*** a lightly edited version of those records, fully vindicates that belief. It is, sadly, the last book that Robert Fitzgerald published in his lifetime, for this gifted and humane poet, scholar and translator, whose translations of the *Odyssey* and the *Iliad* are the most beautiful and exciting produced this century, died in January of [1985].

The idea behind the seminars was to produce something more than the sum of different views. All the participants, moreover, were men of deep learning and wide sympathies, at home in the culture of Europe from Homer to the present, profoundly aware of the ravages caused to any unified concept of culture by the Second World War and what had led up to it. The choice of participants, and therefore of subjects, was inspired: Auerbach's discussion of Pascal and Baudelaire was set alongside Fergusson's thoughts on the relation of will to form in the middle Cantos of Dante's *Purgatorio* and Fitzgerald's discussion of Aristotle's concept of man in Aristotle's *de Anima;* at the end of two years' work six seminars were devoted to the most considerable novel to have come out of the war, Mann's *Doktor Faustus.*

And yet, as Fitzgerald points out in his marginal comments, the ideal never quite materialized. First of all there was the perennial suspicion in which the men of learning held the makers of art, and of the makers for all attempts at synthesis. Eliot was invited to Princeton but was then made to feel that this was not quite the right place for him (they would have welcomed the world's greatest expert on Dante, Fitzgerald observes, but Dante himself would probably have been too much for them). Berryman, having held back throughout an evening's discussion of Baudelaire, burst out suddenly: "Either I do not understand this poem or there has been a series of violent misconceptions."

Nevertheless there are also enormous advantages to group discussions. It is fascinating to listen in not just on the papers but on the discussions which followed, on Berryman's outburst, on Fergusson trying to persuade the unimpressed Princeton *Dantisti* to see things his way, on Curtius rebuking his old pupil Auerbach for wasting his time on Pascal's theology when he might have come closer to the essence of Pascal by looking at his use of participles. Fitzgerald himself is not backward in acquainting the reader with his views: Schorer's "Eng lit" approach he finds banal; Wellek, despite his massive learning, dry; Maritain, superior to everyone. Indeed, part of the excitement generated by the book depends on the fact that though Fitzgerald takes his duties as scribe very seriously, he is as passionately committed as any Greek chorus.

And though he clearly feels that Maritain's seminars were the high point of the sessions, my own impression is that that claim could better be made for the seminars of Fitzgerald himself and Francis Fergusson. The underlying theme of their rich and subtle discourses could perhaps best be summed up thus: the study of the past is not an antiquarian activity; nor is the past important to us to the degree that it is "relevant". Rather, modern culture has narrowed down our notion of what it means to be human, and only by listening with attention to Sophocles, Thucydides, Aristotle, Dante and Aquinas can one learn again the full range of possibilities open to us. In the light of their comments the earlier remarks of Auerbach on Pascal, Baudelaire and Flaubert, of Wellek on Lessing and Herder, suddenly take on a new significance, and we can appreciate the progressive narrowing of philosophical and literary horizons.

This is perhaps the central message of the Princeton seminars. It seems as important to reiterate it today as it was in the immediate post-war years. And yet there is something about the way it comes across that leaves one slightly uneasy. That unease only really comes to the surface when reading the final set of seminars, those devoted to Mann's *Doktor Faustus.* Apart from Erich Kahler's rather banal defence of the novel, all the members of the seminar are at one in their condemnation of it. Mann is castigated as being provincial, ponderous, pretentious and actually knowing nothing about music.

Of course they are partly right. Stravinsky, meeting Mann while he was at work on the novel, noted in his diary that the man was a dreadful bore, interested only in The Future Of Music. But what is worrying is that the members of the seminar, having said that kind of thing, should feel that they had said enough. As with Alasdair MacIntyre's brilliant *After Virtue,* one is left wondering why the rediscovery of Aristotle should have to entail a blindness to the real thrust of post-Romantic and Modernist art and ideas.

Yet Fergusson can't simply be accused of turning his back on the present. ''There may be another reason for my attitude, or feeling'', he says,

> namely that I was brought up with other proph-
> ets of doom, who caught me young, and hit me
> where I really lived. I am thinking primarily
> of Eliot, of course. An early reading of Eliot,
> like an injection of ragweed, has produced in
> me a partial immunity . . .
>
> After thirty years I still hear more music, and
> more of the authentic unheard *mousike* in
> [''Gerontion''] than I do in all the screaming
> *Weheklage.*

In spite of this, though, I am left feeling that neither Fergusson nor the other members of the seminar even begin to do *Doktor Faustus* justice.

In the end the debate cannot be resolved, not because the questions are difficult but because the issues are so deep that how one responds to them depends on the kinds of choices one has made in one's own life and the kinds of aims for which one is struggling. That is why no ''science'' of literary criticism is possible or desirable, and why a book like this is both more instructive than a dozen books on literary theory or the future of the novel, and more exciting than a thriller.

> *Gabriel Josipovici, ''Progressively Narrower,'' in*
> The Times Literary Supplement, *No. 4285, May 17,*
> *1985, p. 560.*

Habitations of the Word

by William Gass

(See also *CLC*, Vols. 1, 2, 8, 11, 15; *Contemporary Authors*, Vols. 17-20, rev. ed.; and *Dictionary of Literary Biography*, Vol. 2.)

An Excerpt from *Habitations of the Word*

It has long been our habit to quote the words, and hence to adopt, or temporarily to borrow, the views of others. In debate I may attribute to historical figures convictions which they might have expressed on some famous occasion, although I was not present to hear them, as Thucydides did in his history, or Plato did when he composed the *Phaedo*. Again, I may cite Homer or Hesiod to give the weight of their authority to my otherwise airy opinions. I implicitly say, by so doing, that I assent, not only to the sense of their sentences, but also to their style. The breath of my lungs unites us in a common course or cause. But where do these words have their home now? Where do they reside? Are they part of my soul's very flesh and blood? Have they been the words that have nourished me from the first and formed my self and established my character, been the bone of my bones, as the very diction and verbal rhythms of the King James Bible shaped the souls of the early settlers of this country— its meanings, sounds, and meters reinforced by every family reading? . . .

Often, of course, the words of others, which I have dragged squalling into my oration like someone else's children, have little substance of their own, but take their authority from the famous, and often imposing, figure of their father. God's word frequently walks lamely enough for the ordinary man to claim it. Because I say so, Zeus thunders. The orders come from me, the Führer screams. It is not the meaning and weight and arrangement—the argument—of the words themselves which persuades. The Sybil's riddles, the Oracles' ambiguities, say: Believe me, because I am in touch with divinity. The highly organized harangues of the politicians say: Believe me, because I can give you what you want, and tell you what you want to hear; my tongue shall lick your ear. The carefully measured considerations of the philosopher say: Believe me, because I am wise; but can the philosopher be wise before his words are? and worse, where in those words can we find the Forms? where is the deep resemblance in these syllables which will spur us to recall and spell out the unspellable Ideas? The well-wrought verses of the poet, too—the periods of the orator, the sophist's sleights of speech—each says: Believe me because I am clever, resonant, beautiful; but the beauty of any such display of talent, and exercise of skill, for Plato, rests on whether its eloquence stirs others to theirs; and be-

cause the beauty of the truly Beautiful depends on whether it manages to be an adequate manifestation of the ultimate Good at which Truth aims.

CHRISTOPHER LEHMANN-HAUPT

Back in 1971, in his first collection of essays, *Fiction and the Figures of Life,* the philosopher-novelist William H. Gass laid down the law that "the esthetic aim of any fiction is the creation of a verbal world, or a significant part of such world, alive through every order of its Being." He continued: "The artist's task is therefore twofold. He must show or exhibit his world, and to do this he must actually make something, not merely describe something that might be made."

What I think he really meant is that the writer's task is onefold—to make his world, he must make words. But whatever he meant, Professor Gass, who teaches at Washington University in St. Louis, has continued ever since to explore the ontology of words, first in a tour de force of an essay, **"On Being Blue,"** then in a second collection, *The World Within the Word.* Now, in the dozen essays that constitute his latest collection, *Habitations of the Word,* he has developed still further his preoccupation with the primacy of language.

He has developed it philosophically. In the collection's longest and most difficult essay, **"Representation and the War for Reality,"** he labors to the conclusion that "however we choose to think about it, the fact remains that a word is closer to its sense than to its reference, even if we can write or say the word without knowing what it means, as if its meaning were as absent as its object usually is, and therefore producing it without thinking anything, the way I might pick a word at random from the dictionary—'phot,' for instance—and say it: 'phot . . . phot, phot, phot . . .' before I learn it is a unit of illumination."

He has developed the critical dimension of his inquiry. In **"Emerson and the Essay,"** he makes us understand as never before how the Concord transcendentalist *essayed to be.* Elsewhere, in readings of Shakespeare, Dickens, Hemingway, Nabokov, Rilke, Henry James, Ford Madox Ford, Gertrude Stein, Sir Thomas Browne, and dozens of others equally varied, he drives the lesson home again and yet again that language in great writing begins and ends with itself.

He has developed his obsession stylistically. His sentences lope and leap, swoop and soar, zig and zag until our senses are filled with their dazzle. They can be exhilarating. Here he illustrates how the air is likely to leak out of a soul that an Emerson essay inflates: "We have scarcely gotten home, our feet wet and chilly from the snow, or our chest asweat from the deep summer heat like a heavy coat we can't remove, when our children's sneezes greet us, skinned knees bleed after waiting all day to do so. There is the bellyache and the burned-out basement bulb, the stalled car and the incontinent cat. The windows frost, the toilets sweat, the body of our spouse is one cold shoulder, and the darkness of our bedroom is soon full of the fallen shadows our failures. Now the quiet night light whispers to us: You are unloved—unlovely—you are old. These white sheets rehearse the corpse they will cover. None of our times change. We are the same age as our essayist. Wrinkles squeeze our eyes shut, and we slide into sleep like a sailor from beneath his national flag. Tomorrow our tumescence must be resumed. Tomorrow, Emerson realizes, he must again be a genius.''

More often, alas, the prose is numbing. I'm not sure what the problem is. Professor Gass may be in over my head. His reach may exceed my grasp. Having apparently long ago devoured all of literature, he seems to be fed up with digesting it for us. The result is bloat. I wouldn't dream of saying it if he hadn't done so first: He's gotten Gassy. Something else he writes: ''I was, almost from birth, and so I suppose by 'bottom nature,' what Gertrude Stein called Ezra Pound—a village explainer—which, she said, was all right if you were a village, but if not, not.'' Enough said.

What remains worthwhile are bits and pieces—the essays on Emerson and Ford Madox Ford, a pyrotechnic display on the uses of the conjunction ''and,'' a survey on how people talk to themselves, a gloss on a speech by Antony in *Antony and Cleopatra*. But one comes away from *Habitations of the Word* wishing that Professor Gass would stop talking about fiction and start doing it again. It's been almost two decades since he published his extraordinary first novel, *Omensetter's Luck,* and his estimable collection of stories, *In the Heart of the Heart of the Country*. Between then and now, only a somewhat pallid novella, *Willie Masters' Lonesome Wife,* has intervened.

If Professor Gass has been preparing us for his next novel, *The Tunnel,* we are as ready now as we are going to be. It will be dominated by ''the trope of its title,'' he explains. ''The text is at once the hollow absence of life, words, and earth, which the narrator is hauling secretly way; then it is the uneasy structure of bedboards, bent flesh, rhetorical flourishes and other fustian forms, which shapes the passage, and which incontinently caves in occasionally, filling the reader's nose with noise, and ears with sand and misunderstanding; while finally it is the shapeless mess of dirt, word-dung, and desire, which has to be taken out and disposed of.''

Or else he is training us still to be better readers. But at this he's reached the point of diminishing returns.

> Christopher Lehmann-Haupt, in a review of ''Habitations of the Word,'' in The New York Times, February 14, 1985, p. C28.

EDMUND WHITE

[*White, an American novelist, dramatist, and nonfiction writer, is noted for his impressionistic style and luxurious prose. In the following excerpt White discusses the themes in several of the essays in* Habitations of the Word *and illustrates Gass's ''elaborate literary style.''*]

Although William Gass has turned his masterly hand to essays frequently in the past decade as he has labored to complete his novel *The Tunnel,* his discursive prose always reminds us that he is an imaginative writer of the highest order. Indeed, among contemporary American writers of fiction, he is matched as a

stylist only by a very select group that includes Eudora Welty, Stanley Elkin, W. M. Spackman and Guy Davenport.

Despite the fact that Gass is a trained philosopher, he never thinks in uprooted, ungrounded abstractions but rather always plants his thoughts firmly in a rough, gravelly matrix of circumstantiality. Thus he writes, in a phrase that both states and illustrates his point, that ''ideas carry bombs in their suitcases.'' Or when he discusses the purely ceremonial nature of consumer culture, he says ''we wipe ourselves with a symbol of softness, push an ad around our face; the scale rolls up a number which means 'overweight,' and the innersoles of our shoes say 'hush!'''

The reader of Gass' essays can never drift off into a trance of comfortable (because empty) generalities, each phrase melting into the next through the smoky dissolves of an exhausted rhetoric. No, in every paragraph Gass writes, the very specificity of his images requires the reader to conjure up a matching picture, to expend an erg of energy, the way a farsighted diner must hold his menu at arm's length in order to order at all.

In [*Habitations of the Word*] Gass has collected 12 essays, one of which is an homage to Emerson (whose sentences rush ''from side to side, rebounding as though from rubber bumpers, hurrying out to edges, sounding alarms'') and another to Ford Madox Ford's neglected historical romance *The Fifth Queen* (''the work is so intensely visual, so alternately light and dark, you might think the words were being laid on the page like Holbein's paint''). Gass' enthusiasm returns the reader to the original text. At least I reread Emerson, surprised to discover that his sort of gloomy stoicism had ever been offered to the American public as *advice,* of all things.

Gass' remaining 10 essays are more broadly philosophical. In one he analyzes all the possible connotations of the word *and* in an exercise reminiscent of his dazzling thematic rhapsody *On Being Blue*. A pair of essays takes up the related subjects **''On Talking to Oneself''** and **''On Reading to Oneself.''**

In several of these pieces Gass reminds us that written words should be pleasing to the ear when spoken. ''Above all,'' he says, ''the written word must be so set down that it rises up immediately in its readers to the level of the ear, and becomes a vital presence in their consciousness. It asks, that is, to be performed; to be returned to the world of orality it came from; it asks to be said, to be sung.'' Certainly Gass' own prose—from his mythic novel, *Omensetter's Luck,* with its extended bravura soliloquy for a sex-crazed man of God to the flat, terse poetry of his hallucinatory story, **''The Pedersen Kid''**—has always invited song. In fact in **''The Pedersen Kid''** (included in the collection *In the Heart of the Heart of the Country*), the breath marks are even notated.

But Gass is not just concerned with word music. He recognizes the intellectual nature of words. Although Gass may not be a Platonist, he has been permanently compromised by the irresistible theory of the Forms, those abstract entities that Plato claimed were far denser with reality than any of their mere instances on earth, so that ''Chair'' must be considered infinitely superior to any actual thing we might sit on. Or as Gass puts it, we are astride mythical horses that ''sink down in the direction of things and their disconnections, to pornograph among the passions'' or we ''rise as if winged toward meanings, ideas, regions of pure relation.''

This tension between the grittiness of the particular and the ethereal dynamism of the general is exactly what animates the best fiction and poetry. Wallace Stevens wrote a late poem called "What We See is What We Think." Conversely, William Carlos Williams declared, "No ideas but in things." Yet both poets point to this busy traffic between the intellectual and the material that constitutes any work of imaginative literature that is more than a list of facts or the exposition of a thesis. In one essay, **"Representation and the War for Reality,"** Gass clarifies the subject by dividing the world into the Thick and the Thin. Thins are reductionists. "Thins firmly believe that explanations should be simpler and quite other than the things explained." They make good scientists and philosophers. By contrast, Thicks are more concerned "with amassing facts rather than discovering laws." They make good novelists and historians. But in practice (at least sound practice), these two extremes come together, since "without arrangement and connection" there is "no history" and "without rhetoric, without pattern, without coherence there is only the ordinary novel."

I don't mean to reduce this rich, energetic book to a single topic, no matter how fertile. Gass attacks Roland Barthes and champions Freud, Rilke, Beckett and Gertrude Stein (I wish he'd write an essay on Wallace Stevens, his perfect subject). He argues that "I love you" depends for its meaning on which organ of the body energizes the words—or at least that is his interpretation of Plato. He flits with the idea proposed by Leibnitz that "we are wholly windowless with regard to one another," yet he offers the possibility that reading a novel permits us to enter an alien system, "to become a different monad for a moment." He reminds us that wisdom is never general but rather something "found by means of a vocalized internal investigation," a sort of sustained dialogue of the soul and self. In **"The Soul Inside the Sentence"** Gass ingeniously elaborates Freud's theories of wish-fulfillment and sublimation as the underpinnings of creativity, but surely any psychoanalytic theory of art that leaves out Freud's notion of the repetition compulsion (proposed in his 1920 essay *Beyond The Pleasure Principle*) can only be partial.

Gass consistently defends an elaborate literary style. Thus Ford Madox Ford did not "have to assume a severe, undecorated, screwed-down style, as if weakness were a show of strength, as if only the simple were sincere, or the plain ennobling." Americans sometimes fall into the trap of imagining that the national style is invariably chaste, business-like. But Gass— like Emerson, Whitman, Melville—belongs to the other American tradition of inspired rhetoric. Perhaps the two great sources of this rhetorical style were the King James Bible and Shakespeare. The decline of the Renaissance ornate style Gass traces to the rise of the bourgeoisie and the novel and laments in a sentence worthy of his models, one I cannot and will not follow:

> The paragraph is replaced by the sentence; the sentence is shortened like a dress; the dress is moreover designed to be as plain as a Mennonite's nightgown; and that majestic, endlessly elaborating language, subtle and continuously discriminating, that joyful, private, yet publicly appointed prose, that mouthmade music, once headlong, resonant, and roaring, is reduced to a mousy squeak by the rising noise of the novel.

(pp. 3-4)

Edmund White, "*The World According to Gass*," in Book World—The Washington Post, *March 3, 1985, pp. 3-4.*

FRANK KERMODE

[*Kermode is an English literary critic who has written and edited a variety of works, including studies of such writers as William Shakespeare, John Donne, D. H. Lawrence, and Wallace Stevens. Among his works of critical theory are* Approaches to Poetics *(1973) and* The Art of Telling: Essays on Fiction *(1983). In the following excerpt Kermode approaches Gass in his role as philosopher-essayist, examining his ideas and praising his sumptuous prose.*]

William H. Gass is not alone among leading American fiction writers in giving some of his time and talent to nonfiction, but nobody does it more energetically. How best may we describe him in this alternative role? He wouldn't mind being called a philosopher but would certainly object to the description "literary critic," for he has small regard for most of the writing done by such persons. The best, most acceptable term is "essayist." Mr. Gass has strong views about the essay and thinks it worthy of his best attention.

Habitations of the Word is his first collection of essays since *The World Within the Word,* published seven years ago. That book contained a number of reviews, but Mr. Gass has a genial contempt for reviewers, and his own specimens clearly indicate his determination to be as unlike them as possible. Not for him the plain expository manner they probably think appropriate to their task; everything must be charged by his virtuoso's passion for language.

So it is in this new collection, and its reviewers have an obvious problem. They may feel obliged to give some account of the gist of Mr. Gass's thinking about his chosen topics, and that could easily be done; but if there's one thing he hates more than another it's a gist. This may be, in part, because summary would falsely suggest that he is often repeating what he has said before, or what others have said in more pedestrian ways. But mostly it is because he won't have what is said separated from the manner of its saying. His hatred of readers who tear through a book looking for gists is well expressed in the following paragraph, specially designed to show how much more than gists there is in his prose.

For the speeding reader, "paragraphs become a country the eye flies over looking for landmarks, reference points, airports, restrooms, passages of sex. The speeding reader guts a book the way the skillful clean fish. The gills are gone, the tail, the scales, the fins; then the fillet slides away swiftly as though fed to a seal; and only the slow reader, one whom those with green teeth chew through like furious worms; only the reader whose finger falters in front of long words, who moves the lips, who dances the text, will notice the odd crowd of images— flier, butcher, seal—which have gathered to comment on the aims and activities of the speeding reader, perhaps like gossips at a wedding. To the speeding reader, this jostle of images, this crazy collision of ideas—of landing strip, kernel, heart, guts, sex—will not be felt or even recognized, because these readers are after what they regard as the inner core of meaning; it is the gist they want, the heart of the matter; they want what can equally well be said in their own, other, and always fewer words: so that the gist of this passage could be said to be: readers who read rapidly read only for the most generalized and stereotyped significances."

And that is by no means all. The seal and the fish turn up again. Sentences of more than 300 words, marked by just this bundling together of metaphors, just this redundancy, just this self-reference or, if you like, self-regard, are quite common. Mr. Gass's gists are always lavishly cocooned.

And that is why he writes essays, not articles. Articles are spiritless, orderly things, not a gist out of place. Essays can be loose, baggy, abundant. Mr. Gass leads off with an essay called **"Emerson and the Essay."** It is given this pole position because it demonstrates what he can do in emulation of the American master of the form; but he probably owes more to other masters. Montaigne's great essay ''On Certain Verses of Virgil'' is important to him, and he admires some 17th-century English writers, notably Thomas Browne. Mr. Gass's own baroque abundance is fully displayed in this Emerson essay, though it seems to me the least successful in the book. It tells us that Mr. Gass, like Emerson, has ''a need to be immense,'' and that, like Emerson again, he will ''essay to be'' by writing essays, which in his case means a good deal of disorder and hectic digression. Insights into Emerson have to fight their way through swathes of gorgeous prose.

Mr. Gass believes sentences have souls. When Emerson says that ''sleep lingers all our lifetime about our eyes, as night hovers all day in the boughs of the fir trees,'' you feel you have heard a sentence with a soul. But souls can be capable of bathos. ''The snip of Atropos is sudden. Quick. Complete. The way the cleaning woman quits'' is a sequence without much soul; though ''the sun comes through the clouds like a melon through a wet sack'' proves Mr. Gass's sentences also have souls, though of a different species from Emerson's.

Everything else in the book is better than its overture.... The tone is a blend of down-to-earth and rhapsodic, even if the subject is **"Tropes of the Text"** or **"Representation and the War for Reality."** Here is one creative writer who won't allow himself to look uncreative. As a writer of fiction he has strong opinions for which, as a philosopher, he finds reasons—reasons which, as an essayist, he adorns and fantasticates.

In a remarkable, summary-defying essay, **"The Habitations of the Word,"** on Plato's *Phaedrus,* Mr. Gass once more complains that reviewers destroy ''the subtlety of subtle texts.'' But in the teeth of these warnings, the reviewer has, after all, to provide a few gists. So here we go. This author has one preoccupation above all; he sees fictions, which are his trade, as constituting their own world of words, not as attempts to represent some external reality. We, as persons, are windowless in respect of one another; in the same way fictions are windowless to the world. Novels are made of language—of ''vestigial twitches of the larynx, gray paradigms of sound''— and of that material they construct world models. Strangely enough, we, the readers, can live in such worlds. This basic position is argued philosophically in **"Tropes of the Text,"** and its psychoanalytic implications are explored in **"The Soul inside the Sentence,"** as they were earlier in **"The Anatomy of Mind,"** an essay in *The World Within the Word.* But this is not mere repetition; each time the gists are given a sumptuous new essayistic dress.

Mr. Gass has a good eye, and a good ear, for other great builders of world models—not only for Ford, but for Sartre, whose *Nausea* he passionately examines, and for Nabokov and Beckett. Any variety of model interests him; he has a fine passage on the epistolary novel from Samuel Richardson to John Barth. All these writers use words, vestigial laryngeal twitches; and what they make of them is worlds, opaque worlds, not transparent upon reality. These sound like fashionable critical opinions, but Mr. Gass is above fashion. He maintains,

for example, that the printed word is still ''only a surrogate for the spoken one.'' So much for Jacques Derrida. He is equally firm in his dismissal of Roland Barthes's *Death of the Author,* for in an essay with the same title, he argues that Barthes's report is much exaggerated. Playing with a celebrated philosophers' puzzle, he affirms that Sir Walter Scott is dead but the author of *Waverley* isn't. He wants to dissociate himself from the view that writers are simply the instruments of earlier texts and inherited cultural presuppositions. Some are, some aren't; some die, some don't; and those that don't are the ones that aren't.

Mr. Gass has a heartwarming respect for authors who live. The most moving parts of his book, I think, are moments when he lingers over a loved sentence or paragraph, perhaps by Rilke or Beckett, Browne or Jeremy Taylor, Joyce or Shakespeare. These are sentences with souls, and therefore alive, with a life not bursting out like a melon from a sack but held forever in its gray paradigms, like the night in the fir-trees. He aspires to such souled sentences himself, and to the construction and study of Gassian world models. It is to that task that he devotes his large reading and his intense, animated philosophical mind. He is a living author, and has splendid aspirations.

Frank Kermode, ''Adornment and Fantastication,'' in The New York Times Book Review, *March 10, 1985, p. 12.*

ROBERT ALTER

[*Alter, an American literary critic, has written several studies of the novel as a genre as well as works on individual authors and reflections on Jewish writing. His works include* Rogues's Progress: Studies in the Picaresque Novel *(1965),* Defenses of the Imagination *(1978), and* Motives for Fiction *(1984). In the following excerpt Alter evaluates the strengths and weaknesses of* Habitations of the Word, *finding that Gass's inventive and eloquent style is often at cross-purposes with his expression of ideas.*]

To the extent that one can discern a general critical argument in [*Habitations of the Word*], there appears to be a shift in emphasis from Gass's earlier essays. A decade ago, he was typically insisting with acerbic wit that novels are made out of nothing but words, or even, that what any writer finally cares about is words and words alone. Now, perhaps because the post-Structuralists have made this stress on the sheer textuality of texts rather uncomfortably fashionable, Gass strives to recover a sense of lived individual experience embodied in, or rather transmuted into, literary texts. In accord with this sense, he passionately argues, contrary to Deconstructive notions, that what is primary in the literary use of language is not writing but the pulsating presence of the spoken word, reworked and heightened in the formal complexities of a literary style.

There is much musing here, in a baroque mood and mode, on the painful transience of human existence, and so the effort to get life into words, **"The Soul inside the Sentence"** (as one of the essays is called), is seen as the most urgent and poignant of undertakings. Here is Gass, sounding this theme at his eloquent best in the long lead-essay on Emerson that is probably the strongest piece in the book:

In fact, in time, the dross body drops away, the peevish tongue is still, greed is gone because the gut is, vanities collapse with the lungs, the long competition with the Great concludes, the very arcs of energy and impotence, of which Emerson so often complains, finally slow and cease like a swing with an empty seat, and our author is at last that: the lonely words of his work.

This is fine writing because the person who has framed these sentences obviously reads with his whole imagination—from the base of the spine, as Nabokov liked to tell his students—and knows what is involved existentially in both writing and reading, and how to translate that knowledge into answering cadences, images, alliterative stresses.

What is peculiar about *Habitations of the Word,* running counter to prevalent conceptions of the kind of writer Gass might be, is that there is so little clear or consecutive thinking in it. It may be possible, by an athletic feat of exegesis, to wrest from these essays a "theoretical position" on mimesis, artifice, and the status of language, but if such a position is there at all, it exists in hints and winks and ellipses and teasing allusions, never as a sustained argument. *Habitations of the Word* virtually invites judgment not as a pursuit of discernible ideas but as a stylistic performance, a series of verbal improvisations on fairly simple themes. Indeed, as one progresses in the volume, it becomes increasingly difficult to make out any real subject in individual essays, or any subject that is more than a banality. Thus, "Tropes of the Text" conveys little more than the idea that different fictional texts offer different metaphors (auto-biography, letters, etc.) for their own textual existence. **"And"** tells us that the English conjunction means different things in different contexts. **"On Talking to Oneself"** argues what we have all known since childhood, that we constantly talk to ourselves in varying voices, emulating different models of oral delivery. **"On Reading to Oneself"** suggests, unexceptionally, that there is a big difference between the leisurely pleasures of reading and the pinched purposefulness of skimming. By the time we get to essays like **"The Origin of Extermination in the Imagination"** and **"The Death of the Author,"** the subject dissolves entirely into the writer's associative gambits, rhetorical gyrations, catalogs of illustrations, and anecdotal asides.

If Gass the essayist is to be judged as a performer, not as an analyst or thinker, how good a show does he put on? He has obviously been reading the English prose masters of the early 17th century, particularly Sir Thomas Browne, whom he quotes several times; and his own self-conscious aim is to write like a contemporary Browne. In bits and pieces, he manages to do this quite wonderfully. (pp. 32, 34)

Between . . . moving moments of genuine eloquence, Gass is almost always lively and inventive, tossing bright images into the air and spinning them in surprising directions. A formidable speed-reader remembered from boyhood "had a head of thin red hair like rust on a saw; he screwed a suggestive little finger into his large fungiform ears. He was made of rust, moss, and wax. . . ." Senescence and death are made vivid to the mind's eye through the following metaphorical terms: "Wrinkles squeeze our eyes shut, and we slide into sleep like a sailor from beneath his national flag."

This last example hints at the defect of a virtue in Gass's style that elsewhere obliterates the virtue altogether. There is often rather too much going on in his games of figuration, which is to say that the gamesman works a little too hard displaying his own adroitness. The frequent result is mere cuteness instead of expressive force, the image calling attention to itself at the expense of the idea, feeling, or object it is supposed to illuminate. (p. 34)

William Gass is clearly a writer willing to take chances with his prose. There are, as I have suggested, real gains in such freewheeling inventiveness. But the casting aside of inhibitions also means that unconscious materials are constantly popping through the surface of the writing, often in ways that subvert its effectiveness. Images of disjunct body parts and disease are frequent, even when the link with their objects of reference is questionable ("thirst and hunger and hope return and return like a tubercular cough"). The prose is blotched with a cloacal obsession, the excretory functions being deemed the aptest image for most things. Thoughts of mortality: "The freshly dead dog us; their corpses fill our thoughts like stool packed in the bowel." The return of the repressed: "that name on the tip of the tongue . . . suddenly explodes like a fart in the mouth." The human predisposition to transform everything: "What I am emptying my bladder of, behind that tree in that neglected park, was once a nice hot cup of green tea." Such images tempt one to psychological conjecture, but I will resist the temptation. The main point, in any case, is that Gass is a spectacular, and spectacularly uneven, writer. Though he works under academic auspices, sometimes with footnotes and with reference to both philosophers and literary theorists, he has increasingly assumed the posture of a zanily serious prose-poet vamping on intellectual themes. At his best, he can call up the power of a master of English prose, but his overreach for originality often carries him to the brink of bad taste, bathos, and plain imprecision. (pp. 34-5)

Robert Alter, "Classical Gass," in The New Republic, *Vol. 192, No. 10, March 11, 1985, pp. 32, 34-5.*

DAVID LEHMAN

[*Lehman is an American poet whose collections include* Some Nerve *(1973) and* Day One *(1979). Lehman has also edited collections of essays on such contemporary poets as John Ashbery, Elizabeth Bishop, and James Merrill. In 1976 Lehman founded Nobaddady Press, a publisher of poetry. Lehman has stated that Gass is among his three favorite critics, citing Gass's use of language as a reason for his admiration. In the following excerpt Lehman praises* Habitations of the Word.]

The essays of William Gass belong in a category all their own. A relentlessly experimental novelist who teaches philosophy at Washington University in St. Louis, Gass writes with extraordinary panache about everything—and nothing. In a typical essay, he mixes a little literary criticism with a lot of rhetorical analysis, stirs in some philosophical extemporizing and coats it all in the most mellifluous and baroque of prose styles. Nobody but Gass would, for example, devote an entire essay—and that a panegyric—to the diverse functions of the word "and": "and" as the glue in a collage or list, the "and" that "separates and joins at the same time," the "and" that implies causality, the adverbial "and." Along the way, he pauses to admire a Gertrude Stein comma that behaves like an "and"—and declares that "one could easily write another essay on the germinal, the spermatic character of this seedy wormlike bit of punctuation."

"And" is one of the best essays in *Habitations of the Word,* Gass's new collection, and that isn't surprising. Gass has been enjoying a lifelong, reciprocal love affair with words, and he is as passionate about them as Humbert Humbert was about his Lolita. If you want to learn how the language really works, check out Gass's analysis of a Shakespearean metaphor in **"Representation and the War for Reality,"** or hear him on the differences between the ampersand and the word "and," or let him guide you to **"The Soul inside the Sentence."**

For Gass, an essay is an invitation to digress. After all, as he writes in **"Emerson and the Essay,"** "what is a stroll without a stop, a calculated dawdle, coffee in a café we've surprised, some delicious detour down a doorway-crowded street, the indulgence of several small delays?" Any subject qualifies as the pretext for a profusion of rich figures of speech, language strutting its stuff. (pp. 80-1)

Gass never runs out of high-octane fuel. In **"The Death of the Author"** he races from Flaubert to Trollope, from Joyce to Nabokov ("the great Vladimir, Napoleon of prose")—all by way of arguing that academically trendy rumors alleging the death of the author have been greatly exaggerated. There's a danger, of course, in reading so rhapsodic a writer. Gass is like an intoxicant. His sentences go straight to your head, and it's more than likely that you'll wake up mildly hung over, not knowing what hit you, not remembering exactly what got proved or debunked. What Gass says about Ford Madox Ford's neglected novel *The Fifth Queen* applies with a vengeance to **Habitations of the Word:** "It must be read with the whole mouth—lips, tongue, teeth—like a long slow bite of wine." (p. 81)

David Lehman, "Verbal Valentines," in Newsweek, *Vol. CV, No. 12, March 25, 1985, pp. 80-1.*

CANDYCE DOSTERT

To read William Gass is to accompany an extraordinary mind on a quest for perfection, an invigorating voyage for the strong of heart. "There are truths," asserts this philosopher/fiction writer/literary critic, and while these truths cannot be named, they can be realized and encountered in language, for the word is the essence of consciousness, and "consciousness is all the holiness we have."

In [*Habitations of the Word*], written for different occasions over the past five years (symposia, commencement addresses, publication in journals), Gass returns to the same themes he explored in his last volume of essays, **The World Within the Word.** Again it is language that is celebrated, examined, and put to use in startling new ways. In this volume we are urged to seek out the "habitation of the word" in the great lines of literature, for there both reader and writer share a moment of immortality. Each of these essays resounds with a faith in the power of language well-used; their various subjects provide Gass with different materials and strategies for coming around to this one injunction: Read; Use language with care and joy; Live it so that you sing the word, dance it, taste it.

"When Ideas and things are separate, the word is torn in two," says Gass in his title essay. In keeping with this vision of the essential unity, in language, of Ideas (or Forms) and things, Gass undertakes this spiritual quest in the most physical terms. His imagery is earthy and sublime, his style one of luxurious excess, where things are called by all their names. His essay devoted to exploring the multiple meanings of the word "and" reveals that he is aware of his place in the tradition of expansive American writers which includes Gertrude Stein and Hemingway as well as Whitman and Melville.

It is a keen pleasure to accompany so erudite and energetic a reader over the terrain of great writers, Henry James, Rilke, Sir Thomas Browne, and Plato among many others. . . .

This volume is a call to join this celebrant of words in realizing the infinite possibilities of the human spirit. It is a challenge only the faint of heart would refuse.

Candyce Dostert, in a review of "Habitations of the Word," in Wilson Library Bulletin, *Vol. 59, No. 9, May, 1985, p. 630.*

SAM TANENHAUS

Habitations of the Word, William Gass's fourth nonfiction book, picks up where **The World Within the Word** left off seven years ago—with essays meant to enliven the form as Montaigne, Emerson, and Woolf enlivened it. This is an ambitious task, but no contemporary American has better credentials than Gass: **Omensetter's Luck** and **In the Heart of the Heart of the Country** fuse the speculative power of a practicing philosopher with the storyteller's instinct for improvisation. Each of these dozen pieces is a performance or foray: he announces a topic, then descants with impressive erudition and unbuttoned ardor for the surprising phrase. The results often dazzle, and they're unfailingly original, in the root sense of the word—they work back toward some point of origin, generally a point where literature departs from the external world to invent a world of its own.

This world is built of language, which as readers we must learn to approach anew, not as a tyrannical code that classfies, and thereby negates, experience, but as an instrument for asserting the anarchic priorities of the self. **"The Soul inside the Sentence"** describes how even novels that faithfully record objective reality subvert it: their verbal reconstitution of the physical universe smuggles nourishment to our most primal appetite—possession. Elsewhere Gass reminds us that our verbal history begins with the noises we utter in infancy—in orality—not with our eventual mastery of language as a written system.

Art is a response to our primitive impulses; it also gratifies an innate desire for order, chiefly through the designs of style. **"The Neglect of Ford Madox Ford's Fifth Queen"** celebrates a "textbook of technique, a catalogue of resources, an art of the English fugue"—a tour de force encapsulating the entire formalist tradition. Passages from *The Golden Bowl* gleam like a gorgeous centerpiece in **"Culture, Self, and Style,"** a tribute to the ways highly wrought prose—its phrases arranged as lovingly as heirlooms—raises our concern with objects to a higher plane, where order prevails. The remarkable **"And"** takes this argument further; a hymn to the versatility of our commonest conjunction, it identifies six different uses in a single sentence by Gertrude Stein.

The polarities of language—the primal and the perfected—meet in their campaign to outwit convention, the jailer of intuition and insight. A high point of **"The Soul inside the Sentence"** is a hilarious dialogue between the id and its various censors, an exchange of wishes and denials that charts the progress of sexual urges from our first thwarted attempts to fondle ourselves, through the mazy stages of lust, up to the sly blandishments of poetry's "How do I love thee, let me count the ways." . . . **"The Origin of Extermination in the Imagination"** gives an extraordinarily vivid account of the ways in which consciousness, seeking to annihilate threatening stimuli, retreats into the sanctuary of mass-produced, civically approved lies. Though Gass deplores the nervelessness of the herd, he's at odds with iconoclasts. In **"The Death of the Author,"** he tackles Roland Barthes, whose essay of the same name is, in Gass's estimation, too quick to carry off the corpse. Ordinary writers, mouthpieces of a generalized language, don't come alive in their texts; but the great author inhabits words by liberating them from their old meanings, "and in that simple rearrangement of the given and the inevitable and the previous, he triumphs, making something new, in Pound's sense, and thus *breaking through the circle of society.*"

Gass himself tries to break through in each sentence. His mission, after all, is to transform arcs of thought into gaudy word rainbows, in defiance of his sworn enemy—the article writer. He succeeds heroically, but not absolutely; sometimes his digressions seem like indulgences, and on occasion his famous prose, with its piled-up lists, preening phrases, and crowded images, buckles under its own elephantine weight. Such are the risks of the grand style. Gass willingly takes them, and well he should; as consistently as any essayist we have, he gives us language that displays, to quote his own prescription for inspired writing, "energy, perception, passion, thought, music, movement, and imagination."

> *Sam Tanenhaus, "Splendor in the Gass," in* The Village Voice, *Vol. XXX, No. 23, June 4, 1985, p. 50.*

Occasional Prose

by Mary McCarthy

(See also *CLC*, Vols. 1, 3, 5, 14, 24; *Contemporary Authors,*
Vols. 5-8, rev. ed.; *Contemporary Authors New Revision Series,* Vol. 16; *Dictionary of Literary Biography,* Vol. 2; and
Dictionary of Literary Biography Yearbook: 1981.)

An Excerpt from *Occasional Prose*

The first real dent on my Cavalier-period armor was
made in my senior year at Vassar in Miss Peebles's
course in Contemporary Prose Fiction, where we studied
"multiplicity" and "stream of consciousness" and were
assigned *The 42nd Parallel* by Dos Passos as an example
of those trends. I fell madly in love with that book—the
first volume of the trilogy that was going to be *U.S.A.*
No doubt the fervor of emotion—an incommunicable
bookish delight—had been preparing in me for some time
through other "social" books, just as two mild bee-
stings may prepare you for a third that is fatal. I had
been telling my friends, and believing, that in politics I
was a royalist—an impractical position, I knew, for an
American, since we did not even have a kingly line to
restore. At the suggestion of one of those anxious friends,
I had read Shaw's *The Intelligent Woman's Guide to
Socialism and Capitalism,* but it rolled right off me,
water off a duck's back. Then came *The 42nd Parallel. . . .*

I went to the library and looked up every line that Dos
Passos had published that was in the card catalogue. I
read them all. The last was a pamphlet on the Sacco-
Vanzetti case, which I found and read in the library
basement, feeling tremendously stirred by Vanzetti's famous words, brand-new, of course, to me, and by the
whole story. But we were in 1933, I realized, and they
had been executed in 1927. So there was nothing to be
done. But I was moved to read up on the Tom Mooney
case too (he at least was still alive) and to become aware
of the *New Republic.* One thing leading to another, soon
after graduation, I was writing little book reviews for
the *New Republic,* then for the *Nation,* and I never looked
back. Like a Japanese paper flower dropped into a glass
of water, my political persona unfolded, magically, from
Dos Passos, though he would have been saddened in
later years to hear what his energy, enthusiasm, and sheer
unwary talent had brought about.

STEFAN KANFER

"I'm not sure she isn't the woman Stendhal," wrote Edmund
Wilson back in 1941, when his young wife began her first
book. Some 40 years, 20 volumes and two husbands later, the

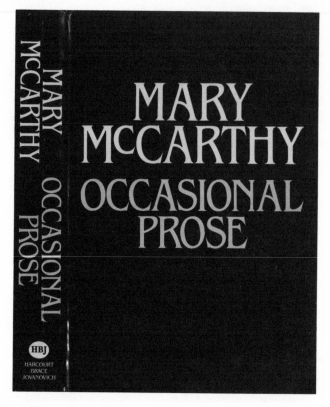

Dust jacket of Occasional Prose, *by Mary McCarthy. Harcourt Brace Jovanovich, 1985. Courtesy of Harcourt Brace
Jovanovich, Inc.*

evidence is in. Mary McCarthy, 72, has her own wise and
distinctive voice, but the cool, analytical approach to art, sex
and politics inescapably suggests the 19th century Frenchman.

In *Occasional Prose,* fugitive pieces range from reportage to
literary criticism to the comparative values of wood ash, manure and seaweed in the garden. All of the works are reminiscent of, in Stendhal's memorable phrase, "a mirror walking
along a main road." McCarthy's reflections begin with a recollection of her colleague Philip Rahv, longtime editor of *Partisan Review.* Thousands of words have been spent discussing
the unrepentant old radical; this obituary captures him in three
sentences: "He never learned to swim . . . He would immerse
his body in the alien element but declined or perhaps feared
to move with it. His resistance to swimming with the tide, his
mistrust of currents, were his strength."

Sudden illuminations occur throughout the collection. In London, an anti-Viet Nam protest is "something like a medieval
carnival in a modern setting, with everybody changing places,
the fool becoming king for a day . . . the police merging with

the populace and even putting on false beards. But no more than a carnival did it 'solve' anything.'' Vladimir Nabokov, she notes, treats the Russian language ''as a national treasure the usurper Bolsheviks appropriated from him, to turn over to the rabble.'' She ponders the absence of important fiction in prewar Germany: ''Common sense tells you the way things *are,* rather than the way your covetous ego or prehensile will would like them to be. And the sparsity of novels, the great carriers of the reality principle, may help to explain German defenselessness in the face of National Socialism.''

In the past, McCarthy's pugnacity sometimes led her to be labeled Mary Mary Quite Contrary, and she still seems to delight in offering a chair for her subject, merely to yank it away at the appropriate moment. In her lecture **"Living with Beautiful Things,"** she discusses collections of great art, then decides, ''By contrast to the ear, the eye is a jealous, concupiscent organ, and some idea of ownership or exclusion enters into our relation with visual beauty.'' From there it is a quick step to the conclusion, ''Quite poisonous people, on the whole, are attracted by the visual arts and can become very knowledgeable about them. This is much less true of literature . . . A bookish man will be an omnivorous reader, obviously, but he will not be greedy: by consuming more reading matter than is customary he does not deprive anyone else of his share . . . The same could be said of music.''

Let home gardeners pore over seed catalogs and boast of home-grown salads; she knows that ''Nature, far from being on your side, is actively against you, attacking with bugs, molds, rot, cankers, neighboring dogs, raccoons, skunks, porcupines, drought, torrential rains, 'black' frosts, snow heaves, winter-kill. And I cannot think that the satisfaction derived is in the results, however beautiful or tasty . . . The fact is that gardening, more than most of our other activities except sometimes love-making, confronts us with the inexplicable.''

Although *Occasional Prose* ranges back to 1968, none of it is dated, and little seems forced by headlines. McCarthy writes, therefore she is, and she is everywhere. In the course of a dissertation on cooking, she quotes a parody of Goethe's *Werther:* ''Charlotte, having seen his body / Borne before her on a shutter, / Like a well-conducted person, / Went on cutting bread and butter.'' Charlotte was a lady after the author's art. Let violence and fatuities pass in review; the well-conducted Mary McCarthy will watch and then slice them into appropriate pieces. Books and events have always been her bread and butter. (pp. 101-02)

Stefan Kanfer, ''Reflections,'' in Time, Vol. 125, No. 15, April 15, 1985, pp. 101-02.

JULIAN MOYNAHAN

The earliest article in *Occasional Prose,* **"On the Demo,"** is from 1968. It describes the big demonstration against the Vietnam War that took place in London that fall. Things came to a head before the fortress-styled United States Embassy in Grosvenor Square. I had witnessed a particularly violent demonstration there that spring, organized by an international roster of student radicals, and can certify the correctness of her remark that ''Grosvenor Square, if not a death-trap, is a box in which pressures build up almost by themselves.'' By the fall, apparently, the demonstrators and the police had learned a little patience with each other; she describes how one constable in the siege line across the front of the embassy flicked his lighter

for one of the cigarette-smoking Maoists opposite him. In March they would have tried to club each other.

This description is typical of her reportorial style—a quick eye for the telling and anomalous detail, along with a tendency to view public events, or at least public events in the 1960's, as theater: ''Indeed, the Demo, which might have been a tragedy, turned into a comedy of manners.'' Come to think of it, ''demo'' is to ''demonstration'' as ''panto'' is to ''pantomime,'' with Tariq Ali, the abrasive Pakistani leader of the Trotskyist faction of demonstrators, playing Turko the Terrible. The abbreviation somehow makes it all more cozy.

Her latest dated essay is a ''postface'' to a new edition of Nicola Chiaromonte's *Paradox of History,* which has not even been published yet. It is the second piece in the book on this too little known Italian intellectual who flew with Malraux during the Spanish Civil War and combined an independent left-wing political stance with a lifelong passion for live theater. As a working drama critic, Chiaromonte distrusted Brecht and the ''alienation effect,'' clung to Pirandello, Shaw and Ibsen as exemplary influences on modern drama, approved the distancing effected by masks, stylized acting and other devices deriving from the Attic stage and yet defined the essence of the play as ''reasoning action.'' Miss McCarthy shows us how these seemingly diverse and contradictory tendencies fit together. We are reminded that she has also been an excellent drama critic, starting out with the old *Partisan Review.*

Some of Miss McCarthy's closest friends passed away during the 1970's and become the subject of her obituary commemorations, which seem to me to be suffused with a downright Irish need to speak ''nice words'' about the departed. These people were of a generation, though they were not a clique, and she is of that generation too, though, being something of a Wunderkind in her literary beginnings, she was actually four or five years younger than any of them.

Her strongest friendship was perhaps with Hannah Arendt, whom she not only describes as an intellectual's intellectual— ''The task that had fallen to her . . . was to apply thought systematically to each and every characteristic experience of her time . . . and, having finally achieved this, to divert thought inward, upon itself, and its own characteristic processes''— but also as ''beautiful . . . alluring, seductive, feminine.'' That may go a little far, though many will remember Arendt's vitality and charm. She was arresting even when quoting passages of technical philosophy in languages unknown to most of her auditors. In the spring of 1959, Mary McCarthy and Hannah Arendt sometimes attended the Gauss Seminars in Criticism, which Richard Blackmur directed at Princeton University. Without saying a word, they were a daunting pair. Their looks spoke volumes, and they always seemed in total agreement.

As a literary critic Miss McCarthy often likes to lay down rules and devise categories (see the pieces **"Politics and the Novel"** and **"Novel, Tale, and Romance"**), but her finest talent is for unraveling difficult texts by paying the closest possible attention to the actual twists and turns of words on the page. Who can forget her superb explication of *Pale Fire* nearly a quarter-century ago, which did so much to firm up Nabokov's post-*Lolita* literary reputation with his American audience? Here she tries something similar with Italo Calvino's *If on a Winter's Night a Traveler* and Joan Didion's *Democracy.*

She is wonderful on the tale in **"Novel, Tale, and Romance."** It's unlikely any other American literary journalist could reveal intimate knowledge of the works of Adalbert Stifter in the original German and then go on to associate him with the northern European forests and wooden house architecture. Her account of the novel, which emphasizes its factuality and ties to common sense and the reality principle, seems unduly restrictive. I would also dissent from her conventional account of how Joyce's heaping up of verbal detritus in *Finnegans Wake* and the overwhelming nature of modern events have stopped the novel dead in its tracks. Nobody can prove it, but these bones live.

Everywhere in *Occasional Prose* appear bracing opinions tartly expressed—Americans are slow, tedious talkers; big-time art collectors are not very nice people; the word "drugget" must never be used for stair carpeting; everybody misuses prepositions because nobody studies Latin in school anymore. In this mood she is reminiscent of Miss Jean Brodie, without that character's feckless right wingery, of course. May she continue to call us all to attention ("No slumping in the back seats!"), showing us the world of her imagination, thought and rich experience.

> Julian Moynahan, "You Pay Attention, You Learn Something," in The New York Times Book Review, May 5, 1985, p. 15.

WEBSTER SCHOTT

Around 32 years ago, a few months after *The Groves of Academe* was published, Gilbert Highet, surveying the world of letters as if from Olympus, concluded, "In America the most effective satirist is Mary McCarthy, who writes a peculiarly cold but skillful prose, as graceful as a deft surgical operation."

Fourteen books later we know there has been much more to Mary McCarthy—she's now 72—than dissections of Colonel Blimp college presidents and sleazy professors of literature who defend themselves against discharge on the grounds they were once communists. Not only has she written rapier novels. She is a clear-eyed, cool-voiced analyst of human behavior and one of the few commentators on the arts for whom the term "critic" seems barely adequate. She is nearly a national cultural asset, and the pieces retrieved for *Occasional Prose* show us why once again.

Gathered from lectures in unlikely places like Kansas, Poughkeepsie, and Aberdeen, from prefaces and postfaces to several books, from such publications as *Saturday Review, The New York Review of Books, The New York Times* and Britain's *Observer* and *Sunday Times,* these 21 selections range from obituaries of friends who fought the battle of liberalism to reports of social disorder visited on us by the Vietnam war, from accounts of Richard Nixon's debasement of our language and the romanticism of Boris Pasternak to insights into the penny-pinching meanness of the French *petite noblesse* and the eccentricities of those who devote their lives to plants.

In a preface to Jean-Francois Revel's *Without Marx or Jesus,* Mary McCarthy tells us, "There is something wonderfully disinterested about Revel's biases, a joy in bias itself as an artistic form . . . He has a Falstaffian side and only cares that his 'slant' should run counter to respectable culture and received opinion. If he has a personal grievance, it is a longstanding, deeply nurtured one against the immovable forces of entrenched beliefs that insult his sense of the self-evident."

We admire in others the qualities we ourselves possess. Revel's independence of mind and his enthusiasm for turning conventional wisdom upside down—maxims like "War is a contin-

uation of politics by other means" reversed into "Foreign policy is an initiation of war by other means"—are essentially what attract us to Mary McCarthy. She is Irish, had a Jewish grandmother, got her Phi Beta Kappa key at Vassar and began her writing career on the *Partisan Review*. She may have both genetic and acquired contrariness. And it has the right targets.

"If I hear often enough 'Poverty is no crime,' I feel an urge to reply 'Poverty *is* a crime,' meaning that it is against the laws of humanity or that to be poor is to be already two-thirds of a criminal in the eyes of the police."

While she doesn't believe that the 1968 Whitehall antiwar demonstration she covered in London gave the U.S. a push toward withdrawal from Vietnam, she suggests "another way of looking at the question." She turns it around. "What would *not* demonstrating have accomplished? . . . Nothing. So given the choice between a problematical nothing and a certain nothing, maybe it was best to demonstrate after all."

This thought follows, by the way, her observation that to ask demonstrators, "What do you hope to accomplish?" had "the effect of a negative password. It virtually invited the bum's rush." Such commonsensical questions were "an unwelcome interruption in a theatre of revolution." McCarthy takes sides but not blindly.

She thinks about writers and writing with this same sort of pollution-free intellect. "In the realm of ideas," she says of her friend Hannah Arendt, "Hannah was a conservationist; she did not believe in throwing away anything that had once been thought. A use might be found for it; in her own way, she was an enthusiastic recycler."

Phillip Rahv, her old mentor at *Partisan Review* and grand pooh-bah of the U.S. literary left, knew America intimately but lived emotionally in the ghetto of his Jewish Ukrainian past. (p. 5)

To read Mary McCarthy is often sheer pleasure. Her mind works like bright light, showing us details that redefine what we thought we had seen before. Her sentences are displays of grace.

Vladimir Nabokov "has been trying throughout his career to make a one-man literary restoration, using his prodigious memory to undo the present." While the Russian Revolution as described by Boris Pasternak "still has some of a Tolstoyan natural force, awesome and fierce . . . in Solzhenitsyn, the savage natural is replaced by the universal ordinary." From Henry James on, our expatriate writing has a "certain Jackie-and-Ari color supplement flavor" as characters appear to be "impersonating figures in a work of art—something few people dare to do at home." During the 1920s "there were more converts made to hedonism than to any other faith, and that may still be the message of the most influential fiction of today, from Mailer to Updike."

Reviewing Italo Calvino's voluptuous *The Castle of Crossed Destinies,* Mary McCarthy notices that "the act of reading, when finally consummated, is seen to be parallel to the act of love." In an essay on the Italian critic and leftist Nicola Chiaromonte, she notes that "the theatre is dependent on numbers, both to produce it and to consume it. Far more than the novel, or say, the sonnet, it is keyed to demand . . . The sociability of the theatre distinguishes it from films, where one sits in the dark . . . One is never lonely in the theatre."

The motor that runs Mary McCarthy is powerful but different. She believes, for example, that fiction may not change societies but changes individuals the way falling in love does. As a result of reading John Dos Passos' *The 42nd Parallel* at the age of 20, she went from political royalist to liberal socialist. She believes that "if beauty is good for something, then it is a mysterious something that we today cannot put our finger on." But she knows that "everyone needs the good, hankers for it, as Plato says, because of the lack of it in the self. This greatly craved goodness is meaning, which is absent from the world, outside the chain of cause and effect and incommensurable with reason."

Mary McCarthy's purpose in writing is exactly this: to find meaning, to make order of human expression and action. I do wish in this particular book she had left out her rewrite of the plot of *La Traviata* for a Metropolitan Opera guide book and had passed up the temptation to memorialize her garden pieces. They're geese among swans. The rest of the essays in *Occasional Prose* are the goodness she and we crave: gorgeous meaning. (pp. 5, 8)

> Webster Schott, "Mary, Mary, Quite Contrary," in Book World—The Washington Post, May 12, 1985, pp. 5, 8.

JACQUELINE AUSTIN

The publication of a book by Mary McCarthy has often signaled a free-for-all. Critics come running, brandishing quotations, bristling political attitudes, yelling "She's wonderful!" "She's silly!" "And what a literary critic!" or "Well, what can you expect from someone who's really just a literary critic?" McCarthy's devotees rave about her wit, knowledge, and courage. Even her detractors admit she's as intelligent as anyone needs to be; they attack her, instead, as too much the protected academic squinting through a text. For me, McCarthy provides an education in transforming the external into the personal, whether I agree with her or not. She makes each moment of reading, experiencing, remembering into an occasion. McCarthy has that rarest of qualities: erudite, she can seem amateur, in the old sense of that word—she does what she does for pleasure. Beside her, many of her sharpest critics seem dried up, punctilious, or crude.

Since 20 of the 21 essays in *Occasional Prose* are reprints, this book may have already run through its quota of immediate topical controversy. It's too bad that some die-hards will still be shaking fingers instead of turning pages and getting down to business. Usually a reader would have every right to expect a book called *Occasional Prose* to be miscellaneous. Here, "occasional" means not scattered, but pertaining to occasions: days marked by devotion and contemplation as well as celebration.

A McCarthy occasion always points at something larger. A 1968 antiwar demonstration in London becomes theater. A postface to a book by Jean-François Revel becomes provocation. A little essay about Alice Brayton becomes a maypole around which people who favor individuality would do well to dance. And so forth. The occasions in this book, unlike those in *The Writing on the Wall* or other McCarthy collections, are mostly poignant. Not that the author's gone soft—she hasn't—but the last 15 years have brought striking changes. The old *Partisan Review* group is passing. Four essays in this collection are obituaries for associates and friends. The deaths of Nicola Chiaromonte, F. W. Dupee, Hannah Arendt, Philip Rahv called

for eulogy over analysis, and McCarthy's eulogies are generous: not mournful, lockstep funerals or encyclopedic assessments, but wakes. In the emotional **"Saying Goodbye to Hannah (1907-1975),"** a friend takes leave of someone who meant so much to her that any expression might fall short, but McCarthy has the presence to mention Arendt's small vanities, her "pupil-like, eager, approval-seeking" attitude toward her husband Heinrich Bluecher, her private evasions, as well as those qualities which made Arendt publicly great. Philip Rahv is similarly described with emotion, but in detail: "Recounting some story, seizing on some item in a newspaper, he would be transported, positively enraptured, with glee and offended disbelief. His black eyes with their large almost bulging whites would roll, and he would shake his head over and over, have a fit of chuckling, nudge you, if you were a man, squeeze your arm, if you were a woman—as though together you and he were watching a circus parade of human behavior, marvelous monstrosities and curious animals, pass through your village."

A new book by Italo Calvino becomes the occasion for what must be McCarthy's version of heaven: she allows herself to give unmitigated, though typically analytical, praise. In **"Acts of Love,"** about Calvino's *If on a winter's night a traveler*, McCarthy rejoices that "We readers have seen pass in review, like a series of floats, to our cries of delight and recognition, a parade of the types and varieties of narrative experience. . . . It is better than a parade. It is a *Summa fictionis* of scholastic rigor and, like all glorious codifications of divine mysteries, it has to do with love . . ." The last time McCarthy allowed herself to effuse this way was in her review of Nabokov's *Pale Fire*. Indeed, Nabokov's butterfly haunts a couple of paragraphs in this review—not because Calvino's so close to Nabokov, but because McCarthy worships both.

The Watergate trials and their perversion of the English language, a particularly good garden book, the rereading of *Anna Karenina* after 30 years, are all occasions, if lesser ones. Marked by traditions, and by personal ceremonies, McCarthy's occasions may not include turkey with all the trimmings or other routines, except if you call the deliberate progression through a loved (or hated) literary work routine, but instead are marked by flags of feeling and intellect. When she loves something, the preferred form is to step back and let the phenomenon reveal itself, as in the obituary or the laudatory review. Otherwise, the McCarthy ceremony often starts—after the date of note is selected—with a speech to the reader about why it's noteworthy. If the occasion is well known, McCarthy can open with an indirect, satirical, or deadpan image; if less well known, she describes it more plainly, as when she outlines why Nicola Chiaromonte was important. The curious but essentially good occasion can receive a more complex version of the laudatory treatment: a retelling of *La Traviata* is as much social analysis as plot summary, and its wit derives from exposing the cultural attitudes inherent in each episode or scene. This is done deftly, sometimes with just one word: "Five months have passed. It is January. Nothing has turned out as a realist might have expected." The scene change involves not just a simple switch of sets, but a discussion about *Manon Lescaut*, about how kept women always stay close to Paris, about today's Auteuil.

The occasion of dislike or disaffection incurs the wittiest treatment. Joan Didion's novel *Democracy* is seen as puzzling, unresolved, sloppy, and McCarthy takes great care to place it in context:

> In sentences of Orwell she heard an echo of
> Hemingway, and in sentences of Adams she

heard a note of the Mailer to come. How the sentences she quotes from Orwell resemble any of Hemingway's or how Adams's forty-foot dynamo foretells Mailer is not elucidated, nor how they relate to their authors' notions of democracy.

In the same way, I have found it hard to make out what connection there can be between Joan Didion's *Democracy,* opening with a memory of the pink dawns of early atomic weapons tests in the Pacific, and Henry Adams's *Democracy,* whch deals with the dirty politics of the second Grant administration . . .

The McCarthy attack often stretches the subject at hand, as though a faulty book merited less attention than the jangling associations it evoked. The *Democracy* review becomes the occasion for debunking Didion's "hypnosis by movies" ("Maybe that is what coming from California, even as far north as Sacramento, does to you"), imperialism, Conrad, the pervasive influence of Hemingway, the pernicious effect of working at *Vogue* for seven years, celebrity, hollowness, enigma: McCarthy stuffs Didion's turkey with her own spicy mixture before serving it up.

Sometimes McCarthy's occasions recur on almost an annual basis, full of surface change—like Christmas or Easter—but really expressions of the same set of feelings. **"Living with Beautiful Things,"** a 1974 essay about the politics of the art object, is practically a preview of McCarthy's 1979 novel *Cannibals and Missionaries* both in concept and anecdote. The characters in *Cannibals*—art collectors, politicians, liberals—exist almost as illustrations of **"Living"** 's particular wry turns of phrase. **"Language and Politics,"** with its dissections of the computerized mouthings of Watergate actors Haldeman and Ehrlichman, recalls McCarthy's scathing attacks on "The Future Past" in her famous essay on David Halberstam. Despite what Edward Grossman, in *Commentary,* and other critics have said about McCarthy's "fluctuations" in attitude, her work is notable for its unity and continuity. Such remarks seem sourgraphish: over the years, McCarthy has cracked quite a few teapots while sampling the delicious tempests they contained, and it's only natural for the owners' tempers to run high.

In the past, she has tended to mock even the most intimate of her associates, as William Barrett describes in *The Truants:*

"In 1948 she brought out a satirical novelette, *The Oasis,* which caricatured the whole *Partisan Review* circle. . . . [They] gathered around like a group of mourners. 'The woman is a thug,' Diana Trilling said. . . . The most upset of all was Philip Rahv, the central figure in the whole caricature, and clearly identifiable through the slightly changed fictitious name. It would not have been so bad if he had merely been represented as evil, but he was made ridiculous, and that wounded him to the quick. . . . What was amazing was that there was no real break in his friendship with Miss McCarthy. For his part he could come to regard her act of writing as the play of a very brilliant child who does not quite know what she was doing. And for her part she probably had not thought that the victim would be so wounded, for it was all in such fun."

Occasional Prose does not wound, it braces. There is no undeserved mockery here, but much wisdom, honest thought, strong writing. And McCarthy's current major project, an "intellectual autobiography," promises even more. The very brilliant child has grown up.

Jacqueline Austin, "A Sense of Occasion," *in* The Village Voice, *Vol. XXX, No. 23, June 4, 1985, p. 47.*

ROBERT LINKOUS

Mary McCarthy's *Occasional Prose* is a grab-bag of trivialities and occasional treasures. . . . The compilation is eclectic, if not eccentric.

McCarthy's more extreme views range from the obscure to the provocative. She observes that tales flourish in northern countries while romances thrived on the Mediterranean littoral, then speculates (without providing satisfactory explanation) that "the deep northern forests and wooden cottage architecture are a reason for the difference." She maintains that "the scarcity of novels, the great carriers of the reality principle, may help to explain German defenselessness in the face of National Socialism." She fancies that museum curators exhibit "no moral effect of the regular exposure to beauty," and that for scholars and specialists "pleasures in the act of reading are perverse to a repellent degree." These last two notions are not without charm, but only the most blatant cynic would avow that they are true without exception.

In *Occasional Prose* much of what is not obscure is merely innocuous. The lectures seldom surpass the level of undergraduate superficiality; many books are mentioned, but few elucidated; McCarthy hastens like a behind-schedule professor bound to get through the prescribed material by the end of the semester. Several of the reviews are little more than flat encapsulations of plot or subject matter, not much livelier than jacket blurbs.

In two of the essays McCarthy displays a penchant for desultory typology. She troubles to differentiate between novels, tales, and romances, uses those differentiations to draw a few nebulous conclusions, and then meanders on, the original premises all but abandoned. Later she explains that there are three types of political novels to be found in American literature, the persuasive (*Uncle Tom's Cabin*), the realistic (about politicians, not persuasive, "except maybe to discourage one from voting at all"), and a type that "ponders large political questions—essentially the nature and effects of power" (too "long-sighted" to coexist with the first two). Again, the utility of the distinctions is barely demonstrated, but then the thesis of the essay, that the American novel is as political as its European counterpart, has already been refuted so comprehensively that it has begun to appear moot.

And even some of the more insightful views are dated. In a 1971 essay McCarthy wrote that there would be no revolution in America because the vast majority of the populace was content with consumer society; as we observe the burgeoning yuppie culture we hardly need to be reminded that this was true.

So there is much that is too old in *Occasional Prose,* and of what isn't, unfortunately, most is too new. The keenest and most amusing piece in the collection is McCarthy's recent review of Joan Didion's *Democracy.* It is couched in mordant, unyielding terms (Too unyielding, in fact? Elsewhere McCarthy praises Italo Calvino's use of similar modernistic techniques.), and brings to light Didion's most annoying faults as a novelist, her evasiveness, her withholding of vital information in order to generate some spurious suspense, "like the working out of a jigsaw puzzle that is slowly being put together with a continual shuffling and re-examination of pieces still on the edges or heaped in the middle of the design.'' Joan Didion, formerly of *Vogue* magazine, 1956 to 1963, is almost as much of an elitist as Ernest Hemingway, McCarthy contends; a mere foible on the part of one of her characters is enough to cause Didion to ''cook him for all eternity.'' But ''that is insufficient evidence for *artistic* damnation . . . I think one has the right to ask to know them better before sending them unpardoned to hell.'' Who can argue? Didion's characters are obsessed, not multi-faceted, served up after most of the flesh and viscera have been removed. . . .

McCarthy delivers arresting commentary on the decline of theatre and language, and her portraits, of Chiaromonte, Hannah Arendt, Philip Rahv, and F. W. Dupee, are poignant and evocative. But when the reader reaches the two ''Nature Pieces'' that conclude the collection, within which McCarthy confesses that ''I lack the strength of character *not* to spray fruit trees'' and shares the idea of using tan duck as a runner for one's stairs, he will ask himself, ''Why the bother?''—if he hasn't long before.

Robert Linkous, in a review of ''Occasional Prose,''
in San Francisco Review of Books, *Summer, 1985,*
p. 10.

JEFFREY MEYERS

Mary McCarthy is the American Rebecca West. Both writers are lucid, intelligent, incisive; severe, irreverent, committed. Both have a steady moral seriousness and a wide range of interests, and are equally at home in art or history. Like Miss West, and also like most contemporary American novelists— Mailer, Baldwin, Updike, Vidal, Capote, Gass, Theroux, Oates—Miss McCarthy is better at nonfiction, which permits her to strengthen her work through the discipline of fact, while using novelistic techniques to describe character and setting.

These essays have a common manner and style, but are rather arbitrarily arranged. They would be more effective if they were divided into sections on literature and politics, as in her collection *On the Contrary,* and if she had placed together the essays on Nicola Chiaromonte and on F. W. Dupee, whose amusing and observant flashes of insight exemplify her own best qualities. Miss McCarthy, now a septuagenarian *éminence grise,* has mellowed considerably. We miss, in these remarkably unvituperative essays, her impressive ferocity. She loyally overrates Philip Rahv (once her lover) and Hannah Arendt (whom she unaccountably calls ''a beautiful woman''). The only negative essay is on Joan Didion's novel *Democracy.*

There are a few lapses in the book. Miss McCarthy writes that the Great War produced only a single major novel in English, Frederic Manning's *The Middle Parts of Fortune,* and seems unaware of Ford's *Parade's End,* Aldington's *Death of a Hero,* and David Jones's *In Parenthesis.* She discusses the paucity of present-day expatriate writers, but does not mention Robert Graves and Gerald Brenan in Spain, Anthony Burgess in Monaco, and V. S. Naipaul in London. And she makes some strange assertions about Hemingway. He actually went to Paris in 1921, lived as a journalist, and did not receive royalties from Scribner's until 1927. He *did* have problems with censorship: ''Up in Michigan'' was excluded from the Liveright edition of *In Our Time,* and *A Farewell to Arms* was banned in both Boston and Italy. And it seems odd to remark that Hemingway is a more elitist writer than, say, Henry James.

The longest and least substantial piece was prompted by the Metropolitan Opera's commission to tell ''in her own words'' the story of *La Traviata:* ''On the theme of that pure maiden, Germont waxes eloquent.'' Miss McCarthy mentions that Violetta is devoured by passion and consumption, but she does not place Verdi's opera in its context by discussing the mystique of tuberculosis, which extends from Schiller and Keats to Orwell and Simone Weil, and reaches its literary and operatic apotheoses in *La dame aux camélias* and *Traviata.*

The four lectures in this collection were probably more impressive when heard than when read. The most perverse talk— on art forgery (portrayed in Wyndham Lewis's *The Revenge for Love*), acquisitiveness (portrayed in D. H. Lawrence's ''Things''), and museums—has an elitist bias but offers no solutions. Miss McCarthy argues that museums make art all but inaccessible, that ''once a work of art enters a museum, instead of belonging to everybody, it belongs to nobody.'' She feels it is essential to be alone in order to commune with a work of art and that the presence of a crowd is a sacrilegious intrusion. Yet this difficulty does not prevent people from praying in a cathedral.

Most of the essays are filled with shrewd insights, informed by the metaphor of theater and unified by the theme of paradox. In **''Language and Politics,''** strongly influenced by Orwell's ''Politics and the English Language,'' Miss McCarthy observes that the Watergate politicians ''would not know *how* to tell the truth if an occasion favoring truth-telling should arise.'' The playwright Pirandello is ''locked into a set of once-current notions and sealed off from posterity as though in a time capsule''; ''nobody breaking with Stalinism ever seemed to suffer regrets''; gardening, like love-making, ''confronts us with the inexplicable.'' (p. 55)

Miss McCarthy writes that while so many Soviet citizens were trying to leave the country, ''Solzhenitsyn insisted on his right to stay *and* to receive the Nobel Prize.'' And in the best essay in the book, a masterly analysis of Solzhenitsyn's complex novel *August 1914,* she shows how the Soviet writer, despite the profound influence of Tolstoy, opposes the master's view of history: He ''holds that leadership is determining in war and uses examples from the tragic Eastern campaign to prove it.'' (p. 56)

Jeffrey Meyers, ''Mistress of Paradox,'' in National
Review, *Vol. XXXVII, No. 17, September 6, 1985,*
pp. 55-6.

DUNCAN FALLOWELL

Some of [*Occasional Prose*] is unreadable, for example the pieces on Solzhenitsyn, Calvino, Joan Didion, and *La Traviata,* which are extensive re-tellings of narrative plots, with a comment thrown in periodically. Mary McCarthy can be very pedestrian and after a while one wonders whether she feels pedestrianism is something to be striven for. She has many prerequisites for being a successful essayist. She is intelligent and reads a lot. She has a degree of commitment, in this case to socialist tradition, and although commitment is usually disastrous in a novel, it gives purpose to an essay. She is cosmopolitan, living half the year in Maine and half the year in Paris, and this prevents her degree of New England commitment from turning into downright fundamentalism. She can be witty—in a ponderously bitchy way. She is well-connected, having been married to Edmund Wilson, which is an advantage when it comes to off-loading one's more turgid produce. And she writes tough, decent prose, never inspired, often adroit.

But her mind is bureaucratic and this gives rise to rigidity of execution. It means, for example, that on examination her tough, decent prose reveals a number of affectations. She uses 'named for' instead of 'named after', as in 'the *Strelitzia* (bird-of-paradise flower) was named for Queen Charlotte, an ardent botanist who was born Mecklenburg-Strelitz.' This mannerism occurs many times, despite the ugly effect—therefore presumably because of that effect. In the same ostentatiously stubborn way did Somerset Maugham, who also prided himself on un-affected prose, persist in using 'of a sudden' for 'suddenly'. Another affectation cropping up here is the split infinitive. Mary McCarthy, Gore Vidal and other Americans increasingly flaunt this device as a way of demonstrating their vigorous independence from the conventions of European English.

Like 'named for', the aggressively split infinitive is an example of inverted pedantry. But Mary McCarthy is also capable of true pedantry—hear her rage against the flabby use of language by politicians and media people, and against the misuse of prepositions by just about everybody. She is a stickler for the accurate use of words and is on fairly solid ground here. But again there is an uncomfortable ostentation about it. Perhaps as a woman, writing and publishing in a man's world, she feels she must be trebly sure of not being caught out. To this end she makes regular appeals to a higher presence described in a mystic tone as 'the big Oxford dictionary'. Hence more affectation. On p. 93 she uses 'perspicuousness', but on p. 250 this returns to 'perspicuity'. On p. 237 there is the horrible word 'better', which she uses instead of 'gambler'. 'Clandestinity' and 'reprehension' are two favourites. The latter crops up so frequently that it must answer a deep need. She uses 'fictions' in the plural, meaning pieces of fiction, but since 'fiction' also means that, what is the point? It comes across as pretentious.

Moving from prose style to content, one encounters the same bureaucratic tendency. This is at its most obvious in a piece called **"Novel, Tale, Romance"**, these being the three categories into which, she has decided, all 'fictions' fall. She bashes away for 26 pages trying to work it but the system of division never begins to make any kind of sense. Moreover, the severity with which she adheres to the original groundplan prevents her from following the fruitful lines of thought which occasionally do appear. One of these is: why does German literature have so few novels and why do almost all of them tend to the extreme, the overloaded, the fantastical? 'The sparsity of novels, the great carriers of the reality principle, may help to explain German defencelessness in the face of National Socialism which—to us, incredibly—was not recognised by most Germans as a monstrosity until Hitler had perished in his bunker.' She uses this idea to reinforce her basic premise, that a novel cannot be called a novel unless it takes place in the soul's front parlour at tea-time. But this is by far the least interesting aspect of the question she's raised. For example, another question immediately suggests itself: why is German literature in general of rather small quantity and of a fantastical inclination? Could the answer be that the German genius is expressed essentially in music and secondarily in philosophy? Is there any connection between this and susceptibility to a perverse afflatus such as National Socialism? Probably. If one views the whole of German philosophy as a hypertrophy of the intellect, which is an easy thing to do, then does it not become less incredible that when such an aberration acts upon a musical spirit, the result should be some sort of impassioned leap away from reality?

The subject on which Mary McCarthy has simply touched will open out in the most fascinating way. That she herself doesn't follow it through produces not a sense of control but a sense of abortion.

She is a very bookish person. And of course a political person too—and here the reedy dryness of tone prevents any pomposity. She at least is never a pompous intellectual. In fact with the passing years Mary McCarthy has become that strange thing, a sentimental intellectual. Her obituaries on dead friends, a mixture of warmth and insight which produces just the right amount of embarrassment in the reader, are among the best pieces here. But she is even better than that when she gets away from books and politics altogether. When she steps down from the platform of her main calling, the self-image weakens, so she loosens up, comes alive, moves about, discovers things. A sense of relish and freshness is communicated—and she's almost as wicked as she used to be. This happens in a marvellous piece about art collectors called **"Living With Beautiful Things"** in which she asks, if paintings and sculpture aad beautiful objects are good for one, why is it that art dealers, art critics and collectors are such terrible types? Big question. Tom Wolfe made a whole book (*The Painted Word*) from much less. And in answering it she produces the richest as well as the most entertaining essay in the book. (pp. 31-2)

Duncan Fallowell, "A Sentimental Intellectual," in The Spectator, Vol. 255, No. 8206, October 19, 1985, pp. 31-2.

MARY GORDON

It begins, **Occasional Prose** . . . , with the deaths of friends. A signal to the reader, a clue to author Mary McCarthy's situation, and the setting of the book within the life. The writer says, in effect, that she is at that point in her life when all her friends are dying. But no voice could be less funereal, less tempted to the warm broth of nostalgia and regret. For this is the voice of Mary McCarthy: combative, adversarial, discriminating, and engaged. It is a voice that we have come to think of as more than a bit symbolic. She is, of course, the *femme de lettres,* and in her case both sides of the phrase have weight. The voice is above all assured, and the assurance is two-fold: an intellectual assurance that allows her to range freely around the culture of the West, not literature only, but philosophy, history, politics, music, gardening, art. But the assurance has a second source; it is the assurance of a woman certain always of her power to attract.

No woman, or man either, starting out now could have it. We feel overmastered by specialists; the generalist has become for us a journalist, pureeing all of culture into an undistinguished slop. (p. 249)

Mary McCarthy's may be the last generation to be comfortable with drawing a firm line between high and popular culture, stepping clearly to one side and declaring itself immune to the other. It is, after all, a question of time and energy: What does one do with a day? We are all of us now capable of admitting that we wouldn't miss an episode of *Hill Street Blues*. But it is not possible to think of Mary McCarthy settling down in front of the tube with a bag of Doritos. In the time we spend on aerobics, she is reading *La Princesse de Clèves*.

But in no sense is she an elitist (a word she would hate). She is in love with excellence, but that passion must share its place with her love of justice. She has never fallen back to the exhausted rear flank of the neoconservatives, who are tired of fighting for a just society and have settled instead for a Florida condo patrolled by armed guards. She is political in a way that seems no longer open to us: politics for her is a world of ideas; its roots are philosophy, not sociology or media studies. And so her work is marked by seriousness, but she is never merely mandarin. Style vivifies her, and the humor bred of a highly developed sense of style. She says of her friend F. W. Dupee: "He was never a bohemian; he was too much attracted to style for that." The same is true of her. Yet she admired her friend for "being on the protective picket line for the students at Columbia in 1968, the day he got a new and expensive set of the finest porcelain teeth—example of rueful courage, since he expected to be hit by a night stick." Like her friend, McCarthy has never stepped back from the fray.

If she is not the smug and punitive reactionary, she is even less the dreary "thinker" making her way at night from the stacks of the university library to some dire flat with roaches on the countertop, a mattress on the floor. "Things" matter to her—"good things," as opposed to "nice things," for which she could muster the highest scorn. She would never deny that she is a materialist, but she sees clearly the problems of materialism in a world where all resources, but especially things of beauty, are finite. This is the problem she addresses in her brilliant **"Living with Beautiful Things."** We have all, more or less since the nineteenth century, acted as if it were true that beauty is truth, truth beauty, and we have, in our largess, extended the equation: beauty is goodness, or at least it leads to it. But to assume that the good beauty leads to is moral in its nature has been, according to McCarthy, the source of our error. The only good that the proximity to beauty seems to bring about is the creation of good taste: a circular movement whose value is limited, and that cannot even be counted on to occur. What does occur in the presence of beauty is some mysterious sense of security and order—but even that is not automatic. "The daily service of beautiful things conduces to decorum; it is a rite, a kind of communion, as we notice whenever we wash a fine wine glass as opposed, say, to a jelly jar. . . . And yet museum attendants seem to be immune to contagion from the god. . . ." The problem with beautiful objects, as McCarthy explains to us, is that their pleasure is the eye's. And, she tells us, "the eye is a jealous, concupiscent organ, and some idea of ownership or exclusion enters into our relation with visual beauty. The eye is a natural collector, acquisitive, undemocratic, loath to share." Listen to the beauty of that last sentence; there is, of course, rhythmic beauty, but it shimmers, too, with elegance of thought. And whereas most modern thought is quite defeating in its murkiness, McCarthy's ideas shine clear. This is precisely because she is never merely abstract; she traverses easily the avenue between the world of

ideas and things, crossing from side to side for clarification, refreshment, to have a good time, or to make a point. Consider her description of Joan Didion's narrative line, which she compares to a French seam: "one big stitch forward, one little stitch back, turn over and repeat on the other side of the cloth. . . ."

This genius of Mary McCarthy's serves her most superbly in the piece that is, for me, the crown of the collection, her reminiscence of Hannah Arendt. For McCarthy, as for many of us, Hannah Arendt seemed to incarnate the perfect blend of the *vita activa* and the *vita contemplativa*. She was the representative of the old, ideal Europe—our own now on the Upper West Side. How easy, then, to reduce her to an icon, to make her *stand for* rather than *be*. From the outset, McCarthy acknowledges her friend's greatness of mind. But she tells us that this kind of homage is not what she's about; she wants to present her friend before us bathed in the intimate light of a friend's mourning. The triumph of the presentation comes from McCarthy's acute selection of details:

> She would press on a visitor assorted nuts, chocolates, candied ginger, tea, coffee, Campari, whiskey, cigarettes, cake, crackers, fruit, cheese, almost all at once, regardless of conventional sequence or, often, of the time of day. It was as if the profusion of edibles, set out, many of them, in little ceremonial-like dishes and containers, were impatient propitiatory offerings to all the queer gods of taste. Someone said that this was the eternal Jewish mother, but it was not that: there was no notion that any of this fodder was good for you; in fact most of it was distinctly bad for you, which she must have known somehow, for she did not insist.

McCarthy speaks of Hannah Arendt's feet: "She liked shoes; in all the years I knew her, I think she only once had a corn." How much this tells us of the ease and caring of two women of genius! (pp. 249, 251)

But Mary McCarthy would have no patience with the kind of romantic backward looking I am tempted to indulge in. The world, she is always telling us, is full of interesting things. It is simply a matter of looking. *Cast a Cold Eye* is the title of one of McCarthy's earlier collections. The eye of *Occasional Prose,* though, is not cold but tender, the reflective vision beautifully matured. (p. 251)

Mary Gordon, "When Beauty Is Truth, Truth Beauty," in Esquire, *Vol. 104, No. 5, November, 1985, pp. 249, 251.*

Appendix

The following is a listing of all sources used in Volume 39 of *Contemporary Literary Criticism*. Included in this list are all copyright and reprint rights and acknowledgments for those essays for which permission was obtained. Every effort has been made to trace copyright, but if omissions have been made, please let us know.

THE EXCERPTS IN CLC, VOLUME 39, WERE REPRINTED FROM THE FOLLOWING PERIODICALS:

America, v. 151, September 1-September 8, 1984 for a review of "The Barracks Thief" by Andre Dubus; v. 153, July 6-July 13, 1985 for a review of "White Noise" by Robert Phillips. © 1984, 1985. All rights reserved. Both reprinted by permission of the respective authors.

The American Book Review, v. 6, November-December, 1983. © 1983 by *The American Book Review.* Reprinted by permission.

The American Poetry Review, v. 13, September-October, 1984 for a review of "The Dead and the Living" by Mary Kinzie. Copyright © 1984 by World Poetry, Inc. Reprinted by permission of the author.

The American Spectator, v. 18, June, 1985; v. 18, September, 1985; v. 18, November, 1985; v. 19, February, 1986. Copyright © *The American Spectator* 1985, 1986. All reprinted by permission.

Ariel, v. 16, October, 1985 for "Keri Hulme's 'The Bone People,' and the Pegasus Award for Maori Literature" by C. K. Stead. Copyright © 1985 C. K. Stead and The Board of Governors, The University of Calgary. Reprinted by permission of the publisher and the author.

The Atlantic Monthly, v. 255, June, 1985 for "The Prisoner of Fame" by Anthony Burgess. Copyright 1985 by The Atlantic Monthly Company, Boston, MA. Reprinted by permission of the author.

Belles Lettres, v. 1, March-April, 1986. Reprinted by permission.

Best Sellers, v. 44, July, 1984; v. 44, December, 1984; v. 45, July, 1985; v. 45, August, 1985; v. 45, February, 1986. Copyright © 1984, 1985, 1986 Helen Dwight Reid Educational Foundation. All reprinted by permission.

The Bloomsbury Review, v. 6, February, 1986 for "E Pluribus Unicorn: Theodore Sturgeon, 1918-1985" by Rodger Rapp. Copyright © by Owaissa Communications Company, Inc. 1986. Reprinted by permission of the author.

Book Week—The Washington Post, November 13, 1983. © 1983, *The Washington Post.* Reprinted by permission.

Book World—The Washington Post, July 29, 1984; August 5, 1984; September 30, 1984; October 28, 1984; November 18, 1984; January 13, 1985; January 20, 1985; February 4, 1985; February 17, 1985; March 3, 1985; May 12, 1985; May 19, 1985; May 26, 1985; June 16, 1985; June 30, 1985; August 25, 1985; November 3, 1985; December 1, 1985; January 5, 1986. © 1984, 1985, 1986, *The Washington Post.* All reprinted by permission.

Booklist, v. 80, July, 1984; v. 81, September 1, 1984; v. 81, October 15, 1984; v. 81, November 1, 1984; v. 81, December 1, 1984; v. 81, March 15, 1985; v. 81, April 1, 1985; v. 81, April 15, 1985; v. 81, May 15, 1985; v. 82, November 15, 1985. Copyright © 1984, 1985 by the American Library Association. All reprinted by permission.

Books and Bookmen, n. 353, February, 1985; n. 354, April, 1985; n. 358, August, 1985. © copyright *Books and Bookmen* 1985. All reprinted with permission of the publisher.

Books in Canada, v. 14, April, 1985 for "Opening Lines" by Richard Plant. Reprinted by permission of the author.

Bookworld, Chicago Tribune, September 8, 1984 for a review of "Low Tide" by Kendall Mitchell; May 19, 1985 for "A Magical Vision of Society in Revolt" by Bruce Allen. Both reprinted by permission of the respective authors.

Boston Globe, July 17, 1985 for "Heinrich Boell, Author, Known as 'Literary Conscience' of W. Germany" by Anna Tomforde. © 1985 Globe Newspaper Co. Reprinted by permission of the author.

Boston Review, v. X, April-May, 1985 for a review of "The Beans of Egypt, Maine" by Megan Marshall. Copyright © 1985 by the Boston Critic, Inc. Reprinted by permission of the author.

The Canadian Forum, v. LXIV, August-September, 1984. Reprinted by permission.

Canadian Theatre Review, n. 45, Winter, 1985. Copyright © 1985, CTR Publications. Reprinted by permission.

Chicago Tribune, March 3, 1985 for "Cowley Provides Guide to Survive Literary Cold Wars" by James R. Mellow. Copyright © 1985 by James R. Mellow. Reprinted by permission of Georges Borchardt, Inc. and the author./ June 9, 1985 for "Agatha Christie Remains Mystery to Her Biographer" by Sara Paretsky; s. 14, June 16, 1985 for "Mailer in the Raw: A Tape Collage Brings Him Roaring to Life" by Seymour Krim; November 10, 1985 for "Last Work Offers an Inward View of Writer, Person" by Constance Markey; November 17, 1985 for "James Jones, a Warrior Who Saw the Insanity of War" by Gerald Nicosia. © copyrighted 1985, Chicago Tribune Company. All rights reserved. All reprinted by permission of the respective authors./ February 24, 1985; s. 4, May 15, 1985. © copyrighted 1985, Chicago Tribune Company. All rights reserved. Both used with permission.

The Christian Science Monitor, April 17, 1985 for "Literary Criticism for Readers—Not Academics" by L. S. Klepp; May 1, 1985 for "A Critic's Plain-Spoken Views of American Literature Since 1941" by Bruce Allen; June 7, 1985 for "Nam Book Year's Best" by Bruce Allen; December 2, 1985 for "Restoring the Reputation of a 'Literary Hardhat'" by James Kaufmann. © 1985 by the respective authors. All rights reserved. All reprinted by permission of the respective authors./ December 9, 1965; May 3, 1984; January 2, 1985. © 1965, 1984, 1985 The Christian Science Publishing Society. All rights reserved. All reprinted by permission from *The Christian Science Monitor.*

Commentary, v. 81, April, 1986 for "E. B. White, Dark & Lite" by Joseph Epstein. Copyright © 1986 by American Jewish Committee. All rights reserved. Reprinted by permission of the publisher and the author.

Commonweal, v. LXXII, May 13, 1960; v. LXXVII, December 14, 1962. Copyright © 1960, 1962 Commonweal Publishing Co., Inc. Both reprinted by permission of Commonweal Foundation./ v. CXII, April 5, 1985; v. CXII, September 20, 1985. Copyright © 1985 Commonweal Foundation. All reprinted by permission of Commonweal Foundation.

Daily News, New York, May 3, 1984; October 12, 1984; March 29, 1985. © 1984, 1985, New York News, Inc. All reprinted by permission.

The Detroit News, November 17, 1985. Copyright 1985, The Evening News Association, Inc. Both reprinted by permission.

The Eagle, Providence, R.I., October 21, 1984 for "The Great Wrong Place" by Les Daniels. Reprinted by permission of the author.

Encounter, v. LXV, July-August, 1985. © 1985 by Encounter Ltd. Both reprinted by permission of the publisher.

Esquire, v. 104, November, 1985 for "When Beauty Is Truth, Truth Beauty" by Mary Gordon. Copyright © 1985 by Mary Gordon. Reprinted by permission of Literistic, Ltd.

Extrapolation, v. 26, Fall, 1985. Copyright 1985 by The Kent State University Press. Reprinted by permission.

Fantasy Review, v. 7, July, 1984 for a review of "Neuromancer" by Lawrence I. Charters; v. 7, December, 1984 for "One of the Year's Best Fantasy Novels" by Chris Morgan; v. 8, May, 1985 for "Theodore Sturgeon: 1918-1985" by Bob Collins; v. 8, May, 1985 for "I Remember Ted" by James Gunn; v. 8, May, 1985 for "Eudiche: Theodore Sturgeon" by Gary K. Wolfe; v. 8, May, 1985 for "Worst Week of My Life" by S. P. Somtow; v. 8, July, 1985 for "Sterling Tries but Fails" by Steve Carper; v. 8, September, 1985 for "The Lore of Old China" by Naomi Galbreath; v. 9, April, 1986 for "Cobra, She Said: An Interim Report on the Fiction of William Gibson" by Tom Maddox. Copyright © 1984, 1985, 1986 by the respective authors. All reprinted by permission of the respective authors.

The Fiddlehead, n. 143, Spring, 1985 for "Dramatic Work: Retrospectives and New Directions" by Richard Paul Knowles. Copyright by the author. Reprinted by permission of the author.

The Georgia Review, v. XXXVI, Spring, 1982; v. XXXVIII, Winter, 1984; v. XXXIX, Spring, 1985; v. XXXIX, Fall, 1985. Copyright, 1982, 1984, 1985, by the University of Georgia. All reprinted by permission.

The Globe & Mail, Toronto, January 13, 1984; February 23, 1984. Both reprinted by permission.

Harper's Magazine, v. 230, April, 1965. Copyright © 1965 by *Harper's Magazine*. All rights reserved. Reprinted by special permission.

The Harvard Advocate, v. CXIX, May, 1986 for ''Philip Larkin: Legacy of the Almost-Instinct'' by Andrew Sullivan. © 1986 by *The Harvard Advocate*. Reprinted by permission of the author.

History Today, v. 35, March, 1985. © History Today Limited 1985. Reprinted by permission.

The Hudson Review, v. XXXIV, Autumn, 1981; v. XXXVII, Autumn, 1984; v. XXXVIII, Summer, 1985. Copyright © 1981, 1984, 1985 by The Hudson Review, Inc. All reprinted by permission.

The Iowa Review, v. 15 (Winter), 1985 for a review of ''The Dead and the Living'' by Carolyne Wright. Copyright © 1985 by The University of Iowa. Reprinted by permission of the publisher and the author.

Kirkus Reviews, v. LII, April 1, 1984; v. LII, August 15, 1984; v. LII, September 15, 1984; v. LII, December 1, 1984; v. LIII, January 1, 1985; v. LIII, January 15, 1985; v. LIII, February 1, 1985; v. LIII, February 15, 1985; v. LIII, March 1, 1985; v. LIII, March 15, 1985; v. LIII, April 1, 1985; v. LIII, April 15, 1985; v. LIII, May 15, 1985; v. LIII, June 15, 1985; v. LIII, August 1, 1985; v. LIII, September 1, 1985; v. LIII, September 15, 1985; v. LIII, October 1, 1985. Copyright © 1984, 1985 The Kirkus Service, Inc. All reprinted by permission.

Kliatt Young Adult Paperback Book Guide, v. XIX, September, 1985. Copyright © by Kliatt Paperback Book Guide. Reprinted by permission.

Library Journal, v. 108, May 1, 1983 for a review of ''The World About Us'' by Robert P. Holley; v. 109, July, 1984 for a review of ''Yin'' by Suzanne Juhasz; v. 109, November 15, 1984 for a review of ''Louise Bogan: A Portrait'' by Suzanne Juhasz; v. 110, January, 1985 for a review of ''The Unlovely Child'' by Joseph A. Lipari; v. 110, February 1, 1985 for a review of ''Easy in the Islands: Stories'' by Patricia Molloy; v. 110, March 1, 1985 for a review of ''The Beans of Egypt, Maine'' by Hugh M. Crane; v. 110, May 15, 1985 for a review of ''Metro: A Novel of the Moscow Underground'' by Mary F. Zirin. Copyright © 1983, 1984, 1985 by Xerox Corporation. All reprinted from *Library Journal*, published by R. R. Bowker Co. (a Xerox company), by permission of the publisher and the respective authors./ v. 110, November 1, 1985 for a review of ''The Bone People'' by Rhoda Yerburgh; v. 110, November 15, 1985 for a review of ''Along with Youth: Hemingway, the Early Years'' by Arthur Waldhorn; v. 110, November 15, 1985 for a review of ''Hemingway: A Biography'' by Arthur Waldhorn. Copyright 1985 by Reed Publishing USA. All reprinted from *Library Journal*, published by R. R. Bowker Company, a Reed Publishing company, by permission of the publisher and the respective authors.

The Listener, v. 114, September 26, 1985 for ''The World Minus Calvino'' by Patchy Wheatley; v. 114, October 24, 1985 for ''The Booker Club'' by Angela Huth; v. 114, December 12, 1985 for '''Colourful, Balding Book-basher''' by Patrick Garland. © British Broadcasting Corp. 1985. All reprinted by permission of the respective authors./ v. 114, December 19 & December 26, 1985 for ''Graves and the Muses'' by Stephen Spender. © British Broadcasting Corp. 1985. Reprinted by permission of A. D. Peters & Co. Ltd.

London Review of Books, December 6 to December 19, 1984 for ''At the Hydropathic'' by T. J. Binyon; February 21, 1985 for ''Amor vincit Vinnie'' by Marilyn Butler; August 1, 1985 for ''Magical Realism'' by D.A.N. Jones; December 19, 1985 for a letter to the editor by Susan Broidy; January 23 to January 30, 1986 for a letter to the editor by Rod Edmond. All appear here by permission of the *London Review of Books* and the respective authors.

Los Angeles Times, July 17, 1985./ November 24, 1984; May 11, 1985; May 18, 1985; September 2, 1985; September 21, 1985; October 2, 1985; December 3, 1985. Copyright, 1984, 1985, *Los Angeles Times*. All reprinted by permission.

Los Angeles Times Book Review, July 1, 1984; July 29, 1984; October 21, 1984; November 18, 1984; December 2, 1984; January 13, 1985; February 24, 1985; March 31, 1985; May 26, 1985; June 2, 1985; June 23, 1985; July 7, 1985; July 14, 1985; July 28, 1985; August 11, 1985; September 8, 1985; October 20, 1985; December 8, 1985; January 26, 1986; May 9, 1986. Copyright, 1984, 1985, 1986, *Los Angeles Times*. All reprinted by permission.

Maclean's Magazine, v. 97, January 30, 1984. © 1984 by *Maclean's Magazine*. Reprinted by permission.

The Magazine of Fantasy and Science Fiction, v. 69, September, 1985 for a review of ''Bridge of Birds'' by Algis Budrys. © 1985 by Mercury Press Inc. Reprinted by permission of *The Magazine of Fantasy and Science Fiction* and the author.

MOTHEROOT Journal, v. 6, Summer, 1985 for ''Kizer: Feminist Poet Pre-Feminism'' by Judith Barrington. © 1985 MOTHEROOT Publications. Reprinted by permission of the publisher and the author.

Ms., v. XIII, July, 1984 for a review of ''The Dead and the Living'' by Paula Bonnell, © 1984, 1986 by Paula Bonnell. Reprinted by permission of Paula Bonnell./ v. XIII, April, 1985 for ''The Pick of the Crop: Five First Novels'' by Diane Cole; v. XIII, April, 1985 for ''Carolyn Chute: Down East Daughter'' by Ann Marie Cunningham; v. XIII, June, 1985 for a review of ''Self-Help'' by Jennifer Crichton;

v. XIII, June, 1985 for a review of "Manny & Rose" by Jennifer Crichton. © 1985 Ms. Magazine Corp. All reprinted by permission of the respective authors.

The Nation, v. 239, August 4 & 11, 1984; v. 239, October 13, 1984; v. 239, December 8, 1984; v. 240, February 2, 1985; v. 240, February 23, 1985; v. 240, April 6, 1985; v. 241, July 20 & 27, 1985. Copyright 1984, 1985 *The Nation* magazine, The Nation Associates, Inc. All reprinted by permission.

National Review, v. XXXVII, September 6, 1985; v. XXXVII, October 18, 1985; v. XXXVII, December 31, 1985; v. XXXVIII, January 31, 1986; v. XXXVIII, January 31, 1986; v. XXXVIII, February 28, 1986. © by National Review, Inc., 150 East 35th Street, New York, NY 10016; 1985, 1986. All reprinted with permission.

The New Criterion, v. IV, December, 1985 for "Italo Calvino, 1923-1985" by James Gardner; v. IV, February, 1986 for "'Trying to Preserve Something'" by Robert Richman; v. IV, February, 1986 for "Philip Larkin, 1922-1985" by Donald Hall; v. IV, February, 1986 for "Larkin's Voice" by X. J. Kennedy. Copyright © 1985, 1986 by The Foundation for Cultural Review. All reprinted by permission of the respective authors.

New Directions for Women, v. 14, July-August, 1985. © copyright 1986 New Directions for Women, Inc. Reprinted by permission.

The New Leader, v. LXIV, December 14, 1981; v. LXVIII, April 22, 1985; v. LXVIII, June 3 & 7, 1985; v. LXVIII, December 16 & 30, 1985. © 1981, 1985 by The American Labor Conference on International Affairs, Inc. All reprinted by permission.

The New Republic, v. 191, August 27, 1984; v. 191, October 8, 1984; v. 192, February 4, 1985; v. 192, March 11, 1985; v. 192, March 18, 1985; v. 192, March 25, 1985; v. 192, May 13, 1985; v. 192, June 10, 1985; v. 192, June 24, 1985; v. 193, December 2, 1985; v. 193, December 9, 1985; v. 194, January 6 & 13, 1986. © 1984, 1985, 1986 The New Republic, Inc. All reprinted by permission of *The New Republic.*

New Statesman, v. 96, September 22, 1978; v. 109, February 1, 1985; v. 109, February 8, 1985; v. 110, July 5, 1985; v. 110, September 27, 1985. © 1978, 1985 The Statesman & Nation Publishing Co. Ltd. All reprinted by permission.

New York Post, May 3, 1984; October 12, 1984; March 9, 1985; March 29, 1985. © 1984, 1985, News America Publishing, Incorporated. All reprinted from the *New York Post* by permission.

The New York Review of Books, v. XV, August 13, 1970; v. XX, December 13, 1973; v. XXV, February 23, 1978; v. XXXI, September 27, 1984; v. XXXII, March 14, 1985; v. XXXII, April 11, 1985; v. XXXII, May 30, 1985; v. XXXII, June 13, 1985; v. XXXII, June 27, 1985; v. XXXII, July 18, 1985; v. XXXII, August 15, 1985; v. XXXII, November 21, 1985; v. XXXII, January 16, 1986; v. XXXIII, February 27, 1986; v. XXXIII, May 29, 1986; v. XXXIII, June 12, 1986. Copyright © 1970, 1973, 1978, 1984, 1985, 1986 Nyrev, Inc. All reprinted with permission from *The New York Review of Books.*

The New York Times, October 16, 1973; January 9, 1978; May 3, 1984; July 23, 1984; September 13, 1984; October 12, 1984; October 28, 1984; December 20, 1984; January 1, 1985; January 4, 1985; January 7, 1985; January 17, 1985; February 14, 1985; February 15, 1985; March 29, 1985; April 13, 1985; April 20, 1985; April 24, 1985; May 9, 1985; May 13, 1985; May 17, 1985; May 21, 1985; May 25, 1985; June 20, 1985; July 17, 1985; August 16, 1985; September 2, 1985; September 20, 1985; October 1, 1985; October 2, 1985; October 21, 1985; November 11, 1985; November 13, 1985; December 3, 1985; December 8, 1985. Copyright © 1973, 1978, 1984, 1985 by The New York Times Company. All reprinted by permission.

The New York Times Book Review, May 1, 1960; October 14, 1962; December 19, 1965; January 1, 1978; November 2, 1980; April 1, 1984; August 19, 1984; September 16, 1984; November 25, 1984; December 23, 1984; January 13, 1985; January 31, 1985; February 10, 1985; February 17, 1985; February 24, 1985; March 3, 1985; March 10, 1985; March 24, 1985; April 21, 1985; April 28, 1985; May 5, 1985; May 12, 1985; May 19, 1985; May 26, 1985; June 2, 1985; June 16, 1985; June 23, 1985; June 30, 1985; July 7, 1985; July 14, 1985; September 15, 1985; October 6, 1985; October 13, 1985; November 10, 1985; November 17, 1985; November 24, 1985; December 8, 1985. Copyright © 1960, 1962, 1965, 1978, 1980, 1984, 1985 by The New York Times Company. All reprinted by permission.

The New Yorker, v. LX, October 22, 1984 for "Hard Times" by Brendan Gill; v. LXI, July 29, 1985 for "Louise Bogan's Story" by William Maxwell. © 1984, 1985 by the respective authors. Both reprinted by permission./ v. LXI, October 14, 1985; v. LXI, October 28, 1985. © 1985 by The New Yorker Magazine, Inc. Both reprinted by permission.

Newsday, August 19, 1984; October 2, 1985. © Newsday, Inc. 1984, 1985. Both reprinted by permission.

Newsweek, v. XCVI, November 3, 1980; v. CIII, May 14, 1984; v. CIV, September 24, 1984; v. CIV, October 22, 1984; v. CV, January 21, 1985; v. CV, February 11, 1985; v. CV, February 25, 1985; v. CV, March 25, 1985; v. CVI, July 8, 1985. Copyright 1980, 1984, 1985, by Newsweek, Inc. All rights reserved. All reprinted by permission.

NOW, September 27-October 3, 1984 for a review of "White Biting Dog" by Jon Kaplan. Reprinted by permission of the publisher and the author.

The Observer, March 3, 1985 for "Laughing It Off" by Anthony Burgess. Reprinted by permission of the author./ March 21, 1971; February 3, 1985; February 24, 1985; June 2, 1985; June 7, 1985; July 21, 1985; July 28, 1985; August 18, 1985; September 22, 1985; December 1, 1985; December 8, 1985. All reprinted by permission of The Observer Limited.

Open Places, n. 40, Fall-Winter, 1985. Copyright 1985 *Open Places*. Reprinted by permission.

Parabola, v. X, May, 1985 for a review of "Love Medicine" by Elaine Jahner. Copyright © 1985 by the Society for the Study of Myth and Tradition. Reprinted by permission of the author.

Partisan Review, v. XXXII, Spring, 1965. Copyright © 1965 by *Partisan Review*. Reprinted by permission of *Partisan Review*.

Poetry, v. CXXXVIII, May, 1981 for "Weighing the Verse" by William H. Pritchard; v. CXLV, October, 1984 for a review of "The Dead and the Living" by Linda Gregerson; v. CXLV, March, 1985 for "Praise" by Edward Hirsch; v. CXLV, March, 1985 for a review of "Yin" by Robert Phillips; v. CXLVII, November, 1985 for a review of "Yin: New Poems" by Grace Schulman. © 1981, 1984, 1985 by The Modern Poetry Association. All reprinted by permission of the Editor of *Poetry* and the respective authors.

Prairie Schooner, v. 59, Spring, 1985. © 1985 by University of Nebraska Press. Reprinted from *Prairie Schooner* by permission of University of Nebraska Press.

Publishers Weekly, v. 223, April 8, 1983; v. 225, April 6, 1984; v. 225, May 11, 1984; v. 225, May 25, 1984; v. 226, November 16, 1984; v. 226, November 30, 1984; v. 227, January 4, 1985; v. 227, January 11, 1985; v. 227, February 1, 1985; v. 227, February 8, 1985; v. 227, March 1, 1985; v. 227, March 15, 1985; v. 227, April 12, 1985; v. 227, April 26, 1985; v. 227, May 10, 1985; v. 227, June 14, 1985. Copyright © 1983, 1984, 1985 by Xerox Corporation. All reprinted from *Publishers Weekly*, published by R. R. Bowker Company, a Xerox company, by permission./ v. 228, September 13, 1985; v. 228, October 4, 1985. Copyright 1985 by Reed Publishing USA. Both reprinted from *Publishers Weekly*, published by R. R. Bowker Company, a Reed Publishing company, by permission.

Punch, v. 288, January 23, 1985. © 1985 by Punch Publications Ltd. All rights reserved. May not be reprinted without permission.

Quill and Quire, v. 50, May, 1984 for "Skvorecky Engineers a Milestone of World Literature" by Mark Czarnecki. Reprinted by permission of *Quill and Quire* and the author.

Review, n. 34, January-June, 1985. Copyright © 1985 by the Center for Inter-American Relations, Inc. Reprinted by permission.

San Francisco Review of Books, May-June, 1985; Summer, 1985. Copyright © by the *San Francisco Review of Books* 1985. Both reprinted by permission.

Saturday Review, v. XLVIII, December 11, 1965; v. 11, January-February, 1985; v. 11, March-April, 1985. © 1965, 1985 *Saturday Review* magazine. All reprinted by permission.

Science Fiction Chronicle, v. 6, July, 1985 for "Ted Sturgeon Eulogies: Ian Ballantine" by Ian Ballantine; v. 6, July, 1985 for "Ted Sturgeon Eulogies: Robert Bloch" by Robert Bloch; v. 6, July, 1985 for "Ted Sturgeon Eulogies: David G. Hartwell" by David G. Hartwell; v. 6, July, 1985 for "Theodore Sturgeon: February 26, 1918 - May 8, 1985" by Damon Knight. Copyright © 1985 by *Science Fiction Chronicle*. All rights reserved. All reprinted by permission of the respective authors.

Science Fiction Review, n. 56, Fall, 1985 for "You Got No Friends in This World: A Quarterly Review Essay of Short Science Fiction" by Orson Scott Card. Copyright © 1985 by the author. Reprinted by permission of the author.

Science-Fiction Studies, v. 13, March, 1986. Copyright © 1986 by SFS Publications. Reprinted by permission.

Southwest Review, v. 66, Spring, 1981. © 1981 by Southern Methodist University. Reprinted by permission.

The Spectator, v. 250, September 15, 1984; v. 255, August 24, 1985; v. 255, October 19, 1985; v. 255, December 7, 1985. © 1984, 1985 by *The Spectator*. All reprinted by permission of *The Spectator*.

Sports Illustrated, v. 62, April 8, 1985. © 1985 Time Inc. Reprinted courtesy of *Sports Illustrated*.

Stand Magazine, Summer (1985) for "Basil Bunting, 1900-1985: A Personal Memoir" by Connie Pickard. Copyright © Connie Pickard. Reprinted by permission.

Sulfur 13, v. V, 1985. Copyright © *Sulfur* 1985. Reprinted by permission.

The Sunday Times, London, December 8, 1985. © Times Newspapers Limited 1985. Reproduced from *The Sunday Times*, London by permission.

Time, v. 124, July 30, 1984; v. 125, January 21, 1985; v. 125, January 28, 1985; v. 125, February 18, 1985; v. 125, April 8, 1985; v. 125, April 15, 1985; v. 125, May 20, 1985; v. 125, May 27, 1985; v. 125, June 10, 1985; v. 126, October 14, 1985. Copyright 1984, 1985 Time Inc. All rights reserved. All reprinted by permission from *Time.*

The Times, London, January 19, 1985; April 19, 1985; July 17, 1985; August 16, 1985; August 21, 1985; October 2, 1985; November 30, 1985. © Times Newspapers Limited 1985. All reprinted by permission.

The Times Literary Supplement, n. 3612, May 21, 1971; n. 3766, May 10, 1974; n. 4051, November 21, 1980; n. 4105, December 4, 1981; n. 4113, January 29, 1982; n. 4262, December 7, 1984; n. 4270, February 1, 1985; n. 4276, March 15, 1985; n. 4285, May 17, 1985; n. 4314, December 6, 1985; n. 4315, December 13, 1985; n. 4320, January 17, 1986; n. 4321, January 24, 1986; n. 4326, February 28, 1986. © Times Newspapers Ltd. (London) 1971, 1974, 1980, 1981, 1982, 1984, 1985, 1986. All reproduced from *The Times Literary Supplement* by permission.

Tribune, v. 49, August 9 & 16, 1985; v. 49, August 30, 1985. Both reprinted by permission of *Tribune,* London.

USA Today, January 11, 1985; March 15, 1985; June 7, 1985. Copyright, 1985 *USA Today.* All reprinted with permission.

The Village Voice, v. XXVIII, October 4, 1983 for "The End of Irony" by Sean Wilentz; v. XXIX, July 3, 1984 for a review of "Neuromancer" by Debra Rae Cohen; v. XXX, February 19, 1985 for "No Deliverance" by Ellen Lesser; v. XXX, April 30, 1985 for "Death by Inches" by Albert Mobilio; v. XXX, May 21, 1985 for "Norman Mailer and the Pot-Roast Theory" by Eliot Fremont-Smith; v. XXX, June 4, 1985 for "A Sense of Occasion" by Jacqueline Austin; v. XXX, June 4, 1985 for "Splendor in the Gass" by Sam Tanenhaus; v. XXX, June 4, 1985 for "Send in the Clone" by Enrique Fernández; v. XXX, July 2, 1985 for "Banal Retentive" by Walter Kendrick; v. XXX, July 30, 1985 for "Death in the Family" by Jacqueline Austin; v. XXX, August 6, 1985 for "Prank Amateurs" by William Grimes; v. XXX, December 3, 1985 for "Southern Comforts" by Ellen Lesser; v. XXX, December 24, 1985 for "Search for Tomorrow" by Diane Jacobs. Copyright © News Group Publications, Inc., 1983, 1984, 1985. All reprinted by permission of *The Village Voice* and the respective authors./ v. XXX, March 19, 1985; v. XXX, March 26, 1985. Copyright © News Group Publications, Inc., 1985. Both reprinted by permission of *The Village Voice.*

The Virginian-Pilot and The Ledger-Star, June 9, 1985. Reprinted by permission.

VLS, n. 24, March, 1984; n. 29, October, 1984; n. 35, May, 1985; n. 36, June, 1985. Copyright © 1984, 1985 News Group Publications, Inc. All reprinted by permission.

The Wall Street Journal, April 2, 1985. © Dow Jones & Company, Inc. 1985. All rights reserved. Reprinted by permission of *The Wall Street Journal.*

The Washington Post, July 17, 1985; August 17, 1985; September 2, 1985; October 2, 1985; December 8, 1985; December 9, 1985. © 1985, Washington Post Co. All reprinted by permission.

Wilson Library Bulletin, v. 59, November, 1984; v. 59, May, 1985. Copyright © 1984, 1985 by the H. W. Wilson Company. Both reprinted by permission.

Winston-Salem Journal, July 14, 1985. Reprinted by permission.

The Women's Review of Books, v. II, July, 1985 for "The Pursuit of Perfection" by Gloria Bowles. Copyright © 1985. All rights reserved. Reprinted by permission of the author.

Women's Wear Daily, May 3, 1984; October 12, 1984; March 29, 1985. Copyright, 1984, 1985 Fairchild Publications. All reprinted by permission.

World Literature Today, v. 52, Autumn, 1978; v. 56, Spring, 1982; v. 57, Winter, 1983; v. 59, Winter, 1985; v. 59, Summer, 1985. Copyright 1978, 1982, 1983, 1985 by the University of Oklahoma Press. All reprinted by permission.

The Yale Review, v. 74, July, 1985. Copyright 1985, by Yale University. Both reprinted by permission of the editors.

THE EXCERPTS IN CLC, VOLUME 39, WERE REPRINTED FROM THE FOLLOWING BOOKS:

Carroll, David. From *The Subject in Question: The Languages of Theory and the Strategies of Fiction*. University of Chicago Press, 1982. © 1982 by The University of Chicago. All rights reserved. Reprinted by permission of The University of Chicago Press and the author.

Fletcher, John. From *Claude Simon and Fiction Now*. Calder and Boyars, 1975. © John Fletcher 1975. All rights reserved. Reprinted by permission of Marion Boyars Publishers Ltd.

Kessler, Jascha. From radio broadcasts on March 31, 1982; September 26, 1984; January, 1985 on KUSC-FM—Los Angeles, CA. All reprinted by permission of Jascha Kessler.

Roudiez, Leon S. From *French Fiction Today: A New Direction*. Rutgers University Press, 1972. Copyright © 1972 by Rutgers University, The State University of New Jersey. Reprinted by permission of Rutgers University Press.

Siegel, Joel. For a television broadcast on October 11, 1984 on WABC-TV—New York, NY. Reprinted by permission of Joel Siegel.

Sontag, Susan. From a preface to *Plays: Mud, The Danube, The Conduct of Life, Sarita*. By Maria Irene Fornes. PAJ Publications, 1986. © 1985 preface copyright by Susan Sontag. All rights reserved. Reprinted by permission.

Stitt, Peter. From *The World's Hieroglyphic Beauty*. University of Georgia Press, 1985. © 1985 the University of Georgia Press. All rights reserved. Reprinted by permission of the University of Georgia Press.

Watkins, Floyd C. From *Then & Now: The Personal Past in the Poetry of Robert Penn Warren*. University Press of Kentucky, 1982. Copyright © 1982 by The University Press of Kentucky. Reprinted by permission.

Appendix

THE EXCERPTS FROM THE AUTHOR'S WORKS IN CLC, VOLUME 39, WERE REPRINTED FROM THE FOLLOWING BOOKS:

Allende, Isabel. From *The House of the Spirits*. Knopf, 1985. Copyright © 1985 by Alfred A. Knopf, Inc.

Chute, Carolyn. From *The Beans of Egypt, Maine*. Ticknor & Fields, 1985. Copyright © 1985 by Carolyn Chute.

DeLillo, Don. From *White Noise*. Penguin Books, 1985. Copyright © Don DeLillo, 1984, 1985.

Durban, Pam. From *All Set About with Fever Trees and Other Stories*. David R. Godine, Publisher, 1985. Copyright © 1985 Pam Durban.

Eberstadt, Fernanda. From *Low Tide*. Alfred A. Knopf, 1985. Copyright © 1985 by Fernanda Eberstadt.

Edgerton, Clyde. From *Raney: A Novel*. Algonquin Books of Chapel Hill, 1985. © 1985 by Clyde Edgerton.

Ellis, Bret Easton. From *Less than Zero*. Simon and Schuster, 1985. Copyright © 1985 by Bret Easton Ellis.

Epstein, Joseph. From *Plausible Prejudices: Essays on American Writing*. W. W. Norton & Company, 1985. Copyright © 1985 by Joseph Epstein.

Erdrich, Louise. From *Love Medicine*. Holt, Rinehart and Winston, 1984. Copyright © 1984 by Louise Erdrich.

Fitzgerald, Robert. From *Enlarging the Change: The Princeton Seminars in Literary Criticism, 1949-1951*. Northeastern University Press, 1985. Copyright © 1985 by Robert Fitzgerald.

Fornes, Maria Irene. From *Plays: Mud, The Danube, The Conduct of Life, Sarita*. PAJ Publications, 1986. © 1986 copyright by PAJ Publications. © 1986 copyright by Maria Irene Fornes.

Frank, Elizabeth. From *Louise Bogan: A Portrait*. Alfred A. Knopf, 1985. Copyright © 1985 by Elizabeth Frank.

Gass, William H. From *Habitations of the Word: Essays*. Simon and Schuster, 1985. Copyright © 1985 by William Gass.

Gébler, Carlo. From *The Eleventh Summer*. E. P. Dutton, 1985. Copyright © 1985 by Carlo Gébler.

Gibson, William. From *Neuromancer*. Ace Science Fiction Books, 1984. Copyright © 1984 by William Gibson.

Giles, Molly. From *Rough Translations: Stories*. The University of Georgia Press, 1985. © 1985 by Molly Giles.

Griffin, Peter. From *Along with Youth: Hemingway, the Early Years*. Oxford University Press, 1985. Copyright © 1985 by Oxford University Press, Inc.

Hass, Robert. From *Twentieth Century Pleasures: Prose on Poetry*. The Ecco Press, 1984. Copyright © 1984 by Robert Hass.

Hempel, Amy. From *Reasons to Live: Stories*. Alfred A. Knopf, 1985. Copyright © 1985 by Amy Hempel.

Holdstock, Robert. From *Mythago Wood*. Arbor House, 1984. Copyright © 1984 by Robert Holdstock.

Hughart, Barry. From *Bridge of Birds: A Novel of an Ancient China That Never Was*. St. Martin's Press, 1984. Copyright © 1984 by Barry Hughart.

Hulme, Keri. From *The Bone People*. Louisiana State University Press, 1985. Copyright © 1983 by Keri Hulme.

Kaletski, Alexander. From *Metro: A Novel of the Moscow Underground*. Viking Penguin, 1985. Copyright © Alexander Kaletski, 1985.

Kizer, Carolyn. From *Yin: New Poems*. BOA Editions, Ltd., 1984. Copyright © 1984 by Carolyn Kizer. All rights reserved. Reprinted by permission of the publisher and the author.

Lemann, Nancy. From *Lives of the Saints: A Novel*. Alfred A. Knopf, 1985. Copyright © 1985 by Nancy Lemann.

Lurie, Alison. From *Foreign Affairs*. Random House, 1984. Copyright © 1984 by Alison Lurie.

MacShane, Frank. From *Into Eternity: The Life of James Jones, American Writer*. Houghton Mifflin Company, 1985. Copyright © 1985 by Frank MacShane.

Manso, Peter. From *Mailer: His Life and Times*. Simon and Schuster, 1985. Copyright © 1985 by Peter Manso.

McCarthy, Mary. From *Occasional Prose*. Harcourt Brace Jovanovich, Publishers, 1985. Copyright © 1985, 1984, 1983, 1981, 1979, 1976, 1975, 1974, 1972, 1971, 1968 by Mary McCarthy.

Meyers, Jeffrey. From *Hemingway: A Biography*. Harper & Row, Publishers, Inc., 1985. Copyright © 1985 by Jeffrey Meyers.

Minus, Ed. From *Kite, a Novel*. Viking, 1985. Copyright © Ed Minus, 1985.

Moore, Lorrie. From *Self-Help*. Alfred A. Knopf, Inc., 1985. Copyright © 1985 by M. L. Moore.

Morgan, Janet. From *Agatha Christie: A Biography*. William Collins Sons & Company, Ltd., 1984. Copyright © 1984 by Janet Morgan.

Olds, Sharon. From *The Dead and the Living: Poems*. Knopf, 1984. Copyright © 1983 by Sharon Olds. All rights reserved. Reprinted by permission of Alfred A. Knopf, Inc.

Pearson, T. R. From *A Short History of a Small Place*. Simon & Schuster, 1985. Copyright © 1985 by T. R. Pearson.

Peters, Joan K. From *Manny & Rose*. St. Martin's Press, 1985. Copyright © 1985 by Joan K. Peters.

Pineda, Cecile. From *Face*. Viking, 1985. Copyright © Cecile Pineda, 1985.

Rosen, R. D. From *Strike Three You're Dead*. Walker and Company, 1984. Copyright © 1984 by Richard Dean Rosen.

Shacochis, Bob. From *Easy in the Islands: Stories*. Crown Publishers, Inc., 1985. Copyright © 1985 by Bob Shacochis.

Simon, Neil. From *Biloxi Blues*. Random House, 1986. Copyright © 1984, 1985 by Neil Simon.

Skvorecky, Josef. From *The Engineer of Human Souls: An Entertainment on the Old Themes of Life, Women, Fate, Dreams, the Working Class, Secret Agents, Love and Death*. Translated by Paul Wilson. Alfred A. Knopf, 1984. English translation copyright © 1984 by Paul Wilson.

Smith, Mary-Ann Tirone. From *The Book of Phoebe*. Doubleday & Company, Inc., 1985. Copyright © 1985 by Mary-Ann Tirone Smith.

Spoto, Donald. From *The Kindness of Strangers: The Life of Tennessee Williams*. Little, Brown and Company, 1985. Copyright © 1985 by Donald Spoto.

Thomas, Ross. From *Briarpatch*. Simon and Schuster, 1984. Copyright © 1984 by Ross Thomas.

Thompson, Judith. From *White Biting Dog. Revised edition*. Playwrights Canada, 1985. Copyright © 1984 Judith Thompson.

Williams, Norman. From *The Unlovely Child*. Alfred A. Knopf, 1985. Copyright © 1984 by Norman Williams. All rights reserved. Reprinted by permission of Alfred A. Knopf, Inc.

Wilson, August. From *Ma Rainey's Black Bottom: A Play in Two Acts*. New American Library, 1985. Copyright © 1981, 1985 by August Wilson.

Wolff, Tobias. From *The Barracks Thief*. The Ecco Press, 1984. Copyright © 1984 by Tobias Wolff.

Cumulative Index to Authors

This index lists all author entries in the Gale Literary Criticism Series and includes cross-references to other Gale sources. For the convenience of the reader, references to the *Yearbook* in the *Contemporary Literary Criticism* series include the page number (in parentheses) after the volume number. References in the index are identified as follows:

AITN: *Authors in the News,* Volumes 1-2
CAAS: *Contemporary Authors Autobiography Series,* Volumes 1-3
CA: *Contemporary Authors* (original series), Volumes 1-117
CANR: *Contemporary Authors New Revision Series,* Volumes 1-17
CAP: *Contemporary Authors Permanent Series,* Volumes 1-2
CA-R: *Contemporary Authors* (revised editions), Volumes 1-44
CLC: *Contemporary Literary Criticism,* Volumes 1-39
CLR: *Children's Literature Review,* Volumes 1-10
DLB: *Dictionary of Literary Biography,* Volumes 1-47
DLB-DS: *Dictionary of Literary Biography Documentary Series,* Volumes 1-4
DLB-Y: *Dictionary of Literary Biography Yearbook,* Volumes 1980-1985
LC: *Literature Criticism from 1400 to 1800,* Volumes 1-3
NCLC: *Nineteenth-Century Literature Criticism,* Volumes 1-12
SAAS: *Something about the Author Autobiography Series,* Volume 1
SATA: *Something about the Author,* Volumes 1-44
TCLC: *Twentieth-Century Literary Criticism,* Volumes 1-20
YABC: *Yesterday's Authors of Books for Children,* Volumes 1-2

Author Index

A. E. 1867-1935 . . . . TCLC 3, 10
See also Russell, George William
See also DLB 19

Abbey, Edward 1927- . . . . CLC 36
See also CANR 2
See also CA 45-48

Abé, Kōbō 1924- . . . . CLC 8, 22
See also CA 65-68

Abell, Kjeld 1901-1961 . . . . CLC 15
See also obituary CA 111

Abish, Walter 1931- . . . . CLC 22
See also CA 101

Abrahams, Peter (Henry) 1919- . . . . . CLC 4
See also CA 57-60

Abrams, M(eyer) H(oward)
1912- . . . . CLC 24
See also CANR 13
See also CA 57-60

Abse, Dannie 1923- . . . . CLC 7, 29
See also CAAS 1
See also CANR 4
See also CA 53-56
See also DLB 27

Achebe, Chinua
1930- . . . . CLC 1, 3, 5, 7, 11, 26
See also CANR 6
See also CA 1-4R
See also SATA 38, 40

Ackroyd, Peter 1917- . . . . CLC 34 (387)
See also CA 25-28R

Acorn, Milton 1923- . . . . CLC 15
See also CA 103
See also AITN 2

Adamov, Arthur 1908-1970 . . . . . CLC 4, 25
See also CAP 2
See also CA 17-18
See also obituary CA 25-28R

Adams, Alice (Boyd) 1926- . . . . . . CLC 6, 13
See also CA 81-84

Adams, Douglas (Noel) 1952- . . . . . . .CLC 27
See also CA 106
See also DLB-Y 83

Adams, Henry (Brooks)
1838-1918 . . . . TCLC 4
See also CA 104
See also DLB 12, 47

Adams, Richard (George)
1920- . . . . CLC 4, 5, 18
See also CANR 3
See also CA 49-52
See also SATA 7
See also AITN 1, 2

Adamson, Joy(-Friederike Victoria)
1910-1980 . . . . .CLC 17
See also CA 69-72
See also obituary CA 93-96
See also SATA 11
See also obituary SATA 22

Addams, Charles (Samuel)
1912- . . . . .CLC 30
See also CANR 12
See also CA 61-64

Adler, C(arole) S(chwerdtfeger)
1932- . . . . .CLC 35
See also CA 89-92
See also SATA 26

Adler, Renata 1938- . . . . CLC 8, 31
See also CANR 5
See also CA 49-52

Ady, Endre 1877-1919 . . . . TCLC 11
See also CA 107

Agee, James 1909-1955 . . . . TCLC 1, 19
See also CA 108
See also DLB 2, 26
See also AITN 1

Agnon, S(hmuel) Y(osef Halevi)
1888-1970 . . . . CLC 4, 8, 14
See also CAP 2
See also CA 17-18
See also obituary CA 25-28R

Ai 1947- . . . . CLC 4, 14
See also CA 85-88

Aiken, Conrad (Potter)
1889-1973 . . . . CLC 1, 3, 5, 10
See also CANR 4
See also CA 5-8R
See also obituary CA 45-48
See also SATA 3, 30
See also DLB 9, 45

Aiken, Joan (Delano) 1924- ....CLC 35
  See also CLR 1
  See also CANR 4
  See also CA 9-12R
  See also SAAS 1
  See also SATA 2, 30

Ajar, Emile 1914-1980
  See Gary, Romain

Akhmatova, Anna
  1888-1966............... CLC 11, 25
  See also CAP 1
  See also CA 19-20
  See also obituary CA 25-28R

Aksakov, Sergei Timofeyvich
  1791-1859.................. NCLC 2

Aksenov, Vassily (Pavlovich) 1932-
  See Aksyonor, Vasily (Pavlovich)

Aksyonov, Vasily (Pavlovich)
  1932-.................... CLC 22, 37
  See also CANR 12
  See also CA 53-56

Akutagawa Ryūnosuke
  1892-1927................. TCLC 16

Alain-Fournier 1886-1914 .... TCLC 6
  See also Fournier, Henri Alban

Alarcón, Pedro Antonio de
  1833-1891 ..... NCLC 1

Albee, Edward (Franklin III)
  1928-..... CLC 1, 2, 3, 5, 9, 11, 13, 25
  See also CANR 8
  See also CA 5-8R
  See also DLB 7
  See also AITN 1

Alberti, Rafael 1902-...............CLC 7
  See also CA 85-88

Alcott, Amos Bronson
  1799-1888................... NCLC 1
  See also DLB 1

Alcott, Louisa May 1832-1888..... NCLC 6
  See also CLR 1
  See also YABC 1
  See also DLB 1, 42

Aldiss, Brian (Wilson) 1925- .... CLC 5, 14
  See also CAAS 2
  See also CANR 5
  See also CA 5-8R
  See also SATA 34
  See also DLB 14

Aleichem, Sholom 1859-1916...... TCLC 1
  See also Rabinovitch, Sholem

Aleixandre, Vicente
  1898-1984................ CLC 9, 36
  See also CA 85-88
  See also obituary CA 114

Alepoudelis, Odysseus 1911-
  See Elytis, Odysseus

Alexander, Lloyd (Chudley)
  1924-.......................CLC 35
  See also CLR 1, 5
  See also CANR 1
  See also CA 1-4R
  See also SATA 3

Alger, Horatio, Jr. 1832-1899..... NCLC 8
  See also SATA 16
  See also DLB 42

Algren, Nelson
  1909-1981............. CLC 4, 10, 33
  See also CA 13-16R
  See also obituary CA 103
  See also DLB 9
  See also DLB-Y 81, 82

Allen, Heywood 1935-
  See Allen, Woody
  See also CA 33-36R

Allen, Roland 1939-
  See Ayckbourn, Alan

Allen, Woody 1935-...............CLC 16
  See also Allen, Heywood
  See also DLB 44

Allende, Isabel 1942-........ CLC 39 (27)

Allingham, Margery (Louise)
  1904-1966...................CLC 19
  See also CANR 4
  See also CA 5-8R
  See also obituary CA 25-28R

Allston, Washington
  1779-1843................. NCLC 2
  See also DLB 1

Almedingen, E. M. 1898-1971......CLC 12
  See also Almedingen, Martha Edith von
  See also SATA 3

Almedingen, Martha Edith von 1898-1971
  See Almedingen, E. M.
  See also CANR 1
  See also CA 1-4R

Alonso, Dámaso 1898-.............CLC 14
  See also CA 110

Alta 1942-.......................CLC 19
  See also CA 57-60

Alter, Robert 1935-......... CLC 34 (515)
  See also CANR 1
  See also CA 49-52

Alther, Lisa 1944-.................CLC 7
  See also CANR 12
  See also CA 65-68

Altman, Robert 1925-.............CLC 16
  See also CA 73-76

Alvarez, A(lfred) 1929-......... CLC 5, 13
  See also CANR 3
  See also CA 1-4R
  See also DLB 14, 40

Amado, Jorge 1912-..............CLC 13
  See also CA 77-80

Ambler, Eric 1909-........... CLC 4, 6, 9
  See also CANR 7
  See also CA 9-12R

Amichai, Yehuda 1924- .... CLC 9, 22
  See also CA 85-88

Amiel, Henri Frédéric
  1821-1881.................. NCLC 4

Amis, Kingsley (William)
  1922-............CLC 1, 2, 3, 5, 8, 13
  See also CANR 8
  See also CA 9-12R
  See also DLB 15, 27
  See also AITN 2

Amis, Martin 1949-......... CLC 4, 9, 38
  See also CANR 8
  See also CA 65-68
  See also DLB 14

Ammons, A(rchie) R(andolph)
  1926-...........CLC 2, 3, 5, 8, 9, 25
  See also CANR 6
  See also CA 9-12R
  See also DLB 5
  See also AITN 1

Anand, Mulk Raj 1905-...........CLC 23
  See also CA 65-68

Anaya, Rudolfo A(lfonso)
  1937-.......................CLC 23
  See also CANR 1
  See also CA 45-48

Andersen, Hans Christian
  1805-1875.................. NCLC 7
  See also CLR 6
  See also YABC 1

Anderson, Jessica (Margaret Queale)
  19??-.......................CLC 37
  See also CANR 4
  See also CA 9-12R

Anderson, Jon (Victor) 1940- ....CLC 9
  See also CA 25-28R

Anderson, Lindsay 1923-.........CLC 20

Anderson, Maxwell 1888-1959 .... TCLC 2
  See also CA 105
  See also DLB 7

Anderson, Poul (William)
  1926-......................CLC 15
  See also CAAS 2
  See also CANR 2, 15
  See also CA 1-4R
  See also SATA 39
  See also DLB 8

Anderson, Robert (Woodruff)
  1917-.......................CLC 23
  See also CA 21-24R
  See also DLB 7
  See also AITN 1

Anderson, Roberta Joan 1943-
  See Mitchell, Joni

Anderson, Sherwood
  1876-1941............... TCLC 1, 10
  See also CA 104
  See also DLB 4, 9
  See also DLB-DS 1

Andrade, Carlos Drummond de
  1902-.......................CLC 18

Andrews, Cicily Fairfield 1892-1983
  See West, Rebecca

Andreyev, Leonid (Nikolaevich)
  1871-1919.................. TCLC 3
  See also CA 104

Andrézel, Pierre 1885-1962
  See Dinesen, Isak
  See also Blixen, Karen (Christentze Dinesen)

Andrić, Ivo 1892-1975 ....CLC 8
  See also CA 81-84
  See also obituary CA 57-60

Angelique, Pierre 1897-1962
  See Bataille, Georges

Angell, Roger 1920-...............CLC 26
  See also CANR 13
  See also CA 57-60

Angelou, Maya 1928- .... CLC 12, 35
  See also CA 65-68
  See also DLB 38

Annensky, Innokenty
　1856-1909................. **TCLC 14**
　See also CA 110

Anouilh, Jean (Marie Lucien Pierre)
　1910-.................**CLC 1, 3, 8, 13**
　See also CA 17-20R

Anthony, Florence 1947-
　See Ai

Anthony (Jacob), Piers 1934-.......**CLC 35**
　See also Jacob, Piers A(nthony)
　D(illingham)
　See also DLB 8

Antoninus, Brother 1912-
　See Everson, William (Oliver)

Antonioni, Michelangelo 1912- .....**CLC 20**
　See also CA 73-76

Antschel, Paul 1920-1970
　See Celan, Paul
　See also CA 85-88

Apollinaire, Guillaume
　1880-1918................. **TCLC 3, 8**
　See also Kostrowitzki, Wilhelm Apollinaris
　de

Appelfeld, Aharon 1932- ....**CLC 23**
　See also CA 112

Apple, Max (Isaac) 1941-....... **CLC 9, 33**
　See also CA 81-84

Aquin, Hubert 1929-1977.........**CLC 15**
　See also CA 105

Aragon, Louis 1897-1982....... **CLC 3, 22**
　See also CA 69-72
　See also obituary CA 108

Arbuthnot, John 1667-1735.........**LC 1**

Archer, Jeffrey (Howard)
　1940-.......................**CLC 28**
　See also CA 77-80

Archer, Jules 1915-................**CLC 12**
　See also CANR 6
　See also CA 9-12R
　See also SATA 4

Arden, John 1930-.........**CLC 6, 13, 15**
　See also CA 13-16R
　See also DLB 13

Arguedas, José María
　1911-1969............... **CLC 10, 18**
　See also CA 89-92

Argueta, Manlio 1936- ....**CLC 31**

Armah, Ayi Kwei 1939-........ **CLC 5, 33**
　See also CA 61-64

Armatrading, Joan 1950-.........**CLC 17**
　See also CA 114

Arnim, Achim von 1781-1831..... **NCLC 5**

Arnold, Matthew 1822-1888...... **NCLC 6**
　See also DLB 32

Arnow, Harriette (Louisa Simpson)
　1908-................... **CLC 2, 7, 18**
　See also CANR 14
　See also CA 9-12R
　See also DLB 6
　See also SATA 42

Arp, Jean 1887-1966..............**CLC 5**
　See also CA 81-84
　See also obituary CA 25-28R

Arquette, Lois S(teinmetz)
　See Duncan (Steinmetz Arquette), Lois
　See also SATA 1

Arrabal, Fernando 1932- ..... **CLC 2, 9, 18**
　See also CANR 15
　See also CA 9-12R

Arrick, Fran ....**CLC 30**

Artaud, Antonin 1896-1948...... **TCLC 3**
　See also CA 104

Arthur, Ruth M(abel)
　1905-1979...................**CLC 12**
　See also CANR 4
　See also CA 9-12R
　See also obituary CA 85-88
　See also SATA 7
　See also obituary SATA 26

Arundel, Honor (Morfydd)
　1919-1973...................**CLC 17**
　See also CAP 2
　See also CA 21-22
　See also obituary CA 41-44R
　See also SATA 4
　See also obituary SATA 24

Asch, Sholem 1880-1957......... **TCLC 3**
　See also CA 105

Ashbery, John (Lawrence)
　1927-..... **CLC 2, 3, 4, 6, 9, 13, 15, 25**
　See also CANR 9
　See also CA 5-8R
　See also DLB 5
　See also DLB-Y 81

Ashton-Warner, Sylvia (Constance)
　1908-1984...................**CLC 19**
　See also CA 69-72
　See also obituary CA 112

Asimov, Isaac
　1920-............ **CLC 1, 3, 9, 19, 26**
　See also CANR 2
　See also CA 1-4R
　See also SATA 1, 26
　See also DLB 8

Aston, James 1906-1964
　See White, T(erence) H(anbury)

Asturias, Miguel Ángel
　1899-1974............... **CLC 3, 8, 13**
　See also CAP 2
　See also CA 25-28
　See also obituary CA 49-52

Atheling, William, Jr. 1921-1975
　See Blish, James (Benjamin)

Atherton, Gertrude (Franklin Horn)
　1857-1948................... **TCLC 2**
　See also CA 104
　See also DLB 9

Atwood, Margaret (Eleanor)
　1939-........**CLC 2, 3, 4, 8, 13, 15, 25**
　See also CANR 3
　See also CA 49-52

Auchincloss, Louis (Stanton)
　1917-................**CLC 4, 6, 9, 18**
　See also CANR 6
　See also CA 1-4R
　See also DLB 2
　See also DLB-Y 80

Auden, W(ystan) H(ugh)
　1907-1973....... **CLC 1, 2, 3, 4, 6, 9,**
　　　　　　　　　　　　　　11, 14
　See also CANR 5
　See also CA 9-12R
　See also obituary CA 45-48
　See also DLB 10, 20

Audiberti, Jacques 1899-1965......**CLC 38**
　See also obituary CA 25-28R

Auel, Jean M(arie) 1936-.........**CLC 31**
　See also CA 103

Austen, Jane 1775-1817.......... **NCLC 1**

Avison, Margaret 1918-......... **CLC 2, 4**
　See also CA 17-20R

Ayckbourn, Alan
　1939-..........**CLC 5, 8, 18, 33**
　See also CA 21-24R
　See also DLB 13

Aymé, Marcel (Andre)
　1902-1967....................**CLC 11**
　See also CA 89-92

Ayrton, Michael 1921-1975.........**CLC 7**
　See also CANR 9
　See also CA 5-8R
　See also obituary CA 61-64

Azorín 1874-1967................**CLC 11**
　See also Martínez Ruiz, José

Azuela, Mariano 1873-1952....... **TCLC 3**
　See also CA 104

"Bab" 1836-1911
　See Gilbert, (Sir) W(illiam) S(chwenck)

Babel, Isaak (Emmanuilovich)
　1894-1941............... **TCLC 2, 13**
　See also CA 104

Babits, Mihály 1883-1941....... **TCLC 14**
　See also CA 114

Bacchelli, Riccardo 1891-.........**CLC 19**
　See also CA 29-32R

Bach, Richard (David) 1936-.......**CLC 14**
　See also CA 9-12R
　See also SATA 13
　See also AITN 1

Bachman, Richard 1947-
　See King, Stephen (Edwin)

Bagehot, Walter 1826-1877...... **NCLC 10**

Bagnold, Enid 1889-1981..........**CLC 25**
　See also CANR 5
　See also CA 5-8R
　See also obituary CA 103
　See also SATA 1, 25
　See also DLB 13

Bagryana, Elisaveta 1893- ....**CLC 10**

Baillie, Joanna 1762-1851 .... **NCLC 2**

Bainbridge, Beryl
　1933-.......**CLC 4, 5, 8, 10, 14, 18, 22**
　See also CA 21-24R
　See also DLB 14

Baker, Elliott 1922-................**CLC 8**
　See also CANR 2
　See also CA 45-48

Baker, Russell (Wayne) 1925-......**CLC 31**
　See also CANR 11
　See also CA 57-60

Bakshi, Ralph 1938-.............**CLC 26**
　See also CA 112

Author Index

Baldwin, James (Arthur)
1924-......CLC 1, 2, 3, 4, 5, 8, 13, 15,
17
See also CANR 3
See also CA 1-4R
See also SATA 9
See also DLB 2, 7, 33

Ballard, J(ames) G(raham)
1930-................CLC 3, 6, 14, 36
See also CANR 15
See also CA 5-8R
See also DLB 14

Balmont, Konstantin Dmitriyevich
1867-1943................. TCLC 11
See also CA 109

Balzac, Honoré de 1799-1850 ..... NCLC 5

Bambara, Toni Cade 1939-........CLC 19
See also CA 29-32R
See also DLB 38

Banks, Iain 1954-............ CLC 34 (29)

Banks, Lynne Reid 1929-.........CLC 23
See also Reid Banks, Lynne

Banks, Russell 1940-..............CLC 37
See also CA 65-68

Banville, Théodore (Faullain) de
1832-1891................... NCLC 9

Baraka, Amiri
1934-........CLC 1, 2, 3, 5, 10, 14, 33
See also Baraka, Imamu Amiri
See also Jones, (Everett) LeRoi
See also DLB 5, 7, 16, 38

Baraka, Imamu Amiri
1934-........CLC 1, 2, 3, 5, 10, 14, 33
See also Baraka, Amiri
See also Jones, (Everett) LeRoi
See also DLB 5, 7, 16, 38

Barbey d'Aurevilly, Jules Amédée
1808-1889................... NCLC 1

Barbusse, Henri 1873-1935 .... TCLC 5
See also CA 105

Barea, Arturo 1897-1957 .... TCLC 14
See also CA 111

Barfoot, Joan 1946-...............CLC 18
See also CA 105

Baring, Maurice 1874-1945 .... TCLC 8
See also CA 105
See also DLB 34

Barker, George (Granville)
1913-.......................CLC 8
See also CANR 7
See also CA 9-12R
See also DLB 20

Barker, Howard 1946- ....CLC 37
See also CA 102
See also DLB 13

Barker, Pat 19??-.................CLC 32

Barnes, Djuna
1892-1982........ CLC 3, 4, 8, 11, 29
See also CANR 16
See also CA 9-12R
See also obituary CA 107
See also DLB 4, 9, 45

Barnes, Peter 1931-...............CLC 5
See also CA 65-68
See also DLB 13

Baroja (y Nessi), Pío
1872-1956.................. TCLC 8
See also CA 104

Barondess, Sue K(aufman) 1926-1977
See Kaufman, Sue
See also CANR 1
See also CA 1-4R
See also obituary CA 69-72

Barrett, (Roger) Syd 1946-
See Pink Floyd

Barrett, William (Christopher)
1913-.......................CLC 27
See also CANR 11
See also CA 13-16R

Barrie, (Sir) J(ames) M(atthew)
1860-1937................... TCLC 2
See also CA 104
See also YABC 1
See also DLB 10

Barrol, Grady 1953-
See Bograd, Larry

Barry, Philip (James Quinn)
1896-1949.................. TCLC 11
See also CA 109
See also DLB 7

Barth, John (Simmons)
1930-......CLC 1, 2, 3, 5, 7, 9, 10, 14,
27
See also CANR 5
See also CA 1-4R
See also DLB 2
See also AITN 1, 2

Barthelme, Donald
1931-...... CLC 1, 2, 3, 5, 6, 8, 13, 23
See also CA 21-24R
See also SATA 7
See also DLB 2
See also DLB-Y 80

Barthelme, Frederick 1943-........CLC 36
See also CA 114
See also DLB-Y 85

Barthes, Roland 1915-1980 ....CLC 24
See also obituary CA 97-100

Bassani, Giorgio 1916- ....CLC 9
See also CA 65-68

Bataille, Georges 1897-1962.......CLC 29
See also CA 101
See also obituary CA 89-92

Baudelaire, Charles
1821-1867................... NCLC 6

Baum, L(yman) Frank
1856-1919.................. TCLC 7
See also CA 108
See also SATA 18
See also DLB 22

Baumbach, Jonathan 1933- ..... CLC 6, 23
See also CANR 12
See also CA 13-16R
See also DLB-Y 80

Baxter, James K(eir)
1926-1972....................CLC 14
See also CA 77-80

Bayer, Sylvia 1909-1981
See Glassco, John

Beagle, Peter S(oyer) 1939- ....CLC 7
See also CANR 4
See also CA 9-12R
See also DLB-Y 80

Beard, Charles A(ustin)
1874-1948.................. TCLC 15
See also CA 115
See also SATA 18
See also DLB 17

Beardsley, Aubrey 1872-1898 ..... NCLC 6

Beattie, Ann 1947-.........CLC 8, 13, 18
See also CA 81-84
See also DLB-Y 82

Beauvoir, Simone de
1908-.......... CLC 1, 2, 4, 8, 14, 31
See also CA 9-12R

Becker, Jurek 1937- .... CLC 7, 19
See also CA 85-88

Becker, Walter 1950-
See Becker, Walter and Fagen, Donald

Becker, Walter 1950- and
Fagen, Donald 1948- ....CLC 26

Beckett, Samuel (Barclay)
1906-......CLC 1, 2, 3, 4, 6, 9, 10, 11,
14, 18, 29
See also CA 5-8R
See also DLB 13, 15

Beckman, Gunnel 1910-.............CLC 26
See also CANR 15
See also CA 33-36R
See also SATA 6

Becque, Henri 1837-1899........ NCLC 3

Beddoes, Thomas Lovell
1803-1849................... NCLC 3

Beecher, John 1904-1980...........CLC 6
See also CANR 8
See also CA 5-8R
See also obituary CA 105
See also AITN 1

Beerbohm, (Sir Henry) Max(imilian)
1872-1956.................. TCLC 1
See also CA 104
See also DLB 34

Behan, Brendan
1923-1964............CLC 1, 8, 11, 15
See also CA 73-76
See also DLB 13

Behn, Aphra 1640?-1689 .... LC 1
See also DLB 39

Belasco, David 1853-1931......... TCLC 3
See also CA 104
See also DLB 7

Belcheva, Elisaveta 1893-
See Bagryana, Elisaveta

Belinski, Vissarion Grigoryevich
1811-1848................... NCLC 5

Belitt, Ben 1911- ....CLC 22
See also CANR 7
See also CA 13-16R
See also DLB 5

Bell, Acton 1820-1849
See Brontë, Anne

Bell, Currer 1816-1855
See Brontë, Charlotte

Bell, Marvin 1937-............. CLC 8, 31
See also CA 21-24R
See also DLB 5

Bellamy, Edward 1850-1898 ...... NCLC 4
See also DLB 12

Belloc, (Joseph) Hilaire (Pierre Sébastien Réné Swanton)
1870-1953 . . . . TCLC **7, 18**
See also CA 106
See also YABC 1
See also DLB 19

Bellow, Saul
1915- . . . . . CLC **1, 2, 3, 6, 8, 10, 13, 15, 25, 33, 34** (545)
See also CA 5-8R
See also DLB 2, 28
See also DLB-Y 82
See also DLB-DS 3
See also AITN 2

Belser, Reimond Karel Maria de 1929-
See Ruyslinck, Ward

Bely, Andrey 1880-1934 . . . . TCLC **7**
See also CA 104

Benary-Isbert, Margot
1889-1979 . . . . CLC **12**
See also CANR 4
See also CA 5-8R
See also obituary CA 89-92
See also SATA 2
See also obituary SATA 21

Benavente (y Martinez), Jacinto
1866-1954 . . . . TCLC **3**
See also CA 106

Benchley, Peter (Bradford)
1940- . . . . CLC **4, 8**
See also CANR 12
See also CA 17-20R
See also SATA 3
See also AITN 2

Benchley, Robert 1889-1945 . . . . . . TCLC **1**
See also CA 105
See also DLB 11

Benedikt, Michael 1935- . . . . CLC **4, 14**
See also CANR 7
See also CA 13-16R
See also DLB 5

Benet, Juan 1927- . . . . CLC **28**

Benét, Stephen Vincent
1898-1943 . . . . TCLC **7**
See also CA 104
See also YABC 1
See also DLB 4

Benn, Gottfried 1886-1956 . . . . TCLC **3**
See also CA 106

Bennett, (Enoch) Arnold
1867-1931 . . . . TCLC **5, 20**
See also CA 106
See also DLB 10, 34

Bennett, George Harold 1930-
See Bennett, Hal
See also CA 97-100

Bennett, Hal 1930- . . . . CLC **5**
See also Bennett, George Harold
See also DLB 33

Bennett, Jay 1912- . . . . CLC **35**
See also CANR 11
See also CA 69-72
See also SATA 27

Bennett, Louise (Simone)
1919- . . . . CLC **28**
See also Bennett-Coverly, Louise Simone

Bennett-Coverly, Louise Simone 1919-
See Bennett, Louise (Simone)
See also CA 97-100

Benson, Jackson J.
1930- . . . . CLC **34** (404)
See also CA 25-28R

Benson, Sally 1900-1972 . . . . CLC **17**
See also CAP 1
See also CA 19-20
See also obituary CA 37-40R
See also SATA 1, 35
See also obituary SATA 27

Benson, Stella 1892-1933 . . . . TCLC **17**
See also DLB 36

Bentley, E(dmund) C(lerihew)
1875-1956 . . . . TCLC **12**
See also CA 108

Bentley, Eric (Russell) 1916- . . . . . . CLC **24**
See also CANR 6
See also CA 5-8R

Berger, John (Peter) 1926- . . . . . . CLC **2, 19**
See also CA 81-84
See also DLB 14

Berger, Melvin (H.) 1927- . . . . CLC **12**
See also CANR 4
See also CA 5-8R
See also SATA 5

Berger, Thomas (Louis)
1924- . . . . CLC **3, 5, 8, 11, 18, 38**
See also CANR 5
See also CA 1-4R
See also DLB 2
See also DLB-Y 80

Bergman, (Ernst) Ingmar
1918- . . . . CLC **16**
See also CA 81-84

Bergstein, Eleanor 1938- . . . . CLC **4**
See also CANR 5
See also CA 53-56

Bernanos, (Paul Louis) Georges
1888-1948 . . . . TCLC **3**
See also CA 104

Bernhard, Thomas 1931- . . . . CLC **3, 32**
See also CA 85-88

Berrigan, Daniel J. 1921- . . . . CLC **4**
See also CAAS 1
See also CANR 11
See also CA 33-36R
See also DLB 5

Berrigan, Edmund Joseph Michael, Jr.
1934-1983
See Berrigan, Ted
See also CANR 14
See also CA 61-64
See also obituary CA 110

Berrigan, Ted 1934-1983 . . . . CLC **37**
See also Berrigan, Edmund Joseph Michael, Jr.
See also DLB 5

Berry, Chuck 1926- . . . . CLC **17**

Berry, Wendell (Erdman)
1934- . . . . CLC **4, 6, 8, 27**
See also CA 73-76
See also DLB 5, 6
See also AITN 1

Berryman, John
1914-1972 . . . . . CLC **1, 2, 3, 4, 6, 8, 10, 13, 25**
See also CAP 1
See also CA 15-16
See also obituary CA 33-36R

Bertolucci, Bernardo 1940- . . . . CLC **16**
See also CA 106

Besant, Annie (Wood)
1847-1933 . . . . TCLC **9**
See also CA 105

Bessie, Alvah 1904-1985 . . . . CLC **23**
See also CANR 2
See also CA 5-8R
See also obituary CA 116
See also DLB 26

Beti, Mongo 1932- . . . . CLC **27**

Betjeman, John
1906-1984 . . . . . . CLC **2, 6, 10, 34** (305)
See also CA 9-12R
See also obituary CA 112
See also DLB 20
See also DLB-Y 84

Betti, Ugo 1892-1953 . . . . TCLC **5**
See also CA 104

Betts, Doris (Waugh)
1932- . . . . CLC **3, 6, 28**
See also CANR 9
See also CA 13-16R
See also DLB-Y 82

Bidart, Frank 19??- . . . . CLC **33**

Bienek, Horst 1930- . . . . CLC **7, 11**
See also CA 73-76

Bierce, Ambrose (Gwinett)
1842-1914? . . . . TCLC **1, 7**
See also CA 104
See also DLB 11, 12, 23

Binyon, T(imothy) J(ohn)
1936- . . . . CLC **34** (32)
See also CA 111

Bioy Casares, Adolfo
1914- . . . . CLC **4, 8, 13**
See also CA 29-32R

Bird, Robert Montgomery
1806-1854 . . . . NCLC **1**

Birdwell, Cleo 1936-
See DeLillo, Don

Birney (Alfred) Earle
1904- . . . . CLC **1, 4, 6, 11**
See also CANR 5
See also CA 1-4R

Bishop, Elizabeth
1911-1979 . . . . . . CLC **1, 4, 9, 13, 15, 32**
See also CA 5-8R
See also obituary CA 89-92
See also obituary SATA 24
See also DLB 5

Bishop, John 1935- . . . . CLC **10**
See also CA 105

Bissett, Bill 1939- . . . . CLC **18**
See also CANR 15
See also CA 69-72

Biyidi, Alexandre 1932-
See Beti, Mongo
See also CA 114

Bjørnson, Bjørnstjerne (Martinius)
    1832-1910................... **TCLC 7**
    See also CA 104

Blackburn, Paul 1926-1971 ....**CLC 9**
    See also CA 81-84
    See also obituary CA 33-36R
    See also DLB 16
    See also DLB-Y 81

Blackmur, R(ichard) P(almer)
    1904-1965................ **CLC 2, 24**
    See also CAP 1
    See also CA 11-12
    See also obituary CA 25-28R

Blackwood, Algernon (Henry)
    1869-1951................... **TCLC 5**
    See also CA 105

Blackwood, Caroline 1931- ...... **CLC 6, 9**
    See also CA 85-88
    See also DLB 14

Blair, Eric Arthur 1903-1950
    See Orwell, George
    See also CA 104
    See also SATA 29

Blais, Marie-Claire
    1939-............ **CLC 2, 4, 6, 13, 22**
    See also CA 21-24R

Blaise, Clark 1940- ....**CLC 29**
    See also CAAS 3
    See also CANR 5
    See also CA 53-56R
    See also AITN 2

Blake, Nicholas 1904-1972
    See Day Lewis, C(ecil)

Blasco Ibáñez, Vicente
    1867-1928................... **TCLC 12**
    See also CA 110

Blatty, William Peter 1928- ....**CLC 2**
    See also CANR 9
    See also CA 5-8R

Blish, James (Benjamin)
    1921-1975....................**CLC 14**
    See also CANR 3
    See also CA 1-4R
    See also obituary CA 57-60
    See also DLB 8

Blixen, Karen (Christentze Dinesen)
    1885-1962
    See Dinesen, Isak
    See also CAP 2
    See also CA 25-28
    See also SATA 44

Bloch, Robert (Albert) 1917-.......**CLC 33**
    See also CANR 5
    See also CA 5-8R
    See also DLB 44
    See also SATA 12

Blok, Aleksandr (Aleksandrovich)
    1880-1921................... **TCLC 5**
    See also CA 104

Bloom, Harold 1930-..............**CLC 24**
    See also CA 13-16R

Blount, Roy (Alton), Jr. 1941- .....**CLC 38**
    See also CANR 10
    See also CA 53-56

Blume, Judy (Sussman Kitchens)
    1938-................... **CLC 12, 30**
    See also CLR 2
    See also CANR 13
    See also CA 29-32R
    See also SATA 2, 31

Blunden, Edmund (Charles)
    1896-1974....................**CLC 2**
    See also CAP 2
    See also CA 17-18
    See also obituary CA 45-48
    See also DLB 20

Bly, Robert (Elwood)
    1926-.......... **CLC 1, 2, 5, 10, 15, 38**
    See also CA 5-8R
    See also DLB 5

Bochco, Steven 1944?-
    See Bochco, Steven and Kozoll, Michael

Bochco, Steven 1944?- and
    Kozoll, Michael 1940?- ....**CLC 35**

Bødker, Cecil 1927-...............**CLC 21**
    See also CANR 13
    See also CA 73-76
    See also SATA 14

Boell, Heinrich (Theodor) 1917-1985
    See Böll, Heinrich
    See also CA 21-24R
    See also obituary CA 116

Bogan, Louise
    1897-1970........... **CLC 4, 39** (383)
    See also CA 73-76
    See also obituary CA 25-28R
    See also DLB 45

Bogarde, Dirk 1921-..............**CLC 19**
    See also Van Den Bogarde, Derek (Jules
        Gaspard Ulric) Niven
    See also DLB 14

Bograd, Larry 1953-..............**CLC 35**
    See also CA 93-96
    See also SATA 33

Böhl de Faber, Cecilia 1796-1877
    See Caballero, Fernán

Boileau-Despréaux, Nicolas
    1636-1711..................... **LC 3**

Böll, Heinrich (Theodor)
    1917-1985...... **CLC 2, 3, 6, 9, 11, 15,**
                                 27, 39 (291)
    See also DLB-Y 85
    See also Boell, Heinrich (Theodor)

Bolt, Robert (Oxton) 1924- ....**CLC 14**
    See also CA 17-20R
    See also DLB 13

Bond, Edward 1934-......**CLC 4, 6, 13, 23**
    See also CA 25-28R
    See also DLB 13

Bonham, Frank 1914-..............**CLC 12**
    See also CANR 4
    See also CA 9-12R
    See also SATA 1

Bonnefoy, Yves 1923- .... **CLC 9, 15**
    See also CA 85-88

Bontemps, Arna (Wendell)
    1902-1973................ **CLC 1, 18**
    See also CLR 6
    See also CANR 4
    See also CA 1-4R
    See also obituary CA 41-44R
    See also SATA 2, 44
    See also obituary SATA 24

Booth, Martin 1944-..............**CLC 13**
    See also CAAS 2
    See also CA 93-96

Booth, Philip 1925-...............**CLC 23**
    See also CANR 5
    See also CA 5-8R
    See also DLB-Y 82

Booth, Wayne C(layson) 1921- .....**CLC 24**
    See also CANR 3
    See also CA 1-4R

Borchert, Wolfgang 1921-1947 .... **TCLC 5**
    See also CA 104

Borges, Jorge Luis
    1899-.......**CLC 1, 2, 3, 4, 6, 8, 9, 10,**
                                 13, 19
    See also CA 21-24R

Borowski, Tadeusz 1922-1951..... **TCLC 9**
    See also CA 106

Borrow, George (Henry)
    1803-1881................... **NCLC 9**
    See also DLB 21

Bosschère, Jean de
    1878-1953.................. **TCLC 19**

Bourget, Paul (Charles Joseph)
    1852-1935.................. **TCLC 12**
    See also CA 107

Bourjaily, Vance (Nye) 1922-........**CLC 8**
    See also CAAS 1
    See also CANR 2
    See also CA 1-4R
    See also DLB 2

Bourne, Randolph S(illiman)
    1886-1918.................. **TCLC 16**

Bowen, Elizabeth (Dorothea Cole)
    1899-1973...... **CLC 1, 3, 6, 11, 15, 22**
    See also CAP 2
    See also CA 17-18
    See also obituary CA 41-44R
    See also DLB 15

Bowering, George 1935-...........**CLC 15**
    See also CANR 10
    See also CA 21-24R

Bowering, Marilyn R(uthe)
    1949-.......................**CLC 32**
    See also CA 101

Bowers, Edgar 1924-...............**CLC 9**
    See also CA 5-8R
    See also DLB 5

Bowie, David 1947-...............**CLC 17**
    See also Jones, David Robert

Bowles, Jane (Sydney)
    1917-1973....................**CLC 3**
    See also CAP 2
    See also CA 19-20
    See also obituary CA 41-44R

Bowles, Paul (Frederick)
    1910-................... **CLC 1, 2, 19**
    See also CAAS 1
    See also CANR 1
    See also CA 1-4R
    See also DLB 5, 6

Box, Edgar 1925-
    See Vidal, Gore

Boyd, William 1952-..............**CLC 28**
    See also CA 114

Boyle, Kay 1903- .... **CLC 1, 5, 19**
See also CAAS 1
See also CA 13-16R
See also DLB 4, 9

Boyle, Patrick .... **CLC 19**

Boyle, T. Coraghessan 1948- ...... **CLC 36**

Brackenridge, Hugh Henry
1748-1816 .... **NCLC 7**
See also DLB 11, 37

Bradbury, Edward P. 1939-
See Moorcock, Michael

Bradbury, Malcolm (Stanley)
1932- .... **CLC 32**
See also CANR 1
See also CA 1-4R
See also DLB 14

Bradbury, Ray (Douglas)
1920- .... **CLC 1, 3, 10, 15**
See also CANR 2
See also CA 1-4R
See also SATA 11
See also DLB 2, 8
See also AITN 1, 2

Bradley, David (Henry), Jr.
1950- .... **CLC 23**
See also CA 104
See also DLB 33

Bradley, Marion Zimmer
1930- .... **CLC 30**
See also CANR 7
See also CA 57-60
See also DLB 8

Bragg, Melvyn 1939- .... **CLC 10**
See also CANR 10
See also CA 57-60
See also DLB 14

Braine, John (Gerard) 1922- ..... **CLC 1, 3**
See also CANR 1
See also CA 1-4R
See also DLB 15

Brammer, Billy Lee 1930?-1978
See Brammer, William

Brammer, William 1930?-1978 ..... **CLC 31**
See also obituary CA 77-80

Brancati, Vitaliano
1907-1954 .... **TCLC 12**
See also CA 109

Brancato, Robin F(idler) 1936- ..... **CLC 35**
See also CANR 11
See also CA 69-72
See also SATA 23

Brand, Millen 1906-1980 .... **CLC 7**
See also CA 21-24R
See also obituary CA 97-100

Brandes, Georg (Morris Cohen)
1842-1927 .... **TCLC 10**
See also CA 105

Branley, Franklyn M(ansfield)
1915- .... **CLC 21**
See also CANR 14
See also CA 33-36R
See also SATA 4

Brathwaite, Edward 1930- .... **CLC 11**
See also CANR 11
See also CA 25-28R

Brautigan, Richard
1935-1984 .... **CLC 1, 3, 5, 9, 12,**
34 (314)
See also CA 53-56
See also obituary CA 113
See also DLB 2, 5
See also DLB-Y 80, 84

Brecht, (Eugen) Bertolt (Friedrich)
1898-1956 .... **TCLC 1, 6, 13**
See also CA 104

Bremer, Fredrika 1801-1865 ..... **NCLC 11**

Brennan, Christopher John
1870-1932 .... **TCLC 17**

Brennan, Maeve 1917- .... **CLC 5**
See also CA 81-84

Brentano, Clemens (Maria)
1778-1842 .... **NCLC 1**

Brenton, Howard 1942- .... **CLC 31**
See also CA 69-72
See also DLB 13

Breslin, James (E.) 1930-
See Breslin, Jimmy
See also CA 73-76

Breslin, Jimmy 1930- .... **CLC 4**
See also Breslin, James (E.)
See also AITN 1

Bresson, Robert 1907- .... **CLC 16**
See also CA 110

Breton, André 1896-1966 ..... **CLC 2, 9, 15**
See also CAP 2
See also CA 19-20
See also obituary CA 25-28R

Breytenbach, Breyten
1939- .... **CLC 23, 37**
See also CA 113

Bridgers, Sue Ellen 1942- .... **CLC 26**
See also CANR 11
See also CA 65-68
See also SAAS 1
See also SATA 22

Bridges, Robert 1844-1930 .... **TCLC 1**
See also CA 104
See also DLB 19

Bridie, James 1888-1951 .... **TCLC 3**
See also Mavor, Osborne Henry
See also DLB 10

Brin, David 1950- .... **CLC 34 (133)**
See also CA 102

Brink, André (Philippus)
1935- .... **CLC 18, 36**
See also CA 104

Brinsmead, H(esba) F(ay)
1922- .... **CLC 21**
See also CANR 10
See also CA 21-24R
See also SATA 18

Brittain, Vera (Mary)
1893?-1970 .... **CLC 23**
See also CAP 1
See also CA 15-16
See also obituary CA 25-28R

Broch, Hermann 1886-1951 ...... **TCLC 20**
See also CA 117

Brock, Rose 1923-
See Hansen, Joseph

Brodsky, Iosif Alexandrovich 1940-
See Brodsky, Joseph
See also CA 41-44R
See also AITN 1

Brodsky, Joseph
1940- .... **CLC 4, 6, 13, 36**
See also Brodsky, Iosif Alexandrovich

Brodsky, Michael (Mark)
1948- .... **CLC 19**
See also CA 102

Bromell, Henry 1947- .... **CLC 5**
See also CANR 9
See also CA 53-56

Bromfield, Louis (Brucker)
1896-1956 .... **TCLC 11**
See also CA 107
See also DLB 4, 9

Broner, E(sther) M(asserman)
1930- .... **CLC 19**
See also CANR 8
See also CA 17-20R
See also DLB 28

Bronk, William 1918- .... **CLC 10**
See also CA 89-92

Brontë, Anne 1820-1849 .... **NCLC 4**
See also DLB 21

Brontë, Charlotte
1816-1855 .... **NCLC 3, 8**
See also DLB 21
See also DLB 39

Brooke, Henry 1703?-1783 .... **LC 1**
See also DLB 39

Brooke, Rupert (Chawner)
1887-1915 .... **TCLC 2, 7**
See also CA 104
See also DLB 19

Brookner, Anita
1938- .... **CLC 32, 34 (136)**
See also CA 114

Brooks, Cleanth 1906- .... **CLC 24**
See also CA 17-20R

Brooks, Gwendolyn
1917- .... **CLC 1, 2, 4, 5, 15**
See also CANR 1
See also CA 1-4R
See also SATA 6
See also DLB 5
See also AITN 1

Brooks, Mel 1926- .... **CLC 12**
See also Kaminsky, Melvin
See also CA 65-68
See also DLB 26

Brooks, Peter 1938- .... **CLC 34 (519)**
See also CANR 1
See also CA 45-48

Brooks, Van Wyck 1886-1963 ...... **CLC 29**
See also CANR 6
See also CA 1-4R
See also DLB 45

Brophy, Brigid (Antonia)
1929- .... **CLC 6, 11, 29**
See also CA 5-8R
See also DLB 14

Brosman, Catharine Savage
1934- .... **CLC 9**
See also CA 61-64

Broughton, T(homas) Alan
    1936-........................CLC 19
  See also CANR 2
  See also CA 45-48

Broumas, Olga 1949- ....CLC 10
  See also CA 85-88

Brown, Claude 1937- ....CLC 30
  See also CA 73-76

Brown, Dee (Alexander) 1908- .....CLC 18
  See also CANR 11
  See also CA 13-16R
  See also SATA 5
  See also DLB-Y 80

Brown, George Mackay 1921-.......CLC 5
  See also CANR 12
  See also CA 21-24R
  See also SATA 35
  See also DLB 14, 27

Brown, Rita Mae 1944- ....CLC 18
  See also CANR 2, 11
  See also CA 45-48

Brown, Rosellen 1939- ....CLC 32
  See also CANR 14
  See also CA 77-80

Brown, Sterling A(llen)
    1901-..................... CLC 1, 23
  See also CA 85-88

Brown, William Wells
    1816?-1884.................. NCLC 2
  See also DLB 3

Browne, Jackson 1950-............CLC 21

Browning, Elizabeth Barrett
    1806-1861................... NCLC 1
  See also DLB 32

Browning, Tod 1882-1962 ....CLC 16

Bruccoli, Matthew J(oseph)
    1931-................... CLC 34 (416)
  See also CANR 7
  See also CA 9-12R

Bruce, Lenny 1925-1966..........CLC 21
  See also Schneider, Leonard Alfred

Brunner, John (Kilian Houston)
    1934-.................. CLC 8, 10
  See also CANR 2
  See also CA 1-4R

Bryan, C(ourtlandt) D(ixon) B(arnes)
    1936-.........................CLC 29
  See also CANR 13
  See also CA 73-76

Bryant, William Cullen
    1794-1878................... NCLC 6
  See also DLB 3, 43

Bryusov, Valery (Yakovlevich)
    1873-1924.................. TCLC 10
  See also CA 107

Buchheim, Lothar-Günther
    1918-.........................CLC 6
  See also CA 85-88

Buchwald, Art(hur) 1925- ....CLC 33
  See also CA 5-8R
  See also SATA 10
  See also AITN 1

Buck, Pearl S(ydenstricker)
    1892-1973............. CLC 7, 11, 18
  See also CANR 1
  See also CA 1-4R
  See also obituary CA 41-44R
  See also SATA 1, 25
  See also DLB 9
  See also AITN 1

Buckler, Ernest 1908-1984........CLC 13
  See also CAP 1
  See also CA 11-12
  See also obituary CA 114

Buckley, William F(rank), Jr.
    1925-.................CLC 7, 18, 37
  See also CANR 1
  See also CA 1-4R
  See also DLB-Y 80
  See also AITN 1

Buechner, (Carl) Frederick
    1926-...................CLC 2, 4, 6, 9
  See also CANR 11
  See also CA 13-16R
  See also DLB-Y 80

Buell, John (Edward) 1927-.......CLC 10
  See also CA 1-4R

Buero Vallejo, Antonio 1916- ......CLC 15
  See also CA 106

Bukowski, Charles 1920- ...... CLC 2, 5, 9
  See also CA 17-20R
  See also DLB 5

Bulgakov, Mikhail (Afanas'evich)
    1891-1940............... TCLC 2, 16
  See also CA 105

Bullins, Ed 1935-.............. CLC 1, 5, 7
  See also CA 49-52
  See also DLB 7, 38

Bulwer-Lytton, (Lord) Edward (George Earle
    Lytton) 1803-1873 .... NCLC 1
  See also Lytton, Edward Bulwer
  See also DLB 21

Bunin, Ivan (Alexeyevich)
    1870-1953.................. TCLC 6
  See also CA 104

Bunting, Basil
    1900-1985........... CLC 10, 39 (297)
  See also CANR 7
  See also CA 53-56
  See also obituary CA 115
  See also DLB 20

Buñuel, Luis 1900-1983 ....CLC 16
  See also CA 101
  See also obituary CA 110

Burgess, Anthony
    1917-.....CLC 1, 2, 4, 5, 8, 10, 13, 15, 22
  See also Wilson, John (Anthony) Burgess
  See also DLB 14
  See also DLB-Y 84
  See also AITN 1

Burke, Kenneth (Duva)
    1897-..................... CLC 2, 24
  See also CA 5-8R
  See also DLB 45

Burney, Fanny 1752-1840 .... NCLC 12
  See also DLB 39

Burns, Robert 1759-1796........... LC 3

Burns, Tex 1908?-
  See L'Amour, Louis (Dearborn)

Burnshaw, Stanley 1906- .... CLC 3, 13
  See also CA 9-12R

Burr, Anne 1937-..................CLC 6
  See also CA 25-28R

Burroughs, Edgar Rice
    1875-1950................... TCLC 2
  See also CA 104
  See also DLB 8
  See also SATA 41

Burroughs, William S(eward)
    1914-............. CLC 1, 2, 5, 15, 22
  See also CA 9-12R
  See also DLB 2, 8, 16
  See also DLB-Y 81
  See also AITN 2

Busch, Frederick 1941-...... CLC 7, 10, 18
  See also CAAS 1
  See also CA 33-36R
  See also DLB 6

Bush, Ronald 19??-......... CLC 34 (523)

Butler, Octavia E(stelle) 1947-......CLC 38
  See also CANR 12
  See also CA 73-76
  See also DLB 33

Butler, Samuel 1835-1902 .... TCLC 1
  See also CA 104
  See also DLB 18

Butor, Michel (Marie François)
    1926-............. CLC 1, 3, 8, 11, 15
  See also CA 9-12R

Buzzati, Dino 1906-1972...........CLC 36
  See also obituary CA 33-36R

Byars, Betsy 1928-................CLC 35
  See also CLR 1
  See also CA 33-36R
  See also SAAS 1
  See also SATA 4

Byatt, A(ntonia) S(usan Drabble)
    1936-.........................CLC 19
  See also CANR 13
  See also CA 13-16R
  See also DLB 14

Byrne, David 1953?-..............CLC 26

Byrne, John Keyes 1926-
  See Leonard, Hugh
  See also CA 102

Byron, George Gordon (Noel), Lord Byron
    1788-1824................NCLC 2, 12

Caballero, Fernán 1796-1877 .... NCLC 10

Cabell, James Branch
    1879-1958................... TCLC 6
  See also CA 105
  See also DLB 9

Cable, George Washington
    1844-1925.................. TCLC 4
  See also CA 104
  See also DLB 12

Cabrera Infante, G(uillermo)
    1929-..................... CLC 5, 25
  See also CA 85-88

Cain, G. 1929-
  See Cabrera Infante, G(uillermo)

Cain, James M(allahan)
    1892-1977.............. CLC 3, 11, 28
    See also CANR 8
    See also CA 17-20R
    See also obituary CA 73-76
    See also AITN 1

Caldwell, Erskine 1903- ...... CLC 1, 8, 14
    See also CAAS 1
    See also CANR 2
    See also CA 1-4R
    See also DLB 9
    See also AITN 1

Caldwell, (Janet Miriam) Taylor (Holland)
    1900-1985........ CLC 2, 28, 39 (301)
    See also CANR 5
    See also CA 5-8R
    See also obituary CA 116

Calisher, Hortense
    1911-................ CLC 2, 4, 8, 38
    See also CANR 1
    See also CA 1-4R
    See also DLB 2

Callaghan, Morley (Edward)
    1903-...................... CLC 3, 14
    See also CA 9-12R

Calvino, Italo
    1923-1985....... CLC 5, 8, 11, 22, 33,
                                    39 (305)
    See also CA 85-88
    See also obituary CA 116

Campana, Dino 1885-1932...... TCLC 20
    See also CA 117

Campbell, John W(ood), Jr.
    1910-1971................... CLC 32
    See also CAP 2
    See also CA 21-22
    See also obituary CA 29-32R
    See also DLB 8

Campbell, (Ignatius) Roy (Dunnachie)
    1901-1957................... TCLC 5
    See also CA 104
    See also DLB 20

Campbell, (William) Wilfred
    1861-1918................. TCLC 9
    See also CA 106

Camus, Albert
    1913-1960...... CLC 1, 2, 4, 9, 11, 14,
                                        32
    See also CA 89-92

Canby, Vincent 1924-............. CLC 13
    See also CA 81-84

Canetti, Elias 1905-........ CLC 3, 14, 25
    See also CA 21-24R

Cape, Judith 1916-
    See Page, P(atricia) K(athleen)

Capek, Karel 1890-1938......... TCLC 6
    See also CA 104

Capote, Truman
    1924-1984........ CLC 1, 3, 8, 13, 19,
                                    34 (320), 38
    See also CA 5-8R
    See also obituary CA 113
    See also DLB 2
    See also DLB-Y 80, 84

Capra, Frank 1897-............... CLC 16
    See also CA 61-64

Caputo, Philip 1941-............. CLC 32
    See also CA 73-76

Cardenal, Ernesto 1925-.......... CLC 31
    See also CANR 2
    See also CA 49-52

Carey, Ernestine Gilbreth 1908-
    See Gilbreth, Frank B(unker), Jr. and
        Carey, Ernestine Gilbreth
    See also CA 5-8R
    See also SATA 2

Carleton, William 1794-1869...... NCLC 3

Carlisle, Henry (Coffin) 1926-...... CLC 33
    See also CANR 15
    See also CA 13-16R

Carman, (William) Bliss
    1861-1929.................. TCLC 7
    See also CA 104

Carpentier (y Valmont), Alejo
    1904-1980............. CLC 8, 11, 38
    See also CANR 11
    See also CA 65-68
    See also obituary CA 97-100

Carr, John Dickson 1906-1977......CLC 3
    See also CANR 3
    See also CA 49-52
    See also obituary CA 69-72

Carr, Virginia Spencer
    1929-.................. CLC 34 (419)
    See also CA 61-64

Carrier, Roch 1937- ....CLC 13

Carroll, James (P.) 1943-.......... CLC 38
    See also CA 81-84

Carroll, Jim 1951-................ CLC 35
    See also CA 45-48

Carroll, Lewis 1832-1898........ NCLC 2
    See also Dodgson, Charles Lutwidge
    See also CLR 2
    See also DLB 18

Carroll, Paul Vincent
    1900-1968................... CLC 10
    See also CA 9-12R
    See also obituary CA 25-28R
    See also DLB 10

Carruth, Hayden
    1921-................ CLC 4, 7, 10, 18
    See also CANR 4
    See also CA 9-12R
    See also DLB 5

Carter, Angela 1940-............... CLC 5
    See also CANR 12
    See also CA 53-56
    See also DLB 14

Carver, Raymond 1938-....... CLC 22, 36
    See also CANR 17
    See also CA 33-36R
    See also DLB-Y 84

Cary, (Arthur) Joyce
    1888-1957.................. TCLC 1
    See also CA 104
    See also DLB 15

Casares, Adolfo Bioy 1914-
    See Bioy Casares, Adolfo

Casey, John 1880-1964
    See O'Casey, Sean

Casey, Michael 1947- .... CLC 2
    See also CA 65-68
    See also DLB 5

Casey, Warren 1935-
    See Jacobs, Jim and Casey, Warren
    See also CA 101

Cassavetes, John 1929-............ CLC 20
    See also CA 85-88

Cassill, R(onald) V(erlin)
    1919-..................... CLC 4, 23
    See also CAAS 1
    See also CANR 7
    See also CA 9-12R
    See also DLB 6

Cassity, (Allen) Turner 1929- ....CLC 6
    See also CANR 11
    See also CA 17-20R

Castaneda, Carlos 1935?-.......... CLC 12
    See also CA 25-28R

Castro, Rosalía de 1837-1885 ..... NCLC 3

Cather, Willa (Sibert)
    1873-1947................ TCLC 1, 11
    See also CA 104
    See also SATA 30
    See also DLB 9
    See also DLB-DS 1

Catton, (Charles) Bruce
    1899-1978................... CLC 35
    See also CANR 7
    See also CA 5-8R
    See also obituary CA 81-84
    See also SATA 2
    See also obituary SATA 24
    See also DLB 17
    See also AITN 1

Caunitz, William 1935-....... CLC 34 (35)

Causley, Charles (Stanley)
    1917-...................... CLC 7
    See also CANR 5
    See also CA 9-12R
    See also SATA 3
    See also DLB 27

Caute, (John) David 1936-........CLC 29
    See also CANR 1
    See also CA 1-4R
    See also DLB 14

Cavafy, C(onstantine) P(eter)
    1863-1933................. TCLC 2, 7
    See also CA 104

Cavanna, Betty 1909-............. CLC 12
    See also CANR 6
    See also CA 9-12R
    See also SATA 1, 30

Cayrol, Jean 1911- .... CLC 11
    See also CA 89-92

Cela, Camilo José 1916-....... CLC 4, 13
    See also CA 21-24R

Celan, Paul 1920-1970 .... CLC 10, 19
    See also Antschel, Paul

Céline, Louis-Ferdinand
    1894-1961........ CLC 1, 3, 4, 7, 9, 15
    See also Destouches, Louis Ferdinand

Cendrars, Blaise 1887-1961........CLC 18
    See also Sauser-Hall, Frédéric

Césaire, Aimé (Fernand)
    1913-..................... CLC 19, 32
    See also CA 65-68

Chabrol, Claude 1930- ....CLC 16
    See also CA 110

Challans, Mary 1905-1983
  See Renault, Mary
  See also CA 81-84
  See also obituary CA 111
  See also SATA 23
  See also obituary SATA 36

Chambers, Aidan 1934- . . . . .CLC 35
  See also CANR 12
  See also CA 25-28R
  See also SATA 1

Chambers, James 1948-
  See Cliff, Jimmy

Chandler, Raymond
  1888-1959. . . . . TCLC 1, 7
  See also CA 104

Chaplin, Charles (Spencer)
  1889-1977. . . . . .CLC 16
  See also CA 81-84
  See also obituary CA 73-76
  See also DLB 44

Chapman, Graham 1941?-
  See Monty Python
  See also CA 116

Chapman, John Jay
  1862-1933. . . . . TCLC 7
  See also CA 104

Char, René (Emile)
  1907- . . . . CLC 9, 11, 14
  See also CA 13-16R

Charyn, Jerome 1937- . . . . CLC 5, 8, 18
  See also CAAS 1
  See also CANR 7
  See also CA 5-8R
  See also DLB-Y 83

Chase, Mary Ellen 1887-1973 . . . . . . .CLC 2
  See also CAP 1
  See also CA 15-16
  See also obituary CA 41-44R
  See also SATA 10

Chateaubriand, François René de
  1768-1848. . . . . NCLC 3

Chatterji, Saratchandra
  1876-1938. . . . . TCLC 13
  See also CA 109

Chatterton, Thomas 1752-1770 . . . . . . LC 3

Chatwin, (Charles) Bruce
  1940- . . . . .CLC 28
  See also CA 85-88

Chayefsky, Paddy 1923-1981 . . . . . . .CLC 23
  See also CA 9-12R
  See also obituary CA 104
  See also DLB 7, 44
  See also DLB-Y 81

Chayefsky, Sidney 1923-1981
  See Chayefsky, Paddy

Cheever, John
  1912-1982. . . . . . CLC 3, 7, 8, 11, 15, 25
  See also CANR 5
  See also CA 5-8R
  See also obituary CA 106
  See also DLB 2
  See also DLB-Y 80, 82

Cheever, Susan 1943- . . . . .CLC 18
  See also CA 103
  See also DLB-Y 82

Chekhov, Anton (Pavlovich)
  1860-1904. . . . . TCLC 3, 10
  See also CA 104

Chernyshevsky, Nikolay Gavrilovich
  1828-1889. . . . . NCLC 1

Cherry, Caroline Janice 1942-
  See Cherryh, C. J.

Cherryh, C. J. 1942- . . . . .CLC 35
  See also DLB-Y 80

Chesnutt, Charles Waddell
  1858-1932. . . . . TCLC 5
  See also CA 106
  See also DLB 12

Chesterton, G(ilbert) K(eith)
  1874-1936. . . . . TCLC 1, 6
  See also CA 104
  See also SATA 27
  See also DLB 10, 19, 34

Ch'ien Chung-shu 1910- . . . . .CLC 22

Child, Lydia Maria 1802-1880 . . . . NCLC 6
  See also DLB 1

Child, Philip 1898-1978 . . . . .CLC 19
  See also CAP 1
  See also CA 13-14

Childress, Alice 1920- . . . . CLC 12, 15
  See also CANR 3
  See also CA 45-48
  See also SATA 7
  See also DLB 7, 38

Chislett, (Margaret) Anne
  1943?- . . . . CLC 34 (144)

Chitty, (Sir) Thomas Willes 1926-
  See Hinde, Thomas
  See also CA 5-8R

Chomette, René 1898-1981
  See Clair, René
  See also obituary CA 103

Chopin, Kate (O'Flaherty)
  1851-1904. . . . . TCLC 5, 14
  See also CA 104
  See also DLB 12

Christie, Agatha (Mary Clarissa)
  1890-1976. . . . . CLC 1, 6, 8, 12,
                                         39 (436)
  See also CANR 10
  See also CA 17-20R
  See also obituary CA 61-64
  See also SATA 36
  See also DLB 13
  See also AITN 1, 2

Christie, (Ann) Philippa 1920-
  See Pearce, (Ann) Philippa
  See also CANR 4

Chulkov, Mikhail Dmitrievich
  1743-1792. . . . . LC 2

Churchill, Caryl 1938- . . . . .CLC 31
  See also CA 102
  See also DLB 13

Churchill, Charles 1731?-1764 . . . . LC 3

Chute, Carolyn 1947- . . . . CLC 39 (37)

Ciardi, John (Anthony)
  1916-1986. . . . . .CLC 10
  See also CAAS 2
  See also CANR 5
  See also CA 5-8R
  See also SATA 1
  See also DLB 5

Cimino, Michael 1943?- . . . . .CLC 16
  See also CA 105

Clair, René 1898-1981 . . . . .CLC 20
  See also Chomette, René

Clampitt, Amy 19??- . . . . .CLC 32
  See also CA 110

Clare, John 1793-1864 . . . . NCLC 9

Clark, (Robert) Brian 1932- . . . . . . .CLC 29
  See also CA 41-44R

Clark, Eleanor 1913- . . . . CLC 5, 19
  See also CA 9-12R
  See also DLB 6

Clark, John Pepper 1935- . . . . . . .CLC 38
  See also CANR 16
  See also CA 65-68

Clark, Mavis Thorpe 1912?- . . . . . . .CLC 12
  See also CANR 8
  See also CA 57-60
  See also SATA 8

Clark, Walter Van Tilburg
  1909-1971. . . . . .CLC 28
  See also CA 9-12R
  See also obituary CA 33-36R
  See also SATA 8
  See also DLB 9

Clarke, Arthur C(harles)
  1917- . . . . CLC 1, 4, 13, 18, 35
  See also CANR 2
  See also CA 1-4R
  See also SATA 13

Clarke, Austin 1896-1974. . . . . CLC 6, 9
  See also CAP 2
  See also CA 29-32
  See also obituary CA 49-52
  See also DLB 10, 20

Clarke, Austin C(hesterfield)
  1934- . . . . .CLC 8
  See also CA 25-28R

Clarke, Shirley 1925- . . . . .CLC 16

Clash, The. .CLC 30

Claudel, Paul (Louis Charles Marie)
  1868-1955. . . . . TCLC 2, 10
  See also CA 104

Clavell, James (duMaresq)
  1924- . . . . CLC 6, 25
  See also CA 25-28R

Cleaver, (Leroy) Eldridge
  1935- . . . . .CLC 30
  See also CANR 16
  See also CA 21-24R

Cleese, John 1939-
  See Monty Python
  See also CA 112, 116

Cleland, John 1709-1789 . . . . LC 2
  See also DLB 39

Clemens, Samuel Langhorne 1835-1910
  See Twain, Mark
  See also CA 104
  See also YABC 2
  See also DLB 11, 12, 23

Cliff, Jimmy 1948-. . . . . .CLC 21

Clifton, Lucille 1936- . . . . .CLC 19
  See also CLR 5
  See also CANR 2
  See also CA 49-52
  See also SATA 20
  See also DLB 5, 41

Clutha, Janet Paterson Frame 1924-
See Frame (Clutha), Janet (Paterson)
See also CANR 2
See also CA 1-4R

Coburn, D(onald) L(ee) 1938-......CLC 10
See also CA 89-92

Cocteau, Jean (Maurice Eugene Clement)
1889-1963............CLC 1, 8, 15, 16
See also CAP 2
See also CA 25-28

Coetzee, J(ohn) M. 1940-......CLC 23, 33
See also CA 77-80

Cohen, Arthur A(llen) 1928-.... CLC 7, 31
See also CANR 1, 17
See also CA 1-4R
See also DLB 28

Cohen, Leonard (Norman)
1934-......................CLC 3, 38
See also CANR 14
See also CA 21-24R

Cohen, Matt 1942-...............CLC 19
See also CA 61-64

Colegate, Isabel 1931-............CLC 36
See also CANR 8
See also CA 17-20R
See also DLB 14

Coleridge, Samuel Taylor
1772-1834.................. NCLC 9

Colette (Sidonie-Gabrielle)
1873-1954.............TCLC 1, 5, 16
See also CA 104

Collier, Christopher 1930-
See Collier, Christopher and Collier, James
L(incoln)
See also CANR 13
See also CA 33-36R
See also SATA 16

Collier, Christopher 1930- and
Collier, James L(incoln)
1928-.......................CLC 30

Collier, James L(incoln) 1928-
See Collier, Christopher and Collier, James
L(incoln)
See also CLR 3
See also CANR 4
See also CA 9-12R
See also SATA 8

Collier, James L(incoln) 1928- and
Collier, Christopher 1930-
See Collier, Christopher and Collier, James
L(incoln)

Collins, Hunt 1926-
See Hunter, Evan

Collins, (William) Wilkie
1824-1889.................. NCLC 1
See also DLB 18

Colman, George 1909-1981
See Glassco, John

Colton, James 1923-
See Hansen, Joseph

Colum, Padraic 1881-1972........CLC 28
See also CA 73-76
See also obituary CA 33-36R
See also SATA 15
See also DLB 19

Colvin, James 1939-
See Moorcock, Michael

Colwin, Laurie 1945- ...... CLC 5, 13, 23
See also CA 89-92
See also DLB-Y 80

Comfort, Alex(ander) 1920-........CLC 7
See also CANR 1
See also CA 1-4R

Compton-Burnett, Ivy
1892-1969..........CLC 1, 3, 10, 15,
34 (494)
See also CANR 4
See also CA 1-4R
See also obituary CA 25-28R
See also DLB 36

Comstock, Anthony
1844-1915................. TCLC 13
See also CA 110

Condon, Richard (Thomas)
1915-...........CLC 4, 6, 8, 10
See also CAAS 1
See also CANR 2
See also CA 1-4R

Connell, Evan S(helby), Jr.
1924-..................... CLC 4, 6
See also CAAS 2
See also CANR 2
See also CA 1-4R
See also DLB 2
See also DLB-Y 81

Connelly, Marc(us Cook)
1890-1980...................CLC 7
See also CA 85-88
See also obituary CA 102
See also obituary SATA 25
See also DLB 7
See also DLB-Y 80

Conrad, Joseph
1857-1924.............TCLC 1, 6, 13
See also CA 104
See also SATA 27
See also DLB 10, 34

Conroy, Pat 1945-................CLC 30
See also CA 85-88
See also DLB 6
See also AITN 1

Constant (de Rebecque), (Henri) Benjamin
1767-1830................. NCLC 6

Cook, Robin 1940-................CLC 14
See also CA 108, 111

Cooke, John Esten 1830-1886 ..... NCLC 5
See also DLB 3

Cooper, James Fenimore
1789-1851.................. NCLC 1
See also SATA 19
See also DLB 3

Coover, Robert (Lowell)
1932-...............CLC 3, 7, 15, 32
See also CANR 3
See also CA 45-48
See also DLB 2
See also DLB-Y 81

Copeland, Stewart (Armstrong) 1952-
See The Police

Coppard, A(lfred) E(dgar)
1878-1957.................. TCLC 5
See also CA 114
See also YABC 1

Coppola, Francis Ford 1939-.......CLC 16
See also CA 77-80
See also DLB 44

Corcoran, Barbara 1911-..........CLC 17
See also CAAS 2
See also CANR 11
See also CA 21-24R
See also SATA 3

Corman, Cid 1924-...............CLC 9
See also Corman, Sidney
See also CAAS 2
See also DLB 5

Corman, Sidney 1924-
See Corman, Cid
See also CA 85-88

Cormier, Robert (Edmund)
1925-................... CLC 12, 30
See also CANR 5
See also CA 1-4R
See also SATA 10

Corn, Alfred (Dewitt III)
1943-......................CLC 33
See also CA 104
See also DLB-Y 80

Cornwell, David (John Moore) 1931-
See le Carré, John
See also CANR 13
See also CA 5-8R

Corso, (Nunzio) Gregory
1930-................... CLC 1, 11
See also CA 5-8R
See also DLB 5, 16

Cortázar, Julio
1914-1984..... CLC 2, 3, 5, 10, 13, 15,
33, 34 (329)
See also CANR 12
See also CA 21-24R

Corvo, Baron 1860-1913
See Rolfe, Frederick (William Serafino
Austin Lewis Mary)

Ćosić, Dobrica 1921-..............CLC 14

Costain, Thomas B(ertram)
1885-1965...................CLC 30
See also CA 5-8R
See also obituary CA 25-28R
See also DLB 9

Costello, Elvis 1955- ....CLC 21

Couperus, Louis (Marie Anne)
1863-1923.................. TCLC 15
See also CA 115

Cousteau, Jacques-Yves 1910-......CLC 30
See also CANR 15
See also CA 65-68
See also SATA 38

Coward, Nöel (Pierce)
1899-1973..............CLC 1, 9, 29
See also CAP 2
See also CA 17-18
See also obituary CA 41-44R
See also DLB 10
See also AITN 1

Cowley, Malcolm 1898- ..... CLC 39 (457)
See also CANR 3
See also CA 5-6R
See also DLB 4
See also DLB-Y 81

Cowper, William 1731-1800 ...... NCLC 8

Author Index

Cox, William Trevor 1928-
 See Trevor, William
 See also CANR 4
 See also CA 9-12R

Cozzens, James Gould
 1903-1978.............. CLC 1, 4, 11
 See also CA 9-12R
 See also obituary CA 81-84
 See also DLB 9
 See also DLB-Y 84
 See also DLB-DS 2

Crane, (Harold) Hart
 1899-1932................. TCLC 2, 5
 See also CA 104
 See also DLB 4

Crane, R(onald) S(almon)
 1886-1967.....................CLC 27
 See also CA 85-88

Crane, Stephen
 1871-1900.............. TCLC 11, 17
 See also CA 109
 See also DLB 12
 See also YABC 2

Craven, Margaret 1901-1980......CLC 17
 See also CA 103

Crawford, F(rancis) Marion
 1854-1909................. TCLC 10
 See also CA 107

Crawford, Isabella Valancy
 1850-1887................. NCLC 12

Crayencour, Marguerite de 1913-
 See Yourcenar, Marguerite

Creasey, John 1908-1973..........CLC 11
 See also CANR 8
 See also CA 5-8R
 See also obituary CA 41-44R

Crébillon, Claude Prosper Jolyot de (fils)
 1707-1777..................... LC 1

Creeley, Robert (White)
 1926-........CLC 1, 2, 4, 8, 11, 15, 36
 See also CA 1-4R
 See also DLB 5, 16

Crews, Harry 1935-........... CLC 6, 23
 See also CA 25-28R
 See also DLB 6
 See also AITN 1

Crichton, (John) Michael
 1942-....................... CLC 2, 6
 See also CANR 13
 See also CA 25-28R
 See also SATA 9
 See also DLB-Y 81
 See also AITN 2

Crispin, Edmund 1921-1978.......CLC 22
 See also Montgomery, Robert Bruce

Cristofer, Michael 1946-..........CLC 28
 See also CA 110
 See also DLB 7

Crockett, David (Davy)
 1786-1836................. NCLC 8
 See also DLB 3, 11

Croker, John Wilson
 1780-1857................. NCLC 10

Cronin, A(rchibald) J(oseph)
 1896-1981....................CLC 32
 See also CANR 5
 See also CA 1-4R
 See also obituary CA 102
 See also obituary SATA 25

Cross, Amanda 1926-
 See Heilbrun, Carolyn G(old)

Crothers, Rachel 1878-1953...... TCLC 19
 See also CA 113
 See also DLB 7

Crowley, Aleister 1875-1947 ...... TCLC 7
 See also CA 104

Crumb, Robert 1943-................CLC 17
 See also CA 106

Cryer, Gretchen 1936?-...........CLC 21
 See also CA 114

Csáth, Géza 1887-1919......... TCLC 13
 See also CA 111

Cudlip, David 1933- .... CLC 34 (38)

Cullen, Countee 1903-1946 ...... TCLC 4
 See also CA 108
 See also SATA 18
 See also DLB 4

Cummings, E(dward) E(stlin)
 1894-1962........ CLC 1, 3, 8, 12, 15
 See also CA 73-76
 See also DLB 4

Cunningham, J(ames) V(incent)
 1911-1985................. CLC 3, 31
 See also CANR 1
 See also CA 1-4R
 See also obituary CA 115
 See also DLB 5

Cunningham, Julia (Woolfolk)
 1916-.......................CLC 12
 See also CANR 4
 See also CA 9-12R
 See also SATA 1, 26

Cunningham, Michael
 1952-.................. CLC 34 (40)

Dąbrowska, Maria (Szumska)
 1889-1965....................CLC 15
 See also CA 106

Dabydeen, David 1956?-..... CLC 34 (147)

Dagerman, Stig (Halvard)
 1923-1954................. TCLC 17

Dahl, Roald 1916- .... CLC 1, 6, 18
 See also CLR 1, 7
 See also CANR 6
 See also CA 1-4R
 See also SATA 1, 26

Dahlberg, Edward
 1900-1977............... CLC 1, 7, 14
 See also CA 9-12R
 See also obituary CA 69-72

Daly, Maureen 1921-..............CLC 17
 See also McGivern, Maureen Daly
 See also SAAS 1
 See also SATA 2

Däniken, Erich von 1935-
 See Von Däniken, Erich

Dannay, Frederic 1905-1982
 See Queen, Ellery
 See also CANR 1
 See also CA 1-4R
 See also obituary CA 107

D'Annunzio, Gabriele
 1863-1938................ TCLC 6
 See also CA 104

Danziger, Paula 1944-.............CLC 21
 See also CA 112, 115
 See also SATA 30, 36

Darío, Rubén 1867-1916......... TCLC 4
 See also Sarmiento, Felix Ruben Garcia
 See also CA 104

Darley, George 1795-1846 .... NCLC 2

Daryush, Elizabeth
 1887-1977................. CLC 6, 19
 See also CANR 3
 See also CA 49-52
 See also DLB 20

Daudet, (Louis Marie) Alphonse
 1840-1897.................. NCLC 1

Daumal, René 1908-1944 .... TCLC 14
 See also CA 114

Davenport, Guy (Mattison, Jr.)
 1927-.................... CLC 6, 14, 38
 See also CA 33-36R

Davidson, Donald (Grady)
 1893-1968.............. CLC 2, 13, 19
 See also CANR 4
 See also CA 5-8R
 See also obituary CA 25-28R
 See also DLB 45

Davidson, Sara 1943- ....CLC 9
 See also CA 81-84

Davie, Donald (Alfred)
 1922-.................CLC 5, 8, 10, 31
 See also CAAS 3
 See also CANR 1
 See also CA 1-4R
 See also DLB 27

Davies, Ray(mond Douglas)
 1944-.......................CLC 21
 See also CA 116

Davies, Rhys 1903-1978 ....CLC 23
 See also CANR 4
 See also CA 9-12R
 See also obituary CA 81-84

Davies, (William) Robertson
 1913-................CLC 2, 7, 13, 25
 See also CANR 17
 See also CA 33-36R

Davies, W(illiam) H(enry)
 1871-1940................. TCLC 5
 See also CA 104
 See also DLB 19

Davis, Rebecca (Blaine) Harding
 1831-1910.................. TCLC 6
 See also CA 104

Davison, Frank Dalby
 1893-1970....................CLC 15
 See also obituary CA 116

Davison, Peter 1928-..............CLC 28
 See also CANR 3
 See also CA 9-12R
 See also DLB 5

Davys, Mary 1674-1732 .... LC 1
 See also DLB 39

Dawson, Fielding 1930-.............CLC 6
 See also CA 85-88

Day, Thomas 1748-1789............LC 1
See also YABC 1
See also DLB 39

Day Lewis, C(ecil)
1904-1972..............CLC 1, 6, 10
See also CAP 1
See also CA 15-16
See also obituary CA 33-36R
See also DLB 15, 20

Dazai Osamu 1909-1948........TCLC 11
See also Tsushima Shūji

De Crayencour, Marguerite 1903-
See Yourcenar, Marguerite

Defoe, Daniel 1660?-1731...........LC 1
See also SATA 22
See also DLB 39

De Hartog, Jan 1914-............CLC 19
See also CANR 1
See also CA 1-4R

Deighton, Len 1929- ....CLC 4, 7, 22
See also CA 9-12R

De la Mare, Walter (John)
1873-1956..................TCLC 4
See also CA 110
See also SATA 16
See also DLB 19

Delaney, Shelagh 1939-...........CLC 29
See also CA 17-20R
See also DLB 13

Delany, Samuel R(ay, Jr.)
1942-.................CLC 8, 14, 38
See also CA 81-84
See also DLB 8, 33

De la Roche, Mazo 1885-1961......CLC 14
See also CA 85-88

Delbanco, Nicholas (Franklin)
1942-.....................CLC 6, 13
See also CAAS 2
See also CA 17-20R
See also DLB 6

Del Castillo, Michel 1933- ....CLC 38
See also CA 109

Delibes (Setien), Miguel
1920-......................CLC 8, 18
See also CANR 1
See also CA 45-48

DeLillo, Don
1936-.....CLC 8, 10, 13, 27, 39 (115)
See also CA 81-84
See also DLB 6

De Lisser, H(erbert) G(eorge)
1878-1944.................TCLC 12
See also CA 109

Deloria, Vine (Victor), Jr.
1933-......................CLC 21
See also CANR 5
See also CA 53-56
See also SATA 21

Del Vecchio, John M(ichael)
1947-......................CLC 29
See also CA 110

Dennis, Nigel (Forbes) 1912-........CLC 8
See also CA 25-28R
See also DLB 13, 15

De Palma, Brian 1940-............CLC 20
See also CA 109

De Quincey, Thomas
1785-1859..................NCLC 4

Deren, Eleanora 1908-1961
See Deren, Maya
See also obituary CA 111

Deren, Maya 1908-1961..........CLC 16
See also Deren, Eleanora

Derleth, August William
1909-1971..................CLC 31
See also CANR 4
See also CA 1-4R
See also obituary CA 29-32R
See also SATA 5
See also DLB 9

Derrida, Jacques 1930-............CLC 24

Desai, Anita 1937-...........CLC 19, 37
See also CA 81-84

De Saint-Luc, Jean 1909-1981
See Glassco, John

De Sica, Vittorio 1902-1974.......CLC 20

Destouches, Louis Ferdinand 1894-1961
See Céline, Louis-Ferdinand
See also CA 85-88

Deutsch, Babette 1895-1982........CLC 18
See also CANR 4
See also CA 1-4R
See also obituary CA 108
See also DLB 45
See also SATA 1
See also obituary SATA 33

De Vries, Peter
1910-........CLC 1, 2, 3, 7, 10, 28
See also CA 17-20R
See also DLB 6
See also DLB-Y 82

Dexter, Pete 1943-...........CLC 34 (43)

Diamond, Neil (Leslie) 1941-......CLC 30
See also CA 108

Dick, Philip K(indred)
1928-1982................CLC 10, 30
See also CANR 2, 16
See also CA 49-52
See also obituary CA 106
See also DLB 8

Dickens, Charles 1812-1870.....NCLC 3, 8
See also SATA 15
See also DLB 21

Dickey, James (Lafayette)
1923-..........CLC 1, 2, 4, 7, 10, 15
See also CANR 10
See also CA 9-12R
See also DLB 5
See also DLB-Y 82
See also AITN 1, 2

Dickey, William 1928-.........CLC 3, 28
See also CA 9-12R
See also DLB 5

Dickinson, Peter (Malcolm de Brissac)
1927-....................CLC 12, 35
See also CA 41-44R
See also SATA 5

Didion, Joan 1934- .... CLC 1, 3, 8, 14, 32
See also CANR 14
See also CA 5-8R
See also DLB 2
See also DLB-Y 81
See also AITN 1

Dillard, Annie 1945-...............CLC 9
See also CANR 3
See also CA 49-52
See also SATA 10
See also DLB-Y 80

Dillard, R(ichard) H(enry) W(ilde)
1937-......................CLC 5
See also CANR 10
See also CA 21-24R
See also DLB 5

Dillon, Eilis 1920- ....CLC 17
See also CAAS 3
See also CANR 4
See also CA 9-12R
See also SATA 2

Dinesen, Isak 1885-1962.......CLC 10, 29
See also Blixen, Karen (Christentze Dinesen)

Disch, Thomas M(ichael)
1940-....................CLC 7, 36
See also CANR 17
See also CA 21-24R
See also DLB 8

Disraeli, Benjamin 1804-1881 ..... NCLC 2
See also DLB 21

Dixon, Paige 1911-
See Corcoran, Barbara

Döblin, Alfred 1878-1957........TCLC 13
See also Doeblin, Alfred

Dobrolyubov, Nikolai Alexandrovich
1836-1861...................NCLC 5

Dobyns, Stephen 1941-...........CLC 37
See also CANR 2
See also CA 45-48

Doctorow, E(dgar) L(aurence)
1931-..........CLC 6, 11, 15, 18, 37
See also CANR 2
See also CA 45-48
See also DLB 2, 28
See also DLB-Y 80
See also AITN 2

Dodgson, Charles Lutwidge 1832-1898
See Carroll, Lewis
See also YABC 2

Doeblin, Alfred 1878-1957
See also CA 110

Doerr, Harriet 1914?-....... CLC 34 (151)

Donleavy, J(ames) P(atrick)
1926-.................CLC 1, 4, 6, 10
See also CA 9-12R
See also DLB 6
See also AITN 2

Donnell, David 1939?-....... CLC 34 (155)

Donoso, José 1924- ....CLC 4, 8, 11, 32
See also CA 81-84

Donovan, John 1928- ....CLC 35
See also CLR 3
See also CA 97-100
See also SATA 29

Doolittle, Hilda 1886-1961
See H(ilda) D(oolittle)
See also CA 97-100
See also DLB 4, 45

Dorn, Ed(ward Merton)
1929-...................CLC 10, 18
See also CA 93-96
See also DLB 5

Dos Passos, John (Roderigo)
    1896-1970..... CLC 1, 4, 8, 11, 15, 25,
                                        34 (419)
    See also CANR 3
    See also CA 1-4R
    See also obituary CA 29-32R
    See also DLB 4, 9
    See also DLB-DS 1

Dostoevski, Fedor Mikhailovich
    1821-1881................NCLC 2, 7

Douglass, Frederick
    1817-1895...................NCLC 7
    See also SATA 29
    See also DLB 1, 43

Dourado, (Waldomiro Freitas) Autran
    1926-........................CLC 23
    See also CA 25-28R

Dowson, Ernest (Christopher)
    1867-1900..................TCLC 4
    See also CA 105
    See also DLB 19

Doyle, (Sir) Arthur Conan
    1859-1930..................TCLC 7
    See also CA 104
    See also SATA 24
    See also DLB 18

Dr. A 1933-
    See Silverstein, Alvin and Virginia
        B(arbara Opshelor) Silverstein

Drabble, Margaret
    1939-..........CLC 2, 3, 5, 8, 10, 22
    See also CA 13-16R
    See also DLB 14

Dreiser, Theodore (Herman Albert)
    1871-1945..............TCLC 10, 18
    See also CA 106
    See also DLB 9, 12
    See also DLB-DS 1

Drexler, Rosalyn 1926-..........CLC 2, 6
    See also CA 81-84

Dreyer, Carl Theodor
    1889-1968....................CLC 16
    See also obituary CA 116

Droste-Hülshoff, Annette Freiin von
    1797-1848...................NCLC 3

Drummond de Andrade, Carlos 1902-
    See Andrade, Carlos Drummond de

Drury, Allen (Stuart) 1918-........CLC 37
    See also CA 57-60

Dryden, John 1631-1700............LC 3

Duberman, Martin 1930-...........CLC 8
    See also CANR 2
    See also CA 1-4R

Dubie, Norman (Evans, Jr.)
    1945-.......................CLC 36
    See also CANR 12
    See also CA 69-72

Du Bois, W(illiam) E(dward) B(urghardt)
    1868-1963..............CLC 1, 2, 13
    See also CA 85-88
    See also SATA 42
    See also DLB 47

Dubus, Andre 1936-..........CLC 13, 36
    See also CANR 17
    See also CA 21-24R

Ducasse, Isidore Lucien 1846-1870
    See Lautréamont, Comte de

Duclos, Charles Pinot 1704-1772.....LC 1

Dudek, Louis 1918-..........CLC 11, 19
    See also CANR 1
    See also CA 45-48

Dudevant, Amandine Aurore Lucile Dupin
    1804-1876
    See Sand, George

Duerrenmatt, Friedrich 1921-
    See also CA 17-20R

Duffy, Maureen 1933-.............CLC 37
    See also CA 25-28R
    See also DLB 14

Dugan, Alan 1923-.............CLC 2, 6
    See also CA 81-84
    See also DLB 5

Duhamel, Georges 1884-1966.......CLC 8
    See also CA 81-84
    See also obituary CA 25-28R

Dujardin, Édouard (Émile Louis)
    1861-1949.................TCLC 13
    See also CA 109

Duke, Raoul 1939-
    See Thompson, Hunter S(tockton)

Dumas, Alexandre (*père*)
    1802-1870.................NCLC 11
    See also SATA 18

Dumas, Alexandre (*fils*)
    1824-1895..................NCLC 9

Dumas, Henry (L.) 1934-1968......CLC 6
    See also CA 85-88
    See also DLB 41

Du Maurier, Daphne 1907-.....CLC 6, 11
    See also CANR 6
    See also CA 5-8R
    See also SATA 27

Dunbar, Paul Laurence
    1872-1906................TCLC 2, 12
    See also CA 104
    See also SATA 34

Duncan (Steinmetz Arquette), Lois
    1934-........................CLC 26
    See also Arquette, Lois S(teinmetz)
    See also CANR 2
    See also CA 1-4R
    See also SATA 1, 36

Duncan, Robert
    1919-.............CLC 1, 2, 4, 7, 15
    See also CA 9-12R
    See also DLB 5, 16, 37

Dunlap, William 1766-1839.......NCLC 2
    See also DLB 30, 37

Dunn, Douglas (Eaglesham)
    1942-........................CLC 6
    See also CANR 2
    See also CA 45-48
    See also DLB 40

Dunn, Stephen 1939-.............CLC 36
    See also CANR 12
    See also CA 33-36R

Dunne, John Gregory 1932-........CLC 28
    See also CANR 14
    See also CA 25-28R
    See also DLB-Y 80

Dunsany, Lord (Edward John Moreton Drax
    Plunkett) 1878-1957........TCLC 2
    See also CA 104
    See also DLB 10

Durang, Christopher (Ferdinand)
    1949-...................CLC 27, 38
    See also CA 105

Duras, Marguerite
    1914-.......CLC 3, 6, 11, 20, 34 (161)
    See also CA 25-28R

Durban, Pam 1947-.........CLC 39 (44)

Durrell, Lawrence (George)
    1912-...........CLC 1, 4, 6, 8, 13, 27
    See also CA 9-12R
    See also DLB 15, 27

Dürrenmatt, Friedrich
    1921-.............CLC 1, 4, 8, 11, 15
    See also Duerrenmatt, Friedrich

Dylan, Bob 1941-..........CLC 3, 4, 6, 12
    See also CA 41-44R
    See also DLB 16

East, Michael 1916-
    See West, Morris L.

Eastlake, William (Derry) 1917-.....CLC 8
    See also CAAS 1
    See also CANR 5
    See also CA 5-8R
    See also DLB 6

Eberhart, Richard 1904- .... CLC 3, 11, 19
    See also CANR 2
    See also CA 1-4R

Eberstadt, Fernanda
    1960-...................CLC 39 (48)

Echegaray (y Eizaguirre), José (María
    Waldo) 1832-1916..........TCLC 4
    See also CA 104

Eckert, Allan W. 1931-............CLC 17
    See also CANR 14
    See also CA 13-16R
    See also SATA 27, 29

Eco, Umberto 1932- ....CLC 28
    See also CANR 12
    See also CA 77-80

Eddison, E(ric) R(ucker)
    1882-1945.................TCLC 15
    See also CA 109

Edel, (Joseph) Leon
    1907-...............CLC 29, 34 (534)
    See also CANR 1
    See also CA 1-4R

Eden, Emily 1797-1869.........NCLC 10

Edgerton, Clyde 1944- ....CLC 39 (52)

Edgeworth, Maria 1767-1849.....NCLC 1
    See also SATA 21

Edmonds, Helen (Woods) 1904-1968
    See Kavan, Anna
    See also CA 5-8R
    See also obituary CA 25-28R

Edmonds, Walter D(umaux)
    1903-........................CLC 35
    See also CANR 2
    See also CA 5-8R
    See also SATA 1, 27
    See also DLB 9

Edson, Russell 1905-..............CLC 13
    See also CA 33-36R

Edwards, G(erald) B(asil)
    1899-1976...................CLC 25
    See also obituary CA 110

Ehle, John (Marsden, Jr.)
1925-.........................CLC 27
See also CA 9-12R

Ehrenbourg, Ilya (Grigoryevich) 1891-1967
See Ehrenburg, Ilya (Grigoryevich)

Ehrenburg, Ilya (Grigoryevich)
1891-1967........... CLC 18, 34 (433)
See also CA 102
See also obituary CA 25-28R

Eich, Guenter 1907-1971
See also CA 111
See also obituary CA 93-96

Eich, Günter 1907-1971 ....CLC 15
See also Eich, Guenter

Eichendorff, Joseph Freiherr von
1788-1857.................. NCLC 8

Eigner, Larry 1927- ....CLC 9
See also Eigner, Laurence (Joel)
See also DLB 5

Eigner, Laurence (Joel) 1927-
See Eigner, Larry
See also CANR 6
See also CA 9-12R

Eiseley, Loren (Corey)
1907-1977.....................CLC 7
See also CANR 6
See also CA 1-4R
See also obituary CA 73-76

Ekeloef, Gunnar (Bengt) 1907-1968
See Ekelöf, Gunnar (Bengt)
See also obituary CA 25-28R

Ekelöf, Gunnar (Bengt)
1907-1968....................CLC 27
See also Ekeloef, Gunnar (Bengt)

Ekwensi, Cyprian (Odiatu Duaka)
1921-........................CLC 4
See also CA 29-32R

Eliade, Mircea 1907-..............CLC 19
See also CA 65-68

Eliot, George 1819-1880.......... NCLC 4
See also DLB 21, 35

Eliot, T(homas) S(tearns)
1888-1965...... CLC 1, 2, 3, 6, 9, 10,
13, 15, 24, 34 (387; 523)
See also CA 5-8R
See also obituary CA 25-28R
See also DLB 7, 10, 45

Elkin, Stanley L(awrence)
1930-............ CLC 4, 6, 9, 14, 27
See also CANR 8
See also CA 9-12R
See also DLB 2, 28
See also DLB-Y 80

Elledge, Scott 19??-......... CLC 34 (425)

Elliott, George P(aul)
1918-1980....................CLC 2
See also CANR 2
See also CA 1-4R
See also obituary CA 97-100

Elliott, Sumner Locke 1917- ....CLC 38
See also CANR 2
See also CA 5-8R

Ellis, A. E. ....CLC 7

Ellis, Bret Easton 1964- ...... CLC 39 (55)

Ellis, (Henry) Havelock
1859-1939................. TCLC 14
See also CA 109

Ellison, Harlan 1934- .... CLC 1, 13
See also CANR 5
See also CA 5-8R
See also DLB 8

Ellison, Ralph (Waldo)
1914-................. CLC 1, 3, 11
See also CA 9-12R
See also DLB 2

Elman, Richard 1934-.............CLC 19
See also CAAS 3
See also CA 17-20R

Éluard, Paul 1895-1952 .... TCLC 7
See also Grindel, Eugene

Elvin, Anne Katharine Stevenson 1933-
See Stevenson, Anne (Katharine)
See also CA 17-20R

Elytis, Odysseus 1911- ....CLC 15
See also CA 102

Emecheta, (Florence Onye) Buchi
1944-........................CLC 14
See also CA 81-84

Emerson, Ralph Waldo
1803-1882.................. NCLC 1
See also DLB 1

Empson, William
1906-1984.......... CLC 3, 8, 19, 33,
34 (335; 538)
See also CA 17-20R
See also obituary CA 112
See also DLB 20

Enchi, Fumiko 1905-..............CLC 31

Ende, Michael 1930-..............CLC 31
See also SATA 42

Endo, Shusaku 1923- .... CLC 7, 14, 19
See also CA 29-32R

Engel, Marian 1933-1985..........CLC 36
See also CANR 12
See also CA 25-28R

Enright, D(ennis) J(oseph)
1920-................. CLC 4, 8, 31
See also CANR 1
See also CA 1-4R
See also SATA 25
See also DLB 27

Ephron, Nora 1941- .... CLC 17, 31
See also CANR 12
See also CA 65-68
See also AITN 2

Epstein, Daniel Mark 1948-........CLC 7
See also CANR 2
See also CA 49-52

Epstein, Jacob 1956-..............CLC 19
See also CA 114

Epstein, Joseph 1937-....... CLC 39 (463)
See also CA 112

Epstein, Leslie 1938-..............CLC 27
See also CA 73-76

Erdman, Paul E(mil) 1932-........CLC 25
See also CANR 13
See also CA 61-64
See also AITN 1

Erdrich, Louise 1954-....... CLC 39 (128)
See also CA 114

Erenburg, Ilya (Grigoryevich) 1891-1967
See Ehrenburg, Ilya (Grigoryevich)

Eseki, Bruno 1919-
See Mphahlele, Ezekiel

Esenin, Sergei (Aleksandrovich)
1895-1925.................. TCLC 4
See also CA 104

Eshleman, Clayton 1935- ....CLC 7
See also CA 33-36R
See also DLB 5

Espriu, Salvador 1913-1985........CLC 9
See also obituary CA 115

Evans, Marian 1819-1880
See Eliot, George

Evans, Mary Ann 1819-1880
See Eliot, George

Evarts, Esther 1900-1972
See Benson, Sally

Everson, R(onald) G(ilmour)
1903-......................CLC 27
See also CA 17-20R

Everson, William (Oliver)
1912-................. CLC 1, 5, 14
See also CA 9-12R
See also DLB 5, 16

Evtushenko, Evgenii (Aleksandrovich) 1933-
See Yevtushenko, Yevgeny

Ewart, Gavin (Buchanan)
1916-......................CLC 13
See also CANR 17
See also CA 89-92
See also DLB 40

Ewers, Hanns Heinz
1871-1943................. TCLC 12
See also CA 109

Ewing, Frederick R. 1918-
See Sturgeon, Theodore (Hamilton)

Exley, Frederick (Earl)
1929-.................... CLC 6, 11
See also CA 81-84
See also DLB-Y 81
See also AITN 2

Ezekiel, Tish O'Dowd
1943-.................. CLC 34 (46)

Fagen, Donald 1948-
See Becker, Walter and Fagen, Donald

Fagen, Donald 1948- and
Becker, Walter 1950-
See Becker, Walter and Fagen, Donald

Fair, Ronald L. 1932-.............CLC 18
See also CA 69-72
See also DLB 33

Fairbairns, Zoë (Ann) 1948- ....CLC 32
See also CA 103

Fairfield, Cicily Isabel 1892-1983
See West, Rebecca

Fallaci, Oriana 1930- ....CLC 11
See also CANR 15
See also CA 77-80

Fargue, Léon-Paul 1876-1947 .... TCLC 11
See also CA 109

Farigoule, Louis 1885-1972
See Romains, Jules

Author Index

Fariña, Richard 1937?-1966 ....CLC 9
See also CA 81-84
See also obituary CA 25-28R

Farley, Walter 1920-..............CLC 17
See also CANR 8
See also CA 17-20R
See also SATA 2, 43
See also DLB 22

Farmer, Philip José 1918- ...... CLC 1, 19
See also CANR 4
See also CA 1-4R
See also DLB 8

Farrell, J(ames) G(ordon)
1935-1979.................CLC 6
See also CA 73-76
See also obituary CA 89-92
See also DLB 14

Farrell, James T(homas)
1904-1979.............CLC 1, 4, 8, 11
See also CANR 9
See also CA 5-8R
See also obituary CA 89-92
See also DLB 4, 9
See also DLB-DS 2

Farrell, M. J. 1904-
See Keane, Molly

Fassbinder, Rainer Werner
1946-1982..................CLC 20
See also CA 93-96
See also obituary CA 106

Fast, Howard (Melvin) 1914-.......CLC 23
See also CANR 1
See also CA 1-4R
See also SATA 7
See also DLB 9

Faulkner, William (Cuthbert)
1897-1962...... CLC 1, 3, 6, 8, 9, 11,
    14, 18, 28
See also CA 81-84
See also DLB 9, 11, 44
See also DLB-DS 2
See also AITN 1

Fauset, Jessie Redmon
1884?-1961..................CLC 19
See also CA 109

Faust, Irvin 1924- ....CLC 8
See also CA 33-36R
See also DLB 2, 28
See also DLB-Y 80

Federman, Raymond 1928- ....CLC 6
See also CANR 10
See also CA 17-20R
See also DLB-Y 80

Feiffer, Jules 1929- .... CLC 2, 8
See also CA 17-20R
See also SATA 8
See also DLB 7, 44

Feinstein, Elaine 1930-............CLC 36
See also CA 69-72
See also CAAS 1
See also DLB 14, 40

Feldman, Irving (Mordecai)
1928-........................CLC 7
See also CANR 1
See also CA 1-4R

Fellini, Federico 1920- ....CLC 16
See also CA 65-68

Felsen, Gregor 1916-
See Felsen, Henry Gregor

Felsen, Henry Gregor 1916-........CLC 17
See also CANR 1
See also CA 1-4R
See also SATA 1

Fenton, James (Martin) 1949-......CLC 32
See also CA 102
See also DLB 40

Ferber, Edna 1887-1968..........CLC 18
See also CA 5-8R
See also obituary CA 25-28R
See also SATA 7
See also DLB 9, 28
See also AITN 1

Ferlinghetti, Lawrence (Monsanto)
1919?-.............CLC 2, 6, 10, 27
See also CANR 3
See also CA 5-8R
See also DLB 5, 16

Ferrier, Susan (Edmonstone)
1782-1854................... NCLC 8

Feuchtwanger, Lion
1884-1958................. TCLC 3
See also CA 104

Fiedler, Leslie A(aron)
1917-................. CLC 4, 13, 24
See also CANR 7
See also CA 9-12R
See also DLB 28

Field, Eugene 1850-1895 .... NCLC 3
See also SATA 16
See also DLB 21, 23, 42

Fielding, Henry 1707-1754........... LC 1
See also DLB 39

Fielding, Sarah 1710-1768 .... LC 1
See also DLB 39

Fierstein, Harvey 1954- ....CLC 33

Figes, Eva 1932-.................CLC 31
See also CANR 4
See also CA 53-56
See also DLB 14

Finch, Robert (Duer Claydon)
1900-........................CLC 18
See also CANR 9
See also CA 57-60

Findley, Timothy 1930-............CLC 27
See also CANR 12
See also CA 25-28R

Fink, Janis 1951-
See Ian, Janis

Firbank, (Arthur Annesley) Ronald
1886-1926.................. TCLC 1
See also CA 104
See also DLB 36

Firbank, Louis 1944-
See Reed, Lou

Fisher, Roy 1930- ....CLC 25
See also CANR 16
See also CA 81-84
See also DLB 40

Fisher, Rudolph 1897-1934 ...... TCLC 11
See also CA 107

Fisher, Vardis (Alvero)
1895-1968....................CLC 7
See also CA 5-8R
See also obituary CA 25-28R
See also DLB 9

FitzGerald, Edward
1809-1883................. NCLC 9
See also DLB 32

Fitzgerald, F(rancis) Scott (Key)
1896-1940.........TCLC 1, 6, 14
See also CA 110
See also DLB 4, 9
See also DLB-Y 81
See also DLB-DS 1
See also AITN 1

Fitzgerald, Penelope 1916-.........CLC 19
See also CA 85-88
See also DLB 14

FitzGerald, Robert D(avid)
1902-........................CLC 19
See also CA 17-20R

Fitzgerald, Robert (Stuart)
1910-1985.......... CLC 39 (318; 470)
See also CANR 1
See also CA 2R
See also obituary CA 114
See also DLB-Y 80

Flanagan, Thomas (James Bonner)
1923-........................CLC 25
See also CA 108
See also DLB-Y 80

Flaubert, Gustave
1821-1880................NCLC 2, 10

Fleming, Ian (Lancaster)
1908-1964.................. CLC 3, 30
See also CA 5-8R
See also SATA 9

Fleming, Thomas J(ames)
1927-........................CLC 37
See also CANR 10
See also CA 5-8R
See also SATA 8

Fo, Dario 1929- ....CLC 32
See also CA 116

Follett, Ken(neth Martin)
1949-........................CLC 18
See also CANR 13
See also CA 81-84
See also DLB-Y 81

Forbes, Esther 1891-1967..........CLC 12
See also CAP 1
See also CA 13-14
See also obituary CA 25-28R
See also DLB 22
See also SATA 2

Forché, Carolyn 1950- ....CLC 25
See also CA 109
See also DLB 5

Ford, Ford Madox
1873-1939............... TCLC 1, 15
See also CA 104
See also DLB 34

Ford, John 1895-1973.............CLC 16
See also obituary CA 45-48

Forester, C(ecil) S(cott)
1899-1966....................CLC 35
See also CA 73-76
See also obituary CA 25-28R
See also SATA 13

Forman, James D(ouglas)
1932-............................CLC 21
See also CANR 4
See also CA 9-12R
See also SATA 8, 21

Fornes, Maria Irene
1930-.....................CLC 39 (135)
See also CA 25-28R
See also DLB 7

Forrest, Leon 1937-.................CLC 4
See also CA 89-92
See also DLB 33

Forster, E(dward) M(organ)
1879-1970...... CLC 1, 2, 3, 4, 9, 10,
13, 15, 22
See also CAP 1
See also CA 13-14
See also obituary CA 25-28R
See also DLB 34

Forster, John 1812-1876.........NCLC 11

Forsyth, Frederick 1938-..... CLC 2, 5, 36
See also CA 85-88

Forten (Grimk), Charlotte L(ottie)
1837-1914..................TCLC 16

Foscolo, Ugo 1778-1827 ....NCLC 8

Fosse, Bob 1925-.................CLC 20
See also Fosse, Robert Louis

Fosse, Robert Louis 1925-
See Bob Fosse
See also CA 110

Foucault, Michel
1926-1984...........CLC 31, 34 (339)
See also CA 105
See also obituary CA 113

**Fouqué, Friedrich (Heinrich Karl) de La
Motte** 1777-1843............NCLC 2

Fournier, Henri Alban 1886-1914
See Alain-Fournier
See also CA 104

Fournier, Pierre 1916-.............CLC 11
See also CANR 16
See also CA 89-92

Fowles, John (Robert)
1926-......CLC 1, 2, 3, 4, 6, 9, 10, 15,
33
See also CA 5-8R
See also DLB 14
See also SATA 22

Fox, Paula 1923-................CLC 2, 8
See also CLR 1
See also CA 73-76
See also SATA 17

Fox, William Price (Jr.) 1926-......CLC 22
See also CANR 11
See also CA 17-20R
See also DLB 2
See also DLB-Y 81

Frame (Clutha), Janet (Paterson)
1924-..................CLC 2, 3, 6, 22
See also Clutha, Janet Paterson Frame

France, Anatole 1844-1924 ....TCLC 9
See also Thibault, Jacques Anatole
Francois

Francis, Dick 1920-............CLC 2, 22
See also CANR 9
See also CA 5-8R

Francis, Robert (Churchill)
1901-........................CLC 15
See also CANR 1
See also CA 1-4R

Frank, Anne 1929-1945 .... TCLC 17
See also CA 113
See also SATA 42

Frank, Elizabeth 1945-...... CLC 39 (383)

Franklin, (Stella Maria Sarah) Miles
1879-1954..................TCLC 7
See also CA 104

Fraser, Antonia (Pakenham)
1932-........................CLC 32
See also CA 85-88
See also SATA 32

Fraser, George MacDonald
1925-.........................CLC 7
See also CANR 2
See also CA 45-48

Frayn, Michael 1933- .... CLC 3, 7, 31
See also CA 5-8R
See also DLB 13, 14

Frederic, Harold 1856-1898...... NCLC 10
See also DLB 12, 23

Fredro, Aleksander 1793-1876 .... NCLC 8

Freeling, Nicolas 1927-.............CLC 38
See also CANR 1, 17
See also CA 49-52

Freeman, Douglas Southall
1886-1953.................. TCLC 11
See also CA 109
See also DLB 17

Freeman, Mary (Eleanor) Wilkins
1852-1930.................. TCLC 9
See also CA 106
See also DLB 12

French, Marilyn 1929- .... CLC 10, 18
See also CANR 3
See also CA 69-72

Freneau, Philip Morin
1752-1832.................. NCLC 1
See also DLB 37, 43

Friedman, B(ernard) H(arper)
1926-........................CLC 7
See also CANR 3
See also CA 1-4R

Friedman, Bruce Jay 1930-...... CLC 3, 5
See also CA 9-12R
See also DLB 2, 28

Friel, Brian 1929-..................CLC 5
See also CA 21-24R
See also DLB 13

Friis-Baastad, Babbis (Ellinor)
1921-1970..................CLC 12
See also CA 17-20R
See also SATA 7

Frisch, Max (Rudolf)
1911-........... CLC 3, 9, 14, 18, 32
See also CA 85-88

Fromentin, Eugène (Samuel Auguste)
1820-1876.................. NCLC 10

Frost, Robert (Lee)
1874-1963...... CLC 1, 3, 4, 9, 10, 13,
15, 26, 34 (468)
See also CA 89-92
See also SATA 14

Fry, Christopher 1907-...... CLC 2, 10, 14
See also CANR 9
See also CA 17-20R
See also DLB 13

Frye, (Herman) Northrop
1912-........................CLC 24
See also CANR 8
See also CA 5-8R

Fuchs, Daniel 1909-...........CLC 8, 22
See also CA 81-84
See also DLB 9, 26, 28

Fuchs, Daniel 1934-.........CLC 34 (545)
See also CANR 14
See also CA 37-40R

Fuentes, Carlos
1928-............ CLC 3, 8, 10, 13, 22
See also CANR 10
See also CA 69-72
See also AITN 2

Fugard, Athol 1932-......CLC 5, 9, 14, 25
See also CA 85-88

Fuller, Charles (H., Jr.) 1939-.....CLC 25
See also CA 108, 112
See also DLB 38

Fuller, (Sarah) Margaret
1810-1850..................NCLC 5
See also Ossoli, Sarah Margaret (Fuller
marchesa d')
See also DLB 1

Fuller, Roy (Broadbent)
1912-........................CLC 4, 28
See also CA 5-8R
See also DLB 15, 20

Futrelle, Jacques 1875-1912...... TCLC 19
See also CA 113

Gadda, Carlo Emilio
1893-1973....................CLC 11
See also CA 89-92

Gaddis, William
1922-...........CLC 1, 3, 6, 8, 10, 19
See also CA 17-20R
See also DLB 2

Gaines, Ernest J. 1933- ..... CLC 3, 11, 18
See also CANR 6
See also CA 9-12R
See also DLB 2, 33
See also DLB-Y 80
See also AITN 1

Gale, Zona 1874-1938............TCLC 7
See also CA 105
See also DLB 9

Gallagher, Tess 1943-.............CLC 18
See also CA 106

Gallant, Mavis 1922-........CLC 7, 18, 38
See also CA 69-72

Gallant, Roy A(rthur) 1924- ....CLC 17
See also CANR 4
See also CA 5-8R
See also SATA 4

Gallico, Paul (William)
1897-1976....................CLC 2
See also CA 5-8R
See also obituary CA 69-72
See also SATA 13
See also DLB 9
See also AITN 1

Galsworthy, John 1867-1933 . . . . . **TCLC 1**
 See also CA 104
 See also DLB 10, 34

Galt, John 1779-1839 . . . . **NCLC 1**

Galvin, James 1951- . . . . **CLC 38**
 See also CA 108

Gann, Ernest K(ellogg) 1910- . . . . . . **CLC 23**
 See also CANR 1
 See also CA 1-4R
 See also AITN 1

García Lorca, Federico
  1899-1936 . . . . **TCLC 1, 7**
 See also CA 104

García Márquez, Gabriel
  1928- . . . . **CLC 2, 3, 8, 10, 15, 27**
 See also CANR 10
 See also CA 33-36R

Gardner, John (Champlin, Jr.)
  1933-1982 . . . . **CLC 2, 3, 5, 7, 8, 10,
                              18, 28, 34** (547)
 See also CA 65-68
 See also obituary CA 107
 See also obituary SATA 31, 40
 See also DLB 2
 See also DLB-Y 82
 See also AITN 1

Gardner, John (Edmund)
  1926- . . . . **CLC 30**
 See also CANR 15
 See also CA 103
 See also AITN 1

Garfield, Leon 1921- . . . . **CLC 12**
 See also CA 17-20R
 See also SATA 1, 32

Garland, (Hannibal) Hamlin
  1860-1940 . . . . **TCLC 3**
 See also CA 104
 See also DLB 12

Garneau, Hector (de) Saint Denys
  1912-1943 . . . . **TCLC 13**
 See also CA 111

Garner, Alan 1935- . . . . **CLC 17**
 See also CANR 15
 See also CA 73-76
 See also SATA 18

Garner, Hugh 1913-1979 . . . . **CLC 13**
 See also CA 69-72

Garnett, David 1892-1981 . . . . **CLC 3**
 See also CA 5-8R
 See also obituary CA 103
 See also DLB 34

Garrett, George (Palmer)
  1929- . . . . **CLC 3, 11**
 See also CANR 1
 See also CA 1-4R
 See also DLB 2, 5
 See also DLB-Y 83

Garrigue, Jean 1914-1972 . . . . **CLC 2, 8**
 See also CA 5-8R
 See also obituary CA 37-40R

Gary, Romain 1914-1980 . . . . **CLC 25**
 See also Kacew, Romain

Gascar, Pierre 1916-
 See Fournier, Pierre

Gaskell, Elizabeth Cleghorn
  1810-1865 . . . . **NCLC 5**
 See also DLB 21

Gass, William H(oward)
  1924- . . . . . **CLC 1, 2, 8, 11, 15, 39** (477)
 See also CA 17-20R
 See also DLB 2

Gautier, Théophile 1811-1872 . . . . . **NCLC 1**

Gaye, Marvin (Pentz)
  1939-1984 . . . . **CLC 26**
 See also obituary CA 112

Gébler, Carlo (Ernest)
  1954- . . . . **CLC 39** (60)

Gee, Maurice (Gough) 1931- . . . . . . **CLC 29**
 See also CA 97-100

Gelbart, Larry (Simon) 1923- . . . . . . **CLC 21**
 See also CA 73-76

Gelber, Jack 1932- . . . . **CLC 1, 6, 14**
 See also CANR 2
 See also CA 1-4R
 See also DLB 7

Gellhorn, Martha (Ellis) 1908- . . . . **CLC 14**
 See also CA 77-80
 See also DLB-Y 82

Genet, Jean 1910- . . . . . **CLC 1, 2, 5, 10, 14**
 See also CA 13-16R

Gent, Peter 1942- . . . . **CLC 29**
 See also CA 89-92
 See also DLB-Y 82
 See also AITN 1

George, Jean Craighead 1919- . . . . . **CLC 35**
 See also CLR 1
 See also CA 5-8R
 See also SATA 2

George, Stefan (Anton)
  1868-1933 . . . . **TCLC 2, 14**
 See also CA 104

Gerhardi, William (Alexander) 1895-1977
 See Gerhardie, William (Alexander)

Gerhardie, William (Alexander)
  1895-1977 . . . . **CLC 5**
 See also CA 25-28R
 See also obituary CA 73-76
 See also DLB 36

Gertler, T(rudy) 1946?- . . . . . . **CLC 34** (49)
 See also CA 116

Gessner, Friedrike Victoria 1910-1980
 See Adamson, Joy(-Friederike Victoria)

Ghelderode, Michel de
  1898-1962 . . . . **CLC 6, 11**
 See also CA 85-88

Ghiselin, Brewster 1903- . . . . **CLC 23**
 See also CANR 13
 See also CA 13-16R

Giacosa, Giuseppe 1847-1906 . . . . . **TCLC 7**
 See also CA 104

Gibbon, Lewis Grassic
  1901-1935 . . . . **TCLC 4**
 See also Mitchell, James Leslie

Gibran, (Gibran) Kahlil
  1883-1931 . . . . **TCLC 1, 9**
 See also CA 104

Gibson, William 1914- . . . . **CLC 23**
 See also CANR 9
 See also CA 9-12R
 See also DLB 7

Gibson, William 1948- . . . . . . **CLC 39** (139)

Gide, André (Paul Guillaume)
  1869-1951 . . . . **TCLC 5, 12**
 See also CA 104

Gifford, Barry (Colby)
  1946- . . . . **CLC 34** (457)
 See also CANR 9
 See also CA 65-68

Gilbert, (Sir) W(illiam) S(chwenck)
  1836-1911 . . . . **TCLC 3**
 See also CA 104
 See also SATA 36

Gilbreth, Ernestine 1908-
 See Carey, Ernestine Gilbreth

Gilbreth, Frank B(unker), Jr. 1911-
 See Gilbreth, Frank B(unker), Jr. and
    Carey, Ernestine Gilbreth
 See also CA 9-12R
 See also SATA 2

Gilbreth, Frank B(unker), Jr. 1911- and
    Carey, Ernestine Gilbreth
  1908- . . . . **CLC 17**

Gilchrist, Ellen 1939- . . . . **CLC 34** (164)
 See also CA 113, 116

Giles, Molly 1942- . . . . **CLC 39** (64)

Gilliam, Terry (Vance) 1940-
 See Monty Python
 See also CA 108, 113

Gilliatt, Penelope (Ann Douglass)
  1932- . . . . **CLC 2, 10, 13**
 See also CA 13-16R
 See also DLB 14
 See also AITN 2

Gilman, Charlotte (Anna) Perkins (Stetson)
  1860-1935 . . . . **TCLC 9**
 See also CA 106

Gilmour, David 1944-
 See Pink Floyd

Gilroy, Frank D(aniel) 1925- . . . . **CLC 2**
 See also CA 81-84
 See also DLB 7

Ginsberg, Allen
  1926- . . . . **CLC 1, 2, 3, 4, 6, 13, 36**
 See also CANR 2
 See also CA 1-4R
 See also DLB 5, 16
 See also AITN 1

Ginzburg, Natalia 1916- . . . . **CLC 5, 11**
 See also CA 85-88

Giono, Jean 1895-1970 . . . . **CLC 4, 11**
 See also CANR 2
 See also CA 45-48
 See also obituary CA 29-32R

Giovanni, Nikki 1943- . . . . **CLC 2, 4, 19**
 See also CLR 6
 See also CA 29-32R
 See also SATA 24
 See also DLB 5
 See also AITN 1

Giovene, Andrea 1904- . . . . **CLC 7**
 See also CA 85-88

Gippius, Zinaida (Nikolayevna) 1869-1945
 See also Hippius, Zinaida
 See also CA 106

Giraudoux, (Hippolyte) Jean
  1882-1944 . . . . **TCLC 2, 7**
 See also CA 104

Author Index

Gironella, José María 1917-........CLC 11
See also CA 101

Gissing, George (Robert)
1857-1903...................TCLC 3
See also CA 105
See also DLB 18

Glanville, Brian (Lester) 1931-......CLC 6
See also CANR 3
See also CA 5-8R
See also DLB 15
See also SATA 42

Glasgow, Ellen (Anderson Gholson)
1873?-1945................TCLC 2, 7
See also CA 104
See also DLB 9, 12

Glassco, John 1909-1981 ....CLC 9
See also CANR 15
See also CA 13-16R
See also obituary CA 102

Glasser, Ronald J. 1940?- ....CLC 37

Glissant, Edouard 1928-...........CLC 10

Glück, Louise 1943- .... CLC 7, 22
See also CA 33-36R
See also DLB 5

Godard, Jean-Luc 1930-...........CLC 20
See also CA 93-96

Godwin, Gail 1937-.......CLC 5, 8, 22, 31
See also CANR 15
See also CA 29-32R
See also DLB 6

Goethe, Johann Wolfgang von
1749-1832..................NCLC 4

Gogarty, Oliver St. John
1878-1957.................TCLC 15
See also CA 109
See also DLB 15, 19

Gogol, Nikolai (Vasilyevich)
1809-1852 .... NCLC 5

Gökçeli, Yasar Kemal 1923-
See Kemal, Yashar

Gold, Herbert 1924- ....CLC 4, 7, 14
See also CANR 17
See also CA 9-12R
See also DLB 2
See also DLB-Y 81

Goldbarth, Albert 1948-........ CLC 5, 38
See also CANR 6
See also CA 53-56

Goldberg, Anatol 19??-...... CLC 34 (433)

Golding, William (Gerald)
1911-.......CLC 1, 2, 3, 8, 10, 17, 27
See also CANR 13
See also CA 5-8R
See also DLB 15

Goldman, Emma 1869-1940 ..... TCLC 13
See also CA 110

Goldman, William (W.) 1931-.......CLC 1
See also CA 9-12R
See also DLB 44

Goldmann, Lucien 1913-1970 ......CLC 24
See also CAP 2
See also CA 25-28

Goldsberry, Steven 1949-..... CLC 34 (54)

Goldsmith, Oliver 1728?-1774........ LC 2
See also SATA 26
See also DLB 39

Gombrowicz, Witold
1904-1969............... CLC 4, 7, 11
See also CAP 2
See also CA 19-20
See also obituary CA 25-28R

Gómez de la Serna, Ramón
1888-1963...................CLC 9
See also obituary CA 116

Goncharov, Ivan Alexandrovich
1812-1891.................. NCLC 1

Goncourt, Edmond (Louis Antoine Huot) de
1822-1896
See Goncourt, Edmond (Louis Antoine
Huot) de and Goncourt, Jules (Alfred
Huot) de

Goncourt, Edmond (Louis Antoine Huot) de
1822-1896 and **Goncourt, Jules (Alfred
Huot) de** 1830-1870 .... NCLC 7

Goncourt, Jules (Alfred Huot) de 1830-1870
See Goncourt, Edmond (Louis Antoine
Huot) de and Goncourt, Jules (Alfred
Huot) de

Goncourt, Jules (Alfred Huot) de 1830-1870
and **Goncourt, Edmond (Louis Antoine
Huot) de** 1822-1896
See Goncourt, Edmond (Louis Antoine
Huot) de and Goncourt, Jules (Alfred
Huot) de

Goodman, Paul
1911-1972.............CLC 1, 2, 4, 7
See also CAP 2
See also CA 19-20
See also obituary CA 37-40R

Gordimer, Nadine
1923-..........CLC 3, 5, 7, 10, 18, 33
See also CANR 3
See also CA 5-8R

Gordon, Caroline
1895-1981.............. CLC 6, 13, 29
See also CAP 1
See also CA 11-12
See also obituary CA 103
See also DLB 4, 9
See also DLB-Y 81

Gordon, Mary (Catherine)
1949-.................... CLC 13, 22
See also CA 102
See also DLB 6
See also DLB-Y 81

Gordon, Sol 1923-................CLC 26
See also CANR 4
See also CA 53-56
See also SATA 11

Gordone, Charles 1925- .... CLC 1, 4
See also CA 93-96
See also DLB 7

Gorenko, Anna Andreyevna 1889?-1966
See Akhmatova, Anna

Gorky, Maxim 1868-1936 .... TCLC 8
See also Peshkov, Alexei Maximovich

Goryan, Sirak 1908-1981
See Saroyan, William

Gotlieb, Phyllis (Fay Bloom)
1926-.......................CLC 18
See also CANR 7
See also CA 13-16R

Gould, Lois 1938?- .... CLC 4, 10
See also CA 77-80

Gourmont, Rémy de
1858-1915.................. TCLC 17
See also CA 109

Goyen, (Charles) William
1915-1983...............CLC 5, 8, 14
See also CANR 6
See also CA 5-8R
See also obituary CA 110
See also DLB 2
See also DLB-Y 83
See also AITN 2

Goytisolo, Juan 1931-.......CLC 5, 10, 23
See also CA 85-88

Grabbe, Christian Dietrich
1801-1836................... NCLC 2

Gracq, Julien 1910-...............CLC 11

Grade, Chaim 1910-1982..........CLC 10
See also CA 93-96
See also obituary CA 107

Graham, R(obert) B(ontine) Cunninghame
1852-1936................ TCLC 19

Graham, W(illiam) S(ydney)
1918-.....................CLC 29
See also CA 73-76
See also DLB 20

Graham, Winston (Mawdsley)
1910-......................CLC 23
See also CANR 2
See also CA 49-52

Granville-Barker, Harley
1877-1946................. TCLC 2
See also CA 104

Grass, Günter (Wilhelm)
1927-.......CLC 1, 2, 4, 6, 11, 15, 22,
                                       32
See also CA 13-16R

Grau, Shirley Ann 1929- .... CLC 4, 9
See also CA 89-92
See also DLB 2
See also AITN 2

Graves, Robert (von Ranke)
1895-1985...........CLC 1, 2, 6, 11,
                                 39 (320)
See also CANR 5
See also CA 5-8R
See also DLB 20
See also DLB-Y 85

Gray, Amlin 1946-................CLC 29

Gray, Francine du Plessix
1930-......................CLC 22
See also CAAS 2
See also CANR 11
See also CA 61-64

Gray, John (Henry)
1866-1934................:...... TCLC 19

Gray, Simon (James Holliday)
1936-..................CLC 9, 14, 36
See also CAAS 3
See also CA 21-24R
See also DLB 13
See also AITN 1

Grayson, Richard (A.) 1951-.......CLC 38
See also CANR 14
See also CA 85-88

Greeley, Andrew M(oran)
    1928-..........................CLC 28
    See also CANR 7
    See also CA 5-8R

Green, Hannah 1932-........ CLC 3, 7, 30
    See also Greenberg, Joanne
    See also CA 73-76

Green, Henry 1905-1974 .... CLC 2, 13
    See also Yorke, Henry Vincent
    See also DLB 15

Green, Julien (Hartridge)
    1900-.....................CLC 3, 11
    See also CA 21-24R
    See also DLB 4

Greenberg, Ivan 1908-1973
    See Rahv, Philip
    See also CA 85-88

Greenberg, Joanne (Goldenberg)
    1932-....................CLC 3, 7, 30
    See also Green, Hannah
    See also CANR 14
    See also CA 5-8R
    See also SATA 25

Greene, Bette 1934-...............CLC 30
    See also CLR 2
    See also CANR 4
    See also CA 53-56
    See also SATA 8

Greene, Gael.....................CLC 8
    See also CANR 10
    See also CA 13-16R

Greene, Graham
    1904-........CLC 1, 3, 6, 9, 14, 18, 27,
                                        37
    See also CA 13-16R
    See also SATA 20
    See also DLB 13, 15
    See also DLB-Y 85
    See also AITN 2

Gregor, Arthur 1923-..............CLC 9
    See also CANR 11
    See also CA 25-28R
    See also SATA 36

Gregory, Lady (Isabella Augusta Persse)
    1852-1932...................TCLC 1
    See also CA 104
    See also DLB 10

Grendon, Stephen 1909-1971
    See Derleth, August (William)

Greve, Felix Paul Berthold Friedrich
    1879-1948
    See Grove, Frederick Philip
    See also CA 104

Grey, (Pearl) Zane
    1872?-1939..................TCLC 6
    See also CA 104
    See also DLB 9

Grieg, (Johan) Nordahl (Brun)
    1902-1943..................TCLC 10
    See also CA 107

Grieve, C(hristopher) M(urray) 1892-1978
    See MacDiarmid, Hugh
    See also CA 5-8R
    See also obituary CA 85-88

Griffin, Gerald 1803-1840 .... NCLC 7

Griffin, Peter 1942-........ CLC 39 (398)

Griffiths, Trevor 1935-............CLC 13
    See also CA 97-100
    See also DLB 13

Grigson, Geoffrey (Edward Harvey)
    1905-1985............ CLC 7, 39 (330)
    See also CA 25-28R
    See also DLB 27

Grillparzer, Franz 1791-1872 ..... NCLC 1

Grimm, Jakob (Ludwig) Karl 1785-1863
    See Grimm, Jakob (Ludwig) Karl and
        Grimm, Wilhelm Karl

Grimm, Jakob (Ludwig) Karl 1785-1863
    and **Grimm, Wilhelm Karl**
    1786-1859...................NCLC 3
    See also SATA 22

Grimm, Wilhelm Karl 1786-1859
    See Grimm, Jakob (Ludwig) Karl and
        Grimm, Wilhelm Karl

Grimm, Wilhelm Karl 1786-1859 and
    Grimm, Jakob (Ludwig) Karl
    1785-1863
    See Grimm, Jakob (Ludwig) Karl and
        Grimm, Wilhelm Karl

Grindel, Eugene 1895-1952
    See also CA 104

Grove, Frederick Philip
    1879-1948 .... TCLC 4
    See also Greve, Felix Paul Berthold
        Friedrich

Grumbach, Doris (Isaac)
    1918-.................... CLC 13, 22
    See also CAAS 2
    See also CANR 9
    See also CA 5-8R

Grundtvig, Nicolai Frederik Severin
    1783-1872..................NCLC 1

Guare, John 1938-......... CLC 8, 14, 29
    See also CA 73-76
    See also DLB 7

Gudjonsson, Halldór Kiljan 1902-
    See Laxness, Halldór (Kiljan)
    See also CA 103

Guest, Barbara 1920-....... CLC 34 (441)
    See also CANR 11
    See also CA 25-28R
    See also DLB 5

Guest, Judith (Ann) 1936-...... CLC 8, 30
    See also CANR 15
    See also CA 77-80

Guild, Nicholas M. 1944-.........CLC 33
    See also CA 93-96

Guillén, Jorge 1893-1984 ....CLC 11
    See also CA 89-92
    See also obituary CA 112

Guillevic, (Eugène) 1907-..........CLC 33
    See also CA 93-96

Gunn, Bill 1934- ....CLC 5
    See also Gunn, William Harrison
    See also DLB 38

Gunn, Thom(son William)
    1929-...............CLC 3, 6, 18, 32
    See also CANR 9
    See also CA 17-20R
    See also DLB 27

Gunn, William Harrison 1934-
    See Gunn, Bill
    See also CANR 12
    See also CA 13-16R
    See also AITN 1

Gurney, A(lbert) R(amsdell), Jr.
    1930-........................CLC 32
    See also CA 77-80

Gustafson, Ralph (Barker)
    1909-.......................CLC 36
    See also CANR 8
    See also CA 21-24R

Guthrie, A(lfred) B(ertram), Jr.
    1901-.......................CLC 23
    See also CA 57-60
    See also DLB 6

Guthrie, Woodrow Wilson 1912-1967
    See Guthrie, Woody
    See also CA 113
    See also obituary CA 93-96

Guthrie, Woody 1912-1967 ....CLC 35
    See also Guthrie, Woodrow Wilson

Guy, Rosa (Cuthbert) 1928-........CLC 26
    See also CANR 14
    See also CA 17-20R
    See also SATA 14
    See also DLB 33

Haavikko, Paavo (Juhani)
    1931-............... CLC 18, 34 (167)
    See also CA 106

Hacker, Marilyn 1942-....... CLC 5, 9, 23
    See also CA 77-80

Haggard, (Sir) H(enry) Rider
    1856-1925.................. TCLC 11
    See also CA 108
    See also SATA 16

Haig-Brown, Roderick L(angmere)
    1908-1976...................CLC 21
    See also CANR 4
    See also CA 5-8R
    See also obituary CA 69-72
    See also SATA 12

Hailey, Arthur 1920-...............CLC 5
    See also CANR 2
    See also CA 1-4R
    See also DLB-Y 82
    See also AITN 2

Haley, Alex (Palmer) 1921- ..... CLC 8, 12
    See also CA 77-80
    See also DLB 38

Hall, Donald (Andrew, Jr.)
    1928-............... CLC 1, 13, 37
    See also CANR 2
    See also CA 5-8R
    See also SATA 23
    See also DLB 5

Hall, (Marguerite) Radclyffe
    1886-1943.................. TCLC 12
    See also CA 110

Halpern, Daniel 1945-.............CLC 14
    See also CA 33-36R

Hamburger, Michael (Peter Leopold)
    1924-....................CLC 5, 14
    See also CANR 2
    See also CA 5-8R
    See also DLB 27

Hamill, Pete 1935-.................CLC 10
See also CA 25-28R

Hamilton, Edmond 1904-1977......CLC 1
See also CANR 3
See also CA 1-4R
See also DLB 8

Hamilton, Gail 1911-
See Corcoran, Barbara

Hamilton, Mollie 1909?-
See Kaye, M(ary) M(argaret)

Hamilton, Virginia (Edith)
1936-.......................CLC 26
See also CLR 1
See also CA 25-28R
See also SATA 4
See also DLB 33

Hammett, (Samuel) Dashiell
1894-1961...........CLC 3, 5, 10, 19
See also CA 81-84
See also AITN 1

Hammon, Jupiter
1711?-1800?................NCLC 5
See also DLB 31

Hamner, Earl (Henry), Jr.
1923-.......................CLC 12
See also CA 73-76
See also DLB 6
See also AITN 2

Hampton, Christopher (James)
1946-.......................CLC 4
See also CA 25-28R
See also DLB 13

Hamsun, Knut 1859-1952.....TCLC 2, 14
See also Pedersen, Knut

Handke, Peter
1942-...........CLC 5, 8, 10, 15, 38
See also CA 77-80

Hanley, James 1901-......CLC 3, 5, 8, 13
See also CA 73-76

Hannah, Barry 1942-.........CLC 23, 38
See also CA 108, 110
See also DLB 6

Hansberry, Lorraine
1930-1965..................CLC 17
See also CA 109
See also obituary CA 25-28R
See also DLB 7, 38
See also AITN 2

Hansen, Joseph 1923-...........CLC 38
See also CANR 16
See also CA 29-32R

Hanson, Kenneth O(stlin)
1922-.......................CLC 13
See also CANR 7
See also CA 53-56

Hardwick, Elizabeth 1916-.........CLC 13
See also CANR 3
See also CA 5-8R
See also DLB 6

Hardy, Thomas
1840-1928............TCLC 4, 10, 18
See also CA 104
See also SATA 25
See also DLB 18, 19

Hare, David 1947-................CLC 29
See also CA 97-100
See also DLB 13

Harlan, Louis R(udolph)
1922-.................. CLC 34 (182)
See also CA 21-24R

Harmon, William (Ruth) 1938-.....CLC 38
See also CANR 14
See also CA 33-36R

Harper, Frances Ellen Watkins
1825-1911.................TCLC 14
See also CA 111

Harper, Michael S(teven)
1938-................... CLC 7, 22
See also CA 33-36R
See also DLB 41

Harris, Christie (Lucy Irwin)
1907-.......................CLC 12
See also CANR 6
See also CA 5-8R
See also SATA 6

Harris, Joel Chandler
1848-1908..................TCLC 2
See also CA 104
See also YABC 1
See also DLB 11, 23, 42

Harris, John (Wyndham Parkes Lucas)
Beynon 1903-1969
See Wyndham, John
See also CA 102
See also obituary CA 89-92

Harris, MacDonald 1921-...........CLC 9
See also Heiney, Donald (William)

Harris, Mark 1922-...............CLC 19
See also CAAS 3
See also CANR 2
See also CA 5-8R
See also DLB 2
See also DLB-Y 80

Harris, (Theodore) Wilson
1921-.......................CLC 25
See also CANR 11
See also CA 65-68

Harrison, James (Thomas) 1937-
See Harrison, Jim
See also CANR 8
See also CA 13-16R

Harrison, Jim 1937-........ CLC 6, 14, 33
See also Harrison, James (Thomas)
See also DLB-Y 82

Harriss, Will(ard Irvin)
1922-.................. CLC 34 (192)
See also CA 111

Harte, (Francis) Bret(t)
1836?-1902..................TCLC 1
See also CA 104
See also SATA 26
See also DLB 12

Hartley, L(eslie) P(oles)
1895-1972................ CLC 2, 22
See also CA 45-48
See also obituary CA 37-40R
See also DLB 15

Hartman, Geoffrey H. 1929-.......CLC 27

Haruf, Kent 19??-.......... CLC 34 (57)

Harwood, Ronald 1934-...........CLC 32
See also CANR 4
See also CA 1-4R
See also DLB 13

Hašek, Jaroslav (Matej Frantisek)
1883-1923..................TCLC 4
See also CA 104

Hass, Robert 1941-...... CLC 18, 39 (145)
See also CA 111

Hauptmann, Gerhart (Johann Robert)
1862-1946..................TCLC 4
See also CA 104

Havel, Václav 1936-..............CLC 25
See also CA 104

Haviaras, Stratis 1935-............CLC 33
See also CA 105

Hawkes, John (Clendennin Burne, Jr.)
1925-......CLC 1, 2, 3, 4, 7, 9, 14, 15,
27
See also CANR 2
See also CA 1-4R
See also DLB 2, 7
See also DLB-Y 80

Hawthorne, Nathaniel
1804-1864...............NCLC 2, 10
See also YABC 2
See also DLB 1

Hayden, Robert (Earl)
1913-1980..........CLC 5, 9, 14, 37
See also CA 69-72
See also obituary CA 97-100
See also SATA 19
See also obituary SATA 26
See also DLB 5

Haywood, Eliza (Fowler)
1693?-1756....................LC 1
See also DLB 39

Hazzard, Shirley 1931-............CLC 18
See also CANR 4
See also CA 9-12R
See also DLB-Y 82

H(ilda) D(oolittle)
1886-1961..........CLC 3, 8, 14, 31,
34 (441)
See also Doolittle, Hilda

Head, Bessie 1937-................CLC 25
See also CA 29-32R

Headon, (Nicky) Topper 1956?-
See The Clash

Heaney, Seamus (Justin)
1939-......... CLC 5, 7, 14, 25, 37
See also CA 85-88
See also DLB 40

Hearn, (Patricio) Lafcadio (Tessima Carlos)
1850-1904..................TCLC 9
See also CA 105
See also DLB 12

Heat Moon, William Least
1939-.......................CLC 29

Hébert, Anne 1916-....... CLC 4, 13, 29
See also CA 85-88

Hecht, Anthony (Evan)
1923-................... CLC 8, 13, 19
See also CANR 6
See also CA 9-12R
See also DLB 5

Hecht, Ben 1894-1964..............CLC 8
See also CA 85-88
See also DLB 7, 9, 25, 26, 28

Heidegger, Martin 1889-1976 ......CLC **24**
  See also CA 81-84
  See also obituary CA 65-68

Heidenstam, (Karl Gustaf) Verner von
  1859-1940.................. TCLC **5**
  See also CA 104

Heifner, Jack 1946-..............CLC **11**
  See also CA 105

Heilbrun, Carolyn G(old)
  1926-.....................CLC **25**
  See also CANR 1
  See also CA 45-48

Heine, Harry 1797-1856
  See Heine, Heinrich

Heine, Heinrich 1797-1856........ NCLC **4**

Heiney, Donald (William) 1921-
  See Harris, MacDonald
  See also CANR 3
  See also CA 1-4R

Heinlein, Robert A(nson)
  1907-............. CLC **1, 3, 8, 14, 26**
  See also CANR 1
  See also CA 1-4R
  See also SATA 9
  See also DLB 8

Heller, Joseph
  1923-.........CLC **1, 3, 5, 8, 11, 36**
  See also CANR 8
  See also CA 5-8R
  See also DLB 2, 28
  See also DLB-Y 80
  See also AITN 1

Hellman, Lillian (Florence)
  1905?-1984.......CLC **2, 4, 8, 14, 18,**
                              34 (347)
  See also CA 13-16R
  See also obituary CA 112
  See also DLB 7
  See also DLB-Y 84
  See also AITN 1, 2

Helprin, Mark 1947-.....CLC **7, 10, 22, 32**
  See also CA 81-84
  See also DLB-Y 85

Hemingway, Ernest (Miller)
  1899-1961...... CLC **1, 3, 6, 8, 10, 13,**
                    19, 30, 34 (477), **39** (398; 427)
  See also CA 77-80
  See also DLB 4, 9
  See also DLB-Y 81
  See also DLB-DS 1
  See also AITN 2

Hempel, Amy 1951-.........CLC **39** (67)

Henley, Beth 1952- ....CLC **23**
  See also Henley, Elizabeth Becker

Henley, Elizabeth Becker 1952-
  See Henley, Beth
  See also CA 107

Henley, William Ernest
  1849-1903.................. TCLC **8**
  See also CA 105
  See also DLB 19

Hennissart, Martha
  See Lathen, Emma
  See also CA 85-88

Henry, O. 1862-1910 .... TCLC **1, 19**
  See also Porter, William Sydney

Hentoff, Nat(han Irving) 1925-.....CLC **26**
  See also CLR 1
  See also CANR 5
  See also CA 1-4R
  See also SATA 27, 42

Heppenstall, (John) Rayner
  1911-1981..................CLC **10**
  See also CA 1-4R
  See also obituary CA 103

Herbert, Frank (Patrick)
  1920-.................. CLC **12, 23, 35**
  See also CANR 5
  See also CA 53-56
  See also SATA 9, 37
  See also DLB 8

Herbert, Zbigniew 1924-...........CLC **9**
  See also CA 89-92

Herbst, Josephine
  1897-1969............. CLC **34** (448)
  See also CA 5-8R
  See also obituary CA 25-28R
  See also DLB 9

Herder, Johann Gottfried von
  1744-1803.................. NCLC **8**

Hergesheimer, Joseph
  1880-1954.................. TCLC **11**
  See also CA 109
  See also DLB 9

Herlagñez, Pablo de 1844-1896
  See Verlaine, Paul (Marie)

Herlihy, James Leo 1927-..........CLC **6**
  See also CANR 2
  See also CA 1-4R

Herriot, James 1916-..............CLC **12**
  See also Wight, James Alfred

Hersey, John (Richard)
  1914-...................CLC **1, 2, 7, 9**
  See also CA 17-20R
  See also SATA 25
  See also DLB 6

Herzen, Aleksandr Ivanovich
  1812-1870.................. NCLC **10**

Herzog, Werner 1942- ....CLC **16**
  See also CA 89-92

Hesse, Hermann
  1877-1962...... CLC **1, 2, 3, 6, 11, 17,**
                                        25
  See also CAP 2
  See also CA 17-18

Heyen, William 1940-......... CLC **13, 18**
  See also CA 33-36R
  See also DLB 5

Heyerdahl, Thor 1914-............CLC **26**
  See also CANR 5
  See also CA 5-8R
  See also SATA 2

Heym, Georg (Theodor Franz Arthur)
  1887-1912.................. TCLC **9**
  See also CA 106

Heyse, Paul (Johann Ludwig von)
  1830-1914.................. TCLC **8**
  See also CA 104

Hibbert, Eleanor (Burford)
  1906-.....................CLC **7**
  See also CANR 9
  See also CA 17-20R
  See also SATA 2

Higgins, George V(incent)
  1939-................CLC **4, 7, 10, 18**
  See also CA 77-80
  See also DLB 2
  See also DLB-Y 81

Highsmith, (Mary) Patricia
  1921-................. CLC **2, 4, 14**
  See also CANR 1
  See also CA 1-4R

Highwater, Jamake 1942-..........CLC **12**
  See also CANR 10
  See also CA 65-68
  See also SATA 30, 32
  See also DLB-Y 85

Hill, Geoffrey 1932-.......... CLC **5, 8, 18**
  See also CA 81-84
  See also DLB 40

Hill, George Roy 1922-............CLC **26**
  See also CA 110

Hill, Susan B. 1942- ....CLC **4**
  See also CA 33-36R
  See also DLB 14

Hilliard, Noel (Harvey) 1929- ......CLC **15**
  See also CANR 7
  See also CA 9-12R

Himes, Chester (Bomar)
  1909-1984............CLC **2, 4, 7, 18**
  See also CA 25-28R
  See also obituary CA 114
  See also DLB 2

Hinde, Thomas 1926- .... CLC **6, 11**
  See also Chitty, (Sir) Thomas Willes

Hine, (William) Daryl 1936- ......CLC **15**
  See also CANR 1
  See also CA 1-4R

Hinton, S(usan) E(loise) 1950-......CLC **30**
  See also CLR 3
  See also CA 81-84
  See also SATA 19

Hippius (Merezhkovsky), Zinaida
  (Nikolayevna) 1869-1945 ..... TCLC **9**
  See also Gippius, Zinaida (Nikolayevna)

Hiraoka, Kimitake 1925-1970
  See Mishima, Yukio
  See also CA 97-100
  See also obituary CA 29-32R

Hirsch, Edward 1950-.............CLC **31**
  See also CA 104

Hitchcock, (Sir) Alfred (Joseph)
  1899-1980...................CLC **16**
  See also obituary CA 97-100
  See also SATA 27
  See also obituary SATA 24

Hoagland, Edward 1932-..........CLC **28**
  See also CANR 2
  See also CA 1-4R
  See also DLB 6

Hoban, Russell C(onwell)
  1925-.....................CLC **7, 25**
  See also CLR 3
  See also CA 5-8R
  See also SATA 1, 40

Hobson, Laura Z(ametkin)
  1900-.....................CLC **7, 25**
  See also CA 17-20R
  See also DLB 28

Hochhuth, Rolf 1931- . . . . **CLC 4, 11, 18**
  See also CA 5-8R

Hochman, Sandra 1936- . . . . **CLC 3, 8**
  See also CA 5-8R
  See also DLB 5

Hochwälder, Fritz 1911- . . . . **CLC 36**
  See also CA 29-32R

Hocking, Mary (Eunice) 1921- . . . . . **CLC 13**
  See also CA 101

Hodgins, Jack 1938- . . . . **CLC 23**
  See also CA 93-96

Hodgson, William Hope
  1877-1918 . . . . **TCLC 13**
  See also CA 111

Hoffman, Daniel (Gerard)
  1923- . . . . **CLC 6, 13, 23**
  See also CANR 4
  See also CA 1-4R
  See also DLB 5

Hoffman, Stanley 1944- . . . . **CLC 5**
  See also CA 77-80

Hoffmann, Ernst Theodor Amadeus
  1776-1822 . . . . **NCLC 2**
  See also SATA 27

Hofmannsthal, Hugo (Laurenz August
  Hofmann Edler) von
  1874-1929 . . . . **TCLC 11**
  See also CA 106

Hogg, James 1770-1835 . . . . **NCLC 4**

Holden, Ursula 1921- . . . . **CLC 18**
  See also CA 101

Holdstock, Robert (P.)
  1948- . . . . **CLC 39 (151)**

Holland, Isabelle 1920- . . . . **CLC 21**
  See also CANR 10
  See also CA 21-24R
  See also SATA 8

Holland, Marcus 1900-1985
  See Caldwell, (Janet Miriam) Taylor
  (Holland)

Hollander, John 1929- . . . . . **CLC 2, 5, 8, 14**
  See also CANR 1
  See also CA 1-4R
  See also SATA 13
  See also DLB 5

Holleran, Andrew 1943?- . . . . **CLC 38**

Hollis, Jim 1916-
  See Summers, Hollis (Spurgeon, Jr.)

Holt, Victoria 1906-
  See Hibbert, Eleanor (Burford)

Holub, Miroslav 1923- . . . . **CLC 4**
  See also CANR 10
  See also CA 21-24R

Honig, Edwin 1919- . . . . **CLC 33**
  See also CANR 4
  See also CA 5-8R
  See also DLB 5

Hood, Hugh (John Blagdon)
  1928- . . . . **CLC 15, 28**
  See also CANR 1
  See also CA 49-52

Hope, A(lec) D(erwent) 1907- . . . . **CLC 3**
  See also CA 21-24R

Hopkins, John (Richard) 1931- . . . . . . **CLC 4**
  See also CA 85-88

Horgan, Paul 1903- . . . . **CLC 9**
  See also CANR 9
  See also CA 13-16R
  See also SATA 13
  See also DLB-Y 85

Horwitz, Julius 1920- . . . . **CLC 14**
  See also CANR 12
  See also CA 9-12R

Hougan, Carolyn 19??- . . . . **CLC 34 (60)**

Household, Geoffrey (Edward West)
  1900- . . . . **CLC 11**
  See also CA 77-80
  See also SATA 14

Housman, A(lfred) E(dward)
  1859-1936 . . . . **TCLC 1, 10**
  See also CA 104
  See also DLB 19

Housman, Laurence
  1865-1959 . . . . **TCLC 7**
  See also CA 106
  See also SATA 25
  See also DLB 10

Howard, Elizabeth Jane
  1923- . . . . **CLC 7, 29**
  See also CANR 8
  See also CA 5-8R

Howard, Maureen 1930- . . . . **CLC 5, 14**
  See also CA 53-56
  See also DLB-Y 83

Howard, Richard 1929- . . . . **CLC 7, 10**
  See also CA 85-88
  See also DLB 5
  See also AITN 1

Howard, Robert E(rvin)
  1906-1936 . . . . **TCLC 8**
  See also CA 105

Howells, William Dean
  1837-1920 . . . . **TCLC 7, 17**
  See also CA 104
  See also DLB 12

Howes, Barbara 1914- . . . . **CLC 15**
  See also CAAS 3
  See also CA 9-12R
  See also SATA 5

Hrabal, Bohumil 1914- . . . . **CLC 13**
  See also CA 106

Huch, Ricarda (Octavia)
  1864-1947 . . . . **TCLC 13**
  See also CA 111

Hueffer, Ford Madox 1873-1939
  See Ford, Ford Madox

Hughart, Barry 1934- . . . . **CLC 39 (155)**

Hughes, Edward James 1930-
  See Hughes, Ted

Hughes, (James) Langston
  1902-1967 . . . . **CLC 1, 5, 10, 15, 35**
  See also CANR 1
  See also CA 1-4R
  See also obituary CA 25-28R
  See also SATA 4, 33
  See also DLB 4, 7

Hughes, Richard (Arthur Warren)
  1900-1976 . . . . **CLC 1, 11**
  See also CANR 4
  See also CA 5-8R
  See also obituary CA 65-68
  See also SATA 8
  See also obituary SATA 25
  See also DLB 15

Hughes, Ted 1930- . . . . . **CLC 2, 4, 9, 14, 37**
  See also CLR 3
  See also CANR 1
  See also CA 1-4R
  See also SATA 27
  See also DLB 40

Hugo, Richard F(ranklin)
  1923-1982 . . . . **CLC 6, 18, 32**
  See also CANR 3
  See also CA 49-52
  See also obituary CA 108
  See also DLB 5

Hugo, Victor Marie
  1802-1885 . . . . **NCLC 3, 10**

Hulme, Keri 1947- . . . . **CLC 39 (158)**

Humphreys, Josephine
  1945- . . . . **CLC 34 (63)**

Hunt, E(verette) Howard (Jr.)
  1918- . . . . **CLC 3**
  See also CANR 2
  See also CA 45-48
  See also AITN 1

Hunt, (James Henry) Leigh
  1784-1859 . . . . **NCLC 1**

Hunter, Evan 1926- . . . . **CLC 1, 11, 31**
  See also CANR 5
  See also CA 5-8R
  See also SATA 25
  See also DLB-Y 82

Hunter, Kristin (Eggleston)
  1931- . . . . **CLC 35**
  See also CLR 3
  See also CANR 13
  See also CA 13-16R
  See also SATA 12
  See also DLB 33
  See also AITN 1

Hunter, Mollie (Maureen McIlwraith)
  1922- . . . . **CLC 21**
  See also McIlwraith, Maureen Mollie
  Hunter

Hurston, Zora Neale
  1901?-1960 . . . . **CLC 7, 30**
  See also CA 85-88

Huston, John (Marcellus)
  1906- . . . . **CLC 20**
  See also CA 73-76
  See also DLB 26

Huxley, Aldous (Leonard)
  1894-1963 . . . . **CLC 1, 3, 4, 5, 8, 11,
                                              18, 35**
  See also CA 85-88
  See also DLB 36

Huysmans, Charles Marie Georges
  1848-1907
  See also Huysmans, Joris-Karl
  See also CA 104

Huysmans, Joris-Karl
  1848-1907 . . . . **TCLC 7**
  See also Huysmans, Charles Marie Georges

Hyde, Margaret O(ldroyd)
  1917- . . . . **CLC 21**
  See also CANR 1
  See also CA 1-4R
  See also SATA 1, 42

Ian, Janis 1951- . . . . **CLC 21**
  See also CA 105

Ibargüengoitia, Jorge
  1928-1983....................CLC 37
  See also obituary CA 113

Ibsen, Henrik (Johan)
  1828-1906...........TCLC 2, 8, 16
  See also CA 104

Ibuse, Masuji 1898-..............CLC 22

Ichikawa, Kon 1915-..............CLC 20

Idle, Eric 1943-
  See Monty Python
  See also CA 116

Ignatow, David 1914-........CLC 4, 7, 14
  See also CAAS 3
  See also CA 9-12R
  See also DLB 5

Immermann, Karl (Lebrecht)
  1796-1840...................NCLC 4

Inge, William (Motter)
  1913-1973..............CLC 1, 8, 19
  See also CA 9-12R
  See also DLB 7

Innaurato, Albert 1948-...........CLC 21
  See also CA 115

Innes, Michael 1906-
  See Stewart, J(ohn) I(nnes) M(ackintosh)

Ionesco, Eugène
  1912-.......CLC 1, 4, 6, 9, 11, 15
  See also CA 9-12R
  See also SATA 7

Irving, John (Winslow)
  1942-.................CLC 13, 23, 38
  See also CA 25-28R
  See also DLB 6
  See also DLB-Y 82

Irving, Washington 1783-1859 .... NCLC 2
  See also YABC 2
  See also DLB 3, 11, 30

Isaacs, Susan 1943-..............CLC 32
  See also CA 89-92

Isherwood, Christopher (William Bradshaw)
  1904-................CLC 1, 9, 11, 14
  See also CA 13-16R
  See also DLB 15

Ishiguro, Kazuo 1954?-...........CLC 27

Ishikawa Takuboku
  1885-1912.................TCLC 15

Ivask, Ivar (Vidrik) 1927- ....CLC 14
  See also CA 37-40R

Jackson, Jesse 1908-1983..........CLC 12
  See also CA 25-28R
  See also obituary CA 109
  See also SATA 2, 29

Jackson, Laura (Riding) 1901-
  See Riding, Laura
  See also CA 65-68

Jackson, Shirley 1919-1965 ....CLC 11
  See also CANR 4
  See also CA 1-4R
  See also obituary CA 25-28R
  See also SATA 2
  See also DLB 6

Jacob, (Cyprien) Max
  1876-1944...................TCLC 6
  See also CA 104

Jacob, Piers A(nthony) D(illingham) 1934-
  See Anthony (Jacob), Piers
  See also CA 21-24R

Jacobs, Jim 1942-
  See Jacobs, Jim and Casey, Warren
  See also CA 97-100

Jacobs, Jim 1942- and
  Casey, Warren 1935-.........CLC 12

Jacobson, Dan 1929-...........CLC 4, 14
  See also CANR 2
  See also CA 1-4R
  See also DLB 14

Jagger, Mick 1944-
  See Jagger, Mick and Richard, Keith

Jagger, Mick 1944- and
  Richard, Keith 1943-.........CLC 17

Jakes, John (William) 1932- ......CLC 29
  See also CANR 10
  See also CA 57-60
  See also DLB-Y 83

James, C(yril) L(ionel) R(obert)
  1901-......................CLC 33

James, Daniel 1911-
  See Santiago, Danny

James, Henry (Jr.)
  1843-1916...............TCLC 2, 11
  See also CA 104
  See also DLB 12

James, M(ontague) R(hodes)
  1862-1936..................TCLC 6
  See also CA 104

James, P(hyllis) D(orothy)
  1920-......................CLC 18
  See also CA 21-24R

James, William 1842-1910....... TCLC 15
  See also CA 109

Jandl, Ernst 1925-......... CLC 34 (194)

Jarrell, Randall
  1914-1965.......... CLC 1, 2, 6, 9, 13
  See also CLR 6
  See also CANR 6
  See also CA 5-8R
  See also obituary CA 25-28R
  See also SATA 7

Jarry, Alfred 1873-1907....... TCLC 2, 14
  See also CA 104

Jean Paul 1763-1825............ NCLC 7

Jeffers, (John) Robinson
  1887-1962...........CLC 2, 3, 11, 15
  See also CA 85-88
  See also DLB 45

Jefferson, Thomas 1743-1826 .... NCLC 11
  See also DLB 31

Jellicoe, (Patricia) Ann 1927-.......CLC 27
  See also CA 85-88
  See also DLB 13

Jennings, Elizabeth (Joan)
  1926-................... CLC 5, 14
  See also CANR 8
  See also CA 61-64
  See also DLB 27

Jennings, Waylon 1937-..........CLC 21

Jensen, Laura (Linnea) 1948- ......CLC 37
  See also CA 103

Jerrold, Douglas 1803-1857....... NCLC 2

Jewett, Sarah Orne 1849-1909 .... TCLC 1
  See also CA 108
  See also SATA 15
  See also DLB 12

Jhabvala, Ruth Prawer
  1927-..................CLC 4, 8, 29
  See also CANR 2
  See also CA 1-4R

Jiles, Paulette 1943-..............CLC 13
  See also CA 101

Jiménez (Mantecón), Juan Ramón
  1881-1958................. TCLC 4
  See also CA 104

Joel, Billy 1949-..................CLC 26
  See also Joel, William Martin

Joel, William Martin 1949-
  See Joel, Billy
  See also CA 108

Johnson, B(ryan) S(tanley William)
  1933-1973................ CLC 6, 9
  See also CANR 9
  See also CA 9-12R
  See also obituary CA 53-56
  See also DLB 14, 40

Johnson, Charles 1948-............CLC 7
  See also CA 116
  See also DLB 33

Johnson, Diane 1934- .... CLC 5, 13
  See also CANR 17
  See also CA 41-44R
  See also DLB-Y 80

Johnson, Eyvind (Olof Verner)
  1900-1976..................CLC 14
  See also CA 73-76
  See also obituary CA 69-72

Johnson, James Weldon
  1871-1938...............TCLC 3, 19
  See also Johnson, James William
  See also CA 104

Johnson, James William 1871-1938
  See Johnson, James Weldon
  See also SATA 31

Johnson, Lionel Pigot
  1867-1902.................TCLC 19
  See also DLB 19

Johnson, Marguerita 1928-
  See Angelou, Maya

Johnson, Pamela Hansford
  1912-1981...............CLC 1, 7, 27
  See also CANR 2
  See also CA 1-4R
  See also obituary CA 104
  See also DLB 15

Johnson, Uwe
  1934-1984.............. CLC 5, 10, 15
  See also CANR 1
  See also CA 1-4R
  See also obituary CA 112

Johnston, Jennifer 1930- ....CLC 7
  See also CA 85-88
  See also DLB 14

Jones, D(ouglas) G(ordon)
  1929-......................CLC 10
  See also CANR 13
  See also CA 29-32R
  See also CA 113

Jones, David
1895-1974............CLC 2, 4, 7, 13
See also CA 9-12R
See also obituary CA 53-56
See also DLB 20

Jones, David Robert 1947-
See Bowie, David
See also CA 103

Jones, Diana Wynne 1934-........CLC 26
See also CANR 4
See also CA 49-52
See also SATA 9

Jones, Gayl 1949- ....CLC 6, 9
See also CA 77-80
See also DLB 33

Jones, James
1921-1977...... CLC 1, 3, 10, 39 (404)
See also CANR 6
See also CA 1-4R
See also obituary CA 69-72
See also DLB 2
See also AITN 1, 2

Jones, (Everett) LeRoi
1934-........CLC 1, 2, 3, 5, 10, 14, 33
See also Baraka, Amiri
See also Baraka, Imamu Amiri
See also CA 21-24R

Jones, Madison (Percy, Jr.)
1925-......................CLC 4
See also CANR 7
See also CA 13-16R

Jones, Mervyn 1922-.............CLC 10
See also CANR 1
See also CA 45-48

Jones, Mick 1956?-
See The Clash

Jones, Nettie 19??-...........CLC 34 (67)

Jones, Preston 1936-1979.........CLC 10
See also CA 73-76
See also obituary CA 89-92
See also DLB 7

Jones, Robert F(rancis) 1934- ....CLC 7
See also CANR 2
See also CA 49-52

Jones, Terry 1942?-
See Monty Python
See also CA 112, 116

Jong, Erica 1942-.........CLC 4, 6, 8, 18
See also CA 73-76
See also DLB 2, 5, 28
See also AITN 1

Jordan, June 1936- ....CLC 5, 11, 23
See also CLR 10
See also CA 33-36R
See also SATA 4
See also DLB 38

Jordan, Pat(rick M.) 1941- ....CLC 37
See also CA 33-36R

Josipovici, G(abriel) 1940- ....CLC 6
See also CA 37-40R
See also DLB 14

Joubert, Joseph 1754-1824....... NCLC 9

Joyce, James (Augustine Aloysius)
1882-1941..............TCLC 3, 8, 16
See also CA 104
See also DLB 10, 19, 36

Just, Ward S(wift) 1935- .... CLC 4, 27
See also CA 25-28R

Justice, Donald (Rodney)
1925-.................... CLC 6, 19
See also CA 5-8R
See also DLB-Y 33

Kacew, Romain 1914-1980
See Gary, Romain
See also CA 108
See also obituary CA 102

Kacewgary, Romain 1914-1980
See Gary, Romain

Kafka, Franz
1883-1924.............TCLC 2, 6, 13
See also CA 105

Kahn, Roger 1927- ....CLC 30
See also CA 25-28R

Kaiser, (Friedrich Karl) Georg
1878-1945.................. TCLC 9
See also CA 106

Kaletski, Alexander 1946- .... CLC 39 (72)

Kallman, Chester (Simon)
1921-1975....................CLC 2
See also CANR 3
See also CA 45-48
See also obituary CA 53-56

Kaminsky, Melvin 1926-
See Brooks, Mel
See also CANR 16

Kane, Paul 1941-
See Simon, Paul

Kanin, Garson 1912-.............CLC 22
See also CANR 7
See also CA 5-8R
See also DLB 7
See also AITN 1

Kaniuk, Yoram 1930-.............CLC 19

Kantor, MacKinlay 1904-1977 ......CLC 7
See also CA 61-64
See also obituary CA 73-76
See also DLB 9

Karamzin, Nikolai Mikhailovich
1766-1826.................. NCLC 3

Karapánou, Margaríta 1946-.......CLC 13
See also CA 101

Karl, Frederick R(obert)
1927-................. CLC 34 (551)
See also CANR 3
See also CA 5-8R

Kassef, Romain 1914-1980
See Gary, Romain

Kaufman, George S(imon)
1889-1961...................CLC 38
See also CA 108
See also obituary CA 93-96
See also DLB 7

Kaufman, Sue 1926-1977........ CLC 3, 8
See also Barondess, Sue K(aufman)

Kavan, Anna 1904-1968........ CLC 5, 13
See also Edmonds, Helen (Woods)
See also CANR 6

Kavanagh, Patrick (Joseph Gregory)
1905-1967...................CLC 22
See also CA 25-28R
See also DLB 15, 20

Kawabata, Yasunari
1899-1972............CLC 2, 5, 9, 18
See also CA 93-96
See also obituary CA 33-36R

Kaye, M(ary) M(argaret)
1909?-......................CLC 28
See also CA 89-92

Kaye, Mollie 1909?-
See Kaye, M(ary) M(argaret)

Kaye-Smith, Sheila
1887-1956.................TCLC 20
See also DLB 36

Kazan, Elia 1909- ....CLC 6, 16
See also CA 21-24R

Kazantzakis, Nikos
1885?-1957..............TCLC 2, 5
See also CA 105

Kazin, Alfred 1915-......CLC 34 (555), 38
See also CANR 1
See also CA 1-4R

Keane, Mary Nesta (Skrine) 1904-
See Keane, Molly
See also CA 108, 114

Keane, Molly 1904-................CLC 31
See also Keane, Mary Nesta (Skrine)

Keates, Jonathan 19??-...... CLC 34 (201)

Keaton, Buster 1895-1966 ....CLC 20

Keaton, Joseph Francis 1895-1966
See Keaton, Buster

Keats, John 1795-1821 .... NCLC 8

Keene, Donald 1922-........ CLC 34 (566)
See also CANR 5
See also CA 1-4R

Keller, Gottfried 1819-1890...... NCLC 2

Kelley, William Melvin 1937- ......CLC 22
See also CA 77-80
See also DLB 33

Kellogg, Marjorie 1922-............CLC 2
See also CA 81-84

Kemal, Yashar 1922- .... CLC 14, 29
See also CA 89-92

Kemelman, Harry 1908-.............CLC 2
See also CANR 6
See also CA 9-12R
See also DLB 28
See also AITN 1

Kendall, Henry 1839-1882....... NCLC 12

Keneally, Thomas (Michael)
1935-.........CLC 5, 8, 10, 14, 19, 27
See also CANR 10
See also CA 85-88

Kennedy, John Pendleton
1795-1870................... NCLC 2
See also DLB 3

Kennedy, Joseph Charles 1929-
See Kennedy, X. J.
See also CANR 4
See also CA 1-4R
See also SATA 14

Kennedy, William
1928-............CLC 6, 28, 34 (205)
See also CANR 14
See also CA 85-88
See also DLB-Y 85

Kennedy, X. J. 1929- ....CLC 8
See also Kennedy, Joseph Charles
See also DLB 5

Kerouac, Jack
1922-1969...... CLC 1, 2, 3, 5, 14, 29
See also Kerouac, Jean-Louis Lebrid de
See also DLB 2, 16
See also DLB-DS 3

Kerouac, Jean-Louis Lebrid de 1922-1969
See Kerouac, Jack
See also CA 5-8R
See also obituary CA 25-28R
See also AITN 1

Kerr, Jean 1923- ....CLC 22
See also CANR 7
See also CA 5-8R

Kerr, M. E. 1927-............ CLC 12, 35
See also Meaker, Marijane
See also SAAS 1

Kerrigan, (Thomas) Anthony
1918-................... CLC 4, 6
See also CANR 4
See also CA 49-52

Kesey, Ken (Elton)
1935-...............CLC 1, 3, 6, 11
See also CA 1-4R
See also DLB 2, 16

Kessler, Jascha (Frederick)
1929-.........................CLC 4
See also CANR 8
See also CA 17-20R

Kettelkamp, Larry 1933-..........CLC 12
See also CANR 16
See also CA 29-32R
See also SATA 2

Kherdian, David 1931-.......... CLC 6, 9
See also CAAS 2
See also CA 21-24R
See also SATA 16

Khlebnikov, Velimir (Vladimirovich)
1885-1922................. TCLC 20
See also CA 117

Khodasevich, Vladislav (Felitsianovich)
1886-1939................. TCLC 15
See also CA 115

Kielland, Alexander (Lange)
1849-1906................. TCLC 5
See also CA 104

Kiely, Benedict 1919- ....CLC 23
See also CANR 2
See also CA 1-4R
See also DLB 15

Kienzle, William X(avier)
1928-.........................CLC 25
See also CAAS 1
See also CANR 9
See also CA 93-96

Killens, John Oliver 1916-........CLC 10
See also CAAS 2
See also CA 77-80
See also DLB 33

King, Francis (Henry) 1923- ....CLC 8
See also CANR 1
See also CA 1-4R
See also DLB 15

King, Stephen (Edwin)
1947-................. CLC 12, 26, 37
See also CANR 1
See also CA 61-64
See also SATA 9
See also DLB-Y 80

Kingman, (Mary) Lee 1919- ....CLC 17
See also Natti, (Mary) Lee
See also CA 5-8R
See also SATA 1

Kingston, Maxine Hong
1940-................... CLC 12, 19
See also CANR 13
See also CA 69-72
See also DLB-Y 80

Kinnell, Galway
1927-........... CLC 1, 2, 3, 5, 13, 29
See also CANR 10
See also CA 9-12R
See also DLB 5

Kinsella, Thomas 1928- .... CLC 4, 19
See also CA 17-20R
See also DLB 27

Kinsella, W(illiam) P(atrick)
1935-.......................CLC 27
See also CA 97-100

Kipling, (Joseph) Rudyard
1865-1936............... TCLC 8, 17
See also CA 105
See also YABC 2
See also DLB 19, 34

Kirkup, James 1927-...............CLC 1
See also CANR 2
See also CA 1-4R
See also SATA 12
See also DLB 27

Kirkwood, James 1930- ....CLC 9
See also CANR 6
See also CA 1-4R
See also AITN 2

Kizer, Carolyn (Ashley)
1925-.............. CLC 15, 39 (168)
See also CA 65-68
See also DLB 5

Klausner, Amos 1939-
See Oz, Amos

Klein, A(braham) M(oses)
1909-1972...................CLC 19
See also CA 101
See also obituary CA 37-40R

Klein, Norma 1938-...............CLC 30
See also CLR 2
See also CANR 15
See also CA 41-44R
See also SAAS 1
See also SATA 7

Klein, T.E.D. 19??-.......... CLC 34 (70)

Kleist, Heinrich von
1777-1811.................... NCLC 2

Klimentev, Andrei Platonovich 1899-1951
See Platonov, Andrei (Platonovich)
See also CA 108

Klinger, Friedrich Maximilian von
1752-1831.................... NCLC 1

Klopstock, Friedrich Gottlieb
1724-1803................... NCLC 11

Knebel, Fletcher 1911-............CLC 14
See also CAAS 3
See also CANR 1
See also CA 1-4R
See also SATA 36
See also AITN 1

Knowles, John 1926-......CLC 1, 4, 10, 26
See also CA 17-20R
See also SATA 8
See also DLB 6

Koch, Kenneth 1925-........... CLC 5, 8
See also CANR 6
See also CA 1-4R
See also DLB 5

Koestler, Arthur
1905-1983....... CLC 1, 3, 6, 8, 15, 33
See also CANR 1
See also CA 1-4R
See also obituary CA 109
See also DLB-Y 83

Kohout, Pavel 1928-..............CLC 13
See also CANR 3
See also CA 45-48

Konrád, György 1933-......... CLC 4, 10
See also CA 85-88

Konwicki, Tadeusz 1926-....... CLC 8, 28
See also CA 101

Kopit, Arthur (Lee)
1937-................. CLC 1, 18, 33
See also CA 81-84
See also DLB 7
See also AITN 1

Kops, Bernard 1926-...............CLC 4
See also CA 5-8R
See also DLB 13

Kornbluth, C(yril) M.
1923-1958................. TCLC 8
See also CA 105
See also DLB 8

Kosinski, Jerzy (Nikodem)
1933-........... CLC 1, 2, 3, 6, 10, 15
See also CANR 9
See also CA 17-20R
See also DLB 2
See also DLB-Y 82

Kostelanetz, Richard (Cory)
1940-.......................CLC 28
See also CA 13-16R

Kostrowitzki, Wilhelm Apollinaris de
1880-1918
See Apollinaire, Guillaume
See also CA 104

Kotlowitz, Robert 1924-...........CLC 4
See also CA 33-36R

Kotzwinkle, William
1938-................. CLC 5, 14, 35
See also CLR 6
See also CANR 3
See also CA 45-48
See also SATA 24

Kozol, Jonathan 1936-............CLC 17
See also CANR 16
See also CA 61-64

Kozoll, Michael 1940?-
See Bochco, Steven and Kozoll, Michael

Kramer, Kathryn 19??- ...... CLC 34 (74)

Krasicki, Ignacy 1735-1801 .... NCLC 8

Krasiński, Zygmunt
　1812-1859..................NCLC 4

Kraus, Karl　1874-1936..........TCLC 5
　See also CA 104

Kristofferson, Kris　1936-..........CLC 26
　See also CA 104

Krleža, Miroslav　1893-1981........CLC 8
　See also CA 97-100
　See also obituary CA 105

Kroetsch, Robert　1927-.........CLC 5, 23
　See also CANR 8
　See also CA 17-20R

Krotkov, Yuri　1917-..............CLC 19
　See also CA 102

Krumgold, Joseph (Quincy)
　1908-1980....................CLC 12
　See also CANR 7
　See also CA 9-12R
　See also obituary CA 101
　See also SATA 1
　See also obituary SATA 23

Krutch, Joseph Wood
　1893-1970....................CLC 24
　See also CANR 4
　See also CA 1-4R
　See also obituary CA 25-28R

Krylov, Ivan Andreevich
　1768?-1844.................NCLC 1

Kubrick, Stanley　1928-............CLC 16
　See also CA 81-84
　See also DLB 26

Kumin, Maxine (Winokur)
　1925-.................CLC 5, 13, 28
　See also CANR 1
　See also CA 1-4R
　See also SATA 12
　See also DLB 5
　See also AITN 2

Kundera, Milan
　1929-...............CLC 4, 9, 19, 32
　See also CA 85-88

Kunitz, Stanley J(asspon)
　1905-.................CLC 6, 11, 14
　See also CA 41-44R

Kunze, Reiner　1933-..............CLC 10
　See also CA 93-96

Kuprin, Aleksandr (Ivanovich)
　1870-1938...................TCLC 5
　See also CA 104

Kurosawa, Akira　1910-...........CLC 16
　See also CA 101

Kuttner, Henry　1915-1958.......TCLC 10
　See also CA 107
　See also DLB 8

Kuzma, Greg　1944-...............CLC 7
　See also CA 33-36R

Labrunie, Gérard　1808-1855
　See Nerval, Gérard de

Laclos, Pierre Ambroise François Choderlos
　de　1741-1803..............NCLC 4

La Fayette, Marie (Madelaine Pioche de la
　Vergne, Comtesse) de
　1634-1693....................LC 2

Laforgue, Jules　1860-1887.......NCLC 5

Lagerkvist, Pär (Fabian)
　1891-1974.............CLC 7, 10, 13
　See also CA 85-88
　See also obituary CA 49-52

Lagerlöf, Selma (Ottiliana Lovisa)
　1858-1940...................TCLC 4
　See also CLR 7
　See also CA 108
　See also SATA 15

La Guma, (Justin) Alex(ander)
　1925-.......................CLC 19
　See also CA 49-52

Lamartine, Alphonse (Marie Louis Prat) de
　1790-1869.................NCLC 11

Lamb, Charles　1775-1834 ....NCLC 10
　See also SATA 17

Lamming, George (William)
　1927-.................... CLC 2, 4
　See also CA 85-88

LaMoore, Louis Dearborn　1908?-
　See L'Amour, Louis (Dearborn)

L'Amour, Louis (Dearborn)
　1908-.......................CLC 25
　See also CANR 3
　See also CA 1-4R
　See also DLB-Y 80
　See also AITN 2

Lampedusa, (Prince) Giuseppe (Maria
　Fabrizio) Tomasi di
　1896-1957.................TCLC 13
　See also CA 111

Lancaster, Bruce　1896-1963 ....CLC 36
　See also CAP-1
　See also CA 9-12R
　See also SATA 9

Landis, John (David)　1950-........CLC 26
　See also CA 112

Landolfi, Tommaso　1908-.........CLC 11

Landwirth, Heinz　1927-
　See Lind, Jakov
　See also CANR 7

Lane, Patrick　1939-..............CLC 25
　See also CA 97-100

Lang, Andrew　1844-1912........TCLC 16
　See also CA 114
　See also SATA 16

Lang, Fritz　1890-1976 ....CLC 20
　See also CA 77-80
　See also obituary CA 69-72

Langer, Elinor　1939-........ CLC 34 (448)

Lanier, Sidney　1842-1881.........NCLC 6
　See also SATA 18

Lapine, James　1949-........ CLC 39 (172)

Larbaud, Valéry　1881-1957.......TCLC 9
　See also CA 106

Lardner, Ring(gold Wilmer)
　1885-1933................TCLC 2, 14
　See also CA 104
　See also DLB 11, 25

Larkin, Philip (Arthur)
　1922-1985...... CLC 3, 5, 8, 9, 13, 18,
　　　　　　　　　　　　　33, 39 (333)
　See also CA 5-8R
　See also obituary CA 117
　See also DLB 27

Larsen, Nella　1893-1964..........CLC 37

Larson, Charles R(aymond)
　1938-......................CLC 31
　See also CANR 4
　See also CA 53-56

Latham, Jean Lee　1902-...........CLC 12
　See also CANR 7
　See also CA 5-8R
　See also SATA 2
　See also AITN 1

Lathen, Emma....................CLC 2
　See also Hennissart, Martha
　See also Latsis, Mary J(ane)

Latsis, Mary J(ane)
　See Lathen, Emma
　See also CA 85-88

Lattimore, Richmond (Alexander)
　1906-1984...................CLC 3
　See also CANR 1
　See also CA 1-4R
　See also obituary CA 112

Laurence, (Jean) Margaret (Wemyss)
　1926-................. CLC 3, 6, 13
　See also CA 5-8R

Lautréamont, Comte de
　1846-1870.................NCLC 12

Lavin, Mary　1912-............ CLC 4, 18
　See also CA 9-12R
　See also DLB 15

Lawrence, D(avid) H(erbert)
　1885-1930..............TCLC 2, 9, 16
　See also CA 104
　See also DLB 10, 19, 36

Lawrence, T(homas) E(dward)
　1888-1935.................TCLC 18
　See also CA 115

Laxness, Halldór (Kiljan)
　1902-.......................CLC 25
　See also Gudjonsson, Halldór Kiljan

Laye, Camara　1928-1980....... CLC 4, 38
　See also CA 85-88
　See also obituary CA 97-100

Layton, Irving (Peter)　1912- .... CLC 2, 15
　See also CANR 2
　See also CA 1-4R

Lazarus, Emma　1849-1887 ....NCLC 8

Leacock, Stephen (Butler)
　1869-1944..................TCLC 2
　See also CA 104

Lear, Edward　1812-1888 ....NCLC 3
　See also CLR 1
　See also SATA 18
　See also DLB 32

Lear, Norman (Milton)　1922- ......CLC 12
　See also CA 73-76

Leavis, F(rank) R(aymond)
　1895-1978...................CLC 24
　See also CA 21-24R.
　See also obituary CA 77-80

Leavitt, David　1961?- .... CLC 34 (77)
　See also CA 116

Lebowitz, Fran(ces Ann)
　1951?-................. CLC 11, 36
　See also CANR 14
　See also CA 81-84

Le Carré, John
        1931-............. **CLC 3, 5, 9, 15, 28**
        See also Cornwell, David (John Moore)

Le Clézio, J(ean) M(arie) G(ustave)
        1940-........................**CLC 31**
        See also CA 116

Leduc, Violette 1907-1972 ....**CLC 22**
        See also CAP 1
        See also CA 13-14
        See also obituary CA 33-36R

Lee, Andrea 1953-.................**CLC 36**

Lee, Don L. 1942-....................**CLC 2**
        See also Madhubuti, Haki R.
        See also CA 73-76

Lee, (Nelle) Harper 1926-..........**CLC 12**
        See also CA 13-16R
        See also SATA 11
        See also DLB 6

Lee, Lawrence 1903-........ **CLC 34** (457)
        See also CA 25-28R

Lee, Manfred B(ennington) 1905-1971
        See Queen, Ellery
        See also CANR 2
        See also CA 1-4R
        See also obituary CA 29-32R

Lee, Stan 1922-...................**CLC 17**
        See also CA 108, 111

Lee, Vernon 1856-1935...........**TCLC 5**
        See also Paget, Violet

Leet, Judith 1935-.................**CLC 11**

Le Fanu, Joseph Sheridan
        1814-1873................... **NCLC 9**
        See also DLB 21

Leffland, Ella 1931-.................**CLC 19**
        See also CA 29-32R
        See also DLB-Y 84

Léger, (Marie-Rene) Alexis Saint-Léger
        1887-1975
        See Perse, St.-John
        See also CA 13-16R
        See also obituary CA 61-64

Le Guin, Ursula K(roeber)
        1929-............ **CLC 8, 13, 22**
        See also CLR 3
        See also CANR 9
        See also CA 21-24R
        See also SATA 4
        See also DLB 8
        See also AITN 1

Lehmann, Rosamond (Nina)
        1901-.........................**CLC 5**
        See also CANR 8
        See also CA 77-80
        See also DLB 15

Leiber, Fritz (Reuter, Jr.)
        1910-.......................**CLC 25**
        See also CANR 2
        See also CA 45-48
        See also DLB 8

Leithauser, Brad 1953-............**CLC 27**
        See also CA 107

Lelchuk, Alan 1938-................**CLC 5**
        See also CANR 1
        See also CA 45-48

Lem, Stanislaw 1921-......... **CLC 8, 15**
        See also CAAS 1
        See also CA 105

Lemann, Nancy 1956-........ **CLC 39** (75)

L'Engle, Madeleine 1918-..........**CLC 12**
        See also CLR 1
        See also CANR 3
        See also CA 1-4R
        See also SATA 1, 27
        See also AITN 2

Lennon, John (Ono)
        1940-1980....................**CLC 35**
        See also Lennon, John (Ono) and
        McCartney, Paul
        See also CA 102

Lennon, John (Ono) 1940-1980 and
        McCartney, Paul 1942-.......**CLC 12**

Lennon, John Winston 1940-1980
        See Lennon, John (Ono)

Lentricchia, Frank (Jr.)
        1940-................. **CLC 34** (571)
        See also CA 25-28R

Lenz, Siegfried 1926- ....**CLC 27**
        See also CA 89-92

Leonard, Elmore
        1925-.............. **CLC 28, 34** (212)
        See also CANR 12
        See also CA 81-84
        See also AITN 1

Leonard, Hugh 1926-............**CLC 19**
        See also Byrne, John Keyes
        See also DLB 13

Lerman, Eleanor 1952-............**CLC 9**
        See also CA 85-88

Lermontov, Mikhail Yuryevich
        1814-1841................... **NCLC 5**

Lesage, Alain-René 1668-1747....... **LC 2**

Lessing, Doris (May)
        1919-........**CLC 1, 2, 3, 6, 10, 15, 22**
        See also CA 9-12R
        See also DLB 15
        See also DLB-Y 85

Lester, Richard 1932-.............**CLC 20**

Leverson, Ada 1865-1936........ **TCLC 18**

Levertov, Denise
        1923-.........**CLC 1, 2, 3, 5, 8, 15, 28**
        See also CANR 3
        See also CA 1-4R
        See also DLB 5

Levi, Primo 1919- ....**CLC 37**
        See also CANR 12
        See also CA 13-16R

Levin, Ira 1929-................. **CLC 3, 6**
        See also CANR 17
        See also CA 21-24R

Levin, Meyer 1905-1981............**CLC 7**
        See also CANR 15
        See also CA 9-12R
        See also obituary CA 104
        See also SATA 21
        See also obituary SATA 27
        See also DLB 9, 28
        See also DLB-Y 81
        See also AITN 1

Levine, Philip
        1928-........... **CLC 2, 4, 5, 9, 14, 33**
        See also CANR 9
        See also CA 9-12R
        See also DLB 5

Lévi-Strauss, Claude 1908- ....**CLC 38**
        See also CANR 6
        See also CA 1-4R

Levitin, Sonia 1934- ....**CLC 17**
        See also CA 29-32R
        See also SATA 4

Lewis, Alun 1915-1944.......... **TCLC 3**
        See also CA 104
        See also DLB 20

Lewis, C(ecil) Day 1904-1972
        See Day Lewis, C(ecil)

Lewis, C(live) S(taples)
        1898-1963........ **CLC 1, 3, 6, 14, 27**
        See also CLR 3
        See also CA 81-84
        See also SATA 13
        See also DLB 15

Lewis, (Harry) Sinclair
        1885-1951................ **TCLC 4, 13**
        See also CA 104
        See also DLB 9
        See also DLB-DS 1

Lewis, Matthew Gregory
        1775-1818................. **NCLC 11**
        See also DLB 39

Lewis, (Percy) Wyndham
        1882?-1957................ **TCLC 2, 9**
        See also CA 104
        See also DLB 15

Lewisohn, Ludwig 1883-1955 .... **TCLC 19**
        See also CA 107
        See also DLB 4, 9, 28

Lezama Lima, José
        1910-1976................. **CLC 4, 10**
        See also CA 77-80

Li Fei-kan 1904-
        See Pa Chin
        See also CA 105

Lie, Jonas (Lauritz Idemil)
        1833-1908................... **TCLC 5**

Lieber, Joel 1936-1971 ....**CLC 6**
        See also CA 73-76
        See also obituary CA 29-32R

Lieber, Stanley Martin 1922-
        See Lee, Stan

Lieberman, Laurence (James)
        1935-.................... **CLC 4, 36**
        See also CANR 8
        See also CA 17-20R

Lightfoot, Gordon (Meredith)
        1938-.......................**CLC 26**
        See also CA 109

Liliencron, Detlev von
        1844-1909................. **TCLC 18**

Lima, José Lezama 1910-1976
        See Lezama Lima, José

Lind, Jakov 1927- ....**CLC 1, 2, 4, 27**
        See also Landwirth, Heinz
        See also CA 9-12R

Lindsay, David 1876-1945 .... **TCLC 15**
        See also CA 113

Lindsay, (Nicholas) Vachel
        1879-1931................. **TCLC 17**
        See also CA 114
        See also SATA 40

Lipsyte, Robert (Michael)
1938- ....CLC 21
See also CANR 8
See also CA 17-20R
See also SATA 5

Liu E 1857-1909 .... TCLC 15
See also CA 115

Lively, Penelope 1933- ....CLC 32
See also CLR 7
See also CA 41-44R
See also SATA 7
See also DLB 14

Livesay, Dorothy 1909-......... CLC 4, 15
See also CA 25-28R
See also AITN 2

Llewellyn, Richard 1906-1983.......CLC 7
See also Llewellyn Lloyd, Richard (Dafydd Vyvyan)
See also DLB 15

Llewellyn Lloyd, Richard (Dafydd Vyvyan)
1906-1983
See Llewellyn, Richard
See also CANR 7
See also CA 53-56
See also obituary CA 111
See also SATA 11

Llosa, Mario Vargas 1936-
See Vargas Llosa, Mario

Lloyd, Richard Llewellyn 1906-
See Llewellyn, Richard

Lockhart, John Gibson
1794-1854................. NCLC 6

Lodge, David (John) 1935-........CLC 36
See also CA 17-20R
See also DLB 14

Logan, John 1923-.................CLC 5
See also CA 77-80
See also DLB 5

Lombino, S. A. 1926-
See Hunter, Evan

London, Jack 1876-1916 ...... TCLC 9, 15
See also London, John Griffith
See also SATA 18
See also DLB 8, 12
See also AITN 2

London, John Griffith 1876-1916
See London, Jack
See also CA 110

Long, Emmett 1925-
See Leonard, Elmore

Longfellow, Henry Wadsworth
1807-1882................. NCLC 2
See also SATA 19
See also DLB 1

Longley, Michael 1939-...........CLC 29
See also CA 102
See also DLB 40

Lopate, Phillip 1943-.............CLC 29
See also CA 97-100
See also DLB-Y 80

López y Fuentes, Gregorio
1897-1966.................CLC 32

Lord, Bette Bao 1938-............CLC 23
See also CA 107

Lorde, Audre (Geraldine)
1934-.......................CLC 18
See also CANR 16
See also CA 25-28R
See also DLB 41

Loti, Pierre 1850-1923 .... TCLC 11
See also Viaud, (Louis Marie) Julien

Lovecraft, H(oward) P(hillips)
1890-1937.................. TCLC 4
See also CA 104

Lowell, Amy 1874-1925 .... TCLC 1, 8
See also CA 104

Lowell, James Russell
1819-1891.................. NCLC 2
See also DLB 1, 11

Lowell, Robert (Traill Spence, Jr.)
1917-1977...... CLC 1, 2, 3, 4, 5, 8, 9,
                              11, 15, 37
See also CA 9-12R
See also obituary CA 73-76
See also DLB 5

Lowndes, Marie (Adelaide Belloc)
1868-1947.................. TCLC 12
See also CA 107

Lowry, (Clarence) Malcolm
1909-1957.................. TCLC 6
See also CA 105
See also DLB 15

Loy, Mina 1882-1966 ....CLC 28
See also CA 113
See also DLB 4

Lucas, George 1944-..............CLC 16
See also CA 77-80

Lucas, Victoria 1932-1963
See Plath, Sylvia

Ludlum, Robert 1927- ....CLC 22
See also CA 33-36R
See also DLB-Y 82

Ludwig, Otto 1813-1865.......... NCLC 4

Lugones, Leopoldo
1874-1938.................. TCLC 15
See also CA 116

Lu Hsün 1881-1936.............. TCLC 3

Lukács, Georg 1885-1971..........CLC 24
See also Lukács, György

Lukács, György 1885-1971
See Lukács, Georg
See also CA 101
See also obituary CA 29-32R

Luke, Peter (Ambrose Cyprian)
1919-.......................CLC 38
See also CA 81-84
See also DLB 13

Lurie, Alison
1926-......... CLC 4, 5, 18, 39 (176)
See also CANR 2, 17
See also CA 1-4R
See also DLB 2

Luzi, Mario 1914-................CLC 13
See also CANR 9
See also CA 61-64

Lytle, Andrew (Nelson) 1902- ......CLC 22
See also CA 9-12R
See also DLB 6

Lytton, Edward Bulwer 1803-1873
See Bulwer-Lytton, (Lord) Edward (George Earle Lytton)
See also SATA 23

Maas, Peter 1929-................CLC 29
See also CA 93-96

Macaulay, (Dame Emile) Rose
1881-1958................. TCLC 7
See also CA 104
See also DLB 36

MacBeth, George (Mann)
1932-...................CLC 2, 5, 9
See also CA 25-28R
See also SATA 4
See also DLB 40

MacCaig, Norman (Alexander)
1910-.......................CLC 36
See also CANR 3
See also CA 9-12R
See also DLB 27

MacDiarmid, Hugh
1892-1978...........CLC 2, 4, 11, 19
See also Grieve, C(hristopher) M(urray)
See also DLB 20

Macdonald, Cynthia 1928-..... CLC 13, 19
See also CANR 4
See also CA 49-52

MacDonald, George
1824-1905.................. TCLC 9
See also CA 106
See also SATA 33
See also DLB 18

MacDonald, John D(ann)
1916-.................... CLC 3, 27
See also CANR 1
See also CA 1-4R
See also DLB 8

Macdonald, (John) Ross
1915-1983...........CLC 1, 2, 3, 14,
                              34 (416)
See also Millar, Kenneth

MacEwen, Gwendolyn 1941-.......CLC 13
See also CANR 7
See also CA 9-12R

Machado (y Ruiz), Antonio
1875-1939.................. TCLC 3
See also CA 104

Machado de Assis, (Joaquim Maria)
1839-1908.................. TCLC 10
See also CA 107

Machen, Arthur (Llewellyn Jones)
1863-1947.................. TCLC 4
See also CA 104
See also DLB 36

MacInnes, Colin 1914-1976 ..... CLC 4, 23
See also CA 69-72
See also obituary CA 65-68
See also DLB 14

MacInnes, Helen (Clark)
1907-1985.......... CLC 27, 39 (349)
See also CANR 1
See also CA 1-4R
See also SATA 22, 44

Macintosh, Elizabeth 1897-1952
See Tey, Josephine
See also CA 110

Author Index

Mackenzie, (Edward Montague) Compton
  1883-1972....................CLC 18
  See also CAP 2
  See also CA 21-22
  See also obituary CA 37-40R
  See also DLB 34

Mac Laverty, Bernard   1942-.......CLC 31
  See also CA 116

MacLean, Alistair (Stuart)
  1922-..................... CLC 3, 13
  See also CA 57-60
  See also SATA 23

MacLeish, Archibald
  1892-1982.............. CLC 3, 8, 14
  See also CA 9-12R
  See also obituary CA 106
  See also DLB 4, 7, 45
  See also DLB-Y 82

MacLennan, (John) Hugh
  1907-..................... CLC 2, 14
  See also CA 5-8R

MacNeice, (Frederick) Louis
  1907-1963.............. CLC 1, 4, 10
  See also CA 85-88
  See also DLB 10, 20

Macpherson, (Jean) Jay   1931-......CLC 14
  See also CA 5-8R

MacShane, Frank   1927-..... CLC 39 (404)
  See also CANR 3
  See also CA 11-12R

Macumber, Mari   1896-1966
  See Sandoz, Mari (Susette)

Madden, (Jerry) David
  1933-..................... CLC 5, 15
  See also CAAS 3
  See also CANR 4
  See also CA 1-4R
  See also DLB 6

Madhubuti, Haki R.   1942-.........CLC 6
  See also Lee, Don L.
  See also DLB 5, 41

Maeterlinck, Maurice
  1862-1949.................. TCLC 3
  See also CA 104

Maginn, William   1794-1842....... NCLC 8

Mahapatra, Jayanta   1928-.........CLC 33
  See also CANR 15
  See also CA 73-76

Mahon, Derek   1941-..............CLC 27
  See also CA 113
  See also DLB 40

Mailer, Norman
  1923-......CLC 1, 2, 3, 4, 5, 8, 11, 14,
                              28, 39 (416)
  See also CA 9-12R
  See also DLB 2, 16, 28
  See also DLB-Y 80, 83
  See also DLB-DS 3
  See also AITN 2

Mais, Roger   1905-1955........... TCLC 8
  See also CA 105

Major, Clarence   1936-......... CLC 3, 19
  See also CA 21-24R
  See also DLB 33

Major, Kevin   1949-..............CLC 26
  See also CA 97-100
  See also SATA 32

Malamud, Bernard
  1914-......CLC 1, 2, 3, 5, 8, 9, 11, 18,
                              27
  See also CA 5-8R
  See also DLB 2, 28
  See also DLB-Y 80

Mallarmé, Stéphane
  1842-1898.................. NCLC 4

Mallet-Joris, Françoise   1930-......CLC 11
  See also CANR 17
  See also CA 65-68

Maloff, Saul   1922-..................CLC 5
  See also CA 33-36R

Malouf, David   1934-..............CLC 28

Malraux, (Georges-) André
  1901-1976........ CLC 1, 4, 9, 13, 15
  See also CAP 2
  See also CA 21-24R
  See also obituary CA 69-72

Malzberg, Barry N.   1939- ....CLC 7
  See also CANR 16
  See also CA 61-64
  See also DLB 8

Mamet, David
  1947-.............CLC 9, 15, 34 (217)
  See also CANR 15
  See also CA 81-84
  See also DLB 7

Mamoulian, Rouben   1898-.........CLC 16
  See also CA 25-28R

Mandelstam, Osip (Emilievich)
  1891?-1938?.............. TCLC 2, 6
  See also CA 104

Manley, (Mary) Delariviere
  1672?-1724.................... LC 1
  See also DLB 39

Mann, (Luiz) Heinrich
  1871-1950.................. TCLC 9
  See also CA 106

Mann, Thomas
  1875-1955.............TCLC 2, 8, 14
  See also CA 104

Manning, Olivia   1915-1980 ..... CLC 5, 19
  See also CA 5-8R
  See also obituary CA 101

Mano, D. Keith   1942-.......... CLC 2, 10
  See also CA 25-28R
  See also DLB 6

Mansfield, Katherine
  1888-1923................. TCLC 2, 8
  See also CA 104

Manso, Peter   1940-......... CLC 39 (416)
  See also CA 29-32R

Marcel, Gabriel (Honore)
  1889-1973...................CLC 15
  See also CA 102
  See also obituary CA 45-48

Marchbanks, Samuel   1913-
  See Davies, (William) Robertson

Marinetti, F(ilippo) T(ommaso)
  1876-1944................. TCLC 10
  See also CA 107

Markandaya, Kamala   1924- .... CLC 8, 38
  See also Taylor, Kamala (Purnaiya)

Markfield, Wallace (Arthur)
  1926-.........................CLC 8
  See also CAAS 3
  See also CA 69-72
  See also DLB 2, 28

Markham, Robert   1922-
  See Amis, Kingsley (William)

Marks, J.   1942-
  See Highwater, Jamake

Marley, Bob   1945-1981 ....CLC 17
  See also Marley, Robert Nesta

Marley, Robert Nesta   1945-1981
  See Marley, Bob
  See also CA 107
  See also obituary CA 103

Marmontel, Jean-François
  1723-1799..................... LC 2

Marquand, John P(hillips)
  1893-1960.................. CLC 2, 10
  See also CA 85-88
  See also DLB 9

Márquez, Gabriel García   1928-
  See García Márquez, Gabriel

Marquis, Don(ald Robert Perry)
  1878-1937.................. TCLC 7
  See also CA 104
  See also DLB 11, 25

Marryat, Frederick   1792-1848 .... NCLC 3
  See also DLB 21

Marsh, (Edith) Ngaio
  1899-1982...................CLC 7
  See also CANR 6
  See also CA 9-12R

Marshall, Garry   1935?- ....CLC 17
  See also CA 111

Marshall, Paule   1929-.............CLC 27
  See also CA 77-80
  See also DLB 33

Marsten, Richard   1926-
  See Hunter, Evan

Martin, Steve   1945?-..............CLC 30
  See also CA 97-100

Martínez Ruiz, José   1874-1967
  See Azorín
  See also CA 93-96

Martínez Sierra, Gregorio   1881-1947
  See Martínez Sierra, Gregorio and Martínez
      Sierra, María (de la O'LeJárraga)
  See also CA 104, 115

Martínez Sierra, Gregorio   1881-1947 and
      **Martínez Sierra, María (de la
      O'LeJárraga)**   1880?-1974 .... TCLC 6

Martínez Sierra, María (de la O'LeJárraga)
      1880?-1974
  See Martínez Sierra, Gregorio and Martínez
      Sierra, María (de la O'LeJárraga)
  See also obituary CA 115

Martínez Sierra, María (de la O'LeJárraga)
      1880?-1974 and **Martínez Sierra,
      Gregorio**   1881-1947
  See Martínez Sierra, Gregorio and Martínez
      Sierra, María (de la O'LeJárraga)

Martinson, Harry (Edmund)
  1904-1978...................CLC 14
  See also CA 77-80

Masaoka Shiki   1867-1902....... TCLC 18

Masefield, John (Edward)
   1878-1967...................CLC 11
   See also CAP 2
   See also CA 19-20
   See also obituary CA 25-28R
   See also SATA 19
   See also DLB 10, 19

Mason, Bobbie Ann 1940-.........CLC 28
   See also CANR 11
   See also CA 53-56

Mason, Nick 1945-
   See Pink Floyd

Mason, Tally 1909-1971
   See Derleth, August (William)

Masters, Edgar Lee
   1868?-1950.................TCLC 2
   See also CA 104

Mastrosimone, William 19??- ......CLC 36

Matheson, Richard (Burton)
   1926-......................CLC 37
   See also CA 97-100
   See also DLB 8, 44

Mathews, Harry 1930-.............CLC 6
   See also CA 21-24R

Matthias, John (Edward) 1941-......CLC 9
   See also CA 33-36R

Matthiessen, Peter
   1927-................CLC 5, 7, 11, 32
   See also CA 9-12R
   See also SATA 27
   See also DLB 6

Maturin, Charles Robert
   1780?-1824..................NCLC 6

Matute, Ana María 1925-.........CLC 11
   See also CA 89-92

Maugham, W(illiam) Somerset
   1874-1965.............CLC 1, 11, 15
   See also CA 5-8R
   See also obituary CA 25-28R
   See also DLB 10, 36

Maupassant, (Henri René Albert) Guy de
   1850-1893..................NCLC 1

Mauriac, Claude 1914-.............CLC 9
   See also CA 89-92

Mauriac, François (Charles)
   1885-1970.................CLC 4, 9
   See also CAP 2
   See also CA 25-28

Mavor, Osborne Henry 1888-1951
   See Bridie, James
   See also CA 104

Maxwell, William (Keepers, Jr.)
   1908-......................CLC 19
   See also CA 93-96
   See also DLB-Y 80

May, Elaine 1932-................CLC 16
   See also DLB 44

Mayakovsky, Vladimir (Vladimirovich)
   1893-1930...............TCLC 4, 18
   See also CA 104

Maynard, Joyce 1953-.............CLC 23
   See also CA 111

Mayne, William (James Carter)
   1928-......................CLC 12
   See also CA 9-12R
   See also SATA 6

Mayo, Jim 1908?-
   See L'Amour, Louis (Dearborn)

Maysles, Albert 1926-
   See Maysles, Albert and Maysles, David
   See also CA 29-32R

Maysles, Albert 1926- and **Maysles, David**
   1932-......................CLC 16

Maysles, David 1932-
   See Maysles, Albert and Maysles, David

Mazer, Norma Fox 1931-..........CLC 26
   See also CANR 12
   See also CA 69-72
   See also SAAS 1
   See also SATA 24

McBain, Ed 1926-
   See Hunter, Evan

McCaffrey, Anne 1926- ....CLC 17
   See also CANR 15
   See also CA 25-28R
   See also SATA 8
   See also DLB 8
   See also AITN 2

McCarthy, Cormac 1933-...........CLC 4
   See also CANR 10
   See also CA 13-16R
   See also DLB 6

McCarthy, Mary (Therese)
   1912-.....CLC 1, 3, 5, 14, 24, 39 (484)
   See also CANR 16
   See also CA 5-8R
   See also DLB 2
   See also DLB-Y 81

McCartney, (James) Paul
   1942-......................CLC 35
   See also Lennon, John (Ono) and
      McCartney, Paul

McClure, Michael 1932-........ CLC 6, 10
   See also CANR 17
   See also CA 21-24R
   See also DLB 16

McCourt, James 1941-.............CLC 5
   See also CA 57-60

McCrae, John 1872-1918........ TCLC 12
   See also CA 109

McCullers, (Lula) Carson
   1917-1967...........CLC 1, 4, 10, 12
   See also CA 5-8R
   See also obituary CA 25-28R
   See also SATA 27
   See also DLB 2, 7

McCullough, Colleen 1938?- ....CLC 27
   See also CANR 17
   See also CA 81-84

McElroy, Joseph 1930-............CLC 5
   See also CA 17-20R

McEwan, Ian 1948-................CLC 13
   See also CA 61-64
   See also DLB 14

McGahern, John 1935-.......... CLC 5, 9
   See also CA 17-20R
   See also DLB 14

McGinley, Phyllis 1905-1978.......CLC 14
   See also CA 9-12R
   See also obituary CA 77-80
   See also SATA 2, 44
   See also obituary SATA 24
   See also DLB 11

McGinniss, Joe 1942- ....CLC 32
   See also CA 25-28R
   See also AITN 2

McGivern, Maureen Daly 1921-
   See Daly, Maureen
   See also CA 9-12R

McGrath, Thomas 1916- ....CLC 28
   See also CANR 6
   See also CA 9-12R
   See also SATA 41

McGuane, Thomas (Francis III)
   1939-..................CLC 3, 7, 18
   See also CANR 5
   See also CA 49-52
   See also DLB 2
   See also DLB-Y 80
   See also AITN 2

McHale, Tom 1941-1982 .... CLC 3, 5
   See also CA 77-80
   See also obituary CA 106
   See also AITN 1

McIlwraith, Maureen Mollie Hunter 1922-
   See Hunter, Mollie
   See also CA 29-32R
   See also SATA 2

McInerney, Jay 1955-........ CLC 34 (81)
   See also CA 116

McIntyre, Vonda N(eel) 1948-......CLC 18
   See also CA 81-84

McKay, Claude 1890-1948........ TCLC 7
   See also CA 104
   See also DLB 4, 45

McKuen, Rod 1933- .... CLC 1, 3
   See also CA 41-44R
   See also AITN 1

McLuhan, (Herbert) Marshall
   1911-1980...................CLC 37
   See also CANR 12
   See also CA 9-12R
   See also obituary CA 102

McManus, Declan Patrick 1955-
   See Costello, Elvis

McMurtry, Larry (Jeff)
   1936-............. CLC 2, 3, 7, 11, 27
   See also CA 5-8R
   See also DLB 2
   See also DLB-Y 80
   See also AITN 2

McNally, Terrence 1939- .... CLC 4, 7
   See also CANR 2
   See also CA 45-48
   See also DLB 7

McPhee, John 1931- ....CLC 36
   See also CA 65-68

McPherson, James Alan 1943- .....CLC 19
   See also CA 25-28R
   See also DLB 38

McPherson, William
   1939-.................... CLC 34 (85)
   See also CA 57-60

McSweeney, Kerry 19??- .... CLC 34 (579)

Mead, Margaret 1901-1978........CLC 37
   See also CANR 4
   See also CA 1-4R
   See also obituary CA 81-84
   See also SATA 20
   See also AITN 1

Meaker, M. J. 1927-
See Kerr, M. E.
See Meaker, Marijane

Meaker, Marijane 1927-
See Kerr, M. E.
See also CA 107
See also SATA 20

Medoff, Mark (Howard)
1940- .... **CLC 6, 23**
See also CANR 5
See also CA 53-56
See also DLB 7
See also AITN 1

Megged, Aharon 1920- ....**CLC 9**
See also CANR 1
See also CA 49-52

Mehta, Ved (Parkash) 1934- ......**CLC 37**
See also CANR 2
See also CA 1-4R

Mellor, John 1953?-
See The Clash

Meltzer, Milton 1915- ....**CLC 26**
See also CA 13-16R
See also SAAS 1
See also SATA 1

Melville, Herman
1819-1891................**NCLC 3, 12**
See also DLB 3

Mencken, H(enry) L(ouis)
1880-1956................ **TCLC 13**
See also CA 105
See also DLB 11, 29

Mercer, David 1928-1980..........**CLC 5**
See also CA 9-12R
See also obituary CA 102
See also DLB 13

Meredith, George 1828-1909 .....**TCLC 17**
See also DLB 18, 35

Meredith, William (Morris)
1919-..................**CLC 4, 13, 22**
See also CANR 6
See also CA 9-12R
See also DLB 5

Mérimée, Prosper 1803-1870......**NCLC 6**

Merrill, James (Ingram)
1926-.......... **CLC 2, 3, 6, 8, 13, 18,**
34 (225)
See also CANR 10
See also CA 13-16R
See also DLB 5
See also DLB-Y 85

Merton, Thomas (James)
1915-1968...... **CLC 1, 3, 11, 34 (460)**
See also CA 5-8R
See also obituary CA 25-28R
See also DLB-Y 81

Merwin, W(illiam) S(tanley)
1927-.........**CLC 1, 2, 3, 5, 8, 13, 18**
See also CANR 15
See also CA 13-16R
See also DLB 5

Metcalf, John 1938-..............**CLC 37**
See also CA 113

Mew, Charlotte (Mary)
1870-1928.................. **TCLC 8**
See also CA 105
See also DLB 19

Mewshaw, Michael 1943-..........**CLC 9**
See also CANR 7
See also CA 53-56
See also DLB-Y 80

Meyers, Jeffrey 1939-....... **CLC 39 (427)**
See also CA 73-76

Meynell, Alice (Christiana Gertrude
Thompson) 1847-1922 .... **TCLC 6**
See also CA 104
See also DLB 19

Michaels, Leonard 1933- .... **CLC 6, 25**
See also CA 61-64

Michaux, Henri 1899-1984..... **CLC 8, 19**
See also CA 85-88
See also obituary CA 114

Michener, James A(lbert)
1907-.................**CLC 1, 5, 11, 29**
See also CA 5-8R
See also DLB 6
See also AITN 1

Mickiewicz, Adam 1798-1855 ..... **NCLC 3**

Middleton, Christopher 1926-......**CLC 13**
See also CA 13-16R
See also DLB 40

Middleton, Stanley 1919- .... **CLC 7, 38**
See also CA 25-28R
See also DLB 14

Miguéis, José Rodrigues 1901- .....**CLC 10**

Miles, Josephine (Louise)
1911-1985.....**CLC 1, 2, 14, 34 (243),**
39 (352)
See also CANR 2
See also CA 1-4R
See also obituary CA 116

Mill, John Stuart 1806-1873 ..... **NCLC 11**

Millar, Kenneth
1915-1983........ **CLC 1, 2, 3, 14, 34**
See Macdonald, Ross
See also CANR 16
See also CA 9-12R
See also obituary CA 110
See also DLB 2
See also DLB-Y 83

Millay, Edna St. Vincent
1892-1950.................. **TCLC 4**
See also CA 104
See also DLB 45

Miller, Arthur
1915-.......... **CLC 1, 2, 6, 10, 15, 26**
See also CANR 2
See also CA 1-4R
See also DLB 7
See also AITN 1

Miller, Henry (Valentine)
1891-1980......... **CLC 1, 2, 4, 9, 14**
See also CA 9-12R
See also obituary CA 97-100
See also DLB 4, 9
See also DLB-Y 80

Miller, Jason 1939?-.................**CLC 2**
See also CA 73-76
See also DLB 7
See also AITN 1

Miller, Walter M(ichael), Jr.
1923-..................... **CLC 4, 30**
See also CA 85-88
See also DLB 8

Millhauser, Steven 1943- ....**CLC 21**
See also CA 108, 110, 111
See also DLB 2

Milne, A(lan) A(lexander)
1882-1956................. **TCLC 6**
See also CLR 1
See also CA 104
See also YABC 1
See also DLB 10

Miłosz, Czesław
1911-............**CLC 5, 11, 22, 31**
See also CA 81-84

Minus, Ed 1938- .... **CLC 39 (79)**

Miró (Ferrer), Gabriel (Francisco Víctor)
1879-1930.................. **TCLC 5**
See also CA 104

Mishima, Yukio
1925-1970......... **CLC 2, 4, 6, 9, 27**
See also Hiraoka, Kimitake

Mistral, Gabriela 1889-1957 ...... **TCLC 2**
See also CA 104

Mitchell, James Leslie 1901-1935
See Gibbon, Lewis Grassic
See also CA 104
See also DLB 15

Mitchell, Joni 1943-................**CLC 12**
See also CA 112

Mitchell (Marsh), Margaret (Munnerlyn)
1900-1949.................. **TCLC 11**
See also CA 109
See also DLB 9

Mitchell, W(illiam) O(rmond)
1914-....................**CLC 25**
See also CANR 15
See also CA 77-80

Mitford, Mary Russell
1787-1855.................. **NCLC 4**

Modiano, Patrick (Jean) 1945- .....**CLC 18**
See also CANR 17
See also CA 85-88

Mohr, Nicholasa 1935-............**CLC 12**
See also CANR 1
See also CA 49-52
See also SATA 8

Mojtabai, A(nn) G(race)
1938-................**CLC 5, 9, 15, 29**
See also CA 85-88

Molnár, Ferenc 1878-1952....... **TCLC 20**
See also CA 109

Momaday, N(avarre) Scott
1934-..................... **CLC 2, 19**
See also CANR 14
See also CA 25-28R
See also SATA 30

Monroe, Harriet 1860-1936...... **TCLC 12**
See also CA 109

Montagu, Elizabeth 1720-1800 .... **NCLC 7**

Montague, John (Patrick)
1929-......................**CLC 13**
See also CANR 9
See also CA 9-12R
See also DLB 40

Montale, Eugenio
1896-1981.............. **CLC 7, 9, 18**
See also CA 17-20R
See also obituary CA 104

Montgomery, Marion (H., Jr.)
 1925- ....CLC 7
 See also CANR 3
 See also CA 1-4R
 See also DLB 6
 See also AITN 1

Montgomery, Robert Bruce 1921-1978
 See Crispin, Edmund
 See also CA 104

Montherlant, Henri (Milon) de
 1896-1972................. CLC 8, 19
 See also CA 85-88
 See also obituary CA 37-40R

Monty Python....................CLC 21
 See also Cleese, John

Mooney, Ted 1951- ....CLC 25

Moorcock, Michael (John)
 1939- .... CLC 5, 27
 See also CANR 2, 17
 See also CA 45-48
 See also DLB 14

Moore, Brian
 1921- ....CLC 1, 3, 5, 7, 8, 19, 32
 See also CANR 1
 See also CA 1-4R

Moore, George (Augustus)
 1852-1933.................. TCLC 7
 See also CA 104
 See also DLB 10, 18

Moore, Lorrie 1957- .... CLC 39 (82)
 See also Moore, Marie Lorena

Moore, Marianne (Craig)
 1887-1972...... CLC 1, 2, 4, 8, 10, 13,
                                        19
 See also CANR 3
 See also CA 1-4R
 See also obituary CA 33-36R
 See also DLB 45
 See also SATA 20

Moore, Marie Lorena 1957-
 See Moore, Lorrie
 See also CA 116

Moore, Thomas 1779-1852........ NCLC 6

Morante, Elsa 1918- ....CLC 8
 See also CA 85-88

Moravia, Alberto
 1907- .... CLC 2, 7, 11, 18, 27
 See also Pincherle, Alberto

Moréas, Jean 1856-1910........ TCLC 18

Morgan, Berry 1919- ....CLC 6
 See also CA 49-52
 See also DLB 6

Morgan, Edwin (George)
 1920- ....CLC 31
 See also CANR 3
 See also CA 7-8R
 See also DLB 27

Morgan, Frederick 1922- ....CLC 23
 See also CA 17-20R

Morgan, Janet 1945- .... CLC 39 (436)
 See also CA 65-68

Morgan, Robin 1941- ....CLC 2
 See also CA 69-72

Morgenstern, Christian (Otto Josef Wolfgang)
 1871-1914.................. TCLC 8
 See also CA 105

Mori Ōgai 1862-1922 .... TCLC 14
 See also Mori Rintaro

Mori Rintaro 1862-1922
 See Mori Ōgai
 See also CA 110

Mörike, Eduard (Friedrich)
 1804-1875................. NCLC 10

Moritz, Karl Philipp 1756-1793 ...... LC 2

Morris, Julian 1916-
 See West, Morris L.

Morris, Steveland Judkins 1950-
 See Wonder, Stevie
 See also CA 111

Morris, William 1834-1896 .... NCLC 4
 See also DLB 18, 35

Morris, Wright
 1910- .... CLC 1, 3, 7, 18, 37
 See also CA 9-12R
 See also DLB 2
 See also DLB-Y 81

Morrison, James Douglas 1943-1971
 See Morrison, Jim
 See also CA 73-76

Morrison, Jim 1943-1971.........CLC 17
 See also Morrison, James Douglas

Morrison, Toni 1931- .... CLC 4, 10, 22
 See also CA 29-32R
 See also DLB 6, 33
 See also DLB-Y 81

Morrison, Van 1945- ....CLC 21
 See also CA 116

Mortimer, John (Clifford)
 1923- ....CLC 28
 See also CA 13-16R
 See also DLB 13

Mortimer, Penelope (Ruth)
 1918- ....CLC 5
 See also CA 57-60

Moss, Howard 1922- .... CLC 7, 14
 See also CANR 1
 See also CA 1-4R
 See also DLB 5

Motley, Willard (Francis)
 1912-1965.....................CLC 18
 See also obituary CA 106

Mott, Michael (Charles Alston)
 1930- .... CLC 15, 34 (460)
 See also CANR 7
 See also CA 5-8R

Mowat, Farley (McGill) 1921- ......CLC 26
 See also CANR 4
 See also CA 1-4R
 See also SATA 3

Mphahlele, Es'kia 1919-
 See Mphahlele, Ezekiel

Mphahlele, Ezekiel 1919- ....CLC 25
 See also CA 81-84

Mrożek, Sławomir 1930- .... CLC 3, 13
 See also CA 13-16R

Mueller, Lisel 1924- ....CLC 13
 See also CA 93-96

Muir, Edwin 1887-1959 .... TCLC 2
 See also CA 104
 See also DLB 20

Mujica Láinez, Manuel
 1910-1984....................CLC 31
 See also CA 81-84
 See also obituary CA 112

Muldoon, Paul 1951- ....CLC 32
 See also CA 113
 See also DLB 40

Mull, Martin 1943- ....CLC 17
 See also CA 105

Munro, Alice 1931- .... CLC 6, 10, 19
 See also CA 33-36R
 See also SATA 29
 See also AITN 2

Munro, H(ector) H(ugh) 1870-1916
 See Saki
 See also CA 104
 See also DLB 34

Murdoch, (Jean) Iris
 1919- ......CLC 1, 2, 3, 4, 6, 8, 11, 15,
                                   22, 31
 See also CANR 8
 See also CA 13-16R
 See also DLB 14

Murphy, Sylvia 19??- .... CLC 34 (91)

Murry, John Middleton
 1889-1957.................. TCLC 16

Musgrave, Susan 1951- ....CLC 13
 See also CA 69-72

Musil, Robert (Edler von)
 1880-1942.................. TCLC 12
 See also CA 109

Musset, (Louis Charles) Alfred de
 1810-1857.................. NCLC 7

Myers, Walter Dean 1937- ....CLC 35
 See also CLR 4
 See also CA 33-36R
 See also SATA 27, 41
 See also DLB 33

Nabokov, Vladimir (Vladimirovich)
 1899-1977....... CLC 1, 2, 3, 6, 8, 11,
                                   15, 23
 See also CA 5-8R
 See also obituary CA 69-72
 See also DLB 2
 See also DLB-Y 80
 See also DLB-DS 3

Nagy, László 1925-1978 ....CLC 7
 See also obituary CA 112

Naipaul, Shiva(dhar Srinivasa)
 1945-1985........... CLC 32, 39 (355)
 See also CA 110, 112
 See also obituary CA 116
 See also DLB-Y 85

Naipaul, V(idiadhar) S(urajprasad)
 1932- .... CLC 4, 7, 9, 13, 18, 37
 See also CANR 1
 See also CA 1-4R
 See also DLB-Y 85

Nakos, Ioulia 1899?-
 See Nakos, Lilika

Nakos, Lilika 1899?- ....CLC 29

Nakou, Lilika 1899?-
 See Nakos, Lilika

Narayan, R(asipuram) K(rishnaswami)
 1906- .... CLC 7, 28
 See also CA 81-84

Nash, (Frediric) Ogden
    1902-1971...................CLC **23**
    See also CAP 1
    See also CA 13-14
    See also obituary CA 29-32R
    See also SATA 2
    See also DLB 11

Nathan, George Jean
    1882-1958.................TCLC **18**
    See also CA 114

Natsume, Kinnosuke 1867-1916
    See Natsume, Sōseki
    See also CA 104

Natsume, Sōseki
    1867-1916...............TCLC **2, 10**
    See also Natsume, Kinnosuke

Natti, (Mary) Lee 1919-
    See Kingman, (Mary) Lee
    See also CANR 2

Naylor, Gloria 1950-..............CLC **28**
    See also CA 107

Neihardt, John G(neisenau)
    1881-1973...................CLC **32**
    See also CAP 1
    See also CA 13-14
    See also DLB 9

Nekrasov, Nikolai Alekseevich
    1821-1878.................NCLC **11**

Nelligan, Émile 1879-1941.......TCLC **14**
    See also CA 114

Nelson, Willie 1933-..............CLC **17**
    See also CA 107

Nemerov, Howard
    1920-................CLC **2, 6, 9, 36**
    See also CANR 1
    See also CA 1-4R
    See also DLB 5, 6
    See also DLB-Y 83

Neruda, Pablo
    1904-1973........CLC **1, 2, 5, 7, 9, 28**
    See also CAP 2
    See also CA 19-20
    See also obituary CA 45-48

Nerval, Gérard de 1808-1855.....NCLC **1**

Nervo, (José) Amado (Ruiz de)
    1870-1919.................TCLC **11**
    See also CA 109

Neufeld, John (Arthur) 1938-......CLC **17**
    See also CANR 11
    See also CA 25-28R
    See also SATA 6

Neville, Emily Cheney 1919-.......CLC **12**
    See also CANR 3
    See also CA 5-8R
    See also SATA 1

Newbound, Bernard Slade 1930-
    See Slade, Bernard
    See also CA 81-84

Newby, P(ercy) H(oward)
    1918-................... CLC **2, 13**
    See also CA 5-8R
    See also DLB 15

Newlove, Donald 1928-.............CLC **6**
    See also CA 29-32R

Newlove, John (Herbert) 1938-.....CLC **14**
    See also CANR 9
    See also CA 21-24R

Newman, Charles 1938-.........CLC **2, 8**
    See also CA 21-24R

Newman, Edwin (Harold)
    1919-....................CLC **14**
    See also CANR 5
    See also CA 69-72
    See also AITN 1

Newton, Suzanne 1936-...........CLC **35**
    See also CANR 14
    See also CA 41-44R
    See also SATA 5

Ngugi, James (Thiong'o)
    1938-...............CLC **3, 7, 13, 36**
    See also Ngugi wa Thiong'o
    See also Wa Thiong'o, Ngugi
    See also CA 81-84

Ngugi wa Thiong'o
    1938-...............CLC **3, 7, 13, 36**
    See also Ngugi, James (Thiong'o)
    See also Wa Thiong'o, Ngugi

Nichol, B(arne) P(hillip) 1944-.....CLC **18**
    See also CA 53-56

Nichols, John (Treadwell)
    1940-.....................CLC **38**
    See also CANR 6
    See also CA 9-12R
    See also DLB-Y 82

Nichols, Peter 1927-..........CLC **5, 36**
    See also CA 104
    See also DLB 13

Nicolas, F.R.E. 1927-
    See Freeling, Nicolas

Niedecker, Lorine 1903-1970.......CLC **10**
    See also CAP 2
    See also CA 25-28

Nietzsche, Friedrich (Wilhelm)
    1844-1900...............TCLC **10, 18**
    See also CA 107

Nightingale, Anne Redmon 1943-
    See Redmon (Nightingale), Anne
    See also CA 103

Nin, Anaïs
    1903-1977........CLC **1, 4, 8, 11, 14**
    See also CA 13-16R
    See also obituary CA 69-72
    See also DLB 2, 4
    See also AITN 2

Nissenson, Hugh 1933-..........CLC **4, 9**
    See also CA 17-20R
    See also DLB 28

Niven, Larry 1938-................CLC **8**
    See also Niven, Laurence Van Cott
    See also DLB 8

Niven, Laurence Van Cott 1938-
    See Niven, Larry
    See also CANR 14
    See also CA 21-24R

Nixon, Agnes Eckhardt 1927-......CLC **21**
    See also CA 110

Norman, Marsha 1947-............CLC **28**
    See also CA 105
    See also DLB-Y 84

Norris, Leslie 1921-................CLC **14**
    See also CANR 14
    See also CAP 1
    See also CA 11-12
    See also DLB 27

North, Andrew 1912-
    See Norton, Andre

North, Christopher 1785-1854
    See Wilson, John

Norton, Alice Mary 1912-
    See Norton, Andre
    See also CANR 2
    See also CA 1-4R
    See also SATA 1, 43

Norton, Andre 1912-..............CLC **12**
    See also Norton, Mary Alice
    See also DLB 8

Norway, Nevil Shute 1899-1960
    See Shute (Norway), Nevil
    See also CA 102
    See also obituary CA 93-96

Nossack, Hans Erich 1901-1978.....CLC **6**
    See also CA 93-96
    See also obituary CA 85-88

Nova, Craig 1945-..............CLC **7, 31**
    See also CANR 2
    See also CA 45-48

Nowlan, Alden (Albert) 1933-......CLC **15**
    See also CANR 5
    See also CA 9-12R

Noyes, Alfred 1880-1958.........TCLC **7**
    See also CA 104
    See also DLB 20

Nunn, Kem 19??-............CLC **34** (94)

Nye, Robert 1939-................CLC **13**
    See also CA 33-36R
    See also SATA 6
    See also DLB 14

Nyro, Laura 1947-................CLC **17**

Oates, Joyce Carol
    1938-.....CLC **1, 2, 3, 6, 9, 11, 15, 19,
                                    33**
    See also CA 5-8R
    See also DLB 2, 5
    See also DLB-Y 81
    See also AITN 1

O'Brien, Darcy 1939-.............CLC **11**
    See also CANR 8
    See also CA 21-24R

O'Brien, Edna
    1932-............ CLC **3, 5, 8, 13, 36**
    See also CANR 6
    See also CA 1-4R
    See also DLB 14

O'Brien, Flann
    1911-1966......... CLC **1, 4, 5, 7, 10**
    See also O Nuallain, Brian

O'Brien, Richard 19??-...........CLC **17**

O'Brien, Tim 1946-............CLC **7, 19**
    See also CA 85-88
    See also DLB-Y 80

O'Casey, Sean
    1880-1964......... CLC **1, 5, 9, 11, 15**
    See also CA 89-92
    See also DLB 10

Ochs, Phil 1940-1976.............CLC **17**
    See also obituary CA 65-68

O'Connor, Edwin (Greene)
    1918-1968...................CLC **14**
    See also CA 93-96
    See also obituary CA 25-28R

O'Connor, (Mary) Flannery
    1925-1964...... CLC 1, 2, 3, 6, 10, 13,
                                    15, 21
    See also CANR 3
    See also CA 1-4R
    See also DLB 2
    See also DLB-Y 80

O'Connor, Frank
    1903-1966............... CLC 14, 23
    See also O'Donovan, Michael (John)

O'Dell, Scott   1903- ....CLC 30
    See also CLR 1
    See also CANR 12
    See also CA 61-64
    See also SATA 12

Odets, Clifford   1906-1963 ...... CLC 2, 28
    See also CA 85-88
    See also DLB 7, 26

O'Donovan, Michael (John)   1903-1966
    See O'Connor, Frank
    See also CA 93-96

Ōe, Kenzaburō   1935- .... CLC 10, 36
    See also CA 97-100

O'Faolain, Julia   1932- .... CLC 6, 19
    See also CAAS 2
    See also CANR 12
    See also CA 81-84
    See also DLB 14

O'Faoláin, Seán
    1900-...............CLC 1, 7, 14, 32
    See also CANR 12
    See also CA 61-64
    See also DLB 15

O'Flaherty, Liam
    1896-1984........... CLC 5, 34 (355)
    See also CA 101
    See also obituary CA 113
    See also DLB 36
    See also DLB-Y 84

O'Grady, Standish (James)
    1846-1928.................. TCLC 5
    See also CA 104

O'Hara, Frank
    1926-1966.............. CLC 2, 5, 13
    See also CA 9-12R
    See also obituary CA 25-28R
    See also DLB 5, 16

O'Hara, John (Henry)
    1905-1970......... CLC 1, 2, 3, 6, 11
    See also CA 5-8R
    See also obituary CA 25-28R
    See also DLB 9
    See also DLB-DS 2

Okigbo, Christopher (Ifenayichukwu)
    1932-1967..................CLC 25
    See also CA 77-80

Olds, Sharon   1942- ...... CLC 32, 39 (186)
    See also CA 101

Olesha, Yuri (Karlovich)
    1899-1960...................CLC 8
    See also CA 85-88

Oliphant, Margaret (Oliphant Wilson)
    1828-1897.................. NCLC 11
    See also DLB 18

Oliver, Mary   1935- ...... CLC 19, 34 (246)
    See also CANR 9
    See also CA 21-24R
    See also DLB 5

Olivier, (Baron) Laurence (Kerr)
    1907-......................CLC 20
    See also CA 111

Olsen, Tillie   1913-............. CLC 4, 13
    See also CANR 1
    See also CA 1-4R
    See also DLB 28
    See also DLB-Y 80

Olson, Charles (John)
    1910-1970...... CLC 1, 2, 5, 6, 9, 11,
                                        29
    See also CAP 1
    See also CA 15-16
    See also obituary CA 25-28R
    See also DLB 5, 16

Olson, Theodore   1937-
    See Olson, Toby

Olson, Toby   1937-................CLC 28
    See also CANR 9
    See also CA 65-68

Ondaatje, (Philip) Michael
    1943-................... CLC 14, 29
    See also CA 77-80

Oneal, Elizabeth   1934-
    See Oneal, Zibby
    See also CA 106
    See also SATA 30

Oneal, Zibby   1934-...............CLC 30
    See also Oneal, Elizabeth

O'Neill, Eugene (Gladstone)
    1888-1953................ TCLC 1, 6
    See also CA 110
    See also AITN 1
    See also DLB 7

Onetti, Juan Carlos   1909- ...... CLC 7, 10
    See also CA 85-88

O'Nolan, Brian   1911-1966
    See O'Brien, Flann

O Nuallain, Brian   1911-1966
    See O'Brien, Flann
    See also CAP 2
    See also CA 21-22
    See also obituary CA 25-28R

Oppen, George
    1908-1984........CLC 7, 13, 34 (358)
    See also CANR 8
    See also CA 13-16R
    See also obituary CA 113
    See also DLB 5

Orlovitz, Gil   1918-1973 ....CLC 22
    See also CA 77-80
    See also obituary CA 45-48
    See also DLB 2, 5

Ortega y Gasset, José
    1883-1955.................. TCLC 9
    See also CA 106

Orton, Joe   1933?-1967 .... CLC 4, 13
    See also Orton, John Kingsley
    See also DLB 13

Orton, John Kingsley   1933?-1967
    See Orton, Joe
    See also CA 85-88

Orwell, George
    1903-1950............. TCLC 2, 6, 15
    See also Blair, Eric Arthur
    See also DLB 15

Osborne, John (James)
    1929-.................CLC 1, 2, 5, 11
    See also CA 13-16R
    See also DLB 13

Osceola   1885-1962
    See Dinesen, Isak
    See also Blixen, Karen (Christentze
        Dinesen)

Oshima, Nagisa   1932-.............CLC 20
    See also CA 116

Ossoli, Sarah Margaret (Fuller marchesa d')
    1810-1850
    See Fuller, (Sarah) Margaret
    See also SATA 25

Otero, Blas de   1916-..............CLC 11
    See also CA 89-92

Owen, Wilfred (Edward Salter)
    1893-1918.................. TCLC 5
    See also CA 104
    See also DLB 20

Owens, Rochelle   1936-..............CLC 8
    See also CAAS 2
    See also CA 17-20R

Owl, Sebastian   1939-
    See Thompson, Hunter S(tockton)

Oz, Amos   1939-...... CLC 5, 8, 11, 27, 33
    See also CA 53-56

Ozick, Cynthia   1928- ....CLC 3, 7, 28
    See also CA 17-20R
    See also DLB 28
    See also DLB-Y 82

Ozu, Yasujiro   1903-1963 ....CLC 16
    See also CA 112

Pa Chin   1904-....................CLC 18
    See also Li Fei-kan

Pack, Robert   1929-...............CLC 13
    See also CANR 3
    See also CA 1-4R
    See also DLB 5

Padgett, Lewis   1915-1958
    See Kuttner, Henry

Padilla, Heberto   1932- ....CLC 38
    See also AITN 1

Page, Jimmy   1944-
    See Page, Jimmy and Plant, Robert

Page, Jimmy   1944-   and
    Plant, Robert   1948- ....CLC 12

Page, P(atricia) K(athleen)
    1916-.................... CLC 7, 18
    See also CANR 4
    See also CA 53-56

Paget, Violet   1856-1935
    See Lee, Vernon
    See also CA 104

Palamas, Kostes   1859-1943 .... TCLC 5
    See also CA 105

Palazzeschi, Aldo   1885-1974 ....CLC 11
    See also CA 89-92
    See also obituary CA 53-56

Paley, Grace   1922- .... CLC 4, 6, 37
    See also CANR 13
    See also CA 25-28R
    See also DLB 28
    See also AITN 1

Author Index

Palin, Michael 1943-
See Monty Python
See also CA 107

Pancake, Breece Dexter 1952-1979
See Pancake, Breece D'J

Pancake, Breece D'J
1952-1979....................CLC 29
See also obituary CA 109

Parker, Dorothy (Rothschild)
1893-1967....................CLC 15
See also CAP 2
See also CA 19-20
See also obituary CA 25-28R
See also DLB 11, 45

Parker, Robert B(rown) 1932-......CLC 27
See also CANR 1
See also CA 49-52

Parkman, Francis 1823-1893.....NCLC 12
See also DLB 1, 30

Parks, Gordon (Alexander Buchanan)
1912-.....................CLC 1, 16
See also CA 41-44R
See also SATA 8
See also DLB 33
See also AITN 2

Parnell, Thomas 1679-1718..........LC 3

Parra, Nicanor 1914- ....CLC 2
See also CA 85-88

Pasolini, Pier Paolo
1922-1975............... CLC 20, 37
See also CA 93-96
See also obituary CA 61-64

Pastan, Linda (Olenik) 1932-.......CLC 27
See also CA 61-64
See also DLB 5

Pasternak, Boris
1890-1960.............. CLC 7, 10, 18
See also obituary CA 116

Patchen, Kenneth
1911-1972............... CLC 1, 2, 18
See also CANR 3
See also CA 1-4R
See also obituary CA 33-36R
See also DLB 16

Pater, Walter (Horatio)
1839-1894..................NCLC 7

Paterson, Katherine (Womeldorf)
1932-................. CLC 12, 30
See also CLR 7
See also CA 21-24R
See also SATA 13

Patmore, Coventry Kersey Dighton
1823-1896..................NCLC 9
See also DLB 35

Paton, Alan (Stewart)
1903-................ CLC 4, 10, 25
See also CAP 1
See also CA 15-16
See also SATA 11

Paulding, James Kirke
1778-1860..................NCLC 2
See also DLB 3

Paulin, Tom 1949-................CLC 37
See also DLB 40

Pavese, Cesare 1908-1950 .... TCLC 3
See also CA 104

Payne, Alan 1932-
See Jakes, John (William)

Paz, Octavio 1914-..... CLC 3, 4, 6, 10, 19
See also CA 73-76

Peake, Mervyn 1911-1968 ....CLC 7
See also CANR 3
See also CA 5-8R
See also obituary CA 25-28R
See also SATA 23
See also DLB 15

Pearce, (Ann) Philippa 1920-......CLC 21
See also Christie, (Ann) Philippa
See also CA 5-8R
See also SATA 1

Pearl, Eric 1934-
See Elman, Richard

Pearson, T(homas) R(eid)
1956-................. CLC 39 (86)

Peck, John 1941-................CLC 3
See also CANR 3
See also CA 49-52

Peck, Richard 1934- ....CLC 21
See also CA 85-88
See also SATA 18

Peck, Robert Newton 1928-........CLC 17
See also CA 81-84
See also SAAS 1
See also SATA 21

Peckinpah, (David) Sam(uel)
1925-1984..................CLC 20
See also CA 109
See also obituary CA 114

Pedersen, Knut 1859-1952
See Hamsun, Knut
See also CA 104

Péguy, Charles (Pierre)
1873-1914.................. TCLC 10
See also CA 107

Percy, Walker
1916-.......... CLC 2, 3, 6, 8, 14, 18
See also CANR 1
See also CA 1-4R
See also DLB 2
See also DLB-Y 80

Pereda, José María de
1833-1906 .... TCLC 16

Perelman, S(idney) J(oseph)
1904-1979........ CLC 3, 5, 9, 15, 23
See also CA 73-76
See also obituary CA 89-92
See also DLB 11, 44
See also AITN 1, 2

Péret, Benjamin 1899-1959 ...... TCLC 20
See also CA 117

Peretz, Isaac Leib
1852?-1915................. TCLC 16
See also CA 109

Perrault, Charles 1628-1703 .... LC 2
See also SATA 25

Perse, St.-John 1887-1975 ...... CLC 4, 11
See also Léger, (Marie-Rene) Alexis Saint-
Léger

Pesetsky, Bette 1932-.............CLC 28

Peshkov, Alexei Maximovich 1868-1936
See Gorky, Maxim
See also CA 105

Peterkin, Julia (Mood)
1880-1961...................CLC 31
See also CA 102
See also DLB 9

Peters, Joan K. 1945-........ CLC 39 (91)

Peters, Robert L(ouis) 1924- ....CLC 7
See also CA 13-16R

Petrakis, Harry Mark 1923- ....CLC 3
See also CANR 4
See also CA 9-12R

Petry, Ann (Lane) 1912-...... CLC 1, 7, 18
See also CANR 4
See also CA 5-8R
See also SATA 5

Phillips, Jayne Anne 1952-..... CLC 15, 33
See also CA 101
See also DLB-Y 80

Phillips, Robert (Schaeffer)
1938-......................CLC 28
See also CANR 8
See also CA 17-20R

Piccolo, Lucio 1901-1969 ....CLC 13
See also CA 97-100

Piercy, Marge
1936-............ CLC 3, 6, 14, 18, 27
See also CAAS 1
See also CA 21-24R

Pincherle, Alberto 1907-
See Moravia, Alberto
See also CA 25-28R

Pineda, Cecile 1942- .... CLC 39 (94)

Piñero, Miguel (Gomez) 1947?-......CLC 4
See also CA 61-64

Pinget, Robert 1919-........ CLC 7, 13, 37
See also CA 85-88

Pink Floyd.......................CLC 35

Pinkwater, D(aniel) M(anus)
1941-......................CLC 35
See also Pinkwater, Manus
See also CLR 4
See also CANR 12
See also CA 29-32R

Pinkwater, Manus 1941-
See Pinkwater, D(aniel) M(anus)
See also SATA 8 ·

Pinsky, Robert 1940-........ CLC 9, 19, 38
See also CA 29-32R
See also DLB-Y 82

Pinter, Harold
1930-........CLC 1, 3, 6, 9, 11, 15, 27
See also CA 5-8R
See also DLB 13

Pirandello, Luigi 1867-1936....... TCLC 4
See also CA 104

Pirsig, Robert M(aynard)
1928-......................CLC 4, 6
See also CA 53-56
See also SATA 39

Plaidy, Jean 1906-
See Hibbert, Eleanor (Burford)

Plant, Robert 1948-
See Page, Jimmy and Plant, Robert

Plante, David (Robert)
1940-.................. CLC 7, 23, 38
See also CANR 12
See also CA 37-40R
See also DLB-Y 83

Plath, Sylvia
1932-1963...... **CLC 1, 2, 3, 5, 9, 11,**
14, 17
See also CAP 2
See also CA 19-20
See also DLB 5, 6

Platonov, Andrei (Platonovich)
1899-1951.................. **TCLC 14**
See also Klimentov, Andrei Platonovich

Platt, Kin 1911-..................**CLC 26**
See also CANR 11
See also CA 17-20R
See also SATA 21

Plimpton, George (Ames)
1927-........................**CLC 36**
See also CA 21-24R
See also SATA 10
See also AITN 1

Plomer, William (Charles Franklin)
1903-1973.................. **CLC 4, 8**
See also CAP 2
See also CA 21-22
See also SATA 24
See also DLB 20

Plumly, Stanley (Ross) 1939-......**CLC 33**
See also CA 108, 110
See also DLB 5

Poe, Edgar Allan 1809-1849 ...... **NCLC 1**
See also SATA 23
See also DLB 3

Pohl, Frederik 1919-..............**CLC 18**
See also CAAS 1
See also CANR 11
See also CA 61-64
See also SATA 24
See also DLB 8

Poirier, Louis 1910-
See Gracq, Julien

Poitier, Sidney 1924?-..............**CLC 26**

Polanski, Roman 1933-............**CLC 16**
See also CA 77-80

Poliakoff, Stephen 1952-...........**CLC 38**
See also CA 106
See also DLB 13

Police, The.......................**CLC 26**

Pollitt, Katha 1949-...............**CLC 28**

Pomerance, Bernard 1940-.........**CLC 13**
See also CA 101

Ponge, Francis (Jean Gaston Alfred)
1899-...................... **CLC 6, 18**
See also CA 85-88

Poole, Josephine 1933-............**CLC 17**
See also CANR 10
See also CA 21-24R
See also SATA 5

Pope, Alexander 1688-1744 .... **LC 3**

Popa, Vasko 1922-................**CLC 19**
See also CA 112

Porter, Katherine Anne
1890-1980..... **CLC 1, 3, 7, 10, 13, 15,**
27
See also CANR 1
See also CA 1-4R
See also obituary CA 101
See also obituary SATA 23, 39
See also DLB 4, 9
See also DLB-Y 80
See also AITN 2

Porter, Peter (Neville Frederick)
1929-.................. **CLC 5, 13, 33**
See also CA 85-88
See also DLB 40

Porter, William Sydney 1862-1910
See Henry, O.
See also CA 104
See also YABC 2
See also DLB 12

Potok, Chaim 1929-.......**CLC 2, 7, 14, 26**
See also CA 17-20R
See also SATA 33
See also DLB 28
See also AITN 1, 2

Pound, Ezra (Loomis)
1885-1972..... **CLC 1, 2, 3, 4, 5, 7, 10,**
13, 18, 34 (503)
See also CA 5-8R
See also obituary CA 37-40R
See also DLB 4, 45

Powell, Anthony (Dymoke)
1905-.......... **CLC 1, 3, 7, 9, 10, 31**
See also CANR 1
See also CA 1-4R
See also DLB 15

Powell, Padgett 1952-........ **CLC 34 (97)**

Powers, J(ames) F(arl)
1917-...................... **CLC 1, 4, 8**
See also CANR 2
See also CA 1-4R

Pownall, David 1938-..............**CLC 10**
See also CA 89-92
See also DLB 14

Powys, John Cowper
1872-1963............... **CLC 7, 9, 15**
See also CA 85-88
See also DLB 15

Powys, T(heodore) F(rancis)
1875-1953.................. **TCLC 9**
See also CA 106
See also DLB 36

Pratt, E(dwin) J(ohn)
1883-1964....................**CLC 19**
See also obituary CA 93-96

Preussler, Otfried 1923-...........**CLC 17**
See also CA 77-80
See also SATA 24

Prévert, Jacques (Henri Marie)
1900-1977....................**CLC 15**
See also CA 77-80
See also obituary CA 69-72
See also obituary SATA 30

Prévost, Abbé (Antoine Francois)
1697-1763..................... **LC 1**

Price, (Edward) Reynolds
1933-.................. **CLC 3, 6, 13**
See also CANR 1
See also CA 1-4R
See also DLB 2

Price, Richard 1949-........... **CLC 6, 12**
See also CANR 3
See also CA 49-52
See also DLB-Y 81

Priestley, J(ohn) B(oynton)
1894-1984....... **CLC 2, 5, 9, 34 (360)**
See also CA 9-12R
See also obituary CA 113
See also DLB 10, 34
See also DLB-Y 84

Prince (Rogers Nelson) 1958?-......**CLC 35**

Prince, F(rank) T(empleton)
1912-........................**CLC 22**
See also CA 101
See also DLB 20

Pritchard, William H(arrison)
1932-.................. **CLC 34 (468)**
See also CA 65-68

Pritchett, V(ictor) S(awdon)
1900-.................. **CLC 5, 13, 15**
See also CA 61-64
See also DLB 15

Procaccino, Michael 1946-
See Cristofer, Michael

Prokosch, Frederic 1908-...........**CLC 4**
See also CA 73-76

Proust, Marcel 1871-1922 ..... **TCLC 7, 13**
See also CA 104

Pryor, Richard 1940- ....**CLC 26**

P'u Sung-ling 1640-1715............. **LC 3**

Puig, Manuel 1932-.......**CLC 3, 5, 10, 28**
See also CANR 2
See also CA 45-48

Purdy, A(lfred) W(ellington)
1918-.................... **CLC 3, 6, 14**
See also CA 81-84

Purdy, James (Amos)
1923-...............**CLC 2, 4, 10, 28**
See also CAAS 1
See also CA 33-36R
See also DLB 2

Pushkin, Alexander (Sergeyevich)
1799-1837.................. **NCLC 3**

Puzo, Mario 1920-.........**CLC 1, 2, 6, 36**
See also CANR 4
See also CA 65-68
See also DLB 6

Pym, Barbara (Mary Crampton)
1913-1980.............**CLC 13, 19, 37**
See also CANR 13
See also CAP 1
See also CA 13-14
See also obituary CA 97-100
See also DLB 14

Pynchon, Thomas (Ruggles, Jr.)
1937-........**CLC 2, 3, 6, 9, 11, 18, 33**
See also CA 17-20R
See also DLB 2

Quasimodo, Salvatore
1901-1968....................**CLC 10**
See also CAP 1
See also CA 15-16
See also obituary CA 25-28R

Queen, Ellery 1905-1982 .... **CLC 3, 11**
See also Dannay, Frederic
See also Lee, Manfred B(ennington)

Queneau, Raymond
1903-1976...............**CLC 2, 5, 10**
See also CA 77-80
See also obituary CA 69-72

Quin, Ann (Marie) 1936-1973.......**CLC 6**
See also CA 9-12R
See also obituary CA 45-48
See also DLB 14

Quinn, Simon 1942-
See Smith, Martin Cruz

Author Index

Quiroga, Horatio (Sylvestre)
    1878-1937.................. TCLC **20**
    See also CA 117

Quoirez, Françoise 1935-
    See Sagan, Françoise
    See also CANR 6
    See also CA 49-52

Rabe, David (William)
    1940-.................... CLC **4, 8, 33**
    See also CA 85-88
    See also DLB 7

Rabinovitch, Sholem 1859-1916
    See Aleichem, Sholom
    See also CA 104

Radcliffe, Ann (Ward)
    1764-1823.................. NCLC **6**
    See also DLB 39

Radnóti, Miklós 1909-1944 ...... TCLC **16**

Rado, James 1939-
    See Ragni, Gerome and
       Rado, James
    See also CA 105

Radomski, James 1932-
    See Rado, James

Radvanyi, Netty Reiling 1900-1983
    See Seghers, Anna
    See also CA 85-88
    See also obituary CA 110

Raeburn, John 1941-........ CLC **34** (477)
    See also CA 57-60

Ragni, Gerome 1942-
    See Ragni, Gerome and Rado, James
    See also CA 105

Ragni, Gerome 1942- and
       Rado, James 1939-........... CLC **17**

Rahv, Philip 1908-1973 .... CLC **24**
    See also Greenberg, Ivan

Raine, Craig 1944- .... CLC **32**
    See also CA 108
    See also DLB 40

Raine, Kathleen (Jessie) 1908-...... CLC **7**
    See also CA 85-88
    See also DLB 20

Rand, Ayn 1905-1982 .... CLC **3, 30**
    See also CA 13-16R
    See also obituary CA 105

Randall, Dudley (Felker) 1914-...... CLC **1**
    See also CA 25-28R
    See also DLB 41

Ransom, John Crowe
    1888-1974......... CLC **2, 4, 5, 11, 24**
    See also CANR 6
    See also CA 5-8R
    See also obituary CA 49-52
    See also DLB 45

Rao, Raja 1909-.................. CLC **25**
    See also CA 73-76

Raphael, Frederic (Michael)
    1931-.................... CLC **2, 14**
    See also CANR 1
    See also CA 1-4R
    See also DLB 14

Rattigan, Terence (Mervyn)
    1911-1977.................... CLC **7**
    See also CA 85-88
    See also obituary CA 73-76
    See also DLB 13

Raven, Simon (Arthur Noel)
    1927-......................... CLC **14**
    See also CA 81-84

Rawlings, Marjorie Kinnan
    1896-1953.................. TCLC **4**
    See also CA 104
    See also YABC 1
    See also DLB 9, 22

Ray, Satyajit 1921-............... CLC **16**

Read, Herbert (Edward)
    1893-1968.................... CLC **4**
    See also CA 85-88
    See also obituary CA 25-28R
    See also DLB 20

Read, Piers Paul 1941-...... CLC **4, 10, 25**
    See also CA 21-24R
    See also SATA 21
    See also DLB 14

Reade, Charles 1814-1884 .... NCLC **2**
    See also DLB 21

Reade, Hamish 1936-
    See Gray, Simon (James Holliday)

Reaney, James 1926-............... CLC **13**
    See also CA 41-44R
    See also SATA 43

Rechy, John (Francisco)
    1934-.................. CLC **1, 7, 14, 18**
    See also CANR 6
    See also CA 5-8R
    See also DLB-Y 82

Redgrove, Peter (William)
    1932-........................ CLC **6**
    See also CANR 3
    See also CA 1-4R
    See also DLB 40

Redmon (Nightingale), Anne
    1943-........................ CLC **22**
    See also Nightingale, Anne Redmon

Reed, Ishmael
    1938-........... CLC **2, 3, 5, 6, 13, 32**
    See also CA 21-24R
    See also DLB 2, 5, 33

Reed, John (Silas) 1887-1920...... TCLC **9**
    See also CA 106

Reed, Lou 1944-.................. CLC **21**

Reid, Christopher 1949-........... CLC **33**
    See also DLB 40

Reid Banks, Lynne 1929-
    See Banks, Lynne Reid
    See also CANR 6
    See also CA 1-4R
    See also SATA 22

Reiner, Max 1900-
    See Caldwell, (Janet Miriam) Taylor
       (Holland)

Remark, Erich Paul 1898-1970
    See Remarque, Erich Maria

Remarque, Erich Maria
    1898-1970.................... CLC **21**
    See also CA 77-80
    See also obituary CA 29-32R

Renard, Jules 1864-1910 .... TCLC **17**

Renault, Mary
    1905-1983............. CLC **3, 11, 17**
    See also Challans, Mary
    See also DLB-Y 83

Rendell, Ruth 1930- .... CLC **28**
    See also CA 109

Renoir, Jean 1894-1979 .... CLC **20**
    See also obituary CA 85-88

Resnais, Alain 1922-.............. CLC **16**

Rexroth, Kenneth
    1905-1982........ CLC **1, 2, 6, 11, 22**
    See also CA 5-8R
    See also obituary CA 107
    See also DLB 16
    See also DLB-Y 82

Reyes y Basoalto, Ricardo Eliecer Neftali
    1904-1973
    See Neruda, Pablo

Reymont, Wladyslaw Stanislaw
    1867-1925.................. TCLC **5**
    See also CA 104

Reynolds, Jonathan 1942?- ..... CLC **6, 38**
    See also CA 65-68

Reznikoff, Charles 1894-1976 ....CLC **9**
    See also CAP 2
    See also CA 33-36
    See also obituary CA 61-64
    See also DLB 28, 45

Rezzori, Gregor von 1914-.........CLC **25**

Rhys, Jean
    1894-1979........ CLC **2, 4, 6, 14, 19**
    See also CA 25-28R
    See also obituary CA 85-88
    See also DLB 36

Ribeiro, Darcy 1922-........ CLC **34** (102)
    See also CA 33-36R

Ribeiro, João Ubaldo (Osorio Pimentel)
    1941-....................... CLC **10**
    See also CA 81-84

Ribman, Ronald (Burt) 1932- ....CLC **7**
    See also CA 21-24R

Rice, Elmer 1892-1967..............CLC **7**
    See also CAP 2
    See also CA 21-22
    See also obituary CA 25-28R
    See also DLB 4, 7

Rice, Tim 1944-
    See Rice, Tim and Webber, Andrew Lloyd
    See also CA 103

Rice, Tim 1944- and
       Webber, Andrew Lloyd
       1948-....................... CLC **21**

Rich, Adrienne (Cecile)
    1929-........... CLC **3, 6, 7, 11, 18, 36**
    See also CA 9-12R
    See also DLB 5

Richard, Keith 1943-
    See Jagger, Mick and Richard, Keith

Richards, I(vor) A(rmstrong)
    1893-1979................ CLC **14, 24**
    See also CA 41-44R
    See also obituary CA 89-92
    See also DLB 27

Richards, Keith 1943-
    See Richard, Keith
    See also CA 107

Richardson, Dorothy (Miller)
    1873-1957.................. TCLC **3**
    See also CA 104
    See also DLB 36

Richardson, Ethel 1870-1946
See Richardson, Henry Handel
See also CA 105

Richardson, Henry Handel
1870-1946. . . . . TCLC 4
See also Richardson, Ethel

Richardson, Samuel 1689-1761. . . . . . . LC 1
See also DLB 39

Richler, Mordecai
1931-. . . . . CLC 3, 5, 9, 13, 18
See also CA 65-68
See also SATA 27
See also AITN 1

Richter, Conrad (Michael)
1890-1968. . . . . .CLC 30
See also CA 5-8R
See also obituary CA 25-28R
See also SATA 3
See also DLB 9

Richter, Johann Paul Friedrich 1763-1825
See Jean Paul

Riding, Laura 1901-. . . . . CLC 3, 7
See also Jackson, Laura (Riding)

Riefenstahl, Berta Helene Amalia 1902-
See Riefenstahl, Leni
See also CA 108

Riefenstahl, Leni 1902-. . . . . .CLC 16
See also Riefenstahl, Berta Helene Amalia

Rilke, Rainer Maria
1875-1926. . . . . .TCLC 1, 6, 19
See also CA 104

Rimbaud, (Jean Nicolas) Arthur
1854-1891. . . . . NCLC 4

Ritsos, Yannis 1909-. . . . . CLC 6, 13, 31
See also CA 77-80

Rivers, Conrad Kent 1933-1968 . . . . .CLC 1
See also CA 85-88
See also DLB 41

Robbe-Grillet, Alain
1922-. . . . . .CLC 1, 2, 4, 6, 8, 10, 14
See also CA 9-12R

Robbins, Harold 1916-. . . . . .CLC 5
See also CA 73-76

Robbins, Thomas Eugene 1936-
See Robbins, Tom
See also CA 81-84

Robbins, Tom 1936-. . . . . CLC 9, 32
See also Robbins, Thomas Eugene
See also DLB-Y 80

Robbins, Trina 1938- . . . . .CLC 21

Roberts, (Sir) Charles G(eorge) D(ouglas)
1860-1943. . . . . TCLC 8
See also CA 105
See also SATA 29

Roberts, Kate 1891-1985 . . . . .CLC 15
See also CA 107
See also obituary CA 116

Roberts, Keith (John Kingston)
1935-. . . . . .CLC 14
See also CA 25-28R

Robinson, Edwin Arlington
1869-1935. . . . . TCLC 5
See also CA 104

Robinson, Jill 1936-. . . . . .CLC 10
See also CA 102

Robinson, Kim Stanley
19??-. . . . . CLC 34 (105)

Robinson, Marilynne 1944-. . . . . . . .CLC 25
See also CA 116

Robinson, Smokey 1940- . . . . .CLC 21

Robinson, William 1940-
See Robinson, Smokey
See also CA 116

Roddenberry, Gene 1921- . . . . .CLC 17

Rodgers, Mary 1931- . . . . .CLC 12
See also CANR 8
See also CA 49-52
See also SATA 8

Rodgers, W(illiam) R(obert)
1909-1969. . . . . .CLC 7
See also CA 85-88
See also DLB 20

Rodriguez, Claudio 1934-. . . . . .CLC 10

Roethke, Theodore (Huebner)
1908-1963. . . . . CLC 1, 3, 8, 11, 19
See also CA 81-84
See also DLB 5

Rogers, Sam 1943-
See Shepard, Sam

Rogers, Will(iam Penn Adair)
1879-1935. . . . . TCLC 8
See also CA 105
See also DLB 11

Rogin, Gilbert 1929-. . . . . .CLC 18
See also CANR 15
See also CA 65-68

Rohmer, Eric 1920-. . . . . .CLC 16
See also Scherer, Jean-Marie Maurice

Roiphe, Anne (Richardson)
1935-. . . . . CLC 3, 9
See also CA 89-92
See also DLB-Y 80

Rolfe, Frederick (William Serafino Austin
Lewis Mary) 1860-1913. . . . . TCLC 12
See also CA 107
See also DLB 34

Rölvaag, O(le) E(dvart)
1876-1931. . . . . TCLC 17
See also DLB 9

Romains, Jules 1885-1972 . . . . .CLC 7
See also CA 85-88

Romero, José Rubén
1890-1952. . . . . TCLC 14
See also CA 114

Rooke, Leon 1934-. . . . . . . CLC 25, 34 (250)
See also CA 25-28R

Rosa, João Guimarães
1908-1967. . . . . .CLC 23
See also obituary CA 89-92

Rosen, Richard (Dean)
1949-. . . . . CLC 39 (194)

Rosenberg, Isaac 1890-1918. . . . . . TCLC 12
See also CA 107
See also DLB 20

Rosenblatt, Joe 1933- . . . . .CLC 15
See also Rosenblatt, Joseph
See also AITN 2

Rosenblatt, Joseph 1933-
See Rosenblatt, Joe
See also CA 89-92

Rosenthal, M(acha) L(ouis)
1917-. . . . . .CLC 28
See also CANR 4
See also CA 1-4R
See also DLB 5

Ross, (James) Sinclair 1908- . . . . . . .CLC 13
See also CA 73-76

Rossetti, Christina Georgina
1830-1894. . . . . NCLC 2
See also SATA 20
See also DLB 35

Rossetti, Dante Gabriel
1828-1882. . . . . NCLC 4
See also DLB 35

Rossetti, Gabriel Charles Dante 1828-1882
See Rossetti, Dante Gabriel

Rossner, Judith (Perelman)
1935-. . . . . CLC 6, 9, 29
See also CA 17-20R
See also DLB 6
See also AITN 2

Rostand, Edmond (Eugène Alexis)
1868-1918. . . . . TCLC 6
See also CA 104

Roth, Henry 1906-. . . . . CLC 2, 6, 11
See also CAP 1
See also CA 11-12
See also DLB 28

Roth, Philip (Milton)
1933-. . . . . . CLC 1, 2, 3, 4, 6, 9, 15, 22,
                               31
See also CANR 1
See also CA 1-4R
See also DLB 2, 28
See also DLB-Y 82

Rothenberg, Jerome 1931-. . . . . .CLC 6
See also CANR 1
See also CA 45-48
See also DLB 5

Roumain, Jacques 1907-1944 . . . . TCLC 19

Rourke, Constance (Mayfield)
1885-1941. . . . . TCLC 12
See also CA 107
See also YABC 1

Roussel, Raymond 1877-1933 . . . . TCLC 20
See also CA 117

Rovit, Earl (Herbert) 1927-. . . . . .CLC 7
See also CA 5-8R

Rowson, Susanna Haswell
1762-1824. . . . . NCLC 5
See also DLB 37

Roy, Gabrielle 1909-1983. . . . . . CLC 10, 14
See also CANR 5
See also CA 53-56
See also obituary CA 110

Różewicz, Tadeusz 1921- . . . . CLC 9, 23
See also CA 108

Ruark, Gibbons 1941-. . . . . .CLC 3
See also CANR 14
See also CA 33-36R

Rubens, Bernice 192?- . . . . CLC 19, 31
See also CA 25-28R
See also DLB 14

Rudkin, (James) David 1936- . . . . . .CLC 14
See also CA 89-92
See also DLB 13

Rudnik, Raphael 1933-............CLC 7
See also CA 29-32R

Ruiz, José Martínez 1874-1967
See Azorín

Rukeyser, Muriel
1913-1980..........CLC 6, 10, 15, 27
See also CA 5-8R
See also obituary CA 93-96
See also obituary SATA 22

Rule, Jane (Vance) 1931-..........CLC 27
See also CANR 12
See also CA 25-28R

Rulfo, Juan 1918- ....CLC 8
See also CA 85-88

Runyon, (Alfred) Damon
1880-1946..................TCLC 10
See also CA 107
See also DLB 11

Rushdie, (Ahmed) Salman
1947-....................CLC 23, 31
See also CA 108, 111

Rushforth, Peter (Scott) 1945-......CLC 19
See also CA 101

Ruskin, John 1819-1900.........TCLC 20
See also CA 114
See also SATA 24

Russ, Joanna 1937-...............CLC 15
See also CANR 11
See also CA 25-28R
See also DLB 8

Russell, George William 1867-1935
See A. E.
See also CA 104

Russell, (Henry) Ken(neth Alfred)
1927-.......................CLC 16
See also CA 105

Ruyslinck, Ward 1929-............CLC 14

Ryan, Cornelius (John)
1920-1974....................CLC 7
See also CA 69-72
See also obituary CA 53-56

Rybakov, Anatoli 1911?- ....CLC 23

Ryga, George 1932-...............CLC 14
See also CA 101

Sabato, Ernesto 1911-......... CLC 10, 23
See also CA 97-100

Sachs, Marilyn (Stickle) 1927-......CLC 35
See also CLR 2
See also CANR 13
See also CA 17-20R
See also SATA 3

Sachs, Nelly 1891-1970...........CLC 14
See also CAP 2
See also CA 17-18
See also obituary CA 25-28R

Sackler, Howard (Oliver)
1929-1982...................CLC 14
See also CA 61-64
See also obituary CA 108
See also DLB 7

Sade, Donatien Alphonse François, Comte de
1740-1814..................NCLC 3

Sadoff, Ira 1945- ....CLC 9
See also CANR 5
See also CA 53-56

Safire, William 1929- ....CLC 10
See also CA 17-20R

Sagan, Carl (Edward) 1934- ....CLC 30
See also CANR 11
See also CA 25-28R

Sagan, Françoise
1935-............. CLC 3, 6, 9, 17, 36
See also Quoirez, Françoise

Sainte-Beuve, Charles Augustin
1804-1869..................NCLC 5

Sainte-Marie, Beverly 1941-
See Sainte-Marie, Buffy
See also CA 107

Sainte-Marie, Buffy 1941- ....CLC 17
See also Sainte-Marie, Beverly

**Saint-Exupéry, Antoine (Jean Baptiste Marie
Roger) de** 1900-1944 .... TCLC 2
See also CA 108
See also SATA 20

Saki 1870-1916.................. TCLC 3
See also Munro, H(ector) H(ugh)

Salama, Hannu 1936-............CLC 18

Salamanca, J(ack) R(ichard)
1922-..................... CLC 4, 15
See also CA 25-28R

Salinas, Pedro 1891-1951....... TCLC 17

Salinger, J(erome) D(avid)
1919-................CLC 1, 3, 8, 12
See also CA 5-8R
See also DLB 2

Salter, James 1925-...............CLC 7
See also CA 73-76

Saltus, Edgar (Evertson)
1855-1921.................. TCLC 8
See also CA 105

Samarakis, Antonis 1919-..........CLC 5
See also CA 25-28R

Sánchez, Luis Rafael 1936- ....CLC 23

Sanchez, Sonia 1934-.............CLC 5
See also CA 33-36R
See also SATA 22
See also DLB 41

Sand, George 1804-1876......... NCLC 2

Sandburg, Carl (August)
1878-1967........ CLC 1, 4, 10, 15, 35
See also CA 5-8R
See also obituary CA 25-28R
See also SATA 8
See also DLB 17

Sandburg, Charles August 1878-1967
See Sandburg, Carl (August)

Sandoz, Mari (Susette)
1896-1966...................CLC 28
See also CANR 17
See also CA 1-4R
See also obituary CA 25-28R
See also SATA 5
See also DLB 9

Saner, Reg(inald Anthony)
1931-.......................CLC 9
See also CA 65-68

Sansom, William 1912-1976..... CLC 2, 6
See also CA 5-8R
See also obituary CA 65-68

Santiago, Danny 1911- ....CLC 33

Santmyer, Helen Hoover 1895-.....CLC 33
See also CANR 15
See also CA 1-4R
See also DLB-Y 84

Santos, Bienvenido N(uqui)
1911-......................CLC 22
See also CA 101

Sarduy, Severo 1937- ....CLC 6
See also CA 89-92

Sargeson, Frank 1903-1982.......CLC 31
See also CA 25-28R
See also CA 106

Sarmiento, Felix Ruben Garcia 1867-1916
See also CA 104

Saroyan, William
1908-1981..........CLC 1, 8, 10, 29,
34 (457)
See also CA 5-8R
See also obituary CA 103
See also SATA 23
See also obituary SATA 24
See also DLB 7, 9
See also DLB-Y 81

Sarraute, Nathalie
1902-...........CLC 1, 2, 4, 8, 10, 31
See also CA 9-12R

Sarton, (Eleanor) May
1912-..................... CLC 4, 14
See also CANR 1
See also CA 1-4R
See also SATA 36
See also DLB-Y 81

Sartre, Jean-Paul
1905-1980...... CLC 1, 4, 7, 9, 13, 18,
24
See also CA 9-12R
See also obituary CA 97-100

Sassoon, Siegfried (Lorraine)
1886-1967....................CLC 36
See also CA 104
See also Obituary CA 25-28R
See also DLB 20

Saura, Carlos 1932-..............CLC 20
See also CA 114

Sauser-Hall, Frédéric-Louis 1887-1961
See Cendrars, Blaise
See also CA 102
See also obituary CA 93-96

Sayers, Dorothy L(eigh)
1893-1957...............TCLC 2, 15
See also CA 104
See also DLB 10, 36

Sayles, John (Thomas)
1950-.................. CLC 7, 10, 14
See also CA 57-60
See also DLB 44

Scammell, Michael 19??- .... CLC 34 (480)

Schaeffer, Susan Fromberg
1941-................ CLC 6, 11, 22
See also CA 49-52
See also SATA 22
See also DLB 28

Schell, Jonathan 1943- ....CLC 35
See also CANR 12
See also CA 73-76

Scherer, Jean-Marie Maurice 1920-
See Rohmer, Eric
See also CA 110

Schevill, James (Erwin) 1920- ......CLC 7
See also CA 5-8R

Schisgal, Murray (Joseph)
1926- ....CLC 6
See also CA 21-24R

Schlee, Ann 1934- ....CLC 35
See also CA 101
See also SATA 36

Schmitz, Ettore 1861-1928
See Svevo, Italo
See also CA 104

Schneider, Leonard Alfred 1925-1966
See Bruce, Lenny
See also CA 89-92

Schnitzler, Arthur 1862-1931 ..... TCLC 4
See also CA 104

Schorer, Mark 1908-1977 ....CLC 9
See also CANR 7
See also CA 5-8R
See also obituary CA 73-76

Schrader, Paul (Joseph) 1946-......CLC 26
See also CA 37-40R
See also DLB 44

Schreiner (Cronwright), Olive (Emilie
Albertina) 1855-1920 .... TCLC 9
See also CA 105
See also DLB 18

Schulberg, Budd (Wilson) 1914- .....CLC 7
See also CA 25-28R
See also DLB 6, 26, 28
See also DLB-Y 81

Schulz, Bruno 1892-1942 .... TCLC 5
See also CA 115

Schulz, Charles M(onroe)
1922- ....CLC 12
See also CANR 6
See also CA 9-12R
See also SATA 10

Schuyler, James (Marcus)
1923- .... CLC 5, 23
See also CA 101
See also DLB 5

Schwartz, Delmore
1913-1966...............CLC 2, 4, 10
See also CAP 2
See also CA 17-18
See also obituary CA 25-28R
See also DLB 28

Schwartz, Lynne Sharon 1939-.....CLC 31
See also CA 103

Schwarz-Bart, André 1928-...... CLC 2, 4
See also CA 89-92

Schwarz-Bart, Simone 1938- ....CLC 7
See also CA 97-100

Schwob, (Mayer André) Marcel
1867-1905..................... TCLC 20
See also CA 117

Sciascia, Leonardo 1921- .... CLC 8, 9
See also CA 85-88

Scoppettone, Sandra 1936-.........CLC 26
See also CA 5-8R
See also SATA 9

Scorsese, Martin 1942-............CLC 20
See also CA 110, 114

Scotland, Jay 1932-
See Jakes, John (William)

Scott, Duncan Campbell
1862-1947................... TCLC 6
See also CA 104

Scott, F(rancis) R(eginald)
1899-1985...................CLC 22
See also CA 101
See also obituary CA 114

Scott, Paul (Mark) 1920-1978 ......CLC 9
See also CA 81-84
See also obituary CA 77-80
See also DLB 14

Scudéry, Madeleine de 1607-1701..... LC 2

Seare, Nicholas 1925-
See Trevanian
See also Whitaker, Rodney

Sebestyen, Igen 1924-
See Sebestyen, Ouida

Sebestyen, Ouida 1924-...........CLC 30
See also CA 107
See also SATA 39

Seelye, John 1931-.................CLC 7
See also CA 97-100

Seferiades, Giorgos Stylianou 1900-1971
See Seferis, George
See also CANR 5
See also CA 5-8R
See also obituary CA 33-36R

Seferis, George 1900-1971 ...... CLC 5, 11
See also Seferiades, Giorgos Stylianou

Segal, Erich (Wolf) 1937-....... CLC 3, 10
See also CA 25-28R

Seger, Bob 1945- ....CLC 35

Seger, Robert Clark 1945-
See Seger, Bob

Seghers, Anna 1900-...............CLC 7
See Radvanyi, Netty

Seidel, Frederick (Lewis) 1936-.....CLC 18
See also CANR 8
See also CA 13-16R
See also DLB-Y 84

Seifert, Jaroslav 1901- ...... CLC 34 (255)

Selby, Hubert, Jr.
1928-...................CLC 1, 2, 4, 8
See also CA 13-16R
See also DLB 2

Sender, Ramón (José)
1902-1982...................CLC 8
See also CANR 8
See also CA 5-8R
See also obituary CA 105

Serling, (Edward) Rod(man) 1924-1975
See also CA 65-68
See also obituary CA 57-60
See also DLB 26
See also AITN 1

Serpières 1907-
See Guillevic, (Eugène)

Service, Robert W(illiam)
1874-1958................... TCLC 15
See also CA 115
See also SATA 20

Seton, Cynthia Propper
1926-1982...................CLC 27
See also CANR-7
See also CA 5-8R
See also obituary CA 108

Settle, Mary Lee 1918-............CLC 19
See also CAAS 1
See also CA 89-92
See also DLB 6

Sexton, Anne (Harvey)
1928-1974....... CLC 2, 4, 6, 8, 10, 15
See also CANR 3
See also CA 1-4R
See also obituary CA 53-56
See also SATA 10
See also DLB 5

Shaara, Michael (Joseph)
1929-.........................CLC 15
See also CA 102
See also DLB-Y 83
See also AITN 1

Shacochis, Bob 1951- .... CLC 39 (198)

Shaffer, Anthony 1926-............CLC 19
See also CA 110
See also CA 116
See also DLB 13

Shaffer, Peter (Levin)
1926-...............CLC 5, 14, 18, 37
See also CA 25-28R
See also DLB 13

Shalamov, Varlam (Tikhonovich)
1907?-1982...................CLC 18
See also obituary CA 105

Shamlu, Ahmad 1925- ....CLC 10

Shange, Ntozake 1948-...... CLC 8, 25, 38
See also CA 85-88
See also DLB 38

Shapcott, Thomas W(illiam)
1935-.........................CLC 38
See also CA 69-72

Shapiro, Karl (Jay) 1913-..... CLC 4, 8, 15
See also CANR 1
See also CA 1-4R

Sharpe, Tom 1928- ....CLC 36
See also CA 114
See also DLB 14

Shaw, (George) Bernard
1856-1950................. TCLC 3, 9
See also CA 104, 109
See also DLB 10

Shaw, Irwin
1913-1984........CLC 7, 23, 34 (368)
See also CA 13-16R
See also obituary CA 112
See also DLB 6
See also DLB-Y 84
See also AITN 1

Shaw, Robert 1927-1978 ....CLC 5
See also CANR 4
See also CA 1-4R
See also obituary CA 81-84
See also DLB 13, 14
See also AITN 1

Sheed, Wilfrid (John Joseph)
1930-..................... CLC 2, 4, 10
See also CA 65-68
See also DLB 6

Sheffey, Asa 1913-1980
See Hayden, Robert (Earl)

Shepard, Jim 19??- ....CLC 36

Shepard, Lucius 19??-....... CLC 34 (108)

Shepard, Sam
1943-.......... CLC **4, 6, 17, 34** (264)
See also CA 69-72
See also DLB 7

Sherburne, Zoa (Morin) 1912- .....CLC **30**
See also CANR 3
See also CA 1-4R
See also SATA 3

Sheridan, Richard Brinsley
1751-1816................... NCLC **5**

Sherman, Martin ....CLC **19**
See also CA 116

Sherwin, Judith Johnson
1936-..................... CLC **7, 15**
See also CA 25-28R

Sherwood, Robert E(mmet)
1896-1955................. TCLC **3**
See also CA 104
See also DLB 7, 26

Shiel, M(atthew) P(hipps)
1865-1947................. TCLC **8**
See also CA 106

Shiga Naoya 1883-1971...........CLC **33**
See also CA 101
See also obituary CA 33-36R

Shimazaki, Haruki 1872-1943
See Shimazaki, Tōson
See also CA 105

Shimazaki, Tōson 1872-1943 ...... TCLC **5**
See Shimazaki, Haruki

Sholokhov, Mikhail (Aleksandrovich)
1905-1984................ CLC **7, 15**
See also CA 101
See also obituary CA 112
See also SATA 36

Shreve, Susan Richards 1939-......CLC **23**
See also CANR 5
See also CA 49-52
See also SATA 41

Shulman, Alix Kates 1932-...... CLC **2, 10**
See also CA 29-32R
See also SATA 7

Shuster, Joe 1914-
See Siegel, Jerome and Shuster, Joe

Shute (Norway), Nevil
1899-1960...................CLC **30**
See also Norway, Nevil Shute

Shuttle, Penelope (Diane) 1947-......CLC **7**
See also CA 93-96
See also DLB 14, 40

Siegel, Jerome 1914-
See Siegel, Jerome and Shuster, Joe
See also CA 116

Siegel, Jerome 1914- and
Shuster, Joe 1914- ....CLC **21**

Sienkiewicz, Henryk (Adam Aleksander Pius)
1846-1916................... TCLC **3**
See also CA 104

Sigal, Clancy 1926- ....CLC **7**
See also CA 1-4R

Silkin, Jon 1930- .... CLC **2, 6**
See also CA 5-8R
See also DLB 27

Silko, Leslie Marmon 1948-........CLC **23**
See also CA 115

Sillanpää, Franz Eemil
1888-1964....................CLC **19**
See also obituary CA 93-96

Sillitoe, Alan 1928- .... CLC **1, 3, 6, 10, 19**
See also CAAS 2
See also CANR 8
See also CA 9-12R
See also DLB 14
See also AITN 1

Silone, Ignazio 1900-1978..........CLC **4**
See also CAP 2
See also CA 25-28
See also obituary CA 81-84

Silver, Joan Micklin 1935-........CLC **20**
See also CA 114

Silverberg, Robert 1935- ....CLC **7**
See also CAAS 3
See also CANR 1
See also CA 1-4R
See also SATA 13
See also DLB 8

Silverstein, Alvin 1933-
See Silverstein, Alvin
and Silverstein, Virginia B(arbara
Opshelor)
See also CANR 2
See also CA 49-52
See also SATA 8

Silverstein, Alvin 1933- and **Silverstein,
Virginia B(arbara Opshelor)**
1937-.......................CLC **17**

Silverstein, Virginia B(arbara Opshelor)
1937-
See Silverstein, Alvin and Silverstein,
Virginia B(arbara Opshelor)
See also CANR 2
See also CA 49-52
See also SATA 8

Simak, Clifford D(onald) 1904-......CLC **1**
See also CANR 1
See also CA 1-4R
See also DLB 8

Simenon, Georges (Jacques Christian)
1903-.............. CLC **1, 2, 3, 8, 18**
See also CA 85-88

Simenon, Paul 1956?-
See The Clash

Simic, Charles 1938-......... CLC **6, 9, 22**
See also CA 29-32R

Simms, William Gilmore
1806-1870................... NCLC **3**
See also DLB 3, 30

Simon, Carly 1945-...............CLC **26**
See also CA 105

Simon, Claude (Henri Eugéne)
1913-.......... CLC **4, 9, 15, 39** (202)
See also CA 89-92

Simon, (Marvin) Neil
1927-......... CLC **6, 11, 31, 39** (216)
See also CA 21-24R
See also DLB 7
See also AITN 1

Simon, Paul 1941-................CLC **17**
See also CA 116

Simonon, Paul 1956?-
See The Clash

Simpson, Louis (Aston Marantz)
1923-.................CLC **4, 7, 9, 32**
See also CANR 1
See also CA 1-4R
See also DLB 5

Simpson, N(orman) F(rederick)
1919-.......................CLC **29**
See also CA 11-14R
See also DLB 13

Sinclair, Andrew (Annandale)
1935-..................... CLC **2, 14**
See also CANR 14
See also CA 9-12R
See also DLB 14

Sinclair, Mary Amelia St. Clair 1865?-1946
See Sinclair, May
See also CA 104

Sinclair, May 1865?-1946...... TCLC **3, 11**
See also Sinclair, Mary Amelia St. Clair
See also DLB 36

Sinclair, Upton (Beall)
1878-1968............. CLC **1, 11, 15**
See also CANR 7
See also CA 5-8R
See also obituary 25-28R
See also SATA 9
See also DLB 9

Singer, Isaac Bashevis
1904-....... CLC **1, 3, 6, 9, 11, 15, 23,**
38
See also CLR 1
See also CANR 1
See also CA 1-4R
See also SATA 3, 27
See also DLB 6, 28
See also AITN 1, 2

Singh, Khushwant 1915-...........CLC **11**
See also CANR 6
See also CA 9-12R

Sinyavsky, Andrei (Donatevich)
1925-.......................CLC **8**
See also CA 85-88

Sissman, L(ouis) E(dward)
1928-1976................ CLC **9, 18**
See also CA 21-24R
See also obituary CA 65-68
See also DLB 5

Sisson, C(harles) H(ubert) 1914-.....CLC **8**
See also CAAS 3
See also CANR 3
See also CA 1-4R
See also DLB 27

Sitwell, (Dame) Edith
1887-1964.................. CLC **2, 9**
See also CA 9-12R
See also DLB 20

Sjoewall, Maj 1935-
See Wahlöö, Per
See also CA 65-68

Sjöwall, Maj 1935-
See Wahlöö, Per

Skelton, Robin 1925-..............CLC **13**
See also CA 5-8R
See also AITN 2
See also DLB 27

Skolimowski, Jerzy 1938-..........CLC **20**

Skolimowski, Yurek 1938-
See Skolimowski, Jerzy

Skrine, Mary Nesta 1904-
See Keane, Molly

Škvorecký, Josef (Vaclav)
1924-..............CLC 15, 39 (220)
See also CAAS 1
See also CANR 10
See also CA 61-64

Slade, Bernard 1930-.............CLC 11
See also Newbound, Bernard Slade

Slaughter, Frank G(ill) 1908-......CLC 29
See also CANR 5
See also CA 5-8R
See also AITN 2

Slavitt, David (R.) 1935-........CLC 5, 14
See also CAAS 3
See also CA 21-24R
See also DLB 5, 6

Slesinger, Tess 1905-1945........TCLC 10
See also CA 107

Slessor, Kenneth 1901-1971........CLC 14
See also CA 102
See also obituary CA 89-92

Smart, Christopher 1722-1771 ....LC 3

Smith, A(rthur) J(ames) M(arshall)
1902-1980.....................CLC 15
See also CANR 4
See also CA 1-4R
See also obituary CA 102

Smith, Betty (Wehner)
1896-1972.....................CLC 19
See also CA 5-8R
See also obituary CA 33-36R
See also SATA 6
See also DLB-Y 82

Smith, Cecil Lewis Troughton 1899-1966
See Forester, C(ecil) S(cott)

Smith, Dave 1942-.................CLC 22
See also Smith, David (Jeddie)
See also DLB 5

Smith, David (Jeddie) 1942-
See Smith, Dave
See also CANR 1
See also CA 49-52

Smith, Florence Margaret 1902-1971
See Smith, Stevie
See also CAP 2
See also CA 17-18
See also obituary CA 29-32R

Smith, Lee 1944-.................CLC 25
See also CA 114
See also DLB-Y 83

Smith, Martin Cruz 1942-.........CLC 25
See also CANR 6
See also CA 85-88

Smith, Martin William 1942-
See Smith, Martin Cruz

Smith, Mary-Ann Tirone
1944-..................CLC 39 (97)

Smith, Patti 1946-.................CLC 12
See also CA 93-96

Smith, Sara Mahala Redway 1900-1972
See Benson, Sally

Smith, Stevie 1902-1971......CLC 3, 8, 25
See also Smith, Florence Margaret
See also DLB 20

Smith, Wilbur (Addison) 1933-.....CLC 33
See also CANR 7
See also CA 13-16R

Smith, William Jay 1918-..........CLC 6
See also CA 5-8R
See also SATA 2
See also DLB 5

Smollett, Tobias (George)
1721-1771....................LC 2
See also DLB 39

Snodgrass, W(illiam) D(e Witt)
1926-..............CLC 2, 6, 10, 18
See also CANR 6
See also CA 1-4R
See also DLB 5

Snow, C(harles) P(ercy)
1905-1980.......CLC 1, 4, 6, 9, 13, 19
See also CA 5-8R
See also obituary CA 101
See also DLB 15

Snyder, Gary 1930-.....CLC 1, 2, 5, 9, 32
See also CA 17-20R
See also DLB 5, 16

Snyder, Zilpha Keatley 1927-......CLC 17
See also CA 9-12R
See also SATA 1, 28

Sokolov, Raymond 1941-...........CLC 7
See also CA 85-88

Sologub, Fyodor 1863-1927.......TCLC 9
See also Teternikov, Fyodor Kuzmich

Solwoska, Mara 1929-
See French, Marilyn

Solzhenitsyn, Aleksandr I(sayevich)
1918-.....CLC 1, 2, 4, 7, 9, 10, 18, 26,
34 (480)
See also CA 69-72
See also AITN 1

Sommer, Scott 1951-..............CLC 25
See also CA 106

Sondheim, Stephen (Joshua)
1930-..............CLC 33, 39 (172)
See also CA 103

Sontag, Susan
1933-...........CLC 1, 2, 10, 13, 31
See also CA 17-20R
See also DLB 2

Sorrentino, Gilbert
1929-...............CLC 3, 7, 14, 22
See also CANR 14
See also CA 77-80
See also DLB 5
See also DLB-Y 80

Soto, Gary 1952-.................CLC 32

Souster, (Holmes) Raymond
1921-...................CLC 5, 14
See also CANR 13
See also CA 13-16R

Southern, Terry 1926- ....CLC 7
See also CANR 1
See also CA 1-4R
See also DLB 2

Southey, Robert 1774-1843 ....NCLC 8

Soyinka, Akin-wande Oluwole 1934-
See Soyinka, Wole

Soyinka, Wole 1934-......CLC 3, 5, 14, 36
See also CA 13-16R

Spacks, Barry 1931-..............CLC 14
See also CA 29-32R

Spark, Muriel (Sarah)
1918-..........CLC 2, 3, 5, 8, 13, 18
See also CANR 12
See also CA 5-8R
See also DLB 15

Spencer, Elizabeth 1921-..........CLC 22
See also CA 13-16R
See also SATA 14
See also DLB 6

Spencer, Scott 1945-.............CLC 30
See also CA 113

Spender, Stephen (Harold)
1909-.............CLC 1, 2, 5, 10
See also CA 9-12R
See also DLB 20

Spicer, Jack 1925-1965........CLC 8, 18
See also CA 85-88
See also DLB 5, 16

Spielberg, Peter 1929-.............CLC 6
See also CANR 4
See also CA 5-8R
See also DLB-Y 81

Spielberg, Steven 1947-...........CLC 20
See also CA 77-80
See also SATA 32

Spillane, Frank Morrison 1918-
See Spillane, Mickey
See also CA 25-28R

Spillane, Mickey 1918-.........CLC 3, 13
See also Spillane, Frank Morrison

Spitteler, Carl (Friedrich Georg)
1845-1924.................TCLC 12
See also CA 109

Spivack, Kathleen (Romola Drucker)
1938-.......................CLC 6
See also CA 49-52

Spoto, Donald 1941-........CLC 39 (444)
See also CANR 11
See also CA 65-68

Springsteen, Bruce 1949-..........CLC 17
See also CA 111

Spurling, Hilary 1940- ......CLC 34 (494)
See also CA 104

Staël-Holstein, Anne Louise Germaine
Necker, Baronne de
1766-1817............... NCLC 3

Stafford, Jean 1915-1979.....CLC 4, 7, 19
See also CANR 3
See also CA 1-4R
See also obituary CA 85-88
See also obituary SATA 22
See also DLB 2

Stafford, William (Edgar)
1914-..................CLC 4, 7, 29
See also CAAS 3
See also CANR 5
See also CA 5-8R
See also DLB 5

Stanton, Maura 1946-.............CLC 9
See also CANR 15
See also CA 89-92

Stark, Richard 1933-
See Westlake, Donald E(dwin)

Stead, Christina (Ellen)
1902-1983.............CLC 2, 5, 8, 32
See also CA 13-16R
See also obituary CA 109

Steffens, (Joseph) Lincoln
1866-1936..................TCLC 20
See also CA 117
See also SAAS 1

Stegner, Wallace (Earle) 1909- ......CLC 9
See also CANR 1
See also CA 1-4R
See also DLB 9
See also AITN 1

Stein, Gertrude 1874-1946......TCLC 1, 6
See also CA 104
See also DLB 4

Steinbeck, John (Ernst)
1902-1968........CLC 1, 5, 9, 13, 21,
34 (404)
See also CANR 1
See also CA 1-4R
See also obituary CA 25-28R
See also SATA 9
See also DLB 7, 9
See also DLB-DS 2

Steiner, George 1929-..............CLC 24
See also CA 73-76

Steiner, Rudolf(us Josephus Laurentius)
1861-1925.................TCLC 13
See also CA 107

Stephens, James 1882?-1950 ......TCLC 4
See also CA 104
See also DLB 19

Steptoe, Lydia 1892-1982
See Barnes, Djuna

Sterling, George 1869-1926 ......TCLC 20
See also CA 117

Stern, Richard G(ustave)
1928-................CLC 4, 39 (234)
See also CANR 1
See also CA 1-4R

Sternberg, Jonas 1894-1969
See Sternberg, Josef von

Sternberg, Josef von
1894-1969...................CLC 20
See also CA 81-84

Sterne, Laurence 1713-1768 ....LC 2
See also DLB 39

Sternheim, (William Adolf) Carl
1878-1942..................TCLC 8
See also CA 105

Stevens, Mark 19??- ....CLC 34 (111)

Stevens, Wallace
1879-1955...............TCLC 3, 12
See also CA 104

Stevenson, Anne (Katharine)
1933-.....................CLC 7, 33
See also Elvin, Anne Katharine Stevenson
See also CANR 9
See also DLB 40

Stevenson, Robert Louis
1850-1894..................NCLC 5
See also CLR 10
See also YABC 2
See also DLB 18

Stewart, J(ohn) I(nnes) M(ackintosh)
1906-..................CLC 7, 14, 32
See also CAAS 3
See also CA 85-88

Stewart, Mary (Florence Elinor)
1916-...................CLC 7, 35
See also CANR 1
See also CA 1-4R
See also SATA 12

Stewart, Will 1908-
See Williamson, Jack

Sting 1951-
See The Police

Stitt, Milan 1941-..................CLC 29
See also CA 69-72

Stoker, Bram (Abraham)
1847-1912.................TCLC 8
See also CA 105
See also SATA 29
See also DLB 36

Stolz, Mary (Slattery) 1920-.......CLC 12
See also CANR 13
See also CA 5-8R
See also SATA 10
See also AITN 1

Stone, Irving 1903-................CLC 7
See also CAAS 3
See also CANR 1
See also CA 1-4R
See also SATA 3
See also AITN 1

Stone, Robert (Anthony)
1937?-...................CLC 5, 23
See also CA 85-88

Stoppard, Tom
1937-........CLC 1, 3, 4, 5, 8, 15, 29,
34 (272)
See also CA 81-84
See also DLB 13
See also DLB-Y 85

Storey, David (Malcolm)
1933-..................CLC 2, 4, 5, 8
See also CA 81-84
See also DLB 13, 14

Storm, Hyemeyohsts 1935-..........CLC 3
See also CA 81-84

Storm, (Hans) Theodor (Woldsen)
1817-1888..................NCLC 1

Storni, Alfonsina 1892-1938.......TCLC 5
See also CA 104

Stout, Rex (Todhunter)
1886-1975...................CLC 3
See also CA 61-64
See also AITN 2

Stow, (Julian) Randolph 1935- .....CLC 23
See also CA 13-16R

Stowe, Harriet (Elizabeth) Beecher
1811-1896..................NCLC 3
See also YABC 1
See also DLB 1, 12, 42

Strachey, (Giles) Lytton
1880-1932.................TCLC 12
See also CA 110

Strand, Mark 1934-...........CLC 6, 18
See also CA 21-24R
See also DLB 5
See also SATA 41

Straub, Peter (Francis) 1943- ......CLC 28
See also CA 85-88
See also DLB-Y 84

Strauss, Botho 1944-..............CLC 22

Straussler, Tomas 1937-
See Stoppard, Tom

Streatfeild, Noel 1897- ....CLC 21
See also CA 81-84
See also SATA 20

Stribling, T(homas) S(igismund)
1881-1965.................CLC 23
See also obituary CA 107
See also DLB 9

Strindberg, (Johan) August
1849-1912.................TCLC 1, 8
See also CA 104

Strugatskii, Arkadii (Natanovich) 1925-
See Strugatskii, Arkadii (Natanovich) and
Strugatskii, Boris (Natanovich)
See also CA 106

Strugatskii, Arkadii (Natanovich) 1925-
and **Strugatskii, Boris**
(Natanovich) 1933-...........CLC 27

Strugatskii, Boris (Natanovich) 1933-
See Strugatskii, Arkadii (Natanovich) and
Strugatskii, Boris (Natanovich)
See also CA 106

Strugatskii, Boris (Natanovich) 1933- and
Strugatskii, Arkadii (Natanovich) 1925-
See Strugatskii, Arkadii (Natanovich) and
Strugatskii, Boris (Natanovich)

Strummer, Joe 1953?-
See The Clash

Stuart, (Hilton) Jesse
1906-1984...........CLC 1, 8, 11, 14,
34 (372)
See also CA 5-8R
See also obituary CA 112
See also SATA 2
See also obituary SATA 36
See also DLB 9
See also DLB-Y 84

Sturgeon, Theodore (Hamilton)
1918-1985..........CLC 22, 39 (360)
See also CA 81-84
See also obituary CA 116
See also DLB 8
See also DLB-Y 85

Styron, William
1925-............CLC 1, 3, 5, 11, 15
See also CANR 6
See also CA 5-8R
See also DLB 2
See also DLB-Y 80

Sudermann, Hermann
1857-1928.................TCLC 15
See also CA 107

Sue, Eugène 1804-1857...........NCLC 1

Sukenick, Ronald 1932- ....CLC 3, 4, 6
See also CA 25-28R
See also DLB-Y 81

Suknaski, Andrew 1942-..........CLC 19
See also CA 101

Summers, Andrew James 1942-
See The Police

Summers, Andy 1942-
See The Police

Summers, Hollis (Spurgeon, Jr.)
1916-......................CLC 10
See also CANR 3
See also CA 5-8R
See also DLB 6

Summers, (Alphonsus Joseph-Mary Augustus)
Montague 1880-1948 ....TCLC 16

Sumner, Gordon Matthew 1951-
See The Police

Susann, Jacqueline 1921-1974.......CLC 3
See also CA 65-68
See also obituary CA 53-56
See also AITN 1

Sutcliff, Rosemary 1920- ....CLC 26
See also CLR 1
See also CA 5-8R
See also SATA 6, 44

Sutro, Alfred 1863-1933.......... TCLC 6
See also CA 105
See also DLB 10

Sutton, Henry 1935-
See Slavitt, David (R.)

Svevo, Italo 1861-1928 .... TCLC 2
See also Schmitz, Ettore

Swados, Elizabeth 1951-...........CLC 12
See also CA 97-100

Swados, Harvey 1920-1972 ....CLC 5
See also CANR 6
See also CA 5-8R
See also obituary CA 37-40R
See also DLB 2

Swarthout, Glendon (Fred)
1918-...........................CLC 35
See also CANR 1
See also CA 1-4R
See also SATA 26

Swenson, May 1919-........... CLC 4, 14
See also CA 5-8R
See also SATA 15
See also DLB 5

Swift, Jonathan 1667-1745.......... LC 1
See also SATA 19
See also DLB 39

Swinburne, Algernon Charles
1837-1909..................... TCLC 8
See also CA 105
See also DLB 35

Swinfen, Ann 19??- .... CLC 34 (576)

Swinnerton, Frank (Arthur)
1884-1982.....................CLC 31
See also obituary CA 108
See also DLB 34

Symons, Arthur (William)
1865-1945................... TCLC 11
See also CA 107
See also DLB 19

Symons, Julian (Gustave)
1912-...................... CLC 2, 14, 32
See also CAAS 3
See also CANR 3
See also CA 49-52

Synge, (Edmund) John Millington
1871-1909................... TCLC 6
See also CA 104
See also DLB 10, 19

Syruc, J. 1911-
See Miłosz, Czesław

Tabori, George 1914- ....CLC 19
See also CANR 4
See also CA 49-52

Tagore, (Sir) Rabindranath
1861-1941................... TCLC 3
See also Thakura, Ravindranatha

Talese, Gaetano 1932-
See Talese, Gay

Talese, Gay 1932- ....CLC 37
See also CANR 9
See also CA 1-4R
See also AITN 1

Tamayo y Baus, Manuel
1829-1898................... NCLC 1

Tanizaki, Jun'ichirō
1886-1965.............CLC 8, 14, 28
See also CA 93-96
See also obituary CA 25-28R

Tarkington, (Newton) Booth
1869-1946................... TCLC 9
See also CA 110
See also SATA 17
See also DLB 9

Tate, (John Orley) Allen
1899-1979...... CLC 2, 4, 6, 9, 11, 14, 24
See also CA 5-8R
See also obituary CA 85-88
See also DLB 4, 45

Tate, James 1943-........... CLC 2, 6, 25
See also CA 21-24R
See also DLB 5

Tavel, Ronald 1940- ....CLC 6
See also CA 21-24R

Taylor, C(ecil) P(hillip)
1929-1981...................CLC 27
See also CA 25-28R
See also obituary CA 105

Taylor, Eleanor Ross 1920-.........CLC 5
See also CA 81-84

Taylor, Elizabeth
1912-1975.............. CLC 2, 4, 29
See also CANR 9
See also CA 13-16R
See also SATA 13

Taylor, Kamala (Purnaiya) 1924-
See Markandaya, Kamala
See also CA 77-80

Taylor, Mildred D(elois) 19??-......CLC 21
See also CA 85-88
See also SATA 15

Taylor, Peter (Hillsman)
1917-...............CLC 1, 4, 18, 37
See also CANR 9
See also CA 13-16R
See also DLB-Y 81

Taylor, Robert Lewis 1912-.......CLC 14
See also CANR 3
See also CA 1-4R
See also SATA 10

Teasdale, Sara 1884-1933........ TCLC 4
See also CA 104
See also DLB 45
See also SATA 32

Tegnér, Esaias 1782-1846........ NCLC 2

Teilhard de Chardin, (Marie Joseph) Pierre
1881-1955................... TCLC 9
See also CA 105

Tennant, Emma 1937- ....CLC 13
See also CANR 10
See also CA 65-68
See also DLB 14

Teran, Lisa St. Aubin de 19??-.....CLC 36

Terkel, Louis 1912-
See Terkel, Studs
See also CA 57-60

Terkel, Studs 1912-...............CLC 38
See also Terkel, Louis
See also AITN 1

Terry, Megan 1932- ....CLC 19
See also CA 77-80
See also DLB 7

Tertz, Abram 1925-
See Sinyavsky, Andrei (Donatevich)

Teternikov, Fyodor Kuzmich 1863-1927
See Sologub, Fyodor
See also CA 104

Tey, Josephine 1897-1952 .... TCLC 14
See also Mackintosh, Elizabeth

Thackeray, William Makepeace
1811-1863................... NCLC 5
See also SATA 23
See also DLB 21

Thakura, Ravindranatha 1861-1941
See Tagore, (Sir) Rabindranath
See also CA 104

Thelwell, Michael (Miles)
1939-.........................CLC 22
See also CA 101

Theroux, Alexander (Louis)
1939-.................... CLC 2, 25
See also CA 85-88

Theroux, Paul
1941-............ CLC 5, 8, 11, 15, 28
See also CA 33-36R
See also DLB 2
See also SATA 44

Thibault, Jacques Anatole Francois
1844-1924
See France, Anatole
See also CA 106

Thiele, Colin (Milton) 1920-........CLC 17
See also CANR 12
See also CA 29-32R
See also SATA 14

Thomas, Audrey (Grace)
1935-................... CLC 7, 13, 37
See also CA 21-24R
See also AITN 2

Thomas, D(onald) M(ichael)
1935-................ CLC 13, 22, 31
See also CANR 17
See also CA 61-64
See also DLB 40

Thomas, Dylan (Marlais)
1914-1953................ TCLC 1, 8
See also CA 104
See also DLB 13, 20

Thomas, Edward (Philip)
1878-1917................ TCLC 10
See also CA 106
See also DLB 19

Author Index

Thomas, John Peter 1928-
  See Thomas, Piri

Thomas, Joyce Carol 1938- ....**CLC 35**
  See also CA 113, 116
  See also SATA 40
  See also DLB 33

Thomas, Lewis 1913- ....**CLC 35**
  See also CA 85-88

Thomas, Piri 1928- ....**CLC 17**
  See also CA 73-76

Thomas, R(onald) S(tuart)
  1913- .... **CLC 6, 13**
  See also CA 89-92
  See also DLB 27

Thomas, Ross (Elmore)
  1926- .... **CLC 39** (246)
  See also CA 33-36R

Thompson, Francis (Joseph)
  1859-1907................... **TCLC 4**
  See also CA 104
  See also DLB 19

Thompson, Hunter S(tockton)
  1939-.................... **CLC 9, 17**
  See also CA 17-20R

Thompson, Judith 1954-..... **CLC 39** (250)

Thoreau, Henry David
  1817-1862.................. **NCLC 7**
  See also DLB 1

Thurber, James (Grover)
  1894-1961.............. **CLC 5, 11, 25**
  See also CANR 17
  See also CA 73-76
  See also SATA 13
  See also DLB 4, 11, 22

Thurman, Wallace 1902-1934..... **TCLC 6**
  See also CA 104

Tieck, (Johann) Ludwig
  1773-1853................... **NCLC 5**

Tillinghast, Richard 1940-........**CLC 29**
  See also CA 29-32R

Tindall, Gillian 1938- ....**CLC 7**
  See also CANR 11
  See also CA 21-24R

Tocqueville, Alexis de
  1805-1859................... **NCLC 7**

Tolkien, J(ohn) R(onald) R(euel)
  1892-1973....... **CLC 1, 2, 3, 8, 12, 38**
  See also CAP 2
  See also CA 17-18
  See also obituary CA 45-48
  See also SATA 2, 32
  See also obituary SATA 24
  See also DLB 15
  See also AITN 1

Toller, Ernst 1893-1939........ **TCLC 10**
  See also CA 107

Tolson, Melvin B(eaunorus)
  1900?-1966...................**CLC 36**
  See also Obituary CA 89-92

Tolstoy, (Count) Alexey Nikolayevich
  1883-1945.................. **TCLC 18**
  See also CA 107

Tolstoy, (Count) Leo (Lev Nikolaevich)
  1828-1910............**TCLC 4, 11, 17**
  See also CA 104
  See also SATA 26

Tomlin, Lily 1939-................**CLC 17**

Tomlin, Mary Jean 1939-
  See Tomlin, Lily

Tomlinson, (Alfred) Charles
  1927-....................**CLC 2, 4, 6, 13**
  See also CA 5-8R
  See also DLB 40

Toole, John Kennedy
  1937-1969....................**CLC 19**
  See also CA 104
  See also DLB-Y 81

Toomer, Jean
  1894-1967............**CLC 1, 4, 13, 22**
  See also CA 85-88
  See also DLB 45

Torrey, E. Fuller 19??-...... **CLC 34** (503)

Tournier, Michel 1924-...... **CLC 6, 23, 36**
  See also CANR 3
  See also CA 49-52
  See also SATA 23

Townshend, Peter (Dennis Blandford)
  1945-......................**CLC 17**
  See also CA 107

Trakl, Georg 1887-1914......... **TCLC 5**
  See also CA 104

Traven, B. 1890-1969......... **CLC 8, 11**
  See also CAP 2
  See also CA 19-20
  See also obituary CA 25-28R
  See also DLB 9

Tremblay, Michel 1942-...........**CLC 29**

Trevanian 1925-........▸........**CLC 29**
  See also Whitaker, Rodney
  See also CA 108

Trevor, William
  1928-................**CLC 7, 9, 14, 25**
  See also Cox, William Trevor
  See also DLB 14

Trilling, Lionel
  1905-1975.............. **CLC 9, 11, 24**
  See also CANR 10
  See also CA 9-12R
  See also obituary CA 61-64
  See also DLB 28

Trogdon, William 1939-
  See Heat Moon, William Least
  See also CA 115

Trollope, Anthony 1815-1882..... **NCLC 6**
  See also SATA 22
  See also DLB 21

Troyat, Henri 1911- ....**CLC 23**
  See also CANR 2
  See also CA 45-48

Trudeau, G(arretson) B(eekman) 1948-
  See Trudeau, Garry
  See also CA 81-84
  See also SATA 35

Trudeau, Garry 1948-.............**CLC 12**
  See also Trudeau, G(arretson) B(eekman)
  See also AITN 2

Truffaut, François 1932-1984......**CLC 20**
  See also CA 81-84
  See also obituary CA 113

Trumbo, Dalton 1905-1976 ....**CLC 19**
  See also CANR 10
  See also CA 21-24R
  See also obituary CA 69-72
  See also DLB 26

Tryon, Thomas 1926- .... **CLC 3, 11**
  See also CA 29-32R
  See also AITN 1

Ts'ao Hsüeh-ch'in 1715?-1763....... **LC 1**

Tsushima Shūji 1909-1948
  See Dazai Osamu
  See also CA 107

Tsvetaeva (Efron), Marina (Ivanovna)
  1892-1941................. **TCLC 7**
  See also CA 104

Tunis, John R(oberts)
  1889-1975...................**CLC 12**
  See also CA 61-64
  See also SATA 30, 37
  See also DLB 22

Tuohy, Frank 1925- ....**CLC 37**
  See also DLB 14

Tuohy, John Francis 1925-
  See Tuohy, Frank
  See also CANR 3
  See also CA 5-8R

Turco, Lewis (Putnam) 1934- ......**CLC 11**
  See also CA 13-16R
  See also DLB-Y 84

Tutuola, Amos 1920-........ **CLC 5, 14, 29**
  See also CA 9-12R

Twain, Mark
  1835-1910............**TCLC 6, 12, 19**
  See also Clemens, Samuel Langhorne
  See also DLB 11

Tyler, Anne 1941- ....**CLC 7, 11, 18, 28**
  See also CANR 11
  See also CA 9-12R
  See also SATA 7
  See also DLB 6
  See also DLB-Y 82

Tyler, Royall 1757-1826.......... **NCLC 3**
  See also DLB 37

Tynan (Hinkson), Katharine
  1861-1931................. **TCLC 3**
  See also CA 104

Unamuno (y Jugo), Miguel de
  1864-1936................. **TCLC 2, 9**
  See also CA 104

Underwood, Miles 1909-1981
  See Glassco, John

Undset, Sigrid 1882-1949......... **TCLC 3**
  See also CA 104

Ungaretti, Giuseppe
  1888-1970............. **CLC 7, 11, 15**
  See also CAP 2
  See also CA 19-20
  See also obituary CA 25-28R

Unger, Douglas 1952-....... **CLC 34** (114)

Unger, Eva 1932-
  See Figes, Eva

Updike, John (Hoyer)
  1932-......**CLC 1, 2, 3, 5, 7, 9, 13, 15,**
               23, 34 (283)
  See also CANR 4
  See also CA 1-4R
  See also DLB 2, 5
  See also DLB-Y 80, 82
  See also DLB-DS 3

Uris, Leon (Marcus) 1924- . . . . . . **CLC 7, 32**
   See also CANR 1
   See also CA 1-4R
   See also AITN 1, 2

Ustinov, Peter (Alexander)
   1921- . . . .**CLC 1**
   See also CA 13-16R
   See also DLB 13
   See also AITN 1

Vaculík, Ludvík 1926- . . . .**CLC 7**
   See also CA 53-56

Valenzuela, Luisa 1938- . . . .**CLC 31**
   See also CA 101

Valera (y Acalá-Galiano), Juan
   1824-1905. . . . . **TCLC 10**
   See also CA 106

Valéry, Paul (Ambroise Toussaint Jules)
   1871-1945. . . . . **TCLC 4, 15**
   See also CA 104

Valle-Inclán (y Montenegro), Ramón (María)
   del 1866-1936 . . . . **TCLC 5**
   See also CA 106

Vallejo, César (Abraham)
   1892-1938 . . . . **TCLC 3**
   See also CA 105

Van Ash, Cay 1918- . . . . **CLC 34** (118)

Vance, Jack 1916?- . . . .**CLC 35**
   See also DLB 8

Vance, John Holbrook 1916?-
   See Vance, Jack
   See also CANR 17
   See also CA 29-32R

Van Den Bogarde, Derek (Jules Gaspard
   Ulric) Niven 1921-
   See Bogarde, Dirk
   See also CA 77-80

Van der Post, Laurens (Jan)
   1906- . . . .**CLC 5**
   See also CA 5-8R

Van Doren, Carl (Clinton)
   1885-1950. . . . . **TCLC 18**
   See also CA 111

Van Doren, Mark
   1894-1972. . . . . **CLC 6, 10**
   See also CANR 3
   See also CA 1-4R
   See also obituary CA 37-40R
   See also DLB 45

Van Druten, John (William)
   1901-1957. . . . . **TCLC 2**
   See also CA 104
   See also DLB 10

Van Duyn, Mona 1921- . . . . **CLC 3, 7**
   See also CANR 7
   See also CA 9-12R
   See also DLB 5

Van Itallie, Jean-Claude 1936- . . . . . .**CLC 3**
   See also CAAS 2
   See also CANR 1
   See also CA 45-48
   See also DLB 7

Van Peebles, Melvin 1932- . . . . . . **CLC 2, 20**
   See also CA 85-88

Van Vechten, Carl 1880-1964 . . . . . .**CLC 33**
   See also obituary CA 89-92
   See also DLB 4, 9

Van Vogt, A(lfred) E(lton)
   1912- . . . .**CLC 1**
   See also CA 21-24R
   See also SATA 14
   See also DLB 8

Varda, Agnès 1928- . . . .**CLC 16**
   See also CA 116

Vargas Llosa, (Jorge) Mario (Pedro)
   1936- . . . . **CLC 3, 6, 9, 10, 15, 31**
   See also CA 73-76

Vassilikos, Vassilis 1933- . . . . **CLC 4, 8**
   See also CA 81-84

Verga, Giovanni 1840-1922 . . . . **TCLC 3**
   See also CA 104

Verhaeren, Émile (Adolphe Gustave)
   1855-1916. . . . . **TCLC 12**
   See also CA 109

Verlaine, Paul (Marie)
   1844-1896. . . . . **NCLC 2**

Verne, Jules (Gabriel)
   1828-1905. . . . . **TCLC 6**
   See also CA 110
   See also SATA 21

Very, Jones 1813-1880 . . . . **NCLC 9**
   See also DLB 1

Vian, Boris 1920-1959 . . . . **TCLC 9**
   See also CA 106

Viaud, (Louis Marie) Julien 1850-1923
   See Loti, Pierre
   See also CA 107

Vicker, Angus 1916-
   See Felsen, Henry Gregor

Vidal, Eugene Luther, Jr. 1925-
   See Vidal, Gore

Vidal, Gore
   1925- . . . .**CLC 2, 4, 6, 8, 10, 22, 33**
   See also CANR 13
   See also CA 5-8R
   See also DLB 6
   See also AITN 1

Viereck, Peter (Robert Edwin)
   1916- . . . .**CLC 4**
   See also CANR 1
   See also CA 1-4R
   See also DLB 5

Vigny, Alfred (Victor) de
   1797-1863. . . . . **NCLC 7**

Villiers de l'Isle Adam, Jean Marie Mathias
   Philippe Auguste, Comte de,
   1838-1889. . . . . **NCLC 3**

Vinge, Joan (Carol) D(ennison)
   1948- . . . .**CLC 30**
   See also CA 93-96
   See also SATA 36

Visconti, Luchino 1906-1976 . . . .**CLC 16**
   See also CA 81-84
   See also obituary CA 65-68

Vittorini, Elio 1908-1966 . . . . . **CLC 6, 9, 14**
   See also obituary CA 25-28R

Vliet, R(ussell) G. 1929- . . . .**CLC 22**
   See also CA 37-40R

Voigt, Cynthia 1942- . . . .**CLC 30**
   See also CA 106
   See also SATA 33

Voinovich, Vladimir (Nikolaevich)
   1932- . . . .**CLC 10**
   See also CA 81-84

Von Daeniken, Erich 1935-
   See Von Däniken, Erich
   See also CANR 17
   See also CA 37-40R
   See also AITN 1

Von Däniken, Erich 1935- . . . .**CLC 30**
   See also Von Daeniken, Erich

Vonnegut, Kurt, Jr.
   1922- . . . **CLC 1, 2, 3, 4, 5, 8, 12, 22**
   See also CANR 1
   See also CA 1-4R
   See also DLB 2, 8
   See also DLB-Y 80
   See also DLB-DS 3
   See also AITN 1

Vorster, Gordon 1924- . . . . . . **CLC 34** (121)

Voznesensky, Andrei 1933- . . . . . **CLC 1, 15**
   See also CA 89-92

Waddington, Miriam 1917- . . . .**CLC 28**
   See also CANR 12
   See also CA 21-24R

Wagman, Fredrica 1937- . . . .**CLC 7**
   See also CA 97-100

Wagner, Richard 1813-1883 . . . . . . **NCLC 9**

Wagoner, David (Russell)
   1926- . . . .**CLC 3, 5, 15**
   See also CAAS 3
   See also CANR 2
   See also CA 1-4R
   See also SATA 14
   See also DLB 5

Wahlöö, Per 1926-1975 . . . .**CLC 7**
   See also CA 61-64

Wahlöö, Peter 1926-1975
   See Wahlöö, Per

Wain, John (Barrington)
   1925- . . . .**CLC 2, 11, 15**
   See also CA 5-8R
   See also DLB 15, 27

Wajda, Andrzej 1926- . . . .**CLC 16**
   See also CA 102

Wakefield, Dan 1932- . . . .**CLC 7**
   See also CA 21-24R

Wakoski, Diane
   1937- . . . . **CLC 2, 4, 7, 9, 11**
   See also CAAS 1
   See also CANR 9
   See also CA 13-16R
   See also DLB 5

Walcott, Derek (Alton)
   1930- . . . . **CLC 2, 4, 9, 14, 25**
   See also CA 89-92
   See also DLB-Y 81

Waldman, Anne 1945- . . . .**CLC 7**
   See also CA 37-40R
   See also DLB 16

Waldo, Edward Hamilton 1918-
   See Sturgeon, Theodore (Hamilton)

Walker, Alice
   1944- . . . . **CLC 5, 6, 9, 19, 27**
   See also CANR 9
   See also CA 37-40R
   See also SATA 31
   See also DLB 6, 33

Author Index

Walker, David Harry 1911-........CLC 14
See also CANR 1
See also CA 1-4R
See also SATA 8

Walker, Edward Joseph 1934-
See Walker, Ted
See also CA 21-24R

Walker, Joseph A. 1935-.........CLC 19
See also CA 89-92
See also DLB 38

Walker, Margaret (Abigail)
1915-.....................CLC 1, 6
See also CA 73-76

Walker, Ted 1934-...............CLC 13
See also Walker, Edward Joseph
See also DLB 40

Wallace, Irving 1916-.........CLC 7, 13
See also CAAS 1
See also CANR 1
See also CA 1-4R
See also AITN 1

Wallant, Edward Lewis
1926-1962.................CLC 5, 10
See also CA 1-4R
See also DLB 2, 28

Walpole, Horace 1717-1797.........LC 2
See also DLB 39

Walpole, (Sir) Hugh (Seymour)
1884-1941...................TCLC 5
See also CA 104
See also DLB 34

Walser, Martin 1927-............CLC 27
See also CANR 8
See also CA 57-60

Walser, Robert 1878-1956.......TCLC 18

Walsh, Gillian Paton 1939-
See Walsh, Jill Paton
See also CA 37-40R
See also SATA 4

Walsh, Jill Paton 1939-...........CLC 35
See also CLR 2

Wambaugh, Joseph (Aloysius, Jr.)
1937-.....................CLC 3, 18
See also CA 33-36R
See also DLB 6
See also DLB-Y 83
See also AITN 1

Ward, Douglas Turner 1930-.......CLC 19
See also CA 81-84
See also DLB 7, 38

Warhol, Andy 1928-..............CLC 20
See also CA 89-92

Warner, Francis (Robert le Plastrier)
1937-.......................CLC 14
See also CANR 11
See also CA 53-56

Warner, Sylvia Townsend
1893-1978.................CLC 7, 19
See also CANR 16
See also CA 61-64
See also obituary CA 77-80
See also DLB 34

Warren, Robert Penn
1905-.......CLC 1, 4, 6, 8, 10, 13, 18,
                                 39 (254)
See also CANR 10
See also CA 13-16R
See also DLB 2
See also DLB-Y 80
See also AITN 1

Washington, Booker T(aliaferro)
1856-1915.........TCLC 10, CLC 34
See also CA 114
See also SATA 28

Wassermann, Jakob
1873-1934..................TCLC 6
See also CA 104

Wasserstein, Wendy 1950-.........CLC 32

Waters, Roger 1944-
See Pink Floyd

Wa Thiong'o, Ngugi
1938-................CLC 3, 7, 13, 36
See also Ngugi, James (Thiong'o)
See also Ngugi wa Thiong'o

Waugh, Auberon (Alexander)
1939-.......................CLC 7
See also CANR 6
See also CA 45-48
See also DLB 14

Waugh, Evelyn (Arthur St. John)
1903-1966......CLC 1, 3, 8, 13, 19, 27
See also CA 85-88
See also obituary CA 25-28R
See also DLB 15

Waugh, Harriet 1944-.............CLC 6
See also CA 85-88

Webb, Charles (Richard) 1939-......CLC 7
See also CA 25-28R

Webb, James H(enry), Jr.
1946-.......................CLC 22
See also CA 81-84

Webb, Phyllis 1927-..............CLC 18
See also CA 104

Webber, Andrew Lloyd 1948-
See Rice, Tim and Webber, Andrew Lloyd

Weber, Lenora Mattingly
1895-1971...................CLC 12
See also CAP 1
See also CA 19-20
See also obituary CA 29-32R
See also SATA 2
See also obituary SATA 26

Wedekind, (Benjamin) Frank(lin)
1864-1918...................TCLC 7
See also CA 104

Weidman, Jerome 1913-............CLC 7
See also CANR 1
See also CA 1-4R
See also DLB 28
See also AITN 2

Weinstein, Nathan Wallenstein 1903?-1940
See West, Nathanael
See also CA 104

Weir, Peter 1944- ....CLC 20
See also CA 113

Weiss, Peter (Ulrich)
1916-1982.................CLC 3, 15
See also CANR 3
See also CA 45-48
See also obituary CA 106

Weiss, Theodore (Russell)
1916-.....................CLC 3, 8, 14
See also CAAS 2
See also CA 9-12R
See also DLB 5

Welch, James 1940-............ CLC 6, 14
See also CA 85-88

Weldon, Fay
1933-............ CLC 6, 9, 11, 19, 36
See also CANR 16
See also CA 21-24R
See also DLB 14

Wellek, René 1903-...............CLC 28
See also CANR 8
See also CA 5-8R

Weller, Michael 1942-.............CLC 10
See also CA 85-88

Weller, Paul 1958-................CLC 26

Welles, (George) Orson
1915-1985..................CLC 20
See also CA 93-96

Wells, H(erbert) G(eorge)
1866-1946...........TCLC 6, 12, 19
See also CA 110
See also SATA 20
See also DLB 34

**Wells, Rosemary...................CLC 12
See also CA 85-88
See also SAAS 1
See also SATA 18

Welty, Eudora (Alice)
1909-.........CLC 1, 2, 5, 14, 22, 33
See also CA 9-12R
See also DLB 2

Werfel, Franz (V.) 1890-1945.....TCLC 8
See also CA 104

Wergeland, Henrik Arnold
1808-1845..................NCLC 5

Wersba, Barbara 1932- ....CLC 30
See also CLR 3
See also CA 29-32R
See also SATA 1

Wertmüller, Lina 1928- ....CLC 16
See also CA 97-100

Wescott, Glenway 1901-...........CLC 13
See also CA 13-16R
See also DLB 4, 9

Wesker, Arnold 1932-..........CLC 3, 5
See also CANR 1
See also CA 1-4R
See also DLB 13

Wesley, Richard (Errol) 1945-.......CLC 7
See also CA 57-60
See also DLB 38

West, Jessamyn 1907-1984......CLC 7, 17
See also CA 9-12R
See also obituary SATA 37
See also DLB 6
See also DLB-Y 84

West, Morris L(anglo)
1916-.....................CLC 6, 33
See also CA 5-8R

West, Nathanael
1903?-1940..............TCLC 1, 14
See Weinstein, Nathan Wallenstein
See also DLB 4, 9, 28

West, Paul 1930- .... CLC 7, 14
  See also CA 13-16R
  See also DLB 14

West, Rebecca 1892-1983..... CLC 7, 9, 31
  See also CA 5-8R
  See also obituary CA 109
  See also DLB 36
  See also DLB-Y 83

Westall, Robert (Atkinson)
  1929- ....CLC 17
  See also CA 69-72
  See also SATA 23

Westlake, Donald E(dwin)
  1933- .... CLC 7, 33
  See also CANR 16
  See also CA 17-20R

Whalen, Philip 1923-.......... CLC 6, 29
  See also CANR 5
  See also CA 9-12R
  See also DLB 16

Wharton, Edith (Newbold Jones)
  1862-1937................. TCLC 3, 9
  See also CA 104
  See also DLB 4, 9, 12

Wharton, William 1925-....... CLC 18, 37
  See also CA 93-96
  See also DLB-Y 80

Wheatley (Peters), Phillis
  1753?-1784.................... LC 3
  See also DLB 31

Wheelock, John Hall
  1886-1978...................CLC 14
  See also CANR 14
  See also CA 13-16R
  See also obituary CA 77-80
  See also DLB 45

Whelan, John 1900-
  See O'Faoláin, Seán

Whitaker, Rodney 1925-
  See Trevanian
  See also CA 29-32R

White, E(lwyn) B(rooks)
  1899-1985.......... CLC 10, 34 (425),
                            39 (369)
  See also CLR 1
  See also CANR 16
  See also CA 13-16R
  See also obituary CA 116
  See also SATA 2, 29, 44
  See also DLB-11, 22
  See also AITN 2

White, Edmund III 1940-..........CLC 27
  See also CANR 3
  See also CA 45-48

White, Patrick (Victor Martindale)
  1912-.......... CLC 3, 4, 5, 7, 9, 18
  See also CA 81-84

White, T(erence) H(anbury)
  1906-1964....................CLC 30
  See also CA 73-76
  See also SATA 12

White, Walter (Francis)
  1893-1955................. TCLC 15
  See also CA 115

Whitehead, E(dward) A(nthony)
  1933-........................CLC 5
  See also CA 65-68

Whitman, Walt 1819-1892....... NCLC 4
  See also SATA 20
  See also DLB 3

Whitemore, Hugh 1936-...........CLC 37

Whittemore, (Edward) Reed (Jr.)
  1919-........................CLC 4
  See also CANR 4
  See also CA 9-12R
  See also DLB 5

Whittier, John Greenleaf
  1807-1892.................. NCLC 8
  See also DLB 1

Wicker, Thomas Grey 1926-
  See Wicker, Tom
  See also CA 65-68

Wicker, Tom 1926-.................CLC 7
  See also Wicker, Thomas Grey

Wideman, John Edgar
  1941-.........CLC 5, 34 (297), 36
  See also CANR 14
  See also CA 85-88
  See also DLB 33

Wiebe, Rudy (H.) 1934-..... CLC 6, 11, 14
  See also CA 37-40R

Wieners, John 1934-...............CLC 7
  See also CA 13-16R
  See also DLB 16

Wiesel, Elie(zer)
  1928-................CLC 3, 5, 11, 37
  See also CANR 8
  See also CA 5-8R
  See also AITN 1

Wight, James Alfred 1916-
  See Herriot, James
  See also CA 77-80
  See also SATA 44

Wilbur, Richard (Purdy)
  1921-.................CLC 3, 6, 9, 14
  See also CANR 2
  See also CA 1-4R
  See also SATA 9
  See also DLB 5

Wild, Peter 1940-.................CLC 14
  See also CA 37-40R
  See also DLB 5

Wilde, Oscar (Fingal O'Flahertie Wills)
  1854-1900................. TCLC 1, 8
  See also CA 104
  See also SATA 24
  See also DLB 10, 19, 34

Wilder, Billy 1906- ....CLC 20
  See also Wilder, Samuel
  See also DLB 26

Wilder, Samuel 1906-
  See Wilder, Billy
  See also CA 89-92

Wilder, Thornton (Niven)
  1897-1975...... CLC 1, 5, 6, 10, 15, 35
  See also CA 13-16R
  See also obituary CA 61-64
  See also DLB 4, 7, 9
  See also AITN 2

Wilhelm, Kate 1928-...............CLC 7
  See also CANR 17
  See also CA 37-40R
  See also DLB 8

Willard, Nancy 1936-.......... CLC 7, 37
  See also CLR 5
  See also CANR 10
  See also CA 89-92
  See also SATA 30, 37
  See also DLB 5

Williams, C(harles) K(enneth)
  1936-........................CLC 33
  See also CA 37-40R
  See also DLB 5

Williams, Charles (Walter Stansby)
  1886-1945................ TCLC 1, 11
  See also CA 104

Williams, (George) Emlyn
  1905-........................CLC 15
  See also CA 104
  See also DLB 10

Williams, John A(lfred)
  1925-.................... CLC 5, 13
  See also CAAS 3
  See also CANR 6
  See also CA 53-56
  See also DLB 2, 33

Williams, Jonathan (Chamberlain)
  1929-........................CLC 13
  See also CANR 8
  See also CA 9-12R
  See also DLB 5

Williams, Joy 1944-...............CLC 31
  See also CA 41-44R

Williams, Norman 1952-..... CLC 39 (100)

Williams, Paulette 1948-
  See Shange, Ntozake

Williams, Tennessee
  1911-1983...... CLC 1, 2, 5, 7, 8, 11,
                15, 19, 30, 39 (444)
  See also CA 5-8R
  See also obituary CA 108
  See also DLB 7
  See also DLB-Y 83
  See also DLB-DS 4
  See also AITN 1, 2

Williams, Thomas (Alonzo)
  1926-........................CLC 14
  See also CANR 2
  See also CA 1-4R

Williams, Thomas Lanier 1911-1983
  See Williams, Tennessee

Williams, William Carlos
  1883-1963...... CLC 1, 2, 5, 9, 13, 22
  See also CA 89-92
  See also DLB 4, 16

Williamson, Jack 1908-............CLC 29
  See also Williamson, John Stewart
  See also DLB 8

Williamson, John Stewart 1908-
  See Williamson, Jack
  See also CA 17-20R

Willingham, Calder (Baynard, Jr.)
  1922-........................CLC 5
  See also CANR 3
  See also CA 5-8R
  See also DLB 2, 44

Wilson, A(ndrew) N(orman)
  1950-........................CLC 33
  See also CA 112
  See also DLB 14

Author Index

Wilson, Andrew 1948-
See Wilson, Snoo

Wilson, Angus (Frank Johnstone)
1913-........ CLC 2, 3, 5, 25, 34 (579)
See also CA 5-8R
See also DLB 15

Wilson, August 1945-....... CLC 39 (275)
See also CA 115

Wilson, Brian 1942-..............CLC 12

Wilson, Colin 1931-............ CLC 3, 14
See also CANR 1
See also CA 1-4R
See also DLB 14

Wilson, Edmund
1895-1972......... CLC 1, 2, 3, 8, 24
See also CANR 1
See also CA 1-4R
See also obituary CA 37-40R

Wilson, Ethel Davis (Bryant)
1888-1980...................CLC 13
See also CA 102

Wilson, John 1785-1854.......... NCLC 5

Wilson, John (Anthony) Burgess 1917-
See Burgess, Anthony
See also CANR 2
See also CA 1-4R

Wilson, Lanford 1937-...... CLC 7, 14, 36
See also CA 17-20R
See also DLB 7

Wilson, Robert (M.) 1944-....... CLC 7, 9
See also CANR 2
See also CA 49-52

Wilson, Sloan 1920-..............CLC 32
See also CANR 1
See also CA 1-4R

Wilson, Snoo 1948-..............CLC 33
See also CA 69-72

**Winchilsea, Anne (Kingsmill) Finch, Countess
of** 1661-1720 .... LC 3

Winters, (Arthur) Yvor
1900-1968............... CLC 4, 8, 32
See also CAP 1
See also CA 11-12
See also obituary CA 25-28R

Wiseman, Frederick 1930-.........CLC 20

Witkiewicz, Stanislaw Ignacy
1885-1939.................. TCLC 8
See also CA 105

Wittig, Monique 1935?-...........CLC 22
See also CA 116

Wittlin, Joseph 1896-1976........CLC 25
See also Wittlin, Józef

Wittlin, Józef 1896-1976
See Wittlin, Joseph
See also CANR 3
See also CA 49-52
See also obituary CA 65-68

Wodehouse, P(elham) G(renville)
1881-1975........ CLC 1, 2, 5, 10, 22
See also CANR 3
See also CA 45-48
See also obituary CA 57-60
See also SATA 22
See also DLB 34
See also AITN 2

Woiwode, Larry (Alfred)
1941-.................... CLC 6, 10
See also CANR 16
See also CA 73-76
See also DLB 6

Wojciechowska, Maia (Teresa)
1927-...........................CLC 26
See also CLR 1
See also CANR 4
See also CA 9-12R
See also SAAS 1
See also SATA 1, 28

Wolf, Christa 1929-.......... CLC 14, 29
See also CA 85-88

Wolfe, Gene (Rodman) 1931- ......CLC 25
See also CANR 6
See also CA 57-60
See also DLB 8

Wolfe, Thomas (Clayton)
1900-1938................ TCLC 4, 13
See also CA 104
See also DLB 9
See also DLB-Y 85
See also DLB-DS 2

Wolfe, Thomas Kennerly, Jr. 1931-
See Wolfe, Tom
See also CANR 9
See also CA 13-16R

Wolfe, Tom 1931- ..... CLC 1, 2, 9, 15, 35
See also Wolfe, Thomas Kennerly, Jr.
See also AITN 2

Wolff, Tobias (Jonathan Ansell)
1945-.................. CLC 39 (283)
See also CA 117

Wolitzer, Hilma 1930-.............CLC 17
See also CA 65-68
See also SATA 31

Wonder, Stevie 1950- ....CLC 12
See also Morris, Steveland Judkins

Wong, Jade Snow 1922-...........CLC 17
See also CA 109

Woodcott, Keith 1934-
See Brunner, John (Kilian Houston)

Woolf, (Adeline) Virginia
1882-1941..............TCLC 1, 5, 20
See also CA 104
See also DLB 36

Woollcott, Alexander (Humphreys)
1887-1943................... TCLC 5
See also CA 105
See also DLB 29

Wordsworth, William
1770-1850.................. NCLC 12

Wouk, Herman 1915-........ CLC 1, 9, 38
See also CANR 6
See also CA 5-8R
See also DLB-Y 82

Wright, Charles 1935- ...... CLC 6, 13, 28
See also CA 29-32R
See also DLB-Y 82

Wright, James (Arlington)
1927-1980............CLC 3, 5, 10, 28
See also CANR 4
See also CA 49-52
See also obituary CA 97-100
See also DLB 5
See also AITN 2

Wright, Judith 1915-..............CLC 11
See also CA 13-16R
See also SATA 14

Wright, Richard (Nathaniel)
1908-1960...... CLC 1, 3, 4, 9, 14, 21
See also CA 108
See also DLB-DS 2

Wright, Richard B(ruce) 1937-......CLC 6
See also CA 85-88

Wright, Rick 1945-
See Pink Floyd

Wright, Stephen 1946- ....CLC 33

Wu Ching-tzu 1701-1754 .... LC 2

Wurlitzer, Rudolph
1938?-.................. CLC 2, 4, 15
See also CA 85-88

Wylie (Benét), Elinor (Morton Hoyt)
1885-1928................... TCLC 8
See also CA 105
See also DLB 9, 45

Wyndham, John 1903-1969.......CLC 19
See also Harris, John (Wyndham Parkes
Lucas) Beynon

Wyss, Johann David
1743-1818................. NCLC 10
See also SATA 27, 29

Yanovsky, Vassily S(emenovich)
1906-................... CLC 2, 18
See also CA 97-100

Yates, Richard 1926-......... CLC 7, 8, 23
See also CANR 10
See also CA 5-8R
See also DLB 2
See also DLB-Y 81

Yeats, William Butler
1865-1939............TCLC 1, 11, 18
See also CANR 10
See also CA 104
See also DLB 10, 19

Yehoshua, Abraham B.
1936-................... CLC 13, 31
See also CA 33-36R

Yep, Laurence (Michael) 1948-.....CLC 35
See also CLR 3
See also CANR 1
See also CA 49-52
See also SATA 7

Yerby, Frank G(arvin)
1916-................... CLC 1, 7, 22
See also CANR 16
See also CA 9-12R

Yevtushenko, Yevgeny (Aleksandrovich)
1933-...............CLC 1, 3, 13, 26
See also CA 81-84

Yglesias, Helen 1915- .... CLC 7, 22
See also CANR 15
See also CA 37-40R

Yorke, Henry Vincent 1905-1974
See Green, Henry
See also CA 85-88
See also obituary CA 49-52

Young, Al 1939-..................CLC 19
See also CA 29-32R
See also DLB 33

Young, Andrew 1885-1971.........CLC 5
See also CANR 7
See also CA 5-8R

Young, Edward 1683-1765........... LC 3

Young, Neil 1945- ....CLC 17
See also CA 110

Yourcenar, Marguerite
1903- .... CLC 19, 38
See also CA 69-72

Yurick, Sol 1925-.................CLC 6
See also CA 13-16R

Zamyatin, Yevgeny Ivanovich
1884-1937................... TCLC 8
See also CA 105

Zangwill, Israel 1864-1926...... TCLC 16
See also CA 109
See also DLB 10

Zappa, Francis Vincent, Jr. 1940-
See Zappa, Frank
See also CA 108

Zappa, Frank 1940- ....CLC 17
See also Zappa, Francis Vincent, Jr.

Zaturenska, Marya
1902-1982................. CLC 6, 11
See also CA 13-16R
See also obituary CA 105

Zelazny, Roger 1937- ....CLC 21
See also CA 21-24R
See also SATA 39
See also DLB 8

Zhdanov, Andrei A(lexandrovich)
1896-1948................. TCLC 18

Zimmerman, Robert 1941-
See Dylan, Bob

Zindel, Paul 1936-............. CLC 6, 26
See also CLR 3
See also CA 73-76
See also SATA 16
See also DLB 7

Zinoviev, Alexander 1922-.........CLC 19
See also CA 116

Zola, Émile 1840-1902 .... TCLC 1, 6
See also CA 104

Zorrilla y Moral, José
1817-1893.................. NCLC 6

Zoshchenko, Mikhail (Mikhailovich)
1895-1958.................. TCLC 15
See also CA 115

Zuckmayer, Carl 1896-1977 ....CLC 18
See also CA 69-72

Zukofsky, Louis
1904-1978....... CLC 1, 2, 4, 7, 11, 18
See also CA 9-12R
See also obituary CA 77-80
See also DLB 5

Zweig, Paul 1935-1984 ...... CLC 34 (378)
See also CA 85-88
See also obituary CA 113

Zweig, Stefan 1881-1942 .... TCLC 17
See also CA 112

Cumulative Index to Critics

Aalfs, Janet
Jane Rule 27:422

Aaron, Daniel
Claude Brown 30:38
Thornton Wilder 15:575

Aaron, Jonathan
Tadeusz Różewicz 23:363

Aaron, Jules
Michael Cristofer 28:96
Jack Heifner 11:264

Abbey, Edward
Wright Morris 37:317
Robert M. Pirsig 6:421

Abbott, James H.
Juan Benet 28:21

Abbott, John Lawrence
Isaac Bashevis Singer 9:487
Sylvia Townsend Warner 7:512

Abbott, Shirley
Eudora Welty 33:425

Abeel, Erica
Pamela Hansford Johnson 7:185

Abel, Elizabeth
Jean Rhys 14:448

Abel, Lionel
Samuel Beckett 2:45
Jack Gelber 6:196
Jean Genet 2:157
Yoram Kaniuk 19:238

Abernethy, Peter L.
Thomas Pynchon 3:410

Abicht, Ludo
Jan de Hartog 19:133

Ableman, Paul
Brian Aldiss 14:14
Martin Amis 38:13, 15
Beryl Bainbridge 22:45
Jurek Becker 19:36
William Boyd 28:39
William S. Burroughs 22:85
J. M. Coetzee 23:125
Len Deighton 22:116
Elaine Feinstein 36:171
William Golding 17:179
Mary Gordon 13:250
Mervyn Jones 10:295
David Lodge 36:273
Michael Moorcock 27:351
Piers Paul Read 25:377
Mary Renault 17:402
Anatoli Rybakov 23:373
Andrew Sinclair 14:489
Scott Sommer 25:424
D. M. Thomas 22:419
Gore Vidal 22:438
A. N. Wilson 33:451

Abley, Mark
Margaret Atwood 25:65
Clark Blaise 29:76
J. M. Coetzee 33:109
Harry Crews 23:136
John le Carré 28:226
Mavis Gallant 38:190
William Mitchell 25:327
Brian Moore 32:312
Michael Ondaatje 29:341, 342
Agnès Varda 16:560
Miriam Waddington 28:440

Abraham, Willie E.
William Melvin Kelley 22:249

Abrahams, Cecil A.
Bessie Head 25:236

Abrahams, William
Elizabeth Bowen 6:95
Hortense Calisher 2:97
Herbert Gold 4:193
A. N. Wilson 33:451
Joyce Carol Oates 2:315
Harold Pinter 9:418
V. S. Pritchett 5:352

Abrahamson, Dick
Fran Arrick 30:19
Sue Ellen Bridgers 26:92
Jean Craighead George 35:179
John Knowles 26:265
Norma Fox Mazer 26:294

Abrams, Elliott
William F. Buckley, Jr. 37:59

Abrams, M. H.
M. H. Abrams 24:18
Northrop Frye 24:209

Abramson, Doris E.
Alice Childress 12:105

Abramson, Jane
Peter Dickinson 12:172
Christie Harris 12:268
S. E. Hinton 30:205
Rosemary Wells 12:638

Achebe, Chinua
Ayi Kwei Armah 33:28
Amos Tutuola 29:435

Acheson, Dean
Art Buchwald 33:92

Acheson, James
William Golding 17:177

Acken, Edgar L.
Ernest K. Gann 23:163

Acker, Robert
Ernst Jandl 34:198

Ackerman, Diane
John Berryman 25:97
Arthur C. Clarke 35:119

Ackroyd, Peter
Brian Aldiss 5:16
Martin Amis 4:19
Miguel Ángel Asturias 8:27
Louis Auchincloss 6:15
W. H. Auden 9:56
Beryl Bainbridge 8:36
James Baldwin 5:43
John Barth 5:51
Donald Barthelme 3:44
Samuel Beckett 4:52
John Berryman 3:72
Richard Brautigan 5:72
Charles Bukowski 5:80
Anthony Burgess 5:87
William S. Burroughs 5:92
Italo Calvino 5:100; 8:132
Richard Condon 6:115
Roald Dahl 6:122
Ed Dorn 10:155
Margaret Drabble 8:183
Douglas Dunn 6:148
Eva Figes 31:163, 165
Bruce Jay Friedman 5:127
John Gardner 7:116
Günter Grass 4:207
MacDonald Harris 9:261
Joseph Heller 5:179
Mark Helprin 10:261
Russell C. Hoban 7:160
Elizabeth Jane Howard 7:164

B. S. Johnson 6:264
Pamela Hansford Johnson 7:184
G. Josipovici 6:270
Thomas Keneally 10:298
Jack Kerouac 5:215
Francis King 8:321
Jerzy Kosinski 10:308
Doris Lessing 6:300
Alison Lurie 4:305
Thomas McGuane 7:212
Stanley Middleton 7:220
Michael Moorcock 5:294;
  27:350
Penelope Mortimer 5:298
Iris Murdoch 4:368
Vladimir Nabokov 6:358
V. S. Naipaul 7:252
Joyce Carol Oates 6:368
Tillie Olsen 13:432
Grace Paley 6:393
Frederik Pohl 18:411
Davi Pownall 10:418, 419
J. B. Priestley 9:441
V. S. Pritchett 5:352
Thomas Pynchon 3:419
Frederic Raphael 14:437
Simon Raven 14:442
Peter Redgrove 6:446
Keith Roberts 14:463
Judith Rossner 9:458
May Sarton 4:472
Tom Sharpe 36:400
David Slavitt 5:392
Wole Soyinka 5:398
David Storey 4:529
Peter Straub 28:409
Glendon Swarthout 35:403
Frank Swinnerton 31:428
Paul Theroux 5:428
Thomas Tryon 11:548
John Updike 7:488; 9:540
Gore Vidal 8:525
Harriet Waugh 6:559
Jerome Weidman 7:518
Arnold Wesker 5:483
Patrick White 4:587
Roger Zelazny 21:469

Acton, Gary
D. M. Pinkwater 35:320

Acton, Harold
Anthony Powell 31:318

Aczel, Tamas
Heinrich Böll 27:63

Adachi, Ken
David Donnell 34:157, 159

Adam, G. F.
Rhys Davies 23:143

Adamic, Louis
Woody Guthrie 35:182

Adamowski, T. H.
Simone de Beauvoir 4:47

Adams, Agatha Boyd
Paul Green 25:197

Adams, Alice
Lisa Alther 7:14
C.D.B. Bryan 29:106
Joyce Carol Oates 33:291
Cynthia Propper Seton 27:429
Joy Williams 31:463

Adams, Franklin P.
James M. Cain 28:43

Adams, George R.
Lorraine Hansberry 17:190
Ann Petry 18:403

Adams, J. Donald
Erich Maria Remarque 21:327

Adams, Jacqueline
Al Young 19:479

Adams, James Truslow
Esther Forbes 12:206

Adams, John
Roy A. Gallant 17:131

Adams, John J.
Jack Vance 35:421, 422

Adams, Laura
Norman Mailer 11:340

Adams, Leonie
John Crowe Ransom 4:428

Adams, M. Ian
Juan Carlos Onetti 10:376

Adams, Mildred
Alejo Carpentier 38:90

Adams, Percy
James Dickey 7:81

Adams, Phoebe-Lou
Chinua Achebe 26:11, 13
Richard Adams 18:2
Joy Adamson 17:3
Nelson Algren 33:17
Beryl Bainbridge 5:40
Ann Beattie 18:38
David Bradley, Jr. 23:81
André Brink 18:68
Robert Cormier 12:133
Margaret Craven 17:80
Roald Dahl 18:109
Peter Davison 28:100
José Donoso 32:154
G. B. Edwards 25:151
John Ehle 27:105
John Fowles 15:234
Dick Francis 22:150
Günter Grass 22:196
Dashiell Hammett 5:161
James Herriot 12:282
George V. Higgins 18:234
Jamake Highwater 12:285
Bohumil Hrabal 13:290
Langston Hughes 35:219
P. D. James 18:275
David Jones 7:189
Garson Kanin 22:232
Jerzy Kosinski 6:285
William Kotzwinkle 14:311
Halldór Laxness 25:292, 300
Harper Lee 12:341
Yukio Mishima 9:385
N. Scott Momaday 19:317
Berry Morgan 6:340
Joyce Carol Oates 6:374
Tillie Olsen 13:433
Sylvia Plath 17:352
Reynolds Price 6:426
Jean Rhys 19:394
Darcy Ribeiro 34:102

João Ubaldo Ribeiro 10:436
Philip Roth 15:452
Françoise Sagan 17:419
Khushwant Singh 11:504
Jean Stafford 19:431
Christina Stead 8:500
Douglas Unger 34:116
R. G. Vliet 22:441
Joseph Wambaugh 18:532

Adams, Richard
Robert Newton Peck 17:338

Adams, Robert M.
Isabel Allende 39:34
Peter Brooks 34:521
Adolfo Bioy Casares 13:87
R. V. Cassill 23:105
John Cheever 25:121
Eleanor Clark 19:105
Malcolm Cowley 39:458
Edward Dahlberg 7:63
William Empson 34:337
Max Frisch 32:194
John Irving 38:254
Peter Matthiessen 11:361
Mary McCarthy 14:362
Alberto Moravia 18:348
Robert M. Pirsig 4:404
Severo Sarduy 6:485
Mary Lee Settle 19:409
Edmund Wilson 24:469

Adams, Robert Martin
John Barth 10:24
Samuel Beckett 14:74
Jorge Luis Borges 10:66
Richard Brautigan 12:61
Anthony Burgess 10:90
Lawrence Durrell 13:185
T. S. Eliot 10:171
William Faulkner 11:201
Carlo Emilio Gadda 11:215
William H. Gass 2:154
José Lezama Lima 10:321
Vladimir Nabokov 11:393
Flann O'Brien 10:363
Thomas Pynchon 11:453
Alain Robbe-Grillet 10:437
J.R.R. Tolkien 12:586
Angus Wilson 2:472

Adams, Robin
Frank Herbert 12:279
Roger Zelazny 21:470

Adams, Robin G.
Joan D. Vinge 30:409

Adams, S. J.
Ezra Pound 13:453

Adams, Stephen D.
James Purdy 28:380

Adams, Timothy Dow
Leon Rooke 25:394

Adcock, Fleur
John Berryman 13:83
Maurice Gee 29:178, 179
Robert Graves 39:328
Robert Lowell 11:331
David Malouf 28:268
Peter Porter 13:453

Addiego, John
Albert Goldbarth 38:203

Adelman, Clifford
John Berryman 3:71

Adelman, George
Frank B. Gilbreth, Jr. and
  Ernestine Gilbreth Carey
  17:156

Adereth, M.
Louis Aragon 22:36

Adkins, Laurence
Eilís Dillon 17:96
Farley Mowat 26:336

Adler, Anne G.
John Jakes 29:250

Adler, Bill
Marvin Gaye 26:132

Adler, Dick
Ross Macdonald 1:185

Adler, Jerry
Leon Uris 32:437

Adler, Joyce
Wilson Harris 25:207

Adler, Renata
Mel Brooks 12:75
Francis Ford Coppola 16:232
Joan Micklin Silver 20:346

Adler, Thomas P.
Edward Albee 11:13
Harold Pinter 15:424
Sam Shepard 17:446
Stephen Sondheim 30:389

Aers, Lesley
Philippa Pearce 21:284

Aeschliman, M. D.
William Mastrosimone 36:291
Tom Stoppard 34:282

Agar, John
Jonathan Baumbach 6:32
Laurie Colwin 5:107
Joy Williams 31:462

Agee, James
Frank Capra 16:156
Charles Chaplin 16:193
Maya Deren 16:251
Carl Theodor Dreyer 16:256
Alfred Hitchcock 16:339, 342
John Huston 20:158, 160
Buster Keaton 20:188
Laurence Olivier 20:234
Billy Wilder 20:456

Agee, Joel
Aharon Appelfeld 23:38
Günter Grass 32:202

Agena, Kathleen
Charles Wright 13:613

Aggeler, Geoffrey
Anthony Burgess 2:86; 5:85;
  13:123; 22:69

Aghazarian, Nancy
Milton Meltzer 26:304

Agius, Ambrose, O.S.B.
Edward Dahlberg 7:64

Ahearn, Kerry
Wallace Stegner **9**:509

Aherne, Michael A.
Allen Drury **37**:108

Ahokas, Jaakko A.
Paavo Haavikko **18**:206; **34**:169
Frans Eemil Sillanpää **19**:418

Ahrold, Robbin
Kurt Vonnegut, Jr. **3**:501

Aidoo, Christina Ama Ata
Ayi Kwei Armah **33**:24

Aiken, Conrad
William Faulkner **8**:206
St.-John Perse **11**:433
I. A. Richards **24**:370
Carl Sandburg **35**:345
Karl Shapiro **15**:475

Aiken, David
Flannery O'Connor **10**:365

Aiken, William
David Kherdian **6**:281

Aithal, Rashmi
Raja Rao **25**:373

Aithal, S. Krishnamoorthy
Raja Rao **25**:373

Aitken, Will
Carlos Saura **20**:319

Ajami, Fouad
V. S. Naipaul **37**:321

Aklujkar, Ashok
R. K. Narayan **28**:301

Alazraki, Jaime
Jorge Luis Borges **19**:45
Pablo Neruda **2**:309; **7**:261

Albers, Randall
Ai **14**:8

Albert, Walter
Blaise Cendrars **18**:90

Albertson, Chris
Laura Nyro **17**:313
Stevie Wonder **12**:662

Aldan, Daisy
Maya Angelou **35**:32
Phyllis Gotlieb **18**:193
Howard Nemerov **36**:306
Joyce Carol Oates **33**:294

Alden, John R.
Bruce Lancaster **36**:245

Alderson, Brian W.
Aidan Chambers **35**:98
Leon Garfield **12**:226
Jean Craighead George **35**:177
William Mayne **12**:395, 401

Alderson, S. William
Andre Norton **12**:464, 466, 470

Alderson, Sue Ann
Muriel Rukeyser **10**:442

Alderson, Valerie
E. M. Almedingen **12**:6
Noel Streatfeild **21**:412

Aldiss, Brian
J. G. Ballard **3**:33
Frank Herbert **12**:272
Jack Williamson **29**:450

Aldiss, Brian W.
Isaac Asimov **26**:38
Philip K. Dick **30**:116
Robert A. Heinlein **26**:162
Jack Williamson **29**:456

Aldrich, Nelson
Piri Thomas **17**:497

Aldridge, John W.
Nelson Algren **33**:17
James Baldwin **4**:42
Donald Barthelme **2**:39
Saul Bellow **2**:49, 50
Louis-Ferdinand Céline **7**:47
John Cheever **3**:105
John Dos Passos **4**:131
James T. Farrell **4**:157
William Faulkner **3**:150
William Gaddis **3**:177; **6**:193
Joseph Heller **5**:177; **36**:224
Ernest Hemingway **3**:231, 233
James Jones **3**:261
Frederick Karl **34**:552
Jerzy Kosinski **2**:231
Richard Kostelanetz **28**:216
Alison Lurie **5**:260
Norman Mailer **1**:193; **2**:258
Mary McCarthy **3**:327, 328
Wright Morris **3**:342; **18**:352
John O'Hara **2**:323
Katherine Anne Porter **3**:392
Philip Roth **4**:459
Alan Sillitoe **3**:447
William Styron **3**:472
John Updike **2**:439
Gore Vidal **22**:431
Robert Penn Warren **1**:356
Eudora Welty **2**:461
Colin Wilson **3**:536
Edmund Wilson **2**:474
P. G. Wodehouse **2**:478

Aldridge, Judith
Ruth M. Arthur **12**:27
Honor Arundel **17**:14, 15, 18

Alegria, Fernando
Jorge Luis Borges **2**:71
Pablo Neruda **28**:309

Alessandri, Tom
Czesław Miłosz **31**:263
Jim Shepard **36**:407

Aletti, Vince
Marvin Gaye **26**:130, 131, 132
Laura Nyro **17**:312
Prince **35**:325
Smokey Robinson **21**:342, 345
Stevie Wonder **12**:656, 660

Alexander, Alex E.
Stephen King **26**:234

Alexander, Edward
Cynthia Ozick **28**:348
Isaac Bashevis Singer **11**:503

Alexander, Jean
Richard Peck **21**:296

Alexander, John R.
Robinson Jeffers **2**:215

Alexander, Michael
Donald Davie **5**:113
Ezra Pound **7**:336

Alexander, William
Carl Sandburg **4**:463

Alexandrova, Vera
Mikhail Sholokhov **7**:420

Alfonso, Barry
Van Morrison **21**:239

Alford, Steven E.
Doris Betts **28**:34

Algren, Nelson
Clancy Sigal **7**:424

Ali, Ahmed
Raja Rao **25**:366

Ali, Tariq
Jules Archer **12**:19

Alig, Tracy
John Gregory Dunne **28**:121

Alkalimat, Abd-Al Hakimu Ibn
C.L.R. James **33**:219

Allaby, Michael
Jacques-Yves Cousteau **30**:107

Allen, Blaine
Monty Python **21**:223

Allen, Bob
Waylon Jennings **21**:206
Willie Nelson **17**:305

Allen, Bruce
Richard Adams **5**:6
Isabel Allende **39**:31
Russell Banks **37**:23
Thomas Berger **38**:42
David Bradley, Jr. **23**:81
Hortense Calisher **38**:74, 76
Raymond Carver **36**:103
J. M. Coetzee **33**:108
Julio Cortázar **5**:110
Malcolm Cowley **39**:460
Stanley Elkin **6**:168
John Gardner **8**:236; **28**:162
Mary Gordon **13**:250
Thomas Keneally **5**:212
Kenneth Koch **5**:219
Peter Matthiessen **7**:211
Wright Morris **18**:354; **37**:317
Iris Murdoch **6**:347
Joyce Carol Oates **6**:369
Kenzaburō Ōe **36**:346
Seán O'Faoláin **32**:343
Manuel Puig **5**:355
John Sayles **10**:460
Isaac Bashevis Singer **6**:509
Paul West **7**:524
Patrick White **5**:485
A. N. Wilson **33**:457
Tobias Wolff **39**:285

Allen, Bruce D.
Jane Rule **27**:417

Allen, Carol J.
Susan Fromberg Schaeffer **11**:491

Allen, Constance
Robin F. Brancato **35**:70

Allen, Dexter
Mary Lee Settle **19**:408

Allen, Dick
Margaret Atwood **2**:20
Wendell Berry **6**:61
Hayden Carruth **7**:40
Paul Goodman **2**:169
Thom Gunn **6**:221
Richard F. Hugo **6**:245
Philip Levine **2**:244
Jayanta Mahapatra **33**:277
Lisel Mueller **13**:400
George Oppen **7**:281
Judith Johnson Sherwin **7**:414

Allen, Don
François Truffaut **20**:397

Allen, Frank
Jayanta Mahapatra **33**:279

Allen, Gay Wilson
Carl Sandburg **10**:447

Allen, Gilbert
Stephen Dobyns **37**:80

Allen, Henry
Robert M. Pirsig **4**:403

Allen, James Sloan
Margaret Mead **37**:281

Allen, John A.
Eudora Welty **14**:564

Allen, John Alexander
Daniel Hoffman **13**:288

Allen, L. David
Arthur C. Clarke **18**:106

Allen, Louis
Shusaku Endo **14**:161
Shiga Naoya **33**:373

Allen, Merritt P.
Walter Farley **17**:116
Andre Norton **12**:455

Allen, Michael
Richard F. Hugo **32**:239

Allen, Michael S.
Richard F. Hugo **32**:247

Allen, Patricia H.
Zilpha Keatley Snyder **17**:469

Allen, Paul
Alan Ayckbourn **33**:45, 46
Howard Barker **37**:34
C. S. Forester **35**:159

Allen, Ralph G.
Eric Bentley **24**:51

Allen, Rodney F.
Thomas J. Fleming **37**:121

Allen, Steve
S. J. Perelman **23**:335

Allen, Tom
Ralph Bakshi **26**:73
Vittorio De Sica **20**:97
Rainer Werner Fassbinder **20**:115
Kon Ichikawa **20**:186
Yasujiro Ozu **16**:450

Pier Paolo Pasolini 20:270
Sidney Poitier 26:361
Carlos Saura 20:321
Jerzy Skolimowski 20:354

Allen, Tom, S. C.
Mel Brooks 12:81

Allen, Walter
A. Alvarez 5:17
Kingsley Amis 1:5
Riccardo Bacchelli 19:31
Saul Bellow 1:30
Elizabeth Bowen 1:40
Paul Bowles 1:41
Truman Capote 1:55
Ivy Compton-Burnett 1:61
James Gould Cozzens 1:66
Edward Dahlberg 1:71
John Dos Passos 1:79; 8:181
Margaret Drabble 22:120
Lawrence Durrell 1:85
James T. Farrell 1:98; 8:205
William Faulkner 1:101
E. M. Forster 1:104
John Fowles 4:170
William Golding 1:120
Nadine Gordimer 33:179
Henry Green 2:178
Graham Greene 1:132
L. P. Hartley 2:181; 22:211
Ernest Hemingway 1:142
Richard Hughes 1:149
Aldous Huxley 1:150
Christopher Isherwood 1:155
Pamela Hansford Johnson
  1:160; 27:217
Doris Lessing 1:173
Richard Llewellyn 7:206
Bernard Malamud 1:197
Olivia Manning 19:300
John P. Marquand 2:271
Carson McCullers 1:208
Henry Miller 1:221
Wright Morris 1:231
John Mortimer 28:282
Iris Murdoch 1:234
P. H. Newby 2:310
Flannery O'Connor 1:255
John O'Hara 1:260
William Plomer 4:406
Anthony Powell 1:277
Henry Roth 2:377; 11:487
J. D. Salinger 1:298
William Sansom 2:383
C. P. Snow 1:316
John Steinbeck 1:325
William Styron 1:330
Frank Swinnerton 31:426
Allen Tate 2:427
Gore Vidal 22:434
Robert Penn Warren 1:355
Evelyn Waugh 1:358
Glenway Wescott 13:592
Rebecca West 7:525
Angus Wilson 2:471

Allen, Ward
Donald Davidson 2:112

Allen, Woody
S. J. Perelman 15:419

Alley, Phillip W.
Franklyn M. Branley 21:18

Allott, Miriam
Graham Greene 18:193

Allsop, Kenneth
J. P. Donleavy 6:139
Eva Figes 31:161
Thomas Hinde 6:238

Alm, Richard S.
Betty Cavanna 12:99
Maureen Daly 17:89
Mary Stolz 12:548

Alma, Roger
Philippa Pearce 21:291

Almansi, Guido
Alan Ayckbourn 18:27
Italo Calvino 22:90
Mario Luzi 13:354

Almon, Bert
Gary Snyder 32:394

Alonso, J. M.
Rafael Alberti 7:11
Jorge Luis Borges 9:117

Alpern, Joyce
Christopher Collier and James
  L. Collier 30:71

Alpert, Hollis
Vincent Canby 13:131
Howard Fast 23:156
C. S. Forester 35:169
Daniel Fuchs 8:220
William Kotzwinkle 14:311
Olivia Manning 19:300
Ernesto Sabato 23:375
Budd Schulberg 7:402
Melvin Van Peebles 20:410

Alstrum, James J.
Ernesto Cardenal 31:74

Altbach, Philip G.
Jonathan Kozol 17:252

Alter, Robert
S. Y. Agnon 4:11
Yehuda Amichai 9:23
John Barth 9:71
Donald Barthelme 8:49
Saul Bellow 3:48, 49; 33:69
Heinrich Böll 27:68
Jorge Luis Borges 2:76; 6:94
R. V. Cassill 23:104
Leslie Epstein 27:130
Leslie A. Fiedler 13:212
William H. Gass 39:480
John Hollander 8:298
Alfred Kazin 38:282
Jerzy Kosinski 2:232
Doris Lessing 22:285
Norman Mailer 3:312; 11:342
Bernard Malamud 3:30, 321;
  27:299, 305
Claude Mauriac 9:366
Elsa Morante 8:402
Alberto Moravia 18:346
Vladimir Nabokov 2:302; 8:414
Hugh Nissenson 4:380
Flann O'Brien 7:269
Amos Oz 33:299
Manuel Puig 10:420
Thomas Pynchon 9:443

Raymond Queneau 10:429
Philip Rahv 24:353
Alain Robbe-Grillet 6:468
Earl Rovit 7:383
André Schwarz-Bart 4:480
Isaac Bashevis Singer 11:501;
  15:507
J.I.M. Stewart 7:465
William Styron 15:527
John Updike 2:444
Kurt Vonnegut, Jr. 8:531
Elie Wiesel 3:526
Abraham B. Yehoshua 13:618;
  31:467

Alterman, Loraine
Ray Davies 21:96
Jesse Jackson 12:291
Gordon Lightfoot 26:279
Carly Simon 26:408
Andrew Lloyd Webber and Tim
  Rice 21:428

Alterman, Peter S.
Samuel R. Delany 38:151

Altieri, Charles
Robert Creeley 2:107
Robert Duncan 15:191
Denise Levertov 28:238
Robert Lowell 15:345
Charles Olson 29:332
Gary Snyder 32:390

Altman, Billy
Elvis Costello 21:75
Ray Davies 21:102
Peter Townshend 17:537, 539
Brian Wilson 12:652

Alvarez, A.
Aharon Appelfeld 23:38
John Berryman 2:58; 3:65
Albert Camus 4:89
William Empson 19:154
Eva Figes 31:168
E. M. Forster 1:109
Carlos Fuentes 22:165
Dashiell Hammett 3:218
Seamus Heaney 25:247
Zbigniew Herbert 9:271
Russell C. Hoban 25:266
Miroslav Holub 4:233
Edwin Honig 33:210
Dan Jacobson 14:289
Philip Larkin 3:275
Robert Lowell 3:300
Hugh MacDiarmid 4:309
Norman Mailer 3:312
Cynthia Ozick 28:351
David Plante 23:346
Sylvia Plath 2:335; 3:388
Jean Rhys 4:445
Jean-Paul Sartre 4:475
Edith Sitwell 9:493
Aleksandr I. Solzhenitsyn 7:436
Robert Stone 23:428
Patrick White 3:521
Elie Wiesel 3:527
Yvor Winters 4:589

Alvia, Sister
Robert Newton Peck 17:339

Aly, Lucile F.
John G. Neihardt 32:336

Amacher, Richard E.
Edward Albee 1:5

Amado, Jorge
João Ubaldo Ribeiro 10:436
João Guimarães Rosa 23:348

Amanuddin, Syed
James Welch 14:559

Amberg, George
Jean Cocteau 16:229

Ambrose, Stephen E.
Cornelius Ryan 7:385

Ambrosetti, Ronald
Eric Ambler 9:20

Ames, Alfred C.
Joy Adamson 17:5

Ames, Carol
John Berryman 25:96

Ames, Evelyn
J. B. Priestley 5:351

Ames, Katrine
Gordon Parks 16:460

Amiel, Barbara
Margaret Atwood 15:37
Jack Hodgins 23:228
Chaim Potok 14:429
A. W. Purdy 14:435
Jane Rule 27:422

Amis, Kingsley
Ray Bradbury 10:68
Arthur C. Clarke 13:155
Ivy Compton-Burnett 1:60
Ilya Ehrenburg 18:132
Leslie A. Fiedler 4:159
Ian Fleming 30:137, 139
Christopher Isherwood 14:278
Philip Larkin 39:335
Philip Roth 1:293
Elizabeth Taylor 29:408
Arnold Wesker 3:517

Amis, Martin
J. G. Ballard 6:27
Saul Bellow 33:70
Malcolm Bradbury 32:56
Peter De Vries 7:77
Bruce Jay Friedman 5:127
Ernest J. Gaines 3:179
John Hawkes 7:141
Philip Larkin 13:337
Norman Mailer 39:424
Peter Manso 39:424
Iris Murdoch 4:367
Vladimir Nabokov 8:412
Shiva Naipaul 32:325; 39:356
Roman Polanski 16:472
Philip Roth 6:475
John Updike 34:293
Fay Weldon 11:565
Angus Wilson 34:582

Ammons, A. R.
Mark Strand 18:514

Amory, Cleveland
Art Buchwald 33:94
Rod McKuen 1:210
Rod Serling 30:357

Amprimoz, Alexandre
Joe Rosenblatt **15**:448

Amy, Jenny L.
Robert Newton Peck **17**:343

Anders, Jaroslaw
Tadeusz Konwicki **28**:209

Andersen, Richard
Robert Coover **32**:124

Anderson, A. J.
Charles Addams **30**:16
Jeffrey Archer **28**:11
Russell Baker **31**:32
Roy Blount, Jr. **38**:46
Art Buchwald **33**:93

Anderson, David
Albert Camus **4**:89, 90
William Golding **3**:197, 198
Jean-Paul Sartre **4**:477

Anderson, David C.
L. E. Sissman **9**:491

Anderson, Elliott
Vladimir Nabokov **3**:354

Anderson, George
Piri Thomas **17**:499

Anderson, H. T.
Herbert Gold **14**:208
Erich Segal **10**:467

Anderson, Isaac
Agatha Christie **12**:114
August Derleth **31**:127, 128
Joseph Krumgold **12**:316

Anderson, Jack
Philip Levine **4**:286
George MacBeth **2**:252

Anderson, James Douglas
Louis R. Harlan **34**:190

Anderson, Jervis
James Baldwin **8**:41
Michael Thelwell **22**:415

Anderson, Joseph L.
Akira Kurosawa **16**:396

Anderson, Lindsay
Luis Buñuel **16**:129
Vittorio De Sica **20**:84
John Ford **16**:305, 306
Elia Kazan **16**:362
Fritz Lang **20**:205
Yasujiro Ozu **16**:447

Anderson, Michael
Edward Bond **6**:85
Tennessee Williams **11**:577

Anderson, Patrick
David Cudlip **34**:39
Allen Drury **37**:110
Ward Just **4**:266

Anderson, Poul
Poul Anderson **15**:14
Fritz Leiber **25**:303
Erich von Däniken **30**:423

Anderson, Quentin
Leon Edel **29**:171
Vladimir Nabokov **3**:351

Anderson, Reed
Juan Goytisolo **10**:244; **23**:184

Anderson, Robert W.
Helen MacInnes **27**:279

Anderson, Sherwood
Carl Sandburg **35**:342

Anderson, William
Stephen Sondheim **30**:397

André, Michael
Robert Creeley **2**:107

Andrejevic, Helen B.
Walter Dean Myers **35**:296

Andrews, James H.
William F. Buckley, Jr. **37**:62

Andrews, Nigel
John Cassavetes **20**:47
Sam Peckinpah **20**:277
Jerzy Skolimowski **20**:350

Andrews, Peter
Philip Caputo **32**:105
Michael Crichton **6**:119
Peter De Vries **28**:108
Ken Follett **18**:157
Arthur Hailey **5**:157
Richard F. Hugo **32**:249
Pat Jordon **37**:194
Peter Maas **29**:305
D. M. Pinkwater **35**:319
Martin Cruz Smith **25**:413
Irving Stone **7**:471

Andrews, Sheryl B.
Barbara Corcoran **17**:70
James D. Forman **21**:119
Virginia Hamilton **26**:149
S. E. Hinton **30**:204
Isabelle Holland **21**:148
Mollie Hunter **21**:158
Andre Norton **12**:460
Barbara Wersba **30**:430

Angell, Roger
Brian De Palma **20**:80
Bob Fosse **20**:126
Steve Martin **30**:249
Gene Roddenberry **17**:413
Paul Schrader **26**:395
Lina Wertmüller **16**:600

Angier, Carole
Stevie Smith **25**:421

Angle, Paul M.
Milton Meltzer **26**:299

Angogo, R.
Chinua Achebe **11**:2

Annan, Gabriele
Aharon Appelfeld **23**:37
Simone de Beauvoir **4**:47
Heinrich Böll **9**:111
Laurie Colwin **23**:129
I. Compton-Burnett **34**:500
Anita Desai **19**:133
Iris Murdoch **11**:388
Jean Rhys **19**:391
Isaac Bashevis Singer **38**:408
Hilary Spurling **34**:500
Sylvia Townsend Warner
19:459

Annan, Noel
E. M. Forster **4**:166

Anozie, Sunday O.
Christopher Okigbo **25**:350

Anselm, Felix
Hermann Hesse **17**:194

Ansen, David
Lillian Hellman **34**:349
George Roy Hill **26**:208
Stephen King **26**:243; **37**:206
Sidney Poitier **26**:362
Prince **35**:328

Ansorge, Peter
Howard Brenton **31**:59
Trevor Griffiths **13**:256
David Hare **29**:213
Sam Shepard **6**:495
Snoo Wilson **33**:460

Anthony, Robert J.
Isaac Asimov **26**:38

Appel, Alfred, Jr.
Fritz Lang **20**:211
Vladimir Nabokov **1**:240; **2**:300

Appel, Benjamin
Nelson Algren **33**:11
Glendon Swarthout **35**:399

Apple, Max
T. Coraghessan Boyle **36**:56
John Gardner **10**:222

Appleyard, Bryan
Alan Ayckbourn **33**:46
Samuel Beckett **29**:64
Stephen Poliakoff **38**:385

Aptheker, Herbert
W.E.B. Du Bois **13**:180

Arau, Anthony
Kamala Markandaya **38**:321

Araújo, Virginia de
Carlos Drummond de Andrade
18:4

Arbuthnot, May Hill
Frank Bonham **12**:53
Franklyn M. Branley **21**:18
Betsy Byars **35**:73
Julia W. Cunningham **12**:164
Maureen Daly **17**:91
Jesse Jackson **12**:290
Joseph Krumgold **12**:320, 321
Madeleine L'Engle **12**:350
Emily Cheney Neville **12**:452
Alvin Silverstein and Virginia
B. Silverstein **17**:455
Mary Stolz **12**:553
Noel Streatfeild **21**:412
Rosemary Sutcliff **26**:436
Jade Snow Wong **17**:566

Archer, Eileen A.
Diana Wynne Jones **26**:228

Archer, Eugene
Ingmar Bergman **16**:46
Bernardo Bertolucci **16**:83
Federico Fellini **16**:271
John Huston **20**:164, 165
Sam Peckinpah **20**:272

Archer, Marguerite
Jean Anouilh **13**:18

Archer, Mildred
John Donovan **35**:142

Archer, Rosanne
Kamala Markandaya **38**:322

Arendt, Hannah
W. H. Auden **6**:21

Argus
Josef von Sternberg **20**:370

Arias, Ron
Rudolfo A. Anaya **23**:25

Aristarco, Guido
Satyajit Ray **16**:474

Arkhurst, Joyce E.
Mildred D. Taylor **21**:419

Arland, Marcel
Françoise Sagan **17**:416

Arlen, M. J.
Art Buchwald **33**:90

Arlen, Michael J.
Alex Haley **12**:254

Armes, Roy
Michelangelo Antonioni **20**:38
Robert Bresson **16**:114
Claude Chabrol **16**:170
Jean Cocteau **16**:228
Federico Fellini **16**:284
Pier Paolo Pasolini **20**:265
Alain Resnais **16**:505
Alain Robbe-Grillet **4**:449
Agnès Varda **16**:556

Armour, Robert A.
Fritz Lang **20**:214

Armour-Hileman, Vicki
Gary Soto **32**:403

Armstrong, Judith
Philippa Pearce **21**:292

Armstrong, Louise
John Donovan **35**:142

Armstrong, Marion
Fletcher Knebel **14**:308

Armstrong, William A.
Sean O'Casey **1**:252; **9**:407

Arnason, David
Amos Tutuola **14**:540

Arnett, Janet
Roderick L. Haig-Brown
21:146

Arnez, Nancy L.
Alex Haley **12**:250

Arnheim, Rudolf
Maya Deren **16**:253

Arnold, A. James
Aimé Césaire **19**:99

Arnold, Armin
Friedrich Dürrenmatt **15**:193

Arnold, Gary
Woody, Allen **16**:4

Arnold, Marilyn
John Gardner **18**:177

Arnolt, Vicki
Hermann Hesse **17**:215

Arnson, Curtis
A. B. Yehoshua **31**:470

Aronowitz, Alfred G.
John Lennon and Paul
McCartney **12**:364
Peter Townshend **17**:526

Aronson, James
Donald Barthelme **1**:18
Saul Bellow **1**:33
James Dickey **1**:73
John Fowles **1**:109
John Knowles **1**:169
John Updike **1**:345
Eudora Welty **1**:363

Aros, Andrew
Christopher Fry **14**:189

Arpin, Gary Q.
John Berryman **10**:48
Edwin Honig **33**:215

Arrowsmith, William
Dino Buzzati **36**:88

Arthos, John
E. E. Cummings **12**:146

Arthur, George
Monty Python **21**:226

Arthur, George W.
Judy Blume **12**:47
Robert Crumb **17**:85

Artinian, Robert W.
Jean-Paul Sartre **24**:411

Arvedson, Peter
Roy A. Gallant **17**:131

Arvin, Newton
Leon Edel **29**:168

Asahina, Robert
Woody Allen **16**:12
Mel Brooks **12**:80
Caryl Churchill **31**:86
Brian De Palma **20**:82
Athol Fugard **25**:175
Jean-Luc Godard **20**:153
Werner Herzog **16**:334
George Roy Hill **26**:208
Steve Martin **30**:249
Pier Paolo Pasolini **20**:270
Eric Rohmer **16**:538
Sam Shepard **34**:270
Joan Micklin Silver **20**:346
Steven Spielberg **20**:366
Lanford Wilson **36**:463

Ascher, Carol
Simone de Beauvoir **31**:39, 42

Ascherson, Neal
Beryl Bainbridge **14**:38
Breyten Breytenbach **37**:49
André Brink **36**:72
Leslie Epstein **27**:129
Rolf Hochhuth **18**:256
György Konrád **10**:304
Tadeusz Konwicki **8**:327

Milan Kundera **4**:278
Tadeusz Różewicz **9**:465
Yevgeny Yevtushenko **1**:382

Aschkenasy, Nehama
Amos Oz **27**:361

Asein, Samuel Omo
Alex La Guma **19**:276
Ezekiel Mphahlele **25**:342
Derek Walcott **25**:451

Ashbery, John
A. R. Ammons **2**:13
Elizabeth Bishop **9**:89
Philip Booth **23**:75
James Schuyler **23**:390

Ashburn, Frank D.
William F. Buckley, Jr. **37**:56

Ashcroft, W. D.
Janet Frame **22**:146

Ashley, L. F.
Rosemary Sutcliff **26**:433

Ashlin, John
William Mayne **12**:390

Ashton, Dore
Octavio Paz **10**:392

Ashton, Thomas L.
C. P. Snow **4**:504

Asimov, Isaac
Arthur C. Clarke **35**:117
Roy A. Gallant **17**:127, 128
Carl Sagan **30**:338

Asinof, Eliot
Pete Hamill **10**:251

Asnani, Shyam M.
Mulk Raj Anand **23**:21

Aspel, Alexander
Ivar Ivask **14**:286

Aspler, Tony
William F. Buckley, Jr. **7**:36
William Gaddis **8**:226
Josef Škvorecký **15**:510

Astor, Judy
Italo Calvino **33**:99
Kamala Markandaya **38**:326

Astrachan, Anthony
Joseph Brodsky **36**:77
John Pepper Clark **38**:113
Agnes Eckhardt Nixon **21**:246
Vladimir Voinovich **10**:509

Atchity, Kenneth
Jorge Luis Borges **2**:71
Virginia Spencer Carr **34**:423
John Dos Passos **34**:423
Leon Edel **29**:174
James Jones **3**:261
Stephen King **26**:241
Robert Penn Warren **4**:581

Athanason, Arthur N.
Pavel Kohout **13**:326

Atheling, William, Jr.
Isaac Asimov **3**:17
Arthur C. Clarke **1**:58
Harlan Ellison **1**:93
Robert A. Heinlein **1**:139;
3:227

Atherton, J. S.
Anaïs Nin **11**:398

Atherton, Stan
Margaret Laurence **6**:290

Athos, John
L. P. Hartley **22**:214

Atkins, Anselm
Robert Bolt **14**:90

Atkins, John
L. P. Hartley **2**:182

Atkinson, Bert
Donald Hall **37**:149

Atkinson, Brooks
Robert Anderson **23**:30
Enid Bagnold **25**:76
Sally Benson **17**:49
Paddy Chayefsky **23**:112
William Gibson **23**:174, 175
Paul Green **25**:195
Lorraine Hansberry **17**:182
Fritz Hochwälder **36**:232
Garson Kanin **22**:230
Jean Kerr **22**:254, 255
Arthur Miller **26**:315
Elmer Rice **7**:361
Irwin Shaw **23**:397
Stephen Sondheim **30**:376, 377

Atkinson, Joan L.
Sue Ellen Bridgers **26**:92

Atkinson, Michael
Robert Bly **10**:58

Atlas, Jacoba
Mel Brooks **12**:78
Joni Mitchell **12**:436

Atlas, James
Russell Banks **37**:27
Samuel Beckett **6**:37
Frank Bidart **33**:76
Marie-Claire Blais **6**:82
C.D.B. Bryan **29**:105
Raymond Carver **22**:102
J. V. Cunningham **3**:122
Peter Davison **28**:102
Alan Dugan **6**:144
Leon Edel **34**:535
John Gardner **34**:548
Paul Goodman **4**:198
Graham Greene **27**:172
Mark Harris **19**:206
John Irving **23**:248
Randall Jarrell **6**:261
Galway Kinnell **5**:217
Thomas McGrath **28**:277
W. S. Merwin **5**:287
Wright Morris **37**:315
John O'Hara **6**:386
Kenneth Rexroth **6**:451
Laura Riding **7**:375
Delmore Schwartz **4**:478
L. E. Sissman **9**:490
Christina Stead **32**:411
James Tate **2**:431
Richard Tillinghast **29**:414
John Updike **34**:294
C. K. Williams **33**:444
Angus Wilson **34**:583
Richard Yates **23**:482

Attanasio, Paul
C.L.R. James **33**:123

Attebery, Brian
Lloyd Alexander **35**:26
James Thurber **25**:437

Atwell, Lee
Michelangelo Antonioni **20**:39
George Roy Hill **26**:199

Atwood, Margaret
Frederick Barthelme **36**:50
Ann Beattie **18**:38
Marie-Claire Blais **6**:80
E. L. Doctorow **18**:126
Janet Frame **22**:148
Susan B. Hill **4**:227
Erica Jong **6**:267
A. G. Mojtabai **5**:293
Tillie Olsen **13**:432
Marge Piercy **14**:420; **27**:381
Sylvia Plath **11**:451
A. W. Purdy **14**:430
James Reaney **13**:472
Adrienne Rich **3**:429; **11**:478;
36:365
Cynthia Propper Seton **27**:425
Audrey Thomas **7**:472; **37**:417

Aubert, Rosemary
Patrick Lane **25**:288

Auchincloss, Eve
Vera Brittain **23**:93
Brigid Brophy **29**:93
Hortense Calisher **38**:71
Bruce Chatwin **28**:71
Mavis Gallant **18**:171
R. K. Narayan **7**:257
Gilbert Rogin **18**:457

Auchincloss, Louis
Katherine Anne Porter **7**:316

Aucouturier, Michel
Aleksandr I. Solzhenitsyn **7**:432

Auden, W. H.
Joseph Brodsky **4**:77
Cleanth Brooks **24**:101
Kenneth Burke **24**:121
William Dickey **28**:116
Loren Eiseley **7**:90
Daniel Hoffman **23**:237
Christopher Isherwood **14**:281
Chester Kallman **2**:221
C. S. Lewis **27**:261
Adrienne Rich **36**:364
J.R.R. Tolkien **1**:336; **12**:564
Andrei Voznesensky **1**:349
James Wright **28**:461

Auriol, Jean-George
René Clair **20**:57

Auster, Paul
John Ashbery **6**:14
John Hollander **8**:300
Laura Riding **7**:375
Giuseppe Ungaretti **7**:484

Austin, Allan E.
Elizabeth Bowen **22**:61
Roy Fuller **28**:155

Austin, Anthony
Ilya Ehrenburg **34**:434
Anatol Goldberg **34**:434

Austin, Jacqueline
Mary McCarthy **39**:487
Joan K. Peters **39**:92

Auty, Martyn
John Landis **26**:273

Avant, John Alfred
Eleanor Bergstein **4**:55
Rosellen Brown **32**:63
Gail Godwin **5**:142
Gayl Jones **6**:266
José Lezama Lima **4**:291
Carson McCullers **12**:427
Joyce Carol Oates **6**:371, 373
Tillie Olsen **4**:386
Patrick White **5**:486

Averill, Deborah
Frank O'Connor **14**:395

Avery, Evelyn Gross
Richard Wright **14**:597

Axel-Lute, Melanie
Will Harriss **34**:193

Axelrod, George
Gore Vidal **4**:556

Axelrod, Rise B.
Anne Sexton **15**:471

Axelrod, Steven
Robert Lowell **2**:249

Axelrod, Steven Gould
Saul Bellow **6**:60
Allen Ginsberg **36**:192
Robert Lowell **37**:235

Axhelm, Peter M.
Saul Bellow **13**:66
Allen Ginsberg **36**:192
William Golding **10**:232

Axthelm, Pete
Peter Gent **29**:180
Robert Lipsyte **21**:210
Gilbert Rogin **18**:457

Ayd, Joseph D., S.J.
Louis Auchincloss **18**:26

Ayer, A. J.
Albert Camus **9**:152

Ayers, William R.
Lewis Thomas **35**:414

Ayling, Ronald
Sean O'Casey **11**:409; **15**:405

Ayo, Nicholas
Edward Lewis Wallant **10**:515

Ayre, John
Austin C. Clarke **8**:143
Mavis Gallant **7**:110
V. S. Naipaul **13**:407
Mordecai Richler **5**:378

Baar, Ron
Ezra Pound **1**:276

Babbitt, Natalie
Joan Aiken **35**:19
Paula Danziger **21**:85
Lois Duncan **26**:106
William Mayne **12**:395
Katherine Paterson **12**:403, 486

Babby, Ellen R.
Michel Tremblay **29**:427

Babenko, Vickie A.
Yevgeny Yevtushenko **13**:620

Bach, Alice
Norma Klein **30**:238
Sandra Scoppettone **26**:400
Jill Paton Walsh **35**:432

Bachem, Michael
Christa Wolf **29**:464

Bachman, Charles R.
Sam Shepard **17**:442

Bachmann, Gideon
Shirley Clarke **16**:215
Federico Fellini **16**:283
Jean Renoir **20**:290
Luchino Visconti **16**:572

Backscheider, Nick
John Updike **5**:452

Backscheider, Paula
John Updike **5**:452

Bacon, Leonard
Eric Bentley **24**:43

Bacon, Martha
John Donovan **35**:140
Walter Farley **17**:118

Bacon, Terry R.
Robert Creeley **11**:137

Bader, Julia
Vladimir Nabokov **23**:303

Baer, Barbara L.
Harriette Arnow **7**:16
Christina Stead **5**:403

Bagchee, Syhamal
John Fowles **33**:166

Bagdikian, Ben H.
Gay Talese **37**:391

Bagnall, Norma
Robert Cormier **30**:84
M. E. Kerr **35**:248
Norma Klein **30**:241

Bagshaw, Marguerite
Farley Mowat **26**:337

Bailey, Anthony
James Baldwin **17**:38
A. J. Cronin **32**:138
John Gregory Dunne **28**:124
David Plante **23**:342

Bailey, Bruce
George Ryga **14**:474

Bailey, Hilary
Maya Angelou **35**:33

Bailey, James
Andrei Voznesensky **15**:553

Bailey, Jennifer
Norman Mailer **28**:255

Bailey, Nancy I.
Roch Carrier **13**:142

Bailey, O. L.
Eric Ambler **6**:2
Robert Bloch **33**:84
Dick Francis **2**:142
Nicolas Freeling **38**:185
Joseph Hansen **38**:237
George V. Higgins **4**:223
Maj Sjöwall **7**:501
Mickey Spillane **3**:469
Per Wahlöö **7**:501

Bailey, Paul
Maya Angelou **35**:33
James Baldwin **15**:43
Elizabeth Bishop **32**:44
Isak Dinesen **29**:164
Gabriel García Márquez **3**:180
Nadine Gordimer **10**:239
Kazuo Ishiguro **27**:202
P. D. James **18**:274
Yasunari Kawabata **2**:223
Louis L'Amour **25**:278
Primo Levi **37**:222
Brian Moore **3**:341
Alberto Moravia **11**:384
James Purdy **2**:351
Barbara Pym **37**:379
Philip Roth **3**:437
Muriel Spark **5**:400
David Storey **2**:426
Elizabeth Taylor **29**:410
Paul Theroux **11**:531
Gore Vidal **6**:550
Tennessee Williams **7**:544

Bailey, Peter
Nikki Giovanni **2**:165
Melvin Van Peebles **2**:447

Bailey, Wilfrid C.
Margaret Mead **37**:278

Bair, Deirdre
Russell Banks **37**:27
Simone de Beauvoir **31**:42
Samuel Beckett **6**:43

Baird, James
Djuna Barnes **8**:49

Baird, Jock
Paul McCartney **35**:293

Bak, Hans
Malcolm Cowley **39**:461

Baker, A. T.
A. R. Ammons **5**:30

Baker, Betty
Scott O'Dell **30**:269

Baker, Carlos
Truman Capote **19**:79
Ernest Hemingway **6**:234;
  30:180
Elizabeth Spencer **22**:401
John Steinbeck **21**:366
Jessamyn West **17**:546

Baker, Charles A.
Robert Altman **16**:25

Baker, D. C.
J.R.R. Tolkien **38**:440

Baker, David
Marvin Bell **31**:51

Baker, Donald W.
Edward Dahlberg **7**:63

Baker, Houston A., Jr.
James Baldwin **1**:16
Arna Bontemps **1**:37
Gwendolyn Brooks **15**:92
Sterling A. Brown **1**:47
W.E.B. Du Bois **1**:80
Ralph Ellison **1**:95; **3**:145
Leon Forrest **4**:163
Langston Hughes **1**:149
LeRoi Jones **1**:163
Ann Petry **1**:266
Ishmael Reed **2**:369; **6**:449
Jean Toomer **1**:341
Richard Wright **1**:380

Baker, Howard
Caroline Gordon **6**:206
Katherine Anne Porter **1**:273

Baker, James R.
William Golding **3**:200; **17**:169,
175

Baker, John Ross
Wayne C. Booth **24**:94

Baker, Kenneth
Walter Abish **22**:18
Leon Rooke **25**:391

Baker, Nina Brown
Madeleine L'Engle **12**:344

Baker, Peter
Lindsay Anderson **20**:12
Vittorio De Sica **20**:89

Baker, Rob
Albert Innaurato **21**:196

Baker, Roger
Poul Anderson **15**:11
Beryl Bainbridge **4**:39
James Blish **14**:83
John Buell **10**:81
Paula Fox **8**:217
Janet Frame **3**:164
Joseph Hansen **38**:237
John Hawkes **1**:139
Jerzy Kosinski **1**:172
Alistair MacLean **13**:359
Larry McMurtry **3**:333
Harold Robbins **5**:378
Herman Wouk **9**:580
Rudolph Wurlitzer **2**:483
Helen Yglesias **7**:558
Roger Zelazny **21**:466

Baker, Ruth
Frank B. Gilbreth, Jr. and
  Ernestine Gilbreth Carey
  17:152

Baker, Sheridan
Alan Paton **25**:358

Baker, William
William Carlos Williams
  13:606

Baker, William E.
Jacques Prévert **15**:437

Critic Index

Bakerman, Jane S.
Nicolas Freeling **38**:187
Toni Morrison **22**:318
Ruth Rendell **28**:385
May Sarton **14**:481

Bakker, J.
William Gaddis **19**:189

Bakshy, Alexander
Frank Capra **16**:153
Charles Chaplin **16**:188
René Clair **20**:57, 58
Rouben Mamoulian **16**:418, 419

Balakian, Anna
Louis Aragon **22**:42
André Breton **9**:132; **15**:90
René Char **9**:164
Monique Wittig **22**:472

Balakian, Nona
Taylor Caldwell **28**:58

Baldanza, Frank
Alberto Moravia **2**:293
Iris Murdoch **1**:235
James Purdy **2**:350; **4**:424; **10**:421

Baldauf, Gretchen S.
C. S. Adler **35**:15
Larry Bograd **35**:63

Baldeshwiler, Eileen
Flannery O'Connor **1**:255

Balducci, Carolyn
M. E. Kerr **12**:297
Norma Klein **30**:237

Baldwin, James
Alex Haley **8**:259
Langston Hughes **35**:216
Norman Mailer **8**:364
Richard Wright **21**:438

Bales, Kent
Richard Brautigan **5**:71

Ballantine, Ian
Theodore Sturgeon **39**:365

Ballantyne, Sheila
Amy Hempel **39**:69

Ballard, J. G.
Philip K. Dick **10**:138
Harlan Ellison **13**:203
Frederik Pohl **18**:410
Robert Silverberg **7**:425

Ballet, Arthur H.
Thornton Wilder **35**:439

Balliett, Whitney
James Baldwin **17**:44
Ann Beattie **18**:40
R. V. Cassill **23**:103
Richard Condon **4**:105
C.L.R. James **33**:224
Pamela Hansford Johnson **27**:218
William Melvin Kelley **22**:247
Walter M. Miller, Jr. **30**:255
Clancy Sigal **7**:424

Ballif, Gene
Jorge Luis Borges **6**:87
Vladimir Nabokov **6**:351
Sylvia Plath **11**:449
Alain Robbe-Grillet **6**:464
Nathalie Sarraute **8**:469

Ballstadt, Carl
Earle Birney **6**:78

Balm, Trixie A.
David Bowie **17**:63

Baltensperger, Peter
Robertson Davies **25**:129

Bambara, Toni Cade
Gwendolyn Brooks **2**:81
June Jordan **23**:256
Ntozake Shange **25**:396

Bamborough, J. B.
F. R. Leavis **24**:300

Banas, Mary
T.E.D. Klein **34**:71

Band, Arnold J.
S. Y. Agnon **14**:2

Bander, Edward J.
Jules Archer **12**:16

Bandler, Michael J.
Roger Kahn **30**:233
Chaim Potok **14**:430; **26**:369
Elie Wiesel **11**:570

Banfield, Beryle
Rosa Guy **26**:143

Bangs, Lester
Chuck Berry **17**:51
David Bowie **17**:63
David Byrne **26**:97
Jimmy Cliff **21**:64
Mick Jagger and Keith Richard **17**:225, 226, 236
John Lennon **35**:266
John Lennon and Paul McCartney **12**:381
Bob Marley **17**:270, 271
Paul McCartney **35**:283
Joni Mitchell **12**:437
Jim Morrison **17**:289, 290, 292
Van Morrison **21**:234, 238
Jimmy Page and Robert Plant **12**:474, 476
Lou Reed **21**:306, 310, 317
Bob Seger **35**:381, 382
Bruce Springsteen **17**:481
Lily Tomlin **17**:523
Peter Townshend **17**:536
Frank Zappa **17**:586, 587, 591

Banks, Joyce
Ruth M. Arthur **12**:28

Banks, R. Jeff
Mickey Spillane **13**:527

Banks, Russell
William McPherson **34**:85
Joyce Carol Oates **19**:355

Bann, Stephen
Lawrence Durrell **27**:99
Elaine Feinstein **36**:172
Ernst Jandl **34**:195
William Kotzwinkle **35**:257
Seán O'Faoláin **32**:341

J.I.M. Stewart **32**:422

Bannerman, David
Allan W. Eckert **17**:104

Bannikov, Nikolai
Anna Akhmatova **25**:29

Banning, Charles Leslie
William Gaddis **10**:210

Baranczak, Stanislaw
Peter Handke **38**:228

Barber, Michael
Simon Raven **14**:443
Gore Vidal **4**:557

Barber, Raymond W.
Jean Lee Latham **12**:324

Barbera, Jack Vincent
John Berryman **8**:88

Barbour, Douglas
Marilyn R. Bowering **32**:47
Matt Cohen **19**:111
Samuel R. Delany **38**:149
Louis Dudek **11**:160
Ursula K. Le Guin **22**:265
Gwendolyn MacEwan **13**:358
B. P. Nichol **18**:368
Michael Ondaatje **14**:407
Joe Rosenblatt **15**:446
Rudy Wiebe **6**:566
Gene Wolfe **25**:472
Roger Zelazny **21**:466

Barbour, Joan
Anne McCaffrey **17**:282

Barclay, Pat
Robertson Davies **7**:72
Farley Mowat **26**:344

Bardeche, Maurice
René Clair **20**:61

Bargad, Warren
Yehuda Amichai **22**:29
Amos Oz **8**:436
Abraham B. Yehoshua **13**:617

Bargainnier, Earl F.
Agatha Christie **12**:126
Peter Dickinson **35**:132

Barge, Laura
Samuel Beckett **10**:34; **11**:39

Bargen, Doris G.
Stanley Elkin **27**:122

Barghoorn, Frederick C.
Aleksandr I. Solzhenitsyn **4**:508

Barish, Jonas A.
Jean-Paul Sartre **24**:408

Barker, A. L.
Edna O'Brien **5**:311

Barker, Felix
Alan Ayckbourn **33**:48

Barker, Frank Granville
Margaret Drabble **10**:163
J. B. Priestly **9**:442

Barker, George
Brian Aldiss **5**:14

Barker, Shirley
Bruce Lancaster **36**:244

Barkham, John
A. J. Cronin **32**:137, 138
Nadine Gordimer **33**:176
Alan Paton **25**:359

Barksdale, Richard K.
Gwendolyn Brooks **5**:75
Langston Hughes **15**:294

Barnard, Caroline King
Sylvia Plath **17**:361

Barnden, Louise
Eva Figes **31**:166

Barnes, Anne
Laurie Colwin **23**:128

Barnes, Bart
Heinrich Böll **39**:295
Helen MacInnes **39**:350
J. B. Priestley **34**:362
Irwin Shaw **34**:368

Barnes, Clive
Enid Bagnold **25**:78
John Bishop **10**:54
Alice Childress **12**:104, 105
Caryl Churchill **31**:85, 89
Michael Cristofer **28**:96
Gretchen Cryer **21**:77, 78, 80
Christopher Durang **38**:171, 173
Lawrence Ferlinghetti **2**:134
Harvey Fierstein **33**:154
Athol Fugard **25**:176
Larry Gelbart **21**:126, 127
Jack Gelber **14**:193
Simon Gray **9**:240
John Guare **29**:203, 207
Peter Handke **38**:217
Lorraine Hansberry **17**:191
David Hare **29**:211
Jack Heifner **11**:264
Arthur Kopit **1**:170; **33**:252
James Lapine **39**:173
Peter Luke **38**:313
David Mamet **34**:219
Mark Medoff **23**:292
Peter Nichols **36**:326, 330
Monty Python **21**:226
John Mortimer **28**:286
Richard O'Brien **17**:322
David Rabe **33**:345
Gerome Ragni and James Rado **17**:378, 380, 383, 386, 387
Anthony Shaffer **19**:413
Sam Shepard **17**:436, 437, 438, 441; **34**:267
Neil Simon **31**:394, 399, 400; **39**:217
Stephen Sondheim **30**:380, 388; **39**:173
Tom Stoppard **1**:328; **34**:274
Elizabeth Swados **12**:556
Lily Tomlin **17**:517
Andrew Lloyd Webber and Tim Rice **21**:425, 427, 430, 432
Michael Weller **10**:525
Hugh Whitemore **37**:447
August Wilson **39**:276
Lanford Wilson **7**:547; **36**:459, 464

Barnes, Harper
James Tate **2**:431

Barnes, Hazel F.
Simone de Beauvoir **31**:44

Barnes, Howard
Irwin Shaw **23**:396
Tennessee Williams **30**:454

Barnes, Hugh
Carlo Gébler **39**:60

Barnes, John A.
John Gardner **30**:157

Barnes, Julian
Richard Brautigan **5**:72; **9**:124
Vincent Canby **13**:131
Agatha Christie **12**:120
James Clavell **6**:114
Len Deighton **7**:76
B. S. Johnson **6**:264
Pamela Hansford Johnson **7**:184
G. Josipovici **6**:270
Richard Llewellyn **7**:207
Alistair MacLean **13**:359
Stanley Middleton **38**:331
Vladimir Nabokov **6**:359
Joyce Carol Oates **9**:402
Chaim Potok **26**:373
Richard Price **12**:490
Richard Stern **39**:243

Barnes, Ken
Bob Seger **35**:380

Barnes, Peter
John Huston **20**:162

Barnes, Regina
James T. Farrell **4**:158
Geoffrey Household **11**:277

Barnett, Abraham
John Ehle **27**:102

Barnett, Ursula A.
J. M. Coetzee **23**:121
Ezekiel Mphahlele **25**:336

Barnouw, Dagmar
Elias Canetti **14**:120
Doris Lessing **6**:295

Barnstone, William
Jorge Luis Borges **6**:93

Barnstone, Willis
Jorge Luis Borges **9**:120

Baro, Gene
Dannie Abse **29**:12
Brigid Brophy **29**:91
R. V. Cassill **23**:103
Carolyn Kizer **15**:308
Henri de Montherlant **19**:324
Auberon Waugh **7**:512

Barolini, Helen
Lucio Piccolo **13**:441

Baron, Alexander
Bernard Malamud **2**:268

Barozzi, Al
John Nichols **38**:343

Barr, Alan P.
Akira Kurosawa **16**:405

Barr, Donald
Robert Bloch **33**:83
Kamala Markandaya **38**:319
Mary Renault **17**:392
George Tabori **19**:435
T. H. White **30**:444

Barrenechea, Ana María
Jorge Luis Borges **1**:38

Barrett, Gerald
Jerzy Kosinski **10**:305

Barrett, Nina
T. Coraghessan Boyle **36**:62

Barrett, William
Nelson Algren **33**:12
Samuel Beckett **2**:48
Albert Camus **2**:99
Arthur C. Clarke **4**:105; **35**:116
Sumner Locke Elliott **38**:177
William Faulkner **3**:154
Leslie A. Fiedler **24**:188
Romain Gary **25**:186
William Golding **17**:168
Martin Heidegger **24**:271
Ernest Hemingway **3**:238
Hermann Hesse **2**:191
Alfred Kazin **38**:274
Fletcher Knebel **14**:308
Halldór Laxness **25**:292
Yukio Mishima **27**:336
John Nichols **38**:338
Philip Rahv **24**:358
Alain Robbe-Grillet **2**:377
Françoise Sagan **17**:423
Leon Uris **7**:491
Yvor Winters **32**:460

Barrington, Judith
Carolyn Kizer **39**:170

Barrow, Craig Wallace
Madeleine L'Engle **12**:351
Paul Muldoon **32**:318

Barrow, Geoffrey R.
Blas de Otero **11**:425

Barry, Elaine
Robert Frost **26**:125

Barry, Iris
Charles Addams **30**:12
Fritz Lang **20**:200, 201
T. H. White **30**:439

Barry, John Brooks
T. S. Eliot **6**:165

Barry, Kevin
John Berryman **6**:65

Barsam, Richard Meran
Leni Riefenstahl **16**:522

Barson, Anthony
Chaim Potok **26**:371

Bartelme, Elizabeth
Alice Walker **27**:454

Barth, J. Robert
Tom Stoppard **34**:274

Barthel, Joan
Joe McGinnis **32**:305

Barthelme, Donald
Werner Herzog **16**:334

Barthes, Roland
Georges Bataille **29**:39
Michel Foucault **31**:171
Raymond Queneau **5**:357

Bartholomay, Julia A.
Howard Nemerov **6**:360

Bartholomew, David
Larry McMurtry **11**:371
Lina Wertmüller **16**:597

Bartkowech, R.
Alain Robbe-Grillet **14**:462

Bartlett, Lee
Robert Bly **38**:54
Lawrence Ferlinghetti **27**:137

Bartley, E. F.
Jacques-Yves Cousteau **30**:105

Bartley, Edward
Donald E. Westlake **33**:438

Barton, Mrs. G. V.
H. F. Brinsmead **21**:28

Barzun, Jaques
Lionel Trilling **11**:539

Baskett, Sam S.
Ronald Bush **34**:530
T. S. Eliot **34**:530

Baskin, Barbara H.
Betsy Byars **35**:72
Virginia Hamilton **26**:156
Zoa Sherburne **30**:363
Barbara Wersba **30**:432

Baskin, John
Helen Hooven Santmyer **33**:360

Basler, Roy P.
Melvin B. Tolson **36**:428

Bass, Judy
Barbara Guest **34**:447
H. D. **34**:447

Bassan, Maurice
Flannery O'Connor **21**:261

Basso, Hamilton
Paul Green **25**:195
Halldór Laxness **25**:291
Andrew Lytle **22**:292

Bassoff, Bruce
William H. Gass **8**:244

Batchelor, John Calvin
Ann Beattie **18**:39
Thomas M. Disch **36**:125
William Golding **17**:179
Mark Helprin **10**:262
Frank Herbert **35**:207
Steven Millhauser **21**:220
Joyce Carol Oates **19**:355
Walker Percy **18**:400
David Plante **23**:344
Peter Rushforth **19**:407

Batchelor, R.
André Malraux **9**:353

Bates, Ernest Sutherland
T. S. Stribling **23**:445
Rebecca West **31**:453

Bates, Evaline
Ezra Pound **3**:397

Bates, Gladys Graham
Sally Benson **17**:48
Laura Z. Hobson **25**:268

Bates, Graham
Pär Lagerkvist **7**:198

Bates, Lewis
E. M. Almedingen **12**:2

Bates, Marston
Peter Matthiessen **32**:286

Bates, Ralph
Edwin Honig **33**:208

Bateson, F. W.
W. H. Auden **6**:24
John Gardner **2**:151

Bateson, John
William Wharton **37**:443

Bati, Anwer
Ken Russell **16**:551

Battcock, Gregory
Andy Warhol **20**:415

Bauer, Arnold
Carl Zuckmayer **18**:555

Bauer, William
John Buell **10**:82

Baugh, Edward
Derek Walcott **25**:450

Bauke, J. P.
Jakov Lind **4**:292

Bauke, Joseph P.
Heinrich Böll **27**:60

Baum, Alwin L.
Alain Robbe-Grillet **14**:458

Baum, Betty
Robert Westall **17**:556

Baumann, Michael L.
B. Traven **8**:520; **11**:535, 537

Baumbach, Elinor
Sylvia Ashton-Warner **19**:22

Baumbach, Jonathan
Thomas Berger **38**:38
Robert Bresson **16**:117
Truman Capote **8**:132
R. V. Cassill **23**:106
Ralph Ellison **1**:95
John Hawkes **4**:212
Stanley Kubrick **16**:377
Norman Mailer **4**:318
Bernard Malamud **1**:197, 199
Mary McCarthy **5**:275
Wright Morris **1**:232
Flannery O'Connor **1**:256
Grace Paley **6**:393
J. D. Salinger **1**:299
Scott Sommer **25**:424
William Styron **1**:330
Peter Taylor **1**:333
Michel Tournier **36**:435
Edward Lewis Wallant **10**:511
Robert Penn Warren **1**:355

Baumgarten, Murray
Jorge Luis Borges **19**:52

Baumgarten, Ruth
Peter Handke **38**:227

Baumgold, Julie
Truman Capote **34**:325

Bauska, Barry
Dick Francis **22**:151

Bawer, Bruce
Robert Creeley **36**:121
E. L. Doctorow **37**:92
Gary Snyder **32**:400
C. K. Williams **33**:448

Baxter, Charles
J. R. Salamanca **15**:464

Baxter, John
John Ford **16**:312
Josef von Sternberg **20**:375

Baxter, Ralph C.
Allan W. Eckert **17**:104

Bayles, Martha
Anita Brookner **34**:141

Bayley, John
Anna Akhmatova **11**:9
W. H. Auden **2**:27, 28
Joseph Brodsky **36**:79
Anthony Burgess **4**:85
D. J. Enright **8**:203
E. M. Forster **22**:136
M. M. Kaye **28**:197
Philip Larkin **33**:267; **39**:340
Robert Lowell **4**:296
Czesław Miłosz **31**:260
Amos Oz **11**:428
Vasko Popa **19**:375
Anthony Powell **10**:417
Christopher Reid **33**:349
Varlam Shalamov **18**:479
Stevie Smith **25**:420
Aleksandr I. Solzhenitsyn
4:511; **7**:444; **10**:479; **18**:499
T. H. White **30**:444
Alexander Zinoviev **19**:486

Baylis, Jamie
Edmund White III **27**:481

Bazarov, Konstantin
Ivo Andrić **8**:20
Heinrich Böll **3**:76
James A. Michener **1**:214
Aleksandr I. Solzhenitsyn
2:411; **10**:483

Bazelon, David T.
Dashiell Hammett **19**:193

Bazin, André
Robert Bresson **16**:111
Luis Buñuel **16**:131
Charles Chaplin **16**:200
Orson Welles **20**:435

Bazzdlo, Gretchen
Lee Kingman **17**:246

Beach, Glyger G.
Ouida Sebestyen **30**:348

Beach, Joseph Warren
John Dos Passos **25**:137
Carl Van Vechten **33**:388

Beacham, Richard
Howard Brenton **31**:67

Beacham, Walton
Erskine Caldwell **8**:124
Paul West **14**:568

Beagle, Peter S.
J.R.R. Tolkien **12**:567

Bean, Robin
Bob Fosse **20**:121
Pier Paolo Pasolini **20**:258, 259
Carlos Saura **20**:313

Beards, Virginia K.
Margaret Drabble **3**:128

Beardsley, Doug
Ralph Gustafson **36**:218

Beardsley, Monroe C.
Wayne C. Booth **24**:99

Beatie, Bruce A.
J.R.R. Tolkien **3**:477

Beattie, Munro
Daryl Hine **15**:282
Irving Layton **15**:323
Dorothy Livesay **15**:341
A.J.M. Smith **15**:516

Beatty, Jack
Ann Beattie **18**:39
Thomas Berger **38**:40
Isabel Colegate **36**:112
Barry Hannah **38**:231
George V. Higgins **18**:235
Ward S. Just **27**:230
Bernard Mac Laverty **31**:256
William Maxwell **19**:308
Alice Munro **19**:346
Shiva Naipaul **32**:326
V. S. Naipaul **18**:362
R. K. Narayan **28**:301
Alexander Theroux **25**:432
Paul Theroux **15**:534; **28**:427
William Trevor **25**:443
William Wharton **37**:435

Beatty, Jerome, Jr.
Larry Kettelkamp **12**:305

Beatty, Patricia V.
John Fowles **33**:169

Beatty, Richmond C.
Donald Davidson **13**:166

Beauchamp, Gorman
E. M. Forster **10**:183

Beauchamp, William
Elizabeth Taylor **4**:541

Beaufort, John
Amlin Gray **29**:201
Sam Shepard **34**:268
Martin Sherman **19**:416
Stephen Sondheim **30**:394
Tom Stoppard **34**:277
Elizabeth Swados **12**:560
Tennessee Williams **19**:473
Lanford Wilson **36**:465

Beaujour, Michel
Georges Bataille **29**:45

Beauman, Sally
Julia O'Faolain **19**:359
Leon Rooke **25**:390
Monique Wittig **22**:473

Beaupre, Lee
Ralph Bakshi **26**:67

Beauvoir, Simone de
Violette Leduc **22**:260
Henri de Montherlant **19**:322

Beaver, Harold
William S. Burroughs **15**:112
Daniel Fuchs **22**:161
Allen Ginsburg **13**:241
Joyce Carol Oates **11**:404
Flannery O'Connor **21**:278
Sharon Olds **32**:346

Bechtel, Louise S.
Margot Benary-Isbert **12**:31, 32
Franklyn M. Branley **21**:16
Walter Farley **17**:117
Henry Gregor Felsen **17**:121,
122
Margaret O. Hyde **21**:171
Carl Sandburg **35**:354
Zoa Sherburne **30**:360
Mary Stolz **12**:546
Noel Streatfeild **21**:399, 400,
401
Rosemary Sutcliff **26**:425, 426
John R. Tunis **12**:596
Lenora Mattingly Weber **12**:632

Beck, Alfred D.
Franklyn M. Branley **21**:16
Margaret O. Hyde **21**:172

Beck, Marilyn
Rod McKuen **1**:210

Beck, Richard
Frans Eemil Sillanpää **19**:417

Beck, Warren
William Faulkner **11**:197;
14:171

Beckelman, June
Jacques Audiberti **38**:22

Becker, Alida
Penelope Lively **32**:277

Becker, Brenda L.
Mary Gordon **22**:187

Becker, George J.
John Dos Passos **15**:183
Upton Sinclair **15**:500
T. S. Stribling **23**:446

Becker, Lucille Frackman
Louis Aragon **3**:14
Michel Butor **11**:80
Henri de Montherlant **19**:325
Georges Simenon **2**:398, 399;
8:488; **18**:481

Becker, May Lamberton
Betty Cavanna **12**:97, 98
Maureen Daly **17**:88
Walter Farley **17**:115
Henry Gregor Felsen **17**:119
Esther Forbes **12**:207
Jesse Jackson **12**:289

Noel Streatfeild **21**:397, 398,
399
John R. Tunis **12**:594, 595
Leonora Mattingly Weber
12:631, 632

Becker, Stephen
Jerome Siegel and Joe Shuster
21:355

Beckett, Samuel
Václav Havel **25**:230
Sean O'Casey **11**:405

Beckham, Barry
Piri Thomas **17**:499

Beckman, Susan
Jack Hodgins **23**:234

Beddow, Reid
Iris Murdoch **22**:328

Bedell, Thomas
John Gardner **30**:155

Bedford, William
Robert Lowell **15**:342
Eugenio Montale **18**:342

Bedient, Calvin
A. R. Ammons **8**:13
John Ashbery **15**:29
W. H. Auden **2**:27
Samuel Beckett **1**:24
Marvin Bell **31**:50
Leonard Cohen **3**:110
Edward Dahlberg **7**:67
Donald Davie **10**:120
Richard Eberhart **11**:178
T. S. Eliot **13**:196
Louise Glück **7**:119
John Hawkes **4**:215
Seamus Heaney **25**:242
Anthony Hecht **19**:209
Joseph Heller **5**:178
Geoffrey Hill **5**:184
Daniel Hoffman **6**:243
Ted Hughes **2**:202; **4**:235
David Ignatow **7**:182
Donald Justice **19**:236
Thomas Kinsella **4**:271; **19**:256
Philip Larkin **5**:228
Robert Lowell **3**:303
George MacBeth **5**:264
James Merrill **8**:381
Joyce Carol Oates **2**:314; **3**:362
Octavio Paz **4**:398
Sylvia Plath **14**:426
Jon Silkin **6**:498
Dave Smith **22**:386
Stevie Smith **25**:416
Mark Strand **18**:520
James Tate **25**:429
R. S. Thomas **6**:532
Charles Tomlinson **4**:545, 547
Mona Van Duy **7**:499
Robert Penn Warren **10**:523;
18:534, 538
John Hall Wheelock **14**:571
Richard Wilbur **9**:568
James Wright **5**:520

Bednarczyk, Tony
Edmund Crispin **22**:111
William X. Kienzle **25**:274

Bedrosian, Margaret
William Saroyan **29**:361

Beer, John
E. M. Forster **22**:131

Beer, Patricia
W. H. Auden **6**:19
Beryl Bainbridge **18**:33
Christopher Fry **14**:188
Seamus Heaney **14**:241
Eleanor Hibbert **7**:156
Lisel Mueller **13**:400
Alice Munro **10**:357
Peter Redgrove **6**:447

Beerman, Hans
Hermann Hesse **17**:199

Beesley, Paddy
Horst Bienek **11**:48

Begley, John
Oriana Fallaci **11**:191

Begley, John J., S.J.
Erich von Däniken **30**:426

Begnal, Michael
Vladimir Nabokov **23**:309

Behar, Jack
T. S. Eliot **13**:198
Rod Serling **30**:355

Behrendt, Stephen
Sharon Olds **39**:192
Richard Tillinghast **29**:417

Beichman, Arnold
Art Buchwald **33**:94
Arthur Koestler **1**:170
Anthony Powell **3**:400

Beidler, Peter G.
Leslie Marmon Silko **23**:407

Beidler, Philip D.
David Rabe **33**:343

Beja, Morris
Lawrence Durrell **4**:145
William Faulkner **3**:153
Nathalie Sarraute **4**:466

Belben, Rosalind
David Plante **23**:347

Belgion, Montgomery
André Malraux **4**:334
I. A. Richards **24**:373

Belitt, Ben
Jorge Luis Borges **2**:75
Robert Lowell **4**:297
Pablo Neruda **1**:247
Ayn Rand **30**:292

Belkind, Allen
Amos Oz **27**:361
Ishmael Reed **13**:480
Kurt Vonnegut, Jr. **22**:447

Bell, Anthea
Katherine Paterson **30**:285
Otfried Preussler **17**:377

Bell, Bernard
William Styron **3**:473

Bell, Bernard W.
Jean Toomer **4**:550; **22**:427

Bell, David
Joyce Carol Oates **19**:356

Bell, De Witt
William Dickey **28**:118

Bell, Frederick J.
Ernest K. Gann **23**:162

Bell, Gene H.
Jorge Luis Borges **9**:118
Alejo Carpentier **8**:135
Vladimir Nabokov **6**:360

Bell, Ian F. A.
Ezra Pound **10**:404

Bell, Lisle
Charles Addams **30**:12, 13
Frank B. Gilbreth, Jr. and
    Ernestine Gilbreth Carey
    17:152
Ogden Nash **23**:316
Frank G. Slaughter **29**:374

Bell, Madison
William Caunitz **34**:35
Lisa St. Aubin de Teran **36**:421

Bell, Marvin
Ted Berrigan **37**:42
F. R. Scott **22**:375
Dave Smith **22**:387
Miriam Waddington **28**:437

Bell, Millicent
Margaret Atwood **2**:19
Lynne Reid Banks **23**:40
Peter De Vries **2**:113
Janet Frame **22**:144
Eugenio Montale **7**:231
John O'Hara **2**:325
Anne Tyler **28**:430

Bell, Pearl K.
Martin Amis **4**:20
John Ashbery **6**:12
Beryl Bainbridge **4**:39
James Baldwin **4**:40; **15**:42
William Barrett **27**:24
Ann Beattie **18**:40
Saul Bellow **8**:70
Thomas Berger **38**:37
Marie-Claire Blais **6**:81
Louise Bogan **4**:69
William F. Buckley, Jr. **7**:35
Anthony Burgess **22**:77
John Cheever **15**:130
Eleanor Clark **5**:106
Arthur A. Cohen **7**:51
Len Deighton **7**:76
William Faulkner **6**:177
Paula Fox **2**:140
Nadine Gordimer **5**:146
Juan Goytisolo **5**:149
Günter Grass **4**:206
Graham Greene **3**:214
Joseph Heller **5**:180; **36**:226
Mark Helprin **22**:222
Josephine Herbst **34**:454
George V. Higgins **7**:157
Maureen Howard **5**:189
John Irving **13**:293
Ruth Prawer Jhabvala **8**:311
Charles Johnson **7**:183
Diane Johnson **5**:199
Uwe Johnson **10**:284

James Jones **10**:291
Milan Kundera **4**:277; **19**:270
Elinor Langer **34**:454
Philip Larkin **13**:337
John le Carré **5**:232
Alison Lurie **4**:307
Bernard Malamud **18**:321
Peter Matthiessen **5**:275
Mary McCarthy **14**:360
John McGahern **5**:281
James A. Michener **29**:313
Steven Millhauser **21**:217
A. G. Mojtabai **9**:385
Toni Morrison **22**:323
V. S. Naipaul **7**:254
Amos Oz **5**:335
Cynthia Ozick **7**:288
Walker Percy **8**:438
Marge Piercy **18**:409
Anthony Powell **3**:403
J. F. Powers **8**:447
Mario Puzo **36**:359
Ishmael Reed **6**:448
Adrienne Rich **6**:459
Jill Robinson **10**:439
Philip Roth **15**:455
J. R. Salamanca **15**:463
Susan Fromberg Schaeffer
    22:367
Anne Sexton **6**:494
Alix Kates Shulman **10**:475
Stephen Spender **5**:402
D. M. Thomas **22**:421
Mario Vargas Llosa **6**:546
Patrick White **3**:523
Edmund Wilson **24**:483
Herman Wouk **38**:451

Bell, Robert
Honor Arundel **17**:12
H. F. Brinsmead **21**:27
Robert Cormier **12**:137
Eilís Dillon **17**:95, 96
Mollie Hunter **21**:163
Madeleine L'Engle **12**:350
William Mayne **12**:390, 399
Robert Westall **17**:555, 557

Bell, Vereen M.
E. M. Forster **1**:107
Ted Hughes **9**:281
Richard F. Hugo **18**:260
Robert Lowell **37**:239

Bellamy, Joe David
Donald Barthelme **13**:60
Sam Shepard **4**:490
Kurt Vonnegut, Jr. **4**:564
Tom Wolfe **35**:462

Bellman, Samuel Irving
Saul Bellow **8**:81
Jorge Luis Borges **6**:91
Jerome Charyn **5**:103
Leonard Cohen **3**:109
Stanley Elkin **6**:169
William Faulkner **3**:152
Leslie A. Fiedler **4**:160, 161
Bruce Jay Friedman **3**:165
William H. Gass **15**:258
Ernest Hemingway **3**:234
Yoram Kaniuk **19**:239
Jack Kerouac **3**:263, 264
Meyer Levin **7**:205

Bernard Malamud **1**:197; **3**:320,
325
Saul Maloff **5**:271
Wallace Markfield **8**:380
James A. Michener **5**:288
Harry Mark Petrakis **3**:382
Philip Roth **3**:435
John Updike **3**:487
Elie Wiesel **5**:490

Belloc, Hilaire
P. G. Wodehouse **22**:479

Bellow, Saul
Camilo José Cela **13**:144
Ilya Ehrenburg **18**:131

Bellows, Silence Buck
Frank B. Gilbreth, Jr. and
    Ernestine Gilbreth Carey
    17:155
Zilpha Keatley Snyder **17**:471

Bell-Villada, Gene H.
Gabriel García Márquez **15**:254
Mario Vargas Llosa **31**:442

Beloff, Max
Paul Scott **9**:477

Beloof, Robert
Stanley J. Kunitz **6**:285
Marianne Moore **4**:360

Belton, John
Claude Chabrol **16**:177

Bemrose, John
Scott Elledge **34**:430
Frank Herbert **35**:206
Leon Rooke **34**:251
D. M. Thomas **31**:434
E. B. White **34**:430

Benchley, Nathaniel
Art Buchwald **33**:92
Robert Newton Peck **17**:337

Bendau, Clifford P.
Colin Wilson **14**:585

Bender, Marylin
Alix Kates Shulman **2**:395

Bender, Rose S.
Babbis Friis-Baastad **12**:214

Bender, William
Neil Diamond **30**:110
Andrew Lloyd Webber and Tim
    Rice **21**:423

Bendiner, Elmer
Piri Thomas **17**:498

Bendow, Burton
Grace Paley **4**:393

Benedict, Joan
Arthur C. Clarke **35**:123

Benedict, Ruth
Margaret Mead **37**:269, 271

Benedikt, Michael
Ted Berrigan **37**:43
David Ignatow **14**:276
Galway Kinnell **2**:230
Charles Simic **22**:379
Richard Wilbur **3**:532

Benestad, Janet P.
M. E. Kerr 12:300

Benet, Rosemary
Enid Bagnold 25:74

Benét, Stephen Vincent
Walter D. Edmonds 35:147, 150
Bruce Lancaster 36:241, 242
Carl Sandburg 35:347, 348

Benét, William Rose
Alvah Bessie 23:60
Sterling A. Brown 23:95
Agatha Christie 12:111
August Derleth 31:136
Robert Francis 15:235
Ogden Nash 23:316
John G. Neihardt 32:331
Carl Sandburg 35:347

Benford, Gregory
Arthur C. Clarke 35:128

Benham, G. F.
Friedrich Dürrenmatt 11:174

Benjamin, Cynthia
Madeleine L'Engle 12:351

Benjamin, David A.
John D. MacDonald 27:274

Benn, M. B.
Michael Hamburger 14:234

Bennett, Bruce
Brad Leithauser 27:240
Mary Oliver 34:247
Katha Pollitt 28:367
Richard Tillinghast 29:416
Nancy Willard 37:463

Bennett, C. S.
Rosemary Sutcliff 26:427

Bennett, Joseph
Philip Booth 23:75
Anthony Hecht 8:266

Bennett, Michael Alan
Walter M. Miller, Jr. 30:258

Bennett, Spencer C.
John Lennon and Paul McCartney 12:365

Bennett, Steven D.
William Kotzwinkle 35:258

Bennett, Virginia
Truman Capote 19:80

Bennett, Wendell C.
Thor Heyerdahl 26:190

Benoff, Symme J.
C. S. Adler 35:11

Bensen, D. R.
Glendon Swarthout 35:399

Bensheimer, Virginia
Mary Oliver 34:247

Bensky, Lawrence M.
Leonard Cohen 38:135

Benson, C. David
Anthony Powell 31:314
P. G. Wodehouse 22:484

Benson, Gerard
Leon Garfield 12:229

Benson, Jackson J.
Ernest Hemingway 6:232
John Steinbeck 9:517

Benson, Mary
Athol Fugard 14:189

Benson, Sheila
Jerzy Skolimowski 20:355

Benson, Thomas W.
Wayne C. Booth 24:89

Benstock, Bernard
William Gaddis 3:177
Flann O'Brien 7:270
Sean O'Casey 5:317

Benston, Alice N.
W. S. Merwin 2:276

Bentkowski, Tom
John Lennon 35:275

Bentley, Allen
Morris L. West 6:564

Bentley, Eric
Robert Anderson 23:29
Sally Benson 17:50
Truman Capote 19:81
Charles Chaplin 16:205
I. A. Richards 24:388
Robert Penn Warren 8:536
Orson Welles 20:434
Tennessee Williams 30:461
Herman Wouk 9:579

Bentley, Joseph
Aldous Huxley 1:152

Bentley, Phyllis
Pearl S. Buck 11:69
Noel Streatfeild 21:394

Benton, Michael
Alan Garner 17:146

Bere, Carol
Ted Hughes 37:174

Berenda, Carlton W.
Nevil Shute 30:372

Berendt, John
Phil Ochs 17:333

Berendzen, Richard
Carl Sagan 30:332, 336

Berets, Ralph
Saul Bellow 15:47
John Fowles 3:163

Berg, Beatrice
Agnes Eckhardt Nixon 21:243

Berg, Rona
Jessica Anderson 37:20

Berg, Stephen
Guillevic 33:191

Berge, Jody
Betsy Byars 35:73

Berger, Arthur Asa
Robert Crumb 17:85
Stan Lee 17:257
Monty Python 21:228
Charles M. Schulz 12:529
Jerome Siegel and Joe Shuster 21:360

Berger, Charles
Olga Broumas 10:77
James Merrill 18:331
Frederick Seidel 18:474

Berger, Harold L.
Frank Herbert 12:278
Walter M. Miller, Jr. 30:261

Berger, John
Lindsay Anderson 20:11

Berger, Joseph
Liam O'Flaherty 34:355

Berger, Matt
Roger Zelazny 21:474

Berger, Peter L.
Andrew M. Greeley 28:171
Shiva Naipaul 32:326

Bergin, Thomas G.
Aldo Palazzeschi 11:432
Lucio Piccolo 13:440
Salvatore Quasimodo 10:429
João Guimarães Rosa 23:349

Bergman, Andrew
Frank Capra 16:159
Isaac Bashevis Singer 11:499

Bergman, Andrew C. J.
Peter Benchley 4:53
Guy Davenport, Jr. 6:124

Bergmann, Linda Shell
Ishmael Reed 13:479
Ronald Sukenick 4:531

Bergonzi, Bernard
Kingsley Amis 2:6, 9
W. H. Auden 6:22
Amiri Baraka 33:52
John Barth 3:39
Heinrich Böll 27:60
Paul Bowles 2:79
Anthony Burgess 2:85
R. V. Cassill 23:106
David Caute 29:108, 121
Donald Davie 10:123
Nigel Dennis 8:173
Ilya Ehrenburg 18:135
Richard Fariña 9:195
Ian Fleming 30:131
John Fowles 2:138
Paula Fox 2:139
Geoffrey H. Hartman 27:189
Aldous Huxley 35:244
B. S. Johnson 6:262
Doris Lessing 3:283
William Maxwell 19:307
Iris Murdoch 2:297
Flann O'Brien 4:383
Anthony Powell 3:400
Thomas Pynchon 3:408
Alain Robbe-Grillet 4:447
Siegfried Sassoon 36:392
Andrew Sinclair 2:401

C. P. Snow 4:501; 13:508
Evelyn Waugh 1:357; 3:510
Angus Wilson 2:473; 25:461

Berke, Roberta
John Ashbery 25:55
Allen Ginsberg 36:187
Charles Olson 29:335
Katha Pollitt 28:366
Craig Raine 32:353

Berkley, Miriam
Cynthia Voigt 30:420

Berkman, Leonard
Tennessee Williams 30:468

Berkman, Sylvia
Peter Matthiessen 32:285

Berkowitz, Gerald M.
Neil Simon 31:396
Tom Stoppard 29:397

Berkson, Bill
Frank O'Hara 2:320
Jerome Rothenberg 6:477

Berkvist, Margaret
Babbis Friis-Baastad 12:213

Berkvist, Robert
Isaac Asimov 26:36
Allan W. Eckert 17:105
Earl Hamner, Jr. 12:258
Robert A. Heinlein 26:161
S. E. Hinton 30:205
Farley Mowat 26:337
Andre Norton 12:456, 457
Kin Platt 26:348, 352
Mary Rodgers 12:493

Berlin, Isaiah
Aldous Huxley 3:254

Berlin, Normand
Roman Polanski 16:469
Tennessee Williams 30:473

Berman, Bruce
Rainer Werner Fassbinder 20:105

Berman, Jeffrey
E. M. Forster 22:129

Berman, Marshall
Studs Terkel 38:421

Berman, Michael
Milan Kundera 19:267

Berman, Neil
Robert Coover 15:143

Berman, Paul
Maria Irene Fornes 39:136
C.L.R. James 33:221
Peter Nichols 36:334
Isaac Bashevis Singer 11:501
Gary Snyder 32:400
Michel Tournier 36:439
Hugh Whitemore 37:447
August Wilson 39:279

Berman, Ronald
William F. Buckley, Jr. 18:81
Ronald Bush 34:532
T. S. Eliot 34:532

Berman, Susan K.
Fredrica Wagman **7**:500

Bermel, Albert
Ed Bullins **1**:47
Jean Genet **10**:227
Christopher Hampton **4**:211
Megan Terry **19**:439

Bermel, Joyce
Hilma Wolitzer **17**:562

Bernard, April
Louise Bogan **39**:385
Elizabeth Frank **39**:385

Bernays, Anne
Alice Adams **6**:1
Stratis Haviaras **33**:203
Alison Lurie **39**:177
Adrienne Rich **11**:474

Berner, Robert L.
André Brink **18**:68; **36**:69
Bessie Head **25**:233
Alan Paton **10**:388

Berner, Steve
Louis L'Amour **25**:281

**Bernetta (Quinn), Sister Mary,
O.S.F.**
Allen Tate **4**:539
See also Quinn, Sister Mary
Bernetta, O.S.F.

Bernhardt, William
François Truffaut **20**:380

Bernikow, Louise
A. S. Byatt **19**:77
Muriel Rukeyser **6**:479

Berns, Walter
Daniel J. Berrigan **4**:57

Bernstein, Burton
George P. Elliott **2**:131

Bernstein, Jeremy
Lewis Thomas **35**:413

Bernstein, Paul
James Clavell **25**:127

Bernstein, Richard
Marguerite Duras **34**:162

Bernstein, Samuel J.
Robert Anderson **23**:33

Bernstein, Theodore M.
Isaac Asimov **26**:36

Berrigan, Daniel, S.J.
Horst Bienek **7**:28
Denise Levertov **28**:243
Thomas Merton **11**:373

Berry, Faith
Amiri Baraka **33**:54

Berry, Jason
Steven Goldsberry **34**:55

Berry, Mabel
Maureen Daly **17**:91

Berry, Margaret
Mulk Raj Anand **23**:12

Berry, Mary Clay
Allen Drury **37**:110

Berry, Patricia
Walter Dean Myers **35**:298

Berry, Wendell
Hayden Carruth **4**:94

Berryman, Charles
E. L. Doctorow **37**:83
Joseph Heller **36**:227
Gore Vidal **22**:435

Berryman, John
Saul Bellow **10**:37
T. S. Eliot **13**:197
Ernest Hemingway **10**:270
Randall Jarrell **13**:299
Ezra Pound **13**:460

Bersani, Leo
Julio Cortázar **2**:104
Jean Genet **2**:158
J.M.G. Le Clézio **31**:243
Norman Mailer **8**:364
Henri de Montherlant **19**:328
Alain Robbe-Grillet **1**:288
Robert Wilson **7**:551

Berthel, John H.
Nevil Shute **30**:367

Berthoff, Warner
Alex Haley **12**:245
Norman Mailer **3**:313
Iris Murdoch **3**:345
Vladimir Nabokov **3**:352
Muriel Spark **3**:464
Edmund Wilson **2**:475; **3**:538

Beschta, James
Norman Williams **39**:101

Bespaloff, Rachel
Albert Camus **9**:139

Bessai, Diane
Austin C. Clarke **8**:142

Besser, Gretchen R.
Julien Green **3**:205

Besser, Gretchen Raus
Nathalie Sarraute **31**:380, 381,
382

Bessie, Alvah
Norman Mailer **3**:319

Best, Alan
Fritz Hochwälder **36**:237

Bester, Alfred
Isaac Asimov **3**:16
Robert A. Heinlein **3**:227

Bester, John
Masuji Ibuse **22**:225, 226
Kenzaburō Ōe **10**:372

Beston, John B.
Patrick White **18**:544

Bethell, Nicholas
Aleksandr I. Solzhenitsyn **7**:441

Betsky, Celia B.
A. Alvarez **5**:19
Max Apple **9**:32
Harriette Arnow **7**:15
Don DeLillo **10**:135
Margaret Drabble **2**:119

John Hawkes **4**:217
Doris Lessing **10**:315
Iris Murdoch **4**:370
Tim O'Brien **19**:358
Marge Piercy **14**:419

Bettelheim, Bruno
Lina Wertmüller **16**:599

Bettersworth, John K.
Milton Meltzer **26**:300

Betts, Doris
Barry Hannah **38**:235

Betts, Whitney
Winston Graham **23**:192

Bevan, A. R.
Mordecai Richler **5**:377

Bevan, David G.
Pier Paolo Pasolini **20**:268

Bevan, Jack
Arthur Gregor **9**:253

Bevington, Helen
Peter Davison **28**:101
Louis Simpson **4**:500

Bewick, E. N.
H. F. Brinsmead **21**:28

Bewick, Elizabeth
Josephine Poole **17**:371

Bewley, Marius
A. R. Ammons **2**:11
John Berryman **2**:56
Kenneth Burke **24**:124
C. Day Lewis **6**:128
Thomas Kinsella **4**:270
Hugh MacDiarmid **2**:253
Sylvia Plath **2**:335
Herbert Read **4**:440
Charles Tomlinson **2**:436

Bezanker, Abraham
Saul Bellow **1**:32
Isaac Bashevis Singer **3**:454

Bianco, David
James Purdy **10**:426

Biasin, Gian-Paolo
Dino Buzzati **36**:86
Umberto Eco **28**:131
Carlo Emilio Gadda **11**:211
Leonardo Sciascia **8**:473

Bibby, Geoffrey
Thor Heyerdahl **26**:192

Bick, Janice
Christie Harris **12**:269

Bickerton, Dorothy
Melvin Berger **12**:41

Bickman, Martin
Alfred Kazin **34**:555

Bidart, Frank
Robert Lowell **9**:336

Bien, Peter
Yannis Ritsos **6**:462

Bienstock, Beverly Gray
John Barth **3**:41

Bier, Jesse
James Thurber **5**:434

Bierhaus, E. G., Jr.
John Osborne **11**:423

Bierman, James
Snoo Wilson **33**:463

Bigger, Charles P.
Walker Percy **8**:440

Bigsby, C.W.E.
Edward Albee **9**:6, 9; **13**:4
James Baldwin **13**:51; **17**:33
Imamu Amiri Baraka **14**:43;
33:58
Lorraine Hansberry **17**:185
Arthur Miller **10**:342; **26**:321
Willard Motley **18**:357

Bilan, R. P.
Margaret Atwood **25**:62
F. R. Leavis **24**:310
Rudy Wiebe **14**:574

Bilik, Dorothy Seidman
Bernard Malamud **27**:296

Bill, Rise
Richard Peck **21**:301

Billings, Robert
Marilyn R. Bowering **32**:47

Billington, Michael
Howard Brenton **31**:56
David Mamet **34**:218
Snoo Wilson **33**:459

Billington, Rachel
Malcolm Bradbury **32**:58

Billman, Carol W.
Arthur Kopit **18**:290
Laurence Yep **35**:474

Binder, Lucia
Cecil Bødker **21**:12

Binding, Paul
Jurek Becker **19**:36
Rolf Hochhuth **18**:256
Brian Moore **19**:334

Binham, Philip
Paavo Haavikko **18**:207, 208;
34:172, 174, 177
Hannu Salama **18**:460

Binns, Ronald
Samuel Beckett **29**:55
John Fowles **4**:171

Binyon, T. J.
Eric Ambler **9**:21
William Boyd **28**:40
Matthew Bruccoli **34**:416
Agatha Christie **39**:436
Peter Dickinson **12**:175, 176
Paul E. Erdman **25**:154
Ross Macdonald **34**:416
Janet Morgan **39**:436
Ruth Rendell **28**:384

Birbalsingh, F. M.
Mordecai Richler **13**:485

Birch, Ian
David Byrne **26**:95

Critic Index

Birchall, Jonathan
Elizabeth Jane Howard 29:246

Bird, Caroline
Milton Meltzer 26:299

Bird, Christopher
Colin Wilson 14:584

Birkerts, Sven
Blaise Cendrars 18:97
Max Frisch 32:193
Brad Leithauser 27:241
Michel Tournier 36:441

Birmingham, Mary Louise
Jesse Jackson 12:289

Birnbaum, Henry
Gil Orlovitz 22:332

Birnbaum, Larry
Frank Zappa 17:595

Birnbaum, Milton
Aldous Huxley 3:255; 4:239

Birnbaum, Phyllis
Shiga Naoya 33:365

Birney, Earle
A.J.M. Smith 15:513

Birney, Hoffman
Bruce Lancaster 36:243

Birrell, Francis
René Clair 20:59
Rouben Mamoulian 16:420

Birstein, Ann
Russell Banks 37:24
Iris Murdoch 4:370
David Plante 23:343
Sylvia Plath 17:352

Bishop, Christopher
Buster Keaton 20:189

Bishop, Claire Huchet
Joseph Krumgold 12:316
Noel Streatfeild 21:401

Bishop, Elizabeth
Flannery O'Connor 15:408

Bishop, Ferman
Allen Tate 2:428

Bishop, John Peale
E. E. Cummings 12:142

Bishop, Lloyd
Henri Michaux 8:390

Bishop, Michael
Arthur C. Clarke 35:125
Guillevic 33:192, 193, 194
Stephen King 26:238
Ursula K. Le Guin 22:275
Fritz Leiber 25:307

Bishop, Morris
Ogden Nash 23:323

Bishop, Tom
Jean Cocteau 8:145
Julio Cortázar 2:103
Raymond Queneau 5:359
Claude Simon 9:482

Biskind, Peter
Elia Kazan 16:371
Sam Peckinpah 20:278
Lina Wertmüller 16:588

Bissell, Claude T.
Hugh Garner 13:234

Bissett, Donald J.
Walter Dean Myers 35:296
Colin Thiele 17:493

Bjorkland, Beth
Ernst Jandl 34:200

Bjornson, Richard
Charles R. Larson 31:240

Black, Campbell
Stanley Middleton 38:330
Mary Renault 17:400
Isaac Bashevis Singer 6:507

Black, Cyril E.
André Malraux 1:203

Black, Susan M.
Art Buchwald 33:89
Pamela Hansford Johnson 27:219
Elizabeth Spencer 22:400

Black, W. E.
John G. Neihardt 32:332

Blackburn, Sara
Lynne Reid Banks 23:41
Marie-Claire Blais 22:58
C.D.B. Bryan 29:102
R. V. Cassill 4:95
Michel del Castillo 38:167
Don DeLillo 27:77
Peter Dickinson 12:169
Rosalyn Drexler 2:120
Maureen Duffy 37:115
Sumner Locke Elliott 38:179
Jim Harrison 6:225
Maxine Hong Kingston 12:313
Alan Lelchuk 5:244
David Madden 5:266
Michael McClure 6:316
Toni Morrison 4:365
Marge Piercy 3:384
Alix Kates Shulman 2:395
Elizabeth Spencer 22:402
Gillian Tindall 7:473
Anne Tyler 28:431
David Wagoner 5:474
Fay Weldon 6:562

Blackburn, Thomas
Sylvia Plath 17:344

Blackburn, Tom
Kingsley Amis 2:6

Blackford, Staige D.
M. M. Kaye 28:201

Blackman, Ruth
Sylvia Ashton-Warner 19:20

Blackman, Ruth Chapin
Ayn Rand 30:294

Blackmon, W. D.
Antonia Fraser 32:185

Blackmur, R(ichard) P.
Cleanth Brooks 24:102
E. E. Cummings 8:154; 12:140
T. S. Eliot 24:159
Archibald MacLeish 14:336
Marianne Moore 13:393
John Crowe Ransom 5:363
I. A. Richards 24:389
Allen Tate 4:536
Lionel Trilling 24:450
Yvor Winters 32:456

Blackwood, Caroline
Ingmar Bergman 16:49

Blades, Joe
Bob Fosse 20:123

Blaha, Franz G.
J. P. Donleavy 4:125

Blair, Karin
Gene Roddenberry 17:408, 411

Blair, Walter
Ogden Nash 23:320

Blais, Marie-Claire
Elizabeth Bishop 13:88

Blaise, Clark
Ved Mehta 37:294
Salman Rushdie 23:365

Blake, George
John Cowper Powys 9:439

Blake, Nicholas
Margery Allingham 19:12
Agatha Christie 12:113

Blake, Patricia
Isabel Allende 39:32
Josephine Herbst 34:453
Elinor Langer 34:453
Cynthia Ozick 28:355
Aleksandr I. Solzhenitsyn 1:319; 7:439
Andrei Voznesensky 1:349

Blake, Percival
Leonardo Sciascia 8:474

Blake, Richard A.
Norman Lear 12:331
George Lucas 16:411
Monty Python 21:224
Peter Shaffer 37:384
Morris L. West 33:433

Blakeston, Oswell
Michael Ayrton 7:19
Peter Dickinson 35:131
Gabriel García Márquez 3:180
Paul Theroux 15:535
Trevanian 29:430
P. G. Wodehouse 2:480

Blamires, David
David Jones 2:216, 217; 4:260; 13:308

Bland, Peter
Norman MacCaig 36:283
Louis Simpson 32:378
Derek Walcott 25:457

Blanford, S. L.
Honor Arundel 17:13

Blaser, Robin
Jack Spicer 18:506

Blasi, Alberto
José Donoso 32:161

Blasing, Mutlu Konuk
Elizabeth Bishop 32:44

Blassingame, Wyatt
Harriette Arnow 7:15

Blaydes, Sophia B.
Simon Gray 9:242

Blazek, Douglas
Robert Creeley 2:107
W. S. Merwin 5:286
Diane Wakoski 4:573

Bleikasten, André
Flannery O'Connor 10:366

Bleiler, E. F.
Isaac Asimov 26:58

Blessing, Richard A.
John Nichols 38:339

Blewitt, Charles G.
Fumiko Enchi 31:140
John Gardner 30:154

Blicksilver, Edith
Leslie Marmon Silko 23:409

Blindheim, Joan Tindale
John Arden 13:26

Blish, James
Poul Anderson 15:11
John Brunner 10:77
Theodore Sturgeon 22:411
Roger Zelazny 21:465

Blishen, Edward
Alan Garner 17:150
William Golding 27:159
William Mayne 12:391, 394
Amos Tutuola 29:441

Bliss, Corinne Demas
Stratis Haviaras 33:205

Bliss, Michael
Hugh Hood 28:195

Bliss, Shepherd
Frederick Wiseman 20:477

Bliven, Naomi
Marie-Claire Blais 22:58
Brigid Brophy 29:93
Louis-Ferdinand Céline 4:103
Agatha Christie 12:125
Isak Dinesen 29:163
Andrea Giovene 7:117
Andrew M. Greeley 28:170
Eugène Ionesco 6:257
Anthony Powell 7:343
Emlyn Williams 15:578
Monique Wittig 22:471

Bloch, Adèle
Michel Butor 8:120
Pär Lagerkvist 7:200

Bloch, Robert
Theodore Sturgeon 39:365

Blodgett, E. D.
D. G. Jones 10:285
Sylvia Plath 3:388

Blodgett, Harriet
  Colin MacInnes **23**:285
  V. S. Naipaul **4**:375

Blomster, W. V.
  Christa Wolf **14**:594

Blomster, Wes
  Günter Grass **32**:201
  Siegfried Lenz **27**:256

Błonski, Jan
  Czesław Miłosz **11**:377

Blonston, Gary
  Tom Robbins **32**:374

Bloom, Harold
  A. R. Ammons **5**:25; **8**:14; **9**:26
  John Ashbery **4**:23; **9**:41; **13**:30;
    15:26, 33
  W. H. Auden **6**:16
  Saul Bellow **6**:50
  Frank Bidart **33**:77
  Jorge Luis Borges **6**:87
  Alfred Corn **33**:114
  James Dickey **10**:141
  Northrop Frye **24**:226
  Allen Ginsberg **6**:199
  Seamus Heaney **25**:246
  Anthony Hecht **13**:269
  Daryl Hine **15**:282
  John Hollander **8**:301, 302;
    14:264
  Galway Kinnell **29**:284
  Philip Levine **9**:332
  Robert Lowell **8**:355
  Archibald MacLeish **8**:363
  Norman Mailer **28**:260
  James Merrill **8**:388
  Howard Moss **7**:249; **14**:375
  Howard Nemerov **36**:300
  Robert Pack **13**:439
  Isaac Bashevis Singer **38**:410
  W. D. Snodgrass **10**:478
  Mark Strand **18**:517
  Robert Penn Warren **8**:539;
    18:535; **39**:265
  Charles Wright **13**:614
  A. B. Yehoshua **31**:474

Bloom, J. Don
  Alvin Silverstein and Virginia
    B. Silverstein **17**:454

Bloom, Janet
  Linda Pastan **27**:368

Bloom, Lynn Z.
  John Nichols **38**:344

Bloom, Robert
  W. H. Auden **1**:10; **11**:13

Blotner, Joseph L.
  Cleanth Brooks **24**:116
  J. D. Salinger **1**:295

Blount, Roy, Jr.
  Steve Martin **30**:248

Blow, Simon
  Julia O'Faolain **19**:360
  Sylvia Plath **11**:451
  Anthony Powell **31**:317
  Isaac Bashevis Singer **6**:510
  Scott Spencer **30**:408
  A. N. Wilson **33**:452

Blue, Adrianne
  Simone de Beauvoir **31**:44
  Buchi Emecheta **14**:160
  Henri Troyat **23**:461
  John Edgar Wideman **34**:300

Bluefarb, Sam
  Leslie A. Fiedler **13**:213
  Bernard Malamud **1**:196; **9**:350
  Chaim Potok **26**:370
  John Steinbeck **5**:407
  Richard Wright **3**:546

Bluestein, Gene
  Bob Dylan **12**:189
  Richard Fariña **9**:195

Bluestone, George
  Nelson Algren **10**:5

Blum, David
  Peter Handke **15**:268

Blum, Morgan
  Peter Taylor **18**:522

Blumberg, Myrna
  Ronald Harwood **32**:225

Blumenberg, Richard M.
  Alain Resnais **16**:510

Blumenfeld, Yorick
  John Berger **19**:37
  Yevgeny Yevtushenko **1**:382

Blumenthal, Eileen
  Jonathan Reynolds **38**:391

Blundell, Janet Boyarin
  Maya Angelou **12**:14; **35**:31, 32

Bly, Robert
  A. R. Ammons **5**:28
  Carlos Castaneda **12**:94
  Gunnar Ekelöf **27**:111, 115
  David Ignatow **14**:274
  Robert Lowell **4**:297
  Pablo Neruda **28**:306, 315
  Francis Ponge **18**:419

Blythe, Ronald
  Roy Fuller **28**:158
  William Golding **17**:178
  Ronald Harwood **32**:224
  Erica Jong **6**:267
  Alice Munro **6**:341
  Joyce Carol Oates **6**:368
  Jean Rhys **19**:391
  Wilbur Smith **33**:375
  David Storey **8**:506
  A. N. Wilson **33**:458

Boak, Denis
  André Malraux **4**:330

Boardman, Gwenn R.
  Yasunari Kawabata **2**:222
  Yukio Mishima **2**:286

Boas, Franz
  Zora Neale Hurston **30**:209

Boatwright, James
  Harry Crews **23**:132
  John Ehle **27**:104
  Paul Horgan **9**:278
  David Leavitt **34**:79
  James McCourt **5**:278
  Gore Vidal **6**:549

  Robert Penn Warren **1**:356
  Marguerite Yourcenar **38**:455

Boatwright, John
  Walker Percy **8**:438

Boatwright, Taliaferro
  Ernest K. Gann **23**:165
  Richard Matheson **37**:245
  Emily Cheney Neville **12**:450

Bobbie, Walter
  Stephen King **12**:309

Bobbitt, Joan
  James Dickey **15**:173
  William Price Fox **22**:140

Bochner, Jay
  Blaise Cendrars **18**:93

Bochtler, Stan
  Cecil Bødker **21**:12

Bock, Philip K.
  John G. Neihardt **32**:335

Bocock, Maclin
  Donald Barthelme **23**:44

Bodart, Joni
  John Gardner **30**:154
  Frank Herbert **12**:272
  Rosemary Wells **12**:638

Bode, Carl
  Katherine Anne Porter **7**:318

Bodo, Maureen
  Gore Vidal **10**:504

Boe, Eugene
  Christina Stead **2**:421

Boek, Jean K.
  Vine Deloria, Jr. **21**:113

Boening, John
  Robert Penn Warren **39**:261

Boeth, Richard
  Len Deighton **22**:114
  John O'Hara **2**:324

Bogan, Louise
  W. H. Auden **1**:9
  Richard Eberhart **19**:140
  Barbara Howes **15**:289
  Patrick Kavanagh **22**:235
  Marianne Moore **13**:396; **19**:338
  W. R. Rodgers **7**:377
  Muriel Rukeyser **15**:456
  Frederick Seidel **18**:474

Bogart, Gary
  Sol Gordon **26**:137
  Kristin Hunter **35**:228
  Robert Newton Peck **17**:340

Bogdanovich, Peter
  Alfred Hitchcock **16**:343

Bogen, Don
  Frank Bidart **33**:80
  Richard F. Hugo **32**:251

Bogstad, Janice M.
  Barbara Wersba **30**:433

Bohn, Chris
  Bob Marley **17**:272

Bohner, Charles H.
  Robert Penn Warren **1**:354

Bok, Sissela
  Vladimir Nabokov **1**:245

Boland, John
  Brian Aldiss **5**:15
  John Dickson Carr **3**:101
  Richard Condon **4**:106
  Harry Kemelman **2**:225
  Michael Moorcock **5**:293

Bold, Alan
  Robert Graves **1**:130

Boles, Paul Darcy
  Truman Capote **19**:81

Bolger, Eugenie
  Hortense Calisher **8**:125
  José Donoso **4**:130

Bollard, Margaret Lloyd
  William Carlos Williams **9**:571

Bolling, Doug
  John Barth **27**:30

Bolling, Douglass
  E. M. Forster **9**:206
  Doris Lessing **3**:290
  Clarence Major **19**:296
  Rudolph Wurlitzer **4**:598;
    15:588
  Al Young **19**:478

Bolotin, Susan
  Eva Figes **31**:167
  Jay McInerney **34**:81
  Gloria Naylor **28**:304

Bolton, Richard R.
  Herman Wouk **9**:580

Bond, Kirk
  Carl Theodor Dreyer **16**:260

Bondy, François
  Günter Grass **2**:173

Bone, Robert
  William Melvin Kelley **22**:247
  Nella Larsen **37**:213
  Paule Marshall **27**:309
  Melvin B. Tolson **36**:430
  Jean Toomer **22**:425

Bone, Robert A.
  James Baldwin **1**:15; **17**:29
  Amiri Baraka **33**:53
  Arna Bontemps **1**:37
  W.E.B. Du Bois **1**:80
  Ralph Ellison **1**:95; **3**:142
  Jessie Redmon Fauset **19**:170
  Langston Hughes **1**:147
  Zora Neale Hurston **7**:171
  Willard Motley **18**:357
  Ann Petry **1**:266
  Jean Toomer **1**:341
  Richard Wright **1**:378
  Frank G. Yerby **1**:381

Bongiorno, Robert
  Carlo Emilio Gadda **11**:209

Boni, John
  Kurt Vonnegut, Jr. **5**:465

Boniol, John Dawson, Jr.
  Melvin Berger **12**:40, 41

Bonnell, Paula
  Sharon Olds **39**:187

Bonner, Joey
  Bette Bao Lord **23**:279

Bonney, Mary Anne
  Erich von Däniken **30**:427
  Jonathan Keates **34**:201
  Ann Schlee **35**:374

Bontemps, Arna
  Langston Hughes **35**:215
  Zora Neale Hurston **30**:213
  Ann Petry **18**:403
  Jean Toomer **13**:551

Booker, Christopher
  Andrea Lee **36**:254
  Tom Wolfe **35**:457

Boon, James A.
  Claude Lévi-Strauss **38**:301

Booth, James A.
  Ayi Kwei Armah **33**:30
  Carl Sagan **30**:338

Booth, Martin
  Thomas M. Disch **36**:126
  Ted Hughes **14**:272
  John Matthias **9**:361
  Christopher Reid **33**:351
  Gilbert Sorrentino **14**:500
  Yevgeny Yevtushenko **26**:469

Booth, Philip
  Hayden Carruth **18**:87
  William Dickey **28**:117
  Richard Eberhart **11**:176;
    19:140
  Randall Jarrell **1**:159
  Maxine Kumin **13**:327
  Mary Oliver **19**:361
  Louis Simpson **7**:426

Booth, Rosemary
  Marilynne Robinson **25**:388

Booth, Wayne C.
  M. H. Abrams **24**:13
  Kenneth Burke **24**:133
  Susan Fromberg Schaeffer
    22:367
  Hunter S. Thompson **17**:507

Borden, Diane M.
  Ingmar Bergman **16**:78

Bordewich, Fergus M.
  Agnes Eckhardt Nixon **21**:246

Bordwell, David
  Charles Chaplin **16**:199
  François Truffaut **20**:389
  Orson Welles **20**:445

Borg, Mary
  Eva Figes **31**:163
  Bessie Head **25**:232
  Elizabeth Jane Howard **29**:245
  Françoise Sagan **17**:426
  Frank Tuohy **37**:428

Borges, Jorge Luis
  Adolfo Bioy Casares **4**:63
  Orson Welles **20**:453

Boring, Phyllis Zatlin
  Miguel Delibes **18**:117

Borinsky, Alicia
  Manuel Puig **5**:355

Borkat, Robert F. Sarfatt
  Robert Frost **9**:222

Borland, Hal
  John Ehle **27**:103
  Farley Mowat **26**:333, 335

Boroff, David
  Hortense Calisher **38**:70
  R. V. Cassill **23**:104, 105
  William Melvin Kelley **22**:247

Boroff, David A.
  John A. Williams **13**:598

Borroff, Marie
  John Hollander **2**:197
  Denise Levertov **2**:243
  William Meredith **4**:348
  James Merrill **2**:274

Borrus, Bruce J.
  Saul Bellow **15**:57

Boruch, Marianne
  Robert Hass **39**:149

Bosley, Keith
  Eugenio Montale **7**:229

Bosmajian, Hamida
  Louis-Ferdinand Céline **3**:103

Bosse, Malcolm
  Walter Dean Myers **35**:297

Boston, Howard
  Eilís Dillon **17**:93, 94
  Jean Lee Latham **12**:323
  Farley Mowat **26**:333

Boston, Richard
  Alison Lurie **39**:183

Bosworth, David
  Robert Stone **23**:430
  Kurt Vonnegut, Jr. **12**:629

Bosworth, Patricia
  Nora Ephron **31**:159

Botsford, Judith
  Franklyn M. Branley **21**:19

Boucher, Anthony
  Margery Allingham **19**:13
  Robert Bloch **33**:83
  Taylor Caldwell **28**:65
  Agatha Christie **12**:115, 116,
    117
  John Creasey **11**:134
  Edmund Crispin **22**:109, 110
  C. Day Lewis **6**:128
  August Derleth **31**:137, 138
  Nicolas Freeling **38**:183
  Jan de Hartog **19**:131
  Evan Hunter **31**:219, 220
  Len Deighton **22**:113, 114
  Eilís Dillon **17**:95
  Howard Fast **23**:158
  Timothy Findley **27**:140
  Thomas J. Fleming **37**:122
  Dick Francis **22**:150
  John Gardner **30**:151, 152
  Winston Graham **23**:193, 194
  Patricia Highsmith **2**:193
  P. D. James **18**:272

M. M. Kaye **28**:198
  Harry Kemelman **2**:225
  Colin MacInnes **23**:282
  Mary Lee Settle **19**:409
  Anthony Shaffer **19**:413
  Mary Stewart **7**:467; **35**:388,
    389, 390, 391
  Julian Symons **2**:426; **14**:523

Boucher, Norman
  Thomas Merton **34**:467
  Michael Mott **34**:467

Bouise, Oscar A.
  Allan W. Eckert **17**:103
  Eleanor Hibbert **7**:155
  Per Wahlöö **7**:501

Boulby, Mark
  Hermann Hesse **11**:272; **17**:207

Boulding, Kenneth E.
  Margaret Mead **37**:276

Boulton, James T.
  Harold Pinter **6**:406

Boumelha, Penny
  Howard Nemerov **36**:309

Bouraoui, H. A.
  Nathalie Sarraute **2**:385

Bourdillon, Jennifer
  Otfried Preussler **17**:374

Bourjaily, Vance
  Kay Boyle **19**:66
  David Bradley, Jr. **23**:80
  Roald Dahl **18**:109
  Jim Harrison **14**:235
  Philip Roth **9**:460
  Helen Hoover Santmyer **33**:358
  John Sayles **14**:483
  George Tabori **19**:436

Bourne, Mike
  Jimmy Page and Robert Plant
    12:476
  Pink Floyd **35**:305
  Frank Zappa **17**:588

Bourne, Randolph
  Carl Van Vechten **33**:385

Bourneuf, Roland
  Hubert Aquin **15**:17

Bousoño, Carlos
  Vicente Aleixandre **36**:30

Boutelle, Ann E.
  Hugh MacDiarmid **2**:253

Boutrous, Lawrence K.
  John Hawkes **3**:223

Bova, Ben
  James A. Michener **29**:314

Bova, Benjamin W.
  Franklyn M. Branley **21**:17

Bowden, J. H.
  Peter De Vries **28**:112

Bowden, Laurie
  Zibby Oneal **30**:280

Bowe, Clotilde Soave
  Natalia Ginzburg **11**:228

Bowen, Barbara C.
  P. G. Wodehouse **10**:538

Bowen, Elizabeth
  Henri de Montherlant **19**:322

Bowen, John
  Arthur Kopit **1**:171
  Randolph Stow **23**:433

Bowen, Robert O.
  Andrew Lytle **22**:293
  Flannery O'Connor **21**:259

Bowen, Roger
  Philip Larkin **18**:297

Bowen, Zack
  Padraic Colum **28**:90

Bowering, George
  Milton Acorn **15**:9
  Margaret Atwood **2**:19
  Margaret Avison **2**:29
  Earle Birney **4**:64
  Leonard Cohen **38**:135
  D. G. Jones **10**:288
  Margaret Laurence **3**:278
  Denise Levertov **15**:336
  Gwendolyn MacEwan **13**:357
  John Newlove **14**:377
  A. W. Purdy **6**:428
  Mordecai Richler **5**:374
  Audrey Thomas **7**:472; **13**:538

Bowering, Marilyn
  Patrick Lane **25**:285

Bowering, Peter
  Aldous Huxley **4**:237

Bowers, A. Joan
  Gore Vidal **8**:526

Bowers, Marvin
  L. E. Sissman **9**:491

Bowie, Malcolm
  Yves Bonnefoy **9**:114

Bowles, Gloria
  Louise Bogan **39**:390
  Elizabeth Frank **39**:390
  Diane Wakoski **7**:505

Bowles, Jerry G.
  Craig Nova **7**:267

Bowra, C. M.
  Rafael Alberti **7**:7

Boxer, David
  Raymond Carver **22**:98

Boyce, Burke
  Esther Forbes **12**:205

Boyd, Alex
  Walter Dean Myers **35**:298

Boyd, Ann S.
  Ian Fleming **30**:145

Boyd, Blanche M.
  Renata Adler **8**:5

Boyd, Celia
  Honor Arundel **17**:16

Boyd, Ernest
  Padraic Colum **28**:86, 87

Boyd, John D.
Theodore Roethke **11**:483

Boyd, Malcolm
Andrew Lloyd Webber and Tim Rice **21**:425

Boyd, Robert
James Purdy **2**:350
Studs Terkel **38**:423

Boyd, William
J. G. Ballard **36**:47
William F. Buckley, Jr. **37**:62
Margaret Drabble **22**:126
Gabriel García Márquez **15**:252
Penelope Gilliatt **13**:238
William Golding **27**:162
Steven Millhauser **21**:221
John Mortimer **28**:288
Irwin Shaw **23**:399
Frank Tuohy **37**:430
Kurt Vonnegut, Jr. **22**:451
Gordon Vorster **34**:122
Stephen Wright **33**:468

Boyer, Robert H.
Roger Zelazny **21**:473

Boyers, Robert
Saul Bellow **3**:57
Ingmar Bergman **16**:79
Alan Dugan **6**:143
Louise Glück **22**:173
Witold Gombrowicz **7**:125; **11**:241
Robinson Jeffers **2**:214; **3**:258
Arthur Koestler **6**:281
Robert Lowell **8**:349; **9**:336
Sylvia Plath **11**:447
Adrienne Rich **7**:364
Theodore Roethke **8**:457
W. D. Snodgrass **2**:406
Gary Snyder **2**:406
Richard Wilbur **6**:569

Boylan, Martin M.
Allen Drury **37**:109

Boyle, Kay
James Baldwin **1**:15
Tom Wicker **7**:534

Boyle, Ted E.
Kingsley Amis **2**:6
Brendan Behan **1**:26

Boylston, Helen Dore
Betty Cavanna **12**:97
Henry Gregor Felsen **17**:120
Lee Kingman **17**:243

Boynton, H. W.
Frank Swinnerton **31**:421

Bozek, Phillip
Hugh MacDiarmid **19**:285

Bracher, Frederick
John Cheever **15**:127
James Gould Cozzens **11**:127

Bracken, Paul
Jonathan Schell **35**:369

Brackman, Jacob
Renata Adler **31**:11
Robert Crumb **17**:84
Melvin Van Peebles **20**:411

Bradbrook, M. C.
T. S. Eliot **1**:91; **2**:130
William Empson **33**:137

Bradbury, John M.
Allen Tate **24**:446

Bradbury, Malcolm
J. G. Ballard **14**:40
Saul Bellow **33**:65
Malcolm Bradbury **32**:55
A. S. Byatt **19**:75
Ivy Compton-Burnett **10**:109
John Dos Passos **8**:181
D. J. Enright **31**:147
E. M. Forster **4**:167; **10**:180
John Fowles **3**:162; **4**:172
William Gaddis **8**:227
Peter Handke **38**:229
Joseph Heller **36**:226
Thomas Hinde **6**:240
Aldous Huxley **4**:244
Alfred Kazin **34**:555
Alison Lurie **39**:182
Michael Mott **15**:379
Iris Murdoch **4**:367; **11**:388
John O'Hara **11**:413
Ezra Pound **34**:508
Piers Paul Read **25**:378
Frank Sargeson **31**:365
C. P. Snow **4**:505
Gilbert Sorrentino **14**:501
Muriel Spark **2**:418
E. Fuller Torrey **34**:508
Lionel Trilling **9**:531
Gore Vidal **33**:411
Evelyn Waugh **8**:543
Angus Wilson **5**:513

Bradbury, Maureen
Phyllis Gotlieb **18**:193

Bradbury, Ray
Ray Bradbury **15**:86

Bradford, Melvin E.
Donald Davidson **2**:111, 112; **13**:167
William Faulkner **1**:102; **3**:155; **18**:149
Walker Percy **3**:381
Allen Tate **2**:429

Bradford, Richard
A. B. Guthrie, Jr. **23**:199
M. E. Kerr **12**:300
James Kirkwood **9**:319
Scott O'Dell **30**:270

Bradford, Roark
Nella Larsen **37**:210

Bradford, Tom
Ray Bradbury **10**:69

Bradley, Jerry
Gary Soto **32**:401

Bradley, Marion Zimmer
Thomas M. Disch **36**:128

Bradley, Sculley
Robert Frost **3**:169

Bradlow, Paul
Frederick Wiseman **20**:469

Brady, Ann P.
T. S. Eliot **15**:213

Brady, Charles A.
David Kherdian **6**:281
C. S. Lewis **14**:322

Brady, Owen
Richard Wright **21**:460

Brady, Patrick
Albert Camus **9**:147

Brady, Veronica
Thomas Keneally **19**:245

Braestrup, Peter
James H. Webb, Jr. **22**:454

Bragdon, Henry Wilkinson
Thomas J. Fleming **37**:126

Bragg, Lois
John Nichols **38**:344

Bragg, Melvyn
Kingsley Amis **13**:14
Saul Bellow **25**:84
William F. Buckley, Jr. **18**:82
E. M. Forster **2**:136
John le Carré **28**:227
Tom Sharpe **36**:401

Bragg, Pamela
Frank Bonham **12**:52

Bragin, John
Jean-Luc Godard **20**:133
Jean Renoir **20**:297

Braginsky, Dorothea D.
Judith Guest **30**:173

Braine, John
Richard Llewellyn **7**:207
Fay Weldon **9**:559

Braithwaite, E. R.
J. G. Ballard **36**:38

Braithwaite, William Stanley
T. S. Stribling **23**:439

Bramwell, Gloria
Richard Wright **21**:439

Branden, Nathaniel
Ayn Rand **30**:296

Brander, Laurence
E. M. Forster **15**:224
Aldous Huxley **18**:269

Brandriff, Welles T.
William Styron **11**:514

Brandt, G. W.
John Arden **13**:23

Brasillach, Robert
René Clair **20**:61

Brater, Enoch
Samuel Beckett **6**:42; **9**:81; **14**:78; **18**:51; **29**:63
Harold Pinter **27**:389
Tom Stoppard **29**:398

Braudy, Leo
John Berger **2**:54
Thomas Berger **3**:63
Bernardo Bertolucci **16**:90
Richard Condon **4**:107
Alfred Hitchcock **16**:347

Norman Mailer **1**:193; **8**:368
Jean Renoir **20**:301
Susan Sontag **31**:415

Braudy, Susan
Nora Ephron **17**:112

Braun, Devra
Lillian Hellman **18**:225

Braun, Eric
John Landis **26**:273
Elaine May **16**:433

Braun, Julie
Philip Roth **4**:453

Braver-Mann, Barnet G.
Charles Chaplin **16**:188

Braybrooke, Neville
Graham Greene **1**:130
François Mauriac **4**:337

Brazier, Chris
David Byrne **26**:94
The Clash **30**:44
Mick Jagger and Keith Richard **17**:239
Bruce Springsteen **17**:482
Paul Weller **26**:443

Brée, Germaine
Louis Aragon **3**:12
Marcel Aymé **11**:21
Samuel Beckett **10**:27
Stanley Burnshaw **13**:128
Albert Camus **1**:54; **11**:93
Louis-Ferdinand Céline **1**:57
Jean Cocteau **1**:59
Georges Duhamel **8**:186
Jean Giono **4**:183
Julien Green **3**:203
André Malraux **1**:202
François Mauriac **4**:337
Raymond Queneau **2**:359
Jules Romains **7**:381
Jean-Paul Sartre **1**:306; **7**:397

Breen, Jon L.
Robert Lipsyte **21**:210

Bregman, Alice Miller
Milton Meltzer **26**:301

Breit, Harvey
James Baldwin **2**:31

Breitrose, Henry
Shirley Clarke **16**:215

Brench, A. C.
Mongo Beti **27**:41

Brendon, Piers
Donald Barthelme **5**:53
Rosalyn Drexler **2**:119
Daphne du Maurier **6**:146
Tom Sharpe **36**:398
Wilbur Smith **33**:376
Robert Penn Warren **4**:582
Morris L. West **33**:432

Brennan, Anthony
W. P. Kinsella **27**:235
John Metcalf **37**:299
Jane Rule **27**:420

Brennan, Anthony S.
Samuel Beckett **14**:80
Clark Blaise **29**:72

Critic Index

Brennan, Thomas
Herman Wouk **38**:449

Brereton, Geoffrey
Lucien Goldmann **24**:239

Breschard, Jack
Billy Joel **26**:213

Breskin, David
Sterling A. Brown **23**:100

Breslin, James E.
T. S. Eliot **6**:166

Breslin, James E. B.
Robert Lowell **37**:241

Breslin, Jimmy
Gore Vidal **8**:525

Breslin, John B.
Charles Addams **30**:16
Gail Godwin **31**:196
Andrew M. Greeley **28**:177
C. S. Lewis **6**:308
Phyllis McGinley **14**:368
Tom McHale **5**:281
Wilfrid Sheed **10**:474
Susan Sontag **13**:516

Breslin, Patrick
Miguel Ángel Asturias **8**:25
Romain Gary **25**:189
Paul Theroux **15**:534

Breslin, Paul
Philip Booth **23**:77
Michael S. Harper **22**:209
Geoffrey Hill **18**:239
Daniel Hoffman **23**:242
William Meredith **22**:303
Charles Olson **29**:334
James Schuyler **23**:391
Robert Penn Warren **39**:255

Bresnick, Paul
James Purdy **10**:425

Breton, André
Luis Buñuel **16**:152

Brew, Claude C.
Tommaso Landolfi **11**:321

Brewer, Joan Scherer
Sol Gordon **26**:138

Brewster, Ben
Yasujiro Ozu **16**:455

Brewster, Dorothy
Doris Lessing **1**:173

Brickell, Herschel
Harriette Arnow **7**:15
Julia Peterkin **31**:303

Bricker, Karin K.
Mavis Thorpe Clark **12**:131

Brickner, Richard P.
Anthony Burgess **2**:86
Jerome Charyn **8**:136
Frederick Exley **11**:186
Frederick Forsyth **2**:137
Herbert Gold **7**:120
Evan Hunter **31**:222
William Kotzwinkle **14**:309
Phillip Lopate **29**:300
Cormac McCarthy **4**:341

Vladimir Nabokov 3:355
Harry Mark Petrakis 3:383
Muriel Spark 3:465
Richard B. Wright 6:581

Bridges, Les
Mickey Spillane **3**:469

Bridges, Linda
Donald Barthelme **5**:55
Alistair MacLean **13**:359
Georges Simenon **8**:487

Brien, Alan
Kingsley Amis **2**:6
Alan Ayckbourn **8**:34
Trevor Griffiths **13**:255
Ann Jellicoe **27**:205
John Osborne **5**:333
Harold Pinter **6**:418
N. F. Simpson **29**:365, 366
Wole Soyinka **14**:505
Tennessee Williams **8**:547

Brien, Dolores Elise
Robert Duncan **15**:188

Brigg, Peter
Arthur C. Clarke **13**:148
Frank Herbert **35**:204

Briggs, Julia
Leon Garfield **12**:234
Diana Wynne Jones **26**:227
Philippa Pearce **21**:290

Briggs, Kenneth A.
Thomas Merton **34**:463
Michael Mott **34**:463

Brignano, Russell Carl
Richard Wright **4**:594

Brink, Andre
James A. Michener **29**:312

Brink, André P.
Breyten Breytenbach **23**:83, 84

Brinkmeyer, Robert H., Jr.
Caroline Gordon **29**:189

Brinnin, John Malcolm
John Ashbery **6**:12
Ben Belitt **22**:49
Allen Ginsberg **6**:201
Galway Kinnell **1**:168
William Meredith **13**:372
Sylvia Plath **1**:269
Muriel Rukeyser **27**:404
William Jay Smith **6**:512

Brinsmead, H. F.
H. F. Brinsmead **21**:28

Brinson, Linda
T. R. Pearson **39**:89

Brinson, Peter
Jean Renoir **20**:289

Bristol, Horace
Pearl S. Buck **7**:33

Britt, Gwenneth
Vittorio De Sica **20**:94

Brittain, Victoria
Ngugi wa Thiong'o **36**:319

Britten, Florence Haxton
Carl Van Vechten **33**:394

Brivic, Sheldon
Richard Wright **9**:585

Brizzi, Mary T.
C. J. Cherryh **35**:109

Brock, H. I.
Zora Neale Hurston **30**:209

Brockway, James
Beryl Bainbridge **10**:16
Angela Carter **5**:102
J. P. Donleavy **4**:126
Mavis Gallant **7**:111
Penelope Gilliatt **10**:230
Julien Green **3**:205
Susan B. Hill **4**:228
Ursula Holden **18**:257
Frederic Raphael **14**:438
Piers Paul Read **10**:435
Muriel Spark **5**:399; **8**:495
Frank Swinnerton **31**:428
Emma Tennant **13**:537

Broderick, Dorothy M.
Fran Arrick **30**:18
H. F. Brinsmead **21**:27
Lois Duncan **26**:101
James D. Forman **21**:119
Nat Hentoff **26**:185
Jesse Jackson **12**:655
Stephen King **26**:239

Brodin, Dorothy
Marcel Aymé **11**:22

Brodrick, Jeffrey
John Gregory Dunne **28**:127

Brodsky, Arnold
Stevie Wonder **12**:655

Brodsky, Joseph
Anna Akhmatova **25**:26
Czesław Miłosz **11**:376
Eugenio Montale **9**:388

Brody, Patricia Ann
Joan Armatrading **17**:9

Brogan, D. W.
Bruce Catton **35**:88

Brogan, Hugh
Peter Ackroyd **34**:389
T. S. Eliot **34**:389
Mervyn Peake **7**:301

Broidy, Susan
Keri Hulme **39**:163

Bromberg, Pam
Lillian Hellman **18**:229

Brombert, Victor
Robert Alter **34**:517
Peter Brooks **34**:520
St.-John Perse **4**:398
Nathalie Sarraute **31**:378
Michel Tournier **36**:439

Bromell, Nicholas
Derek Walcott **25**:456

Bromfield, Louis
Conrad Richter **30**:310, 312

Bromige, David
Leonard Cohen **38**:132

Bromwich, David
Conrad Aiken **5**:10
A. R. Ammons **9**:2
John Ashbery **15**:34
Ben Belitt **22**:54
Elizabeth Bishop **32**:37
Hayden Carruth **10**:100
Leslie Epstein **27**:127
Robert Frost **9**:266
John Hawkes **4**:216
John Hollander **5**:187
Richard Howard **7**:167
Thomas Kinsella **19**:253
Doris Lessing **3**:288
Jay Macpherson **14**:346
Penelope Mortimer **5**:299
Michael Mott **15**:380
Iris Murdoch **3**:348; **6**:347
Howard Nemerov **9**:394
Robert Pinsky **9**:416
Stanley Plumly **33**:315
Eric Rohmer **16**:532
Anne Sexton **10**:467
Charles Simic **9**:479
Stevie Smith **8**:492
Muriel Spark **3**:465
Paul Theroux **5**:427
Robert Penn Warren **13**:572
Elie Wiesel **3**:528
Joy Williams **31**:462
Charles Wright **13**:615

Broner, E. M.
Maxine Hong Kingston **19**:250

Bronowski, J.
Kathleen Raine **7**:352

Bronson, A. A.
Joe Rosenblatt **15**:448

Bronstein, Lynne
Trina Robbins **21**:338

Brook, Stephen
Howard Brenton **31**:69
David Mamet **34**:218
Anthony Powell **31**:321

Brooke, Jocelyn
Elizabeth Bowen **1**:39

Brooke, Nicholas
Anne Stevenson **7**:462

Brooke-Rose, Christine
Ezra Pound **7**:328

Brookner, Anita
Ursula Holden **18**:259
Colleen McCullough **27**:320
Fay Weldon **19**:469

Brooks, Anne
Maureen Daly **17**:87
Mary Stolz **12**:548

Brooks, Cleanth
William Empson **19**:152
William Faulkner **18**:148;
  28:144
Ernest Hemingway **30**:179
Randall Jarrell **1**:159
Alfred Kazin **38**:272
Marianne Moore **10**:347

Walker Percy **6**:399
I. A. Richards **24**:396
Allen Tate **4**:539; **11**:522
Eudora Welty **33**:415
Yvor Winters **32**:458

Brooks, Ellen W.
Doris Lessing **3**:284

Brooks, G. L.
J.R.R. Tolkien **38**:440

Brooks, Gwendolyn
Kristin Hunter **35**:225
Melvin B. Tolson **36**:426

Brooks, Jeremy
A. J. Cronin **32**:140
Michael Frayn **31**:188

Brooks, John
Ernest K. Gann **23**:163

Brooks, Peter
Louis Aragon **22**:39
Roland Barthes **24**:28
J.M.G. Le Clézio **31**:246
Violette Leduc **22**:262
Alain Robbe-Grillet **1**:287

Brooks, Rick
Andre Norton **12**:467

Brooks, Robert M.
Andrew M. Greeley **28**:169

Brooks, Taye
Cecil Bødker **21**:12

Brooks, Thomas R.
Muriel Spark **18**:506

Brooks, Valerie
Beryl Bainbridge **22**:47

Brooks, Van Wyck
Upton Sinclair **15**:497

Broome, Peter
Robert Pinget **7**:306

Brophy, Brigid
Kingsley Amis **2**:5
Simone de Beauvoir **2**:42
Hortense Calisher **2**:95
Ivy Compton-Burnett **3**:111
William Faulkner **1**:102
Ernest K. Gann **23**:167
Jean Genet **2**:157
Joanne Greenberg **30**:162
Ronald Harwood **32**:223
Shirley Hazzard **18**:213
Patricia Highsmith **2**:192
W. Somerset Maugham **1**:204
Henry Miller **2**:281
Françoise Sagan **3**:443; **6**:482
Georges Simenon **2**:397
Elizabeth Taylor **2**:432
Evelyn Waugh **3**:509

Brophy, James D.
W. H. Auden **11**:15

Brose, Margaret
Giuseppe Ungaretti **11**:558;
15:538

Brosman, Catharine Savage
Simone de Beauvoir **31**:39
Jean-Paul Sartre **13**:503

Brosnahan, John
Robert Coover **32**:127
Michael Cunningham **34**:40
Don DeLillo **39**:115
Andrew Holleran **38**:246
John Jakes **29**:250
Stephen King **26**:236
David Leavitt **34**:78
Larry McMurtry **27**:333
Wilbur Smith **33**:377
Gordon Vorster **34**:122

Brothers, Barbara
Elizabeth Bowen **15**:79
Barbara Pym **37**:372

Brotherston, Gordon
Ernesto Cardenal **31**:71
Alejo Carpentier **38**:97

Brotman, Sonia
Margaret O. Hyde **21**:176, 177

Broughton, Glenda
Hilma Wolitzer **17**:563

Broughton, Panthea Reid
William Faulkner **6**:175
Carson McCullers **4**:345

Broun, Heywood
George S. Kaufman **38**:261

Broun, Heywood Hale
Roger Kahn **30**:231

Brousse, Charles
William Mastrosimone **36**:291

Brown, Alan
Marie-Claire Blais **22**:59
Ernest Hemingway **19**:217

Brown, Ashley
Caroline Gordon **6**:204, 206;
13:241
Allen Tate **2**:428

Brown, Calvin S.
Conrad Aiken **3**:4
William Faulkner **18**:149;
28:142

Brown, Chip
Joe McGinniss **32**:303

Brown, Clarence
Jorge Luis Borges **19**:48
Joseph Brodsky **36**:77
Czeslaw Milosz **5**:292
Vladimir Nabokov **1**:242

Brown, Constance A.
Laurence Olivier **20**:239

Brown, Cynthia
Barbara Corcoran **17**:75

Brown, Dee
Vine Deloria, Jr. **21**:112

Brown, Deming
Alexander Zinoviev **19**:487

Brown, E. K.
Louis Dudek **19**:136
E. J. Pratt **19**:382

Brown, Edward Hickman
Nadine Gordimer **33**:180
Doris Lessing **22**:279

Brown, Edward J.
Ilya Ehrenburg **18**:136

Brown, F. J.
Arthur Koestler **3**:271
Alberto Moravia **2**:293
Mario Puzo **1**:282
Muriel Spark **2**:417

Brown, Frederick
Louis Aragon **3**:13
Jean Cocteau **1**:60

Brown, Geoff
Woody Allen **16**:8
Walter Becker and Donald
Fagen **26**:79
Jackson Browne **21**:35
Dario Fo **32**:172
Marvin Gaye **26**:132
Satyajit Ray **16**:495
Smokey Robinson **21**:345, 350
Joan Micklin Silver **20**:342
Peter Weir **20**:425
Brian Wilson **12**:648

Brown, Georgia A.
Lynne Sharon Schwartz **31**:388

Brown, Harry
Hollis Summers **10**:494

Brown, Ivor
J. B. Priestley **2**:346

Brown, J. R.
Michael Frayn **31**:192

Brown, Jennifer
Richard Peck **21**:300

Brown, John L.
Helen MacInnes **27**:281
Marguerite Yourcenar **19**:484

Brown, John Mason
Charles Addams **30**:13
Eric Bentley **24**:46
Paul Green **25**:193
Laura Z. Hobson **25**:270
George S. Kaufman **38**:260,
261
Thornton Wilder **35**:436, 437
Tennessee Williams **30**:457

Brown, John Russell
John Arden **6**:8
John Osborne **5**:332
Harold Pinter **6**:408, 413
Arnold Wesker **5**:482

Brown, Kenneth R.
Sam Peckinpah **20**:275

Brown, Linda
Alan Ayckbourn **33**:43

Brown, Lloyd W.
Imamu Amiri Baraka **3**:35;
33:56
Wilson Harris **25**:212
Langston Hughes **10**:281
Paule Marshall **27**:313

Brown, Margaret Warren
Jean Lee Latham **12**:323

Brown, Merle E.
Kenneth Burke **2**:88
Geoffrey Hill **18**:236
Philip Larkin **18**:295

Brown, Pam
Billy Joel **26**:215

Brown, Ralph Adams
Henry Gregor Felsen **17**:121
Andre Norton **12**:455
John R. Tunis **12**:595

Brown, Richard
Douglas Adams **27**:14
John Kennedy Toole **19**:443

Brown, Robert
Stanley Elkin **14**:157

Brown, Robert McAfee
Elie Wiesel **5**:493; **37**:455

Brown, Rosellen
Margaret Atwood **8**:28; **15**:39
Hortense Calisher **38**:75
Marilyn French **18**:158
Toni Morrison **22**:321
Tim O'Brien **7**:272
May Sarton **4**:471
Judith Johnson Sherwin **7**:414
Diane Wakoski **4**:572

Brown, Royal S.
Brian De Palma **20**:78

Brown, Russell M.
Clark Blaise **29**:69, 73
Robert Kroetsch **5**:221
Leon Rooke **25**:392
Audrey Thomas **37**:418

Brown, Ruth Leslie
John Gardner **2**:151
Gilbert Rogin **18**:457

Brown, Slater
Jerome Siegel and Joe Shuster
21:353

Brown, Spencer
Edward Hoagland **28**:185
John McPhee **36**:297

Brown, Stephen P.
David Brin **34**:135
Kim Stanley Robinson **34**:105
Lucius Shepard **34**:108

Brown, Sterling
Zora Neale Hurston **30**:211

Brown, Steve
Arthur C. Clarke **18**:107

Brown, T.
Louis MacNeice **10**:323

Brown, Terence
Kingsley Amis **2**:6
Seamus Heaney **25**:240
Michael Longley **29**:293
Derek Mahon **27**:288

Brown, William P.
John Brunner **10**:78

Browne, Joseph
Larry McMurtry **27**:334

Browne, Ray B.
Irving Wallace **13**:569

Browne, Robert M.
J. D. Salinger **12**:511

Browning, Dominique
Susan Cheever 18:101

Browning, John
Snoo Wilson 33:466

Browning, Preston M., Jr.
Flannery O'Connor 3:367;
21:275

Brownjohn, Alan
Dannie Abse 7:1; 29:16
Ted Berrigan 37:44
Elizabeth Daryush 19:120
Donald Davie 5:115
C. Day Lewis 6:128
D. J. Enright 31:149, 153
Elaine Feinstein 36:168
Roy Fisher 25:157, 159
Roy Fuller 28:157, 158
W. S. Graham 29:197
Geoffrey Grigson 7:136
Thom Gunn 18:199
Seamus Heaney 7:148
Hermann Hesse 17:215
Geoffrey Hill 18:239
Elizabeth Jennings 14:292
Thomas Kinsella 4:270
Philip Larkin 5:226
Penelope Lively 32:275
Michael Longley 29:291
George MacBeth 9:340
Norman MacCaig 36:283, 284
Derek Mahon 27:287
Stanley Middleton 38:333
Edwin Morgan 31:273
Leslie Norris 14:388
Linda Pastan 27:370
Kenneth Patchen 18:393
Peter Porter 33:326
Anthony Powell 7:341
Craig Raine 32:349
Christopher Reid 33:349
Marilynne Robinson 25:388
Alan Sillitoe 19:420
Louis Simpson 7:428
D. M. Thomas 13:541
Ted Walker 13:567
Yevgeny Yevtushenko 26:467

Brownjohn, Elizabeth
Philip Larkin 5:227

Broyard, Anatole
Walter Abish 22:17
William Barrett 27:19
Frederick Barthelme 36:53
Saul Bellow 2:52; 33:67;
34:545
Roy Blount, Jr. 38:47
Claude Brown 30:39
Rosellen Brown 32:63, 64
William F. Buckley, Jr. 18:83
Frederick Busch 18:84
Hortense Calisher 38:73
Italo Calvino 33:99
Elias Canetti 25:113
Raymond Carver 36:100
John Cheever 25:119
Arthur A. Cohen 31:94
Laurie Colwin 23:129
Pat Conroy 30:76
Len Deighton 22:119
John M. Del Vecchio 29:151
Peter Dickinson 12:176; 35:137

José Donoso 8:179
Lawrence Durrell 27:97
Sumner Locke Elliott 38:180
Nora Ephron 17:111
Jules Feiffer 8:217
Elaine Feinstein 36:169
Ken Follett 18:156
Nicolas Freeling 38:185
Daniel Fuchs 34:545
John Gardner 28:164
John Gardner 30:158
Penelope Gilliatt 10:229
Herbert Gold 14:208
Günter Grass 2:172
Peter Handke 38:221
Lillian Hellman 18:227
Mark Helprin 22:221; 32:230
Richard F. Hugo 32:241
Garson Kanin 22:232
Yoram Kaniuk 19:239
Donald Keene 34:566
Benedict Kiely 23:266
Jerzy Kosinski 10:307
Helen MacInnes 27:283
Bernard Mac Laverty 31:256
Bernard Malamud 2:266
Bobbie Ann Mason 28:272
James A. Michener 29:316
A. G. Mojtabai 15:378
Wright Morris 18:353
Edna O'Brien 13:415
Michael Ondaatje 14:410
Cynthia Ozick 28:351
Robert B. Parker 27:367
Marge Piercy 14:420
David Plante 38:371
Anthony Powell 31:317
V. S. Pritchett 15:442
Barbara Pym 37:372
Anne Redmon 22:342
Jean Rhys 19:393
Marilynne Robinson 25:387
Philip Roth 3:436; 22:356
Françoise Sagan 9:468; 17:427;
36:380
Nathalie Sarraute 8:473
Mark Schorer 9:473
Lynne Sharon Schwartz 31:390
Georges Simenon 8:488
Isaac Bashevis Singer 38:410
Richard Stern 39:240, 241
J.I.M. Stewart 32:421, 422
Peter Taylor 18:527
Lisa St. Aubin de Teran 36:422
Trevanian 29:429, 430
William Trevor 25:445
Anne Tyler 11:553
John Updike 2:440; 9:539;
15:545
Eudora Welty 33:423
Joy Williams 31:463
Hilma Wolitzer 17:563

Bruccoli, Matthew J.
James Gould Cozzens 11:131
Peter Griffin 39:402
Ernest Hemingway 39:402
John O'Hara 3:370

Bruce-Novoa
Gary Soto 32:404

Bruchac, Joseph
Chinua Achebe 26:21

Bruckner, D.J.R.
Carolyn Chute 39:38
Louise Erdrich 39:129
Robert Fitzgerald 39:470
Thomas Merton 34:465
Michael Mott 34:465
J.R.R. Tolkien 38:434

Brudnoy, David
James Baldwin 2:33
Robin Cook 14:131
Bob Fosse 20:123

Bruell, Edwin
Harper Lee 12:342

Brukenfeld, Dick
Joyce Carol Oates 3:364

Brumberg, Abraham
Aleksandr I. Solzhenitsyn
4:514; 18:498

Brumer, Andy
Stephen Dobyns 37:81
Mary Oliver 34:246

Brummell, O. B.
Bob Dylan 12:183

Brunette, Peter
Archibald MacLeish 14:338

Bruning, Peter
Ward Ruyslinck 14:472

Brushwood, John S.
Gregorio López y Fuentes
32:280

Brustein, Robert
Edward Albee 3:6, 7; 25:37
Jean Anouilh 1:6
Enid Bagnold 25:77
James Baldwin 4:40; 17:28
Brendan Behan 1:26
Robert Bolt 14:88
Christopher Durang 27:89, 91
Federico Fellini 16:278
Dario Fo 32:176
Michael Frayn 31:193
Athol Fugard 25:178
Jack Gelber 1:114
Jean Genet 1:115
William Gibson 23:175
John Guare 29:208
A. R. Gurney, Jr. 32:219
John Hare 29:219
Ronald Harwood 32:227
Joseph Heller 3:228
Lillian Hellman 34:350
Rolf Hochhuth 4:230
William Inge 1:153
Eugène Ionesco 1:154
Arthur Kopit 18:287; 33:252
Stanley Kubrick 16:378
David Mamet 34:223
William Mastrosimone 36:290
Mark Medoff 23:294
Arthur Miller 6:330
John Osborne 5:332
Harold Pinter 1:266; 3:385,
386; 15:426; 27:392
David Rabe 33:346
Gerome Ragni and James Rado
17:379
Jonathan Reynolds 38:389

Ronald Ribman 7:357
Jean-Paul Sartre 4:476
Murray Schisgal 6:489
Peter Shaffer 5:386
Sam Shepard 17:442; 34:269
Martin Sherman 19:416
Stephen Sondheim 30:403
Tom Stoppard 3:470; 15:524;
29:406
Ronald Tavel 6:529
C. P. Taylor 27:447
Jean-Claude Van Itallie 3:492
Gore Vidal 4:552, 553
Peter Weiss 3:514
Arnold Wesker 5:482
Tennessee Williams 19:470
Lanford Wilson 36:465

Brutus, Dennis
Alan Paton 25:361

Bruun, Geoffrey
Thomas B. Costain 30:95, 96,
98, 99
Marguerite Yourcenar 19:480

Bryan, C.D.B.
Jonathan Baumbach 23:54
Julio Cortázar 2:103
Norma Klein 30:236
Craig Nova 7:267
Tom Wolfe 35:452

Bryant, J. A., Jr.
Allen Tate 14:530
Eudora Welty 1:361; 5:480

Bryant, Jerry H.
James Baldwin 8:41
John Barth 2:36
Saul Bellow 2:52
William S. Burroughs 2:91
Ronald L. Fair 18:140
Ernest J. Gaines 18:165
Nikki Giovanni 19:191
Joseph Heller 3:228
James Jones 3:261
Norman Mailer 2:260
Bernard Malamud 2:266
Carson McCullers 4:344
Toni Morrison 4:366
Flannery O'Connor 2:317
Walker Percy 2:333
Thomas Pynchon 2:353
Ayn Rand 3:423
Ishmael Reed 32:362
John Updike 2:441
Kurt Vonnegut, Jr. 2:452
John A. Williams 5:497

Bryant, Nelson
Jacques-Yves Cousteau 30:105
James Herriot 12:282

Bryant, Rene Kuhn
Thomas Berger 8:83
Heinrich Böll 6:84
John Fowles 6:187
Paula Fox 8:219
John Hersey 7:154
Doris Lessing 10:316
James A. Michener 5:291

Bryden, Ronald
Peter Barnes **5**:49
David Hare **29**:212
Doris Lessing **6**:299
Kamala Markandaya **38**:324
Shiva Naipaul **32**:324
Peter Nichols **5**:306
Françoise Sagan **17**:421
David Storey **4**:529
Peter Straub **28**:408
Paul West **7**:525

Buache, Freddy
Luis Buñuel **16**:138

Bucco, Martin
René Wellek **28**:452

Buchanan, Cynthia
Norman Mailer **2**:263

Buchen, Irving H.
Carson McCullers **10**:334

Buchholz, Todd G.
Margaret Mead **37**:285

Buchsbaum, Betty
David Kherdian **6**:280

Buck, Philo M., Jr.
Jules Romains **7**:378

Buck, Richard M.
Andre Norton **12**:457

Buckle, Richard
John Betjeman **2**:60

Buckler, Ernest
Hugh Hood **15**:283
Frank Swinnerton **31**:427

Buckler, Robert
Elia Kazan **6**:274
Thomas Williams **14**:582

Buckley, James J., Jr.
Pat Conroy **30**:77

Buckley, John
Jim Harrison **33**:196

Buckley, Kathryn
Joan Barfoot **18**:36

Buckley, Leonard
Ronald Harwood **32**:224

Buckley, P. L.
Helen MacInnes **27**:282

Buckley, Peter
Lily Tomlin **17**:522
Andy Warhol **20**:420

Buckley, Priscilla L.
Eric Ambler **6**:4
Thomas J. Fleming **37**:124

Buckley, Reid
William McPherson **34**:88

Buckley, Tom
Steven Bochco and Michael
Kozoll **35**:48
Michael Cimino **16**:212
Ronald J. Glasser **37**:132
Irving Wallace **13**:570

Buckley, Vincent
T. S. Eliot **3**:138

Buckley, Virginia
Katherine Paterson **12**:487

Buckley, William F., Jr.
William F. Buckley, Jr. **7**:35
Len Deighton **22**:118
Lillian Hellman **14**:257
John le Carré **28**:226
Monty Python **21**:229
Gerome Ragni and James Rado
17:381
Aleksandr I. Solzhenitsyn **4**:511
Hunter S. Thompson **17**:513
Garry Trudeau **12**:590
Tom Wolfe **2**:481

Buckman, Gertrude
Hortense Calisher **38**:67

Buckman, Peter
Elaine Feinstein **36**:168
Tom Sharpe **36**:400

Buckmaster, Henrietta
Kristin Hunter **35**:223
Maxine Hong Kingston **19**:250
Paule Marshall **27**:310
Barbara Pym **19**:387

Bucknall, Barbara J.
Ursula K. LeGuin **13**:349

Budgen, Suzanne
Jean Renoir **20**:299

Budrys, Algis
Piers Anthony **35**:35
Isaac Asimov **26**:52
Robert Bloch **33**:84
Octavia E. Butler **38**:66
John W. Campbell, Jr. **32**:78,
80
C. J. Cherryh **35**:102, 103,
104, 108
Arthur C. Clarke **35**:124
Robert A. Heinlein **26**:174
Barry Hughart **39**:156
Fritz Leiber **25**:307
Frederik Pohl **18**:412
Keith Roberts **14**:464
Kim Stanley Robinson **34**:106
Lucius Shepard **34**:109
Arkadii Strugatskii and Boris
Strugatskii **21**:435
Jack Williamson **29**:457
Gene Wolfe **25**:473, 475
Roger Zelazny **21**:479

Buechner, Frederick
Annie Dillard **9**:178
J.R.R. Tolkien **38**:431

Buell, Ellen Lewis
Lloyd Alexander **35**:22
E. M. Almedingen **12**:3
Isaac Asimov **26**:35
Margot Benary-Isbert **12**:31
Dino Buzzati **36**:83
Betty Cavanna **12**:97, 98
Maureen Daly **17**:90
Walter Farley **17**:115
Henry Gregor Felsen **17**:120,
122
Esther Forbes **12**:207
Roderick L. Haig-Brown
21:134
Lee Kingman **17**:243

Joseph Krumgold **12**:317
Jean Lee Latham **12**:32
Madeleine L'Engle **12**:345
William Mayne **12**:389
Andre Norton **12**:456
Scott O'Dell **30**:267
Otfried Preussler **17**:374
Carl Sandburg **35**:354
Mary Stolz **12**:545, 546, 547,
548, 549, 550, 551, 552
Noel Streatfeild **21**:396, 397,
398, 399
John R. Tunis **12**:593, 594,
595, 596
Jill Paton Walsh **35**:430
Lenora Mattingly Weber **12**:631
Maia Wojciechowska **26**:451

Buell, Frederick
A. R. Ammons **8**:17

Bueno, J.R.T., Jr.
Roderick L. Haig-Brown
21:136

Buffalohead, W. Roger
Vine Deloria, Jr. **21**:110

Buffington, Robert
Wayne C. Booth **24**:92
Cleanth Brooks **24**:111
Frederick Busch **18**:85
Donald Davidson **2**:112
John Crowe Ransom **4**:430,
437

Bufithis, Philip H.
Norman Mailer **11**:342

Bufkin, E. C.
Iris Murdoch **2**:297
P. H. Newby **2**:310

Buford, Bill
Gabriel García Márquez **27**:151

Bugeja, Michael J.
Sharon Olds **39**:193

Buhle, Paul and Fiehrer, Thomas
Ernesto Cardenal **31**:79

Buitenhuis, Peter
Harry Mathews **6**:314
Richard Stern **39**:235, 238
William Trevor **7**:475
Richard Yates **23**:479

Bukoski, Anthony
W. P. Kinsella **27**:237

Bullins, Ed
Alice Childress **12**:106

Bullock, Florence Haxton
John Ehle **27**:102
Laura Z. Hobson **25**:268
Elizabeth Jane Howard **29**:242
Frank Tuohy **37**:426
T. H. White **30**:440

Bulman, Learned T.
Henry Gregor Felsen **17**:122
Margaret O. Hyde **21**:171
Jean Lee Latham **12**:323, 325
Andre Norton **12**:456
Studs Terkel **38**:418

Bumpus, Jerry
Mario Vargas Llosa **15**:552

Bumsted, J. M.
Bruce Catton **35**:95

Bundy, McGeorge
William F. Buckley, Jr. **37**:53

Bunnell, Sterling
Michael McClure **6**:321

Bunster, Elizabeth
Sylvia Murphy **34**:91

Bunting, Basil
Hugh MacDiarmid **4**:313

Bunting, Charles T.
Elizabeth Spencer **22**:403

Bunting, Josiah, III
James H. Webb, Jr. **22**:453

Burbank, Rex
Thornton Wilder **1**:364

Burch, Noel
Alain Resnais **16**:496

Burg, Victor
Richard Elman **19**:150

Burg, Victor Kantor
Pat Jordan **37**:195

Burger, Marjorie
Walter Farley **17**:116, 117

Burger, Nash K.
Walter D. Edmonds **35**:153
Elizabeth Spencer **22**:400

Burger, Otis Kidwell
Lynne Reid Banks **23**:40

Burgess, Anthony
Kingsley Amis **1**:6; **2**:8
James Baldwin **1**:16
Samuel Beckett **1**:23; **3**:44
Saul Bellow **1**:31
Elizabeth Bowen **1**:40; **3**:82
Brigid Brophy **6**:99; **29**:94, 95
William S. Burroughs **1**:48
Italo Calvino **22**:92
Albert Camus **1**:54
Louis-Ferdinand Céline **7**:46
Agatha Christie **1**:58
J. M. Coetzee **23**:126
Ivy Compton-Burnett **1**:62
Don DeLillo **13**:178
Peter De Vries **28**:109
E. L. Doctorow **18**:125
Lawrence Durrell **1**:87
T. S. Eliot **3**:139
E. M. Forster **1**:107
Carlos Fuentes **13**:231
Gabriel García Márquez **27**:156
Jean Genet **1**:115
Penelope Gilliatt **2**:160
William Golding **1**:121
Günter Grass **1**:125; **11**:251
Henry Green **2**:178
Graham Greene **3**:207
Joseph Heller **1**:140
Ernest Hemingway **1**:143;
3:234
Aldous Huxley **1**:151
John Irving **38**:254
Christopher Isherwood **1**:156
Pamela Hansford Johnson **1**:160
Erica Jong **18**:278

Alfred Kazin **34**:562
Arthur Koestler **1**:169; **3**:270
John le Carré **9**:326
Colin MacInnes **4**:314
Norman Mailer **1**:190; **28**:262; **39**:420
Bernard Malamud **1**:199; **3**:322
Olivia Manning **19**:301
Peter Manso **39**:420
Mary McCarthy **1**:206; **24**:345
Henry Miller **1**:224
Manuel Mujica Láinez **31**:285
Iris Murdoch **1**:235
Vladimir Nabokov **1**:244; **3**:352
Flann O'Brien **1**:252
Lucio Piccolo **13**:440
Reynolds Price **13**:464
J. B. Priestley **2**:347
Alain Robbe-Grillet **1**:288
J. D. Salinger **1**:299
William Sansom **2**:383
Alan Sillitoe **1**:307
Josef Škvorecký **39**:231
C. P. Snow **1**:317
Muriel Spark **2**:416
Paul Theroux **11**:528
D. M. Thomas **31**:431
John Wain **2**:458
Evelyn Waugh **1**:359; **3**:510
Angus Wilson **2**:472
Edmund Wilson **3**:538

Burgess, Charles E.
William Inge **8**:308

Burgess, Jackson
Robert Altman **16**:22
Stanley Kubrick **16**:380

Burgess, John
Satyajit Ray **16**:476

Burgin, Richard
Isaac Bashevis Singer **23**:420

Burhans, Clinton S., Jr.
Joseph Heller **3**:230
Ernest Hemingway **8**:283; **30**:188
Kurt Vonnegut, Jr. **8**:530

Burian, Jarka M.
Václav Havel **25**:223

Burjorjee, D. M.
Peter Luke **38**:316

Burk, Anne M.
Fumiko Enchi **31**:140
William Kotzwinkle **35**:254

Burke, Frank
Federico Fellini **16**:298

Burke, Jeffrey
Carolyn G. Heilbrun **25**:256
Thomas Keneally **19**:248
Ted Mooney **25**:330
Alberto Moravia **18**:349
John Nichols **38**:342
Jayne Anne Phillips **15**:420
Richard Price **12**:492
Lewis Thomas **35**:410
Elie Wiesel **37**:453

Burke, Kathleen
René Wellek **28**:454

Burke, Kenneth
Wayne C. Booth **24**:90
William Empson **33**:146
Clifford Odets **28**:325
John Crowe Ransom **24**:363
Theodore Roethke **11**:479
James Thurber **25**:435
Glenway Wescott **13**:590

Burke, Susan E.
Cynthia Propper Seton **27**:424

Burke, William M.
John A. Williams **5**:497

Burkholder, Robert E.
Pat Conroy **30**:78

Burkman, Katherine H.
Harold Pinter **27**:384

Burkom, Selma R.
Doris Lessing **1**:174

Burnett, Constance Buil
Frank B. Gilbreth, Jr. and
Ernestine Gilbreth Carey **17**:153

Burnett, Michael
James Thurber **5**:440

Burnett, W. R.
Mari Sandoz **28**:403

Burnham, David
Clifford Odets **28**:329
Emlyn Williams **15**:577

Burns, Alan
Michael Moorcock **27**:348
Ann Quin **6**:442
C. P. Snow **1**:317

Burns, Gerald
W. H. Auden **4**:33
John Berryman **6**:62, 63
Austin Clarke **9**:169
Donald Hall **37**:141
Seamus Heaney **7**:147
Donald Justice **19**:236
Robert Lowell **5**:256
Frank O'Hara **5**:324
Charles Olson **5**:328
Ezra Pound **5**:348
Gary Snyder **5**:393
William Stafford **4**:520
Diane Wakoski **11**:564

Burns, J.
Noel Hilliard **15**:280

Burns, James
Maurice Gee **29**:177

Burns, John F.
James A. Michener **29**:313

Burns, Landon C., Jr.
Mary Renault **17**:395

Burns, Martin
Kurt Vonnegut, Jr. **12**:608

Burns, Mary M.
Lloyd Alexander **35**:28
Cecil Bødker **21**:14
Alice Childress **12**:107
Barbara Corcoran **17**:77
Peter Dickinson **12**:171; **35**:136

Lois Duncan **26**:102
Jean Craighead George **35**:178
Bette Greene **30**:171
Jamake Highwater **12**:287
Isabelle Holland **21**:154
Mollie Hunter **21**:164
Diana Wynne Jones **26**:230
M. E. Kerr **12**:297, 298
Lee Kingman **17**:247
Jean Lee Latham **12**:325
Norma Fox Mazer **26**:290
Anne McCaffrey **17**:282
Nicholasa Mohr **12**:445
Andre Norton **12**:471
Scott O'Dell **30**:274
Robert Newton Peck **17**:340, 342
Carl Sandburg **35**:357
Ann Schlee **35**:372
Ouida Sebestyen **30**:350
Noel Streatfeild **21**:410
Maia Wojciechowska **26**:457
Laurence Yep **35**:470

Burns, Robert
A. J. Cronin **32**:140

Burns, Stuart L.
Ernest Hemingway **30**:197
Jean Stafford **4**:517

Burns, Wayne
Alex Comfort **7**:52, 53

Burnshaw, Stanley
James Dickey **10**:141

Burroughs, Franklin G.
William Faulkner **3**:157

Burrow, J. W.
Aldous Huxley **3**:254
J.R.R. Tolkien **3**:482

Burroway, Janet
James Leo Herlihy **6**:235
Mary Hocking **13**:284
Masuji Ibuse **22**:227
Paule Marshall **27**:310

Burstein, Janet Handler
Isak Dinesen **29**:160

Burt, Struthers
Kay Boyle **19**:62

Burton, Dwight L.
Betty Cavanna **12**:99
Maureen Daly **17**:88

Burton, Thomas
Alfred Hitchcock **16**:338

Busch, Frederick
Thomas Berger **38**:41
J. G. Farrell **6**:173
John Hawkes **7**:140
William Kotzwinkle **35**:256
Alice Munro **10**:356
John Nichols **38**:341
Jim Shepard **36**:406
Paul Theroux **28**:426
Paul West **7**:523

Bush, Kent
Thor Heyerdahl **26**:190

Bush, Roland E.
Ishmael Reed **3**:424

Busi, Frederick
Alain Resnais **16**:513

Butcher, Patrick
Howard Barker **37**:36

Butkiss, John F.
Lee Kingman **17**:246

Butler, Christopher
I. A. Richards **24**:401

Butler, Colin
Hermann Hesse **17**:214

Butler, Florence W.
Henry Gregor Felsen **17**:120

Butler, G. P.
Siegfried Lenz **27**:251
Martin Walser **27**:466

Butler, Geoff
Rolf Hochhuth **18**:256

Butler, Marilyn
Brigid Brophy **29**:98
Alison Lurie **39**:184
Barbara Pym **37**:370

Butler, Michael
Heinrich Böll **11**:58
Ernst Jandl **34**:197

Butler, Rupert
Laurence Olivier **20**:239

Butler, William Vivian
John Creasey **11**:135

Butscher, Edward
John Berryman **3**:67
Shusaku Endo **14**:162
John Gardner **3**:185
Jerzy Kosinski **6**:282
Richard Kostelanetz **28**:218
John Sayles **14**:483
Philip Whalen **29**:445
James Wright **5**:519
Rudolph Wurlitzer **4**:598

Butt, John
Carlos Fuentes **10**:208

Buttel, Robert
Seamus Heaney **25**:241

Butterick, George
Ed Dorn **18**:129

Butterick, George F.
Charles Olson **29**:327

Butwin, Joseph
Richard Brautigan **12**:62

Byars, Betsy
Jean Craighead George **35**:180
Kin Platt **26**:350

Byatt, A. S.
Malcolm Bradbury **32**:51
Penelope Fitzgerald **19**:174
Antonia Fraser **32**:179
Diane Johnson **13**:305
Pamela Hansford Johnson **27**:221
Amos Oz **11**:429
V. S. Pritchett **15**:440
C. P. Snow **13**:514

Byer, Kathryn Stripling
Carolyn Kizer **15**:309

Byers, Margaret
Elizabeth Jennings **5**:197

Byers, Nancy
Jean Lee Latham **12**:324

Byrd, James W.
Willard Motley **18**:357

Byrd, Max
Jorge Luis Borges **6**:93
Peter DeVries **10**:136

Byrd, Scott
John Barth **1**:17

Byrns, Ruth
August Derleth **31**:131

Byrom, Thomas
Frank O'Hara **13**:423

Byron, Stuart
Woody Allen **16**:12
John Lennon **35**:265

Cabrera, Vicente
Juan Benet **28**:23

Cadogan, Mary
Joan Aiken **35**:17
Antonia Fraser **32**:185
William Mayne **12**:404
Noel Streatfeild **21**:143

Cahill, Daniel J.
E. L. Doctorow **18**:121
Jerzy Kosinski **2**:232

Cahn, Victor L.
Tom Stoppard **29**:397

Cahnman, Werner J.
Primo Levi **37**:221

Caidin, Martin
Ernest K. Gann **23**:166

Cain, James M.
James M. Cain **28**:45

Cain, Joan
Camilo José Cela **13**:147

Cain, William E.
Wayne C. Booth **24**:97

Cairns, Scott C.
Michael S. Harper **22**:209

Calas, Nicholas
André Breton **9**:125

Calder, Angus
T. S. Eliot **2**:128
Alex La Guma **19**:273
Ngugi wa Thiong'o **36**:310

Calder, Robert L.
W. Somerset Maugham **15**:369

Caldicott, Leonie
Michael Frayn **31**:191

Caldwell, James R.
Muriel Rukeyser **27**:407

Caldwell, Joan
Margaret Laurence **13**:344
Audrey Thomas **7**:472

Caldwell, Mark
Thom Gunn **32**:214
Lewis Thomas **35**:415

Caldwell, Stephen
D. Keith Mano **2**:270

Caless, Bryn
Joan Aiken **35**:20
Penelope Lively **32**:275
J.I.M. Stewart **32**:421

Calisher, Hortense
Yukio Mishima **2**:289
Vladimir Nabokov **1**:246
Raja Rao **25**:365
Christina Stead **5**:403

Callaghan, Linda Ward
Gene Roddenberry **17**:414

Callahan, John
Michael S. Harper **7**:138

Callahan, John F.
Alice Walker **5**:476

Callahan, Patrick
Wendell Berry **27**:33

Callahan, Patrick J.
C. S. Lewis **3**:297
George MacBeth **2**:251
Alan Sillitoe **1**:308
Stephen Spender **2**:420

Callan, Edward
W. H. Auden **1**:9, 11; **14**:30
Alan Paton **4**:395; **25**:363

Callan, Richard J.
José Donoso **11**:147
Octavio Paz **19**:364

Callanan, Deirdre G.
Mary Oliver **34**:249

Callenbach, Ernest
Ingmar Bergman **16**:60
Charles Chaplin **16**:198
Shirley Clarke **16**:218
John Ford **16**:309
Alfred Hitchcock **16**:342, 344
Elia Kazan **16**:367
Satyajit Ray **16**:482
Andy Warhol **20**:418
Orson Welles **20**:438

Callendar, Newgate
Eric Ambler **4**:18
Isaac Asimov **9**:49
T. J. Binyon **34**:34
William Peter Blatty **2**:64
Robert Bloch **33**:83, 84
William F. Buckley, Jr. **18**:81,
83
James Carroll **38**:104
Robert Cormier **12**:136
John Creasey **11**:135
Edmund Crispin **22**:111
Rhys Davies **23**:147
Peter Dickinson **12**:170, 171,
177; **35**:131, 132, 136
Paul E. Erdman **25**:153, 154
Howard Fast **23**:160, 161
Dick Francis **22**:152
Nicolas Freeling **38**:185, 186
John Gardner **30**:154, 155

Nicholas M. Guild **33**:186, 187
Joseph Hansen **38**:236, 238,
239, 240
Ronald Harwood **32**:226
Carolyn G. Heilbrun **25**:252,
254
Richard F. Hugo **32**:242
Evan Hunter **11**:279, 280
P. D. James **18**:272
James Jones **3**:262
Harry Kemelman **2**:225
William X. Kienzle **25**:275,
276
Emma Lathen **2**:236
Elmore Leonard **28**:233
Robert Ludlum **22**:289
Ross Macdonald **14**:336
Helen MacInnes **27**:284
Richard Matheson **37**:247
Robert B. Parker **27**:363, 364
Ellery Queen **11**:458
Ruth Rendell **28**:383, 384, 385,
386, 387
Richard Rosen **39**:195
Georges Simenon **2**:399
Martin Cruz Smith **25**:412
Wilbur Smith **33**:375, 376, 377
Mickey Spillane **3**:469
J.I.M. Stewart **14**:512; **32**:420,
421
Julian Symons **32**:425
Trevanian **29**:429
Vassilis Vassilikos **8**:524
Gore Vidal **22**:434
Donald E. Westlake **7**:528,
529; **33**:436, 437, 438

Callery, Sean
Mario Puzo **36**:358

Callow, Philip
Andrew Sinclair **2**:400

Calta, Louis
N. F. Simpson **29**:367

Caltabiano, Frank P.
Edward Albee **25**:39

Calverton, V. F.
Langston Hughes **35**:213

Cambon, Glauco
Michael Hamburger **14**:234
Robert Lowell **8**:348
Eugenio Montale **7**:224
Giuseppe Ungaretti **7**:482;
11:555; **15**:536
Elio Vittorini **14**:543

Cameron, Ann
Tom Robbins **9**:454

Cameron, Barry
John Metcalf **37**:300
A. W. Purdy **14**:432

Cameron, Ben
Edward Albee **25**:38
Howard Brenton **31**:66

Cameron, Eleanor
Lloyd Alexander **35**:25
Julia W. Cunningham **12**:164
Leon Garfield **12**:226
Alan Garner **17**:138
Nat Hentoff **26**:184

Mollie Hunter **21**:159, 160
Joseph Krumgold **12**:320
William Mayne **12**:393
Emily Cheney Neville **12**:452
Philippa Pearce **21**:283
Rosemary Sutcliff **26**:434

Cameron, Elspeth
Margaret Atwood **13**:4
Timothy Findley **27**:145

Cameron, Ian
Michelangelo Antonioni **20**:20
Nagisa Oshima **20**:247

Cameron, J. M.
David Caute **29**:110

Cameron, J. R.
T. H. White **30**:447

Cameron, James
V. S. Naipaul **37**:319

Cameron, Julia
Judith Rossner **6**:469

Camp, Raymond R.
Roderick L. Haig-Brown
21:135

Camp, Richard
Leon Garfield **12**:221

Campbell, Alex
Ian Fleming **30**:142

Campbell, Barbara
Henry Gregor Felsen **17**:124
John Metcalf **37**:303

Campbell, Colin
Muriel Rukeyser **27**:408

Campbell, Don G.
Tobias Wolff **39**:283

Campbell, Donald
Howard Barker **37**:39
Caryl Churchill **31**:83
Norman MacCaig **36**:287
Tom Paulin **37**:354

Campbell, Gregg M.
Bob Dylan **6**:157

Campbell, James
William S. Burroughs **22**:84
Frederick Forsyth **36**:176
Kazuo Ishiguro **27**:202
Bernard Mac Laverty **31**:254
Vladimir Nabokov **23**:314
Ngugi wa Thiong'o **36**:318
Barbara Pym **37**:369

Campbell, Josie P.
E. L. Doctorow **18**:123

Campbell, Mary Jo
Isaac Asimov **26**:51
Arthur C. Clarke **35**:126

Campbell, Patricia
Kin Platt **26**:353

Campbell, Patty
Fran Arrick **30**:17
Sol Gordon **26**:138, 139
Norma Klein **30**:241
Stan Lee **17**:262
Norma Fox Mazer **26**:292

D. M. Pinkwater **35**:318
Kin Platt **26**:353, 355
Sandra Scoppettone **26**:402

Campbell, Peter
Frank Sargeson **31**:371

Camper, Carol
H. D. **31**:212

Canary, Robert H.
Robert Graves **11**:256

Canavan, Francis
Thomas J. Fleming **37**:119

Canby, Henry Seidel
Pearl S. Buck **18**:75

Canby, Peter
Randolph Stow **23**:438

Canby, Vincent
Lindsay Anderson **20**:16
Ralph Bakshi **26**:66, 68, 72, 76
Shirley Clarke **16**:218
Brian De Palma **20**:72, 74, 75, 79, 80
Vittorio De Sica **20**:95, 97
Marguerite Duras **20**:99
Rainer Werner Fassbinder **20**:113, 120
Federico Fellini **16**:290
Bob Fosse **20**:123
George Roy Hill **26**:205, 207
Alfred Hitchcock **16**:359
John Landis **26**:273
Nagisa Oshima **20**:249
Piers Paolo Pasolini **20**:262, 265
Sam Peckinpah **20**:276
Sidney Poitier **26**:357, 359
Richard Pryor **26**:380
Carlos Saura **20**:316
Paul Schrader **26**:391, 394
Martin Scorsese **20**:323, 330
Jerzy Skolimowski **20**:348
François Truffaut **20**:393
Peter Weir **20**:428

Canham, Erwin D.
Russell Baker **31**:27
T. H. White **30**:447

Canham, Patience M.
John Donovan **35**:140

Candlin, Enid Saunders
Bette Bao Lord **23**:280

Cannella, Anthony R.
Richard Condon **10**:111

Cannon, JoAnn
Italo Calvino **11**:92

Cannon, Margaret
Frederick Forsyth **36**:176

Cansler, Ronald Lee
Robert A. Heinlein **3**:227

Cantarella, Helene
Jules Archer **12**:15
Dino Buzzati **36**:87

Cantor, Jay
William F. Buckley, Jr. **37**:63

Cantor, Peter
Frederic Raphael **2**:367

Cantwell, Mary
Alan Sillitoe **19**:421
Julian Symons **32**:428
Fay Weldon **36**:445

Cantwell, Robert
Erskine Caldwell **14**:94
Upton Sinclair **15**:498

Capers, Charlotte
Mary Lee Settle **19**:409

Capey, A. C.
William Golding **17**:177

Capitanchik, Maurice
E. M. Forster **2**:135
Yukio Mishima **6**:338
Michael Moorcock **27**:348

Caplan, Brina
John Gardner **18**:176
Lillian Hellman **18**:226
Larry McMurtry **27**:331
Isaac Bashevis Singer **38**:412
Joy Williams **31**:465

Caplan, Lincoln
Frederick Buechner **6**:103

Caplan, Pat
Colleen McCullough **27**:319

Caplan, Ralph
Kingsley Amis **1**:6

Capouya, Emile
Amiri Baraka **33**:52
Albert Camus **2**:98
Camilo José Cela **13**:145
Robert Coover **7**:57
Michel del Castillo **38**:166
Howard Fast **23**:158
Paul Goodman **7**:129
James Leo Herlihy **6**:234
Ignazio Silone **4**:493
Aleksandr I. Solzhenitsyn **1**:320
Robert Stone **23**:425
Dalton Trumbo **19**:445

Capp, Al
Charles Chaplin **16**:194
Mary McCarthy **5**:276

Capps, Benjamin
Christie Harris **12**:262

Caprio, Betsy
Gene Roddenberry **17**:411

Caputi, Jane E.
Steven Spielberg **20**:363

Caputo, Philip
Thomas McGuane **18**:322

Caputo-Mayr, Maria Luise
Peter Handke **8**:261

Caram, Richard
Anne Stevenson **7**:463

Carb, Alison B.
Joan K. Peters **39**:92

Card, Orson Scott
William Gibson **39**:141
Roger Zelazny **21**:472

Cardinal, Roger
André Breton **15**:86

Cardullo, Robert J.
Robert Altman **16**:37

Carduner, Art
Ingmar Bergman **16**:69

Carens, James F.
Evelyn Waugh **27**:472

Carew, Jan
John Irving **13**:292
George Lamming **2**:235

Carey, John
Richard Bach **14**:35
Lawrence Durrell **4**:147
Richard Eberhart **3**:135
William Empson **8**:201
D. J. Enright **4**:155
Robert Graves **39**:323
Graham Greene **37**:139
Doris Lessing **6**:292
Norman MacCaig **36**:283
John Updike **7**:489

Carey, Julian C.
Langston Hughes **10**:278

Cargas, H. J.
Jacques-Yves Cousteau **30**:105

Cargas, Harry James
Elie Wiesel **37**:452

Cargill, Oscar
Pearl S. Buck **7**:32

Cargin, Peter
Michael Cimino **16**:208

Carhart, Tom
Stephen Wright **33**:467

Carleton, Joyce
Patrick Modiano **18**:338

Carleton, Phillips D.
Halldór Laxness **25**:290
Frans Eemil Sillanpää **19**:417

Carlile, Henry
Stanley Plumly **33**:313

Carls, Alice-Catherine
Tadeusz Rózewicz **23**:363

Carlsen, G. Robert
Frank Herbert **12**:273

Carlson, Dale
M. E. Kerr **12**:296
Rosemary Wells **12**:638

Carlson, Lori M.
Isabel Allende **39**:28

Carlson, Michael
James Fenton **32**:166

Carmer, Carl
A. B. Guthrie, Jr. **23**:197
Zora Neale Hurston **30**:212
George S. Kaufman **38**:257
Bruce Lancaster **36**:244

Carmody, Rev. Francis R., S.J.
Roy A. Gallant **17**:129

Carne, Rosalind
Caryl Churchill **31**:90

Carne-Ross, D. S.
John Gardner **3**:185
Eugenio Montale **7**:222

Carollo, Monica
Margaret O. Hyde **21**:177

Caron, Paul A.
M. E. Kerr **35**:249

Carpenter, Bogdana
Zbigniew Herbert **9**:274

Carpenter, Frederic I.
William Everson **14**:163
Robinson Jeffers **2**:212; **11**:311; **15**:300
Carson McCullers **12**:417
Conrad Richter **30**:313
Jessamyn West **17**:547
Herman Wouk **38**:446

Carpenter, Humphrey
J.R.R. Tolkien **38**:439

Carpenter, John R.
Zbigniew Herbert **9**:274
Greg Kuzma **7**:196
John Logan **5**:255
James Schevill **7**:401
Gary Snyder **2**:407
Diane Wakoski **2**:459
Peter Wild **14**:581
Charles Wright **6**:580

Carpenter, Richard C.
Kay Boyle **19**:63, 64

Carper, Steve
William Gibson **39**:41

Carpio, Rustica C.
Bienvenido N. Santos **22**:363

Carpio, Virginia
Andre Norton **12**:464

Carr, Archie
Peter Matthiessen **32**:285

Carr, John
George Garrett **3**:190

Carr, Patrick
Peter Townshend **17**:540
Neil Young **17**:580

Carr, Roy
John Lennon and Paul McCartney **12**:379

Carr, Terry
Kim Stanley Robinson **34**:107
Lucius Shepard **34**:108

Carroll, David
Chinua Achebe **1**:1
Jean Cayrol **11**:107
Claude Simon **39**:212

Carroll, Michael J.
Molly Giles **39**:66

Carroll, Paul
John Ashbery **2**:16
Robert Creeley **2**:106
James Dickey **2**:116
Allen Ginsberg **2**:163
Frank O'Hara **2**:321
W. D. Snodgrass **2**:405
Philip Whalen **6**:565

Carruth, Hayden
Ai **14**:9
A. R. Ammons **9**:30
W. H. Auden **1**:11
Ted Berrigan **37**:43
John Berryman **2**:56
Earle Birney **6**:75
Robert Bly **15**:68
Edward Brathwaite **11**:67
Charles Bukowski **5**:80
Cid Corman **9**:170
Robert Creeley **8**:153
J. V. Cunningham **3**:121
Babette Deutsch **18**:119
Annie Dillard **9**:177
Robert Duncan **2**:122
Loren Eiseley **7**:91
Clayton Eshleman **7**:97, 98
Robert Frost **10**:198
Tess Gallagher **18**:169
Jean Garrigue **8**:239
Arthur Gregor **9**:251
H. D. **8**:256
Marilyn Hacker **9**:257
Donald Hall **37**:142
Jim Harrison **14**:235
William Heyen **18**:230
John Hollander **8**:301
Edwin Honig **33**:215
Richard Howard **7**:166
David Ignatow **7**:174, 175, 177; **14**:275
June Jordan **11**:312
Denise Levertov **8**:346
Philip Levine **2**:244
Phillip Lopate **29**:299
Audre Lorde **18**:309
Robert Lowell **4**:299; **9**:338
Archibald MacLeish **14**:337
W. S. Merwin **8**:390
Josephine Miles **2**:278
Frederick Morgan **23**:297
Howard Nemerov **2**:306
Charles Olson **9**:412
Robert Pinsky **9**:417
J. F. Powers **1**:280
Kenneth Rexroth **2**:370
Reg Saner **9**:468
Anne Sexton **2**:390; **4**:484
Judith Johnson Sherwin **15**:480
Leslie Marmon Silko **23**:406
W. D. Snodgrass **18**:492
Gilbert Sorrentino **7**:448
Raymond Souster **14**:502
R. G. Vliet **22**:443
David Wagoner **15**:559
Diane Wakoski **2**:459; **4**:574
Theodore Weiss **8**:545
Louis Zukofsky **2**:487

Carson, Dale
Gunnel Beckman **26**:87

Carson, Katharine W.
Claude Simon **9**:485

Carson, Neil
Arthur Miller **26**:327
George Ryga **14**:472, 473

Carson, Rachel L.
Jacques-Yves Cousteau **30**:101

Carson, Tom
The Clash **30**:44, 50
Steve Martin **30**:247
Paul McCartney **35**:287
Van Morrison **21**:239
The Police **26**:363
Richard Pryor **26**:378
Lou Reed **21**:315
Paul Simon **17**:467
Paul Weller **26**:446
Brian Wilson **12**:653
Neil Young **17**:582
Frank Zappa **17**:594

Cart, Michael
Virginia Hamilton **26**:148
S. E. Hinton **30**:204

Carter, Albert Howard, III
Italo Calvino **8**:126
Thomas McGuane **7**:213

Carter, Angela
John Hawkes **27**:197
Thomas Keneally **5**:210
Christina Stead **32**:414

Carter, Anne
Eilís Dillon **17**:100
Josephine Poole **17**:373

Carter, Betty
Robert Cormier **30**:85
Jean Craighead George **35**:179

Carter, Boyd
Gregorio López y Fuentes **32**:280

Carter, Lin
J.R.R. Tolkien **1**:339

Carter, Mary
Maxine Kumin **28**:221

Carter, Paul
Eugenio Montale **9**:387

Carter, Robert A.
Arthur Gregor **9**:253

Carter, Steven R.
Isaac Asimov **19**:28
Julian Symons **14**:523

Carver, Ann Cathey
Lucille Clifton **19**:109

Carver, Raymond
Peter Griffith **39**:399
Ernest Hemingway **39**:399, 430
Jeffrey Meyers **39**:430

Cary, Joseph
Dino Buzzati **36**:94
Eugenio Montale **7**:223; **9**:386
Giuseppe Ungaretti **7**:482
Louis Zukofsky **18**:558

Casari, Laura E.
Adrienne Rich **11**:479

Case, Brian
Steven Bochco and Michael Kozoll **35**:53

Casebeer, Edwin F.
Hermann Hesse **3**:245

Caserio, Robert L.
Gilbert Sorrentino **7**:449

Casey, Carol K.
Eleanor Hibbert **7**:156

Casey, Daniel J.
Benedict Kiely **23**:260

Casey, Ellen Miller
Maya Angelou **35**:31

Casey, Jane Barnes
Peter Taylor **18**:527

Casey, John
T. Alan Broughton **19**:73
John D. MacDonald **27**:275
Breece D'J Pancake **29**:346

Casey, John D.
Jim Harrison **33**:197

Cashin, Edward J.
Walker Percy **14**:411

Caspary, Sister Anita Marie
François Mauriac **4**:337, 338

Casper, Leonard
Flannery O'Connor **6**:375
Bienvenido N. Santos **22**:361, 362, 365

Cassada, Jackie
Piers Anthony **35**:40, 41
Jeffrey Archer **28**:14

Cassal, Gould
Irwin Shaw **23**:395

Cassidy, John
Dannie Abse **29**:21

Cassidy, T. E.
Jessamyn West **17**:545

Cassill, R. V.
Hortense Calisher **38**:71
Mavis Gallant **7**:110
Joanne Greenberg **30**:161
Thomas Hinde **6**:241
William Kotzwinkle **35**:254
James Alan McPherson **19**:309
Tom Robbins **32**:367
Irwin Shaw **7**:413
Wilfrid Sheed **2**:393
Christina Stead **2**:422
Thomas Williams **14**:581

Cassirer, Thomas
Mongo Beti **27**:43

Casson, Lionel
Mary Renault **17**:399

Castor, Gladys Crofoot
Betty Cavanna **12**:98

Catalano, Frank
David Brin **34**:134

Catania, Susan
Alvin Silverstein and Virginia B. Silverstein **17**:452

Catanoy, Nicholas
Mircea Eliade **19**:147, 148

Cate, Curtis
Romain Gary **25**:185

Cathey, Kenneth Clay
Peter Taylor **37**:406

Catinella, Joseph
Christopher Isherwood **1**:157
Joel Lieber **6**:311
Bernard Malamud **1**:201

Catling, Patrick Skene
William Trevor **25**:447

Cattani, Richard J.
Gay Talese **37**:394

Causey, James Y.
Camilo José Cela **4**:95

Caute, David
Breyten Breytenbach **23**:86
Jean Genet **5**:137
Lucien Goldmann **24**:236, 242
Primo Levi **37**:221
Ved Mehta **37**:289
Lionel Trilling **9**:531

Cavan, Romilly
Derek Walcott **4**:574

Caviglia, John
José Donoso **11**:149

Cavitch, David
William Stafford **4**:521

Cawelti, John G.
Dashiell Hammett **19**:195
Mario Puzo **6**:430
Mickey Spillane **3**:468

Cawley, Joseph A., S.J.
Isabelle Holland **21**:150

Caws, Mary Ann
André Breton **2**:81; **9**:125
Yves Bonnefoy **9**:113
Blaise Cendrars **18**:92

Caws, Peter
Michel Foucault **31**:177

Caylor, Lawrence M.
Marion Zimmer Bradley **30**:31

Caywood, Carolyn
Joyce Carol Thomas **35**:406
Joan D. Vinge **30**:415

Cecchetti, Giovanni
Eugenio Montale **7**:221

Cecil, David
Aldous Huxley **3**:252

Cederstrom, Lorelei
Doris Lessing **22**:281

Ceplair, Larry
Alvah Bessie **23**:61

Cerf, Bennett
John O'Hara **2**:324

Cerf, Cristopher
Peter De Vries **28**:105

Cevasco, G. A.
Pearl S. Buck **18**:77

Chabot, C. Barry
Frederick Exley **11**:187

Chabrol, Claude
Alfred Hitchcock **16**:357

Chace, William M.
Ezra Pound **4**:415

Chadwick, Joseph
Julio Cortázar 33:123

Chaillet, Ned
Athol Fugard 9:232
Hugh Leonard 19:281
Stephen Poliakoff 38:383

Chamberlain, Ethel L.
E. M. Almedingen 12:8

Chamberlain, John
James Gould Cozzens 11:131
Aldous Huxley 35:232
Mary McCarthy 3:326
Ayn Rand 30:293
Conrad Richter 30:329
Carl Van Vechten 33:395
Sloan Wilson 32:449

Chamberlain, John R.
Julia Peterkin 31:303, 304

Chamberlin, J. E.
Margaret Atwood 8:28
George MacBeth 5:265
W. S. Merwin 3:338
Charles Tomlinson 4:547;
6:535, 536
David Wagoner 5:475

Chambers, A.
S. E. Hinton 30:204

Chambers, Aidan
Alan Garner 17:145, 147
William Mayne 12:404
Philippa Pearce 21:293
Robert Westall 17:555

Chambers, Colin
Howard Brenton 31:63
Peter Shaffer 18:477

Chambers, D. D.
Alan Paton 25:359

Chambers, D.D.C.
Matt Cohen 19:111

Chambers, Robert D.
Ernest Buckler 13:120
Sinclair Ross 13:492

Chambers, Ross
Samuel Beckett 9:77

Chametzky, Jules
Edward Dahlberg 14:134
Isaac Bashevis Singer 1:313

Champagne, Roland A.
Roland Barthes 24:32
Marguerite Duras 11:167
Romain Gary 25:188

Champlin, Charles
Julio Cortázar 33:135
Don DeLillo 27:84
John Hawkes 27:196
Alison Lurie 39:181
Manuel Puig 28:373
Evelyn Waugh 27:476

Champness, H. M.
Kamala Markandaya 38:320

Chanady, Amaryll B.
Julio Cortázar 34:331

Chancellor, Alexander
Shiva Naipaul 39:357

Chandler, D. G.
Len Deighton 22:117

Chang, Charity
Barbara Corcoran 17:74

Changas, Estelle
Elia Kazan 16:368

Chankin, Donald O.
B. Traven 8:517

Chapin, Katherine Garrison
Allen Tate 4:536

Chapin, Nancy
Jean Craighead George 35:179

Chapla, Bill
Ed Minus 39:80

Chaplin, William H.
John Logan 5:253

Chapman, Abraham
Kristin Hunter 35:225

Chapman, John
Stephen Sondheim 30:376, 378

Chapman, Raymond
Graham Greene 1:133

Chapman, Robert
Anthony Burgess 4:83
Ivy Compton-Burnett 3:112

Chappell, Fred
George Garrett 3:191
Richard Yates 7:554

Chappetta, Robert
Bernardo Bertolucci 16:88
Roman Polanski 16:466

Charles, Faustin
David Dabydeen 34:148

Charnes, Ruth
M. E. Kerr 12:303

Charques, R. D.
Ian Fleming 30:130
Nevil Shute 30:368

Charters, Ann
Charles Olson 5:326

Charters, Lawrence I.
William Gibson 39:139

Charters, Samuel
Robert Creeley 4:117
Robert Duncan 4:142
Larry Eigner 9:180
William Everson 5:121
Lawrence Ferlinghetti 6:182
Allen Ginsberg 4:181
Charles Olson 5:329
Gary Snyder 5:393
Jack Spicer 8:497

Charyn, Jerome
Kōbō Abé 8:1
Martin Amis 9:26
J. G. Ballard 36:41
David Bradley, Jr. 23:79
T. Alan Broughton 19:72
R.H.W. Dillard 5:116

Elizabeth Jane Howard 7:165
Margaríta Karapánou 13:314
William Kotzwinkle 14:311
Richard Price 12:492
James Purdy 10:424; 28:381
Ishmael Reed 32:356
Leon Rooke 34:254
Judith Rossner 9:457
Luis Rafael Sánchez 23:383
Mario Vargas Llosa 31:443
Joseph Wambaugh 18:533
Jerome Weidman 7:518
Donald E. Westlake 33:438
Kate Wilhelm 7:538

Chase, Edward T.
Nat Hentoff 26:181

Chase, Gilbert
Louis Aragon 22:35

Chase, Ilka
Art Buchwald 33:87

Chase, K.
Josephine Miles 34:244

Chase, Mary Ellen
Nadine Gordimer 33:179

Chase, Richard
Saul Bellow 1:27
Philip Rahv 24:351

Chasin, Helen
Laurie Colwin 23:128
Alan Dugan 6:144
May Sarton 4:472

Chaskel, Walter B.
Robert Lipsyte 21:208

Chassler, Philip I.
Meyer Levin 7:205

Chatfield, Hale
Gil Orlovitz 22:334

Chatfield, Jack
William F. Buckley, Jr. 18:83

Chatham, Margaret L.
Isaac Asimov 26:50
Roy A. Gallant 17:133

Chatterton, Wayne
Nelson Algren 33:15

Chaudhuri, Una
Salman Rushdie 31:357

Chazen, Leonard
Anthony Powell 3:402

Cheatwood, Kiarri T-H
Ayi Kwei Armah 5:32

Cheever, John
Saul Bellow 10:43

Cheever, Susan
Susan Isaacs 32:254

Chelton, Mary K.
Jay Bennett 35:46
Anne McCaffrey 17:281

Chemasi, Antonio
Christopher Durang 27:88

Cheney, Brainard
Donald Davidson 2:112
Flannery O'Connor 1:254;
21:261
Julia Peterkin 31:307

Chernaik, Judith
Beryl Bainbridge 14:39
Amos Oz 27:360

Cherry, Kelly
John Betjeman 10:53

Cherry, Kenneth
Vladimir Nabokov 8:413

Cheshire, Ardner R., Jr.
William Styron 11:518

Chesnick, Eugene
John Cheever 7:48
Nadine Gordimer 7:133
Michael Mewshaw 9:376

Chester, Alfred
Terry Southern 7:454

Chettle, Judith
Nadine Gordimer 33:181
Judith Guest 30:176

Cheuse, Alan
Thomas Berger 38:36
Alejo Carpentier 11:100
James Carroll 38:108
Carlos Fuentes 13:231
John Gardner 5:132
Nicholas M. Guild 33:189
Stephen King 26:241
Jerzy Kosinski 15:317
Camara Laye 38:292
Elmore Leonard 28:237; 34:215
André Schwarz-Bart 4:480
Claude Simon 39:215
B. Traven 11:534
John Edgar Wideman 34:298

Chevigny, Bell Gale
Toni Cade Bambara 19:32
Julio Cortázar 15:148
Paule Marshall 27:311
Tillie Olsen 4:387

Chew, Shirley
Wilson Harris 25:211

Chiari, Joseph
Jean Anouilh 8:23
Jean Cocteau 8:144

Chiaromonte, Nicola
Eric Bentley 24:45

Child, Ruth C.
T. S. Eliot 24:169

Childress, Alice
Joyce Carol Thomas 35:405

Childs, E. Ira
Peter Townshend 17:534

Chinn, Nick
Trina Robbins 21:338

Chitre, Dilip
Jayanta Mahapatra 33:277

Chomsky, Noam
Saul Bellow 8:81

Christ, Carol P.
Doris Lessing **22**:283
Ntozake Shange **25**:401

Christ, Ronald
Chinua Achebe **26**:13
Jorge Luis Borges **2**:70, 73;
4:75
José Donoso **8**:178
Gabriel García Márquez **3**:179
Leonard Michaels **25**:315
Pablo Neruda **5**:301; **7**:260
Octavio Paz **3**:375; **4**:397;
6:398
Manuel Puig **5**:354; **28**:370
Luis Rafael Sánchez **23**:384
Mario Vargas Llosa **9**:542

Christensen, Paul
Ed Dorn **18**:128
Charles Olson **29**:331

Christgau, Georgia
Joan Armatrading **17**:8
Bob Marley **17**:273
Prince **35**:323

Christgau, Robert
Chuck Berry **17**:54
Richard Brautigan **9**:124
Jimmy Cliff **21**:62
Mick Jagger and Keith Richard
17:225, 237
C.L.R. James **33**:225
John Lennon **35**:273
John Lennon and Paul
McCartney **12**:358
Carly Simon **26**:407
Patti Smith **12**:539
Peter Townshend **17**:525
Stevie Wonder **12**:658, 659

Christiansen, Robert
Jackson J. Benson **34**:413

Christiansen, Rupert
John Steinbeck **34**:413

Christie, Ian Leslie
Ken Russell **16**:541

Christie, Joseph, S.J.
Allen Drury **37**:109

Christison, Kathleen
Amos Oz **33**:304

Christman, Elizabeth
Graham Greene **37**:140

Christon, Lawrence
Monty Python **21**:229

Christopher, Nicholas
Seamus Heaney **37**:167

Chrzanowski, Joseph
Jorge Luis Borges **19**:49
Carlos Fuentes **22**:167

Chubb, Thomas Caldecot
Thomas B. Costain **30**:97
C. S. Forester **35**:171
Zora Neale Hurston **30**:209

Chupack, Henry
James Purdy **28**:379

Church, D. M.
Arthur Adamov **25**:16
Albert Camus **32**:94

Church, Richard
Robert Frost **26**:113
Erich Maria Remarque **21**:324

Churchill, David
Peter Dickinson **12**:175
Mollie Hunter **21**:161

Churchill, R. C.
John Cowper Powys **15**:433
P. G. Wodehouse **10**:537

Churchill, Winston
Charles Chaplin **16**:189

Ciardi, John
Robert Frost **13**:223
Stanley Kunitz **14**:312
Melvin B. Tolson **36**:425
Richard Wilbur **14**:576
William Carlos Williams
13:602

Cifelli, Edward
John Ciardi **10**:106

Cioffi, Frank
Gilbert Sorrentino **22**:397

Ciplijauskaité, Biruté
Gabriel García Márquez **3**:182

Cismaru, Alfred
Jacques Audiberti **38**:27
Simone de Beauvoir **2**:43
Albert Camus **11**:95
Aimé Césaire **19**:96
Marguerite Duras **6**:149; **11**:164
Eugène Ionesco **9**:289
Robert Pinget **13**:442

Cixous, Helen
Severo Sarduy **6**:485

Claire, Thomas
Albert Camus **9**:150

Claire, William F.
Stanley Kunitz **11**:319
Sylvia Plath **17**:347
Allen Tate **9**:521
Mark Van Doren **6**:541

Clancy, Cathy
Piri Thomas **17**:502

Clancy, James H.
Albert Camus **32**:91

Clancy, Joseph
A. J. Cronin **32**:139

Clancy, Thomas H.
Andrew M. Greeley **28**:170

Clancy, William P.
Carson McCullers **12**:413
Brian Moore **7**:235

Clapp, Susannah
Caroline Blackwood **9**:101
Elaine Feinstein **36**:170
Penelope Fitzgerald **19**:172
Antonia Fraser **32**:184
Maurice Gee **29**:177
Ursula Holden **18**:257
Margaríta Karapánou **13**:315
Seán O'Faoláin **7**:274
George MacBeth **9**:340
David Plante **7**:308

Barbara Pym **19**:386
Cynthia Propper Seton **27**:427,
428
Frank G. Slaughter **29**:378
A. N. Wilson **33**:450
Hilma Wolitzer **17**:562

Clare, Anthony
Susan Sontag **13**:518

Clarens, Carlos
Eric Rohmer **16**:530, 531

Clareson, Thomas D.
James Blish **14**:83
Arthur C. Clarke **35**:120
Thomas M. Disch **36**:124
Aldous Huxley **35**:237
Theodore Sturgeon **39**:367
Gene Wolfe **25**:475, 477

Claridge, Elizabeth
Kamala Markandaya **38**:327

Clark, Barrett H.
Paul Green **25**:192

Clark, Edwin
Carl Van Vechten **33**:390, 393

Clark, Eleanor
A. J. Cronin **32**:133

Clark, G. J.
T. J. Binyon **34**:33

Clark, Gerry
Bernice Rubens **19**:405
Heberto Padilla **38**:349

Clark, Jeff
William Kotzwinkle **35**:255

Clark, J. Michael
Jean Toomer **22**:426

Clark, John R.
Doris Betts **6**:69
Alan Sillitoe **1**:308

Clark, Katerina
Vasily Aksenov **22**:28

Clark, Tom
Ted Berrigan **37**:42
Philip Whalen **29**:447

Clark, Walter Van Tilburg
A. B. Guthrie, Jr. **23**:198

Clarke, Edward J.
Walter D. Edmonds **35**:148

Clarke, Gerald
Edward Albee **25**:37
Larry Gelbart **21**:126
Gore Vidal **2**:449
P. G. Wodehouse **2**:480

Clarke, Henry Leland
Melvin Berger **12**:38

Clarke, Jane H.
Jesse Jackson **12**:289

Clarke, Kenneth
Jesse Stuart **14**:516

Clarke, Loretta
Paul Zindel **6**:587

Clarke, Pauline
Rosemary Sutcliff **26**:437

Clarkson, Paul R.
Robert Kroetsch **23**:269

Clarkson, William
Donald Davie **31**:112
William Harmon **38**:243

Claudel, Alice Moser
David Kherdian **9**:317

Clausen, Christopher
T. S. Eliot **10**:171

Clay, Carolyn
Barry Hannah **38**:232
Mario Vargas Llosa **31**:446

Clay, George R.
Conrad Richter **30**:317

Clayton, John
Richard Brautigan **12**:63

Clayton, John Jacob
Saul Bellow **6**:50

Clements, Bruce
Robert Cormier **12**:137
Richard Peck **21**:297

Clements, Robert J.
Michel del Castillo **38**:168
Pablo Neruda **2**:308
Irving Stone **7**:469
Vassilis Vassilikos **4**:551

Clemons, Walter
Lisa Alther **7**:12
Max Apple **33**:20
James Baldwin **5**:43
Saul Bellow **6**:55
Peter Benchley **8**:82
Jackson J. Benson **34**:409
Anita Brookner **34**:140
G. Cabrera Infante **5**:96
Don DeLillo **39**:120
E. L. Doctorow **6**:133
Nora Ephron **17**:113
J. G. Farrell **6**:173
Joseph Heller **5**:176, 182
George V. Higgins **7**:158
Maureen Howard **5**:189
John Irving **38**:253
Erica Jong **4**:263
Milan Kundera **4**:276
Doris Lessing **6**:302
Alison Lurie **4**:305; **39**:178
Ross Macdonald **1**:185
James McCourt **5**:278
Carson McCullers **1**:210
Vladimir Nabokov **6**:354
Donald Newlove **6**:364
Joyce Carol Oates **2**:316; **3**:363
Flannery O'Connor **2**:317
Grace Paley **4**:391
Robert M. Pirsig **4**:403
Manuel Puig **5**:354
Adrienne Rich **6**:458
Isaac Bashevis Singer **3**:456
Martin Cruz Smith **25**:412
Raymond Sokolov **7**:430
John Steinbeck **34**:409
Peter Taylor **37**:412
Gore Vidal **33**:411

Tom Wicker **7**:534
Richard B. Wright **6**:582

Clerc, Charles
Thomas Pynchon **33**:335

Clery, Val
Brian Moore **32**:307

Clever, Glenn
E. J. Pratt **19**:383

Clifford, Gay
Staley Middleton **7**:221
Bernice Rubens **19**:403

Clifford, Paula M.
Claude Simon **9**:485

Clifford, William
Walter Farley **17**:116

Cline, Edward
John Gardner **30**:156

Cline, Ruth
C. S. Adler **35**:14

Clinton, Craig
John Arden **15**:24

Clinton, Dana G.
Sue Ellen Bridgers **26**:91
Ouida Sebestyen **30**:346

Clinton, Farley
William Safire **10**:447

Cloonan, William
André Malraux **13**:368
Tom Robbins **32**:365

Close, Peter
Jack Vance **35**:423

Cloudsley, Donald H.
Glendon Swarthout **35**:401

Cloutier, Pierre
Hugh Hood **15**:285

Clouzot, Claire
John Cassavetes **20**:45
Andy Warhol **20**:419

Clucas, Humphrey
Philip Larkin **5**:227

Clum, John M.
Paddy Chayefsky **23**:115
Peter Shaffer **14**:487

Clurman, Harold
Edward Albee **2**:2; **5**:14; **25**:37
Robert Anderson **23**:28
Jean Anouilh **3**:12
Fernando Arrabal **2**:15; **9**:41
Alan Ayckbourn **5**:37; **8**:35;
  18:30
Samuel Beckett **2**:47; **6**:33
Howard Brenton **31**:57
Lenny Bruce **21**:52
Ed Bullins **1**:47; **5**:83
Albert Camus **32**:84
Alice Childress **12**:106
D. L. Coburn **10**:108
Padraic Colum **28**:88
E. E. Cummings **8**:160
Christopher Durang **27**:89
Brian Friel **5**:129
Jean Genet **2**:158

William Gibson **23**:174
Trevor Griffiths **13**:256
John Guare **14**:220
Bill Gunn **5**:153
Christopher Hampton **4**:211,
  212
Lorraine Hansberry **17**:190
Lillian Hellman **18**:226
Rolf Hochhuth **4**:230
Fritz Hochwälder **36**:233
William Inge **8**:308
Eugène Ionesco **4**:250
Ann Jellicoe **27**:209
Preston Jones **10**:296
Jean Kerr **22**:254
Arthur Kopit **18**:287, 291
Peter Luke **38**:315
David Mamet **15**:355, 356
Terrence McNally **4**:347;
  7:217, 218
Mark Medoff **6**:322
Arthur Miller **1**:218; **6**:335
Jason Miller **2**:284
Yukio Mishima **27**:337
Sławomir Mrozek **13**:399
Peter Nichols **36**:326
Clifford Odets **2**:320; **28**:330,
  334
John Osborne **5**:330
Miguel Piñero **4**:402
Harold Pinter **6**:405, 410, 415,
  419; **15**:426
David Rabe **4**:426; **8**:450, 451
Terence Rattigan **7**:355
Eric Rohmer **16**:537
Tadeusz Różewicz **23**:361
Anthony Shaffer **19**:413
Peter Shaffer **5**:388
Sam Shepard **6**:496, 497;
  17:437, 442
Neil Simon **11**:496
Bernard Slade **11**:508
John Steinbeck **5**:408
Tom Stoppard **1**:327; **4**:526;
  5:411; **8**:501; **15**:521
David Storey **5**:417; **8**:505
Elizabeth Swados **12**:557
George Tabori **19**:437
Megan Terry **19**:438
Gore Vidal **2**:450
Joseph A. Walker **19**:454, 455
Richard Wesley **7**:519
Morris L. West **33**:428
Thornton Wilder **6**:573; **35**:445
Tennessee Williams **2**:465;
  5:500, 504; **7**:545; **30**:459,
  470
Lanford Wilson **7**:549; **14**:592

Clute, John
Douglas Adams **27**:13
Isaac Asimov **26**:58
Samuel R. Delany **14**:147
Fritz Leiber **25**:308
Cecile Pineda **39**:96
Gene Wolfe **25**:478

Cluysenaar, Anne
Edwin Morgan **31**:273
László Nagy **7**:251
Jon Silkin **6**:498

Coady, Matthew
Monty Python **21**:223

Coale, Samuel
Donald Barthelme **23**:49
John Cheever **25**:118
Jerzy Kosinski **3**:273; **6**:284
Alain Robbe-Grillet **6**:468

Coates, John
Patrick White **18**:545

Coates, Ken
Aleksandr I. Solzhenitsyn
  18:500

Cobb, Carl W.
Vicente Aleixandre **36**:23

Cobb, Jane
Taylor Caldwell **28**:61
Betty Cavanna **12**:97
Henry Gregor Felsen **17**:120
Frank B. Gilbreth, Jr. and
  Ernestine Gilbreth Carey
  17:154, 155
Lee Kingman **17**:243
James Schuyler **23**:387
Zoa Sherburne **30**:361
Mary Stolz **12**:547

Cobb, Richard
René Clair **20**:68

Cockburn, Alexander
P. G. Wodehouse **22**:480

Cocks, Geoffrey
Thomas Pynchon **18**:437

Cocks, Jay
Mel Brooks **12**:77
Michael Cimino **16**:208
Neil Diamond **30**:113
Werner Herzog **16**:326
Richard Lester **20**:231
Gordon Parks **16**:460
Pink Floyd **35**:310
Harold Pinter **3**:388
Prince **35**:329
Lou Reed **21**:316
Bruce Springsteen **17**:480
François Truffaut **20**:383
Frank Zappa **17**:587

Cocks, John C., Jr.
Federico Fellini **16**:274

Cockshott, Gerald
John Ford **16**:307

Coe, Richard L.
Lily Tomlin **17**:521

Coe, Richard N.
Jean Genet **1**:117
Eugène Ionesco **6**:251

Coelho, Joaquim-Francisco
Carlos Drummond de Andrade
  18:4

Coffey, Barbara
François Truffaut **20**:393

Coffey, Warren
Flannery O'Connor **21**:262
Kurt Vonnegut, Jr. **3**:494

Cogell, Elizabeth Cummins
Ursula K. LeGuin **13**:348

Coggeshall, Rosanne
Lee Smith **25**:408, 409

Cogley, John
Dan Wakefield **7**:502

Cogswell, Fred
Earle Birney **1**:34
Phyllis Gotlieb **18**:191
Ralph Gustafson **36**:217
Joe Rosenblatt **15**:446

Cohan, Steven
Iris Murdoch **31**:286

Cohan, Tony
William Caunitz **34**:36

Cohen, Arthur A.
Joseph Brodsky **4**:77
Cynthia Ozick **3**:372
Marguerite Yourcenar **19**:483

Cohen, Dean
J. P. Donleavy **1**:76

Cohen, Debra Rae
William Gibson **39**:139
Anne McCaffrey **17**:283
The Police **26**:365
Carly Simon **26**:413

Cohen, Edwin
Woody Guthrie **35**:194

Cohen, Esther
Ntozake Shange **38**:394

Cohen, F.
Romain Gary **25**:189

Cohen, George
Robin Cook **14**:131
Nicholas M. Guild **33**:188

Cohen, Gerda
Eva Figes **31**:166

Cohen, Henry
Aimé Césaire **19**:96
Anne Hébert **29**:233

Cohen, J. M.
Heberto Padilla **38**:352
Yevgeny Yevtushenko **13**:619

Cohen, Joseph
Cynthia Ozick **28**:356
Siegfried Sassoon **36**:388
A. B. Yehoshua **31**:475

Cohen, Keith
Julio Cortázar **33**:132

Cohen, Larry
Jules Feiffer **2**:133

Cohen, Mitchell
David Byrne **26**:98
John Lennon **35**:274
Paul McCartney **35**:292
Prince **35**:326
Smokey Robinson **21**:351
Brian Wilson **12**:652
Neil Young **17**:578

Cohen, Mitchell S.
Elaine May **16**:433

Cohen, Nathan
Mordecai Richler **5**:371

Cohen, Phyllis
Kin Platt **26**:349
Zoa Sherburne **30**:362

Cohen, Richard
Joseph Heller **36**:229

Cohen, Robert
Farley Mowat **26**:336

Cohen, Ron
Christopher Durang **38**:174
Amlin Gray **29**:201

Cohen, Sarah Blacher
Cynthia Ozick **28**:347
Isaac Bashevis Singer **38**:413

Cohen, Stephen F.
Aleksandr I. Solzhenitsyn **18**:497

Cohn, David L.
Marshall McLuhan **37**:252

Cohn, Dorrit
Alain Robbe-Grillet **1**:289

Cohn, Ellen
Lily Tomlin **17**:517

Cohn, Jeanette
Hilma Wolitzer **17**:564

Cohn, Nik
Mick Jagger and Keith Richard **17**:234
Paul Simon **17**:465
Bruce Springsteen **17**:480

Cohn, Ruby
Edward Albee **1**:4; **2**:4
Fernando Arrabal **18**:20
James Baldwin **2**:32
Imamu Amiri Baraka **2**:35
Djuna Barnes **4**:43
John Dos Passos **4**:133
Lawrence Ferlinghetti **2**:134
John Hawkes **4**:215
Robinson Jeffers **11**:310
Kenneth Koch **5**:219
Robert Lowell **11**:324
Arthur Miller **2**:279
Harold Pinter **6**:405
Kenneth Rexroth **11**:472
Thornton Wilder **15**:569
Tennessee Williams **2**:465

Cohn-Sfetcu, Ofelia
Hubert Aquin **15**:15

Coker, Elizabeth Boatwright
Julia Peterkin **31**:307

Colby, Elbridge
James D. Forman **21**:119

Colby, Harriet
Enid Bagnold **25**:72

Colby, Rob
Olga Broumas **10**:76

Colby, Thomas E.
Hermann Hesse **17**:206

Colcord, Lincoln
C. S. Forester **35**:164, 168

Coldwell, Joan
Marie-Claire Blais **13**:96

Cole, Barry
J.M.G. Le Clézio **31**:245
Ann Quin **6**:442

Cole, Diane
Pat Barker **32**:13
Harriet Doerr **34**:152
Cecile Pineda **39**:95

Cole, John N.
Edward Abbey **36**:20

Cole, Laurence
Jean Rhys **2**:372

Cole, Margaret
Eva Figes **31**:164

Cole, Sheila R.
Julia W. Cunningham **12**:166

Cole, Terry M.
Sonia Levitin **17**:263

Cole, William
Charles Causley **7**:42
Alex Comfort **7**:54
Richard Condon **10**:111
Louis Simpson **7**:429
R. S. Thomas **6**:531

Coleby, John
Howard Barker **37**:34
E. L. Doctorow **15**:180
Robert Nye **13**:413
Stephen Poliakoff **38**:378
David Rudkin **14**:471
Wole Soyinka **36**:411
George Tabori **19**:438
Francis Warner **14**:553

Colegate, Isabel
Susan B. Hill **4**:227
Joyce Carol Oates **6**:369

Coleman, Alexander
Isabel Allende **39**:30
Alejo Carpentier **11**:99
José Donoso **11**:145; **32**:152
Pablo Neruda **2**:309
Nicanor Parra **2**:331
João Guimarães Rosa **23**:350, 352
Marguerite Yourcenar **19**:484

Coleman, Sister Anne Gertrude
Paul Vincent Carroll **10**:95

Coleman, Arthur Prudden
Joseph Wittlin **25**:466

Coleman, John
Chinua Achebe **26**:12
Robert Altman **16**:44
Mel Brooks **12**:79
Isabel Colegate **36**:108
Marguerite Duras **20**:102
George Roy Hill **26**:201
Kon Ichikawa **20**:180
Garson Kanin **22**:231
Elia Kazan **16**:367
Jack Kerouac **2**:227
Pier Paolo Pasolini **20**:266
Pink Floyd **35**:313
Sidney Poitier **26**:361
Simon Raven **14**:439
Satyajit Ray **16**:487
Bernice Rubens **31**:350
Jerzy Skolimowski **20**:354
Leon Uris **7**:490
Orson Welles **20**:452

Coleman, Jonathan
Evan Hunter **31**:227

Coleman, Ray
Joan Armatrading **17**:8
Neil Diamond **30**:113
Billy Joel **26**:215
John Lennon **35**:265
Bob Marley **17**:268, 269

Coleman, Robert
Stephen Sondheim **30**:376

Coleman, Sidney
Roger Zelazny **21**:467

Coles, Don
Clark Blaise **29**:71
Graham Greene **27**:174

Coles, Robert
Eldridge Cleaver **30**:57
Shirley Ann Grau **4**:208
Nat Hentoff **26**:182
Kenneth Koch **8**:324
Jonathan Kozol **17**:249
Cormac McCarthy **4**:343
John McPhee **36**:297
Milton Meltzer **26**:298
Thomas Merton **34**:464
Michael Mott **34**:464
Tillie Olsen **13**:432
Walker Percy **14**:415
Ezra Pound **34**:505
Muriel Rukeyser **10**:442
William Stafford **7**:461
William Styron **1**:331
Gay Talese **37**:400
E. Fuller Torrey **34**:505
C. K. Williams **33**:446
Frederick Wiseman **20**:467
James Wright **3**:544

Coles, W. E., Jr.
Ann Swinfen **34**:577

Colimore, Vincent J.
John Gardner **30**:153

Colley, Iain
John Dos Passos **25**:140

Collier, Carmen P.
Pearl S. Buck **7**:32

Collier, Christopher
Esther Forbes **12**:212

Collier, Eugenia
James Baldwin **2**:33
Melvin Van Peebles **2**:447

Collier, Michael
Delmore Schwartz **10**:463

Collier, Peter
Earl Rovit **7**:383

Collings, Michael R.
Piers Anthony **35**:37
Dino Buzzati **36**:92, 94
Samuel R. Delaney **38**:159
Stephen King **37**:207

Collings, Rex
Wole Soyinka **5**:397

Collins, Anne
André Brink **36**:65

James Clavell **25**:126
Stephen King **12**:311
Manuel Mujica Láinez **31**:283
Joyce Carol Oates **33**:295

Collins, Bill
Jack Vance **35**:427

Collins, Bob
Theodore Sturgeon **39**:360
Gene Wolfe **25**:478

Collins, Glen
Fran Lebowitz **36**:248

Collins, Harold R.
Amos Tutuola **5**:443

Collins, J. A.
Christopher Fry **14**:185

Collins, Michael
Dannie Abse **29**:20
Tom Wolfe **15**:584

Collins, Michael J.
Donald Davie **31**:118

Collins, Ralph L.
Elmer Rice **7**:360

Collins, Robert G.
George Lucas **16**:412

Colman, Cathy
Cecile Pineda **39**:95

Colmer, John
Shirley Hazzard **18**:215

Colombo, John Robert
B. P. Nichol **18**:366

Colum, Mary M.
Vera Brittain **23**:89

Colum, Padraic
Patrick Kavanagh **22**:234
Rosemary Sutcliff **26**:433

Columba, Sister Mary, P.B.V.M.
Rosemary Wells **12**:638

Combs, Richard
Woody Allen **16**:4
Robert Altman **16**:24
John Cassavetes **20**:48, 53
Claude Chabrol **16**:182
Brian De Palma **20**:76
Rainer Werner Fassbinder **20**:107, 117, 120
Werner Herzog **16**:322, 323, 333
Elaine May **16**:431
Gordon Parks **16**:459
Sidney Poitier **26**:361, 362
Paul Schrader **26**:388, 396, 399
Martin Scorsese **20**:330, 331, 332
Peter Shaffer **37**:386
Jerzy Skolimowski **20**:353
François Truffaut **20**:393
Peter Weir **20**:425, 427
Orson Welles **20**:453

Commager, Henry Steele
Bruce Catton **35**:83, 85, 86
Esther Forbes **12**:209
MacKinlay Kantor **7**:194
Carl Sandburg **35**:348, 352

Compton, D. G.
Samuel Beckett **3**:47
Frederick Buechner **2**:84
John Gardner **2**:151
Bernard Kops **4**:274
Vladimir Nabokov **6**:352
Frederic Prokosch **4**:422

Compton, Neil
Marshall McLuhan **37**:259
Tom Wolfe **35**:453

Compton-Burnett, Ivy
Ivy Compton-Burnett **15**:139

Conant, Oliver
Renata Adler **31**:15
Saul Bellow **33**:69
Edna O'Brien **36**:338
Peter Taylor **37**:413

Conarroe, Joel
John Berryman **8**:91; **13**:76
Malcolm Bradbury **32**:57
Alfred Corn **33**:121
Leon Edel **34**:536
Stanley Elkin **27**:124
Richard Howard **7**:167
Carolyn Kizer **39**:169
Brad Leithauser **27**:240
Philip Levine **33**:275
Alison Lurie **39**:178
Howard Nemerov **2**:307
Anne Sexton **2**:391
W. D. Snodgrass **2**:405
Judith Thompson **39**:250

Conaty, Barbara
Carolyn Hougan **34**:60

Condini, N. E.
Denise Levertov **28**:241

Condini, Nereo
Eugenio Montale **7**:230
Octavio Paz **19**:368
David Plante **23**:345
Isaac Bashevis Singer **6**:511
Tom Wolfe **9**:579

Condon, Richard
John le Carré **15**:324

Conley, Timothy K.
William Faulkner **9**:200

Conlogue, Ray
Anne Chislett **34**:144

Conn, Stewart
Elaine Feinstein **36**:169
Anne Stevenson **7**:463

Connell, Evan
Carlos Fuentes **22**:170
Trevanian **29**:431

Connell, Evan S., Jr.
Simone de Beauvoir **2**:43
James Dickey **2**:116
Gilbert Rogin **18**:459
Wilfrid Sheed **2**:392

Connelly, Christopher
Jim Carroll **35**:81
Paul McCartney **35**:293

Connelly, Kenneth
John Berryman **1**:34

Connelly, Robert
Luchino Visconti **16**:565

Conner, John W.
E. M. Almedingen **12**:5
Honor Arundel **17**:15, 16
Jay Bennett **35**:42
Judy Blume **12**:44
Frank Bonham **12**:53
James D. Forman **21**:118
Nikki Giovanni **4**:189
Jesse Jackson **12**:290
Madeleine L'Engle **12**:348, 349, 350
Robert Lipsyte **21**:209
John Neufeld **17**:309
Zoa Sherburne **30**:363
Glendon Swarthout **35**:402
Lenora Mattingly Weber **12**:635
Barbara Wersba **30**:430
Maia Wojciechowska **26**:455, 456

Connole, John M.
Thor Heyerdahl **26**:191
Margaret O. Hyde **21**:172

Connolly, Cyril
Ernest Hemingway **6**:225
Louis MacNeice **4**:315
Ezra Pound **4**:408, 414

Connolly, Francis X.
C. S. Forester **35**:168
T. H. White **30**:441

Connor, Anne
Norma Klein **30**:244

Conover, Roger
Paul Muldoon **32**:316

Conover, Roger L.
Mina Loy **28**:250

Conquest, Robert
Roy Fuller **28**:149
Norman MacCaig **36**:280
Ezra Pound **7**:334
Aleksandr I. Solzhenitsyn **2**:413; **4**:513

Conrad, George
Helen MacInnes **27**:280

Conrad, Peter
Beryl Bainbridge **22**:46
F. R. Leavis **24**:307
David Lodge **36**:272

Conrad, Randall
Luis Buñuel **16**:145

Conrad, Robert C.
Heinrich Böll **27**:65

Conradi, Peter J.
John Fowles **33**:174
Harold Pinter **27**:391

Conron, Brandon
Alice Munro **19**:343

Conroy, Frank
Peter Handke **38**:216

Conroy, Jack
Charles Bukowski **2**:84

Consiglio, Alberto
Rouben Mamoulian **16**:421

Contoski, Victor
Robert Duncan **2**:123
Albert Goldbarth **38**:200
David Ignatow **7**:175
David Kherdian **6**:281
W. S. Merwin **18**:334
Czesław Miłosz **11**:376
Marge Piercy **6**:403; **18**:405; **27**:374
Charles Simic **9**:480

Conway, John D.
Paul Vincent Carroll **10**:98

Coogan, Daniel
Antonia Fraser **32**:184

Coogan, Tim Pat
Brian Moore **19**:332

Cook, Albert
Djuna Barnes **4**:43
André Malraux **4**:327

Cook, Bruce
Kingsley Amis **8**:11
James Baldwin **3**:32; **17**:39
Heinrich Böll **6**:84
William S. Burroughs **1**:49
Evan S. Connell, Jr. **4**:109
Gregory Corso **1**:64
Robert Duncan **1**:83
John Gregory Dunne **28**:122
Allen Ginsberg **1**:118; **36**:194
Lillian Hellman **8**:281
John Jakes **29**:248
Marjorie Kellogg **2**:224
Thomas Keneally **5**:211
Jack Kerouac **1**:166
Jerzy Kosinski **1**:171
Ross Macdonald **2**:256
Norman Mailer **1**:193
Brian Moore **7**:235
Charles Olson **1**:263
Ezra Pound **1**:276
Ayn Rand **30**:299
Budd Schulberg **7**:403
Irwin Shaw **7**:413
Georges Simenon **2**:399
Gary Snyder **1**:318
Glendon Swarthout **35**:401
Dalton Trumbo **19**:446, 448
Arnold Wesker **5**:484
William Carlos Williams **1**:372

Cook, Carole
Robert Coover **32**:122
Janet Frame **22**:149
V. S. Pritchett **15**:443
Lynne Sharon Schwartz **31**:391
Eudora Welty **14**:565

Cook, David
Roald Dahl **18**:108
Camara Laye **4**:283
Ngugi wa Thiong'o **36**:321

Cook, Fred J.
Peter Maas **29**:303

Cook, John
Robert Kroetsch **23**:274
Patrick Lane **25**:286

Cook, Jon
William Empson **34**:539
Pier Paolo Pasolini **37**:351

Cook, Martha E.
Donald Davidson **19**:128

Cook, Reginald L.
Robert Frost **1**:111

Cook, Richard M.
Carson McCullers **12**:429
Edmund Wilson **24**:486

Cook, Roderick
Harry Mathews **6**:314
John McPhee **36**:293
Berry Morgan **6**:340
Paul Theroux **28**:422

Cook, Stanley
William Golding **17**:173
Mollie Hunter **21**:168

Cooke, Alistair
C. S. Lewis **27**:260

Cooke, Judy
Maureen Duffy **37**:116
H. D. **31**:207
Stanley Middleton **38**:333
Peter Rushforth **19**:406
John Updike **23**:477

Cooke, Michael
Eldridge Cleaver **30**:58

Cooke, Michael G.
Ronald L. Fair **18**:141
Alex Haley **12**:246, 252
Gayl Jones **9**:308
Margaríta Karapánou **13**:314
George Lamming **4**:279
Michael Mott **15**:381
Joyce Carol Oates **9**:403
Jean Rhys **4**:445
William Styron **1**:331
John Updike **2**:443
Alice Walker **9**:558
Robert Penn Warren **4**:581

Cookson, William
David Jones **4**:260
Hugh MacDiarmid **4**:310

Cooley, Peter
Stephen Dobyns **37**:75
Daniel Halpern **14**:231
Daniel Hoffman **13**:286
Ted Hughes **2**:201
David Ignatow **14**:275
Stanley Plumly **33**:313
Gary Soto **32**:402
Peter Wild **14**:581

Coolidge, Elizabeth S.
Jill Paton Walsh **35**:431

Coolidge, Olivia
Christopher Collier and James L. Collier **30**:71

Coombs, Orde
James Baldwin **8**:40

Coon, Caroline
Joan Armatrading **17**:8

Cooney, Thomas E.
Sloan Wilson **32**:447

Cooper, Arthur
Richard Adams **5**:5
Ralph Bakshi **26**:70
Richard Condon **6**:115
Michael Crichton **2**:109
J. P. Donleavy **6**:142
Frederick Forsyth **36**:174
Ward S. Just **4**:266; **27**:228
John le Carré **3**:281
James A. Michener **5**:290
Wright Morris **7**:245
Gordon Parks **16**:459
Ishmael Reed **6**:450
Philip Roth **2**:378
Irwin Shaw **7**:414
David Storey **5**:417
Gore Vidal **6**:549
Fay Weldon **6**:563

Cooper, Carolyn
Louise Bennett **28**:30

Cooper, Ilene
C. S. Adler **35**:12, 13, 15
Norma Fox Mazer **26**:294

Cooper, Jane
Muriel Rukeyser **15**:456
Norman Williams **39**:100

Cooper, Keith B.
Milton Meltzer **26**:306

Cooper, Nina
Gabriel Marcel **15**:362

Cooper, Philip
Robert Lowell **4**:300

Cooper, Susan
John Donovan **35**:142
Mollie Hunter **21**:160
Mildred D. Taylor **21**:419
Colin Thiele **17**:494, 495

Cooper, William
C. P. Snow **19**:427

Cooperman, Stanley
Langston Hughes **35**:215
Evan Hunter **31**:218
W. S. Merwin **1**:212
Philip Roth **3**:438
Marguerite Yourcenar **19**:481

Coover, Robert
Julio Cortázar **34**:333
José Donoso **4**:127
Carlos Fuentes **8**:224
Gabriel García Márquez **15**:253
Robert Pinget **37**:365
Manuel Puig **28**:371
Ernesto Sabato **23**:381

Cope, Myron
George Plimpton **36**:352

Copland, R. A.
Noel Hilliard **15**:279

Copland, Ray
Frank Sargeson **31**:368, 370

Coppage, Noel
David Bowie **17**:66
Jackson Browne **21**:42
Neil Diamond **30**:114
Janis Ian **21**:184
Mick Jagger and Keith Richard **17**:233

Waylon Jennings **21**:202, 203, 204, 205
Kris Kristofferson **26**:266, 270
John Lennon **35**:263, 268
Gordon Lightfoot **26**:279, 280, 281, 282, 283
Paul McCartney **35**:282
Joni Mitchell **12**:439
Willie Nelson **17**:304
Laura Nyro **17**:314
Phil Ochs **17**:334
Buffy Sainte-Marie **17**:431
Bob Seger **35**:378, 379
Carly Simon **26**:407
Neil Young **17**:583

Corbeil, Carole
Judith Thompson **39**:251

Corbin, Louise
Jean Renoir **20**:293

Corcoran, Neil
Tom Paulin **37**:353

Cordell, Richard A.
Taylor Caldwell **28**:56, 59
August Derleth **31**:136

Cordesse, Gérard
William S. Burroughs **15**:110

Cording, Robert
Albert Goldbarth **38**:204

Core, George
Virginia Spencer Carr **34**:421
John Dos Passos **34**:421
Clyde Edgerton **39**:54
Scott Elledge **34**:428
Andrew Lytle **22**:293
Edna O'Brien **8**:429
Seán O'Faoláin **7**:273
John Crowe Ransom **2**:364; **5**:366
Jean Rhys **14**:447
William Styron **1**:331
Allen Tate **4**:537
William Trevor **9**:529
E. B. White **34**:428

Coren, Alan
James Thurber **25**:440

Corey, David
Wilbur Smith **33**:377

Corey, Stephen
Robert Pinsky **38**:363
William Stafford **29**:386

Corke, Hilary
Isaac Asimov **26**:37
John Cheever **3**:106
A. N. Wilson **33**:452

Corliss, Richard
Renata Adler **31**:13
Alan Ayckbourn **33**:50
Ingmar Bergman **16**:58
Steven Bochco and Michael Kozoll **35**:49
Larry Gelbart **21**:128
Amlin Gray **29**:200
Stephen King **26**:243
Richard Lester **20**:224
David Mamet **34**:222
Garry Marshall **17**:277

Tom Stoppard **34**:273, 280

Corman, Avery
Joseph Hansen **38**:238

Corman, Cid
Kon Ichikawa **20**:179
George Oppen **13**:433
Philip Whalen **29**:447

Corn, Alfred
Elizabeth Bowen **15**:78
Robert Frost **34**:474
John Hollander **8**:302
Czesław Miłosz **22**:310
Eugenio Montale **18**:339
Frederick Morgan **23**:299
Boris Pasternak **7**:300
William H. Pritchard **34**:474
Reg Saner **9**:469
James Schuyler **23**:390
L. E. Sissman **18**:489

Cornell, George W.
Andrew M. Greeley **28**:174

Cornell, Kenneth
Jacques Audiberti **38**:21

Cornish, Sam
Douglas Unger **34**:117

Cornwell, Ethel F.
Samuel Beckett **3**:45
Nathalie Sarraute **8**:471

Corodimas, Peter
Ira Levin **6**:305
Françoise Sagan **17**:425
Glendon Swarthout **35**:401

Corr, Patricia
Evelyn Waugh **1**:356

Corradi, Juan E.
Joan Didion **32**:145

Corrigan, Mary Ann
Tennessee Williams **11**:571, 575

Corrigan, Matthew
Charles Olson **5**:328

Corrigan, Maureen
T. Gertler **34**:52
Frank Lentricchia **34**:571
Alison Lurie **39**:179

Corrigan, Robert W.
Edward Albee **5**:11
John Arden **6**:9
Saul Bellow **6**:51
Robert Bolt **14**:89
Friedrich Dürrenmatt **8**:196
Michel de Ghelderode **6**:197
Arthur Miller **1**:218
John Osborne **5**:332
Harold Pinter **6**:417
Thornton Wilder **5**:494

Corrigan, Sylvia Robinson
Sylvia Plath **17**:350

Corrington, John William
James Dickey **1**:73
Marion Montgomery **7**:233

Cort, David
Jules Archer **12**:16

Cort, John C.
Helen MacInnes **27**:279

Cortázar, Julio
Jorge Luis Borges **8**:102
Luisa Valenzuela **31**:437

Cortínez, Carlos
Octavio Paz **10**:393

Corwin, Phillip
Kay Boyle **5**:67
Siegfried Lenz **27**:249

Cosgrave, Mary Silva
Maya Angelou **12**:13; **35**:32
Robert Lipsyte **21**:208
Paul Zindel **26**:472

Cosgrave, Patrick
Kingsley Amis **3**:8
J. V. Cunningham **31**:102
Robert Lowell **4**:300
Ruth Rendell **28**:384, 386
Georges Simenon **3**:452
Julian Symons **14**:523

Cosier, Tony
Leonard Cohen **38**:138

Cosman, Max
Sylvia Ashton-Warner **19**:21

Costa, Jean-Charles
Pink Floyd **35**:306

Costello, Bonnie
Elizabeth Bishop **32**:29
Philip Levine **33**:275
Howard Nemerov **36**:307

Cott, Jonathan
Bob Dylan **6**:156
Mick Jagger and Keith Richard **17**:234
John Lennon **35**:261
John Lennon and Paul McCartney **12**:356
Jim Morrison **17**:287
Van Morrison **21**:236
Patti Smith **12**:542
Andrew Lloyd Webber and Tim Rice **21**:423

Cotter, James Finn
Robert Bly **10**:62
Philip Booth **23**:76
Peter Davison **28**:104
William Everson **14**:167
Nikki Giovanni **19**:192
Thom Gunn **18**:204
Daniel Hoffman **23**:243
Denise Levertov **28**:243
Laurence Lieberman **36**:262
Jayanta Mahapatra **33**:280
Josephine Miles **34**:245
Frederick Morgan **23**:298, 300
Howard Nemerov **36**:309
Sharon Olds **39**:189
Robert Phillips **28**:364
Robert Pinsky **19**:371
May Sarton **14**:482
Barry Spacks **14**:511
James Tate **25**:429
Richard Tillinghast **29**:416
Mark Van Doren **6**:542
David Wagoner **15**:559

Critic Index

John Hall Wheelock **14**:571

Cottrell, Robert D.
Simone de Beauvoir **8**:58

Coughlan, Margaret N.
E. M. Almedingen **12**:4

Coult, Tony
Edward Bond **23**:65

Cournos, John
R. V. Cassill **23**:102
Carl Sandburg **35**:354

Courtines, Pierre
Michel del Castillo **38**:166

Courtivron, Isabelle de
Violette Leduc **22**:263

Couto, Maria
Salman Rushdie **23**:367

Covatta, Anthony
Elio Vittorini **6**:551

Coveney, Michael
Athol Fugard **5**:130
Stephen Poliakoff **38**:378, 385
Sam Shepard **6**:496
Snoo Wilson **33**:462

Cowan, Doris
Marian Engel **36**:164

Cowan, Louise
Caroline Gordon **13**:243
John Crowe Ransom **5**:363
Allen Tate **2**:431
Robert Penn Warren **6**:555

Cowan, Michael
Norman Mailer **8**:371

Cowan, Paul
Edmund White III **27**:480

Cowan, Robert
Billy Joel **26**:214

Cowasjee, Saros
Mulk Raj Anand **23**:19

Cowen, Robert C.
Jacques-Yves Cousteau **30**:102
Margaret O. Hyde **21**:174

Cowie, Peter
Michelangelo Antonioni **20**:24
Ingmar Bergman **16**:50, 65
Nagisa Oshima **20**:249, 256
Satyajit Ray **16**:480
Jean Renoir **20**:294, 296
Eric Rohmer **16**:531
Jerzy Skolimowski **20**:353
Orson Welles **20**:451

Cowley, Malcolm
Conrad Aiken **10**:3
Louis Aragon **22**:34, 35
Cleanth Brooks **24**:116
Pearl S. Buck **7**:31; **11**:71
Erskine Caldwell **14**:93
E. E. Cummings **3**:118
John Dos Passos **4**:135
Howard Fast **23**:154
William Faulkner **8**:210; **28**:142
Robert Frost **4**:173
Ernest Hemingway **13**:270; **19**:212

Arthur Koestler **33**:229
Doris Lessing **6**:303
Margaret Mead **37**:272
John O'Hara **2**:325
Ezra Pound **4**:407
Upton Sinclair **15**:500
Allen Tate **24**:439
James Thurber **5**:430

Cowley, Robert
Woody Guthrie **35**:185

Cox, C. B.
James Baldwin **17**:27
William Golding **17**:163
David Lodge **36**:267
Norman MacCaig **36**:283

Cox, David
Wilfrid Sheed **4**:489

Cox, James M.
Robert Frost **26**:118

Cox, Kenneth
Hugh MacDiarmid **4**:311
Ezra Pound **4**:413
C. H. Sisson **8**:490
Louis Zukofsky **7**:562; **11**:582

Cox, Martha Heasley
Nelson Algren **33**:15

Cox, Robert
Breyten Breytenbach **37**:51

Cox, Shelley
Tish O'Dowd Ezekiel **34**:46

Cox, Terrance
W. P. Kinsella **27**:238

Coxe, Louis
David Jones **2**:217
Mary McCarthy **24**:344
Anne Sexton **2**:391

Coxe, Louis O.
Sloan Wilson **32**:445

Coy, Jane
Norma Fox Mazer **26**:291

Coyle, Cathy S.
Paula Danziger **21**:83
Diana Wynne Jones **26**:224

Coyle, William
Frank Herbert **35**:201

Coyne, John R., Jr.
David Caute **29**:116
Frederick Forsyth **5**:125
Dick Francis **2**:142
Nicholas Freeling **38**:184
E. Howard Hunt **3**:251
Ward Just **4**:266
Robert Lipsyte **21**:211
Donald E. Westlake **7**:528
Tom Wolfe **2**:481

Coyne, Patricia S.
Kingsley Amis **3**:10
Erica Jong **4**:265
Joyce Carol Oates **9**:402
Wilfrid Sheed **2**:395
Elizabeth Spencer **22**:402
Morris L. West **6**:564

Crabtree, Paul
Louis Auchincloss **18**:27

Crabbe, Katharyn F.
J.R.R. Tolkien **38**:435

Crace, Jim
William Least Heat Moon **29**:225

Cracroft, Richard H.
A. B. Guthrie, Jr. **23**:199

Craft, Robert
Aldous Huxley **5**:193

Craft, Wallace
Eugenio Montale **7**:230

Crago, Hugh
Andre Norton **12**:460
J.R.R. Tolkien **12**:573

Craib, Roderick
Bernard Malamud **3**:322

Craig, Barbara J.
Sandra Scoppettone **26**:405

Craig, D. A.
Thomas Bernhard **32**:17

Craig, David
Piers Paul Read **25**:375
Frank Sargeson **31**:365

Craig, George
Samuel Beckett **29**:62
Michel Butor **15**:115

Craig, Patricia
Joan Aiken **35**:17, 20
Beryl Bainbridge **18**:33
Joan Barfoot **18**:36
Elizabeth Bowen **22**:67
Rosellen Brown **32**:68
Antonia Fraser **32**:185
Carolyn G. Heilbrun **25**:257
Penelope Lively **32**:274
Bernard Mac Laverty **31**:252
William Mayne **12**:404
Joyce Carol Oates **33**:295
Edna O'Brien **8**:429
Frank O'Connor **23**:330
Julia O'Faolain **19**:360
Katherine Paterson **12**:485
Frederic Raphael **14**:438
Noel Streatfeild **21**:413
Fay Weldon **19**:468
A. N. Wilson **33**:451

Craig, Randall
Jean Genet **2**:160
Stephen Poliakoff **38**:375, 376, 377
Bernard Pomerance **13**:444
Robert Shaw **5**:390
Sam Shepard **4**:489
E. A. Whitehead **5**:489
Snoo Wilson **33**:461

Crain, Jane Larkin
Alice Adams **13**:1
Caroline Blackwood **9**:101
André Brink **18**:66
E. M. Broner **19**:72
Rosellen Brown **32**:63
William F. Buckley, Jr. **18**:81
Sara Davidson **9**:175
Lawrence Durrell **6**:153
Leslie Epstein **27**:129

Thomas J. Fleming **37**:128
Bruce Jay Friedman **5**:126
John Gardner **5**:134
Gail Godwin **8**:248
Shirley Ann Grau **9**:240
Milan Kundera **4**:276
Alan Lelchuk **5**:244
Doris Lessing **6**:299
Grace Paley **4**:394
Walker Percy **6**:401
Kathleen Raine **7**:353
C. P. Snow **6**:518
Muriel Spark **5**:398
Mario Vargas Llosa **6**:545
Gore Vidal **4**:555
David Wagoner **5**:474
Frederick Wiseman **20**:474
Sol Yurick **6**:583

Crane, Hugh M.
Carolyn Chute **39**:41
Andrew M. Greeley **28**:175

Crane, John K.
T. H. White **30**:448

Crane, Lucille
Winston Graham **23**:194

Crane, Peggy
Joy Adamson **17**:6
Jean Rhys **14**:446
Wilbur Smith **33**:376

Crane, R. S.
Cleanth Brooks **24**:104

Crane, Rufus S.
Primo Levi **37**:224

Cranford, Beaufort
John McPhee **36**:299

Crankshaw, Edward
Yuri Krotkov **19**:264
Aleksandr I. Solzhenitsyn **1**:319

Cranston, Maurice
Michel Foucault **31**:178

Cranston, Mechthild
René Char **14**:126

Craven, Avery
Bruce Catton **35**:87

Crawford, John W.
Julia Peterkin **31**:302

Crawford, Pamela
Andy Warhol **20**:418

Creagh, Patrick
Giuseppe Ungaretti **7**:484

Creamer, Robert W.
Roy Blount, Jr. **38**:44
Peter Gent **29**:182
Pat Jordan **37**:195

Creekmore, Hubert
Langston Hughes **35**:214

Creeley, Robert
Robert Duncan **4**:141
William Everson **5**:121
Robert Graves **6**:210
Charles Olson **5**:326; **29**:326
Ezra Pound **3**:395
William Stafford **4**:519

William Carlos Williams **5**:507
Louis Zukofsky **4**:599; **18**:559

Creighton, Joanne V.
Joyce Carol Oates **19**:348

Creighton, Luella
Dalton Trumbo **19**:444

Crenshaw, Brad
Frank Bidart **33**:78

Crew, Gary
Wilson Harris **25**:217

Crews, Frederick
Geoffrey H. Hartman **27**:187

Crews, Frederick C.
E. M. Forster **13**:219
Shirley Ann Grau **4**:207
Philip Roth **2**:379

Crews, Harry
Elliott Baker **8**:39
Roy Blount, Jr. **38**:45
Pat Conroy **30**:80

Crichfield, Grant
E. M. Forster **22**:135
Barry Hannah **23**:210

Crichton, Jennifer
Lorrie Moore **39**:83
Joan K. Peters **39**:91

Crichton, Michael
Frederick Forsyth **2**:136
Kurt Vonnegut, Jr. **3**:495

Crichton, Robert
Pier Paolo Pasolini **37**:341

Crick, Bernard
Arthur Koestler **33**:243

Crick, Francis
Michael McClure **6**:319

Crick, Joyce
Michael Hamburger **5**:159
Botho Strauss **22**:408
Christa Wolf **29**:464

Crider, Bill
Octavia E. Butler **38**:62
Robert Cormier **30**:82
Stephen King **12**:310

Crinklaw, Don
John Gardner **3**:186
David Lodge **36**:268

Crinkley, Richmond
Edward Albee **2**:3

Crisler, Ben
Art Buchwald **33**:88, 89

Crisp, Quentin
Graham Greene **18**:198
Molly Keane **31**:234
Stevie Smith **25**:422

Crist, Judith
Lindsay Anderson **20**:17
Mel Brooks **12**:81
John Cassavetes **20**:52
Julia W. Cunningham **12**:163
George Roy Hill **26**:196
Harry Kemelman **2**:225

Jean Kerr **22**:256
Richard Lester **20**:231
Laurence Olivier **20**:241
Nagisa Oshima **20**:249
Sidney Poitier **26**:358
Satyajit Ray **16**:488
Alain Resnais **16**:514
Ken Russell **16**:547

Croce, A.
John Gregory Dunne **28**:121

Croce, Arlene
Ingmar Bergman **16**:47
Shirley Clarke **16**:217
Vittorio De Sica **20**:88
Jean-Luc Godard **20**:128
John Huston **20**:163
Stanley Kubrick **16**:377
Satyajit Ray **16**:475
Stephen Sondheim **30**:382
François Truffaut **20**:381

Croft, Julian
Robert D. FitzGerald **19**:182

Croft, L. B.
Yevgeny Yevtushenko **13**:620

Cromelin, Richard
Walter Becker and Donald
Fagen **26**:79
David Bowie **17**:58

Cromie, Robert
Allen Drury **37**:105

Crompton, D. W.
William Golding **17**:171

Croome, Lesley
Diana Wynne Jones **26**:225

Crosby, John
Donald E. Westlake **33**:437

Crosland, Margaret
Isabel Colegate **36**:113

Cross, Michael S.
Octavia E. Butler **38**:61
Frank Herbert **12**:279

Cross, Nigel
I. Compton-Burnett **34**:496
Hilary Spurling **34**:496

Cross, Richard K.
Richard Eberhart **19**:143

Crossman, R.H.S.
Arthur Koestler **33**:234

Crossmann, Richard
David Caute **29**:117

Crouch, Marcus
Ruth M. Arthur **12**:28
Margot Benary-Isbert **12**:34
Cecil Bødker **21**:13
Larry Bograd **35**:64
H. F. Brinsmead **21**:32
Peter Dickinson **12**:175
Leon Garfield **12**:228
Alan Garner **17**:144
Diana Wynne Jones **26**:229,
230, 231, 232
Andre Norton **12**:464
Katherine Paterson **30**:285
Philippa Pearce **21**:289

Noel Streatfeild **21**:403
Rosemary Sutcliff **26**:432, 438,
440

Crouch, Stanley
James Baldwin **17**:42
Marvin Gaye **26**:134
Ishmael Reed **13**:480; **32**:359

Crouse, Timothy
Carly Simon **26**:406

Crow, John
Harlan Ellison **13**:203

Crowder, Richard H.
Carl Sandburg **1**:300; **15**:467

Crowe, Linda
Honor Arundel **17**:13

Crowl, Samuel R.
Donald Hall **37**:143

Crowne, Thomas
David Donnell **34**:155

Crowson, Lydia
Jean Cocteau **8**:148

Crowther, Bosley
Jean Cocteau **16**:222, 223, 227
Carl Theodor Dreyer **16**:256
Federico Fellini **16**:270
John Ford **16**:305, 309
John Huston **20**:157, 158, 159,
161
Kon Ichikawa **20**:178
Elia Kazan **16**:360, 363
Norman Lear **12**:326
Laurence Olivier **20**:234
Alain Resnais **16**:498
Carlos Saura **20**:314
Nevil Shute **30**:367
Josef von Sternberg **20**:375
Agnès Varda **16**:554
Andrzej Wajda **16**:577
Jessamyn West **17**:548
Billy Wilder **20**:455, 457, 462

Crozier, Andrew
Ed Dorn **18**:128

Cruickshank, John
Patrick Lane **25**:289

Crump, G. B.
Tom Stoppard **15**:519

Crunk
See also Robert Bly
James Wright **28**:462

Crunk
See also James Wright
Gary Snyder **32**:386

Cruse, Harold
Eldridge Cleaver **30**:63

Cruse, Harold W.
W.E.B. Du Bois **2**:120

Cruttwell, Patrick
Sylvia Ashton-Warner **19**:23
Adolfo Bioy Casares **4**:63
Jerzy Kosinski **3**:274
Iris Murdoch **2**:296
I. A. Richards **24**:392
Patrick White **7**:529

Cryer, Dan
Michael Ende **31**:143

Cuddon, J. A.
Peter De Vries **2**:114
James Purdy **4**:423
Frederic Raphael **2**:367
Ann Schlee **35**:372
Claude Simon **4**:497

Culbertson, Diana
Alberto Moravia **7**:243

Cullen, Elinor S.
Ruth M. Arthur **12**:26

Cullen, John B.
Len Deighton **22**:114

Culler, Jonathan
Harold Bloom **24**:75
Wayne C. Booth **24**:96
Geoffrey H. Hartman **27**:184
Walker Percy **8**:439
George Steiner **24**:433

Culligan, Glendy
Sumner Locke Elliot **38**:178
Rosa Guy **26**:140

Cully, Kevin
Manlio Argueta **31**:21

Culpan, Norman
Mollie Hunter **21**:167
Andre Norton **12**:470, 471
Roger Zelazny **21**:464, 465,
472

Cumare, Rosa
Flann O'Brien **5**:317

Cumming, George M. A., Jr.
Piers Anthony **35**:38

Cumming, Joseph B., Jr.
Richard O'Brien **17**:325

Cummings, Peter
Northrop Frye **24**:225

Cunliffe, Marcus
Peter Griffin **39**:398
Ernest Hemingway **39**:398
Alfred Kazin **34**:556
Ved Mehta **37**:289
Irving Stone **7**:469
Studs Terkel **38**:421

Cunliffe, W. Gordon
Heinrich Böll **11**:57
Günter Grass **1**:126
Uwe Johnson **10**:283

Cunningham, Ann Marie
Carolyn Chute **39**:41

Cunningham, John
Isabelle Holland **21**:150

Cunningham, Laura
Richard Price **6**:427

Cunningham, Valentine
Jeffrey Archer **28**:12
Louis Auchincloss **6**:15
Djuna Barnes **29**:32
John Barth **5**:51
Donald Barthelme **3**:43
Samuel Beckett **29**:67
Richard Brautigan **12**:70

Breyten Breytenbach **37**:47
Pearl S. Buck **18**:80
Alejo Carpentier **8**:134
Margaret Craven **17**:79
Donald Davie **31**:120
Len Deighton **4**:119
Don DeLillo **13**:179
Ilya Ehrenburg **18**:137
Buchi Emecheta **14**:159
Shusaku Endo **7**:96; **14**:161
Louise Erdrich **39**:132
Eva Figes **31**:164
Penelope Fitzgerald **19**:172
Frederick Forsyth **5**:125
Carlo Gébler **39**:62
Andrew Holleran **38**:246
Mervyn Jones **10**:295
Anna Kavan **5**:206
William Kennedy **28**:204
William Kotzwinkle **5**:220
Mary Lavin **4**:282
J.M.G. Le Clézio **31**:248
Colin MacInnes **4**:314
Bernard Mac Laverty **31**:255
Stanley Middleton **7**:220
Yukio Mishima **4**:358
Vladimir Nabokov **3**:355
Hans Erich Nossack **6**:364
David Plante **7**:307
Bernice Rubens **19**:404
Salman Rushdie **23**:366
Ward Ruyslinck **14**:471
Françoise Sagan **9**:468
William Sansom **6**:484
Randolph Stow **23**:437
Emma Tennant **13**:536
Lisa St. Aubin de Teran **36**:422
Paul Theroux **8**:513
Gillian Tindall **7**:474
Ludvík Vaculík **7**:495
Kurt Vonnegut, Jr. **22**:450
Harriet Waugh **6**:559
Arnold Wesker **5**:483
Patrick White **4**:587

Cunningham, William
William Harmon **38**:241

Cuppy, Will
Agatha Christie **12**:112, 113
August Derleth **31**:127

Curley, Thomas
Laura Z. Hobson **25**:272
John Nichols **38**:336

Curley, Thomas F.
Pamela Hansford Johnson
27:218

Curran, Charles
Vera Brittain **23**:93

Curran, Mary Doyle
Nadine Gordimer **33**:180

Curran, Ronald
Joyce Carol Oates **33**:293

Curran, Thomas M.
Shusaku Endo **19**:161

Current-Garcia, Eugene
George Seferis **11**:494

Currie, William
Kōbō Abé **8**:2

Curry, Andrew
Robert Phillips **28**:361

Curtin, Edward J., Jr.
Manlio Argueta **31**:20

Curtis, Anthony
Alan Ayckbourn **18**:30; **33**:41
Caryl Churchill **31**:84
David Hare **29**:213
Ronald Harwood **32**:227
W. Somerset Maugham **15**:365
J. B. Priestley **5**:351
Hugh Whitemore **37**:444 .

Curtis, C. Michael
Sara Davidson **9**:175
Annie Dillard **9**:179
George Plimpton **36**:354

Curtis, Charlotte
Bette Bao Lord **23**:279

Curtis, Jerry L.
Jean Genet **10**:224

Curtis, Penelope
Katherine Paterson **12**:485

Curtis, Simon
Donald Davie **5**:113
Seamus Heaney **7**:151

Curtius, E. R.
William Goyen **14**:209

Cuscuna, Michael
Jim Morrison **17**:289

Cuseo, Allan
Michael Cunningham **34**:42
Sam Shepard **34**:270

Cushing, Edward
Aldous Huxley **35**:233

Cushman, Jerome
Jascha Kessler **4**:270

Cushman, Kathleen
Kurt Vonnegut, Jr. **12**:610

Cushman, Keith
Roger Angell **26**:28
Marilyn French **18**:157
Mark Schorer **9**:474

Cushman, Robert
Edward Bond **23**:71

Cusimano, Jim
Lou Reed **21**:309

Cutler, Bruce
Louis Simpson **7**:428

Cutter, William
S. Y. Agnon **4**:15

Cutts, John
Frank Capra **16**:157
Carl Theodor Dreyer **16**:258
Lorraine Hansberry **17**:184

Cyclops
Larry Gelbart **21**:126, 127
Garry Marshall **17**:275

Czajkowska, Magdalena
Tadeusz Różewicz **9**:463

Czarnecki, Mark
Anne Chislett **34**:144
Mavis Gallant **38**:190
W. P. Kinsella **27**:238
Josef Škvorecký **39**:221
Lewis Thomas **35**:414
Judith Thompson **39**:251
Michel Tremblay **29**:419

Dabney, Lewis H.
William Faulkner **6**:174

Dabney, Lewis M.
Edmund Wilson **24**:482

Dabydeen, David
David Dabydeen **34**:147

Dacey, Philip
Arthur Gregor **9**:255

Daemmrich, Horst S.
Eugène Ionesco **11**:289

Dahlie, Hallvard
Hugh Hood **28**:192
Brian Moore **1**:225; **7**:237
Alice Munro **10**:357

Daiches, David
W. H. Auden **1**:8
Saul Bellow **3**:55
Elizabeth Bowen **1**:39
Anthony Burgess **22**:71
Arthur A. Cohen **31**:92
Ivy Compton-Burnett **1**:60
Elizabeth Daryush **19**:119
C. Day Lewis **1**:72
T. S. Eliot **1**:89
William Empson **3**:147
Christopher Fry **2**:143
Robert Graves **1**:126
Henry Green **2**:178
H. D. **31**:202
Aldous Huxley **1**:149
Hugh MacDiarmid **2**:252
Louis MacNeice **1**:186
Bernard Malamud **3**:323
I. A. Richards **24**:384
Henry Roth **6**:473
Edith Sitwell **2**:403
Stephen Spender **1**:322
Evelyn Waugh **1**:356
René Wellek **28**:443

Daiker, Donald A.
Hugh Nissenson **4**:381

Dale, Peter
John Berryman **2**:58
Basil Bunting **10**:84
Stanley Burnshaw **13**:128,129

Daley, Robert
Mark Harris **19**:200
John R. Tunis **12**:597

Dalgliesh, Alice
Margaret O. Hyde **21**:173
Madeleine L'Engle **12**:346, 347

Dallas, Karl
Jimmy Cliff **21**:63
Janis Ian **21**:185
Joni Mitchell **12**:435
Jim Morrison **17**:287
Phil Ochs **17**:330
Frank Zappa **17**:593

Dalton, David
Mick Jagger and Keith Richard
17:239
Jim Morrison **17**:292
Lou Reed **21**:314
Smokey Robinson **21**:347
Paul Simon **17**:466

Dalton, Elizabeth
E. M. Broner **19**:71
Vladimir Nabokov **1**:245
John Updike **1**:344

Dalton, Margaret
Yevgeny Yevtushenko **26**:461

Daltry, Patience M.
Mary Stewart **35**:391

Daltry, Patrice M.
Lee Kingman **17**:245

Daly, Jay
Roger Zelazny **21**:470

Daly, Maureen
Mary Stolz **12**:551

Daly, Mike
Ray Davies **21**:90

Dame, Enid
Chaim Potok **7**:322

D'Amico, Masolino
Umberto Eco **28**:130

Dana, Robert
Yukio Mishima **2**:286

Dangerfield, George
Taylor Caldwell **28**:55
Rayner Heppenstall **10**:272
Compton Mackenzie **18**:313
Carson McCullers **12**:410
Nevil Shute **30**:367
Noel Streatfeild **21**:397
Frank Swinnerton **31**:424, 425
Carl Van Vechten **33**:394

Daniel, Glyn
Thor Heyerdahl **26**:191

Daniel, Helen
David Malouf **28**:265

Daniel, John
Ann Quin **6**:441
Isaac Bashevis Singer **6**:507

Daniel, Lorne
Andrew Suknaski **19**:432

Daniel, Mary L.
João Guimarães Rosa **23**:354

Daniel, Robert
Yvor Winters **32**:458

Daniel, Robert D.
Walker Percy **14**:414

Daniel, Robert W.
W. D. Snodgrass **10**:478

Daniels, Jonathan
T. S. Stribling **23**:440

Daniels, Les
Trina Robbins **21**:338
Richard Rosen **39**:195
Jerome Siegel and Joe Shuster
21:359

Daniels, Robert V.
Larry Woiwode **10**:540

Danielson, J. David
Simone Schwarz-Bart **7**:404

Danis, Francine
Nancy Willard **37**:462

Danischewsky, Nina
Ruth M. Arthur **12**:26
Peter Dickinson **12**:167

Danner, G. Richard
Eugène Ionesco **15**:298

D'Arazien, Steven
Hunter S. Thompson **9**:528

D'Arcy, David
Shiva Naipaul **32**:328

Dardess, George
Jack Kerouac **5**:213

Dareff, Hal
Jonathan Schell **35**:362

Darling, Cary
Prince **35**:325

Darling, Frances C.
Henry Gregor Felsen **17**:120

Darlington, W. A.
Shelagh Delaney **29**:143

Darnton, John
Shiva Naipaul **32**:325

Darrach, Brad
George V. Higgins **4**:224
Joyce Carol Oates **2**:313
Ezra Pound **7**:336
Irving Stone **7**:471

Darragh, Tim
Kem Nunn **34**:94

Dasenbrock, Reed Way
Ngugi wa Thiong'o **36**:324

Das Gupta, Chidananda
Satyajit Ray **16**:481

Dasgupta, Gautam
John Guare **29**:204
Albert Innaurato **21**:191
Arthur Kopit **33**:248

Datchery, Dick
Agatha Christie **12**:120
Trevanian **29**:430

Dathorne, O. R.
Mongo Beti **27**:45
Christopher Okigbo **25**:347

Dauenhauer, Richard
Paavo Haavikko **18**:206; **34**:170

Dault, Gary Michael
Joe Rosenblatt **15**:447, 448

Dauster, Frank
Gabriel García Márquez **3**:182

Davenport, Basil
Daphne du Maurier **11**:162
Carson McCullers **12**:409
Frank Swinnerton **31**:424

Davenport, G.
J.R.R. Tolkien **3**:482

Davenport, Gary
Seán O'Faoláin **14**:406

Davenport, Gary T.
E. M. Almedingen **12**:4
Matt Cohen **19**:113
Timothy Findley **27**:142
Frank O'Connor **23**:326
Seán O'Faoláin **7**:275

Davenport, Guy
E. M. Almedingen **12**:4
Ayi Kwei Armah **33**:24
Michael Ayrton **7**:17
Beryl Bainbridge **8**:36
Thomas Berger **8**:82
Wendell Berry **8**:85
Richard Brautigan **12**:58
Frederick Buechner **2**:82
Paul Celan **10**:101
Louis-Ferdinand Céline **3**:104
John Cheever **25**:116
Evan S. Connell, Jr. **4**:110
Harry Crews **23**:132
Joan Didion **1**:75
J. P. Donleavy **4**:124
G. B. Edwards **25**:151
Sumner Locke Elliot **38**:179
Günter Grass **22**:197
Donald Hall **13**:260
Miroslav Holub **4**:233
Benedict Kiely **23**:267
Frederick Morgan **23**:296
Michael Mott **15**:379
Charles Olson **6**:388; **9**:412
Nicanor Parra **2**:331
Chaim Potok **2**:338
James Purdy **2**:350
Gilbert Sorrentino **22**:394
J.I.M. Stewart **7**:466
Harriet Waugh **6**:560
Eudora Welty **14**:564
Richard Wilbur **6**:569
Louis Zukofsky **2**:487; **4**:599;
  7:560

Davey, Frank
Margaret Atwood **25**:68
Bill Bissett **18**:58
E. J. Pratt **19**:380
Joe Rosenblatt **15**:446

Daviau, Donald G.
Ernst Jandl **34**:196

David, Jack
B. P. Nichol **18**:369

Davidon, Ann Morrissett
Simone de Beauvoir **8**:57
Grace Paley **4**:391
Gore Vidal **4**:557

Davidson, Andrea
Larry Bograd **35**:63

Davidson, Edward
Carl Van Vechten **33**:390

Davidson, Jim
Thomas W. Shapcott **38**:402

Davidson, Michael
Jack Spicer **18**:509

Davidson, Peter
Sylvia Plath **17**:346

Davidson, Richard B.
Christie Harris **12**:266

Davie, Donald
A. R. Ammons **5**:30
John Berryman **8**:87
Austin Clarke **6**:112
Elizabeth Daryush **19**:120
T. S. Eliot **15**:210
Thom Gunn **18**:202; **32**:212
Donald Hall **37**:143
Michael Hamburger **5**:159
Anthony Hecht **8**:267
John Hollander **8**:299
Galway Kinnell **5**:217
Norman MacCaig **36**:288
John Peck **3**:377
Peter Porter **33**:317
Ezra Pound **13**:456
F. T. Prince **22**:339
Siegfried Sassoon **36**:391
Andrew Sinclair **14**:488
Paul Theroux **11**:529
J.R.R. Tolkien **12**:572

Davie, Michael
Michael Scammell **34**:491
Aleksandr Solzhenitsyn **34**:491

Davies, Brenda
René Clair **20**:65
Jean Renoir **20**:296

Davies, Brian
Robert Bresson **16**:103
Claude Chabrol **16**:168

Davies, Norman
Czesław Miłosz **31**:269

Davies, R. R.
Joanne Greenberg **7**:135
Diane Johnson **5**:198
William Sansom **6**:482

Davies, Ray
Ray Davies **21**:88

Davies, Robertson
Marie-Claire Blais **22**:57
John Fowles **33**:171
William Golding **27**:160
John Irving **23**:248
Iris Murdoch **31**:292

Davies, Russell
Richard Condon **8**:150
Donald Davie **31**:111
Joan Didion **8**:177
Elaine Feinstein **36**:168, 169
Michael Hamburger **14**:234
Thomas Hinde **11**:273
Francis King **8**:321
Fran Lebowitz **36**:249
Norman MacCaig **36**:286
S. J. Perelman **15**:418
Harold Pinter **27**:386
Kate Roberts **15**:445
Josef Škvorecký **15**:511
C. P. Snow **19**:429
Donald Spoto **39**:446
William Trevor **9**:528
John Updike **23**:477
Tennessee Williams **39**:446

Davis, Arthur P.
Arna Bontemps **18**:64
Langston Hughes **35**:219
Nella Larsen **37**:214
Ann Petry **18**:404

Davis, Bolton
Breece D'J Pancake **29**:350

Davis, Charles E.
Eudora Welty **33**:417

Davis, Charles T.
Robert Hayden **5**:68

Davis, Cheri Colby
W. S. Merwin **13**:383; **18**:332

Davis, Christopher
Diana Wynne Jones **26**:225

Davis, Deborah
Julio Cortázar **5**:109

Davis, Dick
Robert Hass **39**:149
Ted Hughes **37**:178
Norman MacCaig **36**:288
Edwin Morgan **31**:276
Tom Paulin **37**:353, 355
Peter Porter **33**:325
Craig Raine **32**:353
Anne Stevenson **33**:381
D. M. Thomas **31**:430

Davis, Elmer
William F. Buckley, Jr. **37**:57

Davis, Elrick B.
A. B. Guthrie, Jr. **23**:197

Davis, Fath
Toni Morrison **4**:366

Davis, George
Claude Brown **30**:40
George Lamming **2**:235
Clarence Major **3**:320

Davis, Gladys
Vera Brittain **23**:90

Davis, Hassoldt
Nevil Shute **30**:365

Davis, Hope Hale
John Cheever **8**:140
Oriana Fallaci **11**:190
Sloan Wilson **32**:448

Davis, Jack L.
Charles R. Larson **31**:239

Davis, James
Gretchen Cryer **21**:78

Davis, Jorja
Sandra Scoppettone **26**:405

Davis, Jorja Perkins
Sol Gordon **26**:139

Davis, L. J.
Richard Brautigan **12**:71
Anthony Burgess **22**:71
Richard Condon **4**:106
Robert Cormier **30**:82
Peter De Vries **7**:78
John Gregory Dunne **28**:121
Stanley Elkin **4**:153
Leon Forrest **4**:163

Lois Gould **4**:200
Hannah Green **3**:202
A. B. Guthrie, Jr. **23**:200
John Hersey **2**:188
Stanley Hoffman **5**:184
James Jones **10**:291
Ward S. Just **27**:226, 227
William Kennedy **6**:274
Richard Kostelanetz **28**:213
Ira Levin **6**:307
Colin MacInnes **23**:284
Larry McMurtry **27**:326
John O'Hara **2**:324
J. F. Powers **8**:448
Philip Roth **2**:379
Françoise Sagan **6**:481
Tom Sharpe **36**:404
Ronald Sukenick **4**:531
Paul Theroux **28**:424
J.R.R. Tolkien **8**:516
Vassilis Vassilikos **8**:524
Herman Wouk **38**:449
Richard B. Wright **6**:582

Davis, Lavinia
Margot Benary-Isbert **12**:31
Maureen Daly **17**:90

Davis, Lavinia R.
Rosemary Sutcliff **26**:425, 426

Davis, M. E.
José María Arguedas **10**:10

Davis, Mary Gould
Betty Cavanna **12**:98
Esther Forbes **12**:207
John R. Tunis **12**:595, 596

Davis, Michael
Pink Floyd **35**:308

Davis, Ossie
Lorraine Hansberry **17**:184

Davis, Paxton
Eric Ambler **9**:18
George Garrett **3**:189
S. E. Hinton **30**:205
Paul Zindel **26**:480

Davis, Richard
Woody Allen **16**:2
Claude Chabrol **16**:169
Larry Gelbart **21**:126
Ken Russell **16**:541

Davis, Richard A.
Sam Shepard **17**:439

Davis, Rick
Richard Brautigan **9**:125
Richard Condon **10**:111

Davis, Robert Gorham
Saul Bellow **2**:49
Paul Bowles **19**:57
John Dos Passos **1**:78
A. B. Guthrie, Jr. **23**:197
Ernest Hemingway **39**:433
Josephine Herbst **34**:451
Elinor Langer **34**:451
Halldór Laxness **25**:291
Jeffrey Meyers **39**:433
Irwin Shaw **23**:396
William Styron **3**:472

Davis, Robert Murray
Anthony Powell **31**:316
John Steinbeck **21**:387
Evelyn Waugh **1**:359

Davis, Stephen
Jimmy Cliff **21**:63, 64
Bob Marley **17**:267
Jimmy Page and Robert Plant **12**:480
Lou Reed **21**:307
Carly Simon **26**:407
Brian Wilson **12**:645

Davis, Thulani
Joyce Carol Thomas **35**:407

Davis, Thurston
John le Carré **28**:229

Davis, William V.
Robert Bly **15**:63, 67

Davison, Peter
Robert Creeley **8**:151
Robert Frost **4**:175
Tess Gallagher **18**:169
Doris Grumbach **13**:257
Robert Hass **18**:209
John Hollander **8**:298
Galway Kinnell **2**:229
Denise Levertov **8**:345
Sylvia Plath **2**:337
Anne Sexton **8**:482
William Stafford **7**:460

Davison, Will
Margaret Mead **37**:280

Davy, Charles
René Clair **20**:61
Rouben Mamoulian **16**:422

Davy, John
Arthur Koestler **1**:169

Dawidoff, Robert
Joyce Carol Oates **33**:293

Dawson, Dorotha
Walter Farley **17**:115
Noel Streatfeild **21**:399

Dawson, Helen
David Storey **4**:529

Dawson, Jan
Robert Altman **16**:20, 21
Rainer Werner Fassbinder **20**:116, 118
Werner Herzog **16**:328
Roman Polanski **16**:470
Jerzy Skolimowski **20**:349
François Truffaut **20**:392
Andrzej Wajda **16**:583

Dawson, Margaret Cheney
Nella Larsen **37**:211
Noel Streatfeild **21**:395

Dawson, Rosemary
Betty Smith **19**:422

Day, A. Grove
James A. Michener **1**:214

Day, Doris M.
Peter Shaffer **14**:487

Day, Douglas
Robert Graves **1**:127

Day, James M.
Paul Horgan **9**:278

Daymond, Douglas M.
Mazo de la Roche **14**:150

Daynard, Jodi
Russell Banks **37**:27
Sylvia Murphy **34**:92

De Aguilar, Helene J. F.
Vicente Aleixandre **36**:28

Deakin, Motley
John Nichols **38**:341

Deal, Borden
Doris Betts **28**:33

Deal, Paula Nespecca
C. J. Cherryh **35**:114

Dean, Joan F.
Peter Shaffer **18**:475

Dean, Joan Fitzpatrick
Tom Stoppard **29**:401

Dean, Leigh
Robert Cormier **30**:87
Lois Duncan **26**:108

DeAndrea, Francis T.
Nicholas M. Guild **33**:188

Deane, Peter
Frank Tuohy **37**:427

Deane, Seamus
Seamus Heaney **7**:150
Thomas Kinsella **19**:253
Derek Mahon **27**:289

Deas, Malcolm
Bruce Chatwin **28**:70

Debicki, Andrew P.
Dámaso Alonso **14**:15
Claudio Rodríguez **10**:439

De Bolt, Joe
John Brunner **8**:110

Debrix, Jean R.
Jean Cocteau **16**:223

DeBuys, William
Paul Horgan **9**:279

Decancq, Roland
Lawrence Durrell **8**:191

De Charmant, Elizabeth
Giorgio Bassani **9**:74

Deck, John
Harry Crews **6**:17
Henry Dumas **6**:145
J. G. Farrell **6**:173
Michael Moorcock **5**:294
John Seelye **7**:406

de Costa, René
Pablo Neruda **28**:311

Decter, Naomi [later Naomi Munson]
Judy Blume **30**:20

Dector, Midge
Leon Uris **7**:491

DeCurtis, Anthony
Leonard Michaels **25**:316

Dee, Jonathan
Raymond Carver **36**:107

Deedy, John
J. P. Donleavy **4**:123
Nora Ephron **17**:114
Upton Sinclair **11**:498

Deemer, Charles
Renata Adler **8**:7
James Baldwin **17**:38
John Cheever **3**:108
Peter Handke **5**:165
Bernard Malamud **3**:324

Deen, Rosemary F.
Randall Jarrell **6**:259
Galway Kinnell **3**:268

Deer, Harriet
Stanley Kubrick **16**:387

Deer, Irving
Stanley Kubrick **16**:387

DeFalco, Joseph
Ernest Hemingway **30**:185

De Feo, Ronald
Martin Amis **4**:21
Beryl Bainbridge **8**:37
Thomas Bernhard **3**:65
William S. Burroughs **2**:93
Dino Buzzati **36**:94
José Donoso **4**:128
Frederick Exley **11**:187
Eva Figes **31**:169
William Gaddis **6**:195
Gabriel García Márquez **2**:149; **10**:216
John Gardner **5**:131, 134
Graham Greene **6**:219
John Hawkes **1**:138
Richard Hughes **11**:278
Dan Jacobson **4**:255
Jerzy Kosinski **1**:172
Iris Murdoch **6**:345
Howard Nemerov **6**:360
Robert Pinget **37**:363
Sylvia Plath **1**:270
Anthony Powell **3**:404
Manuel Puig **28**:369
James Salter **7**:388
Gilbert Sorrentino **3**:461
William Trevor **7**:477
John Updike **5**:460
Mario Vargas Llosa **31**:445
Angus Wilson **5**:514

Deford, Frank
Martin Scorsese **20**:334

Degenfelder, E. Pauline
Larry McMurtry **7**:213

Degnan, James P.
Kingsley Amis **2**:10
Roald Dahl **1**:71
John Knowles **26**:258
J.M.G. Le Clézio **31**:247
Wilfrid Sheed **2**:394

Degnan, James P., Jr.
Betty Smith **19**:424

de Horá, Seán
William Kennedy **34**:210

Deitz, Paula
Frederick Busch **18**:84

De Jonge, Alex
Dick Francis **22**:151
Robert A. Heinlein **26**:165
Frank Herbert **23**:219
Frederik Pohl **18**:413
Aleksandr I. Solzhenitsyn **9**:506
D. M. Thomas **22**:417
Roger Zelazny **21**:471, 472

Dekker, George
Donald Davie **8**:166

Dekle, Bernard
Saul Bellow **1**:32
E. E. Cummings **1**:69
John Dos Passos **1**:80
William Faulkner **1**:102
Robert Frost **1**:111
Langston Hughes **1**:148
John P. Marquand **2**:271
Arthur Miller **1**:219
John O'Hara **1**:262
J. D. Salinger **1**:300
Upton Sinclair **1**:310
Thornton Wilder **1**:366
Tennessee Williams **1**:369
William Carlos Williams **1**:371

DeKoven, Marianne
Grace Paley **37**:331

De la Fuentes, Patricia
Gary Soto **32**:405

Delahanty, Thornton
Rouben Mamoulian **16**:419

Delamater, Jerome H.
Jean-Luc Godard **20**:145

Delaney, Marshall
See Fulford, Robert

Delany, Paul
A. Alvarez **5**:19
Margaret Atwood **4**:24
John Berger **19**:39
Vera Brittain **23**:93
Anthony Powell **31**:322

Delap, Richard
Fritz Leiber **25**:306

De la Roche, Catherine
Jean Renoir **20**:288

De la Torre Bueno, J. R., Jr.
Roderick L. Haig-Brown
21:134, 135, 137

Delattre, Genevieve
Françoise Mallet-Joris **11**:355

De Lauretis, Teresa
Italo Calvino **8**:127; **39**:316

De Laurot, Edouard L.
Paddy Chayefsky **23**:111
Federico Fellini **16**:270

Delbanco, Nicholas
Max Apple **33**:18
Frederick Busch **10**:93
Graham Greene **9**:251
Doris Grumbach **13**:257

Deligiorgis, Stavros
David Kherdian **9**:318

Delius, Anthony
Breyten Breytenbach **23**:86
Alan Paton **25**:361

Della Fazia, Alba
Jean Anouilh **1**:7

Dellar, Fred
Smokey Robinson **21**:345

Dellett, Wendy
Ann Schlee **35**:373

Delong-Tonelli, Beverly J.
Fernando Arrabal **9**:36

Del Rey, Lester
Marion Zimmer Bradley **30**:26, 27
John W. Campbell, Jr. **32**:77
C. J. Cherryh **35**:103, 104, 105
Frederik Pohl **18**:412
Jack Williamson **29**:461
Roger Zelazny **21**:471

De Luca, Geraldine
Aidan Chambers **35**:99
Robert Cormier **30**:83
Mollie Hunter **21**:168
J. D. Salinger **12**:517
Sandra Scoppettone **26**:403

De Man, Paul
Harold Bloom **24**:72
Georg Lukács **24**:323

DeMara, Nicholas A.
Italo Calvino **11**:87

DeMarco, Charles
Allen Drury **37**:112

Demarest, Michael
Michael Crichton **6**:119

DeMaria, Robert
Diane Wakoski **2**:459

De Mauny, Erik
Ilya Ehrenburg **34**:435
Anatol Goldberg **34**:435

Dembo, L. S.
Donald Davie **31**:110
Charles Olson **2**:327
George Oppen **7**:283
Robert Phillips **28**:362
Louis Zukofsky **2**:488

DeMeritt, William
Bernard Mac Laverty **31**:252

Demetz, Peter
Lucien Goldmann **24**:241
Rolf Hochhuth **18**:250
Georg Lukács **24**:328

De Mille, Richard
Carlos Castaneda **12**:95

Demorest, Stephen
David Byrne **26**:95
Lou Reed **21**:313
Neil Young **17**:579

Demos, E. Virginia
Larry Kettelkamp **12**:307

Demos, John
Gunnar Ekelöf **27**:113

DeMott, Benjamin
Margaret Atwood **2**:20
James Baldwin **2**:32
John Barth **14**:58
Thomas Berger **38**:36
Jorge Luis Borges **2**:70
Lenny Bruce **21**:49
Anthony Burgess **13**:126
Vincent Canby **13**:132
Truman Capote **19**:84
Eleanor Clark **19**:107
Robert Coover **15**:142
E. L. Doctorow **18**:124
T. S. Eliot **2**:127
John Fowles **33**:171
John Gardner **28**:165
Barry Hannah **23**:210
Joseph Heller **36**:223
Mark Helprin **32**:230
Nat Hentoff **26**:183
Russell C. Hoban **7**:162; **25**:266
John Irving **23**:250; **38**:252
Doris Lessing **2**:240
Norman Mailer **28**:258
Mary McCarthy **14**:357
Margaret Mead **37**:277
Henry Miller **2**:283
A. G. Mojtabai **29**:318
Philip Roth **9**:462
Josef Škvorecký **15**:512
William Styron **15**:526
Gay Talese **37**:396
Alexander Theroux **25**:433
Paul Theroux **28**:425
William Trevor **14**:537
Anne Tyler **28**:432
John Updike **5**:459
Kurt Vonnegut, Jr. **2**:453
John Wain **15**:562
Derek Walcott **14**:550
William Wharton **37**:436
Patrick White **18**:547
Maia Wojciechowska **26**:456

DeMott, Robert
Mary Oliver **19**:362
Judith Johnson Sherwin **15**:480

Dempsey, David
Patrick Boyle **19**:67
James M. Cain **28**:48
R. V. Cassill **23**:103
Janet Frame **22**:143
Ernest K. Gann **23**:162
Martha Gellhorn **14**:195
Willard Motley **18**:357
Nevil Shute **30**:370
Terry Southern **7**:454
Glendon Swarthout **35**:400
Leon Uris **32**:431
Herman Wouk **38**:448

Dempsey, Michael
Robert Altman **16**:20
Lindsay Anderson **20**:14
Francis Ford Coppola **16**:248
John Huston **20**:171
Richard Lester **20**:226
George Lucas **16**:408
Ken Russell **16**:546
Paul Schrader **26**:387

Demuth, Philip
Jerome Siegel and Joe Shuster
21:363

Denby, David
Woody Allen **16**:2
John Cassavetes **20**:55
Francis Ford Coppola **16**:237, 241, 245
Brian De Palma **20**:81
Bob Fosse **20**:126
Werner Herzog **16**:334
John Landis **26**:272, 274
Richard Lester **20**:232
Richard Pryor **26**:380
Paul Schrader **26**:392, 396, 398
Martin Scorsese **20**:325
Peter Shaffer **37**:382
Joan Micklin Silver **20**:345
Steven Spielberg **20**:366, 367
Andy Warhol **20**:419

Deneau, Daniel P.
Hermann Hesse **3**:249
Jakov Lind **1**:178
Amos Oz **27**:360
Alain Robbe-Grillet **4**:449

Denham, Paul
Louis Dudek **11**:159

Denham, Robert D.
Northrop Frye **24**:227

Denisoff, R. Serge
Woody Guthrie **35**:193

Denison, Paul
Ward S. Just **27**:227

Denne, Constance Ayers
Joyce Carol Oates **6**:372

Denney, Reuel
Conrad Aiken **1**:3

Dennis, Sr. M., R.S.M.
E. M. Almedingen **12**:1

Dennis, Nigel
Louis-Ferdinand Céline **1**:57
William Golding **17**:167
Günter Grass **11**:253
Robert Pinget **7**:305
E. B. White **10**:531

Dennis, Patrick
Françoise Sagan **17**:422

Dennison, George
Claude Brown **30**:37
Paul Goodman **4**:197

Denuel, Eleanor P.
Laura Z. Hobson **25**:273

De Pietro, Thomas
Don DeLillo **39**:124

DeRamus, Betty
Joyce Carol Oates **3**:364

Deredita, John
Pablo Neruda **7**:257
Juan Carlos Onetti **7**:278

Deren, Maya
Maya Deren **16**:252

Der Hovanessian, Diana
Vicente Aleixandre **36**:29
David Kherdian **6**:280

Derman, Lisa
Ken Follett **18**:156

Dershowitz, Alan M.
Peter Matthiessen **32**:293

Desai, Anita
Salman Rushdie **23**:365

De Salvo, Louise A.
Robin F. Brancato **35**:67

De Santana, Hubert
Brian Moore **19**:332

Desilets, E. Michael
Frederick Wiseman **20**:471

Desmond, Harold F., Jr.
Melvin Berger **12**:38

Desmond, J. F.
Truman Capote **38**:87

Des Pres, Terrence
Geoffrey H. Hartman **27**:186
Peter Matthiessen **11**:360
Czesław Miłosz **22**:308

Dessner, Lawrence Jay
Mario Puzo **6**:429

De Téran, Lisa St. Auban
Fernanda Eberstadt **39**:50

De Teresa, Mary
Laura Nyro **17**:318

Detro, Gene
Jackson J. Benson **34**:412
John Steinbeck **34**:412

Detweiler, Robert
John Updike **2**:442

Deutsch, Babette
W. H. Auden **2**:21
Ben Belitt **22**:49
Louise Bogan **4**:68
E. E. Cummings **3**:116
Richard Eberhart **11**:176
T. S. Eliot **2**:125
William Empson **8**:201
Robert Frost **3**:171
Jean Garrigue **8**:239
H. D. **3**:217
Langston Hughes **35**:214
Robinson Jeffers **15**:300
Stanley Kunitz **11**:319
Marianne Moore **2**:290
St.-John Perse **4**:398
Ezra Pound **2**:339
Kathleen Raine **7**:351
John Crowe Ransom **2**:361;
   24:363
Theodore Roethke **3**:432
Carl Sandburg **4**:463; **35**:345
Edith Sitwell **2**:402
Stephen Spender **2**:419
Allen Tate **2**:427
Richard Wilbur **9**:568
William Carlos Williams **2**:466
Marya Zaturenska **11**:579

Deutsch, Herbert
Margaret O. Hyde **21**:173

De Van, Fred
Janis Ian **21**:187
Billy Joel **26**:214
Richard Pryor **26**:378

DeVault, Joseph J.
Mark Van Doren **6**:541

D'Evelyn, Thomas
Robert Fitzgerald **39**:471

Dever, Joe
Edna Ferber **18**:151

Devert, Krystyna
Hermann Hesse **2**:189

Deveson, Richard
Thomas M. Disch **36**:127
Carlo Gébler **39**:61
Brian Moore **32**:313
Bernice Rubens **31**:352

DeView, Lucille
Peter Maas **29**:307

DeVitis, A. A.
Graham Greene **1**:133

Devlin, Diana
Howard Barker **37**:37
Howard Brenton **31**:68
Edna O'Brien **36**:336

Devlin, John
Ramón Sender **8**:478

DeVoto, Bernard
Van Wyck Brooks **29**:80
Erich Maria Remarque **21**:327

De Vries, Daniel
Stanley Kubrick **16**:387

De Vries, Peter
James Thurber **5**:429

De Vries, Hilary
Tom Stoppard **34**:273

Devrnja, Zora
Charles Olson **9**:412
Charles Simic **9**:478

Dew, Robb Forman
Pam Durban **39**:45

Dewart, Leslie
William Barrett **27**:18
Jack Williamson **29**:462

Deweese, Beverly
Marion Zimmer Bradley **30**:32

Deweese, Gene
Arthur C. Clarke **35**:127
Lucius Shepard **34**:109

Dewsnap, Terence
Christopher Isherwood **1**:156

Dey, Susnigdha
Octavio Paz **19**:368

DeYoung, Alan J.
Margaret Mead **37**:282

Dial, John E.
José María Gironella **11**:237

Díaz, Janet Winecoff
Fernando Arrabal **18**:17
Miguel Delibes **18**:111
Ana María Matute **11**:363

Dibbell, Carola
Pat Barker **32**:14

Dick, Bernard F.
Michelangelo Antonioni **20**:41
Thomas J. Fleming **37**:122
William Golding **1**:120
John Hersey **2**:188
Iris Murdoch **6**:342; **22**:331
Robert Pinsky **38**:358
Mary Renault **3**:426
I. A. Richards **14**:454
Stevie Smith **8**:492
Gore Vidal **4**:558

Dick, Kay
Simone de Beauvoir **4**:48

Dickens, Anthony
E. M. Forster **22**:137

Dickens, Byrom
T. S. Stribling **23**:444

Dickens, Monica
Colin Thiele **17**:495

Dickenson, Peter
P. G. Wodehouse **22**:485

Dickey, Chris
Kurt Vonnegut, Jr. **5**:470

Dickey, Christopher
Manlio Argueta **31**:20
Graham Greene **37**:138
Trevanian **29**:432

Dickey, James
Conrad Aiken **1**:3
John Ashbery **2**:16
John Berryman **1**:33
Philip Booth **23**:74
Kenneth Burke **2**:87
Stanley Burnshaw **3**:91
Hayden Carruth **4**:93
E. E. Cummings **1**:68
J. V. Cunningham **3**:120
Robert Duncan **1**:82
Richard Eberhart **3**:133
Ronald G. Everson **27**:133
William Everson **1**:96
Robert Frost **1**:111
Allen Ginsberg **1**:118
Woody Guthrie **35**:193
David Ignatow **4**:247
Robinson Jeffers **2**:214
Galway Kinnell **1**:167
James Kirkup **1**:169
John Logan **5**:252
Louis MacNeice **1**:186
William Meredith **4**:347
James Merrill **2**:272
W. S. Merwin **1**:211
Josephine Miles **1**:215
Marianne Moore **1**:226
Howard Nemerov **2**:305
Mary Oliver **19**:361
Charles Olson **1**:262; **2**:327
Kenneth Patchen **1**:265
Sylvia Plath **2**:337
Herbert Read **4**:439
I. A. Richards **14**:452
Theodore Roethke **1**:290
May Sarton **4**:470
Frederick Seidel **18**:474
Anne Sexton **2**:390
Louis Simpson **4**:497
William Jay Smith **6**:512

William Stafford **4**:519
Allen Tate **6**:527
Derek Walcott **14**:548
Robert Penn Warren **1**:352;
   18:538
Theodore Weiss **3**:515
John Hall Wheelock **14**:571
Reed Whittemore **4**:588
Richard Wilbur **3**:531
William Carlos Williams **1**:370
Yvor Winters **4**:590

Dickey, R. P.
Lawrence Ferlinghetti **6**:183
Robert Lowell **5**:258

Dickey, William
Daniel J. Berrigan **4**:56
John Berryman **13**:75
Hayden Carruth **7**:40
James Dickey **2**:115
William Everson **5**:121
W. S. Merwin **2**:277
George Oppen **7**:281
Richard Wilbur **14**:577

Dickins, Anthony
Vladimir Nabokov **2**:304

Dickinson, Hugh
Eugène Ionesco **6**:250

Dickinson-Brown, R.
Barry Spacks **14**:510
Lewis Turco **11**:551

Dickstein, Lore
Gail Godwin **8**:247
Judith Guest **8**:254
Sue Kaufman **3**:263
Judith Rossner **6**:469
Susan Fromberg Schaeffer
   22:369
Lynne Sharon Schwartz **31**:387
Cynthia Propper Seton **27**:426
Isaac Bashevis Singer **3**:456
Botho Strauss **22**:408

Dickstein, Morris
John Barth **7**:24
Donald Barthelme **6**:29
R. P. Blackmur **2**:61
John Cassavetes **20**:55
Daniel Fuchs **8**:220
John Gardner **3**:184
Günter Grass **11**:252
Galway Kinnell **29**:288
Bernard Malamud **27**:300
Philip Roth **4**:454
Hunter S. Thompson **17**:509
C. K. Williams **33**:442, 445
Tom Wolfe **35**:456
Richard Wright **21**:458
Rudolph Wurlitzer **2**:484

Didion, Joan
Woody Allen **16**:13
John Cheever **8**:137
Elizabeth Hardwick **13**:265
Doris Lessing **2**:240
Norman Mailer **14**:352
V. S. Naipaul **18**:365
J. D. Salinger **12**:511

Dienstag, Eleanor
Sylvia Ashton-Warner **19**:22
Maureen Duffy **37**:113
Lee Kingman **17**:246

Dietemann, Margaret
Arthur Adamov **25**:16

Dietrichson, Jan W.
Daniel Hoffman **23**:239

Diez, Luys A.
Juan Carlos Onetti **7**:280

Digilio, Alice
M. E. Kerr **35**:248
Barbara Pym **37**:379
Cynthia Voight **30**:419
Barbara Wersba **30**:434

Dillard, Annie
Evan S. Connell, Jr. **4**:109

Dillard, R.H.W.
William S. Burroughs **22**:83
W. S. Merwin **8**:389
Wright Morris **18**:351
Vladimir Nabokov **2**:304
Colin Wilson **3**:537

Diller, Edward
Friedrich Dürrenmatt **11**:171

Dillin, Gay Andrews
John Jakes **29**:250

Dillin, John
Jonathan Schell **35**:362

Dillingham, Thomas
Susan Fromberg Schaeffer
6:488

Dillon, Brooke Selby
Marilyn Sachs **35**:334

Dillon, David
William Goyen **14**:211
John Hawkes **4**:218
Edwin O'Connor **14**:393
Tillie Olsen **13**:433
Wallace Stegner **9**:509

Dillon, George
Gil Orlovitz **22**:332

Dillon, Michael
Thornton Wilder **6**:571

Di Martino, Dave
Pink Floyd **35**:311

Dimeo, Steve
George Roy Hill **26**:197

Dimeo, Steven
Ray Bradbury **3**:85

Dimock, Edward C.
Raja Rao **25**:366

Di Napoli, Thomas
Günter Grass **11**:247

Dinchak, Marla
Laurence Yep **35**:471

Dinnage, Rosemary
Peter Ackroyd **34**:396
A. S. Byatt **19**:77
Isak Dinesen **10**:152
T. S. Eliot **34**:396
E. M. Forster **22**:137
Elizabeth Hardwick **13**:264
Doris Lessing **6**:303
Iris Murdoch **22**:328

Barbara Pym 37:378
Elizabeth Taylor **29**:409
Fay Weldon **19**:468
Rebecca West **31**:459

Dinoto, Andrea
Walter Farley **17**:118

Di Piero, W. S.
John Ashbery **4**:22
John Hawkes **9**:269
Seamus Heaney **25**:250
Philip Levine **14**:321
Sam Peckinpah **20**:282
R. G. Vliet **22**:442

Dipple, Elizabeth
Iris Murdoch **31**:289

Dirda, Michael
James Dickey **15**:177
Umberto Eco **28**:132
Henry Green **13**:251
Russell C. Hoban **25**:266
John Knowles **10**:303
Vladimir Nabokov **23**:310
D. M. Pinkwater **35**:320
Gilbert Sorrentino **14**:500
John Updike **34**:285
Jack Vance **35**:426
Alice Walker **19**:452

Disch, Thomas M.
William S. Burroughs **22**:84
Arthur C. Clarke **18**:106
Don DeLillo **39**:121
Philip José Farmer **19**:168
Piers Paul Read **25**:378
Anne Tyler **18**:529
Gene Wolfe **25**:474
Laurence Yep **35**:474

Ditlea, Steve
Willie Nelson **17**:302

Ditsky, John
Richard Brautigan **12**:69
John Hawkes **2**:186
Erica Jong **8**:313
Joyce Carol Oates **2**:316

Dix, Carol
Martin Amis **4**:20

Dix, Winslow
William X. Kienzle **25**:274

Dixon, Bob
Gunnel Beckman **26**:89
Alan Garner **17**:149
Noel Streatfeild **21**:416

Dixon, John W., Jr.
Elie Wiesel **3**:527

DiZazzo, Raymond
Robert L. Peters **7**:303

Djilas, Milovan
Aleksandr I. Solzhenitsyn **2**:408

Djwa, Sandra
Margaret Laurence **13**:341
E. J. Pratt **19**:381
F. R. Scott **22**:376

Dobbs, Kildare
Hugh Hood **28**:187
Margaret Laurence **3**:278
Alice Munro **6**:341

Dobie, Ann B.
Muriel Spark **2**:416

Dobie, J. Frank
Mari Sandoz **28**:403, 404

Dobrez, L.A.C.
Jean Genet **14**:205

Dobson, Joan L.
Margaret O. Hyde **21**:180
Suzanne Newton **35**:301

Dobyns, Stephen
Julio Cortázar **33**:129, 135
James Tate **25**:427

Doctorow, E. L.
E. L. Doctorow **15**:179
Mary Lee Settle **19**:411

Dodd, Wayne
Robert Bly **38**:55
Madeleine L'Engle **12**:350

Dodsworth, Martin
Robert Bly **2**:65
Donald Davie **8**:163; **31**:110
James Dickey **2**:115
Ian Fleming **30**:133
Marianne Moore **2**:291
Edwin Morgan **31**:273
Peter Porter **33**:318

Doerksen, Daniel W.
Margaret Avison **4**:36

Doerner, William R.
James Herriot **12**:282

Doherty, Andy
Frank Zappa **17**:592

Dohmann, Barbara
Jorge Luis Borges **2**:69
Julio Cortázar **2**:101
Gabriel García Márquez **2**:147
Juan Carlos Onetti **7**:276
João Guimarães Rosa **23**:350
Juan Rulfo **8**:461
Mario Vargas Llosa **3**:493

Dolan, Mary
Frank G. Slaughter **29**:377

Doležel, Lubomír
Milan Kundera **32**:257

Dollard, Peter
Wendell Berry **27**:37
Carl Sandburg **35**:360

Dollard, W.A.S.
Winston Graham **23**:191

Dollen, Charles
William Peter Blatty **2**:64
Paul Gallico **2**:147
Ernest K. Gann **23**:167
N. Scott Momaday **2**:289

Dombroski, Robert S.
Carlo Emilio Gadda **11**:208

Domingues, Larry
Jim Shepard **36**:407

Domini, John
Stratis Haviaras **33**:206
Craig Nova **31**:296

Domowitz, Janet
Alice Adams **13**:3

Dompkowski, Judith A.
Matthew Bruccoli **34**:417
Ross Macdonald **34**:417

Donadio, Stephen
John Ashbery **2**:19
James Baldwin **17**:33
Richard Fariña **9**:195
Sandra Hochman **3**:250
Richard Stern **39**:237

Donaghue, Denis
Donald Barthelme **13**:62

Donahue, Deirdre
Bernard Mac Laverty **31**:255
Gloria Naylor **28**:305

Donahue, Francis
Antonio Buero Vallejo **15**:96
Camilo José Cela **4**:97; **13**:147

Donahue, Walter
Sam Shepard **4**:491

Donahugh, Robert H.
Allan W. Eckert **17**:104
Thomas J. Fleming **37**:127
John Knowles **26**:257
Margaret Mead **37**:280

Donald, David
Bruce Catton **35**:85, 89, 93
Margaret Mead **37**:279

Donald, David Herbert
Alex Haley **12**:246

Donald, Miles
Wilbur Smith **33**:374
Alexander Theroux **25**:431
John Updike **23**:465

Donaldson, Margaret
August Derleth **31**:135

Donaldson, Scott
Ernest Hemingway **13**:276
Philip Roth **1**:293

Donato, Eugenio
Claude Lévi-Strauss **38**:299

Donavin, Denise P.
Leon Edel **34**:534
John Ehle **27**:106
Howard Fast **23**:161
Norma Klein **30**:243
Barbara Pym **37**:368

Donegan, Patricia
Ayn Rand **30**:295

Donelson, Kenneth L.
Jay Bennett **35**:45
Robert Cormier **30**:87
James D. Forman **21**:123
Rosa Guy **26**:145
Paul Zindel **26**:472

Donnard, Jean-Hervé
Eugène Ionesco **6**:249

Donnelly, Brian
Derek Mahon **27**:289, 291

Donnelly, Dorothy
Marge Piercy **3**:384
Anne Stevenson **33**:379

Donnelly, John
Thomas Merton **34**:466
Michael Mott **34**:466

Donner, Jorn
Ingmar Bergman **16**:52

Donoghue, Denis
Peter Ackroyd **34**:395
A. R. Ammons **9**:27
John Ashbery **15**:34
W. H. Auden **3**:24
Saul Bellow **2**:51
J. V. Cunningham **31**:101, 103
Elizabeth Bishop **13**:95
R. P. Blackmur **24**:58, 67
Marie-Claire Blais **2**:63
Wayne C. Booth **24**:90
Kenneth Burke **2**:88
Ronald Bush **34**:531
Austin Clarke **9**:167
C. Day Lewis **6**:129
Jacques Derrida **24**:152
Margaret Drabble **22**:127
Richard Eberhart **11**:175
T. S. Eliot **2**:126; **34**:395, 531
Thomas Flanagan **25**:165
John Fowles **10**:188
William H. Gass **11**:225
William Golding **3**:196
Shirley Ann Grau **4**:209
Graham Greene **9**:250; **27**:173
Geoffrey H. Hartman **27**:182, 186
Seamus Heaney **14**:245; **37**:163
Anthony Hecht **8**:269
Paul Horgan **9**:278
Randall Jarrell **1**:160
Robert Lowell **4**:295
James Merrill **2**:274; **18**:331
W. S. Merwin **2**:277
Marianne Moore **2**:291
Joyce Carol Oates **33**:291
Frank O'Connor **23**:331
Seán O'Faoláin **32**:340, 343
Tom Paulin **37**:355
Robert Pinsky **19**:370
David Plante **23**:341
Ezra Pound **2**:340
Philip Rahv **24**:357
I. A. Richards **24**:400
Philip Roth **6**:476
Frederick Seidel **18**:475
Jaroslav Seifert **34**:262
Christina Stead **2**:422
Mark Strand **18**:515
Allen Tate **6**:527; **9**:521; **11**:526
Charles Tomlinson **2**:437
Lionel Trilling **9**:530; **11**:543; **24**:452
Frank Tuohy **37**:430
Gore Vidal **33**:403
Derek Walcott **2**:460; **25**:451
Anne Waldman **7**:507
Robert Penn Warren **4**:579; **13**:581
René Wellek **28**:450
Rebecca West **7**:525
William Carlos Williams **2**:467
Angus Wilson **25**:464
Yvor Winters **32**:463

Donoghue, Susan
Joni Mitchell **12**:435, 436

Donohue, Agnes McNeill
Jessamyn West **17**:553

Donohue, John W.
Earl Hamner **12**:259

Donovan, Diane C.
Lloyd Alexander **35**:28
Sue Ellen Bridgers **26**:92
C. J. Cherryh **35**:107
Stephen King **37**:201

Donovan, Josephine
Sylvia Plath **3**:390

Dooley, D. J.
Earle Birney **6**:71

Dooley, Dennis M.
Robert Penn Warren **10**:517

Dooley, Eugene A.
Evan Hunter **31**:228

Dooley, Patricia
William Kotzwinkle **35**:255
Barbara Wersba **30**:433

Dooley, Roger B.
Thomas J. Fleming **37**:121

Dooley, Susan
Joanne Greenberg **30**:167

Dooley, Tim
Peter Porter **33**:321

Dooley, William Germain
Charles Addams **30**:12

Doreski, William
Louise Glück **22**:175
Charles Simic **22**:383
Richard Tillinghast **29**:415

Dorfman, Ariel
Miguel Ángel Asturias **13**:39

Dorian, Marguerite
Mircea Eliade **19**:147

Dorsey, David
Alex La Guma **19**:277

Dorsey, George A.
Margaret Mead **37**:268

Dorsey, Margaret A.
Lloyd Alexander **35**:25
Gunnel Beckman **26**:86
Babbis Friis-Baastad **12**:214
Larry Kettelkamp **12**:305
Andre Norton **12**:458, 459
Scott O'Dell **30**:273

Dos Passos, John
E. E. Cummings **12**:139

Dostert, Candyce
William H. Gass **39**:482

Doubrovsky, J. S.
Eugène Ionesco **6**:247

Doubrovsky, Serge
Albert Camus **11**:93

Dougherty, Dru
Juan Goytisolo **23**:189
Darcy Ribeiro **34**:102

Doughtie, Edward
James Dickey **15**:176

Douglas, Ann
James T. Farrell **11**:196

Douglas, Donald
Carl Van Vechten **33**:388

Douglas, Ellen
Josephine Humphreys **34**:65
Flannery O'Connor **6**:381
May Sarton **4**:471

Douglas, George H.
Alfred Kazin **38**:278
Edmund Wilson **2**:477

Douglas, Marjory Stoneman
Noel Streatfeild **21**:400

Dowd, Nancy Ellen
Frederick Wiseman **20**:468

Dowell, Bob
Flannery O'Connor **21**:264

Dowie, James Iverne
Helen Hooven Santmyer **33**:357

Dowie, William
Sylvia Plath **17**:364

Dowling, Gordon Graham
Yukio Mishima **6**:337

Downer, Alan S.
Thornton Wilder **5**:495

Downey, Sharon D.
Leon Uris **32**:433

Downing, Robert
Orson Welles **20**:433

Doxey, William S.
Ken Kesey **3**:267
Flannery O'Connor **3**:368

Doyle, Charles
James K. Baxter **14**:60
See also Doyle, Mike

Doyle, Jacqueline
Sean O'Casey **15**:406

Doyle, Mike
Irving Layton **2**:236
A. W. Purdy **6**:428
Raymond Souster **5**:395, 396
See also Doyle, Charles

Doyle, Paul A.
Pearl S. Buck **11**:71
Paul Vincent Carroll **10**:96
R. V. Cassill **23**:104
James T. Farrell **8**:205
MacKinlay Kantor **7**:195
Seán O'Faoláin **1**:259; **7**:273
Anne Tyler **28**:431
Evelyn Waugh **1**:359

Drabble, Margaret
Malcolm Bradbury **32**:52
Michael Frayn **3**:164
John Irving **13**:295
Philip Larkin **8**:333; **9**:323
Iris Murdoch **4**:367
Muriel Spark **8**:494
John Updike **15**:544

Drabelle, Dennis
Edward Abbey **36**:19
David Cudlip **34**:38
Frank Tuohy **37**:433

Dragonwagon, C.
Stevie Wonder **12**:663

Drake, Leah Bodine
Norman MacCaig **36**:280

Drake, Robert
Carson McCullers **12**:426
Flannery O'Connor **21**:264, 273
Reynolds Price **3**:405
Eudora Welty **5**:478

Drake, Sylvie
August Wilson **39**:279

Draper, Charlotte W.
Andre Norton **12**:471

Draper, Gary
Michael Ondaatje **29**:343

Draudt, Manfred
Joe Orton **13**:436

Draya, Ren
Tennessee Williams **15**:579

Dretzsky, George
Marian Engel **36**:162

Drew, Fraser
John Masefield **11**:356

Drexler, Rosalyn
Anaïs Nin **14**:387
Fay Weldon **36**:449

Dries, Linda R.
Allan W. Eckert **17**:105

Driver, Christopher
Yukio Mishima **4**:357
D. M. Thomas **31**:433

Driver, Sam N.
Anna Akhmatova **11**:6

Driver, Tom F.
Samuel Beckett **29**:54
Jean Genet **1**:115
Lorraine Hansberry **17**:182
Arthur Miller **1**:215; **2**:279

Druska, John
John Beecher **6**:49
John Gregory Dunne **28**:125
Mario Puzo **36**:360

Dryden, Edgar A.
John Barth **5**:52

Drzal, Dawn Ann
Amy Hempel **39**:70
Lorrie Moore **39**:84

Duberman, Martin
Ed Bullins **1**:47
Robert Fitzgerald **39**:472
Laura Z. Hobson **7**:163
Albert Innaurato **21**:197
David Mamet **15**:355

Duberman, Martin B.
John Gregory Dunne **28**:120
Nat Hentoff **26**:180

Duberstein, Larry
Joel Lieber **6**:312

Dubois, Larry
William F. Buckley, Jr. **7**:34
Walker Percy **8**:445

Du Bois, W. E. Burghardt
Arna Bontemps **18**:62
Nella Larsen **37**:210
Carl Van Vechten **33**:392
Richard Wright **21**:434

Du Bois, William
James M. Cain **28**:45
Thomas B. Costain **30**:93
A. J. Cronin **32**:136
Howard Fast **23**:158
Laura Z. Hobson **25**:269
Conrad Richter **30**:308, 323

Dubro, Alec
Neil Diamond **30**:111
Kris Kristofferson **26**:267
Jim Morrison **17**:288
Laura Nyro **17**:313

Dubus, Andre
Tobias Wolff **39**:284

Ducan, Jean
Zibby Oneal **30**:280

Ducharme, Edward
Walter M. Miller, Jr. **30**:255

Duchêne, Anne
Beryl Bainbridge **22**:45
Bruce Chatwin **28**:73
Francine du Plessix Gray **22**:200
Mark Helprin **22**:221
Elizabeth Jane Howard **29**:246
Alberto Moravia **18**:347
Rosemary Sutcliff **26**:441
D. M. Thomas **22**:419

Duddy, Thomas A.
Louis Zukofsky **11**:581

Dudek, Louis
Daryl Hine **15**:281
Irving Layton **15**:320
Alden Nowlan **15**:399
James Reaney **13**:474
Raymond Souster **14**:501

Dufault, Peter Kane
Philip Booth **23**:73

Duffey, Bernard
W. H. Auden **4**:3
H. D. **31**:207
Jack Kerouac **1**:66
Carl Sandburg **35**:358

Duffus, R. L.
Walter D. Edmonds **35**:150
Richard Wright **21**:435

Duffy, Dennis
Philip Child **19**:102
Matt Cohen **19**:111

Duffy, Martha
James Baldwin **4**:41
Jean Cocteau **1**:59
Joan Didion **1**:75
Nikki Giovanni **2**:164
Gail Godwin **22**:180
Lillian Hellman **4**:221
D. Keith Mano **10**:328
Tom McHale **5**:281
Grace Paley **4**:393
Walker Percy **2**:334

Sylvia Plath **2**:336
Judith Rossner **6**:470
Bernice Rubens **19**:404
Françoise Sagan **36**:383
Leon Uris **32**:433
Patrick White **3**:523

Duffy, Michael
Walter Becker and Donald Fagen **26**:84

Duguid, Lindsay
Ursula K. Le Guin **22**:274

Duhamel, P. Albert
Flannery O'Connor **1**:253
Paul Scott **9**:477

Dukas, Vytas
Vasily Aksenov **22**:26, 28

Dukes, Ashley
Emlyn Williams **15**:577

Dukore, Bernard F.
Harold Pinter **27**:393

Dullea, Gerard J.
Gregory Corso **11**:123

Dumas, Bethany K.
E. E. Cummings **12**:159

Dunbar, Ernest
Jules Archer **12**:21

Duncan, Erika
William Goyen **8**:251
Anaïs Nin **8**:425

Duncan, Robert
Paul McCartney **35**:285
Richard Pryor **26**:378
John Wieners **7**:536
Frank Zappa **17**:591

Dunham, Vera S.
Yevgeny Yevtushenko **26**:461

Dunlap, John R.
Martin Cruz Smith **25**:414

Dunlea, William
Michel del Castillo **38**:163
Kamala Markandaya **38**:320
Nevil Shute **30**:370
Richard Wright **21**:437

Dunlop, John B.
Vladimir Voinovich **10**:509

Dunn, Douglas
Dannie Abse **29**:20
Giorgio Bassani **9**:77
Donald Davie **31**:112
John Berryman **4**:62
George Mackay Brown **5**:78
Noël Coward **29**:137
Donald Davie **5**:115
Lawrence Durrell **4**:147
D. J. Enright **4**:156; **8**:203
Gavin Ewart **13**:209
James Fenton **32**:165
W. S. Graham **29**:196
Geoffrey Grigson **7**:136
John Hawkes **7**:141
Seamus Heaney **7**:150
Dan Jacobson **14**:290
Erica Jong **6**:268

Michael Longley **29**:292, 294, 296
Norman MacCaig **36**:284, 285, 286
Derek Mahon **27**:287
Christopher Middleton **13**:388
Leslie Norris **14**:387
Sylvia Plath **5**:339
William Plomer **4**:407
Peter Porter **13**:452; **33**:325
Peter Redgrove **6**:446
Kenneth Rexroth **11**:473
Jon Silkin **6**:499
Anne Stevenson **7**:463
Charles Tomlinson **6**:534
Andrew Young **5**:25

Dunn, Tony
Howard Barker **37**:41

Dunne, John Gregory
William F. Buckley, Jr. **37**:61
Danny Santiago **33**:353

Dunning, Jennifer
Albert Innaurato **21**:195

Dunson, Josh
Phil Ochs **17**:330, 333

Dupee, F. W.
Kenneth Koch **5**:218
Robert Lowell **3**:299
Norman Mailer **11**:339
Bernard Malamud **3**:321
W. S. Merwin **3**:338
John Osborne **5**:330
J. F. Powers **4**:418

DuPlessis, Rachel Blau
Edward Albee **13**:6
H. D. **14**:229
Muriel Rukeyser **27**:412

Dupree, Robert S.
Caroline Gordon **13**:245
Allen Tate **6**:525

Duprey, Richard A.
Edward Albee **25**:32
William Gibson **23**:178
Arthur Miller **26**:318

Duran, Daniel Flores
Scott O'Dell **30**:275

Durán, Manuel
Pablo Neruda **28**:312

Durand, Laura G.
Monique Wittig **22**:475

Durbin, Karen
Eleanor Clark **5**:107

Duree, Barbara Joyce
Lenora Mattingly Weber **12**:633

Durgnat, Raymond
Georges Bataille **29**:43
Robert Bresson **16**:110
Tod Browning **16**:122
Luis Buñuel **16**:142, 150
John Cassavetes **20**:44, 45
Claude Chabrol **16**:168
René Clair **20**:66
Shirley Clarke **16**:216
Rainer Werner Fassbinder **20**:119

Federico Fellini **16**:273
Jean-Luc Godard **20**:129
John Huston **20**:168
Kon Ichikawa **20**:177
Richard Lester **20**:219
Roman Polanski **16**:163, 468
Ann Quin **6**:442
Jean Renoir **20**:291, 304
François Truffaut **20**:382
Lina Wertmüller **16**:587

Durham, Frank
Julia Peterkin **31**:306
Elmer Rice **7**:363
T. S. Stribling **23**:447

Durham, Philip
Dashiell Hammett **3**:218; **19**:194

Duroche, L. L.
Martin Heidegger **24**:261

Durrant, Digby
Caroline Blackwood **6**:80
Penelope Fitzgerald **19**:174
Maurice Gee **29**:178
Julia O'Faolain **6**:383

Durrell, Gerald
Joy Adamson **17**:2

Durrell, Lawrence
Odysseus Elytis **15**:219
George Seferis **5**:385

Dusenbury, Winifred L.
William Saroyan **29**:359
Tennessee Williams **30**:464

Dust, Harvey
Jules Archer **12**:17

Dutton, Robert R.
Saul Bellow **25**:86

Duvall, E. S.
Ann Beattie **13**:66

Duvall, Elizabeth
Helen Yglesias **22**:493

Du Verlie, Claude
Claude Simon **4**:497

Dworkin, Ronald
Gay Talese **37**:394

Dworkin, Susan
Gretchen Cryer **21**:80

Dwyer, David J.
Mary Renault **3**:426
Nathalie Sarraute **31**:379

Dyck, J. W.
Boris Pasternak **18**:381

Dyer, Geoff
Lorrie Moore **39**:85

Dyer, Peter John
René Clair **20**:64
Jean Cocteau **16**:227
Pier Paolo Pasolini **20**:260
Jean Renoir **20**:291
Luchino Visconti **16**:563
Billy Wilder **20**:459

Critic Index

Dyson, A. E.
Jorge Luis Borges **19**:50
Ted Hughes **14**:269
Sylvia Plath **11**:446

Dyson, Claire M.
Kin Platt **26**:354

Dyson, Timothy S.
Ronald J. Glasser **37**:134

Dyson, William
Ezra Pound **1**:276

Dzwonkoski, F. Peter, Jr.
T. S. Eliot **6**:163

Eagle, Herbert
Aleksandr I. Solzhenitsyn **9**:504
Ludvík Vaculík **7**:495

Eagle, Robert
Thomas Hinde **11**:274
Alberto Moravia **7**:244
Flann O'Brien **4**:385

Eagleton, Terry
George Barker **8**:45
John Berger **19**:39
Donald Davie **8**:162
Thom Gunn **6**:221
Seamus Heaney **7**:150
Hermann Hesse **11**:272
Elizabeth Jennings **14**:293
William Plomer **8**:447
Stevie Smith **8**:491
Maura Stanton **9**:508
Charles Tomlinson **6**:535
John Wain **11**:561
Andrew Young **5**:525

Eakin, Mary K.
Mary Stolz **12**:553

Earl, Pauline J.
Frank B. Gilbreth, Jr. and
Ernestine Gilbreth Carey
17:156

Earle, Adelaide
Mary Stewart **35**:391

Early, Len
Bill Bissett **18**:59

Earnshaw, Doris Smith
Denise Levertov **28**:242
Joyce Carol Oates **33**:289

Easterbrook, Gregg
Nicholas M. Guild **33**:188

Eastlake, William
A. B. Guthrie, Jr. **23**:198

Eastman, Fred
Marc Connelly **7**:55

Eastman, Max
William F. Buckley, Jr. **37**:55
I. A. Richards **24**:374

Easton, Tom
Piers Anthony **35**:36
David Brin **34**:133
Octavia E. Butler **38**:62
C. J. Cherryh **35**:106, 107,
109, 113, 114
Michael Ende **31**:144
Frank Herbert **35**:206, 207

Stephen King **26**:238
Lucius Shepard **34**:110
Jack Vance **35**:428
Jack Williamson **29**:461

Eaton, Anne T.
Sally Benson **17**:47
Langston Hughes **35**:214
Carl Sandburg **35**:347
John R. Tunis **12**:593

Eaton, Charles Edward
Robert Frost **9**:225

Eaton, Walter Prichard
Padraic Colum **28**:88
Joseph Wood Krutch **24**:285

Eaves, T. C. Duncan
Ezra Pound **34**:507
E. Fuller Torrey **34**:507

Eberhart, Richard
Djuna Barnes **8**:48
William Empson **19**:152
Robert Frost **13**:227
Allen Ginsberg **13**:239
Archibald MacLeish **3**:310
Ezra Pound **7**:324
Kenneth Rexroth **2**:370
Muriel Rukeyser **27**:409

Ebert, Roger
Charles Chaplin **16**:199
John Edgar Wideman **36**:451

Eby, Cecil
Vine Deloria, Jr. **21**:109

Eccleshare, Julia
Diana Wynne Jones **26**:227

Echevarría, Roberto González
Alejo Carpentier **11**:101
Julio Cortázar **10**:114; **13**:158;
34:334
Carlos Fuentes **10**:209
Severo Sarduy **6**:486

Eckley, Grace
Benedict Kiely **23**:259
Edna O'Brien **5**:312

Eckley, Wilton
Harriette Arnow **18**:10

Eckman, Martha
Colin Wilson **14**:583

Eco, Umberto
Italo Calvino **39**:308

Economou, George
Yannis Ritsos **31**:328

Edd, Karl
Arthur C. Clarke **35**:129

Eddins, Dwight
John Fowles **10**:183

Eddy, Elizabeth M.
Jonathan Kozol **17**:250

Edel, Leon
Van Wyck Brooks **29**:85
Lawrence Durrell **1**:85
William Faulkner **1**:100
Ernest Hemingway **10**:265
Alain Robbe-Grillet **1**:286
Nathalie Sarraute **1**:303

Edelberg, Cynthia Dubin
Robert Creeley **15**:151

Edelheit, S. J.
Anthony Burgess **13**:126

Edelman, Diane Gersoni
Walter Dean Myers **35**:298

Edelman, Sarah Prewitt
Robert Lowell **15**:344
Robert Penn Warren **39**:256

Edelson, Edward
Carl Sagan **30**:331

Edelstein, Arthur
William Faulkner **1**:102
Janet Frame **6**:190
Jean Stafford **7**:458
Angus Wilson **2**:472

Edelstein, J. M.
Patricia Highsmith **2**:193
Doris Lessing **22**:279

Edelstein, Mark G.
Flannery O'Connor **6**:381

Edenbaum, Robert I.
Dashiell Hammett **3**:219
John Hawkes **2**:185

Eder, Richard
Vasily Aksyonov **37**:14
Frederick Barthelme **36**:50
T. Coraghessan Boyle **36**:60
Hortense Calisher **38**:73
Raymond Carver **36**:102
Brian Clark **29**:127
Gretchen Cryer **21**:81
Don DeLillo **39**:118
Scott Elledge **34**:428
Joseph Epstein **39**:464
Athol Fugard **14**:191
Albert Innaurato **21**:194
Arthur Kopit **33**:246
Hugh Leonard **19**:283
Iris Murdoch **31**:292
Edna O'Brien **8**:430
Cynthia Ozick **28**:355
Bernard Pomerance **13**:445
Padgett Powell **34**:99
Gerome Ragni and James Rado
17:388
Ntozake Shange **25**:397, 398
Stephen Sondheim **30**:393
Josef Škvorecký **39**:222
Peter Taylor **37**:411
Wendy Wasserstein **32**:439
E. B. White **34**:428
Nancy Willard **37**:465
Lanford Wilson **14**:590

Edinborough, Arnold
Earle Birney **6**:70
Robertson Davies **25**:129
Robert Kroetsch **23**:269
Jay Macpherson **14**:345

Edman, Irwin
Alfred Kazin **38**:272
Ogden Nash **23**:322
Siegfried Sassoon **36**:387

Edmiston, Susan
Maeve Brennan **5**:72

Edmond, Rod
Keri Hulme **39**:165

Edmonds, Ben
Pink Floyd **35**:308
Bob Seger **35**:378

Edmonds, Walter D.
Esther Forbes **12**:204

Edwards, Annabel
Carolyn Chute **39**:41

Edwards, C. Hines, Jr.
James Dickey **4**:121

Edwards, Christopher
Alan Ayckbourn **33**:49

Edwards, Clifford
Andrew Lloyd Webber and Tim
Rice **21**:423

Edwards, Henry
David Bowie **17**:60
Jackson Browne **21**:35
John Lennon **35**:263
Monty Python **21**:224
Lou Reed **21**:304
Bruce Springsteen **17**:479

Edwards, K. Anthony
Henry Gregor Felsen **17**:125

Edwards, Margaret A.
Betty Cavanna **12**:99
Maureen Daly **17**:89
Mary Stolz **12**:546

Edwards, Mary Jane
Paulette Jiles **13**:304
Susan Musgrave **13**:401

Edwards, Michael
René Char **14**:130
Donald Davie **5**:114
Charles Tomlinson **4**:547

Edwards, Owen Dudley
Agatha Christie **39**:438
Janet Morgan **39**:438

Edwards, Page
Richard Grayson **38**:210

Edwards, Paul
Amos Tutuola **14**:540

Edwards, Sharon
Jessamyn West **7**:522

Edwards, Terrance
Ronald Harwood **32**:225

Edwards, Thomas R.
Lisa Alther **7**:14
Kingsley Amis **8**:12
James Baldwin **4**:41
Donald Barthelme **8**:49
Jackson J. Benson **34**:410
Thomas Berger **18**:56
Richard Brautigan **12**:73
Frederick Buechner **2**:83
Charles Bukowski **2**:84
Anthony Burgess **5**:88
Raymond Carver **22**:96
John Cheever **7**:48
Evan S. Connell, Jr. **4**:108
Don DeLillo **27**:76
Joan Didion **32**:148

Stanley Elkin **4**:153
Leslie A. Fiedler **4**:161
Timothy Findley **27**:142
Paula Fox **2**:140
John Gardner **2**:151; **5**:133
Gail Godwin **8**:248
Herbert Gold **4**:193
James Hanley **8**:266
Edward Hoagland **28**:182
Diane Johnson **13**:306
James Jones **10**:293
Yoram Kaniuk **19**:239
Jerzy Kosinski **2**:233
George Lamming **2**:235
Norman Mailer **2**:264
Harry Mathews **6**:616
Peter Matthiessen **7**:211
Mary McCarthy **14**:363
Thomas McGuane **3**:330
Leonard Michaels **6**:324
Brian Moore **7**:237
Alice Munro **19**:347
Craig Nova **31**:298
Joyce Carol Oates **33**:288
Tim O'Brien **19**:358
Ishmael Reed **2**:368
Mordecai Richler **18**:454
Philip Roth **3**:437
André Schwarz-Bart **2**:389
Hubert Selby, Jr. **2**:390
Wilfrid Sheed **4**:488
Gilbert Sorrentino **14**:500
Scott Spencer **30**:407
John Steinbeck **34**:410
John Updike **5**:460; **23**:469
Derek Walcott **4**:576
William Wharton **37**:438
Tom Wolfe **1**:375
Richard Yates **23**:482

Edwards, William D.
Jules Archer **12**:18

Egan, James
Stephen King **37**:201

Eggenschwiler, David
Flannery O'Connor **6**:378
William Styron **5**:419

Egoff, Sheila A.
Julia W. Cunningham **12**:165
Leon Garfield **12**:218
Roderick L. Haig-Brown
21:140
Christie Harris **12**:265
Farley Mowat **26**:338, 339
Rosemary Sutcliff **26**:433, 440
Jill Paton Walsh **35**:433

Egremont, Max
Anna Kavan **13**:317
Seán O'Faoláin **7**:276
Anthony Powell **7**:341; **9**:438
Gillian Tindall **7**:474
Ludvík Vaculík **7**:496

Egudu, Romanus N.
Christopher Okigbo **25**:348,
355

Ehre, Milton
Aleksandr I. Solzhenitsyn **2**:412

Ehrenpreis, Irvin
A. R. Ammons **25**:45
John Ashbery **6**:13
W. H. Auden **9**:58
Ronald Bush **34**:527
Donald Davie **31**:111
T. S. Eliot **13**:200; **34**:527
Ronald Hall **13**:260
Seamus Heaney **37**:162
Anthony Hecht **13**:269
Geoffrey Hill **8**:293
Donald Justice **6**:272
Robert Lowell **1**:180; **8**:353
George Oppen **7**:285
John Updike **5**:455
Robert Penn Warren **18**:537

Ehresmann, Julia M.
Erich von Däniken **30**:427

Eidelman, M.
Anatoli Rybakov **23**:370

Eidus, Janice
Stephen King **37**:206

Einarsson, Stefán
Halldór Laxness **25**:291

Eiseley, Loren
Peter Matthiessen **32**:287
J.R.R. Tolkien **12**:566

Eiseman, Alberta
Betty Cavanna **12**:100
Maureen Daly **17**:89
William Mayne **12**:390
Zoa Sherburne **30**:360, 361
Lenora Mattingly Weber **12**:633

Eisen, Dulcie
Ronald Tavel **6**:529

Eisenberg, J. A.
Isaac Bashevis Singer **1**:310

Eisinger, Chester E.
Carson McCullers **12**:421
Arthur Miller **6**:331

Eisinger, Erica M.
Marguerite Duras **11**:165
Georges Simenon **18**:484

Eisner, Bob
Smokey Robinson **21**:344

Eisner, Lotte H.
René Clair **20**:64
Fritz Lang **20**:210, 213

Eksteins, Modris
Erich Maria Remarque **21**:336

Elderkin, Phil
Russell Baker **31**:28

Eldred, Kate
David Malouf **28**:266

Eldridge, Richard
Jean Toomer **22**:425

Eley, Holly
Laurie Colwin **23**:130
Virginia Hamilton **26**:155, 157

Eliade, Mircea
Mircea Eliade **19**:146

Elias, Robert H.
James Thurber **5**:431

Eliot, T. S.
Djuna Barnes **29**:23
Marianne Moore **13**:392; **19**:336
I. A. Richards **24**:371

Elizondo, Salvador
Octavio Paz **3**:376

Elkin, Judith
Diana Wynne Jones **26**:230

Elkin, Sam
Robert Lipsyte **21**:208

Elkin, Stanley
Frederick Forsyth **2**:136

Elledge, Jim
Stephen Dobyns **37**:82
Robert Hayden **37**:159

Elledge, Scott
Wayne C. Booth **24**:89

Elleman, Barbara
Melvin Berger **12**:42
Robin F. Brancato **35**:66
Barbara Corcoran **17**:77
Paula Danziger **21**:86
Madeleine L'Engle **12**:351
Sonia Levitin **17**:265
Anne McCaffrey **17**:282, 284
Suzanne Newton **35**:301
Katherine Paterson **12**:485;
30:282, 283
Zilpha Keatley Snyder **17**:475

Ellestad, Everett M.
Pär Lagerkvist **13**:333

Elley, Derek
Mel Brooks **12**:79
Werner Herzog **16**:324
Yasujiro Ozu **16**:455
Pier Paolo Pasolini **20**:266, 269
Ken Russell **16**:549
Carlos Saura **20**:315
François Truffaut **20**:404

Ellin, Stanley
James Carroll **38**:106
Robert Cormier **12**:138; **30**:81
Richard Elman **19**:151
John Gardner **30**:157
Evan Hunter **31**:224

Elliott, David
Roman Polanski **16**:470

Elliott, George P.
Jean Giono **4**:187
Robert Graves **2**:176
Norman Mailer **3**:317
Milton Meltzer **26**:305
Susan Sontag **10**:485
Richard Stern **39**:237
David Wagoner **3**:507

Elliott, Janice
Lynne Reid Banks **23**:41
Patricia Highsmith **2**:193
Michael Moorcock **27**:347
Aleksandr I. Solzhenitsyn **1**:321

Elliott, Robert C.
Ursula K. LeGuin **8**:341

Elliott, Susan
Billy Joel **26**:215, 216

Elliott, William I.
Shusaku Endo **7**:95

Ellis, James
John Knowles **1**:169; **26**:248

Ellis, Roger
Michel Tremblay **29**:423

Ellis, W. Geiger
Robert Cormier **30**:91

Ellison, Harlan
Barry N. Malzberg **7**:208
Roman Polanski **16**:464

Ellison, Ralph
Richard Wright **9**:583; **21**:441

Ellmann, Mary
John Barth **2**:39
Vladimir Nabokov **1**:244
Joyce Carol Oates **3**:364
Sylvia Plath **17**:350
Richard Price **12**:490
Aleksandr I. Solzhenitsyn **1**:321
J.R.R. Tolkien **12**:571
Michel Tournier **6**:538
Rebecca West **7**:526
Vassily S. Yanovsky **2**:485

Ellmann, Richard
W. H. Auden **9**:55
Giorgio Bassani **9**:76
Samuel Beckett **2**:47
Elizabeth Daryush **19**:119
Seamus Heaney **37**:168
Alfred Kazin **34**:558

Elman, Richard
William Bronk **10**:73
Frederick Busch **10**:91
Allen Drury **37**:112
Daniel Fuchs **22**:160
Thomas McGuane **18**:323
Margaret Mead **37**:278
Richard Price **12**:490
Françoise Sagan **17**:426
Zilpha Keatley Snyder **17**:471

Elman, Richard M.
Arthur A. Cohen **31**:91
Charles Bukowski **9**:137
Hannah Green **3**:202
Jack Spicer **8**:497
Hunter S. Thompson **9**:526
Rudolf Wurlitzer **2**:482

Elon, Amos
Yehuda Amichai **9**:22

Elsaesser, Thomas
Rainer Werner Fassbinder
20:110

Elsom, John
Alan Ayckbourn **5**:35
Samuel Beckett **6**:43
Edward Bond **6**:85
Michael Frayn **7**:108
Arthur Miller **15**:376
David Rudkin **14**:470
Sam Shepard **6**:496
Tom Stoppard **5**:412
E. A. Whitehead **5**:488

Elstob, Peter
Len Deighton **4**:119

Elston, Nina
Susan Richards Shreve **23**:403

Elton, G. R.
Antonia Fraser **32**:181

Emanuel, James A.
Langston Hughes **1**:147

Emblidge, David
E. L. Doctorow **11**:143

Embree, Ainslie
Ved Mehta **37**:296

Emerson, Donald
Carson McCullers **12**:420

Emerson, Gloria
Michael Cimino **16**:213

Emerson, Ken
David Bowie **17**:61
David Byrne **26**:97
Ray Davies **21**:95, 103
Van Morrison **21**:235
Smokey Robinson **21**:345
Bruce Springsteen **17**:477
Paul Weller **26**:443
Stevie Wonder **12**:657

Emerson, O. B.
Marion Montgomery **7**:232

Emerson, Sally
Douglas Adams **27**:13
Hermann Hesse **25**:261
Molly Keane **31**:233
William Mayne **12**:404
Piers Paul Read **25**:379

Emerson, Stephen
Gilbert Sorrentino **7**:450

Emme, Eugene M.
Arthur C. Clarke **35**:118

Emmons, Winfred S.
Katherine Anne Porter **1**:273

Empson, William
Wayne C. Booth **24**:92
Cleanth Brooks **24**:103

Endres, Robin
Milton Acorn **15**:10

Engel, Bernard F.
Marianne Moore **1**:227

Engel, Eva J.
Hermann Hesse **17**:202

Engel, Howard
Morley Callaghan **14**:102

Engel, Marian
Penelope Gilliatt **2**:160
Margaret Laurence **3**:278
Françoise Mallet-Joris **11**:356
Joyce Carol Oates **6**:372
Françoise Sagan **6**:481
Michel Tournier **6**:537

England, David A.
Garry Marshall **17**:278

Engle, Gary
Robert Altman **16**:22

Engle, Paul
Charles M. Schulz **12**:531

English, Raymond
Carl Zuckmayer **18**:553

Enright, D. J.
John Ashbery **9**:49
Simone de Beauvoir **14**:66
Heinrich Böll **3**:74; **11**:52;
  39:295
Anthony Burgess **4**:80; **15**:103;
  22:75
Stanley Burnshaw **3**:90
James Clavell **6**:114
Lawrence Durrell **6**:151
Max Frisch **32**:192
Witold Gombrowicz **4**:195
Günter Grass **2**:271; **4**:202
Robert Graves **2**:175
Hermann Hesse **3**:243
Keri Hulme **39**:166
Randall Jarrell **9**:296
Yasunari Kawabata **5**:206;
  9:316
Thomas Keneally **14**:302;
  27:233
Carolyn Kizer **15**:308
Milan Kundera **9**:321
Philip Larkin **3**:276
Doris Lessing **3**:282
Norman MacCaig **36**:282
Czesław Miłosz **5**:291
Yukio Mishima **4**:353; **27**:336
Vladimir Nabokov **3**:352
V. S. Naipaul **4**:371
Kenzaburō Ōe **36**:344
Ezra Pound **3**:395
Salman Rushdie **31**:358
Josef Škvorecký **39**:231
Stevie Smith **3**:460
C. P. Snow **9**:496
Muriel Spark **3**:463
George Steiner **24**:429
John Updike **2**:439

Enslin, Theodore
George Oppen **7**:281

Ensslen, Klaus
Alice Walker **27**:451

Envall, Markku
Paavo Haavikko **34**:179

Eoff, Sherman H.
Jean-Paul Sartre **1**:303
Ramón Sender **8**:477

Ephron, Nora
Erich Segal **3**:447
Garry Trudeau **12**:589

Epps, Garrett
Russell Banks **37**:29
Thomas Berger **11**:47; **38**:39
William Brammer **31**:54
Nicholas Delbanco **13**:174
Molly Keane **31**:233
John Sayles **14**:483
Susan Fromberg Schaeffer
  22:368
Alan Sillitoe **19**:421
Gilbert Sorrentino **22**:394
Elizabeth Spencer **22**:406
John Edgar Wideman **34**:299

Epstein, Helen
Isaac Bashevis Singer **23**:422

Epstein, Joseph
Renata Adler **31**:16
Jonathan Baumbach **23**:55
Rosellen Brown **32**:66
Joan Didion **32**:150
E. M. Forster **4**:165
Gabriel García Márquez **27**:154
Nadine Gordimer **18**:188
Mark Harris **19**:205
Joseph Heller **5**:174
John Irving **23**:253
Alan Lelchuk **5**:241
Bernard Malamud **27**:301
Philip Roth **31**:343
Aleksandr I. Solzhenitsyn **2**:409
Stephen Spender **5**:402
Gay Talese **37**:393
E. B. White **39**:377
Edmund Wilson **2**:477; **8**:551
Tom Wolfe **35**:449
Marguerite Yourcenar **38**:457

Epstein, Julia
Anita Brookner **32**:60

Epstein, Lawrence J.
Elie Wiesel **5**:493

Epstein, Leslie
Cynthia Ozick **28**:350
D. M. Thomas **22**:420

Epstein, Seymour
Saul Bellow **13**:72
Dino Buzzati **36**:95
Jerome Charyn **18**:99

Erbes, Bill
C. S. Adler **35**:15

Erickson, Peter
Alice Walker **19**:451

Ericson, Edward, Jr.
Thornton Wilder **10**:533

Ericson, Edward E., Jr.
C. S. Lewis **6**:310
Aleksandr I. Solzhenitsyn
  4:509; **26**:422

Erikson, Kai
Jonathan Schell **35**:366

Erlich, Nancy
Ray Davies **21**:94

Erlich, Richard
Harlan Ellison **13**:203

Erlich, Victor
Joseph Brodsky **6**:96

Ermolaev, Herman
Mikhail Sholokhov **15**:481

Ernst, Margaret
Andre Norton **12**:455

Eron, Carol
John Hawkes **4**:218

Ervine, St. John
Noël Coward **29**:132

Eshleman, Clayton
Aimé Césaire **32**:110
Robert Creeley **36**:120
Robert Hass **39**:145
C. K. Williams **33**:447

Eskin, Stanley G.
Nicholas Delbanco **6**:130

Esmonde, Margaret P.
Ursula K. Le Guin **22**:270
Zilpha Keatley Snyder **17**:474

Esposito, Joseph J.
Larry McMurtry **27**:332

Esslin, Martin
Arthur Adamov **4**:5
Edward Albee **2**:4; **9**:10
John Arden **6**:5
Samuel Beckett **1**:24; **4**:52;
  6:33, 44
Thomas Bernhard **32**:23
Edward Bond **13**:98
Dino Buzzati **36**:85
John Pepper Clark **38**:114
Friedrich Dürrenmatt **4**:139
Max Frisch **3**:167
Jack Gelber **1**:114
Jean Genet **1**:117
Günter Grass **4**:201
Graham Greene **9**:250
Václav Havel **25**:222
Rolf Hochhuth **4**:231
Eugène Ionesco **1**:154; **4**:252
Arthur Kopit **1**:170
Sławomir Mrożek **3**:344
Robert Pinget **7**:306
Harold Pinter **1**:268; **6**:407,
  414; **27**:392
Peter Shaffer **18**:477
Neil Simon **6**:506
N. F. Simpson **29**:369
Wole Soyinka **14**:505
Peter Weiss **3**:515

Estes, Sally
Robert Cormier **30**:90
Danny Santiago **33**:352
Joan D. Vinge **30**:412

Estes, Sally C.
Sol Gordon **26**:138

Estess, Sybil
Elizabeth Bishop **9**:95
Padgett Powell **34**:100

Estess, Ted L.
Samuel Beckett **11**:41
Elie Wiesel **37**:456

Estrin, Barbara L.
Adrienne Rich **18**:450

Esty, William
James Baldwin **17**:21
Flannery O'Connor **21**:255
Rebecca West **31**:456

Etherton, Michael
Ngugi wa Thiong'o **36**:315

Ettin, Andrew V.
James Merrill **2**:273

Evanier, David
Saul Bellow **25**:85
Eldridge Cleaver **30**:56
Leonard Michaels **25**:319
John Updike **15**:547

Evans, Ann
Judy Blume **12**:46
Rosemary Sutcliff **26**:438

Evans, Don
Ed Bullins **5**:82

Evans, Donald T.
Alice Childress **12**:105

Evans, Eli N.
James Dickey **7**:86

Evans, Ernestine
Jessamyn West **17**:544
Jade Snow Wong **17**:565

Evans, Fallon
J. F. Powers **1**:279

Evans, Gareth Lloyd
Edward Albee **25**:34
Harold Pinter **11**:444

Evans, Gwyneth F.
Christie Harris **12**:267

Evans, Joseph T.
Jacques-Yves Cousteau **30**:104

Evans, M. Stanton
Allen Drury **37**:103, 105

Evans, Oliver
Paul Bowles **1**:41
Babette Deutsch **18**:119
Carson McCullers **12**:425

Evans, Patrick
Frank Sargeson **31**:369

Evans, Robley
J.R.R. Tolkien **3**:478

Evans, Sarah Jane
Peter Luke **38**:318

Evans, T. Jeff
Peter De Vries **28**:106

Evans, Timothy
Isaac Bashevis Singer **11**:499

Evans, William R.
Julian Symons **32**:424
Edmund White III **27**:478

Evarts, Prescott, Jr.
John Fowles **2**:138

Everett, Barbara
Peter Ackroyd **34**:399
Donald Davie **31**:119
T. S. Eliot **34**:399

Everman, Welch D.
Richard Kostelanetz **28**:215

Evers, Larry
Charles R. Larson **31**:240

Everson, Edith A.
E. E. Cummings **15**:157

Evett, Robert
Terrence McNally **7**:219
Manuel Mujica Láinez **31**:278
Lanford Wilson **7**:548

Ewart, Gavin
D. J. Enright **31**:150, 154
Roy Fuller **28**:157
Geoffrey Grigson **39**:331
William Sansom **2**:383
Sylvia Townsend Warner
19:461

Ewen, David
Gerome Ragni and James Rado
17:385

Ewers, John C.
Jamake Highwater **12**:286

Ewing, Dorothy
Miguel Delibes **18**:110

Exner, R.
Botho Strauss **22**:407

Eyles, Allen
Francis Ford Coppola **16**:231
John Huston **20**:169
Ken Russell **16**:541

Eyre, Frank
H. F. Brinsmead **21**:30
Peter Dickinson **12**:170
Eilís Dillon **17**:98
Leon Garfield **12**:223
Alan Garner **17**:142
William Mayne **12**:396
Philippa Pearce **21**:287
Colin Thiele **17**:494

Eyster, Warren
James Dickey **1**:74

Faas, Ekbert
Gary Snyder **32**:388

Faase, Thomas P.
Andrew M. Greeley **28**:174

Faber, Nancy W.
Frank Bonham **12**:50

Faber, Roderick Mason
Tennessee Williams **19**:474

Fabian, Hans J.
Fritz Hochwälder **36**:239

Fabio, Sarah Webster
Nikki Giovanni **19**:190

Fabre, Michel
James Baldwin **3**:31
Chester Himes **2**:195

Fadiman, Anne
Fran Lebowitz **11**:322

Fadiman, Clifton
Taylor Caldwell **28**:56, 57
Walter Van Tilburg Clark **28**:76
Howard Fast **23**:155
William Faulkner **28**:139
Arthur Koestler **33**:229
Carson McCullers **12**:409
Mari Sandoz **28**:402
Nevil Shute **30**:366
Carl Van Vechten **33**:394
Rebecca West **31**:455
T. H. White **30**:438

Fadiman, Edwin
Laura Z. Hobson **7**:163

Faery, Rebecca B.
Richard Wilbur **9**:570

Fagan, Carey
John Metcalf **37**:304

Fager, Charles E.
Bob Dylan **12**:185

Fahey, James
Evan S. Connell, Jr. **4**:109

Fahey, Joseph J.
William Barrett **27**:21

Fairchild, B. H., Jr.
Steven Spielberg **20**:364

Fairweather, Eileen
Pat Barker **32**:11

Faith, Rosamond
Rosemary Wells **12**:638

Falck, Colin
A. Alvarez **5**:16
John Berryman **2**:55
William Empson **3**:147
Geoffrey Grigson **7**:136
Thom Gunn **6**:220
Seamus Heaney **7**:149
Ted Hughes **9**:280
Philip Larkin **3**:275, 276
Robert Lowell **2**:245; **5**:256
George MacBeth **9**:340
Paul Muldoon **32**:317
Peter Porter **33**:319
Anne Sexton **8**:483
Charles Tomlinson **2**:436

Falcoff, Mark
Joan Didion **32**:144

Falk, Doris V.
Lillian Hellman **14**:258

Falk, Signi
Tennessee Williams **1**:367

Falke, Wayne
Kenzaburō Ōe **10**:372
Jun'ichirō Tanizaki **14**:525
John Updike **5**:453

Falkenberg, Betty
Walter Abish **22**:21
Beryl Bainbridge **18**:34
Thomas Bernhard **32**:21
Milan Kundera **32**:264
Primo Levi **37**:226
Marge Piercy **18**:408
Patrick White **18**:549

Fallis, Laurence S.
Ruth Prawer Jhabvala **4**:259
Thomas W. Shapcott **38**:404

Fallowell, Duncan
J. G. Ballard **36**:37
Giorgio Bassani **9**:77
John Berger **2**:54
William Peter Blatty **2**:64
Richard Brautigan **12**:72
Taylor Caldwell **28**:66
Robert Coover **3**:114
Mark Helprin **7**:152
Ruth Prawer Jhabvala **8**:312
Anna Kavan **13**:316
Yashar Kemal **29**:266

Jerzy Kosinski **3**:274
Fran Lebowitz **36**:250
Mary McCarthy **39**:489
Iris Murdoch **4**:368
Tim O'Brien **7**:272
Seán O'Faoláin **7**:274
Mervyn Peake **7**:303
David Plante **7**:308
Françoise Sagan **9**:468
James Salter **7**:388
Hubert Selby, Jr. **2**:390
Terry Southern **7**:454
Muriel Spark **3**:465; **8**:493
Auberon Waugh **7**:514

Fallows, James
William Brammer **31**:54
George V. Higgins **18**:233

Fandel, John
E. E. Cummings **3**:120

Fandray, David F.
David Bowie **17**:62

Fanger, Donald
Aleksandr I. Solzhenitsyn **1**:319

Fanning, Peter
Alan Garner **17**:149
Nat Hentoff **26**:185
Paul Zindel **26**:478

Fantoni, Barry
S. J. Perelman **15**:418
Brian Wilson **12**:60

Farber, Jim
Prince **35**:323

Farber, Manny
Maya Deren **16**:251
John Ford **16**:305
Alfred Hitchcock **16**:338, 339
John Huston **20**:159
Akira Kurosawa **16**:394
Paul Schrader **26**:386

Farber, Marjorie
Laura Z. Hobson **25**:269

Farber, Stephen
Lindsay Anderson **20**:15
Francis Ford Coppola **16**:231,
232, 235
Michael Cristofer **28**:94
George Roy Hill **26**:196
Richard Lester **20**:225
Sam Peckinpah **20**:274
Ken Russell **16**:548
Martin Scorsese **20**:327
Steven Spielberg **20**:358
François Truffaut **20**:396
Luchino Visconti **16**:569
Orson Welles **20**:446
Billy Wilder **20**:461, 464, 465

Farmer, Betty Catherine Dobson
Donald Barthelme **13**:58

Farmer, Penelope
Alan Garner **17**:147
Diana Wynne Jones **26**:226,
229
William Mayne **12**:401
Philippa Pearce **21**:289

Farmiloe, Dorothy
Hugh MacLennan **14**:341

Farnsworth, Emily C.
Robert Newton Peck **17**:343

Farnsworth, Robert M.
Melvin B. Tolson **36**:429

Farrell, Diane
Sol Gordon **26**:136
Andre Norton **12**:459
Paul Zindel **26**:470

Farrell, James T.
James M. Cain **11**:84
John Dos Passos **25**:139
Ben Hecht **8**:269
Frank O'Connor **14**:395

Farrell, John P.
Richard Wilbur **3**:532

Farrell, Walter C., Jr.
Langston Hughes **35**:220, 221

Farrelly, John
Andrew Lytle **22**:293

Farrison, W. Edward
Lorraine Hansberry **17**:191

Farwell, Harold
John Barth **5**:50

Farwell, Ruth
George Mackay Brown **5**:77

Farzan, Massud
Ahmad Shamlu **10**:469

Fasick, Adele M.
Roderick L. Haig-Brown
21:139

Fassbinder, Rainer Werner
Claude Chabrol **16**:181

Fast, Howard
Conrad Richter **30**:308

Faulkner, Peter
Angus Wilson **25**:464

Faulkner, William
Erich Maria Remarque **21**:326

Faulks, Sebastian
Anita Brookner **34**:136
Anita Desai **37**:71
Yasunari Kawabata **9**:316

Fawcett, Anthony
Jackson Browne **21**:41

Fawcett, Graham
Anthony Burgess **8**:111

Fay, Eliot G.
Jacques Prévert **15**:437

Feagles, Anita MacRae
Maia Wojciechowska **26**:455

Fearing, Kenneth
George Tabori **19**:435

Featherstone, Joseph
Katherine Anne Porter **3**:392
Frederick Wiseman **20**:468

Featherstone, Simon
Thomas M. Disch **36**:127

Feaver, Vicki
Sylvia Townsend Warner
19:460

Feaver, William
Michael Ayrton **7**:19
Peter Gent **29**:181

Feder, Kenneth L.
Erich von Däniken **30**:426

Feder, Lillian
Conrad Aiken **5**:8
W. H. Auden **4**:33, 34, 35
George Barker **8**:43
Samuel Beckett **6**:37
T. S. Eliot **6**:160
Robert Graves **6**:210
Ted Hughes **9**:281
Robert Lowell **4**:301
Ezra Pound **3**:396; **4**:414

Federman, Raymond
Samuel Beckett **9**:79

Feehan, Paul G.
Woody Guthrie **35**:193

Feeney, Joseph J., S.J.
Jessie Redmon Fauset **19**:171
Isabelle Holland **21**:150

Feidelson, Charles, Jr.
Leon Edel **29**:167

Feied, Frederick
John Dos Passos **1**:80
Jack Kerouac **1**:166

Feifer, George
Aleksandr I. Solzhenitsyn **7**:444

Feiffer, Jules
Richard Lester **20**:223
Jerome Siegel and Joe Shuster
21:356

Fein, Cheri
Bob Shacochis **39**:199

Fein, Richard J.
Robert Lowell **3**:304

Feinberg, Anat
A. B. Yehoshua **31**:469

Feingold, Michael
Dannie Abse **7**:2
E. L. Doctorow **15**:179
Athol Fugard **9**:235
John Guare **8**:252,253
Peter Handke **8**:263
Beth Henley **23**:216, 217
John Hopkins **4**:234
Albert Innaurato **21**:192, 194
Jim Jacobs and Warren Casey
12:294
Ira Levin **3**:294
Miguel Piñero **4**:401
Sam Shepard **17**:444, 445, 447
Elizabeth Swados **12**:557, 561
Tennessee Williams **7**:544

Feinstein, Elaine
Martin Amis **38**:11
Marian Engel **36**:159
Gail Godwin **8**:247
William Golding **2**:169
Nadine Gordimer **3**:202
George MacBeth **5**:265
Olivia Manning **19**:301
Mary McCarthy **3**:329
Grace Paley **6**:339

Christina Stead **5**:403

Feirstein, Frederick
Robert Graves **2**:177

Feld, Michael
Richard Brautigan **12**:63
John Updike **2**:445

Feld, Rose C.
Sally Benson **17**:47
Agatha Christie **12**:114
August Derleth **31**:130
Walter D. Edmonds **35**:152
C. S. Forester **35**:163
Ernest K. Gann **23**:162
Madeleine L'Engle **12**:345
Helen MacInnes **27**:278, 279
Farley Mowat **26**:333
Mary Renault **17**:389
Françoise Sagan **17**:420
Mari Sandoz **28**:400
Mary Stewart **35**:390
Glendon Swarthout **35**:398

Feld, Ross
Paul Blackburn **9**:98
Laurie Colwin **13**:156
William H. Gass **11**:225
Jack Spicer **8**:497
Eudora Welty **14**:566
Tom Wolfe **9**:578

Feldman, Anita
Irwin Shaw **7**:412

Feldman, Hans
Stanley Kubrick **16**:391

Feldman, Irma P.
Helen Yglesia **7**:558

Feldman, Morton
Frank O'Hara **2**:322

Felheim, Marvin
Ben Hecht **8**:272
Lillian Hellman **14**:255
Carson McCullers **1**:208
Eudora Welty **1**:361

Fell, John L.
Rainer Werner Fassbinder
20:117

Fellows, Jo-Ann
Mazo de la Roche **14**:150

Felsen, Henry Gregor
Henry Gregor Felsen **17**:123

Felstiner, John
Pablo Neruda **1**:247; **2**:309;
5:302

Felton, David
Steve Martin **30**:246
Richard Pryor **26**:379
Lily Tomlin **17**:519

Fender, Stephen
Jacob Epstein **19**:162
Richard Price **12**:491
John Sayles **10**:462

Fenin, George N.
Vittorio De Sica **20**:86
Billy Wilder **20**:457, 458

Fenton, Edward
Mollie Hunter **21**:157
Maia Wojciechowska **26**:454

Fenton, James
W. H. Auden **6**:18
Lynne Reid Banks **23**:41
Giorgio Bassani **9**:76
Douglas Dunn **6**:148
Gavin Ewart **13**:210
Josephine Poole **17**:372
George Steiner **24**:435
Charles Tomlinson **6**:534

Fenves, Peter
Samuel Beckett **29**:59

Ferguson, Alan
Ivo Andrić **8**:20

Ferguson, Charles W.
Thomas B. Costain **30**:98

Ferguson, Frances
Randall Jarrell **13**:301
Robert Lowell **4**:302

Ferguson, John
John Pepper Clark **38**:119

Ferguson, Otis C.
Frank Capra **16**:154, 155, 156
Charles Chaplin **16**:190, 192
A. J. Cronin **32**:135
Walter D. Edmonds **35**:146
John Ford **16**:303, 304
Alfred Hitchcock **16**:337
Zora Neale Hurston **30**:211
Rouben Mamoulian **16**:420
Irwin Shaw **23**:395
Orson Welles **20**:432
T. H. White **30**:438

Ferguson, Suzanne
Djuna Barnes **3**:36
Randall Jarrell **2**:209

Fergusson, Francis
René Clair **20**:59

Fernandez, Doreen G.
Bienvenido N. Santos **22**:365

Fernandez, Enrique
Isabel Allende **39**:33

Fernandez, Jaime
Jun'ichirō Tanizaki **8**:511

Fernández-Morera, Dario
Vicente Aleixandre **36**:25

Ferrari, Margaret
Colleen McCullough **27**:317
Marge Piercy **6**:402
Hilma Wolitzer **17**:561

Ferrari, Margaret Burns
Norma Klein **30**:239

Ferrell, Henry C., Jr.
Louis R. Harlan **34**:187

Ferrer, José M.
Garry Marshall **17**:274

Ferrer, Olga Prjevalinskaya
Eugène Ionesco **6**:256

Ferreri, Rosario
Primo Levi **37**:225

Ferres, John H.
Arthur Miller **26**:324

Ferretti, Fred
Norman Lear **12**:326
George Plimpton **36**:357

Ferrier, Carole
Sylvia Plath **17**:369
Diane Wakoski **7**:505

Ferris, Ina
Rudy Wiebe **11**:567

Ferris, Sumner J.
Flannery O'Connor **21**:257

Ferris, William H.
W.E.B. Du Bois **13**:180

Ferrucci, Franco
Italo Calvino **33**:100
Umberto Eco **28**:131

Ferry, David
Theodore Roethke **1**:291

Fetherling, Doug
Hugh Garner **13**:235,236
Patrick Lane **25**:283
A. W. Purdy **14**:435
Mordecai Richler **3**:431
Robin Skelton **13**:506

Fetz, Gerald A.
Martin Walser **27**:463

Feuer, Kathryn B.
Aleksandr I. Solzhenitsyn **7**:445

Feuser, Willfried F.
Chinua Achebe **7**:6

Fialkowski, Barbara
Maxine Kumin **13**:326

Fiamengo, Marya
Susan Musgrave **13**:400

Fickert, Kurt J.
Friedrich Dürrenmatt **4**:139
Hermann Hesse **17**:201

Fiddler, Virginia
Frederick Forsyth **36**:178

Fiedler, Leslie A.
John Barth **3**:38
Saul Bellow **1**:27, 31; **3**:48
Truman Capote **19**:79
Leonard Cohen **3**:109
Bob Dylan **3**:130
Philip José Farmer **19**:164
William Faulkner **1**:101; **3**:149
Allen Ginsberg **2**:162; **3**:193
John Hawkes **3**:221
Ernest Hemingway **1**:143;
    3:232, 33
John Hersey **7**:153
Randall Jarrell **1**:160
Arthur Koestler **33**:237
Robert Lowell **2**:246
Norman Mailer **3**:311
Bernard Malamud **9**:341, 351
Henry Miller **2**:282
Alberto Moravia **2**:293
Wright Morris **1**:232
Vladimir Nabokov **1**:239
Ezra Pound **7**:329
John Crowe Ransom **2**:363

Mordecai Richler **5**:375
Henry Roth **6**:470
J. D. Salinger **12**:512
Jerome Siegel and Joe Shuster
    21:361
Kurt Vonnegut, Jr. **12**:603
Robert Penn Warren **4**:579
Richard Wilbur **3**:530
Herman Wouk **1**:376

Field, Andrew
Djuna Barnes **29**:32
Vladimir Nabokov **1**:242
Yevgeny Yevtushenko **1**:382

Field, Carol
Paule Marshall **27**:308

Field, Colin
H. F. Brinsmead **21**:26
Eilís Dillon **17**:98
William Mayne **12**:392

Field, Ellen Wilson
George Plimpton **36**:357

Field, George Wallis
Hermann Hesse **1**:147

Field, Joyce
Bernard Malamud **9**:348

Field, Leslie
Bernard Malamud **9**:348

Field, Louise Maunsell
Alvah Bessie **23**:59
Taylor Caldwell **28**:57
Edna Ferber **18**:150
Noel Streatfeild **21**:396

Field, Trevor
Julien Green **11**:261

Fields, Beverly
Anne Sexton **2**:391

Fields, Kenneth
J. V. Cunningham **3**:121
Robert Lowell **4**:299
Mina Loy **28**:247
N. Scott Momaday **2**:290
Marya Zaturenska **6**:585

Fiess, Edward
Edmund Wilson **24**:466

Fifer, Elizabeth
Maxine Hong Kingston **12**:314

Figes, Eva
Edward Bond **23**:72

Filer, Malva E.
Julio Cortázar **10**:117

Finch, John
E. E. Cummings **12**:144

Fincke, Gary
Ben Hecht **8**:271

Fincke, Kate
Isabelle Holland **21**:153

Fine, Dennis
Neil Young **17**:573

Finel-Honigman, Irène
Albert Camus **11**:96

Finger, Louis
John Le Carré **9**:326

Finholt, Richard
James Dickey **10**:142
Ralph Ellison **11**:184

Fink, Rita
Alvah Bessie **23**:61

Finkelstein, Sidney
Louis Aragon **22**:36

Finkle, David
John Fowles **9**:215
Mordecai Richler **18**:459

Finlay, John
Elizabeth Daryush **19**:122

Finlayson, Iain
Peter Rushforth **19**:405

Finley, M. I.
Michael Ayrton **7**:17

Finn, James
James Baldwin **17**:23, 24
Peter Matthiessen **32**:285
François Mauriac **4**:339
P. G. Wodehouse **2**:480

Finn, James D.
Dannie Abse **29**:11

Finne, Elisabeth
Günter Grass **32**:201

Firchow, Peter
Lawrence Durrell **27**:96
Aldous Huxley **8**:305

Firchow, Peter E.
W. H. Auden **11**:17
Aldous Huxley **18**:266

Fireside, Bryna J.
Joan Aiken **35**:20
Ann Schlee **35**:374

Fireside, Harvey
Andrei Sinyavsky **8**:489, 490

Firestone, Bruce M.
Anthony Burgess **10**:89

Firkins, O. W.
Carl Sandburg **35**:338

Firmat, Gustavo Pérez
Dámaso Alonso **14**:24

First, Elsa
Carlos Castaneda **12**:91

Fisch, Harold
Aharon Megged **9**:374
A. B. Yehoshua **31**:469

Fischer, John Irwin
Catharine Savage Brosman
    9:135

Fischer, Lucy
René Clair **20**:67

Fischer, Marjorie
Margot Benary-Isbert **12**:30
Joseph Krumgold **12**:317

Fischer, Max
Arthur Koestler **33**:228

Fischer, Michael
Wayne C. Booth **24**:99

Fischler, Alexander
Eugène Ionesco **15**:297

Fisher, Dorothy Canfield
A. B. Guthrie, Jr. **23**:195

Fisher, Elizabeth
Jessamyn West **17**:553

Fisher, Emma
Beryl Bainbridge **18**:32
John Berryman **10**:47
Anaïs Nin **14**:386
Peter Porter **13**:452
R. S. Thomas **13**:544
Yevgeny Yevtushenko **26**:468

Fisher, George William
Richard Grayson **38**:208

Fisher, Margery
Joan Aiken **35**:18, 21
E. M. Almedingen **12**:6
Ruth M. Arthur **12**:25, 26
Honor Arundel **17**:14, 16
Gunnel Beckman **26**:88
Judy Blume **12**:47
Cecil Bødker **21**:11
H. F. Brinsmead **21**:27, 28, 29,
    30, 33
Aidan Chambers **35**:98, 100,
    101
Mavis Thorpe Clark **12**:130,
    131, 132
Robert Cormier **12**:135, 137
Julia W. Cunningham **12**:164,
    165
Maureen Daly **17**:91
Peter Dickinson **12**:169, 174,
    177; **35**:135, 138
Eilís Dillon **17**:95, 96, 97
Walter Farley **17**:118
Esther Forbes **12**:211
Leon Garfield **12**:216, 217,
    218, 223, 227, 231, 233,
    234
Alan Garner **17**:135, 136, 148
S. E. Hinton **30**:206
Mollie Hunter **21**:156, 160, 170
Diana Wynne Jones **26**:224,
    225, 226, 228, 231, 232
Norma Klein **30**:239
William Mayne **12**:389, 405
Emily Cheney Neville **12**:450
Andre Norton **12**:469, 470
Katherine Paterson **12**:485
Philippa Pearce **21**:281, 282,
    287, 288, 290, 291
Richard Peck **21**:298
Josephine Poole **17**:373
Otfried Preussler **17**:375, 376
Zilpha Keatley Snyder **17**:474
Noel Streatfeild **21**:403, 409,
    410, 416
Rosemary Sutcliff **26**:437, 441
Mildred D. Taylor **21**:421
Colin Thiele **17**:493, 494, 495,
    496
J.R.R. Tolkien **12**:586
Rosemary Wells **12**:638
Robert Westall **17**:555, 556,
    559

Laurence Yep **35**:469
Paul Zindel **26**:481

Fisher, Maxine
Paul Zindel **26**:477

Fisher, William J.
William Saroyan **8**:466

Fishman, Charles
A. R. Ammons **25**:47

Fiske, Minnie Maddern
Charles Chaplin **16**:187

Fisketjon, Gary L.
Raymond Carver **22**:97
Thomas McGuane **18**:323

Fison, Peter
C. P. Snow **13**:511

Fitts, Dudley
Peter Davison **28**:99
Langston Hughes **35**:216
Mary Renault **17**:394, 398

Fitzgerald, Edward J.
Howard Fast **23**:156
Mark Harris **19**:200

Fitzgerald, Jennifer
Tom Paulin **37**:356

Fitzgerald, Judith
Margaret Atwood **25**:66
David Donnell **34**:156

Fitzgerald, Penelope
Barbara Pym **19**:388
Stevie Smith **25**:420

Fitzgerald, Robert
Seamus Heaney **7**:151
Robert Lowell **11**:325; **15**:345
Flannery O'Connor **15**:409

Fitzlyon, Kyril
Aleksandr I. Solzhenitsyn **1**:321

Fitzpatrick, Kelly
Nicholas M. Guild **33**:186

Fitzpatrick, Marjorie A.
Marie-Claire Blais **22**:60

Fitzsimmons, Thomas
Elizabeth Hardwick **13**:264

Fiut, Aleksander
Czesław Miłosz **11**:379

Fixler, Michael
Isaac Bashevis Singer **1**:311

Fixx, James F.
Art Buchwald **33**:91

Flagg, Nancy
Jorge Amado **13**:11

Flaherty, Joe
Richard Brautigan **9**:124
James M. Cain **28**:54
Joe McGinniss **32**:300
Edwin Newman **14**:379
George Plimpton **36**:356

Flake, Carol
Paul McCartney **35**:286

Flamm, Dudley
Robert M. Pirsig **4**:404

Flanagan, John T.
John Neihardt **32**:336
Conrad Richter **30**:314, 315
Jessamyn West **17**:551, 552

Flanagan, Kate M.
Sue Ellen Bridgers **26**:91
Walter Dean Myers **35**:296
Marilyn Sachs **35**:335

Flanagan, Margaret
Kent Haruf **34**:57

Flanagan, Thomas
Aharon Appelfeld **23**:36
Benedict Kiely **23**:265

Flanders, Jane
James Dickey **15**:177
Katherine Anne Porter **10**:396;
27:400

Flanner, Janet
André Malraux **4**:326
Carl Van Vechten **33**:386

Flasch, Joy
Melvin B. Tolson **36**:427

Flatto, Eric
Stanley Kubrick **16**:382

Flaxman, Seymour L.
Hermann Hesse **17**:196

Fleckenstein, Joan S.
Edward Albee **11**:13

Fleischer, Leonard
Woody Allen **16**:6
John A. Williams **5**:496

Fleischer, Leonore
Nora Ephron **17**:110

Fleischmann, Mark
Ray Davies **21**:105

Fleischmann, Wolfgang Bernard
René Wellek **28**:446

Fleishman, Avrom
John Fowles **9**:210

Fleming, Alice
Zilpha Keatley Snyder **17**:471

Fleming, Robert E.
Ronald L. Fair **18**:140
John A. Williams **5**:496

Fleming, Thomas
S. E. Hinton **30**:203

Fleming, Thomas J.
Elizabeth Jane Howard **29**:244
Ira Levin **6**:305
Emily Cheney Neville **12**:450
John Nichols **38**:339
Michel Tournier **23**:451

Fleshman, Bob
David Madden **15**:350

Fletcher, Angus
Northrop Frye **24**:219

Fletcher, Connie
Ted Berrigan **37**:44
Robert Bloch **33**:84
Will Harriss **34**:192
Elmore Leonard **28**:234
J.I.M. Stewart **32**:420

Fletcher, John
Arthur Adamov **25**:18
Uwe Johnson **5**:201
Kamala Markandaya **8**:377
Jean-Paul Sartre **7**:398
Claude Simon **39**:206

Fletcher, Peggy
Joe Rosenblatt **15**:447

Flexner, James Thomas
Esther Forbes **12**:209

Flint, F. Cudworth
Ralph Gustafson **36**:211

Flint, R. W.
A. R. Ammons **8**:15; **9**:29
Irving Feldman **7**:102
Anthony Hecht **8**:267
Randall Jarrell **1**:159
James Merrill **34**:229
Robert Pinsky **38**:356
Karl Shapiro **8**:486
Charles Tomlinson **13**:550

Flippo, Chet
Waylon Jennings **21**:201
Kris Kristofferson **26**:268
Willie Nelson **17**:302, 303,
304, 305
Sam Shepard **17**:445

Floan, Howard R.
William Saroyan **1**:301

Flood, Charles Bracelen
Thomas J. Fleming **37**:123

Flood, Jeanne
Brian Moore **5**:294

Flora, Joseph M.
Vardis Fisher **7**:103
Günter Grass **6**:209
J. E. Wideman **5**:490
Nancy Willard **7**:539

Florence, Ronald
Ed Minus **39**:80

Flores, Ralph
Frederick Karl **34**:552

Flower, Dean
Italo Calvino **33**:100
Raymond Carver **22**:97
Dan Jacobson **14**:291
William Kennedy **34**:210
Kamala Markandaya **38**:327
Vladimir Nabokov **15**:393
Marge Piercy **14**:421
Frederic Raphael **14**:438
Hubert Selby, Jr. **8**:477
Helen Yglesias **7**:559
Al Young **19**:479

Flowers, Ann A.
Jay Bennett **35**:45
Robin F. Brancato **35**:70
Betsy Byars **35**:75
Barbara Corcoran **17**:78
Peter Dickinson **35**:131
Lois Duncan **26**:108
Leon Garfield **12**:239
Norma Klein **30**:240
Norma Fox Mazer **26**:291
Katherine Paterson **12**:486

Flowers, Betty
Isaac Asimov **26**:37
Donald Barthelme **5**:56

Flowers, Paul
John Ehle **27**:101

Flowers, Sandra Hollin
Ntozake Shange **25**:403

Fludas, John
Rita Mae Brown **18**:73
Richard Price **12**:491

Foell, Earl W.
Thomas B. Costain **30**:98
Romain Gary **25**:183
Bruce Lancaster **36**:245

Fogelman, Phyllis J.
Mildred D. Taylor **21**:421

Folejewski, Zbigniew
Maria Dabrowska **15**:165, 167
Joseph Wittlin **25**:467

Foley, Ann D.
John McPhee **36**:295

Foley, Barbara
E. L. Doctorow **18**:121

Foley, Michael
Raymond Carver **36**:106

Folkart, Burt A.
Richard Brautigan **34**:314
Philip Larkin **39**:333
Theodore Sturgeon **39**:364

Folsom, James K.
Larry McMurtry **27**:326

Folsom, L. Edwin
W. S. Merwin **13**:384

Fong, Monique
Vittorio De Sica **20**:95

Fontenla, Cesar Santos
Carlos Saura **20**:320

Fontenot, Chester J.
Alex Haley **8**:260
Alice Walker **19**:450

Fontenrose, Joseph
John Steinbeck **21**:372

Foose, Thomas T.
Jean Renoir **20**:287

Foote, Audrey C.
Anthony Burgess **4**:81
Zoë Fairbairns **32**:163
Nathalie Sarraute **2**:386
Christina Stead **5**:404
Mary Stewart **7**:468

Foote, Bud
Charles R. Larson **31**:239

Foote, Jennifer
Richard O'Brien **17**:325

Foote, Timothy
W. H. Auden **3**:26; **6**:24
Anthony Burgess **5**:89
Henry Carlisle **33**:104
Peter De Vries **2**:114
Nicolas Freeling **38**:185, 186
John Gardner **3**:187

John le Carré 5:232
V. S. Pritchett **5**:352
Aleksandr I. Solzhenitsyn **4**:516
Tom Stoppard **4**:525
Tom Wolfe **2**:481

Forbes, Alastair
Lawrence Durrell **13**:189

Forbes, Cheryl
Ralph Bakshi **26**:73

Forbes, Jill
René Clair **20**:66
Rainer Werner Fassbinder
20:116
Joan Micklin Silver **20**:341

Forche, Carolyn
Ai **14**:8

Ford, John
Howard Barker **37**:32
Snoo Wilson **33**:460

Ford, Nick Aaron
Zora Neale Hurston **30**:210
Harper Lee **12**:341
Willard Motley **18**:356
Frank G. Yerby **22**:488

Ford, Richard J.
Hermann Hesse **2**:189

Ford, Thomas W.
A. B. Guthrie, Jr. **23**:202

Foreman, John D.
Evan Hunter **31**:222

Forest, James
Eldridge Cleaver **30**:65
Peter Matthiessen **32**:289

Forman, Jack
Jules Archer **12**:18, 20
Frank Bonham **12**:51
Bette Greene **30**:170
Nat Hentoff **26**:184, 185
Norma Fox Mazer **26**:290
Scott O'Dell **30**:276
Katherine Paterson **12**:485, 486
Richard Peck **21**:300
Kin Platt **26**:352, 354
Barbara Wersba **30**:434
Paul Zindel **26**:477

Fornacca, Daisy
Dino Buzzati **36**:83

Fornatale, Peter
Laura Nyro **17**:314
Brian Wilson **12**:646

Forrest, Alan
W. H. Auden **3**:27
Mario Puzo **2**:352

Forrey, Robert
Ken Kesey **11**:316
Andrew Sinclair **14**:488

Forster, E. M.
Mulk Raj Anand **23**:11

Forster, Leonard
Günter Grass **15**:262

Forster, Margaret
Iain Banks **34**:29

Fortin, René E.
Boris Pasternak **7**:296

Foster, David William
Jorge Luis Borges **3**:78; **6**:89
Camilo José Cela **4**:96
Julio Cortázar **10**:118
Jorge Ibargüengoitia **37**:183
Manuel Mujica Láinez **31**:280
Ernesto Sabato **10**:445

Foster, Francis Smith
Octavia E. Butler **38**:62

Foster, Isabel
Robert Francis **15**:234

Foster, John Wilson
Seamus Heaney **5**:170
Brian Moore **1**:225

Foster, Richard
R. P. Blackmur **24**:61
Norman Mailer **1**:190; **8**:365
I. A. Richards **24**:393
Allen Tate **24**:444

Foster, Richard J.
Arthur Miller **26**:315

Foster, Roy
Brian Moore **19**:333

Foster, Ruel E.
Jesse Stuart **1**:328

Fothergill, C. Z.
N. F. Simpson **29**:370

Fotheringham, Hamish
William Mayne **12**:388

Foulke, Adrienne
Elizabeth Taylor **29**:407

Fowke, Edith
Nevil Shute **30**:370

Fowler, Alastair
Michael Moorcock **27**:351
Charles M. Schulz **12**:532

Fowler, Douglas
Thomas Pynchon **18**:438

Fowler, F. M.
Günter Eich **15**:203

Fowles, John
G. B. Edwards **25**:149

Fowlie, Wallace
Ben Belitt **22**:50
Michel Butor **8**:119
René Char **9**:158
Jean Cocteau **15**:133
Jean Genet **5**:135
Julien Green **11**:258
Henri Michaux **8**:392
Anaïs Nin **4**:378; **11**:398
Jules Romains **7**:379
Marguerite Yourcenar **38**:461

Fox, Charles
Akira Kurosawa **16**:396

Fox, Edward
J. G. Ballard **36**:48

Fox, Gail
Phyllis Webb **18**:542

Fox, Geoff
Bette Greene **30**:170
Rosa Guy **26**:144
Nat Hentoff **26**:187
Scott O'Dell **30**:275

Fox, Hank
Janis Ian **21**:183

Fox, Hugh
William Carlos Williams **5**:509

Fox, Terry Curtis
Rita Mae Brown **18**:73
Marguerite Duras **20**:103
Max Frisch **18**:162
Athol Fugard **14**:192
Jean-Luc Godard **20**:152
Simon Gray **14**:215
John Guare **14**:221
Beth Henley **23**:214
George V. Higgins **18**:235
George Lucas **16**:415
Marsha Norman **28**:317
Harold Pinter **15**:425
Martin Scorsese **20**:333

Fox-Genovese, Elizabeth
Susan Cheever **18**:102
William Gaddis **8**:226
Gail Godwin **22**:183

Fraenkel, Heinrich
Leni Riefenstahl **16**:521

Fraiberg, Louis
Kenneth Burke **24**:130
Joseph Wood Krutch **24**:287
Lionel Trilling **24**:454
Edmund Wilson **24**:476

Fraire, Isabel
Ernesto Cardenal **31**:72

Frakes, J. R.
Frederick Forsyth **36**:175
J.M.G. Le Clézio **31**:246
Robert Ludlum **22**:288

Frakes, James R.
Nelson Algren **4**:17
Wendell Berry **4**:59
E. M. Broner **19**:70
R. V. Cassill **23**:108
Allen Drury **37**:108
Maureen Duffy **37**:115
Bruce Jay Friedman **5**:127
Joanne Greenberg **30**:165
Patricia Highsmith **2**:194
Stanley Hoffman **5**:185
Julius Horwitz **14**:266
Evan Hunter **11**:280; **31**:224
Diane Johnson **5**:198
Peter Maas **29**:307
Michael Mewshaw **9**:376
Ezekiel Mphahlele **25**:332
Muriel Spark **2**:418
Richard G. Stern **4**:522
Glendon Swarthout **35**:403
Richard Tillinghast **29**:408

France, Arthur
Lorraine Hansberry **17**:185

France, Peter
Anne Hébert **13**:267

Francescato, Martha Paley
Julio Cortázar **10**:116

Francis, William A. C.
William Price Fox **22**:139

Francis, Wynne
Louis Dudek **19**:137

Frane, Jeff
Fritz Leiber **25**:310

Frank, Armin Paul
Kenneth Burke **2**:89

Frank, Elizabeth
Robert Pinsky **38**:355

Frank, Joseph
Djuna Barnes **8**:47
R. P. Blackmur **24**:64
Yves Bonnefoy **15**:74
André Malraux **4**:327
Aleksandr I. Solzhenitsyn **7**:443
Lionel Trilling **24**:453

Frank, Margot K.
Vasily Aksyonov **37**:12

Frank, Mike
Joseph Heller **11**:266

Frank, Pat
Leon Uris **32**:431

Frank, Peter
Richard Kostelanetz **28**:219

Frank, Sheldon
Edward Abbey **36**:13
T. Alan Broughton **19**:72
Margaret Laurence **6**:289
Steven Millhauser **21**:218
Hans Erich Nossack **6**:365
Al Young **19**:480

Frankel, Bernice
Mary Stolz **12**:547

Frankel, Charles
William Barrett **27**:17
Arthur Koestler **33**:235

Frankel, Haskel
Jonathan Baumbach **23**:53
Bruce Jay Friedman **3**:165
Joanne Greenberg **30**:161
Ronald Harwood **32**:223
Muriel Spark **2**:417
Glendon Swarthout **35**:401
Peter Ustinov **1**:346
Charles Webb **7**:514
Donald E. Westlake **33**:437

Frankenberg, Lloyd
Marianne Moore **19**:337
Ogden Nash **23**:321

Franklin, Allan
Jorg Luis Borges **9**:116

Franklin, H. Bruce
J. G. Ballard **3**:32
Robert A. Heinlein **26**:175, 179

Franks, Lucinda
Edward Abbey **36**:18
Breece D'J Pancake **29**:350

Fraser, Antonio
Agatha Christie **39**:442
Janet Morgan **39**:442

Critic Index

Fraser, C. Gerald
Julio Cortázar **34**:329
George Oppen **34**:358

Fraser, G. S.
Basil Bunting **10**:86
Robert Creeley **1**:67
C. Day Lewis **6**:127
Nigel Dennis **8**:172
Lawrence Durrell **4**:145; **13**:184
Jean Garrigue **2**:153
W. S. Graham **29**:195
Randall Jarrell **9**:296
Robert Lowell **2**:249; **11**:325
Norman MacCaig **36**:279
Hugh MacDiarmid **11**:337
W. S. Merwin **1**:214
C. P. Snow **4**:502
Gary Snyder **1**:318
Andrei Voznesensky **15**:552
Louis Zukofsky **1**:385

Fraser, George
William Empson **33**:147

Fraser, John
Louis-Ferdinand Céline **1**:56; **4**:102
F. R. Leavis **24**:298
Yvor Winters **4**:592; **8**:552

Fraser, Kathleen
Adrienne Rich **3**:429

Fraser, Keath
Alden Nowlan **15**:398
Sinclair Ross **13**:492

Fraser, Robert
Ayi Kwei Armah **33**:33

Fraser, Russell
Eugenio Montale **18**:341

Fratz, D. Douglas
Frank Herbert **23**:222

Fraustino, Lisa
Suzanne Newton **35**:302

Frayne, John P.
John Ford **16**:320

Frazer, Frances M.
Christie Harris **12**:268

Frazer, Mary
Frederick Wiseman **20**:477

Frazier, Kermit
John Edgar Wideman **36**:452

Fredeman, W. E.
Earle Birney **6**:72

Frederick, Linda J.
Ray Davies **21**:100

Fredericks, Claude
Brewster Ghiselin **23**:169

Fredericks, Pierce
Ernest K. Gann **23**:165

Fredrick, E. Coston
Barbara Corcoran **17**:75

Free, William J.
Federico Fellini **16**:284
Tennessee Williams **15**:581

Freed, Donald
Alberto Moravia **27**:353

Freedberg, Mike
Smokey Robinson **21**:348

Freedberger, Peter
Stan Lee **17**:261

Freedman, Morris
Sylvia Ashton-Warner **19**:23

Freedman, Ralph
Saul Bellow **1**:29
Hermann Hesse **1**:146; **17**:203

Freedman, Richard
A. Alvarez **13**:10
Dino Buzzati **36**:89
Taylor Caldwell **28**:69
Hortense Calisher **2**:96
Sumner Locke Elliot **38**:182
Dick Francis **2**:142
Lois Gould **4**:199
Evan Hunter **31**:226
Robert Ludlum **22**:290
Tim O'Brien **19**:356
S. J. Perelman **9**:416; **23**:337
Wilbur Smith **33**:375
George Steiner **24**:432
Henri Troyat **23**:460
P. G. Wodehouse **5**:517

Freedman, Samuel G.
Stephen Sondheim **30**:402

Freedman, William
Henry Roth **11**:487

Freeman, Anne Hobson
Reynolds Price **13**:463

Freeman, David
Steven Bochco and Michael Kozoll **35**:59

Freeman, E.
Albert Camus **32**:96

Freeman, Gillian
Robert Nye **13**:412

Freeman, Suzanne
Carolyn Chute **39**:39
M. E. Kerr **35**:247
Joyce Maynard **23**:290
Norma Fox Mazer **26**:296
Susan Richards Shreve **23**:404

Freibert, Lucy M.
H. D. **31**:206, 210, 213

Frein, George H.
Vine Deloria, Jr. **21**:112

Fremantle, Anne
W. H. Auden **1**:10
Ernesto Cardenal **31**:71
Thomas J. Fleming **37**:124
Auberon Waugh **7**:513
Vassily S. Yanovsky **18**:551

Fremont-Smith, Eliot
Richard Adams **4**:6
Martin Amis **4**:20; **38**:12
Max Apple **9**:33
Louis Auchincloss **4**:31
Russell Baker **31**:27
Claude Brown **30**:33
Arthur C. Clarke **35**:124

Laurie Colwin **13**:156
E. L. Doctorow **6**:132
Lawrence Durrell **6**:152
Bret Easton Ellis **39**:56
Gael Greene **8**:252
Graham Greene **37**:140
Barry Hannah **23**:211
Joseph Heller **5**:173; **11**:268
Lillian Hellman **4**:221
John Irving **13**:294; **23**:247
Marjorie Kellogg **2**:223
Jascha Kessler **4**:269
Arthur Koestler **3**:271
Jerzy Kosinski **1**:172
John le Carré **9**:327
Alan Lelchuk **5**:243
Norman Mailer **4**:322; **39**:419
Peter Manso **39**:419
Peter Matthiessen **32**:287
Colleen McCullough **27**:318
Joe McGinniss **32**:304
James A. Michener **5**:289
Chaim Potok **26**:368
Richard Price **6**:426; **12**:490
Mario Puzo **36**:361
Judith Rossner **29**:354
Philip Roth **4**:453, 455
Alix Kates Shulman **10**:476
Gay Talese **37**:396
John Updike **23**:468
Gore Vidal **6**:54
Irving Wallace **7**:510
Patrick White **3**:524

French, Allen
Esther Forbes **12**:206

French, Janet
Sue Ellen Bridgers **26**:92
Otfried Preussler **17**:375

French, Marilyn
Margaret Atwood **15**:39
Christa Wolf **29**:466

French, Ned
William H. Gass **15**:255

French, Philip
Bernardo Bertolucci **16**:101
Jorge Luis Borges **4**:75
Truman Capote **8**:132
Eleanor Clark **19**:107
Graham Greene **3**:212; **6**:220
Richard Lester **20**:219
S. J. Perelman **23**:340

French, Roberts W.
Wendell Berry **27**:32
Philip Booth **23**:75
Joyce Carol Oates **1**:251

French, Warren
William Goldman **1**:123
R. K. Narayan **7**:254
James Purdy **2**:349
J. D. Salinger **1**:297; **12**:514
John Steinbeck **1**:324; **5**:406
Thornton Wilder **1**:366
Richard Wright **21**:447

Frenkel, James
Jack Vance **35**:427

Fretz, Sada
Julia W. Cunningham **12**:165
John Donovan **35**:141
John Neufeld **17**:308

Friar, Kimon
Margaríta Karapánou **13**:314
Yannis Ritsos **6**:463; **31**:324, 327
Vassilis Vassilikos **8**:524

Fricke, David
David Byrne **26**:99
The Clash **30**:51
Mick Jagger and Keith Richard **17**:242
Bob Seger **35**:386
Paul Weller **26**:447
Frank Zappa **17**:592

Friebert, Stuart
Ernst Jandl **34**:196

Fried, Lewis
James T. Farrell **11**:191

Friedberg, Maurice
Aleksandr I. Solzhenitsyn **1**:319; **7**:435

Friedenberg, Daniel M.
Michel del Castillo **38**:166

Friedenberg, Edgar Z.
James Baldwin **17**:24
Mark Harris **19**:201
Hermann Hesse **2**:190
Margaret Mead **37**:275
Frederick Wiseman **20**:472

Friedman, Alan
T. Coraghessan Boyle **36**:58
William S. Burroughs **5**:93
John Gardner **7**:112
John Hawkes **27**:198
Erica Jong **18**:279
Yukio Mishima **4**:357
Amos Oz **8**:435
John Rechy **18**:442
Ishmael Reed **2**:367
André Schwarz-Bart **2**:389
John Kennedy Toole **19**:443
Elie Wiesel **3**:528

Friedman, Alan J.
Thomas Pynchon **6**:434

Friedman, Alan Warren
Saul Bellow **8**:69
Lawrence Durrell **1**:87
Bernard Malamud **8**:375

Friedman, Jack
Wendell Berry **4**:59
José Lezama Lima **4**:290

Friedman, John
William Eastlake **8**:200

Friedman, Melvin J.
Bruce Jay Friedman **5**:127
Carolyn G. Heilbrun **25**:252
Eugène Ionesco **6**:256
André Malraux **4**:333
R. K. Narayan **7**:255
Flannery O'Connor **1**:253
Isaac Bashevis Singer **1**:313

Friedman, Norman
E. E. Cummings **1**:69; **12**:149; **15**:153
David Ignatow **7**:174

Friedman, Richard
The Police **26**:365

Friedman, Susan Stanford
H. D. **31**:204, 207

Friedrich, Pia
Pier Paolo Pasolini **37**:349

Friedrichsmeyer, Erhard
Uwe Johnson **15**:302

Friend, Beverly
Octavia E. Butler **38**:65

Frieling, Kenneth
Flannery O'Connor **13**:416

Fries, Maureen
Mary Stewart **35**:394

Friesem, Roberta Ricky
Lenora Mattingly Weber **12**:635

Friesen, Gordon
Phil Ochs **17**:329, 330

Frith, Simon
Elvis Costello **21**:68
Mick Jagger and Keith Richard **17**:240
Bob Marley **17**:272
Smokey Robinson **21**:346
Patti Smith **12**:543
Peter Townshend **17**:538
Paul Weller **26**:445
Neil Young **17**:580

Fritz, Jean
Lloyd Alexander **35**:23, 24, 26, 27
Ruth M. Arthur **12**:24
Judy Blume **30**:23
Betsy Byars **35**:73
Barbara Corcoran **17**:73
Rosa Guy **26**:144
Virginia Hamilton **26**:153, 155
Joseph Krumgold **12**:318
Norma Fox Mazer **26**:293
Milton Meltzer **26**:297
Scott O'Dell **30**:273, 274, 276
Zilpha Keatley Snyder **17**:472
Mary Stolz **12**:553
Mildred D. Taylor **21**:418
Maia Wojciechowska **26**:457
Laurence Yep **35**:470

Frohock, W. M.
James M. Cain **11**:84
Erskine Caldwell **1**:51
James Gould Cozzens **4**:113
John Dos Passos **1**:77
James T. Farrell **1**:97
William Faulkner **1**:99
Ernest Hemingway **1**:141
André Malraux **4**:324; **13**:366
John Steinbeck **1**:323
Robert Penn Warren **1**:351

Frost, Lucy
John Hawkes **3**:223

Fruchtbaum, Harold
Loren Eiseley **7**:90

Frye, Northrop
Charles Chaplin **16**:192
Leonard Cohen **38**:131
R. S. Crane **27**:71
Louis Dudek **11**:158; **19**:136, 137
Northrop Frye **24**:222

Daryl Hine **15**:280
Dorothy Livesay **15**:339
E. J. Pratt **19**:376, 379
A.J.M. Smith **15**:516
Allen Tate **24**:443

Fryer, Jonathan H.
Christopher Isherwood **9**:292

Frykman, Erik
Norman MacCaig **36**:286

Fuchs, Daniel
Saul Bellow **3**:62

Fuchs, Marcia G.
Jonathan Keates **34**:203

Fuchs, Miriam
Djuna Barnes **29**:30

Fuchs, Vivian
Thomas Keneally **10**:299

Fuchs, Wolfgang
Charles M. Schulz **12**:528

Fuentes, Carlos
Luis Buñuel **16**:137
Julio Cortázar **34**:330

Fugard, Athol
Athol Fugard **14**:189

Fulford, Robert
George Bowering **15**:81
Michael Cimino **16**:214
Mavis Gallant **18**:172
Hugh Hood **28**:187
Kevin Major **26**:285
Brian Moore **3**:340
Mordecai Richler **3**:429
Philip Roth **3**:435
Raymond Souster **14**:504

Fullbrook, Kate
Pat Barker **32**:12

Fuller, Edmund
Paul Bowles **1**:41
Frederick Buechner **4**:80
James Gould Cozzens **1**:65
Michel del Castillo **38**:167
Jan de Hartog **19**:130
John Ehle **27**:106
Michael Ende **31**:144
Joseph Epstein **39**:467
James D. Forman **21**:116
Pamela Hansford Johnson **27**:220
James Jones **1**:161
Thomas Keneally **19**:248
Jack Kerouac **1**:165
Bernard Malamud **27**:299
Walter M. Miller, Jr. **30**:253
Alan Paton **4**:395; **25**:360
Mary Renault **17**:392
Carl Sagan **30**:336
Mary Lee Settle **19**:408
Frank G. Slaughter **29**:374
J.R.R. Tolkien **1**:335
Morris L. West **33**:433
Herman Wouk **1**:375

Fuller, Elizabeth Ely
Isak Dinesen **10**:150

Fuller, Henry B.
Rebecca West **31**:451

Fuller, Hoyt W.
Milton Meltzer **26**:299

Fuller, John
Anna Akhmatova **11**:9
Peter Davison **28**:102
Thom Gunn **3**:215
Michael Hamburger **14**:234
Randall Jarrell **2**:208
Diana Wynne Jones **26**:225
Leslie Norris **14**:387
Robert Pinsky **19**:370
William Plomer **4**:406
Ann Quin **6**:441
Kathleen Raine **7**:353
Jon Silkin **6**:499
Andrew Young **5**:523

Fuller, John G.
Colin MacInnes **23**:282

Fuller, John Wesley
Art Buchwald **33**:91

Fuller, Roy
W. H. Auden **3**:25
John Betjeman **34**:306
Aldous Huxley **5**:192
A.J.M. Smith **15**:513
C. P. Snow **19**:427
Stephen Spender **2**:420
Allen Tate **14**:532
Lionel Trilling **9**:530

Fulton, Robin
Pär Lagerkvist **10**:313

Funke, Lewis
John Mortimer **28**:282

Funsten, Kenneth
Robert Creeley **36**:119
James Galvin **38**:198
Darcy Ribeiro **34**:102
Derek Walcott **25**:456

Furbank, P. N.
Donald Davie **31**:115
Margaret Drabble **22**:120
D. J. Enright **31**:146, 150
E. M. Forster **4**:165, 168
William Golding **17**:176
Elizabeth Jennings **14**:291
Uwe Johnson **10**:284
Norman MacCaig **36**:280
Derek Mahon **27**:287
Gore Vidal **4**:556

Furlong, Vivienne
Honor Arundel **17**:18

Furman, Laura
Fernanda Eberstadt **39**:50

Fussell, B. H.
Robert Coover **32**:120
Peter Taylor **4**:543

Fussell, Edwin
Wendell Berry **6**:61
Hayden Carruth **7**:40

Fussell, Paul
Noël Coward **29**:141
Graham Greene **27**:171
Richard F. Hugo **32**:234
Thomas Keneally **8**:318
Siegfried Sassoon **36**:394

Paul Theroux **15**:533
Evelyn Waugh **27**:475, 477
Herman Wouk **38**:450

Fussell, Paul, Jr.
Karl Shapiro **4**:486

Fyne, Robert
Aharon Appelfeld **23**:37

Fytton, Francis
Paul Bowles **2**:78

Fyvel, T. R.
Ilya Ehrenburg **18**:133

Gabbard, Krin
Tess Gallagher **18**:170

Gabel, Lars
Marvin Gaye **26**:133

Gabert, Charla
Robert Coover **32**:122

Gabree, John
Mick Jagger and Keith Richard **17**:223
John Lennon **35**:261
John Lennon and Paul McCartney **12**:364

Gadney, Reg
George V. Higgins **7**:158
Patricia Highsmith **2**:194
Ross Macdonald **2**:257
Alistair MacLean **3**:309

Gaev, A.
Vasily Aksenov **22**:25

Gaffney, Elizabeth
Sharon Olds **32**:347
Mary Oliver **34**:248

Gaffney, James
Ayi Kwei Armah **33**:27

Gagné, Sarah
Melvin Berger **12**:42
Larry Kettelkamp **12**:307
Alvin Silverstein and Virginia B. Silverstein **17**:456

Gaillard, Dawson
Harry Crews **23**:134

Gaillard, Frye
Willie Nelson **17**:304

Gaines, Richard H.
Chester Himes **2**:196

Gaiser, Carolyn
Gregory Corso **1**:63
Nettie Jones **34**:68

Gaither, Frances
Esther Forbes **12**:210

Galassi, Jonathan
John Berryman **6**:63
Frank Bidart **33**:73
Robert Duncan **2**:123
Robert Graves **6**:212
Seamus Heaney **7**:147
Randall Jarrell **9**:297
Czesław Miłosz **22**:309
Eugenio Montale **7**:231
Howard Nemerov **9**:396
George Oppen **13**:434

Galbraith, John Kenneth
Robertson Davies **25**:135
Edwin O'Connor **14**:389
William Safire **10**:446

Galbreath, Naomi
Barry Hughart **39**:156

Gale, David
Suzanne Newton **35**:302

Gale, Zona
August Derleth **31**:129

Gall, Sally M.
Kenneth O. Hanson **13**:263
Eleanor Lerman **9**:329
M. L. Rosenthal **28**:394
Charles Wright **6**:580

Gallagher, Ann Maureen, I.H.M.
Joseph Hansen **38**:240

Gallagher, Bob
Smokey Robinson **21**:347

Gallagher, D. P.
Adolfo Bioy Casares **8**:94;
13:83
Jorge Luis Borges **6**:88
G. Cabrera Infante **5**:96
Gabriel García Márquez **8**:230
Pablo Neruda **7**:257
Octavio Paz **6**:394
Manuel Puig **10**:420
Mario Vargas Llosa **6**:543

Gallagher, David
Alejo Carpentier **38**:94
G. Cabrera Infante **5**:95
Manuel Mujica Láinez **31**:279
Manuel Puig **3**:407

Gallagher, Donat
Jessica Anderson **37**:19

Gallagher, Jerry
John G. Neihardt **32**:336

Gallagher, Michael
Shusaku Endo **7**:95

Gallagher, Michael Paul
Brian Moore **32**:313

Gallagher, Steve
Stephen King **37**:201

Gallagher, Tess
Laura Jensen **37**:187

Gallant, Mavis
Simone de Beauvior **4**:48
Louis-Ferdinand Céline **7**:46
Günter Grass **4**:205
Vladimir Nabokov **2**:303
Marguerite Yourcenar **38**:463

Galler, David
Peter Davison **28**:100
Ted Hughes **2**:198
Howard Nemerov **2**:307

Galligan, Edward L.
Georges Simenon **1**:309

Galloway, David
William Melvin Kelley **22**:251

Galloway, David D.
Saul Bellow **3**:51, 55
Stanley Elkin **4**:152
Dan Jacobson **4**:253
J. D. Salinger **3**:445
William Styron **3**:473
John Updike **3**:486

Galt, George
Leon Rooke **34**:251

Gambaccini, Paul
Smokey Robinson **21**:342

Gambaccini, Peter
Billy Joel **26**:217

Gannett, Lewis
Allen Drury **37**:98

Gannon, Edward, S.J.
André Malraux **4**:326

Gannon, Thomas M.
David Bradley, Jr. **23**:82
John Gregory Dunne **28**:127
James A. Michener **29**:313

Gant, Lisbeth
Ed Bullins **5**:82

Ganz, Arthur
Harold Pinter **6**:416

Ganz, Earl
John Hawkes **1**:139
Flannery O'Connor **2**:318

Garbarini, Vic
Paul McCartney **35**:293

Garber, Frederick
Norman Dubie **36**:138
Richard F. Hugo **32**:236
William Stafford **29**:385

Garber, Meg Elliott
Joanne Greenberg **30**:167

Garcia, Irma
Nicholosa Mohr **12**:447

Gard, Roger
Shirley Hazzard **18**:214

Gardiner, Harold C.
Robert Cormier **12**:134

Gardner, Averil
William Empson **19**:156

Gardner, Craig Shaw
Frank Herbert **35**:200
Laurence Yep **35**:473

Gardner, Erle Stanley
Meyer Levin **7**:203

Gardner, Harvey
Jimmy Breslin **4**:76

Gardner, James
Italo Calvino **39**:313

Gardner, John
Saul Bellow **10**:44
Anthony Burgess **2**:84
Italo Calvino **8**:129; **22**:90
John Cheever **25**:117
E. L. Doctorow **15**:178
John Fowles **9**:215
William H. Gass **1**:114

John Knowles **4**:271
Brian Moore **8**:395
Charles Newman **8**:419
Joyce Carol Oates **19**:354
Walker Percy **8**:442
Philip Roth **2**:379
John Steinbeck **21**:387
William Styron **15**:525
J.R.R. Tolkien **12**:585
Patrick White **9**:567
Thomas Williams **14**:582
Larry Woiwode **6**:578

Gardner, Marilyn
Barbara Corcoran **17**:69
Virginia Hamilton **26**:149
Mary Stolz **12**:554
Maia Wojciechowska **26**:457

Gardner, Peter
Allan W. Eckert **17**:108
John Hersey **9**:277

Gardner, Philip
William Empson **19**:156
D. J. Enright **4**:155; **31**:148
Roy Fisher **25**:160
Philip Larkin **5**:230; **18**:293

Gardner, R. H.
William Inge **19**:228
Arthur Miller **26**:319
Thornton Wilder **35**:444
Tennessee Williams **30**:466

Garebian, Keith
Anne Chislett **34**:146
David Donnell **34**:156
Ralph Gustafson **36**:222
Patrick White **9**:563

Garfield, Brian
Ernest K. Gann **23**:166
Glendon Swarthout **35**:402

Garfield, Evelyn Picon
Julio Cortázar **13**:163

Garfield, Leon
William Mayne **12**:395
Scott O'Dell **30**:276

Garfitt, Roger
George Barker **8**:46
James K. Baxter **14**:60
Martin Booth **13**:103
Joseph Brodsky **6**:96
Robert Creeley **4**:118
Eilís Dillon **17**:99
Douglas Dunn **6**:148
Geoffrey Grigson **7**:136
Donald Hall **13**:259
Anthony Hecht **19**:209
Anna Kavan **5**:206
Reiner Kunze **10**:310
Philip Larkin **8**:332
George MacBeth **5**:263
László Nagy **7**:251
Leslie Norris **14**:388
Julia O'Faolain **6**:383
Vasko Popa **19**:375
Peter Porter **5**:346
Thomas Pynchon **3**:418
Peter Redgrove **6**:445
Bernice Rubens **19**:403
Ward Ruyslinck **14**:471
C. H. Sisson **8**:490

Anne Stevenson **7**:462
Derek Walcott **4**:575

Gargan, Carol
Maya Angelou **35**:30

Garioch, Robert
Elaine Feinstein **36**:168

Garis, Leslie
Doris Lessing **6**:302

Garis, Robert
Herbert Gold **4**:191
Anthony Powell **3**:400

Garland, Patrick
Philip Larkin **39**:338

Garland, Phyl
Marvin Gaye **26**:135
Smokey Robinson **21**:348, 349

Garner, Alan
Leon Garfield **12**:219

Garnet, Eldon
B. P. Nichol **18**:367

Garnett, David
T. H. White **30**:436

Garnick, Vivian
Toni Morrison **10**:355

Garrard, J. G.
Aleksandr I. Solzhenitsyn
2:411; **9**:503

Garrett, George
Truman Capote **38**:78
John Cheever **3**:107
Babette Deutsch **18**:119
Gail Godwin **22**:180
Sue Kaufman **8**:317
Wright Morris **3**:342; **18**:351
Leon Rooke **25**:391

Garrett, J. C.
Aldous Huxley **35**:235

Garrett, John
Edmund Crispin **22**:109
Northrop Frye **24**:207

Garrigue, Jean
Romain Gary **25**:183
Mary McCarthy **14**:357
Marianne Moore **1**:228

Garside, E. B.
Farley Mowat **26**:335

Garson, Helen S.
Truman Capote **19**:85
John Hawkes **9**:268; **27**:192

Garvey, Michael
Studs Terkel **38**:426
William Trevor **25**:444

Garvin, Larry
Piri Thomas **17**:501

Gascoigne, Bamber
Ann Jellicoe **27**:207

Gasparini, Len
Ronald G. Everson **27**:135
Patrick Lane **25**:284, 286

Gasque, Thomas J.
J.R.R. Tolkien **1**:337

Gass, William H.
Donald Barthelme **3**:43
Jorge Luis Borges **3**:76
Robert Coover **3**:113
Leon Edel **29**:169
Gabriel García Márquez **27**:153
William H. Gass **15**:257
Vladimir Nabokov **3**:351
J. F. Powers **1**:281
Philip Roth **3**:437
Isaac Bashevis Singer **3**:454
Susan Sontag **10**:484

Gassner, John
Edward Albee **3**:6, 7
Robert Anderson **23**:30
Jean Anouilh **3**:11, 12
Samuel Beckett **3**:44, 45
Brendan Behan **8**:63
Eric Bentley **24**:47
William Gibson **23**:177
Lillian Hellman **4**:220
William Inge **8**:307
Eugène Ionesco **4**:250
Joseph Wood Krutch **24**:286
Archibald MacLeish **3**:310
Mary McCarthy **24**:342
Arthur Miller **6**:330; **26**:310
Clifford Odets **28**:331
John Osborne **5**:330
Harold Pinter **3**:386
Thornton Wilder **5**:495
Tennessee Williams **5**:498, 500;
30:462

Gaston, Edwin W., Jr.
Conrad Richter **30**:319

Gaston, Karen C.
Gail Godwin **22**:182

Gaston, Paul M.
John Ehle **27**:103

Gates, David
Samuel Beckett **9**:83

Gates, Henry Louis, Jr.
Sterling A. Brown **23**:100

Gathercole, Patricia M.
Tommaso Landolfi **11**:321

Gathorne-Hardy, J.
Vladimir Nabokov **3**:354

Gatt-Rutter, John
Italo Calvino **11**:89; **22**:89
Pier Paolo Pasolini **37**:346

Gauch, Patricia Lee
Walter Dean Myers **35**:297
Robert Newton Peck **17**:343
Marilyn Sachs **35**:333
Ouida Sebestyen **30**:349

Gaudon, Sheila
Julien Gracq **11**:245

Gaull, Marilyn
E. E. Cumming **12**:156

Gault, John
Stephen King **26**:234

Gaurilović, Zoran
Dobrica Ćosić **14**:132

Gavin, Francis
John Gardner **30**:155

Gavin, Willam
Auberon Waugh **7**:514

Gavin, William F.
Michael Frayn **31**:189

Gavronsky, Serge
Aimé Césaire **32**:113

Gay, Robert M.
Walter D. Edmonds **35**:151

Gayle, Addison, Jr.
Gwendolyn Brooks **1**:46
Ernest J. Gaines **18**:167
Zora Neale Hurston **30**:217
Nella Larson **37**:215
Ezekiel Mphahlele **25**:334

Gaylin, Willard
Lewis Thomas **35**:413

Gealy, Marcia B.
Bernard Malamud **18**:317

Gearing, Nigel
Pier Paolo Pasolini **20**:266

Geary, Joyce
Jade Snow Wong **17**:566

Gebhard, Ann
Barbara Corcoran **17**:75

Geddes, Gary
Raymond Souster **5**:395

Geduld, Harry M.
Woody Allen **16**:8

Geering, R. G.
Shirley Hazzard **18**:216
Christina Stead **2**:42

Geeslin, Campbell
Henry Carlisle **33**:105

Geherin, David
John D. MacDonald **27**:276
Robert B. Parker **27**:364

Geherin, David J.
Joan Didion **8**:173

Gehman, Richard B.
Herman Wouk **38**:445

Gehrz, Robert D.
Franklyn M. Branley **21**:21

Geis, Richard E.
Peter Dickinson **12**:172

Geismar, Maxwell
Nelson Algren **4**:16
John Beecher **6**:48
Saul Bellow **1**:27
Cleanth Brooks **24**:107
Camilo José Cela **13**:145
Eldridge Cleaver **30**:54
James Gould Cozzens **1**:66
John Dos Passos **1**:77
William Faulkner **1**:100
William Gaddis **19**:185
Nadine Gordimer **5**:146
Ernest Hemingway **1**:142
John Hersey **1**:144
Norman Mailer **1**:187

Henry Miller **4**:350
Erich Maria Remarque **21**:332
Henry Roth **6**:471
J. D. Salinger **1**:295
William Styron **1**:329
Leon Uris **7**:490
Herman Wouk **1**:376

Gelb, Arthur
Alice Childress **12**:104

Geldrich-Leffman, Hanna
Siegfried Lenz **27**:256

Geldzahler, Henry
Andy Warhol **20**:414

Gelfant, Blanche H.
Yasunari Kawabata **9**:316
Jack Kerouac **5**:213
Jean Stafford **7**:459
James Welch **14**:558

Gellatly, Peter
C. Day Lewis **6**:128

Gellert, Roger
David Caute **29**:109

Gelpi, Albert J.
Philip Booth **23**:74
H. D. **31**:211
William Everson **14**:164
Adrienne Rich **6**:457

Geltman, Max
Arthur Koestler **8**:325
Ezra Pound **5**:349; **7**:338

Gemmil, Janet P.
Raja Rao **25**:367

Gendzier, Irene L.
David Caute **29**:113

Genêt
Dino Buzzati **36**:85
Françoise Sagan **17**:422, 423

Geng, Veronica
Francis Ford Coppola **16**:246
Paula Danziger **21**:83
Nadine Gordimer **5**:148

Geoghegan, Tom
Peter Maas **29**:304

George, Daniel
Elizabeth Jane Howard **29**:242

George, Diana L.
Lionel Trilling **9**:532

George, Donald W.
Stephen Dobyns **37**:76

George, Michael
J. B. Priestley **5**:350

Georgiou, Constantine
James D. Forman **21**:118
Philippa Pearce **21**:283

Gerald, John Bart
Robert Lowell **3**:302
Robert Stone **5**:11

Gerhardt, Lillian N.
Lloyd Alexander **35**:24
Betty Cavanna **12**:101
S. E. Hinton **30**:203
Mollie Hunter **21**:159

Geringer, Laura
Fran Arrick **30**:18
Toni Cade Bambara **19**:34
Thomas M. Disch **36**:125
Norma Fox Mazer **26**:293
Jill Paton Walsh **35**:432

Gerlach, John
Robert Bresson **16**:118

Gerlach, Larry R.
Thomas J. Fleming **37**:127

German, Howard
Iris Murdoch **15**:383

Gerould, Daniel C.
Vasily Aksenov **22**:26
Tadeusz Rózewicz **9**:463

Gerrard, Charlotte F.
Eugène Ionesco **9**:286

Gerrity, Thomas W.
Jakov Lind **27**:272

Gerrold, David
Gene Roddenberry **17**:403

Gerson, Ben
David Bowie **17**:59
Kris Kristofferson **26**:267
John Lennon and Paul
McCartney **12**:366, 377

Gerson, Villiers
Isaac Asimov **26**:35
Robert A. Heinlein **26**:161
John Wyndham **19**:474

Gersoni-Edelman, Diane
Paul Zindel **26**:471

Gersoni-Stavn, Diane
See Stavn, Diane Gersoni

Gerstein, Evelyn
Fritz Lang **20**:201

Gersten, Russell
Smokey Robinson **21**:343

Gerstenberger, Donna
Djuna Barnes **29**:26
Iris Murdoch **6**:348

Gertel, Zunilda
José Donoso **4**:128
Juan Carlos Onetti **7**:278

Gervais, Marc
Pier Paolo Pasolini **20**:260

Getz, Thomas H.
Geoffrey Hill **18**:241

Gewen, Barry
Fran Lebowitz **36**:249
Norman Mailer **39**:416
Peter Manso **39**:416
Studs Terkel **38**:428

Giacoman, Helmy F.
Alejo Carpentier **11**:97

Gianakaris, C. J.
Arthur Miller **15**:376
Peter Shaffer **37**:388

Giannaris, George
Vassilis Vassilikos **8**:524

Critic Index

Giannetti, Louis D.
Federico Fellini **16**:295

Giannone, Richard
Kurt Vonnegut, Jr. **12**:620;
22:447

Gianturo, Elio
Dino Buzzati **36**:88

Giard, Robert
Claude Chabrol **16**:169, 175

Gibb, Hugh
Thomas McGrath **28**:275

Gibbons, Boyd
James A. Michener **11**:374

Gibbons, Kathryn Gibbs
H. D. **31**:203

Gibbons, Reginald
Robert Hayden **14**:241
Czesław Miłosz **31**:266
Theodore Weiss **14**:553

Gibbs, Beverly J.
Juan Carlos Onetti **10**:374

Gibbs, Robert
Margaret Avison **2**:29
Ronald G. Everson **27**:134

Gibbs, Vernon
Jimmy Cliff **21**:62

Gibbs, Wolcott
Charles Addams **30**:12
Robert Anderson **23**:29
Sally Benson **17**:50
Garson Kanin **22**:229
George S. Kaufman **38**:264,
266, 267
Emlyn Williams **15**:576
Tennessee Williams **30**:455

Gibian, George
Varlam Shalamov **18**:478
Aleksandr I. Solzhenitsyn **7**:447

Gibson, Arthur
Ingmar Bergman **16**:62

Gibson, Donald B.
James Baldwin **3**:32
Imamu Amiri Baraka **5**:46
Ralph Ellison **3**:143
Langston Hughes **5**:19
Jean Toomer **13**:551

Gibson, Kenneth
Roch Carrier **13**:143

Gibson, Margaret
James Galvin **38**:197
Judith Wright **11**:578

Gibson, Morgan
Kenneth Rexroth **22**:343

Gibson, Shirley Mann
Marie-Claire Blais **22**:59

Giddings, Paula
Nikki Giovanni **19**:191
Margaret Walker **1**:351

Giddins, Gary
James M. Cain **28**:53
Elias Canetti **25**:114
Philip Roth **31**:341

Gide, André
Hermann Hesse **11**:270
Pär Lagerkvist **7**:199

Gidley, Mick
William Faulkner **3**:156

Gies, Judith
Frederick Busch **18**:86
André Dubus **36**:146
Gail Godwin **31**:198
Francine du Plessix Gray
22:201
Jayne Anne Phillips **33**:305
Susan Fromberg Schaeffer
22:368
Lynne Sharon Schwartz **31**:389

Gifford, Henry
Joseph Brodsky **13**:117
Marianne Moore **4**:361

Gifford, Terry
Ted Hughes **37**:175

Gifford, Thomas
Stephen King **26**:240

Gilbert, Elliot L.
Leonard Michaels **25**:315

Gilbert, Harriett
J. G. Ballard **36**:44
André Brink **36**:70
Italo Calvino **33**:98, 100
Julio Cortázar **33**:132
André Dubus **36**:148
Louise Erdrich **39**:131
Ruth Prawer Jhabvala **29**:261
David Plante **38**:371
Ntozake Shange **25**:397
J.I.M. Stewart **32**:421
D. M. Thomas **31**:435

Gilbert, James
Renata Adler **31**:13

Gilbert, Sandra M.
Maya Angelou **12**:13
Norman Dubie **36**:130
Jean Garrigue **8**:239
Sandra Hochman **8**:297
Diane Johnson **5**:200
Kenneth Koch **8**:323
Eleanor Lerman **9**:329
Audre Lorde **18**:308
Sylvia Plath **17**:361
Anne Sexton **4**:484
Kathleen Spivack **6**:521
Diane Wakoski **9**:554

Gilbert, W. Stephen
Howard Barker **37**:33
Caryl Churchill **31**:82, 84
Brian Clark **29**:126
Peter Handke **5**:163
Richard O'Brien **17**:322, 324
J. B. Priestley **5**:350
David Storey **5**:416

Gilbert, Zack
Leon Forrest **4**:164

Gilboy, J. Thomas
David Cudlip **34**:39

Gilder, Joshua
Dee Brown **18**:71
Jerzy Kosinski **15**:316
Alberto Moravia **27**:356

Gilder, Rosamond
Garson Kanin **22**:229
Clifford Odets **28**:330
Tennessee Williams **30**:458

Giles, Dennis
Jean-Luc Godard **20**:151

Giles, James R.
Richard Wright **21**:452

Giles, Mary E.
Juan Goytisolo **10**:243

Gilkes, Michael
Wilson Harris **25**:210, 211, 218

Gill, Brendan
Edward Albee **5**:12; **25**:36
Alan Ayckbourn **5**:36; **8**:34;
18:29
John Bishop **10**:54
Anne Burr **6**:104
D. L. Coburn **10**:107
Noel Coward **9**:172, 173
James Gould Cozzens **11**:126
Michael Cristofer **28**:96
Christopher Durang **27**:93
Athol Fugard **25**:174, 178
Ernest K. Gann **23**:165
Larry Gelbart **21**:128
William Gibson **23**:180
Charles Gordone **1**:125
John Guare **14**:221
Bill Gunn **5**:152
A. R. Gurney, Jr. **32**:221
Lorraine Hansberry **17**:189
Lillian Hellman **18**:227
Beth Henley **23**:216
John Hopkins **4**:233
Preston Jones **10**:296
Jean Kerr **22**:259
James Kirkwood **9**:319
Pavel Kohout **13**:323
Arthur Kopit **33**:251
Ira Levin **6**:306
David Mamet **9**:360; **34**:220
Terrence McNally **7**:219
Mark Medoff **23**:293
Arthur Miller **6**:334
Peter Nichols **5**:307; **36**:330
Clifford Odets **2**:319
John O'Hara **6**:385
Dorothy Parker **15**:414
Harold Pinter **15**:425
Roman Polanski **16**:464
Gerome Ragni and James Rado
17:388
Ronald Ribman **7**:358
William Saroyan **8**:468
Murray Schisgal **6**:490
Rod Serling **30**:354, 355
Peter Shaffer **5**:386
Sam Shepard **17**:437
Martin Sherman **19**:416
Neil Simon **6**:505; **11**:495
Isaac Bashevis Singer **15**:509
Stephen Sondheim **30**:399
Elizabeth Spencer **22**:399
John Steinbeck **5**:408
Milan Stitt **29**:390
Tom Stoppard **4**:526; **5**:413;
8:504; **15**:521; **29**:396
David Storey **2**:424
C. P. Taylor **27**:446

Lily Tomlin **17**:518
Gore Vidal **2**:449
Andy Warhol **20**:419
Thornton Wilder **35**:445
Tennessee Williams **5**:503;
8:548
August Wilson **39**:277
Lanford Wilson **7**:547
Robert Wilson **7**:550

Gill, Richard T.
Frank O'Connor **23**:325

Gillen, Francis
Donald Barthelme **2**:40

Gillespie, Beryl C.
Barbara Corcoran **17**:78

Gillespie, Bruce
Philip K. Dick **30**:121

Gillespie, John
Scott O'Dell **30**:268
Kin Platt **26**:350

Gillespie, John T.
Frank Bonham **12**:51, 55
Alice Childress **12**:107

Gillespie, Robert
Eric Ambler **6**:2
Jorge Luis Borges **6**:91
John le Carré **9**:326

Gillett, Charlie
Jimmy Cliff **21**:60

Gillett, John
Kon Ichikawa **20**:178, 180
Fritz Lang **20**:209
Yasujiro Ozu **16**:446
Satyajit Ray **16**:477
Josef von Sternberg **20**:374
Billy Wilder **20**:458

Gilliatt, Penelope
Woody Allen **16**:2, 7
Robert Altman **16**:30
Ralph Bakshi **26**:70
Samuel Beckett **4**:49
Claude Chabrol **16**:179
Shirley Clarke **16**:216
Noel Coward **9**:172
Brian De Palma **20**:76
Rainer Werner Fassbinder
20:108, 112, 114, 115
Jean-Luc Godard **20**:141
Werner Herzog **16**:326
John Huston **20**:173
Buster Keaton **20**:195
John Landis **26**:272
Richard Lester **20**:230
Monty Python **21**:224
Joe Orton **4**:387
Roman Polanski **16**:472
Satyajit Ray **16**:487
Ken Russell **16**:550
Carlos Saura **20**:317
Melvin Van Peebles **20**:409,
412
Lina Wertmüller **16**:589, 595
Vassily S. Yanovsky **18**:550

Gillis, William
Friedrich Dürrenmatt **11**:170

Gilman, Harvey
Howard Nemerov **6**:362

Gilman, Richard
Richard Adams **4**:7
Edward Albee **5**:10
John Arden **6**:6
James Baldwin **15**:41; **17**:35, 44
Imamu Amiri Baraka **5**:44
Donald Barthelme **2**:40
Samuel Beckett **29**:66
Saul Bellow **6**:49
Thomas Bernhard **32**:22
Heinrich Böll **27**:67
Eldridge Cleaver **30**:55, 68
J. P. Donleavy **6**:140
Bruce Jay Friedman **5**:126
Max Frisch **32**:192
Carlos Fuentes **22**:163
William H. Gass **2**:154
Jack Gelber **1**:114; **6**:196
Günter Grass **32**:203
Graham Greene **6**:214
A. R. Gurney, Jr. **32**:220
Woody Guthrie **35**:188
Rolf Hochhuth **11**:274
Eugène Ionesco **6**:249
Kenneth Koch **5**:218
Norman Mailer **2**:260; **8**:367
Bernard Malamud **18**:320
William Maxwell **19**:307
Michael McClure **10**:331
Arthur Miller **6**:326, 327
Marsha Norman **28**:320
Sean O'Casey **5**:319
Walker Percy **18**:399
Harold Pinter **6**:405, 406, 410
Reynolds Price **6**:424
John Rechy **7**:356
Jonathan Reynolds **38**:390
Philip Roth **3**:438; **22**:358
Howard Sackler **14**:478
Irwin Shaw **23**:398
Robert Shaw **5**:390
Neil Simon **6**:502
Susan Sontag **31**:406
George Steiner **24**:425
John Updike **2**:440
Tennessee Williams **5**:499
Edmund Wilson **24**:478
Richard Wright **21**:440

Gilmore, Mikal
Bob Marley **17**:269, 270
Lou Reed **21**:316, 320
Bruce Springsteen **17**:486
Stevie Wonder **12**:660

Gilroy, Harry
Frank B. Gilbreth, Jr. and Ernestine Gilbreth Carey **17**:153
Thor Heyerdahl **26**:189

Gilsdorf, Jeanette
Robert Creeley **4**:118

Giltrow, Janet
Marilyn R. Bowering **32**:48

Gimelson, Deborah
Frederick Barthelme **36**:51

Gindin, James
Kingsley Amis **2**:4
Saul Bellow **3**:54
Truman Capote **3**:100
Margaret Drabble **10**:165
E. M. Forster **3**:160

John Fowles **10**:189
William Golding **2**:165; **3**:198
Rosamond Lehmann **5**:238
Doris Lessing **2**:238; **22**:278
Iris Murdoch **2**:295; **3**:347
John Osborne **2**:327
Philip Roth **3**:436
Alan Sillitoe **3**:447, 448
David Storey **2**:423; **4**:528
John Wain **2**:457
Angus Wilson **2**:470; **3**:534

Gingell, S.
William Mitchell **25**:325

Gingher, Robert S.
John Updike **5**:454

Gingrich, Arnold
Chester Himes **2**:196

Ginsberg, Allen
Gregory Corso **11**:123
Jack Kerouac **2**:228; **14**:306
Ezra Pound **18**:420

Gioia, Dana
John Ashbery **25**:56
Margaret Atwood **25**:69
Joseph Brodsky **36**:79
Alfred Corn **33**:118
Thom Gunn **32**:214
Maxine Kumin **28**:225
Frederick Morgan **23**:301
Katha Pollitt **28**:368
Craig Raine **32**:354

Giovanni, Nikki
Virginia Hamilton **26**:149
Alice Walker **5**:476

Gipson, Carolyn
W.E.B. Du Bois **2**:120

Girard, René
Claude Lévi-Strauss **38**:304

Girson, Rochelle
Peter S. Beagle **7**:25

Girvin, Peter
A. J. Cronin **32**:138

Gish, Robert F.
A. B. Guthrie, Jr. **23**:200
Conrad Richter **30**:328

Gitlin, Todd
James Baldwin **2**:32
Robert Bly **2**:66
Steven Bochco and Michael Kozoll **35**:54
Bob Dylan **4**:150
Paul Goodman **7**:130
Denise Levertov **2**:243
Marge Piercy **3**:383

Gitomer, Irene
Mary Stewart **35**:390

Gitzen, Julian
Robert Bly **10**:56
Seamus Heaney **5**:172
Ted Hughes **4**:237
Denise Levertov **5**:250
Peter Redgrove **6**:446
R. S. Thomas **6**:531
Charles Tomlinson **2**:437; **4**:548
Ted Walker **13**:566

Giuliano, William
Antonio Buero Vallejo **15**:98

Givner, Joan
Katherine Anne Porter **7**:319; **10**:398; **13**:450; **15**:432
Eudora Welty **5**:479

Gladstein, Mimi R.
Ayn Rand **30**:302

Glaessner, Verina
François Truffaut **20**:404

Glanville, Brian
George Plimpton **36**:353

Glassco, John
Jane Rule **27**:418

Glasser, Perry
Kent Haruf **34**:58

Glasser, William
J. D. Salinger **8**:464

Glassman, Peter
Shirley Ann Grau **9**:240
R. G. Vliet **22**:441

Glastonbury, Marion
Isabel Allende **39**:34
Lynne Reid Banks **23**:43
John Gregory Dunne **28**:128
Max Frisch **32**:192
Russell C. Hoban **25**:264
Thomas Keneally **27**:233
Lisa St. Aubin de Teran **36**:420, 423
Martin Walser **27**:467

Glatstein, Jacob
Marianne Moore **4**:358

Glauber, Robert H.
Mary Oliver **19**:361

Glazer, Mitchell
Paul McCartney **35**:284

Gleason, George
Jean Craighead George **35**:178
Sonia Levitin **17**:266
Robert Newton Peck **17**:342

Gleason, Judith
Aimé Césaire **19**:95
Donald Hall **37**:145

Gleason, Judith Illsley
Chinua Achebe **7**:3

Gleason, Ralph J.
Nelson Algren **10**:7
Lenny Bruce **21**:43
Bob Dylan **6**:156; **12**:181
Martin Mull **17**:299
Paul Simon **17**:459

Gleicher, David
Margaret Atwood **3**:19

Glen, Duncan
Hugh MacDiarmid **4**:311

Glendinning, Victoria
Martin Amis **38**:14
Margaret Atwood **15**:38
Elizabeth Bowen **22**:64
Melvyn Bragg **10**:72
Anthony Burgess **5**:87

Angela Carter **5**:101
Bruce Chatwin **28**:72
Roald Dahl **6**:122
Anita Desai **19**:134
Zöe Fairbairns **32**:162
Elaine Feinstein **36**:169
Penelope Fitzgerald **19**:173
Thomas Flanagan **25**:164
Doris Grumbach **13**:258
James Hanley **13**:262
Chester Himes **7**:159
Russell C. Hoban **7**:160; **25**:264
Ursula Holden **18**:258
Elizabeth Jane Howard **7**:164
Alison Lurie **18**:310
Olivia Manning **19**:303
Joyce Carol Oates **11**:404
Edna O'Brien **13**:416
Barbara Pym **13**:471
Jane Rule **27**:418
Françoise Sagan **9**:468
Alan Sillitoe **6**:500
Stevie Smith **25**:420
J.I.M. Stewart **7**:466
Glendon Swarthout **35**:403
Fay Weldon **11**:565
Eudora Welty **14**:565

Glenn, Jerry
Paul Celan **10**:102, 104; **19**:89

Glenn, Jules
Anthony Shaffer **19**:414

Glick, William
Walter Farley **17**:115

Glicksberg, Charles I.
Arthur Adamov **4**:6
Kenneth Burke **24**:119
Albert Camus **1**:52
Jean Genet **5**:136
Hermann Hesse **3**:244
Aldous Huxley **3**:254
Eugène Ionesco **9**:288; **11**:290
Robinson Jeffers **3**:260
Arthur Koestler **33**:238
Joseph Wood Krutch **24**:281
André Malraux **1**:201
Kenneth Patchen **18**:392
Edmund Wilson **24**:464

Glimm, James York
Thomas Merton **3**:337; **11**:372

Gloag, Julian
Michael Frayn **31**:189

Gloster, Hugh M.
Arna Bontemps **18**:63
Jessie Redmon Fauset **19**:170
Carl Van Vechten **33**:395
Frank G. Yerby **22**:487

Glover, Al
Michael McClure **6**:320

Glover, Elaine
John Fowles **6**:188
Nadine Gordimer **7**:131
Joseph Heller **8**:279
Tim O'Brien **7**:271

Glover, Tony
Chuck Berry **17**:53
Waylon Jennings **21**:202
Patti Smith **12**:534

Critic Index

Glover, Willis B.
J.R.R. Tolkien **1**:340

Glusman, John A.
Stephen Wright **33**:468

Goatley, James L.
Roy A. Gallant **17**:132

Gobeil, Madeleine
Marie-Claire Blais **22**:60

Godard, B.
Audrey Thomas **13**:540

Godard, Barbara
Audrey Thomas **37**:420

Goddard, Donald
Lothar-Günther Buchheim
6:102

Goddard, Rosalind K.
Milton Meltzer **26**:301

Godden, Rumer
Kamala Markandaya **38**:320,
321
Carson McCullers **12**:418

Godfrey, Dave
Joan Barfoot **18**:35
Hugh MacLennan **14**:343

Godsell, Geoffrey
Allen Drury **37**:100

Godshalk, William L.
Kurt Vonnegut, Jr. **3**:500

Godwin, Gail
Beryl Bainbridge **5**:39
Ann Beattie **13**:64
Julien Green **3**:205
Doris Grumbach **13**:258
Shirley Hazzard **18**:220
Joy Williams **31**:461
Vassily S. Yanovsky **18**:552

Goetz, David R.
William Mastrosimone **36**:291

Goetz, Ronald
Larry Gelbart **21**:128

Goetz-Stankiewicz, Marketa
Václav Havel **25**:225, 229

Going, William T.
T. S. Stribling **23**:448

Goitein, Denise
Nathalie Sarraute **10**:457

Gold, Arthur R.
Arthur A. Cohen **31**:92

Gold, Herbert
Mel Brooks **12**:78
Richard Condon **10**:111
John Dos Passos **4**:136
Doris Grumbach **22**:205
Alistair MacLean **13**:364
James Purdy **28**:376
Aleksandr I. Solzhenitsyn **2**:409
Terry Southern **7**:454
Gore Vidal **6**:550
Donald E. Westlake **33**:440

Gold, Ivan
Pat Barker **32**:13
R. V. Cassill **23**:106
John Ehle **27**:107
Shusaku Endo **14**:162
Richard Grayson **38**:211
Barry Hannah **38**:232
George V. Higgins **10**:273
Paul Horgan **9**:279
Evan Hunter **31**:225
Jerzy Kosinski **15**:316
Kenzaburō Ōe **36**:348
Frederic Raphael **14**:437
Ishmael Reed **32**:360
Susan Fromberg Schaeffer
22:369
Robert Stone **23**:424
John Updike **2**:440
John A. Williams **13**:599
Sloan Wilson **32**:447
Helen Yglesias **7**:558

Gold, Pat
Taylor Caldwell **28**:68
Thomas J. Fleming **37**:128

Gold, Peter
José María Arguedas **18**:5

Gold, Renee
Marge Piercy **27**:378

Gold, Richard
Jim Carroll **35**:80

Gold, Sylviane
Peter Nichols **36**:333
Lanford Wilson **36**:465

Goldberg, Isaac
Gregorio López y Fuentes
32:278

Goldberg, Joe
Neil Diamond **30**:112

Goldberg, Michael
Jim Carroll **35**:80
The Clash **30**:46
Prince **35**:328

Goldberg, Steven
Bob Dylan **6**:154

Goldberg, Vicki
Paul Theroux **11**:530

Goldberger, Judith
Marilyn Sachs **35**:334

Golden, Bernette
Kristin Hunter **35**:226

Golden, Dorothy S.
Josephine Humphreys **34**:66

Golden, Robert E.
Thomas Pynchon **3**:409

Goldensohn, Lorrie
Ben Belitt **22**:54
Norman Dubie **36**:131, 135
Albert Goldbarth **38**:201
Ira Sadoff **9**:466
Maura Stanton **9**:508

Goldfarb, Clare R.
Aleksandr I. Solzhenitsyn **7**:443

Goldhurst, William
John Steinbeck **21**:378

Goldknopf, David
Kurt Vonnegut, Jr. **12**:600

Goldman, Albert
Lenny Bruce **21**:45, 53
Bob Dylan **3**:130; **12**:186
John Lennon and Paul
McCartney **12**:367
John Nichols **38**:337

Goldman, Arnold
Amos Tutuola **29**:435

Goldman, Eric F.
John Steinbeck **21**:370
Dalton Trumbo **19**:445

Goldman, Mark
Bernard Malamud **1**:197

Goldman, Merle
Jules Archer **12**:19

Goldman, Michael
Joyce Carol Oates **3**:361

Goldman, Rowena
Howard Barker **37**:36
Snoo Wilson **33**:465

Goldman, Vivien
Jimmy Cliff **21**:64

Goldman, William
Ross Macdonald **1**:185

Goldmann, Lucien
Witold Gombrowicz **11**:239
Georg Lukács **24**:324

Goldsmith, Arnold L.
Leslie A. Fiedler **24**:203
John Steinbeck **9**:515
Morris L. West **33**:429

Goldsmith, Barbara
Norman Mailer **39**:418
Peter Manso **39**:418

Goldsmith, Claire K.
Alvin Silverstein and Virginia
B. Silverstein **17**:455

Goldsmith, David H.
Kurt Vonnegut, Jr. **4**:562

Goldstein, Eric
Susan Cheever **18**:102

Goldstein, Laurence
Robert Frost **13**:230
Edwin Honig **33**:212, 213
David Ignatow **4**:248
Adrienne Rich **7**:372
James Wright **3**:541

Goldstein, Malcolm
Thornton Wilder **1**:365

Goldstein, Marilyn
Milton Meltzer **26**:298

Goldstein, Patrick
Elvis Costello **21**:69

Goldstein, Rebecca
Mary-Ann Tirone Smith **39**:99

Goldstein, Richard
Bob Dylan **3**:130; **12**:182
John Lennon and Paul
McCartney **12**:357
Edmund White III **27**:480

Goldstein, Toby
The Clash **30**:43
Jonathan Kozol **17**:252
Paul McCartney **35**:286
Jim Morrison **17**:294

Goldstone, Richard H.
Thornton Wilder **6**:574

Goldwasser, Noë
Smokey Robinson **21**:345

Golffing, Francis
Salvatore Quasimodo **10**:429

Gomez, Joseph A.
Ken Russell **16**:550

Gömöri, George
Tadeusz Konwicki **28**:207
László Nagy **7**:251

Goodenough, Ward
Margaret Mead **37**:285

Goodfellow, Patricia
A. J. Cronin **32**:141

Goodfield, June
Ronald J. Glasser **37**:133

Goodfriend, James
Laura Nyro **17**:314

Goodheart, Eugene
John Fowles **33**:175
F. R. Leavis **24**:311
Cynthia Ozick **3**:372
Theodore Roethke **1**:292
John Seelye **7**:405
William Carlos Williams **5**:510

Goodman, Charlotte
Joyce Carol Oates **15**:400

Goodman, Ellen
Maureen Daly **17**:91

Goodman, Henry
Elia Kazan **16**:367

Goodman, James
George Seferis **5**:385

Goodman, Jan M.
Lois Duncan **26**:107

Goodman, Joseph
John Edgar Wideman **36**:452

Goodman, Lord
John Mortimer **28**:288

Goodman, Paul
James Baldwin **17**:23
Ernest Hemingway **1**:144

Goodman, Robert L.
David Kherdian **6**:280

Goodman, Walter
Thomas Berger **8**:83
Peter Handke **38**:226
Josephine Herbst **34**:450
Elinor Langer **34**:450

Goodrich, Norma L.
Jean Giono **4**:187; **11**:230

Goodrick, Susan
Robert Crumb **17**:86

Goodsell, James Nelson
Jules Archer **12**:18
Allan W. Eckert **17**:106, 107
Piri Thomas **17**:498

Goodstein, Jack
Alain Robbe-Grillet **2**:376

Goodwin, June
Laurence Yep **35**:468

Goodwin, Michael
Chuck Berry **17**:51
John Brunner **10**:80
Samuel R. Delany **14**:143
Joanna Russ **15**:461
Andy Warhol **20**:420

Goodwin, Polly
Honor Arundel **17**:12
Eilís Dillon **17**:94
James D. Forman **21**:117
Lee Kingman **17**:245
Emily Cheney Neville **12**:450
Zoa Sherburne **30**:361
Barbara Wersba **30**:430

Goodwin, Stephen
Eleanor Clark **19**:108
Ella Leffland **19**:280
Leonard Michaels **25**:317
Walker Percy **2**:335
Peter Taylor **1**:334
John Kennedy Toole **19**:442

Goodwyn, Larry
Larry McMurtry **27**:328

Goodyear, Russell H.
Robin F.Brancato **35**:69

Gooneratne, Yasmine
Ruth Prawer Jhabvala **29**:259

Gordimer, Nadine
Chinua Achebe **3**:2
Simone de Beauvoir **14**:67
Breyten Breytenbach **37**:48
J. M. Coetzee **33**:109
V. S. Naipaul **4**:372
James Ngugi **3**:358
Alan Paton **25**:359, 362
Wole Soyinka **36**:414

Gordon, Andrew
Ishmael Reed **2**:368

Gordon, Caroline
Flannery O'Connor **15**:411;
21:255

Gordon, Cecelia
Ruth M. Arthur **12**:27

Gordon, David
Margaret Drabble **22**:121

Gordon, David J.
Herbert Gold **4**:192
William Golding **1**:122
Uwe Johnson **5**:200
Maxine Kumin **28**:221
Brian Moore **1**:225
Vladimir Nabokov **1**:245
Tom Stoppard **1**:328

Gordon, Giles
Caryl Churchill **31**:90
Simon Gray **36**:210

Gordon, Jaimy
Richard Grayson **38**:212
David Plante **38**:369

Gordon, Jan B.
Richard Adams **5**:4
John Braine **3**:86
Doris Lessing **6**:292
Iris Murdoch **3**:349

Gordon, Lenore
Sandra Scoppettone **26**:402

Gordon, Leonard A.
Ved Mehta **37**:292

Gordon, Leonore
Norma Fox Mazer **26**:293

Gordon, Lois
Donald Barthelme **23**:49
Arthur Miller **26**:322

Gordon, Mary
Diane Johnson **13**:306
Maxine Hong Kingston **19**:249
Mary McCarthy **14**:359; **39**:490
Edna O'Brien **13**:416; **36**:339
Walker Percy **18**:401
David Plante **23**:346

Gordon, Philip
Ayn Rand **30**:300

Gorman, Herbert
Taylor Caldwell **28**:57

Gornick, Vivian
Rosellen Brown **32**:70
J. M. Coetzee **33**:111
Paula Fox **2**:140
Nadine Gordimer **18**:190
Doris Grumbach **22**:205
Lillian Hellman **8**:282; **18**:227
Jonathan Kozol **17**:253
Phillip Lopate **29**:298
Alberto Moravia **18**:347
Grace Paley **4**:391
Marge Piercy **18**:407
David Plante **38**:368
Anne Tyler **28**:432
Gregor von Rezzori **25**:384
Helen Yglesias **22**:494

Gorra, Michael
Pat Barker **32**:13
Thomas Berger **38**:40
T. Coraghessan Boyle **36**:62
Bernard Mac Laverty **31**:257
Jayne Anne Phillips **33**:307
David Plante **38**:366
Anthony Powell **31**:319
Barbara Pym **37**:375
Salman Rushdie **31**:360
Lynne Sharon Schwartz **31**:392

Gose, Elliot
Marie-Claire Blais **13**:96
Gwendolyn MacEwan **13**:357

Goskowski, Francis
Rosa Guy **26**:146
Andrea Lee **36**:257

Gosse, Van
The Clash **30**:48

Gossett, Louise Y.
William Goyen **14**:209
Flannery O'Connor **1**:256

Gossman, Ann
Lawrence Durrell **1**:87
Iris Murdoch **15**:387

Gostnell, David
Alvin Silverstein and Virginia
B. Silverstein **17**:456

Gott, Richard
Carlos Castaneda **12**:86

Gottesman, Ronald
Frederick Karl **34**:553

Gottfried, Martin
Enid Bagnold **25**:78
Gretchen Cryer **21**:79
Charles Fuller **25**:180
William Gibson **23**:179
John Guare **14**:222; **29**:204
A. R. Gurney, Jr. **32**:216, 217
Peter Handke **38**:217
Lorraine Hansberry **17**:189
Jean Kerr **22**:257
Peter Luke **38**:314
Bernard Pomerance **13**:445
Howard Sackler **14**:479
Ntozake Shange **25**:396
Sam Shepard **17**:436
Neil Simon **31**:395
Stephen Sondheim **30**:380, 381,
383, 388, 389
Milan Stitt **29**:389
George Tabori **19**:438
Michel Tremblay **29**:418
Andrew Lloyd Webber and Tim
Rice **21**:425, 431
Tennessee Williams **30**:469
Lanford Wilson **7**:547

Gottlieb, Annie
Maya Angelou **12**:11
Henry Bromell **5**:74
Anita Brookner **32**:59
Marian Engel **36**:158
Louis-Ferdinand Céline **4**:104
Lois Gould **10**:241
Nat Hentoff **26**:186
Charles Johnson **7**:183
Stephen King **37**:203
Joyce Maynard **23**:288
Gloria Naylor **28**:305
Tillie Olsen **4**:386
Sandra Scoppettone **26**:401,
404
Lee Smith **25**:408

Gottlieb, Elaine
Isaac Bashevis Singer **6**:507

Gottlieb, Gerald
Russell Baker **31**:26
Jean Craighead George **35**:176
John R. Tunis **12**:599
Maia Wojciechowska **26**:452

Gottschalk, Jane
Ralph Ellison **11**:181

Gotz, David M.
Pink Floyd **35**:316

Gould, Gerald
Edna Ferber **18**:150

Gould, Jack
John Lennon and Paul
McCartney **12**:354

Gould, Jean
Elmer Rice **7**:363

Gould, Lois
Paddy Chayefsky **23**:119

Gould, Stephen Jay
John McPhee **36**:298

Goulianos, Joan Rodman
Lawrence Durrell **8**:193

Govan, Sandra Y.
Samuel R. Delany **38**:160

Govier, Katharine
Marian Engel **36**:163

Gow, Gordon
Lindsay Anderson **20**:18
Michelangelo Antonioni **20**:40
John Cassavetes **20**:45
Claude Chabrol **16**:170
René Clair **20**:66
Vittorio De Sica **20**:88, 91
Bob Fosse **20**:125
George Roy Hill **26**:200, 204
Alfred Hitchcock **16**:353
John Huston **20**:168
Elia Kazan **16**:374
Peter Nichols **36**:328
Nagisa Oshima **20**:246
Sidney Poitier **26**:358
Satyajit Ray **16**:479
Alain Resnais **16**:510
Ken Russell **16**:542, 543
Jerzy Skolimowski **20**:352
Steven Spielberg **20**:359
C. P. Taylor **27**:442
Agnès Varda **16**:555
Peter Weir **20**:428
Orson Welles **20**:439, 452

Gower, Herschel
Peter Taylor **18**:525

Goyen, William
Truman Capote **19**:81
Peter Matthiessen **32**:285
Anaïs Nin **4**:379

Goytisolo, Juan
Carlos Fuentes **10**:204

Grace, Sherrill
Margaret Atwood **25**:64

Grace, William J.
T. H. White **30**:440, 441

Grady, R. F., S.J.
Mary Stewart **35**:393

Grady, Wayne
Matt Cohen **19**:116
Ralph Gustafson **36**:221
Farley Mowat **26**:347
Audrey Thomas **37**:423

Graff, Gerald
Geoffrey H. Hartman **27**:185

Graff, Gerald E.
Donald Barthelme **6**:30
Saul Bellow **6**:54
Stanley Elkin **6**:169
Norman Mailer **8**:372
I. A. Richards **24**:394

Graham, Desmond
Jorge Luis Borges **8**:103
Breyten Breytenbach **23**:84
James Hanley **13**:262
Anthony Hecht **13**:269
Philip Larkin **5**:229
Robert Lowell **11**:329
John Montague **13**:392
Eugenio Montale **9**:388
Edwin Morgan **31**:274
Linda Pastan **27**:370
Peter Porter **13**:453

Graham, John
John Hawkes **3**:221
Ernest Hemingway **3**:236
Gibbons Ruark **3**:441

Graham, Kenneth
Richard Adams **5**:5
Eva Figes **31**:162
Pamela Hansford Johnson **27**:221
Yashar Kemal **29**:265
Kamala Markandaya **38**:324
Laurens Van der Post **5**:463

Graham, Maryemma
Frank G. Yerby **22**:491

Graham-Yooll, Andrew
Gabriel García Márquez **15**:253

Grahn, Judy
Alta **19**:19

Granahan, Paul
Piers Anthony **35**:37
C. J. Cherryh **35**:113
Arthur C. Clarke **35**:129
Gene Wolfe **25**:477

Granahan, Tom
Heberto Padilla **38**:354

Grande, Brother Luke M., F.S.C.
Marion Montgomery **7**:232

Granetz, Marc
Donald Barthelme **13**:61
John Gardner **18**:183
Sloan Wilson **32**:448

Granfield, Linda
Kevin Major **26**:286

Grange, Joseph
Carlos Castaneda **12**:86

Grant, Annette
Shirley Ann Grau **4**:209
Edward Hoagland **28**:180

Grant, Damian
W. H. Auden **6**:17
Seamus Heaney **5**:172
Sylvia Plath **2**:337
Peter Porter **5**:347

Grant, Joy
Elizabeth Taylor **29**:411

Grant, Judith Skelton
Robertson Davies **13**:173

Grant, Patrick
Robert Graves **11**:257

Grant, Roberta
Molly Giles **39**:65

Grant, Steve
Howard Barker **37**:36, 39
Howard Brenton **31**:64
David Hare **29**:216
Stephen Poliakoff **38**:383
C. P. Taylor **27**:441
Snoo Wilson **33**:461

Grau, Shirley Ann
William Goyen **8**:250
Marion Montgomery **7**:233

Graustark, Barbara
Jim Carroll **35**:79

Grave, Elizabeth F.
Franklyn M. Branley **21**:16

Gravel, George E.
Joanne Greenberg **30**:160

Graver, Lawrence
Samuel Beckett **6**:40
Doris Lessing **2**:242
Carson McCullers **1**:209
Iris Murdoch **3**:347
Gilbert Sorrentino **22**:392
Muriel Spark **2**:417
Paul Theroux **8**:513
William Trevor **7**:475

Graves, Elizabeth Minot
Lee Kingman **17**:246
Sonia Levitin **17**:263
Zilpha Keatley Snyder **17**:471

Graves, Peter
Jurek Becker **19**:36
Christa Wolf **14**:595

Graves, Peter J.
Friedrich Dürrenmatt **15**:196

Graves, Robert
Robert Frost **26**:121
Yevgeny Yevtushenko **1**:382

Graves, Tom
Stephen Wright **33**:469

Grawe, Christian
Botho Strauss **22**:407

Gray, Francine du Plessix
Oriana Fallaci **11**:190
Max Frisch **14**:184
Mary Gordon **22**:184
Stratis Haviaras **33**:203

Gray, Hildagarde
C. S. Adler **35**:12
Gunnel Beckman **26**:89
Jay Bennett **35**:45
Robin F. Brancato **35**:67
Lois Duncan **26**:105
Norma Fox Mazer **26**:289
Katherine Paterson **12**:485

Gray, J. Glenn
Martin Heidegger **24**:263

Gray, James
Pearl S. Buck **7**:32
August Derleth **31**:130, 132
Ralph Gustafson **36**:213
Jules Roains **7**:381
Henri Troyat **23**:459

Gray, John
Paul Bowles **2**:79

Gray, Mrs. John G.
Jules Archer **12**:20
Jean Craighead George **35**:178
M. E. Kerr **12**:298

Gray, Larry
John Knowles **26**:262

Gray, Paul
Lisa Alther **7**:12
Roger Angell **26**:30
Samuel Beckett **6**:44
Adolfo Bioy Casares **8**:94
Vance Bourjaily **8**:104
Jimmy Breslin **4**:76
William F. Buckley, Jr. **7**:35
James Carroll **38**:107
Alex Comfort **7**:54
Evan S. Connell, Jr. **6**:116
Peter De Vries **7**:78
Pete Dexter **34**:45
Thomas M. Disch **7**:86
Scott Elledge **34**:427
Carolyn Forché **25**:170
John Gardner **5**:132
William H. Gass **8**:246
Joanne Greenberg **30**:165
Russell C. Hoban **7**:160
Maureen Howard **5**:189
John Irving **38**:253
Elia Kazan **6**:274
William Kennedy **28**:206
Stephen King **26**:242
Maxine Hong Kingston **12**:312
Norman Mailer **28**:259
Bernard Malamud **27**:307
Peter Matthiessen **5**:274
Ted Mooney **25**:329
V. S. Naipaul **7**:253
Seán O'Faoláin **7**:274
Cynthia Ozick **7**:288
Reynolds Price **6**:425
Gregor von Rezzori **25**:385
Marilynne Robinson **25**:386
Robert Stone **5**:409
Julian Symons **32**:428
John Updike **5**:457
Sylvia Townsend Warner **19**:459
James Welch **6**:561
Fay Weldon **6**:562
Morris L. West **33**:431
William Wharton **37**:437
E. B. White **34**:427

Gray, Paul Edward
Agatha Christie **39**:441
Eleanor Clark **19**:106
Bret Easton Ellis **39**:57
John Fowles **1**:109
Janet Morgan **39**:441
Iris Murdoch **1**:236
Joyce Carol Oates **1**:251
Bob Shacochis **39**:200
Eudora Welty **1**:363
E. B. White **39**:377

Gray, Richard
Erskine Caldwell **14**:96
Truman Capote **38**:85
Donald Davidson **19**:124
William Faulkner **11**:202
Carson McCullers **12**:430
John Crowe Ransom **11**:469
William Styron **11**:520

Tennessee Williams **11**:577

Gray, Ronald
Heinrich Böll **9**:112

Grayden, Robin
Waylon Jennings **21**:204
Kris Kristofferson **26**:270

Greacen, Robert
W. H. Auden **3**:25
Samuel Beckett **4**:50
Margaret Drabble **2**:117
Bernard Kops **4**:274
Doris Lessing **3**:287
Norman MacCaig **36**:287
Harold Robbins **5**:378
Isaac Bashevis Singer **3**:457
Vassilis Vassilikos **4**:551

Grealish, Gerald
Gilbert Sorrentino **14**:498

Grebanier, Bernard
Thornton Wilder **1**:365

Grebstein, Sheldon Norman
Nelson Algren **33**:12
Ernest Hemingway **3**:235
Bernard Malamud **11**:348
John O'Hara **1**:261

Grecco, Stephen
Howard Brenton **31**:69

Greco, Mike
Ralph Bakshi **26**:75

Greeley, Andrew M.
Richard Bach **14**:36
William X. Kienzle **25**:276
Francine du Plessix Gray **22**:199

Green, Alan
Peter De Vries **3**:126
Michael Frayn **3**:164

Green, Benny
August Derleth **31**:139
John Fowles **6**:186
Compton Mackenzie **18**:316
Brian Moore **7**:238
V. S. Naipaul **18**:359
John O'Hara **6**:383
S. J. Perelman **15**:417
Charles M. Schulz **12**:533
Noel Streatfeild **21**:417
Julian Symons **32**:427

Green, Calvin
Pier Paolo Pasolini **20**:264
Eric Rohmer **16**:529

Green, Dorothy
Christina Stead **32**:409

Green, Gerald
Thomas Berger **3**:63

Green, Graham
A. J. Cronin **32**:132

Green, Harris
Jim Jacobs and Warren Casey **12**:293

Green, James L.
John Hawkes **14**:237

Green, Jim
Ray Davies **21**:103

Green, Kate
Anne Sexton **15**:473

Green, Laurence
Joan Micklin Silver **20**:342

Green, Marc
Robert Altman **16**:43

Green, Martin
Malcolm Bradbury **32**:53
E. L. Doctorow **6**:138
B. S. Johnson **6**:263
Doris Lessing **15**:333
Anthony Powell **31**:315
Philip Roth **15**:449
J. D. Salinger **1**:298

Green, Michelle
Joyce Maynard **23**:289

Green, Paul
Eric Bentley **24**:47

Green, Peter
William Golding **17**:162
R. K. Narayan **28**:301
Gore Vidal **22**:433

Green, Philip
E. E. Cummings **12**:147

Green, Randall
John Hawkes **4**:217
Aleksandr I. Solzhenitsyn **4**:512

Green, Robert J.
Roch Carrier **13**:141
Athol Fugard **9**:233

Green, Robin
Stan Lee **17**:257

Green, Roger Lancelyn
Alan Garner **17**:135

Green, Roland
Piers Anthony **35**:41
Isaac Asimov **26**:58
Marion Zimmer Bradley **30**:29, 32
Robert Holdstock **39**:153
Roger Zelazny **21**:478

Green, Timothy
W. H. Auden **14**:27

Greenberg, Clement
Arthur Koestler **33**:231

Greenberg, Joanne
Colleen McCullough **27**:321

Greenberg, Judith L.
Patrick Modiano **18**:338

Greenberg, Martin
Reiner Kunze **10**:310

Greenberg, Martin Harry
Robert A. Heinlein **26**:170

Greenblatt, Stephen Jay
Evelyn Waugh **13**:585

Greenburg, Dan
Roy Blount, Jr. **38**:47

Greene, A. C.
Jim Harrison **33**:200

Greene, Daniel
Don L. Lee **2**:237

Greene, Daniel St. Albin
William Kennedy **28**:203

Greene, Douglas G.
Edmund Crispin **22**:111

Greene, George
Paul West **7**:522

Greene, Graham
Sally Benson **17**:47
Frank Capra **16**:154, 155
R. K. Narayan **28**:299

Greene, James
Eugenio Montale **9**:388

Greene, Naomi
Simone de Beauvoir **31**:36

Greene, Robert W.
René Char **14**:124
Francis Ponge **18**:417
Raymond Queneau **10**:430

Greene, Ronald
Kim Stanley Robinson **34**:105

Greenfeld, Josh
Emily Cheney Neville **12**:451
Philip Roth **2**:378
Paul Zindel **6**:586

Greenfield, Jeff
Art Buchwald **33**:94
Jonathan Kozol **17**:255
John Lennon and Paul
McCartney **12**:378
Dan Wakefield **7**:503

Greenfield, Jerome
A. B. Yehoshua **31**:468

Greenfield, Robert
Bernice Rubens **31**:352

Greenland, Colin
J. G. Ballard **36**:44
William Gibson **39**:140
Robert Holdstock **39**:152

Greenlaw, M. Jean
John Knowles **26**:265
Suzanne Newton **35**:301
Mary Stewart **35**:397
Laurence Yep **35**:473

Greenman, Myron
Donald Barthelme **6**:29

Greenspan, Miriam
Maxine Hong Kingston **12**:313

Greenspun, Roger
Bernardo Bertolucci **16**:94
Brian De Palma **20**:74
Marguerite Duras **20**:98
Federico Fellini **16**:283
Bob Fosse **20**:122
Alfred Hitchcock **16**:354
Akira Kurosawa **16**:404
Fritz Lang **20**:211
Jean Renoir **20**:303
Carlos Saura **20**:314, 315
Jerzy Skolimowski **20**:349, 353

Melvin Van Peebles **20**:411

Greenstein, Michael
Dorothy Livesay **15**:342

Greenway, John
Woody Guthrie **35**:183, 186
Norman Mailer **2**:262
Joseph Wambaugh **18**:532

Greenwell, Bill
John Cheever **25**:122
Evan Hunter **31**:226
Bette Pesetsky **28**:358
Lynne Sharon Schwartz **31**:389
Christina Stead **32**:413

Greenwell, Scott L.
Mari Sandoz **28**:405

Greenwood, Gillian
Howard Barker **37**:35
Jayne Anne Phillips **33**:308

Greenya, John R.
Ronald L. Fair **18**:139
Budd Schulberg **7**:403

Gregerson, Linda
Sharon Olds **39**:189
Mary Oliver **34**:248

Greggs, R.
Robert Westall **17**:559

Gregor, Ian
William Golding **27**:165
Graham Greene **6**:214

Gregor, Ulrich
Leni Riefenstahl **16**:521

Gregory, Charles
Robert Altman **16**:27

Gregory, Helen
Betty Cavanna **12**:103
H. D. **31**:202

Gregory, Hilda
Joyce Carol Oates **1**:251; **2**:315
Mark Strand **6**:522
Nancy Willard **7**:540

Gregory, Horace
Morley Callaghan **14**:99
H. D. **31**:202
Laura Riding **7**:373

Gregory, Kristiana
Kim Stanley Robinson **34**:107

Gregory, Sister M., O.P.
Shelagh Delaney **29**:146

Greider, William
William Safire **10**:447

Greiling, Franziska Lynne
John Knowles **26**:256

Greiner, Donald J.
Djuna Barnes **8**:48
Frederick Busch **10**:91
Robert Frost **26**:127
John Hawkes **1**:138; **4**:213; **7**:145; **27**:192
John Updike **23**:472
Kurt Vonnegut, Jr. **3**:499

Grella, George
Ian Fleming **3**:158
Dashiell Hammett **19**:197

Grene, Marjorie
Jacques Derrida **24**:135
Martin Heidegger **24**:270

Grenier, Cynthia
Satyajit Ray **16**:476
Helen Hooven Santmyer **33**:361

Gresham, William Lindsay
Edward Hoagland **28**:179

Gretlund, Jan Nordby
Katherine Anne Porter **27**:402

Grier, Edward F.
Jonathan Williams **13**:600

Grier, Peter
Fran Lebowitz **36**:249
Tom Wolfe **35**:460

Griffin, Bryan
John Irving **13**:27

Griffin, Robert J.
Cid Corman **9**:169

Griffith, Albert J.
Carson McCullers **1**:209
Peter Taylor **1**:334; **4**:542; **18**:526
John Updike **5**:455

Griffiths, Eric
William Empson **34**:540

Griffiths, Gareth
Ayi Kwei Armah **33**:25

Grigg, John
Ved Mehta **37**:292

Grigsby, Gordon K.
Kenneth Rexroth **1**:284

Grigsby John L.
Frank Herbert **23**:222

Grigson, Geoffrey
G. B. Edwards **25**:152
Yasunari Kawabata **18**:280
Robert Lowell **3**:302
Kathleen Raine **7**:351
George Steiner **24**:431

Grillo, Jean Bergantini
Steven Bochco and Michael
Kozoll **35**:50

Grimes, Ann
Joyce Maynard **23**:289

Grimes, William
Alexander Kaletski **39**:73

Grimwood, Michael
William Faulkner **14**:174

Griswold, Jerry
Ken Kesey **3**:268

Groberg, Nancy
Mark Harris **19**:199

Groden, Michael
William Faulkner **9**:198

Gropper, Esther C.
Hermann Hesse **2**:189; **3**:244

Grosholz, Emily
  Donald Davie **31**:124
  Richard F. Hugo **18**:264
  Mary Oliver **19**:363
  Dave Smith **22**:388

Gross, Amy
  Lily Tomlin **17**:516

Gross, Barry
  Arthur Miller **10**:344

Gross, Beverly
  John Barth **14**:49
  Jonathan Baumbach **6**:32
  Saul Bellow **2**:52
  B. H. Friedman **7**:109
  Peter Spielberg **6**:514

Gross, Harvey
  T. S. Eliot **6**:161
  André Malraux **4**:335
  Ezra Pound **4**:414

Gross, John
  Martin Amis **38**:18
  Louise Bogan **39**:384
  Breyten Breytenbach **37**:50
  Anita Brookner **34**:138
  Agatha Christie **39**:439
  Anita Desai **37**:72
  William Empson **34**:336, 538
  D. J. Enright **31**:155
  Elizabeth Frank **39**:384
  Janet Morgan **39**:439
  Ezra Pound **34**:506
  V. S. Pritchett **15**:441
  George Steiner **24**:426
  E. Fuller Torrey **34**:506
  A. N. Wilson **33**:457
  Marguerite Yourcenar **38**:461

Gross, Leonard
  Michael Cristofer **28**:97

Gross, Michael
  David Bowie **17**:62

Gross, Theodore L.
  J. D. Salinger **1**:300

Grosskurth, Phyllis
  Margaret Atwood **2**:20
  Mavis Gallant **38**:189
  Mary McCarthy **24**:349
  Gabrielle Roy **14**:463

Grossman, Edward
  Simone de Beauvoir **2**:44
  Saul Bellow **8**:80
  Thomas Berger **3**:63
  Heinrich Böll **3**:75
  Joseph Heller **5**:181
  Doris Lessing **3**:287
  Vladimir Nabokov **3**:355
  Kurt Vonnegut, Jr. **5**:466

Grossman, Elizabeth
  Zöe Fairbairns **32**:163

Grossman, Jan
  Václav Havel **25**:219

Grossman, Jill
  William Kotzwinkle **35**:259

Grossman, Joel
  Philip Roth **9**:459

Grossman, Loyd
  Pink Floyd **35**:306
  Peter Townshend **17**:536

Grossman, William L.
  João Guimarães Rosa **23**:349

Grossvogel, David I.
  Agatha Christie **12**:127
  Julio Cortázar **10**:112
  Jean Genet **14**:196

Groth, Janet
  John Cheever **8**:136

Groves, Margaret
  Nathalie Sarraute **4**:470

Gruen, John
  Charles Addams **30**:15

Grumbach, Doris
  Maya Angelou **12**:12
  Simone de Beauvoir **4**:49
  Kay Boyle **5**:66
  Frederick Busch **18**:85
  Hortense Calisher **8**:124
  R. V. Cassill **23**:109
  Arthur A. Cohen **7**:50
  Joan Didion **8**:175
  E. L. Doctorow **6**:131
  Daphne du Maurier **11**:164
  Stanley Elkin **4**:154; **14**:158
  Marian Engel **36**:162
  Leslie A. Fiedler **13**:214
  Nadine Gordimer **18**:188
  Francine du Plessix Gray
    22:201
  Stratis Haviaras **33**:204
  Susan B. Hill **4**:288
  Maureen Howard **5**:188
  Ward S. Just **27**:228
  Garson Kanin **22**:232
  Alison Lurie **4**:307
  Cormac McCarthy **4**:342
  Mary McCarthy **5**:276
  Margaret Mead **37**:282
  A. G. Mojtabai **9**:385
  Brian Moore **5**:297
  Penelope Mortimer **5**:299
  John Nichols **38**:343
  Tim O'Brien **19**:357
  Julia O'Faolain **6**:383
  Aldo Palazzeschi **11**:431
  Bette Pesetsky **28**:359
  Jayne Anne Phillips **15**:421
  Judith Rossner **9**:457
  J. R. Salamanca **4**:461
  May Sarton **4**:471; **14**:480
  Ntozake Shange **38**:392
  Clancy Sigal **7**:425
  Henri Troyat **23**:458
  Anne Tyler **7**:479
  John Updike **15**:546
  Nancy Willard **7**:538, 539
  Hilma Wolitzer **17**:561, 564
  Helen Yglesias **22**:492
  Sol Yurick **6**:584

Grunfeld, Frederick V.
  John Lennon and Paul
    McCartney **12**:361

Grunwald, Beverly
  Maureen Daly **17**:90

Grunwald, Henry
  Jaroslav Seifert **34**:259

Gubar, Susan
  H. D. **14**:225

Gubbins, Bill
  Brian Wilson **12**:648

Guerard, Albert, Jr.
  C. S. Lewis **27**:259

Guerard, Albert J.
  Donald Barthelme **5**:53
  Jerome Charyn **5**:103
  John Hawkes **2**:183; **3**:222;
    15:278; **27**:190
  Alfred Kazin **38**:274
  Ayn Rand **30**:293

Guereschi, Edward
  Joyce Carol Oates **15**:403
  Glendon Swarthout **35**:404
  Guernsey, Bruce **Thomas W.**
    Shapcott:38

  403 **Guernsey, Otis L., Jr.**
  Sally Benson **17**:49

Guerrard, Philip
  Mervyn Peake **7**:301

Guggenheim, Michel
  Françoise Sagan **17**:421

Guicharnaud, Jacques
  Arthur Adamov **25**:13
  Fernando Arrabal **18**:16
  Jacques Audiberti **38**:22
  Michel de Ghelderode **11**:226
  Eugène Ionesco **6**:254
  Henri de Montherlant **19**:326
  Jean-Paul Sartre **1**:304
  Claude Simon **15**:485

Guicharnaud, June
  Michel de Ghelderode **11**:226

Guidry, Frederick H.
  Thor Heyerdahl **26**:193

Guild, Nicholas
  Paul Theroux **11**:530
  Richard Yates **23**:480

Guillory, Daniel L.
  Josephine Miles **34**:244

Guimond, James
  Gilbert Sorrentino **3**:461

Guinn, John
  Andrew M. Greeley **28**:178

Guiton, Margaret Otis
  Louis Aragon **3**:12
  Marcel Aymé **11**:21
  Albert Camus **1**:54
  Louis-Ferdinand Céline **1**:57
  Jean Cocteau **1**:59
  Georges Duhamel **8**:186
  Jean Giono **4**:183
  Julien Green **3**:203
  André Malraux **1**:202
  François Mauriac **4**:337
  Raymond Queneau **2**:359
  Jules Romains **7**:381
  Jean-Paul Sartre **1**:306

Gullason, Thomas A.
  Jackson J. Benson **34**:414
  Carson McCullers **4**:344
  Flannery O'Connor **1**:259
  John Steinbeck **34**:414

Gullette, David
  Mark Strand **18**:518

Gullon, Agnes
  Pablo Neruda **7**:260

Gunn, Edward
  Djuna Barnes **4**:44

Gunn, James
  Isaac Asimov **19**:29; **26**:59, 63
  Theodore Sturgeon **39**:361
  Joan D. Vinge **30**:410
  Gene Wolfe **25**:474

Gunn, Thom
  J. V. Cunningham **31**:98
  Donald Davie **31**:109
  William Dickey **28**:117
  Roy Fuller **28**:148
  Barbara Howes **15**:289
  David Ignatow **7**:173
  Donald Justice **19**:232
  W. S. Merwin **13**:383
  Christopher Middleton **13**:387
  Howard Nemerov **9**:393
  Charles Olson **11**:414
  Louis Simpson **7**:426, 427

Gunston, David
  Leni Riefenstahl **16**:520

Guptara, Prabhu S.
  David Dabydeen **34**:150
  Anita Desai **37**:68

Guralnick, Peter
  Waylon Jennings **21**:205
  Willie Nelson **17**:304

Gurewitsch, M. Anatole
  William Gaddis **6**:195

Gurian, Jay
  Thomas Berger **18**:55

Gurko, Leo
  Ernest Hemingway **6**:226
  John P. Marquand **10**:331
  John Steinbeck **21**:383
  Edward Lewis Wallant **5**:477

Gurko, Miriam
  Carl Sandburg **35**:357

Gussenhoven, Frances
  Joseph Heller **36**:231

Gussow, Adam
  Czesław Miłosz **31**:265

Gussow, Mel
  Howard Barker **37**:37
  Samuel Beckett **29**:65
  Ed Bullins **1**:47
  Michael Cristofer **28**:95, 97
  Christopher Durang **27**:87
  Harvey Fierstein **33**:152
  Dario Fo **32**:173, 175
  Charles Fuller **25**:180
  Charles Gordone **1**:125
  A. R. Gurney, Jr. **32**:218

Albert Innaurato **21**:190, 191, 193
David Rabe **33**:342
Howard Sackler **14**:480
Ntozake Shange **25**:399
Sam Shepard **17**:438
Milan Stitt **29**:389
Tom Stoppard **29**:395
Elizabeth Swados **12**:558
Wendy Wasserstein **32**:441
Snoo Wilson **33**:465

Gustafson, Ralph
Ronald G. Everson **27**:134

Gustafson, Richard
Reg Saner **9**:469

Gustainis, J. Justin
Thomas J. Fleming **37**:127
Stephen King **12**:311
Steven Millhauser **21**:217
Amos Oz **11**:429

Gutcheon, Beth
Doris Betts **28**:35
Agnes Eckhardt Nixon **21**:245

Gutowski, John A.
Joan Micklin Silver **20**:345

Guttenplan, Don David
Arna Bontemps **18**:65

Gutteridge, Don
Clark Blaise **29**:70
Patrick Lane **25**:289

Guy, David
Virginia Hamilton **26**:158
David Malouf **28**:268
Ed Minus **39**:81

Guzman, Pablo
Prince **35**:323

Guzman, Richard R.
Raja Rao **25**:370

Gwynn, Frederick L.
J. D. Salinger **1**:295

Gysin, Fritz
Jean Toomer **13**:552

Gyurko, Lanin A.
Julio Cortázar **5**:108; **10**:112; **13**:159; **33**:126
Carlos Fuentes **22**:165

Haas, Diane
Judy Blume **12**:46
Barbara Wersba **30**:432

Haas, Joseph
Bob Dylan **12**:180
Jerome Weidman **7**:517

Haavikko, Paavo
Paavo Haavikko **34**:175

Haberl, Franz P.
Max Frisch **9**:218; **14**:184
Botho Strauss **22**:408
Peter Weiss **15**:565

Haberland, Jody
Jane Rule **27**:417

Hack, Richard
Kenneth Patchen **2**:332
Colin Wilson **3**:537

Hackett, C. A.
Henri Michaux **19**:311

Hackett, Francis
Carl Sandburg **35**:338

Hackney, Louise Wallace
John Ford **16**:303

Hadas, Moses
Mary Renault **17**:392
Marguerite Yourcenar **19**:481

Hadas, Pamela White
Marianne Moore **10**:348

Hadas, Rachel
Yannis Ritsos **13**:487; **31**:330
Robert Penn Warren **18**:534

Hadgraft, Cecil
David Malouf **28**:267

Haedens, Kléber
J.M.G. Le Clézio **31**:243

Haenicke, Diether H.
Heinrich Böll **6**:83
Paul Celan **10**:101
Friedrich Dürrenmatt **8**:194
Günter Eich **15**:204
Max Frisch **9**:217
Günter Grass **6**:207
Uwe Johnson **5**:201
Reiner Kunze **10**:310
Anna Seghers **7**:408
Martin Walser **27**:460
Carl Zuckmayer **18**:553

Haffenden, John
John Berryman **10**:45
Robert Lowell **11**:330

Haft, Cynthia
Aleksandr I. Solzhenitsyn **7**:435

Hafter, Ronald
René Wellek **28**:448

Hagan, Candace
Philip Roth **15**:453

Hagan, Patti
Barbara Corcoran **17**:73

Haglin, Donna
Henry Gregor Felsen **17**:123

Hagopian, John V.
James Baldwin **1**:15
William Faulkner **3**:157
J. F. Powers **1**:282

Hague, René
David Jones **7**:189

Hahn, Claire
William Everson **5**:122
Carolyn Forché **25**:170
Jean Garrigue **8**:239
Audre Lorde **18**:309

Hahn, Emily
Martha Gellhorn **14**:196

Haight, Amanda
Anna Akhmatova **25**:26

Hainsworth, J. D.
John Arden **13**:24

Hájek, Igor
Bohumil Hrabal **13**:291

Hajewski, Thomas
Siegfried Lenz **27**:254

Halderman, Marjorie
Larry Kettelkamp **12**:304

Hale, Nancy
Hortense Calisher **38**:70
Jessamyn West **7**:522; **17**:552, 554

Hale, Thomas A.
Aimé Césaire **19**:97

Hale, William Harlan
Bruce Catton **35**:83

Hales, David
Berry Morgan **6**:340

Haley, Beverly
Ouida Sebestyen **30**:350

Haley, Beverly A.
Paul Zindel **26**:472

Halio, Jay L.
Lawrence Durrell **27**:95
William Gaddis **10**:212
John Gardner **10**:220
Ernest Hemingway **6**:230
John Knowles **26**:246
Mary McCarthy **5**:276
Chaim Potok **26**:373
Reynolds Price **13**:464
Isaac Bashevis Singer **1**:314; **6**:509
C. P. Snow **6**:517
Aleksandr I. Solzhenitsyn **7**:434
Alice Walker **5**:476
Paul West **14**:569

Hall, Donald
Roger Angell **26**:31
Russell Edson **13**:191
Robert Frost **34**:469
Allen Ginsberg **3**:195
Thom Gunn **18**:202
Mark Harris **19**:205
Seamus Heaney **14**:242, 245
Geoffrey Hill **18**:241
Edward Hoagland **28**:185
Richard F. Hugo **18**:263
Roger Kahn **30**:232
Philip Larkin **39**:342
Robert Lowell **15**:344
Norman MacCaig **36**:279
Peter Matthiessen **11**:361
Thomas McGrath **28**:278
Rod McKuen **3**:333
Marianne Moore **4**:362
William H. Pritchard **34**:469
Kenneth Rexroth **22**:349
David Wagoner **15**:559
Thomas Williams **14**:583

Hall, Elizabeth
Frank Herbert **12**:275
Stephen King **12**:309

Hall, James
Saul Bellow **3**:50
Elizabeth Bowen **3**:82
William Faulkner **3**:152
Graham Greene **3**:207
Iris Murdoch **2**:296

J. D. Salinger **3**:444
Robert Penn Warren **4**:577

Hall, James B.
Mario Puzo **1**:282

Hall, Joan Joffe
Wendell Berry **4**:59
Marie-Claire Blais **6**:81
Shirley Ann Grau **4**:210
Ursula K. LeGuin **8**:342
Robert Stone **5**:410
John Updike **5**:458
Jessamyn West **17**:550

Hall, John
Gary Snyder **1**:318

Hall, Linda B.
Carlos Fuentes **8**:222
Gabriel García Márquez **10**:214
Maxine Hong Kingston **12**:314

Hall, Mordaunt
Tod Browning **16**:121
Frank Capra **16**:153

Hall, Richard
Breyten Breytenbach **23**:86
Bruce Chatwin **28**:73

Hall, Richard W.
Ezra Pound **5**:348

Hall, Stanley B.
Arthur C. Clarke **35**:120

Hall, Stephen
R. H. W. Dillard **5**:116

Hall, Vernon, Jr.
Paule Marshall **27**:309

Hall, Wade
Jesse Stuart **11**:511

Hallberg, Peter
Halldór Laxness **25**:293

Halle, Louis J.
William Golding **17**:157

Haller, Robert S.
Martin Booth **13**:104
Alan Sillitoe **6**:500

Haller, Scot
Beth Henley **23**:214
John Irving **23**:248

Halliday, Bob
Samuel Beckett **29**:66
Guy Davenport **38**:146

Halliday, Mark
Eleanor Lerman **9**:329

Halman, Talat Sait
Yashar Kemal **14**:299, 300, 301; **29**:268

Halpern, Daniel
David Wagoner **5**:475

Halpern, Joseph
Jean-Paul Sartre **24**:416

Halpern, Sue M.
Tom Robbins **32**:368

Halsey, Martha T.
Antonio Buero Vallejo **15**:99

Haltrecht, Monty
Chaim Potok **26**:376

Hamalian, Leo
Jean-Luc Godard **20**:141

Haman, A. C.
Margaret O. Hyde **21**:176

Hamblen, Abigail Ann
Flannery O'Connor **21**:270

Hamburger, Michael
Wendell Berry **27**:36
Paul Celan **19**:93
Günter Grass **32**:197
Martin Heidegger **24**:255
Ernst Jandl **34**:195
Siegfried Lenz **27**:247
Robert Pinsky **19**:370

Hamel, Guy
William Mitchell **25**:328

Hamill, Pete
Seán O'Faoláin **7**:272
Gay Talese **37**:391, 394
Leon Uris **7**:492

Hamill, Sam
Greg Kuzma **7**:197

Hamilton, Alice
Samuel Beckett **10**:31
John Updike **2**:443; **5**:449

Hamilton, Daphne Ann
Melvin Berger **12**:41, 42
Franklyn M. Branley **21**:22
Roy A. Gallant **17**:132

Hamilton, Ian
Kingsley Amis **2**:6
Martin Amis **38**:16
Nicolas Freeling **38**:184
Joseph Hansen **38**:237
John Landis **26**:273
Philip Larkin **39**:337
Robert Lowell **2**:246; **4**:303
Norman MacCaig **36**:282, 284
Louis MacNeice **4**:317
James Merrill **34**:231
Christopher Middleton **13**:387

Hamilton, James Shelley
René Clair **20**:58, 61
John Ford **16**:303
Rouben Mamoulian **16**:420
Jean Renoir **20**:286

Hamilton, Kenneth
Samuel Beckett **10**:31
John Updike **2**:443; **5**:449

Hamilton, Lynne
Judy Blume **30**:23

Hamilton, Mary
Paul Vincent Carroll **10**:98

Hamilton, William
Albert Camus **1**:52
Paul Goodman **7**:128

Hamilton-Paterson, James
Anne McCaffrey **17**:281

Hamley, Dennis
H. F. Brinsmead **21**:32
Diana Wynne Jones **26**:229

Hamlin, William C.
Leonard Michaels **25**:315

Hammond, Graham
Diana Wynne Jones **26**:227

Hammond, John G.
Robert Creeley **8**:151

Hammond, Jonathan
Howard Barker **37**:32
Athol Fugard **9**:229
Stephen Poliakoff **38**:376, 377, 378
Snoo Wilson **33**:461

Hammond, Kristin E.
Kin Platt **26**:351

Hammond, Nancy C.
C. S. Adler **35**:14
Robert Cormier **30**:91
M. E. Kerr **35**:250
D. M. Pinkwater **35**:320
Laurence Yep **35**:474

Hamner, Robert D.
V. S. Naipaul **13**:402
Derek Walcott **25**:453

Hampl, Patricia
Carolyn Kizer **39**:170

Hampshire, Stuart
Christopher Isherwood **11**:296

Hampson, John
Edmund Crispin **22**:108

Hanckel, Frances
Isabelle Holland **21**:150

Hancock, Geoff
John Metcalf **37**:304

Handa, Carolyn
Conrad Aiken **10**:1

Handlin, Oscar
Bruce Catton **35**:84
Yuri Krotkov **19**:264
Hunter S. Thompson **17**:503

Handy, William J.
John Crowe Ransom **24**:365

Handzo, Stephen
Michelangelo Antonioni **20**:36
Frank Capra **16**:160

Haney, Robert W.
Erich Maria Remarque **21**:333

Hanley, Clifford
Martin Walser **27**:455

Hanley, Karen Stang
C. S. Adler **35**:15
Lloyd Alexander **35**:28

Hanly, Elizabeth
Jorge Ibargüengoitia **37**:185

Hann, Sandra
Aidan Chambers **35**:101

Hanna, Clifford
Jessica Anderson **37**:20

Hanna, Thomas L.
Albert Camus **9**:143

Hannabuss, C. Stuart
Leon Garfield **12**:230, 234
Andre Norton **12**:463
Josephine Poole **17**:372
J.R.R. Tolkien **12**:575

Hannah, Barry
William Eastlake **8**:200

Hanne, Michael
Elio Vittorini **9**:551

Hanscom, Leslie
E. B. White **39**:373

Hansen, Arlen J.
Richard Brautigan **3**:90

Hansen, Arthur G.
Richard Bach **14**:35

Hansen, I. V.
Maia Wojciechowska **26**:458

Hansen, Olaf
Peter Handke **10**:259

Hansen, Ron
Stephen King **26**:239

Hanson, Jarice
Steven Bochco and Michael Kozoll **35**:57

Harada, Violet H.
Barbara Corcoran **17**:77

Harbaugh, William H.
Louis R. Harlan **34**:185

Harcourt, Joan
Roch Carrier **13**:141

Harcourt, Peter
Ingmar Bergman **16**:50, 72
Luis Buñuel **16**:141
Federico Fellini **16**:290
Jean-Luc Godard **20**:143
Richard Lester **20**:221
Jean Renoir **20**:292, 305
Alain Resnais **16**:511

Hardee, Ethel R.
Robert Newton Peck **17**:337

Harder, Worth T.
Herbert Read **4**:443

Hardgrave, Robert L., Jr.
Ved Mehta **37**:296

Hardie, Alec M.
Edmund Blunden **2**:65

Hardin, Nancy Shields
Margaret Drabble **3**:129
Doris Lessing **6**:297

Harding, D. W.
Roy Fuller **4**:178
F. R. Leavis **24**:292
I. A. Richards **24**:377

Hardison, O. B., Jr.
Paul Bowles **19**:59
Larry McMurtry **7**:215

Hardré, Jacques
Jean-Paul Sartre **24**:403

Hardwick, Elizabeth
Renata Adler **8**:6
Elizabeth Bishop **32**:40
Lillian Hellman **14**:257
Doris Lessing **3**:285
Flannery O'Connor **15**:408
Marge Piercy **3**:383
Sylvia Plath **17**:355
Alexsandr I. Solzhenitsyn **10**:480
Susan Sontag **31**:416

Hardwick, Mollie
Roald Dahl **18**:108
Penelope Fitzgerald **19**:174

Hardy, Barbara
A. Alvarez **5**:18

Hardy, John Edward
Cleanth Brooks **24**:107
Katherine Anne Porter **15**:428

Hardy, Melody
Arthur C. Clarke **4**:105
Howard Fast **23**:159

Hare, David
Noël Coward **29**:139
Nicolas Freeling **38**:184
Ngaio Marsh **7**:209

Hargrove, Nancy D.
T. S. Eliot **6**:165

Harker, Jonathan
Roman Polanski **16**:462
Satyajit Ray **16**:475

Harker, Ronald
Mary Renault **17**:401

Harkins, William E.
Jaroslav Seifert **34**:256

Harlow, Robert
Jack Hodgins **23**:231

Harmon, Daniel
Waylon Jennings **21**:201

Harmon, Elva
Eilís Dillon **17**:96
William Mayne **12**:392

Harmon, William
Jim Harrison **33**:198
James Wright **28**:468
Louis Zukofsky **18**:560

Haro, Robert P.
Piri Thomas **17**:498

Harold, Brent
William Faulkner **11**:199
Vladimir Nabokov **6**:356

Harper, Howard M., Jr.
John Barth **1**:18
Saul Bellow **1**:33
Jerzy Kosinski **1**:172
Vladimir Nabokov **1**:245
Philip Roth **1**:293

Harper, Michael F.
Robert Alter **34**:515
Joyce Carol Oates **33**:297

Harper, Michael S.
Sterling A. Brown 23:100
Robert Hayden 9:269; 14:241;
37:152
Ntozake Shange 25:398

Harper, Ralph
Eric Ambler 4:18

Harper, Robert D.
Wright Morris 18:349

Harper, Roy
Jimmy Page and Robert Plant
12:481

Harrell, Don
James A. Michener 29:316

Harrigan, Brian
Paul Weller 26:442

Harrington, Curtis
Josef von Sternberg 20:371

Harrington, Michael
James Merrill 34:235
Czesław Miłosz 22:305
Theodore Roethke 3:433

Harrington, Stephanie
Norman Lear 12:327, 334
Agnes Eckhardt Nixon 21:242

Harris, Bertha
Rita Mae Brown 18:72
Carolyn Chute 39:38
John Hawkes 27:196
Jane Rule 27:418

Harris, Bruce
John Lennon 35:261
John Lennon and Paul
McCartney 12:371
Jimmy Page and Robert Plant
12:475
Carly Simon 26:406
Neil Young 17:569

Harris, Helen
Penelope Gilliatt 13:239
Ian McEwan 13:371

Harris, Jane Gary
Boris Pasternak 10:382

Harris, Janet
June Jordan 11:312

Harris, John
Robertson Davies 25:134

Harris, Karen
Robin F. Brancato 35:66
Barbara Corcoran 17:78
Robert Cormier 30:85
Barbara Wersba 30:431

Harris, Karen H.
Betsy Byars 35:72
Virginia Hamilton 26:156
Zoa Sherburne 30:363
Barbara Wersba 30:432

Harris, Leo
Peter Dickinson 35:130
Ngaio Marsh 7:209
Julian Symons 2:426

Harris, Lis
Truman Capote 3:100
Amos Oz 11:429
Grace Paley 4:392
Georges Simenon 18:486

Harris, Marie
Marge Piercy 6:403

Harris, Mark
Roger Angell 26:33
E. L. Doctorow 18:125
George Plimpton 36:352
Mordecai Richler 18:455
Isaac Bashevis Singer 23:422

Harris, Michael
Thomas Berger 5:60
Andre Dubus 13:183
John Gardner 5:133

Harris, Norman
Ishmael Reed 32:356

Harris, Robert R.
John Gardner 28:163
Cynthia Ozick 28:349
Grace Paley 37:334
William Wharton 18:542
Richard Yates 23:483

Harris, Wilson
George Lamming 4:279
V. S. Naipaul 4:374

Harrison, Barbara F.
Jean Craighead George 35:178

Harrison, Barbara Grizzuti
Joan Didion 14:153
Ruth Prawer Jhabvala 4:257
Iris Murdoch 6:343
George Plimpton 36:355
Adrienne Rich 18:448
Gay Talese 37:399

Harrison, Bernard
Muriel Spark 18:502

Harrison, Ed
Bob Seger 35:382

Harrison, G. B.
Thomas B. Costain 30:96

Harrison, George
Nevil Shute 30:369

Harrison, Jim
Barry Hannah 23:207
Peter Matthiessen 11:360;
32:291
Larry McMurtry 2:272
Farley Mowat 26:340

Harrison, Joseph G.
Thomas J. Fleming 37:120
Arthur Koestler 33:235
Mary Renault 17:395

Harrison, Keith
Margot Benary-Isbert 12:34
John Berryman 3:69
Marge Piercy 14:422

Harrison, M. J.
Henri Troyat 23:461

Harrison, M. John
Thomas M. Disch 36:123

Harrison, Robert
Julian Symons 32:425

Harrison, Tony
Lorine Niedecker 10:360

Harrison-Ford, Carl
Thomas W. Shapcott 38:400

Harron, Mary
Joan Armatrading 17:10

Harsent, David
Joe Orton 13:437

Harss, Luis
Jorge Luis Borges 2:69
Julio Cortázar 2:101
Gabriel García Márquez 2:147
Juan Carlos Onetti 7:276
João Guimarães Rosa 23:350
Juan Rulfo 8:461
Mario Vargas Llosa 3:493

Hart, Elizabeth
August Derleth 31:128

Hart, Henry
Carlos Saura 20:314
Billy Wilder 20:457, 458, 459

Hart, Jane
Carson McCullers 12:416

Hart, Jeffrey
E. L. Doctorow 6:136
Robert Frost 15:243
Allen Ginsberg 36:199
Robert Graves 39:327
Ernest Hemingway 34:478
John Raeburn 34:478
Auberon Waugh 7:514

Hart, John E.
Jack Kerouac 3:264

Hart, Johnny
Charles M. Schulz 12:527

Hart, Kevin
Thomas W. Shapcott 38:402

Hart, Marc
William X. Kienzle 25:276

Hart-Davis, Rupert
Agatha Christie 12:114

Harte, Barbara
Janet Frame 3:164

Harte, Joe
David Dabydeen 34:150

Hartfelder, William A., Jr.
Elie Wiesel 37:457

Harth, Erica
Simone de Beauvoir 14:68

Hartley, Anthony
Ian Fleming 30:131

Hartley, George
Philip Larkin 5:230

Hartley, Lodwick
Katherine Anne Porter 13:446

Hartley, Lois
Raja Rao 25:366

Hartman, Charles
Shirley Clarke 16:218

Hartman, Geoffrey
Kenneth Burke 24:132
Ross Macdonald 2:257

Hartman, Geoffrey H.
A. R. Ammons 2:13
Harold Bloom 24:76
J. V. Cunningham 31:101
Jacques Derrida 24:153
Northrop Frye 24:216
André Malraux 9:358
Lionel Trilling 24:457

Hartos, Marsha
Norma Klein 30:243

Hartshorne, Thomas L.
Kurt Vonnegut, Jr. 22:444

Hartt, Julian N.
Mary Renault 3:426

Hartung, Charles V.
Cleanth Brooks 24:103

Hartung, Philip T.
John Ford 16:304
Laurence Olivier 20:238
Gordon Parks 16:458
Budd Schulberg 7:402
Rod Serling 30:354, 357

Hartwell, David G.
Theodore Sturgeon 39:366

Harvey, David D.
Herbert Read 4:440

Harvey, G. M.
John Betjeman 10:52

Harvey, James
Jonathan Baumbach 23:53

Harvey, John
F. R. Leavis 24:313
V. S. Pritchett 15:442

Harvey, Lawrence E.
Samuel Beckett 9:80

Harvey, Robert D.
Howard Nemerov 2:306

Harvey, Stephen
Anita Brookner 32:60
David Mamet 34:222

Haskell, Ann S.
D. M. Pinkwater 35:317

Haskell, Molly
Woody Allen 16:6
Marguerite Duras 20:100
Elaine May 16:434, 436
François Truffaut 20:397

Haskins, Jim
Pat Conroy 30:77

Hasley, Louis
Peter De Vries 1:72
Joseph Heller 5:173
S. J. Perelman 3:381
James Thurber 11:532
E. B. White 10:526

Critic Index

Hass, Robert
  Joseph Brodsky **36**:78
  Stephen Dobyns **37**:79
  Robert Lowell **9**:336
  James Wright **28**:463

Hass, Victor P.
  August Derleth **31**:138
  Rosa Guy **26**:141
  Evan Hunter **31**:220

Hassall, Anthony J.
  Randolph Stow **23**:433

Hassan, Ihab
  John Barth **2**:36
  Samuel Beckett **1**:23
  Saul Bellow **1**:29
  Thomas Berger **18**:53
  André Breton **2**:81
  Frederick Buechner **4**:79
  William S. Burroughs **2**:91
  Truman Capote **1**:55
  J. P. Donleavy **1**:75
  Ralph Ellison **1**:94
  Jean Genet **2**:159
  Allen Ginsberg **2**:164
  Herbert Gold **4**:190
  Ernest Hemingway **3**:237
  Norman Mailer **1**:188, 189;
    4:319
  Bernard Malamud **1**:195, 196
  Carson McCullers **1**:207, 208
  Henry Miller **1**:222
  Vladimir Nabokov **1**:239
  James Purdy **28**:378
  Alain Robbe-Grillet **2**:375
  J. D. Salinger **1**:296; **3**:446
  Nathalie Sarraute **2**:385
  Jean Stafford **7**:455
  William Styron **1**:330; **11**:514
  Kurt Vonnegut, Jr. **12**:610

Hassett, John J.
  José Donoso **4**:129

Hassler, Donald M.
  Theodore Sturgeon **22**:412

Hatch, James V.
  Alice Childress **12**:106

Hatch, Robert
  Ralph Bakshi **26**:67
  Anne Burr **6**:104
  Francis Ford Coppola **16**:234
  Shelagh Delaney **29**:145
  Rainer Werner Fassbinder
    20:115, 119
  Federico Fellini **16**:300
  Ian Fleming **30**:134
  Larry Gelbart **21**:130
  Werner Herzog **16**:326
  Alfred Hitchcock **16**:340
  Fletcher Knebel **14**:307
  George Lucas **16**:412
  Nagisa Oshima **20**:257
  Pink Floyd **35**:314
  Richard Pryor **26**:382
  Carlos Saura **20**:317
  François Truffaut **20**:408
  Orson Welles **20**:439
  Lina Wertmüller **16**:597
  Frederick Wiseman **20**:467
  Richard Wright **21**:436

Hatch, Ronald
  David Donnell **34**:159
  Mavis Gallant **38**:191

Hatcher, Harlan
  Julia Peterkin **31**:305

Hatcher, Robert D., Jr.
  John McPhee **36**:299

Hatfield, H. C.
  George Tabori **19**:435

Hatfield, Henry
  Günter Grass **2**:173; **22**:189,
    195

Hattersley, Roy
  J. B. Priestley **34**:365

Hattman, John W.
  Wendell Berry **27**:32

Hauck, Richard Boyd
  Kurt Vonnegut, Jr. **5**:465

Haugaard, Kay
  Betty Cavanna **12**:102

Haugh, Robert
  John Updike **7**:489

Haugh, Robert F.
  Nadine Gordimer **18**:184

Hauptman, Ira
  John Buell **10**:81

Hauser, Frank
  Ogden Nash **23**:322

Hausermann, H. W.
  Herbert Read **4**:438, 439

Havard, Robert G.
  Jorge Guillén **11**:262

Haverstick, S. Alexander
  John Knowles **4**:271

Havighurst, Walter
  Allan W. Eckert **17**:105
  Edna Ferber **18**:152
  James A. Michener **29**:309
  William Mitchell **25**:321
  Scott O'Dell **30**:268
  Betty Smith **19**:423

Haviland, Virginia
  E. M. Almedingen **12**:5
  Ruth M. Arthur **12**:25
  Margot Benary-Isbert **12**:30
  Betty Cavanna **12**:100
  Mavis Thorpe Clark **12**:130,
    131
  Barbara Corcoran **17**:70
  Julia W. Cunningham **12**:165
  Eilís Dillon **17**:93
  Leon Garfield **12**:218
  Jean Craighead George **35**:177
  Virginia Hamilton **26**:147
  Christie Harris **12**:264
  Jamake Highwater **12**:287
  Margaret O. Hyde **21**:179
  Larry Kettelkamp **12**:304
  Joseph Krumgold **12**:317
  Jean Lee Latham **12**:323
  John Neufeld **17**:307
  Andre Norton **12**:456, 466
  Scott O'Dell **30**:274

  Philippa Pearce **21**:288
  Josephine Poole **17**:372
  Mary Rodgers **12**:494
  Zilpha Keatley Snyder **17**:472
  Mary Stolz **12**:546, 550, 555
  Colin Thiele **17**:494
  Jill Paton Walsh **35**:432
  Laurence Yep **35**:469

Hawkes, David
  Ch'ien Chung-shu **22**:105

Hawkes, John
  Djuna Barnes **29**:25
  John Barth **10**:21
  John Hawkes **15**:277
  Flannery O'Connor **1**:254

Hawkes, Terence
  David Lodge **36**:274

Hawkins, Desmond
  Pamela Hansford Johnson
    27:214

Hawkins, Robert F.
  Vittorio De Sica **20**:85

Hawley, Lucy V.
  Walter Dean Myers **35**:299
  Marilyn Sachs **35**:335

Haworth, David
  Bernice Rubens **19**:402
  Morris L. West **6**:563

Hawtree, Christopher
  Carlo Gébler **39**:61

Hay, John
  Eleanor Clark **19**:104
  Peter Matthiessen **32**:289
  John McPhee **36**:295

Hay, Linda
  Marian Engel **36**:160

Hay, Samuel A.
  Ed Bullins **5**:83

Hay, Sara Henderson
  Brewster Ghiselin **23**:169

Hayakawa, S. Ichiyé
  E. E. Cummings **12**:144
  T. S. Eliot **24**:162

Haycraft, Howard
  Agatha Christie **12**:118
  August Derleth **31**:137

Hayden, Brad
  Richard Brautigan **12**:72

Hayden, Robert
  Robert Hayden **37**:150

Hayes, Alfred
  Ernesto Sabato **23**:375

Hayes, Brian P.
  Joyce Carol Oates **1**:252

Hayes, E. Nelson
  J. R. Salamanca **4**:461

Hayes, Harold
  Joy Adamson **17**:6

Hayes, Noreen
  J.R.R. Tolkien **1**:336

Hayes, Richard
  Robert Anderson **23**:28
  Sally Benson **17**:50
  Paul Bowles **19**:57
  Truman Capote **19**:80
  William Gibson **23**:176
  Nadine Gordimer **33**:178
  Fritz Hochwälder **36**:233
  Mary McCarthy **24**:342
  Clifford Odets **28**:334

Hayes, Sarah
  Rosemary Sutcliff **26**:437

Hayman, David
  Samuel Beckett **11**:34
  Louis-Ferdinand Céline **7**:42

Hayman, Ronald
  Alan Ayckbourn **33**:42
  Howard Barker **37**:34
  Robert Duncan **7**:88
  Roy Fisher **25**:158
  Robert Frost **4**:174
  Allen Ginsberg **6**:198
  David Hare **29**:215
  Arthur Miller **6**:331
  Charles Olson **5**:327
  Anne Sexton **4**:482
  Peter Shaffer **14**:485
  David Storey **5**:414
  Charles Tomlinson **4**:544
  Tom Wolfe **15**:586

Haynes, Elizabeth
  Andre Norton **12**:459

Haynes, Muriel
  Shirley Ann Grau **4**:208
  Lillian Hellman **4**:222
  Thomas Keneally **5**:210

Hays, H. R.
  Robert Bloch **33**:82
  Edwin Honig **33**:209

Hays, Peter L.
  Henry Miller **9**:379

Hayward, Henry S.
  James Clavell **25**:127

Hayward, Max
  Andrei Voznesensky **1**:349

Hazard, Lucy Lockwood
  John G. Neihardt **32**:331

Hazelton, Lesley
  Amos Oz **27**:359

Hazo, Samuel
  John Berryman **2**:57
  Philip Booth **23**:74
  Linda Pastan **27**:369
  Yannis Ritsos **31**:326

Hazzard, Shirley
  Jean Rhys **2**:371
  Patrick White **3**:522

Headings, Philip R.
  T. S. Eliot **1**:91

Heald, Tim
  Brian Moore **19**:333

Healey, James
Catharine Savage Brosman
9:135
Michael Casey 2:100
Leonard Cohen 3:110

Healey, Robert
Thomas J. Fleming 37:120

Healey, Robert C.
Chinua Achebe 26:12
Evan Hunter 31:219
Gregor von Rezzori 25:381

Healy, Michael
Wilbur Smith 33:378

Heaney, Seamus
David Jones 7:187
Paul Muldoon 32:319

Hearne, Betsy
Virginia Hamilton 26:157
Robert Lipsyte 21:212
D. M. Pinkwater 35:318
Marilyn Sachs 35:334
Kin Platt 26:352

Hearne, John
Wilson Harris 25:205

Hearron, Thomas
Richard Brautigan 5:68

Heath, Jeffrey M.
Evelyn Waugh 8:543

Heath, Melville
Howard Fast 23:156
Bruce Lancaster 36:244

Heath, Stephen
Nagisa Oshima 20:251, 252

Heath, Susan
Martin Amis 9:25
John Hersey 7:154
Yasunari Kawabata 5:208
John Knowles 4:272
Yukio Mishima 6:337
Anaïs Nin 4:379
Richard Price 12:489
V. S. Pritchett 5:353
Kurt Vonnegut, Jr. 3:503

Heath, William
Paul Blackburn 9:100

Hecht, Anthony
Peter Ackroyd 34:392
W. H. Auden 2:22
T. S. Eliot 34:392
Ted Hughes 2:198
James Merrill 2:273
Marianne Moore 2:291
Howard Nemerov 2:306
L. E. Sissman 9:489
Richard Wilbur 9:570

Heck, Francis S.
Marguerite Duras 11:166

Heckard, Margaret
William H. Gass 8:244

Heckman, Don
John Lennon and Paul
McCartney 12:358

Hector, Mary Louise
Margot Benary-Isbert 12:32, 33
Mary Stolz 12:552

Hedden, Worth Tuttle
Zora Neale Hurston 30:214

Heffernan, Michael
Albert Goldbarth 5:143
Gibbons Ruark 3:441
Dave Smith 22:384

Heffernan, Thomas Farel
Robert Newton Peck 17:339

Heffernan, Tom
Norma Fox Mazer 26:290

Hegel, Robert E.
Ch'ien Chung-shu 22:106

Heidenry, John
Agatha Christie 6:110
Robert M. Pirsig 4:405

Heifetz, Henry
Bernardo Bertolucci 16:84

Heilbrun, Carolyn
Nat Hentoff 26:182

Heilbrun, Carolyn G.
Christopher Isherwood 14:279
C. P. Snow 19:428
Noel Streatfeild 21:407

Heilbut, Anthony
Stanley Elkin 9:191

Heilman, Robert B.
Edward Albee 5:11
Max Frisch 3:168
Harold Pinter 3:386
Katherine Anne Porter 15:426
Tennessee Williams 30:465

Heim, Michael Henry
Josef Škvorecký 39:224

Heimberg, Martha
Shirley Hazzard 18:220
John Updike 15:547
Tom Wolfe 15:586

Heims, Neil
Paul Goodman 4:198

Heinegg, Peter
Morris L. West 33:431

Heineman, Alan
Janis Ian 21:183
Pink Floyd 35:305
Frank Zappa 17:586

Heiney, Donald
Jean Anouilh 8:22
Natalia Ginzburg 11:227
Alberto Moravia 2:294
Elio Vittorini 9:546, 548

Heins, Ethel L.
Lloyd Alexander 35:26, 27
Ruth M. Arthur 12:24
Betsy Byars 35:71, 72
Barbara Corcoran 17:70
Julia W. Cunningham 12:166
Peter Dickinson 12:177
Eilís Dillon 17:97
Lois Duncan 26:104
Leon Garfield 12:231

Rosa Guy 26:141, 144
Virginia Hamilton 26:157
Isabelle Holland 21:148
Lee Kingman 17:246, 247
Joseph Krumgold 12:318
Norma Fox Mazer 26:292
Walter Dean Myers 35:296
Emily Cheney Neville 12:451
Scott O'Dell 30:274
Katherine Paterson 12:487
Marilyn Sachs 35:333
Zilpha Keatley Snyder 17:469,
471
Cynthia Voight 30:420
Laurence Yep 35:472

Heins, Paul
Lloyd Alexander 35:25
Frank Bonham 12:50
Betsy Byars 35:73
Christopher Collier and James
L. Collier 30:73
Robert Cormier 12:136
Julia W. Cunningham 12:164,
166
Peter Dickinson 12:171
John Donovan 35:139, 141
James D. Forman 21:116
Alan Garner 17:142
Rosa Guy 26:143
Kristin Hunter 35:226
Mollie Hunter 21:164
Madeleine L'Engle 12:347
William Mayne 12:398, 402
Milton Meltzer 26:303, 308
Nicholasa Mohr 12:446
Scott O'Dell 30:268, 271, 278
Katherine Paterson 30:284
Philippa Pearce 21:289
Ouida Sebestyen 30:346
Zilpha Keatley Snyder 17:471
Colin Thiele 17:496
Jill Paton Walsh 35:429
Barbara Wersba 30:434
Laurence Yep 35:468

Heiserman, Arthur
J. D. Salinger 12:496

Held, George
Jim Harrison 33:198

Heldman, Irma Pascal
Joan Aiken 35:18
Robert Ludlum 22:289

Helfgott, Barbara
Sue Ellen Bridgers 26:90

Helfgott, Barbara Cutler
Marilyn Sachs 35:336

Helgesen, Sally
Anita Brookner 34:142

Heller, Amanda
Max Apple 9:32
C.D.B. Bryan 29:103
John Cheever 8:138
Don DeLillo 8:171
Joan Didion 8:175
William Gaddis 6:194
Mary Gordon 13:249
Mark Helprin 7:152
Colleen McCullough 27:319
Leonard Michaels 6:325

Luisa Valenzuela 31:436
Fay Weldon 11:566
Larry Woiwode 6:579

Heller, Erich
Martin Heidegger 24:269

Heller, Joseph
Alfred Kazin 38:275

Heller, M. Kay
C. S. Adler 35:12

Heller, Michael
William Bronk 10:75
Cid Corman 9:170
George Oppen 7:284; 13:434
Charles Reznikoff 9:449

Hellmann, John
Mick Jagger and Keith Richard
17:226
Hunter S. Thompson 17:511
Tom Wolfe 35:460

Helm.
Rod Serling 30:354

Helm, Thomas E.
Colleen McCullough 27:322

Helms, Alan
John Ashbery 2:18
Robert Bly 10:61
Richard F. Hugo 18:261
Galway Kinnell 13:321
Philip Levine 4:287
William Meredith 13:373

Helms, Randel
J.R.R. Tolkien 12:578

Helwig, David
David Donnell 34:158

Hemenway, Leone R.
Melvin Berger 12:39

Hemenway, Robert
Zora Neale Hurston 7:170;
30:219

Hemesath, James B.
Jim Harrison 33:199

Hemley, Robin
Richard Grayson 38:211

Hemming, John
Bruce Chatwin 28:72
Thor Heyerdahl 26:194

Hemmings, F.W.J.
José Donoso 32:152
Mary Stewart 7:467

Hemmings, John
J.M.G. Le Clézio 31:246

Henault, Marie
Peter Viereck 4:559

Henderson, Alice Corbin
Padraic Colum 28:85

Henderson, David w.
David Leavitt 34:78

Henderson, Katherine Usher
Joan Didion 32:142

Henderson, Stephen E.
Sterling A. Brown 23:96, 99

Henderson, Tony
Patricia Highsmith 4:226

Hendin, Josephine
Truman Capote 38:85
Gail Godwin 31:195
Joe McGinniss 32:305

Hendin, Josephine Gattuso
John Barth 3:42
Donald Barthelme 6:28
Richard Brautigan 1:45
William S. Burroughs 5:92
Janet Frame 2:142
John Hawkes 15:276
John Hersey 2:188
Marjorie Kellogg 2:224
Robet Kotlowitz 4:275
Doris Lessing 3:286
Michael McClure 6:316
Joyce Carol Oates 6:371; 9:404
Flannery O'Connor 6:375;
   13:421; 21:274
Thomas Pynchon 6:436
Hubert Selby, Jr. 1:307; 4:482
Paul Theroux 5:427
John Updike 9:536
Kurt Vonnegut, Jr. 4:569

Hendley, W. Clark
Philip Roth 31:347

Hendrick, George
Mazo de la Roche 14:148
Jack Kerouac 2:227
Katherine Anne Porter 1:273

Hendricks, Flora
Jessamyn West 17:544

Hendricks, Sharon
Melvin Berger 12:42

Henighan, T. J.
Richard Hughes 1:149

Henkel, Wayne J.
John Knowles 4:272

Henkels, Robert
Robert Pinget 37:362

Henkels, Robert M.
Robert Pinget 37:365

Henkels, Robert M., Jr.
Robert Pinget 13:443, 444;
   37:360
Raymond Queneau 10:430

Henkin, Bill
Richard O'Brien 17:325

Henniger, Gerd
Francis Ponge 18:416

Henniker-Heaton, Peter
Arthur C. Clarke 35:119

Henninger, Francis J.
Albert Camus 4:93

Henry, Avril
William Golding 10:237

Henry, Gerrit
Russell Edson 13:190
W. S. Merwin 5:287

Henry, Parrish Dice
Samuel Beckett 29:61

Henry, William A. III
Neil Simon 39:219

Hentoff, Margaret
Paul Zindel 6:586

Hentoff, Margot
Joan Didion 8:174

Hentoff, Nat
Claude Brown 30:34
Lenny Bruce 21:44, 47, 51
Eldridge Cleaver 30:59
Bob Dylan 12:180
Paul Goodman 4:197
Woody Guthrie 35:185
Alex Haley 12:243
Jonathan Kozol 17:250
Robert Lipsyte 21:207
Colin MacInnes 4:314

Henze, Shelly Temchin
Rita Mae Brown 18:74

Hepburn, Neil
Martin Amis 38:12
Rayner Heppenstall 10:273
Patricia Highsmith 14:260
Mary Hocking 13:285
Ursula Holden 18:257
Thomas Keneally 5:211; 10:299
David Lodge 36:271
Tim O'Brien 7:272
David Plante 7:308
Frederic Raphael 14:437
William Sansom 6:484
Tom Sharpe 36:401
William Trevor 7:477
John Updike 7:489
Elio Vittorini 14:547
Fay Weldon 9:559

Hepner, Arthur
John R. Tunis 12:594

Herberg, Will
Herman Wouk 38:448

Herbert, Cynthia
Hilma Wolitzer 17:562

Herbert, Kevin
Mary Renault 17:394

Herbert, Rosemary
Piers Anthony 35:35
C. J. Cherryh 35:106
Jack Vance 35:422
Roger Zelazny 21:479

Herbold, Tony
Dannie Abse 7:2
Michael Hamburger 5:159

Herman, Gary
Peter Townshend 17:528

Herman, Gertrude B.
Maia Wojciechowska 26:458

Hermann, John
J. D. Salinger 12:510

Hern, Nicholas
Peter Handke 15:265

Hernández, Ana María
Julio Cortázar 13:162

Hernlund, Patricia
Richard Brautigan 5:67

Herr, Marian
Otfried Preussler 17:374

Herr, Paul
James Purdy 2:347

Herrera, Philip
Daphne du Maurier 6:147

Herrick, Robert
Julia Peterkin 31:303
T. S. Stribling 23:440

Herrick, William
Manuel Puig 28:373

Herring, Reginald
John Gardner 30:152

Herrnstein, R. J.
Carl Sagan 30:334

Herron, Ima Honaker
William Inge 19:228

Hershinow, Sheldon J.
Bernard Malamud 27:295

Hertz, Peter D.
Hermann Hesse 17:212

Hertzel, Leo J.
J. F. Powers 1:281

Herzberger, David K.
Juan Benet 28:15

Herzog, Arthur
Aldous Huxley 35:239

Heseltine, Harry
Frank Dalby Davison 15:170

Hess, John
Botho Strauss 22:407

Hess, Linda
Kamala Markandaya 38:324
Shiva Naipaul 32:323

Hesse, Eva
Ezra Pound 7:329

Hesseltine, William B.
MacKinlay Kantor 7:194

Hettinga, Donald R.
Tom Robbins 32:367

Hewes, Henry
Edward Albee 2:2; 13:3
Robert Anderson 23:32
Robert Bolt 14:91
Ed Bullins 5:84
Truman Capote 19:81
William Gibson 23:177
Günter Grass 2:173
Jim Jacobs and Warren Casey
   12:293
Garson Kanin 22:230
Jean Kerr 22:257
Terrence McNally 7:216
Alan Paton 25:361
David Rabe 4:425
Gerome Ragni and James Rado
   17:379
Anthony Shaffer 19:413
Peter Shaffer 5:388

Stephen Sondheim 30:382
Tom Stoppard 4:524
Melvin Van Peebles 2:447
Gore Vidal 2:450
Joseph A. Walker 19:454
Tennessee Williams 2:465

Hewison, Robert
Jeffrey Archer 28:13
Ursula K. Le Guin 22:275

Hewitt, M. R.
Rosa Guy 26:142

Hewitt, Nicholas
Louis-Ferdinand Céline 15:125

Hewitt, Paulo
Prince 35:324
Paul Weller 26:444, 446, 447

Heyen, William
Robert Bly 5:61
Louise Bogan 4:68
John Cheever 3:106
E. E. Cummings 3:118
James Dickey 2:117
Richmond Lattimore 3:278
Denise Levertov 1:177
Hugh MacDiarmid 2:253
Arthur Miller 6:336
Frederick Morgan 23:296
Theodore Roethke 3:433
M. L. Rosenthal 28:393
Anne Sexton 6:491
W. D. Snodgrass 6:513
William Stafford 4:520
Lewis Turco 11:550
John Updike 3:485
Richard Wilbur 3:533
William Carlos Wiliams 2:468

Heymann, Hans G.
Horst Bienek 7:29

Heywood, Christopher
Peter Abrahams 4:1
Nadine Gordimer 33:182

Hibben, Sheila
Zora Neale Hurston 30:211

Hibberd, Dominic
William Mayne 12:406

Hibbett, Howard
Kōbō Abé 22:12

Hichens, Gordon
Shirley Clarke 16:217

Hickey, Dave
B. H. Friedman 7:108

Hickman, Janet
Mollie Hunter 21:169

Hicks, Granville
Louis Auchincloss 4:28, 30;
   9:52, 53; 18:24
James Baldwin 2:31
Amiri Baraka 33:52
Peter S. Beagle 7:25
James M. Cain 28:49
Taylor Caldwell 28:60
Hortense Calisher 38:69
Truman Capote 19:80
R. V. Cassill 23:102
James Clavell 25:124

James Gould Cozzens **1**:66
José Donoso **32**:151
Walter D. Edmonds **35**:154
Leslie A. Fiedler **24**:189
Herbert Gold **4**:189
Shirley Ann Grau **4**:207
Mark Harris **19**:200
Aldous Huxley **35**:233, 235
Dan Jacobson **14**:290
Elia Kazan **6**:273
Alfred Kazin **38**:270
Ken Kesey **6**:277
John Knowles **26**:254
Arthur Koestler **33**:230, 238
Richard Kostelanetz **28**:212
Jonathan Kozol **17**:248
Meyer Levin **7**:204
Bernard Malamud **1**:200;
  11:345
Harry Mathews **6**:314
Czesław Miłosz **22**:305
Wright Morris **37**:310
John Nichols **38**:338
Flannery O'Connor **1**:258
Grace Paley **37**:331
Katherine Ann Porter **7**:312
Reynolds Price **3**:404, 405
Ann Quin **6**:442
Ayn Rand **30**:294
Mary Renault **17**:397
Conrad Richter **30**:322
J. D. Salinger **12**:502
Upton Sinclair **15**:499
Robert Stone **23**:424
Randolph Stow **23**:432
John Updike **23**:463
Kurt Vonnegut, Jr. **2**:451;
  12:602
Auberon Waugh **7**:514
Eudora Welty **14**:561
Glenway Wescott **13**:590
Herman Wouk **1**:376
Richard Wright **21**:435, 440

Hicks, Lorne
Patrick Lane **25**:284

Hieatt, Constance B.
John Fowles **15**:231

Hiesberger, Jean Marie
Charles M. Schulz **12**:533

Higgins, Bertram
Fritz Lang **20**:200

Higgins, James
Jonathan Kozol **17**:255

Higgins, R. A.
Peter Gent **29**:182

Higham, Charles
Alfred Hitchcock **16**:342
Andrzej Wajda **16**:578
Orson Welles **20**:443

Highet, Gilbert
Henry Miller **1**:224
Ezra Pound **1**:276

Highsmith, Patricia
Georges Simenon **2**:398

Highwater, Jamake Mamake
Joan Armatrading **17**:7

Hilburn, Robert
Chuck Berry **17**:54
Waylon Jennings **21**:200

Hildick, Wallace
William Mayne **12**:390

Hiley, Jim
Peter Nichols **36**:332

Hill, Ann Maxwell
Barry Hughart **39**:156

Hill, Art
Roger Angell **26**:32

Hill, Donald L.
Richard Wilbur **3**:530

Hill, Douglas
Margaret Atwood **25**:61
Joan Barfoot **18**:35
John Gardner **28**:161
Michel Tremblay **29**:423

Hill, Eldon C.
Helen Hooven Santmyer **33**:357

Hill, Frances
Penelope Lively **32**:276

Hill, Frank Ernest
Erich Maria Remarque **21**:325
Carl Sandburg **35**:345

Hill, Gladwin
John Gregory Dunne **28**:121

Hill, Helen G.
Norman Mailer **4**:321

Hill, Jane Bowers
John Irving **38**:250

Hill, Michael
Prince **35**:327

Hill, Reginald
Nicolas Freeling **38**:188
John Gardner **30**:157
John le Carré **28**:228
Morris L. West **33**:434

Hill, Robert W.
Laurence Lieberman **36**:262

Hill, Susan
Maureen Duffy **37**:115
Penelope Lively **32**:273
Daphne du Maurier **6**:146
Bruce Springsteen **17**:486
Paul Theroux **28**:424

Hill, William B.
Peter De Vries **10**:137
Bruce Lancaster **36**:245

Hill, William B., S.J.
Taylor Caldwell **28**:65
Robert Cormier **12**:133
Paul Gallico **2**:147
Evan Hunter **31**:222
Bernard Malamud **5**:269
Anthony Powell **10**:417
Muriel Spark **2**:418

Hilliard, Stephen S.
Philip Larkin **9**:323

Hillier, Bevis
John Betjeman **34**:312

Hillman, Martin
Len Deighton **22**:118

Hills, Rust
Joy Williams **31**:461

Hillyer, Robert
Siegfried Sassoon **36**:388

Hilton, James
C. S. Forester **35**:169
Jan de Hartog **19**:130
Nevil Shute **30**:368

Hilton, Robert M.
Henry Gregor Felsen **17**:124

Hilty, Hans Rudolf
Odysseus, Elytis **15**:218

Himes, Geoffrey
Seger, Bob **35**:385

Himmelblau, Jack
Miguel Ángel Asturias **8**:25

Hinchcliffe, P. M.
Ethel Davis Wilson **13**:610

Hinchliffe, Arnold P.
John Arden **13**:28
Edward Bond **6**:86
T. S. Eliot **13**:195
Harold Pinter **1**:267

Hinden, Michael
John Barth **3**:41

Hindus, Milton
Louis-Ferdinand Céline **1**:56;
  15:122
Isaac Bashevis Singer **23**:413

Hinerfeld, Susan Slocum
Harriet Doerr **34**:152
Ntozake Shange **38**:393

Hines, Theodore C.
Isaac Asimov **26**:37

Hingley, Ronald
Anna Akhmatova **25**:30
Aleksandr I. Solzhenitsyn
  1:319; **4**:515; **7**:445
Andrei Voznesensky **1**:349

Hinkemeyer, Joan
John Jakes **29**:249

Hinman, Myra
D. J. Enright **31**:150

Hinton, David B.
Leni Riefenstahl **16**:525

Hinz, Evelyn J.
Doris Lessing **6**:293
Anaïs Nin **1**:248; **4**:377

Hipkiss, Robert A.
Ernest Hemingway **3**:242
Jack Kerouac **29**:269

Hippisley, Anthony
Yuri Olesha **8**:433

Hirsch, Corinne
Isabelle Holland **21**:151

Hirsch, Edward
Robert Hass **39**:148
Robert Hayden **37**:159
Geoffrey Hill **8**:296
Isaac Bashevis Singer **11**:499
Charles Tomlinson **13**:546
James Wright **28**:467
Paul Zweig **34**:379

Hirsch, Foster
Federico Fellini **16**:295
Ernest Hemingway **1**:144
Mary McCarthy **3**:328
Laurence Olivier **20**:242
Tennessee Williams **5**:505;
  19:471

Hirt, Andrew J.
Rod McKuen **3**:332

Hislop, Alan
Richard Elman **19**:150
Jerzy Kosinski **2**:233
Wright Morris **3**:344
Frederic Prokosch **4**:422

Hislop, Ian
J.R.R. Tolkien **38**:439, 441
Fay Weldon **36**:447

Hiss, Tony
Patti Smith **12**:536

Hitchcock, George
Diane Wakoski **7**:503

Hitchcock, James
Andrew M. Greeley **28**:173

Hitchens, Gordon
Vittorio De Sica **20**:91
Orson Welles **20**:437

Hitrec, Joseph
Ivo Andrić **8**:19
Kamala Markandaya **38**:323

Hjortsberg, William
Angela Carter **5**:101
Rosalyn Drexler **2**:120
Steven Millhauser **21**:215

Hoag, David G.
Melvin Berger **12**:40
Franklyn M. Branley **21**:18, 19,
  20, 22
Roy A. Gallant **17**:132

Hoagland, Edward
Roger Angell **26**:31
Erskine Caldwell **8**:123
Peter Matthiessen **11**:359
Joe McGinniss **32**:302
John McPhee **36**:295, 296
V. S. Naipaul **37**:328
William Saroyan **8**:468; **10**:454
Kurt Vonnegut, Jr. **22**:449

Hoare, Ian
Smokey Robinson **21**:346

Hoban, Russell
Leon Garfield **12**:232
William Mayne **12**:403

Hobbs, Glenda
Harriette Arnow **18**:14, 16

Hobbs, John
Galway Kinnell **13**:318

Critic Index

Hobbs, Mary
Gunnel Beckman **26**:88

Hoberman, J.
Jean-Luc Godard **20**:155
Georg Lukács **24**:338
Nagisa Oshima **20**:256
Pier Paolo Pasolini **20**:270
Satyajit Ray **16**:495
Martin Scorsese **20**:333

Hobsbaum, Philip
F. R. Leavis **24**:308
Sylvia Plath **17**:353

Hobson, Harold
Alan Ayckbourn **33**:47
Howard Brenton **31**:58, 66
Caryl Churchill **31**:82
Michael Frayn **31**:192
Christopher Fry **14**:188
Simon Gray **14**:215; **36**:205
Peter Nichols **36**:327
Edna O'Brien **36**:335
Stephen Poliakoff **38**:374, 375

Hobson, Laura Z.
Norman Lear **12**:327
Joyce Carol Oates **33**:286

Hobson, Wilder
Evan Hunter **31**:219

Hochman, Baruch
S. Y. Agnon **4**:12
Isaac Bashevis Singer **1**:312

Hodgart, Matthew
Kingsley Amis **5**:23
Heinrich Böll **27**:60
V. S. Pritchett **5**:353
J.R.R. Tolkien **12**:568

Hodgart, Patricia
Paul Bowles **2**:78

Hodgens, Richard
John W. Campbell **32**:77

Hodges, Elizabeth
Rosemary Sutcliff **26**:426

Hodgkin, Thomas
C.L.R. James **33**:221

Hodgson, Maria
Dirk Bogarde **19**:42

Hoeksema, Thomas
Ishmael Reed **3**:424

Hoellering, Franz
Alfred Hitchcock **16**:338

Hoerchner, Susan
Denise Levertov **5**:247

Hofeldt, Roger L.
Larry Gelbart **21**:129

Hoffa, William Walter
Ezra Pound **2**:343

Hoffman, Barbara
Nora Ephron **17**:112

Hoffman, Charles W.
Max Frisch **32**:188

Hoffman, Daniel
A. R. Ammons **2**:11
W. H. Auden **2**:25
Richard Eberhart **3**:133, 134
Ted Hughes **2**:198
Robert Lowell **2**:247
Carl Sandburg **15**:468
Robin Skelton **13**:507
Anne Stevenson **33**:380
Julian Symons **32**:426

Hoffman, Eva
Marguerite Duras **34**:162
Tadeusz Konwicki **28**:208
Josef Škvorecký **39**:223
Anne Tyler **18**:529

Hoffman, Frederick J.
Conrad Aiken **1**:2
James Baldwin **1**:15
Samuel Beckett **1**:21
Saul Bellow **1**:30
John Dos Passos **1**:79
Jaes T. Farrell **4**:157
William Faulkner **1**:100
John Hawkes **4**:212
Ernest Hemingway **1**:142
Aldous Huxley **11**:281
Flannery O'Connor **15**:410
Katherine Anne Porter **1**:272
Theodore Roethke **3**:434
Philip Roth **4**:451
John Steinbeck **1**:325
William Styron **15**:524
Robert Penn Warren **1**:353

Hoffman, Lyla
James D. Forman **21**:123
Milton Meltzer **26**:304, 306

Hoffman, Marvin
Herman Wouk **38**:453

Hoffman, Michael J.
Henry Miller **1**:224

Hoffman, Nancy Y.
Anaïs Nin **4**:380
Flannery O'Connor **3**:369

Hoffman, Roy
Mary Stewart **35**:376

Hoffman, Stanley
Paul Zindel **26**:475

Hoffman, Stanton
John Rechy **14**:443

Hoffman, Valerie
Thomas J. Fleming **37**:127

Hofmann, Michael
Elizabeth Bishop **32**:43

Hofstadter, Marc
Yves Bonnefoy **15**:73

Hogan, Charles A.
Jonathan Schell **35**:362

Hogan, Lesley
Leon Rooke **25**:392

Hogan, Paula
Margaret O. Hyde **21**:178

Hogan, Randolph
Larry Kettelkamp **12**:305

Hogan, Randy
Donald E. Westlake **33**:439

Hogan, Richard
Kris Kristofferson **26**:269
Paul Weller **26**:445

Hogan, Robert
Paul Vincent Carroll **10**:97
Hugh Leonard **19**:280
Arthur Miller **1**:216
Elmer Rice **7**:361

Hogan, William
Jessamyn West **17**:548

Hoggart, Richard
W. H. Auden **1**:9
Graham Greene **6**:217
Carolyn G. Heilbrun **25**:252

Hokenson, Jan
Louis-Ferdinand Céline **9**:152

Holahan, Susan
Frank O'Hara **5**:324

Holbert, Cornelia
Kenzaburō Ōe **10**:373

Holberton, Paul
Mary Renault **17**:401

Holbrook, Stewart
Woody Guthrie **35**:182

Holden, Anthony
Rayner Heppenstall **10**:272
Daniel Hoffman **13**:286

Holden, David
Piers Paul Read **4**:445

Holden, Jonathan
John Ashbery **15**:30
Stephen Dunn **36**:156
Nancy Willard **7**:540

Holden, Raymond
Carl Sandburg **35**:342

Holden, Stephen
Jackson Browne **21**:35
Neil Diamond **30**:112, 114
Bob Dylan **12**:191
Marvin Gaye **26**:133
Janis Ian **21**:187
Billy Joel **26**:213, 222
Kris Kristofferson **26**:268
John Lennon and Paul
  McCartney **12**:372
Gordon Lightfoot **26**:279, 280
Paul McCartney **35**:284, 288, 290
Joni Mitchell **12**:438
Van Morrison **21**:234
Martin Mull **17**:298
Laura Nyro **17**:319
The Police **26**:366
Prince **35**:326
Lou Reed **21**:304
Smokey Robinson **21**:349, 351
Buffy Sainte-Marie **17**:431
Carly Simon **26**:408, 409, 412
Paul Simon **17**:463, 464, 467
Patti Smith **12**:535
Elizabeth Swados **12**:561
Lily Tomlin **17**:522
Neil Young **17**:572

Holder, Alan
Robert Lowell **5**:256

Holder, Stephen C.
John Brunner **8**:107

Holditch, W. Kenneth
Tennessee Williams **19**:471

Holland, Bette
Eleanor Clark **5**:106

Holland, Isabelle
Isabelle Holland **21**:148, 154

Holland, Jack
Derek Mahon **27**:292

Holland, Laurence B.
Wright Morris **18**:353

Holland, Mary
Tom Paulin **37**:355

Holland, Norman N.
Federico Fellini **16**:272
Stanley Kubrick **16**:377
Alain Resnais **16**:497

Holland, Philip
Leon Garfield **12**:236

Holland, Robert
Elizabeth Bishop **13**:95
Marilyn Hacker **9**:258
Richard F. Hugo **18**:263
Cynthia Macdonald **13**:356
David Slavitt **14**:491
James Welch **14**:559

Hollander, Deborah
Norma Klein **30**:242

Hollander, John
A. R. Ammons **2**:12
Howard Moss **7**:247
S. J. Perelman **15**:419

Holley, Robert P.
Claude Simon **39**:215

Hollindale, Peter
Mollie Hunter **21**:164

Hollinghurst, Alan
Martin Amis **38**:14
William Boyd **28**:37
Brigid Brophy **29**:98
Donald Justice **19**:236
Paul Muldoon **32**:320
Paul Theroux **28**:425
Michel Tournier **23**:455
Gore Vidal **22**:439
Edmund White III **27**:482

Hollington, Michael
Günter Grass **11**:250; **32**:199

Hollingworth, Roy
Ray Davies **21**:92
Neil Diamond **30**:111
Jim Jacobs and Warren Casey **12**:295
John Lennon **35**:263
Andrew Lloyd Webber and Tim
  Rice **21**:428
Pink Floyd **35**:306

Hollis, Christopher
Evelyn Waugh **19**:461

Hollis, James R.
Harold Pinter 11:439

Hollo, Anselm
Paavo Haavikko 34:168

Holloway, John
Northrop Frye 24:211

Hollowell, John
Truman Capote 19:82

Holman, C. Hugh
John P. Marquand 10:328
Robert Penn Warren 4:576

Holmes, Carol
Joseph McElroy 5:279

Holmes, Charles M.
Aldous Huxley 11:283

Holmes, Charles S.
James Thurber 5:439, 441

Holmes, Deborah A.
Marshall McLuhan 37:256

Holmes, H. H.
Isaac Asimov 26:36
Roy A. Gallant 17:126
Robert A. Heinlein 26:161
Fritz Leiber 25:301
Andre Norton 12:456
Jack Williamson 29:450
John Wyndham 19:474

Holmes, John
August Derleth 31:137
M. L. Rosenthal 28:389

Holmes, John Clellon
Jack Kerouac 2:227

Holmes, Kay
Emma Lathen 2:236

Holmstrom, Lakshmi
R. K. Narayan 28:296

Holroyd, Michael
William Gerhardie 5:139

Holsaert, Eunice
Madeleine L'Engle 12:344

Holt, John
Jonathan Kozol 17:249

Holte, James Craig
Ralph Bakshi 26:74

Holtz, William
Joseph Wood Krutch 24:289

Holtze, Sally Holmes
Sue Ellen Bridges 26:90
Sonia Levitin 17:266
Mildred D. Taylor 21:419
Paul Zindel 26:478

Holzapfel, Tamara
Ernesto Sabato 23:377

Holzhauer, Jean
Jean Kerr 22:256

Holzinger, Walter
Pablo Neruda 9:396

Homan, Richard L.
David Rabe 33:341

Homann, Frederick A., S.J.
Elie Wiesel 37:456

Homberger, Eric
Kurt Vonnegut, Jr. 22:446

Honig, Edwin
Edmund Wilson 24:475

Hood, Eric
Rosemary Sutcliff 26:426

Hood, Robert
James D. Forman 21:118
Jean Craighead George 35:175
Emily Cheney Neville 12:449

Hood, Stuart
Nicolas Freeling 38:184
Josef Škvorecký 15:510
Aleksandr I. Solzhenitsyn 1:319

Hook, Sidney
Eric Bentley 24:44
David Caute 29:120
Martin Heidegger 24:257

Hooks, Wayne
Piers Anthony 35:40

Hooper, William Bradley
Barry Gifford 34:458
Norma Klein 30:243
Lawrence Lee 34:458
Paule Marshall 27:314
William McPherson 34:85
Gloria Naylor 28:304
Barbara Pym 37:367
William Saroyan 34:458
Wilbur Smith 33:378

Hoops, Jonathan
Ingmar Bergman 16:58
Agnès Varda 16:558

Hope, Christopher
Nadine Gordimer 5:147; 18:187
Paul Muldoon 32:318
V. S. Naipaul 18:361
Louis Simpson 9:486
Derek Walcott 9:556

Hope, Francis
D. J. Enright 31:147
John Gardner 30:151
Norman MacCaig 36:282
Mary McCarthy 24:346
Sylvia Plath 17:345
Frank Tuohy 37:427

Hope, Mary
Richard Brautigan 12:74
André Brink 36:70
Brigid Brophy 11:68
Bruce Chatwin 28:72
Eilís Dillon 17:100
Martha Gellhorn 14:195
James Hanley 13:261
Benedict Kiely 23:265
Stanley Middleton 38:335
Tom Sharpe 36:402
Fay Weldon 11:566

Hope-Wallace, Philip
Orson Welles 20:433

Hopkins, Crale D.
Lawrence Ferlinghetti 10:174

Hopkins, Elaine R.
Michel Tremblay 29:427

Hopkins, J.G.E.
Maureen Daly 17:87

Hopkins, Jerry
Jim Morrison 17:288

Hopkins, Thomas
Jean M. Auel 31:23

Hopkinson, Shirley L.
E. M. Almedingen 12:3

Horak, Jan-Christopher
Werner Herzog 16:330

Horchler, Richard
Arthur A. Cohen 31:93
John Neufeld 17:307
James Purdy 28:378
Frank Tuohy 37:426

Horgan, John
Tom Paulin 37:356

Horia, Vintila
Mircea Eliade 19:144

Horn, Carole
Caroline Blackwood 6:80

Horn, Richard
Henry Green 13:253

Hornak, Paul T.
G. Cabrera Infante 25:104
Colin Wilson 14:585

Horne, Philip
Ann Schlee 35:374
Lisa St. Aubin de Teran 36:420

Horner, Patrick J.
Randall Jarrell 13:303

Hornsey, Richard
James Galvin 38:197

Hornyansky, Michael
F. R. Scott 22:376

Horovitz, Carolyn
Esther Forbes 12:210
Joseph Krumgold 12:318
Madeleine L'Engle 12:347
Rosemary Sutcliff 26:428

Horowitz, Michael
Jack Kerouac 5:214

Horowitz, Susan
Ann Beattie 8:54

Horton, Andrew
James Welch 14:560

Horton, Andrew S.
Ken Kesey 6:278
John Updike 7:487

Horvath, Violet M.
André Malraux 4:332

Horwich, Richard
John McPhee 36:296

Horwitz, Carey
Donald Barthelme 23:47

Horwood, Harold
E. J. Pratt 19:377

Hosek, Chaviva
Marilyn R. Bowering 32:47

Hosking, Geoffrey
Aleksandr I. Solzhenitsyn 18:499
Vladimir Voinovich 10:507
Alexander Zinoviev 19:488

Hoskins, Cathleen
Leon Rooke 25:394

Hough, Graham
Alan Paton 25:362
John Crowe Ransom 24:365

Hough, Lynn Harold
Joseph Wood Krutch 24:281

Hough, Marianne
Zoa Sherburne 30:362

Hough, Raymond L.
Erich von Däniken 30:423

House, John
Evan Hunter 31:229
Tom Robbins 32:374

Houston, Beverle
Bernardo Bertolucci 16:92
John Cassavetes 20:50
Roman Polanski 16:466

Houston, James
Jean Craighead George 35:177

Houston, Penelope
Michelangelo Antonioni 20:23, 29
Charles Chaplin 16:197
Paddy Chayefsky 23:115
John Ford 16:308
Alfred Hitchcock 16:341, 342, 344
Elia Kazan 16:362
Buster Keaton 20:189, 193
Richard Lester 20:223
Laurence Olivier 20:239
Satyajit Ray 16:480
Alain Resnais 16:498
Eric Rohmer 16:528
Orson Welles 20:434, 435
Billy Wilder 20:456

Houston, Robert
Raymond Carver 22:103
Luis Rafael Sánchez 23:385
Mary Lee Settle 19:411

Houston, Stan
Isaac Bashevis Singer 15:509

Howard, Anthony
Joe McGinniss 32:300

Howard, Ben
Michael Benedikt 14:81
Ed Dorn 18:129
Loren Eiseley 7:92
Marilyn Hacker 5:155
Ted Hughes 37:172
F. T. Prince 22:339
Anne Sexton 6:494
John Wain 15:560

Howard, Elizabeth J.
John Gardner 30:151

Critic Index

Howard, Esther
Edmund Crispin 22:109

Howard, Ivor
Larry Gelbart 21:125

Howard, Jane
C.D.B. Bryan 29:102
Maxine Kumin 5:222
Margaret Mead 37:279

Howard, Joseph Kinsey
A. B. Guthrie, Jr. 23:196

Howard, Lawrence A.
Robert Newton Peck 17:340

Howard, Leon
Wright Morris 1:232

Howard, Lillie P.
Zora Neale Hurston 30:225

Howard, Maureen
Donald Barthelme 8:50
Samuel Beckett 11:43
Jorge Luis Borges 1:38
Paul Bowles 2:79
Isak Dinesen 10:150
Margaret Drabble 2:117;
  10:163, 165
Eva Figes 31:170
Mavis Gallant 38:193
Mary Gordon 13:249
Peter Handke 8:261; 38:222
Lillian Hellman 8:281
P. D. James 18:275
Doris Lessing 6:301
Toni Morrison 10:356
Joyce Carol Oates 15:402
Philip Roth 1:292
Isaac Bashevis Singer 11:502
Paul Theroux 15:533
John Updike 9:537
Kurt Vonnegut, Jr. 1:347
Eudora Welty 22:458
Tennessee Williams 1:369

Howard, Michael
Len Deighton 22:116
Evelyn Waugh 27:474

Howard, Philip
Douglas Adams 27:12

Howard, Richard
Walter Abish 22:16
A. R. Ammons 2:12; 5:24
John Ashbery 2:17, 18; 13:30
W. H. Auden 2:26; 3:23
Imamu Amiri Baraka 10:18
Donald Barthelme 13:61
Roland Barthes 24:28
Marvin Bell 8:67
Frank Bidart 33:73
Robert Bly 5:61
Louise Bogan 39:388
Millen Brand 7:29
Amy Clampitt 32:116
Alfred Corn 33:114
Gregory Corso 1:63
Robert Creeley 15:150
James Dickey 7:79
Norman Dubie 36:129
Irving Feldman 7:102
Michel Foucault 31:176
Elizabeth Frank 39:388

Louise Glück 22:173
Paul Goodman 7:128
Daryl Hine 15:281
Daniel Hoffman 6:244; 23:238
John Hollander 5:185
Richard F. Hugo 32:235
Uwe Johnson 5:201
Alfred Kazin 34:558
Galway Kinnell 5:215
Kenneth Koch 5:219
Denise Levertov 5:245
Philip Levine 5:251
John Logan 5:252, 254
William Meredith 4:348;
  13:372; 22:301
James Merrill 2:274
W. S. Merwin 2:277; 5:284
Howard Moss 7:249
Frank O'Hara 5:323
Sylvia Plath 5:338
Katha Pollitt 28:367
Adrienne Rich 3:428
Raphael Rudnik 7:384
Gary Snyder 5:393
William Stafford 7:460
Mark Strand 18:515
Jun'ichirō Tanizaki 28:420
Allen Tate 4:538
Peter Taylor 18:523, 524
Mona Van Duyn 3:491
David Wagoner 5:473
Robert Penn Warren 6:557
Theodore Weiss 3:516
C. K. Williams 33:441
James Wright 5:518; 10:547
Vassily S. Yanovsky 2:485
Marguerite Yourcenar 38:460

Howard, Thomas
Frederick Buechner 2:82

Howarth, David
Gavin Ewart 13:209

Howarth, R. G.
Frank Dalby Davison 15:170

Howarth, William
Jackson J. Benson 34:406
John Steinbeck 34:406

Howe, Fanny
Laura Jensen 37:187
Clarence Major 19:299

Howe, Irving
James Baldwin 3:31; 17:21
Jurek Becker 19:36
Saul Bellow 3:49, 60; 8:79
Raymond Carver 36:100
Louis-Ferdinand Céline 3:101
James Gould Cozzens 4:111
Ralph Ellison 3:141
William Faulkner 3:151
Leslie A. Fiedler 24:190
Paula Fox 2:139
Robert Frost 3:170
Daniel Fuchs 8:221; 22:155,
  156
Henry Green 13:252
James Hanley 8:265
Ernest Hemingway 3:232
Arthur Koestler 15:312
György Konrád 4:273
Jerzy Kosinski 1:171

Primo Levi 37:228
Georg Lukács 24:337
Norman Mailer 3:311
Bernard Malamud 8:376
Czesław Miłosz 22:311
Octavio Paz 3:377
Sylvia Plath 1:270; 3:391
Ezra Pound 2:344
V. S. Pritchett 13:467
Philip Rahv 24:360
Ishmael Reed 13:477
Philip Roth 2:380; 3:440
Delmore Schwartz 10:466
Varlam Shalamov 18:479
Ignazio Silone 4:492, 494
Isaac Bashevis Singer 1:311;
  23:413
Lionel Trilling 9:533
Edmund Wilson 3:538; 24:489
Richard Wright 3:545; 9:585;
  21:437

Howe, Parkman
Jim Harrison 14:235

Howe, Russell Warren
Alex Haley 12:247

Howell, Christopher
Harry Martinson 14:356

Howell, Elmo
Flannery O'Connor 3:369
Eudora Welty 22:456

Howell, Margaret C.
C. S. Adler 35:14

Howes, Victor
Rosellen Brown 32:66
Peter Davison 28:100
Howard Fast 23:159
Robert Francis 15:236
Joanne Greenberg 30:163
Kenneth Rexroth 22:349
Muriel Rukeyser 15:457
May Swenson 14:521
James Tate 25:427

Howlett, Ivan
John Osborne 5:333

Howley, Edith C.
Isabelle Holland 21:147
Robert Newton Peck 17:338

Howley, Veronica
Barbara Corcoran 17:76

Hoy, David
Jacques Derrida 24:155
Michel Foucault 34:342

Hoy, David Couzens
Lucien Goldmann 24:251

Hoyem, Andrew
Larry Eigner 9:180

Hoyenga, Betty
Kay Boyle 1:42

Hoyt, Charles Alva
Bernard Malamud 1:196
Muriel Spark 2:414
Edward Lewis Wallant 5:477

Hubbard, Henry W.
Roy A. Gallant 17:128

Hubbell, Albert
Farley Mowat 26:329

Hubbell, Jay B.
John Hall Wheelock 14:570

Hubert, Renée Riese
André Breton 2:80
Alain Robbe-Grillet 4:449
Nathalie Sarraute 4:470

Hubin, Allen J.
Michael Crichton 6:119
Edmund Crispin 22:110
Peter Dickinson 12:168, 169
Nicolas Freeling 38:184
John Gardner 30:152
Joseph Hansen 38:236
Harry Kemelman 2:225
Ruth Rendell 28:383
Julian Symons 14:523
Donald E. Westlake 33:436

Huck, Charlotte S.
Julia W. Cunningham 12:164
Joseph Krumgold 12:320

Huck, Janet
Prince 35:331

Hudacs, Martin J.
William Caunitz 34:36
Nicholas M. Guild 33:189

Huddy, Mrs. D.
Eilís Dillon 17:98

Hudnall, Clayton
Peter Ackroyd 34:402
T. S. Eliot 34:402

Hudson, Charles
Wendell Berry 27:38

Hudson, Christopher
John Montague 13:390

Hudson, Liam
William H. Gass 15:256

Hudson, Peggy
Earl Hamner, Jr. 12:259
Norman Lear 12:330

Hudson, Theodore R.
Imamu Amiri Baraka 14:44
Langston Hughes 35:218

Hudzik, Robert
Laura Jensen 37:191

Huebner, Theodore
Anna Seghers 7:408

Huff, Theodore
Charles Chaplin 16:194

Huffman, James R.
Andrew Lloyd Webber and Tim
  Rice 21:427

Huggins, Nathan Irvin
Arna Bontemps 18:65
Carl Van Vechten 33:399

Hugh-Jones, Stephen
Len Deighton 22:114

Hughes, Carl Milton
Chester Himes 4:229
Willard Motley 18:355
Ann Petry 1:266
Richard Wright 1:377
Frank G. Yerby 1:381

Hughes, Catharine
Edward Albee **2**:3; **9**:6
Robert Anderson **23**:33
Samuel Beckett **2**:47
Daniel J. Berrigan **4**:57
Ed Bullins **5**:82
D. L. Coburn **10**:108
Allen Ginsberg **2**:164
Charles Gordone **4**:199
Rolf Hochhuth **4**:232
Albert Innaurato **21**:192
James Kirkwood **9**:320
Carson McCullers **12**:419
Mark Medoff **6**:323
Stephen Poliakoff **38**:381
David Rabe **4**:427
Robert Shaw **5**:391
Sam Shepard **17**:438; **34**:270
Neil Simon **11**:496
Milan Stitt **29**:390
Tom Stoppard **34**:281
Megan Terry **19**:439
Michael Weller **10**:526
Tennessee Williams **2**:466;
  5:502
Lanford Wilson **14**:590

Hughes, Catharine R.
Anthony Shaffer **19**:413
Megan Terry **19**:440
Douglas Turner Ward **19**:457

Hughes, D. J.
Edwin Honig **33**:211

Hughes, Daniel
John Berryman **3**:70

Hughes, David
Gabriel García Márquez **27**:152

Hughes, Dorothy B.
John Gardner **30**:152
Mary Stewart **35**:391
Donald E. Westlake **7**:528

Hughes, Douglas A.
Elizabeth Bowen **15**:77

Hughes, H. Stuart
David Caute **29**:120
Primo Levi **37**:225

Hughes-Hallett, Lucy
Elizabeth Taylor **29**:411

Hughes, James
Louis Auchincloss **9**:53

Hughes, John W.
Dannie Abse **7**:1
Joy Adamson **17**:4
John Ashbery **2**:17
W. H. Auden **2**:26
John Ciardi **10**:106

Hughes, Langston
James Baldwin **17**:21

Hughes, Olga R.
Boris Pasternak **7**:297

Hughes, R. E.
Graham Greene **1**:131

Hughes, Riley
Taylor Caldwell **28**:60, 62
Robert Cormier **12**:133
Ernest K. Gann **23**:164
Evan Hunter **31**:219

Hughes, Robert
Elia Kazan **16**:363

Hughes, Roger
Monty Python **21**:226

Hughes, Serge
Dino Buzzati **36**:85

Hughes, Ted
Joy Adamson **17**:3
Yehuda Amichai **22**:30
Leon Garfield **12**:219
Sylvia Plath **1**:270
Clancy Sigal **7**:423
Isaac Bashevis Singer **15**:503

Hughes-Hallett, Lucy
Thomas Keneally **14**:302
Bernard Slade **11**:508

Hughson, Lois
John Dos Passos **4**:136

Hugo, Richard
Theodore Roethke **8**:458

Hulbert, Ann
Ann Beattie **13**:65
André Brink **36**:72
Rosellen Brown **32**:68
John Cheever **25**:120
Eleanor Clark **19**:107
Joan Didion **14**:152
Harriet Doerr **34**:154
Mavis Gallant **18**:172
Molly Keane **31**:235
Patrick White **18**:548

Hulbert, Debra
Diane Wakoski **4**:572

Hulcoop, John
Phyllis Webb **18**:540

Hull, Elizabeth Anne
Robert Heinlein **14**:254

Hull, Robert A.
Lou Reed **21**:321

Hull, Robot A.
David Byrne **26**:98
Lou Reed **21**:305
Smokey Robinson **21**:350

Hulse, Michael
Roy Fisher **25**:161
Craig Raine **32**:351
Christopher Reid **33**:351

Hume, Kathryn
C. S. Lewis **6**:308

Humes, Walter M.
Robert Cormier **12**:137

Hummer, T. R.
Louis Simpson **32**:382

Humphrey, Robert
William Faulkner **1**:98

Humphreys, Hubert
Jules Archer **12**:19

Humphries, Patrick
The Clash **30**:47
Pink Floyd **35**:313

Humphries, Rolfe
Langston Hughes **35**:214

Hungerford, Alice N.
John Donovan **35**:139
Henry Gregor Felsen **17**:122,
  123

Hungerford, Edward B.
Robert Lipsyte **21**:207

Hunt, Albert
John Arden **6**:5

Hunt, David
Lillian Hellman **14**:257

Hunt, George W., S. J.
John Updike **15**:543

Hunt, Peter
Peter Dickinson **12**:176
Leon Garfield **12**:233
William Mayne **12**:406

Hunt, Tim
Jack Kerouac **29**:273

Hunter, Carol
Louise Erdrich **39**:134

Hunter, Evan
Martin Amis **38**:15
William F. Buckley, Jr. **37**:60
Allen Drury **37**:111
John Gregory Dunne **28**:125
George V. Higgins **18**:234
Peter Maas **29**:306
Irwin Shaw **23**:401
Leon Uris **32**:436

Hunter, Jim
Anne Tyler **11**:552

Hunter, Kristin
Ann Beattie **8**:55
Virginia Hamilton **26**:152
Ouida Sebestyen **30**:345

Hunter, Mollie
Mollie Hunter **21**:161

Hunter, Tim
Stanley Kubrick **16**:382

Hunter, William
Charles Chaplin **16**:189
Fritz Lang **20**:202

Hunting, Constance
Mina Loy **28**:253

Huntington, John
Arthur C. Clarke **18**:105
Ursula K. Le Guin **22**:268

Hurd, Pearl Strachan
Philip Booth **23**:73

Hurren, Kenneth
Samuel Beckett **6**:43
Christopher Fry **2**:144
John Hopkins **4**:234
Peter Nichols **5**:306
Harold Pinter **6**:418
Peter Shaffer **5**:388
Neil Simon **6**:505
Tom Stoppard **4**:527
David Storey **5**:415
James Thurber **11**:534

Hurst, Fannie
Zora Neale Hurston **30**:208

Hurwitz, K. Sue
Piers Anthony **35**:36
C. J. Cherryh **35**:108

Hush, Michele
Brian Wilson **12**:645

Huss, Roy
Michelangelo Antonioni **20**:37

Hussain, Riaz
Philip K. Dick **10**:138

Hutchens, John
Carl Theodor Dreyer **16**:256

Hutchens, John K.
Jessamyn West **17**:546
P. G. Wodehouse **2**:481

Hutchings, W.
Kingsley Amis **13**:12

Hutchins, James N.
Pat Conroy **30**:77

Hutchinson, Joanne
Ivy Compton-Burnett **15**:139

Hutchinson, Tom
Douglas Adams **27**:14

Hutchison, Alexander
Luchino Visconti **16**:571

Hutchison, David
Robert Altman **16**:20

Hutchison, Joanna
Peter Dickinson **12**:172

Hutchison, Paul E.
Kathryn Kramer **34**:74

Hutchison, Percy
A. J. Cronin **32**:129, 130, 131,
  132
August Derleth **31**:130
C. S. Forester **35**:160
Zora Neale Hurston **30**:212
Carl Sandburg **35**:346

Huth, Angela
Martin Amis **38**:18
Thomas M. Disch **36**:126
Maurice Gee **29**:178
Keri Hulme **39**:161
John Irving **13**:297
Penelope Lively **32**:275
Piers Paul Read **25**:380
Bernice Rubens **31**:351
Lynne Sharon Schwartz **31**:389
Michel Tournier **23**:456
A. N. Wilson **33**:454

Hutman, Norma L.
John Gardner **18**:173

Hutton, Muriel
Noel Streatfeild **21**:410

Hux, Samuel
John Dos Passos **8**:182
M. L. Rosenthal **28**:392

Huxley, Elspeth
Joy Adamson **17**:5

Huxley, Julian
Joy Adamson **17**:4
Aldous Huxley **3**:253

Hydak, Michael G.
Art Buchwald **33**:95

Hyde, Austin T., Jr.
Alvin Silverstein and Virginia
B. Silverstein **17**:456

Hyde, Lewis
Vicente Aleixandre **9**:18
Allen Ginsberg **36**:193
Heberto Padilla **38**:348

Hyde, Virginia M.
W. H. Auden **3**:23

Hyman, Esther
Nella Larsen **37**:212

Hyman, Nicholas
Ngugi wa Thiong'o **36**:319

Hyman, Sidney
Russell Baker **31**:25
Allen Drury **37**:101

Hyman, Stanley Edgar
W. H. Auden **2**:22
James Baldwin **2**:32
Djuna Barnes **3**:36
John Barth **2**:35
R. P. Blackmur **24**:56
Kenneth Burke **24**:126
Dino Buzzati **36**:89
James M. Cain **28**:45
Truman Capote **3**:99
James Gould Cozzens **11**:124
E. E. Cummings **3**:117
T. S. Eliot **6**:159
William Faulkner **3**:152
Janet Frame **2**:141
Bruce Jay Friedman **3**:165
William Golding **2**:168
Ernest Hemingway **3**:234
Norman Mailer **2**:258
Bernard Malamud **2**:265
Wallace Markfield **8**:378
Henry Miller **2**:283
Marianne Moore **2**:291
Vladimir Nabokov **2**:299
Flannery O'Connor **1**:257
Seán O'Faoláin **7**:273
J. F. Powers **4**:419
James Purdy **2**:348
Thomas Pynchon **2**:353
John Crowe Ransom **2**:363
I. A. Richards **24**:389
Alain Robbe-Grillet **2**:374
J. D. Salinger **3**:444
Isaac Bashevis Singer **3**:452
John Steinbeck **5**:405
Jun'ichiro Tanizaki **8**:510
John Updike **2**:440
Edmund Wilson **24**:472
Yvor Winters **4**:589
Joseph Wittlin **25**:467
Herman Wouk **9**:579

Hyman, Timothy
Federico Fellini **16**:288
Salman Rushdie **31**:354

Hynes, Emerson
August Derleth **31**:137

Hynes, Joseph
Graham Greene **9**:244
Evelyn Waugh **3**:511

Hynes, Samuel
W. H. Auden **1**:11; **3**:24
C. Day Lewis **10**:130, 131
T. S. Eliot **10**:172
Sumner Locke Elliott **38**:177
E. M. Forster **3**:161
William Golding **1**:122; **27**:169
Graham Greene **6**:219; **27**:177
Louis MacNeice **4**:317; **10**:326
Jean Rhys **19**:393
Stephen Spender **5**:401; **10**:488
J.I.M. Stewart **7**:464
Vassily S. Yanovsky **18**:550

Ianni, L. A.
Lawrence Ferlinghetti **2**:133

Iannone, Carol
Grace Paley **37**:337

Ianzito, Ben
Margaret O. Hyde **21**:175

Idol, John
Flannery O'Connor **3**:366

Ignatow, David
Wendell Berry **27**:35
Michael S. Harper **22**:209
Denise Levertov **8**:347
George Oppen **7**:282
Gil Orlovitz **22**:333
Charles Simic **22**:380
Diane Wakoski **7**:506
Paul Zweig **34**:378

Inge, M. Thomas
Donald Davidson **13**:168

Ingoldby, Grace
Manlio Argueta **31**:21
Maurice Gee **29**:179

Ingram, Phyllis
Betty Cavanna **12**:102

Ingrams, Richard
John Betjeman **34**:311

Innaurato, Albert
Albert Innaurato **21**:197

Innes, C. D.
Martin Walser **27**:464

Innes, Michael
J.I.M. Stewart **32**:419

Innis, Doris
Jesse Jackson **12**:289

Ionesco, Eugene
Peter Porter **33**:317

Irby, James E.
Julio Cortázar **15**:146

Irele, Abiola
Chinua Achebe **7**:3
Camara Laye **38**:284
Amos Tutuola **29**:439

Iribarne, Louis
Czesław Miłosz **22**:307

Irvine, Lorna
Marian Engel **36**:165

Irving, Edward B., Jr.
J.R.R. Tolkien **38**:438

Irving, John
John Cheever **11**:121
Toni Morrison **22**:321
Craig Nova **31**:298
Jayne Anne Phillips **15**:420

Irwin, Colin
Billy Joel **26**:214, 220
Kris Kristofferson **26**:268
Gordon Lightfoot **26**:281, 282
Carly Simon **26**:410
Paul Simon **17**:466

Irwin, John T.
George P. Elliott **2**:131
William Faulkner **14**:168
William Heyen **13**:281
David Ignatow **7**:177
Louis MacNeice **1**:187
Thomas Merton **3**:336
Stanley Plumly **33**:311
William Jay Smith **6**:512
David Wagoner **3**:508
Theodore Weiss **3**:517

Irwin, Michael
A. S. Byatt **19**:76
Isak Dinesen **10**:149
Andrea Lee **36**:254
Chaim Potok **26**:373
V. S. Pritchett **13**:467
Paul Theroux **11**:528
John Updike **9**:539

Isaac, Dan
Rainer Werner Fassbinder
20:119
Isaac Bashevis Singer **3**:453
Elie Wiesel **5**:493

Isaac, Erich
John le Carré **28**:231
Chaim Potok **26**:374

Isaac, Rael Jean
John le Carré **28**:231

Isaacs, Edith J. R.
Clifford Odets **28**:325, 327

Isaacs, Elizabeth
Yvor Winters **32**:466

Isaacs, Harold R.
Lorraine Hansberry **17**:183

Isaacs, Hermine Rich
Orson Welles **20**:431

Isaacs, James
Jimmy Cliff **21**:60
Lou Reed **21**:309

Isaacs, Neil D.
George Roy Hill **26**:200

Isaacs, Susan
Hortense Calisher **38**:76
Ntozake Shange **38**:393

Isbell, Harold
John Logan **5**:253

Isherwood, Christopher
Katherine Anne Porter **13**:446

Ishiguro, Hidé
Yukio Mishima **9**:384

Isler, Scott
David Byrne **26**:95, 98
Paul McCartney **35**:285
Jim Morrison **17**:294
Lou Reed **21**:316, 320

Isola, Carolanne
Anne McCaffrey **17**:283

Israel, Callie
Roderick L. Haig-Brown
21:139

Issacs, Susan
Jean M. Auel **31**:24

Italia, Paul G.
James Dickey **10**:139

Itzin, Catherine
Jack Gelber **6**:197

Ivask, Ivar
Paavo Haavikko **34**:174

Iverson, Lucille
Judith Leet **11**:323

Ives, John
Sonia Levitin **17**:265
Josephine Poole **17**:372
Roger Zelazny **21**:465

Iwamoto, Yoshio
Yasunari Kawabata **18**:281
Yukio Mishima **9**:381

Iwasaki, Akira
Akira Kurosawa **16**:397

Iyer, Pico
Jim Harrison **33**:199
Barbara Pym **37**:379

Izard, Anne
Babbis Friis-Baastad **12**:213
John R. Tunis **12**:597

Jablons, Pam
Ved Mehta **37**:293

Jack, Aparna
Kamala Markandaya **38**:326

Jack, Peter Monro
Alfred Kazin **38**:270
Ogden Nash **23**:318

Jackel, David
Matt Cohen **19**:112
James Reaney **13**:476
Robin Skelton **13**:508
Raymond Souster **14**:505

Jackson, Al
Andre Norton **12**:463

Jackson, Angela
Lucille Clifton **19**:109
Henry Dumas **6**:145

Jackson, Blyden
Gwendolyn Brooks **5**:75
Sterling A. Brown **23**:98
Robert Hayden **5**:169
Langston Hughes **5**:191
Margaret Walker **6**:554

Jackson, Brian
Philippa Pearce **21**:283

Jackson, David
James Merrill 34:241

Jackson, Esther Merle
Tennessee Williams 7:540

Jackson, Jane B.
Richard Peck 21:300

Jackson, Joseph Henry
Howard Fast 23:154
Roderick L. Haig-Brown
21:135
Irving Stone 7:468

Jackson, Katherine Gauss
Isabel Colegate 36:109
Evan Hunter 31:222
Elizabeth Taylor 29:408

Jackson, Marni
Nora Ephron 31:158

Jackson, Miles M.
Rosa Guy 26:141

Jackson, Paul R.
Henry Miller 14:370, 374

Jackson, Richard
Stephen Dobyns 37:78
Robert Pack 13:439
Robert Penn Warren 13:578
Charles Wright 13:614

Jackson, Richard L.
Ramón Gómez de la Serna
9:239

Jackson, Robert Louis
Aleksandr I. Solzhenitsyn 7:446

Jackson, Seán Wyse
Dirk Bogarde 19:43
D. M. Thomas 22:418

Jacob, Gilles
Robert Bresson 16:110
François Truffaut 20:383

Jacob, John
Thomas McGrath 28:278
Jonathan Williams 13:601

Jacobs, Barry
Halldór Laxness 25:292

Jacobs, Diane
Claude Chabrol 16:178
Keri Hulme 39:164
Lina Wertmüller 16:592

Jacobs, Lewis
Charles Chaplin 16:191
Rouben Mamoulian 16:422

Jacobs, Nicolas
David Jones 4:261

Jacobs, Rita D.
Saul Bellow 10:42

Jacobs, Ronald M.
Samuel R. Delany 8:168

Jacobs, William Jay
C. S. Forester 35:172
S. E. Hinton 30:204
John R. Tunis 12:598

Jacobsen, Josephine
Peter Davison 28:100
Arthur Gregor 9:256
Daniel Hoffman 6:242
David Ignatow 4:249
Denise Levertov 3:293
Howard Moss 14:375
James Schevill 7:401
Mona Van Duyn 7:498

Jacobson, Dan
S. Y. Agnon 14:1
James Baldwin 17:22
D. J. Enright 4:155; 31:147
Ian Fleming 30:131
Andrei Sinyavsky 8:490

Jacobson, Irving
Arthur Miller 6:333; 10:345

Jacobus, John
Charles M. Schulz 12:531

Jacobus, Lee A.
Imamu Amiri Baraka 5:46

Jacoby, Susan
Andrea Lee 36:253
Gore Vidal 22:435

Jacoby, Tamar
Athol Fugard 25:174
Maxine Hong Kingston 19:250

Jaehne, Karen
Werner Herzog 16:329

Jaffe, Daniel
A. R. Ammons 2:12
John Berryman 2:57
Philip Booth 23:76
William Melvin Kelley 22:248
Norman MacCaig 36:283
Sylvia Plath 17:346
Gary Snyder 2:406
Hollis Summers 10:493
R. G. Vliet 22:441

Jaffe, Harold
Peter S. Beagle 7:26
Ernesto Cardenal 31:79
Kenneth Rexroth 2:369

Jaffee, Cyrisse
Robin F. Brancato 35:65
Betty Cavanna 12:102
Paula Danziger 21:84
Lois Duncan 26:106
Stan Lee 17:261
Hilma Wolitzer 17:563
Paul Zindel 26:478

Jahiel, Edwin
Marguerite Duras 6:150
Antonis Samarakis 5:381
Vassilis Vassilikos 4:552

Jahn, Janheing
Camara Laye 4:282

Jahn, Mike
Chuck Berry 17:53
Mick Jagger and Keith Richard
17:229
Jim Morrison 17:291
Paul Simon 17:464

Jahner, Elaine
Louise Erdrich 39:133
Leslie Marmon Silko 23:408
Wole Soyinka 36:412

Jajko, Pamela
Robin F. Brancato 35:66

Jamal, Zahir
Gail Godwin 22:181
Olivia Manning 19:302
Alberto Moravia 11:384
William Trevor 14:535
John Wain 15:561

James, Caryn
Robert Coover 32:127
Stanley Elkin 27:124

James, Clive
W. H. Auden 3:28
John Berryman 25:89
John Betjeman 6:66
Ronald Bush 34:524
T. S. Eliot 34:524
Lillian Hellman 8:280
Philip Larkin 5:225, 229;
33:262, 266
John le Carré 9:327
Norman Mailer 3:317
Aleksandr I. Solzhenitsyn 7:436
Tom Stoppard 29:393
Evelyn Waugh 19:465
Edmund Wilson 24:481
Yvor Winters 8:553
Alexander Zinoviev 19:490

James, D. G.
I. A. Richards 24:381

James, Jamie
Jim Carroll 35:78
Toby Olson 28:345

James, John
David Hare 29:219

James, Kathryn C.
Christie Harris 12:263

James, Louis
Louise Bennett 28:30
Wilson Harris 25:210
Jean Rhys 14:447
Derek Walcott 25:449

James, Stuart
James A. Michener 5:290

Jameson, Fredric
Larry Niven 8:426
Jean-Paul Sartre 24:412, 421

Jameson, Richard T.
Steven Bochco and Michael
Kozoll 35:49

Janes, Annette V.
Thomas W. Shapcott 38:404

Janeway, Elizabeth
Sylvia Ashton-Warner 19:22
Pamela Hansford Johnson
7:184; 27:217
Jean Kerr 22:255, 256
Françoise Sagan 17:417, 420
Elizabeth Spencer 22:399
John Steinbeck 21:369
Elizabeth Taylor 29:408

Jessamyn West 7:519
Rebecca West 31:456

Janeway, Michael
Anne Tyler 7:479
Tom Wicker 7:533

Janiera, Armando Martins
Kōbō Abé 8:1
Jun'ichirō Tanizaki 8:510

Jannone, Claudia
Philip José Farmer 19:166

Janovicky, Karel
Jaroslav Seifert 34:259

Janson, Michael
Alta 19:19

Jarrell, Randall
Conrad Aiken 3:3
W. H. Auden 2:21
Ben Belitt 22:49
John Berryman 13:75
Elizabeth Bishop 1:34; 4:65
R. P. Blackmur 2:61
Alex Comfort 7:54
R. S. Crane 27:70
E. E. Cummings 3:116
Robert Frost 1:109; 3:169
Robert Graves 1:126; 2:174
David Ignatow 7:173
Robinson Jeffers 2:213
Robert Lowell 1:178; 2:246
Josephine Miles 1:215
Marianne Moore 1:226; 2:290;
19:338
Ezra Pound 2:340
John Crowe Ransom 2:361
Theodore Roethke 3:432
Muriel Rukeyser 6:478
Carl Sandburg 4:462
Karl Shapiro 4:485
Christina Stead 2:420
Richard Wilbur 3:530
William Carlos Williams 1:369;
2:467
Yvor Winters 32:454, 459

Jarrett-Kerr, Martin
F. R. Leavis 24:295

Jaspers, Karl
Czesław Miłosz 22:304

Jastrow, Robert
Arthur C. Clarke 35:117

Jaszi, Peter
Stanley Kubrick 16:382

Jayne, Edward
Roland Barthes 24:39

Jeanneret, F.
Adolfo Bioy Casares 13:87

Jeavons, Clyde
Sidney Poitier 26:359

Jebb, Julian
Bernardo Bertolucci 16:91
Anita Brookner 34:137
Anita Loos 32:259
François Truffaut 20:406
Evelyn Waugh 27:471

Jeffares, A. N.
Molly Keane **31**:234
Seán O'Faoláin **32**:342

Jefferies, Ian
Stanley Middleton **38**:329

Jefferson, Margo
Beryl Bainbridge **5**:39
James Baldwin **17**:43
Rosalyn Drexler **6**:142
Nadine Gordimer **7**:133
Jack Heifner **11**:264
Carolyn G. Heilbrun **25**:254
Elizabeth Jane Howard **7**:164
Gayl Jones **6**:265
Nettie Jones **34**:68
V. S. Naipaul **7**:253
Juan Carlos Onetti **7**:280
Salman Rushdie **31**:354

Jefferson, Margot
Molly Keane **31**:235

Jefferson, M. L.
Ann Schlee **35**:376

Jeffords, Ed
Jim Morrison **17**:289

Jeffrey, David L.
Jack Hodgins **23**:230

Jeffreys, Susan
Erich von Däniken **30**:427
Ann Schlee **35**:374

Jelenski, K. A.
Witold Gombrowicz **7**:123

Jelliffe, R. A.
Robert A. Heinlein **26**:161

Jellinck, Frank
Rex Stout **3**:472

Jemie, Onwuchekwa
Langston Hughes **35**:219

Jenkins, Alan
Lawrence Durrell **27**:95
Bret Easton Ellis **39**:58
Derek Walcott **25**:457

Jenkins, Cecil
André Malraux **4**:336

Jenkins, David
A. R. Ammons **5**:28
Patrick Boyle **19**:68

Jenkins, J. S.
Eilís Dillon **17**:97

Jenkins, Peter
Simon Gray **14**:215

Jenkins, Steve
Pink Floyd **35**:314

Jennings, Elizabeth
Robert Frost **3**:171
Seamus Heaney **37**:165

Jerome, Judson
John Ciardi **10**:105
William Dickey **28**:118
Edwin Honig **33**:211
Marge Piercy **27**:376

Jervis, Steven A.
Evelyn Waugh **1**:359

Joad, C.E.M.
Margaret Mead **37**:273

Jochmans, Betty
Agatha Christie **8**:142

Joe, Radcliffe
Gerome Ragni and James Rado
17:388

Johannesson, Eric O.
Isak Dinesen **29**:153

Johansen, Nancy K.
Betsy Byars **35**:74

John, Roland
Stanley J. Kunitz **6**:287

Johnsen, William F.
Frank Lentricchia **34**:573

Johnson, Abby Ann Arthur
Penelope Gilliatt **10**:229

Johnson, Albert
Lindsay Anderson **20**:14
John Cassavetes **20**:44, 45
Shirley Clarke **16**:217

Johnson, Alexandra
Isaac Bashevis Singer **15**:507
Elie Wiesel **37**:450

Johnson, Ann S.
David Garnett **3**:188

Johnson, Becky
Kristin Hunter **35**:230

Johnson, Carol
Donald Davie **31**:108

Johnson, Carolyn
Hilma Wolitzer **17**:562

Johnson, Colton
Anthony Kerrigan **6**:276

Johnson, Curtis
Guy Davenport, Jr. **6**:125

Johnson, Cynthia
Margaret O. Hyde **21**:177

Johnson, Diane
Beryl Bainbridge **14**:37
Donald Barthelme **13**:59
Saul Bellow **25**:83
C.D.B. Bryan **29**:104
Don DeLillo **8**:172; **39**:123
Joan Didion **8**:176
E. L. Doctorow **37**:80
Nadine Gordimer **5**:147
Edward Hoagland **28**:184
Erica Jong **8**:315
Maxine Hong Kingston **12**:313
Doris Lessing **3**:286; **10**:316
Norman Mailer **14**:354
James Alan McPherson **19**:310
Toni Morrison **10**:355
Joyce Carol Oates **3**:361;
33:290
Jean Rhys **6**:453
Muriel Spark **3**:465
Alexander Theroux **25**:431
D. M. Thomas **31**:431
Gore Vidal **10**:502
Paul West **7**:524

Johnson, Douglas
Louis-Ferdinand Céline **7**:45
Claude Mauriac **9**:367

Johnson, Ernest A., Jr.
Miguel Delibes **18**:109

Johnson, Gerald W.
Ved Mehta **37**:287

Johnson, Greg
Joyce Carol Oates **15**:401
John Updike **9**:538

Johnson, Halvard
Gary Snyder **1**:318

Johnson, Helen Armstead
Joseph A. Walker **19**:454

Johnson, Ira D.
Glenway Wescott **13**:592

Johnson, James Weldon
Sterling A. Brown **23**:95
Carl Van Vechten **33**:391

Johnson, James William
Katherine Anne Porter **7**:311

Johnson, Joyce
Ayi Kwei Armah **33**:36
Louise Bogan **39**:383
Elizabeth Frank **39**:383

Johnson, Kenneth
Richard Wilbur **6**:570

Johnson, Lee R.
Eilís Dillon **17**:99

Johnson, Manly
David Ignatow **14**:277
Thomas W. Shapcott **38**:404

Johnson, Marigold
Lynne Reid Banks **23**:43
Pamela Hansford Johnson
27:223
Bernard Malamud **3**:324

Johnson, Nora
Jeffrey Archer **28**:13
Laura Z. Hobson **25**:272
Garson Kanin **22**:233
Norma Klein **30**:240
Darcy O'Brien **11**:405
Françoise Sagan **36**:381

Johnson, Pamela Hansford
Allen Drury **37**:100
Winston Graham **23**:192
Doris Lessing **22**:277
Colin MacInnes **23**:281
Olivia Manning **19**:302
Mary McCarthy **24**:343
Françoise Sagan **17**:419

Johnson, Patricia A.
Langston Hughes **35**:220, 221

Johnson, Patricia J.
J.M.G. Le Clézio **31**:250

Johnson, Paul
Ian Fleming **30**:134
Lillian Hellman **34**:349
Michael Scammell **34**:482
Aleksandr Solzhenitsyn **34**:482

Johnson, Priscilla
Judith Guest **30**:176

Johnson, R. E., Jr.
Agnes Eckhardt Nixon **21**:248

Johnson, Richard
W. H. Auden **2**:26

Johnson, Richard A.
Turner Cassity **6**:107
Anthony Hecht **8**:268
Delmore Schwartz **2**:387

Johnson, Robert K.
Francis Ford Coppola **16**:244
Neil Simon **31**:403

Johnson, Rosemary
John Ashbery **13**:35
May Swenson **14**:520

Johnson, Sidney M.
Hermann Hesse **17**:197

Johnson, Thomas S.
Bob Dylan **12**:194

Johnson, Tom
Archibald Macleish **14**:338
Howard Nemerov **36**:303

Johnson, Wayne L.
Ray Bradbury **15**:85

Johnson, William
Robert Altman **16**:20
Kon Ichikawa **20**:179, 184
Eric Rohmer **16**:532
Martin Scorsese **20**:326
Jerzy Skolimowski **20**:354
Orson Welles **20**:439, 442

Johnson-Masters, Virginia
Gay Talese **37**:401

Johnston, Albert H.
Nora Ephron **17**:110
Patti Smith **12**:541

Johnston, Ann
Kevin Major **26**:287

Johnston, Arnold
William Golding **3**:198

Johnston, Clarie
Nagisa Oshima **20**:250

Johnston, Dillon
Austin Clarke **6**:111
Albert Goldbarth **5**:143
Seamus Heaney **7**:147
Paul Muldoon **32**:315

Johnston, George Sim
Saul Bellow **33**:71
Joseph Epstein **39**:468
Alfred Kazin **34**:563
Tom Wolfe **35**:466

Johnston, Kenneth G.
William Faulkner **11**:199

Johnston, Neal
Elmore Leonard **28**:236; **34**:215

Johnston, Sheila
Paul McCartney **35**:293

Johnstone, J. K.
E. M. Forster **3**:160

Joly, Jacques
Jean Renoir **20**:294

Jonas, George
Margaret Atwood **3**:19
Gwendolyn MacEwan **13**:357
Raymond Souster **14**:504

Jonas, Gerald
Douglas Adams **27**:12
Poul Anderson **15**:14
Isaac Asimov **9**:49; **19**:27;
  26:59
Arthur C. Clarke **13**:155;
  35:123, 126
Samuel R. Delany **8**:168, 169;
  14:148; **38**:162
Thomas M. Disch **36**:124
Harlan Ellison **13**:203
William Gibson **39**:142
Robert A. Heinlein **26**:174
Frank Herbert **12**:278, 279;
  23:221; **35**:205, 207
Arthur Koestler **33**:242
Ursula K. LeGuin **8**:343
Stanislaw Lem **15**:330
Barry N. Malzberg **7**:209
Vonda N. McIntyre **18**:326
Larry Niven **8**:426
Andre Norton **12**:470
Frederik Pohl **18**:412
Keith Roberts **14**:464
Joanna Russ **15**:461, 462
Arkadii Strugatskii and Boris
  Strugatskii **27**:438
Kate Wilhelm **7**:538
Jack Williamson **29**:461
Gene Wolfe **25**:473
Roger Zelazny **21**:469

Jones, A. R.
James Baldwin **17**:27
Sylvia Plath **9**:430

Jones, Allan
David Bowie **17**:63, 65
Elvis Costello **21**:66, 68, 69,
  74, 75
Ray Davies **21**:100, 101, 102
Mick Jagger and Keith Richard
  17:235
Laura Nyro **17**:315, 317, 319
Richard O'Brien **17**:324
Pink Floyd **35**:307, 312
Lou Reed **21**:308, 312, 314
Carly Simon **26**:410
Neil Young **17**:576, 577, 580

Jones, Alun R.
Rhys Davies **23**:148
Philip Larkin **13**:335
Eudora Welty **1**:362; **2**:460

Jones, Ann
Joe McGinniss **32**:306

Jones, Bedwyr Lewis
Kate Roberts **15**:445

Jones, Bernard
John Cowper Powys **9**:441

Jones, Brian
Howard Nemerov **2**:306
Peter Porter **33**:318

Jones, C. A.
Edwin Honig **33**:213

Jones, Chris
Athol Fugard **25**:173

Jones, D. A. N.
Isabel Allende **39**:36
Howard Barker **37**:31
Marie-Claire Blais **22**:58
Dirk Bogarde **19**:41
William Boyd **28**:37
Ed Bullins **1**:47
John Fowles **6**:184
Julius Horwitz **14**:266
Mervyn Jones **10**:295
Yoram Kaniuk **19**:239
William Kennedy **34**:211
Milan Kundera **19**:267
Colin MacInnes **23**:286
Stanley Middleton **38**:329, 334
V. S. Naipaul **37**:325
Richard Stern **39**:239
Amos Tutuola **29**:441
John Wain **11**:564
Fay Weldon **11**:565
Vassily S. Yanovsky **18**:551

Jones, D. Allan
John Barth **5**:52

Jones, D. G.
Earle Birney **6**:76; **11**:49
Philip Child **19**:102
Phyllis Gotlieb **18**:192
Anne Hébert **4**:219
Irving Layton **2**:237
Miriam Waddington **28**:437

Jones, Daniel R.
Edward Bond **23**:70

Jones, David R.
Saul Bellow **13**:69

Jones, Du Pre
Sam Peckinpah **20**:272

Jones, E.B.C.
Noel Streatfeild **21**:395

Jones, Edward T.
John Updike **3**:487

Jones, Eldred D.
Wole Soyinka **36**:409

Jones, Ernest
William Maxwell **19**:306
Aldo Palazzeschi **11**:431
Budd Schulberg **7**:403
Elizabeth Spencer **22**:398

Jones, F. Whitney
Ernesto Cardenal **31**:72

Jones, Frank N.
Evan Hunter **31**:221

Jones, Granville H.
Jack Kerouac **2**:226

Jones, Howard Mumford
Alvah Bessie **23**:58
Leon Edel **29**:169
Alfred Kazin **38**:269
Olivia Manning **19**:299
Philip Rahv **24**:352

Jones, James H.
Louis R. Harlan **34**:183

Jones, John Bush
Simon Gray **36**:203
Harold Pinter **9**:418

Jones, John M.
Kate Roberts **15**:445

Jones, LeRoi
Robert Creeley **15**:149

Jones, Lewis
Seán O'Faoláin **32**:340
Michel Tournier **36**:436
Fay Weldon **36**:445

Jones, Linda T.
Katherine Paterson **30**:284

Jones, Louisa E.
Raymond Queneau **10**:431

Jones, Madison
Andrew Lytle **22**:295

Jones, Margaret E. W.
Ana María Matute **11**:362, 365

Jones, Mervyn
Nadine Gordimer **33**:184
Ved Mehta **37**:291
Peter Nichols **36**:331
Philip Roth **31**:345

Jones, Nettie
Nettie Jones **34**:69

Jones, Patricia
June Jordan **23**:257

Jones, Rhodri
Leon Garfield **12**:227, 235

Jones, Rhonda
Ezekiel Mphahlele **25**:335

Jones, Richard
Graham Greene **14**:218
L. P. Hartley **2**:182
Anthony Powell **7**:346

Jones, Robert F.
Sumner Locke Elliott **38**:179
James Jones **3**:262

Jones, Roger
Saul Bellow **10**:39
Gary Snyder **32**:394

Jones, Sherman
Louis R. Harlan **34**:188

Jones, Sumie
Jun'ichirō Tanizaki **14**:527

Jong, Erica
Sara Davidson **9**:174
Doris Lessing **3**:287
Marge Piercy **27**:373
Anne Sexton **4**:483; **8**:484
Eleanor Ross Taylor **5**:425

Joost, Nicholas
T. S. Eliot **9**:190
Ernest Hemingway **19**:217
Carl Sandburg **35**:353

Jordan, Alice M.
Henry Gregor Felsen **17**:120
Esther Forbes **12**:207
Lee Kingman **17**:243
Andre Norton **12**:455
John R. Tunis **12**:593

Jordan, Ann
Jean Craighead George **35**:179

Jordan, Clive
Martin Amis **4**:19
Maureen Duffy **37**:114
Elaine Feinstein **36**:168
Masuji Ibuse **22**:226
Dan Jacobson **4**:253
G. Josipovici **6**:271
Milan Kundera **19**:266
Yukio Mishima **4**:356
Thomas Pynchon **6**:432
Gillian Tindall **7**:473
Ludvík Vaculík **7**:494
Kurt Vonnegut, Jr. **4**:567

Jordan, Elaine
Anita Brookner **32**:60

Jordan, Francis X.
Barry Gifford **34**:459
Lawrence Lee **34**:459
Scott O'Dell **30**:276
William Saroyan **34**:459
Gore Vidal **10**:51

Jordan, June
Maya Angelou **12**:13
Millen Brand **7**:30
John Donovan **35**:140
Nikki Giovanni **2**:165
Zora Neale Hurston **7**:171
Gayl Jones **9**:306
Marge Piercy **6**:402
Richard Wright **14**:595

Jose, Nicholas
Noel Hilliard **15**:280

Joseph, Gerhard
John Barth **1**:17

Joseph, Michael
Margery Allingham **19**:12
John Wyndham **19**:475

Josephs, Allen
Manlio Argueta **31**:19
Juan Benet **28**:22
Manuel Puig **28**:374
Luisa Valenzuela **31**:438

Josephy, Alvin M., Jr.
Mari Sandoz **28**:404

Josipovici, Gabriel
Saul Bellow **3**:54; **25**:85
Robert Fitzgerald **39**:475
William Golding **27**:168
Vladimir Nabokov **3**:353

Joyce, Joyce Ann
Amiri Baraka **33**:61

Joye, Barbara
Ishmael Reed **13**:476
John A. Williams **13**:598

Joyner, Nancy
Andrew Lytle **22**:297

Judd, Inge
Martin Walser **27**:467

Judell, Brandon
William Kotzwinkle **35**:257

Judson, Horace
Allen Drury **37**:106

Juhasz, Suzanne
Alta **19**:18
Louise Bogan **39**:383
Elizabeth Frank **39**:383
Carolyn Kizer **39**:169
Marge Piercy **27**:380

Julian, Janet
Piers Anthony **35**:35, 37

Jumper, Will C.
Robert Lowell **1**:178

Jürma, Mall
Ivar Ivask **14**:287

Jury, Floyd D.
Margaret O. Hyde **21**:180

Justice, Donald
J. V. Cunningham **31**:99

Justus, James H.
John Berryman **4**:60
John Crowe Ransom **4**:431
Karl Shapiro **4**:487
Robert Penn Warren **4**:578, 582

Kabakoff, Jacob
Aharon Megged **9**:375

Kabatchnik, Amnon
William F. Buckley, Jr. **7**:36

Kadish, Doris Y.
Jean Genet **14**:203

Kadison, Chris
Ted Berrigan **37**:45

Kael, Pauline
Woody Allen **16**:4
Robert Altman **16**:23, 28
Michelangelo Antonioni **20**:30, 38
Ingmar Bergman **16**:70
Bernardo Bertolucci **16**:89
Mel Brooks **12**:76
Luis Buñuel **16**:137
John Cassavetes **20**:46, 48
Jimmy Cliff **21**:59
Francis Ford Coppola **16**:233, 240
Brian De Palma **20**:75, 77, 79, 81, 83
Marguerite Duras **20**:102
Federico Fellini **16**:280, 282
Bob Fosse **20**:122
Larry Gelbart **21**:130
Jean-Luc Godard **20**:137, 138, 154
Werner Herzog **16**:325
George Roy Hill **26**:205
John Huston **20**:170, 173
Elia Kazan **16**:364, 373
Stanley Kubrick **16**:378, 393
John Landis **26**:275
Richard Lester **20**:226, 229
George Lucas **16**:409
Norman Mailer **3**:315
Steve Martin **30**:251
Elaine May **16**:432
Sam Peckinpah **20**:281
Sidney Poitier **26**:360
Richard Pryor **26**:381
Satyajit Ray **16**:485, 488
Jean Renoir **20**:296

Erich Rohmer **16**:537
Ken Russell **16**:543
Paul Schrader **26**:389, 394, 399
Martin Scorsese **20**:335
Peter Shaffer **37**:385
Steven Spielberg **20**:357, 360, 366
François Truffaut **20**:383, 384, 385, 392, 404
Agnès Varda **16**:559
Luchino Visconti **16**:570, 575
Peter Weir **20**:429
Lina Wertmüller **16**:591
Frederick Wiseman **20**:469

Kaeppler, Adrienne
Thor Heyerdahl **26**:193

Kaftan, Robert
Morris L. West **33**:432

Kagan, Norman
Stanley Kubrick **16**:385

Kagan, Shel
Frank Zappa **17**:593

Kahn, Lothar
Arthur Koestler **3**:271
Siegfried Lenz **27**:251
Jakov Lind **4**:293
André Schwarz-Bart **4**:479
Isaac Bashevis Singer **23**:416
Peter Weiss **3**:515
Elie Wiesel **3**:527; **37**:452, 455

Kahn, Roger
Robert Lipsyte **21**:211

Kaiser, Marjorie
Joan Aiken **35**:21

Kaiser, Walter
George Seferis **11**:493

Kakish, William
Peter Hundke **10**:260

Kakutani, Michiko
William Boyd **28**:41
André Brink **36**:69
Ronald Bush **34**:524
Peter De Vries **28**:111
T. S. Eliot **34**:524
Frederick Forsyth **36**:177
T. Gertler **34**:49
Barbara Guest **34**:442
Jim Harrison **33**:199
H. D. **34**:442
Amy Hempel **39**:68
Keri Hulme **39**:161
Susan Isaacs **32**:255
Nancy Lemann **39**:75
Jay McInerney **34**:82
V. S. Naipaul **37**:324
Joyce Carol Oates **33**:294
Cynthia Ozick **28**:355
Grace Paley **37**:333
Jayne Anne Phillips **33**:305
Anthony Powell **31**:322
John Updike **34**:285
Robert Penn Warren **39**:264
Fay Weldon **36**:448
Nancy Willard **37**:464

Kalb, Marvin L.
Aleksandr I. Solzhenitsyn **26**:414

Kalem, T. E.
Edward Albee **2**:2; **5**:12
Kingsley Amis **3**:8
Samuel Beckett **2**:47
Ed Bullins **5**:84
Anne Burr **6**:104
Friedrich Dürrenmatt **4**:141
Jules Feiffer **8**:216
Robert Graves **2**:177
Bill Gunn **5**:152
John Hopkins **4**:234
Albert Innaurato **21**:192
Ira Levin **3**:294
Paul McCartney **35**:278
Terrence McNally **7**:217
Jason Miller **2**:284
Peter Nichols **5**:307
Sean O'Casey **5**:319
Murray Schisgal **6**:490
Sam Shepard **34**:267
Neil Simon **6**:506
Isaac Bashevis Singer **6**:511
Aleksandr I. Solzhenitsyn **1**:321
Stephen Sondheim **30**:381, 384
Tom Stoppard **4**:526
David Storey **2**:424, 425; **4**:530
C. P. Taylor **27**:446
Thornton Wilder **6**:572
Tennessee Williams **7**:545
Robert Wilson **7**:550

Kallan, Richard A.
Leon Uris **32**:433

Kalstone, David
A. R. Ammons **2**:12
John Ashbery **2**:17; **13**:31
John Berryman **3**:69
Elizabeth Bishop **13**:95
Alfred Corn **33**:114
A. D. Hope **3**:250
Philip Levine **5**:250
Robert Lowell **11**:326
James Merrill **2**:273, 275; **13**:378
Robert Pinsky **19**:371
Adrienne Rich **11**:475
James Schuyler **5**:383

Kameen, Paul
Daniel J. Berrigan **4**:57
Robert Lowell **3**:303

Kamin, Ira
Charles Bukowski **9**:137

Kaminsky, Stuart M.
Elaine May **16**:435

Kamla, Thomas A.
Hermann Hesse **25**:259

Kane, B. M.
Christa Wolf **14**:594

Kane, Patricia
Chester Himes **7**:159

Kanfer, Stefan
Truman Capote **19**:85
Jerzy Kosinski **6**:285
Mary McCarthy **39**:484
Terrence McNally **7**:218
William McPherson **34**:86
Brian Moore **7**:237
Paul Simon **17**:458

Isaac Bashevis Singer **3**:453; **6**:510
John Steinbeck **5**:408
Dalton Trumbo **19**:447
Gore Vidal **22**:438

Kanigel, Robert
Margaret Mead **37**:283

Kannenstine, Louis F.
Djuna Barnes **29**:30

Kanon, Joseph
Robert Altman **16**:29
Louis Auchincloss **4**:29
Carlos Castaneda **12**:88
Daphne du Maurier **6**:147
Penelope Gilliatt **2**:160
Steven Millhauser **21**:216
Jacqueline Susann **3**:475
Hunter S. Thompson **17**:505
John Updike **2**:444

Kantra, Robert A.
Samuel Beckett **3**:46

Kao, Donald
Laurence Yep **35**:471

Kapai, Leela
Paule Marshall **27**:311

Kaplan, Abraham
John Ford **16**:306

Kaplan, Fred
Francis Ford Coppola **16**:239
Bob Fosse **20**:125
Roman Polanski **16**:470
François Truffaut **20**:381

Kaplan, George
Alfred Hitchcock **16**:349

Kaplan, Howard
T. Coraghessan Boyle **36**:61

Kaplan, Johanna
Dan Jacobson **4**:254
Cynthia Ozick **7**:287
Chaim Potok **26**:374

Kaplan, Jon
Judith Thompson **39**:252

Kaplan, Samuel
John Neufeld **17**:311

Kaplan, Stephen
Stanley Kubrick **16**:382

Kaplan, Sydney Janet
Doris Lessing **6**:296

Kaplow, Jeffrey J.
David Caute **29**:110

Kapp, Isa
Thomas Berger **18**:57
John Cheever **11**:120
Joan Didion **32**:149
Oriana Fallaci **11**:189
Jascha Kessler **4**:269
Andrea Lee **36**:257
Grace Paley **4**:394
Barbara Pym **37**:374
Philip Roth **4**:459; **22**:356
Eudora Welty **22**:458

Kappel, Lawrence
Thomas Pynchon **18**:439

Karanikas, Alexander
Donald Davidson **19**:123

Karatnycky, Adrian
Frederick Forsyth **36**:176

Kardokas, Christine
Zilpha Keatley Snyder **17**:475

Kareda, Urjo
Marian Engel **36**:164
Alice Munro **19**:345
Audrey Thomas **37**:422

Karimi-Hakkak, Ahmad
Ahmad Shamlu **10**:470

Karl, Frederick R.
Samuel Beckett **1**:20
Elizabeth Bowen **1**:40
John Braine **1**:43
Ivy Compton-Burnett **1**:60
Lawrence Durrell **1**:83
E. M. Forster **1**:103
William Golding **1**:119
Henry Green **2**:178
Graham Greene **1**:132
L. P. Hartley **2**:181
Joseph Heller **1**:140
Aldous Huxley **1**:150
Christopher Isherwood **1**:155
Pamela Hansford Johnson **1**:160
Doris Lessing **1**:173, 175
Iris Murdoch **1**:233
P. H. Newby **2**:310
Anthony Powell **1**:277
William Sansom **2**:383
C. P. Snow **1**:314, 315, 316
Muriel Spark **2**:414
Evelyn Waugh **1**:357
Angus Wilson **2**:471

Karlen, Arno
Edward Dahlberg **7**:62

Karlinsky, Simon
Vladimir Nabokov **1**:241; **2**:305
John Rechy **7**:357
Aleksandr I. Solzhenitsyn **2**:408
Edmund White III **27**:478
Yevgeny Yevtushenko **1**:382

Karloff, Boris
Charles Addams **30**:11

Karp, David
James Baldwin **17**:21
Meyer Levin **7**:203

Karriker, Alexandra Heidi
Vasily Aksyonov **37**:13

Kasack, Wolfgang
Aleksandr I. Solzhenitsyn **7**:434

Kasindorf, Martin
Christopher Hampton **4**:212
Norman Lear **12**:335

Kasper, Rosemary
M. E. Kerr **35**:249

Kass, Judith M.
Robert Altman **16**:38, 40

Katope, Christopher G.
Jessamyn West **17**:548

Kattan, Naim
Mordecai Richler **5**:373

Katz, Bill
Roderick L. Haig-Brown
21:138

Katz, Claire
Flannery O'Connor **6**:379, 380

Katz, Donald R.
Thomas McGuane **18**:325

Katz, Jonathan
Albert Goldbarth **5**:144

Kauf, R.
Fritz Hochwälder **36**:239

Kauffmann, Stanley
Kōbō Abé **22**:11
Edward Albee **2**:3; **5**:11, 14;
25:38
Robert Altman **16**:29, 44
Lindsay Anderson **20**:16
Fernando Arrabal **2**:15; **9**:41
Alan Ayckbourn **5**:37
Ralph Bakshi **26**:67, 69, 71
Ingmar Bergman **16**:57
John Berryman **3**:69
Bernardo Bertolucci **16**:90, 94,
100
Mel Brooks **12**:80
Ed Bullins **7**:36
Luis Buñuel **16**:135
Anthony Burgess **2**:86
John Cassavetes **20**:47, 49
Charles Chaplin **16**:203, 206
Michael Cimino **16**:213
D. L. Coburn **10**:108
Francis Ford Coppola **16**:234
Vittorio De Sica **20**:95, 96
E. L. Doctorow **6**:133
Carl Theodor Dreyer **16**:262
Nora Ephron **31**:160
Rainer Werner Fassbinder
20:109, 113
Federico Fellini **16**:279, 281,
283
Bob Fosse **20**:122, 124, 127
Athol Fugard **5**:130; **9**:230
Larry Gelbart **21**:128
Jean-Luc Godard **20**:139, 140
John Guare **14**:220
Peter Handke **5**:164; **38**:215,
219, 227
Lorraine Hansberry **17**:184
David Hare **29**:211
Beth Henley **23**:217
James Leo Herlihy **6**:234
Werner Herzog **16**:327, 334
George Roy Hill **26**:202, 209
John Huston **20**:175
Buster Keaton **20**:194
James Kirkwood **9**:319
Jerzy Kosinski **1**:171; **2**:233
Stanley Kubrick **16**:382, 383,
390
J.M.G. Le Clézio **31**:242
Richard Lester **20**:224, 228,
231
George Lucas **16**:407, 408, 411
Steve Martin **30**:251
Elaine May **16**:435
Albert Maysles and David
Maysles **16**:439
Arthur Miller **2**:280
Henry Miller **4**:350

Henri de Montherlant **19**:326
Monty Python **21**:225
Peter Nichols **5**:307
Hugh Nissenson **9**:399
Marsha Norman **28**:320
Edna O'Brien **3**:365
Clifford Odets **28**:336
John O'Hara **2**:325
Nagisa Oshima **20**:255
Yasujiro Ozu **16**:448
Pier Paolo Pasolini **20**:260
Miguel Piñero **4**:402
Harold Pinter **3**:386, 387;
6:417; **15**:421
Roman Polanski **16**:464
Bernard Pomerance **13**:446
Richard Pryor **26**:379, 382
David Rabe **4**:425, 426; **8**:450
Terence Rattigan **7**:356
Satyajit Ray **16**:486
Jean Renoir **20**:300, 302
Gregor von Rezzori **25**:383
Eric Rohmer **16**:531, 537
Ken Russell **16**:543, 547
Françoise Sagan **17**:424
James Salter **7**:387
Carlos Saura **20**:317
Paul Schrader **26**:385, 389
André Schwarz-Bart **2**:388
Martin Scorsese **20**:325, 335
Rod Serling **30**:354
Peter Shaffer **37**:385
Irwin Shaw **7**:412
Sam Shepard **17**:434, 446
Joan Micklin Silver **20**:341
Elizabeth Spencer **22**:401
Steven Spielberg **20**:360, 367
John Steinbeck **5**:408
Tom Stoppard **4**:527; **15**:524
Elizabeth Swados **12**:560
François Truffaut **20**:386, 389
Melvin Van Peebles **20**:410
Gore Vidal **2**:450
Luchino Visconti **16**:567, 570
Kurt Vonnegut, Jr. **2**:452
Andrzej Wajda **16**:584
Joseph A. Walker **19**:455
Orson Welles **20**:453
Lina Wertmüller **16**:587, 591,
598
Billy Wilder **20**:465
Tennessee Williams **5**:504;
7:545
August Wilson **39**:281
Lanford Wilson **14**:593
Robert Wilson **9**:576

Kaufman, Donald L.
Norman Mailer **2**:263

Kaufman, James
James Jones **39**:408
Frank MacShane **39**:408

Kaufman, Joanne
William Kotzwinkle **35**:258

Kaufman, Marjorie
Thomas Pynchon **18**:432

Kaufman, Michael T.
Salman Rushdie **31**:356

Kaufmann, James
Elmore Leonard **34**:213

Kaufmann, R. J.
F. R. Leavis **24**:299

Kavanagh, Julie
Marilynne Robinson **25**:387

Kavanagh, P. J.
Czesław Miłosz **31**:263
Siegfried Sassoon **36**:396

Kavanaugh, Patrick
Frank O'Connor **14**:400

Kaveney, Roz
Don DeLillo **39**:126
Doris Lessing **15**:332
Frederik Pohl **18**:412

Kay, George
Eugenio Montale **18**:340

Kaye, Frances W.
W. P. Kinsella **27**:237

Kaye, Howard
Yvor Winters **4**:593

Kaye, Lenny
Jimmy Cliff **21**:59
Mick Jagger and Keith Richard
17:224, 239
Paul McCartney **35**:281
Jim Morrison **17**:292
Jimmy Page and Robert Plant
12:475
Lou Reed **21**:303, 314
Smokey Robinson **21**:347
Paul Simon **17**:446
Peter Townshend **17**:532
Stevie Wonder **12**:656

Kaye, Marilyn
Franklyn M. Branley **21**:23
Betsy Byars **35**:75, 76
Aidan Chambers **35**:99
Christopher Collier and James
L. Collier **30**:75
Isabelle Holland **21**:154
Kristin Hunter **35**:230
M. E. Kerr **35**:248, 249
Cynthia Voigt **30**:417, 419

Kaysen, Xana
Jerzy Kosinski **10**:309

Kazin, Alfred
Renata Adler **8**:7
James Baldwin **1**:13; **13**:52
Amiri Baraka **33**:56
Donald Barthelme **13**:54
Brendan Behan **1**:25
Saul Bellow **1**:28; **3**:61
R. P. Blackmur **24**:55
Jane Bowles **3**:84
Paul Bowles **1**:41
William S. Burroughs **5**:91
Albert Camus **2**:97
Elias Canetti **25**:113
Truman Capote **38**:84
Louis-Ferdinand Céline **9**:158
John Cheever **3**:108
James Gould Cozzens **4**:116
A. J. Cronin **32**:134
E. E. Cummings **8**:155
Joan Didion **3**:127
Lawrence Durrell **1**:83
Leon Edel **29**:167

Ralph Ellison **1**:93; **3**:146
Frederick Exley **6**:170
William Faulkner **28**:137
Gabriel García Márquez **2**:149
William H. Gass **8**:240
Paul Goodman **4**:195
Graham Greene **1**:131
Barbara Guest **34**:445
H. D. **34**:445
Joseph Heller **11**:265
Ernest Hemingway **3**:242
Edward Hoagland **28**:181
Maureen Howard **14**:268
Aldous Huxley **35**:234
David Ignatow **4**:249
Jack Kerouac **1**:165
Alan Lelchuk **5**:241
Robert Lowell **1**:179
Georg Lukács **24**:321
Norman Mailer **1**:187
Bernard Malamud **1**:194; **3**:326
Wallace Markfield **8**:379
John P. Marquand **2**:271
Mary McCarthy **3**:329
Carson McCullers **4**:345
Czesław Miłosz **31**:264
Vladimir Nabokov **3**:356; **8**:418
V. S. Naipaul **4**:373; **9**:393
Joyce Carol Oates **2**:313; **3**:363
Flannery O'Connor **1**:259;
　3:370
Julia O'Faolain **19**:359
John O'Hara **1**:260; **3**:371
Alan Paton **25**:357
Walker Percy **2**:334
Ann Petry **1**:266
Thomas Pynchon **3**:419
Kenneth Rexroth **1**:284
Philip Roth **1**:292
J. D. Salinger **1**:295, 296;
　3:446, 458
Karl Shapiro **4**:484
Isaac Bashevis Singer **1**:310;
　3:457; **9**:487
C. P. Snow **1**:314
Aleksandr I. Solzhenitsyn
　2:410; **4**:515
Susan Sontag **13**:515
John Steinbeck **13**:530
Allen Tate **24**:440
Peter Taylor **4**:543
Paul Theroux **8**;514
John Updike **3**:488; **9**:538;
　23:471
Carl Van Vechten **33**:395
Kurt Vonnegut, Jr. **3**:505
Robert Penn Warren **1**:352;
　4:582
Edmund Wilson **2**:475; **24**:475
Abraham B. Yehoshua **13**:618

Kazin, Pearl
Brigid Brophy **29**:91

Keane, Patrick
Galway Kinnell **5**:216

Kearns, Edward
Richard Wright **1**:379

Kearns, George
Walter Abish **22**:23
Elizabeth Bowen **22**:68
T. Coraghessan Boyle **36**:60
Alfred Corn **33**:115
Julio Cortázar **33**:130

Guy Davenport **38**:139
Fumiko Enchi **31**:141
Athol Fugard **25**:176
Luis Rafael Sánchez **23**:385
Danny Santiago **33**:353
D. M. Thomas **31**:434

Kearns, Kathleen
T. Coraghessan Boyle **36**:57
Anita Brookner **32**:61

Kearns, Lionel
Earle Birney **6**:77

Keates, Jonathan
Gunnel Beckman **26**:88
Dirk Bogarde **19**:42
Jorge Luis Borges **6**:94
John Fowles **10**:187
Roy Fuller **28**:157
Anthony Hecht **19**:208
John Hersey **7**:155
Ursula Holden **18**:257
Thomas W. Shapcott **38**:404
Tom Sharpe **36**:403
Peter Straub **28**:409

Keating, H.R.F.
Jessica Anderson **37**:19
Robert B. Parker **27**:364

Keating, L. Clark
Marie-Claire Blais **22**:58

Keating, Peter
Erica Jong **8**:315

Kee, Robert
Enid Bagnold **25**:75
Agatha Christie **12**:115

Keefe, Joan
Flann O'Brien **10**:362

Keehan, Anne
Evan Hunter **31**:221

Keeley, Edmund
Odysseus Elytis **15**:221
Stratis Haviaras **33**:204
Yannis Ritsos **31**:328
George Seferis **11**:492

Keen, Sam
Carlos Castaneda **12**:93

Keenan, Hugh T.
J.R.R. Tolkien **1**:336

Keene, Donald
Yukio Mishima **2**:287; **4**:354
Jun'ichirō Tanizaki **8**:509

Keene, Frances
Françoise Sagan **17**:417

Keeney, Willard
Eudora Welty **1**:361

Keffer, Charles J.
Jeffrey Archer **28**:11
Robin Cook **14**:131
Susan Isaacs **32**:253

Kehoe, William
August Derleth **31**:137

Keils, R. M.
Vladimir Nabokov **11**:391

Keith, Philip
J. E. Wideman **5**:489

Keith, W. J.
Louis Dudek **19**:138
Robert Frost **26**:128
Roderick L. Haig-Brown
　21:141
Hugh Hood **28**:194
Rudy Wiebe **14**:573

Keitnor, Wendy
Ralph Gustafson **36**:217, 220

Kelleher, Ed
David Bowie **17**:58
Carly Simon **26**:408

Kelleher, Victor
Muriel Spark **13**:523

Kellen, Konrad
Lina Wertmüller **16**:596

Keller, Jane Carter
Flannery O'Connor **3**:365

Keller, Karl
Aimé Césaire **32**:110, 112
Robert Creeley **36**:119
Robert Frost **34**:472
William H. Pritchard **34**:472
Ntozake Shange **38**:395

Keller, Marcia
Agatha Christie **12**:117

Kelley, Welbourn
Julia Peterkin **31**:305

Kellman, Steven
Max Frisch **14**:184

Kellman, Steven G.
Milan Kundera **32**:267
Aharon Megged **9**:374
Iris Murdoch **15**:385
Amos Oz **33**:302
Robert Pinget **13**:442

Kellogg, Gene
Graham Greene **3**:208
François Mauriac **4**:339
Flannery O'Connor **3**:365
J. F. Powers **4**:419
Evelyn Waugh **3**:511

Kelly, Aileen
Michael Scammell **34**:483
Aleksandr Solzhenitsyn **34**:483
Henri Troyat **23**:462

Kelly, Ernece B.
Maya Angelou **12**:9

Kelly, Frank
Andrew Holleran **38**:245
David Madden **15**:350
T. H. White **30**:451

Kelly, James
Rhys Davies **23**:146
Ernest K. Gann **23**:165
Evan Hunter **31**:218
Pamela Hansford Johnson
　27:216
Irwin Shaw **7**:411
Richard Stern **39**:235

Kelly, Thomas
Bernard Mac Laverty **31**:254

Kelman, Ken
Carl Theodor Dreyer **16**:259
Leni Riefenstahl **16**:522

Kemball-Cook, Jessica
Andre Norton **12**:465

Kemme, Tom
Shusaku Endo **19**:161
Cay Van Ash **34**:118

Kemp, Barbara
Françoise Sagan **17**:427

Kemp, John C.
Robert Frost **15**:245

Kemp, Peter
Douglas Adams **27**:11
Elizabeth Bishop **32**:39
Frederick Busch **18**:84
I. Compton-Burnett **34**:494
Roald Dahl **18**:108
Lawrence Durrell **13**:189
Buchi Emecheta **14**:160
Robert Graves **39**:328
Thom Gunn **32**:213
John Hawkes **27**:200
Thomas Keneally **27**:231
Philip Larkin **39**:341
Doris Lessing **22**:286
David Malouf **28**:269
Iris Murdoch **22**:326
Barbara Pym **19**:387; **37**:377
Bernice Rubens **31**:350
Tom Sharpe **36**:401
Scott Sommer **25**:424
Hilary Spurling **34**:494
D. M. Thomas **22**:417
William Trevor **25**:444
Frank Tuohy **37**:432
Fay Weldon **19**:468

Kemper, Robert Graham
Robert Anderson **23**:31

Kempton, Kenneth Payson
C. S. Forester **35**:161, 162

Kempton, Murray
Gore Vidal **4**:554

Kempton, Sally
John Knowles **26**:258

Kendall, Elaine
Nelson Algren **33**:17
William Kennedy **34**:206
Françoise Sagan **36**:381

Kendall, Paul M.
Thomas B. Costain **30**:99

Kendle, Burton
John Cheever **15**:128

Kendle, Judith
Morley Callaghan **14**:102

Kendrick, Walter
Robert Bloch **33**:84
Agatha Christie **39**:443
Leon Edel **34**:536
Stephen King **37**:198
Janet Morgan **39**:443
Judith Rossner **29**:355
Susan Sontag **31**:411, 417
Tobias Wolff **39**:284
Stephen Wright **33**:469

Keneas, Alex
Ira Levin 6:305

Kenefick, Madeleine
Gayl Jones 6:265
Cynthia Ozick 7:290

Kennard, Jean E.
Anthony Burgess 10:86
William Golding 10:233
Joseph Heller 8:275
James Purdy 10:421
Kurt Vonnegut, Jr. 12:611

Kennaway, James
Simon Raven 14:439

Kennebeck, Edwin
Heinrich Böll 27:55
Kamala Markandaya 38:321
Walter M. Miller, Jr. 30:253
James Schuyler 23:387
Terry Southern 7:453
Marguerite Yourcenar 19:482

Kennedy, Andrew K.
John Arden 6:10
Samuel Beckett 6:46
T. S. Eliot 6:166
John Osborne 11:422
Harold Pinter 6:419

Kennedy, Dorothy Mintzlaff
Raymond Federman 6:181
Howard Nemerov 6:363

Kennedy, Eileen
Molly Giles 39:66
Penelope Gilliatt 10:230
Norma Klein 30:237
Susan Richards Shreve 23:402
Sloan Wilson 32:449

Kennedy, Eugene
James Carroll 38:106
Thomas Merton 34:466
Michael Mott 34:466

Kennedy, Harlan
Michelangelo Antonioni 20:42
Federico Fellini 16:300
Werner Herzog 16:330

Kennedy, John S.
John Steinbeck 1:323; 13:532

Kennedy, P. C.
Frank Swinnerton 31:423

Kennedy, Randall
Philip Caputo 32:104

Kennedy, Ray
Joseph Wambaugh 3:509

Kennedy, Raymond
Richard Wright 21:435

Kennedy, Richard S.
Aldous Huxley 35:241

Kennedy, Sighle
Arthur Miller 26:311

Kennedy, Susan
Rita Mae Brown 18:75
Susan Cheever 18:101
Anne Redmon 22:342
J.I.M. Stewart 14:512

Kennedy, William
Jorge Amado 13:11
Thomas Bernhard 3:64
Carlos Castaneda 12:92
Robertson Davies 2:113
Don DeLillo 10:134
Gabriel García Márquez 8:232
John Gardner 7:111
Joseph Heller 5:179
Elia Kazan 6:273
Jerzy Kosinski 15:316
William Kotzwinkle 5:219
Peter Matthiessen 7:211
Steven Millhauser 21:219
Mordecai Richler 5:378
Piri Thomas 17:500
Mario Vargas Llosa 31:444

Kennedy, William V.
Thomas J. Fleming 37:122

Kennedy, X. J.
A. R. Ammons 2:13
Edward Dahlberg 7:62
Philip Larkin 39:344
Eleanor Lerman 9:328
James Merrill 2:275
Robert Pack 13:438
David Wagoner 15:558

Kennelly, Brendan
Seamus Heaney 37:163
Patrick Kavanagh 22:236

Kennely, Patricia
Jim Morrison 17:288, 289

Kenner, Hugh
W. H. Auden 2:29
Samuel Beckett 11:43; 29:53
Ben Belitt 22:54
Saul Bellow 25:81
R. P. Blackmur 24:60
Robert Bly 10:62
Guy Davenport, Jr. 14:142;
    38:141
John Dos Passos 8:182
William Empson 33:145
Leslie A. Fiedler 24:196
H. D. 31:204
Ernest Hemingway 8:285
Irving Layton 15:319
J.M.G. Le Clézio 31:245
Marshall McLuhan 37:265
James Merrill 34:234
Marianne Moore 4:360; 13:397;
    19:340
Vladimir Nabokov 6:357
George Oppen 7:283, 285
Sylvia Plath 17:366
Ezra Pound 2:345; 4:412; 7:325
Mary Renault 11:472
W. D. Snodgrass 18:492
Richard G. Stern 4:522
William Carlos Williams 2:469;
    13:605
James Wright 10:546
Louis Zukofsky 7:561, 562

Kennerly, Sarah Law
Jay Bennett 35:43, 44
Lois Duncan 26:104
Kin Platt 26:349, 350

Kenney, Edwin J., Jr.
Elizabeth Bowen 11:61
Iris Murdoch 6:345

Kenney, Harry C.
Farley Mowat 26:335

Kenny, Anthony
Ved Mehta 37:290

Kenny, Kevin
Norma Klein 30:243
D. M. Pinkwater 35:320
Kin Platt 26:356

Kenny, Mary
Benedict Kiely 23:265

Kenny, Shirley Strum
Antonia Fraser 32:183

Kent, Cerrulia
Laura Z. Hobson 7:164

Kent, George E.
James Baldwin 1:15
Gwendolyn Brooks 1:46; 15:94
Nikki Giovanni 19:192
Chester Himes 4:229
Ishmael Reed 13:477

Kent, Heddie
Franklyn M. Branley 21:20

Keon, Carol
Pat Jordan 37:194

Kerans, James
Jean Renoir 20:289

Kerensky, Oleg
Alan Ayckbourn 33:40
Howard Brenton 31:61
Simon Gray 36:201
Stephen Poliakoff 38:379

Kermode, Frank
W. H. Auden 2:25; 14:33
Beryl Bainbridge 8:37; 22:46
Roland Barthes 24:25
Samuel Beckett 2:46
T. S. Eliot 2:126, 128
E. M. Forster 10:178
Northrop Frye 24:208, 213
William H. Gass 39:479
William Golding 2:167, 169;
    17:161, 167; 27:164
Nadine Gordimer 10:240
Graham Greene 6:215
Peter Handke 5:165
Edwin Honig 33:210
Christopher Isherwood 11:296
Stanley Kunitz 14:312
C. S. Lewis 27:264
Marshall McLuhan 37:254
Henry Miller 2:282
Iris Murdoch 2:298
Philip Rahv 24:355
I. A. Richards 14:453
Philip Roth 3:440
J. D. Salinger 12:497
Susan Sontag 31:413
Muriel Spark 2:414, 415, 418;
    18:500
Edmund Wilson 24:478
Marguerite Yourcenar 19:483

Kern, Anita
Buchi Emecheta 14:159

Kern, Edith
Samuel Beckett 2:47; 14:70

Kern, Gary
Aleksandr I. Solzhenitsyn
    26:420

Kern, Robert
Richard Brautigan 12:71
Gary Snyder 9:500

Kernan, Alvin B.
Bernard Malamud 27:303
Philip Roth 4:453
Evelyn Waugh 1:358

Kernan, Margot S.
Claude Chabrol 16:172

Kerr, Baine
N. Scott Momaday 19:318

Kerr, Elizabeth M.
William Faulkner 14:178

Kerr, John Austin, Jr.
José Rodrigues Miguéis 10:341

Kerr, Peter
Michel Foucault 34:339

Kerr, Walter
Edward Albee 25:33
Enid Bagnold 25:75, 76
Sally Benson 17:50
Albert Camus 32:85
Alice Childress 12:106
Michael Cristofer 28:95
Gretchen Cryer 21:79, 80, 82
Shelagh Delaney 29:144
Harvey Fierstein 33:154
Charles Fuller 25:182
William Gibson 23:173, 174
Charles Gordone 1:124
Simon Gray 36:208
David Hare 29:211, 218
Jan de Hartog 19:130
Lorraine Hansberry 17:184, 190
Beth Henley 23:215, 217
Jim Jacobs and Warren Casey
    12:292
George S. Kaufman 38:267
Peter Luke 38:314
Marsha Norman 28:318
Clifford Odets 28:334
Harold Pinter 1:267
Gerome Ragni and James Rado
    17:386, 387
Jonathan Reynolds 38:388
Martin Sherman 19:415
Neil Simon 6:503; 31:402
Stephen Sondheim 30:379, 380,
    399
Megan Terry 19:440
Kurt Vonnegut, Jr. 12:605
Douglas Turner Ward 19:458
Andrew Lloyd Webber and Tim
    Rice 21:426, 432
Michael Weller 10:526
Tennessee Williams 19:473
Lanford Wilson 36:463

Kerrane, Kevin
Robert Coover 7:59

Kerridge, Roy
Colin MacInnes 23:286

Kerrigan, Anthony
Jorge Luis Borges 4:74; 9:115;
    13:109
Camilo José Cela 13:145

Kerrigan, John
Paul Muldoon **32**:321

Kerr-Jarrett, Peter
Octavio Paz **6**:397

Kersh, Gerald
José Donoso **32**:152

Kertes, Joseph
Leonard Cohen **38**:137

Kertzer, Jon
Matt Cohen **19**:114
Michael Ondaatje **29**:339

Kessler, Edward
Daniel Hoffman **6**:242
Charles Wright **6**:580

Kessler, Jascha
Vicente Aleixandre **36**:27
Yehuda Amichai **22**:31
A. R. Ammons **5**:28
Imamu Amiri Baraka **2**:34
Samuel Beckett **29**:60
Elizabeth Bishop **32**:36
Sterling A. Brown **23**:101
Charles Bukowski **5**:79
Ernesto Cardenal **31**:78
Robert Creeley **36**:116
James Dickey **7**:79
Loren Eiseley **7**:91
Louise Erdrich **39**:131
Irving Feldman **7**:101
Lawrence Ferlinghetti **10**:174
Eva Figes **31**:169
Allen Ginsberg **36**:197
Robert Graves **2**:176
Sandra Hochman **8**:297
Edwin Honig **33**:216
Ted Hughes **2**:201
June Jordan **5**:203
Yoram Kaniuk **19**:241
Anthony Kerrigan **4**:269
György Konrád **10**:304
Maxine Kumin **28**:222
Don L. Lee **2**:238
Thomas Merton **3**:335
Czesław Miłosz **31**:267
Pablo Neruda **28**:315
Robert Pack **13**:438
Kenneth Patchen **18**:394
Octavio Paz **10**:388
John Crowe Ransom **11**:467
Muriel Rukeyser **15**:460
Peter Shaffer **37**:383
Karl Shapiro **8**:485; **15**:478
Josef Škvorecký **39**:230
Gary Soto **32**:401
Muriel Spark **8**:492
May Swenson **14**:521
D. M. Thomas **31**:433
John Wain **11**:561, 563
Robert Penn Warren **4**:578;
39:258
Nancy Willard **37**:464
C. K. Williams **33**:444
Charles Wright **28**:460
James Wright **28**:467
Louis Zukofsky **7**:560

Ketterer, David
Ursula K. Le Guin **22**:267
Theodore Sturgeon **22**:411

Kettle, Arnold
John Berger **2**:55
Ivy Compton-Burnett **3**:111
E. M. Forster **3**:159
Graham Greene **3**:206
Aldous Huxley **3**:252

Key, Jan
Aidan Chambers **35**:100

Keyes, Mary
Phyllis Gotlieb **18**:192

Keyser, Barbara Y.
Muriel Spark **8**:494

Keyser, Lester J.
Federico Fellini **16**:294

Khan, Naseem
Simon Gray **36**:209

Kherdian, David
Philip Whalen **6**:565

Kibera, Leonard
Alex La Guma **19**:275

Kibler, Louis
Alberto Moravia **11**:382; **18**:344

Kibler, Myra L.
Robert Cormier **30**:86

Kidder, Rushworth M.
E. E. Cummings **8**:161; **15**:155,
158

Kidel, Mark
Bob Dylan **12**:198
The Police **26**:364

Kieffer, Eduardo Gudiño
Jorge Luis Borges **9**:117

Kieley, Benedict
Brendan Behan **11**:44
John Montague **13**:391

Kiely, Robert
Richard Adams **18**:2
Louis Auchincloss **18**:26
Russell Banks **37**:24
Maeve Brennan **5**:73
Frederick Busch **18**:85
Hortense Calisher **2**:96
Susan Cheever **18**:101
Michael Frayn **7**:106
Gabriel García Márquez **2**:148
William H. Gass **2**:155
Bernard Malamud **3**:323
Joyce Carol Oates **19**:356
Anne Redmon **22**:342
Philip Roth **31**:340
Angus Wilson **25**:463

Kieran, Margaret Ford
Walter Farley **17**:117
Mary Stolz **12**:547

Kiernan, Robert F.
John Barth **3**:42
Gore Vidal **33**:405

Kiernan, V. G.
Antonia Fraser **32**:178

Kilgore, Kathryn
Juan Benet **28**:22
Adrienne Rich **36**:367

Killam, G. D.
Chinua Achebe **1**:1; **26**:22
Ngugi wa Thiong'o **36**:317

Killinger, John
Fernando Arrabal **9**:37

Kilpatrick, Thomas L.
T. J. Binyon **34**:33

Kilroy, Thomas
Samuel Beckett **3**:45

Kimball, Arthur G.
Yasunari Kawabata **9**:309
Kenzaburō Ōe **36**:344
Jun'ichirō Tanizaki **14**:526

Kimmel, Eric A.
Emily Cheney Neville **12**:452

Kimzey, Ardis
Leslie Norris **14**:388

Kinder, Marsha
Michelangelo Antonioni **20**:31
Ingmar Bergman **16**:75
Bernardo Bertolucci **16**:92
Luis Buñuel **16**:144
John Cassavetes **20**:50, 52
Richard Lester **20**:223
Roman Polanski **16**:466
Carlos Saura **20**:320
Peter Weir **20**:429

Kindilien, Glenn A.
Saul Bellow **10**:44

King, Adele
Camara Laye **38**:288

King, Bruce
Chinua Achebe **26**:19, 25
Jayanta Mahapatra **33**:278
Nadine Gordimer **10**:240
Ruth Prawer Jhabvala **8**:312
V. S. Naipaul **9**:392
Frank Sargeson **31**:371
Derek Walcott **25**:452

King, Cameron
Derek Walcott **25**:449

King, Charles L.
Ramón Sender **8**:479

King, Cynthia
Christopher Collier and James
L. Collier **30**:73
Ouida Sebestyen **30**:346

King, Dolores
Margaret O. Hyde **21**:177

King, Edmund L.
Vicente Aleixandre **36**:25
Jorge Guillén **11**:263

King, Florence
Nancy Lemann **39**:78

King, Francis
Vasily Aksyonov **37**:14
Louis Auchincloss **18**:26
William Boyd **28**:39
Malcolm Bradbury **32**:57
Bruce Chatwin **28**:74
Isabel Colegate **36**:111, 112
Rhys Davies **23**:148
Margaret Drabble **22**:125

Maureen Duffy **37**:117
Lawrence Durrell **27**:98
Shusaku Endo **14**:161
Herbert Gold **14**:208
Graham Greene **18**:195
Aldous Huxley **5**:193
John Irving **23**:253
Kazuo Ishiguro **27**:203
M. M. Kaye **28**:198
Penelope Lively **32**:274
Bernard Mac Laverty **31**:256
Bobbie Ann Mason **28**:274
Brian Moore **32**:309
Iris Murdoch **11**:388
Shiva Naipaul **32**:327
David Plante **38**:372
Barbara Pym **19**:388
Tom Sharpe **36**:401, 403
Muriel Spark **13**:525
Robert Stone **23**:430
Lisa St. Aubin de Teran **36**:423
Fay Weldon **19**:469
Morris L. West **33**:434
A. N. Wilson **33**:452, 456

King, James
F. R. Scott **22**:373

King, Larry L.
Roy Blount, Jr. **38**:46
John Nicols **38**:341
Kurt Vonnegut, Jr. **12**:602

King, Michael
Albert Goldbarth **38**:202

King, Nicholas
Rebecca West **31**:458

King, P. R.
Thom Gunn **32**:207
Ted Hughes **37**:171
Philip Larkin **33**:256
Tom Paulin **37**:352

King, Stephen
Theodore Sturgeon **39**:364

King, Thomas M.
Jean-Paul Sartre **7**:394

Kingsbury, Mary
M. E. Kerr **12**:298

Kingston, Carolyn T.
Margot Benary-Isbert **12**:35
Emily Cheney Neville **12**:453
Scott O'Dell **30**:271

Kingston, Maxine Hong
Bienvenido N. Santos **22**:366

Kington, Miles
Peter Nichols **36**:332

Kinkead, Gwen
Penelope Gilliatt **2**:161

Kinkead-Weekes, Mark
William Golding **27**:165

Kinnamon, Keneth
James Baldwin **13**:52
Richard Wright **21**:451

Kinney, Arthur F.
William Faulkner **28**:141
Dorothy Parker **15**:415

Kinney, Jeanne
Louise Erdrich **39**:129
Carson McCullers **4**:344;
12:427

Kinsella, Anna M.
Alberto Moravia **7**:242

Kinsella, Thomas
Austin Clarke **6**:111

Kinsey, Helen E.
Margot Benary-Isbert **12**:33

Kinzie, Mary
Jorge Luis Borges **2**:73
Rosellen Brown **32**:67
Stephen Dobyns **37**:77
Albert Goldbarth **38**:201
Marilyn Hacker **23**:206
Ted Hughes **14**:271
Laura Jensen **37**:191
Howard Nemerov **36**:306
Sharon Olds **39**:188
Robert Pinsky **38**:356
Gary Snyder **32**:395
Charles Wright **28**:459

Kirby, David
A. R. Ammons **25**:44
Stephen Dunn **36**:155
William Harmon **38**:244

Kirby, Emma
Lenora Mattingly Weber **12**:633

Kirby, Fred
Jim Carroll **35**:77

Kirby, Martin
Walker Percy **8**:440

Kirby-Smith, H. T., Jr.
Elizabeth Bishop **4**:66
Arthur Gregor **9**:254

Kirk, Elizabeth D.
J.R.R. Tolkien **1**:341

Kirk, John M.
Mario Vargas Llosa **15**:549

Kirk, Ron
Michael Moorcock **27**:349

Kirk, Russell
Ray Bradbury **10**:68

Kirke, Ron
D. M. Thomas **22**:418

Kirkham, Michael
Donald Davie **31**:118
Charles Tomlinson **4**:543

Kirkpatrick, Stephen
James Tate **25**:428

Kirsch, Bob
Neil Diamond **30**:112
Paul McCartney **35**:283

Kirsch, Robert
Jascha Kessler **4**:270

Kirton, Mary
Roderick L. Haig-Brown
21:142

Kirwan, Jack
James A. Michener **29**:316

Kish, A. V.
Mark Helprin **22**:221
Helen Yglesias **22**:493

Kish, Anne V.
Jim Harrison **14**:237

Kisner, Sister Madeleine
T. S. Eliot **15**:216

Kissel, Howard
Harvey Fierstein **33**:156
James Lapine **39**:174
Neil Simon **31**:398; **39**:219
Stephen Sondheim **30**:392;
39:174
Tom Stoppard **34**:276
Andrew Lloyd Webber and Tim
Rice **21**:433
August Wilson **39**:277

Kissel, Susan
Robert Coover **15**:145

Kitchen, Paddy
J. M. Coetzee **23**:122
Eva Figes **31**:163, 164
Judith Guest **30**:173
Bessie Head **25**:238
Fay Weldon **36**:447

Kitchin, Laurence
John Arden **13**:24
Arnold Wesker **5**:481

Kitching, Jessie B.
E. M. Almedingen **12**:3

Kitman, Marvin
Larry Gelbart **21**:131
Garry Marshall **17**:277
Arthur Miller **26**:326

Kitses, Jim
Elia Kazan **16**:369

Kitta, Donna
Mary-Ann Tirone Smith **39**:98

Kittrel, William
Edna Ferber **18**:151

Kizer, Carolyn
Ted Hughes **2**:201
Robert Penn Warren **39**:263

Klaidman, Stephen
Juan Goytisolo **5**:150

Klappert, Peter
Daniel Mark Epstein **7**:97
Kathleen Spivack **6**:520

Klarmann, Adolf D.
Friedrich Dürrenmatt **11**:168

Klaw, Barbara
Evan Hunter **31**:218

Klaw, Spencer
Herman Wouk **38**:144

Klein, A. M.
A.J.M. Smith **15**:512

Klein, Arnold
William Wharton **37**:440

Klein, Gillian Parker
François Truffaut **20**:398

Klein, Joe
William Brammer **31**:55
Philip Caputo **32**:106
John M. Del Vecchio **29**:150
Ronald J. Glasser **37**:134

Klein, Julia M.
Marilyn French **18**:159
Erica Jong **18**:279
James Purdy **28**:381

Klein, Marcus
Saul Bellow **1**:29
Stanley Elkin **27**:121
Ralph Ellison **1**:94

Klein, T.E.D.
T.E.D. Klein **34**:72

Klein, Theodore
Albert Camus **11**:95

Kleinbard, David
Guillevic **33**:191

Kleinberg, Seymour
Phillip Lopate **29**:301
Isaac Bashevis Singer **3**:458

Kleinzahler, August
Basil Bunting **39**:298

Klemtner, Susan Strehle
John Fowles **15**:232
William Gaddis **10**:212

Klepp, L. S.
Joseph Epstein **39**:467

Kley, Ronald J.
Margaret O. Hyde **21**:175

Kliman, Bernice W.
Philip Roth **3**:438

Klin, George
Yoram Kaniuk **19**:240

Kline, T. Jefferson
André Malraux **15**:353

Kling, Vincent
Rainer Werner Fassbinder
20:111

Klingel, Gilbert
Jacques-Yves Cousteau **30**:102

Klinkowitz, Jerome
Walter Abish **22**:22
Russell Banks **37**:25
Imamu Amiri Baraka **5**:45
Donald Barthelme **3**:43; **5**:52;
6:29; **13**:60; **23**:46
Jonathan Baumbach **6**:32
Robert Coover **32**:122
Guy Davenport **38**:148
Peter Handke **38**:223
Erica Jong **6**:269
Jerzy Kosinski **3**:272
Clarence Major **19**:294, 295
Flann O'Brien **7**:269
Ishmael Reed **32**:361
Tom Robbins **32**:368
Gilbert Sorrentino **3**:462;
22:392
Steven Spielberg **20**:365
Ronald Sukenick **3**:475; **4**:530
Hunter S. Thompson **17**:510

Kurt Vonnegut, Jr. 1:348;
3:500; **4**:563
Thomas Williams **14**:583

Klockner, Karen M.
Madeleine L'Engle **12**:352
Katherine Paterson **30**:283
Cynthia Voigt **30**:418

Kloman, William
Laura Nyro **17**:312
Gerome Ragni and James Rado
17:380

Klotman, Phyllis R.
Ronald L. Fair **18**:142
Langston Hughes **15**:292
Toni Morrison **22**:314

Klug, M. A.
Saul Bellow **15**:50

Kluger, Richard
Jerome Siegel and Joe Shuster
21:357

Kmetz, Gail Kessler
Muriel Spark **8**:493

Knapp, Bettina Liebowitz
Jean Anouilh **8**:24
Jean Cocteau **8**:145
Georges Duhamel **8**:187
Marguerite Duras **6**:151
Jean Genet **1**:116
Yukio Mishima **27**:343
Anna Kavan **13**:317
Robert Pinget **7**:305
Nathalie Sarraute **8**:469
Marguerite Yourcenar **38**:457

Knapp, James F.
T. S. Eliot **6**:163
Ken Kesey **11**:317
Delmore Schwartz **2**:387

Knapp, John V.
John Hawkes **7**:145

Knelman, Martin
W. Somerset Maugham **11**:370
William Mitchell **25**:326
Harold Pinter **9**:421
Mordecai Richler **5**:377
Michel Tremblay **29**:419

Knickerbocker, Brad
Allan W. Eckert **17**:108

Knieger, Bernard
S. Y. Agnon **8**:8

Knight, Arthur
Woody Allen **16**:1
Gordon Parks **16**:457

Knight, Damon
Brian Aldiss **14**:10
Isaac Asimov **3**:16
Ray Bradbury **3**:84
John W. Campbell, Jr. **32**:75
Robert A. Heinlein **3**:224
Richard Matheson **37**:245
Theodore Sturgeon **39**:366

Knight, G. Wilson
Sean O'Casey **11**:406
John Cowper Powys **7**:347

Knight, Karl F.
John Crowe Ransom **4**:428

Knight, Max
Günter Grass **32**:197

Knight, Susan
Frederick Busch **7**:38
John Gardner **3**:186
József Lengyel **7**:202

Knipp, Thomas R.
John Pepper Clark **38**:126

Knittel, Robert
Riccardo Bacchelli **19**:31

Knobler, Peter
Jackson Browne **21**:39
Bob Dylan **12**:189
Van Morrison **21**:237
Phil Ochs **17**:333
Bruce Springsteen **17**:476, 484

Knoll, Robert E.
Kay Boyle **19**:64
Wright Morris **18**:351, 355
Ezra Pound **3**:398

Knoll, Robert F.
Ken Russell **16**:542

Knopf, Terry Ann
Agnes Eckhardt Nixon **21**:243,
245

Knopp, Josephine
Elie Wiesel **5**:491

Knorr, Walter L.
E. L. Doctorow **11**:142

Knowles, A. Sidney, Jr.
Marie-Claire Blais **2**:63
Frederic Prokosch **4**:421

Knowles, Dorothy
Eugène Ionesco **11**:290

Knowles, George W.
Marie-Claire Blais **13**:96

Knowles, John
C.D.B. Bryan **29**:100
Pamela Hansford Johnson
27:221
Françoise Sagan **17**:423

Knowles, Richard Paul
Judith Thompson **39**:253

Knowlton, James
Walter Abish **22**:21
Peter Handke **38**:223

Knox, Bernard
Primo Levi **37**:230

Knox, George
Kenneth Burke **24**:129

Knox, Wendy
Carolyn Forché **25**:168

Knudsen, Erika
Elisaveta Bagryana **10**:11

Kobel, Peter
Steven Goldsberry **34**:54

Kobler, John
Jerome Siegel and Joe Shuster
21:353

Kobler, Turner S.
Rebecca West **7**:526

Koch, Christopher
Richard Elman **19**:149
Michael Frayn **31**:190

Koch, Kenneth
Frank O'Hara **2**:322
James Schuyler **23**:387

Koch, Stephen
Tish O'Dowd Ezekiel **34**:46
Peter Handke **38**:229
Hermann Hesse **3**:243
Reynolds Price **6**:425
Nathalie Sarraute **8**:472; **31**:385
Christina Stead **5**:404
Gore Vidal **4**:554
Andy Warhol **20**:420
Marguerite Yourcenar **38**:456,
463

Koch, Vivienne
August Derleth **31**:136
W. S. Graham **29**:192

Kochan, Lionel
Ilya Ehrenburg **34**:436
Anatol Goldberg **34**:436

Kodjak, Andrej
Aleksandr I. Solzhenitsyn
18:495

Koenig, Peter William
William Gaddis **10**:209

Koenig, Rhoda
Roald Dahl **18**:108
Peter De Vries **28**:110
E. L. Doctorow **37**:96
Michael Ende **31**:144
Nora Ephron **31**:158
T. Gertler **34**:50
Mark Helprin **22**:220
Paul Theroux **15**:535
Gore Vidal **33**:411

Koepf, Michael
Raymond Carver **22**:102

Koester, Rudolf
Hermann Hesse **17**:205

Koethe, John
John Ashbery **2**:17; **3**:15
Sandra Hochman **3**:250
James Schuyler **23**:388
Theodore Weiss **3**:517

Koff, Jan
Josef Škvorecký **39**:226

Kofsky, Frank
Lenny Bruce **21**:56
Mick Jagger and Keith Richard
17:220

Kogan, Rick
Richard Price **12**:489

Koger, Grove
Kristin Hunter **35**:229

Kohler, Dayton
Walter D. Edmonds **35**:148
Carson McCullers **12**:413
Conrad Richter **30**:311
Jesse Stuart **14**:513

Kohn, Hans
E. M. Almedingen **12**:2

Kolb, Muriel
Lois Duncan **26**:102
Alvin Silverstein and Virginia
B. Silverstein **17**:451

Kolker, Robert Phillip
Robert Altman **16**:30
Ken Russell **16**:545
Martin Scorsese **20**:336

Kolodin, Irving
Buffy Sainte-Marie **17**:430

Kolodny, Annette
Thomas Pynchon **3**:412

Kolonosky, Walter F.
Vasily Aksenov **22**:27
Vladimir Voinovich **10**:508

Koltz, Newton
Wright Morris **3**:343
Patrick White **3**:524

Koniczek, Ryszard
Andrzej Wajda **16**:584

Koning, Hans
Jerzy Kosinski **15**:315
Aleksandr I. Solzhenitsyn
18:498

Koningsberger, Hans
John Huston **20**:171

Kooi, Cynthia
Louise Erdrich **39**:129

Koon, William
William Price Fox **22**:140

Koper, Peter T.
Ursula K. Le Guin **22**:271

Kopff, E. Christian
J.R.R. Tolkien **38**:442

Kopkind, Andrew
Lenny Bruce **21**:57
John Lennon **35**:262
Prince **35**:330

Koprowski, Jan
Joseph Wittlin **25**:471

Korenblum, Toba
Thor Heyerdahl **26**:194

Korg, Jacob
Bernard Malamud **2**:269
Rebecca West **31**:458

Korges, James
Erskine Caldwell **1**:51

Korn, Eric
Martin Amis **38**:16
Philip K. Dick **10**:138
G. B. Edwards **25**:150
Harlan Ellison **13**:203
Rayner Heppenstall **10**:272
John Irving **23**:252
Jack Kerouac **14**:307
Richard O'Brien **17**:323
Judith Rossner **9**:457
Claude Simon **9**:482
Gore Vidal **10**:502
Fay Weldon **11**:566

William Wharton **18**:543
Tom Wolfe **15**:587
Roger Zelazny **21**:470

Kornblatt, Joyce
Joy Williams **31**:464

Kornblum, William
Peter Maas **29**:306

Kornfeld, Matilda
Zilpha Keatley Snyder **17**:473

Kornfeld, Melvin
Jurek Becker **7**:27

Kosek, Steven
Kurt Vonnegut, Jr. **4**:569

Koslow, Jules
Jorge Ibargüengoitia **37**:184

Kostach, Myrna
Rudy Wiebe **6**:566

Kostelanetz, Anne
Nathalie Sarraute **31**:377

Kostelanetz, Richard
R. P. Blackmur **2**:61
Ralph Ellison **3**:141
Ezra Pound **2**:344

Kostis, Nicholas
Julien Green **11**:259

Kostolefsky, Joseph
Frank Capra **16**:156

Kotin, Armine
Jean Arp **5**:33

Kotlowitz, Robert
Gerome Ragni and James Rado
17:382
Howard Sackler **14**:479

Kott, Jan
Andrei Sinyavsky **8**:488

Kotzwinkle, William
Max Apple **33**:20
Jay McInerney **34**:82

Kouidis, Virginia M.
Mina Loy **28**:248

Kountz, Peter
Thomas Merton **11**:372
Frank Zappa **17**:589

Kovács, Katherine Singer
Jorge Luis Borges **19**:49

Kovanda, Karel
Ilya Ehrenburg **34**:434
Anatol Goldberg **34**:434

Kovar, Helen M.
Christie Harris **12**:261

Kozak, Ellen M.
Gene Roddenberry **17**:413

Kozak, Roman
John Lennon **35**:272

Kozarek, Linda
Norma Klein **30**:239

Kozloff, Max
Agnès Varda **16**:557

Kozol, Jonathan
　Marjorie Kellogg **2**:223

Kracauer, Siegfried
　Fritz Lang **20**:202
　Leni Riefenstahl **16**:519
　Josef von Sternberg **20**:370

Kraemer, Chuck
　Frederick Wiseman **20**:475

Krall, Flo
　Jean Craighead George **35**:179

Kramer, Aaron
　Stanley J. Kunitz **6**:287

Kramer, Hilton
　William Barrett **27**:22
　Donald Barthelme **8**:50
　Bruce Chatwin **28**:71
　Guy Davenport **38**:142
　E. L. Doctorow **6**:137
　Alfred Kazin **38**:275
　Robert Lowell **8**:357
　Archibald MacLeish **8**:362
　Mary McCarthy **5**:276
　Marianne Moore **19**:342
　L. E. Sissman **9**:492
　Allen Tate **11**:527; **14**:530
　Robert Penn Warren **8**:538

Kramer, Jane
　André Brink **36**:67
　Maxine Hong Kingston **12**:312
　V. S. Naipaul **18**:363

Kramer, Lawrence
　William Stafford **29**:382

Kramer, Mark
　Joe McGinniss **32**:304

Kramer, Nora
　Betty Cavanna **12**:99

Kramer, Peter G.
　William Goyen **5**:149

Krance, Charles
　Louis-Ferdinand Céline **9**:153

Krasny, Michael
　Ishmael Reed **32**:361

Krasso, Nicolas
　George Steiner **24**:430

Kraus, Elisabeth
　John Hawkes **7**:146

Kraus, W. Keith
　Kristin Hunter **35**:228

Krause, Walter
　James D. Forman **21**:121

Krebs, Albin
　Truman Capote **34**:320

Kreidl, John Francis
　Alain Resnais **16**:514

Kreitzman, Ruth
　Bernardo Bertolucci **16**:86

Krensky, Stephen
　Frank Bonham **12**:55
　Christopher Collier and James
　　L. Collier **30**:73
　Robert Lipsyte **21**:212

Kresh, Paul
　Neil Diamond **30**:111
　Isaac Bashevis Singer **23**:417

Kreyling, Michael
　Eudora Welty **22**:459

Kreymborg, Alfred
　Mina Loy **28**:247

Krickel, Edward
　James Gould Cozzens **1**:67
　William Saroyan **1**:302

Kridl, Manfred
　Maria Dabrowska **15**:165

Kriegel, Harriet
　Nora Ephron **17**:112

Kriegel, Leonard
　Virginia Spencer Carr **34**:422
　John Dos Passos **34**:422
　T. S. Eliot **8**:166
　James T. Farrell **11**:193
　Günter Grass **2**:172
　James Jones **10**:293
　Iris Murdoch **1**:234
　Ezra Pound **7**:333
　Harvey Swados **5**:423
　Edmund Wilson **2**:475

Krieger, Murray
　Northrop Frye **24**:223
　I. A. Richards **24**:391

Krim
　James Jones **10**:290

Krim, Seymour
　William Barrett **27**:23
　Leslie A. Fiedler **24**:193
　Mark Helprin **32**:232
　Ernest Hemingway **19**:219
　James Jones **39**:411
　Jack Kerouac **14**:303
　Frank MacShane **39**:411
　Norman Mailer **39**:422
　Peter Manso **39**:422

Krispyn, Egbert
　Günter Eich **15**:202

Krist, Gary
　James Purdy **28**:381

Kroll, Ernest
　Peter Viereck **4**:559

Kroll, Jack
　Edward Albee **2**:1
　Jean Anouilh **3**:12
　W. H. Auden **3**:27
　Alan Ayckbourn **5**:36
　Saul Bellow **6**:55
　Mel Brooks **12**:80
　Ed Bullins **1**:47
　Anne Burr **6**:103, 104
　Truman Capote **34**:325
　Brian Clark **29**:127
　Rosalyn Drexler **2**:119
　Frederick Exley **6**:171
　Jules Feiffer **8**:216
　Harvey Fierstein **33**:157
　Jean Genet **2**:158
　Amlin Gray **29**:201
　Simon Gray **36**:210
　John Guare **8**:253; **29**:206

Bill Gunn **5**:152
David Hare **29**:216
Ted Hughes **2**:200
Arthur Kopit **33**:254
Stanley J. Kunitz **6**:286
John Landis **26**:276
James Lapine **39**:174
Ira Levin **6**:306
David Mamet **9**:360; **34**:221
Steve Martin **30**:251
Terrence McNally **7**:218
Mark Medoff **6**:322
Arthur Miller **2**:280; **6**:334
Jason Miller **2**:284
Rochelle Owens **8**:434
Miguel Piñero **4**:402
Dave Rabe **33**:346
Terence Rattigan **7**:355
Jonathan Reynolds **6**:451
Ronald Ribman **7**:358
Tadeusz Rózewicz **23**:362
Murray Schisgal **6**:490
Sam Shepard **34**:267
Neil Simon **6**:504; **31**:398, 399,
　400
Stephen Sondheim **30**:388, 394;
　39:174
Tom Stoppard **5**:414; **29**:402;
　34:274, 279
David Storey **2**:424, 426
Elizabeth Swados **12**:559
Lily Tomlin **17**:518
Kurt Vonnegut, Jr. **2**:452
Andrew Lloyd Webber and Tim
　Rice **21**:426, 433
August Wilson **39**:278
Lanford Wilson **7**:548

Kroll, Judith
　Sylvia Plath **17**:359

Kroll, Steven
　Irvin Faust **8**:215
　Elizabeth Jane Howard **29**:245
　Thomas McGuane **3**:330
　Dan Wakefield **7**:503
　Irving Wallace **7**:510

Kronenberger, Louis
　Babette Deutsch **18**:118
　Edna Ferber **18**:150
　Henri de Montherlant **19**:322
　Erich Maria Remarque **21**:325
　Tennessee Williams **30**:455

Krouse, Agate Nesaule
　Agatha Christie **12**:119
　Robert B. Parker **27**:364
　J.I.M. Stewart **14**:512
　Fay Weldon **19**:466

Krulik, Ted
　Richard Matheson **37**:248

Krumgold, Joseph
　Joseph Krumgold **12**:319

Krupka, Mary Lee
　Margot Benary-Isbert **12**:33, 34

Krupnick, Mark L.
　Philip Rahv **24**:354

Krutch, Joseph Wood
　Brigid Brophy **11**:67
　Erskine Caldwell **8**:122
　Paul Green **25**:194, 195
　George S. Kaufman **38**:260,
　　262, 263
　Mary McCarthy **24**:341
　Clifford Odets **28**:323, 324,
　　326, 327, 331
　Erich Maria Remarque **21**:326
　Elmer Rice **7**:360
　Irwin Shaw **23**:394
　Frank Swinnerton **31**:425
　Carl Van Vechten **33**:387
　T. H. White **30**:443
　Thornton Wilder **35**:436
　Emlyn Williams **15**:576, 577
　Tennessee Williams **30**:456,
　　461

Krynski, Magnus Jan
　Tadeusz Rózewicz **23**:359

Krysl, Marilyn
　Marilyn Hacker **23**:204

Krystal, Arthur
　T.E.D. Klein **34**:72

Krza, Paul
　Edward Abbey **36**:20

Krzyzanowski, Jerzy R.
　Tadeusz Konwicki **8**:325

Kubal, David
　Raymond Carver **22**:104
　G. B. Edwards **25**:152
　Barbara Pym **37**:368
　Richard Stern **39**:244

Kucewicz, William
　Len Deighton **22**:117

Kuczkowski, Richard
　Anthony Burgess **13**:125
　Don DeLillo **13**:179
　Susan Sontag **10**:485

Kuehl, Linda
　Doris Lessing **3**:282
　Iris Murdoch **3**:345; **15**:381
　Marge Piercy **3**:384
　Muriel Spark **2**:417
　Eudora Welty **5**:479
　Thomas Williams **14**:582

Kuehn, Robert E.
　Aldous Huxley **11**:284

Kuhn, Doris Young
　Julia W. Cunningham **12**:164
　Joseph Krumgold **12**:320

Kuhn, Ira
　Uwe Johnson **15**:304

Kuhn, Reinhard
　J.M.G. Le Clézio **31**:248
　Henri Michaux **19**:312, 313

Kuitunen, Maddalena
　Dino Buzzati **36**:90

Kulshrestha, Chirantan
　Mulk Raj Anand **23**:21

Kuncewicz, Maria
　Maria Dąbrowska **15**:166

Kunitz, Isadora
Margaret O. Hyde **21**:174
Alvin Silverstein and Virginia
B. Silverstein **17**:454

Kunitz, Stanley
John Berryman **8**:86
Robert Creeley **8**:152
Carolyn Forché **25**:168
Robert Frost **9**:223
Jean Garrigue **8**:240
H. D. **8**:255; **31**:201
Robert Lowell **9**:334
Marianne Moore **8**:397; **10**:346
John Crowe Ransom **11**:467
Theodore Roethke **8**:458

Kunz, Don
James Welch **14**:559

Kunzle, David
Stan Lee **17**:258

Kupferberg, Herbert
Yoram Kaniuk **19**:238

Kurzweil, Edith
Claude Lévi-Strauss **38**:306

Kussi, Peter
Milan Kundera **32**:260

Kustow, Michael
Jean-Luc Godard **20**:130
Arnold Wesker **3**:519

Kuzma, Greg
Barry Spacks **14**:510

Kyle, Carol A.
John Barth **9**:65

Labaree, Mary Fleming
Nella Larsen **37**:212

LaBarre, Weston
Carlos Castaneda **12**:88

Laber, Jeri
Ilya Ehrenburg **18**:132
Aleksandr I. Solzhenitsyn
2:411; **4**:514

Labrie, Ross
Thomas Merton **11**:373

Lacey, Henry C.
Amiri Baraka **33**:60

La Charité, Virginia
René Char **9**:167; **11**:113;
14:128
Henri Michaux **19**:314

Lachtman, Howard
Martin Cruz Smith **25**:414

Lacy, Allen
William Barrett **27**:20
Harry Crews **23**:136
Gilbert Sorrentino **14**:501

La Faille, Eugene E.
Piers Anthony **35**:39
Isaac Asimov **26**:58
Kim Stanley Robinson **34**:105
Jack Vance **35**:427

La Farge, Oliver
Howard Fast **23**:153
Robert Lewis Taylor **14**:534

Lafore, Laurence
David Caute **29**:111
Rhys Davies **23**:146
Shirley Hazzard **18**:214
William Maxwell **19**:307
James Alan McPherson **19**:309
R. K. Narayan **28**:295
Paul Theroux **28**:423
Irving Wallace **7**:509
Jessamyn West **17**:550

LaFrance, Marston
Evelyn Waugh **1**:358

LaHood, M. J.
William S. Burroughs **22**:85

LaHood, Marvin J.
Conrad Richter **30**:317, 325

Lahr, John
Edward Bond **13**:103
Noël Coward **29**:139
Dario Fo **32**:172
Andrew Holleran **38**:246
Arthur Kopit **1**:171
Darcy O'Brien **11**:405
Joe Orton **4**:388; **13**:435, 436
John Osborne **11**:422
Harold Pinter **6**:411
Richard Price **12**:489
Mordecai Richler **18**:454
Sam Shepard **4**:491; **17**:447
Stephen Sondheim **30**:394

Laidlaw, Marc
Stephen King **12**:311

Laing, Alexander
Esther Forbes **12**:208
C. S. Forester **35**:161

Laing, R. D.
Michel Foucault **31**:173

Laitinen, Kai
Paavo Haavikko **18**:205; **34**:173
Hannu Salama **18**:460

Lake, Steve
Ray Davies **21**:96
Gordon Lightfoot **26**:280
Phil Ochs **17**:332
Lou Reed **21**:307
Patti Smith **12**:536

Lall, Arthur
Kamala Markandaya **38**:323

Lalley, Francis A.
Vine Deloria, Jr. **21**:112

Lalley, J. M.
A. B. Guthrie, Jr. **23**:195

Lally, Michael
Charles Bukowski **9**:138
Larry Eigner **9**:182
Kenneth Koch **8**:323
Howard Moss **7**:249
Anne Sexton **6**:493

Lamb, Sister Avila
Piers Anthony **35**:38
David Brin **34**:134

Lambert, Gail Tansill
Fran Arrick **30**:18

Lambert, Gavin
Lindsay Anderson **20**:11
Robert Bresson **16**:102
Luis Buñuel **16**:129
Charles Chaplin **16**:195
Agatha Christie **8**:142
René Clair **20**:63, 64
John Huston **20**:160, 161, 162
Stanley Kubrick **16**:376, 377
Fritz Lang **20**:205
John O'Hara **6**:384
Jean Renoir **20**:288

Lambert, J. W.
Dannie Abse **29**:17
Edward Albee **2**:4
Alan Ayckbourn **5**:35
Howard Barker **37**:32
Peter Barnes **5**:50
Thomas Bernhard **32**:20
Edward Bond **4**:70; **6**:84
Caryl Churchill **31**:83
A. E. Ellis **7**:95
Dario Fo **32**:172
Michael Frayn **7**:108
Athol Fugard **5**:130
Trevor Griffiths **13**:256
David Hare **29**:211
Peter Luke **38**:318
John Osborne **2**:328
J. B. Priestley **34**:363
Sam Shepard **6**:496
Bernard Slade **11**:508
Tom Stoppard **3**:470; **5**:413
David Storey **2**:425; **4**:530
Arnold Wesker **3**:518

Lambert, Marguerite M.
Larry Bograd **35**:64

Lamie, Edward L.
John Brunner **8**:110

Lamming, George
Ishmael Reed **3**:424
Derek Walcott **4**:574

Lamont, Rosette C.
Fernando Arrabal **9**:35
Eugène Ionesco **1**:155; **6**:252,
256; **9**:287
Boris Pasternak **18**:387

Lamott, Kenneth
Maureen Duffy **37**:113
Siegfried Lenz **27**:244

Lamport, Felicia
Hortense Calisher **38**:70
Sumner Locke Elliott **38**:176
Laura Z. Hobson **25**:272
S. J. Perelman **5**:337

Lancaster, Bruce
Thomas J. Fleming **37**:118
Halldór Laxness **25**:291

Landau, Deborah
Van Morrison **21**:233

Landau, Elaine
Virginia Hamilton **26**:150

Landau, Jon
Bob Dylan **12**:190
Marvin Gaye **26**:131
George Roy Hill **26**:202
Mick Jagger and Keith Richard
17:221, 224, 233
John Lennon **35**:265, 269, 279

John Lennon and Paul
McCartney **12**:377
Joni Mitchell **12**:438
Van Morrison **21**:231, 232
Jimmy Page and Robert Plant
12:475
Sam Peckinpah **20**:278
Martin Scorsese **20**:324
Bob Seger **35**:379
Paul Simon **17**:461
Bruce Springsteen **17**:478
Andrew Lloyd Webber and Tim
Rice **21**:429
Stevie Wonder **12**:655, 657

Landess, Thomas
Thomas Merton **1**:211

Landess, Thomas H.
John Berryman **2**:60
Caroline Gordon **6**:205; **13**:247
Andrew Lytle **22**:294
William Meredith **4**:349
Marion Montgomery **7**:234
Julia Peterkin **31**:308, 311
William Jay Smith **6**:512
Allen Tate **4**:540
Mona Van Duyn **3**:491
Eudora Welty **1**:363
James Wright **3**:541

Landis, Joan Hutton
Ben Belitt **22**:52

Landy, Francis
A. Alvarez **13**:9

Lane, Helen R.
Carlos Fuentes **22**:165

Lane, James B.
Harold Robbins **5**:379
Piri Thomas **17**:499

Lane, John Francis
Michelangelo Antonioni **20**:38
Vittorio De Sica **20**:90

Lane, M. Travis
Marilyn Bowering **32**:46
Ralph Gustafson **36**:213, 215,
221

Lane, Patrick
Andrew Suknaski **19**:433

Lanes, Jerrold
Michel del Castillo **38**:164

Lanes, Selma G.
Richard Adams **4**:9
Paula Danziger **21**:84

Lang, Doug
Donald Justice **19**:233
Cynthia MacDonald **19**:291

Lang, Olga
Pa Chin **18**:371

Langbaum, Robert
Samuel Beckett **9**:85
Truman Capote **38**:80
Isak Dinesen **29**:156
E. M. Forster **1**:107
Galway Kinnell **13**:321
M. L. Rosenthal **28**:390

Lange, Victor
Heinrich Böll **27**:62
Martin Heidegger **24**:279

Langer, Elinor
Marge Piercy **18**:408

Langer, Lawrence L.
Simone de Beauvoir **31**:35
Paul Celan **19**:91
Elie Wiesel **37**:450

Langford, Paul
Leon Garfield **12**:233

Langguth, A. J.
Gay Talese **37**:392

Langlois, Jim
William Kotzwinkle **35**:254

Langlois, Walter
Pearl S. Buck **18**:77
André Malraux **9**:355

Langton, Jane
Paula Danziger **21**:85
Virginia Hamilton **26**:151
William Mayne **12**:402
Richard Peck **21**:301
Mary Rodgers **12**:493
Zilpha Keatley Snyder **17**:472,
473, 474
Cynthia Voigt **30**:420
Jill Paton Walsh **35**:433
Rosemary Wells **12**:637

Lant, Jeffrey
Jonathan Kozol **17**:253

Lantz, Fran
D. M. Pinkwater **35**:318

Lanyi, Ronald Levitt
Trina Robbins **21**:339

Laqueur, Walter
Anatoli Rybakov **23**:370

Lardner, David
Alfred Hitchcock **16**:339

Lardner, John
Irwin Shaw **7**:409

Lardner, Rex
Winston Graham **23**:191
Frank G. Slaughter **29**:377

Lardner, Susan
Toni Cade Bambara **19**:34
John Gregory Dunne **28**:124
Mary Gordon **22**:186
György Konrád **10**:305
Thomas McGuane **18**:324
Joyce Carol Oates **9**:404
Wilfrid Sheed **2**:393

Larkin, Joan
Rita Mae Brown **18**:73
Hortense Calisher **4**:88
June Jordan **23**:256
Audre Lorde **18**:307

Larkin, Philip
Dick Francis **22**:153
Barbara Pym **19**:386

LaRocque, Geraldine E.
Jay Bennett **35**:42
Madeleine L'Engle **12**:348

Larrabee, Eric
Cornelius Ryan **7**:385

Larrieu, Kay
H. D. **34**:443
Barbara Guest **34**:443
Larry Woiwode **10**:542

Larsen, Anne
Lisa Alther **7**:11
William Kotzwinkle **14**:310
Leonard Michaels **6**:325

Larsen, Eric
Charles Newman **8**:419

Larsen, Ernest
Jerome Charyn **18**:100
Gilbert Sorrentino **14**:499

Larson, Charles
Hyemeyohsts Storm **3**:470

Larson, Charles R.
Peter Abrahams **4**:2
Chinua Achebe **5**:1
Rudolfo A. Anaya **23**:25
Ayi Kwei Armah **5**:31; **33**:27,
29
John Pepper Clark **38**:118
J. M. Coetzee **23**:122
Leslie A. Fiedler **4**:163; **13**:211
Bessie Head **25**:235, 239
Camara Laye **4**:284
Jayanta Mahapatra **33**:277
Kamala Markandaya **8**:377
Peter Matthiessen **7**:210
V. S. Naipaul **7**:253; **18**:359
R. K. Narayan **7**:255
James Ngugi **7**:263
Raja Rao **25**:369
Simone Schwarz-Bart **7**:404
Leslie Marmon Silko **23**:406
Raymond Sokolov **7**:430
Wole Soyinka **5**:396
Jean Toomer **13**:556
Amos Tutuola **5**:445; **29**:442
Ngugi Wa Thiong'o **13**:583,
584
James Welch **6**:561

Larson, James
Gunnar Ekelöf **27**:118

Lasagna, Louis
Michael Crichton **2**:108
Margaret O. Hyde **21**:174

LaSalle, Peter
Frederick Barthelme **36**:52
J. M. Coetzee **23**:124
J. F. Powers **8**:448
Cynthia Propper Seton **27**:426
Michel Tournier **36**:435

Lasansky, Terry Andrews
W. P. Kinsella **27**:236

Laschever, Sara
Gordon Vorster **34**:122

Lasdun, James
Anita Brookner **34**:140
J. M. Coetzee **33**:108
Elaine Feinstein **36**:172
Pamela Hansford Johnson
27:223
Alison Lurie **39**:185

Peter Porter **33:320
Josef Škvorecký **39**:232
Fay Weldon **36**:444

Lask, I. M.
S. Y. Agnon **4**:10

Lask, Thomas
Franklyn M. Branley **21**:15
Richard Brautigan **12**:60
Dino Buzzati **36**:88
Ronald J. Glasser **37**:130
Kenneth O. Hanson **13**:263
Bohumil Hrabal **13**:291
David Ignatow **7**:177
P. D. James **18**:273
William Kotzwinkle **35**:253
J.M.G. Le Clézio **31**:246
Ross Macdonald **1**:185
Clarence Major **19**:294
Frederick Morgan **23**:298
Grace Paley **37**:331
Linda Pastan **27**:368
M. L. Rosenthal **28**:391
John Sayles **14**:484
Georges Simenon **8**:486
Josef Škvorecký **15**:510
W. D. Snodgrass **2**:405
Piri Thomas **17**:502

Laska, P. J.
Imamu Amiri Baraka **10**:21

Laski, Audrey
Bette Greene **30**:169

Laski, Marghanita
Peter Dickinson **35**:131, 132,
136
Frederick Forsyth **36**:175
John Gardner **30**:154
Joseph Hansen **38**:237, 238
Patricia Highsmith **14**:260
John le Carré **28**:230
Ruth Rendell **28**:384
J.I.M. Stewart **32**:421
Glendon Swarthout **35**:404
Mario Vargas Llosa **31**:447

Lassell, Michael
Tennessee Williams **11**:573

Lasson, Robert
Mario Puzo **2**:352

Last, B. W.
Ngugi wa Thiong'o **36**:320

Last, Rex
Christa Wolf **29**:467

Latham, Aaron
Jack Kerouac **2**:228

Latham, David
Hugh Hood **28**:191

Lathen, Emma
Agatha Christie **12**:123

Latiak, Dorothy S.
Jules Archer **12**:17

Latimer, Jonathan P.
Francis Ford Coppola **16**:236

Latimer, Margery
Molly Keane **31**:230

Latrell, Craig
Harold Pinter **9**:421

Latshaw, Jessica
Christie Harris **12**:268

Lattimore, Richmond
John Berryman **2**:59
Philip Booth **23**:76
Jorge Luis Borges **2**:73
Edgar Bowers **9**:121
Joseph Brodsky **6**:97
Michael Casey **2**:100
Alan Dugan **6**:144
Daniel Hoffman **6**:243
John Hollander **14**:265
Galway Kinnell **13**:318
Vladimir Nabokov **8**:407
Adrienne Rich **7**:364
I. A. Richards **14**:453
L. E. Sissman **9**:491
Andrei Voznesensky **15**:557

Lattin, Vernon E.
N. Scott Momaday **19**:320

Lauder, Robert E.
Ingmar Bergman **16**:77
John Cassavetes **20**:52, 328
Christopher Durang **27**:91
Jean-Paul Sartre **24**:405

Laughlin, Rosemary M.
John Fowles **2**:138

Laughner, Peter
Lou Reed **21**:310

Laurence, Margaret
Chinua Achebe **7**:3
William Mitchell **25**:322
Wole Soyinka **14**:507
Amos Tutuola **14**:538

Laut, Stephen J., S.J.
R. V. Cassill **23**:105
John Gardner **10**:220

Lavender, Ralph
Alan Garner **17**:150
Diana Wynne Jones **26**:227
Otfried Preussler **17**:375
Robert Westall **17**:557

Lavers, Annette
Sylvia Plath **9**:425

Lavers, Norman
John Hawkes **2**:186

Lavine, Stephen David
Philip Larkin **8**:336

Law, Richard
Joan D. Vinge **30**:416
Robert Penn Warren **13**:570

Lawall, Sarah N.
Yves Bonnefoy **9**:113; **15**:72
Guillevic **33**:193, 194
Francis Ponge **18**:413

Lawhead, Terry
Lois Duncan **26**:108
Milton Meltzer **26**:309

Lawler, Daniel F., S.J.
Eleanor Hibbert **7**:156

Lawler, James R.
René Char **11**:117

Critic Index

Lawless, Ken
J. P. Donleavy **10**:155

Lawrence, D. H.
Edward Dahlberg **7**:61
Ernest Hemingway **10**:263
Carl Van Vechten **33**:393

Lawrence, Isabelle
Lee Kingman **17**:244

Lawrence, Leota S.
C.L.R. James **33**:220

Lawrence, Peter C.
Jean Lee Latham **12**:324

Laws, Frederick
Sally Benson **17**:47

Laws, Page R.
Uwe Johnson **15**:307

Lawson, Lewis A.
William Faulkner **3**:153
Flannery O'Connor **1**:255
Eudora Welty **14**:567

Lawton, A.
Yevgeny Yevtushenko **13**:620

Lazarus, H. P.
Budd Schulberg **7**:401

Lazenby, Francis D.
Milton Meltzer **26**:300

Lazere, Donald
Albert Camus **14**:107

Lea, Sydney
Philip Levine **14**:319
Frederick Morgan **23**:299

Leach, Edmund
Carlos Castaneda **12**:85
Claude Lévi-Strauss **38**:303

Leader, Zachary
Garson Kanin **22**:233

Leaf, David
Brian Wilson **12**:652

Leahy, Jack
David Wagoner **5**:474

Leak, Thomas
Michael Shaara **15**:474

Leal, Luis
Juan Rulfo **8**:462

Leamer, Laurence
Allen Drury **37**:109

Leaming, Barbara
Rainer Werner Fassbinder **20**:114

Leapman, Michael
Maurice Gee **29**:179

Lear, Norman
Norman Lear **12**:328

Learmont, Lavinia Marina
Hermann Hesse **2**:191

Leary, Lewis
Lionel Trilling **9**:534

Leary, Timothy
Bob Dylan **12**:193

Leavell, Frank H.
Jesse Stuart **14**:514

Leavis, F. R.
Van Wyck Brooks **29**:84
John Dos Passos **11**:152
T. S. Eliot **24**:171
C. P. Snow **13**:512

Leavitt, David
E. L. Doctorow **37**:95
Sharon Olds **39**:187

Leavitt, Harvey
Richard Brautigan **5**:67

Leb, Joan P.
Laura Z. Hobson **25**:272

LeBeau, Bryan F.
Alfred Kazin **34**:559

Lebel, J.-P.
Buster Keaton **20**:190

Leber, Michele M.
Judith Guest **30**:174
Jane Rule **27**:417
Sandra Scoppettone **26**:404

Lebowitz, Alan
Ernest Hemingway **1**:144

Lebowitz, Naomi
Stanley Elkin **4**:152
E. M. Forster **4**:166
J. F. Powers **1**:279

Lechlitner, Ruth
Ben Belitt **22**:48
August Derleth **31**:132

Lecker, Robert
Clark Blaise **29**:74
Ralph Gustafson **36**:219
Jack Hodgins **23**:233
Hugh Hood **15**:286

Lecker, Robert A.
John Metcalf **37**:302

LeClair, Thomas
Isaac Asimov **26**:51
Russell Banks **37**:22
John Barth **7**:23
Saul Bellow **6**:53
Anthony Burgess **1**:48
R. V. Cassill **23**:109
Carlos Castaneda **12**:95
Jerome Charyn **5**:103; **8**:135
Don DeLillo **10**:135; **13**:179
J. P. Donleavy **1**:76; **4**:124;
   6:141; **10**:154
Stanley Elkin **6**:170; **9**:190;
   27:125
Sumner Locke Elliott **38**:180
John Gardner **8**:236; **18**:179,
   183
John Hawkes **7**:141, 144
Joseph Heller **8**:278
Flannery O'Connor **13**:420
Walker Percy **6**:400; **14**:412
David Plante **7**:307
Thomas Pynchon **6**:435
Tom Robbins **9**:454
Marilynne Robinson **25**:389
Michael Shaara **15**:474
Ronald Sukenick **6**:523

Harvey Swados **5**:420

LeClair, Tom
Max Apple **33**:21
Don DeLillo **39**:117
William Wharton **37**:442

LeClercq, Diane
Patricia Highsmith **2**:194
Susan B. Hill **4**:226
William Sansom **6**:483

Ledbetter, J. T.
Galway Kinnell **13**:320
Mark Van Doren **6**:542

Lee, A. Robert
Chester Himes **18**:249

Lee, Alvin
James Reaney **13**:472

Lee, Brian
James Baldwin **17**:35

Lee, Charles
Taylor Caldwell **28**:60, 62
Hortense Calisher **38**:68
Thomas B. Costain **30**:94, 96
A. J. Cronin **32**:137
Ernest K. Gann **23**:163
Earl Hamner, Jr. **12**:257
Laura Z. Hobson **25**:271
Mary Renault **17**:391
Frank G. Slaughter **29**:375, 376
T. H. White **30**:442

Lee, Dennis
David Donnell **34**:156
Paulette Giles **13**:304
A. W. Purdy **6**:428

Lee, Don L.
Nikki Giovanni **4**:189
Conrad Kent Rivers **1**:285

Lee, Dorothy
Joseph A. Walker **19**:455

Lee, Dorothy H.
Harriette Arnow **18**:13

Lee, Felicia
John Edgar Wideman **34**:300

Lee, Hermione
Isabel Allende **39**:33
J. G. Ballard **14**:40
Pat Barker **32**:12
Jurek Becker **19**:36
Elizabeth Bowen **11**:65; **22**:63
Malcolm Bradbury **32**:57
Brigid Brophy **29**:97
Anita Brookner **34**:137
Penelope Fitzgerald **19**:173
Nadine Gordimer **18**:189
Jonathan Keates **34**:201
Thomas Keneally **14**:302
Flannery O'Connor **15**:413
Julia O'Faolain **19**:360
Jayne Anne Phillips **33**:308
Marilynne Robinson **25**:387
Andrew Sinclair **14**:490
J.I.M. Stewart **14**:513
Lisa St. Aubin de Teran **36**:419
Anne Tyler **28**:434

Lee, James W.
John Braine **1**:43

Lee, Judith Yaross
Philip Roth **22**:354

Lee, L. L.
Thomas Berger **18**:54
Walter Van Tilburg Clark **28**:79

Lee, Lance
Thom Gunn **18**:201

Lee, Robert A.
Alistair MacLean **13**:359

Lee, S. E.
Thomas W. Shapcott **38**:398,
   399

Lee, Stan
Stan Lee **17**:261

Leech, Margaret
Esther Forbes **12**:206

Leedom-Ackerman, Joanne
Howard Fast **23**:160

Leeds, Barry H.
Ken Kesey **6**:278
Norman Mailer **1**:191
D. Keith Mano **2**:270

Leeming, Glenda
John Arden **6**:9

Leepson, Marc
Sloan Wilson **32**:449

Leer, Norman
Bernard Malamud **8**:374

Lees, Gene
John Lennon and Paul
   McCartney **12**:358
Gerome Ragni and James Rado
   17:383

Lees-Milne, James
I. Compton-Burnett **34**:497
Hilary Spurling **34**:497

Leet, Herbert L.
Frank B. Gilbreth and
   Ernestine Gilbreth Carey
   17:155

Leet, Judith
May Sarton **14**:482

Leffland, Ella
Lois Gould **10**:242

Legates, Charlotte
Aldous Huxley **11**:287

Le Guin, Ursula K.
Italo Calvino **22**:89; **33**:101
Philip K. Dick **30**:125
John Gardner **18**:181
Doris Lessing **15**:334
Arkadii Strugatskii and Boris
   Strugatskii **27**:435

Legum, Colin
David Caute **29**:123

Lehan, Richard
Walker Percy **2**:332
Wilfrid Sheed **2**:392
Susan Sontag **1**:322

Critic Index

Lehman, David
W. H. Auden **11**:20
Ted Berrigan **37**:44
Frank Bidart **33**:81
Bret Easton Ellis **39**:58
Nicolas Freeling **38**:187
William H. Gass **39**:481
Michael S. Harper **22**:208
Evan Hunter **31**:227
David Ignatow **7**:182
William McPherson **34**:88
Charles Reznikoff **9**:449
Ira Sadoff **9**:466

Lehmann, A. G.
Georg Lukács **24**:333

Lehmann, John
W. Somerset Maugham **11**:370
Edith Sitwell **2**:403

Lehmann, Rosamond
Mary Renault **17**:390
Conrad Richter **30**:308

Lehmann-Haupt, Christopher
Isabel Allende **39**:29
Roger Angell **26**:28
Aharon Appelfeld **23**:35
Louis Auchincloss **18**:25
Amiri Baraka **33**:60
Thomas Berger **18**:56; **38**:41
Peter Brooks **34**:520
Rosellen Brown **32**:67
Italo Calvino **22**:92
Truman Capote **19**:85
Henry Carlisle **33**:104
James Carroll **38**:107
Jerome Charyn **18**:99
Susan Cheever **18**:100
James Clavell **25**:126
J. M. Coetzee **33**:106
Michael Crichton **2**:109
Robert Crumb **17**:82
Don DeLillo **27**:80; **39**:116
E. L. Doctorow **37**:91
Rosalyn Drexler **2**:119
Stanley Elkin **14**:157
Sumner Locke Elliott **38**:180
Nora Ephron **31**:157
William Price Fox **22**:139
Marilyn French **18**:159
Robert Frost **34**:470
John Gardner **18**:180
William H. Gass **39**:477
Gail Godwin **31**:197
Francine du Plessix Gray
22:200
Graham Greene **27**:172; **37**:139
Judith Guest **30**:175
Pete Hamill **10**:251
Barry Hannah **23**:210; **38**:232,
233
Ernest Hemingway **39**:428
George V. Higgins **18**:234
John Irving **38**:251
P. D. James **18**:276
James Jones **39**:406
William Kennedy **28**:205
John Knowles **26**:262
Andrea Lee **36**:256
Ella Leffland **19**:277, 278
Siegfried Lenz **27**:248
Elmore Leonard **34**:213
Hugh Leonard **19**:282

Bette Bao Lord **23**:280
Robert Ludlum **22**:291
Alison Lurie **39**:177
Peter Maas **29**:308
Frank MacShane **39**:406
Norman Mailer **28**:257; **39**:417
Clarence Major **19**:291
Peter Manso **39**:417
Peter Matthiessen **32**:292
Jeffrey Meyers **39**:428
Ted Mooney **25**:330
Joe McGinniss **32**:301
Brian Moore **32**:308
Wright Morris **37**:314
Farley Mowat **26**:345
Iris Murdoch **22**:329
Charles Newman **2**:311
T. R. Pearson **39**:88
Robert Newton Peck **17**:336
Bette Pesetsky **28**:357, 359
George Plimpton **36**:354, 355,
356
Chaim Potok **26**:372
William H. Pritchard **34**:470
Richard Price **12**:488
Mario Puzo **36**:361
Thomas Pynchon **33**:338
Piers Paul Read **25**:376, 378
Gregor von Rezzori **25**:382
Mordecai Richler **18**:452
Philip Roth **31**:340
Salman Rushdie **31**:356
Peter Rushforth **19**:406
Jaroslav Seifert **34**:260
Irwin Shaw **23**:399
Lee Smith **25**:407
Martin Cruz Smith **25**:412
Richard Stern **39**:242
Paul Theroux **28**:428
Lewis Thomas **35**:410, 412
Hunter S. Thompson **17**:504
Anne Tyler **28**:431
Leon Uris **32**:432
Gore Vidal **33**:403, 409
Kurt Vonnegut, Jr. **22**:450
Jill Paton Walsh **35**:431
John Edgar Wideman **36**:456
Helen Yglesias **22**:492
Al Young **19**:479

Lehrmann, Charles C.
Romain Gary **25**:185

Leib, Mark
Sylvia Plath **3**:389

Leiber, Fritz
T.E.D. Klein **34**:71
Fritz Leiber **25**:304

Leiber, Justin
Fritz Leiber **25**:309

Leibold, Cynthia K.
Suzanne Newton **35**:303

Leibowitz, Herbert
Elizabeth Bishop **13**:91
Robert Bly **2**:66
Edward Dahlberg **14**:136
Jean Garrigue **2**:153
Philip Levine **14**:320
Robert Lowell **4**:297
Josephine Miles **2**:278
Kenneth Rexroth **6**:451

Theodore Roethke **3**:434
Delmore Schwartz **2**:388
Judith Johnson Sherwin **15**:479
Isaac Bashevis Singer **3**:453
W. D. Snodgrass **2**:405
Gary Snyder **5**:395
Mona Van Duyn **3**:492
Jonathan Williams **13**:600
William Carlos Williams **9**:574;
22:468
Edmund Wilson **3**:540

Leibowitz, Herbert A.
Frank O'Hara **2**:321

Leichtling, Jerry
Jackson Browne **21**:35

Leigh, David J., S.J.
Ernest Hemingway **6**:233
Tadeusz Konwicki **28**:211

Leighton, Jean
Simone de Beauvoir **31**:33

Leitch, David
Romain Gary **25**:187

Leiter, Robert
Janet Frame **6**:190
Nadine Gordimer **7**:132
Cormac McCarthy **4**:342
Jean Rhys **6**:453
Clancy Sigal **7**:424
Larry Woiwode **10**:541

Leiter, Robert A.
William Maxwell **19**:308

Leith, Linda
Hubert Aquin **15**:17
Marie-Claire Blais **22**:59
Matt Cohen **19**:112
Mavis Gallant **38**:195

Leithauser, Brad
Marianne Moore **19**:340
Jean Stafford **19**:431
Evelyn Waugh **19**:465

Lejeune, Anthony
Agatha Christie **12**:117
Ian Fleming **30**:138
Paul Gallico **2**:147
Anthony Powell **7**:345
P. G. Wodehouse **2**:480

Lejeune, C. A.
René Clair **20**:59
Jean Cocteau **16**:224
Elia Kazan **16**:360

Lekachman, Robert
William F. Buckley, Jr. **18**:83
Richard Elman **19**:151
Paul E. Erdman **25**:156
Ken Follett **18**:156
Robert Ludlum **22**:290
Martin Cruz Smith **25**:413

Lelchuk, Alan
Bernard Malamud **27**:298
Isaac Bashevis Singer **11**:500

Lellis, George
Rainer Werner Fassbinder
20:107
Martin Scorsese **20**:324

Lelyveld, Joseph
Breyten Breytenbach **37**:51
Buchi Emecheta **14**:160

Lem, Stanislaw
Philip K. Dick **30**:117
Arkadii Strugatskii and Boris
Strugatskii **27**:436

LeMaster, J. R.
Jesse Stuart **8**:507; **11**:509

Lemay, Harding
John Knowles **26**:246
J. R. Salamanca **4**:461

Lembeck, Carolyn S.
Kevin Major **26**:286

Lembke, Russell W.
George S. Kaufman **38**:264

Lembo, Diana
Scott O'Dell **30**:268

Lemmons, Philip
Brian Moore **8**:396
William Trevor **7**:478

Lemon, Lee T.
Kenneth Burke **2**:87, 89
Louis-Ferdinand Céline **3**:105
Guy Davenport, Jr. **6**:124
Judith Guest **8**:254
Jack Kerouac **5**:213
Jerzy Kosinski **10**:306
Joyce Carol Oates **6**:369
John Rechy **1**:283
Andrew Sinclair **14**:488
C. P. Snow **4**:503
Patrick White **5**:485
Yvor Winters **4**:591

Lenardon, Robert J.
Mary Renault **17**:401

Lenburg, Greg
Steve Martin **30**:250

Lenburg, Jeff
Steve Martin **30**:250

L'Engle, Madeleine
James D. Forman **21**:115
Mary Stolz **12**:552

Lenhart, Maria
Laurence Yep **35**:470

Lennox, John Watt
Anne Hébert **13**:266

Lensing, George
James Dickey **4**:120
Robert Lowell **1**:183
Louis Simpson **4**:498
Louis Zukofsky **1**:385

Lensing, George S.
William Stafford **29**:380

Lenski, Branko
Miroslav Krleža **8**:329

Lent, Henry B.
John R. Tunis **12**:596

Lentfoehr, Sister Therese
David Kherdian **6**:281

Lentricchia, Frank
Northrop Frye **24**:229

Lenz, Joseph M.
Frank Herbert **35**:199

Leonard, George
Robert Coover **32**:125

Leonard, John
Lisa Alther **7**:12
Max Apple **33**:19
Louis Auchincloss **18**:25
Saul Bellow **6**:56
John Berger **19**:41
E. M. Broner **19**:71
T. Alan Broughton **19**:73
Anthony Burgess **22**:75
Jerome Charyn **18**:98
John Cheever **3**:107; **8**:139;
    25:120
Arthur C. Clarke **35**:120
Arthur A. Cohen **31**:93
Anita Desai **19**:135
Joan Didion **1**:74; **14**:151
Sumner Locke Elliott **38**:178
Nora Ephron **17**:113
Thomas Flanagan **25**:166
Dick Francis **22**:153
Max Frisch **18**:162
Francine du Plessix Gray
    22:201
Shirley Hazzard **18**:218
Carolyn G. Heilbrun **25**:256
Frank Herbert **23**:219, 221
Maxine Hong Kingston **19**:249
Doris Lessing **3**:285
Jakov Lind **27**:271
Robert Ludlum **22**:289
Alison Lurie **4**:306
Larry McMurtry **2**:271
Margaret Mead **37**:275
V. S. Naipaul **18**:361
Joyce Carol Oates **19**:355
Marge Piercy **27**:372
Thomas Pynchon **3**:414
Wilfrid Sheed **2**:393
Gilbert Sorrentino **14**:499
Gay Talese **37**:398
Alexander Theroux **25**:433
Trevanian **29**:431
Anne Tyler **18**:529
Joseph Wambaugh **18**:532
Donald E. Westlake **33**:439
John Edgar Wideman **36**:451,
    454
Alexander Zinoviev **19**:486

Leonard, Vickie
Marge Piercy **27**:380

Leonard, William J.
Hugh Leonard **19**:283

Leonberger, Janet
Richard Peck **21**:298

Leone, Arthur T.
Jill Paton Walsh **35**:429

Leonhardt, Rudolf Walter
Martin Walser **27**:456

LePellec, Yves
John Updike **15**:540

Le Pelley, Guernsey
William F. Buckley, Jr. **18**:82
G. B. Edwards **25**:150

Leppard, David
Joan Didion **32**:144

Lerman, Leo
Enid Bagnold **25**:74
Gay Talese **37**:390

Lerman, Sue
Agnès Varda **16**:559

Lerner, Laurence
Geoffrey H. Hartman **27**:179
Craig Raine **32**:353
René Wellek **28**:445
A. N. Wilson **33**:455

Lerner, Max
James M. Cain **28**:47
Arthur Koestler **33**:233

Lernoux, Penny
Mario Vargas Llosa **9**:544

LeSage, Laurent
Roland Barthes **24**:25
Marie-Claire Blais **22**:57
Robert Pinget **7**:305
Françoise Sagan **17**:423

Le Shan, Eda J.
Sol Gordon **26**:136

Leslie, Omolara
Chinua Achebe **3**:2
Charles R. Larson **31**:237
Christopher Okigbo **25**:353

Lesser, Ellen
Carolyn Chute **39**:40
Pam Durban **39**:46
Molly Giles **39**:65

Lesser, Rika
Paul Celan **19**:94

Lesser, Wendy
Isabel Colegate **36**:114
David Leavitt **34**:78
Kem Nunn **34**:94

Lessing, Doris
Kurt Vonnegut, Jr. **2**:456

Lester, Julius
Pete Dexter **34**:43
Henry Dumas **6**:146
Lorraine Hansberry **17**:192

Lester, Margot
Dan Jacobson **4**:256
Hugh Nissenson **9**:400

Lester-Massman, Elli
John Edgar Wideman **34**:298

Le Stourgeon, Diana E.
Rosamond Lehmann **5**:235

Letson, Russell
Philip José Farmer **19**:167

Letter, Robert
August Wilson **39**:282

Leung, Paul
Margaret O. Hyde **21**:179

Levene, Mark
Arthur Koestler **33**:240

Levensohn, Alan
Brigid Brophy **29**:96
Christina Stead **2**:422

Levenson, Christopher
Patrick Lane **25**:287

Levenson, J. C.
Saul Bellow **1**:29

Levenson, Michael
Herbert Gold **7**:121
Tom McHale **5**:282
John Updike **5**:460

Leventhal, A. J.
Samuel Beckett **11**:32

Lever, Karen M.
John Fowles **15**:234

Leverence, John
Irving Wallace **13**:567

Leverich, Kathleen
Robin F. Brancato **35**:69
Jean Craighead George **35**:179
Cynthia Voigt **30**:417, 418

Levertov, Denise
Imamu Amiri Baraka **14**:42
Russell Edson **13**:190
Guillevic **33**:190
H. D. **14**:223
David Ignatow **7**:173
Gilbert Sorrentino **22**:391
John Wieners **7**:535
Nancy Willard **37**:461

Levett, Karl
Stephen Sondheim **30**:400

Levey, Michael
William Faulkner **1**:102
W. Somerset Maugham **1**:204

Levi, Peter
Peter Ackroyd **34**:388
Donald Davie **31**:115
T. S. Eliot **34**:388
David Jones **4**:261; **13**:307
Shiva Naipaul **32**:327
Peter Porter **33**:324
F. T. Prince **22**:338
Yannis Ritsos **31**:325
Siegfried Sassoon **36**:393
George Seferis **5**:384
Jaroslav Seifert **34**:261
Yevgeny Yevtushenko **1**:381

Leviant, Curt
S. Y. Agnon **4**:12
Jakov Lind **4**:292
Chaim Potok **26**:369
Isaac Bashevis Singer **3**:453
Elie Wiesel **3**:530

Levin, Bernard
Breyten Breytenbach **37**:50
Scott Elledge **34**:432
Howard Fast **23**:157
Michael Scammell **34**:481
Aleksandr I. Solzhenitsyn
    7:436; **34**:481
E. B. White **34**:432

Levin, Betty
Virginia Hamilton **26**:155

Levin, Dan
Yasunari Kawabata **2**:223

Levin, David
James Baldwin **17**:26

Levin, Elena
Yevgeny Yevtushenko **1**:382

Levin, Harry
Robert Fitzgerald **39**:472

Levin, Irene S.
Elizabeth Swados **12**:558

Levin, Martin
Brian Aldiss **5**:14
Jeffrey Archer **28**:13
J. G. Ballard **14**:39
Patrick Boyle **19**:67
Art Buchwald **33**:88
A. S. Byatt **19**:75
James M. Cain **28**:49
Taylor Caldwell **2**:95; **28**:63, 67
Henry Carlisle **33**:103
Austin C. Clarke **8**:143
James Clavell **25**:125
Robert Cormier **12**:134
Margaret Craven **17**:79
Harry Crews **23**:131
Don DeLillo **27**:76
Stephen Dobyns **37**:76
Allen Drury **37**:107
Allan W. Eckert **17**:107
John Ehle **27**:105
Thomas J. Fleming **37**:121, 126
William Price Fox **22**:139
George MacDonald Fraser
    7:106
Paul Gallico **2**:147
Ernest K. Gann **23**:166
Natalia Ginzburg **5**:141
Winston Graham **23**:192
Doris Grumbach **22**:204
A. R. Gurney, Jr. **32**:217
Earl Hamner, Jr. **12**:258
Fletcher Knebel **14**:309
William Kotzwinkle **5**:220;
    35:255
Richard Llewellyn **7**:207
Robert Ludlum **22**:288
Kamala Markandaya **38**:324
Richard Matheson **37**:247
John McGahern **5**:280
Walter M. Miller, Jr. **30**:254
Alice Munro **6**:341
Leslie Norris **14**:388
Craig Nova **7**:267
Marge Piercy **27**:372
J. B. Priestley **2**:347
Ann Quin **6**:441
Frederic Raphael **14**:437
Jean Rhys **2**:371
Judith Rossner **6**:468
Susan Richards Shreve **23**:402
Frank G. Slaughter **29**:377, 378
David Slavitt **14**:491
Lee Smith **25**:406
Wilbur Smith **33**:374, 375
Terry Southern **7**:452
Scott Spencer **30**:404
David Storey **4**:530
Jesse Stuart **8**:507
Hollis Summers **10**:493
Glendon Swarthout **35**:400, 403
Elizabeth Taylor **4**:541
Fredrica Wagman **7**:500
David Harry Walker **14**:552
Morris L. West **33**:430, 431
Donald E. Westlake **33**:437

Thomas Williams **14**:581
Sloan Wilson **32**:447
P. G. Wodehouse **2**:479; **5**:516
Hilma Wolitzer **17**:561
John Wyndham **19**:475
Louis Zukofsky **2**:487

Levin, Meyer
Elmer Rice **7**:358
Henry Roth **6**:472

Levin, Milton
Noel Coward **1**:64

Levine, Bernice
Maia Wojciechowska **26**:454

Levine, George
John Gardner **7**:113
Paul Goodman **2**:171
Juan Carlos Onetti **7**:279
Thomas Pynchon **3**:414

Levine, Joan
Franklyn M. Branley **21**:20

Levine, Joan Goldman
Richard Peck **21**:297

Levine, Judith
André Dubus **36**:148

Levine, June Perry
Vladimir Nabokov **6**:352;
  11:396

Levine, Norman
Clark Blaise **29**:71
Frank Sargeson **31**:365

Levine, Paul
Truman Capote **1**:55; **3**:99
J. D. Salinger **12**:498

Levine, Suzanne Jill
Severo Sarduy **6**:486
Mario Vargas Llosa **6**:547

Levinson, Daniel
Walter Abish **22**:17

Levitas, Gloria
Jay Bennett **35**:44
Frank Bonham **12**:54
Hortense Calisher **38**:69
Lois Duncan **26**:103
Sonia Levitin **17**:263

Levitas, Mitchel
James D. Forman **21**:117

Levitin, Alexis
J.R.R. Tolkien **12**:574

Levitin, Sonia
Sonia Levitin **17**:264

Levitt, Morton P.
Michel Butor **3**:92
Claude Simon **4**:495

Levitt, Paul M.
Brendan Behan **11**:45
Jorge Luis Borges **9**:116
Michel de Ghelderode **11**:226

Levitzky, Sergei
Aleksandr I. Solzhenitsyn **4**:507

Levy, Alan
Art Buchwald **33**:87

Levy, Eric P.
Samuel Beckett **18**:49

Levy, Francis
Thomas Berger **3**:64
Ruth Prawer Jhabvala **4**:257
Megan Terry **19**:441
Frank Tuohy **37**:432

Levy, Frank
Norman Lear **12**:330

Levy, Jacques
Sam Shepard **17**:435

Levy, Paul
Kingsley Amis **13**:14
James Baldwin **15**:41
A. S. Byatt **19**:77
Roald Dahl **6**:122
E. L. Doctorow **11**:141
Doris Lessing **6**:301
William Styron **15**:529

Levy, William Turner
Padraic Colum **28**:90

Lewald, H. Ernest
Ernesto Sabato **10**:446; **23**:376

Lewin, Leonard C.
Art Buchwald **33**:90

Lewis, Alan
David Bowie **17**:59
Marvin Gaye **26**:131
Neil Young **17**:569, 570, 571

Lewis, Allan
Robert Anderson **23**:32
Paddy Chayefsky **23**:114
William Gibson **23**:180
William Inge **19**:227
Clifford Odets **28**:339

Lewis, Anthony R.
Joan D. Vinge **30**:410

Lewis, C. S.
J.R.R. Tolkien **1**:336; **12**:563

Lewis, Caroline
Bob Fosse **20**:124

Lewis, Constance
Ivy Compton-Burnett **15**:141

Lewis, David Levering
Maya Angelou **35**:31

Lewis, Gwyneth
Alfred Corn **33**:120

Lewis, J. Patrick
Howard Nemerov **36**:309

Lewis, Janet
Caroline Gordon **6**:206

Lewis, Lloyd
Carl Sandburg **35**:351

Lewis, Maggie
W. P. Kinsella **27**:239
V. S. Naipaul **37**:329
Anthony Powell **31**:318

Lewis, Marshall
Leni Riefenstahl **16**:520

Lewis, Marvin A.
Rudolfo Anaya **23**:26

Lewis, Naomi
Joan Aiken **35**:18
Betsy Byars **35**:72
Leon Garfield **12**:217
Alan Garner **17**:134
Noel Streatfeild **21**:399, 401
Rosemary Sutcliff **26**:425
J.R.R. Tolkien **38**:432
Jill Paton Walsh **35**:431, 432,
  434

Lewis, Paula Gilbert
Anne Hébert **29**:239
Gabrielle Roy **10**:440
Michel Tremblay **29**:424

Lewis, Peter
Horst Bienek **11**:48
J. M. Coetzee **23**:124
Autran Dourado **23**:152
Eva Figes **31**:165
Yashar Kemal **29**:267

Lewis, Peter Elfed
Marvin Bell **8**:65
Ruth Prawer Jhabvala **8**:313

Lewis, R.W.B.
R. P. Blackmur **24**:57
Graham Greene **1**:131
Peter Griffin **39**:401
Ernest Hemingway **39**:401, 431
André Malraux **4**:328
Jeffrey Meyers **39**:431
John Steinbeck **9**:512
Lionel Trilling **24**:449

Lewis, Robert W.
Edward Lewis Wallant **10**:516

Lewis, Robert W., Jr.
Ernest Hemingway **1**:142

Lewis, Robin Jared
E. M. Forster **22**:132

Lewis, Roger
Malcolm Bradbury **32**:56
John Irving **38**:254
J.I.M. Stewart **32**:422

Lewis, Sinclair
P. G. Wodehouse **22**:478

Lewis, Stuart
Bruce Jay Friedman **3**:166

Lewis, Theophilus
Gretchen Cryer **21**:78
Langston Hughes **35**:218
Gerome Ragni and James Rado
  17:382
Neil Simon **6**:502, 503
Douglas Turner Ward **19**:457

Lewis, Tom J.
Stanislaw Lem **8**:344

Lewis, Wyndham
William Faulkner **28**:135
Ezra Pound **7**:322

Ley, Charles David
Vicente Aleixandre **9**:10

Ley, Willy
Arthur C. Clarke **35**:118

Leyda, Jay
Akira Kurosawa **16**:395

Lhamon, W. T., Jr.
Anthony Burgess **5**:89
Bob Dylan **6**:158; **12**:192
John Gardner **3**:187
William Kennedy **6**:275
Joseph McElroy **5**:280
Robert M. Pirsig **4**:405
Thomas Pynchon **3**:412; **18**:430
Kurt Vonnegut, Jr. **4**:568

L'heureux, John
John Gardner **34**:550
Bernard Malamud **27**:306

Libby, Anthony
Robert Bly **15**:62
Robert Hass **39**:148
Theodore Roethke **11**:484
William Carlos Williams **2**:470

Libby, Margaret Sherwood
Lloyd Alexander **35**:24
Margot Benary-Isbert **12**:33
Franklyn M. Branley **21**:16
Betty Cavanna **12**:100
Maureen Daly **17**:90
Eilís Dillon **17**:93
James D. Forman **21**:115
Leon Garfield **12**:215
Jean Craighead George **35**:176
Christie Harris **12**:261
Margaret O. Hyde **21**:174
Jean Lee Latham **12**:323
Philippa Pearce **21**:281
Noel Streatfeild **21**:402
Rosemary Sutcliff **26**:426, 427

Libby, Marion Vlastos
Margaret Drabble **5**:117

Libera, Sharon Mayer
Frank Bidart **33**:74

Liberman, M. M.
Katherine Anne Porter **1**:274;
  7:318
Jean Stafford **4**:517

Libhart, Byron R.
Julien Green **11**:260

Librach, Ronald S.
Ingmar Bergman **16**:81

Lichtenberg, Jacqueline
Gene Roddenberry **17**:407

Lichtenstein, Grace
Roger Kahn **30**:231

Lichtheim, George
Lucien Goldmann **24**:234
Georg Lukács **24**:319

Liddell, Robert
Ivy Compton-Burnett **15**:135

Lidoff, Joan
Christina Stead **32**:416

Lieber, Joel
Richard Elman **19**:150
Lois Gould **4**:199

Lieber, Todd M.
Ralph Ellison **3**:144
Robert Frost **9**:221
John Steinbeck **5**:406

Lieberman, Laurence
Rafael Alberti 7:10
A. R. Ammons 2:11
John Ashbery 9:44
W. H. Auden 2:28
John Berryman 1:33
Edward Brathwaite 11:67
James Dickey 1:73; 2:115
Arthur Gregor 9:252
Michael S. Harper 22:207
Anthony Hecht 8:268
Zbigniew Herbert 9:271
Edwin Honig 33:212
Richard Howard 7:165
Richard F. Hugo 18:259
Galway Kinnell 1:168
Stanley J. Kunitz 6:286
W. S. Merwin 1:212; 3:338
Leonard Michaels 25:314
Frederick Morgan 23:296
Howard Moss 7:248
Howard Nemerov 2:307
Kenneth Patchen 18:394
John Peck 3:378
Kenneth Rexroth 2:371
Muriel Rukeyser 27:409
W. D. Snodgrass 2:405
William Stafford 4:520, 521
Mark Strand 6:521
Melvin B. Tolson 36:426
Ted Walker 13:565
Theodore Weiss 3:517
Reed Whittemore 4:588

Lifton, Robert Jay
Albert Camus 2:99
Masuji Ibuse 22:224
Kurt Vonnegut, Jr. 2:455

Liggett, Priscilla
Larry Bograd 35:63

Light, Carolyn M.
Madeleine L'Engle 12:347

Lillard, Richard G.
Barry Gifford 34:458
Lawrence Lee 34:458
William Saroyan 34:458

Lima, Robert
Jorge Luis Borges 6:88
Ira Levin 6:306
Colin Wilson 3:538

Lindabury, Richard V.
Philip Booth 23:73

Lindberg, Gary
Jack Kerouac 29:277

Lindberg-Seyersted, Brita
Bernard Malamud 9:343

Lindblad, Ishrat
Pamela Hansford Johnson
27:223

Lindborg, Henry J.
Doris Lessing 6:299

Lindegren, Eric
Gunnar Ekelöf 27:109

Lindeman, Jack
Robert Francis 15:235
Edwin Honig 33:210

Lindfors, Bernth
Chinua Achebe 7:4
Ayi Kwei Armah 33:32
Wole Soyinka 36:412
Amos Tutuola 29:439

Lindner, Carl M.
Robert Frost 3:175
James Thurber 5:440

Lindop, Grevel
Dannie Abse 29:20
John Berryman 3:66
Bob Dylan 4:148
Philip Larkin 33:261

Lindquist, Jennie D.
Margot Benary-Isbert 12:32
Walter Farley 17:116
Lee Kingman 17:244
William Mayne 12:387
Zoa Sherburne 30:361
Mary Stolz 12:546, 550
Lenora Mattingly Weber 12:633

Lindsay, Leon
James Carroll 38:105

Lindsey, Almont
Milton Meltzer 26:299

Lindsey, Byron
Joseph Brodsky 13:116

Lindsey, David A.
Jules Archer 12:22

Lindskoog, Kathryn Ann
C. S. Lewis 27:262

Lindstrom, Naomi
Bob Dylan 12:191

Linehan, Eugene J., S.J.
Taylor Caldwell 2:95
A. J. Cronin 32:140
Allen Drury 37:107
James Herriot 12:283
Irving Wallace 7:509

Lingeman, Richard R.
Richard Bach 14:36
Russell Baker 31:30
James Herriot 12:283
Mary McCarthy 14:362
Charles M. Schulz 12:531
Erich Segal 10:466
William Saroyan 29:360
Garry Trudeau 12:590

Linkous, Robert
Mary McCarthy 39:488

Linney, Romulus
Claude Brown 30:34

Lipari, Joseph A.
James Galvin 38:198
Robert Hayden 37:159
M. L. Rosenthal 28:398
Norman Williams 39:100

Lipking, Lawrence
R. S. Crane 27:72

Lippi, Tom
Milan Kundera 32:263

Lippit, Noriko Mizuta
Yukio Mishima 27:345
Jun'ichirō Tanizaki 28:416

Lippmann, Walter
Van Wyck Brooks 29:78

Lipsius, Frank
Herbert Gold 7:121
Bernard Malamud 2:268
Henry Miller 2:283
Thomas Pynchon 6:434

Lipson, Eden Ross
Larry McMurtry 27:333

Lipsyte, Robert
Judy Blume 30:23
Robert Lipsyte 21:213
Walter Dean Myers 35:295
Robert Newton Peck 17:339

Lisca, Peter
John Steinbeck 21:380

Lissner, John
Janis Ian 21:185

Listri, Pier Francesco
Allen Tate 6:525

Litsinger, Kathryn A.
Andre Norton 12:465

Litt, Dorothy E.
John Mortimer 28:286

Littell, Philip
Rebecca West 31:450

Littell, Robert
Howard Fast 23:154
Robert Frost 15:240
Jean Toomer 13:550

Little, Roger
St.-John Perse 4:400; 11:433, 436

Little, Stuart W.
Gay Talese 37:393

Littlejohn, David
James Baldwin 5:40
Imamu Amiri Baraka 5:44
Samuel Beckett 2:45
Jorge Luis Borges 2:68
Cleanth Brooks 24:108
Gwendolyn Brooks 5:75
Lawrence Durrell 4:144
Ralph Ellison 11:179
Jean Genet 2:157
John Hawkes 2:183
Robert Hayden 5:168
Joseph Heller 3:229
Chester Himes 7:159
Langston Hughes 5:190
Robinson Jeffers 2:214
John Oliver Killens 10:300
Henry Miller 2:281, 283
Ann Petry 7:304
Jean Toomer 13:551
J. E. Wideman 5:489
Richard Wright 9:583

Littler, Frank
Isabel Colegate 36:109
Nigel Dennis 8:173
Maureen Duffy 37:114

Litvinoff, Emanuel
Arthur Koestler 33:235

Litwak, Leo E.
Hunter S. Thompson 17:503

Litz, A. Walton
Peter Ackroyd 34:394
T. S. Eliot 34:394

Liv, Gwen
Barbara Corcoran 17:70

Lively, Penelope
Penelope Fitzgerald 19:175
Russell C. Hoban 25:265
Kazuo Ishiguro 27:204
Doris Lessing 22:287
Michael Moorcock 27:352
Barbara Pym 37:369
Ann Schlee 35:374
D. M. Thomas 22:422
Angus Wilson 25:461

Livesay, Dorothy
Milton Acorn 15:8
Louis Dudek 11:159
E. J. Pratt 19:378

Livingstone, Leon
Azorín 11:25

Llorens, David
Nikki Giovanni 19:190

Lloyd, Christopher
Siegfried Sassoon 36:397

Lloyd, Paul M.
Michael Ende 31:144
J.R.R. Tolkien 38:441

Lloyd, Peter
Leonardo Sciascia 9:476

Lloyd-Jones, Hugh
Marguerite Yourcenar 38:462

Loake, Jonathan
Lisa St. Aubin de Teran 36:422

Lobb, Edward
T. S. Eliot 24:185

Lobdell, Jared C.
August Derleth 31:138

Locke, Alain
Langston Hughes 35:212

Locke, Richard
Donald Barthelme 8:52
Ann Beattie 18:37
Thomas Berger 8:83
Heinrich Böll 3:73
John Cheever 8:139
Joan Didion 8:175
Peter Handke 38:216, 226
Barry Hannah 23:209
Joseph Heller 11:268
John le Carré 5:233
Vladimir Nabokov 2:303; 8:418
Thomas Pynchon 2:356
John Updike 1:345; 9:540
Mario Vargas Llosa 31:448

Lockerbie, D. Bruce
C. S. Lewis 1:177

Lockhart, Marilyn
Norma Klein 30:242

Locklin, Gerald
Richard Brautigan 12:67

Lockwood, William J.
Ed Dorn **10**:159

Loder, Kurt
John Lennon **35**:276
Pink Floyd **35**:309, 314
Prince **35**:329

Lodge, David
Kingsley Amis **2**:10
William S. Burroughs **2**:92
Mary Gordon **13**:250
Graham Greene **1**:134; **3**:206
Ted Hughes **2**:199
Milan Kundera **32**:265
Doris Lessing **15**:332
Norman Mailer **4**:321
Alain Robbe-Grillet **4**:447
Wilfrid Sheed **2**:394
Muriel Spark **13**:525
John Updike **34**:295

Loewinsohn, Ron
Frederick Barthelme **36**:53
Richard Brautigan **12**:59
Padgett Powell **34**:98

Loftis, John E.
John Nichols **38**:345

Logan, John
E. E. Cummings **3**:117

Logan, William
Gabriel García Márquez **15**:253
Albert Goldbarth **38**:207
Robert Hayden **14**:240
Laura Jensen **37**:190
Michael Ondaatje **14**:410
James Tate **25**:428
Derek Walcott **14**:548

Loggins, Vernon
Julia Peterkin **31**:305

Lohrke, Eugene
Rhys Davies **23**:140

Loke, Margarett
Scott O'Dell **30**:275

Lomas, Herbert
Roy Fuller **4**:179
John Gardner **7**:115
Paul Goodman **4**:196
John Hawkes **7**:143
Robert M. Pirsig **6**:421
Ezra Pound **3**:398

Londré, Felicia Hardison
Mark Medoff **23**:294

Long, John Allan
Anne Tyler **28**:430

Long, Margo Alexander
John Neufeld **17**:311

Long, Robert Emmet
Ernest Hemingway **3**:237
Robert Phillips **28**:362
Edmund Wilson **8**:550

Long, Sidney
Lloyd Alexander **35**:25

Longley, Edna
Douglas Dunn **6**:147
Seamus Heaney **5**:170
Thomas Kinsella **19**:256
Marge Piercy **18**:409

Longley, John Lewis, Jr.
Robert Penn Warren **1**:355

Longstreth, T. Morris
Frank B. Gilbreth and
Ernestine Gilbreth Carey
17:154
Jean Lee Latham **12**:322
Farley Mowat **26**:330

Longsworth, Polly
Madeleine L'Engle **12**:349

Lopez, Daniel
Bernardo Bertolucci **16**:97

Loprete, Nicholas J.
Richard Grayson **38**:211
William Saroyan **10**:457

Lorch, Thomas M.
Edward Lewis Wallant **10**:512

Lord, James
Henri Troyat **23**:460

Lorich, Bruce
Samuel Beckett **6**:34

Lorrah, Jean
Marion Zimmer Bradley **30**:29

Losinski, Julie
Christie Harris **12**:263

Lothian, Helen M.
Christie Harris **12**:262

Lotz, Jim
Farley Mowat **26**:334

Loubère, J.A.E.
Claude Simon **15**:490

Louch, A. R.
René Wellek **28**:453

Lounsberry, Barbara
Gay Talese **37**:403

Lourie, Richard
Joseph Brodsky **13**:114

Love, Keith
E. B. White **39**:369

Love, Theresa R.
Zora Neale Hurston **30**:218

Lovecraft, H. P.
August Derleth **31**:126, 127

Loveman, Amy
C. S. Forester **35**:159
William Maxwell **19**:305

Lovering, Joseph P.
Pat Jordon **37**:195

Lovett, R. M.
Carl Van Vechten **33**:387

Low, Alice
Isabelle Holland **21**:147

Lowell, Amy
Robert Frost **13**:222
Carl Sandburg **35**:340

Lowell, Robert
W. H. Auden **1**:9
John Berryman **2**:57
Elizabeth Bishop **32**:28
Randall Jarrell **2**:207; **13**:298
Stanley J. Kunitz **6**:285

Sylvia Plath **17**:347
I. A. Richards **14**:452
Allen Tate **4**:535

Lowenkopf, Shelly
Cecile Pineda **39**:96

Lowenkron, David Henry
Samuel Beckett **6**:40

Lowenthal, Lawrence D.
Arthur Miller **15**:374

Lowie, Robert H.
Margaret Mead **37**:270

Lownsbrough, John
A. G. Mojtabai **29**:319

Lowrie, Rebecca
Maureen Daly **17**:88

Lowrey, Burling
S. J. Perelman **23**:336

Lowry, Beverly
Ellen Gilchrist **34**:166
D. M. Thomas **22**:421

Lowry, Margerie Bonner
Edward Hoagland **28**:180

Lubbers, Klaus
Carson McCullers **12**:423

Lubbock, Richard
Joan D. Vinge **30**:411

Lubow, Arthur
Michael Cimino **16**:211
Fran Lebowitz **36**:247
George Lucas **16**:414

Lucas, Alec
Roderick L. Haig-Brown
21:142
Farley Mowat **26**:341

Lucas, John
Donald Davie **31**:124
Thom Gunn **32**:214
Stanley Middleton **38**:332
Edwin Morgan **31**:276
Peter Porter **33**:324
Ezra Pound **7**:332
Anne Stevenson **33**:382
William Trevor **25**:442

Luccock, Halford E.
Taylor Caldwell **28**:55

Lucey, Beatus T., O.S.B.
Daphne du Maurier **6**:146

Luchting, Wolfgang A.
José María Arguedas **10**:9
José Donoso **4**:126, 127
Gabriel García Márquez **2**:150
Alain Resnais **16**:499
Luisa Valenzuela **31**:438
Mario Vargas Llosa **10**:496

Lucid, Luellen
Aleksandr I. Solzhenitsyn
10:480

Lucid, Robert F.
Ernest Hemingway **6**:232
Norman Mailer **4**:323

Lucie-Smith, Edward
Sylvia Plath **9**:424

Luckett, Richard
Lenny Bruce **21**:51
Anthony Powell **7**:339
Robert Penn Warren **6**:555
Edmund Wilson **3**:540

Luckey, Eleanore Braun
Honor Arundel **17**:19

Luddy, Thomas E.
Edwin Morgan **31**:273

Ludlow, Colin
David Hare **29**:214
David Mamet **15**:356
Stephen Poliakoff **38**:382
Tom Stoppard **15**:520

Ludwig, Jack
Bernard Malamud **2**:269
Mordecai Richler **18**:452

Ludwig, Linda
Doris Lessing **6**:301

Lueders, Edward
Jorge Luis Borges **2**:72
George MacBeth **2**:252
Carl Van Vechten **33**:397

Lugg, Andrew M.
Andy Warhol **20**:417

Lukács, Georg
Aleksandr I. Solzhenitsyn
26:416

Lukacs, John
Russell Baker **31**:31
Aleksandr I. Solzhenitsyn **7**:438

Lukacs, Paul
Anthony Burgess **13**:125

Lukas, Betty
Jeffrey Archer **28**:13

Lukens, Rebecca J.
Mavis Thorpe Clark **12**:132
Madeleine L'Engle **12**:351

Lukowsky, Wes
Roger Kahn **30**:234

Lumley, Frederick
Terence Rattigan **7**:354

Lumport, Felicia
Jessamyn West **7**:520

Lund, Mary
Marian Engel **36**:161

Lundquist, James
J. D. Salinger **12**:518
Kurt Vonnegut, Jr. **12**:615

Lunn, Janet
Kevin Major **26**:286

Lupack, Alan C.
Gwendolyn Brooks **15**:95

Lupoff, Richard
John W. Campbell, Jr. **32**:76
Kurt Vonnegut, Jr. **12**:629

Luria-Sukenick, Lynn
Max Apple **33**:20

Lurie, Alison
Richard Adams **5**:7
Peter Davison **28**:101
Iris Murdoch **3**:348

Critic Index

Lurie, Nancy Oestreich
Vine Deloria, Jr. **21**:108

Luschei, Martin
Walker Percy **3**:378

Lustig, Irma S.
Sean O'Casey **9**:411

Luttwak, Edward
Bernard Malamud **3**:325

Lyall, Gavin
Edmund Crispin **22**:110

Lydenberg, Robin
Jorge Luis Borges **13**:111, 113

Lydon, Michael
Chuck Berry **17**:52

Lydon, Susan
Leslie Epstein **27**:132
John Lennon and Paul
McCartney **12**:362
Toni Morrison **22**:322

Lye, John
A. W. Purdy **14**:433

Lyell, Frank H.
Harper Lee **12**:340

Lyles, Jean Caffey
Richard Bach **14**:35

Lyles, W. H.
Stephen King **12**:310

Lynch, Dennis Daley
William Stafford **7**:462

Lynch, Josephine E.
Noel Streatfeild **21**:399

Lynch, Michael
Richard Howard **7**:168
Michael McClure **10**:332

Lynch, William S.
C. S. Forester **35**:167

Lynd, Helen Merrell
Muriel Rukeyser **27**:409

Lyne, Oliver
Ted Hughes **9**:282

Lynen, John F.
Robert Frost **1**:110

Lynes, Carlos, Jr.
Arthur Adamov **25**:11

Lynes, Russell
Charles Addams **30**:15
Scott Elledge **34**:429
E. B. White **34**:429

Lynn, Elizabeth A.
Octavia E. Butler **38**:62

Lynn, Kenneth S.
Virginia Spencer Carr **34**:420
John Dos Passos **34**:420
Ernest Hemingway **30**:199
Alfred Kazin **34**:560

Lyon, George W., Jr.
Allen Ginsberg **3**:194

Lyon, James K.
Paul Celan **19**:87

Lyon, Laurence Gill
Jean-Paul Sartre **18**:463

Lyon, Melvin
Edward Dahlberg **1**:72

Lyon, Thomas J.
Gary Snyder **32**:393

Lyons, Bonnie
Margaret Atwood **8**:33
Henry Roth **2**:378; **6**:473
Delmore Schwartz **10**:463

Lyons, Donald
Luchino Visconti **16**:574

Lyons, Eugene
Walker Percy **6**:399
John Updike **3**:486

Lyons, Gene
Peter Ackroyd **34**:392
Jeffrey Archer **28**:11
Peter Benchley **8**:82
Roy Blount, Jr. **38**:45
Len Deighton **7**:75
Allen Drury **37**:107
Clyde Edgerton **39**:52
T. S. Eliot **34**:392
Louise Erdrich **39**:132
John Gardner **30**:155
John Hersey **9**:277
John Irving **23**:249
Elia Kazan **6**:274
George MacBeth **9**:340
Helen Hooven Santmyer **33**:358
Peter Straub **28**:410
Hunter S. Thompson **17**:515
John Updike **13**:562; **23**:470
Irving Wallace **7**:510
Robert Penn Warren **8**:540
Richard Yates **7**:555

Lyons, John O.
Vladimir Nabokov **1**:241

Lytle, Andrew
Caroline Gordon **29**:184
Allen Tate **4**:535

Maas, Peter
Frederick Forsyth **36**:177

MacAdam, Alfred J.
José Donoso **32**:155, 160, 161
G. Cabrera Infante **25**:102
Thomas Pynchon **11**:455
João Guimarães Rosa **23**:356

MacAndrew, Andrew R.
Yuri Olesha **8**:430

Macaulay, Jeannette
Camara Laye **4**:285

Macauley, Robie
Toni Cade Bambara **19**:33
R. P. Blackmur **2**:61
Shirley Hazzard **18**:214
James Alan McPherson **19**:310
Jean Rhys **14**:446
M. L. Rosenthal **28**:390
René Wellek **28**:447
Patrick White **9**:566

MacBeth, George
Robert Nye **13**:412

MacBride, James
James M. Cain **28**:48
Helen MacInnes **27**:279
Jessamyn West **17**:544

MacBrudnoy, David
George MacDonald Fraser
7:106

MacCabe, Colin
Jean-Luc Godard **20**:146

MacCaig, Norman
D. J. Enright **31**:146

MacCallum, Hugh
Leonard Cohen **38**:136

MacCann, Donnarae
Christopher Collier and James
L. Collier **30**:73

MacCarthy, Desmond
T. S. Eliot **24**:161
George S. Kaufman **38**:259

Maccoby, Hyam
Ezra Pound **18**:420

MacDiarmid, Hugh
Norman MacCaig **36**:280
Ezra Pound **4**:413

Macdonald, Dwight
Charles Addams **30**:14
Charles Chaplin **16**:199
James Gould Cozzens **4**:111
Federico Fellini **16**:274
Rouben Mamoulian **16**:424
Marshall McLuhan **37**:255
Czesław Miłosz **22**:305
Philip Roth **1**:293
Tom Wolfe **35**:450

MacDonald, John D.
James M. Cain **11**:87

Macdonald, Rae McCarthy
Alice Munro **10**:357

Macdonald, Ross
Nelson Algren **10**:8
Dashiell Hammett **5**:160

MacDonald, Ruth K.
Marilyn Sachs **35**:335

MacDonald, S. Yvonne
Christie Harris **12**:266

MacDonald, Scott
Erskine Caldwell **14**:96

Macdonald, Susan
Pier Paolo Pasolini **20**:262

MacDougall, Ruth Doan
Michael Cunningham **34**:41
Harriet Doerr **34**:152
Sylvia Murphy **34**:92

MacDuffie, Bruce L.
Milton Meltzer **26**:299

MacFadden, Patrick
Albert Maysles and David
Maysles **16**:438, 440
Pier Paolo Pasolini **20**:260

MacFall, Russell
August Derleth **31**:138

Macfarlane, David
Margaret Atwood **25**:65
Clark Blaise **29**:76
Brian Moore **32**:311

MacInnes, Colin
James Baldwin **1**:14; **17**:25
Brendan Behan **15**:44
Shelagh Delaney **29**:143
Alex Haley **12**:244
Gay Talese **37**:393

MacIntyre, Alasdair
Arthur Koestler **1**:170

MacIntyre, Jean
Barbara Corcoran **17**:77

Maciuszko, George J.
Czesław Miłosz **5**:292

Mackay, Barbara
Imamu Amiri Baraka **10**:19
Ed Bullins **7**:37
James Kirkwood **9**:319

MacKay, L. A.
Robert Finch **18**:154

MacKendrick, Louis K.
Hugh Hood **28**:193
Robert Kroetsch **23**:272

MacKenzie, Nancy K.
Babette Deutsch **18**:120

MacKenzie, Robert
Norman Lear **12**:337

MacKethan, Lucinda H.
Lee Smith **25**:409

MacKinnon, Alex
Earle Birney **6**:79

Macklin, Elizabeth
Heberto Padilla **38**:350

Macklin, F. A.
Leon Uris **32**:432

Macklin, F. Anthony
Robert Altman **16**:34
Stanley Kubrick **16**:381
Gore Vidal **2**:449

MacLaren, I. S.
A.J.M. Smith **15**:517

Maclean, Alasdair
Elizabeth Jennings **14**:292
D. M. Thomas **13**:541

MacLean, Kenneth
William Heyen **18**:229

MacLeish, Archibald
Ezra Pound **3**:399
Carl Sandburg **35**:356

MacLeish, Roderick
Eric Ambler **6**:3
Richard Condon **8**:150
Len Deighton **7**:74
Ken Follett **18**:155
Frederick Forsyth **36**:177
George V. Higgins **4**:224

MacLeod, Anne Scott
Robert Cormier **30**:88

MacManus, Patricia
Shirley Hazzard **18**:214
Grace Paley **37**:330
Françoise Sagan **17**:424

Macmillan, Carrie
Jane Rule **27**:421

Mac Namara, Desmond
Jessamyn West **17**:550

Macnaughton, W. R.
Ernest Hemingway **8**:286

MacPike, Loralee
Thomas J. Fleming **37**:129
Zibby Oneal **30**:279
Cynthia Propper Seton **27**:429
Fay Weldon **19**:470

MacQuown, Vivian J.
Mary Stolz **12**:552

Macrae, Alasdair D. F.
Edwin Morgan **31**:276
D. M. Thomas **31**:430

Macri, F. M.
Anne Hébert **29**:229

MacShane, Frank
Jorge Luis Borges **2**:76
Italo Calvino **22**:93
Edward Dahlberg **1**:71; **14**:138
Barbara Howes **15**:290
Clarence Major **19**:292
W. S. Merwin **1**:212
Alberto Moravia **18**:348
Pablo Neruda **9**:399
Leslie Marmon Silko **23**:407

MacSkimming, Roy
Jack Hodgins **23**:228
Michael Ondaatje **29**:340

MacSween, R. J.
Ivy Compton-Burnett **10**:110
Evelyn Waugh **19**:462

MacTaggart, Garaud
Jimmy Cliff **21**:65

MacWillie, Joan
Noel Streatfeild **21**:396

Madden, David
James M. Cain **3**:96; **11**:86
William Gaddis **1**:113
Wright Morris **1**:230; **3**:343
Sam Shepard **17**:434

Madden, David W.
Thomas Berger **38**:42

Madden, Susan B.
D. M. Pinkwater **35**:319, 320

Maddocks, Fiona
Maya Angelou **35**:33

Maddocks, Melvin
Richard Adams **4**:7
Kingsley Amis **2**:7, 8
John Beecher **6**:48
Jackson J. Benson **34**:408
Heinrich Böll **3**:75
Paul Bowles **2**:78
Truman Capote **34**:324
Padraic Colum **28**:89
J. P. Donleavy **6**:142

Ernest J. Gaines **3**:179
John Gardner **2**:152
Judith Guest **30**:172
Mark Harris **19**:201
Joseph Heller **5**:176
Thomas Keneally **5**:209, 212
Doris Lessing **2**:239; **6**:298, 303
Jakov Lind **27**:271
Bernard Malamud **2**:267
S. J. Perelman **23**:337
Anthony Powell **31**:318
Thomas Pynchon **2**:354
Piers Paul Read **4**:444
Erich Maria Remarque **21**:333
Philip Roth **4**:456
Cornelius Ryan **7**:385
Josef Škvorecký **39**:232
John Steinbeck **34**:408
William Wharton **37**:437
Angus Wilson **3**:536

Maddox, Brenda
Arthur C. Clarke **35**:118

Maddox, Tom
William Gibson **39**:142

Madison, Charles
James A. Michener **29**:317

Madison, Charles A.
Isaac Bashevis Singer **23**:414

Madsen, Alan
Andre Norton **12**:457

Madsen, Axel
Jerzy Skolimowski **20**:347

Madsen, Børge Gedsø
Kjeld Abell **15**:1

Maes-Jelinek, Hena
Wilson Harris **25**:212

Magalaner, Marvin
E. M. Forster **1**:103
Aldous Huxley **1**:150

Magee, Bryan
Martin Heidegger **24**:271

Magee, William H.
Philip Child **19**:100

Magid, Marion
Shelagh Delaney **29**:145
Tennessee Williams **30**:465

Magid, Nora L.
Mordecai Richler **9**:450; **18**:456
Françoise Sagan **17**:416
Herman Wouk **38**:445

Magliola, Robert
Jorge Luis Borges **10**:68

Magnarelli, Sharon
Luisa Valenzuela **31**:439

Magner, James E., Jr.
John Crowe Ransom **4**:431

Magnússon, Sigurður A.
Halldór Laxness **25**:299

Magny, Claude-Edmonde
John Dos Passos **15**:182
William Faulkner **18**:143
André Malraux **15**:351

Maguire, C. E.
Siegfried Sassoon **36**:390

Maguire, Clinton J.
Farley Mowat **26**:337

Maguire, Gregory
Aidan Chambers **35**:101
Joanne Greenberg **30**:168

Maguire, Robert A.
Tadeusz Różewicz **23**:359

Mahlendorf, Ursula
Horst Bienek **7**:28
Christa Wolf **29**:465

Mahon, Derek
Patrick Boyle **19**:68
Austin Clarke **9**:168
Donald Davie **10**:125
Frederick Exley **11**:186
John le Carré **5**:233
József Lengyel **7**:202
Hugh MacDiarmid **19**:289
John Montague **13**:390
Brian Moore **8**:394
Edna O'Brien **8**:429
Tom Paulin **37**:354
Craig Raine **32**:348

Mahon, Vincent
Marilyn French **18**:157

Mahood, M. M.
R. K. Narayan **28**:297

Maida, Patricia D.
Flannery O'Connor **10**:364

Mailer, Norman
Bernardo Bertolucci **16**:92

Maini, Darshan Singhi
Anita Desai **37**:65

Maio, Kathleen
Joseph Hansen **38**:240
Richard Rosen **39**:196

Mairowitz, David Zane
Edward Bond **6**:86
Caryl Churchill **31**:83

Mais, S.P.B.
Siegfried Sassoon **36**:385

Maitland, Jeffrey
William H. Gass **11**:224

Maitland, Sara
Thomas M. Disch **36**:127
Edna O'Brien **36**:336
Flann O'Brien **5**:314

Majdiak, Daniel
John Barth **1**:17

Majeski, Jane
Arthur Koestler **8**:324

Majkut, Denise R.
Bob Dylan **4**:148

Major, Clarence
Ralph Ellison **3**:146
Rudolph Wurlitzer **15**:588

Makeig, Hester
Nicolas Freeling **38**:184

Malabre, Alfred L., Jr.
Paul E. Erdman **25**:153

Malamut, Bruce
Jimmy Cliff **21**:63
Steve Martin **30**:246
Pink Floyd **35**:306
Lou Reed **21**:312
Peter Townshend **17**:536

Malanga, Gerard
Jim Carroll **35**:77
Anne Waldman **7**:508

Malcolm, Donald
James Baldwin **17**:22
Allen Drury **37**:101
Mark Harris **19**:200

Malcolm, Janet
Milan Kundera **32**:262
Ved Mehta **37**:295
Maia Wojciechowska **26**:453

Malin, Irving
Kōbō Abé **22**:15
Walter Abish **22**:18
Jonathan Baumbach **23**:52, 55
Saul Bellow **13**:70
Paul Bowles **19**:61
Frederick Busch **7**:39
Hortense Calisher **4**:87
Jerome Charyn **18**:98
Eleanor Clark **5**:105
B. H. Friedman **7**:109
John Hawkes **4**:217
Joseph Heller **5**:182
Ken Kesey **6**:278
Carson McCullers **4**:344
Flannery O'Connor **2**:317
Walker Percy **8**:445
James Purdy **2**:347
Philip Roth **15**:449
Isaac Bashevis Singer **23**:415
Muriel Spark **5**:398; **8**:496
Peter Spielberg **6**:519
Harvey Swados **5**:421
Elie Wiesel **5**:490

Malkin, Lawrence
Harold Pinter **6**:418

Malko, George
Frederick Buechner **4**:80

Malkoff, Karl
Robert Duncan **15**:189
Kenneth Rexroth **1**:284
Theodore Roethke **1**:291
May Swenson **4**:533

Mallalieu, H. B.
John Gardner **7**:116
Pablo Neruda **7**:261
David Pownall **10**:419

Mallerman, Tony
Satyajit Ray **16**:479

Mallet, Gina
Iris Murdoch **1**:237
Tennessee Williams **7**:545

Malley, Terrence
Richard Brautigan **3**:88

Mallon, Thomas
Donald Spoto **39**:452
Gore Vidal **33**:404
Tennessee Williams **39**:452

Critic Index

Malmfelt, A. D.
Brian De Palma **20**:73

Malmström, Gunnel
Pär Lagerkvist **13**:330

Maloff, Saul
Nelson Algren **4**:18; **33**:14
Louis Auchincloss **4**:30
James Baldwin **17**:23
Heinrich Böll **9**:110
Frederick Busch **7**:38
Edward Dahlberg **7**:68
Carlos Fuentes **22**:164
Ernest Hemingway **3**:236
Nat Hentoff **26**:188
Ward S. Just **27**:226
Milan Kundera **9**:321
Norman Mailer **2**:264
Milton Meltzer **26**:303
Vladimir Nabokov **6**:356
Flannery O'Connor **3**:365
Clifford Odets **2**:319
Sylvia Plath **2**:336; **17**:358
Philip Roth **3**:435; **4**:455
Alan Sillitoe **1**:307
Josef Škvorecký **15**:512
Richard Stern **39**:236
Studs Terkel **38**:240
Calder Willingham **5**:512
Maia Wojciechowska **26**:450

Malone, Hank
Richard Grayson **38**:208

Malone, Michael
Thomas Berger **18**:57
William F. Buckley, Jr. **37**:61
Ernest K. Gann **23**:168
Barry Hannah **23**:209
Helen Hooven Santmyer **33**:359
Kurt Vonnegut, Jr. **22**:449

Maloney, Douglas J.
Frederick Exley **6**:171

Maloney, Russell
Ogden Nash **23**:320

Maltin, Leonard
Woody Allen **16**:5

Malzberg, Barry N.
Ursula K. LeGuin **13**:349

Mamber, Stephen
Albert Mayslés and David
Maysles **16**:441, 442
Frederick Wiseman **20**:470,
473, 476

Maminski, Dolores
Jay Bennett **35**:46

Mandel, Eli
Leonard Cohen **38**:131, 136
Andrew Suknaki **19**:432

Mandel, Siegfried
Uwe Johnson **5**:200
Mary Renault **17**:393

Mandelbaum, Allen
Giuseppe Ungaretti **7**:481

Mandelbaum, Bernard
Elie Wiesel **11**:570

Mandelbaum, Sara
Adrienne Rich **36**:366

Mander, Gertrud
Peter Weiss **15**:566

Mander, John
Günter Grass **6**:208

Mandić, Oleg
Lucien Goldmann **24**:235

Manfred, Freya
Erica Jong **18**:277

Mangelsdorff, Rich
Michael McClure **6**:318

Mangione, Jerry
Andrea Giovene **7**:116

Manguel, Alberto
André Brink **36**:69
Lawrence Durrell **27**:100
Audrey Thomas **37**:423

Manheimer, Joan
Margaret Drabble **22**:123

Mankiewicz, Don
Jessamyn West **17**:546

Mankiewicz, Don M.
Laura Z. Hobson **25**:271

Manlove, C. N.
J.R.R. Tolkien **12**:580

Mann, Charles W., Jr.
Jonathan Kozol **17**:248

Mann, Elizabeth C.
Mary Stolz **12**:551

Mann, Golo
W. H. Auden **3**:29

Mann, Jeanette W.
Jean Stafford **7**:458

Mann, Jessica
John Gardner **30**:156

Mann, Thomas
Hermann Hesse **11**:270

Mannes, Marya
Françoise Sagan **17**:422

Manning, Olivia
Louis Aragon **22**:36
Beryl Bainbridge **14**:36
Sylvia Townend Warner **7**:511

Manning, Robert J.
Art Buchwald **33**:91

Mano, D. Keith
Richard Adams **4**:9
J. G. Ballard **3**:34
Thomas Berger **5**:60
Daniel J. Berrigan **4**:58
Jorge Luis Borges **2**:71
Philip Caputo **32**:103, 105
John Cheever **3**:108
Evan S. Connell, Jr. **6**:117
Peter DeVries **10**:136
J. P. Donleavy **4**:125
Richard Elman **19**:151
Irvin Faust **8**:214
Gabriel García Márquez **27**:157
William Gerhardie **5**:140
James Hanley **3**:221
Joseph Heller **5**:180

George V. Higgins **4**:224
B. S. Johnson **6**:263, 264
Erica Jong **8**:315
Ward S. Just **27**:229
Yuri Krotkov **19**:264
Siegfried Lenz **27**:250
James A. Michener **11**:376
Vladimir Nabokov **2**:301
Hugh Nissenson **9**:400
Richard O'Brien **17**:325
John O'Hara **2**:325
Philip Roth **4**:458
William Saroyan **10**:456
Alexander Theroux **2**:433
Michel Tournier **36**:434
John Updike **2**:444; **5**:456
Patrick White **3**:525
Elie Wiesel **37**:459
Tennessee Williams **7**:546

Mansbridge, Francis
Rudy Wiebe **14**:573

Mansell, Mark
Isaac Asimov **26**:50
Harlan Ellison **13**:208

Mansfield, Katherine
Enid Bagnold **25**:71

Manso, Susan
Anaïs Nin **8**:424

Mansur, Carole
Fran Lebowitz **36**:250

Manthorne, Jane
Frank Bonham **12**:50, 51
Mavis Thorpe Clark **12**:130
Allan W. Eckert **17**:106
James D. Forman **21**:117
James Herriot **12**:283
Andre Norton **12**:457
Maia Wojciechowska **26**:455

Manuel, Bruce
Wright Morris **37**:314
Jonathan Schell **35**:365

Manuel, Diane Casselberry
Chaim Potok **26**:375
Morris L. West **33**:432

Manvell, Roger
René Clair **20**:63
John Gardner **30**:158
Fritz Lang **20**:204
Jean Cocteau **16**:227
Leni Riefenstahl **16**:521
Thomas W. Shapcott **38**:405
Wilbur Smith **33**:376
Agnès Varda **16**:554
Andrzej Wajda **16**:577
Orson Welles **20**:433, 447

Mao, Nathan K.
Pa Chin **18**:373

Maples, Houston L.
Joseph Krumgold **12**:318
William Mayne **12**:392
Maia Wojciechowska **26**:451

Marafino, Elizabeth A.
Sonia Levitin **17**:265

Marcello, J. J. Armas
Mario Vargas Llosa **10**:499

Marciniak, Ed
Frank Bonham **12**:50

Marcorelles, Louis
René Clair **20**:65
Elia Kazan **16**:373
Eric Rohmer **16**:528

Marcotte, Edward
Alain Robbe-Grillet **6**:467

Marcus, Adrianne
Anna Kavan **13**:316
Jon Silkin **2**:395
William Stafford **4**:520

Marcus, Frank
Stephen Poliakoff **38**:382

Marcus, Greil
Wendell Berry **8**:85
E. L. Doctorow **6**:134
Bob Dylan **12**:197
John Irving **13**:294, 295, 296
John Lennon **35**:269
John Lennon and Paul
McCartney **12**:382
Richard Price **12**:490
John Sayles **10**:460
Patti Smith **12**:535
Raymond Sokolov **7**:431
Robert Wilson **9**:576

Marcus, Mordecai
William Everson **1**:96
Robert Frost **9**:224
Ted Hughes **2**:203
Bernard Malamud **1**:199
Nancy Willard **37**:462

Marcus, Steven
William Golding **2**:165
Dashiell Hammett **10**:252
Bernard Malamud **2**:265
Irving Stone **7**:470
Evelyn Waugh **27**:470

Marcus, Susan F.
Bette Greene **30**:171

Marder, Irving
Ernest Hemingway **39**:432
James Jones **39**:412
Frank MacShane **39**:412
Jeffrey Meyers **39**:432

Marder, Joan V.
Rosemary Sutcliff **26**:434

Maremaa, Thomas
Robert Crumb **17**:84

Margaronis, Maria
Jonathan Schell **35**:370

Margolies, Edward
John Ehle **27**:103
Chester Himes **18**:244
Richard Wright **21**:443

Margolis, John D.
Joseph Wood Krutch **24**:290

Margolis, Richard J.
Margaret Mead **37**:277

Marguerite, Sister M., R.S.M.
Eleanor Hibbert **7**:155
Erich von Däniken **30**:422

Mariani, John
Aleksandr I. Solzhenitsyn 7:440

Mariani, Paul
Robert Penn Warren 8:536
William Carlos Williams 9:572

Marill-Albérès, René
Jean-Paul Sartre 1:304

Marine, Gene
Lenny Bruce 21:49

Marinucci, Ron
Isaac Asimov 19:29

Marius, Richard
Frederick Buechner 4:79

Mark, M.
Carly Simon 26:411
Bruce Springsteen 17:483

Mark, Rachel
Tom Wolfe 15:587

Marken, Jack W.
N. Scott Momaday 19:320

Marker, Frederick J.
Kjeld Abell 15:3

Markey, Constance
Italo Calvino 39:309

Markmann, Charles Lam
Julien Green 3:205
Joyce Carol Oates 2:313

Markos, Donald
Hannah Green 3:202

Markos, Donald W.
James Dickey 1:74

Markow, Alice Bradley
Doris Lessing 6:297

Marks, Emerson R.
René Wellek 28:452

Marks, Lawrence
Robert Graves 39:323

Marks, Mitchell
Frederick Busch 7:38

Marling, William
Edward Abbey 36:13, 18

Marnell, Francis X.
Helen Hooven Santmyer 33:361

Marnham, Patrick
Graham Greene 37:137
Paul Theroux 15:535

Marowitz, Charles
John Arden 13:23
Howard Brenton 31:60
Ed Bullins 1:47
Peter Nichols 36:327
John Osborne 5:331
Tom Stoppard 1:327
Tennessee Williams 11:576

Marquard, Jean
André Brink 18:69
Bessie Head 25:237

Marranca, Bonnie
Peter Handke 8:261; 10:256

Mars-Jones, Adam
Anita Brookner 34:139
John Gregory Dunne 28:128
Edna O'Brien 36:341
Cynthia Ozick 28:350

Marsden, Michael T.
Louis L'Amour 25:277, 278

Marsh, Dave
Jackson Browne 21:38
Jimmy Cliff 21:61
Bob Dylan 12:192
Marvin Gaye 26:135
John Lennon 35:264, 270
Steve Martin 30:246
Van Morrison 21:233
Jimmy Page and Robert Plant
12:480
Bob Seger 35:379, 380, 383,
384, 387
Patti Smith 12:539
Bruce Springsteen 17:486
Peter Townshend 17:527, 531,
533, 535, 541
Paul Weller 26:443, 444
Brian Wilson 12:654
Neil Young 17:574

Marsh, Fred T.
A. J. Cronin 32:130
Walter D. Edmonds 35:146
C. S. Forester 35:161, 163, 164
Arthur Koestler 33:228
Andrew Lytle 22:292
Carson McCullers 12:409
Nevil Shute 30:365

Marsh, Irving T.
Roger Kahn 30:230
Jean Lee Latham 12:323

Marsh, Jeffrey
Carl Sagan 30:340

Marsh, Meredith
Raymond Carver 22:101
Ted Mooney 25:330

Marsh, Pamela
Art Buchwald 33:92
Agatha Christie 1:58
Jan de Hartog 19:131
Michael Ende 31:143
Ronald L. Fair 18:140
Michael Frayn 31:190
Romain Gary 25:186
Joseph Krumgold 12:317
John McPhee 36:293
Robert Newton Peck 17:336
Josephine Poole 17:372
Mary Stewart 35:390
Mary Stolz 12:552
Leon Uris 32:432

Marshak, Sondra
Gene Roddenberry 17:407

Marshall, Donald
Geoffrey H. Hartman 27:184
Stanislaw Lem 8:343

Marshall, Donald G.
Jacques Derrida 24:151

Marshall, Elizabeth B.
Manuel Puig 28:372

Marshall, Eliot
Margaret Mead 37:283

Marshall, Margaret
René Clair 20:60
A. B. Guthrie, Jr. 23:196
Josef von Sternberg 20:370

Marshall, Megan
Carolyn Chute 39:42
Julian Symons 32:426
Thornton Wilder 15:575

Marshall, Tom
Margaret Atwood 8:29; 25:63
Leonard Cohen 38:137
William Heyen 13:282
Gwendolyn MacEwen 13:358
Michael Ondaatje 29:341
P. K. Page 7:292
Leon Rooke 25:393

Mars-Jones, Adam
Judith Rossner 29:356

Marten, Harry
Paul Bowles 19:60
Stanley Kunitz 14:313
Denise Levertov 15:338
Muriel Rukeyser 15:457
Anne Stevenson 33:381

Martin, Allie Beth
Walter Farley 17:118

Martin, B. J.
Noel Streatfeild 21:412

Martin, Brian
Bruce Chatwin 28:72
Alan Sillitoe 19:422
D. M. Thomas 22:418

Martin, Bruce K.
Philip Larkin 13:338
John Steinbeck 21:376

Martin, David
Nevil Shute 30:371

Martin, Dolores M.
G. Cabrera Infante 25:103

Martin, D. R.
David Brin 34:134

Martin, Gerald
Miguel Angel Asturias 13:37

Martin, Graham
Roy Fuller 4:177
Robert Pinget 13:444

Martin, James
Stanley Plumly 33:311
May Sarton 14:480

Martin, Jane
Rhys Davies 23:143
Pamela Hansford Johnson
27:215

Martin, Jay
Robert Lowell 1:181

Martin, Jean
Hortense Calisher 38:68

Martin, John
Russell Baker 31:26

Martin, Judith
Erica Jong 18:278

Martin, Mick
Edward Bond 23:71

Martin, Murray S.
Frank Sargeson 31:373

Martin, Robert A.
Arthur Miller 10:346

Martin, Robert K.
Richard Howard 10:274

Martin, Ruby
Mildred D. Taylor 21:419

Martin, Sandra
Hugh Garner 13:237
Jane Rule 27:419

Martin, Terence
Ken Kesey 11:314

Martin, Valerie
Nancy Lemann 39:77

Martin, Wallace
D. J. Enright 8:204

Martin, Wendy
Adrienne Rich 36:374

Martineau, Stephen
Susan Musgrave 13:401
James Reaney 13:475

Martinez, Z. Nelly
José Donoso 8:178

Martins, Wilson
Carlos Drummond de Andrade
18:5
João Guimarães Rosa 23:355

Martinson, Steven D.
Günter Eich 15:205

Martone, J.
Robert Bly 38:53

Martone, John
Robert Creeley 36:122
Richard Kostelanetz 28:218

Marty, Martin E.
Studs Terkel 38:418

Martz, Louis L.
Ted Berrigan 37:44
Robert Creeley 1:67
Phyllis Gotlieb 18:192
John Hollander 14:261
X. J. Kennedy 8:320
Philip Levine 33:274
Robert Lowell 1:181
Lisel Mueller 13:400
Joyce Carol Oates 9:403
Robert Pinsky 9:417
Ezra Pound 1:276
Reg Saner 9:469
Jon Silkin 2:396
William Stafford 4:521
Mark Strand 18:515
John Wain 2:458
Al Young 19:477

Martz, William J.
John Berryman 1:34

Critic Index

Marusiak, Joe
Galway Kinnell **29**:286

Marvin, K. Shattuck
Thomas B. Costain **30**:93

Marwell, Patricia McCue
Jules Archer **12**:22

Marx, Leo
Alfred Kazin **38**:273, 276

Marx, Paul
Nadine Gordimer **33**:185

Marz, Charles
John Dos Passos **25**:147

Marzan, Julio
V. S. Naipaul **37**:322

Mascaro, Phyllis
Suzanne Newton **35**:301

Masek, Linda
Joseph Hansen **38**:237

Masing-Delic, Irene
Boris Pasternak **18**:389

Masinton, Charles G.
J. P. Donleavy **10**:153

Maskell, Duke
E. M. Forster **1**:108; **9**:203

Maslin, Janet
Elvis Costello **21**:72
Ray Davies **21**:105
Marguerite Duras **20**:103
Rainer Werner Fassbinder **20**:114
Alex Haley **12**:254
Werner Herzog **16**:328
John Landis **26**:274, 276
Gordon Lightfoot **26**:278
Joni Mitchell **12**:440, 443
Laura Nyro **17**:318
Mary Rodgers **12**:495
Buffy Sainte-Marie **17**:431
Carly Simon **26**:411
Paul Simon **17**:466
Bruce Springsteen **17**:480
Lina Wertmüller **16**:589
Neil Young **17**:573

Mason, Ann L.
Günter Grass **4**:204; **11**:247

Mason, Clifford
William Melvin Kelley **22**:249

Mason, John Hope
David Hare **29**:220

Mason, Margaret
Judy Blume **30**:22

Mason, Michael
Donald Barthelme **8**:53
John Cheever **15**:131
Robert Coover **15**:143
George V. Higgins **10**:273
Colin MacInnes **23**:286
Peter Straub **28**:409

Massa, Robert
Edna O'Brien **36**:341

Massey, Ian
Ray Davies **21**:96

Massie, Allan
Anthony Powell **31**:321
David Harry Walker **14**:552

Massingham, Harold
George Mackay Brown **5**:76

Mast, Gerald
Buster Keaton **20**:194

Masterman, Len
Roman Polanski **16**:468

Masters, Anthony
David Rudkin **14**:470
C. P. Taylor **27**:444

Match, Richard
Ernest K. Gann **23**:163
Winston Graham **23**:191
Frank G. Slaughter **29**:374, 375
Sloan Wilson **32**:444

Mathes, Miriam S.
Lloyd Alexander **35**:22
Kin Platt **26**:348

Mathes, William
Claude Brown **30**:35

Mathews, F. X.
P. H. Newby **13**:408, 410

Mathews, Laura
James Hanley **13**:261
Richard Price **12**:491

Mathews, Richard
Brian Aldiss **14**:10
Piers Anthony **35**:39
Anthony Burgess **22**:72

Mathewson, Joseph
J.R.R. Tolkien **12**:566

Mathewson, Rufus W., Jr.
Boris Pasternak **7**:299
Mikhail Sholokhov **7**:421
Aleksandr I. Solzhenitsyn **7**:441

Mathewson, Ruth
Alejo Carpentier **8**:134
Joan Didion **8**:176
J. P. Donleavy **10**:154
Margaret Drabble **8**:184
Paula Fox **8**:219
James Hanley **13**:260
Colleen McCullough **27**:320
Leslie Marmon Silko **23**:407
Christina Stead **8**:500
Robert Penn Warren **8**:540

Mathias, Roland
Dannie Abse **29**:12

Mathy, Francis
Shiga Naoya **33**:363

Matlaw, Myron
Alan Paton **10**:387

Matson, Marshall
Margaret Atwood **15**:36

Matthews, Anne E.
Margaret O. Hyde **21**:177

Matthews, Barbara
Peter Straub **28**:411

Matthews, Charles
John Hawkes **2**:183

Matthews, Desmond, S.J.
Pat Jordan **37**:193

Matthews, Dorothy
J.R.R. Tolkien **12**:583

Matthews, Herbert L.
Ved Mehta **37**:288

Matthews, J. H.
André Breton **2**:80

Matthews, James H.
Frank O'Connor **14**:396; **23**:329

Matthews, Nancie
Isaac Asimov **26**:35
Noel Streatfeild **21**:401

Matthews, Pete
Walter Becker and Donald Fagen **26**:83

Matthews, Robin
Robin Skelton **13**:507

Matthews, Steve
Robin F. Brancato **35**:69

Matthews, T. S.
Edmund Wilson **8**:551

Matthews, Virginia H.
Betty Cavanna **12**:98

Matthias, John
Elizabeth Daryush **6**:123
Michael Hamburger **5**:158
Elizabeth Jennings **14**:293
David Jones **7**:189
Edwin Morgan **31**:273
Anne Stevenson **7**:463
D. M. Thomas **13**:542
R. S. Thomas **6**:530

Matyas, Cathy
Ralph Gustafson **36**:222

Maugham, W. Somerset
Noël Coward **29**:131

Maunder, Gabrielle
Ruth M. Arthur **12**:27
Alvin Silverstein and Virginia B. Silverstein **17**:450

Maurer, Robert
A. Alvarez **5**:17
Thomas Bernhard **32**:16
Robertson Davies **7**:73
José Donoso **8**:180
Stanley Elkin **27**:120
Leslie A. Fiedler **24**:198
MacDonald Harris **9**:258
Pablo Neruda **9**:398
Clancy Sigal **7**:425

Maurer, Robert E.
E. E. Cummings **8**:155

Mauriac, Claude
Roland Barthes **24**:22
Georges Bataille **29**:38
Samuel Beckett **2**:44
Albert Camus **2**:97
Henry Miller **2**:281
Alain Robbe-Grillet **2**:373
Nathalie Sarraute **2**:383
Georges Simenon **2**:396

Maurois, André
Aldous Huxley **3**:253
Jules Romains **7**:381

Maury, Lucien
Pär Lagerkvist **7**:198

Maxwell, D. E. S.
Brian Friel **5**:128

Maxwell, Emily
Isaac Asimov **26**:36
Maia Wojciechowska **26**:449

Maxwell, Gavin
Farley Mowat **26**:336

Maxwell, William
Louise Bogan **39**:393
Scott Elledge **34**:431
Elizabeth Frank **39**:393
Eudora Welty **33**:424
E. B. White **34**:431

May, Charles Paul
Joy Adamson **17**:1

May, Clifford D.
Art Buchwald **33**:95

May, Derwent
D. J. Enright **31**:153
Nadine Gordimer **5**:145
Seamus Heaney **37**:166
Alfred Hitchcock **16**:340
Ted Hughes **14**:270
Alison Lurie **4**:305
Tadeusz Różewicz **9**:463
Louis Simpson **9**:485

May, Gita
Michel del Castillo **38**:168

May, Jill P.
Robert Newton Peck **17**:341

May, John R.
Kurt Vonnegut, Jr. **2**:455

May, Keith M.
Aldous Huxley **4**:242

May, Yolanta
Emma Tennant **13**:536

Mayberry, George
Howard Fast **23**:155

Mayer, David
Ronald Harwood **32**:225, 226
Thornton Wilder **15**:574

Mayer, Glenn
Taylor Caldwell **28**:67

Mayer, Hans
Friedrich Dürrenmatt **4**:140
Witold Gombrowicz **4**:193
Günter Grass **4**:202
Jean-Paul Sartre **4**:473

Mayer, Peter
Vine Deloria, Jr. **21**:111

Mayer, Thomas
Maya Deren **16**:253

Mayfield, Julian
Eldridge Cleaver **30**:57

Mayhew, Alice
Graham Greene **1**:134
Claude Mauriac **9**:363

Maynard, Robert C.
Alex Haley **8**:259
Garry Trudeau **12**:588

Maynard, Theodore
Thomas B. Costain **30**:95

Mayne, Richard
Saul Bellow **8**:70
J.M.G. Le Clézio **31**:242
J.I.M. Stewart **7**:465

Mayne, William
Eilís Dillon **17**:95

Mayo, Clark
Kurt Vonnegut, Jr. **12**:617

Mayo, E. L.
Richard F. Hugo **32**:235

Mayoux, Jean-Jacques
Samuel Beckett **18**:41

Mays, Milton A.
Wayne C. Booth **24**:84

Mazrui, Ali A.
Alex Haley **12**:249

Mazzaro, Jerome
Elizabeth Bishop **9**:88
Donald Davie **31**:116
Norman Dubie **36**:135
Brewster Ghiselin **23**:172
David Ignatow **7**:175, 178
Randall Jarrell **6**:259
Robert Lowell **4**:295, 298
Cynthia Macdonald **19**:291
Joyce Carol Oates **3**:359
Robert Phillips **28**:363
Marge Piercy **27**:375
Ezra Pound **4**:417
John Crowe Ransom **2**:366
W. D. Snodgrass **6**:514
R. G. Vliet **22**:443
William Carlos Williams **5**:508

Mazzocco, Robert
John Ashbery **3**:15
Chester Kallman **2**:221
Philip Levine **5**:251
Mario Luzi **13**:354
William Meredith **4**:348
James Merrill **34**:232
Anne Sexton **6**:492
Eleanor Ross Taylor **5**:426
Gore Vidal **6**:548
Derek Walcott **14**:551

McAleer, John
Barbara Pym **37**:368

McAleer, John J.
MacKinlay Kantor **7**:195
Alain Robbe-Grillet **10**:438

McAllister, H. S.
Carlos Castaneda **12**:92

McAllister, Mick
Michael McClure **6**:319

McAlpin, Sara, B.V.M.
Eudora Welty **33**:421

McAlpine, Mary
Audrey Thomas **37**:415

McAneny, Marguerite
Richard Kostelanetz **28**:213

McArthur, Colin
Roman Polanski **16**:464
Andrzej Wajda **16**:579

McAuley, Gay
Jean Genet **10**:225
Peter Handke **10**:254

McBride, James
Frank Bonham **12**:49

McBride, Joseph
John Ford **16**:310, 314
Alfred Hitchcock **16**:348
Sidney Poitier **26**:358
Orson Welles **20**:447, 450
Billy Wilder **20**:462, 463, 464

McBroom, Gerry
Joanne Greenberg **30**:166
Barbara Wersba **30**:435

McCabe, Bernard
Jonathan Baumbach **23**:52, 54
Wilfrid Sheed **10**:474

McCaffery, Larry
Donald Barthelme **5**:55
T. Coraghessan Boyle **36**:63
Robert Coover **32**:126
William H. Gass **8**:242

McCaffery, Mark M.
Jim Shepard **36**:406

McCahill, Alice
Elizabeth Taylor **2**:432

McCall, Dorothy
Jean-Paul Sartre **7**:388; **13**:498

McCalla, Nelle
Maureen Daly **17**:89

McCallister, Myrna J.
François Sagan **36**:383

McCandlish, George
Jan de Hartog **19**:132

McCann, Garth
Edward Abbey **36**:14

McCann, John J.
Arthur Adamov **25**:21

McCann, Sean
Brendan Behan **15**:46

McCarriston, Linda
Sharon Olds **39**:186

McCarten, John
Robert Bolt **14**:88
Alfred Hitchcock **16**:339
Langston Hughes **35**:216
Jean Kerr **22**:256
Douglas Turner Ward **19**:456

McCarthy, Abigail
Cynthia Propper Seton **27**:428
John Updike **15**:546

McCarthy, Colman
P. G. Wodehouse **5**:516

McCarthy, Dermot
Bill Bissett **18**:62

McCarthy, Harold T.
Henry Miller **9**:377
Richard Wright **3**:545

McCarthy, Mary
Alvah Bessie **23**:59
William S. Burroughs **2**:90
Ivy Compton-Burnett **3**:112
Joan Didion **32**:147
Mary McCarthy **14**:361
Vladimir Nabokov **2**:301
Clifford Odets **28**:336
J. D. Salinger **3**:444
Nathalie Sarraute **2**:384
Monique Wittig **22**:472

McCarthy, Paul
John Steinbeck **21**:389

McCartney, Barney C.
Ezekiel Mphahlele **25**:333

McCarty, John Alan
Roman Polanski **16**:467

McCawley, Dwight L.
Theodore Roethke **19**:401

McClain, Harriet
Paula Danziger **21**:86

McClain, John
Larry Gelbart **21**:124
Jean Kerr **22**:255
Stephen Sondheim **30**:376

McClain, Ruth Rambo
Toni Morrison **4**:365

McClanahan, Ed
Richard Brautigan **12**:64

McClatchy, J. D.
A. R. Ammons **5**:31
Alfred Corn **33**:113
Stephen Dobyns **37**:78
Norman Dubie **36**:133
Lawrence Durrell **27**:97
Louise Glück **7**:119; **22**:177
Marilyn Hacker **23**:205
Anthony Hecht **19**:210
Edward Hirsch **31**:216
Richard Howard **7**:167
Ted Hughes **37**:179
Laura Jensen **37**:192
Donald Justice **19**:237
Laurence Lieberman **36**:259
Robert Lowell **8**:355
James Merrill **6**:324
Howard Moss **14**:376
Robert Pinsky **9**:417
Sylvia Plath **5**:346
Ira Sadoff **9**:466
Anne Sexton **15**:471
Charles Simic **22**:383
W. D. Snodgrass **18**:490
Maura Stanton **9**:507
Diane Wakoski **7**:504
Robert Penn Warren **6**:557
Theodore Weiss **8**:546
Philip Whalen **29**:447
Edmund White III **27**:479
Charles Wright **6**:581

McCleary, Dorothy
Eilís Dillon **17**:94

McClellan, Edwin
Yukio Mishima **6**:338

McClellan, Joseph
Mary Stewart **35**:395

McClelland, David
Flann O'Brien **5**:315
Patti Smith **12**:536

McClintock, Michael W.
C. J. Cherryh **35**:109

McCloskey, Mark
Robert Francis **15**:235

McClure, Michael
Sam Shepard **17**:441

McCluskey, John
James Baldwin **17**:39

McCluskey, Sally
John G. Neihardt **32**:335

McComas, J. Frances
Frank Herbert **12**:270

McConnell, Frank
John Barth **7**:25; **14**:57
Saul Bellow **6**:54
Michel Foucault **31**:180
John Gardner **7**:115
Andrew M. Greeley **28**:175
Graham Greene **14**:217; **18**:198
Norman Mailer **14**:353
Tom Robbins **32**:371

McConnell, Ruth M.
William Kotzwinkle **35**:254
Katherine Paterson **30**:288
Laurence Yep **35**:474

McConnell-Mammarella, Joan
Carlo Emilio Gadda **11**:210

McConville, Edward
John Sayles **10**:461

McCord, David
Ogden Nash **23**:321

McCorkle, Elizabeth
Milton Meltzer **26**:305

McCormack, W. J.
Elizabeth Bowen **22**:66

McCormick, E. H.
James K. Baxter **14**:59
Frank Sargeson **31**:364

McCormick, Lynde
Bruce Springsteen **17**:479

McCormick, Ruth
Nagisa Oshima **20**:249, 252

McCourt, James
Noël Coward **29**:141
Eric Rohmer **16**:538

McCown, Robert, S. J.
Flannery O'Connor **21**:255

McCracken, Samuel
Jonathan Schell **35**:368

McCue, Michael
Margaret Craven **17**:80
Anne McCaffrey **17**:283
John Neufeld **17**:310
Laurence Yep **35**:470

McCullers, Carson
Carson McCullers **12**:417

McCullough, Frank
George Garrett 3:189

McCutcheon, R. S.
Alvin Silverstein and Virginia
B. Silverstein 17:455

McDaniel, John N.
Philip Roth 31:334

McDaniel, Richard Bryan
Chinua Achebe 7:6

McDiarmid, Matthew P.
Hugh MacDiarmid 11:334

McDonald, Edward R.
Friedrich Dürrenmatt 15:199

McDonald, Henry
William Price Fox 22:142
John Gardner 30:156

McDonald, James L.
John Barth 2:38
John Knowles 26:255

McDonald, Marcia
John Crowe Ransom 24:367

McDonald, Susan S.
Harriet Waugh 6:560

McDonnell, Christine
Roy A. Gallant 17:133
Zibby Oneal 30:280
Noel Streatfeild 21:417

McDonnell, Jane Taylor
Galway Kinnell 2:230

McDonnell, John V.
William Barrett 27:18

McDonnell, Peter J.
Noel Streatfeild 21:400

McDonnell, Thomas P.
David Lodge 36:267
Conrad Richter 30:318

McDonough, Jack
Jackson Browne 21:36
Jim Carroll 35:78

McDowell, Danièle
Michel Tournier 23:452

McDowell, Edwin
Richard Brautigan 34:315
Helen MacInnes 39:349
Glendon Swarthout 35:402

McDowell, Frederick P. W.
John Braine 1:43
Lawrnce Durrell 1:87
E. M. Forster 1:107; 10:181
Caroline Gordon 29:186
Doris Lessing 1:175
Iris Murdoch 1:236
Frederic Raphael 2:366
Muriel Spark 2:416

McDowell, Myles
Leon Garfield 12:228
William Mayne 12:404

McDowell, Robert
Chinua Achebe 26:14
A. R. Ammons 25:42
William Least Heat Moon
29:224
Laura Jensen 37:190
Thomas Merton 11:374

Stanley Plumly 33:315
Louis Simpson 32:381

McDowell, Robert E.
Thomas Keneally 10:298

McElroy, Joseph
Samuel Beckett 2:48
Italo Calvino 5:99
Vladimir Nabokov 2:304

McElroy, Wendy
Gabriel García Márquez 10:217

McEvilly, Wayne
Anaïs Nin 1:248

McEvoy, Ruth M.
Henry Gregory Felsen 17:121

McEwan, Ian
David Hare 29:215
Milan Kundera 32:264

McEwen, Joe
Smokey Robinson 21:350

McFadden, George
Wayne C. Booth 24:91
Robert Lowell 9:333

McFee, Michael
Laurence Lieberman 36:263
Dave Smith 22:389
William Stafford 29:387

McFee, William
Edna Ferber 18:151
C. S. Forester 35:162, 163, 164

McFerran, Douglas
Carlos Castaneda 12:93

McGann, Jerome
Robert Creeley 2:106; 8:151
David Jones 7:188
X. J. Kennedy 8:320
Eleanor Lerman 9:331

McGann, Jerome J.
Michael Benedikt 14:81
Harold Bloom 24:70
Turner Cassity 6:107
Daniel Mark Epstein 7:97
A. D. Hope 3:251
Donald Justice 6:272
Galway Kinnell 13:320
Muriel Rukeyser 6:479
Judith Johnson Sherwin 7:415

McGann, Kevin
Ayn Rand 30:302

McGarry, Susan Lloyd
Richard Grayson 38:209

McGee, David
Kris Kristofferson 26:269
Bruce Springsteen 17:479

McGeehin, R.
Mary Renault 17:402

McGerr, Celia
René Clair 20:69

McGhan, Barry
Andre Norton 12:459

McGilchrist, Iain
W. H. Auden 9:57

McGinley, Karen
Sandra Scoppettone 26:401

McGinley, Phyllis
Margery Allingham 19:13

McGinnis, Wayne D.
Roman Polanski 16:471
Kurt Vonnegut, Jr. 8:529

McGinniss, Joe
Nora Ephron 17:113
George V. Higgins 4:222

McGovern, Hugh
Rhys Davies 23:146
Sumner Locke Elliott 38:177
George Tabori 19:436

McGowan, Sarah M.
Don DeLillo 27:79

McGrath, Joan
Gwendolyn MacEwen 13:358

McGregor, Craig
Bob Dylan 4:148

McGrory, Mary
Taylor Caldwell 28:59
Helen MacInnes 27:280
Frank G. Slaughter 29:373

McGuane, Thomas
Richard Brautigan 1:44
John Hawkes 2:185

McGuinness, Arthur E.
Seamus Heaney 14:242

McGuinness, Frank
Kingsley Amis 1:6
Andrew Sinclair 2:400
Frank Tuohy 37:428

McGuire, Alice Brooks
Betty Cavanna 12:98
Jean Lee Latham 12:322

McGuire, Paul, III
Marion Zimmer Bradley 30:27

McHaffie, Margaret
Christa Wolf 29:465

McHale, Tom
Diane Johnson 5:198
D. Keith Mano 2:270
J. F. Powers 8:447

McHargue, Georgess
Joan Aiken 35:17
Lloyd Alexander 35:27
Barbara Corcoran 17:71, 74
Peter Dickinson 35:132
Nicholasa Mohr 12:447
John Neufeld 17:308
Scott O'Dell 30:277
Zilpha Keatley Snyder 17:473
Barbara Wersba 30:432, 434
Laurence Yep 35:469

McHenry, Susan
June Jordan 23:256

McHugh, Joseph J.
Phillip Lopate 29:299

McInerney, Jay
Don DeLillo 39:122
Lorrie Moore 39:83

McInerney, John
John Knowles 10:303
Douglas Unger 34:116

McInerny, Ralph
Anthony Burgess 4:80

McInnes, Neil
David Caute 29:116

McIntyre, Jean
Sue Ellen Bridgers 26:91

McKay, Nellie Y.
Jean Toomer 22:428

McKay, Ruth Capers
Frank Swinnerton 31:423

McKegney, Michael
Claude Chabrol 16:171

McKenna, Andrew J.
Patrick Modiano 18:338

McKenzie, Alan T.
John Updike 5:452

McKenzie, Barbara
Mary McCarthy 24:344

McKeown, Thomas
Donald Davie 31:110

McKillop, Alan D.
Wayne C. Booth 24:88

McKinley, Hugh
Anthony Kerrigan 6:275

McKinley, Robin
Laurence Yep 35:473

McKinnon, William T.
Louis MacNeice 10:324

McLachlan, Ian
Timothy Findley 27:144

McLane, Daisann
Laura Nyro 17:320
Neil Young 17:579

McLatchie, Ian B.
W. P. Kinsella 27:238

McLaughlin, Pat
Charles M. Schulz 12:533

McLay, C. M.
Margaret Laurence 3:278
Ethel Davis Wilson 13:609

McLay, Catherine
William Mitchell 25:324

McLean, David G.
Lewis Turco 11:551

McLean, Scott
Frank Herbert 35:208
Gary Snyder 33:389

McLellan, Joseph
Richard Adams 18:1
Richard Bach 14:36
Russell Baker 31:29
Donald Barthelme 8:52
John Berryman 8:90
Dee Brown 18:70
Max Frisch 18:163
Arthur Hailey 5:156
Robert Heinlein 8:275

George V. Higgins **10**:274
John le Carré **15**:324
Phillip Lopate **29**:300
J. B. Priestley **34**:362
John Sayles **7**:399
J.R.R. Tolkien **8**:515
Trevanian **29**:431
T. H. White **30**:450

McLennan, Winona
Alvin Silverstein and Virginia
B. Silverstein **17**:453

McLeod, A. L.
Thomas Keneally **19**:248
Patrick White **7**:531

McLeod, Alan L.
Thomas Keneally **19**:243

McLuhan, H. M.
F. R. Leavis **24**:294

McLuhan, Herbert Marshall
John Dos Passos **11**:154

McLure, G.
C.L.R. James **33**:218

McMahon, Erik S.
Günter Grass **22**:197

McMahon, Joseph H.
Jean-Paul Sartre **7**:389
Michel Tournier **23**:451, 453

McMahon, Patricia
Alan Garner **17**:151

McMahon-Hill, Gillian
Russell C. Hoban **7**:161

McManus, Jeanne
Rosellen Brown **32**:69

McMichael, Charles T.
Aldous Huxley **35**:243

McMichael, James
May Sarton **4**:471

McMillan, George
Leon Uris **32**:431

McMullen, Roy
Nathalie Sarraute **2**:385

McMurray, George R.
José Donoso **32**:154, 156
Gabriel García Márquez **27**:147

McMurtry, Larry
Vardis Fisher **7**:103
Ernest J. Gaines **11**:217
Ward Just **4**:265
John McPhee **36**:298
Wright Morris **18**:353
Susan Richards Shreve **23**:404

McNally, John
Carson McCullers **12**:429

McNamara, Eugene
Hugh Hood **28**:189

McNamee, Kenneth
T.E.D. Klein **34**:72

McNeil, Helen
Mary Gordon **22**:186
Olivia Manning **19**:304
Jean Rhys **19**:392
Philip Roth **15**:454
Colin Wilson **14**:584

McNeil, Nicholas J., S.J.
Eleanor Hibbert **7**:156

McNeill, William H.
Charles M. Schulz **12**:524

McNelly, Willis E.
Ray Bradbury **10**:70
Robert Heinlein **8**:274
Frank Herbert **12**:277
Kurt Vonnegut, Jr. **2**:452

McNevin, Tom
George V. Higgins **18**:235

McNulty, Faith
Judy Blume **30**:24
Paula Danziger **21**:85
Isabelle Holland **21**:150
Ann Schlee **35**:374

McNulty, John
Sloan Wilson **32**:444

McPheeters, D. W.
Camilo José Cela **4**:98

McPheron, Judith
Jamake Highwater **12**:287

McPherson, Hugo
Morley Callaghan **14**:99
Mordecai Richler **5**:374
Gabrielle Roy **14**:465

McPherson, James
Richard Pryor **26**:377

McPherson, James Alan
Breece D'J Pancake **29**:345

McPherson, Sandra
William Heyen **13**:283
Ted Hughes **37**:176

McPherson, William
Margaret Atwood **8**:30
Paula Fox **8**:218
John Gardner **8**:235
Günter Grass **11**:252
Maxine Hong Kingston **12**:312
Maxine Kumin **5**:222
Ross Macdonald **14**:328
Lewis Thomas **35**:410
John Updike **5**:457; **13**:563

McRobbie, Angela
Pat Barker **32**:14
Anita Brookner **34**:137
Maureen Duffy **37**:116
Zoë Fairbairns **32**:163
Michel Tournier **36**:438
Gore Vidal **33**:408

McRobbie, Kenneth
Seamus Heaney **14**:242

McShane, Joseph M., S.J.
Louis R. Harlan **34**:186

McSweeney, Kerry
Brian Moore **19**:330; **32**:313
V. S. Naipaul **9**:391
Anthony Powell **9**:435
Simon Raven **14**:439

McVay, Douglas
Claude Chabrol **16**:182
Vittorio De Sica **20**:91
Satyajit Ray **16**:475

McWilliams, Dean
Michel Butor **3**:94; **15**:115
Marguerite Duras **3**:129; **20**:100

McWilliams, Donald E.
Frederick Wiseman **20**:471

McWilliams, Nancy R.
John Steinbeck **5**:405

McWilliams, W. C.
Mary Renault **11**:472

McWilliams, Wilson C.
John Steinbeck **5**:405

Meades, Jonathan
Simone de Beauvoir **2**:43
Jorge Luis Borges **1**:39; **3**:77;
4:74
Louis-Ferdinand Céline **3**:105
Iris Murdoch **2**:297
Vladimir Nabokov **2**:302; **3**:354
Alain Robbe-Grillet **1**:289;
2:376; **4**:448
Keith Roberts **14**:463
Kurt Vonnegut, Jr. **2**:455

Means, Howard
Roger Kahn **30**:233

Meckier, Jerome
Aldous Huxley **11**:285; **18**:267
Evelyn Waugh **3**:512; **19**:462

Mecklin, John
Jonathan Schell **35**:361

Medawar, Peter B.
Arthur Koestler **6**:281; **8**:324
Lewis Thomas **35**:416

Medjuck, Joe
Monty Python **21**:223

Mednick, Liz
Rita Mae Brown **18**:73
Susan Sontag **13**:518

Medvedev, R. A.
Mikhail Sholokhov **15**:483

Meehan, Thomas
Peter De Vries **28**:112
Bob Dylan **12**:180
Monty Python **21**:227

Meek, Margaret
Peter Dickinson **12**:175
Alan Garner **17**:138, 148, 149,
150
Mollie Hunter **21**:170
William Mayne **12**:391, 394,
399, 405
Rosemary Sutcliff **26**:428
Robert Westall **17**:559

Meerloo, Joost A. M.
Aldous Huxley **35**:236

Meeter, Glenn
Kurt Vonnegut, Jr. **4**:566

Megaw, Moira
W. H. Auden **6**:24

Megged, Aharon
S. Y. Agnon **4**:14

Meggers, Betty J.
Margaret Mead **37**:274

Mehrer, Sophia B.
Milton Meltzer **26**:297

Meiners, R. K.
James Dickey **7**:81
Robert Lowell **1**:182
Delmore Schwartz **2**:387
Allen Tate **4**:536; **24**:447

Meinke, Peter
W. H. Auden **6**:20
John Beecher **6**:48
John Dos Passos **4**:136
H. D. **8**:256
Marilyn Hacker **5**:155
Ted Hughes **4**:236
Philip Levine **5**:250
William Meredith **13**:372
Howard Nemerov **2**:307
Muriel Rukeyser **6**:478
Anne Sexton **4**:483
Diane Wakoski **7**:504
Robert Penn Warren **6**:555
Charles Wright **6**:579

Meisel, Perry
Joni Mitchell **12**:440

Meisler, Stanley
Howard Fast **23**:157

Mekas, Jonas
Andy Warhol **20**:415

Melanson, Jim
Richard O'Brien **17**:322

Meldrum, Barbara
Conrad Richter **30**:329

Mélèse, Pierre
Jacques Audiberti **38**:22

Mellard, James M.
Bernard Malamud **1**:198;
27:296
François Mauriac **9**:367
Kurt Vonnegut, Jr. **3**:504;
4:565

Mellen, Joan
Ingmar Bergman **16**:71
Luis Buñuel **16**:135
Jean-Luc Godard **20**:142
Kon Ichikawa **20**:185
Akira Kurosawa **16**:403
Elaine May **16**:434
Nagisa Oshima **20**:253, 255
Eric Rohmer **16**:533
Carlos Saura **20**:314

Mellers, Wilfrid
Bob Dylan **12**:187
John Lennon and Paul
McCartney **12**:374

Mellor, Anne K.
Nathalie Sarraute **31**:377

Mellor, Isha
Sol Yurick **6**:583

Mellors, John
Martin Amis **4**:20; **38**:12
Louis Auchincloss **6**:15
Beryl Bainbridge **10**:17
Lynne Reid Banks **23**:42
Thomas Berger **5**:60
Caroline Blackwood **9**:101

Dirk Bogarde **19**:43
Elizabeth Bowen **22**:64
Melvyn Bragg **10**:72
Angela Carter **5**:102
Isabel Colegate **36**:111
Peter De Vries **7**:77
Peter Dickinson **35**:135
Shusaku Endo **7**:96; **14**:160
Elaine Feinstein **36**:170, 171
Penelope Fitzgerald **19**:173
John Fowles **6**:188
Athol Fugard **25**:173
Maurice Gee **29**:177
Herbert Gold **14**:208
John Hawkes **7**:141
Bessie Head **25**:237
Mark Helprin **10**:260
Rolf Hochhuth **18**:256
Ursula Holden **18**:258
Jorge Ibargüengoitia **37**:183
Dan Jacobson **4**:253
Ruth Prawer Jhabvala **8**:312
G. Josipovici **6**:270
Jonathan Keates **34**:202
Yashar Kemal **29**:266
Penelope Lively **32**:273, 274, 276
Bernard Malamud **5**:269
Olivia Manning **19**:303
Ian McEwan **13**:370
Stanley Middleton **7**:219; **38**:331, 334
Yukio Mishima **4**:357
Brian Moore **19**:334
Alberto Moravia **7**:244
Iris Murdoch **4**:369
Craig Nova **31**:296
Julia O'Faolain **6**:382; **19**:360
Seán O'Faoláin **14**:407
V. S. Pritchett **5**:353
Frederic Raphael **14**:438
Piers Paul Read **4**:444; **10**:435; **25**:379, 380
Philip Roth **31**:346
J. R. Salamanca **15**:464
William Sansom **6**:484
Nathalie Sarraute **10**:460
Ann Schlee **35**:373, 375
Penelope Shuttle **7**:422
Alan Sillitoe **6**:499; **19**:420
Wole Soyinka **5**:398
Richard G. Stern **4**:523
David Storey **8**:504
Peter Straub **28**:409
Lisa St. Aubin de Teran **36**:420
Frank Tuohy **37**:431
Ludvík Vaculík **7**:495
John Wain **15**:561
Charles Webb **7**:516
Patrick White **5**:48
A. N. Wilson **33**:451

Mellow, James R.
Malcolm Cowley **39**:460

Mellown, Elgin W.
Jean Rhys **2**:373
John Wain **2**:458

Melly, George
Jean Arp **5**:33

Melnyk, George
Andrew Suknaski **19**:432

Meltzer, R.
John Lennon and Paul McCartney **12**:382
Jim Morrison **17**:290
Patti Smith **12**:538

Melville, Robert
Herbert Read **4**:438
Susan Sontag **13**:515

Melzer, Annabelle Henkin
Louis Aragon **22**:41

Menand, Louis
Frank Lentricchia **34**:572
Norman Mailer **39**:422
Peter Manso **39**:422

Mendelsohn, John
Walter Becker and Donald Fagen **26**:80
Paul McCartney **35**:280

Mendelsohn, John Ned
David Bowie **17**:57, 58
Ray Davies **21**:91
Jimmy Page and Robert Plant **12**:473, 474
Peter Townshend **17**:527
Neil Young **17**:570

Mendelsohn, Michael J.
Clifford Odets **28**:337

Mendelson, David
Eugène Ionesco **6**:255

Mendelson, Edward
John Berryman **4**:61
Thomas Pynchon **3**:415; **6**:439; **33**:329

Mengel, Robert M.
Peter Matthiessen **32**:288

Mengeling, Marvin E.
Ray Bradbury **1**:42

Menkiti, Ifeanyi A.
Chinua Achebe **26**:20

Mephisto
Maya Deren **16**:252

Mercer, Peter
John Barth **9**:61

Merchant, Paul
Howard Brenton **31**:63

Merchant, W. Moelwyn
R. S. Thomas **13**:542

Mercier, Jean F.
Ruth M. Arthur **12**:27
Melvin Berger **12**:42
Betty Cavanna **12**:103
Jamake Highwater **12**:288
M. E. Kerr **12**:300
Madeleine L'Engle **12**:352
Katherine Paterson **12**:484, 486
Rosemary Wells **12**:637

Mercier, Vivian
Samuel Beckett **6**:38; **14**:79
Michel Butor **11**:78
Padraic Colum **28**:89
Harry Crews **6**:118
J. P. Donleavy **4**:125
Thomas Flanagan **25**:163

E. M. Forster **2**:135
George V. Higgins **4**:222
Aldous Huxley **5**:193
Iris Murdoch **4**:368
Raymond Queneau **5**:360
Alain Robbe-Grillet **6**:465
Nathalie Sarraute **4**:466
Claude Simon **4**:496

Mercurio, Gregory
Frank Herbert **35**:204

Meredith, William
John Berryman **2**:59; **3**:68; **25**:88
Anthony Hecht **8**:268
Robert Lowell **2**:248
Muriel Rukeyser **10**:442

Merguerian, Karen
James D. Forman **21**:122

Merideth, Robert
Norman Mailer **1**:192

Meritt, Carole
Alex Haley **12**:250

Merivale, Patricia
Vladimir Nabokov **1**:242

Merkin, Daphne
Ann Beattie **13**:65
André Brink **18**:68
Michael Brodsky **19**:69
A. S. Byatt **19**:77
Vincent Canby **13**:132
Joan Didion **14**:152
Jacob Epstein **19**:162
Romain Gary **25**:188
Penelope Gilliatt **13**:239
Thomas Keneally **14**:302
Ella Leffland **19**:278
Phillip Lopate **29**:300
A. G. Mojtabai **15**:378
Vladimir Nabokov **23**:311
Breece D'J Pancake **29**:349
Jayne Anne Phillips **15**:421
Chaim Potok **7**:321
V. S. Pritchett **15**:443
Philip Roth **15**:452
Christina Stead **32**:411
John Updike **13**:559; **15**:546
Angus Wilson **25**:463

Mermier, G.
Romain Gary **25**:189, 190

Mermier, Guy
Françoise Sagan **17**:424

Mernit, Susan
June Jordan **23**:255

Merriam, Eve
Jacques Prévert **15**:440

Merrick, Gordon
Truman Capote **19**:82

Merrill, Anthony
Paul Green **25**:196

Merrill, George
Isaac Asimov **26**:37

Merrill, James
Francis Ponge **18**:415

Merrill, Reed B.
William H. Gass **8**:245

Merrill, Robert
Vladimir Nabokov **15**:396
Kurt Vonnegut, Jr. **8**:534

Merrill, Thomas F.
Allen Ginsberg **1**:118
Charles Olson **11**:417; **29**:336

Merry, Bruce
Mario Luzi **13**:352
Elio Vittorini **14**:544

Mersand, Joseph
Elmer Rice **7**:359

Mersmann, James F.
Robert Bly **5**:62
Robert Duncan **4**:142
Allen Ginsberg **4**:182
Denise Levertov **5**:247
Diane Wakoski **7**:507

Merton, John Kenneth
Pamela Hansford Johnson **27**:214

Merton, Thomas
Roland Barthes **24**:37
Albert Camus **1**:52
J. F. Powers **1**:281
John Crowe Ransom **24**:362

Mertz, Barbara
Jean M. Auel **31**:23

Meryl, Jay
Norma Klein **30**:242

Meserve, Walter
James Baldwin **17**:36

Mesher, David R.
Bernard Malamud **9**:346; **11**:353

Mesic, Michael
James Dickey **4**:121
Chester Kallman **2**:221

Mesic, Penelope
Russell C. Hoban **25**:267

Meškys, Edmund R.
Franklyn M. Branley **21**:18, 19

Mesnet, Marie-Béatrice
Graham Greene **3**:210

Messer, Bill
Peter Dickinson **12**:171

Metcalf, Paul
Charles Olson **9**:413

Metzger, C. R.
Lawrence Ferlinghetti **10**:176

Metzger, Norman
Franklyn M. Branley **21**:24

Mews, Siegfried
Carl Zuckmayer **18**:553, 557

Mewshaw, Michael
Jeffrey Archer **28**:14
Jonathan Baumbach **6**:31
Doris Betts **3**:73
Robertson Davies **7**:74
William Eastlake **8**:200

B. H. Friedman **7**:108
Graham Greene **18**:195
Jack Hodgins **23**:230
Robert F. Jones **7**:192
Stephen King **12**:310
David Slavitt **5**:391
Raymond Sokolov **7**:430
Peter Spielberg **6**:519
Robert Lewis Taylor **14**:534
Paul Theroux **5**:427

Meyer, Ellen Hope
Erica Jong **4**:264
Joyce Carol Oates **2**:315

Meyer, Gerard Previn
Thomas McGrath **28**:276

Meyer, Karl E.
Garry Marshall **17**:278
Frederick Wiseman **20**:475

Meyer, Marianne
Joan Armatrading **17**:10

Meyer, Michael
Harry Martinson **14**:356

Meyer, Thomas
Lorine Niedecker **10**:360
Toby Olson **28**:344

Meyers, Jeffrey
Peter Ackroyd **34**:398
T. S. Eliot **34**:398
E. M. Forster **3**:162; **4**:169
Peter Griffin **39**:402
Ernest Hemingway **39**:402, 432
James Jones **39**:414
Doris Lessing **2**:241
Frank MacShane **39**:414
André Malraux **4**:333
Mary McCarthy **39**:489
Jeffrey Meyers **39**:432
Ezra Pound **34**:507
E. Fuller Torrey **34**:507

Meyers, Richard
Steven Bochco and Michael
   Kozoll **35**:50

Meyers, Robert B.
Robert Altman **16**:26

Mezan, Peter
Ken Russell **16**:544

Mezei, Kathy
Anne Hébert **29**:232, 236

Mezey, Robert
Jerome Rothenberg **6**:478
Gary Snyder **9**:498

Micciche, Pauline F.
Roger Zelazny **21**:464

Michaels, Leonard
John Barth **2**:37
Samuel Beckett **11**:43
Thomas Berger **11**:46
Jorge Luis Borges **2**:77
Dashiell Hammett **5**:160
Peter Handke **8**:264
Joseph Heller **11**:269
Erica Jong **8**:314
Bernard Malamud **3**:324
Peter Matthiessen **11**:361
Vladimir Nabokov **8**:417

Robert Stone **23**:427

Michaels, Robert G.
Woody Allen **16**:3

Michalczyk, John J.
Fernando Arrabal **18**:23

Michałek, Bolesław
Andrzej Wajda **16**:581

Michaud, Charles
Evan Hunter **31**:229

Michel, Sonya
Joan Micklin Silver **20**:342

Michelson, Aaron I.
Robin F. Brancato **35**:70
Martha Gellhorn **14**:196

Michelson, Bruce
Richard Wilbur **14**:579

Michelson, Peter
Leslie A. Fiedler **24**:199

Michener, Charles
Albert Maysles and David
   Maysles **16**:444
Stephen Sondheim **30**:384

Michener, Charles T.
Anthony Powell **3**:402; **7**:343

Michener, James
Herman Wouk **38**:452

Mickelson, Anne Z.
Toni Morrison **22**:315

Middlebrook, Diane
Allen Ginsberg **6**:199

Middleton, Christopher
Herman Hesse **25**:258

Middleton, Victoria
A. G. Mojtabai **29**:319

Miesel, Sandra
Poul Anderson **15**:11

Mihailovich, Vasa D.
Miroslav Krleža **8**:330
Vasko Popa **19**:373, 375

Miklitsch, Robert
Robert Hass **18**:211

Milano, Paolo
Riccardo Bacchelli **19**:32

Milbauer, Jerry
The Police **26**:364

Milch, Robert J.
Chaim Potok **2**:338

Milder, Robert
Flannery O'Connor **13**:417

Mileck, Joseph
Hermann Hesse **17**:198

Miles, G. E.
Betty Smith **19**:423

Miles, Jack
Josephine Miles **39**:353

Miles, Keith
Günter Grass **15**:259

Miles, William
Langston Hughes **1**:148

Milford, Nancy
Louise Bogan **4**:69

Milivojević, D.
Vasily Aksyonov **37**:12

Millar, Daniel
Jean Renoir **20**:297

Millar, Gavin
Robert Altman **16**:42
Lindsay Anderson **20**:13
Ingmar Bergman **16**:80
Claude Chabrol **16**:172, 184
Michael Cimino **16**:210

Millar, Margaret
Daphne du Maurier **6**:146

Millar, Neil
John McPhee **36**:294
David Harry Walker **14**:552

Millar, Sylvia
Erskine Caldwell **14**:95
Carlos Saura **20**:315

Miller, Adam David
Maya Angelou **35**:31
Alex Haley **12**:249

Miller, Alice
Rosemary Wells **12**:637

Miller, Arthur
Thornton Wilder **35**:438

Miller, Baxter
Langston Hughes **10**:282

Miller, Brown
Robert Bly **38**:56

Miller, Charles
Chinua Achebe **26**:13
Ayi Kwei Armah **33**:23

Miller, Charles L.
Joy Adamson **17**:4

Miller, Dan
Robert Bloch **33**:84
Marion Zimmer Bradley **30**:26
John W. Campbell **32**:78
Jack Vance **35**:419
Roger Zelazny **21**:469

Miller, David M.
Michael Hamburger **5**:158
Frank Herbert **35**:196

Miller, Faren
Gene Wolfe **25**:478

Miller, Gabriel
Alvah Bessie **23**:61
Daniel Fuchs **22**:157
Alfred Hitchcock **16**:353

Miller, Henry
Luis Buñuel **16**:127
Blaise Cendrars **18**:91
Anaïs Nin **14**:379

Miller, James E.
John Berryman **25**:98

Miller, James E., Jr.
William Faulkner **6**:180
J. D. Salinger **1**:298; **12**:496

Miller, Jane
Elaine Feinstein **36**:167
Ursula Holden **18**:257
Julius Horwitz **14**:267
Alain Robbe-Grillet **14**:462
Simone Schwarz-Bart **7**:404

Miller, Jeanne-Marie A.
Imamu Amiri Baraka **2**:35
Gwendolyn Brooks **1**:46; **4**:78
Charles Gordone **4**:198

Miller, Jim
Manlio Argueta **31**:19
Julio Cortázar **33**:136
Ray Davies **21**:94
Max Frisch **32**:194
Paul McCartney **35**:283, 289
Wright Morris **37**:313
Van Morrison **21**:236
Jimmy Page and Robert Plant
   12:477
Prince **35**:331
Smokey Robinson **21**:350
Bruce Springsteen **17**:482, 485
Brian Wilson **12**:644, 648
Neil Young **17**:571

Miller, Jim Wayne
Jesse Stuart **11**:513

Miller, Jonathan
Lenny Bruce **21**:44

Miller, Jordan Y.
Lorraine Hansberry **17**:188

Miller, Karl
Kingsley Amis **13**:14
Martin Amis **4**:21
Beryl Bainbridge **22**:44
James Baldwin **17**:28
John Berger **19**:38
Paula Fox **8**:218
Ted Hughes **4**:236
Dan Jacobson **4**:256
Hugh MacDiarmid **2**:254
Flann O'Brien **5**:316
Barbara Pym **13**:470
Anne Roiphe **9**:456
Emma Tennant **13**:537
Paul Theroux **11**:530
Michel Tournier **6**:538

Miller, Marjorie Mithoff
Isaac Asimov **26**:39

Miller, Mark Crispin
Steven Bochco and Michael
   Kozoll **35**:50
Sam Peckinpah **20**:279

Miller, Mary Jane
Harold Pinter **27**:385

Miller, Merle
C. S. Forester **35**:170
Leon Uris **32**:430

Miller, Michael H.
Rosa Guy **26**:142

Miller, Neil
Julio Cortázar **2**:103

Miller, Nolan
Henry Bromell **5**:73
Tillie Olsen **13**:433

Critic Index

Miller, Perry
Arthur Koestler **33**:234

Miller, R. Baxter
Langston Hughes **15**:293

Miller, Sara
Sue Ellen Bridgers **26**:91
Anne McCaffrey **17**:283

Miller, Stephen
Saul Bellow **25**:84
Zbigniew Herbert **9**:272

Miller, Tom P.
William Stafford **4**:521

Miller, Vincent
T. S. Eliot **9**:182
Ezra Pound **13**:462

Millgate, Michael
James Gould Cozzens **4**:114
John Dos Passos **4**:133
William Faulkner **28**:139

Millichap, Joseph R.
Carson McCullers **12**:428

Milliken, Elizabeth
Tish O'Dowd Ezekiel **34**:47

Milliken, James M., Jr.
Bret Easton Ellis **39**:58

Milliken, Stephen F.
Chester Himes **18**:247

Millken, Elizabeth
Pat Jordan **37**:196

Mills, James
George V. Higgins **4**:222

Mills, John
John Arden **13**:26
John Metcalf **37**:301
Leon Rooke **25**:391
Kurt Vonnegut, Jr. **22**:450

Mills, Mary
Mary Stewart **35**:397

Mills, Nicolaus
Joan Micklin Silver **20**:344

Mills, Ralph J., Jr.
Yves Bonnefoy **9**:112
René Char **9**:160
Lucille Clifton **19**:109
Stephen Dobyns **37**:75
Richard Eberhart **3**:134, 135
David Ignatow **7**:174, 179
Galway Kinnell **29**:279
Maxine Kumin **5**:222
Denise Levertov **2**:243; **3**:293
Philip Levine **4**:287
Kathleen Raine **7**:351
Theodore Roethke **1**:291
Anne Stevenson **7**:462
Jonathan Williams **13**:600

Millstein, Gilbert
Lenny Bruce **21**:43
Irvin Faust **8**:215
Langston Hughes **35**:215
Milton Meltzer **26**:304
John R. Tunis **12**:598

Milne, Gordon
Allen Drury **37**:104

Milne, Tom
Robert Altman **16**:42
Ingmar Bergman **16**:54, 55
Robert Bresson **16**:112, 119
Mel Brooks **12**:79
Claude Chabrol **16**:175, 178
René Clair **20**:68
Francis Ford Coppola **16**:232
Vittorio De Sica **20**:97
Bob Fosse **20**:121
Jean-Luc Godard **20**:129, 131
George Roy Hill **26**:197, 205
Kon Ichikawa **20**:179, 181, 183
Stanley Kubrick **16**:379
Akira Kurosawa **16**:404
Rouben Mamoulian **16**:424
John Osborne **5**:330
Yasujiro Ozu **16**:447
Gordon Parks **16**:459
Sam Peckinpah **20**:273
Roman Polanski **16**:463
Satyajit Ray **16**:483, 487, 488, 495
Jean Renoir **20**:292, 293
Martin Scorsese **20**:330, 331
Steven Spielberg **20**:357, 358
Josef von Sternberg **20**:377
Andrzej Wajda **16**:578
Peter Weir **20**:425
Orson Welles **20**:442

Milne, W. Gordon
John Dos Passos **4**:134

Milner, Joseph O.
Sue Ellen Bridgers **26**:93
Ouida Sebestyen **30**:350

Milner, Philip
Toby Olson **28**:342

Milner-Gulland, Robin
Andrei Voznesensky **1**:349
Yevgeny Yevtushenko **1**:381

Milord, James E.
Thomas Merton **34**:462
Michael Mott **34**:462

Milosh, Joseph
John Gardner **10**:220

Miłosz, Czesław
Joseph Brodsky **36**:74
Tadeusz Różewicz **23**:358

Milton, Edith
Beryl Bainbridge **10**:17
Frederick Buechner **9**:136
André Dubus **36**:144
Leslie Epstein **27**:131
Gail Godwin **22**:181
Nadine Gordimer **18**:190
Andrew Holleran **38**:246
Kazuo Ishiguro **27**:203
Alison Lurie **18**:311
Olivia Manning **19**:303
V. S. Naipaul **18**:361
David Plante **38**:365
Barbara Pym **37**:371
Bernice Rubens **31**:351
Jane Rule **27**:420
Alan Sillitoe **10**:477
William Styron **15**:528
D. M. Thomas **22**:420

Milton, John R.
Walter Van Tilburg Clark **28**:82
Vardis Fisher **7**:105
A. B. Guthrie, Jr. **23**:201
N. Scott Momaday **2**:290
James Welch **14**:558

Milton, Joyce
Jules Feiffer **8**:217
Virginia Hamilton **26**:156
Isabelle Holland **21**:151
M. E. Kerr **35**:249
Norma Fox Mazer **26**:291
Scott O'Dell **30**:273
Zibby Oneal **30**:279
Richard Peck **21**:299
Kin Platt **26**:355
Paul Zindel **26**:476

Milun, Richard A.
William Faulkner **6**:177

Milward, John
David Bowie **17**:65
Billy Joel **26**:222
The Police **26**:364
Prince **35**:328

Mindlin, M.
Yehuda Amichai **9**:22

Minemier, Betty
Jacques-Yves Cousteau **30**:106

Miner, Earl
Kōbō Abé **22**:11
Yukio Mishima **27**:337

Miner, Robert G., Jr.
Charles M. Schulz **12**:529

Miner, Valerie
Carolyn Chute **39**:43
William Wharton **37**:442

Mines, Samuel
Jack Williamson **29**:456

Minogue, Valerie
Michel Butor **11**:82
Alain Robbe-Grillet **10**:437
Nathalie Sarraute **10**:458; **31**:382

Mintz, Alan L.
Andrew M. Greeley **28**:172
Yoram Kaniuk **19**:240
A. B. Yehoshua **31**:471

Minudri, Regina
Charles Addams **30**:16

Miroff, Bruce
Neil Young **17**:569

Mirsky, Jonathan
Jonathan Schell **35**:363

Mirsky, Mark J.
John Hawkes **7**:145
Elie Wiesel **37**:456

Mirsky, Mark Jay
Samuel Beckett **6**:38
Anthony Burgess **4**:83
Günter Grass **4**:205
Flann O'Brien **5**:314
Manuel Puig **3**:407

Mishima, Yukio
Yasunari Kawabata **18**:280

Mitchell, A.C.W.
Kenneth Slessor **14**:497

Mitchell, Chuck
Walter Becker and Donald Fagen **26**:79

Mitchell, Deborah
Roy Fisher **25**:159

Mitchell, Gregg
Paul Simon **17**:460
Bruce Springsteen **17**:476, 478

Mitchell, Henry
S. J. Perelman **23**:338
E. B. White **39**:374

Mitchell, Judith N.
Rosa Guy **26**:146
Paul Zindel **26**:481

Mitchell, Judy
Bette Green **30**:171

Mitchell, Julian
Ivy Compton-Burnett **10**:110

Mitchell, Juliet
Norman Mailer **1**:192

Mitchell, Kendall
Fernanda Eberstadt **39**:48

Mitchell, Lisa
Stevie Smith **25**:421

Mitchell, Loften
Alice Childress **12**:104

Mitchell, Louis D.
Virginia Hamilton **26**:150
Evan Hunter **31**:223

Mitchell, Marilyn L.
John Steinbeck **9**:516

Mitchell, Penelope M.
Roy A. Gallant **17**:128, 130
Christie Harris **12**:263

Mitchell, Roger
Richard F. Hugo **32**:242
Thomas McGrath **28**:279

Mitchell, W.J.T.
Hubert Selby, Jr. **4**:481

Mitchison, Naomi
W. H. Auden **9**:57
Arthur Koestler **33**:227
Mildred D. Taylor **21**:421

Mitgang, Herbert
Giorgio Bassani **9**:75
Jackson J. Benson **34**:406
John Betjeman **34**:305
Italo Calvino **39**:305
Virginia Spencer Carr **34**:419
John Dos Passos **34**:419
John Ehle **27**:102
Robert Fitzgerald **39**:318
James A. Michener **29**:311
Michael Mott **15**:379
J. B. Priestley **34**:360
Carl Sandburg **15**:468
Leonardo Sciascia **9**:475
John Steinbeck **34**:406
Gay Talese **37**:391
Studs Terkel **38**:419
E. B. White **39**:371

Mittleman, Leslie B.
Kingsley Amis **8**:11

Mitton, Pat
Christie Harris **12**:265

Mitz, Rick
Larry Gelbart **21**:132

Mix, David
Gordon Lightfoot **26**:282

Miyoshi, Masao
Yasunari Kawabata **9**:311
Donald Keene **34**:567
Yukio Mishima **27**:338

Mizejewski, Linda
James Dickey **15**:174

Mizener, Arthur
James Gould Cozzens **4**:115
John Dos Passos **4**:133
Anthony Hecht **8**:266
F. R. Leavis **24**:294
Anthony Powell **10**:408
J. D. Salinger **12**:501
James Thurber **5**:439
Edmund Wilson **2**:475
Sloan Wilson **32**:445

Mo, Timothy
Eva Figes **31**:164
Jennifer Johnston **7**:186
John le Carré **5**:234
Colin MacInnes **4**:35
Wilfrid Sheed **4**:489
Harriet Waugh **6**:559

Mobilio, Albert
Don DeLillo **39**:125

Moeller, Hans-Bernhard
Peter Weiss **15**:563

Moers, Ellen
Lillian Hellman **2**:187
Adrienne Rich **18**:447

Moffatt, Gregory T., S.J.
Michael Cunningham **34**:41

Moffett, Judith
Thomas M. Disch **36**:127
Daniel Hoffman **13**:287
James Merrill **13**:376; **18**:329

Mohs, Mayo
Andrew M. Greeley **28**:176
Elie Wiesel **37**:451

Moir, Hughes
Christopher Collier and James
L. Collier **30**:72

Mojtabai, A. G.
Yasunari Kawabata **5**:208
Yashar Kemal **29**:267
Thomas Keneally **5**:211
Joyce Carol Oates **15**:402
Amos Oz **27**:358
Anne Tyler **18**:530
Richard Yates **8**:555

Mok, Michael
Aleksandr I. Solzhenitsyn **2**:409

Mole, John
Dannie Abse **29**:19
Thom Gunn **32**:214
Ted Hughes **14**:271; **37**:178
Michael Longley **29**:295
Norman MacCaig **36**:288
Derek Mahon **27**:293
Paul Muldoon **32**:321
Tom Paulin **37**:354
Christopher Reid **33**:351
Louis Simpson **7**:428
Anne Stevenson **33**:382
R. S. Thomas **6**:530; **13**:545
Frank Tuohy **37**:430
Theodore Weiss **14**:555

Molesworth, Charles
John Ashbery **15**:26
John Berryman **2**:56; **8**:89
Robert Bly **15**:64; **38**:55
Hayden Carruth **18**:89
Ronald G. Everson **27**:135
Leslie A. Fiedler **24**:200
Louise Glück **22**:175
Marilyn Hacker **23**:205
Robert Hass **18**:210
Ted Hughes **4**:236
Erica Jong **18**:278
Donald Justice **19**:233
Galway Kinnell **3**:269; **29**:282
Richard Kostelanetz **28**:217
Laurence Lieberman **36**:260
Leslie Norris **14**:387
Michael Ondaatje **14**:410
Marge Piercy **14**:421
Robert Pinsky **19**:369; **38**:359
Anne Sexton **8**:483
Charles Simic **22**:381
Gary Snyder **32**:396
Charles Tomlinson **4**:548

Molin, Sven Eric
René Wellek **28**:444

Molina, Ida
Antonio Buero Vallejo **15**:103

Moll, Denise L.
Jay Bennett **35**:46

Molloy, F. C.
John McGahern **9**:370

Molloy, Patricia
Bob Shacochis **39**:199

Molnar, Thomas
Françoise Sagan **17**:419

Moloney, Michael F.
François Mauriac **4**:337

Molyneux, Robert
Erich von Däniken **30**:424, 425

Momaday, N. Scott
Dee Brown **18**:70
Vine Deloria, Jr. **21**:110
Jamake Highwater **12**:288
Leslie Marmon Silko **23**:411

Momberger, Philip
William Faulkner **6**:179

Monaco, James
Woody Allen **16**:15
John Cassavetes **20**:54
Claude Chabrol **16**:182
Francis Ford Coppola **16**:248
Jean-Luc Godard **20**:148

Richard Lester **20**:228
Gordon Parks **16**:460
Alain Resnais **16**:511
Martin Scorsese **20**:333
Andrew Sinclair **14**:489
Steven Spielberg **20**:359, 365
François Truffaut **20**:399
Melvin Van Peebles **20**:412

Monagan, John S.
Anthony Powell **7**:342

Monaghan, Charles
Richard Stern **39**:235

Monas, Sidney
Joseph Brodsky **36**:80
Ilya Ehrenburg **18**:134
Aleksandr I. Solzhenitsyn
4:511; **26**:415
Andrei Voznesensky **15**:552

Mondello, Salvatore
Stan Lee **17**:259

Monegal, Emir Rodríguez-
See Rodríguez-Monegal, Emir

Monet, Christina
Mark Medoff **6**:323

Monguió, Luis
Rafael Alberti **7**:8

Monheit, Albert
Roy A. Gallant **17**:126

Monk, Patricia
Robertson Davies **25**:132, 136

Monley, Keith
Frederick Busch **18**:86
Ella Leffland **19**:279

Monogue, Valerie
Harold Pinter **6**:404

Monroe, Harriet
Robert Frost **26**:112
H. D. **31**:201
Marianne Moore **19**:335
John G. Neihardt **32**:329, 330

Monsman, Gerald
J.R.R. Tolkien **1**:339

Monson, Dianne L.
Betsy Byars **35**:73

Montagnes, Anne
Phyllis Gotlieb **18**:192
Brian Moore **5**:297
Audrey Thomas **13**:538

Montague, John
Thomas Kinsella **19**:251
Hugh MacDiarmid **11**:333

Monteiro, George
Bob Dylan **4**:149
Robert Frost **4**:174; **10**:199
Ernest Hemingway **6**:231

Montgomery, Marion
T. S. Eliot **6**:163
Robert Frost **10**:195
Flannery O'Connor **1**:258

Montgomery, Niall
Flann O'Brien **7**:269

Montrose, David
Malcolm Bradbury **32**:57
William Golding **27**:164
Alfred Kazin **34**:562
Bette Pesetsky **28**:358
Siegfried Sassoon **36**:396
Gore Vidal **33**:404
Angus Wilson **34**:580

Moody, Charlotte
Molly Keane **31**:233

Moody, Christopher
Aleksandr I. Solzhenitsyn
26:418

Moody, David
Thomas W. Shapcott **38**:397

Moody, Jennifer
Lois Duncan **26**:108

Moody, John
Jaroslav Seifert **34**:259

Moody, Michael
Mario Vargas Llosa **9**:544

Moody, Richard
Lillian Hellman **18**:221

Moon, Bucklin
Langston Hughes **35**:214

Moon, Eric
Colin MacInnes **23**:283
Frederic Raphael **14**:436

Moon, Samuel
Anne Hébert **29**:228

Mooney, Bel
Doris Lessing **22**:286

Mooney, Philip
Albert Camus **14**:115

Mooney, Stephen
Josephine Miles **14**:368

Moorcock, Michael
Angus Wilson **3**:535

Moore, Anne Carroll
Margot Benary-Isbert **12**:30

Moore, Brian
Robertson Davies **2**:113

Moore, D. B.
Louis MacNeice **4**:316

Moore, David W.
Isaac Asimov **26**:58

Moore, Emily R.
Mildred D. Taylor **21**:419

Moore, Ernest
Gregorio López y Fuentes
32:278

Moore, Gerald
Chinua Achebe **11**:1
Camara Laye **38**:287
Ezekiel Mphahlele **25**:343

Moore, Harry T.
Arthur Adamov **4**:5
Kay Boyle **5**:65
August Derleth **31**:132, 133,
134
John Dos Passos **4**:132
E. M. Forster **1**:106

Critic Index

Herbert Gold **4**:190
H. D. **31**:203
Rolf Hochhuth **18**:250
Eugène Ionesco **4**:252
James Jones **3**:262
Meyer Levin **7**:204
Henry Miller **4**:350
Alain Robbe-Grillet **2**:374
Nathalie Sarraute **2**:384
Georges Simenon **2**:397
Claude Simon **4**:494
John Steinbeck **5**:405

Moore, Honor
Marilyn Hacker **5**:156
June Jordan **5**:203

Moore, Hugo
Hugh MacDiarmid **4**:311

Moore, Jack B.
Carson McCullers **12**:425
Frank Yerby **7**:556

Moore, John Rees
James Baldwin **2**:31
Samuel Beckett **10**:29
J. P. Donleavy **1**:76; **4**:124
Robert Penn Warren **6**:558

Moore, L. Hugh
Robert Stone **23**:425

Moore, Marianne
E. E. Cummings **12**:141
George Plimpton **36**:351
Ezra Pound **7**:322
Edith Sitwell **9**:493
William Carlos Williams **13**:601

Moore, Maxine
Isaac Asimov **9**:49

Moore, Michael
William Wharton **18**:543

Moore, Rayburn S.
Elizabeth Spencer **22**:402

Moore, Richard
George Garrett **3**:192
Maxine Kumin **28**:220

Moore, Stephen C.
John Cheever **7**:49
Robert Lowell **3**:301

Moore, T. Inglis
Kenneth Slessor **14**:495

Moorehead, Caroline
Joyce Maynard **23**:291
David Plante **23**:347
Martin Cruz Smith **25**:414

Moorhead, Wendy
Laurence Yep **35**:469

Moorhouse, Geoffrey
Ved Mehta **37**:294

Moorehouse, Val
Richard Kostelanetz **28**:218

Moorman, Charles
C. S. Lewis **14**:323
J.R.R. Tolkien **1**:337

Moramarco, Fred
John Ashbery **4**:22; **9**:42
Ted Berrigan **37**:44
Robert Creeley **1**:67
Allen Ginsberg **36**:188
David Ignatow **7**:181
Galway Kinnell **2**:229
James Merrill **34**:226
W. S. Merwin **1**:213
Frank O'Hara **13**:424
Ezra Pound **18**:425
James Schevill **7**:401
C. K. Williams **33**:442

Moran, Ronald
Wendell Berry **4**:59
Robert Creeley **4**:117
David Ignatow **4**:248
Marge Piercy **6**:402
Louis Simpson **4**:498
William Stafford **29**:380
James Tate **6**:528

Moran, Terence
Jay McInerney **34**:83

Moravia, Alberto
Truman Capote **13**:132

Mordas, Phyllis G.
Melvin Berger **12**:40

Morel, Jean-Pierre
André Breton **15**:88

Morello-Frosch, Marta
Julio Cortázar **2**:104
Gabriel García Márquez **3**:183

Morgan, Al
Art Buchwald **33**:88, 89
Evan Hunter **31**:220

Morgan, Chris
Robert Holdstock **39**:151

Morgan, Constance
Helen MacInnes **27**:280

Morgan, Edmund S.
Thomas J. Fleming **37**:126

Morgan, Edwin
John Berryman **10**:47
James Blish **14**:83
Malcolm Bradbury **32**:51
Anthony Burgess **15**:104
Ilya Ehrenburg **18**:137
Eva Figes **31**:163
Roy Fuller **28**:153
W. S. Graham **29**:194
Halldór Laxness **25**:292
Norman MacCaig **36**:281
Hugh MacDiarmid **11**:338
Eugenio Montale **9**:387
Piers Paul Read **25**:376
Frank Sargeson **31**:365
Rudolph Wurlitzer **15**:587
Yevgeny Yevtushenko **26**:468

Morgan, Ellen
Doris Lessing **3**:288

Morgan, John
Günter Grass **6**:209

Morgan, Robert
Geoffrey Hill **8**:294

Morgan, Speer
Wendell Berry **27**:33
Dan Jacobson **4**:256

Morgan, Ted
Edward Abbey **36**:14
Harry Crews **23**:136
Norman Mailer **14**:354
Farley Mowat **26**:346
Alice Munro **19**:346

Morgans, Patricia A.
Walter Dean Myers **35**:299

Morgenstern, Dan
Andrew Lloyd Webber and Tim Rice **21**:426
Frank Zappa **17**:587

Morgenstern, Joseph
Gordon Parks **16**:458
Melvin Van Peebles **20**:410

Moritz, A. F.
Andrew Suknaski **19**:433

Moritz, Albert
Robert Kroetsch **23**:276

Morley, Christopher
Enid Bagnold **25**:72, 73
Ogden Nash **23**:321

Morley, Patricia
John Metcalf **37**:299

Morley, Patricia A.
Margaret Atwood **13**:41
David Donnell **34**:159
Hugh Hood **28**:190
Patrick White **7**:529

Morley, Sheridan
Terence Rattigan **7**:354

Morner, Claudia
Douglas Adams **27**:13
Piers Anthony **35**:38

Morrell, A. C.
Jean Rhys **19**:390

Morris, Alice
Hortense Calisher **38**:68
Christina Stead **2**:422

Morris, C. B.
Rafael Alberti **7**:9
Vicente Aleixandre **9**:12

Morris, Christopher D.
John Barth **7**:23

Morris, Edmund
Fernanda Eberstadt **39**:49

Morris, George
Paddy Chayefsky **23**:117
Brian De Palma **20**:82
Eric Rohmer **16**:539
Martin Scorsese **20**:329
Billy Wilder **20**:466

Morris, Gregory
Breece D'J Pancake **29**:350

Morris, H. H.
Dashiell Hammett **10**:253

Morris, Harry
Louise Bogan **4**:68
James Dickey **1**:73
Jean Garrigue **2**:154
John Hollander **2**:197
George MacBeth **2**:251
Louis Simpson **4**:498
John Steinbeck **21**:370

Morris, Ivan
Yasunari Kawabata **2**:222

Morris, Jan
Laurens van der Post **5**:464

Morris, Jeff
Robert Francis **15**:238

Morris, John N.
Ai **14**:7
Kenneth O. Hanson **13**:263
Donald Justice **6**:271
Adrienne Rich **7**:370
Mark Strand **6**:521
Nancy Willard **7**:539
Charles Wright **6**:580; **13**:612

Morris, Mervyn
Louise Bennett **28**:26

Morris, Richard B.
Bruce Lancaster **36**:244

Morris, Robert K.
Anthony Burgess **4**:81; **5**:86
Lawrence Durrell **4**:146
John Fowles **6**:189
James Hanley **5**:167
Doris Lessing **6**:290
Olivia Manning **5**:271
Anthony Powell **1**:278; **3**:404; **7**:345
V. S. Pritchett **5**:354
C. P. Snow **6**:515
Thornton Wilder **6**:578

Morris, Wesley
John Crowe Ransom **4**:433

Morris, Willie
Irwin Shaw **34**:369

Morris, Wright
Ernest Hemingway **1**:141

Morrison, Blake
Beryl Bainbridge **14**:37
William Boyd **28**:40
André Brink **18**:69
Raymond Carver **36**:105
J. M. Coetzee **23**:121
Donald Davie **10**:124
Jacob Epstein **19**:162
Roy Fuller **28**:156
Gabriel García Márquez **15**:252
Allen Ginsberg **36**:198
Patricia Highsmith **14**:261
Ted Hughes **37**:172
Thomas Keneally **14**:301
Philip Larkin **33**:267; **39**:337
Eugenio Montale **18**:343
Anaïs Nin **14**:386
Robert Pinsky **19**:370
Frederic Raphael **14**:438
Christopher Reid **33**:348
Salman Rushdie **31**:353
Andrew Sinclair **14**:489

Derek Walcott **25**:457
Yevgeny Yevtushenko **13**:620

Morrison, Harriet
Frank Bonham **12**:53

Morrison, Hobe
Stephen Sondheim **30**:378, 379

Morrison, J. Allan
Leon Garfield **12**:226, 234

Morrison, J. M.
Hugh MacDiarmid **2**:254

Morrison, John W.
Jun'ichiro Tanizaki **8**:509

Morrison, Lillian
Eilís Dillon **17**:93
Mary Stolz **12**:549, 551

Morrison, Michael
Andrew M. Greeley **28**:169

Morrison, Patt
John Betjeman **34**:308

Morrison, Philip
Franklyn M. Branley **21**:17
Jacques-Yves Cousteau **30**:106
Roy A. Gallant **17**:129
Christie Harris **12**:262
Thor Heyerdahl **26**:191
Larry Kettelkamp **12**:304

Morrison, Phylis
Franklyn M. Branley **21**:17
Jacques-Yves Cousteau **30**:106
Roy A. Gallant **17**:129
Christie Harris **12**:262
Larry Kettelkamp **12**:304

Morrison, Theodore
Robert Frost **1**:111

Morrison, Toni
Jean Toomer **22**:428

Morrissette, Bruce
Alain Robbe-Grillet **1**:27;
14:455

Morrissey, Daniel
John Updike **7**:488

Morrow, Lance
John Fowles **6**:187
Erica Jong **8**:314
Yasunari Kawabata **5**:208
James A. Michener **5**:290
Yukio Mishima **4**:356, 358

Morsberger, Robert E.
Jackson J. Benson **34**:415
John Steinbeck **34**:415

Morse, David
Smokey Robinson **21**:344

Morse, J. Mitchell
Kingsley Amis **2**:6
James Baldwin **2**:32
Richard Elman **19**:150
Bruce Jay Friedman **3**:165
Joanne Greenberg **7**:134
J.M.G. Le Clézio **31**:245
Jakov Lind **2**:245
Mary McCarthy **1**:207
Vladimir Nabokov **2**:299
Peter Weiss **3**:514

Morse, John
Gilbert Sorrentino **22**:395

Morse, Jonathan
John Dos Passos **11**:156

Morse, Samuel French
W. H. Auden **6**:18
Margaret Avison **2**:29
John Berryman **3**:65
Brewster Ghiselin **23**:170
Robert Lowell **3**:301
Louis Zukofsky **1**:385

Morthland, John
The Clash **30**:47
Jimmy Cliff **21**:63
Waylon Jennings **21**:204
Bob Marley **17**:269

Mortifoglio, Richard
Marvin Gaye **26**:133
Laura Nyro **17**:320

Mortimer, John
James Thurber **5**:433

Mortimer, Penelope
Elizabeth Bishop **9**:89
Nadine Gordimer **7**:132
Fay Weldon **6**:562
Tom Wolfe **15**:586

Mortimer, Peter
C. P. Taylor **27**:444

Mortimer, Raymond
Enid Bagnold **25**:72
Frank Swinnerton **31**:422

Mortimore, Roger
Carlos Saura **20**:315

Morton, Brian
I. Compton-Burnett **34**:495
Stephen King **37**:199
Hilary Spurling **34**:495

Morton, Desmond
Thomas Flanagan **25**:166

Morton, Donald E.
Vladimir Nabokov **15**:390

Morton, Frederic
Richard Elman **19**:149
Romain Gary **25**:184
Erich Maria Remarque **21**:331
Henri Troyat **23**:459
Morris L. West **33**:427
Elie Wiesel **37**:459

Moscoso-Gongora, Peter
José Lezama Lima **10**:319

Moser, Gerald M.
José Rodrigues Miguéis **10**:340

Moses, Carole
Ernest Hemingway **19**:220

Moses, Edwin
Albert Camus **9**:148

Moses, Joseph
E. L. Doctorow **11**:140

Moses, Robbie Odom
Edward Albee **11**:12

Moses, Wilson J.
W.E.B. DuBois **13**:182

Mosher, Harold F., Jr.
Paul Simon **17**:462

Mosher, John
Alfred Hitchcock **16**:338

Moshos, Fran
Ouida Sebestyen **30**:346

Moskowitz, Moshe
Chaim Grade **10**:248

Moskowitz, Sam
John W. Campbell, Jr. **32**:71,
72
Fritz Leiber **25**:301
Theodore Sturgeon **22**:410
Jack Williamson **29**:454
John Wyndham **19**:474

Mosley, Nicholas
J. P. Donleavy **10**:155
D. J. Enright **31**:152
Iris Murdoch **31**:290

Moss, Chuck
Stephen King **37**:207

Moss, Mrs. E. D.
Philippa Pearce **21**:282

Moss, Elaine
Margaret Craven **17**:80
Diana Wynne Jones **26**:231
Madeleine L'Engle **12**:347
Rosemary Sutcliff **26**:438

Moss, Howard
W. H. Auden **6**:20
Elizabeth Bishop **1**:35; **9**:91
Elizabeth Bowen **1**:41; **3**:84
Graham Greene **6**:217
Flann O'Brien **1**:252
Katherine Anne Porter **1**:272
Jean Rhys **6**:454
Nathalie Sarraute **1**:302
Eudora Welty **2**:463

Moss, Leonard
Arthur Miller **1**:217

Moss, Robert
David Caute **29**:118
Frank Tuohy **37**:429

Moss, Robert F.
John Berryman **13**:76
Paddy Chayefsky **23**:119
Lawrence Durrell **6**:153
John O'Hara **6**:384
Richard Wright **14**:596

Moss, Stanley
Stanley J. Kunitz **6**:286

Mossman, Elliott
Boris Pasternak **10**:382

Motion, Andrew
William Boyd **28**:38
Thomas M. Disch **36**:126
Buchi Emecheta **14**:159
D. J. Enright **31**:154
Roy Fisher **25**:157
Max Frisch **32**:191
W. S. Graham **29**:197
John Hollander **14**:265
Thomas Keneally **19**:247
Philip Larkin **33**:263

Michael Longley **29**:294
Derek Mahon **27**:292
Paul Muldoon **32**:319
Seán O'Faoláin **14**:407
Tom Paulin **37**:353
Craig Raine **32**:350
Piers Paul Read **25**:380
James Schuyler **23**:390
D. M. Thomas **22**:418
Yevgeny Yevtushenko **26**:467

Motley, Joel
Leon Forrest **4**:164

Mott, Frank Luther
John G. Neihardt **32**:330

Mott, Michael
A. R. Ammons **8**:15
Geoffrey Grigson **7**:135
Elizabeth Jennings **14**:292
David Jones **7**:186
D. M. Thomas **13**:541
Charles Tomlinson **13**:545

Mottram, Eric
Fielding Dawson **6**:126
Roy Fisher **25**:157
Carolyn Kizer **15**:309
Michael McClure **6**:317
Arthur Miller **1**:218
Gilbert Sorrentino **7**:449
Diane Wakoski **4**:572
Jonathan Williams **13**:601

Moulton, Priscilla L.
E. M. Almedingen **12**:1
Jean Craighead George **35**:176
Christie Harris **12**:262
Lee Kingman **17**:245
Mary Renault **17**:397

Mount, Ferdinand
Harry Crews **23**:133
Peter Handke **10**:257
V. S. Naipaul **37**:327
Bernice Rubens **19**:403

Movius, Geoffrey H.
William Carlos Williams **9**:575

Mowbray, S. M.
Zoë Fairbairns **32**:163
David Plante **23**:345

Moyer, Charles R.
Jonathan Kozol **17**:250

Moyer, Kermit
Robert Altman **16**:34

Moyles, R. G.
Kevin Major **26**:284

Moynahan, Julian
Louis Auchincloss **9**:54
André Brink **36**:66
Frederick Buechner **9**:137
Anthony Burgess **8**:113
R. V. Cassill **23**:109
J. P. Donleavy **4**:126
André Dubus **36**:145
Thomas Flanagan **25**:163
Ernest J. Gaines **11**:218
John Gardner **28**:161
Francine du Plessix Gray
22:200
John Irving **13**:293

Jack Kerouac **2**:228
Ken Kesey **6**:277
John Knowles **26**:264
John le Carré **15**:326
Tom McHale **3**:331
Mary McCarthy **39**:485
A. G. Mojtabai **15**:378
Brian Moore **3**:341; **8**:394
Edna O'Brien **36**:340
Seán O'Faoláin **7**:274; **14**:404
Philip Rahv **24**:353
Anne Roiphe **9**:455
Judith Rossner **29**:353
Karl Shapiro **15**:477
Wilfrid Sheed **10**:472
Susan Richards Shreve **23**:404
James Tate **2**:431
Douglas Unger **34**:115
John Wain **15**:562
William Wharton **18**:542

Moynihan, Julian
Alan Sillitoe **19**:421
C. P. Snow **19**:428
James Thurber **11**:532

Mozejko, Edward
Elisaveta Bagryana **10**:13

Muchnic, Helen
Ilya Ehrenburg **18**:137
Mikhail Sholokhov **7**:418, 421
Aleksandr I. Solzhenitsyn **9**:507

Mudrick, Marvin
Donald Barthelme **2**:39
Harold Bloom **24**:82
William S. Burroughs **2**:90
E. M. Forster **2**:135
John Fowles **2**:137
Jerzy Kosinski **2**:231
Doris Lessing **2**:239
Norman Mailer **1**:192
Bernard Malamud **1**:200
Vladimir Nabokov **3**:355
V. S. Naipaul **37**:323
Joyce Carol Oates **2**:314
Nathalie Sarraute **2**:384; **4**:468
David Wagoner **3**:508

Mudrovic, Mike
Claudio Rodríguez **10**:440

Mueller, Lisel
Robert Bly **1**:37
Louise Glück **7**:118; **22**:174
Michael S. Harper **7**:138
Jim Harrison **6**:223
Anthony Hecht **8**:268
W. S. Merwin **1**:212
Sharon Olds **32**:345
Marge Piercy **6**:401
Peter Viereck **4**:559
Alice Walker **6**:553
Reed Whittemore **4**:588

Mugerauer, Robert
Martin Heidegger **24**:266

Muggeridge, John
John Metcalf **37**:301

Muggeridge, Malcolm
Paul Scott **9**:478
P. G. Wodehouse **22**:483

Muir, Edwin
Dannie Abse **29**:12
Djuna Barnes **29**:25
T. S. Eliot **24**:158

Muirhead, L. Russell
C. S. Forester **35**:165

Mukherjee, Bharati
Michael Ondaatje **29**:342

Mukherjee, Meenakshi
Anita Desai **37**:64

Muldoon, Paul
Seamus Heaney **37**:164

Mulhallen, Karen
Robert Kroetsch **23**:273
Audrey Thomas **13**:538

Mulherin, Kathy
Eva Figes **31**:162

Mulkeen, Anne
L. P. Hartley **22**:215

Mullan, Fitzhugh
Lewis Thomas **35**:412

Mullen, Patrick B.
E. E. Cummings **12**:157

Mullen, R. D.
Jack Vance **35**:419
Roger Zelazny **21**:468, 470

Mullen, Richard
Elizabeth Bishop **32**:34

Mullen, Richard D.
James Blish **14**:82

Muller, Al
Laurence Yep **35**:473

Muller, Gilbert H.
William Faulkner **8**:212
Studs Terkel **38**:425

Muller, H. J.
R. P. Blackmur **24**:54

Müller-Bergh, Klaus
G. Cabrera Infante **25**:102, 104
José Lezama Lima **4**:288

Mullin, John
T. H. White **30**:449

Mullin, Michael
Orson Welles **20**:451

Mumford, Olive
Larry Kettelkamp **12**:304

Munk, Erika
Martin Duberman **8**:185
Peter Handke **15**:268
David Rudkin **14**:471
Nathalie Sarraute **31**:385
Tom Stoppard **29**:405
Elizabeth Swados **12**:560, 561
Lanford Wilson **14**:591

Murch, A. E.
Edmund Crispin **22**:110

Murch, Anne C.
Arthur Kopit **18**:287

Murchison, John C.
Jorge Luis Borges **2**:71, 75

Murchison, W., Jr.
John Dickson Carr **3**:101

Murchland, Bernard
Albert Camus **2**:97
Jean-Paul Sartre **7**:396

Murdoch, Brian
Heinrich Böll **15**:68
Siegfried Lenz **27**:252

Murdoch, Charles
John Glassco **9**:236

Murdoch, Iris
A. S. Byatt **19**:76
Elias Canetti **25**:106

Murdock, Kenneth B.
Esther Forbes **12**:203

Murillo, L. A.
Jorge Luis Borges **4**:70

Murphy, Brian
Luis Buñuel **16**:134
Eric Rohmer **16**:529

Murphy, Catherine A.
Mary Lavin **18**:306

Murphy, Mrs. J. M.
Honor Arundel **17**:14

Murphy, Reverend James M.
Carlos Fuentes **13**:232

Murphy, Joan
Colin Thiele **17**:495

Murphy, L. J.
Isaac Asimov **26**:59

Murphy, Peggy
James Carroll **38**:104

Murphy, Richard
Thom Gunn **18**:203
Patrick Kavanagh **22**:235
Philip Larkin **5**:231

Murphy, Robert
Allan W. Eckert **17**:104

Murphy, Sylvia
Sylvia Murphy **34**:93

Murr, Judy Smith
John Gardner **10**:219

Murra, John V.
Amos Tutuola **14**:537

Murray, Atholl C.C.
David Jones **7**:188

Murray, Brian
Frederick Barthelme **36**:54
Ezra Pound **34**:510
E. Fuller Torrey **34**:510

Murray, Charles Shaar
Peter Townshend **17**:533

Murray, Donald C.
James Baldwin **13**:53

Murray, Edward
Samuel Beckett **6**:35
William Faulkner **6**:176
Ernest Hemingway **6**:229
Eugène Ionesco **6**:251
Arthur Miller **6**:327, 332

Clifford Odets **28**:337
Alain Robbe-Grillet **6**:466
Tennessee Williams **5**:501

Murray, G. E.
Ai **14**:9
Russell Banks **37**:23
Marvin Bell **31**:49
Alfred Corn **33**:118
Robert Hayden **37**:158
Anthony Hecht **13**:269
Howard Moss **14**:376
Michael Ondaatje **14**:410
Robert Pack **13**:439
Robert Phillips **28**:364
Louis Simpson **32**:377
William Stafford **29**:386
Derek Walcott **14**:550

Murray, Jack
Alain Robbe-Grillet **1**:287

Murray, James G.
A. J. Cronin **32**:139

Murray, John J.
Robert Penn Warren **4**:579

Murray, Michael
Edward Albee **2**:3
Lenny Bruce **21**:52

Murray, Michele
Robert Cormier **12**:134
Paula Fox **2**:140
Doris Grumbach **22**:204
Susan B. Hill **4**:227
William Melvin Kelley **22**:246
Robert Kotlowitz **4**:275
Pär Lagerkvist **7**:200
Mary Lavin **4**:282
William Mayne **12**:399
Grace Paley **4**:392
Frank Tuohy **37**:426

Murray, Peggy
Piers Anthony **35**:38

Murray, Philip
Aldous Huxley **3**:256

Murray, Thomas J.
Mary Lavin **18**:302

Murray, William J.
Melvin Berger **12**:38

Murry, John Middleton
I. A. Richards **24**:372
Siegfried Sassoon **36**:386

Murtaugh, Daniel M.
Marie-Claire Blais **4**:67
Eilís Dillon **17**:100
Wilfrid Sheed **2**:393
John Updike **23**:470

Murtaugh, Kristen
Italo Calvino **22**:94

Mus, David
T. S. Eliot **2**:129

Musher, Andrea
Diane Wakoski **7**:505

Muske, Carol
Jon Anderson **9**:31
Lucille Clifton **19**:110
Adrienne Rich **18**:448; **36**:378
Charles Wright **13**:613

Mutiso, Gideon-Cyrus M.
Alex La Guma **19**:272

Myers, Andrew B.
Alan Garner **17**:137

Myers, Christine
Zoa Sherburne **30**:361

Myers, David
Max Frisch **32**:195

Myers, David A.
Kurt Vonnegut, Jr. **22**:446

Myers, George Jr.
Ted Berrigan **37**:45

Myers, Oliver T.
José Donoso **32**:153

Myers, Robert J.
Lothar-Günther Buchheim
6:100

Myers, Tim
Arthur C. Clarke **18**:107
Nicholas Delbanco **13**:175

Myerson, Jonathan
David Hare **29**:221

Myles, Lynda
George Lucas **16**:416

Myrsiades, Kostas
Stratis Haviaras **33**:202
Yannis Ritsos **6**:463; **13**:487,
488

Mysak, Joe
Russell Baker **31**:31

Nabokov, Peter
Peter Matthiessen **32**:296

Nadeau, Maurice
Louis Aragon **3**:13
Simone de Beauvoir **1**:19
Samuel Beckett **1**:22
Michel Butor **1**:49
Albert Camus **1**:54
Louis-Ferdinand Céline **1**:56
Jean Genet **1**:115
Jean Giono **4**:185
Raymond Queneau **2**:359
Alain Robbe-Grillet **1**:288
Françoise Sagan **3**:444
Nathalie Sarraute **1**:303
Jean-Paul Sartre **1**:305
Claude Simon **4**:495

Nadeau, Robert L.
Djuna Barnes **11**:29
Don DeLillo **27**:80
Tom Robbins **32**:372

Nadel, Norman
Irwin Shaw **23**:398
Neil Simon **31**:394

Naha, Ed
The Police **26**:363
Monty Python **21**:225

Nahal, Chaman
Ernest Hemingway **30**:191

Nahrgang, W. Lee
Fritz Hochwälder **36**:239

Naiden, James N.
Thomas McGrath **28**:277
Lorine Niedecker **10**:360

Naik, M. K.
Mulk Raj Anand **23**:18

Naipaul, Shiva
Miguel Ángel Asturias **8**:27
José Donoso **4**;130

Naipaul, V. S.
Jorge Luis Borges **2**:77
David Caute **29**:108
C.L.R. James **33**:219
R. K. Narayan **28**:293, 298
P. H. Newby **13**:407
Jean Rhys **2**:372
Françoise Sagan **17**:422

Nairn, Tom
Marshall McLuhan **37**:263

Naison, Mark
C.L.R. James **33**:223

Nalley, Richard
Donald Hall **13**:259

Namjoshi, Suniti
Jay Macpherson **14**:347
P. K. Page **18**:377

Nance, William L.
Truman Capote **13**:133

Nance, William L., S.M.
Katherine Anne Porter **7**:314

Napier, Stuart
Frank Herbert **35**:205

Napolin, Leah
E. M. Broner **19**:71

Nardi, Marcia
Babette Deutsch **18**:118

Nardin, Jane
Evelyn Waugh **8**:544

Nardo, A. K.
C. S. Lewis **14**:325

Naremore, James
John Huston **20**:172
Philip Larkin **5**:226

Nassar, Eugene Paul
Ezra Pound **7**:335

Natanson, Maurice
Jean-Paul Sartre **24**:407

Nathan, George Jean
Noel Coward **9**:171
Lillian Hellman **18**:220
Arthur Miller **26**:314
Terence Rattigan **7**:353
Elmer Rice **7**:359
George Tabori **19**:437
Tennessee Williams **30**:460

Nathan, John
Kenzaburō Ōe **36**:346

Nathan, Leonard
Gunnar Ekelöf **27**:118

Natov, Roni
Leon Garfield **12**:239

Naughton, John
A. Alvarez **13**:9
Jeffrey Archer **28**:12
Beryl Bainbridge **18**:33
John Berger **19**:38
Cecil Bødker **21**:13
Arthur A. Cohen **31**:94
Isabel Colegate **36**:111
Autran Dourado **23**:152
Romain Gary **25**:188
Ursula Holden **18**:258
Penelope Lively **32**:274
Bernard Mac Laverty **31**:253
Stanley Middleton **38**:332
Fay Weldon **36**:443

Navarro, Carlos
Jorge Luis Borges **3**:79

Navasky, Victor S.
Jules Archer **12**:21
Meyer Levin **7**:204

Navone, John J.
Federico Fellini **16**:273

Nazareth, Peter
Charles R. Larson **31**:239
James Ngugi **7**:266

Nebecker, Helen E.
Shirley Jackson **11**:302

Necker, Walter
Joy Adamson **17**:2

Needham, Dorothy
Jacques-Yves Cousteau **30**:106

Needleman, Ruth
Octavio Paz **3**:375

Neeper, Cary
Arthur C. Clarke **35**:125

Neil, Boyd
Mavis Gallant **38**:193
Michel Tremblay **29**:424

Neil, J. Meredith
Jack Kerouac **14**:306

Neill, Edward
Peter Ackroyd **34**:387
T. S. Eliot **34**:387

Neimark, Paul G.
Agatha Christie **1**:58

Neiswender, Rosemary
E. M. Almedingen **12**:4
Yevgeny Yevtushenko **26**:462

Nekrich, Alexsandr
Alexander Zinoviev **19**:485

Nelsen, Don
Simon Gray **36**:207
Beth Henley **23**:215
Ntozake Shange **25**:397

Nelson, Alix
Nora Ephron **17**:111
Richard Peck **21**:298
Kin Platt **26**:351
Mary Rodgers **12**:494

Nelson, Anne
Jonathan Kozol **17**:254

Nelson, Byron
Howard Barker **37**:40

Nelson, Donald F.
Martin Walser **27**:456

Nelson, Dorothy H.
Esther Forbes **12**:211

Nelson, Elizabeth
Thomas J. Fleming **37**:125

Nelson, Howard
Robert Bly **10**:54; **38**:56
Robert Francis **15**:237

Nelson, Hugh
Harold Pinter **6**:413

Nelson, John A.
Nat Hentoff **26**:186

Nelson, Joyce
Frank Capra **16**:161
Kurt Vonnegut, Jr. **4**:562

Nelson, Paul
David Bowie **17**:64
Jackson Browne **21**:40
Janis Ian **21**:186
Billy Joel **26**:221
John Lennon and Paul
McCartney **12**:378
Willie Nelson **17**:303
Lou Reed **21**:310, 311
Paul Simon **17**:465
Patti Smith **12**:538
Bruce Springsteen **17**:484
Neil Young **17**:576, 581

Nelson, Raymond
Van Wyck Brooks **29**:87
Chester Himes **2**:196

Nelson, Robert C.
Vine Deloria, Jr. **21**:111

Nemerov, Howard
Conrad Aiken **3**:4
Kingsley Amis **2**:5
Djuna Barnes **3**:36
Ben Belitt **22**:50
Kenneth Burke **2**:89
James Dickey **4**:120
Daniel Hoffman **13**:286
Harry Mathews **6**:315
Marianne Moore **4**:359
Howard Moss **7**:247
Kathleen Raine **7**:353

Nesbitt, Bruce
Earle Birney **11**:49

Nesbitt, John D.
Louis L'Amour **25**:279, 281

Nesin, Jeff
Lou Reed **21**:321

Ness, David E.
Lorraine Hansberry **17**:191

Nettelbeck, Colin W.
Louis-Ferdinand Céline **3**:103

Nettleford, Rex
Louise Bennett **28**:28

Neubauer, John
Georg Lukács **24**:335

Critic Index

Neuberger, Richard L.
Allen Drury 37:99

Neufeld, John
Kristin Hunter 35:226
Maia Wojciechowska 26:455

Neufeldt, Leonard
David Wagoner 15:560

Neumark, Victoria
Carlos Fuentes 13:232

Nevans, Ronald
Barry Hannah 23:212
Bette Bao Lord 23:278

Neves, John
Martin Walser 27:466

Neville, Robert
Helen MacInnes 27:281

Nevins, Allan
Walter D. Edmonds 35:144,
145, 147, 152
Howard Fast 23:155
Carl Sandburg 35:349

Nevins, Francis M., Jr.
Ellery Queen 3:421; 11:458
Rex Stout 3:471

Nevius, Blake
Ivy Compton-Burnett 1:62

New, W. H.
Ethel Davis Wilson 13:608

New, William H.
Margaret Avison 4:36
Robertson Davies 7:73
Simon Gray 9:241
Hugh Hood 15:286
William Mitchell 25:322, 323
Alden Nowlan 15:399

Newberry, Wilma
Ramón Gómez de la Serna
9:237

Newby, I. A.
Louis R. Harlan 34:189

Newby, P. H.
Penelope Fitzgerald 19:174

Newcomb, Horace
Larry Gelbart 21:127

Newfield, Jack
Bob Dylan 12:183

Newlin, Margaret
H. D. 14:225
Sylvia Plath 3:389

Newlove, Donald
Frederick Barthelme 36:49
Peter Benchley 4:53
Joseph Brodsky 4:78
Howard Fast 23:159
Günter Grass 22:195
Thomas Kinsella 4:271
W. S. Merwin 5:287
J. D. Salinger 8:463
Trevanian 29:431

Newman, Anne R.
Elizabeth Bishop 15:59

Newman, Barbara
Jamake Highwater 12:288

Newman, Charles
James Baldwin 13:48
Donald Barthelme 23:48
Saul Bellow 6:59
Sylvia Plath 9:421
Philip Roth 4:457

Newman, Christina
Brian Moore 8:395

Newman, Michael
W. H. Auden 6:25

Newton, David E.
Isaac Asimov 26:57
Franklyn M. Branley 21:22, 23
Roy A. Gallant 17:130, 133

Newton, Edmund
Wendy Wasserstein 32:439

Newton, Francis
John Lennon and Paul
McCartney 12:353

Neyman, Mark
Allan W. Eckert 17:108

Nichol, B. P.
Earle Birney 6:76

Nicholas, Brian
Graham Greene 6:214

Nicholas, Charles A.
N. Scott Momaday 19:317

Nicholas, Robert L.
Antonio Buero Vallejo 15:97

Nicholaus, Charles
Van Morrison 21:236

Nicholls, Peter
Stephen King 37:206
William Kotzwinkle 35:258
Gene Wolfe 25:476

Nichols, Bill
Bernardo Bertolucci 16:85

Nichols, Kathleen L.
Ernest Hemingway 19:221

Nichols, Lewis
George S. Kaufman 38:264
Irwin Shaw 23:396

Nichols, Ruth
Diana Wynne Jones 26:228

Nichols, Stephen G., Jr.
John Hawkes 3:221

Nicholson, C. E.
Theodore Roethke 11:486

Nicholson, Kris
Neil Young 17:575

Nickerson, Edward A.
Robinson Jeffers 15:301

Nickerson, Susan L.
Piers Anthony 35:37, 39
C. J. Cherryh 35:113
Marion Zimmer Bradley 30:32
Anne McCaffrey 17:282, 283,
284
Jack Williamson 29:461

Nicol, Charles
Kingsley Amis 5:22
J. G. Ballard 36:39
Brigid Brophy 6:100
Anthony Burgess 5:90
John Cheever 11:121; 25:116
Peter De Vries 7:77
John Gardner 30:153
Dashiell Hammett 5:162
John Hawkes 4:218; 7:144
John Irving 13:293; 23:252
Alfred Kazin 38:278
Milan Kundera 9:320; 19:268
Norman Mailer 4:323
Vladimir Nabokov 1:244
Kurt Vonnegut, Jr. 3:504;
8:534; 12:602

Nicosia, Gerald
James Jones 39:407
Frank McShane 39:407

Niemeyer, Gerhart
Aleksandr I. Solzhenitsyn 7:439

Niester, Alan
Frank Zappa 17:590

Nightingale, Benedict
Piers Anthony 35:34
Alan Ayckbourn 5:35; 18:30;
33:41
Howard Barker 37:38
Edward Bond 4:70
Howard Brenton 31:63, 64, 68
David Caute 29:114
Caryl Churchill 31:87, 88
A. E. Ellis 7:93
Dario Fo 32:173, 174
Michael Frayn 7:107; 31:190
Simon Gray 36:205, 206
John Hopkins 4:234
David Mercer 5:284
Slawomir Mrozek 13:399
Peter Nichols 5:305, 306;
36:328, 329
Joe Orton 13:435
John Osborne 5:333
Stephen Poliakoff 38:375, 377,
384
J. B. Priestley 5:350
Gerome Ragni and James Rado
17:382
Anthony Shaffer 19:415
Sam Shepard 34:271
Neil Simon 6:504
Tom Stoppard 5:412; 29:395,
398, 402; 34:272, 277
David Storey 5:415
C. P. Taylor 27:443
Wendy Wasserstein 32:441
E. A. Whitehead 5:488
Snoo Wilson 33:463, 465

Nigro, Kirsten F.
José Donoso 32:153

Nilsen, Aileen Pace
Maya Angelou 12:14
Gunnel Beckman 26:89
Jay Bennett 35:45
Judy Blume 12:44
Robert Cormier 30:85, 87
James D. Forman 21:123
Rosa Guy 26:145

M. E. Kerr 12:300
Norma Klein 30:239
Norma Fox Mazer 26:291
Nicholosa Mohr 12:447
Sandra Scoppettone 26:401
John R. Tunis 12:599

Nimmo, Dorothy
C. S. Adler 35:12
Joan Aiken 35:20
Judy Blume 12:45
S. E. Hinton 30:205
Diana Wynne Jones 26:233
Philippa Pearce 21:290

Nissenson, Hugh
Chaim Potok 2:338; 7:321;
26:368
A. B. Yehoshua 31:468

Nist, John
Carlos Drummond de Andrade
18:3, 4

Nist, Joan
Laurence Yep 35:474

Nitchie, George W.
Robert Lowell 8:350
George MacBeth 2:251
Marianne Moore 8:397

Niven, Alastair
C.L.R. James 33:223

Nixon, Agnes Eckhardt
Agnes Eckhardt Nixon 21:241,
244

Nixon, Rob
André Brink 36:70

Nkosi, Lewis
André Brink 18:68
Alex La Guma 19:272
Ngugi wa Thiong'o 36:313

Nnolim, Charles E.
Mongo Beti 27:47

Noah, Carolyn
Suzanne Newton 35:301

Noble, David W.
James Baldwin 4:40

Nokes, David
Michael Mewshaw 9:377

Nolan, Mary L.
John Donovan 35:143

Nolan, Paul T.
Marc Connelly 7:55

Nolan, Tom
Neil Diamond 30:112
T. R. Pearson 39:90

Noland, W. Richard
Elliott Baker 8:38

Nolen, William A.
Colleen McCullough 27:321

Nomad, Max
Ignazio Silone 4:493

Noonan, Tom
Rainer Werner Fassbinder
20:118

Nordberg, Robert B.
Ward S. Just **27**:226
Jonathan Kozol **17**:252

Nordell, Roderick
John Ehle **27**:105
William Golding **17**:172
Mark Harris **19**:201
Nat Hentoff **26**:185
Peter Matthiessen **32**:294
Margaret Mead **37**:281
Jerome Siegel and Joe Shuster
21:357

Nordyke, Lewis
Glendon Swarthout **35**:399
Robert Lewis Taylor **14**:533

Norman, Albert H.
Richard Brautigan **12**:58

Norman, Doreen
Otfried Preussler **17**:375

Norman, Gurney
Richard Brautigan **12**:64

Norman, Marsha
Lillian Hellman **34**:352

Norman, Mary Anne
Dee Brown **18**:71

Norris, Christopher
William Empson **33**:150;
34:543

Norris, Hoke
Frank Tuohy **37**:427

Norris, Jerrie
Rosa Guy **26**:144

Norris, Ken
George Bowering **15**:81

Norris, Leslie
Andrew Young **5**:525

Norrish, P. J.
Henri de Montherlant **19**:329

Norsworthy, James
Kin Platt **26**:353

Norsworthy, James A.
Cecil Bødker **21**:14
Jamake Highwater **12**:286
Zilpha Keatley Snyder **17**:474

North, R. J.
Andre Malraux **13**:367

Northey, Margot
Matt Cohen **19**:115
Anne Hébert **29**:235
Mordecai Richler **18**:451

Norton, Dale
Alex Haley **12**:248

Norton, Elliot
Lily Tomlin **17**:517

Norwood, Gilbert
Agatha Christie **12**:113

Norwood, W. D., Jr.
C. S. Lewis **1**:177

Nossiter, Bernard D.
Ved Mehta **37**:290

Noth, Dominique Paul
Garry Trudeau **12**:589

Notken, Debbie
Marion Zimmer Bradley **30**:29
C. J. Cherryh **35**:107

Notley, Alice
James Schuyler **23**:391

Nott, Kathleen
Alejo Carpentier **38**:91
Graham Greene **14**:217
Arthur Koestler **33**:236

Nouryeh, Christopher
Ben Belitt **22**:54

Novak, Barbara
Audrey Thomas **37**:418

Novak, Michael
Norman Lear **12**:338

Novak, Michael Paul
Robert Hayden **5**:169

Novak, William
Grace Paley **6**:391
Susan Fromberg Schaeffer
6:488
A. B. Yehoshua **31**:470

Novick, Julius
Edward Albee **9**:10
John Bishop **10**:54
Gretchen Cryer **21**:81
Charles Fuller **25**:181
Simon Gray **9**:242
Albert Innaurato **21**:199
Hugh Leonard **19**:284
David Mamet **9**:360
Sean O'Casey **11**:411
David Rabe **4**:425
Howard Sackler **14**:478
Neil Simon **11**:496
Isaac Bashevis Singer **15**:509
Tom Stoppard **4**:525; **8**:504
David Storey **8**:505
Tennessee Williams **8**:548
Lanford Wilson **14**:592

Nowell-Smith, Geoffrey
Michelangelo Antonioni **20**:27
Bernardo Bertolucci **16**:100
Luis Buñuel **16**:131
Richard Lester **20**:218
Pier Paolo Pasolini **20**:259
Luchino Visconti **16**:573

Nowicki, R. E.
Josephine Miles **39**:353

Nowlan, Alden
Ralph Gustafson **36**:212
Hugh Hood **15**:283

Nuechterlein, James
Bruce Catton **35**:95

Nugent, Frank S.
Tod Browning **16**:121
John Ford **16**:304
Jean Renoir **20**:287

Nugent, Robert
René Char **11**:111

Nwoga, Donatus I.
Christopher Okigbo **25**:350

Nyabongo, V. S.
Alice Walker **6**:554

Nyamfukudza, S.
Ayi Kwei Armah **33**:29

Nye, Robert
Brigid Brophy **6**:98
Eva Figes **31**:162
E. M. Forster **3**:162
David Garnett **3**:189
Graham Greene **3**:214
Hermann Hesse **17**:218
Mollie Hunter **21**:159
Bernard Malamud **5**:269
Stanley Middleton **38**:331
Michael Moorcock **27**:347
Anthony Powell **3**:402
John Cowper Powys **7**:349
William Sansom **6**:483
Tom Sharpe **36**:402
Penelope Shuttle **7**:422

Nye, Russel
John Lennon and Paul
McCartney **12**:366

Nygaard, Anita
Joy Adamson **17**:5

Nyren, D.
Marie-Claire Blais **13**:97

Nyren, Dorothy
Frederick Barthelme **36**:49
Russell Edson **13**:190

Oakley, Helen
Lenora Mattingly Weber **12**:633

Oates, Joyce Carol
Harriette Arnow **2**:14
James Baldwin **5**:42
Stephen Bochco and Michael
Kozoll **35**:60
Paul Bowles **19**:60
Brigid Brophy **29**:97
I. Compton-Burnett **34**:499
Frederick Busch **7**:38
James M. Cain **3**:95
Hortense Calisher **38**:74
Carlos Castaneda **12**:88
John Cheever **11**:120
Laurie Colwin **23**:129
Robert Coover **7**:58
Alfred Corn **33**:116
Julio Cortázar **33**:123
Robert Creeley **8**:152
Roald Dahl **1**:177
Robertson Davies **25**:132
James Dickey **7**:83
Joan Didion **8**:175
Margaret Drabble **2**:118; **5**:117
André Dubus **13**:183; **36**:146
Marion Engel **36**:159
James T. Farrell **4**:158
Eva Figes **31**:169
Carolyn Forché **25**:170
Janet Frame **2**:141
Tess Gallagher **18**:170
Gail Godwin **5**:142; **22**:179
William Golding **17**:180
William Goyen **8**:250
Joanne Greenberg **30**:162
Jim Harrison **6**:224
Anne Hébert **13**:268; **29**:238

Carolyn G. Heilbrun **25**:252
David Ignatow **14**:276
Maxine Kumin **5**:222
Philip Larkin **8**:337
Mary Lavin **4**:282
Stanislaw Lem **15**:328
Doris Lessing **2**:241
Philip Levine **4**:286, 288
Alison Lurie **18**:310
Norman Mailer **11**:341
Bernard Malamud **3**:323
Leonard Michaels **25**:314
Brian Moore **32**:309
Berry Morgan **6**:339
Alice Munro **6**:342; **19**:346
Iris Murdoch **1**:237; **11**:389;
31:293
Vladimir Nabokov **2**:304
R. K. Narayan **28**:295
Charles Newman **2**:312; **8**:419
Flannery O'Connor **1**:258
Mary Oliver **19**:362
Breece D'J Pancake **29**:346
Robert Phillips **28**:362
Sylvia Plath **2**:338; **5**:340
Gilbert Rogin **18**:458
Philip Roth **4**:454
J. R. Salamanca **15**:463
Anne Sexton **6**:492
Stevie Smith **25**:422
Hilary Spurling **34**:499
Jean Stafford **19**:430
Elizabeth Taylor **2**:433
Peter Taylor **1**:335
Paul Theroux **8**:512
Lewis Thomas **35**:408
William Trevor **9**:529
John Updike **2**:441; **13**:561
Gore Vidal **33**:410
Kurt Vonnegut, Jr. **12**:603
Fay Weldon **9**:559
Eudora Welty **1**:363
Richard Yates **7**:554

Oberbeck, S. K.
Kingsley Amis **2**:7
Amiri Baraka **33**:55
Frederick Forsyth **5**:125
John Hawkes **1**:137
John Hersey **7**:154
John Irving **13**:293
Norman Mailer **2**:264
Joyce Carol Oates **2**:315
Georges Simenon **2**:398
Glendon Swarthout **35**:403
Erich von Däniken **30**:424
Kurt Vonnegut, Jr. **3**:502
Stevie Wonder **12**:655

Oberg, Arthur
Marvin Bell **31**:46
John Berryman **4**:66; **25**:93
Galway Kinnell **3**:270
Greg Kuzma **7**:197
Philip Levine **2**:244
John Matthias **9**:362
Josephine Miles **14**:369
Joyce Carol Oates **6**:367
Robert Pack **13**:438
Sylvia Plath **14**:422; **17**:349
Anne Sexton **4**:482
Mona Van Duyn **7**:498
Derek Walcott **9**:556

Critic Index

Oberhelman, Harley D.
José Donoso **11**:146
Ernesto Sabato **23**:378

Obolensky, Laura
Andrea Lee **36**:256

O'Brien, Conor Cruise
See also **O'Donnell, Donat**
Jimmy Breslin **4**:76
Thomas Flanagan **25**:166
Graham Greene **3**:214
Seamus Heaney **7**:149

O'Brien, D. V.
Evan Hunter **31**:228

O'Brien, Darcy
Patrick Kavanagh **22**:241
Edna O'Brien **36**:336

O'Brien, Edna
Françoise Sagan **17**:428

O'Brien, Geoffrey
Peter Dickinson **35**:138
Jun'ichirō Tanizaki **28**:419

O'Brien, James H.
Liam O'Flaherty **5**:321

O'Brien, John
Robert Coover **32**:125
Clarence Major **19**:293
Gilbert Sorrentino **7**:450

O'Brien, Kate
Elias Canetti **14**:118
Rhys Davies **23**:142

O'Brien, Tim
Craig Nova **31**:297

O'Brien, Tom
Farley Mowat **26**:346
William Wharton **37**:441

Obstfeld, Raymond
Elmore Leonard **28**:236

Obuchowski, Chester W.
Pierre Gascar **11**:220

Obuchowski, Mary Dejong
Yasunari Kawabata **9**:316

Obuke, Okpure O.
John Pepper Clark **38**:124

Occhiogrosso, Frank
Georges Simenon **18**:481

Ochshorn, Susan
Ann Schlee **35**:372

O'Connell, Kay Webb
Jean Craighead George **35**:180
Marilyn Sachs **35**:335

O'Connell, Margaret F.
Franklyn M. Branley **21**:18

O'Connell, Robert W.
Margaret O. Hyde **21**:174

O'Connell, Shaun
Harry Crews **23**:134
Seamus Heaney **25**:248
Marjorie Kellogg **2**:224
Gilbert Sorrentino **7**:447

O'Connor, Flannery
Flannery O'Connor **21**:254

O'Connor, Garry
Jean Anouilh **8**:24

O'Connor, Gerald
J.R.R. Tolkien **12**:576

O'Connor, John J.
Steven Bochco and Michael
Kozoll **35**:52
Larry Gelbart **21**:126
Earl Hamner, Jr. **12**:258
Norman Lear **12**:333, 334, 337
Garry Marshall **17**:275, 276
Lanford Wilson **7**:547

O'Connor, Mary
Caroline Gordon **6**:203

O'Connor, William Van
Kingsley Amis **1**:5
Donald Davie **5**:113
D. J. Enright **4**:154
Leslie A. Fiedler **24**:189
Elizabeth Jennings **5**:197
Philip Larkin **3**:275
Iris Murdoch **1**:234
Robert Phillips **28**:361
Ezra Pound **1**:275
John Wain **2**:458

O'Daniel, Therman B.
Ralph Ellison **1**:95

Oddo, Sandra Schmidt
John McPhee **36**:295

Odell, Brian Neal
Arna Bontemps **18**:64

Oderman, Kevin
Gary Snyder **32**:393

O'Doherty, Brian
Flann O'Brien **5**:314

O'Donnell, Donat
Seán O'Faoláin **14**:402
George Steiner **24**:424

O'Donnell, Patrick
John Hawkes **27**:199
Philip Roth **31**:338

O'Donnell, Thomas D.
Michel Butor **11**:81
Claude Simon **15**:495

O'Donovan, Patrick
Allen Drury **37**:99
Aldous Huxley **35**:239

O'Faolain, Julia
Margaret Atwood **25**:69
Beryl Bainbridge **10**:15; **18**:33
Mark Helprin **10**:260
Bernard Mac Laverty **31**:253
Alice Munro **19**:346
Edna O'Brien **5**:311
Seán O'Faoláin **32**:342
Isaac Bashevis Singer **9**:489

O'Faoláin, Seán
Daphne du Maurier **11**:162
William Faulkner **28**:143
Ernest Hemingway **13**:272

Offerman, Sister Mary Columba
Gunnel Beckman **26**:87

Offit, Sidney
H. F. Brinsmead **21**:28

O'Flaherty, Patrick
Farley Mowat **26**:338

Ogilvie, John T.
Robert Frost **26**:116

Oglesby, Leora
Frank Bonham **12**:50

Ogunyemi, Chikwenye Okonjo
Toni Morrison **10**:354
Amos Tutuola **14**:542

O'Hara, J. D.
Kingsley Amis **8**:11
Donald Barthelme **5**:54
Ann Beattie **8**:54
Samuel Beckett **6**:39; **14**:73;
29:58
Jorge Luis Borges **2**:77
Kay Boyle **5**:66
Richard Brautigan **12**:58
Anthony Burgess **5**:86, 88
Italo Calvino **22**:93
Louis-Ferdinand Céline **4**:103
John Cheever **15**:129
Laurie Colwin **13**:156
Robert Crumb **17**:82
Roald Dahl **6**:121
Edward Dahlberg **7**:71
Don DeLillo **13**:178; **27**:78, 79
William Gaddis **19**:186
Lawrence Durrell **6**:152
William Golding **17**:170
Peter Handke **15**:268
George V. Higgins **4**:223
José Lezama Lima **4**:288
Steven Millhauser **21**:216, 218
Vladimir Nabokov **1**:246
Judith Rossner **6**:469
C. P. Snow **9**:498
Gore Vidal **22**:436
Kurt Vonnegut, Jr. **12**:608
René Wellek **28**:451
Paul West **14**:569

O'Hara, T.
Derek Walcott **4**:575

O'Hara, Tim
Ronald Sukenick **4**:531

O'Hearn, Walter
Farley Mowat **26**:333

Ohmann, Carol B.
Alex Haley **12**:244
J. D. Salinger **12**:516
Muriel Spark **2**:414

Ohmann, Richard M.
Pär Lagerkvist **7**:199
J. D. Salinger **12**:516

Ojaide, Tanure
Wole Soyinka **36**:415

Oka, Takashi
Yukio Mishima **27**:336

Okam, Hilary
Aimé Césaire **19**:98

O'Keeffe, Timothy
Patrick White **3**:521

Okenimkpe, Michael
Ngugi wa Thiong'o **36**:321

Okrent, Daniel
Roger Kahn **30**:234

Okri, Ben
Mongo Beti **27**:53
Anita Desai **19**:134

Okun, Milton
Phil Ochs **17**:330
Buffy Sainte-Marie **17**:430

Olander, Joseph D.
Robert A. Heinlein **26**:170

Olcott, Anthony
Vasily Aksyonov **37**:12
André Brink **36**:71

Olcott, Lynn
Steven Goldsberry **34**:56

Olderman, Raymond M.
John Barth **3**:40
Peter S. Beagle **7**:26
Stanley Elkin **4**:153; **27**:121
John Hawkes **3**:222
Joseph Heller **3**:229
Ken Kesey **3**:266
Thomas Pynchon **3**:411
Kurt Vonnegut, Jr. **3**:505

Oldfield, Michael
Jim Morrison **17**:291
Jimmy Page and Robert Plant
12:477
Bob Seger **35**:379, 380, 381,
385
Carly Simon **26**:408

Oldham, Andrew
Brian Wilson **12**:640

Oldsey, Bernard S.
William Golding **2**:167

Oliphant, Dave
Albert Goldbarth **5**:143

Oliva, Leo E.
Vine Deloria, Jr. **21**:112

Oliver, Edith
Howard Barker **37**:38
Ed Bullins **5**:83; **7**:36
Anne Burr **6**:103
Alice Childress **12**:105
Caryl Churchill **31**:81
Gretchen Cryer **21**:78, 81
Shelagh Delaney **29**:145
Christopher Durang **27**:88, 90
Harvey Fierstein **33**:157
Dario Fo **32**:174
Athol Fugard **14**:191
Charles Fuller **25**:181
Jack Gelber **14**:193
Simon Gray **14**:214, 215
John Guare **8**:253; **14**:220, 221
A. R. Gurney, Jr. **32**:216, 219,
220
Christopher Hampton **4**:211
Beth Henley **23**:214
Albert Innaurato **21**:194
Jim Jacobs and Warren Casey
12:292
Arthur Kopit **18**:286; **33**:253

David Mamet **15**:355, 358
William Mastrosimone **36**:289
Mark Medoff **6**:322
Rochelle Owens **8**:434
Stephen Poliakoff **38**:381
Gerome Ragni and James Rado **17**:379
Terence Rattigan **7**:355
Jonathan Reynolds **6**:451; **38**:387, 390
Sam Shepard **6**:497; **17**:435, 442
Stephen Sondheim **30**:398
Tom Stoppard **3**:470; **4**:525
Elizabeth Swados **12**:557, 559
George Tabori **19**:437
Megan Terry **19**:440
Kurt Vonnegut, Jr. **12**:605
Derek Walcott **2**:460; **14**:551
Joseph A. Walker **19**:455
Douglas Turner Ward **19**:457, 458
Wendy Wasserstein **32**:440, 441
Richard Wesley **7**:518
Hugh Whitemore **37**:444
Thornton Wilder **35**:445
Lanford Wilson **14**:591

Oliver, Raymond
J. V. Cunningham **31**:105
Arthur Gregor **9**:255
George Steiner **24**:434

Oliver, Roland
Shiva Naipaul **32**:325

Oliver, Roy
Arthur A. Cohen **7**:51

Olivier, Edith
Esther Forbes **12**:203

Olmert, Michael
Philip Roth **4**:452

Olney, James
Chinua Achebe **1**:2
Loren Eiseley **7**:92
Wole Soyinka **36**:414

Olsen, Gary R.
Hermann Hesse **6**:238

Olsen, Miken
Norma Fox Mazer **26**:291

Olshaker, Mark
Rod Serling **30**:358

Olshen, Barry N.
John Fowles **9**:210; **33**:163

Olson, Carol Booth
A. G. Mojtabai **15**:377

Olson, David B.
Robert Penn Warren **10**:518

Olson, Elder
William Empson **33**:142

Olson, Lawrence
Yukio Mishima **2**:288

Olson, Patricia
Morris L. West **33**:434

Olson, Paul A.
Amy Clampitt **32**:115

Olson, Ray
Bret Easton Ellis **39**:56
Amy Hempel **39**:69
Lorrie Moore **39**:83

Olson, Toby
Diane Wakoski **7**:505

O'Malley, Casey
M. E. Kerr **35**:250

O'Malley, Michael
Erich Maria Remarque **21**:334

O'Malley, William J., S.J.
Carl Sagan **30**:338

O'Mealy, R. G.
Robert Hayden **37**:159

O'Mealy, Robert
Carlo Gébler **39**:62

O'Mealy, Robert G.
Sterling A. Brown **23**:98
Robert Hayden **14**:240
Michael Thelwell **22**:416

O'Neal, Susan
Kristin Hunter **35**:225
Robert Lipsyte **21**:208

O'Neill, Kathleen
Michel Butor **11**:80

O'Neill, T.
Pier Paolo Pasolini **37**:343

O'Neill, Tom
Giuseppe Ungaretti **11**:557; **15**:537

O'Neill, William L.
Andrew M. Greeley **28**:171

Onley, Gloria
Margaret Atwood **4**:25; **13**:42

Onyeama, Dillibe
Alex Haley **12**:252

Opdahl, Keith
Saul Bellow **3**:51; **15**:55
Jim Harrison **14**:236

Oppenheim, Jane
Len Deighton **22**:114
Susan Isaacs **32**:256

Oppenheim, Shulamith
Leon Garfield **12**:230

Oppenheimer, Dan
Paul Weller **26**:442

Oppenheimer, George
Sumner Locke Elliott **38**:178

Oppenheimer, Joel
Robert Creeley **15**:153
Lawrence Ferlinghetti **27**:136
Anthony Hecht **19**:208
Philip Roth **4**:457
William Saroyan **10**:456; **29**:362
L. E. Sissman **18**:489
Andrei Voznesensky **15**:557

Orange, John
David Donnell **34**:156
Hugh Hood **28**:193

Ordóñez, Elizabeth
Ana María Matute **11**:366

O'Reilly, Jane
T. Gertler **34**:51

O'Reilly, Timothy
Frank Herbert **12**:279; **23**:224

Orenstein, Gloria Feman
Fernando Arrabal **18**:20

Orfalea, Greg
William Stafford **29**:383

Orgel, Doris
Emily Cheney Neville **12**:453
Barbara Wersba **30**:431

Oriard, Michael
Don DeLillo **13**:175

Orme, John
Bob Marley **17**:273

Ormerod, Beverley
Édouard Glissant **10**:230

Ormerod, David
V. S. Naipaul **4**:371

Ornstein, Jacob
Camilo José Cela **4**:95

O'Rourke, William
James Carroll **38**:110
Rosalyn Drexler **2**:120
Craig Nova **7**:267

Orr, Gregory
Robert Bly **38**:50
Josephine Miles **34**:244

Orr, Leonard
Richard Condon **4**:107

Orr, Nancy Young
Barbara Corcoran **17**:69

Ortega, Julio
José María Arguedas **18**:7, 8

Orth, Maureen
Bob Dylan **3**:130
Stevie Wonder **12**:657

Ortiz, Alfonso
Vine Deloria, Jr. **21**:111

Ortiz, Gloria M.
Pablo Neruda **7**:260

Ortiz, Miguel A.
Alice Childress **12**:108
Nicholosa Mohr **12**:448

Ortiz, Simon J.
Leslie Marmon Silko **23**:412

Ortmayer, Roger
Federico Fellini **16**:286

Orton, Gavin
Eyvind Johnson **14**:294

Orwell, George
Alex Comfort **7**:52
Graham Greene **6**:216
Arthur Koestler **33**:227
P. G. Wodehouse **22**:480

Osborn, John Jay, Jr.
George V. Higgins **18**:234

Osborn, Neal J.
Kenneth Burke **2**:87

Osborne, Charles
William Faulkner **1**:102
W. Somerset Maugham **1**:204

Osborne, David
Albert Camus **2**:99

Osborne, John
Noël Coward **29**:140
Joe McGinniss **32**:299

Osborne, Linda B.
Sylvia Ashton-Warner **19**:24
Ella Leffland **19**:278

Osborne, Linda Barrett
Betsy Byars **35**:74
Zibby Oneal **30**:281

Osborne, Trudie
Madeleine L'Engle **12**:345

Osgood, Eugenia V.
Julien Gracq **11**:244

Osler, Ruth
Roderick L. Haig-Brown **21**:139

Osnos, Peter
Andrea Lee **36**:252
Martin Cruz Smith **25**:413

Ostriker, Alicia
Ai **4**:16
Louise Bogan **39**:387
Cid Corman **9**:170
Alan Dugan **2**:121
Elizabeth Frank **39**:387
Paul Goodman **7**:131
William Harmon **38**:242
John Hollander **14**:262
Maxine Kumin **28**:224
Sylvia Plath **17**:348
Adrienne Rich **36**:372
Susan Sontag **31**:405
May Swenson **14**:518
Anne Waldman **7**:508

Ostroff, Anthony
Donald Justice **6**:271
Kathleen Spivack **6**:520
Mark Van Doren **6**:542

Ostrom, Alan
William Carlos Williams **1**:370

Ostrovsky, Erika
Louis-Ferdinand Céline **4**:98

O'Toole, Lawrence
Werner Herzog **16**:335
John Landis **26**:274
Paul Schrader **26**:398

Ott, Bill
Maya Angelou **35**:30
T. J. Binyon **34**:32
Pete Dexter **34**:43
Stephen King **26**:240
Ross Thomas **39**:247
Sloan Wilson **32**:449

Ottaway, Robert
John Cheever **25**:122

Otten, Anna
  Heinrich Böll **2**:66
  Michel Butor **8**:120; **15**:120
  Robert Pinget **37**:363
  Alain Robbe-Grillet **6**:467;
    8:453
  Nathalie Sarraute **2**:386;
    31:380, 382
  Claude Simon **4**:497; **39**:215

Ottenberg, Eve
  Rosellen Brown **32**:65
  Erskine Caldwell **14**:95
  Elizabeth Jane Howard **29**:247
  William Kotzwinkle **35**:256
  Vonda N. McIntyre **18**:327
  James Schuyler **23**:389
  Alexander Theroux **25**:432

Oughton, John
  Marilyn Bowering **32**:48

Overbey, David L.
  Luis Buñuel **16**:151
  Claude Chabrol **16**:178
  Werner Herzog **16**:324, 333
  Fritz Lang **20**:212
  Richard Lester **20**:227

Överland, Orm
  Arthur Miller **15**:371

Oviedo, José Miguel
  Mario Vargas Llosa **10**:497,
    500

Owen, Carys T.
  Louis-Ferdinand Céline **9**:155

Owen, I. M.
  Robertson Davies **7**:72
  Thomas Flanagan **25**:164
  Mavis Gallant **18**:173
  Audrey Thomas **37**:417

Owen, Ivon
  Robertson Davies **13**:171

Owen, Roger
  David Caute **29**:124

Owens, Brad
  Mark Harris **19**:205
  Lewis Thomas **35**:411
  John Kennedy Toole **19**:442

Owens, Iris
  Lois Gould **4**:200

Owens, Rochelle
  Diane Wakoski **7**:505

Owens, Tony J.
  William Faulkner **18**:145

Ower, John
  Frank Herbert **12**:273
  Mordecai Richler **9**:451
  Edith Sitwell **9**:494

Ower, John B.
  Edith Sitwell **2**:404

Ownbey, Steve
  George V. Higgins **10**:273
  Georges Simenon **8**:486

Owomoyela, Oyekan
  Chester Himes **7**:159

Oxenhandler, Neal
  Jean Cocteau **16**:225
  Jean Genet **14**:203
  Robert Pinget **37**:361

Oxley, Brian
  Geoffrey Hill **18**:240

Ozick, Cynthia
  Saul Bellow **10**:43; **33**:67
  Frederick Buechner **2**:83
  Truman Capote **38**:82
  J. M. Coetzee **33**:107
  Mark Harris **19**:202
  Bernard Malamud **11**:346
  Hugh Nissenson **4**:380
  Isaac Bashevis Singer **38**:407

Pa Chin
  Pa Chin **18**:371

Pace, David
  Claude Lévi-Strauss **38**:309

Pace, Eric
  Paul E. Erdman **25**:154
  Heinrich Böll **39**:293
  Joseph Wambaugh **3**:508

Pace, Mary Kathleen
  Suzanne Newton **35**:300

Pacernick, Gary
  Millen Brand **7**:30

Pacey, Desmond
  Ralph Gustafson **36**:213
  F. R. Scott **22**:371
  Miriam Waddington **28**:436

Pachter, Henry
  Paul Goodman **7**:129

Pachter, Henry M.
  Hermann Hesse **6**:236

Pacifici, Sergio J.
  Dino Buzzati **36**:87, 90
  Elio Vittorini **14**:543

Pack, Robert
  James Schevill **7**:400
  Mark Strand **18**:514
  Nancy Willard **37**:463

Packard, Nancy H.
  Grace Paley **6**:393

Packard, Rosalie
  Art Buchwald **33**:90

Packard, William
  Kenneth Patchen **18**:394

Paddock, Lisa
  William Faulkner **18**:147

Page, James A.
  James Baldwin **3**:32
  Ralph Ellison **3**:145
  Richard Wright **3**:546

Page, Malcolm
  John Arden **13**:25
  Alan Ayckbourn **33**:48

Pagès, Irène M.
  Simone de Beauvoir **14**:68

Paige, Nancy E.
  Zoa Sherburne **30**:362

Palandri, Angela Jung
  Ch'ien Chung-shu **22**:107

Palencia-Roth, Michael
  Günter Grass **22**:191

Palevsky, Joan
  Isak Dinesen **10**:148

Paley, Bruce
  Waylon Jennings **21**:205

Paley, Maggie
  Laura Nyro **17**:313

Palley, Julian
  Azorín **11**:25

Palmer, Eustace
  Chinua Achebe **7**:5
  Ayi Kwei Armah **33**:35
  Mongo Beti **27**:49
  James Ngugi **7**:265
  Ngugi wa Thiong'o **36**:315
  Amos Tutuola **29**:437

Palmer, James W.
  Francis Ford Coppola **16**:242

Palmer, Penelope
  Charles Tomlinson **6**:536

Palmer, R. Roderick
  Haki R. Madhubuti **6**:313
  Sonia Sanchez **5**:382

Palmer, Robert
  Ray Davies **21**:92, 93
  Smokey Robinson **21**:346, 349
  Sam Shepard **17**:445

Palmer, Tony
  Bob Dylan **12**:196
  Jimmy Page and Robert Plant
    12:481

Pancella, John R.
  Robert Newton Peck **17**:340

Panek, LeRoy L.
  Ian Fleming **30**:147

Paniagua, Lita
  Luis Buñuel **16**:134

Panichas, George A.
  F. R. Leavis **24**:306

Pannick, David
  John Mortimer **28**:287

Pannick, Gerald J.
  R. P. Blackmur **24**:68

Panshin, Alexei
  C. J. Cherryh **35**:104
  Robert A. Heinlein **3**:224
  Fritz Leiber **25**:305

Panshin, Cory
  C. J. Cherryh **35**:104
  Fritz Leiber **25**:305

Panter-Downes, Mollie
  Robert Bolt **14**:91
  John Le Carré **9**:327

Paolucci, Anne
  Federico Fellini **16**:278

Papatzonis, Takis
  Giuseppe Ungaretti **11**:557

Parachini, Allan
  Waylon Jennings **21**:202
  Garry Trudeau **12**:589

Parameswaran, Uma
  Derek Walcott **9**:557

Pareles, Jon
  Joan Armatrading **17**:9
  Walter Becker and Donald
    Fagen **26**:84
  David Byrne **26**:96, 98
  Elvis Costello **21**:70
  Ray Davies **21**:104
  Bob Dylan **12**:197
  Mick Jagger and Keith Richard
    17:240
  Kris Kristofferson **26**:269
  Joni Mitchell **12**:443
  Prince **35**:332
  William Trevor **25**:446
  Frank Zappa **17**:593, 594

Parente, Diane A.
  James Dickey **10**:142
  Isabelle Holland **21**:149

Parente, Margaret
  Scott O'Dell **30**:277

Parente, William J.
  Alexsandr I. Solzhenitsyn
    10:479

Paretsky, Sara
  Agatha Christie **39**:442
  Janet Morgan **39**:442

Parham, Sidney F.
  Peter Weiss **15**:568

Parini, Jay
  Alfred Corn **33**:120
  Peter Davison **28**:103
  Louise Glück **22**:176
  Thom Gunn **32**:210
  Daniel Halpern **14**:232
  Seamus Heaney **25**:244
  Edward Hirsch **31**:215
  Brad Leithauser **27**:241
  Christopher Middleton **13**:388
  Joyce Carol Oates **33**:296
  Katha Pollitt **28**:367
  Susan Sontag **31**:418
  Anne Stevenson **33**:381
  Robert Penn Warren **39**:258

Parish, Maggie
  Barbara Wersba **30**:433

Parish, Margaret
  Barbara Wersba **30**:433

Parisi, John
  M. L. Rosenthal **28**:398

Parisi, Joseph
  Vicente Aleixandre **36**:32
  James Carroll **38**:105
  Robert Frost **34**:473
  X. J. Kennedy **8**:320
  Carolyn Kizer **39**:169
  Josephine Miles **34**:244
  William H. Pritchard **34**:473
  Susan Fromberg Schaeffer
    11:491
  Mark Van Doren **6**:543
  Robert Penn Warren **18**:536

Park, Clara Claiborne
Brigid Brophy **6**:99
Maxine Kumin **28**:224
James Merrill **13**:377; **18**:330
Stanley Plumly **33**:312
Manuel Puig **28**:371
Luisa Valenzuela **31**:437
Richard Wilbur **9**:568

Park, John G.
Shirley Jackson **11**:302

Park, Sue Simpson
Gwendolyn Brooks **15**:94
Joyce Carol Oates **11**:400

Parke, Andrea
Mary Stolz **12**:548

Parker, A. A.
Edwin Honig **33**:214

Parker, Barbara
Kem Nunn **34**:94

Parker, Dorothy
S. J. Perelman **23**:335
P. G. Wodehouse **22**:478

Parker, Dorothy L.
Pamela Hansford Johnson
27:221

Parker, Geoffrey
Jonathan Keates **34**:202

Parker, John M.
Autran Dourado **23**:151

Parkes, K. S.
Martin Walser **27**:463

Parkes, Stuart
Martin Walser **27**:462

Parkhill-Rathbone, James
C. P. Snow **1**:317; **6**:518

Parkinson, Robert C.
Frank Herbert **12**:271

Parkinson, Thomas
Robert Lowell **1**:179, 180
Gary Snyder **1**:317; **32**:398

Parks, John G.
Lewis Thomas **35**:410

Parr, J. L.
Calder Willingham **5**:510

Parrinder, Patrick
Philip K. Dick **10**:138
B. S. Johnson **9**:302
David Lodge **36**:270
V. S. Naipaul **18**:360
Frederik Pohl **18**:411

Parris, Robert
Françoise Sagan **17**:418

Parrish, Anne
Esther Forbes **12**:202

Parrish, Paul A.
Elizabeth Bowen **11**:59

Parry, Idris
Elias Canetti **25**:108
Hermann Hesse **25**:261

Parsons, Ann
William Carlos Williams **2**:469

Parsons, Gordon
Ruth M. Arthur **12**:27
Leon Garfield **12**:231, 241
Mollie Hunter **21**:156, 158, 167

Parsons, I. M.
Agatha Christie **12**:112

Parsons, Jerry L.
Jack Vance **35**:421, 422, 427

Parsons, Robert A.
Robert Holdstock **39**:153

Parsons, Thornton H.
John Crowe Ransom **2**:364

Parton, Margaret
Timothy Findley **27**:140
Kamala Markandaya **38**:323

Partridge, Marianne
Patti Smith **12**:538

Partridge, Ralph
Agatha Christie **12**:113, 114
Edmund Crispin **22**:108, 109

Partridge, Robert
Willie Nelson **17**:304

Pascal, Roy
Georg Lukács **24**:332

Pascal, Sylvia
Stephen King **26**:239

Pascale, Jim
Sumner Locke Elliott **38**:181

Paschall, Douglas
Theodore Roethke **3**:434

Pasinetti, P. M.
Eleanor Clark **19**:105

Pasolli, Robert
Sam Shepard **17**:434

Pasquariello, Ronald D., F.M.S.
Elie Wiesel **37**:457

Paterson, Gary H.
Kevin Major **26**:285
Norma Fox Mazer **26**:296

Paterson, Katherine
Anita Desai **19**:135
Virginia Hamilton **26**:158
Bette Bao Lord **23**:278
Rosemary Wells **12**:639

Patrouch, Joseph F., Jr.
Isaac Asimov **19**:24
Stephen King **37**:204

Patten, Brian
Isaac Asimov **3**:17
Kurt Vonnegut, Jr. **3**:504

Patten, Frederick
Stephen King **12**:310
Andre Norton **12**:471
Roger Zelazny **21**:468

Patten, Karl
Graham Greene **1**:131

Patterson, Lindsay
Eldridge Cleaver **30**:62

Patterson, Mary Louise
Andrea Lee **36**:253

Patterson, Patricia
Paul Schrader **26**:386

Patterson, Rob
Martin Mull **17**:300

Pattison, Barrie
Brian De Palma **20**:77

Pattow, Donald J.
Dashiell Hammett **19**:198

Paul, Jay S.
William Goyen **14**:211, 212

Paul, Louis
John Steinbeck **21**:365

Paul, Sherman
Paul Goodman **1**:123
Charles Olson **11**:420
Boris Pasternak **7**:295
Edmund Wilson **1**:373

Pauli, David N.
Scott O'Dell **30**:277

Paulin, Tom
Kingsley Amis **13**:15
Martin Amis **38**:13
Robin Cook **14**:131
Robert Coover **15**:145
Thomas Flanagan **25**:167
John Fowles **10**:189
Patricia Highsmith **14**:261
Dan Jacobson **14**:290
Benedict Kiely **23**:264
Jerzy Kosinski **10**:308
Seán O'Faoláin **14**:406
Jim Shepard **36**:405
William Trevor **14**:536
Ian McEwan **13**:370
Barbara Pym **13**:469

Pauls, Ted
Roger Zelazny **21**:464

Pauly, Rebecca M.
Kurt Vonnegut, Jr. **12**:609

Pauly, Thomas H.
John Ford **16**:313

Pautz, Peter D.
Robert Bloch **33**:84

Pavletich, Aida
Joan Armatrading **17**:11
Janis Ian **21**:188
Laura Nyro **17**:321
Buffy Sainte-Marie **17**:431

Pawel, Ernst
Heinrich Böll **2**:67; **9**:109
Peter Handke **38**:221
Hermann Hesse **2**:192
Jakov Lind **2**:245
Martin Walser **27**:467

Paxford, Sandra
Noel Streatfeild **21**:410

Payne, James Robert
Imamu Amiri Baraka **14**:48

Payne, Jocelyn
David Slavitt **14**:491

Payne, Margaret
Mildred D. Taylor **21**:421

Payne, Robert
Winston Graham **23**:193
Kamala Markandaya **38**:322
Yuri Olesha **8**:432
Boris Pasternak **7**:292
Mary Renault **17**:397
Rosemary Sutcliff **26**:432

Paz, Octavio
Elizabeth Bishop **9**:89
André Breton **9**:129
Alexsandr I. Solzhenitsyn
10:478
William Carlos Williams **5**:508

Peabody, Richard, Jr.
Leon Edel **34**:537
Scott Sommer **25**:426

Peacock, Allen
Frederick Busch **18**:86

Peacock, R.
T. S. Eliot **24**:184

Pearce, Howard D.
Paul Green **25**:198, 199

Pearce, Philippa
Alan Garner **17**:136
Philippa Pearce **21**:288

Pearce, Richard
Saul Bellow **8**:72
John Dos Passos **8**:181
John Hawkes **9**:266
Henry Roth **6**:473
William Styron **11**:515

Pearce, Roy Harvey
Robert Frost **26**:120

Pearlman, Sandy
Ray Davies **21**:89
Jim Morrison **17**:287
Lou Reed **21**:302

Pearson, Alan
Joe Rosenblatt **15**:447

Pearson, Carol
Joseph Heller **11**:265

Pearson, Gabriel
John Berryman **2**:55
T. S. Eliot **13**:192
Leslie A. Fiedler **24**:202

Pearson, Haydn S.
Roderick L. Haig-Brown
21:137, 138

Pearson, Ian
W. P. Kinsella **27**:238

Pearson, Norman Holmes
Ezra Pound **2**:340

Pearson, Richard
Taylor Caldwell **39**:303
Robert Graves **39**:324
Jesse Stuart **34**:373

Pease, Howard
Henry Gregor Felsen **17**:121
John R. Tunis **12**:596

Critic Index

Peavy, Charles D.
Larry McMurtry 27:324
Hubert Selby, Jr. 1:306
Melvin Van Peebles 20:410

Pechter, William S.
Lindsay Anderson 20:16
Ingmar Bergman 16:48
Frank Capra 16:158
John Cassavetes 20:49
Francis Ford Coppola 16:234,
238
Federico Fellini 16:282
Elaine May 16:432
Satyajit Ray 16:482, 494
Jean Renoir 20:298
Andrew Lloyd Webber and Tim
Rice 21:429
Orson Welles 20:448
Lina Wertmüller 16:589

Peck, Richard
Robert Cormier 12:135
Lois Duncan 26:104
Katherine Paterson 12:485
Richard Peck 21:30

Peckham, Morse
Wayne C. Booth 24:98

Peden, William
James Baldwin 8:40
Doris Betts 6:70; 28:33
Paul Bowles 19:58
Ed Bullins 7:37
John Cheever 7:49
Laurie Colwin 5:108
James T. Farrell 8:205
Ernest J. Gaines 11:217
Mavis Gallant 18:170
Shirley Ann Grau 9:240
Chester Himes 7:159
Langston Hughes 10:281
Grace Paley 6:392
Ann Petry 7:305
William Saroyan 8:468
Mary Lee Settle 19:409
Irwin Shaw 7:411
Isaac Bashevis Singer 6:509
Jesse Stuart 8:507
Peter Taylor 18:523
Tennessee Williams 5:502
Richard Wright 14:596

Peel, Mark
John Lennon 35:275
Paul McCartney 35:291
Prince 35:331
Bob Seger 35:386

Peel, Marie
John Osborne 2:329
Peter Redgrove 6:445, 446
Penelope Shuttle 7:423
Alan Sillitoe 3:448
David Storey 2:425
R. S. Thomas 6:531

Peet, Creighton
Franklyn M. Branley 21:15
Robert A. Heinlein 26:160

Pekar, Harvey
Robert Crumb 17:82
Frank Zappa 17:585

Pelham, Philip
Dick Francis 22:151

Pelli, Moshe
S. Y. Agnn 8:8

Pelorus
Judy Blume 12:45
Robert Cormier 12:135
Alan Garner 17:147

Peltier, Ed
Peter Weir 20:424

Pemberton, Clive
Leon Garfield 12:219

Pendergast, Constance
Mavis Gallant 18:171

Pendleton, Dennis
Douglas Unger 34:114

Penner, Allen R.
Alan Sillitoe 1:308

Penner, Dick
Vladimir Nabokov 15:395

Penner, Jonathan
Margaret Atwood 25:69
Hortense Calisher 38:73
André Dubus 36:143
Carlos Fuentes 22:171
Graham Greene 18:196
Jonathan Keates 34:203
William Kennedy 28:204
V. S. Pritchett 15:443
Philip Roth 15:450
Susan Richards Shreve 23:483
Richard Yates 23:480

Pennington, Jane
Walter Dean Myers 35:296

Pennington, Lee
Jesse Stuart 11:508; 34:373

Penta, Anne Constance
Jane Rule 27:417

Peppard, Murray B.
Friedrich Dürrenmatt 1:81

Pepper, Nancy
Anaïs Nin 11:399

Perazzini, Randolph
Robert Frost 13:229

Percy, Walker
Walter M. Miller, Jr. 4:352
Marion Montgomery 7:232
Jean-Paul Sartre 13:506
John Kennedy Toole 19:441
Eudora Welty 1:362

Percy, William
Joy Adamson 17:2

Perebinossoff, Phillipe R.
Jean Renoir 20:308

Perera, Victor
Miguel Ángel Asturias 3:18

Pérez, Genaro J.
Juan Goytisolo 23:185

Perez, Gilberto
Beryl Bainbridge 10:16
Ingmar Bergman 16:81
Werner Herzog 16:335
Yuri Krotkov 19:266
Alan Sillitoe 10:477
Anne Tyler 11:553

Pérez Firmat, Gustavo
José Lezama Lima 10:319

Perkins, David
W. H. Auden 11:19
Richard Eberhart 11:179
Howard Nemerov 36:304
Ezra Pound 3:397
Carl Sandburg 10:449

Perkins, Elizabeth
Christina Stead 32:412

Perkins, Huel D.
Kristin Hunter 35:227
John A. Williams 13:599

Perlberg, Mark
Larry Eigner 9:181
Michael S. Harper 7:138
George Oppen 7:285

Perloff, Marjorie
Donald Hall 37:143

Perloff, Marjorie G.
John Berryman 2:59
Aimé Césaire 32:112
Ed Dorn 10:156
Clayton Eshleman 7:99
Thom Gunn 3:216
Seamus Heaney 25:250
Ted Hughes 2:204; 4:235
Richard F. Hugo 6:244
Erica Jong 6:270
Galway Kinnell 2:230
Denise Levertov 2:243
Philip Levine 33:273
Robert Lowell 1:181
Frank O'Hara 2:322; 5:325;
13:425
Charles Olson 11:415
Sylvia Plath 9:432; 17:368
Ezra Pound 10:400
Adrienne Rich 7:369; 36:369
Françoise Sagan 6:482
May Sarton 14:481
Mark Van Doren 10:496
Mona Van Duyn 3:492
Diane Wakoski 7:504
John Wieners 7:537
James Wright 3:542, 544

Perrick, Eve
Ira Levin 3:294

Perrin, Noel
James Gould Cozzens 11:132
Walter D. Edmonds 35:155
Wright Morris 37:314

Perrine, Laurence
John Ciardi 10:105

Perry, Charles
Andrew Lloyd Webber and Tim
Rice 21:431

Perry, Frank
C. S. Adler 35:13

Perry, Nick
J. G. Ballard 36:35

Perry, R. C.
Rolf Hochhuth 11:276

Perry, Ruth
Doris Lessing 15:330

Pershing, Amy
Pete Dexter 34:44

Peseroff, Joyce
Sharon Olds 32:346

Peter, John
Alan Ayckbourn 33:42
Edward Bond 13:102
William Golding 17:158
Stephen Poliakoff 38:383

Peterkiewicz, Jerzy
Witold Gombrowicz 4:195
Alain Robbe-Grillet 4:447

Peterkin, Julia
Paul Green 25:194

Peterman, Michael A.
Farley Mowat 26:340

Peters, Andrew
Steven Goldsberry 34:55

Peters, Daniel James
Thomas Pynchon 3:412

Peters, Jonathan
Chinua Achebe 26:25

Peters, Julie Stone
Maxine Kumin 28:223

Peters, Margot
Agatha Christie 12:119
Robert B. Parker 27:364
J.I.M. Stewart 14:512

Peters, Robert
Ted Berrigan 37:45
Charles Bukowski 5:80
Clayton Eshleman 7:99
Michael McClure 6:317
W. D. Snodgrass 18:492
Gary Snyder 32:397
Anne Waldman 7:508
Robert Penn Warren 39:263

Peters, Robert L.
Hollis Summers 10:493

Peters, Ted
Erich von Däniken 30:424

Petersen, Carol
Max Frisch 18:160

Petersen, Clarence
Nora Ephron 17:110
Charles M. Schulz 12:527
Wilfrid Sheed 2:392

Petersen, Fred
Ernesto Sabato 23:376

Petersen, Gwenn Boardman
Yukio Mishima 27:341
Jun'ichirō Tanizaki 28:415

Peterson, Levi S.
Edward Abbey 36:11
A. B. Guthrie, Jr. 23:200

Peterson, Linda Kauffmann
Betsy Byars **35**:75

Peterson, Mary
Jayne Anne Phillips **15**:419

Peterson, Maurice
Sidney Poitier **26**:360

Peterson, Richard F.
Mary Lavin **18**:303

Peterson, Susan
Steve Martin **30**:246

Peterson, Virgilia
Sylvia Ashton-Warner **19**:22
Hortense Calisher **38**:72
Jan de Hartog **19**:131
Michel del Castillo **38**:165
Elizabeth Jane Howard **29**:243
Primo Levi **37**:222
Betty Smith **19**:424
George Tabori **19**:436
Henri Troyat **23**:458
Jessamyn West **17**:548
Monique Wittig **22**:471

Petit, Christopher
Peter Townshend **17**:539

Petric, Vlada
Carl Theodor Dreyer **16**:266

Petrie, Graham
Jean Renoir **20**:302
Eric Rohmer **16**:529
François Truffaut **20**:386

Petrie, Paul
A. Alvarez **5**:16

Petroski, Catherine
Penelope Gilliatt **13**:237

Petrović, Njegoš M.
Dobrica Ćosić **14**:132

Petticoffer, Dennis
Richard Brautigan **12**:73

Pettigrew, John
D. J. Enright **31**:146

Pettingell, Phoebe
John Ashbery **25**:54
Ernesto Cardenal **31**:79
Alfred Corn **33**:117
Allen Ginsberg **36**:192
Donald Hall **1**:137
Anthony Hecht **19**:207
Edward Hirsch **31**:214
John Hollander **14**:266
Barbara Howes **15**:289
Brad Leithauser **27**:241
Philip Levine **9**:332; **14**:320
Robert Lowell **8**:353
James Merrill **13**:382
Howard Nemerov **36**:301, 309
Carl Sandburg **35**:358
John Wain **11**:563
Robert Penn Warren **39**:257

Pettit, Arthur G.
Sam Peckinpah **20**:280

Pettit, Michael
Paul Bowles **19**:59

Pettit, Philip
J.R.R. Tolkien **3**:483

Petts, Margo
H. F. Brinsmead **21**:32

Pevear, Richard
A. R. Ammons **3**:10
Wendell Berry **27**:38
Charles Causley **7**:42
Guy Davenport, Jr. **14**:139
Richmond Lattimore **3**:277
Denise Levertov **3**:292
Hugh MacDiarmid **4**:313
James Merrill **3**:334
Pablo Neruda **5**:301
George Oppen **7**:286
Peter Porter **13**:452
Ezra Pound **2**:343
Louis Zukofsky **7**:563

Pew, Thomas W., Jr.
Gary Snyder **32**:394

Peyre, Henri
Marcel Aymé **11**:21
Simone de Beauvoir **1**:19
Albert Camus **1**:53; **14**:106
Louis-Ferdinand Céline **1**:57
René Char **9**:162
Georges Duhamel **8**:186
Romain Gary **25**:184, 186
Jean Giono **4**:185
Julien Green **3**:203
Violette Leduc **22**:261
André Malraux **1**:201
François Mauriac **4**:338
Henri de Montherlant **19**:324
Raymond Queneau **5**:358
Alain Robbe-Grillet **4**:446
Jules Romains **7**:383
Nathalie Sarraute **4**:464
Jean-Paul Sartre **1**:305
Claude Simon **4**:494
Henri Troyat **23**:458, 459, 460

Pfaff, William
Alejo Carpentier **38**:89

Pfeffercorn, Eli
Abraham B. Yehoshua **13**:616

Pfeiffer, John
Jean M. Auel **31**:22
Franklyn M. Branley **21**:16

Pfeiffer, John R.
John Brunner **8**:105
Octavia E. Butler **38**:66

Pfeil, Fred
John Berger **19**:40
Luis Rafael Sánchez **23**:385

Pfeiler, William K.
Erich Maria Remarque **21**:329

Phelan, Kappo
Tennessee Williams **30**:456

Phelps, Donald
Fielding Dawson **6**:125
Gilbert Sorrentino **7**:451

Phelps, Paul B.
Bienvenido N. Santos **22**:366

Phelps, Robert
Helen MacInnes **27**:280
Walter M. Miller, Jr. **30**:254
Dan Wakefield **7**:502

Phelps, William Lyon
Van Wyck Brooks **29**:79

Philip, Neil
Iain Banks **34**:30
Maureen Duffy **37**:117
Elaine Feinstein **36**:171
Ted Hughes **37**:178
Diana Wynne Jones **26**:230
Rosemary Sutcliff **26**:440, 441
Jill Paton Walsh **35**:434

Phillips, Allen W.
Octavio Paz **3**:376

Phillips, Cassandra
Raymond Carver **22**:98

Phillips, Delbert
Yevgeny Yevtushenko **3**:547

Phillips, Frank Lamont
Maya Angelou **12**:12

Phillips, Gene D.
Ken Russell **16**:551

Phillips, James A.
Vine Deloria, Jr. **21**:109
Pat Jordan **37**:194

Phillips, James E.
Laurence Olivier **20**:237

Phillips, Jayne Anne
Don DeLillo **39**:119

Phillips, Klaus
Jurek Becker **19**:35

Phillips, Michael Joseph
Richard Kostelanetz **28**:218

Phillips, Norma
Alan Sillitoe **6**:501

Phillips, Robert
A. R. Ammons **25**:45
John Berryman **25**:90
Philip Booth **23**:77
Hortense Calisher **8**:125
Arthur A. Cohen **7**:52
Don DeLillo **39**:126
James T. Farrell **4**:158
Allen Ginsberg **6**:199
William Goyen **5**:148, 149;
14:213
William Heyen **18**:231
Richard Howard **10**:275
James Jones **39**:405
Carolyn Kizer **39**:170
Robert Lowell **4**:303
Frank MacShane **39**:405
Bernard Malamud **3**:325
Carson McCullers **4**:345;
12:432
James Alan McPherson **19**:310
Brian Moore **7**:239
Joyce Carol Oates **11**:404;
33:288
Jayne Anne Phillips **33**:308
Anne Sexton **15**:470
Patrick White **4**:586
Marya Zaturenska **11**:579

Phillips, Robert L., Jr.
Eudora Welty **33**:419

Phillips, Steven R.
Ernest Hemingway **3**:241

Phillips, William
Susan Sontag **31**:409
Edmund Wilson **24**:474

Phillipson, John S.
Vine Deloria, Jr. **21**:109
Howard Fast **23**:161

Phillipson, Michael
Lucien Goldmann **24**:250

Philpott, Joan
Josephine Humphreys **34**:63

Piacentino, Edward J.
T. S. Stribling **23**:449

Piazza, Paul
Christopher Isherwood **14**:281
John Knowles **26**:263

Picard, Raymond
Roland Barthes **24**:23

Piccarella, John
David Byrne **26**:96
The Clash **30**:45, 49
Pink Floyd **35**:315
Smokey Robinson **21**:351

Piccione, Anthony
Stanley Plumly **33**:310

Piccoli, Raffaello
Riccardo Bacchelli **19**:30

Pichaske, David R.
John Lennon and Paul
McCartney **12**:373

Pick, Robert
Ronald Harwood **32**:222
Erich Maria Remarque **21**:329
Frank Yerby **7**:556

Pickar, G. B.
Martin Walser **27**:461

Pickar, Gertrud B.
Max Frisch **14**:181

Pickar, Gertrud Bauer
Martin Walser **27**:458

Pickard, Connie
Basil Bunting **39**:299

Pickering, Felix
Benedict Kiely **23**:264

Pickering, James S.
Alvin Silverstein and Virginia
B. Silverstein **17**:450

Pickering, Sam, Jr.
Anthony Powell **7**:338
P. G. Wodehouse **5**:517

Pickering, Samuel
Alan Garner **17**:151

Pickering, Samuel F., Jr.
Peter Matthiessen **32**:290
Joyce Carol Oates **6**:369

Pickford, John
J. B. Priestley **34**:366

Pickrel, Paul
Heinrich Böll **27**:54
L. P. Hartley **22**:211
Kamala Markandaya **38**:322
Aldo Palazzeschi **11**:431
Sylvia Townsend Warner **7**:511

Critic Index

Picon, Gaëtan
Jean Anouilh **13**:21
Michel Butor **8**:119
Albert Camus **9**:144
Henri Michaux **8**:392

Piehl, Kathy
Thomas J. Fleming **37**:129
M. E. Kerr **35**:250

Piehler, Heide
D. M. Pinkwater **35**:320

Pierce, Hazel
Isaac Asimov **26**:41

Piercy, Marge
Alta **19**:18
Margaret Atwood **3**:20
Margaret Laurence **6**:289
Judith Rossner **29**:353
Joanna Russ **15**:461
Alice Walker **9**:557

Pietrzyk, Leslie
Pam Durban **39**:46

Pifer, Ellen
Vladimir Nabokov **23**:312

Pigaga, Thom
John Hollander **2**:197

Piggott, Stuart
David Jones **4**:261

Pike, B. A.
Margery Allingham **19**:13, 14, 15, 16, 17, 18

Pike, C. R.
Arkadii Strugatskii and Boris Strugatskii **27**:437

Pilger, John
Michael Cimino **16**:211
Joan Didion **32**:145

Pinchin, Jane Lagoudis
Lawrence Durrell **13**:186
E. M. Forster **13**:220

Pinckney, Darryl
James Baldwin **17**:44
Russell Banks **37**:25
Imamu Amiri Baraka **14**:48
Bret Easton Ellis **39**:59
Jacob Epstein **19**:163
Gayl Jones **9**:307
Nettie Jones **34**:69
June Jordan **23**:257
Paule Marshall **27**:315
Jay McInerney **34**:84
Toni Morrison **22**:322
John Rechy **18**:442
Michael Thelwell **22**:415
Jean Toomer **22**:429
Richard Wright **9**:585

Pinckney, Josephine
Zora Neale Hurston **30**:208

Pincus, Richard Eliot
Theodore Sturgeon **22**:412

Pinkerton, Jan
Peter Taylor **1**:333

Pinsker, Sanford
Leslie A. Fiedler **24**:204
Joanne Greenberg **30**:166
Frederick Karl **34**:551
Alfred Kazin **34**:561
Bernard Malamud **3**:322; **18**:321
Joyce Carol Oates **11**:402
Philip Roth **31**:337
Isaac Bashevis Singer **3**:454
John Updike **7**:489

Pinsky, Robert
John Berryman **8**:93
Frank Bidart **33**:75
Elizabeth Bishop **15**:61; **32**:33, 38
J. V. Cunningham **31**:104
Seamus Heaney **25**:249; **37**:167
Ted Hughes **9**:282
Philip Larkin **33**:268
Philip Levine **9**:332
Cynthia MacDonald **13**:355
Theodore Roethke **8**:461
Raphael Rudnik **7**:384
Mark Strand **18**:517

Piper, John
John Betjeman **34**:307

Pipes, Charles D.
Eva Figes **31**:162

Pipkin, Vicki
Neil Diamond **30**:113

Pippett, Aileen
Isabel Colegate **36**:110
Julia W. Cunningham **12**:163
Frank Tuohy **37**:428

Pippett, Roger
John Mortimer **28**:282

Pirie, Bruce
Timothy Findley **27**:142

Pit
Richard O'Brien **17**:323

Pitou, Spire
Jean Cayrol **11**:110

Pittock, Malcolm
Ivy Compton-Burnett **10**:108

Pivovarnick, John
Louis L'Amour **25**:282

Plaice, S. N.
Siegfried Lenz **27**:255

Planchart, Alejandro Enrique
John Lennon and Paul McCartney **12**:359

Plant, Richard
Heinrich Böll **27**:58
Anne Chislett **34**:145
Eleanor Clark **19**:105
Mavis Gallant **38**:192
Gregor von Rezzori **25**:381
Judith Thompson **39**:253
Henri Troyat **23**:457

Plater, William M.
Thomas Pynchon **18**:433

Plath, Sara
Ted Berrigan **37**:45
Sharon Olds **32**:345

Platt, Charles
William Gibson **39**:140

Platypus, Bill
C. S. Forester **35**:173

Platzner, Robert L.
J. G. Ballard **36**:44

Pleasants, Ben
Lisa St. Aubin de Teran **36**:421

Pleszczynski, Wladyslaw
James A. Michener **29**:317

Plomer, William
C. S. Forester **35**:161
Ayn Rand **30**:292
Rebecca West **31**:453

Plumb, J. H.
Antonia Fraser **32**:185

Plumb, Robert K.
Roy A. Gallant **17**:126

Plumly, Stanley
Alfred Corn **33**:116
Carolyn Forché **25**:169
Marilyn Hacker **23**:205
Lisel Mueller **13**:399
Charles Simic **22**:381
James Tate **25**:428
C. K. Williams **33**:445

Plummer, William
Jerome Charyn **18**:99
John M. Del Vecchio **29**:149
Stanley Elkin **14**:157
Jerzy Kosinski **10**:306

Poague, Leland A.
Frank Capra **16**:162
Bob Dylan **6**:156

Pochoda, Elizabeth
Djuna Barnes **11**:30
Milan Kundera **19**:268
Tim O'Brien **19**:357

Pochoda, Elizabeth Turner
Anna Kavan **13**:316
Tadeusz Konwicki **8**:327
Alan Lelchuk **5**:245
Joyce Carol Oates **6**:373

Podhoretz, John
David Lodge **36**:276

Podhoretz, Norman
James Baldwin **1**:13, 14
Saul Bellow **1**:28
Albert Camus **1**:52
J. P. Donleavy **1**:75
George P. Elliott **2**:130
William Faulkner **1**:98
William Golding **17**:160
Paul Goodman **1**:123
Joseph Heller **1**:139
Thomas Hinde **6**:239
Jack Kerouac **1**:165
Milan Kundera **32**:268
Norman Mailer **1**:188
Bernard Malamud **1**:194
Mary McCarthy **1**:205
John O'Hara **1**:260
Philip Roth **1**:292
Nathalie Sarraute **1**:302
John Updike **1**:343

Edmund Wilson **1**:372, 373

Poger, Sidney
T. S. Eliot **15**:212

Poggi, Gianfranco
Luchino Visconti **16**:563

Poggioli, Renato
Eugenio Montale **7**:221

Pogrebin, Letty Cottin
Laurie Colwin **23**:130
Norma Klein **30**:235
Richard Peck **21**:295

Poirier, Richard
John Barth **3**:40
Saul Bellow **8**:74
Jorge Luis Borges **3**:77
T. S. Eliot **3**:140
Robert Frost **4**:176; **9**:226
Geoffrey H. Hartman **27**:180
Lillian Hellman **4**:221
John Hollander **14**:264
Jonathan Kozol **17**:251
John Lennon and Paul McCartney **12**:368
Norman Mailer **2**:263, 265; **3**:314; **4**:322; **14**:349; **28**:262
Vladimir Nabokov **6**:354
Thomas Pynchon **2**:355; **3**:409; **18**:429
Robert Stone **23**:429
William Styron **3**:474
Gore Vidal **4**:553
Rudolph Wurlitzer **2**:482; **4**:597

Polacheck, Janet G.
Jules Archer **12**:18
James D. Forman **21**:120
Milton Meltzer **26**:300

Poland, Nancy
Margaret Drabble **5**:118

Polar, Antonio Cornejo
José María Arguedas **18**:7

Polishook, Irwin
Allan W. Eckert **17**:107

Politzer, Heinz
Jerome Siegel and Joe Shuster **21**:355

Polk, James
Leslie Marmon Silko **23**:411

Pollack, Pamela D.
Gunnel Beckman **26**:88
Robert Cormier **30**:81
Rosa Guy **26**:143
Norma Fox Mazer **26**:291
Richard Peck **21**:299
Maia Wojciechowska **26**:455

Pollak, Richard
Jan de Hartog **19**:132

Pollitt, Katha
Alice Adams **13**:1, 2
Margaret Atwood **8**:30
Pat Barker **32**:15
Saul Bellow **25**:82
Louise Bogan **39**:391
Anita Desai **19**:133
Norman Dubie **36**:134
Leslie Epstein **27**:128

Carolyn Forché **25**:171
Elizabeth Frank **39**:391
Gail Godwin **22**:180
Barbara Guest **34**:444
H. D. **34**:444
Carolyn G. Heilbrun **25**:257
Sandra Hochman **8**:298
Maureen Howard **14**:268
Susan Isaacs **32**:254
Dan Jacobson **14**:291
Yashar Kemal **14**:300
William X. Kienzle **25**:275
Norma Klein **30**:239
Ella Leffland **19**:279
David Malouf **28**:266
Cynthia Ozick **28**:352
Marge Piercy **27**:377
James Purdy **10**:425
Françoise Sagan **17**:428
Lynne Sharon Schwartz **31**:388
Susan Richards Shreve **23**:402
Lee Smith **25**:409
Scott Spencer **30**:405
Anne Tyler **7**:479
Alice Walker **27**:448
William Wharton **18**:542

Pollnitz, Christopher
Thomas W. Shapcott **38**:402

Pollock, Bruce
Jim Carroll **35**:81
Mick Jagger and Keith Richard
17:235
Paul Simon **17**:465

Pollock, Zailig
A. M. Klein **19**:262

Polner, Murray
Ronald J. Glasser **37**:131
Roger Kahn **30**:232

Polt, Harriet
Ralph Bakshi **26**:69
Bernard Malamud **18**:322

Polt, Harriet R.
René Clair **20**:66

Pond, Steve
Paul Weller **26**:447

Ponnuthurai, Charles Sarvan
Chinua Achebe **5**:3

Pontac, Perry
Miguel Piñero **4**:401

Pool, Gail
Barbara Pym **37**:377
Anne Sexton **10**:468

Poole, Adrian
Stanley Middleton **38**:333

Poole, Michael
John Fowles **33**:172

Poore, C. G.
Ogden Nash **23**:317, 318

Poore, Charles
Charles Addams **30**:13
Jessica Anderson **37**:18
Gregorio López y Fuentes
32:278
Erich Maria Remarque **21**:330
Wilfrid Sheed **2**:392

Jessamyn West **17**:549

Popkin, Henry
Albert Camus **9**:145; **32**:84
Arthur Miller **26**:319

Pops, Martin L.
Charles Olson **29**:327

Porsild, A. E.
Farley Mowat **26**:332

Portales, Marco
Louise Erdrich **39**:130

Portch, Stephen R.
Flannery O'Connor **15**:412

Porter, Carolyn
Lina Wertmüller **16**:593

Porter, Katherine Anne
Kay Boyle **19**:61
Ezra Pound **7**:325
Eudora Welty **33**:414

Porter, M. Gilbert
Saul Bellow **2**:54; **8**:72

Porter, Michael
Horst Bienek **11**:48

Porter, Peter
W. H. Auden **14**:31
Amy Clampitt **32**:118
Gavin Ewart **13**:208
James Fenton **32**:166
Roy Fisher **25**:161
Seamus Heaney **14**:244
Ted Hughes **14**:273
Norman MacCaig **36**:285
Derek Mahon **27**:291
Sylvia Plath **17**:352
Craig Raine **32**:350
Christopher Reid **33**:350
Jaroslav Seifert **34**:256
Stevie Smith **3**:460
Judith Wright **11**:578

Porter, Raymond J.
Brendan Behan **8**:64

Porter, Robert
Milan Kundera **4**:276

Porter, Thomas E.
John Ehle **27**:103

Porterfield, Christopher
Kingsley Amis **2**:8
Robert Frost **34**:473
Christopher Fry **2**:143
Ted Hughes **2**:199
William H. Pritchard **34**:473
Donald E. Westlake **7**:528
William Wharton **37**:442

Posnock, Ross
Frank Lentricchia **34**:574

Poss, Stanley
John Hollander **8**:301
Philip Larkin **13**:337
Cynthia Macdonald **13**:355
P. H. Newby **2**:310
Adrienne Rich **7**:370
Theodore Roethke **8**:460
Nancy Willard **7**:539

Postell, Frances
Christie Harris **12**:263

Poster, Mark
Michel Foucault **31**:181

Postlewait, Thomas
Samuel Beckett **18**:46

Potamkin, Harry Allan
Carl Theodor Dreyer **16**:255
Langston Hughes **35**:212

Potok, Chaim
Paul West **7**:523

Potoker, Edward Martin
Michael Mott **15**:379
Judith Rossner **9**:456
Ronald Sukenick **6**:524

Potter, David M.
Bruce Catton **35**:88, 90

Potter, Lois
Antonia Fraser **32**:186

Potter, Vilma Ruskin
Robert Hayden **37**:157

Potts, Charles
Thomas McGrath **28**:277

Potts, Paul
George Barker **8**:43

Potts, Stephen W.
Stanislaw Lem **15**:330

Pouillon, Jean
William Faulkner **8**:208

Pound, Ezra
Robert Frost **15**:239
Mina Loy **28**:245
Marianne Moore **19**:335
William Carlos Williams
13:602

Povey, John
Chinua Achebe **26**:20
John Pepper Clark **38**:116

Povey, John F.
Chinua Achebe **1**:1; **7**:6
Cyprian Ekwensi **4**:151
Ngugi wa Thiong'o **36**:318
Wole Soyinka **14**:506

Powdermaker, Hortense
Margaret Mead **37**:272

Powell, Anthony
Evelyn Waugh **3**:513

Powell, Bertie J.
Lorraine Hansberry **17**:193

Powell, Dilys
Elia Kazan **16**:361

Powell, Grosvenor E.
J. V. Cunningham **31**:99
Yvor Winters **32**:465

Powell, Meghan
Stan Lee **17**:262

Powell, Michael
Martin Scorsese **20**:340

Powell, Neil
Donald Davie **31**:117
Thom Gunn **3**:216

Power, K. C.
Michael McClure **6**:321

Power, Victor
Hugh Leonard **19**:281

Powers, Kim
Harvey Fierstein **33**:154

Powers, Thomas
Donald Hall **37**:148
Richard Kostelanetz **28**:213
Tom Wolfe **15**:583

Prado, Holly
Mary Oliver **34**:247
Adrienne Rich **36**:374
Ntozake Shange **38**:394

Prasad, Madhusudan
Anita Desai **37**:68
Jayanta Mahapatra **33**:281

Pratt, Annis
Doris Lessing **3**:288; **6**:292

Pratt, Fletcher
C. S. Forester **35**:167

Pratt, John Clark
John Steinbeck **1**:326

Pratt, Linda Ray
Sylvia Plath **3**:390

Pratt, Sarah
V. S. Pritchett **13**:468

Pratt, William
John Berryman **10**:45
Joseph Brodsky **6**:97
Daniel Halpern **14**:232
Ezra Pound **18**:427
Andrei Voznesensky **15**:554

Prawer, Siegbert S.
Ernst Jandl **34**:195

Prendergast, Christopher
Roland Barthes **24**:36

Prendowska, Krystyna
Jerzy Kosinski **15**:313

Prescott, Anne Lake
Rosellen Brown **32**:65

Prescott, Orville
Michael Ayrton **7**:17
James Clavell **25**:125
Earl Hamner, Jr. **12**:257
Kamala Markandaya **38**:323
James A. Michener **29**:310
Erich Maria Remarque **21**:330
Conrad Richter **30**:310, 314
Betty Smith **19**:422
J.I.M. Stewart **7**:466
Robert Penn Warren **8**:543

Prescott, Peter S.
Alice Adams **6**:1
Richard Adams **4**:7
Renata Adler **31**:14
Eric Ambler **6**:3
Kingsley Amis **3**:8
Martin Amis **4**:20
Donald Barthelme **5**:54
William Peter Blatty **2**:64
Vance Bourjaily **8**:104
Kay Boyle **5**:65

Robin F. Brancato **35**:67
Richard Brautigan **5**:71
Lothar-Günther Buchheim
  6:101
Anthony Burgess **5**:85
James Carroll **38**:104
William Caunitz **34**:36
Agatha Christie **12**:120
Carolyn Chute **39**:40
Robert Coover **32**:120
Michael Crichton **6**:119
Robertson Davies **7**:73
Len Deighton **7**:75
Don DeLillo **8**:171
Peter De Vries **7**:78
John Dos Passos **4**:137
Lawrence Durrell **6**:151
Leslie A. Fiedler **4**:161
John Fowles **6**:186
Michael Frayn **3**:165
Ronald J. Glasser **37**:131, 132
Nadine Gordimer **5**:146
Graham Greene **3**:213
Judith Guest **30**:175
Lillian Hellman **4**:221
Mark Helprin **32**:231
George V. Higgins **4**:223
Edward Hoagland **28**:182
Russell C. Hoban **7**:161
Geoffrey Household **11**:277
Dan Jacobson **4**:254
Diane Johnson **5**:198
Robert F. Jones **7**:193
Roger Kahn **30**:232
Thomas Keneally **8**:318
William Kennedy **6**:275;
  28:205, 206
John Knowles **26**:265
Jerzy Kosinski **6**:285
Charles R. Larson **31**:239
John Le Carré **5**:232, 234
Elmore Leonard **34**:214
Doris Lessing **2**:241
Peter Matthiessen **5**:274
Cormac McCarthy **4**:341
John McGahern **5**:280
A. G. Mojtabai **9**:385
Brian Moore **7**:236; **32**:308
Toni Morrison **4**:365
Penelope Mortimer **5**:299
Joyce Carol Oates **6**:374
Flann O'Brien **5**:314
Robert B. Parker **27**:367
Padgett Powell **34**:98
Reynolds Price **6**:425
Thomas Pynchon **33**:338
Philip Roth **2**:378; **4**:455; **6**:475
Jonathan Schell **35**:363
Cynthia Propper Seton **27**:425
Isaac Bashevis Singer **3**:458
Aleksandr I. Solzhenitsyn **4**:516
Muriel Spark **5**:399
Richard Stern **39**:243
Robert Stone **5**:409
Harvey Swados **5**:422
Paul Theroux **5**:428
Michel Tournier **6**:537
William Trevor **7**:478
Frank Tuohy **37**:433
John Updike **5**:455, 458
Gore Vidal **4**:554
Alice Walker **27**:449
Jessamyn West **7**:521

William Wharton **37**:439
Patrick White **3**:524
P. G. Wodehouse **5**:515
Larry Woiwode **6**:579
Richard Yates **7**:555

Presley, Delma Eugene
John Fowles **3**:163
Carson McCullers **4**:346

Press, John
John Betjeman **6**:67
Philip Larkin **8**:339
Norman MacCaig **36**:280
Louis MacNeice **4**:316

Preston, Don
Agnes Eckhardt Nixon **21**:252

Prestwich, J. O.
Rosemary Sutcliff **26**:426

Preuss, Paul
David Brin **34**:135

Prevet, James E.
Andrew Holleran **38**:247

Price, Derek de Solla
John Brunner **10**:80
Ursula K. LeGuin **8**:343

Price, James
Martin Amis **9**:26
Beryl Bainbridge **8**:37
Caroline Blackwood **9**:101
Frank Capra **16**:157
Margaret Drabble **8**:184
Stanley Middleton **38**:330

Price, John D.
St.-John Perse **11**:434

Price, L. Brian
Jean Genet **14**:203

Price, Martin
Robert Bolt **14**:87
Alejo Carpentier **38**:91
Mavis Gallant **18**:171
Marjorie Kellogg **2**:224
David Lodge **36**:269, 271
Iris Murdoch **1**:236; **3**:349
Joyce Carol Oates **1**:251
Nathalie Sarraute **4**:469
C. P. Snow **1**:317
David Storey **4**:530
Angus Wilson **5**:514

Price, R.G.G.
Kingsley Amis **2**:7
Paul Bowles **2**:78
Dino Buzzati **36**:88
Isabel Colegate **36**:110
L. P. Hartley **2**:182
Ruth Prawer Jhabvala **29**:253
Robert Kroetsch **23**:270
Josephine Poole **17**:371
Bernice Rubens **31**:350
Elizabeth Taylor **2**:432

Price, Reynolds
Cleanth Brooks **24**:107
Lucille Clifton **19**:110
William Faulkner **1**:102; **3**:151
Francine du Plessix Gray
  22:202
Graham Greene **3**:212

Mark Helprin **22**:220
Toni Morrison **10**:355
Walker Percy **8**:442
Elizabeth Spencer **22**:405
James Welch **6**:560
Eudora Welty **2**:463

Priebe, Richard
Wole Soyinka **3**:463

Priest, Christopher
Joan D. Vinge **30**:411

Priestley, J. B.
Alejo Carpentier **38**:92
T. S. Eliot **3**:135
William Faulkner **3**:150
Ernest Hemingway **3**:232
F. R. Leavis **24**:296
Ezra Pound **3**:394

Priestley, Michael
John Irving **23**:244

Prigozy, Ruth
Larry McMurtry **3**:333

Primeau, Ronald
John Brunner **8**:109

Prince, Peter
Martin Amis **4**:19
Charles Bukowski **5**:80
Anthony Burgess **4**:84
John Fowles **6**:184
Ronald Harwood **32**:224
Thomas Hinde **11**:273
Yashar Kemal **14**:299
Thomas Keneally **5**:210
Larry McMurtry **27**:333
Patrick Modiano **18**:338
Alice Munro **6**:341
David Pownall **10**:419
Piers Paul Read **4**:444; **25**:377
Philip Roth **3**:439

Pring-Mill, Robert
Ernesto Cardenal **31**:76
Pablo Neruda **28**:310

Pringle, David
J. G. Ballard **14**:40; **36**:35

Pringle, John Douglas
Hugh MacDiarmid **4**:312

Pritchard, R. E.
L. P. Hartley **22**:219

Pritchard, William H.
Dannie Abse **7**:1; **29**:19
Margaret Atwood **3**:19
Wendell Berry **8**:85
John Berryman **3**:72; **8**:90
Henry Bromell **5**:74
Anthony Burgess **1**:48; **4**:84
Jerome Charyn **18**:99
Donald Davie **8**:162, 163;
  31:125
Stephen Dunn **36**:154
Joseph Epstein **39**:465
John Fowles **9**:214; **10**:189
Allen Ginsberg **3**:195
Robert Graves **2**:177
Marilyn Hacker **9**:257
William Harmon **38**:244

Seamus Heaney **14**:242
John Hollander **5**:187
Ted Hughes **9**:281
Richard F. Hugo **6**:244; **18**:260
William Kennedy **34**:208
Philip Larkin **39**:339
Alan Lelchuk **5**:245
Denise Levertov **2**:242; **15**:338
Philip Levine **2**:244
Robert Lowell **1**:184
Louis MacNeice **4**:316
William McPherson **34**:86
Wright Morris **18**:354
Iris Murdoch **8**:406; **31**:295
Vladimir Nabokov **3**:353
Howard Nemerov **6**:363
Anthony Powell **7**:339
Padgett Powell **34**:99
Thomas Pynchon **3**:418
Piers Paul Read **25**:379
Kenneth Rexroth **2**:369
Adrienne Rich **3**:427; **6**:459
Susan Fromberg Schaeffer
  6:489
Cynthia Propper Seton **27**:428
Anne Sexton **15**:473
L. E. Sissman **18**:488
Aleksandr I. Solzhenitsyn **4**:510
Kathleen Spivack **6**:520
Richard G. Stern **4**:523
Robert Stone **5**:410
May Swenson **4**:532
James Tate **25**:429
Elizabeth Taylor **2**:433
Paul Theroux **11**:531
John Updike **3**:487
Robert Penn Warren **39**:256,
  264
Richard Wilbur **6**:571
James Wright **3**:544
Rudolph Wurlitzer **4**:597
Richard Yates **7**:556

Pritchett, V. S.
Kingsley Amis **13**:15
Simone de Beauvoir **4**:48;
  14:67
Samuel Beckett **4**:50
Saul Bellow **25**:80
Heinrich Böll **27**:64
Bruce Chatwin **28**:74
Rhys Davies **23**:141
Leon Edel **29**:174
Max Frisch **14**:183
Ernest K. Gann **23**:166
William Golding **2**:168; **17**:160,
  166
Juan Goytisolo **5**:151; **10**:245
Aldous Huxley **35**:240
Ruth Prawer Jhabvala **29**:261
Patrick Kavanagh **22**:234
Alfred Kazin **38**:277
Molly Keane **31**:235
Arthur Koestler **15**:309
Mary Lavin **18**:301
John le Carré **15**:326
Compton Mackenzie **18**:313
Norman Mailer **2**:262
Carson McCullers **12**:415
William Maxwell **19**:305
John Mortimer **28**:289
Vladimir Nabokov **6**:356
Flann O'Brien **10**:364

Flannery O'Connor **21**:267
Frank O'Connor **14**:395
John Cowper Powys **15**:435
Gregor von Rezzori **25**:382
Michael Scammell **34**:492
Aleksandr I. Solzhenitsyn
1:320; **34**:492
Paul Theroux **8**:513
James Thurber **5**:433
William Trevor **14**:536
Henri Troyat **23**:461
John Updike **23**:471
Gore Vidal **8**:529
Evelyn Waugh **27**:475

Procopiow, Norma
Marilyn Hacker **5**:155
Eleanor Lerman **9**:329
Anne Sexton **4**:483

Proffer, Carl R.
Michael Scammell **34**:487
Aleksandr I. Solzhenitsyn
9:506; **34**:487

Profumo, David
Graham Greene **37**:139

Pronko, Leonard Cabell
Arthur Adamov **25**:12
Jacques Audiberti **38**:23
Jean Anouilh **13**:16
Jean Genet **14**:201
Eugène Ionesco **1**:154

Proteus
Agatha Christie **12**:112
Edna Ferber **18**:151

Prothro, Laurie
May Sarton **14**:482

Prouse, Derek
Elia Kazan **16**:364
Laurence Olivier **20**:237

Prucha, Francis Paul
Vine Deloria, Jr. **21**:113

Pruette, Lorne
Ayn Rand **30**:292

Pryce-Jones, Alan
Michael Ayrton **7**:16
John Betjeman **6**:69
Italo Calvino **5**:98
John le Carré **28**:230
Vladimir Nabokov **1**:246
John Nichols **38**:338

Pryce-Jones, David
Siegfried Lenz **27**:250

Pryor, Thomas M.
Sally Benson **17**:49

Pryse, Marjorie
Helen Yglesias **7**:558; **22**:493

Przekop, Benjamin Paul John
Richard Matheson **37**:247

Puckett, Harry
T. S. Eliot **10**:167

Puckette, Charles McD.
Julia Peterkin **31**:302
T. S. Stribling **23**:439

Puetz, Manfred
John Barth **9**:72
Thomas Pynchon **6**:434

Pugh, Anthony R.
Alain Robbe-Grillet **4**:450

Pulleine, Tim
Woody Allen **16**:9
Claude Chabrol **16**:184
Carlos Saura **20**:319
Peter Weir **20**:428

Punnett, Spencer
Edwin Newman **14**:378

Purcell, H. D.
George MacDonald Fraser
7:106

Purcell, J. M.
Carolyn G. Heilbrun **25**:255

Purcell, Patricia
Anne Hébert **29**:227

Purdy, A. W.
Earle Birney **6**:73
Leonard Cohen **38**:132

Purdy, Al
Bill Bissett **18**:59

Purdy, Strother
Luis Buñuel **16**:133

Purdy, Theodore, Jr.
William Maxwell **19**:304

Purtill, Richard
J.R.R. Tolkien **12**:577

Puterbaugh, Parke
Paul McCartney **35**:291

Putney, Michael
Hunter S. Thompson **17**:504

Puzo, Mario
James Baldwin **17**:34

Pybus, Rodney
Paul Muldoon **32**:320
Christina Stead **32**:409

Pye, Ian
John Lennon **35**:270, 272

Pye, Michael
George Lucas **16**:416

Pym, Christopher
Mary Stewart **35**:389
Julian Symons **14**:522

Pym, John
René Clair **20**:69
John Landis **26**:277

Pyros, J.
Michael McClure **6**:320

Quacinella, Lucy
Lina Wertmüller **16**:596

Quammen, David
Michael Ende **31**:143
Bobbie Ann Mason **28**:272
Bette Pesetsky **28**:357
Leon Rooke **25**:392
Danny Santiago **33**:352
Joy Williams **31**:464

Quance, Robert A.
Miguel Delibes **18**:115

Quant, Leonard
Robert Altman **16**:35

Quart, Barbara Koenig
T. Gertler **34**:52
Norma Klein **30**:243
Cynthia Ozick **28**:354
Bette Pesetsky **28**:359

Quennell, Peter
Robert Graves **6**:210

Quigly, Isabel
Danny Abse **29**:12
Robert Bresson **16**:104
Frank Capra **16**:157
Claude Chabrol **16**:168
Natalia Ginzburg **11**:230
Jean-Luc Godard **20**:130
Pamela Hansford Johnson **1**:160
Noel Streatfeild **21**:411
Elio Vittorini **14**:547
Paul Zindel **26**:474

Quilligan, Maureen
Marion Zimmer Bradley **30**:31

Quinn, Sister Bernetta, O.S.F.
Alan Dugan **2**:121
David Jones **4**:259
Ezra Pound **4**:416; **7**:326
William Stafford **7**:460
Allen Tate **4**:539
Derek Walcott **2**:460
See also Bernetta (Quinn),
Sister Mary, O.S.F.

Quinn, James P.
Edward Albee **5**:11

Quinn, Joseph L.
Brigid Brophy **29**:92

Quinn, Mary Ellen
Fernanda Eberstadt **39**:49
Tish O'Dowd Ezekiel **34**:46
Bob Shacochis **39**:198

Quinn, Michael
William Golding **17**:164

Quinn, Vincent
H. D. **14**:224

Quinton, Anthony
William Barrett **27**:21

Quirino, Leonard
Tennessee Williams **30**:470

R
David Jones **4**:259
Arthur Koestler **6**:281
Aleksandr I. Solzhenitsyn **4**:506

Raab, Lawrence
Norman Dubie **36**:131

Raban, Jonathan
A. Alvarez **5**:18
Kingsley Amis **8**:11
Beryl Bainbridge **5**:40
John Barth **1**:17
Saul Bellow **1**:32
E. L. Doctorow **11**:141
Stanley Elkin **6**:169
James Fenton **32**:167

Eva Figes **31**:162
Nadine Gordimer **5**:145
Erica Jong **4**:265
David Lodge **36**:270
Mary McCarthy **1**:207
Ian McEwan **13**:369
John McGahern **9**:369
Stanley Middleton **7**:220
Brian Moore **1**:225
Iris Murdoch **4**:369
Vladimir Nabokov **6**:359
Jean Rhys **6**:456
Frank Sargeson **31**:366
Tom Sharpe **36**:400
Richard G. Stern **4**:523
Paul Theroux **28**:425
Hunter S. Thompson **17**:505
William Trevor **7**:476
Angus Wilson **25**:458

Rabassa, Gregory
Ernesto Cardenal **31**:72
Alejo Carpentier **11**:99
Julio Cortázar **15**:147
Gabriel García Márquez **3**:180;
27:148
João Guimarães Rosa **23**:353
Gilbert Sorrentino **22**:392
Mario Vargas Llosa **15**:551

Rabinovitz, Rubin
Kingsley Amis **5**:20
Samuel Beckett **6**:40, 41
Norman Mailer **5**:267
Iris Murdoch **1**:235; **2**:297
C. P. Snow **4**:500
Angus Wilson **5**:512

Rabinowitz, Dorothy
Beryl Bainbridge **8**:36
Elliott Baker **8**:40
Giorgio Bassani **9**:77
Maeve Brennan **5**:72
Anthony Burgess **5**:88
Hortense Calisher **4**:87; **8**:124
John Cheever **3**:107
Laurie Colwin **23**:128
Lois Gould **4**:201
Peter Handke **5**:165
Mark Helprin **7**:152
Dan Jacobson **4**:254
Ruth Prawer Jhabvala **4**:256,
257; **8**:311
Robert Kotlowitz **4**:275
Mary Lavin **4**:281
Doris Lessing **3**:241
Meyer Levin **7**:205
Larry McMurtry **11**:371
Brian Moore **7**:237
Wright Morris **3**:344
Edna O'Brien **5**:312
John O'Hara **6**:384
Grace Paley **4**:392
S. J. Perelman **5**:337
Philip Roth **3**:437
Anne Sexton **10**:468
John Updike **2**:445
Gore Vidal **4**:553
Dan Wakefield **7**:503
Joseph Wambaugh **3**:509
Harriet Waugh **6**:560
Arnold Wesker **5**:482

Rabinowitz, Morris
James D. Forman **21**:121

Critic Index

Rabkin, David
  Alex La Guma 19:273

Rabkin, Eric S.
  Donald Barthelme 13:58
  Robert A. Heinlein 26:166
  Frederik Pohl 18:410

Rabkin, Gerald
  Paul Green 25:198
  Derek Walcott 9:556

Rachewiltz, Boris de
  Ezra Pound 7:331

Rachleff, Owen S.
  Woody Allen 16:9

Rachlis, Kit
  Jackson Browne 21:41
  Elvis Costello 21:70, 72
  Bob Seger 35:381
  Neil Young 17:582

Rackham, Jeff
  John Fowles 2:138

Radcliff-Umstead, Douglas
  Alberto Moravia 11:381

Rader, Dotson
  Hubert Selby, Jr. 4:481
  Yevgeny Yevtushenko 3:547

Radford, C. B.
  Simone de Beauvoir 4:45, 46

Radhuber, S. G.
  Stanley Plumly 33:310

Radin, Victoria
  Sara Davidson 9:175

Radke, Judith J.
  Pierre Gascar 11:221

Radley, Philippe
  Andrei Voznesensky 15:554

Radner, Rebecca
  Gail Godwin 31:198
  Lenora Mattingly Weber 12:635

Radowsky, Colby
  Laurence Yep 35:472

Radtke, Karen K.
  C. S. Adler 35:15

Radu, Kenneth
  Christie Harris 12:264

Rae, Bruce
  John R. Tunis 12:593

Rae, Simon
  Donald Davie 31:119

Raeburn, John
  Frank Capra 16:163

Rafalko, Robert
  Eric Ambler 9:22

Rafalko, Robert J.
  Philip K. Dick 10:138

Raff, Emanuel
  Henry Gregor Felsen 17:124

Raffel, Burton
  Czesław Miłosz 31:259
  J.R.R. Tolkien 1:337
  Louis Zukofsky 11:580

Rafferty, Terrence
  Barry Hannah 38:233

Raftery, Gerald
  Ayn Rand 30:300

Ragusa, Olga
  Italo Calvino 22:91
  Alberto Moravia 2:292
  Pier Paolo Pasolini 37:341

Rahv, Betty T.
  Albert Camus 9:148
  Alain Robbe-Grillet 8:451
  Nathalie Sarraute 8:469
  Jean-Paul Sartre 7:395

Rahv, Philip
  Louis Aragon 22:34
  Saul Bellow 2:50
  Richard Brautigan 12:57
  Leon Edel 29:171
  T. S. Eliot 2:126
  Leslie A. Fiedler 24:195
  Ernest Hemingway 3:231
  Arthur Koestler 33:232
  F. R. Leavis 24:304
  Arthur Miller 2:278
  Delmore Schwartz 10:462
  Aleksandr I. Solzhenitsyn
    2:411; 26:422

Raidy, William A.
  Sam Shepard 17:449

Raine, Craig
  James Fenton 32:165
  Geoffrey Hill 18:237
  Ted Hughes 14:272
  Harold Pinter 6:419
  Anne Stevenson 33:380
  Ted Walker 13:566

Raine, Kathleen
  Brewster Ghiselin 23:170
  David Jones 2:216; 7:191
  St.-John Perse 4:399
  Herbert Read 4:440

Rainer, Dachine
  Rebecca West 7:525

Raines, Charles A.
  Woody Guthrie 35:185

Raizada, Harish
  R. K. Narayan 28:294

Rama Rau, Santha
  Khushwant Singh 11:504

Rambali, Paul
  Elvis Costello 21:67

Rampersad, Arnold
  Claude Brown 30:40
  Alex Haley 12:247

Ramras-Rauch, Gila
  S. Y. Agnon 4:14
  Yehuda Amichai 22:32
  Yoram Kaniuk 19:241

Ramsey, Jarold
  Leslie Marmon Silko 23:411

Ramsey, Nancy
  Margaret Atwood 25:70

Ramsey, Paul
  Robert Bly 5:62
  Edgar Bowers 9:121
  Hayden Carruth 10:100
  Norman Dubie 36:130
  Larry Eigner 9:181
  William Harmon 38:243
  John Hollander 14:265
  Eleanor Lerman 9:328
  W. S. Merwin 5:286
  N. Scott Momaday 19:318
  Michael Mott 15:380
  Howard Nemerov 9:394
  Linda Pastan 27:369
  Richard Wilbur 14:577

Ramsey, R. H.
  Robert Kroetsch 23:271

Ramsey, Roger
  Friedrich Dürrenmatt 4:140
  Pär Lagerkvist 10:311

Ramsey, S. A.
  Randolph Stow 23:438

Ranbom, Sheppard J.
  Philip Roth 15:453

Rand, Richard A.
  John Hollander 5:187

Randall, Dudley
  Robert Hayden 5:168
  Audre Lorde 18:307
  Margaret Walker 6:554

Randall, Francis B.
  Ch'ien Chung-shu 22:105
  Yevgeny Yevtushenko 26:468

Randall, Julia
  Howard Nemerov 2:308
  Gabrielle Roy 10:441

Randall, Margaret
  Judith Johnson Sherwin 15:479

Randall-Tsuruta, Dorothy
  Joyce Carol Thomas 35:406

Ranger, Terence
  David Caute 29:122

Ranjbaran, Esmaeel
  Ahmad Shamlu 10:469

Rank, Hugh
  Walter M. Miller, Jr. 30:257
  Edwin O'Connor 14:390

Ranly, Ernest W.
  Kurt Vonnegut, Jr. 2:453

Ransom, John Crowe
  Kenneth Burke 24:122
  Donald Davidson 13:167
  T. S. Eliot 24:165
  William Empson 33:138
  Randall Jarrell 1:159
  Marianne Moore 19:337
  I. A. Richards 24:382, 385
  Allen Tate 4:535
  Yvor Winters 32:454

Ransom, W. M.
  Galway Kinnell 3:268

Rao, K. B.
  Salman Rushdie 23:367

Rao, K. S. Narayana
  R. K. Narayan 28:299

Raper, Tod
  Rod Serling 30:354

Raphael, Frederic
  James Baldwin 17:41
  Michael Frayn 7:107
  Jakov Lind 4:293

Raphael, Isabel
  David Caute 29:124

Rapisarda, Martin
  David Lodge 36:276

Rapp, Rodger
  Theodore Sturgeon 39:367

Rascoe, Judith
  Laurie Colwin 5:107
  John Gregory Dunne 28:123
  Dick Francis 22:150

Rasi, Humberto M.
  Jorge Luis Borges 2:74

Raskin, A. H.
  Milton Meltzer 26:298

Rasmussen, Douglas B.
  Ayn Rand 30:304

Raspa, Anthony
  Anne Hébert 29:231

Rasso, Pamela S.
  William Heyen 13:284

Rasula, Jed
  Robert White 36:120

Ratcliff, Michael
  Michael Frayn 31:193
  Thomas Keneally 14:303

Rathbone, Richard
  Breyten Breytenbach 23:86

Rathburn, Norma
  Margot Benary-Isbert 12:32

Ratiner, Steven
  Marvin Bell 31:51

Ratner, Marc L.
  John Hawkes 14:237
  William Styron 5:418

Ratner, Rochelle
  Yehuda Amichai 22:33
  Rosellen Brown 32:66
  Clayton Eshleman 7:100
  Carolyn Forché 25:171
  Phillip Lopate 29:302
  Sharon Olds 32:345
  Susan Fromberg Schaeffer
    22:370
  Patti Smith 12:541

Rave, Eugene S.
  Barbara Corcoran 17:78

Raven, Simon
  Alvah Bessie 23:60
  David Caute 29:108
  Isabel Colegate 36:109
  Ian Fleming 30:133
  Dan Jacobson 14:289
  John Knowles 26:245

Anthony Powell **31**:313

Ravenscroft, Arthur
Chinua Achebe **11**:1
Bessie Head **25**:233
Wole Soyinka **36**:417

Rawley, James
James Baldwin **15**:43
Donald Barthelme **13**:63

Rawlings, Donn
John Nichols **38**:344

Rawlins, Jack P.
John W. Campbell **32**:81

Rawson, Judy
Dino Buzzati **36**:95

Ray, David
E. E. Cummings **12**:151

Ray, Robert
James Baldwin **2**:34
J.I.M. Stewart **7**:466

Ray, Sheila G.
E. M. Almedingen **12**:7

Rayburn, Bill
Peter Griffin **39**:399
Ernest Hemingway **39**:399, 429
Jeffrey Meyers **39**:429

Rayme, Anne C.
Larry Kettelkamp **12**:307

Raymond, John
Noël Coward **29**:133
Daphne du Maurier **11**:163
Pamela Hansford Johnson **27**:216
Françoise Sagan **17**:417
Georges Simenon **3**:449

Raynor, Henry
Laurence Olivier **20**:236

Raynor, Vivien
Evan S. Connell, Jr. **6**:115
Iris Murdoch **3**:348
Edna O'Brien **3**:364

Rayns, Tony
Shirley Clarke **16**:219
Elvis Costello **21**:71
Maya Deren **16**:253
Rainer Werner Fassbinder **20**:107, 108
Werner Herzog **16**:321, 322
Richard O'Brien **17**:323
Nagisa Oshima **20**:251

Raysor, Thomas M.
M. H. Abrams **24**:11

Rea, Dorothy
Auberon Waugh **7**:514

Read, Esther H.
Melvin Berger **12**:40

Read, Forrest, Jr.
Ezra Pound **7**:327

Read, Herbert
Georg Lukács **24**:317
Allen Tate **4**:535

Read, Malcolm
Siegfried Lenz **27**:252

Read, S. E.
Robertson Davies **13**:172

Reading, Peter
Geoffrey Grigson **39**:332

Reagan, Dale
Robert Kroetsch **23**:273

Real, Jere
Noël Coward **29**:135
Peter Shaffer **5**:388

Reaney, James
Jay Macpherson **14**:345

Reardon, Betty S.
James D. Forman **21**:122
Jessamyn West **17**:554

Rebay, Luciano
Alberto Moravia **7**:239

Rebovich, David Paul
Carl Sagan **30**:342

Rechnitz, Robert M.
Carson McCullers **1**:209

Rechy, John
Bret Easton Ellis **39**:56
Peter Matthiessen **32**:289
William McPherson **34**:87

Reck, Rima Drell
Albert Camus **32**:86
Louis-Ferdinand Céline **7**:44
Françoise Mallet-Joris **11**:355

Reck, Tom S.
James M. Cain **28**:50

Redding, Saunders
John Ehle **27**:105
Shirley Ann Grau **4**:208
Ezekiel Mphahlele **25**:333
Richard Wright **1**:377

Redfern, W. D.
Jean Giono **4**:186

Redman, Ben Ray
Vera Brittain **23**:91
Thomas B. Costain **30**:93
C. S. Forester **35**:160, 163
Erich Maria Remarque **21**:328
Nevil Shute **30**:364
Dalton Trumbo **19**:444
Frank Tuohy **37**:425
Marguerite Yourcenar **19**:482

Redman, Eric
André Brink **18**:69

Redmon, Anne
Judy Blume **12**:45

Redmond, Eugene B.
Clarence Major **19**:293

Reed, Bill
Frank Zappa **17**:586

Reed, Diana
J. G. Ballard **6**:28
John Wyndham **19**:476

Reed, Henry
Rhys Davies **23**:142
Mary Renault **17**:391

Reed, Ishmael
Claude Brown **30**:38
Chester Himes **2**:195
John Edgar Wideman **36**:457

Reed, J. D.
Jim Harrison **33**:196
Richard F. Hugo **32**:235
Mark Stevens **34**:112

Reed, John
Arthur Hailey **5**:156
Ngugi Wa Thiong'o **13**:583

Reed, John R.
William Dickey **3**:127
D. J. Enright **4**:155
William Heyen **18**:233
Daniel Hoffman **6**:243
John Hollander **8**:302
Richard Howard **7**:169; **10**:276
Judith Leet **11**:323
James Merrill **8**:388
Charles Reznikoff **9**:450
David Wagoner **3**:508
Philip Whalen **6**:566

Reed, Peter J.
Kurt Vonnegut, Jr. **3**:495; **12**:626

Reed, Rex
Laura Nyro **17**:313
Gordon Parks **16**:460
Stephen Sondheim **30**:385
Tennessee Williams **2**:464

Reedy, Gerard
James Carroll **38**:103
C. S. Lewis **6**:308
Walker Percy **18**:402

Reedy, Gerard C.
Richard Price **12**:490

Rees, David
Judy Blume **30**:21
Rhys Davies **23**:147
C. S. Forester **35**:171
Rosa Guy **26**:145
Piers Paul Read **25**:375
Paul Zindel **26**:478

Rees, David L.
Philippa Pearce **21**:285
Otfried Preussler **17**:375
Colin Thiele **17**:494

Rees, Goronwy
Rhys Davies **23**:146
Richard Hughes **11**:278
Erich Maria Remarque **21**:328

Rees, Samuel
David Jones **13**:309

Reeve, Benjamin
Grace Paley **4**:393

Reeve, F. D.
Joseph Brodsky **6**:98
Aleksandr I. Solzhenitsyn **1**:319
Alexander Zinoviev **19**:489

Regan, Robert Alton
John Updike **5**:454

Regier, W. G.
W. H. Auden **3**:22
Michael Benedikt **4**:54
Kenneth O. Hanson **13**:263
Howard Moss **14**:375
Howard Nemerov **9**:395
Pablo Neruda **5**:305
Francis Ponge **6**:423

Rehder, Jesse
Randolph Stow **23**:432

Rehmus, E. E.
Gordon Vorster **34**:123

Reibetanz, John
Philip Larkin **8**:334

Reichek, Morton A.
Chaim Grade **10**:249

Reid, Alastair
Jorge Luis Borges **2**:73
Hayden Carruth **18**:89
Bruce Chatwin **28**:71
Pablo Neruda **5**:302
John Updike **13**:561

Reid, Alfred S.
Karl Shapiro **15**:476

Reid, B. L.
V. S. Pritchett **13**:465

Reid, Beryl
Barbara Corcoran **17**:74
Lee Kingman **17**:246
Sonia Levitin **17**:264

Reid, Christopher
Ted Hughes **14**:272
Michael Ondaatje **29**:343

Reid, David
Leonard Michaels **25**:318

Reid, Ian
Frank Sargeson **31**:365, 366

Reigo, Ants
A. W. Purdy **14**:434

Reilly, Alayne P.
Yevgeny Yevtushenko **26**:463

Reilly, John H.
Arthur Adamov **25**:19

Reilly, John M.
Chester Himes **18**:245
B. Traven **11**:538

Reilly, Peter
Joan Armatrading **17**:10
Jimmy Cliff **21**:61
Ray Davies **21**:101
Neil Diamond **30**:113
Janis Ian **21**:184, 185, 186, 187, 188
Billy Joel **26**:213, 214, 215, 216, 217, 221
Kris Kristofferson **26**:269
Paul McCartney **35**:288
Joni Mitchell **12**:436
Monty Python **21**:227
Lou Reed **21**:312
Smokey Robinson **21**:345, 346
Carly Simon **26**:410, 411, 412, 413
Paul Simon **17**:460

Critic Index

Stephen Sondheim **30**:389, 399
Frank Zappa **17**:592

Reilly, Robert J.
C. S. Lewis **3**:298
J.R.R. Tolkien **1**:337; **3**:477

Reingold, Stephen C.
Carl Sagan **30**:335

Reinhardt, Max
Charles Chaplin **16**:187

Reisz, Karel
Vittorio De Sica **20**:86
Elia Kazan **16**:361

Reitberger, Reinhold
Chares M. Schulz **12**:528

Reiter, Seymour
Sean O'Casey **5**:319

Reitman, David
Frank Zappa **17**:588

Reitt, Barbara B.
John Steinbeck **21**:392

Remini, Robert V.
Gore Vidal **8**:526

Remnick, David
Truman Capote **34**:322
Robert Graves **39**:326
Shiva Naipaul **39**:356

Renault, Gregory
Samuel R. Delany **38**:157

Renault, Mary
William Golding **17**:161

Rendle, Adrian
Aidan Chambers **35**:97
Sam Shepard **17**:433
Tom Stoppard **3**:470

Renek, Morris
Erskine Caldwell **8**:123

Renner, Charlotte
John Barth **27**:29

Rennert, Maggie
Mary Stewart **35**:390

Rennie, Neil
Peter Porter **33**:319
Robin Skelton **13**:507

Renoir, Jean
Charles Chaplin **16**:194

Renshaw, Robert
J.R.R. Tolkien **1**:336

Resnik, Henry S.
Amiri Baraka **33**:54
Jonathan Baumbach **23**:54
Nora Ephron **17**:110
Richard Fariña **9**:195
John Irving **13**:292
William Melvin Kelley **22**:248
Wilfrid Sheed **2**:392
J.R.R. Tolkien **12**:566

Restak, Richard
Carl Sagan **30**:333

Restivo, Angelo
Rudolfo A. Anaya **23**:26

Reuss, Richard A.
Woody Guthrie **35**:189

Rexine, John E.
Vassilis Vassilikos **4**:552

Rexroth, Kenneth
Philip Booth **23**:74
Robert Creeley **4**:116
Robert Duncan **1**:82; **2**:123
T. S. Eliot **2**:127
William Everson **1**:96; **14**:162
Leslie A. Fiedler **24**:197
Carolyn Forché **25**:169
Allen Ginsberg **2**:164; **3**:193,
194
William Golding **3**:196
Paul Goodman **2**:169
Robinson Jeffers **2**:211
Pär Lagerkvist **13**:334
Denise Levertov **1**:175; **2**:243;
3:292
Thomas McGrath **28**:276
W. S. Merwin **2**:278; **3**:338
Henry Miller **1**:219
Marianne Moore **2**:292
Kenneth Patchen **2**:332
Laura Riding **3**:432
Muriel Rukeyser **6**:478; **27**:407,
414
Carl Sandburg **1**:300; **4**:463
Isaac Bashevis Singer **3**:452
Edith Sitwell **2**:403
Gary Snyder **2**:407
Jean Toomer **4**:548
Philip Whalen **6**:565
William Carlos Williams **1**:371;
2:469
Yvor Winters **4**:594

Reynal, Eugene
Margery Allingham **19**:11

Reynolds, Gary K.
Anne McCaffrey **17**:284

Reynolds, Horace
August Derleth **31**:134
Woody Guthrie **35**:182
Olivia Manning **19**:299

Reynolds, Quentin
Erich Maria Remarque **21**:330

Reynolds, R. C.
Larry McMurtry **7**:215

Reynolds, Siân
Simone de Beauvoir **31**:38

Reynolds, Stanley
Iain Banks **34**:29
José Donoso **32**:161
Frederick Exley **11**:186
Wilson Harris **25**:209
Anna Kavan **5**:205
Yashar Kemal **29**:265
William Kennedy **28**:204
Violette Leduc **22**:262
Stanley Middleton **38**:330
John Mortimer **28**:287
Chaim Potok **26**:369
Tom Sharpe **36**:399, 402
Paul Theroux **28**:428
Robert Penn Warren **4**:582
A. N. Wilson **33**:454
Tom Wolfe **35**:465

Rezos, Ray
Kris Kristofferson **26**:266

Rheuban, Joyce
Josef von Sternberg **20**:375

Rhoads, Kenneth W.
William Saroyan **10**:455

Rhode, Eric
James Baldwin **17**:40
Robert Bresson **16**:105, 113
Vittorio De Sica **20**:89
Satyajit Ray **16**:477, 479
François Truffaut **20**:381

Rhodes, H. Winston
Frank Sargeson **31**:361, 366,
367

Rhodes, Joseph, Jr.
W.E.B. Du Bois **2**:120

Rhodes, Richard
Chester Himes **2**:194
MacKinlay Kantor **7**:196
Paule Marshall **27**:310
Michael Shaara **15**:474
Wilfrid Sheed **2**:394
Studs Terkel **38**:420

Riasanovsky, Nicholas N.
Henri Troyat **23**:462

Ribalow, Harold U.
Lloyd Alexander **35**:22
Meyer Levin **7**:205
Henry Roth **6**:471
Arnold Wesker **3**:518

Ribalow, Menachem
S. Y. Agnon **4**:10

Ribe, Neil
C. S. Lewis **27**:266

Rice, Edward
Thomas Merton **3**:337

Rice, Elmer
Howard Fast **23**:155

Rice, Jennings
Walter D. Edmonds **35**:153

Rice, Julian C.
Ingmar Bergman **16**:76
LeRoi Jones **1**:163
Martin Scorsese **20**:327

Rice, Susan
Gordon Parks **16**:457

Rich, Adrienne
Elizabeth Bishop **32**:38
Hayden Carruth **18**:87
Jean Garrigue **8**:239
Paul Goodman **2**:170
Robert Lowell **3**:304
Robin Morgan **2**:294
Adrienne Rich **36**:370
Eleanor Ross Taylor **5**:425

Rich, Alan
Alan Ayckbourn **8**:34
Enid Bagnold **25**:79
Jules Feiffer **8**:216
Jack Gelber **14**:194
Simon Gray **9**:241
John Guare **8**:253

Albert Innaurato **21**:191, 193
Preston Jones **10**:297
Stephen Sondheim **30**:396
Tom Stoppard **8**:501, 503
Elizabeth Swados **12**:558
Tennessee Williams **7**:545
Lanford Wilson **7**:549

Rich, Frank
Caryl Churchill **31**:85, 87, 89
Christopher Durang **27**:90;
38:171, 173
Harvey Fierstein **33**:156
Dario Fo **32**:175
Michael Frayn **31**:192
Athol Fugard **25**:177
Charles Fuller **25**:181
Amlin Gray **29**:200
Simon Gray **36**:208
John Guare **29**:205, 208
David Hare **29**:217
Ronald Harwood **32**:227
Albert Innaurato **21**:198
Jean Kerr **22**:258
Arthur Kopit **33**:252
Hugh Leonard **19**:284
David Mamet **34**:220
Garry Marshall **17**:276, 278
William Mastrosimone **36**:289
Peter Nichols **36**:330
Marsha Norman **28**:319
David Rabe **33**:345
Ntozake Shange **25**:400
Sam Shepard **34**:267
Neil Simon **31**:400, 401; **39**:217
Stephen Sondheim **30**:400, 402
Donald Spoto **39**:444
Tom Stoppard **34**:274, 275
C. P. Taylor **27**:445
Fay Weldon **36**:444
Hugh Whitemore **37**:447
August Wilson **39**:277
Tennessee Williams **39**:444
Lanford Wilson **36**:459, 461,
464

Rich, Nancy B.
Carson McCullers **10**:336

Richards, David
August Wilson **39**:278

Richards, I. A.
William Empson **33**:149
E. M. Forster **13**:215

Richards, Jeffrey
Frank Capra **16**:160

Richards, Lewis A.
William Faulkner **3**:153

Richards, Marily
Vine Deloria, Jr. **21**:114

Richardson, D. E.
Wendell Berry **27**:35
Catharine Savage Brosman
9:135
Donald Davie **31**:112

Richardson, H. Edward
Jesse Stuart **34**:374

Richardson, Jack
John Barth 3:39
Saul Bellow 8:71
Brian Clark 29:128
Eldridge Cleaver 30:62
T. S. Eliot 9:182
Trevor Griffiths 13:257
Jack Kerouac 2:227
Arthur Miller 2:280
Vladimir Nabokov 2:300
Peter Shaffer 5:389
Tom Stoppard 4:527
Megan Terry 19:438
Thornton Wilder 35:445

Richardson, Joanna
François Sagan 36:382

Richardson, Maurice
Vasily Aksenov 22:25
Brigid Brophy 29:92
Bruce Chatwin 28:70
Isabel Colegate 36:108
John Knowles 26:246
David Lodge 36:266
Randolph Stow 23:432
Glendon Swarthout 35:400
J.R.R. Tolkien 12:565
Frank Tuohy 37:426
T. H. White 30:444

Richardson, Tony
Luis Buñuel 16:128
John Huston 20:163
Akira Kurosawa 16:395
Jean Renoir 20:288
Josef von Sternberg 20:373
Orson Welles 20:433

Richart, Bette
Phyllis McGinley 14:364

Richie, Donald
Kon Ichikawa 20:177
Donald Keene 34:569
Akira Kurosawa 16:396, 398
Yukio Mishima 2:288; 4:357
Nagisa Oshima 20:246
Yasujiro Ozu 16:450

Richie, Fimie
Luisa Valenzuela 31:437

Richie, Mary
Penelope Mortimer 5:300

Richler, Mordecai
Daniel Fuchs 22:156
Joseph Heller 36:228
Alfred Kazin 38:280
Ken Kesey 3:267
Bernard Malamud 2:267
Mordecai Richler 18:458
Jerome Siegel and Joe Shuster
21:361
Isaac Bashevis Singer 15:508
Alexander Theroux 2:433
Paul Theroux 28:425

Richman, Michele H.
Georges Bataille 29:49

Richman, Robert
John Ashbery 25:57
John Gardner 18:180
Philip Larkin 39:343

Richman, Sidney
Bernard Malamud 1:198

Richmond, Al
Alvah Bessie 23:60

Richmond, Jane
E. L. Doctorow 6:131
Thomas McGuane 3:329

Richmond, Velma Bourgeois
Muriel Spark 3:464

Richter, David H.
Jerzy Kosinski 6:283

Richter, Frederick
Kenzaburō Ōe 10:373

Rickey, Carrie
Sidney Poitier 26:361

Ricks, Christopher
Peter Ackroyd 34:390
Giorgio Bassani 9:75
Samuel Beckett 2:48
Harold Bloom 24:80
Ronald Bush 34:526
Charles Causley 7:41
Robert Creeley 2:108
Donald Davie 31:109, 121
Leon Edel 29:173
T. S. Eliot 34:390, 526
William Empson 34:541
William Golding 17:169
Nadine Gordimer 7:131
Marilyn Hacker 5:155
Geoffrey H. Hartman 27:178
Anthony Hecht 19:207
Geoffrey Hill 8:293
Richard Howard 7:167
Galway Kinnell 5:217
David Lodge 36:266
Robert Lowell 1:181; 9:335
Louis MacNeice 1:186
Marshall McLuhan 37:258
Reynolds Price 6:423
Christina Stead 8:499
Peter Taylor 18:524
John Updike 1:346
Robert Penn Warren 6:556
Patrick White 4:586

Ricou, L. R.
Miriam Waddington 28:438

Ricou, Laurence
Jack Hodgins 23:230
Robert Kroetsch 23:270

Ricou, Laurie
Andrew Suknaski 19:434

Riddel, Joseph N.
C. Day Lewis 10:125
Jacques Derrida 24:146
T. S. Eliot 13:195
Geoffrey H. Hartman 27:179

Rideout, Walter B.
John Dos Passos 4:131
Howard Fast 23:157
Randall Jarrell 2:207
Norman Mailer 4:318
Henry Roth 2:377
Upton Sinclair 11:497

Ridge, Lola
Frank Swinnerton 31:421

Ridington, Edith Farr
Taylor Caldwell 28:65

Ridley, Clifford A.
Neil Simon 31:395
Julian Symons 2:426

Ridolfino, Carole
Jean Craighead George 35:177

Riefenstahl, Leni
Leni Riefenstahl 16:521

Rieff, David
Anthony Burgess 13:124
Ilya Ehrenburg 18:138

Riegel, Richard
Jim Carroll 35:79
The Clash 30:43

Riegelhaupt, Joyce F.
Darcy Ribeiro 34:104

Riemer, Jack
Ernesto Cardenal 31:70
Chaim Potok 14:430
Elie Wiesel 11:570; 37:451,
457

Riera, Emilio G.
Luis Buñuel 16:130

Ries, Frank W. D.
Jean Cocteau 15:134

Ries, Lawrence R.
William Golding 10:239
Ted Hughes 9:283
John Osborne 11:424
Anthony Powell 9:439
Alan Sillitoe 10:476
John Wain 11:561

Riesman, David
Margaret Mead 37:273

Riesman, Paul
Carlos Castaneda 12:87

Riggan, William
Thomas Berger 38:41
John Updike 34:291

Righter, William
André Malraux 4:329

Righton, Barbara
Peter Straub 28:411

Riley, Brooks
Lina Wertmüller 16:593

Riley, Clayton
Charles Gordone 1:124
Melvin Van Peebles 20:412

Riley, Craig
John Gardner 34:550

Riley, Jocelyn
Cynthia Propper Seton 27:428

Riley, Peter
Jack Spicer 18:512

Rimanelli, Giose
Alberto Moravia 18:343

Rimer, J. Thomas
Shusaku Endo 19:160
Masuji Ibuse 22:227
Yasunari Kawabata 18:283

Rimland, Ingrid
Denise Levertov 28:243

Rimmon-Kenan, Shlomith
Jorge Luis Borges 19:54

Rinear, David L.
Arthur Kopit 18:289

Ringel, Fred J.
Vera Brittain 23:88

Ringel, Harry
Alfred Hitchcock 16:352

Ringer, Agnes C.
John Knowles 26:263

Ringrose, Christopher Xerxes
Ralph Gustafson 36:214

Rinsler, Norma
Louis Aragon 22:40

Rinzler, Alan
Bob Dylan 12:198

Rinzler, Carol Eisen
Judith Rossner 6:469
Fay Weldon 36:449

Ripley, John
Michel Tremblay 29:419

Ripley, Josephine
Frank B. Gilbreth, Jr. and
Ernestine Gilbreth Carey
17:155

Risdon, Ann
T. S. Eliot 9:190

Risk, Mirna
Primo Levi 37:223

Ritchie, Barbara
Milton Meltzer 26:301

Ritholz, Robert E.A.P.
Martin Mull 17:299

Ritter, Jess
Kurt Vonnegut, Jr. 4:563

Ritter, Karen
Virginia Hamilton 26:152
Lee Kingman 17:247
Norma Fox Mazer 26:294

Ritterman, Pamela
Richard Brautigan 12:57

Ritvo, Harriet
Judith Rossner 29:354

Riva, Raymond T.
Samuel Beckett 1:25

Rivas, Daniel E.
Romain Gary 25:191

Rivera, Francisco
José Donoso 4:129

Rivers, Cheryl
Susan Cheever 18:102

Rivers, Elias L.
G. Cabrera Infante 25:102

Rivett, Kenneth
Arthur Koestler 33:233

Critic Index

Rizza, Peggy
  Elizabeth Bishop 4:66

Rizzardi, Alfredo
  Allen Tate 4:538

Robbe-Grillet, Alain
  Samuel Beckett 10:25

Robbins, Henry
  Stanley Elkin 14:158

Robbins, Ira A.
  David Bowie 17:66
  The Clash 30:51
  Elvis Costello 21:72, 74, 75

Robbins, Jack Alan
  Louis Auchincloss 4:28
  Herbert Gold 4:189
  Bernard Malamud 1:200
  Flannery O'Connor 1:258

Roberts, Cecil
  W. Somerset Maugham 11:370

Roberts, David
  R. V. Cassill 4:94; 23:106
  Carl Sagan 30:338

Roberts, John
  Zora Neale Hurston 30:224

Roberts, Mark
  Wayne C. Booth 24:86

Roberts, Neil
  Ted Hughes 37:175

Roberts, Paul
  William Mitchell 25:327

Roberts, Philip
  Edward Bond 23:67

Roberts, R. Ellis
  Pamela Hansford Johnson
  27:215

Roberts, Sheila
  Breyten Breytenbach 23:86
  J. M. Coetzee 23:123
  Athol Fugard 25:176

Roberts, Thomas J.
  Italo Calvino 8:129

Robertson, Anthony
  Hugh Hood 28:188

Robertson, Deborah G.
  Kathryn Kramer 34:74

Robertson, P.
  Otfried Preussler 17:375

Robertson, R. T.
  Mulk Raj Anand 23:20

Robins, Corinne
  Leonard Michaels 25:319

Robins, Dave
  Michael Frayn 31:191

Robins, Wayne
  Joni Mitchell 12:438
  Neil Young 17:574

Robinson, Beryl
  Virginia Hamilton 26:150
  Milton Meltzer 26:301
  Andre Norton 12:462
  Robert Newton Peck 17:337,
  340
  Mary Rodgers 12:494
  Ann Schlee 35:371

Robinson, Christopher
  Odysseus Elytis 15:219

Robinson, David
  Robert Altman 16:19
  Luis Buñuel 16:130
  Orson Welles 20:434

Robinson, Debbie
  Roy A. Gallant 17:130

Robinson, Harlow
  Czesław Miłosz 31:259

Robinson, Henry Morton
  T. H. White 30:443

Robinson, Hubbell
  Gordon Parks 16:459

Robinson, James K.
  Robert Francis 15:239
  John Hollander 14:263
  David Ignatow 14:275
  Archibald MacLeish 14:338
  Josephine Miles 14:370
  David Wagoner 15:559

Robinson, Janice S.
  H. D. 31:212

Robinson, Jill
  Alice Adams 6:2
  Anna Kavan 5:206
  Fran Lebowitz 11:322
  Larry McMurtry 11:371

Robinson, Louie
  Norman Lear 12:332

Robinson, Paul
  Andrew Holleran 38:245
  Gay Talese 37:394

Robinson, Robert
  Saul Bellow 6:54

Robinson, Spider
  Frank Herbert 23:223
  Frederik Pohl 18:413
  Roger Zelazny 21:479

Robinson, Ted
  Ogden Nash 23:317

Robinson, W. R.
  George Garrett 3:190

Robson, Jeremy
  W. H. Auden 4:33
  Leonard Cohen 3:110

Robson, W. W.
  Yvor Winters 32:464, 465

Rochman, Hazel
  Lloyd Alexander 35:27
  Robert Cormier 30:90
  Walter Dean Myers 35:297,
  298
  Ouida Sebestyen 30:350
  Joyce Carol Thomas 35:405

Rockett, W. H.
  George Ryga 14:473

Rockman, Arnold
  Marshall McLuhan 37:264

Rocks, James E.
  T. S. Stribling 23:448

Rockwell, John
  Ray Davies 21:106
  Peter Handke 5:164
  Gerome Ragni and James Rado
  17:384
  Lou Reed 21:306
  Patti Smith 12:537
  Stephen Sondheim 30:401
  Bruce Springsteen 17:478
  Stevie Wonder 12:661

Rodgers, Audrey T.
  T. S. Eliot 6:162, 166

Rodgers, Bernard F., Jr.
  Philip Roth 22:350

Rodman, Selden
  William F. Buckley, Jr. 37:56
  Alejo Carpentier 38:89
  Carlos Fuentes 10:207
  Gabriel García Márquez 27:157
  John Gardner 28:166
  Carl Sandburg 35:351
  Mario Vargas Llosa 31:447
  Derek Walcott 14:551

Rodrigues, Eusebio L.
  Saul Bellow 3:56; 6:52

Rodríguez-Monegal, Emir
  Alejo Carpentier 38:91
  Adolfo Bioy Casares 13:84
  Jorge Luis Borges 2:72; 3:80
  Gabriel García Márquez 3:183
  Juan Carlos Onetti 7:276, 279

Rodriguez-Peralta, Phyllis
  José María Arguedas 10:8

Rodway, Allan
  Samuel Beckett 4:51
  Tom Stoppard 8:502

Roe, Shirley
  Roy A. Gallant 17:131

Roethke, Theodore
  Ben Belitt 22:48

Roffman, Rosaly DeMaios
  Donald Keene 34:569

Rogan, Helen
  Maeve Brennan 5:73
  John Gardner 5:134
  Evan Hunter 31:226
  Jennifer Johnston 7:186
  Irving Wallace 7:510

Rogers, D.
  I. A. Richards 14:455

Rogers, Deborah C.
  J.R.R. Tolkien 12:584

Rogers, Del Marie
  Reynolds Price 6:423

Rogers, Ivor A.
  Robert Heinlein 14:251

Rogers, John Williams
  Bruce Lancaster 36:243

Rogers, Linda
  Margaret Atwood 4:27
  Paulette Jiles 13:304
  Susan Musgrave 13:400
  Angus Wilson 5:515

Rogers, Michael
  Peter Benchley 4:54
  Richard Brautigan 12:70
  Bob Dylan 12:187
  John Gardner 3:188
  Richard Price 12:489
  Piers Paul Read 4:445

Rogers, Norma
  Alice Childress 12:106

Rogers, Pat
  Daphne du Maurier 11:163
  A. N. Wilson 33:457

Rogers, Philip
  Chinua Achebe 11:3

Rogers, Thomas
  R. V. Cassill 23:107
  Vladimir Nabokov 6:358
  Tom Stoppard 1:328

Rogers, Timothy
  Alan Garner 17:135

Rogers, W. G.
  Pearl S. Buck 7:33
  James Clavell 25:125
  Allen Drury 37:102, 105
  C. S. Forester 35:172
  Joanne Greenberg 7:134
  Irwin Shaw 23:398

Rogge, Whitney
  Cecil Bødker 21:13

Roggersdorf, Wilhelm
  Erich von Däniken 30:422

Roginski, Ed
  Peter Weir 20:426

Rogoff, Gordon
  David Mamet 9:361

Rogoff, Leonard
  Lee Smith 25:406

Rogow, Roberta
  William Kotzwinkle 35:257

Rohlehr, Gordon
  V. S. Naipaul 4:372

Rohmann, Gloria P.
  Cynthia Voigt 30:420

Rohmer, Eric
  Ingmar Bergman 16:45
  Alfred Hitchcock 16:357

Rohter, Larry
  Carlos Fuentes 8:223
  Yashar Kemal 14:300

Roiphe, Anne
  Earl Hamner, Jr. 12:259

Rolens, Linda
  Margaret Atwood 25:70

Rollins, Ronald G.
Sean O'Casey **9**:409

Rolo, Charles
Arthur Koestler **33**:234

Rolo, Charles J.
Marcel Aymé **11**:21
Brigid Brophy **29**:91
William Gaddis **19**:185
Romain Gary **25**:185
Martha Gellhorn **14**:195
Aldous Huxley **35**:235
Pär Lagerkvist **7**:198
Françoise Sagan **17**:420
Irwin Shaw **7**:411

Rolph, C. H.
Peter Maas **29**:305

Roman, Diane
Paul Vincent Carroll **10**:98

Romano, John
James Baldwin **17**:42
Donald Barthelme **23**:47
Ann Beattie **8**:56
Thomas Berger **11**:47
Frederick Busch **10**:92
Laurie Colwin **13**:156
John Gardner **18**:182
Graham Greene **18**:196
Barry Hannah **23**:212
Ella Leffland **19**:279
Mary McCarthy **24**:347
Joyce Carol Oates **9**:406
Alan Paton **25**:363
Walker Percy **18**:398
Sylvia Plath **5**:342
John Updike **15**:544
Gore Vidal **10**:501

Rome, Florence
Muriel Spark **3**:465

Romer, Samuel
Alvah Bessie **23**:59

Rompers, Terry
Jim Morrison **17**:294

Ronge, Peter
Eugène Ionesco **6**:249

Rooke, Constance
P. K. Page **18**:380
Katherine Anne Porter **15**:430

Roosevelt, Karyl
Diane Johnson **13**:304
Michael Ondaatje **29**:339

Root, William Pitt
Sonia Sanchez **5**:382
Anne Sexton **4**:483
Peter Wild **14**:580

Rorabacher, Louise E.
Frank Dalby Davison **15**:171

Roraback, Dick
Peter Gent **29**:183

Rorem, Ned
Paul Bowles **2**:79
Tennessee Williams **5**:502

Rorty, Richard
Jacques Derrida **24**:143

Roscoe, Adrian
Ezekiel Mphahlele **25**:341
Ngugi wa Thiong'o **36**:311

Roscoe, Adrian A.
Chinua Achebe **26**:17
John Pepper Clark **38**:120

Rose, Barbara
Tom Wolfe **35**:455

Rose, Ellen Cronan
Margaret Drabble **22**:125
Doris Lessing **6**:300

Rose, Ernst
Hermann Hesse **1**:145

Rose, Frank
David Byrne **26**:95
Pat Conroy **30**:79
Pink Floyd **35**:309
Lou Reed **21**:312
Peter Townshend **17**:540

Rose, Karel
Norma Fox Mazer **26**:292

Rose, Kate
Richard Brautigan **12**:59

Rose, Lois
J. G. Ballard **3**:33
Arthur C. Clarke **4**:104
Robert A. Heinlein **3**:226
C. S. Lewis **3**:297
Walter M. Miller, Jr. **4**:352

Rose, Marilyn
Julien Green **3**:204

Rose, Marilyn Gaddis
Robert Pinget **13**:441

Rose, Mark
J. G. Ballard **36**:42
Frank Herbert **35**:200

Rose, Phyllis
Margaret Drabble **22**:126
Cynthia Ozick **28**:353
Jean Rhys **19**:394

Rose, Stephen
J. G. Ballard **3**:33
Arthur C. Clarke **4**:104
Robert A. Heinlein **3**:226
C. S. Lewis **3**:297
Walter M. Miller, Jr. **4**:352

Rose, Willie Lee
Alex Haley **8**:260

Rosen, Carol
Sam Shepard **17**:448

Rosen, Charles
M. H. Abrams **24**:12

Rosen, Marjorie
Elaine May **16**:433
Albert Maysles and David
Maysles **16**:444

Rosen, Norma
Paula Fox **8**:218
Judith Guest **30**:174
Françoise Sagan **17**:425

Rosen, R. D.
S. J. Perelman **23**:339
James Tate **6**:528

Rosen, Winifred
Richard Peck **21**:299

Rosenbaum, Jean
Marge Piercy **18**:404; **27**:373

Rosenbaum, Jonathan
Robert Altman **16**:31, 39
Robert Bresson **16**:118
John Cassavetes **20**:50
Carl Theodor Dreyer **16**:268
Rainer Werner Fassbinder
20:108
Yasujiro Ozu **16**:454
Sidney Poitier **26**:360
Roman Polanski **16**:472
Richard Pryor **26**:383
Jean Renoir **20**:304

Rosenbaum, Olga
Bernice Rubens **19**:404

Rosenbaum, Ron
Richard Condon **4**:106

Rosenbaum, S. P.
E. M. Forster **22**:130

Rosenberg, Harold
Stanley Kubrick **16**:390
André Malraux **4**:334
Marshall McLuhan **37**:259
Muriel Rukeyser **27**:403
Anna Seghers **7**:407

Rosenberg, Ross
Philip José Farmer **19**:168

Rosenberger, Coleman
John Ehle **27**:101
Ernest K. Gann **23**:164
Bruce Lancaster **36**:243
Carson McCullers **12**:412
Conrad Richter **30**:316

Rosenblatt, Jon
Sylvia Plath **17**:364

Rosenblatt, Roger
Renata Adler **8**:5
Allen Ginsberg **36**:196
Norman Lear **12**:332
Amos Oz **33**:300
Ishmael Reed **32**:356
Ludvík Vaculík **7**:496
Thornton Wilder **6**:572

Rosenblum, Michael
Vladimir Nabokov **15**:394

Rosenfeld, Alvin H.
Saul Bellow **15**:52
Herbert Gold **7**:122
Primo Levi **37**:224, 227
Jakov Lind **4**:293
Nelly Sachs **14**:476
William Styron **15**:529

Rosenfeld, Isaac
Nadine Gordimer **33**:177

Rosenfeld, Megan
Lillian Hellman **34**:347

Rosenfeld, Paul
Ernest Hemingway **19**:210

Rosenfeld, Sidney
Elias Canetti **14**:124

Rosenfeld, Stella P.
Thomas Bernhard **32**:26

Rosengarten, Herbert
Margaret Atwood **8**:33
William Mitchell **25**:323

Rosenman, John B.
Ray Bradbury **15**:84

Rosenstone, Robert A.
Frank Zappa **17**:585

Rosenthal, David H.
Louis-Ferdinand Céline **7**:45
Austin C. Clarke **8**:143
Nicanor Parra **2**:331

Rosenthal, Lucy
Hortense Calisher **2**:96
Norma Klein **30**:237
Richard Llewellyn **7**:207
Sylvia Plath **2**:336
Cynthia Propper Seton **27**:425
Alix Kates Shulman **2**:395

Rosenthal, M. L.
Yehuda Amichai **9**:25
A. R. Ammons **2**:13
Imamu Amiri Baraka **2**:34;
10:19
John Berryman **2**:56
John Betjeman **2**:60
Kay Boyle **1**:42
John Ciardi **10**:105
Austin Clarke **6**:110
Robert Creeley **2**:105; **36**:122
E. E. Cummings **1**:68
James Dickey **2**:115; **7**:81
Robert Duncan **2**:122
Richard Eberhart **11**:178
T. S. Eliot **2**:125
D. J. Enright **4**:155
Robert Frost **1**:110
Allen Ginsberg **1**:118; **2**:162
Paul Goodman **1**:124; **4**:196
Thom Gunn **18**:203
Michael Hamburger **14**:234
Jim Harrison **6**:223
Daniel Hoffman **23**:237
Ted Hughes **2**:197; **9**:280
Randall Jarrell **13**:299
X. J. Kennedy **8**:320
Galway Kinnell **1**:168
Thomas Kinsella **4**:270; **19**:254
Philip Larkin **3**:275, 277
Denise Levertov **2**:242
Robert Lowell **1**:179; **2**:247
George MacBeth **2**:251
Hugh MacDiarmid **2**:253
W. S. Merwin **1**:211
Marianne Moore **1**:226
Charles Olson **2**:326
Robert L. Peters **7**:304
Sylvia Plath **2**:335
Ezra Pound **1**:274; **7**:332
Kenneth Rexroth **1**:283
Theodore Roethke **3**:432
Delmore Schwartz **2**:387
Anne Sexton **2**:391
Karl Shapiro **4**:484
Charles Tomlinson **2**:436
Reed Whittemore **4**:588
Richard Wilbur **14**:577
C. K. Williams **33**:442

Critic Index

William Carlos Williams 1:370

Rosenthal, Michael
David Lodge 36:277

Rosenthal, R.
Paula Fox 2:139

Rosenthal, Raymond
David Caute 29:112
Edward Dahlberg 7:66
Tennessee Williams 8:547

Rosenthal, Stuart
Tod Browning 16:123

Rosenthal, T. G.
Michael Ayrton 7:20
Colin MacInnes 23:283

Rosenzweig, A. L.
Peter Dickinson 12:169

Rosenzweig, Paul
William Faulkner 14:176
John Hawkes 27:194

Roshwald, Miriam
S. Y. Agnon 8:9

Roskolenko, John
John Edgar Wideman 36:450

Ross, Alan
Kingsley Amis 2:7
Alberto Moravia 7:244
Satyajit Ray 16:486

Ross, Alec
David Bowie 17:66, 67

Ross, Anne
Mary Stewart 35:389

Ross, Catherine
Jane Rule 27:422

Ross, Catherine Sheldrick
Hugh MacLennan 14:344

Ross, Charles S.
Tom Wolfe 35:458

Ross, Gary
Margaret Atwood 4:27

Ross, James
Reynolds Price 6:426

Ross, Jerome
Paddy Chayefsky 23:111

Ross, Joan
Alberto Moravia 27:353

Ross, Mary
Vera Brittain 23:91
R. V. Cassill 23:102
A. J. Cronin 32:135
Madeleine L'Engle 12:344
Mary Stewart 35:389
Rebecca West 31:454

Ross, Morton L.
Norman Mailer 1:192

Ross, Nancy Wilson
Sylvia Ashton-Warner 19:20
Ruth Prawer Jhabvala 29:252
Thomas Merton 34:462
Yukio Mishima 27:335
Michael Mott 34:462

Ross, Peter
T. Coraghessan Boyle 36:63

Ross, Robert
Tess Gallagher 18:168, 169

Rossardi, Orlando
Heberto Padilla 38:350

Rosser, Harry L.
Julio Cortázar 33:130

Rossi, Ino
Claude Lévi-Strauss 38:308

Rossi, Louis R.
Salvatore Quasimodo 10:427

Rossman, Charles
F. R. Leavis 24:309

Rosten, Norman
Lucille Clifton 19:109
James Tate 2:431

Roston, Murray
Aldous Huxley 18:270

Roszak, Theodore
Paul Goodman 2:170

Roth, Philip
Edward Albee 9:1
James Baldwin 17:27
Saul Bellow 6:52
Milan Kundera 32:259
Norman Mailer 5:268
Bernard Malamud 5:269; 8:376
J. D. Salinger 8:464
Fredrica Wagman 7:500

Roth, Susan A.
Barbara Wersba 30:429

Rotha, Paul
Buster Keaton 20:189

Rothberg, Abraham
Graham Greene 3:211
Gary Snyder 9:499
Aleksandr I. Solzhenitsyn
4:507; 7:437

Rothchild, Paul
Jim Morrison 17:285

Rothenberg, Randall
Craig Nova 31:297

Rothenbuecher, Bea
Roman Polanski 16:469

Rother, James
Vladimir Nabokov 11:391
Thomas Pynchon 11:453

Rothery, Agnes
Frans Eemil Sillanpää 19:418

Rothman, Nathan
Nadine Gordimer 33:177

Rothman, Nathan L.
Kay Boyle 19:63
A. J. Cronin 32:136
Evan Hunter 31:217
Jessamyn West 17:543
Frank Yerby 7:556

Rothschild, Elaine
Elaine May 16:431

Rothstein, Edward
Agatha Christie 8:141
Philip Roth 22:359
Scott Spencer 30:406

Rothwell, Kenneth S.
John G. Neihardt 32:333

Rotondaro, Fred
Robert Kroetsch 23:269
Robert Lipsyte 21:211

Rottenberg, Annette T.
Taylor Caldwell 28:63

Rottensteiner, Franz
Philip José Farmer 19:165

Roud, Richard
Michelangelo Antonioni 20:19
Bernardo Bertolucci 16:86
Marguerite Duras 20:101
Jean-Luc Godard 20:132
François Truffaut 20:382, 405
Luchino Visconti 16:566

Roudiez, Leon S.
Louis Aragon 22:35
Michel Butor 8:114
Jean Cocteau 15:132
Claude Mauriac 9:363
Claude Simon 39:203, 212
Michel Tournier 36:438

Roueché, Berton
Trevanian 29:432

Rout, Kathleen
Flannery O'Connor 15:412

Routh, Michael
Graham Greene 9:246

Rovit, Earl
Leslie A. Fiedler 24:205
Ernest Hemingway 30:182

Rovit, Earl H.
Saul Bellow 1:31; 8:71; 13:71
Kay Boyle 19:66
Ralph Ellison 1:93
John Hawkes 2:184
Norman Mailer 8:372
Bernard Malamud 1:195

Rowan, Diana
Heinrich Böll 11:58

Rowan, Louis
Diane Wakoski 7:506

Rowan, Thomas
J. F. Powers 1:281

Rowell, Charles H.
Sterling A. Brown 23:96

Rowland, Richard
Carl Theodor Dreyer 16:257

Rowland, Stanley J., Jr.
Walter M. Miller, Jr. 30:255

Rowley, Brian A.
Erich Maria Remarque 21:334

Rowley, Peter
Paula Fox 2:139
John Knowles 4:272

Rowse, A. L.
Vladimir Nabokov 23:309
Flannery O'Connor 2:318
Barbara Pym 13:469

Roy, Emil
John Arden 15:18
Sean O'Casey 15:403

Roy, Joy K.
James Herriot 12:284

Royal, Robert
Mario Puzo 36:363

Royte, Elizabeth
Michael Cunningham 34:42

Ruark, Gibbons
Andrei Voznesensky 1:349

Ruark, Robert
Lenny Bruce 21:45

Ruben, Elaine
Maureen Howard 5:189

Rubens, Linda Morgan
Vine Deloria, Jr. 21:114

Rubenstein, Joshua
Anatoli Rybakov 23:373

Rubenstein, Roberta
Robert Altman 16:21
Margaret Atwood 8:31
Paddy Chayefsky 23:119
Gail Godwin 22:182
Bessie Head 25:232
Doris Lessing 6:303; 10:316
Kamala Markandaya 38:325

Rubin, Jay
Donald Keene 34:568

Rubin, Louis, Jr.
William Melvin Kelley 22:246

Rubin, Louis D., Jr.
Donald Davidson 19:126
William Faulkner 1:101
Carson McCullers 10:338
John Crowe Ransom 4:428;
5:365
Carl Sandburg 10:450
Susan Sontag 10:484
William Styron 3:473
Allen Tate 9:523; 14:533
Robert Penn Warren 1:353;
4:577
Eudora Welty 1:361

Rubin, Steven J.
Richard Wright 21:461

Rubins, Josh
Brigid Brophy 11:69
Raymond Carver 36:104
Agatha Christie 6:108
Don DeLillo 27:86
Jacob Epstein 19:162
Helen MacInnes 27:282
Gilbert Sorrentino 22:396
William Trevor 14:537

Rubinstein, E.
Buster Keaton 20:195

Ruby, Kathryn
Linda Pastan 27:369

Ruby, Michael
    Charles M. Schulz **12**:528

Rucker, Rudy
    Tom Robbins **32**:373

Ruddick, Sara
    Carolyn G. Heilbrun **25**:254

Rudin, Ellen
    Emily Cheney Neville **12**:449
    Katherine Paterson **30**:283

Rudman, Mark
    Robert Lowell **37**:238
    James Tate **25**:429

Rudolf, Anthony
    Yehuda Amichai **22**:32
    Jonathan Schell **35**:367

Rueckert, William
    Wright Morris **7**:245

Ruegg, Maria
    Jacques Derrida **24**:149

Ruffin, Carolyn F.
    Sylvia Ashton-Warner **19**:23
    Vonda N. McIntyre **18**:327
    John McPhee **36**:294

Rugg, Winifred King
    C. S. Forester **35**:169

Rugoff, Milton
    Irwin Shaw **23**:397

Rukeyser, Muriel
    Gunnar Ekelöf **27**:113
    John Crowe Ransom **11**:466

Rule, Jane
    Rita Mae Brown **18**:72

Rule, Philip C.
    Thomas J. Fleming **37**:124

Rumeau-Smith, M.
    Michel del Castillo **38**:168

Rumens, Carol
    Maurice Gee **29**:178
    Colleen McCullough **27**:322
    Leonard Michaels **25**:319
    Alice Walker **27**:449

Runciman, Lex
    Richard F. Hugo **32**:251

Ruoff, A. LaVonne
    Leslie Marmon Silko **23**:408

Rupp, Richard H.
    John Updike **1**:343

Ruppert, Peter
    Max Frisch **18**:161

Rushdie, Salman
    Italo Calvino **33**:97
    Gabriel García Márquez **27**:150
    Günter Grass **22**:197
    Siegfried Lenz **27**:255
    Salman Rushdie **31**:356
    Ernesto Sabato **23**:382
    Michel Tournier **23**:453
    Mario Vargas Llosa **31**:448

Rushing, Andrea Benton
    Audre Lorde **18**:309

Ruskamp, Judith S.
    Henri Michaux **8**:392

Russ, C.A.H.
    Siegfried Lenz **27**:244

Russ, Joanna
    Poul Anderson **15**:15
    Isaac Asimov **19**:28
    Octavia E. Butler **38**:62
    Ursula K. Le Guin **22**:274
    Adrienne Rich **18**:447
    Robert Silverberg **7**:425
    Kate Wilhelm **7**:537
    Gene Wolfe **25**:472

Russ, Lavinia
    Ruth M. Arthur **12**:25
    Judy Blume **12**:44
    M. E. Kerr **12**:298

Russell, Barry
    Howard Brenton **31**:58

Russell, Brandon
    Robert Holdstock **39**:151
    Joyce Carol Oates **33**:296

Russell, Charles
    John Barth **7**:22
    Richard Brautigan **9**:123
    Jerzy Kosinski **6**:284
    Vladimir Nabokov **6**:353
    Ronald Sukenick **6**:523

Russell, Delbert W.
    Anne Hébert **29**:240

Russell, Gillian Harding
    David Donnell **34**:158

Russell, J.
    Honor Arundel **17**:18

Russell, John
    André Malraux **9**:357
    Anthony Powell **3**:402

Russell, Julia G.
    Honor Arundel **17**:15
    Virginia Hamilton **26**:148

Russell, Mariann
    Melvin B. Tolson **36**:430

Rustin, Bayard
    Eldridge Cleaver **30**:67

Ruth, John
    Jay Bennett **35**:45

Rutherford, Anna
    Janet Frame **22**:145

Ryan, Alan
    David Caute **29**:118
    Walter D. Edmonds **35**:157
    Brian Moore **32**:311

Ryan, Allan A., Jr.
    Frederick Forsyth **36**:175
    Nicholas M. Guild **33**:187
    Robert Ludlum **22**:289

Ryan, Frank L.
    Daniel J. Berrigan **4**:56
    C. S. Forester **35**:173
    Anne Hébert **4**:220
    Françoise Sagan **17**:426

Ryan, Judith
    Christa Wolf **29**:467

Ryan, Marjorie
    Diane Johnson **5**:198

Ryan, Richard W.
    Isaac Asimov **26**:37
    Anne McCaffrey **17**:281

Ryan, Stephen P.
    Leslie A. Fiedler **24**:190

Rybus, Rodney
    Seamus Heaney **25**:250

Ryf, Robert S.
    Henry Green **2**:179
    B. S. Johnson **9**:299
    Doris Lessing **10**:313
    Vladimir Nabokov **6**:353
    Flann O'Brien **7**:268

Ryle, John
    John Berger **19**:40
    Penelope Fitzgerald **19**:173
    Mark Helprin **10**:261

Rysten, Felix
    Jean Giono **11**:232

Rzhevsky, Leonid
    Aleksandr I. Solzhenitsyn
        26:417

Saal, Hubert
    Paul McCartney **35**:278
    Mary Renault **17**:393
    Irwin Shaw **7**:411

Saal, Rollene W.
    Kristin Hunter **35**:224
    Anne Tyler **28**:429

Sabin, Edwin L.
    Lenora Mattingly Weber **12**:631

Sabiston, Elizabeth
    Philip Roth **6**:475
    Ludvík Vaculík **7**:497

Sabor, Peter
    Ezekiel Mphahlele **25**:345

Sabri, M. Arjamand
    Thomas Pynchon **3**:417

Sacharoff, Mark
    Elias Canetti **3**:98

Sachner, Mark J.
    Samuel Beckett **14**:71

Sachs, Marilyn
    Nicholasa Mohr **12**:445, 446
    Robert Newton Peck **17**:338

Sack, John
    Ward S. Just **27**:225

Sacks, Peter
    James Merrill **34**:239

Sackville-West, Edward
    Ivy Compton-Burnett **15**:137

Saddler, Allen
    Ann Jellicoe **27**:210
    C. P. Taylor **27**:442

Sadker, David Miller
    Bette Greene **30**:170
    Kristin Hunter **35**:229

Sadker, Myra Pollack
    Bette Greene **30**:170
    Kristin Hunter **35**:229

Sadler, Frank
    Jack Spicer **18**:508

Sadoff, Dianne F.
    Gail Godwin **8**:247

Sadoff, Ira
    Tess Gallagher **18**:168
    Robert Hass **18**:210
    Philip Levine **14**:315

Sáez, Richard
    James Merrill **6**:323

Safir, Margery
    Pablo Neruda **28**:312

Sagalyn, Raphael
    James H. Webb, Jr. **22**:453

Sagan, Carl
    Paul West **14**:568

Sagar, Keith
    Ted Hughes **2**:203

Sage, Lorna
    Brian Aldiss **14**:14
    John Barth **27**:28
    Simone de Beauvoir **31**:43
    Olga Broumas **10**:76
    Italo Calvino **39**:307
    David Caute **29**:124
    Bruce Chatwin **28**:74
    Isabel Colegate **36**:112
    Maureen Duffy **37**:116
    Elaine Feinstein **36**:169
    John Hawkes **27**:201
    Patricia Highsmith **14**:261
    Erica Jong **6**:267
    Thomas Keneally **27**:232
    Alison Lurie **39**:183
    Iris Murdoch **11**:384
    Vladimir Nabokov **8**:412
    Edna O'Brien **36**:336
    Sylvia Plath **11**:450
    Philip Roth **15**:455
    Françoise Sagan **17**:429; **36**:382
    Christina Stead **32**:413
    Fay Weldon **36**:447
    Angus Wilson **34**:580

Sage, Victor
    David Storey **8**:505

Said, Edward
    V. S. Naipaul **37**:319

Said, Edward W.
    R. P. Blackmur **2**:61
    Jacques Derrida **24**:140
    Michel Foucault **34**:340
    Lucien Goldmann **24**:238
    Paul Goodman **2**:169
    V. S. Naipaul **18**:364

Saikowski, Charlotte
    Primo Levi **37**:222

Sail, Lawrence
    James Fenton **32**:166
    Craig Raine **32**:349

Sailsbury, M. B.
    Franklyn M. Branley **21**:16

Critic Index

Sainer, Arthur
Martin Duberman 8:185
Max Frisch 18:163
Jack Gelber 14:194
Simon Gray 9:242
Michael McClure 6:317
Miguel Piñero 4:401

St. Aubyn, F. C.
Albert Camus 32:93

St. John, David
Marvin Bell 31:49, 50
Norman Dubie 36:141
Philip Levine 33:272
Stanley Plumly 33:315
C. K. Williams 33:448
Charles Wright 28:458

St. John-Stevas, Norman
C. S. Lewis 6:308

St. Martin, Hardie
Blas de Otero 11:424

Sakurai, Emiko
Fumiko Enchi 31:140
Kenzaburō Ōe 10:374
Kenneth Rexroth 11:474
Shiga Naoya 33:370

Salamon, Julie
Harriet Doerr 34:154

Salamon, Lynda B.
Sylvia Plath 17:350

Salamone, Anthony
Howard Fast 23:160

Sale, Roger
Richard Adams 18:2
E. M. Almedingen 12:3
A. Alvarez 13:10
Kingsley Amis 5:22
Saul Bellow 6:61
Thomas Berger 8:84
Richard Brautigan 12:70
Frederick Buechner 2:83; 6:103
Anthony Burgess 5:87
Frederick Busch 10:94
Agatha Christie 8:141
Richard Condon 8:150
Robertson Davies 7:72
E. L. Doctorow 6:135
Margaret Drabble 2:118, 119;
    8:183; 22:122
George P. Elliott 2:131
Frederick Exley 6:172
Leslie A. Fiedler 4:162
B. H. Friedman 7:109
Paula Fox 2:141
Herbert Gold 7:121
Witold Gombrowicz 7:122
Joanne Greenberg 30:163
Dashiell Hammett 5:161
John Hawkes 4:214
Mark Helprin 10:261
Maureen Howard 5:188; 14:267
Zora Neale Hurston 30:222
Alfred Kazin 38:281
Ken Kesey 6:278
Richard Kostelanetz 28:215
John le Carré 5:234
Alan Lelchuk 5:240
Doris Lessing 2:239, 242;
    6:299, 304

Alison Lurie 4:306
Ross Macdonald 2:255
David Madden 5:266
Norman Mailer 2:261; 4:319
Peter Matthiessen 7:212
Iris Murdoch 8:404
Tim O'Brien 7:271
Grace Paley 6:392
J. F. Powers 8:447
Richard Price 6:427
Mario Puzo 36:359
Judith Rossner 6:470
Philip Roth 2:381; 6:476
Andrew Sinclair 2:400
Isaac Bashevis Singer 9:487
Richard Stern 39:242
Robert Stone 5:410
Paul Theroux 5:428
J.R.R. Tolkien 1:338; 38:433
Lionel Trilling 24:458
Anne Tyler 11:553
John Updike 23:467
Luisa Valenzuela 31:436
Mario Vargas Llosa 6:547
Kurt Vonnegut, Jr. 8:532
David Wagoner 5:475
James Welch 14:558
René Wellek 28:449
William Wharton 37:437
Monique Wittig 22:474
Larry Woiwode 10:541

Salemi, Joseph S.
William Gaddis 19:187

Sales, Grover
Jean M. Auel 31:23

Salisbury, David F.
Ernest K. Gann 23:168

Salisbury, Harrison E.
Aleksandr I. Solzhenitsyn 4:511

Salisbury, Stephan
Howard Fast 23:159

Salkey, Andrew
Ngugi Wa Thiong'o 13:584

Salmans, Sandra
Scott Sommer 25:425

Salmon, Sheila
Barbara Corcoran 17:77

Salomon, I. L.
Robert Duncan 4:142

Salomon, Louis B.
Carson McCullers 12:408

Salter, D.P.M.
Saul Bellow 2:53

Salter, Denis
Jack Hodgins 23:229

Salter, Mary Jo
Bret Easton Ellis 39:58

Salvadore, Maria
Betsy Byars 35:76

Salvadori, Massimo
William F. Buckley, Jr. 37:58

Salvatore, Caroline
Chaim Potok 26:368

Salvesen, Christopher
Jane Rule 27:416

Salway, Lance
Robert Cormier 12:136
Peter Dickinson 12:168
Alan Garner 17:147
S. E. Hinton 30:206
Barbara Wersba 30:433
Robert Westall 17:556

Salzman, Eric
David Byrne 26:99
Andrew Lloyd Webber and Tim
    Rice 21:431
Frank Zappa 17:591

Salzman, Jack
John Dos Passos 4:138
Jack Kerouac 2:229
Tillie Olsen 4:386

Samet, Tom
Henry Roth 11:488

Sammons, Jeffrey L.
Hermann Hesse 11:271

Sampley, Arthur M.
Robert Frost 1:112

Sampson, Edward C.
E. B. White 10:529

Samuels, Charles Thomas
Richard Adams 4:7
Michelangelo Antonioni 20:33
Donald Barthelme 3:43
Robert Bresson 16:115
Lillian Hellman 2:187
Alfred Hitchcock 16:348
Stanley Kubrick 16:384
Christina Stead 2:421; 32:408
John Updike 1:344; 2:442
Kurt Vonnegut, Jr. 2:454

Samuels, Wilfred D.
John Edgar Wideman 36:455

Samuelson, David N.
Arthur C. Clarke 18:103
Robert A. Heinlein 26:164, 167
Walter M. Miller, Jr. 30:260,
    261

Sanborn, Sara
Anthony Burgess 4:84
Rosalyn Drexler 6:143
Alison Lurie 4:305
Joyce Carol Oates 3:363

Sandars, N. K.
David Jones 4:260

Sandeen, Ernest
R. P. Blackmur 2:62

Sander, Ellen
Mick Jagger and Keith Richard
    17:223
John Lennon and Paul
    McCartney 12:364
Paul McCartney 35:278
Joni Mitchell 12:435
Paul Simon 17:459
Neil Young 17:569
Frank Zappa 17:585

Sanders, Charles
Theodore Roethke 19:402

Sanders, Charles L.
Norman Lear 12:330

Sanders, David
John Hersey 1:144; 7:153
Frederick Morgan 23:300
Robert Phillips 28:365

Sanders, Ed
Allen Ginsberg 4:181

Sanders, Frederick L.
Conrad Aiken 3:5

Sanders, Ivan
Dobrica Ćosić 14:132
György Konrád 4:273; 10:304
Milan Kundera 4:278
József Lengyel 7:202
Amos Oz 8:436

Sanders, Peter L.
Robert Graves 2:176

Sanders, Ronald
Richard Wright 21:442

Sanderson, Ivan
Farley Mowat 26:334

Sanderson, Stewart F.
Compton Mackenzie 18:315

Sandhuber, Holly
Lois Duncan 26:107

Sandler, Linda
Margaret Atwood 8:29, 30
Ernest Buckler 13:123

Sandoe, James
Margery Allingham 19:13
Robert Bloch 33:83
August Derleth 31:138
Roy Fuller 28:148
Evan Hunter 31:219, 220
M. M. Kaye 28:198
Mary Stewart 35:388

Sandow, Gregory
Michael Moorcock 27:352

Sandrof, Ivan
Jean Lee Latham 12:324

Sands, Douglas B.
Franklyn M. Branley 21:19

Sandwell, B. K.
Mazo de la Roche 14:148

Sandy, Stephen
Peter Davison 28:104

Saner, Reg
William Dickey 28:119

Sanfield, Steve
Michael McClure 6:320

Sanhuber, Holly
Christopher Collier and James
    L. Collier 30:74

Santha, Rama Rau
Ruth Prawer Jhabvala 29:253

Santí, Enrico-Mario
G. Cabrera Infante 25:100

Sargeant, Winthrop
Vittorio De Sica 20:87
Robert Lewis Taylor 14:534

Sargent, David
　Robert Wilson **9**:576

Sargo, Tina Mendes
　Luchino Visconti **16**:566

Sarland, Charles
　William Mayne **12**:402

Sarlin, Bob
　Chuck Berry **17**:54
　Janis Ian **21**:186
　Mick Jagger and Keith Richard **17**:229
　Van Morrison **21**:235
　Laura Nyro **17**:316
　Neil Young **17**:572

Sarotte, Georges-Michel
　William Inge **19**:229
　John Rechy **18**:442

Saroyan, Aram
　Kenneth Koch **8**:323
　Phillip Lopate **29**:299
　Frank O'Hara **13**:424
　Anne Waldman **7**:508

Saroyan, William
　Flann O'Brien **10**:362

Sarratt, Janet P.
　Milton Meltzer **26**:302

Sarrett, Ethel Shapiro
　Richard Grayson **38**:210

Sarris, Andrew George
　Woody Allen **16**:7, 11
　Robert Altman **16**:36, 38, 43
　Ralph Bakshi **26**:68
　Mel Brooks **12**:75
　Michael Cimino **16**:209
　Francis Ford Coppola **16**:245
　Brian De Palma **20**:80
　Rainer Werner Fassbinder **20**:115
　Federico Fellini **16**:271, 297
　John Ford **16**:308
　Bob Fosse **20**:127
　Jean-Luc Godard **20**:137, 153
　Werner Herzog **16**:333
　George Roy Hill **26**:203, 206, 208
　Alfred Hitchcock **16**:341, 357
　Kristin Hunter **35**:224
　John Huston **20**:174
　Elia Kazan **16**:364, 366
　Buster Keaton **20**:196
　Stanley Kubrick **16**:380
　Akira Kurosawa **16**:406
　John Landis **26**:275
　Richard Lester **20**:231, 232
　Norman Mailer **3**:315
　Sam Peckinpah **20**:282
　Roman Polanski **16**:473
　Jean Renoir **20**:308
　Alain Resnais **16**:504, 518
　Carlos Saura **20**:318
　Paul Schrader **26**:390, 393, 396
　Wilfrid Sheed **4**:487
　Joan Micklin Silver **20**:344
　Jerzy Skolimowski **20**:354
　François Truffaut **20**:383, 404, 406, 407
　Lina Wertmüller **16**:599
　Billy Wilder **20**:461, 466

Sartre, Jean-Paul
　Georges Bataille **29**:34
　Albert Camus **14**:104
　Aimé Césaire **32**:108
　John Dos Passos **11**:153
　William Faulkner **9**:197
　Jean Genet **2**:155

Sato, Hiroko
　Nella Larsen **37**:213

Saunders, Charles
　May Swenson **14**:522

Saunders, Mike
　Ray Davies **21**:92, 93

Saunders, William S.
　James Wright **28**:466

Sauvage, Leo
　Charles Fuller **25**:182
　David Hare **29**:217
　Beth Henley **23**:217
　David Mamet **34**:222
　Tom Stoppard **34**:280
　Hugh Whitemore **37**:446

Sauzey, François
　Jean-Paul Sartre **18**:473

Savage, D. S.
　E. M. Forster **13**:216
　Christopher Isherwood **14**:286
　Pamela Hansford Johnson **27**:215
　Mary Renault **17**:391

Savage, Jon
　Lou Reed **21**:316

Savage, Lois E.
　Norma Klein **30**:237
　Noel Streatfeild **21**:412

Savory, Teo
　Guillevic **33**:192

Savvas, Minas
　Yannis Ritsos **13**:487

Sawyer, Roland
　Thor Heyerdahl **26**:190

Saxon, Wolfgang
　Robert Graves **39**:320
　Jesse Stuart **34**:372

Sayre, Henry M.
　John Ashbery **15**:31

Sayre, Joel
　Garson Kanin **22**:231

Sayre, Nora
　Enid Bagnold **25**:77
　Marguerite Duras **20**:99
　Marian Engel **36**:157
　Iris Murdoch **1**:236
　Richard O'Brien **17**:325
　Anne Roiphe **3**:434
　Elizabeth Taylor **2**:432
　James Thurber **25**:439
　Kurt Vonnegut, Jr. **3**:502

Sayre, Robert
　Lucien Goldmann **24**:246

Sayre, Robert F.
　James Baldwin **1**:15

Scaduto, Anthony
　Bob Dylan **4**:148

Scammell, Michael
　Ilya Ehrenburg **34**:438
　Anatol Goldberg **34**:438

Scammell, William
　John Berger **19**:40
　Patrick White **18**:547

Scanlan, Margaret
　Iris Murdoch **15**:387

Scanlan, Tom
　Thornton Wilder **35**:446

Scanlon, Laura Polla
　John Donovan **35**:139
　Barbara Wersba **30**:430
　Maia Wojciechowska **26**:454

Scannell, Vernon
　Martin Booth **13**:103
　Randall Jarrell **9**:298
　George MacBeth **9**:341
　Piers Paul Read **25**:375

Scarbrough, George
　Babette Deutsch **18**:119
　James Schevill **7**:400

Scarf, Maggie
　Lillian Hellman **18**:228
　Susan Sontag **10**:487

Schaap, Dick
　Peter Gent **29**:181
　George Plimpton **36**:354
　Mario Puzo **2**:351

Schaar, John H.
　Jonathan Schell **35**:364

Schacht, Chuck
　Mollie Hunter **21**:169
　Diana Wynne Jones **26**:229

Schaefer, J. O'Brien
　Margaret Drabble **5**:119

Schaeffer, Susan Fromberg
　Nancy Willard **37**:465

Schafer, William J.
　Mark Harris **19**:202
　David Wagoner **3**:507

Schaffer, Michael
　Bruce Catton **35**:94

Schaffner, Nicholas
　Ray Davies **21**:107
　John Lennon and Paul McCartney **12**:385

Schaire, Jeffrey
　Pat Barker **32**:13
　Umberto Eco **28**:133
　Leon Rooke **34**:251

Schakne, Ann
　Roderick L. Haig-Brown **21**:136

Schaller, Joseph G., S.J.
　Carolyn Hougan **34**:61

Schamschula, Walter
　Václav Havel **25**:223

Schanzer, George O.
　Manuel Mujica Láinez **31**:281

Schapiro, Leonard
　Aleksandr I. Solzhenitsyn **7**:440

Schatt, Stanley
　Langston Hughes **10**:279
　Isaac Bashevis Singer **3**:459
　Kurt Vonnegut, Jr. **1**:348; **4**:560; **12**:614

Schaub, Thomas Hill
　Thomas Pynchon **18**:430

Schechner, Mark
　Lionel Trilling **11**:540

Schechner, Richard
　Edward Albee **11**:10
　Eugène Ionesco **6**:253

Scheer, George F.
　Thomas J. Fleming **37**:125

Scheerer, Constance
　Sylvia Plath **9**:432

Schein, Harry
　Carl Theodor Dreyer **16**:258

Schemering, Christopher
　Sumner Locke Elliott **38**:181
　Joseph Hansen **38**:238

Schene, Carol
　Norma Klein **30**:240

Scherman, David E.
　Milton Meltzer **26**:305

Schevill, James
　Peter Davison **28**:99
　Richard F. Hugo **32**:234
　Kenneth Patchen **18**:395

Schickel, Richard
　Woody Allen **16**:3
　Robert Altman **16**:24
　Michelangelo Antonioni **20**:30
　Louis Auchincloss **9**:54
　Ingmar Bergman **16**:58, 63
　John Cassavetes **20**:47
　Charles Chaplin **16**:202
　Francis Ford Coppola **16**:236
　Joan Didion **1**:75
　Nora Ephron **31**:159
　Jean-Luc Godard **20**:143
　John Landis **26**:271
　Norman Lear **12**:333
　Alan Lelchuk **5**:242
　Richard Lester **20**:227
　Ross Macdonald **1**:185
　Garry Marshall **17**:276
　Steve Martin **30**:251
　Monty Python **21**:228
　Thomas Pynchon **2**:358
　Satyajit Ray **16**:481
　Alain Resnais **16**:504
　Eric Rohmer **16**:530
　Carlos Saura **20**:318
　Peter Shaffer **5**:387
　Glendon Swarthout **35**:402
　Luchino Visconti **16**:567
　Andy Warhol **20**:420
　Frederick Wiseman **20**:470, 475

Schickele, Peter
　John Lennon and Paul McCartney **12**:355

Critic Index

Schieder, Rupert
Jack Hodgins **23**:232, 235

Schier, Donald
André Breton **2**:81

Schier, Flint
Michel Foucault **31**:186

Schiff, Jeff
Mary Oliver **19**:362

Schillaci, Peter P.
Luis Buñuel **16**:140

Schiller, Barbara
Brigid Brophy **11**:68
Mary Stewart **35**:389

Schiller, Jerome P.
I. A. Richards **24**:395

Schindenhette, Susan
Ntozake Shange **38**:396

Schine, Cathleen
Roy Blount, Jr. **38**:46

Schirmer, Gregory A.
Scott Elledge **34**:430
Seamus Heaney **25**:243
M. L. Rosenthal **28**:395
E. B. White **34**:430

Schjeldahl, Peter
Paul Blackburn **9**:100
André Breton **2**:80; **9**:129
Russell Edson **13**:191
Gerome Ragni and James Rado
17:384
James Schevill **7**:400
Diane Wakoski **11**:564

Schlant, Ernestine
Christa Wolf **14**:593

Schlesinger, Arthur, Jr.
Woody Allen **16**:11
David Caute **29**:119
Michael Cimino **16**:209
Bob Fosse **20**:127
Mary McCarthy **24**:343
Paul Schrader **26**:391

Schlesinger, Arthur M., Jr.
Marshall McLuhan **37**:262

Schlotter, Charles
T. Coraghessan Boyle **36**:62
William Caunitz **34**:36

Schlueter, June
Samuel Beckett **18**:43
Peter Handke **15**:269
Arthur Miller **10**:346
Tom Stoppard **15**:522

Schlueter, Paul
Pär Lagerkvist **7**:201
Doris Lessing **1**:174; **3**:283
Mary McCarthy **1**:205
Gabrielle Roy **14**:469
Robert Lewis Taylor **14**:535

Schmering, Chris
Satyajit Ray **16**:494

Schmerl, Rudolf B.
Aldous Huxley **3**:255

Schmidt, Arthur
Joni Mitchell **12**:437
Brian Wilson **12**:641, 645
Frank Zappa **17**:589

Schmidt, Elizabeth
Margaret Craven **17**:80

Schmidt, Michael
Donald Davie **8**:165
Philip Larkin **18**:300
George MacBeth **2**:252
Edwin Morgan **31**:275
Peter Porter **33**:319
Jon Silkin **2**:396
Stevie Smith **25**:419
Charles Tomlinson **13**:548
Yevgeny Yevtushenko **26**:466

Schmidt, Nancy J.
Amos Tutuola **29**:442

Schmidt, Pilar
Lenora Mattingly Weber **12**:634

Schmidt, Sandra
Hortense Calisher **38**:71
James D. Forman **21**:116

Schmieder, Rob
Joseph Hansen **38**:239

Schmitt, James
Fritz Hochwälder **36**:236

Schmitz, Eugenia E.
Isabelle Holland **21**:153

Schmitz, Neil
Donald Barthelme **1**:19
Richard Brautigan **3**:90
Robert Coover **3**:113; **7**:58
Thomas Pynchon **6**:435
Ishmael Reed **5**:368; **6**:448
Jonathan Schell **35**:366
Al Young **19**:478

Schneck, Stephen
Richard Brautigan **1**:44
LeRoi Jones **1**:162

Schneckloth, Tim
Frank Zappa **17**:592

Schneidau, Herbert N.
Ezra Pound **4**:408

Schneider, Alan
Edward Albee **11**:10

Schneider, Duane
Anaïs Nin **1**:248; **11**:396

Schneider, Duane B.
Gilbert Sorrentino **22**:391

Schneider, Elisabeth
T. S. Eliot **3**:140

Schneider, Harold W.
Muriel Spark **13**:519

Schneider, Isidor
Kenneth Burke **24**:118
Margaret Mead **37**:270

Schneider, Mary W.
Muriel Spark **18**:504

Schneider, Richard J.
William H. Gass **8**:240

Schoeck, R. J.
Allen Tate **24**:442

Schoenbaum, S.
Leon Rooke **34**:253

Schoenbrun, David
Francine du Plessix Gray
22:199
Cornelius Ryan **7**:385

Schoenstein, Ralph
Garry Trudeau **12**:590

Schoenwald, Richard L.
Ogden Nash **23**:322

Schoffman, Stuart
Nora Ephron **31**:158
John Gardner **34**:549
Richard Grayson **38**:210

Scholes, Robert
Jorge Luis Borges **10**:63
Robert Coover **32**:120
Lawrence Durrell **8**:190
Gail Godwin **22**:179
John Hawkes **9**:262; **15**:273
Robert A. Heinlein **26**:166
Frank Herbert **12**:276
Ursula K. Le Guin **22**:266
Iris Murdoch **22**:324
Sylvia Plath **17**:351
Frederik Pohl **18**:410
Ishmael Reed **5**:370
Kurt Vonnegut, Jr. **2**:451;
4:561

Schonberg, Harold C.
T. H. White **30**:450

Schopen, Bernard A.
John Updike **23**:464

Schorer, Mark
Truman Capote **3**:98
Walter Van Tilburg Clark **28**:77
Leon Edel **29**:168
Martha Gellhorn **14**:195
Lillian Hellman **4**:221
Carson McCullers **4**:344
Katherine Anne Porter **7**:312
John Steinbeck **21**:367
René Wellek **28**:443

Schott, Webster
Richard Adams **5**:6
Louis Auchincloss **4**:31
W. H. Auden **2**:25
Donald Barthelme **2**:41
Saul Bellow **8**:69
William Peter Blatty **2**:63
Vance Bourjaily **8**:103
Vincent Canby **13**:131
James Carroll **38**:104, 109
R. V. Cassill **23**:107, 108
James Clavell **6**:113; **25**:126
J. M. Coetzee **23**:126
Robert Coover **7**:57
Michael Crichton **2**:108
Thomas J. Fleming **37**:123
John Gardner **10**:223
Andrew M. Greeley **28**:175
Shirley Hazzard **18**:219
William Kennedy **34**:206
John Knowles **26**:261
Ira Levin **6**:305

David Madden **15**:350
Mary McCarthy **39**:486
Colleen McCullough **27**:319
Larry McMurtry **2**:272
Ted Mooney **25**:329
Toni Morrison **22**:320
Sylvia Plath **2**:338
Raymond Queneau **10**:432
Philip Roth **3**:436
Susan Fromberg Schaeffer
11:492
Georges Simenon **2**:398
Harvey Swados **5**:421
Thomas Tryon **11**:548
Elio Vittorini **6**:551
Jessamyn West **7**:520
Patrick White **18**:549
Tennessee Williams **5**:506

Schow, H. Wayne
Günter Grass **11**:248

Schrader, George Alfred
Norman Mailer **14**:348

Schrader, Paul
Robert Bresson **16**:115
Brian De Palma **20**:72
Carl Theodor Dreyer **16**:263
Albert Maysles and David
Maysles **16**:440
Yasujiro Ozu **16**:449
Sam Peckinpah **20**:273

Schraepen, Edmond
William Carlos Williams **9**:575

Schraibman, Joseph
Juan Goytisolo **23**:188, 189

Schramm, Richard
Philip Levine **2**:244
Howard Moss **7**:248

Schrank, Bernice
Sean O'Casey **11**:411

Schraufnagel, Noel
Kristin Hunter **35**:226
Frank G. Yerby **22**:491

Schreiber, Jan
Elizabeth Daryush **6**:122

Schreiber, Le Anne
Jerome Charyn **8**:135
David Lodge **36**:274
Adrienne Rich **36**:367
Marilynne Robinson **25**:386

Schreiber, Ron
Marge Piercy **27**:379

Schroeder, Andreas
Michael Ondaatje **14**:408

Schroth, Raymond A., S.J.
Andrew M. Greeley **28**:170,
173
Norman Mailer **2**:261; **3**:312
Walter M. Miller, Jr. **30**:256

Schruers, Fred
Joan Armatrading **17**:9
Ray Davies **21**:98
Neil Young **17**:576

Schubert, Peter Z.
Josef Škvorecký **39**:221

Schulberg, Budd
Laura Z. Hobson **25**:270

Schulder, Diane
Marge Piercy **3**:385

Schuler, Barbara
Peter Taylor **1**:333

Schulman, Grace
Jorge Luis Borges **13**:110
Richard Eberhart **3**:134
Carolyn Kizer **39**:171
Pablo Neruda **5**:302
Amos Oz **33**:301
Octavio Paz **6**:395
Adrienne Rich **3**:427
Mark Van Doren **6**:541
Richard Wilbur **9**:569

Schulps, Dave
Elvis Costello **21**:67
Ray Davies **21**:106
Van Morrison **21**:238
Peter Townshend **17**:537

Schultheis, Anne Marie
Luisa Valenzuela **31**:439

Schulz, Charles M.
Charles M. Schulz **12**:527

Schulz, Max F.
John Barth **9**:68
Norman Mailer **1**:190
Bernard Malamud **1**:199
Kurt Vonnegut, Jr. **1**:347

Schumacher, Dorothy
Margaret O. Hyde **21**:171

Schumer, Fran
T. R. Pearson **39**:89

Schürer, Ernst
Fritz Hochwälder **36**:235

Schusler, Kris
Robert Lewis Taylor **14**:534

Schuster, Arian
Richard Brautigan **12**:74

Schuster, Edgar H.
Harper Lee **12**:341

Schwaber, Paul
Robert Lowell **1**:184

Schwartz, Alvin
Jerome Siegel and Joe Shuster **21**:362

Schwartz, Barry N.
Eugène Ionesco **15**:296

Schwartz, Delmore
R. P. Blackmur **24**:53
John Dos Passos **15**:180
T. S. Eliot **24**:166
Randall Jarrell **1**:159
Robinson Jeffers **11**:304
Edmund Wilson **24**:468
Yvor Winters **32**:451

Schwartz, Edward
Katherine Anne Porter **7**:309

Schwartz, Harry
Ronald J. Glasser **37**:133

Schwartz, Howard
Yehuda Amichai **22**:31
David Ignatow **7**:178

Schwartz, Joseph
A. G. Mojtabai **29**:320

Schwartz, Julius
Roy A. Gallant **17**:127

Schwartz, Kessel
Vicente Aleixandre **9**:15; **36**:28
Manlio Argueta **31**:19
Juan Benet **28**:21
Adolfo Bioy Casares **8**:94
Antonio Buero Vallejo **15**:96
Gabriel García Márquez **10**:215
Juan Goytisolo **23**:182, 183
Manuel Mujica Láinez **31**:282
Juan Rulfo **8**:462

Schwartz, Lloyd
Elizabeth Bishop **9**:93, 97

Schwartz, Lynne Sharon
Beryl Bainbridge **5**:40
Rosellen Brown **32**:68
Eleanor Clark **19**:107
Natalia Ginzburg **5**:141
Susan Fromberg Schaeffer **11**:491
Alix Kates Shulman **10**:475
Anne Tyler **11**:552
Fay Weldon **9**:560

Schwartz, Nancy Lynn
E. M. Broner **19**:72
Jill Robinson **10**:438

Schwartz, Paul J.
Samuel Beckett **6**:41
Alain Robbe-Grillet **8**:453

Schwartz, Ronald
Alejo Carpentier **38**:100
Miguel Delibes **8**:169
José Donoso **32**:159
José María Gironella **11**:234
Juan Goytisolo **23**:181

Schwartz, Sanford
Milton Meltzer **26**:302
John Updike **34**:288

Schwartz, Sheila
E. M. Broner **19**:72

Schwartz, Tony
Steve Martin **30**:247

Schwartz, Wendy
Marge Piercy **27**:379

Schwartzenburg, Dewey
Carl Sagan **30**:337

Schwarz, Alfred
Jean-Paul Sartre **18**:469

Schwarz, Egon
Hermann Hesse **17**:211

Schwarzbach, F. S.
Thomas Pynchon **9**:443

Schwarzchild, Bettina
James Purdy **2**:349

Schweitzer, Darrell
Samuel R. Delany **38**:159
Jack Vance **35**:428
Roger Zelazny **21**:474, 478

Schwerer, Armand
Diane Wakoski **7**:506

Scigaj, Leonard M.
Frank Herbert **35**:201

Scobbie, Irene
Pär Lagerkvist **10**:312
Leon Rooke **25**:393

Scobie, Stephen
Bill Bissett **18**:59
John Glassco **9**:237
John Newlove **14**:377
B. P. Nichol **18**:366, 368
Michael Ondaatje **14**:408
Leon Rooke **25**:393

Scobie, Stephen A. C.
F. R. Scott **22**:375

Scobie, W. I.
Melvin Van Peebles **2**:448
Derek Walcott **2**:459

Scofield, Martin
T. S. Eliot **9**:186

Scoggin, Margaret C.
Walter Farley **17**:116
Henry Gregor Felsen **17**:120
Mary Stolz **12**:547, 549, 550, 552
John R. Tunis **12**:594

Scoppa, Bud
Walter Becker and Donald Fagen **26**:79
Jackson Browne **21**:34
Mick Jagger and Keith Richard **17**:228
John Lennon and Paul McCartney **12**:366
Jimmy Page and Robert Plant **12**:479
Neil Young **17**:572, 575

Scott, Alexander
Hugh MacDiarmid **4**:310

Scott, Carolyn D.
Graham Greene **1**:130

Scott, Helen G.
Alfred Hitchcock **16**:346

Scott, J. D.
Gil Orlovitz **22**:334
Andrew Sinclair **2**:400

Scott, James B.
Djuna Barnes **29**:26

Scott, John
Ch'ien Chung-shu **22**:106

Scott, Lael
Mary Stolz **12**:554

Scott, Malcolm
Jean Giono **11**:232

Scott, Nathan A., Jr.
Elizabeth Bishop **32**:41
Charles M. Schulz **12**:522
Lionel Trilling **24**:460
Richard Wright **1**:378

Scott, Paul
Ved Mehta **37**:292

Scott, Peter Dale
John Newlove **14**:377
Mordecai Richler **5**:372

Scott, Tom
Hugh MacDiarmid **4**:309
Ezra Pound **4**:413

Scott, Wendy
Jacques Audiberti **38**:31

Scott, Winfield Townley
Edwin Honig **33**:211
David Ignatow **7**:173
James Purdy **28**:377
Louis Simpson **7**:426

Scott-James, R. A.
Edith Sitwell **9**:493

Scouffas, George
J. F. Powers **1**:280

Scruggs, Charles W.
Ishmael Reed **32**:358
Jean Toomer **4**:549

Scruton, Roger
Lucien Goldmann **24**:254
Marge Piercy **27**:381
Harold Pinter **27**:396
Sylvia Plath **5**:340
Tom Stoppard **29**:403

Scrutton, Mary
Vera Brittain **23**:92

Scudder, Vida D.
T. H. White **30**:438

Sculatti, Gene
Brian Wilson **12**:642

Scupham, Peter
W. H. Auden **6**:16
Elizabeth Daryush **19**:121
Robert Graves **6**:211
H. D. **8**:257
Elizabeth Jennings **14**:293
David Jones **4**:262
D. M. Thomas **13**:542

Seabrook, W. B.
Nella Larsen **37**:212

Sealy, Douglas
Benedict Kiely **23**:265
Michael Longley **29**:294

Searle, Leroy
Dannie Abse **7**:2
Erica Jong **4**:264

Searles, Baird
Anna Kavan **5**:205
Andre Norton **12**:459

Searles, George J.
Joseph Heller **8**:279

Seaver, Richard
Louis-Ferdinand Céline **1**:57

Seay, James
James Wright **3**:543

Secher, Andy
Pink Floyd **35**:313

Sedgwick, Ellery
Esther Forbes **12**:208

Critic Index

See, Carolyn
Josephine Herbst **34**:453
Elinor Langer **34**:453
Kem Nunn **34**:95

Seebohm, Caroline
Isaac Asimov **19**:29
Dirk Bogarde **19**:42
Andrew Holleran **38**:247
Kamala Markandaya **8**:377

Seed, David
Isaac Bashevis Singer **9**:487

Seed, John
Donald Davie **31**:117

Seeger, Pete
Woody Guthrie **35**:188

Seelye, John
Donald Barthelme **2**:41
Richard Lester **20**:218, 219
Norman Mailer **3**:316
Marge Piercy **3**:383
Charles M. Schulz **12**:531
James Thurber **5**:439
David Wagoner **5**:474

Segal, Erich
Robert Lowell **15**:348

Segal, Lore
Joan Didion **1**:75
James D. Forman **21**:116

Segel, Harold
Gregor von Rezzori **25**:384

Segel, Harold B.
Vasily Aksenov **22**:27
Czesław Miłosz **22**:312

Segovia, Tomás
Octavio Paz **3**:376

Seib, Kenneth
Richard Brautigan **1**:44

Seibles, Timothy S.
James Baldwin **15**:43

Seiden, Melvin
Vladimir Nabokov **2**:302

Seidensticker, Edward
Kōbō Abé **22**:12
Yukio Mishima **27**:337

Seidlin, Oskar
Hermann Hesse **17**:216

Seidman, Hugh
Edward Hirsch **31**:214
Denise Levertov **15**:338
Mary Oliver **19**:362
Linda Pastan **27**:371

Seidman, Robert
John Berger **19**:39

Seitz, Michael
Luchino Visconti **16**:574

Seitz, Michael H.
Richard Pryor **26**:383

Selby, Herbert, Jr.
Richard Price **6**:427

Seldes, Gilbert
Charles Chaplin **16**:188

Seligson, Tom
Piri Thomas **17**:500
Hunter S. Thompson **9**:527

Sellick, Robert
Shirley Hazzard **18**:218

Sellin, Eric
Samuel Beckett **2**:47
Camara Laye **38**:286

Seltzer, Alvin J.
William S. Burroughs **22**:80

Selz, Thalia
Jonathan Baumbach **23**:55

Selzer, David
Peter Porter **5**:346

Semkow, Julie
Joan Micklin Silver **20**:341

Semple, Robert B., Jr.
Allen Drury **37**:103

Sena, Vinad
T. S. Eliot **6**:159

Senkewicz, Robert M.
Bruce Catton **35**:95

Senna, Carl
Julio Cortázar **33**:135
Piers Paul Read **25**:376

Sennwald, Andre
Rouben Mamoulian **16**:421

Serchuk, Peter
Richard F. Hugo **32**:243
Laurence Lieberman **36**:261

Sergay, Timothy
Vasily Aksyonov **37**:13

Sergeant, Howard
Dannie Abse **29**:17
Siegfried Sassoon **36**:391

Servodidio, Mirella D'Ambrosio
Azorín **11**:24

Sesonske, Alexander
Jean Renoir **20**:309

Sessions, William A.
Julia Peterkin **31**:312

Seton, Cynthia Propper
Marilyn French **18**:158
Doris Grumbach **22**:206
Barbara Pym **19**:387
Muriel Spark **18**:505

Settle, Mary Lee
Russell Baker **31**:30

Severin, Timothy
Thor Heyerdahl **26**:193

Sewell, Elizabeth
Muriel Rukeyser **15**:458

Seybolt, Cynthia T.
Jules Archer **12**:21, 22

Seydor, Paul
Sam Peckinpah **20**:283

Seyler, Harry E.
Allen Drury **37**:111

Seymour, Miranda
Italo Calvino **33**:99
Eva Figes **31**:168

Seymour-Smith, Martin
David Caute **29**:113
J. M. Coetzee **23**:126
D. J. Enright **31**:150
Roy Fuller **28**:150
Robert Graves **1**:128

Sgammato, Joseph
Alfred Hitchcock **16**:351

Shack, Neville
William McPherson **34**:89

Shadoian, Jack
Donald Barthelme **1**:18

Shaffer, Dallas Y.
Jules Archer **12**:16
Frank Bonham **12**:53

Shaffer, Peter
Peter Shaffer **37**:382

Shah, Diane K.
Richard O'Brien **17**:325

Shahane, Vasant A.
Ruth Prawer Jhabvala **29**:257

Shahane, Vasant Anant
Khushwant Singh **11**:504

Shakespeare, Nicholas
Morris L. West **33**:434

Shands, Annette Oliver
Gwendolyn Brooks **4**:78, 79
Don L. Lee **2**:238

Shanks, Edward
Siegfried Sassoon **36**:387

Shanley, J. P.
Rod Serling **30**:353

Shannon, James P.
J. F. Powers **1**:279

Shannon, William H.
Thomas Merton **34**:461
Michael Mott **34**:461

Shapcott, Thomas
Frank O'Hara **2**:323
W. R. Rodgers **7**:377
Thomas W. Shapcott **38**:402

Shapiro, Alan
Donald Davie **31**:125

Shapiro, Anna
Russell Banks **37**:26
Truman Capote **38**:87
Don DeLillo **39**:124
Susan Isaacs **32**:256
Stephen King **37**:205
J.I.M. Stewart **32**:423

Shapiro, Charles
Meyer Levin **7**:203
David Madden **5**:265
John Nichols **38**:337
Joyce Carol Oates **3**:363
Anthony Powell **1**:277
Harvey Swados **5**:420
Jerome Weidman **7**:517

Shapiro, David
John Ashbery **25**:49
Elizabeth Bishop **15**:60
Hayden Carruth **10**:100
X. J. Kennedy **8**:320
Josephine Miles **14**:370
Eric Rohmer **16**:539

Shapiro, Jane
Rosalyn Drexler **6**:143

Shapiro, Karl
W. H. Auden **1**:8; **3**:21
T. S. Eliot **3**:136
Rod McKuen **1**:210
Henry Miller **4**:349
Chaim Potok **26**:367
Ezra Pound **3**:394
Melvin B. Tolson **36**:426
William Carlos Williams **5**:506
Tom Wolfe **35**:451

Shapiro, Laura
Elizabeth Swados **12**:560

Shapiro, Lillian L.
Rosa Guy **26**:145
Kristin Hunter **35**:229

Shapiro, Marianne
Elio Vittorini **14**:546

Shapiro, Paula Meinetz
Alice Walker **6**:553

Shapiro, Susin
Joan Armatrading **17**:7
Jimmy Cliff **21**:61
Janis Ian **21**:184
Lou Reed **21**:315
Carly Simon **26**:409

Shapiro, Walter
Thomas J. Fleming **37**:128
M. M. Kaye **28**:202

Sharma, Govind Narain
Ngugi wa Thiong'o **36**:314

Sharma, P. P.
Arthur Miller **15**:370

Sharman, Vincent
Ralph Gustafson **36**:220

Sharp, Christopher
Ntozake Shange **25**:397
Sam Shepard **34**:267

Sharp, Sister Corona
Friedrich Dürrenmatt **15**:201
Eugène Ionesco **15**:297

Sharp, Francis Michael
Thomas Bernhard **32**:25

Sharp, Jonathan
Alvah Bessie **23**:61

Sharpe, David F.
Henry Carlisle **33**:103

Sharpe, Patricia
Margaret Drabble **10**:162

Sharpe, Tom
Nicolas Freeling **38**:186

Sharrock, Roger
T. S. Eliot **24**:179

Shattan, Joseph
Saul Bellow 8:80

Shattuck, Roger
Renata Adler 31:15
Jean Arp 5:32
Saul Bellow 6:57
Alain Robbe-Grillet 2:376
Octavio Paz 19:365
Nathalie Sarraute 31:384
Michel Tournier 36:436

Shaughnessy, Mary Rose
Edna Ferber 18:152

Shaw, Arnold
Chuck Berry 17:53

Shaw, Bob
Michael Moorcock 27:350

Shaw, Evelyn
Melvin Berger 12:37

Shaw, Greg
Monty Python 21:224
Brian Wilson 12:647

Shaw, Irwin
James Jones 10:290

Shaw, Peter
Robert Lowell 8:351
Hugh Nissenson 9:400
Ezra Pound 18:422

Shaw, Robert B.
A. R. Ammons 3:11
W. H. Auden 2:26
Wendell Berry 8:85
Rosellen Brown 32:63
Stanley Burnshaw 3:91
Alfred Corn 33:117
Peter Davison 28:101
Babette Deutsch 18:120
James Dickey 2:117
William Dickey 28:119
Robert Duncan 7:88
Stephen Dunn 36:155
Robert Francis 15:238
Brewster Ghiselin 23:171
Allen Ginsberg 6:201
John Glassco 9:236
W. S. Graham 29:196
William Harmon 38:242
Richard Howard 7:166
Barbara Howes 15:289
David Ignatow 4:248
Stanley Kunitz 14:313
Philip Larkin 8:338
Brad Leithauser 27:242
Robert Lowell 37:236
William Meredith 4:348
Frederick Morgan 23:299
Howard Nemerov 36:302
Adrienne Rich 6:457
M. L. Rosenthal 28:392
Raphael Rudnik 7:384
Charles Simic 6:501; 9:479;
    22:381
Louis Simpson 32:377
Allen Tate 2:430
Mark Van Doren 6:541
Eudora Welty 14:566
James Wright 28:468
Marya Zaturenska 6:585

Shaw, Russell
Pink Floyd 35:309

Shaw, Spencer G.
Lloyd Alexander 35:28

Shaw, Valerie
Fay Weldon 36:448

Shawe-Taylor, Desmond
Pamela Hansford Johnson
    27:212

Shayon, Robert Lewis
Norman Lear 12:329
Gene Roddenberry 17:403
Rod Serling 30:352, 357

Shea, Robert J.
Budd Schulberg 7:403

Shear, Walter
Bernard Malamud 1:197

Shearer, Ann
Christa Wolf 29:465

Shechner, Mark
Arthur A. Cohen 31:94
Allen Ginsberg 36:185
Tadeusz Konwicki 8:328
Philip Rahv 24:356
Mordecai Richler 18:453
Philip Roth 15:451
Isaac Bashevis Singer 15:508

Shedlin, Michael
Woody Allen 16:2

Sheean, Vincent
Alvah Bessie 23:59

Sheed, Wilfrid
Renata Adler 31:12
Edward Albee 1:4
Roger Angell 26:33
James Baldwin 1:16; 8:42
Robert Coover 7:58
Robert Frost 1:110
William Golding 1:121
Joseph Heller 5:182
Ernest Hemingway 39:434
James Jones 1:162
Norman Mailer 1:193; 4:320
Terrence McNally 7:216
Jeffrey Meyers 39:434
Arthur Miller 1:217
Alberto Moravia 2:292
Iris Murdoch 1:236
P. H. Newby 13:409
John Osborne 1:263
Walker Percy 2:332
S. J. Perelman 23:339
Neil Simon 6:503
William Styron 1:330
James Thurber 25:436
John Updike 1:343
Kurt Vonnegut, Jr. 1:347
Douglas Turner Ward 19:456
Evelyn Waugh 3:512
Arnold Wesker 3:518
Tennessee Williams 1:369
P. G. Wodehouse 22:482
Tom Wolfe 2:481

Sheehan, Donald
John Berryman 1:34
Richard Howard 7:166
Robert Lowell 1:181

Sheehan, Edward R. F.
Edwin O'Connor 14:392

Sheehan, Ethna
E. M. Almedingen 12:1
Lois Duncan 26:101
Christie Harris 12:261
Mollie Hunter 21:156
Philippa Pearce 21:281

Sheils, Merrill
Frank Herbert 35:206

Shelton, Austin J.
Chinua Achebe 7:4

Shelton, Frank W.
Robert Coover 7:60
Harry Crews 23:137
E. L. Doctorow 37:88
Ernest Hemingway 10:269

Shelton, Robert
Joan Armatrading 17:10
Bob Dylan 12:179

Shepard, Paul
Peter Matthiessen 5:273

Shepard, Ray Anthony
Alice Childress 12:107
Nicholasa Mohr 12:446

Shepard, Richard F.
Lois Duncan 26:102
Sam Shepard 17:433
Elie Wiesel 37:458

Shepherd, Allen
Harry Crews 23:133
Reynolds Price 3:405, 406
Robert Penn Warren 1:355

Shepherd, Naomi
S. Y. Agnon 14:1

Shepherd, R.
Raja Rao 25:368

Shepley, John
Alberto Moravia 27:356

Sheppard, R. Z.
Louis Auchincloss 4:30
Russell Baker 31:28
Saul Bellow 6:55
William Peter Blatty 2:64
Lothar-Günther Buchheim
    6:101
Anthony Burgess 5:85
Philip Caputo 32:106
Don DeLillo 39:120
Peter De Vries 2:114
E. L. Doctorow 6:133
Nora Ephron 17:113
Paul E. Erdman 25:154
Thomas J. Fleming 37:121
Barbara Guest 34:443
Alex Haley 8:260
H. D. 34:443
Frank Herbert 12:270
James Leo Herlihy 6:235
Dan Jacobson 4:254
Bernard Malamud 2:266
S. J. Perelman 5:338
Padgett Powell 34:97
Ishmael Reed 5:370
Harvey Swados 5:422

Michel Tournier 6:537
Anne Tyler 28:433
Douglas Unger 34:115
Mario Vargas Llosa 6:545
Gore Vidal 6:548
Paul West 7:523
Hilma Wolitzer 17:561

Sheps, G. David
Mordecai Richler 13:481

Sher, John Lear
Zoa Sherburne 30:362

Sheridan, Alan
Michel Foucault 31:184

Sheridan, Martin
Jerome Siegel and Joe Shuster
    21:354

Sheridan, Nancy
Betsy Byars 35:75

Sheridan, Robert N.
Henry Gregor Felsen 17:124

Sherman, Beatrice
Margery Allingham 19:13
Sally Benson 17:48
Zora Neale Hurston 30:213
Dalton Trumbo 19:445
T. H. White 30:439, 440

Sherman, Bill
Trina Robbins 21:341

Sherman, Paul
Charles Olson 29:329

Sherman, Stuart
Carl Sandburg 35:343

Sherman, Susan
Adrienne Rich 36:371

Sherrard, Philip
Yannis Ritsos 31:327

Sherrard-Smith, Barbara
Zilpha Keatley Snyder 17:472

Sherrell, Richard E.
Arthur Adamov 25:15

Sherrill, Robert
C.D.B. Bryan 29:103
Art Buchwald 33:95
Peter Matthiessen 32:292
Joe McGinniss 32:301
Jonathan Schell 35:363
Gay Talese 37:395
Studs Terkel 38:425

Sherry, Vincent B., Jr.
W. S. Merwin 18:335

Sherwood, Martin
Isaac Asimov 26:39
Roger Zelazny 21:468

Sherwood, R. E.
Buster Keaton 20:188

Sherwood, Robert E.
Carl Sandburg 35:350, 353

Sherwood, Terry G.
Ken Kesey 1:167

Shetley, Vernon
A. R. Ammons **25**:45
John Ashbery **25**:59
Norman Dubie **36**:138
Laura Jensen **37**:190
Galway Kinnell **29**:286
James Merrill **34**:235
James Schuyler **23**:392

Shewey, Don
Joan Armatrading **17**:11
William Least Heat Moon
29:224
Janis Ian **21**:188
Billy Joel **26**:216, 221
John Lennon **35**:275
David Plante **38**:371
Lou Reed **21**:319
Wole Soyinka **36**:413
Frank Zappa **17**:594

Shideler, Ross
Gunnar Ekelöf **27**:117

Shifreen, Lawrence J.
Henry Miller **14**:372

Shimuhara, Nobuo
Margaret Mead **37**:277

Shinn, Thelma J.
Flannery O'Connor **6**:375
Ann Petry **7**:304
William Saroyan **10**:452

Shipp, Randy
Robert Lewis Taylor **14**:535

Shippey, T. A.
Samuel R. Delany **14**:147
Robert Nye **13**:414
Frederik Pohl **18**:410
Mary Lee Settle **19**:410
John Steinbeck **13**:535
Arkadii Strugatskii and Boris
Strugatskii **27**:432
Roger Zelazny **21**:469

Shippey, Tom
Fritz Leiber **25**:305

Shippey, Thomas
Lothar-Günther Buchheim
6:100

Shiras, Mary
William Meredith **22**:301

Shirley, John
Jack Vance **35**:421

Shively, Charley
Albert Goldbarth **38**:204

Shivers, Alfred S.
Jessamyn West **7**:520

Shlaes, Amity
Christa Wolf **29**:467

Shockley, Ann Allen
Claude Brown **30**:38

Shockley, Martin
John Steinbeck **21**:368

Shoemaker, Alice
William Faulkner **14**:175

Shore, Rima
Yevgeny Yevtushenko **13**:619

Shores, Edward
George Roy Hill **26**:210

Shorris, Earl
Donald Barthelme **2**:42
Arthur A. Cohen **31**:95
John Gardner **3**:184
William H. Gass **2**:155
Thomas Pynchon **3**:414

Shorris, Sylvia
Russell Banks **37**:24

Short, Robert L.
Charles M. Schulz **12**:522, 525

Shorter, Eric
Alan Ayckbourn **5**:36; **18**:29
Agatha Christie **12**:118
Ronald Harwood **32**:224
Hugh Leonard **19**:282
Thornton Wilder **15**:574

Shorter, Kingsley
Siegfried Lenz **27**:249
Frank Tuohy **37**:429

Shoukri, Doris Enright-Clark
Marguerite Duras **3**:129

Showalter, Dennis E.
Robert Heinlein **14**:246

Showalter, Elaine
Mary McCarthy **3**:329

Showers, Paul
Art Buchwald **33**:93
Peter De Vries **2**:114
James Herriot **12**:283
John Seelye **7**:407
Alvin Silverstein and Virginia
B. Silverstein **17**:454

Shrapnel, Norman
Stanley Middleton **38**:330
Marge Piercy **18**:406

Shreve, Susan Richards
Andrea Lee **36**:255

Shrimpton, Nicholas
Anita Brookner **32**:59
J. M. Coetzee **23**:124
Zoë Fairbairns **32**:162
M. M. Kaye **28**:200
David Lodge **36**:273
Bernice Rubens **19**:405
Tom Sharpe **36**:402
Irwin Shaw **23**:401
C. P. Snow **19**:428
D. M. Thomas **22**:417
Donald E. Westlake **33**:439
A. N. Wilson **33**:453

Shub, Anatole
Vasily Aksyonov **37**:15
Paddy Chayefsky **23**:113

Shuey, Andrea Lee
M. M. Kaye **28**:202

Shulman, Alix Kates
Grace Paley **37**:335

Shuman, R. Baird
William Inge **1**:153
Clifford Odets **2**:318, 320

Shuttleworth, Martin
Christina Stead **2**:421

Shuttleworth, Paul
Leon Uris **7**:492

Shwartz, Susan M.
Marion Zimmer Bradley **30**:30

Siaulys, Tony
Sonia Levitin **17**:266

Sibbald, K. M.
Jorge Guillén **11**:263

Sibley, Brian
J.R.R. Tolkien **38**:431

Sibley, Francis M.
Chinua Achebe **26**:22

Sibley, William F.
Shiga Naoya **33**:371

Sicherman, Barbara
Taylor Caldwell **28**:67

Sicherman, Carol M.
Saul Bellow **10**:37

Siconolfi, Michael T., S.J.
Audre Lorde **18**:309

Sidnell, M. J.
Ronald G. Everson **27**:133

Siebert, Sara L.
Maureen Daly **17**:89

Siegal, R. A.
Judy Blume **12**:47

Siegel, Ben
Saul Bellow **8**:78
Bernard Malamud **1**:195
Isaac Bashevis Singer **1**:313

Siegel, Eve
Margaret Atwood **25**:68

Siegel, Joel E.
Robert Altman **16**:33
Albert Maysles and David
Maysles **16**:445
August Wilson **39**:276

Siegel, Mark
Tom Robbins **32**:369

Siegel, Paul N.
Norman Mailer **5**:266

Siegel, Robert
Philip Booth **23**:76
Al Young **19**:480

Siemens, William L.
Julio Cortázar **5**:110

Sievers, W. David
Tennessee Williams **30**:460

Sigal, Clancy
Kingsley Amis **3**:9; **5**:22
Patrick Boyle **19**:67
Melvyn Bragg **10**:72
E. L. Doctorow **18**:127
Penelope Lively **32**:276
Piers Paul Read **25**:376
Alan Sillitoe **3**:448
James Thurber **25**:440

Sigerson, Davitt
Paul McCartney **35**:289
Brian Wilson **12**:653

Siggins, Clara M.
Taylor Caldwell **2**:95
Alan Garner **17**:146
Lillian Hellman **4**:221
Saul Maloff **5**:270

Signoriello, John
Mollie Hunter **21**:157

Šilbajoris, Rimvydas
Boris Pasternak **10**:387

Silber, Irwin
Bob Dylan **12**:181

Silber, Joan
Cynthia Propper Seton **27**:430
Scott Sommer **25**:426

Silbersack, John
Fritz Leiber **25**:308

Silenieks, Juris
Édouard Glissant **10**:231

Silet, Charles L. P.
David Kherdian **9**:317, 318

Silkin, Jon
Geoffrey Hill **5**:183

Silko, Leslie Marmon
Dee Brown **18**:71
Harriet Doerr **34**:153

Sillanpoa, Wallace P.
Pier Paolo Pasolini **37**:347

Silva, Candelaria
Maya Angelou **35**:32

Silver, Adele Z.
E. M. Broner **19**:70

Silver, Charles
Orson Welles **20**:446

Silver, David
Peter Townshend **17**:527

Silver, George A.
John Berger **19**:37

Silver, Linda
Lois Duncan **26**:103

Silver, Linda R.
Zibby Oneal **30**:279
Sandra Scoppettone **26**:402

Silver, Philip
Dámaso Alonso **14**:22

Silverberg, Robert
Jack Vance **35**:419

Silverman, Hugh J.
Jean-Paul Sartre **18**:472

Silverman, Malcolm
Jorge Amado **13**:11
Autran Dourado **23**:149

Silverman, Michael
Nagisa Oshima **20**:253

Silverstein, Norman
James Dickey **7**:81
Buster Keaton **20**:195

Silvert, Conrad
Peter Matthiessen **7**:210

Silverton, Pete
Elvis Costello **21**:73

Silvey, Anita
Gunnel Beckman **26**:86
S. E. Hinton **30**:205
Milton Meltzer **26**:303
Otfried Preussler **17**:377
Mildred D. Taylor **21**:418

Simels, Steve
Jackson Browne **21**:40
The Clash **30**:43
Jimmy Cliff **21**:64
Ray Davies **21**:95, 100
Billy Joel **26**:223
John Lennon **35**:269, 270, 274
Monty Python **21**:230
Martin Mull **17**:300
Jimmy Page and Robert Plant **12**:476
Pink Floyd **35**:309
The Police **26**:365
Lou Reed **21**:305, 308
Gene Roddenberry **17**:414
Patti Smith **12**:537
Bruce Springsteen **17**:485
Peter Townshend **17**:535
Brian Wilson **12**:651
Neil Young **17**:579

Simels, Steven
Jim Carroll **35**:80

Simenon, Georges
Georges Simenon **3**:451

Simic, Charles
Vasko Popa **19**:374

Simmons, Dee Dee
Betsy Byars **35**:71

Simmons, Ernest J.
Mikhail Sholokhov **7**:416, 420

Simmons, John S.
Robert Lipsyte **21**:209

Simmons, Ruth J. S.
Aimé Césaire **19**:97

Simmons, Tom
Richard F. Hugo **18**:263

Simms, Michael
Albert Goldbarth **38**:206

Simon, John
Edward Albee **2**:1; **5**:13; **11**:11; **13**:3, 4; **25**:36
Vicente Aleixandre **36**:30
Woody Allen **16**:7, 13
Robert Altman **16**:33, 36
Lindsay Anderson **20**:14
Jean Anouilh **13**:22
Michelangelo Antonioni **20**:40
Alan Ayckbourn **8**:34; **18**:29; **33**:50
Ralph Bakshi **26**:70, 72
James Baldwin **17**:40
Howard Barker **37**:38
Peter Barnes **5**:49
Samuel Beckett **3**:47; **29**:66
Ingmar Bergman **16**:77
Thomas Bernhard **32**:26
Bernardo Bertolucci **16**:100
Robert Bolt **14**:88

Mel Brooks **12**:80
Ed Bullins **5**:84; **7**:36
Anne Burr **6**:104
John Cassavetes **20**:51
Claude Chabrol **16**:179
Caryl Churchill **31**:89
Francis Ford Coppola **16**:240
Michael Cristofer **28**:96, 97
Shelagh Delaney **29**:147
Brian De Palma **20**:74, 76
Martin Duberman **8**:185
Christopher Durang **27**:89, 92; **38**:172, 174
Marguerite Duras **20**:98
Rainer Werner Fassbinder **20**:112
Jules Feiffer **2**:133
Federico Fellini **16**:289, 297, 300
Lawrence Ferlinghetti **2**:134
Harvey Fierstein **33**:153
Dario Fo **32**:176
Bob Fosse **20**:124
Athol Fugard **9**:230; **14**:191; **25**:177
Peter Gent **29**:182
Frank D. Gilroy **2**:161
Jean-Luc Godard **20**:135
Charles Gordone **1**:124
Günter Grass **11**:252
Simon Gray **14**:215; **36**:207
John Guare **14**:222
Bill Gunn **5**:153
A. R. Gurney, Jr. **32**:218, 219, 220, 221
Christopher Hampton **4**:211
David Hare **29**:218
Joseph Heller **11**:265
Lillian Hellman **8**:281; **18**:226
Beth Henley **23**:216
George Roy Hill **26**:203, 210
Alfred Hitchcock **16**:353
Rolf Hochhuth **11**:275
Bohumil Hrabal **13**:290
William Inge **8**:308
Albert Innaurato **21**:197, 198
Ann Jellicoe **27**:210
Jean Kerr **22**:259
Pavel Kohout **13**:323
Arthur Kopit **1**:171; **18**:291; **33**:247, 251, 253
Stanley Kubrick **16**:390
Richard Lester **20**:230, 231
Denise Levertov **15**:336
Ira Levin **3**:294
Robert Lowell **4**:299; **11**:324
Peter Luke **38**:317
Norman Mailer **2**:259; **3**:316
David Mamet **15**:356, 358; **34**:221
William Mastrosimone **36**:289
Elaine May **16**:436
Albert Maysles and David Maysles **16**:444
Marshall McLuhan **37**:253
Terrence McNally **4**:347; **7**:217, 218, 219
Mark Medoff **6**:321, 322; **23**:293
Christopher Middleton **13**:387
Arthur Miller **2**:279, 280; **6**:335
Jason Miller **2**:284, 285
Czesław Miłosz **22**:310

Vladimir Nabokov **23**:314
Peter Nichols **36**:331, 333
Marsha Norman **28**:317, 319
Joyce Carol Oates **11**:400
Joe Orton **4**:387
John Osborne **2**:328; **11**:421
Nagisa Oshima **20**:245, 256
Rochelle Owens **8**:434
Gordon Parks **16**:460
Pier Paolo Pasolini **20**:262
Sam Peckinpah **20**:274
S. J. Perelman **5**:337
Harold Pinter **3**:386, 387; **11**:443; **15**:425
Sylvia Plath **17**:345
Roman Polanski **16**:471
Stephen Poliakoff **38**:384
Bernard Pomerance **13**:446
David Rabe **8**:449, 451; **33**:346
Gerome Ragni and James Rado **17**:381, 388
Satyajit Ray **16**:489
Jean Renoir **20**:307
Jonathan Reynolds **6**:452; **38**:389, 390
Yannis Ritsos **31**:329
Eric Rohmer **16**:538
Howard Sackler **14**:478
Carlos Saura **20**:318
Murray Schisgal **6**:490
Peter Shaffer **5**:387, 389; **37**:384
Ntozake Shange **8**:484; **25**:398, 399
Sam Shepard **6**:497; **17**:435, 449; **34**:269
Martin Sherman **19**:415
Joan Micklin Silver **20**:343
Neil Simon **6**:506; **11**:495, 496; **31**:402
Isaac Bashevis Singer **15**:509
Bernard Slade **11**:507
Steven Spielberg **20**:361
Donald Spoto **39**:447
John Steinbeck **5**:408
George Steiner **24**:427
Tom Stoppard **3**:470; **4**:525, 526; **5**:412; **8**:504; **29**:396; **34**:278
David Storey **4**:528; **5**:415, 417
Elizabeth Swados **12**:559, 562
Ronald Tavel **6**:529
C. P. Taylor **27**:446
François Truffaut **20**:385, 405
John Updike **34**:286
Melvin Van Peebles **2**:448
Gore Vidal **2**:450; **4**:554; **10**:503
Andrzej Wajda **16**:578
Derek Walcott **2**:460; **14**:550
Wendy Wasserstein **32**:440
Andrew Lloyd Webber and Tim Rice **21**:430
Peter Weiss **3**:513
Fay Weldon **36**:445
Michael Weller **10**:526
Lina Wertmüller **16**:590, 598
Morris L. West **33**:428
Hugh Whitemore **37**:444
Billy Wilder **20**:460
Thornton Wilder **10**:535
Tennessee Williams **2**:464; **5**:501; **7**:544; **8**:549; **11**:571; **39**:447

Lanford Wilson **14**:591, 592; **36**:460, 461, 462, 464
Robert Wilson **7**:550, 551

Simon, John K.
Michel Butor **15**:112

Simon, Kate
Rhys Davies **23**:145

Simon, Linda
Saul Bellow **34**:546
Daniel Fuchs **34**:546

Simonds, C. H.
Joan Didion **1**:74
Gay Talese **37**:392

Simonds, Katharine
Sally Benson **17**:47

Simonsuuri, Kirsti
Paavo Haavikko **34**:176

Simpson, Allen
Albert Camus **11**:96

Simpson, Claude M., Jr.
Woody Guthrie **35**:184

Simpson, Clinton
Ilya Ehrenburg **18**:130

Simpson, Elaine
Andre Norton **12**:456

Simpson, Louis
Robert Bly **2**:65
J. V. Cunningham **31**:97
Donald Davie **31**:123
Allen Ginsberg **13**:241
Ronald J. Glasser **37**:131
James Merrill **8**:380
Kenneth Rexroth **2**:370
W. D. Snodgrass **2**:405
C. K. Williams **33**:446

Simpson, Mona
Carolyn Hougan **34**:60
Tobias Wolff **39**:286

Simpson, Sarah
Kristin Hunter **35**:230

Sims, Rudine
Ouida Sebestyen **30**:347

Simson, Eve
Norma Klein **30**:242

Sinclair, Dorothy
Erich Segal **10**:467
David Slavitt **14**:491

Sinclair, Karen
Ursula K. LeGuin **13**:350

Siner, Robin
Margaret O. Hyde **21**:179

Singer, Alexander
René Clair **20**:63

Singer, Isaac B.
Otfried Preussler **17**:376

Singer, Marilyn
Frank Bonham **12**:54

Singer, Marilyn R.
Jean Craighead George **35**:178
Norma Klein **30**:236
Paul Zindel **26**:471

Singh, G.
Eugenio Montale **7**:223, 226
Ezra Pound **2**:342, 344; **7**:334

Singh, Rahul
M. M. Kaye **28**:200

Singleton, Mary Ann
Doris Lessing **22**:280

Sinha, Krishna Nandan
Mulk Raj Anand **23**:15

Sinyavsky, Andrei
Anna Akhmatova **25**:24
Robert Frost **4**:174
Yevgeny Yevtushenko **26**:465

Sire, James W.
C. S. Lewis **1**:177

Sirkin, Elliott
Christopher Durang **38**:172
Tom Stoppard **34**:281
Wendy Wasserstein **32**:442

Sisco, Ellen
Jamake Highwater **12**:286

Sisk, John P.
Mark Harris **19**:200
J. F. Powers **1**:280
Philip Rahv **24**:354

Sissman, L. E.
Kingsley Amis **2**:7; **5**:22
Martin Amis **4**:21
Jimmy Breslin **4**:76
Michael Crichton **6**:119
J. P. Donleavy **4**:126
J. G. Farrell **6**:174
Natalia Ginzburg **5**:141
Joseph Heller **8**:278
Dan Jacobson **4**:255
Joe McGinniss **32**:300
Thomas McGuane **3**:329
Tom McHale **3**:332; **5**:282
Brian Moore **7**:237
Gilbert Rogin **18**:458
Anne Roiphe **3**:434
John Updike **2**:441
Evelyn Waugh **3**:513
Fay Weldon **6**:563
Emlyn Williams **15**:578
Edmund Wilson **2**:478
Al Young **19**:477

Sisson, C. H.
H. D. **8**:257

Sitterly, Bancroft W.
Roy A. Gallant **17**:127

Sjöberg, Leif
Gunnar Ekelöf **27**:111, 113, 115
Eyvind Johnson **14**:296, 297
Harry Martinson **14**:355, 356

Skau, Michael
Lawrence Ferlinghetti **10**:177

Skelton, Robin
Ralph Gustafson **36**:212, 215
Patrick Kavanagh **22**:236
Anthony Kerrigan **6**:276
Dorothy Livesay **4**:294
Derek Mahon **27**:286
John Metcalf **37**:307

John Newlove **14**:378
Jane Rule **27**:417

Skerrett, Joseph T., Jr.
Ralph Ellison **11**:182

Skiles, Don
Jonathan Baumbach **23**:56

Skirius, A. John
Carlos Fuentes **22**:168

Sklar, Robert
Thomas Pynchon **33**:327
J.R.R. Tolkien **12**:568

Skloot, Floyd
Laura Jensen **37**:186
Thomas Kinsella **19**:255

Skodnick, Roy
Gilbert Sorrentino **7**:448

Skoller, Don
Carl Theodor Dreyer **16**:262

Skow, Jack
John Gardner **5**:132
Robert Graves **2**:176

Skow, John
Richard Adams **5**:5
Richard Brautigan **3**:86
Arthur A. Cohen **7**:52
Richard Condon **4**:107; **6**:115
Julio Cortázar **5**:109
Robertson Davies **2**:113
Allen Drury **37**:108
Lawrence Durrell **6**:152
Barry Hannah **23**:208
Charles Johnson **7**:183
Robert F. Jones **7**:193
Sue Kaufman **3**:263
Yasunari Kawabata **5**:208
Milan Kundera **4**:277
John D. MacDonald **3**:307
Iris Murdoch **4**:370
Vladimir Nabokov **6**:354
Harold Robbins **5**:379
Susan Fromberg Schaeffer **6**:488
Irving Stone **7**:471
Kurt Vonnegut, Jr. **4**:568
Morris L. West **6**:564
Patrick White **3**:525

Skretvedt, Randy
Steve Martin **30**:250

Škvorecký, Josef
Pavel Kohout **13**:325
Jaroslav Seifert **34**:262

Slade, Joseph W.
James T. Farrell **11**:192
Thomas Pynchon **33**:332

Sladek, John
Thomas Berger **38**:42

Slansky, Paul
Martin Mull **17**:300

Slate, Ron
Stephen Dobyns **37**:76
Stephen Dunn **36**:153

Slater, Candace
Elizabeth Bishop **13**:88
Salvatore Espriu **9**:193

Slater, Jack
Stevie Wonder **12**:662

Slater, Joseph
Nelly Sachs **14**:475

Slaughter, Frank G.
Millen Brand **7**:29
Margaret O. Hyde **21**:172

Slavitt, David R.
George Garrett **11**:220
Maureen Howard **14**:267
Ann Quin **6**:441

Slethaug, Gordon E.
John Barth **2**:38

Slick, Sam L.
Jorge Ibargüengoitia **37**:182

Sloan, James Park
Alice Childress **15**:131
David Madden **15**:350

Sloman, Larry
Lou Reed **21**:306

Slomovitz, Philip
Zora Neale Hurston **30**:213

Slonim, Marc
Ilya Ehrenburg **18**:133
Mikhail Sholokhov **7**:415, 418
Aleksandr I. Solzhenitsyn **1**:320
Arkadii Strugatskii and Boris Strugatskii **27**:432
Henri Troyat **23**:458
Yevgeny Yevtushenko **26**:460
Marguerite Yourcenar **19**:482

Sloss, Henry
Richard Howard **10**:276
James Merrill **8**:381, 384
Reynolds Price **3**:406
Philip Roth **1**:293

Slotkin, Richard
Christopher Collier and James L. Collier **30**:74

Slung, Michele
Betsy Byars **35**:74
Bette Greene **30**:171
Jorge Ibargüengoitia **37**:184
P. D. James **18**:273
Stephen King **26**:237; **37**:198
Helen MacInnes **27**:284
Cynthia Voigt **30**:419

Slusser, George Edgar
Arthur C. Clarke **13**:151
Samuel R. Delany **14**:143
Harlan Ellison **13**:204
Robert Heinlein **14**:246
Ursula K. LeGuin **13**:345

Small, Robert C.
Joanne Greenberg **30**:167
Zibby Oneal **30**:281

Smalley, Webster
Langston Hughes **35**:217

Smedman, Sarah M.
Katherine Paterson **30**:288

Smelser, Marshall
Thomas J. Fleming **37**:123

Smeltzer, Sister Mary Etheldra
Larry Kettelkamp **12**:306

Smith, A.J.M.
Earle Birney **6**:74
Stanley Kunitz **14**:312
Irving Layton **15**:318
P. K. Page **7**:291
F. R. Scott **22**:373
A.J.M. Smith **15**:515

Smith, Anne
Lisa St. Aubin de Teran **36**:419

Smith, Annette
Aimé Césaire **32**:110

Smith, Barbara
Ishmael Reed **6**:447
Alice Walker **6**:553

Smith, Bradford
Roderick L. Haig-Brown **21**:136
Bruce Lancaster **36**:241

Smith, C.E.J.
Mavis Thorpe Clark **12**:130
Leon Garfield **12**:231

Smith, Chris
Claude Brown **30**:41

Smith, Dave
Philip Booth **23**:77
Harry Crews **6**:118
Stephen Dunn **36**:154
Brewster Ghiselin **23**:171
Albert Goldbarth **5**:144
Daniel Halpern **14**:232
William Heyen **18**:232
Richard F. Hugo **32**:244, 249
Philip Levine **33**:270
Laurence Lieberman **36**:260
Cynthia Macdonald **19**:290
Craig Nova **31**:299
Linda Pastan **27**:370
Louis Simpson **7**:429; **32**:375
Barry Spacks **14**:511
Robert Penn Warren **13**:581; **39**:268
James Wright **28**:469

Smith, David E.
E. E. Cummings **8**:158

Smith, Dinitia
Alice Walker **27**:451

Smith, Ethanne
Franklyn M. Branley **21**:21

Smith, Eleanor T.
Jessamyn West **17**:547

Smith, F. C.
Henry Gregor Felsen **17**:121

Smith, Gene
Ian Fleming **30**:138

Smith, Grover
T. S. Eliot **15**:206
Archibald MacLeish **8**:359

Smith, H. Allen
Jacqueline Susann **3**:476

Smith, Harrison
Taylor Caldwell **28**:61
Ilya Ehrenburg **18**:132
Madeleine L'Engle **12**:345
Mary Renault **17**:392
Elizabeth Spencer **22**:398
Jessamyn West **17**:546

Smith, Iain Crichton
Hugh MacDiarmid **11**:336

Smith, Irene
Noel Streatfeild **21**:398

Smith, Jack
Josef von Sternberg **20**:373

Smith, Janet Adam
Richard Adams **4**:8
Lloyd Alexander **35**:23
Farley Mowat **26**:331
J.R.R. Tolkien **2**:435

Smith, Jay
Woody Guthrie **35**:184

Smith, Jennifer Farley
Margaret Craven **17**:79
Allan W. Eckert **17**:108

Smith, Joan
Piri Thomas **17**:502

Smith, Julian
Nevil Shute **30**:373

Smith, Larry
Lawrence Ferlinghetti **27**:138

Smith, Leslie
Edward Bond **23**:68

Smith, Liz
Truman Capote **8**:133

Smith, Martin Cruz
John le Carré **28**:228

Smith, Mason
Richard Brautigan **12**:60

Smith, Maxwell A.
Jean Giono **4**:184
François Mauriac **4**:340

Smith, Michael
Rosalyn Drexler **2**:119
Anthony Kerrigan **6**:275
John Metcalf **37**:303
Tom Stoppard **1**:327
Robert Wilson **7**:549

Smith, Nancy
Larry Bograd **35**:64

Smith, Patricia Keeney
Anne Chislett **34**:146
Ralph Gustafson **36**:221
William Mastrosimone **36**:292

Smith, Patti
Lou Reed **21**:308

Smith, Phillip E., II
Charles Olson **11**:420

Smith, Raymond J.
James Dickey **10**:141

Smith, R. J.
Prince **35**:330

Smith, Robert
Jimmy Page and Robert Plant
12:481

Smith, Robert P., Jr.
Mongo Beti **27**:46, 53

Smith, Robert W.
Varlam Shalamov **18**:479

Smith, Roger H.
John D. MacDonald **3**:307

Smith, Sherwin D.
Charles M. Schulz **12**:530

Smith, Sidonie Ann
Maya Angelou **12**:10

Smith, Stan
Sylvia Plath **17**:357

Smith, Starr E.
Virginia Spencer Carr **34**:419
John Dos Passos **34**:419

Smith, Stephen
J.M.G. Le Clézio **31**:251
Michel Tournier **23**:456

Smith, Stevie
Edna Ferber **18**:152

Smith, William James
Frank O'Connor **23**:325
Kurt Vonnegut, Jr. **12**:601
Sloan Wilson **32**:446

Smith, William Jay
Elizabeth Bishop **13**:89
Louis MacNeice **4**:315
Frederick Seidel **18**:474
Sylvia Townsend Warner
19:459

Smothers, Joyce
Norma Klein **30**:240, 241

Smucker, Tom
Steven Bochco and Michael
Kozoll **35**:53

Smyth, Pat
William Mayne **12**:395

Smyth, Paul
William Harmon **38**:242
Derek Walcott **4**:575

Snelling, O. F.
Ian Fleming **30**:135

Snider, David
Piers Anthony **35**:40

Sniderman, Stephen L.
Joseph Heller **3**:230

Snitow, Ann
Nettie Jones **34**:67

Snodgrass, W. D.
Theodore Roethke **8**:455

Snow, C. P.
Malcolm Bradbury **32**:49
Norman Mailer **4**:322

Snow, George E.
Allen Drury **37**:106
Aleksandr I. Solzhenitsyn **4**:507

Snow, Helen F.
Pearl S. Buck **7**:33

Snow, Philip
Thor Heyerdahl **26**:193

Snowden, J. A.
Sean O'Casey **9**:406

Snyder, Emine
Ezekiel Mphahlele **25**:334

Snyder, Louis
Stephen Sondheim **30**:387

Snyder, Patrick
John Lennon **35**:268
Paul McCartney **35**:280

Snyder, Stephen
Pier Paolo Pasolini **20**:271

Snyder-Scumpy, Patrick
Martin Mull **17**:297, 298

Soares, Manuela
Agnes Eckhardt Nixon **21**:251

Sobejano, Gonzalo
Dámaso Alonso **14**:20

Sobran, M. J., Jr.
Norman Lear **12**:338

Socken, Paul G.
Anne Hébert **13**:268; **29**:239
Gabrielle Roy **14**:469

Soderbergh, Peter A.
Upton Sinclair **11**:497

Sodowsky, Alice
George Lucas **16**:409

Sodowsky, Roland
George Lucas **16**:409

Soete, Mary
Bette Pesetsky **28**:358

Sohlich, W. F.
Jacques Audiberti **38**:29

Soile, Sola
Chinua Achebe **11**:4

Sokel, Walter Herbert
Heinrich Böll **9**:102

Sokolov, Raymond A.
André Brink **18**:67
E. L. Doctorow **6**:132
Julius Horwitz **14**:267
Dan Jacobson **4**:254
Gayl Jones **6**:265
Thomas Keneally **8**:319
József Lengyel **7**:202
John Sayles **7**:400
Hilma Wolitzer **17**:563

Solecki, Sam
Earle Birney **11**:50
Robertson Davies **25**:133
Doris Lessing **22**:286
Josef Škvorecký **39**:228

Solnick, Bruce B.
George Garrett **11**:220

Solomon, Barbara Probst
Juan Goytisolo **5**:151
J.M.G. Le Clézio **31**:247
João Ubaldo Ribeiro **10**:436
Mario Vargas Llosa **10**:500

Solomon, Linda
David Bowie **17**:61

Solomon, Norman
Jonathan Kozol **17**:253

Solomon, Philip H.
Louis-Ferdinand Céline **15**:123

Solomon, Stanley J.
Francis Ford Coppola **16**:244

Solotaroff, Ted
Roger Angell **26**:29
William Trevor **25**:446

Solotaroff, Theodore
Saul Bellow **1**:33
Paul Bowles **1**:41
Anthony Burgess **1**:48
William S. Burroughs **1**:48
Albert Camus **9**:146
Philip Caputo **32**:102
Alex Comfort **7**:54
George P. Elliott **2**:130
John Fowles **6**:185
Herbert Gold **7**:120
Paul Goodman **1**:123
Günter Grass **1**:125
Stanislaw Lem **8**:344
Bernard Malamud **1**:196, 200
Henry Miller **1**:219
Flannery O'Connor **1**:256
Katherine Anne Porter **1**:271
V. S. Pritchett **5**:352
James Purdy **2**:348
Philip Roth **4**:451
Jean-Paul Sartre **1**:304
Hubert Selby, Jr. **8**:474
Susan Sontag **1**:322
George Steiner **24**:427
Vladimir Voinovich **10**:508
Richard Wright **1**:377
Richard Yates **7**:553

Solt, Marilyn Leathers
Betsy Byars **35**:75

Solvick, Stanley D.
Bruce Catton **35**:94

Solzhenitsyn, Alexander
Mikhail Sholokhov **15**:480

Somer, John
Kurt Vonnegut, Jr. **4**:566

Somers, Paul P., Jr.
Ernest Hemingway **8**:283

Sommer, Sally R.
Alice Childress **12**:108

Sommers, Joseph
Miguel Ángel Asturias **13**:39

Somtow, S. P.
Theodore Sturgeon **39**:363

Sondheim, Stephen
Stephen Sondheim **30**:386

Sondrup, Steven P.
Ernst Jandl **34**:200

Sonkiss, Lois
Jamake Highwater **12**:286

Sonnenfeld, Albert
Heinrich Böll **9**:107
Albert Camus **32**:87

Critic Index

Sonntag, Jacob
Amos Oz **8**:435
Isaac Bashevis Singer **3**:456
Arnold Wesker **3**:519

Sontag, Susan
James Baldwin **4**:40
Roland Barthes **24**:26
Ingmar Bergman **16**:56
Robert Bresson **16**:106
Albert Camus **4**:88
Elias Canetti **25**:110
Maria Irene Fornes **39**:138
Paul Goodman **2**:170
Rolf Hochhuth **4**:230
Eugène Ionesco **4**:251
Claude Lévi-Strauss **38**:294
Alain Resnais **16**:501
Nathalie Sarraute **4**:465
Jean-Paul Sartre **4**:475
Peter Weiss **15**:564

Sonthoff, Helen W.
Phyllis Webb **18**:540
Ethel Davis Wilson **13**:606

Sorban, M. J., Jr.
Woody Allen **16**:8

Sorenson, Marian
Allan W. Eckert **17**:103
Lee Kingman **17**:245

Sorenson, Somner
Carl Sandburg **35**:356

Sorrentino, Gilbert
Paul Blackburn **9**:99
Richard Brautigan **12**:57
Italo Calvino **22**:94
Robert Creeley **2**:106
Robert Duncan **2**:122
William Gaddis **8**:227
Charles Olson **2**:327
Manuel Puig **28**:374
Luis Rafael Sánchez **23**:383
John Wieners **7**:535, 536
Louis Zukofsky **7**:563

Soskin, William
James M. Cain **28**:44
Taylor Caldwell **28**:59
Esther Forbes **12**:204
Carl Sandburg **35**:351
T. H. White **30**:437

Sotiron, Michael
Hugh Garner **13**:237

Soule, Stephen W.
Anthony Burgess **5**:90

Soupault, Philippe
René Clair **20**:60

Sourian, Peter
Albert Camus **2**:98
Eleanor Clark **5**:105
Bette Greene **30**:169, 170
Jack Kerouac **2**:227
Norman Lear **12**:336
Eric Rohmer **16**:535
William Saroyan **8**:468
Vassilis Vassilikos **4**:552

Southerland, Ellease
Zora Neale Hurston **7**:171

Southern, David
Michael McClure **6**:320

Southern, Jane
Helen MacInnes **27**:281

Southern, Terry
William Golding **17**:165
Peter Matthiessen **32**:286
John Rechy **1**:283
Kurt Vonnegut, Jr. **12**:601

Southron, Jane Spence
Enid Bagnold **25**:73
Thomas B. Costain **30**:92
Pamela Hansford Johnson
27:213, 214
Molly Keane **31**:232

Southworth, James G.
E. E. Cummings **3**:115
Robert Frost **3**:168
Robinson Jeffers **3**:257
Archibald MacLeish **3**:309
Laura Riding **7**:373

Souza, Eunice de
Ruth Prawer Jhabvala **29**:258

Souza, Raymond D.
Alejo Carpentier **38**:95
G. Cabrera Infante **25**:100
Octavio Paz **10**:392
Ernesto Sabato **10**:444; **23**:381

Sowton, Ian
Patrick Lane **25**:288
F. R. Scott **22**:373

Soyinka, Wole
Mongo Beti **27**:48

Spackman, W. M.
I. Compton-Burnett **34**:499
Hilary Spurling **34**:499

Spacks, Patricia Meyer
Kingsley Amis **5**:24
Nicholas Delbanco **6**:130
Hannah Green **3**:202
Joseph Heller **5**:183
Jennifer Johnston **7**:186
D. Keith Mano **10**:328
Alberto Moravia **2**:294
Iris Murdoch **6**:347
J. R. Salamanca **15**:463
Anne Sexton **8**:483
Andrew Sinclair **2**:402
Muriel Spark **2**:419; **5**:400
Peter Spielberg **6**:520
J.R.R. Tolkien **1**:336
Elio Vittorini **6**:551
Eudora Welty **2**:464
Paul West **7**:524
Patrick White **4**:587
Joy Williams **31**:464

Spain, Francis Lander
Margot Benary-Isbert **12**:31

Spann, Marcella
Ezra Pound **4**:413

Spanos, William V.
Martin Heidegger **24**:277
Yannis Ritsos **6**:460
Jean-Paul Sartre **18**:466

Sparshott, Francis
Northrop Frye **24**:231

Spaulding, Martha
Laurie Colwin **13**:156
Kamala Markandaya **8**:377
J.R.R. Tolkien **8**:516

Spears, Monroe K.
W. H. Auden **2**:22
John Berryman **2**:57
Cleanth Brooks **24**:114
James Dickey **2**:116
T. S. Eliot **2**:127
Robert Graves **11**:254
Daniel Hoffman **23**:242
Ted Hughes **2**:199
David Jones **2**:217
Madison Jones **4**:263
Maxine Kumin **28**:222
Ursula K. Le Guin **22**:269
Robert Lowell **2**:248
Ezra Pound **2**:342
John Crowe Ransom **2**:366
Karl Shapiro **4**:487
Allen Tate **2**:430; **24**:441
John Kennedy Toole **19**:443
Robert Penn Warren **1**:355;
4:579; **18**:539
René Wellek **28**:445

Spector, Ivar
Mikhail Sholokhov **7**:420

Spector, Robert D.
Robert Alter **34**:516
William Bronk **10**:73
Len Deighton **22**:114
Stephen Dobyns **37**:74
Robert Duncan **7**:87
D. J. Enright **4**:156
Louise Glück **22**:173
Edwin Honig **33**:209
David Ignatow **7**:174
Carolyn Kizer **15**:308
Halldór Laxness **25**:293
Kenneth Rexroth **2**:371

Speer, Diane Parkin
Robert Heinlein **8**:275

Spence, Jon
Katherine Anne Porter **7**:320

Spence, Jonathan
Kazuo Ishiguro **27**:204

Spencer, Benjamin T.
Edward Dahlberg **7**:70

Spencer, Brent
Donald Hall **37**:145

Spencer, Elizabeth
Elizabeth Spencer **22**:403

Spencer, Jack
André Schwarz-Bart **2**:388

Spencer, Marjorie
Prince **35**:327

Spencer, Sharon
Djuna Barnes **3**:38
Jorge Luis Borges **3**:77
Julio Cortázar **3**:114
Carlos Fuentes **3**:175
Anaïs Nin **4**:376; **14**:381
Alain Robbe-Grillet **4**:448

Spendal, R. J.
James Wright **10**:546

Spender, Stephen
A. R. Ammons **2**:12
W. H. Auden **3**:25, 27
James Baldwin **17**:25
T. S. Eliot **24**:163
James Fenton **32**:169
Günter Grass **22**:196
Robert Graves **2**:177; **39**:327
Thom Gunn **3**:216
Ted Hughes **2**:200
Aldous Huxley **3**:253; **5**:192;
8:304
David Jones **13**:312
Arthur Koestler **15**:311
F. R. Leavis **24**:293
Philip Levine **4**:287
James Merrill **3**:335
W. S. Merwin **3**:340
Eugenio Montale **7**:225
Elsa Morante **8**:403
Alberto Moravia **27**:356
Sylvia Plath **9**:429
William Plomer **4**:406
Peter Porter **33**:323
Nelly Sachs **14**:475
James Schuyler **5**:383; **23**:389
Gore Vidal **2**:450; **8**:527
Christa Wolf **29**:464
James Wright **3**:541

Sperone, Al J.
Joseph Heller **36**:230

Spice, Nicholas
Michel Tournier **36**:438

Spicer, Edward H.
Carlos Castaneda **12**:85

Spiegel, Alan
Stanley Kubrick **16**:392
Jean-Paul Sartre **7**:398

Spiegelman, Willard
John Betjeman **10**:53
Richard Howard **7**:169
James Merrill **8**:384
Adrienne Rich **7**:370

Spieler, F. Joseph
Robert Wilson **9**:577

Spilka, Mark
Ernest Hemingway **10**:263
Doris Lessing **6**:300
Erich Segal **3**:446
John Steinbeck **21**:385

Spina, James
Jimmy Page and Robert Plant
12:482

Spinrad, Norman
Jack Vance **35**:417

Spitz, David
William Golding **17**:172

Spitz, Robert Stephen
Pete Hamill **10**:251

Spitzer, Jane Stewart
Leon Uris **32**:437

Spitzer, Nicholas R.
Waylon Jennings **21**:202

Spitzer, Susan
Margaret Drabble **22**:122

Spivack, Kathleen
Robert Lowell **2**:248

Spivey, Herman E.
William Faulkner **6**:176

Spivey, Ted R.
Conrad Aiken **5**:9
Romain Gary **25**:189
Flannery O'Connor **1**:255

Spiwack, David
Jackson Browne **21**:36

Spoliar, Nicholas
Richard Stern **39**:244

Spraggins, Mary Beth Pringle
Monique Wittig **22**:476

Sprague, Rosemary
Marianne Moore **4**:362

Sprague, Susan
Mavis Thorpe Clark **12**:132
Barbara Corcoran **17**:77

Springer, Cole
Frank Zappa **17**:593

Sproul, Kathleen
Nevil Shute **30**:368

Spurling, Hilary
James Fenton **32**:167
Anthony Powell **10**:417

Spurling, John
Peter Barnes **5**:50
Samuel Beckett **6**:42
Peter Benchley **4**:54
Malcolm Bradbury **32**:51
Howard Brenton **31**:58
Graham Greene **37**:135, 138
Anna Kavan **13**:315
Francis King **8**:322
David Mercer **5**:284
Joe McGinniss **32**:301
Kamala Markandaya **38**:325
Yukio Mishima **9**:384
Peter Nichols **5**:308
David Plante **7**:307
Anne Redmon **22**:341
Peter Shaffer **5**:388
Elie Wiesel **5**:491

Squillace, Jacques
Eldridge Cleaver **30**:69

Squires, Radcliffe
Brewster Ghiselin **23**:169
Caroline Gordon **6**:204
Randall Jarrell **6**:260
Robinson Jeffers **11**:305
Mario Luzi **13**:353
Frederic Prokosh **4**:420
Allen Tate **2**:429; **4**:540; **11**:524
Robert Penn Warren **18**:537

Sragow, Michael
Roy Blount, Jr. **38**:44
Brian De Palma **20**:83
George Roy Hill **26**:209
Stephen King **26**:243
Steve Martin **30**:251

Srivastava, Narsingh
W. H. Auden **14**:26

Stabb, Martin S.
Jorge Luis Borges **19**:44
José Donoso **11**:149

Stableford, Brian M.
Douglas Adams **27**:15
James Blish **14**:84
Ann Swinfen **34**:577

Stade, George
Kingsley Amis **8**:10
E. E. Cummings **3**:119
Guy Davenport, Jr. **14**:142
Don DeLillo **27**:78
E. L. Doctorow **6**:132; **18**:126
John Gregory Dunne **28**:126
Leslie Epstein **27**:131
Max Frisch **18**:163
John Gardner **3**:186
Robert Graves **1**:129
Barry Hannah **38**:234
William Kennedy **34**:207
Jerzy Kosinski **3**:272
Alan Lelchuk **5**:243
Elmore Leonard **28**:235
Doris Lessing **15**:331
Joseph McElroy **5**:279
Henry Miller **14**:371
Steven Millhauser **21**:219
Iris Murdoch **22**:328
Jean Rhys **6**:452
Wilfrid Sheed **4**:488
Muriel Spark **2**:416
John Updike **5**:458
Gore Vidal **33**:409
Kurt Vonnegut, Jr. **3**:501

Stadnychenko, Tamara
Ayn Rand **30**:304

Stafford, I. Elizabeth
Lee Kingman **17**:244

Stafford, Jean
Harry Crews **23**:132
M. E. Kerr **12**:296, 298
James A. Michener **5**:289
Jessamyn West **17**:552
Paul West **7**:523

Stafford, William E.
Millen Brand **7**:29
William Dickey **28**:117
Richard Eberhart **19**:142
Loren Eiseley **7**:93
Barbara Howes **15**:289
David Kherdian **6**:280
Kenneth Rexroth **2**:370
M. L. Rosenthal **28**:393
Louis Simpson **7**:427
May Swenson **14**:518
Theodore Weiss **8**:546

Staley, Thomas F.
Margaret Drabble **22**:127

Stallings, Sylvia
Doris Betts **28**:33

Stallknecht, Newton P.
Amos Tutuola **5**:445

Stallman, Robert W.
Ernest Hemingway **13**:271;
19:212

Stambolian, George
Sam Shepard **4**:490

Stamelman, Richard
Yves Bonnefoy **15**:75
Francis Ponge **18**:415

Stamford, Anne Marie
Taylor Caldwell **28**:68
Leslie Epstein **27**:127
Isabelle Holland **21**:149

Stamm, Michael E.
Robert Bloch **33**:85
Stephen King **37**:204, 205

Stamm, Rudolf
Harold Pinter **27**:388

Stamp, Gavin
John Betjeman **34**:310

Stampfel, Peter
Samuel R. Delaney **38**:154

Stampfer, Judah
Saul Bellow **6**:60
Philip Roth **6**:476

Standard, Elinore
Virginia Hamilton **26**:147

Staneck, Lou Willet
John Neufeld **17**:310

Stanford, Alfred
Thor Heyerdahl **26**:189

Stanford, Ann
May Swenson **4**:533

Stanford, Derek
A. Alvarez **13**:9
Earle Birney **4**:64
Robert Creeley **2**:106
C. Day Lewis **1**:72
Lawrence Durrell **4**:147
Geoffrey Hill **18**:238
Aldous Huxley **5**:192
Elizabeth Jennings **5**:197
Patrick Kavanagh **22**:244
Norman MacCaig **36**:284
Hugh MacDiarmid **4**:313
Louis MacNeice **1**:187
Robert Nye **13**:413
William Plomer **4**:406
Craig Raine **32**:349
Carl Sandburg **15**:470
Stephen Spender **1**:322; **2**:419
Yevgeny Yevtushenko **3**:547

Stanford, Don
Yvor Winters **32**:462

Stanford, Donald E.
Elizabeth Daryush **19**:122
Caroline Gordon **6**:202
Marianne Moore **4**:364
Katherine Anne Porter **27**:402
Ezra Pound **10**:407
Allen Tate **2**:430
Yvor Winters **4**:591

Stange, Maren
Susan Sontag **10**:486

Stanhope, Henry
Wilbur Smith **33**:377

Stankiewicz, Marketa Goetz
Pavel Kohout **13**:323
Sławomir Mrożek **3**:345

Stanleigh, Bertram
Frank Zappa **17**:584

Stanlis, Peter L.
Robert Frost **3**:174

Stannard, Martin
Evelyn Waugh **13**:588

Stansky, Peter
Antonia Fraser **32**:184

Stanton, Michael N.
E. M. Forster **22**:135

Staples, Hugh B.
Randall Jarrell **6**:261
Robert Lowell **2**:246

Stark, Andy
Norman Mailer **39**:425
Peter Manso **39**:425

Stark, Freya
Paul Bowles **19**:58

Stark, John O.
John Barth **7**:22
Jorge Luis Borges **8**:94
E. L. Doctorow **6**:131
William Gaddis **8**:228
Vladimir Nabokov **8**:407

Stark, Myra
Adrienne Rich **11**:477

Starobinski, Jean
Michel Foucault **31**:178

Starr, Carol
John Neufeld **17**:310

Starr, Kevin
Jackson J. Benson **34**:407
James M. Cain **28**:52
E. L. Doctorow **6**:136
John Dos Passos **8**:181
John Steinbeck **34**:407

Starr, Roger
Anthony Powell **3**:403

Stasio, Marilyn
Anne Burr **6**:105
Maria Irene Fornes **39**:136
John Hopkins **4**:234
Terrence McNally **4**:346, 347
Jason Miller **2**:284
David Rabe **4**:426
Murray Schisgal **6**:491
Melvin Van Peebles **2**:448

States, Bert O.
R. S. Crane **27**:74
Harold Pinter **6**:412

Stathis, James J.
William Gaddis **19**:186

Stauffer, Donald A.
Rebecca West **31**:455

Stauffer, Helen Winter
Mari Sandoz **28**:406

Stavin, Robert H.
Alvin Silverstein and Virginia
B. Silverstein **17**:450

Stavn, Diane G.
Nat Hentoff **26**:183

Stavn, Diane Gersoni
Frank Bonham 12:51
Barbara Corcoran 17:72
Mollie Hunter 21:157
M. E. Kerr 12:297
Joseph Krumgold 12:320
Emily Cheney Neville 12:451
Barbara Wersba 30:431

Stavrou, C. N.
Edward Albee 5:12
Tennessee Williams 30:463

Stead, C. K.
Keri Hulme 39:159

Steck, Henry J.
Jules Archer 12:20

Steck, John A.
Al Young 19:480

Steegmuller, Francis
Patrick Modiano 18:338

Steel, Ronald
Pavel Kohout 13:323

Steele, Timothy
W. S. Merwin 18:336

Steene, Birgitta
Ingmar Bergman 16:54, 59, 64

Stefanile, Felix
William Bronk 10:73
Lewis Turco 11:552

Stegner, Page
J.M.G. Le Clézio 31:244
Peter Matthiessen 32:294
Vladimir Nabokov 1:239

Stegner, Wallace
Jackson J. Benson 34:405
Walter Van Tilburg Clark 28:81
N. Scott Momaday 19:318
John Steinbeck 34:405

Stein, Benjamin
Joan Didion 8:177
John Gregory Dunne 28:123

Stein, Charles
Jerome Rothenberg 6:477

Stein, Elliott
Andrzej Wajda 16:584

Stein, Howard F.
Alex Haley 12:251

Stein, Robert A.
J. V. Cunningham 3:122

Stein, Robert J.
Margaret O. Hyde 21:176, 179

Stein, Ruth M.
Jamake Highwater 12:287
Norma Fox Mazer 26:293
Anne McCaffrey 17:283, 284
Robert Newton Peck 17:342

Steinbeck, Nancy
Kin Platt 26:356

Steinberg, Karen
Martin Cruz Smith 25:414

Steinberg, Karen Matlaw
Yuri Krotkov 19:265
Anatoli Rybakov 23:372

Steinberg, M. W.
John Arden 15:23
Robertson Davies 7:72
A. M. Klein 19:258, 261
Arthur Miller 1:215

Steiner, Carlo
Giuseppe Ungaretti 7:483

Steiner, George
Jorge Luis Borges 2:70
Malcolm Bradbury 32:52
Anthony Burgess 22:78
Guy Davenport 38:144
C. Day Lewis 6:126
Lawrence Durrell 4:144
Elaine Feinstein 36:173
Michel Foucault 31:174
Paul Goodman 7:127
Graham Greene 6:220
Martin Heidegger 24:275
Aldous Huxley 5:194
Thomas Keneally 8:318; 10:298
F. R. Leavis 24:303
Claude Levi-Strauss 38:296
Georg Lukács 24:318
Robert M. Pirsig 4:403
Sylvia Plath 11:445
Jean-Paul Sartre 7:397
Aleksandr I. Solzhenitsyn 4:516
John Updike 5:459
Patrick White 4:583
Sloan Wilson 32:447
Marguerite Yourcenar 38:454

Stekert, Ellen J.
Woody Guthrie 35:187

Stendahl, Brita
Gunnar Ekelöf 27:116

Stengel, Richard
Brian Moore 19:333

Stenson, Leah Deland
Sol Gordon 26:137

Stepanchev, Stephen
John Ashbery 2:16
Imamu Amiri Baraka 2:34
Ted Berrigan 37:43
Elizabeth Bishop 4:65
Robert Bly 2:65
James M. Cain 28:47
Robert Creeley 2:105
James Dickey 2:115
Alan Dugan 2:121
Robert Duncan 2:122
Jean Garrigue 2:153
Allen Ginsberg 2:162
Randall Jarrell 2:208
Robert Lowell 2:247
W. S. Merwin 2:276
Lilika Nakos 29:321
Charles Olson 2:325
Kenneth Rexroth 2:369
Karl Shapiro 4:485
Irwin Shaw 23:397
Louis Simpson 4:498
William Stafford 4:519
May Swenson 4:532
Richard Wilbur 6:568

Stephen, Sidney J.
A. M. Klein 19:260

Stephens, Donald
Dorothy Livesay 4:294
Sinclair Ross 13:490
Rudy Wiebe 6:567

Stephens, George D.
Thornton Wilder 35:442

Stephens, Martha
Richard Wright 1:379

Stephens, Robert O.
Ernest Hemingway 3:239

Stephenson, Edward R.
John Hawkes 15:277

Stephenson, William
James Dickey 4:122

Stepto, R. B.
Maya Angelou 35:30

Stepto, Robert B.
Michael S. Harper 7:139
Richard Wright 21:455

Sterba, James P.
Jacques-Yves Cousteau 30:109

Sterling, Dorothy
Virginia Hamilton 26:148

Stern, Daniel
James Baldwin 17:33
Paul Bowles 2:79
Leonard Cohen 38:132
Margaret Drabble 22:120
Joanne Greenberg 7:134
Marjorie Kellogg 2:223
Jakov Lind 4:292
Bernard Malamud 3:324
Chaim Potok 2:339
Ann Quin 6:441
Richard Stern 39:237
Piri Thomas 17:497
Paul West 7:523
Elie Wiesel 3:529

Stern, David
Robert Kotlowitz 4:275
Amos Oz 5:334

Stern, Frederick C.
Thomas McGrath 28:278

Stern, Gerald
Gil Orlovitz 22:335

Stern, J. P.
Günter Grass 22:192
Eric Rohmer 16:537

Stern, James
William Golding 17:158
Nadine Gordimer 33:177, 179

Stern, Margaret
Helen MacInnes 27:278

Stern, Richard
Studs Terkel 38:419

Sterne, Richard C.
Octavio Paz 10:391

Sterne, Richard Clark
Jerome Weidman 7:517

Sternhell, Carol
Simone de Beauvoir 31:43
Kathryn Kramer 34:75
Lynne Sharon Schwartz 31:390
Fay Weldon 36:446

Sternlicht, Stanford
C. S. Forester 35:173

Sterritt, David
William Kotzwinkle 35:256
James Lapine 39:172
Stephen Sondheim 39:172

Stetler, Charles
Richard Brautigan 12:67
James Purdy 4:423

Steuding, Bob
Gary Snyder 32:387

Stevens, George
T. S. Stribling 23:443

Stevens, Georgiana G.
Vera Brittain 23:90

Stevens, Mark
David Byrne 26:94

Stevens, Peter
A. R. Ammons 8:14
Margaret Atwood 4:24
Patrick Lane 25:283
Dorothy Livesay 15:339
A. W. Purdy 3:408

Stevens, Shane
Eldridge Cleaver 30:56, 65
Ronald L. Fair 18:139
Ronald Harwood 32:223
William Kennedy 28:203
John Rechy 7:356
Paul Theroux 28:423

Stevens, Wallace
Marianne Moore 10:347

Stevenson, Anne
Elizabeth Bishop 1:35
Peter Davison 28:103
W. S. Graham 29:196
Michael Hamburger 14:235
Seamus Heaney 25:242
Barbara Howes 15:290
Elizabeth Jennings 14:292, 293
Primo Levi 37:223
Paul Muldoon 32:318
Tom Paulin 37:352
Marge Piercy 27:376
David Plante 23:343
Peter Porter 13:453
F. T. Prince 22:338
Christopher Reid 33:349
Muriel Rukeyser 15:457
May Swenson 14:521
R. S. Thomas 13:544
Charles Tomlinson 13:548

Stevenson, David L.
James Jones 3:260
Jack Kerouac 2:226
William Styron 1:329

Stevenson, Drew
C. S. Adler 35:12, 14
Jay Bennett 35:45
Lois Duncan 26:105
Kin Platt 26:355
Laurence Yep 35:472

Stevenson, Patrick
W. R. Rodgers **7**:377

Stevenson, Warren
Hugh MacLennan **14**:343

Stevick, Philip
Max Apple **33**:20
John Barth **14**:57
Donald Barthelme **8**:53
Wayne C. Booth **24**:93
William S. Burroughs **5**:93
William H. Gass **8**:247
Jerzy Kosinski **6**:283
Jan Stafford **4**:518
Kurt Vonnegut, Jr. **5**:465

Stewart, Alastair
Kon Ichikawa **20**:176

Stewart, Alfred D.
Jack Williamson **29**:457

Stewart, Corbet
Paul Celan **10**:102

Stewart, David H.
George Steiner **24**:437

Stewart Douglas
Robert D. FitzGerald **19**:175

Stewart, Garrett
Buster Keaton **20**:197
Steven Spielberg **20**:361

Stewart, Harry E.
Jean Genet **10**:225; **14**:201

Stewart, Ian
Françoise Sagan **17**:428

Stewart, J.I.M.
I. Compton-Burnett **34**:498
Compton Mackenzie **18**:316
Hilary Spurling **34**:498
Angus Wilson **34**:581

Stewart, John L.
John Crowe Ransom **2**:362;
24:367

Stewart, Mary
Mary Stewart **35**:391

Stewart, Robert Sussman
Heinrich Böll **2**:67

Stewart, Ruth Weeden
William Mayne **12**:387

Stille, Alexander
T. Coraghessan Boyle **36**:57
Michael Ende **31**:143
Pier Paolo Pasolini **37**:348

Stiller, Nikki
Louis Simpson **9**:486

Stillman, Clara Gruening
C.L.R. James **33**:218

Stillwell, Robert
Edwin Honig **33**:213

Stilwell, Robert L.
A. R. Ammons **3**:10
Sylvia Plath **1**:269
Jon Silkin **2**:395
James Wright **3**:540

Stimpfle, Nedra
Kristin Hunter **35**:228

Stimpson, Catharine R.
Thom Gunn **18**:199
Tillie Olsen **13**:432
Marge Piercy **6**:403
J.R.R. Tolkien **1**:338
Edmund White III **27**:481

Stineback, David C.
Allen Tate **9**:525

Stinnett, Caskie
S. J. Perelman **15**:419

Stinson, John J.
Anthony Burgess **4**:82

Stitt, Peter
A. R. Ammons **25**:41
John Ashbery **13**:34
Marvin Bell **31**:50
Wendell Berry **27**:35
John Berryman **10**:46
Frank Bidart **33**:77
Robert Bly **38**:54
Amy Clampitt **32**:117
Stephen Dobyns **37**:79, 80
Norman Dubie **36**:134, 135,
139
Stephen Dunn **36**:152, 155
Daniel Halpern **14**:232
William Harmon **38**:244
William Heyen **13**:282; **18**:232
Edward Hirsch **31**:215
Richard F. Hugo **32**:243
David Ignatow **14**:277
Galway Kinnell **29**:284
Philip Levine **33**:271, 274
Laurence Lieberman **36**:261
James Merrill **18**:330
Linda Pastan **27**:370
Stanley Plumly **33**:312, 314
Katha Pollitt **28**:367
Louis Simpson **7**:429; **32**:376,
378
Dave Smith **22**:387
William Stafford **29**:387
Mark Strand **18**:521
Robert Penn Warren **10**:519;
39:259, 269, 270
Charles Wright **13**:614; **28**:458
James Wright **10**:542

Stock, Irvin
Saul Bellow **2**:50
Mary McCarthy **1**:206

Stock, Robert
Theodore Weiss **14**:555

Stocking, George W., Jr.
Margaret Mead **37**:280

Stocking, Marion Kingston
Galway Kinnell **1**:168
Gary Snyder **1**:318

Stoelting, Winifred L.
Ernest J. Gaines **18**:165

Stokes, Eric
Kamala Markandaya **8**:378

Stokes, Geoffrey
Martin Amis **38**:15
John Cheever **25**:120
Len Deighton **22**:117
Stanley Elkin **14**:158
Mark Helprin **32**:233
Edward Hoagland **28**:186
John le Carré **15**:325
James Merrill **34**:226
Paul Muldoon **32**:321
Phil Ochs **17**:335
Frank O'Connor **23**:332
Robert Stone **23**:428
Richard Yates **23**:482

Stokes, Thomas L.
Bruce Catton **35**:82

Stoler, Peter
Douglas Adams **27**:15
Carl Sagan **30**:333

Stoltzfus, Ben F.
Ernest Hemingway **13**:279
Alain Robbe-Grillet **1**:285;
14:456

Stolz, Herbert J.
Larry Kettelkamp **12**:307

Stone, Chuck
Garry Trudeau **12**:590

Stone, Elizabeth
John Fowles **9**:213
John Gardner **8**:234
Cynthia Macdonald **13**:355;
19:290
Judith Rossner **29**:352
Joan Micklin Silver **20**:344
Lily Tomlin **17**:520

Stone, Laurie
Margaret Atwood **15**:38
Rosellen Brown **32**:65
Raymond Carver **36**:101
Max Frisch **9**:217
Elizabeth Hardwick **13**:266
Shirley Hazzard **18**:219
Mary McCarthy **24**:348
Anaïs Nin **8**:423
Anne Roiphe **9**:455
Judith Rossner **29**:356
Dalton Trumbo **19**:447
Tom Wolfe **15**:584

Stone, Norman
Michael Scammell **34**:489
Aleksandr Solzhenitsyn **34**:489

Stone, Robert
William Kotzwinkle **14**:309
Peter Matthiessen **5**:274

Stone, Rochelle K.
Tadeusz Różewicz **23**:362

Stone, Wilfred
E. M. Forster **15**:229

Stone, William B.
Alice Munro **19**:347

Stoneback, H. R.
William Faulkner **8**:213

Stonehill, Brian
André Dubus **36**:147
Vladimir Nabokov **23**:310

Stones, Rosemary
Virginia Hamilton **26**:152
Philippa Pearce **21**:291

Stonier, G. W.
Charles Chaplin **16**:187

Storch, R. F.
Harold Pinter **6**:409

Storey, Mark
Stevie Smith **25**:418

Storey, Robert
David Mamet **15**:357

Storr, Catherine
Eilís Dillon **17**:98
Leon Garfield **12**:221

Story, Jack Trevor
C. P. Snow **6**:517

Stothard, Peter
Lawrence Durrell **13**:188

Stott, Jon C.
Kevin Major **26**:288
Scott O'Dell **30**:271

Stouck, David
Marie-Claire Blais **2**:63
Hugh MacLennan **2**:257

Stourton, James
Monty Python **21**:228

Stout, Janis P.
Larry McMurtry **27**:329

Stout, Rex
Laura Z. Hobson **25**:270

Stover, Leon E.
Frank Herbert **12**:276

Stow, Randolph
Claude Simon **39**:211

Stowers, Bonnie
Hortense Calisher **4**:88
Saul Maloff **5**:271

Strachan, Don
Thomas M. Disch **36**:127
Nettie Jones **34**:69
John Edgar Wideman **34**:298

Strachan, W. J.
Sylvia Townsend Warner
19:460

Stracley, Julia
Rhys Davies **23**:142

Strakhovsky, Leonid I.
Anna Akhmatova **25**:23

Strandberg, Victor H.
Cynthia Ozick **28**:353
John Updike **13**:557
Robert Penn Warren **13**:573

Stratford, Philip
Graham Greene **6**:212

Straub, Peter
Michael Ayrton **7**:19
Beryl Bainbridge **8**:36
James Baldwin **4**:43
J. G. Ballard **3**:35
Donald Barthelme **3**:44

Critic Index

John Gregory Dunne **28**:123
Brian Glanville **6**:202
Hermann Hesse **6**:237
Julius Horwitz **14**:266
Jack Kerouac **3**:266
Francis King **8**:321
Margaret Laurence **6**:290
Olivia Manning **5**:273
Thomas McGuane **7**:213
Michael Mewshaw **9**:376
James A. Michener **5**:291
Anaïs Nin **8**:419
Joyce Carol Oates **9**:402
Flann O'Brien **4**:385
Simon Raven **14**:442
Simone Schwarz-Bart **7**:404
Isaac Bashevis Singer **6**:509
Richard G. Stern **4**:523
John Updike **5**:457
Morris L. West **6**:563

Strauch, Carl F.
J. D. Salinger **12**:505

Strauss, Harold
James M. Cain **28**:44
Taylor Caldwell **28**:56
Rhys Davies **23**:141
Arthur Koestler **33**:228
Ayn Rand **30**:291
Dalton Trumbo **19**:44

Strauss, Theodore
Rouben Mamoulian **16**:424

Strauss, Victor
Brigid Brophy **29**:95

Strawson, Galen
Michel Tournier **23**:454

Strawson, P. F.
George Steiner **24**:436

Strebel, Elizabeth Grottle
Jean Renoir **20**:309

Street, Douglas O.
Lawrence Ferlinghetti **6**:183

Strehle, Susan
John Gardner **10**:218

Strell, Lois A.
Piers Anthony **35**:38
Norma Klein **30**:243

Stresau, Hermann
Thornton Wilder **15**:571

Strick, Philip
Ingmar Bergman **16**:80
Philip K. Dick **30**:126
Werner Herzog **16**:330
Kon Ichikawa **20**:182
Nagisa Oshima **20**:246
Pier Paolo Pasolini **20**:264
Jerzy Skolimowski **20**:348
Andrzej Wajda **16**:580
Peter Weir **20**:424

Strickland, Geoffrey
Michel Tournier **36**:433

Strickland, Margaret
Norma Klein **30**:239

Stringer, William H.
Russell Baker **31**:25

Strong, Jonathan
David Plante **23**:342

Strong, Kenneth
Shiga Naoya **33**:369

Strong, L.A.G.
John Masefield **11**:356

Strong, Ray
Antonia Fraser **32**:179

Stroud, Janet G.
Judith Guest **30**:173

Stroupe, John H.
Jean Anouilh **13**:22

Strouse, Jean
Russell Banks **37**:28
Rosellen Brown **32**:64
Bob Dylan **12**:185
Joyce Maynard **23**:290

Strout, Cushing
William Styron **5**:420

Strozier, Robert M.
Peter De Vries **7**:78
S. J. Perelman **5**:337
P. G. Wodehouse **5**:517

Struthers, J. R. (Tim)
Jack Hodgins **23**:235
Hugh Hood **28**:191

Struve, Gleb
Ilya Ehrenburg **18**:131
Vladimir Nabokov **1**:241

Struve, Nikita
Aleksandr I. Solzhenitsyn **7**:433

Stuart, Alexander
Ralph Bakshi **26**:72
Richard O'Brien **17**:323
Pier Paolo Pasolini **20**:266

Stuart, Dabney
Ted Hughes **2**:201
Edwin Morgan **31**:273

Stubblefield, Charles
Sylvia Plath **1**:270

Stubbs, G. T.
Rosemary Sutcliff **26**:433

Stubbs, Harry C.
Isaac Asimov **26**:51
Melvin Berger **12**:38
Franklyn M. Branley **21**:20, 21, 23
Roy A. Gallant **17**:129, 131, 132
Alvin Silverstein and Virginia B. Silverstein **17**:451, 454

Stubbs, Helen
William Mayne **12**:399

Stubbs, Jean
Julio Cortázar **2**:102
Daphne du Maurier **6**:147
George Garrett **3**:193
Elizabeth Hardwick **13**:265
Eleanor Hibbert **7**:155
Anaïs Nin **8**:421

Stubbs, John C.
John Hawkes **1**:138

Stubbs, Patricia
Muriel Spark **3**:466

Stubing, John L.
Len Deighton **22**:119
Evan Hunter **31**:228

Stuckey, Sterling
Sterling A. Brown **23**:98

Stuckey, W. J.
Pearl S. Buck **18**:76
Caroline Gordon **29**:186

Stuewe, Paul
Joan Barfoot **18**:35
Ernest K. Gann **23**:167
John Gardner **30**:157
Jim Harrison **33**:197
Stephen King **26**:237
Ted Mooney **25**:330
Manuel Mujica Láinez **31**:284
Ernesto Sabato **23**:382
Françoise Sagan **36**:383

Stull, William L.
William S. Burroughs **15**:111

Stumpf, Thomas
Hayden Carruth **7**:41
Daniel Mark Epstein **7**:97
Ishmael Reed **5**:368
Muriel Rukeyser **6**:479

Stupple, A. James
Ray Bradbury **10**:69

Sturgeon, Ray
Joni Mitchell **12**:443

Sturgeon, Theodore
Poul Anderson **15**:10
Isaac Asimov **3**:16
Marion Zimmer Bradley **30**:26
John W. Campbell, Jr. **32**:76
Michael Crichton **2**:108
Harlan Ellison **13**:202
Robert A. Heinlein **26**:178
Frank Herbert **12**:276; **35**:204
Barry N. Malzberg **7**:208

Sturm, T. L.
Robert D. FitzGerald **19**:180

Sturrock, John
Jorge Amado **13**:12
Roland Barthes **24**:33
Jorge Luis Borges **13**:105
Peter De Vries **3**:125
Gabriel García Márquez **8**:233; **10**:217
J.M.G. Le Clézio **31**:248
Robert Pinget **37**:358
Alain Robbe-Grillet **8**:454
Nathalie Sarraute **31**:381
Claude Simon **15**:486
Michel Tournier **23**:453
Monique Wittig **22**:476

Styron, William
Philip Caputo **32**:103
Peter Matthiessen **32**:290
Terry Southern **7**:453

Subiotto, Arrigo
Max Frisch **32**:190

Subramani
W. Somerset Maugham **15**:368

Sucharitkul, Somtow
Samuel R. Delaney **38**:162
Michael Ende **31**:142
Gene Wolfe **25**:476

Suczek, Barbara
John Lennon and Paul McCartney **12**:369

Suderman, Elmer F.
John Updike **2**:443; **3**:488

Sugg, Alfred R.
Richard Lester **20**:222

Sugrue, Thomas
Riccardo Bacchelli **19**:31
Rhys Davies **23**:145
Ogden Nash **23**:318, 319
Mary Renault **17**:390
T. H. White **30**:442

Suhl, Benjamin
Jean-Paul Sartre **24**:410

Sukenick, Lynn
Maya Angelou **12**:12
Doris Lessing **3**:288
Anaïs Nin **8**:421
Robert L. Peters **7**:303

Sukenick, Ronald
Carlos Castaneda **12**:89
Rudolph Wurlitzer **2**:483

Suleiman, Jo-Ann D.
Thor Heyerdahl **26**:194
Erich von Däniken **30**:428

Sullivan, Andrew
Philip Larkin **39**:345

Sullivan, Anita T.
Ray Bradbury **3**:85

Sullivan, Dan
Edward Albee **25**:40
Charles Fuller **25**:179
Sam Shepard **34**:265

Sullivan, Eugene V., Jr.
Aidan Chambers **35**:99

Sullivan, Francis
James Carroll **38**:102

Sullivan, Jack
Richard Condon **8**:150
Robin Cook **14**:131
Guy Davenport, Jr. **14**:142
André Dubus **36**:144
Paul Horgan **9**:279
Susan Isaacs **32**:253
Stephen King **12**:309
John Knowles **26**:263
Wright Morris **18**:354
J. B. Priestley **9**:442
Susan Richards Shreve **23**:404
Peter Straub **28**:410
Julian Symons **14**:524
Joan D. Vinge **30**:411

Sullivan, John T.
Keri Hulme **39**:166

Sullivan, Kevin
Thomas Kinsella **19**:251
Flann O'Brien **5**:316
Sean O'Casey **5**:320
Frank O'Connor **23**:326
Gil Orlovitz **22**:333

Sullivan, Mary
B. S. Johnson **6**:262
William Sansom **6**:483
Fay Weldon **6**:562

Sullivan, Nancy
May Swenson **4**:534

Sullivan, Patrick
Frederick Wiseman **20**:473

Sullivan, Peggy
Gunnel Beckman **26**:87
Barbara Corcoran **17**:72
Lois Duncan **26**:101, 102
Lee Kingman **17**:244
Richard Peck **21**:295

Sullivan, Richard
A. J. Cronin **32**:139
Harper Lee **12**:340
Colin MacInnes **23**:282
William Maxwell **19**:306
William Mitchell **25**:321
Piers Paul Read **25**:376
Betty Smith **19**:423
Mary Stolz **12**:547

Sullivan, Rosemary
Marie-Claire Blais **6**:81
Patrick Lane **25**:286
P. K. Page **18**:378
Theodore Roethke **19**:398

Sullivan, Ruth
Ken Kesey **6**:278

Sullivan, Tom R.
William Golding **8**:249
Michel Tournier **6**:538

Sullivan, Victoria
Saul Bellow **8**:76

Sullivan, Walter
Donald Barthelme **1**:19
Saul Bellow **8**:81
Elizabeth Bowen **11**:64
Eleanor Clark **19**:106
Harry Crews **23**:131
Guy Davenport, Jr. **6**:124
Margaret Drabble **8**:184
Andre Dubus **13**:182
George Garnett **11**:219
William Golding **2**:166, 168
Graham Greene **6**:219
Richard Hughes **11**:278
Bernard Malamud **1**:200
William Maxwell **19**:309
Joyce Carol Oates **6**:368; **9**:405
Flannery O'Connor **2**:317;
21:268
John O'Hara **6**:385
Reynolds Price **13**:464
V. S. Pritchett **13**:465
Jean Rhys **6**:456
Alan Sillitoe **6**:501
William Trevor **14**:535
Anne Tyler **11**:553

Sullivan, Wilson
Irving Stone **7**:470

Sullivan, Zohreh Tawakuli
Iris Murdoch **6**:346; **11**:386

Sullivan-Daly, Tess
Michael Mott **15**:380

Sultan, Stanley
Ezra Pound **7**:331

Sultana, Donald
A. N. Wilson **33**:453

Sultanik, Aaron
E. L. Doctorow **18**:120
Lina Wertmüller **16**:595

Suplee, Curt
Thomas Berger **11**:46

Surette, Leon
George Bowering **15**:84
Ezra Pound **34**:511
E. Fuller Torrey **34**:511

Sussex, Elizabeth
Lindsay Anderson **20**:15
Satyajit Ray **16**:482
Agnès Varda **16**:555
Lina Wertmüller **16**:586
Billy Wilder **20**:460

Sussman, Vic
Fran Lebowitz **36**:248

Sutcliffe, Thomas
Robert Stone **23**:430
Peter Straub **28**:411

Suter, Anthony
Basil Bunting **10**:83, 84

Suther, Judith D.
Eugène Ionesco **11**:292

Sutherland, Bruce
Conrad Richter **30**:308

Sutherland, Donald
Rafael Alberti **7**:10
Octavio Paz **10**:389
St.-John Perse **4**:399
Francis Ponge **6**:422

Sutherland, Fraser
Elizabeth Spencer **22**:405

Sutherland, J. A.
Philip José Farmer **19**:168

Sutherland, John
Vasily Aksyonov **37**:16
Len Deighton **22**:118
Robert Finch **18**:153
Günter Grass **32**:204
Jorge Ibargüengoitia **37**:184
Ruth Prawer Jhabvala **29**:262
P. K. Page **18**:376
Anatoli Rybakov **23**:374
Ross Thomas **39**:249
A. N. Wilson **33**:454

Sutherland, Kathryn
Eva Figes **31**:168

Sutherland, Ronald
Roch Carrier **13**:140
Hugh MacLennan **14**:342

Sutherland, Sam
The Clash **30**:46
Elvis Costello **21**:67
Bob Seger **35**:385

Sutherland, Steve
Prince **35**:326

Sutherland, Stuart
A. Alvarez **13**:8
Peter De Vries **10**:137; **28**:107

Sutherland, Zena
Charles Addams **30**:16
C. S. Adler **35**:11, 13, 14
Joan Aiken **35**:16
Fran Arrick **30**:17
E. M. Almedingen **12**:3, 4, 7
Honor Arundel **17**:13
Gunnel Beckman **26**:87
Jay Bennett **35**:44
Melvin Berger **12**:39, 40, 41
Judy Blume **12**:44
Larry Bograd **35**:62, 63
Frank Bonham **12**:49, 50, 51,
52, 53, 54, 55
H. F. Brinsmead **21**:26
Betsy Byars **35**:73, 74
Betty Cavanna **12**:102
Aidan Chambers **35**:100
Alice Childress **12**:107
Mavis Thorpe Clark **12**:132
Christopher Collier and James
L. Collier **30**:71, 72, 73
Barbara Corcoran **17**:74, 76, 78
Robert Cormier **30**:87, 90
Paula Danziger **21**:84, 85
Lois Duncan **26**:101, 103, 106,
108
Babbis Friis-Baastad **12**:214
Roy A. Gallant **17**:132
Sol Gordon **26**:137
Rosa Guy **26**:142, 144, 145
Virginia Hamilton **26**:149
Nat Hentoff **26**:184
Isabelle Holland **21**:148, 149,
153, 154
Langston Hughes **35**:219
Mollie Hunter **21**:157
Margaret O. Hyde **21**:178, 179,
180
Jesse Jackson **12**:290, 291
Diana Wynne Jones **26**:226
M. E. Kerr **12**:298; **35**:248
Larry Kettelkamp **12**:305, 306,
307
Lee Kingman **17**:247
Joseph Krumgold **12**:318, 321
Madeleine L'Engle **12**:350
Sonia Levitin **17**:264, 265
Robert Lipsyte **21**:212
Anne McCaffrey **17**:282, 284
Milton Meltzer **26**:298, 302,
307
Nicholosa Mohr **12**:447
Walter Dean Myers **35**:295,
298
John Neufeld **17**:308, 310
Emily Cheney Neville **12**:450,
451, 452
Suzanne Newton **35**:301
Scott O'Dell **30**:276
Zibby Oneal **30**:280
Katherine Paterson **12**:484,
486; **30**:283, 288
Richard Peck **21**:296, 298, 299,
300
Robert Newton Peck **17**:338,
339, 340, 342
Kin Platt **26**:350, 351, 352,
353, 354, 356

D. M. Pinkwater **35**:318
Josephine Poole **17**:373
Marilyn Sachs **35**:335
Ann Schlee **35**:372
Ouida Sebestyen **30**:347
Alvin Silverstein and Virginia
B. Silverstein **17**:451, 454,
455
Zilpha Keatley Snyder **17**:470,
473, 475
Mary Stolz **12**:551, 553, 554,
555
Noel Streatfeild **21**:403, 408,
409, 412, 415
Rosemary Sutcliff **26**:436
Mildred D. Taylor **21**:419
Colin Thiele **17**:495, 496
Joyce Carol Thomas **35**:407
John R. Tunis **12**:599
Cynthia Voigt **30**:417, 418
Lenora Mattingly Weber **12**:634
Rosemary Wells **12**:639
Barbara Wersba **30**:432
Jessamyn West **17**:552
Hilma Wolitzer **17**:563
Laurence Yep **35**:471, 472, 473
Paul Zindel **26**:470, 472, 474

Sutton, Graham
W. Somerset Maugham **11**:367

Sutton, Horace
S. J. Perelman **23**:335

Sutton, Martyn
Joan Armatrading **17**:10

Sutton, Roger
Robert Cormier **30**:89
Laurence Yep **35**:473

Sutton, Roger D.
Robin F. Brancato **35**:69

Sutton, Walter
Allen Ginsberg **4**:181
Robert Lowell **4**:303
Thomas Merton **3**:336
Marianne Moore **4**:364
Ezra Pound **3**:395

Suvin, Darko
Eric Bentley **24**:49
Arkadii Strugatskii and Boris
Strugatskii **27**:432

Svensson, Frances
Vine Deloria, Jr. **21**:114

Swados, Harvey
Walter Van Tilburg Clark **28**:78
Howard Fast **23**:156
David Ignatow **4**:249

Swanbrow, Diane J.
John Knowles **26**:263

Swann, Brian
Theodore Roethke **19**:396

Swanson, Stevenson
Joseph Epstein **39**:463

Sward, Robert
Philip Whalen **29**:445

Swartley, Ariel
Joan Armatrading 17:8
Walter Becker and Donald
Fagen 26:85
Joni Mitchell 12:442
Bruce Springsteen 17:490

Swartney, Joyce
Charles M. Schulz 12:533

Swayze, Walter E.
Robertson Davies 25:131

Sweeney, Francis
Thomas J. Fleming 37:125

Sweeney, Patricia Runk
M. E. Kerr 12:301

Sweet, Louise
Frederick Wiseman 20:477

Sweeting, Adam
The Clash 30:50
Paul Weller 26:447

Swenson, John
Ray Davies 21:99
Paul McCartney 35:292
Willie Nelson 17:303
Peter Townshend 17:533, 540
Frank Zappa 17:591

Swenson, May
Ben Belitt 22:49
Robin Morgan 2:294
Muriel Rukeyser 27:408
Anne Sexton 2:392
W. D. Snodgrass 2:406

Swerdlow, Joel
John Nichols 38:343

Swift, John N.
John Cheever 15:129

Swift, Jonathan
Gerome Ragni and James Rado
17:385

Swift, Pat
George Barker 8:44

Swigg, Richard
E. M. Forster 9:209
Philip Larkin 9:324

Swigger, Ronald T.
Raymond Queneau 2:359

Swindell, Larry
Scott Spencer 30:407

Swinden, Patrick
D. J. Enright 31:155
C. P. Snow 4:503

Swing, Raymond
John R. Tunis 12:596

Swingewood, Alan
Lucien Goldmann 24:244

Swink, Helen
William Faulkner 3:154

Swiss, Thomas
James Galvin 38:198
Donald Justice 19:234
Laurence Lieberman 36:264

Swope, Donald B.
Peter Gent 29:180

Sykes, Christopher
Aldous Huxley 4:244; 8:303;
35:236

Sykes, Gerald
Jessie Redmon Fauset 19:169
William Gibson 23:173
Pamela Hansford Johnson
27:219, 220
Nevil Shute 30:369

Sykes, S. W.
Claude Simon 9:483

Sylvester, R. D.
Joseph Brodsky 13:114

Sylvester, William
Daniel Hoffman 23:239

Symons, Julian
Eric Ambler 4:18
W. H. Auden 2:28
Beryl Bainbridge 18:34
John Berryman 2:59
Edward Brathwaite 11:66
John Dickson Carr 3:101
John Cheever 8:140
Agatha Christie 6:107; 8:140;
12:121, 126
John Creasey 11:134
C. Day Lewis 6:129
Len Deighton 4:119
Thomas M. Disch 36:126
Friedrich Dürrenmatt 4:141
James Fenton 32:164, 169
Ian Fleming 3:159
Dick Francis 22:154
Roy Fuller 4:178
Graham Greene 27:175
Dashiell Hammett 3:219
Lillian Hellman 4:222
Patricia Highsmith 2:193; 4:225
Chester Himes 4:229
Evan Hunter 11:279; 31:224
P. D. James 18:276
Eliabeth Jennings 14:292
Pamela Hansford Johnson
27:222
John le Carré 3:282
John D. MacDonald 3:307
Ross Macdonald 3:307
Mary McCarthy 3:326
Henry Miller 2:281
Edwin Morgan 31:272
Ellery Queen 3:421
Simon Raven 14:442
Kenneth Rexroth 11:473
Laura Riding 3:431
Tadeusz Różewicz 23:358
Georges Simenon 3:451; 8:487;
18:485
Louis Simpson 4:498
Maj Sjöwall 7:501
C. P. Snow 4:500
Mickey Spillane 3:469
J.I.M. Stewart 14:511
Rex Stout 3:471
William Styron 15:528
Per Wahlöö 7:501
Robert Penn Warren 4:577
Patrick White 3:523

Angus Wilson 3:536
Yevgeny Yevtushenko 26:462

Syrkin, Marie
Henry Roth 6:472

Szanto, George H.
Alain Robbe-Grillet 1:288

Szirtes, George
Peter Porter 33:322

Szogyi, Alex
Lillian Hellman 2:187
Isaac Bashevis Singer 11:501

Szporluk, Mary Ann
Vladimir Voinovich 10:504

Szuhay, Joseph A.
Sandra Scoppettone 26:405

Tabachnick, Stephen E.
Conrad Aiken 5:9

Taëni, Rainer
Rolf Hochhuth 18:252

Tager, Marcia
Amy Hempel 39:70

Tagliabue, John
Muriel Rukeyser 27:414

Tait, Michael
James Reaney 13:472

Takiff, Jonathan
Lily Tomlin 17:521

Talbot, Daniel
Richard Matheson 37:244

Talbot, Emile J.
Marie-Claire Blais 22:60
Roch Carrier 13:144
J.M.G. Le Clézio 31:250, 251

Talbott, Strobe
Aleksandr I. Solzhenitsyn 4:516

Talese, Gay
Mario Puzo 36:362

Taliaferro, Frances
Frederick Barthelme 36:51
Anita Brookner 32:61
Frederick Busch 18:85
Laurie Colwin 13:157
Andre Dubus 13:184
Stanley Elkin 27:125
Nadine Gordimer 5:147
Maureen Howard 14:268
Milan Kundera 32:262
Tom McHale 5:283
Brian Moore 32:312
Barbara Pym 37:376
Françoise Sagan 36:380
Mark Stevens 34:111

Tallant, Robert
Doris Betts 28:32
Elizabeth Spencer 22:399

Tallenay, J. L.
Charles Chaplin 16:195

Tallman, Warren
Earle Birney 11:50
Ernest Buckler 13:118
Robert Creeley 11:135
Robert Duncan 15:187
Jack Kerouac 14:304

John Rechy 14:445
Mordecai Richler 3:430
Sinclair Ross 13:490

Tambling, Jeremy
Brian Aldiss 14:15
J.I.M. Stewart 14:513

Tamkin, Linda
Anaïs Nin 14:387

Tanenhaus, Sam
Guy Davenport 38:146
William H. Gass 39:482

Tannen, Deborah
Lilika Nakos 29:321, 323

Tanner, Alain
Luchino Visconti 16:561

Tanner, Stephen L.
Ernest Hemingway 8:288

Tanner, Tony
Walter Abish 22:19
John Barth 1:17; 2:37; 14:55
Donald Barthelme 2:40
Richard Brautigan 12:66
William S. Burroughs 2:92
William Gaddis 3:177
John Gardner 2:152
John Hawkes 2:185; 7:143
Ernest Hemingway 10:266
Norman Mailer 1:189
Bernard Malamud 2:267
James Purdy 2:351; 4:422
Thomas Pynchon 6:430, 432;
33:335
Philip Roth 22:357
Susan Sontag 1:322
John Updike 2:445
Kurt Vonnegut, Jr. 12:606

Taplin, Oliver
Edward Bond 23:67

Tapply, Robert S.
Roy A. Gallant 17:128

Tapscott, Stephen
Friedrich Dürrenmatt 11:173
Hugh MacDiarmid 19:288
Stevie Smith 25:417

Tarantino, Michael
Marguerite Duras 20:100, 101
Elaine May 16:437

Targan, Barry
Scott Sommer 25:425

Tarkka, Pekka
Hannu Salama 18:461

Tarn, Nathaniel
William H. Gass 1:114

Tarratt, Margaret
Nagisa Oshima 20:246
Gordon Parks 16:459
Luchino Visconti 16:568
Frederick Wiseman 20:474

Tarshis, Jerome
J. G. Ballard 3:34

Tartt, Alison
H. D. 31:212

Tate, Allen
　Edward Dahlberg **14**:134
　Donald Davidson **13**:167
　John Crowe Ransom **2**:363;
　　5:364
　I. A. Richards **24**:387
　T. S. Stribling **23**:443
　Melvin B. Tolson **36**:425
　Eudora Welty **1**:362

Tate, Claudia
　Keri Hulme **39**:162
　Nella Larsen **37**:216

Tate, George S.
　Halldór Laxness **25**:299

Tate, Greg
　Amiri Baraka **33**:62

Tate, J. O.
　Flannery O'Connor **13**:421
　Thomas Pynchon **33**:340
　Alexander Theroux **25**:434

Tate, Robert S., Jr.
　Albert Camus **1**:54

Tatham, Campbell
　John Barth **1**:18
　Raymond Federman **6**:181
　Thomas Pynchon **2**:354

Tatum, Charles M.
　José Donoso **11**:146

Taubman, Howard
　Enid Bagnold **25**:77
　James Baldwin **17**:27, 31
　Larry Gelbart **21**:125
　William Gibson **23**:179
　Garson Kanin **22**:230
　Arthur Kopit **18**:286
　Gerome Ragni and James Rado
　　17:379
　Stephen Sondheim **30**:379

Taubman, Robert
　John Barth **27**:29
　Patrick Boyle **19**:67
　Anita Brookner **32**:59
　William S. Burroughs **22**:85
　D. J. Enright **31**:146
　John Fowles **33**:173
　Michael Frayn **31**:189
　Nicolas Freeling **38**:184
　Iris Murdoch **31**:291
　Cynthia Ozick **7**:287
　Sylvia Plath **17**:345
　Lisa St. Aubin de Teran **36**:420
　D. M. Thomas **22**:419
　John Updike **23**:477

Taus, Roger
　William Everson **14**:167

Tavris, Carol
　Kate Wilhelm **7**:538

Tax, Jeremiah
　Richard Rosen **39**:197
　Nancy Willard **37**:466

Tax, Meredith
　Julian Symons **32**:429

Tax, Sol
　Margaret Mead **37**:274

Taxel, Joseph
　Christopher Collier and James
　　L. Collier **30**:73, 74

Taylor, Angus
　Philip K. Dick **30**:122

Taylor, Clyde
　Imamu Amiri Baraka **5**:47

Taylor, D. W.
　Eilís Dillon **17**:99

Taylor, David
　John Rechy **18**:443

Taylor, Eleanor Ross
　Elizabeth Bishop **15**:59
　Sylvia Plath **17**:347

Taylor, F. H. Griffin
　George Garrett **3**:192; **11**:219
　Robert Lowell **1**:181
　Theodore Weiss **3**:516

Taylor, Gordon O.
　Mary McCarthy **14**:358
　Tennessee Williams **30**:458

Taylor, Harry H.
　William Golding **17**:170

Taylor, Henry
　Ben Belitt **22**:50
　Marvin Bell **8**:64
　Irving Feldman **7**:103
　X. J. Kennedy **8**:319
　William Meredith **13**:373
　Howard Nemerov **6**:363
　Flannery O'Connor **1**:258
　Richard Tillinghast **29**:415
　John Hall Wheelock **14**:570
　James Wright **5**:521

Taylor, Jane
　Galway Kinnell **1**:168

Taylor, John Russell
　Lindsay Anderson **20**:17
　Robert Anderson **23**:32
　Michelangelo Antonioni **20**:28
　John Arden **6**:4
　Alan Ayckbourn **5**:34; **33**:43,
　　44
　Howard Barker **37**:36
　Brendan Behan **11**:44
　Ingmar Bergman **16**:50
　Edward Bond **4**:69
　Howard Brenton **31**:57
　Robert Bresson **16**:108
　Mel Brooks **12**:78
　Luis Buñuel **16**:132
　David Caute **29**:115
　Claude Chabrol **16**:180
　Caryl Churchill **31**:87
　Brian Clark **29**:128, 129
　Shelagh Delaney **29**:146
　Vittorio De Sica **20**:90
　Marguerite Duras **20**:99
　Federico Fellini **16**:274, 281,
　　288
　Simon Gray **36**:200, 207
　David Hare **29**:220
　Alfred Hitchcock **16**:344
　John Huston **20**:170, 171
　Ann Jellicoe **27**:207
　Stanley Kubrick **16**:388

　Fritz Lang **20**:208
　Hugh Leonard **19**:282
　David Mercer **5**:283
　John Mortimer **28**:283
　Peter Nichols **5**:305
　Joe Orton **4**:388
　Pier Paolo Pasolini **20**:266
　Harold Pinter **11**:436
　Terence Rattigan **7**:354
　Satyajit Ray **16**:490
　Alain Resnais **16**:502
　Peter Shaffer **14**:484, 485;
　　18:477
　Ntozake Shange **25**:399
　Robert Shaw **5**:390
　N. F. Simpson **29**:367
　Tom Stoppard **4**:524
　David Storey **4**:528
　C. P. Taylor **27**:440, 442
　Andy Warhol **20**:423
　E. A. Whitehead **5**:488
　Billy Wilder **20**:461
　Snoo Wilson **33**:463

Taylor, Joseph H.
　Milton Meltzer **26**:298

Taylor, Katharine
　Sylvia Ashton-Warner **19**:21

Taylor, Lewis Jerome, Jr.
　Walker Percy **6**:399

Taylor, Mark
　W. H. Auden **3**:27
　John Berryman **3**:72
　Tom McHale **5**:282
　Walker Percy **3**:378
　Earl Rovit **7**:383
　Edmund Wilson **8**:550
　Richard Yates **8**:555

Taylor, Michael
　Marian Engel **36**:160
　Timothy Findley **27**:141
　Brian Moore **32**:310
　Leon Rooke **25**:391
　Gillian Tindall **7**:474

Taylor, Mildred D.
　Mildred D. Taylor **21**:419

Taylor, Millicent
　Thomas B. Costain **30**:99, 100

Taylor, Nora E.
　Isabelle Holland **21**:149, 151
　Mary Stewart **35**:393
　Noel Streatfeild **21**:404

Taylor, Rebecca
　C. J. Cherryh **35**:106

Taylor, Rebecca Sue
　C. J. Cherryh **35**:106

Taylor, Rhoda E.
　Margaret O. Hyde **21**:178

Taylor, Stephen
　John Huston **20**:169

Taylor, William L.
　J.R.R. Tolkien **12**:569

Tazewell, William L.
　Tobias Wolff **39**:286

Tchen, John
　Milton Meltzer **26**:307

Teachout, Terry
　William F. Buckley, Jr. **37**:60
　Joseph Hansen **38**:239
　James Jones **39**:413
　Frank MacShane **39**:413
　Ayn Rand **30**:303
　Donald Spoto **39**:452
　Tennessee Williams **39**:452

Teale, Edwin Way
　Edward Abbey **36**:12

Tearson, Michael
　Jim Carroll **35**:80
　Janis Ian **21**:187

Tebbel, John
　Charles M. Schulz **12**:527

Téchiné, André
　Carl Theodor Dreyer **16**:268

Teich, Nathaniel
　Pier Paolo Pasolini **20**:267

Temple, Joanne
　John Berryman **3**:72

Temple, Ruth Z.
　C. S. Lewis **14**:321
　Nathalie Sarraute **1**:303; **2**:386

Templeton, Joan
　Sean O'Casey **11**:406

Tenenbaum, Louis
　Italo Calvino **5**:97

Tennant, Catherine
　Joyce Maynard **23**:289

Tennant, Emma
　J. G. Ballard **6**:28
　Italo Calvino **5**:100
　Elaine Feinstein **36**:170
　Thomas Hinde **6**:242
　Penelope Mortimer **5**:298

Teo, Elizabeth A.
　Jade Snow Wong **17**:567

Terbille, Charles I.
　Saul Bellow **6**:52
　Joyce Carol Oates **6**:371

Teresa, Vincent
　Mario Puzo **2**:352

Terras, Rita
　Christa Wolf **29**:463

Terrell, Carroll F.
　Ezra Pound **34**:503
　E. Fuller Torrey **34**:503

Terrien, Samuel
　Fernando Arrabal **2**:15

Terrill, Mary
　Carl Van Vechten **33**:385

Terris, Susan
　Robin F. Brancato **35**:65
　Rosemary Wells **12**:639

Terris, Virginia R.
　Muriel Rukeyser **27**:410

Terry, Arthur
　Vicente Aleixandre **9**:17
　Salvador Espriu **9**:192
　Octavio Paz **10**:393

Terry, C. V.
  Frank B. Gilbreth, Jr. and
    Ernestine Gilbreth Carey
    17:154
  A. J. Cronin 32:136

Terry, Sara
  Helen MacInnes 27:283

Terzian, Philip
  Anthony Powell 31:316

Tessitore, John
  Francis Ford Coppola 16:247

Testa, Bart
  Gordon Lightfoot 26:281
  Frank Zappa 17:591

Testa, Daniel
  Rudolfo A. Anaya 23:22

Tetlow, Joseph A.
  William X. Kienzle 25:274

Teunissen, John T.
  Doris Lessing 6:293

Thackery, Joseph C.
  Czesław Miłosz 31:261

Thackrey, Ted, Jr.
  Taylor Caldwell 39:301

Thale, Jerome
  C. P. Snow 19:425

Thane, Elswyth
  Thomas J. Fleming 37:120

Tharp, Mike
  Roy Blount, Jr. 38:44

Thatcher, A.
  Paul Zindel 26:481

Thayer, C. G.
  Antonia Fraser 32:183

Theall, Donald F.
  Arthur C. Clarke 35:123

Thelwell, Mike
  James Baldwin 17:36

Therese, Sister M.
  Marianne Moore 1:229

Theroux, Paul
  Breyten Breytenbach 23:85
  Frederick Buechner 2:83
  Anthony Burgess 5:89
  Henry Carlisle 33:103
  John Cheever 7:48
  John Pepper Clark 38:120
  Peter De Vries 3:126; 7:76
  Maureen Duffy 37:116
  Lawrence Durrell 6:151
  George MacDonald Fraser
    7:106
  Nadine Gordimer 5:147
  Shirley Ann Grau 4:209
  Graham Greene 3:213
  Ernest Hemingway 6:229
  Susan B. Hill 4:226
  Erica Jong 4:264
  Yashar Kemal 14:299
  John Knowles 4:272
  Milan Kundera 4:276
  David Lodge 36:275
  Mary McCarthy 5:277

  Joe McGinniss 32:303
  Yukio Mishima 4:356
  Brian Moore 3:341; 7:236
  V. S. Naipaul 4:373, 374;
    7:252
  Christopher Okigbo 25:349
  Cynthia Ozick 7:288
  S. J. Perelman 9:415
  Jean Rhys 2:372
  Georges Simenon 18:487
  Gilbert Sorrentino 22:391
  David Storey 4:529
  Peter Taylor 4:542
  John Updike 13:563
  Gore Vidal 22:437
  Kurt Vonnegut, Jr. 5:470

Theroux, Phyllis
  Jean Kerr 22:258

Thesen, Sharon Fawcett
  Gilbert Sorrentino 14:498

Thiébaux, Marcelle
  Stratis Haviaras 33:206

Thiher, Allen
  Fernando Arrabal 9:33
  Luis Buñuel 16:149
  Louis-Ferdinand Céline 4:101
  Michel del Castillo 38:169
  Henri de Montherlant 19:328
  François Truffaut 20:402

Thody, Philip
  Roland Barthes 24:30
  Albert Camus 4:91; 14:116
  Jean-Paul Sartre 4:476; 24:407

Thomas, Audrey
  Marian Engel 36:159
  Anne Hébert 29:240

Thomas, Brian
  P. G. Wodehouse 22:485

Thomas, Carolyn
  David Jones 7:191

Thomas, Clara
  Margaret Laurence 3:281;
    13:342

Thomas, D. M.
  Anna Akhmatova 25:29
  Martin Booth 13:103
  Eva Figes 31:167
  Francine du Plessix Gray
    22:202
  Yuri Krotkov 19:265
  John Matthias 9:362
  Elie Wiesel 37:453, 458

Thomas, David
  James Baldwin 5:43

Thomas, David P.
  Christopher Isherwood 1:157

Thomas, Della
  Charles Addams 30:15

Thomas, Dylan
  Amos Tutuola 29:434

Thomas, Harry
  Laurence Lieberman 36:261

Thomas, Jo
  Philip Larkin 39:334

Thomas, John
  Bernardo Bertolucci 16:84
  Tod Browning 16:122
  Jean-Luc Godard 20:134

Thomas, John Alfred
  Josef von Sternberg 20:369

Thomas, Keith
  Antonia Fraser 32:180

Thomas, M. Wynn
  Katherine Anne Porter 10:394

Thomas, Michael M.
  Paul E. Erdman 25:155

Thomas, Noel L.
  Martin Walser 27:464

Thomas, Paul
  Rainer Werner Fassbinder
    20:109
  Lina Wertmüller 16:593

Thomas, Peter
  John Betjeman 6:65
  Robert Kroetsch 5:220; 23:275

Thomas, Ross
  Matthew Bruccoli 34:417
  Herbert Gold 14:209
  Ross Macdonald 34:417
  Mario Puzo 36:362
  Studs Terkel 38:424

Thomas, S. L.
  John R. Tunis 12:592

Thompson, Betty
  Nadine Gordimer 33:181

Thompson, Craig
  Vera Brittain 23:91

Thompson, Dody Weston
  Pearl S. Buck 18:78

Thompson, E. P.
  Donald Davie 31:114

Thompson, Eric
  Matt Cohen 19:112
  T. S. Eliot 2:125; 24:172

Thompson, Howard
  Robert Altman 16:19
  Gretchen Cryer 21:79
  Brian De Palma 20:73
  Garry Marshall 17:274
  Martin Scorsese 20:324
  Jerzy Skolimowski 20:347
  Andy Warhol 20:417

Thompson, Jean C.
  Barbara Wersba 30:430

Thompson, John
  James Baldwin 17:34
  John Berryman 3:71
  Bruce Chatwin 28:73
  Irving Feldman 7:102
  Daniel Fuchs 22:156
  Natalia Ginzburg 5:141
  Nadine Gordimer 18:191
  Joseph Heller 5:176
  Robert Lowell 9:338
  Peter Matthiessen 32:287
  Amos Oz 5:335
  John Updike 13:560

  Richard Yates 23:480

Thompson, Kent
  John Gardner 28:162
  Hugh Hood 15:284; 28:188

Thompson, Lawrence
  Robert Frost 13:224

Thompson, Leslie M.
  Stephen Spender 10:487

Thompson, Mildred
  June Jordan 23:255

Thompson, Raymond H.
  C. J. Cherryh 35:114

Thompson, R. J.
  John Hawkes 4:214
  Mary Lavin 4:282

Thompson, Robert B.
  Robert Frost 13:230

Thompson, Susan
  S. E. Hinton 30:206

Thompson, Toby
  Bruce Jay Friedman 5:126

Thompson, Tyler
  Vine Deloria, Jr. 21:109

Thomsen, Christian Braad
  Rainer Werner Fassbinder
    20:105

Thomson, David
  Paddy Chayefsky 23:118
  Fritz Lang 20:213
  Peter Shaffer 37:387

Thomson, George H.
  J.R.R. Tolkien 1:335

Thomson, Jean C.
  H. F. Brinsmead 21:28
  Barbara Corcoran 17:72
  Eilís Dillon 17:97
  James D. Forman 21:117
  Leon Garfield 12:216
  Madeleine L'Engle 12:347
  John Neufeld 17:307, 308
  Philippa Pearce 21:282

Thomson, Peter
  Harold Pinter 15:422

Thomson, R.D.B.
  Andrei Voznesensky 15:554

Thorburn, David
  Renata Adler 8:7
  Ann Beattie 8:57
  Judith Guest 8:254
  Norman Mailer 3:315
  Thomas Pynchon 3:416

Thornber, Robin
  Alan Ayckbourn 33:42

Thorp, Katherine
  Isaac Asimov 26:57

Thorp, Willard
  W. D. Snodgrass 2:404

Thorpe, Michael
  J. G. Ballard 36:42
  André Brink 36:68
  Doris Lessing 3:291
  Shiva Naipaul 32:324

Thurley, Geoffrey
Galway Kinnell **29**:280
Charles Simic **22**:379
Philip Whalen **29**:445

Thurman, Judith
Joyce Carol Oates **6**:374
Jean Rhys **6**:456
Laura Riding **7**:374
Susan Fromberg Schaeffer **22**:368
Agnès Varda **16**:560

Thurston, Frederick
Walter D. Edmonds **35**:146

Thurston, Robert
Fritz Leiber **25**:304

Thwaite, Ann
E. M. Almedingen **12**:5

Thwaite, Anthony
Kōbō Abé **22**:14
Joan Aiken **35**:20
W. H. Auden **6**:24
Charles Causley **7**:41
Anita Desai **37**:72
Douglas Dunn **6**:148
Shusaku Endo **19**:160
D. J. Enright **31**:145
Michael Frayn **31**:189
Geoffrey Grigson **7**:136
Seamus Heaney **7**:147; **25**:249
David Jones **7**:187
Yashar Kemal **14**:301
Thomas Keneally **19**:242
Philip Larkin **13**:335
David Lodge **36**:277
Derek Mahon **27**:287
Stanley Middleton **38**:334, 335
Sylvia Murphy **34**:91
R. K. Narayan **7**:256
Darcy O'Brien **11**:405
Sylvia Plath **14**:426
Peter Porter **33**:318
Ann Schlee **35**:373
Tom Sharpe **36**:399, 400
C. P. Snow **4**:503
Snoo Wilson **33**:466

Tibbetts, John
Frank Capra **16**:165
Josef von Sternberg **20**:377

Tick, Edward
Mario Vargas Llosa **31**:446

Tickell, Paul
Frank Zappa **17**:595

Tiedman, Richard
Jack Vance **35**:424

Tiessen, Hildegard E.
Rudy Wiebe **14**:572

Tiffin, Chris
Thomas Keneally **19**:243

Tiger, Virginia
William Golding **27**:166

Tilden, David
M. M. Kaye **28**:198

Tilden, Freeman
Edward Abbey **36**:12

Tillinghast, Richard
Sterling A. Brown **23**:101
Amy Clampitt **32**:117
Robert Creeley **36**:119
James Galvin **38**:199
Jim Harrison **33**:197
Galway Kinnell **29**:289
James Merrill **2**:274
Frederick Morgan **23**:300
Sharon Olds **39**:190
Katha Pollitt **28**:368
Adrienne Rich **3**:427
Louis Simpson **32**:381
Charles Wright **28**:460

Tillman, Nathaniel
Melvin B. Tolson **36**:424

Tilton, John W.
Anthony Burgess **15**:104
Kurt Vonnegut, Jr. **12**:614

Timmerman, John H.
C. S. Lewis **14**:324

Timms, David
Philip Larkin **5**:223

Timpe, Eugene F.
Hermann Hesse **17**:210

Tindal, Gillian
Louis-Ferdinand Céline **7**:45
Leon Garfield **12**:227

Tindall, William York
Samuel Beckett **1**:22

Tinkle, Lon
A. J. Cronin **32**:137
Jean Lee Latham **12**:324
Hollis Summers **10**:493

Tintner, Adeline R.
Philip Roth **22**:355
François Truffaut **20**:406

Tipmore, David
Joyce Maynard **23**:288

Tisdale, Bob
John Hawkes **4**:215

Tiven, Jon
Paul McCartney **35**:287, 288, 292
Monty Python **21**:226
The Police **26**:363, 364

Tiven, Sally
Paul McCartney **35**:288, 292

Toback, James
Kenzaburō Ōe **36**:343

Tobias, Richard
Thomas Kinsella **19**:256

Tobias, Richard C.
James Thurber **5**:435

Tobin, Patricia
William Faulkner **3**:155

Tobin, Richard L.
Lothar-Günther Buchheim **6**:101

Todd, Richard
Renata Adler **8**:4
Louis Auchincloss **9**:54
Donald Barthelme **8**:49
Saul Bellow **6**:55, 61
Thomas Berger **3**:64
Eleanor Bergstein **4**:55
Vance Bourjaily **8**:104
E. L. Doctorow **6**:138
Andre Dubus **13**:183
Bruce Jay Friedman **5**:126
John Hawkes **4**:216
Sue Kaufman **8**:317
William Kotzwinkle **5**:220
Cormac McCarthy **4**:343
Robert Newton Peck **17**:337
Walker Percy **8**:443
Marge Piercy **6**:402
Robert M. Pirsig **6**:420
Judith Rossner **6**:470
John Updike **7**:489
Kurt Vonnegut, Jr. **3**:501
Richard Yates **7**:555

Todisco, Paula
James D. Forman **21**:122
Norma Klein **30**:241
Mary Stewart **35**:396

Toeplitz, Krzysztof-Teodor
Jerzy Skolimowski **20**:348
Andrzej Wajda **16**:579

Toerien, Barend J.
Breyten Breytenbach **23**:83, 84
J. M. Coetzee **23**:122

Toledano, Ralph de
Hugh Whitemore **37**:445

Toliver, Harold E.
Robert Frost **4**:175

Tolkien, J.R.R.
C. S. Lewis **27**:259

Tolomeo, Diane
Flannery O'Connor **21**:276

Toloudis, Constantin
Jacques Audiberti **38**:32

Tolson, Jay
T. Coraghessan Boyle **36**:59
Jakov Lind **27**:272

Tomalin, Claire
Beryl Bainbridge **10**:15
Charles Newman **2**:311
Paul Theroux **5**:427

Tomforde, Anna
Heinrich Böll **39**:291

Tonks, Rosemary
Adrienne Rich **3**:428

Took, Barry
Monty Python **21**:228

Toolan, David S.
Tom Wicker **7**:535

Toomajian, Janice
Isaac Asimov **26**:59

Toomey, Philippa
Peter Luke **38**:318

Torchiana, Donald T.
W. D. Snodgrass **2**:404

Tosches, Nick
Mick Jagger and Keith Richard **17**:240
Waylon Jennings **21**:204, 205
Jim Morrison **17**:293
Lou Reed **21**:304
Andrew Lloyd Webber and Tim Rice **21**:423

Totton, Nick
Beryl Bainbridge **8**:37
J. G. Ballard **14**:39
Heinrich Böll **9**:111
Patrick Boyle **19**:68
Malcolm Bradbury **32**:53
André Brink **18**:67
Gail Godwin **8**:249
James Hanley **8**:265
Mary Hocking **13**:285
Francis King **8**:322
Alistair MacLean **13**:364
Michael Moorcock **27**:349
Iris Murdoch **8**:405
Vladimir Nabokov **8**:417
David Pownall **10**:419
Frederic Raphael **14**:437
Piers Paul Read **10**:434
Elizabeth Taylor **29**:410

Tovey, Roberta
William Kotzwinkle **14**:311
Tadeusz Rózewicz **23**:361

Towers, Robert
Renata Adler **8**:4
Russell Banks **37**:30
Donald Barthelme **13**:59
Ann Beattie **18**:38
William Boyd **28**:41
Michael Brodsky **19**:69
Anthony Burgess **22**:76
Italo Calvino **33**:101
Raymond Carver **22**:101
John Cheever **8**:138; **11**:122
Don DeLillo **27**:84
E. L. Doctorow **18**:127; **37**:94
Stanley Elkin **9**:191
Louise Erdrich **39**:132
John Gardner **8**:233
Graham Greene **18**:197
Lillian Hellman **18**:228
Mark Helprin **22**:222; **32**:229
John Irving **23**:251
Ruth Prawer Jhabvala **29**:263
Diane Johnson **13**:305
Alfred Kazin **38**:280
William Kennedy **34**:209
Doris Lessing **15**:335
Bernard Malamud **18**:319
Bobbie Ann Mason **28**:273
Ian McEwan **13**:371
Larry McMurtry **7**:214
Leonard Michaels **25**:317
Lorrie Moore **39**:84
R. K. Narayan **28**:302
Flannery O'Connor **13**:422
Grace Paley **37**:339
Breece D'J Pancake **29**:348
Walker Percy **8**:444; **18**:401
David Plante **38**:367
Anthony Powell **9**:435
Padgett Powell **34**:100
V. S. Pritchett **15**:444
Ishmael Reed **32**:360

Philip Roth **9**:461; **15**:451
Salman Rushdie **23**:366
James Salter **7**:387
Wilfrid Sheed **10**:473
Josef Škvorecký **39**:226
Scott Sommer **25**:425
Mark Stevens **34**:112
Peter Taylor **37**:412
Paul Theroux **8**:512; **28**:427
Douglas Unger **34**:116
John Updike **13**:559
Kurt Vonnegut, Jr. **8**:533
Alice Walker **27**:451
Rebecca West **9**:562
William Wharton **18**:543;
  37:440

Townley, Rod
Agnes Eckhardt Nixon **21**:247

Towns, Saundra
Gwendolyn Brooks **15**:93

Townsend, John Rowe
Joan Aiken **35**:19
Honor Arundel **17**:18
H. F. Brinsmead **21**:31
Peter Dickinson **12**:172
John Donovan **35**:141
Esther Forbes **12**:211
Leon Garfield **12**:222, 224
Alan Garner **17**:143
Virginia Hamilton **26**:153
S. E. Hinton **30**:204
Jesse Jackson **12**:291
Madeleine L'Engle **12**:350
William Mayne **12**:397
Andre Norton **12**:460
Scott O'Dell **30**:269
Philippa Pearce **21**:289
Rosemary Sutcliff **26**:435
Jill Paton Walsh **35**:430
Barbara Wersba **30**:430
Paul Zindel **26**:471

Townsend, R. C.
William Golding **17**:168

Townshend, Peter
Peter Townshend **17**:534

Toynbee, Philip
D. J. Enright **31**:153
Arthur Koestler **1**:170; **33**:230
Mary Renault **17**:399
Mordecai Richler **5**:375

Trachtenberg, Alan
Henry Miller **4**:351
Tom Wolfe **9**:578

Tracy, Honor
Janet Frame **22**:144
Nadine Gordimer **33**:180
Graham Greene **3**:206

Tracy, Phil
Kingsley Amis **3**:9

Tracy, Robert
Benedict Kiely **23**:267

Trakin, Roy
Lou Reed **21**:321

Traschen, Isadore
William Faulkner **9**:201
Robert Frost **26**:122

Traub, James
Evelyn Waugh **27**:476

Traubitz, Nancy Baker
Tennessee Williams **15**:578

Traum, Happy
Van Morrison **21**:231

Trease, Geoffrey
H. F. Brinsmead **21**:26
Leon Garfield **12**:216, 217
William Mayne **12**:390

Treece, Henry
Herbert Read **4**:437

Treglown, Jeremy
Brian Aldiss **14**:14
Howard Barker **37**:33
Samuel Beckett **29**:57
Brigid Brophy **11**:68
Anthony Burgess **22**:75
Len Deighton **22**:116
Parel Kohout **13**:325
Olivia Manning **19**:302
Stanley Middleton **38**:331
Joyce Carol Oates **11**:403
Barbara Pym **13**:470
Tom Robbins **9**:454
J.I.M. Stewart **14**:512
A. N. Wilson **33**:450
Snoo Wilson **33**:462

Trenner, Richard
E. L. Doctorow **37**:89

Trensky, Paul I.
Václav Havel **25**:220

Trevor, William
Elizabeth Bowen **22**:64
Margaret Drabble **22**:122
Michael Frayn **31**:189
Frank O'Connor **23**:331
Frank Sargeson **31**:364

Trewin, J. C.
Robert Bolt **14**:89
Agatha Christie **12**:125

Trickett, Rachel
Olivia Manning **19**:302
James Purdy **2**:349
Andrew Sinclair **2**:401
Wallace Stegner **9**:508
Angus Wilson **2**:473

Trilling, Diana
Margery Allingham **19**:12
Ilya Ehrenburg **18**:131
Esther Forbes **12**:209
Martha Gellhorn **14**:194
Aldous Huxley **8**:304
Frank O'Connor **14**:395
Jean Rhys **19**:392
Irwin Shaw **7**:410
Betty Smith **19**:422

Trilling, Lionel
E. M. Forster **1**:104
Robert Graves **2**:174

Trilling, Roger
Bob Marley **17**:270

Trimbur, John
Lawrence Ferlinghetti **27**:137

Trimpi, Helen P.
Edgar Bowers **9**:121, 122

Tripp, John
Dannie Abse **29**:18

Tritel, Barbara
J.R.R. Tolkien **38**:441

Trodd, Kenith
Andrew Sinclair **2**:400

Troeger, Thomas H.
Czesław Miłosz **31**:266

Trombetta, Jim
Lou Reed **21**:314

Trotsky, Leon
André Malraux **13**:364

Trotter, David
Leon Edel **29**:175

Trotter, Stewart
Jean Genet **5**:137
Graham Greene **6**:220

Trowbridge, Clinton
John Updike **2**:442

Troy, William
Carl Theodor Dreyer **16**:256
Fritz Lang **20**:202
Josef von Sternberg **20**:370

True, Michael D.
Daniel J. Berrigan **4**:58
Robert Francis **15**:236
Paul Goodman **2**:169
Flannery O'Connor **13**:422;
  21:271
Karl Shapiro **15**:477

Trueblood, Valerie
Margaret Atwood **13**:43
Tess Gallagher **18**:168
Gilbert Sorrentino **14**:499
Derek Walcott **14**:548

Trueheart, Charles
John Barth **27**:25
Craig Nova **31**:299

Truesdale, David A.
Marion Zimmer Bradley **30**:28
C. J. Cherryh **35**:105

Truffaut, François
Ingmar Bergman **16**:70
Luis Buñuel **16**:136
Frank Capra **16**:161
Charles Chaplin **16**:198
John Ford **16**:314
Alfred Hitchcock **16**:341, 346
Elia Kazan **16**:366
Fritz Lang **20**:208
Agnès Varda **16**:553
Billy Wilder **20**:457

Trumbull, Robert
Thor Heyerdahl **26**:193

Truscott, Lucian K.
Bob Dylan **3**:131

Trussler, Simon
John Arden **15**:19

Tsuruta, Kinya
Shusaku Endo **7**:96

Tsvetaeva, Marina
Boris Pasternak **18**:386

Tube, Henry
Vasily Aksenov **22**:26
Alejo Carpentier **38**:93
Masuji Ibuse **22**:226

Tuch, Ronald
Charles Chaplin **16**:204

Tucker, Carll
Imamu Amiri Baraka **10**:19
Ed Bullins **7**:37
Jules Feiffer **8**:216
Richard Howard **7**:169
Albert Innaurato **21**:191
Robert Lowell **9**:338
Archibald MacLeish **8**:363

Tucker, Chris
Kurt Vonnegut, Jr. **22**:451

Tucker, James
Anthony Powell **7**:338; **10**:409

Tucker, Ken
T. Coraghessan Boyle **36**:59
Allen Ginsberg **36**:195
Stephen King **37**:205
Elmore Leonard **28**:234

Tucker, Kenneth
Joan Armatrading **17**:9
Walter Becker and Donald
  Fagen **26**:83
David Byrne **26**:96
Waylon Jennings **21**:203
Steve Martin **30**:249
Prince **35**:324
Carly Simon **26**:410, 413
Patti Smith **12**:543
Neil Young **17**:576, 580

Tucker, Martin
Chinua Achebe **3**:1
Ayi Kwei Armah **33**:25
Malcolm Bradbury **32**:50
André Brink **18**:67
Brigid Brophy **29**:93
Claude Brown **30**:35
Cyprian Ekwensi **4**:152
Nadine Gordimer **3**:201
Jan de Hartog **19**:131, 132
Ernest Hemingway **3**:234
Jerzy Kosinski **1**:172
Camara Laye **38**:291
Bernard Malamud **3**:322
Ezekiel Mphahlele **25**:346
James Ngugi **3**:357
Cynthia Ozick **7**:287
Alan Paton **4**:395
William Plomer **4**:406
James Purdy **28**:377
Raja Rao **25**:365
Ishmael Reed **13**:477
Wole Soyinka **3**:462; **36**:408
Amos Tutuola **5**:443
Laurens van der Post **5**:463

Tucker, Nicholas
Honor Arundel **17**:16
Judy Blume **12**:45
Virginia Hamilton **26**:151
Barbara Wersba **30**:434

Tulip, James
David Malouf **28**:269
Thomas W. Shapcott **38**:398,
399, 401, 404

Tunis, John R.
Maia Wojciechowska **26**:449,
454

Tunney, Gene
Budd Schulberg **7**:402

Tunstall, Caroline
William Brammer **31**:53
Taylor Caldwell **28**:61

Tuohy, Frank
Nora Ephron **31**:159
Nadine Gordimer **18**:188
Ruth Prawer Jhabvala **29**:262
Patrick Kavanagh **22**:244
Jakov Lind **27**:270
Seán O'Faoláin **14**:405
Isaac Bashevis Singer **38**:409
Randolph Stow **23**:437

Turan, Kenneth
Roy Blount, Jr. **38**:48
Gene Roddenberry **17**:414
Elie Wiesel **11**:570

Turco, Lewis
Edward Brathwaite **11**:67
Robert Hayden **9**:270
Donald Justice **19**:232

Turin, Michele
Alix Kates Shulman **10**:476

Turkington, Kate
Chinua Achebe **26**:16

Turnbull, Colin M.
Christie Harris **12**:262

Turnbull, Martin
François Mauriac **4**:340

Turnell, Martin
Graham Greene **1**:134

Turner, Alice K.
Jamake Highwater **12**:285
Colleen McCullough **27**:318

Turner, Darwin T.
Zora Neale Hurston **30**:214
Ishmael Reed **13**:477
Alice Walker **9**:558
Richard Wright **21**:450
Frank G. Yerby **22**:488, 489,
490

Turner, E. S.
Jeffrey Archer **28**:11
Art Buchwald **33**:93
Mircea Eliade **19**:148
Daphne du Maurier **11**:164
Monty Python **21**:223

Turner, George
Philip K. Dick **30**:115

Turner, Gil
Bob Dylan **12**:179

Turner, R. H.
Claude Chabrol **16**:167

Turner, Steve
Peter Townshend **17**:537

Turoff, Robert David
Milton Meltzer **26**:306

Tuska, Jon
Louis L'Amour **25**:279

Tuttle, Lisa
Douglas Adams **27**:11

Tuttleton, James W.
Louis Auchincloss **4**:29

Tvardovsky, Alexander
Aleksandr I. Solzhenitsyn
26:415

Twichell, Ethel R.
C. S. Adler **35**:15
Norma Fox Mazer **26**:295
Milton Meltzer **26**:308
Walter Dean Myers **35**:297
Katherine Paterson **30**:288
Marilyn Sachs **35**:334

Tyler, Anne
Richard Adams **18**:2
Renata Adler **31**:14
Toni Cade Bambara **19**:33
Thomas Berger **38**:38
Anita Brookner **34**:141
John Cheever **11**:121
Anita Desai **19**:134
Joan Didion **14**:151; **32**:146
E. L. Doctorow **37**:94
Lawrence Durrell **27**:99
Sumner Locke Elliott **38**:181
Jacob Epstein **19**:162
Marilyn French **10**:191
Mavis Gallant **18**:172; **38**:194
Penelope Gilliatt **13**:238
Gail Godwin **31**:196
Nadine Gordimer **33**:181
Caroline Gordon **29**:188
Lois Gould **10**:241
John Irving **23**:244
Sue Kaufman **8**:317
Molly Keane **31**:234
Thomas Keneally **10**:299
Maxine Hong Kingston **19**:250
Nancy Lemann **39**:76
Paule Marshall **27**:315
Bobbie Ann Mason **28**:271
Joyce Maynard **23**:289
Ian McEwan **13**:370
Leonard Michaels **25**:318
Suzanne Newton **35**:302
Grace Paley **37**:335
Katherine Paterson **30**:283
Jayne Anne Phillips **33**:306
Barbara Pym **37**:374
Bernice Rubens **19**:404
Mary Lee Settle **19**:410
Alix Kates Shulman **10**:475
Susan Sontag **13**:516
Scott Spencer **30**:405
Elizabeth Taylor **29**:412
Paul Theroux **11**:529
D. M. Thomas **31**:432
William Trevor **7**:478
Angus Wilson **25**:462
Marguerite Yourcenar **38**:459

Tyler, Karen B.[eyard-]
Norma Klein **30**:239

Tyler, Parker
Charles Chaplin **16**:196
Laurence Olivier **20**:235
Agnès Varda **16**:554
Andy Warhol **20**:416
Orson Welles **20**:438

Tyler, Ralph
Richard Adams **5**:5
Agatha Christie **6**:109
S. J. Perelman **9**:416
Jean Rhys **6**:455

Tyler, Tony
John Lennon and Paul
McCartney **12**:379

Tymn, Marshall B.
Roger Zelazny **21**:473

Tyms, James D.
Langston Hughes **5**:191

Tynan, Kenneth
Enid Bagnold **25**:76
Lenny Bruce **21**:47
William Gibson **23**:175, 177
Roman Polanski **16**:463
N. F. Simpson **29**:364, 366
Stephen Sondheim **30**:377
Tom Stoppard **15**:518
Tennessee Williams **30**:462

Tyrmand, Leopold
Witold Gombrowicz **7**:124

Tyrrell, Connie
Franklyn M. Branley **21**:23

Tyrrell, William Blake
Gene Roddenberry **17**:407

Tyson, Christy
Piers Anthony **35**:39

Tytell, John
William S. Burroughs **22**:86
Allen Ginsberg **36**:180
Jack Kerouac **3**:264; **29**:272

Ueda, Makoto
Shiga Naoya **33**:366
Jun'ichirō Tanizaki **28**:413

Ugarte, Michael
Juan Goytisolo **23**:187

Uglow, Jennifer
Caroline Gordon **29**:188
Russell C. Hoban **25**:264
Marge Piercy **18**:408

Uhelski, Jaan
Jimmy Page and Robert Plant
12:478

Uibopuu, Valev
Ivar Ivask **14**:287

Ulam, Adam
Agatha Christie **12**:120
Michael Scammell **34**:490
Aleksandr Solzhenitsyn **34**:490

Ulanov, Ann Belford
Margaret Mead **37**:280

Ulfers, Friedrich
Paul Celan **19**:92

Ullman, Montague
Melvin Berger **12**:42
Larry Kettelkamp **12**:308

Ulrich, Mabel S.
A. J. Cronin **32**:133

Underdown, David
Antonia Fraser **32**:183

Underwood, Tim
Jack Vance **35**:422

Unger, Arthur
Alex Haley **12**:253

Unger, Leonard
T. S. Eliot **1**:90

Unsworth, Robert
Larry Bograd **35**:63
Mavis Thorpe Clark **12**:131
James D. Forman **21**:122
Rosa Guy **26**:144
Sonia Levitin **17**:265

Unterecker, John
Lawrence Durrell **1**:84
Ezra Pound **4**:415
Kenneth Rexroth **2**:370

Untermeyer, Louis
Robert Francis **15**:235
Robert Frost **13**:223; **15**:239
Ogden Nash **23**:319
Muriel Rukeyser **27**:403
Carl Sandburg **35**:339, 341

Updike, John
Walter Abish **22**:16
Peter Ackroyd **34**:402
Vasily Aksyonov **37**:16
Michael Ayrton **7**:20
Roland Barthes **24**:29
Ann Beattie **8**:55
Samuel Beckett **6**:45
Saul Bellow **6**:56
Heinrich Böll **27**:68
Jorge Luis Borges **8**:100
William S. Burroughs **22**:83
Italo Calvino **5**:101; **8**:130
Albert Camus **9**:149
Bruce Chatwin **28**:75
John Cheever **7**:50; **25**:121
Julio Cortázar **5**:109
Don DeLillo **10**:135
Margaret Drabble **8**:183
André Dubus **36**:149
T. S. Eliot **34**:402
Shusaku Endo **19**:160, 161
Daniel Fuchs **8**:221
Witold Gombrowicz **7**:124
Günter Grass **2**:172; **4**:206;
32:204
Peter Handke **38**:220
Barry Hannah **23**:207
William Least Heat Moon
29:223
Ernest Hemingway **8**:285
Ruth Prawer Jhabvala **8**:312;
29:263
Gayl Jones **6**:266; **9**:307
Erica Jong **4**:263
Tadeusz Konwicki **28**:210
Jerzy Kosinski **6**:282
Milan Kundera **19**:269
Alex La Guma **19**:275

Ursula K. Le Guin 22:275
Stanislaw Lem 15:329
Alberto Moravia 7:243
Wright Morris 7:245
Iris Murdoch 6:344; 22:330;
  31:294
Vladimir Nabokov 2:301;
  3:351; 6:355; 8:414, 415,
  416, 417; 11:395
V. S. Naipaul 13:407
R. K. Narayan 7:256; 28:296,
  303
Flann O'Brien 7:269, 270
Tim O'Brien 19:358
John O'Hara 11:414
Robert Pinget 7:306; 37:359,
  364
Harold Pinter 15:423
Raymond Queneau 5:359, 362
Jean Rhys 19:395
Alain Robbe-Grillet 8:452
Carl Sagan 30:335
Françoise Sagan 6:481
J. D. Salinger 12:513
Simone Schwarz-Bart 7:405
L. E. Sissman 18:487
Wole Soyinka 14:509
Muriel Spark 5:400
Christina Stead 8:499, 500
James Thurber 5:433
William Trevor 25:444
Anne Tyler 7:479; 18:530;
  28:434
Sylvia Townsend Warner
  7:512; 19:460
Edmund Wilson 8:551

Uphaus, Robert W.
Kurt Vonnegut, Jr. 5:469

Urang, Gunnar
C. S. Lewis 3:298
J.R.R. Tolkien 2:434

Urbanska, Wanda
Clyde Edgerton 39:53

Urbanski, Marie Mitchell Oleson
Joyce Carol Oates 11:402

Urbas, Jeannette
Gabrielle Roy 14:468

Uroff, Margaret D.
Sylvia Plath 3:391; 17:354

Uroff, Margaret Dickie
Caroline Gordon 29:188

Ury, Claude
Jules Archer 12:17

Usborne, Richard
MacDonald Harris 9:261

Uscatescu, George
Mircea Eliade 19:145

Useem, Michael
Jonathan Schell 35:368

Usmiani, Renate
Friedrich Dürrenmatt 8:194
Michel Tremblay 29:425

Uyl, Douglas Den
Ayn Rand 30:304

Uys, Stanley
Breyten Breytenbach 23:85

Vaidyanathan, T. G.
Ernest Hemingway 30:195

Vaizey, John
Kingsley Amis 5:22

Valdés, Richard A.
Manuel Mujica Láinez 31:283

Valdéz, Jorge H.
G. Cabrera Infante 25:105
Julio Cortázar 13:165

Valentine, Dean
Albert Innaurato 21:195
Arthur Kopit 33:247

Valgemae, Mardi
Sławomir Mrozek 13:398
Jean-Claude Van Itallie 3:493

Vallee, Lillian
Czesław Miłosz 22:305

Valley, John A.
Alberto Moravia 7:243

Vallis, Val
Judith Wright 11:578

Van Brunt, H. L.
Jim Harrison 6:224

Van Buren, Alice
Janet Frame 2:142

Vance, Joel
Chuck Berry 17:56
David Bowie 17:63
Jimmy Cliff 21:63
Marvin Gaye 26:132
Bob Marley 17:268
Monty Python 21:225
Lou Reed 21:313
Bob Seger 35:382
Paul Simon 17:467

Van Cleave, Kit
Julia Peterkin 31:310

Vande Kieft, Ruth M.
Flannery O'Connor 1:258
Eudora Welty 1:360

Vandenbroucke, Russell
Athol Fugard 9:230

Van den Haag, Ernest
William F. Buckley, Jr. 7:34

Van den Heuvel, Cor
James Wright 10:545

Vanderbilt, Kermit
Norman Mailer 3:319
William Styron 3:474

Vanderwerken, David L.
Richard Brautigan 5:69

Van Doren, Carl
Esther Forbes 12:205, 208
Carl Van Vechten 33:385

Van Doren, Dorothy
A. J. Cronin 32:129

Van Doren, Mark
Djuna Barnes 29:24
René Clair 20:62
E. E. Cummings 12:139
Robert Frost 13:223; 15:241
Robinson Jeffers 11:304

John Cowper Powys 7:346

Van Duyn, Mona
Margaret Atwood 2:19
Adrienne Rich 3:427
Anne Sexton 2:391

Van Dyne, Susan R.
Adrienne Rich 18:445

Van Gelder, Lawrence
Charles Fuller 25:179
John Landis 26:271
Nagisa Oshima 20:250

Van Gelder, Lindsay
Joan D. Vinge 30:410

Van Gelder, Robert
August Derleth 31:133

Van Ghent, Dorothy
Alejo Carpentier 38:90

Vanjak, Gloria
Jim Morrison 17:290

Van Matre, Lynn
Lily Tomlin 17:517

Vanocur, Sander
Fletcher Knebel 14:307

Van Rjndt, Philippe
Morris L. West 33:433

Vansittart, Peter
José Donoso 32:152
Lawrence Durrell 13:189
D. J. Enright 31:147
Winston Graham 23:193
Piers Paul Read 10:436
Elizabeth Taylor 29:410
Jill Paton Walsh 35:430

Van Slyke, Berenice
John G. Neihardt 32:330

Van Spanckeren, Kathryn
John Gardner 28:166

Van Vechten, Carl
Carl Van Vechten 33:396

Van Wert, William F.
Kōbō Abé 22:14
Marguerite Duras 20:103
Alain Resnais 16:516

Van Wyngarden, Bruce
Andrea Lee 36:258

Vardi, Dov
Aharon Appelfeld 23:35
Abraham B. Yehoshua 13:617

Vargas Llosa, Mario
José María Arguedas 18:9
Gabriel García Márquez 3:181

Vargo, Edward P.
John Updike 7:486

Vas, Robert
Lindsay Anderson 20:12
Robert Bresson 16:105

Vas Dias, Robert
Toby Olson 28:342

Vásquez Amaral, José
Julio Cortázar 13:157

Vassal, Jacques
Janis Ian 21:183
Phil Ochs 17:331
Buffy Sainte-Marie 17:431

Vassallo, Carol
Virginia Hamilton 26:151

Vaughan, Alden T.
Maia Wojciechowska 26:451

Vaughan, Dai
Carl Theodor Dreyer 16:265

Vaughan, Stephen
Thomas Keneally 14:302
Ann Schlee 35:372

Veidemanis, Gladys
William Golding 17:169

Veit, Henri C.
Stephen Dobyns 37:75

Velie, Alan R.
James Welch 14:561

Venable, Gene
Fletcher Knebel 14:309
James H. Webb, Jr. 22:453

Venclova, Tomas
Aleksandr I. Solzhenitsyn
  18:497

Vendler, Helen
A. R. Ammons 2:14; 25:46
John Ashbery 25:51
Margaret Atwood 8:29
John Berryman 3:68; 10:46
Frank Bidart 33:77, 79
Elizabeth Bishop 9:90
Harold Bloom 24:81
Olga Broumas 10:77
Hayden Carruth 7:41
Amy Clampitt 32:114
Lucille Clifton 19:109
E. E. Cummings 3:119
D. J. Enright 8:203
Robert Frost 34:471
Allen Ginsberg 2:163; 3:195
Louise Glück 7:118; 22:174,
  177
Seamus Heaney 7:152
John Hollander 5:187
Ted Hughes 37:180
Richard F. Hugo 6:245
Randall Jarrell 9:295
Erica Jong 4:263
Maxine Kumin 13:326
Brad Leithauser 27:242
Philip Levine 33:272
Audre Lorde 18:308
Robert Lowell 37:232
Haki R. Madhubuti 6:313
Mary McCarthy 3:328
James Merrill 2:275; 18:328
W. S. Merwin 18:332
Josephine Miles 14:369
Czesław Miłosz 31:267
Marianne Moore 19:341
Howard Moss 7:250
Howard Nemerov 36:301
Joyce Carol Oates 3:361
Frank O'Hara 5:323
Octavio Paz 4:397
Sylvia Plath 17:353

William H. Pritchard **34**:471
Adrienne Rich **7**:367; **18**:444;
　36:368, 377
I. A. Richards **14**:454
Irwin Shaw **7**:414
David Slavitt **14**:490
Dave Smith **22**:384, 387
Allen Tate **2**:429
Charles Tomlinson **6**:535
Diane Wakoski **7**:504
Derek Walcott **25**:455
Robert Penn Warren **10**:525;
　18:533
Charles Wright **6**:581; **28**:456

Ventimiglia, Peter James
Albert Innaurato **21**:196

Venturi, Lauro
Jean Renoir **20**:288

Venuti, Lawrence
Dino Buzzati **36**:92
Rod Serling **30**:358

Verani, Hugo J.
Juan Carlos Onetti **7**:277

Verderese, Carol
Clyde Edgerton **39**:54
Bob Shacochis **39**:199

Vernon, Grenville
George S. Kaufman **38**:259,
　262
Clifford Odets **28**:324, 328

Vernon, John
Michael Benedikt **4**:54
William S. Burroughs **15**:108
James Dickey **7**:82
Norman Dubie **36**:133
Richard F. Hugo **18**:264
David Ignatow **4**:247
James Merrill **3**:334
W. S. Merwin **1**:213
Thomas Pynchon **11**:452
C. K. Williams **33**:443

Verschoyle, Derek
Rayner Heppenstall **10**:271

Vesselo, Arthur
Laurence Olivier **20**:235

Vickery, John B.
John Updike **5**:451

Vickery, Olga W.
John Hawkes **4**:213

Vickery, R. C.
Jules Archer **12**:23

Vidal, Gore
Louis Auchincloss **4**:31
John Barth **14**:51
Italo Calvino **5**:98; **39**:310
John Dos Passos **4**:132
William H. Gass **11**:224
E. Howard Hunt **3**:251
Doris Lessing **15**:333
Norman Mailer **2**:265
Carson McCullers **12**:418
Henry Miller **2**:282
Yukio Mishima **2**:287
Vladimir Nabokov **23**:304
Anaïs Nin **4**:376

John O'Hara **2**:323
Thomas Pynchon **11**:452
Ayn Rand **30**:295
Alain Robbe-Grillet **2**:375
Aleksandr I. Solzhenitsyn **4**:510
Susan Sontag **2**:414
Donald Spoto **39**:448
Tennessee Williams **7**:546;
　39:448

Vidal-Hall, Judith
Leon Garfield **12**:230

Viereck, Peter
Robert Frost **26**:114

Vigderman, Patricia
Andrea Lee **36**:257
Bobbi Ann Mason **28**:273
Breece D'J Pancake **29**:348

Viguers, Ruth Hill
Lloyd Alexander **35**:23, 24
E. M. Almedingen **12**:2
Ruth M. Arthur **12**:24
Margot Benary-Isbert **12**:33
Betty Cavanna **12**:100
Eilís Dillon **17**:95
Lois Duncan **26**:100, 101
Leon Garfield **12**:218
Jean Craighead George **35**:175,
　176
Christie Harris **12**:261, 262
Isabelle Holland **21**:147
Lee Kingman **17**:244, 245
Joseph Krumgold **12**:320
Madeleine L'Engle **12**:345, 346
William Mayne **12**:393
Emily Cheney Neville **12**:450,
　451
Scott O'Dell **30**:268
Philippa Pearce **21**:283
Josephine Poole **17**:370
Zoa Sherburne **30**:361
Zilpha Keatley Snyder **17**:469,
　470
Mary Stolz **12**:553
Noel Streatfeild **21**:404, 408
Lenora Mattingly Weber **12**:632

Vilhjalmsson, Thor
Gabriel García Márquez **2**:150

Viljanen, Lauri
Frans Eemil Sillanpää **19**:417

Villani, Sergio
Romain Gary **25**:190

Vince, Thomas L.
Rosa Guy **26**:140

Vincent, Celeste H.
Franklyn M. Branley **21**:18

Vincent, Chris
Carolyn Chute **39**:42
Norman Mailer **39**:424
Peter Manso **39**:424

Vincent, Emily
Isabelle Holland **21**:153

Vine, Richard
Stanley Kunitz **11**:319

Vinge, Joan D.
Jack Vance **35**:427

Vining, Mark
Smokey Robinson **21**:344

Vinson, Joe
Isabelle Holland **21**:151

Vintcent, Brian
Marie-Claire Blais **4**:67
Roch Carrier **13**:143
Anne Hébert **4**:220

Vinton, Iris
Robert A. Heinlein **26**:160

Viorst, Judith
Lois Gould **10**:243

Vivas, Eliseo
F. R. Leavis **24**:297
I. A. Richards **24**:379
George Steiner **24**:432
Allen Tate **24**:443
René Wellek **28**:442

Vogel, Christine B.
Barbara Pym **37**:376
Frank G. Slaughter **29**:378

Vogel, Dan
William Faulkner **6**:177, 178
Arthur Miller **6**:333
John Steinbeck **21**:369
Robert Penn Warren **6**:556
Tennessee Williams **5**:504

Volpe, Edmond L.
James Jones **1**:162

Vonalt, Larry P.
John Berryman **3**:66; **4**:60
Marianne Moore **1**:230

Von Däniken, Erich
Erich von Däniken **30**:421

Von Dare, Greg
Cay Van Ash **34**:119

Von Hallberg, Robert
Charles Olson **6**:386
W. D. Snodgrass **18**:495
William Carlos Williams
　22:464

Von Hoffman, Nicholas
Aldous Huxley **35**:245

Vonnegut, Kurt, Jr.
Robert Altman **16**:32
Heinrich Böll **27**:61
Joseph Heller **5**:175
Hermann Hesse **17**:219
Stanislaw Lem **15**:328
Hunter S. Thompson **17**:506
Tom Wolfe **35**:449

Von Obenauer, Heidi
Noel Streatfeild **21**:412

Von Tersch, Gary
Buffy Sainte-Marie **17**:431

Voorhees, Richard J.
P. G. Wodehouse **1**:374

Vopat, Carole Gottlieb
Jack Kerouac **3**:265

Voss, Arthur
James T. Farrell **11**:191
John O'Hara **11**:413
Dorothy Parker **15**:414
Jean Stafford **19**:430

Wachtel, Eleanor
Audrey Thomas **37**:419

Wachtel, Nili
Isaac Bashevis Singer **15**:504
A. B. Yehoshua **31**:472

Waddington, C. H.
Lewis Thomas **35**:409

Waddington, Miriam
Joan Barfoot **18**:35
Hugh Garner **13**:234
Ralph Gustafson **36**:212
A. M. Klein **19**:258

Wade, Barbara
Leon Rooke **25**:394

Wade, David
J.R.R. Tolkien **2**:434

Wade, Mason
August Derleth **31**:131

Wade, Michael
Peter Abrahams **4**:2

Wade, Rosalind
Iain Banks **34**:30
Lynne Reid Banks **23**:42
Isabel Colegate **36**:110
Elaine Feinstein **36**:170
L. P. Hartley **22**:215
Ronald Harwood **32**:226
Stanley Middleton **38**:331, 334
David Plante **38**:373

Waelti-Walters, Jennifer R.
Michel Butor **15**:113
J.M.G. Le Clézio **31**:248

Wagenaar, Dick
Yasunari Kawabata **18**:281

Wagenknecht, Edward
Frank G. Slaughter **29**:376

Waggoner, Diana
William Mayne **12**:406

Waggoner, Hyatt H.
E. E. Cummings **3**:117
Robert Duncan **2**:122
T. S. Eliot **2**:127
Robert Frost **3**:173
H. D. **3**:217
Robinson Jeffers **2**:214
Robert Lowell **3**:300
Archibald MacLeish **3**:310
Marianne Moore **2**:292
Ezra Pound **2**:341
John Crowe Ransom **2**:363
Theodore Roethke **3**:432
Carl Sandburg **4**:463
Karl Shapiro **4**:485
Lewis Turco **11**:549
Richard Wilbur **3**:532
William Carlos Williams **2**:468

Wagner, Dave
Robert L. Peters **7**:303

Critic Index

Wagner, Dick
Yukio Mishima 9:381

Wagner, Geoffrey
R. P. Blackmur 2:61
Jerome Siegel and Joe Shuster
21:354
Josef von Sternberg 20:372

Wagner, Jean
Jean Toomer 22:423

Wagner, Linda W.
Margaret Atwood 25:66
John Dos Passos 25:142
Louise Glück 22:176
Ernest Hemingway 30:198
Adrienne Rich 36:366
William Stafford 29:379

Wagner, Linda Welshimer
William Faulkner 1:103
Robert Hass 18:208
Ernest Hemingway 6:231;
19:215
Denise Levertov 1:176; 5:247
Philip Levine 9:332
Phyllis McGinley 14:365
W. S. Merwin 13:383
Joyce Carol Oates 19:349
Diane Wakoski 9:554, 555

Waidson, H. M.
Heinrich Böll 11:55; 27:56

Wain, John
Sylvia Ashton-Warner 19:20
William Barrett 27:19
R. P. Blackmur 24:62
William S. Burroughs 5:91
Eleanor Clark 19:105
Edward Dahlberg 7:66
William Empson 33:141
C. Day Lewis 6:127
Günter Grass 2:173; 4:202
Michael Hamburger 5:158
Ben Hecht 8:270
Ernest Hemingway 3:233
Aldous Huxley 5:192
C. S. Lewis 27:261
Archibald MacLeish 14:336
Ved Mehta 37:290
Edwin Morgan 31:277
Flann O'Brien 4:383
Sylvia Plath 17:345
I. A. Richards 24:390
C. P. Snow 4:500
Edmund Wilson 24:476

Wainwright, Andy
Earle Birney 6:77
Marian Engel 36:158

Wainwright, Jeffrey
W. S. Graham 29:198
Ezra Pound 7:332

Wainwright, Loudon
Studs Terkel 38:427

Wakefield, Dan
Edward Hoagland 28:181
Garson Kanin 22:232
Norma Klein 30:240
Agnes Eckhardt Nixon 21:250
J. D. Salinger 12:500
Harvey Swados 5:422

John R. Tunis 12:597
Leon Uris 7:490

Wakoski, Diane
Clayton Eshleman 7:98
Albert Goldbarth 38:205
David Ignatow 4:248
John Logan 5:255
Robert Lowell 4:304
Anaïs Nin 4:377
Jerome Rothenberg 6:477
Charles Simic 22:379

Walcott, Derek
C.L.R. James 33:222

Walcott, James
Leonard Michaels 25:318

Walcott, Ronald
Hal Bennett 5:57, 59
Charles Gordone 4:199

Walcutt, Charles Child
James Gould Cozzens 4:114
John O'Hara 1:262

Waldeland, Lynne
John Cheever 25:118

Waldemar, Carla
Anaïs Nin 11:399

Waldhorn, Arthur
Peter Griffin 39:399
Ernest Hemingway 39:399, 429
Jeffrey Meyers 39:429

Waldmeir, Joseph
Jackson J. Benson 34:414
John Steinbeck 34:414
John Updike 5:450

Waldron, Edward E.
Langston Hughes 15:291

Waldron, Randall H.
Norman Mailer 3:314

Waldrop, Howard
Samuel R. Delaney 38:154

Waldrop, Rosemary
Hans Erich Nossack 6:365

Walkarput, W.
Vladimir Nabokov 11:392

Walker, Alice
Ai 4:16
Alice Childress 15:132
Buchi Emecheta 14:159
Rosa Guy 26:141
Virginia Hamilton 26:148
Zora Neale Hurston 30:223
Flannery O'Connor 6:381
Derek Walcott 4:576

Walker, Carolyn
Joyce Carol Oates 3:360

Walker, Cheryl
Richard Brautigan 12:68
Stephen Dunn 36:152
Adrienne Rich 3:428
Robert Penn Warren 6:558

Walker, David
Anne Hébert 13:268; 29:231

Walker, Evelyn
Scott O'Dell 30:278

Walker, Greta
Babbis Friis-Baastad 12:214

Walker, Jeanne Murray
Samuel R. Delany 38:154

Walker, Jim
Clarence Major 19:292

Walker, John
Manuel Mujica Láinez 31:284

Walker, Keith
John Rechy 14:445

Walker, Martin
Robert Ludlum 22:291

Walker, Michael
Claude Chabrol 16:173
Jerzy Skolimowski 20:350

Walker, Robert G.
Ernest Hemingway 8:287

Walker, Stanley
Mari Sandoz 28:402

Walker, Ted
Andrew Young 5:523

Wall, Cheryl A.
Zora Neale Hurston 30:225

Wall, Chris
Allen Drury 37:112
Kent Haruf 34:59

Wall, James M.
Andrew Lloyd Webber and Tim
Rice 21:429

Wall, John
Prince 35:323

Wall, Richard
Behan, Brendan 15:46

Wall, Stephen
Isabel Colegate 36:109, 110
P. H. Newby 13:408
Richard Stern 39:239

Wallace, Herbert W.
Alvin Silverstein and Virginia
B. Silverstein 17:455

Wallace, Irving
Irving Wallace 13:568

Wallace, Margaret
Dee Brown 18:70
Roderick L. Haig-Brown
21:135
Zora Neale Hurston 30:209
Molly Keane 31:232
Bruce Lancaster 36:242
Mari Sandoz 28:401
Frank G. Slaughter 29:372, 373

Wallace, Michele
Ntozake Shange 8:485

Wallace, Ronald
Stephen Dunn 36:152
John Hawkes 15:274
Vladimir Nabokov 23:304

Wallace, Willard M.
Thomas J. Fleming 37:118
Robert Newton Peck 17:340

Wallace-Crabbe, Chris
Kenneth Slessor 14:492

Wallenstein, Barry
James T. Farrell 11:195
Donald Hall 37:147
Ted Hughes 2:200

Waller, Claudia Joan
José Lezama Lima 10:317

Waller, G. F.
Joyce Carol Oates 19:350
Paul Theroux 8:514

Waller, Gary F.
T. Alan Broughton 19:74
William Maxwell 19:309

Walley, David G.
Peter Townshend 17:526
Frank Zappa 17:585, 588

Wallis, Bruce
Katherine Anne Porter 15:430

Wallis, C. G.
Jean Cocteau 16:220

Wallrich, William J.
Franklyn M. Branley 21:16

Walls, Richard C.
Bob Seger 35:385

Walpole, Hugh
A. J. Cronin 32:128

Walrond, Eric
Carl Van Vechten 33:392

Walsh, Chad
Robert Bly 2:66
Stanley Burnshaw 13:129
Robert Graves 6:212
Ted Hughes 2:197
Aldous Huxley 35:238
Fletcher Knebel 14:308
Philip Larkin 5:228
C. S. Lewis 27:265
David Lodge 36:267
Cynthia Macdonald 13:355
Archibald MacLeish 3:311
Frederick Morgan 23:298
Howard Nemerov 2:306
Conrad Richter 30:317
Frank G. Slaughter 29:376
Jerome Weidman 7:517

Walsh, Jill Paton
H. F. Brinsmead 21:30
Mollie Hunter 21:160
Diana Wynne Jones 26:225
Norma Fox Mazer 26:289
Rosemary Sutcliff 26:437

Walsh, John
Malcolm Bradbury 32:55
Jorge Ibargüengoitia 37:183
Bernard Mac Laverty 31:255

Walsh, Moira
Gordon Parks 16:458

Walsh, Nina M.
Alvin Silverstein and Virginia
B. Silverstein 17:452

Walsh, Patricia L.
John M. Del Vecchio **29**:151

Walsh, Paul
Judith Thompson **39**:252

Walsh, Thomas F.
Katherine Anne Porter **13**:449

Walsh, William
Earle Birney **6**:78
D. J. Enright **31**:151
Robert Finch **18**:155
A. M. Klein **19**:261
F. R. Leavis **24**:301
R. K. Narayan **7**:254; **28**:290
Thomas Tryon **11**:548
Patrick White **3**:521; **4**:583,
584; **7**:532; **9**:567; **18**:546

Walsten, David M.
Yukio Mishima **2**:286

Walt, James
Jean Cayrol **11**:110
Ward Just **4**:266
Violette Leduc **22**:262
John O'Hara **6**:385
J. R. Salamanca **4**:462

Walter, James F.
John Barth **10**:22

Walter, Sydney Schubert
Sam Shepard **17**:435

Walters, Jennifer R.
Michel Butor **3**:93

Walters, Margaret
Brigid Brophy **6**:99
John Irving **38**:254

Walton, Alan Hull
Colin Wilson **3**:537; **14**:585

Walton, Eda Lou
Nella Larsen **37**:211
Conrad Richter **30**:306, 307

Walton, Edith H.
Enid Bagnold **25**:73
Sally Benson **17**:46, 48
Maureen Daly **17**:87
August Derleth **31**:128, 129,
131, 135
Esther Forbes **12**:204
Pamela Hansford Johnson
27:213
Mary Renault **17**:390
Rebecca West **31**:454

Walton, Richard J.
Jules Archer **12**:20

Walton, Todd
Scott Sommer **25**:426

Walzer, Judith B.
Marge Piercy **18**:407

Walzer, Michael
J. D. Salinger **12**:503

Wanamaker, John
Joy Adamson **17**:6

Wand, David Hsin-Fu
Marianne Moore **13**:396

Ward, A. C.
W. H. Auden **1**:8
Samuel Beckett **1**:21
Edmund Blunden **2**:65
Ivy Compton-Burnett **1**:62
Noel Coward **1**:64
T. S. Eliot **1**:90
E. M. Forster **1**:104
Christopher Fry **2**:143
Robert Graves **1**:128
Graham Greene **1**:132
Aldous Huxley **1**:150
W. Somerset Maugham **1**:204
Iris Murdoch **1**:234
J. B. Priestley **2**:346
Edith Sitwell **2**:403
C. P. Snow **1**:316
Evelyn Waugh **1**:358
Arnold Wesker **3**:518
P. G. Wodehouse **1**:374

Ward, Allen
John Ehle **27**:102

Ward, Andrew
Bob Dylan **12**:197

Ward, Christopher
Walter D. Edmonds **35**:146

Ward, David E.
Ezra Pound **1**:275

Ward, Ed
Jimmy Cliff **21**:60
Bob Marley **17**:268
Paul Weller **26**:444

Ward, Elizabeth
Pat Barker **32**:12
Keri Hulme **39**:162

Ward, J. A.
S. J. Perelman **9**:414

Ward, Jeff
Lou Reed **21**:307

Ward, Leo
Harper Lee **12**:341

Ward, Margaret Joan
Morley Callahan **3**:97

Ward, P.
N. Scott Momaday **19**:318

Ward, Peter
Thomas W. Shapcott **38**:399

Ward, Robert
Thomas W. Shapcott **38**:398
Bruce Springsteen **17**:479
Lily Tomlin **17**:523

Wardle, Irving
Alan Ayckbourn **33**:42
David Caute **29**:113
Caryl Churchill **31**:82, 85
Michael Frayn **31**:191
David Hare **29**:212
Ann Jellicoe **27**:209, 210
Hugh Leonard **19**:282
Richard O'Brien **17**:324
Donald Spoto **39**:451
Hugh Whitemore **37**:445
Tennessee Williams **39**:451
Snoo Wilson **33**:460

Wards, Jeff
Pink Floyd **35**:307

Ware, Cade
Leon Uris **32**:432

Warkentin, Germaine
A. W. Purdy **3**:408
F. R. Scott **22**:377

Warme, Lars G.
Eyvind Johnson **14**:297

Warner, Alan
Patrick Kavanagh **22**:238
Ken Russell **16**:543

Warner, Edwin
Jorge Luis Borges **2**:71

Warner, John M.
John Hawkes **3**:223

Warner, Jon M.
George MacBeth **5**:263

Warner, Rex
E. M. Forster **1**:105

Warner, Sam Bass, Jr.
James Carroll **38**:110

Warner, Sylvia Townsend
T. H. White **30**:451

Warnke, Frank J.
Heinrich Böll **27**:61
William Golding **17**:166
Richard Yates **7**:553

Warnock, Mary
Brigid Brophy **6**:98
Lawrence Durrell **27**:94
Iris Murdoch **8**:404

Warren, Austin
T. S. Eliot **24**:177
E. M. Forster **15**:223

Warren, Robert Penn
James Dickey **10**:140
William Faulkner **28**:141
Robert Frost **26**:114
Caroline Gordon **29**:187
Alex Haley **12**:243
Ernest Hemingway **30**:179
Andrew Lytle **22**:296
Katherine Anne Porter **13**:447;
27:401
T. S. Stribling **23**:440
Eudora Welty **1**:362; **14**:562

Warrick, Patricia S.
Isaac Asimov **26**:53
Philip K. Dick **30**:126
Frank Herbert **23**:219

Warrick, Ruth
Agnes Eckhardt Nixon **21**:252

Warsh, Lewis
Richard Brautigan **3**:86
B. P. Nichol **18**:366

Warshow, Paul
Buster Keaton **20**:197

Warshow, Robert
Arthur Miller **1**:215; **26**:312

Washburn, Martin
Richard Adams **4**:7
Anthony Burgess **4**:84
Nicholas Delbanco **6**:129
John Gardner **3**:187
Lois Gould **4**:200
Juan Goytisolo **5**:150
Günter Grass **4**:206
Dan Jacobson **4**:255
György Konrád **4**:273
Denise Levertov **3**:293
Alison Lurie **4**:306
Lewis Thomas **35**:409

Washburn, Wilcomb E.
Peter Matthiessen **32**:295

Washington, Mary Helen
Arna Bontemps **18**:66
David Bradley, Jr. **23**:80
Nella Larsen **37**:218
Alice Walker **6**:554; **19**:452

Washington, Peter
Roy Fuller **28**:154
Seamus Heaney **7**:149
Peter Porter **13**:451
Stevie Smith **8**:491
R. S. Thomas **13**:544

Wasilewski, W. H.
Theodore Roethke **11**:486

Wasserman, Debbi
Murray Schisgal **6**:490
Sam Shepard **4**:489
Tom Stoppard **4**:525
Richard Wesley **7**:519

Wasserman, Jerry
Leon Rooke **25**:393

Wasserstrom, William
Van Wyck Brooks **29**:86

Waterhouse, Keith
Lynne Reid Banks **23**:40
Harper Lee **12**:341
Doris Lessing **22**:277
Colin MacInnes **23**:282

Waterhouse, Michael
William Golding **27**:161

Waterman, Andrew
Daniel Hoffman **13**:286
John Matthias **9**:361

Waterman, Arthur
Conrad Aiken **3**:5

Waters, Chris
Tim O'Brien **7**:271

Waters, Harry F.
Steven Bochco and Michael
Kozoll **35**:48
Larry Gelbart **21**:131
Norman Lear **12**:335, 338
Garry Marshall **17**:276
Agnes Eckhardt Nixon **21**:242

Waters, Kate
Sandra Scoppettone **26**:404

Waters, Michael
Robert Hass **18**:209

Waterston, Elizabeth
Irving Layton **2**:236

Watkins, Alan
A. N. Wilson 33:455

Watkins, Floyd C.
Robert Frost 9:219
Ernest Hemingway 3:239
Robert Penn Warren 39:260

Watkins, Mel
James Baldwin 2:33
David Bradley, Jr. 23:79
Frederick Forsyth 36:176
Ernest J. Gaines 11:218
John Gardner 30:158
John Jakes 29:250
Robert Lipsyte 21:213
Simone Schwarz-Bart 7:404
Michael Thelwell 22:416
Alice Walker 5:476; 27:450
John Edgar Wideman 36:454
Al Young 19:479

Watkins, Tony
Alan Garner 17:141, 150

Watson, Edward A.
James Baldwin 17:31

Watson, Elizabeth Porges
C. S. Adler 35:12

Watson, George
T. S. Eliot 24:181

Watson, Ian
Marion Zimmer Bradley 30:28
Elias Canetti 14:119

Watson, J. P.
J.R.R. Tolkien 2:434

Watson, Robert
Richard Tillinghast 29:415

Watson, Wilbur
Henri Troyat 23:458

Watt, Donald
Isaac Asimov 26:45

Watt, Donald J.
Aldous Huxley 18:266

Watt, Douglas
Lenny Bruce 21:48
Gretchen Cryer 21:80
Christopher Durang 38:170
James Lapine 39:173
David Mamet 34:218
David Rabe 33:344
Sam Shepard 34:265
Neil Simon 31:398, 399; 39:216
Stephen Sondheim 30:380, 383, 387; 39:173
Andrew Lloyd Webber and Tim Rice 21:424
August Wilson 39:276

Watt, F. W.
A. M. Klein 19:260
Raymond Souster 14:504

Watt, Ian
John Fowles 2:137

Watt, Roderick H.
Uwe Johnson 15:305

Watterson, William C.
Guy Davenport 38:140

Watts, Emily Stipes
H. D. 31:205

Watts, Harold H.
Robert Frost 15:241
Aldous Huxley 1:151
Gabriel Marcel 15:359
Ezra Pound 7:323

Watts, Michael
Walter Becker and Donald Fagen 26:81, 83
David Bowie 17:60
Jackson Browne 21:35
Ray Davies 21:98
Mick Jagger and Keith Richard 17:230, 242
Waylon Jennings 21:201, 202
John Lennon 35:266
Jim Morrison 17:290
Van Morrison 21:237
Martin Mull 17:299
Lou Reed 21:306
Carly Simon 26:409
Paul Simon 17:460
Bruce Springsteen 17:478
Neil Young 17:571, 575

Watts, Richard
Jean Kerr 22:257
Lanford Wilson 7:548

Watts, Richard, Jr.
Robert Anderson 23:30, 31
Enid Bagnold 25:76
Paddy Chayefsky 23:114
Sumner Locke Elliott 38:176
George S. Kaufman 38:268
Neil Simon 31:393, 394
Stephen Sondheim 30:378, 379
Tennessee Williams 30:455

Waugh, Auberon
Kōbō Abé 22:13
Michael Ayrton 7:18
John Betjeman 34:309
Frederick Forsyth 36:174
Romain Gary 25:187
James Leo Herlihy 6:235
Elizabeth Jane Howard 7:164
Ruth Prawer Jhabvala 29:256
Shiva Naipaul 32:323
Tom Robbins 9:453
Tom Sharpe 36:398
Gillian Tindall 7:474
William Trevor 7:476
P. G. Wodehouse 5:516

Waugh, Coulton
Jerome Siegel and Joe Shuster 21:354

Waugh, Evelyn
Graham Greene 14:216
Aldous Huxley 11:281
Christopher Isherwood 14:278

Waugh, Harriet
Jessica Anderson 37:20
Peter Dickinson 35:136
Antonia Fraser 32:186
David Lodge 36:277
Stanley Middleton 38:335
Ruth Rendell 28:386, 387, 388
Ann Schlee 35:376
Emma Tennant 13:536

Fay Weldon 36:446

Wax, Rosalie H.
Margaret Mead 37:281

Way, Brian
Edward Albee 9:2

Wayman, Tom
Miriam Waddington 28:437

Weales, Gerald
Edward Albee 9:4
Beryl Bainbridge 4:39
Eric Bentley 24:48
Elizabeth Bowen 6:95
Ivy Compton-Burnett 1:63
J. P. Donleavy 4:123
Christopher Durang 27:92, 93
Charles Fuller 25:181
Amlin Gray 29:201
A. R. Gurney, Jr. 32:218
Lorraine Hansberry 17:183, 187
John Hawkes 1:139; 4:213
John Huston 20:168
William Inge 19:226
Robert Lowell 4:299
Peter Luke 38:315
Norman Mailer 3:319; 4:319
Bernard Malamud 1:201
William Mastrosimone 36:290
Mark Medoff 6:322; 23:294
Arthur Miller 1:218
Marsha Norman 28:318
Clifford Odets 28:335, 340
Harold Pinter 9:420
James Purdy 2:348; 4:422
David Rabe 4:427
Gerome Ragni and James Rado 17:380
Ronald Ribman 7:357
Peter Shaffer 5:390
Sam Shepard 4:489; 17:436
Wole Soyinka 3:463; 36:417
Milan Stitt 29:390
Donald Spoto 39:450
Tom Stoppard 1:327; 8:502
David Storey 2:424
James Thurber 5:430
Douglas Turner Ward 19:456
Robert Penn Warren 1:356
Thornton Wilder 10:536; 35:442
Tennessee Williams 1:368; 2:466; 19:470; 39:450
Lanford Wilson 36:460, 462
Sloan Wilson 32:445

Weatherby, Harold L.
Andrew Lytle 22:298

Weatherby, Lonnie
Jorge Ibargüengoitia 37:183

Weatherhead, A. Kingsley
Robert Duncan 1:82; 7:88
Marianne Moore 4:360
Charles Olson 1:263
Stephen Spender 1:323
William Carlos Williams 1:371

Weathers, Winston
Par Lägerkvist 7:200

Weaver, Carolyn
Ntozake Shange 38:396

Weaver, John D.
Lenny Bruce 21:47

Weaver, Mike
William Carlos Williams 13:603

Weaver, Robert
John Metcalf 37:298

Webb, Bernice Larson
Ian Fleming 30:143

Webb, Julian
Philip Roth 31:346

Webb, Phyllis
D. G. Jones 10:285

Weber, Brom
Thomas Berger 5:60
Edward Dahlberg 7:69
Bernard Kops 4:274
C. P. Snow 4:503
John Updike 2:442

Weber, Bruce
Raymond Carver 36:105

Weber, Robert C.
Robert Duncan 15:189

Weber, Ronald
Saul Bellow 1:32
John Knowles 26:249
Tom Wolfe 35:453, 466

Webster, Grant
Allen Tate 2:427

Webster, Harvey Curtis
James Baldwin 17:20
Dino Buzzati 36:85
L. P. Hartley 22:212
Maxine Kumin 13:329
Bernice Rubens 19:404
C. P. Snow 13:514

Webster, Ivan
James Baldwin 4:43
Gayl Jones 6:266

Wedgwood, C. V.
Antonia Fraser 32:180, 181

Weeks, Brigitte
Joan Aiken 35:18
Judy Blume 12:46
Betsy Byars 35:72
Marilyn French 10:191
Gail Godwin 31:195
M. M. Kaye 28:199
M. E. Kerr 12:301
Iris Murdoch 8:405
Scott Spencer 30:406

Weeks, Edward
Margaret Atwood 4:25
Jorge Luis Borges 1:39
Brigid Brophy 29:96
Lothar-Günther Buchheim 6:102
Pearl S. Buck 7:33
Bruce Catton 35:92
Len Deighton 22:115
Daphne du Maurier 6:147; 11:163
Loren Eiseley 7:91
Howard Fast 23:155
Edna Ferber 18:152
Esther Forbes 12:208

Frank B. Gilbreth, Jr. and
  Ernestine Gilbreth Carey
  17:153
Nadine Gordimer **33**:179
James Herriot **12**:283
Garson Kanin **22**:231
Yasunari Kawabata **5**:208
Madeleine L'Engle **12**:344
Peter Matthiessen **5**:273, 275;
  32:285
Iris Murdoch **6**:344
Vladimir Nabokov **6**:357
May Sarton **14**:480
André Schwarz-Bart **4**:480
Michael Shaara **15**:474
Irwin Shaw **7**:413
Mikhail Sholokhov **7**:418
Joseph Wambaugh **3**:509
Jessamyn West **7**:519; **17**:545
Herman Wouk **1**:377

Weeks, Ramona
Lucille Clifton **19**:108

Weeks, Robert P.
Ernest Hemingway **19**:214

Weesner, Theodore
Robert Cormier **12**:134

Wegner, Robert E.
E. E. Cummings **12**:153

Weibel, Kay
Mickey Spillane **13**:525

Weigel, Jack W.
Erich von Däniken **30**:422

Weigel, John A.
Lawrence Durrell **1**:86

Weightman, J. G.
David Caute **29**:110
N. F. Simpson **29**:365

Weightman, John
Alan Ayckbourn **5**:37
Simone de Beauvoir **4**:49
Albert Camus **2**:98
Louis-Ferdinand Céline **4**:100
Marguerite Duras **6**:149; **34**:162
A. E. Ellis **7**:94
Romain Gary **25**:191
Jean Genet **5**:136, 139
Jean-Luc Godard **20**:140
Anne Hébert **29**:239
J.M.G. Le Clézio **31**:244
André Malraux **9**:359
Peter Nichols **5**:308
Francis Ponge **6**:422
Gerome Ragni and James Rado
  17:382
Alain Robbe-Grillet **2**:377
Nathalie Sarraute **4**:468, 469
Jean-Paul Sartre **9**:473
Tom Stoppard **5**:412
David Storey **5**:416
Michel Tournier **23**:454; **36**:440
Gore Vidal **4**:555
Monique Wittig **22**:473
Marguerite Yourcenar **38**:459

Weil, Dorothy
Arna Bontemps **18**:63

Weil, Henry
Philip Roth **22**:358

Weiland, Steven
Wendell Berry **27**:36

Weiler, A. H.
Jean Cocteau **16**:223
Werner Herzog **16**:321
Elia Kazan **16**:362
Alain Resnais **16**:496
Jack Williamson **29**:449
Maia Wojciechowska **26**:453

Weinberg, Helen
Saul Bellow **2**:53
Ralph Ellison **11**:180
Herbert Gold **4**:192
Norman Mailer **2**:261
Philip Roth **4**:452

Weinberg, Herman G.
Josef von Sternberg **20**:374

Weinberger, David
M. M. Kaye **28**:200
Farley Mowat **26**:345
Lewis Thomas **35**:411

Weinberger, Deborah
Adolfo Bioy Casares **13**:86

Weinberger, Eliot
Robert Bly **15**:63

Weinberger, G. J.
E. E. Cummings **8**:160

Weinfield, Henry
Gilbert Sorrentino **7**:448, 449

Weingarten, Sherwood L.
Monty Python **21**:224

Weingartner, Charles
Carl Sagan **30**:336

Weinkauf, Mary S.
Piers Anthony **35**:39, 41
Fritz Leiber **25**:307

Weinstein, Shirley
Maia Wojciechowska **26**:458

Weintraub, Stanley
William Golding **2**:167
C. P. Snow **9**:497, 498

Weir, Alison
Bernard Mac Laverty **31**:254

Weir, Dana
Dave Smith **22**:386

Weir, Emily, C.H.S.
Mary Stewart **35**:394

Weir, Sister Emily
Mary Stewart **35**:393

Weisberg, Robert
Stanley Burnshaw **3**:92
Randall Jarrell **2**:211
Richmond Lattimore **3**:277

Weisberger, Bernard A.
Studs Terkel **38**:423

Weiskopf, F. C.
Joseph Wittlin **25**:467

Weisman, Kathryn
Margaret O. Hyde **21**:179
Larry Kettelkamp **12**:308

Weismiller, Edward
J. V. Cunningham **31**:96

Weiss, Jonathan M.
Gabrielle Roy **14**:470

Weiss, Nancy Quint
H. F. Brinsmead **21**:26

Weiss, Paulette
Jim Morrison **17**:294

Weiss, Penelope
Edwin Honig **33**:211

Weiss, Peter
Peter Weiss **15**:563

Weiss, Theodore
Dannie Abse **29**:22
Cleanth Brooks **24**:111
Donald Davie **5**:115
Ezra Pound **10**:405
M. L. Rosenthal **28**:396

Weiss, Victoria L.
Marguerite Duras **6**:150

Weissenberger, Klaus
Paul Celan **19**:93

Weixlmann, Joe
John Barth **14**:54
Ronald L. Fair **18**:142

Weixlmann, Sher
John Barth **14**:54

Welburn, Ron
Imamu Amiri Baraka **2**:35
Don L. Lee **2**:237
Clarence Major **19**:291
Dudley Randall **1**:283

Welch, Chris
David Bowie **17**:64
Jimmy Page and Robert Plant
  12:476, 478
Peter Townshend **17**:524, 538

Welch, Elizabeth H.
Jules Archer **12**:19

Welch, Robert D.
Ernesto Cardenal **31**:71

Welcome, John
Dick Francis **22**:152, 153
P. D. James **18**:272

Welding, Pete
Chuck Berry **17**:52
Jimmy Cliff **21**:62
Gordon Lightfoot **26**:278

Weldon, Fay
Françoise Sagan **36**:382

Wellek, René
R. P. Blackmur **2**:62
Cleanth Brooks **24**:111
Van Wyck Brooks **29**:82
Kenneth Burke **2**:89
F. R. Leavis **24**:302
I. A. Richards **24**:395

Weller, Richard H.
Margaret O. Hyde **21**:175

Weller, Sheila
Ann Beattie **8**:55
Gael Greene **8**:252
Diane Wakoski **7**:507

Wells, H. G.
Frank Swinnerton **31**:420

Wells, John
Bob Dylan **12**:200

Wellwarth, George
Arthur Adamov **4**:5
Edward Albee **2**:1
John Arden **6**:8
Jacques Audiberti **38**:25
Samuel Beckett **2**:46
Brendan Behan **8**:63
Friedrich Dürrenmatt **4**:138
Max Frisch **3**:166
Jean Genet **2**:157
Michel de Ghelderode **6**:197
Fritz Hochwälder **36**:233
Eugène Ionesco **4**:251
Arthur Kopit **18**:287
Bernard Kops **4**:274
John Mortimer **28**:283
John Osborne **2**:327
Harold Pinter **3**:385
N. F. Simpson **29**:368
Arnold Wesker **3**:518

Welsh, Mary
Noel Streatfeild **21**:401

Welty, Eudora
Margery Allingham **19**:12
Elizabeth Bowen **6**:94; **22**:65
Annie Dillard **9**:175
E. M. Forster **3**:161
Ross Macdonald **2**:255
S. J. Perelman **23**:334, 337
Katherine Anne Porter **27**:398
V. S. Pritchett **13**:467
Jessamyn West **17**:544
Patrick White **5**:485

Welz, Becky
Betty Cavanna **12**:101

Wendell, Carolyn
C. J. Cherryh **35**:114
Vonda N. McIntyre **18**:326

Werner, Alfred
Hermann Hesse **17**:195
Primo Levi **37**:220

Werner, C.
Amiri Baraka **33**:62

Werner, Craig
Tom Stoppard **15**:520

Wernick, Robert
Wright Morris **3**:343

Wersba, Barbara
Julia W. Cunningham **12**:164,
  165, 166
Leon Garfield **12**:222
Norma Fox Mazer **26**:290
Scott O'Dell **30**:274
Philippa Pearce **21**:283
Noel Streatfeild **21**:409
Jill Paton Walsh **35**:430

Wertham, Fredric
Jerome Siegel and Joe Shuster
  21:355

Wertime, Richard A.
Guy Davenport, Jr. **14**:139
Hubert Selby, Jr. **8**:475

Critic Index

Weschler, Lawrence
  Mel Brooks 12:82

Wescott, Glenway
  Katherine Anne Porter 7:313

Wesker, Arnold
  James Fenton 32:167
  William Styron 15:531

Wesling, Donald
  Robert Bly 38:50, 53
  Ed Dorn 10:157

Wesolek, George
  E. E. Cummings 12:152

West, Anthony
  Jorge Amado 13:11
  Yehuda Amichai 9:22
  Jessica Anderson 37:18
  Enid Bagnold 25:74
  James Baldwin 17:20
  Heinrich Böll 27:55
  Paul Bowles 19:58
  Alejo Carpentier 38:95
  Michel del Castillo 38:164, 167
  Bruce Catton 35:87
  Carlos Fuentes 22:164
  Yukio Mishima 27:336
  Edwin O'Connor 14:389
  Leonardo Sciascia 9:474
  Elizabeth Spencer 22:398
  Sylvia Townsend Warner 7:512

West, David S.
  Ralph Gustafson 36:219
  Robert Kroetsch 23:275

West, Martha Ullman
  David Leavitt 34:79
  Lee Smith 25:409

West, Paul
  Walter Abish 22:20
  Isabel Allende 39:35
  Miguel Ángel Asturias 3:18
  Michael Ayrton 7:18
  Samuel Beckett 2:48
  Earle Birney 6:72
  Heinrich Böll 3:74
  Michel Butor 8:113
  Alejo Carpentier 11:99
  Camilo José Cela 13:146
  Louis-Ferdinand Céline 1:57
  Jean Cocteau 15:132
  Evan S. Connell, Jr. 4:108
  Julio Cortázar 2:103
  Guy Davenport, Jr. 6:123
  Len Deighton 22:115
  José Donoso 4:127
  Richard Elman 19:151
  Howard Fast 23:158
  Gabriel García Márquez 10:215
  John Gardner 2:150
  William H. Gass 11:224
  William Golding 1:122
  Peter Handke 5:166
  MacDonald Harris 9:261
  Wilson Harris 25:202
  Uwe Johnson 5:202
  Robert Kroetsch 23:270
  Primo Levi 37:227
  Jakov Lind 2:245
  David Lodge 36:269
  Charles Newman 2:311

  Robert Nye 13:413
  Sylvia Plath 1:271
  André Schwarz-Bart 2:389
  Josef Škvorecký 39:223
  Gilbert Sorrentino 22:394
  Allen Tate 11:526
  Robert Penn Warren 1:353

West, Ray B.
  Katherine Ann Porter 1:272

West, Rebecca
  Carl Sandburg 35:343
  Frank Swinnerton 31:422

West, Richard
  Michael Cimino 16:211

Westall, Robert
  Robert Westall 17:557

Westbrook, Max
  Saul Bellow 1:30
  William Faulkner 1:101
  Ernest Hemingway 1:143
  J. D. Salinger 1:299
  John Steinbeck 1:326
  Robert Penn Warren 1:355

Westbrook, Perry D.
  Mary Ellen Chase 2:100
  R. K. Narayan 28:293

Westbrook, Wayne W.
  Louis Auchincloss 4:30

Westburg, Faith
  Adolfo Bioy Casares 4:64
  Jerzy Kosinski 3:274

Westerbeck, Colin L., Jr.
  Robert Altman 16:42
  Lindsay Anderson 20:17
  Ralph Bakshi 26:76
  Mel Brooks 12:76, 77
  Charles Chaplin 16:204
  Vittorio De Sica 20:96
  Bob Fosse 20:123
  Werner Herzog 16:327, 336
  Sidney Poitier 26:357, 359
  Richard Pryor 26:383
  Paul Schrader 26:397
  Steven Spielberg 20:359
  Lina Wertmüller 16:587

Westervelt, Linda A.
  John Barth 14:52

Westfall, Jeff
  Theodore Roethke 19:401

Westhuis, Mary G.
  Robert Newton Peck 17:342

Westlake, Donald E.
  Gael Greene 8:252
  Elmore Leonard 34:214

Weston, Jeremy
  Roger Zelazny 21:470

Weston, John
  Nat Hentoff 26:183
  Paul Zindel 6:586

Weston, John C.
  Hugh MacDiarmid 11:335

Weston, Robert V.
  Andrew Lytle 22:299

Weston, Susan B.
  Galway Kinnell 29:281

Wetzsteon, Ross
  Charles Gordone 1:124
  Stratis Haviaras 33:204
  Edward Hoagland 28:184
  Albert Innaurato 21:192
  May Sarton 4:472
  Irwin Shaw 23:399
  Lily Tomlin 17:518

Wevers, Lydia
  Frank Sargeson 31:369

Wexler, Eric
  Ronald Bush 34:524
  Ilya Ehrenburg 34:434
  T. S. Eliot 34:524
  John Gardner 34:548
  Anatol Goldberg 34:434
  Frederick Karl 34:551

Weyant, Jill
  William Melvin Kelley 22:250

Wheatcroft, Geoffrey
  David Caute 29:123

Wheatley, Patchy
  Italo Calvino 39:308

Whedon, Julia
  Judy Blume 12:46
  Lois Duncan 26:104
  Penelope Gilliatt 2:160

Wheeler, Charles
  Jeffrey Archer 28:12
  Paul E. Erdman 25:155
  William Safire 10:447

Wheeler, Elizabeth
  Louise Bogan 39:390
  Elizabeth Frank 39:390

Wheelock, Carter
  Jorge Luis Borges 2:76; 3:81;
    4:72; 6:90; 13:104
  Julio Cortázar 5:109

Wheelock, John Hall
  Allen Tate 4:536

Whelan, Gloria
  Margaret Laurence 13:342

Whelton, Clark
  Joan Micklin Silver 20:343

Whichard, Nancy Winegardner
  Patrick White 4:583

Whicher, George F.
  Ogden Nash 23:319

Whicher, Stephen E.
  E. E. Cummings 3:116

Whipple, T. K.
  Erskine Caldwell 14:93
  Robert Frost 26:110

Whissen, Thomas R.
  Isak Dinesen 10:144, 149

Whitaker, Jennifer Seymour
  Alberto Moravia 7:243

Whitaker, John T.
  Arthur Koestler 33:229

Whitaker, Muriel
  Kevin Major 26:288

Whitaker, Thomas R.
  Conrad Aiken 3:3

White, Charles, S. J.
  Mircea Eliade 19:147

White, David A.
  Martin Heidegger 24:274

White, E. B.
  James Thurber 5:432

White, Edmund
  John Ashbery 6:11; 15:33
  James Baldwin 17:41
  Amy Clampitt 32:116
  Edward Dahlberg 7:65
  Thomas M. Disch 7:87
  E. L. Doctorow 37:96
  Lawrence Durrell 6:153
  William H. Gass 39:478
  Jean Genet 5:138
  Russell C. Hoban 7:161
  Eugène Ionesco 11:290
  James Jones 39:409
  Yasunari Kawabata 5:207
  Marjorie Kellogg 2:224
  Fran Lebowitz 11:322
  José Lezama Lima 4:290
  Frank MacShane 39:409
  Harry Mathews 6:315
  William Maxwell 19:308
  James Merrill 18:328
  Yukio Mishima 4:355
  Howard Moss 7:248
  Vladimir Nabokov 2:304
  Ishmael Reed 32:355
  James Schuyler 5:383
  Muriel Spark 18:505
  Donald Spoto 39:445
  Jun'ichirō Tanizaki 28:420
  Gore Vidal 8:527
  Paul West 14:569
  Tennessee Williams 5:503;
    39:445
  Marguerite Yourcenar 38:462

White, Edward M.
  Stratis Haviaras 33:206

White, Gavin
  Farley Mowat 26:336

White, Gertrude M.
  W. D. Snodgrass 10:477;
    18:494

White, Jean M.
  Stephen Dobyns 37:78, 82
  Dick Francis 2:143
  Nicolas Freeling 38:186
  Joseph Hansen 38:237, 238
  Carolyn G. Heilbrun 25:256
  Evan Hunter 31:223, 224, 226
  P. D. James 18:272
  Ross Macdonald 3:308
  Richard Rosen 39:197
  George Simenon 2:398
  Maj Sjöwall 7:502
  Per Wahlöö 7:502
  Donald E. Westlake 7:529;
    33:440

White, John
  Michael Ayrton **7**:18
  Louis R. Harlan **34**:191

White, John J.
  MacDonald Harris **9**:259

White, John P.
  David Lodge **36**:270

White, Jon Manchip
  Gore Vidal **22**:437

White, Olive B.
  T. H. White **30**:441

White, Patricia O.
  Samuel Beckett **1**:25

White, Ray Lewis
  Gore Vidal **2**:448

White, Robert J.
  Pier Paolo Pasolini **20**:269

White, Sarah
  Anne Stevenson **33**:382

White, Ted
  Jerome Siegel and Joe Shuster
    21:358

White, Timothy
  Jackson Browne **21**:37
  Billy Joel **26**:222
  Bob Marley **17**:268, 269, 271,
    272
  Bob Seger **35**:384

White, Victor
  Thornton Wilder **10**:536

White, William Allen
  Mari Sandoz **28**:400

White, William Luther
  C. S. Lewis **3**:295

Whitebait, William
  Jean Cocteau **16**:226

Whitehall, Richard
  George Roy Hill **26**:196
  John Huston **20**:168
  Jean Renoir **20**:291

Whitehead, James
  Jim Harrison **6**:224
  Stanley J. Kunitz **6**:287
  Adrienne Rich **3**:427
  Gibbons Ruark **3**:441

Whitehead, John
  Louis MacNeice **1**:186

Whitehead, Peter
  Pier Paolo Pasolini **20**:263

Whitehead, Phillip
  Vera Brittain **23**:93

Whitehead, Ralph, Jr.
  Hunter S. Thompson **17**:514

Whitehead, Ted
  Woody Allen **16**:9
  Michael Cimino **16**:210
  Peter Townshend **17**:539

Whitehead, Winifred
  Eilís Dillon **17**:100

Whiteman, Bruce
  Marilyn R. Bowering **32**:48
  David Donnell **34**:158

Whitlock, Pamela
  Eilís Dillon **17**:93

Whitman, Alden
  Henry Carlisle **33**:104
  Antonia Fraser **32**:184
  Norman Mailer **14**:353

Whitman, Digby B.
  John Donovan **35**:140

Whitman, Ruth
  Adrienne Rich **6**:459
  Anne Sexton **6**:494

Whitney, Phyllis A.
  Mary Stolz **12**:551

Whittemore, Bernice
  Ilya Ehrenburg **18**:130

Whittemore, Reed
  Allen Ginsberg **2**:163
  James Kirkwood **9**:320
  Larry McMurtry **27**:329
  Ogden Nash **23**:323
  Charles Olson **2**:326
  Tom Robbins **9**:453

Whittington-Egan, Richard
  Truman Capote **8**:133
  Rayner Heppenstall **10**:272

Whitton, Kenneth S.
  Friedrich Dürrenmatt **15**:198

Whitty, John
  Tennessee Williams **11**:575

Wickenden, Dan
  Brigid Brophy **11**:68; **29**:91
  Roy Fuller **28**:149
  Jessamyn West **17**:545

Wickenden, Dorothy
  Raymond Carver **36**:103
  Isabel Colegate **36**:113
  André Dubus **36**:146
  Ella Leffland **19**:280
  Alison Lurie **39**:180
  Gloria Naylor **28**:305
  Susan Fromberg Schaeffer
    22:369

Wickes, George
  Henry Miller **1**:221
  Anaïs Nin **1**:247

Wideman, John
  Toni Cade Bambara **19**:34
  Breyten Breytenbach **37**:48
  Richard Wright **14**:596

Widmer, Kingsley
  John Dos Passos **4**:133
  Leslie A. Fiedler **4**:160
  Allen Ginsberg **13**:239
  Herbert Gold **4**:191
  Jack Kerouac **14**:305
  Henry Miller **1**:220

Wiegand, William
  J. D. Salinger **1**:295
  Jerome Weidman **7**:516

Wiegner, Kathleen
  Michael Benedikt **14**:82
  Judith Leet **11**:323
  Diane Wakoski **9**:555

Wiemer, Bob
  Richard Rosen **39**:195

Wier, Allen
  Laurie Colwin **23**:129

Wiersma, Stanley M.
  Christopher Fry **2**:144; **10**:202

Wiesel, Elie
  Richard Elman **19**:148
  Chaim Grade **10**:246
  Anatoli Rybakov **23**:372

Wieseltier, Leon
  Yehuda Amichai **9**:24
  Harold Bloom **24**:79
  Nadine Gordimer **33**:183
  Czesław Miłosz **31**:265
  Gregor von Rezzori **25**:383
  Salman Rushdie **31**:357
  Isaac Bashevis Singer **11**:502
  Elie Wiesel **3**:529
  A. B. Yehoshua **31**:475

Wiggins, William H., Jr.
  John Oliver Killens **10**:300

Wightman, G.B.H.
  W. S. Graham **29**:197

Wilbur, Richard
  Elizabeth Bishop **32**:33
  Barbara Howes **15**:288

Wilce, Gillian
  Beryl Bainbridge **18**:32
  Isabel Colegate **36**:111
  Pamela Hansford Johnson
    27:222
  Gay Talese **37**:402

Wilcher, Robert
  Samuel Beckett **11**:35

Wilcox, Barbara
  Joyce Maynard **23**:290

Wilcox, Thomas W.
  Anthony Powell **7**:341

Wild, John
  William Barrett **27**:16

Wilde, Alan
  Donald Barthelme **13**:55
  Christopher Isherwood **1**:156;
    9:290

Wilder, Cherry
  Marion Zimmer Bradley **30**:28

Wilder, Thornton
  Thornton Wilder **35**:441

Wilder, Virginia
  M. E. Kerr **12**:301

Wildgen, Kathryn E.
  François Mauriac **9**:368

Wilding, Michael
  L. P. Hartley **2**:182
  Jack Kerouac **5**:215
  Christina Stead **2**:422, 423;
    32:406

Wildman, John Hazard
  Mary Lavin **4**:281
  Joyce Carol Oates **6**:367
  Reynolds Price **6**:423
  Muriel Spark **13**:520

Wilentz, Amy
  Frederick Busch **18**:85

Wilentz, Sean
  Robert Penn Warren **39**:262

Wiley, Bell I.
  Bruce Catton **35**:86

Wiley, Marion E.
  Elias Canetti **25**:108

Wilford, John Noble
  James A. Michener **29**:315

Wilgus, Neal
  Piers Anthony **35**:41

Wilhelm, James J.
  Ezra Pound **4**:418

Wilkes, G. A.
  Robert D. FitzGerald **19**:178

Wilkes, Paul
  Shusaku Endo **14**:162

Wilkie, Brian
  C.D.B. Bryan **29**:101

Wilkie, Roy
  J. G. Ballard **36**:33

Wilkinson, Burke
  Allen Drury **37**:110
  C. S. Forester **35**:171
  Ernest K. Gann **23**:164

Wilkinson, Doris Y.
  Chester Himes **7**:159

Wilkinson, Marguerite
  Siegfried Sassoon **36**:385

Wilkinson, Theon
  M. M. Kaye **28**:199

Will, Frederic
  Martin Heidegger **24**:258

Willard, Mark
  Jack Vance **35**:423

Willard, Nancy
  Pierre Gascar **11**:222
  Pablo Neruda **1**:246; **28**:307
  Ntozake Shange **38**:395
  J.R.R. Tolkien **8**:515

Willbanks, Ray
  Randolph Stow **23**:434

Willett, Holly
  Nat Hentoff **26**:186

Willett, Ralph
  Clifford Odets **2**:319

Willey, Basil
  I. A. Richards **24**:399

Williams, A. R.
  Diana Wynne Jones **26**:232

Williams, Anne
  Richard Wilbur **14**:578

Critic Index

Williams, David
Kon Ichikawa 20:183
Peter Porter 33:320
Christina Stead 2:423
John Wyndham 19:476

Williams, Forrest
Federico Fellini 16:279

Williams, Frank
Alexander Kaletski 39:74

Williams, Gary Jay
Brian Clark 29:126
Jean Kerr 22:258

Williams, Gladys
Leon Garfield 12:226

Williams, H. Moore
Ruth Prawer Jhabvala 29:253

Williams, Hugo
Horst Bienek 7:29
Richard Brautigan 12:60
William S. Burroughs 5:92
Czesław Miłosz 31:264
Paul Muldoon 32:315
James Schuyler 23:392
Derek Walcott 25:448
Morris L. West 33:430
Philip Whalen 29:447

Williams, John
Henry Miller 1:223

Williams, Jonathan
Richard Brautigan 3:87
Rod McKuen 3:333
Anne Sexton 4:482

Williams, Linda L.
Bernardo Bertolucci 16:99

Williams, Liz
Sandra Scoppettone 26:404

Williams, Lloyd
James Ngugi 7:262

Williams, Martin
Lenny Bruce 21:44

Williams, Miller
Donald Davidson 2:111
John Crowe Ransom 4:434
Hollis Summers 10:493
Andrei Voznesensky 1:349

Williams, Nick B.
T.E.D. Klein 34:70

Williams, Nigel
Ronald Harwood 32:226

Williams, Oscar
Muriel Rukeyser 27:407

Williams, Paul
Ray Davies 21:88, 90
Mick Jagger and Keith Richard 17:231
Jim Morrison 17:285
Bruce Springsteen 17:482
Brian Wilson 12:641
Neil Young 17:568, 577

Williams, R. V.
James Clavell 25:128

Williams, Raymond L.
Manuel Puig 28:372
Aleksandr I. Solzhenitsyn 2:407

Williams, Regina
Rosa Guy 26:143

Williams, Richard
Joan Armatrading 17:7
Chuck Berry 17:52
Allen Ginsberg 6:201
Van Morrison 21:232
Laura Nyro 17:313
Lou Reed 21:303, 304
Smokey Robinson 21:343, 344, 348
Carly Simon 26:407
Paul Simon 17:461
Bruce Springsteen 17:477
Andrew Lloyd Webber and Tim Rice 21:422
Richard Wilbur 6:568
Brian Wilson 12:644, 646, 650
Neil Young 17:569

Williams, Robert V.
Ogden Nash 23:324

Williams, Sherley Anne
James Baldwin 3:32
Imamu Amiri Baraka 3:35; 10:20
Ralph Ellison 3:144
Zora Neale Hurston 30:222
Haki R. Madhubuti 6:313

Williams, Sherwood
William Wharton 37:440

Williams, Stanley T.
Mari Sandoz 28:400

Williams, Tennessee
Paul Bowles 19:56
William Inge 8:307
Carson McCullers 12:412

Williams, T. Harry
Bruce Catton 35:89, 91, 92

Williams, William Carlos
David Ignatow 14:274
Marianne Moore 10:348
Kenneth Patchen 18:391
Carl Sandburg 15:466

Williams, Wirt
William Brammer 31:54

Williamson, Alan
Jon Anderson 9:31
Frank Bidart 33:74
Robert Bly 5:65; 15:68
Alfred Corn 33:116, 119
Robert Creeley 15:153
Louise Glück 22:176
Ted Hughes 37:177
Galway Kinnell 5:216
Robert Lowell 4:304
Robert Phillips 28:364
Charles Simic 22:380
Louis Simpson 32:380
L. E. Sissman 18:489
Gary Snyder 5:394
Barry Spacks 14:510
Allen Tate 14:528
Richard Tillinghast 29:414, 416

C. K. Williams 33:442
James Wright 3:541; 5:519, 521; 28:472

Williamson, Chilton, Jr.
Norman Lear 12:331

Williamson, Jack
Robert A. Heinlein 26:170

Williamson, Michael
Leon Rooke 34:251

Williamson, Norma B.
Joanne Greenberg 30:167
Lisa St. Aubin de Teran 36:421

Williamson, Susan
Walter Dean Myers 35:299

Willis, David K.
Art Buchwald 33:93

Willis, Don
Fritz Lang 20:215
Josef von Sternberg 20:378

Willis, Donald C.
Luis Buñuel 16:151
Frank Capra 16:161
Yasojiro Ozu 16:455

Willis, Ellen
David Bowie 17:59
Bob Dylan 3:131; 12:183, 186
Lou Reed 21:317
Paul Simon 17:459
Stevie Wonder 12:658

Willis, J. H., Jr.
William Empson 3:147

Willison, Marilyn
Norma Klein 30:240

Wills, Garry
James Baldwin 17:25
Andrew M. Greeley 28:174
Thomas Keneally 5:210
James A. Michener 11:375
Vladimir Nabokov 3:356
Hunter S. Thompson 17:514

Willson, Robert F., Jr.
Stephen Dunn 36:151

Wilmer, Clive
Thom Gunn 32:209
Czesław Miłosz 22:310

Wilmington, Michael
John Ford 16:310, 314
Billy Wilder 20:462, 463

Wilms, Denise Murko
Lloyd Alexander 35:27
Jules Archer 12:23
Cecil Bødker 21:13
Frank Bonham 12:55
Betty Cavanna 12:103
Barbara Corcoran 17:78
Roy A. Gallant 17:133
Margaret O. Hyde 21:180
Larry Kettelkamp 12:306
Norma Klein 30:243
Sonia Levitin 17:266
Walter Dean Myers 35:296
Marilyn Sachs 35:334
Ouida Sebestyen 30:349
Noel Streatfeild 21:415

Piri Thomas 17:502
Cynthia Voigt 30:418

Wilner, Eleanor
Adrienne Rich 7:369

Wilson, A. N.
Martin Amis 38:18
Peter Dickinson 35:135
Thomas Keneally 27:234
Philip Larkin 39:334
Barbara Pym 19:388
J.I.M. Stewart 32:420
J.R.R. Tolkien 38:433

Wilson, Angus
Kingsley Amis 3:9
L. P. Hartley 2:181
Christopher Isherwood 11:294
John Cowper Powys 15:433

Wilson, Arthur
Carl Sandburg 35:341

Wilson, Barbara Ker
Noel Streatfeild 21:404

Wilson, Bryan
Kenneth Rexroth 11:473

Wilson, Carter
Rudolfo A. Anaya 23:24

Wilson, Clifford
Farley Mowat 26:330

Wilson, Colin
Jorge Luis Borges 3:78
Christopher Isherwood 11:297

Wilson, David
Dirk Bogarde 19:43
Garson Kanin 22:232
Yashar Kemal 29:266
Nagisa Oshima 20:248
Salman Rushdie 23:364
Ken Russell 16:547
François Truffaut 20:389
Joseph Wambaugh 18:533

Wilson, Dawn
Conrad Richter 30:323

Wilson, Douglas
Ernest Hemingway 3:241

Wilson, Edmund
W. H. Auden 2:21; 4:33
Marie-Claire Blais 2:62; 4:66
Kay Boyle 19:62
Van Wyck Brooks 29:81
James M. Cain 28:48
Morley Callaghan 3:97
Agatha Christie 12:114
Walter Van Tilburg Clark 28:77
John Dos Passos 4:130
T. S. Eliot 24:160
Anne Hébert 4:219
Ernest Hemingway 30:178
Joseph Wood Krutch 24:286
Hugh MacLennan 2:257
André Malraux 13:365
William Maxwell 19:305
Carson McCullers 12:410
Katherine Anne Porter 7:309
Aleksandr I. Solzhenitsyn 2:407
John Steinbeck 13:529
J.R.R. Tolkien 2:433

Carl Van Vechten 33:386
Evelyn Waugh 13:584; 27:469
Angus Wilson 2:470

Wilson, Edwin
Harvey Fierstein 33:154, 157
Mark Medoff 23:293
Stephen Sondheim 30:393, 399
Milan Stitt 29:390
Tom Stoppard 34:275

Wilson, Ellen
Guy Davenport 38:144

Wilson, Evie
Margaret Craven 17:80
Anne McCaffrey 17:283
John Neufeld 17:310
Laurence Yep 35:470

Wilson, Frank
Françoise Sagan 17:427
Susan Sontag 13:519

Wilson, George
Fritz Lang 20:213

Wilson, J. C.
Wright Morris 7:246

Wilson, Jane
Andrew Sinclair 2:401

Wilson, Jason
Octavio Paz 19:365

Wilson, Jay
Andy Warhol 20:416

Wilson, John
Robert Creeley 36:117

Wilson, Keith
David Kherdian 6:280

Wilson, Kevin
Bette Greene 30:170

Wilson, Michiko N.
Kenzaburō Ōe 36:349

Wilson, Milton
Milton Acorn 15:8
Earl Birney 6:74, 75
Leonard Cohen 38:130, 135
Ralph Gustafson 36:212
A.J.M. Smith 15:514

Wilson, Raymond J.
Isaac Asimov 19:26

Wilson, Reuel K.
Tadeusz Konwicki 8:328
Stanislaw Lem 15:326

Wilson, Robert
Isabel Allende 39:34
Robert Cormier 30:87
Joseph Epstein 39:466
Mark Harris 19:206
Breece D'J Pancake 29:347
Richard Yates 23:483

Wilson, Robley, Jr.
Marvin Bell 31:46
Daniel J. Berrigan 4:56
T. Coraghessan Boyle 36:58
Richard Howard 7:165
Philip Levine 4:285

Wilson, Sandy
A. R. Gurney, Jr. 32:217
Peter Luke 38:317

Wilson, William E.
Jessamyn West 17:545

Wilson-Beach, Fay
Ouida Sebestyen 30:348

Wilton, Shirley
Joan Aiken 35:18
Isabelle Holland 21:151

Wimble, Barton
Allan W. Eckert 17:108

Wimsatt, Margaret
Margaret Atwood 3:19
Rosellen Brown 32:63
Robertson Davies 13:173
Graham Greene 3:208
Danny Santiago 33:353
Eudora Welty 33:425

Wimsatt, W. K.
Northrop Frye 24:214

Wimsatt, W. K., Jr.
René Wellek 28:441

Wincelberg, Shimon
Max Apple 33:21
Elie Wiesel 37:454

Winch, Terence
Max Apple 33:19
Russell Banks 37:23
Jonathan Baumbach 23:56
Ann Beattie 13:64
Benedict Kiely 23:267
W. S. Merwin 8:388, 390
Flann O'Brien 10:363
William Trevor 25:443

Winchell, Mark Royden
Robert Penn Warren 13:579

Winder, David
James A. Michener 29:312

Windsor, Philip
Josef Skvorecký 15:511
Aleksandr I. Solzhenitsyn 7:441

Winegarten, Renee
Ruth Prawer Jhabvala 4:258
Bernard Malamud 3:324; 8:375
André Malraux 1:203
Grace Paley 6:392

Winehouse, Bernard
Conrad Aiken 10:2

Winer, Linda
Christopher Durang 38:174

Winfrey, Carey
James H. Webb, Jr. 22:454

Wing, George Gordon
Octavio Paz 3:376

Winks, Robin
Donald E. Westlake 33:437

Winks, Robin W.
William F. Buckley, Jr. 18:82
Len Deighton 7:75
Peter Dickinson 35:137

Howard Fast 23:160
John Gardner 30:157
Evan Hunter 31:227
P. D. James 18:273
Elmore Leonard 28:234
Robert B. Parker 27:363, 364
David Harry Walker 14:552

Winner, Langdon
Paul McCartney 35:278

Winner, Viola Hopkins
R. P. Blackmur 24:66

Winnington, Richard
Vittorio De Sica 20:85
Alfred Hitchcock 16:340

Winsten, Archer
Julia Peterkin 31:304

Winston, Joan
Gene Roddenberry 17:407

Winston, Richard
Thomas B. Costain 30:97
Mary Renault 17:393, 399
T. H. White 30:446

Winter, Douglas E.
Stephen King 37:200, 203

Winter, Thomas
Anthony Burgess 4:81

Winterich, John T.
Frank B. Gilbreth, Jr. and
Ernestine Gilbreth Carey
17:152, 154
Nevil Shute 30:369

Winters, Yvor
J. V. Cunningham 31:97, 101
Elizabeth Daryush 19:119
Robert Frost 10:192
Mina Loy 28:246
John Crowe Ransom 24:364

Wintle, Justin
Jonathan Keates 34:201
Padgett Powell 34:101

Wintz, Cary D.
Langston Hughes 10:279

Wirth-Nesher, Hana
Amos Oz 11:427

Wise, William
Richard Matheson 37:245

Wisse, Ruth R.
Saul Bellow 8:68
Leslie Epstein 27:128
Chaim Grade 10:246
Joanne Greenberg 30:167
Amos Oz 33:303
Cynthia Ozick 7:289
Chaim Potok 26:375

Wistrich, Robert
A. E. Ellis 7:93

Witcover, Jules
Hunter S. Thompson 17:507

Witemeyer, Hugh
Guy Davenport, Jr. 14:141

Witherington, Paul
John Knowles 26:252
Bernard Malamud 11:352

Witt, Harold
Conrad Aiken 1:4

Witte, Stephen
George Lucas 16:409

Wittels, Anne F.
Michael Cunningham 34:40

Wittke, Paul
Stephen Sondheim 30:397

Wixson, Douglas Charles, Jr.
Thornton Wilder 10:531

Wohlers, H. C.
Melvin Berger 12:40

Wohlgelernter, Maurice
Frank O'Connor 23:327

Wohlsen, Theodore O., Jr.
Fritz Hochwälder 36:239

Woiwode, L.
John Cheever 3:107

Woiwode, Larry
Wendell Berry 27:37

Wojahn, David
Norman Dubie 36:140
Stanley Plumly 33:316
C. K. Williams 33:447

Wojciechowska, Maia
Maia Wojciechowska 26:451

Wojnaroski, Janet B.
Margaret O. Hyde 21:180

Wolcott, James
John Barth 27:26
Steven Bochco and Michael
Kozoll 35:52
William F. Buckley, Jr. 7:35
Peter De Vries 28:110
E. L. Doctorow 37:93
Mary Gordon 22:185
Alex Haley 12:253
Peter Handke 10:255
Barry Hannah 38:235
John Hawkes 27:197
Norman Lear 12:333, 337, 338
Fran Lebowitz 36:248
Nancy Lemann 39:77
John le Carré 28:229
Norman Mailer 14:351
Laura Nyro 17:319
Jimmy Page and Robert Plant
12:480
David Plante 38:368
Mordecai Richler 18:456
Wilfrid Sheed 10:472
Lily Tomlin 17:516
Anne Tyler 18:530
John Updike 34:284
Gore Vidal 8:528
Frederick Wiseman 20:476
Tom Wolfe 35:464

Wolf, Barbara
Yukio Mishima 2:288; 6:338

Wolf, L. N.
C. S. Forester 35:172

Wolf, Manfred
Brigid Brophy 11:68

Wolf, William
Ralph Bakshi **26**:73
Gordon Parks **1**:265

Wolfe, Don M.
Shirley Hazzard **18**:213

Wolfe, Gary K.
Joanne Greenberg **30**:163
Theodore Sturgeon **39**:362
Kurt Vonnegut, Jr. **3**:495

Wolfe, George H.
William Faulkner **9**:203

Wolfe, H. Leslie
Laurence Lieberman **4**:291

Wolfe, Kary K.
Joanne Greenberg **30**:163

Wolfe, Morris
Matt Cohen **19**:111
John Metcalf **37**:307

Wolfe, Peter
Richard Adams **5**:6
A. Alvarez **5**:20
Maeve Brennan **5**:72
Laurie Colwin **5**:108
John Fowles **33**:159
Dashiell Hammett **19**:199
John Knowles **26**:258
Jakov Lind **1**:177
Ross Macdonald **14**:329
Walker Percy **2**:333
Mary Renault **3**:425
Georges Simenon **18**:487
Charles Webb **7**:515
Patrick White **3**:522

Wolfe, Tom
James M. Cain **28**:49
John Lennon and Paul
  McCartney **12**:355, 363
S. J. Perelman **23**:338

Wolff, Ellen
Kris Kristofferson **26**:268

Wolff, Geoffrey
John Barth **14**:56
Frederick Buechner **2**:83
Raymond Carver **22**:96
Arthur A. Cohen **7**:52
Julio Cortázar **3**:115
J. P. Donleavy **6**:140
George P. Elliott **2**:131
John Fowles **33**:173
Paula Fox **8**:217
John Gardner **2**:152
Barry Hannah **23**:212
Edward Hoagland **28**:180, 182
James Jones **3**:261
Jerzy Kosinski **1**:171; **3**:272;
  6:282
J.M.G. Le Clézio **31**:246
Norman Mailer **39**:419
D. Keith Mano **2**:270
Peter Manso **39**:419
Peter Matthiessen **5**:273
Wright Morris **7**:247
Donald Newlove **6**:363
Ezra Pound **2**:342
Thomas Pynchon **2**:356
Isaac Bashevis Singer **3**:456
Richard Stern **39**:245

Wolfley, Lawrence C.
Thomas Pynchon **9**:444

Wolitzer, Hilma
Jessica Anderson **37**:21
Joanne Greenberg **30**:166
Richard Yates **8**:556

Wolkenfeld, J. S.
Isaac Bashevis Singer **1**:311

Wolkoff, Lewis H.
Anne McCaffrey **17**:281
Roger Zelazny **21**:470, 471

Woll, Josephine
Varlam Shalamov **18**:480

Wollen, Peter
John Ford **16**:310

Wollheim, Donald A.
Isaac Asimov **1**:8
Ray Bradbury **1**:42
Arthur C. Clarke **1**:59
Harlan Ellison **1**:93
Philip Jose Farmer **1**:97
Edmond Hamilton **1**:137
Robert A. Heinlein **1**:139
Andre Norton **12**:466
Clifford D. Simak **1**:309
A. E. Van Vogt **1**:347
Kurt Vonnegut, Jr. **1**:348

Womack, John, Jr.
Peter Matthiessen **32**:290

Wong, Jade Snow
Jade Snow Wong **17**:566

Wong, Sharon
John Ehle **27**:105

Wood, Adolf
Louis Auchincloss **18**:25

Wood, Anne
Leon Garfield **12**:232

Wood, Charles
Kurt Vonnegut, Jr. **4**:565

Wood, Clement
Carl Sandburg **35**:342

Wood, Gayle
Margaret Atwood **15**:37

Wood, Karen
Kurt Vonnegut, Jr. **4**:565

Wood, Michael
Miguel Ángel Asturias **3**:18
J. G. Ballard **14**:39
John Barth **2**:37; **27**:27
Donald Barthelme **2**:41
Georges Bataille **29**:48
Samuel Beckett **29**:58
John Betjeman **6**:66
Adolfo Bioy Casares **4**:63
Elizabeth Bishop **9**:95
Harold Bloom **24**:74
Jorge Luis Borges **2**:72
Anthony Burgess **8**:112
Italo Calvino **8**:131; **22**:95
Elias Canetti **25**:109
Alejo Carpentier **11**:101
Evan S. Connell, Jr. **6**:116
Francis Ford Coppola **16**:246
Julio Cortázar **2**:105

Jacques Derrida **24**:138
Lawrence Durrell **6**:153
T. S. Eliot **10**:169
Stanley Elkin **4**:154
William Empson **8**:201
Ken Follett **18**:156
Carlos Fuentes **8**:225; **22**:171
Gabriel García Márquez **15**:254
John Gardner **5**:131; **8**:235
Juan Goytisolo **5**:150
Judith Guest **8**:253
Peter Handke **38**:217
Barry Hannah **23**:209
John Hawkes **4**:219
Seamus Heaney **7**:147
John Hollander **14**:263
Erica Jong **4**:264
William Melvin Kelley **22**:249
John le Carré **15**:324
Violette Leduc **22**:263
Stanislaw Lem **8**:345
John Lennon and Paul
  McCartney **12**:365
José Lezama Lima **4**:289
Ross Macdonald **14**:328
Norman Mailer **3**:316
Thomas McGuane **3**:330
A. G. Mojtabai **9**:385
Brian Moore **8**:395
Alberto Moravia **27**:355
Berry Morgan **6**:340
Vladimir Nabokov **2**:303
Pablo Neruda **5**:303
Hans Erich Nossack **6**:365
Craig Nova **31**:296
Robert Nye **13**:413
Joyce Carol Oates **2**:316
Heberto Padilla **38**:354
Grace Paley **4**:392
Octavio Paz **4**:396
Peter Porter **13**:451
Ezra Pound **2**:345
Anthony Powell **3**:403
Manuel Puig **3**:407; **28**:371
Thomas Pynchon **2**:357; **33**:339
Raymond Queneau **10**:432
Jean Rhys **14**:446
Philip Roth **4**:456
Luis Rafael Sánchez **23**:386
Severo Sarduy **6**:487
Isaac Bashevis Singer **3**:459
Susan Sontag **13**:517
Muriel Spark **5**:399; **8**:495
Richard Stern **39**:240
Robert Stone **23**:426
J.R.R. Tolkien **12**:570
Charles Tomlinson **6**:534
John Updike **2**:445
Mario Vargas Llosa **6**:546;
  31:443
Gore Vidal **8**:525
Kurt Vonnegut, Jr. **3**:503
Eudora Welty **2**:463
Angus Wilson **3**:535
Rudolph Wurlitzer **2**:483
Roger Zelazny **21**:468

Wood, Peter
Peter De Vries **2**:114
Alberto Moravia **2**:293

Wood, Robin
Robert Altman **16**:31
Michelangelo Antonioni **20**:34

Ingmar Bergman **16**:60
Frank Capra **16**:164
Claude Chabrol **16**:173
Carl Theodor Dreyer **16**:264
John Ford **16**:311
Alfred Hitchcock **16**:354
Rouben Mamoulian **16**:428
Pier Paolo Pasolini **20**:268
Satyajit Ray **16**:483

Wood, Scott
Rudolfo A. Anaya **23**:22

Wood, Susan
Alice Adams **13**:2
Margaret Atwood **15**:36
T. Alan Broughton **19**:74
Art Buchwald **33**:94
Norman Dubie **36**:133
Penelope Gilliatt **10**:230
Peter Handke **38**:222
Robert Hass **18**:210
Howard Nemerov **36**:302
Joyce Carol Oates **33**:287
David Plante **23**:343
John Wain **11**:564

Wood, William C.
Wallace Markfield **8**:380

Woodbery, W. Potter
John Crowe Ransom **11**:467

Woodburn, James A.
Carl Sandburg **35**:344

Woodburn, John
Nevil Shute **30**:367

Woodcock, George
Margaret Atwood **25**:65
Earle Birney **6**:71, 75; **11**:51
Camilo José Cela **13**:145
Louis-Ferdinand Céline **9**:158
Matt Cohen **19**:113
Robert Finch **18**:154
Roy Fuller **28**:151, 154
Hugh Garner **13**:236
Jean Genet **5**:138
Jack Hodgins **23**:229, 232
W. P. Kinsella **27**:235
Patrick Lane **25**:284
Irving Layton **15**:321
Denise Levertov **5**:246
Hugh MacDiarmid **2**:255
Hugh MacLennan **14**:339
Brian Moore **1**:225; **3**:341
R. K. Narayan **28**:300
Alden Nowlan **15**:399
Joyce Carol Oates **33**:289
A. W. Purdy **14**:431
Herbert Read **4**:441
Kenneth Rexroth **2**:70, 371
Mordecai Richler **5**:375
Gabrielle Roy **14**:469
A.J.M. Smith **15**:515
Andrew Suknaski **19**:432
Audrey Thomas **37**:416
Rudy Wiebe **11**:569

Woodfield, James
Christopher Fry **10**:200; **14**:187

Woodhouse, J. R.
Italo Calvino **22**:87

Woodruff, Stuart C.
Shirley Jackson **11**:301

Woods, Crawford
Ross Macdonald **3**:308
Isaac Bashevis Singer **3**:457
Hunter S. Thompson **9**:526

Woods, George A.
Charles Addams **30**:15
Jay Bennett **35**:42
Margaret O. Hyde **21**:172

Woods, Katherine
A. J. Cronin **32**:135
August Derleth **31**:134
Nevil Shute **30**:366
Henri Troyat **23**:457

Woods, Richard, O.P.
Gay Talese **37**:401

Woods, William C.
Lisa Alther **7**:13
Leon Uris **7**:492

Woods, William Crawford
Jim Harrison **6**:225

Woodward, C. Vann
Louis R. Harlan **34**:184
William Styron **3**:473
Eudora Welty **33**:424

Woodward, Helen Beal
Vera Brittain **23**:93
Frank B. Gilbreth, Jr. and
Ernestine Gilbreth Carey
17:155
Jean Kerr **22**:255
Ayn Rand **30**:294

Woodward, Kathleen
William Carlos Williams
22:464

Wooldridge, C. Nordhielm
Fran Arrick **30**:17, 19
Robin F. Brancato **35**:67
Norma Klein **30**:241
Norma Fox Mazer **26**:295

Woolf, Jenny
Joan Aiken **35**:21

Woolf, Virginia
E. M. Forster **15**:222
Ernest Hemingway **19**:211

Woollcott, Alexander
Dorothy Parker **15**:414

Wooster, Martin Morse
C. J. Cherryh **35**:106

Wooten, Anna
Louise Glück **7**:119

Worden, Blair
Antonia Fraser **32**:182, 187

Wordsworth, Christopher
Thor Heyerdahl **26**:192
Stanley Middleton **38**:332
Ann Schlee **35**:371
Jill Paton Walsh **35**:434

Worsley, T. C.
Ann Jellicoe **27**:206
Stephen Spender **10**:488
Martin Walser **27**:455

Worth, Katharine J.
Edward Bond **13**:99

Worthen, John
Edward Bond **23**:63

Worton, Michael J.
René Char **11**:115

Wray, Wendell
Joyce Carol Thomas **35**:406

Wrenn, John H.
John Dos Passos **1**:77

Wright, Barbara
Romain Gary **25**:188
Michel Tournier **23**:452

Wright, Basil
Luis Buñuel **16**:129
Charles Chaplin **16**:192

Wright, Cuthbert
Compton MacKenzie **18**:313

Wright, David
C. Day Lewis **6**:126
Seamus Heaney **25**:249
Hugh MacDiarmid **19**:289

Wright, Elsa Gress
Carl Theodor Dreyer **16**:262

Wright, Carolyne
Sharon Olds **39**:191

Wright, George T.
W. H. Auden **1**:10
T. S. Eliot **3**:137

Wright, Gordon
David Caute **29**:109

Wright, Hilary
Rosemary Sutcliff **26**:439

Wright, James
Richard F. Hugo **6**:244
Pablo Neruda **28**:306, 308
Gary Snyder **32**:386

Wright, John M.
David Malouf **28**:268

Wright, John S.
Robert Hayden **37**:154

Wright, Judith
Robert D. FitzGerald **19**:176
Kenneth Slessor **14**:493

Wright, Lawrence
Richard Brautigan **34**:316

Wright, Madeleine
Nathalie Sarraute **31**:379

Wright, Richard
Arna Bontemps **18**:63
Michel del Castillo **38**:165
Zora Neale Hurston **30**:211
Carson McCullers **12**:408

Wulf, Deirdre
Zoa Sherburne **30**:362

Wunderlich, Lawrence
Fernando Arrabal **2**:16

Wyatt, David M.
Ernest Hemingway **8**:288;
19:223
Robert Penn Warren **8**:541

Wyatt, E.V.R.
Jade Snow Wong **17**:566

Wyld, Lionel D.
Walter D. Edmonds **35**:153,
155

Wylder, Delbert E.
William Eastlake **8**:198

Wylie, Andrew
Giuseppe Ungaretti **11**:556

Wylie, John Cook
Earl Hamner, Jr. **12**:257

Wylie, Philip
Sally Benson **17**:49

Wyllie, John Cook
John Ehle **27**:103
Earl Hamner, Jr. **12**:257

Wymard, Eleanor B.
Annie Dillard **9**:177
John Irving **23**:246

Wyndham, Francis
Caroline Blackwood **6**:79
Elizabeth Bowen **15**:78
Agatha Christie **12**:120
Aldous Huxley **18**:265
Ruth Rendell **28**:387

Yablonsky, Victoria
Robin F. Brancato **35**:70

Yacowar, Maurice
Woody Allen **16**:16
Alfred Hitchcock **16**:351

Yagoda, Ben
James Carroll **38**:106
Margaret Drabble **10**:164
Henry Green **13**:254
Tom Wolfe **15**:585

Yakir, Dan
Peter Weir **20**:428

Yamanouchi, Hisaaki
Kōbō Abé **22**:13
Yasunari Kawabata **18**:285
Yukio Mishima **27**:339
Kenzaburō Ōe **36**:348
Shiga Naoya **33**:370

Yamashita, Sumi
Agatha Christie **12**:117

Yannella, Philip R.
Pablo Neruda **5**:301
Louis Zukofsky **18**:557

Yardley, Jonathan
Chinua Achebe **3**:2
Isabel Allende **39**:30
Kingsley Amis **2**:8
Martin Amis **38**:19
Roger Angell **26**:30, 32
Russell Banks **37**:26
Frederick Barthelme **36**:52
Hal Bennett **5**:59
Wendell Berry **4**:59; **6**:62
Doris Betts **3**:73; **28**:34, 35
C.D.B. Bryan **29**:101, 106
Frederick Buechner **6**:102
James Carroll **38**:108
Malcolm Cowley **39**:457
Harry Crews **6**:117, 118

Don DeLillo **27**:83; **39**:117
Peter De Vries **7**:77; **28**:111
James Dickey **2**:116
E. L. Doctorow **37**:91
Harriet Doerr **34**:151
John Gregory Dunne **28**:122
John Ehle **27**:106
Frederick Exley **6**:171
William Faulkner **3**:158
Leslie A. Fiedler **13**:213
Ellen Gilchrist **34**:165
Brian Glanville **6**:202
Gail Godwin **31**:194, 197
Judith Guest **30**:174
James Hanley **5**:167, 168
Barry Hannah **23**:208
Jim Harrison **6**:224
William Least Heat Moon
29:222
John Hersey **9**:277
George V. Higgins **7**:157
Josephine Humphreys **34**:64
Susan Isaacs **32**:255
Diane Johnson **5**:199
Madison Jones **4**:263
Pat Jordan **37**:193
Ward Just **4**:266; **27**:228, 229
Thomas Keneally **8**:319; **10**:299
John Knowles **4**:271; **10**:303
Elmore Leonard **28**:235
Robert Lipsyte **21**:210
John D. MacDonald **27**:275
Bernard Malamud **2**:267
Saul Maloff **5**:271
Cormac McCarthy **4**:342
James A. Michener **11**:375
A. G. Mojtabai **5**:293; **29**:319
Wright Morris **37**:316
Toni Morrison **4**:365
John Nichols **38**:342
Joyce Carol Oates **33**:297
Katherine Paterson **30**:287
T. R. Pearson **39**:87
Robert Newton Peck **17**:337
Walker Percy **3**:381
Jayne Anne Phillips **33**:306
David Plante **23**:342, 345;
38:365
Piers Paul Read **4**:444
J. R. Salamanca **4**:462
John Seelye **7**:406
Irwin Shaw **34**:370
Wilfrid Sheed **2**:394; **4**:488
Robert Stone **23**:428
Peter Taylor **37**:410
Studs Terkel **38**:426
Lewis Thomas **35**:415
Ross Thomas **39**:247
James Thurber **25**:438
Thomas Tryon **3**:483
Gore Vidal **33**:408
Jerome Weidman **7**:518
Eudora Welty **2**:462
Tom Wicker **7**:533
John Edgar Wideman **36**:456
Calder Willingham **5**:511, 512

Ya Salaam, Kalumu
Nikki Giovanni **4**:189

Yates, Diane C.
Marion Zimmer Bradley **30**:29

Critic Index

Yates, Donald A.
Jorge Amado **13**:11
John Dickson Carr **3**:100
Autran Dourado **23**:149
Carlos Fuentes **13**:232
João Guimarães Rosa **23**:352

Yates, Irene
Julia Peterkin **31**:305

Yates, Jessica
Ann Swinfen **34**:576
J.R.R. Tolkien **38**:432, 442

Yates, John
Francis Ford Coppola **16**:241

Yates, Nona
David Leavitt **34**:79

Yates, Norris W.
Günter Grass **4**:203
James Thurber **5**:433

Yates, Richard
Aidan Chambers **35**:98

Yatron, Michael
Carl Sandburg **35**:355

Yenser, Stephen
Ai **14**:9
A. R. Ammons **25**:43
Stephen Dunn **36**:154
Galway Kinnell **29**:285
Philip Levine **14**:315
Robert Lowell **3**:305
James Merrill **3**:335
Robert Pinsky **19**:372
Adrienne Rich **11**:479
James Schuyler **23**:390
W. D. Snodgrass **18**:493
Robert Penn Warren **8**:537, 540

Yerburgh, Mark R.
Amiri Baraka **33**:61

Yerburgh, Rhoda
Keri Hulme **39**:161
Nancy Willard **37**:464

Yglesias, Helen
Cynthia Propper Seton **27**:427
Ludvík Vaculík **7**:494

Yglesias, Jose
Christina Stead **2**:421
Mario Vargas Llosa **6**:547
William Wharton **37**:443

Yglesias, Luis E.
Pablo Neruda **7**:262; **9**:398
Kenneth Rexroth **22**:348

Yoder, Edwin M.
MacKinlay Kantor **7**:195

Yoder, Jon A.
Upton Sinclair **15**:501

Yohalem, John
Clark Blaise **29**:72
Richard Brautigan **5**:70
James McCourt **5**:277
Charles Webb **7**:516
Edmund White III **27**:479

Yoke, Carl B.
Joan D. Vinge **30**:412
Roger Zelazny **21**:474

Yolen, Jane
Jamake Highwater **12**:287
Mollie Hunter **21**:158
Zilpha Keatley Snyder **17**:470

York, David Winston
Chaim Potok **26**:374

Yoshida, Sanroku
Kenzaburō Ōe **36**:350

Young, Alan
Donald Justice **19**:236
Christopher Middleton **13**:389
Edwin Morgan **31**:276
James Schuyler **23**:388

Young, Alan R.
Ernest Buckler **13**:118, 119

Young, B. A.
Eva Figes **31**:161

Young, Charles M.
Mel Brooks **12**:83
Patti Smith **12**:543

Young, Colin
Kon Ichikawa **20**:177

Young, David
John Ashbery **25**:54
Robert Francis **15**:236
Craig Raine **32**:350

Young, Desmond
Jacques-Yves Cousteau **30**:103

Young, Dora Jean
Katherine Paterson **12**:484

Young, Dudley
Carlos Castaneda **12**:84

Young, Israel G.
Bob Dylan **12**:180

Young, J. R.
Waylon Jennings **21**:201

Young, James O.
Jessie Redmon Fauset **19**:170

Young, Jon
Joan Armatrading **17**:10
Chuck Berry **17**:55
Carly Simon **26**:411

Young, Kenneth
Compton Mackenzie **18**:314

Young, Marguerite
John Gardner **30**:154
Carson McCullers **12**:411
Mark Van Doren **10**:495

Young, Peter
Andrei Voznesensky **1**:348

Young, Philip
Ernest Hemingway **13**:273;
30:193, 194

Young, Scott
Farley Mowat **26**:331

Young, Stanley
August Derleth **31**:131
Conrad Richter **30**:307

Young, Stark
Eric Bentley **24**:45
Paul Green **25**:196
Clifford Odets **28**:323, 327, 328
Irwin Shaw **23**:395
Emlyn Williams **15**:576

Young, Thomas Daniel
Donald Davidson **13**:168
Andrew Lytle **22**:298
John Crowe Ransom **4**:433, 436
Peter Taylor **37**:409

Young, Tracy
Lily Tomlin **17**:520

Young, Vernon
Woody Allen **16**:10
Yehuda Amichai **22**:31
W. H. Auden **2**:28
Ingmar Bergman **16**:66
Wendell Berry **27**:35
George Mackay Brown **5**:77
Charles Chaplin **16**:197
Walter Van Tilburg Clark **28**:78
J. V. Cunningham **3**:121
Peter Davison **28**:102
Vittorio De Sica **20**:86, 90
William Dickey **3**:126
Isak Dinesen **29**:164
Gunnar Ekelöf **27**:116
Odysseus Elytis **15**:220
Lawrence Ferlinghetti **6**:183
Brewster Ghiselin **23**:171
William Heyen **18**:231
John Hollander **2**:197
Richard F. Hugo **6**:245; **32**:239
John Huston **20**:172
Donald Justice **19**:232
Galway Kinnell **13**:320
Akira Kurosawa **16**:397
Laurence Lieberman **4**:291
Michael Longley **29**:296
Robert Lowell **5**:258
Cynthia Macdonald **19**:291
Jayanta Mahapatra **33**:276
Peter Matthiessen **32**:291
William Meredith **22**:303
W. S. Merwin **13**:384
Josephine Miles **14**:369
Michael Mott **15**:380
Pablo Neruda **1**:247
Robert Pack **13**:439
Nicanor Parr **2**:331
Roman Polanski **16**:469
Yannis Ritsos **6**:464; **31**:329
Carlos Saura **20**:319
Martin Scorsese **20**:329
Frederick Seidel **18**:475
Jon Silkin **2**:396
Charles Simic **22**:382
David Slavitt **14**:490
Susan Sontag **31**:408
Maura Stanton **9**:508
James Tate **2**:432
Diane Wakoski **2**:459; **4**:573
Ted Walker **13**:566
Peter Weir **20**:429

Youngblood, Gene
Stanley Kubrick **16**:391

Younge, Shelia F.
Joan Armatrading **17**:8

Youree, Beverly B.
Melvin Berger **12**:41

Yourgrau, Barry
William Price Fox **22**:141
Mordecai Richler **18**:452
Peter Rushforth **19**:406

Yucht, Alice H.
Richard Peck **21**:296

Yuill, W. E.
Heinrich Böll **11**:52

Yurchenco, Henrietta
Woody Guthrie **35**:184, 189

Yurieff, Zoya
Joseph Wittlin **25**:468

Zabel, Morton Dauwen
Glenway Wescott **13**:591

Zabriskie, George
Marshall McLuhan **37**:256

Zacharias, Lee
Truman Capote **13**:139

Zahn, Grace M.
Zoa Sherburne **30**:361

Zahorski, Kenneth J.
Roger Zelazny **21**:473

Zaiss, David
Roy Fisher **25**:158

Zak, Michele Wender
Doris Lessing **6**:294

Zaller, Robert
Bernardo Bertolucci **16**:94
Anaïs Nin **4**:377

Zamora, Carlos
Gary Soto **32**:403

Zamora, Lois Parkinson
Julio Cortázar **33**:124, 134

Zarookian, Cherie
Barbara Corcoran **17**:71

Zatlin, Linda G.
Isaac Bashevis Singer **1**:312

Zaturenska, Marya
Laura Riding **7**:373

Zavatsky, Bill
Robert Bly **38**:51
Ed Dorn **10**:157

Zebrowski, George
Arkadii Strugatskii and Boris Strugatskii **27**:436

Zebrun, Gary
Robert Hayden **37**:153

Zehender, Ted
Tod Browning **16**:123

Zehr, David E.
Ernest Hemingway **8**:286

Zeidner, Lisa
André Dubus **36**:148

Zeik, Michael
Thomas Merton **3**:337

Zelazny, Roger
Philip K. Dick **30**:120

Zelenko, Barbara
Nora Ephron **17**:111

Zeller, Bernhard
Hermann Hesse **2**:190

Zeman, Marvin
Jean Renoir **20**:300

Zern, Ed
Roderick L. Haig-Brown **21**:136

Zetterberg, Bettijane
Hilma Wolitzer **17**:562

Zeugner, John F.
Gabriel Marcel **15**:364
Walker Percy **18**:396

Zibart, Eve
Penelope Gilliatt **13**:238

Ziegfeld, Richard E.
Kurt Vonnegut, Jr. **22**:447

Ziff, Larzer
Leslie A. Fiedler **24**:205
Edmund Wilson **24**:488

Zilkha, Michael
Mark Medoff **6**:323

Zimbardo, Rose A.
Edward Albee **13**:3

Zimmerman, Eugenia N.
Jean-Paul Sartre **9**:472

Zimmerman, Paul
R. K. Narayan **7**:256

Zimmerman, Paul D.
John Gregory Dunne **28**:121
E. M. Forster **2**:135
Lois Gould **4**:199
Stanley Kubrick **16**:383
Robert Lipsyte **21**:211
Leni Riefenstahl **16**:524
Melvin Van Peebles **20**:412

Zimmerman, Ulf
Rolf Hochhuth **18**:255
Martin Walser **27**:463, 464, 466

Ziner, Feenie
Frank Bonham **12**:53
Rosemary Sutcliff **26**:437

Zinnes, Harriet
Robert Bly **1**:37
Robert Duncan **1**:83
Anaïs Nin **4**:379; **8**:425
Ezra Pound **3**:399
May Swenson **4**:533, 534
Mona Van Duyn **7**:499

Zinsser, William
Stephen Sondheim **30**:377
James Thurber **25**:439

Ziolkowski, Theodore
Heinrich Böll **2**:67; **6**:83
Günter Grass **22**:195
Hermann Hesse **1**:145, 146;
3:248; **17**:209; **25**:260
Hans Erich Nossack **6**:364

Zipes, Jack D.
Christa Wolf **14**:593

Zirin, Mary F.
Alexander Kaletski **39**:72

Zivanovic, Judith
Jean-Paul Sartre **9**:470

Zivkovic, Peter D.
W. H. Auden **3**:23

Zivley, Sherry Lutz
Sylvia Plath **9**:431

Zoglin, Richard
Hugh Whitemore **37**:445

Zolf, Larry
Mordecai Richler **5**:376

Zonderman, Jon
Robert Coover **32**:124

Zorach, Cecile Cazort
Heinrich Böll **15**:70

Zoss, Betty
Jesse Jackson **12**:290

Zucker, David
Delmore Schwartz **10**:464

Zuckerman, Albert J.
Vassilis Vassilikos **4**:551

Zuckerman, Lord
Jonathan Schell **35**:369

Zuger, David
Adrienne Rich **7**:372

Zukofsky, Louis
Charles Chaplin **16**:190

Zunser, Jesse
Akira Kurosawa **16**:394

Zvirin, Stephanie
Fran Arrick **30**:19
Jay Bennett **35**:45
Larry Bograd **35**:62, 63, 64

Erich von Däniken **30**:427
Lois Duncan **26**:108
Sol Gordon **26**:138
Nat Hentoff **26**:187
Norma Klein **30**:242
Norma Fox Mazer **26**:295
Walter Dean Myers **35**:298
Katherine Paterson **30**:288
D. M. Pinkwater **35**:319

Zweig, Paul
Richard Adams **5**:6
A. R. Ammons **5**:29
John Ashbery **2**:18
Julio Cortázar **33**:125
James Dickey **15**:178
William Dickey **3**:126
Clayton Eshleman **7**:100
Allen Ginsberg **13**:240
Günter Grass **11**:254
John Hollander **5**:186
David Ignatow **7**:181
Thomas Keneally **27**:232
Kenneth Koch **8**:322
Violette Leduc **22**:263
Philip Levine **4**:286
Jakov Lind **27**:272
Peter Matthiessen **11**:358;
32:296
Leonard Michaels **6**:325
Czesław Miłosz **5**:292; **22**:312
Vladimir Nabokov **3**:354
Pablo Neruda **5**:303
Joyce Carol Oates **15**:402
Frank O'Hara **13**:424
George Oppen **7**:284
Charles Simic **6**:502
William Stafford **7**:461
Diane Wakoski **4**:571
James Wright **3**:542

Critic Index